THE OFFICIAL® 2001 PRICE GUIDE TO BASKETBALL CARDS

BY

DR. JAMES BECKETT

TENTH EDITION

HC

HOUSE OF COLLECTIBLES

THE CROWN PUBLISHING GROUP • NEW YORK

Important Notice: All of the information, including valuations, in this book has been compiled from the most reliable sources, and every effort has been made to eliminate errors and questionable data. Nevertheless, the possibility of error in a work of such scope always exists. The publisher will not be held responsible for losses which may occur in the purchase, sale or other transaction of items because of information contained herein. Readers who feel they have discovered errors are invited to write and inform us, so that they may be corrected in subsequent editions. Those seeking further information on the topics covered in this book are advised to refer to the complete line of *Official Price Guides* published by the House of Collectibles.

Published by:
House of Collectibles
The Crown Publishing Group
New York, New York

Distributed by The Crown Publishing Group,
a division of Random House, Inc.,
New York, and simultaneously in Canada by
Random House of Canada Limited, Toronto.

www.randomhouse.com

Manufactured in the United States of America

ISSN: 1062-6980

ISBN: 0-676-60193-6

10 9 8 7 6 5 4 3 2 1

Tenth Edition: December 2000

Table of Contents

About the Author

Jim Beckett, the leading authority on sport card values in the United States, maintains a wide range of activities in the world of sports. He possesses one of the finest collections of sports cards and autographs in the world, has made numerous appearances on radio and television, and has been frequently cited in many national publications. He was awarded the first "Special Achievement Award" for Contributions to the Hobby by the National Sports Collectors Convention in 1980, the "Jock-Jaspersen Award" for Hobby Dedication in 1983, and the "Buck Barker, Spirit of the Hobby Award" in 1991.

Dr. Beckett is the author of *Beckett Baseball Card Price Guide, The Official Price Guide to Baseball Cards, The Sport Americana Price Guide to Baseball Collectibles, The Sport Americana Baseball Memorabilia and Autograph Price Guide, Beckett Football Card Price Guide, The Official Price Guide to Football Cards, Beckett Hockey Card Price Guide, The Official Price Guide to Hockey Cards, Beckett Basketball Card Price Guide, The Official Price Guide to Basketball Cards, and The Sport Americana Baseball Card Alphabetical Checklist*. In addition, he is the founder, publisher, and editor of *Beckett Baseball Card Monthly, Beckett Basketball Monthly, Beckett Football Card Monthly, Beckett Hockey Collector, Beckett Sports Collectibles and Autographs* and *Beckett Racing & Motorsports Marketplace* magazines.

Jim Beckett received his Ph.D. in Statistics from Southern Methodist University in 1975. Prior to starting Beckett Publications in 1984, Dr. Beckett served as an Associate Professor of Statistics at Bowling Green State University and as a Vice President of a consulting firm in Dallas, Texas. He currently resides in Dallas.

How to Use This Book

Isn't it great? Every year this book gets bigger and bigger with all the new sets coming out. But even more exciting is that every year there are more attractive choices and, subsequently, more interest in the cards we love so much. This edition has been enhanced and expanded from the previous edition. The cards you collect — who appears on them, what they look like, where they are from, and (most important to most of you) what their current values are — are enumerated within. Many of the features contained in the other *Beckett Price Guides* have been incorporated into this volume since condition grading, terminology, and many other aspects of collecting are common to the card hobby in general. We hope you find the book both interesting and useful in your collecting pursuits.

The Beckett Guide has been successful where other attempts have failed because it is complete, current, and valid. This Price Guide contains not just one, but three prices by condition for all the basketball cards listed. These account for most of the basketball cards in existence. The prices were added to the card lists just prior to printing and reflect not the author's opinions or desires but the going retail prices for each card, based on the marketplace (sports memorabilia conventions and shows, sports card shops, hobby papers, current mail-order catalogs, local club meetings, auction results, and other first-hand reportings of actually realized prices).

What is the best price guide available on the market today? Of course card sellers will prefer the price guide with the highest prices, while card buyers will naturally prefer the one with the lowest prices. Accuracy, however, is the true test. Use the price guide used by more collectors and dealers than all the others combined. Look for the Beckett name. I won't put my name on anything I won't stake my reputation on. Not the lowest and not the highest — but the most accurate, with integrity.

To facilitate your use of this book, read the complete introductory section on the following pages before going to the pricing pages. Every collectible field has its own terminology; we've tried to capture most of these terms and definitions in our glossary. Please read carefully the section on grading and the condition of your cards, as you will not be able to determine which price column is appropriate for a given card without first knowing its condition.

Introduction

Welcome to the exciting world of sports card collecting, one of America's most popular avocations. You have made a good choice in buying this book, since it will open up to you the entire panorama of this field in the simplest, most concise way.

The growth of *Beckett Baseball Card Monthly, Beckett Basketball Monthly, Beckett Football Card Monthly, Beckett Hockey Collector, Beckett Sports Collectibles and Autographs* and *Beckett Racing & Motorsports Marketplace* is another indication of the unprecedented popularity of sports cards. Founded in 1984 by Dr. James Beckett, the author of this Price Guide, *Beckett Baseball Card Monthly* contains the most extensive and accepted monthly Price Guide, collectible glossy superstar covers, colorful feature articles, "Hot List," Convention Calendar, tips for beginners, "Readers Write" letters to and responses from the editor, information on errors and varieties, autograph collecting tips and profiles of the sport's Hottest stars. Published every month, *BBCM* is the hobby's largest paid circulation periodical. The other five magazines were built on the success of *BBCM*.

So collecting sports cards — while still pursued as a hobby with youthful exuberance by kids in the neighborhood — has also taken on the trappings of an industry, with thousands of full- and part-time card dealers, as well as vendors of supplies, clubs and conventions. In fact, each year since 1980 thousands of hobbyists have assembled for a National Sports Collectors Convention, at which hundreds of dealers have displayed their wares, seminars have been conducted, autographs penned by sports notables, and millions of cards changed hands.

The Beckett Guide is the best annual guide available to the exciting world of basketball cards. Read it and use it. May your enjoyment and your card collection increase in the coming months and years.

How to Collect

Each collection is personal and reflects the individuality of its owner. There are no set rules on how to collect cards. Since card collecting is a hobby or leisure pastime, what you collect, how much you collect, and how much time and money you spend collecting are entirely up to you. The funds you have available for collecting and your own personal taste should determine how you collect. The information and ideas presented here are intended to help you get the most enjoyment from this hobby.

It is impossible to collect every card ever produced. Therefore, beginners as well as intermediate and advanced collectors usually specialize in some way. One of the reasons this hobby is popular is that individual collectors can define and tailor their collecting methods to match their own tastes. To give you some ideas of the various approaches to collecting, we will list some of the more popular areas of specialization.

Many collectors select complete sets from particular years. For example, they may concentrate on assembling complete sets from all the years since their birth or since they became avid sports fans. They may try to collect a card for every player during that specified period of time. Many others wish to acquire only certain players. Usually such players are the superstars of the sport, but occasionally collectors will specialize in all the cards of players who attended a particular college or came from a certain town. Some collectors are only interested in the first cards or Rookie Cards of certain players.

Another fun way to collect cards is by team. Most fans have a favorite team, and it is natural for that loyalty to be translated into a desire for cards of the players on that favorite team. For most of the recent years, team sets (all the cards from a given team for that year) are readily available at a reasonable price. *The Sport Americana Team Football* and *Basketball Card Checklist* will open up this field to the collector.

Obtaining Cards

Several avenues are open to card collectors. Cards still can be purchased in the traditional way: by the pack at the local discount, grocery or convenience stores. But there are also thousands of card shops across the country that specialize in selling cards individually or by the pack, box, or set. Another alternative is the thousands of card shows held each month around the country, which feature anywhere from five to 800 tables of sports cards and memorabilia for sale.

For many years, it has been possible to purchase complete sets of cards through mail-order advertisers found in traditional sports media publications, such as *The Sporting News, Basketball Digest, Street & Smith* yearbooks, and others. These sets also are advertised in the card collecting periodicals. Many collectors will begin by subscribing to at least one of the hobby periodicals, all with good up-to-date information. In fact, subscription offers can be found in the advertising section of this book.

Most serious card collectors obtain old (and new) cards from one or more of several main sources: (1) trading or buying from other collectors or dealers; (2) responding to sale or auction ads in the hobby publications; (3) buying at a local hobby store; and/or (4) attending sports collectibles shows or conventions.

We advise that you try all four methods since each has its own distinct advantages: (1) trading is a great way to make new friends; (2) hobby periodicals help you keep up with what's going on in the hobby (including when and where the conventions are happening); (3) stores provide the opportunity to enjoy personalized service and consider a great diversity of material in a relaxed sports-oriented atmosphere; and (4) shows allow you to choose from multiple dealers and thousands of cards under one roof in a competitive situation.

Preserving Your Cards

Cards are fragile. They must be handled properly in order to retain their value. Careless handling can easily result in creased or bent cards. It is, however, not recommended that tweezers or tongs be used to pick up your cards since such utensils might mar or indent card surfaces and thus reduce those cards' conditions and values. In general, your cards should be handled directly as little as possible. This is sometimes easier to say than to do.

Although there are still many who use custom boxes, storage trays, or even shoe boxes, plastic sheets are the preferred method of many collectors for storing cards. A collection stored in plastic pages in a three-ring album allows you to view your collection at any time without the need to touch the card itself. Cards can also be kept in single holders (of various types and thicknesses) designed for the enjoyment of each card individually. For a large collection, some collectors may use a combination of the above methods. When purchasing plastic sheets for your cards, be sure that you find the pocket size that fits the cards snugly. Don't put your 1969-70 Topps in a sheet designed to fit 1992-93 Topps.

Most hobby and collectibles shops and virtually all collectors' conventions will have these plastic pages available in quantity for the various sizes offered, or you can purchase them directly from the advertisers in this book. Also, remember that pocket size isn't the only factor to consider when looking for plastic sheets. Other factors such as safety, economy, appearance, availability, or personal preference also may indicate which types of sheets a collector may want to buy.

Damp, sunny and/or hot conditions — no, this is not a weather forecast — are three elements to avoid in extremes if you are interested in preserving your collection. Too much (or too little) humidity can cause gradual deterioration of a card. Direct, bright sun (or fluorescent light) over time will bleach out the color of a card. Extreme heat accelerates the decomposition of the card. On the other hand, many cards have lasted more than 50 years without much scientific intervention. So be cautious, even if the above factors typically present a problem only when present in the extreme. It never hurts to be prudent.

Collecting vs. Investing

Collecting individual players and collecting complete sets are both popular vehicles for investment and speculation. Most investors and speculators stock up on complete sets or on quantities of players they think have good investment potential.

There is obviously no guarantee in this book, or anywhere else for that matter, that cards will outperform the stock market or other investment alternatives in the future. After all, basketball cards do not pay quarterly dividends and cards cannot be sold at their "current values" as easily as stocks or bonds.

Nevertheless, investors have noticed a favorable long-term trend in the past performance of sports collectibles, and certain cards and sets have outperformed just about any other investment in some years. Many hobbyists maintain that the best investment is and always will be the building of a collection, which traditionally has held up better than outright speculation.

Some of the obvious questions are: Which cards? When to buy? When to sell? The best investment you can make is in your own education. The more you know about your collection and the hobby, the more informed the decisions you will be able to make. We're not selling investment tips. We're selling information about the current value of basketball cards. It's up to you to use that information to your best advantage.

Glossary/Legend

Our glossary defines terms frequently used in the card collecting hobby. Many of these terms are also common to other types of sports memorabilia collecting. Some terms may have several meanings depending on use and context.

ABA - American Basketball Association.

ACC - Accomplishment.

ACO - Assistant Coach Card.

AL - Active Leader.

ART - All-Rookie Team.

AS - All-Star.

ASA - All-Star Advice.

ASW - All-Star Weekend.

AUTO - Autograph.

AW - Award Winner.

B - Bronze.

BC - Bonus Card.

BRICK - A group or "lot" or cards, usually 50 or more having common characteristics, that is intended to be bought, sold, or traded as a unit.

BT - Beam Team or Breakaway Threats.

CB - Collegiate Best.

CBA - Continental Basketball Association.

CL - Checklist card. A card that lists in order the cards and players in the set or series. Older checklist cards in Mint condition that have not been checked off are very desirable and command large premiums.

CO - Coach card.

COIN - A small disc of metal or plastic portraying a player in its center.

COLLECTOR - A person who engages in the hobby of collecting cards primarily for his own enjoyment, with any profit motive being secondary.

COMBINATION CARD - A single card depicting two or more players (not including team cards).

COMMON CARD - The typical card of any set; it has no premium value accruing from subject matter, numerical scarcity, popular demand, or anomaly.

CONVENTION ISSUE - A set produced in conjunction with a sports collectibles convention to commemorate or promote the show. Most recent convention issues could also be classified as promo sets.

COR - Corrected card. A version of an error card that was fixed by the manufacturer.

COUPON - See Tab.

CY - City Lights.

DEALER - A person who engages in buying, selling, and trading sports collectibles or supplies. A dealer may also be a collector, but as a dealer, he anticipates a profit.

DIE-CUT - A card with part of its stock partially cut for ornamental reasons.

DISC - A circular-shaped card.

DISPLAY SHEET - A clear, plastic page that is punched for insertion into a binder (with standard three-ring spacing) containing pockets for displaying cards. Many different styles of sheets exist with pockets of varying sizes to hold the many differing card formats. The vast majority of current cards measure 2 1/2 by 3 1/2 inches and fit in nine-pocket sheets.

DP - Double Print. A card that was printed in approximately double the quantity compared to other cards in the same series, or draft pick card.

ERR - Error card. A card with erroneous information, spelling, or depiction on either side of the card. Most errors are never corrected by the producing card company.

EXCH - An exchange card that is inserted into packs that can be redeemed for something else–usually a set or autograph.

FIN - Finals.

FLB - Flashback.

FPM - Future Playoff MVP's.

FSL - Future Scoring Leaders.

FULL SHEET - A complete sheet of cards that has not been cut into individual cards by the manufacturer. Also called an uncut sheet.

G - Gold.

GQ - Gentleman's Quarterly.

GRA - Grace.

HL - Highlight card.

HOF - Hall of Fame, or Hall of Famer (also abbreviated HOFer).

HOR - Horizontal pose on a card as opposed to the standard vertical orientation found on most cards.

IA - In Action card. A special type of card depicting a player in an action photo, such as the 1982 Topps cards.

INSERT - A card of a different type, e.g., a poster, or any other sports collectible contained and sold in the same package along with a card or cards of a major set.

IS - Inside Stuff.

ISSUE - Synonymous with set, but usually used in conjunction with a manufacturer, e.g., a Topps issue.

JWA - John Wooden Award.

KID - Kid Picture card.

LEGITIMATE ISSUE - A set produced to promote or boost sales of a product or service, e.g., bubble gum, cereal, cigarettes, etc. Most collector issues are not legitimate issues in this sense.

LID - A circular-shaped card (possibly with tab) that forms the top of the container for the product being promoted.

MAG - Magic of SkyBox cards.

MAJOR SET - A set produced by a national manufacturer of cards, containing a large number of cards. Usually 100 or more different cards comprise a major set.

MC - Members Choice.

MEM - Memorial.

MO - McDonald's Open.

MINI - A small card or stamp (the 1991-92 SkyBox Canadian set, for example).

MVP - Most Valuable Player.

NNO - No number on back.

NY - New York.

OBVERSE - The front, face, or pictured side of the card.

OLY - Olympic card.

PANEL - An extended card that is composed of multiple individual cards.

PC - Poster card.

PERIPHERAL SET - A loosely defined term that applies to any non-regular issue set. This term most often is used to describe food issue, giveaway, regional or sendaway sets that contain a fairly small number of cards and are not accepted by the hobby as major sets.

PF - Pacific Finest.

POY - Player of the Year.

PREMIUM - A card, sometimes on photographic stock, that is purchased or obtained in conjunction with (or redeemed for) another card or product. This term applies mainly to older products, as newer cards distributed in this manner are generally lumped together as peripheral sets.

PREMIUM CARDS - A class of products introduced recently, intended to have higher quality card stock and photography than regular cards, but more limited production and higher cost. Defining what is and isn't a premium card is somewhat subjective.

PROMOTIONAL SET - A set, usually containing a small number of cards, issued by a national card producer and distributed in limited quantities or to a select group of people, such as major show attendees or dealers with wholesale accounts. Presumably, the purpose of a promo set is to stir up demand for an upcoming set. Also called a preview, prototype, promo, or test set.

QP - Quadruple Print. A card that was printed in approximately four times the quantity compared to other cards in the same series.

RARE - A card or series of cards of very limited availability. Unfortunately, "rare" is a subjective term sometimes used indiscriminately. Using the strict definitions, rare cards are harder to obtain than scarce cards.

RC - Rookie Card. A player's first appearance on a regular issue card from one of the major card companies. Each company has only one regular issue set per season, and that is the widely available traditional set. With a few exceptions, each player has only one RC in any given set. A Rookie Card cannot be an All-Star, Highlight, In Action, League Leader, Super Action or

Team Leader card. It can, however, be a coach card or draft pick card.

REGIONAL - A card issued and distributed only in a limited geographical area of the country. The producer may or may not be a major, national producer of trading cards. The key is whether the set was distributed nationally in any form or not.

REVERSE - The back or narrative side of the card.

REV NEG - Reversed or flopped photo side of the card. This is a common type of error card, but only some are corrected.

RIS - Rising Star.

ROY - Rookie of the Year.

S - Silver.

SA - Super Action card. Similar to an In Action card.

SAL - SkyBox Salutes.

SASE - Self-addressed, stamped envelope.

SCARCE - A card or series of cards of limited availability. This subjective term is sometimes used indiscriminately to promote or hype value. Using strict definitions, scarce cards are easier to obtain than rare cards.

SERIES - The entire set of cards issued by a particular producer in a particular year, e.g., the 1978-79 Topps series. Also, within a particular set, series can refer to a group of (consecutively numbered) cards printed at the same time, e.g., the first series of the 1972-73 Topps set (#1 through #132).

SET - One each of an entire run of cards of the same type, produced by a particular manufacturer during a single season. In other words, if you have a complete set of 1989-90 Fleer cards, then you have every card from #1 up to and including #132; i.e., all the different cards that were produced.

SHOOT - Shooting Star.

SHOW - A large gathering of dealers and collectors at a single location for the purpose of buying, selling, and trading sports cards and memorabilia. Conventions are open to the public and sometimes also feature autograph guests, door prizes, films, contests, etc. (Or, Showcase, as in 1996–97 Flair Showcase).

SKED - Schedules.

SP - Single or Short Print. A card which was printed in lesser quantity compared to the other cards in the same series (also see DP). This term can be used only in a relative sense and in reference to one particular set. For instance, the 1989-90 Hoops Pistons Championship card (#353A) is less common than the other cards in that set, but it isn't necessarily scarcer than regular cards of any other set.

SPECIAL CARD - A card that portrays something other than a single player or team.

SS - Star Stats.

STANDARD SIZE - The standard size for sports cards is 2 1/2 by 3 1/2 inches. All exceptions, such as 1969-70 Topps, are noted in card descriptions.

STAR CARD - A card that portrays a player of some repute, usually determined by his ability, but sometimes referring to sheer popularity.

STAY - Stay in School.

STICKER - A card-like item with a removable layer that can be affixed to another surface. Example: 1986-87 through 1989-90 Fleer bonus cards.

STOCK - The cardboard or paper on which the card is printed.

STY - Style.

SUPERSTAR CARD - A card that portrays a superstar, e.g., a Hall of Fame member or a player whose current performance may eventually warrant serious Hall of Fame consideration.

SY - Schoolyard Stars.

TC - Team card or team checklist card.

TD - Triple Double. A term used for having double digit totals in three categories.

TEAM CARD - A card that depicts an entire team, notably the 1989-90 and 1990-91 NBA Hoops Detroit Pistons championship cards and the 1991-92 NBA Hoops subset.

TEST SET - A set, usually containing a small number of cards, issued by a national producer and distributed in a limited section of the country or to a select group of people. Presumably, the purpose of a test set is to measure market appeal for a particular type of card. Also called a promo or prototype set.

TFC - Team Fact card.

TL - Team Leader.

TO - Tip-off.

TR - Traded card.

TRIB - Tribune.

TRV - Trivia.

TT - Team Tickets card.

UER - Uncorrected Error card.

USA - Team USA.

VAR - Variation card. One of two or more cards from the same series, with the same card number (or player with identical pose, if the series is unnumbered) differing from one another in some aspect, from the printing, stock or other feature of the card. This is often caused when the manufacturer of the cards notices an error in a particular card, corrects the error and then resumes the print run. In this case there will be two versions or variations of the same card. Sometimes one of the variations is relatively scarce. Variations also can result from accidental or deliberate design changes, information updates, photo substitutions, etc.

VERT - Vertical pose on a card.

XRC - Extended Rookie Card. A player's first appearance on a card, but issued in a set that was not distributed nationally nor in packs. In basketball sets, this term only refers to the 1983, '84 and '85 Star Company sets.

YB - Yearbook.

20A - Twenty assist club.

50P - Fifty point club.

6M - Sixth Man.

! - Condition sensitive card or set *(see Grading Your Cards)*.

* - Multisport set.

Understanding Card Values

Determining Value

Why are some cards more valuable than others? Obviously, the economic laws of supply and demand are applicable to card collecting just as they are to any other field where a commodity is bought, sold or traded in a free, unregulated market.

Supply (the number of cards available on the market) is less than the total number of cards originally produced since attrition diminishes that original quantity. Each year a percentage of cards is typically thrown away, destroyed or otherwise lost to collectors. This percentage is much, much smaller today than it was in the past because more and more people have become increasingly aware of the value of their cards.

For those who collect only Mint condition cards, the supply of older cards can be quite small indeed. Until recently, collectors were not so conscious of the need to preserve the condition of their cards. For this reason, it is difficult to know exactly how many 1957-58 Topps are currently available, Mint or otherwise. It is generally accepted that there are fewer 1957-58 Topps available than

1969-70, 1979-80 or 1992-93 Topps cards. If demand were equal for each of these sets, the law of supply and demand would increase the price for the least available sets.

Demand, however, is never equal for all sets, so price correlations can be complicated. The demand for a card is influenced by many factors. These include: (1) the age of the card; (2) the number of cards printed; (3) the player(s) portrayed on the card; (4) the attractiveness and popularity of the set; and (5) the physical condition of the card.

In general, (1) the older the card, (2) the fewer the number of the cards printed, (3) the more famous, popular and talented the player, (4) the more attractive and popular the set, and (5) the better the condition of the card, the higher the value of the card will be. There are exceptions to all but one of these factors: the condition of the card. Given two cards similar in all respects except condition, the one in the best condition will always be valued higher.

While those guidelines help to establish the value of a card, the countless exceptions and peculiarities make any simple, direct mathematical formula to determine card values impossible.

Regional Variation

Since the market varies from region to region, card prices of local players may be higher. This is known as a regional premium. How significant the premium is — and if there is any premium at all — depends on the local popularity of the team and the player.

The largest regional premiums usually do not apply to superstars, who often are so well known nationwide that the prices of their key cards are too high for local dealers to realize a premium.

Lesser stars often command the strongest premiums. Their popularity is concentrated in their home region, creating local demand that greatly exceeds overall demand.

Regional premiums can apply to popular retired players and sometimes can be found in the areas where the players grew up or starred in college.

A regional discount is the converse of a regional premium. Regional discounts occur when a player has been so popular in his region for so long that local collectors and dealers have accumulated quantities of his cards. The abundant supply may make the cards available in that area at the lowest prices anywhere.

Set Prices

A somewhat paradoxical situation exists in the price of a complete set vs. the combined cost of the individual cards in the set. In nearly every case, the sum of the prices for the individual cards is higher than the cost for the complete set. This is prevalent especially in the cards of the past few years. The reasons for this apparent anomaly stem from the habits of collectors and from the carrying costs to dealers. Today, each card in a set normally is produced in the same quantity as all others in its set.

Many collectors pick up only stars, superstars and particular teams. As a result, the dealer is left with a shortage of certain player cards and an abundance of others. He therefore incurs an expense in simply "carrying" these less desirable cards in stock. On the other hand, if he sells a complete set, he gets rid of large numbers of cards at one time. For this reason, he generally is willing to receive less money for a complete set. By doing this, he recovers all of his costs and also makes a profit.

Set prices do not include rare card varieties, unless specifically stated. Of course, the prices for sets do include one example of each type for the given set, but this is the least expensive variety.

For some sets, a complete set price is not listed. This is due to sets currently not trading on the market in that form. Usually, the sets that have low serial number print runs do not have complete set prices.

Scarce Series

Only a select few basketball sets contain scarce series: 1948 Bowman, 1970-71 and 1972-73 Topps, 1983-84, 1984-85 and 1985-86 Star. The 1948 Bowman set was printed on two 36-card sheets, the second of which was issued in significantly lower quantities. The two Topps scarce series are only marginally tougher than the set as a whole. The Star Company scarcities relate to particular team sets that, to different extents, were less widely distributed.

We are always looking for information or photographs of printing sheets of cards for research. Each year, we try to update the hobby's knowledge of distribution anomalies. Please let us know at the address in this book if you have firsthand knowledge that would be helpful in this pursuit.

Grading Your Cards

Each hobby has its own grading terminology — stamps, coins, comic books, record collecting, etc. Collectors of sports cards are no exception. The one invariable criterion for determining the value of a card is its condition: the better the condition of the card, the more valuable it is. Condition grading, however, is subjective. Individual card dealers and collectors differ in the strictness of their grading, but the stated condition of a card should be determined without regard to whether it is being bought or sold.

No allowance is made for age. A 1961-62 Fleer card is judged by the same standards as a 1991-92 Fleer card. But there are specific sets and cards that are condition sensitive (marked with "!" in the Price Guide) because of their border color, consistently poor centering, etc. Such cards and sets sometimes command premiums above the listed percentages in Mint condition.

Centering

Current centering terminology uses numbers representing the percentage of border on either side of the main design. Obviously, centering is diminished in importance for borderless cards such as Stadium Club.

Slightly Off-Center (60/40): A slightly off-center card is one that upon close inspection is found to have one border bigger than the opposite border. This degree once was offensive only to purists, but now some hobbyists try to avoid cards that are anything other than perfectly centered.

Off-Center (70/30): An off-center card has one border that is noticeably more than twice as wide as the opposite border.

Badly Off-Center (80/20 or worse): A badly off-center card has virtually no border on one side of the card.

Miscut: A miscut card actually shows part of the adjacent card in its larger border and consequently a corresponding amount of its card is cut off.

Corner Wear

Corner wear is the most scrutinized grading criteria in the hobby. These are the major categories of corner wear:

Corner with a slight touch of wear: The corner still is sharp, but there is a slight touch of wear showing. On a dark-bordered card, this shows as a dot of white.

Fuzzy corner: The corner still comes to a point, but the point has just begun to fray. A slightly "dinged" corner is considered the same as a fuzzy corner.

Slightly rounded corner: The fraying of the corner has increased to where there is only a hint of a point. Mild layering may be evident. A "dinged" corner is considered the same as a slightly rounded corner.

Centering

Well-centered

Slightly off-centered

Off-centered

Badly off-centered

Miscut

Corner Wear

The partial cards here have been photographed at 300%. This was done in order to magnify each card's corner wear to such a degree that differences could be shown on a printed page.

This 1986-87 Fleer Mark Aguirre card has a touch of wear. Notice the extremely slight fraying on the corner.

This 1986-87 Fleer Isiah Thomas card has a fuzzy corner. Notice that there is no longer a sharp corner.

This 1986-87 Fleer Wayman Tisdale card has a slightly rounded corner evident by the lack of a sharp point and heavy wear on both edges.

This 1986-87 Fleer Herb Williams card displays a badly rounded corner. Notice a large portion of missing cardboard accompanied by heavy wear and excessive fraying.

This 1986-87 Fleer Maurice Cheeks card displays several creases of varying degrees. Light creases (middle of the card) may not break the card's surface, while heavy creases (right side) will.

Rounded corner: The point is completely gone. Some layering is noticeable.

Badly rounded corner: The corner is completely round and rough. Severe layering is evident.

Creases

A third common defect is the crease. The degree of creasing in a card is difficult to show in a drawing or picture. On giving the specific condition of an expensive card for sale, the seller should note any creases additionally. Creases can be categorized as to severity according to the following scale:

Light Crease: A light crease is a crease that is barely noticeable upon close inspection. In fact, when cards are in plastic sheets or holders, a light crease may not be seen (until the card is taken out of the holder). A light crease on the front is much more serious than a light crease on the card back only.

Medium Crease: A medium crease is noticeable when held and studied at arm's length by the naked eye, but does not overly detract from the appearance of the card. It is an obvious crease, but not one that breaks the picture surface of the card.

Heavy Crease: A heavy crease is one that has torn or broken through the card's picture surface, e.g., puts a tear in the photo surface.

Alterations

Deceptive Trimming: This occurs when someone alters the card in order (1) to shave off edge wear, (2) to improve the sharpness of the corners, or (3) to improve centering — obviously their objective is to falsely increase the perceived value of the card to an unsuspecting buyer. The shrinkage usually is evident only if the trimmed card is compared to an adjacent full-sized card or if the trimmed card is itself measured.

Obvious Trimming: Obvious trimming is noticeable and unfortunate. It is usually performed by non-collectors who give no thought to the present or future value of their cards.

Deceptively Retouched Borders: This occurs when the borders (especially on those cards with dark borders) are touched up on the edges and corners with magic marker or crayons of appropriate color in order to make the card appear to be Mint.

Categorization of Defects

Miscellaneous Flaws

The following are common minor flaws that, depending on severity, lower a card's condition by one to four grades and often render it no better than Excellent-Mint: bubbles (lumps in surface), gum and wax stains, diamond cutting (slanted borders), notching, off-centered backs, paper wrinkles, scratched-off cartoons or puzzles on back, rubber band marks, scratches, surface impressions and warping.

The following are common serious flaws that, depending on severity, lower a card's condition at least four grades and often render it no better than Good: chemical or sun fading, erasure marks, mildew, miscutting (severe off-centering), holes, bleached or retouched borders, tape marks, tears, trimming, water or coffee stains and writing.

Condition Guide

Grades

Mint (Mt) - A card with no flaws or wear. The card has four perfect corners, 55/45 or better centering from top to bottom and from left to right, original gloss, smooth edges and original color borders. A Mint card does not have print spots, color or focus imperfections.

Near Mint-Mint (NrMt-Mt) - A card with one minor flaw. Any one of the following would lower a Mint card to Near Mint-Mint: one corner with a slight touch of wear, barely noticeable print spots, color or focus imperfections. The card must have 60/40 or better centering in both directions, original gloss, smooth edges and original color borders.

Near Mint (NrMt) - A card with one minor flaw. Any one of the following would lower a Mint card to Near Mint: one fuzzy corner or two to four corners with slight touches of wear, 70/30 to 60/40 centering, slightly rough edges, minor print spots, color or focus imperfections. The card must have original gloss and original color borders.

Excellent-Mint (ExMt) - A card with two or three fuzzy, but not rounded, corners and centering no worse than 80/20. The card may have no more than two of the following: slightly rough edges, very slightly discolored borders, minor print spots, color or focus imperfections. The card must have original gloss.

Excellent (Ex) - A card with four fuzzy but definitely not rounded corners and centering no worse than 80/20. The card may have a small amount of original gloss lost, rough edges, slightly discolored borders and minor print spots, color or focus imperfections.

Very Good (Vg) - A card that has been handled but not abused: slightly rounded corners with slight layering, slight notching on edges, a significant amount of gloss lost from the surface but no scuffing and moderate discoloration of borders. The card may have a few light creases.

Good (G), Fair (F), Poor (P) - A well-worn, mishandled or abused card: badly rounded and layered corners, scuffing, most or all original gloss missing, seriously discolored borders, moderate or heavy creases, and one or more serious flaws. The grade of Good, Fair or Poor depends on the severity of wear and flaws. Good, Fair and Poor cards generally are used only as fillers.

The most widely used grades are defined above. Obviously, many cards will not perfectly fit one of the definitions.

Therefore, categories between the major grades known as in-between grades are used, such as Good to Very Good (G-Vg), Very Good to Excellent (VgEx), and Excellent-Mint to Near Mint (ExMt-NrMt). Such grades indicate a card with all qualities of the lower category but with at least a few qualities of the higher category.

This Price Guide book lists each card and set in three grades, with the middle grade valued at about 40-45% of the top grade, and the bottom grade valued at about 10-15% of the top grade.

The value of cards that fall between the listed columns can also be calculated using a percentage of the top grade. For example, a card that falls between the top and middle grades (Ex, ExMt or NrMt in most cases) will generally be valued at anywhere from 50% to 90% of the top grade.

Similarly, a card that falls between the middle and bottom grades (G-Vg, Vg or VgEx in most cases) will generally be valued at anywhere from 20% to 40% of the top grade.

There are also cases where cards are in better condition than the top grade or worse than the bottom grade. Cards that grade worse than the lowest grade are generally valued at 5-10% of the top grade.

When a card exceeds the top grade by one — such as NrMt-Mt when the top grade is NrMt, or Mint when the top grade is NrMt-Mt — a premium of up to 50% is possible, with 10-20% the usual norm.

When a card exceeds the top grade by two — such as Mint when the top grade is NrMt, or NrMt-Mt when the top grade is ExMt — a premium of 25-50% is the usual norm. But certain condition sensitive cards or sets, particularly those from the pre-war era, can bring premiums of up to 100% or even more.

Unopened packs, boxes and factory-collated sets are considered Mint in their unknown (and presumed perfect) state. Once opened, however, each card can be graded (and valued) in its own right by taking into account any defects that may be present in spite of the fact that the card has never been handled.

Selling Your Cards

Just about every collector sells cards or will sell cards eventually. Someday you may be interested in selling your duplicates or maybe even your whole collection. You may sell to other collectors, friends or dealers. You may even sell cards you purchased from a certain dealer back to that same dealer. In any event, it helps to know some of the mechanics of the typical transaction between buyer and seller.

Dealers will buy cards in order to resell them to other collectors who are interested in the cards. Dealers will always pay a higher percentage for items that (in their opinion) can be resold quickly, and a much lower percentage for those items that are perceived as having low demand and hence are slow moving. In either case, dealers must buy at a price that allows for the expense of doing business and a margin for profit.

If you have cards for sale, the best advice we can give is that you get several offers for your cards — either from card shops or at a card show — and take the best offer, all things considered. Note, the "best" offer may not be the one for the highest amount. And remember, if a dealer really wants your cards, he won't let you get away without making his best competitive offer. Another alternative is to place your cards in an auction as one or several lots.

Many people think nothing of going into a department store and paying $15 for an item of clothing for which the store paid $5. But if you were selling your $15 card to a dealer and he offered you $5 for it, you might think his markup unreasonable. To complete the analogy: most department stores (and card dealers) that consistently pay $10 for $15 items eventually go out of business. An exception is when the dealer has lined up a willing buyer for the item(s) you are attempting to sell, or if the cards are so Hot that it's likely he'll have to hold the cards for only a short period of time.

In those cases, an offer of up to 75 percent of book value still will allow the dealer to make a reasonable profit considering the short time he will need to hold the merchandise. In general, however, most cards and collections will bring offers in the range of 25 to 50 percent of retail price. Also consider that most material from the past five to 10 years is plentiful. If that's what you're selling, don't be surprised if your best offer is well below that range.

Interesting Notes

The first card numerically of an issue is the single card most likely to obtain excessive wear. Consequently, you typically will find the price on the #1 card (in NrMt or Mint condition) somewhat higher than might otherwise be the case. Similarly, but to a lesser extent (because normally the less important, reverse side of the card is the one exposed), the last card numerically in an issue also is prone to abnormal wear. This extra wear and tear occurs because the first and last cards are exposed to the elements (human element included) more than any other cards. They are generally end cards in any brick formations, rubber bandings, stackings on wet surfaces, and like activities.

Sports cards have no intrinsic value. The value of a card, like the value of other collectibles, can be determined only by you and your enjoyment in viewing and possessing these cardboard treasures.

Remember, the buyer ultimately determines the price of each card. You are the determining price factor because you have the ability to say "No" to the price of any card by not exchanging your hard-earned money for a given card. When the cost of a trading card exceeds the enjoyment you will receive from it, your answer should be "No." We assess and report the prices. You set them!

We are always interested in receiving the price input of collectors and dealers from around the country. We happily credit all contributors. We welcome your opinions, since your contributions assist us in ensuring a better guide each year. If you would like to join our survey list for the next editions of this book and others authored by Dr. Beckett, please send your name and address to Dr. James Beckett, 15850 Dallas Parkway, Dallas, Texas 75248.

History of Basketball Cards

The earliest basketball collectibles known are team postcards issued at the turn of the 20th century. Many of these postcards feature collegiate or high school teams of that day. Postcards were intermittently issued throughout the first half of the 20th century, with the bulk of them coming out in the 1920s and '30s. Unfortunately, the cataloging of these collectibles is sporadic at best. In addition, many collectors consider these postcards as memorabilia more so than trading cards, thus their exclusion from this book.

In 1910, College Athlete Felts (catalog number B-33) made their debut. Of a total of 270 felts, 20 featured basketball plays.

The first true basketball trading cards were issued by Murad cigarettes in 1911. The "College Series" cards depict a number of various sports and colleges, including four basketball cards (Luther, Northwestern, Williams and Xavier). In addition to these small (2-by-3 inch) cards, Murad issued a large (8-by-5 inch) basketball card featuring Williams college (catalog number T-6) as part of another multisport set.

The first basketball cards ever to be issued in gum packs were distributed in 1933 by Goudey in its multisport Sport Kings set, which was the first issue to list individual and professional players. Four cards from the complete 48-card set feature Original Celtics basketball players Nat Holman, Ed Wachter, Joe Lapchick and Eddie Burke.

The period of growth that the NBA experienced from 1948 to 1951 marked the first initial boom, both for that sport and the cards that chronicle it. In 1948, Bowman created the first trading card set exclusively devoted to basketball cards, ushering in the modern era of hoops collectibles. The 72-card Bowman set contains the Rookie Card of HOFer George Mikan, one of the most valuable, and important, basketball cards in the hobby. Mikan, pro basketball's first dominant big man, set the stage for Bill Russell, Wilt Chamberlain and all the other legendary centers who have played the game since.

In addition to the Bowman release, Topps included 11 basketball cards in its 252-card multisport 1948 Magic Photo set. Five of the cards feature individual players (including collegiate great "Easy" Ed Macauley), another five feature colleges, and one additional card highlights a Manhattan-Dartmouth game. These 11 cards represent Topps first effort to produce basketball trading cards. Kellogg's also created an 18-card multisport set of trading cards in 1948 that were inserted into boxes of Pep cereal. The only basketball card in the set features Mikan. Throughout 1948 and 1949, the Exhibit Supply Company of Chicago issued oversized thick-stock multisport trading cards in conjunction with the 1948 Olympic games. Six basketball players were featured, including HOFers Mikan and Joe Fulks, among others. The cards were distributed through penny arcade machines.

In 1950-51, Scott's Chips issued a 13-card set featuring the Minneapolis Lakers. The cards were issued in Scott's Potato and Cheese Potato Chip boxes. The cards are extremely scarce today due to the fact that many were redeemed back in 1950-51 in exchange for game tickets and signed team pictures. This set contains possibly the scarcest Mikan issue in existence. In 1951, a Philadelphia-based meat company called Berk Ross issued a four-series, 72-

card multisport set. The set contains five different basketball players, including the first cards of HOFers Bob Cousy and Bill Sharman.

Wheaties issued an oversized six-card multisport set on the backs of its cereal boxes in 1951. The only basketball player featured in the set is Mikan.

In 1952, Wheaties expanded the cereal box set to 30 cards, including six issues featuring basketball players of that day. Of these six cards, two feature Mikan (a portrait and an action shot). The 1952 cards are significantly smaller than the previous year's issue. That same year, the 32-card Bread for Health set was issued. The set was one of the few trading card issues of that decade exclusively devoted to the sport of basketball. The cards are actually bread end labels and were probably meant to be housed in an album. To date, the only companies known to have issued this set are Fisher's Bread in the New Jersey, New York and Pennsylvania areas and NBC Bread in the Michigan area.

One must skip ahead to 1957-58 to find the next major basketball issue, again produced by Topps. Its 80-card basketball set from that year is recognized within the hobby as the second major modern basketball issue, including Rookie Cards of all-time greats such as Bill Russell, Bob Cousy and Bob Pettit.

In 1960, Post cereal created a nine-card multisport set by devoting most of the back of the actual cereal boxes to full color picture frames of the athletes. HOFers Cousy and Pettit are the two featured basketball players.

In 1961-62, Fleer issued the third major modern basketball set. The 66-card set contains the Rookie Cards of all-time greats such as Wilt Chamberlain, Oscar Robertson and Jerry West. That same year, Bell Brand Potato Chips inserted trading cards (one per bag) featuring the L.A. Lakers team of that year and including scarce, early issues of HOFers West and Elgin Baylor.

From 1963 to 1968 no major companies manufactured basketball cards. Kahn's (an Ohio-based meat company) issued small regional basketball sets from 1957-58 through 1965-66 (including the first cards of Jerry West and Oscar Robertson in its 1960-61 set). All the Kahn's sets feature members of the Cincinnati Royals, except for the few issues featuring the Lakers' West.

In 1968, Topps printed a very limited quantity of standard-size black-and-white test issue cards, preluding its 1969-70 nationwide return to the basketball card market.

The 1969-70 Topps set began a 13-year run of producing nationally distributed basketball card sets which ended in 1981-82. This was about the time the league's popularity bottomed out and was about to begin its ascent to the lofty level it's at today.

Topps' run included several sets that are troublesome for today's collectors. The 1969-70, 1970-71 and 1976-77 sets are larger than standard size, thus making them hard to store and preserve. The 1980-81 set consists of standard-size panels containing three cards each. Completing and cataloging the 1980-81 set (which features the classic Larry Bird RC/Magic Johnson RC/Julius Erving panel) is challenging, to say the least.

In 1983, this basketball card void was filled by the Star Company, a small company which issued three attractive sets of basketball cards, along with a plethora of peripheral sets. Star's 1983-84 premiere offering was issued in four groups, with the first series (cards 1-100) very difficult to obtain, as many of the early team subsets were miscut and destroyed before release. The 1984-85 and 1985-86 sets were more widely and evenly distributed. Even so, players' initial appearances on any of the three Star Company sets are considered Extended Rookie Cards, not regular Rookie Cards, because of the relatively limited distribution. Chief among these is Michael Jordan's 1984-85 Star XRC, the most valuable sports card issued in a 1980s major set.

Then, in 1986, Fleer took over the rights to produce cards for the NBA.

Their 1986-87, 1987-88 and 1988-89 sets each contain 132 attractive, colorful cards depicting mostly stars and superstars. They were sold in the familiar wax pack format (12 cards and one sticker per pack). Fleer increased its set size to 168 in 1989-90, and was joined by NBA Hoops, which produced a 300-card first series (containing David Robinson's only Rookie Card) and a 52-card second series. The demand for all three Star Company sets, along with the first four Fleer sets and the premiere NBA Hoops set, skyrocketed during the early part of 1990.

The basketball card market stabilized somewhat in 1990-91, with both Fleer and Hoops stepping up production tremendously. A new major set, SkyBox, also made a splash in the market with its unique "high-tech" cards featuring computer-generated backgrounds. Because of overproduction, none of the three major 1990-91 sets has experienced significant price growth, although the increased competition has led to higher quality and more innovative products.

Another milestone in 1990-91 was the first-time inclusion of current rookies in update sets (NBA Hoops and SkyBox Series II, Fleer Update). The NBA Hoops and SkyBox issues contain just the 11 lottery picks, while Fleer's 100-card boxed set includes all rookies of any significance. A small company called "Star Pics" (not to be confused with Star Company) tried to fill this niche by printing a 70-card set in late 1990, but because the set was not licensed by the NBA, it is not considered a major set by the majority of collectors. It does, however, contain the first nationally distributed cards of 1990-91 rookies such as Derrick Coleman and Kendall Gill, among others.

In 1991-92, the draft pick set market that Star Pics opened in 1990-91 expanded to include several competitors. More significantly, that season brought with it the three established NBA card brands plus Upper Deck, known throughout the hobby for its high quality card stock and photography in other sports. Upper Deck's first basketball set probably captured NBA action better than any previous set. But its value — like all other major 1990-91 and 1991-92 NBA sets — declined because of overproduction.

On the bright side, the historic entrance of NBA players to Olympic competition kept interest in basketball cards going long after the Chicago Bulls won their second straight NBA championship. So for at least one year, the basketball card market — probably the most seasonal of the four major team sports — remained in the spotlight for an extended period of time.

The 1992-93 season will be remembered as the year of Shaq — the debut campaign of the most heralded rookie in many years. Shaquille O'Neal headlined the most promising rookie class in NBA history, sparking unprecedented interest in basketball cards. Among O'Neal's many talented rookie companions were Alonzo Mourning, Jim Jackson and Latrell Sprewell.

Classic Games, known primarily for producing draft picks and minor league baseball cards, signed O'Neal to an exclusive contract through 1992, thus postponing the appearances of O'Neal's NBA-licensed cards.

Shaquille's Classic and NBA cards, particularly the inserts, became some of the most sought-after collectibles in years. As a direct result of O'Neal and his fellow rookie standouts, the basketball card market achieved a new level of popularity in 1993.

The hobby rode that crest of popularity throughout the 1993-94 season. Michael Jordan may have retired, but his absence only spurred interest in some of his tougher inserts. Another strong rookie class followed Shaq, and Reggie Miller elevated his collectibility to a superstar level. Hakeem Olajuwon, by leading the Rockets to an NBA title, boosted his early cards to levels surpassed only by Jordan.

No new cardmakers came on board, but super premium Topps Finest raised the stakes, and the parallel set came into its own.

In 1994-95, the return of Michael Jordan, coupled with the high impact splash of Detroit Pistons rookie Grant Hill, kept collector interest high. In addition, the NBA granted all the licensed manufacturers the opportunity to create a fourth brand of basketball cards that year, allowing each company to create a selection of clearly defined niche products at different price points. The manufacturers also expanded the calendar release dates with 1994-95 cards being released on a consistent basis from August, 1994 all the way through June, 1995. The super-premium card market expanded greatly as the battle for the best selling five dollar (or more) pack reached epic levels by season's end. The key new super premium products included the premier of SP, Embossed and Emotion. This has continued through 1996 with the release of SPX, which contained only one card per pack.

The collecting year of 1996-97 brought even more to the table with a prominent motif of tough parallel sets and an influx of autographs available at lower ratio pulls. One of the greatest rookie classes in some time also carried the collecting season with players showing great promise: Allen Iverson, Kobe Bryant, Stephon Marbury, Antoine Walker and Shareef Abdur-Rahim. Topps Chrome was also introduced bringing about a rookie frenzy not seen since the 1986-87 Fleer set.

In 1997-98, Kobe Bryant was deemed the next Michael Jordan and his cards escalated throughout the year. In addition, a stronger than expected rookie class gave collector's some new blood to chase after, including Tim Duncan, Keith Van Horn, Ron Mercer and Tim Thomas. Autographs and serial-numbered inserts were the key inserts to chase featuring numbering as low as one of one.

The 1998-99 season brought about a huge change in Basketball. The player's strike crushed a growing basketball market and sent manufacturer's scrambling. On top of this, Michael Jordan decided to retire (again), sending another direct hit to the hobby. Many releases were cut back - or cut period. There was a bright spot once the season began though - a great rookie class led by Vince Carter. The hobby benefited by combining the great class, with shorter print run products. The top of the class was the 1998-99 SP Authentic release, which serially numbered the rookies to 3500. The San Antonio Spurs were crowned NBA Champions, leading to a spike in Tim Duncan cards. The top hobby card of the season was the SP Authentic Vince Carter RC.

If the beginning of the 1998-99 season was at rock bottom, the 1999-00 season was one of transition. Vince Carter became the new hobby hero and the NBA Champion Lakers helped the state of the hobby with their two horses, Kobe Bryant and Shaquille O'Neal. Another solid rookie class emerged, led by Steve Francis and Elton Brand, who shared Rookie of the Year honors. The 1999-00 card releases all combined elements of short-printed or serially numbered rookies, autographs and game-worn materials. SP Authentic again led the way for consumer dollars, but many other brands also did extremely well, including E-X, Flair Showcase and SPx, which combined rookie serial numbered cards with autographs. The top hobby card of the season was the SPx Steve Francis RC, which was autographed to 500.

Additional Reading

Each year Beckett Publications produces comprehensive annual price guides for each of the four major sports: *Beckett Baseball Card Price Guide, Beckett Football Card Price Guide, Beckett Basketball Card Price Guide,* and *Beckett Hockey Card Price Guide.* The aim of these annual guides is to provide information and accurate pricing on a wide array of sports cards, ranging from main issues by the major card manufacturers to various regional, promotional, and food issues. Also alphabetical checklists, such as *Beckett Basketball Card Alphabetical Checklist # 1*, are published to assist the collector in identifying all the cards of a particular player. The seasoned collector will find these tools valuable sources of information that will enable him to pursue his hobby interests.

In addition, abridged editions of the Beckett Price Guides have been published for each of the four major sports as part of the House of Collectible series: *The Official Price Guide to Baseball Cards, The Official Price Guide to Football Cards, The Official Price Guide to Basketball Cards,* and *The Official Price Guide to Hockey Cards.* Published in a convenient mass-market paperback format, these price guides provide information and accurate pricing on all the main issues by the major card manufacturers.

Advertising

Within this Price Guide you will find advertisements for sports memorabilia material, mail order, and retail sports collectibles establishments. All advertisements were accepted in good faith based on the reputation of the advertiser; however, neither the author, the publisher, the distributors, nor the other advertisers in this Price Guide accept any responsibility for any particular advertiser not complying with the terms of his or her ad.

Readers also should be aware that prices in advertisements are subject to change over the annual period before a new edition of this volume is issued each spring. When replying to an advertisement late in the basketball year, the reader should take this into account, and contact the dealer by phone or in writing for up-to-date price information. Should you come into contact with any of the advertisers in this guide as a result of their advertisement herein, please mention this source as your contact.

Prices in This Guide

Prices found in this guide reflect current retail rates just prior to the printing of this book. They do not reflect the FOR SALE prices of the author, the publisher, the distributors, the advertisers, or any card dealers associated with this guide. No one is obligated in any way to buy, sell or trade his or her cards based on these prices. The price listings were compiled by the author from actual buy/sell transactions at sports conventions, sports card shops, buy/sell advertisements in the hobby papers, for sale prices from dealer catalogs and price lists, and discussions with leading hobbyists in the U.S. and Canada. All prices are in U.S. dollars.

Acknowledgments

A great deal of diligence, hard work, and dedicated effort went into this year's volume. The high standards to which we hold ourselves, however, could not have been met without the expert input and generous amount of time contributed by many people. Our sincere thanks are extended to each and every one of you.

A complete list of these invaluable contributors appears after the price guide.

1998-99 Black Diamond

	MINT	NRMT
COMPLETE SET (120)	150.00	70.00
COMPLETE SET w/o RC (90)	40.00	18.00
COMMON MJ (1-13/22)	3.00	1.35
COMMON CARD (14-90)	.20	.09
COMMON CARD (91-120)	1.00	.45
SEMISTARS	.25	.11
SEMISTARS RC	1.25	.55
UNLISTED STARS	.50	.23
UNLISTED STARS RC	2.50	1.10

RC STATED ODDS 1:4 HOB/RET

Card	MINT	NRMT
❑ 1 Michael Jordan	3.00	1.35
❑ 2 Michael Jordan	3.00	1.35
❑ 3 Michael Jordan	3.00	1.35
❑ 4 Michael Jordan	3.00	1.35
❑ 5 Michael Jordan	3.00	1.35
❑ 6 Michael Jordan	3.00	1.35
❑ 7 Michael Jordan	3.00	1.35
❑ 8 Michael Jordan	3.00	1.35
❑ 9 Michael Jordan	3.00	1.35
❑ 10 Michael Jordan	3.00	1.35
❑ 11 Michael Jordan	3.00	1.35
❑ 12 Michael Jordan	3.00	1.35
❑ 13 Michael Jordan	3.00	1.35
❑ 14 Dikembe Mutombo	.25	.11
❑ 15 Steve Smith	.25	.11
❑ 16 Mookie Blaylock	.20	.09
❑ 17 Antoine Walker	.75	.35
❑ 18 Kenny Anderson	.25	.11
❑ 19 Ron Mercer	.75	.35
❑ 20 Glen Rice	.25	.11
❑ 21 Derrick Coleman	.25	.11
❑ 22 Michael Jordan	3.00	1.35
❑ 23 Toni Kukoc	.60	.25
❑ 24 Brent Barry	.20	.09
❑ 25 Brevin Knight	.20	.09
❑ 26 Derek Anderson	.60	.25
❑ 27 Shawn Kemp	.75	.35
❑ 28 Shawn Bradley	.20	.09
❑ 29 Michael Finley	.50	.23
❑ 30 Nick Van Exel	.25	.11
❑ 31 Chauncey Billups	.20	.09
❑ 32 Antonio McDyess	.50	.23
❑ 33 Grant Hill	2.50	1.10
❑ 34 Jerry Stackhouse	.25	.11
❑ 35 Bison Dele	.20	.09
❑ 36 John Starks	.20	.09
❑ 37 Chris Mills	.20	.09
❑ 38 Scottie Pippen	1.50	.70
❑ 39 Hakeem Olajuwon	.75	.35
❑ 40 Charles Barkley	.75	.35
❑ 41 Antonio Davis	.20	.09
❑ 42 Reggie Miller	.50	.23
❑ 43 Mark Jackson	.20	.09
❑ 44 Eddie Jones	1.00	.45
❑ 45 Shaquille O'Neal	2.50	1.10
❑ 46 Kobe Bryant	4.00	1.80
❑ 47 Rodney Rogers	.20	.09
❑ 48 Maurice Taylor	.50	.23
❑ 49 Tim Hardaway	.50	.23
❑ 50 Jamal Mashburn	.25	.11
❑ 51 Alonzo Mourning	.50	.23
❑ 52 Ray Allen	.60	.25
❑ 53 Terrell Brandon	.25	.11
❑ 54 Glenn Robinson	.25	.11
❑ 55 Joe Smith	.25	.11
❑ 56 Stephon Marbury	1.25	.55
❑ 57 Kevin Garnett	3.00	1.35
❑ 58 Kerry Kittles	.25	.11
❑ 59 Jayson Williams	.25	.11
❑ 60 Keith Van Horn	1.25	.55
❑ 61 Patrick Ewing	.50	.23
❑ 62 Allan Houston	.50	.23
❑ 63 Latrell Sprewell	1.00	.45
❑ 64 Anfernee Hardaway	1.50	.70
❑ 65 Horace Grant	.25	.11
❑ 66 Allen Iverson	2.00	.90
❑ 67 Tim Thomas	.75	.35
❑ 68 Jason Kidd	1.50	.70
❑ 69 Danny Manning	.25	.11
❑ 70 Tom Gugliotta	.25	.11
❑ 71 Damon Stoudamire	.50	.23
❑ 72 Rasheed Wallace	.50	.23
❑ 73 Isaiah Rider	.25	.11
❑ 74 Corliss Williamson	.20	.09
❑ 75 Chris Webber	1.50	.70
❑ 76 Tim Duncan	2.50	1.10
❑ 77 David Robinson	.75	.35
❑ 78 Sean Elliott	.20	.09
❑ 79 Gary Payton	.75	.35
❑ 80 Vin Baker	.25	.11
❑ 81 John Wallace	.20	.09
❑ 82 Tracy McGrady	2.00	.90
❑ 83 Jeff Hornacek	.25	.11
❑ 84 Karl Malone	.75	.35
❑ 85 John Stockton	.50	.23
❑ 86 Bryant Reeves	.20	.09
❑ 87 Shareef Abdur-Rahim	1.25	.55
❑ 88 Rod Strickland	.25	.11
❑ 89 Juwan Howard	.25	.11
❑ 90 Mitch Richmond	.50	.23
❑ 91 Michael Olowokandi RC	4.00	1.80
❑ 92 Dirk Nowitzki RC	10.00	4.50
❑ 93 Raef LaFrentz RC	5.00	2.20
❑ 94 Mike Bibby RC	8.00	3.60
❑ 95 Ricky Davis RC	5.00	2.20
❑ 96 Jason Williams RC	15.00	6.75
❑ 97 Al Harrington RC	8.00	3.60
❑ 98 Bonzi Wells RC	10.00	4.50
❑ 99 Keon Clark RC	2.50	1.10
❑ 100 Rashard Lewis RC	10.00	4.50
❑ 101 Paul Pierce RC	12.00	5.50
❑ 102 Antawn Jamison RC	12.00	5.50
❑ 103 Nazr Mohammed RC	1.25	.55
❑ 104 Brian Skinner RC	2.50	1.10
❑ 105 Corey Benjamin RC	2.50	1.10
❑ 106 Predrag Stojakovic RC	4.00	1.80
❑ 107 Bryce Drew RC	2.50	1.10
❑ 108 Matt Harpring RC	2.50	1.10
❑ 109 Toby Bailey RC	1.00	.45
❑ 110 Tyronn Lue RC	1.25	.55
❑ 111 Michael Dickerson RC	5.00	2.20
❑ 112 Roshown McLeod RC	1.25	.55
❑ 113 Felipe Lopez RC	3.00	1.35
❑ 114 Michael Doleac RC	2.50	1.10
❑ 115 Ruben Patterson RC	5.00	2.20
❑ 116 Robert Traylor RC	2.50	1.10
❑ 117 Sam Jacobson RC	1.00	.45
❑ 118 Larry Hughes RC	15.00	6.75
❑ 119 Pat Garrity RC	1.25	.55
❑ 120 Vince Carter RC	50.00	22.00

1998-99 Black Diamond Double Diamond

	MINT	NRMT
COMPLETE SET (120)	250.00	110.00
COMMON CARD (1-90)	.40	.18
COMMON CARD (91-120)	1.25	.55

*STARS: .75X TO 2X BASE CARD HI
*RCs: .5X TO 1.25X BASE HI
STARS: PRINT RUN 3000 SERIAL #'d SETS
RCs: PRINT RUN 2500 SERIAL #'d SETS

1998-99 Black Diamond Triple Diamond

	MINT	NRMT
COMPLETE SET (120)	400.00	180.00
COMMON CARD (1-90)	.75	.35
COMMON CARD (91-120)	1.50	.70

*STARS: 1.5X TO 4X BASE CARD HI
*RCs: .6X TO 1.5X BASE CARD HI
STARS: PRINT RUN 1500 SERIAL #'d SETS
RCs: PRINT RUN 1000 SERIAL #'d SETS

1998-99 Black Diamond Quadruple Diamond

	MINT	NRMT
COMMON MJ (1-13/22)	60.00	27.00
COMMON CARD (14-90)	6.00	2.70
COMMON CARD (91-120)	10.00	4.50

*STARS: 12.5X TO 30X BASE CARD HI
*RCs: 4X TO 10X HI
RANDOM INSERTS IN PACKS
STARS: PRINT RUN 150 SERIAL #'d SETS
RCs: PRINT RUN 50 SERIAL #'d SETS

1998-99 Black Diamond Diamond Dominance

	MINT	NRMT
COMPLETE SET (30)	250.00	110.00
COMMON CARD (D1-D30)	2.00	.90

UNLISTED STARS.................... 3.00 1.35
RANDOM INSERTS IN HOB/RET PACKS
STATED PRINT RUN 1000 SERIAL #'d SETS
COMMON EMERALD (D1-30) .. 8.00 3.60
*EMERALD: 1.5X TO 4X HI COLUMN
EMERALD: RANDOM INSERTS IN PACKS
EMERALD: PRINT RUN 100 SERIAL #'d SETS

❑ D1 Steve Smith .... 2.00 .90
❑ D2 Paul Pierce 15.00 6.75
❑ D3 Glen Rice .... 2.00 .90
❑ D4 Toni Kukoc 4.00 1.80
❑ D5 Shawn Kemp 5.00 2.20
❑ D6 Michael Finley.............. 3.00 1.35
❑ D7 Antonio McDyess 3.00 1.35
❑ D8 Grant Hill..................... 15.00 6.75
❑ D9 Antawn Jamison 15.00 6.75
❑ D10 Scottie Pippen 10.00 4.50
❑ D11 Reggie Miller.............. 3.00 1.35
❑ D12 Michael Olowokandi 5.00 2.20
❑ D13 Shaquille O'Neal........ 15.00 6.75
❑ D14 Alonzo Mourning.......... 3.00 1.35
❑ D15 Ray Allen 4.00 1.80
❑ D16 Stephon Marbury 8.00 3.60
❑ D17 Keith Van Horn 8.00 3.60
❑ D18 Allan Houston 3.00 1.35
❑ D19 Anfernee Hardaway .. 10.00 4.50
❑ D20 Allen Iverson............. 12.00 5.50
❑ D21 Jason Kidd 10.00 4.50
❑ D22 Damon Stoudamire...... 3.00 1.35
❑ D23 Chris Webber 10.00 4.50
❑ D24 Tim Duncan 15.00 6.75
❑ D25 Gary Payton 5.00 2.20
❑ D26 Vince Carter 80.00 36.00
❑ D27 Karl Malone 6.00 2.70
❑ D28 Mike Bibby 12.00 5.50
❑ D29 Mitch Richmond 3.00 1.35
❑ D30 Michael Jordan 50.00 22.00

1998-99 Black Diamond MJ Sheer Brilliance

MINT NRMT
COMPLETE SET (30) 1200.00 550.00
COMMON CARD (B1-B30) 50.00 22.00
RANDOM INSERTS IN HOBBY PACKS
STATED PRINT RUN 230 SERIAL #'d SETS
COMMON MJ EXT.(B1-30) .. 500.00 220.00
RANDOM INSERTS IN PACKS
STATED PRINT RUN 23 SERIAL #'d SETS

❑ B1 Michael Jordan 50.00 22.00
❑ B2 Michael Jordan 50.00 22.00
❑ B3 Michael Jordan 50.00 22.00
❑ B4 Michael Jordan 50.00 22.00
❑ B5 Michael Jordan 50.00 22.00
❑ B6 Michael Jordan 50.00 22.00
❑ B7 Michael Jordan 50.00 22.00
❑ B8 Michael Jordan 50.00 22.00
❑ B9 Michael Jordan 50.00 22.00
❑ B10 Michael Jordan 50.00 22.00
❑ B11 Michael Jordan 50.00 22.00
❑ B12 Michael Jordan 50.00 22.00
❑ B13 Michael Jordan 50.00 22.00
❑ B14 Michael Jordan 50.00 22.00
❑ B15 Michael Jordan 50.00 22.00
❑ B16 Michael Jordan 50.00 22.00
❑ B17 Michael Jordan 50.00 22.00
❑ B18 Michael Jordan 50.00 22.00
❑ B19 Michael Jordan 50.00 22.00
❑ B20 Michael Jordan 50.00 22.00
❑ B21 Michael Jordan 50.00 22.00
❑ B22 Michael Jordan 50.00 22.00
❑ B23 Michael Jordan 50.00 22.00
❑ B24 Michael Jordan 50.00 22.00
❑ B25 Michael Jordan 50.00 22.00
❑ B26 Michael Jordan 50.00 22.00
❑ B27 Michael Jordan 50.00 22.00
❑ B28 Michael Jordan 50.00 22.00
❑ B29 Michael Jordan 50.00 22.00
❑ B30 Michael Jordan 50.00 22.00

1998-99 Black Diamond UD Authentics

MINT NRMT
COMPLETE SET (5) 150.00 70.00
COMMON CARD 20.00 9.00
RANDOM INSERTS IN HOB/RET PACKS
STATED PRINT RUN 475 SETS

❑ AJ Antawn Jamison 60.00 27.00
❑ BW Bonzi Wells 30.00 13.50
❑ LH Larry Hughes 60.00 27.00
❑ MB Mike Bibby 40.00 18.00
❑ RT Robert Traylor 20.00 9.00

1999-00 Black Diamond

MINT NRMT
COMPLETE SET (120) 60.00 27.00
COMPLETE SET w/o RC (90) 25.00 11.00
COMMON CARD (1-90) .... .15 .07
COMMON CARD (91-120)........... .60 .25
SEMISTARS............................ .20 .09
SEMISTARS RC....................... .75 .35
UNLISTED STARS.................... .40 .18
UNLISTED STARS RC............ 1.00 .45
RC SUBSET: STATED ODDS 1:3 H/R
MJ FINAL FLOOR LISTED UNDER 99-00 UD

❑ 1 Dikembe Mutombo .... .20 .09
❑ 2 Alan Henderson .... .15 .07
❑ 3 Roshown McLeod .... .15 .07
❑ 4 Kenny Anderson .... .20 .09
❑ 5 Paul Pierce .... .75 .35
❑ 6 Antoine Walker .... .50 .23
❑ 7 Eddie Jones .... .75 .35
❑ 8 Elden Campbell.............. .15 .07
❑ 9 David Wesley .... .15 .07
❑ 10 Toni Kukoc .... .50 .23
❑ 11 Randy Brown................ .15 .07
❑ 12 Dickey Simpkins .... .15 .07
❑ 13 Shawn Kemp................. .60 .25
❑ 14 Zydrunas Ilgauskas........ .15 .07
❑ 15 Brevin Knight................ .15 .07
❑ 16 Michael Finley .... .40 .18
❑ 17 Dirk Nowitzki .... .60 .25
❑ 18 Robert Pack .... .15 .07
❑ 19 Antonio McDyess .... .40 .18
❑ 20 Nick Van Exel .... .20 .09
❑ 21 Ron Mercer .... .50 .23
❑ 22 Grant Hill .... 2.00 .90
❑ 23 Lindsey Hunter .... .15 .07
❑ 24 Jerry Stackhouse .... .20 .09
❑ 25 Antawn Jamison .... .75 .35
❑ 26 John Starks .... .15 .07
❑ 27 Donyell Marshall .... .15 .07
❑ 28 Hakeem Olajuwon.......... .60 .25
❑ 29 Charles Barkley............. .60 .25
❑ 30 Cuttino Mobley .... .40 .18
❑ 31 Reggie Miller .... .40 .18
❑ 32 Rik Smits .... .15 .07
❑ 33 Jalen Rose .... .40 .18
❑ 34 Maurice Taylor .... .40 .18
❑ 35 Tyrone Nesby RC .... .15 .07
❑ 36 Michael Olowokandi .... .20 .09
❑ 37 Shaquille O'Neal .... 2.00 .90
❑ 38 Kobe Bryant 3.00 1.35
❑ 39 Glen Rice .... .20 .09
❑ 40 P.J. Brown...................... .15 .07
❑ 41 Tim Hardaway .... .40 .18
❑ 42 Alonzo Mourning............ .40 .18
❑ 43 Jamal Mashburn .... .20 .09
❑ 44 Glenn Robinson .... .20 .09
❑ 45 Ray Allen........................ .40 .18
❑ 46 Tim Thomas .... .50 .23
❑ 47 Kevin Garnett 2.50 1.10
❑ 48 Joe Smith .... .20 .09
❑ 49 Terrell Brandon .... .20 .09
❑ 50 Stephon Marbury............ .75 .35
❑ 51 Jayson Williams .... .20 .09
❑ 52 Keith Van Horn .... .75 .35
❑ 53 Latrell Sprewell .... .75 .35
❑ 54 Allan Houston .... .40 .18
❑ 55 Patrick Ewing .... .40 .18
❑ 56 Marcus Camby .... .40 .18
❑ 57 Darrell Armstrong .... .20 .09
❑ 58 Charles Outlaw .... .15 .07
❑ 59 Michael Doleac .... .15 .07
❑ 60 Allen Iverson .... 1.50 .70
❑ 61 Theo Ratliff .... .15 .07
❑ 62 Larry Hughes............... 1.00 .45
❑ 63 Anfernee Hardaway ...... 1.25 .55
❑ 64 Jason Kidd .... 1.25 .55
❑ 65 Tom Gugliotta .... .20 .09
❑ 66 Brian Grant .... .20 .09
❑ 67 Damon Stoudamire .... .40 .18
❑ 68 Rasheed Wallace .... .40 .18
❑ 69 Jason Williams .... 1.00 .45
❑ 70 Chris Webber .... 1.25 .55
❑ 71 Vlade Divac.................... .15 .07
❑ 72 Tim Duncan................. 2.00 .90
❑ 73 David Robinson.............. .60 .25
❑ 74 Avery Johnson .... .15 .07
❑ 75 Sean Elliott .... .15 .07
❑ 76 Gary Payton .... .60 .25
❑ 77 Vin Baker........................ .20 .09
❑ 78 Brent Barry .... .15 .07
❑ 79 Vince Carter 4.00 1.80
❑ 80 Tracy McGrady .... 1.25 .55
❑ 81 Doug Christie .... .15 .07
❑ 82 Karl Malone .... .60 .25
❑ 83 John Stockton .... .40 .18
❑ 84 Bryon Russell .... .15 .07
❑ 85 Shareef Abdur-Rahim ...... .75 .35
❑ 86 Mike Bibby...................... .50 .23
❑ 87 Felipe Lopez .... .15 .07
❑ 88 Juwan Howard .... .20 .09
❑ 89 Rod Strickland................ .20 .09
❑ 90 Mitch Richmond .... .40 .18
❑ 91 Elton Brand RC 10.00 4.50
❑ 92 Steve Francis RC 12.00 5.50
❑ 93 Baron Davis RC 2.50 1.10
❑ 94 Lamar Odom RC............ 8.00 3.60
❑ 95 Jonathan Bender RC...... 5.00 2.20
❑ 96 Wally Szczerbiak RC...... 4.00 1.80
❑ 97 Richard Hamilton RC 2.50 1.10
❑ 98 Andre Miller RC............. 3.00 1.35
❑ 99 Shawn Marion RC.......... 3.00 1.35
❑ 100 Jason Terry RC............ 1.50 .70
❑ 101 Trajan Langdon RC...... 1.50 .70
❑ 102 Aleksandar Radojevic RC .60 .25
❑ 103 Corey Maggette RC 4.00 1.80
❑ 104 William Avery RC .... 1.50 .70
❑ 105 Ron Artest RC.............. 2.50 1.10
❑ 106 Adrian Griffin RC.......... 1.25 .55
❑ 107 James Posey RC .... 2.00 .90
❑ 108 Quincy Lewis RC.......... 1.00 .45
❑ 109 Dion Glover RC............ 1.00 .45
❑ 110 Jeff Foster RC............. 1.00 .45
❑ 111 Kenny Thomas RC ...... 1.50 .70

Card	MINT	NRMT
❑ 112 Devean George RC	2.00	.90
❑ 113 Tim James RC	1.25	.55
❑ 114 Vonteego Cummings RC	1.50	.70
❑ 115 Jumaine Jones RC	.75	.35
❑ 116 Scott Padgett RC	1.00	.45
❑ 117 Obinna Ekezie RC	.75	.35
❑ 118 Ryan Robertson RC	.75	.35
❑ 119 Chucky Atkins RC	1.25	.55
❑ 120 A.J. Bramlett RC	.60	.25

1999-00 Black Diamond Diamond Cut

	MINT	NRMT
COMPLETE SET (120)	150.00	70.00
COMMON CARD (1-120)	.40	.18

*STARS: 1X TO 2.5X BASE CARD HI
*RCs: .6X TO 1.5X BASE HI
STARS: STATED ODDS 1:6 H/R
RCs: STATED ODDS 1:12 H/R

1999-00 Black Diamond Final Cut

	MINT	NRMT
COMMON CARD (1-90)	5.00	2.20
COMMON CARD (91-120)	15.00	6.75

*STARS: 12.5X TO 30X BASE CARD HI
*RCs: 8X TO 20X BASE HI
STARS: PRINT RUN 100 SERIAL #'d SETS
RCs: PRINT RUN 50 SERIAL #'d SETS
RANDOM INSERTS IN PACKS

1999-00 Black Diamond A Piece of History

	MINT	NRMT
COMMON CARD	15.00	6.75
H: STATED ODDS 1:144		
H/R: STATED ODDS 1:336		
COMMON DOUBLE	30.00	13.50
*DOUBLE: .75X TO 2X BASE HI		
DOUBLE H: STATED ODDS 1:864		
DOUBLE H/R: STATED ODDS 1:1008		

Card	MINT	NRMT
❑ AH Allan Houston H/R	30.00	13.50
❑ AW Antoine Walker H	25.00	11.00
❑ BD Baron Davis H	25.00	11.00
❑ CB Charles Barkley H/R	40.00	18.00
❑ CM Corey Maggette H/R	30.00	13.50
❑ CW Chris Webber H	50.00	22.00
❑ DG Devean George H	25.00	11.00
❑ DR David Robinson H/R	30.00	13.50
❑ GP Gary Payton H	40.00	18.00
❑ HO Hakeem Olajuwon H	40.00	18.00
❑ JB Jonathan Bender H	40.00	18.00
❑ JS John Stockton H/R	30.00	13.50
❑ JT Jason Terry H/R	25.00	11.00
❑ JW Jason Williams H	40.00	18.00
❑ KG Kevin Garnett H	40.00	18.00
❑ KM Karl Malone H	30.00	13.50
❑ KT Kenny Thomas H/R	20.00	9.00
❑ MF Michael Finley H/R	15.00	6.75
❑ PP Paul Pierce H/R	25.00	11.00
❑ RM Reggie Miller H	40.00	18.00
❑ SA Shareef Abdur-Rahim H/R	40.00	18.00
❑ SF Steve Francis H	60.00	27.00
❑ SO Shaquille O'Neal H/R	50.00	22.00
❑ TB Terrell Brandon H	15.00	6.75
❑ WS Wally Szczerbiak H/R	40.00	18.00

1999-00 Black Diamond A Piece of History Triple

	MINT	NRMT
COMMON CARD	50.00	22.00

STATED PRINT RUN 25 SERIAL #'d SETS
RANDOM INSERTS IN PACKS

Card	MINT	NRMT
❑ AH Allan Houston H/R	100.00	45.00
❑ AW Antoine Walker H	100.00	45.00
❑ BD Baron Davis H	120.00	55.00
❑ CB Charles Barkley H/R		
❑ CM Corey Maggette H/R	150.00	70.00
❑ CW Chris Webber H	250.00	110.00
❑ DG Devean George H	60.00	27.00
❑ DR David Robinson H/R	150.00	70.00
❑ GP Gary Payton H	120.00	55.00
❑ HO Hakeem Olajuwon H	120.00	55.00
❑ JB Jonathan Bender H	150.00	70.00
❑ JS John Stockton H/R		
❑ JT Jason Terry H/R	60.00	27.00
❑ JW Jason Williams H	250.00	110.00
❑ KG Kevin Garnett H	400.00	180.00
❑ KM Karl Malone H	150.00	70.00
❑ KT Kenny Thomas H/R	60.00	27.00
❑ MF Michael Finley H/R	120.00	55.00
❑ PP Paul Pierce H/R	200.00	90.00
❑ RM Reggie Miller H	250.00	110.00
❑ SA Shareef Abdur-Rahim H/R		
❑ SF Steve Francis H	500.00	220.00
❑ SO Shaquille O'Neal H/R	200.00	90.00
❑ TB Terrell Brandon H	50.00	22.00
❑ WS Wally Szczerbiak H/R	150.00	70.00

1999-00 Black Diamond Diamonation

	MINT	NRMT
COMPLETE SET (10)	15.00	6.75
COMMON CARD (D1-D10)	.60	.25

STATED ODDS 1:8 HOB/RET

Card	MINT	NRMT
❑ D1 Vince Carter	6.00	2.70
❑ D2 Tim Duncan	3.00	1.35
❑ D3 Kobe Bryant	5.00	2.20
❑ D4 Stephon Marbury	1.25	.55
❑ D5 Ron Mercer	.75	.35
❑ D6 Allen Iverson	2.50	1.10
❑ D7 Shareef Abdur-Rahim	1.25	.55
❑ D8 Kevin Garnett	4.00	1.80
❑ D9 Jason Kidd	2.00	.90
❑ D10 Allan Houston	.60	.25

1999-00 Black Diamond Jordan Diamond Gallery

	MINT	NRMT
COMPLETE SET (10)	40.00	18.00
COMMON CARD (DG1-DG10)	5.00	2.20

STATED ODDS 1:12 HOB/RET
UNPRICED GOLD VERSION SERIAL #'d TO 1

Card	MINT	NRMT
❑ DG1 Michael Jordan	5.00	2.20
❑ DG2 Michael Jordan	5.00	2.20
❑ DG3 Michael Jordan	5.00	2.20
❑ DG4 Michael Jordan	5.00	2.20
❑ DG5 Michael Jordan	5.00	2.20
❑ DG6 Michael Jordan	5.00	2.20
❑ DG7 Michael Jordan	5.00	2.20
❑ DG8 Michael Jordan	5.00	2.20
❑ DG9 Michael Jordan	5.00	2.20
❑ DG10 Michael Jordan	5.00	2.20

1999-00 Black Diamond Might

	MINT	NRMT
COMPLETE SET (20)	10.00	4.50
COMMON CARD (DM1-20)	.30	.14

UNLISTED STARS	.50	.23
STATED ODDS 1:3 HOB/RET		

❑ DM1 Shaquille O'Neal	2.50	1.10
❑ DM2 Allan Houston	.50	.23
❑ DM3 Keith Van Horn	1.00	.45
❑ DM4 Antonie Walker	.60	.25
❑ DM5 Latrell Sprewell	1.00	.45
❑ DM6 Hakeem Olajuwon	.75	.35
❑ DM7 David Robinson	.75	.35
❑ DM8 Antonio McDyess	.50	.23
❑ DM9 Shawn Kemp	.75	.35
❑ DM10 Ray Allen	.50	.23
❑ DM11 Karl Malone	.75	.35
❑ DM12 Tim Hardaway	.50	.23
❑ DM13 Mike Bibby	.60	.25
❑ DM14 Antawn Jamison	1.00	.45
❑ DM15 Dikembe Mutombo	.30	.14
❑ DM16 Michael Finley	.50	.23
❑ DM17 Juwan Howard	.30	.14
❑ DM18 Maurice Taylor	.50	.23
❑ DM19 Gary Payton	.75	.35
❑ DM20 Shareef Abdur-Rahim	1.00	.45

1999-00 Black Diamond Myriad

	MINT	NRMT
COMPLETE SET (10)	40.00	18.00
COMMON CARD (M1-M10)	2.00	.90
STATED ODDS 1:24 HOB/RET		

Card	MINT	NRMT
❑ M1 Kobe Bryant	10.00	4.50
❑ M2 Tim Duncan	6.00	2.70
❑ M3 Kevin Garnett	8.00	3.60
❑ M4 Keith Van Horn	2.50	1.10
❑ M5 Vince Carter	12.00	5.50
❑ M6 Grant Hill	6.00	2.70
❑ M7 Anfernee Hardaway	4.00	1.80
❑ M8 Karl Malone	2.00	.90
❑ M9 Allen Iverson	5.00	2.20
❑ M10 Jason Williams	3.00	1.35

1999-00 Black Diamond Skills

	MINT	NRMT
COMPLETE SET (10)	20.00	9.00
COMMON CARD (DS1-10)	1.25	.55
STATED ODDS 1:24 HOB/RET		

Card	MINT	NRMT
❑ DS1 Stephon Marbury	2.50	1.10
❑ DS2 Grant Hill	6.00	2.70
❑ DS3 Reggie Miller	1.25	.55
❑ DS4 Jason Kidd	4.00	1.80
❑ DS5 Mike Bibby	1.50	.70
❑ DS6 John Stockton	1.25	.55
❑ DS7 Jason Williams	3.00	1.35
❑ DS8 Shaquille O'Neal	6.00	2.70
❑ DS9 Antonio McDyess	1.25	.55
❑ DS10 Hakeem Olajuwon	2.00	.90

1948 Bowman

	EX-MT	VG-E
COMPLETE SET (72)	8000.00	3600.00
COMMON CARD (1-36)	60.00	27.00
COMMON CARD (37-72)	90.00	40.00
PLAY (5/11/17/23/29/35)	50.00	22.00
PLAY (41/47/53/59/65/71)	75.00	34.00
LO SEMISTARS (1-36)	75.00	34.00
HI SEMISTARS (37-72)	125.00	55.00
CARDS PRICED IN EX-MT CONDITION		

Card	EX-MT	VG-E
❑ 1 Ernie Calverley RC !	200.00	60.00
❑ 2 Ralph Hamilton	60.00	27.00
❑ 3 Gale Bishop	60.00	27.00
❑ 4 Fred Lewis CO RC	75.00	34.00
❑ 5 Basketball Play Single cut off post	50.00	22.00
❑ 6 Bob Ferrick RC	75.00	34.00
❑ 7 John Logan	60.00	27.00
❑ 8 Mel Riebe	60.00	27.00
❑ 9 Andy Phillip RC	150.00	70.00
❑ 10 Bob Davies RC !	150.00	70.00
❑ 11 Basketball Play Single cut with return pass to post	50.00	22.00
❑ 12 Kenny Sailors RC	75.00	34.00
❑ 13 Paul Armstrong	60.00	27.00
❑ 14 Howard Dallmar RC	75.00	34.00
❑ 15 Bruce Hale RC	75.00	34.00
❑ 16 Sid Hertzberg	75.00	34.00
❑ 17 Basketball Play Single cut	50.00	22.00
❑ 18 Red Rocha	60.00	27.00
❑ 19 Eddie Ehlers	60.00	27.00
❑ 20 Ellis(Gene) Vance	60.00	27.00
❑ 21 Andrew(Fuzzy) Levane RC	75.00	34.00
❑ 22 Earl Shannon	60.00	27.00
❑ 23 Basketball Play Double cut off post	50.00	22.00
❑ 24 Leo(Crystal) Klier	60.00	27.00
❑ 25 George Senesky	60.00	27.00
❑ 26 Price Brookfield	60.00	27.00
❑ 27 John Norlander	60.00	27.00
❑ 28 Don Putman	60.00	27.00
❑ 29 Basketball Play Double post	50.00	22.00
❑ 30 Jack Garfinkel	60.00	27.00
❑ 31 Chuck Gilmur	60.00	27.00
❑ 32 William Holzman RC !	350.00	160.00
❑ 33 Jack Smiley	60.00	27.00
❑ 34 Joe Fulks RC !	350.00	160.00
❑ 35 Basketball Play Screen play	50.00	22.00
❑ 36 Hal Tidrick	60.00	27.00
❑ 37 Don(Swede) Carlson	90.00	40.00
❑ 38 Buddy Jeanette RC CO	135.00	60.00
❑ 39 Ray Kuka	90.00	40.00
❑ 40 Stan Miasek	90.00	40.00
❑ 41 Basketball Play Double screen	75.00	34.00
❑ 42 George Nostrand	90.00	40.00
❑ 43 Chuck Halbert RC	125.00	55.00
❑ 44 Arnie Johnson	90.00	40.00
❑ 45 Bob Doll	90.00	40.00
❑ 46 Horace McKinney RC	135.00	60.00
❑ 47 Basketball Play Out of bounds	75.00	34.00
❑ 48 Ed Sadowski	125.00	55.00
❑ 49 Bob Kinney	90.00	40.00
❑ 50 Charles(Hawk) Black	90.00	40.00
❑ 51 Jack Dwan	75.00	34.00
❑ 52 Cornelius Simmons RC	125.00	55.00
❑ 53 Basketball Play Out of bounds	75.00	34.00
❑ 54 Bud Palmer RC	150.00	70.00
❑ 55 Max Zaslofsky RC !	300.00	135.00
❑ 56 Lee Roy Robbins	90.00	40.00
❑ 57 Arthur Spector	90.00	40.00
❑ 58 Arnie Risen RC	175.00	80.00
❑ 59 Basketball Play Out of bounds play	75.00	34.00
❑ 60 Ariel Maughan	90.00	40.00
❑ 61 Dick O'Keefe	90.00	40.00
❑ 62 Herman Schaefer	90.00	40.00
❑ 63 John Mahnken	90.00	40.00
❑ 64 Tommy Byrnes	90.00	40.00
❑ 65 Basketball Play Held ball	75.00	34.00
❑ 66 Jim Pollard RC !	400.00	180.00
❑ 67 Lee Mogus	90.00	40.00
❑ 68 Lee Knorek	90.00	40.00
❑ 69 George Mikan RC !	3000.00	1350.00
❑ 70 Walter Budko	90.00	40.00
❑ 71 Basketball Play Guards Play	75.00	34.00
❑ 72 Carl Braun RC !	500.00	150.00

1996-97 Bowman's Best

	MINT	NRMT
COMPLETE SET (125)	60.00	27.00
COMMON CARD (1-80/TB1-20)	.25	.11
COMMON CARD (R1-R25)	.50	.23
SEMISTARS	.40	.18
SEMISTARS RC	.60	.25
UNLISTED STARS	.60	.25
UNLISTED STARS RC	1.00	.45
SUBSET CARDS HALF VALUE OF BASE CARDS		

Card	MINT	NRMT
❑ 1 Scottie Pippen	2.00	.90
❑ 2 Glen Rice	.40	.18
❑ 3 Bryant Stith	.25	.11
❑ 4 Dino Radja	.25	.11
❑ 5 Horace Grant	.40	.18
❑ 6 Mahmoud Abdul-Rauf	.25	.11
❑ 7 Mookie Blaylock	.25	.11
❑ 8 Clifford Robinson	.25	.11
❑ 9 Vin Baker	.40	.18
❑ 10 Grant Hill	3.00	1.35
❑ 11 Terrell Brandon	.40	.18
❑ 12 P.J. Brown	.25	.11
❑ 13 Kendall Gill	.40	.18
❑ 14 Brent Barry	.25	.11
❑ 15 Hakeem Olajuwon	1.00	.45
❑ 16 Allan Houston	.60	.25

		MINT	NRMT
❑ 17	Elden Campbell	.25	.11
❑ 18	Latrell Sprewell	1.25	.55
❑ 19	Jerry Stackhouse	.60	.25
❑ 20	Robert Horry	.25	.11
❑ 21	Mitch Richmond	.60	.25
❑ 22	Gary Payton	1.00	.45
❑ 23	Rik Smits	.25	.11
❑ 24	Jim Jackson	.25	.11
❑ 25	Damon Stoudamire	1.00	.45
❑ 26	Bobby Phills	.25	.11
❑ 27	Chris Webber	2.00	.90
❑ 28	Shawn Bradley	.25	.11
❑ 29	Arvydas Sabonis	.40	.18
❑ 30	John Stockton	.60	.25
❑ 31	Anfernee Hardaway	2.00	.90
❑ 32	Christian Laettner	.40	.18
❑ 33	Juwan Howard	.40	.18
❑ 34	Anthony Mason	.40	.18
❑ 35	Tom Gugliotta	.40	.18
❑ 36	Avery Johnson	.25	.11
❑ 37	Cedric Ceballos	.25	.11
❑ 38	Patrick Ewing	.60	.25
❑ 39	Joe Smith	.60	.25
❑ 40	Dennis Rodman	1.25	.55
❑ 41	Alonzo Mourning	.60	.25
❑ 42	Kevin Garnett	4.00	1.80
❑ 43	Antonio McDyess	1.00	.45
❑ 44	Detlef Schrempf	.40	.18
❑ 45	Reggie Miller	.60	.25
❑ 46	Charles Barkley	1.00	.45
❑ 47	Derrick Coleman	.40	.18
❑ 48	Brian Grant	.60	.25
❑ 49	Kenny Anderson	.40	.18
❑ 50	Otis Thorpe	.25	.11
❑ 51	Rod Strickland	.40	.18
❑ 52	Eric Williams	.25	.11
❑ 53	Rony Seikaly	.25	.11
❑ 54	Danny Manning	.40	.18
❑ 55	Karl Malone	1.00	.45
❑ 56	B.J. Armstrong	.25	.11
❑ 57	Greg Anthony	.25	.11
❑ 58	Larry Johnson	.40	.18
❑ 59	Loy Vaught	.25	.11
❑ 60	Sean Elliott	.25	.11
❑ 61	Dikembe Mutombo	.40	.18
❑ 62	Clarence Weatherspoon	.25	.11
❑ 63	Jamal Mashburn	.40	.18
❑ 64	Bryant Reeves	.25	.11
❑ 65	Vlade Divac	.25	.11
❑ 66	Shawn Kemp	1.00	.45
❑ 67	LaPhonso Ellis	.25	.11
❑ 68	Tyrone Hill	.25	.11
❑ 69	David Robinson	1.00	.45
❑ 70	Shaquille O'Neal	3.00	1.35
❑ 71	Doug Christie	.25	.11
❑ 72	Jayson Williams	.40	.18
❑ 73	Michael Finley	.75	.35
❑ 74	Tim Hardaway	.60	.25
❑ 75	Clyde Drexler	.60	.25
❑ 76	Joe Dumars	.60	.25
❑ 77	Glenn Robinson	.60	.25
❑ 78	Dana Barros	.25	.11
❑ 79	Jason Kidd	2.00	.90
❑ 80	Michael Jordan	8.00	3.60
❑ R1	Allen Iverson RC	10.00	4.50
❑ R2	Stephon Marbury RC	5.00	2.20
❑ R3	Shareef Abdur-Rahim RC	5.00	2.20
❑ R4	Marcus Camby RC	2.50	1.10
❑ R5	Ray Allen RC	3.00	1.35
❑ R6	Antoine Walker RC	3.00	1.35
❑ R7	Lorenzen Wright RC	.60	.25
❑ R8	Kerry Kittles RC	2.00	.90
❑ R9	Samaki Walker RC	.50	.23
❑ R10	Tony Delk RC	.60	.25
❑ R11	Vitaly Potapenko RC	.50	.23
❑ R12	Jerome Williams RC	1.50	.70
❑ R13	Todd Fuller RC	.50	.23
❑ R14	Erick Dampier RC	.60	.25
❑ R15	Derek Fisher RC	1.50	.70
❑ R16	Donald Whiteside RC	.50	.23
❑ R17	John Wallace RC	1.00	.45
❑ R18	Steve Nash RC	.60	.25
❑ R19	Brian Evans RC	.50	.23
❑ R20	Jermaine O'Neal RC	2.00	.90
❑ R21	Roy Rogers RC	.50	.23
❑ R22	Priest Lauderdale RC	.50	.23
❑ R23	Kobe Bryant RC	30.00	13.50
❑ R24	Martin Muursepp RC	.50	.23
❑ R25	Zydrunas Ilgauskas RC	3.00	1.35
❑ TB1	Avery Johnson RET	.25	.11
❑ TB2	Chris Webber RET	.75	.35
❑ TB3	Sean Elliott RET	.25	.11
❑ TB4	Joe Dumars RET	.40	.18
❑ TB5	Grant Hill RET	2.00	.90
❑ TB6	Gary Payton RET	.60	.25
❑ TB7	Shawn Kemp RET	.60	.25
❑ TB8	Shaquille O'Neal	1.25	.55
❑ TB9	Eddie Jones RET	.60	.25
❑ TB10	John Wallace RET	.40	.18
❑ TB11	Patrick Ewing RET	.40	.18
❑ TB12	Jerry Stackhouse RET	.40	.18
❑ TB13	Allen Iverson RET	3.00	1.35
❑ TB14	Latrell Sprewell RET	.60	.25
❑ TB15	Dino Radja RET	.25	.11
❑ TB16	David Wesley RET	.25	.11
❑ TB17	Joe Smith RET	.40	.18
❑ TB18	D.Stoudamire RET	.60	.25
❑ TB19	Marcus Camby RET	.75	.35
❑ TB20	Juwan Howard RET	.25	.11

1996-97 Bowman's Best Refractors

	MINT	NRMT
COMPLETE SET (125)	600.00	275.00
COMMON CARD (1-80/TB1-20)	1.50	.70
COMMON CARD (R1-R25)	2.50	1.10

*STARS: 4X TO 10X BASE CARD HI
*RCs: 2X TO 5X BASE HI
STATED ODDS 1:12 HOBBY, 1:20 RETAIL

1996-97 Bowman's Best Atomic Refractors

	MINT	NRMT
COMPLETE SET (125)	2000.00	900.00
COMMON CARD (1-80/TB1-20)	5.00	2.20
COMMON CARD (R1-R25)	5.00	2.20
SEMISTARS	8.00	3.60
UNLISTED STARS	12.00	5.50

*STARS: 8X TO 20X HI COLUMN
*RCs: 4X TO 10X HI
SUBSET CARDS HALF VALUE OF BASE CARDS
STATED ODDS 1:24 HOBBY, 1:40 RETAIL

		MINT	NRMT
❑ R1	Allen Iverson	100.00	45.00
❑ R2	Stephon Marbury	60.00	27.00
❑ R3	Shareef Abdur-Rahim	60.00	27.00
❑ R4	Marcus Camby	30.00	13.50
❑ R5	Ray Allen	40.00	18.00
❑ R6	Antoine Walker	40.00	18.00
❑ R8	Kerry Kittles	20.00	9.00
❑ R15	Derek Fisher	15.00	6.75
❑ R17	John Wallace	10.00	4.50
❑ R18	Steve Nash	6.00	2.70
❑ R20	Jermaine O'Neal	20.00	9.00
❑ R23	Kobe Bryant	250.00	110.00
❑ R25	Zydrunas Ilgauskas	20.00	9.00

1996-97 Bowman's Best Cuts

	MINT	NRMT
COMPLETE SET (20)	150.00	70.00
COMMON CARD (BC1-BC20)	3.00	1.35

STATED ODDS 1:24 HOBBY, 1:40 RETAIL
*REFRACTORS: .75X TO 2X HI COLUMN
REF: STATED ODDS 1:96 HOB, 1:160 RET
*ATOMIC REFRACTORS: 1.5X TO 4X HI
ATO: STATED ODDS 1:192 HOB, 1:320 RET

		MINT	NRMT
❑ BC1	Karl Malone	5.00	2.20
❑ BC2	Michael Jordan	40.00	18.00
❑ BC3	Juwan Howard	3.00	1.35
❑ BC4	Charles Barkley	5.00	2.20
❑ BC5	Jerry Stackhouse	3.00	1.35
❑ BC6	Anfernee Hardaway	10.00	4.50
❑ BC7	Shaquille O'Neal	15.00	6.75
❑ BC8	Alonzo Mourning	3.00	1.35
❑ BC9	Shawn Kemp	5.00	2.20
❑ BC10	Scottie Pippen	10.00	4.50
❑ BC11	David Robinson	5.00	2.20
❑ BC12	Kevin Garnett	20.00	9.00
❑ BC13	Patrick Ewing	3.00	1.35
❑ BC14	Hakeem Olajuwon	5.00	2.20
❑ BC15	Damon Stoudamire	5.00	2.20
❑ BC16	Grant Hill	15.00	6.75
❑ BC17	Dennis Rodman	6.00	2.70
❑ BC18	Chris Webber	10.00	4.50
❑ BC19	Gary Payton	5.00	2.20
❑ BC20	John Stockton	3.00	1.35

1996-97 Bowman's Best Honor Roll

	MINT	NRMT
COMPLETE SET (10)	120.00	55.00
COMMON CARD (HR1-HR10)	6.00	2.70

STATED ODDS 1:48 HOBBY, 1:80 RETAIL
*REFRACTORS: 1.25X TO 3X HI COLUMN
REF: STATED ODDS 1:192 HOB, 1:320 RET
*ATOMIC REFRACTORS: 2.5X TO 6X HI
ATO: STATED ODDS 1:384 HOB, 1:640 RET

		MINT	NRMT
❑ HR1	Charles Barkley John Stockton	10.00	4.50
❑ HR2	Michael Jordan Hakeem Olajuwon	50.00	22.00
❑ HR3	Patrick Ewing Karl Malone	10.00	4.50
❑ HR4	Dennis Rodman Arvydas Sabonis	8.00	3.60

		MINT	NRMT
❑ HR5	Scottie Pippen David Robinson	20.00	9.00
❑ HR6	Glen Rice Shawn Kemp	6.00	2.70
❑ HR7	Shaquille O'Neal Alonzo Mourning	25.00	11.00
❑ HR8	Anfernee Hardaway Chris Webber	30.00	13.50
❑ HR9	Grant Hill Juwan Howard	15.00	6.75
❑ HR10	Kevin Garnett Jerry Stackhouse	30.00	13.50

1996-97 Bowman's Best Picks

	MINT	NRMT
COMPLETE SET (10)	60.00	27.00
COMMON CARD (BP1-BP10)	1.25	.55
SEMISTARS	2.00	.90
UNLISTED STARS	3.00	1.35

STATED ODDS 1:24 HOBBY, 1:40 RETAIL
*REFRACTORS: .75X TO 2X HI COLUMN
REF: STATED ODDS 1:96 HOB, 1:160 RET
*ATOMIC REFRACTORS: 1.5X TO 4X HI
ATO: STATED ODDS 1:192 HOB, 1:320 RET

		MINT	NRMT
❑ BP1	Stephon Marbury	10.00	4.50
❑ BP2	Marcus Camby	5.00	2.20
❑ BP3	Lorenzen Wright	1.25	.55
❑ BP4	John Wallace	2.00	.90
❑ BP5	Ray Allen	6.00	2.70
❑ BP6	Kerry Kittles	3.00	1.35
❑ BP7	Shareef Abdur-Rahim	10.00	4.50
❑ BP8	Todd Fuller	1.25	.55
❑ BP9	Allen Iverson	15.00	6.75
❑ BP10	Kobe Bryant	30.00	13.50

1996-97 Bowman's Best Shots

	MINT	NRMT
COMPLETE SET (10)	50.00	22.00
COMMON CARD (BS1-BS10)	2.50	1.10

STATED ODDS 1:12 HOBBY, 1:20 RETAIL
*REFRACTORS: .75X TO 2X HI COLUMN
REF: STATED ODDS 1:48 HOB, 1:80 RET
*ATOMIC REFRACTORS: 1.5X TO 4X HI
ATO: STATED ODDS 1:96 HOB, 1:160 RET

		MINT	NRMT
❑ BS1	Scottie Pippen	5.00	2.20
❑ BS2	Gary Payton	2.50	1.10
❑ BS3	Shaquille O'Neal	8.00	3.60
❑ BS4	Hakeem Olajuwon	2.50	1.10
❑ BS5	Kevin Garnett	10.00	4.50
❑ BS6	Michael Jordan	20.00	9.00
❑ BS7	Anfernee Hardaway	5.00	2.20
❑ BS8	Grant Hill	8.00	3.60
❑ BS9	Shawn Kemp	2.50	1.10
❑ BS10	Dennis Rodman	3.00	1.35

1997-98 Bowman's Best

	MINT	NRMT
COMPLETE SET (125)	50.00	22.00
COMMON CARD (1-100)	.20	.09
COMMON CARD (101-125)	.40	.18
SEMISTARS	.25	.11
SEMISTARS RC	.60	.25
UNLISTED STARS	.40	.18
UNLISTED STARS RC	.75	.35

SUBSET CARDS HALF VALUE OF BASE CARDS

		MINT	NRMT
❑ 1	Scottie Pippen	1.25	.55
❑ 2	Michael Finley	.40	.18
❑ 3	David Wesley	.20	.09
❑ 4	Brent Barry	.20	.09
❑ 5	Gary Payton	.60	.25
❑ 6	Christian Laettner	.25	.11
❑ 7	Grant Hill	2.00	.90
❑ 8	Glenn Robinson	.25	.11
❑ 9	Reggie Miller	.40	.18
❑ 10	Tyus Edney	.20	.09
❑ 11	Jim Jackson	.20	.09
❑ 12	John Stockton	.40	.18
❑ 13	Karl Malone	.60	.25
❑ 14	Samaki Walker	.20	.09
❑ 15	Bryant Stith	.20	.09
❑ 16	Clyde Drexler	.40	.18
❑ 17	Danny Ferry	.20	.09
❑ 18	Shawn Bradley	.20	.09
❑ 19	Bryant Reeves	.20	.09
❑ 20	John Starks	.20	.09
❑ 21	Joe Dumars	.40	.18
❑ 22	Checklist	.20	.09
❑ 23	Antonio McDyess	.50	.23
❑ 24	Jeff Hornacek	.25	.11
❑ 25	Terrell Brandon	.25	.11
❑ 26	Kendall Gill	.25	.11
❑ 27	LaPhonso Ellis	.20	.09
❑ 28	Shaquille O'Neal	2.00	.90
❑ 29	Mahmoud Abdul-Rauf	.20	.09
❑ 30	Eric Williams	.20	.09
❑ 31	Lorenzen Wright	.20	.09
❑ 32	Shareef Abdur-Rahim	1.25	.55
❑ 33	Avery Johnson	.20	.09
❑ 34	Juwan Howard	.25	.11
❑ 35	Vin Baker	.25	.11
❑ 36	Dikembe Mutombo	.25	.11
❑ 37	Patrick Ewing	.40	.18
❑ 38	Allen Iverson	2.00	.90
❑ 39	Alonzo Mourning	.40	.18
❑ 40	Travis Knight	.20	.09
❑ 41	Ray Allen	.60	.25
❑ 42	Detlef Schrempf	.25	.11
❑ 43	Kevin Johnson	.25	.11
❑ 44	David Robinson	.60	.25
❑ 45	Tim Hardaway	.40	.18
❑ 46	Shawn Kemp	.60	.25
❑ 47	Marcus Camby	.50	.23
❑ 48	Rony Seikaly	.20	.09
❑ 49	Eddie Jones	.75	.35
❑ 50	Rik Smits	.20	.09
❑ 51	Jayson Williams	.25	.11
❑ 52	Malik Sealy	.20	.09
❑ 53	Chris Mullin	.40	.18
❑ 54	Larry Johnson	.25	.11
❑ 55	Isaiah Rider	.25	.11
❑ 56	Dennis Rodman	.75	.35
❑ 57	Bob Sura	.20	.09
❑ 58	Hakeem Olajuwon	.60	.25
❑ 59	Steve Smith	.25	.11
❑ 60	Michael Jordan	5.00	2.20
❑ 61	Jerry Stackhouse	.25	.11
❑ 62	Joe Smith	.25	.11
❑ 63	Walt Williams	.20	.09
❑ 64	Anthony Peeler	.20	.09
❑ 65	Charles Barkley	.60	.25
❑ 66	Erick Dampier	.20	.09
❑ 67	Horace Grant	.25	.11
❑ 68	Anthony Mason	.25	.11
❑ 69	Anfernee Hardaway	1.25	.55
❑ 70	Elden Campbell	.20	.09
❑ 71	Cedric Ceballos	.20	.09
❑ 72	Allan Houston	.40	.18
❑ 73	Kerry Kittles	.40	.18
❑ 74	Antoine Walker	.75	.35
❑ 75	Sean Elliott	.20	.09
❑ 76	Jamal Mashburn	.25	.11
❑ 77	Mitch Richmond	.40	.18
❑ 78	Damon Stoudamire	.50	.23
❑ 79	Tom Gugliotta	.25	.11
❑ 80	Jason Kidd	1.25	.55
❑ 81	Chris Webber	1.25	.55
❑ 82	Glen Rice	.25	.11
❑ 83	Loy Vaught	.20	.09
❑ 84	Olden Polynice	.20	.09
❑ 85	Kenny Anderson	.25	.11
❑ 86	Stephon Marbury	1.25	.55
❑ 87	Calbert Cheaney	.20	.09
❑ 88	Kobe Bryant	3.00	1.35
❑ 89	Arvydas Sabonis	.25	.11
❑ 90	Kevin Garnett	2.50	1.10
❑ 91	Grant Hill BP	1.25	.55
❑ 92	Clyde Drexler BP	.25	.11
❑ 93	Patrick Ewing BP	.25	.11
❑ 94	Shawn Kemp BP	.40	.18
❑ 95	Shaquille O'Neal BP	.75	.35
❑ 96	Michael Jordan BP	2.50	1.10
❑ 97	Karl Malone BP	.40	.18
❑ 98	Allen Iverson BP	.75	.35
❑ 99	Shareef Abdur-Rahim BP	.60	.25
❑ 100	Dikembe Mutombo BP	.20	.09
❑ 101	Bobby Jackson RC	.60	.25
❑ 102	Tony Battie RC	.75	.35
❑ 103	Keith Booth RC	.40	.18
❑ 104	Keith Van Horn RC	4.00	1.80
❑ 105	Paul Grant RC	.40	.18
❑ 106	Tim Duncan RC	10.00	4.50
❑ 107	Scot Pollard RC	.60	.25
❑ 108	Maurice Taylor RC	1.50	.70
❑ 109	Antonio Daniels RC	.75	.35
❑ 110	Austin Croshere RC	2.00	.90
❑ 111	Tracy McGrady RC	8.00	3.60
❑ 112	Charles O'Bannon RC	.40	.18
❑ 113	Rodrick Rhodes RC	.40	.18

❑ 114 Johnny Taylor RC	.40	.18
❑ 115 Danny Fortson RC	.75	.35
❑ 116 Chauncey Billups RC	1.00	.45
❑ 117 Tim Thomas RC	2.50	1.10
❑ 118 Derek Anderson RC	2.00	.90
❑ 119 Ed Gray RC	.40	.18
❑ 120 Jacque Vaughn RC	.60	.25
❑ 121 Kelvin Cato RC	.75	.35
❑ 122 Tariq Abdul-Wahad RC	.60	.25
❑ 123 Ron Mercer RC	2.50	1.10
❑ 124 Brevin Knight RC	1.25	.55
❑ 125 Adonal Foyle RC	.60	.25

1997-98 Bowman's Best Refractors

	MINT	NRMT
COMPLETE SET (125)	500.00	220.00
COMMON CARD (1-125)	2.00	.90

*STARS: 4X TO 10X BASE CARD HI
*RCs: 1.5X TO 4X BASE HI
STATED ODDS 1:12 HOB, 1:20 RET

1997-98 Bowman's Best Atomic Refractors

	MINT	NRMT
COMPLETE SET (125)	1500.00	700.00
COMMON CARD (1-125)	4.00	1.80

*STARS: 8X TO 20X BASE CARD HI
*RCs: 3X TO 8X BASE HI
STATED ODDS 1:24 HOB, 1:40 RET

1997-98 Bowman's Best Autographs

	MINT	NRMT
COMPLETE SET (11)	350.00	160.00
COMMON CARD	12.00	5.50

STATED ODDS 1:373 HOB, 1:745 RET
*REFRACTORS: 1X TO 2.5X HI COLUMN
REF: STATED ODDS 1:1,987 H, 1:3,974 R
*ATOMIC REFRACTORS: 1.5X TO 4X HI
ATO: STATED ODDS 1:5,961 H, 1:11,922 R

❑ 8 Glenn Robinson	30.00	13.50
❑ 13 Karl Malone	60.00	27.00
❑ 36 Dikembe Mutombo	15.00	6.75
❑ 59 Steve Smith	15.00	6.75
❑ 77 Mitch Richmond	25.00	11.00
❑ 102 Tony Battie	12.00	5.50
❑ 104 Keith Van Horn	60.00	27.00
❑ 116 Chauncey Billups	20.00	9.00
❑ 123 Ron Mercer	40.00	18.00
❑ 125 Adonal Foyle	20.00	9.00
❑ KM Karl Malone MVP	80.00	36.00

1997-98 Bowman's Best Cuts

	MINT	NRMT
COMPLETE SET (10)	75.00	34.00
COMMON CARD (BC1-BC10)	3.00	1.35

STATED ODDS 1:24 HOB, 1:40 RET
*REFRACTORS: .6X TO 1.5X HI COLUMN
REF: STATED ODDS 1:48 HOB, 1:80 RET

*ATOMIC REFRACTORS: 1.25X TO 3X HI
ATO: STATED ODDS 1:96 HOB, 1:160 RET

❑ BC1 Vin Baker	3.00	1.35
❑ BC2 Patrick Ewing	3.00	1.35
❑ BC3 Scottie Pippen	10.00	4.50
❑ BC4 Karl Malone	5.00	2.20
❑ BC5 Kevin Garnett	20.00	9.00
❑ BC6 Anfernee Hardaway	10.00	4.50
❑ BC7 Shawn Kemp	5.00	2.20
❑ BC8 Charles Barkley	5.00	2.20
❑ BC9 Stephon Marbury	10.00	4.50
❑ BC10 Shaquille O'Neal	15.00	6.75

1997-98 Bowman's Best Mirror Image

	MINT	NRMT
COMPLETE SET (10)	150.00	70.00
COMMON CARD (MI1-MI10)	6.00	2.70

STATED ODDS 1:48 HOB, 1:80 RET
*REFRACTORS: .6X TO 1.5X HI COLUMN
REF: STATED ODDS 1:96 HOB, 1:160 RET
*ATOMIC REFRACTORS: 1.25X TO 3X HI
ATO: STATED ODDS 1:192 HOB, 1:320 RET

❑ MI1 Michael Jordan Ron Mercer Stephon Marbury Gary Payton	50.00	22.00
❑ MI2 Tim Thomas Chris Webber Shaquille O'Neal Adonal Foyle	20.00	9.00
❑ MI3 Tim Hardaway Allen Iverson Bobby Jackson Jason Kidd	20.00	9.00
❑ MI4 Scottie Pippen Keith Van Horn Kobe Bryant Cedric Ceballos	40.00	18.00
❑ MI5 Grant Hill Tracy McGrady Shareef Abdur-Rahim Kevin Garnett	40.00	18.00
❑ MI6 Shawn Kemp Marcus Camby Tim Duncan David Robinson	25.00	11.00
❑ MI7 Ray Allen Steve Smith Shandon Anderson Sean Elliott	6.00	2.70
❑ MI8 Chauncey Billups Terrell Brandon Antonio Daniels Kevin Johnson	6.00	2.70
❑ MI9 Kerry Kittles Reggie Miller Tony Battie Hakeem Olajuwon	6.00	2.70
❑ MI10 Larry Johnson Antoine Walker Maurice Taylor Vin Baker	6.00	2.70

1997-98 Bowman's Best Picks

	MINT	NRMT
COMPLETE SET (10)	30.00	13.50
COMMON CARD (BP1-BP10)	2.00	.90
UNLISTED STARS	3.00	1.35

STATED ODDS 1:24 HOB, 1:40 RET
*REFRACTORS: .6X TO 1.5X HI COLUMN
REF: STATED ODDS 1:48 HOB, 1:80 RET
*ATOMIC REFRACTORS: 1.25X TO 3X HI
ATO: STATED ODDS 1:96 HOB, 1:160 RET

❑ BP1 Adonal Foyle	2.00	.90
❑ BP2 Maurice Taylor	3.00	1.35
❑ BP3 Austin Croshere	4.00	1.80
❑ BP4 Tracy McGrady	15.00	6.75
❑ BP5 Antonio Daniels	3.00	1.35
❑ BP6 Tony Battie	2.00	.90
❑ BP7 Chauncey Billups	3.00	1.35
❑ BP8 Tim Duncan	15.00	6.75
❑ BP9 Ron Mercer	5.00	2.20
❑ BP10 Keith Van Horn	8.00	3.60

1997-98 Bowman's Best Techniques

	MINT	NRMT
COMPLETE SET (10)	40.00	18.00
COMMON CARD (T1-T10)	1.00	.45
UNLISTED STARS	1.50	.70

STATED ODDS 1:12 HOB, 1:20 RET
*REFRACTORS: 1X TO 2.5X HI COLUMN

REF: STATED ODDS 1:48 HOB, 1:80 RET
*ATOMIC REFRACTORS: 2X TO 5X HI
ATO: STATED ODDS 1:96 HOB, 1:160 RET

❑ T1 Dikembe Mutombo	1.00	.45
❑ T2 Michael Jordan	20.00	9.00
❑ T3 Grant Hill	8.00	3.60
❑ T4 Kobe Bryant	12.00	5.50
❑ T5 Gary Payton	2.50	1.10
❑ T6 Glen Rice	1.00	.45
❑ T7 Dennis Rodman	3.00	1.35
❑ T8 Hakeem Olajuwon	2.50	1.10
❑ T9 Allen Iverson	8.00	3.60
❑ T10 John Stockton	1.50	.70

1998-99 Bowman's Best

	MINT	NRMT
COMPLETE SET (125)	120.00	55.00
COMPLETE SET w/o SP (100)	20.00	9.00
COMMON CARD (1-100)	.15	.07
COMMON CARD (101-125)	1.00	.45
SEMISTARS	.20	.09
SEMISTARS RC	1.25	.55
UNLISTED STARS	.40	.18
UNLISTED STARS RC	2.00	.90

ROOKIES STATED ODDS 1:4

❑ 1 Jason Kidd	1.25	.55
❑ 2 Dikembe Mutombo	.20	.09
❑ 3 Chris Mullin	.40	.18
❑ 4 Terrell Brandon	.20	.09
❑ 5 Cedric Ceballos	.15	.07
❑ 6 Rod Strickland	.20	.09
❑ 7 Darrell Armstrong	.20	.09
❑ 8 Anfernee Hardaway	1.25	.55
❑ 9 Eddie Jones	.75	.35
❑ 10 Allen Iverson	1.50	.70
❑ 11 Kenny Anderson	.20	.09
❑ 12 Toni Kukoc	.50	.23
❑ 13 Lawrence Funderburke	.15	.07
❑ 14 P.J. Brown	.15	.07
❑ 15 Jeff Hornacek	.20	.09
❑ 16 Mookie Blaylock	.15	.07
❑ 17 Avery Johnson	.15	.07
❑ 18 Donyell Marshall	.15	.07
❑ 19 Detlef Schrempf	.20	.09
❑ 20 Joe Dumars	.40	.18
❑ 21 Charles Barkley	.60	.25
❑ 22 Maurice Taylor	.40	.18
❑ 23 Chauncey Billups	.15	.07
❑ 24 Lee Mayberry	.15	.07
❑ 25 Glen Rice	.20	.09
❑ 26 John Stockton	.40	.18
❑ 27 Rik Smits	.15	.07
❑ 28 Laphonso Ellis	.15	.07
❑ 29 Kerry Kittles	.20	.09
❑ 30 Damon Stoudamire	.40	.18
❑ 31 Kevin Garnett	2.50	1.10
❑ 32 Chris Mills	.15	.07
❑ 33 Kendall Gill	.20	.09
❑ 34 Tim Thomas	.60	.25
❑ 35 Derek Anderson	.50	.23
❑ 36 Billy Owens	.15	.07
❑ 37 Bobby Jackson	.15	.07
❑ 38 Allan Houston	.40	.18
❑ 39 Horace Grant	.20	.09
❑ 40 Ray Allen	.50	.23
❑ 41 Shawn Bradley	.15	.07
❑ 42 Arvydas Sabonis	.20	.09
❑ 43 Rex Chapman	.15	.07
❑ 44 Larry Johnson	.20	.09
❑ 45 Jayson Williams	.20	.09
❑ 46 Joe Smith	.20	.09
❑ 47 Ron Mercer	.60	.25
❑ 48 Rodney Rogers	.15	.07
❑ 49 Corliss Williamson	.15	.07
❑ 50 Tim Duncan	2.00	.90
❑ 51 Rasheed Wallace	.40	.18
❑ 52 Vin Baker	.20	.09
❑ 53 Reggie Miller	.40	.18
❑ 54 Patrick Ewing	.40	.18
❑ 55 Michael Finley	.40	.18
❑ 56 Bryant Reeves	.15	.07
❑ 57 Glenn Robinson	.20	.09
❑ 58 Walter McCarty	.15	.07
❑ 59 Brent Barry	.15	.07
❑ 60 John Starks	.15	.07
❑ 61 Clarence Weatherspoon	.15	.07
❑ 62 Calbert Cheaney	.15	.07
❑ 63 Lamond Murray	.15	.07
❑ 64 Zydrunas Ilgauskas	.15	.07
❑ 65 Anthony Mason	.20	.09
❑ 66 Bryon Russell	.15	.07
❑ 67 Dean Garrett	.15	.07
❑ 68 Tom Gugliotta	.20	.09
❑ 69 Dennis Rodman	.75	.35
❑ 70 Keith Van Horn	1.00	.45
❑ 71 Jamal Mashburn	.20	.09
❑ 72 Steve Smith	.20	.09
❑ 73 David Wesley	.15	.07
❑ 74 Chris Webber	1.25	.55
❑ 75 Isaiah Rider	.20	.09
❑ 76 Stephon Marbury	1.00	.45
❑ 77 Tim Hardaway	.40	.18
❑ 78 Jerry Stackhouse	.20	.09
❑ 79 John Wallace	.15	.07
❑ 80 Karl Malone	.60	.25
❑ 81 Juwan Howard	.20	.09
❑ 82 Antonio McDyess	.40	.18
❑ 83 David Robinson	.60	.25
❑ 84 Bobby Phills	.15	.07
❑ 85 Scottie Pippen	1.25	.55
❑ 86 Brevin Knight	.15	.07
❑ 87 Alan Henderson	.15	.07
❑ 88 Kobe Bryant	3.00	1.35
❑ 89 Shawn Kemp	.60	.25
❑ 90 Antoine Walker	.60	.25
❑ 91 Tracy McGrady	1.50	.70
❑ 92 Hakeem Olajuwon	.60	.25
❑ 93 Mark Jackson	.15	.07
❑ 94 Bison Dele	.15	.07
❑ 95 Gary Payton	.60	.25
❑ 96 Ron Harper	.20	.09
❑ 97 Shareef Abdur-Rahim	1.00	.45
❑ 98 Alonzo Mourning	.40	.18
❑ 99 Grant Hill	2.00	.90
❑ 100 Shaquille O'Neal	2.00	.90
❑ 101 Michael Olowokandi RC	3.00	1.35
❑ 102 Mike Bibby RC	6.00	2.70
❑ 103 Raef LaFrentz RC	4.00	1.80
❑ 104 Antawn Jamison RC	10.00	4.50
❑ 105 Vince Carter RC	50.00	22.00
❑ 106 Robert Traylor RC	2.00	.90
❑ 107 Jason Williams RC	12.00	5.50
❑ 108 Larry Hughes RC	12.00	5.50
❑ 109 Dirk Nowitzki RC	8.00	3.60
❑ 110 Paul Pierce RC	10.00	4.50
❑ 111 Bonzi Wells RC	8.00	3.60
❑ 112 Michael Doleac RC	2.00	.90
❑ 113 Keon Clark RC	2.00	.90
❑ 114 Michael Dickerson RC	4.00	1.80
❑ 115 Matt Harpring RC	2.00	.90
❑ 116 Bryce Drew RC	2.00	.90
❑ 117 Pat Garrity RC	1.25	.55
❑ 118 Roshown McLeod RC	1.25	.55
❑ 119 Ricky Davis RC	4.00	1.80
❑ 120 Brian Skinner RC	2.00	.90
❑ 121 Tyronn Lue RC	1.25	.55
❑ 122 Felipe Lopez RC	2.50	1.10
❑ 123 Al Harrington RC	6.00	2.70
❑ 124 Corey Benjamin RC	2.00	.90
❑ 125 Nazr Mohammed RC	1.00	.45

1998-99 Bowman's Best Refractors

	MINT	NRMT
COMPLETE SET (125)	800.00	350.00
COMMON CARD (1-100)	3.00	1.35
COMMON CARD (101-125)	2.50	1.10

*STARS: 8X TO 20X BASE CARD HI
*RCs: 1X TO 2.5X BASE HI
STATED PRINT RUN 400 SERIAL #'d SETS
STATED ODDS 1:25

1998-99 Bowman's Best Atomic Refractors

	MINT	NRMT
COMMON CARD (1-125)	6.00	2.70

*STARS: 15X TO 40X BASE CARD HI
*RCs: 2.5X TO 6X BASE HI
STATED PRINT RUN 100 SERIAL #'d SETS
STATED ODDS 1:100

1998-99 Bowman's Best Autographs

	MINT	NRMT
COMPLETE SET (9)	600.00	275.00
COMMON CARD (A1-A10)	15.00	6.75

VETERAN STATED ODDS 1:628
ROOKIE STATED ODDS 1:598
*REF: .75X TO 2X HI COLUMN
VETERAN REF: STATED ODDS 1:3358

RC REF: STATED ODDS 1:4172
*ATO.REF: 1.5X TO 3X HI
VETERAN ATO.REF: STATED ODDS 1:10073
RC ATO.REF: STATED ODDS 1:12515
CARD A7 DOES NOT EXIST

		MINT	NRMT
❑ A1	Kobe Bryant	125.00	55.00
❑ A2	Tim Duncan	120.00	55.00
❑ A3	Eddie Jones	40.00	18.00
❑ A4	Gary Payton	40.00	18.00
❑ A5	Antoine Walker	20.00	9.00
❑ A6	Antawn Jamison	40.00	18.00
❑ A7	Does not exist		
❑ A8	Mike Bibby	30.00	13.50
❑ A9	Vince Carter	350.00	160.00
❑ A10	Michael Doleac	15.00	6.75

1998-99 Bowman's Best Franchise Best

	MINT	NRMT
COMPLETE SET (10)	40.00	18.00
COMMON CARD (F1-F10)	2.00	.90
STATED ODDS 1:23		

		MINT	NRMT
❑ FB1	Michael Jordan	15.00	6.75
❑ FB2	Karl Malone	2.00	.90
❑ FB3	Antoine Walker	2.00	.90
❑ FB4	Grant Hill	6.00	2.70
❑ FB5	Kevin Garnett	8.00	3.60
❑ FB6	Shaquille O'Neal	6.00	2.70
❑ FB7	Gary Payton	2.00	.90
❑ FB8	Keith Van Horn	3.00	1.35
❑ FB9	Tim Duncan	6.00	2.70
❑ FB10	Allen Iverson	5.00	2.20

1998-99 Bowman's Best Mirror Image

	MINT	NRMT
COMPLETE SET (20)	50.00	22.00
COMMON CARD (MI1-MI20)	1.00	.45
SEMISTARS	1.50	.70
STATED ODDS 1:12		
COMP.REF.SET (20)	600.00	275.00
COMMON REF. (MI1-20)	12.00	5.50
*REF: 5X TO 12X HI COLUMN		
REF: PRINT RUN 100 SERIAL #'d SETS		
REF: STATED ODDS 1:628		
COMMON ATO.REF (MI1-20)	25.00	11.00
*ATO.REF: 12.5X TO 25X HI		
ATO.REF: PRINT RUN 25 SERIAL #'d SETS		
ATO.REF: STATED ODDS 1:2504		

		MINT	NRMT
❑ MI1	Tim Hardaway / Brevin Knight	1.50	.70
❑ MI2	Gary Payton / Damon Stoudamire	2.00	.90
❑ MI3	Anfernee Hardaway / Allen Iverson	8.00	3.60
❑ MI4	John Stockton / Stephon Marbury	4.00	1.80
❑ MI5	Ray Allen / Kerry Kittles	2.00	.90
❑ MI6	Eddie Jones / Kobe Bryant	10.00	4.50
❑ MI7	Steve Smith / Ron Mercer	2.00	.90
❑ MI8	Isaiah Rider / Michael Finley	1.50	.70
❑ MI9	Latrell Sprewell / Antoine Walker	4.00	1.80
❑ MI10	Detlef Schrempf / Shareef Abdur-Rahim	3.00	1.35
❑ MI11	Grant Hill / Tim Thomas	5.00	2.20
❑ MI12	Scottie Pippen / Kevin Garnett	8.00	3.60
❑ MI13	Jayson Williams / Juwan Howard	1.50	.70
❑ MI14	Vin Baker / Antonio McDyess	2.00	.90
❑ MI15	Shawn Kemp / Keith Van Horn	3.00	1.35
❑ MI16	Karl Malone / Tim Duncan	6.00	2.70
❑ MI17	Alonzo Mourning / Zydrunas Ilgauskas	1.50	.70
❑ MI18	Shaquille O'Neal / Bryant Reeves	6.00	2.70
❑ MI19	Dikembe Mutombo / Theo Ratliff	1.00	.45
❑ MI20	David Robinson / Greg Ostertag	2.00	.90

1998-99 Bowman's Best Performers

	MINT	NRMT
COMPLETE SET (10)	20.00	9.00
COMMON CARD (BP1-BP10)	.60	.25
SEMISTARS	1.00	.45
STATED ODDS 1:12		
COMP.REF.SET (10)	150.00	70.00
COMMON REF. (BP1-10)	5.00	2.20
*REF: 3X TO 8X HI COLUMN		
REF: PRINT RUN 200 SERIAL #'d SETS		
REF: STATED ODDS 1:628		
COMP.ATO.REF.SET (10)	500.00	220.00
COMMON ATO.REF. (BP1-10)	15.00	6.75
*ATO.REF: 10X TO 25X HI		
ATO.REF: PRINT RUN 50 SERIAL #'d SETS		
ATO.REF: STATED ODDS 1:2504		

		MINT	NRMT
❑ BP1	Shaquille O'Neal	5.00	2.20
❑ BP2	Kevin Garnett	6.00	2.70
❑ BP3	Dikembe Mutombo	.60	.25
❑ BP4	Grant Hill	5.00	2.20
❑ BP5	Tim Duncan	5.00	2.20
❑ BP6	Antawn Jamison	2.50	1.10
❑ BP7	Raef LaFrentz	1.00	.45
❑ BP8	Mike Bibby	1.50	.70
❑ BP9	Paul Pierce	2.50	1.10
❑ BP10	Jason Williams	3.00	1.35

1999-00 Bowman's Best

	MINT	NRMT
COMPLETE SET (133)	80.00	36.00
COMMON CARD (1-100)	.15	.07
COMMON RC (101-133)	.60	.25
SEMISTARS	.20	.09
SEMISTARS RC	.75	.35
UNLISTED STARS	.40	.18
UNLISTED STARS RC	1.00	.45

		MINT	NRMT
❑ 1	Vince Carter	4.00	1.80
❑ 2	Dikembe Mutombo	.20	.09
❑ 3	Steve Nash	.15	.07
❑ 4	Matt Harpring	.15	.07
❑ 5	Stephon Marbury	.75	.35
❑ 6	Chris Webber	1.25	.55
❑ 7	Jason Kidd	1.25	.55
❑ 8	Theo Ratliff	.15	.07
❑ 9	Damon Stoudamire	.40	.18
❑ 10	Shareef Abdur-Rahim	.75	.35
❑ 11	Rod Strickland	.20	.09
❑ 12	Jeff Hornacek	.20	.09
❑ 13	Vin Baker	.20	.09
❑ 14	Joe Smith	.20	.09
❑ 15	Alonzo Mourning	.40	.18
❑ 16	Isaiah Rider	.20	.09
❑ 17	Shaquille O'Neal	2.00	.90
❑ 18	Chris Mullin	.40	.18
❑ 19	Charles Barkley	.60	.25
❑ 20	Grant Hill	2.00	.90
❑ 21	Chris Mills	.15	.07
❑ 22	Antonio McDyess	.40	.18
❑ 23	Brevin Knight	.15	.07
❑ 24	Toni Kukoc	.50	.23
❑ 25	Antoine Walker	.50	.23
❑ 26	Eddie Jones	.75	.35
❑ 27	Tim Thomas	.50	.23
❑ 28	Latrell Sprewell	.75	.35
❑ 29	Larry Hughes	1.00	.45
❑ 30	Tim Duncan	2.00	.90
❑ 31	Horace Grant	.20	.09
❑ 32	John Stockton	.40	.18
❑ 33	Mike Bibby	.50	.23
❑ 34	Mitch Richmond	.40	.18
❑ 35	Allan Houston	.40	.18
❑ 36	Terrell Brandon	.20	.09
❑ 37	Glenn Robinson	.20	.09
❑ 38	Tyrone Nesby RC	.15	.07
❑ 39	Glen Rice	.20	.09
❑ 40	Hakeem Olajuwon	.60	.25
❑ 41	Jerry Stackhouse	.20	.09
❑ 42	Elden Campbell	.15	.07
❑ 43	Ron Harper	.20	.09
❑ 44	Kenny Anderson	.20	.09
❑ 45	Michael Finley	.40	.18
❑ 46	Scottie Pippen	1.25	.55
❑ 47	Lindsey Hunter	.15	.07
❑ 48	Michael Olowokandi	.20	.09
❑ 49	P.J. Brown	.15	.07
❑ 50	Keith Van Horn	.75	.35

❑ 51 Michael Doleac .... .15 .07
❑ 52 Anfernee Hardaway ...... 1.25 .55
❑ 53 Rasheed Wallace .... .40 .18
❑ 54 Nick Anderson................. .15 .07
❑ 55 Gary Payton .... .60 .25
❑ 56 Tracy McGrady .... 1.25 .55
❑ 57 Ray Allen......................... .40 .18
❑ 58 Kobe Bryant 3.00 1.35
❑ 59 Ron Mercer .... .50 .23
❑ 60 Shawn Kemp.................... .60 .25
❑ 61 Anthony Mason .... .20 .09
❑ 62 Tim Hardaway.................. .40 .18
❑ 63 Antawn Jamison .... .75 .35
❑ 64 Mark Jackson .... .15 .07
❑ 65 Tom Gugliotta .... .20 .09
❑ 66 Marcus Camby .... .40 .18
❑ 67 Kerry Kittles.................... .20 .09
❑ 68 Vlade Divac...................... .15 .07
❑ 69 Avery Johnson .... .15 .07
❑ 70 Karl Malone...................... .60 .25
❑ 71 Juwan Howard .... .20 .09
❑ 72 Alan Henderson .... .15 .07
❑ 73 Hersey Hawkins .... .20 .09
❑ 74 Darrell Armstrong .... .20 .09
❑ 75 Allen Iverson .... 1.50 .70
❑ 76 Maurice Taylor .... .40 .18
❑ 77 Gary Trent........................ .15 .07
❑ 78 John Starks...................... .15 .07
❑ 79 Paul Pierce .... .75 .35
❑ 80 Kevin Garnett 2.50 1.10
❑ 81 Patrick Ewing .... .40 .18
❑ 82 Steve Smith...................... .20 .09
❑ 83 Jason Williams .... 1.00 .45
❑ 84 David Robinson................ .60 .25
❑ 85 Charles Oakley .... .15 .07
❑ 86 Bryant Reeves.................. .15 .07
❑ 87 Nick Van Exel .... .20 .09
❑ 88 Reggie Miller.................... .40 .18
❑ 89 Chris Gatling.................... .15 .07
❑ 90 Brian Grant .... .20 .09
❑ 91 Allen Iverson BP .... .75 .35
❑ 92 Tim Duncan BP............. 1.00 .45
❑ 93 Keith Van Horn BP .... .40 .18
❑ 94 Kevin Garnett BP .... 1.25 .55
❑ 95 Kobe Bryant BP............. 1.50 .70
❑ 96 Elton Brand BP 5.00 2.20
❑ 97 Baron Davis BP............. 1.50 .70
❑ 98 Lamar Odom BP 4.00 1.80
❑ 99 Wally Szczerbiak BP...... 2.00 .90
❑ 100 Jason Terry BP .... .75 .35
❑ 101 Elton Brand RC 10.00 4.50
❑ 102 Steve Francis RC 12.00 5.50
❑ 103 Baron Davis RC 2.50 1.10
❑ 104 Lamar Odom RC.......... 8.00 3.60
❑ 105 Jonathan Bender RC.... 5.00 2.20
❑ 106 Wally Szczerbiak RC.... 4.00 1.80
❑ 107 Richard Hamilton RC .. 2.50 1.10
❑ 108 Andre Miller RC........... 3.00 1.35
❑ 109 Shawn Marion RC........ 3.00 1.35
❑ 110 Jason Terry RC............ 1.50 .70
❑ 111 Trajan Langdon RC...... 1.50 .70
❑ 112 Aleksandar Radojevic RC .60 .25
❑ 113 Corey Maggette RC 4.00 1.80
❑ 114 William Avery RC .... 1.50 .70
❑ 115 DeMarco Johnson RC.... .75 .35
❑ 116 Ron Artest RC.............. 2.50 1.10
❑ 117 Cal Bowdler RC............ 1.00 .45
❑ 118 James Posey RC .... 2.00 .90
❑ 119 Quincy Lewis RC.......... 1.00 .45
❑ 120 Dion Glover RC............ 1.00 .45
❑ 121 Jeff Foster RC .... 1.00 .45
❑ 122 Kenny Thomas RC ...... 1.50 .70
❑ 123 Devean George RC...... 2.00 .90
❑ 124 Tim James RC .... 1.25 .55
❑ 125 Vonteego Cummings RC 1.50 .70
❑ 126 Jumaine Jones RC .... .75 .35
❑ 127 Scott Padgett RC .... 1.00 .45
❑ 128 Anthony Carter RC 2.50 1.10
❑ 129 Chris Herren RC .... .60 .25
❑ 130 Todd MacCulloch RC .. 1.00 .45
❑ 131 John Celestand RC...... 1.00 .45
❑ 132 Adrian Griffin RC......... 1.25 .55
❑ 133 Mirsad Turkcan RC .... .60 .25

1999-00 Bowman's Best Atomic Refractors

	MINT	NRMT
COMMON CARD (1-133)..........	6.00	2.70

*STARS: 15X TO 40X BASE CARD HI
*RCs: 5X TO 12X BASE HI
STATED ODDS 1:33
STATED PRINT RUN 100 SERIAL #'d SETS

❑ 1 Vince Carter 200.00 90.00

1999-00 Bowman's Best Refractors

	MINT	NRMT
COMMON CARD (1-133)..........	2.50	1.10

*STARS: 6X TO 15X BASE CARD HI
*RCs: 2X TO 5X BASE HI
STATED ODDS 1:8
STATED PRINT RUN 400 SERIAL #'d SETS

❑ 1 Vince Carter 100.00 45.00

1999-00 Bowman's Best Autographs

	MINT	NRMT
COMPLETE SET (11)	120.00	55.00
COMMON CARD (BBA1-11)	6.00	2.70

STATED ODDS 1:79

❑ BBA1 Mitch Richmond 12.00 5.50
❑ BBA2 Damon Stoudamire 20.00 9.00
❑ BBA3 Antoine Walker........ 15.00 6.75
❑ BBA4 Antonio McDyess.... 15.00 6.75
❑ BBA5 Trajan Langdon 12.00 5.50
❑ BBA6 Jumaine Jones.......... 6.00 2.70
❑ BBA7 Andre Miller 25.00 11.00
❑ BBA8 Richard Hamilton 12.00 5.50
❑ BBA9 Jonathan Bender 30.00 13.50
❑ BBA10 William Avery 6.00 2.70
❑ BBA11 Shawn Marion 20.00 9.00

1999-00 Bowman's Best Class Photo

	MINT	NRMT
COMPLETE SET (3)	250.00	110.00

STATED ODDS 1:100
REF: STATED ODDS 1:3478
REF: PRINT RUN 125 SERIAL #'d SETS
AR: STATED ODDS 1:12420
AR: PRINT RUN 35 SERIAL #'d SETS

❑ CS1 Draft Picks 10.00 4.50
Richard Hamilton
Corey Maggette
Lamar Odom
Wally Szczerbiak
Jonathan Bender
Trajan Langdon
Aleksandar Radojevic
Baron Davis
Shawn Marion
Jason Terry
Andre Miller
Steve Francis
Elton Brand

❑ CS1 Draft Picks Refractor 80.00 36.00
Richard Hamilton
Corey Maggette
Lamar Odom
Wally Szczerbiak
Jonathan Bender
Trajan Langdon
Aleksandar Radojevic
Baron Davis
Shawn Marion
Jason Terry
Andre Miller
Steve Francis
Elton Brand

❑ CS1 Draft Picks Atomic Refractor 200.00
90.00
Richard Hamilton
Corey Maggette
Lamar Odom
Wally Szczerbiak
Jonathan Bender
Trajan Langdon
Aleksandar Radojevic
Baron Davis
Shawn Marion
Jason Terry
Andre Miller
Steve Francis
Elton Brand

1999-00 Bowman's Best Franchise Favorites

	MINT	NRMT
COMPLETE SET (3)	4.00	1.80
COMMON CARD (FR1A-FR1C)	1.00	.45

STATED ODDS 1:14
DUNCAN AU: STATED ODDS 1:2174
GERVIN AU: STATED ODDS 1:966
COMBO AU: STATED ODDS 1:8694

❑ FR1A Tim Duncan	2.50	1.10
❑ FR1B George Gervin	1.00	.45
❑ FR1C Tim Duncan George Gervin	4.00	1.80
❑ FRA1A Tim Duncan AU	150.00	70.00
❑ FRA1B George Gervin AU	20.00	9.00
❑ FRA1C Tim Duncan George Gervin Autograph	250.00	110.00

1999-00 Bowman's Best Franchise Foundations

	MINT	NRMT
COMPLETE SET (13)	50.00	22.00
COMMON CARD (FF1-FF13)	1.25	.55

STATED ODDS 1:21

❑ FF1 Allen Iverson	5.00	2.20
❑ FF2 Tim Duncan	6.00	2.70
❑ FF3 Kevin Garnett	8.00	3.60
❑ FF4 Shareef Abdur-Rahim	2.50	1.10
❑ FF5 Kobe Bryant	10.00	4.50
❑ FF6 Grant Hill	6.00	2.70
❑ FF7 Keith Van Horn	2.50	1.10
❑ FF8 Vince Carter	12.00	5.50
❑ FF9 Antoine Walker	1.50	.70
❑ FF10 Shaquille O'Neal	6.00	2.70
❑ FF11 Jason Williams	3.00	1.35
❑ FF12 Stephon Marbury	2.50	1.10
❑ FF13 Antonio McDyess	1.25	.55

1999-00 Bowman's Best Franchise Futures

	MINT	NRMT
COMPLETE SET (10)	30.00	13.50
COMMON CARD (FFT1-FFT10)	1.50	.70

STATED ODDS 1:27

❑ FFT1 Elton Brand	10.00	4.50
❑ FFT2 Steve Francis	12.00	5.50
❑ FFT3 Baron Davis	2.50	1.10
❑ FFT4 Lamar Odom	8.00	3.60
❑ FFT5 Jonathan Bender	5.00	2.20
❑ FFT6 Wally Szczerbiak	4.00	1.80
❑ FFT7 Richard Hamilton	2.50	1.10
❑ FFT8 Andre Miller	3.00	1.35
❑ FFT9 Shawn Marion	3.00	1.35
❑ FFT10 Jason Terry	1.50	.70

1999-00 Bowman's Best Rookie Locker Room Collection

	MINT	NRMT
COMPLETE SET (9)	450.00	200.00
COMMON CARD	15.00	6.75

AU STATED ODDS 1:174
JERSEY STATED ODDS 1:197

❑ LRCA1 Elton Brand AU	60.00	27.00
❑ LRCA2 Steve Francis AU	80.00	36.00
❑ LRCA3 Wally Szczerbiak AU	40.00	18.00
❑ LRCA4 Baron Davis AU	15.00	6.75
❑ LRCA5 Corey Maggette AU	25.00	11.00
❑ LRCJ1 Elton Brand	120.00	55.00
❑ LRCJ2 Steve Francis	150.00	70.00
❑ LRCJ3 Wally Szczerbiak	40.00	18.00
❑ LRCJ4 Baron Davis	30.00	13.50

1999-00 Bowman's Best Techniques

	MINT	NRMT
COMPLETE SET (13)	30.00	13.50
COMMON CARD (BT1-BT13)	.75	.35
UNLISTED STARS	1.25	.55

STATED ODDS 1:21

❑ BT1 Tim Duncan	6.00	2.70
❑ BT2 Tim Hardaway	1.25	.55
❑ BT3 Shaquille O'Neal	6.00	2.70
❑ BT4 Vince Carter	12.00	5.50
❑ BT5 Dikembe Mutombo	.75	.35
❑ BT6 Grant Hill	6.00	2.70
❑ BT7 Gary Payton	2.00	.90
❑ BT8 Jason Williams	3.00	1.35

❑ BT9 Stephon Marbury	2.50	1.10
❑ BT10 Reggie Miller	1.25	.55
❑ BT11 Scottie Pippen	4.00	1.80
❑ BT12 John Stockton	1.25	.55
❑ BT13 Karl Malone	2.00	.90

1999-00 Bowman's Best World's Best

	MINT	NRMT
COMPLETE SET (9)	12.00	5.50
COMMON CARD (WB1-WB9)	.75	.35
UNLISTED STARS	1.25	.55

STATED ODDS 1:30

❑ WB1 Allan Houston	1.25	.55
❑ WB2 Kevin Garnett	8.00	3.60
❑ WB3 Gary Payton	2.00	.90
❑ WB4 Steve Smith	.75	.35
❑ WB5 Tim Hardaway	1.25	.55
❑ WB6 Tim Duncan	6.00	2.70
❑ WB7 Jason Kidd	4.00	1.80
❑ WB8 Tom Gugliotta	.75	.35
❑ WB9 Vin Baker	.75	.35

1994-95 Collector's Choice

	MINT	NRMT
COMPLETE SET (420)	30.00	13.50
COMPLETE SERIES 1 (210)	12.00	5.50
COMPLETE SERIES 2 (210)	18.00	8.00

COMMON CARD (1-420)	.05	.02
SEMISTARS	.10	.05
UNLISTED STARS	.20	.09
SUBSET CARDS HALF VALUE OF BASE CARDS		

❑ 1	Anfernee Hardaway	.60	.25
❑ 2	Mark Macon	.05	.02
❑ 3	Steve Smith	.10	.05
❑ 4	Chris Webber	.60	.25
❑ 5	Donald Royal	.05	.02
❑ 6	Avery Johnson	.05	.02
❑ 7	Kevin Johnson	.10	.05
❑ 8	Doug Christie	.05	.02
❑ 9	Derrick McKey	.05	.02
❑ 10	Dennis Rodman	.40	.18
❑ 11	Scott Skiles UER	.05	.02
	(Listed as playing with Cavaliers instead of Pacers in '87-'88, '88-'89)		
❑ 12	Isiah Thomas	.20	.09
❑ 13	Kendall Gill	.10	.05
❑ 14	Jeff Hornacek	.10	.05
❑ 15	Latrell Sprewell	.40	.18
❑ 16	Lucious Harris	.05	.02
❑ 17	Chris Mullin	.20	.09
❑ 18	John Williams	.05	.02
❑ 19	Tony Campbell	.05	.02
❑ 20	LaPhonso Ellis	.05	.02
❑ 21	Gerald Wilkins	.05	.02
❑ 22	Clyde Drexler	.20	.09
❑ 23	Michael Jordan	2.50	1.10
❑ 24	George Lynch	.05	.02
❑ 25	Mark Price	.05	.02
❑ 26	James Robinson	.05	.02
❑ 27	Elmore Spencer	.05	.02
❑ 28	Stacey King	.05	.02
❑ 29	Corie Blount	.05	.02
❑ 30	Dell Curry	.05	.02
❑ 31	Reggie Miller	.20	.09
❑ 32	Karl Malone	.30	.14
❑ 33	Scottie Pippen	.60	.25
❑ 34	Hakeem Olajuwon	.30	.14
❑ 35	Clarence Weatherspoon	.05	.02
❑ 36	Kevin Edwards	.05	.02
❑ 37	Pete Myers	.05	.02
❑ 38	Jeff Turner	.05	.02
❑ 39	Ennis Whatley	.05	.02
❑ 40	Calbert Cheaney	.05	.02
❑ 41	Glen Rice	.10	.05
❑ 42	Vin Baker	.20	.09
❑ 43	Grant Long	.05	.02
❑ 44	Derrick Coleman	.10	.05
❑ 45	Rik Smits	.05	.02
❑ 46	Chris Smith	.05	.02
❑ 47	Carl Herrera	.05	.02
❑ 48	Bob Martin	.05	.02
❑ 49	Terrell Brandon	.10	.05
❑ 50	David Robinson	.30	.14
❑ 51	Danny Ferry	.05	.02
❑ 52	Buck Williams	.05	.02
❑ 53	Josh Grant	.05	.02
❑ 54	Ed Pinckney	.05	.02
❑ 55	Dikembe Mutombo	.10	.05
❑ 56	Clifford Robinson	.10	.05
❑ 57	Luther Wright	.05	.02
❑ 58	Scott Burrell	.05	.02
❑ 59	Stacey Augmon	.05	.02
❑ 60	Jeff Malone	.05	.02
❑ 61	Byron Houston	.05	.02
❑ 62	Anthony Peeler	.05	.02
❑ 63	Michael Adams	.05	.02
❑ 64	Negele Knight	.05	.02
❑ 65	Terry Cummings	.05	.02
❑ 66	Christian Laettner	.10	.05
❑ 67	Tracy Murray	.05	.02
❑ 68	Sedale Threatt	.05	.02
❑ 69	Dan Majerle	.10	.05
❑ 70	Frank Brickowski	.05	.02
❑ 71	Ken Norman	.05	.02
❑ 72	Charles Smith	.05	.02
❑ 73	Adam Keefe	.05	.02
❑ 74	P.J. Brown	.05	.02
❑ 75	Kevin Duckworth	.05	.02
❑ 76	Shawn Bradley UER	.05	.02
	Bradely on back		
❑ 77	Darnell Mee	.05	.02
❑ 78	Nick Anderson	.05	.02
❑ 79	Mark West	.05	.02
❑ 80	B.J. Armstrong	.05	.02
❑ 81	Dennis Scott	.05	.02
❑ 82	Lindsey Hunter	.10	.05
❑ 83	Derek Strong	.05	.02
❑ 84	Mike Brown	.05	.02
❑ 85	Antonio Harvey	.05	.02
❑ 86	Anthony Bonner	.05	.02
❑ 87	Sam Cassell	.20	.09
❑ 88	Harold Miner	.05	.02
❑ 89	Spud Webb	.05	.02
❑ 90	Mookie Blaylock	.05	.02
❑ 91	Greg Anthony	.05	.02
❑ 92	Richard Petruska	.05	.02
❑ 93	Sean Rooks	.05	.02
❑ 94	Ervin Johnson	.05	.02
❑ 95	Randy Brown	.05	.02
❑ 96	Orlando Woolridge	.05	.02
❑ 97	Charles Oakley	.05	.02
❑ 98	Craig Ehlo	.05	.02
❑ 99	Derek Harper	.05	.02
❑ 100	Doug Edwards	.05	.02
❑ 101	Muggsy Bogues	.10	.05
❑ 102	Mitch Richmond	.20	.09
❑ 103	Mahmoud Abdul-Rauf	.05	.02
❑ 104	Joe Dumars	.20	.09
❑ 105	Eric Riley	.05	.02
❑ 106	Terry Mills	.05	.02
❑ 107	Toni Kukoc	.30	.14
❑ 108	Jon Koncak	.05	.02
❑ 109	Haywoode Workman	.05	.02
❑ 110	Todd Day	.05	.02
❑ 111	Detlef Schrempf	.10	.05
❑ 112	David Wesley	.05	.02
❑ 113	Mark Jackson	.05	.02
❑ 114	Doug Overton	.05	.02
❑ 115	Vinny Del Negro	.05	.02
❑ 116	Loy Vaught	.05	.02
❑ 117	Mike Peplowski	.05	.02
❑ 118	Bimbo Coles	.05	.02
❑ 119	Rex Walters	.05	.02
❑ 120	Sherman Douglas	.05	.02
❑ 121	David Benoit	.05	.02
❑ 122	John Salley	.05	.02
❑ 123	Cedric Ceballos	.05	.02
❑ 124	Chris Mills	.10	.05
❑ 125	Robert Horry	.05	.02
❑ 126	Johnny Newman	.05	.02
❑ 127	Malcolm Mackey	.05	.02
❑ 128	Terry Dehere	.05	.02
❑ 129	Dino Radja	.05	.02
❑ 130	Tree Rollins	.05	.02
❑ 131	Xavier McDaniel	.05	.02
❑ 132	Bobby Hurley	.05	.02
❑ 133	Alonzo Mourning	.25	.11
❑ 134	Isaiah Rider	.10	.05
❑ 135	Antoine Carr	.05	.02
❑ 136	Robert Pack	.05	.02
❑ 137	Walt Williams	.05	.02
❑ 138	Tyrone Corbin	.05	.02
❑ 139	Popeye Jones	.05	.02
❑ 140	Shawn Kemp	.30	.14
❑ 141	Thurl Bailey	.05	.02
❑ 142	James Worthy	.20	.09
❑ 143	Scott Haskin	.05	.02
❑ 144	Hubert Davis	.05	.02
❑ 145	A.C. Green	.10	.05
❑ 146	Dale Davis	.05	.02
❑ 147	Nate McMillan	.05	.02
❑ 148	Chris Morris	.05	.02
❑ 149	Will Perdue	.05	.02
❑ 150	Felton Spencer	.05	.02
❑ 151	Rod Strickland	.10	.05
❑ 152	Blue Edwards	.05	.02
❑ 153	John Williams	.05	.02
❑ 154	Rodney Rogers	.05	.02
❑ 155	Acie Earl	.05	.02
❑ 156	Hersey Hawkins	.10	.05
❑ 157	Jamal Mashburn	.20	.09
❑ 158	Don MacLean	.05	.02
❑ 159	Micheal Williams	.05	.02
❑ 160	Kenny Gattison	.05	.02
❑ 161	Rich King	.05	.02
❑ 162	Allan Houston	.30	.14
❑ 163	Hoop-it up	.05	.02
	Men's Champions		
❑ 164	Hoop-it up	.05	.02
	Women's Champions Lisa Harrison		
❑ 165	Hoop-it up	.05	.02
	Slam-Dunk Champions Corey Etheridge		
❑ 166	Danny Manning TO	.05	.02
❑ 167	Robert Parish TO	.05	.02
❑ 168	Alonzo Mourning TO	.20	.09
❑ 169	Scottie Pippen TO	.30	.14
❑ 170	Mark Price TO	.05	.02
❑ 171	Jamal Mashburn TO	.10	.05
❑ 172	Dikembe Mutombo TO	.05	.02
❑ 173	Joe Dumars TO	.10	.05
❑ 174	Chris Webber TO	.25	.11
❑ 175	Hakeem Olajuwon TO	.20	.09
❑ 176	Reggie Miller TO	.10	.05
❑ 177	Ron Harper TO	.05	.02
❑ 178	Nick Van Exel TO	.10	.05
❑ 179	Steve Smith TO	.05	.02
❑ 180	Vin Baker TO	.10	.05
❑ 181	Isaiah Rider TO	.05	.02
❑ 182	Derrick Coleman TO	.05	.02
❑ 183	Patrick Ewing TO	.10	.05
❑ 184	Shaquille O'Neal TO	.40	.18
❑ 185	Clarence Weatherspoon TO	.05	.02
❑ 186	Charles Barkley TO	.20	.09
❑ 187	Clyde Drexler TO	.10	.05
❑ 188	Mitch Richmond TO	.10	.05
❑ 189	David Robinson TO	.20	.09
❑ 190	Shawn Kemp TO	.20	.09
❑ 191	Karl Malone TO	.20	.09
❑ 192	Tom Gugliotta TO	.05	.02
❑ 193	Kenny Anderson ASA	.05	.02
❑ 194	Alonzo Mourning ASA	.20	.09
❑ 195	Mark Price ASA	.05	.02
❑ 196	John Stockton ASA	.10	.05
❑ 197	Shaquille O'Neal ASA	.40	.18
❑ 198	Latrell Sprewell ASA	.20	.09
❑ 199	Charles Barkley PRO	.20	.09
❑ 200	Chris Webber PRO	.25	.11
❑ 201	Patrick Ewing PRO	.10	.05
❑ 202	Dennis Rodman PRO	.20	.09
❑ 203	Shawn Kemp PRO	.20	.09
❑ 204	Michael Jordan PRO	1.25	.55
❑ 205	Shaquille O'Neal PRO	.40	.18
❑ 206	Larry Johnson PRO	.05	.02
❑ 207	Tim Hardaway CL	.10	.05
❑ 208	John Stockton CL	.10	.05
❑ 209	Harold Miner CL	.05	.02
❑ 210	B.J. Armstrong CL	.05	.02
❑ 211	Vernon Maxwell	.05	.02
❑ 212	John Stockton	.20	.09
❑ 213	Luc Longley	.05	.02
❑ 214	Sam Perkins	.10	.05
❑ 215	Pooh Richardson	.05	.02
❑ 216	Tyrone Corbin	.05	.02
❑ 217	Mario Elie	.05	.02
❑ 218	Bobby Phills	.05	.02
❑ 219	Grant Hill RC	2.00	.90
❑ 220	Gary Payton	.30	.14
❑ 221	Tom Hammonds	.05	.02
❑ 222	Danny Ainge	.05	.02
❑ 223	Gary Grant	.05	.02
❑ 224	Jim Jackson	.10	.05
❑ 225	Chris Gatling	.05	.02
❑ 226	Sergei Bazarevich	.05	.02
❑ 227	Tony Dumas RC	.05	.02
❑ 228	Andrew Lang	.05	.02
❑ 229	Wesley Person RC	.20	.09
❑ 230	Terry Porter	.05	.02
❑ 231	Duane Causwell	.05	.02
❑ 232	Shaquille O'Neal	1.00	.45
❑ 233	Antonio Davis	.05	.02
❑ 234	Charles Barkley	.30	.14
❑ 235	Tony Massenburg	.05	.02
❑ 236	Ricky Pierce	.05	.02
❑ 237	Scott Skiles	.05	.02
❑ 238	Jalen Rose RC	.75	.35
❑ 239	Charlie Ward RC	.20	.09
❑ 240	Michael Jordan	1.25	.55
❑ 241	Elden Campbell	.05	.02
❑ 242	Bill Cartwright	.05	.02
❑ 243	Armon Gilliam	.05	.02

Card	MINT	NRMT
❑ 244 Rick Fox	.05	.02
❑ 245 Tim Breaux	.05	.02
❑ 246 Monty Williams RC	.05	.02
❑ 247 Dominique Wilkins	.20	.09
❑ 248 Robert Parish	.10	.05
❑ 249 Mark Jackson	.05	.02
❑ 250 Jason Kidd RC	1.50	.70
❑ 251 Andres Guibert	.05	.02
❑ 252 Matt Geiger	.05	.02
❑ 253 Stanley Roberts	.05	.02
❑ 254 Jack Haley	.05	.02
❑ 255 David Wingate	.05	.02
❑ 256 John Crotty	.05	.02
❑ 257 Brian Grant RC	.50	.23
❑ 258 Otis Thorpe	.05	.02
❑ 259 Clifford Rozier RC	.05	.02
❑ 260 Grant Long	.05	.02
❑ 261 Eric Mobley RC	.05	.02
❑ 262 Dickey Simpkins RC	.05	.02
❑ 263 J.R. Reid	.05	.02
❑ 264 Kevin Willis	.05	.02
❑ 265 Scott Brooks	.05	.02
❑ 266 Glenn Robinson RC	.60	.25
❑ 267 Dana Barros	.05	.02
❑ 268 Ken Norman	.05	.02
❑ 269 Herb Williams	.05	.02
❑ 270 Dee Brown	.05	.02
❑ 271 Steve Kerr	.05	.02
❑ 272 Jon Barry	.05	.02
❑ 273 Sean Elliott	.10	.05
❑ 274 Elliot Perry	.05	.02
❑ 275 Kenny Smith	.05	.02
❑ 276 Sean Rooks	.05	.02
❑ 277 Gheorghe Muresan	.05	.02
❑ 278 Juwan Howard RC	.50	.23
❑ 279 Steve Smith	.10	.05
❑ 280 Anthony Bowie	.05	.02
❑ 281 Moses Malone	.20	.09
❑ 282 Olden Polynice	.05	.02
❑ 283 Jo Jo English	.05	.02
❑ 284 Marty Conlon	.05	.02
❑ 285 Sam Mitchell	.05	.02
❑ 286 Doug West	.05	.02
❑ 287 Cedric Ceballos	.05	.02
❑ 288 Lorenzo Williams	.05	.02
❑ 289 Harold Ellis	.05	.02
❑ 290 Doc Rivers	.10	.05
❑ 291 Keith Tower	.05	.02
❑ 292 Mark Bryant	.05	.02
❑ 293 Oliver Miller	.05	.02
❑ 294 Michael Adams	.05	.02
❑ 295 Tree Rollins	.05	.02
❑ 296 Eddie Jones RC	1.25	.55
❑ 297 Malik Sealy	.05	.02
❑ 298 Blue Edwards	.05	.02
❑ 299 Brooks Thompson RC	.05	.02
❑ 300 Benoit Benjamin	.05	.02
❑ 301 Avery Johnson	.05	.02
❑ 302 Larry Johnson	.10	.05
❑ 303 John Starks	.05	.02
❑ 304 Byron Scott	.10	.05
❑ 305 Eric Murdock	.05	.02
❑ 306 Jay Humphries	.05	.02
❑ 307 Kenny Anderson	.10	.05
❑ 308 Brian Williams	.05	.02
❑ 309 Nick Van Exel	.20	.09
❑ 310 Tim Hardaway	.20	.09
❑ 311 Lee Mayberry	.05	.02
❑ 312 Vlade Divac	.05	.02
❑ 313 Donyell Marshall RC	.20	.09
❑ 314 Anthony Mason	.10	.05
❑ 315 Danny Manning	.10	.05
❑ 316 Tyrone Hill	.05	.02
❑ 317 Vincent Askew	.05	.02
❑ 318 Khalid Reeves RC	.05	.02
❑ 319 Ron Harper	.10	.05
❑ 320 Brent Price	.05	.02
❑ 321 Byron Houston	.05	.02
❑ 322 Lamond Murray RC	.10	.05
❑ 323 Bryant Stith	.05	.02
❑ 324 Tom Gugliotta	.10	.05
❑ 325 Jerome Kersey	.05	.02
❑ 326 B.J. Tyler RC	.05	.02
❑ 327 Antonio Lang	.05	.02
❑ 328 Carlos Rogers RC	.05	.02
❑ 329 Wayman Tisdale	.05	.02
❑ 330 Kevin Gamble	.05	.02
❑ 331 Eric Piatkowski RC	.05	.02
❑ 332 Mitchell Butler	.05	.02
❑ 333 Patrick Ewing	.20	.09
❑ 334 Doug Smith	.05	.02
❑ 335 Joe Kleine	.05	.02
❑ 336 Keith Jennings	.05	.02
❑ 337 Bill Curley RC	.05	.02
❑ 338 Johnny Newman	.05	.02
❑ 339 Howard Eisley RC	.05	.02
❑ 340 Willie Anderson	.05	.02
❑ 341 Aaron McKie RC	.05	.02
❑ 342 Tom Chambers	.05	.02
❑ 343 Scott Williams	.05	.02
❑ 344 Harvey Grant	.05	.02
❑ 345 Billy Owens	.05	.02
❑ 346 Sharone Wright RC	.05	.02
❑ 347 Michael Cage	.05	.02
❑ 348 Vern Fleming	.05	.02
❑ 349 Darrin Hancock RC	.05	.02
❑ 350 Matt Fish	.05	.02
❑ 351 Rony Seikaly	.05	.02
❑ 352 Victor Alexander	.05	.02
❑ 353 Anthony Miller RC	.05	.02
❑ 354 Horace Grant	.10	.05
❑ 355 Jayson Williams	.10	.05
❑ 356 Dale Ellis	.05	.02
❑ 357 Sarunas Marciulionis	.05	.02
❑ 358 Anthony Avent	.05	.02
❑ 359 Rex Chapman	.05	.02
❑ 360 Askia Jones RC	.05	.02
❑ 361 Charles Outlaw RC	.05	.02
❑ 362 Chuck Person	.05	.02
❑ 363 Dan Schayes	.05	.02
❑ 364 Morlon Wiley	.05	.02
❑ 365 Dontonio Wingfield RC	.05	.02
❑ 366 Tony Smith	.05	.02
❑ 367 Bill Wennington	.05	.02
❑ 368 Bryon Russell	.05	.02
❑ 369 Geert Hammink	.05	.02
❑ 370 Eric Montross RC	.05	.02
❑ 371 Cliff Levingston	.05	.02
❑ 372 Stacey Augmon BP	.05	.02
❑ 373 Eric Montross BP	.05	.02
❑ 374 Alonzo Mourning BP	.20	.09
❑ 375 Scottie Pippen BP	.30	.14
❑ 376 Mark Price BP	.05	.02
❑ 377 Jason Kidd BP	.60	.25
❑ 378 Jalen Rose BP	.10	.05
❑ 379 Grant Hill BP	1.00	.45
❑ 380 Latrell Sprewell BP	.20	.09
❑ 381 Hakeem Olajuwon BP	.20	.09
❑ 382 Reggie Miller BP	.10	.05
❑ 383 Lamond Murray BP	.05	.02
❑ 384 Eddie Jones BP	.60	.25
❑ 385 Khalid Reeves BP	.05	.02
❑ 386 Glenn Robinson BP	.30	.14
❑ 387 Donyell Marshall BP	.10	.05
❑ 388 Derrick Coleman BP	.05	.02
❑ 389 Patrick Ewing BP	.10	.05
❑ 390 Shaquille O'Neal BP	.40	.18
❑ 391 Sharone Wright BP	.05	.02
❑ 392 Charles Barkley BP	.20	.09
❑ 393 Aaron McKie BP	.05	.02
❑ 394 Brian Grant BP	.10	.05
❑ 395 David Robinson BP	.20	.09
❑ 396 Shawn Kemp BP	.20	.09
❑ 397 Karl Malone BP	.20	.09
❑ 398 Tom Gugliotta BP	.05	.02
❑ 399 Hakeem Olajuwon TRIV	.20	.09
❑ 400 Shaquille O'Neal TRIV	.40	.18
❑ 401 Chris Webber TRIV	.25	.11
❑ 402 Michael Jordan TRIV	1.25	.55
❑ 403 David Robinson TRIV	.20	.09
❑ 404 Shawn Kemp TRIV	.20	.09
❑ 405 Patrick Ewing TRIV	.10	.05
❑ 406 Charles Barkley TRIV	.20	.09
❑ 407 Glenn Robinson DC	.30	.14
❑ 408 Jason Kidd DC	.60	.25
❑ 409 Grant Hill DC	1.00	.45
❑ 410 Donyell Marshall DC	.10	.05
❑ 411 Sharone Wright DC	.05	.02
❑ 412 Lamond Murray DC	.05	.02
❑ 413 Brian Grant DC	.10	.05
❑ 414 Eric Montross DC	.05	.02
❑ 415 Eddie Jones DC	.60	.25
❑ 416 Carlos Rogers DC	.05	.02
❑ 417 Shawn Kemp CL	.05	.02
❑ 418 Bobby Hurley CL	.05	.02
❑ 419 Shawn Bradley CL	.05	.02
❑ 420 Michael Jordan CL	.75	.35

1994-95 Collector's Choice Silver Signature

	MINT	NRMT
COMPLETE SET (420)	100.00	45.00
COMPLETE SERIES 1 (210)	40.00	18.00
COMPLETE SERIES 2 (210)	60.00	27.00
COMMON SILVER (1-420)	.10	.05

*STARS: 1.5X TO 3X BASE CARD HI
*RCs: 1.25X TO 2.5X BASE HI
ONE PER PACK
THREE PER RETAIL JUMBO PACK

1994-95 Collector's Choice Gold Signature

	MINT	NRMT
COMPLETE SET (420)	800.00	350.00
COMPLETE SERIES 1 (210)	300.00	135.00
COMPLETE SERIES 2 (210)	500.00	220.00
COMMON GOLD (1-420)	1.25	.55

*STARS: 15X TO 30X BASE CARD HI
*RCs: 12.5X TO 25X BASE HI
SER.1/2 STATED ODDS 1:35 HOB/RET

1994-95 Collector's Choice Blow-Ups

	MINT	NRMT
COMPLETE SET (5)	10.00	4.50
COMMON CARD (40/76/132)	.50	.23

ONE PER SER.2 HOBBY BOX
AU CARDS RANDOMLY INSERTED

Card	MINT	NRMT
❑ 23 Michael Jordan BB	8.00	3.60
❑ 40 Calbert Cheaney	.50	.23
❑ 76 Shawn Bradley	.50	.23
❑ 132 Bobby Hurley	.50	.23
❑ 140 Shawn Kemp	1.00	.45
❑ A23 Michael Jordan AU	5000.00	2200.00
❑ A40 Calbert Cheaney AU	30.00	13.50
❑ A76 Shawn Bradley AU	30.00	13.50
❑ A132 Bobby Hurley AU	30.00	13.50
❑ A140 Shawn Kemp AU	150.00	70.00

1994-95 Collector's Choice Crash the Game Assists

	MINT	NRMT
COMPLETE SET (15)	12.00	5.50

*SINGLES: 3X TO 8X BASE CARD HI
SER.1 STATED ODDS 1:20 RETAIL

COMP.AST.RED.SET (15)	6.00	2.70

*RED.CARDS: .2X TO .5X HI COLUMN
ONE EXCH.SET PER WINNER CARD BY MAIL

Card	MINT	NRMT
❑ A1 Michael Adams	.40	.18
❑ A2 Kenny Anderson	.75	.35

		MINT	NRMT
❑ A3	Mookie Blaylock	.40	.18
❑ A4	Muggsy Bogues	.75	.35
❑ A5	Sherman Douglas	.40	.18
❑ A6	Anfernee Hardaway	5.00	2.20
❑ A7	Tim Hardaway	1.50	.70
❑ A8	Lindsey Hunter	.75	.35
❑ A9	Mark Jackson	.40	.18
❑ A10	Kevin Johnson	.75	.35
❑ A11	Eric Murdock	.40	.18
❑ A12	Mark Price	.40	.18
❑ A13	John Stockton	1.50	.70
❑ A14	Rod Strickland	.75	.35
❑ A15	Micheal Williams	.40	.18

1994-95 Collector's Choice Crash the Game Rebounds

	MINT	NRMT
COMPLETE SET (15)	15.00	6.75
*SINGLES: 2.5X TO 6X BASE CARD HI		
SER.2 STATED ODDS 1:20 RETAIL		
COMP.REB.RED.SET (15)	8.00	3.60
*RED.CARDS: .2X TO .5X HI COLUMN		
ONE EXCH.SET PER WINNER CARD BY MAIL		

		MINT	NRMT
❑ R1	Derrick Coleman	.60	.25
❑ R2	Patrick Ewing	1.25	.55
❑ R3	Horace Grant	.60	.25
❑ R4	Shawn Kemp	2.00	.90
❑ R5	Karl Malone	2.00	.90
❑ R6	Alonzo Mourning	1.50	.70
❑ R7	Dikembe Mutombo	.60	.25
❑ R8	Charles Oakley	.30	.14
❑ R9	Hakeem Olajuwon	2.00	.90
❑ R10	Shaquille O'Neal	6.00	2.70
❑ R11	Olden Polynice	.30	.14
❑ R12	David Robinson	2.00	.90
❑ R13	Dennis Rodman	2.50	1.10
❑ R14	Otis Thorpe	.30	.14
❑ R15	Kevin Willis	.30	.14

1994-95 Collector's Choice Crash the Game Rookie Scoring

	MINT	NRMT
COMPLETE SET (15)	15.00	6.75

	MINT	NRMT
*SINGLES: 1X TO 2.5X BASE CARD HI		
SER.2 STATED ODDS 1:20 HOBBY		
COMP.ROOK.RED.SET (15)	8.00	3.60
*RED.CARDS: .2X TO .5X HI COLUMN		
ONE EXCH.SET PER WINNER CARD BY MAIL		

		MINT	NRMT
❑ S1	Tony Dumas	.15	.07
❑ S2	Brian Grant	1.25	.55
❑ S3	Grant Hill	5.00	2.20
❑ S4	Juwan Howard	1.25	.55
❑ S5	Eddie Jones	3.00	1.35
❑ S6	Jason Kidd	4.00	1.80
❑ S7	Donyell Marshall	.50	.23
❑ S8	Eric Montross	.15	.07
❑ S9	Lamond Murray	.25	.11
❑ S10	Khalid Reeves	.15	.07
❑ S11	Glenn Robinson	1.50	.70
❑ S12	Jalen Rose	2.00	.90
❑ S13	Dickey Simpkins	.15	.07
❑ S14	Charlie Ward	.50	.23
❑ S15	Sharone Wright	.15	.07

1994-95 Collector's Choice Crash the Game Scoring

	MINT	NRMT
COMPLETE SET (15)	15.00	6.75
*SINGLES: 2.5X TO 6X BASE CARD HI		
SER.1 STATED ODDS 1:20 HOBBY		
COMP.SCOR.RED.SET (15)	8.00	3.60
*RED.CARDS: .2X TO .5X HI COLUMN		
ONE EXCH.SET PER WINNER CARD BY MAIL		

		MINT	NRMT
❑ S1	Charles Barkley	2.00	.90
❑ S2	Derrick Coleman	.60	.25
❑ S3	Joe Dumars	1.25	.55
❑ S4	Patrick Ewing	1.25	.55
❑ S5	Karl Malone	2.00	.90
❑ S6	Reggie Miller	1.25	.55
❑ S7	Shaquille O'Neal	6.00	2.70
❑ S8	Hakeem Olajuwon	2.00	.90
❑ S9	Scottie Pippen	4.00	1.80
❑ S10	Glen Rice	.60	.25
❑ S11	Mitch Richmond	1.25	.55
❑ S12	David Robinson	2.00	.90
❑ S13	Latrell Sprewell	2.50	1.10
❑ S14	Chris Webber	4.00	1.80
❑ S15	Dominique Wilkins	1.25	.55

1994-95 Collector's Choice Draft Trade

	MINT	NRMT
COMPLETE SET (10)	8.00	3.60
*SINGLES: .6X TO 1.5X BASE CARD HI		
ONE SET PER DRAFT TRADE CARD BY MAIL		
DT CARD: SER.1 STATED ODDS 1:36		

		MINT	NRMT
❑ 1	Glenn Robinson	1.00	.45
❑ 2	Jason Kidd	2.50	1.10
❑ 3	Grant Hill	3.00	1.35
❑ 4	Donyell Marshall	.30	.14
❑ 5	Juwan Howard	.75	.35
❑ 6	Sharone Wright	.10	.05
❑ 7	Lamond Murray	.15	.07
❑ 8	Brian Grant	.75	.35
❑ 9	Eric Montross	.10	.05
❑ 10	Eddie Jones	2.00	.90
❑ NNO	Draft Trade Card	.25	.11

1995-96 Collector's Choice

	MINT	NRMT
COMPLETE SET (410)	35.00	16.00
COMP.FACTORY SET (419)	35.00	16.00
COMPLETE SERIES 1 (210)	15.00	6.75
COMPLETE SERIES 2 (200)	20.00	9.00
COMMON CARD (1-410)	.05	.02
SEMISTARS	.10	.05
UNLISTED STARS	.20	.09
SUBSET CARDS HALF VALUE OF BASE CARDS		

		MINT	NRMT
❑ 1	Rod Strickland	.10	.05
❑ 2	Larry Johnson	.10	.05
❑ 3	Mahmoud Abdul-Rauf	.05	.02
❑ 4	Joe Dumars	.20	.09
❑ 5	Jason Kidd	.60	.25
❑ 6	Avery Johnson	.05	.02
❑ 7	Dee Brown	.05	.02
❑ 8	Brian Williams	.05	.02
❑ 9	Nick Van Exel	.10	.05
❑ 10	Dennis Rodman	.40	.18
❑ 11	Rony Seikaly	.05	.02
❑ 12	Harvey Grant	.05	.02
❑ 13	Craig Ehlo	.05	.02
❑ 14	Derek Harper	.05	.02
❑ 15	Oliver Miller	.05	.02

Drafted by the Raptors
❑ 16 Dennis Scott .05 .02
❑ 17 Ed Pinckney .05 .02
Drafted by the Raptors
❑ 18 Eric Piatkowski .05 .02
❑ 19 B.J. Armstrong .05 .02
❑ 20 Tyrone Hill .05 .02
❑ 21 Malik Sealy .05 .02
❑ 22 Clyde Drexler .20 .09
❑ 23 Aaron McKie .05 .02
❑ 24 Harold Miner .05 .02
❑ 25 Bobby Hurley .05 .02
❑ 26 Dell Curry .05 .02
❑ 27 Micheal Williams .05 .02
❑ 28 Adam Keefe .05 .02
❑ 29 Antonio Harvey .05 .02
Drafted by the Grizzlies
❑ 30 Billy Owens .05 .02
❑ 31 Nate McMillan .05 .02
❑ 32 J.R. Reid .05 .02
❑ 33 Grant Hill 1.00 .45
❑ 34 Charles Barkley .30 .14
❑ 35 Tyrone Corbin .05 .02
Traded to the Kings
❑ 36 Don MacLean .05 .02
❑ 37 Kenny Smith .05 .02
❑ 38 Juwan Howard .20 .09
❑ 39 Charles Smith .05 .02
❑ 40 Shawn Kemp .30 .14
❑ 41 Dana Barros .05 .02
❑ 42 Vin Baker .20 .09
❑ 43 Armon Gilliam .05 .02
❑ 44 Spud Webb .05 .02
Traded to the Hawks
❑ 45 Michael Jordan 2.50 1.10
❑ 46 Scott Williams .05 .02
❑ 47 Vlade Divac .05 .02
❑ 48 Roy Tarpley .05 .02
❑ 49 Bimbo Coles .05 .02
❑ 50 David Robinson .30 .14
❑ 51 Terry Dehere .05 .02
❑ 52 Bobby Phills .05 .02
❑ 53 Sherman Douglas .05 .02
❑ 54 Rodney Rogers .05 .02
Traded to the Clippers
❑ 55 Detlef Schrempf .10 .05
❑ 56 Calbert Cheaney .05 .02
❑ 57 Tom Gugliotta .10 .05
❑ 58 Jeff Turner .05 .02
❑ 59 Mookie Blaylock .05 .02
❑ 60 Bill Curley .05 .02
❑ 61 Chris Dudley .05 .02
❑ 62 Popeye Jones .05 .02
❑ 63 Scott Burrell .05 .02
❑ 64 Dale Davis .05 .02
❑ 65 Mitchell Butler .05 .02
❑ 66 Pervis Ellison .05 .02
❑ 67 Todd Day .05 .02
❑ 68 Carl Herrera .05 .02
❑ 69 Jeff Hornacek .10 .05
❑ 70 Vincent Askew .05 .02
❑ 71 A.C. Green .10 .05
❑ 72 Kevin Gamble .05 .02
❑ 73 Chris Gatling .05 .02
❑ 74 Otis Thorpe .05 .02
❑ 75 Michael Cage .05 .02
❑ 76 Carlos Rogers .05 .02
❑ 77 Gheorghe Muresan .05 .02
❑ 78 Olden Polynice .05 .02
❑ 79 Grant Long .05 .02
❑ 80 Allan Houston .25 .11
❑ 81 Charles Outlaw .05 .02
❑ 82 Clarence Weatherspoon .05 .02
❑ 83 Tony Dumas .05 .02
❑ 84 Herb Williams .05 .02
❑ 85 P.J. Brown .05 .02
❑ 86 Robert Horry .05 .02
❑ 87 Byron Scott .05 .02
Drafted by the Grizzlies
❑ 88 Horace Grant .10 .05
❑ 89 Dominique Wilkins .20 .09
❑ 90 Doug West .05 .02
❑ 91 Antoine Carr .05 .02
❑ 92 Dickey Simpkins .05 .02
Washington Bulls
❑ 93 Elden Campbell .05 .02
❑ 94 Kevin Johnson .10 .05
❑ 95 Rex Chapman .05 .02
Traded to the Heat
❑ 96 John Williams .05 .02
❑ 97 Tim Hardaway .20 .09
❑ 98 Rik Smits .05 .02
❑ 99 Rex Walters .05 .02
❑ 100 Robert Parish .10 .05
❑ 101 Isaiah Rider .10 .05
❑ 102 Sarunas Marciulionis .05 .02
❑ 103 Andrew Lang .05 .02
❑ 104 Eric Mobley .05 .02
❑ 105 Randy Brown .05 .02
❑ 106 John Stockton .20 .09
❑ 107 Lamond Murray .05 .02
❑ 108 Will Perdue .05 .02
❑ 109 Wayman Tisdale .05 .02
❑ 110 John Starks .05 .02
❑ 111 John Salley .05 .02
❑ 112 Lucious Harris .05 .02
❑ 113 Jeff Malone .05 .02
❑ 114 Anthony Bowie .05 .02
❑ 115 Vinny Del Negro .05 .02
❑ 116 Michael Adams .05 .02
❑ 117 Chris Mullin .20 .09
❑ 118 Benoit Benjamin .05 .02
Drafted by the Grizzlies
❑ 119 Byron Houston .05 .02
❑ 120 LaPhonso Ellis .05 .02
❑ 121 Doug Overton .05 .02
❑ 122 Jerome Kersey .05 .02
Drafted by the Grizzlies
❑ 123 Greg Minor .05 .02
❑ 124 Christian Laettner .10 .05
❑ 125 Mark Price .05 .02
❑ 126 Kevin Willis .05 .02
❑ 127 Kenny Anderson .10 .05
❑ 128 Marty Conlon .05 .02
❑ 129 Blue Edwards .05 .02
Drafted by the Grizzlies
❑ 130 Dan Schayes .05 .02
❑ 131 Duane Ferrell .05 .02
❑ 132 Charles Oakley .05 .02
❑ 133 Brian Grant .20 .09
❑ 134 Reggie Williams .05 .02
❑ 135 Steve Kerr .05 .02
❑ 136 Khalid Reeves .05 .02
❑ 137 David Benoit .05 .02
❑ 138 Derrick Coleman .10 .05
❑ 139 Anthony Peeler .05 .02
❑ 140 Jim Jackson .05 .02
❑ 141 Stacey Augmon .05 .02
❑ 142 Sam Cassell .10 .05
❑ 143 Derrick McKey .05 .02
❑ 144 Danny Ferry .05 .02
❑ 145 Anfernee Hardaway .60 .25
❑ 146 Clifford Robinson .05 .02
❑ 147 B.J. Tyler .05 .02
Drafted by the Raptors
❑ 148 Mark West .05 .02
❑ 149 David Wingate .05 .02
Traded to the Sonics
❑ 150 Willie Anderson .05 .02
Drafted by the Raptors
❑ 151 Hersey Hawkins .10 .05
Traded to the Sonics
❑ 152 Bryant Stith .05 .02
❑ 153 Dan Majerle .05 .02
❑ 154 Chris Smith .05 .02
❑ 155 Donyell Marshall .10 .05
❑ 156 Loy Vaught .05 .02
❑ 157 Reggie Miller .20 .09
❑ 158 Hubert Davis .05 .02
❑ 159 Ron Harper .10 .05
❑ 160 Lee Mayberry .05 .02
❑ 161 Eddie Jones .40 .18
❑ 162 Shawn Bradley .05 .02
❑ 163 Nick Anderson .05 .02
❑ 164 Ervin Johnson .05 .02
❑ 165 Walt Williams .05 .02
❑ 166 Steve Smith FF .05 .02
❑ 167 Dino Radja FF .05 .02
❑ 168 Alonzo Mourning FF .10 .05
❑ 169 Michael Jordan FF 1.25 .55
❑ 170 Tyrone Hill FF .05 .02
❑ 171 Jamal Mashburn FF .05 .02
❑ 172 Dikembe Mutombo FF .05 .02
❑ 173 Grant Hill FF .75 .35
with Michael Jordan
❑ 174 Latrell Sprewell FF .20 .09
❑ 175 Hakeem Olajuwon FF .20 .09
❑ 176 Reggie Miller FF .10 .05
❑ 177 Pooh Richardson FF .05 .02
❑ 178 Cedric Ceballos FF .05 .02
❑ 179 Glen Rice FF .05 .02
❑ 180 Glenn Robinson FF .10 .05
❑ 181 Isaiah Rider FF .05 .02
❑ 182 Derrick Coleman FF .05 .02
❑ 183 Patrick Ewing FF .10 .05
❑ 184 Shaquille O'Neal FF .40 .18
❑ 185 Dana Barros FF .05 .02
❑ 186 Dan Majerle FF .05 .02
❑ 187 Clifford Robinson FF .05 .02
❑ 188 Mitch Richmond FF .10 .05
❑ 189 David Robinson FF .20 .09
❑ 190 Gary Payton FF .20 .09
❑ 191 Oliver Miller FF .05 .02
❑ 192 Karl Malone FF .20 .09
❑ 193 Kevin Pritchard FF .05 .02
❑ 194 Chris Webber FF .25 .11
❑ 195 Michael Jordan PD 1.25 .55
❑ 196 Hakeem Olajuwon PD .20 .09
❑ 197 Vin Baker PD .10 .05
❑ 198 Grant Hill PD .60 .25
❑ 199 Clyde Drexler PD .10 .05
❑ 200 Chris Webber PD .25 .11
❑ 201 Shawn Kemp PD .20 .09
❑ 202 Shaquille O'Neal PD .40 .18
❑ 203 Stacey Augmon PD .05 .02
❑ 204 David Benoit PD .05 .02
❑ 205 Rodney Rogers PD .05 .02
❑ 206 Latrell Sprewell PD .20 .09
❑ 207 Brian Grant PD .10 .05
❑ 208 Lamond Murray PD .05 .02
❑ 209 Shawn Kemp CL .05 .02
❑ 210 Michael Jordan CL .60 .25
❑ 211 Cory Alexander RC .05 .02
❑ 212 Vernon Maxwell .05 .02
❑ 213 George Lynch .05 .02
❑ 214 Terry Mills .05 .02
❑ 215 Scottie Pippen .60 .25
❑ 216 Donald Royal .05 .02
❑ 217 Wesley Person .10 .05
❑ 218 Antonio Davis .05 .02
❑ 219 Glenn Robinson .20 .09
❑ 220 Jerry Stackhouse RC .60 .25
❑ 221 James Robinson .05 .02
❑ 222 Chris Mills .05 .02
❑ 223 Chuck Person .05 .02
❑ 224 Duane Causwell .05 .02
❑ 225 Gary Payton .30 .14
❑ 226 Eric Montross .05 .02
❑ 227 Felton Spencer .05 .02
❑ 228 Scott Skiles .05 .02
❑ 229 Latrell Sprewell .40 .18
❑ 230 Sedale Threatt .05 .02
❑ 231 Mark Bryant .05 .02
❑ 232 Buck Williams .05 .02
❑ 233 Brian Williams .05 .02
❑ 234 Sharone Wright .05 .02
❑ 235 Karl Malone .30 .14
❑ 236 Kevin Edwards .05 .02
❑ 237 Muggsy Bogues .05 .02
❑ 238 Mario Elie .05 .02
❑ 239 Rasheed Wallace RC .75 .35
❑ 240 George Zidek RC .05 .02
❑ 241 Cedric Ceballos .05 .02
❑ 242 Alan Henderson RC .20 .09
❑ 243 Joe Kleine .05 .02
❑ 244 Patrick Ewing .20 .09
❑ 245 Sasha Danilovic RC .05 .02
❑ 246 Bill Wennington .05 .02
❑ 247 Steve Smith .10 .05
❑ 248 Bryant Stith .05 .02
❑ 249 Dino Radja .05 .02
❑ 250 Monty Williams .05 .02
❑ 251 Andrew DeClercq RC .05 .02
❑ 252 Sean Elliott .05 .02
❑ 253 Rick Fox .05 .02
❑ 254 Lionel Simmons .05 .02
❑ 255 Dikembe Mutombo .10 .05
❑ 256 Lindsey Hunter .05 .02

❑ 257 Terrell Brandon .10 .05
❑ 258 Shawn Respert RC .05 .02
❑ 259 Rodney Rogers .05 .02
❑ 260 Bryon Russell .05 .02
❑ 261 David Wesley .05 .02
❑ 262 Ken Norman .05 .02
❑ 263 Mitch Richmond .20 .09
❑ 264 Sam Perkins .10 .05
❑ 265 Hakeem Olajuwon .30 .14
❑ 266 Brian Shaw .05 .02
❑ 267 B.J. Armstrong .05 .02
❑ 268 Jalen Rose .25 .11
❑ 269 Bryant Reeves RC .20 .09
❑ 270 Cherokee Parks RC .05 .02
❑ 271 Dennis Rodman .40 .18
❑ 272 Kendall Gill .10 .05
❑ 273 Elliot Perry .05 .02
❑ 274 Anthony Mason .10 .05
❑ 275 Kevin Garnett RC 2.50 1.10
❑ 276 Damon Stoudamire RC 1.00 .45
❑ 277 Lawrence Moten RC .05 .02
❑ 278 Ed O'Bannon RC .05 .02
❑ 279 Toni Kukoc .25 .11
❑ 280 Greg Ostertag RC .05 .02
❑ 281 Tom Hammonds .05 .02
❑ 282 Yinka Dare .05 .02
❑ 283 Michael Smith .05 .02
❑ 284 Clifford Rozier .05 .02
❑ 285 Gary Trent RC .05 .02
❑ 286 Shaquille O'Neal 1.00 .45
❑ 287 Luc Longley .05 .02
❑ 288 Bob Sura RC .10 .05
❑ 289 Dana Barros .05 .02
❑ 290 Lorenzo Williams .05 .02
❑ 291 Haywoode Workman .05 .02
❑ 292 Randolph Childress RC .05 .02
❑ 293 Doc Rivers .05 .02
❑ 294 Chris Webber .60 .25
❑ 295 Kurt Thomas RC .10 .05
❑ 296 Greg Anthony .05 .02
❑ 297 Tyus Edney RC .05 .02
❑ 298 Danny Manning .10 .05
❑ 299 Brent Barry RC .20 .09
❑ 300 Joe Smith RC .60 .25
❑ 301 Pooh Richardson .05 .02
❑ 302 Mark Jackson .05 .02
❑ 303 Richard Dumas .05 .02
❑ 304 Michael Finley RC .75 .35
❑ 305 Theo Ratliff RC .25 .11
❑ 306 Gary Grant .05 .02
❑ 307 Jamal Mashburn .10 .05
❑ 308 Corliss Williamson RC .40 .18
❑ 309 Eric Williams RC .10 .05
❑ 310 Zan Tabak .05 .02
❑ 311 Eric Murdock .05 .02
❑ 312 Sherrell Ford RC .05 .02
❑ 313 Terry Davis .05 .02
❑ 314 Vern Fleming .05 .02
❑ 315 Jason Caffey RC .10 .05
❑ 316 Mario Bennett RC .05 .02
❑ 317 David Vaughn RC .05 .02
❑ 318 Loren Meyer RC .05 .02
❑ 319 Travis Best RC .10 .05
❑ 320 Byron Scott .05 .02
❑ 321 Mookie Blaylock SR .05 .02
❑ 322 Dee Brown SR .05 .02
❑ 323 Alonzo Mourning SR .10 .05
❑ 324 Michael Jordan SR 1.25 .55
❑ 325 Terrell Brandon SR .05 .02
❑ 326 Jim Jackson SR .05 .02
❑ 327 Dikembe Mutombo SR .05 .02
❑ 328 Grant Hill SR .60 .25
❑ 329 Joe Smith SR UER .30 .14
Team stats say Seattle
Should be Golden State
❑ 330 Clyde Drexler SR .10 .05
❑ 331 Reggie Miller SR .10 .05
❑ 332 Lamond Murray SR .05 .02
❑ 333 Nick Van Exel SR .05 .02
❑ 334 Glen Rice SR .05 .02
❑ 335 Glenn Robinson SR .10 .05
❑ 336 Christian Laettner SR .05 .02
❑ 337 Kenny Anderson SR .05 .02
❑ 338 Patrick Ewing SR .10 .05
❑ 339 Shaquille O'Neal SR .40 .18
❑ 340 Jerry Stackhouse SR .30 .14
❑ 341 Charles Barkley SR .20 .09
❑ 342 Clifford Robinson SR .05 .02
❑ 343 Brian Grant SR .10 .05
❑ 344 David Robinson SR .20 .09
❑ 345 Shawn Kemp SR .20 .09
❑ 346 Damon Stoudamire SR .60 .25
❑ 347 Karl Malone SR .20 .09
❑ 348 Bryant Reeves SR .10 .05
❑ 349 Juwan Howard SR .10 .05
❑ 350 Nick Anderson .05 .02
Dee Brown PT
Orlando vs. Boston East Conf
1st Round
❑ 351 Rik Smits PT .05 .02
Indiana vs Atlanta East Conf.
1st Round
❑ 352 Herb Williams .05 .02
Greg Dreiling PT
New York vs Cleveland East Conf.
1st Round
❑ 353 Michael Jordan PT 1.25 .55
Chicago vs Charlotte East Conf.
1st Round
❑ 354 David Robinson PT .20 .09
San Antonio vs Denver West Conf.
1st Round
❑ 355 Terry Porter .10 .05
Kevin Johnson PT
Phoenix vs Portland West Conf.
1st Round
❑ 356 Clyde Drexler PT .10 .05
Houston vs Utah West Conf.
1st Round
❑ 357 Cedric Ceballos PT .05 .02
L.A. Lakers vs Seattle West Conf.
1st Round
❑ 358 Horace Grant .05 .02
Group PT
Orlando vs Chicago
East Conf.
Semifinals
❑ 359 Reggie Miller PT .10 .05
Indiana vs New York East Conf.
Semifinals
❑ 360 Avery Johnson .10 .05
Nick Van Exel PT
SA vs L.A. Lakers
West Conf. Semifinals
❑ 361 Hakeem Olajuwon .20 .09
Robert Horry PT
Houston vs Phoenix
West Conf. Semifinals
❑ 362 Rik Smits PT .05 .02
Orlando vs Indiana
East Conf. Finals
❑ 363 David Robinson .20 .09
Hakeem Olajuwon PT
Houston vs San Antonio
West Conf. Finals
❑ 364 Robert Horry PT .05 .02
Houston vs Orlando
NBA Finals
❑ 365 Kenny Smith PT .05 .02
Houston Rockets
1995 NBA Champs
❑ 366 Stacey Augmon LOVE .05 .02
❑ 367 Sherman Douglas LOVE .05 .02
❑ 368 Larry Johnson LOVE .05 .02
❑ 369 Scottie Pippen LOVE .30 .14
❑ 370 Tyrone Hill LOVE .05 .02
❑ 371 Jamal Mashburn LOVE .05 .02
❑ 372 M. Abdul-Rauf LOVE .05 .02
❑ 373 Grant Hill LOVE .60 .25
❑ 374 Latrell Sprewell LOVE .20 .09
❑ 375 Sam Cassell LOVE .05 .02
❑ 376 Rik Smits LOVE .05 .02
❑ 377 Terry Dehere LOVE .05 .02
❑ 378 Eddie Jones LOVE .20 .09
❑ 379 Billy Owens LOVE .05 .02
❑ 380 Vin Baker LOVE .10 .05
❑ 381 Isaiah Rider LOVE .05 .02
❑ 382 Kenny Anderson LOVE .05 .02
❑ 383 John Starks LOVE .05 .02
❑ 384 A. Hardaway LOVE .40 .18
❑ 385 Sharone Wright LOVE .05 .02
❑ 386 Charles Barkley LOVE .20 .09
❑ 387 Clifford Robinson LOVE .05 .02
❑ 388 Walt Williams LOVE .05 .02
❑ 389 Sean Elliott LOVE .05 .02
❑ 390 Gary Payton LOVE .20 .09
❑ 391 Carlos Rogers LOVE .05 .02
❑ 392 John Stockton LOVE .10 .05
❑ 393 Greg Anthony LOVE .05 .02
❑ 394 Chris Webber LOVE .25 .11
❑ 395 Gary Payton PG .20 .09
❑ 396 Mookie Blaylock PG .05 .02
❑ 397 Charles Barkley PG .20 .09
❑ 398 Grant Hill PG .60 .25
❑ 399 Anfernee Hardaway PG .40 .18
❑ 400 Kenny Anderson PG .05 .02
❑ 401 Mark Jackson PG .05 .02
❑ 402 Karl Malone PG .20 .09
❑ 403 Avery Johnson PG .05 .02
❑ 404 Larry Johnson 40 .05 .02
Top Scorers
❑ 405 Nick Van Exel 40 .05 .02
Top Shooters
❑ 406 Vin Baker 40 .10 .05
Top Rebounders
❑ 407 Jason Kidd 40 .25 .11
Top Passers
❑ 408 David Robinson 40 .20 .09
Top Defenders
❑ 409 Shawn Kemp CL .05 .02
❑ 410 Michael Jordan CL .60 .25
❑ NNO Bulls Comm. Card 6.00 2.70
Issued with Factory set

1995-96 Collector's Choice Player's Club

	MINT	NRMT
COMPLETE SET (410)	70.00	32.00
COMPLETE SERIES 1 (210)	30.00	13.50
COMPLETE SERIES 2 (200)	40.00	18.00
COMMON CARD (1-410)	.15	.07

*STARS: 1.5X TO 3X BASE CARD HI
*RCs: 1.25X TO 2.5X BASE HI
ONE PER PACK

1995-96 Collector's Choice Player's Club Platinum

	MINT	NRMT
COMPLETE SET (410)	800.00	350.00
COMPLETE SERIES 1 (210)	300.00	135.00
COMPLETE SERIES 2 (200)	500.00	220.00
COMMON CARD (1-410)	1.50	.70

*STARS: 15X TO 30X BASE CARD HI
*RCs: 10X TO 20X BASE HI
SER.1/2 STATED ODDS 1:35

1995-96 Collector's Choice Crash the Game Assists/Rebounds

	MINT	NRMT
COMPLETE SILVER SET (90)	60.00	27.00

*SINGLES: 1.25X TO 3X BASE CARD HI
*GOLD CARDS: 2X TO 4X HI COLUMN
EACH PLAYER HAS THREE DIFF.SILV.CARDS
EACH PLAYER HAS THREE DIFF.GOLD CARDS
SER.2 STATED ODDS 1:5
GOLD: SER.2 STATED ODDS 1:49
COMP.SILVER RED.SET (30).. 8.00 3.60
*SIL.RED.CARDS: .2X TO .5X HI COLUMN
*GOLD RED: 2X TO 4X SILVER RED.
ONE RED.SET PER WINNER BY MAIL

	MINT	NRMT
❑ C1 Michael Jordan 1/30 L	8.00	3.60
❑ C1B Michael Jordan 2/22 L	8.00	3.60
❑ C1C Michael Jordan 3/19 L	8.00	3.60
❑ C2 Tim Hardaway 2/4 L	.60	.25
❑ C2B Tim Hardaway 3/12 L	.60	.25
❑ C2C Tim Hardaway 4/11 W	.60	.25
❑ C3 Juwan Howard 2/2 L	.60	.25
❑ C3B Juwan Howard 2/21 L	.60	.25
❑ C3C Juwan Howard 3/30 L	.60	.25
❑ C4 Shawn Kemp 1/29 L	1.00	.45
❑ C4B Shawn Kemp 3/15 W	1.00	.45
❑ C4C Shawn Kemp 4/3 L	1.00	.45
❑ C5 Nick Van Exel 2/4 L	.30	.14
❑ C5B Nick Van Exel 2/21 L	.30	.14
❑ C5C Nick Van Exel 4/14 L	.30	.14
❑ C6 Mookie Blaylock 2/16 L	.15	.07
❑ C6B Mookie Blaylock 3/8 L	.15	.07
❑ C6C Mookie Blaylock 4/20 L	.15	.07
❑ C7 John Stockton 2/13 W	.60	.25
❑ C7B John Stockton 3/6 W	.60	.25
❑ C7C John Stockton 4/14 W	.60	.25
❑ C8 Scottie Pippen 1/28 L	2.00	.90
❑ C8B Scottie Pippen 3/15 L	2.00	.90
❑ C8C Scottie Pippen 4/11 L	2.00	.90
❑ C9 Vin Baker 2/3 L	.60	.25
❑ C9B Vin Baker 3/4 W	.60	.25
❑ C9C Vin Baker 4/5 W	.60	.25
❑ C10 Lamond Murray 2/3 L	.15	.07
❑ C10B Lamond Murray 2/17 L	.15	.07
❑ C10C Lamond Murray 3/30 L	.15	.07
❑ C11 David Robinson 2/15 W	1.00	.45
❑ C11B David Robinson 3/14 W	1.00	.45
❑ C11C David Robinson 4/13 W	1.00	.45
❑ C12 Jason Kidd 2/6 L	2.00	.90
❑ C12B Jason Kidd 3/19 L	2.00	.90
❑ C12C Jason Kidd 4/13 W	2.00	.90
❑ C13 Rod Strickland 2/15 L	.30	.14
❑ C13B Rod Strickland 3/8 W	.30	.14
❑ C13C Rod Strickland 4/5 L	.30	.14
❑ C14 Glen Rice 1/29 L	.30	.14
❑ C14B Glen Rice 2/28 L	.30	.14
❑ C14C Glen Rice 4/2 L	.30	.14
❑ C15 A. Hardaway 2/4 W	2.00	.90
❑ C15B A. Hardaway 3/31 L	2.00	.90
❑ C15C A. Hardaway 4/21 W	2.00	.90
❑ C16 H. Olajuwon 2/15 L	1.00	.45
❑ C16B H. Olajuwon 3/8 L	1.00	.45
❑ C16C H. Olajuwon 4/15 W	1.00	.45
❑ C17 K. Anderson 2/14 W	.30	.14
❑ C17B K. Anderson 2/29 W	.30	.14
❑ C17C K. Anderson 3/29 L	.30	.14
❑ C18 Sharone Wright 2/14 L	.15	.07
❑ C18B Sharone Wright 3/22 L	.15	.07
❑ C18C Sharone Wright 4/17 L	.15	.07
❑ C19 D. Mutombo 2/16 L	.30	.14
❑ C19B D. Mutombo 3/2 W	.30	.14
❑ C19C D. Mutombo 4/5 W	.30	.14
❑ C20 Muggsy Bogues 2/1	.15	.07
❑ C20B Muggsy Bogues 2/21 L	.15	.07
❑ C20C Muggsy Bogues 3/20 L	.15	.07
❑ C21 Reggie Miller 2/18 L	.60	.25
❑ C21B Reggie Miller 3/5 L	.60	.25
❑ C21C Reggie Miller 4/8 L	.60	.25
❑ C22 Danny Manning 2/6 L	.30	.14
❑ C22B Danny Manning 3/3 L	.30	.14
❑ C22C Danny Manning 4/16 L	.30	.14
❑ C23 C. Laettner 2/5 L	.30	.14
❑ C23B C. Laettner 3/10 L	.30	.14
❑ C23C C. Laettner 3/27 W	.30	.14
❑ C24 Eric Montross 2/14 L	.15	.07
❑ C24B Eric Montross 3/8 L	.15	.07
❑ C24C Eric Montross 3/31 L	.15	.07
❑ C25 Patrick Ewing 2/21 L	.60	.25
❑ C25B Patrick Ewing 3/29 W	.60	.25
❑ C25C Patrick Ewing 4/3 W	.60	.25
❑ C26 D. Stoudamire 1/30 L	3.00	1.35
❑ C26B D. Stoudamire 3/10 L	3.00	1.35
❑ C26C D. Stoudamire 3/22 W	3.00	1.35
❑ C27 Bryant Reeves 2/28 L	.60	.25
❑ C27B Bryant Reeves 3/31 L	.60	.25
❑ C27C Bryant Reeves 4/9 L	.60	.25
❑ C28 Joe Dumars 2/15 L	.60	.25
❑ C28B Joe Dumars 3/22 L	.60	.25
❑ C28C Joe Dumars 4/13 L	.60	.25
❑ C29 Tyrone Hill 2/6 L	.15	.07
❑ C29B Tyrone Hill 3/10 L	.15	.07
❑ C29C Tyrone Hill 4/20 L	.15	.07
❑ C30 Brian Grant 2/13 L	.60	.25
❑ C30B Brian Grant 3/20 L	.60	.25
❑ C30C Brian Grant 4/21 L	.60	.25

1995-96 Collector's Choice Crash the Game Scoring

	MINT	NRMT
COMPLETE SILVER SET (81)	60.00	27.00

*SINGLES: 1.25X TO 3X BASE CARD HI
*GOLD CARDS: 2X TO 4X HI COLUMN
EACH PLAYER HAS THREE DIFF.SILV.CARDS
EACH PLAYER HAS THREE DIFF.GOLD CARDS
SER.1 STATED ODDS 1:5
GOLD: SER.1 STATED ODDS 1:50
COMP.SILVER RED.SET (30) 10.00 4.50
*SIL.RED.CARDS: .2X TO .5X HI COLUMN
*GOLD RED: 2X TO 4X SILVER RED.
ONE RED.SET PER WINNER BY MAIL

	MINT	NRMT
❑ C1 Michael Jordan HOU W	8.00	3.60
❑ C1B Michael Jordan NY W	8.00	3.60
❑ C1C Michael Jordan ORL W	8.00	3.60
❑ C2 Kenny Anderson CLE L	.30	.14
❑ C2B Kenny Anderson LAC L	.30	.14
❑ C2C Kenny Anderson MIA L	.30	.14
❑ C3 Charles Barkley CLE L	1.00	.45
❑ C3B Charles Barkley GS W	1.00	.45
❑ C3C Charles Barkley SA W	1.00	.45
❑ C4 Dana Barros ATL L	.15	.07
❑ C4B Dana Barros BOS W	.15	.07
❑ C4C Dana Barros LAL L	.15	.07
❑ C5 A. Hardaway CHI W	2.00	.90
❑ C5B A. Hardaway SA W	2.00	.90
❑ C5C A. Hardaway MIL W	2.00	.90
❑ C6 Mookie Blaylock DAL L	.15	.07
❑ C6B Mookie Blaylock DET L	.15	.07
❑ C6C Mookie Blaylock TOR L	.15	.07
❑ C7 Lamond Murray ATL L	.15	.07
❑ C7B Lamond Murray MIN L	.15	.07
❑ C7C Lamond Murray VAN L	.15	.07
❑ C8 Karl Malone HOU L	1.00	.45
❑ C8B Karl Malone NY L	1.00	.45
❑ C8C Karl Malone POR W	1.00	.45
❑ C9 A. Mourning CHI L	.60	.25
❑ C9B A. Mourning IND L	.60	.25
❑ C9C A. Mourning WASH W	.60	.25
❑ C10 H. Olajuwon LAL W	1.00	.45
❑ C10B H.Olajuwon ORL W	1.00	.45
❑ C10C H. Olajuwon POR W	1.00	.45
❑ C11 Mark Price CHI L	.15	.07
❑ C11B Mark Price NJ L	.15	.07
❑ C11C Mark Price SEA L	.15	.07
❑ C12 Isaiah Rider BOS L	.30	.14
❑ C12B Isaiah Rider PHO L	.30	.14
❑ C12C Isaiah Rider SAC L	.30	.14
❑ C13 Glen Rice NJ W	.30	.14
❑ C13B Glen Rice SAC W	.30	.14
❑ C13C Glen Rice WASH W	.30	.14
❑ C14 Mitch Richmond LAL L	.60	.25
❑ C14B Mitch Richmond MIN W	.60	.25
❑ C14C Mitch Richmond NJ L	.60	.25
❑ C15 Chris Webber GS W	2.00	.90
❑ C15B Chris Webber IND L	2.00	.90
❑ C15C Chris Webber PHI L	2.00	.90
❑ C16 Nick Van Exel DAL L	.30	.14
❑ C16B Nick Van Exel MIL L	.30	.14
❑ C16C Nick Van Exel SAC L	.30	.14
❑ C17 M. Abdul-Rauf CHA L	.15	.07
❑ C17B M. Abdul-Rauf PHO W	.15	.07
❑ C17C M. Abdul-Rauf SEA	.15	.07
❑ C18 D. Wilkins PHI L	.60	.25
❑ C18B D. Wilkins POR L	.60	.25
❑ C18C D. Wilkins TOR L	.60	.25
❑ C19 Patrick Ewing BOS W	.60	.25
❑ C19B Patrick Ewing CHA L	.60	.25
❑ C19C Patrick Ewing PHO L	.60	.25
❑ C20 D. Robinson DEN	1.00	.45
❑ C20B David Robinson SEA W	1.00	.45
❑ C20C D. Robinson WASH W	1.00	.45
❑ C21 Shawn Kemp DEN L	1.00	.45
❑ C21B Shawn Kemp DET L	1.00	.45
❑ C21C Shawn Kemp UTAH L	1.00	.45
❑ C22 Jason Kidd IND W	2.00	.90
❑ C22B Jason Kidd LAC L	2.00	.90
❑ C22C Jason Kidd SA L	2.00	.90
❑ C23 Glenn Robinson ATL W	.60	.25
❑ C23B Glenn Robinson CHA L	.60	.25
❑ C23C Glenn Robinson VAN L	.60	.25
❑ C24 Reggie Miller MIN L	.60	.25
❑ C24B Reggie Miller NY L	.60	.25
❑ C24C Reggie Miller ORL L	.60	.25
❑ C25 Joe Dumars CLE L	.60	.25
❑ C25B Joe Dumars MIL L	.60	.25
❑ C25C Joe Dumars UTAH L	.60	.25
❑ C26 Latrell Sprewell DAL L	1.25	.55
❑ C26B Latrell Sprewell HOU L	1.25	.55
❑ C26C Latrell Sprewell MIA L	1.25	.55
❑ C27 C. Robinson LAC L	.15	.07
❑ C27B C. Robinson PHI L	.15	.07
❑ C27C C. Robinson UTAH W	.15	.07
❑ XC28 D. Stoudamire EXCH	3.00	1.35
❑ XC29 Bryant Reeves EXCH	.60	.25
❑ XC30 Michael Jordan EXCH	8.00	3.60

1995-96 Collector's Choice Debut Trade

	MINT	NRMT
COMPLETE SET (30)	4.00	1.80
COMMON CARD (T1-T30)	.05	.02
SEMISTARS	.15	.07
UNLISTED STARS	.30	.14
COMP.PLAY.CLUB SET (30)..	10.00	4.50

*PLAY.CLUB STARS: 1X TO 2X HI COLUMN
*PLAY.CLUB RCs: .75X TO 1.5X HI

COMP.PLAY.PLAT.SET (30)..	40.00	18.00

*PLAY.PLAT.STARS: 10X TO 20X HI COLUMN
*PLAY.PLAT.RCs: 6X TO 12X HI
ONE SET PER DEBUT TRADE CARD VIA MAIL
TRADE: SER.2 STATED ODDS 1:30
PC TRADE: SER.2 STATED ODDS 1:144
PCP TRADE: SER.2 STATED ODDS 1:720

❑ T1 Magic Johnson	1.00	.45
❑ T2 Arvydas Sabonis	.50	.23
❑ T3 Kenny Anderson	.15	.07
❑ T4 Antonio McDyess	1.50	.70
❑ T5 Sherman Douglas	.05	.02
❑ T6 Spud Webb	.05	.02
❑ T7 Glen Rice	.15	.07
❑ T8 Todd Day	.05	.02
❑ T9 John Williams	.05	.02
❑ T10 Chris Morris	.05	.02
❑ T11 Shawn Bradley	.05	.02
❑ T12 Dan Majerle	.05	.02
❑ T13 George McCloud	.05	.02
❑ T14 Derrick Coleman	.15	.07
❑ T15 Kendall Gill	.15	.07
❑ T16 Ricky Pierce	.05	.02
❑ T17 Robert Pack	.05	.02
❑ T18 Alonzo Mourning	.30	.14
❑ T19 Matt Geiger	.05	.02
❑ T20 Don MacLean	.05	.02
❑ T21 Willie Anderson	.05	.02
❑ T22 Oliver Miller	.05	.02
❑ T23 Tracy Murray	.05	.02
❑ T24 Ed Pinckney	.05	.02
❑ T25 Alvin Robertson	.05	.02
❑ T26 Anthony Avent	.05	.02
❑ T27 Blue Edwards	.05	.02
❑ T28 Kenny Gattison	.05	.02
❑ T29 Chris King	.05	.02
❑ T30 Eric Murdock	.05	.02

1995-96 Collector's Choice Draft Trade

	MINT	NRMT
COMPLETE SET (10)	12.00	5.50
COMMON CARD (D1-D10)	.25	.11
SEMISTARS	.50	.23
UNLISTED STARS	1.00	.45

ONE SET PER DRAFT TRADE CARD VIA MAIL
TRADE: SER.1 STATED ODDS 1:144

❑ D1 Joe Smith	1.50	.70
❑ D2 Antonio McDyess	2.50	1.10
❑ D3 Jerry Stackhouse	1.50	.70
❑ D4 Rasheed Wallace	2.00	.90
❑ D5 Kevin Garnett	6.00	2.70
❑ D6 Bryant Reeves	.50	.23

❑ D7 Damon Stoudamire	2.50	1.10
❑ D8 Shawn Respert	.25	.11
❑ D9 Ed O'Bannon	.25	.11
❑ D10 Kurt Thomas	.25	.11

1995-96 Collector's Choice Jordan He's Back

	MINT	NRMT
COMPLETE SET (5)	6.00	2.70
COMMON JORDAN (M1-M5)	1.50	.70

ONE PER SPECIAL RETAIL PACK

❑ M1 Michael Jordan First Game Back	1.50	.70
❑ M2 Michael Jordan Buzzer beater versus Hawks	1.50	.70
❑ M3 Michael Jordan Versus Knicks	1.50	.70
❑ M4 Michael Jordan Playoffs versus Charlotte	1.50	.70
❑ M5 Michael Jordan Playoffs versus Orlando Switch to #23	1.50	.70

1996-97 Collector's Choice

	MINT	NRMT
COMPLETE SET (400)	30.00	13.50
COMP.FACT.SET (406)	35.00	16.00
COMPLETE SERIES 1 (200)..	15.00	6.75
COMPLETE SERIES 2 (200)..	15.00	6.75
COMMON CARD (1-400)	.05	.02
COMMON PENNY! (113-117)	.40	.18
SEMISTARS	.10	.05
UNLISTED STARS	.20	.09

SUBSET CARDS HALF VALUE OF BASE CARDS

COMP.UPDATE SET (30)	12.00	5.50
COMMON UPDATE (401-430)	.40	.18
UPDATE SEMISTARS	.60	.25
UPDATE UNLISTED STARS	1.00	.45

ONE UPDATE SET VIA TRADE CARD
UPDATE TRADE: STATED ODDS 1:71
F1-F4: RANDOM INS.IN FACT.SETS

❑ 1 Mookie Blaylock	.05	.02
❑ 2 Grant Long	.05	.02
❑ 3 Christian Laettner	.10	.05
❑ 4 Craig Ehlo	.05	.02
❑ 5 Ken Norman	.05	.02
❑ 6 Stacey Augmon	.05	.02
❑ 7 Dana Barros	.05	.02
❑ 8 Dino Radja	.05	.02
❑ 9 Rick Fox	.05	.02
❑ 10 Eric Montross	.05	.02
❑ 11 David Wesley	.05	.02
❑ 12 Eric Williams	.05	.02
❑ 13 Glen Rice	.10	.05
❑ 14 Dell Curry	.05	.02
❑ 15 Matt Geiger	.05	.02
❑ 16 Scott Burrell	.05	.02
❑ 17 George Zidek	.05	.02
❑ 18 Muggsy Bogues	.05	.02
❑ 19 Ron Harper	.10	.05
❑ 20 Steve Kerr	.05	.02
❑ 21 Toni Kukoc	.25	.11
❑ 22 Dennis Rodman	.40	.18
❑ 23 Michael Jordan	2.50	1.10
❑ 24 Luc Longley	.05	.02
❑ 25 Michael Jordan Vlade Divac VT	1.25	.55
❑ 26 Michael Jordan Bulls VT	1.25	.55
❑ 27 Luc Longley VT	.05	.02
❑ 28 Scottie Pippen VT	.30	.14
❑ 29 Toni Kukoc Juwan Howard VT	.10	.05
❑ 30 Terrell Brandon	.10	.05
❑ 31 Bobby Phills	.05	.02
❑ 32 Tyrone Hill	.05	.02
❑ 33 Michael Cage	.05	.02
❑ 34 Bob Sura	.05	.02
❑ 35 Tony Dumas	.05	.02
❑ 36 Jim Jackson	.05	.02
❑ 37 Loren Meyer	.05	.02
❑ 38 Cherokee Parks	.05	.02
❑ 39 Jamal Mashburn	.10	.05
❑ 40 Popeye Jones	.05	.02
❑ 41 LaPhonso Ellis	.05	.02
❑ 42 Jalen Rose	.20	.09
❑ 43 Antonio McDyess	.30	.14
❑ 44 Tom Hammonds	.05	.02
❑ 45 Mahmoud Abdul-Rauf	.05	.02
❑ 46 Dale Ellis	.05	.02
❑ 47 Joe Dumars	.20	.09
❑ 48 Theo Ratliff	.10	.05
❑ 49 Lindsey Hunter	.05	.02
❑ 50 Terry Mills	.05	.02
❑ 51 Don Reid	.05	.02
❑ 52 B.J. Armstrong	.05	.02
❑ 53 Bimbo Coles	.05	.02
❑ 54 Joe Smith	.20	.09
❑ 55 Chris Mullin	.20	.09
❑ 56 Rony Seikaly	.05	.02
❑ 57 Donyell Marshall	.05	.02
❑ 58 Hakeem Olajuwon	.30	.14
❑ 59 Robert Horry	.05	.02
❑ 60 Mario Elie	.05	.02
❑ 61 Mark Bryant	.05	.02
❑ 62 Chucky Brown	.05	.02
❑ 63 Rik Smits	.05	.02
❑ 64 Derrick McKey	.05	.02
❑ 65 Eddie Johnson	.05	.02
❑ 66 Mark Jackson	.05	.02
❑ 67 Ricky Pierce	.05	.02
❑ 68 Travis Best	.05	.02
❑ 69 Rodney Rogers	.05	.02
❑ 70 Brent Barry	.05	.02
❑ 71 Lamond Murray	.05	.02
❑ 72 Eric Piatkowski	.05	.02
❑ 73 Pooh Richardson	.05	.02
❑ 74 Cedric Ceballos	.05	.02
❑ 75 Eddie Jones	.40	.18
❑ 76 Anthony Peeler	.05	.02
❑ 77 George Lynch	.05	.02
❑ 78 Vlade Divac	.05	.02
❑ 79 Rex Chapman	.05	.02
❑ 80 Sasha Danilovic	.05	.02
❑ 81 Kurt Thomas	.05	.02
❑ 82 Keith Askins	.05	.02
❑ 83 Walt Williams	.05	.02
❑ 84 Vin Baker	.10	.05
❑ 85 Shawn Respert	.05	.02

❑ 86 Sherman Douglas .05 .02
❑ 87 Marty Conlon .05 .02
❑ 88 Johnny Newman .05 .02
❑ 89 Kevin Garnett 1.25 .55
❑ 90 Andrew Lang .05 .02
❑ 91 Terry Porter .05 .02
❑ 92 Sam Mitchell .05 .02
❑ 93 Tom Gugliotta .10 .05
❑ 94 Spud Webb .05 .02
❑ 95 Kendall Gill .10 .05
❑ 96 Vern Fleming .05 .02
❑ 97 Shawn Bradley .05 .02
❑ 98 Yinka Dare .05 .02
❑ 99 Jayson Williams .10 .05
❑ 100 Kevin Edwards .05 .02
❑ 101 Charles Oakley .05 .02
❑ 102 Anthony Mason .10 .05
❑ 103 John Starks .05 .02
❑ 104 J.R. Reid .05 .02
❑ 105 Hubert Davis .05 .02
❑ 106 Gary Grant .05 .02
❑ 107 Nick Anderson .05 .02
❑ 108 Donald Royal .05 .02
❑ 109 Brian Shaw .05 .02
❑ 110 Brooks Thompson .05 .02
❑ 111 Anfernee Hardaway .60 .25
❑ 112 Dennis Scott .05 .02
❑ 113 Anfernee Hardaway PEN .40 .18
❑ 114 Anfernee Hardaway PEN .40 .18
❑ 115 Anfernee Hardaway PEN .40 .18
❑ 116 Anfernee Hardaway PEN .40 .18
❑ 117 Anfernee Hardaway PEN .40 .18
❑ 118 Derrick Coleman .10 .05
❑ 119 Rex Walters .05 .02
❑ 120 Sean Higgins .05 .02
❑ 121 Clarence Weatherspoon .05 .02
❑ 122 Jerry Stackhouse .20 .09
❑ 123 Elliot Perry .05 .02
❑ 124 Wayman Tisdale .05 .02
❑ 125 Wesley Person .05 .02
❑ 126 Charles Barkley .30 .14
❑ 127 A.C. Green .10 .05
❑ 128 Harvey Grant .05 .02
❑ 129 Arvydas Sabonis .10 .05
❑ 130 Aaron McKie .05 .02
❑ 131 Gary Trent .05 .02
❑ 132 Buck Williams .05 .02
❑ 133 Billy Owens .05 .02
❑ 134 Brian Grant .20 .09
❑ 135 Corliss Williamson .05 .02
❑ 136 Tyus Edney .05 .02
❑ 137 Olden Polynice .05 .02
❑ 138 Avery Johnson .05 .02
❑ 139 Vinny Del Negro .05 .02
❑ 140 Sean Elliott .05 .02
❑ 141 Chuck Person .05 .02
❑ 142 Will Perdue .05 .02
❑ 143 Nate McMillan .05 .02
❑ 144 Vincent Askew .05 .02
❑ 145 Detlef Schrempf .10 .05
❑ 146 Hersey Hawkins .10 .05
❑ 147 Sharone Wright .05 .02
❑ 148 Zan Tabak .05 .02
❑ 149 Oliver Miller .05 .02
❑ 150 Doug Christie .05 .02
❑ 151 Damon Stoudamire .30 .14
❑ 152 Jeff Hornacek .10 .05
❑ 153 Chris Morris .05 .02
❑ 154 Antoine Carr .05 .02
❑ 155 Karl Malone .30 .14
❑ 156 Adam Keefe .05 .02
❑ 157 Greg Anthony .05 .02
❑ 158 Blue Edwards .05 .02
❑ 159 Bryant Reeves .05 .02
❑ 160 Anthony Avent .05 .02
❑ 161 Lawrence Moten .05 .02
❑ 162 Calbert Cheaney .05 .02
❑ 163 Chris Webber .60 .25
❑ 164 Tim Legler .05 .02
❑ 165 Gheorghe Muresan .05 .02
❑ 166 Stacey Augmon FUND .05 .02
❑ 167 Dee Brown FUND .05 .02
❑ 168 Glen Rice FUND .05 .02
❑ 169 Scottie Pippen FUND .30 .14
❑ 170 Danny Ferry FUND .05 .02
❑ 171 Jason Kidd FUND .20 .09
❑ 172 LaPhonso Ellis FUND .05 .02
❑ 173 Grant Hill FUND .60 .25
❑ 174 Chris Mullin FUND .10 .05
❑ 175 Clyde Drexler FUND .10 .05
❑ 176 Rik Smits FUND .05 .02
❑ 177 Loy Vaught FUND .05 .02
❑ 178 Nick Van Exel FUND .05 .02
❑ 179 Alonzo Mourning FUND .10 .05
❑ 180 Glenn Robinson FUND .10 .05
❑ 181 Isaiah Rider FUND .05 .02
❑ 182 Ed O'Bannon FUND .05 .02
❑ 183 Patrick Ewing FUND .10 .05
❑ 184 Shaquille O'Neal FUND .40 .18
❑ 185 Derrick Coleman FUND .05 .02
❑ 186 Danny Manning FUND .05 .02
❑ 187 Clifford Robinson FUND .05 .02
❑ 188 Mitch Richmond FUND .10 .05
❑ 189 David Robinson FUND .20 .09
❑ 190 Shawn Kemp FUND .20 .09
❑ 191 Oliver Miller FUND .05 .02
❑ 192 John Stockton FUND .10 .05
❑ 193 Greg Anthony FUND .05 .02
❑ 194 Rasheed Wallace FUND .20 .09
❑ 195 Michael Jordan FUND 1.25 .55
❑ 196 Michael Jordan .20 .09
Matt Geiger CL
❑ 197 Eddie Jones .05 .02
Antonio McDyess CL
❑ 198 Anfernee Hardaway .20 .09
Kevin Garnett CL
❑ 199 Damon Stoudamire CL .05 .02
Avery Johnson CL
❑ 200 David Robinson CL .05 .02
Chris Mullin CL
❑ 201 Alan Henderson .05 .02
❑ 202 Steve Smith .10 .05
❑ 203 Donnie Boyce RC .05 .02
❑ 204 Priest Lauderdale RC .05 .02
❑ 205 Dikembe Mutombo .10 .05
❑ 206 Dee Brown .05 .02
❑ 207 Junior Burrough .05 .02
❑ 208 Todd Day .05 .02
❑ 209 Pervis Ellison .05 .02
❑ 210 Greg Minor .05 .02
❑ 211 Antoine Walker RC .75 .35
❑ 212 Rafael Addison .05 .02
❑ 213 Tony Delk RC .10 .05
❑ 214 Vlade Divac .05 .02
❑ 215 Anthony Goldwire .05 .02
❑ 216 Anthony Mason .10 .05
❑ 217 Dickey Simpkins .05 .02
❑ 218 Randy Brown .05 .02
❑ 219 Jud Buechler .05 .02
❑ 220 Jason Caffey .05 .02
❑ 221 Scottie Pippen .60 .25
❑ 222 Bill Wennington .05 .02
❑ 223 Danny Ferry .05 .02
❑ 224 Antonio Lang .05 .02
❑ 225 Chris Mills .05 .02
❑ 226 Vitaly Potapenko RC .05 .02
❑ 227 Terry Davis .05 .02
❑ 228 Chris Gatling .05 .02
❑ 229 Jason Kidd .60 .25
❑ 230 George McCloud .05 .02
❑ 231 Eric Montross .05 .02
❑ 232 Samaki Walker RC .05 .02
❑ 233 Mark Jackson .05 .02
❑ 234 Ervin Johnson .05 .02
❑ 235 Sarunas Marciulionis .05 .02
❑ 236 Eric Murdock .05 .02
❑ 237 Ricky Pierce .05 .02
❑ 238 Bryant Stith .05 .02
❑ 239 Stacey Augmon .05 .02
❑ 240 Grant Hill 1.00 .45
❑ 241 Otis Thorpe .05 .02
❑ 242 Jerome Williams RC .30 .14
❑ 243 Andrew DeClercq .05 .02
❑ 244 Todd Fuller RC .05 .02
❑ 245 Mark Price .05 .02
❑ 246 Clifford Rozier .05 .02
❑ 247 Latrell Sprewell .40 .18
❑ 248 Charles Barkley .30 .14
❑ 249 Clyde Drexler .20 .09
❑ 250 Othella Harrington RC .20 .09
❑ 251 Sam Mack .05 .02
❑ 252 Kevin Willis .05 .02
❑ 253 Erick Dampier RC .10 .05
❑ 254 Antonio Davis .05 .02
❑ 255 Dale Davis .05 .02
❑ 256 Duane Ferrell .05 .02
❑ 257 Reggie Miller .20 .09
❑ 258 Jalen Rose .20 .09
❑ 259 Reggie Williams .05 .02
❑ 260 Terry Dehere .05 .02
❑ 261 Charles Outlaw .05 .02
❑ 262 Stanley Roberts .05 .02
❑ 263 Malik Sealy .05 .02
❑ 264 Loy Vaught .05 .02
❑ 265 Lorenzen Wright RC .10 .05
❑ 266 Corie Blount .05 .02
❑ 267 Kobe Bryant RC 5.00 2.20
❑ 268 Elden Campbell .05 .02
❑ 269 Derek Fisher RC .30 .14
❑ 270 Shaquille O'Neal 1.00 .45
❑ 271 Nick Van Exel .10 .05
❑ 272 P.J. Brown .05 .02
❑ 273 Tim Hardaway .20 .09
❑ 274 Voshon Lenard RC .10 .05
❑ 275 Dan Majerle .10 .05
❑ 276 Alonzo Mourning .20 .09
❑ 277 Martin Muursepp RC .05 .02
❑ 278 Ray Allen RC .75 .35
❑ 279 Elliot Perry .05 .02
❑ 280 Glenn Robinson .20 .09
❑ 281 Stephon Marbury RC 1.25 .55
❑ 282 Cherokee Parks .05 .02
❑ 283 Doug West .05 .02
❑ 284 Micheal Williams .05 .02
❑ 285 Kerry Kittles RC .40 .18
❑ 286 Ed O'Bannon .05 .02
❑ 287 Robert Pack .05 .02
❑ 288 Khalid Reeves .05 .02
❑ 289 David Benoit .05 .02
❑ 290 Patrick Ewing .20 .09
❑ 291 Allan Houston .20 .09
❑ 292 Larry Johnson .10 .05
❑ 293 Dontae' Jones RC .05 .02
❑ 294 Walter McCarty RC .05 .02
❑ 295 John Wallace RC .20 .09
❑ 296 Charlie Ward .05 .02
❑ 297 Brian Evans RC .05 .02
❑ 298 Horace Grant .10 .05
❑ 299 Jon Koncak .05 .02
❑ 300 Felton Spencer .05 .02
❑ 301 Allen Iverson RC 2.00 .90
❑ 302 Don MacLean .05 .02
❑ 303 Scott Williams .05 .02
❑ 304 Sam Cassell .10 .05
❑ 305 Michael Finley .25 .11
❑ 306 Robert Horry .05 .02
❑ 307 Kevin Johnson .10 .05
❑ 308 Joe Kleine .05 .02
❑ 309 Danny Manning .10 .05
❑ 310 Steve Nash RC .10 .05
❑ 311 John Williams .05 .02
❑ 312 Kenny Anderson .10 .05
❑ 313 Randolph Childress .05 .02
❑ 314 Chris Dudley .05 .02
❑ 315 Jermaine O'Neal RC .40 .18
❑ 316 Isaiah Rider .10 .05
❑ 317 Clifford Robinson .05 .02
❑ 318 Rasheed Wallace .25 .11
❑ 319 Mahmoud Abdul-Rauf .05 .02
❑ 320 Duane Causwell .05 .02
❑ 321 Bobby Hurley .05 .02
❑ 322 Mitch Richmond .20 .09
❑ 323 Lionel Simmons .05 .02
❑ 324 Michael Smith .05 .02
❑ 325 Dominique Wilkins .20 .09
❑ 326 Cory Alexander .05 .02
❑ 327 Greg Anderson .05 .02
❑ 328 Carl Herrera .05 .02
❑ 329 David Robinson .30 .14
❑ 330 Charles Smith .05 .02
❑ 331 Craig Ehlo .05 .02
❑ 332 Sherrell Ford .05 .02
❑ 333 Shawn Kemp .30 .14
❑ 334 Jim McIlvaine .05 .02
❑ 335 Gary Payton .30 .14
❑ 336 Sam Perkins .10 .05
❑ 337 Eric Snow .05 .02
❑ 338 David Wingate .05 .02

❑ 339 Marcus Camby RC .... .60 .25
❑ 340 Acie Earl .... .05 .02
❑ 341 Carlos Rogers .... .05 .02
❑ 342 Greg Ostertag .... .05 .02
❑ 343 Bryon Russell .... .05 .02
❑ 344 John Stockton .... .20 .09
❑ 345 Jamie Watson .... .05 .02
❑ 346 Shareef Abdur-Rahim RC 1.25 .55
❑ 347 Doug Edwards .... .05 .02
❑ 348 George Lynch .... .05 .02
❑ 349 Eric Mobley .... .05 .02
❑ 350 Anthony Peeler .... .05 .02
❑ 351 Roy Rogers RC .... .05 .02
❑ 352 Juwan Howard .... .10 .05
❑ 353 Harvey Grant .... .05 .02
❑ 354 Tracy Murray .... .05 .02
❑ 355 Rod Strickland .... .10 .05
❑ 356 Anfernee Hardaway .... 1.25 .55
Michael Jordan ONE
❑ 357 Hakeem Olajuwon .... .60 .25
Shaquille O'Neal ONE
❑ 358 Joe Smith .... .20 .09
Shawn Kemp ONE
❑ 359 Detlef Schrempf .... .10 .05
Toni Kukoc ONE
❑ 360 Jim Jackson .... .10 .05
Jerry Stackhouse ONE
❑ 361 Kobe Bryant .... 1.25 .55
Shareef Abdur-Rahim ONE
❑ 362 Nick Anderson .... .75 .35
Michael Jordan AJ
❑ 363 Joe Dumars .... .75 .35
Michael Jordan AJ
❑ 364 John Starks .... .75 .35
Michael Jordan AJ
❑ 365 Reggie Miller .... 1.00 .45
Michael Jordan AJ
❑ 366 Gary Payton .... 1.00 .45
Michael Jordan AJ
❑ 367 Mookie Blaylock PLAY .. .05 .02
❑ 368 Dino Radja .... .05 .02
Rick Fox
David Wesley PLAY
❑ 369 Glen Rice PLAY .... .05 .02
❑ 370 Michael Jordan .... 1.25 .55
Scottie Pippen PLAY
❑ 371 Terrell Brandon PLAY .... .05 .02
❑ 372 Jason Kidd PLAY .... .20 .09
❑ 373 Antonio McDyess PLAY .20 .09
❑ 374 Grant Hill PLAY .... .60 .25
❑ 375 Joe Smith PLAY .... .10 .05
❑ 376 Charles Barkley .... .75 .35
Hakeem Olajuwon
Clyde Drexler PLAY
❑ 377 Reggie Miller PLAY .... .10 .05
❑ 378 L.A. Clippers PLAY .... .05 .02
❑ 379 Nick Van Exel PLAY .... .05 .02
❑ 380 Alonzo Mourning PLAY .. .10 .05
❑ 381 Ray Allen PLAY .... .30 .14
❑ 382 Stephon Marbury PLAY 1.00 .45
❑ 383 Shawn Bradley PLAY .... .05 .02
❑ 384 Patrick Ewing PLAY ...... .10 .05
❑ 385 A.Hardaway PLAY .... .40 .18
❑ 386 Jerry Stackhouse PLAY .10 .05
❑ 387 Danny Manning PLAY .... .05 .02
❑ 388 Clifford Robinson PLAY .05 .02
❑ 389 Tyus Edney PLAY .... .05 .02
❑ 390 San Antonio Spurs PLAY .05 .02
❑ 391 Shawn Kemp PLAY .... .20 .09
❑ 392 Toronto Raptors PLAY .. .05 .02
❑ 393 John Stockton PLAY ...... .10 .05
❑ 394 Greg Anthony PLAY ...... .05 .02
❑ 395 Gheorghe Muresan PLAY .05 .02
❑ 396 Checklist .... .05 .02
❑ 397 Checklist .... .05 .02
❑ 398 Checklist .... .05 .02
❑ 399 Checklist .... .05 .02
❑ 400 Checklist .... .05 .02
❑ 401 Henry James TRADE .... .40 .18
❑ 402 Shawn Bradley TRADE .. .40 .18
❑ 403 Sasha Danilovic TRADE .40 .18
❑ 404 Michael Finley TRADE 1.00 .45
❑ 405 A.C. Green TRADE .... .60 .25
❑ 406 Derek Harper TRADE .... .40 .18
❑ 407 Khalid Reeves TRADE .. .40 .18
❑ 408 Aaron McKie TRADE .... .40 .18
❑ 409 Matt Maloney TRADE .... .60 .25
❑ 410 Darrick Martin TRADE .... .40 .18
❑ 411 Robert Horry TRADE .... .40 .18
❑ 412 Travis Knight TRADE .... .40 .18
❑ 413 Isaac Austin TRADE ...... .40 .18
❑ 414 Jamal Mashburn TRADE .60 .25
❑ 415 Armon Gilliam TRADE .. .40 .18
❑ 416 Chris Carr TRADE .... .40 .18
❑ 417 Dean Garrett TRADE .... .40 .18
❑ 418 Shane Heal TRADE ...... .40 .18
❑ 419 Sam Cassell TRADE ...... .60 .25
❑ 420 Chris Gatling TRADE .... .40 .18
❑ 421 Jim Jackson TRADE ...... .40 .18
❑ 422 Chris Childs TRADE ...... .40 .18
❑ 423 Rony Seikaly TRADE .... .40 .18
❑ 424 Gerald Wilkins TRADE .. .40 .18
❑ 425 Cedric Ceballos TRADE .40 .18
❑ 426 Tony Dumas TRADE ...... .40 .18
❑ 427 Jason Kidd TRADE 2.50 1.10
❑ 428 Popeye Jones TRADE .. .40 .18
❑ 429 Walt Williams TRADE .... .40 .18
❑ 430 Jaren Jackson TRADE .. .60 .25
❑ NNO Update Trade Card .. 15.00 6.75
❑ NNO Michael Jordan 5x7 MM5.00 .20
❑ NNO Michael Jordan 5x7 DD5.00 2.20

1996-97 Collector's Choice Crash the Game Scoring 1

	MINT	NRMT
COMPLETE SILVER SET (60)	50.00	22.00
COMMON CARD (C1-C30)	.40	.18
SEMISTARS	.60	.25
UNLISTED STARS	1.00	.45

SER.1 STATED ODDS 1:5
*GOLD CARDS: 2.5X TO 5X HI COLUMN
GOLD: SER.1 STATED ODDS 1:49
*SILVER RED.CARDS: .75X TO 1.25X HI
*GOLD RED.CARDS: 3X TO 6X HI
ONE RED.CARD PER WINNER BY MAIL
EACH PLAYER HAS TWO DIFF.SILVER CARDS
EACH PLAYER HAS TWO DIFF.GOLD CARDS

❑ C1 Mookie Blaylock 11/4 L .... .40 .18
❑ C1B Mookie Blaylock 12/16 L .40 .18
❑ C2 Dino Radja 11/18 L .... .40 .18
❑ C2B Dino Radja 1/6 L .... .40 .18
❑ C3 Glen Rice 11/18 L .... .60 .25
❑ C3B Glen Rice 1/27 W .... .60 .25
❑ C4 Scottie Pippen 12/2 L 3.00 1.35
❑ C4B Scottie Pippen 1/13 L .. 2.50 1.10
❑ C5 Terrell Brandon 11/4 L .... .60 .25
❑ C5B Terrell Brandon 1/13 L .. .60 .25
❑ C6 Jason Kidd 12/9 L 3.00 1.35
❑ C6B Jason Kidd 12/23 L .... 1.25 .55
❑ C7 A. McDyess 11/11 L ...... 1.50 .70
❑ C7B A. McDyess 12/23 L .... 1.25 .55
❑ C8 Joe Dumars 12/9 L .... 1.00 .45
❑ C8B Joe Dumars 1/13 L ...... 1.00 .45
❑ C9 Joe Smith 12/2 L .... 1.00 .45
❑ C9B Joe Smith 12/23 W ...... 1.00 .45
❑ C10 H. Olajuwon 11/4 W .... 1.50 .70
❑ C10B H. Olajuwon 12/23 W 3.00 1.35
❑ C11 Reggie Miller 12/9 L .... 1.00 .45
❑ C11B Reggie Miller 1/27 W 1.00 .45
❑ C12 Loy Vaught 11/18 L ...... .40 .18
❑ C12B Loy Vaught 1/6 L .... .40 .18
❑ C13 Cedric Ceballos 12/2 L .. .40 .18
❑ C13B Cedric Ceballos 1/27 L .40 .18
❑ C14 Alonzo Mourning 11/11 L 1.00 .45
❑ C14B Alonzo Mourning 1/6 W 1.00 .45
❑ C15 Vin Baker 12/9 L .... .60 .25
❑ C15B Vin Baker 1/27 L .... .60 .25
❑ C16 Kevin Garnett 11/18 L .. 6.00 2.70
❑ C16B Kevin Garnett 1/13 L 4.00 1.80
❑ C17 Ed O'Bannon 12/2 L ...... .40 .18
❑ C17B Ed O'Bannon 1/6 L ...... .40 .18
❑ C18 Patrick Ewing 11/4 W .. 1.00 .45
❑ C18B Patrick Ewing 1/13 L 1.00 .45
❑ C19 A. Hardaway 12/23 L .. 3.00 1.35
❑ C19B A. Hardaway 1/27 W 6.00 2.70
❑ C20 C. Weatherspoon 12/16 L .40 .18
❑ C20B C. Weatherspoon 1/13 W .40 .18
❑ C21 Kevin Johnson 11/11 L .. .60 .25
❑ C21B Kevin Johnson 1/27 L .. .60 .25
❑ C22 Clifford Robinson 12/16 L .40 .18
❑ C22B Clifford Robinson 1/6 L .40 .18
❑ C23 Mitch Richmond 12/16 W 1.00 .45
❑ C23B Mitch Richmond 1/27 W 1.00 .45
❑ C24 Sean Elliott 11/4 L .... .40 .18
❑ C24B Sean Elliott 1/6 L .... .40 .18
❑ C25 Shawn Kemp 12/16 L .. 1.50 .70
❑ C25B Shawn Kemp 1/13 L .. 2.50 1.10
❑ C26 D. Stoudamire 12/9 W 1.50 .70
❑ C26B D. Stoudamire 1/6 L .. 2.00 .90
❑ C27 John Stockton 11/11 L 1.00 .45
❑ C27B John Stockton 12/23 L 1.00 .45
❑ C28 Bryant Reeves 12/2 L .... .40 .18
❑ C28B Bryant Reeves 1/27 W .40 .18
❑ C29 Rasheed Wallace 11/18 L 1.25 .55
❑ C29B Rasheed Wallace 1/13 L .. .60 .25
❑ C30 Michael Jordan 11/11 W 12.00 5.50
❑ C30B Michael Jordan 12/23 W 15.00 6.75

1996-97 Collector's Choice Crash the Game Scoring 2

	MINT	NRMT
COMPLETE SILVER SET (60)	50.00	22.00
COMMON CARD (C1-C30)	.40	.18
SEMISTARS	.60	.25
UNLISTED STARS	1.00	.45

SER.2 STATED ODDS 1:5
*GOLD CARDS: 2.5X TO 5X HI COLUMN
GOLD: SER.2 STATED ODDS 1:49
*SILVER RED.CARDS: .75X TO 1.25X HI
*GOLD RED.CARDS: 3X TO 6X HI
ONE RED.CARD PER WINNER BY MAIL
EACH PLAYER HAS TWO DIFF.SILVER CARDS
EACH PLAYER HAS TWO DIFF.GOLD CARDS

❑ C1 Steve Smith 2/17 L .... .60 .25
❑ C1B Steve Smith 4/14 W ...... .60 .25
❑ C2 Dana Barros 3/3 L .... .40 .18
❑ C2B Dana Barros 3/31 L ...... .40 .18
❑ C3 Tony Delk 2/24 L .... .40 .18
❑ C3B Tony Delk 4/7 L .... .40 .18
❑ C4 Toni Kukoc 3/10 L .... 1.25 .55
❑ C4B Toni Kukoc 3/31 L .... .60 .25
❑ C5 Bobby Phills 2/24 L .... .40 .18
❑ C5B Bobby Phills 3/17 L ...... .40 .18

❑ C6 Jamal Mashburn 3/3 L .... .60 .25
❑ C6B Jamal Mashburn 3/31 L .60 .25
❑ C7 LaPhonso Ellis 2/24 W .... .40 .18
❑ C7B LaPhonso Ellis 3/31 L .. .40 .18
❑ C8 Jerome Williams 2/17 L 1.00 .45
❑ C8B Jerome Williams 4/7 L 1.00 .45
❑ C9 Latrell Sprewell 3/3 L .... 2.00 .90
❑ C9B Latrell Sprewell 4/7 L .... .60 .25
❑ C10 Clyde Drexler 2/24 L.... 1.00 .45
❑ C10B Clyde Drexler 4/7 L .. 1.00 .45
❑ C11 Dale Davis 3/3 L .... .40 .18
❑ C11B Dale Davis 3/24 L....... .40 .18
❑ C12 Brent Barry 3/3 L .... .40 .18
❑ C12B Brent Barry 4/14 L ...... .40 .18
❑ C13 Nick Van Exel 3/10 L ..... .60 .25
❑ C13B Nick Van Exel 4/7 L ..... .60 .25
❑ C14 Sasha Danilovic 2/17 L.. .40 .18
❑ C14B Sasha Danilovic 3/17 L .40 .18
❑ C15 Glenn Robinson 2/24 L 1.00 .45
❑ C15B Glenn Robinson 3/17 L 1.00 .45
❑ C16 Stephon Marbury 2/17 L 3.00 1.35
❑ C16B Stephon Marbury 3/31 L 4.00 1.80
❑ C17 Shawn Bradley 3/10 W.. .40 .18
❑ C17B Shawn Bradley 3/24 L .40 .18
❑ C18 John Wallace 3/3 L......... .60 .25
❑ C18B John Wallace 4/14 L..... .60 .25
❑ C19 A. Hardaway 2/24 L 3.00 1.35
❑ C19B A. Hardaway 4/14 L .. 4.00 1.80
❑ C20 J. Stackhouse 3/10 W.. 1.00 .45
❑ C20B J. Stackhouse 3/31 W 1.00 .45
❑ C21 Danny Manning 2/17 L .. .40 .18
❑ C21B Danny Manning 3/24 L .60 .25
❑ C22 Arvydas Sabonis 2/24 L .40 .18
❑ C22B Arvydas Sabonis 3/31 L .40 .18
❑ C23 Brian Grant 3/3 L .... 1.00 .45
❑ C23B Brian Grant 3/31 L .... 1.00 .45
❑ C24 David Robinson 2/24 L 1.50 .70
❑ C24B David Robinson 3/24 L 1.25 .55
❑ C25 Gary Payton 3/3 L........ 1.50 .70
❑ C25B Gary Payton 4/14 L .. 1.25 .55
❑ C26 Marcus Camby 3/3 L .. 1.50 .70
❑ C26B Marcus Camby 4/7 L 2.00 .90
❑ C27 Karl Malone 2/24 W .... 1.50 .70
❑ C27B Karl Malone 4/14 W .. 1.50 .70
❑ C28 S.Abdur-Rahim 2/24 L 3.00 1.35
❑ C28B S.Abdur-Rahim 3/17 L 2.50 1.10
❑ C29 Juwan Howard 2/17 L.... .60 .25
❑ C29B Juwan Howard 4/7 L .. .60 .25
❑ C30 Michael Jordan 3/3 W 12.00 5.50
❑ C30B Michael Jordan 4/14 W 15.00 6.75

1996-97 Collector's Choice Draft Trade

	MINT	NRMT
COMPLETE SET (10)	10.00	4.50
COMMON CARD (DR1-DR10)	.75	.35

ONE SET PER DRAFT TRADE CARD VIA MAIL
TRADE: SER.1 STATED ODDS 1:144

❑ DR1 Allen Iverson 4.00 1.80
❑ DR2 Marcus Camby........... 1.25 .55
❑ DR3 Shareef Abdur-Rahim 2.50 1.10
❑ DR4 Stephon Marbury 2.50 1.10
❑ DR5 Ray Allen .... 1.50 .70
❑ DR6 Antoine Walker........... 1.50 .70
❑ DR7 Lorenzen Wright........... .75 .35
❑ DR8 Kerry Kittles .... .75 .35
❑ DR9 Samaki Walker............. .75 .35
❑ DR10 Erick Dampier .... .75 .35
❑ NNO Exp. Draft Trade Card 1.00 .45

1996-97 Collector's Choice Game Face

	MINT	NRMT
COMPLETE SET (10)	10.00	4.50
COMMON CARD (GF1-GF10)	.30	.14
SEMISTARS	.40	.18
UNLISTED STARS	.60	.25

ONE PER SPECIAL SER.1 RETAIL PACK

❑ GF1 Anfernee Hardaway .... 2.00 .90
❑ GF2 Michael Jordan........... 8.00 3.60
❑ GF3 Shawn Kemp .... 1.00 .45
❑ GF4 Alonzo Mourning .... .60 .25
❑ GF5 Cherokee Parks .... .30 .14
❑ GF6 Avery Johnson .... .30 .14
❑ GF7 LaPhonso Ellis .... .30 .14
❑ GF8 Rasheed Wallace......... .75 .35
❑ GF9 Jim Jackson .... .30 .14
❑ GF10 Larry Johnson .... .40 .18

1996-97 Collector's Choice Jordan A Cut Above

	MINT	NRMT
COMPLETE SET (10)	20.00	9.00
COMMON JORDAN (CA1-CA10)	2.50	1.10

ONE PER SPECIAL SER.1 RETAIL PACK

❑ CA1 Michael Jordan........... 2.50 1.10
1985 Rookie of the Year
❑ CA2 Michael Jordan........... 2.50 1.10
8-Time Scoring Leader
❑ CA3 Michael Jordan........... 2.50 1.10
8-Time All-NBA First Team
❑ CA4 Michael Jordan........... 2.50 1.10
Defensive POY
❑ CA5 Michael Jordan........... 2.50 1.10
10-Time All-Star
❑ CA6 Michael Jordan........... 2.50 1.10
2-Time All-Star Game MVP
❑ CA7 Michael Jordan........... 2.50 1.10
4-Time MVP
❑ CA8 Michael Jordan........... 2.50 1.10
4-Time Champion
❑ CA9 Michael Jordan........... 2.50 1.10
4-Time Finals MVP
❑ CA10 Michael Jordan.......... 2.50 1.10
Continuing Excellence

1996-97 Collector's Choice Memorable Moments

	MINT	NRMT
COMPLETE SET (10)	12.00	5.50
COMMON CARD (1-10)	.50	.23
SEMISTARS	.60	.25

ONE PER SPECIAL SER.2 RETAIL PACK

❑ 1 Michael Jordan 8.00 3.60
❑ 2 Nick Van Exel .... .50 .23
❑ 3 Karl Malone..................... 1.00 .45
❑ 4 Latrell Sprewell .... 1.25 .55
❑ 5 Anfernee Hardaway .... 2.00 .90
❑ 6 Glenn Robinson .... .60 .25
❑ 7 Shaquille O'Neal 3.00 1.35
❑ 8 Damon Stoudamire .... 1.00 .45
❑ 9 Clyde Drexler .... .60 .25
❑ 10 Shawn Kemp.................. 1.00 .45

1996-97 Collector's Choice Mini-Cards

	MINT	NRMT
COMPLETE SET (60)	20.00	9.00
COMPLETE SERIES 1 (30)	8.00	3.60
COMPLETE SERIES 2 (30)	12.00	5.50
COMMON CARD (1-60)	.10	.05
SEMISTARS	.20	.09
UNLISTED STARS	.30	.14

ONE PER BOTH SERIES PACKS
TWO PER SPECIAL SER.1 RETAIL PACK
*GOLD: 5X TO 10X HI COLUMN
GOLD: SER.1/2 STATED ODDS 1:35
ORDERED BY FAR LEFT NUMBER ON BACK
NUMBER M106 NEVER ISSUED
SURA AND STITH NUMBERED M112
SKIP-NUMBERED SET

❑ M2 Rex Walters .... .20 .09
Jeff Hornacek
Mookie Blaylock

❑ M5 Detlef Schrempf .... .20 .09
Toni Kukoc
Dino Radja
❑ M6 Ashraf Amaya.......... .10 .05
Sharone Wright
Eric Williams
❑ M10 Tyus Edney .... .10 .05
Ed O'Bannon
George Zidek
❑ M13 Theo Ratliff.......... .20 .09
Shawn Bradley
Luc Longley
❑ M22 Bobby Phills .... .10 .05
Avery Johnson
Mahmoud Abdul-Rauf
❑ M23 Popeye Jones .... .10 .05
Chris Morris
Tom Hammonds
❑ M25 Bobby Hurley .... 1.50 .70
Christian Laettner
Grant Hill
❑ M28 Sherman Douglas .... .10 .05
Derrick Coleman
Rony Seikaly
❑ M30 Nick Van Exel.......... .30 .14
John Starks
Sam Cassell
❑ M33 Matt Geiger .... .10 .05
Dennis Scott
Travis Best
❑ M36 Cedric Ceballos .... .20 .09
Isaiah Rider
Brent Barry
❑ M37 Jason Kidd.......... .30 .14
Kevin Johnson
Lamond Murray
❑ M38 Chris Mullin .... .20 .09
Jayson Williams
Terry Dehere
❑ M39 Arvedas Sabonis .... .20 .09
Sasha Danilovic
Vlade Divac
❑ M43 Tyrone Hill .... .10 .05
Brian Grant
Kurt Thomas
❑ M44 Derrick McKey .... .10 .05
Robert Horry
Keith Askins
❑ M46 Randolph Childress ...... .40 .18
David Robinson
Shawn Respert
❑ M49 Todd Day .... .10 .05
Oliver Miller
Andrew Lang
❑ M56 Dell Curry.......... .10 .05
Bimbo Coles
Charles Oakley
❑ M57 Rasheed Wallace.......... .40 .18
Jerry Stackhouse
J.R. Reid
❑ M66 Joe Dumars .... .30 .14
Clyde Drexler
A.C. Green
❑ M67 Kendall Gill.......... .20 .09
Nick Anderson
Aaron McKie
❑ M75 Danny Ferry .... .10 .05
Mark Jackson
Doc Rivers
❑ M78 Michael Jordan.......... 5.00 2.20
Anfernee Hardaway
Shawn Kemp
❑ M79 Jalen Rose.......... .60 .25
Chris Webber
Jimmy King
❑ M83 Dennis Rodman .... 1.50 .70
Charles Barkley
Karl Malone
❑ M85 Stacey Augmon .... .20 .09
Larry Johnson
Greg Anthony
❑ M86 Nate McMillan .... .20 .09
Tom Gugliotta
Blue Edwards
❑ M90 Jim Jackson .... .30 .14
Glenn Robinson
Calbert Cheaney
❑ M92 Ken Norman.......... .10 .05
Doug West
Kevin Edwards
❑ M93 Steve Smith .... .30 .14
Tim Hardaway
BJ Armstrong
❑ M99 Glen Rice .... .30 .14
Danny Manning
Sam Perkins
❑ M102 Steve Kerr .... .20 .09
Reggie Miller
Dana Barros
❑ M109 Samaki Walker.......... .30 .14
Lorenzen Wright
Greg Minor
❑ M110 LaPhonso Ellis .... .10 .05
Kevin Willis
Clarence Weatherspoon
❑ M111 Antonio McDyess....... .60 .25
Latrell Sprewell
Jason Caffey
❑ M112A Bryant Stith .... .10 .05
Vinny Del Negro
Kenny Anderson
❑ M112B Bob Sura .... .10 .05
Rodney Rogers
Olden Polynice
❑ M113 Lindsey Hunter.......... .30 .14
Eddie Jones
Ron Harper
❑ M115 Otis Thorpe .... .30 .14
John Stockton
Antoine Carr
❑ M125 Rik Smits .... .60 .25
Hakeem Olajuwon
Gheorghe Muresan
❑ M129 Kobe Bryant 6.00 2.70
Jermaine O'Neal
Kevin Garnett
❑ M135 Alonzo Mourning .... .50 .23
Dikembe Mutombo
Patrick Ewing
❑ M137 Vin Baker .... 1.00 .45
Jamal Mashburn
Scottie Pippen
❑ M140 Stephon Marbury ...... 1.00 .45
Darrin Hancock
Wesley Person
❑ M146 Allan Houston.......... .75 .35
Marcus Camby
Kerry Kittles
❑ M148 John Wallace .... .60 .25
Walter McCarty
Antoine Walker
❑ M149 Horace Grant .... .20 .09
Elden Campbell
Dale Davis
❑ M150 Donald Royal .... .10 .05
Tim Legler
Mario Elie
❑ M151 Brian Shaw.......... .10 .05
Antonio Davis
P.J. Brown
❑ M152 Allen Iverson 4.00 1.80
Joe Smith
Shaquille O'Neal
❑ M159 Cliff Robinson.......... .50 .23
Scott Burrell
Ray Allen
❑ M161 Mitch Richmond .... .30 .14
Will Perdue
Hersey Hawkins
❑ M167 Gary Payton .... .40 .18
Terrell Brandon
Sean Elliott
❑ M170 Doug Christie .... .10 .05
Johnny Newman
Tony Dumas
❑ M175 Shareef Abdur-Rahim .75 .35
Chris Mills
Khalid Reeves
❑ M176 Lawrence Moten.......... .10 .05
Michael Smith
Bryon Russell
❑ M177 Bryant Reeves .... .40 .18
Michael Finley
Damon Stoudamire
❑ M178 Juwan Howard .... .30 .14
Loy Vaught
Terry Mills

1996-97 Collector's Choice Stick-Ums 1

	MINT	NRMT
COMPLETE SET (30)	8.00	3.60
COMMON STICKER (S1-S30)....	.15	.07
SEMISTARS..........	.20	.09
UNLISTED STARS..........	.30	.14
SER.1 STATED ODDS 1:4		

❑ S1 Mookie Blaylock .... .15 .07
❑ S2 Dana Barros .... .15 .07
❑ S3 Scott Burrell .... .15 .07
❑ S4 Dennis Rodman .... .60 .25
❑ S5 Terrell Brandon.......... .20 .09
❑ S6 Jamal Mashburn .... .20 .09
❑ S7 LaPhonso Ellis .... .15 .07
❑ S8 Grant Hill.......... 1.50 .70
❑ S9 Joe Smith .... .30 .14
❑ S10 Hakeem Olajuwon .... .50 .23
❑ S11 Rik Smits.......... .15 .07
❑ S12 Brent Barry .... .15 .07
❑ S13 Nick Van Exel .... .20 .09
❑ S14 Sasha Danilovic .... .15 .07
❑ S15 Vin Baker .... .20 .09
❑ S16 Kevin Garnett .... 2.00 .90
❑ S17 Shawn Bradley .... .15 .07
❑ S18 Patrick Ewing .... .30 .14
❑ S19 Anfernee Hardaway .... 1.00 .45
❑ S20 Clarence Weatherspoon .15 .07
❑ S21 Charles Barkley .... .50 .23
❑ S22 Clifford Robinson .... .15 .07
❑ S23 Mitch Richmond .... .30 .14
❑ S24 David Robinson .... .50 .23
❑ S25 Shawn Kemp .... .50 .23
❑ S26 Damon Stoudamire....... .50 .23
❑ S27 Karl Malone.......... .50 .23
❑ S28 Bryant Reeves .... .15 .07
❑ S29 Gheorghe Muresan....... .15 .07
❑ S30 Michael Jordan 4.00 1.80

1996-97 Collector's Choice Stick-Ums 2

	MINT	NRMT
COMPLETE SET (30)	8.00	3.60
COMMON STICKER (S1-S30)	.15	.07
SEMISTARS	.20	.09
UNLISTED STARS	.30	.14
SER.2 STATED ODDS 1:3		
COMPLETE BASE SET (30)	4.00	1.80
COMMON BASE (B1-B30)	.10	.05
*BASE STARS: .2X TO .5X HI COLUMN		
BASE: SER.2 STATED ODDS 1:4		

	MINT	NRMT
❑ S1 Steve Smith	.20	.09
❑ S2 Dino Radja	.15	.07
❑ S3 Glen Rice	.20	.09
❑ S4 Toni Kukoc	.40	.18
❑ S5 Bobby Phills	.15	.07
❑ S6 Jason Kidd	1.00	.45
❑ S7 Antonio McDyess	.50	.23
❑ S8 Joe Dumars	.30	.14
❑ S9 Latrell Sprewell	.60	.25
❑ S10 Clyde Drexler	.30	.14
❑ S11 Reggie Miller	.30	.14
❑ S12 Loy Vaught	.15	.07
❑ S13 Eddie Jones	.60	.25
❑ S14 Alonzo Mourning	.30	.14
❑ S15 Glenn Robinson	.30	.14
❑ S16 Tom Gugliotta	.20	.09
❑ S17 Ed O'Bannon	.15	.07
❑ S18 John Starks	.15	.07
❑ S19 Anfernee Hardaway	1.00	.45
❑ S20 Jerry Stackhouse	.30	.14
❑ S21 Kevin Johnson	.20	.09
❑ S22 Arvydas Sabonis	.20	.09
❑ S23 Brian Grant	.30	.14
❑ S24 Sean Elliott	.15	.07
❑ S25 Gary Payton	.50	.23
❑ S26 Zan Tabak	.15	.07
❑ S27 John Stockton	.30	.14
❑ S28 Greg Anthony	.15	.07
❑ S29 Juwan Howard	.20	.09
❑ S30 Michael Jordan	4.00	1.80

1997-98 Collector's Choice

	MINT	NRMT
COMPLETE SET (400)	30.00	13.50
COMP.FACTORY SET (415)	40.00	18.00
COMPLETE SERIES 1 (200)	15.00	6.75
COMPLETE SERIES 2 (200)	15.00	6.75
COMMON CARD (1-400)	.05	.02
COMMON MJ C23 (186-195)	1.00	.45
COMMON MJ MAGIC (386-395)	1.00	.45
SEMISTARS	.10	.05
UNLISTED STARS	.20	.09
SUBSET CARDS HALF VALUE OF BASE CARDS		

	MINT	NRMT
❑ 1 Mookie Blaylock	.05	.02
❑ 2 Dikembe Mutombo	.10	.05
❑ 3 Eldridge Recasner	.05	.02
❑ 4 Christian Laettner	.10	.05
❑ 5 Tyrone Corbin	.05	.02
❑ 6 Antoine Walker	.40	.18
❑ 7 Eric Williams	.05	.02
❑ 8 Dana Barros	.05	.02
❑ 9 David Wesley	.05	.02
❑ 10 Dino Radja	.05	.02
❑ 11 Vlade Divac	.05	.02
❑ 12 Dell Curry	.05	.02
❑ 13 Muggsy Bogues	.05	.02
❑ 14 Tony Smith	.05	.02
❑ 15 Glen Rice	.10	.05
❑ 16 Anthony Mason	.10	.05
❑ 17 Dennis Rodman	.40	.18
❑ 18 Brian Williams	.05	.02
❑ 19 Toni Kukoc	.25	.11
❑ 20 Jason Caffey	.05	.02
❑ 21 Steve Kerr	.05	.02
❑ 22 Luc Longley	.05	.02
❑ 23 Michael Jordan	2.50	1.10
❑ 24 Chris Mills	.05	.02
❑ 25 Tyrone Hill	.05	.02
❑ 26 Vitaly Potapenko	.05	.02
❑ 27 Bob Sura	.05	.02
❑ 28 Robert Pack	.05	.02
❑ 29 Ed O'Bannon	.05	.02
❑ 30 Michael Finley	.20	.09
❑ 31 Shawn Bradley	.05	.02
❑ 32 Khalid Reeves	.05	.02
❑ 33 Antonio McDyess	.25	.11
❑ 34 Ervin Johnson	.05	.02
❑ 35 Dale Ellis	.05	.02
❑ 36 Bryant Stith	.05	.02
❑ 37 Tom Hammonds	.05	.02
❑ 38 Otis Thorpe	.05	.02
❑ 39 Lindsey Hunter	.05	.02
❑ 40 Grant Long	.05	.02
❑ 41 Aaron McKie	.05	.02
❑ 42 Randolph Childress	.05	.02
❑ 43 Scott Burrell	.05	.02
❑ 44 Bimbo Coles	.05	.02
❑ 45 B.J. Armstrong	.05	.02
❑ 46 Mark Price	.05	.02
❑ 47 Latrell Sprewell	.40	.18
❑ 48 Felton Spencer	.05	.02
❑ 49 Charles Barkley	.30	.14
❑ 50 Mario Elie	.05	.02
❑ 51 Clyde Drexler	.20	.09
❑ 52 Kevin Willis	.05	.02
❑ 53 Antonio Davis	.05	.02
❑ 54 Reggie Miller	.20	.09
❑ 55 Dale Davis	.05	.02
❑ 56 Mark Jackson	.05	.02
❑ 57 Erick Dampier	.05	.02
❑ 58 Pooh Richardson	.05	.02
❑ 59 Terry Dehere	.05	.02
❑ 60 Brent Barry	.05	.02
❑ 61 Loy Vaught	.05	.02
❑ 62 Lorenzen Wright	.05	.02
❑ 63 Eddie Jones	.40	.18
❑ 64 Kobe Bryant	1.50	.70
❑ 65 Elden Campbell	.05	.02
❑ 66 Corie Blount	.05	.02
❑ 67 Shaquille O'Neal	1.00	.45
❑ 68 Dan Majerle	.10	.05
❑ 69 P.J. Brown	.05	.02
❑ 70 Tim Hardaway	.20	.09
❑ 71 Isaac Austin	.05	.02
❑ 72 Jamal Mashburn	.10	.05
❑ 73 Ray Allen	.30	.14
❑ 74 Glenn Robinson	.10	.05
❑ 75 Armon Gilliam	.05	.02
❑ 76 Johnny Newman	.05	.02
❑ 77 Elliot Perry	.05	.02
❑ 78 Sherman Douglas	.05	.02
❑ 79 Doug West	.05	.02
❑ 80 Kevin Garnett	1.25	.55
❑ 81 Sam Mitchell	.05	.02
❑ 82 Tom Gugliotta	.10	.05
❑ 83 Terry Porter	.05	.02
❑ 84 Chris Carr	.05	.02
❑ 85 Kevin Edwards	.05	.02
❑ 86 Jayson Williams	.10	.05
❑ 87 Kendall Gill	.10	.05
❑ 88 Kerry Kittles	.20	.09
❑ 89 Chris Gatling	.05	.02
❑ 90 John Starks	.05	.02
❑ 91 Charlie Ward	.05	.02
❑ 92 Larry Johnson	.10	.05
❑ 93 Charles Oakley	.05	.02
❑ 94 Chris Childs	.05	.02
❑ 95 Allan Houston	.20	.09
❑ 96 Horace Grant	.10	.05
❑ 97 Darrell Armstrong	.10	.05
❑ 98 Rony Seikaly	.05	.02
❑ 99 Dennis Scott	.05	.02
❑ 100 Anfernee Hardaway	.60	.25
❑ 101 Brian Shaw	.05	.02
❑ 102 Jerry Stackhouse	.10	.05
❑ 103 Rex Walters	.05	.02
❑ 104 Don MacLean	.05	.02
❑ 105 Derrick Coleman	.10	.05
❑ 106 Lucious Harris	.05	.02
❑ 107 Clarence Weatherspoon	.05	.02
❑ 108 Cedric Ceballos	.05	.02
❑ 109 Danny Manning	.10	.05
❑ 110 Jason Kidd	.60	.25
❑ 111 Loren Meyer	.05	.02
❑ 112 Wesley Person	.05	.02
❑ 113 Steve Nash	.05	.02
❑ 114 Isaiah Rider	.10	.05
❑ 115 Stacey Augmon	.05	.02
❑ 116 Arvydas Sabonis	.10	.05
❑ 117 Kenny Anderson	.10	.05
❑ 118 Jermaine O'Neal	.10	.05
❑ 119 Gary Trent	.05	.02
❑ 120 Michael Smith	.05	.02
❑ 121 Kevin Gamble	.05	.02
❑ 122 Olden Polynice	.05	.02
❑ 123 Billy Owens	.05	.02
❑ 124 Corliss Williamson	.05	.02
❑ 125 Cory Alexander	.05	.02
❑ 126 Vinny Del Negro	.05	.02
❑ 127 Sean Elliott	.05	.02
❑ 128 Will Perdue	.05	.02
❑ 129 Carl Herrera	.05	.02
❑ 130 Shawn Kemp	.30	.14
❑ 131 Hersey Hawkins	.10	.05
❑ 132 Nate McMillan	.05	.02
❑ 133 Craig Ehlo	.05	.02
❑ 134 Detlef Schrempf	.10	.05
❑ 135 Sam Perkins	.10	.05
❑ 136 Sharone Wright	.05	.02
❑ 137 Doug Christie	.05	.02
❑ 138 Popeye Jones	.05	.02
❑ 139 Shawn Respert	.05	.02
❑ 140 Marcus Camby	.25	.11
❑ 141 Adam Keefe	.05	.02
❑ 142 Karl Malone	.30	.14
❑ 143 John Stockton	.20	.09
❑ 144 Greg Ostertag	.05	.02
❑ 145 Chris Morris	.05	.02
❑ 146 Shareef Abdur-Rahim	.60	.25
❑ 147 Roy Rogers	.05	.02
❑ 148 George Lynch	.05	.02
❑ 149 Anthony Peeler	.05	.02
❑ 150 Lee Mayberry	.05	.02
❑ 151 Calbert Cheaney	.05	.02
❑ 152 Harvey Grant	.05	.02
❑ 153 Rod Strickland	.10	.05
❑ 154 Tracy Murray	.05	.02
❑ 155 Chris Webber	.60	.25
❑ 156 Atlanta Hawks GN	.05	.02
Mookie Blaylock		
Christian Laettner		
Dikembe Mutombo		
Steve Smith		
❑ 157 Boston Celtics GN	.20	.09
Antoine Walker		
Dana Barros		
David Wesley		
❑ 158 Charlotte Hornets GN	.10	.05
Glen Rice		
Anthony Mason		
Tony Delk		
Vlade Divac		
❑ 159 Chicago Bulls GN	1.25	.55
Michael Jordan		
Toni Kukoc		
Scottie Pippen		
Dennis Rodman		
❑ 160 Cleveland Cavaliers GN	.05	.02
Tyrone Hill		
Terrell Brandon		
Bob Sura		
❑ 161 Dallas Mavericks GN	.05	.02
Shawn Bradley		
Michael Finley		
Ed O'Bannon		

Robert Pack
❑ 162 Denver Nuggets GN ...... .20 .09
Antoino McDyess
Ervin Johnson
Dale Ellis
LaPhonso Ellis
❑ 163 Detroit Pistons GN .... .60 .25
Grant Hill
Joe Dumars
Theo Ratliff
Lindsey Hunter
❑ 164 Golden St. Warriors GN .05 .02
Latrell Sprewell
Chris Mullin
Joe Smith
❑ 165 Houston Rockets GN .... .20 .09
Hakeem Olajuwon
Clyde Drexler
Charles Barkley
Kevin Willis
❑ 166 Indiana Pacers GN .... .10 .05
Reggie Miller
Antonio Davis
Dale Davis
❑ 167 Los Angeles Clippers GN .05 .02
Loy Vaught
Terry Dehere
Pooh Richardson
Brent Barry
❑ 168 Los Angeles Lakers GN .20 .09
Eddie Jones
Shaquille O'Neal
Kobe Bryant
Nick Van Exel
❑ 169 Miami Heat GN .... .10 .05
Tim Hardaway
Alonzo Mourning
P.J. Brown
Jamal Mashburn
❑ 170 Milwaukee Bucks GN .... .05 .02
Vin Baker
Ray Allen
Elliot Perry
Johnny Newman
Glenn Robinson
❑ 171 Minnesota T'wolves GN .60 .25
Kevin Garnett
Stephon Marbury
Terry Porter
Tom Gugliotta
❑ 172 New Jersey Nets GN...... .10 .05
Kendall Gill
Jim Jackson
Chris Gatling
Jayson Williams
❑ 173 New York Knicks GN...... .10 .05
Patrick Ewing
Allan Houston
Charles Oakley
Larry Johnson
Charlie Ward
❑ 174 Orlando Magic GN .... .40 .18
Anfernee Hardaway
Horace Grant
Brian Shaw
Rony Seikaly
❑ 175 Philadelphia 76ers GN .. .40 .18
Allen Iverson
Jerry Stackhouse
Derrick Coleman
Rex Walters
❑ 176 Phoenix Suns GN .... .20 .09
Jason Kidd
Danny Manning
Wesley Person
Kevin Johnson
❑ 177 Portland Trail Blazers GN .10 .05
Rasheed Wallace
Kenny Anderson
Isaiah Rider
Arvydas Sabonis
❑ 178 Sacramento Kings GN .. .10 .05
Mitch Richmond
Olden Polynice
Billy Owens
Mahmoud Abdul-Rauf
❑ 179 San Antonio Spurs GN .. .05 .02
Sean Elliott
Avery Johnson
David Robinson
Cory Alexander
❑ 180 Seattle Supersonics GN .20 .09
Gary Payton
Detlef Schrempf
Shawn Kemp
Hersey Hawkins
❑ 181 Toronto Raptors GN ...... .20 .09
Damon Stoudamire
Marcus Camby
Zan Tabak
Doug Christie
❑ 182 Utah Jazz GN .... .20 .09
Karl Malone
John Stockton
Jeff Hornacek
❑ 183 Vancouver Grizzlies GN .30 .14
Shareef Abdur-Rahim
Roy Rogers
Anthony Peeler
Bryant Reeves
❑ 184 Washington Wizards GN .25 .11
Chris Webber
Juwan Howard
Calbert Cheaney
Rod Strickland
❑ 185 1997 NBA Finals .... 1.25 .55
Game Night
Michael Jordan
Karl Malone
Dennis Rodman
John Stockton
❑ 186 Michael Jordan .... 1.00 .45
Catch 23 Fast Break
❑ 187 Michael Jordan .... 1.00 .45
Catch 23 Finger Roll
❑ 188 Michael Jordan .... 1.00 .45
Catch 23 Favorite Pastimes
❑ 189 Michael Jordan .... 1.00 .45
Catch 23 Championship Drive
❑ 190 Michael Jordan .... 1.00 .45
Catch 23 Road Show
❑ 191 Michael Jordan .... 1.00 .45
Catch 23 Media Circus
❑ 192 Michael Jordan .... 1.00 .45
Catch 23 Jump Shot
❑ 193 Michael Jordan .... 1.00 .45
Catch 23 Shake and Bake
❑ 194 Michael Jordan .... 1.00 .45
Catch 23 Strong Finish
❑ 195 Michael Jordan .... 1.00 .45
Catch 23 Leader
❑ 196 Checklist #1................. .05 .02
❑ 197 Checklist #2................. .05 .02
❑ 198 Checklist #3................. .05 .02
❑ 199 Checklist #4................. .05 .02
❑ 200 Checklist #5................. .05 .02
❑ 201 Steve Smith................. .10 .05
❑ 202 Chris Crawford RC .... .05 .02
❑ 203 Ed Gray RC.................. .05 .02
❑ 204 Alan Henderson .... .05 .02
❑ 205 Walter McCarty .... .05 .02
❑ 206 Dee Brown .... .05 .02
❑ 207 Chauncey Billups RC .... .25 .11
❑ 208 Ron Mercer RC .... .60 .25
❑ 209 Travis Knight .... .05 .02
❑ 210 Andrew DeClercq .... .05 .02
❑ 211 Tyus Edney .... .05 .02
❑ 212 Matt Geiger .... .05 .02
❑ 213 Tony Delk .... .05 .02
❑ 214 J.R. Reid .... .05 .02
❑ 215 Bobby Phills .... .05 .02
❑ 216 David Wesley .... .05 .02
❑ 217 Ron Harper .... .10 .05
❑ 218 Scottie Pippen............... .60 .25
❑ 219 Scott Burrell.................. .05 .02
❑ 220 Keith Booth RC .... .05 .02
❑ 221 Bill Wennington .... .05 .02
❑ 222 Shawn Kemp .... .30 .14
❑ 223 Zydrunas Ilgauskas .... .05 .02
❑ 224 Brevin Knight RC.......... .30 .14
❑ 225 Danny Ferry .... .05 .02
❑ 226 Derek Anderson RC ...... .50 .23
❑ 227 Wesley Person .... .05 .02
❑ 228 A.C. Green .... .10 .05
❑ 229 Samaki Walker .... .05 .02
❑ 230 Hubert Davis .... .05 .02
❑ 231 Erick Strickland RC .... .10 .05
❑ 232 Dennis Scott .... .05 .02
❑ 233 Tony Battie RC .... .20 .09
❑ 234 LaPhonso Ellis .... .05 .02
❑ 235 Eric Williams .... .05 .02
❑ 236 Bobby Jackson RC .... .10 .05
❑ 237 Anthony Goldwire .... .05 .02
❑ 238 Danny Fortson RC .... .20 .09
❑ 239 Joe Dumars.................. .20 .09
❑ 240 Grant Hill .... 1.00 .45
❑ 241 Malik Sealy .... .05 .02
❑ 242 Brian Williams .... .05 .02
❑ 243 Theo Ratliff .... .05 .02
❑ 244 Scot Pollard RC............ .10 .05
❑ 245 Erick Dampier .... .05 .02
❑ 246 Duane Ferrell .... .05 .02
❑ 247 Joe Smith .... .10 .05
❑ 248 Todd Fuller .... .05 .02
❑ 249 Adonal Foyle RC .... .10 .05
❑ 250 Othella Harrington......... .05 .02
❑ 251 Matt Maloney................ .05 .02
❑ 252 Hakeem Olajuwon......... .30 .14
❑ 253 Rodrick Rhodes RC ...... .05 .02
❑ 254 Eddie Johnson .... .05 .02
❑ 255 Brent Price .... .05 .02
❑ 256 Austin Croshere RC ...... .50 .23
❑ 257 Derrick McKey.............. .05 .02
❑ 258 Chris Mullin .... .20 .09
❑ 259 Rik Smits..................... .05 .02
❑ 260 Jalen Rose .... .20 .09
❑ 261 Darrick Martin .... .05 .02
❑ 262 Lamond Murray............. .05 .02
❑ 263 Maurice Taylor RC .... .40 .18
❑ 264 Rodney Rogers .... .05 .02
❑ 265 James Robinson .... .05 .02
❑ 266 Rick Fox .... .05 .02
❑ 267 Nick Van Exel .... .10 .05
❑ 268 Sean Rooks.................. .05 .02
❑ 269 Derek Fisher .... .05 .02
❑ 270 Jon Barry..................... .05 .02
❑ 271 Robert Horry .... .05 .02
❑ 272 Terry Mills .... .05 .02
❑ 273 Charles Smith RC .... .05 .02
❑ 274 Alonzo Mourning .... .20 .09
❑ 275 Voshon Lenard .... .05 .02
❑ 276 Todd Day..................... .05 .02
❑ 277 Ervin Johnson .... .05 .02
❑ 278 Terrell Brandon .... .10 .05
❑ 279 Michael Curry .... .05 .02
❑ 280 Andrew Lang................ .05 .02
❑ 281 Tyrone Hill................... .05 .02
❑ 282 Stephon Marbury.......... .60 .25
❑ 283 Cherokee Parks .... .05 .02
❑ 284 Stanley Roberts............ .05 .02
❑ 285 Paul Grant RC.............. .05 .02
❑ 286 David Benoit .... .05 .02
❑ 287 Lucious Harris .... .05 .02
❑ 288 Don MacLean .... .05 .02
❑ 289 Sam Cassell .... .10 .05
❑ 290 Keith Van Horn RC ...... 1.00 .45
❑ 291 Patrick Ewing .... .20 .09
❑ 292 Walter McCarty .... .05 .02
❑ 293 Chris Dudley .... .05 .02
❑ 294 Chris Mills .... .05 .02
❑ 295 Buck Williams .... .05 .02
❑ 296 Nick Anderson.............. .05 .02
❑ 297 Derek Strong................ .05 .02
❑ 298 Gerald Wilkins.............. .05 .02
❑ 299 Johnny Taylor RC .... .05 .02
❑ 300 Derek Harper................ .05 .02
❑ 301 Anthony Parker RC .... .05 .02
❑ 302 Allen Iverson .... 1.00 .45
❑ 303 Jim Jackson .... .05 .02
❑ 304 Eric Montross .... .05 .02
❑ 305 Tim Thomas RC .... .60 .25
❑ 306 Kebu Stewart RC .... .05 .02
❑ 307 Rex Chapman .... .05 .02
❑ 308 Tom Chambers .... .05 .02
❑ 309 Kevin Johnson.............. .10 .05
❑ 310 John Williams .... .05 .02
❑ 311 Clifford Robinson.......... .05 .02
❑ 312 Antonio McDyess .... .25 .11

❑ 313 Rasheed Wallace	.20	.09
❑ 314 Brian Grant	.10	.05
❑ 315 Dontonio Wingfield	.05	.02
❑ 316 Kelvin Cato RC	.20	.09
❑ 317 Mahmoud Abdul-Rauf	.05	.02
❑ 318 L. Funderburke RC	.10	.05
❑ 319 Mitch Richmond	.20	.09
❑ 320 Tariq Abdul-Wahad RC	.10	.05
❑ 321 Terry Dehere	.05	.02
❑ 322 Michael Stewart RC	.05	.02
❑ 323 Tim Duncan RC	2.50	1.10
❑ 324 Avery Johnson	.05	.02
❑ 325 David Robinson	.30	.14
❑ 326 Charles Smith	.05	.02
❑ 327 Chuck Person	.05	.02
❑ 328 Monty Williams	.05	.02
❑ 329 Jim McIlvaine	.05	.02
❑ 330 Gary Payton	.30	.14
❑ 331 Eric Snow	.05	.02
❑ 332 Dale Ellis	.05	.02
❑ 333 Vin Baker	.10	.05
❑ 334 Walt Williams	.05	.02
❑ 335 Tracy McGrady RC	2.00	.90
❑ 336 Damon Stoudamire	.25	.11
❑ 337 Carlos Rogers	.05	.02
❑ 338 John Wallace	.05	.02
❑ 339 Shandon Anderson	.05	.02
❑ 340 Jeff Hornacek	.10	.05
❑ 341 Howard Eisley	.05	.02
❑ 342 Jacque Vaughn RC	.10	.05
❑ 343 Bryon Russell	.05	.02
❑ 344 Antoine Carr	.05	.02
❑ 345 Antonio Daniels RC	.20	.09
❑ 346 Pete Chilcutt	.05	.02
❑ 347 Blue Edwards	.05	.02
❑ 348 Bryant Reeves	.05	.02
❑ 349 Chris Robinson RC	.05	.02
❑ 350 Otis Thorpe	.05	.02
❑ 351 Tim Legler	.05	.02
❑ 352 Juwan Howard	.10	.05
❑ 353 God Shammgod RC	.05	.02
❑ 354 Gheorghe Muresan	.05	.02
❑ 355 Chris Whitney	.05	.02
❑ 356 Dikembe Mutombo HP	.05	.02
❑ 357 Antoine Walker HP	.20	.09
❑ 358 Glen Rice HP	.05	.02
❑ 359 Scottie Pippen HP	.30	.14
❑ 360 Derek Anderson HP	.20	.09
❑ 361 Michael Finley HP	.10	.05
❑ 362 LaPhonso Ellis HP	.05	.02
❑ 363 Grant Hill HP	.60	.25
❑ 364 Joe Smith HP	.05	.02
❑ 365 Charles Barkley HP	.20	.09
❑ 366 Reggie Miller HP	.10	.05
❑ 367 Loy Vaught HP	.05	.02
❑ 368 Shaquille O'Neal HP	.40	.18
❑ 369 Alonzo Mourning HP	.10	.05
❑ 370 Glenn Robinson HP	.05	.02
❑ 371 Kevin Garnett HP	.60	.25
❑ 372 Kendall Gill HP	.05	.02
❑ 373 Allan Houston HP	.10	.05
❑ 374 Anfernee Hardaway HP	.40	.18
❑ 375 Tim Thomas HP	.60	.25
❑ 376 Jason Kidd HP	.20	.09
❑ 377 Kenny Anderson HP	.05	.02
❑ 378 Mitch Richmond HP	.10	.05
❑ 379 Tim Duncan HP	1.25	.55
❑ 380 Gary Payton HP	.20	.09
❑ 381 Marcus Camby HP	.10	.05
❑ 382 Karl Malone HP	.20	.09
❑ 383 Shareef Abdur-Rahim HP	.30	.14
❑ 384 Chris Webber HP	.25	.11
❑ 385 Michael Jordan HP	1.25	.55
❑ 386 Michael Jordan MM	1.00	.45
❑ 387 Michael Jordan MM	1.00	.45
❑ 388 Michael Jordan MM	1.00	.45
❑ 389 Michael Jordan MM	1.00	.45
❑ 390 Michael Jordan MM	1.00	.45
❑ 391 Michael Jordan MM	1.00	.45
❑ 392 Michael Jordan MM	1.00	.45
❑ 393 Michael Jordan MM	1.00	.45
❑ 394 Michael Jordan MM	1.00	.45
❑ 395 Michael Jordan MM	1.00	.45
❑ 396 Checklist #1	.05	.02
❑ 397 Checklist #2	.05	.02
❑ 398 Checklist #3	.05	.02
❑ 399 Checklist #4	.05	.02
❑ 400 Checklist #5	.05	.02

1997-98 Collector's Choice Crash the Game Scoring

	MINT	NRMT
COMPLETE SET (60)	50.00	22.00
COMMON CARD (C1-C30)	.40	.18
SEMISTARS	.60	.25
UNLISTED STARS	1.00	.45
EACH PLAYER HAS TWO DIFF.CARDS		
SER.1 STATED ODDS 1:5		
COMP.RED.SET (30)	15.00	6.75
COMMON RED.(R1-R30)	.20	.09
*RED.CARDS: .2X TO .5X HI COLUMN		
ONE RED.SET PER WINNER BY MAIL		
ONE RED.SET PER 15 NON-WIN BY MAIL		

❑ C1A D. Mutombo 11/17 L	.60	.25
❑ C1B D.Mutombo 1/12 L	.60	.25
❑ C2A Dana Barros 12/1 L	.40	.18
❑ C2B Dana Barros 12/22 L	.40	.18
❑ C3A Glen Rice 12/15 W	.60	.25
❑ C3B Glen Rice 1/19 W	.60	.25
❑ C4A Scottie Pippen 11/10 L	3.00	1.35
❑ C4B Scottie Pippen 1/5 L	2.50	1.10
❑ C5A Terrell Brandon 11/17 L	.60	.25
❑ C5B Terrell Brandon 1/5 L	.60	.25
❑ C6A Shawn Bradley 12/1 L	.40	.18
❑ C6B Shawn Bradley 12/22 L	.40	.18
❑ C7A Antonio McDyess 12/8 L	1.25	.55
❑ C7B Antonio McDyess 1/19 L	1.00	.45
❑ C8A Lindsey Hunter 12/8 L	.40	.18
❑ C8B Lindsey Hunter 12/22 L	.40	.18
❑ C9A Joe Smith 11/17 L	.60	.25
❑ C9B Joe Smith 1/19 W	.60	.25
❑ C10A H. Olajuwon 11/17 L	1.50	.70
❑ C10B H. Olajuwon 1/5 L	1.50	.70
❑ C11A Reggie Miller 11/24 W	1.00	.45
❑ C11B Reggie Miller 12/29 L	1.00	.45
❑ C12A Rodney Rogers 11/24 L	.40	.18
❑ C12B Rodney Rogers 1/19 L	.40	.18
❑ C13A Nick Van Exel 12/1 L	.60	.25
❑ C13B Nick Van Exel 1/5 L	.60	.25
❑ C14A Tim Hardaway 12/8 L	1.00	.45
❑ C14B Tim Hardaway 12/29 L	1.00	.45
❑ C15A G. Robinson 11/17 L	.60	.25
❑ C15B Glenn Robinson 1/5 L	.60	.25
❑ C16A Kevin Garnett 11/10 L	6.00	2.70
❑ C16B Kevin Garnett 12/15 L	5.00	2.20
❑ C17A Kerry Kittles 11/24 L	1.00	.45
❑ C17B Kerry Kittles 12/29 L	1.00	.45
❑ C18A Larry Johnson 12/1 L	.60	.25
❑ C18B Larry Johnson 1/12 L	.60	.25
❑ C19A A.Hardaway 11/24 L	3.00	1.35
❑ C19B A.Hardaway 1/5 L	3.00	1.35
❑ C20A Allen Iverson 12/1 L	5.00	2.20
❑ C20B Allen Iverson 1/12 W	6.00	2.70
❑ C21A Jason Kidd 11/24 L	3.00	1.35
❑ C21B Jason Kidd 12/29 L	1.50	.70
❑ C22A A. Sabonis 11/17 L	.60	.25
❑ C22B A. Sabonis 1/19 W	.60	.25
❑ C23A Mitch Richmond 12/8 W	1.00	.45
❑ C23B Mitch Richmond 1/5 L	1.00	.45
❑ C24A D. Robinson 11/10 W	1.50	.70
❑ C24B D. Robinson 12/29 L	1.25	.55
❑ C25A Gary Payton 12/1 L	1.50	.70
❑ C25B Gary Payton 12/22 L	1.25	.55
❑ C26A Marcus Camby 12/15 L	1.25	.55
❑ C26B Marcus Camby 1/12 L	1.00	.45
❑ C27A Karl Malone 12/8 W	1.50	.70
❑ C27B Karl Malone 1/19 W	2.00	.90
❑ C28A Bryant Reeves 11/17 L	.40	.18
❑ C28B Bryant Reeves 1/5 L	.40	.18
❑ C29A Chris Webber 12/8 W	3.00	1.35
❑ C29B Chris Webber 1/12 W	3.00	1.35
❑ C30A M. Jordan 11/24 W	12.00	5.50
❑ C30B M. Jordan 12/29 W	15.00	6.75

1997-98 Collector's Choice Draft Trade

	MINT	NRMT
COMPLETE SET (10)	8.00	3.60
COMMON CARD (1-10)	.50	.23
UNLISTED STARS	.75	.35
RED.THROUGH CHECK.CHALLENGE		

❑ 1 Tim Duncan	4.00	1.80
❑ 2 Keith Van Horn	2.00	.90
❑ 3 Chauncey Billups	.75	.35
❑ 4 Antonio Daniels	.75	.35
❑ 5 Tony Battie	.50	.23
❑ 6 Ron Mercer	1.25	.55
❑ 7 Tim Thomas	1.25	.55
❑ 8 Adonal Foyle	.50	.23
❑ 9 Tracy McGrady	4.00	1.80
❑ 10 Danny Fortson	.50	.23

1997-98 Collector's Choice Memorable Moments

	MINT	NRMT
COMPLETE SET (10)	20.00	9.00
COMMON CARD (1-10)	1.00	.45
ONE PER SPECIAL RETAIL PACK		

❑ 1 Michael Jordan	8.00	3.60
❑ 2 Grant Hill	3.00	1.35
❑ 3 Anfernee Hardaway	2.00	.90
❑ 4 Kobe Bryant	5.00	2.20
❑ 5 Kevin Garnett	4.00	1.80
❑ 6 Jason Kidd	2.00	.90
❑ 7 Karl Malone	1.00	.45
❑ 8 Hakeem Olajuwon	1.00	.45
❑ 9 Gary Payton	1.00	.45
❑ 10 Dennis Rodman	1.25	.55

1997-98 Collector's Choice Miniatures

	MINT	NRMT
COMPLETE SET (30)	10.00	4.50
COMMON CARD (M1-M30)	.10	.05
SEMISTARS	.15	.07
UNLISTED STARS	.25	.11
SER.2 STATED ODDS 1:3		
FIVE PER FACTORY SET		

❑ M1 Mookie Blaylock	.10	.05

		MINT	NRMT
❑ M2	Chauncey Billups	.15	.07
❑ M3	Glen Rice	.15	.07
❑ M4	Scottie Pippen	.75	.35
❑ M5	Bob Sura	.10	.05
❑ M6	Erick Strickland	.10	.05
❑ M7	Tony Battie	.10	.05
❑ M8	Joe Dumars	.25	.11
❑ M9	Adonal Foyle	.10	.05
❑ M10	Charles Barkley	.40	.18
❑ M11	Dale Davis	.10	.05
❑ M12	Lamond Murray	.10	.05
❑ M13	Kobe Bryant	2.00	.90
❑ M14	Tim Hardaway	.25	.11
❑ M15	Glenn Robinson	.15	.07
❑ M16	Kevin Garnett	1.50	.70
❑ M17	Keith Van Horn	.60	.25
❑ M18	Patrick Ewing	.25	.11
❑ M19	Anfernee Hardaway	.75	.35
❑ M20	Tim Thomas	.40	.18
❑ M21	Jason Kidd	.75	.35
❑ M22	Isaiah Rider	.15	.07
❑ M23	Mahmoud Abdul-Rauf	.10	.05
❑ M24	Tim Duncan	1.25	.55
❑ M25	Detlef Schrempf	.15	.07
❑ M26	Damon Stoudamire	.30	.14
❑ M27	John Stockton	.25	.11
❑ M28	Bryant Reeves	.10	.05
❑ M29	Juwan Howard	.15	.07
❑ M30	Michael Jordan	3.00	1.35

1997-98 Collector's Choice MJ Bullseye

	MINT	NRMT
COMPLETE SET (30)	125.00	55.00
COMMON JORDAN (B1-B30)	5.00	2.20
ONE WEEK/TARGET PER CARD		
SER.2 STATED ODDS 1:5		
COMP.REW.RED.SET (13)	40.00	18.00
COMMON REW. (R1-R13)	4.00	1.80
REW.RED.PER WINNER BY MAIL		

		MINT	NRMT
❑ B1	Michael Jordan 2/9 1,750 W	5.00	2.20
❑ B2	Michael Jordan 2/9 2,000 W	5.00	2.20
❑ B3	Michael Jordan 2/16 1,750 L	5.00	2.20
❑ B4	Michael Jordan 2/23 1,750 L	5.00	2.20
❑ B5	Michael Jordan 2/16 2,000 L	5.00	2.20
❑ B6	Michael Jordan 2/9 2,250 W	5.00	2.20
❑ B7	Michael Jordan 2/16 2,250 W	5.00	2.20
❑ B8	Michael Jordan 2/23 2,000 L	5.00	2.20
❑ B9	Michael Jordan 2/23 2,250 W	5.00	2.20
❑ B10	Michael Jordan 2/9 2,500 W	5.00	2.20
❑ B11	Michael Jordan 3/9 1,750 L	5.00	2.20
❑ B12	Michael Jordan 3/9 2,000 L	5.00	2.20
❑ B13	Michael Jordan 3/16 1,750 W	5.00	2.20
❑ B14	Michael Jordan 3/23 1,750 W	5.00	2.20
❑ B15	Michael Jordan 3/16 2,000 W	5.00	2.20
❑ B16	Michael Jordan 3/9 2,250 W	5.00	2.20
❑ B17	Michael Jordan 3/16 2,250 W	5.00	2.20
❑ B18	Michael Jordan 3/23 2,000 W	5.00	2.20
❑ B19	Michael Jordan 3/23 2,250 W	5.00	2.20
❑ B20	Michael Jordan 3/9 2,500 L	5.00	2.20
❑ B21	Michael Jordan 3/30 1,750 W	5.00	2.20
❑ B22	Michael Jordan 4/6 1,750 L	5.00	2.20
❑ B23	Michael Jordan 4/13 1,750 W	5.00	2.20
❑ B24	Michael Jordan 3/30 2,000 W	5.00	2.20
❑ B25	Michael Jordan 4/6 2,000 L	5.00	2.20
❑ B26	Michael Jordan 4/13 2,000 W	5.00	2.20
❑ B27	Michael Jordan 3/30 2,250 W	5.00	2.20
❑ B28	Michael Jordan 4/6 2,250 W	5.00	2.20
❑ B29	Michael Jordan 4/13 2,250 W	5.00	2.20
❑ B30	Michael Jordan 3/30 2,500 W	5.00	2.20

1997-98 Collector's Choice Star Attractions

	MINT	NRMT
COMPLETE SET (20)	50.00	22.00
COMPLETE SERIES 1 (10)	30.00	13.50
COMPLETE SERIES 2 (10)	20.00	9.00
COMMON CARD (SA1-SA20)	.75	.35
ONE PER SPECIAL RETAIL PACK		
*GOLD: 2.5X TO 5X HI COLUMN		
GOLD: SER.1/2 STATED ODDS 1:20 SPEC.		

		MINT	NRMT
❑ SA1	Michael Jordan	20.00	9.00
❑ SA2	Joe Smith	.75	.35
❑ SA3	Karl Malone	1.25	.55
❑ SA4	Chauncey Billups	.75	.35
❑ SA5	Charles Barkley	1.25	.55
❑ SA6	Shaquille O'Neal	4.00	1.80
❑ SA7	Jason Kidd	2.50	1.10
❑ SA8	Chris Webber	2.50	1.10
❑ SA9	Allen Iverson	4.00	1.80
❑ SA10	Patrick Ewing	.75	.35
❑ SA11	Tim Duncan	4.00	1.80
❑ SA12	Kevin Garnett	5.00	2.20
❑ SA13	Tony Battie	.75	.35
❑ SA14	Gary Payton	1.25	.55
❑ SA15	Hakeem Olajuwon	1.25	.55
❑ SA16	Antonio Daniels	.75	.35
❑ SA17	Grant Hill	4.00	1.80
❑ SA18	Anfernee Hardaway	2.50	1.10
❑ SA19	Scottie Pippen	2.50	1.10
❑ SA20	Keith Van Horn	2.00	.90

1997-98 Collector's Choice StarQuest

	MINT	NRMT
COMPLETE SET (180)	600.00	275.00
COMPLETE SERIES 1 (90)	300.00	135.00
COMPLETE SERIES 2 (90)	300.00	135.00
COMMON (1-45/91-135)	.15	.07
COMMON (46-65/136-155)	1.50	.70
COMMON (66-80/156-170)	5.00	2.20
COMMON (81-90/171-180)	6.00	2.70
SEMISTARS (1-45/91-135)	.20	.09
SEMISTARS (46-65/136-155)	2.00	.90
STARS (1-45/91-135)	.30	.14
STARS (46-65/136-155)	3.00	1.35
STARS (66-80/156-170)	5.00	2.20
STARS (81-90/171-180)	6.00	2.70
1-45/91-135 SER.1/2 STATED ODDS 1:1		
46-65/136-155 SER.1/2 STATED ODDS 1:21		
66-80/156-170 SER.1/2 STATED ODDS 1:71		
81-90/171-180 SER.1/2 STATED ODDS 1:145		
SQ PREFIX ON CARD NUMBERS		

		MINT	NRMT
❑ 1	Dale Davis	.15	.07
❑ 2	Jamal Mashburn	.20	.09
❑ 3	Christian Laettner	.20	.09
❑ 4	Billy Owens	.15	.07
❑ 5	Vlade Divac	.15	.07
❑ 6	Sean Elliott	.15	.07
❑ 7	Marcus Camby	.40	.18
❑ 8	Dana Barros	.15	.07
❑ 9	Rod Strickland	.20	.09
❑ 10	Jim Jackson	.15	.07
❑ 11	Tyrone Hill	.15	.07
❑ 12	Ervin Johnson	.15	.07
❑ 13	Antoine Walker	.60	.25
❑ 14	Lorenzen Wright	.15	.07
❑ 15	Shawn Bradley	.15	.07
❑ 16	John Starks	.15	.07
❑ 17	Corliss Williamson	.15	.07
❑ 18	Steve Smith	.20	.09
❑ 19	Chris Mills	.15	.07
❑ 20	Vinny Del Negro	.15	.07
❑ 21	Jayson Williams	.20	.09
❑ 22	Anthony Mason	.20	.09
❑ 23	Dennis Scott	.15	.07
❑ 24	Mark Jackson	.15	.07
❑ 25	Dino Radja	.15	.07
❑ 26	Greg Ostertag	.15	.07
❑ 27	Anthony Peeler	.15	.07

❑ 28 Toni Kukoc .40 .18
❑ 29 Michael Finley .30 .14
❑ 30 Brent Barry .15 .07
❑ 31 Wesley Person .15 .07
❑ 32 Horace Grant .20 .09
❑ 33 Walt Williams .15 .07
❑ 34 Bryant Stith .15 .07
❑ 35 Ray Allen .50 .23
❑ 36 Otis Thorpe .15 .07
❑ 37 Rasheed Wallace .30 .14
❑ 38 Charles Oakley .15 .07
❑ 39 Robert Pack .15 .07
❑ 40 Kendall Gill .20 .09
❑ 41 Lindsey Hunter .15 .07
❑ 42 Cedric Ceballos .15 .07
❑ 43 Allan Houston .30 .14
❑ 44 Bryant Reeves .15 .07
❑ 45 Derrick Coleman .20 .09
❑ 46 Isaiah Rider 2.00 .90
❑ 47 Detlef Schrempf 2.00 .90
❑ 48 Antonio McDyess 4.00 1.80
❑ 49 Glenn Robinson 2.00 .90
❑ 50 Damon Stoudamire 4.00 1.80
❑ 51 Terrell Brandon 2.00 .90
❑ 52 Joe Smith 2.00 .90
❑ 53 Tom Gugliotta 2.00 .90
❑ 54 Loy Vaught 1.50 .70
❑ 55 Kenny Anderson 2.00 .90
❑ 56 Dikembe Mutombo 2.00 .90
❑ 57 Tim Hardaway 3.00 1.35
❑ 58 Chris Webber 10.00 4.50
❑ 59 Nick Van Exel 2.00 .90
❑ 60 Kerry Kittles 3.00 1.35
❑ 61 Chris Mullin 3.00 1.35
❑ 62 Stephon Marbury 10.00 4.50
❑ 63 Juwan Howard 2.00 .90
❑ 64 Larry Johnson 2.00 .90
❑ 65 Shareef Abdur-Rahim 10.00 4.50
❑ 66 Dennis Rodman 10.00 4.50
❑ 67 Vin Baker 5.00 2.20
❑ 68 Clyde Drexler 5.00 2.20
❑ 69 Eddie Jones 10.00 4.50
❑ 70 Jerry Stackhouse 5.00 2.20
❑ 71 Karl Malone 8.00 3.60
❑ 72 Mitch Richmond 5.00 2.20
❑ 73 Glen Rice 5.00 2.20
❑ 74 Jason Kidd 15.00 6.75
❑ 75 Latrell Sprewell 10.00 4.50
❑ 76 David Robinson 8.00 3.60
❑ 77 Charles Barkley 8.00 3.60
❑ 78 Gary Payton 8.00 3.60
❑ 79 Scottie Pippen 15.00 6.75
❑ 80 Reggie Miller 6.00 2.70
❑ 81 Alonzo Mourning 6.00 2.70
❑ 82 Allen Iverson 30.00 13.50
❑ 83 Michael Jordan 80.00 36.00
❑ 84 Shawn Kemp 10.00 4.50
❑ 85 Kevin Garnett 40.00 18.00
❑ 86 Grant Hill 30.00 13.50
❑ 87 Anfernee Hardaway 20.00 9.00
❑ 88 Shaquille O'Neal 30.00 13.50
❑ 89 John Stockton 6.00 2.70
❑ 90 Hakeem Olajuwon 10.00 4.50
❑ 91 Billy Owens .15 .07
❑ 92 Derek Anderson .40 .18
❑ 93 Hersey Hawkins .20 .09
❑ 94 Bryon Russell .15 .07
❑ 95 Rik Smits .15 .07
❑ 96 Tracy McGrady 1.25 .55
❑ 97 Kendall Gill .20 .09
❑ 98 Tim Thomas .50 .23
❑ 99 Robert Horry .15 .07
❑ 100 Marcus Camby .40 .18
❑ 101 Rodney Rogers .15 .07
❑ 102 Danny Manning .20 .09
❑ 103 John Starks .15 .07
❑ 104 Mahmoud Abdul-Rauf .15 .07
❑ 105 Chris Childs .15 .07
❑ 106 Antonio Davis .15 .07
❑ 107 Lamond Murray .15 .07
❑ 108 Nick Anderson .15 .07
❑ 109 Antoine Walker .60 .25
❑ 110 Christian Laettner .20 .09
❑ 111 Gary Trent .15 .07
❑ 112 Tony Battie .15 .07
❑ 113 Vlade Divac .15 .07
❑ 114 Kevin Johnson .20 .09
❑ 115 Erick Strickland .15 .07
❑ 116 Ray Allen .50 .23
❑ 117 Antonio Daniels .20 .09
❑ 118 Sean Elliott .15 .07
❑ 119 Horace Grant .20 .09
❑ 120 Walt Williams .15 .07
❑ 121 Rony Seikaly .15 .07
❑ 122 Allan Houston .30 .14
❑ 123 Michael Finley .30 .14
❑ 124 Rasheed Wallace .30 .14
❑ 125 Doug Christie .15 .07
❑ 126 Danny Ferry .15 .07
❑ 127 Arvydas Sabonis .20 .09
❑ 128 Shandon Anderson .15 .07
❑ 129 Otis Thorpe .15 .07
❑ 130 Adonal Foyle .15 .07
❑ 131 Bryant Reeves .15 .07
❑ 132 Theo Ratliff .15 .07
❑ 133 Matt Maloney .15 .07
❑ 134 Voshon Lenard .15 .07
❑ 135 Danny Fortson .15 .07
❑ 136 Joe Smith 2.00 .90
❑ 137 Mookie Blaylock 1.50 .70
❑ 138 Loy Vaught 1.50 .70
❑ 139 Tom Gugliotta 2.00 .90
❑ 140 Damon Stoudamire 4.00 1.80
❑ 141 Antonio McDyess 4.00 1.80
❑ 142 Kobe Bryant 25.00 11.00
❑ 143 Juwan Howard 2.00 .90
❑ 144 Tim Hardaway 3.00 1.35
❑ 145 Ron Mercer 6.00 2.70
❑ 146 Joe Dumars 3.00 1.35
❑ 147 Clyde Drexler 3.00 1.35
❑ 148 Shareef Abdur-Rahim 10.00 4.50
❑ 149 LaPhonso Ellis 1.50 .70
❑ 150 Dikembe Mutombo 2.00 .90
❑ 151 Chauncey Billups 2.00 .90
❑ 152 Chris Webber 10.00 4.50
❑ 153 Glenn Robinson 2.00 .90
❑ 154 Patrick Ewing 3.00 1.35
❑ 155 Stephon Marbury 10.00 4.50
❑ 156 Keith Van Horn 12.00 5.50
❑ 157 Karl Malone 8.00 3.60
❑ 158 Terrell Brandon 5.00 2.20
❑ 159 Sam Cassell 5.00 2.20
❑ 160 Jerry Stackhouse 5.00 2.20
❑ 161 Vin Baker 5.00 2.20
❑ 162 Jason Kidd 15.00 6.75
❑ 163 Charles Barkley 8.00 3.60
❑ 164 Reggie Miller 5.00 2.20
❑ 165 Alonzo Mourning 5.00 2.20
❑ 166 Scottie Pippen 15.00 6.75
❑ 167 Glen Rice 5.00 2.20
❑ 168 Allen Iverson 30.00 13.50
❑ 169 David Robinson 8.00 3.60
❑ 170 Shawn Kemp 10.00 4.50
❑ 171 Michael Jordan 100.00 45.00
❑ 172 Tim Duncan 30.00 13.50
❑ 173 Anfernee Hardaway 15.00 6.75
❑ 174 Shaquille O'Neal 30.00 13.50
❑ 175 John Stockton 6.00 2.70
❑ 176 Gary Payton 10.00 4.50
❑ 177 Mitch Richmond 6.00 2.70
❑ 178 Kevin Garnett 40.00 18.00
❑ 179 Hakeem Olajuwon 10.00 4.50
❑ 180 Grant Hill 30.00 13.50

1997-98 Collector's Choice Stick-Ums

	MINT	NRMT
COMPLETE SET (30)	8.00	3.60
COMMON CARD (S1-S30)	.10	.05
SEMISTARS	.15	.07
UNLISTED STARS	.25	.11

SER.1 STATED ODDS 1:3

❑ S1 Steve Smith .15 .07
❑ S2 Antoine Walker .50 .23
❑ S3 Anthony Mason .15 .07
❑ S4 Dennis Rodman .50 .23
❑ S5 Terrell Brandon .15 .07
❑ S6 Michael Finley .25 .11
❑ S7 Antonio McDyess .30 .14

❑ S8 Grant Hill 1.25 .55
❑ S9 Joe Smith .15 .07
❑ S10 Hakeem Olajuwon .40 .18
❑ S11 Reggie Miller .25 .11
❑ S12 Loy Vaught .10 .05
❑ S13 Shaquille O'Neal 1.25 .55
❑ S14 Alonzo Mourning .25 .11
❑ S15 Vin Baker .15 .07
❑ S16 Stephon Marbury .75 .35
❑ S17 Jim Jackson .10 .05
❑ S18 John Starks .10 .05
❑ S19 Anfernee Hardaway .75 .35
❑ S20 Allen Iverson 1.25 .55
❑ S21 Jason Kidd .75 .35
❑ S22 Kenny Anderson .15 .07
❑ S23 Mitch Richmond .25 .11
❑ S24 David Robinson .40 .18
❑ S25 Shawn Kemp .40 .18
❑ S26 Damon Stoudamire .30 .14
❑ S27 Karl Malone .40 .18
❑ S28 Bryant Reeves .10 .05
❑ S29 Juwan Howard .15 .07
❑ S30 Michael Jordan 3.00 1.35

1997-98 Collector's Choice The Jordan Dynasty

	MINT	NRMT
COMPLETE SET (5)	60.00	27.00
COMMON CARD (1-5)	15.00	6.75

RANDOM INSERTS IN SER.1 PACKS
STATED PRINT RUN 23,000 EACH

❑ 1 Michael Jordan 15.00 6.75
1990-91 NBA Champs
❑ 2 Michael Jordan 15.00 6.75
1991-92 NBA Champs
❑ 3 Michael Jordan 15.00 6.75
1992-93 NBA Champs
❑ 4 Michael Jordan 15.00 6.75
1995-96 NBA Champs
❑ 5 Michael Jordan 15.00 6.75
1996-97 NBA Champs

1994-95 Emotion

	MINT	NRMT
COMPLETE SET (121)	50.00	22.00
COMMON CARD (1-121)	.15	.07

SEMISTARS	.30	.14
UNLISTED STARS	.60	.25

SUBSET CARDS HALF VALUE OF BASE CARDS

Card		
❑ 1 Stacey Augmon	.15	.07
❑ 2 Mookie Blaylock	.15	.07
❑ 3 Steve Smith	.30	.14
❑ 4 Greg Minor RC	.15	.07
❑ 5 Eric Montross RC	.15	.07
❑ 6 Dino Radja	.15	.07
❑ 7 Dominique Wilkins	.60	.25
❑ 8 Muggsy Bogues	.30	.14
❑ 9 Larry Johnson	.30	.14
❑ 10 Alonzo Mourning	.75	.35
❑ 11 B.J. Armstrong	.15	.07
❑ 12 Toni Kukoc	1.00	.45
❑ 13 Scottie Pippen	2.00	.90
❑ 14 Dickey Simpkins RC	.15	.07
❑ 15 Tyrone Hill	.15	.07
❑ 16 Chris Mills	.30	.14
❑ 17 Mark Price	.15	.07
❑ 18 Tony Dumas RC	.15	.07
❑ 19 Jim Jackson	.30	.14
❑ 20 Jason Kidd RC	5.00	2.20
❑ 21 Jamal Mashburn	.60	.25
❑ 22 LaPhonso Ellis	.15	.07
❑ 23 Dikembe Mutombo	.30	.14
❑ 24 Rodney Rogers	.15	.07
❑ 25 Jalen Rose RC	2.50	1.10
❑ 26 Bill Curley RC	.15	.07
❑ 27 Joe Dumars	.60	.25
❑ 28 Grant Hill RC	6.00	2.70
❑ 29 Tim Hardaway	.60	.25
❑ 30 Donyell Marshall RC	.60	.25
❑ 31 Chris Mullin	.60	.25
❑ 32 Carlos Rogers RC	.15	.07
❑ 33 Clifford Rozier RC	.15	.07
❑ 34 Latrell Sprewell	1.25	.55
❑ 35 Sam Cassell	.60	.25
❑ 36 Clyde Drexler	.60	.25
❑ 37 Robert Horry	.15	.07
❑ 38 Hakeem Olajuwon	1.00	.45
❑ 39 Mark Jackson	.15	.07
❑ 40 Reggie Miller	.60	.25
❑ 41 Rik Smits	.15	.07
❑ 42 Lamond Murray RC	.30	.14
❑ 43 Eric Piatkowski RC	.15	.07
❑ 44 Loy Vaught	.15	.07
❑ 45 Cedric Ceballos	.15	.07
❑ 46 Eddie Jones RC	4.00	1.80
❑ 47 George Lynch	.15	.07
❑ 48 Nick Van Exel	.60	.25
❑ 49 Harold Miner	.15	.07
❑ 50 Khalid Reeves RC	.15	.07
❑ 51 Glen Rice	.30	.14
❑ 52 Kevin Willis	.15	.07
❑ 53 Vin Baker	.60	.25
❑ 54 Eric Mobley RC	.15	.07
❑ 55 Eric Murdock	.15	.07
❑ 56 Glenn Robinson RC	2.00	.90
❑ 57 Tom Gugliotta	.30	.14
❑ 58 Christian Laettner	.30	.14
❑ 59 Isaiah Rider	.30	.14
❑ 60 Kenny Anderson	.30	.14
❑ 61 Derrick Coleman	.30	.14
❑ 62 Yinka Dare	.15	.07
❑ 63 Patrick Ewing	.60	.25
❑ 64 John Starks	.15	.07
❑ 65 Charlie Ward RC	.60	.25
❑ 66 Monty Williams RC	.15	.07
❑ 67 Nick Anderson	.15	.07
❑ 68 Horace Grant	.30	.14
❑ 69 Anfernee Hardaway	2.00	.90
❑ 70 Shaquille O'Neal	3.00	1.35
❑ 71 Brooks Thompson	.15	.07
❑ 72 Dana Barros	.15	.07
❑ 73 Shawn Bradley	.15	.07
❑ 74 B.J. Tyler	.15	.07
❑ 75 Clarence Weatherspoon	.15	.07
❑ 76 Sharone Wright RC	.15	.07
❑ 77 Charles Barkley	1.00	.45
❑ 78 Kevin Johnson	.30	.14
❑ 79 Dan Majerle	.30	.14
❑ 80 Danny Manning	.30	.14
❑ 81 Wesley Person RC	.60	.25
❑ 82 Aaron McKie RC	.15	.07
❑ 83 Clifford Robinson	.30	.14
❑ 84 Rod Strickland	.30	.14
❑ 85 Brian Grant RC	1.50	.70
❑ 86 Bobby Hurley	.15	.07
❑ 87 Mitch Richmond	.60	.25
❑ 88 Sean Elliott	.30	.14
❑ 89 David Robinson	1.00	.45
❑ 90 Dennis Rodman	1.25	.55
❑ 91 Shawn Kemp	1.00	.45
❑ 92 Gary Payton	1.00	.45
❑ 93 Dontonio Wingfield	.15	.07
❑ 94 Jeff Hornacek	.30	.14
❑ 95 Karl Malone	1.00	.45
❑ 96 John Stockton	.60	.25
❑ 97 Calbert Cheaney	.15	.07
❑ 98 Juwan Howard RC	1.50	.70
❑ 99 Chris Webber	2.00	.90
❑ 100 Michael Jordan	12.00	5.50
❑ 101 Brian Grant ROO	.30	.14
❑ 102 Grant Hill ROO	3.00	1.35
❑ 103 Juwan Howard ROO	1.25	.55
❑ 104 Eddie Jones ROO	2.00	.90
❑ 105 Jason Kidd ROO	2.00	.90
❑ 106 Eric Montross ROO	.15	.07
❑ 107 Lamond Murray ROO	.15	.07
❑ 108 Wesley Person ROO	.30	.14
❑ 109 Glenn Robinson ROO	1.00	.45
❑ 110 Sharone Wright ROO	.15	.07
❑ 111 Anfernee Hardaway MAS	1.25	.55
❑ 112 Shawn Kemp MAS	.60	.25
❑ 113 Karl Malone MAS	.60	.25
❑ 114 Alonzo Mourning MAS	.60	.25
❑ 115 Shaquille O'Neal MAS	1.25	.55
❑ 116 Hakeem Olajuwon MAS	.60	.25
❑ 117 Scottie Pippen MAS	1.00	.45
❑ 118 David Robinson MAS	.60	.25
❑ 119 Latrell Sprewell MAS	.60	.25
❑ 120 Chris Webber MAS	.75	.35
❑ 121 Checklist	.15	.07
❑ NNO Grant Hill SkyMotion Exchange	75.00	34.00
❑ NNO Grant Hil David Robinson Promo	5.00	l2.20

1994-95 Emotion N-Tense

	MINT	NRMT
COMPLETE SET (10)	80.00	36.00
COMMON CARD (N1-N10)	4.00	1.80

STATED ODDS 1:18

Card		
❑ N1 Charles Barkley	6.00	2.70
❑ N2 Patrick Ewing	4.00	1.80
❑ N3 Michael Jordan	50.00	22.00
❑ N4 Shawn Kemp	6.00	2.70
❑ N5 Karl Malone	6.00	2.70
❑ N6 Alonzo Mourning	5.00	2.20
❑ N7 Shaquille O'Neal	20.00	9.00
❑ N8 Hakeem Olajuwon	6.00	2.70
❑ N9 David Robinson	6.00	2.70
❑ N10 Glenn Robinson	5.00	2.20

1994-95 Emotion X-Cited

	MINT	NRMT
COMPLETE SET (20)	60.00	27.00

*SINGLES: 1.5X TO 4X BASE CARD HI
STATED ODDS 1:4

Card		
❑ X1 Kenny Anderson	1.25	.55
❑ X2 Anfernee Hardaway	8.00	3.60
❑ X3 Tim Hardaway	2.50	1.10
❑ X4 Grant Hill	12.00	5.50
❑ X5 Jim Jackson	1.25	.55
❑ X6 Eddie Jones	8.00	3.60
❑ X7 Jason Kidd	10.00	4.50
❑ X8 Dan Majerle	1.25	.55
❑ X9 Jamal Mashburn	2.50	1.10
❑ X10 Lamond Murray	1.25	.55
❑ X11 Gary Payton	4.00	1.80
❑ X12 Wesley Person	2.50	1.10
❑ X13 Scottie Pippen	8.00	3.60
❑ X14 Mark Price	.60	.25
❑ X15 Mitch Richmond	2.50	1.10
❑ X16 Isaiah Rider	1.25	.55
❑ X17 Latrell Sprewell	5.00	2.20
❑ X18 John Stockton	2.50	1.10
❑ X19 Rod Strickland	1.25	.55
❑ X20 Nick Van Exel	2.50	1.10

1995-96 E-XL

	MINT	NRMT
COMPLETE SET (100)	50.00	22.00
COMMON CARD (1-100)	.25	.11
SEMISTARS	.40	.18
UNLISTED STARS	.60	.25

Card	MINT	NRMT
❑ 1 Stacey Augmon	.25	.11
❑ 2 Mookie Blaylock	.25	.11
❑ 3 Christian Laettner	.40	.18
❑ 4 Dana Barros	.25	.11
❑ 5 Dino Radja	.25	.11
❑ 6 Eric Williams RC	.40	.18
❑ 7 Kenny Anderson	.40	.18
❑ 8 Larry Johnson	.40	.18
❑ 9 Glen Rice	.40	.18
❑ 10 Michael Jordan	8.00	3.60
❑ 11 Toni Kukoc	.75	.35
❑ 12 Scottie Pippen	2.00	.90
❑ 13 Dennis Rodman	1.25	.55
❑ 14 Terrell Brandon	.40	.18
❑ 15 Bobby Phills	.25	.11
❑ 16 Bob Sura RC	.40	.18
❑ 17 Jim Jackson	.25	.11
❑ 18 Jason Kidd	2.00	.90
❑ 19 Jamal Mashburn	.40	.18
❑ 20 Mahmoud Abdul-Rauf	.25	.11
❑ 21 Antonio McDyess RC	3.00	1.35
❑ 22 Dikembe Mutombo	.40	.18
❑ 23 Joe Dumars	.60	.25
❑ 24 Grant Hill	3.00	1.35
❑ 25 Allan Houston	.75	.35
❑ 26 Joe Smith RC	2.00	.90
❑ 27 Latrell Sprewell	1.25	.55
❑ 28 Kevin Willis	.25	.11
❑ 29 Sam Cassell	.40	.18
❑ 30 Clyde Drexler	.60	.25
❑ 31 Robert Horry	.25	.11
❑ 32 Hakeem Olajuwon	1.00	.45
❑ 33 Derrick McKey	.25	.11
❑ 34 Reggie Miller	.60	.25
❑ 35 Rik Smits	.25	.11
❑ 36 Brent Barry RC	.60	.25
❑ 37 Loy Vaught	.25	.11
❑ 38 Brian Williams	.25	.11
❑ 39 Cedric Ceballos	.25	.11
❑ 40 Magic Johnson	2.00	.90
❑ 41 Nick Van Exel	.40	.18
❑ 42 Tim Hardaway	.60	.25
❑ 43 Alonzo Mourning	.60	.25
❑ 44 Kurt Thomas RC	.40	.18
❑ 45 Walt Williams	.25	.11
❑ 46 Vin Baker	.60	.25
❑ 47 Shawn Respert RC	.25	.11
❑ 48 Glenn Robinson	.60	.25
❑ 49 Kevin Garnett RC	10.00	4.50
❑ 50 Tom Gugliotta	.40	.18
❑ 51 Isaiah Rider	.40	.18
❑ 52 Shawn Bradley	.25	.11
❑ 53 Chris Childs	.25	.11
❑ 54 Ed O'Bannon RC	.25	.11
❑ 55 Patrick Ewing	.60	.25
❑ 56 Anthony Mason	.40	.18
❑ 57 Charles Oakley	.25	.11
❑ 58 Horace Grant	.40	.18
❑ 59 Anfernee Hardaway	2.00	.90
❑ 60 Shaquille O'Neal	3.00	1.35
❑ 61 Derrick Coleman	.40	.18
❑ 62 Jerry Stackhouse RC	2.00	.90
❑ 63 Clarence Weatherspoon	.25	.11
❑ 64 Charles Barkley	1.00	.45
❑ 65 Michael Finley RC	2.50	1.10
❑ 66 Kevin Johnson	.40	.18
❑ 67 Clifford Robinson	.25	.11
❑ 68 Arvydas Sabonis RC	1.00	.45
❑ 69 Rod Strickland	.40	.18
❑ 70 Tyus Edney RC	.25	.11
❑ 71 Billy Owens	.25	.11
❑ 72 Mitch Richmond	.60	.25
❑ 73 Sean Elliott	.25	.11
❑ 74 Avery Johnson	.25	.11
❑ 75 David Robinson	1.00	.45
❑ 76 Shawn Kemp	1.00	.45
❑ 77 Gary Payton	1.00	.45
❑ 78 Detlef Schrempf	.40	.18
❑ 79 Tracy Murray	.25	.11
❑ 80 Damon Stoudamire RC	3.00	1.35
❑ 81 Sharone Wright	.25	.11
❑ 82 Jeff Hornacek	.40	.18
❑ 83 Karl Malone	1.00	.45
❑ 84 John Stockton	.60	.25
❑ 85 Greg Anthony	.25	.11
❑ 86 Bryant Reeves RC	.60	.25
❑ 87 Byron Scott	.25	.11
❑ 88 Juwan Howard	.60	.25
❑ 89 Gheorghe Muresan	.25	.11
❑ 90 Rasheed Wallace RC	2.50	1.10
❑ 91 Steve Smith UNT	.25	.11
❑ 92 Dikembe Mutombo UNT	.25	.11
❑ 93 Brent Barry UNT	.40	.18
❑ 94 Glenn Robinson UNT	.40	.18
❑ 95 Armon Gilliam UNT	.25	.11
❑ 96 Nick Anderson UNT	.25	.11
❑ 97 Gary Trent UNT	.25	.11
❑ 98 Brian Grant UNT	.40	.18
❑ 99 Bryant Reeves UNT	.40	.18
❑ 100 Checklist	.25	.11
❑ NNO Grant Hill Promo	5.00	2.20

1995-96 E-XL Blue

	MINT	NRMT
COMPLETE SET (100)	100.00	45.00
COMMON CARD (1-100)	.30	.14

*STARS:1.25X TO 2.5X BASE CARD HI
*RCs: 1X TO 2X BASE HI
ONE OR MORE BLUES PER PACK

1995-96 E-XL A Cut Above

	MINT	NRMT
COMPLETE SET (10)	150.00	70.00
COMMON CARD (1-10)	10.00	4.50

STATED ODDS 1:130

Card	MINT	NRMT
❑ 1 Scottie Pippen	25.00	11.00
❑ 2 Jason Kidd	25.00	11.00
❑ 3 Grant Hill	40.00	18.00
❑ 4 Joe Smith	10.00	4.50
❑ 5 Hakeem Olajuwon	12.00	5.50
❑ 6 Magic Johnson	15.00	6.75
❑ 7 Shaquille O'Neal	40.00	18.00
❑ 8 Jerry Stackhouse	10.00	4.50
❑ 9 Charles Barkley	12.00	5.50
❑ 10 David Robinson	12.00	5.50

1995-96 E-XL Natural Born Thrillers

	MINT	NRMT
COMPLETE SET (10)	200.00	90.00
COMMON CARD (1-10)	6.00	2.70

STATED ODDS 1:48

Card	MINT	NRMT
❑ 1 Michael Jordan	100.00	45.00
❑ 2 Antonio McDyess	15.00	6.75
❑ 3 Grant Hill	30.00	13.50
❑ 4 Clyde Drexler	6.00	2.70
❑ 5 Kevin Garnett	40.00	18.00
❑ 6 Anfernee Hardaway	20.00	9.00
❑ 7 Jerry Stackhouse	10.00	4.50
❑ 8 Michael Finley	12.00	5.50
❑ 9 Shawn Kemp	10.00	4.50
❑ 10 Damon Stoudamire	15.00	6.75
❑ NNO Jerry Stackhouse Promo	3.00	1.35

1995-96 E-XL No Boundaries

	MINT	NRMT
COMPLETE SET (10)	70.00	32.00
COMMON CARD (1-10)	3.00	1.35

STATED ODDS 1:18 HOBBY

Card	MINT	NRMT
❑ 1 Michael Jordan	40.00	18.00
❑ 2 Antonio McDyess	8.00	3.60
❑ 3 Hakeem Olajuwon	5.00	2.20
❑ 4 Magic Johnson	10.00	4.50
❑ 5 Vin Baker	3.00	1.35
❑ 6 Patrick Ewing	3.00	1.35
❑ 7 Anfernee Hardaway	10.00	4.50
❑ 8 Jerry Stackhouse	5.00	2.20
❑ 9 Gary Payton	5.00	2.20
❑ 10 Damon Stoudamire	8.00	3.60

1995-96 E-XL Unstoppable

	MINT	NRMT
COMPLETE SET (20)	50.00	22.00
COMMON CARD (1-20)	1.25	.55
SEMISTARS	1.50	.70
UNLISTED STARS	2.50	1.10

STATED ODDS 1:6

Card	MINT	NRMT
❑ 1 Alan Henderson	1.50	.70
❑ 2 Glen Rice	1.50	.70
❑ 3 Scottie Pippen	8.00	3.60
❑ 4 Dennis Rodman	5.00	2.20
❑ 5 Terrell Brandon	1.50	.70
❑ 6 Jason Kidd	8.00	3.60
❑ 7 Grant Hill	12.00	5.50

	MINT	NRMT
❑ 8 Joe Smith	4.00	1.80
❑ 9 Sam Cassell	1.50	.70
❑ 10 Reggie Miller	2.50	1.10
❑ 11 Alonzo Mourning	2.50	1.10
❑ 12 Shaquille O'Neal	12.00	5.50
❑ 13 Charles Barkley	4.00	1.80
❑ 14 Clifford Robinson	1.25	.55
❑ 15 Sean Elliott	1.25	.55
❑ 16 David Robinson	4.00	1.80
❑ 17 Shawn Kemp	4.00	1.80
❑ 18 Karl Malone	4.00	1.80
❑ 19 John Stockton	2.50	1.10
❑ 20 Juwan Howard	2.50	1.10

1996-97 E-X2000

	MINT	NRMT
COMPLETE SET (82)	150.00	70.00
COMMON CARD (1-82)	.50	.23
COMMON RC	2.00	.90
SEMISTARS	.60	.25
UNLISTED STARS	1.00	.45

EMERALD EXCH: STATED ODDS 1:500
CONDITION SENSITIVE SET

	MINT	NRMT
❑ 1 Christian Laettner	.60	.25
❑ 2 Dikembe Mutombo	.60	.25
❑ 3 Steve Smith	.60	.25
❑ 4 Antoine Walker RC	8.00	3.60
❑ 5 David Wesley	.50	.23
❑ 6 Tony Delk RC	2.00	.90
❑ 7 Anthony Mason	.60	.25
❑ 8 Glen Rice	.60	.25
❑ 9 Michael Jordan	15.00	6.75
❑ 10 Scottie Pippen	3.00	1.35
❑ 11 Dennis Rodman	2.00	.90
❑ 12 Terrell Brandon	.60	.25
❑ 13 Chris Mills	.50	.23
❑ 14 Shawn Bradley	.50	.23
❑ 15 Michael Finley	1.25	.55
❑ 16 Dale Ellis	.50	.23
❑ 17 Antonio McDyess	1.50	.70
❑ 18 Joe Dumars	1.00	.45
❑ 19 Grant Hill	5.00	2.20
❑ 20 Chris Mullin	1.00	.45
❑ 21 Joe Smith	1.00	.45
❑ 22 Latrell Sprewell	2.00	.90
❑ 23 Charles Barkley	1.50	.70
❑ 24 Clyde Drexler	1.00	.45
❑ 25 Hakeem Olajuwon	1.50	.70
❑ 26 Erick Dampier RC	2.00	.90
❑ 27 Reggie Miller	1.00	.45
❑ 28 Loy Vaught	.50	.23
❑ 29 Lorenzen Wright RC	2.00	.90
❑ 30 Kobe Bryant RC	120.00	55.00
❑ 31 Eddie Jones	2.00	.90
❑ 32 Shaquille O'Neal	5.00	2.20
❑ 33 Nick Van Exel	.60	.25
❑ 34 Tim Hardaway	1.00	.45
❑ 35 Jamal Mashburn	.60	.25
❑ 36 Alonzo Mourning	1.00	.45
❑ 37 Ray Allen RC	8.00	3.60
❑ 38 Vin Baker	.60	.25
❑ 39 Glenn Robinson	1.00	.45
❑ 40 Kevin Garnett	6.00	2.70
❑ 41 Tom Gugliotta	.60	.25
❑ 42 Stephon Marbury RC	12.00	5.50
❑ 43 Kendall Gill	.60	.25
❑ 44 Jim Jackson	.50	.23
❑ 45 Kerry Kittles RC	4.00	1.80
❑ 46 Patrick Ewing	1.00	.45
❑ 47 Larry Johnson	.60	.25
❑ 48 John Wallace RC	2.00	.90
❑ 49 Nick Anderson	.50	.23
❑ 50 Horace Grant	.60	.25
❑ 51 Anfernee Hardaway	3.00	1.35
❑ 52 Derrick Coleman	.60	.25
❑ 53 Allen Iverson RC	25.00	11.00
❑ 54 Jerry Stackhouse	1.00	.45
❑ 55 Cedric Ceballos	.50	.23
❑ 56 Kevin Johnson	.60	.25
❑ 57 Jason Kidd	3.00	1.35
❑ 58 Clifford Robinson	.50	.23
❑ 59 Arvydas Sabonis	.60	.25
❑ 60 Rasheed Wallace	1.25	.55
❑ 61 Mahmoud Abdul-Rauf	.50	.23
❑ 62 Brian Grant	1.00	.45
❑ 63 Mitch Richmond	1.00	.45
❑ 64 Sean Elliott	.50	.23
❑ 65 David Robinson	1.50	.70
❑ 66 Dominique Wilkins	1.00	.45
❑ 67 Shawn Kemp	1.50	.70
❑ 68 Gary Payton	1.50	.70
❑ 69 Detlef Schrempf	.60	.25
❑ 70 Marcus Camby RC	6.00	2.70
❑ 71 Damon Stoudamire	1.50	.70
❑ 72 Walt Williams	.50	.23
❑ 73 Shandon Anderson RC	3.00	1.35
❑ 74 Karl Malone	1.50	.70
❑ 75 John Stockton	1.00	.45
❑ 76 Shareef Abdur-Rahim RC	12.00	5.50
❑ 77 Bryant Reeves	.50	.23
❑ 78 Roy Rogers RC	2.00	.90
❑ 79 Juwan Howard	.60	.25
❑ 80 Chris Webber	3.00	1.35
❑ 81 Checklist	.50	.23
❑ 82 Checklist	.50	.23
❑ NNO Grant Hill1 Blow-Up/3000	40.00	8.00
❑ NNO Grant Hill Promo	5.00	2.20
❑ NNO Grant Hill Autographed ball	300.00	135.00

1996-97 E-X2000 Credentials

	MINT	NRMT
COMPLETE SET (80)	2000.00	900.00
COMMON CARD (1-80)	6.00	2.70
SEMISTARS	10.00	4.50
UNLISTED STARS	15.00	6.75

*STARS: 6X TO 15X BASE CARD HI
*RCs: 2X TO 5X BASE HI
RANDOM INSERTS IN PACKS
STATED PRINT RUN 499 SERIAL #'d SETS
CONDITION SENSITIVE SET

	MINT	NRMT
❑ 4 Antoine Walker	50.00	22.00
❑ 30 Kobe Bryant	700.00	325.00
❑ 37 Ray Allen	50.00	22.00
❑ 42 Stephon Marbury	100.00	45.00
❑ 53 Allen Iverson	200.00	90.00
❑ 70 Marcus Camby	40.00	18.00
❑ 76 Shareef Abdur-Rahim	100.00	45.00

1996-97 E-X2000 A Cut Above

	MINT	NRMT
COMPLETE SET (10)	500.00	220.00
COMMON CARD (1-10)	15.00	6.75

STATED ODDS 1:288

	MINT	NRMT
❑ 1 Kevin Garnett	80.00	36.00
❑ 2 Anfernee Hardaway	40.00	18.00
❑ 3 Grant Hill	60.00	27.00
❑ 4 Allen Iverson	60.00	27.00
❑ 5 Michael Jordan	200.00	90.00
❑ 6 Shawn Kemp	20.00	9.00
❑ 7 Hakeem Olajuwon	20.00	9.00
❑ 8 Shaquille O'Neal	60.00	27.00
❑ 9 Glenn Robinson	15.00	6.75
❑ 10 Dennis Rodman	25.00	11.00

1996-97 E-X2000 Net Assets

	MINT	NRMT
COMPLETE SET (20)	150.00	70.00
COMMON CARD (1-20)	2.00	.90
SEMISTARS	3.00	1.35

STATED ODDS 1:20

	MINT	NRMT
❑ 1 Ray Allen	6.00	2.70
❑ 2 Charles Barkley	5.00	2.20
❑ 3 Patrick Ewing	3.00	1.35
❑ 4 Kevin Garnett	20.00	9.00
❑ 5 Anfernee Hardaway	10.00	4.50
❑ 6 Grant Hill	15.00	6.75
❑ 7 Allen Iverson	15.00	6.75
❑ 8 Michael Jordan	40.00	18.00
❑ 9 Jason Kidd	10.00	4.50
❑ 10 Kerry Kittles	3.00	1.35
❑ 11 Karl Malone	5.00	2.20
❑ 12 Alonzo Mourning	3.00	1.35
❑ 13 Shaquille O'Neal	15.00	6.75
❑ 14 Gary Payton	5.00	2.20
❑ 15 Bryant Reeves	2.00	.90
❑ 16 David Robinson	5.00	2.20
❑ 17 Dennis Rodman	6.00	2.70
❑ 18 Joe Smith	3.00	1.35
❑ 19 Damon Stoudamire	5.00	2.20
❑ 20 Chris Webber	10.00	4.50

1996-97 E-X2000 Star Date 2000

	MINT	NRMT
COMPLETE SET (15)	40.00	18.00
COMMON CARD (1-15)	1.00	.45
SEMISTARS	1.50	.70
STATED ODDS 1:9		
❑ 1 Shareef Abdur-Rahim	5.00	2.20
❑ 2 Ray Allen	3.00	1.35
❑ 3 Kobe Bryant	12.00	5.50
❑ 4 Marcus Camby	2.50	1.10
❑ 5 Erick Dampier	1.00	.45
❑ 6 Juwan Howard	1.50	.70
❑ 7 Allen Iverson	8.00	3.60
❑ 8 Jason Kidd	5.00	2.20
❑ 9 Kerry Kittles	1.50	.70
❑ 10 Stephon Marbury	5.00	2.20
❑ 11 Jamal Mashburn	1.50	.70
❑ 12 Antonio McDyess	2.50	1.10
❑ 13 Joe Smith	1.50	.70
❑ 14 Damon Stoudamire	2.50	1.10
❑ 15 Antoine Walker	3.00	1.35

1997-98 E-X2001

	MINT	NRMT
COMPLETE SET (82)	60.00	27.00
COMMON CARD (1-61)	.30	.14
COMMON CARD (62-80)	.75	.35
SEMISTARS	.40	.18
SEMISTARS RC	1.00	.45
UNLISTED STARS	.60	.25
UNLISTED STARS RC	1.50	.70
❑ 1 Grant Hill	3.00	1.35
❑ 2 Kevin Garnett	4.00	1.80
❑ 3 Allen Iverson	3.00	1.35
❑ 4 Anfernee Hardaway	2.00	.90
❑ 5 Dennis Rodman	1.25	.55
❑ 6 Shawn Kemp	1.00	.45
❑ 7 Shaquille O'Neal	3.00	1.35
❑ 8 Kobe Bryant	6.00	2.70
❑ 9 Michael Jordan	8.00	3.60
❑ 10 Marcus Camby	.75	.35
❑ 11 Scottie Pippen	2.00	.90
❑ 12 Antoine Walker	1.25	.55
❑ 13 Stephon Marbury	2.00	.90
❑ 14 Shareef Abdur-Rahim	2.00	.90
❑ 15 Jerry Stackhouse	.40	.18
❑ 16 Eddie Jones	1.25	.55
❑ 17 Charles Barkley	1.00	.45
❑ 18 David Robinson	1.00	.45
❑ 19 Karl Malone	1.00	.45
❑ 20 Damon Stoudamire	.75	.35
❑ 21 Patrick Ewing	.60	.25
❑ 22 Kerry Kittles	.60	.25
❑ 23 Gary Payton	1.00	.45
❑ 24 Glenn Robinson	.40	.18
❑ 25 Hakeem Olajuwon	1.00	.45
❑ 26 John Starks	.30	.14
❑ 27 John Stockton	.60	.25
❑ 28 Vin Baker	.40	.18
❑ 29 Reggie Miller	.60	.25
❑ 30 Clyde Drexler	.60	.25
❑ 31 Alonzo Mourning	.60	.25
❑ 32 Juwan Howard	.40	.18
❑ 33 Ray Allen	1.00	.45
❑ 34 Christian Laettner	.40	.18
❑ 35 Terrell Brandon	.40	.18
❑ 36 Sean Elliott	.30	.14
❑ 37 Rod Strickland	.40	.18
❑ 38 Rodney Rogers	.30	.14
❑ 39 Donyell Marshall	.30	.14
❑ 40 David Wesley	.30	.14
❑ 41 Sam Cassell	.40	.18
❑ 42 Cedric Ceballos	.30	.14
❑ 43 Mahmoud Abdul-Rauf	.30	.14
❑ 44 Rik Smits	.30	.14
❑ 45 Lindsey Hunter	.30	.14
❑ 46 Michael Finley	.60	.25
❑ 47 Steve Smith	.40	.18
❑ 48 Larry Johnson	.40	.18
❑ 49 Dikembe Mutombo	.40	.18
❑ 50 Tom Gugliotta	.40	.18
❑ 51 Joe Dumars	.60	.25
❑ 52 Glen Rice	.40	.18
❑ 53 Bryant Reeves	.30	.14
❑ 54 Tim Hardaway	.60	.25
❑ 55 Isaiah Rider	.40	.18
❑ 56 Rasheed Wallace	.60	.25
❑ 57 Jason Kidd	2.00	.90
❑ 58 Joe Smith	.40	.18
❑ 59 Chris Webber	2.00	.90
❑ 60 Mitch Richmond	.60	.25
❑ 61 Antonio McDyess	.75	.35
❑ 62 Bobby Jackson RC	1.00	.45
❑ 63 Derek Anderson RC	3.00	1.35
❑ 64 Kelvin Cato RC	1.50	.70
❑ 65 Jacque Vaughn RC	1.00	.45
❑ 66 Tariq Abdul-Wahad RC	1.00	.45
❑ 67 Johnny Taylor RC	.75	.35
❑ 68 Chris Anstey RC	.75	.35
❑ 69 Maurice Taylor RC	2.50	1.10
❑ 70 Antonio Daniels RC	1.50	.70
❑ 71 Chauncey Billups RC	1.50	.70
❑ 72 Austin Croshere RC	3.00	1.35
❑ 73 Brevin Knight RC	1.50	.70
❑ 74 Keith Van Horn RC	6.00	2.70
❑ 75 Tim Duncan RC	20.00	9.00
❑ 76 Danny Fortson RC	1.50	.70
❑ 77 Tim Thomas RC	4.00	1.80
❑ 78 Tony Battie RC	1.50	.70
❑ 79 Tracy McGrady RC	15.00	6.75
❑ 80 Ron Mercer RC	4.00	1.80
❑ 81 Checklist (1-82)	.30	.14
❑ 82 Checklist (inserts)	.30	.14
❑ S1 Grant Hill SAMPLE	8.00	3.60

1997-98 E-X2001 Essential Credentials Future

	MINT	NRMT
COMMON CARD (1-80)	40.00	18.00
SEMISTARS	50.00	22.00
UNPRICED CARDS 66-80 SERIAL #'d 15-1		
RANDOM INSERTS IN PACKS		
PRINT RUNS IN PARENTHESIS BELOW		
❑ 1 Grant Hill (80	300.00	135.00

	MINT	NRMT
❑ 2 Kevin Garnett (79)	400.00	180.00
❑ 3 Allen Iverson (78)	300.00	135.00
❑ 4 Anfernee Hardaway (77)	200.00	90.00
❑ 5 Dennis Rodman (76)	125.00	55.00
❑ 6 Shawn Kemp (75)	100.00	45.00
❑ 7 Shaquille O'Neal (74)	300.00	135.00
❑ 8 Kobe Bryant (73)	600.00	275.00
❑ 9 Michael Jordan (72)	1200.00	550.00
❑ 10 Marcus Camby (71)	80.00	36.00
❑ 11 Scottie Pippen (70)	200.00	90.00
❑ 12 Antoine Walker (69)	120.00	55.00
❑ 13 Stephon Marbury (68)	200.00	90.00
❑ 14 Shareef Abdur-Rahim (67)	200.00	90.00
❑ 15 Jerry Stackhouse (66)	50.00	22.00
❑ 16 Eddie Jones (65)	125.00	55.00
❑ 17 Charles Barkley (64)	100.00	45.00
❑ 18 David Robinson (63)	100.00	45.00
❑ 19 Karl Malone (62)	100.00	45.00
❑ 20 Damon Stoudamire (61)	80.00	36.00
❑ 21 Patrick Ewing (60)	80.00	36.00
❑ 22 Kerry Kittles (59)	70.00	32.00
❑ 23 Gary Payton (58)	125.00	55.00
❑ 24 Glenn Robinson (57)	50.00	22.00
❑ 25 Hakeem Olajuwon (56)	100.00	45.00
❑ 26 John Starks (55)	40.00	18.00
❑ 27 John Stockton (54)	80.00	36.00
❑ 28 Vin Baker (53)	50.00	22.00
❑ 29 Reggie Miller (52)	80.00	36.00
❑ 30 Clyde Drexler (51)	100.00	45.00
❑ 31 Alonzo Mourning (50)	80.00	36.00
❑ 32 Juwan Howard (49)	50.00	22.00
❑ 33 Ray Allen (48)	150.00	70.00
❑ 34 Christian Laettner (47)	50.00	22.00
❑ 35 Terrell Brandon (46)	60.00	27.00
❑ 36 Sean Elliott (45)	40.00	18.00
❑ 37 Rod Strickland (44)	50.00	22.00
❑ 38 Rodney Rogers (43)	40.00	18.00
❑ 39 Donyell Marshall (42)	40.00	18.00
❑ 40 David Wesley (41)	40.00	18.00
❑ 41 Sam Cassell (40)	60.00	27.00
❑ 42 Cedric Ceballos (39)	40.00	18.00
❑ 43 Mahmoud Abdul-Rauf (38)	40.00	18.00
❑ 44 Rik Smits (37)	60.00	27.00
❑ 45 Lindsey Hunter (36)	60.00	27.00
❑ 46 Michael Finley (35)	100.00	45.00
❑ 47 Steve Smith (34)	60.00	27.00
❑ 48 Larry Johnson (33)	60.00	27.00
❑ 49 Dikembe Mutombo (32)	50.00	22.00
❑ 50 Tom Gugliotta (31)	70.00	32.00
❑ 51 Joe Dumars (30)	80.00	36.00
❑ 52 Glen Rice (29)	80.00	36.00
❑ 53 Bryant Reeves (28)	40.00	18.00
❑ 54 Tim Hardaway (27)	120.00	55.00
❑ 55 Isaiah Rider (26)	80.00	36.00
❑ 56 Rasheed Wallace (25)	100.00	45.00
❑ 57 Jason Kidd (24)	500.00	220.00
❑ 58 Joe Smith (23)	120.00	55.00
❑ 59 Chris Webber (22)	400.00	180.00
❑ 60 Mitch Richmond (21)	150.00	70.00
❑ 61 Antonio McDyess (20)	200.00	90.00
❑ 62 Bobby Jackson (19)	125.00	55.00
❑ 63 Derek Anderson (18)	200.00	90.00
❑ 64 Kelvin Cato (17)	100.00	45.00
❑ 65 Jacque Vaughn (16)	80.00	36.00
❑ 66 Tariq Abdul-Wahad (15)		
❑ 67 Johnny Taylor (14)		
❑ 68 Chris Anstey (13)		
❑ 69 Maurice Taylor (12)		

❑ 70 Antonio Daniels (11)
❑ 71 Chauncey Billups (10)
❑ 72 Austin Croshere (9)
❑ 73 Brevin Knight (8)
❑ 74 Keith Van Horn (7)
❑ 75 Tim Duncan (6)
❑ 76 Danny Fortson (5)
❑ 77 Tim Thomas (4)
❑ 78 Tony Battie (3)
❑ 79 Tracy McGrady (2)
❑ 80 Ron Mercer (1)

1997-98 E-X2001 Essential Credentials Now

	MINT	NRMT
COMMON CARD (1-80)	40.00	18.00
SEMISTARS	50.00	22.00

UNPRICED CARDS 1-15 SERIAL #'d 1-15
RANDOM INSERTS IN PACKS
PRINT RUNS IN PARENTHESIS BELOW

❑ 1 Grant Hill (1)
❑ 2 Kevin Garnett (2)
❑ 3 Allen Iverson (3)
❑ 4 Anfernee Hardaway (4)
❑ 5 Dennis Rodman (5)
❑ 6 Shawn Kemp (6)
❑ 7 Shaquille O'Neal (7)
❑ 8 Kobe Bryant (8)
❑ 9 Michael Jordan (9)
❑ 10 Marcus Camby (10)
❑ 11 Scottie Pippen (11)
❑ 12 Antoine Walker (12)
❑ 13 Stephon Marbury (13)
❑ 14 Shareef Abdur-Rahim (14)
❑ 15 Jerry Stackhouse (15)

	MINT	NRMT
❑ 16 Eddie Jones (16)	450.00	200.00
❑ 17 Charles Barkley (17)	325.00	145.00
❑ 18 David Robinson (18)	325.00	145.00
❑ 19 Karl Malone (19)	325.00	145.00
❑ 20 Damon Stoudamire (20)	200.00	90.00
❑ 21 Patrick Ewing (21)	200.00	90.00
❑ 22 Kerry Kittles (22)	150.00	70.00
❑ 23 Gary Payton (23)	200.00	90.00
❑ 24 Glenn Robinson (24)	60.00	27.00
❑ 25 Hakeem Olajuwon (25)	200.00	90.00
❑ 26 John Starks (26)	60.00	27.00
❑ 27 John Stockton (27)	200.00	90.00
❑ 28 Vin Baker (28)	40.00	18.00
❑ 29 Reggie Miller (29)	200.00	90.00
❑ 30 Clyde Drexler (30)	175.00	80.00
❑ 31 Alonzo Mourning (31)	100.00	45.00
❑ 32 Juwan Howard (32)	50.00	22.00
❑ 33 Ray Allen (33)	150.00	70.00
❑ 34 Christian Laettner (34)	60.00	27.00
❑ 35 Terrell Brandon (35)	80.00	36.00
❑ 36 Sean Elliott (36)	40.00	18.00
❑ 37 Rod Strickland (37)	50.00	22.00
❑ 38 Rodney Rogers (38)	40.00	18.00
❑ 39 Donyell Marshall (39)	60.00	27.00
❑ 40 David Wesley (40)	40.00	18.00
❑ 41 Sam Cassell (41)	50.00	22.00
❑ 42 Cedric Ceballos (42)	40.00	18.00
❑ 43 Mahmoud Abdul-Rauf (43)	40.00	18.00
❑ 44 Rik Smits (44)	40.00	18.00
❑ 45 Lindsey Hunter (45)	40.00	18.00
❑ 46 Michael Finley (46)	80.00	36.00
❑ 47 Steve Smith (47)	50.00	22.00
❑ 48 Larry Johnson (48)	50.00	22.00
❑ 49 Dikembe Mutombo (49)	50.00	22.00
❑ 50 Tom Gugliotta (50)	50.00	22.00
❑ 51 Joe Dumars (51)	50.00	22.00
❑ 52 Glen Rice (52)	60.00	27.00
❑ 53 Bryant Reeves (53)	40.00	18.00
❑ 54 Tim Hardaway (54)	100.00	45.00
❑ 55 Isaiah Rider (55)	50.00	22.00
❑ 56 Rasheed Wallace (56)	50.00	22.00
❑ 57 Jason Kidd (57)	200.00	90.00
❑ 58 Joe Smith (58)	50.00	22.00
❑ 59 Chris Webber (59)	250.00	110.00
❑ 60 Mitch Richmond (60)	80.00	36.00
❑ 61 Antonio McDyess (61)	100.00	45.00
❑ 62 Bobby Jackson (62)	50.00	22.00
❑ 63 Derek Anderson (63)	125.00	55.00
❑ 64 Kelvin Cato (64)	40.00	18.00
❑ 65 Jacque Vaughn (65)	40.00	18.00
❑ 66 Tariq Abdul-Wahad (66)	40.00	18.00
❑ 67 Johnny Taylor (67)	40.00	18.00
❑ 68 Chris Anstey (68)	40.00	18.00
❑ 69 Maurice Taylor (69)	60.00	27.00
❑ 70 Antonio Daniels (70)	50.00	22.00
❑ 71 Chauncey Billups (71)	50.00	22.00
❑ 72 Austin Croshere (72)	80.00	36.00
❑ 73 Brevin Knight (73)	50.00	22.00
❑ 74 Keith Van Horn (74)	150.00	70.00
❑ 75 Tim Duncan (75)	300.00	135.00
❑ 76 Danny Fortson (76)	40.00	18.00
❑ 77 Tim Thomas (77)	100.00	45.00
❑ 78 Tony Battie (78)	50.00	22.00
❑ 79 Tracy McGrady (79)	300.00	135.00
❑ 80 Ron Mercer (80)	100.00	45.00

1997-98 E-X2001 Gravity Denied

	MINT	NRMT
COMPLETE SET (20)	150.00	70.00
COMMON CARD (1-20)	3.00	1.35

STATED ODDS 1:24

	MINT	NRMT
❑ 1 Vin Baker	3.00	1.35
❑ 2 Charles Barkley	5.00	2.20
❑ 3 Tony Battie	3.00	1.35
❑ 4 Kobe Bryant	25.00	11.00
❑ 5 Patrick Ewing	3.00	1.35
❑ 6 Kevin Garnett	20.00	9.00
❑ 7 Anfernee Hardaway	10.00	4.50
❑ 8 Grant Hill	15.00	6.75
❑ 9 Michael Jordan	50.00	22.00
❑ 10 Shawn Kemp	5.00	2.20
❑ 11 Kerry Kittles	3.00	1.35
❑ 12 Karl Malone	5.00	2.20
❑ 13 Tracy McGrady	15.00	6.75
❑ 14 Hakeem Olajuwon	5.00	2.20
❑ 15 Shaquille O'Neal	15.00	6.75
❑ 16 Scottie Pippen	10.00	4.50
❑ 17 Jerry Stackhouse	3.00	1.35
❑ 18 Tim Thomas	5.00	2.20
❑ 19 Antoine Walker	6.00	2.70
❑ 20 Chris Webber	10.00	4.50

1997-98 E-X2001 Jambalaya

	MINT	NRMT
COMPLETE SET (15)	2500.00	1100.00
COMMON CARD (1-15)	50.00	22.00

STATED ODDS 1:720

	MINT	NRMT
❑ 1 Allen Iverson	200.00	90.00
❑ 2 Anfernee Hardaway	125.00	55.00
❑ 3 Dennis Rodman	80.00	36.00
❑ 4 Grant Hill	200.00	90.00
❑ 5 Kevin Garnett	250.00	110.00
❑ 6 Michael Jordan	700.00	325.00
❑ 7 Shaquille O'Neal	200.00	90.00
❑ 8 Tim Duncan	200.00	90.00
❑ 9 Keith Van Horn	100.00	45.00
❑ 10 Stephon Marbury	120.00	55.00
❑ 11 Shareef Abdur-Rahim	120.00	55.00
❑ 12 Kobe Bryant	300.00	135.00
❑ 13 Damon Stoudamire	50.00	22.00
❑ 14 Scottie Pippen	120.00	55.00
❑ 15 Eddie Jones	80.00	36.00

1997-98 E-X2001 Star Date 2001

	MINT	NRMT
COMPLETE SET (15)	50.00	22.00
COMMON CARD (1-15)	1.25	.55
SEMISTARS	1.50	.70
UNLISTED STARS	2.50	1.10

STATED ODDS 1:12

	MINT	NRMT
❑ 1 Shareef Abdur-Rahim	4.00	1.80
❑ 2 Tony Battie	1.25	.55
❑ 3 Kobe Bryant	10.00	4.50
❑ 4 Antonio Daniels	1.50	.70
❑ 5 Tim Duncan	12.00	5.50
❑ 6 Adonal Foyle	1.25	.55
❑ 7 Allen Iverson	6.00	2.70
❑ 8 Matt Maloney	1.25	.55
❑ 9 Stephon Marbury	4.00	1.80
❑ 10 Tracy McGrady	12.00	5.50
❑ 11 Ron Mercer	4.00	1.80
❑ 12 Tim Thomas	4.00	1.80
❑ 13 Keith Van Horn	6.00	2.70
❑ 14 Jacque Vaughn	1.25	.55
❑ 15 Antoine Walker	2.50	1.10

1998-99 E-X Century

	MINT	NRMT
COMPLETE SET (1-90)	120.00	55.00
COMMON CARD (1-60)	.25	.11
COMMON CARD (61-90)	1.00	.45
SEMISTARS	.30	.14
SEMISTARS RC	1.25	.55
UNLISTED STARS	.50	.23
UNLISTED STARS RC	2.00	.90

RC STATED ODDS 1:1.5

	MINT	NRMT
❑ 1 Keith Van Horn	1.25	.55
❑ 2 Scottie Pippen	1.50	.70
❑ 3 Tim Thomas	.75	.35
❑ 4 Stephon Marbury	1.25	.55
❑ 5 Allen Iverson	2.00	.90
❑ 6 Grant Hill	2.50	1.10
❑ 7 Tim Duncan	2.50	1.10
❑ 8 Latrell Sprewell	1.00	.45
❑ 9 Ron Mercer	.75	.35
❑ 10 Kobe Bryant	4.00	1.80
❑ 11 Antoine Walker	.75	.35
❑ 12 Reggie Miller	.50	.23
❑ 13 Kevin Garnett	3.00	1.35
❑ 14 Shaquille O'Neal	2.50	1.10
❑ 15 Karl Malone	.75	.35
❑ 16 Dennis Rodman	1.00	.45
❑ 17 Tracy McGrady	2.00	.90
❑ 18 Anfernee Hardaway	1.50	.70
❑ 19 Shareef Abdur-Rahim	1.25	.55
❑ 20 Marcus Camby	.50	.23
❑ 21 Eddie Jones	1.00	.45
❑ 22 Vin Baker	.30	.14
❑ 23 Charles Barkley	.75	.35
❑ 24 Patrick Ewing	.50	.23
❑ 25 Jason Kidd	1.50	.70
❑ 26 Mitch Richmond	.50	.23
❑ 27 Tim Hardaway	.50	.23
❑ 28 Glen Rice	.30	.14
❑ 29 Shawn Kemp	.75	.35
❑ 30 John Stockton	.50	.23
❑ 31 Ray Allen	.60	.25
❑ 32 Brevin Knight	.25	.11
❑ 33 David Robinson	.75	.35
❑ 34 Juwan Howard	.30	.14
❑ 35 Alonzo Mourning	.50	.23
❑ 36 Hakeem Olajuwon	.75	.35
❑ 37 Gary Payton	.75	.35
❑ 38 Damon Stoudamire	.50	.23
❑ 39 Steve Smith	.30	.14
❑ 40 Chris Webber	1.50	.70
❑ 41 Michael Finley	.50	.23
❑ 42 Jayson Williams	.30	.14
❑ 43 Maurice Taylor	.50	.23
❑ 44 Jalen Rose	.50	.23
❑ 45 Sam Cassell	.30	.14
❑ 46 Jerry Stackhouse	.30	.14
❑ 47 Toni Kukoc	.60	.25
❑ 48 Charles Oakley	.25	.11
❑ 49 Jim Jackson	.25	.11
❑ 50 Dikembe Mutombo	.30	.14
❑ 51 Wesley Person	.25	.11
❑ 52 Antonio Daniels	.25	.11
❑ 53 Isaiah Rider	.30	.14
❑ 54 Tom Gugliotta	.30	.14
❑ 55 Antonio McDyess	.50	.23
❑ 56 Jeff Hornacek	.30	.14
❑ 57 Joe Dumars	.50	.23
❑ 58 Jamal Mashburn	.30	.14
❑ 59 Donyell Marshall	.25	.11
❑ 60 Glenn Robinson	.30	.14
❑ 61 Jelani McCoy RC	1.00	.45
❑ 62 Predrag Stojakovic RC	3.00	1.35
❑ 63 Randell Jackson RC	1.00	.45
❑ 64 Brad Miller RC	1.00	.45
❑ 65 Corey Benjamin RC	2.00	.90
❑ 66 Toby Bailey RC	1.00	.45
❑ 67 Nazr Mohammed RC	1.25	.55
❑ 68 Dirk Nowitzki RC	8.00	3.60
❑ 69 Andrae Patterson RC	1.00	.45
❑ 70 Michael Dickerson RC	4.00	1.80
❑ 71 Cory Carr RC	1.00	.45
❑ 72 Brian Skinner RC	2.00	.90
❑ 73 Pat Garrity RC	1.25	.55
❑ 74 Ricky Davis RC	4.00	1.80
❑ 75 Roshown McLeod RC	1.25	.55
❑ 76 Matt Harpring RC	2.00	.90
❑ 77 Jason Williams RC	12.00	5.50
❑ 78 Keon Clark RC	2.00	.90
❑ 79 Al Harrington RC	6.00	2.70
❑ 80 Felipe Lopez RC	2.50	1.10
❑ 81 Michael Doleac RC	2.00	.90
❑ 82 Paul Pierce RC	10.00	4.50
❑ 83 Robert Traylor RC	2.00	.90
❑ 84 Raef LaFrentz RC	4.00	1.80
❑ 85 Michael Olowokandi RC	3.00	1.35
❑ 86 Mike Bibby RC	6.00	2.70
❑ 87 Antawn Jamison RC	10.00	4.50
❑ 88 Bonzi Wells RC	8.00	3.60
❑ 89 Vince Carter RC	65.00	29.00
❑ 90 Larry Hughes RC	12.00	5.50

1998-99 E-X Century Essential Credentials Future

	MINT	NRMT
COMMON CARD (1-90)	25.00	11.00
SEMISTARS	30.00	13.50
UNLISTED STARS	40.00	18.00

UNPRICED CARDS 76-90 SERIAL #'d 15-1
RANDOM INSERTS IN PACKS
PRINT RUNS IN PARENTHESIS BELOW

	MINT	NRMT
❑ 1 Keith Van Horn (90)	80.00	36.00
❑ 2 Scottie Pippen (89)	100.00	45.00
❑ 3 Tim Thomas (88)	50.00	22.00
❑ 4 Stephon Marbury (87)	80.00	36.00
❑ 5 Allen Iverson (86)	120.00	55.00
❑ 6 Grant Hill (85)	150.00	70.00
❑ 7 Tim Duncan (84)	150.00	70.00
❑ 8 Latrell Sprewell (83)	80.00	36.00
❑ 9 Ron Mercer (82)	50.00	22.00
❑ 10 Kobe Bryant (81)	300.00	135.00
❑ 11 Antoine Walker (80)	50.00	22.00
❑ 12 Reggie Miller (79)	40.00	18.00
❑ 13 Kevin Garnett (78)	200.00	90.00
❑ 14 Shaquille O'Neal (77)	150.00	70.00
❑ 15 Karl Malone (76)	50.00	22.00
❑ 16 Dennis Rodman (75)	100.00	45.00
❑ 17 Tracy McGrady (74)	200.00	90.00
❑ 18 Anfernee Hardaway (73)	150.00	70.00
❑ 19 Shareef Abdur-Rahim (72)	125.00	55.00
❑ 20 Marcus Camby (71)	50.00	22.00
❑ 21 Eddie Jones (70)	100.00	45.00
❑ 22 Vin Baker (69)	30.00	13.50
❑ 23 Charles Barkley (68)	80.00	36.00
❑ 24 Patrick Ewing (67)	60.00	27.00
❑ 25 Jason Kidd (66)	150.00	70.00
❑ 26 Mitch Richmond (65)	40.00	18.00
❑ 27 Tim Hardaway (64)	50.00	22.00
❑ 28 Glen Rice (63)	30.00	13.50
❑ 29 Shawn Kemp (62)	100.00	45.00
❑ 30 John Stockton (61)	50.00	22.00
❑ 31 Ray Allen (60)	80.00	36.00
❑ 32 Brevin Knight (59)	25.00	11.00
❑ 33 David Robinson (58)	100.00	45.00
❑ 34 Juwan Howard (57)	30.00	13.50
❑ 35 Alonzo Mourning (56)	60.00	27.00
❑ 36 Hakeem Olajuwon (55)	100.00	45.00
❑ 37 Gary Payton (54)	100.00	45.00
❑ 38 Damon Stoudamire (53)	60.00	27.00
❑ 39 Steve Smith (52)	30.00	13.50
❑ 40 Chris Webber (51)	200.00	90.00
❑ 41 Michael Finley (50)	50.00	22.00
❑ 42 Jayson Williams (49)	30.00	13.50
❑ 43 Maurice Taylor (48)	50.00	22.00
❑ 44 Jalen Rose (47)	40.00	18.00
❑ 45 Sam Cassell (46)	30.00	13.50
❑ 46 Jerry Stackhouse (45)	50.00	22.00
❑ 47 Toni Kukoc (44)	175.00	80.00
❑ 48 Charles Oakley (43)	25.00	11.00
❑ 49 Jim Jackson (42)	25.00	11.00
❑ 50 Dikembe Mutombo (41)	30.00	13.50
❑ 51 Wesley Person (40)	25.00	11.00
❑ 52 Antonio Daniels (39)	25.00	11.00
❑ 53 Isaiah Rider (38)	50.00	22.00
❑ 54 Tom Gugliotta (37)	50.00	22.00
❑ 55 Antonio McDyess (36)	80.00	36.00
❑ 56 Jeff Hornacek (35)	30.00	13.50
❑ 57 Joe Dumars (34)	60.00	27.00
❑ 58 Jamal Mashburn (33)	50.00	22.00
❑ 59 Donyell Marshall (32)	25.00	11.00
❑ 60 Glenn Robinson (31)	50.00	22.00
❑ 61 Jelani McCoy (30)	25.00	11.00
❑ 62 Predrag Stojakovic (29)	40.00	18.00
❑ 63 Randell Jackson (28)	25.00	11.00
❑ 64 Brad Miller (27)	25.00	11.00
❑ 65 Corey Benjamin (26)	50.00	22.00
❑ 66 Toby Bailey (25)	25.00	11.00
❑ 67 Nazr Mohammed (24)	50.00	22.00
❑ 68 Dirk Nowitzki (23)	200.00	90.00
❑ 69 Andrae Patterson (22)	40.00	18.00
❑ 70 Michael Dickerson (21)	100.00	45.00
❑ 71 Cory Carr (20)	50.00	22.00
❑ 72 Brian Skinner (19)	60.00	27.00
❑ 73 Pat Garrity (18)	60.00	27.00
❑ 74 Ricky Davis (17)	120.00	55.00
❑ 75 Roshown McLeod (16)	60.00	27.00
❑ 76 Matt Harpring (15)		
❑ 77 Jason Williams (14)		
❑ 78 Keon Clark (13)		
❑ 79 Al Harrington (12)		
❑ 80 Felipe Lopez (11)		
❑ 81 Michael Doleac (10)		
❑ 82 Paul Pierce (9)		
❑ 83 Robert Traylor (8)		
❑ 84 Raef LaFrentz (7)		
❑ 85 Michael Olowokandi (6)		
❑ 86 Mike Bibby (5)		
❑ 87 Antawn Jamison (4)		
❑ 88 Bonzi Wells (3)		
❑ 89 Vince Carter (2)		
❑ 90 Larry Hughes (1)		

1998-99 E-X Century Essential Credentials Now

	MINT	NRMT
COMMON CARD (1-90)	20.00	9.00
SEMISTARS	25.00	11.00
UNLISTED STARS	30.00	13.50

UNPRICED CARDS 1-15 SERIAL #'d 1-15
RANDOM INSERTS IN PACKS
PRINT RUNS IN PARENTHESIS BELOW

❑ 1 Keith Van Horn (1)

Card	MINT	NRMT
❑ 2 Scottie Pippen (2)		
❑ 3 Tim Thomas (3)		
❑ 4 Stephon Marbury (4)		
❑ 5 Allen Iverson (5)		
❑ 6 Grant Hill (6)		
❑ 7 Tim Duncan (7)		
❑ 8 Latrell Sprewell (8)		
❑ 9 Ron Mercer (9)		
❑ 10 Kobe Bryant (10)		
❑ 11 Antoine Walker (11)		
❑ 12 Reggie Miller (12)		
❑ 13 Kevin Garnett (13)		
❑ 14 Shaquille O'Neal (14)		
❑ 15 Karl Malone (15)		
❑ 16 Dennis Rodman (16)	350.00	160.00
❑ 17 Tracy McGrady (17)	400.00	180.00
❑ 18 Anfernee Hardaway (18)	400.00	180.00
❑ 19 Shareef Abdur-Rahim (19)	300.00	135.00
❑ 20 Marcus Camby (20)	150.00	70.00
❑ 21 Eddie Jones (21)	200.00	90.00
❑ 22 Vin Baker (22)	60.00	27.00
❑ 23 Charles Barkley (23)	160.00	70.00
❑ 24 Patrick Ewing (24)	100.00	45.00
❑ 25 Jason Kidd (25)	300.00	135.00
❑ 26 Mitch Richmond (26)	80.00	36.00
❑ 27 Tim Hardaway (27)	100.00	45.00
❑ 28 Glen Rice (28)	60.00	27.00
❑ 29 Shawn Kemp (29)	150.00	70.00
❑ 30 John Stockton (30)	125.00	55.00
❑ 31 Ray Allen (31)	100.00	45.00
❑ 32 Brevin Knight (32)	20.00	9.00
❑ 33 David Robinson (33)	150.00	70.00
❑ 34 Juwan Howard (34)	50.00	22.00
❑ 35 Alonzo Mourning (35)	80.00	36.00
❑ 36 Hakeem Olajuwon (36)	120.00	55.00
❑ 37 Gary Payton (37)	125.00	55.00
❑ 38 Damon Stoudamire (38)	80.00	36.00
❑ 39 Steve Smith (39)	25.00	11.00
❑ 40 Chris Webber (40)	250.00	110.00
❑ 41 Michael Finley (41)	60.00	27.00
❑ 42 Jayson Williams (42)	25.00	11.00
❑ 43 Maurice Taylor (43)	60.00	27.00
❑ 44 Jalen Rose (44)	30.00	13.50
❑ 45 Sam Cassell (45)	25.00	11.00
❑ 46 Jerry Stackhouse (46)	40.00	18.00
❑ 47 Toni Kukoc (47)	150.00	70.00
❑ 48 Charles Oakley (48)	20.00	9.00
❑ 49 Jim Jackson (49)	20.00	9.00
❑ 50 Dikembe Mutombo (50)	25.00	11.00
❑ 51 Wesley Person (51)	20.00	9.00
❑ 52 Antonio Daniels (52)	20.00	9.00
❑ 53 Isaiah Rider (53)	25.00	11.00
❑ 54 Tom Gugliotta (54)	25.00	11.00
❑ 55 Antonio McDyess (55)	60.00	27.00
❑ 56 Jeff Hornacek (56)	25.00	11.00
❑ 57 Joe Dumars (57)	25.00	11.00
❑ 58 Jamal Mashburn (58)	25.00	11.00
❑ 59 Donyell Marshall (59)	20.00	9.00
❑ 60 Glenn Robinson (60)	25.00	11.00
❑ 61 Jelani McCoy (61)	20.00	9.00
❑ 62 Predrag Stojakovic (62)	30.00	13.50
❑ 63 Randell Jackson (63)	20.00	9.00
❑ 64 Brad Miller (64)	20.00	9.00
❑ 65 Corey Benjamin (65)	25.00	11.00
❑ 66 Toby Bailey (66)	20.00	9.00
❑ 67 Nazr Mohammed (67)	20.00	9.00
❑ 68 Dirk Nowitzki (68)	120.00	55.00
❑ 69 Andrae Patterson (69)	20.00	9.00
❑ 70 Michael Dickerson (70)	40.00	18.00
❑ 71 Cory Carr (71)	20.00	9.00
❑ 72 Brian Skinner (72)	25.00	11.00
❑ 73 Pat Garrity (73)	20.00	9.00
❑ 74 Ricky Davis (74)	50.00	22.00
❑ 75 Roshown McLeod (75)	20.00	9.00
❑ 76 Matt Harpring (76)	25.00	11.00
❑ 77 Jason Williams (77)	120.00	55.00
❑ 78 Keon Clark (78)	25.00	11.00
❑ 79 Al Harrington (79)	60.00	27.00
❑ 80 Felipe Lopez (80)	25.00	11.00
❑ 81 Michael Doleac (81)	20.00	9.00
❑ 82 Paul Pierce (82)	100.00	45.00
❑ 83 Robert Traylor (83)	25.00	11.00
❑ 84 Raef LaFrentz (84)	40.00	18.00
❑ 85 Michael Olowokandi (85)	30.00	13.50
❑ 86 Mike Bibby (86)	60.00	27.00
❑ 87 Antawn Jamison (87)	100.00	45.00
❑ 88 Bonzi Wells (88)	80.00	36.00
❑ 89 Vince Carter (89)	400.00	180.00
❑ 90 Larry Hughes (90)	120.00	55.00

1998-99 E-X Century Authen-Kicks

	MINT	NRMT
COMPLETE SET (12)	1100.00	500.00
COMMON CARD (1-12)	60.00	27.00

RANDOM INSERTS IN PACKS
PRINT RUNS IN PARENTHESIS BELOW

Card	MINT	NRMT
❑ 1 Antawn Jamison (225)	120.00	55.00
❑ 2 Tracy McGrady (225)	150.00	70.00
❑ 3 Ron Mercer (180)	100.00	45.00
❑ 4 Antoine Walker (125)	120.00	55.00
❑ 5 Mike Bibby (165)	80.00	36.00
❑ 6 Michael Dickerson (230)	60.00	27.00
❑ 7 Larry Hughes (115)	125.00	55.00
❑ 8 Raef LaFrentz (160)	80.00	36.00
❑ 9 Keith Van Horn (125)	125.00	55.00
❑ 9AU Keith Van Horn (44)	500.00	220.00
❑ 10 Tim Thomas (215)	60.00	27.00
❑ 11 Allen Iverson (165)	250.00	110.00
❑ 12 Robert Traylor (215)	60.00	27.00

1998-99 E-X Century Dunk 'N Go Nuts

	MINT	NRMT
COMPLETE SET (20)	200.00	90.00
COMMON CARD (1-20)	2.50	1.10
SEMISTARS	3.00	1.35

STATED ODDS 1:36

Card	MINT	NRMT
❑ 1 Tim Thomas	5.00	2.20
❑ 2 Grant Hill	15.00	6.75
❑ 3 Shareef Abdur-Rahim	8.00	3.60
❑ 4 Tim Duncan	15.00	6.75
❑ 5 Allen Iverson	12.00	5.50
❑ 6 Kobe Bryant	25.00	11.00
❑ 7 Antoine Walker	5.00	2.20
❑ 8 Kevin Garnett	20.00	9.00
❑ 9 Shaquille O'Neal	15.00	6.75
❑ 10 Tracy McGrady	12.00	5.50
❑ 11 Antawn Jamison	8.00	3.60
❑ 12 Vince Carter	40.00	18.00
❑ 13 Robert Traylor	2.50	1.10
❑ 14 Scottie Pippen	10.00	4.50
❑ 15 Michael Jordan	50.00	22.00
❑ 16 Michael Olowokandi	3.00	1.35
❑ 17 Anfernee Hardaway	10.00	4.50
❑ 18 Michael Dickerson	3.00	1.35
❑ 19 Ron Mercer	5.00	2.20
❑ 20 Felipe Lopez	2.50	1.10

1998-99 E-X Century Generation E-X

	MINT	NRMT
COMPLETE SET (15)	60.00	27.00
COMMON CARD (1-15)	2.00	.90

STATED ODDS 1:18

Card	MINT	NRMT
❑ 1 Larry Hughes	6.00	2.70
❑ 2 Michael Olowokandi	2.00	.90
❑ 3 Tim Duncan	8.00	3.60
❑ 4 Vince Carter	25.00	11.00
❑ 5 Antawn Jamison	5.00	2.20
❑ 6 Kevin Garnett	10.00	4.50
❑ 7 Al Harrington	3.00	1.35
❑ 8 Mike Bibby	3.00	1.35
❑ 9 Raef LaFrentz	2.00	.90
❑ 10 Ron Mercer	2.50	1.10
❑ 11 Tracy McGrady	6.00	2.70
❑ 12 Kobe Bryant	12.00	5.50
❑ 13 Keith Van Horn	4.00	1.80
❑ 14 Stephon Marbury	4.00	1.80
❑ 15 Allen Iverson	10.00	4.50

1999-00 E-X

	MINT	NRMT
COMPLETE SET (90)	250.00	110.00
COMPLETE SET w/o RC (60)	30.00	13.50
COMMON CARD (1-60)	.25	.11
COMMON RC (61-90)	3.00	1.35
SEMISTARS	.30	.14
SEMISTARS RC	4.00	1.80
UNLISTED STARS	.50	.23
UNLISTED STARS RC	5.00	2.20

RCs: PRINT RUN 3499 SERIAL #'d SETS
RCs: RANDOM INSERTS IN PACKS

Card	MINT	NRMT
❑ 1 Stephon Marbury	1.00	.45
❑ 2 Antawn Jamison	1.00	.45
❑ 3 Patrick Ewing	.50	.23
❑ 4 Nick Anderson	.25	.11
❑ 5 Charles Barkley	.75	.35
❑ 6 Marcus Camby	.50	.23
❑ 7 Ron Mercer	.60	.25
❑ 8 Avery Johnson	.25	.11
❑ 9 Maurice Taylor	.50	.23
❑ 10 Isaiah Rider	.30	.14
❑ 11 Dirk Nowitzki	.75	.35
❑ 12 Damon Stoudamire	.50	.23
❑ 13 Alonzo Mourning	.50	.23
❑ 14 Jason Kidd	1.50	.70
❑ 15 Juwan Howard	.30	.14
❑ 16 Vince Carter	5.00	2.20
❑ 17 Tim Duncan	2.50	1.10
❑ 18 Paul Pierce	1.00	.45
❑ 19 Tim Hardaway	.50	.23
❑ 20 Grant Hill	2.50	1.10
❑ 21 Keith Van Horn	1.00	.45
❑ 22 Shaquille O'Neal	2.50	1.10

		MINT	NRMT
❑ 23	Jason Williams	1.25	.55
❑ 24	Shareef Abdur-Rahim	1.00	.45
❑ 25	Kobe Bryant	4.00	1.80
❑ 26	David Robinson	.75	.35
❑ 27	Anfernee Hardaway	1.50	.70
❑ 28	Vin Baker	.30	.14
❑ 29	Hakeem Olajuwon	.75	.35
❑ 30	Michael Olowokandi	.30	.14
❑ 31	Mike Bibby	.60	.25
❑ 32	Tracy McGrady	1.50	.70
❑ 33	Antoine Walker	.60	.25
❑ 34	Larry Hughes	1.25	.55
❑ 35	Chris Webber	1.50	.70
❑ 36	Ray Allen	.50	.23
❑ 37	Danny Fortson	.25	.11
❑ 38	Shawn Kemp	.75	.35
❑ 39	Michael Doleac	.25	.11
❑ 40	Gary Payton	.75	.35
❑ 41	Toni Kukoc	.60	.25
❑ 42	Kevin Garnett	3.00	1.35
❑ 43	Steve Smith	.30	.14
❑ 44	Scottie Pippen	1.50	.70
❑ 45	Allen Iverson	2.00	.90
❑ 46	Latrell Sprewell	1.00	.45
❑ 47	Matt Harpring	.25	.11
❑ 48	Lindsey Hunter	.25	.11
❑ 49	Karl Malone	.75	.35
❑ 50	Michael Finley	.50	.23
❑ 51	Jerry Stackhouse	.30	.14
❑ 52	Cedric Ceballos	.25	.11
❑ 53	Brent Barry	.25	.11
❑ 54	Elden Campbell	.25	.11
❑ 55	Glenn Robinson	.30	.14
❑ 56	Eddie Jones	1.00	.45
❑ 57	Reggie Miller	.50	.23
❑ 58	Mitch Richmond	.50	.23
❑ 59	Raef LaFrentz	.50	.23
❑ 60	John Starks	.25	.11
❑ 61	Elton Brand RC	50.00	22.00
❑ 62	William Avery RC	8.00	3.60
❑ 63	Cal Bowdler RC	5.00	2.20
❑ 64	Dion Glover RC	5.00	2.20
❑ 65	Lamar Odom RC	40.00	18.00
❑ 66	Richard Hamilton RC	12.00	5.50
❑ 67	Kenny Thomas RC	8.00	3.60
❑ 68	Shawn Marion RC	15.00	6.75
❑ 69	Baron Davis RC	12.00	5.50
❑ 70	Wally Szczerbiak RC	20.00	9.00
❑ 71	Scott Padgett RC	5.00	2.20
❑ 72	Jason Terry RC	8.00	3.60
❑ 73	Trajan Langdon RC	8.00	3.60
❑ 74	Andre Miller RC	15.00	6.75
❑ 75	Jeff Foster RC	5.00	2.20
❑ 76	Tim James RC	6.00	2.70
❑ 77	Aleksandar Radojevic RC	3.00	1.35
❑ 78	Quincy Lewis RC	5.00	2.20
❑ 79	James Posey RC	10.00	4.50
❑ 80	Steve Francis RC	60.00	27.00
❑ 81	Jonathan Bender RC	25.00	11.00
❑ 82	Corey Maggette RC	20.00	9.00
❑ 83	Obinna Ekezie RC	4.00	1.80
❑ 84	Laron Profit RC	5.00	2.20
❑ 85	Devean George RC	10.00	4.50
❑ 86	Ron Artest RC	12.00	5.50
❑ 87	Rafer Alston RC	6.00	2.70
❑ 88	Vonteego Cummings RC	8.00	3.60
❑ 89	Evan Eschmeyer RC	3.00	1.35
❑ 90	Jumaine Jones RC	4.00	1.80
❑ S16	Vince Carter PROMO	5.00	2.20

1999-00 E-X Essential Credentials Future

	MINT	NRMT
COMMON CARD (1-90)	30.00	13.50
SEMISTARS	40.00	18.00
UNLISTED STARS	50.00	22.00

UNPRICED CARDS 47-60 SERIAL #'d 14-1
UNPRICED CARDS 77-90 SERIAL #'d 14-1
RANDOM INSERTS IN PACKS
PRINT RUNS IN PARENTHESIS BELOW

		MINT	NRMT
❑ 1	Stephon Marbury (60)	80.00	36.00
❑ 2	Antawn Jamison (59)	100.00	45.00
❑ 3	Patrick Ewing (58)	50.00	22.00
❑ 4	Nick Anderson (57)	30.00	13.50
❑ 5	Charles Barkley (56)	80.00	36.00
❑ 6	Marcus Camby (55)	50.00	22.00
❑ 7	Ron Mercer (54)	60.00	27.00
❑ 8	Avery Johnson (53)	30.00	13.50
❑ 9	Maurice Taylor (52)	50.00	22.00
❑ 10	Isaiah Rider (51)	40.00	18.00
❑ 11	Dirk Nowitzki (50)	80.00	36.00
❑ 12	Damon Stoudamire (49)	50.00	22.00
❑ 13	Alonzo Mourning (48)	50.00	22.00
❑ 14	Jason Kidd (47)	150.00	70.00
❑ 15	Juwan Howard (46)	40.00	18.00
❑ 16	Vince Carter (45)	500.00	220.00
❑ 17	Tim Duncan (44)	250.00	110.00
❑ 18	Paul Pierce (43)	100.00	45.00
❑ 19	Tim Hardaway (42)	50.00	22.00
❑ 20	Grant Hill (41)	250.00	110.00
❑ 21	Keith Van Horn (40)	100.00	45.00
❑ 22	Shaquille O'Neal (39)	300.00	135.00
❑ 23	Jason Williams (38)	150.00	70.00
❑ 24	Shareef Abdur-Rahim (37)	120.00	55.00
❑ 25	Kobe Bryant (36)	500.00	220.00
❑ 26	David Robinson (35)	100.00	45.00
❑ 27	Anfernee Hardaway (34)	200.00	90.00
❑ 28	Vin Baker (33)	40.00	18.00
❑ 29	Hakeem Olajuwon (32)	100.00	45.00
❑ 30	Michael Olowokandi (31)	40.00	18.00
❑ 31	Mike Bibby (30)	80.00	36.00
❑ 32	Tracy McGrady (29)	250.00	110.00
❑ 33	Antoine Walker (28)	100.00	45.00
❑ 34	Larry Hughes (27)	200.00	90.00
❑ 35	Chris Webber (26)	250.00	110.00
❑ 36	Ray Allen (25)	80.00	36.00
❑ 37	Danny Fortson (24)	30.00	13.50
❑ 38	Shawn Kemp (23)	120.00	55.00
❑ 39	Michael Doleac (22)	30.00	13.50
❑ 40	Gary Payton (21)	120.00	55.00
❑ 41	Toni Kukoc (20)	150.00	70.00
❑ 42	Kevin Garnett (19)	600.00	275.00
❑ 43	Steve Smith (18)	40.00	18.00
❑ 44	Scottie Pippen (17)	300.00	135.00
❑ 45	Allen Iverson (16)	400.00	180.00
❑ 46	Latrell Sprewell (15)	250.00	110.00
❑ 47	Matt Harpring (14)		
❑ 48	Lindsey Hunter (13)		
❑ 49	Karl Malone (12)		
❑ 50	Michael Finley (11)		
❑ 51	Jerry Stackhouse (10)		
❑ 52	Cedric Ceballos (9)		
❑ 53	Brent Barry (8)		
❑ 54	Elden Campbell (7)		
❑ 55	Glenn Robinson (6)		
❑ 56	Eddie Jones (5)		
❑ 57	Reggie Miller (4)		
❑ 58	Mitch Richmond (3)		
❑ 59	Raef LaFrentz (2)		
❑ 60	John Starks (1)		
❑ 61	Elton Brand (30)	400.00	180.00
❑ 62	William Avery (29)	60.00	27.00
❑ 63	Cal Bowdler (28)	50.00	22.00
❑ 64	Dion Glover (27)	40.00	18.00
❑ 65	Lamar Odom (26)	300.00	135.00
❑ 66	Richard Hamilton (25)	100.00	45.00
❑ 67	Kenny Thomas (24)	60.00	27.00
❑ 68	Shawn Marion (23)	120.00	55.00
❑ 69	Baron Davis (22)	100.00	45.00
❑ 70	Wally Szczerbiak (21)	150.00	70.00
❑ 71	Scott Padgett (20)	50.00	22.00
❑ 72	Jason Terry (19)	80.00	36.00
❑ 73	Trajan Langdon (18)	80.00	36.00
❑ 74	Andre Miller (17)	150.00	70.00
❑ 75	Jeff Foster (16)	50.00	22.00
❑ 76	Tim James (15)	60.00	27.00
❑ 77	Aleksandar Radojevic (14)		
❑ 78	Quincy Lewis (13)		
❑ 79	James Posey (12)		
❑ 80	Steve Francis (11)		
❑ 81	Jonathan Bender (10)		
❑ 82	Corey Maggette (9)		
❑ 83	Obinna Ekezie (8)		
❑ 84	Laron Profit (7)		
❑ 85	Devean George (6)		
❑ 86	Ron Artest (5)		
❑ 87	Rafer Alston (4)		
❑ 88	Vonteego Cummings (3)		
❑ 89	Evan Eschmeyer (2)		
❑ 90	Jumaine Jones (1)		

1999-00 E-X Essential Credentials Now

	MINT	NRMT
COMMON CARD (1-90)	30.00	13.50
SEMISTARS	40.00	18.00
UNLISTED STARS	50.00	22.00

UNPRICED CARDS 1-14 SERIAL #'d 1-14
UNPRICED CARDS 61-74 SERIAL #'d 1-14
RANDOM INSERTS IN PACKS
PRINT RUNS IN PARENTHESIS BELOW

		MINT	NRMT
❑ 1	Stephon Marbury (1)		
❑ 2	Antawn Jamison (2)		
❑ 3	Patrick Ewing (3)		
❑ 4	Nick Anderson (4)		
❑ 5	Charles Barkley (5)		
❑ 6	Marcus Camby (6)		
❑ 7	Ron Mercer (7)		
❑ 8	Avery Johnson (8)		
❑ 9	Maurice Taylor (9)		
❑ 10	Isaiah Rider (10)		
❑ 11	Dirk Nowitzki (11)		
❑ 12	Damon Stoudamire (12)		
❑ 13	Alonzo Mourning (13)		
❑ 14	Jason Kidd (14)		
❑ 15	Juwan Howard (15)	60.00	27.00
❑ 16	Vince Carter (16)	1000.00	450.00
❑ 17	Tim Duncan (17)	500.00	220.00
❑ 18	Paul Pierce (18)	200.00	90.00
❑ 19	Tim Hardaway (19)	100.00	45.00
❑ 20	Grant Hill (20)	500.00	220.00
❑ 21	Keith Van Horn (21)	150.00	70.00
❑ 22	Shaquille O'Neal (22)	400.00	180.00
❑ 23	Jason Williams (23)	200.00	90.00
❑ 24	Shareef Abdur-Rahim (24)	150.00	70.00
❑ 25	Kobe Bryant (25)	600.00	275.00
❑ 26	David Robinson (26)	120.00	55.00
❑ 27	Anfernee Hardaway (27)	250.00	110.00
❑ 28	Vin Baker (28)	40.00	18.00
❑ 29	Hakeem Olajuwon (29)	120.00	55.00
❑ 30	Michael Olowokandi (30)	40.00	18.00
❑ 31	Mike Bibby (31)	80.00	36.00
❑ 32	Tracy McGrady (32)	200.00	90.00
❑ 33	Antoine Walker (33)	80.00	36.00
❑ 34	Larry Hughes (34)	150.00	70.00
❑ 35	Chris Webber (35)	200.00	90.00
❑ 36	Ray Allen (36)	60.00	27.00
❑ 37	Danny Fortson (37)	30.00	13.50
❑ 38	Shawn Kemp (38)	100.00	45.00
❑ 39	Michael Doleac (39)	30.00	13.50
❑ 40	Gary Payton (40)	80.00	36.00
❑ 41	Toni Kukoc (41)	80.00	36.00
❑ 42	Kevin Garnett (42)	300.00	135.00
❑ 43	Steve Smith (43)	40.00	18.00
❑ 44	Scottie Pippen (44)	150.00	70.00
❑ 45	Allen Iverson (45)	200.00	90.00
❑ 46	Latrell Sprewell (46)	100.00	45.00
❑ 47	Matt Harpring (47)	30.00	13.50
❑ 48	Lindsey Hunter (48)	30.00	13.50
❑ 49	Karl Malone (49)	80.00	36.00
❑ 50	Michael Finley (50)	50.00	22.00
❑ 51	Jerry Stackhouse (51)	40.00	18.00
❑ 52	Cedric Ceballos (52)	30.00	13.50
❑ 53	Brent Barry (53)	30.00	13.50
❑ 54	Elden Campbell (54)	30.00	13.50
❑ 55	Glenn Robinson (55)	40.00	18.00
❑ 56	Eddie Jones (56)	100.00	45.00
❑ 57	Reggie Miller (57)	50.00	22.00
❑ 58	Mitch Richmond (58)	50.00	22.00
❑ 59	Raef LaFrentz (59)	40.00	18.00
❑ 60	John Starks (60)	30.00	13.50
❑ 61	Elton Brand (1)		
❑ 62	William Avery (2)		
❑ 63	Cal Bowdler (3)		
❑ 64	Dion Glover (4)		
❑ 65	Lamar Odom (5)		
❑ 66	Richard Hamilton (6)		
❑ 67	Kenny Thomas (7)		
❑ 68	Shawn Marion (8)		
❑ 69	Baron Davis (9)		
❑ 70	Wally Szczerbiak (10)		
❑ 71	Scott Padgett (11)		
❑ 72	Jason Terry (12)		
❑ 73	Trajan Langdon (13)		

Card	MINT	NRMT
❑ 74 Andre Miller (14)		
❑ 75 Jeff Foster (15)	60.00	27.00
❑ 76 Tim James (16)	60.00	27.00
❑ 77 Aleksandar Radojevic (17)	50.00	22.00
❑ 78 Quincy Lewis (18)	50.00	22.00
❑ 79 James Posey (19)	100.00	45.00
❑ 80 Steve Francis (20)	600.00	275.00
❑ 81 Jonathan Bender (21)	200.00	90.00
❑ 82 Corey Maggette (22)	150.00	70.00
❑ 83 Obinna Ekezie (23)	30.00	13.50
❑ 84 Laron Profit (24)	40.00	18.00
❑ 85 Devean George (25)	80.00	36.00
❑ 86 Ron Artest (26)	100.00	45.00
❑ 87 Rafer Alston (27)	50.00	22.00
❑ 88 Vonteego Cummings (28)	60.00	27.00
❑ 89 Evan Eschmeyer (29)	30.00	13.50
❑ 90 Jumaine Jones (30)	30.00	13.50

1999-00 E-X E-Xceptional Red

	MINT	NRMT
COMPLETE SET (15)	80.00	36.00
COMMON CARD (XC1-XC15)	3.00	1.35
STATED ODDS 1:16		
COMMON GREEN (XC1-XC15)	8.00	3.60
*GREEN: 1X TO 2.5X HI COLUMN		
GREEN: PRINT RUN 500 SERIAL #'d SETS		
GREEN: RANDOM INSERTS IN PACKS		
COMMON BLUE (XC1-XC15)	12.00	5.50
*BLUE: 1.5X TO 4X HI		
BLUE: PRINT RUN 250 SERIAL #'d SETS		
BLUE: RANDOM INSERTS IN PACKS		

Card	MINT	NRMT
❑ XC1 Jason Williams	4.00	1.80
❑ XC2 Kevin Garnett	10.00	4.50
❑ XC3 Allen Iverson	6.00	2.70
❑ XC4 Paul Pierce	3.00	1.35
❑ XC5 Keith Van Horn	3.00	1.35
❑ XC6 Grant Hill	8.00	3.60
❑ XC7 Scottie Pippen	5.00	2.20
❑ XC8 Stephon Marbury	3.00	1.35
❑ XC9 Tim Duncan	8.00	3.60
❑ XC10 Kobe Bryant	12.00	5.50
❑ XC11 Vince Carter	15.00	6.75
❑ XC12 Shaquille O'Neal	8.00	3.60
❑ XC13 Steve Francis	10.00	4.50
❑ XC14 Elton Brand	8.00	3.60
❑ XC15 Lamar Odom	6.00	2.70

1999-00 E-X E-Xciting

	MINT	NRMT
COMPLETE SET (10)	60.00	27.00
COMMON CARD (XCT1-XCT10)	3.00	1.35
STATED ODDS 1:24		

Card	MINT	NRMT
❑ XCT1 Jason Williams	4.00	1.80
❑ XCT2 Vince Carter	15.00	6.75
❑ XCT3 Allen Iverson	6.00	2.70
❑ XCT4 Kevin Garnett	10.00	4.50
❑ XCT5 Shaquille O'Neal	8.00	3.60
❑ XCT6 Larry Hughes	4.00	1.80
❑ XCT7 Tim Duncan	8.00	3.60
❑ XCT8 Kobe Bryant	12.00	5.50
❑ XCT9 Grant Hill	8.00	3.60
❑ XCT10 Paul Pierce	3.00	1.35

1999-00 E-X E-Xplosive

	MINT	NRMT
COMPLETE SET (10)	25.00	11.00
COMMON CARD (XP1-XP10)	1.50	.70
UNLISTED STARS	2.50	1.10
STATED PRINT RUN 1999 SERIAL #'d SETS		
FIRST 99 ARE AUTOGRAPHED		
RANDOM INSERTS IN PACKS		

Card	MINT	NRMT
❑ XP1 William Avery	2.50	1.10
❑ XP1 William Avery AU	25.00	11.00
❑ XP2 Baron Davis	3.00	1.35
❑ XP2 Baron Davis AU	50.00	22.00
❑ XP3 Richard Hamilton	3.00	1.35
❑ XP3 Richard Hamilton AU	50.00	22.00
❑ XP4 Trajan Langdon	2.50	1.10
❑ XP4 Trajan Langdon AU	30.00	13.50
❑ XP5 Wally Szczerbiak	5.00	2.20
❑ XP5 Wally Szczerbiak AU	60.00	27.00
❑ XP6 Jason Terry	2.50	1.10
❑ XP6 Jason Terry AU	25.00	11.00
❑ XP7 Shawn Marion	4.00	1.80
❑ XP7 Shawn Marion AU	60.00	27.00
❑ XP8 James Posey	2.50	1.10
❑ XP8 James Posey AU	40.00	18.00
❑ XP9 Lamar Odom	10.00	4.50
❑ XP9 Lamar Odom AU	150.00	70.00
❑ XP10 Quincy Lewis	1.50	.70
❑ XP10 Quincy Lewis AU	20.00	9.00

1999-00 E-X Generation E-X

	MINT	NRMT
COMPLETE SET (15)	30.00	13.50
COMMON CARD (GX1-GX15)	.60	.25
UNLISTED STARS	1.00	.45
STATED ODDS 1:8		

Card	MINT	NRMT
❑ GX1 Michael Olowokandi	.60	.25
❑ GX2 Kobe Bryant	8.00	3.60
❑ GX3 Allen Iverson	4.00	1.80
❑ GX4 Tim Duncan	5.00	2.20
❑ GX5 Vince Carter	10.00	4.50
❑ GX6 Paul Pierce	2.00	.90
❑ GX7 Jason Williams	2.50	1.10
❑ GX8 Steve Francis	10.00	4.50
❑ GX9 Lamar Odom	6.00	2.70

Card	MINT	NRMT
❑ GX10 Elton Brand	8.00	3.60
❑ GX11 Larry Hughes	2.50	1.10
❑ GX12 Antawn Jamison	2.00	.90
❑ GX13 Mike Bibby	1.25	.55
❑ GX14 Keith Van Horn	2.00	.90
❑ GX15 Raef LaFrentz	1.00	.45

1999-00 E-X Genuine Coverage

	MINT	NRMT
COMPLETE SET (20)	700.00	325.00
COMMON CARD (GC1-GC20)	20.00	9.00
SEMISTARS	25.00	11.00
STATED ODDS 1:72		

Card	MINT	NRMT
❑ GC1 Shaquille O'Neal	100.00	45.00
❑ GC2 Vince Carter	200.00	90.00
❑ GC3 Jason Kidd	50.00	22.00
❑ GC4 Karl Malone	40.00	18.00
❑ GC5 Joe Smith	25.00	11.00
❑ GC6 Terrell Brandon	20.00	9.00
❑ GC7 John Stockton	50.00	22.00
❑ GC8 Lamar Odom	80.00	36.00
❑ GC9 Shareef Abdur-Rahim	50.00	22.00
❑ GC10 David Robinson	50.00	22.00
❑ GC11 Larry Hughes	60.00	27.00
❑ GC12 Michael Olowokandi	20.00	9.00
❑ GC13 Antonio McDyess	25.00	11.00
❑ GC14 Mike Bibby	30.00	13.50
❑ GC15 Stephon Marbury	40.00	18.00
❑ GC16 Michael Finley	25.00	11.00
❑ GC17 Gary Payton	40.00	18.00
❑ GC18 Keith Van Horn	30.00	13.50
❑ GC19 Jamal Mashburn	20.00	9.00
❑ GC20 Grant Hill	60.00	27.00

1993-94 Finest

	MINT	NRMT
COMPLETE SET (220)	100.00	45.00
COMMON CARD (1-220)	.25	.11
SEMISTARS	.40	.18
UNLISTED STARS	.75	.35
SUBSET CARDS HALF VALUE OF BASE CARDS		

Card	MINT	NRMT
❑ 1 Michael Jordan	12.00	5.50
❑ 2 Larry Bird	2.50	1.10
❑ 3 Shaquille O'Neal	5.00	2.20

❑ 4 Benoit Benjamin .25 .11
❑ 5 Ricky Pierce .25 .11
❑ 6 Ken Norman .25 .11
❑ 7 Victor Alexander .25 .11
❑ 8 Mark Jackson .40 .18
❑ 9 Mark West .25 .11
❑ 10 Don MacLean .25 .11
❑ 11 Reggie Miller .75 .35
❑ 12 Sarunas Marciulionis .25 .11
❑ 13 Craig Ehlo .25 .11
❑ 14 Toni Kukoc RC 5.00 2.20
❑ 15 Glen Rice .40 .18
❑ 16 Otis Thorpe .40 .18
❑ 17 Reggie Williams .25 .11
❑ 18 Charles Smith .25 .11
❑ 19 Micheal Williams .25 .11
❑ 20 Tom Chambers .25 .11
❑ 21 David Robinson 1.50 .70
❑ 22 Jamal Mashburn RC 4.00 1.80
❑ 23 Clifford Robinson .40 .18
❑ 24 Acie Earl RC .25 .11
❑ 25 Danny Ferry .25 .11
❑ 26 Bobby Hurley RC .40 .18
❑ 27 Eddie Johnson .25 .11
❑ 28 Detlef Schrempf .40 .18
❑ 29 Mike Brown .25 .11
❑ 30 Latrell Sprewell 2.50 1.10
❑ 31 Derek Harper .40 .18
❑ 32 Stacey Augmon .25 .11
❑ 33 Pooh Richardson .25 .11
❑ 34 Larry Krystkowiak .25 .11
❑ 35 Pervis Ellison .25 .11
❑ 36 Jeff Malone .25 .11
❑ 37 Sean Elliott .40 .18
❑ 38 John Paxson .25 .11
❑ 39 Robert Parish .40 .18
❑ 40 Mark Aguirre .25 .11
❑ 41 Danny Ainge .40 .18
❑ 42 Brian Shaw .25 .11
❑ 43 LaPhonso Ellis .25 .11
❑ 44 Carl Herrera .25 .11
❑ 45 Terry Cummings .25 .11
❑ 46 Chris Dudley .25 .11
❑ 47 Anthony Mason .40 .18
❑ 48 Chris Morris .25 .11
❑ 49 Todd Day .25 .11
❑ 50 Nick Van Exel RC 5.00 2.20
❑ 51 Larry Nance .25 .11
❑ 52 Derrick McKey .25 .11
❑ 53 Muggsy Bogues .40 .18
❑ 54 Andrew Lang .25 .11
❑ 55 Chuck Person .25 .11
❑ 56 Michael Adams .25 .11
❑ 57 Spud Webb .40 .18
❑ 58 Scott Skiles .25 .11
❑ 59 A.C. Green .40 .18
❑ 60 Terry Mills .25 .11
❑ 61 Xavier McDaniel .25 .11
❑ 62 B.J. Armstrong .25 .11
❑ 63 Donald Hodge .25 .11
❑ 64 Gary Grant .25 .11
❑ 65 Billy Owens .25 .11
❑ 66 Greg Anthony .25 .11
❑ 67 Jay Humphries .25 .11
❑ 68 Lionel Simmons .25 .11
❑ 69 Dana Barros .25 .11
❑ 70 Steve Smith .75 .35
❑ 71 Ervin Johnson RC .40 .18
❑ 72 Sleepy Floyd .25 .11
❑ 73 Blue Edwards .25 .11
❑ 74 Clyde Drexler .75 .35
❑ 75 Elden Campbell .25 .11
❑ 76 Hakeem Olajuwon 1.50 .70
❑ 77 Clarence Weatherspoon .25 .11
❑ 78 Kevin Willis .25 .11
❑ 79 Isaiah Rider RC 5.00 2.20
❑ 80 Derrick Coleman .40 .18
❑ 81 Nick Anderson .40 .18
❑ 82 Bryant Stith .25 .11
❑ 83 Johnny Newman .25 .11
❑ 84 Calbert Cheaney RC 1.50 .70
❑ 85 Oliver Miller .25 .11
❑ 86 Loy Vaught .25 .11
❑ 87 Isiah Thomas .75 .35
❑ 88 Dee Brown .25 .11
❑ 89 Horace Grant .40 .18
❑ 90 Patrick Ewing AF .40 .18
❑ 91 Clarence Weatherspoon AF .25 .11
❑ 92 Rony Seikaly AF .25 .11
❑ 93 Dino Radja AF .25 .11
❑ 94 Kenny Anderson AF .25 .11
❑ 95 John Starks AF .25 .11
❑ 96 Tom Gugliotta AF .40 .18
❑ 97 Steve Smith AF .40 .18
❑ 98 Derrick Coleman AF .25 .11
❑ 99 Shaquille O'Neal AF 3.00 1.35
❑ 100 Brad Daugherty CF .25 .11
❑ 101 Horace Grant CF .25 .11
❑ 102 Dominique Wilkins CF .40 .18
❑ 103 Joe Dumars CF .40 .18
❑ 104 Alonzo Mourning CF .75 .35
❑ 105 Scottie Pippen CF 2.50 1.10
❑ 106 Reggie Miller CF .40 .18
❑ 107 Mark Price CF .25 .11
❑ 108 Ken Norman CF .25 .11
❑ 109 Larry Johnson CF .40 .18
❑ 110 Jamal Mashburn MF .75 .35
❑ 111 Christian Laettner MF .25 .11
❑ 112 Karl Malone MF .75 .35
❑ 113 Dennis Rodman MF .75 .35
❑ 114 Mahmoud Abdul-Rauf MF .25 .11
❑ 115 Hakeem Olajuwon MF .75 .35
❑ 116 Jim Jackson MF .25 .11
❑ 117 John Stockton MF .40 .18
❑ 118 David Robinson MF .75 .35
❑ 119 Dikembe Mutombo MF .25 .11
❑ 120 Vlade Divac PF .25 .11
❑ 121 Dan Majerle PF .25 .11
❑ 122 Chris Mullin PF .40 .18
❑ 123 Shawn Kemp PF .75 .35
❑ 124 Danny Manning PF .25 .11
❑ 125 Charles Barkley PF .75 .35
❑ 126 Mitch Richmond PF .40 .18
❑ 127 Tim Hardaway PF .40 .18
❑ 128 Detlef Schrempf PF .25 .11
❑ 129 Clyde Drexler PF .40 .18
❑ 130 Christian Laettner .40 .18
❑ 131 Rodney Rogers RC 2.00 .90
❑ 132 Rik Smits .40 .18
❑ 133 Chris Mills RC 2.00 .90
❑ 134 Corie Blount RC .25 .11
❑ 135 Mookie Blaylock .40 .18
❑ 136 Jim Jackson .40 .18
❑ 137 Tom Gugliotta .75 .35
❑ 138 Dennis Scott .25 .11
❑ 139 Vin Baker RC 4.00 1.80
❑ 140 Gary Payton 1.50 .70
❑ 141 Sedale Threatt .25 .11
❑ 142 Orlando Woolridge .25 .11
❑ 143 Avery Johnson .25 .11
❑ 144 Charles Oakley .40 .18
❑ 145 Harvey Grant .25 .11
❑ 146 Bimbo Coles .25 .11
❑ 147 Vernon Maxwell .25 .11
❑ 148 Danny Manning .40 .18
❑ 149 Hersey Hawkins .40 .18
❑ 150 Kevin Gamble .25 .11
❑ 151 Johnny Dawkins .25 .11
❑ 152 Olden Polynice .25 .11
❑ 153 Kevin Edwards .25 .11
❑ 154 Willie Anderson .25 .11
❑ 155 Wayman Tisdale .25 .11
❑ 156 Popeye Jones RC .25 .11
❑ 157 Dan Majerle .40 .18
❑ 158 Rex Chapman .25 .11
❑ 159 Shawn Kemp 1.50 .70
❑ 160 Eric Murdock .25 .11
❑ 161 Randy White .25 .11
❑ 162 Larry Johnson .75 .35
❑ 163 Dominique Wilkins .75 .35
❑ 164 Dikembe Mutombo .40 .18
❑ 165 Patrick Ewing .75 .35
❑ 166 Jerome Kersey .25 .11
❑ 167 Dale Davis .25 .11
❑ 168 Ron Harper .40 .18
❑ 169 Sam Cassell RC 5.00 2.20
❑ 170 Bill Cartwright .25 .11
❑ 171 John Williams .25 .11
❑ 172 Dino Radja RC .25 .11
❑ 173 Dennis Rodman 2.00 .90
❑ 174 Kenny Anderson .40 .18
❑ 175 Robert Horry .40 .18
❑ 176 Chris Mullin .75 .35
❑ 177 John Salley .25 .11
❑ 178 Scott Burrell RC 1.50 .70
❑ 179 Mitch Richmond .75 .35
❑ 180 Lee Mayberry .25 .11
❑ 181 James Worthy .75 .35
❑ 182 Rick Fox .25 .11
❑ 183 Kevin Johnson .40 .18
❑ 184 Lindsey Hunter RC 2.00 .90
❑ 185 Marlon Maxey .25 .11
❑ 186 Sam Perkins .40 .18
❑ 187 Kevin Duckworth .25 .11
❑ 188 Jeff Hornacek .40 .18
❑ 189 Anfernee Hardaway RC 25.00 11.00
❑ 190 Rex Walters RC .25 .11
❑ 191 Mahmoud Abdul-Rauf .25 .11
❑ 192 Terry Dehere RC .25 .11
❑ 193 Brad Daugherty .25 .11
❑ 194 John Starks .40 .18
❑ 195 Rod Strickland .40 .18
❑ 196 Luther Wright RC .25 .11
❑ 197 Vlade Divac .40 .18
❑ 198 Tim Hardaway .75 .35
❑ 199 Joe Dumars .75 .35
❑ 200 Charles Barkley 1.50 .70
❑ 201 Alonzo Mourning 1.50 .70
❑ 202 Doug West .25 .11
❑ 203 Anthony Avent .25 .11
❑ 204 Lloyd Daniels .25 .11
❑ 205 Mark Price .25 .11
❑ 206 Rumeal Robinson .25 .11
❑ 207 Kendall Gill .40 .18
❑ 208 Scottie Pippen 3.00 1.35
❑ 209 Kenny Smith .25 .11
❑ 210 Walt Williams .25 .11
❑ 211 Hubert Davis .25 .11
❑ 212 Chris Webber RC 25.00 11.00
❑ 213 Rony Seikaly .25 .11
❑ 214 Sam Bowie .25 .11
❑ 215 Karl Malone 1.50 .70
❑ 216 Malik Sealy .25 .11
❑ 217 Dale Ellis .25 .11
❑ 218 Harold Miner .25 .11
❑ 219 John Stockton .75 .35
❑ 220 Shawn Bradley RC 2.00 .90

1993-94 Finest Refractors

	MINT	NRMT
COMPLETE SET (220)	1200.00	550.00
COMMON CARD (1-220)	3.00	1.35
SP (10/28/35/40/47/49/53)	5.00	2.20
SP (56/57/107/190/204/218)	5.00	2.20
SP (7/33/36/41/66/78/89)	8.00	3.60
SP (91/116/128/142/147)	8.00	3.60
SP (155/180/211/217)	8.00	3.60
SP (12/48/64/170/182)	20.00	9.00

*STARS: 6X TO 15X HI COLUMN
*RC's: 2.5X TO 6X HI
STATED ODDS 1:9 HOBBY, 1:4 JUMBO
ASTERISK CARDS: PERCEIVED SCARCITY

	MINT	NRMT
❑ 14 Toni Kukoc	30.00	13.50
❑ 22 Jamal Mashburn	20.00	9.00
❑ 50 Nick Van Exel	25.00	11.00
❑ 79 Isaiah Rider	20.00	9.00
❑ 84 Calbert Cheaney *	20.00	9.00
❑ 133 Chris Mills *	20.00	9.00
❑ 139 Vin Baker *	25.00	11.00
❑ 169 Sam Cassell	20.00	9.00
❑ 189 Anfernee Hardaway	120.00	55.00
❑ 212 Chris Webber *	120.00	55.00

1993-94 Finest Main Attraction

	MINT	NRMT
COMPLETE SET (27)	50.00	22.00

*SINGLES: .75X TO 2X BASE CARD HI
ONE PER JUMBO PACK

	MINT	NRMT
❑ 1 Dominique Wilkins	1.50	.70
❑ 2 Dino Radja	.50	.23
❑ 3 Larry Johnson	1.50	.70
❑ 4 Scottie Pippen	6.00	2.70
❑ 5 Mark Price	.50	.23
❑ 6 Jamal Mashburn	3.00	1.35
❑ 7 Mahmoud Abdul-Rauf	.50	.23
❑ 8 Joe Dumars	1.50	.70
❑ 9 Chris Webber	12.00	5.50
❑ 10 Hakeem Olajuwon	3.00	1.35
❑ 11 Reggie Miller	1.50	.70
❑ 12 Danny Manning	.75	.35
❑ 13 Doug Christie	.75	.35
❑ 14 Steve Smith	1.50	.70
❑ 15 Eric Murdock	.50	.23
❑ 16 Isaiah Rider	3.00	1.35
❑ 17 Derrick Coleman	.75	.35
❑ 18 Patrick Ewing	1.50	.70
❑ 19 Shaquille O'Neal	10.00	4.50
❑ 20 Shawn Bradley	4.00	1.80
❑ 21 Charles Barkley	3.00	1.35
❑ 22 Clyde Drexler	1.50	.70
❑ 23 Mitch Richmond	1.50	.70
❑ 24 David Robinson	3.00	1.35
❑ 25 Shawn Kemp	3.00	1.35
❑ 26 Karl Malone	3.00	1.35
❑ 27 Tom Gugliotta	1.50	.70

1994-95 Finest

	MINT	NRMT
COMPLETE SET (1-331)	300.00	135.00
COMP.SERIES 1 (165)	100.00	45.00
COMP.SERIES 2 (166)	200.00	90.00
COMMON CARD (1-165)	.60	.25
COMMON CARD (166-331)	.30	.14
SEMISTARS SER.1	1.25	.55
SEMISTARS SER.2	.60	.25
UNLISTED STARS SER.1	2.50	1.10
UNLISTED STARS SER.2	1.25	.55

	MINT	NRMT
❑ 1 Chris Mullin CY	1.25	.55
❑ 2 Anthony Mason CY	.60	.25
❑ 3 John Salley CY	.60	.25
❑ 4 Jamal Mashburn CY	1.25	.55
❑ 5 Mark Jackson CY	.60	.25
❑ 6 Mario Elie CY	.60	.25
❑ 7 Kenny Anderson CY	.60	.25
❑ 8 Rod Strickland CY	.60	.25
❑ 9 Kenny Smith CY	.60	.25
❑ 10 Olden Polynice CY	.60	.25
❑ 11 Derek Harper	.60	.25
❑ 12 Danny Ainge	.60	.25
❑ 13 Dino Radja	.60	.25
❑ 14 Eric Murdock	.60	.25
❑ 15 Sean Rooks	.60	.25
❑ 16 Dell Curry	.60	.25
❑ 17 Victor Alexander	.60	.25
❑ 18 Rodney Rogers	.60	.25
❑ 19 John Salley	.60	.25
❑ 20 Brad Daugherty	.60	.25
❑ 21 Elmore Spencer	.60	.25
❑ 22 Mitch Richmond	2.50	1.10
❑ 23 Rex Walters	.60	.25
❑ 24 Antonio Davis	.60	.25
❑ 25 B.J. Armstrong	.60	.25
❑ 26 Andrew Lang	.60	.25
❑ 27 Carl Herrera	.60	.25
❑ 28 Kevin Edwards	.60	.25
❑ 29 Micheal Williams	.60	.25
❑ 30 Clyde Drexler	2.50	1.10
❑ 31 Dana Barros	.60	.25
❑ 32 Shaquille O'Neal	12.00	5.50
❑ 33 Patrick Ewing	2.50	1.10
❑ 34 Charles Barkley	4.00	1.80
❑ 35 J.R. Reid	.60	.25
❑ 36 Lindsey Hunter	1.25	.55
❑ 37 Jeff Malone	.60	.25
❑ 38 Rik Smits	.60	.25
❑ 39 Brian Williams	.60	.25
❑ 40 Shawn Kemp	4.00	1.80
❑ 41 Terry Porter	.60	.25
❑ 42 James Worthy	2.50	1.10
❑ 43 Rex Chapman	.60	.25
❑ 44 Stanley Roberts	.60	.25
❑ 45 Chris Smith	.60	.25
❑ 46 Dee Brown	.60	.25
❑ 47 Chris Gatling	.60	.25
❑ 48 Donald Hodge	.60	.25
❑ 49 Bimbo Coles	.60	.25
❑ 50 Derrick Coleman	1.25	.55
❑ 51 Muggsy Bogues CY	.60	.25
❑ 52 Reggie Williams CY	.60	.25
❑ 53 David Wingate CY	.60	.25
❑ 54 Sam Cassell CY	1.25	.55
❑ 55 Sherman Douglas CY	.60	.25
❑ 56 Keith Jennings	.60	.25
❑ 57 Kenny Gattison	.60	.25
❑ 58 Brent Price	.60	.25
❑ 59 Luc Longley	.60	.25
❑ 60 Jamal Mashburn	2.50	1.10
❑ 61 Doug West	.60	.25
❑ 62 Walt Williams	.60	.25
❑ 63 Tracy Murray	.60	.25
❑ 64 Robert Pack	.60	.25
❑ 65 Johnny Dawkins	.60	.25
❑ 66 Vin Baker	2.50	1.10
❑ 67 Sam Cassell	2.50	1.10
❑ 68 Dale Davis	.60	.25
❑ 69 Terrell Brandon	1.25	.55
❑ 70 Billy Owens	.60	.25
❑ 71 Ervin Johnson	.60	.25
❑ 72 Allan Houston	4.00	1.80
❑ 73 Craig Ehlo	.60	.25
❑ 74 Loy Vaught	.60	.25
❑ 75 Scottie Pippen	8.00	3.60
❑ 76 Sam Bowie	.60	.25
❑ 77 Anthony Mason	1.25	.55
❑ 78 Felton Spencer	.60	.25
❑ 79 P.J. Brown	.60	.25
❑ 80 Christian Laettner	1.25	.55
❑ 81 Todd Day	.60	.25
❑ 82 Sean Elliott	1.25	.55
❑ 83 Grant Long	.60	.25
❑ 84 Xavier McDaniel	.60	.25
❑ 85 David Benoit	.60	.25
❑ 86 Larry Stewart	.60	.25
❑ 87 Donald Royal	.60	.25
❑ 88 Duane Causwell	.60	.25
❑ 89 Vlade Divac	.60	.25
❑ 90 Derrick McKey	.60	.25
❑ 91 Kevin Johnson	1.25	.55
❑ 92 LaPhonso Ellis	.60	.25
❑ 93 Jerome Kersey	.60	.25
❑ 94 Muggsy Bogues	1.25	.55
❑ 95 Tom Gugliotta	1.25	.55
❑ 96 Jeff Hornacek	1.25	.55
❑ 97 Kevin Willis	.60	.25
❑ 98 Chris Mills	1.25	.55
❑ 99 Sam Perkins	1.25	.55
❑ 100 Alonzo Mourning	3.00	1.35
❑ 101 Derrick Coleman CY	.60	.25
❑ 102 Glen Rice CY	.60	.25
❑ 103 Kevin Willis CY	.60	.25
❑ 104 Chris Webber CY	4.00	1.80
❑ 105 Terry Mills CY	.60	.25
❑ 106 Tim Hardaway CY	1.25	.55
❑ 107 Nick Anderson CY	.60	.25
❑ 108 Terry Cummings CY	.60	.25
❑ 109 Hersey Hawkins CY	.60	.25
❑ 110 Ken Norman CY	.60	.25
❑ 111 Nick Anderson	.60	.25
❑ 112 Tim Perry	.60	.25
❑ 113 Terry Dehere	.60	.25
❑ 114 Chris Morris	.60	.25
❑ 115 John Williams	.60	.25
❑ 116 Jon Barry	.60	.25
❑ 117 Rony Seikaly	.60	.25
❑ 118 Detlef Schrempf	1.25	.55
❑ 119 Terry Cummings	.60	.25
❑ 120 Chris Webber	8.00	3.60
❑ 121 David Wingate	.60	.25
❑ 122 Popeye Jones	.60	.25
❑ 123 Sherman Douglas	.60	.25
❑ 124 Greg Anthony	.60	.25
❑ 125 Mookie Blaylock	.60	.25
❑ 126 Don MacLean	.60	.25
❑ 127 Lionel Simmons	.60	.25
❑ 128 Scott Brooks	.60	.25
❑ 129 Jeff Turner	.60	.25
❑ 130 Bryant Stith	.60	.25
❑ 131 Shawn Bradley	.60	.25
❑ 132 Byron Scott	1.25	.55
❑ 133 Doug Christie	.60	.25
❑ 134 Dennis Rodman	5.00	2.20
❑ 135 Dan Majerle	1.25	.55
❑ 136 Gary Grant	.60	.25
❑ 137 Bryon Russell	.60	.25
❑ 138 Will Perdue	.60	.25
❑ 139 Gheorghe Muresan	.60	.25
❑ 140 Kendall Gill	1.25	.55
❑ 141 Isaiah Rider	1.25	.55
❑ 142 Terry Mills	.60	.25
❑ 143 Willie Anderson	.60	.25
❑ 144 Hubert Davis	.60	.25
❑ 145 Lucious Harris	.60	.25
❑ 146 Spud Webb	.60	.25
❑ 147 Glen Rice	1.25	.55
❑ 148 Dennis Scott	.60	.25

Card	MINT	NRMT
❑ 149 Robert Horry	.60	.25
❑ 150 John Stockton	2.50	1.10
❑ 151 Stacey Augmon CY	.60	.25
❑ 152 Chris Mills CY	.60	.25
❑ 153 Elden Campbell CY	.60	.25
❑ 154 Jay Humphries CY	.60	.25
❑ 155 Reggie Miller CY	1.25	.55
❑ 156 George Lynch	.60	.25
❑ 157 Tyrone Hill	.60	.25
❑ 158 Lee Mayberry	.60	.25
❑ 159 Jon Koncak	.60	.25
❑ 160 Joe Dumars	2.50	1.10
❑ 161 Vernon Maxwell	.60	.25
❑ 162 Joe Kleine	.60	.25
❑ 163 Acie Earl	.60	.25
❑ 164 Steve Kerr	.60	.25
❑ 165 Rod Strickland	1.25	.55
❑ 166 Glenn Robinson RC	8.00	3.60
❑ 167 Anfernee Hardaway	5.00	2.20
❑ 168 Latrell Sprewell	2.50	1.10
❑ 169 Sergei Bazarevich	.30	.14
❑ 170 Hakeem Olajuwon	2.00	.90
❑ 171 Nick Van Exel	1.25	.55
❑ 172 Buck Williams	.30	.14
❑ 173 Antoine Carr	.30	.14
❑ 174 Corie Blount	.30	.14
❑ 175 Dominique Wilkins	1.25	.55
❑ 176 Yinka Dare	.30	.14
❑ 177 Byron Houston	.30	.14
❑ 178 LaSalle Thompson	.30	.14
❑ 179 Doug Smith	.30	.14
❑ 180 David Robinson	2.00	.90
❑ 181 Eric Piatkowski RC	.30	.14
❑ 182 Scott Skiles	.30	.14
❑ 183 Scott Burrell	.30	.14
❑ 184 Mark West	.30	.14
❑ 185 Billy Owens	.30	.14
❑ 186 Brian Grant RC	5.00	2.20
❑ 187 Scott Williams	.30	.14
❑ 188 Gerald Madkins	.30	.14
❑ 189 Reggie Williams	.30	.14
❑ 190 Danny Manning	.60	.25
❑ 191 Mike Brown	.30	.14
❑ 192 Charles Smith	.30	.14
❑ 193 Elden Campbell	.30	.14
❑ 194 Ricky Pierce	.30	.14
❑ 195 Karl Malone	2.00	.90
❑ 196 Brooks Thompson	.30	.14
❑ 197 Alaa Abdelnaby	.30	.14
❑ 198 Tyrone Corbin	.30	.14
❑ 199 Johnny Newman	.30	.14
❑ 200 Grant Hill CB	10.00	4.50
❑ 201 Kenny Anderson CB	.30	.14
❑ 202 Olden Polynice CB	.30	.14
❑ 203 Horace Grant CB	.30	.14
❑ 204 Muggsy Bogues CB	.30	.14
❑ 205 Mark Price CB	.30	.14
❑ 206 Tom Gugliotta CB	.30	.14
❑ 207 Christian Laettner CB	.30	.14
❑ 208 Eric Montross CB	.30	.14
❑ 209 Sam Cassell CB	.60	.25
❑ 210 Charles Oakley	.30	.14
❑ 211 Harold Ellis	.30	.14
❑ 212 Nate McMillan	.30	.14
❑ 213 Chuck Person	.30	.14
❑ 214 Harold Miner	.30	.14
❑ 215 Clarence Weatherspoon	.30	.14
❑ 216 Robert Parish	.60	.25
❑ 217 Michael Cage	.30	.14
❑ 218 Kenny Smith	.30	.14
❑ 219 Larry Krystkowiak	.30	.14
❑ 220 Dikembe Mutombo	.60	.25
❑ 221 Wayman Tisdale	.30	.14
❑ 222 Kevin Duckworth	.30	.14
❑ 223 Vern Fleming	.30	.14
❑ 224 Eric Mobley RC	.30	.14
❑ 225 Patrick Ewing CB	.60	.25
❑ 226 Clifford Robinson CB	.30	.14
❑ 227 Eric Murdock CB	.30	.14
❑ 228 Derrick Coleman CB	.30	.14
❑ 229 Otis Thorpe CB	.30	.14
❑ 230 Alonzo Mourning CB	1.25	.55
❑ 231 Donyell Marshall CB	.60	.25
❑ 232 Dikembe Mutombo CB	.30	.14
❑ 233 Rony Seikaly CB	.30	.14
❑ 234 Chris Mullin CB	.60	.25
❑ 235 Reggie Miller	1.25	.55
❑ 236 Benoit Benjamin	.30	.14
❑ 237 Sean Rooks	.30	.14
❑ 238 Terry Davis	.30	.14
❑ 239 Anthony Avent	.30	.14
❑ 240 Grant Hill RC	70.00	32.00
❑ 241 Randy Woods	.30	.14
❑ 242 Tom Chambers	.30	.14
❑ 243 Michael Adams	.30	.14
❑ 244 Monty Williams RC	.30	.14
❑ 245 Chris Mullin	1.25	.55
❑ 246 Bill Wennington	.30	.14
❑ 247 Mark Jackson	.30	.14
❑ 248 Blue Edwards	.30	.14
❑ 249 Jalen Rose RC	15.00	6.75
❑ 250 Glenn Robinson CB	1.50	.70
❑ 251 Kevin Willis CB	.30	.14
❑ 252 B.J. Armstrong CB	.30	.14
❑ 253 Jim Jackson CB	.30	.14
❑ 254 Steve Smith CB	.30	.14
❑ 255 Chris Webber CB	2.00	.90
❑ 256 Glen Rice CB	.30	.14
❑ 257 Derek Harper CB	.30	.14
❑ 258 Jalen Rose CB	2.00	.90
❑ 259 Juwan Howard CB	1.25	.55
❑ 260 Kenny Anderson	.60	.25
❑ 261 Calbert Cheaney	.30	.14
❑ 262 Bill Cartwright	.30	.14
❑ 263 Mario Elie	.30	.14
❑ 264 Chris Dudley	.30	.14
❑ 265 Jim Jackson	.60	.25
❑ 266 Antonio Harvey	.30	.14
❑ 267 Bill Curley RC	.30	.14
❑ 268 Moses Malone	1.25	.55
❑ 269 A.C. Green	.60	.25
❑ 270 Larry Johnson	.60	.25
❑ 271 Marty Conlon	.30	.14
❑ 272 Greg Graham	.30	.14
❑ 273 Eric Montross RC	.30	.14
❑ 274 Stacey King	.30	.14
❑ 275 Charles Barkley CB	1.25	.55
❑ 276 Chris Morris CB	.30	.14
❑ 277 Robert Horry CB	.30	.14
❑ 278 Dominique Wilkins CB	.60	.25
❑ 279 Latrell Sprewell CB	1.25	.55
❑ 280 Shaquille O'Neal CB	3.00	1.35
❑ 281 Wesley Person CB	.60	.25
❑ 282 Mahmoud Abdul-Rauf CB	.30	.14
❑ 283 Jamal Mashburn CB	.60	.25
❑ 284 Dale Ellis CB	.30	.14
❑ 285 Gary Payton	2.00	.90
❑ 286 Jason Kidd RC	25.00	11.00
❑ 287 Ken Norman	.30	.14
❑ 288 Juwan Howard RC	4.00	1.80
❑ 289 Lamond Murray RC	2.00	.90
❑ 290 Clifford Robinson	.60	.25
❑ 291 Frank Brickowski	.30	.14
❑ 292 Adam Keefe	.30	.14
❑ 293 Ron Harper	.60	.25
❑ 294 Tom Hammonds	.30	.14
❑ 295 Otis Thorpe	.30	.14
❑ 296 Rick Mahorn	.30	.14
❑ 297 Alton Lister	.30	.14
❑ 298 Vinny Del Negro	.30	.14
❑ 299 Danny Ferry	.30	.14
❑ 300 John Starks	.30	.14
❑ 301 Duane Ferrell	.30	.14
❑ 302 Hersey Hawkins	.60	.25
❑ 303 Khalid Reeves RC	.30	.14
❑ 304 Anthony Peeler	.30	.14
❑ 305 Tim Hardaway	1.25	.55
❑ 306 Rick Fox	.30	.14
❑ 307 Jay Humphries	.30	.14
❑ 308 Brian Shaw	.30	.14
❑ 309 Dan Schayes	.30	.14
❑ 310 Stacey Augmon	.30	.14
❑ 311 Oliver Miller	.30	.14
❑ 312 Pooh Richardson	.30	.14
❑ 313 Donyell Marshall RC	4.00	1.80
❑ 314 Aaron McKie RC	.30	.14
❑ 315 Mark Price	.30	.14
❑ 316 B.J. Tyler RC	.30	.14
❑ 317 Olden Polynice	.30	.14
❑ 318 Avery Johnson	.30	.14
❑ 319 Derek Strong	.30	.14
❑ 320 Toni Kukoc	2.00	.90
❑ 321 Charlie Ward RC	4.00	1.80
❑ 322 Wesley Person RC	4.00	1.80
❑ 323 Eddie Jones RC	15.00	6.75
❑ 324 Horace Grant	.60	.25
❑ 325 Mahmoud Abdul-Rauf	.30	.14
❑ 326 Sharone Wright RC	.30	.14
❑ 327 Kevin Gamble	.30	.14
❑ 328 Sarunas Marciulionis	.30	.14
❑ 329 Harvey Grant	.30	.14
❑ 330 Bobby Hurley	.30	.14
❑ 331 Michael Jordan	25.00	11.00

1994-95 Finest Refractors

	MINT	NRMT
COMPLETE SET (331)	2700.00	1200.00
COMP.SERIES 1 (165)	1200.00	550.00
COMP.SERIES 2 (166)	1500.00	700.00
COMMON CARD (1-331)	6.00	2.70
SP (39,138,143,156)	10.00	4.50
SP (2,135,149,164)	12.00	5.50
SP (4,27,38,140,162)	15.00	6.75
SP (1,18,139,153)	20.00	9.00

*SER.1 STARS: 4X TO 10X BASE CARD HI
*SER.2 STARS: 8X TO 20X BASE
SER.1/2 STATED ODDS 1:12
CONDITION SENSITIVE SET
ASTERISK CARDS: PERCEIVED SCARCITY

Card	MINT	NRMT
❑ 102 Glen Rice CY *	100.00	45.00
❑ 104 Chris Webber CY *	80.00	36.00
❑ 106 Tim Hardaway CY *	25.00	11.00
❑ 120 Chris Webber *	150.00	70.00
❑ 150 John Stockton *	60.00	27.00
❑ 155 Reggie Miller CY *	40.00	18.00
❑ 166 Glenn Robinson	80.00	36.00
❑ 186 Brian Grant	30.00	13.50
❑ 200 Grant Hill CB	100.00	45.00
❑ 240 Grant Hill	300.00	135.00
❑ 249 Jalen Rose	80.00	36.00
❑ 250 Glenn Robinson CB	20.00	9.00
❑ 258 Jalen Rose CB	20.00	9.00
❑ 286 Jason Kidd	150.00	70.00
❑ 288 Juwan Howard	30.00	13.50
❑ 289 Lamond Murray	15.00	6.75
❑ 313 Donyell Marshall	25.00	11.00
❑ 321 Charlie Ward	15.00	6.75
❑ 322 Wesley Person	25.00	11.00
❑ 323 Eddie Jones	120.00	55.00
❑ 331 Michael Jordan	250.00	110.00

1994-95 Finest Cornerstone

	MINT	NRMT
COMPLETE SET (15)	80.00	36.00
COMMON CARD (1-15)	3.00	1.35
SEMISTARS	4.00	1.80
UNLISTED STARS	5.00	2.20

SER.2 STATED ODDS 1:24

Card	MINT	NRMT
❑ CS1 Shaquille O'Neal	25.00	11.00
❑ CS2 Alonzo Mourning	6.00	2.70
❑ CS3 Patrick Ewing	5.00	2.20
❑ CS4 Karl Malone	8.00	3.60
❑ CS5 Kenny Anderson	4.00	1.80

	MINT	NRMT
❑ CS6 Latrell Sprewell	10.00	4.50
❑ CS7 Dikembe Mutombo	4.00	1.80
❑ CS8 Charles Barkley	8.00	3.60
❑ CS9 John Stockton	5.00	2.20
❑ CS10 Reggie Miller	5.00	2.20
❑ CS11 Jamal Mashburn	4.00	1.80
❑ CS12 Anfernee Hardaway	15.00	6.75
❑ CS13 Jim Jackson	3.00	1.35
❑ CS14 David Robinson	8.00	3.60
❑ CS15 Hakeem Olajuwon	8.00	3.60

1994-95 Finest Iron Men

	MINT	NRMT
COMPLETE SET (10)	30.00	13.50
COMMON CARD (1-10)	1.00	.45
SEMISTARS	2.00	.90
SER.1 STATED ODDS 1:24		
❑ 1 Shaquille O'Neal	15.00	6.75
❑ 2 Kenny Anderson	2.00	.90
❑ 3 Jim Jackson	2.00	.90
❑ 4 Clarence Weatherspoon	1.00	.45
❑ 5 Karl Malone	5.00	2.20
❑ 6 Dan Majerle	2.00	.90
❑ 7 Anfernee Hardaway	10.00	4.50
❑ 8 David Robinson	5.00	2.20
❑ 9 Latrell Sprewell	6.00	2.70
❑ 10 Hakeem Olajuwon	5.00	2.20

1994-95 Finest Lottery Prize

	MINT	NRMT
COMPLETE SET (22)	50.00	22.00
COMMON CARD (1-22)	.75	.35
SEMISTARS	1.50	.70
UNLISTED STARS	2.50	1.10
SER.2 STATED ODDS 1:6		
❑ LP1 Patrick Ewing	2.50	1.10
❑ LP2 Chris Mullin	2.50	1.10
❑ LP3 David Robinson	4.00	1.80
❑ LP4 Scottie Pippen	8.00	3.60
❑ LP5 Kevin Johnson	1.50	.70
❑ LP6 Danny Manning	1.50	.70
❑ LP7 Mitch Richmond	2.50	1.10
❑ LP8 Derrick Coleman	1.50	.70
❑ LP9 Gary Payton	4.00	1.80

	MINT	NRMT
❑ LP10 Mahmoud Abdul-Rauf	.75	.35
❑ LP11 Larry Johnson	1.50	.70
❑ LP12 Kenny Anderson	1.50	.70
❑ LP13 Dikembe Mutombo	1.50	.70
❑ LP14 Stacey Augmon	.75	.35
❑ LP15 Shaquille O'Neal	12.00	5.50
❑ LP16 Alonzo Mourning	3.00	1.35
❑ LP17 Clarence Weatherspoon	.75	.35
❑ LP18 Robert Horry	.75	.35
❑ LP19 Chris Webber	8.00	3.60
❑ LP20 Anfernee Hardaway	8.00	3.60
❑ LP21 Jamal Mashburn	2.50	1.10
❑ LP22 Vin Baker	2.50	1.10

1994-95 Finest Marathon Men

	MINT	NRMT
COMPLETE SET (20)	50.00	22.00
COMMON CARD (1-20)	1.25	.55
SEMISTARS	3.00	1.35
SER.1 STATED ODDS 1:12		
❑ 1 Latrell Sprewell	10.00	4.50
❑ 2 Gary Payton	8.00	3.60
❑ 3 Kenny Anderson	3.00	1.35
❑ 4 Jim Jackson	3.00	1.35
❑ 5 Lindsey Hunter	3.00	1.35
❑ 6 Rod Strickland	3.00	1.35
❑ 7 Hersey Hawkins	3.00	1.35
❑ 8 Gerald Wilkins	1.25	.55
❑ 9 B.J. Armstrong	1.25	.55
❑ 10 Anfernee Hardaway	15.00	6.75
❑ 11 Stacey Augmon	1.25	.55
❑ 12 Eric Murdock	1.25	.55
❑ 13 Clarence Weatherspoon	1.25	.55
❑ 14 Karl Malone	8.00	3.60
❑ 15 Charles Oakley	1.25	.55
❑ 16 Rick Fox	1.25	.55
❑ 17 Otis Thorpe	1.25	.55
❑ 18 Dikembe Mutombo	3.00	1.35
❑ 19 Mike Brown	1.25	.55
❑ 20 A.C. Green	3.00	1.35

1994-95 Finest Rack Pack

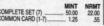

	MINT	NRMT
COMPLETE SET (7)	50.00	22.00
COMMON CARD (1-7)	1.25	.55

	MINT	NRMT
SEMISTARS	3.00	1.35
SER.2 STATED ODDS 1:72		
❑ RP1 Grant Hill	30.00	13.50
❑ RP2 Wesley Person	3.00	1.35
❑ RP3 Juwan Howard	6.00	2.70
❑ RP4 Lamond Murray	1.25	.55
❑ RP5 Glenn Robinson	8.00	3.60
❑ RP6 Donyell Marshall	3.00	1.35
❑ RP7 Jason Kidd	20.00	9.00

1995-96 Finest

	MINT	NRMT
COMPLETE SET (251)	220.00	100.00
COMP.SERIES 1 (140)	180.00	80.00
COMP.SERIES 2 (111)	40.00	18.00
COMMON CARD (1-250/252)	.30	.14
COMMON RC	1.50	.70
SEMISTARS	.60	.25
UNLISTED STARS	1.25	.55

UER CL 111 SHOULD BE NUMBERED 140
NUMBER 251 NEVER ISSUED

	MINT	NRMT
❑ 1 Hakeem Olajuwon	2.00	.90
❑ 2 Stacey Augmon	.30	.14
❑ 3 John Starks	.30	.14
❑ 4 Sharone Wright	.30	.14
❑ 5 Jason Kidd	4.00	1.80
❑ 6 Lamond Murray	.30	.14
❑ 7 Kenny Anderson	.60	.25
❑ 8 James Robinson	.30	.14
❑ 9 Wesley Person	.60	.25
❑ 10 Latrell Sprewell	2.50	1.10
❑ 11 Sean Elliott	.30	.14
❑ 12 Greg Anthony	.30	.14
❑ 13 Kendall Gill	.60	.25
❑ 14 Mark Jackson	.30	.14
❑ 15 John Stockton	1.25	.55
❑ 16 Steve Smith	.60	.25
❑ 17 Bobby Hurley	.30	.14
❑ 18 Ervin Johnson	.30	.14
❑ 19 Elden Campbell	.30	.14
❑ 20 Vin Baker	1.25	.55
❑ 21 Micheal Williams	.30	.14
❑ 22 Steve Kerr	.30	.14
❑ 23 Kevin Duckworth	.30	.14
❑ 24 Willie Anderson	.30	.14
❑ 25 Joe Dumars	1.25	.55
❑ 26 Dale Ellis	.30	.14
❑ 27 Bimbo Coles	.30	.14

❑ 28 Nick Anderson .30 .14
❑ 29 Dee Brown .30 .14
❑ 30 Tyrone Hill .30 .14
❑ 31 Reggie Miller 1.25 .55
❑ 32 Shaquille O'Neal 6.00 2.70
❑ 33 Brian Grant 1.25 .55
❑ 34 Charles Barkley 2.00 .90
❑ 35 Cedric Ceballos .30 .14
❑ 36 Rex Walters .30 .14
❑ 37 Kenny Smith .30 .14
❑ 38 Popeye Jones .30 .14
❑ 39 Harvey Grant .30 .14
❑ 40 Gary Payton 2.00 .90
❑ 41 John Williams .30 .14
❑ 42 Sherman Douglas .30 .14
❑ 43 Oliver Miller .30 .14
❑ 44 Kevin Willis .30 .14
❑ 45 Isaiah Rider .60 .25
❑ 46 Gheorghe Muresan .30 .14
❑ 47 Blue Edwards .30 .14
❑ 48 Jeff Hornacek .60 .25
❑ 49 J.R. Reid .30 .14
❑ 50 Glenn Robinson 1.25 .55
❑ 51 Dell Curry .30 .14
❑ 52 Greg Graham .30 .14
❑ 53 Ron Harper .60 .25
❑ 54 Derek Harper .30 .14
❑ 55 Dikembe Mutombo .60 .25
❑ 56 Terry Mills .30 .14
❑ 57 Victor Alexander .30 .14
❑ 58 Malik Sealy .30 .14
❑ 59 Vincent Askew .30 .14
❑ 60 Mitch Richmond 1.25 .55
❑ 61 Duane Ferrell .30 .14
❑ 62 Dickey Simpkins .30 .14
❑ 63 Pooh Richardson .30 .14
❑ 64 Khalid Reeves .30 .14
❑ 65 Dino Radja .30 .14
❑ 66 Lee Mayberry .30 .14
❑ 67 Kenny Gattison .30 .14
❑ 68 Joe Kleine .30 .14
❑ 69 Tony Dumas .30 .14
❑ 70 Nick Van Exel .60 .25
❑ 71 Armon Gilliam .30 .14
❑ 72 Craig Ehlo .30 .14
❑ 73 Adam Keefe .30 .14
❑ 74 Chris Dudley .30 .14
❑ 75 Clyde Drexler 1.25 .55
❑ 76 Jeff Turner .30 .14
❑ 77 Calbert Cheaney .30 .14
❑ 78 Vinny Del Negro .30 .14
❑ 79 Tim Perry .30 .14
❑ 80 Tim Hardaway 1.25 .55
❑ 81 B.J. Armstrong .30 .14
❑ 82 Muggsy Bogues .30 .14
❑ 83 Mark Macon .30 .14
❑ 84 Doug West .30 .14
❑ 85 Jalen Rose 1.50 .70
❑ 86 Chris Mills .30 .14
❑ 87 Charles Oakley .30 .14
❑ 88 Andrew Lang .30 .14
❑ 89 Olden Polynice .30 .14
❑ 90 Sam Cassell .60 .25
❑ 91 Todd Day .30 .14
❑ 92 P.J. Brown .30 .14
❑ 93 Benoit Benjamin .30 .14
❑ 94 Sam Perkins .60 .25
❑ 95 Eddie Jones 2.50 1.10
❑ 96 Robert Parish .60 .25
❑ 97 Avery Johnson .30 .14
❑ 98 Lindsey Hunter .30 .14
❑ 99 Billy Owens .30 .14
❑ 100 Shawn Bradley .30 .14
❑ 101 Dale Davis .30 .14
❑ 102 Terry Dehere .30 .14
❑ 103 A.C. Green .60 .25
❑ 104 Christian Laettner .60 .25
❑ 105 Horace Grant .60 .25
❑ 106 Rony Seikaly .30 .14
❑ 107 Reggie Williams .30 .14
❑ 108 Toni Kukoc 1.50 .70
❑ 109 Terrell Brandon .60 .25
❑ 110 Clifford Robinson .30 .14
❑ 111 Joe Smith RC 5.00 2.20
❑ 112 Antonio McDyess RC 8.00 3.60
❑ 113 Jerry Stackhouse RC 8.00 3.60
❑ 114 Rasheed Wallace RC 12.00 5.50
❑ 115 Kevin Garnett RC 100.00 45.00
❑ 116 Bryant Reeves RC 2.50 1.10
❑ 117 Damon Stoudamire RC 10.00 4.50
❑ 118 Shawn Respert RC 1.50 .70
❑ 119 Ed O'Bannon RC 1.50 .70
❑ 120 Kurt Thomas RC 1.50 .70
❑ 121 Gary Trent RC 4.00 1.80
❑ 122 Cherokee Parks RC 1.50 .70
❑ 123 Corliss Williamson RC 5.00 2.20
❑ 124 Eric Williams RC 2.50 1.10
❑ 125 Brent Barry RC 4.00 1.80
❑ 126 Alan Henderson RC 4.00 1.80
❑ 127 Bob Sura RC 3.00 1.35
❑ 128 Theo Ratliff RC 5.00 2.20
❑ 129 Randolph Childress RC 1.50 .70
❑ 130 Jason Caffey RC 3.00 1.35
❑ 131 Michael Finley RC 12.00 5.50
❑ 132 George Zidek RC 1.50 .70
❑ 133 Travis Best RC 1.50 .70
❑ 134 Loren Meyer RC 1.50 .70
❑ 135 David Vaughn RC 1.50 .70
❑ 136 Sherrell Ford RC 1.50 .70
❑ 137 Mario Bennett RC 1.50 .70
❑ 138 Greg Ostertag RC 1.50 .70
❑ 139 Cory Alexander RC 1.50 .70
❑ 140 Checklist UER #111 .30 .14
❑ 141 Chucky Brown .30 .14
❑ 142 Eric Mobley .30 .14
❑ 143 Tom Hammonds .30 .14
❑ 144 Chris Webber 4.00 1.80
❑ 145 Carlos Rogers .30 .14
❑ 146 Chuck Person .30 .14
❑ 147 Brian Williams .30 .14
❑ 148 Kevin Gamble .30 .14
❑ 149 Dennis Rodman 2.50 1.10
❑ 150 Pervis Ellison .30 .14
❑ 151 Jayson Williams .60 .25
❑ 152 Buck Williams .30 .14
❑ 153 Allan Houston 1.50 .70
❑ 154 Tom Gugliotta .60 .25
❑ 155 Charles Smith .30 .14
❑ 156 Chris Gatling .30 .14
❑ 157 Darrin Hancock .30 .14
❑ 158 Blue Edwards .30 .14
❑ 159 Shawn Kemp 2.00 .90
❑ 160 Michael Cage .30 .14
❑ 161 Sedale Threatt .30 .14
❑ 162 Byron Scott .30 .14
❑ 163 Elliot Perry .30 .14
❑ 164 Jim Jackson .30 .14
❑ 165 Wayman Tisdale .30 .14
❑ 166 Vernon Maxwell .30 .14
❑ 167 Brian Shaw .30 .14
❑ 168 Haywoode Workman .30 .14
❑ 169 Mookie Blaylock .30 .14
❑ 170 Donald Royal .30 .14
❑ 171 Lorenzo Williams .30 .14
❑ 172 Eric Piatkowski UER .30 .14
Name spelled Paitkowski on back
❑ 173 Sarunas Marciulionis .30 .14
❑ 174 Otis Thorpe .30 .14
❑ 175 Rex Chapman .30 .14
❑ 176 Felton Spencer .30 .14
❑ 177 John Salley .30 .14
❑ 178 Pete Chilcutt .30 .14
❑ 179 Scottie Pippen 4.00 1.80
❑ 180 Robert Pack .30 .14
❑ 181 Dana Barros .30 .14
❑ 182 Mahmoud Abdul-Rauf .30 .14
❑ 183 Eric Murdock .30 .14
❑ 184 Anthony Mason .60 .25
❑ 185 Will Perdue .30 .14
❑ 186 Jeff Malone .30 .14
❑ 187 Anthony Peeler .30 .14
❑ 188 Chris Childs .30 .14
❑ 189 Glen Rice .60 .25
❑ 190 Grant Hill 6.00 2.70
❑ 191 Michael Smith .30 .14
❑ 192 Sean Rooks .30 .14
❑ 193 Clifford Rozier .30 .14
❑ 194 Rik Smits .30 .14
❑ 195 Spud Webb .30 .14
❑ 196 Aaron McKie .30 .14
❑ 197 Nate McMillan .30 .14
❑ 198 Bobby Phills .30 .14
❑ 199 Dennis Scott .30 .14
❑ 200 Mark West .30 .14
❑ 201 George McCloud .30 .14
❑ 202 B.J. Tyler .30 .14
❑ 203 Lionel Simmons .30 .14
❑ 204 Loy Vaught .30 .14
❑ 205 Kevin Edwards .30 .14
❑ 206 Eric Montross .30 .14
❑ 207 Kenny Gattison .30 .14
❑ 208 Mario Elie .30 .14
❑ 209 Karl Malone 2.00 .90
❑ 210 Ken Norman .30 .14
❑ 211 Antonio Davis .30 .14
❑ 212 Doc Rivers .30 .14
❑ 213 Hubert Davis .30 .14
❑ 214 Jamal Mashburn .60 .25
❑ 215 Donyell Marshall .60 .25
❑ 216 Sasha Danilovic RC .30 .14
❑ 217 Danny Manning .60 .25
❑ 218 Scott Burrell .30 .14
❑ 219 Vlade Divac .30 .14
❑ 220 Marty Conlon .30 .14
❑ 221 Clarence Weatherspoon .30 .14
❑ 222 Terry Porter .30 .14
❑ 223 Luc Longley .30 .14
❑ 224 Juwan Howard 1.25 .55
❑ 225 Danny Ferry .30 .14
❑ 226 Rod Strickland .60 .25
❑ 227 Bryant Stith .30 .14
❑ 228 Derrick McKey .30 .14
❑ 229 Michael Jordan 15.00 6.75
❑ 230 Jamie Watson .30 .14
❑ 231 Rick Fox .30 .14
❑ 232 Scott Williams .30 .14
❑ 233 Larry Johnson .60 .25
❑ 234 Anfernee Hardaway 4.00 1.80
❑ 235 Hersey Hawkins .60 .25
❑ 236 Robert Horry .30 .14
❑ 237 Kevin Johnson .60 .25
❑ 238 Rodney Rogers .30 .14
❑ 239 Detlef Schrempf .60 .25
❑ 240 Derrick Coleman .60 .25
❑ 241 Walt Williams .30 .14
❑ 242 LaPhonso Ellis .30 .14
❑ 243 Patrick Ewing 1.25 .55
❑ 244 Grant Long .30 .14
❑ 245 David Robinson 2.00 .90
❑ 246 Chris Mullin 1.25 .55
❑ 247 Alonzo Mourning 1.25 .55
❑ 248 Dan Majerle .30 .14
❑ 249 Johnny Newman .30 .14
❑ 250 Chris Morris .30 .14
❑ 252 Magic Johnson 4.00 1.80

1995-96 Finest Refractors

	MINT	NRMT
COMPLETE SET (221)	1300.00	575.00
COMPLETE SERIES 1 (110)	500.00	220.00
COMPLETE SERIES 2 (111)	800.00	350.00
COMMON CARD	2.50	1.10
SEMISTARS	6.00	2.70
UNLISTED STARS	12.00	5.50

*STARS: 5X TO 10X HI COLUMN
SER.1/2 STATED ODDS: 1:12 HOB, 1:18 RET

❑ 229 Michael Jordan 200.00 90.00
❑ 252 Magic Johnson 6P 20.00 9.00

1995-96 Finest Dish and Swish

	MINT	NRMT
COMPLETE SET (29)	200.00	90.00
COMMON CARD (DS1-DS29)	2.00	.90
SEMISTARS	3.00	1.35
UNLISTED STARS	5.00	2.20

SER.1 STATED ODDS 1:24

		MINT	NRMT
❑ DS1	Mookie Blaylock / Steve Smith	2.00	.90
❑ DS2	Sherman Douglas / Dino Radja	2.00	.90
❑ DS3	Muggsy Bogues / Larry Johnson	3.00	1.35
❑ DS4	Scottie Pippen / Michael Jordan	60.00	27.00
❑ DS5	Mark Price / Chris Mills	2.00	.90
❑ DS6	Jason Kidd / Jamal Mashburn	15.00	6.75
❑ DS7	Mahmoud Abdul-Rauf / Dikembe Mutombo	2.00	.90
❑ DS8	Grant Hill / Joe Dumars	25.00	11.00
❑ DS9	Tim Hardaway / Chris Mullin	5.00	2.20
❑ DS10	Clyde Drexler / Hakeem Olajuwon	10.00	4.50
❑ DS11	Mark Jackson / Reggie Miller	5.00	2.20
❑ DS12	Pooh Richardson / Lamond Murray	2.00	.90
❑ DS13	Nick Van Exel / Cedric Ceballos	3.00	1.35
❑ DS14	Glen Rice / Khalid Reeves	5.00	2.20
❑ DS15	Glenn Robinson / Eric Murdock	5.00	2.20
❑ DS16	Tom Gugliotta / Christian Laettner	5.00	2.20
❑ DS17	Kenny Anderson / Derrick Coleman	3.00	1.35
❑ DS18	Patrick Ewing / Derek Harper	5.00	2.20
❑ DS19	Anfernee Hardaway / Shaquille O'Neal	30.00	13.50
❑ DS20	Dana Barros / Clarence Weatherspoon	2.00	.90
❑ DS21	Kevin Johnson / Charles Barkley	8.00	3.60
❑ DS22	Rod Strickland / Clifford Robinson	3.00	1.35
❑ DS23	Mitch Richmond / Walt Williams	5.00	2.20
❑ DS24	Avery Johnson / David Robinson	8.00	3.60
❑ DS25	Gary Payton / Shawn Kemp	15.00	6.75
❑ DS26	B.J.Armstrong / Oliver Miller	2.00	.90
❑ DS27	John Stockton / Karl Malone	12.00	5.50
❑ DS28	Greg Anthony / Byron Scott	2.00	.90
❑ DS29	Juwan Howard / Chris Webber	15.00	6.75

1995-96 Finest Hot Stuff

	MINT	NRMT
COMPLETE SET (15)	60.00	27.00
COMMON CARD (HS1-HS15)	1.00	.45
SEMISTARS	1.25	.55
UNLISTED STARS	2.00	.90

SER.1 STATED ODDS 1:9

		MINT	NRMT
❑ HS1	Michael Jordan	25.00	11.00
❑ HS2	Grant Hill	10.00	4.50
❑ HS3	Clyde Drexler	2.00	.90
❑ HS4	Anfernee Hardaway	6.00	2.70
❑ HS5	Sean Elliott	1.00	.45
❑ HS6	Latrell Sprewell	4.00	1.80
❑ HS7	Larry Johnson	1.25	.55
❑ HS8	Eddie Jones	4.00	1.80
❑ HS9	Karl Malone	3.00	1.35
❑ HS10	John Starks	1.00	.45
❑ HS11	Scottie Pippen	6.00	2.70
❑ HS12	Shawn Kemp	3.00	1.35
❑ HS13	Chris Webber	6.00	2.70
❑ HS14	Isaiah Rider	1.25	.55
❑ HS15	Robert Horry	1.00	.45

1995-96 Finest Mystery

	MINT	NRMT
COMPLETE SET (44)	45.00	20.00
COMP.BORDER.SER.1 (22)	30.00	13.50
COMP.BRONZE SER.2 (22)	15.00	6.75
COMMON BORDER (M1-M22)	.50	.23
COMMON BRONZE (M23-M44)	.40	.18
SEMISTARS SER.1	.60	.25
SEMISTARS SER.2	.50	.23
UNLISTED STARS SER.1	1.00	.45
UNLISTED STARS SER.2	.75	.35
COMP.BDLS/SILV.SET (44)	300.00	135.00
COMP.BDLS.SER.1 (22)	200.00	90.00
COMP.SILVER SER.2 (22)	100.00	45.00

*BDLS./SILVER: 2X TO 5X HI COLUMN
*SILVER RCs: 1.5X TO 4X HI
BDLS: SER.1 STATED ODDS 1:24
SILVER: SER.2 STATED ODDS 1:24

	MINT	NRMT
COMP.REF/GOLD SET (44)	1300.00	575.00
COMP.BDLS.REF.SER.1 (22)	1000.00	450.00
COMP.GOLD SER.2 (22)	300.00	135.00
COMMON BDLS.REF (M1-M22)	12.00	5.50
COMMON GOLD (M23-M44)	8.00	3.60

*BDLS.REF: 12.5X TO 25X HI
*GOLD STARS: 10X TO 20X HI
*GOLD RCs: 6X TO 12X HI
BDLS.REF: SER.1 STATED ODDS 1:96
GOLD: SER.2 STATED ODDS 1:96
CONDITION SENSITIVE SET

		MINT	NRMT
❑ M1	Michael Jordan	12.00	5.50
❑ M2	Grant Hill	5.00	2.20
❑ M3	Anfernee Hardaway	3.00	1.35
❑ M4	Shawn Kemp	1.50	.70
❑ M5	Kenny Anderson	.50	.23
❑ M6	Charles Barkley	1.50	.70
❑ M7	Latrell Sprewell	2.00	.90
❑ M8	Chris Webber	3.00	1.35
❑ M9	Jason Kidd	3.00	1.35
❑ M10	Glenn Robinson	1.00	.45
❑ M11	David Robinson	1.50	.70
❑ M12	Karl Malone	1.50	.70
❑ M13	Larry Johnson	.60	.25
❑ M14	Reggie Miller	1.00	.45
❑ M15	Scottie Pippen	3.00	1.35
❑ M16	Patrick Ewing	1.00	.45
❑ M17	Mitch Richmond	1.00	.45
❑ M18	Glen Rice	.60	.25
❑ M19	Jamal Mashburn	.60	.25
❑ M20	Juwan Howard	1.00	.45
❑ M21	Hakeem Olajuwon	1.50	.70
❑ M22	Shaquille O'Neal	5.00	2.20
❑ M23	Alonzo Mourning	.75	.35
❑ M24	Dennis Rodman	2.00	.90
❑ M25	Joe Dumars	.75	.35
❑ M26	Tim Hardaway	.75	.35
❑ M27	Clyde Drexler	.75	.35
❑ M28	Jerry Stackhouse	2.00	.90
❑ M29	John Stockton	.75	.35
❑ M30	Derrick Coleman	.50	.23
❑ M31	Michael Finley	2.50	1.10
❑ M32	Glen Rice	.50	.23
❑ M33	Mahmoud Abdul-Rauf	.40	.18
❑ M34	Anthony Mason	.50	.23
❑ M35	Nick Van Exel	.50	.23
❑ M36	Vin Baker	.75	.35
❑ M37	Horace Grant	.50	.23
❑ M38	John Starks	.40	.18
❑ M39	Clarence Weatherspoon	.40	.18
❑ M40	Kevin Johnson	.50	.23
❑ M41	Joe Smith	2.00	.90
❑ M42	Dikembe Mutombo	.50	.23
❑ M43	Damon Stoudamire	3.00	1.35
❑ M44	Antonio McDyess	3.00	1.35

1995-96 Finest Rack Pack

	MINT	NRMT
COMPLETE SET (7)	60.00	27.00
COMMON CARD (RP1-RP7)	4.00	1.80

SER.2 STATED ODDS 1:72 HOB, 1:96 RET

		MINT	NRMT
❑ RP1	Jerry Stackhouse	10.00	4.50
❑ RP2	Brent Barry	4.00	1.80
❑ RP3	Damon Stoudamire	15.00	6.75
❑ RP4	Joe Smith	10.00	4.50
❑ RP5	Michael Finley	12.00	5.50
❑ RP6	Antonio McDyess	15.00	6.75
❑ RP7	Rasheed Wallace	12.00	5.50

1995-96 Finest Veteran/Rookie

	MINT	NRMT
COMPLETE SET (29)	250.00	110.00
COMMON CARD (RV1-RV29)	2.00	.90
SEMISTARS	3.00	1.35
UNLISTED STARS	5.00	2.20

SER.2 STATED ODDS 1:24 HOB, 1:18 RET

		MINT	NRMT
❑ RV1	Joe Smith Latrell Sprewell	20.00	9.00
❑ RV2	Antonio McDyess Dikembe Mutombo	15.00	6.75
❑ RV3	Jerry Stackhouse Clarence Weatherspoon	10.00	4.50
❑ RV4	Rasheed Wallace Chris Webber	25.00	11.00
❑ RV5	Kevin Garnett Tim Gugliotta	40.00	18.00
❑ RV6	Bryant Reeves Greg Anthony	5.00	2.20
❑ RV7	Damon Stoudamire Willie Anderson	12.00	5.50
❑ RV8	Shawn Respert Vin Baker	10.00	4.50
❑ RV9	Ed O'Bannon Armon Gilliam	2.00	.90
❑ RV10	Kurt Thomas Alonzo Mourning	5.00	2.20
❑ RV11	Gary Trent Rod Strickland	3.00	1.35
❑ RV12	Cherokee Parks Jamal Mashburn	3.00	1.35
❑ RV13	Corliss Williamson Mitch Richmond	5.00	2.20
❑ RV14	Eric Williams Dino Radja	2.00	.90
❑ RV15	Brent Barry Loy Vaught	3.00	1.35
❑ RV16	Alan Henderson Mookie Blaylock	3.00	1.35
❑ RV17	Bob Sura Terrell Brandon	3.00	1.35
❑ RV18	Theo Ratliff Grant Hill	25.00	11.00
❑ RV19	Randolph Childress Rod Strickland	3.00	1.35
❑ RV20	Jason Caffey Michael Jordan	50.00	22.00
❑ RV21	Michael Finley Kevin Johnson	12.00	5.50
❑ RV22	George Zidek Larry Johnson	3.00	1.35
❑ RV23	Travis Best Reggie Miller	5.00	2.20
❑ RV24	Loren Meyer Jason Kidd	12.00	5.50
❑ RV25	David Vaughn Shaquille O'Neal	25.00	11.00
❑ RV26	Sherell Ford Shawn Kemp	8.00	3.60
❑ RV27	Mario Bennett Charles Barkley	10.00	4.50
❑ RV28	Greg Ostertag Karl Malone	10.00	4.50
❑ RV29	Cory Alexander David Robinson	8.00	3.60

1996-97 Finest

	MINT	NRMT
COMPLETE SET (291)	800.00	350.00
COMPLETE SERIES 1 (146)	400.00	180.00
COMPLETE SERIES 2 (145)	400.00	180.00
COMP.BRONZE SET (200)	150.00	70.00
COMP.BRONZE SER.1 (100)	120.00	55.00
COMP.BRONZE SER.2 (100)	40.00	18.00
COMMON BRONZE	.30	.14
COMMON BRONZE RC	1.50	.70
SEMISTARS BRONZE	.40	.18
SEMISTARS BRONZE RC	2.00	.90
UNLISTED STARS BRONZE	.60	.25
UNLISTED STARS BRONZE RC	3.00	1.35
COMP.SILVER SET (54)	120.00	55.00
COMP.SILVER SER.1 (27)	40.00	18.00
COMP.SILVER SER.2 (27)	80.00	36.00
COMMON SILVER	1.00	.45
SEMISTARS SILVER	1.25	.55
UNLISTED STARS SILVER	2.00	.90
SILVER: SER.1/2 STATED ODDS 1:4		
COMP.GOLD SET (37)	550.00	250.00
COMP.GOLD SER.1 (19)	250.00	110.00
COMP.GOLD SER.2 (18)	300.00	135.00
COMMON GOLD	4.00	1.80
SEMISTARS GOLD	5.00	2.20
UNLISTED STARS GOLD	6.00	2.70

GOLD: SER.1/2 STATED ODDS 1:24
CARD NUMBERS 7 AND 134 DO NOT EXIST
LAETTNER B, EWING G AND HORNACEK G NUMBERED 136
NUMBER 269 PART OF GOLD SET
NUMBER 289 PART OF SILVER SET
CONDITION SENSITIVE SET

		MINT	NRMT
❑ 1	Scottie Pippen B	2.00	.90
❑ 2	Tim Legler B	.30	.14
❑ 3	Rex Walters B	.30	.14
❑ 4	Calbert Cheaney B	.30	.14
❑ 5	Dennis Rodman B	1.25	.55
❑ 6	Tyrone Hill B	.30	.14
❑ 8	Dell Curry B	.30	.14
❑ 9	Olden Polynice B	.30	.14
❑ 10	John Wallace B RC	2.00	.90
❑ 11	Martin Muursepp B RC	1.50	.70
❑ 12	Chuck Person B	.30	.14
❑ 13	Grant Hill B	3.00	1.35
❑ 14	Shawn Kemp B	1.00	.45
❑ 15	B.J. Armstrong B	.30	.14
❑ 16	Gary Trent B	.30	.14
❑ 17	Scott Williams B	.30	.14
❑ 18	Dino Radja B	.30	.14
❑ 19	Roy Rogers B RC	1.50	.70
❑ 20	Tony Delk B RC	2.00	.90
❑ 21	Clifford Robinson B	.30	.14
❑ 22	Ray Allen B RC	6.00	2.70
❑ 23	Clyde Drexler B	.60	.25
❑ 24	Elliot Perry B	.30	.14
❑ 25	Gary Payton B	1.00	.45
❑ 26	Dale Davis B	.30	.14
❑ 27	Horace Grant B	.40	.18
❑ 28	Brian Evans B RC	1.50	.70
❑ 29	Joe Smith B	.60	.25
❑ 30	Reggie Miller B	.60	.25
❑ 31	Jermaine O'Neal B RC	4.00	1.80
❑ 32	Avery Johnson B	.30	.14
❑ 33	Ed O'Bannon B	.30	.14
❑ 34	Cedric Ceballos B	.30	.14
❑ 35	Jamal Mashburn B	.40	.18
❑ 36	Michael Williams B	.30	.14
❑ 37	Detlef Schrempf B	.40	.18
❑ 38	Damon Stoudamire B	1.00	.45
❑ 39	Jason Kidd B	2.00	.90
❑ 40	Tom Gugliotta B	.40	.18
❑ 41	Arvydas Sabonis B	.40	.18
❑ 42	Samaki Walker B RC	1.50	.70
❑ 43	Derek Fisher B RC	4.00	1.80
❑ 44	Patrick Ewing B	.60	.25
❑ 45	Bryant Reeves B	.30	.14
❑ 46	Mookie Blaylock B	.30	.14
❑ 47	George Zidek B	.30	.14
❑ 48	Jerry Stackhouse B	.60	.25
❑ 49	Vin Baker B	.40	.18
❑ 50	Michael Jordan B	8.00	3.60
❑ 51	Terrell Brandon B	.40	.18
❑ 52	Karl Malone B	1.00	.45
❑ 53	Lorenzen Wright B RC	1.50	.70
❑ 54	S. Abdur-Rahim B RC	10.00	4.50
❑ 55	Kurt Thomas B	.30	.14
❑ 56	Glen Rice B	.40	.18
❑ 57	Shawn Bradley B	.30	.14
❑ 58	Todd Fuller B RC	1.50	.70
❑ 59	Dale Ellis B	.30	.14
❑ 60	David Robinson B	1.00	.45
❑ 61	Doug Christie B	.30	.14
❑ 62	Stephon Marbury B RC	10.00	4.50
❑ 63	Hakeem Olajuwon B	1.00	.45
❑ 64	Lindsey Hunter B	.30	.14
❑ 65	Anfernee Hardaway B	2.00	.90
❑ 66	Kevin Garnett B	4.00	1.80
❑ 67	Kendall Gill B	.40	.18
❑ 68	Sean Elliott B	.30	.14
❑ 69	Allen Iverson B RC	15.00	6.75
❑ 70	Erick Dampier B RC	1.50	.70
❑ 71	Jerome Williams B RC	4.00	1.80
❑ 72	Charles Jones B	.30	.14
❑ 73	Danny Manning B	.40	.18
❑ 74	Kobe Bryant B RC	80.00	36.00
❑ 75	Steve Nash B RC	2.00	.90
❑ 76	Sam Perkins B	.40	.18
❑ 77	Horace Grant B	.40	.18
❑ 78	Alonzo Mourning B	.60	.25
❑ 79	Kerry Kittles B RC	4.00	1.80
❑ 80	LaPhonso Ellis B	.30	.14
❑ 81	Michael Finley B	.75	.35
❑ 82	Marcus Camby B RC	5.00	2.20
❑ 83	Antonio McDyess B	1.00	.45
❑ 84	Antoine Walker B RC	6.00	2.70
❑ 85	Juwan Howard B	.40	.18
❑ 86	Bryon Russell B	.30	.14
❑ 87	Walter McCarty B RC	1.50	.70
❑ 88	Priest Lauderdale B RC	1.50	.70
❑ 89	Clarence Weatherspoon B	.30	.14
❑ 90	John Stockton B	.60	.25
❑ 91	Mitch Richmond B	.60	.25
❑ 92	Dontae' Jones B RC	1.50	.70
❑ 93	Michael Smith B	.30	.14
❑ 94	Brent Barry B	.30	.14
❑ 95	Chris Mills B	.30	.14
❑ 96	Dee Brown B	.30	.14
❑ 97	Terry Dehere B	.30	.14
❑ 98	Danny Ferry B	.30	.14
❑ 99	Gheorghe Muresan B	.30	.14
❑ 100	Checklist B	.30	.14
❑ 101	Jim Jackson S	1.00	.45
❑ 102	Cedric Ceballos S	1.00	.45
❑ 103	Glen Rice S	1.25	.55
❑ 104	Tom Gugliotta S	1.25	.55
❑ 105	Mario Elie S	1.00	.45
❑ 106	Nick Anderson S	1.00	.45
❑ 107	Glenn Robinson S	1.25	.55
❑ 108	Terrell Brandon S	1.25	.55
❑ 109	Tim Hardaway S	2.00	.90
❑ 110	John Stockton S	2.00	.90
❑ 111	Brent Barry S	1.00	.45
❑ 112	Mookie Blaylock S	1.00	.45
❑ 113	Tyus Edney S	1.00	.45
❑ 114	Gary Payton S	3.00	1.35
❑ 115	Joe Smith S	2.00	.90
❑ 116	Karl Malone S	3.00	1.35
❑ 117	Dino Radja S	1.00	.45
❑ 118	Alonzo Mourning S	2.00	.90
❑ 119	Bryant Stith S	1.00	.45

❑ 120 Derrick McKey S	1.00	.45
❑ 121 Clyde Drexler S	2.00	.90
❑ 122 Michael Finley S	2.50	1.10
❑ 123 Sean Elliott S	1.00	.45
❑ 124 Hakeem Olajuwon S	3.00	1.35
❑ 125 Joe Dumars S	2.00	.90
❑ 126 Shawn Bradley S	1.00	.45
❑ 127 Michael Jordan S	25.00	11.00
❑ 128 Latrell Sprewell G	12.00	5.50
❑ 129 Anfernee Hardaway G	20.00	9.00
❑ 130 Grant Hill G	30.00	13.50
❑ 131 Damon Stoudamire G	10.00	4.50
❑ 132 David Robinson G	10.00	4.50
❑ 133 Scottie Pippen G	20.00	9.00
❑ 135 Jason Kidd G	20.00	9.00
❑ 136A Jeff Hornacek G	4.00	1.80
❑ 136B Patrick Ewing G UER Should be card number 134	6.00	2.70
❑ 136C C. Laettner B UER Should be card number 7	5.00	2.20
❑ 137 Jerry Stackhouse G	6.00	2.70
❑ 138 Kevin Garnett G	40.00	18.00
❑ 139 Mitch Richmond G	6.00	2.70
❑ 140 Juwan Howard G	5.00	2.20
❑ 141 Reggie Miller G	6.00	2.70
❑ 142 Christian Laettner G	5.00	2.20
❑ 143 Vin Baker G	5.00	2.20
❑ 144 Shawn Kemp G	10.00	4.50
❑ 145 Dennis Rodman G	12.00	5.50
❑ 146 Shaquille O'Neal G	30.00	13.50
❑ 147 Mookie Blaylock B	.30	.14
❑ 148 Derek Harper B	.30	.14
❑ 149 Gerald Wilkins B	.30	.14
❑ 150 Adam Keefe B	.30	.14
❑ 151 Billy Owens B	.30	.14
❑ 152 Terrell Brandon B	.40	.18
❑ 153 Antonio Davis B	.30	.14
❑ 154 Muggsy Bogues B	.30	.14
❑ 155 Cherokee Parks B	.30	.14
❑ 156 Rasheed Wallace B	.75	.35
❑ 157 Lee Mayberry B	.30	.14
❑ 158 Craig Ehlo B	.30	.14
❑ 159 Todd Fuller B	.30	.14
❑ 160 Charles Barkley B	1.00	.45
❑ 161 Glenn Robinson B	.60	.25
❑ 162 Charles Oakley B	.30	.14
❑ 163 Chris Webber B	2.00	.90
❑ 164 Frank Brickowski B	.30	.14
❑ 165 Mark Jackson B	.30	.14
❑ 166 Jayson Williams B	.40	.18
❑ 167 C. Weatherspoon B	.30	.14
❑ 168 Toni Kukoc B	.75	.35
❑ 169 Alan Henderson B	.30	.14
❑ 170 Tony Delk B	.30	.14
❑ 171 Jamal Mashburn B	.40	.18
❑ 172 Vinny Del Negro B	.30	.14
❑ 173 Greg Ostertag B	.30	.14
❑ 174 Shawn Bradley B	.30	.14
❑ 175 Gheorghe Muresan B	.30	.14
❑ 176 Brent Price B	.30	.14
❑ 177 Rick Fox B	.30	.14
❑ 178 Stacey Augmon B	.30	.14
❑ 179 P.J. Brown B	.30	.14
❑ 180 Jim Jackson B	.30	.14
❑ 181 Hersey Hawkins B	.40	.18
❑ 182 Danny Manning B	.40	.18
❑ 183 Dennis Scott B	.30	.14
❑ 184 Tom Gugliotta B	.40	.18
❑ 185 Tyrone Hill B	.30	.14
❑ 186 Malik Sealy B	.30	.14
❑ 187 John Starks B	.30	.14
❑ 188 Mark Price B	.30	.14
❑ 189 Elden Campbell B	.30	.14
❑ 190 Mahmoud Abdul-Rauf B	.30	.14
❑ 191 Will Perdue B	.30	.14
❑ 192 Nate McMillan B	.30	.14
❑ 193 Robert Horry B	.30	.14
❑ 194 Dino Radja B	.30	.14
❑ 195 Loy Vaught B	.30	.14
❑ 196 Dikembe Mutombo B	.40	.18
❑ 197 Eric Montross B	.30	.14
❑ 198 Sasha Danilovic B	.30	.14
❑ 199 Kenny Anderson B	.40	.18
❑ 200 Sean Elliott B	.30	.14
❑ 201 Mark West B	.30	.14
❑ 202 Vlade Divac B	.30	.14
❑ 203 Joe Dumars B	.60	.25
❑ 204 Allan Houston B	.60	.25
❑ 205 Kevin Garnett B	4.00	1.80
❑ 206 Rod Strickland B	.40	.18
❑ 207 Robert Parish B	.40	.18
❑ 208 Jalen Rose B	.60	.25
❑ 209 Armon Gilliam B	.30	.14
❑ 210 Kerry Kittles B	1.50	.70
❑ 211 Derrick Coleman B	.40	.18
❑ 212 Greg Anthony B	.30	.14
❑ 213 Joe Smith B	.60	.25
❑ 214 Steve Smith B	.40	.18
❑ 215 Tim Hardaway B	.60	.25
❑ 216 Tyus Edney B	.30	.14
❑ 217 Steve Nash B	.30	.14
❑ 218 Anthony Mason B	.40	.18
❑ 219 Otis Thorpe B	.30	.14
❑ 220 Eddie Jones B	1.25	.55
❑ 221 Rik Smits B	.30	.14
❑ 222 Isaiah Rider B	.40	.18
❑ 223 Bobby Phills B	.30	.14
❑ 224 Antoine Walker B	.60	.25
❑ 225 Rod Strickland B	.40	.18
❑ 226 Hubert Davis B	.30	.14
❑ 227 Eric Williams B	.30	.14
❑ 228 Danny Manning B	.40	.18
❑ 229 Dominique Wilkins B	.60	.25
❑ 230 Brian Shaw B	.30	.14
❑ 231 Larry Johnson B	.40	.18
❑ 232 Kevin Willis B	.30	.14
❑ 233 Bryant Stith B	.30	.14
❑ 234 Blue Edwards B	.30	.14
❑ 235 Robert Pack B	.30	.14
❑ 236 Brian Grant B	.60	.25
❑ 237 Latrell Sprewell B	1.25	.55
❑ 238 Glen Rice B	.40	.18
❑ 239 Jerome Williams B	.60	.25
❑ 240 Allen Iverson B	6.00	2.70
❑ 241 Popeye Jones B	.30	.14
❑ 242 Clifford Robinson B	.30	.14
❑ 243 Shaquille O'Neal B	4.00	1.80
❑ 244 Vitaly Potapenko B RC	1.50	.70
❑ 245 Ervin Johnson B	.30	.14
❑ 246 Checklist	.30	.14
❑ 247 Scottie Pippen S	6.00	2.70
❑ 248 Jason Kidd S	6.00	2.70
❑ 249 Antonio McDyess S	3.00	1.35
❑ 250 Latrell Sprewell S	4.00	1.80
❑ 251 Lorenzen Wright S	1.00	.45
❑ 252 Ray Allen S	5.00	2.20
❑ 253 Stephon Marbury S	8.00	3.60
❑ 254 Patrick Ewing S	2.00	.90
❑ 255 Anfernee Hardaway S	6.00	2.70
❑ 256 Kenny Anderson S	1.25	.55
❑ 257 David Robinson S	3.00	1.35
❑ 258 Marcus Camby S	4.00	1.80
❑ 259 Shareef Abdur-Rahim S	8.00	3.60
❑ 260 Dennis Rodman S	4.00	1.80
❑ 261 Juwan Howard S	1.25	.55
❑ 262 Damon Stoudamire S	3.00	1.35
❑ 263 Shawn Kemp S	3.00	1.35
❑ 264 Mitch Richmond S	2.00	.90
❑ 265 Jerry Stackhouse S	2.00	.90
❑ 266 Horace Grant S	1.25	.55
❑ 267 Kerry Kittles S	2.50	1.10
❑ 268 Vin Baker S	1.25	.55
❑ 269 Kobe Bryant G	120.00	55.00
❑ 270 Reggie Miller S	2.00	.90
❑ 271 Grant Hill S	10.00	4.50
❑ 272 Oliver Miller S	1.00	.45
❑ 273 Chris Webber S	6.00	2.70
❑ 274 Dikembe Mutombo G	5.00	2.20
❑ 275 Antonio McDyess G	10.00	4.50
❑ 276 Clyde Drexler G	6.00	2.70
❑ 277 Brent Barry G	4.00	1.80
❑ 278 Tim Hardaway G	6.00	2.70
❑ 279 Glenn Robinson G	5.00	2.20
❑ 280 Allen Iverson G	40.00	18.00
❑ 281 Hakeem Olajuwon G	10.00	4.50
❑ 282 Marcus Camby G	12.00	5.50
❑ 283 John Stockton G	6.00	2.70
❑ 284 Shareef Abdur-Rahim G	25.00	11.00
❑ 285 Karl Malone G	10.00	4.50
❑ 286 Gary Payton G	10.00	4.50
❑ 287 Stephon Marbury G	25.00	11.00
❑ 288 Alonzo Mourning G	6.00	2.70
❑ 289 Shaquille O'Neal S	10.00	4.50
❑ 290 Charles Barkley G	10.00	4.50
❑ 291 Michael Jordan G	80.00	36.00

1996-97 Finest Refractors

	MINT	NRMT
COMPLETE SET (291)	3200.00	1450.00
COMP.SERIES 1 (146)	1800.00	800.00
COMP.SERIES 2 (145)	1400.00	650.00
COMP.BRNZ.SET (200)	1300.00	575.00
COMP.BRNZ.SER.1 (100)	1000.00	450.00
COMP.BRNZ.SER.2 (100)	300.00	135.00
COMMON BRONZE	2.50	1.10
SEMISTARS BRONZE	4.00	1.80
UNLISTED STARS BRONZE	8.00	3.60

*BRONZE STARS: 5X TO 12X BASIC CARDS
*BRONZE RCs: 2.5X TO 6X HI
*BRONZE SER.2 RCs: 3X TO 8X HI
BRONZE: SER.1/2 STATED ODDS 1:12

COMP.SILVER SET (54)	650.00	300.00
COMP.SILVER SER.1 (27)	200.00	90.00
COMP.SILVER SER.2 (27)	300.00	135.00
COMMON SILVER	4.00	1.80
SEMISTARS SILVER	5.00	2.20
UNLISTED STARS SILVER	8.00	3.60

*SILVER STARS: 1.5X TO 4X BASIC CARDS
*SILVER RCs: 1.25X TO 3X BASIC CARDS
SILVER: SER.1/2 STATED ODDS 1:48

COMP.GOLD SET (37)	1400.00	650.00
COMP.GOLD SER.1 (19)	600.00	275.00
COMP.GOLD SER.2 (18)	800.00	350.00
COMMON GOLD	12.00	5.50
SEMISTARS GOLD	15.00	6.75
UNLISTED STARS GOLD	20.00	9.00

*GOLD STARS/RCs: 1X TO 2.5X BASIC CARDS
GOLD: SER.1/2 STATED ODDS 1:288
CARD NUMBERS 7 AND 134 DO NOT EXIST
LAETTNER B, EWING G AND HORNACEK G NUMBERED 136
NUMBER 269 PART OF GOLD SET
NUMBER 289 PART OF SILVER SET
CONDITION SENSITIVE SET

❑ 22 Ray Allen B	40.00	18.00
❑ 54 Shareef Abdur-Rahim B	50.00	22.00
❑ 62 Stephon Marbury B	60.00	27.00
❑ 69 Allen Iverson B	120.00	55.00
❑ 74 Kobe Bryant B	300.00	135.00
❑ 82 Marcus Camby B	30.00	13.50
❑ 84 Antoine Walker B	40.00	18.00

1997-98 Finest

	MINT	NRMT
COMPLETE SET (326)	850.00	375.00
COMPLETE SERIES 1 (173)	350.00	160.00
COMPLETE SERIES 2 (153)	500.00	220.00
COMP.BRONZE SET (220)	130.00	57.50
COMP.BRONZE SER.1 (120)	80.00	36.00
COMP.BRONZE SER.2 (100)	50.00	22.00
COMMON BRONZE	.25	.11
COMMON BRONZE RC	.75	.35
SEMISTARS BRONZE	.30	.14
SEMISTARS BRONZE RC	1.00	.45
UNLISTED STARS BRONZE	.50	.23
UNLISTED STARS BRONZE RC	1.50	.70

COMP.SILVER SET (66) 150.00 70.00
COMP.SILVER SER.1 (33) 80.00 36.00
COMP.SILVER SER.2 (33) 60.00 27.00
COMMON SILVER .60 .25
SEMISTARS SILVER 1.00 .45
UNLISTED STARS SILVER 1.50 .70
SILVER: SER.1/2 STATED ODDS 1:4
COMP.GOLD SET (40) 600.00 275.00
COMP.GOLD SER.1 (20) 200.00 90.00
COMP.GOLD SER.2 (20) 400.00 180.00
COMMON GOLD 3.00 1.35
SEMISTARS GOLD 4.00 1.80
UNLISTED STARS GOLD 6.00 2.70
GOLD: SER.1/2 STATED ODDS 1:24

❑ 1 Scottie Pippen B 1.50 .70
❑ 2 Tim Hardaway B .50 .23
❑ 3 Charles Outlaw B .25 .11
❑ 4 Rik Smits B .25 .11
❑ 5 Dale Ellis B .25 .11
❑ 6 Clyde Drexler B .50 .23
❑ 7 Steve Smith B .30 .14
❑ 8 Nick Anderson B .25 .11
❑ 9 Juwan Howard B .30 .14
❑ 10 Cedric Ceballos B .25 .11
❑ 11 Shawn Bradley B .25 .11
❑ 12 Loy Vaught B .25 .11
❑ 13 Todd Day B .25 .11
❑ 14 Glen Rice B .30 .14
❑ 15 Bryant Stith B .25 .11
❑ 16 Bob Sura B .25 .11
❑ 17 Derrick McKey B .25 .11
❑ 18 Ray Allen B .75 .35
❑ 19 Stephon Marbury B 1.50 .70
❑ 20 David Robinson B .75 .35
❑ 21 Anthony Peeler B .25 .11
❑ 22 Isaiah Rider B .30 .14
❑ 23 Mookie Blaylock B .25 .11
❑ 24 Damon Stoudamire B .60 .25
❑ 25 Rod Strickland B .30 .14
❑ 26 Glenn Robinson B .30 .14
❑ 27 Chris Webber B 1.50 .70
❑ 28 Christian Laettner B .30 .14
❑ 29 Joe Dumars B .50 .23
❑ 30 Mark Price B .25 .11
❑ 31 Jamal Mashburn B .30 .14
❑ 32 Danny Manning B .30 .14
❑ 33 John Stockton B .50 .23
❑ 34 Detlef Schrempf B .30 .14
❑ 35 Tyus Edney B .25 .11
❑ 36 Chris Childs B .25 .11
❑ 37 Dana Barros B .25 .11
❑ 38 Bobby Phills B .25 .11
❑ 39 Michael Jordan B 6.00 2.70
❑ 40 Grant Hill B 2.50 1.10
❑ 41 Brent Barry B .25 .11
❑ 42 Rony Seikaly B .25 .11
❑ 43 Shareef Abdur-Rahim B 1.50 .70
❑ 44 Dominique Wilkins B .50 .23
❑ 45 Vin Baker B .30 .14
❑ 46 Kendall Gill B .30 .14
❑ 47 Muggsy Bogues B .25 .11
❑ 48 Hakeem Olajuwon B .75 .35
❑ 49 Reggie Miller B .50 .23
❑ 50 Shaquille O'Neal B 2.50 1.10
❑ 51 Antonio McDyess B .60 .25
❑ 52 Michael Finley B .50 .23
❑ 53 Jerry Stackhouse B .30 .14
❑ 54 Brian Grant B .30 .14
❑ 55 Greg Anthony B .25 .11
❑ 56 Patrick Ewing B .50 .23
❑ 57 Allen Iverson B 2.50 1.10
❑ 58 Rasheed Wallace B .50 .23
❑ 59 Shawn Kemp B .75 .35
❑ 60 Bryant Reeves B .25 .11
❑ 61 Kevin Garnett B 3.00 1.35
❑ 62 Allan Houston B .50 .23
❑ 63 Stacey Augmon B .25 .11
❑ 64 Rick Fox B .25 .11
❑ 65 Derek Harper B .25 .11
❑ 66 Lindsey Hunter B .25 .11
❑ 67 Eddie Jones B 1.00 .45
❑ 68 Joe Smith B .30 .14
❑ 69 Alonzo Mourning B .50 .23
❑ 70 LaPhonso Ellis B .25 .11
❑ 71 Tyrone Hill B .25 .11
❑ 72 Charles Barkley B .75 .35
❑ 73 Malik Sealy B .25 .11
❑ 74 Shandon Anderson B .25 .11
❑ 75 Arvydas Sabonis B .30 .14
❑ 76 Tom Gugliotta B .30 .14
❑ 77 Anfernee Hardaway B 1.50 .70
❑ 78 Sean Elliott B .25 .11
❑ 79 Marcus Camby B .60 .25
❑ 80 Gary Payton B .75 .35
❑ 81 Kerry Kittles B .50 .23
❑ 82 Dikembe Mutombo B .30 .14
❑ 83 Antoine Walker B 1.00 .45
❑ 84 Terrell Brandon B .30 .14
❑ 85 Otis Thorpe B .25 .11
❑ 86 Mark Jackson B .25 .11
❑ 87 A.C. Green B .30 .14
❑ 88 John Starks B .25 .11
❑ 89 Kenny Anderson B .30 .14
❑ 90 Karl Malone B .75 .35
❑ 91 Mitch Richmond B .50 .23
❑ 92 Derrick Coleman B .30 .14
❑ 93 Horace Grant B .30 .14
❑ 94 John Williams B .25 .11
❑ 95 Jason Kidd B 1.50 .70
❑ 96 Mahmoud Abdul-Rauf B .25 .11
❑ 97 Walt Williams B .25 .11
❑ 98 Anthony Mason B .30 .14
❑ 99 Latrell Sprewell B 1.00 .45
❑ 100 Checklist .25 .11
❑ 101 Tim Duncan B RC 25.00 11.00
❑ 102 Keith Van Horn B RC 6.00 2.70
❑ 103 Chauncey Billups B RC 2.00 .90
❑ 104 Antonio Daniels B RC 1.50 .70
❑ 105 Tony Battie B RC 1.50 .70
❑ 106 Tim Thomas B RC 5.00 2.20
❑ 107 Tracy McGrady B RC 20.00 9.00
❑ 108 Adonal Foyle B RC 1.00 .45
❑ 109 Maurice Taylor B RC 3.00 1.35
❑ 110 Austin Croshere B RC 4.00 1.80
❑ 111 Bobby Jackson B RC 1.00 .45
❑ 112 Olivier Saint-Jean B RC .75 .35
❑ 113 John Thomas B RC .75 .35
❑ 114 Derek Anderson B RC 4.00 1.80
❑ 115 Brevin Knight B RC 2.50 1.10
❑ 116 Charles Smith B RC .75 .35
❑ 117 Johnny Taylor B RC .75 .35
❑ 118 Jacque Vaughn B RC 1.00 .45
❑ 119 Anthony Parker B RC .75 .35
❑ 120 Paul Grant B RC .75 .35
❑ 121 Stephon Marbury S 5.00 2.20
❑ 122 Terrell Brandon S 1.00 .45
❑ 123 Dikembe Mutombo S 1.00 .45
❑ 124 Patrick Ewing S 1.50 .70
❑ 125 Scottie Pippen S 5.00 2.20
❑ 126 Antoine Walker S 3.00 1.35
❑ 127 Karl Malone S 2.50 1.10
❑ 128 Sean Elliott S .60 .25
❑ 129 Chris Webber S 5.00 2.20
❑ 130 Shawn Kemp S 2.50 1.10
❑ 131 Hakeem Olajuwon S 2.50 1.10
❑ 132 Tim Hardaway S 1.50 .70
❑ 133 Glen Rice S 1.00 .45
❑ 134 Vin Baker S 1.00 .45
❑ 135 Jim Jackson S .60 .25
❑ 136 Kevin Garnett S 10.00 4.50
❑ 137 Kobe Bryant S 15.00 6.75
❑ 138 Damon Stoudamire S 2.00 .90
❑ 139 Larry Johnson S 1.00 .45
❑ 140 Latrell Sprewell S 3.00 1.35
❑ 141 Lorenzen Wright S .60 .25
❑ 142 Toni Kukoc S 2.00 .90
❑ 143 Allen Iverson S 8.00 3.60
❑ 144 Elden Campbell S .60 .25
❑ 145 Tom Gugliotta S 1.00 .45
❑ 146 David Robinson S 2.50 1.10
❑ 147 Jayson Williams S 1.00 .45
❑ 148 Shaquille O'Neal S 8.00 3.60
❑ 149 Grant Hill S 8.00 3.60
❑ 150 Reggie Miller S 1.50 .70
❑ 151 Clyde Drexler S 1.50 .70
❑ 152 Ray Allen S 2.50 1.10
❑ 153 Eddie Jones S 3.00 1.35
❑ 154 Michael Jordan G 80.00 36.00
❑ 155 Dominique Wilkins G 6.00 2.70
❑ 156 Charles Barkley G 10.00 4.50
❑ 157 Jerry Stackhouse G 4.00 1.80
❑ 158 Juwan Howard G 4.00 1.80
❑ 159 Marcus Camby G 8.00 3.60
❑ 160 Christian Laettner G 4.00 1.80
❑ 161 Anthony Mason G 4.00 1.80
❑ 162 Joe Smith G 4.00 1.80
❑ 163 Kerry Kittles G 6.00 2.70
❑ 164 Mitch Richmond G 6.00 2.70
❑ 165 Shareef Abdur-Rahim G 20.00 9.00
❑ 166 Alonzo Mourning G 6.00 2.70
❑ 167 Dennis Rodman G 12.00 5.50
❑ 168 Antonio McDyess G 8.00 3.60
❑ 169 Shawn Bradley G 3.00 1.35
❑ 170 Anfernee Hardaway G 20.00 9.00
❑ 171 Jason Kidd G 20.00 9.00
❑ 172 Gary Payton G 10.00 4.50
❑ 173 John Stockton G 6.00 2.70
❑ 174 Allan Houston B .50 .23
❑ 175 Bob Sura B .25 .11
❑ 176 Clyde Drexler B .50 .23
❑ 177 Glenn Robinson B .30 .14
❑ 178 Joe Smith B .30 .14
❑ 179 Larry Johnson B .30 .14
❑ 180 Mitch Richmond B .50 .23
❑ 181 Rony Seikaly B .25 .11
❑ 182 Tyrone Hill B .25 .11
❑ 183 Allen Iverson B 2.50 1.10
❑ 184 Brent Barry B .25 .11
❑ 185 Damon Stoudamire B .60 .25
❑ 186 Grant Hill B 2.50 1.10
❑ 187 John Stockton B .50 .23
❑ 188 Latrell Sprewell B 1.00 .45
❑ 189 Mookie Blaylock B .25 .11
❑ 190 Samaki Walker B .25 .11
❑ 191 Vin Baker B .30 .14
❑ 192 Alonzo Mourning B .50 .23
❑ 193 Brevin Knight B .50 .23
❑ 194 Danny Manning B .30 .14
❑ 195 Hakeem Olajuwon B .75 .35
❑ 196 Johnny Taylor B .25 .11
❑ 197 Lorenzen Wright B .25 .11
❑ 198 Olden Polynice B .25 .11
❑ 199 Scottie Pippen B 1.50 .70
❑ 200 Lindsey Hunter B .25 .11
❑ 201 Anfernee Hardaway B 1.50 .70
❑ 202 Greg Anthony B .25 .11
❑ 203 David Robinson B .75 .35
❑ 204 Horace Grant B .30 .14
❑ 205 Calbert Cheaney B .25 .11
❑ 206 Loy Vaught B .25 .11
❑ 207 Tariq Abdul-Wahad B .25 .11
❑ 208 Sean Elliott B .25 .11
❑ 209 Rodney Rogers B .25 .11
❑ 210 Anthony Mason B .30 .14
❑ 211 Bryant Reeves B .25 .11
❑ 212 David Wesley B .25 .11
❑ 213 Isaiah Rider B .30 .14
❑ 214 Karl Malone B .75 .35
❑ 215 Mahmoud Abdul-Rauf B .25 .11
❑ 216 Patrick Ewing B .50 .23
❑ 217 Shaquille O'Neal B 2.50 1.10
❑ 218 Antoine Walker B 1.00 .45
❑ 219 Charles Barkley B .75 .35
❑ 220 Dennis Rodman B 1.00 .45
❑ 221 Jamal Mashburn B .30 .14
❑ 222 Kendall Gill B .30 .14
❑ 223 Malik Sealy B .25 .11
❑ 224 Rasheed Wallace B .50 .23
❑ 225 Shareef Abdur-Rahim B 1.50 .70
❑ 226 Antonio Daniels B .30 .14
❑ 227 Charles Oakley B .25 .11
❑ 228 Derek Anderson B .75 .35
❑ 229 Jason Kidd B 1.50 .70
❑ 230 Kenny Anderson B .30 .14
❑ 231 Marcus Camby B .60 .25
❑ 232 Ray Allen B .75 .35
❑ 233 Shawn Bradley B .25 .11
❑ 234 Antonio McDyess B .60 .25
❑ 235 Chauncey Billups B .30 .14
❑ 236 Detlef Schrempf B .30 .14
❑ 237 Jayson Williams B .30 .14
❑ 238 Kerry Kittles B .50 .23
❑ 239 Jalen Rose B .50 .23
❑ 240 Reggie Miller B .50 .23
❑ 241 Shawn Kemp B .75 .35
❑ 242 Arvydas Sabonis B .30 .14
❑ 243 Tom Gugliotta B .30 .14

❑ 244 Dikembe Mutombo B...... .30 .14
❑ 245 Jeff Hornacek B............. .30 .14
❑ 246 Kevin Garnett B........... 3.00 1.35
❑ 247 Matt Maloney B............. .25 .11
❑ 248 Rex Chapman B .... .25 .11
❑ 249 Stephon Marbury B...... 1.50 .70
❑ 250 Austin Croshere B.......... .75 .35
❑ 251 Chris Childs B .... .25 .11
❑ 252 Eddie Jones B............. 1.00 .45
❑ 253 Jerry Stackhouse B........ .30 .14
❑ 254 Kevin Johnson B........... .30 .14
❑ 255 Maurice Taylor B........... .50 .23
❑ 256 Chris Mullin B .... .50 .23
❑ 257 Terrell Brandon B .... .30 .14
❑ 258 Avery Johnson B........... .25 .11
❑ 259 Chris Webber B........... 1.50 .70
❑ 260 Gary Payton B............... .75 .35
❑ 261 Jim Jackson B................ .25 .11
❑ 262 Kobe Bryant B............. 5.00 2.20
❑ 263 Michael Finley B .... .50 .23
❑ 264 Rod Strickland B .... .30 .14
❑ 265 Tim Hardaway B .... .50 .23
❑ 266 B.J. Armstrong B........... .25 .11
❑ 267 Christian Laettner B ...... .30 .14
❑ 268 Glen Rice B.................... .30 .14
❑ 269 Joe Dumars B .... .50 .23
❑ 270 LaPhonso Ellis B........... .25 .11
❑ 271 Michael Jordan B 6.00 2.70
❑ 272 Ron Mercer B RC 4.00 1.80
❑ 273 Checklist B .... .25 .11
❑ 274 Anfernee Hardaway S.. 5.00 2.20
❑ 275 Dennis Rodman S........ 3.00 1.35
❑ 276 Gary Payton S............. 2.50 1.10
❑ 277 Jamal Mashburn S ...... 1.00 .45
❑ 278 Shareef Abdur-Rahim S 5.00 2.20
❑ 279 Steve Smith S .... 1.00 .45
❑ 280 Tony Battie S............... 1.00 .45
❑ 281 Alonzo Mourning S ...... 1.50 .70
❑ 282 Bobby Jackson S .... .60 .25
❑ 283 Christian Laettner S .... 1.00 .45
❑ 284 Jerry Stackhouse S...... 1.00 .45
❑ 285 Terrell Brandon S .... 1.00 .45
❑ 286 Chauncey Billups S...... 1.00 .45
❑ 287 Michael Jordan S 20.00 9.00
❑ 288 Glenn Robinson S........ 1.00 .45
❑ 289 Jason Kidd S............... 5.00 2.20
❑ 290 Joe Smith S................. 1.00 .45
❑ 291 Michael Finley S .... 1.50 .70
❑ 292 Rod Strickland S .... 1.00 .45
❑ 293 Ron Mercer S 2.50 1.10
❑ 294 Tracy McGrady S 8.00 3.60
❑ 295 Adonal Foyle S .... .60 .25
❑ 296 Marcus Camby S.......... 2.00 .90
❑ 297 John Stockton S .... 1.50 .70
❑ 298 Kerry Kittles S .... 1.50 .70
❑ 299 Mitch Richmond S........ 1.50 .70
❑ 300 Shawn Bradley S........... .60 .25
❑ 301 Anthony Mason S .... 1.00 .45
❑ 302 Antonio Daniels S .... 1.00 .45
❑ 303 Antonio McDyess S...... 2.00 .90
❑ 304 Charles Barkley S 2.50 1.10
❑ 305 Keith Van Horn S 4.00 1.80
❑ 306 Tim Duncan S 8.00 3.60
❑ 307 Dikembe Mutombo G .. 4.00 1.80
❑ 308 Grant Hill G 30.00 13.50
❑ 309 Shaquille O'Neal G 30.00 13.50
❑ 310 Keith Van Horn G 15.00 6.75
❑ 311 Shawn Kemp G......... 10.00 4.50
❑ 312 Antoine Walker G 12.00 5.50
❑ 313 Hakeem Olajuwon G.. 10.00 4.50
❑ 314 Vin Baker G................. 4.00 1.80
❑ 315 Patrick Ewing G........... 6.00 2.70
❑ 316 Tracy McGrady G 30.00 13.50
❑ 317 Glen Rice G.................. 4.00 1.80
❑ 318 Reggie Miller G 6.00 2.70
❑ 319 Kevin Garnett G 40.00 18.00
❑ 320 Allen Iverson G 30.00 13.50
❑ 321 Karl Malone G........... 10.00 4.50
❑ 322 Scottie Pippen G 20.00 9.00
❑ 323 Kobe Bryant G........... 50.00 22.00
❑ 324 Stephon Marbury G.... 20.00 9.00
❑ 325 Tim Duncan G............ 30.00 13.50
❑ 326 Chris Webber G 20.00 9.00

1997-98 Finest Embossed

	MINT	NRMT
COMPLETE SET (106)	1100.00	500.00
COMPLETE SERIES 1 (53) ..	400.00	180.00
COMPLETE SERIES 2 (53) ..	700.00	325.00
COMP.SILVER SER.1 (33) ..	120.00	55.00
COMP.SILVER SER.2 (33) ..	100.00	45.00
COMMON SILVER	1.00	.45

*SILVER: .5X TO 1.25X BASE HI
SILVER: SER.1/2 STATED ODDS 1:16

COMP.GOLD SER.1 (20)......	300.00	135.00
COMP.GOLD SER.2 (20)......	600.00	275.00
COMMON GOLD	5.00	2.20

*GOLD STARS/RCs: .6X TO 1.5X BASE HI
GOLD: SER.1/2 STATED ODDS 1:96

1997-98 Finest Embossed Refractors

	MINT	NRMT
COMMON SILVER	8.00	3.60

*SILVER: 5X TO 12X BASE HI
SILVER: SER.1/2 STATED ODDS 1:192
STATED PRINT RUN 263 SERIAL #'d SETS

COMMON GOLD	60.00	27.00

*GOLD STARS/RC's: 6X TO 15X BASE HI
GOLD: SER.1/2 STATED ODDS 1:1152
STATED PRINT RUN 74 SERIAL #'d SETS

❑ 154 Michael Jordan G .. 1800.00 800.00

1997-98 Finest Refractors

	MINT	NRMT
COMPLETE SET (326)	4400.00	2000.00
COMPLETE SERIES 1 (173)	2000.00	900.00
COMPLETE SERIES 2 (153)	2400.00	1100.00
COMP.BRONZE SET (220)	1400.00	650.00
COMP.BRONZE SER.1 (120)	800.00	350.00
COMP.BRONZE SER.2 (100)	600.00	275.00
COMMON BRONZE................	2.50	1.10

*BRONZE STARS: 4X TO 10X BASIC CARDS
*BRONZE RCs: 4X TO 10X BASE
BRONZE: SER.1/2 STATED ODDS 1:12

COMP.SILVER SET (66)	550.00	250.00
COMP.SILVER SER.1 (33) ..	300.00	135.00

COMP.SILVER SER.2 (33) ..	250.00	110.00
COMMON SILVER	3.00	1.35

*SILVER: 1.5X TO 4X BASIC CARDS
SILVER: SER.1/2 STATED ODDS 1:48
STATED PRINT RUN 1090 SERIAL #'d SETS

COMP.GOLD SET (40)	2400.00	1100.00
COMP.GOLD SER.1 (20)......	800.00	350.00
COMP.GOLD SER.2 (20)....	1600.00	700.00
COMMON GOLD (154-173)....	12.00	5.50

*GOLD STARS/RCs: 1.5X TO 4X BASIC CARDS
GOLD: SER.1/2 STATED ODDS 1:288
STATED PRINT RUN 289 SERIAL #'d SETS

❑ 101 Tim Duncan B 120.00 55.00
❑ 102 Keith Van Horn B 60.00 27.00
❑ 106 Tim Thomas B............ 40.00 18.00
❑ 107 Tracy McGrady B 120.00 55.00
❑ 110 Austin Croshere B...... 30.00 13.50
❑ 114 Derek Anderson B...... 30.00 13.50
❑ 272 Ron Mercer B 40.00 18.00

1998-99 Finest

	MINT	NRMT
COMPLETE SET (250)	110.00	50.00
COMPLETE SERIES 1 (125)..	30.00	13.50
COMPLETE SERIES 2 (125)..	80.00	36.00
COMMON CARD (1-225)...........	.25	.11
COMMON CARD (226-250)........	.75	.35
SEMISTARS..........................	.30	.14
SEMISTARS RC..........................	1.00	.45
UNLISTED STARS......................	.50	.23
UNLISTED STARS RC.............	1.50	.70

❑ 1 Chris Mills .... .25 .11
❑ 2 Matt Maloney...................... .25 .11
❑ 3 Sam Mitchell .... .25 .11
❑ 4 Corliss Williamson.............. .25 .11
❑ 5 Bryant Reeves..................... .25 .11
❑ 6 Juwan Howard .... .30 .14
❑ 7 Eddie Jones .... 1.00 .45
❑ 8 Ray Allen............................. .60 .25
❑ 9 Larry Johnson .... .30 .14
❑ 10 Travis Best .... .25 .11
❑ 11 Isaiah Rider......................... .30 .14
❑ 12 Hakeem Olajuwon............... .75 .35
❑ 13 Gary Trent............................ .25 .11
❑ 14 Kevin Garnett 3.00 1.35
❑ 15 Dikembe Mutombo .... .30 .14
❑ 16 Brevin Knight....................... .25 .11

	No.	Player	Mint	Nrmt
❑	17	Keith Van Horn	1.25	.55
❑	18	Theo Ratliff	.25	.11
❑	19	Tim Hardaway	.50	.23
❑	20	Blue Edwards	.25	.11
❑	21	David Wesley	.25	.11
❑	22	Jaren Jackson	.25	.11
❑	23	Nick Anderson	.25	.11
❑	24	Rodney Rogers	.25	.11
❑	25	Antonio Davis	.25	.11
❑	26	Clarence Weatherspoon	.25	.11
❑	27	Kelvin Cato	.25	.11
❑	28	Tracy McGrady	2.00	.90
❑	29	Mookie Blaylock	.25	.11
❑	30	Ron Harper	.30	.14
❑	31	Allan Houston	.50	.23
❑	32	Brian Williams	.25	.11
❑	33	John Stockton	.50	.23
❑	34	Hersey Hawkins	.30	.14
❑	35	Donyell Marshall	.25	.11
❑	36	Mark Strickland	.25	.11
❑	37	Rod Strickland	.30	.14
❑	38	Cedric Ceballos	.25	.11
❑	39	Danny Fortson	.30	.14
❑	40	Shaquille O'Neal	2.50	1.10
❑	41	Kendall Gill	.30	.14
❑	42	Allen Iverson	2.00	.90
❑	43	Travis Knight	.25	.11
❑	44	Cedric Henderson	.25	.11
❑	45	Steve Kerr	.25	.11
❑	46	Antonio McDyess	.50	.23
❑	47	Darrick Martin	.25	.11
❑	48	Shandon Anderson	.25	.11
❑	49	Shareef Abdur-Rahim	1.25	.55
❑	50	Antoine Carr	.25	.11
❑	51	Jason Kidd	1.50	.70
❑	52	Calbert Cheaney	.25	.11
❑	53	Antoine Walker	.75	.35
❑	54	Greg Anthony	.25	.11
❑	55	Jeff Hornacek	.30	.14
❑	56	Reggie Miller	.50	.23
❑	57	Lawrence Funderburke	.25	.11
❑	58	Derek Strong	.25	.11
❑	59	Robert Horry	.25	.11
❑	60	Shawn Bradley	.25	.11
❑	61	Matt Bullard	.25	.11
❑	62	Terrell Brandon	.30	.14
❑	63	Dan Majerle	.30	.14
❑	64	Jim Jackson	.25	.11
❑	65	Anthony Peeler	.25	.11
❑	66	Charles Outlaw	.25	.11
❑	67	Khalid Reeves	.25	.11
❑	68	Toni Kukoc	.60	.25
❑	69	Mario Elie	.25	.11
❑	70	Derek Anderson	.60	.25
❑	71	Jalen Rose	.50	.23
❑	72	Tyrone Corbin	.25	.11
❑	73	Anthony Mason	.30	.14
❑	74	Lamond Murray	.25	.11
❑	75	Tom Gugliotta	.30	.14
❑	76	Arvydas Sabonis	.30	.14
❑	77	Brian Shaw	.25	.11
❑	78	Rick Fox	.25	.11
❑	79	Danny Manning	.30	.14
❑	80	Lindsey Hunter	.25	.11
❑	81	Michael Jordan	6.00	2.70
❑	82	LaPhonso Ellis	.25	.11
❑	83	David Robinson	.75	.35
❑	84	Christian Laettner	.30	.14
❑	85	Armon Gilliam	.25	.11
❑	86	Sherman Douglas	.25	.11
❑	87	Charlie Ward	.25	.11
❑	88	Shawn Kemp	.75	.35
❑	89	Gary Payton	.75	.35
❑	90	Doug Christie	.25	.11
❑	91	Voshon Lenard	.25	.11
❑	92	Detlef Schrempf	.30	.14
❑	93	Walter McCarty	.25	.11
❑	94	Sam Cassell	.30	.14
❑	95	Jerry Stackhouse	.30	.14
❑	96	Billy Owens	.25	.11
❑	97	Matt Geiger	.25	.11
❑	98	Avery Johnson	.25	.11
❑	99	Bobby Jackson	.25	.11
❑	100	Rex Chapman	.25	.11
❑	101	Andrew DeClercq	.25	.11
❑	102	Vlade Divac	.25	.11
❑	103	Erick Strickland	.25	.11
❑	104	Dean Garrett	.25	.11
❑	105	Grant Long	.25	.11
❑	106	Adonal Foyle	.25	.11
❑	107	Isaac Austin	.25	.11
❑	108	Michael Curry	.25	.11
❑	109	Darrell Armstrong	.30	.14
❑	110	Aaron McKie	.25	.11
❑	111	Stacey Augmon	.25	.11
❑	112	Anthony Johnson	.25	.11
❑	113	Vinny Del Negro	.25	.11
❑	114	Reggie Slater	.25	.11
❑	115	Lee Mayberry	.25	.11
❑	116	Tracy Murray	.25	.11
❑	117	Scottie Pippen	1.50	.70
❑	118	Sam Perkins	.30	.14
❑	119	Derek Fisher	.30	.14
❑	120	Mark Bryant	.25	.11
❑	121	Dale Davis	.25	.11
❑	122	B.J. Armstrong	.25	.11
❑	123	Charles Barkley	.75	.35
❑	124	Horace Grant	.30	.14
❑	125	Checklist	.25	.11
❑	126	Alonzo Mourning	.50	.23
❑	127	Kerry Kittles	.30	.14
❑	128	Eldridge Recasner	.25	.11
❑	129	Dell Curry	.25	.11
❑	130	Jamal Mashburn	.30	.14
❑	131	Eric Piatkowski	.25	.11
❑	132	Othella Harrington	.25	.11
❑	133	Pete Chilcutt	.25	.11
❑	134	Dennis Rodman	1.00	.45
❑	135	Patrick Ewing	.50	.23
❑	136	Danny Schayes	.25	.11
❑	137	John Williams	.25	.11
❑	138	Joe Smith	.30	.14
❑	139	Tariq Abdul-Wahad	.25	.11
❑	140	Vin Baker	.30	.14
❑	141	Elden Campbell	.25	.11
❑	142	Chris Carr	.25	.11
❑	143	John Starks	.25	.11
❑	144	Felton Spencer	.25	.11
❑	145	Mark Jackson	.25	.11
❑	146	Dana Barros	.25	.11
❑	147	Eric Williams	.25	.11
❑	148	Wesley Person	.25	.11
❑	149	Joe Dumars	.50	.23
❑	150	Steve Smith	.30	.14
❑	151	Randy Brown	.25	.11
❑	152	A.C. Green	.30	.14
❑	153	Dee Brown	.25	.11
❑	154	Brian Grant	.30	.14
❑	155	Tim Thomas	.75	.35
❑	156	Howard Eisley	.25	.11
❑	157	Malik Sealy	.25	.11
❑	158	Maurice Taylor	.50	.23
❑	159	Tyrone Hill	.25	.11
❑	160	Chris Gatling	.25	.11
❑	161	Rodrick Rhodes	.25	.11
❑	162	Muggsy Bogues	.25	.11
❑	163	Kenny Anderson	.30	.14
❑	164	Zydrunas Ilgauskas	.25	.11
❑	165	Grant Hill	2.50	1.10
❑	166	Lorenzen Wright	.25	.11
❑	167	Tony Battie	.30	.14
❑	168	Bobby Phills	.25	.11
❑	169	Michael Finley	.50	.23
❑	170	Anfernee Hardaway	1.50	.70
❑	171	Terry Porter	.25	.11
❑	172	P.J. Brown	.25	.11
❑	173	Clifford Robinson	.25	.11
❑	174	Olden Polynice	.25	.11
❑	175	Kobe Bryant	4.00	1.80
❑	176	Sean Elliott	.25	.11
❑	177	Latrell Sprewell	1.00	.45
❑	178	Rik Smits	.25	.11
❑	179	Darrell Armstrong	.30	.14
❑	180	Stephon Marbury	1.25	.55
❑	181	Brent Price	.25	.11
❑	182	Danny Fortson	.30	.14
❑	183	Vitaly Potapenko	.25	.11
❑	184	Anthony Parker	.25	.11
❑	185	Glenn Robinson	.30	.14
❑	186	Erick Dampier	.25	.11
❑	187	George McCloud	.25	.11
❑	188	Rasheed Wallace	.50	.23
❑	189	Aaron Williams	.25	.11
❑	190	Tim Duncan	2.50	1.10
❑	191	Chauncey Billups	.25	.11
❑	192	Jim McIlvaine	.25	.11
❑	193	Chris Mullin	.50	.23
❑	194	George Lynch	.25	.11
❑	195	Damon Stoudamire	.50	.23
❑	196	Bryon Russell	.25	.11
❑	197	Luc Longley	.25	.11
❑	198	Ron Mercer	.75	.35
❑	199	Alan Henderson	.25	.11
❑	200	Jayson Williams	.30	.14
❑	201	Ben Wallace	.25	.11
❑	202	Elliot Perry	.25	.11
❑	203	Walt Williams	.25	.11
❑	204	Cherokee Parks	.25	.11
❑	205	Brent Barry	.25	.11
❑	206	Hubert Davis	.25	.11
❑	207	Terry Davis	.25	.11
❑	208	Loy Vaught	.25	.11
❑	209	Adam Keefe	.25	.11
❑	210	Karl Malone	.75	.35
❑	211	Chuck Person	.25	.11
❑	212	Chris Childs	.25	.11
❑	213	Rony Seikaly	.25	.11
❑	214	Ervin Johnson	.25	.11
❑	215	Derrick McKey	.25	.11
❑	216	Jerome Williams	.30	.14
❑	217	Glen Rice	.30	.14
❑	218	Steve Nash	.25	.11
❑	219	Nick Van Exel	.30	.14
❑	220	Chris Webber	1.50	.70
❑	221	Marcus Camby	.50	.23
❑	222	Antonio Daniels	.25	.11
❑	223	Mitch Richmond	.50	.23
❑	224	Otis Thorpe	.25	.11
❑	225	Charles Oakley	.25	.11
❑	226	Michael Olowokandi RC	2.50	1.10
❑	227	Mike Bibby RC	5.00	2.20
❑	228	Raef LaFrentz RC	3.00	1.35
❑	229	Antawn Jamison RC	8.00	3.60
❑	230	Vince Carter RC	50.00	22.00
❑	231	Robert Traylor RC	1.50	.70
❑	232	Jason Williams RC	10.00	4.50
❑	233	Larry Hughes RC	10.00	4.50
❑	234	Dirk Nowitzki RC	6.00	2.70
❑	235	Paul Pierce RC	8.00	3.60
❑	236	Bonzi Wells RC	6.00	2.70
❑	237	Michael Doleac RC	1.50	.70
❑	238	Keon Clark RC	1.50	.70
❑	239	Michael Dickerson RC	3.00	1.35
❑	240	Matt Harpring RC	1.50	.70
❑	241	Bryce Drew RC	1.50	.70
❑	242	Pat Garrity RC	1.00	.45
❑	243	Roshown McLeod RC	1.00	.45
❑	244	Ricky Davis RC	3.00	1.35
❑	245	Brian Skinner RC	1.50	.70
❑	246	Tyronn Lue RC	1.00	.45
❑	247	Felipe Lopez RC	2.00	.90
❑	248	Sam Jacobson RC	.75	.35
❑	249	Corey Benjamin RC	1.50	.70
❑	250	Nazr Mohammed RC	1.00	.45

1998-99 Finest No Protector

	MINT	NRMT
COMPLETE SET (250)	230.00	105.00
COMPLETE SERIES 1 (125)	80.00	36.00

COMPLETE SERIES 2 (125)	150.00	70.00
COMMON CARD (1-225)	1.00	.45
COMMON CARD (226-250)	1.25	.55

*STARS: 1.5X TO 4X BASE CARD HI
*RCs: .6X TO 1.5X BASE HI
SER.1/2 STATED ODDS 1:4 H/R

1998-99 Finest No Protector Refractors

	MINT	NRMT
COMPLETE SET (250)	1600.00	700.00
COMPLETE SERIES 1 (125)	600.00	275.00
COMPLETE SERIES 2 (125)	1000.00	450.00
COMMON CARD (1-225)	5.00	2.20
COMMON CARD (226-250)	5.00	2.20

*STARS: 8X TO 20X BASE CARD HI
*RCs: 2.5X TO 6X BASE HI
SER.1/2 STATED ODDS 1:24 H/R

1998-99 Finest Refractors

	MINT	NRMT
COMPLETE SET (250)	800.00	350.00
COMPLETE SERIES 1 (125)	300.00	135.00
COMPLETE SERIES 2 (125)	500.00	220.00
COMMON CARD (1-250)	2.50	1.10

*REF.STARS: 4X TO 10X BASE CARD HI
*REF.RCs: 1.25X TO 3X BASE
REF: SER.1/2 STATED ODDS 1:12 H/R

❑ 227 Mike Bibby	15.00	6.75
❑ 229 Antawn Jamison	30.00	13.50
❑ 230 Vince Carter	150.00	70.00
❑ 232 Jason Williams	40.00	18.00
❑ 233 Larry Hughes	40.00	18.00
❑ 234 Dirk Nowitzki	25.00	11.00
❑ 235 Paul Pierce	30.00	13.50
❑ 236 Bonzi Wells	20.00	9.00

1998-99 Finest Arena Stars

	MINT	NRMT
COMPLETE SET (20)	120.00	55.00
COMMON CARD (AS1-20)	2.50	1.10
UNLISTED STARS	3.00	1.35

SER.2 STATED ODDS 1:48 H/R

❑ AS1 Shaquille O'Neal	15.00	6.75
❑ AS2 Stephon Marbury	8.00	3.60
❑ AS3 Allen Iverson	12.00	5.50
❑ AS4 John Stockton	3.00	1.35
❑ AS5 Kobe Bryant	25.00	11.00
❑ AS6 Alonzo Mourning	3.00	1.35
❑ AS7 Damon Stoudamire	3.00	1.35
❑ AS8 Scottie Pippen	10.00	4.50
❑ AS9 Tim Hardaway	3.00	1.35
❑ AS10 Karl Malone	5.00	2.20
❑ AS11 Tim Duncan	15.00	6.75
❑ AS12 Gary Payton	5.00	2.20
❑ AS13 Antoine Walker	5.00	2.20
❑ AS14 Keith Van Horn	8.00	3.60
❑ AS15 Juwan Howard	2.50	1.10
❑ AS16 David Robinson	5.00	2.20
❑ AS17 Michael Finley	2.50	1.10
❑ AS18 Shareef Abdur-Rahim	8.00	3.60
❑ AS19 Michael Jordan	40.00	18.00
❑ AS20 Vin Baker	2.50	1.10

1998-99 Finest Centurions

	MINT	NRMT
COMPLETE SET (20)	250.00	110.00
COMMON CARD (C1-C20)	4.00	1.80
SEMISTARS	5.00	2.20
UNLISTED STARS	6.00	2.70

SER.1 STATED ODDS 1:91 H/R
STATED PRINT RUN 500 SERIAL #'d SETS

COMP.REF.SET (20)	1000.00	450.00
COMMON REF. (C1-C20)	15.00	6.75

*REF: 1.5X TO 4X HI COLUMN
REF: SER.1 STATED ODDS 1:609 H/R
REF: PRINT RUN 75 SERIAL #'d SETS

❑ C1 Grant Hill	30.00	13.50
❑ C2 Tim Thomas	10.00	4.50
❑ C3 Eddie Jones	12.00	5.50
❑ C4 Michael Finley	6.00	2.70
❑ C5 Shaquille O'Neal	30.00	13.50
❑ C6 Kobe Bryant	50.00	22.00
❑ C7 Keith Van Horn	15.00	6.75
❑ C8 Tim Duncan	30.00	13.50
❑ C9 Antoine Walker	10.00	4.50
❑ C10 Shareef Abdur-Rahim	15.00	6.75
❑ C11 Stephon Marbury	15.00	6.75
❑ C12 Kevin Garnett	40.00	18.00
❑ C13 Ray Allen	8.00	3.60
❑ C14 Kerry Kittles	5.00	2.20
❑ C15 Allen Iverson	25.00	11.00
❑ C16 Damon Stoudamire	6.00	2.70
❑ C17 Brevin Knight	4.00	1.80
❑ C18 Bryant Reeves	4.00	1.80
❑ C19 Ron Mercer	10.00	4.50
❑ C20 Zydrunas Ilgauskas	4.00	1.80

1998-99 Finest Court Control

	MINT	NRMT
COMPLETE SET (20)	200.00	90.00
COMMON CARD (CC1-20)	3.00	1.35
SEMISTARS	4.00	1.80
UNLISTED STARS	5.00	2.20

SER.2 STATED ODDS 1:76 H/R
STATED PRINT RUN 750 SERIAL #'d SETS

COMP.REF.SET (20)	600.00	275.00
COMMON REF. (CC1-20)	10.00	4.50

*REF: 1.25X TO 3X HI COLUMN
REF: SER.2 STATED ODDS 1:379 H/R
REF: PRINT RUN 150 SERIAL #'d SETS

❑ CC1 Shareef Abdur-Rahim	10.00	4.50
❑ CC2 Keith Van Horn	10.00	4.50
❑ CC3 Tim Duncan	20.00	9.00
❑ CC4 Antoine Walker	6.00	2.70
❑ CC5 Stephon Marbury	10.00	4.50
❑ CC6 Kevin Garnett	25.00	11.00
❑ CC7 Grant Hill	20.00	9.00
❑ CC8 Michael Finley	5.00	2.20
❑ CC9 Ron Mercer	6.00	2.70
❑ CC10 Damon Stoudamire	5.00	2.20
❑ CC11 Michael Olowokandi	5.00	2.20
❑ CC12 Mike Bibby	8.00	3.60
❑ CC13 Antawn Jamison	12.00	5.50
❑ CC14 Vince Carter	60.00	27.00
❑ CC15 Jason Williams	15.00	6.75
❑ CC16 Larry Hughes	15.00	6.75
❑ CC17 Paul Pierce	12.00	5.50
❑ CC18 Michael Dickerson	5.00	2.20
❑ CC19 Bryce Drew	4.00	1.80
❑ CC20 Felipe Lopez	3.00	1.35

1998-99 Finest Hardwood Honors

	MINT	NRMT
COMPLETE SET (20)	150.00	70.00
COMMON CARD (H1-H20)	2.00	.90
SEMISTARS	2.50	1.10
UNLISTED STARS	4.00	1.80
SER.1 STATED ODDS 1:33 H/R		

❑ H1 Michael Jordan	50.00	22.00
❑ H2 Shaquille O'Neal	20.00	9.00
❑ H3 Karl Malone	6.00	2.70
❑ H4 Eddie Jones	8.00	3.60
❑ H5 Dikembe Mutombo	2.50	1.10
❑ H6 Wesley Person	2.00	.90
❑ H7 Glen Rice	2.50	1.10
❑ H8 David Robinson	6.00	2.70
❑ H9 Rik Smits	2.00	.90
❑ H10 Steve Smith	2.50	1.10
❑ H11 Allen Iverson	15.00	6.75
❑ H12 Jayson Williams	2.50	1.10
❑ H13 Nick Anderson	2.00	.90
❑ H14 Tim Duncan	20.00	9.00
❑ H15 Jason Kidd	12.00	5.50
❑ H16 Alonzo Mourning	4.00	1.80
❑ H17 Sam Cassell	2.50	1.10
❑ H18 Alan Henderson	2.00	.90
❑ H19 Gary Payton	6.00	2.70
❑ H20 Scottie Pippen	12.00	5.50

1998-99 Finest Mystery Finest

	MINT	NRMT
COMPLETE SET (40)	450.00	200.00
COMPLETE SERIES 1 (20)	250.00	110.00
COMPLETE SERIES 2 (20)	200.00	90.00
COMMON CARD (M1-M40)	3.00	1.35
SER.1 STATED ODDS 1:33 H/R		
SER.2 STATED ODDS 1:36 H/R		
COMP.REF.SET (40)	900.00	400.00
COMP.REF.SERIES 1 (20)	500.00	220.00
COMP.REF.SERIES 2 (20)	400.00	180.00
COMMON REF (M1-M40)	6.00	2.70
*REF.: .75X TO 2X HI COLUMN		
REF: SER.1 STATED ODDS 1:133 H/R		
REF: SER.2 STATED ODDS 1:144 H/R		

❑ M1 Michael Jordan Kobe Bryant	50.00	22.00
❑ M2 Kobe Bryant Shaquille O'Neal	40.00	18.00
❑ M3 Shaquille O'Neal David Robinson	20.00	9.00
❑ M4 David Robinson Tim Duncan	15.00	6.75
❑ M5 Tim Duncan Keith Van Horn	12.00	5.50
❑ M6 Keith Van Horn Scottie Pippen	10.00	4.50
❑ M7 Scottie Pippen Shareef Abdur-Rahim	15.00	6.75
❑ M8 Shareef Abdur-Rahim Grant Hill	20.00	9.00
❑ M9 Grant Hill Kevin Garnett	30.00	13.50
❑ M10 Kevin Garnett Stephon Marbury	20.00	9.00
❑ M11 Stephon Marbury Gary Payton	12.00	5.50
❑ M12 Gary Payton Vin Baker	4.00	1.80
❑ M13 Vin Baker Karl Malone	4.00	1.80
❑ M14 Karl Malone Shawn Kemp	6.00	2.70
❑ M15 Shawn Kemp Tim Thomas	4.00	1.80
❑ M16 Tim Thomas Antoine Walker	3.00	1.35
❑ M17 Antoine Walker Ron Mercer	4.00	1.80
❑ M18 Ron Mercer Kerry Kittles	4.00	1.80
❑ M19 Kerry Kittles Eddie Jones	3.00	1.35
❑ M20 Eddie Jones Michael Jordan	30.00	13.50
❑ M21 Alonzo Mourning Scottie Pippen	10.00	4.50
❑ M22 Scottie Pippen Antoine Walker	12.00	5.50
❑ M23 Antoine Walker Shareef Abdur-Rahim	10.00	4.50
❑ M24 Shareef Abdur-Rahim Kevin Garnett	25.00	11.00
❑ M25 Kevin Garnett Keith Van Horn	15.00	6.75
❑ M26 Keith Van Horn Tim Thomas	6.00	2.70
❑ M27 Tim Thomas Grant Hill	10.00	4.50
❑ M28 Grant Hill Anfernee Hardaway	15.00	6.75
❑ M29 Anfernee Hardaway Kerry Kittles	10.00	4.50
❑ M30 Kerry Kittles Jayson Williams	3.00	1.35
❑ M31 Jayson Williams Karl Malone	5.00	2.20
❑ M32 Karl Malone John Stockton	6.00	2.70
❑ M33 John Stockton Gary Payton	6.00	2.70
❑ M34 Gary Payton Ron Mercer	5.00	2.20
❑ M35 Ron Mercer Stephon Marbury	6.00	2.70
❑ M36 Stephon Marbury Allen Iverson	20.00	9.00
❑ M37 Allen Iverson Kobe Bryant	30.00	13.50
❑ M38 Kobe Bryant Tim Duncan	30.00	13.50
❑ M39 Tim Duncan Shaquille O'Neal	25.00	11.00
❑ M40 Shaquille O'Neal Alonzo Mourning	15.00	6.75

1998-99 Finest Oversized

	MINT	NRMT
COMPLETE SET (14)	40.00	18.00
COMPLETE SERIES 1 (7)	25.00	11.00
COMPLETE SERIES 2 (7)	15.00	6.75
COMMON CARD (1-14)	.75	.35
UNLISTED STARS	1.25	.55
SER.1 STATED ODDS 1:3 BOXES		
SER.2 STATED ODDS ONE PER BOX		
COMP.REF.SET (14)	80.00	36.00
COMP.REF.SER.1 (7)	50.00	22.00
COMP.REF.SER.2 (7)	30.00	13.50
COMMON REF (1-14)	1.50	.70
*REF: .75X TO 2X HI COLUMN		
REF: SER.1/2 STATED ODDS 1:12 BOXES		

❑ 1 Kevin Garnett	12.00	5.50
❑ 2 Keith Van Horn	5.00	2.20
❑ 3 Shaquille O'Neal	10.00	4.50
❑ 4 Shareef Abdur-Rahim	5.00	2.20
❑ 5 Antoine Walker	3.00	1.35
❑ 6 Gary Payton	3.00	1.35
❑ 7 Scottie Pippen	6.00	2.70
❑ 8 Alonzo Mourning	1.25	.55
❑ 9 Kerry Kittles	.75	.35
❑ 10 Kobe Bryant	10.00	4.50
❑ 11 Stephon Marbury	3.00	1.35
❑ 12 Tim Duncan	6.00	2.70
❑ 13 Ron Mercer	2.00	.90
❑ 14 Karl Malone	2.00	.90

1999-00 Finest

	MINT	NRMT
COMPLETE SET (266)	350.00	160.00
COMPLETE SERIES 1 (133)	80.00	36.00
COMPLETE SERIES 2 (133)	300.00	135.00
COMP.SERIES 2 w/o RC (118)	50.00	22.00
COMMON CARD (1-266)	.25	.11
COMMON SUBSET	.40	.18
COMMON RC (110-124)	1.00	.45
COMMON RC (252-266)	6.00	2.70
SEMISTARS	.30	.14
SEMISTARS SER.1 RC	1.25	.55
SEMISTARS SER.2 RC	8.00	3.60
UNLISTED STARS	.50	.23
UNLISTED STARS SUBSET	.75	.35
UNLISTED STARS SER.1 RC	1.50	.70
UNLISTED STARS SER.2 RC	10.00	4.50
SUBSET CARDS INSERTED ONE PER PACK		
SER.2 RCs PRINT RUN 2000 SERIAL #'d SETS		
SER.2 RCs STATED ODDS 1:14, 1:6 HTA		

❑ 1 Shareef Abdur-Rahim	1.00	.45
❑ 2 Kevin Willis	.25	.11
❑ 3 Sean Elliott	.25	.11
❑ 4 Vlade Divac	.25	.11
❑ 5 Tom Gugliotta	.30	.14
❑ 6 Matt Harpring	.25	.11
❑ 7 Kerry Kittles	.30	.14
❑ 8 Joe Smith	.30	.14
❑ 9 Jamal Mashburn	.30	.14
❑ 10 Tyrone Nesby RC	.25	.11
❑ 11 Alan Henderson	.25	.11
❑ 12 Vitaly Potapenko	.25	.11
❑ 13 Dickey Simpkins	.25	.11
❑ 14 Michael Finley	.50	.23
❑ 15 Lindsey Hunter	.25	.11
❑ 16 Antawn Jamison	1.00	.45
❑ 17 Reggie Miller	.50	.23
❑ 18 Maurice Taylor	.50	.23
❑ 19 Clarence Weatherspoon	.25	.11
❑ 20 Sam Mitchell	.25	.11
❑ 21 Latrell Sprewell	1.00	.45
❑ 22 Michael Doleac	.25	.11

❑ 23 Rex Chapman .25 .11
❑ 24 Predrag Stojakovic .30 .14
❑ 25 Vladimir Stepania .25 .11
❑ 26 Tracy McGrady 1.50 .70
❑ 27 Cherokee Parks .25 .11
❑ 28 LaPhonso Ellis .25 .11
❑ 29 Hakeem Olajuwon .75 .35
❑ 30 Adonal Foyle .25 .11
❑ 31 Bryant Stith .25 .11
❑ 32 Andrew DeClercq .25 .11
❑ 33 Toni Kukoc .60 .25
❑ 34 Kenny Anderson .30 .14
❑ 35 Mike Bibby .60 .25
❑ 36 Glen Rice .30 .14
❑ 37 Avery Johnson .25 .11
❑ 38 Arvydas Sabonis .30 .14
❑ 39 Kornel David RC .25 .11
❑ 40 Hubert Davis .25 .11
❑ 41 Grant Hill 2.50 1.10
❑ 42 Donyell Marshall .25 .11
❑ 43 Jalen Rose .50 .23
❑ 44 Derrick Coleman .30 .14
❑ 45 P.J. Brown .25 .11
❑ 46 Vin Baker .30 .14
❑ 47 Clifford Robinson .25 .11
❑ 48 Allan Houston .50 .23
❑ 49 Kendall Gill .30 .14
❑ 50 Matt Geiger .25 .11
❑ 51 Larry Hughes 1.25 .55
❑ 52 Corliss Williamson .25 .11
❑ 53 Darrell Armstrong .30 .14
❑ 54 Bobby Jackson .25 .11
❑ 55 Bryon Russell .25 .11
❑ 56 Juwan Howard .30 .14
❑ 57 Dikembe Mutombo .30 .14
❑ 58 Eddie Jones 1.00 .45
❑ 59 Randy Brown .25 .11
❑ 60 Dirk Nowitzki .75 .35
❑ 61 Jerome Williams .30 .14
❑ 62 Scottie Pippen 1.50 .70
❑ 63 Dale Davis .25 .11
❑ 64 Kobe Bryant 4.00 1.80
❑ 65 Robert Traylor .25 .11
❑ 66 Tim Hardaway .50 .23
❑ 67 Michael Olowokandi .30 .14
❑ 68 Walter McCarty .25 .11
❑ 69 Damon Stoudamire .50 .23
❑ 70 Othella Harrington .25 .11
❑ 71 Chauncey Billups .25 .11
❑ 72 John Starks .25 .11
❑ 73 Ricky Davis .50 .23
❑ 74 Glenn Robinson .30 .14
❑ 75 Dean Garrett .25 .11
❑ 76 Chris Childs .25 .11
❑ 77 Shawn Kemp .75 .35
❑ 78 Allen Iverson 2.00 .90
❑ 79 Brian Grant .30 .14
❑ 80 David Robinson .75 .35
❑ 81 Tracy Murray .25 .11
❑ 82 Howard Eisley .25 .11
❑ 83 Doug Christie .25 .11
❑ 84 Gary Payton .75 .35
❑ 85 John Stockton .50 .23
❑ 86 Rod Strickland .30 .14
❑ 87 Tyrone Corbin .25 .11
❑ 88 Antonio Daniels .25 .11
❑ 89 Dee Brown .25 .11
❑ 90 Antoine Walker .60 .25
❑ 91 Theo Ratliff .25 .11
❑ 92 Larry Johnson .30 .14
❑ 93 Stephon Marbury 1.00 .45
❑ 94 Brevin Knight .25 .11
❑ 95 Antonio McDyess .50 .23
❑ 96 Bison Dele .25 .11
❑ 97 Cuttino Mobley .50 .23
❑ 98 Haywoode Workman .25 .11
❑ 99 J.R. Reid .25 .11
❑ 100 Travis Best .25 .11
❑ 101 Chris Webber GEM 2.50 1.10
❑ 102 Grant Hill GEM 4.00 1.80
❑ 103 Kevin Garnett GEM 5.00 2.20
❑ 104 Jason Kidd GEM 2.50 1.10
❑ 105 Gary Payton GEM 1.25 .55
❑ 106 Shaquille O'Neal GEM 4.00 1.80
❑ 107 Alonzo Mourning GEM .75 .35
❑ 108 Karl Malone GEM 1.25 .55
❑ 109 John Stockton GEM .75 .35
❑ 110 Elton Brand RC 15.00 6.75
❑ 111 Baron Davis RC 4.00 1.80
❑ 112 Aleksandar Radojevic RC 1.00 .45
❑ 113 Cal Bowdler RC 1.50 .70
❑ 114 Jumaine Jones RC 1.25 .55
❑ 115 Jason Terry RC 2.50 1.10
❑ 116 Trajan Langdon RC 2.50 1.10
❑ 117 Dion Glover RC 1.50 .70
❑ 118 Jeff Foster RC 1.50 .70
❑ 119 Lamar Odom RC 12.00 5.50
❑ 120 Wally Szczerbiak RC 6.00 2.70
❑ 121 Shawn Marion RC 5.00 2.20
❑ 122 Kenny Thomas RC 2.50 1.10
❑ 123 Devean George RC 3.00 1.35
❑ 124 Scott Padgett RC 1.50 .70
❑ 125 Tim Duncan SEN 4.00 1.80
❑ 126 Jason Williams SEN 2.00 .90
❑ 127 Paul Pierce SEN 1.50 .70
❑ 128 Kobe Bryant SEN 6.00 2.70
❑ 129 Keith Van Horn SEN 1.50 .70
❑ 130 Vince Carter SEN 8.00 3.60
❑ 131 Matt Harpring SEN .40 .18
❑ 132 Antawn Jamison SEN 1.50 .70
❑ 133 Tracy McGrady SEN 2.50 1.10
❑ 134 Tim Duncan 2.50 1.10
❑ 135 Tariq Abdul-Wahad .25 .11
❑ 136 Luc Longley .25 .11
❑ 137 Steve Smith .30 .14
❑ 138 Alonzo Mourning .50 .23
❑ 139 Kevin Garnett 3.00 1.35
❑ 140 Christian Laettner .30 .14
❑ 141 Rik Smits .25 .11
❑ 142 Cedric Henderson .25 .11
❑ 143 Jim Jackson .25 .11
❑ 144 Dan Majerle .30 .14
❑ 145 Bryant Reeves .25 .11
❑ 146 Antonio Davis .25 .11
❑ 147 Michael Smith .25 .11
❑ 148 Charlie Ward .25 .11
❑ 149 Chris Mullin .50 .23
❑ 150 Danny Manning .30 .14
❑ 151 Eric Williams .25 .11
❑ 152 Hersey Hawkins .30 .14
❑ 153 Isaiah Rider .30 .14
❑ 154 Shandon Anderson .25 .11
❑ 155 Jason Kidd 1.50 .70
❑ 156 Chris Whitney .25 .11
❑ 157 Brent Barry .25 .11
❑ 158 Patrick Ewing .50 .23
❑ 159 George Lynch .25 .11
❑ 160 Dickey Simpkins .25 .11
❑ 161 Derek Anderson .50 .23
❑ 162 Ron Mercer .60 .25
❑ 163 David Wesley .25 .11
❑ 164 Mookie Blaylock .25 .11
❑ 165 Terrell Brandon .30 .14
❑ 166 Detlef Schrempf .30 .14
❑ 167 Olden Polynice .25 .11
❑ 168 Jayson Williams .30 .14
❑ 169 Eric Piatkowski .25 .11
❑ 170 A.C. Green .30 .14
❑ 171 Chris Mills .25 .11
❑ 172 Chris Webber 1.50 .70
❑ 173 Jeff Hornacek .30 .14
❑ 174 Calbert Cheaney .25 .11
❑ 175 Wesley Person .25 .11
❑ 176 Corey Benjamin .25 .11
❑ 177 Loy Vaught .25 .11
❑ 178 Keith Closs .25 .11
❑ 179 Charles Outlaw .25 .11
❑ 180 Mitch Richmond .50 .23
❑ 181 Charles Oakley .25 .11
❑ 182 Felipe Lopez .25 .11
❑ 183 Eric Snow .25 .11
❑ 184 Paul Pierce 1.00 .45
❑ 185 Elden Campbell .25 .11
❑ 186 Shaquille O'Neal 2.50 1.10
❑ 187 Charles Barkley .75 .35
❑ 188 Mark Jackson .25 .11
❑ 189 Scott Burrell .25 .11
❑ 190 Anfernee Hardaway 1.50 .70
❑ 191 Samaki Walker .25 .11
❑ 192 Karl Malone .75 .35
❑ 193 Jermaine O'Neal .30 .14
❑ 194 Mario Elie .25 .11
❑ 195 Malik Sealy .25 .11
❑ 196 Voshon Lenard .25 .11
❑ 197 Chris Gatling .25 .11
❑ 198 Walt Williams .25 .11
❑ 199 Nick Van Exel .30 .14
❑ 200 Bimbo Coles .25 .11
❑ 201 John Wallace .25 .11
❑ 202 Anthony Mason .30 .14
❑ 203 Steve Nash .25 .11
❑ 204 Erick Dampier .25 .11
❑ 205 Cedric Ceballos .25 .11
❑ 206 Derek Fisher .30 .14
❑ 207 Marcus Camby .50 .23
❑ 208 Tyrone Hill .25 .11
❑ 209 Nick Anderson .25 .11
❑ 210 Sam Cassell .30 .14
❑ 211 Raef LaFrentz .50 .23
❑ 212 Ruben Patterson .50 .23
❑ 213 Rick Fox .25 .11
❑ 214 Jason Williams 1.25 .55
❑ 215 Vince Carter 5.00 2.20
❑ 216 Michael Dickerson .50 .23
❑ 217 Steve Kerr .25 .11
❑ 218 Rasheed Wallace .50 .23
❑ 219 Keith Van Horn 1.00 .45
❑ 220 Bob Sura .25 .11
❑ 221 Ray Allen .50 .23
❑ 222 Jerry Stackhouse .30 .14
❑ 223 Shawn Bradley .25 .11
❑ 224 Horace Grant .30 .14
❑ 225 Tim Duncan USA 4.00 1.80
❑ 226 Kevin Garnett USA 5.00 2.20
❑ 227 Jason Kidd USA 2.50 1.10
❑ 228 Steve Smith USA .40 .18
❑ 229 Allan Houston USA .75 .35
❑ 230 Tom Gugliotta USA .40 .18
❑ 231 Gary Payton USA 1.25 .55
❑ 232 Tim Hardaway USA .75 .35
❑ 233 Vin Baker USA .40 .18
❑ 234 Karl Malone CAT 1.25 .55
❑ 235 Vince Carter CAT 8.00 3.60
❑ 236 Jason Williams CAT 2.00 .90
❑ 237 Alonzo Mourning CAT .75 .35
❑ 238 Anfernee Hardaway CAT 2.50 1.10
❑ 239 Mitch Richmond CAT .75 .35
❑ 240 Steve Smith CAT .40 .18
❑ 241 Charles Barkley CAT 1.25 .55
❑ 242 Ron Mercer CAT 1.00 .45
❑ 243 Shaquille O'Neal EDGE 4.00 1.80
❑ 244 Jason Kidd EDGE 2.50 1.10
❑ 245 Kevin Garnett EDGE 5.00 2.20
❑ 246 Tim Duncan EDGE 4.00 1.80
❑ 247 Ray Allen EDGE .75 .35
❑ 248 Chris Webber EDGE 2.50 1.10
❑ 249 Jerry Stackhouse EDGE .40 .18
❑ 250 Keith Van Horn EDGE 1.50 .70
❑ 251 Patrick Ewing EDGE .75 .35
❑ 252 Steve Francis RC 150.00 70.00
❑ 253 Jonathan Bender RC 50.00 22.00
❑ 254 Richard Hamilton RC 25.00 11.00
❑ 255 Andre Miller RC 30.00 13.50
❑ 256 Corey Maggette RC 40.00 18.00
❑ 257 William Avery RC 15.00 6.75
❑ 258 Ron Artest RC 25.00 11.00
❑ 259 James Posey RC 15.00 6.75
❑ 260 Quincy Lewis RC 8.00 3.60
❑ 261 Tim James RC 12.00 5.50
❑ 262 Vonteego Cummings RC 15.00 6.75
❑ 263 Anthony Carter RC 25.00 11.00
❑ 264 Mirsad Turkcan RC 6.00 2.70
❑ 265 Adrian Griffin RC 12.00 5.50
❑ 266 Ryan Robertson RC 8.00 3.60

1999-00 Finest Refractors

	MINT	NRMT
COMPLETE SET (266)	1300.00	575.00
COMPLETE SERIES 1 (133)	500.00	220.00
COMPLETE SERIES 2 (133)	800.00	350.00
COMMON CARD (1-266)	2.00	.90
COMMON RC (110-124)	3.00	1.35
COMMON RC (252-266)	8.00	3.60

*STARS: 3X TO 8X BASE CARD HI
*SER.1 RCs: 1.25X TO 3X HI

*SER.2 RCs: .5X TO 1.25X HI
*SUBSETS: 2X TO 5X HI
SER.1/2 STATED ODDS 1:12, 1:5 HTA
SER.2 RCs: PRINT RUN 200 SERIAL #'d SETS
SER.2 RCs STATED ODDS 1:138, 1:64 HTA

	MINT	NRMT
❑ 110 Elton Brand	50.00	22.00
❑ 111 Baron Davis	12.00	5.50
❑ 119 Lamar Odom	40.00	18.00
❑ 120 Wally Szczerbiak	20.00	9.00
❑ 121 Shawn Marion	15.00	6.75
❑ 252 Steve Francis	350.00	160.00
❑ 253 Jonathan Bender	60.00	27.00
❑ 254 Richard Hamilton	30.00	13.50
❑ 255 Andre Miller	40.00	18.00
❑ 256 Corey Maggette	50.00	22.00
❑ 258 Ron Artest	30.00	13.50
❑ 263 Anthony Carter	30.00	13.50

1999-00 Finest Refractors Gold

	MINT	NRMT
COMMON CARD (1-266)	6.00	2.70

*STARS: 10X TO 25X BASE CARD HI
*SER.1 RCs: 4X TO 10X BASE HI
*SER.2 RCs: .75X TO 2X BASE HI
*SUBSETS: 6X TO 15X BASE HI
SER.1 STATED ODDS 1:62, 1:28 HTA
SER.2 STATED ODDS 1:31, 1:14 HTA
STATED PRINT RUN 100 SERIAL #'d SETS

	MINT	NRMT
❑ 252 Steve Francis	400.00	180.00

1999-00 Finest 24-Karat Touch

	MINT	NRMT
COMPLETE SET (10)	12.00	5.50
COMMON CARD (KT1-KT10)	1.00	.45
UNLISTED STARS	1.50	.70

SER.2 STATED ODDS 1:30, 1:15 HTA

COMP.REF.SET (10)	60.00	27.00
COMMON REF (GT1-GT10)	5.00	2.20

*REF: 2X TO 5X HI COLUMN
REF: SER.2 STATED ODDS 1:300, 1:150 HTA

	MINT	NRMT
❑ KT1 Reggie Miller	1.50	.70
❑ KT2 Keith Van Horn	3.00	1.35
❑ KT3 Allan Houston	1.50	.70
❑ KT4 Patrick Ewing	1.50	.70
❑ KT5 Anfernee Hardaway	5.00	2.20
❑ KT6 Steve Smith	1.00	.45
❑ KT7 Glen Rice	1.00	.45
❑ KT8 Ray Allen	1.50	.70
❑ KT9 Charles Barkley	2.50	1.10
❑ KT10 Mitch Richmond	1.50	.70

1999-00 Finest Box Office Draws

	MINT	NRMT
COMPLETE SET (10)	30.00	13.50
COMMON CARD (BOD1-BOD10)	1.25	.55
UNLISTED STARS	1.50	.70

SER.2 STATED ODDS 1:30, 1:15 HTA

COMP.REF.SET (10)	150.00	70.00
COMMON REF (BOD1-10)	6.00	2.70

*REF: 2X TO 5X HI COLUMN
REF: SER.2 STATED ODDS 1:300, 1:150 HTA

	MINT	NRMT
❑ BOD1 Shaquille O'Neal	8.00	3.60
❑ BOD2 Patrick Ewing	1.50	.70
❑ BOD3 Karl Malone	2.50	1.10
❑ BOD4 Jason Williams	4.00	1.80
❑ BOD5 Charles Barkley	2.50	1.10
❑ BOD6 Tim Duncan	8.00	3.60
❑ BOD7 Kevin Garnett	10.00	4.50
❑ BOD8 Alonzo Mourning	1.50	.70
❑ BOD9 Mitch Richmond	1.25	.55
❑ BOD10 Elton Brand	8.00	3.60

1999-00 Finest Double Double

	MINT	NRMT
COMPLETE SET (15)	50.00	22.00
COMMON CARD (D1-D15)	1.00	.45
UNLISTED STARS	1.50	.70

SER.2 STATED ODDS 1:20, 1:10 HTA

COMP.REF.SET (15)	250.00	110.00
COMMON REF (D1-D15)	5.00	2.20

*REF: 2X TO 5X HI COLUMN
REF: SER.2 STATED ODDS 1:200, 1:100 HTA

	MINT	NRMT
❑ D1 Jason Kidd	5.00	2.20
❑ D2 Kobe Bryant	12.00	5.50
❑ D3 Antoine Walker	2.00	.90
❑ D4 Chris Webber	5.00	2.20
❑ D5 Anfernee Hardaway	5.00	2.20
❑ D6 Shawn Kemp	2.50	1.10
❑ D7 Tim Duncan	8.00	3.60
❑ D8 Antonio McDyess	1.50	.70
❑ D9 Grant Hill	8.00	3.60
❑ D10 Karl Malone	2.50	1.10
❑ D11 Shaquille O'Neal	8.00	3.60
❑ D12 Allen Iverson	6.00	2.70
❑ D13 Jayson Williams	1.00	.45
❑ D14 Keith Van Horn	3.00	1.35
❑ D15 Gary Payton	2.50	1.10

1999-00 Finest Double Feature

	MINT	NRMT
COMPLETE SET (14)	50.00	22.00
COMMON CARD (DF1-DF14)	2.00	.90
UNLISTED STARS	2.50	1.10

SER.1 STATED ODDS 1:26, 1:12 HTA
RIGHT/LEFT VARIATIONS EQUAL VALUE
*DUAL REF: .75X TO 2X HI COLUMN
DUAL REF: SER.1 ODDS 1:78, 1:36 HTA

	MINT	NRMT
❑ DF1 Hakeem Olajuwon / Scottie Pippen	5.00	2.20
❑ DF2 Paul Pierce / Antoine Walker	3.00	1.35
❑ DF3 Shareef Abdur-Rahim / Mike Bibby	4.00	1.80
❑ DF4 Alonzo Mourning / Tim Hardaway	2.50	1.10
❑ DF5 Glenn Robinson / Ray Allen	2.50	1.10
❑ DF6 Kevin Garnett / Joe Smith	8.00	3.60
❑ DF7 Keith Van Horn / Stephon Marbury	5.00	2.20
❑ DF8 Chris Webber / Jason Williams	6.00	2.70
❑ DF9 Tim Duncan / David Robinson	6.00	2.70
❑ DF10 Gary Payton / Vin Baker	2.50	1.10
❑ DF11 Karl Malone / John Stockton	4.00	1.80
❑ DF12 Jason Kidd / Tom Gugliotta	4.00	1.80
❑ DF13 Mitch Richmond / Juwan Howard	2.00	.90
❑ DF14 Kobe Bryant / Shaquille O'Neal	15.00	6.75

1999-00 Finest Dunk Masters

	MINT	NRMT
COMPLETE SET (15)	150.00	70.00
COMMON CARD (DM1-DM15)	3.00	1.35
UNLISTED STARS	4.00	1.80

SER.1 STATED ODDS 1:73, 1:34 HTA
STATED PRINT RUN 750 SERIAL #'d SETS
*REFRACTORS: 1.5X TO 4X HI COLUMN
REF: SER.1 ODDS 1:364, 1:168 HTA
REF: PRINT RUN 150 SERIAL #'d SETS

	MINT	NRMT
❑ DM1 Kobe Bryant	30.00	13.50
❑ DM2 Shaquille O'Neal	20.00	9.00
❑ DM3 Chris Webber	12.00	5.50
❑ DM4 Antonio McDyess	4.00	1.80
❑ DM5 Michael Finley	3.00	1.35
❑ DM6 Shawn Kemp	6.00	2.70
❑ DM7 Tracy McGrady	12.00	5.50
❑ DM8 Antoine Walker	5.00	2.20
❑ DM9 Alonzo Mourning	4.00	1.80
❑ DM10 Ray Allen	4.00	1.80
❑ DM11 Kevin Garnett	25.00	11.00
❑ DM12 Allen Iverson	15.00	6.75
❑ DM13 Vince Carter	40.00	18.00
❑ DM14 Tim Duncan	20.00	9.00
❑ DM15 Scottie Pippen	12.00	5.50

1999-00 Finest Future's Finest

	MINT	NRMT
COMPLETE SET (15)	100.00	45.00
COMMON CARD (FF1-FF15)	1.25	.55
SEMISTARS	2.50	1.10
UNLISTED STARS	4.00	1.80

SER.1 STATED ODDS 1:73, 1:34 HTA
STATED PRINT RUN 750 SERIAL #'d SETS
*REFRACTORS: 1.5X TO 4X HI COLUMN
REF: SER. ODDS 1:364, 1:168 HTA
REF: PRINT RUN 150 SERIAL #'d SETS

	MINT	NRMT
❑ FF1 Elton Brand	20.00	9.00
❑ FF2 Steve Francis	25.00	11.00
❑ FF3 Baron Davis	5.00	2.20
❑ FF4 Lamar Odom	15.00	6.75
❑ FF5 Jonathan Bender	10.00	4.50
❑ FF6 Wally Szczerbiak	8.00	3.60
❑ FF7 Richard Hamilton	5.00	2.20
❑ FF8 Andre Miller	6.00	2.70
❑ FF9 Shawn Marion	6.00	2.70
❑ FF10 Jason Terry	4.00	1.80
❑ FF11 Trajan Langdon	4.00	1.80
❑ FF12 Aleksandar Radojevic	1.25	.55
❑ FF13 Corey Maggette	8.00	3.60
❑ FF14 William Avery	4.00	1.80
❑ FF15 Cal Bowdler	2.50	1.10

1999-00 Finest Heirs to Air

	MINT	NRMT
COMPLETE SET (10)	40.00	18.00
COMMON CARD (HA1-HA10)	1.00	.45
SEMISTARS	1.25	.55
UNLISTED STARS	2.00	.90

SER.2 STATED ODDS 1:36, 1:16 HTA

	MINT	NRMT
❑ HA1 Michael Finley	2.00	.90
❑ HA2 Brent Barry	1.00	.45
❑ HA3 Corey Maggette	4.00	1.80
❑ HA4 Ron Mercer	2.50	1.10
❑ HA5 Eddie Jones	4.00	1.80
❑ HA6 Tracy McGrady	6.00	2.70
❑ HA7 Vince Carter	20.00	9.00
❑ HA8 Jerry Stackhouse	1.25	.55
❑ HA9 Ray Allen	2.00	.90
❑ HA10 Kobe Bryant	15.00	6.75

1999-00 Finest Leading Indicators

	MINT	NRMT
COMPLETE SET (10)	40.00	18.00
COMMON CARD (L1-L10)	2.00	.90

SER.1 STATED ODDS 1:30, 1:14 HTA

	MINT	NRMT
❑ L1 Stephon Marbury	4.00	1.80
❑ L2 Paul Pierce	4.00	1.80
❑ L3 Jason Kidd	6.00	2.70
❑ L4 Gary Payton	3.00	1.35
❑ L5 Keith Van Horn	4.00	1.80
❑ L6 Reggie Miller	2.00	.90
❑ L7 Jason Williams	5.00	2.20
❑ L8 Vince Carter	20.00	9.00
❑ L9 Ray Allen	2.00	.90
❑ L10 Kobe Bryant	15.00	6.75

1999-00 Finest New Millennium

	MINT	NRMT
COMPLETE SET (10)	60.00	27.00
COMMON CARD (NM1-NM10)	3.00	1.35

SER.1 STATED ODDS 1:55, 1:25 HTA
STATED PRINT RUN 1500 SERIAL #'d SETS
*REFRACTORS: 1.25X TO 3X HI COLUMN
REF: SER.1 ODDS 1:273, 1:126 HTA
REF: PRINT RUN 300 SERIAL #'d SETS

	MINT	NRMT
❑ NM1 Jason Williams	6.00	2.70
❑ NM2 Vince Carter	25.00	11.00
❑ NM3 Paul Pierce	5.00	2.20
❑ NM4 Mike Bibby	3.00	1.35
❑ NM5 Elton Brand	12.00	5.50
❑ NM6 Steve Francis	15.00	6.75
❑ NM7 Baron Davis	3.00	1.35
❑ NM8 Lamar Odom	10.00	4.50
❑ NM9 Jonathan Bender	6.00	2.70
❑ NM10 Wally Szczerbiak	5.00	2.20

1999-00 Finest Next Generation

	MINT	NRMT
COMPLETE SET (15)	30.00	13.50
COMMON CARD (NG1-NG15)	1.00	.45
UNLISTED STARS	1.50	.70
SER.2 STATED ODDS 1:20, 1:10 HTA		
COMP.REF.SET (15)	150.00	70.00
COMMON REF (NG1-NG15)	5.00	2.20

*REF: 2X TO 5X HI COLUMN
REF: SER.2 STATED ODDS 1:200, 1:100 HTA

	MINT	NRMT
❑ NG1 Steve Francis	10.00	4.50
❑ NG2 Jonathan Bender	4.00	1.80
❑ NG3 Richard Hamilton	2.00	.90
❑ NG4 Andre Miller	2.50	1.10
❑ NG5 Corey Maggette	3.00	1.35
❑ NG6 William Avery	1.50	.70
❑ NG7 Ron Artest	2.00	.90
❑ NG8 Wally Szczerbiak	3.00	1.35
❑ NG9 Quincy Lewis	1.00	.45
❑ NG10 Devean George	1.50	.70
❑ NG11 Vonteego Cummings	1.50	.70
❑ NG12 Lamar Odom	6.00	2.70
❑ NG13 Shawn Marion	2.50	1.10
❑ NG14 Elton Brand	8.00	3.60
❑ NG15 Baron Davis	2.00	.90

1999-00 Finest Producers

	MINT	NRMT
COMPLETE SET (10)	30.00	13.50
COMMON CARD (FP1-FP10)	2.00	.90

SER.1 STATED ODDS 1:22, 1:10 HTA
*REFRACTORS: 1.25X TO 3X HI COLUMN
REF: SER.1 ODDS 1:109, 1:50 HTA

Card	MINT	NRMT
❑ FP1 Shaquille O'Neal	6.00	2.70
❑ FP2 Chris Webber	4.00	1.80
❑ FP3 Karl Malone	2.00	.90
❑ FP4 Allen Iverson	5.00	2.20
❑ FP5 Kevin Garnett	8.00	3.60
❑ FP6 Jason Kidd	4.00	1.80
❑ FP7 Grant Hill	6.00	2.70
❑ FP8 Shareef Abdur-Rahim	2.50	1.10
❑ FP9 Gary Payton	2.00	.90
❑ FP10 Charles Barkley	2.00	.90

1999-00 Finest Salute

	MINT	NRMT
COMPLETE SET (6)	400.00	180.00
COMPLETE SERIES 1 (3)	200.00	90.00
COMPLETE SERIES 2 (3)	200.00	90.00

SER.1 STATED ODDS 1:108, 1:50 HTA
REF: SER.1 ODDS 1:5,305, 1:2,333 HTA
GR: SER.1 ODDS 1:16,992, 1:7,423 HTA
SER.2 STATED ODDS 1:100, 1:50 HTA
REF: SER.2 ODDS 1:4,616, 1:2,194 HTA
GR: SER.2 ODDS 1:8,539, 1:3,790 HTA
GR: PRINT RUN 50 SERIAL #'d SETS

Card	MINT	NRMT
❑ FS1 Vince Carter Tim Duncan Allen Iverson	10.00	4.50
❑ FS1 Vince Carter Tim Duncan Allen Iverson Refractor	60.00	27.00
❑ FS1 Vince Carter Tim Duncan Allen Iverson Gold Refractor	200.00	90.00
❑ FS2 Draft Picks Elton Brand Steve Francis Baron Davis Lamar Odom Jonathan Bender Wally Szczerbiak	10.00	4.50
❑ FS2 Draft Picks REF Elton Brand Steve Francis Baron Davis Lamar Odom Jonathan Bender Wally Szczerbiak	60.00	27.00
❑ FS2 Draft Picks GR Elton Brand Steve Francis Baron Davis Lamar Odom Jonathan Bender Wally Szczerbiak	200.00	90.00

1999-00 Finest Team Finest Blue

	MINT	NRMT
COMPLETE SET (20)	130.00	57.50
COMPLETE SERIES 1 (10)	50.00	22.00
COMPLETE SERIES 2 (10)	80.00	36.00
COMMON CARD (TF1-TF20)	2.50	1.10

SER.1 STATED ODDS 1:55, 1:25 HTA
SER.2 STATED ODDS 1:28, 1:13 HTA
STATED PRINT RUN 1500 SERIAL #'d SETS
*BLUE REF: 1.25X TO 3X BASIC BLUE
BLUE REF: SER.1 ODDS 1:546, 1:252 HTA
BLUE REF: SER.2 ODDS 1:276, 1:127 HTA
BLUE REF: PRINT RUN 150 SERIAL #'d SETS
*RED: .75X TO 2X BASIC BLUE
RED: SER.1 STATED ODDS 1:18 HTA
RED: SER.2 STATED ODDS 1:9 HTA
RED: PRINT RUN 500 SERIAL #'d SETS
*RED REF: 3X TO 8X BASIC BLUE
RED REF: SER.1 STATED ODDS 1:175 HTA
RED REF: SER.2 STATED ODDS 1:89 HTA
RED REF: PRINT RUN 50 SERIAL #'d SETS
*GOLD: 1X TO 2.5X BASIC BLUE
GOLD: SER.1 STATED ODDS 1:35 HTA
GOLD: SER.2 STATED ODDS 1:18 HTA
GOLD: PRINT RUN 250 SERIAL #'d SETS
*GOLD REF: 8X TO 20X BASIC BLUE
GOLD REF: SER.1 STATED ODDS 1:352 HTA
GOLD REF: SER.2 STATED ODDS 1:180 HTA
GOLD REF: PRINT RUN 25 SERIAL #'d SETS

Card	MINT	NRMT
❑ TF1 Shareef Abdur-Rahim	5.00	2.20
❑ TF2 Stephon Marbury	5.00	2.20
❑ TF3 Shawn Kemp	4.00	1.80
❑ TF4 Allen Iverson	10.00	4.50
❑ TF5 Antoine Walker	3.00	1.35
❑ TF6 Hakeem Olajuwon	4.00	1.80
❑ TF7 Tim Duncan	12.00	5.50
❑ TF8 Karl Malone	4.00	1.80
❑ TF9 Grant Hill	12.00	5.50
❑ TF10 Keith Van Horn	5.00	2.20
❑ TF11 Alonzo Mourning	2.50	1.10
❑ TF12 Jason Kidd	8.00	3.60
❑ TF13 Chris Webber	8.00	3.60
❑ TF14 Shaquille O'Neal	12.00	5.50
❑ TF15 Gary Payton	4.00	1.80
❑ TF16 Kevin Garnett	15.00	6.75
❑ TF17 Antonio McDyess	2.50	1.10
❑ TF18 Kobe Bryant	20.00	9.00
❑ TF19 Scottie Pippen	8.00	3.60
❑ TF20 Vince Carter	25.00	11.00

1994-95 Flair

	MINT	NRMT
COMPLETE SET (326)	60.00	27.00
COMPLETE SERIES 1 (175)	20.00	9.00
COMPLETE SERIES 2 (151)	40.00	18.00
COMMON CARD (1-325)	.20	.09
SEMISTARS	.40	.18
UNLISTED STARS	.60	.25

SUBSET CARDS HALF VALUE OF BASE CARDS

Card	MINT	NRMT
❑ 1 Stacey Augmon	.20	.09
❑ 2 Mookie Blaylock	.20	.09
❑ 3 Craig Ehlo	.20	.09
❑ 4 Jon Koncak	.20	.09
❑ 5 Andrew Lang	.20	.09
❑ 6 Dee Brown	.20	.09
❑ 7 Sherman Douglas	.20	.09
❑ 8 Acie Earl	.20	.09
❑ 9 Rick Fox	.20	.09
❑ 10 Kevin Gamble	.20	.09
❑ 11 Xavier McDaniel	.20	.09
❑ 12 Dino Radja	.20	.09
❑ 13 Tony Bennett	.20	.09
❑ 14 Dell Curry	.20	.09
❑ 15 Kenny Gattison	.20	.09
❑ 16 Hersey Hawkins	.40	.18
❑ 17 Larry Johnson	.40	.18
❑ 18 Alonzo Mourning	.75	.35
❑ 19 David Wingate	.20	.09
❑ 20 B.J. Armstrong	.20	.09
❑ 21 Steve Kerr	.20	.09
❑ 22 Toni Kukoc	1.00	.45
❑ 23 Pete Myers	.20	.09
❑ 24 Scottie Pippen	2.00	.90
❑ 25 Bill Wennington	.20	.09
❑ 26 Terrell Brandon	.40	.18
❑ 27 Brad Daugherty	.20	.09
❑ 28 Tyrone Hill	.20	.09
❑ 29 Bobby Phills	.20	.09
❑ 30 Mark Price	.20	.09
❑ 31 Gerald Wilkins	.20	.09
❑ 32 John Williams	.20	.09
❑ 33 Lucious Harris	.20	.09
❑ 34 Jim Jackson	.40	.18
❑ 35 Jamal Mashburn	.60	.25
❑ 36 Sean Rooks	.20	.09
❑ 37 Doug Smith	.20	.09
❑ 38 Mahmoud Abdul-Rauf	.20	.09
❑ 39 LaPhonso Ellis	.20	.09
❑ 40 Dikembe Mutombo	.40	.18
❑ 41 Robert Pack	.20	.09
❑ 42 Rodney Rogers	.20	.09
❑ 43 Brian Williams	.20	.09
❑ 44 Reggie Williams	.20	.09
❑ 45 Joe Dumars	.60	.25
❑ 46 Allan Houston	1.00	.45
❑ 47 Lindsey Hunter	.40	.18
❑ 48 Terry Mills	.20	.09
❑ 49 Victor Alexander	.20	.09
❑ 50 Chris Gatling	.20	.09
❑ 51 Billy Owens	.20	.09
❑ 52 Latrell Sprewell	1.25	.55
❑ 53 Chris Webber	2.00	.90
❑ 54 Sam Cassell	.60	.25
❑ 55 Carl Herrera	.20	.09
❑ 56 Robert Horry	.20	.09
❑ 57 Hakeem Olajuwon	1.00	.45
❑ 58 Kenny Smith	.20	.09
❑ 59 Otis Thorpe	.20	.09
❑ 60 Antonio Davis	.20	.09
❑ 61 Dale Davis	.20	.09
❑ 62 Reggie Miller	.60	.25
❑ 63 Byron Scott	.40	.18
❑ 64 Rik Smits	.20	.09
❑ 65 Haywoode Workman	.20	.09
❑ 66 Terry Dehere	.20	.09
❑ 67 Harold Ellis	.20	.09
❑ 68 Gary Grant	.20	.09
❑ 69 Elmore Spencer	.20	.09
❑ 70 Loy Vaught	.20	.09
❑ 71 Elden Campbell	.20	.09

❑ 72 Doug Christie .20 .09
❑ 73 Vlade Divac .20 .09
❑ 74 George Lynch .20 .09
❑ 75 Anthony Peeler .20 .09
❑ 76 Nick Van Exel .60 .25
❑ 77 James Worthy .60 .25
❑ 78 Bimbo Coles .20 .09
❑ 79 Harold Miner .20 .09
❑ 80 John Salley .20 .09
❑ 81 Rony Seikaly .20 .09
❑ 82 Steve Smith .40 .18
❑ 83 Vin Baker .60 .25
❑ 84 Jon Barry .20 .09
❑ 85 Todd Day .20 .09
❑ 86 Lee Mayberry .20 .09
❑ 87 Eric Murdock .20 .09
❑ 88 Mike Brown .20 .09
❑ 89 Christian Laettner .40 .18
❑ 90 Isaiah Rider .40 .18
❑ 91 Doug West .20 .09
❑ 92 Micheal Williams .20 .09
❑ 93 Kenny Anderson .40 .18
❑ 94 Benoit Benjamin .20 .09
❑ 95 P.J. Brown .20 .09
❑ 96 Derrick Coleman .40 .18
❑ 97 Kevin Edwards .20 .09
❑ 98 Hubert Davis .20 .09
❑ 99 Patrick Ewing .60 .25
❑ 100 Derek Harper .20 .09
❑ 101 Anthony Mason .40 .18
❑ 102 Charles Oakley .20 .09
❑ 103 Charles Smith .20 .09
❑ 104 John Starks .20 .09
❑ 105 Nick Anderson .20 .09
❑ 106 Anfernee Hardaway 2.00 .90
❑ 107 Shaquille O'Neal 3.00 1.35
❑ 108 Dennis Scott .20 .09
❑ 109 Jeff Turner .20 .09
❑ 110 Dana Barros .20 .09
❑ 111 Shawn Bradley .20 .09
❑ 112 Jeff Malone .20 .09
❑ 113 Tim Perry .20 .09
❑ 114 Clarence Weatherspoon .20 .09
❑ 115 Danny Ainge .20 .09
❑ 116 Charles Barkley 1.00 .45
❑ 117 A.C. Green .40 .18
❑ 118 Kevin Johnson .40 .18
❑ 119 Dan Majerle .40 .18
❑ 120 Clyde Drexler .60 .25
❑ 121 Harvey Grant .20 .09
❑ 122 Jerome Kersey .20 .09
❑ 123 Clifford Robinson .40 .18
❑ 124 Rod Strickland .40 .18
❑ 125 Buck Williams .20 .09
❑ 126 Randy Brown .20 .09
❑ 127 Olden Polynice .20 .09
❑ 128 Mitch Richmond .60 .25
❑ 129 Lionel Simmons .20 .09
❑ 130 Spud Webb .20 .09
❑ 131 Walt Williams .20 .09
❑ 132 Willie Anderson .20 .09
❑ 133 Vinny Del Negro .20 .09
❑ 134 Sean Elliott .40 .18
❑ 135 Avery Johnson .20 .09
❑ 136 J.R. Reid .20 .09
❑ 137 David Robinson 1.00 .45
❑ 138 Dennis Rodman 1.25 .55
❑ 139 Kendall Gill .40 .18
❑ 140 Ervin Johnson .20 .09
❑ 141 Shawn Kemp 1.00 .45
❑ 142 Nate McMillan .20 .09
❑ 143 Gary Payton 1.00 .45
❑ 144 Sam Perkins .40 .18
❑ 145 David Benoit .20 .09
❑ 146 Jeff Hornacek .40 .18
❑ 147 Jay Humphries .20 .09
❑ 148 Karl Malone 1.00 .45
❑ 149 Bryon Russell .20 .09
❑ 150 Felton Spencer .20 .09
❑ 151 John Stockton .60 .25
❑ 152 Rex Chapman .20 .09
❑ 153 Calbert Cheaney .20 .09
❑ 154 Tom Gugliotta .40 .18
❑ 155 Don MacLean .20 .09
❑ 156 Gheorghe Muresan .20 .09
❑ 157 Doug Overton .20 .09
❑ 158 Brent Price .20 .09
❑ 159 Derrick Coleman USA .20 .09
❑ 160 Joe Dumars USA .40 .18
❑ 161 Tim Hardaway USA .40 .18
❑ 162 Kevin Johnson USA .20 .09
❑ 163 Larry Johnson USA .20 .09
❑ 164 Shawn Kemp USA .60 .25
❑ 165 Dan Majerle USA .20 .09
❑ 166 Reggie Miller USA .40 .18
❑ 167 Alonzo Mourning USA .60 .25
❑ 168 Shaquille O'Neal USA 1.25 .55
❑ 169 Mark Price USA .20 .09
❑ 170 Steve Smith USA .20 .09
❑ 171 Isiah Thomas USA .40 .18
❑ 172 Dominique Wilkins USA .40 .18
❑ 173 Checklist .20 .09
❑ 174 Checklist .20 .09
❑ 175 Checklist .20 .09
❑ 176 Tyrone Corbin .20 .09
❑ 177 Grant Long .20 .09
❑ 178 Ken Norman .20 .09
❑ 179 Steve Smith .40 .18
❑ 180 Blue Edwards .20 .09
❑ 181 Pervis Ellison .20 .09
❑ 182 Greg Minor RC .20 .09
❑ 183 Eric Montross RC .20 .09
❑ 184 Derek Strong .20 .09
❑ 185 David Wesley .20 .09
❑ 186 Dominique Wilkins .60 .25
❑ 187 Michael Adams .20 .09
❑ 188 Muggsy Bogues .40 .18
❑ 189 Scott Burrell .20 .09
❑ 190 Darrin Hancock .20 .09
❑ 191 Robert Parish .40 .18
❑ 192 Jud Buechler .20 .09
❑ 193 Ron Harper .40 .18
❑ 194 Larry Krystkowiak .20 .09
❑ 195 Will Perdue .20 .09
❑ 196 Dickey Simpkins RC .20 .09
❑ 197 Michael Cage .20 .09
❑ 198 Tony Campbell .20 .09
❑ 199 Danny Ferry .20 .09
❑ 200 Chris Mills .40 .18
❑ 201 Popeye Jones .20 .09
❑ 202 Jason Kidd RC 5.00 2.20
❑ 203 Roy Tarpley .20 .09
❑ 204 Lorenzo Williams .20 .09
❑ 205 Dale Ellis .20 .09
❑ 206 Tom Hammonds .20 .09
❑ 207 Jalen Rose RC 2.50 1.10
❑ 208 Reggie Slater .20 .09
❑ 209 Bryant Stith .20 .09
❑ 210 Rafael Addison .20 .09
❑ 211 Bill Curley RC .20 .09
❑ 212 Johnny Dawkins .20 .09
❑ 213 Grant Hill RC 8.00 3.60
❑ 214 Mark Macon .20 .09
❑ 215 Oliver Miller .20 .09
❑ 216 Ivano Newbill .20 .09
❑ 217 Mark West .20 .09
❑ 218 Tom Gugliotta .40 .18
❑ 219 Tim Hardaway .60 .25
❑ 220 Keith Jennings .20 .09
❑ 221 Dwayne Morton .20 .09
❑ 222 Chris Mullin .60 .25
❑ 223 Ricky Pierce .20 .09
❑ 224 Carlos Rogers RC .20 .09
❑ 225 Clifford Rozier RC .20 .09
❑ 226 Rony Seikaly .20 .09
❑ 227 Tim Breaux .20 .09
❑ 228 Scott Brooks .20 .09
❑ 229 Mario Elie .20 .09
❑ 230 Vernon Maxwell .20 .09
❑ 231 Zan Tabak .20 .09
❑ 232 Mark Jackson .20 .09
❑ 233 Derrick McKey .20 .09
❑ 234 Tony Massenburg .20 .09
❑ 235 Lamond Murray RC .40 .18
❑ 236 Charles Outlaw .20 .09
❑ 237 Eric Piatkowski RC .20 .09
❑ 238 Pooh Richardson .20 .09
❑ 239 Malik Sealy .20 .09
❑ 240 Cedric Ceballos .20 .09
❑ 241 Eddie Jones RC 4.00 1.80
❑ 242 Anthony Miller .20 .09
❑ 243 Tony Smith .20 .09
❑ 244 Sedale Threatt .20 .09
❑ 245 Ledell Eackles .20 .09
❑ 246 Kevin Gamble .20 .09
❑ 247 Matt Geiger .20 .09
❑ 248 Brad Lohaus .20 .09
❑ 249 Billy Owens .20 .09
❑ 250 Khalid Reeves RC .20 .09
❑ 251 Glen Rice .40 .18
❑ 252 Kevin Willis .20 .09
❑ 253 Marty Conlon .20 .09
❑ 254 Eric Mobley RC .20 .09
❑ 255 Johnny Newman .20 .09
❑ 256 Ed Pinckney .20 .09
❑ 257 Glenn Robinson RC 2.00 .90
❑ 258 Pat Durham .20 .09
❑ 259 Howard Eisley .20 .09
❑ 260 Winston Garland .20 .09
❑ 261 Stacey King .20 .09
❑ 262 Donyell Marshall RC .60 .25
❑ 263 Sean Rooks .20 .09
❑ 264 Chris Smith .20 .09
❑ 265 Chris Childs RC .60 .25
❑ 266 Sleepy Floyd .20 .09
❑ 267 Armon Gilliam .20 .09
❑ 268 Sean Higgins .20 .09
❑ 269 Rex Walters .20 .09
❑ 270 Greg Anthony .20 .09
❑ 271 Charlie Ward RC .60 .25
❑ 272 Herb Williams .20 .09
❑ 273 Monty Williams RC .20 .09
❑ 274 Anthony Avent .20 .09
❑ 275 Anthony Bowie .20 .09
❑ 276 Horace Grant .40 .18
❑ 277 Donald Royal .20 .09
❑ 278 Brian Shaw .20 .09
❑ 279 Brooks Thompson .20 .09
❑ 280 Derrick Alston .20 .09
❑ 281 Willie Burton .20 .09
❑ 282 Greg Graham .20 .09
❑ 283 B.J. Tyler RC .20 .09
❑ 284 Scott Williams .20 .09
❑ 285 Sharone Wright RC .20 .09
❑ 286 Joe Kleine .20 .09
❑ 287 Danny Manning .40 .18
❑ 288 Elliot Perry .20 .09
❑ 289 Wesley Person RC .60 .25
❑ 290 Trevor Ruffin RC .20 .09
❑ 291 Wayman Tisdale .20 .09
❑ 292 Mark Bryant .20 .09
❑ 293 Chris Dudley .20 .09
❑ 294 Aaron McKie RC .20 .09
❑ 295 Tracy Murray .20 .09
❑ 296 Terry Porter .20 .09
❑ 297 James Robinson .20 .09
❑ 298 Alaa Abdelnaby .20 .09
❑ 299 Duane Causwell .20 .09
❑ 300 Brian Grant RC 1.50 .70
❑ 301 Bobby Hurley .20 .09
❑ 302 Michael Smith RC .20 .09
❑ 303 Terry Cummings .20 .09
❑ 304 Moses Malone .60 .25
❑ 305 Julius Nwosu .20 .09
❑ 306 Chuck Person .20 .09
❑ 307 Doc Rivers .40 .18
❑ 308 Vincent Askew .20 .09
❑ 309 Sarunas Marciulionis .20 .09
❑ 310 Detlef Schrempf .40 .18
❑ 311 Dontonio Wingfield .20 .09
❑ 312 Antoine Carr .20 .09
❑ 313 Tom Chambers .20 .09
❑ 314 John Crotty .20 .09
❑ 315 Adam Keefe .20 .09
❑ 316 Jamie Watson RC .20 .09
❑ 317 Mitchell Butler .20 .09
❑ 318 Kevin Duckworth .20 .09
❑ 319 Juwan Howard RC 1.50 .70
❑ 320 Jim McIlvaine .20 .09
❑ 321 Scott Skiles .20 .09
❑ 322 Anthony Tucker RC .20 .09
❑ 323 Chris Webber 2.00 .90
❑ 324 Checklist .20 .09
❑ 325 Checklist .20 .09
❑ 326 Michael Jordan 12.00 5.50

1994-95 Flair Center Spotlight

	MINT	NRMT
COMPLETE SET (6)	40.00	18.00
*SINGLES: 3X TO 8X BASE CARD HI		
SER.1 STATED ODDS 1:25		

	MINT	NRMT
❑ 1 Patrick Ewing	5.00	2.20
❑ 2 Alonzo Mourning	6.00	2.70
❑ 3 Hakeem Olajuwon	8.00	3.60
❑ 4 Shaquille O'Neal	25.00	11.00
❑ 5 David Robinson	8.00	3.60
❑ 6 Chris Webber	15.00	6.75

1994-95 Flair Hot Numbers

	MINT	NRMT
COMPLETE SET (20)	60.00	27.00
*SINGLES: 1.5X TO 4X BASE CARD HI		
SER.1 STATED ODDS 1:6		

	MINT	NRMT
❑ 1 Vin Baker	2.50	1.10
❑ 2 Sam Cassell	2.50	1.10
❑ 3 Patrick Ewing	2.50	1.10
❑ 4 Anfernee Hardaway	8.00	3.60
❑ 5 Robert Horry	.75	.35
❑ 6 Shawn Kemp	4.00	1.80
❑ 7 Toni Kukoc	4.00	1.80
❑ 8 Jamal Mashburn	2.50	1.10
❑ 9 Reggie Miller	2.50	1.10
❑ 10 Dikembe Mutombo	1.50	.70
❑ 11 Hakeem Olajuwon	4.00	1.80
❑ 12 Shaquille O'Neal	12.00	5.50
❑ 13 Scottie Pippen	8.00	3.60
❑ 14 Isaiah Rider	1.50	.70
❑ 15 David Robinson	4.00	1.80
❑ 16 Latrell Sprewell	5.00	2.20
❑ 17 John Starks	.75	.35
❑ 18 John Stockton	2.50	1.10
❑ 19 Nick Van Exel	2.50	1.10
❑ 20 Chris Webber	8.00	3.60

1994-95 Flair Playmakers

	MINT	NRMT
COMPLETE SET (10)	10.00	4.50
*SINGLES: .75X TO 2X BASE CARD HI		
SER.2 STATED ODDS 1:4		

	MINT	NRMT
❑ 1 Kenny Anderson	.75	.35
❑ 2 Mookie Blaylock	.40	.18
❑ 3 Sam Cassell	1.25	.55
❑ 4 Anfernee Hardaway	4.00	1.80
❑ 5 Robert Pack	.40	.18
❑ 6 Scottie Pippen	4.00	1.80
❑ 7 Mark Price	.40	.18
❑ 8 Mitch Richmond	1.25	.55
❑ 9 John Stockton	1.25	.55
❑ 10 Nick Van Exel	1.25	.55

1994-95 Flair Rejectors

	MINT	NRMT
COMPLETE SET (6)	50.00	22.00
*SINGLES: 4X TO 10X BASE CARD HI		
SER.2 STATED ODDS 1:25		

	MINT	NRMT
❑ 1 Patrick Ewing	6.00	2.70
❑ 2 Alonzo Mourning	8.00	3.60
❑ 3 Dikembe Mutombo	4.00	1.80
❑ 4 Hakeem Olajuwon	10.00	4.50
❑ 5 Shaquille O'Neal	30.00	13.50
❑ 6 David Robinson	10.00	4.50

1994-95 Flair Scoring Power

	MINT	NRMT
COMPLETE SET (10)	30.00	13.50
*SINGLES: 1.5X TO 4X BASE CARD HI		
SER.1 STATED ODDS 1:8		

	MINT	NRMT
❑ 1 Charles Barkley	4.00	1.80
❑ 2 Patrick Ewing	2.50	1.10
❑ 3 Karl Malone	4.00	1.80
❑ 4 Hakeem Olajuwon	4.00	1.80
❑ 5 Shaquille O'Neal	12.00	5.50
❑ 6 Scottie Pippen	8.00	3.60
❑ 7 Mitch Richmond	2.50	1.10
❑ 8 David Robinson	4.00	1.80

	MINT	NRMT
❑ 9 Latrell Sprewell	5.00	2.20
❑ 10 Dominique Wilkins	2.50	1.10

1994-95 Flair Wave of the Future

	MINT	NRMT
COMPLETE SET (10)	30.00	13.50
*SINGLES: 1X TO 2.5X BASE CARD HI		
SER.2 STATED ODDS 1:7		

	MINT	NRMT
❑ 1 Brian Grant	4.00	1.80
❑ 2 Grant Hill	15.00	6.75
❑ 3 Juwan Howard	4.00	1.80
❑ 4 Eddie Jones	10.00	4.50
❑ 5 Jason Kidd	12.00	5.50
❑ 6 Donyell Marshall	1.50	.70
❑ 7 Eric Montross	.50	.23
❑ 8 Lamond Murray	1.00	.45
❑ 9 Wesley Person	1.50	.70
❑ 10 Glenn Robinson	5.00	2.20

1995-96 Flair

	MINT	NRMT
COMPLETE SET (250)	80.00	36.00
COMPLETE SERIES 1 (150)	40.00	18.00
COMPLETE SERIES 2 (100)	40.00	18.00
COMMON CARD (1-150)	.30	.14
COMMON CARD (151-250)	.20	.09
SEMISTARS SER.1	.60	.25
SEMISTARS SER.2	.40	.18
UNLISTED STARS SER.1	1.00	.45

UNLISTED STARS SER.2 .60 .25

❑ 1 Stacey Augmon .30 .14
❑ 2 Mookie Blaylock .30 .14
❑ 3 Grant Long .30 .14
❑ 4 Steve Smith .60 .25
❑ 5 Dee Brown .30 .14
❑ 6 Sherman Douglas .30 .14
❑ 7 Eric Montross .30 .14
❑ 8 Dino Radja .30 .14
❑ 9 David Wesley .30 .14
❑ 10 Muggsy Bogues .30 .14
❑ 11 Scott Burrell .30 .14
❑ 12 Dell Curry .30 .14
❑ 13 Larry Johnson .60 .25
❑ 14 Alonzo Mourning 1.00 .45
❑ 15 Michael Jordan 12.00 5.50
❑ 16 Steve Kerr .30 .14
❑ 17 Toni Kukoc 1.25 .55
❑ 18 Scottie Pippen 3.00 1.35
❑ 19 Terrell Brandon .60 .25
❑ 20 Tyrone Hill .30 .14
❑ 21 Chris Mills .30 .14
❑ 22 Bobby Phills .30 .14
❑ 23 Mark Price .30 .14
❑ 24 John Williams .30 .14
❑ 25 Jim Jackson .30 .14
❑ 26 Popeye Jones .30 .14
❑ 27 Jason Kidd 3.00 1.35
❑ 28 Jamal Mashburn .60 .25
❑ 29 Lorenzo Williams .30 .14
❑ 30 Mahmoud Abdul-Rauf .30 .14
❑ 31 Dikembe Mutombo .60 .25
❑ 32 Robert Pack .30 .14
❑ 33 Jalen Rose 1.25 .55
❑ 34 Bryant Stith .30 .14
❑ 35 Reggie Williams .30 .14
❑ 36 Joe Dumars 1.00 .45
❑ 37 Grant Hill 5.00 2.20
❑ 38 Allan Houston 1.25 .55
❑ 39 Lindsey Hunter .30 .14
❑ 40 Terry Mills .30 .14
❑ 41 Chris Gatling .30 .14
❑ 42 Tim Hardaway 1.00 .45
❑ 43 Donyell Marshall .60 .25
❑ 44 Chris Mullin 1.00 .45
❑ 45 Carlos Rogers .30 .14
❑ 46 Clifford Rozier .30 .14
❑ 47 Latrell Sprewell 2.00 .90
❑ 48 Sam Cassell .60 .25
❑ 49 Clyde Drexler 1.00 .45
❑ 50 Mario Elie .30 .14
❑ 51 Robert Horry .30 .14
❑ 52 Hakeem Olajuwon 1.50 .70
❑ 53 Kenny Smith .30 .14
❑ 54 Antonio Davis .30 .14
❑ 55 Dale Davis .30 .14
❑ 56 Mark Jackson .30 .14
❑ 57 Derrick McKey .30 .14
❑ 58 Reggie Miller 1.00 .45
❑ 59 Rik Smits .30 .14
❑ 60 Lamond Murray .30 .14
❑ 61 Pooh Richardson .30 .14
❑ 62 Malik Sealy .30 .14
❑ 63 Loy Vaught .30 .14
❑ 64 Elden Campbell .30 .14
❑ 65 Cedric Ceballos .30 .14
❑ 66 Vlade Divac .30 .14
❑ 67 Eddie Jones 2.00 .90
❑ 68 Nick Van Exel .60 .25
❑ 69 Bimbo Coles .30 .14
❑ 70 Billy Owens .30 .14
❑ 71 Khalid Reeves .30 .14
❑ 72 Glen Rice .60 .25
❑ 73 Kevin Willis .30 .14
❑ 74 Vin Baker 1.00 .45
❑ 75 Todd Day .30 .14
❑ 76 Eric Murdock .30 .14
❑ 77 Glenn Robinson 1.00 .45
❑ 78 Tom Gugliotta .60 .25
❑ 79 Christian Laettner .60 .25
❑ 80 Isaiah Rider .60 .25
❑ 81 Doug West .30 .14
❑ 82 Kenny Anderson .60 .25
❑ 83 P.J. Brown .30 .14
❑ 84 Derrick Coleman .60 .25
❑ 85 Armon Gilliam .30 .14
❑ 86 Chris Morris .30 .14
❑ 87 Hubert Davis .30 .14
❑ 88 Patrick Ewing 1.00 .45
❑ 89 Derek Harper .30 .14
❑ 90 Anthony Mason .60 .25
❑ 91 Charles Oakley .30 .14
❑ 92 Charles Smith .30 .14
❑ 93 John Starks .30 .14
❑ 94 Nick Anderson .30 .14
❑ 95 Horace Grant .60 .25
❑ 96 Anfernee Hardaway 3.00 1.35
❑ 97 Shaquille O'Neal 5.00 2.20
❑ 98 Dennis Scott .30 .14
❑ 99 Brian Shaw .30 .14
❑ 100 Dana Barros .30 .14
❑ 101 Shawn Bradley .30 .14
❑ 102 Clarence Weatherspoon .30 .14
❑ 103 Sharone Wright .30 .14
❑ 104 Charles Barkley 1.50 .70
❑ 105 A.C. Green .60 .25
❑ 106 Kevin Johnson .60 .25
❑ 107 Dan Majerle .30 .14
❑ 108 Danny Manning .60 .25
❑ 109 Elliot Perry .30 .14
❑ 110 Wesley Person .60 .25
❑ 111 Terry Porter .30 .14
❑ 112 Clifford Robinson .30 .14
❑ 113 Rod Strickland .60 .25
❑ 114 Otis Thorpe .30 .14
❑ 115 Buck Williams .30 .14
❑ 116 Brian Grant 1.00 .45
❑ 117 Bobby Hurley .30 .14
❑ 118 Olden Polynice .30 .14
❑ 119 Mitch Richmond 1.00 .45
❑ 120 Walt Williams .30 .14
❑ 121 Vinny Del Negro .30 .14
❑ 122 Sean Elliott .30 .14
❑ 123 Avery Johnson .30 .14
❑ 124 David Robinson 1.50 .70
❑ 125 Dennis Rodman 2.00 .90
❑ 126 Shawn Kemp 1.50 .70
❑ 127 Nate McMillan .30 .14
❑ 128 Gary Payton 1.50 .70
❑ 129 Sam Perkins .60 .25
❑ 130 Detlef Schrempf .60 .25
❑ 131 B.J. Armstrong .30 .14
❑ 132 Jerome Kersey .30 .14
❑ 133 Oliver Miller .30 .14
❑ 134 John Salley .30 .14
❑ 135 David Benoit .30 .14
❑ 136 Antoine Carr .30 .14
❑ 137 Jeff Hornacek .60 .25
❑ 138 Karl Malone 1.50 .70
❑ 139 John Stockton 1.00 .45
❑ 140 Greg Anthony .30 .14
❑ 141 Benoit Benjamin .30 .14
❑ 142 Blue Edwards .30 .14
❑ 143 Byron Scott .30 .14
❑ 144 Calbert Cheaney .30 .14
❑ 145 Juwan Howard 1.00 .45
❑ 146 Gheorghe Muresan .30 .14
❑ 147 Scott Skiles .30 .14
❑ 148 Chris Webber 3.00 1.35
❑ 149 Checklist .30 .14
❑ 150 Checklist .30 .14
❑ 151 Stacey Augmon .20 .09
❑ 152 Mookie Blaylock .20 .09
❑ 153 Andrew Lang .20 .09
❑ 154 Steve Smith .40 .18
❑ 155 Dana Barros .20 .09
❑ 156 Rick Fox .20 .09
❑ 157 Kendall Gill .40 .18
❑ 158 Khalid Reeves .20 .09
❑ 159 Glen Rice .40 .18
❑ 160 Dennis Rodman 2.00 .90
❑ 161 Dan Majerle .20 .09
❑ 162 Tony Dumas .20 .09
❑ 163 Dale Ellis .20 .09
❑ 164 Otis Thorpe .20 .09
❑ 165 Rony Seikaly .20 .09
❑ 166 Sam Cassell .40 .18
❑ 167 Clyde Drexler .60 .25
❑ 168 Robert Horry .20 .09
❑ 169 Hakeem Olajuwon 1.00 .45
❑ 170 Ricky Pierce .20 .09
❑ 171 Rodney Rogers .20 .09
❑ 172 Brian Williams .20 .09
❑ 173 Magic Johnson 2.00 .90
❑ 174 Alonzo Mourning .60 .25
❑ 175 Lee Mayberry .20 .09
❑ 176 Terry Porter .20 .09
❑ 177 Shawn Bradley .20 .09
❑ 178 Jayson Williams .40 .18
❑ 179 Gary Grant .20 .09
❑ 180 Jon Koncak .20 .09
❑ 181 Derrick Coleman .40 .18
❑ 182 Vernon Maxwell .20 .09
❑ 183 John Williams .20 .09
❑ 184 Aaron McKie .20 .09
❑ 185 Michael Smith .20 .09
❑ 186 Chuck Person .20 .09
❑ 187 Hersey Hawkins .40 .18
❑ 188 Shawn Kemp 1.00 .45
❑ 189 Gary Payton 1.00 .45
❑ 190 Detlef Schrempf .40 .18
❑ 191 Chris Morris .20 .09
❑ 192 Robert Pack .20 .09
❑ 193 Willie Anderson EXP .20 .09
❑ 194 Oliver Miller EXP .20 .09
❑ 195 Alvin Robertson EXP .20 .09
❑ 196 Greg Anthony EXP .20 .09
❑ 197 Blue Edwards EXP .20 .09
❑ 198 Byron Scott EXP .20 .09
❑ 199 Cory Alexander RC .20 .09
❑ 200 Brent Barry RC .60 .25
❑ 201 Travis Best RC .40 .18
❑ 202 Jason Caffey RC .40 .18
❑ 203 Sasha Danilovic RC .20 .09
❑ 204 Tyus Edney RC .20 .09
❑ 205 Michael Finley RC 2.50 1.10
❑ 206 Kevin Garnett RC 10.00 4.50
❑ 207 Alan Henderson RC .60 .25
❑ 208 Antonio McDyess RC 3.00 1.35
❑ 209 Loren Meyer RC .20 .09
❑ 210 Lawrence Moten RC .20 .09
❑ 211 Ed O'Bannon RC .20 .09
❑ 212 Greg Ostertag RC .20 .09
❑ 213 Cherokee Parks RC .20 .09
❑ 214 Theo Ratliff RC .75 .35
❑ 215 Bryant Reeves RC .60 .25
❑ 216 Shawn Respert RC .20 .09
❑ 217 Arvydas Sabonis RC 1.00 .45
❑ 218 Joe Smith RC 2.00 .90
❑ 219 Jerry Stackhouse RC 2.00 .90
❑ 220 Damon Stoudamire RC 3.00 1.35
❑ 221 Bob Sura RC .40 .18
❑ 222 Kurt Thomas RC .40 .18
❑ 223 Gary Trent RC .20 .09
❑ 224 David Vaughn RC .20 .09
❑ 225 Rasheed Wallace RC 2.50 1.10
❑ 226 Eric Williams RC .40 .18
❑ 227 Corliss Williamson RC 1.25 .55
❑ 228 George Zidek RC .20 .09
❑ 229 Vin Baker STY .40 .18
❑ 230 Charles Barkley STY .60 .25
❑ 231 Patrick Ewing STY .40 .18
❑ 232 Anfernee Hardaway STY 1.00 .45
❑ 233 Grant Hill STY 1.50 .70
❑ 234 Larry Johnson STY .20 .09
❑ 235 Michael Jordan STY 4.00 1.80
❑ 236 Jason Kidd STY 1.00 .45
❑ 237 Karl Malone STY .60 .25
❑ 238 Jamal Mashburn STY .20 .09
❑ 239 Reggie Miller STY .40 .18
❑ 240 Shaquille O'Neal STY 1.50 .70
❑ 241 Scottie Pippen STY 1.00 .45
❑ 242 Mitch Richmond STY .40 .18
❑ 243 Clifford Robinson STY .20 .09
❑ 244 David Robinson STY .60 .25
❑ 245 Glenn Robinson STY .40 .18
❑ 246 John Stockton STY .40 .18
❑ 247 Nick Van Exel STY .20 .09
❑ 248 Chris Webber STY 1.00 .45
❑ 249 Checklist .20 .09
❑ 250 Checklist .20 .09

1995-96 Flair Anticipation

	MINT	NRMT
COMPLETE SET (10)	100.00	45.00
COMMON CARD (1-10)	4.00	1.80
SER.2 STATED ODDS 1:36		

	MINT	NRMT
❑ 1 Grant Hill	20.00	9.00
❑ 2 Michael Jordan	50.00	22.00
❑ 3 Shawn Kemp	6.00	2.70
❑ 4 Jason Kidd	12.00	5.50
❑ 5 Alonzo Mourning	4.00	1.80
❑ 6 Hakeem Olajuwon	6.00	2.70
❑ 7 Shaquille O'Neal	20.00	9.00
❑ 8 Glenn Robinson	4.00	1.80
❑ 9 Joe Smith	6.00	2.70
❑ 10 Jerry Stackhouse	6.00	2.70

1995-96 Flair Center Spotlight

	MINT	NRMT
COMPLETE SET (6)	20.00	9.00
COMMON CARD (1-6)	1.25	.55
SEMISTARS	4.00	1.80
SER.1 STATED ODDS 1:18		

	MINT	NRMT
❑ 1 Vlade Divac	1.25	.55
❑ 2 Patrick Ewing	4.00	1.80
❑ 3 Alonzo Mourning	4.00	1.80
❑ 4 Hakeem Olajuwon	5.00	2.20
❑ 5 Shaquille O'Neal	15.00	6.75
❑ 6 David Robinson	5.00	2.20

1995-96 Flair Class of '95

	MINT	NRMT
COMPLETE SET (15)	20.00	9.00
COMMON CARD (R1-R15)	.25	.11
SEMISTARS	.50	.23
UNLISTED STARS	.75	.35
RANDOM INSERTS IN SER.1 PACKS		

	MINT	NRMT
❑ R1 Brent Barry	.75	.35
❑ R2 Kevin Garnett	10.00	4.50
❑ R3 Antonio McDyess	4.00	1.80
❑ R4 Ed O'Bannon	.25	.11
❑ R5 Cherokee Parks	.25	.11
❑ R6 Bryant Reeves	.50	.23
❑ R7 Shawn Respert	.25	.11
❑ R8 Joe Smith	2.50	1.10
❑ R9 Jerry Stackhouse	2.50	1.10
❑ R10 Damon Stoudamire	4.00	1.80
❑ R11 Kurt Thomas	.25	.11
❑ R12 Gary Trent	.25	.11
❑ R13 Rasheed Wallace	3.00	1.35
❑ R14 Eric Williams	.25	.11
❑ R15 Corliss Williamson	.75	.35

1995-96 Flair Hot Numbers

	MINT	NRMT
COMPLETE SET (15)	200.00	90.00
COMMON CARD (1-15)	2.50	1.10
SEMISTARS	6.00	2.70
SER.1 STATED ODDS 1:36		

	MINT	NRMT
❑ 1 Charles Barkley	10.00	4.50
❑ 2 Grant Hill	30.00	13.50
❑ 3 Eddie Jones	12.00	5.50
❑ 4 Michael Jordan	80.00	36.00
❑ 5 Shawn Kemp	10.00	4.50
❑ 6 Jason Kidd	20.00	9.00
❑ 7 Karl Malone	10.00	4.50
❑ 8 Alonzo Mourning	6.00	2.70
❑ 9 Dikembe Mutombo	2.50	1.10
❑ 10 Hakeem Olajuwon	10.00	4.50
❑ 11 Shaquille O'Neal	30.00	13.50
❑ 12 Glenn Robinson	6.00	2.70
❑ 13 Dennis Rodman	12.00	5.50
❑ 14 Latrell Sprewell	12.00	5.50
❑ 15 Chris Webber	20.00	9.00

1995-96 Flair New Heights

	MINT	NRMT
COMPLETE SET (10)	70.00	32.00
COMMON CARD (1-10)	2.00	.90
UNLISTED STARS	3.00	1.35
SER.2 STATED ODDS 1:18 HOBBY		

	MINT	NRMT
❑ 1 Anfernee Hardaway	10.00	4.50
❑ 2 Grant Hill	15.00	6.75
❑ 3 Larry Johnson	2.00	.90
❑ 4 Michael Jordan	40.00	18.00
❑ 5 Shawn Kemp	5.00	2.20
❑ 6 Karl Malone	5.00	2.20
❑ 7 Hakeem Olajuwon	5.00	2.20
❑ 8 David Robinson	5.00	2.20
❑ 9 Glenn Robinson	3.00	1.35
❑ 10 Chris Webber	10.00	4.50

1995-96 Flair Perimeter Power

	MINT	NRMT
COMPLETE SET (15)	15.00	6.75
COMMON CARD (1-15)	.60	.25
SEMISTARS	.75	.35
UNLISTED STARS	1.25	.55
SER.1 STATED ODDS 1:12		

	MINT	NRMT
❑ 1 Dana Barros	.60	.25
❑ 2 Clyde Drexler	1.25	.55
❑ 3 Anfernee Hardaway	4.00	1.80
❑ 4 Tim Hardaway	1.25	.55
❑ 5 Dan Majerle	.60	.25
❑ 6 Jamal Mashburn	.75	.35
❑ 7 Reggie Miller	1.25	.55
❑ 8 Gary Payton	2.00	.90
❑ 9 Scottie Pippen	4.00	1.80
❑ 10 Glen Rice	.75	.35
❑ 11 Mitch Richmond	1.25	.55
❑ 12 Steve Smith	.75	.35
❑ 13 John Starks	.60	.25
❑ 14 John Stockton	1.25	.55
❑ 15 Nick Van Exel	.75	.35

1995-96 Flair Play Makers

	MINT	NRMT
COMPLETE SET (10)	150.00	70.00
COMMON CARD (1-10)	6.00	2.70
SEMISTARS	8.00	3.60
UNLISTED STARS	12.00	5.50
SER.2 STATED ODDS 1:54		

	MINT	NRMT
❑ 1 Clyde Drexler	12.00	5.50
❑ 2 Anfernee Hardaway	40.00	18.00
❑ 3 Jamal Mashburn	6.00	2.70
❑ 4 Reggie Miller	12.00	5.50
❑ 5 Gary Payton	20.00	9.00
❑ 6 Scottie Pippen	40.00	18.00
❑ 7 Mitch Richmond	12.00	5.50

Card	Mint	NRMT
❑ 8 David Robinson	20.00	9.00
❑ 9 Jerry Stackhouse	20.00	9.00
❑ 10 Nick Van Exel	8.00	3.60

1995-96 Flair Wave of the Future

	MINT	NRMT
COMPLETE SET (10)	25.00	11.00
COMMON CARD (1-10)	.75	.35
SEMISTARS	1.50	.70
SER.2 STATED ODDS 1:12		

Card	Mint	NRMT
❑ 1 Tyus Edney	.75	.35
❑ 2 Michael Finley	3.00	1.35
❑ 3 Kevin Garnett	12.00	5.50
❑ 4 Antonio McDyess	4.00	1.80
❑ 5 Ed O'Bannon	.75	.35
❑ 6 Arvydas Sabonis	1.50	.70
❑ 7 Joe Smith	2.50	1.10
❑ 8 Jerry Stackhouse	2.50	1.10
❑ 9 Damon Stoudamire	4.00	1.80
❑ 10 Rasheed Wallace	3.00	1.35

1996-97 Flair Showcase Row 2

	MINT	NRMT
COMPLETE SET (90)	60.00	27.00
COMMON CARD (1-90)	.30	.14
SEMISTARS	.50	.23
UNLISTED STARS	.75	.35
1-30 ODDS 1.5:1		
31-60 ODDS 1:2		
61-90 ODDS 1:1.5		

Card	Mint	NRMT
❑ 1 Anfernee Hardaway	2.50	1.10
❑ 2 Mitch Richmond	.75	.35
❑ 3 Allen Iverson RC	8.00	3.60
❑ 4 Charles Barkley	1.25	.55
❑ 5 Juwan Howard	.50	.23
❑ 6 David Robinson	1.25	.55
❑ 7 Gary Payton	1.25	.55
❑ 8 Kerry Kittles RC	1.50	.70
❑ 9 Dennis Rodman	1.50	.70
❑ 10 Shaquille O'Neal	4.00	1.80
❑ 11 Stephon Marbury RC	5.00	2.20
❑ 12 John Stockton	.75	.35
❑ 13 Glenn Robinson	.75	.35
❑ 14 Hakeem Olajuwon	1.25	.55
❑ 15 Jason Kidd	2.50	1.10
❑ 16 Jerry Stackhouse	.75	.35
❑ 17 Joe Smith	.75	.35
❑ 18 Reggie Miller	.75	.35
❑ 19 Grant Hill	4.00	1.80
❑ 20 Damon Stoudamire	1.25	.55
❑ 21 Kevin Garnett	5.00	2.20
❑ 22 Clyde Drexler	.75	.35
❑ 23 Michael Jordan	10.00	4.50
❑ 24 Antonio McDyess	1.25	.55
❑ 25 Chris Webber	2.50	1.10
❑ 26 Antoine Walker RC	3.00	1.35
❑ 27 Scottie Pippen	2.50	1.10
❑ 28 Karl Malone	1.25	.55
❑ 29 Shareef Abdur-Rahim RC	5.00	2.20
❑ 30 Shawn Kemp	1.25	.55
❑ 31 Kobe Bryant RC	20.00	9.00
❑ 32 Derrick Coleman	.50	.23
❑ 33 Alonzo Mourning	.75	.35
❑ 34 Anthony Mason	.50	.23
❑ 35 Ray Allen RC	3.00	1.35
❑ 36 Arvydas Sabonis	.50	.23
❑ 37 Brian Grant	.75	.35
❑ 38 Bryant Reeves	.30	.14
❑ 39 Christian Laettner	.50	.23
❑ 40 Tom Gugliotta	.50	.23
❑ 41 Latrell Sprewell	1.50	.70
❑ 42 Erick Dampier RC	.50	.23
❑ 43 Gheorghe Muresan	.30	.14
❑ 44 Glen Rice	.50	.23
❑ 45 Patrick Ewing	.75	.35
❑ 46 Jim Jackson	.30	.14
❑ 47 Michael Finley	.75	.35
❑ 48 Toni Kukoc	1.00	.45
❑ 49 Marcus Camby RC	2.50	1.10
❑ 50 Kenny Anderson	.50	.23
❑ 51 Mark Price	.30	.14
❑ 52 Tim Hardaway	.75	.35
❑ 53 Mookie Blaylock	.30	.14
❑ 54 Steve Smith	.50	.23
❑ 55 Terrell Brandon	.50	.23
❑ 56 Lorenzen Wright RC	.50	.23
❑ 57 Sasha Danilovic	.30	.14
❑ 58 Jeff Hornacek	.50	.23
❑ 59 Eddie Jones	1.50	.70
❑ 60 Vin Baker	.50	.23
❑ 61 Chris Childs	.30	.14
❑ 62 Clifford Robinson	.30	.14
❑ 63 Anthony Peeler	.30	.14
❑ 64 Dino Radja	.30	.14
❑ 65 Joe Dumars	.75	.35
❑ 66 Loy Vaught	.30	.14
❑ 67 Rony Seikaly	.30	.14
❑ 68 Vitaly Potapenko RC	.30	.14
❑ 69 Chris Gatling	.30	.14
❑ 70 Dale Ellis	.30	.14
❑ 71 Allan Houston	.75	.35
❑ 72 Doug Christie	.30	.14
❑ 73 LaPhonso Ellis	.30	.14
❑ 74 Kendall Gill	.50	.23
❑ 75 Rik Smits	.30	.14
❑ 76 Bobby Phills	.30	.14
❑ 77 Malik Sealy	.30	.14
❑ 78 Sean Elliott	.30	.14
❑ 79 Vlade Divac	.30	.14
❑ 80 David Wesley	.30	.14
❑ 81 Dominique Wilkins	.75	.35
❑ 82 Danny Manning	.50	.23
❑ 83 Detlef Schrempf	.50	.23
❑ 84 Hersey Hawkins	.50	.23
❑ 85 Lindsey Hunter	.30	.14
❑ 86 Mahmoud Abdul-Rauf	.30	.14
❑ 87 Shawn Bradley	.30	.14
❑ 88 Horace Grant	.50	.23
❑ 89 Cedric Ceballos	.30	.14
❑ 90 Jamal Mashburn	.50	.23
❑ NNO Jerry Stackhouse Promo 3-card strip	3.00	1.35

1996-97 Flair Showcase Row 1

	MINT	NRMT
COMPLETE SET (90)	80.00	36.00
COMMON CARD (1-90)	.50	.23
*STARS/RC's: .6X TO 1.5X ROW 2		
1-30 ODDS 1:2.5		
31-60 ODDS 1:2		
61-90 ODDS 1:3.5		

1996-97 Flair Showcase Row 0

	MINT	NRMT
COMPLETE SET (90)	900.00	400.00
COMMON CARD (1-30)	10.00	4.50
*STARS 1-30: 5X TO 12X ROW 2		
*RC's 1-30: 2.5X TO 6X HI		
1-30 ODDS 1:24		
COMMON CARD (31-60)	3.00	1.35
*STARS 31-60: 4X TO 10X ROW 2		
*RC's 31-60: 1.5X TO 4X ROW 2		
31-60 ODDS 1:10		
COMMON CARD (61-90)	.60	.25
*STARS/RC's 61-90: .75X TO 2X ROW 2		
61-90 ODDS 1:5		

Card	Mint	NRMT
❑ 31 Kobe Bryant	100.00	45.00

1996-97 Flair Showcase Class of '96

	MINT	NRMT
COMPLETE SET (20)	30.00	13.50
COMMON CARD (1-20)	.60	.25
SEMISTARS	1.00	.45
UNLISTED STARS	1.50	.70
STATED ODDS 1:5		

Card	Mint	NRMT
❑ 1 Shareef Abdur-Rahim	5.00	2.20
❑ 2 Ray Allen	3.00	1.35
❑ 3 Shandon Anderson	1.50	.70
❑ 4 Kobe Bryant	15.00	6.75
❑ 5 Marcus Camby	2.50	1.10
❑ 6 Erick Dampier	.60	.25
❑ 7 Derek Fisher	1.50	.70
❑ 8 Todd Fuller	.60	.25
❑ 9 Othella Harrington	1.00	.45

❑ 10 Allen Iverson	8.00	3.60
❑ 11 Kerry Kittles	1.50	.70
❑ 12 Travis Knight	.60	.25
❑ 13 Matt Maloney	.60	.25
❑ 14 Stephon Marbury	5.00	2.20
❑ 15 Steve Nash	.60	.25
❑ 16 Jermaine O'Neal	1.50	.70
❑ 17 Vitaly Potapenko	.60	.25
❑ 18 Roy Rogers	.60	.25
❑ 19 Antoine Walker	3.00	1.35
❑ 20 Lorenzen Wright	.60	.25

1996-97 Flair Showcase Hot Shots

	MINT	NRMT
COMPLETE SET (20)	500.00	220.00
COMMON CARD (1-20)	10.00	4.50

STATED ODDS 1:90

❑ 1 Michael Jordan	150.00	70.00
❑ 2 Kevin Garnett	60.00	27.00
❑ 3 Damon Stoudamire	15.00	6.75
❑ 4 Anfernee Hardaway	30.00	13.50
❑ 5 Shaquille O'Neal	50.00	22.00
❑ 6 Grant Hill	50.00	22.00
❑ 7 Dennis Rodman	20.00	9.00
❑ 8 Shawn Kemp	15.00	6.75
❑ 9 Scottie Pippen	30.00	13.50
❑ 10 Juwan Howard	10.00	4.50
❑ 11 Jason Kidd	30.00	13.50
❑ 12 Hakeem Olajuwon	15.00	6.75
❑ 13 Karl Malone	15.00	6.75
❑ 14 Joe Smith	10.00	4.50
❑ 15 David Robinson	15.00	6.75
❑ 16 Jerry Stackhouse	10.00	4.50
❑ 17 Antonio McDyess	15.00	6.75
❑ 18 Clyde Drexler	10.00	4.50
❑ 19 Gary Payton	15.00	6.75
❑ 20 Eddie Jones	20.00	9.00

1997-98 Flair Showcase Row 3

	MINT	NRMT
COMPLETE SET (80)	50.00	22.00
COMMON CARD (1-80)	.30	.14
SEMISTARS	.50	.23
UNLISTED STARS	.75	.35

1-20 STATED ODDS 1:0.9
21-40 STATED ODDS 1:1.1
41-60 STATED ODDS 1:1.5
61-80 STATED ODDS 1:2
UNPRICED MASTERPIECES SERIAL #'d TO 1
MASTERPIECES: RANDOM INS.IN PACKS

❑ 1 Michael Jordan	10.00	4.50
❑ 2 Grant Hill	4.00	1.80
❑ 3 Allen Iverson	4.00	1.80
❑ 4 Kevin Garnett	5.00	2.20
❑ 5 Tim Duncan RC	10.00	4.50
❑ 6 Shawn Kemp	1.25	.55
❑ 7 Shaquille O'Neal	4.00	1.80
❑ 8 Antoine Walker	1.50	.70
❑ 9 Shareef Abdur-Rahim	2.50	1.10
❑ 10 Damon Stoudamire	1.00	.45
❑ 11 Anfernee Hardaway	2.50	1.10
❑ 12 Keith Van Horn RC	4.00	1.80
❑ 13 Dennis Rodman	1.50	.70
❑ 14 Ron Mercer RC	2.50	1.10
❑ 15 Stephon Marbury	2.50	1.10
❑ 16 Scottie Pippen	2.50	1.10
❑ 17 Kerry Kittles	.75	.35
❑ 18 Kobe Bryant	6.00	2.70
❑ 19 Marcus Camby	1.00	.45
❑ 20 Chauncey Billups RC	1.00	.45
❑ 21 Tracy McGrady RC	8.00	3.60
❑ 22 Joe Smith	.50	.23
❑ 23 Brevin Knight RC	1.25	.55
❑ 24 Danny Fortson RC	.75	.35
❑ 25 Tim Thomas RC	2.50	1.10
❑ 26 Gary Payton	1.25	.55
❑ 27 David Robinson	1.25	.55
❑ 28 Hakeem Olajuwon	1.25	.55
❑ 29 Antonio Daniels RC	.75	.35
❑ 30 Antonio McDyess	1.00	.45
❑ 31 Eddie Jones	1.50	.70
❑ 32 Adonal Foyle RC	.50	.23
❑ 33 Glenn Robinson	.50	.23
❑ 34 Charles Barkley	1.25	.55
❑ 35 Vin Baker	.50	.23
❑ 36 Jerry Stackhouse	.50	.23
❑ 37 Ray Allen	1.25	.55
❑ 38 Derek Anderson RC	2.00	.90
❑ 39 Isaac Austin	.30	.14
❑ 40 Tony Battie RC	.75	.35
❑ 41 Tariq Abdul-Wahad RC	.50	.23
❑ 42 Dikembe Mutombo	.50	.23
❑ 43 Clyde Drexler	.75	.35
❑ 44 Chris Mullin	.75	.35
❑ 45 Tim Hardaway	.75	.35
❑ 46 Terrell Brandon	.50	.23
❑ 47 John Stockton	.75	.35
❑ 48 Patrick Ewing	.75	.35
❑ 49 Horace Grant	.50	.23
❑ 50 Tom Gugliotta	.50	.23
❑ 51 Mookie Blaylock	.30	.14
❑ 52 Mitch Richmond	.75	.35
❑ 53 Anthony Mason	.50	.23
❑ 54 Michael Finley	.75	.35
❑ 55 Jason Kidd	2.50	1.10
❑ 56 Karl Malone	1.25	.55
❑ 57 Reggie Miller	.75	.35
❑ 58 Steve Smith	.50	.23
❑ 59 Glen Rice	.50	.23
❑ 60 Bryant Stith	.30	.14
❑ 61 Loy Vaught	.30	.14
❑ 62 Brian Grant	.50	.23
❑ 63 Joe Dumars	.75	.35
❑ 64 Juwan Howard	.50	.23
❑ 65 Rik Smits	.30	.14
❑ 66 Alonzo Mourning	.75	.35
❑ 67 Allan Houston	.75	.35
❑ 68 Chris Webber	2.50	1.10
❑ 69 Kendall Gill	.50	.23
❑ 70 Rony Seikaly	.30	.14
❑ 71 Kenny Anderson	.50	.23
❑ 72 John Wallace	.30	.14
❑ 73 Bryant Reeves	.30	.14
❑ 74 Brian Williams	.30	.14
❑ 75 Larry Johnson	.50	.23
❑ 76 Shawn Bradley	.30	.14
❑ 77 Kevin Johnson	.50	.23
❑ 78 Rod Strickland	.50	.23
❑ 79 Rodney Rogers	.30	.14
❑ 80 Rasheed Wallace	.75	.35
❑ NNO Grant Hill Promo 4-card strip	5.00	2.20

1997-98 Flair Showcase Row 2

	MINT	NRMT
COMPLETE SET (80)	150.00	70.00
COMMON CARD (1-80)	.50	.23

*STARS: .6X TO 1.5X ROW 3
*RCs: .75X TO 2X ROW 3
1-20 STATED ODDS 1:3
21-40 STATED ODDS 1:2.5
41-60 STATED ODDS 1:4
61-80 STATED ODDS 1:3.5

1997-98 Flair Showcase Row 1

	MINT	NRMT
COMPLETE SET (80)	500.00	220.00
COMMON CARD (1-20)	3.00	1.35
*STARS/RCs 1-20: 1.5X TO 4X ROW 3		
1-20 STATED ODDS 1:16		
COMMON CARD (21-40)	1.50	.70
*STARS/RCs 21-40: 2X TO 5X ROW 3		
21-40 STATED ODDS 1:24		
COMMON CARD (41-60)	.75	.35
*STARS 41-60: 1X TO 2.5X ROW 3		
*RCs 41-60: 1.25X TO 3X ROW 3		
41-60 STATED ODDS 1:6		
COMMON CARD (61-80)	1.00	.45

*STARS 61-80: 1.25X TO 3X ROW 3
61-80 STATED ODDS 1:10

1997-98 Flair Showcase Row 0

	MINT	NRMT
COMMON CARD (1-20)	10.00	4.50
*STARS 1-20: 6X TO 15X ROW 3		
*RCs 1-20: 4X TO 10X ROW 3		
STATED PRINT RUN 250 SERIAL #'d SETS		
COMMON CARD (21-40)	3.00	1.35
*STARS 21-40: 4X TO 10X ROW 3		
*RCs 21-40: 3X TO 8X ROW 3		
STATED PRINT RUN 500 SERIAL #'d SETS		
COMMON CARD (41-60)	2.00	.90
STARS 41-60: 2.5X TO 6X ROW 3		
*RCs 41-60: 2.5X TO 6X ROW 3		
STATED PRINT RUN 1000 SERIAL #'d SETS		
COMMON CARD (61-80)	1.25	.55
*STARS 61-80: 1.5X TO 4X ROW 3		
STATED PRINT RUN 2000 SERIAL #'d SETS		
RANDOM INSERTS IN PACKS		

	MINT	NRMT
❑ 1 Michael Jordan	150.00	70.00

1997-98 Flair Showcase Wave of the Future

	MINT	NRMT
COMPLETE SET (12)	20.00	9.00
COMMON CARD (1-12)	2.00	.90
SEMISTARS	3.00	1.35
UNLISTED STARS	5.00	2.20
STATED ODDS 1:20		

	MINT	NRMT
❑ 1 Corey Beck	2.00	.90
❑ 2 Maurice Taylor	5.00	2.20
❑ 3 Chris Anstey	2.00	.90
❑ 4 Keith Booth	2.00	.90
❑ 5 Anthony Parker	2.00	.90
❑ 6 Austin Croshere	6.00	2.70
❑ 7 Jacque Vaughn	2.00	.90
❑ 8 God Shammgod	2.00	.90
❑ 9 Bobby Jackson	2.00	.90
❑ 10 Johnny Taylor	2.00	.90
❑ 11 Ed Gray	2.00	.90
❑ 12 Kelvin Cato	2.00	.90

1998-99 Flair Showcase Row 3

	MINT	NRMT
COMPLETE SET (90)	60.00	27.00
COMMON CARD (1-90)	.15	.07
COMMON RC	.50	.23
SEMISTARS	.20	.09
SEMISTARS RC	.60	.25
UNLISTED STARS	.40	.18
UNLISTED STARS RC	1.00	.45
1-30 STATED ODDS 1:0.8		
31-60 STATED ODDS 1:1		
61-90 STATED ODDS 1:1.2		
UNPRICED MASTERPIECES SERIAL #'d TO 1		
MASTERPIECES: RANDOM INS.IN PACKS		

	MINT	NRMT
❑ 1 Keith Van Horn	1.00	.45
❑ 2 Kobe Bryant	3.00	1.35
❑ 3 Tim Duncan	2.00	.90
❑ 4 Kevin Garnett	2.50	1.10
❑ 5 Grant Hill	2.00	.90
❑ 6 Allen Iverson	1.50	.70
❑ 7 Shaquille O'Neal	2.00	.90
❑ 8 Antoine Walker	.60	.25
❑ 9 Shareef Abdur-Rahim	1.00	.45
❑ 10 Stephon Marbury	1.00	.45
❑ 11 Ray Allen	.50	.23
❑ 12 Shawn Kemp	.60	.25
❑ 13 Tim Thomas	.60	.25
❑ 14 Scottie Pippen	1.25	.55
❑ 15 Latrell Sprewell	.75	.35
❑ 16 Dirk Nowitzki RC	4.00	1.80
❑ 17 Antawn Jamison RC	5.00	2.20
❑ 18 Anfernee Hardaway	1.25	.55
❑ 19 Larry Hughes RC	6.00	2.70
❑ 20 Robert Traylor RC	1.00	.45
❑ 21 Kerry Kittles	.20	.09
❑ 22 Ron Mercer	.60	.25
❑ 23 Michael Olowokandi RC	1.50	.70
❑ 24 Jason Kidd	1.25	.55
❑ 25 Vince Carter RC	25.00	11.00
❑ 26 Charles Barkley	.60	.25
❑ 27 Antonio McDyess	.40	.18
❑ 28 Mike Bibby RC	3.00	1.35
❑ 29 Paul Pierce RC	5.00	2.20
❑ 30 Raef LaFrentz RC	2.00	.90
❑ 31 Reggie Miller	.40	.18
❑ 32 Michael Finley	.40	.18
❑ 33 Eddie Jones	.75	.35
❑ 34 Tim Hardaway	.40	.18
❑ 35 Glenn Robinson	.20	.09
❑ 36 Brevin Knight	.15	.07
❑ 37 Gary Payton	.60	.25
❑ 38 David Robinson	.60	.25
❑ 39 Karl Malone	.60	.25
❑ 40 Derek Anderson	.50	.23
❑ 41 Patrick Ewing	.40	.18
❑ 42 Juwan Howard	.20	.09
❑ 43 Jayson Williams	.20	.09
❑ 44 Terrell Brandon	.20	.09
❑ 45 Hakeem Olajuwon	.60	.25
❑ 46 Isaac Austin	.15	.07
❑ 47 Glen Rice	.20	.09
❑ 48 Maurice Taylor	.40	.18
❑ 49 Damon Stoudamire	.40	.18
❑ 50 Brian Skinner RC	1.00	.45
❑ 51 Nazr Mohammed RC	.50	.23
❑ 52 Tom Gugliotta	.20	.09
❑ 53 Al Harrington RC	3.00	1.35
❑ 54 Pat Garrity RC	.60	.25
❑ 55 Jason Williams RC	6.00	2.70
❑ 56 Tracy McGrady	1.50	.70
❑ 57 Keon Clark RC	1.00	.45
❑ 58 Vin Baker	.20	.09
❑ 59 Bonzi Wells RC	4.00	1.80
❑ 60 John Stockton	.40	.18
❑ 61 Isaiah Rider	.20	.09
❑ 62 Alonzo Mourning	.40	.18
❑ 63 Allan Houston	.40	.18
❑ 64 Dennis Rodman	.75	.35
❑ 65 Felipe Lopez RC	1.25	.55
❑ 66 Joe Smith	.20	.09
❑ 67 Chris Webber	1.25	.55
❑ 68 Mitch Richmond	.40	.18
❑ 69 Brent Barry	.15	.07
❑ 70 Mookie Blaylock	.15	.07
❑ 71 Donyell Marshall	.15	.07
❑ 72 Anthony Mason	.20	.09
❑ 73 Rod Strickland	.20	.09
❑ 74 Roshown McLeod RC	.60	.25
❑ 75 Matt Harpring RC	1.00	.45
❑ 76 Detlef Schrempf	.20	.09
❑ 77 Michael Dickerson RC	2.00	.90
❑ 78 Michael Doleac RC	1.00	.45
❑ 79 John Starks	.15	.07
❑ 80 Ricky Davis RC	2.00	.90
❑ 81 Steve Smith	.20	.09
❑ 82 Voshon Lenard	.15	.07
❑ 83 Toni Kukoc	.50	.23
❑ 84 Steve Nash	.15	.07
❑ 85 Vlade Divac	.15	.07
❑ 86 Rasheed Wallace	.40	.18
❑ 87 Bryon Russell	.15	.07
❑ 88 Antonio Daniels	.15	.07
❑ 89 Rik Smits	.15	.07
❑ 90 Joe Dumars	.40	.18

1998-99 Flair Showcase Row 2

	MINT	NRMT
COMPLETE SET (90)	120.00	55.00
COMMON CARD (1-90)	.30	.14
*STARS: .75X TO 2X ROW 3		
*RCs: .6X TO 1.5X ROW 3		
1-30: STATED ODDS 1:3		
31-60: STATED ODDS 1:1.3		
61-90: STATED ODDS 1:2		

1998-99 Flair Showcase Row 1

	MINT	NRMT
COMMON CARD (1-30)	1.50	.70
*STARS: 4X TO 10X ROW 3		
*RCs: 5X TO 12X ROW 3		
1-30: STATED ODDS 1:23		
1:30: PRINT RUN 1500 SERIAL #'d SETS		
COMMON CARD (31-60)	1.25	.55
*STARS: 3X TO 8X ROW 3		
*RCs: 3X TO 8X ROW 3		
31-60: STATED ODDS 1:11		
31-60: PRINT RUN 3000 SERIAL #'d SETS		
COMMON CARD (61-90)	1.00	.45

*STARS: 2.5X TO 6X ROW 3
*RCs: 2X TO 5X ROW 3
61-90: STATED ODDS 1:6
61-90: PRINT RUN 6000 SERIAL #'d SETS

1998-99 Flair Showcase Class of '98

	MINT	NRMT
COMPLETE SET (15)	250.00	110.00
COMMON CARD (1-15)	4.00	1.80
SEMISTARS	6.00	2.70
UNLISTED STARS	8.00	3.60

RANDOM INSERTS IN PACKS
STATED PRINT RUN 500 SERIAL #'d SETS

Card	MINT	NRMT
❑ 1 Michael Olowokandi	8.00	3.60
❑ 2 Mike Bibby	12.00	5.50
❑ 3 Raef LaFrentz	8.00	3.60
❑ 4 Antawn Jamison	20.00	9.00
❑ 5 Vince Carter	150.00	70.00
❑ 6 Robert Traylor	4.00	1.80
❑ 7 Jason Williams	25.00	11.00
❑ 8 Larry Hughes	25.00	11.00
❑ 9 Dirk Nowitzki	20.00	9.00
❑ 10 Paul Pierce	20.00	9.00
❑ 11 Bonzi Wells	20.00	9.00
❑ 12 Michael Doleac	6.00	2.70
❑ 13 Michael Dickerson	8.00	3.60
❑ 14 Pat Garrity	4.00	1.80
❑ 15 Al Harrington	15.00	6.75

1998-99 Flair Showcase takeit2.net

	MINT	NRMT
COMPLETE SET (15)	150.00	70.00
COMMON CARD (1-15)	5.00	2.20

RANDOM INSERTS IN PACKS
STATED PRINT RUN 1000 SERIAL #'d SETS

Card	MINT	NRMT
❑ 1 Scottie Pippen	10.00	4.50
❑ 2 Tim Duncan	15.00	6.75
❑ 3 Keith Van Horn	8.00	3.60
❑ 4 Grant Hill	15.00	6.75
❑ 5 Kobe Bryant	25.00	11.00
❑ 6 Antoine Walker	5.00	2.20
❑ 7 Kevin Garnett	20.00	9.00
❑ 8 Allen Iverson	12.00	5.50
❑ 9 Shareef Abdur-Rahim	8.00	3.60

Card	MINT	NRMT
❑ 10 Anfernee Hardaway	10.00	4.50
❑ 11 Stephon Marbury	8.00	3.60
❑ 12 Ron Mercer	5.00	2.20
❑ 13 Michael Jordan	50.00	22.00
❑ 14 Shaquille O'Neal	15.00	6.75
❑ 15 Shawn Kemp	5.00	2.20

1999-00 Flair Showcase

	MINT	NRMT
COMPLETE SET (130)	400.00	180.00
COMPLETE SET w/o RC (100)	30.00	13.50
COMMON CARD (1-100)	.25	.11
COMMON RC (101-130)	4.00	1.80
SEMISTARS	.30	.14
SEMISTARS RC	5.00	2.20
UNLISTED STARS	.50	.23
UNLISTED STARS RC	6.00	2.70

RCs: PRINT RUN 2000 SERIAL #'d SETS
RCs: RANDOM INSERTS IN PACKS
UNPRICED MASTERPIECES SERIAL #'d TO 1

Card	MINT	NRMT
❑ 1 Vince Carter	5.00	2.20
❑ 2 Anfernee Hardaway	1.50	.70
❑ 3 Nick Van Exel	.30	.14
❑ 4 Kerry Kittles	.30	.14
❑ 5 Michael Doleac	.25	.11
❑ 6 Sean Elliott	.25	.11
❑ 7 Shaquille O'Neal	2.50	1.10
❑ 8 Avery Johnson	.25	.11
❑ 9 Brian Grant	.30	.14
❑ 10 Jerome Williams	.30	.14
❑ 11 Larry Hughes	1.25	.55
❑ 12 Jerry Stackhouse	.30	.14
❑ 13 Alonzo Mourning	.50	.23
❑ 14 Antonio McDyess	.50	.23
❑ 15 Jason Kidd	1.50	.70
❑ 16 Bryon Russell	.25	.11
❑ 17 Hakeem Olajuwon	.75	.35
❑ 18 Juwan Howard	.30	.14
❑ 19 Paul Pierce	1.00	.45
❑ 20 Vin Baker	.30	.14
❑ 21 Larry Johnson	.30	.14
❑ 22 Gary Trent	.25	.11
❑ 23 Jayson Williams	.30	.14
❑ 24 Tim Hardaway	.50	.23
❑ 25 Dirk Nowitzki	.75	.35
❑ 26 Jamal Mashburn	.30	.14
❑ 27 Glenn Robinson	.30	.14
❑ 28 Shawn Bradley	.25	.11
❑ 29 Tom Gugliotta	.30	.14
❑ 30 Vlade Divac	.25	.11
❑ 31 David Robinson	.75	.35
❑ 32 Matt Geiger	.25	.11
❑ 33 Grant Hill	2.50	1.10
❑ 34 Maurice Taylor	.50	.23
❑ 35 Toni Kukoc	.60	.25
❑ 36 Cedric Ceballos	.25	.11
❑ 37 Patrick Ewing	.50	.23
❑ 38 Ray Allen	.50	.23
❑ 39 Michael Finley	.50	.23
❑ 40 Robert Traylor	.25	.11
❑ 41 Brevin Knight	.25	.11
❑ 42 Marcus Camby	.50	.23
❑ 43 Sam Cassell	.30	.14
❑ 44 Antawn Jamison	1.00	.45
❑ 45 Steve Smith	.30	.14
❑ 46 Darrell Armstrong	.30	.14
❑ 47 Mookie Blaylock	.25	.11
❑ 48 Derek Anderson	.50	.23
❑ 49 Hersey Hawkins	.30	.14
❑ 50 Kobe Bryant	4.00	1.80
❑ 51 Shawn Kemp	.75	.35
❑ 52 Scottie Pippen	1.50	.70
❑ 53 Chris Webber	1.50	.70
❑ 54 Damon Stoudamire	.50	.23
❑ 55 Donyell Marshall	.25	.11
❑ 56 Isaiah Rider	.30	.14
❑ 57 Karl Malone	.75	.35
❑ 58 Kevin Garnett	3.00	1.35
❑ 59 Mario Elie	.25	.11
❑ 60 Michael Dickerson	.50	.23
❑ 61 Jahidi White	.25	.11
❑ 62 Joe Smith	.30	.14
❑ 63 Kenny Anderson	.30	.14
❑ 64 Reggie Miller	.50	.23
❑ 65 Ruben Patterson	.50	.23
❑ 66 Shareef Abdur-Rahim	1.00	.45
❑ 67 Allen Iverson	2.00	.90
❑ 68 Glen Rice	.30	.14
❑ 69 Nick Anderson	.25	.11
❑ 70 Rex Chapman	.25	.11
❑ 71 Ron Mercer	.60	.25
❑ 72 Tim Duncan	2.50	1.10
❑ 73 Al Harrington	.60	.25
❑ 74 Brent Barry	.25	.11
❑ 75 Eddie Jones	1.00	.45
❑ 76 Mike Bibby	.60	.25
❑ 77 Anthony Mason	.30	.14
❑ 78 Michael Olowokandi	.30	.14
❑ 79 Matt Harpring	.25	.11
❑ 80 Stephon Marbury	1.00	.45
❑ 81 Tracy McGrady	1.50	.70
❑ 82 Allan Houston	.50	.23
❑ 83 Lindsey Hunter	.25	.11
❑ 84 Tariq Abdul-Wahad	.25	.11
❑ 85 Antoine Walker	.60	.25
❑ 86 Charles Barkley	.75	.35
❑ 87 Gary Payton	.75	.35
❑ 88 John Stockton	.50	.23
❑ 89 Mitch Richmond	.50	.23
❑ 90 Terrell Brandon	.30	.14
❑ 91 Charles Oakley	.25	.11
❑ 92 Bryant Reeves	.25	.11
❑ 93 Dikembe Mutombo	.30	.14
❑ 94 Elden Campbell	.25	.11
❑ 95 Jalen Rose	.50	.23
❑ 96 Jason Williams	1.25	.55
❑ 97 Keith Van Horn	1.00	.45
❑ 98 Latrell Sprewell	1.00	.45
❑ 99 Raef LaFrentz	.50	.23
❑ 100 Rasheed Wallace	.50	.23
❑ 101 Cal Bowdler RC	6.00	2.70
❑ 102 Dion Glover RC	6.00	2.70
❑ 103 Jason Terry RC	10.00	4.50
❑ 104 Adrian Griffin RC	8.00	3.60
❑ 105 Baron Davis RC	15.00	6.75
❑ 106 Michael Ruffin RC	5.00	2.20
❑ 107 Elton Brand RC	60.00	27.00
❑ 108 Ron Artest RC	15.00	6.75
❑ 109 Andre Miller RC	20.00	9.00
❑ 110 Trajan Langdon RC	10.00	4.50
❑ 111 James Posey RC	12.00	5.50
❑ 112 Vonteego Cummings RC	10.00	4.50
❑ 113 Kenny Thomas RC	10.00	4.50
❑ 114 Steve Francis RC	80.00	36.00
❑ 115 Jonathan Bender RC	30.00	13.50

❑ 116 Lamar Odom RC	50.00	22.00
❑ 117 Devean George RC	12.00	5.50
❑ 118 Tim James RC	8.00	3.60
❑ 119 Anthony Carter RC	15.00	6.75
❑ 120 Wally Szczerbiak RC	25.00	11.00
❑ 121 William Avery RC	10.00	4.50
❑ 122 Evan Eschmeyer RC	4.00	1.80
❑ 123 Corey Maggette RC	25.00	11.00
❑ 124 Jumaine Jones RC	5.00	2.20
❑ 125 Shawn Marion RC	20.00	9.00
❑ 126 Ryan Robertson RC	5.00	2.20
❑ 127 Aleksandar Radojevic RC	4.00	1.80
❑ 128 Quincy Lewis RC	6.00	2.70
❑ 129 Scott Padgett RC	6.00	2.70
❑ 130 Richard Hamilton RC	15.00	6.75
❑ P1 Vince Carter PROMO	6.00	2.70

1999-00 Flair Showcase Legacy Collection

	MINT	NRMT
COMMON CARD (1-130)	25.00	11.00
SEMISTARS	40.00	18.00
UNLISTED STARS	60.00	27.00

STATED PRINT RUN 20 SERIAL #'d SETS
RANDOM INSERTS IN PACKS

Card	MINT	NRMT
❑ 1 Vince Carter	600.00	275.00
❑ 2 Anfernee Hardaway	200.00	90.00
❑ 3 Nick Van Exel	40.00	18.00
❑ 4 Kerry Kittles	40.00	18.00
❑ 5 Michael Doleac	25.00	11.00
❑ 6 Sean Elliott	25.00	11.00
❑ 7 Shaquille O'Neal	300.00	135.00
❑ 8 Avery Johnson	25.00	11.00
❑ 9 Brian Grant	40.00	18.00
❑ 10 Jerome Williams	40.00	18.00
❑ 11 Larry Hughes	150.00	70.00
❑ 12 Jerry Stackhouse	40.00	18.00
❑ 13 Alonzo Mourning	60.00	27.00
❑ 14 Antonio McDyess	60.00	27.00
❑ 15 Jason Kidd	200.00	90.00
❑ 16 Bryon Russell	25.00	11.00
❑ 17 Hakeem Olajuwon	100.00	45.00
❑ 18 Juwan Howard	40.00	18.00
❑ 19 Paul Pierce	120.00	55.00
❑ 20 Vin Baker	40.00	18.00
❑ 21 Larry Johnson	40.00	18.00
❑ 22 Gary Trent	25.00	11.00
❑ 23 Jayson Williams	40.00	18.00
❑ 24 Tim Hardaway	60.00	27.00
❑ 25 Dirk Nowitzki	100.00	45.00
❑ 26 Jamal Mashburn	40.00	18.00
❑ 27 Glenn Robinson	40.00	18.00
❑ 28 Shawn Bradley	25.00	11.00
❑ 29 Tom Gugliotta	40.00	18.00
❑ 30 Vlade Divac	25.00	11.00
❑ 31 David Robinson	100.00	45.00
❑ 32 Matt Geiger	25.00	11.00
❑ 33 Grant Hill	300.00	135.00
❑ 34 Maurice Taylor	60.00	27.00
❑ 35 Toni Kukoc	150.00	70.00
❑ 36 Cedric Ceballos	25.00	11.00
❑ 37 Patrick Ewing	60.00	27.00
❑ 38 Ray Allen	60.00	27.00
❑ 39 Michael Finley	60.00	27.00
❑ 40 Robert Traylor	25.00	11.00
❑ 41 Brevin Knight	25.00	11.00
❑ 42 Marcus Camby	60.00	27.00
❑ 43 Sam Cassell	40.00	18.00
❑ 44 Antawn Jamison	120.00	55.00
❑ 45 Steve Smith	40.00	18.00
❑ 46 Darrell Armstrong	40.00	18.00
❑ 47 Mookie Blaylock	25.00	11.00
❑ 48 Derek Anderson	60.00	27.00
❑ 49 Hersey Hawkins	40.00	18.00
❑ 50 Kobe Bryant	500.00	220.00
❑ 51 Shawn Kemp	100.00	45.00
❑ 52 Scottie Pippen	200.00	90.00
❑ 53 Chris Webber	200.00	90.00
❑ 54 Damon Stoudamire	60.00	27.00
❑ 55 Donyell Marshall	25.00	11.00
❑ 56 Isaiah Rider	40.00	18.00
❑ 57 Karl Malone	100.00	45.00
❑ 58 Kevin Garnett	400.00	180.00
❑ 59 Mario Elie	25.00	11.00
❑ 60 Michael Dickerson	60.00	27.00
❑ 61 Jahidi White	25.00	11.00
❑ 62 Joe Smith	40.00	18.00
❑ 63 Kenny Anderson	40.00	18.00
❑ 64 Reggie Miller	60.00	27.00
❑ 65 Ruben Patterson	60.00	27.00
❑ 66 Shareef Abdur-Rahim	120.00	55.00
❑ 67 Allen Iverson	250.00	110.00
❑ 68 Glen Rice	40.00	18.00
❑ 69 Nick Anderson	25.00	11.00
❑ 70 Rex Chapman	25.00	11.00
❑ 71 Ron Mercer	80.00	36.00
❑ 72 Tim Duncan	300.00	135.00
❑ 73 Al Harrington	80.00	36.00
❑ 74 Brent Barry	25.00	11.00
❑ 75 Eddie Jones	120.00	55.00
❑ 76 Mike Bibby	80.00	36.00
❑ 77 Anthony Mason	40.00	18.00
❑ 78 Michael Olowokandi	40.00	18.00
❑ 79 Matt Harpring	25.00	11.00
❑ 80 Stephon Marbury	120.00	55.00
❑ 81 Tracy McGrady	200.00	90.00
❑ 82 Allan Houston	60.00	27.00
❑ 83 Lindsey Hunter	25.00	11.00
❑ 84 Tariq Abdul-Wahad	25.00	11.00
❑ 85 Antoine Walker	80.00	36.00
❑ 86 Charles Barkley	100.00	45.00
❑ 87 Gary Payton	100.00	45.00
❑ 88 John Stockton	60.00	27.00
❑ 89 Mitch Richmond	60.00	27.00
❑ 90 Terrell Brandon	40.00	18.00
❑ 91 Charles Oakley	25.00	11.00
❑ 92 Bryant Reeves	25.00	11.00
❑ 93 Dikembe Mutombo	40.00	18.00
❑ 94 Elden Campbell	25.00	11.00
❑ 95 Jalen Rose	60.00	27.00
❑ 96 Jason Williams	150.00	70.00
❑ 97 Keith Van Horn	120.00	55.00
❑ 98 Latrell Sprewell	120.00	55.00
❑ 99 Raef LaFrentz	60.00	27.00
❑ 100 Rasheed Wallace	60.00	27.00
❑ 101 Cal Bowdler	40.00	18.00
❑ 102 Dion Glover	40.00	18.00
❑ 103 Jason Terry	60.00	27.00
❑ 104 Adrian Griffin	40.00	18.00
❑ 105 Baron Davis	80.00	36.00
❑ 106 Michael Ruffin	25.00	11.00
❑ 107 Elton Brand	300.00	135.00
❑ 108 Ron Artest	80.00	36.00
❑ 109 Andre Miller	100.00	45.00
❑ 110 Trajan Langdon	60.00	27.00
❑ 111 James Posey	60.00	27.00
❑ 112 Vonteego Cummings	60.00	27.00
❑ 113 Kenny Thomas	60.00	27.00
❑ 114 Steve Francis	400.00	180.00
❑ 115 Jonathan Bender	150.00	70.00
❑ 116 Lamar Odom	250.00	110.00
❑ 117 Devean George	60.00	27.00
❑ 118 Tim James	40.00	18.00
❑ 119 Anthony Carter	80.00	36.00
❑ 120 Wally Szczerbiak	120.00	55.00
❑ 121 William Avery	60.00	27.00
❑ 122 Evan Eschmeyer	25.00	11.00
❑ 123 Corey Maggette	120.00	55.00
❑ 124 Jumaine Jones	40.00	18.00
❑ 125 Shawn Marion	100.00	45.00
❑ 126 Ryan Robertson	25.00	11.00
❑ 127 Aleksandar Radojevic	25.00	11.00
❑ 128 Quincy Lewis	40.00	18.00
❑ 129 Scott Padgett	40.00	18.00
❑ 130 Richard Hamilton	80.00	36.00

1999-00 Flair Showcase Ball of Fame

	MINT	NRMT
COMPLETE SET (15)	12.00	5.50
COMMON CARD (BF1-BF15)	.30	.14
UNLISTED STARS	.50	.23

STATED ODDS 1:5

Card	MINT	NRMT
❑ BF1 Lamar Odom	2.50	1.10
❑ BF2 Steve Francis	4.00	1.80
❑ BF3 Elton Brand	3.00	1.35
❑ BF4 Wally Szczerbiak	1.25	.55
❑ BF5 Shawn Marion	1.00	.45
❑ BF6 Jason Terry	.50	.23
❑ BF7 Richard Hamilton	.75	.35
❑ BF8 Andre Miller	1.00	.45
❑ BF9 Corey Maggette	1.25	.55
❑ BF10 Baron Davis	.75	.35
❑ BF11 Vonteego Cummings	.50	.23
❑ BF12 Kenny Thomas	.50	.23
❑ BF13 Jumaine Jones	.30	.14
❑ BF14 Trajan Langdon	.50	.23
❑ BF15 Jonathan Bender	1.50	.70

1999-00 Flair Showcase ConVINCEing

	MINT	NRMT
COMPLETE SET (10)	25.00	11.00
COMMON CARD (C1-C10)	3.00	1.35

STATED ODDS 1:10

Card	MINT	NRMT
❑ C1 Vince Carter	3.00	1.35
❑ C2 Vince Carter	3.00	1.35
❑ C3 Vince Carter	3.00	1.35
❑ C4 Vince Carter	3.00	1.35
❑ C5 Vince Carter	3.00	1.35
❑ C6 Vince Carter	3.00	1.35
❑ C7 Vince Carter	3.00	1.35
❑ C8 Vince Carter	3.00	1.35
❑ C9 Vince Carter	3.00	1.35
❑ C10 Vince Carter	3.00	1.35

1999-00 Flair Showcase Elevators

	MINT	NRMT
COMPLETE SET (10)	30.00	13.50
COMMON CARD (E1-E10)	2.00	.90

STATED ODDS 1:20

Card	MINT	NRMT
❑ E1 Vince Carter	10.00	4.50
❑ E2 Lamar Odom	4.00	1.80
❑ E3 Allen Iverson	4.00	1.80
❑ E4 Kobe Bryant	8.00	3.60
❑ E5 Grant Hill	5.00	2.20
❑ E6 Eddie Jones	2.00	.90
❑ E7 Scottie Pippen	3.00	1.35
❑ E8 Kevin Garnett	6.00	2.70
❑ E9 Steve Francis	6.00	2.70
❑ E10 Keith Van Horn	2.00	.90

1999-00 Flair Showcase Feel the Game

	MINT	NRMT
COMPLETE SET (15)	650.00	300.00
COMMON CARD	25.00	11.00

STATED ODDS 1:120
NNO CARDS LISTED BELOW ALPHABETICALLY

	MINT	NRMT
❑ 1 William Avery	25.00	11.00
❑ 2 Vince Carter	200.00	90.00
❑ 3 Vonteego Cummings	25.00	11.00
❑ 4 Patrick Ewing	50.00	22.00
❑ 5 Brian Grant	25.00	11.00
❑ 6 Karl Malone	40.00	18.00
❑ 7 Shawn Marion	40.00	18.00
❑ 8 Alonzo Mourning	40.00	18.00
❑ 9 Lamar Odom	60.00	27.00
❑ 10 Shaquille O'Neal	120.00	55.00
❑ 11 Paul Pierce	40.00	18.00
❑ 12 David Robinson	40.00	18.00
❑ 13 Damon Stoudamire	30.00	13.50
❑ 14 Kenny Thomas	25.00	11.00
❑ 15 Antoine Walker	30.00	13.50

1999-00 Flair Showcase Fresh Ink

	MINT	NRMT
COMMON CARD	5.00	2.20
SEMISTARS	8.00	3.60

STATED ODDS 1:39
NNO CARDS LISTED BELOW ALPHABETICALLY

	MINT	NRMT
❑ 1 Tariq Abdul-Wahad	5.00	2.20
❑ 2 Ron Artest	15.00	6.75
❑ 3 William Avery	10.00	4.50
❑ 4 Tony Battie	5.00	2.20
❑ 5 Cal Bowdler	5.00	2.20
❑ 6 Vince Carter	200.00	90.00
❑ 7 Dion Glover	8.00	3.60
❑ 8 Chris Herren	5.00	2.20
❑ 9 Juwan Howard	15.00	6.75
❑ 10 Eddie Jones	20.00	9.00
❑ 11 Jumaine Jones	5.00	2.20
❑ 12 Brevin Knight	5.00	2.20
❑ 13 Toni Kukoc	15.00	6.75
❑ 14 Trajan Langdon	12.00	5.50
❑ 15 Quincy Lewis	8.00	3.60
❑ 16 Corey Maggette	25.00	11.00
❑ 17 Stephon Marbury	30.00	13.50
❑ 18 Tracy McGrady	40.00	18.00
❑ 19 Ron Mercer	12.00	5.50
❑ 20 Andre Miller	15.00	6.75
❑ 21 Lamar Odom	50.00	22.00
❑ 22 Hakeem Olajuwon	25.00	11.00
❑ 23 Scott Padgett	10.00	4.50
❑ 24 Scottie Pippen	120.00	55.00
❑ 25 James Posey	8.00	3.60
❑ 26 Aleksandar Radojevic	5.00	2.20
❑ 27 Glen Rice	15.00	6.75
❑ 28 Wally Szczerbiak	25.00	11.00
❑ 29 Jason Terry	10.00	4.50
❑ 30 Kenny Thomas	10.00	4.50
❑ 31 Jerome Williams	8.00	3.60

1999-00 Flair Showcase Fresh Ink Rock Steady

	MINT	NRMT
COMMON CARD	60.00	27.00

STATED PRINT RUN 25 SERIAL #'d SETS
RANDOM INSERTS IN PACKS
NNO CARDS LISTED BELOW ALPHABETICALLY

	MINT	NRMT
❑ 1 Vince Carter	1000.00	450.00
❑ 2 Chris Herren	60.00	27.00
❑ 3 Ron Mercer	150.00	70.00
❑ 4 Lamar Odom	300.00	135.00
❑ 5 Scottie Pippen	400.00	180.00
❑ 6 Aleksandar Radojevic	60.00	27.00
❑ 7 Kenny Thomas	60.00	27.00

1999-00 Flair Showcase Guaranteed Fresh

	MINT	NRMT
COMPLETE SET (10)	15.00	6.75
COMMON CARD (GF1-GF10)	1.25	.55

STATED ODDS 1:10

	MINT	NRMT
❑ GF1 Vince Carter	6.00	2.70
❑ GF2 Shaquille O'Neal	3.00	1.35
❑ GF3 Kevin Garnett	4.00	1.80
❑ GF4 Kobe Bryant	5.00	2.20
❑ GF5 Paul Pierce	1.25	.55
❑ GF6 Jason Williams	1.50	.70
❑ GF7 Stephon Marbury	1.25	.55
❑ GF8 Lamar Odom	2.50	1.10
❑ GF9 Keith Van Horn	1.25	.55
❑ GF10 Wally Szczerbiak	1.25	.55

1999-00 Flair Showcase License to Skill

	MINT	NRMT
COMPLETE SET (10)	30.00	13.50
COMMON CARD (LS1-LS10)	1.25	.55

STATED ODDS 1:20

	MINT	NRMT
❑ LS1 Vince Carter	10.00	4.50
❑ LS2 Shaquille O'Neal	5.00	2.20
❑ LS3 Tim Duncan	5.00	2.20
❑ LS4 Keith Van Horn	2.00	.90
❑ LS5 Grant Hill	5.00	2.20
❑ LS6 Allen Iverson	4.00	1.80
❑ LS7 Antoine Walker	1.25	.55
❑ LS8 Scottie Pippen	3.00	1.35
❑ LS9 Kobe Bryant	8.00	3.60
❑ LS10 Lamar Odom	4.00	1.80

1999-00 Flair Showcase Next

	MINT	NRMT
COMPLETE SET (20)	12.00	5.50
COMMON CARD (N1-N20)	.25	.11
SEMISTARS	.40	.18
UNLISTED STARS	.50	.23

STATED ODDS 1:2.5

	MINT	NRMT
❑ N1 Vince Carter	5.00	2.20
❑ N2 James Posey	.50	.23
❑ N3 Jonathan Bender	1.25	.55
❑ N4 Corey Maggette	1.00	.45
❑ N5 Devean George	.50	.23
❑ N6 Trajan Langdon	.50	.23
❑ N7 Shawn Marion	.75	.35
❑ N8 William Avery	.40	.18
❑ N9 Adrian Griffin	.40	.18
❑ N10 Quincy Lewis	.40	.18
❑ N11 Kenny Thomas	.50	.23
❑ N12 Lamar Odom	2.00	.90
❑ N13 Dion Glover	.25	.11
❑ N14 Elton Brand	2.50	1.10
❑ N15 Andre Miller	.75	.35

❑ N16 Jason Terry	.50	.23
❑ N17 Richard Hamilton	.60	.25
❑ N18 Steve Francis	3.00	1.35
❑ N19 Baron Davis	.60	.25
❑ N20 Wally Szczerbiak	1.00	.45

1999-00 Flair Showcase Rookie Showcase Firsts

	MINT	NRMT
COMMON CARD (1-30)	3.00	1.35
SEMISTARS	6.00	2.70
UNLISTED STARS	10.00	4.50

STATED PRINT RUN 500 SERIAL #'d SETS
RANDOM INSERTS IN PACKS

❑ 1 Cal Bowdler	6.00	2.70
❑ 2 Dion Glover	6.00	2.70
❑ 3 Jason Terry	10.00	4.50
❑ 4 Adrian Griffin	6.00	2.70
❑ 5 Baron Davis	12.00	5.50
❑ 6 Michael Ruffin	3.00	1.35
❑ 7 Elton Brand	50.00	22.00
❑ 8 Ron Artest	12.00	5.50
❑ 9 Andre Miller	15.00	6.75
❑ 10 Trajan Langdon	10.00	4.50
❑ 11 James Posey	10.00	4.50
❑ 12 Vonteego Cummings	10.00	4.50
❑ 13 Kenny Thomas	10.00	4.50
❑ 14 Steve Francis	60.00	27.00
❑ 15 Jonathan Bender	25.00	11.00
❑ 16 Lamar Odom	40.00	18.00
❑ 17 Devean George	10.00	4.50
❑ 18 Tim James	6.00	2.70
❑ 19 Anthony Carter	12.00	5.50
❑ 20 Wally Szczerbiak	20.00	9.00
❑ 21 William Avery	10.00	4.50
❑ 22 Evan Eschmeyer	3.00	1.35
❑ 23 Corey Maggette	20.00	9.00
❑ 24 Jumaine Jones	6.00	2.70
❑ 25 Shawn Marion	15.00	6.75
❑ 26 Ryan Robertson	3.00	1.35
❑ 27 Aleksandar Radojevic	3.00	1.35
❑ 28 Quincy Lewis	6.00	2.70
❑ 29 Scott Padgett	6.00	2.70
❑ 30 Richard Hamilton	12.00	5.50

1961-62 Fleer

	NRMT	VG-E
COMPLETE SET (66)	4000.00	1800.00
COMMON CARD (1-66)	15.00	6.75
SEMISTARS	20.00	9.00
UNLISTED STARS	25.00	11.00

CONDITION SENSITIVE SET
1961-62 THRU 1976-77 PRICED IN NM

❑ 1 Al Attles RC !	125.00	38.00
❑ 2 Paul Arizin	50.00	22.00
❑ 3 Elgin Baylor RC !	300.00	135.00
❑ 4 Walt Bellamy RC !	60.00	27.00
❑ 5 Arlen Bockhorn	15.00	6.75
❑ 6 Bob Boozer RC !	25.00	11.00
❑ 7 Carl Braun	30.00	13.50
❑ 8 Wilt Chamberlain RC !	1000.00	450.00
❑ 9 Larry Costello	20.00	9.00
❑ 10 Bob Cousy	200.00	90.00
❑ 11 Walter Dukes	20.00	9.00
❑ 12 Wayne Embry RC	35.00	16.00
❑ 13 Dave Gambee	15.00	6.75
❑ 14 Tom Gola	40.00	18.00
❑ 15 Sihugo Green RC	20.00	9.00
❑ 16 Hal Greer RC	80.00	36.00
❑ 17 Richie Guerin RC	40.00	18.00
❑ 18 Cliff Hagan	50.00	22.00
❑ 19 Tom Heinsohn	100.00	45.00
❑ 20 Bailey Howell RC	45.00	20.00
❑ 21 Rod Hundley	75.00	34.00
❑ 22 K.C. Jones RC	110.00	50.00
❑ 23 Sam Jones RC	110.00	50.00
❑ 24 Phil Jordan	15.00	6.75
❑ 25 John Kerr	50.00	22.00
❑ 26 Rudy LaRusso RC	35.00	16.00
❑ 27 George Lee	15.00	6.75
❑ 28 Bob Leonard	20.00	9.00
❑ 29 Clyde Lovellette	50.00	22.00
❑ 30 John McCarthy	15.00	6.75
❑ 31 Tom Meschery RC	25.00	11.00
❑ 32 Willie Naulls	25.00	11.00
❑ 33 Don Ohl RC	25.00	11.00
❑ 34 Bob Pettit	90.00	40.00
❑ 35 Frank Ramsey	40.00	18.00
❑ 36 Oscar Robertson RC !	400.00	180.00
❑ 37 Guy Rodgers RC	25.00	11.00
❑ 38 Bill Russell	400.00	180.00
❑ 39 Dolph Schayes	55.00	25.00
❑ 40 Frank Selvy	20.00	9.00
❑ 41 Gene Shue	25.00	11.00
❑ 42 Jack Twyman	40.00	18.00
❑ 43 Jerry West RC !	600.00	275.00
❑ 44 Len Wilkens RC ! UER (Misspelled Wilkins on card front)	175.00	80.00
❑ 45 Paul Arizin IA	25.00	11.00
❑ 46 Elgin Baylor IA	100.00	45.00
❑ 47 Wilt Chamberlain IA	350.00	160.00
❑ 48 Larry Costello IA	20.00	9.00
❑ 49 Bob Cousy IA	125.00	55.00
❑ 50 Walter Dukes IA	15.00	6.75
❑ 51 Tom Gola IA	25.00	11.00
❑ 52 Richie Guerin IA	20.00	9.00
❑ 53 Cliff Hagan IA	25.00	11.00
❑ 54 Tom Heinsohn IA	50.00	22.00
❑ 55 Bailey Howell IA	25.00	11.00
❑ 56 John Kerr IA	30.00	13.50
❑ 57 Rudy LaRusso IA	20.00	9.00
❑ 58 Clyde Lovellette IA	30.00	13.50
❑ 59 Bob Pettit IA	50.00	22.00
❑ 60 Frank Ramsey IA	25.00	11.00
❑ 61 Oscar Robertson IA	175.00	80.00
❑ 62 Bill Russell IA	200.00	90.00
❑ 63 Dolph Schayes IA	35.00	16.00
❑ 64 Gene Shue IA	20.00	9.00
❑ 65 Jack Twyman IA	25.00	11.00
❑ 66 Jerry West IA	300.00	90.00

1986-87 Fleer

	NRMT-MT	EXC
COMPLETE w/Stickers (143)	2200.00	1000.00
COMP.SET (132)	1800.00	800.00
COMMON CARD (1-132)	2.00	.90
CL (132) !	10.00	4.50
SEMISTARS	2.50	1.10
UNLISTED STARS	3.00	1.35

BEWARE COUNTERFEITS
CONDITION SENSITIVE SET

❑ 1 Kareem Abdul-Jabbar	12.00	5.50
❑ 2 Alvan Adams	2.00	.90
❑ 3 Mark Aguirre RC	3.00	1.35
❑ 4 Danny Ainge RC	8.00	3.60
❑ 5 John Bagley RC**	2.00	.90
❑ 6 Thurl Bailey RC**	2.00	.90
❑ 7 Charles Barkley RC	80.00	36.00
❑ 8 Benoit Benjamin RC	2.50	1.10
❑ 9 Larry Bird	40.00	18.00
❑ 10 Otis Birdsong	2.00	.90
❑ 11 Rolando Blackman RC	2.50	1.10
❑ 12 Manute Bol RC	2.00	.90
❑ 13 Sam Bowie RC**	2.00	.90
❑ 14 Joe Barry Carroll	2.00	.90
❑ 15 Tom Chambers RC	4.00	1.80
❑ 16 Maurice Cheeks	2.00	.90
❑ 17 Michael Cooper	2.50	1.10
❑ 18 Wayne Cooper	2.00	.90
❑ 19 Pat Cummings	2.00	.90
❑ 20 Terry Cummings RC	3.00	1.35
❑ 21 Adrian Dantley	2.50	1.10
❑ 22 Brad Davis RC**	2.00	.90
❑ 23 Walter Davis	2.00	.90
❑ 24 Darryl Dawkins	2.50	1.10
❑ 25 Larry Drew	2.00	.90
❑ 26 Clyde Drexler RC	40.00	18.00
❑ 27 Joe Dumars RC	20.00	9.00
❑ 28 Mark Eaton RC**	2.00	.90
❑ 29 James Edwards	2.00	.90
❑ 30 Alex English	2.50	1.10
❑ 31 Julius Erving	15.00	6.75
❑ 32 Patrick Ewing RC !	50.00	22.00
❑ 33 Vern Fleming RC**	2.00	.90
❑ 34 Sleepy Floyd RC**	2.00	.90
❑ 35 World B. Free	2.00	.90
❑ 36 George Gervin	4.00	1.80
❑ 37 Artis Gilmore	2.50	1.10
❑ 38 Mike Gminski	2.00	.90
❑ 39 Rickey Green	2.00	.90
❑ 40 Sidney Green	2.00	.90
❑ 41 David Greenwood	2.00	.90
❑ 42 Darrell Griffith	2.00	.90
❑ 43 Bill Hanzlik	2.00	.90
❑ 44 Derek Harper RC !	6.00	2.70
❑ 45 Gerald Henderson	2.00	.90
❑ 46 Roy Hinson	2.00	.90
❑ 47 Craig Hodges RC**	2.00	.90
❑ 48 Phil Hubbard	2.00	.90
❑ 49 Jay Humphries RC**	2.00	.90
❑ 50 Dennis Johnson	2.00	.90
❑ 51 Eddie Johnson RC	3.00	1.35
❑ 52 Frank Johnson RC**	2.00	.90
❑ 53 Magic Johnson	25.00	11.00
❑ 54 Marques Johnson (Decimal point missing, rookie year scoring avg.)	2.00	.90
❑ 55 Steve Johnson UER (photo actually David Greenwood)	2.00	.90
❑ 56 Vinnie Johnson	2.00	.90
❑ 57 Michael Jordan RC !	1600.00	700.00
❑ 58 Clark Kellogg RC**	2.00	.90
❑ 59 Albert King	2.00	.90
❑ 60 Bernard King	2.50	1.10
❑ 61 Bill Laimbeer	2.50	1.10
❑ 62 Allen Leavell	2.00	.90
❑ 63 Lafayette Lever RC**	2.00	.90
❑ 64 Alton Lister	2.00	.90
❑ 65 Lewis Lloyd	2.00	.90
❑ 66 Maurice Lucas	2.00	.90
❑ 67 Jeff Malone RC	2.00	.90
❑ 68 Karl Malone RC	80.00	36.00
❑ 69 Moses Malone	3.00	1.35
❑ 70 Cedric Maxwell	2.00	.90
❑ 71 Rodney McCray RC**	2.00	.90
❑ 72 Xavier McDaniel RC	2.50	1.10
❑ 73 Kevin McHale	3.00	1.35
❑ 74 Mike Mitchell	2.00	.90
❑ 75 Sidney Moncrief	2.50	1.10
❑ 76 Johnny Moore	2.00	.90
❑ 77 Chris Mullin RC !	20.00	9.00
❑ 78 Larry Nance RC	4.00	1.80
❑ 79 Calvin Natt	2.00	.90
❑ 80 Norm Nixon	2.00	.90

❑ 81 Charles Oakley RC 6.00 2.70
❑ 82 Hakeem Olajuwon RC 60.00 27.00
❑ 83 Louis Orr 2.00 .90
❑ 84 Robert Parish UER 3.00 1.35
(Misspelled Parrish on both sides)
❑ 85 Jim Paxson 2.00 .90
❑ 86 Sam Perkins RC 6.00 2.70
❑ 87 Ricky Pierce RC 2.50 1.10
❑ 88 Paul Pressey RC** 2.00 .90
❑ 89 Kurt Rambis RC 2.00 .90
❑ 90 Robert Reid 2.00 .90
❑ 91 Doc Rivers RC 6.00 2.70
❑ 92 Alvin Robertson RC 2.00 .90
❑ 93 Cliff Robinson 2.00 .90
❑ 94 Tree Rollins 2.00 .90
❑ 95 Dan Roundfield 2.00 .90
❑ 96 Jeff Ruland 2.00 .90
❑ 97 Ralph Sampson RC 2.50 1.10
❑ 98 Danny Schayes RC** 2.00 .90
❑ 99 Byron Scott RC 4.00 1.80
❑ 100 Purvis Short 2.00 .90
❑ 101 Jerry Sichting 2.00 .90
❑ 102 Jack Sikma 2.00 .90
❑ 103 Derek Smith 2.00 .90
❑ 104 Larry Smith 2.00 .90
❑ 105 Rory Sparrow 2.00 .90
❑ 106 Steve Stipanovich 2.00 .90
❑ 107 Terry Teagle 2.00 .90
❑ 108 Reggie Theus 2.50 1.10
❑ 109 Isiah Thomas RC ! 25.00 11.00
❑ 110 LaSalle Thompson RC** 2.00 .90
❑ 111 Mychal Thompson 2.00 .90
❑ 112 Sedale Threatt RC** 2.00 .90
❑ 113 Wayman Tisdale RC 2.50 1.10
❑ 114 Andrew Toney 2.00 .90
❑ 115 Kelly Tripucka 2.00 .90
❑ 116 Mel Turpin 2.00 .90
❑ 117 Kiki Vandeweghe RC 2.50 1.10
❑ 118 Jay Vincent 2.00 .90
❑ 119 Bill Walton 4.00 1.80
(Missing decimal points on four lines of FG Percentage)
❑ 120 Spud Webb RC ! 6.00 2.70
❑ 121 Dominique Wilkins RC ! 25.00 11.00
❑ 122 Gerald Wilkins RC 2.50 1.10
❑ 123 Buck Williams RC 4.00 1.80
❑ 124 Gus Williams 2.00 .90
❑ 125 Herb Williams RC** 2.00 .90
❑ 126 Kevin Willis RC 6.00 2.70
❑ 127 Randy Wittman 2.00 .90
❑ 128 Al Wood 2.00 .90
❑ 129 Mike Woodson 2.00 .90
❑ 130 Orlando Woolridge RC** 2.00 .90
❑ 131 James Worthy RC 20.00 9.00
❑ 132 Checklist 1-132 10.00 4.50

1986-87 Fleer Stickers

	NRMT-MT	EXC
COMPLETE SET (11)	400.00	180.00
COMMON STICKER (1-11)	2.00	.90
ONE PER PACK		
CONDITION SENSITIVE SET		

❑ 1 Kareem Abdul-Jabbar 4.00 1.80
❑ 2 Larry Bird 15.00 6.75
❑ 3 Adrian Dantley 2.00 .90
❑ 4 Alex English 2.00 .90
❑ 5 Julius Erving 5.00 2.20
❑ 6 Patrick Ewing 8.00 3.60
❑ 7 Magic Johnson 12.00 5.50
❑ 8 Michael Jordan 350.00 160.00
❑ 9 Hakeem Olajuwon 12.00 5.50
❑ 10 Isiah Thomas 5.00 2.20
❑ 11 Dominique Wilkins 4.00 1.80

1987-88 Fleer

	MINT	NRMT
COMPLETE w/Stickers (143)	325.00	145.00
COMPLETE SET (132)	250.00	110.00
COMMON CARD (1-132)	1.50	.70
CL (132) !	3.00	1.35
SEMISTARS	2.00	.90
UNLISTED STARS	2.50	1.10
CONDITION SENSITIVE SET		

❑ 1 Kareem Abdul-Jabbar 8.00 3.60
❑ 2 Alvan Adams 1.50 .70
❑ 3 Mark Aguirre 2.00 .90
❑ 4 Danny Ainge 2.00 .90
❑ 5 John Bagley 1.50 .70
❑ 6 Thurl Bailey UER 1.50 .70
(reverse negative)
❑ 7 Greg Ballard 1.50 .70
❑ 8 Gene Banks 1.50 .70
❑ 9 Charles Barkley 20.00 9.00
❑ 10 Benoit Benjamin 1.50 .70
❑ 11 Larry Bird 30.00 13.50
❑ 12 Rolando Blackman 1.50 .70
❑ 13 Manute Bol 1.50 .70
❑ 14 Tony Brown 1.50 .70
❑ 15 Michael Cage RC** 1.50 .70
❑ 16 Joe Barry Carroll 1.50 .70
❑ 17 Bill Cartwright 2.00 .90
❑ 18 Terry Catledge RC 1.50 .70
❑ 19 Tom Chambers 1.50 .70
❑ 20 Maurice Cheeks 1.50 .70
❑ 21 Michael Cooper 2.00 .90
❑ 22 Dave Corzine 1.50 .70
❑ 23 Terry Cummings 2.00 .90
❑ 24 Adrian Dantley 1.50 .70
❑ 25 Brad Daugherty RC 2.50 1.10
❑ 26 Walter Davis 1.50 .70
❑ 27 Johnny Dawkins RC 1.50 .70
❑ 28 James Donaldson 1.50 .70
❑ 29 Larry Drew 1.50 .70
❑ 30 Clyde Drexler 12.00 5.50
❑ 31 Joe Dumars 4.00 1.80
❑ 32 Mark Eaton 1.50 .70
❑ 33 Dale Ellis RC 2.50 1.10
❑ 34 Alex English 2.00 .90
❑ 35 Julius Erving 12.00 5.50
❑ 36 Mike Evans 1.50 .70
❑ 37 Patrick Ewing 12.00 5.50
❑ 38 Vern Fleming 1.50 .70
❑ 39 Sleepy Floyd 1.50 .70
❑ 40 Artis Gilmore 2.00 .90
❑ 41 Mike Gminski UER 1.50 .70
(reversed negative)
❑ 42 A.C. Green RC 6.00 2.70
❑ 43 Rickey Green 1.50 .70
❑ 44 Sidney Green 1.50 .70
❑ 45 David Greenwood 1.50 .70
❑ 46 Darrell Griffith 1.50 .70
❑ 47 Bill Hanzlik 1.50 .70
❑ 48 Derek Harper 2.00 .90
❑ 49 Ron Harper RC 6.00 2.70
❑ 50 Gerald Henderson 1.50 .70
❑ 51 Roy Hinson 1.50 .70
❑ 52 Craig Hodges 1.50 .70
❑ 53 Phil Hubbard 1.50 .70
❑ 54 Dennis Johnson 1.50 .70
❑ 55 Eddie Johnson 2.00 .90
❑ 56 Magic Johnson 25.00 11.00
❑ 57 Steve Johnson 1.50 .70
❑ 58 Vinnie Johnson 1.50 .70
❑ 59 Michael Jordan 200.00 90.00
❑ 60 Jerome Kersey RC** 1.50 .70
❑ 61 Bill Laimbeer 2.00 .90
❑ 62 Lafayette Lever UER 1.50 .70
(Photo actually Otis Smith)
❑ 63 Cliff Levingston RC** 1.50 .70
❑ 64 Alton Lister 1.50 .70
❑ 65 John Long 1.50 .70
❑ 66 John Lucas 1.50 .70
❑ 67 Jeff Malone 1.50 .70
❑ 68 Karl Malone 20.00 9.00
❑ 69 Moses Malone 2.50 1.10
❑ 70 Cedric Maxwell 1.50 .70
❑ 71 Tim McCormick 1.50 .70
❑ 72 Rodney McCray 1.50 .70
❑ 73 Xavier McDaniel 1.50 .70
❑ 74 Kevin McHale 2.50 1.10
❑ 75 Nate McMillan RC 2.50 1.10
❑ 76 Sidney Moncrief 1.50 .70
❑ 77 Chris Mullin 4.00 1.80
❑ 78 Larry Nance 2.00 .90
❑ 79 Charles Oakley 2.50 1.10
❑ 80 Hakeem Olajuwon 20.00 9.00
❑ 81 Robert Parish UER 2.50 1.10
(Misspelled Parrish on both sides)
❑ 82 Jim Paxson 1.50 .70
❑ 83 John Paxson RC 2.50 1.10
❑ 84 Sam Perkins 2.50 1.10
❑ 85 Chuck Person RC 2.50 1.10
❑ 86 Jim Petersen 1.50 .70
❑ 87 Ricky Pierce 1.50 .70
❑ 88 Ed Pinckney RC 1.50 .70
❑ 89 Terry Porter RC 2.50 1.10
(College Wisconsin, should be Wisconsin - Stevens Point)
❑ 90 Paul Pressey 1.50 .70
❑ 91 Robert Reid 1.50 .70
❑ 92 Doc Rivers 2.50 1.10
❑ 93 Alvin Robertson 1.50 .70
❑ 94 Tree Rollins 1.50 .70
❑ 95 Ralph Sampson 1.50 .70
❑ 96 Mike Sanders 1.50 .70
❑ 97 Detlef Schrempf RC 10.00 4.50
❑ 98 Byron Scott 2.00 .90
❑ 99 Jerry Sichting 1.50 .70
❑ 100 Jack Sikma 1.50 .70
❑ 101 Larry Smith 1.50 .70
❑ 102 Rory Sparrow 1.50 .70
❑ 103 Steve Stipanovich 1.50 .70
❑ 104 Jon Sundvold 1.50 .70
❑ 105 Reggie Theus 2.00 .90
❑ 106 Isiah Thomas 6.00 2.70
❑ 107 LaSalle Thompson 1.50 .70
❑ 108 Mychal Thompson 1.50 .70
❑ 109 Otis Thorpe RC 5.00 2.20
❑ 110 Sedale Threatt 1.50 .70
❑ 111 Waymon Tisdale 1.50 .70
❑ 112 Kelly Tripucka 1.50 .70
❑ 113 Trent Tucker RC** 1.50 .70
❑ 114 Terry Tyler 1.50 .70
❑ 115 Darnell Valentine 1.50 .70
❑ 116 Kiki Vandeweghe 1.50 .70
❑ 117 Darrell Walker RC** 1.50 .70
❑ 118 Dominique Wilkins 4.00 1.80
❑ 119 Gerald Wilkins 1.50 .70
❑ 120 Buck Williams 2.00 .90
❑ 121 Herb Williams 1.50 .70
❑ 122 John Williams RC 1.50 .70
❑ 123 John Williams RC 2.00 .90
❑ 124 Kevin Willis 2.00 .90

Card	MINT	NRMT
❑ 125 David Wingate RC	1.50	.70
❑ 126 Randy Wittman	1.50	.70
❑ 127 Leon Wood	1.50	.70
❑ 128 Mike Woodson	1.50	.70
❑ 129 Orlando Woolridge	1.50	.70
❑ 130 James Worthy	4.00	1.80
❑ 131 Danny Young RC**	1.50	.70
❑ 132 Checklist 1-132	3.00	1.35

1987-88 Fleer Stickers

	MINT	NRMT
COMPLETE SET (11)	80.00	36.00
COMMON STICKER (1-11)	.50	.23
ONE PER PACK		

Card	MINT	NRMT
❑ 1 Magic Johnson	6.00	2.70
❑ 2 Michael Jordan (In text, votes misspelled as voites)	60.00	27.00
❑ 3 Hakeem Olajuwon UER (Misspelled Olajuwan on card back)	5.00	2.20
❑ 4 Larry Bird	8.00	3.60
❑ 5 Kevin McHale	.50	.23
❑ 6 Charles Barkley	5.00	2.20
❑ 7 Dominique Wilkins	1.00	.45
❑ 8 Kareem Abdul-Jabbar	2.00	.90
❑ 9 Mark Aguirre	.50	.23
❑ 10 Chuck Person	.50	.23
❑ 11 Alex English	.50	.23

1988-89 Fleer

	MINT	NRMT
COMPLETE w/Stickers (143)	225.00	100.00
COMPLETE SET (132)	200.00	90.00
COMMON CARD (1-132)	.50	.23
CL (132)	.50	.23
SEMISTARS	.75	.35
UNLISTED STARS	1.50	.70
CONDITION SENSITIVE SET		

Card	MINT	NRMT
❑ 1 Antoine Carr RC**	.75	.35
❑ 2 Cliff Levingston	.50	.23
❑ 3 Doc Rivers	.75	.35
❑ 4 Spud Webb	.75	.35
❑ 5 Dominique Wilkins	1.50	.70
❑ 6 Kevin Willis	.75	.35
❑ 7 Randy Wittman	.50	.23
❑ 8 Danny Ainge	.75	.35
❑ 9 Larry Bird	12.00	5.50
❑ 10 Dennis Johnson	.50	.23
❑ 11 Kevin McHale	1.50	.70
❑ 12 Robert Parish	1.50	.70
❑ 13 Tyrone Bogues RC	2.00	.90
❑ 14 Dell Curry RC	1.50	.70
❑ 15 Dave Corzine	.50	.23
❑ 16 Horace Grant RC	5.00	2.20
❑ 17 Michael Jordan	60.00	27.00
❑ 18 Charles Oakley	.75	.35
❑ 19 John Paxson	.75	.35
❑ 20 Scottie Pippen RC ! UER (Misspelled Pippin on card back)	40.00	18.00
❑ 21 Brad Sellers RC	.50	.23
❑ 22 Brad Daugherty	.50	.23
❑ 23 Ron Harper	.75	.35
❑ 24 Larry Nance	.50	.23
❑ 25 Mark Price RC	2.00	.90
❑ 26 Hot Rod Williams	.50	.23
❑ 27 Mark Aguirre	.50	.23
❑ 28 Rolando Blackman	.50	.23
❑ 29 James Donaldson	.50	.23
❑ 30 Derek Harper	.75	.35
❑ 31 Sam Perkins	.75	.35
❑ 32 Roy Tarpley RC	.50	.23
❑ 33 Michael Adams RC	.50	.23
❑ 34 Alex English	.75	.35
❑ 35 Lafayette Lever	.50	.23
❑ 36 Blair Rasmussen RC	.50	.23
❑ 37 Danny Schayes	.50	.23
❑ 38 Jay Vincent	.50	.23
❑ 39 Adrian Dantley	.50	.23
❑ 40 Joe Dumars	1.50	.70
❑ 41 Vinnie Johnson	.50	.23
❑ 42 Bill Laimbeer	.75	.35
❑ 43 Dennis Rodman RC !	15.00	6.75
❑ 44 John Salley RC	.75	.35
❑ 45 Isiah Thomas	1.50	.70
❑ 46 Winston Garland RC	.50	.23
❑ 47 Rod Higgins	.50	.23
❑ 48 Chris Mullin	1.50	.70
❑ 49 Ralph Sampson	.50	.23
❑ 50 Joe Barry Carroll	.50	.23
❑ 51 Sleepy Floyd	.50	.23
❑ 52 Rodney McCray	.50	.23
❑ 53 Hakeem Olajuwon	5.00	2.20
❑ 54 Purvis Short	.50	.23
❑ 55 Vern Fleming	.50	.23
❑ 56 John Long	.50	.23
❑ 57 Reggie Miller RC !	25.00	11.00
❑ 58 Chuck Person	.75	.35
❑ 59 Steve Stipanovich	.50	.23
❑ 60 Waymon Tisdale	.50	.23
❑ 61 Benoit Benjamin	.50	.23
❑ 62 Michael Cage	.50	.23
❑ 63 Mike Woodson	.50	.23
❑ 64 Kareem Abdul-Jabbar	4.00	1.80
❑ 65 Michael Cooper	.50	.23
❑ 66 A.C. Green	.75	.35
❑ 67 Magic Johnson	10.00	4.50
❑ 68 Byron Scott	.75	.35
❑ 69 Mychal Thompson	.50	.23
❑ 70 James Worthy	1.50	.70
❑ 71 Duane Washington	.50	.23
❑ 72 Kevin Williams	.50	.23
❑ 73 Randy Breuer RC**	.50	.23
❑ 74 Terry Cummings	.75	.35
❑ 75 Paul Pressey	.50	.23
❑ 76 Jack Sikma	.50	.23
❑ 77 John Bagley	.50	.23
❑ 78 Roy Hinson	.50	.23
❑ 79 Buck Williams	.75	.35
❑ 80 Patrick Ewing	3.00	1.35
❑ 81 Sidney Green	.50	.23
❑ 82 Mark Jackson RC	2.50	1.10
❑ 83 Kenny Walker RC	.50	.23
❑ 84 Gerald Wilkins	.50	.23
❑ 85 Charles Barkley	5.00	2.20
❑ 86 Maurice Cheeks	.50	.23
❑ 87 Mike Gminski	.50	.23
❑ 88 Cliff Robinson	.50	.23
❑ 89 Armon Gilliam RC	1.50	.70
❑ 90 Eddie Johnson	.50	.23
❑ 91 Mark West RC	.50	.23
❑ 92 Clyde Drexler	3.00	1.35
❑ 93 Kevin Duckworth RC	.50	.23
❑ 94 Steve Johnson	.50	.23
❑ 95 Jerome Kersey	.50	.23
❑ 96 Terry Porter (College Wisconsin, should be Wisconsin Stevens Point)	.50	.23
❑ 97 Joe Kleine RC	.50	.23
❑ 98 Reggie Theus	.75	.35
❑ 99 Otis Thorpe	.75	.35
❑ 100 Kenny Smith RC (College NC State, should be North Carolina)	1.50	.70
❑ 101 Greg Anderson RC	.50	.23
❑ 102 Walter Berry RC	.50	.23
❑ 103 Frank Brickowski RC	.50	.23
❑ 104 Johnny Dawkins	.50	.23
❑ 105 Alvin Robertson	.50	.23
❑ 106 Tom Chambers (Born 6/2/59, should be 6/21/59)	.50	.23
❑ 107 Dale Ellis	.75	.35
❑ 108 Xavier McDaniel	.50	.23
❑ 109 Derrick McKey RC	1.50	.70
❑ 110 Nate McMillan UER (Photo actually Kevin Williams)	.50	.23
❑ 111 Thurl Bailey	.50	.23
❑ 112 Mark Eaton	.50	.23
❑ 113 Bobby Hansen RC**	.50	.23
❑ 114 Karl Malone	5.00	2.20
❑ 115 John Stockton RC !	25.00	11.00
❑ 116 Bernard King	.50	.23
❑ 117 Jeff Malone	.50	.23
❑ 118 Moses Malone	1.50	.70
❑ 119 John Williams	.50	.23
❑ 120 Michael Jordan AS	40.00	18.00
❑ 121 Mark Jackson AS	1.50	.70
❑ 122 Byron Scott AS	.50	.23
❑ 123 Magic Johnson AS	4.00	1.80
❑ 124 Larry Bird AS	5.00	2.20
❑ 125 Dominique Wilkins AS	.75	.35
❑ 126 Hakeem Olajuwon AS	2.00	.90
❑ 127 John Stockton AS	5.00	2.20
❑ 128 Alvin Robertson AS	.50	.23
❑ 129 Charles Barkley AS (Back says Buck Williams is member of Jets, should be Nets)	2.00	.90
❑ 130 Patrick Ewing AS	1.50	.70
❑ 131 Mark Eaton AS	.50	.23
❑ 132 Checklist 1-132	.50	.23

1988-89 Fleer Stickers

	MINT	NRMT
COMPLETE SET (11)	30.00	13.50
COMMON STICKER (1-11)	.25	.11
ONE PER PACK		

Card	MINT	NRMT
❑ 1 Mark Aguirre	.25	.11
❑ 2 Larry Bird	5.00	2.20
❑ 3 Clyde Drexler	1.25	.55
❑ 4 Alex English	.25	.11
❑ 5 Patrick Ewing	1.25	.55
❑ 6 Magic Johnson	4.00	1.80
❑ 7 Michael Jordan	25.00	11.00

	MINT	NRMT
❑ 8 Karl Malone	2.00	.90
❑ 9 Kevin McHale	.25	.11
❑ 10 Isiah Thomas	.60	.25
❑ 11 Dominique Wilkins	.25	.11

1989-90 Fleer

	MINT	NRMT
COMPLETE w/Stickers (179)	50.00	22.00
COMPLETE SET (168)	30.00	13.50
COMMON CARD (1-168)	.15	.07
SEMISTARS	.25	.11
UNLISTED STARS	.50	.23

	MINT	NRMT
❑ 1 John Battle RC	.15	.07
❑ 2 Jon Koncak RC	.15	.07
❑ 3 Cliff Levingston	.15	.07
❑ 4 Moses Malone	.50	.23
❑ 5 Doc Rivers	.25	.11
❑ 6 Spud Webb UER (Points per 48 minutes incorrect at 2.6)	.25	.11
❑ 7 Dominique Wilkins	.50	.23
❑ 8 Larry Bird	3.00	1.35
❑ 9 Dennis Johnson	.15	.07
❑ 10 Reggie Lewis RC	.75	.35
❑ 11 Kevin McHale	.50	.23
❑ 12 Robert Parish	.25	.11
❑ 13 Ed Pinckney	.15	.07
❑ 14 Brian Shaw RC	.50	.23
❑ 15 Rex Chapman RC	.75	.35
❑ 16 Kurt Rambis	.15	.07
❑ 17 Robert Reid	.15	.07
❑ 18 Kelly Tripucka	.15	.07
❑ 19 Bill Cartwright UER (First season 1978-80, should be 1979-80)	.15	.07
❑ 20 Horace Grant	.25	.11
❑ 21 Michael Jordan	15.00	6.75
❑ 22 John Paxson	.15	.07
❑ 23 Scottie Pippen	5.00	2.20
❑ 24 Brad Sellers	.15	.07
❑ 25 Brad Daugherty	.15	.07
❑ 26 Craig Ehlo RC**	.15	.07
❑ 27 Ron Harper	.25	.11
❑ 28 Larry Nance	.25	.11
❑ 29 Mark Price	.25	.11
❑ 30 Mike Sanders	.15	.07
❑ 31A John Williams ERR	.50	.23
❑ 31B John Williams COR	.15	.07
❑ 32 Rolando Blackman UER (Career blocks and points listed as 1961 and 2127, should be 196 and 12,127)	.15	.07
❑ 33 Adrian Dantley	.15	.07
❑ 34 James Donaldson	.15	.07
❑ 35 Derek Harper	.25	.11
❑ 36 Sam Perkins	.25	.11
❑ 37 Herb Williams	.15	.07
❑ 38 Michael Adams	.15	.07
❑ 39 Walter Davis	.15	.07
❑ 40 Alex English	.15	.07
❑ 41 Lafayette Lever	.15	.07
❑ 42 Blair Rasmussen	.15	.07
❑ 43 Danny Schayes	.15	.07
❑ 44 Mark Aguirre	.15	.07
❑ 45 Joe Dumars	.50	.23
❑ 46 James Edwards	.15	.07
❑ 47 Vinnie Johnson	.15	.07
❑ 48 Bill Laimbeer	.25	.11
❑ 49 Dennis Rodman	3.00	1.35
❑ 50 Isiah Thomas	.50	.23
❑ 51 John Salley	.15	.07
❑ 52 Manute Bol	.15	.07
❑ 53 Winston Garland	.15	.07
❑ 54 Rod Higgins	.15	.07
❑ 55 Chris Mullin	.50	.23
❑ 56 Mitch Richmond RC	4.00	1.80
❑ 57 Terry Teagle	.15	.07
❑ 58 Derrick Chievous UER (Stats correctly say 81 games in '88-89, text says 82)	.15	.07
❑ 59 Sleepy Floyd	.15	.07
❑ 60 Tim McCormick	.15	.07
❑ 61 Hakeem Olajuwon	1.25	.55
❑ 62 Otis Thorpe	.25	.11
❑ 63 Mike Woodson	.15	.07
❑ 64 Vern Fleming	.15	.07
❑ 65 Reggie Miller	2.00	.90
❑ 66 Chuck Person	.25	.11
❑ 67 Detlef Schrempf	.25	.11
❑ 68 Rik Smits RC	1.00	.45
❑ 69 Benoit Benjamin	.15	.07
❑ 70 Gary Grant RC	.15	.07
❑ 71 Danny Manning RC	1.00	.45
❑ 72 Ken Norman RC	.15	.07
❑ 73 Charles Smith RC	.50	.23
❑ 74 Reggie Williams RC	.15	.07
❑ 75 Michael Cooper	.15	.07
❑ 76 A.C. Green	.25	.11
❑ 77 Magic Johnson	2.50	1.10
❑ 78 Byron Scott	.25	.11
❑ 79 Mychal Thompson	.15	.07
❑ 80 James Worthy	.50	.23
❑ 81 Kevin Edwards RC	.15	.07
❑ 82 Grant Long RC	.15	.07
❑ 83 Rony Seikaly RC	.50	.23
❑ 84 Rory Sparrow	.15	.07
❑ 85 Greg Anderson UER (Stats show 1988-89 as 19888-89)	.15	.07
❑ 86 Jay Humphries	.15	.07
❑ 87 Larry Krystkowiak RC	.15	.07
❑ 88 Ricky Pierce	.15	.07
❑ 89 Paul Pressey	.15	.07
❑ 90 Alvin Robertson	.15	.07
❑ 91 Jack Sikma	.15	.07
❑ 92 Steve Johnson	.15	.07
❑ 93 Rick Mahorn	.15	.07
❑ 94 David Rivers	.15	.07
❑ 95 Joe Barry Carroll	.15	.07
❑ 96 Lester Conner UER (Garden State in stats, should be Golden State)	.15	.07
❑ 97 Roy Hinson	.15	.07
❑ 98 Mike McGee	.15	.07
❑ 99 Chris Morris RC	.25	.11
❑ 100 Patrick Ewing	.75	.35
❑ 101 Mark Jackson	.25	.11
❑ 102 Johnny Newman RC	.15	.07
❑ 103 Charles Oakley	.25	.11
❑ 104 Rod Strickland RC	2.50	1.10
❑ 105 Trent Tucker	.15	.07
❑ 106 Kiki Vandeweghe	.15	.07
❑ 107A Gerald Wilkins (U. of Tennessee)	.15	.07
❑ 107B Gerald Wilkins (U. of Tenn.)	.15	.07
❑ 108 Terry Catledge	.15	.07
❑ 109 Dave Corzine	.15	.07
❑ 110 Scott Skiles RC	.25	.11
❑ 111 Reggie Theus	.25	.11
❑ 112 Ron Anderson RC**	.15	.07
❑ 113 Charles Barkley	1.25	.55
❑ 114 Scott Brooks RC	.15	.07
❑ 115 Maurice Cheeks	.15	.07
❑ 116 Mike Gminski	.15	.07
❑ 117 Hersey Hawkins RC UER (Born 9/29/65, should be 9/9/65)	1.00	.45
❑ 118 Christian Welp	.15	.07
❑ 119 Tom Chambers	.15	.07
❑ 120 Armon Gilliam	.15	.07
❑ 121 Jeff Hornacek RC	1.00	.45
❑ 122 Eddie Johnson	.25	.11
❑ 123 Kevin Johnson RC	1.50	.70
❑ 124 Dan Majerle RC	1.00	.45
❑ 125 Mark West	.15	.07
❑ 126 Richard Anderson	.15	.07
❑ 127 Mark Bryant RC	.15	.07
❑ 128 Clyde Drexler	.75	.35
❑ 129 Kevin Duckworth	.15	.07
❑ 130 Jerome Kersey	.15	.07
❑ 131 Terry Porter	.15	.07
❑ 132 Buck Williams	.25	.11
❑ 133 Danny Ainge	.25	.11
❑ 134 Ricky Berry	.15	.07
❑ 135 Rodney McCray	.15	.07
❑ 136 Jim Petersen	.15	.07
❑ 137 Harold Pressley	.15	.07
❑ 138 Kenny Smith	.15	.07
❑ 139 Wayman Tisdale	.15	.07
❑ 140 Willie Anderson RC	.15	.07
❑ 141 Frank Brickowski	.15	.07
❑ 142 Terry Cummings	.25	.11
❑ 143 Johnny Dawkins	.15	.07
❑ 144 Vernon Maxwell RC	.75	.35
❑ 145 Michael Cage	.15	.07
❑ 146 Dale Ellis	.25	.11
❑ 147 Alton Lister	.15	.07
❑ 148 Xavier McDaniel UER (All-Rookie team in 1985, not 1988)	.15	.07
❑ 149 Derrick McKey	.15	.07
❑ 150 Nate McMillan	.25	.11
❑ 151 Thurl Bailey	.15	.07
❑ 152 Mark Eaton	.15	.07
❑ 153 Darrell Griffith	.15	.07
❑ 154 Eric Leckner	.15	.07
❑ 155 Karl Malone	1.25	.55
❑ 156 John Stockton	2.00	.90
❑ 157 Mark Alarie	.15	.07
❑ 158 Ledell Eackles RC	.15	.07
❑ 159 Bernard King	.15	.07
❑ 160 Jeff Malone	.15	.07
❑ 161 Darrell Walker	.15	.07
❑ 162A John Williams ERR	.50	.23
❑ 162B John Williams COR	.15	.07
❑ 163 Karl Malone AS, John Stockton, Mark Eaton	.50	.23
❑ 164 Hakeem Olajuwon AS, Clyde Drexler AS	.50	.23
❑ 165 Dominique Wilkins AS, Moses Malone AS	.50	.23
❑ 166 Brad Daugherty AS, Mark Price AS, Larry Nance AS UER (Bio says Nance had 204 blocks, should be 206)	.15	.07
❑ 167 Patrick Ewing AS, Mark Jackson AS	.50	.23
❑ 168 Checklist 1-168	.15	.07

1989-90 Fleer Stickers

	MINT	NRMT
COMPLETE SET (11)	20.00	9.00
COMMON STICKER (1-11)	.15	.07
SEMISTARS	.20	.09
UNLISTED STARS	.50	.23

ONE PER WAX PACK

❑ 1 Karl Malone	.75	.35
❑ 2 Hakeem Olajuwon	.75	.35
❑ 3 Michael Jordan	15.00	6.75
❑ 4 Charles Barkley	.75	.35
❑ 5 Magic Johnson	1.50	.70
❑ 6 Isiah Thomas	.50	.23
❑ 7 Patrick Ewing	.50	.23
❑ 8 Dale Ellis	.15	.07
❑ 9 Chris Mullin	.50	.23
❑ 10 Larry Bird	2.00	.90
❑ 11 Tom Chambers	.15	.07

1990-91 Fleer

	MINT	NRMT
COMPLETE SET (198)	6.00	2.70
COMMON CARD (1-198)	.05	.02
SEMISTARS	.08	.04
UNLISTED STARS	.15	.07

Card	MINT	NRMT
❑ 1 John Battle UER (Drafted in '84, should be '85)	.05	.02
❑ 2 Cliff Levingston	.05	.02
❑ 3 Moses Malone	.15	.07
❑ 4 Kenny Smith	.05	.02
❑ 5 Spud Webb	.08	.04
❑ 6 Dominique Wilkins	.15	.07
❑ 7 Kevin Willis	.08	.04
❑ 8 Larry Bird	.60	.25
❑ 9 Dennis Johnson	.05	.02
❑ 10 Joe Kleine	.05	.02
❑ 11 Reggie Lewis	.08	.04
❑ 12 Kevin McHale	.08	.04
❑ 13 Robert Parish	.08	.04
❑ 14 Jim Paxson	.08	.04
❑ 15 Ed Pinckney	.05	.02
❑ 16 Muggsy Bogues	.08	.04
❑ 17 Rex Chapman	.15	.07
❑ 18 Dell Curry	.05	.02
❑ 19 Armon Gilliam	.05	.02
❑ 20 J.R. Reid RC	.05	.02
❑ 21 Kelly Tripucka	.05	.02
❑ 22 B.J. Armstrong RC	.05	.02
❑ 23A Bill Cartwright ERR (No decimal points in FGP and FTP)	.50	.23
❑ 23B Bill Cartwright COR	.05	.02
❑ 24 Horace Grant	.08	.04
❑ 25 Craig Hodges	.05	.02
❑ 26 Michael Jordan UER (Led NBA in scoring 4 years, not 3)	4.00	1.80
❑ 27 Stacey King RC UER (Comma missing between progressed and Stacy)	.05	.02
❑ 28 John Paxson	.08	.04
❑ 29 Will Perdue	.05	.02
❑ 30 Scottie Pippen UER (Born AR, not AK)	.60	.25
❑ 31 Brad Daugherty	.05	.02
❑ 32 Craig Ehlo	.05	.02
❑ 33 Danny Ferry RC	.08	.04
❑ 34 Steve Kerr	.15	.07
❑ 35 Larry Nance	.05	.02
❑ 36 Mark Price UER (Drafted by Cleveland, should be Dallas)	.08	.04
❑ 37 Hot Rod Williams	.05	.02
❑ 38 Rolando Blackman	.05	.02
❑ 39A Adrian Dantley ERR (No decimal points in FGP and FTP)	.50	.23
❑ 39B Adrian Dantley COR	.05	.02
❑ 40 Brad Davis	.05	.02
❑ 41 James Donaldson UER (Text says in committed, should be is committed)	.05	.02
❑ 42 Derek Harper	.08	.04
❑ 43 Sam Perkins UER (First line of text should be intact)	.08	.04
❑ 44 Bill Wennington	.05	.02
❑ 45 Herb Williams	.05	.02
❑ 46 Michael Adams	.05	.02
❑ 47 Walter Davis	.05	.02
❑ 48 Alex English UER (Stats missing from '76-77 through '79-80)	.05	.02
❑ 49 Bill Hanzlik	.05	.02
❑ 50 Lafayette Lever UER (Born AR, not AK)	.05	.02
❑ 51 Todd Lichti RC	.05	.02
❑ 52 Blair Rasmussen	.05	.02
❑ 53 Dan Schayes	.05	.02
❑ 54 Mark Aguirre	.05	.02
❑ 55 Joe Dumars	.15	.07
❑ 56 James Edwards	.05	.02
❑ 57 Vinnie Johnson	.05	.02
❑ 58 Bill Laimbeer	.08	.04
❑ 59 Dennis Rodman UER (College misspelled as coilege on back)	.40	.18
❑ 60 John Salley	.05	.02
❑ 61 Isiah Thomas	.15	.07
❑ 62 Manute Bol	.05	.02
❑ 63 Tim Hardaway RC	1.00	.45
❑ 64 Rod Higgins	.05	.02
❑ 65 Sarunas Marciulionis RC	.05	.02
❑ 66 Chris Mullin	.15	.07
❑ 67 Mitch Richmond	.20	.09
❑ 68 Terry Teagle	.05	.02
❑ 69 Anthony Bowie RC UER (Seasons, not seeasons)	.05	.02
❑ 70 Sleepy Floyd	.05	.02
❑ 71 Buck Johnson	.05	.02
❑ 72 Vernon Maxwell	.05	.02
❑ 73 Hakeem Olajuwon	.25	.11
❑ 74 Otis Thorpe	.08	.04
❑ 75 Mitchell Wiggins	.05	.02
❑ 76 Vern Fleming	.05	.02
❑ 77 George McCloud RC	.15	.07
❑ 78 Reggie Miller	.20	.09
❑ 79 Chuck Person	.08	.04
❑ 80 Mike Sanders	.05	.02
❑ 81 Detlef Schrempf	.08	.04
❑ 82 Rik Smits	.15	.07
❑ 83 LaSalle Thompson	.05	.02
❑ 84 Benoit Benjamin	.05	.02
❑ 85 Winston Garland	.05	.02
❑ 86 Ron Harper	.08	.04
❑ 87 Danny Manning	.08	.04
❑ 88 Ken Norman	.05	.02
❑ 89 Charles Smith	.05	.02
❑ 90 Michael Cooper	.05	.02
❑ 91 Vlade Divac RC	.30	.14
❑ 92 A.C. Green	.08	.04
❑ 93 Magic Johnson	.50	.23
❑ 94 Byron Scott	.08	.04
❑ 95 Mychal Thompson UER (Missing '78-79 stats from Portland)	.05	.02
❑ 96 Orlando Woolridge	.05	.02
❑ 97 James Worthy	.15	.07
❑ 98 Sherman Douglas RC	.08	.04
❑ 99 Kevin Edwards	.05	.02
❑ 100 Grant Long	.05	.02
❑ 101 Glen Rice RC	.60	.25
❑ 102 Rony Seikaly UER (Ron on front)	.08	.04
❑ 103 Billy Thompson	.05	.02
❑ 104 Jeff Grayer RC	.05	.02
❑ 105 Jay Humphries	.05	.02
❑ 106 Ricky Pierce	.05	.02
❑ 107 Paul Pressey	.05	.02
❑ 108 Fred Roberts	.05	.02
❑ 109 Alvin Robertson	.05	.02
❑ 110 Jack Sikma	.05	.02
❑ 111 Randy Breuer	.05	.02
❑ 112 Tony Campbell	.05	.02
❑ 113 Tyrone Corbin	.05	.02
❑ 114 Sam Mitchell RC UER (Mercer University, not Mercer College)	.05	.02
❑ 115 Tod Murphy UER (Born Long Beach, not Lakewood)	.05	.02
❑ 116 Pooh Richardson RC	.08	.04
❑ 117 Mookie Blaylock RC	.30	.14
❑ 118 Sam Bowie	.05	.02
❑ 119 Lester Conner	.05	.02
❑ 120 Dennis Hopson	.05	.02
❑ 121 Chris Morris	.08	.04
❑ 122 Charles Shackleford	.05	.02
❑ 123 Purvis Short	.05	.02
❑ 124 Maurice Cheeks	.05	.02
❑ 125 Patrick Ewing	.15	.07
❑ 126 Mark Jackson	.08	.04
❑ 127A Johnny Newman ERR (Jr. misprinted as J. on card back)	.50	.23
❑ 127B Johnny Newman COR	.05	.02
❑ 128 Charles Oakley	.08	.04
❑ 129 Trent Tucker	.05	.02
❑ 130 Kenny Walker	.05	.02
❑ 131 Gerald Wilkins	.05	.02
❑ 132 Nick Anderson RC	.30	.14
❑ 133 Terry Catledge	.05	.02
❑ 134 Sidney Green	.05	.02
❑ 135 Otis Smith	.05	.02
❑ 136 Reggie Theus	.08	.04
❑ 137 Sam Vincent	.05	.02
❑ 138 Ron Anderson	.05	.02
❑ 139 Charles Barkley UER (FG Percentage .545.)	.25	.11
❑ 140 Scott Brooks UER ('89-89 Philadelphia in wrong typeface)	.05	.02
❑ 141 Johnny Dawkins	.05	.02
❑ 142 Mike Gminski	.05	.02
❑ 143 Hersey Hawkins	.08	.04
❑ 144 Rick Mahorn	.05	.02
❑ 145 Derek Smith	.05	.02
❑ 146 Tom Chambers	.05	.02
❑ 147 Jeff Hornacek	.08	.04
❑ 148 Eddie Johnson	.08	.04
❑ 149 Kevin Johnson	.15	.07
❑ 150A Dan Majerle ERR (Award in 1988; three-time selection)	.75	.35
❑ 150B Dan Majerle COR (Award in 1989; three-time selection)	.15	.07
❑ 151 Tim Perry	.05	.02
❑ 152 Kurt Rambis	.05	.02
❑ 153 Mark West	.05	.02
❑ 154 Clyde Drexler	.15	.07
❑ 155 Kevin Duckworth	.05	.02
❑ 156 Byron Irvin	.05	.02
❑ 157 Jerome Kersey	.05	.02
❑ 158 Terry Porter	.05	.02
❑ 159 Clifford Robinson RC	.25	.11
❑ 160 Buck Williams	.05	.02
❑ 161 Danny Young	.05	.02
❑ 162 Danny Ainge	.08	.04
❑ 163 Antoine Carr	.05	.02
❑ 164 Pervis Ellison RC	.08	.04
❑ 165 Rodney McCray	.05	.02
❑ 166 Harold Pressley	.05	.02
❑ 167 Wayman Tisdale	.05	.02
❑ 168 Willie Anderson	.05	.02
❑ 169 Frank Brickowski	.05	.02
❑ 170 Terry Cummings	.05	.02
❑ 171 Sean Elliott RC	.30	.14
❑ 172 David Robinson	.50	.23
❑ 173 Rod Strickland	.15	.07
❑ 174 David Wingate	.05	.02
❑ 175 Dana Barros RC	.15	.07

Card	MINT	NRMT
❑ 176 Michael Cage UER (Born AR, not AK)	.05	.02
❑ 177 Dale Ellis	.08	.04
❑ 178 Shawn Kemp RC	1.50	.70
❑ 179 Xavier McDaniel	.05	.02
❑ 180 Derrick McKey	.05	.02
❑ 181 Nate McMillan	.08	.04
❑ 182 Thurl Bailey	.05	.02
❑ 183 Mike Brown	.05	.02
❑ 184 Mark Eaton	.05	.02
❑ 185 Blue Edwards RC	.05	.02
❑ 186 Bobby Hansen	.05	.02
❑ 187 Eric Leckner	.05	.02
❑ 188 Karl Malone	.25	.11
❑ 189 John Stockton	.20	.09
❑ 190 Mark Alarie	.05	.02
❑ 191 Ledell Eackles	.05	.02
❑ 192A Harvey Grant (First name on card front in black)	.75	.35
❑ 192B Harvey Grant (First name on card front in white)	.05	.02
❑ 193 Tom Hammonds RC	.05	.02
❑ 194 Bernard King	.05	.02
❑ 195 Jeff Malone	.05	.02
❑ 196 Darrell Walker	.05	.02
❑ 197 Checklist 1-99	.05	.02
❑ 198 Checklist 100-198	.05	.02

1990-91 Fleer All-Stars

	MINT	NRMT
COMPLETE SET (12)	18.00	8.00

*SINGLES: 1.25X TO 3X BASE CARD HI
RANDOM INSERTS IN WAX PACKS

Card	MINT	NRMT
❑ 1 Charles Barkley	.75	.35
❑ 2 Larry Bird	2.00	.90
❑ 3 Hakeem Olajuwon	.75	.35
❑ 4 Magic Johnson	1.50	.70
❑ 5 Michael Jordan	15.00	6.75
❑ 6 Isiah Thomas	.50	.23
❑ 7 Karl Malone	.75	.35
❑ 8 Tom Chambers	.15	.07
❑ 9 John Stockton	.60	.25
❑ 10 David Robinson	1.50	.70
❑ 11 Clyde Drexler	.50	.23
❑ 12 Patrick Ewing	.50	.23

1990-91 Fleer Rookie Sensations

	MINT	NRMT
COMPLETE SET (10)	15.00	6.75

*SINGLES: 2.5X TO 6X BASE CARD HI
RANDOM INSERTS IN CELLO PACKS

Card	MINT	NRMT
❑ 1 David Robinson UER (Text has 1988-90 season, should be 1989-90)	8.00	3.60
❑ 2 Sean Elliott UER (Misspelled Elliot on card front)	2.00	.90
❑ 3 Glen Rice	4.00	1.80
❑ 4 J.R. Reid	.50	.23
❑ 5 Stacey King	.30	.14
❑ 6 Pooh Richardson	.50	.23

Card	MINT	NRMT
❑ 7 Nick Anderson	2.00	.90
❑ 8 Tim Hardaway	6.00	2.70
❑ 9 Vlade Divac	2.00	.90
❑ 10 Sherman Douglas	.50	.23

1990-91 Fleer Update

	MINT	NRMT
COMPLETE SET (100)	8.00	3.60
COMMON CARD (U1-U100)	.05	.02
SEMISTARS	.15	.07
UNLISTED STARS	.30	.14

Card	MINT	NRMT
❑ U1 Jon Koncak	.05	.02
❑ U2 Tim McCormick	.05	.02
❑ U3 Doc Rivers	.15	.07
❑ U4 Rumeal Robinson RC	.05	.02
❑ U5 Trevor Wilson	.05	.02
❑ U6 Dee Brown RC	.30	.14
❑ U7 Dave Popson	.05	.02
❑ U8 Kevin Gamble	.05	.02
❑ U9 Brian Shaw	.30	.14
❑ U10 Michael Smith	.05	.02
❑ U11 Kendall Gill RC	.60	.25
❑ U12 Johnny Newman	.05	.02
❑ U13 Steve Scheffler RC	.05	.02
❑ U14 Dennis Hopson	.05	.02
❑ U15 Cliff Levingston	.05	.02
❑ U16 Chucky Brown RC	.05	.02
❑ U17 John Morton	.05	.02
❑ U18 Gerald Paddio RC	.05	.02
❑ U19 Alex English	.05	.02
❑ U20 Fat Lever	.05	.02
❑ U21 Rodney McCray	.05	.02
❑ U22 Roy Tarpley	.05	.02
❑ U23 Randy White RC	.05	.02
❑ U24 Anthony Cook RC	.05	.02
❑ U25 Chris Jackson RC	.30	.14
❑ U26 Marcus Liberty RC	.05	.02
❑ U27 Orlando Woolridge	.05	.02
❑ U28 William Bedford RC	.05	.02
❑ U29 Lance Blanks RC	.05	.02
❑ U30 Scott Hastings	.05	.02
❑ U31 Tyrone Hill RC	.15	.07
❑ U32 Les Jepsen	.05	.02
❑ U33 Steve Johnson	.05	.02
❑ U34 Kevin Pritchard	.05	.02
❑ U35 Dave Jamerson RC	.05	.02
❑ U36 Kenny Smith	.05	.02
❑ U37 Greg Dreiling RC	.05	.02
❑ U38 Kenny Williams RC	.05	.02
❑ U39 Micheal Williams UER	.15	.07
❑ U40 Gary Grant	.05	.02
❑ U41 Bo Kimble RC	.05	.02
❑ U42 Loy Vaught RC	.50	.23
❑ U43 Elden Campbell RC	.60	.25
❑ U44 Sam Perkins	.15	.07
❑ U45 Tony Smith RC	.05	.02
❑ U46 Terry Teagle	.05	.02
❑ U47 Willie Burton RC	.05	.02
❑ U48 Bimbo Coles RC	.30	.14
❑ U49 Terry Davis RC	.05	.02
❑ U50 Alec Kessler RC	.05	.02
❑ U51 Greg Anderson	.05	.02
❑ U52 Frank Brickowski	.05	.02
❑ U53 Steve Henson RC	.05	.02
❑ U54 Brad Lohaus	.05	.02
❑ U55 Dan Schayes	.05	.02
❑ U56 Gerald Glass RC	.05	.02
❑ U57 Felton Spencer RC	.15	.07
❑ U58 Doug West RC	.15	.07
❑ U59 Jud Buechler RC	.15	.07
❑ U60 Derrick Coleman RC	.60	.25
❑ U61 Tate George RC	.05	.02
❑ U62 Reggie Theus	.15	.07
❑ U63 Greg Grant RC	.05	.02
❑ U64 Jerrod Mustaf RC	.05	.02
❑ U65 Eddie Lee Wilkins RC**	.05	.02
❑ U66 Michael Ansley	.05	.02
❑ U67 Jerry Reynolds	.05	.02
❑ U68 Dennis Scott RC	.40	.18
❑ U69 Manute Bol	.05	.02
❑ U70 Armon Gilliam	.05	.02
❑ U71 Brian Oliver	.05	.02
❑ U72 Kenny Payne RC	.05	.02
❑ U73 Jayson Williams RC	1.00	.45
❑ U74 Kenny Battle RC	.05	.02
❑ U75 Cedric Ceballos RC	.50	.23
❑ U76 Negele Knight RC	.05	.02
❑ U77 Xavier McDaniel	.05	.02
❑ U78 Alaa Abdelnaby RC	.05	.02
❑ U79 Danny Ainge	.15	.07
❑ U80 Mark Bryant	.05	.02
❑ U81 Drazen Petrovic RC	.15	.07
❑ U82 Anthony Bonner RC	.05	.02
❑ U83 Duane Causwell RC	.05	.02
❑ U84 Bobby Hansen	.05	.02
❑ U85 Eric Leckner	.05	.02
❑ U86 Travis Mays RC	.05	.02
❑ U87 Lionel Simmons RC	.15	.07
❑ U88 Sidney Green	.05	.02
❑ U89 Tony Massenburg	.05	.02
❑ U90 Paul Pressey	.05	.02
❑ U91 Dwayne Schintzius RC	.05	.02
❑ U92 Gary Payton RC	5.00	2.20
❑ U93 Olden Polynice	.05	.02
❑ U94 Jeff Malone	.05	.02
❑ U95 Walter Palmer	.05	.02
❑ U96 Delaney Rudd	.05	.02
❑ U97 Pervis Ellison	.15	.07
❑ U98 A.J. English RC	.05	.02
❑ U99 Greg Foster RC	.15	.07
❑ U100 Checklist 1-100	.05	.02

1991-92 Fleer

	MINT	NRMT
COMPLETE SET (400)	10.00	4.50
COMPLETE SERIES 1 (240)	5.00	2.20

COMPLETE SERIES 2 (160) 5.00 2.20
COMMON CARD (1-400) .05 .02
SEMISTARS .08 .04
UNLISTED STARS .15 .07
SUBSET CARDS HALF VALUE OF BASE CARDS

❑ 1 John Battle .05 .02
❑ 2 Jon Koncak .05 .02
❑ 3 Rumeal Robinson .05 .02
❑ 4 Spud Webb .08 .04
❑ 5 Bob Weiss CO .05 .02
❑ 6 Dominique Wilkins .15 .07
❑ 7 Kevin Willis .05 .02
❑ 8 Larry Bird .60 .25
❑ 9 Dee Brown .05 .02
❑ 10 Chris Ford CO .05 .02
❑ 11 Kevin Gamble .05 .02
❑ 12 Reggie Lewis .08 .04
❑ 13 Kevin McHale .08 .04
❑ 14 Robert Parish .08 .04
❑ 15 Ed Pinckney .05 .02
❑ 16 Brian Shaw .05 .02
❑ 17 Muggsy Bogues .08 .04
❑ 18 Rex Chapman .08 .04
❑ 19 Dell Curry .05 .02
❑ 20 Kendall Gill .08 .04
❑ 21 Eric Leckner .05 .02
❑ 22 Gene Littles CO .05 .02
❑ 23 Johnny Newman .05 .02
❑ 24 J.R. Reid .05 .02
❑ 25 B.J. Armstrong .05 .02
❑ 26 Bill Cartwright .05 .02
❑ 27 Horace Grant .08 .04
❑ 28 Phil Jackson CO .08 .04
❑ 29 Michael Jordan 2.00 .90
❑ 30 Cliff Levingston .05 .02
❑ 31 John Paxson .05 .02
❑ 32 Will Perdue .05 .02
❑ 33 Scottie Pippen .50 .23
❑ 34 Brad Daugherty .05 .02
❑ 35 Craig Ehlo .05 .02
❑ 36 Danny Ferry .05 .02
❑ 37 Larry Nance .08 .04
❑ 38 Mark Price .05 .02
❑ 39 Darnell Valentine .05 .02
❑ 40 Hot Rod Williams .05 .02
❑ 41 Lenny Wilkens CO .08 .04
❑ 42 Richie Adubato CO .05 .02
❑ 43 Rolando Blackman .05 .02
❑ 44 James Donaldson .05 .02
❑ 45 Derek Harper .08 .04
❑ 46 Rodney McCray .05 .02
❑ 47 Randy White .05 .02
❑ 48 Herb Williams .05 .02
❑ 49 Chris Jackson .05 .02
❑ 50 Marcus Liberty .05 .02
❑ 51 Todd Lichti .05 .02
❑ 52 Blair Rasmussen .05 .02
❑ 53 Paul Westhead CO .05 .02
❑ 54 Reggie Williams .05 .02
❑ 55 Joe Wolf .05 .02
❑ 56 Orlando Woolridge .05 .02
❑ 57 Mark Aguirre .05 .02
❑ 58 Chuck Daly CO .08 .04
❑ 59 Joe Dumars .15 .07
❑ 60 James Edwards .05 .02
❑ 61 Vinnie Johnson .05 .02
❑ 62 Bill Laimbeer .08 .04
❑ 63 Dennis Rodman .30 .14
❑ 64 Isiah Thomas .15 .07
❑ 65 Tim Hardaway .25 .11
❑ 66 Rod Higgins .05 .02
❑ 67 Tyrone Hill .08 .04
❑ 68 Sarunas Marciulionis .05 .02
❑ 69 Chris Mullin .15 .07
❑ 70 Don Nelson CO .08 .04
❑ 71 Mitch Richmond .15 .07
❑ 72 Tom Tolbert .05 .02
❑ 73 Don Chaney CO .05 .02
❑ 74 Eric(Sleepy) Floyd .05 .02
❑ 75 Buck Johnson .05 .02
❑ 76 Vernon Maxwell .05 .02
❑ 77 Hakeem Olajuwon .25 .11
❑ 78 Kenny Smith .05 .02
❑ 79 Larry Smith .05 .02
❑ 80 Otis Thorpe .08 .04
❑ 81 Vern Fleming .05 .02
❑ 82 Bob Hill CO RC .05 .02
❑ 83 Reggie Miller .15 .07
❑ 84 Chuck Person .05 .02
❑ 85 Detlef Schrempf .08 .04
❑ 86 Rik Smits .08 .04
❑ 87 LaSalle Thompson .05 .02
❑ 88 Micheal Williams .05 .02
❑ 89 Gary Grant .05 .02
❑ 90 Ron Harper .08 .04
❑ 91 Bo Kimble .05 .02
❑ 92 Danny Manning .08 .04
❑ 93 Ken Norman .05 .02
❑ 94 Olden Polynice .05 .02
❑ 95 Mike Schuler CO .05 .02
❑ 96 Charles Smith .05 .02
❑ 97 Vlade Divac .08 .04
❑ 98 Mike Dunleavy CO .05 .02
❑ 99 A.C. Green .08 .04
❑ 100 Magic Johnson .50 .23
❑ 101 Sam Perkins .08 .04
❑ 102 Byron Scott .08 .04
❑ 103 Terry Teagle .05 .02
❑ 104 James Worthy .15 .07
❑ 105 Willie Burton .05 .02
❑ 106 Bimbo Coles .05 .02
❑ 107 Sherman Douglas .05 .02
❑ 108 Kevin Edwards .05 .02
❑ 109 Grant Long .05 .02
❑ 110 Kevin Loughery CO .05 .02
❑ 111 Glen Rice .15 .07
❑ 112 Rony Seikaly .05 .02
❑ 113 Frank Brickowski .05 .02
❑ 114 Dale Ellis .08 .04
❑ 115 Del Harris CO .05 .02
❑ 116 Jay Humphries .05 .02
❑ 117 Fred Roberts .05 .02
❑ 118 Alvin Robertson .05 .02
❑ 119 Dan Schayes .05 .02
❑ 120 Jack Sikma .05 .02
❑ 121 Tony Campbell .05 .02
❑ 122 Tyrone Corbin .05 .02
❑ 123 Sam Mitchell .05 .02
❑ 124 Tod Murphy .05 .02
❑ 125 Pooh Richardson .05 .02
❑ 126 Jimmy Rodgers CO .05 .02
❑ 127 Felton Spencer .05 .02
❑ 128 Mookie Blaylock .08 .04
❑ 129 Sam Bowie .05 .02
❑ 130 Derrick Coleman .08 .04
❑ 131 Chris Dudley .05 .02
❑ 132 Bill Fitch CO .05 .02
❑ 133 Chris Morris .05 .02
❑ 134 Drazen Petrovic .08 .04
❑ 135 Maurice Cheeks .05 .02
❑ 136 Patrick Ewing .15 .07
❑ 137 Mark Jackson .08 .04
❑ 138 Charles Oakley .08 .04
❑ 139 Pat Riley CO .08 .04
❑ 140 Trent Tucker .05 .02
❑ 141 Kiki Vandeweghe .05 .02
❑ 142 Gerald Wilkins .05 .02
❑ 143 Nick Anderson .08 .04
❑ 144 Terry Catledge .05 .02
❑ 145 Matt Guokas CO .05 .02
❑ 146 Jerry Reynolds .05 .02
❑ 147 Dennis Scott .08 .04
❑ 148 Scott Skiles .05 .02
❑ 149 Otis Smith .05 .02
❑ 150 Ron Anderson .05 .02
❑ 151 Charles Barkley .25 .11
❑ 152 Johnny Dawkins .05 .02
❑ 153 Armon Gilliam .05 .02
❑ 154 Hersey Hawkins .08 .04
❑ 155 Jim Lynam CO .05 .02
❑ 156 Rick Mahorn .05 .02
❑ 157 Brian Oliver .05 .02
❑ 158 Tom Chambers .05 .02
❑ 159 Cotton Fitzsimmons CO .05 .02
❑ 160 Jeff Hornacek .08 .04
❑ 161 Kevin Johnson .15 .07
❑ 162 Negele Knight .05 .02
❑ 163 Dan Majerle .08 .04
❑ 164 Xavier McDaniel .05 .02
❑ 165 Mark West .05 .02
❑ 166 Rick Adelman CO .05 .02
❑ 167 Danny Ainge .08 .04
❑ 168 Clyde Drexler .15 .07
❑ 169 Kevin Duckworth .05 .02
❑ 170 Jerome Kersey .05 .02
❑ 171 Terry Porter .05 .02
❑ 172 Clifford Robinson .08 .04
❑ 173 Buck Williams .05 .02
❑ 174 Antoine Carr .05 .02
❑ 175 Duane Causwell .05 .02
❑ 176 Jim Les RC .05 .02
❑ 177 Travis Mays .05 .02
❑ 178 Dick Motta CO .05 .02
❑ 179 Lionel Simmons .05 .02
❑ 180 Rory Sparrow .05 .02
❑ 181 Wayman Tisdale .05 .02
❑ 182 Willie Anderson .05 .02
❑ 183 Larry Brown CO .05 .02
❑ 184 Terry Cummings .05 .02
❑ 185 Sean Elliott .08 .04
❑ 186 Paul Pressey .05 .02
❑ 187 David Robinson .30 .14
❑ 188 Rod Strickland .15 .07
❑ 189 Benoit Benjamin .05 .02
❑ 190 Eddie Johnson .08 .04
❑ 191 K.C. Jones CO .08 .04
❑ 192 Shawn Kemp .40 .18
❑ 193 Derrick McKey .05 .02
❑ 194 Gary Payton .40 .18
❑ 195 Ricky Pierce .05 .02
❑ 196 Sedale Threatt .05 .02
❑ 197 Thurl Bailey .05 .02
❑ 198 Mark Eaton .05 .02
❑ 199 Blue Edwards .05 .02
❑ 200 Jeff Malone .05 .02
❑ 201 Karl Malone .25 .11
❑ 202 Jerry Sloan CO .08 .04
❑ 203 John Stockton .15 .07
❑ 204 Ledell Eackles .05 .02
❑ 205 Pervis Ellison .05 .02
❑ 206 A.J. English .05 .02
❑ 207 Harvey Grant .05 .02
❑ 208 Bernard King .05 .02
❑ 209 Wes Unseld CO .08 .04
❑ 210 Kevin Johnson AS .08 .04
❑ 211 Michael Jordan AS 1.00 .45
❑ 212 Dominique Wilkins AS .08 .04
❑ 213 Charles Barkley AS .15 .07
❑ 214 Hakeem Olajuwon AS .15 .07
❑ 215 Patrick Ewing AS .08 .04
❑ 216 Tim Hardaway AS .15 .07
❑ 217 John Stockton AS .08 .04
❑ 218 Chris Mullin AS .08 .04
❑ 219 Karl Malone AS .15 .07
❑ 220 Michael Jordan LL 1.00 .45
❑ 221 John Stockton LL .08 .04
❑ 222 Alvin Robertson LL .05 .02
❑ 223 Hakeem Olajuwon LL .15 .07
❑ 224 Buck Williams LL .05 .02
❑ 225 David Robinson LL .15 .07
❑ 226 Reggie Miller LL .08 .04
❑ 227 Blue Edwards SD .05 .02
❑ 228 Dee Brown SD .05 .02
❑ 229 Rex Chapman SD .05 .02
❑ 230 Kenny Smith SD .05 .02
❑ 231 Shawn Kemp SD .15 .07
❑ 232 Kendall Gill SD .05 .02
❑ 233 '91 All Star Game .50 .23
Enemies - A Love Story
(East Bench Scene)
❑ 234 Clyde Drexler ASG .15 .07
Kevin McHale ASG
❑ 235 Alvin Robertson ASG .05 .02
❑ 236 Patrick Ewing ASG .08 .04
Karl Malone ASG
❑ 237 '91 All Star Game .25 .11
Just Me and the Boys
Michael Jordan
Magic Johnson
David Robinson
Patrick Ewing
❑ 238 Michael Jordan ASG .50 .23
❑ 239 Checklist 1-120 .05 .02
❑ 240 Checklist 121-240 .05 .02
❑ 241 Stacey Augmon RC .15 .07
❑ 242 Maurice Cheeks .05 .02

❑ 243 Paul Graham RC .... .05 .02
❑ 244 Rodney Monroe RC ...... .05 .02
❑ 245 Blair Rasmussen .... .05 .02
❑ 246 Alexander Volkov .... .05 .02
❑ 247 John Bagley .... .05 .02
❑ 248 Rick Fox RC .... .15 .07
❑ 249 Rickey Green .... .05 .02
❑ 250 Joe Kleine .... .05 .02
❑ 251 Stojko Vrankovic .... .05 .02
❑ 252 Allan Bristow CO .... .05 .02
❑ 253 Kenny Gattison .... .05 .02
❑ 254 Mike Gminski .... .05 .02
❑ 255 Larry Johnson RC .... .60 .25
❑ 256 Bobby Hansen .... .05 .02
❑ 257 Craig Hodges .... .05 .02
❑ 258 Stacey King .... .05 .02
❑ 259 Scott Williams RC .... .05 .02
❑ 260 John Battle .... .05 .02
❑ 261 Winston Bennett .... .05 .02
❑ 262 Terrell Brandon RC .... .50 .23
❑ 263 Henry James .... .05 .02
❑ 264 Steve Kerr .... .08 .04
❑ 265 Jimmy Oliver RC .... .05 .02
❑ 266 Brad Davis .... .05 .02
❑ 267 Terry Davis .... .05 .02
❑ 268 Donald Hodge RC .... .05 .02
❑ 269 Mike Iuzzolino RC .... .05 .02
❑ 270 Fat Lever .... .05 .02
❑ 271 Doug Smith RC .... .05 .02
❑ 272 Greg Anderson .... .05 .02
❑ 273 Kevin Brooks RC .... .05 .02
❑ 274 Walter Davis .... .05 .02
❑ 275 Winston Garland .... .05 .02
❑ 276 Mark Macon RC .... .05 .02
❑ 277 Dikembe Mutombo RC .. .50 .23
(Fleer '91 on front)
❑ 277B Dikembe Mutombo RC .50 .23
(Fleer '91-92 on front)
❑ 278 William Bedford .... .05 .02
❑ 279 Lance Blanks .... .05 .02
❑ 280 John Salley .... .05 .02
❑ 281 Charles Thomas RC ...... .05 .02
❑ 282 Darrell Walker .... .05 .02
❑ 283 Orlando Woolridge .... .05 .02
❑ 284 Victor Alexander RC ...... .05 .02
❑ 285 Vincent Askew RC .... .05 .02
❑ 286 Mario Elie RC .... .15 .07
❑ 287 Alton Lister .... .05 .02
❑ 288 Billy Owens RC .... .15 .07
❑ 289 Matt Bullard RC .... .05 .02
❑ 290 Carl Herrera RC .... .05 .02
❑ 291 Tree Rollins .... .05 .02
❑ 292 John Turner .... .05 .02
❑ 293 Dale Davis RC UER ...... .15 .07
(Photo on back actually Sean Green)
❑ 294 Sean Green RC .... .05 .02
❑ 295 Kenny Williams .... .05 .02
❑ 296 James Edwards .... .05 .02
❑ 297 LeRon Ellis RC .... .05 .02
❑ 298 Doc Rivers .... .08 .04
❑ 299 Loy Vaught .... .05 .02
❑ 300 Elden Campbell .... .08 .04
❑ 301 Jack Haley .... .05 .02
❑ 302 Keith Owens .... .05 .02
❑ 303 Tony Smith .... .05 .02
❑ 304 Sedale Threatt .... .05 .02
❑ 305 Keith Askins RC .... .05 .02
❑ 306 Alec Kessler .... .05 .02
❑ 307 John Morton .... .05 .02
❑ 308 Alan Ogg .... .05 .02
❑ 309 Steve Smith RC .... .60 .25
❑ 310 Lester Conner .... .05 .02
❑ 311 Jeff Grayer .... .05 .02
❑ 312 Frank Hamblen CO .... .05 .02
❑ 313 Steve Henson .... .05 .02
❑ 314 Larry Krystkowiak .... .05 .02
❑ 315 Moses Malone .... .15 .07
❑ 316 Thurl Bailey .... .05 .02
❑ 317 Randy Breuer .... .05 .02
❑ 318 Scott Brooks .... .05 .02
❑ 319 Gerald Glass .... .05 .02
❑ 320 Luc Longley RC .... .15 .07
❑ 321 Doug West .... .05 .02
❑ 322 Kenny Anderson RC ...... .30 .14
❑ 323 Tate George .... .05 .02
❑ 324 Terry Mills RC .... .15 .07
❑ 325 Greg Anthony RC .... .15 .07
❑ 326 Anthony Mason RC .... .30 .14
❑ 327 Tim McCormick .... .05 .02
❑ 328 Xavier McDaniel .... .05 .02
❑ 329 Brian Quinnett .... .05 .02
❑ 330 John Starks RC .... .15 .07
❑ 331 Stanley Roberts RC ...... .05 .02
❑ 332 Jeff Turner .... .05 .02
❑ 333 Sam Vincent .... .05 .02
❑ 334 Brian Williams RC .... .15 .07
❑ 335 Manute Bol .... .05 .02
❑ 336 Kenny Payne .... .05 .02
❑ 337 Charles Shackleford ...... .05 .02
❑ 338 Jayson Williams .... .15 .07
❑ 339 Cedric Ceballos .... .08 .04
❑ 340 Andrew Lang .... .05 .02
❑ 341 Jerrod Mustaf .... .05 .02
❑ 342 Tim Perry .... .05 .02
❑ 343 Kurt Rambis .... .05 .02
❑ 344 Alaa Abdelnaby .... .05 .02
❑ 345 Robert Pack RC .... .08 .04
❑ 346 Danny Young .... .05 .02
❑ 347 Anthony Bonner .... .05 .02
❑ 348 Pete Chilcutt RC .... .05 .02
❑ 349 Rex Hughes CO .... .05 .02
❑ 350 Mitch Richmond .... .15 .07
❑ 351 Dwayne Schintzius .... .05 .02
❑ 352 Spud Webb .... .08 .04
❑ 353 Antoine Carr .... .05 .02
❑ 354 Sidney Green .... .05 .02
❑ 355 Vinnie Johnson .... .05 .02
❑ 356 Greg Sutton .... .05 .02
❑ 357 Dana Barros .... .05 .02
❑ 358 Michael Cage .... .05 .02
❑ 359 Marty Conlon RC .... .05 .02
❑ 360 Rich King RC .... .05 .02
❑ 361 Nate McMillan .... .05 .02
❑ 362 David Benoit RC .... .08 .04
❑ 363 Mike Brown .... .05 .02
❑ 364 Tyrone Corbin .... .05 .02
❑ 365 Eric Murdock RC .... .05 .02
❑ 366 Delaney Rudd .... .05 .02
❑ 367 Michael Adams .... .05 .02
❑ 368 Tom Hammonds .... .05 .02
❑ 369 Larry Stewart RC .... .05 .02
❑ 370 Andre Turner .... .05 .02
❑ 371 David Wingate .... .05 .02
❑ 372 Dominique Wilkins TL .... .08 .04
❑ 373 Larry Bird TL .... .30 .14
❑ 374 Rex Chapman TL .... .05 .02
❑ 375 Michael Jordan TL .... 1.00 .45
❑ 376 Brad Daugherty TL .... .05 .02
❑ 377 Derek Harper TL .... .05 .02
❑ 378 Dikembe Mutombo TL .... .15 .07
❑ 379 Joe Dumars TL .... .08 .04
❑ 380 Chris Mullin TL .... .08 .04
❑ 381 Hakeem Olajuwon TL ..... .15 .07
❑ 382 Chuck Person TL .... .05 .02
❑ 383 Charles Smith TL .... .05 .02
❑ 384 James Worthy TL .... .08 .04
❑ 385 Glen Rice TL .... .08 .04
❑ 386 Alvin Robertson TL .... .05 .02
❑ 387 Tony Campbell TL .... .05 .02
❑ 388 Derrick Coleman TL ...... .05 .02
❑ 389 Patrick Ewing TL .... .08 .04
❑ 390 Scott Skiles TL .... .05 .02
❑ 391 Charles Barkley TL .... .15 .07
❑ 392 Kevin Johnson TL .... .08 .04
❑ 393 Clyde Drexler TL .... .08 .04
❑ 394 Lionel Simmons TL .... .05 .02
❑ 395 David Robinson TL .... .15 .07
❑ 396 Ricky Pierce TL .... .05 .02
❑ 397 John Stockton TL .... .08 .04
❑ 398 Michael Adams TL .... .05 .02
❑ 399 Checklist .... .05 .02
❑ 400 Checklist .... .05 .02

1991-92 Fleer Dikembe Mutombo

	MINT	NRMT
COMPLETE SET (12)	5.00	2.20
COMMON MUTOMBO (1-12)	.50	.23
CERTIFIED AUTOGRAPH (AU)	60.00	27.00

RANDOM INSERTS IN ALL SER.2 PACKS

❑ 1 Dikembe Mutombo .... .50 .23
Childhood in Zaire
❑ 2 Dikembe Mutombo .... .50 .23
Georgetown Start
❑ 3 Dikembe Mutombo .... .50 .23
Arrival on college scene
❑ 4 Dikembe Mutombo .... .50 .23
Capping college career
❑ 5 Dikembe Mutombo .... .50 .23
NBA Draft
❑ 6 Dikembe Mutombo .... .50 .23
First NBA games
❑ 7 Dikembe Mutombo .... .50 .23
Offensive skills
❑ 8 Dikembe Mutombo .... .50 .23
What he has meant to the Nuggets
❑ 9 Dikembe Mutombo .... .50 .23
Work Habits
❑ 10 Dikembe Mutombo .... .50 .23
Charmed Denver
❑ 11 Dikembe Mutombo .... .50 .23
The Future
❑ 12 Dikembe Mutombo .... .50 .23
The Mutombo Legend

1991-92 Fleer Pro-Visions

	MINT	NRMT
COMPLETE SET (6)	4.00	1.80

*SINGLES: .6X TO 1.5X BASE CARD HI
RANDOM INSERTS IN ALL SER.1 PACKS

❑ 1 David Robinson .... .50 .23
❑ 2 Michael Jordan 3.00 1.35
❑ 3 Charles Barkley .... .40 .18
❑ 4 Patrick Ewing .... .25 .11
❑ 5 Karl Malone .... .40 .18
❑ 6 Magic Johnson .... .75 .35

1991-92 Fleer Rookie Sensations

	MINT	NRMT
COMPLETE SET (10)	8.00	3.60
COMMON CARD (1-10)	.50	.23
SEMISTARS	.75	.35
UNLISTED STARS	1.50	.70

RANDOM INSERTS IN SER.1 CELLO PACKS

❑ 1 Lionel Simmons	.50	.23
❑ 2 Dennis Scott	.75	.35
❑ 3 Derrick Coleman	1.50	.70
❑ 4 Kendall Gill	1.50	.70
❑ 5 Travis Mays	.50	.23
❑ 6 Felton Spencer	.50	.23
❑ 7 Willie Burton	.50	.23
❑ 8 Chris Jackson	.50	.23
❑ 9 Gary Payton	6.00	2.70
❑ 10 Dee Brown	.50	.23

1991-92 Fleer Schoolyard

	MINT	NRMT
COMPLETE SET (6)	8.00	3.60
COMMON CARD (1-6)	.75	.35
SEMISTARS	1.50	.70

ONE PER SER.1 RACK PACK

❑ 1 Chris Mullin	1.50	.70
❑ 2 Isiah Thomas	1.50	.70
❑ 3 Kevin McHale	1.50	.70
❑ 4 Kevin Johnson	1.50	.70
❑ 5 Karl Malone	6.00	2.70
❑ 6 Alvin Robertson	.75	.35

1991-92 Fleer Dominique Wilkins

	MINT	NRMT
COMPLETE SET (12)	4.00	1.80
COMMON WILKINS (1-12)	.40	.18
CERTIFIED AUTOGRAPH (AU)	80.00	36.00

RANDOM INSERTS IN ALL SER.2 PACKS

❑ 1 Dominique Wilkins Overview	.40	.18
❑ 2 Dominique Wilkins College	.40	.18
❑ 3 Dominique Wilkins Early years	.40	.18
❑ 4 Dominique Wilkins Early Career	.40	.18
❑ 5 Dominique Wilkins Dominique Emerges	.40	.18
❑ 6 Dominique Wilkins Another milestone	.40	.18
❑ 7 Dominique Wilkins Wilkins continues to shine	.40	.18
❑ 8 Dominique Wilkins Best all-round season	.40	.18
❑ 9 Dominique Wilkins Charitable Causes	.40	.18
❑ 10 Dominique Wilkins Durability	.40	.18
❑ 11 Dominique Wilkins Career Numbers	.40	.18
❑ 12 Dominique Wilkins Future	.40	.18

1992-93 Fleer

	MINT	NRMT
COMPLETE SET (444)	30.00	13.50
COMPLETE SERIES 1 (264)	15.00	6.75
COMPLETE SERIES 2 (180)	15.00	6.75
COMMON CARD (1-444)	.05	.02
SEMISTARS	.10	.05
UNLISTED STARS	.25	.11

SUBSET CARDS HALF VALUE OF BASE CARDS
SLM DNK AUs: SER.2 STATED ODDS 1:5,000

❑ 1 Stacey Augmon	.10	.05
❑ 2 Duane Ferrell	.05	.02
❑ 3 Paul Graham	.05	.02
❑ 4A Jon Koncak (Shooting pose on back)	.05	.02
❑ 4B Jon Koncak (No ball visible in photo on back)	.05	.02
❑ 5 Blair Rasmussen	.05	.02
❑ 6 Rumeal Robinson	.05	.02
❑ 7 Bob Weiss CO	.05	.02
❑ 8 Dominique Wilkins	.25	.11
❑ 9 Kevin Willis	.05	.02
❑ 10 John Bagley	.05	.02
❑ 11 Larry Bird	1.00	.45
❑ 12 Dee Brown	.05	.02
❑ 13 Chris Ford CO	.05	.02
❑ 14 Rick Fox	.10	.05
❑ 15 Kevin Gamble	.05	.02
❑ 16 Reggie Lewis	.10	.05
❑ 17 Kevin McHale	.25	.11
❑ 18 Robert Parish	.10	.05
❑ 19 Ed Pinckney	.05	.02
❑ 20 Muggsy Bogues	.10	.05
❑ 21 Allan Bristow CO	.05	.02
❑ 22 Dell Curry	.05	.02
❑ 23 Kenny Gattison	.05	.02
❑ 24 Kendall Gill	.10	.05
❑ 25 Larry Johnson	.30	.14
❑ 26 Johnny Newman	.05	.02
❑ 27 J.R. Reid	.05	.02
❑ 28 B.J. Armstrong	.05	.02
❑ 29 Bill Cartwright	.05	.02
❑ 30 Horace Grant	.10	.05
❑ 31 Phil Jackson CO	.10	.05
❑ 32 Michael Jordan	3.00	1.35
❑ 33 Stacey King	.05	.02
❑ 34 Cliff Levingston	.05	.02
❑ 35 John Paxson	.05	.02
❑ 36 Scottie Pippen	.75	.35
❑ 37 Scott Williams	.05	.02
❑ 38 John Battle	.05	.02
❑ 39 Terrell Brandon	.25	.11
❑ 40 Brad Daugherty	.05	.02
❑ 41 Craig Ehlo	.05	.02
❑ 42 Larry Nance	.05	.02
❑ 43 Mark Price	.05	.02
❑ 44 Mike Sanders	.05	.02
❑ 45 Lenny Wilkens CO	.10	.05
❑ 46 John Hot Rod Williams	.05	.02
❑ 47 Richie Adubato CO	.05	.02
❑ 48 Terry Davis	.05	.02
❑ 49 Derek Harper	.10	.05
❑ 50 Donald Hodge	.05	.02
❑ 51 Mike Iuzzolino	.05	.02
❑ 52 Rodney McCray	.05	.02
❑ 53 Doug Smith	.05	.02
❑ 54 Greg Anderson	.05	.02
❑ 55 Winston Garland	.05	.02
❑ 56 Dan Issel CO	.05	.02
❑ 57 Chris Jackson	.05	.02
❑ 58 Marcus Liberty	.05	.02
❑ 59 Mark Macon	.05	.02
❑ 60 Dikembe Mutombo	.25	.11
❑ 61 Reggie Williams	.05	.02
❑ 62 Mark Aguirre	.05	.02
❑ 63 Joe Dumars	.25	.11
❑ 64 Bill Laimbeer	.10	.05
❑ 65 Olden Polynice	.05	.02
❑ 66 Dennis Rodman	.50	.23
❑ 67 Ron Rothstein CO	.05	.02
❑ 68 John Salley	.05	.02
❑ 69 Isiah Thomas	.25	.11
❑ 70 Darrell Walker	.05	.02
❑ 71 Orlando Woolridge	.05	.02
❑ 72 Victor Alexander	.05	.02
❑ 73 Mario Elie	.10	.05
❑ 74 Tim Hardaway	.30	.14
❑ 75 Tyrone Hill	.05	.02
❑ 76 Sarunas Marciulionis	.05	.02
❑ 77 Chris Mullin	.25	.11
❑ 78 Don Nelson CO	.10	.05
❑ 79 Billy Owens	.10	.05
❑ 80 Sleepy Floyd UER (Went past 4000 assist mark, not 2000)	.05	.02
❑ 81 Avery Johnson	.05	.02
❑ 82 Buck Johnson	.05	.02
❑ 83 Vernon Maxwell	.05	.02
❑ 84 Hakeem Olajuwon	.40	.18
❑ 85 Kenny Smith	.05	.02
❑ 86 Otis Thorpe	.10	.05
❑ 87 Rudy Tomjanovich CO	.10	.05
❑ 88 Dale Davis	.05	.02
❑ 89 Vern Fleming	.05	.02
❑ 90 Bob Hill CO	.05	.02
❑ 91 Reggie Miller	.25	.11
❑ 92 Chuck Person	.05	.02
❑ 93 Detlef Schrempf	.10	.05
❑ 94 Rik Smits	.10	.05
❑ 95 LaSalle Thompson	.05	.02

❑ 96 Micheal Williams .05 .02
❑ 97 Larry Brown CO .10 .05
❑ 98 James Edwards .05 .02
❑ 99 Gary Grant .05 .02
❑ 100 Ron Harper .10 .05
❑ 101 Danny Manning .10 .05
❑ 102 Ken Norman .05 .02
❑ 103 Doc Rivers .10 .05
❑ 104 Charles Smith .05 .02
❑ 105 Loy Vaught .05 .02
❑ 106 Elden Campbell .10 .05
❑ 107 Vlade Divac .10 .05
❑ 108 A.C. Green .10 .05
❑ 109 Sam Perkins .10 .05
❑ 110 Randy Pfund CO RC .05 .02
❑ 111 Byron Scott .10 .05
❑ 112 Terry Teagle .05 .02
❑ 113 Sedale Threatt .05 .02
❑ 114 James Worthy .25 .11
❑ 115 Willie Burton .05 .02
❑ 116 Bimbo Coles .05 .02
❑ 117 Kevin Edwards .05 .02
❑ 118 Grant Long .05 .02
❑ 119 Kevin Loughery CO .05 .02
❑ 120 Glen Rice .25 .11
❑ 121 Rony Seikaly .05 .02
❑ 122 Brian Shaw .05 .02
❑ 123 Steve Smith .30 .14
❑ 124 Frank Brickowski .05 .02
❑ 125 Mike Dunleavy CO .05 .02
❑ 126 Blue Edwards .05 .02
❑ 127 Moses Malone .25 .11
❑ 128 Eric Murdock .05 .02
❑ 129 Fred Roberts .05 .02
❑ 130 Alvin Robertson .05 .02
❑ 131 Thurl Bailey .05 .02
❑ 132 Tony Campbell .05 .02
❑ 133 Gerald Glass .05 .02
❑ 134 Luc Longley .10 .05
❑ 135 Sam Mitchell .05 .02
❑ 136 Pooh Richardson .05 .02
❑ 137 Jimmy Rodgers CO .05 .02
❑ 138 Felton Spencer .05 .02
❑ 139 Doug West .05 .02
❑ 140 Kenny Anderson .25 .11
❑ 141 Mookie Blaylock .10 .05
❑ 142 Sam Bowie .05 .02
❑ 143 Derrick Coleman .10 .05
❑ 144 Chuck Daly CO .10 .05
❑ 145 Terry Mills .05 .02
❑ 146 Chris Morris .05 .02
❑ 147 Drazen Petrovic .05 .02
❑ 148 Greg Anthony .05 .02
❑ 149 Rolando Blackman .05 .02
❑ 150 Patrick Ewing .25 .11
❑ 151 Mark Jackson .10 .05
❑ 152 Anthony Mason .25 .11
❑ 153 Xavier McDaniel .05 .02
❑ 154 Charles Oakley .10 .05
❑ 155 Pat Riley CO .10 .05
❑ 156 John Starks .10 .05
❑ 157 Gerald Wilkins .05 .02
❑ 158 Nick Anderson .10 .05
❑ 159 Anthony Bowie .05 .02
❑ 160 Terry Catledge .05 .02
❑ 161 Matt Guokas CO .05 .02
❑ 162 Stanley Roberts .05 .02
❑ 163 Dennis Scott .10 .05
❑ 164 Scott Skiles .05 .02
❑ 165 Brian Williams .05 .02
❑ 166 Ron Anderson .05 .02
❑ 167 Manute Bol .05 .02
❑ 168 Johnny Dawkins .05 .02
❑ 169 Armon Gilliam .05 .02
❑ 170 Hersey Hawkins .10 .05
❑ 171 Jeff Hornacek .10 .05
❑ 172 Andrew Lang .05 .02
❑ 173 Doug Moe CO .05 .02
❑ 174 Tim Perry .05 .02
❑ 175 Jeff Ruland .05 .02
❑ 176 Charles Shackleford .05 .02
❑ 177 Danny Ainge .10 .05
❑ 178 Charles Barkley .40 .18
❑ 179 Cedric Ceballos .10 .05
❑ 180 Tom Chambers .05 .02
❑ 181 Kevin Johnson .25 .11
❑ 182 Dan Majerle .10 .05
❑ 183 Mark West UER .05 .02
(Needs 33 blocks to reach 1000, not 31)
❑ 184 Paul Westphal CO .05 .02
❑ 185 Rick Adelman CO .05 .02
❑ 186 Clyde Drexler .25 .11
❑ 187 Kevin Duckworth .05 .02
❑ 188 Jerome Kersey .05 .02
❑ 189 Robert Pack .05 .02
❑ 190 Terry Porter .05 .02
❑ 191 Clifford Robinson .10 .05
❑ 192 Rod Strickland .25 .11
❑ 193 Buck Williams .10 .05
❑ 194 Anthony Bonner .05 .02
❑ 195 Duane Causwell .05 .02
❑ 196 Mitch Richmond .25 .11
❑ 197 Garry St. Jean CO RC .05 .02
❑ 198 Lionel Simmons .05 .02
❑ 199 Wayman Tisdale .05 .02
❑ 200 Spud Webb .10 .05
❑ 201 Willie Anderson .05 .02
❑ 202 Antoine Carr .05 .02
❑ 203 Terry Cummings .10 .05
❑ 204 Sean Elliott .10 .05
❑ 205 Dale Ellis .05 .02
❑ 206 Vinnie Johnson .05 .02
❑ 207 David Robinson .40 .18
❑ 208 Jerry Tarkanian CO RC .05 .02
❑ 209 Benoit Benjamin .05 .02
❑ 210 Michael Cage .05 .02
❑ 211 Eddie Johnson .05 .02
❑ 212 George Karl CO .10 .05
❑ 213 Shawn Kemp .50 .23
❑ 214 Derrick McKey .05 .02
❑ 215 Nate McMillan .05 .02
❑ 216 Gary Payton .50 .23
❑ 217 Ricky Pierce .05 .02
❑ 218 David Benoit .05 .02
❑ 219 Mike Brown .05 .02
❑ 220 Tyrone Corbin .05 .02
❑ 221 Mark Eaton .05 .02
❑ 222 Jay Humphries .05 .02
❑ 223 Larry Krystkowiak .05 .02
❑ 224 Jeff Malone .05 .02
❑ 225 Karl Malone .40 .18
❑ 226 Jerry Sloan CO .10 .05
❑ 227 John Stockton .25 .11
❑ 228 Michael Adams .05 .02
❑ 229 Rex Chapman .05 .02
❑ 230 Ledell Eackles .05 .02
❑ 231 Pervis Ellison .05 .02
❑ 232 A.J. English .05 .02
❑ 233 Harvey Grant .05 .02
❑ 234 LaBradford Smith .05 .02
❑ 235 Larry Stewart .05 .02
❑ 236 Wes Unseld CO .10 .05
❑ 237 David Wingate .05 .02
❑ 238 Michael Jordan LL 1.50 .70
Scoring
❑ 239 Dennis Rodman LL .25 .11
Rebounding
❑ 240 John Stockton LL .10 .05
Assists/Steals
❑ 241 Buck Williams LL .05 .02
Field Goal Percentage
❑ 242 Mark Price LL .05 .02
Free Throw Percentage
❑ 243 Dana Barros LL .05 .02
Three Point Percentage
❑ 244 David Robinson LL .25 .11
Shots Blocked
❑ 245 Chris Mullin LL .10 .05
Minutes Played
❑ 246 Michael Jordan MVP 1.50 .70
❑ 247 Larry Johnson ROY UER .25 .11
(Scoring average was 19.2, not 19.7)
❑ 248 David Robinson .25 .11
Defensive Player of the Year
❑ 249 Detlef Schrempf .05 .02
Sixth Man of the Year
❑ 250 Clyde Drexler PV .10 .05
❑ 251 Tim Hardaway PV .25 .11
❑ 252 Kevin Johnson PV .10 .05
❑ 253 Larry Johnson PV UER .25 .11
(Scoring average was 19.2, not 19.7)
❑ 254 Scottie Pippen PV .40 .18
❑ 255 Isiah Thomas PV .10 .05
❑ 256 Larry Bird SY .50 .23
❑ 257 Brad Daugherty SY .05 .02
❑ 258 Kevin Johnson SY .10 .05
❑ 259 Larry Johnson SY .25 .11
❑ 260 Scottie Pippen SY .40 .18
❑ 261 Dennis Rodman SY .25 .11
❑ 262 Checklist 1 .05 .02
❑ 263 Checklist 2 .05 .02
❑ 264 Checklist 3 .05 .02
❑ 265 Charles Barkley SD .25 .11
❑ 266 Shawn Kemp SD .25 .11
❑ 267 Dan Majerle SD .05 .02
❑ 268 Karl Malone SD .25 .11
❑ 269 Buck Williams SD .05 .02
❑ 270 Clyde Drexler SD .10 .05
❑ 271 Sean Elliott SD .05 .02
❑ 272 Ron Harper SD .05 .02
❑ 273 Michael Jordan SD 1.50 .70
❑ 274 James Worthy SD .10 .05
❑ 275 Cedric Ceballos SD .05 .02
❑ 276 Larry Nance SD .05 .02
❑ 277 Kenny Walker SD .05 .02
❑ 278 Spud Webb SD .05 .02
❑ 279 Dominique Wilkins SD .10 .05
❑ 280 Terrell Brandon SD .10 .05
❑ 281 Dee Brown SD .05 .02
❑ 282 Kevin Johnson SD .10 .05
❑ 283 Doc Rivers SD .05 .02
❑ 284 Byron Scott SD .05 .02
❑ 285 Manute Bol SD .05 .02
❑ 286 Dikembe Mutombo SD .10 .05
❑ 287 Robert Parish SD .05 .02
❑ 288 David Robinson SD .25 .11
❑ 289 Dennis Rodman SD .25 .11
❑ 290 Blue Edwards SD .05 .02
❑ 291 Patrick Ewing SD .10 .05
❑ 292 Larry Johnson SD .25 .11
❑ 293 Jerome Kersey SD .05 .02
❑ 294 Hakeem Olajuwon SD .25 .11
❑ 295 Stacey Augmon SD .05 .02
❑ 296 Derrick Coleman SD .05 .02
❑ 297 Kendall Gill SD .05 .02
❑ 298 Shaquille O'Neal SD 1.25 .55
❑ 299 Scottie Pippen SD .40 .18
❑ 300 Darryl Dawkins SD .10 .05
❑ 301 Mookie Blaylock .10 .05
❑ 302 Adam Keefe RC .05 .02
❑ 303 Travis Mays .05 .02
❑ 304 Morlon Wiley .05 .02
❑ 305 Sherman Douglas .05 .02
❑ 306 Joe Kleine .05 .02
❑ 307 Xavier McDaniel .05 .02
❑ 308 Tony Bennett RC .05 .02
❑ 309 Tom Hammonds .05 .02
❑ 310 Kevin Lynch .05 .02
❑ 311 Alonzo Mourning RC 1.25 .55
❑ 312 David Wingate .05 .02
❑ 313 Rodney McCray .05 .02
❑ 314 Will Perdue .05 .02
❑ 315 Trent Tucker .05 .02
❑ 316 Corey Williams RC .05 .02
❑ 317 Danny Ferry .05 .02
❑ 318 Jay Guidinger RC .05 .02
❑ 319 Jerome Lane .05 .02
❑ 320 Gerald Wilkins .05 .02
❑ 321 Steve Bardo RC .05 .02
❑ 322 Walter Bond RC .05 .02
❑ 323 Brian Howard RC .05 .02
❑ 324 Tracy Moore RC .05 .02
❑ 325 Sean Rooks RC .05 .02
❑ 326 Randy White .05 .02
❑ 327 Kevin Brooks .05 .02
❑ 328 LaPhonso Ellis RC .25 .11
❑ 329 Scott Hastings .05 .02
❑ 330 Todd Lichti .05 .02
❑ 331 Robert Pack .05 .02
❑ 332 Bryant Stith RC .10 .05
❑ 333 Gerald Glass .05 .02
❑ 334 Terry Mills .05 .02
❑ 335 Isaiah Morris RC .05 .02
❑ 336 Mark Randall .05 .02

❑ 337 Danny Young	.05	.02
❑ 338 Chris Gatling	.05	.02
❑ 339 Jeff Grayer	.05	.02
❑ 340 Byron Houston RC	.05	.02
❑ 341 Keith Jennings RC	.05	.02
❑ 342 Alton Lister	.05	.02
❑ 343 Latrell Sprewell RC	2.00	.90
❑ 344 Scott Brooks	.05	.02
❑ 345 Matt Bullard	.05	.02
❑ 346 Carl Herrera	.05	.02
❑ 347 Robert Horry RC	.25	.11
❑ 348 Tree Rollins	.05	.02
❑ 349 Greg Dreiling	.05	.02
❑ 350 George McCloud	.05	.02
❑ 351 Sam Mitchell	.05	.02
❑ 352 Pooh Richardson	.05	.02
❑ 353 Malik Sealy RC	.10	.05
❑ 354 Kenny Williams	.05	.02
❑ 355 Jaren Jackson RC	.10	.05
❑ 356 Mark Jackson	.10	.05
❑ 357 Stanley Roberts	.05	.02
❑ 358 Elmore Spencer RC	.05	.02
❑ 359 Kiki Vandeweghe	.05	.02
❑ 360 John S. Williams	.05	.02
❑ 361 Randy Woods RC	.05	.02
❑ 362 Duane Cooper RC	.05	.02
❑ 363 James Edwards	.05	.02
❑ 364 Anthony Peeler RC	.10	.05
❑ 365 Tony Smith	.05	.02
❑ 366 Keith Askins	.05	.02
❑ 367 Matt Geiger RC	.10	.05
❑ 368 Alec Kessler	.05	.02
❑ 369 Harold Miner RC	.10	.05
❑ 370 John Salley	.05	.02
❑ 371 Anthony Avent RC	.05	.02
❑ 372 Todd Day RC	.10	.05
❑ 373 Blue Edwards	.05	.02
❑ 374 Brad Lohaus	.05	.02
❑ 375 Lee Mayberry RC	.05	.02
❑ 376 Eric Murdock	.05	.02
❑ 377 Dan Schayes	.05	.02
❑ 378 Lance Blanks	.05	.02
❑ 379 Christian Laettner RC	.50	.23
❑ 380 Bob McCann RC	.05	.02
❑ 381 Chuck Person	.05	.02
❑ 382 Brad Sellers	.05	.02
❑ 383 Chris Smith RC	.05	.02
❑ 384 Micheal Williams	.05	.02
❑ 385 Rafael Addison	.05	.02
❑ 386 Chucky Brown	.05	.02
❑ 387 Chris Dudley	.05	.02
❑ 388 Tate George	.05	.02
❑ 389 Rick Mahorn	.05	.02
❑ 390 Rumeal Robinson	.05	.02
❑ 391 Jayson Williams	.10	.05
❑ 392 Eric Anderson RC	.05	.02
❑ 393 Rolando Blackman	.05	.02
❑ 394 Tony Campbell	.05	.02
❑ 395 Hubert Davis RC	.10	.05
❑ 396 Doc Rivers	.10	.05
❑ 397 Charles Smith	.05	.02
❑ 398 Herb Williams	.05	.02
❑ 399 Litterial Green RC	.05	.02
❑ 400 Greg Kite	.05	.02
❑ 401 Shaquille O'Neal RC	6.00	2.70
❑ 402 Jerry Reynolds	.05	.02
❑ 403 Jeff Turner	.05	.02
❑ 404 Greg Grant	.05	.02
❑ 405 Jeff Hornacek	.10	.05
❑ 406 Andrew Lang	.05	.02
❑ 407 Kenny Payne	.05	.02
❑ 408 Tim Perry	.05	.02
❑ 409 C. Weatherspoon RC	.25	.11
❑ 410 Danny Ainge	.10	.05
❑ 411 Charles Barkley	.40	.18
❑ 412 Negele Knight	.05	.02
❑ 413 Oliver Miller RC	.10	.05
❑ 414 Jerrod Mustaf	.05	.02
❑ 415 Mark Bryant	.05	.02
❑ 416 Mario Elie	.10	.05
❑ 417 Dave Johnson RC	.05	.02
❑ 418 Tracy Murray RC	.10	.05
❑ 419 Reggie Smith RC	.05	.02
❑ 420 Rod Strickland	.25	.11
❑ 421 Randy Brown	.05	.02
❑ 422 Pete Chilcutt	.05	.02
❑ 423 Jim Les	.05	.02
❑ 424 Walt Williams RC	.25	.11
❑ 425 Lloyd Daniels RC	.05	.02
❑ 426 Vinny Del Negro	.05	.02
❑ 427 Dale Ellis	.05	.02
❑ 428 Sidney Green	.05	.02
❑ 429 Avery Johnson	.05	.02
❑ 430 Dana Barros	.05	.02
❑ 431 Rich King	.05	.02
❑ 432 Isaac Austin RC	.10	.05
❑ 433 John Crotty RC	.05	.02
❑ 434 Stephen Howard RC	.05	.02
❑ 435 Jay Humphries	.05	.02
❑ 436 Larry Krystkowiak	.05	.02
❑ 437 Tom Gugliotta RC	.75	.35
❑ 438 Buck Johnson	.05	.02
❑ 439 Charles Jones	.05	.02
❑ 440 Don MacLean RC	.05	.02
❑ 441 Doug Overton	.05	.02
❑ 442 Brent Price RC	.10	.05
❑ 443 Checklist 1	.05	.02
❑ 444 Checklist 2	.05	.02
❑ SD266 Shawn Kemp AU (Certified Autograph)	150.00	70.00
❑ SD277 Darrell Walker AU (Certified Autograph)	30.00	13.50
❑ SD300 Darryl Dawkins AU (Certified Autograph)	40.00	18.00
❑ NNO Slam Dunk Wrapper Exchange	3.00	1.35

1992-93 Fleer All-Stars

	MINT	NRMT
COMPLETE SET (24)	100.00	45.00
COMMON CARD (1-24)	1.00	.45
SEMISTARS	2.50	1.10
UNLISTED STARS	4.00	1.80

SER.1 STATED ODDS 1:9
CONDITION SENSITIVE SET

❑ 1 Michael Adams	1.00	.45
❑ 2 Charles Barkley	6.00	2.70
❑ 3 Brad Daugherty	1.00	.45
❑ 4 Joe Dumars	4.00	1.80
❑ 5 Patrick Ewing	4.00	1.80
❑ 6 Michael Jordan	50.00	22.00
❑ 7 Reggie Lewis	2.50	1.10
❑ 8 Scottie Pippen	12.00	5.50
❑ 9 Mark Price	1.00	.45
❑ 10 Dennis Rodman	8.00	3.60
❑ 11 Isiah Thomas	4.00	1.80
❑ 12 Kevin Willis	1.00	.45
❑ 13 Clyde Drexler	4.00	1.80
❑ 14 Tim Hardaway	5.00	2.20
❑ 15 Jeff Hornacek	2.50	1.10
❑ 16 Dan Majerle	2.50	1.10
❑ 17 Karl Malone	6.00	2.70
❑ 18 Chris Mullin	4.00	1.80
❑ 19 Dikembe Mutombo	4.00	1.80
❑ 20 Hakeem Olajuwon	6.00	2.70
❑ 21 David Robinson	6.00	2.70
❑ 22 John Stockton	4.00	1.80
❑ 23 Otis Thorpe	2.50	1.10
❑ 24 James Worthy	4.00	1.80

1992-93 Fleer Larry Johnson

	MINT	NRMT
COMPLETE SET (12)	10.00	4.50
COMMON L.JOHNSON (1-12)	1.25	.55
SER.1 STATED ODDS 1:18		
CERTIFIED AUTOGRAPH (AU)	60.00	27.00
COMMON SEND-OFF (13-15)	4.00	1.80

THREE CARDS PER 10 SER.1 WRAPPERS

❑ 1 Larry Johnson (Holding up Hornets' home jersey)	1.25	.55
❑ 2 Larry Johnson (Driving through traffic against Knicks)	1.25	.55
❑ 3 Larry Johnson (Turned to the side, holding ball over head)	1.25	.55
❑ 4 Larry Johnson (Shooting jumpshot)	1.25	.55
❑ 5 Larry Johnson (Smiling, holding ball at chest level)	1.25	.55
❑ 6 Larry Johnson (Dribbling into a no-look pass)	1.25	.55
❑ 7 Larry Johnson (Posting up down low)	1.25	.55
❑ 8 Larry Johnson (Shooting ball in lane)	1.25	.55
❑ 9 Larry Johnson (Going for tip-in in home jersey)	1.25	.55
❑ 10 Larry Johnson (In warm-up suit)	1.25	.55
❑ 11 Larry Johnson (High-fiving during pre-game introductions)	1.25	.55
❑ 12 Larry Johnson (Dribbling with his left hand)	1.25	.55
❑ 13 Larry Johnson (Going up for a rebound)	4.00	1.80
❑ 14 Larry Johnson (Away from ball photo)	4.00	1.80
❑ 15 Larry Johnson (Charlotte skyline in background)	4.00	1.80

1992-93 Fleer Rookie Sensations

	MINT	NRMT
COMPLETE SET (12)	25.00	11.00

*SINGLES: 8X TO 20X BASE CARD HI
SER.1 STATED ODDS 1:5 CELLO

❑ 1 Greg Anthony	1.00	.45
❑ 2 Stacey Augmon	2.00	.90
❑ 3 Terrell Brandon	5.00	2.20
❑ 4 Rick Fox	2.00	.90
❑ 5 Larry Johnson	6.00	2.70
❑ 6 Mark Macon	1.00	.45

❑ 7 Dikembe Mutombo	5.00	2.20
❑ 8 Billy Owens	2.00	.90
❑ 9 Stanley Roberts	1.00	.45
❑ 10 Doug Smith	1.00	.45
❑ 11 Steve Smith	6.00	2.70
❑ 12 Larry Stewart	1.00	.45

1992-93 Fleer Sharpshooters

	MINT	NRMT
COMPLETE SET (18)	20.00	9.00

*SINGLES: 6X TO 15X BASE CARD HI
SER.2 STATED ODDS 1:3

❑ 1 Reggie Miller	4.00	1.80
❑ 2 Dana Barros	.75	.35
❑ 3 Jeff Hornacek	1.50	.70
❑ 4 Drazen Petrovic	.75	.35
❑ 5 Glen Rice	4.00	1.80
❑ 6 Terry Porter	.75	.35
❑ 7 Mark Price	.75	.35
❑ 8 Michael Adams	.75	.35
❑ 9 Hersey Hawkins	1.50	.70
❑ 10 Chuck Person	.75	.35
❑ 11 John Stockton	4.00	1.80
❑ 12 Dale Ellis	.75	.35
❑ 13 Clyde Drexler	4.00	1.80
❑ 14 Mitch Richmond	4.00	1.80
❑ 15 Craig Ehlo	.75	.35
❑ 16 Dell Curry	.75	.35
❑ 17 Chris Mullin	4.00	1.80
❑ 18 Rolando Blackman	.75	.35

1992-93 Fleer Team Leaders

	MINT	NRMT
COMPLETE SET (27)	200.00	90.00
COMMON CARD (1-27)	2.00	.90
SEMISTARS	4.00	1.80
UNLISTED STARS	10.00	4.50

ONE TL OR JOHNSON PER SER.1 RACK PACK
CONDITION SENSITIVE SET

❑ 1 Dominique Wilkins	10.00	4.50
❑ 2 Reggie Lewis	4.00	1.80
❑ 3 Larry Johnson	4.00	1.80
❑ 4 Michael Jordan	120.00	55.00
❑ 5 Mark Price	2.00	.90
❑ 6 Terry Davis	2.00	.90
❑ 7 Dikembe Mutombo	10.00	4.50
❑ 8 Isiah Thomas	10.00	4.50
❑ 9 Chris Mullin	10.00	4.50
❑ 10 Hakeem Olajuwon	15.00	6.75
❑ 11 Reggie Miller	10.00	4.50
❑ 12 Danny Manning	4.00	1.80
❑ 13 James Worthy	10.00	4.50
❑ 14 Glen Rice	10.00	4.50
❑ 15 Alvin Robertson	2.00	.90
❑ 16 Tony Campbell	2.00	.90
❑ 17 Derrick Coleman	4.00	1.80
❑ 18 Patrick Ewing	10.00	4.50
❑ 19 Scott Skiles	2.00	.90
❑ 20 Hersey Hawkins	4.00	1.80
❑ 21 Kevin Johnson	10.00	4.50
❑ 22 Clyde Drexler	10.00	4.50
❑ 23 Mitch Richmond	10.00	4.50
❑ 24 David Robinson	15.00	6.75
❑ 25 Ricky Pierce	2.00	.90
❑ 26 Karl Malone	15.00	6.75
❑ 27 Pervis Ellison	2.00	.90

1992-93 Fleer Total D

	MINT	NRMT
COMPLETE SET (15)	60.00	27.00
COMMON CARD (1-15)	1.25	.55
SEMISTARS	2.00	.90
UNLISTED STARS	3.00	1.35

SER.2 STATED ODDS 1:5 CELLO
CONDITION SENSITIVE SET

❑ 1 David Robinson	5.00	2.20
❑ 2 Dennis Rodman	6.00	2.70
❑ 3 Scottie Pippen	10.00	4.50
❑ 4 Joe Dumars	3.00	1.35
❑ 5 Michael Jordan	40.00	18.00
❑ 6 John Stockton	3.00	1.35
❑ 7 Patrick Ewing	3.00	1.35
❑ 8 Micheal Williams	1.25	.55
❑ 9 Larry Nance	1.25	.55
❑ 10 Buck Williams	2.00	.90
❑ 11 Alvin Robertson	1.25	.55
❑ 12 Dikembe Mutombo	3.00	1.35
❑ 13 Mookie Blaylock	2.00	.90
❑ 14 Hakeem Olajuwon	5.00	2.20
❑ 15 Rony Seikaly	1.25	.55

1993-94 Fleer

	MINT	NRMT
COMPLETE SET (400)	20.00	9.00
COMPLETE SERIES 1 (240)	10.00	4.50
COMPLETE SERIES 2 (160)	10.00	4.50
COMMON CARD (1-400)	.05	.02
SEMISTARS	.10	.05
UNLISTED STARS	.25	.11

SUBSET CARDS HALF VALUE OF BASE CARDS

❑ 1 Stacey Augmon	.05	.02
❑ 2 Mookie Blaylock	.10	.05
❑ 3 Duane Ferrell	.05	.02
❑ 4 Paul Graham	.05	.02
❑ 5 Adam Keefe	.05	.02
❑ 6 Jon Koncak	.05	.02
❑ 7 Dominique Wilkins	.25	.11
❑ 8 Kevin Willis	.05	.02
❑ 9 Alaa Abdelnaby	.05	.02
❑ 10 Dee Brown	.05	.02
❑ 11 Sherman Douglas	.05	.02
❑ 12 Rick Fox	.05	.02
❑ 13 Kevin Gamble	.05	.02
❑ 14 Reggie Lewis	.10	.05
❑ 15 Xavier McDaniel	.05	.02
❑ 16 Robert Parish	.10	.05
❑ 17 Muggsy Bogues	.10	.05
❑ 18 Dell Curry	.05	.02
❑ 19 Kenny Gattison	.05	.02
❑ 20 Kendall Gill	.10	.05
❑ 21 Larry Johnson	.25	.11
❑ 22 Alonzo Mourning	.40	.18
❑ 23 Johnny Newman	.05	.02
❑ 24 David Wingate	.05	.02
❑ 25 B.J. Armstrong	.05	.02
❑ 26 Bill Cartwright	.05	.02
❑ 27 Horace Grant	.10	.05
❑ 28 Michael Jordan	3.00	1.35
❑ 29 Stacey King	.05	.02
❑ 30 John Paxson	.05	.02
❑ 31 Will Perdue	.05	.02
❑ 32 Scottie Pippen	.75	.35
❑ 33 Scott Williams	.05	.02
❑ 34 Terrell Brandon	.10	.05
❑ 35 Brad Daugherty	.05	.02
❑ 36 Craig Ehlo	.05	.02
❑ 37 Danny Ferry	.05	.02
❑ 38 Larry Nance	.05	.02
❑ 39 Mark Price	.05	.02
❑ 40 Mike Sanders	.05	.02
❑ 41 Gerald Wilkins	.05	.02
❑ 42 John Williams	.05	.02
❑ 43 Terry Davis	.05	.02
❑ 44 Derek Harper	.10	.05
❑ 45 Mike Iuzzolino	.05	.02
❑ 46 Jim Jackson	.10	.05
❑ 47 Sean Rooks	.05	.02
❑ 48 Doug Smith	.05	.02
❑ 49 Randy White	.05	.02
❑ 50 Mahmoud Abdul-Rauf	.05	.02
❑ 51 LaPhonso Ellis	.05	.02
❑ 52 Marcus Liberty	.05	.02
❑ 53 Mark Macon	.05	.02
❑ 54 Dikembe Mutombo	.10	.05
❑ 55 Robert Pack	.05	.02
❑ 56 Bryant Stith	.05	.02

❑ 57	Reggie Williams	.05	.02
❑ 58	Mark Aguirre	.05	.02
❑ 59	Joe Dumars	.25	.11
❑ 60	Bill Laimbeer	.05	.02
❑ 61	Terry Mills	.05	.02
❑ 62	Olden Polynice	.05	.02
❑ 63	Alvin Robertson	.05	.02
❑ 64	Dennis Rodman	.50	.23
❑ 65	Isiah Thomas	.25	.11
❑ 66	Victor Alexander	.05	.02
❑ 67	Tim Hardaway	.25	.11
❑ 68	Tyrone Hill	.05	.02
❑ 69	Byron Houston	.05	.02
❑ 70	Sarunas Marciulionis	.05	.02
❑ 71	Chris Mullin	.25	.11
❑ 72	Billy Owens	.05	.02
❑ 73	Latrell Sprewell	.60	.25
❑ 74	Scott Brooks	.05	.02
❑ 75	Matt Bullard	.05	.02
❑ 76	Carl Herrera	.05	.02
❑ 77	Robert Horry	.10	.05
❑ 78	Vernon Maxwell	.05	.02
❑ 79	Hakeem Olajuwon	.40	.18
❑ 80	Kenny Smith	.05	.02
❑ 81	Otis Thorpe	.10	.05
❑ 82	Dale Davis	.05	.02
❑ 83	Vern Fleming	.05	.02
❑ 84	George McCloud	.05	.02
❑ 85	Reggie Miller	.25	.11
❑ 86	Sam Mitchell	.05	.02
❑ 87	Pooh Richardson	.05	.02
❑ 88	Detlef Schrempf	.10	.05
❑ 89	Rik Smits	.10	.05
❑ 90	Gary Grant	.05	.02
❑ 91	Ron Harper	.10	.05
❑ 92	Mark Jackson	.10	.05
❑ 93	Danny Manning	.10	.05
❑ 94	Ken Norman	.05	.02
❑ 95	Stanley Roberts	.05	.02
❑ 96	Loy Vaught	.05	.02
❑ 97	John Williams	.05	.02
❑ 98	Elden Campbell	.05	.02
❑ 99	Doug Christie	.05	.02
❑ 100	Duane Cooper	.05	.02
❑ 101	Vlade Divac	.10	.05
❑ 102	A.C. Green	.10	.05
❑ 103	Anthony Peeler	.05	.02
❑ 104	Sedale Threatt	.05	.02
❑ 105	James Worthy	.25	.11
❑ 106	Bimbo Coles	.05	.02
❑ 107	Grant Long	.05	.02
❑ 108	Harold Miner	.05	.02
❑ 109	Glen Rice	.10	.05
❑ 110	John Salley	.05	.02
❑ 111	Rony Seikaly	.05	.02
❑ 112	Brian Shaw	.05	.02
❑ 113	Steve Smith	.25	.11
❑ 114	Anthony Avent	.05	.02
❑ 115	Jon Barry	.05	.02
❑ 116	Frank Brickowski	.05	.02
❑ 117	Todd Day	.05	.02
❑ 118	Blue Edwards	.05	.02
❑ 119	Brad Lohaus	.05	.02
❑ 120	Lee Mayberry	.05	.02
❑ 121	Eric Murdock	.05	.02
❑ 122	Thurl Bailey	.05	.02
❑ 123	Christian Laettner	.10	.05
❑ 124	Luc Longley	.10	.05
❑ 125	Chuck Person	.05	.02
❑ 126	Felton Spencer	.05	.02
❑ 127	Doug West	.05	.02
❑ 128	Micheal Williams	.05	.02
❑ 129	Rafael Addison	.05	.02
❑ 130	Kenny Anderson	.10	.05
❑ 131	Sam Bowie	.05	.02
❑ 132	Chucky Brown	.05	.02
❑ 133	Derrick Coleman	.10	.05
❑ 134	Chris Dudley	.05	.02
❑ 135	Chris Morris	.05	.02
❑ 136	Rumeal Robinson	.05	.02
❑ 137	Greg Anthony	.05	.02
❑ 138	Rolando Blackman	.05	.02
❑ 139	Tony Campbell	.05	.02
❑ 140	Hubert Davis	.05	.02
❑ 141	Patrick Ewing	.25	.11
❑ 142	Anthony Mason	.10	.05
❑ 143	Charles Oakley	.10	.05
❑ 144	Doc Rivers	.10	.05
❑ 145	Charles Smith	.05	.02
❑ 146	John Starks	.10	.05
❑ 147	Nick Anderson	.10	.05
❑ 148	Anthony Bowie	.05	.02
❑ 149	Shaquille O'Neal	1.25	.55
❑ 150	Donald Royal	.05	.02
❑ 151	Dennis Scott	.05	.02
❑ 152	Scott Skiles	.05	.02
❑ 153	Tom Tolbert	.05	.02
❑ 154	Jeff Turner	.05	.02
❑ 155	Ron Anderson	.05	.02
❑ 156	Johnny Dawkins	.05	.02
❑ 157	Hersey Hawkins	.10	.05
❑ 158	Jeff Hornacek	.10	.05
❑ 159	Andrew Lang	.05	.02
❑ 160	Tim Perry	.05	.02
❑ 161	Clarence Weatherspoon	.05	.02
❑ 162	Danny Ainge	.10	.05
❑ 163	Charles Barkley	.40	.18
❑ 164	Cedric Ceballos	.10	.05
❑ 165	Tom Chambers	.05	.02
❑ 166	Richard Dumas	.05	.02
❑ 167	Kevin Johnson	.10	.05
❑ 168	Negele Knight	.05	.02
❑ 169	Dan Majerle	.10	.05
❑ 170	Oliver Miller	.05	.02
❑ 171	Mark West	.05	.02
❑ 172	Mark Bryant	.05	.02
❑ 173	Clyde Drexler	.25	.11
❑ 174	Kevin Duckworth	.05	.02
❑ 175	Mario Elie	.05	.02
❑ 176	Jerome Kersey	.05	.02
❑ 177	Terry Porter	.05	.02
❑ 178	Clifford Robinson	.10	.05
❑ 179	Rod Strickland	.10	.05
❑ 180	Buck Williams	.05	.02
❑ 181	Anthony Bonner	.05	.02
❑ 182	Duane Causwell	.05	.02
❑ 183	Mitch Richmond	.25	.11
❑ 184	Lionel Simmons	.05	.02
❑ 185	Wayman Tisdale	.05	.02
❑ 186	Spud Webb	.10	.05
❑ 187	Walt Williams	.05	.02
❑ 188	Antoine Carr	.05	.02
❑ 189	Terry Cummings	.05	.02
❑ 190	Lloyd Daniels	.05	.02
❑ 191	Vinny Del Negro	.05	.02
❑ 192	Sean Elliott	.10	.05
❑ 193	Dale Ellis	.05	.02
❑ 194	Avery Johnson	.05	.02
❑ 195	J.R. Reid	.05	.02
❑ 196	David Robinson	.40	.18
❑ 197	Michael Cage	.05	.02
❑ 198	Eddie Johnson	.05	.02
❑ 199	Shawn Kemp	.40	.18
❑ 200	Derrick McKey	.05	.02
❑ 201	Nate McMillan	.05	.02
❑ 202	Gary Payton	.40	.18
❑ 203	Sam Perkins	.10	.05
❑ 204	Ricky Pierce	.05	.02
❑ 205	David Benoit	.05	.02
❑ 206	Tyrone Corbin	.05	.02
❑ 207	Mark Eaton	.05	.02
❑ 208	Jay Humphries	.05	.02
❑ 209	Larry Krystkowiak	.05	.02
❑ 210	Jeff Malone	.05	.02
❑ 211	Karl Malone	.40	.18
❑ 212	John Stockton	.25	.11
❑ 213	Michael Adams	.05	.02
❑ 214	Rex Chapman	.05	.02
❑ 215	Pervis Ellison	.05	.02
❑ 216	Harvey Grant	.05	.02
❑ 217	Tom Gugliotta	.25	.11
❑ 218	Buck Johnson	.05	.02
❑ 219	LaBradford Smith	.05	.02
❑ 220	Larry Stewart	.05	.02
❑ 221	B.J. Armstrong LL	.05	.02
	3-Pt Field Goal Percentage Leader		
❑ 222	Cedric Ceballos LL	.05	.02
	FG Percentage Leader		
❑ 223	Larry Johnson LL	.10	.05
	Minutes Played Leader		
❑ 224	Michael Jordan LL	1.50	.70
	Scoring/Steals Leader		
❑ 225	Hakeem Olajuwon LL	.25	.11
	Shot Block Leader		
❑ 226	Mark Price LL	.05	.02
	FT Percentage Leader		
❑ 227	Dennis Rodman LL	.25	.11
	Rebounding Leader		
❑ 228	John Stockton LL	.10	.05
	Assists Leader		
❑ 229	Charles Barkley AW	.25	.11
	Most Valuable Player		
❑ 230	Hakeem Olajuwon AW	.25	.11
	Defensive POY		
❑ 231	Shaquille O'Neal AW	.50	.23
	Rookie of the Year		
❑ 232	Clifford Robinson AW	.05	.02
	Sixth Man Award		
❑ 233	Shawn Kemp PV	.25	.11
❑ 234	Alonzo Mourning PV	.25	.11
❑ 235	Hakeem Olajuwon PV	.25	.11
❑ 236	John Stockton PV	.10	.05
❑ 237	Dominique Wilkins PV	.10	.05
❑ 238	Checklist 1-85	.05	.02
❑ 239	Checklist 86-165	.05	.02
❑ 240	Checklist 166-240 UER	.05	.02
	(237 listed as Cliff Robinson; should be Dominique Wilkins)		
❑ 241	Doug Edwards RC	.05	.02
❑ 242	Craig Ehlo	.05	.02
❑ 243	Andrew Lang	.05	.02
❑ 244	Ennis Whatley	.05	.02
❑ 245	Chris Corchiani	.05	.02
❑ 246	Acie Earl RC	.05	.02
❑ 247	Jimmy Oliver	.05	.02
❑ 248	Ed Pinckney	.05	.02
❑ 249	Dino Radja RC	.05	.02
❑ 250	Matt Wenstrom RC	.05	.02
❑ 251	Tony Bennett	.05	.02
❑ 252	Scott Burrell RC	.25	.11
❑ 253	LeRon Ellis	.05	.02
❑ 254	Hersey Hawkins	.10	.05
❑ 255	Eddie Johnson	.05	.02
❑ 256	Corie Blount RC	.05	.02
❑ 257	Jo Jo English RC	.05	.02
❑ 258	Dave Johnson	.05	.02
❑ 259	Steve Kerr	.10	.05
❑ 260	Toni Kukoc RC	1.00	.45
❑ 261	Pete Myers	.05	.02
❑ 262	Bill Wennington	.05	.02
❑ 263	John Battle	.05	.02
❑ 264	Tyrone Hill	.05	.02
❑ 265	Gerald Madkins RC	.05	.02
❑ 266	Chris Mills RC	.25	.11
❑ 267	Bobby Phills	.05	.02
❑ 268	Greg Dreiling	.05	.02
❑ 269	Lucious Harris RC	.05	.02
❑ 270	Donald Hodge	.05	.02
❑ 271	Popeye Jones RC	.05	.02
❑ 272	Tim Legler RC	.05	.02
❑ 273	Fat Lever	.05	.02
❑ 274	Jamal Mashburn RC	.50	.23
❑ 275	Darren Morningstar RC	.05	.02
❑ 276	Tom Hammonds	.05	.02
❑ 277	Darnell Mee RC	.05	.02
❑ 278	Rodney Rogers RC	.25	.11
❑ 279	Brian Williams	.05	.02
❑ 280	Greg Anderson	.05	.02
❑ 281	Sean Elliott	.10	.05
❑ 282	Allan Houston RC	1.00	.45
❑ 283	Lindsey Hunter RC	.25	.11
❑ 284	Marcus Liberty	.05	.02
❑ 285	Mark Macon	.05	.02
❑ 286	David Wood	.05	.02
❑ 287	Jud Buechler	.05	.02
❑ 288	Chris Gatling	.05	.02
❑ 289	Josh Grant RC	.05	.02
❑ 290	Jeff Grayer	.05	.02
❑ 291	Avery Johnson	.05	.02
❑ 292	Chris Webber RC	2.50	1.10
❑ 293	Sam Cassell RC	.60	.25
❑ 294	Mario Elie	.05	.02
❑ 295	Richard Petruska RC	.05	.02
❑ 296	Eric Riley RC	.05	.02
❑ 297	Antonio Davis RC	.10	.05
❑ 298	Scott Haskin RC	.05	.02
❑ 299	Derrick McKey	.05	.02

Card	Player	MINT	NRMT
❑ 300	Byron Scott	.10	.05
❑ 301	Malik Sealy	.05	.02
❑ 302	LaSalle Thompson	.05	.02
❑ 303	Kenny Williams	.05	.02
❑ 304	Haywoode Workman	.05	.02
❑ 305	Mark Aguirre	.05	.02
❑ 306	Terry Dehere RC	.05	.02
❑ 307	Bob Martin RC	.05	.02
❑ 308	Elmore Spencer	.05	.02
❑ 309	Tom Tolbert	.05	.02
❑ 310	Randy Woods	.05	.02
❑ 311	Sam Bowie	.05	.02
❑ 312	James Edwards	.05	.02
❑ 313	Antonio Harvey RC	.05	.02
❑ 314	George Lynch RC	.05	.02
❑ 315	Tony Smith	.05	.02
❑ 316	Nick Van Exel RC	.60	.25
❑ 317	Manute Bol	.05	.02
❑ 318	Willie Burton	.05	.02
❑ 319	Matt Geiger	.05	.02
❑ 320	Alec Kessler	.05	.02
❑ 321	Vin Baker RC	.60	.25
❑ 322	Ken Norman	.05	.02
❑ 323	Dan Schayes	.05	.02
❑ 324	Derek Strong RC	.05	.02
❑ 325	Mike Brown	.05	.02
❑ 326	Brian Davis RC	.05	.02
❑ 327	Tellis Frank	.05	.02
❑ 328	Marlon Maxey	.05	.02
❑ 329	Isaiah Rider RC	.50	.23
❑ 330	Chris Smith	.05	.02
❑ 331	Benoit Benjamin	.05	.02
❑ 332	P.J. Brown RC	.25	.11
❑ 333	Kevin Edwards	.05	.02
❑ 334	Armon Gilliam	.05	.02
❑ 335	Rick Mahorn	.05	.02
❑ 336	Dwayne Schintzius	.05	.02
❑ 337	Rex Walters RC	.05	.02
❑ 338	David Wesley RC	.25	.11
❑ 339	Jayson Williams	.10	.05
❑ 340	Anthony Bonner	.05	.02
❑ 341	Herb Williams	.05	.02
❑ 342	Litterial Green	.05	.02
❑ 343	Anfernee Hardaway RC	2.50	1.10
❑ 344	Greg Kite	.05	.02
❑ 345	Larry Krystkowiak	.05	.02
❑ 346	Todd Lichti	.05	.02
❑ 347	Keith Tower RC	.05	.02
❑ 348	Dana Barros	.05	.02
❑ 349	Shawn Bradley RC	.25	.11
❑ 350	Michael Curry RC	.05	.02
❑ 351	Greg Graham RC	.05	.02
❑ 352	Warren Kidd RC	.05	.02
❑ 353	Moses Malone	.25	.11
❑ 354	Orlando Woolridge	.05	.02
❑ 355	Duane Cooper	.05	.02
❑ 356	Joe Courtney RC	.05	.02
❑ 357	A.C. Green	.10	.05
❑ 358	Frank Johnson	.05	.02
❑ 359	Joe Kleine	.05	.02
❑ 360	Malcolm Mackey RC	.05	.02
❑ 361	Jerrod Mustaf	.05	.02
❑ 362	Chris Dudley	.05	.02
❑ 363	Harvey Grant	.05	.02
❑ 364	Tracy Murray	.05	.02
❑ 365	James Robinson RC	.05	.02
❑ 366	Reggie Smith	.05	.02
❑ 367	Kevin Thompson RC	.05	.02
❑ 368	Randy Breuer	.05	.02
❑ 369	Randy Brown	.05	.02
❑ 370	Evers Burns RC	.05	.02
❑ 371	Pete Chilcutt	.05	.02
❑ 372	Bobby Hurley RC	.10	.05
❑ 373	Jim Les	.05	.02
❑ 374	Mike Peplowski RC	.05	.02
❑ 375	Willie Anderson	.05	.02
❑ 376	Sleepy Floyd	.05	.02
❑ 377	Negele Knight	.05	.02
❑ 378	Dennis Rodman	.50	.23
❑ 379	Chris Whitney RC	.05	.02
❑ 380	Vincent Askew	.05	.02
❑ 381	Kendall Gill	.10	.05
❑ 382	Ervin Johnson RC	.10	.05
❑ 383	Chris King RC	.05	.02
❑ 384	Rich King	.05	.02
❑ 385	Steve Scheffler	.05	.02
❑ 386	Detlef Schrempf	.10	.05
❑ 387	Tom Chambers	.05	.02
❑ 388	John Crotty	.05	.02
❑ 389	Bryon Russell RC	.25	.11
❑ 390	Felton Spencer	.05	.02
❑ 391	Luther Wright RC	.05	.02
❑ 392	Mitchell Butler RC	.05	.02
❑ 393	Calbert Cheaney RC	.10	.05
❑ 394	Kevin Duckworth	.05	.02
❑ 395	Don MacLean	.05	.02
❑ 396	Gheorghe Muresan RC	.25	.11
❑ 397	Doug Overton	.05	.02
❑ 398	Brent Price	.05	.02
❑ 399	Checklist	.05	.02
❑ 400	Checklist	.05	.02

1993-94 Fleer All-Stars

	MINT	NRMT
COMPLETE SET (24)	80.00	36.00

*SINGLES: 4X TO 10X BASE CARD HI
SER.1 STATED ODDS 1:10 HOBBY

Card	Player	MINT	NRMT
❑ 1	Brad Daugherty	.50	.23
❑ 2	Joe Dumars	2.50	1.10
❑ 3	Patrick Ewing	2.50	1.10
❑ 4	Larry Johnson	2.50	1.10
❑ 5	Michael Jordan	30.00	13.50
❑ 6	Larry Nance	.50	.23
❑ 7	Shaquille O'Neal	12.00	5.50
❑ 8	Scottie Pippen UER (Name spelled Pipen on front)	8.00	3.60
❑ 9	Mark Price	.50	.23
❑ 10	Detlef Schrempf	1.00	.45
❑ 11	Isiah Thomas	2.50	1.10
❑ 12	Dominique Wilkins	2.50	1.10
❑ 13	Charles Barkley	4.00	1.80
❑ 14	Clyde Drexler	2.50	1.10
❑ 15	Sean Elliott	1.00	.45
❑ 16	Tim Hardaway	2.50	1.10
❑ 17	Shawn Kemp	4.00	1.80
❑ 18	Dan Majerle	1.00	.45
❑ 19	Karl Malone	4.00	1.80
❑ 20	Danny Manning	1.00	.45
❑ 21	Hakeem Olajuwon	4.00	1.80
❑ 22	Terry Porter	.50	.23
❑ 23	David Robinson	4.00	1.80
❑ 24	John Stockton	2.50	1.10

1993-94 Fleer Clyde Drexler

	MINT	NRMT
COMPLETE SET (12)	5.00	2.20
COMMON DREXLER (1-12)	.50	.23
SER.1 STATED ODDS 1:6		
CERTIFIED AUTOGRAPH (AU)	100.00	45.00
DREXLER AU: SER.1 STATED ODDS 1:7,000		
COMMON SEND-OFF (13-15)	2.00	.90
THREE CARDS PER 10 SER.1 WRAPPERS		

Card	Player	MINT	NRMT
❑ 1	Clyde Drexler (Ball in right hand, pointing with left)	.50	.23
❑ 2	Clyde Drexler (Holding ball aloft with right hand)	.50	.23
❑ 3	Clyde Drexler (Wearing red shoes, left-hand dribble)	.50	.23
❑ 4	Clyde Drexler (Wearing red shoes, right-hand dribble)	.50	.23
❑ 5	Clyde Drexler (Making ready to slam dunk with both hands)	.50	.23
❑ 6	Clyde Drexler (Wearing white shoes, right-hand dribble)	.50	.23
❑ 7	Clyde Drexler (Right-hand dribble; half of ball visible)	.50	.23
❑ 8	Clyde Drexler (Right hand under ball, left hand alongside)	.50	.23
❑ 9	Clyde Drexler (Receiving or passing ball)	.50	.23
❑ 10	Clyde Drexler (Both hands above head; right hand near ball)	.50	.23
❑ 11	Clyde Drexler (Left foot off floor; right-hand dribble)	.50	.23
❑ 12	Clyde Drexler (In NBA All-Star uniform)	.50	.23
❑ 13	Clyde Drexler (Right-hand dribble, looking over defense)	2.00	.90
❑ 14	Clyde Drexler (Dribbling down court with right hand)	2.00	.90
❑ 15	Clyde Drexler (Shooting, with Pippen defending)	2.00	.90
❑ 16	Clyde Drexler (Bringing ball upcourt black uniform)	2.00	.90

1993-94 Fleer First Year Phenoms

	MINT	NRMT
COMPLETE SET (10)	8.00	3.60

*SINGLES: .5X TO 1.25X BASE CARD HI
SER.2 STATED ODDS 1:4 HOBBY, 1:3 CELLO

Card	Player	MINT	NRMT
❑ 1	Shawn Bradley	.30	.14
❑ 2	Anfernee Hardaway	3.00	1.35

		MINT	NRMT
❑ 3	Lindsey Hunter	.30	.14
❑ 4	Bobby Hurley	.15	.07
❑ 5	Toni Kukoc	1.25	.55
❑ 6	Jamal Mashburn	.60	.25
❑ 7	Dino Radja	.05	.02
❑ 8	Isaiah Rider	.60	.25
❑ 9	Nick Van Exel	.75	.35
❑ 10	Chris Webber	3.00	1.35

1993-94 Fleer Internationals

	MINT	NRMT
COMPLETE SET (12)	4.00	1.80
COMMON CARD (1-12)	.25	.11
SEMISTARS	.60	.25
UNLISTED STARS	1.25	.55

SER.1 STATED ODDS 1:10

		MINT	NRMT
❑ 1	Alaa Abdelnaby	.25	.11
❑ 2	Vlade Divac	.60	.25
❑ 3	Patrick Ewing	1.25	.55
❑ 4	Carl Herrera	.25	.11
❑ 5	Luc Longley	.60	.25
❑ 6	Sarunas Marciulionis	.25	.11
❑ 7	Dikembe Mutombo	.60	.25
❑ 8	Rumeal Robinson	.25	.11
❑ 9	Detlef Schrempf	.60	.25
❑ 10	Rony Seikaly	.25	.11
❑ 11	Rik Smits	.60	.25
❑ 12	Dominique Wilkins	1.25	.55

1993-94 Fleer Living Legends

	MINT	NRMT
COMPLETE SET (6)	25.00	11.00

*SINGLES: 2.5X TO 6X BASE CARD HI
SER.2 STATED ODDS 1:37 HOB, 1:24 JUM

		MINT	NRMT
❑ 1	Charles Barkley	2.50	1.10
❑ 2	Larry Bird	6.00	2.70
❑ 3	Patrick Ewing	1.50	.70
❑ 4	Michael Jordan	20.00	9.00
❑ 5	Hakeem Olajuwon	2.50	1.10
❑ 6	Dominique Wilkins	1.50	.70

1993-94 Fleer Lottery Exchange

	MINT	NRMT
COMPLETE SET (11)	20.00	9.00

*SINGLES: 1.25X TO 3X BASE CARD HI
ONE SET PER EXCHANGE CARD BY MAIL
EXCH.CARD: SER.1 STATED ODDS 1:180

		MINT	NRMT
❑ 1	Chris Webber	8.00	3.60
❑ 2	Shawn Bradley	.75	.35
❑ 3	Anfernee Hardaway	8.00	3.60
❑ 4	Jamal Mashburn	1.50	.70
❑ 5	Isaiah Rider	1.50	.70
❑ 6	Calbert Cheaney	.30	.14
❑ 7	Bobby Hurley	.30	.14
❑ 8	Vin Baker	2.00	.90
❑ 9	Rodney Rogers	.75	.35
❑ 10	Lindsey Hunter	.75	.35
❑ 11	Allan Houston	3.00	1.35
❑ NNO	Expired Exchange Card	.50	.23

1993-94 Fleer NBA Superstars

	MINT	NRMT
COMPLETE SET (20)	15.00	6.75

*SINGLES: 1.25X TO 3X BASE CARD HI
RANDOM INSERTS IN SER.2 HOBBY PACKS

		MINT	NRMT
❑ 1	Mahmoud Abdul-Rauf	.15	.07
❑ 2	Charles Barkley	1.25	.55
❑ 3	Derrick Coleman	.30	.14
❑ 4	Clyde Drexler	.75	.35
❑ 5	Joe Dumars	.75	.35
❑ 6	Patrick Ewing	.75	.35
❑ 7	Michael Jordan	10.00	4.50
❑ 8	Shawn Kemp	1.25	.55
❑ 9	Christian Laettner	.30	.14
❑ 10	Karl Malone	1.25	.55
❑ 11	Danny Manning	.30	.14
❑ 12	Reggie Miller	.75	.35
❑ 13	Alonzo Mourning	1.25	.55
❑ 14	Chris Mullin	.75	.35
❑ 15	Hakeem Olajuwon	1.25	.55
❑ 16	Shaquille O'Neal	4.00	1.80
❑ 17	Mark Price	.15	.07
❑ 18	Mitch Richmond	.75	.35
❑ 19	David Robinson	1.25	.55
❑ 20	Dominique Wilkins	.75	.35

1993-94 Fleer Rookie Sensations

	MINT	NRMT
COMPLETE SET (24)	50.00	22.00

*SINGLES: 6X TO 15X BASE CARD HI
SER.1 STATED ODDS 1:5 CELLO

		MINT	NRMT
❑ 1	Anthony Avent	.75	.35
❑ 2	Doug Christie	.75	.35
❑ 3	Lloyd Daniels	.75	.35
❑ 4	Hubert Davis	.75	.35
❑ 5	Todd Day	.75	.35
❑ 6	Richard Dumas	.75	.35
❑ 7	LaPhonso Ellis	.75	.35
❑ 8	Tom Gugliotta	4.00	1.80
❑ 9	Robert Horry	1.50	.70
❑ 10	Byron Houston	.75	.35
❑ 11	Jim Jackson UER (Text on back states he played in Big East; he played in Big Ten)	1.50	.70
❑ 12	Adam Keefe	.75	.35
❑ 13	Christian Laettner	1.50	.70
❑ 14	Lee Mayberry	.75	.35
❑ 15	Oliver Miller	.75	.35
❑ 16	Harold Miner	.75	.35
❑ 17	Alonzo Mourning	6.00	2.70
❑ 18	Shaquille O'Neal	20.00	9.00
❑ 19	Anthony Peeler	.75	.35
❑ 20	Sean Rooks	.75	.35
❑ 21	Latrell Sprewell	10.00	4.50
❑ 22	Bryant Stith	.75	.35
❑ 23	Clarence Weatherspoon	.75	.35
❑ 24	Walt Williams	.75	.35

1993-94 Fleer Sharpshooters

	MINT	NRMT
COMPLETE SET (10)	30.00	13.50

*SINGLES: 3X TO 8X BASE CARD HI
RANDOM INSERTS IN SER.2 HOBBY PACKS

		MINT	NRMT
❑ 1	Tom Gugliotta	2.00	.90
❑ 2	Jim Jackson	.75	.35
❑ 3	Michael Jordan	25.00	11.00
❑ 4	Dan Majerle	.75	.35
❑ 5	Mark Price	.40	.18
❑ 6	Glen Rice	.75	.35
❑ 7	Mitch Richmond	2.00	.90

❑ 8 Latrell Sprewell	5.00	2.20
❑ 9 John Starks	.75	.35
❑ 10 Dominique Wilkins	2.00	.90

1993-94 Fleer Towers of Power

	MINT	NRMT
COMPLETE SET (30)	60.00	27.00
*STARS: 4X TO 10X BASE CARD HI		
*RCs: 2.5X TO 6X BASE HI		
SER.2 STATED ODDS 2:3 CELLO		
❑ 1 Charles Barkley	4.00	1.80
❑ 2 Shawn Bradley	1.50	.70
❑ 3 Derrick Coleman	1.00	.45
❑ 4 Brad Daugherty	.50	.23
❑ 5 Dale Davis	.50	.23
❑ 6 Vlade Divac	1.00	.45
❑ 7 Patrick Ewing	2.50	1.10
❑ 8 Horace Grant	1.00	.45
❑ 9 Tom Gugliotta	2.50	1.10
❑ 10 Larry Johnson	2.50	1.10
❑ 11 Shawn Kemp	4.00	1.80
❑ 12 Christian Laettner	1.00	.45
❑ 13 Karl Malone	4.00	1.80
❑ 14 Danny Manning	1.00	.45
❑ 15 Jamal Mashburn	3.00	1.35
❑ 16 Oliver Miller	.50	.23
❑ 17 Alonzo Mourning	4.00	1.80
❑ 18 Dikembe Mutombo	1.00	.45
❑ 19 Ken Norman	.50	.23
❑ 20 Hakeem Olajuwon	4.00	1.80
❑ 21 Shaquille O'Neal	12.00	5.50
❑ 22 Robert Parish	1.00	.45
❑ 23 Olden Polynice	.50	.23
❑ 24 Clifford Robinson	1.00	.45
❑ 25 David Robinson	4.00	1.80
❑ 26 Dennis Rodman	5.00	2.20
❑ 27 Rony Seikaly	.50	.23
❑ 28 Wayman Tisdale	.50	.23
❑ 29 Chris Webber	15.00	6.75
❑ 30 Dominique Wilkins	2.50	1.10

1994-95 Fleer

	MINT	NRMT
COMPLETE SET (390)	24.00	11.00
COMPLETE SERIES 1 (240)	12.00	5.50
COMPLETE SERIES 2 (150)	12.00	5.50
COMMON CARD (1-390)	.05	.02
SEMISTARS	.10	.05
UNLISTED STARS	.25	.11
❑ 1 Stacey Augmon	.05	.02
❑ 2 Mookie Blaylock	.05	.02
❑ 3 Craig Ehlo	.05	.02
❑ 4 Duane Ferrell	.05	.02
❑ 5 Adam Keefe	.05	.02
❑ 6 Jon Koncak	.05	.02
❑ 7 Andrew Lang	.05	.02
❑ 8 Danny Manning	.10	.05
❑ 9 Kevin Willis	.05	.02
❑ 10 Dee Brown	.05	.02
❑ 11 Sherman Douglas	.05	.02
❑ 12 Acie Earl	.05	.02
❑ 13 Rick Fox	.05	.02
❑ 14 Kevin Gamble	.05	.02
❑ 15 Xavier McDaniel	.05	.02
❑ 16 Robert Parish	.10	.05
❑ 17 Ed Pinckney	.05	.02
❑ 18 Dino Radja	.05	.02
❑ 19 Muggsy Bogues	.10	.05
❑ 20 Frank Brickowski	.05	.02
❑ 21 Scott Burrell	.05	.02
❑ 22 Dell Curry	.05	.02
❑ 23 Kenny Gattison	.05	.02
❑ 24 Hersey Hawkins	.10	.05
❑ 25 Eddie Johnson	.05	.02
❑ 26 Larry Johnson	.10	.05
❑ 27 Alonzo Mourning	.30	.14
❑ 28 David Wingate	.05	.02
❑ 29 B.J. Armstrong	.05	.02
❑ 30 Horace Grant	.10	.05
❑ 31 Steve Kerr	.05	.02
❑ 32 Toni Kukoc	.40	.18
❑ 33 Luc Longley	.05	.02
❑ 34 Pete Myers	.05	.02
❑ 35 Scottie Pippen	.75	.35
❑ 36 Bill Wennington	.05	.02
❑ 37 Scott Williams	.05	.02
❑ 38 Terrell Brandon	.10	.05
❑ 39 Brad Daugherty	.05	.02
❑ 40 Tyrone Hill	.05	.02
❑ 41 Chris Mills	.10	.05
❑ 42 Larry Nance	.05	.02
❑ 43 Bobby Phills	.05	.02
❑ 44 Mark Price	.05	.02
❑ 45 Gerald Wilkins	.05	.02
❑ 46 John Williams	.05	.02
❑ 47 Lucious Harris	.05	.02
❑ 48 Donald Hodge	.05	.02
❑ 49 Jim Jackson	.10	.05
❑ 50 Popeye Jones	.05	.02
❑ 51 Tim Legler	.05	.02
❑ 52 Fat Lever	.05	.02
❑ 53 Jamal Mashburn	.25	.11
❑ 54 Sean Rooks	.05	.02
❑ 55 Doug Smith	.05	.02
❑ 56 Mahmoud Abdul-Rauf	.05	.02
❑ 57 LaPhonso Ellis	.05	.02
❑ 58 Dikembe Mutombo	.10	.05
❑ 59 Robert Pack	.05	.02
❑ 60 Rodney Rogers	.05	.02
❑ 61 Bryant Stith	.05	.02
❑ 62 Brian Williams	.05	.02
❑ 63 Reggie Williams	.05	.02
❑ 64 Greg Anderson	.05	.02
❑ 65 Joe Dumars	.25	.11
❑ 66 Sean Elliott	.10	.05
❑ 67 Allan Houston	.40	.18
❑ 68 Lindsey Hunter	.10	.05
❑ 69 Terry Mills	.05	.02
❑ 70 Victor Alexander	.05	.02
❑ 71 Chris Gatling	.05	.02
❑ 72 Tim Hardaway	.25	.11
❑ 73 Keith Jennings	.05	.02
❑ 74 Avery Johnson	.05	.02
❑ 75 Chris Mullin	.25	.11
❑ 76 Billy Owens	.05	.02
❑ 77 Latrell Sprewell	.50	.23
❑ 78 Chris Webber	.75	.35
❑ 79 Scott Brooks	.05	.02
❑ 80 Sam Cassell	.25	.11
❑ 81 Mario Elie	.05	.02
❑ 82 Carl Herrera	.05	.02
❑ 83 Robert Horry	.05	.02
❑ 84 Vernon Maxwell	.05	.02
❑ 85 Hakeem Olajuwon	.40	.18
❑ 86 Kenny Smith	.05	.02
❑ 87 Otis Thorpe	.05	.02
❑ 88 Antonio Davis	.05	.02
❑ 89 Dale Davis	.05	.02
❑ 90 Vern Fleming	.05	.02
❑ 91 Derrick McKey	.05	.02
❑ 92 Reggie Miller	.25	.11
❑ 93 Pooh Richardson	.05	.02
❑ 94 Byron Scott	.10	.05
❑ 95 Rik Smits	.05	.02
❑ 96 Haywoode Workman	.05	.02
❑ 97 Terry Dehere	.05	.02
❑ 98 Harold Ellis	.05	.02
❑ 99 Gary Grant	.05	.02
❑ 100 Ron Harper	.10	.05
❑ 101 Mark Jackson	.05	.02
❑ 102 Stanley Roberts	.05	.02
❑ 103 Elmore Spencer	.05	.02
❑ 104 Loy Vaught	.05	.02
❑ 105 Dominique Wilkins	.25	.11
❑ 106 Elden Campbell	.05	.02
❑ 107 Doug Christie	.05	.02
❑ 108 Vlade Divac	.05	.02
❑ 109 George Lynch	.05	.02
❑ 110 Anthony Peeler	.05	.02
❑ 111 Tony Smith	.05	.02
❑ 112 Sedale Threatt	.05	.02
❑ 113 Nick Van Exel	.25	.11
❑ 114 James Worthy	.25	.11
❑ 115 Bimbo Coles	.05	.02
❑ 116 Grant Long	.05	.02
❑ 117 Harold Miner	.05	.02
❑ 118 Glen Rice	.10	.05
❑ 119 John Salley	.05	.02
❑ 120 Rony Seikaly	.05	.02
❑ 121 Brian Shaw	.05	.02
❑ 122 Steve Smith	.10	.05
❑ 123 Vin Baker	.25	.11
❑ 124 Jon Barry	.05	.02
❑ 125 Todd Day	.05	.02
❑ 126 Blue Edwards	.05	.02
❑ 127 Lee Mayberry	.05	.02
❑ 128 Eric Murdock	.05	.02
❑ 129 Ken Norman	.05	.02
❑ 130 Derek Strong	.05	.02
❑ 131 Thurl Bailey	.05	.02
❑ 132 Stacey King	.05	.02
❑ 133 Christian Laettner	.10	.05
❑ 134 Chuck Person	.05	.02
❑ 135 Isaiah Rider	.10	.05
❑ 136 Chris Smith	.05	.02
❑ 137 Doug West	.05	.02
❑ 138 Micheal Williams	.05	.02
❑ 139 Kenny Anderson	.10	.05
❑ 140 Benoit Benjamin	.05	.02
❑ 141 P.J. Brown	.05	.02
❑ 142 Derrick Coleman	.10	.05
❑ 143 Kevin Edwards	.05	.02
❑ 144 Armon Gilliam	.05	.02
❑ 145 Chris Morris	.05	.02
❑ 146 Johnny Newman	.05	.02
❑ 147 Greg Anthony	.05	.02
❑ 148 Anthony Bonner	.05	.02
❑ 149 Hubert Davis	.05	.02
❑ 150 Patrick Ewing	.25	.11
❑ 151 Derek Harper	.05	.02
❑ 152 Anthony Mason	.10	.05
❑ 153 Charles Oakley	.05	.02
❑ 154 Doc Rivers	.10	.05
❑ 155 Charles Smith	.05	.02
❑ 156 John Starks	.05	.02
❑ 157 Nick Anderson	.05	.02
❑ 158 Anthony Avent	.05	.02
❑ 159 Anfernee Hardaway	.75	.35
❑ 160 Shaquille O'Neal	1.25	.55
❑ 161 Donald Royal	.05	.02
❑ 162 Dennis Scott	.05	.02
❑ 163 Scott Skiles	.05	.02
❑ 164 Jeff Turner	.05	.02
❑ 165 Dana Barros	.05	.02
❑ 166 Shawn Bradley	.05	.02
❑ 167 Greg Graham	.05	.02
❑ 168 Eric Leckner	.05	.02

❑ 169 Jeff Malone .05 .02
❑ 170 Moses Malone .25 .11
❑ 171 Tim Perry .05 .02
❑ 172 Clarence Weatherspoon .05 .02
❑ 173 Orlando Woolridge .05 .02
❑ 174 Danny Ainge .05 .02
❑ 175 Charles Barkley .40 .18
❑ 176 Cedric Ceballos .05 .02
❑ 177 A.C. Green .10 .05
❑ 178 Kevin Johnson .10 .05
❑ 179 Joe Kleine .05 .02
❑ 180 Dan Majerle .10 .05
❑ 181 Oliver Miller .05 .02
❑ 182 Mark West .05 .02
❑ 183 Clyde Drexler .25 .11
❑ 184 Harvey Grant .05 .02
❑ 185 Jerome Kersey .05 .02
❑ 186 Tracy Murray .05 .02
❑ 187 Terry Porter .05 .02
❑ 188 Clifford Robinson .10 .05
❑ 189 James Robinson .05 .02
❑ 190 Rod Strickland .10 .05
❑ 191 Buck Williams .05 .02
❑ 192 Duane Causwell .05 .02
❑ 193 Bobby Hurley .05 .02
❑ 194 Olden Polynice .05 .02
❑ 195 Mitch Richmond .25 .11
❑ 196 Lionel Simmons .05 .02
❑ 197 Wayman Tisdale .05 .02
❑ 198 Spud Webb .05 .02
❑ 199 Walt Williams .05 .02
❑ 200 Trevor Wilson .05 .02
❑ 201 Willie Anderson .05 .02
❑ 202 Antoine Carr .05 .02
❑ 203 Terry Cummings .05 .02
❑ 204 Vinny Del Negro .05 .02
❑ 205 Dale Ellis .05 .02
❑ 206 Negele Knight .05 .02
❑ 207 J.R. Reid .05 .02
❑ 208 David Robinson .40 .18
❑ 209 Dennis Rodman .50 .23
❑ 210 Vincent Askew .05 .02
❑ 211 Michael Cage .05 .02
❑ 212 Kendall Gill .10 .05
❑ 213 Shawn Kemp .40 .18
❑ 214 Nate McMillan .05 .02
❑ 215 Gary Payton .40 .18
❑ 216 Sam Perkins .10 .05
❑ 217 Ricky Pierce .05 .02
❑ 218 Detlef Schrempf .10 .05
❑ 219 David Benoit .05 .02
❑ 220 Tom Chambers .05 .02
❑ 221 Tyrone Corbin .05 .02
❑ 222 Jeff Hornacek .10 .05
❑ 223 Jay Humphries .05 .02
❑ 224 Karl Malone .40 .18
❑ 225 Bryon Russell .05 .02
❑ 226 Felton Spencer .05 .02
❑ 227 John Stockton .25 .11
❑ 228 Michael Adams .05 .02
❑ 229 Rex Chapman .05 .02
❑ 230 Calbert Cheaney .05 .02
❑ 231 Kevin Duckworth .05 .02
❑ 232 Pervis Ellison .05 .02
❑ 233 Tom Gugliotta .10 .05
❑ 234 Don MacLean .05 .02
❑ 235 Gheorghe Muresan .05 .02
❑ 236 Brent Price .05 .02
❑ 237 Toronto Raptors Logo Card .05 .02
❑ 238 Checklist .05 .02
❑ 239 Checklist .05 .02
❑ 240 Checklist .05 .02
❑ 241 Sergei Bazarevich .05 .02
❑ 242 Tyrone Corbin .05 .02
❑ 243 Grant Long .05 .02
❑ 244 Ken Norman .05 .02
❑ 245 Steve Smith .10 .05
❑ 246 Fred Vinson .05 .02
❑ 247 Blue Edwards .05 .02
❑ 248 Greg Minor RC .05 .02
❑ 249 Eric Montross RC .05 .02
❑ 250 Derek Strong .05 .02
❑ 251 David Wesley .05 .02
❑ 252 Dominique Wilkins .25 .11
❑ 253 Michael Adams .05 .02
❑ 254 Tony Bennett .05 .02
❑ 255 Darrin Hancock RC .05 .02
❑ 256 Robert Parish .10 .05
❑ 257 Corie Blount .05 .02
❑ 258 Jud Buechler .05 .02
❑ 259 Greg Foster .05 .02
❑ 260 Ron Harper .10 .05
❑ 261 Larry Krystkowiak .05 .02
❑ 262 Will Perdue .05 .02
❑ 263 Dickey Simpkins RC .05 .02
❑ 264 Michael Cage .05 .02
❑ 265 Tony Campbell .05 .02
❑ 266 Terry Davis .05 .02
❑ 267 Tony Dumas RC .05 .02
❑ 268 Jason Kidd RC 2.00 .90
❑ 269 Roy Tarpley .05 .02
❑ 270 Morlon Wiley .05 .02
❑ 271 Lorenzo Williams .05 .02
❑ 272 Dale Ellis .05 .02
❑ 273 Tom Hammonds .05 .02
❑ 274 Cliff Levingston .05 .02
❑ 275 Darnell Mee .05 .02
❑ 276 Jalen Rose RC 1.00 .45
❑ 277 Reggie Slater .05 .02
❑ 278 Bill Curley RC .05 .02
❑ 279 Johnny Dawkins .05 .02
❑ 280 Grant Hill RC 2.50 1.10
❑ 281 Eric Leckner .05 .02
❑ 282 Mark Macon .05 .02
❑ 283 Oliver Miller .05 .02
❑ 284 Mark West .05 .02
❑ 285 Manute Bol .05 .02
❑ 286 Tom Gugliotta .10 .05
❑ 287 Ricky Pierce .05 .02
❑ 288 Carlos Rogers RC .05 .02
❑ 289 Clifford Rozier RC .05 .02
❑ 290 Rony Seikaly .05 .02
❑ 291 Tim Breaux .05 .02
❑ 292 Chris Jent .05 .02
❑ 293 Eric Riley .05 .02
❑ 294 Zan Tabak .05 .02
❑ 295 Duane Ferrell .05 .02
❑ 296 Mark Jackson .05 .02
❑ 297 John Williams .05 .02
❑ 298 Matt Fish .05 .02
❑ 299 Tony Massenburg .05 .02
❑ 300 Lamond Murray RC .10 .05
❑ 301 Charles Outlaw RC .05 .02
❑ 302 Eric Piatkowski RC .05 .02
❑ 303 Pooh Richardson .05 .02
❑ 304 Randy Woods .05 .02
❑ 305 Sam Bowie .05 .02
❑ 306 Cedric Ceballos .05 .02
❑ 307 Antonio Harvey .05 .02
❑ 308 Eddie Jones RC 1.50 .70
❑ 309 Anthony Miller RC .05 .02
❑ 310 Ledell Eackles .05 .02
❑ 311 Kevin Gamble .05 .02
❑ 312 Brad Lohaus .05 .02
❑ 313 Billy Owens .05 .02
❑ 314 Khalid Reeves RC .05 .02
❑ 315 Kevin Willis .05 .02
❑ 316 Marty Conlon .05 .02
❑ 317 Eric Mobley RC .05 .02
❑ 318 Johnny Newman .05 .02
❑ 319 Ed Pinckney .05 .02
❑ 320 Glenn Robinson RC .75 .35
❑ 321 Mike Brown .05 .02
❑ 322 Pat Durham .05 .02
❑ 323 Howard Eisley RC .05 .02
❑ 324 Andres Guibert .05 .02
❑ 325 Donyell Marshall RC .25 .11
❑ 326 Sean Rooks .05 .02
❑ 327 Yinka Dare RC .05 .02
❑ 328 Sleepy Floyd .05 .02
❑ 329 Sean Higgins .05 .02
❑ 330 Rick Mahorn .05 .02
❑ 331 Rex Walters .05 .02
❑ 332 Jayson Williams .10 .05
❑ 333 Charlie Ward RC .25 .11
❑ 334 Herb Williams .05 .02
❑ 335 Monty Williams RC .05 .02
❑ 336 Anthony Bowie .05 .02
❑ 337 Horace Grant .10 .05
❑ 338 Geert Hammink .05 .02
❑ 339 Tree Rollins .05 .02
❑ 340 Brian Shaw .05 .02
❑ 341 Brooks Thompson RC .05 .02
❑ 342 Derrick Alston RC .05 .02
❑ 343 Willie Burton .05 .02
❑ 344 Jaren Jackson .05 .02
❑ 345 B.J. Tyler RC .05 .02
❑ 346 Scott Williams .05 .02
❑ 347 Sharone Wright RC .05 .02
❑ 348 Antonio Lang RC .05 .02
❑ 349 Danny Manning .10 .05
❑ 350 Elliot Perry .05 .02
❑ 351 Wesley Person RC .25 .11
❑ 352 Trevor Ruffin .05 .02
❑ 353 Dan Schayes .05 .02
❑ 354 Aaron Swinson RC .05 .02
❑ 355 Wayman Tisdale .05 .02
❑ 356 Mark Bryant .05 .02
❑ 357 Chris Dudley .05 .02
❑ 358 James Edwards .05 .02
❑ 359 Aaron McKie RC .05 .02
❑ 360 Alaa Abdelnaby .05 .02
❑ 361 Frank Brickowski .05 .02
❑ 362 Randy Brown .05 .02
❑ 363 Brian Grant RC .60 .25
❑ 364 Michael Smith RC .05 .02
❑ 365 Henry Turner .05 .02
❑ 366 Sean Elliott .10 .05
❑ 367 Avery Johnson .05 .02
❑ 368 Moses Malone .25 .11
❑ 369 Julius Nwosu .05 .02
❑ 370 Chuck Person .05 .02
❑ 371 Chris Whitney .05 .02
❑ 372 Bill Cartwright .05 .02
❑ 373 Byron Houston .05 .02
❑ 374 Ervin Johnson .05 .02
❑ 375 Sarunas Marciulionis .05 .02
❑ 376 Antoine Carr .05 .02
❑ 377 John Crotty .05 .02
❑ 378 Adam Keefe .05 .02
❑ 379 Jamie Watson RC .05 .02
❑ 380 Mitchell Butler .05 .02
❑ 381 Juwan Howard RC .60 .25
❑ 382 Jim McIlvaine RC .05 .02
❑ 383 Doug Overton .05 .02
❑ 384 Scott Skiles .05 .02
❑ 385 Larry Stewart .05 .02
❑ 386 Kenny Walker .05 .02
❑ 387 Chris Webber .75 .35
❑ 388 Vancouver Grizzlies Logo Card .05 .02
❑ 389 Checklist .05 .02
❑ 390 Checklist .05 .02

1994-95 Fleer All-Defensive

	MINT	NRMT
COMPLETE SET (10)	6.00	2.70

*SINGLES: 1.25X TO 3X BASE CARD HI
SER.1 STATED ODDS 1:9 HOBBY/RETAIL

❑ 1 Mookie Blaylock .15 .07
❑ 2 Charles Oakley .15 .07
❑ 3 Hakeem Olajuwon 1.25 .55
❑ 4 Gary Payton 1.25 .55
❑ 5 Scottie Pippen 2.50 1.10
❑ 6 Horace Grant .30 .14
❑ 7 Nate McMillan .15 .07

		MINT	NRMT
❑ 8	David Robinson	1.25	.55
❑ 9	Dennis Rodman	1.50	.70
❑ 10	Latrell Sprewell	1.50	.70

1994-95 Fleer All-Stars

	MINT	NRMT
COMPLETE SET (26)	25.00	11.00

*SINGLES: 2.5X TO 6X BASE CARD HI
SER.1 STATED ODDS 1:2 HOBBY

		MINT	NRMT
❑ 1	Kenny Anderson	.60	.25
❑ 2	B.J. Armstrong	.30	.14
❑ 3	Mookie Blaylock	.30	.14
❑ 4	Derrick Coleman	.60	.25
❑ 5	Patrick Ewing	1.50	.70
❑ 6	Horace Grant	.60	.25
❑ 7	Alonzo Mourning	2.00	.90
❑ 8	Charles Oakley	.30	.14
❑ 9	Shaquille O'Neal	8.00	3.60
❑ 10	Scottie Pippen	5.00	2.20
❑ 11	Mark Price	.30	.14
❑ 12	John Starks	.30	.14
❑ 13	Dominique Wilkins	1.50	.70
❑ 14	Charles Barkley	2.50	1.10
❑ 15	Clyde Drexler	1.50	.70
❑ 16	Kevin Johnson	.60	.25
❑ 17	Shawn Kemp	2.50	1.10
❑ 18	Karl Malone	2.50	1.10
❑ 19	Danny Manning	.60	.25
❑ 20	Hakeem Olajuwon	2.50	1.10
❑ 21	Gary Payton	2.50	1.10
❑ 22	Mitch Richmond	1.50	.70
❑ 23	Clifford Robinson	.60	.25
❑ 24	David Robinson	2.50	1.10
❑ 25	Latrell Sprewell	3.00	1.35
❑ 26	John Stockton	1.50	.70

1994-95 Fleer Award Winners

	MINT	NRMT
COMPLETE SET (4)	3.00	1.35

*SINGLES: 1.5X TO 4X BASE CARD HI
SER.1 STATED ODDS 1:22 HOBBY/RETAIL

		MINT	NRMT
❑ 1	Dell Curry	.20	.09
❑ 2	Don MacLean	.20	.09
❑ 3	Hakeem Olajuwon	1.50	.70
❑ 4	Chris Webber	3.00	1.35

1994-95 Fleer Career Achievement

	MINT	NRMT
COMPLETE SET (6)	15.00	6.75

*SINGLES: 5X TO 12X BASE CARD HI
SER.1 STATED ODDS 1:37 HOBBY/RETAIL

		MINT	NRMT
❑ 1	Patrick Ewing	3.00	1.35
❑ 2	Karl Malone	5.00	2.20
❑ 3	Hakeem Olajuwon	5.00	2.20
❑ 4	Robert Parish	1.25	.55
❑ 5	Scottie Pippen	10.00	4.50
❑ 6	Dominique Wilkins	3.00	1.35

1994-95 Fleer First Year Phenoms

	MINT	NRMT
COMPLETE SET (10)	15.00	6.75

*SINGLES: 1X TO 2.5X BASE CARD HI
SER.2 STATED ODDS 1:5 HOBBY/RETAIL

		MINT	NRMT
❑ 1	Grant Hill	6.00	2.70
❑ 2	Jason Kidd	5.00	2.20
❑ 3	Donyell Marshall	.60	.25
❑ 4	Eric Montross	.15	.07
❑ 5	Lamond Murray	.25	.11
❑ 6	Wesley Person	.60	.25
❑ 7	Khalid Reeves	.15	.07
❑ 8	Glenn Robinson	2.00	.90
❑ 9	Jalen Rose	2.50	1.10
❑ 10	Sharone Wright	.15	.07

1994-95 Fleer League Leaders

	MINT	NRMT
COMPLETE SET (8)	5.00	2.20

*SINGLES: 1.25X TO 3X BASE CARD HI
SER.1 STATED ODDS 1:11 HOBBY/RETAIL

		MINT	NRMT
❑ 1	Mahmoud Abdul-Rauf	.15	.07
❑ 2	Nate McMillan	.15	.07
❑ 3	Tracy Murray	.15	.07
❑ 4	Dikembe Mutombo	.30	.14
❑ 5	Shaquille O'Neal	4.00	1.80
❑ 6	David Robinson	1.25	.55
❑ 7	Dennis Rodman	1.50	.70
❑ 8	John Stockton	.75	.35

1994-95 Fleer Lottery Exchange

	MINT	NRMT
COMPLETE SET (11)	20.00	9.00

*SINGLES: 1.25X TO 3X BASE CARD HI
ONE SET PER EXCHANGE CARD BY MAIL
EXCH.CARD: SER.1 STATED ODDS 1:175

		MINT	NRMT
❑ 1	Glenn Robinson	2.50	1.10
❑ 2	Jason Kidd	6.00	2.70
❑ 3	Grant Hill	8.00	3.60
❑ 4	Donyell Marshall	.75	.35
❑ 5	Juwan Howard	2.00	.90
❑ 6	Sharone Wright	.15	.07
❑ 7	Lamond Murray	.30	.14
❑ 8	Brian Grant	2.00	.90
❑ 9	Eric Montross	.15	.07
❑ 10	Eddie Jones	5.00	2.20
❑ 11	Carlos Rogers	.15	.07
❑ NNO	Lottery Exchange Card	1.00	.45

1994-95 Fleer Pro-Visions

	MINT	NRMT
COMPLETE SET (9)	3.00	1.35

*SINGLES: .6X TO 1.5X BASE CARD HI
SER.1 STATED ODDS 1:5 HOBBY/RETAIL

		MINT	NRMT
❑ 1	Jamal Mashburn	.40	.18
❑ 2	John Starks	.10	.05

	MINT	NRMT
❑ 3 Toni Kukoc	.60	.25
❑ 4 Derrick Coleman	.15	.07
❑ 5 Chris Webber	1.25	.55
❑ 6 Dennis Rodman	.75	.35
❑ 7 Gary Payton	.60	.25
❑ 8 Anfernee Hardaway	1.25	.55
❑ 9 Dan Majerle	.15	.07

1994-95 Fleer Rookie Sensations

	MINT	NRMT
COMPLETE SET (25)	25.00	11.00

*SINGLES: 3X TO 8X BASE CARD HI
SER.1 STATED ODDS 1:3 CELLO

	MINT	NRMT
❑ 1 Vin Baker	2.00	.90
❑ 2 Shawn Bradley	.40	.18
❑ 3 P.J. Brown	.40	.18
❑ 4 Sam Cassell	2.00	.90
❑ 5 Calbert Cheaney	.40	.18
❑ 6 Antonio Davis	.40	.18
❑ 7 Acie Earl	.40	.18
❑ 8 Harold Ellis	.40	.18
❑ 9 Anfernee Hardaway	6.00	2.70
❑ 10 Allan Houston	3.00	1.35
❑ 11 Lindsey Hunter	.75	.35
❑ 12 Bobby Hurley	.40	.18
❑ 13 Popeye Jones	.40	.18
❑ 14 Toni Kukoc	3.00	1.35
❑ 15 George Lynch	.40	.18
❑ 16 Jamal Mashburn	2.00	.90
❑ 17 Chris Mills	.75	.35
❑ 18 Gheorghe Muresan	.40	.18
❑ 19 Dino Radja	.40	.18
❑ 20 Isaiah Rider	.75	.35
❑ 21 James Robinson	.40	.18
❑ 22 Rodney Rogers	.40	.18
❑ 23 Bryon Russell	.40	.18
❑ 24 Nick Van Exel	2.00	.90
❑ 25 Chris Webber	6.00	2.70

1994-95 Fleer Sharpshooters

	MINT	NRMT
COMPLETE SET (10)	15.00	6.75

*SINGLES: 6X TO 15X BASE CARD HI
SER.2 STATED ODDS 1:7 RETAIL

	MINT	NRMT
❑ 1 Dell Curry	.75	.35
❑ 2 Joe Dumars	4.00	1.80
❑ 3 Dale Ellis	.75	.35
❑ 4 Dan Majerle	1.50	.70
❑ 5 Reggie Miller	4.00	1.80
❑ 6 Mark Price	.75	.35
❑ 7 Glen Rice	1.50	.70
❑ 8 Mitch Richmond	4.00	1.80
❑ 9 Dennis Scott	.75	.35
❑ 10 Latrell Sprewell	8.00	3.60

1994-95 Fleer Superstars

	MINT	NRMT
COMPLETE SET (6)	15.00	6.75

*SINGLES: 5X TO 12X BASE CARD HI
SER.2 STATED ODDS 1:37 HOBBY/RETAIL

	MINT	NRMT
❑ 1 Charles Barkley	5.00	2.20
❑ 2 Patrick Ewing	3.00	1.35
❑ 3 Hakeem Olajuwon	5.00	2.20
❑ 4 Robert Parish	1.25	.55
❑ 5 Scottie Pippen	10.00	4.50
❑ 6 Dominique Wilkins	3.00	1.35

1994-95 Fleer Team Leaders

	MINT	NRMT
COMPLETE SET (9)	3.00	1.35
COMMON CARD (1-9)	.25	.11
SEMISTARS	.50	.23

SER.2 STATED ODDS 1:3 HOBBY/RETAIL

	MINT	NRMT
❑ 1 Mookie Blaylock Dominique Wilkins Alonzo Mourning	.50	.23
❑ 2 Scottie Pippen Mark Price Jamal Mashburn	1.00	.45
❑ 3 Dikembe Mutombo ERR Joe Dumars Detroit Pistons Latrell Sprewell Card has Dumars with Rockets	.50	.23
❑ 3A Dikembe Mutombo COR Joe Dumars Latrell Sprewell	.50	.23
❑ 4 Hakeem Olajuwon Reggie Miller Loy Vaught	.75	.35
❑ 5 Vlade Divac Glen Rice Vin Baker	.50	.23
❑ 6 Isaiah Rider Kenny Anderson Patrick Ewing	.25	.11
❑ 7 Shaquille O'Neal Clarence Weatherspoon Charles Barkley	2.00	.90
❑ 8 Rod Strickland Mitch Richmond David Robinson	.75	.35
❑ 9 Shawn Kemp John Stockton Rex Chapman	.75	.35

1994-95 Fleer Total D

	MINT	NRMT
COMPLETE SET (10)	8.00	3.60

*SINGLES: 2X TO 5X BASE CARD HI
SER.2 STATED ODDS 1:7 HOBBY

	MINT	NRMT
❑ 1 Mookie Blaylock	.25	.11
❑ 2 Nate McMillan	.25	.11
❑ 3 Dikembe Mutombo	.50	.23
❑ 4 Charles Oakley	.25	.11
❑ 5 Hakeem Olajuwon	2.00	.90
❑ 6 Gary Payton	2.00	.90
❑ 7 Scottie Pippen	4.00	1.80
❑ 8 David Robinson	2.00	.90
❑ 9 Latrell Sprewell	2.50	1.10
❑ 10 John Stockton	1.25	.55

1994-95 Fleer Towers of Power

	MINT	NRMT
COMPLETE SET (10)	20.00	9.00

*SINGLES: 3X TO 8X BASE CARD HI
SER.2 STATED ODDS 1:5 CELLO

	MINT	NRMT
❑ 1 Charles Barkley	3.00	1.35
❑ 2 Patrick Ewing	2.00	.90
❑ 3 Shawn Kemp	3.00	1.35
❑ 4 Karl Malone	3.00	1.35
❑ 5 Alonzo Mourning	2.50	1.10

	MINT	NRMT
❑ 6 Dikembe Mutombo	.75	.35
❑ 7 Hakeem Olajuwon	3.00	1.35
❑ 8 Shaquille O'Neal	10.00	4.50
❑ 9 David Robinson	3.00	1.35
❑ 10 Chris Webber	6.00	2.70

1994-95 Fleer Triple Threats

	MINT	NRMT
COMPLETE SET (10)	5.00	2.20

*SINGLES: .75X TO 2X BASE CARD HI
SER.1 STATED ODDS 1:9 HOBBY/RETAIL

	MINT	NRMT
❑ 1 Mookie Blaylock	.10	.05
❑ 2 Patrick Ewing	.50	.23
❑ 3 Shawn Kemp	.75	.35
❑ 4 Karl Malone	.75	.35
❑ 5 Reggie Miller	.50	.23
❑ 6 Hakeem Olajuwon	.75	.35
❑ 7 Shaquille O'Neal	2.50	1.10
❑ 8 Scottie Pippen	1.50	.70
❑ 9 David Robinson	.75	.35
❑ 10 Latrell Sprewell	1.00	.45

1994-95 Fleer Young Lions

	MINT	NRMT
COMPLETE SET (6)	6.00	2.70

*SINGLES: 1.25X TO 3X BASE CARD HI
SER.2 STATED ODDS 1:5 HOBBY/RETAIL

	MINT	NRMT
❑ 1 Vin Baker	.75	.35
❑ 2 Anfernee Hardaway	2.50	1.10
❑ 3 Larry Johnson	.30	.14
❑ 4 Alonzo Mourning	1.00	.45
❑ 5 Shaquille O'Neal	4.00	1.80
❑ 6 Chris Webber	2.50	1.10

1995-96 Fleer

	MINT	NRMT
COMPLETE SET (350)	40.00	18.00
COMPLETE SERIES 1 (200)	20.00	9.00
COMPLETE SERIES 2 (150)	20.00	9.00
COMMON CARD (1-350)	.10	.05
SEMISTARS	.15	.07
UNLISTED STARS	.25	.11

SUBSET CARDS HALF VALUE OF BASE CARDS

	MINT	NRMT
❑ 1 Stacey Augmon	.10	.05
❑ 2 Mookie Blaylock	.10	.05
❑ 3 Craig Ehlo	.10	.05
❑ 4 Andrew Lang	.10	.05
❑ 5 Grant Long	.10	.05
❑ 6 Ken Norman	.10	.05
❑ 7 Steve Smith	.15	.07
❑ 8 Dee Brown	.10	.05
❑ 9 Sherman Douglas	.10	.05
❑ 10 Eric Montross	.10	.05
❑ 11 Dino Radja	.10	.05
❑ 12 David Wesley	.10	.05
❑ 13 Dominique Wilkins	.25	.11
❑ 14 Muggsy Bogues	.10	.05
❑ 15 Scott Burrell	.10	.05
❑ 16 Dell Curry	.10	.05
❑ 17 Hersey Hawkins	.15	.07
❑ 18 Larry Johnson	.15	.07
❑ 19 Alonzo Mourning	.25	.11
❑ 20 Robert Parish	.15	.07
❑ 21 B.J. Armstrong	.10	.05
❑ 22 Michael Jordan	3.00	1.35
❑ 23 Steve Kerr	.10	.05
❑ 24 Toni Kukoc	.30	.14
❑ 25 Will Perdue	.10	.05
❑ 26 Scottie Pippen	.75	.35
❑ 27 Terrell Brandon	.15	.07
❑ 28 Tyrone Hill	.10	.05
❑ 29 Chris Mills	.10	.05
❑ 30 Bobby Phills	.10	.05
❑ 31 Mark Price	.10	.05
❑ 32 John Williams	.10	.05
❑ 33 Lucious Harris	.10	.05
❑ 34 Jim Jackson	.10	.05
❑ 35 Popeye Jones	.10	.05
❑ 36 Jason Kidd	.75	.35
❑ 37 Jamal Mashburn	.15	.07
❑ 38 George McCloud	.10	.05
❑ 39 Roy Tarpley	.10	.05
❑ 40 Lorenzo Williams	.10	.05
❑ 41 Mahmoud Abdul-Rauf	.10	.05
❑ 42 Dale Ellis	.10	.05
❑ 43 LaPhonso Ellis	.10	.05
❑ 44 Dikembe Mutombo	.15	.07
❑ 45 Robert Pack	.10	.05
❑ 46 Rodney Rogers	.10	.05
❑ 47 Jalen Rose	.30	.14
❑ 48 Bryant Stith	.10	.05
❑ 49 Reggie Williams	.10	.05
❑ 50 Joe Dumars	.25	.11
❑ 51 Grant Hill	1.25	.55
❑ 52 Allan Houston	.30	.14
❑ 53 Lindsey Hunter	.10	.05
❑ 54 Oliver Miller	.10	.05
❑ 55 Terry Mills	.10	.05
❑ 56 Mark West	.10	.05
❑ 57 Chris Gatling	.10	.05
❑ 58 Tim Hardaway	.25	.11
❑ 59 Donyell Marshall	.15	.07
❑ 60 Chris Mullin	.25	.11
❑ 61 Carlos Rogers	.10	.05
❑ 62 Clifford Rozier	.10	.05
❑ 63 Rony Seikaly	.10	.05
❑ 64 Latrell Sprewell	.50	.23
❑ 65 Sam Cassell	.15	.07
❑ 66 Clyde Drexler	.25	.11
❑ 67 Mario Elie	.10	.05
❑ 68 Carl Herrera	.10	.05
❑ 69 Robert Horry	.10	.05
❑ 70 Vernon Maxwell	.10	.05
❑ 71 Hakeem Olajuwon	.40	.18
❑ 72 Kenny Smith	.10	.05
❑ 73 Dale Davis	.10	.05
❑ 74 Mark Jackson	.10	.05
❑ 75 Derrick McKey	.10	.05
❑ 76 Reggie Miller	.25	.11
❑ 77 Sam Mitchell	.10	.05
❑ 78 Byron Scott	.10	.05
❑ 79 Rik Smits	.10	.05
❑ 80 Terry Dehere	.10	.05
❑ 81 Tony Massenburg	.10	.05
❑ 82 Lamond Murray	.10	.05
❑ 83 Pooh Richardson	.10	.05
❑ 84 Malik Sealy	.10	.05
❑ 85 Loy Vaught	.10	.05
❑ 86 Elden Campbell	.10	.05
❑ 87 Cedric Ceballos	.10	.05
❑ 88 Vlade Divac	.10	.05
❑ 89 Eddie Jones	.50	.23
❑ 90 Anthony Peeler	.10	.05
❑ 91 Sedale Threatt	.10	.05
❑ 92 Nick Van Exel	.15	.07
❑ 93 Bimbo Coles	.10	.05
❑ 94 Matt Geiger	.10	.05
❑ 95 Billy Owens	.10	.05
❑ 96 Khalid Reeves	.10	.05
❑ 97 Glen Rice	.15	.07
❑ 98 John Salley	.10	.05
❑ 99 Kevin Willis	.10	.05
❑ 100 Vin Baker	.25	.11
❑ 101 Marty Conlon	.10	.05
❑ 102 Todd Day	.10	.05
❑ 103 Lee Mayberry	.10	.05
❑ 104 Eric Murdock	.10	.05
❑ 105 Glenn Robinson	.25	.11
❑ 106 Winston Garland	.10	.05
❑ 107 Tom Gugliotta	.15	.07
❑ 108 Christian Laettner	.15	.07
❑ 109 Isaiah Rider	.15	.07
❑ 110 Sean Rooks	.10	.05
❑ 111 Doug West	.10	.05
❑ 112 Kenny Anderson	.15	.07
❑ 113 Benoit Benjamin	.10	.05
❑ 114 P.J. Brown	.10	.05
❑ 115 Derrick Coleman	.15	.07
❑ 116 Armon Gilliam	.10	.05
❑ 117 Chris Morris	.10	.05
❑ 118 Rex Walters	.10	.05
❑ 119 Hubert Davis	.10	.05
❑ 120 Patrick Ewing	.25	.11
❑ 121 Derek Harper	.10	.05
❑ 122 Anthony Mason	.15	.07
❑ 123 Charles Oakley	.10	.05
❑ 124 Charles Smith	.10	.05
❑ 125 John Starks	.10	.05
❑ 126 Nick Anderson	.10	.05
❑ 127 Anthony Bowie	.10	.05
❑ 128 Horace Grant	.15	.07
❑ 129 Anfernee Hardaway	.75	.35
❑ 130 Shaquille O'Neal	1.25	.55
❑ 131 Donald Royal	.10	.05
❑ 132 Dennis Scott	.10	.05
❑ 133 Brian Shaw	.10	.05
❑ 134 Derrick Alston	.10	.05
❑ 135 Dana Barros	.10	.05
❑ 136 Shawn Bradley	.10	.05
❑ 137 Willie Burton	.10	.05
❑ 138 Clarence Weatherspoon	.10	.05
❑ 139 Scott Williams	.10	.05
❑ 140 Sharone Wright	.10	.05
❑ 141 Danny Ainge	.10	.05
❑ 142 Charles Barkley	.40	.18
❑ 143 A.C. Green	.15	.07
❑ 144 Kevin Johnson	.15	.07
❑ 145 Dan Majerle	.10	.05
❑ 146 Danny Manning	.15	.07
❑ 147 Elliot Perry	.10	.05
❑ 148 Wesley Person	.15	.07
❑ 149 Wayman Tisdale	.10	.05
❑ 150 Chris Dudley	.10	.05
❑ 151 Jerome Kersey	.10	.05
❑ 152 Aaron McKie	.10	.05
❑ 153 Terry Porter	.10	.05

❑ 154 Clifford Robinson .10 .05
❑ 155 James Robinson .10 .05
❑ 156 Rod Strickland .15 .07
❑ 157 Otis Thorpe .10 .05
❑ 158 Buck Williams .10 .05
❑ 159 Brian Grant .25 .11
❑ 160 Bobby Hurley .10 .05
❑ 161 Olden Polynice .10 .05
❑ 162 Mitch Richmond .25 .11
❑ 163 Michael Smith .10 .05
❑ 164 Spud Webb .10 .05
❑ 165 Walt Williams .10 .05
❑ 166 Terry Cummings .10 .05
❑ 167 Vinny Del Negro .10 .05
❑ 168 Sean Elliott .10 .05
❑ 169 Avery Johnson .10 .05
❑ 170 Chuck Person .10 .05
❑ 171 J.R. Reid .10 .05
❑ 172 Doc Rivers .10 .05
❑ 173 David Robinson .40 .18
❑ 174 Dennis Rodman .50 .23
❑ 175 Vincent Askew .10 .05
❑ 176 Kendall Gill .15 .07
❑ 177 Shawn Kemp .40 .18
❑ 178 Sarunas Marciulionis .10 .05
❑ 179 Nate McMillan .10 .05
❑ 180 Gary Payton .40 .18
❑ 181 Sam Perkins .15 .07
❑ 182 Detlef Schrempf .15 .07
❑ 183 David Benoit .10 .05
❑ 184 Antoine Carr .10 .05
❑ 185 Blue Edwards .10 .05
❑ 186 Jeff Hornacek .15 .07
❑ 187 Adam Keefe .10 .05
❑ 188 Karl Malone .40 .18
❑ 189 Felton Spencer .10 .05
❑ 190 John Stockton .25 .11
❑ 191 Rex Chapman .10 .05
❑ 192 Calbert Cheaney .10 .05
❑ 193 Juwan Howard .25 .11
❑ 194 Don MacLean .10 .05
❑ 195 Gheorghe Muresan .10 .05
❑ 196 Scott Skiles .10 .05
❑ 197 Chris Webber .75 .35
❑ 198 Checklist .10 .05
❑ 199 Checklist .10 .05
❑ 200 Checklist .10 .05
❑ 201 Stacey Augmon .10 .05
❑ 202 Mookie Blaylock .10 .05
❑ 203 Grant Long .10 .05
❑ 204 Ken Norman .10 .05
❑ 205 Steve Smith .15 .07
❑ 206 Spud Webb .10 .05
❑ 207 Dana Barros .10 .05
❑ 208 Rick Fox .10 .05
❑ 209 Kendall Gill .15 .07
❑ 210 Khalid Reeves .10 .05
❑ 211 Glen Rice .15 .07
❑ 212 Luc Longley .10 .05
❑ 213 Dennis Rodman .50 .23
❑ 214 Dan Majerle .10 .05
❑ 215 Tony Dumas .10 .05
❑ 216 Tom Hammonds .10 .05
❑ 217 Elmore Spencer .10 .05
❑ 218 Otis Thorpe .10 .05
❑ 219 B.J. Armstrong .10 .05
❑ 220 Sam Cassell .15 .07
❑ 221 Clyde Drexler .25 .11
❑ 222 Mario Elie .10 .05
❑ 223 Robert Horry .10 .05
❑ 224 Hakeem Olajuwon .40 .18
❑ 225 Kenny Smith .10 .05
❑ 226 Antonio Davis .10 .05
❑ 227 Eddie Johnson .10 .05
❑ 228 Ricky Pierce .10 .05
❑ 229 Eric Piatkowski .10 .05
❑ 230 Rodney Rogers .10 .05
❑ 231 Brian Williams .10 .05
❑ 232 Corie Blount .10 .05
❑ 233 George Lynch .10 .05
❑ 234 Kevin Gamble .10 .05
❑ 235 Alonzo Mourning .25 .11
❑ 236 Eric Mobley .10 .05
❑ 237 Terry Porter .10 .05
❑ 238 Micheal Williams .10 .05
❑ 239 Kevin Edwards .10 .05
❑ 240 Vern Fleming .10 .05
❑ 241 Charlie Ward .10 .05
❑ 242 Jon Koncak .10 .05
❑ 243 Richard Dumas .10 .05
❑ 244 Jeff Malone .10 .05
❑ 245 Vernon Maxwell .10 .05
❑ 246 John Williams .10 .05
❑ 247 Harvey Grant .10 .05
❑ 248 Dontonio Wingfield .10 .05
❑ 249 Tyrone Corbin .10 .05
❑ 250 Sarunas Marciulionis .10 .05
❑ 251 Will Perdue .10 .05
❑ 252 Hersey Hawkins .15 .07
❑ 253 Ervin Johnson .10 .05
❑ 254 Shawn Kemp .40 .18
❑ 255 Gary Payton .40 .18
❑ 256 Sam Perkins .15 .07
❑ 257 Detlef Schrempf .15 .07
❑ 258 Chris Morris .10 .05
❑ 259 Robert Pack .10 .05
❑ 260 Willie Anderson ET .10 .05
❑ 261 Jimmy King ET .10 .05
❑ 262 Oliver Miller ET .10 .05
❑ 263 Tracy Murray ET .10 .05
❑ 264 Ed Pinckney ET .10 .05
❑ 265 Alvin Robertson ET .10 .05
❑ 266 Carlos Rogers ET .10 .05
❑ 267 John Salley ET .10 .05
❑ 268 Damon Stoudamire ET .75 .35
❑ 269 Zan Tabak ET .10 .05
❑ 270 Ashraf Amaya ET .10 .05
❑ 271 Greg Anthony ET .10 .05
❑ 272 Benoit Benjamin ET .10 .05
❑ 273 Blue Edwards ET .10 .05
❑ 274 Kenny Gattison ET .10 .05
❑ 275 Antonio Harvey ET .10 .05
❑ 276 Chris King ET .10 .05
❑ 277 Lawrence Moten ET .10 .05
❑ 278 Bryant Reeves ET .15 .07
❑ 279 Byron Scott ET .10 .05
❑ 280 Cory Alexander RC .10 .05
❑ 281 Jerome Allen RC .10 .05
❑ 282 Brent Barry RC .25 .11
❑ 283 Mario Bennett RC .10 .05
❑ 284 Travis Best RC .15 .07
❑ 285 Junior Burrough RC .10 .05
❑ 286 Jason Caffey RC .15 .07
❑ 287 Randolph Childress RC .10 .05
❑ 288 Sasha Danilovic RC .10 .05
❑ 289 Mark Davis RC .10 .05
❑ 290 Tyus Edney RC .10 .05
❑ 291 Michael Finley RC 1.00 .45
❑ 292 Sherrell Ford RC .10 .05
❑ 293 Kevin Garnett RC 3.00 1.35
❑ 294 Alan Henderson RC .25 .11
❑ 295 Frankie King RC .10 .05
❑ 296 Jimmy King RC .10 .05
❑ 297 Donny Marshall RC .10 .05
❑ 298 Antonio McDyess RC 1.25 .55
❑ 299 Loren Meyer RC .10 .05
❑ 300 Lawrence Moten RC .10 .05
❑ 301 Ed O'Bannon RC .10 .05
❑ 302 Greg Ostertag RC .10 .05
❑ 303 Cherokee Parks RC .10 .05
❑ 304 Theo Ratliff RC .30 .14
❑ 305 Bryant Reeves RC .25 .11
❑ 306 Shawn Respert RC .10 .05
❑ 307 Lou Roe RC .10 .05
❑ 308 Arvydas Sabonis RC .40 .18
❑ 309 Joe Smith RC .75 .35
❑ 310 Jerry Stackhouse RC .75 .35
❑ 311 Damon Stoudamire RC 1.25 .55
❑ 312 Bob Sura RC .15 .07
❑ 313 Kurt Thomas RC .15 .07
❑ 314 Gary Trent RC .10 .05
❑ 315 David Vaughn RC .10 .05
❑ 316 Rasheed Wallace RC 1.00 .45
❑ 317 Eric Williams RC .15 .07
❑ 318 Corliss Williamson RC .50 .23
❑ 319 George Zidek RC .10 .05
❑ 320 Mookie Blaylock FF .10 .05
❑ 321 Dino Radja FF .10 .05
❑ 322 Larry Johnson FF .10 .05
❑ 323 Michael Jordan FF 1.50 .70
❑ 324 Tyrone Hill FF .10 .05
❑ 325 Jason Kidd FF .30 .14
❑ 326 Dikembe Mutombo FF .10 .05
❑ 327 Grant Hill FF .75 .35
❑ 328 Joe Smith FF .40 .18
❑ 329 Hakeem Olajuwon FF .25 .11
❑ 330 Reggie Miller FF .15 .07
❑ 331 Loy Vaught FF .10 .05
❑ 332 Nick Van Exel FF .10 .05
❑ 333 Alonzo Mourning FF .15 .07
❑ 334 Glenn Robinson FF .15 .07
❑ 335 Kevin Garnett FF 1.25 .55
❑ 336 Kenny Anderson FF .10 .05
❑ 337 Patrick Ewing FF .15 .07
❑ 338 Shaquille O'Neal FF .50 .23
❑ 339 Jerry Stackhouse FF .40 .18
❑ 340 Charles Barkley FF .25 .11
❑ 341 Clifford Robinson FF .10 .05
❑ 342 Mitch Richmond FF .15 .07
❑ 343 David Robinson FF .25 .11
❑ 344 Shawn Kemp FF .25 .11
❑ 345 Damon Stoudamire FF .75 .35
❑ 346 Karl Malone FF .25 .11
❑ 347 Bryant Reeves FF .15 .07
❑ 348 Chris Webber FF .30 .14
❑ 349 Checklist (201-319) .10 .05
❑ 350 Checklist (320-350/ins.) .10 .05

1995-96 Fleer All-Stars

	MINT	NRMT
COMPLETE SET (13)	5.00	2.20
COMMON CARD (1-13)	.25	.11
SEMISTARS	.30	.14
UNLISTED STARS	.60	.25

SER.1 STATED ODDS 1:3 HOBBY/RETAIL

❑ 1 Grant Hill 2.00 .90
Charles Barkley
❑ 2 Scottie Pippen 1.00 .45
Shawn Kemp
❑ 3 Shaquille O'Neal 2.00 .90
Hakeem Olajuwon
❑ 4 Anfernee Hardaway 1.25 .55
Dan Majerle
❑ 5 Reggie Miller 1.00 .45
Latrell Sprewell
❑ 6 Vin Baker .60 .25
Cedric Ceballos
❑ 7 Tyrone Hill .30 .14
Karl Malone
❑ 8 Larry Johnson .25 .11
Detlef Schrempf
❑ 9 Patrick Ewing .60 .25
David Robinson
❑ 10 Alonzo Mourning .60 .25
Dikembe Mutombo
❑ 11 Dana Barros .30 .14
Gary Payton
❑ 12 Joe Dumars .60 .25
John Stockton
❑ 13 Mitch Richmond AS MVP .60 .25

1995-96 Fleer Class Encounters

	MINT	NRMT
COMPLETE SET (40)	20.00	9.00
COMMON CARD (1-40)	.25	.11
SEMISTARS	.40	.18

	MINT	NRMT
UNLISTED STARS	.75	.35
SER.2 STATED ODDS 1:2 HOBBY/RETAIL		

❑ 1 Derrick Alston	.25	.11
❑ 2 Brian Grant	.75	.35
❑ 3 Grant Hill	4.00	1.80
❑ 4 Juwan Howard	.75	.35
❑ 5 Eddie Jones	1.50	.70
❑ 6 Jason Kidd	2.50	1.10
❑ 7 Donyell Marshall	.40	.18
❑ 8 Anthony Miller	.25	.11
❑ 9 Eric Mobley	.25	.11
❑ 10 Eric Montross	.25	.11
❑ 11 Lamond Murray	.25	.11
❑ 12 Wesley Person	.40	.18
❑ 13 Eric Piatkowski	.25	.11
❑ 14 Khalid Reeves	.25	.11
❑ 15 Glenn Robinson	.75	.35
❑ 16 Carlos Rogers	.25	.11
❑ 17 Jalen Rose	1.00	.45
❑ 18 Clifford Rozier	.25	.11
❑ 19 Michael Smith	.25	.11
❑ 20 Sharone Wright	.25	.11
❑ 21 Brent Barry	.75	.35
❑ 22 Jason Caffey	.25	.11
❑ 23 Randolph Childress	.25	.11
❑ 24 Kevin Garnett	6.00	2.70
❑ 25 Alan Henderson	.40	.18
❑ 26 Antonio McDyess	2.50	1.10
❑ 27 Ed O'Bannon	.25	.11
❑ 28 Cherokee Parks	.25	.11
❑ 29 Theo Ratliff	.75	.35
❑ 30 Bryant Reeves	.40	.18
❑ 31 Shawn Respert	.25	.11
❑ 32 Joe Smith	1.50	.70
❑ 33 Jerry Stackhouse	1.50	.70
❑ 34 Damon Stoudamire	2.50	1.10
❑ 35 Bob Sura	.40	.18
❑ 36 Kurt Thomas	.25	.11
❑ 37 Gary Trent	.25	.11
❑ 38 Rasheed Wallace	2.00	.90
❑ 39 Eric Williams	.25	.11
❑ 40 Corliss Williamson	.75	.35

1995-96 Fleer Double Doubles

	MINT	NRMT
COMPLETE SET (12)	4.00	1.80
COMMON CARD (1-12)	.25	.11
SEMISTARS	.40	.18
UNLISTED STARS	.50	.23
SER.1 STATED ODDS 1:3 HOBBY/RETAIL		

❑ 1 Vin Baker	.50	.23
❑ 2 Vlade Divac	.25	.11
❑ 3 Patrick Ewing	.50	.23
❑ 4 Tyrone Hill	.25	.11
❑ 5 Popeye Jones	.25	.11
❑ 6 Shawn Kemp	.75	.35
❑ 7 Karl Malone	.75	.35
❑ 8 Dikembe Mutombo	.40	.18
❑ 9 Hakeem Olajuwon	.75	.35
❑ 10 Shaquille O'Neal	2.50	1.10
❑ 11 David Robinson	.75	.35
❑ 12 John Stockton	.50	.23

1995-96 Fleer End to End

	MINT	NRMT
COMPLETE SET (20)	25.00	11.00
COMMON CARD (1-20)	.25	.11
SEMISTARS	.40	.18
UNLISTED STARS	.75	.35
SER.2 STATED ODDS 1:4 HOBBY/RETAIL		

❑ 1 Mookie Blaylock	.25	.11
❑ 2 Vlade Divac	.25	.11
❑ 3 Clyde Drexler	.75	.35
❑ 4 Patrick Ewing	.75	.35
❑ 5 Horace Grant	.25	.11
❑ 6 Anfernee Hardaway	2.50	1.10
❑ 7 Grant Hill	4.00	1.80
❑ 8 Eddie Jones	1.50	.70
❑ 9 Michael Jordan	10.00	4.50
❑ 10 Jason Kidd	2.50	1.10
❑ 11 Alonzo Mourning	.75	.35
❑ 12 Dikembe Mutombo	.40	.18
❑ 13 Hakeem Olajuwon	1.25	.55
❑ 14 Shaquille O'Neal	4.00	1.80
❑ 15 Gary Payton	1.25	.55
❑ 16 Scottie Pippen	2.50	1.10
❑ 17 David Robinson	1.25	.55
❑ 18 Latrell Sprewell	1.50	.70
❑ 19 John Stockton	.75	.35
❑ 20 Rod Strickland	.40	.18

1995-96 Fleer Flair Hardwood Leaders

	MINT	NRMT
COMPLETE SET (27)	15.00	6.75
COMMON CARD (1-27)	.25	.11
SEMISTARS	.40	.18
UNLISTED STARS	.60	.25
ONE PER SER.1 PACK		

❑ 1 Mookie Blaylock	.25	.11
❑ 2 Dominique Wilkins	.60	.25
❑ 3 Alonzo Mourning	.60	.25
❑ 4 Michael Jordan	8.00	3.60
❑ 5 Mark Price	.25	.11
❑ 6 Jim Jackson	.25	.11
❑ 7 Dikembe Mutombo	.40	.18
❑ 8 Grant Hill	3.00	1.35
❑ 9 Tim Hardaway	.60	.25

❑ 10 Hakeem Olajuwon	1.00	.45
❑ 11 Reggie Miller	.60	.25
❑ 12 Loy Vaught	.25	.11
❑ 13 Cedric Ceballos	.25	.11
❑ 14 Glen Rice	.40	.18
❑ 15 Glenn Robinson	.60	.25
❑ 16 Christian Laettner	.40	.18
❑ 17 Derrick Coleman	.40	.18
❑ 18 Patrick Ewing	.60	.25
❑ 19 Shaquille O'Neal	3.00	1.35
❑ 20 Dana Barros	.25	.11
❑ 21 Charles Barkley	1.00	.45
❑ 22 Clifford Robinson	.25	.11
❑ 23 Mitch Richmond	.60	.25
❑ 24 David Robinson	1.00	.45
❑ 25 Gary Payton	1.00	.45
❑ 26 Karl Malone	1.00	.45
❑ 27 Chris Webber	2.00	.90

1995-96 Fleer Franchise Futures

	MINT	NRMT
COMPLETE SET (9)	40.00	18.00
COMMON CARD (1-9)	1.50	.70
SEMISTARS	2.00	.90
UNLISTED STARS	3.00	1.35
SER.1 STATED ODDS 1:37 HOBBY/RETAIL		

❑ 1 Vin Baker	3.00	1.35
❑ 2 Anfernee Hardaway	10.00	4.50
❑ 3 Jim Jackson	1.50	.70
❑ 4 Jamal Mashburn	2.00	.90
❑ 5 Alonzo Mourning	3.00	1.35
❑ 6 Dikembe Mutombo	2.00	.90
❑ 7 Shaquille O'Neal	15.00	6.75
❑ 8 Nick Van Exel	2.00	.90
❑ 9 Chris Webber	10.00	4.50

1995-96 Fleer Rookie Phenoms

	MINT	NRMT
COMPLETE SET (10)	50.00	22.00
COMMON CARD (1-10)	1.00	.45
UNLISTED STARS	3.00	1.35
SER.2 STATED ODDS 1:24 HOBBY		
COMP.HOT PACK SET (10)	20.00	9.00
HP CARDS: .1X TO .3X HI COLUMN		
HP: SER.2 STATED ODDS 1:72 HOBBY		

	MINT	NRMT
❑ 1 Kevin Garnett	25.00	11.00
❑ 2 Antonio McDyess	8.00	3.60
❑ 3 Ed O'Bannon	1.00	.45
❑ 4 Bryant Reeves	3.00	1.35
❑ 5 Shawn Respert	1.00	.45
❑ 6 Joe Smith	5.00	2.20
❑ 7 Jerry Stackhouse	5.00	2.20
❑ 8 Damon Stoudamire	8.00	3.60
❑ 9 Gary Trent	1.00	.45
❑ 10 Rasheed Wallace	6.00	2.70

1995-96 Fleer Rookie Sensations

	MINT	NRMT
COMPLETE SET (15)	25.00	11.00
COMMON CARD (1-15)	.75	.35
SEMISTARS	1.50	.70
UNLISTED STARS	2.50	1.10

SER.1 STATED ODDS 1:5 CELLO

	MINT	NRMT
❑ 1 Brian Grant	2.50	1.10
❑ 2 Grant Hill	12.00	5.50
❑ 3 Juwan Howard	2.50	1.10
❑ 4 Eddie Jones	5.00	2.20
❑ 5 Jason Kidd	8.00	3.60
❑ 6 Donyell Marshall	1.50	.70
❑ 7 Eric Montross	.75	.35
❑ 8 Lamond Murray	.75	.35
❑ 9 Wesley Person	1.50	.70
❑ 10 Khalid Reeves	.75	.35
❑ 11 Glenn Robinson	2.50	1.10
❑ 12 Jalen Rose	3.00	1.35
❑ 13 Clifford Rozier	.75	.35
❑ 14 Michael Smith	.75	.35
❑ 15 Sharone Wright	.75	.35

1995-96 Fleer Stackhouse's Scrapbook

	MINT	NRMT
COMPLETE SET (8)	25.00	11.00
COMP.FLEER SER.1 (2)	3.00	1.35
COMP.ULTRA SER.2 (2)	3.00	1.35
COMP.FLAIR SER.3 (2)	12.00	5.50
COMP.METAL SER.4 (2)	8.00	3.60
COMMON FLEER (S1-S2)	2.00	.90
COMMON ULTRA (S3-S4)	2.50	1.10
COMMON FLAIR (S5-S6)	6.00	2.70
COMMON METAL (S7-S8)	3.00	1.35

SER.2 STATED ODDS 1:24 FLEER PRODUCTS

	MINT	NRMT
❑ S1 Jerry Stackhouse	2.50	1.10
❑ S2 Jerry Stackhouse	2.50	1.10

1995-96 Fleer Total D

	MINT	NRMT
COMPLETE SET (12)	12.00	5.50
COMMON CARD (1-12)	.25	.11
SEMISTARS	.40	.18
UNLISTED STARS	.60	.25

SER.1 STATED ODDS 1:5 HOBBY/RETAIL

	MINT	NRMT
❑ 1 Mookie Blaylock	.25	.11
❑ 2 Patrick Ewing	.60	.25
❑ 3 Michael Jordan	8.00	3.60
❑ 4 Alonzo Mourning	.60	.25
❑ 5 Dikembe Mutombo	.40	.18
❑ 6 Hakeem Olajuwon	1.00	.45
❑ 7 Shaquille O'Neal	3.00	1.35
❑ 8 Gary Payton	1.00	.45
❑ 9 Scottie Pippen	2.00	.90
❑ 10 David Robinson	1.00	.45
❑ 11 Dennis Rodman	1.25	.55
❑ 12 John Stockton	.60	.25

1995-96 Fleer Total O

	MINT	NRMT
COMPLETE SET (10)	40.00	18.00
COMMON CARD (1-10)	.75	.35
SEMISTARS	1.00	.45
UNLISTED STARS	1.50	.70

SER.2 STATED ODDS 1:12 RETAIL

	MINT	NRMT
COMP.HOT PACK SET (10)	25.00	11.00

HP CARDS: .25X TO .6X HI COLUMN
HP: SER.2 STATED ODDS 1:72 RETAIL

	MINT	NRMT
❑ 1 Grant Hill	8.00	3.60
❑ 2 Michael Jordan	25.00	11.00
❑ 3 Jamal Mashburn	.75	.35
❑ 4 Reggie Miller	1.50	.70
❑ 5 Hakeem Olajuwon	2.50	1.10
❑ 6 Shaquille O'Neal	8.00	3.60
❑ 7 Mitch Richmond	1.50	.70
❑ 8 David Robinson	2.50	1.10
❑ 9 Glenn Robinson	1.50	.70
❑ 10 Jerry Stackhouse	2.50	1.10

1995-96 Fleer Towers of Power

	MINT	NRMT
COMPLETE SET (10)	75.00	34.00
COMMON CARD (1-10)	5.00	2.20

SER.2 STATED ODDS 1:54 HOBBY/RETAIL

	MINT	NRMT
❑ 1 Shawn Kemp	8.00	3.60
❑ 2 Karl Malone	8.00	3.60
❑ 3 Antonio McDyess	12.00	5.50
❑ 4 Alonzo Mourning	5.00	2.20
❑ 5 Hakeem Olajuwon	8.00	3.60
❑ 6 Shaquille O'Neal	25.00	11.00
❑ 7 David Robinson	8.00	3.60
❑ 8 Glenn Robinson	5.00	2.20
❑ 9 Joe Smith	8.00	3.60
❑ 10 Chris Webber	15.00	6.75

1996-97 Fleer

	MINT	NRMT
COMPLETE SET (300)	35.00	16.00
COMPLETE SERIES 1 (150)	15.00	6.75
COMPLETE SERIES 2 (150)	20.00	9.00
COMMON CARD (1-300)	.10	.05
SEMISTARS	.15	.07
UNLISTED STARS	.25	.11

SUBSET CARDS HALF VALUE OF BASE CARDS

❑ 1 Stacey Augmon .10 .05
❑ 2 Mookie Blaylock .10 .05
❑ 3 Christian Laettner .15 .07
❑ 4 Grant Long .10 .05
❑ 5 Steve Smith .15 .07
❑ 6 Rick Fox .10 .05
❑ 7 Dino Radja .10 .05
❑ 8 Eric Williams .10 .05
❑ 9 Kenny Anderson .15 .07
❑ 10 Dell Curry .10 .05
❑ 11 Larry Johnson .15 .07
❑ 12 Glen Rice .15 .07
❑ 13 Michael Jordan 3.00 1.35
❑ 14 Toni Kukoc .30 .14
❑ 15 Scottie Pippen .75 .35
❑ 16 Dennis Rodman .50 .23
❑ 17 Terrell Brandon .15 .07
❑ 18 Chris Mills .10 .05
❑ 19 Bobby Phills .10 .05
❑ 20 Bob Sura .10 .05
❑ 21 Jim Jackson .10 .05
❑ 22 Jason Kidd .75 .35
❑ 23 Jamal Mashburn .15 .07
❑ 24 George McCloud .10 .05
❑ 25 Mahmoud Abdul-Rauf .10 .05
❑ 26 Antonio McDyess .40 .18
❑ 27 Dikembe Mutombo .15 .07
❑ 28 Jalen Rose .25 .11
❑ 29 Bryant Stith .10 .05
❑ 30 Joe Dumars .25 .11
❑ 31 Grant Hill 1.25 .55
❑ 32 Allan Houston .25 .11
❑ 33 Theo Ratliff .15 .07
❑ 34 Otis Thorpe .10 .05
❑ 35 Chris Mullin .25 .11
❑ 36 Joe Smith .25 .11
❑ 37 Latrell Sprewell .50 .23
❑ 38 Kevin Willis .10 .05
❑ 39 Sam Cassell .15 .07
❑ 40 Clyde Drexler .25 .11
❑ 41 Robert Horry .10 .05
❑ 42 Hakeem Olajuwon .40 .18
❑ 43 Dale Davis .10 .05
❑ 44 Mark Jackson .10 .05
❑ 45 Derrick McKey .10 .05
❑ 46 Reggie Miller .25 .11
❑ 47 Rik Smits .10 .05
❑ 48 Brent Barry .10 .05
❑ 49 Malik Sealy .10 .05
❑ 50 Loy Vaught .10 .05
❑ 51 Brian Williams .10 .05
❑ 52 Elden Campbell .10 .05
❑ 53 Cedric Ceballos .10 .05
❑ 54 Vlade Divac .10 .05
❑ 55 Eddie Jones .50 .23
❑ 56 Nick Van Exel .15 .07
❑ 57 Tim Hardaway .25 .11
❑ 58 Alonzo Mourning .25 .11
❑ 59 Kurt Thomas .10 .05
❑ 60 Walt Williams .10 .05
❑ 61 Vin Baker .15 .07
❑ 62 Sherman Douglas .10 .05
❑ 63 Glenn Robinson .25 .11
❑ 64 Kevin Garnett 1.50 .70
❑ 65 Tom Gugliotta .15 .07
❑ 66 Isaiah Rider .15 .07
❑ 67 Shawn Bradley .10 .05
❑ 68 Chris Childs .10 .05
❑ 69 Armon Gilliam .10 .05
❑ 70 Ed O'Bannon .10 .05
❑ 71 Patrick Ewing .25 .11
❑ 72 Derek Harper .10 .05
❑ 73 Anthony Mason .15 .07
❑ 74 Charles Oakley .10 .05
❑ 75 John Starks .10 .05
❑ 76 Nick Anderson .10 .05
❑ 77 Horace Grant .15 .07
❑ 78 Anfernee Hardaway .75 .35
❑ 79 Shaquille O'Neal 1.25 .55
❑ 80 Dennis Scott .10 .05
❑ 81 Derrick Coleman .15 .07
❑ 82 Vernon Maxwell .10 .05
❑ 83 Jerry Stackhouse .25 .11
❑ 84 Clarence Weatherspoon .10 .05
❑ 85 Charles Barkley .40 .18
❑ 86 Michael Finley .30 .14
❑ 87 Kevin Johnson .15 .07
❑ 88 Wesley Person .10 .05
❑ 89 Clifford Robinson .10 .05
❑ 90 Arvydas Sabonis .15 .07
❑ 91 Rod Strickland .15 .07
❑ 92 Gary Trent .10 .05
❑ 93 Tyus Edney .10 .05
❑ 94 Brian Grant .25 .11
❑ 95 Billy Owens .10 .05
❑ 96 Mitch Richmond .25 .11
❑ 97 Vinny Del Negro .10 .05
❑ 98 Sean Elliott .10 .05
❑ 99 Avery Johnson .10 .05
❑ 100 David Robinson .40 .18
❑ 101 Hersey Hawkins .15 .07
❑ 102 Shawn Kemp .40 .18
❑ 103 Gary Payton .40 .18
❑ 104 Detlef Schrempf .15 .07
❑ 105 Oliver Miller .10 .05
❑ 106 Tracy Murray .10 .05
❑ 107 Damon Stoudamire .40 .18
❑ 108 Sharone Wright .10 .05
❑ 109 Jeff Hornacek .15 .07
❑ 110 Karl Malone .40 .18
❑ 111 John Stockton .25 .11
❑ 112 Greg Anthony .10 .05
❑ 113 Bryant Reeves .10 .05
❑ 114 Byron Scott .10 .05
❑ 115 Calbert Cheaney .10 .05
❑ 116 Juwan Howard .15 .07
❑ 117 Gheorghe Muresan .10 .05
❑ 118 Rasheed Wallace .30 .14
❑ 119 Chris Webber .75 .35
❑ 120 Mookie Blaylock HL .10 .05
❑ 121 Dino Radja HL .10 .05
❑ 122 Larry Johnson HL .10 .05
❑ 123 Michael Jordan HL 1.50 .70
❑ 124 Terrell Brandon HL .10 .05
❑ 125 Jason Kidd HL .25 .11
❑ 126 Antonio McDyess HL .25 .11
❑ 127 Grant Hill HL .75 .35
❑ 128 Latrell Sprewell HL .25 .11
❑ 129 Hakeem Olajuwon HL .25 .11
❑ 130 Reggie Miller HL .15 .07
❑ 131 Loy Vaught HL .10 .05
❑ 132 Cedric Ceballos HL .10 .05
❑ 133 Alonzo Mourning HL .15 .07
❑ 134 Vin Baker HL .10 .05
❑ 135 Isaiah Rider HL .10 .05
❑ 136 Armon Gilliam HL .10 .05
❑ 137 Patrick Ewing HL .15 .07
❑ 138 Shaquille O'Neal HL .50 .23
❑ 139 Jerry Stackhouse HL .15 .07
❑ 140 Charles Barkley HL .25 .11
❑ 141 Clifford Robinson HL .10 .05
❑ 142 Mitch Richmond HL .15 .07
❑ 143 David Robinson HL .25 .11
❑ 144 Shawn Kemp HL .25 .11
❑ 145 Damon Stoudamire HL .25 .11
❑ 146 Karl Malone HL .25 .11
❑ 147 Bryant Reeves HL .10 .05
❑ 148 Juwan Howard HL .10 .05
❑ 149 Checklist .10 .05
❑ 150 Checklist .10 .05
❑ 151 Alan Henderson .10 .05
❑ 152 Priest Lauderdale RC .10 .05
❑ 153 Dikembe Mutombo .15 .07
❑ 154 Dana Barros .10 .05
❑ 155 Todd Day .10 .05
❑ 156 Brett Szabo RC .10 .05
❑ 157 Antoine Walker RC 1.00 .45
❑ 158 Scott Burrell .10 .05
❑ 159 Tony Delk RC .15 .07
❑ 160 Vlade Divac .10 .05
❑ 161 Matt Geiger .10 .05
❑ 162 Anthony Mason .15 .07
❑ 163 Malik Rose RC .15 .07
❑ 164 Ron Harper .15 .07
❑ 165 Steve Kerr .10 .05
❑ 166 Luc Longley .10 .05
❑ 167 Danny Ferry .10 .05
❑ 168 Tyrone Hill .10 .05
❑ 169 Vitaly Potapenko RC .10 .05
❑ 170 Tony Dumas .10 .05
❑ 171 Chris Gatling .10 .05
❑ 172 Oliver Miller .10 .05
❑ 173 Eric Montross .10 .05
❑ 174 Samaki Walker RC .10 .05
❑ 175 Darvin Ham RC .10 .05
❑ 176 Mark Jackson .10 .05
❑ 177 Ervin Johnson .10 .05
❑ 178 Stacey Augmon .10 .05
❑ 179 Joe Dumars .25 .11
❑ 180 Grant Hill 1.25 .55
❑ 181 Grant Long .10 .05
❑ 182 Terry Mills .10 .05
❑ 183 Otis Thorpe .10 .05
❑ 184 Jerome Williams RC .40 .18
❑ 185 B.J. Armstrong .10 .05
❑ 186 Todd Fuller RC .10 .05
❑ 187 Ray Owes RC .10 .05
❑ 188 Mark Price .10 .05
❑ 189 Felton Spencer .10 .05
❑ 190 Charles Barkley .40 .18
❑ 191 Mario Elie .10 .05
❑ 192 Othella Harrington RC .25 .11
❑ 193 Matt Maloney RC .15 .07
❑ 194 Brent Price .10 .05
❑ 195 Kevin Willis .10 .05
❑ 196 Travis Best .10 .05
❑ 197 Erick Dampier RC .15 .07
❑ 198 Antonio Davis .10 .05
❑ 199 Jalen Rose .25 .11
❑ 200 Pooh Richardson .10 .05
❑ 201 Rodney Rogers .10 .05
❑ 202 Lorenzen Wright RC .15 .07
❑ 203 Kobe Bryant RC 8.00 3.60
❑ 204 Derek Fisher RC .40 .18
❑ 205 Travis Knight RC .10 .05
❑ 206 Shaquille O'Neal 1.25 .55
❑ 207 Byron Scott .10 .05
❑ 208 P.J. Brown .10 .05
❑ 209 Sasha Danilovic .10 .05
❑ 210 Dan Majerle .15 .07
❑ 211 Martin Muursepp RC .10 .05
❑ 212 Ray Allen RC 1.00 .45
❑ 213 Armon Gilliam .10 .05
❑ 214 Andrew Lang .10 .05
❑ 215 Moochie Norris RC .15 .07
❑ 216 Kevin Garnett 1.50 .70
❑ 217 Tom Gugliotta .15 .07
❑ 218 Shane Heal RC .10 .05
❑ 219 Stephon Marbury RC 1.50 .70
❑ 220 Stojko Vrankovic .10 .05
❑ 221 Kerry Kittles RC .50 .23
❑ 222 Robert Pack .10 .05
❑ 223 Jayson Williams .15 .07
❑ 224 Allan Houston .25 .11
❑ 225 Larry Johnson .15 .07
❑ 226 Dontae' Jones RC .10 .05
❑ 227 Walter McCarty RC .10 .05
❑ 228 John Wallace RC .25 .11
❑ 229 Charlie Ward .10 .05
❑ 230 Brian Evans RC .10 .05
❑ 231 Amal McCaskill RC .10 .05
❑ 232 Brian Shaw .10 .05
❑ 233 Mark Davis .10 .05
❑ 234 Lucious Harris .10 .05
❑ 235 Allen Iverson RC 2.50 1.10
❑ 236 Sam Cassell .15 .07
❑ 237 Robert Horry .10 .05
❑ 238 Danny Manning .15 .07
❑ 239 Steve Nash RC .15 .07
❑ 240 Kenny Anderson .15 .07
❑ 241 Aleksandar Djordjevic RC .10 .05
❑ 242 Jermaine O'Neal RC .50 .23
❑ 243 Isaiah Rider .15 .07
❑ 244 Rasheed Wallace .30 .14
❑ 245 Mahmoud Abdul-Rauf .10 .05
❑ 246 Michael Smith .10 .05
❑ 247 Corliss Williamson .10 .05
❑ 248 Vernon Maxwell .10 .05
❑ 249 Charles Smith .10 .05
❑ 250 Dominique Wilkins .25 .11
❑ 251 Craig Ehlo .10 .05
❑ 252 Jim McIlvaine .10 .05
❑ 253 Sam Perkins .15 .07
❑ 254 Marcus Camby RC .75 .35
❑ 255 Popeye Jones .10 .05
❑ 256 Donald Whiteside RC .10 .05
❑ 257 Walt Williams .10 .05

Card	MINT	NRMT
❑ 258 Jeff Hornacek	.15	.07
❑ 259 Karl Malone	.40	.18
❑ 260 Bryon Russell	.10	.05
❑ 261 John Stockton	.25	.11
❑ 262 Shareef Abdur-Rahim RC	1.50	.70
❑ 263 Anthony Peeler	.10	.05
❑ 264 Roy Rogers RC	.10	.05
❑ 265 Tim Legler	.10	.05
❑ 266 Tracy Murray	.10	.05
❑ 267 Rod Strickland	.15	.07
❑ 268 Ben Wallace RC	.10	.05
❑ 269 Kevin Garnett CB	.75	.35
❑ 270 Allan Houston CB	.15	.07
❑ 271 Eddie Jones CB	.25	.11
❑ 272 Jamal Mashburn CB	.10	.05
❑ 273 Antonio McDyess CB	.25	.11
❑ 274 Glenn Robinson CB	.15	.07
❑ 275 Joe Smith CB	.15	.07
❑ 276 Steve Smith CB	.10	.05
❑ 277 Jerry Stackhouse CB	.15	.07
❑ 278 Damon Stoudamire CB	.25	.11
❑ 279 Hakeem Olajuwon AS	.25	.11
❑ 280 Charles Barkley AS	.25	.11
❑ 281 Patrick Ewing AS	.15	.07
❑ 282 Michael Jordan AS	1.50	.70
❑ 283 Clyde Drexler AS	.15	.07
❑ 284 Karl Malone AS	.25	.11
❑ 285 John Stockton AS	.15	.07
❑ 286 David Robinson AS	.25	.11
❑ 287 Scottie Pippen AS	.40	.18
❑ 288 Shawn Kemp AS	.25	.11
❑ 289 Shaquille O'Neal AS	.50	.23
❑ 290 Mitch Richmond AS	.15	.07
❑ 291 Reggie Miller AS	.15	.07
❑ 292 Alonzo Mourning AS	.15	.07
❑ 293 Gary Payton AS	.25	.11
❑ 294 Anfernee Hardaway AS	.50	.23
❑ 295 Grant Hill AS	.75	.35
❑ 296 Dennis Rodman AS	.25	.11
❑ 297 Juwan Howard AS	.10	.05
❑ 298 Jason Kidd AS	.25	.11
❑ 299 Checklist	.10	.05
❑ 300 Checklist	.10	.05

1996-97 Fleer Decade of Excellence

	MINT	NRMT
COMPLETE SET (20)	150.00	70.00
COMPLETE SERIES 1 (10)	100.00	45.00
COMPLETE SERIES 2 (10)	50.00	22.00
COMMON CARD (1-20)	5.00	2.20
SEMISTARS	8.00	3.60

SER.1/2 STATED ODDS 1:72 HOBBY

Card	MINT	NRMT
❑ 1 Clyde Drexler	8.00	3.60
❑ 2 Joe Dumars	5.00	2.20
❑ 3 Derek Harper	5.00	2.20
❑ 4 Michael Jordan	80.00	36.00
❑ 5 Karl Malone	12.00	5.50
❑ 6 Chris Mullin	5.00	2.20
❑ 7 Charles Oakley	5.00	2.20
❑ 8 Sam Perkins	5.00	2.20
❑ 9 Ricky Pierce	5.00	2.20
❑ 10 Buck Williams	5.00	2.20
❑ 11 Charles Barkley	12.00	5.50
❑ 12 Patrick Ewing	8.00	3.60
❑ 13 Eddie Johnson	5.00	2.20
❑ 14 Hakeem Olajuwon	12.00	5.50
❑ 15 Robert Parish	5.00	2.20
❑ 16 Byron Scott	5.00	2.20
❑ 17 Wayman Tisdale	5.00	2.20
❑ 18 Gerald Wilkins	5.00	2.20
❑ 19 Herb Williams	5.00	2.20
❑ 20 Kevin Willis	5.00	2.20

1996-97 Fleer Franchise Futures

	MINT	NRMT
COMPLETE SET (10)	15.00	6.75
COMMON CARD (1-10)	1.25	.55

SER.1 STATED ODDS 1:54 HOBBY

Card	MINT	NRMT
❑ 1 Kevin Garnett	8.00	3.60
❑ 2 Anfernee Hardaway	4.00	1.80
❑ 3 Grant Hill	6.00	2.70
❑ 4 Juwan Howard	1.25	.55
❑ 5 Jason Kidd	4.00	1.80
❑ 6 Antonio McDyess	2.00	.90
❑ 7 Glenn Robinson	1.25	.55
❑ 8 Joe Smith	1.25	.55
❑ 9 Jerry Stackhouse	1.25	.55
❑ 10 Damon Stoudamire	2.00	.90

1996-97 Fleer Game Breakers

	MINT	NRMT
COMPLETE SET (15)	150.00	70.00
COMMON PAIR (1-15)	3.00	1.35

SER.1 STATED ODDS 1:48 RETAIL

Card	MINT	NRMT
❑ 1 Michael Jordan Scottie Pippen	80.00	36.00
❑ 2 Jim Jackson Jason Kidd	12.00	5.50
❑ 3 Grant Hill Allan Houston	20.00	9.00
❑ 4 Joe Smith Latrell Sprewell	8.00	3.60
❑ 5 Clyde Drexler Hakeem Olajuwon	10.00	4.50
❑ 6 Cedric Ceballos Nick Van Exel	3.00	1.35
❑ 7 Tim Hardaway Alonzo Mourning	3.00	1.35
❑ 8 Vin Baker Glenn Robinson	3.00	1.35
❑ 9 Kevin Garnett Isaiah Rider	20.00	9.00
❑ 10 Anfernee Hardaway Shaquille O'Neal	30.00	13.50
❑ 11 Jerry Stackhouse Clarence Weahterspoon	3.00	1.35
❑ 12 Charles Barkley Michael Finley	10.00	4.50
❑ 13 Sean Elliott David Robinson	6.00	2.70
❑ 14 Shawn Kemp Gary Payton	8.00	3.60
❑ 15 Karl Malone John Stockton	10.00	4.50

1996-97 Fleer Lucky 13

	MINT	NRMT
COMPLETE SET (13)	40.00	18.00
COMMON CARD (1-13)	1.00	.45
SEMISTARS	1.25	.55
UNLISTED STARS	2.00	.90

EXCH.CARDS: SER.1 STATED ODDS 1:30

Card	MINT	NRMT
❑ 1 Allen Iverson	10.00	4.50
❑ 2 Marcus Camby	3.00	1.35
❑ 3 Shareef Abdur-Rahim	6.00	2.70
❑ 4 Stephon Marbury	6.00	2.70
❑ 5 Ray Allen	4.00	1.80
❑ 6 Antoine Walker	4.00	1.80
❑ 7 Lorenzen Wright	1.00	.45
❑ 8 Kerry Kittles	2.00	.90
❑ 9 Samaki Walker	1.00	.45
❑ 10 Erick Dampier	1.00	.45
❑ 11 Todd Fuller	1.00	.45
❑ 12 Vitaly Potapenko	1.00	.45
❑ 13 Kobe Bryant	30.00	13.50
❑ NNO Expired Trade Cards	.30	.14

1996-97 Fleer Rookie Rewind

	MINT	NRMT
COMPLETE SET (15)	25.00	11.00
COMMON CARD (1-15)	1.00	.45
SEMISTARS	1.50	.70
UNLISTED STARS	2.50	1.10

SER.1 STATED ODDS 1:24 HOBBY/RETAIL

❑ 1 Brent Barry	1.00	.45
❑ 2 Tyus Edney	1.00	.45
❑ 3 Michael Finley	3.00	1.35
❑ 4 Kevin Garnett	15.00	6.75
❑ 5 Antonio McDyess	4.00	1.80
❑ 6 Bryant Reeves	1.00	.45
❑ 7 Arvydas Sabonis	1.50	.70
❑ 8 Joe Smith	2.50	1.10
❑ 9 Jerry Stackhouse	2.50	1.10
❑ 10 Damon Stoudamire	4.00	1.80
❑ 11 Bob Sura	1.00	.45
❑ 12 Kurt Thomas	1.00	.45
❑ 13 Gary Trent	1.00	.45
❑ 14 Rasheed Wallace	3.00	1.35
❑ 15 Eric Williams	1.00	.45

1996-97 Fleer Rookie Sensations

	MINT	NRMT
COMPLETE SET (15)	150.00	70.00
COMMON CARD (1-15)	3.00	1.35
SEMISTARS	4.00	1.80
UNLISTED STARS	6.00	2.70

SER.2 STATED ODDS 1:90 HOBBY/RETAIL

❑ 1 Shareef Abdur-Rahim	20.00	9.00
❑ 2 Ray Allen	12.00	5.50
❑ 3 Kobe Bryant	60.00	27.00
❑ 4 Marcus Camby	10.00	4.50
❑ 5 Erick Dampier	3.00	1.35
❑ 6 Tony Delk	3.00	1.35
❑ 7 Allen Iverson	30.00	13.50
❑ 8 Kerry Kittles	6.00	2.70
❑ 9 Stephon Marbury	20.00	9.00
❑ 10 Steve Nash	3.00	1.35
❑ 11 Roy Rogers	3.00	1.35
❑ 12 Antoine Walker	12.00	5.50
❑ 13 Samaki Walker	3.00	1.35
❑ 14 John Wallace	4.00	1.80
❑ 15 Lorenzen Wright	3.00	1.35

1996-97 Fleer Stackhouse's All-Fleer

	MINT	NRMT
COMPLETE SET (12)	20.00	9.00
COMMON CARD (1-12)	1.00	.45

SER.1 STATED ODDS 1:12 HOBBY/RETAIL
ONE PER SPECIAL SER.1 RETAIL PACK

❑ 1 Charles Barkley	1.25	.55
❑ 2 Anfernee Hardaway	2.50	1.10
❑ 3 Grant Hill	4.00	1.80
❑ 4 Michael Jordan	10.00	4.50
❑ 5 Shawn Kemp	1.25	.55
❑ 6 Jason Kidd	2.50	1.10
❑ 7 Karl Malone	1.25	.55
❑ 8 Hakeem Olajuwon	1.25	.55
❑ 9 Shaquille O'Neal	4.00	1.80
❑ 10 Gary Payton	1.25	.55
❑ 11 Scottie Pippen	2.50	1.10
❑ 12 David Robinson	1.25	.55

1996-97 Fleer Stackhouse's Scrapbook

	MINT	NRMT
COMPLETE SET (2)	5.00	2.20
COMMON STACK. (S9-S10)	2.50	1.10

SER.1 STATED ODDS 1:24 HOB/RET

❑ S9 Jerry Stackhouse	2.50	1.10
❑ S10 Jerry Stackhouse	2.50	1.10

1996-97 Fleer Swing Shift

	MINT	NRMT
COMPLETE SET (15)	12.00	5.50
COMMON CARD (1-15)	.40	.18
SEMISTARS	.50	.23
UNLISTED STARS	.75	.35

SER.2 STATED ODDS 1:6 HOBBY/RETAIL

❑ 1 Ray Allen	1.50	.70
❑ 2 Charles Barkley	1.25	.55
❑ 3 Michael Finley	1.00	.45
❑ 4 Anfernee Hardaway	2.50	1.10
❑ 5 Grant Hill	4.00	1.80
❑ 6 Jim Jackson	.40	.18
❑ 7 Eddie Jones	1.50	.70
❑ 8 Kerry Kittles	.75	.35
❑ 9 Reggie Miller	.75	.35
❑ 10 Gary Payton	1.25	.55
❑ 11 Scottie Pippen	2.50	1.10
❑ 12 Mitch Richmond	.75	.35
❑ 13 Steve Smith	.50	.23
❑ 14 Latrell Sprewell	1.50	.70
❑ 15 Jerry Stackhouse	.75	.35

1996-97 Fleer Thrill Seekers

	MINT	NRMT
COMPLETE SET (15)	400.00	180.00
COMMON CARD (1-15)	10.00	4.50

SER.2 STATED ODDS 1:240 HOBBY

❑ 1 Shareef Abdur-Rahim	30.00	13.50
❑ 2 Charles Barkley	15.00	6.75
❑ 3 Anfernee Hardaway	30.00	13.50
❑ 4 Grant Hill	50.00	22.00
❑ 5 Allen Iverson	50.00	22.00
❑ 6 Michael Jordan	120.00	55.00
❑ 7 Shawn Kemp	15.00	6.75
❑ 8 Jason Kidd	30.00	13.50
❑ 9 Stephon Marbury	30.00	13.50
❑ 10 Antonio McDyess	15.00	6.75
❑ 11 Reggie Miller	10.00	4.50
❑ 12 Alonzo Mourning	10.00	4.50
❑ 13 Shaquille O'Neal	50.00	22.00
❑ 14 David Robinson	15.00	6.75
❑ 15 Damon Stoudamire	15.00	6.75

1996-97 Fleer Total O

	MINT	NRMT
COMPLETE SET (10)	100.00	45.00
COMMON CARD (1-10)	4.00	1.80

SER.2 STATED ODDS 1:44 RETAIL

❑ 1 Anfernee Hardaway	12.00	5.50
❑ 2 Grant Hill	20.00	9.00
❑ 3 Juwan Howard	4.00	1.80
❑ 4 Michael Jordan	50.00	22.00
❑ 5 Shawn Kemp	6.00	2.70
❑ 6 Karl Malone	6.00	2.70
❑ 7 Alonzo Mourning	4.00	1.80
❑ 8 Hakeem Olajuwon	6.00	2.70
❑ 9 Shaquille O'Neal	20.00	9.00
❑ 10 Jerry Stackhouse	4.00	1.80

1996-97 Fleer Towers of Power

	MINT	NRMT
COMPLETE SET (10)	30.00	13.50
COMMON CARD (1-10)	2.00	.90

SER.2 STATED ODDS 1:30 HOBBY/RETAIL

❑ 1 Shareef Abdur-Rahim	6.00	2.70
❑ 2 Marcus Camby	3.00	1.35
❑ 3 Patrick Ewing	2.00	.90
❑ 4 Kevin Garnett	12.00	5.50
❑ 5 Shawn Kemp	3.00	1.35
❑ 6 Hakeem Olajuwon	3.00	1.35
❑ 7 Shaquille O'Neal	10.00	4.50
❑ 8 David Robinson	3.00	1.35
❑ 9 Dennis Rodman	4.00	1.80
❑ 10 Joe Smith	2.00	.90

1997-98 Fleer

	MINT	NRMT
COMPLETE SET (350)	40.00	18.00
COMPLETE SERIES 1 (200)	20.00	9.00
COMPLETE SERIES 2 (150)	20.00	9.00
COMMON CARD (1-350)	.10	.05
SEMISTARS	.15	.07
UNLISTED STARS	.25	.11

❑ 1 Anfernee Hardaway	.75	.35
❑ 2 Mitch Richmond	.25	.11
❑ 3 Allen Iverson	1.25	.55
❑ 4 Chris Webber	.75	.35
❑ 5 Sasha Danilovic	.10	.05
❑ 6 Avery Johnson	.10	.05
❑ 7 Kenny Anderson	.15	.07
❑ 8 Antoine Walker	.50	.23
❑ 9 Nick Van Exel	.15	.07
❑ 10 Mookie Blaylock	.10	.05
❑ 11 Wesley Person	.10	.05
❑ 12 Vlade Divac	.10	.05
❑ 13 Glenn Robinson	.15	.07
❑ 14 Chris Mills	.10	.05
❑ 15 Latrell Sprewell	.50	.23
❑ 16 Jayson Williams	.15	.07
❑ 17 Travis Best	.10	.05
❑ 18 Charlie Ward	.10	.05
❑ 19 Theo Ratliff	.10	.05
❑ 20 Gary Payton	.40	.18
❑ 21 Marcus Camby	.30	.14
❑ 22 Clyde Drexler	.25	.11
❑ 23 Michael Jordan	3.00	1.35
❑ 24 Antonio McDyess	.30	.14
❑ 25 Stephon Marbury	.75	.35
❑ 26 Isaac Austin	.10	.05
❑ 27 Shareef Abdur-Rahim	.75	.35
❑ 28 Malik Sealy	.10	.05
❑ 29 Arvydas Sabonis	.15	.07
❑ 30 Kerry Kittles	.25	.11
❑ 31 Reggie Miller	.25	.11
❑ 32 Karl Malone	.40	.18
❑ 33 Grant Hill	1.25	.55
❑ 34 Hakeem Olajuwon	.40	.18
❑ 35 Danny Ferry	.10	.05
❑ 36 Dominique Wilkins	.25	.11
❑ 37 Armon Gilliam	.10	.05
❑ 38 Danny Manning	.15	.07
❑ 39 Larry Johnson	.15	.07
❑ 40 Dino Radja	.10	.05
❑ 41 Jason Caffey	.10	.05
❑ 42 Jerry Stackhouse	.15	.07
❑ 43 Alonzo Mourning	.25	.11
❑ 44 Shawn Bradley	.10	.05
❑ 45 Bo Outlaw	.10	.05
❑ 46 Bryon Russell	.10	.05
❑ 47 Doug West	.10	.05
❑ 48 Lawrence Moten	.10	.05
❑ 49 Dale Ellis	.10	.05
❑ 50 Kobe Bryant	2.00	.90
❑ 51 Carlos Rogers	.10	.05
❑ 52 Todd Fuller	.10	.05
❑ 53 Tyus Edney	.10	.05
❑ 54 Horace Grant	.15	.07
❑ 55 Dikembe Mutombo	.15	.07
❑ 56 Jim McIlvaine	.10	.05
❑ 57 Harvey Grant	.10	.05
❑ 58 Dean Garrett	.10	.05
❑ 59 Samaki Walker	.10	.05
❑ 60 Johnny Newman	.10	.05
❑ 61 Antonio Davis	.10	.05
❑ 62 Jamal Mashburn	.15	.07
❑ 63 Muggsy Bogues	.10	.05
❑ 64 Rod Strickland	.15	.07
❑ 65 Craig Ehlo	.10	.05
❑ 66 Rex Walters	.10	.05
❑ 67 Bob Sura	.10	.05
❑ 68 Travis Knight	.10	.05
❑ 69 Toni Kukoc	.30	.14
❑ 70 Antoine Carr	.10	.05
❑ 71 Mario Elie	.10	.05
❑ 72 Popeye Jones	.10	.05
❑ 73 David Wesley	.10	.05
❑ 74 John Wallace	.10	.05
❑ 75 Calbert Cheaney	.10	.05
❑ 76 Grant Long	.10	.05
❑ 77 Will Perdue	.10	.05
❑ 78 Rasheed Wallace	.25	.11
❑ 79 Chris Gatling	.10	.05
❑ 80 Corliss Williamson	.10	.05
❑ 81 B.J. Armstrong	.10	.05
❑ 82 Brian Shaw	.10	.05
❑ 83 Darrick Martin	.10	.05
❑ 84 Vinny Del Negro	.10	.05
❑ 85 Tony Delk	.10	.05
❑ 86 Greg Anthony	.10	.05
❑ 87 Mark Davis	.10	.05
❑ 88 Anthony Goldwire	.10	.05
❑ 89 Rex Chapman	.10	.05
❑ 90 Stojko Vrankovic	.10	.05
❑ 91 Dennis Rodman	.50	.23
❑ 92 Detlef Schrempf	.15	.07
❑ 93 Henry James	.10	.05
❑ 94 Tracy Murray	.10	.05
❑ 95 Voshon Lenard	.10	.05
❑ 96 Sharone Wright	.10	.05
❑ 97 Ed O'Bannon	.10	.05
❑ 98 Gerald Wilkins	.10	.05
❑ 99 Kevin Willis	.10	.05
❑ 100 Shaquille O'Neal	1.25	.55
❑ 101 Jim Jackson	.10	.05
❑ 102 Mark Price	.10	.05
❑ 103 Patrick Ewing	.25	.11
❑ 104 Lorenzen Wright	.10	.05
❑ 105 Tyrone Hill	.10	.05
❑ 106 Ray Allen	.40	.18
❑ 107 Jermaine O'Neal	.15	.07
❑ 108 Anthony Mason	.15	.07
❑ 109 Mahmoud Abdul-Rauf	.10	.05
❑ 110 Terry Mills	.10	.05
❑ 111 Gheorghe Muresan	.10	.05
❑ 112 Mark Jackson	.10	.05
❑ 113 Greg Ostertag	.10	.05
❑ 114 Kevin Johnson	.15	.07
❑ 115 Anthony Peeler	.10	.05
❑ 116 Rony Seikaly	.10	.05
❑ 117 Keith Askins	.10	.05
❑ 118 Todd Day	.10	.05
❑ 119 Chris Childs	.10	.05
❑ 120 Chris Carr	.10	.05
❑ 121 Erick Strickland RC	.15	.07
❑ 122 Elden Campbell	.10	.05
❑ 123 Elliot Perry	.10	.05
❑ 124 Pooh Richardson	.10	.05
❑ 125 Juwan Howard	.15	.07
❑ 126 Ervin Johnson	.10	.05
❑ 127 Eric Montross	.10	.05
❑ 128 Otis Thorpe	.10	.05
❑ 129 Hersey Hawkins	.15	.07
❑ 130 Bimbo Coles	.10	.05
❑ 131 Olden Polynice	.10	.05
❑ 132 Christian Laettner	.15	.07
❑ 133 Sean Elliott	.10	.05
❑ 134 Othella Harrington	.10	.05
❑ 135 Erick Dampier	.10	.05
❑ 136 Vitaly Potapenko	.10	.05
❑ 137 Doug Christie	.10	.05
❑ 138 Luc Longley	.10	.05
❑ 139 Clarence Weatherspoon	.10	.05
❑ 140 Gary Trent	.10	.05
❑ 141 Shandon Anderson	.10	.05
❑ 142 Sam Perkins	.15	.07
❑ 143 Derek Harper	.10	.05
❑ 144 Robert Horry	.10	.05
❑ 145 Roy Rogers	.10	.05
❑ 146 John Starks	.10	.05
❑ 147 Tyrone Corbin	.10	.05
❑ 148 Andrew Lang	.10	.05
❑ 149 Derek Strong	.10	.05
❑ 150 Joe Smith	.15	.07
❑ 151 Ron Harper	.15	.07
❑ 152 Sam Cassell	.15	.07
❑ 153 Brent Barry	.10	.05
❑ 154 LaPhonso Ellis	.10	.05
❑ 155 Matt Geiger	.10	.05
❑ 156 Steve Nash	.10	.05
❑ 157 Michael Smith	.10	.05
❑ 158 Eric Williams	.10	.05
❑ 159 Tom Gugliotta	.15	.07
❑ 160 Monty Williams	.10	.05
❑ 161 Lindsey Hunter	.10	.05
❑ 162 Oliver Miller	.10	.05
❑ 163 Brent Price	.10	.05
❑ 164 Derrick McKey	.10	.05
❑ 165 Robert Pack	.10	.05
❑ 166 Derrick Coleman	.15	.07
❑ 167 Isaiah Rider	.15	.07
❑ 168 Dan Majerle	.15	.07
❑ 169 Jeff Hornacek	.15	.07
❑ 170 Terrell Brandon	.15	.07
❑ 171 Nate McMillan	.10	.05
❑ 172 Cedric Ceballos	.10	.05
❑ 173 Derek Fisher	.10	.05
❑ 174 Rodney Rogers	.10	.05
❑ 175 Blue Edwards	.10	.05
❑ 176 Brooks Thompson	.10	.05
❑ 177 Sherman Douglas	.10	.05
❑ 178 Sam Mitchell	.10	.05
❑ 179 Charles Oakley	.10	.05
❑ 180 Greg Minor	.10	.05
❑ 181 Chris Mullin	.25	.11
❑ 182 P.J. Brown	.10	.05
❑ 183 Stacey Augmon	.10	.05
❑ 184 Don MacLean	.10	.05
❑ 185 Aaron McKie	.10	.05
❑ 186 Dale Davis	.10	.05
❑ 187 Vernon Maxwell	.10	.05
❑ 188 Dell Curry	.10	.05
❑ 189 Kendall Gill	.15	.07
❑ 190 Billy Owens	.10	.05
❑ 191 Steve Kerr	.10	.05
❑ 192 Matt Maloney	.10	.05
❑ 193 Dennis Scott	.10	.05
❑ 194 A.C. Green	.15	.07
❑ 195 George McCloud	.10	.05
❑ 196 Walt Williams	.10	.05
❑ 197 Eldridge Recasner	.10	.05
❑ 198 Checklist (Hawks/Bucks)	.10	.05
❑ 199 Checklist (T'wolves/Wizards)	.10	.05
❑ 200 Checklist	.10	.05

Card	MINT	NRMT
(inserts)		
❑ 201 Tim Duncan RC	3.00	1.35
❑ 202 Tim Thomas RC	.75	.35
❑ 203 Clifford Rozier	.10	.05
❑ 204 Bryant Reeves	.10	.05
❑ 205 Glen Rice	.15	.07
❑ 206 Darrell Armstrong	.15	.07
❑ 207 Juwan Howard	.15	.07
❑ 208 John Stockton	.25	.11
❑ 209 Antonio McDyess	.30	.14
❑ 210 James Cotton RC	.10	.05
❑ 211 Brian Grant	.15	.07
❑ 212 Chris Whitney	.10	.05
❑ 213 Antonio Davis	.10	.05
❑ 214 Kendall Gill	.15	.07
❑ 215 Adonal Foyle RC	.15	.07
❑ 216 Dean Garrett	.10	.05
❑ 217 Dennis Scott	.10	.05
❑ 218 Zydrunas Ilgauskas	.10	.05
❑ 219 Antonio Daniels RC	.25	.11
❑ 220 Derek Harper	.10	.05
❑ 221 Travis Knight	.10	.05
❑ 222 Bobby Hurley	.10	.05
❑ 223 Greg Anderson	.10	.05
❑ 224 Rod Strickland	.15	.07
❑ 225 David Benoit	.10	.05
❑ 226 Tracy McGrady RC	2.50	1.10
❑ 227 Brian Williams	.10	.05
❑ 228 James Robinson	.10	.05
❑ 229 Randy Brown	.10	.05
❑ 230 Greg Foster	.10	.05
❑ 231 Reggie Miller	.25	.11
❑ 232 Eric Montross	.10	.05
❑ 233 Malik Rose	.10	.05
❑ 234 Charles Barkley	.40	.18
❑ 235 Tony Battie RC	.25	.11
❑ 236 Terry Mills	.10	.05
❑ 237 Jerald Honeycutt RC	.10	.05
❑ 238 Bubba Wells RC	.10	.05
❑ 239 John Wallace	.10	.05
❑ 240 Jason Kidd	.75	.35
❑ 241 Mark Price	.10	.05
❑ 242 Ron Mercer RC	.75	.35
❑ 243 Derrick Coleman	.15	.07
❑ 244 Fred Hoiberg	.10	.05
❑ 245 Wesley Person	.10	.05
❑ 246 Eddie Jones	.50	.23
❑ 247 Allan Houston	.25	.11
❑ 248 Keith Van Horn RC	1.25	.55
❑ 249 Johnny Newman	.10	.05
❑ 250 Kevin Garnett	1.50	.70
❑ 251 Latrell Sprewell	.50	.23
❑ 252 Tracy Murray	.10	.05
❑ 253 Charles O'Bannon RC	.10	.05
❑ 254 Lamond Murray	.10	.05
❑ 255 Jerry Stackhouse	.15	.07
❑ 256 Rik Smits	.10	.05
❑ 257 Alan Henderson	.10	.05
❑ 258 Tariq Abdul-Wahad RC	.15	.07
❑ 259 Nick Anderson	.10	.05
❑ 260 Calbert Cheaney	.10	.05
❑ 261 Scottie Pippen	.75	.35
❑ 262 Rodrick Rhodes RC	.10	.05
❑ 263 Derek Anderson RC	.60	.25
❑ 264 Dana Barros	.10	.05
❑ 265 Todd Day	.10	.05
❑ 266 Michael Finley	.25	.11
❑ 267 Kevin Edwards	.10	.05
❑ 268 Terrell Brandon	.15	.07
❑ 269 Bobby Phills	.10	.05
❑ 270 Kelvin Cato RC	.25	.11
❑ 271 Vin Baker	.15	.07
❑ 272 Eric Washington RC	.25	.11
❑ 273 Jim Jackson	.10	.05
❑ 274 Joe Dumars	.25	.11
❑ 275 David Robinson	.40	.18
❑ 276 Jayson Williams	.15	.07
❑ 277 Travis Best	.10	.05
❑ 278 Kurt Thomas	.10	.05
❑ 279 Otis Thorpe	.10	.05
❑ 280 Damon Stoudamire	.30	.14
❑ 281 John Williams	.10	.05
❑ 282 Loy Vaught	.10	.05
❑ 283 Charles Outlaw	.10	.05
❑ 284 Todd Fuller	.10	.05
❑ 285 Terry Dehere	.10	.05
❑ 286 Clarence Weatherspoon	.10	.05
❑ 287 Danny Fortson RC	.25	.11
❑ 288 Howard Eisley	.10	.05
❑ 289 Steve Smith	.15	.07
❑ 290 Chris Webber	.75	.35
❑ 291 Shawn Kemp	.40	.18
❑ 292 Sam Cassell	.15	.07
❑ 293 Rick Fox	.10	.05
❑ 294 Walter McCarty	.10	.05
❑ 295 Mark Jackson	.10	.05
❑ 296 Chris Mills	.10	.05
❑ 297 Jacque Vaughn RC	.15	.07
❑ 298 Shawn Respert	.10	.05
❑ 299 Scott Burrell	.10	.05
❑ 300 Allen Iverson	1.25	.55
❑ 301 Charles Smith RC	.10	.05
❑ 302 Ervin Johnson	.10	.05
❑ 303 Hubert Davis	.10	.05
❑ 304 Eddie Johnson	.10	.05
❑ 305 Erick Dampier	.10	.05
❑ 306 Eric Williams	.10	.05
❑ 307 Anthony Johnson RC	.10	.05
❑ 308 David Wesley	.10	.05
❑ 309 Eric Piatkowski	.10	.05
❑ 310 Austin Croshere RC	.60	.25
❑ 311 Malik Sealy	.10	.05
❑ 312 George McCloud	.10	.05
❑ 313 Anthony Parker RC	.10	.05
❑ 314 Cedric Henderson RC	.15	.07
❑ 315 John Thomas RC	.10	.05
❑ 316 Cory Alexander	.10	.05
❑ 317 Johnny Taylor RC	.10	.05
❑ 318 Chris Mullin	.25	.11
❑ 319 J.R. Reid	.10	.05
❑ 320 George Lynch	.10	.05
❑ 321 L. Funderburke RC	.15	.07
❑ 322 God Shammgod RC	.10	.05
❑ 323 Bobby Jackson RC	.15	.07
❑ 324 Khalid Reeves	.10	.05
❑ 325 Zan Tabak	.10	.05
❑ 326 Chris Gatling	.10	.05
❑ 327 Alvin Williams RC	.10	.05
❑ 328 Scot Pollard RC	.15	.07
❑ 329 Kerry Kittles	.25	.11
❑ 330 Tim Hardaway	.25	.11
❑ 331 Maurice Taylor RC	.50	.23
❑ 332 Keith Booth RC	.10	.05
❑ 333 Chris Morris	.10	.05
❑ 334 Bryant Stith	.10	.05
❑ 335 Terry Cummings	.10	.05
❑ 336 Ed Gray RC	.10	.05
❑ 337 Eric Snow	.10	.05
❑ 338 Clifford Robinson	.10	.05
❑ 339 Chris Dudley	.10	.05
❑ 340 Chauncey Billups RC	.30	.14
❑ 341 Paul Grant RC	.10	.05
❑ 342 Tyrone Hill	.10	.05
❑ 343 Joe Smith	.15	.07
❑ 344 Sean Rooks	.10	.05
❑ 345 Harvey Grant	.10	.05
❑ 346 Dale Davis	.10	.05
❑ 347 Brevin Knight RC	.40	.18
❑ 348 Serge Zwikker RC	.10	.05
❑ 349 Checklist (Hawks/Kings)	.10	.05
❑ 350 Checklist (Spurs/Wizards/Inserts)	.10	.05

1997-98 Fleer Crystal Collection

	MINT	NRMT
COMPLETE SET (350)	240.00	110.00
COMPLETE SERIES 1 (197)	120.00	55.00
COMPLETE SERIES 2 (148)	120.00	55.00
COMMON CARD	.50	.23

*STARS: 2X TO 5X BASE CARD HI
*RCs: 1.5X TO 4X BASE HI
SER.1/2 STATED ODDS 1:2 HOB

1997-98 Fleer Tiffany Collection

	MINT	NRMT
COMPLETE SET (345)	1800.00	800.00
COMPLETE SERIES 1 (197)	800.00	350.00
COMPLETE SERIES 2 (148)	1000.00	450.00
COMMON CARD (1-197)	3.00	1.35
COMMON CARD (200-348)	4.00	1.80

*SER.1 STARS: 12.5X TO 30X BASE CARD HI
*SER.2 STARS: 15X TO 40X BASE HI
*RCs: 8X TO 20X BASE HI
SER.1/2 STATED ODDS 1:20 HOBBY

1997-98 Fleer Decade of Excellence

	MINT	NRMT
COMPLETE SET (12)	100.00	45.00
COMMON CARD (1-12)	3.00	1.35
UNLISTED STARS	5.00	2.20

SER.1 STATED ODDS 1:36 HOBBY

	MINT	NRMT
COMP.RARE TRAD. SET (12)	400.00	180.00
COMMON RARE TRAD. (1-12)	12.00	5.50

*RARE TRAD: 2X TO 4X HI COLUMN
RARE TRAD: SER.1 STATED ODDS 1:360 HOB

Card	MINT	NRMT
❑ 1 Charles Barkley	8.00	3.60
❑ 2 Clyde Drexler	5.00	2.20
❑ 3 Patrick Ewing	5.00	2.20
❑ 4 Kevin Johnson	3.00	1.35
❑ 5 Michael Jordan	60.00	27.00
❑ 6 Karl Malone	8.00	3.60
❑ 7 Reggie Miller	5.00	2.20
❑ 8 Hakeem Olajuwon	8.00	3.60
❑ 9 Scottie Pippen	15.00	6.75
❑ 10 Dennis Rodman	10.00	4.50
❑ 11 John Stockton	5.00	2.20
❑ 12 Dominique Wilkins	5.00	2.20

1997-98 Fleer Flair Hardwood Leaders

	MINT	NRMT
COMPLETE SET (29)	40.00	18.00
COMMON CARD (1-29)	.50	.23
SEMISTARS	.60	.25
UNLISTED STARS	1.00	.45

SER.1 STATED ODDS 1:6 HOBBY/RETAIL

❑ 1	Christian Laettner	.50	.23
❑ 2	Antoine Walker	2.00	.90
❑ 3	Glen Rice	.60	.25
❑ 4	Michael Jordan	15.00	6.75
❑ 5	Terrell Brandon	.50	.23
❑ 6	Michael Finley	1.00	.45
❑ 7	Antonio McDyess	1.25	.55
❑ 8	Grant Hill	5.00	2.20
❑ 9	Latrell Sprewell	2.00	.90
❑ 10	Hakeem Olajuwon	1.50	.70
❑ 11	Reggie Miller	1.00	.45
❑ 12	Loy Vaught	.50	.23
❑ 13	Shaquille O'Neal	5.00	2.20
❑ 14	Alonzo Mourning	1.00	.45
❑ 15	Vin Baker	.60	.25
❑ 16	Kevin Garnett	6.00	2.70
❑ 17	Kerry Kittles	1.00	.45
❑ 18	Patrick Ewing	1.00	.45
❑ 19	Anfernee Hardaway	3.00	1.35
❑ 20	Jerry Stackhouse	.60	.25
❑ 21	Jason Kidd	3.00	1.35
❑ 22	Kenny Anderson	.50	.23
❑ 23	Mitch Richmond	1.00	.45
❑ 24	David Robinson	1.50	.70
❑ 25	Shawn Kemp	1.50	.70
❑ 26	Damon Stoudamire	1.25	.55
❑ 27	Karl Malone	1.50	.70
❑ 28	Shareef Abdur-Rahim	3.00	1.35
❑ 29	Chris Webber	3.00	1.35

1997-98 Fleer Franchise Futures

	MINT	NRMT
COMPLETE SET (10)	60.00	27.00
COMMON CARD (1-10)	3.00	1.35

SER.1 STATED ODDS 1:36 RETAIL

❑ 1	Shareef Abdur-Rahim	10.00	4.50
❑ 2	Ray Allen	5.00	2.20
❑ 3	Kobe Bryant	25.00	11.00
❑ 4	Kevin Garnett	20.00	9.00
❑ 5	Grant Hill	15.00	6.75
❑ 6	Juwan Howard	3.00	1.35
❑ 7	Allen Iverson	15.00	6.75
❑ 8	Kerry Kittles	3.00	1.35
❑ 9	Joe Smith	3.00	1.35
❑ 10	Damon Stoudamire	4.00	1.80

1997-98 Fleer Game Breakers

	MINT	NRMT
COMPLETE SET (12)	450.00	200.00
COMMON CARD (1-12)	20.00	9.00

SER.1 STATED ODDS 1:288 HOBBY/RETAIL

❑ 1	Michael Jordan Dennis Rodman	120.00	55.00
❑ 2	Joe Dumars Grant Hill	50.00	22.00
❑ 3	Joe Smith Latrell Sprewell	30.00	13.50
❑ 4	Charles Barkley Hakeem Olajuwon	30.00	13.50

❑ 5	Eddie Jones Shaquille O'Neal	60.00	27.00
❑ 6	Kevin Garnett Stephon Marbury	50.00	22.00
❑ 7	Nick Anderson Anfernee Hardaway	30.00	13.50
❑ 8	Allen Iverson Jerry Stackhouse	30.00	13.50
❑ 9	Shawn Kemp Gary Payton	30.00	13.50
❑ 10	Marcus Camby Damon Stoudamire	20.00	9.00
❑ 11	Karl Malone John Stockton	25.00	11.00
❑ 12	Juwan Howard Chris Webber	30.00	13.50

1997-98 Fleer Goudey Greats

	MINT	NRMT
COMPLETE SET (15)	12.00	5.50
COMMON CARD (1-15)	.60	.25

SER.2 STATED ODDS 1:4 HOBBY/RETAIL

❑ 1	Ray Allen	1.00	.45
❑ 2	Clyde Drexler	.60	.25
❑ 3	Patrick Ewing	.60	.25
❑ 4	Anfernee Hardaway	2.00	.90
❑ 5	Grant Hill	3.00	1.35
❑ 6	Stephon Marbury	2.00	.90
❑ 7	Alonzo Mourning	.60	.25
❑ 8	Shaquille O'Neal	3.00	1.35
❑ 9	Gary Payton	1.00	.45
❑ 10	Scottie Pippen	2.00	.90
❑ 11	David Robinson	1.00	.45
❑ 12	Joe Smith	.60	.25
❑ 13	John Stockton	.60	.25
❑ 14	Damon Stoudamire	.75	.35
❑ 15	Antoine Walker	1.25	.55

1997-98 Fleer Key Ingredients

	MINT	NRMT
COMPLETE SET (15)	6.00	2.70
COMMON CARD (1-15)	.30	.14

SER.1 STATED ODDS 1:2 RETAIL

COMP.GOLD SET (15)	40.00	18.00
COMMON GOLD (1-15)	2.00	.90

*GOLD: 3X TO 6X HI COLUMN
GOLD: SER.1 STATED ODDS 1:18 HOB/RET

❑ 1	Charles Barkley	.50	.23
❑ 2	Marcus Camby	.40	.18
❑ 3	Anfernee Hardaway	1.00	.45
❑ 4	Juwan Howard	.30	.14
❑ 5	Shawn Kemp	.50	.23
❑ 6	Karl Malone	.50	.23
❑ 7	Stephon Marbury	1.00	.45
❑ 8	Alonzo Mourning	.30	.14
❑ 9	Shaquille O'Neal	1.50	.70
❑ 10	Scottie Pippen	1.00	.45
❑ 11	Mitch Richmond	.30	.14
❑ 12	David Robinson	.50	.23
❑ 13	Joe Smith	.30	.14
❑ 14	Jerry Stackhouse	.30	.14
❑ 15	Antoine Walker	.60	.25

1997-98 Fleer Million Dollar Moments

	MINT	NRMT
COMPLETE SET (45)	5.00	2.20
COMMON CARD (1-45)	.05	.02
SEMISTARS	.10	.05
UNLISTED STARS	.15	.07

*STARS: .25X TO .6X BASE CARD HI
ONE PER FLEER/ULTRA PACK

❑ 1	Checklist (1-50)	.05	.02
❑ 2	Mark Jackson	.05	.02
❑ 3	Charles Barkley	.25	.11
❑ 4	Terrell Brandon	.10	.05
❑ 5	Wayman Tisdale	.05	.02
❑ 6	Clyde Drexler	.15	.07
❑ 7	Patrick Ewing	.15	.07
❑ 8	Kevin Garnett	1.00	.45
❑ 9	Tom Gugliotta	.10	.05
❑ 10	Anfernee Hardaway	.75	.35
❑ 11	Tim Hardaway	.15	.07
❑ 12	Grant Hill	1.00	.45
❑ 13	Allen Iverson	1.00	.45
❑ 14	Shawn Kemp	.50	.23
❑ 15	Jason Kidd	.15	.07
❑ 16	Charles Oakley	.05	.02
❑ 17	Karl Malone	.20	.09
❑ 18	Alonzo Mourning	.15	.07
❑ 19	Shaquille O'Neal	.60	.25
❑ 20	Hakeem Olajuwon	.40	.18
❑ 21	Chris Webber	.40	.18
❑ 22	Scottie Pippen	.50	.23

❑ 23 Glen Rice	.10	.05
❑ 24 Mitch Richmond	.15	.07
❑ 25 David Robinson	.25	.11
❑ 26 Dennis Rodman	.60	.25
❑ 27 Jerry Stackhouse	.10	.05
❑ 28 John Stockton	.15	.07
❑ 29 Mookie Blaylock	.05	.02
❑ 30 Muggsy Bogues	.05	.02
❑ 31 Kobe Bryant	1.25	.55
❑ 32 Rex Chapman	.05	.02
❑ 33 Joe Dumars	.15	.07
❑ 34 Dale Ellis	.05	.02
❑ 35 Horace Grant	.10	.05
❑ 36 Jeff Hornacek	.10	.05
❑ 37 Damon Stoudamire	.30	.14
❑ 38 Kevin Johnson	.10	.05
❑ 39 Larry Johnson	.10	.05
❑ 40 Toni Kukoc	.10	.05
❑ 41 Danny Manning	.10	.05
❑ 42 Stephon Marbury	.60	.25
❑ 43 Reggie Miller	.15	.07
❑ 44 Chris Mullin	.15	.07
❑ 45 Dikembe Mutombo	.10	.05

1997-98 Fleer Rookie Rewind

	MINT	NRMT
COMPLETE SET (10)	15.00	6.75
COMMON CARD (1-10)	.40	.18
SEMISTARS	.60	.25
UNLISTED STARS	1.00	.45

SER.1 STATED ODDS 1:4 HOBBY/RETAIL

❑ 1 Shareef Abdur-Rahim	3.00	1.35
❑ 2 Ray Allen	1.50	.70
❑ 3 Kobe Bryant	8.00	3.60
❑ 4 Marcus Camby	1.25	.55
❑ 5 Allen Iverson	5.00	2.20
❑ 6 Kerry Kittles	1.00	.45
❑ 7 Matt Maloney	.40	.18
❑ 8 Stephon Marbury	3.00	1.35
❑ 9 Roy Rogers	.40	.18
❑ 10 Antoine Walker	2.00	.90

1997-98 Fleer Rookie Sensations

	MINT	NRMT
COMPLETE SET (10)	25.00	11.00
COMMON CARD (1-10)	1.25	.55
UNLISTED STARS	2.00	.90

SER.2 STATED ODDS 1:8 HOBBY/RETAIL

❑ 1 Derek Anderson	2.50	1.10
❑ 2 Tony Battie	1.25	.55
❑ 3 Chauncey Billups	2.00	.90
❑ 4 Austin Croshere	2.50	1.10
❑ 5 Antonio Daniels	2.00	.90
❑ 6 Tim Duncan	10.00	4.50
❑ 7 Tracy McGrady	10.00	4.50
❑ 8 Ron Mercer	3.00	1.35
❑ 9 Tim Thomas	3.00	1.35
❑ 10 Keith Van Horn	5.00	2.20

1997-98 Fleer Soaring Stars

	MINT	NRMT
COMPLETE SET (20)	15.00	6.75
COMMON CARD (1-20)	.20	.09
SEMISTARS	.25	.11
UNLISTED STARS	.40	.18

SER.2 STATED ODDS 1:2 RETAIL

COMP.HIGH FLY (20)	60.00	27.00
COMMON HIGH FLY (1-20)	1.00	.45

*HIGH FLY STARS: 2X TO 4X HI COLUMN
HIGH FLY: SER.2 STATED ODDS 1:24 H/R

❑ 1 Shareef Abdur-Rahim	1.25	.55
❑ 2 Ray Allen	.60	.25
❑ 3 Charles Barkley	.60	.25
❑ 4 Kobe Bryant	3.00	1.35
❑ 5 Marcus Camby	.50	.23
❑ 6 Kevin Garnett	2.50	1.10
❑ 7 Tim Hardaway	.40	.18
❑ 8 Eddie Jones	.75	.35
❑ 9 Michael Jordan	5.00	2.20
❑ 10 Shawn Kemp	.60	.25
❑ 11 Jason Kidd	1.25	.55
❑ 12 Kerry Kittles	.40	.18
❑ 13 Karl Malone	.60	.25
❑ 14 Antonio McDyess	.50	.23
❑ 15 Glen Rice	.25	.11
❑ 16 Mitch Richmond	.40	.18
❑ 17 Latrell Sprewell	.75	.35
❑ 18 Jerry Stackhouse	.20	.09
❑ 19 Antoine Walker	.75	.35
❑ 20 Chris Webber	1.25	.55

1997-98 Fleer Thrill Seekers

	MINT	NRMT
COMPLETE SET (10)	200.00	90.00
COMMON CARD (1-10)	4.00	1.80

SER.2 STATED ODDS 1:288 HOBBY/RETAIL

❑ 1 Shareef Abdur-Rahim	15.00	6.75
❑ 2 Kobe Bryant	40.00	18.00
❑ 3 Tim Duncan	25.00	11.00
❑ 4 Anfernee Hardaway	15.00	6.75
❑ 5 Grant Hill	25.00	11.00
❑ 6 Allen Iverson	25.00	11.00
❑ 7 Michael Jordan	60.00	27.00
❑ 8 Stephon Marbury	15.00	6.75
❑ 9 Dennis Rodman	10.00	4.50
❑ 10 Joe Smith	4.00	1.80

1997-98 Fleer Total O

	MINT	NRMT
COMPLETE SET (10)	50.00	22.00
COMMON CARD (1-10)	1.25	.55

SER.2 STATED ODDS 1:18 RETAIL

❑ 1 Anfernee Hardaway	5.00	2.20
❑ 2 Grant Hill	8.00	3.60
❑ 3 Juwan Howard	1.25	.55
❑ 4 Allen Iverson	8.00	3.60
❑ 5 Michael Jordan	20.00	9.00
❑ 6 Karl Malone	2.50	1.10
❑ 7 Stephon Marbury	5.00	2.20
❑ 8 Hakeem Olajuwon	2.50	1.10
❑ 9 Shaquille O'Neal	8.00	3.60
❑ 10 Damon Stoudamire	2.00	.90

1997-98 Fleer Towers of Power

	MINT	NRMT
COMPLETE SET (12)	30.00	13.50
COMMON CARD (1-12)	1.50	.70

SER.2 STATED ODDS 1:18 HOBBY/RETAIL

❑ 1 Shareef Abdur-Rahim	5.00	2.20
❑ 2 Marcus Camby	2.00	.90
❑ 3 Patrick Ewing	1.50	.70
❑ 4 Kevin Garnett	10.00	4.50
❑ 5 Shawn Kemp	2.50	1.10
❑ 6 Karl Malone	2.50	1.10

Card	MINT	NRMT
❑ 7 Hakeem Olajuwon	2.50	1.10
❑ 8 Shaquille O'Neal	8.00	3.60
❑ 9 Dennis Rodman	3.00	1.35
❑ 10 Joe Smith	1.50	.70
❑ 11 Antoine Walker	3.00	1.35
❑ 12 Chris Webber	5.00	2.20

1997-98 Fleer Zone

	MINT	NRMT
COMPLETE SET (15)	120.00	55.00
COMMON CARD (1-15)	3.00	1.35

SER.2 STATED ODDS 1:36 HOBBY

Card	MINT	NRMT
❑ 1 Shareef Abdur-Rahim	10.00	4.50
❑ 2 Kobe Bryant	25.00	11.00
❑ 3 Marcus Camby	4.00	1.80
❑ 4 Tim Duncan	15.00	6.75
❑ 5 Kevin Garnett	20.00	9.00
❑ 6 Anfernee Hardaway	10.00	4.50
❑ 7 Grant Hill	15.00	6.75
❑ 8 Juwan Howard	3.00	1.35
❑ 9 Allen Iverson	15.00	6.75
❑ 10 Michael Jordan	40.00	18.00
❑ 11 Hakeem Olajuwon	5.00	2.20
❑ 12 Gary Payton	5.00	2.20
❑ 13 Scottie Pippen	10.00	4.50
❑ 14 Glen Rice	3.00	1.35
❑ 15 Keith Van Horn	8.00	3.60

1998-99 Fleer

	MINT	NRMT
COMPLETE SET (150)	20.00	9.00
COMMON CARD (1-150)	.10	.05
SEMISTARS	.15	.07
UNLISTED STARS	.25	.11

Card	MINT	NRMT
❑ 1 Kobe Bryant	2.00	.90
❑ 2 Corliss Williamson	.10	.05
❑ 3 Allen Iverson	1.00	.45
❑ 4 Michael Finley	.25	.11
❑ 5 Juwan Howard	.15	.07
❑ 6 Marcus Camby	.25	.11
❑ 7 Toni Kukoc	.30	.14
❑ 8 Antoine Walker	.40	.18
❑ 9 Stephon Marbury	.60	.25
❑ 10 Tim Hardaway	.25	.11
❑ 11 Zydrunas Ilgauskas	.10	.05
❑ 12 John Stockton	.25	.11
❑ 13 Glenn Robinson	.15	.07
❑ 14 Isaiah Rider	.15	.07
❑ 15 Danny Fortson	.15	.07
❑ 16 Donyell Marshall	.10	.05
❑ 17 Chris Mullin	.25	.11
❑ 18 Shareef Abdur-Rahim	.60	.25
❑ 19 Bobby Phills	.10	.05
❑ 20 Gary Payton	.40	.18
❑ 21 Derrick Coleman	.15	.07
❑ 22 Larry Johnson	.15	.07
❑ 23 Michael Jordan	3.00	1.35
❑ 24 Danny Manning	.15	.07
❑ 25 Nick Anderson	.10	.05
❑ 26 Chris Gatling	.10	.05
❑ 27 Steve Smith	.15	.07
❑ 28 Chris Whitney	.10	.05
❑ 29 Terrell Brandon	.15	.07
❑ 30 Rasheed Wallace	.25	.11
❑ 31 Reggie Miller	.25	.11
❑ 32 Karl Malone	.40	.18
❑ 33 Grant Hill	1.25	.55
❑ 34 Hakeem Olajuwon	.40	.18
❑ 35 Erick Dampier	.10	.05
❑ 36 Vin Baker	.15	.07
❑ 37 Tim Thomas	.40	.18
❑ 38 Mark Price	.10	.05
❑ 39 Shawn Bradley	.10	.05
❑ 40 Calbert Cheaney	.10	.05
❑ 41 Glen Rice	.15	.07
❑ 42 Kevin Willis	.10	.05
❑ 43 Chris Carr	.10	.05
❑ 44 Keith Van Horn	.60	.25
❑ 45 Jamal Mashburn	.15	.07
❑ 46 Eddie Jones	.50	.23
❑ 47 Brevin Knight	.10	.05
❑ 48 Olden Polynice	.10	.05
❑ 49 Bobby Jackson	.10	.05
❑ 50 David Robinson	.40	.18
❑ 51 Patrick Ewing	.25	.11
❑ 52 Samaki Walker	.10	.05
❑ 53 Antonio Daniels	.10	.05
❑ 54 Rodney Rogers	.10	.05
❑ 55 Dikembe Mutombo	.15	.07
❑ 56 Tracy McGrady	1.00	.45
❑ 57 Walt Williams	.10	.05
❑ 58 Walter McCarty	.10	.05
❑ 59 Detlef Schrempf	.15	.07
❑ 60 Ervin Johnson	.10	.05
❑ 61 Michael Smith	.10	.05
❑ 62 Clifford Robinson	.10	.05
❑ 63 Brian Williams	.10	.05
❑ 64 Shandon Anderson	.10	.05
❑ 65 P.J. Brown	.10	.05
❑ 66 Scottie Pippen	.75	.35
❑ 67 Anthony Peeler	.10	.05
❑ 68 Tony Delk	.10	.05
❑ 69 David Wesley	.10	.05
❑ 70 John Starks	.10	.05
❑ 71 Nick Van Exel	.15	.07
❑ 72 Kerry Kittles	.15	.07
❑ 73 Tony Battie	.15	.07
❑ 74 Lamond Murray	.10	.05
❑ 75 Anfernee Hardaway	.75	.35
❑ 76 Jalen Rose	.25	.11
❑ 77 Derek Anderson	.30	.14
❑ 78 Avery Johnson	.10	.05
❑ 79 Michael Stewart	.10	.05
❑ 80 Brian Shaw	.10	.05
❑ 81 Chauncey Billups	.10	.05
❑ 82 Kenny Anderson	.15	.07
❑ 83 Bryon Russell	.10	.05
❑ 84 Jason Kidd	.75	.35
❑ 85 Tyrone Hill	.10	.05
❑ 86 Jim McIlvaine	.10	.05
❑ 87 Brian Grant	.15	.07
❑ 88 Bryant Stith	.10	.05
❑ 89 Brent Price	.10	.05
❑ 90 John Wallace	.10	.05
❑ 91 Dennis Rodman	.50	.23
❑ 92 Alonzo Mourning	.25	.11
❑ 93 Bimbo Coles	.10	.05
❑ 94 Chris Anstey	.10	.05
❑ 95 Lindsey Hunter	.10	.05
❑ 96 Ed Gray	.10	.05
❑ 97 Chris Mills	.10	.05
❑ 98 Rick Fox	.10	.05
❑ 99 Lorenzen Wright	.10	.05
❑ 100 Kevin Garnett	1.50	.70
❑ 101 Shawn Kemp	.40	.18
❑ 102 Mark Jackson	.10	.05
❑ 103 Sam Cassell	.15	.07
❑ 104 Monty Williams	.10	.05
❑ 105 Ron Mercer	.40	.18
❑ 106 Bryant Reeves	.10	.05
❑ 107 Tracy Murray	.10	.05
❑ 108 Ray Allen	.30	.14
❑ 109 Maurice Taylor	.25	.11
❑ 110 Jerome Williams	.15	.07
❑ 111 Horace Grant	.15	.07
❑ 112 Tariq Abdul-Wahad	.10	.05
❑ 113 Travis Knight	.10	.05
❑ 114 Kendall Gill	.15	.07
❑ 115 Aaron McKie	.10	.05
❑ 116 Dean Garrett	.10	.05
❑ 117 Jeff Hornacek	.15	.07
❑ 118 Todd Fuller	.10	.05
❑ 119 Arvydas Sabonis	.15	.07
❑ 120 Voshon Lenard	.10	.05
❑ 121 Steve Nash	.10	.05
❑ 122 Cedric Henderson	.10	.05
❑ 123 Rodrick Rhodes	.10	.05
❑ 124 Mookie Blaylock	.10	.05
❑ 125 Hersey Hawkins	.15	.07
❑ 126 Doug Christie	.10	.05
❑ 127 Eric Piatkowski	.10	.05
❑ 128 Sean Elliott	.10	.05
❑ 129 Anthony Mason	.15	.07
❑ 130 Allan Houston	.25	.11
❑ 131 Antonio Davis	.10	.05
❑ 132 Hubert Davis	.10	.05
❑ 133 Rod Strickland PF	.10	.05
❑ 134 Jason Kidd PF	.40	.18
❑ 135 Mark Jackson PF	.10	.05
❑ 136 Marcus Camby PF	.15	.07
❑ 137 Dikembe Mutombo PF	.10	.05
❑ 138 Shawn Bradley PF	.10	.05
❑ 139 Dennis Rodman PF	.25	.11
❑ 140 Jayson Williams PF	.10	.05
❑ 141 Tim Duncan PF	.60	.25
❑ 142 Michael Jordan PF	1.50	.70
❑ 143 Shaquille O'Neal PF	.60	.25
❑ 144 Karl Malone PF	.25	.11
❑ 145 Mookie Blaylock PF	.10	.05
❑ 146 Brevin Knight PF	.10	.05
❑ 147 Doug Christie PF	.10	.05
❑ 148 Checklist	.10	.05
❑ 149 Checklist	.10	.05
❑ 150 Checklist	.10	.05
❑ S44 Keith Van Horn SAMPLE	2.00	.90

1998-99 Fleer Vintage '61

	MINT	NRMT
COMPLETE SET (147)	70.00	32.00
COMMON CARD (1-147)	.30	.14

*STARS: 1.5X TO 3X BASE CARD HI
ONE PER HOBBY PACK

1998-99 Fleer Classic '61

	MINT	NRMT
COMMON CARD (1-147)	25.00	11.00

*STARS: 100X TO 250X BASE CARD HI
*PF: 125X TO 300X BASE SUBSET
STATED PRINT RUN 61 SERIAL #'d SETS
RANDOM INSERTS IN HOBBY PACKS

❑ 1 Kobe Bryant	400.00	180.00
❑ 23 Michael Jordan	800.00	350.00
❑ 142 Michael Jordan PF	600.00	275.00

1998-99 Fleer Electrifying

	MINT	NRMT
COMPLETE SET (10)	120.00	55.00
COMMON CARD (1-10)	6.00	2.70

STATED ODDS 1:72 HOB/RET

❑ 1 Kobe Bryant	30.00	13.50
❑ 2 Kevin Garnett	25.00	11.00
❑ 3 Anfernee Hardaway	12.00	5.50
❑ 4 Grant Hill	20.00	9.00
❑ 5 Allen Iverson	15.00	6.75
❑ 6 Michael Jordan	50.00	22.00
❑ 7 Shawn Kemp	6.00	2.70
❑ 8 Stephon Marbury	10.00	4.50
❑ 9 Gary Payton	6.00	2.70
❑ 10 Dennis Rodman	8.00	3.60

1998-99 Fleer Great Expectations

	MINT	NRMT
COMPLETE SET (10)	30.00	13.50
COMMON CARD (1-10)	2.00	.90

STATED ODDS 1:20 HOB/RET

❑ 1 Shareef Abdur-Rahim	4.00	1.80
❑ 2 Ray Allen	2.00	.90
❑ 3 Kobe Bryant	12.00	5.50
❑ 4 Tim Duncan	8.00	3.60
❑ 5 Kevin Garnett	10.00	4.50
❑ 6 Grant Hill	8.00	3.60
❑ 7 Allen Iverson	6.00	2.70
❑ 8 Stephon Marbury	4.00	1.80

❑ 9 Keith Van Horn	4.00	1.80
❑ 10 Antoine Walker	2.50	1.10

1998-99 Fleer Lucky 13

	MINT	NRMT
COMPLETE SET (13)	250.00	110.00
COMMON CARD (1-13)	5.00	2.20
SEMISTARS	6.00	2.70
UNLISTED STARS	8.00	3.60

STATED ODDS 1:96 HOB/RET
EXPIRATION: 6/1/99

❑ 1 Michael Olowokandi	8.00	3.60
❑ 2 Mike Bibby	12.00	5.50
❑ 3 Raef Lafrentz	8.00	3.60
❑ 4 Antawn Jamison	20.00	9.00
❑ 5 Vince Carter	150.00	70.00
❑ 6 Robert Traylor	5.00	2.20
❑ 7 Jason Williams	25.00	11.00
❑ 8 Larry Hughes	25.00	11.00
❑ 9 Dirk Nowitzki	15.00	6.75
❑ 10 Paul Pierce	20.00	9.00
❑ 11 Bonzi Wells	15.00	6.75
❑ 12 Michael Doleac	6.00	2.70
❑ 13 Keon Clark	6.00	2.70
❑ NNO Expired Trade Cards	.50	.23

1998-99 Fleer Playmakers Theatre

	MINT	NRMT
COMPLETE SET (15)	2300.00	1050.00
COMMON CARD (1-15)	50.00	22.00

STATED PRINT RUN 100 SERIAL #'d SETS
RANDOM INSERTS IN HOB/RET PACKS

❑ 1 Shareef Abdur-Rahim	100.00	45.00
❑ 2 Ray Allen	50.00	22.00
❑ 3 Kobe Bryant	300.00	135.00
❑ 4 Tim Duncan	200.00	90.00
❑ 5 Kevin Garnett	250.00	110.00
❑ 6 Anfernee Hardaway	125.00	55.00
❑ 7 Grant Hill	200.00	90.00
❑ 8 Allen Iverson	150.00	70.00
❑ 9 Michael Jordan	600.00	275.00
❑ 10 Karl Malone	60.00	27.00
❑ 11 Stephon Marbury	100.00	45.00
❑ 12 Shaquille O'Neal	200.00	90.00
❑ 13 Scottie Pippen	125.00	55.00
❑ 14 Keith Van Horn	100.00	45.00
❑ 15 Antoine Walker	60.00	27.00

1998-99 Fleer Rookie Rewind

	MINT	NRMT
COMPLETE SET (10)	25.00	11.00
COMMON CARD (1-10)	1.50	.70
UNLISTED STARS	2.50	1.10

STATED ODDS 1:36 HOB/RET

❑ 1 Derek Anderson	3.00	1.35
❑ 2 Tim Duncan	12.00	5.50
❑ 3 Cedric Henderson	1.50	.70
❑ 4 Zydrunas Ilgauskas	1.50	.70
❑ 5 Bobby Jackson	1.50	.70
❑ 6 Brevin Knight	1.50	.70
❑ 7 Ron Mercer	4.00	1.80
❑ 8 Maurice Taylor	2.50	1.10
❑ 9 Tim Thomas	4.00	1.80
❑ 10 Keith Van Horn	6.00	2.70

1998-99 Fleer Timeless Memories

	MINT	NRMT
COMPLETE SET (10)	10.00	4.50
COMMON CARD (1-10)	.75	.35

STATED ODDS 1:12 HOB/RET

❑ 1 Shareef Abdur-Rahim	2.00	.90
❑ 2 Ray Allen	1.00	.45

Card	MINT	NRMT
❑ 3 Vin Baker	.75	.35
❑ 4 Anfernee Hardaway	2.50	1.10
❑ 5 Tim Hardaway	.75	.35
❑ 6 Shaquille O'Neal	4.00	1.80
❑ 7 Scottie Pippen	2.50	1.10
❑ 8 David Robinson	1.25	.55
❑ 9 Dennis Rodman	1.50	.70
❑ 10 Antoine Walker	1.25	.55

1999-00 Fleer

	MINT	NRMT
COMPLETE SET (220)	30.00	13.50
COMMON CARD (1-200)	.10	.05
COMMON RC (201-220)	.25	.11
SEMISTARS	.15	.07
SEMISTARS RC	.30	.14
UNLISTED STARS	.25	.11
UNLISTED STARS RC	.40	.18

NNO CL STATED ODDS 1:6

Card	MINT	NRMT
❑ 1 Vince Carter	2.00	.90
❑ 2 Kobe Bryant	2.50	1.10
❑ 3 Keith Van Horn	.50	.23
❑ 4 Tim Duncan	1.25	.55
❑ 5 Grant Hill	1.25	.55
❑ 6 Kevin Garnett	1.50	.70
❑ 7 Anfernee Hardaway	.75	.35
❑ 8 Jason Williams	.60	.25
❑ 9 Paul Pierce	.50	.23
❑ 10 Mookie Blaylock	.10	.05
❑ 11 Shawn Bradley	.10	.05
❑ 12 Kenny Anderson	.15	.07
❑ 13 Chauncey Billups	.10	.05
❑ 14 Elden Campbell	.10	.05
❑ 15 Jason Caffey	.10	.05
❑ 16 Brent Barry	.10	.05
❑ 17 Charles Barkley	.40	.18
❑ 18 Derek Anderson	.25	.11
❑ 19 Darrick Martin	.10	.05
❑ 20 Bison Dele	.10	.05
❑ 21 Rick Fox	.10	.05
❑ 22 Antonio Davis	.10	.05
❑ 23 Terrell Brandon	.15	.07
❑ 24 P.J. Brown	.10	.05
❑ 25 Toby Bailey	.10	.05
❑ 26 Ray Allen	.25	.11
❑ 27 Brian Grant	.15	.07
❑ 28 Scott Burrell	.10	.05
❑ 29 Tariq Abdul-Wahad	.10	.05
❑ 30 Marcus Camby	.25	.11
❑ 31 John Stockton	.25	.11
❑ 32 Nick Anderson	.10	.05
❑ 33 Antonio Daniels	.10	.05
❑ 34 Matt Geiger	.10	.05
❑ 35 Vin Baker	.15	.07
❑ 36 Dee Brown	.10	.05
❑ 37 Shandon Anderson	.10	.05
❑ 38 Calbert Cheaney	.10	.05
❑ 39 Shareef Abdur-Rahim	.50	.23
❑ 40 LaPhonso Ellis	.10	.05
❑ 41 Cedric Ceballos	.10	.05
❑ 42 Tony Battie	.10	.05
❑ 43 Keon Clark	.10	.05
❑ 44 Derrick Coleman	.15	.07
❑ 45 Erick Dampier	.10	.05
❑ 46 Corey Benjamin	.10	.05
❑ 47 Michael Dickerson	.25	.11
❑ 48 Cedric Henderson	.10	.05
❑ 49 Lamond Murray	.10	.05
❑ 50 Horace Grant	.15	.07
❑ 51 Shaquille O'Neal	1.25	.55
❑ 52 Dale Davis	.10	.05
❑ 53 Dean Garrett	.10	.05
❑ 54 Tim Hardaway	.25	.11
❑ 55 Gerald Brown RC	.10	.05
❑ 56 Sam Cassell	.15	.07
❑ 57 Jim Jackson	.10	.05
❑ 58 Kendall Gill	.15	.07
❑ 59 Eric Williams	.10	.05
❑ 60 Chris Childs	.10	.05
❑ 61 Vlade Divac	.10	.05
❑ 62 Darrell Armstrong	.15	.07
❑ 63 Mario Elie	.10	.05
❑ 64 Tyrone Hill	.10	.05
❑ 65 Dale Ellis	.10	.05
❑ 66 Doug Christie	.10	.05
❑ 67 Howard Eisley	.10	.05
❑ 68 Juwan Howard	.15	.07
❑ 69 Mike Bibby	.30	.14
❑ 70 Alan Henderson	.10	.05
❑ 71 Michael Finley	.25	.11
❑ 72 Dana Barros	.10	.05
❑ 73 Danny Fortson	.10	.05
❑ 74 Ricky Davis	.25	.11
❑ 75 Adonal Foyle	.10	.05
❑ 76 Cory Carr	.10	.05
❑ 77 Bryce Drew	.10	.05
❑ 78 Shawn Kemp	.40	.18
❑ 79 Tyrone Nesby RC	.10	.05
❑ 80 Lindsey Hunter	.10	.05
❑ 81 Ruben Patterson	.25	.11
❑ 82 Al Harrington	.30	.14
❑ 83 Bobby Jackson	.10	.05
❑ 84 Dan Majerle	.15	.07
❑ 85 Rex Chapman	.10	.05
❑ 86 Dell Curry	.10	.05
❑ 87 Walt Williams	.10	.05
❑ 88 Kerry Kittles	.15	.07
❑ 89 Isaiah Rider	.15	.07
❑ 90 Patrick Ewing	.25	.11
❑ 91 Lawrence Funderburke	.10	.05
❑ 92 Isaac Austin	.10	.05
❑ 93 Sean Elliott	.10	.05
❑ 94 Larry Hughes	.60	.25
❑ 95 Hersey Hawkins	.15	.07
❑ 96 Tracy McGrady	.75	.35
❑ 97 Jeff Hornacek	.15	.07
❑ 98 Randell Jackson	.10	.05
❑ 99 J.R. Henderson	.10	.05
❑ 100 Roshown McLeod	.10	.05
❑ 101 Steve Nash	.10	.05
❑ 102 Ron Mercer	.30	.14
❑ 103 Raef LaFrentz	.25	.11
❑ 104 Eddie Jones	.50	.23
❑ 105 Antawn Jamison	.50	.23
❑ 106 Kornel David RC	.10	.05
❑ 107 Othella Harrington	.10	.05
❑ 108 Brevin Knight	.10	.05
❑ 109 Michael Olowokandi	.15	.07
❑ 110 Christian Laettner	.15	.07
❑ 111 J.R. Reid	.10	.05
❑ 112 Reggie Miller	.25	.11
❑ 113 Andrae Patterson	.10	.05
❑ 114 Jamal Mashburn	.15	.07
❑ 115 Glenn Robinson	.15	.07
❑ 116 Pat Garrity	.10	.05
❑ 117 Stephon Marbury	.50	.23
❑ 118 Arvydas Sabonis	.15	.07
❑ 119 Allan Houston	.25	.11
❑ 120 Predrag Stojakovic	.15	.07
❑ 121 Michael Doleac	.10	.05
❑ 122 Avery Johnson	.10	.05
❑ 123 Allen Iverson	1.00	.45
❑ 124 Rashard Lewis	.40	.18
❑ 125 Charles Oakley	.10	.05
❑ 126 Karl Malone	.40	.18
❑ 127 Tracy Murray	.10	.05
❑ 128 Felipe Lopez	.10	.05
❑ 129 Dikembe Mutombo	.15	.07
❑ 130 Dirk Nowitzki	.40	.18
❑ 131 Vitaly Potapenko	.10	.05
❑ 132 Antonio McDyess	.25	.11
❑ 133 Anthony Mason	.15	.07
❑ 134 Donyell Marshall	.10	.05
❑ 135 Ron Harper	.15	.07
❑ 136 Cuttino Mobley	.25	.11
❑ 137 Wesley Person	.10	.05
❑ 138 Rodney Rogers	.10	.05
❑ 139 Jerry Stackhouse	.15	.07
❑ 140 Glen Rice	.15	.07
❑ 141 Chris Mullin	.25	.11
❑ 142 Anthony Peeler	.10	.05
❑ 143 Alonzo Mourning	.25	.11
❑ 144 Tom Gugliotta	.15	.07
❑ 145 Tim Thomas	.30	.14
❑ 146 Damon Stoudamire	.25	.11
❑ 147 Jayson Williams	.15	.07
❑ 148 Larry Johnson	.15	.07
❑ 149 Chris Webber	.75	.35
❑ 150 Matt Harpring	.10	.05
❑ 151 David Robinson	.40	.18
❑ 152 George Lynch	.10	.05
❑ 153 Gary Payton	.40	.18
❑ 154 John Wallace	.10	.05
❑ 155 Greg Ostertag	.10	.05
❑ 156 Mitch Richmond	.25	.11
❑ 157 Cherokee Parks	.10	.05
❑ 158 Steve Smith	.15	.07
❑ 159 Gary Trent	.10	.05
❑ 160 Antoine Walker	.30	.14
❑ 161 Johnny Taylor	.10	.05
❑ 162 Brad Miller	.10	.05
❑ 163 Chris Mills	.10	.05
❑ 164 Charles Jones	.10	.05
❑ 165 Hakeem Olajuwon	.40	.18
❑ 166 Bob Sura	.10	.05
❑ 167 Brian Skinner	.10	.05
❑ 168 Korleone Young	.10	.05
❑ 169 Tyronn Lue	.10	.05
❑ 170 Jalen Rose	.25	.11
❑ 171 Joe Smith	.15	.07
❑ 172 Clarence Weatherspoon	.10	.05
❑ 173 Jason Kidd	.75	.35
❑ 174 Robert Traylor	.10	.05
❑ 175 Rasheed Wallace	.25	.11
❑ 176 Latrell Sprewell	.50	.23
❑ 177 Corliss Williamson	.10	.05
❑ 178 Charles Outlaw	.10	.05
❑ 179 Malik Rose	.10	.05
❑ 180 Nazr Mohammed	.10	.05
❑ 181 Olden Polynice	.10	.05
❑ 182 Kevin Willis	.10	.05
❑ 183 Bryon Russell	.10	.05
❑ 184 Bryant Reeves	.10	.05
❑ 185 Rod Strickland	.15	.07
❑ 186 Samaki Walker	.10	.05
❑ 187 Nick Van Exel	.15	.07
❑ 188 David Wesley	.10	.05
❑ 189 John Starks	.10	.05
❑ 190 Toni Kukoc	.30	.14
❑ 191 Scottie Pippen	.75	.35
❑ 192 Zydrunas Ilgauskas	.10	.05
❑ 193 Maurice Taylor	.25	.11
❑ 194 Rik Smits	.10	.05
❑ 195 Clifford Robinson	.10	.05
❑ 196 Bonzi Wells	.40	.18
❑ 197 Charlie Ward	.10	.05
❑ 198 Detlef Schrempf	.15	.07
❑ 199 Theo Ratliff	.10	.05
❑ 200 Rodrick Rhodes	.10	.05
❑ 201 Ron Artest RC	1.00	.45
❑ 202 William Avery RC	.60	.25
❑ 203 Elton Brand RC	4.00	1.80
❑ 204 Baron Davis RC	1.00	.45
❑ 205 Jumaine Jones RC	.30	.14
❑ 206 Andre Miller RC	1.25	.55
❑ 207 Lee Nailon RC	.25	.11
❑ 208 James Posey RC	.75	.35
❑ 209 Jason Terry RC	.60	.25
❑ 210 Kenny Thomas RC	.60	.25
❑ 211 Steve Francis RC	5.00	2.20
❑ 212 Wally Szczerbiak RC	1.50	.70
❑ 213 Richard Hamilton RC	1.00	.45
❑ 214 Jonathan Bender RC	2.00	.90
❑ 215 Shawn Marion RC	1.25	.55
❑ 216 Aleksandar Radojevic RC	.25	.11
❑ 217 Tim James RC	.50	.23
❑ 218 Trajan Langdon RC	.60	.25
❑ 219 Lamar Odom RC	3.00	1.35

	MINT	NRMT
❑ 220 Corey Maggette RC	1.50	.70
❑ NNO Checklist #2	.10	.05
❑ NNO Checklist #3	.10	.05
❑ NNO Checklist #1	.10	.05

1999-00 Fleer Roundball Collection

	MINT	NRMT
COMPLETE SET (220)	80.00	36.00
COMMON CARD (1-220)	.25	.11

*STARS: 1X TO 2.5X BASE CARD HI
*RCs: .75X TO 2X BASE HI
ONE PER RETAIL PACK

1999-00 Fleer Supreme Court Collection

	MINT	NRMT
COMMON CARD (1-220)	25.00	11.00
SEMISTARS	40.00	18.00
UNLISTED STARS	60.00	27.00

STATED PRINT RUN 20 SERIAL #'d SETS
RANDOM INSERTS IN HOB PACKS

	MINT	NRMT
❑ 1 Vince Carter	600.00	275.00
❑ 2 Kobe Bryant	500.00	220.00
❑ 3 Keith Van Horn	120.00	55.00
❑ 4 Tim Duncan	300.00	135.00
❑ 5 Grant Hill	300.00	135.00
❑ 6 Kevin Garnett	400.00	180.00
❑ 7 Anfernee Hardaway	200.00	90.00
❑ 8 Jason Williams	150.00	70.00
❑ 9 Paul Pierce	120.00	55.00
❑ 10 Mookie Blaylock	25.00	11.00
❑ 11 Shawn Bradley	25.00	11.00
❑ 12 Kenny Anderson	40.00	18.00
❑ 13 Chauncey Billups	25.00	11.00
❑ 14 Elden Campbell	25.00	11.00
❑ 15 Jason Caffey	25.00	11.00
❑ 16 Brent Barry	25.00	11.00
❑ 17 Charles Barkley	100.00	45.00
❑ 18 Derek Anderson	60.00	27.00
❑ 19 Darrick Martin	25.00	11.00
❑ 20 Bison Dele	25.00	11.00
❑ 21 Rick Fox	25.00	11.00
❑ 22 Antonio Davis	25.00	11.00
❑ 23 Terrell Brandon	40.00	18.00
❑ 24 P.J. Brown	25.00	11.00
❑ 25 Toby Bailey	25.00	11.00
❑ 26 Ray Allen	60.00	27.00
❑ 27 Brian Grant	40.00	18.00
❑ 28 Scott Burrell	25.00	11.00
❑ 29 Tariq Abdul-Wahad	25.00	11.00
❑ 30 Marcus Camby	60.00	27.00
❑ 31 John Stockton	60.00	27.00
❑ 32 Nick Anderson	25.00	11.00
❑ 33 Antonio Daniels	25.00	11.00
❑ 34 Matt Geiger	25.00	11.00
❑ 35 Vin Baker	40.00	18.00
❑ 36 Dee Brown	25.00	11.00
❑ 37 Shandon Anderson	25.00	11.00
❑ 38 Calbert Cheaney	25.00	11.00
❑ 39 Shareef Abdur-Rahim	120.00	55.00
❑ 40 LaPhonso Ellis	25.00	11.00
❑ 41 Cedric Ceballos	25.00	11.00
❑ 42 Tony Battie	25.00	11.00
❑ 43 Keon Clark	25.00	11.00
❑ 44 Derrick Coleman	40.00	18.00
❑ 45 Erick Dampier	25.00	11.00
❑ 46 Corey Benjamin	25.00	11.00
❑ 47 Michael Dickerson	60.00	27.00
❑ 48 Cedric Henderson	25.00	11.00
❑ 49 Lamond Murray	25.00	11.00
❑ 50 Horace Grant	40.00	18.00
❑ 51 Shaquille O'Neal	300.00	135.00
❑ 52 Dale Davis	25.00	11.00
❑ 53 Dean Garrett	25.00	11.00
❑ 54 Tim Hardaway	60.00	27.00
❑ 55 Gerald Brown	25.00	11.00
❑ 56 Sam Cassell	40.00	18.00
❑ 57 Jim Jackson	25.00	11.00
❑ 58 Kendall Gill	40.00	18.00
❑ 59 Eric Williams	25.00	11.00
❑ 60 Chris Childs	25.00	11.00
❑ 61 Vlade Divac	25.00	11.00
❑ 62 Darrell Armstrong	40.00	18.00
❑ 63 Mario Elie	25.00	11.00
❑ 64 Tyrone Hill	25.00	11.00
❑ 65 Dale Ellis	25.00	11.00
❑ 66 Doug Christie	25.00	11.00
❑ 67 Howard Eisley	25.00	11.00
❑ 68 Juwan Howard	40.00	18.00
❑ 69 Mike Bibby	80.00	36.00
❑ 70 Alan Henderson	25.00	11.00
❑ 71 Michael Finley	60.00	27.00
❑ 72 Dana Barros	25.00	11.00
❑ 73 Danny Fortson	25.00	11.00
❑ 74 Ricky Davis	60.00	27.00
❑ 75 Adonal Foyle	25.00	11.00
❑ 76 Cory Carr	25.00	11.00
❑ 77 Bryce Drew	25.00	11.00
❑ 78 Shawn Kemp	100.00	45.00
❑ 79 Tyrone Nesby	25.00	11.00
❑ 80 Lindsey Hunter	25.00	11.00
❑ 81 Ruben Patterson	60.00	27.00
❑ 82 Al Harrington	80.00	36.00
❑ 83 Bobby Jackson	25.00	11.00
❑ 84 Dan Majerle	40.00	18.00
❑ 85 Rex Chapman	25.00	11.00
❑ 86 Dell Curry	25.00	11.00
❑ 87 Walt Williams	25.00	11.00
❑ 88 Kerry Kittles	40.00	18.00
❑ 89 Isaiah Rider	40.00	18.00
❑ 90 Patrick Ewing	60.00	27.00
❑ 91 Lawrence Funderburke	25.00	11.00
❑ 92 Isaac Austin	25.00	11.00
❑ 93 Sean Elliott	25.00	11.00
❑ 94 Larry Hughes	150.00	70.00
❑ 95 Hersey Hawkins	40.00	18.00
❑ 96 Tracy McGrady	200.00	90.00
❑ 97 Jeff Hornacek	40.00	18.00
❑ 98 Randell Jackson	25.00	11.00
❑ 99 J.R. Henderson	25.00	11.00
❑ 100 Roshown McLeod	25.00	11.00
❑ 101 Steve Nash	25.00	11.00
❑ 102 Ron Mercer	80.00	36.00
❑ 103 Raef LaFrentz	60.00	27.00
❑ 104 Eddie Jones	120.00	55.00
❑ 105 Antawn Jamison	120.00	55.00
❑ 106 Kornel David	25.00	11.00
❑ 107 Othella Harrington	25.00	11.00
❑ 108 Brevin Knight	25.00	11.00
❑ 109 Michael Olowokandi	40.00	18.00
❑ 110 Christian Laettner	40.00	18.00
❑ 111 J.R. Reid	25.00	11.00
❑ 112 Reggie Miller	60.00	27.00
❑ 113 Andrae Patterson	25.00	11.00
❑ 114 Jamal Mashburn	40.00	18.00
❑ 115 Glenn Robinson	40.00	18.00
❑ 116 Pat Garrity	25.00	11.00
❑ 117 Stephon Marbury	120.00	55.00
❑ 118 Arvydas Sabonis	40.00	18.00
❑ 119 Allan Houston	60.00	27.00
❑ 120 Predrag Stojakovic	40.00	18.00
❑ 121 Michael Doleac	25.00	11.00
❑ 122 Avery Johnson	25.00	11.00
❑ 123 Allen Iverson	250.00	110.00
❑ 124 Rashard Lewis	100.00	45.00
❑ 125 Charles Oakley	25.00	11.00
❑ 126 Karl Malone	100.00	45.00
❑ 127 Tracy Murray	25.00	11.00
❑ 128 Felipe Lopez	25.00	11.00
❑ 129 Dikembe Mutombo	40.00	18.00
❑ 130 Dirk Nowitzki	100.00	45.00
❑ 131 Vitaly Potapenko	25.00	11.00
❑ 132 Antonio McDyess	60.00	27.00
❑ 133 Anthony Mason	40.00	18.00
❑ 134 Donyell Marshall	25.00	11.00
❑ 135 Ron Harper	40.00	18.00
❑ 136 Cuttino Mobley	60.00	27.00
❑ 137 Wesley Person	25.00	11.00
❑ 138 Rodney Rogers	25.00	11.00
❑ 139 Jerry Stackhouse	40.00	18.00
❑ 140 Glen Rice	40.00	18.00
❑ 141 Chris Mullin	60.00	27.00
❑ 142 Anthony Peeler	25.00	11.00
❑ 143 Alonzo Mourning	60.00	27.00
❑ 144 Tom Gugliotta	40.00	18.00
❑ 145 Tim Thomas	80.00	36.00
❑ 146 Damon Stoudamire	60.00	27.00
❑ 147 Jayson Williams	40.00	18.00
❑ 148 Larry Johnson	40.00	18.00
❑ 149 Chris Webber	200.00	90.00
❑ 150 Matt Harpring	25.00	11.00
❑ 151 David Robinson	100.00	45.00
❑ 152 George Lynch	25.00	11.00
❑ 153 Gary Payton	100.00	45.00
❑ 154 John Wallace	25.00	11.00
❑ 155 Greg Ostertag	25.00	11.00
❑ 156 Mitch Richmond	60.00	27.00
❑ 157 Cherokee Parks	25.00	11.00
❑ 158 Steve Smith	40.00	18.00
❑ 159 Gary Trent	25.00	11.00
❑ 160 Antoine Walker	80.00	36.00
❑ 161 Johnny Taylor	25.00	11.00
❑ 162 Brad Miller	25.00	11.00
❑ 163 Chris Mills	25.00	11.00
❑ 164 Charles Jones	25.00	11.00
❑ 165 Hakeem Olajuwon	100.00	45.00
❑ 166 Bob Sura	25.00	11.00
❑ 167 Brian Skinner	25.00	11.00
❑ 168 Korleone Young	25.00	11.00
❑ 169 Tyronn Lue	25.00	11.00
❑ 170 Jalen Rose	60.00	27.00
❑ 171 Joe Smith	40.00	18.00
❑ 172 Clarence Weatherspoon	25.00	11.00
❑ 173 Jason Kidd	200.00	90.00
❑ 174 Robert Traylor	25.00	11.00
❑ 175 Rasheed Wallace	60.00	27.00
❑ 176 Latrell Sprewell	120.00	55.00
❑ 177 Corliss Williamson	25.00	11.00
❑ 178 Charles Outlaw	25.00	11.00
❑ 179 Malik Rose	25.00	11.00
❑ 180 Nazr Mohammed	25.00	11.00
❑ 181 Olden Polynice	25.00	11.00
❑ 182 Kevin Willis	25.00	11.00
❑ 183 Bryon Russell	25.00	11.00
❑ 184 Bryant Reeves	25.00	11.00
❑ 185 Rod Strickland	40.00	18.00
❑ 186 Samaki Walker	25.00	11.00
❑ 187 Nick Van Exel	40.00	18.00
❑ 188 David Wesley	25.00	11.00
❑ 189 John Starks	25.00	11.00
❑ 190 Toni Kukoc	100.00	45.00
❑ 191 Scottie Pippen	200.00	90.00
❑ 192 Zydrunas Ilgauskas	25.00	11.00
❑ 193 Maurice Taylor	60.00	27.00
❑ 194 Rik Smits	25.00	11.00
❑ 195 Clifford Robinson	25.00	11.00
❑ 196 Bonzi Wells	100.00	45.00
❑ 197 Charlie Ward	25.00	11.00
❑ 198 Detlef Schrempf	40.00	18.00
❑ 199 Theo Ratliff	25.00	11.00
❑ 200 Rodrick Rhodes	25.00	11.00
❑ 201 Ron Artest	80.00	36.00
❑ 202 William Avery	60.00	27.00
❑ 203 Elton Brand	300.00	135.00
❑ 204 Baron Davis	80.00	36.00
❑ 205 Jumaine Jones	40.00	18.00
❑ 206 Andre Miller	100.00	45.00
❑ 207 Lee Nailon	25.00	11.00
❑ 208 James Posey	60.00	27.00
❑ 209 Jason Terry	60.00	27.00
❑ 210 Kenny Thomas	60.00	27.00
❑ 211 Steve Francis	400.00	180.00
❑ 212 Wally Szczerbiak	120.00	55.00
❑ 213 Richard Hamilton	80.00	36.00
❑ 214 Jonathan Bender	150.00	70.00

❑ 215 Shawn Marion	100.00	45.00
❑ 216 Aleksandar Radojevic	25.00	11.00
❑ 217 Tim James	40.00	18.00
❑ 218 Trajan Langdon	60.00	27.00
❑ 219 Lamar Odom	250.00	110.00
❑ 220 Corey Maggette	120.00	55.00

1999-00 Fleer Fresh Ink

	MINT	NRMT
COMPLETE SET (15)	200.00	90.00
COMMON CARD	10.00	4.50
SEMISTARS	15.00	6.75

NNO CARDS LISTED BELOW ALPHABETICALLY
RANDOM INSERTS IN PACKS
STATED PRINT RUN 400 SERIAL #'d SETS
SOME CARDS AVAILABLE VIA REDEMPTION

❑ 1 Corey Benjamin	15.00	6.75
❑ 2 Mike Bibby	30.00	13.50
❑ 3 Michael Dickerson	20.00	9.00
❑ 4 Michael Doleac	10.00	4.50
❑ 5 Bryce Drew	15.00	6.75
❑ 6 Pat Garrity	10.00	4.50
❑ 7 Matt Harpring	10.00	4.50
❑ 8 Larry Hughes	40.00	18.00
❑ 9 Antawn Jamison	30.00	13.50
❑ 10 Raef LaFrentz	20.00	9.00
❑ 11 Felipe Lopez	10.00	4.50
❑ 12 Jelani McCoy	10.00	4.50
❑ 13 Brad Miller	10.00	4.50
❑ 14 Michael Olowokandi	10.00	4.50
❑ 15 Robert Traylor	10.00	4.50

1999-00 Fleer Game Breakers

	MINT	NRMT
COMPLETE SET (15)	700.00	325.00
COMMON CARD (1-15)	20.00	9.00

STATED PRINT RUN 100 SERIAL #'d SETS
RANDOM INSERTS IN PACKS

❑ 1 Shareef Abdur-Rahim	30.00	13.50
❑ 2 Kobe Bryant	120.00	55.00
❑ 3 Vince Carter	150.00	70.00
❑ 4 Tim Duncan	80.00	36.00
❑ 5 Kevin Garnett	100.00	45.00
❑ 6 Anfernee Hardaway	50.00	22.00
❑ 7 Grant Hill	80.00	36.00
❑ 8 Allen Iverson	60.00	27.00
❑ 9 Shawn Kemp	25.00	11.00
❑ 10 Stephon Marbury	30.00	13.50
❑ 11 Ron Mercer	20.00	9.00
❑ 12 Shaquille O'Neal	80.00	36.00
❑ 13 Keith Van Horn	30.00	13.50
❑ 14 Antoine Walker	20.00	9.00
❑ 15 Jason Williams	40.00	18.00

1999-00 Fleer Masters of the Hardwood

	MINT	NRMT
COMPLETE SET (15)	30.00	13.50
COMMON CARD (1-15)	1.25	.55

STATED ODDS 1:18

❑ 1 Shareef Abdur-Rahim	2.00	.90
❑ 2 Mike Bibby	1.25	.55
❑ 3 Kobe Bryant	8.00	3.60
❑ 4 Tim Duncan	5.00	2.20
❑ 5 Kevin Garnett	6.00	2.70
❑ 6 Anfernee Hardaway	3.00	1.35
❑ 7 Grant Hill	5.00	2.20
❑ 8 Allen Iverson	4.00	1.80
❑ 9 Karl Malone	1.25	.55
❑ 10 Stephon Marbury	2.00	.90
❑ 11 Tracy McGrady	3.00	1.35
❑ 12 Ron Mercer	1.25	.55
❑ 13 Scottie Pippen	3.00	1.35
❑ 14 Antoine Walker	1.25	.55
❑ 15 Jason Williams	2.50	1.10

1999-00 Fleer Net Effect

	MINT	NRMT
COMPLETE SET (10)	100.00	45.00
COMMON CARD (1-10)	6.00	2.70

STATED ODDS 1:96

❑ 1 Kobe Bryant	25.00	11.00
❑ 2 Vince Carter	30.00	13.50
❑ 3 Tim Duncan	15.00	6.75
❑ 4 Kevin Garnett	20.00	9.00
❑ 5 Grant Hill	15.00	6.75
❑ 6 Allen Iverson	12.00	5.50
❑ 7 Shaquille O'Neal	15.00	6.75
❑ 8 Paul Pierce	6.00	2.70
❑ 9 Scottie Pippen	10.00	4.50
❑ 10 Keith Van Horn	6.00	2.70

1999-00 Fleer Rookie Sensations

	MINT	NRMT
COMPLETE SET (20)	15.00	6.75
COMMON CARD (1-20)	.30	.14
SEMISTARS	.50	.23
UNLISTED STARS	.75	.35

STATED ODDS 1:6

❑ 1 Mike Bibby	1.00	.45
❑ 2 Vince Carter	8.00	3.60
❑ 3 Ricky Davis	.75	.35
❑ 4 Michael Dickerson	.75	.35
❑ 5 Michael Doleac	.30	.14
❑ 6 Matt Harpring	.30	.14
❑ 7 Larry Hughes	2.00	.90
❑ 8 Randell Jackson	.30	.14
❑ 9 Antawn Jamison	1.50	.70
❑ 10 Raef LaFrentz	.75	.35
❑ 11 Felipe Lopez	.30	.14
❑ 12 Roshown McLeod	.30	.14
❑ 13 Brad Miller	.30	.14
❑ 14 Cuttino Mobley	.75	.35
❑ 15 Dirk Nowitzki	1.25	.55
❑ 16 Michael Olowokandi	.50	.23
❑ 17 Paul Pierce	1.50	.70
❑ 18 Predrag Stojakovic	.50	.23
❑ 19 Robert Traylor	.30	.14
❑ 20 Jason Williams	2.00	.90

1998-99 Fleer Brilliants

	MINT	NRMT
COMPLETE SET (125)	80.00	36.00
COMPLETE SET w/o SP (100)	30.00	13.50
COMMON CARD (1-100)	.25	.11
COMMON RC (101-125)	.60	.25
SEMISTARS	.30	.14
SEMISTARS RC	.75	.35
UNLISTED STARS	.50	.23
UNLISTED STARS RC	1.25	.55

RC's: STATED ODDS 1:2

❑ 1 Tim Duncan	2.50	1.10
❑ 2 Dikembe Mutombo	.30	.14
❑ 3 Steve Nash	.25	.11
❑ 4 Charles Barkley	.75	.35
❑ 5 Eddie Jones	1.00	.45
❑ 6 Ray Allen	.60	.25
❑ 7 Stephon Marbury	1.25	.55
❑ 8 Anfernee Hardaway	1.50	.70
❑ 9 Gary Payton	.75	.35
❑ 10 Ron Mercer	.75	.35
❑ 11 Nick Van Exel	.30	.14
❑ 12 Brent Barry	.25	.11
❑ 13 Allan Houston	.50	.23
❑ 14 Avery Johnson	.25	.11
❑ 15 Shareef Abdur-Rahim	1.25	.55
❑ 16 Rod Strickland	.30	.14
❑ 17 Vin Baker	.30	.14
❑ 18 Patrick Ewing	.50	.23
❑ 19 Maurice Taylor	.50	.23
❑ 20 Shawn Kemp	.75	.35
❑ 21 Michael Finley	.50	.23
❑ 22 Reggie Miller	.50	.23
❑ 23 Joe Smith	.30	.14
❑ 24 Toni Kukoc	.60	.25
❑ 25 Blue Edwards	.25	.11
❑ 26 Joe Dumars	.50	.23
❑ 27 Tom Gugliotta	.30	.14
❑ 28 Terrell Brandon	.30	.14
❑ 29 Erick Dampier	.25	.11
❑ 30 Antonio McDyess	.50	.23
❑ 31 Donyell Marshall	.25	.11
❑ 32 Jeff Hornacek	.30	.14
❑ 33 David Wesley	.25	.11
❑ 34 Derek Anderson	.60	.25
❑ 35 Ron Harper	.30	.14
❑ 36 John Starks	.25	.11
❑ 37 Kenny Anderson	.30	.14
❑ 38 Anthony Mason	.30	.14
❑ 39 Brevin Knight	.25	.11

❑ 40 Antoine Walker .75 .35
❑ 41 Mookie Blaylock .25 .11
❑ 42 LaPhonso Ellis .25 .11
❑ 43 Tim Hardaway .50 .23
❑ 44 Jim Jackson .25 .11
❑ 45 Matt Maloney .25 .11
❑ 46 Lamond Murray .25 .11
❑ 47 Voshon Lenard .25 .11
❑ 48 Isaiah Rider .30 .14
❑ 49 Tracy Murray .25 .11
❑ 50 Grant Hill 2.50 1.10
❑ 51 Vlade Divac .25 .11
❑ 52 Glenn Robinson .30 .14
❑ 53 Tony Battie .30 .14
❑ 54 Bobby Jackson .25 .11
❑ 55 Jayson Williams .30 .14
❑ 56 Doug Christie .25 .11
❑ 57 Glen Rice .30 .14
❑ 58 Tim Thomas .75 .35
❑ 59 Lindsey Hunter .25 .11
❑ 60 Scottie Pippen 1.50 .70
❑ 61 Marcus Camby .50 .23
❑ 62 Clifford Robinson .25 .11
❑ 63 John Wallace .25 .11
❑ 64 Larry Johnson .30 .14
❑ 65 Bryon Russell .25 .11
❑ 66 Isaac Austin .25 .11
❑ 67 Sam Cassell .30 .14
❑ 68 Allen Iverson 2.00 .90
❑ 69 Chauncey Billups .25 .11
❑ 70 Kobe Bryant 4.00 1.80
❑ 71 Kevin Willis .25 .11
❑ 72 Jason Kidd 1.50 .70
❑ 73 Chris Webber 1.50 .70
❑ 74 Rasheed Wallace .50 .23
❑ 75 Karl Malone .75 .35
❑ 76 Shawn Bradley .25 .11
❑ 77 Kerry Kittles .30 .14
❑ 78 Mitch Richmond .50 .23
❑ 79 Antonio Daniels .25 .11
❑ 80 Kevin Garnett 3.00 1.35
❑ 81 Nick Anderson .25 .11
❑ 82 David Robinson .75 .35
❑ 83 Jamal Mashburn .30 .14
❑ 84 Rodney Rogers .25 .11
❑ 85 Michael Stewart .25 .11
❑ 86 Rik Smits .25 .11
❑ 87 Billy Owens .25 .11
❑ 88 Damon Stoudamire .50 .23
❑ 89 Theo Ratliff .25 .11
❑ 90 Keith Van Horn 1.25 .55
❑ 91 Hakeem Olajuwon .75 .35
❑ 92 Alonzo Mourning .50 .23
❑ 93 Steve Smith .30 .14
❑ 94 Mark Jackson .25 .11
❑ 95 Cedric Ceballos .25 .11
❑ 96 Bryant Reeves .25 .11
❑ 97 Juwan Howard .30 .14
❑ 98 Detlef Schrempf .30 .14
❑ 99 John Stockton .50 .23
❑ 100 Shaquille O'Neal 2.50 1.10
❑ 101 Michael Olowokandi RC 2.00 .90
❑ 102 Mike Bibby RC 4.00 1.80
❑ 103 Raef LaFrentz RC 2.50 1.10
❑ 104 Antawn Jamison RC 6.00 2.70
❑ 105 Vince Carter RC 30.00 13.50
❑ 106 Robert Traylor RC 1.25 .55
❑ 107 Jason Williams RC 8.00 3.60
❑ 108 Larry Hughes RC 8.00 3.60
❑ 109 Dirk Nowitzki RC 5.00 2.20
❑ 110 Paul Pierce RC 6.00 2.70
❑ 111 Bonzi Wells RC 5.00 2.20
❑ 112 Michael Doleac RC 1.25 .55
❑ 113 Keon Clark RC 1.25 .55
❑ 114 Michael Dickerson RC 2.50 1.10
❑ 115 Matt Harpring RC 1.25 .55
❑ 116 Bryce Drew RC 1.25 .55
❑ 117 Pat Garrity RC .75 .35
❑ 118 Roshown McLeod RC .75 .35
❑ 119 Ricky Davis RC 2.50 1.10
❑ 120 Rashard Lewis RC 5.00 2.20
❑ 121 Tyronn Lue RC .75 .35
❑ 122 Al Harrington RC 4.00 1.80
❑ 123 Corey Benjamin RC 1.25 .55
❑ 124 Felipe Lopez RC 1.50 .70
❑ 125 Korleone Young RC .60 .25

1998-99 Fleer Brilliants 24-Karat Gold

	MINT	NRMT
COMMON CARD (1-100)	25.00	11.00
COMMON CARD (101-125)	40.00	18.00
SEMISTARS	50.00	22.00
UNLISTED STARS	80.00	36.00

RANDOM INSERTS IN PACKS
STATED PRINT RUN 24 SERIAL #'d SETS

❑ 1 Tim Duncan 400.00 180.00
❑ 2 Dikembe Mutombo 50.00 22.00
❑ 3 Steve Nash 25.00 11.00
❑ 4 Charles Barkley 120.00 55.00
❑ 5 Eddie Jones 150.00 70.00
❑ 6 Ray Allen 100.00 45.00
❑ 7 Stephon Marbury 200.00 90.00
❑ 8 Anfernee Hardaway 250.00 110.00
❑ 9 Gary Payton 120.00 55.00
❑ 10 Ron Mercer 120.00 55.00
❑ 11 Nick Van Exel 50.00 22.00
❑ 12 Brent Barry 25.00 11.00
❑ 13 Allan Houston 80.00 36.00
❑ 14 Avery Johnson 25.00 11.00
❑ 15 Shareef Abdur-Rahim 200.00 90.00
❑ 16 Rod Strickland 50.00 22.00
❑ 17 Vin Baker 50.00 22.00
❑ 18 Patrick Ewing 80.00 36.00
❑ 19 Maurice Taylor 80.00 36.00
❑ 20 Shawn Kemp 120.00 55.00
❑ 21 Michael Finley 80.00 36.00
❑ 22 Reggie Miller 80.00 36.00
❑ 23 Joe Smith 50.00 22.00
❑ 24 Toni Kukoc 150.00 70.00
❑ 25 Blue Edwards 25.00 11.00
❑ 26 Joe Dumars 80.00 36.00
❑ 27 Tom Gugliotta 50.00 22.00
❑ 28 Terrell Brandon 50.00 22.00
❑ 29 Erick Dampier 25.00 11.00
❑ 30 Antonio McDyess 80.00 36.00
❑ 31 Donyell Marshall 25.00 11.00
❑ 32 Jeff Hornacek 50.00 22.00
❑ 33 David Wesley 25.00 11.00
❑ 34 Derek Anderson 100.00 45.00
❑ 35 Ron Harper 50.00 22.00
❑ 36 John Starks 25.00 11.00
❑ 37 Kenny Anderson 50.00 22.00
❑ 38 Anthony Mason 50.00 22.00
❑ 39 Brevin Knight 25.00 11.00
❑ 40 Antoine Walker 120.00 55.00
❑ 41 Mookie Blaylock 25.00 11.00
❑ 42 LaPhonso Ellis 25.00 11.00
❑ 43 Tim Hardaway 80.00 36.00
❑ 44 Jim Jackson 25.00 11.00
❑ 45 Matt Maloney 25.00 11.00
❑ 46 Lamond Murray 25.00 11.00
❑ 47 Voshon Lenard 25.00 11.00
❑ 48 Isaiah Rider 50.00 22.00
❑ 49 Tracy Murray 25.00 11.00
❑ 50 Grant Hill 400.00 180.00
❑ 51 Vlade Divac 25.00 11.00
❑ 52 Glenn Robinson 50.00 22.00
❑ 53 Tony Battie 50.00 22.00
❑ 54 Bobby Jackson 25.00 11.00
❑ 55 Jayson Williams 50.00 22.00
❑ 56 Doug Christie 25.00 11.00
❑ 57 Glen Rice 50.00 22.00
❑ 58 Tim Thomas 120.00 55.00
❑ 59 Lindsey Hunter 25.00 11.00
❑ 60 Scottie Pippen 250.00 110.00
❑ 61 Marcus Camby 80.00 36.00
❑ 62 Clifford Robinson 25.00 11.00
❑ 63 John Wallace 25.00 11.00
❑ 64 Larry Johnson 50.00 22.00
❑ 65 Bryon Russell 25.00 11.00
❑ 66 Isaac Austin 25.00 11.00
❑ 67 Sam Cassell 50.00 22.00
❑ 68 Allen Iverson 300.00 135.00
❑ 69 Chauncey Billups 25.00 11.00
❑ 70 Kobe Bryant 600.00 275.00
❑ 71 Kevin Willis 25.00 11.00
❑ 72 Jason Kidd 250.00 110.00
❑ 73 Chris Webber 250.00 110.00
❑ 74 Rasheed Wallace 80.00 36.00
❑ 75 Karl Malone 120.00 55.00
❑ 76 Shawn Bradley 25.00 11.00
❑ 77 Kerry Kittles 50.00 22.00
❑ 78 Mitch Richmond 80.00 36.00
❑ 79 Antonio Daniels 25.00 11.00
❑ 80 Kevin Garnett 500.00 220.00
❑ 81 Nick Anderson 25.00 11.00
❑ 82 David Robinson 120.00 55.00
❑ 83 Jamal Mashburn 50.00 22.00
❑ 84 Rodney Rogers 25.00 11.00
❑ 85 Michael Stewart 25.00 11.00
❑ 86 Rik Smits 25.00 11.00
❑ 87 Billy Owens 25.00 11.00
❑ 88 Damon Stoudamire 80.00 36.00
❑ 89 Theo Ratliff 25.00 11.00
❑ 90 Keith Van Horn 200.00 90.00
❑ 91 Hakeem Olajuwon 120.00 55.00
❑ 92 Alonzo Mourning 80.00 36.00
❑ 93 Steve Smith 50.00 22.00
❑ 94 Mark Jackson 25.00 11.00
❑ 95 Cedric Ceballos 25.00 11.00
❑ 96 Bryant Reeves 25.00 11.00
❑ 97 Juwan Howard 50.00 22.00
❑ 98 Detlef Schrempf 50.00 22.00
❑ 99 John Stockton 80.00 36.00
❑ 100 Shaquille O'Neal 400.00 180.00
❑ 101 Michael Olowokandi 80.00 36.00
❑ 102 Mike Bibby 125.00 55.00
❑ 103 Raef LaFrentz 80.00 36.00
❑ 104 Antawn Jamison 200.00 90.00
❑ 105 Vince Carter 1000.00 450.00
❑ 106 Robert Traylor 40.00 18.00
❑ 107 Jason Williams 250.00 110.00
❑ 108 Larry Hughes 250.00 110.00
❑ 109 Dirk Nowitzki 150.00 70.00
❑ 110 Paul Pierce 200.00 90.00
❑ 111 Bonzi Wells 150.00 70.00
❑ 112 Michael Doleac 50.00 22.00
❑ 113 Keon Clark 50.00 22.00
❑ 114 Michael Dickerson 80.00 36.00
❑ 115 Matt Harpring 50.00 22.00
❑ 116 Bryce Drew 50.00 22.00
❑ 117 Pat Garrity 40.00 18.00
❑ 118 Roshown McLeod 40.00 18.00
❑ 119 Ricky Davis 80.00 36.00
❑ 120 Rashard Lewis 150.00 70.00
❑ 121 Tyronn Lue 40.00 18.00
❑ 122 Al Harrington 120.00 55.00
❑ 123 Corey Benjamin 50.00 22.00
❑ 124 Felipe Lopez 50.00 22.00
❑ 125 Korleone Young 40.00 18.00

1998-99 Fleer Brilliants Blue

	MINT	NRMT
COMPLETE SET (125)	120.00	55.00
COMMON CARD (1-100)	.50	.23
COMMON CARD (101-125)	1.00	.45

*STARS: .75X TO 2X BASE CARD HI
*RCs: .5X TO 1.25X BASE
STARS: STATED ODDS 1:3
RCs: STATED ODDS 1:6

1998-99 Fleer Brilliants Gold

	MINT	NRMT
COMMON CARD (1-125)	8.00	3.60

*STARS: 12.5X TO 30X BASE CARD HI
*RCs: 5X TO 12X BASE HI
RANDOM INSERTS IN PACKS
STATED PRINT RUN 99 SERIAL #'d SETS

	MINT	NRMT
❑ 105 Vince Carter	500.00	220.00

1998-99 Fleer Brilliants Illuminators

	MINT	NRMT
COMPLETE SET (15)	60.00	27.00
COMMON CARD (1-15)	1.25	.55
SEMISTARS	1.50	.70
UNLISTED STARS	2.50	1.10

STATED ODDS 1:10

	MINT	NRMT
❑ 1 Michael Olowokandi	2.50	1.10
❑ 2 Mike Bibby	4.00	1.80
❑ 3 Antawn Jamison	6.00	2.70
❑ 4 Vince Carter	30.00	13.50
❑ 5 Robert Traylor	1.25	.55
❑ 6 Larry Hughes	8.00	3.60
❑ 7 Paul Pierce	6.00	2.70
❑ 8 Raef LaFrentz	2.50	1.10
❑ 9 Dirk Nowitzki	5.00	2.20
❑ 10 Corey Benjamin	1.50	.70
❑ 11 Michael Dickerson	2.50	1.10
❑ 12 Roshown McLeod	1.25	.55
❑ 13 Ricky Davis	2.50	1.10
❑ 14 Tyronn Lue	1.25	.55
❑ 15 Al Harrington	4.00	1.80

1998-99 Fleer Brilliants Shining Stars

	MINT	NRMT
COMPLETE SET (15)	100.00	45.00
COMMON CARD (1-15)	4.00	1.80

STATED ODDS 1:20

	MINT	NRMT
COMP.PULSARS SET (15)	600.00	275.00
COMMON PULSAR (1-15)	25.00	11.00

*PULSARS: 2.5X TO 6X HI COLUMN
PULSARS: STATED ODDS 1:400

	MINT	NRMT
❑ 1 Tim Thomas	4.00	1.80
❑ 2 Antoine Walker	4.00	1.80
❑ 3 Tim Duncan	12.00	5.50
❑ 4 Keith Van Horn	6.00	2.70
❑ 5 Grant Hill	12.00	5.50
❑ 6 Shaquille O'Neal	12.00	5.50
❑ 7 Kevin Garnett	15.00	6.75
❑ 8 Allen Iverson	10.00	4.50
❑ 9 Shareef Abdur-Rahim	6.00	2.70
❑ 10 Shawn Kemp	4.00	1.80
❑ 11 Anfernee Hardaway	8.00	3.60
❑ 12 Scottie Pippen	8.00	3.60
❑ 13 Stephon Marbury	6.00	2.70
❑ 14 Kobe Bryant	20.00	9.00
❑ 15 Ron Mercer	4.00	1.80

1999-00 Fleer Focus

	MINT	NRMT
COMPLETE SET (150)	300.00	135.00
COMPLETE SET w/o RC (100)	20.00	9.00
COMMON CARD (1-100)	.15	.07
COMMON RC (101-150)	2.50	1.10
SEMISTARS	.20	.09
SEMISTARS RC	3.00	1.35
UNLISTED STARS	.40	.18
UNLISTED STARS RC	4.00	1.80

*RC PORTRAIT: .75X TO 1.5X BASE RC
RCs: FIRST 999 ARE PORTRAIT PHOTO
RCs: REMAINING 3000 ARE ACTION PHOTO
UNPRICED MASTERPIECES SERIAL #'d TO 1

	MINT	NRMT
❑ 1 Anfernee Hardaway	1.25	.55
❑ 2 Derek Anderson	.40	.18
❑ 3 Jayson Williams	.20	.09
❑ 4 Ron Mercer	.50	.23
❑ 5 Jerry Stackhouse	.20	.09
❑ 6 Tariq Abdul-Wahad	.15	.07
❑ 7 Sean Elliott	.15	.07
❑ 8 Lindsey Hunter	.15	.07
❑ 9 Larry Johnson	.20	.09
❑ 10 Steve Smith	.20	.09
❑ 11 Raef LaFrentz	.40	.18
❑ 12 Jalen Rose	.40	.18
❑ 13 Stephon Marbury	.75	.35
❑ 14 Detlef Schrempf	.20	.09
❑ 15 Rod Strickland	.20	.09
❑ 16 Paul Pierce	.75	.35
❑ 17 Maurice Taylor	.40	.18
❑ 18 Allen Iverson	1.50	.70
❑ 19 Mitch Richmond	.40	.18
❑ 20 Gary Trent	.15	.07
❑ 21 Reggie Miller	.40	.18
❑ 22 Kerry Kittles	.20	.09
❑ 23 Rasheed Wallace	.40	.18
❑ 24 Steve Nash	.15	.07
❑ 25 Scottie Pippen	1.25	.55
❑ 26 Joe Smith	.20	.09
❑ 27 Jason Williams	1.00	.45
❑ 28 Michael Finley	.40	.18
❑ 29 Hakeem Olajuwon	.60	.25
❑ 30 Kevin Garnett	2.50	1.10
❑ 31 Darrell Armstrong	.20	.09
❑ 32 David Robinson	.60	.25
❑ 33 Anthony Mason	.20	.09
❑ 34 Jamal Mashburn	.20	.09
❑ 35 Gary Payton	.60	.25
❑ 36 Bryon Russell	.15	.07
❑ 37 Cedric Ceballos	.15	.07
❑ 38 Michael Dickerson	.40	.18
❑ 39 Robert Traylor	.15	.07
❑ 40 Vin Baker	.20	.09
❑ 41 Shawn Kemp	.60	.25
❑ 42 Charles Barkley	.60	.25
❑ 43 Glenn Robinson	.20	.09
❑ 44 Vince Carter	4.00	1.80
❑ 45 Zydrunas Ilgauskas	.15	.07
❑ 46 Sam Cassell	.20	.09
❑ 47 Tracy McGrady	1.25	.55
❑ 48 Chris Mills	.15	.07
❑ 49 Antawn Jamison	.75	.35
❑ 50 Nick Anderson	.15	.07
❑ 51 Avery Johnson	.15	.07
❑ 52 Brent Barry	.15	.07
❑ 53 Alonzo Mourning	.40	.18
❑ 54 Karl Malone	.60	.25
❑ 55 Toni Kukoc	.50	.23
❑ 56 Ray Allen	.40	.18
❑ 57 Charles Oakley	.15	.07
❑ 58 Cuttino Mobley	.40	.18
❑ 59 Kenny Anderson	.20	.09
❑ 60 Tom Gugliotta	.20	.09
❑ 61 Antoine Walker	.50	.23
❑ 62 Kobe Bryant	3.00	1.35
❑ 63 Larry Hughes	1.00	.45
❑ 64 Vlade Divac	.15	.07
❑ 65 Juwan Howard	.20	.09
❑ 66 Isaiah Rider	.20	.09
❑ 67 Antonio McDyess	.40	.18
❑ 68 Rik Smits	.15	.07
❑ 69 Keith Van Horn	.75	.35
❑ 70 Doug Christie	.15	.07
❑ 71 Elden Campbell	.15	.07
❑ 72 Shaquille O'Neal	2.00	.90
❑ 73 Matt Geiger	.15	.07
❑ 74 Chris Webber	1.25	.55
❑ 75 Troy Hudson	.15	.07
❑ 76 Eddie Jones	.75	.35
❑ 77 Tim Hardaway	.40	.18
❑ 78 Hersey Hawkins	.20	.09
❑ 79 Shareef Abdur-Rahim	.75	.35
❑ 80 Christian Laettner	.20	.09
❑ 81 Latrell Sprewell	.75	.35
❑ 82 Damon Stoudamire	.40	.18
❑ 83 Jason Caffey	.15	.07
❑ 84 Michael Olowokandi	.20	.09
❑ 85 Horace Grant	.20	.09
❑ 86 Grant Hill	2.00	.90
❑ 87 Patrick Ewing	.40	.18
❑ 88 Clifford Robinson	.15	.07
❑ 89 Ricky Davis	.40	.18
❑ 90 Glen Rice	.20	.09
❑ 91 Matt Harpring	.15	.07
❑ 92 Mike Bibby	.50	.23
❑ 93 Dikembe Mutombo	.20	.09
❑ 94 Chris Mullin	.40	.18
❑ 95 Marcus Camby	.40	.18
❑ 96 Jason Kidd	1.25	.55
❑ 97 John Starks	.15	.07
❑ 98 Terrell Brandon	.20	.09
❑ 99 Tim Duncan	2.00	.90
❑ 100 John Stockton	.40	.18
❑ 101 Ron Artest RC	10.00	4.50
❑ 102 William Avery RC	6.00	2.70
❑ 103 Jonathan Bender RC	20.00	9.00
❑ 104 Carl Bowdler RC	4.00	1.80
❑ 105 Elton Brand RC	50.00	22.00
❑ 106 Vonteego Cummings RC	6.00	2.70
❑ 107 Baron Davis RC	10.00	4.50
❑ 108 Jeff Foster RC	4.00	1.80
❑ 109 Steve Francis RC	60.00	27.00
❑ 110 Devean George RC	8.00	3.60
❑ 111 Dion Glover RC	4.00	1.80
❑ 112 Richard Hamilton RC	10.00	4.50
❑ 113 Tim James RC	5.00	2.00
❑ 114 Trajan Langdon RC	6.00	2.70
❑ 115 Quincy Lewis RC	4.00	1.80
❑ 116 Corey Maggette RC	15.00	6.75
❑ 117 Shawn Marion RC	12.00	5.50
❑ 118 Andre Miller RC	12.00	5.50
❑ 119 Lamar Odom RC	40.00	18.00
❑ 120 Scott Padgett RC	4.00	1.80

Card	Mint	Nrmt
❑ 121 James Posey RC	8.00	3.60
❑ 122 Aleksandar Radojevic RC	2.50	1.10
❑ 123 Wally Szczerbiak RC	15.00	6.75
❑ 124 Jason Terry RC	6.00	2.70
❑ 125 Kenny Thomas RC	6.00	2.70
❑ 127 Rick Hughes RC	2.50	1.10
❑ 126 Jumaine Jones RC	3.00	1.35
❑ 128 John Celestand RC	4.00	1.80
❑ 129 Adrian Griffin RC	5.00	2.20
❑ 130 Michael Ruffin RC	3.00	1.35
❑ 131 Chris Herren RC	2.50	1.10
❑ 132 Evan Eschmeyer RC	2.50	1.10
❑ 133 Tim Young RC	2.50	1.10
❑ 134 Obinna Ekezie RC	3.00	1.35
❑ 135 Laron Profit RC	4.00	1.80
❑ 136 AJ Bramlett RC	2.50	1.10
❑ 137 Eddie Robinson RC	6.00	2.70
❑ 138 Ryan Bowen RC	2.50	1.10
❑ 139 Chucky Atkins RC	5.00	2.20
❑ 140 Ryan Robertson RC	3.00	1.35
❑ 141 Derrick Dial RC	2.50	1.10
❑ 142 Todd MacCulloch RC	4.00	1.80
❑ 143 DeMarco Johnson RC	3.00	1.35
❑ 144 Anthony Carter RC	10.00	4.50
❑ 145 Lazaro Borrell RC	2.50	1.10
❑ 146 Rafer Alston RC	5.00	2.20
❑ 147 Nikita Morgunov RC	2.50	1.10
❑ 148 Rodney Buford RC	2.50	1.10
❑ 149 Milt Palacio RC	2.50	1.10
❑ 150 Jermaine Jackson RC	2.50	1.10

1999-00 Fleer Focus Masterpiece Mania

	MINT	NRMT
COMMON CARD (1-100)	2.00	.90
COMMON CARD (101-150)	2.50	1.10

*STARS: 5X TO 12X BASE CARD HI
*RCs: .4X TO 1X BASE HI
RANDOM INSERTS IN HOBBY PACKS
STATED PRINT RUN 300 SERIAL #'d SETS

1999-00 Fleer Focus Feel the Game

	MINT	NRMT
COMPLETE SET (10)	500.00	220.00
COMMON CARD (1-10)	20.00	9.00
SEMISTARS	25.00	11.00

STATED ODDS 1:288

Card	Mint	Nrmt
❑ 1 Vince Carter	300.00	135.00
❑ 2 Kevin Garnett	100.00	45.00
❑ 3 Paul Pierce	30.00	13.50
❑ 4 Grant Hill	60.00	27.00
❑ 5 Tim Hardaway	25.00	11.00
❑ 6 Jayson Williams	25.00	11.00
❑ 7 Bryon Russell	20.00	9.00
❑ 8 Bryant Reeves	20.00	9.00
❑ 9 Keith Van Horn	30.00	13.50
❑ 10 Vin Baker	25.00	11.00

1999-00 Fleer Focus Focus Pocus

	MINT	NRMT
COMPLETE SET (10)	40.00	18.00
COMMON CARD (FP1-FP10)	2.50	1.10

STATED ODDS 1:20

Card	Mint	Nrmt
❑ FP1 Vince Carter	12.00	5.50
❑ FP2 Tim Duncan	6.00	2.70
❑ FP3 Shaquille O'Neal	6.00	2.70
❑ FP4 Paul Pierce	2.50	1.10
❑ FP5 Kobe Bryant	10.00	4.50
❑ FP6 Kevin Garnett	8.00	3.60
❑ FP7 Keith Van Horn	2.50	1.10
❑ FP8 Jason Williams	3.00	1.35
❑ FP9 Grant Hill	6.00	2.70
❑ FP10 Allen Iverson	5.00	2.20

1999-00 Fleer Focus Fresh Ink

	MINT	NRMT
COMMON CARD	5.00	2.20
SEMISTARS	8.00	3.60

NNO CARDS LISTED BELOW ALPHABETICALLY
STATED ODDS 1:96

Card	Mint	Nrmt
❑ 1 Charles Barkley	150.00	70.00
❑ 2 Vince Carter	200.00	90.00
❑ 3 Obinna Ekezie	5.00	2.20
❑ 4 Jeff Foster	8.00	3.60
❑ 5 Devean George	8.00	3.60
❑ 6 Tim Hardaway	15.00	6.75
❑ 7 Matt Harpring	5.00	2.20
❑ 8 Al Harrington	15.00	6.75
❑ 9 Juwan Howard	15.00	6.75
❑ 10 Eddie Jones	30.00	13.50
❑ 11 Shawn Kemp	20.00	9.00
❑ 12 Brevin Knight	10.00	4.50
❑ 13 Trajan Langdon	12.00	5.50
❑ 14 Stephon Marbury	40.00	18.00
❑ 15 Shawn Marion	15.00	6.75
❑ 16 Tracy McGrady	40.00	18.00
❑ 17 Roshown McLeod	5.00	2.20
❑ 18 Brad Miller	5.00	2.20
❑ 19 Alonzo Mourning	50.00	22.00
❑ 20 Shaquille O'Neal	200.00	90.00
❑ 21 Scott Padgett	8.00	3.60
❑ 22 Michael Ruffin	5.00	2.20
❑ 23 Damon Stoudamire	15.00	6.75
❑ 24 Wally Szczerbiak	30.00	13.50
❑ 25 Jason Terry	8.00	3.60
❑ 26 Keith Van Horn	30.00	13.50
❑ 27 Chris Webber	80.00	36.00

1999-00 Fleer Focus Ray of Light

	MINT	NRMT
COMPLETE SET (15)	50.00	22.00
COMMON CARD (RL1-RL15)	1.25	.55
UNLISTED STARS	2.00	.90

STATED ODDS 1:20

Card	Mint	Nrmt
❑ RL1 Andre Miller	4.00	1.80
❑ RL2 Baron Davis	3.00	1.35
❑ RL3 Corey Maggette	5.00	2.20
❑ RL4 Dion Glover	1.25	.55
❑ RL5 Elton Brand	12.00	5.50
❑ RL6 Jason Terry	2.00	.90
❑ RL7 Jonathan Bender	6.00	2.70
❑ RL8 Lamar Odom	10.00	4.50
❑ RL9 Richard Hamilton	3.00	1.35
❑ RL10 Shawn Marion	4.00	1.80
❑ RL11 Steve Francis	15.00	6.75
❑ RL12 Tim James	2.00	.90
❑ RL13 Trajan Langdon	2.00	.90
❑ RL14 Wally Szczerbiak	5.00	2.20
❑ RL15 William Avery	2.00	.90

1999-00 Fleer Focus Soar Subjects

	MINT	NRMT
COMPLETE SET (15)	25.00	11.00
COMMON CARD (SS1-SS15)	.75	.35

STATED ODDS 1:6

	MINT	NRMT
COMMON VIVID (SS1-SS15)	25.00	11.00

*VIVID: 12.5X TO 30X HI COLUMN
VIVID: RANDOM INSERTS IN PACKS
VIVID: PRINT RUN 50 SERIAL #'d SETS

Card	Mint	Nrmt
❑ SS1 Allen Iverson	2.50	1.10
❑ SS2 Anfernee Hardaway	2.00	.90
❑ SS3 Paul Pierce	1.25	.55
❑ SS4 Antoine Walker	.75	.35
❑ SS5 Grant Hill	3.00	1.35
❑ SS6 Keith Van Horn	1.25	.55
❑ SS7 Kevin Garnett	4.00	1.80

Card	Mint	Nrmt
❑ SS8 Kobe Bryant	5.00	2.20
❑ SS9 Larry Hughes	1.50	.70
❑ SS10 Jason Williams	1.50	.70
❑ SS11 Scottie Pippen	2.00	.90
❑ SS12 Shaquille O'Neal	3.00	1.35
❑ SS13 Vince Carter	6.00	2.70
❑ SS14 Stephon Marbury	1.25	.55
❑ SS15 Tim Duncan	3.00	1.35

1999-00 Fleer Force

	MINT	NRMT
COMPLETE SET (235)	400.00	180.00
COMPLETE SET w/o RC (200)	30.00	13.50
COMMON CARD (1-200)	.15	.07
COMMON RC (201-235)	5.00	2.20
SEMISTARS	.20	.09
SEMISTARS RC	6.00	2.70
UNLISTED STARS	.40	.18
UNLISTED STARS RC	8.00	3.60

RCs: PRINT RUN 1600 SERIAL #'d SETS
RCs: RANDOM INSERTS IN PACKS
SGT.CARTER CARD: STATED ODDS 1:300
CARTER AU: PRINT RUN 300 SETS

Card	Mint	Nrmt
❑ 1 Vince Carter	4.00	1.80
❑ 2 Kobe Bryant	3.00	1.35
❑ 3 Keith Van Horn	.75	.35
❑ 4 Tim Duncan	2.00	.90
❑ 5 Grant Hill	2.00	.90
❑ 6 Kevin Garnett	2.50	1.10
❑ 7 Anfernee Hardaway	1.25	.55
❑ 8 Jason Williams	1.00	.45
❑ 9 Paul Pierce	.75	.35
❑ 10 Mookie Blaylock	.15	.07
❑ 11 Shawn Bradley	.15	.07
❑ 12 Kenny Anderson	.20	.09
❑ 13 Chauncey Billups	.15	.07
❑ 14 Elden Campbell	.15	.07
❑ 15 Jason Caffey	.15	.07
❑ 16 Brent Barry	.15	.07
❑ 17 Charles Barkley	.60	.25
❑ 18 Derek Anderson	.40	.18
❑ 19 Darrick Martin	.15	.07
❑ 20 Michael Curry	.15	.07
❑ 21 Rick Fox	.15	.07
❑ 22 Antonio Davis	.15	.07
❑ 23 Terrell Brandon	.20	.09
❑ 24 P.J. Brown	.15	.07
❑ 25 Toby Bailey	.15	.07
❑ 26 Ray Allen	.40	.18
❑ 27 Brian Grant	.20	.09
❑ 28 Scott Burrell	.15	.07
❑ 29 Tariq Abdul-Wahad	.15	.07
❑ 30 Marcus Camby	.40	.18
❑ 31 John Stockton	.40	.18
❑ 32 Nick Anderson	.15	.07
❑ 33 Jamie Feick RC	5.00	2.20
❑ 34 Matt Geiger	.15	.07
❑ 35 Vin Baker	.20	.09
❑ 36 Dee Brown	.15	.07
❑ 37 Shandon Anderson	.15	.07
❑ 38 Vernon Maxwell	.15	.07
❑ 39 Shareef Abdur-Rahim	.75	.35
❑ 40 LaPhonso Ellis	.15	.07
❑ 41 Cedric Ceballos	.15	.07
❑ 42 Tony Battie	.15	.07
❑ 43 Keon Clark	.15	.07
❑ 44 Derrick Coleman	.20	.09
❑ 45 Erick Dampier	.15	.07
❑ 46 Corey Benjamin	.15	.07
❑ 47 Michael Dickerson	.40	.18
❑ 48 Cedric Henderson	.15	.07
❑ 49 Lamond Murray	.15	.07
❑ 50 Jerome Williams	.20	.09
❑ 51 Shaquille O'Neal	2.00	.90
❑ 52 Dale Davis	.15	.07
❑ 53 Dean Garrett	.15	.07
❑ 54 Tim Hardaway	.40	.18
❑ 55 Dennis Rodman	3.00	1.35
❑ 56 Sam Cassell	.20	.09
❑ 57 Jim Jackson	.15	.07
❑ 58 Kendall Gill	.20	.09
❑ 59 Eric Williams	.15	.07
❑ 60 Chris Childs	.15	.07
❑ 61 Vlade Divac	.15	.07
❑ 62 Darrell Armstrong	.20	.09
❑ 63 Mario Elie	.15	.07
❑ 64 Jaren Jackson	.15	.07
❑ 65 Dale Ellis	.15	.07
❑ 66 Doug Christie	.15	.07
❑ 67 Howard Eisley	.15	.07
❑ 68 Juwan Howard	.20	.09
❑ 69 Mike Bibby	.50	.23
❑ 70 Alan Henderson	.15	.07
❑ 71 Michael Finley	.40	.18
❑ 72 Dana Barros	.15	.07
❑ 73 Troy Hudson	.15	.07
❑ 74 Ricky Davis	.40	.18
❑ 75 John Amaechi RC	.50	.23
❑ 76 Erick Strickland	.15	.07
❑ 77 Bryce Drew	.15	.07
❑ 78 Shawn Kemp	.60	.25
❑ 79 Tyrone Nesby RC	.15	.07
❑ 80 Lindsey Hunter	.15	.07
❑ 81 Ruben Patterson	.40	.18
❑ 82 Al Harrington	.50	.23
❑ 83 Bobby Jackson	.15	.07
❑ 84 Dan Majerle	.20	.09
❑ 85 Rex Chapman	.15	.07
❑ 86 Dell Curry	.15	.07
❑ 87 Robert Pack	.15	.07
❑ 88 Kerry Kittles	.20	.09
❑ 89 Isaiah Rider	.20	.09
❑ 90 Patrick Ewing	.40	.18
❑ 91 Lawrence Funderburke	.15	.07
❑ 92 Isaac Austin	.15	.07
❑ 93 Sean Elliott	.15	.07
❑ 94 Larry Hughes	1.00	.45
❑ 95 Jelani McCoy	.15	.07
❑ 96 Tracy McGrady	1.25	.55
❑ 97 Jeff Hornacek	.20	.09
❑ 98 Jahidi White	.15	.07
❑ 99 Danny Manning	.20	.09
❑ 100 Roshown McLeod	.15	.07
❑ 101 Steve Nash	.15	.07
❑ 102 Ron Mercer	.50	.23
❑ 103 Raef LaFrentz	.40	.18
❑ 104 Eddie Jones	.75	.35
❑ 105 Antawn Jamison	.75	.35
❑ 106 Chucky Atkins RC	.50	.23
❑ 107 Othella Harrington	.15	.07
❑ 108 Brevin Knight	.15	.07
❑ 109 Michael Olowokandi	.20	.09
❑ 110 Christian Laettner	.20	.09
❑ 111 J.R. Reid	.15	.07
❑ 112 Reggie Miller	.40	.18
❑ 113 Lazaro Borrell RC	5.00	2.20
❑ 114 Jamal Mashburn	.20	.09
❑ 115 Glenn Robinson	.20	.09
❑ 116 Pat Garrity	.15	.07
❑ 117 Stephon Marbury	.75	.35
❑ 118 Arvydas Sabonis	.20	.09
❑ 119 Allan Houston	.40	.18
❑ 120 Predrag Stojakovic	.20	.09
❑ 121 Michael Doleac	.15	.07
❑ 122 Avery Johnson	.15	.07
❑ 123 Allen Iverson	1.50	.70
❑ 124 Rashard Lewis	.60	.25
❑ 125 Charles Oakley	.15	.07
❑ 126 Karl Malone	.60	.25
❑ 127 Tracy Murray	.15	.07
❑ 128 Felipe Lopez	.15	.07
❑ 129 Dikembe Mutombo	.20	.09
❑ 130 Dirk Nowitzki	.60	.25
❑ 131 Vitaly Potapenko	.15	.07
❑ 132 Antonio McDyess	.40	.18
❑ 133 Anthony Mason	.20	.09
❑ 134 Donyell Marshall	.15	.07
❑ 135 Dickey Simpkins	.15	.07
❑ 136 Cuttino Mobley	.40	.18
❑ 137 Wesley Person	.15	.07
❑ 138 Rodney Rogers	.15	.07
❑ 139 Jerry Stackhouse	.20	.09
❑ 140 Glen Rice	.20	.09
❑ 141 Chris Mullin	.40	.18
❑ 142 Anthony Peeler	.15	.07
❑ 143 Alonzo Mourning	.40	.18
❑ 144 Tom Gugliotta	.20	.09
❑ 145 Tim Thomas	.50	.23
❑ 146 Damon Stoudamire	.40	.18
❑ 147 Jayson Williams	.20	.09
❑ 148 Larry Johnson	.20	.09
❑ 149 Chris Webber	1.25	.55
❑ 150 Matt Harpring	.15	.07
❑ 151 David Robinson	.60	.25
❑ 152 George Lynch	.15	.07
❑ 153 Gary Payton	.60	.25
❑ 154 John Wallace	.15	.07
❑ 155 Greg Ostertag	.15	.07
❑ 156 Mitch Richmond	.40	.18
❑ 157 Cherokee Parks	.15	.07
❑ 158 Steve Smith	.20	.09
❑ 159 Gary Trent	.15	.07
❑ 160 Antoine Walker	.50	.23
❑ 161 Chris Herren RC	.15	.07
❑ 162 Ron Harper	.20	.09
❑ 163 Chris Mills	.15	.07
❑ 164 Fred Hoiberg	.15	.07
❑ 165 Hakeem Olajuwon	.60	.25
❑ 166 Bob Sura	.15	.07
❑ 167 Brian Skinner	.15	.07
❑ 168 Loy Vaught	.15	.07
❑ 169 A.C. Green	.20	.09
❑ 170 Jalen Rose	.40	.18
❑ 171 Joe Smith	.20	.09
❑ 172 Clarence Weatherspoon	.15	.07
❑ 173 Jason Kidd	1.25	.55
❑ 174 Robert Traylor	.15	.07
❑ 175 Rasheed Wallace	.40	.18
❑ 176 Latrell Sprewell	.75	.35
❑ 177 Corliss Williamson	.15	.07
❑ 178 Charles Outlaw	.15	.07
❑ 179 Malik Rose	.15	.07
❑ 180 Nazr Mohammed	.15	.07
❑ 181 Eric Murdock	.15	.07
❑ 182 Kevin Willis	.15	.07
❑ 183 Bryon Russell	.15	.07
❑ 184 Bryant Reeves	.15	.07
❑ 185 Rod Strickland	.20	.09
❑ 186 Samaki Walker	.15	.07
❑ 187 Nick Van Exel	.20	.09
❑ 188 David Wesley	.15	.07
❑ 189 John Starks	.15	.07
❑ 190 Toni Kukoc	.50	.23
❑ 191 Scottie Pippen	1.25	.55
❑ 192 Johnny Newman	.15	.07
❑ 193 Maurice Taylor	.40	.18
❑ 194 Rik Smits	.15	.07
❑ 195 Clifford Robinson	.15	.07
❑ 196 Bonzi Wells	.60	.25
❑ 197 Charlie Ward	.15	.07
❑ 198 Detlef Schrempf	.20	.09
❑ 199 Theo Ratliff	.15	.07
❑ 200 Kelvin Cato	.15	.07
❑ 201 Ron Artest RC	20.00	9.00
❑ 202 William Avery RC	12.00	5.50
❑ 203 Elton Brand RC	80.00	36.00
❑ 204 Baron Davis RC	20.00	9.00
❑ 205 Jumaine Jones RC	6.00	2.70
❑ 206 Andre Miller RC	25.00	11.00
❑ 207 Eddie Robinson RC	12.00	5.50
❑ 208 James Posey RC	15.00	6.75
❑ 209 Jason Terry RC	12.00	5.50
❑ 210 Kenny Thomas RC	12.00	5.50
❑ 211 Steve Francis RC	100.00	45.00
❑ 212 Wally Szczerbiak RC	30.00	13.50
❑ 213 Richard Hamilton RC	20.00	9.00
❑ 214 Jonathan Bender RC	40.00	18.00
❑ 215 Shawn Marion RC	25.00	11.00
❑ 216 Aleksandar Radojevic RC	5.00	2.20
❑ 217 Tim James RC	10.00	4.50
❑ 218 Trajan Langdon RC	12.00	5.50
❑ 219 Lamar Odom RC	60.00	27.00
❑ 220 Corey Maggette RC	30.00	13.50
❑ 221 Dion Glover RC	8.00	3.60
❑ 222 Cal Bowdler RC	8.00	3.60
❑ 223 Vonteego Cummings RC	12.00	5.50
❑ 224 Devean George RC	15.00	6.75
❑ 225 Anthony Carter RC	20.00	9.00

❑ 226 Laron Profit RC 10.00 4.50
❑ 227 Quincy Lewis RC.......... 8.00 3.60
❑ 228 John Celestand RC...... 8.00 3.60
❑ 229 Obinna Ekezie RC........ 6.00 2.70
❑ 230 Scott Padgett RC 8.00 3.60
❑ 231 Michael Ruffin RC 6.00 2.70
❑ 232 Jeff Foster RC............. 8.00 3.60
❑ 233 Jermaine Jackson RC .. 5.00 2.20
❑ 234 Adrian Griffin RC 10.00 4.50
❑ 235 Todd MacCulloch RC .. 8.00 3.60
❑ NNO Vince Carter 150.00 70.00
Sgt.Carter Jersey
❑ NNO Vince Carter 500.00 220.00
Sgt.Carter Auto/300

1999-00 Fleer Force Forcefield

	MINT	NRMT
COMMON CARD (1-200)	.60	.25
COMMON CARD (201-235)	8.00	3.60

*STARS: 1.25X TO 3X BASE CARD HI
*RCs: .5X TO 1.25X BASE HI
STARS: STATED ODDS 1:12
RCs: PRINT RUN 100 SERIAL #'d SETS
RCs: RANDOM INSERTS IN PACKS

❑ 201 Ron Artest 30.00 13.50
❑ 203 Elton Brand 120.00 55.00
❑ 204 Baron Davis................ 30.00 13.50
❑ 206 Andre Miller................ 40.00 18.00
❑ 211 Steve Francis 150.00 70.00
❑ 212 Wally Szczerbiak........ 50.00 22.00
❑ 213 Richard Hamilton........ 30.00 13.50
❑ 214 Jonathan Bender........ 60.00 27.00
❑ 215 Shawn Marion 40.00 18.00
❑ 219 Lamar Odom 100.00 45.00
❑ 220 Corey Maggette.......... 50.00 22.00
❑ 225 Anthony Carter 30.00 13.50

1999-00 Fleer Force Air Force One Five

	MINT	NRMT
COMPLETE SET (15)	50.00	22.00
COMMON CARD (AF1-AF15)	4.00	1.80

STATED ODDS 1:24

COMP.FF.SET (15)	1000.00	450.00
COMMON FF (AF1-AF15)	80.00	36.00

FF: PRINT RUN 150 SERIAL #'d SETS
FF: RANDOM INSERTS IN PACKS

❑ AF1 Vince Carter 4.00 1.80
❑ AF2 Vince Carter 4.00 1.80
❑ AF3 Vince Carter 4.00 1.80
❑ AF4 Vince Carter 4.00 1.80
❑ AF5 Vince Carter 4.00 1.80
❑ AF6 Vince Carter 4.00 1.80
❑ AF7 Vince Carter 4.00 1.80
❑ AF8 Vince Carter 4.00 1.80
❑ AF9 Vince Carter 4.00 1.80
❑ AF10 Vince Carter 4.00 1.80
❑ AF11 Vince Carter 4.00 1.80
❑ AF12 Vince Carter 4.00 1.80
❑ AF13 Vince Carter 4.00 1.80
❑ AF14 Vince Carter 4.00 1.80
❑ AF15 Vince Carter 4.00 1.80

1999-00 Fleer Force Attack Force

	MINT	NRMT
COMPLETE SET (20)	20.00	9.00
COMMON CARD (A1-A20)	.40	.18
UNLISTED STARS	.60	.25

STATED ODDS 1:6

COMPLETE FF SET (20)	40.00	18.00
COMMON FF (AF1-AF20)	.75	.35

*FF: .75X TO 2X BASE CARD HI
FF: STATED ODDS 1:24

❑ A1 Vince Carter 6.00 2.70
❑ A2 Lamar Odom................. 2.50 1.10
❑ A3 Stephon Marbury .... 1.25 .55
❑ A4 Jason Terry..................... .60 .25
❑ A5 Richard Hamilton .... .75 .35
❑ A6 Steve Francis 4.00 1.80
❑ A7 Wally Szczerbiak .... 1.25 .55
❑ A8 Tracy McGrady .... 2.00 .90
❑ A9 Michael Finley.................. .60 .25
❑ A10 Baron Davis .... .75 .35
❑ A11 Shawn Marion............. 1.00 .45
❑ A12 Jonathan Bender .... 1.50 .70
❑ A13 Elton Brand.................. 3.00 1.35
❑ A14 Shareef Abdur-Rahim .. 1.25 .55
❑ A15 Keith Van Horn .... 1.25 .55
❑ A16 Jerry Stackhouse .... .40 .18
❑ A17 Antonio McDyess .... .60 .25
❑ A18 Antoine Walker .... .75 .35
❑ A19 Steve Smith .... .40 .18
❑ A20 Ron Artest...................... .75 .35

1999-00 Fleer Force Forceful

	MINT	NRMT
COMPLETE SET (15)	80.00	36.00
COMMON CARD (F1-F15)	2.00	.90

STATED ODDS 1:36

COMPLETE FF SET (15)	150.00	70.00
COMMON FF (F1-F15)	4.00	1.80

*FF: .75X TO 2X BASE CARD HI
FF: STATED ODDS 1:144

❑ F1 Vince Carter 20.00 9.00
❑ F2 Lamar Odom 8.00 3.60
❑ F3 Shaquille O'Neal 10.00 4.50
❑ F4 Alonzo Mourning .... 2.00 .90
❑ F5 Kevin Garnett 12.00 5.50
❑ F6 Tim Duncan.................. 10.00 4.50
❑ F7 Kobe Bryant 15.00 6.75
❑ F8 Allen Iverson 8.00 3.60
❑ F9 Jason Williams 5.00 2.20
❑ F10 Paul Pierce 4.00 1.80
❑ F11 Shareef Abdur-Rahim .. 4.00 1.80
❑ F12 Stephon Marbury 4.00 1.80
❑ F13 Grant Hill.................... 10.00 4.50
❑ F14 Keith Van Horn 4.00 1.80
❑ F15 Karl Malone.................. 3.00 1.35

1999-00 Fleer Force Mission Accomplished

	MINT	NRMT
COMPLETE SET (15)	30.00	13.50
COMMON CARD (MA1-MA15)	1.00	.45

STATED ODDS 1:12

COMPLETE FF SET (15)	60.00	27.00
COMMON FF (MA1-MA15)	2.00	.90

*FF: .75X TO 2X BASE CARD HI
FF: STATED ODDS 1:48

❑ MA1 Vince Carter............... 8.00 3.60
❑ MA2 Lamar Odom 3.00 1.35
❑ MA3 Allen Iverson 3.00 1.35
❑ MA4 Tim Duncan 4.00 1.80
❑ MA5 Charles Barkley .... 1.25 .55
❑ MA6 Jason Kidd................. 2.50 1.10
❑ MA7 Steve Francis............. 5.00 2.20
❑ MA8 Elton Brand 4.00 1.80
❑ MA9 Kevin Garnett............. 5.00 2.20
❑ MA10 Baron Davis .... 1.00 .45
❑ MA11 Paul Pierce .... 1.50 .70
❑ MA12 Scottie Pippen 2.50 1.10
❑ MA13 Chris Webber........... 2.50 1.10
❑ MA14 Anfernee Hardaway .. 2.50 1.10
❑ MA15 David Robinson .... 1.25 .55

1999-00 Fleer Force Operation Invasion

	MINT	NRMT
COMPLETE SET (15)	50.00	22.00
COMMON CARD (OI1-OI15)	1.25	.55

STATED ODDS 1:24

COMPLETE FF SET (15)	100.00	45.00
COMMON FF (OI1-OI15)	2.50	1.10

*FF: .75X TO 2X BASE CARD HI
FF: STATED ODDS 1:96

❑ OI1 Vince Carter 12.00 5.50
❑ OI2 Lamar Odom 5.00 2.20
❑ OI3 Kobe Bryant............... 10.00 4.50
❑ OI4 Tim Duncan 6.00 2.70

❑ OI5 Paul Pierce	2.50	1.10
❑ OI6 Kevin Garnett	8.00	3.60
❑ OI7 Grant Hill	6.00	2.70
❑ OI8 Allen Iverson	5.00	2.20
❑ OI9 Jason Williams	4.00	1.80
❑ OI10 Ron Mercer	1.50	.70
❑ OI11 Shaquille O'Neal	6.00	2.70
❑ OI12 Keith Van Horn	2.50	1.10
❑ OI13 Shareef Abdur-Rahim	2.50	1.10
❑ OI14 Alonzo Mourning	1.25	.55
❑ OI15 Stephon Marbury	2.50	1.10

1999-00 Fleer Force Special Forces

	MINT	NRMT
COMPLETE SET (15)	30.00	13.50
COMMON CARD (SF1-SF15)	.75	.35
STATED ODDS 1:12		
COMPLETE FF SET (15)	60.00	27.00
COMMON FF (SF1-SF15)	1.50	.70
*FF: .75X TO 2X BASE CARD HI		
FF: STATED ODDS 1:48		

❑ SF1 Vince Carter	8.00	3.60
❑ SF2 Lamar Odom	3.00	1.35
❑ SF3 Keith Van Horn	1.50	.70
❑ SF4 Stephon Marbury	1.50	.70
❑ SF5 Scottie Pippen	2.50	1.10
❑ SF6 Ray Allen	.75	.35
❑ SF7 Chris Webber	2.50	1.10
❑ SF8 Jason Williams	2.00	.90
❑ SF9 Karl Malone	1.25	.55
❑ SF10 Patrick Ewing	.75	.35
❑ SF11 Elton Brand	4.00	1.80
❑ SF12 Grant Hill	4.00	1.80
❑ SF13 Eddie Jones	1.50	.70
❑ SF14 Shaquille O'Neal	4.00	1.80
❑ SF15 Kobe Bryant	6.00	2.70

1999-00 Fleer Mystique

	MINT	NRMT
COMPLETE SET (150)	300.00	135.00
COMPLETE SET w/o SP (100)	30.00	13.50
COMMON CARD (1-100)	.25	.11
COMMON RC (101-140)	3.00	1.35
COMMON STAR (141-150)	2.50	1.10
SEMISTARS	.30	.14
SEMISTARS RC	4.00	1.80
UNLISTED STARS	.50	.23
UNLISTED STARS RC	5.00	2.20

RCs: PRINT RUN 2999 SERIAL #'d SETS
STARS: PRINT RUN 2500 SERIAL #'d SETS
RCs/STARS: RANDOM INSERTS IN PACKS

❑ 1 Allen Iverson	2.00	.90
❑ 2 Grant Hill	2.50	1.10
❑ 3 Antawn Jamison	1.00	.45
❑ 4 Glenn Robinson	.30	.14
❑ 5 Kenny Anderson	.30	.14
❑ 6 Dikembe Mutombo	.30	.14
❑ 7 Gary Trent	.25	.11
❑ 8 Brevin Knight	.25	.11
❑ 9 Chucky Brown	.25	.11
❑ 10 Derek Anderson	.50	.23
❑ 11 Ricky Davis	.50	.23
❑ 12 Chris Webber	1.50	.70
❑ 13 Jalen Rose	.50	.23
❑ 14 Antoine Walker	.60	.25
❑ 15 Michael Dickerson	.50	.23
❑ 16 Tim Hardaway	.50	.23
❑ 17 Toni Kukoc	.60	.25
❑ 18 Raef LaFrentz	.50	.23
❑ 19 Anthony Mason	.30	.14
❑ 20 John Stockton	.50	.23
❑ 21 Hakeem Olajuwon	.75	.35
❑ 22 Shaquille O'Neal	2.50	1.10
❑ 23 Scottie Pippen	1.50	.70
❑ 24 Maurice Taylor	.50	.23
❑ 25 Tariq Abdul-Wahad	.25	.11
❑ 26 Tracy McGrady	1.50	.70
❑ 27 Joe Smith	.30	.14
❑ 28 Rod Strickland	.30	.14
❑ 29 Ruben Patterson	.50	.23
❑ 30 Tom Gugliotta	.30	.14
❑ 31 Ray Allen	.50	.23
❑ 32 Elden Campbell	.25	.11
❑ 33 Lindsey Hunter	.25	.11
❑ 34 Larry Johnson	.30	.14
❑ 35 Michael Olowokandi	.30	.14
❑ 36 Mario Elie	.25	.11
❑ 37 Anfernee Hardaway	1.50	.70
❑ 38 Juwan Howard	.30	.14
❑ 39 Karl Malone	.75	.35
❑ 40 Alonzo Mourning	.50	.23
❑ 41 Billy Owens	.25	.11
❑ 42 Mitch Richmond	.50	.23
❑ 43 Darrell Armstrong	.30	.14
❑ 44 Jason Williams	1.25	.55
❑ 45 Mookie Blaylock	.25	.11
❑ 46 Gary Payton	.75	.35
❑ 47 Brian Grant	.30	.14
❑ 48 Paul Pierce	1.00	.45
❑ 49 Michael Finley	.50	.23
❑ 50 Reggie Miller	.50	.23
❑ 51 Corliss Williamson	.25	.11
❑ 52 Shandon Anderson	.25	.11
❑ 53 Stephon Marbury	1.00	.45
❑ 54 Sam Cassell	.30	.14
❑ 55 Bryon Russell	.25	.11
❑ 56 Rasheed Wallace	.50	.23
❑ 57 Jayson Williams	.30	.14
❑ 58 Damon Stoudamire	.50	.23
❑ 59 Terrell Brandon	.30	.14
❑ 60 Loy Vaught	.25	.11
❑ 61 Kobe Bryant	4.00	1.80
❑ 62 Vlade Divac	.25	.11
❑ 63 Derek Fisher	.30	.14
❑ 64 Isaiah Rider	.30	.14
❑ 65 Eddie Jones	1.00	.45
❑ 66 Kevin Garnett	3.00	1.35
❑ 67 David Robinson	.75	.35
❑ 68 Marcus Camby	.50	.23
❑ 69 Glen Rice	.30	.14
❑ 70 Mike Bibby	.60	.25
❑ 71 Patrick Ewing	.50	.23
❑ 72 Robert Traylor	.25	.11
❑ 73 Tim Duncan	2.50	1.10
❑ 74 Michael Doleac	.25	.11
❑ 75 Steve Smith	.30	.14
❑ 76 Allan Houston	.50	.23
❑ 77 Jamal Mashburn	.30	.14
❑ 78 Brent Barry	.25	.11
❑ 79 Charles Barkley	.75	.35
❑ 80 Ron Mercer	.60	.25
❑ 81 Jerry Stackhouse	.30	.14
❑ 82 Keith Van Horn	1.00	.45
❑ 83 Hersey Hawkins	.30	.14
❑ 84 Avery Johnson	.25	.11
❑ 85 Cedric Ceballos	.25	.11
❑ 86 P.J. Brown	.25	.11
❑ 87 Doug Christie	.25	.11
❑ 88 Shawn Kemp	.75	.35
❑ 89 Dirk Nowitzki	.75	.35
❑ 90 Erick Dampier	.25	.11
❑ 91 Antonio McDyess	.50	.23
❑ 92 Mark Jackson	.25	.11
❑ 93 Clifford Robinson	.25	.11
❑ 94 Vince Carter	5.00	2.20
❑ 95 Shareef Abdur-Rahim	1.00	.45
❑ 96 Vin Baker	.30	.14
❑ 97 Larry Hughes	1.25	.55
❑ 98 Jason Kidd	1.50	.70
❑ 99 Kerry Kittles	.30	.14
❑ 100 Latrell Sprewell	1.00	.45
❑ 101 Lamar Odom RC	40.00	18.00
❑ 102 Elton Brand RC	50.00	22.00
❑ 103 Baron Davis RC	12.00	5.50
❑ 104 Jason Terry RC	8.00	3.60
❑ 105 Corey Maggette RC	20.00	9.00
❑ 106 Wally Szczerbiak RC	20.00	9.00
❑ 107 Richard Hamilton RC	12.00	5.50
❑ 108 Milt Palacio RC	3.00	1.35
❑ 109 Ron Artest RC	12.00	5.50
❑ 110 Eddie Robinson RC	8.00	3.60
❑ 111 Jumaine Jones RC	4.00	1.80
❑ 112 Andre Miller RC	15.00	6.75
❑ 113 Chucky Atkins RC	6.00	2.70
❑ 114 Kenny Thomas RC	8.00	3.60
❑ 115 Scott Padgett RC	5.00	2.20
❑ 116 Devean George RC	10.00	4.50
❑ 117 Tim Young RC	3.00	1.35
❑ 118 Tim James RC	6.00	2.70
❑ 119 Quincy Lewis RC	5.00	2.20
❑ 120 James Posey RC	10.00	4.50
❑ 121 Shawn Marion RC	15.00	6.75
❑ 122 Aleksandar Radojevic RC	3.00	1.35
❑ 123 Trajan Langdon RC	8.00	3.60
❑ 124 Laron Profit RC	5.00	2.20
❑ 125 Jonathan Bender RC	25.00	11.00
❑ 126 William Avery RC	8.00	3.60
❑ 127 Cal Bowdler RC	5.00	2.20
❑ 128 Dion Glover RC	5.00	2.20
❑ 129 Jeff Foster RC	5.00	2.20
❑ 130 Steve Francis RC	60.00	27.00
❑ 131 Adrian Griffin RC	6.00	2.70
❑ 132 Vonteego Cummings RC	8.00	3.60
❑ 133 Rafer Alston RC	6.00	2.70
❑ 134 Michael Ruffin RC	4.00	1.80
❑ 135 Chris Herren RC	3.00	1.35
❑ 136 Jermaine Jackson RC	3.00	1.35
❑ 137 Lazaro Borrell RC	3.00	1.35
❑ 138 Obinna Ekezie RC	4.00	1.80
❑ 139 Rick Hughes RC	3.00	1.35
❑ 140 Todd MacCulloch RC	5.00	2.20
❑ 141 Kobe Bryant STAR	15.00	6.75
❑ 142 Vince Carter STAR	20.00	9.00
❑ 143 Tim Duncan STAR	10.00	4.50
❑ 144 Kevin Garnett STAR	12.00	5.50
❑ 145 Allen Iverson STAR	8.00	3.60
❑ 146 Keith Van Horn STAR	4.00	1.80
❑ 147 Grant Hill STAR	10.00	4.50
❑ 148 Stephon Marbury STAR	4.00	1.80

	MINT	NRMT
❑ 149 Antoine Walker STAR	2.50	1.10
❑ 150 Shaquille O'Neal STAR	10.00	4.50

1999-00 Fleer Mystique Gold

	MINT	NRMT
COMPLETE SET (100)	100.00	45.00
COMMON CARD (1-100)	.75	.35

*GOLD: 1.25X TO 3X BASE CARD HI
GOLD: STATED ODDS 1:4

1999-00 Fleer Mystique Feel the Game

	MINT	NRMT
COMPLETE SET (11)	500.00	220.00
COMMON CARD	25.00	11.00

STATED ODDS 1:120
NNO CARDS LISTED BELOW ALPHABETICAL-LY

	MINT	NRMT
❑ 1 Vince Carter	200.00	90.00
❑ 2 Brian Grant	25.00	11.00
❑ 3 Raef LaFrentz	25.00	11.00
❑ 4 Karl Malone	40.00	18.00
❑ 5 Alonzo Mourning	40.00	18.00
❑ 6 Shaquille O'Neal	100.00	45.00
❑ 7 Gary Payton	50.00	22.00
❑ 8 David Robinson	50.00	22.00
❑ 9 Glenn Robinson	25.00	11.00
❑ 10 Joe Smith	25.00	11.00
❑ 11 John Stockton	50.00	22.00

1999-00 Fleer Mystique Fresh Ink

	MINT	NRMT
COMMON CARD	5.00	2.20
SEMISTARS	8.00	3.60

STATED ODDS 1:40
NNO CARDS LISTED BELOW ALPHABETICAL-LY

	MINT	NRMT
❑ 1 Ray Allen	25.00	11.00
❑ 2 Ron Artest	15.00	6.75
❑ 3 William Avery	8.00	3.60
❑ 4 Jonathan Bender	25.00	11.00
❑ 5 Mike Bibby	10.00	4.50

	MINT	NRMT
❑ 6 Cal Bowdler	5.00	2.20
❑ 7 Vince Carter	200.00	90.00
❑ 8 John Celestand	5.00	2.20
❑ 9 Vonteego Cummings	10.00	4.50
❑ 10 Baron Davis	15.00	6.75
❑ 11 Michael Dickerson	10.00	4.50
❑ 12 Michael Doleac	5.00	2.20
❑ 13 Evan Eschmeyer	5.00	2.20
❑ 14 Michael Finley	15.00	6.75
❑ 15 Steve Francis	150.00	70.00
❑ 16 Pat Garrity	5.00	2.20
❑ 17 Dion Glover	8.00	3.60
❑ 18 Brian Grant	10.00	4.50
❑ 19 Richard Hamilton	15.00	6.75
❑ 20 Tim Hardaway	15.00	6.75
❑ 21 Jumaine Jones	5.00	2.20
❑ 22 Shawn Kemp	15.00	6.75
❑ 23 Raef LaFrentz	10.00	4.50
❑ 24 Quincy Lewis	8.00	3.60
❑ 25 Stephon Marbury	25.00	11.00
❑ 26 Antonio McDyess	15.00	6.75
❑ 27 Andre Miller	12.00	5.50
❑ 28 Cuttino Mobley	10.00	4.50
❑ 29 Alonzo Mourning	40.00	18.00
❑ 30 Shaquille O'Neal	250.00	110.00
❑ 31 Lamar Odom	40.00	18.00
❑ 32 Hakeem Olajuwon	40.00	18.00
❑ 33 Michael Olowokandi	8.00	3.60
❑ 34 James Posey	8.00	3.60
❑ 35 Aleksandar Radojevic	5.00	2.20
❑ 36 Kenny Thomas	8.00	3.60
❑ 37 Robert Traylor	5.00	2.20
❑ 38 Keith Van Horn	25.00	11.00

1999-00 Fleer Mystique Point Perfect

	MINT	NRMT
COMPLETE SET (10)	40.00	18.00
COMMON CARD (PP1-PP10)	2.00	.90

STATED PRINT RUN 1999 SERIAL #'d SETS
RANDOM INSERTS IN PACKS

	MINT	NRMT
❑ PP1 Mike Bibby	3.00	1.35
❑ PP2 Stephon Marbury	5.00	2.20
❑ PP3 Jason Williams	6.00	2.70
❑ PP4 Jason Kidd	8.00	3.60
❑ PP5 William Avery	2.00	.90
❑ PP6 Allen Iverson	10.00	4.50
❑ PP7 Andre Miller	4.00	1.80
❑ PP8 Baron Davis	3.00	1.35
❑ PP9 Steve Francis	15.00	6.75
❑ PP10 Jason Terry	2.00	.90

1999-00 Fleer Mystique Raise the Roof

	MINT	NRMT
COMPLETE SET (10)	600.00	275.00
COMMON CARD (RR1-RR10)	30.00	13.50

STATED PRINT RUN 100 SERIAL #'d SETS
RANDOM INSERTS IN PACKS

	MINT	NRMT
❑ RR1 Grant Hill	80.00	36.00
❑ RR2 Keith Van Horn	30.00	13.50
❑ RR3 Tim Duncan	80.00	36.00
❑ RR4 Kobe Bryant	120.00	55.00
❑ RR5 Vince Carter	150.00	70.00
❑ RR6 Allen Iverson	60.00	27.00
❑ RR7 Kevin Garnett	100.00	45.00
❑ RR8 Shaquille O'Neal	80.00	36.00
❑ RR9 Paul Pierce	30.00	13.50
❑ RR10 Anfernee Hardaway	50.00	22.00

1999-00 Fleer Mystique Slamboree

	MINT	NRMT
COMPLETE SET (10)	60.00	27.00
COMMON CARD (S1-S10)	4.00	1.80

STATED PRINT RUN 999 SERIAL #'d SETS
RANDOM INSERTS IN PACKS

	MINT	NRMT
❑ S1 Antoine Walker	4.00	1.80
❑ S2 Shareef Abdur-Rahim	6.00	2.70
❑ S3 Antawn Jamison	6.00	2.70
❑ S4 Tracy McGrady	10.00	4.50
❑ S5 Larry Hughes	8.00	3.60
❑ S6 Wally Szczerbiak	6.00	2.70
❑ S7 Corey Maggette	6.00	2.70
❑ S8 Lamar Odom	12.00	5.50
❑ S9 Elton Brand	15.00	6.75
❑ S10 Stephon Marbury	6.00	2.70

1989-90 Hoops

	MINT	NRMT
COMPLETE SET (352)	25.00	11.00
COMPLETE SERIES 1 (300)	20.00	9.00
COMPLETE SERIES 2 (52)	5.00	2.20

Card		
COMMON CARD (1-352)	.05	.02
COMMON SP	.15	.07
SEMISTARS	.10	.05
SEMISTARS SP	.25	.11
UNLISTED STARS	.25	.11
SUBSET CARDS HALF VALUE OF BASE CARDS		
BEWARE ROBINSON 138 COUNTERFEIT		
❑ 1 Joe Dumars	.25	.11
❑ 2 Tree Rollins	.05	.02
❑ 3 Kenny Walker	.05	.02
❑ 4 Mychal Thompson	.05	.02
❑ 5 Alvin Robertson SP	.15	.07
❑ 6 Vinny Del Negro RC	.25	.11
❑ 7 Greg Anderson SP	.15	.07
❑ 8 Rod Strickland RC	.75	.35
❑ 9 Ed Pinckney	.05	.02
❑ 10 Dale Ellis	.10	.05
❑ 11 Chuck Daly CO RC	.25	.11
❑ 12 Eric Leckner	.05	.02
❑ 13 Charles Davis	.05	.02
❑ 14 Cotton Fitzsimmons CO (No NBA logo on back in bottom right)	.05	.02
❑ 15 Byron Scott	.10	.05
❑ 16 Derrick Chievous	.05	.02
❑ 17 Reggie Lewis RC	.25	.11
❑ 18 Jim Paxson	.05	.02
❑ 19 Tony Campbell RC	.05	.02
❑ 20 Rolando Blackman	.05	.02
❑ 21 Michael Jordan AS	1.50	.70
❑ 22 Cliff Levingston	.05	.02
❑ 23 Roy Tarpley	.05	.02
❑ 24 Harold Pressley UER (Cinderella misspelled as cindarella)	.05	.02
❑ 25 Larry Nance	.10	.05
❑ 26 Chris Morris RC	.10	.05
❑ 27 Bob Hansen UER (Drafted in '84, should say '83)	.05	.02
❑ 28 Mark Price AS	.05	.02
❑ 29 Reggie Miller	.60	.25
❑ 30 Karl Malone	.40	.18
❑ 31 Sidney Lowe SP	.15	.07
❑ 32 Ron Anderson	.05	.02
❑ 33 Mike Gminski	.05	.02
❑ 34 Scott Brooks RC	.05	.02
❑ 35 Kevin Johnson RC	.50	.23
❑ 36 Mark Bryant RC	.05	.02
❑ 37 Rik Smits RC	.30	.14
❑ 38 Tim Perry RC	.05	.02
❑ 39 Ralph Sampson	.05	.02
❑ 40 Danny Manning RC UER (Missing 1988 in draft info)	.30	.14
❑ 41 Kevin Edwards RC	.05	.02
❑ 42 Paul Mokeski	.05	.02
❑ 43 Dale Ellis AS	.05	.02
❑ 44 Walter Berry	.05	.02
❑ 45 Chuck Person	.10	.05
❑ 46 Rick Mahorn SP	.15	.07
❑ 47 Joe Kleine	.05	.02
❑ 48 Brad Daugherty AS	.05	.02
❑ 49 Mike Woodson	.05	.02
❑ 50 Brad Daugherty	.05	.02
❑ 51 Shelton Jones SP	.15	.07
❑ 52 Michael Adams	.05	.02
❑ 53 Wes Unseld CO	.05	.02
❑ 54 Rex Chapman RC	.25	.11
❑ 55 Kelly Tripucka	.05	.02
❑ 56 Rickey Green	.05	.02
❑ 57 Frank Johnson SP	.15	.07
❑ 58 Johnny Newman RC	.05	.02
❑ 59 Billy Thompson	.05	.02
❑ 60 Stu Jackson CO	.05	.02
❑ 61 Walter Davis	.05	.02
❑ 62 Brian Shaw RC SP UER (Gary Grant led rookies in assists, not Shaw)	.25	.11
❑ 63 Gerald Wilkins	.05	.02
❑ 64 Armon Gilliam	.05	.02
❑ 65 Maurice Cheeks SP	.15	.07
❑ 66 Jack Sikma	.05	.02
❑ 67 Harvey Grant RC	.05	.02
❑ 68 Jim Lynam CO	.05	.02
❑ 69 Clyde Drexler AS	.10	.05
❑ 70 Xavier McDaniel	.05	.02
❑ 71 Danny Young	.05	.02
❑ 72 Fennis Dembo	.05	.02
❑ 73 Mark Acres SP	.15	.07
❑ 74 Brad Lohaus SP RC	.15	.07
❑ 75 Manute Bol	.05	.02
❑ 76 Purvis Short	.05	.02
❑ 77 Allen Leavell	.05	.02
❑ 78 Johnny Dawkins SP	.15	.07
❑ 79 Paul Pressey	.05	.02
❑ 80 Patrick Ewing	.25	.11
❑ 81 Bill Wennington RC	.25	.11
❑ 82 Danny Schayes	.05	.02
❑ 83 Derek Smith	.05	.02
❑ 84 Moses Malone AS	.10	.05
❑ 85 Jeff Malone	.05	.02
❑ 86 Otis Smith SP RC	.15	.07
❑ 87 Trent Tucker	.05	.02
❑ 88 Robert Reid	.05	.02
❑ 89 John Paxson	.05	.02
❑ 90 Chris Mullin	.25	.11
❑ 91 Tom Garrick	.05	.02
❑ 92 Willis Reed CO SP UER (Gambling, should be Grambling)	.25	.11
❑ 93 Dave Corzine SP	.15	.07
❑ 94 Mark Alarie	.05	.02
❑ 95 Mark Aguirre	.05	.02
❑ 96 Charles Barkley AS	.20	.09
❑ 97 Sidney Green SP	.15	.07
❑ 98 Kevin Willis	.10	.05
❑ 99 Dave Hoppen	.05	.02
❑ 100 Terry Cummings SP	.25	.11
❑ 101 Dwayne Washington SP	.15	.07
❑ 102 Larry Brown CO	.10	.05
❑ 103 Kevin Duckworth	.05	.02
❑ 104 Uwe Blab SP	.15	.07
❑ 105 Terry Porter	.05	.02
❑ 106 Craig Ehlo RC**	.05	.02
❑ 107 Don Casey CO	.05	.02
❑ 108 Pat Riley CO	.25	.11
❑ 109 John Salley	.05	.02
❑ 110 Charles Barkley	.40	.18
❑ 111 Sam Bowie SP	.15	.07
❑ 112 Earl Cureton	.05	.02
❑ 113 Craig Hodges UER (3-pointing shooting)	.05	.02
❑ 114 Benoit Benjamin	.05	.02
❑ 115A Spud Webb ERR SP (Signed 9/27/89)	.25	.11
❑ 115B Spud Webb COR (Second series; signed 9/26/85)	.10	.05
❑ 116 Karl Malone AS	.25	.11
❑ 117 Sleepy Floyd	.05	.02
❑ 118 John Williams	.05	.02
❑ 119 Michael Holton	.05	.02
❑ 120 Alex English	.05	.02
❑ 121 Dennis Johnson	.05	.02
❑ 122 Wayne Cooper SP	.15	.07
❑ 123A Don Chaney CO (Line next to NBA coaching record)	.05	.02
❑ 123B Don Chaney CO (No line)	.05	.02
❑ 124 A.C. Green	.10	.05
❑ 125 Adrian Dantley	.05	.02
❑ 126 Del Harris CO	.05	.02
❑ 127 Dick Harter CO	.05	.02
❑ 128 Reggie Williams RC	.05	.02
❑ 129 Bill Hanzlik	.05	.02
❑ 130 Dominique Wilkins	.25	.11
❑ 131 Herb Williams	.05	.02
❑ 132 Steve Johnson SP	.15	.07
❑ 133 Alex English AS	.05	.02
❑ 134 Darrell Walker	.05	.02
❑ 135 Bill Laimbeer	.10	.05
❑ 136 Fred Roberts RC**	.05	.02
❑ 137 Hersey Hawkins RC	.30	.14
❑ 138 David Robinson SP RC !	10.00	4.50
❑ 139 Brad Sellers SP	.15	.07
❑ 140 John Stockton	.60	.25
❑ 141 Grant Long RC	.05	.02
❑ 142 Marc Iavaroni SP	.15	.07
❑ 143 Steve Alford SP RC	.15	.07
❑ 144 Jeff Lamp SP	.15	.07
❑ 145 Buck Williams SP UER (Won ROY in '81& should say '82)	.25	.11
❑ 146 Mark Jackson AS	.05	.02
❑ 147 Jim Petersen	.05	.02
❑ 148 Steve Stipanovich SP	.15	.07
❑ 149 Sam Vincent SP RC	.15	.07
❑ 150 Larry Bird	1.00	.45
❑ 151 Jon Koncak RC	.05	.02
❑ 152 Olden Polynice RC	.10	.05
❑ 153 Randy Breuer	.05	.02
❑ 154 John Battle RC	.05	.02
❑ 155 Mark Eaton	.05	.02
❑ 156 Kevin McHale AS UER (No TM on Celtics logo on back)	.10	.05
❑ 157 Jerry Sichting SP	.15	.07
❑ 158 Pat Cummings SP	.15	.07
❑ 159 Patrick Ewing AS	.10	.05
❑ 160 Mark Price	.10	.05
❑ 161 Jerry Reynolds CO	.05	.02
❑ 162 Ken Norman RC	.05	.02
❑ 163 John Bagley SP UER (Picked in '83, should say '82)	.15	.07
❑ 164 Christian Welp SP	.15	.07
❑ 165 Reggie Theus SP	.25	.11
❑ 166 Magic Johnson AS	.40	.18
❑ 167 John Long UER (Picked in '79, should say '78)	.05	.02
❑ 168 Larry Smith SP	.15	.07
❑ 169 Charles Shackleford RC	.05	.02
❑ 170 Tom Chambers	.05	.02
❑ 171A John MacLeod CO SP ERR (NBA logo in wrong place)	.15	.07
❑ 171B John MacLeod CO COR (Second series)	.05	.02
❑ 172 Ron Rothstein CO	.05	.02
❑ 173 Joe Wolf	.05	.02
❑ 174 Mark Eaton AS	.05	.02
❑ 175 Jon Sundvold	.05	.02
❑ 176 Scott Hastings SP	.15	.07
❑ 177 Isiah Thomas AS	.10	.05
❑ 178 Hakeem Olajuwon AS	.25	.11
❑ 179 Mike Fratello CO	.10	.05
❑ 180 Hakeem Olajuwon	.40	.18
❑ 181 Randolph Keys	.05	.02
❑ 182 Richard Anderson UER (Trail Blazers on front should be all caps)	.05	.02
❑ 183 Dan Majerle RC	.30	.14
❑ 184 Derek Harper	.10	.05
❑ 185 Robert Parish	.10	.05
❑ 186 Ricky Berry SP	.15	.07
❑ 187 Michael Cooper	.05	.02
❑ 188 Vinnie Johnson	.10	.05
❑ 189 James Donaldson	.05	.02
❑ 190 Clyde Drexler UER (4th pick, should be 14th)	.25	.11
❑ 191 Jay Vincent SP	.15	.07
❑ 192 Nate McMillan	.10	.05
❑ 193 Kevin Duckworth AS	.05	.02
❑ 194 Ledell Eackles RC	.05	.02
❑ 195 Eddie Johnson	.10	.05
❑ 196 Terry Teagle	.05	.02
❑ 197 Tom Chambers AS	.05	.02
❑ 198 Joe Barry Carroll	.05	.02
❑ 199 Dennis Hopson RC	.05	.02
❑ 200 Michael Jordan	3.00	1.35

❑ 201 Jerome Lane RC .05 .02
❑ 202 Greg Kite RC** .05 .02
❑ 203 David Rivers SP .15 .07
❑ 204 Sylvester Gray .05 .02
❑ 205 Ron Harper .10 .05
❑ 206 Frank Brickowski .05 .02
❑ 207 Rory Sparrow .05 .02
❑ 208 Gerald Henderson .05 .02
❑ 209 Rod Higgins UER .05 .02
('85-86 stats should#(also include San#(Antonio and Seattle)
❑ 210 James Worthy .25 .11
❑ 211 Dennis Rodman 1.00 .45
❑ 212 Ricky Pierce .05 .02
❑ 213 Charles Oakley .10 .05
❑ 214 Steve Colter .05 .02
❑ 215 Danny Ainge .10 .05
❑ 216 Lenny Wilkens CO UER .10 .05
(No NBA logo on back in bottom right)
❑ 217 Larry Nance AS .05 .02
❑ 218 Muggsy Bogues .10 .05
❑ 219 James Worthy AS .10 .05
❑ 220 Lafayette Lever .05 .02
❑ 221 Quintin Dailey SP .15 .07
❑ 222 Lester Conner .05 .02
❑ 223 Jose Ortiz .05 .02
❑ 224 Micheal Williams RC SP .25 .11
UER (Misspelled Michael on card)
❑ 225 Wayman Tisdale .05 .02
❑ 226 Mike Sanders SP .15 .07
❑ 227 Jim Farmer SP .15 .07
❑ 228 Mark West .05 .02
❑ 229 Jeff Hornacek RC .30 .14
❑ 230 Chris Mullin AS .10 .05
❑ 231 Vern Fleming .05 .02
❑ 232 Kenny Smith .05 .02
❑ 233 Derrick McKey .05 .02
❑ 234 Dominique Wilkins AS .10 .05
❑ 235 Willie Anderson RC .05 .02
❑ 236 Keith Lee SP .15 .07
❑ 237 Buck Johnson RC .05 .02
❑ 238 Randy Wittman .05 .02
❑ 239 Terry Catledge SP .15 .07
❑ 240 Bernard King .05 .02
❑ 241 Darrell Griffith .05 .02
❑ 242 Horace Grant .10 .05
❑ 243 Rony Seikaly RC .25 .11
❑ 244 Scottie Pippen 1.50 .70
❑ 245 Michael Cage UER .05 .02
(Picked in '85& should say '84)
❑ 246 Kurt Rambis .05 .02
❑ 247 Morlon Wiley SP RC .15 .07
❑ 248 Ronnie Grandison .05 .02
❑ 249 Scott Skiles SP RC .25 .11
❑ 250 Isiah Thomas .25 .11
❑ 251 Thurl Bailey .05 .02
❑ 252 Doc Rivers .10 .05
❑ 253 Stuart Gray SP .15 .07
❑ 254 John Williams .05 .02
❑ 255 Bill Cartwright .05 .02
❑ 256 Terry Cummings AS .05 .02
❑ 257 Rodney McCray .05 .02
❑ 258 Larry Krystkowiak RC .05 .02
❑ 259 Will Perdue RC .05 .02
❑ 260 Mitch Richmond RC 1.25 .55
❑ 261 Blair Rasmussen .05 .02
❑ 262 Charles Smith RC .25 .11
❑ 263 Tyrone Corbin SP RC .15 .07
❑ 264 Kelvin Upshaw .05 .02
❑ 265 Otis Thorpe .10 .05
❑ 266 Phil Jackson CO .25 .11
❑ 267 Jerry Sloan CO .10 .05
❑ 268 John Shasky .05 .02
❑ 269A B. Bickerstaff CO SP .15 .07
ERR (Born 2/11/44)
❑ 269B B. Bickerstaff CO .05 .02
COR (Second series; Born 11/2/43)
❑ 270 Magic Johnson .75 .35
❑ 271 Vernon Maxwell RC .25 .11
❑ 272 Tim McCormick .05 .02
❑ 273 Don Nelson CO .10 .05
❑ 274 Gary Grant RC .05 .02
❑ 275 Sidney Moncrief SP .15 .07
❑ 276 Roy Hinson .05 .02
❑ 277 Jimmy Rodgers CO .05 .02
❑ 278 Antoine Carr .05 .02
❑ 279A Orlando Woolridge SP .15 .07
ERR (No Trademark)
❑ 279B Orlando Woolridge .05 .02
COR (Second series)
❑ 280 Kevin McHale .25 .11
❑ 281 LaSalle Thompson .05 .02
❑ 282 Detlef Schrempf .10 .05
❑ 283 Doug Moe CO .05 .02
❑ 284A James Edwards .05 .02
(Small black line next to card number)
❑ 284B James Edwards .05 .02
(No small black line)
❑ 285 Jerome Kersey .05 .02
❑ 286 Sam Perkins .10 .05
❑ 287 Sedale Threatt .05 .02
❑ 288 Tim Kempton SP .15 .07
❑ 289 Mark McNamara .05 .02
❑ 290 Moses Malone .25 .11
❑ 291 Rick Adelman CO UER .05 .02
(Chemekata misspelled as Chemketa)
❑ 292 Dick Versace CO .05 .02
❑ 293 Alton Lister SP .15 .07
❑ 294 Winston Garland .05 .02
❑ 295 Kiki Vandeweghe .05 .02
❑ 296 Brad Davis .05 .02
❑ 297 John Stockton AS .25 .11
❑ 298 Jay Humphries .05 .02
❑ 299 Dell Curry .05 .02
❑ 300 Mark Jackson .10 .05
❑ 301 Morlon Wiley .05 .02
❑ 302 Reggie Theus .10 .05
❑ 303 Otis Smith .05 .02
❑ 304 Tod Murphy RC .05 .02
❑ 305 Sidney Green .05 .02
❑ 306 Shelton Jones .05 .02
❑ 307 Mark Acres .05 .02
❑ 308 Terry Catledge .05 .02
❑ 309 Larry Smith .05 .02
❑ 310 David Robinson IA 2.00 .90
❑ 311 Johnny Dawkins .05 .02
❑ 312 Terry Cummings .10 .05
❑ 313 Sidney Lowe .05 .02
❑ 314 Bill Musselman CO .05 .02
❑ 315 Buck Williams UER .10 .05
(Won ROY in '81& should say '82)
❑ 316 Mel Turpin .05 .02
❑ 317 Scott Hastings .05 .02
❑ 318 Scott Skiles .10 .05
❑ 319 Tyrone Corbin .05 .02
❑ 320 Maurice Cheeks .05 .02
❑ 321 Matt Guokas CO .05 .02
❑ 322 Jeff Turner .05 .02
❑ 323 David Wingate .05 .02
❑ 324 Steve Johnson .05 .02
❑ 325 Alton Lister .05 .02
❑ 326 Ken Bannister .05 .02
❑ 327 Bill Fitch CO UER .05 .02
(Copyright missing on bottom of back)
❑ 328 Sam Vincent .05 .02
❑ 329 Larry Drew .05 .02
❑ 330 Rick Mahorn .05 .02
❑ 331 Christian Welp .05 .02
❑ 332 Brad Lohaus .05 .02
❑ 333 Frank Johnson .05 .02
❑ 334 Jim Farmer .05 .02
❑ 335 Wayne Cooper .05 .02
❑ 336 Mike Brown RC .05 .02
❑ 337 Sam Bowie .05 .02
❑ 338 Kevin Gamble RC .05 .02
❑ 339 Jerry Ice Reynolds RC .05 .02
❑ 340 Mike Sanders .05 .02
❑ 341 Bill Jones UER .05 .02
(Center on front& should be F)
❑ 342 Greg Anderson .05 .02
❑ 343 Dave Corzine .05 .02
❑ 344 Micheal Williams UER .05 .02
(Misspelled Michael on card)
❑ 345 Jay Vincent .05 .02
❑ 346 David Rivers .05 .02
❑ 347 Caldwell Jones UER .05 .02
(He was not starting center on '83 Sixers)
❑ 348 Brad Sellers .05 .02
❑ 349 Scott Roth .05 .02
❑ 350 Alvin Robertson .05 .02
❑ 351 Steve Kerr RC .50 .23
❑ 352 Stuart Gray .05 .02
❑ 353A World Champions SP 4.00 1.80
❑ 353B World Champions UER .50 .23
(George Blaha misspelled Blanha)

1990-91 Hoops

	MINT	NRMT
COMPLETE SET (440)	15.00	6.75
COMPLETE SERIES 1 (336)	10.00	4.50
COMPLETE SERIES 2 (104)	5.00	2.20
COMMON CARD (1-440)	.05	.02
COMMON SP	.10	.05
SEMISTARS	.08	.04
UNLISTED STARS	.15	.07

SUBSET CARDS HALF VALUE OF BASE CARDS

❑ 1 Charles Barkley AS SP .25 .11
❑ 2 Larry Bird AS SP .60 .25
❑ 3 Joe Dumars AS SP .15 .07
❑ 4 Patrick Ewing AS SP .15 .07
(A-S blocks listed as 1& should be 5) UER
❑ 5 Michael Jordan AS SP 2.00 .90
(Won Slam Dunk in '87 and '88& not '86 and '88) UER
❑ 6 Kevin McHale AS SP .08 .04
❑ 7 Reggie Miller AS SP .15 .07
❑ 8 Robert Parish AS SP .10 .05
❑ 9 Scottie Pippen AS SP .60 .25
❑ 10 Dennis Rodman AS SP .40 .18
❑ 11 Isiah Thomas AS SP .15 .07
❑ 12 Dominique Wilkins AS SP .15 .07
❑ 13A All-Star Checklist SP .25 .11
ERR (No card number)
❑ 13B All-Star Checklist SP .10 .05
COR (Card number on back)
❑ 14 Rolando Blackman AS SP .10 .05
❑ 15 Tom Chambers AS SP .10 .05
❑ 16 Clyde Drexler AS SP .08 .04
❑ 17 A.C. Green AS SP .10 .05
❑ 18 Magic Johnson AS SP .50 .23
❑ 19 Kevin Johnson AS SP .15 .07
❑ 20 Lafayette Lever AS SP .10 .05
❑ 21 Karl Malone AS SP .25 .11
❑ 22 Chris Mullin AS SP .15 .07
❑ 23 Hakeem Olajuwon AS SP .25 .11
❑ 24 David Robinson AS SP .50 .23
❑ 25 John Stockton AS SP .20 .09
❑ 26 James Worthy AS SP .15 .07
❑ 27 John Battle .05 .02
❑ 28 Jon Koncak .05 .02
❑ 29 Cliff Levingston SP .10 .05
❑ 30 John Long SP .10 .05
❑ 31 Moses Malone .15 .07

❑ 32 Doc Rivers .08 .04
❑ 33 Kenny Smith SP .10 .05
❑ 34 Alexander Volkov .05 .02
❑ 35 Spud Webb .08 .04
❑ 36 Dominique Wilkins .15 .07
❑ 37 Kevin Willis .08 .04
❑ 38 John Bagley .05 .02
❑ 39 Larry Bird .60 .25
❑ 40 Kevin Gamble .05 .02
❑ 41 Dennis Johnson SP .05 .02
❑ 42 Joe Kleine .05 .02
❑ 43 Reggie Lewis .08 .04
❑ 44 Kevin McHale .08 .04
❑ 45 Robert Parish .08 .04
❑ 46 Jim Paxson SP .08 .04
❑ 47 Ed Pinckney .05 .02
❑ 48 Brian Shaw .15 .07
❑ 49 Richard Anderson SP .10 .05
❑ 50 Muggsy Bogues .08 .04
❑ 51 Rex Chapman .15 .07
❑ 52 Dell Curry .05 .02
❑ 53 Kenny Gattison RC .05 .02
❑ 54 Armon Gilliam .05 .02
❑ 55 Dave Hoppen .05 .02
❑ 56 Randolph Keys .05 .02
❑ 57 J.R. Reid RC .05 .02
❑ 58 Robert Reid SP .10 .05
❑ 59 Kelly Tripucka .05 .02
❑ 60 B.J. Armstrong RC .05 .02
❑ 61 Bill Cartwright .05 .02
❑ 62 Charles Davis SP .10 .05
❑ 63 Horace Grant .08 .04
❑ 64 Craig Hodges .05 .02
❑ 65 Michael Jordan 2.00 .90
❑ 66 Stacey King RC .05 .02
❑ 67 John Paxson .08 .04
❑ 68 Will Perdue .05 .02
❑ 69 Scottie Pippen .60 .25
❑ 70 Winston Bennett .05 .02
❑ 71 Chucky Brown RC .05 .02
❑ 72 Derrick Chievous .05 .02
❑ 73 Brad Daugherty .05 .02
❑ 74 Craig Ehlo .05 .02
❑ 75 Steve Kerr .15 .07
❑ 76 Paul Mokeski SP .10 .05
❑ 77 John Morton .05 .02
❑ 78 Larry Nance .05 .02
❑ 79 Mark Price .08 .04
❑ 80 Hot Rod Williams .05 .02
❑ 81 Steve Alford .05 .02
❑ 82 Rolando Blackman .05 .02
❑ 83 Adrian Dantley SP .05 .02
❑ 84 Brad Davis .05 .02
❑ 85 James Donaldson .05 .02
❑ 86 Derek Harper .08 .04
❑ 87 Sam Perkins SP .08 .04
❑ 88 Roy Tarpley .05 .02
❑ 89 Bill Wennington SP .10 .05
❑ 90 Herb Williams .05 .02
❑ 91 Michael Adams .05 .02
❑ 92 Joe Barry Carroll SP .10 .05
❑ 93 Walter Davis UER .05 .02
(Born NC& not PA)
❑ 94 Alex English SP .05 .02
❑ 95 Bill Hanzlik .05 .02
❑ 96 Jerome Lane .05 .02
❑ 97 Lafayette Lever SP .10 .05
❑ 98 Todd Lichti RC .05 .02
❑ 99 Blair Rasmussen .05 .02
❑ 100 Danny Schayes SP .10 .05
❑ 101 Mark Aguirre .05 .02
❑ 102 William Bedford RC .05 .02
❑ 103 Joe Dumars .15 .07
❑ 104 James Edwards .05 .02
❑ 105 Scott Hastings .05 .02
❑ 106 Gerald Henderson SP .10 .05
❑ 107 Vinnie Johnson .05 .02
❑ 108 Bill Laimbeer .08 .04
❑ 109 Dennis Rodman .40 .18
❑ 110 John Salley .05 .02
❑ 111 Isiah Thomas UER .15 .07
(No position listed on the card)
❑ 112 Manute Bol SP .10 .05
❑ 113 Tim Hardaway RC 1.00 .45
❑ 114 Rod Higgins .05 .02
❑ 115 Sarunas Marciulionis RC .05 .02
❑ 116 Chris Mullin UER .15 .07
(Born Brooklyn& NY& not New York& NY)
❑ 117 Jim Petersen .05 .02
❑ 118 Mitch Richmond .20 .09
❑ 119 Mike Smrek .05 .02
❑ 120 Terry Teagle SP .10 .05
❑ 121 Tom Tolbert RC .05 .02
❑ 122 Christian Welp SP .10 .05
❑ 123 Byron Dinkins SP .10 .05
❑ 124 Eric(Sleepy) Floyd .05 .02
❑ 125 Buck Johnson .05 .02
❑ 126 Vernon Maxwell .05 .02
❑ 127 Hakeem Olajuwon .25 .11
❑ 128 Larry Smith .05 .02
❑ 129 Otis Thorpe .08 .04
❑ 130 Mitchell Wiggins SP .10 .05
❑ 131 Mike Woodson .05 .02
❑ 132 Greg Dreiling RC .05 .02
❑ 133 Vern Fleming .05 .02
❑ 134 Rickey Green SP .10 .05
❑ 135 Reggie Miller .20 .09
❑ 136 Chuck Person .08 .04
❑ 137 Mike Sanders .05 .02
❑ 138 Detlef Schrempf .08 .04
❑ 139 Rik Smits .15 .07
❑ 140 LaSalle Thompson .05 .02
❑ 141 Randy Wittman .05 .02
❑ 142 Benoit Benjamin .05 .02
❑ 143 Winston Garland .05 .02
❑ 144 Tom Garrick .05 .02
❑ 145 Gary Grant .05 .02
❑ 146 Ron Harper .08 .04
❑ 147 Danny Manning .08 .04
❑ 148 Jeff Martin .05 .02
❑ 149 Ken Norman .05 .02
❑ 150 David Rivers SP .10 .05
❑ 151 Charles Smith .05 .02
❑ 152 Joe Wolf SP .10 .05
❑ 153 Michael Cooper SP .10 .05
❑ 154 Vlade Divac RC UER .30 .14
(Height 6'11~& should be 7'1~)
❑ 155 Larry Drew .05 .02
❑ 156 A.C. Green .08 .04
❑ 157 Magic Johnson .50 .23
❑ 158 Mark McNamara SP .10 .05
❑ 159 Byron Scott .08 .04
❑ 160 Mychal Thompson .05 .02
❑ 161 Jay Vincent SP .10 .05
❑ 162 Orlando Woolridge SP .10 .05
❑ 163 James Worthy .15 .07
❑ 164 Sherman Douglas RC .08 .04
❑ 165 Kevin Edwards .05 .02
❑ 166 Tellis Frank SP .10 .05
❑ 167 Grant Long .05 .02
❑ 168 Glen Rice RC .60 .25
❑ 169A Rony Seikaly .08 .04
(Athens)
❑ 169B Rony Seikaly .08 .04
(Beirut)
❑ 170 Rory Sparrow SP .10 .05
❑ 171A Jon Sundvold .05 .02
(First series)
❑ 171B Billy Thompson .05 .02
(Second series)
❑ 172A Billy Thompson .05 .02
(First series)
❑ 172B Jon Sundvold .05 .02
(Second series)
❑ 173 Greg Anderson .05 .02
❑ 174 Jeff Grayer RC .05 .02
❑ 175 Jay Humphries .05 .02
❑ 176 Frank Kornet .05 .02
❑ 177 Larry Krystkowiak .05 .02
❑ 178 Brad Lohaus .05 .02
❑ 179 Ricky Pierce .05 .02
❑ 180 Paul Pressey SP .10 .05
❑ 181 Fred Roberts .05 .02
❑ 182 Alvin Robertson .05 .02
❑ 183 Jack Sikma .05 .02
❑ 184 Randy Breuer .05 .02
❑ 185 Tony Campbell .05 .02
❑ 186 Tyrone Corbin .05 .02
❑ 187 Sidney Lowe SP .10 .05
❑ 188 Sam Mitchell RC .05 .02
❑ 189 Tod Murphy .05 .02
❑ 190 Pooh Richardson RC .08 .04
❑ 191 Scott Roth SP .05 .02
❑ 192 Brad Sellers SP .10 .05
❑ 193 Mookie Blaylock RC .30 .14
❑ 194 Sam Bowie .05 .02
❑ 195 Lester Conner .05 .02
❑ 196 Derrick Gervin .05 .02
❑ 197 Jack Haley RC .05 .02
❑ 198 Roy Hinson .05 .02
❑ 199 Dennis Hopson SP .10 .05
❑ 200 Chris Morris .08 .04
❑ 201 Purvis Short SP .10 .05
❑ 202 Maurice Cheeks .05 .02
❑ 203 Patrick Ewing .15 .07
❑ 204 Stuart Gray .05 .02
❑ 205 Mark Jackson .08 .04
❑ 206 Johnny Newman SP .10 .05
❑ 207 Charles Oakley .08 .04
❑ 208 Trent Tucker .05 .02
❑ 209 Kiki Vandeweghe .05 .02
❑ 210 Kenny Walker .05 .02
❑ 211 Eddie Lee Wilkins .05 .02
❑ 212 Gerald Wilkins .05 .02
❑ 213 Mark Acres .05 .02
❑ 214 Nick Anderson RC .30 .14
❑ 215 Michael Ansley UER .05 .02
(Ranked first& not third)
❑ 216 Terry Catledge .05 .02
❑ 217 Dave Corzine SP .10 .05
❑ 218 Sidney Green SP .10 .05
❑ 219 Jerry Reynolds .05 .02
❑ 220 Scott Skiles .05 .02
❑ 221 Otis Smith .05 .02
❑ 222 Reggie Theus SP .08 .04
❑ 223A Sam Vincent 1.50 .70
(Shows Michael Jordan)
❑ 223B Sam Vincent .05 .02
(Second series and shows Sam dribbling)
❑ 224 Ron Anderson .05 .02
❑ 225 Charles Barkley .25 .11
❑ 226 Scott Brooks SP UER .10 .05
(Born French Camp& not Lathron& Cal.)
❑ 227 Johnny Dawkins .05 .02
❑ 228 Mike Gminski .05 .02
❑ 229 Hersey Hawkins .08 .04
❑ 230 Rick Mahorn .05 .02
❑ 231 Derek Smith SP .10 .05
❑ 232 Bob Thornton .05 .02
❑ 233 Kenny Battle RC .05 .02
❑ 234A Tom Chambers .05 .02
(First series; Forward on front)
❑ 234B Tom Chambers .05 .02
(Second series; Guard on front)
❑ 235 Greg Grant SP RC .10 .05
❑ 236 Jeff Hornacek .08 .04
❑ 237 Eddie Johnson .08 .04
❑ 238A Kevin Johnson .15 .07
(First series; Guard on front)
❑ 238B Kevin Johnson .15 .07
(Second series; Forward on front)
❑ 239 Dan Majerle .15 .07
❑ 240 Tim Perry .05 .02
❑ 241 Kurt Rambis .05 .02
❑ 242 Mark West .05 .02
❑ 243 Mark Bryant .05 .02
❑ 244 Wayne Cooper .05 .02
❑ 245 Clyde Drexler .15 .07
❑ 246 Kevin Duckworth .05 .02
❑ 247 Jerome Kersey .05 .02
❑ 248 Drazen Petrovic RC .08 .04
❑ 249A Terry Porter ERR .50 .23
(No NBA symbol on back)
❑ 249B Terry Porter COR .05 .02
❑ 250 Clifford Robinson RC .25 .11
❑ 251 Buck Williams .05 .02
❑ 252 Danny Young .05 .02
❑ 253 Danny Ainge SP UER .08 .04
(Middle name Ray mis-

spelled as Rae on back)
❑ 254 Randy Allen SP .10 .05
❑ 255 Antoine Carr .05 .02
❑ 256 Vinny Del Negro SP .10 .05
❑ 257 Pervis Ellison SP RC .10 .05
❑ 258 Greg Kite SP .10 .05
❑ 259 Rodney McCray SP .10 .05
❑ 260 Harold Pressley SP .10 .05
❑ 261 Ralph Sampson .05 .02
❑ 262 Wayman Tisdale .05 .02
❑ 263 Willie Anderson .05 .02
❑ 264 Uwe Blab SP .10 .05
❑ 265 Frank Brickowski SP .10 .05
❑ 266 Terry Cummings .05 .02
❑ 267 Sean Elliott RC .30 .14
❑ 268 Caldwell Jones SP .10 .05
❑ 269 Johnny Moore SP .10 .05
❑ 270 David Robinson .50 .23
❑ 271 Rod Strickland .15 .07
❑ 272 Reggie Williams .05 .02
❑ 273 David Wingate SP .10 .05
❑ 274 Dana Barros RC UER .15 .07
(Born April& not March)
❑ 275 Michael Cage UER .05 .02
(Drafted '84& not '85)
❑ 276 Quintin Dailey .05 .02
❑ 277 Dale Ellis .08 .04
❑ 278 Steve Johnson SP .10 .05
❑ 279 Shawn Kemp RC 1.50 .70
❑ 280 Xavier McDaniel .05 .02
❑ 281 Derrick McKey .05 .02
❑ 282 Nate McMillan .08 .04
❑ 283 Olden Polynice .05 .02
❑ 284 Sedale Threatt .05 .02
❑ 285 Thurl Bailey .05 .02
❑ 286 Mike Brown .05 .02
❑ 287 Mark Eaton UER .05 .02
(72nd pick& not 82nd)
❑ 288 Blue Edwards RC .05 .02
❑ 289 Darrell Griffith .05 .02
❑ 290 Robert Hansen SP .10 .05
❑ 291 Eric Leckner SP .10 .05
❑ 292 Karl Malone .25 .11
❑ 293 Delaney Rudd .05 .02
❑ 294 John Stockton .20 .09
❑ 295 Mark Alarie .05 .02
❑ 296 Ledell Eackles SP .10 .05
❑ 297 Harvey Grant .05 .02
❑ 298A Tom Hammonds RC .05 .02
(No rookie logo on front)
❑ 298B Tom Hammonds RC .05 .02
(Rookie logo on front)
❑ 299 Charles Jones .05 .02
❑ 300 Bernard King .05 .02
❑ 301 Jeff Malone SP .10 .05
❑ 302 Mel Turpin SP .10 .05
❑ 303 Darrell Walker .05 .02
❑ 304 John Williams .05 .02
❑ 305 Bob Weiss CO .05 .02
❑ 306 Chris Ford CO .05 .02
❑ 307 Gene Littles CO .05 .02
❑ 308 Phil Jackson CO .15 .07
❑ 309 Lenny Wilkens CO .08 .04
❑ 310 Richie Adubato CO .05 .02
❑ 311 Doug Moe CO SP .10 .05
❑ 312 Chuck Daly CO .08 .04
❑ 313 Don Nelson CO .08 .04
❑ 314 Don Chaney CO .05 .02
❑ 315 Dick Versace CO .05 .02
❑ 316 Mike Schuler CO .05 .02
❑ 317 Pat Riley CO SP .15 .07
❑ 318 Ron Rothstein CO .05 .02
❑ 319 Del Harris CO .05 .02
❑ 320 Bill Musselman CO .05 .02
❑ 321 Bill Fitch CO .05 .02
❑ 322 Stu Jackson CO .05 .02
❑ 323 Matt Guokas CO .05 .02
❑ 324 Jim Lynam CO .05 .02
❑ 325 Cotton Fitzsimmons CO .05 .02
❑ 326 Rick Adelman CO .05 .02
❑ 327 Dick Motta CO .05 .02
❑ 328 Larry Brown CO .08 .04
❑ 329 K.C. Jones CO .05 .02
❑ 330 Jerry Sloan CO .08 .04
❑ 331 Wes Unseld CO .05 .02
❑ 332 Checklist 1 SP .10 .05
❑ 333 Checklist 2 SP .10 .05
❑ 334 Checklist 3 SP .10 .05
❑ 335 Checklist 4 SP .10 .05
❑ 336 Danny Ferry SP RC .25 .11
❑ 337 Pistons Celebrate .15 .07
Dennis Rodman
❑ 338 Buck Williams FIN .15 .07
Dennis Rodman
❑ 339 Joe Dumars FIN .15 .07
❑ 340 Jerome Kersey FIN .08 .04
Isiah Thomas
❑ 341A V. Johnson FIN ERR .05 .02
No headline on back
❑ 341B Vinnie Johnson COR .05 .02
❑ 342 Pistons Celebrate UER .05 .02
James Edwards
Player named as Sidney
Green is really
David Greenwood
❑ 343 K.C. Jones CO .05 .02
❑ 344 Wes Unseld CO .05 .02
❑ 345 Don Nelson CO .08 .04
❑ 346 Bob Weiss CO .05 .02
❑ 347 Chris Ford CO .05 .02
❑ 348 Phil Jackson CO .15 .07
❑ 349 Lenny Wilkens CO .08 .04
❑ 350 Don Chaney CO .05 .02
❑ 351 Mike Dunleavy CO .05 .02
❑ 352 Matt Guokas CO .05 .02
❑ 353 Rick Adelman CO .05 .02
❑ 354 Jerry Sloan CO .08 .04
❑ 355 Dominique Wilkins TC .08 .04
❑ 356 Larry Bird TC .30 .14
❑ 357 Rex Chapman TC .05 .02
❑ 358 Michael Jordan TC 1.00 .45
❑ 359 Mark Price TC .05 .02
❑ 360 Rolando Blackman TC .05 .02
❑ 361 Michael Adams TC UER .05 .02
(Westhead should be
card 422& not 440)
❑ 362 Joe Dumars TC UER .08 .04
(Gerald Henderson's name
and number not listed)
❑ 363 Chris Mullin TC .08 .04
❑ 364 Hakeem Olajuwon TC .15 .07
❑ 365 Reggie Miller TC .15 .07
❑ 366 Danny Manning TC .05 .02
❑ 367 Magic Johnson TC UER .25 .11
(Dunleavy listed as 439&
should be 351)
❑ 368 Rony Seikaly TC .05 .02
❑ 369 Alvin Robertson TC .05 .02
❑ 370 Pooh Richardson TC .05 .02
❑ 371 Chris Morris TC .05 .02
❑ 372 Patrick Ewing TC .08 .04
❑ 373 Nick Anderson TC .15 .07
❑ 374 Charles Barkley TC .15 .07
❑ 375 Kevin Johnson TC .08 .04
❑ 376 Clyde Drexler TC .08 .04
❑ 377 Wayman Tisdale TC .05 .02
❑ 378 David Robinson TC .25 .11
(Basketball fully
visible)
❑ 378B David Robinson TC .30 .14
(Basketball partially
visible)
❑ 379 Xavier McDaniel TC .05 .02
❑ 380 Karl Malone TC .15 .07
❑ 381 Bernard King TC .05 .02
❑ 382 Michael Jordan 1.00 .45
Playground
❑ 383 Karl Malone horseback .15 .07
❑ 384 European Imports .05 .02
(Vlade Divac
Sarunas Marciulionis)
❑ 385 Super Streaks 1.00 .45
Stay In School
(Magic Johnson and
Michael Jordan)
❑ 386 Johnny Newman .05 .02
(Stay in School)
❑ 387 Dell Curry .05 .02
(Stay in School)
❑ 388 Patrick Ewing .08 .04
(Don't Foul Out)
❑ 389 Isiah Thomas .08 .04
(Don't Foul Out)
❑ 390 Derrick Coleman LS RC .30 .14
❑ 391 Gary Payton LS RC 1.25 .55
❑ 392 Chris Jackson LS RC .05 .02
❑ 393 Dennis Scott LS RC .20 .09
❑ 394 Kendall Gill LS RC .30 .14
❑ 395 Felton Spencer LS RC .08 .04
❑ 396 Lionel Simmons LS RC .08 .04
❑ 397 Bo Kimble LS RC .05 .02
❑ 398 Willie Burton LS RC .05 .02
❑ 399 Rumeal Robinson LS RC .05 .02
❑ 400 Tyrone Hill LS RC .05 .02
❑ 401 Tim McCormick .05 .02
❑ 402 Sidney Moncrief .05 .02
❑ 403 Johnny Newman .05 .02
❑ 404 Dennis Hopson .05 .02
❑ 405 Cliff Levingston .05 .02
❑ 406A Danny Ferry ERR .30 .14
(No position on
front of card)
❑ 406B Danny Ferry COR .15 .07
❑ 407 Alex English .05 .02
❑ 408 Lafayette Lever .05 .02
❑ 409 Rodney McCray .05 .02
❑ 410 Mike Dunleavy CO .05 .02
❑ 411 Orlando Woolridge .05 .02
❑ 412 Joe Wolf .05 .02
❑ 413 Tree Rollins .05 .02
❑ 414 Kenny Smith .05 .02
❑ 415 Sam Perkins .08 .04
❑ 416 Terry Teagle .05 .02
❑ 417 Frank Brickowski .05 .02
❑ 418 Danny Schayes .05 .02
❑ 419 Scott Brooks .05 .02
❑ 420 Reggie Theus .08 .04
❑ 421 Greg Grant .05 .02
❑ 422 Paul Westhead CO .05 .02
❑ 423 Greg Kite .05 .02
❑ 424 Manute Bol .05 .02
❑ 425 Rickey Green .05 .02
❑ 426 Ed Nealy .05 .02
❑ 427 Danny Ainge .08 .04
❑ 428 Bobby Hansen .05 .02
❑ 429 Eric Leckner .05 .02
❑ 430 Rory Sparrow .05 .02
❑ 431 Bill Wennington .05 .02
❑ 432 Paul Pressey .05 .02
❑ 433 David Greenwood .05 .02
❑ 434 Mark McNamara .05 .02
❑ 435 Sidney Green .05 .02
❑ 436 Dave Corzine .05 .02
❑ 437 Jeff Malone .05 .02
❑ 438 Pervis Ellison .06 .04
❑ 439 Checklist 5 .05 .02
❑ 440 Checklist 6 .05 .02
❑ NNO David Robinson and 1.25 .55
All-Rookie Team
(No stats on back)
❑ NNO David Robinson and 5.00 2.20
All-Rookie Team
(Stats on back)

1991-92 Hoops

PATRICK EWING

	MINT	NRMT
COMPLETE SET (590)	25.00	11.00
COMPLETE SERIES 1 (330)	10.00	4.50
COMPLETE SERIES 2 (260)	15.00	6.75

COMMON CARD (1-590)	.05	.02
SEMISTARS	.10	.05
UNLISTED STARS	.25	.11
SUBSET CARDS HALF VALUE OF BASE CARDS		

Card	Mint	NRMT
❑ 1 John Battle	.05	.02
❑ 2 Moses Malone UER (119 rebounds 1982-83& should be 1194)	.25	.11
❑ 3 Sidney Moncrief	.05	.02
❑ 4 Doc Rivers	.10	.05
❑ 5 Rumeal Robinson UER (Back says 11th pick in 1990& should be 10th)	.05	.02
❑ 6 Spud Webb	.10	.05
❑ 7 Dominique Wilkins	.25	.11
❑ 8 Kevin Willis	.05	.02
❑ 9 Larry Bird	1.00	.45
❑ 10 Dee Brown	.05	.02
❑ 11 Kevin Gamble	.05	.02
❑ 12 Joe Kleine	.05	.02
❑ 13 Reggie Lewis	.10	.05
❑ 14 Kevin McHale	.10	.05
❑ 15 Robert Parish	.10	.05
❑ 16 Ed Pinckney	.05	.02
❑ 17 Brian Shaw	.05	.02
❑ 18 Muggsy Bogues	.10	.05
❑ 19 Rex Chapman	.10	.05
❑ 20 Dell Curry	.05	.02
❑ 21 Kendall Gill	.10	.05
❑ 22 Mike Gminski	.05	.02
❑ 23 Johnny Newman	.05	.02
❑ 24 J.R. Reid	.05	.02
❑ 25 Kelly Tripucka	.05	.02
❑ 26 B.J. Armstrong (B.J. on front& Benjamin Roy on back)	.05	.02
❑ 27 Bill Cartwright	.05	.02
❑ 28 Horace Grant	.10	.05
❑ 29 Craig Hodges	.05	.02
❑ 30 Michael Jordan	3.00	1.35
❑ 31 Stacey King	.05	.02
❑ 32 Cliff Levingston	.05	.02
❑ 33 John Paxson	.05	.02
❑ 34 Scottie Pippen	.75	.35
❑ 35 Chucky Brown	.05	.02
❑ 36 Brad Daugherty	.05	.02
❑ 37 Craig Ehlo	.05	.02
❑ 38 Danny Ferry	.05	.02
❑ 39 Larry Nance	.10	.05
❑ 40 Mark Price	.05	.02
❑ 41 Darnell Valentine	.05	.02
❑ 42 Hot Rod Williams	.05	.02
❑ 43 Rolando Blackman	.05	.02
❑ 44 Brad Davis	.05	.02
❑ 45 James Donaldson	.05	.02
❑ 46 Derek Harper	.10	.05
❑ 47 Fat Lever	.05	.02
❑ 48 Rodney McCray	.05	.02
❑ 49 Roy Tarpley	.05	.02
❑ 50 Herb Williams	.05	.02
❑ 51 Michael Adams	.05	.02
❑ 52 Chris Jackson UER (Born in Mississippi& not Michigan)	.05	.02
❑ 53 Jerome Lane	.05	.02
❑ 54 Todd Lichti	.05	.02
❑ 55 Blair Rasmussen	.05	.02
❑ 56 Reggie Williams	.05	.02
❑ 57 Joe Wolf	.05	.02
❑ 58 Orlando Woolridge	.05	.02
❑ 59 Mark Aguirre	.05	.02
❑ 60 Joe Dumars	.25	.11
❑ 61 James Edwards	.05	.02
❑ 62 Vinnie Johnson	.05	.02
❑ 63 Bill Laimbeer	.10	.05
❑ 64 Dennis Rodman	.50	.23
❑ 65 John Salley	.05	.02
❑ 66 Isiah Thomas	.25	.11
❑ 67 Tim Hardaway	.40	.18
❑ 68 Rod Higgins	.05	.02
❑ 69 Tyrone Hill	.10	.05
❑ 70 Alton Lister	.05	.02
❑ 71 Sarunas Marciulionis	.05	.02
❑ 72 Chris Mullin	.25	.11
❑ 73 Mitch Richmond	.25	.11
❑ 74 Tom Tolbert	.05	.02
❑ 75 Eric(Sleepy) Floyd	.05	.02
❑ 76 Buck Johnson	.05	.02
❑ 77 Vernon Maxwell	.05	.02
❑ 78 Hakeem Olajuwon	.40	.18
❑ 79 Kenny Smith	.05	.02
❑ 80 Larry Smith	.05	.02
❑ 81 Otis Thorpe	.10	.05
❑ 82 David Wood RC	.05	.02
❑ 83 Vern Fleming	.05	.02
❑ 84 Reggie Miller	.25	.11
❑ 85 Chuck Person	.05	.02
❑ 86 Mike Sanders	.05	.02
❑ 87 Detlef Schrempf	.10	.05
❑ 88 Rik Smits	.10	.05
❑ 89 LaSalle Thompson	.05	.02
❑ 90 Micheal Williams	.05	.02
❑ 91 Winston Garland	.05	.02
❑ 92 Gary Grant	.05	.02
❑ 93 Ron Harper	.10	.05
❑ 94 Danny Manning	.10	.05
❑ 95 Jeff Martin	.05	.02
❑ 96 Ken Norman	.05	.02
❑ 97 Olden Polynice	.05	.02
❑ 98 Charles Smith	.05	.02
❑ 99 Vlade Divac	.10	.05
❑ 100 A.C. Green	.10	.05
❑ 101 Magic Johnson	.75	.35
❑ 102 Sam Perkins	.10	.05
❑ 103 Byron Scott	.10	.05
❑ 104 Terry Teagle	.05	.02
❑ 105 Mychal Thompson	.05	.02
❑ 106 James Worthy	.25	.11
❑ 107 Willie Burton	.05	.02
❑ 108 Bimbo Coles	.05	.02
❑ 109 Terry Davis	.05	.02
❑ 110 Sherman Douglas	.05	.02
❑ 111 Kevin Edwards	.05	.02
❑ 112 Alec Kessler	.05	.02
❑ 113 Glen Rice	.25	.11
❑ 114 Rony Seikaly	.05	.02
❑ 115 Frank Brickowski	.05	.02
❑ 116 Dale Ellis	.10	.05
❑ 117 Jay Humphries	.05	.02
❑ 118 Brad Lohaus	.05	.02
❑ 119 Fred Roberts	.05	.02
❑ 120 Alvin Robertson	.05	.02
❑ 121 Danny Schayes	.05	.02
❑ 122 Jack Sikma	.05	.02
❑ 123 Randy Breuer	.05	.02
❑ 124 Tony Campbell	.05	.02
❑ 125 Tyrone Corbin	.05	.02
❑ 126 Gerald Glass	.05	.02
❑ 127 Sam Mitchell	.05	.02
❑ 128 Tod Murphy	.05	.02
❑ 129 Pooh Richardson	.05	.02
❑ 130 Felton Spencer	.05	.02
❑ 131 Mookie Blaylock	.10	.05
❑ 132 Sam Bowie	.05	.02
❑ 133 Jud Buechler	.05	.02
❑ 134 Derrick Coleman	.10	.05
❑ 135 Chris Dudley	.05	.02
❑ 136 Chris Morris	.05	.02
❑ 137 Drazen Petrovic	.10	.05
❑ 138 Reggie Theus	.10	.05
❑ 139 Maurice Cheeks	.05	.02
❑ 140 Patrick Ewing	.25	.11
❑ 141 Mark Jackson	.10	.05
❑ 142 Charles Oakley	.10	.05
❑ 143 Trent Tucker	.05	.02
❑ 144 Kiki Vandeweghe	.05	.02
❑ 145 Kenny Walker	.05	.02
❑ 146 Gerald Wilkins	.05	.02
❑ 147 Nick Anderson	.10	.05
❑ 148 Michael Ansley	.05	.02
❑ 149 Terry Catledge	.05	.02
❑ 150 Jerry Reynolds	.05	.02
❑ 151 Dennis Scott	.10	.05
❑ 152 Scott Skiles	.05	.02
❑ 153 Otis Smith	.05	.02
❑ 154 Sam Vincent	.05	.02
❑ 155 Ron Anderson	.05	.02
❑ 156 Charles Barkley	.40	.18
❑ 157 Manute Bol	.05	.02
❑ 158 Johnny Dawkins	.05	.02
❑ 159 Armon Gilliam	.05	.02
❑ 160 Rickey Green	.05	.02
❑ 161 Hersey Hawkins	.10	.05
❑ 162 Rick Mahorn	.05	.02
❑ 163 Tom Chambers	.05	.02
❑ 164 Jeff Hornacek	.10	.05
❑ 165 Kevin Johnson	.25	.11
❑ 166 Andrew Lang	.05	.02
❑ 167 Dan Majerle	.10	.05
❑ 168 Xavier McDaniel	.05	.02
❑ 169 Kurt Rambis	.05	.02
❑ 170 Mark West	.05	.02
❑ 171 Danny Ainge	.10	.05
❑ 172 Mark Bryant	.05	.02
❑ 173 Walter Davis	.05	.02
❑ 174 Clyde Drexler	.25	.11
❑ 175 Kevin Duckworth	.05	.02
❑ 176 Jerome Kersey	.05	.02
❑ 177 Terry Porter	.05	.02
❑ 178 Clifford Robinson	.10	.05
❑ 179 Buck Williams	.05	.02
❑ 180 Anthony Bonner	.05	.02
❑ 181 Antoine Carr	.05	.02
❑ 182 Duane Causwell	.05	.02
❑ 183 Bobby Hansen	.05	.02
❑ 184 Travis Mays	.05	.02
❑ 185 Lionel Simmons	.05	.02
❑ 186 Rory Sparrow	.05	.02
❑ 187 Wayman Tisdale	.05	.02
❑ 188 Willie Anderson	.05	.02
❑ 189 Terry Cummings	.05	.02
❑ 190 Sean Elliott	.10	.05
❑ 191 Sidney Green	.05	.02
❑ 192 David Greenwood	.05	.02
❑ 193 Paul Pressey	.05	.02
❑ 194 David Robinson	.50	.23
❑ 195 Dwayne Schintzius	.05	.02
❑ 196 Rod Strickland	.25	.11
❑ 197 Benoit Benjamin	.05	.02
❑ 198 Michael Cage	.05	.02
❑ 199 Eddie Johnson	.10	.05
❑ 200 Shawn Kemp	.60	.25
❑ 201 Derrick McKey	.05	.02
❑ 202 Gary Payton	.60	.25
❑ 203 Ricky Pierce	.05	.02
❑ 204 Sedale Threatt	.05	.02
❑ 205 Thurl Bailey	.05	.02
❑ 206 Mike Brown	.05	.02
❑ 207 Mark Eaton	.05	.02
❑ 208 Blue Edwards UER (Forward/guard on front& guard on back)	.05	.02
❑ 209 Darrell Griffith	.05	.02
❑ 210 Jeff Malone	.05	.02
❑ 211 Karl Malone	.40	.18
❑ 212 John Stockton	.25	.11
❑ 213 Ledell Eackles	.05	.02
❑ 214 Pervis Ellison	.05	.02
❑ 215 A.J. English	.05	.02
❑ 216 Harvey Grant (Shown boxing out twin brother Horace)	.05	.02
❑ 217 Charles Jones	.05	.02
❑ 218 Bernard King	.05	.02
❑ 219 Darrell Walker	.05	.02
❑ 220 John Williams	.05	.02
❑ 221 Bob Weiss CO	.05	.02
❑ 222 Chris Ford CO	.05	.02
❑ 223 Gene Littles CO	.05	.02
❑ 224 Phil Jackson CO	.10	.05
❑ 225 Lenny Wilkens CO	.10	.05
❑ 226 Richie Adubato CO	.05	.02
❑ 227 Paul Westhead CO	.05	.02
❑ 228 Chuck Daly CO	.10	.05
❑ 229 Don Nelson CO	.10	.05
❑ 230 Don Chaney CO	.05	.02
❑ 231 Bob Hill RC CO UER (Coached under Ted Owens& not Ted Owen)	.05	.02
❑ 232 Mike Schuler CO	.05	.02
❑ 233 Mike Dunleavy CO	.05	.02
❑ 234 Kevin Loughery CO	.05	.02
❑ 235 Del Harris CO	.05	.02
❑ 236 Jimmy Rodgers CO	.05	.02
❑ 237 Bill Fitch CO	.05	.02
❑ 238 Pat Riley CO	.10	.05
❑ 239 Matt Guokas CO	.05	.02

❑ 240 Jim Lynam CO .05 .02
❑ 241 Cotton Fitzsimmons CO .05 .02
❑ 242 Rick Adelman CO .05 .02
❑ 243 Dick Motta CO .05 .02
❑ 244 Larry Brown CO .05 .02
❑ 245 K.C. Jones CO .10 .05
❑ 246 Jerry Sloan CO .10 .05
❑ 247 Wes Unseld CO .10 .05
❑ 248 Charles Barkley AS .25 .11
❑ 249 Brad Daugherty AS .05 .02
❑ 250 Joe Dumars AS .10 .05
❑ 251 Patrick Ewing AS .10 .05
❑ 252 Hersey Hawkins AS .05 .02
❑ 253 Michael Jordan AS 1.50 .70
❑ 254 Bernard King AS .05 .02
❑ 255 Kevin McHale AS .05 .02
❑ 256 Robert Parish AS .05 .02
❑ 257 Ricky Pierce AS .05 .02
❑ 258 Alvin Robertson AS .05 .02
❑ 259 Dominique Wilkins AS .10 .05
❑ 260 Chris Ford CO AS .05 .02
❑ 261 Tom Chambers AS .05 .02
❑ 262 Clyde Drexler AS .10 .05
❑ 263 Kevin Duckworth AS .05 .02
❑ 264 Tim Hardaway AS .25 .11
❑ 265 Kevin Johnson AS .10 .05
❑ 266 Magic Johnson AS .40 .18
❑ 267 Karl Malone AS .25 .11
❑ 268 Chris Mullin AS .10 .05
❑ 269 Terry Porter AS .05 .02
❑ 270 David Robinson AS .25 .11
❑ 271 John Stockton AS .10 .05
❑ 272 James Worthy AS .10 .05
❑ 273 Rick Adelman CO AS .05 .02
❑ 274 Atlanta Hawks .05 .02
Team Card UER
(Actually began as
Tri-Cities Blackhawks)
❑ 275 Boston Celtics .05 .02
Team Card UER
(No NBA Hoops logo
on card front)
❑ 276 Charlotte Hornets .05 .02
Team Card
❑ 277 Chicago Bulls .05 .02
Team Card
❑ 278 Cleveland Cavaliers .05 .02
Team Card
❑ 279 Dallas Mavericks .05 .02
Team Card
❑ 280 Denver Nuggets .05 .02
Team Card
❑ 281 Detroit Pistons .05 .02
Team Card UER
(Pistons not NBA Final-
ists until 1988; Ft.
Ft. Wayne Pistons in
Finals in 1955 and 1956)
❑ 282 Golden State Warriors .05 .02
Team Card
❑ 283 Houston Rockets .05 .02
Team Card
❑ 284 Indiana Pacers .05 .02
Team Card
❑ 285 Los Angeles Clippers .05 .02
Team Card
❑ 286 Los Angeles Lakers .05 .02
Team Card
❑ 287 Miami Heat .05 .02
Team Card
❑ 288 Milwaukee Bucks .05 .02
Team Card
❑ 289 Minnesota Timberwolves .05 .02
Team Card
❑ 290 New Jersey Nets .05 .02
Team Card
❑ 291 New York Knicks .05 .02
Team Card UER
(Golden State not men-
tioned as an active
charter member of NBA)
❑ 292 Orlando Magic .05 .02
Team Card
❑ 293 Philadelphia 76ers .05 .02
Team Card
❑ 294 Phoenix Suns .05 .02
Team Card
❑ 295 Portland Trail Blazers .05 .02
Team Card
❑ 296 Sacramento Kings .05 .02
Team Card
❑ 297 San Antonio Spurs .05 .02
Team Card
❑ 298 Seattle Supersonics .05 .02
Team Card
❑ 299 Utah Jazz .05 .02
Team Card
❑ 300 Washington Bullets .05 .02
Team Card
❑ 301 James Naismith .10 .05
Centennial Card
❑ 302 Kevin Johnson IS .10 .05
❑ 303 Reggie Miller IS .10 .05
❑ 304 Hakeem Olajuwon IS .25 .11
❑ 305 Robert Parish IS .05 .02
❑ 306 Scoring Leaders 1.00 .45
Michael Jordan
Karl Malone
❑ 307 3-Point FG Percent .05 .02
League Leaders
Jim Les
Trent Tucker
❑ 308 Free Throw Percent .10 .05
League Leaders
Reggie Miller
Jeff Malone
❑ 309 Blocks League Leaders .25 .11
Hakeem Olajuwon
David Robinson
❑ 310 Steals League Leaders .05 .02
Alvin Robertson
John Stockton
❑ 311 Rebounds LL UER .50 .23
David Robinson
Dennis Rodman
(Robinson credited as
playing for Houston)
❑ 312 Assists League Leaders .10 .05
John Stockton
Magic Johnson
❑ 313 Field Goal Percent .10 .05
League Leaders
Buck Williams
Robert Parish
❑ 314 Larry Bird UER .50 .23
Milestone
(Should be card 315 to
fit Milestone sequence)
❑ 315 Alex English .10 .05
Moses Malone
Milestone UER
(Should be card 314 and
be a League Leader card)
❑ 316 Magic Johnson .40 .18
Milestone
❑ 317 Michael Jordan 1.50 .70
Milestone
❑ 318 Moses Malone .10 .05
Milestone
❑ 319 Larry Bird .50 .23
NBA Yearbook
Look Back
❑ 320 Maurice Cheeks .05 .02
NBA Yearbook
Look Back
❑ 321 Magic Johnson .40 .18
NBA Yearbook
Look Back
❑ 322 Bernard King .05 .02
NBA Yearbook
Look Back
❑ 323 Moses Malone .10 .05
NBA Yearbook
Look Back
❑ 324 Robert Parish .05 .02
NBA Yearbook
Look Back
❑ 325 All-Star Jam .10 .05
Jammin' With Will Smith
(Stay in School)
❑ 326 All-Star Jam .10 .05
Jammin' With The Boys
and Will Smith
(Stay in School)
❑ 327 David Robinson .25 .11
Leave Alcohol Out
❑ 328 Checklist 1 .05 .02
❑ 329 Checklist 2 UER .05 .02
(Card front is from 330)
❑ 330 Checklist 3 UER .05 .02
(Card front is from 329;
card 327 listed oper-
ation& should be
celebration)
❑ 331 Maurice Cheeks .05 .02
❑ 332 Duane Ferrell .05 .02
❑ 333 Jon Koncak .05 .02
❑ 334 Gary Leonard .05 .02
❑ 335 Travis Mays .05 .02
❑ 336 Blair Rasmussen .05 .02
❑ 337 Alexander Volkov .05 .02
❑ 338 John Bagley .05 .02
❑ 339 Rickey Green UER .05 .02
(Ricky on front)
❑ 340 Derek Smith .05 .02
❑ 341 Stojko Vrankovic .05 .02
❑ 342 Anthony Frederick RC .05 .02
❑ 343 Kenny Gattison .05 .02
❑ 344 Eric Leckner .05 .02
❑ 345 Will Perdue .05 .02
❑ 346 Scott Williams RC .05 .02
❑ 347 John Battle .05 .02
❑ 348 Winston Bennett .05 .02
❑ 349 Henry James .05 .02
❑ 350 Steve Kerr .10 .05
❑ 351 John Morton .05 .02
❑ 352 Terry Davis .05 .02
❑ 353 Randy White .05 .02
❑ 354 Greg Anderson .05 .02
❑ 355 Anthony Cook .05 .02
❑ 356 Walter Davis .05 .02
❑ 357 Winston Garland .05 .02
❑ 358 Scott Hastings .05 .02
❑ 359 Marcus Liberty .05 .02
❑ 360 William Bedford .05 .02
❑ 361 Lance Blanks .05 .02
❑ 362 Brad Sellers .05 .02
❑ 363 Darrell Walker .05 .02
❑ 364 Orlando Woolridge .05 .02
❑ 365 Vincent Askew RC .05 .02
❑ 366 Mario Elie RC .25 .11
❑ 367 Jim Petersen .05 .02
❑ 368 Matt Bullard RC .05 .02
❑ 369 Gerald Henderson .05 .02
❑ 370 Dave Jamerson .05 .02
❑ 371 Tree Rollins .05 .02
❑ 372 Greg Dreiling .05 .02
❑ 373 George McCloud .05 .02
❑ 374 Kenny Williams .05 .02
❑ 375 Randy Wittman .05 .02
❑ 376 Tony Brown .05 .02
❑ 377 Lanard Copeland .05 .02
❑ 378 James Edwards .05 .02
❑ 379 Bo Kimble .05 .02
❑ 380 Doc Rivers .10 .05
❑ 381 Loy Vaught .05 .02
❑ 382 Elden Campbell .25 .11
❑ 383 Jack Haley .05 .02
❑ 384 Tony Smith .05 .02
❑ 385 Sedale Threatt .05 .02
❑ 386 Keith Askins RC .05 .02
❑ 387 Grant Long .05 .02
❑ 388 Alan Ogg .05 .02
❑ 389 Jon Sundvold .05 .02
❑ 390 Lester Conner .05 .02
❑ 391 Jeff Grayer .05 .02
❑ 392 Steve Henson .05 .02
❑ 393 Larry Krystkowiak .05 .02
❑ 394 Moses Malone .25 .11
❑ 395 Scott Brooks .05 .02
❑ 396 Tellis Frank .05 .02
❑ 397 Doug West .05 .02
❑ 398 Rafael Addison RC .05 .02
❑ 399 Dave Feitl RC .05 .02
❑ 400 Tate George .05 .02
❑ 401 Terry Mills RC .25 .11
❑ 402 Tim McCormick .05 .02
❑ 403 Xavier McDaniel .05 .02

❑ 404 Anthony Mason RC .50 .23
❑ 405 Brian Quinnett .05 .02
❑ 406 John Starks RC .25 .11
❑ 407 Mark Acres .05 .02
❑ 408 Greg Kite .05 .02
❑ 409 Jeff Turner .05 .02
❑ 410 Morlon Wiley .05 .02
❑ 411 Dave Hoppen .05 .02
❑ 412 Brian Oliver .05 .02
❑ 413 Kenny Payne .05 .02
❑ 414 Charles Shackleford .05 .02
❑ 415 Mitchell Wiggins .05 .02
❑ 416 Jayson Williams .25 .11
❑ 417 Cedric Ceballos .10 .05
❑ 418 Negele Knight .05 .02
❑ 419 Andrew Lang .05 .02
❑ 420 Jerrod Mustaf .05 .02
❑ 421 Ed Nealy .05 .02
❑ 422 Tim Perry .05 .02
❑ 423 Alaa Abdelnaby .05 .02
❑ 424 Wayne Cooper .05 .02
❑ 425 Danny Young .05 .02
❑ 426 Dennis Hopson .05 .02
❑ 427 Les Jepsen .05 .02
❑ 428 Jim Les RC .05 .02
❑ 429 Mitch Richmond .25 .11
❑ 430 Dwayne Schintzius .05 .02
❑ 431 Spud Webb .10 .05
❑ 432 Jud Buechler .05 .02
❑ 433 Antoine Carr .05 .02
❑ 434 Tom Garrick .05 .02
❑ 435 Sean Higgins RC .05 .02
❑ 436 Avery Johnson .10 .05
❑ 437 Tony Massenburg .05 .02
❑ 438 Dana Barros .05 .02
❑ 439 Quintin Dailey .05 .02
❑ 440 Bart Kofoed RC .05 .02
❑ 441 Nate McMillan .05 .02
❑ 442 Delaney Rudd .05 .02
❑ 443 Michael Adams .05 .02
❑ 444 Mark Alarie .05 .02
❑ 445 Greg Foster .05 .02
❑ 446 Tom Hammonds .05 .02
❑ 447 Andre Turner .05 .02
❑ 448 David Wingate .05 .02
❑ 449 Dominique Wilkins SC .10 .05
❑ 450 Kevin Willis SC .05 .02
❑ 451 Larry Bird SC .50 .23
❑ 452 Robert Parish SC .05 .02
❑ 453 Rex Chapman SC .05 .02
❑ 454 Kendall Gill SC .05 .02
❑ 455 Michael Jordan SC 1.50 .70
❑ 456 Scottie Pippen SC .40 .18
❑ 457 Brad Daugherty SC .05 .02
❑ 458 Larry Nance SC .05 .02
❑ 459 Rolando Blackman SC .05 .02
❑ 460 Derek Harper SC .05 .02
❑ 461 Chris Jackson SC .05 .02
❑ 462 Todd Lichti SC .05 .02
❑ 463 Joe Dumars SC .10 .05
❑ 464 Isiah Thomas SC .10 .05
❑ 465 Tim Hardaway SC .25 .11
❑ 466 Chris Mullin SC .10 .05
❑ 467 Hakeem Olajuwon SC .25 .11
❑ 468 Otis Thorpe SC .05 .02
❑ 469 Reggie Miller SC .10 .05
❑ 470 Detlef Schrempf SC .05 .02
❑ 471 Ron Harper SC .05 .02
❑ 472 Charles Smith SC .05 .02
❑ 473 Magic Johnson SC .40 .18
❑ 474 James Worthy SC .10 .05
❑ 475 Sherman Douglas SC .05 .02
❑ 476 Rony Seikaly SC .05 .02
❑ 477 Jay Humphries SC .05 .02
❑ 478 Alvin Robertson SC .05 .02
❑ 479 Tyrone Corbin SC .05 .02
❑ 480 Pooh Richardson SC .05 .02
❑ 481 Sam Bowie SC .05 .02
❑ 482 Derrick Coleman SC .05 .02
❑ 483 Patrick Ewing SC .10 .05
❑ 484 Charles Oakley SC .05 .02
❑ 485 Dennis Scott SC .05 .02
❑ 486 Scott Skiles SC .05 .02
❑ 487 Charles Barkley SC .25 .11
❑ 488 Hersey Hawkins SC .05 .02
❑ 489 Tom Chambers SC .05 .02
❑ 490 Kevin Johnson SC .10 .05
❑ 491 Clyde Drexler SC .10 .05
❑ 492 Terry Porter SC .05 .02
❑ 493 Lionel Simmons SC .05 .02
❑ 494 Wayman Tisdale SC .05 .02
❑ 495 Terry Cummings SC .05 .02
❑ 496 David Robinson SC .25 .11
❑ 497 Shawn Kemp SC .25 .11
❑ 498 Ricky Pierce SC .05 .02
❑ 499 Karl Malone SC .25 .11
❑ 500 John Stockton SC .10 .05
❑ 501 Harvey Grant SC .05 .02
❑ 502 Bernard King SC .05 .02
❑ 503 Travis Mays Art .05 .02
❑ 504 Kevin McHale Art .05 .02
❑ 505 Muggsy Bogues Art .05 .02
❑ 506 Scottie Pippen Art .40 .18
❑ 507 Brad Daugherty Art .05 .02
❑ 508 Derek Harper Art .05 .02
❑ 509 Chris Jackson Art .05 .02
❑ 510 Isiah Thomas Art .10 .05
❑ 511 Tim Hardaway Art .25 .11
❑ 512 Otis Thorpe Art .05 .02
❑ 513 Chuck Person Art .05 .02
❑ 514 Ron Harper Art .05 .02
❑ 515 James Worthy Art .10 .05
❑ 516 Sherman Douglas Art .05 .02
❑ 517 Dale Ellis Art .05 .02
❑ 518 Tony Campbell Art .05 .02
❑ 519 Derrick Coleman Art .05 .02
❑ 520 Gerald Wilkins Art .05 .02
❑ 521 Scott Skiles Art .05 .02
❑ 522 Manute Bol Art .05 .02
❑ 523 Tom Chambers Art .05 .02
❑ 524 Terry Porter Art .05 .02
❑ 525 Lionel Simmons Art .05 .02
❑ 526 Sean Elliott Art .05 .02
❑ 527 Shawn Kemp Art .25 .11
❑ 528 John Stockton Art .10 .05
❑ 529 Harvey Grant Art .05 .02
❑ 530 Michael Adams .05 .02
All-Time Active Leader
Three-Point Field Goals
❑ 531 Charles Barkley .25 .11
All-Time Active Leader
Field Goal Percentage
❑ 532 Larry Bird .50 .23
All-Time Active Leader
Free Throw Percentage
❑ 533 Maurice Cheeks .05 .02
All-Time Active Leader
Steals
❑ 534 Mark Eaton .05 .02
All-Time Active Leader
Blocks
❑ 535 Magic Johnson .40 .18
All-Time Active Leader
Assists
❑ 536 Michael Jordan 1.50 .70
All-Time Active Leader
Scoring Average
❑ 537 Moses Malone .10 .05
All-Time Active Leader
Rebounds
❑ 538 Sam Perkins FIN .05 .02
❑ 539 Scottie Pippen FIN .25 .11
James Worthy
❑ 540 Vlade Divac FIN .05 .02
❑ 541 John Paxson FIN .05 .02
❑ 542 Michael Jordan FIN 1.50 .70
Magic Johnson)
❑ 543 Michael Jordan FIN 1.50 .70
NBA Champs, kissing trophy)
❑ 544 Otis Smith .05 .02
Stay in School
❑ 545 Jeff Turner .05 .02
Stay in School
❑ 546 Larry Johnson RC 1.00 .45
❑ 547 Kenny Anderson RC .50 .23
❑ 548 Billy Owens RC .25 .11
❑ 549 Dikembe Mutombo RC .75 .35
❑ 550 Steve Smith RC 1.00 .45
❑ 551 Doug Smith RC .05 .02
❑ 552 Luc Longley RC .25 .11
❑ 553 Mark Macon RC .05 .02
❑ 554 Stacey Augmon RC .25 .11
❑ 555 Brian Williams RC .25 .11
❑ 556 Terrell Brandon RC .75 .35
❑ 557 Walter Davis .05 .02
Team USA 1976
❑ 558 Vern Fleming .05 .02
Team USA 1984
❑ 559 Joe Kleine .05 .02
Team USA 1984
❑ 560 Jon Koncak .05 .02
Team USA 1984
❑ 561 Sam Perkins .05 .02
Team USA 1984
❑ 562 Alvin Robertson .05 .02
Team USA 1984
❑ 563 Wayman Tisdale .05 .02
Team USA 1984
❑ 564 Jeff Turner .05 .02
Team USA 1984
❑ 565 Willie Anderson .05 .02
Team USA 1988
❑ 566 Stacey Augmon .25 .11
Team USA 1988
❑ 567 Bimbo Coles .05 .02
Team USA 1988
❑ 568 Jeff Grayer .05 .02
Team USA 1988
❑ 569 Hersey Hawkins .05 .02
Team USA 1988
❑ 570 Dan Majerle .05 .02
Team USA 1988
❑ 571 Danny Manning .05 .02
Team USA 1988
❑ 572 J.R. Reid .05 .02
Team USA 1988
❑ 573 Mitch Richmond .50 .23
Team USA 1988
❑ 574 Charles Smith .05 .02
Team USA 1988
❑ 575 Charles Barkley .75 .35
Team USA 1992
❑ 576 Larry Bird 2.00 .90
Team USA 1992
❑ 577 Patrick Ewing .50 .23
Team USA 1992
❑ 578 Magic Johnson 1.50 .70
Team USA 1992
❑ 579 Michael Jordan 6.00 2.70
Team USA 1992
❑ 580 Karl Malone .75 .35
Team USA 1992
❑ 581 Chris Mullin .25 .11
Team USA 1992
❑ 582 Scottie Pippen 1.50 .70
Team USA 1992
❑ 583 David Robinson 1.00 .45
Team USA 1992
❑ 584 John Stockton .50 .23
Team USA 1992
❑ 585 Chuck Daly CO .10 .05
Team USA 1992
❑ 586 Lenny Wilkens CO .10 .05
Team USA 1992
❑ 587 P.J. Carlesimo RC CO .05 .02
Team USA 1992
❑ 588 Mike Krzyzewski RC CO .40 .18
Team USA 1992
❑ 589 Checklist Card 1 .05 .02
❑ 590 Checklist Card 2 .05 .02
❑ CC1 Dr.James Naismith 1.00 .45
❑ XX Head of the Class 20.00 9.00
Kenny Anderson
Larry Johnson
Dikembe Mutombo
Billy Owens
Doug Smith
Steve Smith
❑ NNO Team USA SP .50 .23
Title Card
❑ NNO Centennial Card 1.00 .45
(Sendaway)

1991-92 Hoops All-Star MVP's

	MINT	NRMT
COMPLETE SET (6)	20.00	9.00
*SINGLES: 2X TO 5X BASE CARD HI		
TWO PER SER.2 RACK PACK		
❑ 7 Isiah Thomas (Numbered VII)	1.25	.55
❑ 8 Tom Chambers (Numbered VIII)	.25	.11
❑ 9 Michael Jordan (Numbered IX)	15.00	6.75
❑ 10 Karl Malone (Numbered X)	2.00	.90
❑ 11 Magic Johnson (Numbered XI)	4.00	1.80
❑ 12 Charles Barkley (Numbered XII)	2.00	.90

1991-92 Hoops Slam Dunk

	MINT	NRMT
COMPLETE SET (6)	15.00	6.75
*SINGLES: 2X TO 5X BASE CARD HI		
TWO PER SER.1 RACK PACK		
❑ 1 Larry Nance (Numbered I)	.50	.23
❑ 2 Dominique Wilkins (Numbered II)	1.25	.55
❑ 3 Spud Webb (Numbered III)	.50	.23
❑ 4 Michael Jordan (Numbered IV)	15.00	6.75
❑ 5 Kenny Walker (Numbered V)	.25	.11
❑ 6 Dee Brown (Numbered VI)	.25	.11

1992-93 Hoops

	MINT	NRMT
COMPLETE SET (490)	35.00	16.00
COMPLETE SERIES 1 (350)	15.00	6.75
COMPLETE SERIES 2 (140)	20.00	9.00
COMMON CARD (1-350)	.05	.02
COMMON CARD (351-490)	.10	.05
SEMISTARS SER.1	.10	.05
SEMISTARS SER.2	.20	.09
UNLISTED STARS SER.1	.25	.11
UNLISTED STARS SER.2	.40	.18

SUBSET CARDS HALF VALUE OF BASE CARDS
AC1: SER.2 STATED ODDS 1:21
SU1: SER.2 STATED ODDS 1:92, 1:5,732 AU
TR1: SER.2 STATED ODDS 1:32
BAR.PLASTIC: SER.1 STATED ODDS 1:720
MAGIC AU: SER.1 STATED ODDS 1:14,400
EWING AU: SER.1 STATED ODDS: 1:14,400

	MINT	NRMT
❑ 1 Stacey Augmon	.10	.05
❑ 2 Maurice Cheeks	.05	.02
❑ 3 Duane Ferrell	.05	.02
❑ 4 Paul Graham	.05	.02
❑ 5 Jon Koncak	.05	.02
❑ 6 Blair Rasmussen	.05	.02
❑ 7 Rumeal Robinson	.05	.02
❑ 8 Dominique Wilkins	.25	.11
❑ 9 Kevin Willis	.05	.02
❑ 10 Larry Bird	1.00	.45
❑ 11 Dee Brown	.05	.02
❑ 12 Sherman Douglas	.05	.02
❑ 13 Rick Fox	.10	.05
❑ 14 Kevin Gamble	.05	.02
❑ 15 Reggie Lewis	.10	.05
❑ 16 Kevin McHale	.25	.11
❑ 17 Robert Parish	.10	.05
❑ 18 Ed Pinckney UER (Wrong trade info& Kleine to Sacramento and Lohaus to Boston)	.05	.02
❑ 19 Muggsy Bogues	.10	.05
❑ 20 Dell Curry	.05	.02
❑ 21 Kenny Gattison	.05	.02
❑ 22 Kendall Gill	.10	.05
❑ 23 Mike Gminski	.05	.02
❑ 24 Larry Johnson	.30	.14
❑ 25 Johnny Newman	.05	.02
❑ 26 J.R. Reid	.05	.02
❑ 27 B.J. Armstrong	.05	.02
❑ 28 Bill Cartwright	.05	.02
❑ 29 Horace Grant	.10	.05
❑ 30 Michael Jordan	3.00	1.35
❑ 31 Stacey King	.05	.02
❑ 32 John Paxson	.05	.02
❑ 33 Will Perdue	.05	.02
❑ 34 Scottie Pippen	.75	.35
❑ 35 Scott Williams	.05	.02
❑ 36 John Battle	.05	.02
❑ 37 Terrell Brandon	.25	.11
❑ 38 Brad Daugherty	.05	.02
❑ 39 Craig Ehlo	.05	.02
❑ 40 Danny Ferry	.05	.02
❑ 41 Henry James	.05	.02
❑ 42 Larry Nance	.05	.02
❑ 43 Mark Price	.05	.02
❑ 44 Hot Rod Williams	.05	.02
❑ 45 Rolando Blackman	.05	.02
❑ 46 Terry Davis	.05	.02
❑ 47 Derek Harper	.10	.05
❑ 48 Mike Iuzzolino	.05	.02
❑ 49 Fat Lever	.05	.02
❑ 50 Rodney McCray	.05	.02
❑ 51 Doug Smith	.05	.02
❑ 52 Randy White	.05	.02
❑ 53 Herb Williams	.05	.02
❑ 54 Greg Anderson	.05	.02
❑ 55 Winston Garland	.05	.02
❑ 56 Chris Jackson	.05	.02
❑ 57 Marcus Liberty	.05	.02
❑ 58 Todd Lichti	.05	.02
❑ 59 Mark Macon	.05	.02
❑ 60 Dikembe Mutombo	.25	.11
❑ 61 Reggie Williams	.05	.02
❑ 62 Mark Aguirre	.05	.02
❑ 63 William Bedford	.05	.02
❑ 64 Joe Dumars	.25	.11
❑ 65 Bill Laimbeer	.10	.05
❑ 66 Dennis Rodman	.50	.23
❑ 67 John Salley	.05	.02
❑ 68 Isiah Thomas	.25	.11
❑ 69 Darrell Walker	.05	.02
❑ 70 Orlando Woolridge	.05	.02
❑ 71 Victor Alexander	.05	.02
❑ 72 Mario Elie	.10	.05
❑ 73 Chris Gatling	.05	.02
❑ 74 Tim Hardaway	.30	.14
❑ 75 Tyrone Hill	.05	.02
❑ 76 Alton Lister	.05	.02
❑ 77 Sarunas Marciulionis	.05	.02
❑ 78 Chris Mullin	.25	.11
❑ 79 Billy Owens	.10	.05
❑ 80 Matt Bullard	.05	.02
❑ 81 Sleepy Floyd	.05	.02
❑ 82 Avery Johnson	.05	.02
❑ 83 Buck Johnson	.05	.02
❑ 84 Vernon Maxwell	.05	.02
❑ 85 Hakeem Olajuwon	.40	.18
❑ 86 Kenny Smith	.05	.02
❑ 87 Larry Smith	.05	.02
❑ 88 Otis Thorpe	.10	.05
❑ 89 Dale Davis	.05	.02
❑ 90 Vern Fleming	.05	.02
❑ 91 George McCloud	.05	.02
❑ 92 Reggie Miller	.25	.11
❑ 93 Chuck Person	.05	.02
❑ 94 Detlef Schrempf	.10	.05
❑ 95 Rik Smits	.10	.05
❑ 96 LaSalle Thompson	.05	.02
❑ 97 Micheal Williams	.05	.02
❑ 98 James Edwards	.05	.02
❑ 99 Gary Grant	.05	.02
❑ 100 Ron Harper	.10	.05
❑ 101 Danny Manning	.10	.05
❑ 102 Ken Norman	.05	.02
❑ 103 Olden Polynice	.05	.02
❑ 104 Doc Rivers	.10	.05
❑ 105 Charles Smith	.05	.02
❑ 106 Loy Vaught	.05	.02
❑ 107 Elden Campbell	.10	.05
❑ 108 Vlade Divac	.10	.05
❑ 109 A.C. Green	.10	.05
❑ 110 Sam Perkins	.10	.05
❑ 111 Byron Scott	.10	.05
❑ 112 Tony Smith	.05	.02
❑ 113 Terry Teagle	.05	.02
❑ 114 Sedale Threatt	.05	.02
❑ 115 James Worthy	.25	.11
❑ 116 Willie Burton	.05	.02
❑ 117 Bimbo Coles	.05	.02
❑ 118 Kevin Edwards	.05	.02
❑ 119 Alec Kessler	.05	.02
❑ 120 Grant Long	.05	.02
❑ 121 Glen Rice	.25	.11
❑ 122 Rony Seikaly	.05	.02
❑ 123 Brian Shaw	.05	.02
❑ 124 Steve Smith	.30	.14
❑ 125 Frank Brickowski	.05	.02
❑ 126 Dale Ellis	.05	.02
❑ 127 Jeff Grayer	.05	.02
❑ 128 Jay Humphries	.05	.02
❑ 129 Larry Krystkowiak	.05	.02
❑ 130 Moses Malone	.25	.11
❑ 131 Fred Roberts	.05	.02
❑ 132 Alvin Robertson	.05	.02
❑ 133 Dan Schayes	.05	.02
❑ 134 Thurl Bailey	.05	.02
❑ 135 Scott Brooks	.05	.02
❑ 136 Tony Campbell	.05	.02
❑ 137 Gerald Glass	.05	.02
❑ 138 Luc Longley	.10	.05
❑ 139 Sam Mitchell	.05	.02

❑ 140 Pooh Richardson .05 .02
❑ 141 Felton Spencer .05 .02
❑ 142 Doug West .05 .02
❑ 143 Rafael Addison .05 .02
❑ 144 Kenny Anderson .25 .11
❑ 145 Mookie Blaylock .10 .05
❑ 146 Sam Bowie .05 .02
❑ 147 Derrick Coleman .10 .05
❑ 148 Chris Dudley .05 .02
❑ 149 Terry Mills .05 .02
❑ 150 Chris Morris .05 .02
❑ 151 Drazen Petrovic .05 .02
❑ 152 Greg Anthony .05 .02
❑ 153 Patrick Ewing .25 .11
❑ 154 Mark Jackson .10 .05
❑ 155 Anthony Mason .25 .11
❑ 156 Xavier McDaniel .05 .02
❑ 157 Charles Oakley .10 .05
❑ 158 John Starks .10 .05
❑ 159 Gerald Wilkins .05 .02
❑ 160 Nick Anderson .10 .05
❑ 161 Terry Catledge .05 .02
❑ 162 Jerry Reynolds .05 .02
❑ 163 Stanley Roberts .05 .02
❑ 164 Dennis Scott .10 .05
❑ 165 Scott Skiles .05 .02
❑ 166 Jeff Turner .05 .02
❑ 167 Sam Vincent .05 .02
❑ 168 Brian Williams .05 .02
❑ 169 Ron Anderson .05 .02
❑ 170 Charles Barkley .40 .18
❑ 171 Manute Bol .05 .02
❑ 172 Johnny Dawkins .05 .02
❑ 173 Armon Gilliam .05 .02
❑ 174 Hersey Hawkins .10 .05
❑ 175 Brian Oliver .05 .02
❑ 176 Charles Shackleford .05 .02
❑ 177 Jayson Williams .10 .05
❑ 178 Cedric Ceballos .10 .05
❑ 179 Tom Chambers .05 .02
❑ 180 Jeff Hornacek .10 .05
❑ 181 Kevin Johnson .25 .11
❑ 182 Negele Knight .05 .02
❑ 183 Andrew Lang .05 .02
❑ 184 Dan Majerle .10 .05
❑ 185 Tim Perry .05 .02
❑ 186 Mark West .05 .02
❑ 187 Alaa Abdelnaby .05 .02
❑ 188 Danny Ainge .10 .05
❑ 189 Clyde Drexler .25 .11
❑ 190 Kevin Duckworth .05 .02
❑ 191 Jerome Kersey .05 .02
❑ 192 Robert Pack .05 .02
❑ 193 Terry Porter .05 .02
❑ 194 Clifford Robinson .10 .05
❑ 195 Buck Williams .10 .05
❑ 196 Anthony Bonner .05 .02
❑ 197 Duane Causwell .05 .02
❑ 198 Pete Chilcutt .05 .02
❑ 199 Dennis Hopson .05 .02
❑ 200 Mitch Richmond .25 .11
❑ 201 Lionel Simmons .05 .02
❑ 202 Wayman Tisdale .05 .02
❑ 203 Spud Webb .10 .05
❑ 204 Willie Anderson .05 .02
❑ 205 Antoine Carr .05 .02
❑ 206 Terry Cummings .10 .05
❑ 207 Sean Elliott .10 .05
❑ 208 Sidney Green .05 .02
❑ 209 David Robinson .40 .18
❑ 210 Rod Strickland .25 .11
❑ 211 Greg Sutton .05 .02
❑ 212 Dana Barros .05 .02
❑ 213 Benoit Benjamin .05 .02
❑ 214 Michael Cage .05 .02
❑ 215 Eddie Johnson .05 .02
❑ 216 Shawn Kemp .50 .23
❑ 217 Derrick McKey .05 .02
❑ 218 Nate McMillan .05 .02
❑ 219 Gary Payton .50 .23
❑ 220 Ricky Pierce .05 .02
❑ 221 David Benoit .05 .02
❑ 222 Mike Brown .05 .02
❑ 223 Tyrone Corbin .05 .02
❑ 224 Mark Eaton .05 .02
❑ 225 Blue Edwards .05 .02
❑ 226 Jeff Malone .05 .02
❑ 227 Karl Malone .40 .18
❑ 228 Eric Murdock .05 .02
❑ 229 John Stockton .25 .11
❑ 230 Michael Adams .05 .02
❑ 231 Rex Chapman .05 .02
❑ 232 Ledell Eackles .05 .02
❑ 233 Pervis Ellison .05 .02
❑ 234 A.J. English .05 .02
❑ 235 Harvey Grant .05 .02
❑ 236 Charles Jones .05 .02
❑ 237 LaBradford Smith .05 .02
❑ 238 Larry Stewart .05 .02
❑ 239 Bob Weiss CO .05 .02
❑ 240 Chris Ford CO .05 .02
❑ 241 Allan Bristow CO .05 .02
❑ 242 Phil Jackson CO .10 .05
❑ 243 Lenny Wilkens CO .10 .05
❑ 244 Richie Adubato CO .05 .02
❑ 245 Dan Issel CO .05 .02
❑ 246 Ron Rothstein CO .05 .02
❑ 247 Don Nelson CO .10 .05
❑ 248 Rudy Tomjanovich CO .10 .05
❑ 249 Bob Hill CO .05 .02
❑ 250 Larry Brown CO .10 .05
❑ 251 Randy Pfund CO RC .05 .02
❑ 252 Kevin Loughery CO .05 .02
❑ 253 Mike Dunleavy CO .05 .02
❑ 254 Jimmy Rodgers CO .05 .02
❑ 255 Chuck Daly CO .10 .05
❑ 256 Pat Riley CO .10 .05
❑ 257 Matt Guokas CO .05 .02
❑ 258 Doug Moe CO .05 .02
❑ 259 Paul Westphal CO .05 .02
❑ 260 Rick Adelman CO .05 .02
❑ 261 Garry St. Jean CO RC .05 .02
❑ 262 Jerry Tarkanian CO RC .05 .02
❑ 263 George Karl CO .10 .05
❑ 264 Jerry Sloan CO .10 .05
❑ 265 Wes Unseld CO .10 .05
❑ 266 Atlanta Hawks Team Card .05 .02
❑ 267 Boston Celtics Team Card .05 .02
❑ 268 Charlotte Hornets Team Card .05 .02
❑ 269 Chicago Bulls Team Card .05 .02
❑ 270 Cleveland Cavaliers Team Card .05 .02
❑ 271 Dallas Mavericks Team Card .05 .02
❑ 272 Denver Nuggets Team Card .05 .02
❑ 273 Detroit Pistons Team Card .05 .02
❑ 274 Golden State Warriors Team Card .05 .02
❑ 275 Houston Rockets Team Card .05 .02
❑ 276 Indiana Pacers Team Card .05 .02
❑ 277 Los Angeles Clippers Team Card .05 .02
❑ 278 Los Angeles Lakers Team Card .05 .02
❑ 279 Miami Heat Team Card .05 .02
❑ 280 Milwaukee Bucks Team Card .05 .02
❑ 281 Minnesota Timberwolves Team Card .05 .02
❑ 282 New Jersey Nets Team Card .05 .02
❑ 283 New York Knicks Team Card .05 .02
❑ 284 Orlando Magic Team Card .05 .02
❑ 285 Philadelphia 76ers Team Card .05 .02
❑ 286 Phoenix Suns Team Card .05 .02
❑ 287 Portland Trail Blazers Team Card .05 .02
❑ 288 Sacramento Kings Team Card .05 .02
❑ 289 San Antonio Spurs Team Card .05 .02
❑ 290 Seattle Supersonics Team Card .05 .02
❑ 291 Utah Jazz Team Card .05 .02
❑ 292 Washington Bullets Team Card .05 .02
❑ 293 Michael Adams AS .05 .02
❑ 294 Charles Barkley AS .25 .11
❑ 295 Brad Daugherty AS .05 .02
❑ 296 Joe Dumars AS .10 .05
❑ 297 Patrick Ewing AS .10 .05
❑ 298 Michael Jordan AS 1.50 .70
❑ 299 Reggie Lewis AS .05 .02
❑ 300 Scottie Pippen AS .40 .18
❑ 301 Mark Price AS .05 .02
❑ 302 Dennis Rodman AS .25 .11
❑ 303 Isiah Thomas AS .10 .05
❑ 304 Kevin Willis AS .05 .02
❑ 305 Phil Jackson CO AS .10 .05
❑ 306 Clyde Drexler AS .10 .05
❑ 307 Tim Hardaway AS .25 .11
❑ 308 Jeff Hornacek AS .05 .02
❑ 309 Magic Johnson AS .40 .18
❑ 310 Dan Majerle AS .05 .02
❑ 311 Karl Malone AS .25 .11
❑ 312 Chris Mullin AS .10 .05
❑ 313 Dikembe Mutombo AS .10 .05
❑ 314 Hakeem Olajuwon AS .25 .11
❑ 315 David Robinson AS .25 .11
❑ 316 John Stockton AS .10 .05
❑ 317 Otis Thorpe AS .05 .02
❑ 318 James Worthy AS .10 .05
❑ 319 Don Nelson CO AS .10 .05
❑ 320 Scoring League Leaders Michael Jordan Karl Malone 1.00 .45
❑ 321 Three-Point Field Goal Percent League Leaders Dana Barros Drazen Petrovic .05 .02
❑ 322 Free Throw Percent League Leaders Mark Price Larry Bird .30 .14
❑ 323 Blocks League Leaders David Robinson Hakeem Olajuwon .25 .11
❑ 324 Steals League Leaders John Stockton Micheal Williams .25 .11
❑ 325 Rebounds League Leaders Dennis Rodman Kevin Willis .25 .11
❑ 326 Assists League Leaders John Stockton Kevin Johnson .25 .11
❑ 327 Field Goal Percent League Leaders Buck Williams Otis Thorpe .05 .02
❑ 328 Magic Moments 1980 .25 .11
❑ 329 Magic Moments 1985 .25 .11
❑ 330 Magic Moments 87&88 .25 .11
❑ 331 Magic Numbers .25 .11
❑ 332 Drazen Petrovic Inside Stuff .05 .02
❑ 333 Patrick Ewing Inside Stuff .10 .05
❑ 334 David Robinson Stay in School .25 .11
❑ 335 Kevin Johnson Stay in School .10 .05
❑ 336 Charles Barkley Tournament of The Americas .25 .11
❑ 337 Larry Bird Tournament of The Americas .50 .23
❑ 338 Clyde Drexler Tournament of The Americas .10 .05
❑ 339 Patrick Ewing .10 .05

Tournament of
The Americas
❑ 340 Magic Johnson .40 .18
Tournament of
The Americas
❑ 341 Michael Jordan 1.50 .70
Tournament of
The Americas
❑ 342 Christian Laettner RC .50 .23
Tournament of
The Americas
❑ 343 Karl Malone .25 .11
Tournament of
The Americas
❑ 344 Chris Mullin .10 .05
Tournament of
The Americas
❑ 345 Scottie Pippen .40 .18
Tournament of
The Americas
❑ 346 David Robinson .25 .11
Tournament of
The Americas
❑ 347 John Stockton .10 .05
Tournament of
The Americas
❑ 348 Checklist 1 .05 .02
❑ 349 Checklist 2 .05 .02
❑ 350 Checklist 3 .05 .02
❑ 351 Mookie Blaylock .20 .09
❑ 352 Adam Keefe RC .10 .05
❑ 353 Travis Mays .10 .05
❑ 354 Morlon Wiley .10 .05
❑ 355 Joe Kleine .10 .05
❑ 356 Bart Kofoed .10 .05
❑ 357 Xavier McDaniel .10 .05
❑ 358 Tony Bennett RC .10 .05
❑ 359 Tom Hammonds .10 .05
❑ 360 Kevin Lynch .10 .05
❑ 361 Alonzo Mourning RC 2.00 .90
❑ 362 Rodney McCray .10 .05
❑ 363 Trent Tucker .10 .05
❑ 364 Corey Williams RC .10 .05
❑ 365 Steve Kerr .20 .09
Traded to Orlando
❑ 366 Jerome Lane .10 .05
❑ 367 Bobby Phills RC .40 .18
❑ 368 Mike Sanders .10 .05
❑ 369 Gerald Wilkins .10 .05
❑ 370 Donald Hodge .10 .05
❑ 371 Brian Howard RC .10 .05
❑ 372 Tracy Moore RC .10 .05
❑ 373 Sean Rooks RC .10 .05
❑ 374 Kevin Brooks .10 .05
❑ 375 LaPhonso Ellis RC .40 .18
❑ 376 Scott Hastings .10 .05
❑ 377 Robert Pack .10 .05
❑ 378 Bryant Stith RC .20 .09
❑ 379 Robert Werdann RC .10 .05
❑ 380 Lance Blanks .10 .05
Traded to Minnesota
❑ 381 Terry Mills .10 .05
❑ 382 Isaiah Morris RC .10 .05
❑ 383 Olden Polynice .10 .05
❑ 384 Brad Sellers .10 .05
Traded to Minnesota
❑ 385 Jud Buechler .10 .05
❑ 386 Jeff Grayer .10 .05
❑ 387 Byron Houston RC .10 .05
❑ 388 Keith Jennings RC .10 .05
❑ 389 Latrell Sprewell RC 3.00 1.35
❑ 390 Scott Brooks .10 .05
❑ 391 Carl Herrera .10 .05
❑ 392 Robert Horry RC .40 .18
❑ 393 Tree Rollins .10 .05
❑ 394 Kennard Winchester .10 .05
❑ 395 Greg Dreiling .10 .05
❑ 396 Sean Green .10 .05
❑ 397 Sam Mitchell .10 .05
❑ 398 Pooh Richardson .10 .05
❑ 399 Malik Sealy RC .20 .09
❑ 400 Kenny Williams .10 .05
❑ 401 Jaren Jackson RC .20 .09
❑ 402 Mark Jackson .20 .09
❑ 403 Stanley Roberts .10 .05
❑ 404 Elmore Spencer RC .10 .05
❑ 405 Kiki Vandeweghe .10 .05
❑ 406 John Williams .10 .05
❑ 407 Randy Woods RC .10 .05
❑ 408 Alex Blackwell RC .10 .05
❑ 409 Duane Cooper RC .10 .05
❑ 410 Anthony Peeler RC .20 .09
❑ 411 Keith Askins .10 .05
❑ 412 Matt Geiger RC .20 .09
❑ 413 Harold Miner RC .20 .09
❑ 414 John Salley .10 .05
❑ 415 Alaa Abdelnaby .10 .05
Traded to Boston
❑ 416 Todd Day RC .20 .09
❑ 417 Blue Edwards .10 .05
❑ 418 Brad Lohaus .10 .05
❑ 419 Lee Mayberry RC .10 .05
❑ 420 Eric Murdock .10 .05
❑ 421 Christian Laettner .75 .35
❑ 422 Bob McCann RC .10 .05
❑ 423 Chuck Person .10 .05
❑ 424 Chris Smith RC .10 .05
❑ 425 Gundars Vetra RC .10 .05
❑ 426 Micheal Williams .10 .05
❑ 427 Chucky Brown .10 .05
❑ 428 Tate George .10 .05
❑ 429 Rick Mahorn .10 .05
❑ 430 Rumeal Robinson .10 .05
❑ 431 Jayson Williams .20 .09
❑ 432 Eric Anderson RC .10 .05
❑ 433 Rolando Blackman .10 .05
❑ 434 Tony Campbell .10 .05
❑ 435 Hubert Davis RC .20 .09
❑ 436 Bo Kimble .10 .05
❑ 437 Doc Rivers .20 .09
❑ 438 Charles Smith .10 .05
❑ 439 Anthony Bowie .10 .05
❑ 440 Litterial Green RC .10 .05
❑ 441 Greg Kite .10 .05
❑ 442 Shaquille O'Neal RC 10.00 4.50
❑ 443 Donald Royal .10 .05
❑ 444 Greg Grant .10 .05
❑ 445 Jeff Hornacek .20 .09
❑ 446 Andrew Lang .10 .05
❑ 447 Kenny Payne .10 .05
❑ 448 Tim Perry .10 .05
❑ 449 Clarence Weatherspoon RC .40 .18
❑ 450 Danny Ainge .20 .09
❑ 451 Charles Barkley .60 .25
❑ 452 Tim Kempton .10 .05
❑ 453 Oliver Miller RC .20 .09
❑ 454 Mark Bryant .10 .05
❑ 455 Mario Elie .20 .09
❑ 456 Dave Jamerson RC .10 .05
❑ 457 Tracy Murray RC .20 .09
❑ 458 Rod Strickland .40 .18
❑ 459 Vincent Askew .10 .05
Traded to Seattle
❑ 460 Randy Brown .10 .05
❑ 461 Marty Conlon .10 .05
❑ 462 Jim Les .10 .05
❑ 463 Walt Williams RC .40 .18
❑ 464 William Bedford .10 .05
❑ 465 Lloyd Daniels RC .10 .05
❑ 466 Vinny Del Negro .10 .05
❑ 467 Dale Ellis .10 .05
❑ 468 Larry Smith .10 .05
❑ 469 David Wood .10 .05
❑ 470 Rich King .10 .05
❑ 471 Isaac Austin RC .20 .09
❑ 472 John Crotty RC .10 .05
❑ 473 Stephen Howard RC .10 .05
❑ 474 Jay Humphries .10 .05
❑ 475 Larry Krystkowiak .10 .05
❑ 476 Tom Gugliotta RC 1.25 .55
❑ 477 Buck Johnson .10 .05
❑ 478 Don MacLean RC .10 .05
❑ 479 Doug Overton .10 .05
❑ 480 Brent Price RC .20 .09
❑ 481 David Robinson TRIV .40 .18
Blocks
❑ 482 Magic Johnson TRIV .60 .25
Assists
❑ 483 John Stockton TRIV .20 .09
Steals
❑ 484 Patrick Ewing TRIV .20 .09
Points
❑ 485 Answer Card TRIV .40 .18
Magic Johnson
David Robinson
Patrick Ewing
John Stockton
❑ 486 John Stockton .20 .09
Stay in School
❑ 487 Ahmad Rashad .20 .09
Willow Bay
Inside Stuff
❑ 488 Rookie Checklist .10 .05
❑ 489 Checklist 1 .10 .05
❑ 490 Checklist 2 .10 .05
❑ AC1 Patrick Ewing Art .50 .23
❑ SU1 John Stockton AU 300.00 135.00
(Certified autograph)
❑ SU1 John Stockton Game 1.50 .70
His Ultimate Game
❑ TR1 NBA Championship 3.00 1.35
Michael Jordan
Clyde Drexler
❑ NNO Team USA 1.50 .70
❑ NNO Barcelona Plastic 30.00 13.50
❑ NNO M.Johnson Comm 1.00 .45
❑ NNO M.Johnson AU 200.00 90.00
❑ NNO Patrick Ewing Game .50 .23
His Ultimate Game
❑ NNO Patrick Ewing AU 250.00 110.00
(Certified autograph)

1992-93 Hoops Draft Redemption

	MINT	NRMT
COMPLETE SET (10)	55.00	25.00
COMMON CARD (A-J)	1.50	.70
SEMISTARS	2.00	.90
UNLISTED STARS	3.00	1.35

ONE SET PER EXCHANGE CARD BY MAIL
EXCH.CARD: SER.1 STATED ODDS 1:360

❑ A Shaquille O'Neal 50.00 22.00
❑ B Alonzo Mourning 10.00 4.50
❑ C Christian Laettner 4.00 1.80
❑ D LaPhonso Ellis 3.00 1.35
❑ E Tom Gugliotta 6.00 2.70
❑ F Walt Williams 2.00 .90
❑ G Todd Day 2.00 .90
❑ H Clarence Weatherspoon 2.00 .90
❑ I Adam Keefe 1.50 .70
❑ J Robert Horry 3.00 1.35
❑ NNO Draft Redemption Card 1.00 .45
(Stamped)
❑ NNO Draft Redemption Card 3.00 1.35
(Unstamped)

1992-93 Hoops Magic's All-Rookies

	MINT	NRMT
COMPLETE SET (10)	100.00	45.00
COMMON CARD (1-10)	2.00	.90
SEMISTARS	4.00	1.80
UNLISTED STARS	6.00	2.70

SER.2 STATED ODDS 1:30

❑ 1 Shaquille O'Neal 80.00 36.00

Card	MINT	NRMT
❑ 2 Alonzo Mourning	20.00	9.00
❑ 3 Christian Laettner	8.00	3.60
❑ 4 LaPhonso Ellis	6.00	2.70
❑ 5 Tom Gugliotta	12.00	5.50
❑ 6 Walt Williams	4.00	1.80
❑ 7 Todd Day	4.00	1.80
❑ 8 Clarence Weatherspoon	4.00	1.80
❑ 9 Robert Horry	6.00	2.70
❑ 10 Harold Miner	2.00	.90

1992-93 Hoops More Magic Moments

	MINT	NRMT
COMPLETE SET (3)	70.00	32.00
COMMON MAGIC (M1-M3)	25.00	11.00

SER.2 STATED ODDS 1:195

Card	MINT	NRMT
❑ M1 Magic in Training Camp Fall 1992	25.00	11.00
❑ M2 L.A. Lakers vs. Philadelphia October 20& 1992	25.00	11.00
❑ M3 L.A. Lakers vs. Cleveland October 30& 1992	25.00	11.00

1992-93 Hoops Supreme Court

	MINT	NRMT
COMPLETE SET (10)	30.00	13.50

*SINGLES: 2.5X TO 6X BASE CARD HI
SER.2 STATED ODDS 1:11

Card	MINT	NRMT
❑ SC1 Michael Jordan	20.00	9.00
❑ SC2 Scottie Pippen	5.00	2.20
❑ SC3 David Robinson	2.50	1.10
❑ SC4 Patrick Ewing	1.50	.70
❑ SC5 Clyde Drexler	1.50	.70
❑ SC6 Karl Malone	2.50	1.10
❑ SC7 Charles Barkley	2.50	1.10
❑ SC8 John Stockton	1.50	.70
❑ SC9 Chris Mullin	1.50	.70
❑ SC10 Magic Johnson	2.50	1.10

1993-94 Hoops

	MINT	NRMT
COMPLETE SET (421)	20.00	9.00
COMPLETE SERIES 1 (300)	12.00	5.50
COMPLETE SERIES 2 (121)	8.00	3.60
COMMON CARD (1-421)	.05	.02
SEMISTARS	.10	.05
UNLISTED STARS	.25	.11

SUBSET CARDS HALF VALUE OF BASE CARDS
DR1: SER.2 STATED ODDS 1:18
BOTH AUs: SER.2 STATED ODDS 1:13,886

Card	MINT	NRMT
❑ 1 Stacey Augmon	.05	.02
❑ 2 Mookie Blaylock	.10	.05
❑ 3 Duane Ferrell	.05	.02
❑ 4 Paul Graham	.05	.02
❑ 5 Adam Keefe	.05	.02
❑ 6 Blair Rasmussen	.05	.02
❑ 7 Dominique Wilkins	.25	.11
❑ 8 Kevin Willis	.05	.02
❑ 9 Alaa Abdelnaby	.05	.02
❑ 10 Dee Brown	.05	.02
❑ 11 Sherman Douglas	.05	.02
❑ 12 Rick Fox	.05	.02
❑ 13 Kevin Gamble	.05	.02
❑ 14 Joe Kleine	.05	.02
❑ 15 Xavier McDaniel	.05	.02
❑ 16 Robert Parish	.10	.05
❑ 17 Tony Bennett	.05	.02
❑ 18 Muggsy Bogues	.10	.05
❑ 19 Dell Curry	.05	.02
❑ 20 Kenny Gattison	.05	.02
❑ 21 Kendall Gill	.10	.05
❑ 22 Larry Johnson	.25	.11
❑ 23 Alonzo Mourning	.40	.18
❑ 24 Johnny Newman	.05	.02
❑ 25 B.J. Armstrong	.05	.02
❑ 26 Bill Cartwright	.05	.02
❑ 27 Horace Grant	.10	.05
❑ 28 Michael Jordan	3.00	1.35
❑ 29 Stacey King	.05	.02
❑ 30 John Paxson	.05	.02
❑ 31 Will Perdue	.05	.02
❑ 32 Scottie Pippen	.75	.35
❑ 33 Scott Williams	.05	.02
❑ 34 Moses Malone	.25	.11
❑ 35 John Battle	.05	.02
❑ 36 Terrell Brandon	.10	.05
❑ 37 Brad Daugherty	.05	.02
❑ 38 Craig Ehlo	.05	.02
❑ 39 Danny Ferry	.05	.02
❑ 40 Larry Nance	.05	.02
❑ 41 Mark Price	.05	.02
❑ 42 Gerald Wilkins	.05	.02
❑ 43 John Williams	.05	.02
❑ 44 Terry Davis	.05	.02
❑ 45 Derek Harper	.10	.05
❑ 46 Donald Hodge	.05	.02
❑ 47 Mike Iuzzolino	.05	.02
❑ 48 Jim Jackson	.10	.05
❑ 49 Sean Rooks	.05	.02
❑ 50 Doug Smith	.05	.02
❑ 51 Randy White	.05	.02
❑ 52 Mahmoud Abdul-Rauf	.05	.02
❑ 53 LaPhonso Ellis	.05	.02
❑ 54 Marcus Liberty	.05	.02
❑ 55 Mark Macon	.05	.02
❑ 56 Dikembe Mutombo	.10	.05
❑ 57 Robert Pack	.05	.02
❑ 58 Bryant Stith	.05	.02
❑ 59 Reggie Williams	.05	.02
❑ 60 Mark Aguirre	.05	.02
❑ 61 Joe Dumars	.25	.11
❑ 62 Bill Laimbeer	.05	.02
❑ 63 Terry Mills	.05	.02
❑ 64 Olden Polynice	.05	.02
❑ 65 Alvin Robertson	.05	.02
❑ 66 Dennis Rodman	.50	.23
❑ 67 Isiah Thomas	.25	.11
❑ 68 Victor Alexander	.05	.02
❑ 69 Tim Hardaway	.25	.11
❑ 70 Tyrone Hill	.05	.02
❑ 71 Byron Houston	.05	.02
❑ 72 Sarunas Marciulionis	.05	.02
❑ 73 Chris Mullin	.25	.11
❑ 74 Billy Owens	.05	.02
❑ 75 Latrell Sprewell	.60	.25
❑ 76 Scott Brooks	.05	.02
❑ 77 Matt Bullard	.05	.02
❑ 78 Carl Herrera	.05	.02
❑ 79 Robert Horry	.10	.05
❑ 80 Vernon Maxwell	.05	.02
❑ 81 Hakeem Olajuwon	.40	.18
❑ 82 Kenny Smith	.05	.02
❑ 83 Otis Thorpe	.10	.05
❑ 84 Dale Davis	.05	.02
❑ 85 Vern Fleming	.05	.02
❑ 86 George McCloud	.05	.02
❑ 87 Reggie Miller	.25	.11
❑ 88 Sam Mitchell	.05	.02
❑ 89 Pooh Richardson	.05	.02
❑ 90 Detlef Schrempf	.10	.05
❑ 91 Malik Sealy	.05	.02
❑ 92 Rik Smits	.10	.05
❑ 93 Gary Grant	.05	.02
❑ 94 Ron Harper	.10	.05
❑ 95 Mark Jackson	.10	.05
❑ 96 Danny Manning	.10	.05
❑ 97 Ken Norman	.05	.02
❑ 98 Stanley Roberts	.05	.02
❑ 99 Elmore Spencer	.05	.02
❑ 100 Loy Vaught	.05	.02
❑ 101 John Williams	.05	.02
❑ 102 Randy Woods	.05	.02
❑ 103 Benoit Benjamin	.05	.02
❑ 104 Elden Campbell	.05	.02
❑ 105 Doug Christie UER (Has uniform number on front and 35 on back)	.05	.02
❑ 106 Vlade Divac	.10	.05
❑ 107 Anthony Peeler	.05	.02
❑ 108 Tony Smith	.05	.02
❑ 109 Sedale Threatt	.05	.02
❑ 110 James Worthy	.25	.11
❑ 111 Bimbo Coles	.05	.02
❑ 112 Grant Long	.05	.02
❑ 113 Harold Miner	.05	.02
❑ 114 Glen Rice	.10	.05
❑ 115 John Salley	.05	.02
❑ 116 Rony Seikaly	.05	.02
❑ 117 Brian Shaw	.05	.02
❑ 118 Steve Smith	.25	.11
❑ 119 Anthony Avent	.05	.02
❑ 120 Jon Barry	.05	.02
❑ 121 Frank Brickowski	.05	.02
❑ 122 Todd Day	.05	.02
❑ 123 Blue Edwards	.05	.02
❑ 124 Brad Lohaus	.05	.02

❑	125	Lee Mayberry	.05	.02
❑	126	Eric Murdock	.05	.02
❑	127	Derek Strong RC	.05	.02
❑	128	Thurl Bailey	.05	.02
❑	129	Christian Laettner	.10	.05
❑	130	Luc Longley	.10	.05
❑	131	Marlon Maxey	.05	.02
❑	132	Chuck Person	.05	.02
❑	133	Chris Smith	.05	.02
❑	134	Doug West	.05	.02
❑	135	Micheal Williams	.05	.02
❑	136	Rafael Addison	.05	.02
❑	137	Kenny Anderson	.10	.05
❑	138	Sam Bowie	.05	.02
❑	139	Chucky Brown	.05	.02
❑	140	Derrick Coleman	.10	.05
❑	141	Chris Morris	.05	.02
❑	142	Rumeal Robinson	.05	.02
❑	143	Greg Anthony	.05	.02
❑	144	Rolando Blackman	.05	.02
❑	145	Hubert Davis	.05	.02
❑	146	Patrick Ewing	.25	.11
❑	147	Anthony Mason	.10	.05
❑	148	Charles Oakley	.10	.05
❑	149	Doc Rivers	.10	.05
❑	150	Charles Smith	.05	.02
❑	151	John Starks	.10	.05
❑	152	Nick Anderson	.10	.05
❑	153	Anthony Bowie	.05	.02
❑	154	Litterial Green	.05	.02
❑	155	Shaquille O'Neal	1.25	.55
❑	156	Donald Royal	.05	.02
❑	157	Dennis Scott	.05	.02
❑	158	Scott Skiles	.05	.02
❑	159	Tom Tolbert	.05	.02
❑	160	Jeff Turner	.05	.02
❑	161	Ron Anderson	.05	.02
❑	162	Johnny Dawkins	.05	.02
❑	163	Hersey Hawkins	.10	.05
❑	164	Jeff Hornacek	.10	.05
❑	165	Andrew Lang	.05	.02
❑	166	Tim Perry	.05	.02
❑	167	Clarence Weatherspoon	.05	.02
❑	168	Danny Ainge	.10	.05
❑	169	Charles Barkley	.40	.18
❑	170	Cedric Ceballos	.10	.05
❑	171	Richard Dumas	.05	.02
❑	172	Kevin Johnson	.10	.05
❑	173	Dan Majerle	.10	.05
❑	174	Oliver Miller	.05	.02
❑	175	Mark West	.05	.02
❑	176	Clyde Drexler	.25	.11
❑	177	Kevin Duckworth	.05	.02
❑	178	Mario Elie	.05	.02
❑	179	Dave Johnson	.05	.02
❑	180	Jerome Kersey	.05	.02
❑	181	Tracy Murray	.05	.02
❑	182	Terry Porter	.05	.02
❑	183	Clifford Robinson	.10	.05
❑	184	Rod Strickland	.10	.05
❑	185	Buck Williams	.05	.02
❑	186	Anthony Bonner	.05	.02
❑	187	Randy Brown	.05	.02
❑	188	Duane Causwell	.05	.02
❑	189	Pete Chilcutt	.05	.02
❑	190	Mitch Richmond	.25	.11
❑	191	Lionel Simmons	.05	.02
❑	192	Wayman Tisdale	.05	.02
❑	193	Spud Webb	.10	.05
❑	194	Walt Williams	.05	.02
❑	195	Willie Anderson	.05	.02
❑	196	Antoine Carr	.05	.02
❑	197	Terry Cummings	.05	.02
❑	198	Lloyd Daniels	.05	.02
❑	199	Sean Elliott	.10	.05
❑	200	Dale Ellis	.05	.02
❑	201	Avery Johnson	.05	.02
❑	202	J.R. Reid	.05	.02
❑	203	David Robinson	.40	.18
❑	204	Dana Barros	.05	.02
❑	205	Michael Cage	.05	.02
❑	206	Eddie Johnson	.05	.02
❑	207	Shawn Kemp	.40	.18
❑	208	Derrick McKey	.05	.02
❑	209	Nate McMillan	.05	.02
❑	210	Gary Payton	.40	.18
❑	211	Sam Perkins	.10	.05
❑	212	Ricky Pierce	.05	.02
❑	213	David Benoit	.05	.02
❑	214	Tyrone Corbin	.05	.02
❑	215	Mark Eaton	.05	.02
❑	216	Jay Humphries	.05	.02
❑	217	Jeff Malone	.05	.02
❑	218	Karl Malone	.40	.18
❑	219	John Stockton	.25	.11
❑	220	Michael Adams	.05	.02
❑	221	Rex Chapman	.05	.02
❑	222	Pervis Ellison	.05	.02
❑	223	Harvey Grant	.05	.02
❑	224	Tom Gugliotta	.25	.11
❑	225	Don MacLean	.05	.02
❑	226	Doug Overton	.05	.02
❑	227	Brent Price	.05	.02
❑	228	LaBradford Smith	.05	.02
❑	229	Larry Stewart	.05	.02
❑	230	Lenny Wilkens CO	.10	.05
❑	231	Chris Ford CO	.05	.02
❑	232	Allan Bristow CO	.05	.02
❑	233	Phil Jackson CO	.10	.05
❑	234	Mike Fratello CO	.10	.05
❑	235	Quinn Buckner CO	.05	.02
❑	236	Dan Issel CO	.05	.02
❑	237	Don Chaney CO	.05	.02
❑	238	Don Nelson CO	.10	.05
❑	239	Rudy Tomjanovich CO	.10	.05
❑	240	Larry Brown CO	.10	.05
❑	241	Bob Weiss CO	.05	.02
❑	242	Randy Pfund CO	.05	.02
❑	243	Kevin Loughery CO	.05	.02
❑	244	Mike Dunleavy CO	.05	.02
❑	245	Sidney Lowe CO	.05	.02
❑	246	Chuck Daly CO	.10	.05
❑	247	Pat Riley CO	.10	.05
❑	248	Brian Hill CO	.05	.02
❑	249	Fred Carter CO	.05	.02
❑	250	Paul Westphal CO	.05	.02
❑	251	Rick Adelman CO	.05	.02
❑	252	Garry St. Jean CO	.05	.02
❑	253	John Lucas CO	.05	.02
❑	254	George Karl CO	.10	.05
❑	255	Jerry Sloan CO	.10	.05
❑	256	Wes Unseld CO	.10	.05
❑	257	Michael Jordan AS	1.50	.70
❑	258	Isiah Thomas AS	.10	.05
❑	259	Scottie Pippen AS	.40	.18
❑	260	Larry Johnson AS	.10	.05
❑	261	Dominique Wilkins AS	.10	.05
❑	262	Joe Dumars AS	.10	.05
❑	263	Mark Price AS	.05	.02
❑	264	Shaquille O'Neal AS	.50	.23
❑	265	Patrick Ewing AS	.10	.05
❑	266	Larry Nance AS	.05	.02
❑	267	Detlef Schrempf AS	.05	.02
❑	268	Brad Daugherty AS	.05	.02
❑	269	Charles Barkley AS	.25	.11
❑	270	Clyde Drexler AS	.10	.05
❑	271	Sean Elliott AS	.05	.02
❑	272	Tim Hardaway AS	.10	.05
❑	273	Shawn Kemp AS	.25	.11
❑	274	Dan Majerle AS	.05	.02
❑	275	Karl Malone AS	.25	.11
❑	276	Danny Manning AS	.05	.02
❑	277	Hakeem Olajuwon AS	.25	.11
❑	278	Terry Porter AS	.05	.02
❑	279	David Robinson AS	.25	.11
❑	280	John Stockton AS	.10	.05
❑	281	East Team Photo	.05	.02
❑	282	West Team Photo	.05	.02
❑	283	Scoring	.75	.35
		Michael Jordan		
		Dominique Wilkins		
		Karl Malone		
❑	284	Rebounding	.50	.23
		Dennis Rodman		
		Shaquille O'Neal		
		Dikembe Mutombo		
❑	285	Field Goal Percentage	.05	.02
		Cedric Ceballos		
		Brad Daugherty		
		Dale Davis		
❑	286	Assists	.10	.05
		John Stockton		
		Tim Hardaway		
		Scott Skiles		
❑	287	Free Throw Percentage	.05	.02
		Mark Price		
		Mahmoud Abdul-Rauf		
		Eddie Johnson		
❑	288	3-point FG Percentage	.05	.02
		B.J. Armstrong		
		Chris Mullin		
		Kenny Smith		
❑	289	Steals	.75	.35
		Michael Jordan		
		Mookie Blaylock		
		John Stockton		
❑	290	Blocks	.40	.18
		Hakeem Olajuwon		
		Shaquille O'Neal		
		Dikembe Mutombo		
❑	291	Boys and Girls Club	.10	.05
		David Robinson		
❑	292	B.J. Armstrong TRIB	.05	.02
❑	293	Scottie Pippen TRIB	.40	.18
❑	294	Kevin Johnson TRIB	.05	.02
❑	295	Charles Barkley TRIB	.25	.11
❑	296	Richard Dumas TRIB	.05	.02
❑	297	Horace Grant CL	.05	.02
❑	298	David Robinson CL	.05	.02
❑	299	David Robinson CL	.05	.02
❑	300	David Robinson CL	.05	.02
❑	301	Craig Ehlo	.05	.02
❑	302	Jon Koncak	.05	.02
❑	303	Andrew Lang	.05	.02
❑	304	Chris Corchiani	.05	.02
❑	305	Acie Earl RC	.05	.02
❑	306	Dino Radja RC	.05	.02
❑	307	Scott Burrell RC	.25	.11
❑	308	Hersey Hawkins	.10	.05
❑	309	Eddie Johnson	.05	.02
❑	310	David Wingate	.05	.02
❑	311	Corie Blount RC	.05	.02
❑	312	Steve Kerr	.10	.05
❑	313	Toni Kukoc RC	1.00	.45
❑	314	Pete Myers	.05	.02
❑	315	Jay Guidinger	.05	.02
❑	316	Tyrone Hill	.05	.02
❑	317	Gerald Madkins RC	.05	.02
❑	318	Chris Mills RC	.25	.11
❑	319	Bobby Phills	.05	.02
❑	320	Lucious Harris RC	.05	.02
❑	321	Popeye Jones RC	.05	.02
❑	322	Fat Lever	.05	.02
❑	323	Jamal Mashburn RC	.50	.23
❑	324	Darren Morningstar RC	.05	.02
		(See also 334)		
❑	325	Kevin Brooks	.05	.02
❑	326	Tom Hammonds	.05	.02
❑	327	Darnell Mee RC	.05	.02
❑	328	Rodney Rogers RC	.25	.11
❑	329	Brian Williams	.05	.02
❑	330	Greg Anderson	.05	.02
❑	331	Sean Elliott	.10	.05
❑	332	Allan Houston RC	1.00	.45
❑	333	Lindsey Hunter RC	.25	.11
❑	334	David Wood UER	.05	.02
		(Card misnumbered 324)		
❑	335	Jud Buechler	.05	.02
❑	336	Chris Gatling	.05	.02
❑	337	Josh Grant RC	.05	.02
❑	338	Jeff Grayer	.05	.02
❑	339	Keith Jennings	.05	.02
❑	340	Avery Johnson	.05	.02
❑	341	Chris Webber RC	2.50	1.10
❑	342	Sam Cassell RC	.60	.25
❑	343	Mario Elie	.05	.02
❑	344	Eric Riley RC	.05	.02
❑	345	Antonio Davis RC	.10	.05
❑	346	Scott Haskin RC	.05	.02
❑	347	Gerald Paddio	.05	.02
❑	348	LaSalle Thompson	.05	.02
❑	349	Ken Williams	.05	.02
❑	350	Mark Aguirre	.05	.02
❑	351	Terry Dehere RC	.05	.02
❑	352	Henry James	.05	.02
❑	353	Sam Bowie	.05	.02
❑	354	George Lynch RC	.05	.02
❑	355	Kurt Rambis	.05	.02

Card	MINT	NRMT
❑ 356 Nick Van Exel RC	.60	.25
❑ 357 Trevor Wilson	.05	.02
❑ 358 Keith Askins	.05	.02
❑ 359 Manute Bol	.05	.02
❑ 360 Willie Burton	.05	.02
❑ 361 Matt Geiger	.05	.02
❑ 362 Alec Kessler	.05	.02
❑ 363 Vin Baker RC	.60	.25
❑ 364 Ken Norman	.05	.02
❑ 365 Dan Schayes	.05	.02
❑ 366 Mike Brown	.05	.02
❑ 367 Isaiah Rider RC	.50	.23
❑ 368 Benoit Benjamin	.05	.02
❑ 369 P.J. Brown RC	.25	.11
❑ 370 Kevin Edwards	.05	.02
❑ 371 Armon Gilliam	.05	.02
❑ 372 Rick Mahorn	.05	.02
❑ 373 Dwayne Schintzius	.05	.02
❑ 374 Rex Walters RC	.05	.02
❑ 375 Jayson Williams	.10	.05
❑ 376 Eric Anderson	.05	.02
❑ 377 Anthony Bonner	.05	.02
❑ 378 Tony Campbell	.05	.02
❑ 379 Herb Williams	.05	.02
❑ 380 Anfernee Hardaway RC	2.50	1.10
❑ 381 Greg Kite	.05	.02
❑ 382 Larry Krystkowiak	.05	.02
❑ 383 Todd Lichti	.05	.02
❑ 384 Dana Barros	.05	.02
❑ 385 Shawn Bradley RC	.25	.11
❑ 386 Greg Graham RC	.05	.02
❑ 387 Warren Kidd RC	.05	.02
❑ 388 Eric Leckner	.05	.02
❑ 389 Moses Malone	.25	.11
❑ 390 A.C. Green	.10	.05
❑ 391 Frank Johnson	.05	.02
❑ 392 Joe Kleine	.05	.02
❑ 393 Malcolm Mackey RC	.05	.02
❑ 394 Jerrod Mustaf	.05	.02
❑ 395 Mark Bryant	.05	.02
❑ 396 Chris Dudley	.05	.02
❑ 397 Harvey Grant	.05	.02
❑ 398 James Robinson RC	.05	.02
❑ 399 Reggie Smith	.05	.02
❑ 400 Randy Brown	.05	.02
❑ 401 Bobby Hurley RC	.10	.05
❑ 402 Jim Les	.05	.02
❑ 403 Vinny Del Negro	.05	.02
❑ 404 Sleepy Floyd	.05	.02
❑ 405 Dennis Rodman	.50	.23
❑ 406 Chris Whitney RC	.05	.02
❑ 407 Vincent Askew	.05	.02
❑ 408 Kendall Gill	.10	.05
❑ 409 Ervin Johnson RC	.10	.05
❑ 410 Rich King	.05	.02
❑ 411 Detlef Schrempf	.10	.05
❑ 412 Tom Chambers	.05	.02
❑ 413 John Crotty	.05	.02
❑ 414 Felton Spencer	.05	.02
❑ 415 Luther Wright RC	.05	.02
❑ 416 Calbert Cheaney RC	.10	.05
❑ 417 Kevin Duckworth	.05	.02
❑ 418 Gheorghe Muresan RC	.25	.11
❑ 419 David Robinson CL	.05	.02
❑ 420 David Robinson CL	.05	.02
❑ 421 David Robinson CL	.05	.02
❑ DR1 David Robinson Commemorative 1989 Rookie Card	.40	.18
❑ MB1 Magic Johnson Larry Bird Commemorative	.50	.23
❑ NNO David Robinson Autograph Card	100.00	45.00
❑ NNO David Robinson Expired Voucher	10.00	4.50
❑ NNO Magic Johnson Larry Bird Autograph Card	400.00	180.00
❑ NNO Magic Johnson Larry Bird Expired Voucher	30.00	13.50

1993-94 Hoops Fifth Anniversary Gold

	MINT	NRMT
COMPLETE SET (421)	60.00	27.00
COMPLETE SERIES 1 (300)	35.00	16.00
COMPLETE SERIES 2 (121)	25.00	11.00
COMMON CARD (1-421)	.10	.05

*STARS: 1.25X TO 2.5X BASE CARD HI
*RCs: 1X TO 2X BASE HI
ONE PER PACK
TWO PER JUMBO PACK

1993-94 Hoops Admiral's Choice

	MINT	NRMT
COMPLETE SET (5)	3.00	1.35

*SINGLES: .5X TO 1.25X BASE CARD HI
SER.2 STATED ODDS 1:12

Card	MINT	NRMT
❑ AC1 Shawn Kemp	.50	.23
❑ AC2 Derrick Coleman	.15	.07
❑ AC3 Kenny Anderson	.15	.07
❑ AC4 Shaquille O'Neal	1.50	.70
❑ AC5 Chris Webber	3.00	1.35

1993-94 Hoops David's Best

	MINT	NRMT
COMPLETE SET (5)	2.00	.90
COMMON D.ROB. (DB1-DB5)	.50	.23

SER.1 STATED ODDS 1:10

Card	MINT	NRMT
❑ DB1 David Robinson (Vs. Lakers)	.50	.23
❑ DB2 David Robinson (Vs. Magic)	.50	.23
❑ DB3 David Robinson (Vs. Trail Blazers)	.50	.23
❑ DB4 David Robinson (Vs. Warriors)	.50	.23
❑ DB5 David Robinson (Vs. Hornets)	.50	.23

1993-94 Hoops Draft Redemption

	MINT	NRMT
COMPLETE SET (11)	40.00	18.00
COMMON CARD (LP1-LP11)	1.00	.45
SEMISTARS	1.50	.70
UNLISTED STARS	2.50	1.10

ONE SET PER EXCHANGE CARD BY MAIL
EXCH.CARD: SER.1 STATED ODDS 1:360

Card	MINT	NRMT
❑ LP1 Chris Webber	15.00	6.75
❑ LP2 Shawn Bradley	2.50	1.10
❑ LP3 Anfernee Hardaway	15.00	6.75
❑ LP4 Jamal Mashburn	3.00	1.35
❑ LP5 Isaiah Rider	3.00	1.35
❑ LP6 Calbert Cheaney	1.50	.70
❑ LP7 Bobby Hurley	1.00	.45
❑ LP8 Vin Baker	4.00	1.80
❑ LP9 Rodney Rogers	1.50	.70
❑ LP10 Lindsey Hunter	1.50	.70
❑ LP11 Allan Houston	6.00	2.70
❑ NNO Redeemed Lottery Card	.25	.11
❑ NNO Unred. Lottery Card	1.50	.70

1993-94 Hoops Face to Face

	MINT	NRMT
COMPLETE SET (12)	30.00	13.50
COMMON CARD (1-12)	.75	.35
SEMISTARS	1.25	.55
UNLISTED STARS	2.00	.90

SER.1 STATED ODDS 1:20
FTF PREFIX ON CARD NUMBERS

Card	MINT	NRMT
❑ 1 Shaquille O'Neal David Robinson	6.00	2.70
❑ 2 Alonzo Mourning Patrick Ewing	3.00	1.35
❑ 3 Christian Laettner Shawn Kemp	2.50	1.10
❑ 4 Jim Jackson Clyde Drexler	2.00	.90
❑ 5 LaPhonso Ellis Larry Johnson	1.25	.55
❑ 6 Clarence Weatherspoon Charles Barkley	2.50	1.10
❑ 7 Tom Gugliotta Karl Malone	3.00	1.35

		MINT	NRMT
❑ 8	Walt Williams Magic Johnson	4.00	1.80
❑ 9	Robert Horry Scottie Pippen	3.00	1.35
❑ 10	Harold Miner Michael Jordan	15.00	6.75
❑ 11	Todd Day Chris Mullin	2.00	.90
❑ 12	Richard Dumas Dominique Wilkins	.75	.35

1993-94 Hoops Magic's All-Rookies

	MINT	NRMT
COMPLETE SET (10)	40.00	18.00
COMMON CARD (1-10)	1.00	.45
SEMISTARS	1.50	.70
UNLISTED STARS	2.50	1.10

SER.2 STATED ODDS 1:30

		MINT	NRMT
❑ 1	Chris Webber	15.00	6.75
❑ 2	Shawn Bradley	2.50	1.10
❑ 3	Anfernee Hardaway	15.00	6.75
❑ 4	Jamal Mashburn	4.00	1.80
❑ 5	Isaiah Rider	4.00	1.80
❑ 6	Calbert Cheaney	1.50	.70
❑ 7	Bobby Hurley	1.00	.45
❑ 8	Vin Baker	4.00	1.80
❑ 9	Lindsey Hunter	1.50	.70
❑ 10	Toni Kukoc	6.00	2.70

1993-94 Hoops Scoops

	MINT	NRMT
COMPLETE SET (28)	1.00	.45
COMMON CARD (HS1-HS28)	.05	.02
SEMISTARS	.10	.05
UNLISTED STARS	.25	.11

RANDOM INSERTS IN SER.2 PACKS
*GOLD CARDS:1.25X TO 2.5X HI COLUMN

		MINT	NRMT
❑ HS1	Dominique Wilkins	.25	.11
❑ HS2	Robert Parish	.10	.05
❑ HS3	Alonzo Mourning	.25	.11
❑ HS4	Scottie Pippen	.25	.11
❑ HS5	Larry Nance	.05	.02
❑ HS6	Derek Harper	.10	.05
❑ HS7	Reggie Williams	.05	.02
❑ HS8	Bill Laimbeer	.05	.02
❑ HS9	Tim Hardaway	.25	.11
❑ HS10	Hakeem Olajuwon UER (Robert Horry is featured player)	.25	.11
❑ HS11	LaSalle Thompson	.05	.02
❑ HS12	Danny Manning	.10	.05
❑ HS13	James Worthy	.25	.11
❑ HS14	Grant Long	.05	.02
❑ HS15	Blue Edwards	.05	.02
❑ HS16	Christian Laettner	.10	.05
❑ HS17	Derrick Coleman	.10	.05
❑ HS18	Patrick Ewing	.25	.11
❑ HS19	Nick Anderson	.05	.02
❑ HS20	C. Weatherspoon	.05	.02
❑ HS21	Charles Barkley	.25	.11
❑ HS22	Clifford Robinson	.10	.05
❑ HS23	Lionel Simmons	.05	.02
❑ HS24	David Robinson	.25	.11
❑ HS25	Shawn Kemp	.25	.11
❑ HS26	Karl Malone	.25	.11
❑ HS27	Rex Chapman	.05	.02
❑ HS28	Answer Card	.05	.02

1993-94 Hoops Supreme Court

	MINT	NRMT
COMPLETE SET (11)	10.00	4.50

*SINGLES: .75X TO 2X BASE CARD HI
SER.2 STATED ODDS 1:11

		MINT	NRMT
❑ SC1	Charles Barkley	.75	.35
❑ SC2	David Robinson	.75	.35
❑ SC3	Patrick Ewing	.50	.23
❑ SC4	Shaquille O'Neal	2.50	1.10
❑ SC5	Larry Johnson	.50	.23
❑ SC6	Karl Malone	.75	.35
❑ SC7	Alonzo Mourning	.75	.35
❑ SC8	John Stockton	.50	.23
❑ SC9	Hakeem Olajuwon UER (Name spelled Olajwon on front)	.75	.35
❑ SC10	Scottie Pippen	1.50	.70
❑ SC11	Michael Jordan	6.00	2.70

1994-95 Hoops

	MINT	NRMT
COMPLETE SET (450)	24.00	11.00
COMPLETE SERIES 1 (300)	12.00	5.50
COMPLETE SERIES 2 (150)	12.00	5.50
COMMON CARD (1-450)	.05	.02
SEMISTARS	.10	.05
UNLISTED STARS	.25	.11

SUBSET CARDS HALF VALUE OF BASE CARDS

		MINT	NRMT
❑ 1	Stacey Augmon	.05	.02
❑ 2	Mookie Blaylock	.05	.02
❑ 3	Doug Edwards	.05	.02
❑ 4	Craig Ehlo	.05	.02
❑ 5	Jon Koncak	.05	.02
❑ 6	Danny Manning	.10	.05
❑ 7	Kevin Willis	.05	.02
❑ 8	Dee Brown	.05	.02
❑ 9	Sherman Douglas	.05	.02
❑ 10	Acie Earl	.05	.02
❑ 11	Kevin Gamble	.05	.02
❑ 12	Xavier McDaniel	.05	.02
❑ 13	Robert Parish	.10	.05
❑ 14	Dino Radja	.05	.02
❑ 15	Tony Bennett	.05	.02
❑ 16	Muggsy Bogues	.10	.05
❑ 17	Scott Burrell	.05	.02
❑ 18	Dell Curry	.05	.02
❑ 19	Hersey Hawkins	.10	.05
❑ 20	Eddie Johnson	.05	.02
❑ 21	Larry Johnson	.10	.05
❑ 22	Alonzo Mourning	.30	.14
❑ 23	B.J. Armstrong	.05	.02
❑ 24	Corie Blount	.05	.02
❑ 25	Bill Cartwright	.05	.02
❑ 26	Horace Grant	.10	.05
❑ 27	Toni Kukoc	.40	.18
❑ 28	Luc Longley	.05	.02
❑ 29	Pete Myers	.05	.02
❑ 30	Scottie Pippen	.75	.35
❑ 31	Scott Williams	.05	.02
❑ 32	Terrell Brandon	.10	.05
❑ 33	Brad Daugherty	.05	.02
❑ 34	Tyrone Hill	.05	.02
❑ 35	Chris Mills	.10	.05
❑ 36	Larry Nance	.05	.02
❑ 37	Bobby Phills	.05	.02
❑ 38	Mark Price	.05	.02
❑ 39	Gerald Wilkins	.05	.02
❑ 40	John Williams	.05	.02
❑ 41	Terry Davis	.05	.02
❑ 42	Lucious Harris	.05	.02
❑ 43	Jim Jackson	.10	.05
❑ 44	Popeye Jones	.05	.02
❑ 45	Tim Legler	.05	.02
❑ 46	Jamal Mashburn	.25	.11
❑ 47	Sean Rooks	.05	.02
❑ 48	Mahmoud Abdul-Rauf	.05	.02
❑ 49	LaPhonso Ellis	.05	.02
❑ 50	Dikembe Mutombo	.10	.05
❑ 51	Robert Pack	.05	.02
❑ 52	Rodney Rogers	.05	.02
❑ 53	Bryant Stith	.05	.02
❑ 54	Brian Williams	.05	.02
❑ 55	Reggie Williams	.05	.02
❑ 56	Greg Anderson	.05	.02
❑ 57	Joe Dumars	.25	.11
❑ 58	Sean Elliott	.10	.05
❑ 59	Allan Houston	.40	.18
❑ 60	Lindsey Hunter	.10	.05
❑ 61	Mark Macon	.05	.02
❑ 62	Terry Mills	.05	.02
❑ 63	Victor Alexander	.05	.02
❑ 64	Chris Gatling	.05	.02
❑ 65	Tim Hardaway	.25	.11
❑ 66	Avery Johnson	.05	.02
❑ 67	Sarunas Marciulionis	.05	.02
❑ 68	Chris Mullin	.25	.11
❑ 69	Billy Owens	.05	.02
❑ 70	Latrell Sprewell	.50	.23
❑ 71	Chris Webber	.75	.35
❑ 72	Matt Bullard	.05	.02
❑ 73	Sam Cassell	.25	.11
❑ 74	Mario Elie	.05	.02
❑ 75	Carl Herrera	.05	.02
❑ 76	Robert Horry	.05	.02
❑ 77	Vernon Maxwell	.05	.02
❑ 78	Hakeem Olajuwon	.40	.18
❑ 79	Kenny Smith	.05	.02
❑ 80	Otis Thorpe	.05	.02
❑ 81	Antonio Davis	.05	.02

❑ 82 Dale Davis	.05	.02
❑ 83 Vern Fleming	.05	.02
❑ 84 Scott Haskin	.05	.02
❑ 85 Derrick McKey	.05	.02
❑ 86 Reggie Miller	.25	.11
❑ 87 Byron Scott	.10	.05
❑ 88 Rik Smits	.05	.02
❑ 89 Haywoode Workman	.05	.02
❑ 90 Terry Dehere	.05	.02
❑ 91 Harold Ellis	.05	.02
❑ 92 Gary Grant	.05	.02
❑ 93 Ron Harper	.10	.05
❑ 94 Mark Jackson	.05	.02
❑ 95 Stanley Roberts	.05	.02
❑ 96 Loy Vaught	.05	.02
❑ 97 Dominique Wilkins	.25	.11
❑ 98 Elden Campbell	.05	.02
❑ 99 Doug Christie	.05	.02
❑ 100 Vlade Divac	.05	.02
❑ 101 Reggie Jordan	.05	.02
❑ 102 George Lynch	.05	.02
❑ 103 Anthony Peeler	.05	.02
❑ 104 Sedale Threatt	.05	.02
❑ 105 Nick Van Exel	.25	.11
❑ 106 James Worthy	.25	.11
❑ 107 Bimbo Coles	.05	.02
❑ 108 Matt Geiger	.05	.02
❑ 109 Grant Long	.05	.02
❑ 110 Harold Miner	.05	.02
❑ 111 Glen Rice	.10	.05
❑ 112 John Salley	.05	.02
❑ 113 Rony Seikaly	.05	.02
❑ 114 Brian Shaw	.05	.02
❑ 115 Steve Smith	.10	.05
❑ 116 Vin Baker	.25	.11
❑ 117 Jon Barry	.05	.02
❑ 118 Todd Day	.05	.02
❑ 119 Lee Mayberry	.05	.02
❑ 120 Eric Murdock	.05	.02
❑ 121 Ken Norman	.05	.02
❑ 122 Mike Brown	.05	.02
❑ 123 Stacey King	.05	.02
❑ 124 Christian Laettner	.10	.05
❑ 125 Chuck Person	.05	.02
❑ 126 Isaiah Rider	.10	.05
❑ 127 Chris Smith	.05	.02
❑ 128 Doug West	.05	.02
❑ 129 Micheal Williams	.05	.02
❑ 130 Kenny Anderson	.10	.05
❑ 131 Benoit Benjamin	.05	.02
❑ 132 P.J. Brown	.05	.02
❑ 133 Derrick Coleman	.10	.05
❑ 134 Kevin Edwards	.05	.02
❑ 135 Armon Gilliam	.05	.02
❑ 136 Chris Morris	.05	.02
❑ 137 Rex Walters	.05	.02
❑ 138 David Wesley	.05	.02
❑ 139 Greg Anthony	.05	.02
❑ 140 Anthony Bonner	.05	.02
❑ 141 Hubert Davis	.05	.02
❑ 142 Patrick Ewing	.25	.11
❑ 143 Derek Harper	.05	.02
❑ 144 Anthony Mason	.10	.05
❑ 145 Charles Oakley	.05	.02
❑ 146 Charles Smith	.05	.02
❑ 147 John Starks	.05	.02
❑ 148 Nick Anderson	.05	.02
❑ 149 Anthony Avent	.05	.02
❑ 150 Anthony Bowie	.05	.02
❑ 151 Anfernee Hardaway	.75	.35
❑ 152 Shaquille O'Neal	1.25	.55
❑ 153 Donald Royal	.05	.02
❑ 154 Dennis Scott	.05	.02
❑ 155 Scott Skiles	.05	.02
❑ 156 Jeff Turner	.05	.02
❑ 157 Dana Barros	.05	.02
❑ 158 Shawn Bradley	.05	.02
❑ 159 Greg Graham	.05	.02
❑ 160 Warren Kidd	.05	.02
❑ 161 Eric Leckner	.05	.02
❑ 162 Jeff Malone	.05	.02
❑ 163 Tim Perry	.05	.02
❑ 164 Clarence Weatherspoon	.05	.02
❑ 165 Danny Ainge	.05	.02
❑ 166 Charles Barkley	.40	.18
❑ 167 Cedric Ceballos	.05	.02
❑ 168 A.C. Green	.10	.05
❑ 169 Kevin Johnson	.10	.05
❑ 170 Malcolm Mackey	.05	.02
❑ 171 Dan Majerle	.10	.05
❑ 172 Oliver Miller	.05	.02
❑ 173 Mark West	.05	.02
❑ 174 Clyde Drexler	.25	.11
❑ 175 Chris Dudley	.05	.02
❑ 176 Harvey Grant	.05	.02
❑ 177 Tracy Murray	.05	.02
❑ 178 Terry Porter	.05	.02
❑ 179 Clifford Robinson	.10	.05
❑ 180 James Robinson	.05	.02
❑ 181 Rod Strickland	.10	.05
❑ 182 Buck Williams	.05	.02
❑ 183 Duane Causwell	.05	.02
❑ 184 Bobby Hurley	.05	.02
❑ 185 Olden Polynice	.05	.02
❑ 186 Mitch Richmond	.25	.11
❑ 187 Lionel Simmons	.05	.02
❑ 188 Wayman Tisdale	.05	.02
❑ 189 Spud Webb	.05	.02
❑ 190 Walt Williams	.05	.02
❑ 191 Willie Anderson	.05	.02
❑ 192 Lloyd Daniels	.05	.02
❑ 193 Vinny Del Negro	.05	.02
❑ 194 Dale Ellis	.05	.02
❑ 195 J.R. Reid	.05	.02
❑ 196 David Robinson	.40	.18
❑ 197 Dennis Rodman	.50	.23
❑ 198 Kendall Gill	.10	.05
❑ 199 Ervin Johnson	.05	.02
❑ 200 Shawn Kemp	.40	.18
❑ 201 Chris King	.05	.02
❑ 202 Nate McMillan	.05	.02
❑ 203 Gary Payton	.40	.18
❑ 204 Sam Perkins	.10	.05
❑ 205 Ricky Pierce	.05	.02
❑ 206 Detlef Schrempf	.10	.05
❑ 207 David Benoit	.05	.02
❑ 208 Tom Chambers	.05	.02
❑ 209 Tyrone Corbin	.05	.02
❑ 210 Jeff Hornacek	.10	.05
❑ 211 Karl Malone	.40	.18
❑ 212 Bryon Russell	.05	.02
❑ 213 Felton Spencer	.05	.02
❑ 214 John Stockton	.25	.11
❑ 215 Luther Wright	.05	.02
❑ 216 Michael Adams	.05	.02
❑ 217 Mitchell Butler	.05	.02
❑ 218 Rex Chapman	.05	.02
❑ 219 Calbert Cheaney	.05	.02
❑ 220 Pervis Ellison	.05	.02
❑ 221 Tom Gugliotta	.10	.05
❑ 222 Don MacLean	.05	.02
❑ 223 Gheorghe Muresan	.05	.02
❑ 224 Kenny Anderson AS	.05	.02
❑ 225 B.J. Armstrong AS	.05	.02
❑ 226 Mookie Blaylock AS	.05	.02
❑ 227 Derrick Coleman AS	.05	.02
❑ 228 Patrick Ewing AS	.10	.05
❑ 229 Horace Grant AS	.05	.02
❑ 230 Alonzo Mourning AS	.25	.11
❑ 231 Shaquille O'Neal AS	.50	.23
❑ 232 Charles Oakley AS	.05	.02
❑ 233 Scottie Pippen AS	.40	.18
❑ 234 Mark Price AS	.05	.02
❑ 235 John Starks AS	.05	.02
❑ 236 Dominique Wilkins AS	.10	.05
❑ 237 East Team	.05	.02
❑ 238 Charles Barkley AS	.25	.11
❑ 239 Clyde Drexler AS	.10	.05
❑ 240 Kevin Johnson AS	.05	.02
❑ 241 Shawn Kemp AS	.25	.11
❑ 242 Karl Malone AS	.25	.11
❑ 243 Danny Manning AS	.05	.02
❑ 244 Hakeem Olajuwon AS	.25	.11
❑ 245 Gary Payton AS	.25	.11
❑ 246 Mitch Richmond AS	.10	.05
❑ 247 Clifford Robinson AS	.05	.02
❑ 248 David Robinson AS	.25	.11
❑ 249 Latrell Sprewell AS	.25	.11
❑ 250 John Stockton AS	.10	.05
❑ 251 West Team	.05	.02
❑ 252 Tracy Murray LL B.J. Armstrong Reggie Miller	.05	.02
❑ 253 John Stockton LL Muggsy Bogues Mookie Blaylock	.10	.05
❑ 254 Dikembe Mutombo LL Hakeem Olajuwon Houston Rockets David Robinson	.25	.11
❑ 255 Mahmoud Abdul-Rauf LL Reggie Miller Indiana Pacers Ricky Pierce	.05	.02
❑ 256 Dennis Rodman LL Shaquille O'Neal Kevin Willis	.40	.18
❑ 257 David Robinson LL Shaquille O'Neal Hakeem Olajuwon	.40	.18
❑ 258 Nate McMillan LL Scottie Pippen Mookie Blaylock	.25	.11
❑ 259 Chris Webber AW	.30	.14
❑ 260 Hakeem Olajuwon AW	.25	.11
❑ 261 Hakeem Olajuwon AW	.25	.11
❑ 262 Dell Curry AW	.05	.02
❑ 263 Scottie Pippen AW	.40	.18
❑ 264 Anfernee Hardaway AW	.50	.23
❑ 265 Don MacLean AW	.05	.02
❑ 266 Hakeem Olajuwon FIN	.25	.11
❑ 267 Derek Harper FIN	.05	.02
❑ 268 Sam Cassell FIN	.10	.05
❑ 269 Hakeem Olajuwon Tribute	.25	.11
❑ 270 Patrick Ewing FIN Hakeem Olajuwon	.10	.05
❑ 271 Carl Herrera FIN	.05	.02
❑ 272 Vernon Maxwell FIN	.05	.02
❑ 273 Hakeem Olajuwon FIN	.25	.11
❑ 274 Lenny Wilkens CO	.10	.05
❑ 275 Chris Ford CO	.05	.02
❑ 276 Allan Bristow CO	.05	.02
❑ 277 Phil Jackson CO	.10	.05
❑ 278 Mike Fratello CO	.10	.05
❑ 279 Dick Motta CO	.05	.02
❑ 280 Dan Issel CO	.10	.05
❑ 281 Don Chaney CO	.05	.02
❑ 282 Don Nelson CO	.10	.05
❑ 283 Rudy Tomjanovich CO	.10	.05
❑ 284 Larry Brown CO	.10	.05
❑ 285 Del Harris CO UER (Back refers to Ralph Sampson and Akeem Olajuwon as part of '80-'81 Rockets)	.05	.02
❑ 286 Kevin Loughery CO	.05	.02
❑ 287 Mike Dunleavy CO	.05	.02
❑ 288 Sidney Lowe CO	.05	.02
❑ 289 Pat Riley CO	.10	.05
❑ 290 Brian Hill CO	.05	.02
❑ 291 John Lucas CO	.10	.05
❑ 292 Paul Westphal CO	.05	.02
❑ 293 Garry St. Jean CO	.05	.02
❑ 294 George Karl CO	.10	.05
❑ 295 Jerry Sloan CO	.10	.05
❑ 296 Magic Johnson Commemorative	.75	.35
❑ 297 Denzel Washington	.10	.05
❑ 298 Checklist	.05	.02
❑ 299 Checklist	.05	.02
❑ 300 Checklist	.05	.02
❑ 301 Sergei Bazarevich	.05	.02
❑ 302 Tyrone Corbin	.05	.02
❑ 303 Grant Long	.05	.02
❑ 304 Ken Norman	.05	.02
❑ 305 Steve Smith	.10	.05
❑ 306 Blue Edwards	.05	.02
❑ 307 Greg Minor RC	.05	.02
❑ 308 Eric Montross RC	.05	.02
❑ 309 Dominique Wilkins	.25	.11
❑ 310 Michael Adams	.05	.02
❑ 311 Darrin Hancock RC	.05	.02
❑ 312 Robert Parish	.10	.05
❑ 313 Ron Harper	.10	.05
❑ 314 Dickey Simpkins RC	.05	.02
❑ 315 Michael Cage	.05	.02
❑ 316 Tony Dumas RC	.05	.02
❑ 317 Jason Kidd RC	2.00	.90

❑ 318 Roy Tarpley	.05	.02
❑ 319 Dale Ellis	.05	.02
❑ 320 Jalen Rose RC	1.00	.45
❑ 321 Bill Curley RC	.05	.02
❑ 322 Grant Hill RC	2.50	1.10
❑ 323 Oliver Miller	.05	.02
❑ 324 Mark West	.05	.02
❑ 325 Tom Gugliotta	.10	.05
❑ 326 Ricky Pierce	.05	.02
❑ 327 Carlos Rogers RC	.05	.02
❑ 328 Clifford Rozier RC	.05	.02
❑ 329 Rony Seikaly	.05	.02
❑ 330 Tim Breaux	.05	.02
❑ 331 Duane Ferrell	.05	.02
❑ 332 Mark Jackson	.05	.02
❑ 333 Lamond Murray RC	.10	.05
❑ 334 Charles Outlaw RC	.05	.02
❑ 335 Eric Platkowski RC	.05	.02
❑ 336 Pooh Richardson	.05	.02
❑ 337 Malik Sealy	.05	.02
❑ 338 Cedric Ceballos	.05	.02
❑ 339 Eddie Jones RC	1.50	.70
❑ 340 Anthony Miller RC	.05	.02
❑ 341 Kevin Gamble	.05	.02
❑ 342 Brad Lohaus	.05	.02
❑ 343 Billy Owens	.05	.02
❑ 344 Khalid Reeves RC	.05	.02
❑ 345 Kevin Willis	.05	.02
❑ 346 Eric Mobley RC	.05	.02
❑ 347 Johnny Newman	.05	.02
❑ 348 Ed Pinckney	.05	.02
❑ 349 Glenn Robinson RC	.75	.35
❑ 350 Howard Eisley RC	.05	.02
❑ 351 Donyell Marshall RC	.25	.11
❑ 352 Yinka Dare RC	.05	.02
❑ 353 Charlie Ward RC	.25	.11
❑ 354 Monty Williams RC	.05	.02
❑ 355 Horace Grant	.10	.05
❑ 356 Brian Shaw	.05	.02
❑ 357 Brooks Thompson RC	.05	.02
❑ 358 Derrick Alston RC	.05	.02
❑ 359 B.J. Tyler RC	.05	.02
❑ 360 Scott Williams	.05	.02
❑ 361 Sharone Wright RC	.05	.02
❑ 362 Antonio Lang RC	.05	.02
❑ 363 Danny Manning	.10	.05
❑ 364 Wesley Person RC	.25	.11
❑ 365 Wayman Tisdale	.05	.02
❑ 366 Trevor Ruffin RC	.05	.02
❑ 367 Aaron McKie RC	.05	.02
❑ 368 Brian Grant RC	.60	.25
❑ 369 Michael Smith RC	.05	.02
❑ 370 Sean Elliott	.10	.05
❑ 371 Avery Johnson	.05	.02
❑ 372 Chuck Person	.05	.02
❑ 373 Bill Cartwright	.05	.02
❑ 374 Sarunas Marciulionis	.05	.02
❑ 375 Dontonio Wingfield RC	.05	.02
❑ 376 Antoine Carr	.05	.02
❑ 377 Jamie Watson RC	.05	.02
❑ 378 Juwan Howard RC	.60	.25
❑ 379 Jim McIlvaine RC	.05	.02
❑ 380 Scott Skiles	.05	.02
❑ 381 Anthony Tucker RC	.05	.02
❑ 382 Chris Webber	.75	.35
❑ 383 Bill Fitch CO	.05	.02
❑ 384 Bill Blair CO	.05	.02
❑ 385 Butch Beard CO	.05	.02
❑ 386 P.J. Carlesimo CO	.05	.02
❑ 387 Bob Hill CO	.05	.02
❑ 388 Jim Lynam CO	.05	.02
❑ 389 Checklist 4	.05	.02
❑ 390 Checklist 5	.05	.02
❑ 391 Atlanta Hawks TC	.05	.02
❑ 392 Boston Celtics TC	.05	.02
❑ 393 Charlotte Hornets TC	.05	.02
❑ 394 Chicago Bulls TC	.05	.02
❑ 395 Cleveland Cavaliers TC	.05	.02
❑ 396 Dallas Mavericks TC	.05	.02
❑ 397 Denver Nuggets TC	.05	.02
❑ 398 Detroit Pistons TC	.05	.02
❑ 399 Golden State Warriors TC	.05	.02
❑ 400 Houston Rockets TC	.05	.02
❑ 401 Indiana Pacers TC	.05	.02
❑ 402 Los Angeles Clippers TC	.05	.02
❑ 403 Los Angeles Lakers TC	.05	.02
❑ 404 Miami Heat TC	.05	.02
❑ 405 Milwaukee Bucks TC	.05	.02
❑ 406 Minnesota Timberwolves TC	.05	.02
❑ 407 New Jersey Nets TC	.05	.02
❑ 408 New York Knicks TC	.05	.02
❑ 409 Orlando Magic TC	.05	.02
❑ 410 Philadelphia 76ers TC	.05	.02
❑ 411 Phoenix Suns TC	.05	.02
❑ 412 Portland Trail Blazers TC	.05	.02
❑ 413 Sacramento Kings TC	.05	.02
❑ 414 San Antonio Spurs TC	.05	.02
❑ 415 Seattle Supersonics TC	.05	.02
❑ 416 Utah Jazz TC	.05	.02
❑ 417 Washington Bullets TC	.05	.02
❑ 418 Toronto Raptors TC	.05	.02
❑ 419 Vancouver Grizzlies TC	.05	.02
❑ 420 NBA Logo Card	.05	.02
❑ 421 Glenn Robinson TOP Chris Webber	.40	.18
❑ 422 Jason Kidd TOP Shawn Bradley	.40	.18
❑ 423 Grant Hill TOP Anfernee Hardaway	1.00	.45
❑ 424 Donyell Marshall TOP Jamal Mashburn	.25	.11
❑ 425 Juwan Howard TOP Isaiah Rider	.25	.11
❑ 426 Sharone Wright TOP Calbert Cheaney	.05	.02
❑ 427 Lamond Murray TOP Bobby Hurley	.05	.02
❑ 428 Brian Grant TOP Vin Baker	.25	.11
❑ 429 Eric Montross TOP Rodney Rogers	.05	.02
❑ 430 Eddie Jones TOP Lindsey Hunter	.40	.18
❑ 431 Craig Ehlo GM	.05	.02
❑ 432 Dino Radja GM	.05	.02
❑ 433 Toni Kukoc GM	.25	.11
❑ 434 Mark Price GM	.05	.02
❑ 435 Latrell Sprewell GM	.25	.11
❑ 436 Sam Cassell GM	.10	.05
❑ 437 Vernon Maxwell GM	.05	.02
❑ 438 Haywoode Workman GM	.05	.02
❑ 439 Harold Ellis GM	.05	.02
❑ 440 Cedric Ceballos GM	.05	.02
❑ 441 Vlade Divac GM	.05	.02
❑ 442 Nick Van Exel GM	.10	.05
❑ 443 John Starks GM	.05	.02
❑ 444 Scott Williams GM	.05	.02
❑ 445 Clifford Robinson GM	.05	.02
❑ 446 Spud Webb GM	.05	.02
❑ 447 Avery Johnson GM	.05	.02
❑ 448 Dennis Rodman GM	.25	.11
❑ 449 Sarunas Marciulionis GM	.05	.02
❑ 450 Nate McMillan GM	.05	.02
❑ NNO Shaq Sheet Wrapper Exchange Autograph	400.00	180.00
❑ NNO G.Hill Wrapper Exch.	6.00	2.70
❑ NNO Shaq Sheet Wrap.Exch.	30.00	13.50

1994-95 Hoops Big Numbers

	MINT	NRMT
COMPLETE SET (12)	40.00	18.00

*SINGLES: 4X TO 10X BASE CARD HI
SER.1 STATED ODDS 1:30
*RAINBOW CARDS: EQUAL VALUE TO SILVER
ONE RAINBOW PER SER.1 RETAIL PACK

Card	MINT	NRMT
❑ BN1 David Robinson	4.00	1.80
❑ BN2 Jamal Mashburn	2.50	1.10
❑ BN3 Hakeem Olajuwon	4.00	1.80
❑ BN4 Patrick Ewing	2.50	1.10
❑ BN5 Shaquille O'Neal	12.00	5.50
❑ BN6 Latrell Sprewell	5.00	2.20
❑ BN7 Chris Webber	8.00	3.60
❑ BN8 Anfernee Hardaway	8.00	3.60
❑ BN9 Scottie Pippen	8.00	3.60
❑ BN10 Isaiah Rider	1.00	.45
❑ BN11 Alonzo Mourning	3.00	1.35
❑ BN12 Charles Barkley	4.00	1.80

1994-95 Hoops Draft Redemption

	MINT	NRMT
COMPLETE SET (11)	20.00	9.00
COMMON CARD (1-11)	.50	.23
SEMISTARS	1.00	.45

ONE SET PER EXCHANGE CARD BY MAIL
EXCH.CARD: SER.1 STATED ODDS 1:360

Card	MINT	NRMT
❑ 1 Glenn Robinson	3.00	1.35
❑ 2 Jason Kidd	8.00	3.60
❑ 3 Grant Hill	10.00	4.50
❑ 4 Donyell Marshall	1.00	.45
❑ 5 Juwan Howard	2.50	1.10
❑ 6 Sharone Wright	.50	.23
❑ 7 Lamond Murray	.50	.23
❑ 8 Brian Grant	2.50	1.10
❑ 9 Eric Montross	.50	.23
❑ 10 Eddie Jones	6.00	2.70
❑ 11 Carlos Rogers	.50	.23
❑ NNO Expired Exchange Card	1.00	.45

1994-95 Hoops Magic's All-Rookies

	MINT	NRMT
COMPLETE SET (10)	10.00	4.50

		MINT	NRMT
COMMON CARD (AR1-AR10)		.40	.18
SEMISTARS		.50	.23
SER.2 STATED ODDS 1:12			
COMPLETE FOIL SET (10)		25.00	11.00
*FOIL CARDS:1.25X TO 2.5X HI COLUMN			
SER.2 STATED ODDS 1:36			
FAR PREFIX ON CARD NUMBER			
❑ AR1	Glenn Robinson	1.50	.70
❑ AR2	Jason Kidd	4.00	1.80
❑ AR3	Grant Hill	5.00	2.20
❑ AR4	Donyell Marshall	.50	.23
❑ AR5	Juwan Howard	1.25	.55
❑ AR6	Sharone Wright	.40	.18
❑ AR7	Brian Grant	1.25	.55
❑ AR8	Eddie Jones	3.00	1.35
❑ AR9	Jalen Rose	2.00	.90
❑ AR10	Wesley Person	.50	.23

1994-95 Hoops Power Ratings

		MINT	NRMT
COMPLETE SET (54)		8.00	3.60
*SINGLES: .75X TO 2X BASE CARD HI			
ONE PER SERIES 2 PACK			
❑ PR1	Mookie Blaylock	.10	.05
❑ PR2	Stacey Augmon	.10	.05
❑ PR3	Dino Radja	.10	.05
❑ PR4	Dominique Wilkins	.50	.23
❑ PR5	Larry Johnson	.20	.09
❑ PR6	Alonzo Mourning	.60	.25
❑ PR7	Toni Kukoc	.75	.35
❑ PR8	Scottie Pippen	1.50	.70
❑ PR9	John Williams	.10	.05
❑ PR10	Mark Price	.10	.05
❑ PR11	Jim Jackson	.20	.09
❑ PR12	Jamal Mashburn	.50	.23
❑ PR13	Dale Ellis	.10	.05
❑ PR14	LaPhonso Ellis	.10	.05
❑ PR15	Joe Dumars	.50	.23
❑ PR16	Lindsey Hunter	.20	.09
❑ PR17	Latrell Sprewell	1.00	.45
❑ PR18	Chris Mullin	.50	.23
❑ PR19	Vernon Maxwell	.10	.05
❑ PR20	Hakeem Olajuwon	.75	.35
❑ PR21	Mark Jackson	.10	.05
❑ PR22	Reggie Miller	.50	.23
❑ PR23	Pooh Richardson	.10	.05
❑ PR24	Loy Vaught	.10	.05
❑ PR25	Vlade Divac	.10	.05
❑ PR26	Nick Van Exel	.50	.23
❑ PR27	Glen Rice	.20	.09
❑ PR28	Billy Owens	.10	.05
❑ PR29	Vin Baker	.50	.23
❑ PR30	Eric Murdock	.10	.05
❑ PR31	Christian Laettner	.20	.09
❑ PR32	Isaiah Rider	.20	.09
❑ PR33	Kenny Anderson	.20	.09
❑ PR34	Derrick Coleman	.20	.09
❑ PR35	Patrick Ewing	.50	.23
❑ PR36	John Starks	.10	.05
❑ PR37	Nick Anderson	.10	.05
❑ PR38	Anfernee Hardaway	1.50	.70
❑ PR39	Shawn Bradley	.10	.05
❑ PR40	C. Weatherspoon	.10	.05
❑ PR41	Charles Barkley	.75	.35
❑ PR42	Kevin Johnson	.20	.09
❑ PR43	Clyde Drexler	.50	.23
❑ PR44	Clifford Robinson	.20	.09
❑ PR45	Mitch Richmond	.50	.23
❑ PR46	Olden Polynice	.10	.05
❑ PR47	Sean Elliott	.20	.09
❑ PR48	Chuck Person	.10	.05
❑ PR49	Shawn Kemp	.75	.35
❑ PR50	Gary Payton	.75	.35
❑ PR51	Jeff Hornacek	.20	.09
❑ PR52	Karl Malone	.75	.35
❑ PR53	Rex Chapman	.10	.05
❑ PR54	Don MacLean	.10	.05

1994-95 Hoops Predators

		MINT	NRMT
COMPLETE SET (8)		3.00	1.35
*SINGLES: .75X TO 2X BASE CARD HI			
SER.2 STATED ODDS 1:12			
❑ P1	Mahmoud Abdul-Rauf	.10	.05
❑ P2	Dikembe Mutombo	.20	.09
❑ P3	Shaquille O'Neal	2.50	1.10
❑ P4	Tracy Murray	.10	.05
❑ P5	David Robinson	.75	.35
❑ P6	Dennis Rodman	1.00	.45
❑ P7	Nate McMillan	.10	.05
❑ P8	John Stockton	.50	.23
❑ NNO	David Robinson Jumbo	.15	.07

1994-95 Hoops Supreme Court

		MINT	NRMT
COMPLETE SET (50)		20.00	9.00
*SINGLES: 1.25X TO 3X BASE CARD HI			
SER.1 STATED ODDS 1:4			
❑ SC1	Mookie Blaylock	.15	.07
❑ SC2	Danny Manning	.30	.14
❑ SC3	Dino Radja	.15	.07
❑ SC4	Larry Johnson	.30	.14
❑ SC5	Alonzo Mourning	1.00	.45
❑ SC6	B.J. Armstrong	.15	.07
❑ SC7	Horace Grant	.30	.14
❑ SC8	Toni Kukoc	1.25	.55
❑ SC9	Brad Daugherty	.15	.07
❑ SC10	Mark Price	.15	.07
❑ SC11	Jim Jackson	.30	.14
❑ SC12	Jamal Mashburn	.75	.35
❑ SC13	Dikembe Mutombo	.30	.14
❑ SC14	Joe Dumars	.75	.35
❑ SC15	Lindsey Hunter	.30	.14
❑ SC16	Tim Hardaway	.75	.35
❑ SC17	Chris Mullin	.75	.35
❑ SC18	Sam Cassell	.75	.35
❑ SC19	Hakeem Olajuwon	1.25	.55
❑ SC20	Reggie Miller	.75	.35
❑ SC21	Dominique Wilkins	.75	.35
❑ SC22	Nick Van Exel	.75	.35
❑ SC23	Harold Miner	.15	.07
❑ SC24	Steve Smith	.30	.14
❑ SC25	Vin Baker	.75	.35
❑ SC26	Christian Laettner	.30	.14
❑ SC27	Isaiah Rider	.30	.14
❑ SC28	Kenny Anderson	.30	.14
❑ SC29	Derrick Coleman	.30	.14
❑ SC30	Patrick Ewing	.75	.35
❑ SC31	John Starks	.15	.07
❑ SC32	Anfernee Hardaway	2.50	1.10
❑ SC33	Shaquille O'Neal	4.00	1.80
❑ SC34	Shawn Bradley	.15	.07
❑ SC35	C. Weatherspoon	.15	.07
❑ SC36	Charles Barkley	1.25	.55
❑ SC37	Kevin Johnson	.30	.14
❑ SC38	Oliver Miller	.15	.07
❑ SC39	Clyde Drexler	.75	.35
❑ SC40	Clifford Robinson	.30	.14
❑ SC41	Mitch Richmond	.75	.35
❑ SC42	Bobby Hurley	.15	.07
❑ SC43	David Robinson	1.25	.55
❑ SC44	Dennis Rodman	1.50	.70
❑ SC45	Gary Payton	1.25	.55
❑ SC46	Shawn Kemp	1.25	.55
❑ SC47	John Stockton	.75	.35
❑ SC48	Karl Malone	1.25	.55
❑ SC49	Calbert Cheaney	.15	.07
❑ SC50	Tom Gugliotta	.30	.14

1995-96 Hoops

		MINT	NRMT
COMPLETE SET (400)		35.00	16.00
COMPLETE SERIES 1 (250)		20.00	9.00
COMPLETE SERIES 2 (150)		15.00	6.75
COMMON CARD (1-400)		.10	.05
SEMISTARS		.15	.07
UNLISTED STARS		.25	.11
SUBSET CARDS HALF VALUE OF BASE CARDS			
HILL TRIB: SER.1 STATED ODDS 1:360			
❑ 1	Stacey Augmon	.10	.05
❑ 2	Mookie Blaylock	.10	.05
❑ 3	Craig Ehlo	.10	.05
❑ 4	Andrew Lang	.10	.05
❑ 5	Grant Long	.10	.05
❑ 6	Ken Norman	.10	.05
❑ 7	Steve Smith	.15	.07
❑ 8	Dee Brown	.10	.05
❑ 9	Sherman Douglas	.10	.05
❑ 10	Pervis Ellison	.10	.05
❑ 11	Eric Montross	.10	.05
❑ 12	Dino Radja	.10	.05
❑ 13	Dominique Wilkins	.25	.11
❑ 14	Muggsy Bogues	.10	.05

No.	Card	Mint	Ex
❑ 15	Scott Burrell	.10	.05
❑ 16	Dell Curry	.10	.05
❑ 17	Hersey Hawkins	.15	.07
❑ 18	Larry Johnson	.15	.07
❑ 19	Alonzo Mourning	.25	.11
❑ 20	B.J. Armstrong	.10	.05
❑ 21	Michael Jordan	3.00	1.35
❑ 22	Toni Kukoc	.30	.14
❑ 23	Will Perdue	.10	.05
❑ 24	Scottie Pippen	.75	.35
❑ 25	Dickey Simpkins	.10	.05
❑ 26	Terrell Brandon	.15	.07
❑ 27	Tyrone Hill	.10	.05
❑ 28	Chris Mills	.10	.05
❑ 29	Bobby Phills	.10	.05
❑ 30	Mark Price	.10	.05
❑ 31	John Williams	.10	.05
❑ 32	Tony Dumas	.10	.05
❑ 33	Jim Jackson	.10	.05
❑ 34	Popeye Jones	.10	.05
❑ 35	Jason Kidd	.75	.35
❑ 36	Jamal Mashburn	.15	.07
❑ 37	Roy Tarpley	.10	.05
❑ 38	Mahmoud Abdul-Rauf	.10	.05
❑ 39	LaPhonso Ellis	.10	.05
❑ 40	Dikembe Mutombo	.15	.07
❑ 41	Robert Pack	.10	.05
❑ 42	Rodney Rogers	.10	.05
❑ 43	Jalen Rose	.30	.14
❑ 44	Bryant Stith	.10	.05
❑ 45	Joe Dumars	.25	.11
❑ 46	Grant Hill	1.25	.55
❑ 47	Allan Houston	.30	.14
❑ 48	Lindsey Hunter	.10	.05
❑ 49	Oliver Miller	.10	.05
❑ 50	Terry Mills	.10	.05
❑ 51	Chris Gatling	.10	.05
❑ 52	Tim Hardaway	.25	.11
❑ 53	Donyell Marshall	.15	.07
❑ 54	Chris Mullin	.25	.11
❑ 55	Carlos Rogers	.10	.05
❑ 56	Clifford Rozier	.10	.05
❑ 57	Rony Seikaly	.10	.05
❑ 58	Latrell Sprewell	.50	.23
❑ 59	Sam Cassell	.15	.07
❑ 60	Clyde Drexler	.25	.11
❑ 61	Robert Horry	.10	.05
❑ 62	Vernon Maxwell	.10	.05
❑ 63	Hakeem Olajuwon	.40	.18
❑ 64	Kenny Smith	.10	.05
❑ 65	Dale Davis	.10	.05
❑ 66	Mark Jackson	.10	.05
❑ 67	Derrick McKey	.10	.05
❑ 68	Reggie Miller	.25	.11
❑ 69	Byron Scott	.10	.05
❑ 70	Rik Smits	.10	.05
❑ 71	Terry Dehere	.10	.05
❑ 72	Lamond Murray	.10	.05
❑ 73	Eric Piatkowski	.10	.05
❑ 74	Pooh Richardson	.10	.05
❑ 75	Malik Sealy	.10	.05
❑ 76	Loy Vaught	.10	.05
❑ 77	Elden Campbell	.10	.05
❑ 78	Cedric Ceballos	.10	.05
❑ 79	Vlade Divac	.10	.05
❑ 80	Eddie Jones	.50	.23
❑ 81	Sedale Threatt	.10	.05
❑ 82	Nick Van Exel	.15	.07
❑ 83	Bimbo Coles	.10	.05
❑ 84	Harold Miner	.10	.05
❑ 85	Billy Owens	.10	.05
❑ 86	Khalid Reeves	.10	.05
❑ 87	Glen Rice	.15	.07
❑ 88	Kevin Willis	.10	.05
❑ 89	Vin Baker	.25	.11
❑ 90	Marty Conlon	.10	.05
❑ 91	Todd Day	.10	.05
❑ 92	Eric Mobley	.10	.05
❑ 93	Eric Murdock	.10	.05
❑ 94	Glenn Robinson	.25	.11
❑ 95	Winston Garland	.10	.05
❑ 96	Tom Gugliotta	.15	.07
❑ 97	Christian Laettner	.15	.07
❑ 98	Isaiah Rider	.15	.07
❑ 99	Sean Rooks	.10	.05
❑ 100	Doug West	.10	.05
❑ 101	Kenny Anderson	.15	.07
❑ 102	Benoit Benjamin	.10	.05
❑ 103	Derrick Coleman	.15	.07
❑ 104	Kevin Edwards	.10	.05
❑ 105	Armon Gilliam	.10	.05
❑ 106	Chris Morris	.10	.05
❑ 107	Patrick Ewing	.25	.11
❑ 108	Derek Harper	.10	.05
❑ 109	Anthony Mason	.15	.07
❑ 110	Charles Oakley	.10	.05
❑ 111	Charles Smith	.10	.05
❑ 112	John Starks	.10	.05
❑ 113	Monty Williams	.10	.05
❑ 114	Nick Anderson	.10	.05
❑ 115	Horace Grant	.15	.07
❑ 116	Anfernee Hardaway	.75	.35
❑ 117	Shaquille O'Neal	1.25	.55
❑ 118	Dennis Scott	.10	.05
❑ 119	Brian Shaw	.10	.05
❑ 120	Dana Barros	.10	.05
❑ 121	Shawn Bradley	.10	.05
❑ 122	Willie Burton	.10	.05
❑ 123	Jeff Malone	.10	.05
❑ 124	Clarence Weatherspoon	.10	.05
❑ 125	Sharone Wright	.10	.05
❑ 126	Charles Barkley	.40	.18
❑ 127	A.C. Green	.15	.07
❑ 128	Kevin Johnson	.15	.07
❑ 129	Dan Majerle	.10	.05
❑ 130	Danny Manning	.15	.07
❑ 131	Elliot Perry	.10	.05
❑ 132	Wesley Person	.15	.07
❑ 133	Chris Dudley	.10	.05
❑ 134	Clifford Robinson	.10	.05
❑ 135	James Robinson	.10	.05
❑ 136	Rod Strickland	.15	.07
❑ 137	Otis Thorpe	.10	.05
❑ 138	Buck Williams	.10	.05
❑ 139	Brian Grant	.25	.11
❑ 140	Olden Polynice	.10	.05
❑ 141	Mitch Richmond	.25	.11
❑ 142	Michael Smith	.10	.05
❑ 143	Spud Webb	.10	.05
❑ 144	Walt Williams	.10	.05
❑ 145	Vinny Del Negro	.10	.05
❑ 146	Sean Elliott	.10	.05
❑ 147	Avery Johnson	.10	.05
❑ 148	Chuck Person	.10	.05
❑ 149	David Robinson	.40	.18
❑ 150	Dennis Rodman	.50	.23
❑ 151	Kendall Gill	.15	.07
❑ 152	Ervin Johnson	.10	.05
❑ 153	Shawn Kemp	.40	.18
❑ 154	Nate McMillan	.10	.05
❑ 155	Gary Payton	.40	.18
❑ 156	Detlef Schrempf	.15	.07
❑ 157	Dontonio Wingfield	.10	.05
❑ 158	David Benoit	.10	.05
❑ 159	Jeff Hornacek	.15	.07
❑ 160	Karl Malone	.40	.18
❑ 161	Felton Spencer	.10	.05
❑ 162	John Stockton	.25	.11
❑ 163	Jamie Watson	.10	.05
❑ 164	Rex Chapman	.10	.05
❑ 165	Calbert Cheaney	.10	.05
❑ 166	Juwan Howard	.25	.11
❑ 167	Don MacLean	.10	.05
❑ 168	Gheorghe Muresan	.10	.05
❑ 169	Scott Skiles	.10	.05
❑ 170	Chris Webber	.75	.35
❑ 171	Lenny Wilkens CO	.15	.07
❑ 172	Allan Bristow CO	.10	.05
❑ 173	Phil Jackson CO	.15	.07
❑ 174	Mike Fratello CO	.15	.07
❑ 175	Dick Motta CO	.10	.05
❑ 176	Bernie Bickerstaff CO	.10	.05
❑ 177	Doug Collins CO	.10	.05
❑ 178	Rick Adelman CO	.10	.05
❑ 179	Rudy Tomjanovich CO	.15	.07
❑ 180	Larry Brown CO	.15	.07
❑ 181	Bill Fitch CO	.10	.05
❑ 182	Del Harris CO	.10	.05
❑ 183	Mike Dunleavy CO	.10	.05
❑ 184	Bill Blair CO	.10	.05
❑ 185	Butch Beard CO	.10	.05
❑ 186	Pat Riley CO	.15	.07
❑ 187	Brian Hill CO	.10	.05
❑ 188	John Lucas CO	.15	.07
❑ 189	Paul Westphal CO	.10	.05
❑ 190	P.J. Carlesimo CO	.10	.05
❑ 191	Garry St. Jean CO	.10	.05
❑ 192	Bob Hill CO	.10	.05
❑ 193	George Karl CO	.15	.07
❑ 194	Brendan Malone CO	.10	.05
❑ 195	Jerry Sloan CO	.15	.07
❑ 196	Kevin Pritchard	.10	.05
❑ 197	Jim Lynam CO	.10	.05
❑ 198	Brian Grant SS	.15	.07
❑ 199	Grant Hill SS	.75	.35
❑ 200	Juwan Howard SS	.15	.07
❑ 201	Eddie Jones SS	.25	.11
❑ 202	Jason Kidd SS	.30	.14
❑ 203	Donyell Marshall SS	.10	.05
❑ 204	Eric Montross SS	.10	.05
❑ 205	Glenn Robinson SS	.15	.07
❑ 206	Jalen Rose SS	.25	.11
❑ 207	Sharone Wright SS	.10	.05
❑ 208	Dana Barros MS	.10	.05
❑ 209	Joe Dumars MS	.15	.07
❑ 210	A.C. Green MS	.10	.05
❑ 211	Grant Hill MS	.75	.35
❑ 212	Karl Malone MS	.25	.11
❑ 213	Reggie Miller MS	.15	.07
❑ 214	Glen Rice MS	.10	.05
❑ 215	John Stockton MS	.15	.07
❑ 216	Lenny Wilkens MS	.15	.07
❑ 217	Dominique Wilkins MS	.15	.07
❑ 218	Kenny Anderson BB	.10	.05
❑ 219	Mookie Blaylock BB	.10	.05
❑ 220	Larry Johnson BB	.10	.05
❑ 221	Shawn Kemp BB	.25	.11
❑ 222	Toni Kukoc BB	.25	.11
❑ 223	Jamal Mashburn BB	.10	.05
❑ 224	Glen Rice BB	.10	.05
❑ 225	Mitch Richmond BB	.15	.07
❑ 226	Latrell Sprewell BB	.25	.11
❑ 227	Rod Strickland BB	.10	.05
❑ 228	Michael Adams PL Darrick Martin	.10	.05
❑ 229	Craig Ehlo PL Jerome Harmon	.10	.05
❑ 230	Mario Elie PL George McCloud	.10	.05
❑ 231	Anthony Mason PL Chucky Brown	.10	.05
❑ 232	John Starks PL Tim Legler	.10	.05
❑ 233	Muggsy Bogues CA	.10	.05
❑ 234	Joe Dumars CA	.15	.07
❑ 235	LaPhonso Ellis CA	.10	.05
❑ 236	Patrick Ewing CA	.15	.07
❑ 237	Grant Hill CA	.75	.35
❑ 238	Kevin Johnson CA	.10	.05
❑ 239	Dan Majerle CA	.10	.05
❑ 240	Karl Malone CA	.25	.11
❑ 241	Hakeem Olajuwon CA	.25	.11
❑ 242	David Robinson CA	.25	.11
❑ 243	Dana Barros TT	.10	.05
❑ 244	Scott Burrell TT	.10	.05
❑ 245	Reggie Miller TT	.15	.07
❑ 246	Glen Rice TT	.10	.05
❑ 247	John Stockton TT	.15	.07
❑ 248	Checklist #1	.10	.05
❑ 249	Checklist #2	.10	.05
❑ 250	Checklist #3	.10	.05
❑ 251	Alan Henderson RC	.25	.11
❑ 252	Junior Burrough RC	.10	.05
❑ 253	Eric Williams RC	.15	.07
❑ 254	George Zidek RC	.10	.05
❑ 255	Jason Caffey RC	.15	.07
❑ 256	Donny Marshall RC	.10	.05
❑ 257	Bob Sura RC	.15	.07
❑ 258	Loren Meyer RC	.10	.05
❑ 259	Cherokee Parks RC	.10	.05
❑ 260	Antonio McDyess RC	1.25	.55
❑ 261	Theo Ratliff RC	.30	.14
❑ 262	Lou Roe RC	.10	.05
❑ 263	Andrew DeClercq RC	.10	.05
❑ 264	Joe Smith RC	.75	.35
❑ 265	Travis Best RC	.15	.07
❑ 266	Brent Barry RC	.25	.11
❑ 267	Frankie King RC	.10	.05

❑ 268 Sasha Danilovic RC ...... .10 .05
❑ 269 Kurt Thomas RC .... .15 .07
❑ 270 Shawn Respert RC .... .10 .05
❑ 271 Jerome Allen RC .... .10 .05
❑ 272 Kevin Garnett RC 3.00 1.35
❑ 273 Ed O'Bannon RC .... .10 .05
❑ 274 David Vaughn RC .... .10 .05
❑ 275 Jerry Stackhouse RC .... .75 .35
❑ 276 Mario Bennett RC .... .10 .05
❑ 277 Michael Finley RC .... 1.00 .45
❑ 278 Randolph Childress RC .. .10 .05
❑ 279 Arvydas Sabonis RC ...... .40 .18
❑ 280 Gary Trent RC .... .10 .05
❑ 281 Tyus Edney RC .... .10 .05
❑ 282 Corliss Williamson RC .... .50 .23
❑ 283 Cory Alexander RC .... .10 .05
❑ 284 Sherrell Ford RC .... .10 .05
❑ 285 Jimmy King RC .... .10 .05
❑ 286 Damon Stoudamire RC 1.25 .55
❑ 287 Greg Ostertag RC .... .10 .05
❑ 288 Lawrence Moten RC .... .10 .05
❑ 289 Bryant Reeves RC .... .25 .11
❑ 290 Rasheed Wallace RC .. 1.00 .45
❑ 291 Spud Webb .... .10 .05
❑ 292 Dana Barros .... .10 .05
❑ 293 Rick Fox .... .10 .05
❑ 294 Kendall Gill .... .15 .07
❑ 295 Khalid Reeves .... .10 .05
❑ 296 Glen Rice .... .15 .07
❑ 297 Luc Longley .... .10 .05
❑ 298 Dennis Rodman .... .50 .23
❑ 299 Dan Majerle .... .10 .05
❑ 300 Lorenzo Williams .... .10 .05
❑ 301 Dale Ellis .... .10 .05
❑ 302 Reggie Williams .... .10 .05
❑ 303 Otis Thorpe .... .10 .05
❑ 304 B.J. Armstrong .... .10 .05
❑ 305 Pete Chilcutt .... .10 .05
❑ 306 Mario Elie .... .10 .05
❑ 307 Antonio Davis .... .10 .05
❑ 308 Ricky Pierce .... .10 .05
❑ 309 Rodney Rogers .... .10 .05
❑ 310 Brian Williams .... .10 .05
❑ 311 Corie Blount .... .10 .05
❑ 312 George Lynch .... .10 .05
❑ 313 Alonzo Mourning .... .25 .11
❑ 314 Lee Mayberry .... .10 .05
❑ 315 Terry Porter .... .10 .05
❑ 316 P.J. Brown .... .10 .05
❑ 317 Hubert Davis .... .10 .05
❑ 318 Charlie Ward .... .10 .05
❑ 319 Jon Koncak .... .10 .05
❑ 320 Derrick Coleman .... .15 .07
❑ 321 Richard Dumas .... .10 .05
❑ 322 Vernon Maxwell .... .10 .05
❑ 323 Wayman Tisdale .... .10 .05
❑ 324 Dontonio Wingfield .... .10 .05
❑ 325 Tyrone Corbin .... .10 .05
❑ 326 Bobby Hurley .... .10 .05
❑ 327 Will Perdue .... .10 .05
❑ 328 J.R. Reid .... .10 .05
❑ 329 Hersey Hawkins .... .15 .07
❑ 330 Sam Perkins .... .15 .07
❑ 331 Adam Keefe .... .10 .05
❑ 332 Chris Morris .... .10 .05
❑ 333 Robert Pack .... .10 .05
❑ 334 M.L. Carr CO .... .10 .05
❑ 335 Pat Riley CO .... .15 .07
❑ 336 Don Nelson CO .... .15 .07
❑ 337 Brian Winters CO .... .10 .05
❑ 338 Willie Anderson ET .... .10 .05
❑ 339 Acie Earl ET .... .10 .05
❑ 340 Jimmy King ET .... .10 .05
❑ 341 Oliver Miller ET .... .10 .05
❑ 342 Tracy Murray ET .... .10 .05
❑ 343 Ed Pinckney ET .... .10 .05
❑ 344 Alvin Robertson ET .... .10 .05
❑ 345 Carlos Rogers ET .... .10 .05
❑ 346 John Salley ET .... .10 .05
❑ 347 Damon Stoudamire ET .. .75 .35
❑ 348 Zan Tabak ET .... .10 .05
❑ 349 Greg Anthony ET .... .10 .05
❑ 350 Blue Edwards ET .... .10 .05
❑ 351 Kenny Gattison ET .... .10 .05
❑ 352 Antonio Harvey ET .... .10 .05
❑ 353 Chris King ET .... .10 .05
❑ 354 Darrick Martin ET .... .10 .05
❑ 355 Lawrence Moten ET ...... .10 .05
❑ 356 Bryant Reeves ET .... .15 .07
❑ 357 Byron Scott ET .... .10 .05
❑ 358 Michael Jordan ES ...... 1.50 .70
❑ 359 Dikembe Mutombo ES .. .10 .05
❑ 360 Grant Hill ES .... .75 .35
❑ 361 Robert Horry ES .... .10 .05
❑ 362 Alonzo Mourning ES ...... .15 .07
❑ 363 Vin Baker ES .... .15 .07
❑ 364 Isaiah Rider ES .... .10 .05
❑ 365 Charles Oakley ES .... .10 .05
❑ 366 Shaquille O'Neal ES ...... .50 .23
❑ 367 Jerry Stackhouse ES ...... .40 .18
❑ 368 C. Weatherspoon ES .... .10 .05
❑ 369 Charles Barkley ES .... .25 .11
❑ 370 Sean Elliott ES .... .10 .05
❑ 371 Shawn Kemp ES .... .25 .11
❑ 372 Chris Webber ES .... .30 .14
❑ 373 Spud Webb RH .... .10 .05
❑ 374 Muggsy Bogues RH ...... .10 .05
❑ 375 Toni Kukoc RH .... .25 .11
❑ 376 Dennis Rodman RH ...... .25 .11
❑ 377 Jamal Mashburn RH ...... .10 .05
❑ 378 Jalen Rose RH .... .25 .11
❑ 379 Clyde Drexler RH .... .15 .07
❑ 380 Mark Jackson RH .... .10 .05
❑ 381 Cedric Ceballos RH .... .10 .05
❑ 382 Nick Van Exel RH .... .10 .05
❑ 383 John Starks RH .... .10 .05
❑ 384 Vernon Maxwell RH ...... .10 .05
❑ 385 Shawn Kemp RH .... .25 .11
❑ 386 Gary Payton RH .... .25 .11
❑ 387 Karl Malone RH .... .25 .11
❑ 388 Mookie Blaylock WD ...... .10 .05
❑ 389 Muggsy Bogues WD ...... .10 .05
❑ 390 Jason Kidd WD .... .30 .14
❑ 391 Tim Hardaway WD .... .15 .07
❑ 392 Nick Van Exel WD .... .10 .05
❑ 393 Kenny Anderson WD ...... .10 .05
❑ 394 Anfernee Hardaway WD .50 .23
❑ 395 Rod Strickland WD .... .10 .05
❑ 396 Avery Johnson WD .... .10 .05
❑ 397 John Stockton WD .... .15 .07
❑ 398 Grant Hill SPEC .... .75 .35
❑ 399 Checklist (251-367) .... .10 .05
❑ 400 Checklist (368-400/Ins.) .10 .05
❑ NNO Grant Hill 20.00 9.00
Co-ROY Exchange
❑ NNO Grant Hill .... 1.00 .45
Sweepstakes
❑ NNO Grant Hill Tribute 40.00 18.00

1995-96 Hoops Block Party

	MINT	NRMT
COMPLETE SET (25)	4.00	1.80
COMMON CARD (1-25)	.15	.07
SEMISTARS	.25	.11
UNLISTED STARS	.40	.18

SER.1 STATED ODDS 1:2 HOBBY/RETAIL

❑ 1 Oliver Miller .... .15 .07
❑ 2 Dennis Rodman .... .75 .35
❑ 3 Scottie Pippen .... 1.25 .55
❑ 4 Dikembe Mutombo .... .25 .11
❑ 5 Vlade Divac .... .15 .07
❑ 6 Brian Grant .... .40 .18
❑ 7 Alonzo Mourning .... .40 .18
❑ 8 Hakeem Olajuwon .... .60 .25
❑ 9 Patrick Ewing .... .40 .18
❑ 10 Shawn Kemp .... .60 .25
❑ 11 Vin Baker .... .40 .18
❑ 12 Horace Grant .... .25 .11
❑ 13 Dale Davis .... .15 .07
❑ 14 Juwan Howard .... .40 .18
❑ 15 Eddie Jones .... .75 .35
❑ 16 Eric Montross .... .15 .07
❑ 17 Tyrone Hill .... .15 .07
❑ 18 Tom Gugliotta .... .25 .11
❑ 19 Shawn Bradley .... .15 .07
❑ 20 Dan Majerle .... .15 .07
❑ 21 Loy Vaught .... .15 .07
❑ 22 Donyell Marshall .... .25 .11
❑ 23 Chris Webber .... 1.25 .55
❑ 24 Derrick Coleman .... .25 .11
❑ 25 Walt Williams .... .15 .07

1995-96 Hoops Grant Hill Dunks/Slams

	MINT	NRMT
COMPLETE SET (10)	40.00	18.00
COMPLETE DUNKS SET (5)	20.00	9.00
COMPLETE SLAMS SET (5)	20.00	9.00
COMMON DUNK/SLAM (D1-D5)	5.00	2.20

DUNK: SER.1 STATED ODDS 1:36 RETAIL
SLAM: SER.1 STATED ODDS 1:36 HOBBY

❑ S1 Grant Hill 5.00 2.20
S-Card
❑ S2 Grant Hill 5.00 2.20
L-Card
❑ S3 Grant Hill 5.00 2.20
A-Card
❑ S4 Grant Hill 5.00 2.20
M-Card
❑ S5 Grant Hill 5.00 2.20
!-Card
❑ D1 Grant Hill 5.00 2.20
D-Card
❑ D2 Grant Hill 5.00 2.20
U-Card
❑ D3 Grant Hill 5.00 2.20
N-Card
❑ D4 Grant Hill 5.00 2.20
K-Card
❑ D5 Grant Hill 5.00 2.20
!!!-Card

1995-96 Hoops Grant's All-Rookies

	MINT	NRMT
COMPLETE SET (10)	60.00	27.00
COMMON CARD (AR1-AR10)	1.50	.70
SEMISTARS	2.50	1.10

SER.2 STATED ODDS 1:64 HOBBY/RETAIL

❑ AR1 Cherokee Parks .... 1.50 .70
❑ AR2 Antonio McDyess 10.00 4.50
❑ AR3 Theo Ratliff 2.50 1.10
❑ AR4 Joe Smith 6.00 2.70
❑ AR5 Shawn Respert .... 1.50 .70

❑ AR6 Kevin Garnett	25.00	11.00
❑ AR7 Ed O'Bannon	1.50	.70
❑ AR8 Jerry Stackhouse	6.00	2.70
❑ AR9 Damon Stoudamire	10.00	4.50
❑ AR10 Rasheed Wallace	8.00	3.60

1995-96 Hoops HoopStars

	MINT	NRMT
COMPLETE SET (12)	15.00	6.75
COMMON CARD (HS1-HS12)	.60	.25
SEMISTARS	.75	.35
UNLISTED STARS	1.25	.55

SER.2 STATED ODDS 1:16 HOBBY/RETAIL

❑ HS1 Scottie Pippen	4.00	1.80
❑ HS2 Jim Jackson	.60	.25
❑ HS3 Antonio McDyess	3.00	1.35
❑ HS4 Clyde Drexler	1.25	.55
❑ HS5 Alonzo Mourning	1.25	.55
❑ HS6 Glenn Robinson	1.25	.55
❑ HS7 Patrick Ewing	1.25	.55
❑ HS8 Anfernee Hardaway	4.00	1.80
❑ HS9 Shawn Kemp	2.00	.90
❑ HS10 Karl Malone	2.00	.90
❑ HS11 Juwan Howard	1.25	.55
❑ HS12 Rasheed Wallace	2.50	1.10

1995-96 Hoops Hot List

	MINT	NRMT
COMPLETE SET (10)	50.00	22.00
COMMON CARD (1-10)	1.25	.55
UNLISTED STARS	2.00	.90

SER.2 STATED ODDS 1:32 HOBBY

❑ 1 Michael Jordan	25.00	11.00
❑ 2 Jason Kidd	6.00	2.70
❑ 3 Jamal Mashburn	1.25	.55
❑ 4 Grant Hill	10.00	4.50
❑ 5 Joe Smith	3.00	1.35
❑ 6 Hakeem Olajuwon	3.00	1.35
❑ 7 Glenn Robinson	2.00	.90
❑ 8 Shaquille O'Neal	10.00	4.50
❑ 9 Jerry Stackhouse	3.00	1.35
❑ 10 David Robinson	3.00	1.35

1995-96 Hoops Number Crunchers

	MINT	NRMT
COMPLETE SET (25)	10.00	4.50

*SINGLES: .6X TO 1.5X BASE CARD HI
SER.1 STATED ODDS 1:2 HOBBY/RETAIL

❑ 1 Michael Jordan	5.00	2.20
❑ 2 Shaquille O'Neal	2.00	.90
❑ 3 Grant Hill	2.00	.90
❑ 4 Detlef Schrempf	.25	.11
❑ 5 Kenny Anderson	.25	.11
❑ 6 Anfernee Hardaway	1.25	.55
❑ 7 Latrell Sprewell	.75	.35
❑ 8 Jamal Mashburn	.25	.11
❑ 9 Nick Van Exel	.25	.11
❑ 10 Charles Barkley	.60	.25
❑ 11 Mitch Richmond	.40	.18
❑ 12 David Robinson	.60	.25
❑ 13 Gary Payton	.60	.25
❑ 14 Rod Strickland	.25	.11
❑ 15 Glenn Robinson	.40	.18
❑ 16 Reggie Miller	.40	.18
❑ 17 Karl Malone	.60	.25
❑ 18 Jim Jackson	.15	.07
❑ 19 Clyde Drexler	.40	.18
❑ 20 Glen Rice	.25	.11
❑ 21 Isaiah Rider	.25	.11
❑ 22 Cedric Ceballos	.15	.07
❑ 23 John Stockton	.40	.18
❑ 24 Jason Kidd	1.25	.55
❑ 25 Mookie Blaylock	.15	.07

1995-96 Hoops Power Palette

	MINT	NRMT
COMPLETE SET (10)	60.00	27.00
COMMON CARD (1-10)	2.00	.90

SER.2 STATED ODDS 1:32 RETAIL

❑ 1 Michael Jordan	25.00	11.00
❑ 2 Jason Kidd	6.00	2.70
❑ 3 Grant Hill	10.00	4.50
❑ 4 Joe Smith	3.00	1.35
❑ 5 Hakeem Olajuwon	3.00	1.35
❑ 6 Glenn Robinson	2.00	.90
❑ 7 Anfernee Hardaway	6.00	2.70
❑ 8 Shaquille O'Neal	10.00	4.50
❑ 9 Jerry Stackhouse	3.00	1.35
❑ 10 Charles Barkley	3.00	1.35

1995-96 Hoops SkyView

	MINT	NRMT
COMPLETE SET (10)	100.00	45.00
COMMON CARD (SV1-SV10)	4.00	1.80

SER.2 STATED ODDS 1:480 HOBBY/RETAIL

❑ SV1 Michael Jordan	60.00	27.00
❑ SV2 Jason Kidd	12.00	5.50
❑ SV3 Grant Hill	20.00	9.00
❑ SV4 Joe Smith	6.00	2.70
❑ SV5 Hakeem Olajuwon	6.00	2.70
❑ SV6 Glenn Robinson	4.00	1.80
❑ SV7 Anfernee Hardaway	12.00	5.50
❑ SV8 Shaquille O'Neal	20.00	9.00
❑ SV9 Jerry Stackhouse	6.00	2.70
❑ SV10 Charles Barkley	6.00	2.70

1995-96 Hoops Slamland

	MINT	NRMT
COMPLETE SET (50)	5.00	2.20

*SINGLES: .4X TO 1X BASE CARD HI
ONE PER SER.2 PACK

❑ SL1 Stacey Augmon	.10	.05
❑ SL2 Steve Smith	.15	.07
❑ SL3 Eric Montross	.10	.05
❑ SL4 Dino Radja	.10	.05
❑ SL5 Dell Curry	.10	.05
❑ SL6 Larry Johnson	.15	.07

❑ SL7 Scottie Pippen .75 .35
❑ SL8 Dennis Rodman .50 .23
❑ SL9 Tyrone Hill .10 .05
❑ SL10 Jim Jackson .10 .05
❑ SL11 Jamal Mashburn .15 .07
❑ SL12 Dikembe Mutombo .15 .07
❑ SL13 Joe Dumars .25 .11
❑ SL14 Grant Hill 1.25 .55
❑ SL15 Allan Houston .30 .14
❑ SL16 Donyell Marshall .15 .07
❑ SL17 Latrell Sprewell .50 .23
❑ SL18 Sam Cassell .15 .07
❑ SL19 Hakeem Olajuwon .40 .18
❑ SL20 Reggie Miller .25 .11
❑ SL21 Loy Vaught .10 .05
❑ SL22 Vlade Divac .10 .05
❑ SL23 Eddie Jones .50 .23
❑ SL24 Alonzo Mourning .25 .11
❑ SL25 Kevin Willis .10 .05
❑ SL26 Vin Baker .25 .11
❑ SL27 Glenn Robinson .25 .11
❑ SL28 Tom Gugliotta .15 .07
❑ SL29 Kenny Anderson .15 .07
❑ SL30 Derrick Coleman .15 .07
❑ SL31 Patrick Ewing .25 .11
❑ SL32 John Starks .10 .05
❑ SL33 Dennis Scott .10 .05
❑ SL34 Jerry Stackhouse .75 .35
❑ SL35 Charles Barkley .40 .18
❑ SL36 Kevin Johnson .15 .07
❑ SL37 Danny Manning .15 .07
❑ SL38 Clifford Robinson .10 .05
❑ SL39 Brian Grant .25 .11
❑ SL40 Mitch Richmond .25 .11
❑ SL41 Walt Williams .10 .05
❑ SL42 David Robinson .40 .18
❑ SL43 Gary Payton .40 .18
❑ SL44 Detlef Schrempf .15 .07
❑ SL45 Damon Stoudamire 1.25 .55
❑ SL46 Karl Malone .40 .18
❑ SL47 John Stockton .25 .11
❑ SL48 Bryant Reeves .25 .11
❑ SL49 Juwan Howard .25 .11
❑ SL50 Chris Webber .75 .35

1995-96 Hoops Top Ten

	MINT	NRMT
COMPLETE SET (10)	30.00	13.50
COMMON CARD (AR1-AR10)	1.00	.45
SEMISTARS	1.25	.55

SER.1 STATED ODDS 1:12 HOBBY/RETAIL

❑ AR1 Shaquille O'Neal 6.00 2.70
❑ AR2 Grant Hill 6.00 2.70
❑ AR3 Chris Webber 4.00 1.80
❑ AR4 Jamal Mashburn 1.00 .45
❑ AR5 Anfernee Hardaway 4.00 1.80
❑ AR6 Alonzo Mourning 1.25 .55
❑ AR7 Michael Jordan 15.00 6.75
❑ AR8 Charles Barkley 2.00 .90
❑ AR9 Glenn Robinson 1.25 .55
❑ AR10 Jason Kidd 4.00 1.80

1996-97 Hoops

	MINT	NRMT
COMPLETE SET (350)	30.00	13.50
COMPLETE SERIES 1 (200)	15.00	6.75
COMPLETE SERIES 2 (150)	15.00	6.75
COMMON CARD (1-350)	.10	.05
SEMISTARS	.15	.07
UNLISTED STARS	.25	.11

SUBSET CARDS HALF VALUE OF BASE CARDS
HILL Z-F: SER.1 STATED ODDS 1:360 H/R

❑ 1 Stacey Augmon .10 .05
❑ 2 Mookie Blaylock .10 .05
❑ 3 Alan Henderson .10 .05
❑ 4 Christian Laettner .15 .07
❑ 5 Grant Long .10 .05
❑ 6 Steve Smith .15 .07
❑ 7 Dana Barros .10 .05
❑ 8 Todd Day .10 .05
❑ 9 Rick Fox .10 .05
❑ 10 Eric Montross .10 .05
❑ 11 Dino Radja .10 .05
❑ 12 Eric Williams .10 .05
❑ 13 Kenny Anderson .15 .07
❑ 14 Scott Burrell .10 .05
❑ 15 Dell Curry .10 .05
❑ 16 Matt Geiger .10 .05
❑ 17 Larry Johnson .15 .07
❑ 18 Glen Rice .15 .07
❑ 19 Ron Harper .15 .07
❑ 20 Michael Jordan 3.00 1.35
❑ 21 Steve Kerr .10 .05
❑ 22 Toni Kukoc .30 .14
❑ 23 Luc Longley .10 .05
❑ 24 Scottie Pippen .75 .35
❑ 25 Dennis Rodman .50 .23
❑ 26 Terrell Brandon .15 .07
❑ 27 Danny Ferry .10 .05
❑ 28 Tyrone Hill .10 .05
❑ 29 Chris Mills .10 .05
❑ 30 Bobby Phills .10 .05
❑ 31 Bob Sura .10 .05
❑ 32 Tony Dumas .10 .05
❑ 33 Jim Jackson .10 .05
❑ 34 Popeye Jones .10 .05
❑ 35 Jason Kidd .75 .35
❑ 36 Jamal Mashburn .15 .07
❑ 37 George McCloud .10 .05
❑ 38 Cherokee Parks .10 .05
❑ 39 Mahmoud Abdul-Rauf .10 .05
❑ 40 LaPhonso Ellis .10 .05
❑ 41 Antonio McDyess .40 .18
❑ 42 Dikembe Mutombo .15 .07
❑ 43 Jalen Rose .25 .11
❑ 44 Bryant Stith .10 .05
❑ 45 Joe Dumars .25 .11
❑ 46 Grant Hill 1.25 .55
❑ 47 Allan Houston .25 .11
❑ 48 Lindsey Hunter .10 .05
❑ 49 Terry Mills .10 .05
❑ 50 Theo Ratliff .15 .07
❑ 51 Otis Thorpe .10 .05
❑ 52 B.J. Armstrong .10 .05
❑ 53 Donyell Marshall .10 .05
❑ 54 Chris Mullin .25 .11
❑ 55 Joe Smith .25 .11
❑ 56 Rony Seikaly .10 .05
❑ 57 Latrell Sprewell .50 .23
❑ 58 Mark Bryant .10 .05
❑ 59 Sam Cassell .15 .07
❑ 60 Clyde Drexler .25 .11
❑ 61 Mario Elie .10 .05
❑ 62 Robert Horry .10 .05
❑ 63 Hakeem Olajuwon .40 .18
❑ 64 Travis Best .10 .05
❑ 65 Antonio Davis .10 .05
❑ 66 Mark Jackson .10 .05
❑ 67 Derrick McKey .10 .05
❑ 68 Reggie Miller .25 .11
❑ 69 Rik Smits .10 .05
❑ 70 Brent Barry .10 .05
❑ 71 Terry Dehere .10 .05
❑ 72 Pooh Richardson .10 .05
❑ 73 Rodney Rogers .10 .05
❑ 74 Loy Vaught .10 .05
❑ 75 Brian Williams .10 .05
❑ 76 Elden Campbell .10 .05
❑ 77 Cedric Ceballos .10 .05
❑ 78 Vlade Divac .10 .05
❑ 79 Eddie Jones .50 .23
❑ 80 Anthony Peeler .10 .05
❑ 81 Nick Van Exel .15 .07
❑ 82 Sasha Danilovic .10 .05
❑ 83 Tim Hardaway .25 .11
❑ 84 Alonzo Mourning .25 .11
❑ 85 Kurt Thomas .10 .05
❑ 86 Walt Williams .10 .05
❑ 87 Vin Baker .15 .07
❑ 88 Sherman Douglas .10 .05
❑ 89 Johnny Newman .10 .05
❑ 90 Shawn Respert .10 .05
❑ 91 Glenn Robinson .25 .11
❑ 92 Kevin Garnett 1.50 .70
❑ 93 Tom Gugliotta .15 .07
❑ 94 Andrew Lang .10 .05
❑ 95 Sam Mitchell .10 .05
❑ 96 Isaiah Rider .15 .07
❑ 97 Shawn Bradley .10 .05
❑ 98 P.J. Brown .10 .05
❑ 99 Chris Childs .10 .05
❑ 100 Armon Gilliam .10 .05
❑ 101 Ed O'Bannon .10 .05
❑ 102 Jayson Williams .15 .07
❑ 103 Hubert Davis .10 .05
❑ 104 Patrick Ewing .25 .11
❑ 105 Anthony Mason .15 .07
❑ 106 Charles Oakley .10 .05
❑ 107 John Starks .10 .05
❑ 108 Charlie Ward .10 .05
❑ 109 Nick Anderson .10 .05
❑ 110 Horace Grant .15 .07
❑ 111 Anfernee Hardaway .75 .35
❑ 112 Shaquille O'Neal 1.25 .55
❑ 113 Dennis Scott .10 .05
❑ 114 Brian Shaw .10 .05
❑ 115 Derrick Coleman .15 .07
❑ 116 Vernon Maxwell .10 .05
❑ 117 Trevor Ruffin .10 .05
❑ 118 Jerry Stackhouse .25 .11
❑ 119 Clarence Weatherspoon .10 .05
❑ 120 Charles Barkley .40 .18
❑ 121 Michael Finley .30 .14
❑ 122 A.C. Green .15 .07
❑ 123 Kevin Johnson .15 .07
❑ 124 Danny Manning .15 .07
❑ 125 Wesley Person .10 .05
❑ 126 John Williams .10 .05
❑ 127 Harvey Grant .10 .05
❑ 128 Aaron McKie .10 .05
❑ 129 Clifford Robinson .10 .05
❑ 130 Arvydas Sabonis .15 .07
❑ 131 Rod Strickland .15 .07
❑ 132 Gary Trent .10 .05
❑ 133 Tyus Edney .10 .05
❑ 134 Brian Grant .25 .11
❑ 135 Billy Owens .10 .05
❑ 136 Olden Polynice .10 .05
❑ 137 Mitch Richmond .25 .11
❑ 138 Corliss Williamson .10 .05
❑ 139 Vinny Del Negro .10 .05
❑ 140 Sean Elliott .10 .05
❑ 141 Avery Johnson .10 .05

❑ 142 Chuck Person .10 .05
❑ 143 David Robinson .40 .18
❑ 144 Charles Smith .10 .05
❑ 145 Sherrell Ford .10 .05
❑ 146 Hersey Hawkins .15 .07
❑ 147 Shawn Kemp .40 .18
❑ 148 Nate McMillan .10 .05
❑ 149 Gary Payton .40 .18
❑ 150 Detlef Schrempf .15 .07
❑ 151 Oliver Miller .10 .05
❑ 152 Tracy Murray .10 .05
❑ 153 Carlos Rogers .10 .05
❑ 154 Damon Stoudamire .40 .18
❑ 155 Zan Tabak .10 .05
❑ 156 Sharone Wright .10 .05
❑ 157 Antoine Carr .10 .05
❑ 158 Jeff Hornacek .15 .07
❑ 159 Adam Keefe .10 .05
❑ 160 Karl Malone .40 .18
❑ 161 Chris Morris .10 .05
❑ 162 John Stockton .25 .11
❑ 163 Greg Anthony .10 .05
❑ 164 Blue Edwards .10 .05
❑ 165 Chris King .10 .05
❑ 166 Lawrence Moten .10 .05
❑ 167 Bryant Reeves .10 .05
❑ 168 Byron Scott .10 .05
❑ 169 Calbert Cheaney .10 .05
❑ 170 Juwan Howard .15 .07
❑ 171 Tim Legler .10 .05
❑ 172 Gheorghe Muresan .10 .05
❑ 173 Rasheed Wallace .30 .14
❑ 174 Chris Webber .75 .35
❑ 175 Steve Smith BF .10 .05
❑ 176 Michael Jordan BF 1.50 .70
❑ 177 Scottie Pippen BF .40 .18
❑ 178 Dennis Rodman BF .25 .11
❑ 179 Allan Houston BF .15 .07
❑ 180 Hakeem Olajuwon BF .25 .11
❑ 181 Patrick Ewing BF .15 .07
❑ 182 Anfernee Hardaway BF .50 .23
❑ 183 Shaquille O'Neal BF .50 .23
❑ 184 Charles Barkley BF .25 .11
❑ 185 Arvydas Sabonis BF .10 .05
❑ 186 David Robinson BF .25 .11
❑ 187 Shawn Kemp BF .25 .11
❑ 188 Gary Payton BF .25 .11
❑ 189 Karl Malone BF .25 .11
❑ 190 Kenny Anderson PLA .10 .05
❑ 191 Toni Kukoc PLA .25 .11
❑ 192 Brent Barry PLA .10 .05
❑ 193 Cedric Ceballos PLA .10 .05
❑ 194 Shawn Bradley PLA .10 .05
❑ 195 Charles Oakley PLA .10 .05
❑ 196 Dennis Scott PLA .10 .05
❑ 197 Clifford Robinson PLA .10 .05
❑ 198 Mitch Richmond PLA .15 .07
❑ 199 Checklist .10 .05
❑ 200 Checklist .10 .05
❑ 201 Dikembe Mutombo .15 .07
❑ 202 Dee Brown .10 .05
❑ 203 David Wesley .10 .05
❑ 204 Vlade Divac .10 .05
❑ 205 Anthony Mason .15 .07
❑ 206 Chris Gatling .10 .05
❑ 207 Eric Montross .10 .05
❑ 208 Ervin Johnson .10 .05
❑ 209 Stacey Augmon .10 .05
❑ 210 Joe Dumars .25 .11
❑ 211 Grant Hill 1.25 .55
❑ 212 Charles Barkley .40 .18
❑ 213 Jalen Rose .25 .11
❑ 214 Lamond Murray .10 .05
❑ 215 Shaquille O'Neal 1.25 .55
❑ 216 P.J. Brown .10 .05
❑ 217 Dan Majerle .15 .07
❑ 218 Armon Gilliam .10 .05
❑ 219 Andrew Lang .10 .05
❑ 220 Kevin Garnett 1.50 .70
❑ 221 Tom Gugliotta .15 .07
❑ 222 Cherokee Parks .10 .05
❑ 223 Doug West .10 .05
❑ 224 Kendall Gill .15 .07
❑ 225 Robert Pack .10 .05
❑ 226 Allan Houston .25 .11
❑ 227 Larry Johnson .15 .07
❑ 228 Rony Seikaly .10 .05
❑ 229 Gerald Wilkins .10 .05
❑ 230 Michael Cage .10 .05
❑ 231 Lucious Harris .10 .05
❑ 232 Sam Cassell .15 .07
❑ 233 Robert Horry .10 .05
❑ 234 Kenny Anderson .15 .07
❑ 235 Isaiah Rider .15 .07
❑ 236 Rasheed Wallace .30 .14
❑ 237 Mahmoud Abdul-Rauf .10 .05
❑ 238 Vernon Maxwell .10 .05
❑ 239 Dominique Wilkins .25 .11
❑ 240 Jim McIlvaine .10 .05
❑ 241 Hubert Davis .10 .05
❑ 242 Popeye Jones .10 .05
❑ 243 Walt Williams .10 .05
❑ 244 Karl Malone .40 .18
❑ 245 John Stockton .25 .11
❑ 246 Anthony Peeler .10 .05
❑ 247 Tracy Murray .10 .05
❑ 248 Rod Strickland .15 .07
❑ 249 Lenny Wilkens CO .15 .07
❑ 250 M.L. Carr CO .10 .05
❑ 251 Dave Cowens CO .10 .05
❑ 252 Phil Jackson CO .15 .07
❑ 253 Mike Fratello CO .15 .07
❑ 254 Jim Cleamons CO .10 .05
❑ 255 Dick Motta CO .10 .05
❑ 256 Doug Collins CO .10 .05
❑ 257 Rick Adelman CO .10 .05
❑ 258 Rudy Tomjanovich CO .15 .07
❑ 259 Larry Brown CO .15 .07
❑ 260 Bill Fitch CO .10 .05
❑ 261 Del Harris CO .10 .05
❑ 262 Pat Riley CO .15 .07
❑ 263 Chris Ford CO .10 .05
❑ 264 Flip Saunders CO .10 .05
❑ 265 John Calipari CO .15 .07
❑ 266 Jeff Van Gundy CO .10 .05
❑ 267 Brian Hill CO .10 .05
❑ 268 Johnny Davis CO .10 .05
❑ 269 Danny Ainge CO .15 .07
❑ 270 P.J. Carlesimo CO .10 .05
❑ 271 Garry St. Jean CO .10 .05
❑ 272 Bob Hill CO .10 .05
❑ 273 George Karl CO .15 .07
❑ 274 Darrell Walker CO .10 .05
❑ 275 Jerry Sloan CO .15 .07
❑ 276 Brian Winters CO .10 .05
❑ 277 Jim Lynam CO .10 .05
❑ 278 Shareef Abdur-Rahim RC 1.50 .70
❑ 279 Ray Allen RC 1.00 .45
❑ 280 Shandon Anderson RC .30 .14
❑ 281 Kobe Bryant RC 8.00 3.60
❑ 282 Marcus Camby RC .75 .35
❑ 283 Erick Dampier RC .15 .07
❑ 284 Emanual Davis RC .10 .05
❑ 285 Tony Delk RC .15 .07
❑ 286 Brian Evans RC .10 .05
❑ 287 Derek Fisher RC .40 .18
❑ 288 Todd Fuller RC .10 .05
❑ 289 Dean Garrett RC .10 .05
❑ 290 Reggie Geary RC .10 .05
❑ 291 Darvin Ham RC .10 .05
❑ 292 Othella Harrington RC .25 .11
❑ 293 Shane Heal RC .10 .05
❑ 294 Mark Hendrickson RC .10 .05
❑ 295 Allen Iverson RC 2.50 1.10
❑ 296 Dontae' Jones RC .10 .05
❑ 297 Kerry Kittles RC .50 .23
❑ 298 Priest Lauderdale RC .10 .05
❑ 299 Matt Maloney RC .15 .07
❑ 300 Stephon Marbury RC 1.50 .70
❑ 301 Walter McCarty RC .10 .05
❑ 302 Jeff McInnis RC .10 .05
❑ 303 Martin Muursepp RC .10 .05
❑ 304 Steve Nash RC .15 .07
❑ 305 Moochie Norris RC .15 .07
❑ 306 Jermaine O'Neal RC .50 .23
❑ 307 Vitaly Potapenko RC .10 .05
❑ 308 Virginius Praskevicius RC .10 .05
❑ 309 Roy Rogers RC .10 .05
❑ 310 Malik Rose RC .15 .07
❑ 311 James Scott RC .10 .05
❑ 312 Antoine Walker RC 1.00 .45
❑ 313 Samaki Walker RC .10 .05
❑ 314 Ben Wallace RC .10 .05
❑ 315 John Wallace RC .25 .11
❑ 316 Jerome Williams RC .40 .18
❑ 317 Lorenzen Wright RC .15 .07
❑ 318 Charles Barkley ST .25 .11
❑ 319 Derrick Coleman ST .10 .05
❑ 320 Michael Finley ST .25 .11
❑ 321 Stephon Marbury ST 1.25 .55
❑ 322 Reggie Miller ST .15 .07
❑ 323 Alonzo Mourning ST .15 .07
❑ 324 Shaquille O'Neal ST .50 .23
❑ 325 Gary Payton ST .25 .11
❑ 326 Dennis Rodman ST .25 .11
❑ 327 Damon Stoudamire ST .25 .11
❑ 328 Vin Baker CBG .10 .05
❑ 329 Clyde Drexler CBG .15 .07
❑ 330 Patrick Ewing CBG .15 .07
❑ 331 Anfernee Hardaway CBG .50 .23
❑ 332 Grant Hill CBG .75 .35
❑ 333 Juwan Howard CBG .10 .05
❑ 334 Larry Johnson CBG .10 .05
❑ 335 Michael Jordan CBG 1.50 .70
❑ 336 Shawn Kemp CBG .25 .11
❑ 337 Jason Kidd CBG .25 .11
❑ 338 Karl Malone CBG .25 .11
❑ 339 Reggie Miller CBG .15 .07
❑ 340 Hakeem Olajuwon CBG .25 .11
❑ 341 Scottie Pippen CBG .40 .18
❑ 342 Mitch Richmond CBG .15 .07
❑ 343 David Robinson CBG .25 .11
UER back David Robininson
❑ 344 Dennis Rodman CBG .25 .11
❑ 345 Joe Smith CBG .15 .07
❑ 346 Jerry Stackhouse CBG .15 .07
❑ 347 John Stockton CBG .15 .07
❑ 348 Jerry Stackhouse BG .15 .07
❑ 349 Checklist .10 .05
201-350/inserts
❑ 350 Checklist (inserts) .10 .05
❑ NNO Grant Hill 5.00 2.20
Jerry Stackhouse Promo
❑ NNO G.Hill Z-Force Preview 20.00 9.00

1996-97 Hoops Silver

	MINT	NRMT
COMPLETE SET (98)	50.00	22.00
COMMON CARD (1-98)	.30	.14

*SILVER: 1.5X TO 3X BASE CARD HI
ONE PER SPECIAL SER.1 RETAIL PACK

1996-97 Hoops Fly With

	MINT	NRMT
COMPLETE SET (10)	20.00	9.00
COMMON CARD (1-10)	2.50	1.10

SER.2 STATED ODDS 1:24 RETAIL

❑ 1 Charles Barkley 4.00 1.80
❑ 2 Juwan Howard 2.50 1.10
❑ 3 Jason Kidd 8.00 3.60
❑ 4 Alonzo Mourning 2.50 1.10
❑ 5 Gary Payton 4.00 1.80
❑ 6 David Robinson 4.00 1.80
❑ 7 Dennis Rodman 5.00 2.20
❑ 8 Joe Smith 2.50 1.10
❑ 9 Jerry Stackhouse 2.50 1.10
❑ 10 Damon Stoudamire 4.00 1.80

1996-97 Hoops Grant's All-Rookies

	MINT	NRMT
COMPLETE SET (11)	200.00	90.00
COMMON CARD (1-11)	5.00	2.20
SEMISTARS	8.00	3.60

SER.2 STATED ODDS 1:360 HOBBY/RETAIL
STATED PRINT RUN 996 SETS

	MINT	NRMT
❑ 1 Shareef Abdur-Rahim	25.00	11.00
❑ 2 Ray Allen	15.00	6.75
❑ 3 Kobe Bryant	60.00	27.00
❑ 4 Marcus Camby	12.00	5.50
❑ 5 Grant Hill	25.00	11.00
❑ 6 Allen Iverson	40.00	18.00
❑ 7 Kerry Kittles	8.00	3.60
❑ 8 Stephon Marbury	25.00	11.00
❑ 9 Antoine Walker	15.00	6.75
❑ 10 Samaki Walker	5.00	2.20
❑ 11 Lorenzen Wright	5.00	2.20

1996-97 Hoops Head to Head

	MINT	NRMT
COMPLETE SET (10)	40.00	18.00
COMMON PAIR (HH1-HH10)	1.50	.70

SER.1 STATED ODDS 1:24 HOBBY/RETAIL

	MINT	NRMT
❑ HH1 Larry Johnson Glenn Rice	1.50	.70
❑ HH2 Michael Jordan Scottie Pippen	20.00	9.00
❑ HH3 Jason Kidd Grant Hill	8.00	3.60
❑ HH4 Clyde Drexler Hakeem Olajuwon	4.00	1.80
❑ HH5 Vin Baker Glenn Robinson	1.50	.70
❑ HH6 Anfernee Hardaway Shaquille O'Neal	8.00	3.60
❑ HH7 Antonio McDyess Jerry Stackhouse	3.00	1.35
❑ HH8 Sean Elliott David Robinson	2.50	1.10
❑ HH9 Joe Smith Damon Stoudamire	4.00	1.80
❑ HH10 Karl Malone John Stockton	2.50	1.10

1996-97 Hoops HIPnotized

	MINT	NRMT
COMPLETE SET (20)	12.00	5.50
COMMON CARD (H1-H20)	.30	.14
SEMISTARS	.50	.23
UNLISTED STARS	.75	.35

SER.1 STATED ODDS 1:4 HOBBY/RETAIL

	MINT	NRMT
❑ H1 Steve Smith	.50	.23
❑ H2 Dana Barros	.30	.14
❑ H3 Larry Johnson	.50	.23
❑ H4 Dennis Rodman	1.50	.70
❑ H5 Terrell Brandon	.50	.23
❑ H6 Jason Kidd	2.50	1.10
❑ H7 Grant Hill	4.00	1.80
❑ H8 Clyde Drexler	.75	.35
❑ H9 Reggie Miller	.75	.35
❑ H10 Alonzo Mourning	.75	.35
❑ H11 Glenn Robinson	.75	.35
❑ H12 Patrick Ewing	.75	.35
❑ H13 Shaquille O'Neal	4.00	1.80
❑ H14 Jerry Stackhouse	.75	.35
❑ H15 Charles Barkley	1.25	.55
❑ H16 Clifford Robinson	.30	.14
❑ H17 Mitch Richmond	.75	.35
❑ H18 David Robinson	1.25	.55
❑ H19 Gary Payton	1.25	.55
❑ H20 Juwan Howard	.50	.23

1996-97 Hoops Hot List

	MINT	NRMT
COMPLETE SET (20)	150.00	70.00
COMMON CARD (1-20)	2.00	.90
SEMISTARS	2.50	1.10
UNLISTED STARS	4.00	1.80

SER.2 STATED ODDS 1:48 HOBBY

	MINT	NRMT
❑ 1 Vin Baker	2.50	1.10
❑ 2 Patrick Ewing	4.00	1.80
❑ 3 Michael Finley	5.00	2.20
❑ 4 Kevin Garnett	25.00	11.00
❑ 5 Anfernee Hardaway	12.00	5.50
❑ 6 Grant Hill	20.00	9.00
❑ 7 Allan Houston	4.00	1.80
❑ 8 Michael Jordan	50.00	22.00
❑ 9 Shawn Kemp	6.00	2.70
❑ 10 Christian Laettner	2.50	1.10
❑ 11 Karl Malone	6.00	2.70
❑ 12 Antonio McDyess	6.00	2.70
❑ 13 Reggie Miller	4.00	1.80
❑ 14 Hakeem Olajuwon	6.00	2.70
❑ 15 Shaquille O'Neal	20.00	9.00
❑ 16 Scottie Pippen	12.00	5.50
❑ 17 Mitch Richmond	4.00	1.80
❑ 18 Isaiah Rider	2.50	1.10
❑ 19 Rod Strickland	2.00	.90
❑ 20 Chris Webber	12.00	5.50

1996-97 Hoops Rookie Headliners

	MINT	NRMT
COMPLETE SET (10)	40.00	18.00
COMMON CARD (1-10)	1.25	.55
SEMISTARS	1.50	.70
UNLISTED STARS	4.00	1.80

SER.1 STATED ODDS 1:72 HOBBY

	MINT	NRMT
❑ 1 Antonio McDyess	6.00	2.70
❑ 2 Joe Smith	4.00	1.80
❑ 3 Brent Barry	1.25	.55
❑ 4 Kevin Garnett	25.00	11.00
❑ 5 Jerry Stackhouse	4.00	1.80
❑ 6 Michael Finley	5.00	2.20
❑ 7 Arvydas Sabonis	1.50	.70
❑ 8 Tyus Edney	1.25	.55
❑ 9 Damon Stoudamire	6.00	2.70
❑ 10 Bryant Reeves	1.25	.55

1996-97 Hoops Rookies

	MINT	NRMT
COMPLETE SET (30)	40.00	18.00
COMMON CARD (1-30)	.50	.23
SEMISTARS	1.00	.45
UNLISTED STARS	1.50	.70

SER.2 STATED ODDS 1:6 HOBBY/RETAIL

	MINT	NRMT
❑ 1 Shareef Abdur-Rahim	5.00	2.20
❑ 2 Ray Allen	3.00	1.35
❑ 3 Kobe Bryant	15.00	6.75
❑ 4 Marcus Camby	2.50	1.10
❑ 5 Erick Dampier	.50	.23
❑ 6 Emanual Davis	.50	.23
❑ 7 Tony Delk	.50	.23

❑ 8 Brian Evans	.50	.23
❑ 9 Derek Fisher	1.50	.70
❑ 10 Todd Fuller	.50	.23
❑ 11 Othella Harrington	1.00	.45
❑ 12 Allen Iverson	8.00	3.60
❑ 13 Dontae' Jones	.50	.23
❑ 14 Kerry Kittles	1.50	.70
❑ 15 Priest Lauderdale	.50	.23
❑ 16 Matt Maloney	.50	.23
❑ 17 Stephon Marbury	5.00	2.20
❑ 18 Walter McCarty	.50	.23
❑ 19 Jeff McInnis	.50	.23
❑ 20 Martin Muursepp	.50	.23
❑ 21 Steve Nash	.50	.23
❑ 22 Moochie Norris	.50	.23
❑ 23 Jermaine O'Neal	1.50	.70
❑ 24 Vitaly Potapenko	.50	.23
❑ 25 Roy Rogers	.50	.23
❑ 26 Antoine Walker	3.00	1.35
❑ 27 Samaki Walker	.50	.23
❑ 28 John Wallace	1.00	.45
❑ 29 Jerome Williams	1.50	.70
❑ 30 Lorenzen Wright	.50	.23

1996-97 Hoops Starting Five

	MINT	NRMT
COMPLETE SET (29)	30.00	13.50
COMMON CARD (1-29)	.50	.23
SEMISTARS	.75	.35
UNLISTED STARS	1.25	.55

SER.2 STATED ODDS 1:12 HOBBY/RETAIL

❑ 1 Mookie Blaylock	.75	.35
Christian Laettner		
Dikembe Mutombo		
Ken Norman		
Steve Smith		
Atlanta Hawks		
❑ 2 Dana Barros	.50	.23
Dee Brown		
Todd Day		
Rick Fox		
Dino Radja		
Boston Celtics		
❑ 3 Tyrone Bogues	.75	.35
Dell Curry		
Vlade Divac		
Anthony Mason		
Glen Rice		
Charlotte Hornets		
❑ 4 Michael Jordan	10.00	4.50
Toni Kukoc		
Luc Longley		
Scottie Pippen		
Dennis Rodman		
Chicago Bulls		
❑ 5 Terrell Brandon	.75	.35
Tyrone Hill		
Chris Mills		
Bobby Phills		
Vitaly Potapenko		
Cleveland Cavaliers		
❑ 6 Chris Gatling	2.50	1.10
Jim Jackson		
Jason Kidd		
Jamal Mashburn		
Oliver Miller		
Dallas Mavericks		
❑ 7 LaPhonso Ellis	1.50	.70
Mark Jackson		
Ervin Johnson		
Antonio McDyess		
Bryant Stith		
Denver Nuggets		
❑ 8 Stacey Augmon	6.00	2.70
Joe Dumars		
Grant Hill		
Lindsey Hunter		
Otis Thorpe		
Detroit Pistons		
❑ 9 Chris Mullin	1.50	.70
Mark Price		
Felton Spencer		
Joe Smith		
Latrell Sprewell		
Golden State Warriors		
❑ 10 Charles Barkley	1.50	.70
Clyde Drexler		
Hakeem Olajuwon		
Brent Price		
Kevin Willis		
Houston Rockets		
❑ 11 Dale Davis	1.25	.55
Duane Ferrell		
Reggie Miller		
Jalen Rose		
Rik Smits		
Indiana Pacers		
❑ 12 Terry Dehere	.50	.23
Charles Outlaw		
Pooh Richardson		
Rodney Rogers		
Loy Vaught		
Los Angeles Clippers		
❑ 13 Elden Campbell	6.00	2.70
Cedric Ceballos		
Eddie Jones		
Shaquille O'Neal		
Nick Van Exel		
Los Angeles Lakers		
❑ 14 P.J. Brown	1.25	.55
Tim Hardaway		
Dan Majerle		
Alonzo Mourning		
Kurt Thomas		
Miami Heat		
❑ 15 Ray Allen	1.50	.70
Vin Baker		
Sherman Douglas		
Andrew Lang		
Glenn Robinson		
Milwaukee Bucks		
❑ 16 Kevin Garnett	4.00	1.80
Tom Gugliotta		
Stephon Marbury		
Cherokee Parks		
James Robinson		
Minnesota Timberwolves		
❑ 17 Shawn Bradley	.50	.23
Kendall Gill		
Ed O'Bannon		
Khalid Reeves		
Jayson Williams		
New Jersey Nets		
❑ 18 Patrick Ewing	1.25	.55
Allan Houston		
Larry Johnson		
Charles Oakley		
John Starks		
New York Knicks		
❑ 19 Nick Anderson	4.00	1.80
Horace Grant		
Anfernee Hardaway		
Dennis Scott		
Rony Seikaly		
Orlando Magic		
❑ 20 Michael Cage	2.00	.90
Derrick Coleman		
Allen Iverson		
Jerry Stackhouse		
Clarence Weatherspoon		
Philadelphia 76'ers		
❑ 21 Sam Cassell	.75	.35
Michael Finley		
Robert Horry		
Kevin Johnson		
Danny Manning		
Phoenix Suns		
❑ 22 Kenny Anderson	.50	.23
Isaiah Rider		
Clifford Robinson		
Arvydas Sabonis		
Rasheed Wallace		
Portland Trail Blazers		
❑ 23 Mahmoud Abdul-Rauf	.50	.23
Brian Grant		
Billy Owens		
Olden Polynice		
Mitch Richmond		
Sacramento Kings		
❑ 24 Avery Johnson	1.50	.70
Vernon Maxwell		
David Robinson		
Charles Smith		
Dominique Wilkins		
San Antonio Spurs		
❑ 25 Hersey Hawkins	2.00	.90
Shawn Kemp		
Gary Payton		
Sam Perkins		
Detlef Schrempf		
Seattle Supersonics		
❑ 26 Marcus Camby	1.50	.70
Hubert Davis		
Popeye Jones		
Damon Stoudamire		
Walt Williams		
Toronto Raptors		
❑ 27 Jeff Hornacek	1.50	.70
Adam Keefe		
Karl Malone		
Greg Ostertag		
John Stockton		
Utah Jazz		
❑ 28 Shareef Abdur-Rahim	4.00	1.80
George Lynch		
Lee Mayberry		
Anthony Peeler		
Bryant Reeves		
Vancouver Grizzlies		
❑ 29 Calbert Cheaney	1.25	.55
Juwan Howard		
Gheorghe Muresan		
Rod Strickland		
Chris Webber		
Washington Bullets		

1996-97 Hoops Superfeats

	MINT	NRMT
COMPLETE SET (10)	80.00	36.00
COMMON CARD (1-10)	2.00	.90
SEMISTARS	3.00	1.35

SER.1 STATED ODDS 1:36 RETAIL

❑ 1 Michael Jordan	60.00	27.00
❑ 2 Jason Kidd	10.00	4.50
❑ 3 Grant Hill	15.00	6.75

	Player	MINT	NRMT
❑ 4	Hakeem Olajuwon	5.00	2.20
❑ 5	Alonzo Mourning	3.00	1.35
❑ 6	Anthony Mason	2.00	.90
❑ 7	Anfernee Hardaway	10.00	4.50
❑ 8	Jerry Stackhouse	3.00	1.35
❑ 9	Shawn Kemp	5.00	2.20
❑ 10	Damon Stoudamire	5.00	2.20

1997-98 Hoops

	MINT	NRMT
COMPLETE SET (330)	30.00	13.50
COMPLETE SERIES 1 (165)	12.00	5.50
COMPLETE SERIES 2 (165)	18.00	8.00
COMMON CARD (1-330)	.10	.05
SEMISTARS	.15	.07
UNLISTED STARS	.25	.11

	Player	MINT	NRMT
❑ 1	Michael Jordan LL	1.50	.70
❑ 2	Dennis Rodman LL	.25	.11
❑ 3	Mark Jackson LL	.10	.05
❑ 4	Shawn Bradley LL	.10	.05
❑ 5	Glen Rice LL	.10	.05
❑ 6	Mookie Blaylock LL	.10	.05
❑ 7	Gheorghe Muresan LL	.10	.05
❑ 8	Mark Price LL	.10	.05
❑ 9	Tyrone Corbin	.10	.05
❑ 10	Christian Laettner	.15	.07
❑ 11	Priest Lauderdale	.10	.05
❑ 12	Dikembe Mutombo	.15	.07
❑ 13	Steve Smith	.15	.07
❑ 14	Todd Day	.10	.05
❑ 15	Rick Fox	.10	.05
❑ 16	Brett Szabo	.10	.05
❑ 17	Antoine Walker	.50	.23
❑ 18	David Wesley	.10	.05
❑ 19	Muggsy Bogues	.10	.05
❑ 20	Dell Curry	.10	.05
❑ 21	Tony Delk	.10	.05
❑ 22	Anthony Mason	.15	.07
❑ 23	Glen Rice	.15	.07
❑ 24	Malik Rose	.10	.05
❑ 25	Steve Kerr	.10	.05
❑ 26	Toni Kukoc	.30	.14
❑ 27	Luc Longley	.10	.05
❑ 28	Robert Parish	.15	.07
❑ 29	Scottie Pippen	.75	.35
❑ 30	Dennis Rodman	.50	.23
❑ 31	Terrell Brandon	.15	.07
❑ 32	Danny Ferry	.10	.05
❑ 33	Tyrone Hill	.10	.05
❑ 34	Bobby Phills	.10	.05
❑ 35	Vitaly Potapenko	.10	.05
❑ 36	Shawn Bradley	.10	.05
❑ 37	Sasha Danilovic	.10	.05
❑ 38	Derek Harper	.10	.05
❑ 39	Martin Muursepp	.10	.05
❑ 40	Robert Pack	.10	.05
❑ 41	Khalid Reeves	.10	.05
❑ 42	Vincent Askew	.10	.05
❑ 43	Dale Ellis	.10	.05
❑ 44	LaPhonso Ellis	.10	.05
❑ 45	Antonio McDyess	.30	.14
❑ 46	Bryant Stith	.10	.05
❑ 47	Joe Dumars	.25	.11
❑ 48	Grant Hill	1.25	.55
❑ 49	Lindsey Hunter	.10	.05
❑ 50	Aaron McKie	.10	.05
❑ 51	Theo Ratliff	.10	.05
❑ 52	Scott Burrell	.10	.05
❑ 53	Todd Fuller	.10	.05
❑ 54	Chris Mullin	.25	.11
❑ 55	Mark Price	.10	.05
❑ 56	Joe Smith	.15	.07
❑ 57	Latrell Sprewell	.50	.23
❑ 58	Clyde Drexler	.25	.11
❑ 59	Mario Elie	.10	.05
❑ 60	Othella Harrington	.10	.05
❑ 61	Matt Maloney	.10	.05
❑ 62	Hakeem Olajuwon	.40	.18
❑ 63	Kevin Willis	.10	.05
❑ 64	Travis Best	.10	.05
❑ 65	Erick Dampier	.10	.05
❑ 66	Antonio Davis	.10	.05
❑ 67	Dale Davis	.10	.05
❑ 68	Mark Jackson	.10	.05
❑ 69	Reggie Miller	.25	.11
❑ 70	Brent Barry	.10	.05
❑ 71	Darrick Martin	.10	.05
❑ 72	Charles Outlaw	.10	.05
❑ 73	Loy Vaught	.10	.05
❑ 74	Lorenzen Wright	.10	.05
❑ 75	Kobe Bryant	2.00	.90
❑ 76	Derek Fisher	.10	.05
❑ 77	Robert Horry	.10	.05
❑ 78	Eddie Jones	.50	.23
❑ 79	Travis Knight	.10	.05
❑ 80	George McCloud	.10	.05
❑ 81	Shaquille O'Neal	1.25	.55
❑ 82	P.J. Brown	.10	.05
❑ 83	Tim Hardaway	.25	.11
❑ 84	Voshon Lenard	.10	.05
❑ 85	Jamal Mashburn	.15	.07
❑ 86	Alonzo Mourning	.25	.11
❑ 87	Ray Allen	.40	.18
❑ 88	Vin Baker	.15	.07
❑ 89	Sherman Douglas	.10	.05
❑ 90	Armon Gilliam	.10	.05
❑ 91	Glenn Robinson	.15	.07
❑ 92	Kevin Garnett	1.50	.70
❑ 93	Dean Garrett	.10	.05
❑ 94	Tom Gugliotta	.15	.07
❑ 95	Stephon Marbury	.75	.35
❑ 96	Doug West	.10	.05
❑ 97	Chris Gatling	.10	.05
❑ 98	Kendall Gill	.15	.07
❑ 99	Kerry Kittles	.25	.11
❑ 100	Jayson Williams	.15	.07
❑ 101	Chris Childs	.10	.05
❑ 102	Patrick Ewing	.25	.11
❑ 103	Allan Houston	.25	.11
❑ 104	Larry Johnson	.15	.07
❑ 105	Charles Oakley	.10	.05
❑ 106	John Starks	.10	.05
❑ 107	John Wallace	.10	.05
❑ 108	Nick Anderson	.10	.05
❑ 109	Horace Grant	.15	.07
❑ 110	Anfernee Hardaway	.75	.35
❑ 111	Rony Seikaly	.10	.05
❑ 112	Derek Strong	.10	.05
❑ 113	Derrick Coleman	.15	.07
❑ 114	Allen Iverson	1.25	.55
❑ 115	Doug Overton	.10	.05
❑ 116	Jerry Stackhouse	.15	.07
❑ 117	Rex Walters	.10	.05
❑ 118	Cedric Ceballos	.10	.05
❑ 119	Kevin Johnson	.15	.07
❑ 120	Jason Kidd	.75	.35
❑ 121	Steve Nash	.10	.05
❑ 122	Wesley Person	.10	.05
❑ 123	Kenny Anderson	.15	.07
❑ 124	Jermaine O'Neal	.15	.07
❑ 125	Isaiah Rider	.15	.07
❑ 126	Arvydas Sabonis	.15	.07
❑ 127	Gary Trent	.10	.05
❑ 128	Tyus Edney	.10	.05
❑ 129	Brian Grant	.15	.07
❑ 130	Olden Polynice	.10	.05
❑ 131	Mitch Richmond	.25	.11
❑ 132	Corliss Williamson	.10	.05
❑ 133	Vinny Del Negro	.10	.05
❑ 134	Sean Elliott	.10	.05
❑ 135	Avery Johnson	.10	.05
❑ 136	Will Perdue	.10	.05
❑ 137	Dominique Wilkins	.25	.11
❑ 138	Craig Ehlo	.10	.05
❑ 139	Hersey Hawkins	.15	.07
❑ 140	Shawn Kemp	.40	.18
❑ 141	Jim McIlvaine	.10	.05
❑ 142	Sam Perkins	.15	.07
❑ 143	Detlef Schrempf	.15	.07
❑ 144	Marcus Camby	.30	.14
❑ 145	Doug Christie	.10	.05
❑ 146	Popeye Jones	.10	.05
❑ 147	Damon Stoudamire	.30	.14
❑ 148	Walt Williams	.10	.05
❑ 149	Jeff Hornacek	.15	.07
❑ 150	Karl Malone	.40	.18
❑ 151	Greg Ostertag	.10	.05
❑ 152	Bryon Russell	.10	.05
❑ 153	John Stockton	.25	.11
❑ 154	Shareef Abdur-Rahim	.75	.35
❑ 155	Greg Anthony	.10	.05
❑ 156	Anthony Peeler	.10	.05
❑ 157	Bryant Reeves	.10	.05
❑ 158	Roy Rogers	.10	.05
❑ 159	Calbert Cheaney	.10	.05
❑ 160	Juwan Howard	.15	.07
❑ 161	Gheorghe Muresan	.10	.05
❑ 162	Rod Strickland	.15	.07
❑ 163	Chris Webber	.75	.35
❑ 164	Checklist	.10	.05
❑ 165	Checklist	.10	.05
❑ 166	Tim Duncan RC	3.00	1.35
❑ 167	Chauncey Billups RC	.30	.14
❑ 168	Keith Van Horn RC	1.25	.55
❑ 169	Tracy McGrady RC	2.50	1.10
❑ 170	John Thomas RC	.10	.05
❑ 171	Tim Thomas RC	.75	.35
❑ 172	Ron Mercer RC	.75	.35
❑ 173	Scot Pollard RC	.15	.07
❑ 174	Jason Lawson RC	.10	.05
❑ 175	Keith Booth RC	.10	.05
❑ 176	Adonal Foyle RC	.15	.07
❑ 177	Bubba Wells RC	.10	.05
❑ 178	Derek Anderson RC	.60	.25
❑ 179	Rodrick Rhodes RC	.10	.05
❑ 180	Kelvin Cato RC	.25	.11
❑ 181	Serge Zwikker RC	.10	.05
❑ 182	Ed Gray RC	.10	.05
❑ 183	Brevin Knight RC	.40	.18
❑ 184	Alvin Williams RC	.10	.05
❑ 185	Paul Grant RC	.10	.05
❑ 186	Austin Croshere RC	.60	.25
❑ 187	Chris Crawford RC	.10	.05
❑ 188	Anthony Johnson RC	.10	.05
❑ 189	James Cotton RC	.10	.05
❑ 190	James Collins RC	.10	.05
❑ 191	Tony Battie RC	.25	.11
❑ 192	Tariq Abdul-Wahad RC	.15	.07
❑ 193	Danny Fortson RC	.25	.11
❑ 194	Maurice Taylor RC	.50	.23
❑ 195	Bobby Jackson RC	.15	.07
❑ 196	Charles Smith RC	.10	.05
❑ 197	Johnny Taylor RC	.10	.05
❑ 198	Jerald Honeycutt RC	.10	.05
❑ 199	Marko Milic RC	.10	.05
❑ 200	Anthony Parker RC	.10	.05
❑ 201	Jacque Vaughn RC	.15	.07
❑ 202	Antonio Daniels RC	.25	.11
❑ 203	Charles O'Bannon RC	.10	.05
❑ 204	God Shammgod RC	.10	.05
❑ 205	Kebu Stewart RC	.10	.05

❑ 206 Mookie Blaylock .10 .05
❑ 207 Chucky Brown .10 .05
❑ 208 Alan Henderson .10 .05
❑ 209 Dana Barros .10 .05
❑ 210 Tyus Edney .10 .05
❑ 211 Travis Knight .10 .05
❑ 212 Walter McCarty .10 .05
❑ 213 Vlade Divac .10 .05
❑ 214 Matt Geiger .10 .05
❑ 215 Bobby Phills .10 .05
❑ 216 J.R. Reid .10 .05
❑ 217 David Wesley .10 .05
❑ 218 Scott Burrell .10 .05
❑ 219 Ron Harper .15 .07
❑ 220 Michael Jordan 3.00 1.35
❑ 221 Bill Wennington .10 .05
❑ 222 Mitchell Butler .10 .05
❑ 223 Zydrunas Ilgauskas .10 .05
❑ 224 Shawn Kemp .40 .18
❑ 225 Wesley Person .10 .05
❑ 226 Shawnelle Scott RC .10 .05
❑ 227 Bob Sura .10 .05
❑ 228 Hubert Davis .10 .05
❑ 229 Michael Finley .25 .11
❑ 230 Dennis Scott .10 .05
❑ 231 Erick Strickland RC .15 .07
❑ 232 Samaki Walker .10 .05
❑ 233 Dean Garrett .10 .05
❑ 234 Priest Lauderdale .10 .05
❑ 235 Eric Williams .10 .05
❑ 236 Grant Long .10 .05
❑ 237 Malik Sealy .10 .05
❑ 238 Brian Williams .10 .05
❑ 239 Muggsy Bogues .10 .05
❑ 240 Bimbo Coles .10 .05
❑ 241 Brian Shaw .10 .05
❑ 242 Joe Smith .15 .07
❑ 243 Latrell Sprewell .50 .23
❑ 244 Charles Barkley .40 .18
❑ 245 Emanual Davis .10 .05
❑ 246 Brent Price .10 .05
❑ 247 Reggie Miller .25 .11
❑ 248 Chris Mullin .25 .11
❑ 249 Jalen Rose .25 .11
❑ 250 Rik Smits .10 .05
❑ 251 Mark West .10 .05
❑ 252 Lamond Murray .10 .05
❑ 253 Pooh Richardson .10 .05
❑ 254 Rodney Rogers .10 .05
❑ 255 Stojko Vrankovic .10 .05
❑ 256 Jon Barry .10 .05
❑ 257 Corie Blount .10 .05
❑ 258 Elden Campbell .10 .05
❑ 259 Rick Fox .10 .05
❑ 260 Nick Van Exel .15 .07
❑ 261 Isaac Austin .10 .05
❑ 262 Dan Majerle .15 .07
❑ 263 Terry Mills .10 .05
❑ 264 Mark Strickland RC .10 .05
❑ 265 Terrell Brandon .15 .07
❑ 266 Tyrone Hill .10 .05
❑ 267 Ervin Johnson .10 .05
❑ 268 Andrew Lang .10 .05
❑ 269 Elliot Perry .10 .05
❑ 270 Chris Carr .10 .05
❑ 271 Reggie Jordan .10 .05
❑ 272 Sam Mitchell .10 .05
❑ 273 Stanley Roberts .10 .05
❑ 274 Michael Cage .10 .05
❑ 275 Sam Cassell .15 .07
❑ 276 Lucious Harris .10 .05
❑ 277 Kerry Kittles .25 .11
❑ 278 Don MacLean .10 .05
❑ 279 Chris Dudley .10 .05
❑ 280 Chris Mills .10 .05
❑ 281 Charlie Ward .10 .05
❑ 282 Buck Williams .10 .05
❑ 283 Herb Williams .10 .05
❑ 284 Derek Harper .10 .05
❑ 285 Mark Price .10 .05
❑ 286 Gerald Wilkins .10 .05
❑ 287 Allen Iverson 1.25 .55
❑ 288 Jim Jackson .10 .05
❑ 289 Eric Montross .10 .05
❑ 290 Jerry Stackhouse .15 .07
❑ 291 Clarence Weatherspoon .10 .05
❑ 292 Tom Chambers .10 .05
❑ 293 Rex Chapman .10 .05
❑ 294 Danny Manning .15 .07
❑ 295 Antonio McDyess .30 .14
❑ 296 Clifford Robinson .10 .05
❑ 297 Stacey Augmon .10 .05
❑ 298 Brian Grant .15 .07
❑ 299 Rasheed Wallace .25 .11
❑ 300 Mahmoud Abdul-Rauf .10 .05
❑ 301 Terry Dehere .10 .05
❑ 302 Billy Owens .10 .05
❑ 303 Michael Smith .10 .05
❑ 304 Cory Alexander .10 .05
❑ 305 Chuck Person .10 .05
❑ 306 David Robinson .40 .18
❑ 307 Charles Smith .10 .05
❑ 308 Monty Williams .10 .05
❑ 309 Vin Baker .15 .07
❑ 310 Jerome Kersey .10 .05
❑ 311 Nate McMillan .10 .05
❑ 312 Gary Payton .40 .18
❑ 313 Eric Snow .10 .05
❑ 314 Carlos Rogers .10 .05
❑ 315 Zan Tabak .10 .05
❑ 316 John Wallace .10 .05
❑ 317 Sharone Wright .10 .05
❑ 318 Shandon Anderson .10 .05
❑ 319 Antoine Carr .10 .05
❑ 320 Howard Eisley .10 .05
❑ 321 Chris Morris .10 .05
❑ 322 Pete Chilcutt .10 .05
❑ 323 George Lynch .10 .05
❑ 324 Chris Robinson .10 .05
❑ 325 Otis Thorpe .10 .05
❑ 326 Harvey Grant .10 .05
❑ 327 Darvin Ham .10 .05
❑ 328 Juwan Howard .15 .07
❑ 329 Ben Wallace .10 .05
❑ 330 Chris Webber .75 .35
❑ NNO Grant Hill Promo 3.00 1.35

1997-98 Hoops Chairman of the Boards

	MINT	NRMT
COMPLETE SET (10)	15.00	6.75
COMMON CARD (CB1-CB10)	.50	.23
SEMISTARS	.60	.25
UNLISTED STARS	1.00	.45

SER.2 STATED ODDS 1:9 HOBBY/RETAIL

❑ CB1 Shaquille O'Neal 5.00 2.20
❑ CB2 Dikembe Mutombo .50 .23
❑ CB3 Dennis Rodman 2.00 .90
❑ CB4 Patrick Ewing 1.00 .45
❑ CB5 Charles Barkley 1.50 .70
❑ CB6 Karl Malone 1.50 .70
❑ CB7 Rasheed Wallace 1.00 .45
❑ CB8 Chris Webber 3.00 1.35
❑ CB9 Tim Duncan 5.00 2.20
❑ CB10 Kevin Garnett 6.00 2.70

1997-98 Hoops Chill with Hill

	MINT	NRMT
COMPLETE SET (10)	15.00	6.75
COMMON HILL (1-10)	2.00	.90

SER.1 STATED ODDS 1:10 HOB/RET

❑ 1 Grant Hill 2.00 .90
Tonight's the night
❑ 2 Grant Hill 2.00 .90
Stars from different worlds
❑ 3 Grant Hill 2.00 .90
Lots of questions
❑ 4 Grant Hill 2.00 .90
Another Challenge
❑ 5 Grant Hill 2.00 .90
Obey your thirst
❑ 6 Grant Hill 2.00 .90
All-Star Game
❑ 7 Grant Hill 2.00 .90
In the rafters at Cameron
❑ 8 Grant Hill 2.00 .90
The importance of education
❑ 9 Grant Hill 2.00 .90
I start preparing mentally..
❑ 10 Grant Hill 2.00 .90
I wouldn't trade this..

1997-98 Hoops Dish N Swish

	MINT	NRMT
COMPLETE SET (10)	50.00	22.00
COMMON CARD (DS1-DS10)	1.25	.55
UNLISTED STARS	2.00	.90

SER.1 STATED ODDS 1:18 RETAIL

❑ DS1 Mookie Blaylock 1.25 .55
❑ DS2 Terrell Brandon 1.25 .55
❑ DS3 Anfernee Hardaway 6.00 2.70
❑ DS4 Allen Iverson 10.00 4.50
❑ DS5 Michael Jordan 30.00 13.50
❑ DS6 Jason Kidd 6.00 2.70
❑ DS7 Stephon Marbury 6.00 2.70
❑ DS8 Gary Payton 3.00 1.35
❑ DS9 John Stockton 2.00 .90
❑ DS10 Damon Stoudamire 2.50 1.10

1997-98 Hoops Frequent Flyer Club

	MINT	NRMT
COMPLETE SET (20)	100.00	45.00
COMMON CARD (FF1-FF20)	1.25	.55
SEMISTARS	1.50	.70
UNLISTED STARS	2.50	1.10

SER.1 STATED ODDS 1:36 HOBBY

COMP.UPGRADE SET (20)	400.00	180.00
COMMON UPGRADE (FF1-FF20)	6.00	2.70

*UPGRADE: 1.5X TO 4X HI COLUMN
UPGRADE: SER.1 STATED ODDS 1:360 HOB

❑ FF1 Christian Laettner	1.50	.70
❑ FF2 Antoine Walker	5.00	2.20
❑ FF3 Glen Rice	1.50	.70
❑ FF4 Michael Jordan	30.00	13.50
❑ FF5 Dennis Rodman	5.00	2.20
❑ FF6 Grant Hill	12.00	5.50
❑ FF7 Latrell Sprewell	5.00	2.20
❑ FF8 Charles Barkley	4.00	1.80
❑ FF9 Kobe Bryant	20.00	9.00
❑ FF10 Shaquille O'Neal	12.00	5.50
❑ FF11 Ray Allen	4.00	1.80
❑ FF12 Kevin Garnett	15.00	6.75
❑ FF13 Kerry Kittles	2.50	1.10
❑ FF14 Anfernee Hardaway	8.00	3.60
❑ FF15 Jerry Stackhouse	1.50	.70
❑ FF16 Cedric Ceballos	1.25	.55
❑ FF17 Shawn Kemp	4.00	1.80
❑ FF18 Marcus Camby	3.00	1.35
❑ FF19 Juwan Howard	1.50	.70
❑ FF20 Chris Webber	8.00	3.60

1997-98 Hoops Great Shots

	MINT	NRMT
COMPLETE SET (30)	6.00	2.70
COMMON CARD (1-30)	.10	.05
SEMISTARS	.12	.05
UNLISTED STARS	.15	.07

ONE PER SERIES 2 PACK

❑ 1 Dikembe Mutombo	.12	.05
❑ 2 Antoine Walker	.30	.14
❑ 3 Glen Rice	.12	.05
❑ 4 Dennis Rodman	.30	.14
❑ 5 Derek Anderson Brevin Knight	.15	.07
❑ 6 Michael Finley	.15	.07
❑ 7 Danny Fortson Tony Battie Bobby Jackson	.15	.07
❑ 8 Grant Hill	.75	.35
❑ 9 Joe Smith	.12	.05
❑ 10 Charles Barkley	.25	.11
❑ 11 Reggie Miller	.15	.07
❑ 12 Lamond Murray	.10	.05
❑ 13 Kobe Bryant	1.25	.55
❑ 14 Alonzo Mourning	.15	.07
❑ 15 Ray Allen	.25	.11
❑ 16 Kevin Garnett	1.00	.45
❑ 17 Stephon Marbury	.50	.23
❑ 18 Kerry Kittles	.15	.07
❑ 19 Patrick Ewing	.15	.07
❑ 20 Anfernee Hardaway	.50	.23
❑ 21 Allen Iverson	.75	.35
❑ 22 Jason Kidd	.50	.23
❑ 23 Rasheed Wallace	.15	.07
❑ 24 Mitch Richmond	.15	.07
❑ 25 David Robinson	.25	.11
❑ 26 Gary Payton	.25	.11
❑ 27 Damon Stoudamire	.20	.09
❑ 28 John Stockton	.15	.07
❑ 29 Shareef Abdur-Rahim	.50	.23
❑ 30 Chris Webber	.50	.23

1997-98 Hoops High Voltage

	MINT	NRMT
COMPLETE SET (20)	120.00	55.00
COMMON CARD (HV1-HV20)	2.50	1.10

SER.2 STATED ODDS 1:36 HOBBY

COMP.500 SET (20)	600.00	275.00
COMMON 500 (HV1-20)	12.00	5.50

*500 STARS: 2.5X TO 5X HI COLUMN
500: RANDOM INSERTS IN PACKS
500: STATED PRINT RUN 500 SERIAL #'d SETS

❑ HV1 Kobe Bryant	20.00	9.00
❑ HV2 Eddie Jones	5.00	2.20
❑ HV3 Ray Allen	4.00	1.80
❑ HV4 Anfernee Hardaway	8.00	3.60
❑ HV5 Grant Hill	12.00	5.50
❑ HV6 Shareef Abdur-Rahim	8.00	3.60
❑ HV7 Marcus Camby	3.00	1.35
❑ HV8 Allen Iverson	12.00	5.50
❑ HV9 Kerry Kittles	2.50	1.10
❑ HV10 Kevin Garnett	15.00	6.75
❑ HV11 Stephon Marbury	8.00	3.60
❑ HV12 Chris Webber	8.00	3.60
❑ HV13 Antoine Walker	5.00	2.20
❑ HV14 Michael Jordan	30.00	13.50
❑ HV15 Tim Duncan	12.00	5.50
❑ HV16 Dennis Rodman	5.00	2.20
❑ HV17 Scottie Pippen	8.00	3.60
❑ HV18 Shawn Kemp	4.00	1.80
❑ HV19 Hakeem Olajuwon	4.00	1.80
❑ HV20 Karl Malone	4.00	1.80

1997-98 Hoops HOOPerstars

	MINT	NRMT
COMPLETE SET (10)	250.00	110.00
COMMON CARD (H1-H10)	8.00	3.60

SER.1 STATED ODDS 1:288 HOBBY/RETAIL

❑ H1 Michael Jordan	80.00	36.00
❑ H2 Grant Hill	30.00	13.50
❑ H3 Shaquille O'Neal	30.00	13.50
❑ H4 Ray Allen	10.00	4.50
❑ H5 Stephon Marbury	20.00	9.00
❑ H6 Anfernee Hardaway	20.00	9.00
❑ H7 Allen Iverson	30.00	13.50
❑ H8 Shawn Kemp	10.00	4.50
❑ H9 Marcus Camby	8.00	3.60
❑ H10 Shareef Abdur-Rahim	20.00	9.00

1997-98 Hoops 911

	MINT	NRMT
COMPLETE SET (10)	250.00	110.00
COMMON CARD (N1-N10)	8.00	3.60

SER.2 STATED ODDS 1:288 HOB/RET

❑ N1 Michael Jordan	80.00	36.00
❑ N2 Grant Hill	30.00	13.50
❑ N3 Shawn Kemp	10.00	4.50
❑ N4 Stephon Marbury	20.00	9.00
❑ N5 Damon Stoudamire	8.00	3.60
❑ N6 Shaquille O'Neal	30.00	13.50
❑ N7 Shareef Abdur-Rahim	20.00	9.00
❑ N8 Allen Iverson	30.00	13.50
❑ N9 Antoine Walker	12.00	5.50
❑ N10 Anfernee Hardaway	20.00	9.00

1997-98 Hoops Rock the House

	MINT	NRMT
COMPLETE SET (10)	70.00	32.00
COMMON CARD (RH1-RH10)	1.50	.70

SER.2 STATED ODDS 1:18 RETAIL

❑ RH1 Anfernee Hardaway	6.00	2.70
❑ RH2 Stephon Marbury	6.00	2.70
❑ RH3 Grant Hill	10.00	4.50
❑ RH4 Shaquille O'Neal	10.00	4.50
❑ RH5 Kerry Kittles	1.50	.70

Card	MINT	NRMT
❑ RH6 Michael Jordan	30.00	13.50
❑ RH7 Ray Allen	3.00	1.35
❑ RH8 Damon Stoudamire	2.50	1.10
❑ RH9 Kevin Garnett	12.00	5.50
❑ RH10 Shawn Kemp	3.00	1.35

1997-98 Hoops Rookie Headliners

	MINT	NRMT
COMPLETE SET (10)	50.00	22.00
COMMON CARD (RH1-RH10)	1.25	.55
SEMISTARS	1.50	.70
UNLISTED STARS	2.50	1.10

SER.1 STATED ODDS 1:48 HOBBY/RETAIL

Card	MINT	NRMT
❑ RH1 Antoine Walker	5.00	2.20
❑ RH2 Matt Maloney	1.25	.55
❑ RH3 Kobe Bryant	20.00	9.00
❑ RH4 Ray Allen	4.00	1.80
❑ RH5 Stephon Marbury	8.00	3.60
❑ RH6 Kerry Kittles	2.50	1.10
❑ RH7 John Wallace	1.25	.55
❑ RH8 Allen Iverson	12.00	5.50
❑ RH9 Marcus Camby	3.00	1.35
❑ RH10 Shareef Abdur-Rahim	8.00	3.60

1997-98 Hoops Talkin' Hoops

	MINT	NRMT
COMPLETE SET (30)	10.00	4.50
COMMON CARD (TH1-TH30)	.15	.07
SEMISTARS	.20	.09
UNLISTED STARS	.30	.14

ONE PER SER.1 PACK

Card	MINT	NRMT
❑ TH1 Christian Laettner	.20	.09
❑ TH2 Antoine Walker	.60	.25
❑ TH3 Glen Rice	.20	.09
❑ TH4 Dennis Rodman	.60	.25
❑ TH5 Scottie Pippen	1.00	.45
❑ TH6 Terrell Brandon	.20	.09
❑ TH7 Michael Finley	.30	.14
❑ TH8 Grant Hill	1.50	.70
❑ TH9 Joe Smith	.20	.09
❑ TH10 Charles Barkley	.50	.23
❑ TH11 Hakeem Olajuwon	.50	.23
❑ TH12 Reggie Miller	.30	.14
❑ TH13 Loy Vaught	.15	.07
❑ TH14 Shaquille O'Neal	1.50	.70
❑ TH15 Kobe Bryant	2.50	1.10
❑ TH16 Kevin Garnett	2.00	.90
❑ TH17 Tom Gugliotta	.20	.09
❑ TH18 Kerry Kittles	.30	.14
❑ TH19 John Wallace	.15	.07
❑ TH20 Patrick Ewing	.30	.14
❑ TH21 Jerry Stackhouse	.20	.09
❑ TH22 David Robinson	.50	.23
❑ TH23 Gary Payton	.50	.23
❑ TH24 Shawn Kemp	.50	.23
❑ TH25 Damon Stoudamire	.40	.18
❑ TH26 John Stockton	.30	.14
❑ TH27 Karl Malone	.50	.23
❑ TH28 Shareef Abdur-Rahim	1.00	.45
❑ TH29 Juwan Howard	.20	.09
❑ TH30 Chris Webber	1.00	.45

1997-98 Hoops Top of the World

	MINT	NRMT
COMPLETE SET (15)	50.00	22.00
COMMON CARD (TW1-TW15)	1.50	.70
SEMISTARS	2.50	1.10
UNLISTED STARS	4.00	1.80

SER.2 STATED ODDS 1:48 HOB/RET

Card	MINT	NRMT
❑ TW1 Tim Duncan	20.00	9.00
❑ TW2 Tim Thomas	6.00	2.70
❑ TW3 Tony Battie	1.50	.70
❑ TW4 Keith Van Horn	10.00	4.50
❑ TW5 Antonio Daniels	2.50	1.10
❑ TW6 Derek Anderson	5.00	2.20
❑ TW7 Chauncey Billups	2.50	1.10
❑ TW8 Tracy McGrady	20.00	9.00
❑ TW9 Danny Fortson	1.50	.70
❑ TW10 Austin Croshere	5.00	2.20
❑ TW11 Tariq Abdul-Wahad	1.50	.70
❑ TW12 Adonal Foyle	1.50	.70
❑ TW13 Rodrick Rhodes	1.50	.70
❑ TW14 Ron Mercer	6.00	2.70
❑ TW15 Charles Smith	1.50	.70

1998-99 Hoops

	MINT	NRMT
COMPLETE SET (167)	20.00	9.00
COMMON CARD (1-167)	.10	.05
SEMISTARS	.15	.07
UNLISTED STARS	.25	.11

SUBSET CARDS HALF VALUE OF BASE CARDS
UNPRICED STARTING FIVE SERIAL #'d TO 5
START.FIVE: RANDOM INS.IN HOB.PACKS

Card	MINT	NRMT
❑ 1 Kobe Bryant	2.00	.90
❑ 2 Glenn Robinson	.15	.07
❑ 3 Derek Anderson	.30	.14
❑ 4 Terry Dehere	.10	.05
❑ 5 Jalen Rose	.25	.11
❑ 6 Zydrunas Ilgauskas	.10	.05
❑ 7 Scott Williams	.10	.05
❑ 8 Toni Kukoc	.30	.14
❑ 9 John Stockton	.25	.11
❑ 10 Kevin Garnett	1.50	.70
❑ 11 Jerome Williams	.15	.07
❑ 12 Anthony Mason	.15	.07
❑ 13 Harvey Grant	.10	.05
❑ 14 Mookie Blaylock	.10	.05
❑ 15 Tyrone Hill	.10	.05
❑ 16 Dale Davis	.10	.05
❑ 17 Eric Washington	.10	.05
❑ 18 Aaron McKie	.10	.05
❑ 19 Jermaine O'Neal	.15	.07
❑ 20 Anfernee Hardaway	.75	.35
❑ 21 Derrick Coleman	.15	.07
❑ 22 Allan Houston	.25	.11
❑ 23 Michael Jordan	3.00	1.35
❑ 24 Jason Kidd	.75	.35
❑ 25 Tyrone Corbin	.10	.05
❑ 26 Jacque Vaughn	.10	.05
❑ 27 Bobby Jackson	.10	.05
❑ 28 Chris Anstey	.10	.05
❑ 29 Brent Barry	.10	.05
❑ 30 Shareef Abdur-Rahim	.60	.25
❑ 31 Jeff Hornacek	.15	.07
❑ 32 Ed Gray	.10	.05
❑ 33 Grant Hill	1.25	.55
❑ 34 Steve Smith	.15	.07
❑ 35 Rony Seikaly	.10	.05
❑ 36 Mark Jackson	.10	.05
❑ 37 Shawn Bradley	.10	.05
❑ 38 Corie Blount	.10	.05
❑ 39 Erick Dampier	.10	.05
❑ 40 Kerry Kittles	.15	.07
❑ 41 David Wesley	.10	.05
❑ 42 Horace Grant	.15	.07
❑ 43 Bobby Hurley	.10	.05
❑ 44 Tariq Abdul-Wahad	.10	.05
❑ 45 Brian Williams	.10	.05
❑ 46 Ray Allen	.30	.14
❑ 47 Kenny Anderson	.15	.07
❑ 48 Rodrick Rhodes	.10	.05
❑ 49 Greg Foster	.10	.05
❑ 50 Tim Duncan	1.25	.55
❑ 51 Steve Nash	.10	.05
❑ 52 Kelvin Cato	.10	.05
❑ 53 Donyell Marshall	.10	.05
❑ 54 Marcus Camby	.25	.11
❑ 55 Kevin Willis	.10	.05
❑ 56 Michael Finley	.25	.11
❑ 57 Muggsy Bogues	.10	.05
❑ 58 Mark Price	.10	.05
❑ 59 Larry Johnson	.15	.07
❑ 60 Karl Malone	.40	.18
❑ 61 Greg Ostertag	.10	.05
❑ 62 Sean Elliott	.10	.05
❑ 63 Johnny Taylor	.10	.05
❑ 64 Howard Eisley	.10	.05
❑ 65 Chris Childs	.10	.05
❑ 66 Walt Williams	.10	.05
❑ 67 Tracy Murray	.10	.05
❑ 68 Patrick Ewing	.25	.11
❑ 69 Olden Polynice	.10	.05
❑ 70 Allen Iverson	1.00	.45
❑ 71 David Robinson	.40	.18
❑ 72 Calbert Cheaney	.10	.05
❑ 73 Lamond Murray	.10	.05
❑ 74 Scot Pollard	.10	.05
❑ 75 Alonzo Mourning	.25	.11
❑ 76 Tracy McGrady	1.00	.45
❑ 77 Jim McIlvaine	.10	.05
❑ 78 Bob Sura	.10	.05
❑ 79 Anthony Peeler	.10	.05
❑ 80 Keith Van Horn	.60	.25

		MINT	NRMT
❑ 81	Maurice Taylor	.25	.11
❑ 82	Charles Smith	.10	.05
❑ 83	Dikembe Mutombo	.15	.07
❑ 84	Nick Anderson	.10	.05
❑ 85	Austin Croshere	.30	.14
❑ 86	Armon Gilliam	.10	.05
❑ 87	Eddie Jones	.50	.23
❑ 88	Glen Rice	.15	.07
❑ 89	Sam Cassell	.15	.07
❑ 90	Stephon Marbury	.60	.25
❑ 91	Elliot Perry UER Back spelled Elliott	.10	.05
❑ 92	Jamal Mashburn	.15	.07
❑ 93	Adonal Foyle	.10	.05
❑ 94	Avery Johnson	.10	.05
❑ 95	Micheal Williams	.10	.05
❑ 96	Danny Fortson	.15	.07
❑ 97	Brevin Knight	.10	.05
❑ 98	Ron Harper	.15	.07
❑ 99	Chauncey Billups	.10	.05
❑ 100	Shaquille O'Neal	1.25	.55
❑ 101	Brent Price	.10	.05
❑ 102	Tim Thomas	.40	.18
❑ 103	Khalid Reeves	.10	.05
❑ 104	Chris Gatling	.10	.05
❑ 105	Terry Cummings	.10	.05
❑ 106	Vin Baker	.15	.07
❑ 107	Bryant Reeves	.10	.05
❑ 108	John Starks	.10	.05
❑ 109	Juwan Howard	.15	.07
❑ 110	Antoine Walker	.40	.18
❑ 111	Rodney Rogers	.10	.05
❑ 112	Nick Van Exel	.15	.07
❑ 113	Chris Whitney	.10	.05
❑ 114	Bobby Phills	.10	.05
❑ 115	Travis Knight	.10	.05
❑ 116	Robert Horry	.10	.05
❑ 117	Erick Strickland	.10	.05
❑ 118	Dontae Jones	.10	.05
❑ 119	Tony Battie	.15	.07
❑ 120	Lindsey Hunter	.10	.05
❑ 121	Reggie Miller	.25	.11
❑ 122	John Wallace	.10	.05
❑ 123	Ron Mercer	.40	.18
❑ 124	Antonio Daniels	.10	.05
❑ 125	Paul Grant	.10	.05
❑ 126	Voshon Lenard	.10	.05
❑ 127	Shawn Kemp	.40	.18
❑ 128	Antonio Davis	.10	.05
❑ 129	Hakeem Olajuwon	.40	.18
❑ 130	Danny Manning	.15	.07
❑ 131	Bimbo Coles	.10	.05
❑ 132	Tim Hardaway	.25	.11
❑ 133	Lorenzo Williams	.10	.05
❑ 134	Dan Majerle	.15	.07
❑ 135	Bryant Stith	.10	.05
❑ 136	Randy Brown	.10	.05
❑ 137	Hubert Davis	.10	.05
❑ 138	Gary Payton	.40	.18
❑ 139	Rasheed Wallace	.25	.11
❑ 140	Chris Robinson	.10	.05
❑ 141	Doug Christie	.10	.05
❑ 142	Brian Grant	.15	.07
❑ 143	Isaiah Rider	.15	.07
❑ 144	Kendall Gill	.15	.07
❑ 145	Lorenzen Wright	.10	.05
❑ 146	Ervin Johnson	.10	.05
❑ 147	Monty Williams	.10	.05
❑ 148	Keith Closs	.10	.05
❑ 149	Tony Delk	.10	.05
❑ 150	Hersey Hawkins	.15	.07
❑ 151	Dean Garrett	.10	.05
❑ 152	Cedric Henderson	.10	.05
❑ 153	Detlef Schrempf	.15	.07
❑ 154	Dana Barros	.10	.05
❑ 155	Dee Brown	.10	.05
❑ 156	Jayson Williams SO	.10	.05
❑ 157	Charles Barkley SO	.25	.11
❑ 158	Damon Stoudamire SO	.15	.07
❑ 159	Scottie Pippen SO	.40	.18
❑ 160	Joe Smith SO	.10	.05
❑ 161	Antonio McDyess SO	.15	.07
❑ 162	Jerry Stackhouse SO	.10	.05
❑ 163	Dennis Rodman SO	.25	.11
❑ 164	Shaquille O'Neal SO	.50	.23
❑ 165	Grant Hill SO	.75	.35
❑ 166	Checklist	.10	.05
❑ 167	Checklist	.10	.05

1998-99 Hoops Bams

	MINT	NRMT
COMPLETE SET (10)	700.00	325.00
COMMON CARD (1-10)	40.00	18.00

STATED PRINT RUN 250 SERIAL #'d SETS
RANDOM INSERTS IN PACKS

		MINT	NRMT
❑ 1	Michael Jordan	250.00	110.00
❑ 2	Kobe Bryant	120.00	55.00
❑ 3	Allen Iverson	60.00	27.00
❑ 4	Shaquille O'Neal	80.00	36.00
❑ 5	Tim Duncan	80.00	36.00
❑ 6	Shareef Abdur-Rahim	40.00	18.00
❑ 7	Keith Van Horn	40.00	18.00
❑ 8	Grant Hill	80.00	36.00
❑ 9	Anfernee Hardaway	50.00	22.00
❑ 10	Kevin Garnett	100.00	45.00

1998-99 Hoops Slam Bams

	MINT	NRMT
COMPLETE SET (10)	1500.00	700.00
COMMON CARD (1-10)	80.00	36.00

STARS: 1X TO 2X BAMS INSERT
STATED PRINT RUN 100 SERIAL #'d SETS
RANDOM INSERTS IN HOBBY PACKS

		MINT	NRMT
❑ 1	Michael Jordan	600.00	275.00
❑ 2	Kobe Bryant	300.00	135.00

1998-99 Hoops Freshman Flashback

	MINT	NRMT
COMPLETE SET (10)	80.00	36.00
COMMON CARD (1-10)	5.00	2.20
SEMISTARS	6.00	2.70
UNLISTED STARS	8.00	3.60

STATED PRINT RUN 1000 SERIAL #'d SETS
RANDOM INSERTS IN PACKS

		MINT	NRMT
❑ 1	Tim Duncan	40.00	18.00
❑ 2	Keith Van Horn	20.00	9.00
❑ 3	Tim Thomas	12.00	5.50
❑ 4	Antonio Daniels	5.00	2.20

		MINT	NRMT
❑ 5	Brevin Knight	5.00	2.20
❑ 6	Danny Fortson	6.00	2.70
❑ 7	Maurice Taylor	8.00	3.60
❑ 8	Chauncey Billups	5.00	2.20
❑ 9	Bobby Jackson	5.00	2.20
❑ 10	Derek Anderson	10.00	4.50

1998-99 Hoops Prime Twine

	MINT	NRMT
COMPLETE SET (10)	200.00	90.00
COMMON CARD (1-10)	12.00	5.50

STATED PRINT RUN 500 SERIAL #'d SETS
RANDOM INSERTS IN PACKS

		MINT	NRMT
❑ 1	Dennis Rodman	25.00	11.00
❑ 2	Allen Iverson	50.00	22.00
❑ 3	Karl Malone	20.00	9.00
❑ 4	Antonio McDyess	12.00	5.50
❑ 5	Damon Stoudamire	12.00	5.50
❑ 6	Eddie Jones	25.00	11.00
❑ 7	Scottie Pippen	40.00	18.00
❑ 8	Shawn Kemp	20.00	9.00
❑ 9	Antoine Walker	20.00	9.00
❑ 10	Stephon Marbury	30.00	13.50

1998-99 Hoops Pump Up The Jam

	MINT	NRMT
COMPLETE SET (10)	10.00	4.50

COMMON CARD (1-10) .... .40 .18
STATED ODDS 1:4 HOB/RET

❑ 1 Stephon Marbury .... 1.00 .45
❑ 2 Allen Iverson .... 1.50 .70
❑ 3 Grant Hill .... 2.00 .90
❑ 4 Kobe Bryant 3.00 1.35
❑ 5 Michael Jordan 5.00 2.20
❑ 6 Antoine Walker .... .60 .25
❑ 7 Shareef Abdur-Rahim ...... 1.00 .45
❑ 8 Shawn Kemp .... .60 .25
❑ 9 Anfernee Hardaway .... 1.25 .55
❑ 10 Antonio McDyess .... .40 .18

1998-99 Hoops Rejectors

	MINT	NRMT
COMPLETE SET (10)	60.00	27.00
COMMON CARD (1-10)	1.50	.70
SEMISTARS	2.00	.90
UNLISTED STARS	3.00	1.35

STATED PRINT RUN 2,500 SERIAL #'d SETS
RANDOM INSERTS IN PACKS

❑ 1 Dikembe Mutombo .... 2.00 .90
❑ 2 Marcus Camby 3.00 1.35
❑ 3 Shaquille O'Neal 15.00 6.75
❑ 4 Tim Duncan 15.00 6.75
❑ 5 Shawn Bradley .... 1.50 .70
❑ 6 Chris Webber 10.00 4.50
❑ 7 Patrick Ewing 3.00 1.35
❑ 8 Kevin Garnett 20.00 9.00
❑ 9 David Robinson 5.00 2.20
❑ 10 Michael Stewart .... 1.50 .70

1998-99 Hoops Shout Outs

	MINT	NRMT
COMPLETE SET (30)	10.00	4.50
COMMON CARD (1-30)	.10	.05
SEMISTARS	.15	.07
UNLISTED STARS	.25	.11

ONE PER PACK

❑ 1 Shareef Abdur-Rahim .... .60 .25
❑ 2 Chauncey Billups .... .10 .05
❑ 3 Terrell Brandon UER.......... .15 .07
Back spelled Terrrell
❑ 4 Patrick Ewing .... .25 .11
❑ 5 Michael Finley .... .25 .11
❑ 6 Adonal Foyle .... .10 .05
❑ 7 Kevin Garnett .... 1.50 .70
❑ 8 Anfernee Hardaway .... .75 .35
❑ 9 Tim Hardaway .... .25 .11
❑ 10 Grant Hill .... 1.25 .55
❑ 11 Tim Thomas .... .40 .18
❑ 12 Bobby Jackson .... .10 .05
❑ 13 Michael Jordan 3.00 1.35
❑ 14 Shawn Kemp .... .40 .18
❑ 15 Jason Kidd .... .75 .35
❑ 16 Karl Malone .... .40 .18
❑ 17 Stephon Marbury .... .60 .25
❑ 18 Anthony Mason .... .15 .07
❑ 19 Reggie Miller .... .25 .11
❑ 20 Dikembe Mutombo .... .15 .07
❑ 21 Kobe Bryant .... 2.00 .90
❑ 22 Hakeem Olajuwon .... .40 .18
❑ 23 Gary Payton .... .40 .18
❑ 24 Michael Stewart .... .10 .05
❑ 25 David Robinson .... .40 .18
❑ 26 Maurice Taylor .... .25 .11
❑ 27 Keith Van Horn .... .60 .25
❑ 28 Antoine Walker .... .40 .18
❑ 29 Rasheed Wallace .... .25 .11
❑ 30 Juwan Howard .... .15 .07

1999-00 Hoops

	MINT	NRMT
COMPLETE SET (185)	30.00	13.50
COMMON CARD (1-165)	.10	.05
COMMON RC (166-185)	.25	.11
SEMISTARS	.15	.07
SEMISTARS RC	.30	.14
UNLISTED STARS	.25	.11
UNLISTED STARS RC	.40	.18

UNPRICED STARTING FIVE SERIAL #'d TO 5
START.FIVE: RANDOM INS.IN HOB.PACKS

❑ 1 Paul Pierce .... .50 .23
❑ 2 Ray Allen .... .25 .11
❑ 3 Jason Williams .... .60 .25
❑ 4 Sean Elliott .... .10 .05
❑ 5 Al Harrington .... .30 .14
❑ 6 Bobby Phills .... .10 .05
❑ 7 Tyronn Lue .... .10 .05
❑ 8 James Cotton .... .10 .05
❑ 9 Anthony Peeler .... .10 .05
❑ 10 LaPhonso Ellis .... .10 .05
❑ 11 Voshon Lenard .... .10 .05
❑ 12 Kornel David RC .... .10 .05
❑ 13 Michael Finley .... .25 .11
❑ 14 Danny Fortson .... .10 .05
❑ 15 Antawn Jamison .... .50 .23
❑ 16 Reggie Miller .... .25 .11
❑ 17 Shaquille O'Neal .... 1.25 .55
❑ 18 P.J. Brown .... .10 .05
❑ 19 Roshown McLeod .... .10 .05
❑ 20 Larry Johnson .... .15 .07
❑ 21 Rashard Lewis .... .40 .18
❑ 22 Tracy McGrady .... .75 .35
❑ 23 Predrag Stojakovic .... .15 .07
❑ 24 Tracy Murray .... .10 .05
❑ 25 Gary Payton .... .40 .18
❑ 26 Ricky Davis .... .25 .11
❑ 27 Kobe Bryant .... 2.00 .90
❑ 28 Avery Johnson .... .10 .05
❑ 29 Kevin Garnett .... 1.50 .70
❑ 30 Charles Jones .... .10 .05
❑ 31 Brevin Knight .... .10 .05
❑ 32 Lindsey Hunter .... .10 .05
❑ 33 Felipe Lopez .... .10 .05
❑ 34 Rik Smits .... .10 .05
❑ 35 Maurice Taylor .... .25 .11
❑ 36 Corey Benjamin .... .10 .05
❑ 37 Ervin Johnson .... .10 .05
❑ 38 Steve Smith .... .15 .07
❑ 39 Austin Croshere .... .25 .11
❑ 40 Matt Geiger .... .10 .05
❑ 41 Tom Gugliotta .... .15 .07
❑ 42 Radoslav Nesterovic .... .10 .05
❑ 43 Juwan Howard .... .15 .07
❑ 44 Keon Clark .... .10 .05
❑ 45 Latrell Sprewell .... .50 .23
❑ 46 George Lynch .... .10 .05
❑ 47 Greg Ostertag .... .10 .05
❑ 48 J.R. Henderson .... .10 .05
❑ 49 Kerry Kittles .... .15 .07
❑ 50 Matt Harpring .... .10 .05
❑ 51 Duane Causwell .... .10 .05
❑ 52 Andrae Patterson .... .10 .05
❑ 53 Jerry Stackhouse .... .15 .07
❑ 54 Adonal Foyle .... .10 .05
❑ 55 Bryce Drew .... .10 .05
❑ 56 Chris Childs .... .10 .05
❑ 57 Charles Smith .... .10 .05
❑ 58 Rony Seikaly .... .10 .05
❑ 59 Chauncey Billups .... .10 .05
❑ 60 Grant Hill .... 1.25 .55
❑ 61 Marlon Garnett RC .... .10 .05
❑ 62 Tim Hardaway .... .25 .11
❑ 63 Vlade Divac .... .10 .05
❑ 64 Chris Gatling .... .10 .05
❑ 65 Glenn Robinson .... .15 .07
❑ 66 Michael Olowokandi .... .15 .07
❑ 67 Elliot Perry .... .10 .05
❑ 68 Howard Eisley .... .10 .05
❑ 69 Glen Rice .... .15 .07
❑ 70 Marcus Camby .... .25 .11
❑ 71 Theo Ratliff .... .10 .05
❑ 72 Brian Skinner .... .10 .05
❑ 73 Kenny Anderson .... .15 .07
❑ 74 Jamal Mashburn .... .15 .07
❑ 75 Vladimir Stepania .... .10 .05
❑ 76 Jayson Williams .... .15 .07
❑ 77 Brian Grant .... .15 .07
❑ 78 Raef LaFrentz .... .25 .11
❑ 79 John Starks .... .10 .05
❑ 80 Mike Bibby .... .30 .14
❑ 81 Stephon Marbury .... .50 .23
❑ 82 Armon Gilliam .... .10 .05
❑ 83 Sam Jacobson .... .10 .05
❑ 84 Derrick Coleman .... .15 .07
❑ 85 Allan Houston .... .25 .11
❑ 86 Miles Simon .... .10 .05
❑ 87 Allen Iverson .... 1.00 .45
❑ 88 Derek Anderson .... .25 .11
❑ 89 Chris Anstey .... .10 .05
❑ 90 Larry Hughes .... .60 .25
❑ 91 Vitaly Potapenko .... .10 .05
❑ 92 Cherokee Parks .... .10 .05
❑ 93 Donyell Marshall .... .10 .05
❑ 94 Danny Manning .... .15 .07
❑ 95 Bryon Russell .... .10 .05
❑ 96 Randell Jackson .... .10 .05
❑ 97 Antoine Walker .... .30 .14
❑ 98 Dirk Nowitzki .... .40 .18
❑ 99 Karl Malone .... .40 .18
❑ 100 Vince Carter 2.50 1.10
❑ 101 Eddie Jones .... .50 .23
❑ 102 Bryant Stith .... .10 .05
❑ 103 Korleone Young .... .10 .05
❑ 104 Tim Duncan .... 1.25 .55
❑ 105 Jerome Kersey .... .10 .05
❑ 106 Bonzi Wells .... .40 .18
❑ 107 Wesley Person .... .10 .05
❑ 108 Steve Nash .... .10 .05
❑ 109 Tyrone Nesby RC .... .10 .05
❑ 110 Doug Christie .... .10 .05
❑ 111 David Robinson .... .40 .18
❑ 112 Ruben Patterson .... .25 .11
❑ 113 Dikembe Mutombo .... .15 .07

- ❑ 114 Ron Mercer .30 .14
- ❑ 115 Elden Campbell .10 .05
- ❑ 116 Kevin Willis .10 .05
- ❑ 117 Hakeem Olajuwon .40 .18
- ❑ 118 Shawn Kemp .40 .18
- ❑ 119 Eric Montross .10 .05
- ❑ 120 Shareef Abdur-Rahim .50 .23
- ❑ 121 Bob Sura .10 .05
- ❑ 122 James Robinson .10 .05
- ❑ 123 Shawn Bradley .10 .05
- ❑ 124 Robert Traylor .10 .05
- ❑ 125 Dean Garrett .10 .05
- ❑ 126 Keith Van Horn .50 .23
- ❑ 127 Patrick Ewing .25 .11
- ❑ 128 Isaac Austin .10 .05
- ❑ 129 Jason Kidd .75 .35
- ❑ 130 Isaiah Rider .15 .07
- ❑ 131 Jerome James RC .10 .05
- ❑ 132 John Stockton .25 .11
- ❑ 133 Jason Caffey .10 .05
- ❑ 134 Bryant Reeves .10 .05
- ❑ 135 Michael Dickerson .25 .11
- ❑ 136 Chris Mullin .25 .11
- ❑ 137 Rasheed Wallace .25 .11
- ❑ 138 Cuttino Mobley .25 .11
- ❑ 139 Antonio McDyess .25 .11
- ❑ 140 Chris Webber .75 .35
- ❑ 141 Jelani McCoy .10 .05
- ❑ 142 Damon Stoudamire .25 .11
- ❑ 143 Gerald Brown .10 .05
- ❑ 144 Cory Carr .10 .05
- ❑ 145 Brent Barry .10 .05
- ❑ 146 Alan Henderson .10 .05
- ❑ 147 Nazr Mohammed .10 .05
- ❑ 148 Bison Dele .10 .05
- ❑ 149 Scottie Pippen .75 .35
- ❑ 150 Michael Doleac .10 .05
- ❑ 151 Nick Anderson .10 .05
- ❑ 152 Alonzo Mourning .25 .11
- ❑ 153 Jahidi White .10 .05
- ❑ 154 Jalen Rose .25 .11
- ❑ 155 Brad Miller .10 .05
- ❑ 156 Andrew DeClercq .10 .05
- ❑ 157 Erick Strickland .10 .05
- ❑ 158 Toni Kukoc .30 .14
- ❑ 159 Pat Garrity .10 .05
- ❑ 160 Bobby Jackson .10 .05
- ❑ 161 Steve Kerr .10 .05
- ❑ 162 Toby Bailey .10 .05
- ❑ 163 Charles Oakley .10 .05
- ❑ 164 Rod Strickland .15 .07
- ❑ 165 Rodrick Rhodes .10 .05
- ❑ 166 Ron Artest RC 1.00 .45
- ❑ 167 William Avery RC .60 .25
- ❑ 168 Elton Brand RC 4.00 1.80
- ❑ 169 Baron Davis RC 1.00 .45
- ❑ 170 John Celestand RC .40 .18
- ❑ 171 Jumaine Jones RC .30 .14
- ❑ 172 Andre Miller RC 1.25 .55
- ❑ 173 Lee Nailon RC .25 .11
- ❑ 174 James Posey RC .75 .35
- ❑ 175 Jason Terry RC .60 .25
- ❑ 176 Kenny Thomas RC .60 .25
- ❑ 177 Steve Francis RC 5.00 2.20
- ❑ 178 Wally Szczerbiak RC 1.50 .70
- ❑ 179 Richard Hamilton RC 1.00 .45
- ❑ 180 Jonathan Bender RC 2.00 .90
- ❑ 181 Shawn Marion RC 1.25 .55
- ❑ 182 Aleksandar Radojevic RC .25 .11
- ❑ 183 Tim James RC .50 .23
- ❑ 184 Trajan Langdon RC .60 .25
- ❑ 185 Corey Maggette RC 1.50 .70

1999-00 Hoops Calling Card

	MINT	NRMT
COMPLETE SET (15)	20.00	9.00
COMMON CARD (1-15)	.40	.18
UNLISTED STARS	.60	.25

STATED ODDS 1:8 HOB/RET

- ❑ CC1 Kobe Bryant 5.00 2.20
- ❑ CC2 Kevin Garnett 4.00 1.80
- ❑ CC3 Tim Hardaway .60 .25

- ❑ CC4 Grant Hill 3.00 1.35
- ❑ CC5 Allen Iverson 2.50 1.10
- ❑ CC6 Karl Malone 1.00 .45
- ❑ CC7 Shawn Kemp 1.00 .45
- ❑ CC8 Stephon Marbury 1.25 .55
- ❑ CC9 Shaquille O'Neal 3.00 1.35
- ❑ CC10 Hakeem Olajuwon 1.00 .45
- ❑ CC11 Ray Allen .60 .25
- ❑ CC12 Damon Stoudamire .60 .25
- ❑ CC13 Jason Williams 1.50 .70
- ❑ CC14 Keith Van Horn 1.25 .55
- ❑ CC15 Dikembe Mutombo .40 .18

1999-00 Hoops Dunk Mob

	MINT	NRMT
COMPLETE SET (10)	80.00	36.00
COMMON CARD (DM1-DM10)	2.50	1.10
UNLISTED STARS	4.00	1.80

STATED ODDS 1:144 HOB/RET

- ❑ DM1 Shaquille O'Neal 20.00 9.00
- ❑ DM2 Stephon Marbury 8.00 3.60
- ❑ DM3 Paul Pierce 8.00 3.60
- ❑ DM4 Antawn Jamison 8.00 3.60
- ❑ DM5 Michael Olowokandi 2.50 1.10
- ❑ DM6 Scottie Pippen 12.00 5.50
- ❑ DM7 Antonio McDyess 4.00 1.80
- ❑ DM8 Vince Carter 40.00 18.00
- ❑ DM9 Ron Mercer 5.00 2.20
- ❑ DM10 Shawn Kemp 6.00 2.70

1999-00 Hoops Name Plates

	MINT	NRMT
COMPLETE SET (10)	4.00	1.80
COMMON CARD (NP1-NP10)	.20	.09

STATED ODDS 1:4 HOB/RET

- ❑ NP1 Shareef Abdur-Rahim .60 .25
- ❑ NP2 Allen Iverson 1.25 .55
- ❑ NP3 Karl Malone .50 .23
- ❑ NP4 Gary Payton .50 .23
- ❑ NP5 Hakeem Olajuwon .50 .23
- ❑ NP6 Glenn Robinson .20 .09
- ❑ NP7 Kevin Garnett 2.00 .90
- ❑ NP8 Anfernee Hardaway 1.00 .45
- ❑ NP9 David Robinson .50 .23
- ❑ NP10 Shaquille O'Neal 1.50 .70

1999-00 Hoops Pure Players

	MINT	NRMT
COMPLETE SET (10)	150.00	70.00
COMMON CARD (PP1-PP10)	8.00	3.60

STATED PRINT RUN 500 SERIAL #'d SETS
RANDOM INSERTS IN PACKS

COMPLETE 100 SET (10)	400.00	180.00
COMMON 100 (PP1-PP10)	20.00	9.00

*100 STARS: 1X TO 2.5X HI COLUMN
100: PRINT RUN 100 SERIAL #'d SETS
100: RANDOM INSERTS IN HOB.PACKS

- ❑ PP1 Tim Duncan 30.00 13.50
- ❑ PP2 Keith Van Horn 12.00 5.50
- ❑ PP3 Stephon Marbury 12.00 5.50
- ❑ PP4 Grant Hill 30.00 13.50
- ❑ PP5 Kobe Bryant 50.00 22.00
- ❑ PP6 Kevin Garnett 40.00 18.00
- ❑ PP7 Allen Iverson 25.00 11.00
- ❑ PP8 Antoine Walker 8.00 3.60
- ❑ PP9 Shareef Abdur-Rahim 12.00 5.50
- ❑ PP10 Anfernee Hardaway 20.00 9.00

1999-00 Hoops Y2K Corps

	MINT	NRMT
COMPLETE SET (10)	15.00	6.75
COMMON CARD (BB1-BB10)	.40	.18
SEMISTARS	.50	.23
UNLISTED STARS	1.00	.45
STATED ODDS 1:16 HOB/RET		

	MINT	NRMT
❑ BB1 Michael Olowokandi	.50	.23
❑ BB2 Mike Bibby	1.25	.55
❑ BB3 Jason Williams	2.50	1.10
❑ BB4 Dirk Nowitzki	1.50	.70
❑ BB5 Vince Carter	10.00	4.50
❑ BB6 Robert Traylor	.40	.18
❑ BB7 Larry Hughes	2.50	1.10
❑ BB8 Paul Pierce	2.00	.90
❑ BB9 Matt Harpring	.40	.18
❑ BB10 Michael Dickerson	1.00	.45

1999-00 Hoops Decade

	MINT	NRMT
COMPLETE SET (180)	30.00	13.50
COMMON CARD (1-180)	.10	.05
COMMON RC	.25	.11
SEMISTARS	.15	.07
SEMISTARS RC	.30	.14
UNLISTED STARS	.25	.11
UNLISTED STARS RC	.40	.18

	MINT	NRMT
❑ 1 David Robinson	.40	.18
❑ 2 Mookie Blaylock	.10	.05
❑ 3 Jaren Jackson	.10	.05
❑ 4 Andre Miller RC	1.25	.55
❑ 5 Michael Olowokandi	.15	.07
❑ 6 Glenn Robinson	.15	.07
❑ 7 Steve Smith	.15	.07
❑ 8 Eric Snow	.10	.05
❑ 9 Antoine Walker	.30	.14
❑ 10 Nick Anderson	.10	.05
❑ 11 Jonathan Bender RC	2.00	.90
❑ 12 Sean Elliott	.10	.05
❑ 13 Danny Fortson	.10	.05
❑ 14 Adonal Foyle	.10	.05
❑ 15 Richard Hamilton RC	1.00	.45
❑ 16 Shawn Kemp	.40	.18
❑ 17 Christian Laettner	.15	.07
❑ 18 Rashard Lewis	.40	.18
❑ 19 Danny Manning	.15	.07
❑ 20 Mitch Richmond	.25	.11
❑ 21 Shawn Bradley	.10	.05
❑ 22 Tim Duncan	1.25	.55
❑ 23 Tim Hardaway	.25	.11
❑ 24 Antawn Jamison	.50	.23
❑ 25 Jeff Hornacek	.15	.07
❑ 26 Jumaine Jones RC	.30	.14
❑ 27 Corey Maggette RC	1.50	.70
❑ 28 Vitaly Potapenko	.10	.05
❑ 29 Jerry Stackhouse	.15	.07
❑ 30 Jason Terry RC	.60	.25
❑ 31 Baron Davis RC	1.00	.45
❑ 32 Matt Harpring	.10	.05
❑ 33 Glen Rice	.15	.07
❑ 34 Vladimir Stepania	.10	.05
❑ 35 Jayson Williams	.15	.07
❑ 36 Wally Szczerbiak RC	1.50	.70
❑ 37 Michael Doleac	.10	.05
❑ 38 Hersey Hawkins	.15	.07
❑ 39 Allan Houston	.25	.11
❑ 40 Hakeem Olajuwon	.40	.18
❑ 41 Damon Stoudamire	.25	.11
❑ 42 Jelani McCoy	.10	.05
❑ 43 Aleksandar Radojevic RC	.25	.11
❑ 44 Cal Bowdler RC	.40	.18
❑ 45 Tyronn Lue	.10	.05
❑ 46 Andrae Patterson	.10	.05
❑ 47 Karl Malone	.40	.18
❑ 48 Alonzo Mourning	.25	.11
❑ 49 Vince Carter	2.50	1.10
❑ 50 Darrell Armstrong	.15	.07
❑ 51 Terrell Brandon	.15	.07
❑ 52 John Celestand RC	.40	.18
❑ 53 Grant Hill	1.25	.55
❑ 54 Stephon Marbury	.50	.23
❑ 55 Tracy McGrady	.75	.35
❑ 56 Reggie Miller	.25	.11
❑ 57 Clifford Robinson	.10	.05
❑ 58 Arvydas Sabonis	.15	.07
❑ 59 William Avery RC	.60	.25
❑ 60 Calbert Cheaney	.10	.05
❑ 61 Jermaine Jackson RC	.25	.11
❑ 62 Allen Iverson	1.00	.45
❑ 63 Larry Johnson	.15	.07
❑ 64 Toni Kukoc	.30	.14
❑ 65 Raef LaFrentz	.25	.11
❑ 66 Isaiah Rider	.15	.07
❑ 67 Jeff Foster RC	.40	.18
❑ 68 Juwan Howard	.15	.07
❑ 69 Kerry Kittles	.15	.07
❑ 70 Brevin Knight	.10	.05
❑ 71 Voshon Lenard	.10	.05
❑ 72 Latrell Sprewell	.50	.23
❑ 73 Maurice Taylor	.25	.11
❑ 74 Chris Webber	.75	.35
❑ 75 Jerome Williams	.15	.07
❑ 76 Scott Padgett RC	.40	.18
❑ 77 Vin Baker	.15	.07
❑ 78 Chris Childs	.10	.05
❑ 79 Erick Dampier	.10	.05
❑ 80 Anfernee Hardaway	.75	.35
❑ 81 Jamal Mashburn	.15	.07
❑ 82 Todd Fuller	.10	.05
❑ 83 Eric Piatkowski	.10	.05
❑ 84 Gary Trent	.10	.05
❑ 85 Kevin Garnett	1.50	.70
❑ 86 Chris Mullin	.25	.11
❑ 87 Charles Oakley	.10	.05
❑ 88 Detlef Schrempf	.15	.07
❑ 89 Elton Brand RC	4.00	1.80
❑ 90 Patrick Ewing	.25	.11
❑ 91 Devean George RC	.75	.35
❑ 92 Brian Grant	.15	.07
❑ 93 Larry Hughes	.60	.25
❑ 94 Dan Majerle	.15	.07
❑ 95 Shawn Marion RC	1.25	.55
❑ 96 Cuttino Mobley	.25	.11
❑ 97 Paul Pierce	.50	.23
❑ 98 Bryant Reeves	.10	.05
❑ 99 Keith Van Horn	.50	.23
❑ 100 Corliss Williamson	.10	.05
❑ 101 Tariq Abdul-Wahad	.10	.05
❑ 102 Brent Barry	.10	.05
❑ 103 Elden Campbell	.10	.05
❑ 104 Mark Jackson	.10	.05
❑ 105 Lamond Murray	.10	.05
❑ 106 Bryon Russell	.10	.05
❑ 107 Jason Williams	.60	.25
❑ 108 Ray Allen	.25	.11
❑ 109 Ron Artest RC	1.00	.45
❑ 110 Charles Barkley	.40	.18
❑ 111 Cedric Ceballos	.10	.05
❑ 112 Jason Kidd	.75	.35
❑ 113 Donyell Marshall	.10	.05
❑ 114 John Stockton	.25	.11
❑ 115 Mike Bibby	.30	.14
❑ 116 Ricky Davis	.25	.11
❑ 117 Steve Francis RC	5.00	2.20
❑ 118 Tom Gugliotta	.15	.07
❑ 119 Laron Profit RC	.40	.18
❑ 120 Joe Smith	.15	.07
❑ 121 Doug Christie	.10	.05
❑ 122 Kenny Anderson	.15	.07
❑ 123 Michael Dickerson	.25	.11
❑ 124 Zydrunas Ilgauskas	.10	.05
❑ 125 Bobby Jackson	.10	.05
❑ 126 Quincy Lewis RC	.40	.18
❑ 127 Shandon Anderson	.10	.05
❑ 128 Charles Outlaw	.10	.05
❑ 129 Scottie Pippen	.75	.35
❑ 130 Rodney Rogers	.10	.05
❑ 131 Rik Smits	.10	.05
❑ 132 Chauncey Billups	.10	.05
❑ 133 Chris Crawford	.10	.05
❑ 134 Kornel David RC	.10	.05
❑ 135 Tony Delk	.10	.05
❑ 136 Kendall Gill	.15	.07
❑ 137 Trajan Langdon RC	.60	.25
❑ 138 Ron Mercer	.30	.14
❑ 139 Othella Harrington	.10	.05
❑ 140 Gheorghe Muresan	.10	.05
❑ 141 Isaac Austin	.10	.05
❑ 142 Dion Glover RC	.40	.18
❑ 143 Avery Johnson	.10	.05
❑ 144 Antonio McDyess	.25	.11
❑ 145 Steve Nash	.10	.05
❑ 146 Tyrone Nesby RC	.10	.05
❑ 147 Shaquille O'Neal	1.25	.55
❑ 148 James Posey RC	.75	.35
❑ 149 Rod Strickland	.15	.07
❑ 150 Kobe Bryant	2.00	.90
❑ 151 Michael Finley	.25	.11
❑ 152 Anthony Mason	.15	.07
❑ 153 Dikembe Mutombo	.15	.07
❑ 154 John Starks	.10	.05
❑ 155 Kenny Thomas RC	.60	.25
❑ 156 Matt Geiger	.10	.05
❑ 157 Tim James RC	.50	.23
❑ 158 Eddie Jones	.50	.23
❑ 159 Lamar Odom RC	3.00	1.35
❑ 160 Nick Van Exel	.15	.07
❑ 161 Sam Cassell	.15	.07
❑ 162 Vonteego Cummings RC	.60	.25
❑ 163 Lindsey Hunter	.10	.05
❑ 164 Dirk Nowitzki	.40	.18
❑ 165 Gary Payton	.40	.18
❑ 166 Shareef Abdur-Rahim	.50	.23
❑ 167 Jalen Rose	.25	.11
❑ 168 Robert Traylor	.10	.05
❑ 169 Derek Anderson	.25	.11
❑ 170 Corey Benjamin	.10	.05
❑ 171 Marcus Camby	.25	.11
❑ 172 Vlade Divac	.10	.05
❑ 173 Mario Elie	.10	.05
❑ 174 Felipe Lopez	.10	.05
❑ 175 Rafer Alston RC	.50	.23
❑ 176 Antonio Davis	.10	.05
❑ 177 Howard Eisley	.10	.05
❑ 178 Theo Ratliff	.10	.05
❑ 179 Tim Thomas	.30	.14
❑ 180 Rasheed Wallace	.25	.11

1999-00 Hoops Decade Hoopla

	MINT	NRMT
COMPLETE SET (180)	100.00	45.00
COMMON CARD (1-180)	.40	.18
*STARS: 1.5X TO 4X BASE CARD HI		
*RCs: .75X TO 2X BASE HI		
STATED ODDS 1:3		

1999-00 Hoops Decade Hoopla Plus

	MINT	NRMT
COMMON CARD (1-180)	2.00	.90

*STARS: 6X TO 15X BASE CARD HI
*RCs: 3X TO 8X BASE HI
STATED ODDS 1:30

1999-00 Hoops Decade Draft Day Dominance

	MINT	NRMT
COMPLETE SET (10)	30.00	13.50
COMMON CARD (DD1-10)	.75	.35
STATED ODDS 1:32		
COMP.PARALLEL SET (10)	60.00	27.00
COMMON PARALLEL (DD1-10)	1.50	.70

*PARALLEL: .75X TO 2X HI COLUMN
PARALLEL: RANDOM INSERTS IN PACKS
PARALLEL: PRINT RUN 1989 SERIAL #'d SETS

	MINT	NRMT
❑ DD1 David Robinson	2.00	.90
❑ DD2 Gary Payton	2.00	.90
❑ DD3 Dikembe Mutombo	.75	.35
❑ DD4 Shaquille O'Neal	6.00	2.70
❑ DD5 Anfernee Hardaway	4.00	1.80
❑ DD6 Grant Hill	6.00	2.70
❑ DD7 Antonio McDyess	.75	.35
❑ DD8 Kobe Bryant	10.00	4.50
❑ DD9 Keith Van Horn	2.50	1.10
❑ DD10 Vince Carter	12.00	5.50

1999-00 Hoops Decade Genuine Coverage

	MINT	NRMT
COMPLETE SET (10)	500.00	220.00
COMMON CARD (1-10)	25.00	11.00

STATED ODDS 1:893
NNO CARDS LISTED BELOW ALPHABETICALLY

	MINT	NRMT
❑ 1 Shareef Abdur-Rahim	80.00	36.00
❑ 2 Ray Allen	80.00	36.00
❑ 3 Patrick Ewing	60.00	27.00
❑ 4 Grant Hill	120.00	55.00
❑ 5 Juwan Howard	25.00	11.00
❑ 6 Antonio McDyess	50.00	22.00

	MINT	NRMT
❑ 7 Hakeem Olajuwon	60.00	27.00
❑ 8 David Robinson	60.00	27.00
❑ 9 Keith Van Horn	50.00	22.00
❑ 10 Antoine Walker	40.00	18.00

1999-00 Hoops Decade New Style

	MINT	NRMT
COMPLETE SET (15)	20.00	9.00
COMMON CARD (NS1-15)	.50	.23
UNLISTED STARS	1.00	.45
STATED ODDS 1:18		
COMP.PARALLEL SET (15)	50.00	22.00
COMMON PARALLEL (NS1-15)	1.25	.55

*PARALLEL: 1X TO 2.5X HI COLUMN
PARALLEL: RANDOM INSERTS IN PACKS
PARALLEL: PRINT RUN 1989 SERIAL #'d SETS

	MINT	NRMT
❑ NS1 Steve Francis	6.00	2.70
❑ NS2 Lamar Odom	4.00	1.80
❑ NS3 Wally Szczerbiak	2.00	.90
❑ NS4 Elton Brand	5.00	2.20
❑ NS5 Baron Davis	1.25	.55
❑ NS6 Corey Maggette	2.00	.90
❑ NS7 Trajan Langdon	1.00	.45
❑ NS8 Cal Bowdler	.50	.23
❑ NS9 Richard Hamilton	1.25	.55
❑ NS10 Ron Artest	1.25	.55
❑ NS11 Jason Terry	1.00	.45
❑ NS12 Jonathan Bender	2.50	1.10
❑ NS13 Andre Miller	1.50	.70
❑ NS14 Shawn Marion	1.50	.70
❑ NS15 William Avery	1.00	.45

1999-00 Hoops Decade Retrospection Collection

	MINT	NRMT
COMPLETE SET (10)	100.00	45.00
COMMON CARD (RC1-10)	4.00	1.80
STATED ODDS 1:108		
COMP.PARALLEL SET (10)	500.00	220.00
COMMON PARALLEL (RC1-10)	20.00	9.00

*PARALLEL: 2X TO 5X HI COLUMN
PARALLEL: RANDOM INSERTS IN PACKS
PARALLEL: PRINT RUN 89 SERIAL #'d SETS

	MINT	NRMT
❑ RC1 Kevin Garnett	20.00	9.00
❑ RC2 Kobe Bryant	25.00	11.00
❑ RC3 Allen Iverson	12.00	5.50
❑ RC4 Vince Carter	30.00	13.50
❑ RC5 Jason Williams	8.00	3.60
❑ RC6 Ron Mercer	4.00	1.80
❑ RC7 Tim Duncan	15.00	6.75
❑ RC8 Anfernee Hardaway	10.00	4.50
❑ RC9 Scottie Pippen	10.00	4.50
❑ RC10 Shaquille O'Neal	15.00	6.75

1999-00 Hoops Decade Up Tempo

	MINT	NRMT
COMPLETE SET (15)	20.00	9.00
COMMON CARDS (UT1-15)	.75	.35
STATED ODDS 1:9		
COMP.PARALLEL SET (15)	80.00	36.00
COMMON PARALLEL (UT1-15)	3.00	1.35

*PARALLEL: 1.5X TO 4X HI COLUMN
PARALLEL: RANDOM INSERTS IN PACKS
PARALLEL: PRINT RUN 1989 SERIAL #'d SETS

	MINT	NRMT
❑ UT1 Allen Iverson	2.50	1.10
❑ UT2 Kevin Garnett	4.00	1.80
❑ UT3 Shaquille O'Neal	3.00	1.35
❑ UT4 Tim Duncan	3.00	1.35
❑ UT5 Stephon Marbury	1.25	.55
❑ UT6 Keith Van Horn	1.25	.55
❑ UT7 Paul Pierce	1.25	.55
❑ UT8 Vince Carter	6.00	2.70
❑ UT9 Antawn Jamison	1.25	.55
❑ UT10 Larry Hughes	1.50	.70
❑ UT11 Jason Williams	1.50	.70
❑ UT12 Antoine Walker	.75	.35
❑ UT13 Grant Hill	3.00	1.35
❑ UT14 Steve Francis	4.00	1.80
❑ UT15 Lamar Odom	2.50	1.10

1995-96 Metal

	MINT	NRMT
COMPLETE SET (220)	40.00	18.00
COMPLETE SERIES 1 (120)	20.00	9.00
COMPLETE SERIES 2 (100)	20.00	9.00
COMMON CARD (1-220)	.15	.07
SEMISTARS	.25	.11

UNLISTED STARS .40 .18
SUBSET CARDS HALF VALUE OF BASE CARDS

	Card	MINT	NRMT
❑	1 Stacey Augmon	.15	.07
❑	2 Mookie Blaylock	.15	.07
❑	3 Grant Long	.15	.07
❑	4 Steve Smith	.25	.11
❑	5 Dee Brown	.15	.07
❑	6 Sherman Douglas	.15	.07
❑	7 Eric Montross	.15	.07
❑	8 Dino Radja	.15	.07
❑	9 Muggsy Bogues	.15	.07
❑	10 Scott Burrell	.15	.07
❑	11 Larry Johnson	.25	.11
❑	12 Alonzo Mourning	.40	.18
❑	13 Michael Jordan	5.00	2.20
❑	14 Toni Kukoc	.50	.23
❑	15 Scottie Pippen	1.25	.55
❑	16 Terrell Brandon	.25	.11
❑	17 Tyrone Hill	.15	.07
❑	18 Mark Price	.15	.07
❑	19 John Williams	.15	.07
❑	20 Jim Jackson	.15	.07
❑	21 Popeye Jones	.15	.07
❑	22 Jason Kidd	1.25	.55
❑	23 Jamal Mashburn	.25	.11
❑	24 Mahmoud Abdul-Rauf	.15	.07
❑	25 Dikembe Mutombo	.25	.11
❑	26 Robert Pack	.15	.07
❑	27 Jalen Rose	.50	.23
❑	28 Joe Dumars	.40	.18
❑	29 Grant Hill	2.00	.90
❑	30 Lindsey Hunter	.15	.07
❑	31 Terry Mills	.15	.07
❑	32 Tim Hardaway	.40	.18
❑	33 Donyell Marshall	.25	.11
❑	34 Chris Mullin	.40	.18
❑	35 Clifford Rozier	.15	.07
❑	36 Latrell Sprewell	.75	.35
❑	37 Sam Cassell	.25	.11
❑	38 Clyde Drexler	.40	.18
❑	39 Robert Horry	.15	.07
❑	40 Hakeem Olajuwon	.60	.25
❑	41 Kenny Smith	.15	.07
❑	42 Dale Davis	.15	.07
❑	43 Mark Jackson	.15	.07
❑	44 Derrick McKey	.15	.07
❑	45 Reggie Miller	.40	.18
❑	46 Rik Smits	.15	.07
❑	47 Lamond Murray	.15	.07
❑	48 Pooh Richardson	.15	.07
❑	49 Malik Sealy	.15	.07
❑	50 Loy Vaught	.15	.07
❑	51 Elden Campbell	.15	.07
❑	52 Cedric Ceballos	.15	.07
❑	53 Vlade Divac	.15	.07
❑	54 Eddie Jones	.75	.35
❑	55 Nick Van Exel	.25	.11
❑	56 Bimbo Coles	.15	.07
❑	57 Billy Owens	.15	.07
❑	58 Khalid Reeves	.15	.07
❑	59 Glen Rice	.25	.11
❑	60 Kevin Willis	.15	.07
❑	61 Vin Baker	.40	.18
❑	62 Todd Day	.15	.07
❑	63 Eric Murdock	.15	.07
❑	64 Glenn Robinson	.40	.18
❑	65 Tom Gugliotta	.25	.11
❑	66 Christian Laettner	.25	.11
❑	67 Isaiah Rider	.25	.11
❑	68 Kenny Anderson	.25	.11
❑	69 P.J. Brown	.15	.07
❑	70 Derrick Coleman	.25	.11
❑	71 Patrick Ewing	.40	.18
❑	72 Anthony Mason	.25	.11
❑	73 Charles Oakley	.15	.07
❑	74 John Starks	.15	.07
❑	75 Nick Anderson	.15	.07
❑	76 Horace Grant	.25	.11
❑	77 Anfernee Hardaway	1.25	.55
❑	78 Shaquille O'Neal	2.00	.90
❑	79 Dennis Scott	.15	.07
❑	80 Dana Barros	.15	.07
❑	81 Shawn Bradley	.15	.07
❑	82 Clarence Weatherspoon	.15	.07
❑	83 Sharone Wright	.15	.07
❑	84 Charles Barkley	.60	.25
❑	85 Kevin Johnson	.25	.11
❑	86 Dan Majerle	.15	.07
❑	87 Danny Manning	.25	.11
❑	88 Wesley Person	.25	.11
❑	89 Clifford Robinson	.15	.07
❑	90 Rod Strickland	.25	.11
❑	91 Otis Thorpe	.15	.07
❑	92 Buck Williams	.15	.07
❑	93 Brian Grant	.40	.18
❑	94 Olden Polynice	.15	.07
❑	95 Mitch Richmond	.40	.18
❑	96 Walt Williams	.15	.07
❑	97 Sean Elliott	.15	.07
❑	98 Avery Johnson	.15	.07
❑	99 David Robinson	.60	.25
❑	100 Dennis Rodman	.75	.35
❑	101 Shawn Kemp	.60	.25
❑	102 Nate McMillan	.15	.07
❑	103 Gary Payton	.60	.25
❑	104 Detlef Schrempf	.25	.11
❑	105 B.J. Armstrong	.15	.07
❑	106 Oliver Miller	.15	.07
❑	107 John Salley	.15	.07
❑	108 David Benoit	.15	.07
❑	109 Jeff Hornacek	.25	.11
❑	110 Karl Malone	.60	.25
❑	111 John Stockton	.40	.18
❑	112 Greg Anthony	.15	.07
❑	113 Benoit Benjamin	.15	.07
❑	114 Byron Scott	.15	.07
❑	115 Calbert Cheaney	.15	.07
❑	116 Juwan Howard	.40	.18
❑	117 Gheorghe Muresan	.15	.07
❑	118 Chris Webber	1.25	.55
❑	119 Checklist	.15	.07
❑	120 Checklist	.15	.07
❑	121 Stacey Augmon	.15	.07
❑	122 Mookie Blaylock	.15	.07
❑	123 Alan Henderson RC	.40	.18
❑	124 Andrew Lang	.15	.07
❑	125 Ken Norman	.15	.07
❑	126 Steve Smith	.25	.11
❑	127 Dana Barros	.15	.07
❑	128 Rick Fox	.15	.07
❑	129 Eric Williams RC	.25	.11
❑	130 Kendall Gill	.25	.11
❑	131 Khalid Reeves	.15	.07
❑	132 Glen Rice	.25	.11
❑	133 George Zidek RC	.15	.07
❑	134 Dennis Rodman	.75	.35
❑	135 Danny Ferry	.15	.07
❑	136 Dan Majerle	.15	.07
❑	137 Chris Mills	.15	.07
❑	138 Bobby Phills	.15	.07
❑	139 Bob Sura RC	.25	.11
❑	140 Tony Dumas	.15	.07
❑	141 Dale Ellis	.15	.07
❑	142 Don MacLean	.15	.07
❑	143 Antonio McDyess RC	2.00	.90
❑	144 Bryant Stith	.15	.07
❑	145 Allan Houston	.50	.23
❑	146 Theo Ratliff RC	.50	.23
❑	147 Otis Thorpe	.15	.07
❑	148 B.J. Armstrong	.15	.07
❑	149 Rony Seikaly	.15	.07
❑	150 Joe Smith RC	1.25	.55
❑	151 Sam Cassell	.25	.11
❑	152 Clyde Drexler	.40	.18
❑	153 Robert Horry	.15	.07
❑	154 Hakeem Olajuwon	.60	.25
❑	155 Antonio Davis	.15	.07
❑	156 Ricky Pierce	.15	.07
❑	157 Brent Barry RC	.40	.18
❑	158 Terry Dehere	.15	.07
❑	159 Rodney Rogers	.15	.07
❑	160 Brian Williams	.15	.07
❑	161 Magic Johnson	1.25	.55
❑	162 Sasha Danilovic RC	.15	.07
❑	163 Alonzo Mourning	.40	.18
❑	164 Kurt Thomas RC	.25	.11
❑	165 Sherman Douglas	.15	.07
❑	166 Shawn Respert RC	.15	.07
❑	167 Kevin Garnett RC	5.00	2.20
❑	168 Terry Porter	.15	.07
❑	169 Shawn Bradley	.15	.07
❑	170 Kevin Edwards	.15	.07
❑	171 Ed O'Bannon RC	.15	.07
❑	172 Jayson Williams	.25	.11
❑	173 Derek Harper	.15	.07
❑	174 Charles Smith	.15	.07
❑	175 Brian Shaw	.15	.07
❑	176 Derrick Coleman	.25	.11
❑	177 Vernon Maxwell	.15	.07
❑	178 Trevor Ruffin	.15	.07
❑	179 Jerry Stackhouse RC	1.25	.55
❑	180 Michael Finley RC	1.50	.70
❑	181 A.C. Green	.25	.11
❑	182 John Williams	.15	.07
❑	183 Aaron McKie	.15	.07
❑	184 Arvydas Sabonis RC	.60	.25
❑	185 Gary Trent RC	.15	.07
❑	186 Tyus Edney RC	.15	.07
❑	187 Sarunas Marciulionis	.15	.07
❑	188 Michael Smith	.15	.07
❑	189 Corliss Williamson RC	.75	.35
❑	190 Vinny Del Negro	.15	.07
❑	191 Hersey Hawkins	.25	.11
❑	192 Shawn Kemp	.60	.25
❑	193 Gary Payton	.60	.25
❑	194 Sam Perkins	.25	.11
❑	195 Detlef Schrempf	.25	.11
❑	196 Willie Anderson	.15	.07
❑	197 Oliver Miller	.15	.07
❑	198 Tracy Murray	.15	.07
❑	199 Alvin Robertson	.15	.07
❑	200 Damon Stoudamire RC	2.00	.90
❑	201 Chris Morris	.15	.07
❑	202 Greg Anthony	.15	.07
❑	203 Blue Edwards	.15	.07
❑	204 Eric Murdock	.15	.07
❑	205 Bryant Reeves RC	.40	.18
❑	206 Byron Scott	.15	.07
❑	207 Robert Pack	.15	.07
❑	208 Rasheed Wallace RC	1.50	.70
❑	209 Anfernee Hardaway NB	.75	.35
❑	210 Grant Hill NB	1.25	.55
❑	211 Larry Johnson NB	.15	.07
❑	212 Michael Jordan NB	2.50	1.10
❑	213 Jason Kidd NB	.50	.23
❑	214 Karl Malone NB	.40	.18
❑	215 Shaquille O'Neal NB	.75	.35
❑	216 Scottie Pippen NB	.60	.25
❑	217 David Robinson NB	.40	.18
❑	218 Glenn Robinson NB	.25	.11
❑	219 Checklist	.15	.07
❑	220 Checklist	.15	.07

1995-96 Metal Silver Spotlight

	MINT	NRMT
COMPLETE SET (120)	60.00	27.00
COMMON CARD (1-120)	.50	.23

*STARS: 1.5X TO 3X BASE CARD HI
ONE PER SERIES 1 PACK

1995-96 Metal Maximum Metal

	MINT	NRMT
COMPLETE SET (10)	80.00	36.00
COMMON CARD (1-10)	3.00	1.35

SER.1 STATED ODDS 1:36 HOBBY/RETAIL

❑ 1 Charles Barkley	5.00	2.20
❑ 2 Patrick Ewing	3.00	1.35
❑ 3 Grant Hill	15.00	6.75
❑ 4 Michael Jordan	40.00	18.00
❑ 5 Shawn Kemp	5.00	2.20
❑ 6 Karl Malone	5.00	2.20
❑ 7 Hakeem Olajuwon	5.00	2.20
❑ 8 Shaquille O'Neal	15.00	6.75
❑ 9 Mitch Richmond	3.00	1.35
❑ 10 David Robinson	5.00	2.20

1995-96 Metal Metal Force

	MINT	NRMT
COMPLETE SET (15)	150.00	70.00
COMMON CARD (1-15)	3.00	1.35
SEMISTARS	4.00	1.80
UNLISTED STARS	6.00	2.70

SER.2 STATED ODDS 1:54 RETAIL

❑ 1 Vin Baker	6.00	2.70
❑ 2 Charles Barkley	10.00	4.50
❑ 3 Cedric Ceballos	3.00	1.35
❑ 4 Grant Hill	30.00	13.50
❑ 5 Larry Johnson	4.00	1.80
❑ 6 Magic Johnson	20.00	9.00
❑ 7 Shawn Kemp	10.00	4.50
❑ 8 Karl Malone	10.00	4.50
❑ 9 Jamal Mashburn	4.00	1.80
❑ 10 Scottie Pippen	20.00	9.00
❑ 11 Glenn Robinson	6.00	2.70
❑ 12 Dennis Rodman	12.00	5.50
❑ 13 Joe Smith	8.00	3.60
❑ 14 Jerry Stackhouse	8.00	3.60
❑ 15 Chris Webber	20.00	9.00

1995-96 Metal Molten Metal

	MINT	NRMT
COMPLETE SET (10)	150.00	70.00
COMMON CARD (1-10)	4.00	1.80
SEMISTARS	6.00	2.70
UNLISTED STARS	10.00	4.50

SER.1 STATED ODDS 1:72 HOBBY/RETAIL

❑ 1 Anfernee Hardaway	30.00	13.50
❑ 2 Grant Hill	50.00	22.00
❑ 3 Robert Horry	4.00	1.80
❑ 4 Eddie Jones	20.00	9.00
❑ 5 Toni Kukoc	12.00	5.50
❑ 6 Jamal Mashburn	6.00	2.70
❑ 7 Alonzo Mourning	10.00	4.50
❑ 8 Glenn Robinson	10.00	4.50
❑ 9 Latrell Sprewell	20.00	9.00
❑ 10 Chris Webber	30.00	13.50

1995-96 Metal Rookie Roll Call

	MINT	NRMT
COMPLETE SET (10)	5.00	2.20
COMMON CARD (R1-R10)	.25	.11
SEMISTARS	.30	.14
UNLISTED STARS	.50	.23
COMP.SILV.SPOT.SET (10)	20.00	9.00

*SILV.SPOTLIGHT: 1.25X TO 2.5X HI COLUMN
RANDOM INSERTS IN ALL SER.1 PACKS

❑ R1 Brent Barry	.25	.11
❑ R2 Antonio McDyess	2.50	1.10
❑ R3 Ed O'Bannon	.25	.11
❑ R4 Cherokee Parks	.25	.11
❑ R5 Bryant Reeves	.30	.14
❑ R6 Shawn Respert	.25	.11
❑ R7 Joe Smith	1.50	.70
❑ R8 Jerry Stackhouse	1.50	.70
❑ R9 Gary Trent	.25	.11
❑ R10 Rasheed Wallace	2.00	.90

1995-96 Metal Scoring Magnets

	MINT	NRMT
COMPLETE SET (8)	150.00	70.00
COMMON CARD (1-8)	8.00	3.60

SER.2 STATED ODDS 1:54 HOBBY

❑ 1 Anfernee Hardaway	15.00	6.75
❑ 2 Grant Hill	25.00	11.00
❑ 3 Magic Johnson	15.00	6.75
❑ 4 Michael Jordan	60.00	27.00
❑ 5 Jason Kidd	15.00	6.75
❑ 6 Hakeem Olajuwon	8.00	3.60
❑ 7 Shaquille O'Neal	25.00	11.00
❑ 8 David Robinson	8.00	3.60

1995-96 Metal Slick Silver

	MINT	NRMT
COMPLETE SET (10)	40.00	18.00
COMMON CARD (1-10)	1.00	.45
SEMISTARS	1.25	.55
UNLISTED STARS	2.00	.90

SER.1 STATED ODDS 1:7 HOBBY/RETAIL

❑ 1 Kenny Anderson	1.00	.45
❑ 2 Anfernee Hardaway	6.00	2.70
❑ 3 Michael Jordan	25.00	11.00
❑ 4 Jason Kidd	6.00	2.70
❑ 5 Reggie Miller	2.00	.90
❑ 6 Gary Payton	3.00	1.35
❑ 7 Mitch Richmond	2.00	.90
❑ 8 Latrell Sprewell	4.00	1.80
❑ 9 John Stockton	2.00	.90
❑ 10 Nick Van Exel	1.25	.55

1995-96 Metal Steel Towers

	MINT	NRMT
COMPLETE SET (10)	12.00	5.50
COMMON CARD (1-10)	.50	.23
SEMISTARS	1.00	.45
UNLISTED STARS	1.50	.70

SER.1 STATED ODDS 1:4 RETAIL

❑ 1 Shawn Bradley	.50	.23
❑ 2 Vlade Divac	.50	.23
❑ 3 Patrick Ewing	1.50	.70
❑ 4 Alonzo Mourning	1.50	.70
❑ 5 Dikembe Mutombo	1.00	.45
❑ 6 Hakeem Olajuwon	2.50	1.10
❑ 7 Shaquille O'Neal	8.00	3.60
❑ 8 David Robinson	2.50	1.10
❑ 9 Rik Smits	.50	.23
❑ 10 Kevin Willis	.50	.23

1995-96 Metal Tempered Steel

	MINT	NRMT
COMPLETE SET (12)	30.00	13.50
COMMON CARD (1-12)	1.25	.55
SEMISTARS	1.50	.70
UNLISTED STARS	2.50	1.10

SER.2 STATED ODDS 1:12 HOBBY/RETAIL

❑ 1 Sasha Danilovic	1.25	.55
❑ 2 Tyus Edney	1.25	.55
❑ 3 Michael Finley	5.00	2.20
❑ 4 Kevin Garnett	15.00	6.75
❑ 5 Antonio McDyess	6.00	2.70
❑ 6 Bryant Reeves	1.50	.70
❑ 7 Arvydas Sabonis	2.50	1.10
❑ 8 Joe Smith	4.00	1.80
❑ 9 Jerry Stackhouse	4.00	1.80
❑ 10 Damon Stoudamire	6.00	2.70
❑ 11 Rasheed Wallace	5.00	2.20
❑ 12 Eric Williams	1.25	.55

1996-97 Metal

	MINT	NRMT
COMPLETE SET (250)	45.00	20.00
COMPLETE SERIES 1 (150)	25.00	11.00
COMPLETE SERIES 2 (100)	20.00	9.00

COMMON CARD (1-250)	.15	.07
SEMISTARS	.20	.09
UNLISTED STARS	.40	.18

SUBSET CARDS HALF VALUE OF BASE CARDS

❑ 1 Mookie Blaylock	.15	.07
❑ 2 Christian Laettner	.20	.09
❑ 3 Steve Smith	.20	.09
❑ 4 Dana Barros	.15	.07
❑ 5 Rick Fox	.15	.07
❑ 6 Dino Radja	.15	.07
❑ 7 Eric Williams	.15	.07
❑ 8 Dell Curry	.15	.07
❑ 9 Matt Geiger	.15	.07
❑ 10 Glen Rice	.20	.09
❑ 11 Michael Jordan	5.00	2.20
❑ 12 Toni Kukoc	.50	.23
❑ 13 Luc Longley	.15	.07
❑ 14 Scottie Pippen	1.25	.55
❑ 15 Dennis Rodman	.75	.35
❑ 16 Terrell Brandon	.20	.09
❑ 17 Danny Ferry	.15	.07
❑ 18 Chris Mills	.15	.07
❑ 19 Bobby Phills	.15	.07
❑ 20 Bob Sura	.15	.07
❑ 21 Jim Jackson	.15	.07
❑ 22 Jason Kidd	1.25	.55
❑ 23 Jamal Mashburn	.20	.09
❑ 24 George McCloud	.15	.07
❑ 25 LaPhonso Ellis	.15	.07
❑ 26 Antonio McDyess	.60	.25
❑ 27 Bryant Stith	.15	.07
❑ 28 Joe Dumars	.40	.18
❑ 29 Grant Hill	2.00	.90
❑ 30 Theo Ratliff	.20	.09
❑ 31 Otis Thorpe	.15	.07
❑ 32 Chris Mullin	.40	.18
❑ 33 Joe Smith	.40	.18
❑ 34 Latrell Sprewell	.75	.35
❑ 35 Sam Cassell	.20	.09
❑ 36 Clyde Drexler	.40	.18
❑ 37 Robert Horry	.15	.07
❑ 38 Hakeem Olajuwon	.60	.25
❑ 39 Antonio Davis	.15	.07
❑ 40 Dale Davis	.15	.07
❑ 41 Derrick McKey	.15	.07
❑ 42 Reggie Miller	.40	.18
❑ 43 Rik Smits	.15	.07
❑ 44 Brent Barry	.15	.07
❑ 45 Malik Sealy	.15	.07
❑ 46 Loy Vaught	.15	.07
❑ 47 Elden Campbell	.15	.07
❑ 48 Cedric Ceballos	.15	.07
❑ 49 Eddie Jones	.75	.35
❑ 50 Nick Van Exel	.20	.09
❑ 51 Sasha Danilovic	.15	.07
❑ 52 Tim Hardaway	.40	.18
❑ 53 Alonzo Mourning	.40	.18
❑ 54 Kurt Thomas	.15	.07
❑ 55 Vin Baker	.20	.09
❑ 56 Sherman Douglas	.15	.07
❑ 57 Glenn Robinson	.40	.18
❑ 58 Kevin Garnett	2.50	1.10
❑ 59 Tom Gugliotta	.20	.09
❑ 60 Doug West	.15	.07
❑ 61 Shawn Bradley	.15	.07
❑ 62 Ed O'Bannon	.15	.07
❑ 63 Jayson Williams	.20	.09
❑ 64 Patrick Ewing	.40	.18
❑ 65 Charles Oakley	.15	.07
❑ 66 John Starks	.15	.07
❑ 67 Nick Anderson	.15	.07
❑ 68 Horace Grant	.20	.09
❑ 69 Anfernee Hardaway	1.25	.55
❑ 70 Dennis Scott	.15	.07
❑ 71 Brian Shaw	.15	.07
❑ 72 Derrick Coleman	.20	.09
❑ 73 Jerry Stackhouse	.40	.18
❑ 74 Clarence Weatherspoon	.15	.07
❑ 75 Charles Barkley	.60	.25
❑ 76 Michael Finley	.50	.23
❑ 77 Kevin Johnson	.20	.09
❑ 78 Wesley Person	.15	.07
❑ 79 Aaron McKie	.15	.07
❑ 80 Clifford Robinson	.15	.07
❑ 81 Arvydas Sabonis	.20	.09
❑ 82 Gary Trent	.15	.07
❑ 83 Tyus Edney	.15	.07
❑ 84 Brian Grant	.40	.18
❑ 85 Billy Owens	.15	.07
❑ 86 Olden Polynice	.15	.07
❑ 87 Mitch Richmond	.40	.18
❑ 88 Vinny Del Negro	.15	.07
❑ 89 Sean Elliott	.15	.07
❑ 90 Avery Johnson	.15	.07
❑ 91 David Robinson	.60	.25
❑ 92 Hersey Hawkins	.20	.09
❑ 93 Shawn Kemp	.60	.25
❑ 94 Gary Payton	.60	.25
❑ 95 Sam Perkins	.20	.09
❑ 96 Detlef Schrempf	.20	.09
❑ 97 Doug Christie	.15	.07
❑ 98 Damon Stoudamire	.60	.25
❑ 99 Sharone Wright	.15	.07
❑ 100 Jeff Hornacek	.20	.09
❑ 101 Karl Malone	.60	.25
❑ 102 John Stockton	.40	.18
❑ 103 Greg Anthony	.15	.07
❑ 104 Blue Edwards	.15	.07
❑ 105 Bryant Reeves	.15	.07
❑ 106 Juwan Howard	.20	.09
❑ 107 Gheorghe Muresan	.15	.07
❑ 108 Chris Webber	1.25	.55
❑ 109 Kenny Anderson OTM	.15	.07
❑ 110 Stacey Augmon OTM	.15	.07
❑ 111 Chris Childs OTM	.15	.07
❑ 112 Vlade Divac OTM	.15	.07
❑ 113 Allan Houston OTM	.20	.09
❑ 114 Mark Jackson OTM	.15	.07
❑ 115 Larry Johnson OTM	.15	.07
❑ 116 Grant Long OTM	.15	.07
❑ 117 Anthony Mason OTM	.15	.07
❑ 118 Dikembe Mutombo OTM	.15	.07
❑ 119 Shaquille O'Neal OTM	.75	.35
❑ 120 Isaiah Rider OTM	.15	.07
❑ 121 Rod Strickland OTM	.15	.07
❑ 122 Rasheed Wallace OTM	.40	.18
❑ 123 Jalen Rose OTM	.20	.09
❑ 124 Anfernee Hardaway MET	.75	.35
❑ 125 Tim Hardaway MET	.20	.09
❑ 126 Allan Houston MET	.20	.09
❑ 127 Eddie Jones MET	.40	.18
❑ 128 Michael Jordan MET	2.50	1.10
❑ 129 Reggie Miller MET	.20	.09
❑ 130 Glen Rice MET	.15	.07
❑ 131 Mitch Richmond MET	.20	.09
❑ 132 Steve Smith MET	.15	.07
❑ 133 John Stockton MET	.20	.09
❑ 134 Stephon Marbury FF RC	2.50	1.10
❑ 135 S. Abdur-Rahim FF RC	2.50	1.10
❑ 136 Ray Allen FF RC	1.50	.70
❑ 137 Kobe Bryant FF RC	15.00	6.75
❑ 138 Steve Nash FF RC	.20	.09
❑ 139 Grant Hill MS	1.25	.55
❑ 140 Jason Kidd MS	.40	.18
❑ 141 Karl Malone MS	.40	.18
❑ 142 Hakeem Olajuwon MS	.40	.18
❑ 143 Shaquille O'Neal MS	.75	.35
❑ 144 Gary Payton MS	.40	.18
❑ 145 Scottie Pippen MS	.60	.25
❑ 146 Jerry Stackhouse MS	.20	.09
❑ 147 Damon Stoudamire MS	.40	.18
❑ 148 Rod Strickland MS	.15	.07

❑ 149 Checklist (1-102) .15 .07
❑ 150 Checklist 103-150/inserts .15 .07
❑ 151 Tyrone Corbin .15 .07
❑ 152 Dikembe Mutombo .20 .09
❑ 153 Antoine Walker RC 1.50 .70
❑ 154 David Wesley .15 .07
❑ 155 Vlade Divac .15 .07
❑ 156 Anthony Mason .20 .09
❑ 157 Ron Harper .20 .09
❑ 158 Steve Kerr .15 .07
❑ 159 Robert Parish .20 .09
❑ 160 Tyrone Hill .15 .07
❑ 161 Vitaly Potapenko RC .15 .07
❑ 162 Sam Cassell .20 .09
❑ 163 Chris Gatling .15 .07
❑ 164 Samaki Walker RC .15 .07
❑ 165 Dale Ellis .15 .07
❑ 166 Mark Jackson .15 .07
❑ 167 Ervin Johnson .15 .07
❑ 168 Grant Hill 2.00 .90
❑ 169 Lindsey Hunter .15 .07
❑ 170 Todd Fuller RC .15 .07
❑ 171 Mark Price .15 .07
❑ 172 Charles Barkley .60 .25
❑ 173 Othella Harrington RC .40 .18
❑ 174 Matt Maloney RC .20 .09
❑ 175 Kevin Willis .15 .07
❑ 176 Travis Best .15 .07
❑ 177 Erick Dampier RC .20 .09
❑ 178 Jalen Rose .40 .18
❑ 179 Rodney Rogers .15 .07
❑ 180 Lorenzen Wright RC .20 .09
❑ 181 Kobe Bryant 6.00 2.70
❑ 182 Robert Horry .15 .07
❑ 183 Shaquille O'Neal 2.00 .90
❑ 184 P.J. Brown .15 .07
❑ 185 Dan Majerle .20 .09
❑ 186 Ray Allen .75 .35
❑ 187 Armon Gilliam .15 .07
❑ 188 Andrew Lang .15 .07
❑ 189 Stephon Marbury 1.25 .55
❑ 190 Stojko Vrankovic .15 .07
❑ 191 Kendall Gill .20 .09
❑ 192 Kerry Kittles RC .75 .35
❑ 193 Robert Pack .15 .07
❑ 194 Chris Childs .15 .07
❑ 195 Allan Houston .40 .18
❑ 196 Larry Johnson .20 .09
❑ 197 John Wallace RC .40 .18
❑ 198 Rony Seikaly .15 .07
❑ 199 Gerald Wilkins .15 .07
❑ 200 Lucious Harris .15 .07
❑ 201 Allen Iverson RC 4.00 1.80
❑ 202 Cedric Ceballos .15 .07
❑ 203 Jason Kidd 1.25 .55
❑ 204 Danny Manning .20 .09
❑ 205 Steve Nash .15 .07
❑ 206 Kenny Anderson .20 .09
❑ 207 Isaiah Rider .20 .09
❑ 208 Rasheed Wallace .50 .23
❑ 209 Mahmoud Abdul-Rauf .15 .07
❑ 210 Corliss Williamson .15 .07
❑ 211 Vernon Maxwell .15 .07
❑ 212 Dominique Wilkins .40 .18
❑ 213 Craig Ehlo .15 .07
❑ 214 Jim McIlvaine .15 .07
❑ 215 Marcus Camby RC 1.25 .55
❑ 216 Hubert Davis .15 .07
❑ 217 Walt Williams .15 .07
❑ 218 Shandon Anderson RC .50 .23
❑ 219 Bryon Russell .15 .07
❑ 220 Shareef Abdur-Rahim 1.25 .55
❑ 221 Roy Rogers RC .15 .07
❑ 222 Tracy Murray .15 .07
❑ 223 Rod Strickland .20 .09
❑ 224 Kevin Garnett MET 1.25 .55
❑ 225 Karl Malone MET .40 .18
❑ 226 Alonzo Mourning MET .20 .09
❑ 227 Hakeem Olajuwon MET .40 .18
❑ 228 Gary Payton MET .40 .18
❑ 229 Scottie Pippen MET .60 .25
❑ 230 David Robinson MET .40 .18
❑ 231 Dennis Rodman MET .40 .18
❑ 232 Latrell Sprewell MET .40 .18
❑ 233 Jerry Stackhouse MET .20 .09
❑ 234 Marcus Camby FF .50 .23
❑ 235 Todd Fuller FF .15 .07
❑ 236 Allen Iverson FF 1.50 .70
❑ 237 Kerry Kittles FF .40 .18
❑ 238 Roy Rogers FF .15 .07
❑ 239 Anfernee Hardaway MS .75 .35
❑ 240 Juwan Howard MS .15 .07
❑ 241 Michael Jordan MS 2.50 1.10
❑ 242 Shawn Kemp MS .40 .18
❑ 243 Gary Payton MS .40 .18
❑ 244 Mitch Richmond MS .20 .09
❑ 245 Glenn Robinson MS .20 .09
❑ 246 John Stockton MS .20 .09
❑ 247 Damon Stoudamire MS .40 .18
❑ 248 Chris Webber MS .50 .23
❑ 249 Checklist .15 .07
❑ 250 Checklist .15 .07

1996-97 Metal Precious Metal

	MINT	NRMT
COMPLETE SET (98)	900.00	400.00
COMMON CARD (151-248)	4.00	1.80
SEMISTARS	5.00	2.20
UNLISTED STARS	10.00	4.50
SER.2 STATED ODDS 1:36 HOBBY		

❑ 151 Tyrone Corbin 4.00 1.80
❑ 152 Dikembe Mutombo 5.00 2.20
❑ 153 Antoine Walker 20.00 9.00
❑ 154 David Wesley 4.00 1.80
❑ 155 Vlade Divac 4.00 1.80
❑ 156 Anthony Mason 5.00 2.20
❑ 157 Ron Harper 5.00 2.20
❑ 158 Steve Kerr 4.00 1.80
❑ 159 Robert Parish 5.00 2.20
❑ 160 Tyrone Hill 4.00 1.80
❑ 161 Vitaly Potapenko 4.00 1.80
❑ 162 Sam Cassell 5.00 2.20
❑ 163 Chris Gatling 4.00 1.80
❑ 164 Samaki Walker 4.00 1.80
❑ 165 Dale Ellis 4.00 1.80
❑ 166 Mark Jackson 4.00 1.80
❑ 167 Ervin Johnson 4.00 1.80
❑ 168 Grant Hill 50.00 22.00
❑ 169 Lindsey Hunter 4.00 1.80
❑ 170 Todd Fuller 4.00 1.80
❑ 171 Mark Price 4.00 1.80
❑ 172 Charles Barkley 15.00 6.75
❑ 173 Othella Harrington 10.00 4.50
❑ 174 Matt Maloney 4.00 1.80
❑ 175 Kevin Willis 4.00 1.80
❑ 176 Travis Best 4.00 1.80
❑ 177 Erick Dampier 4.00 1.80
❑ 178 Jalen Rose 10.00 4.50
❑ 179 Rodney Rogers 4.00 1.80
❑ 180 Lorenzen Wright 4.00 1.80
❑ 181 Kobe Bryant 80.00 36.00
❑ 182 Robert Horry 4.00 1.80
❑ 183 Shaquille O'Neal 50.00 22.00
❑ 184 P.J. Brown 4.00 1.80
❑ 185 Dan Majerle 5.00 2.20
❑ 186 Ray Allen 20.00 9.00
❑ 187 Armon Gilliam 4.00 1.80
❑ 188 Andrew Lang 4.00 1.80
❑ 189 Stephon Marbury 30.00 13.50
❑ 190 Stojko Vrankovic 4.00 1.80
❑ 191 Kendall Gill 5.00 2.20
❑ 192 Kerry Kittles 10.00 4.50
❑ 193 Robert Pack 4.00 1.80
❑ 194 Chris Childs 4.00 1.80
❑ 195 Allan Houston 10.00 4.50
❑ 196 Larry Johnson 5.00 2.20
❑ 197 John Wallace 5.00 2.20
❑ 198 Rony Seikaly 4.00 1.80
❑ 199 Gerald Wilkins 4.00 1.80
❑ 200 Lucious Harris 4.00 1.80
❑ 201 Allen Iverson 50.00 22.00
❑ 202 Cedric Ceballos 4.00 1.80
❑ 203 Jason Kidd 30.00 13.50
❑ 204 Danny Manning 5.00 2.20
❑ 205 Steve Nash 4.00 1.80
❑ 206 Kenny Anderson 5.00 2.20
❑ 207 Isaiah Rider 5.00 2.20
❑ 208 Rasheed Wallace 12.00 5.50
❑ 209 Mahmoud Abdul-Rauf 4.00 1.80
❑ 210 Corliss Williamson 4.00 1.80
❑ 211 Vernon Maxwell 4.00 1.80
❑ 212 Dominique Wilkins 10.00 4.50
❑ 213 Craig Ehlo 4.00 1.80
❑ 214 Jim McIlvaine 4.00 1.80
❑ 215 Marcus Camby 12.00 5.50
❑ 216 Hubert Davis 4.00 1.80
❑ 217 Walt Williams 4.00 1.80
❑ 218 Shandon Anderson 10.00 4.50
❑ 219 Bryon Russell 4.00 1.80
❑ 220 Shareef Abdur-Rahim 30.00 13.50
❑ 221 Roy Rogers 4.00 1.80
❑ 222 Tracy Murray 4.00 1.80
❑ 223 Rod Strickland 5.00 2.20
❑ 224 Kevin Garnett MET 60.00 27.00
❑ 225 Karl Malone MET 15.00 6.75
❑ 226 Alonzo Mourning MET 5.00 2.20
❑ 227 Hakeem Olajuwon MET 15.00 6.75
❑ 228 Gary Payton MET 15.00 6.75
❑ 229 Scottie Pippen MET 30.00 13.50
❑ 230 David Robinson MET 15.00 6.75
❑ 231 Dennis Rodman MET 20.00 9.00
❑ 232 Latrell Sprewell MET 20.00 9.00
❑ 233 Jerry Stackhouse MET 5.00 2.20
❑ 234 Marcus Camby FF 10.00 4.50
❑ 235 Todd Fuller FF 4.00 1.80
❑ 236 Allen Iverson FF 25.00 11.00
❑ 237 Kerry Kittles FF 10.00 4.50
❑ 238 Roy Rogers FF 4.00 1.80
❑ 239 Anfernee Hardaway MS 30.00 13.50
❑ 240 Juwan Howard MS 4.00 1.80
❑ 241 Michael Jordan MS 100.00 45.00
❑ 242 Shawn Kemp MS 15.00 6.75
❑ 243 Gary Payton MS 15.00 6.75
❑ 244 Mitch Richmond MS 5.00 2.20
❑ 245 Glenn Robinson MS 5.00 2.20
❑ 246 John Stockton MS 5.00 2.20
❑ 247 Damon Stoudamire MS 15.00 6.75
❑ 248 Chris Webber MS 30.00 13.50

1996-97 Metal Cyber-Metal

	MINT	NRMT
COMPLETE SET (20)	40.00	18.00
COMMON CARD (1-20)	1.25	.55
SEMISTARS	1.50	.70
SER.2 STATED ODDS 1:6 HOBBY/RETAIL		

❑ 1 Shareef Abdur-Rahim 5.00 2.20

	MINT	NRMT
❑ 2 Ray Allen	3.00	1.35
❑ 3 Vin Baker	1.50	.70
❑ 4 Charles Barkley	2.50	1.10
❑ 5 Kobe Bryant	15.00	6.75
❑ 6 Patrick Ewing	1.50	.70
❑ 7 Jason Kidd	5.00	2.20
❑ 8 Karl Malone	2.50	1.10
❑ 9 Stephon Marbury	5.00	2.20
❑ 10 Reggie Miller	1.50	.70
❑ 11 Alonzo Mourning	1.50	.70
❑ 12 Hakeem Olajuwon	2.50	1.10
❑ 13 Gary Payton	2.50	1.10
❑ 14 Scottie Pippen	5.00	2.20
❑ 15 Mitch Richmond	1.50	.70
❑ 16 David Robinson	2.50	1.10
❑ 17 Joe Smith	1.25	.55
❑ 18 Latrell Sprewell	3.00	1.35
❑ 19 John Stockton	1.50	.70
❑ 20 Chris Webber	5.00	2.20

1996-97 Metal Decade of Excellence

	MINT	NRMT
COMPLETE SET (10)	50.00	22.00
COMMON CARD (M1-M10)	2.50	1.10
UNLISTED STARS	3.00	1.35

SER.1 STATED ODDS 1:100 HOBBY/RETAIL

	MINT	NRMT
❑ M1 Clyde Drexler	3.00	1.35
❑ M2 Joe Dumars	3.00	1.35
❑ M3 Derek Harper	2.50	1.10
❑ M4 Michael Jordan	40.00	18.00
❑ M5 Karl Malone	5.00	2.20
❑ M6 Chris Mullin	3.00	1.35
❑ M7 Charles Oakley	2.50	1.10
❑ M8 Sam Perkins	2.50	1.10
❑ M9 Ricky Pierce	2.50	1.10
❑ M10 Buck Williams	2.50	1.10

1996-97 Metal Freshly Forged

	MINT	NRMT
COMPLETE SET (15)	80.00	36.00
COMMON CARD (1-15)	2.00	.90

SER.2 STATED ODDS 1:24 HOBBY/RETAIL

	MINT	NRMT
❑ 1 Shareef Abdur-Rahim	6.00	2.70
❑ 2 Ray Allen	4.00	1.80
❑ 3 Kobe Bryant	15.00	6.75
❑ 4 Marcus Camby	3.00	1.35
❑ 5 Kevin Garnett	12.00	5.50
❑ 6 Anfernee Hardaway	6.00	2.70
❑ 7 Grant Hill	10.00	4.50
❑ 8 Allen Iverson	10.00	4.50
❑ 9 Jason Kidd	6.00	2.70
❑ 10 Stephon Marbury	6.00	2.70
❑ 11 Glenn Robinson	2.00	.90
❑ 12 Joe Smith	2.00	.90
❑ 13 Jerry Stackhouse	2.00	.90
❑ 14 Damon Stoudamire	3.00	1.35
❑ 15 Antoine Walker	4.00	1.80

1996-97 Metal Maximum Metal

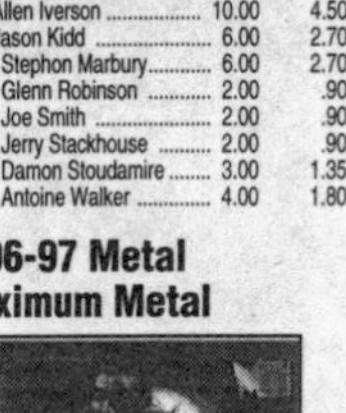

	MINT	NRMT
COMPLETE SET (20)	300.00	135.00
COMPLETE SERIES 1 (10)	250.00	110.00
COMPLETE SERIES 2 (10)	60.00	27.00
COMMON CARD (1-20)	5.00	2.20

1-10: SER.1 STATED ODDS 1:180 HOBBY
11-20: SER.2 STATED ODDS 1:120 RETAIL

	MINT	NRMT
❑ 1 Charles Barkley	12.00	5.50
❑ 2 Anfernee Hardaway	25.00	11.00
❑ 3 Grant Hill	40.00	18.00
❑ 4 Michael Jordan	100.00	45.00
❑ 5 Jason Kidd	25.00	11.00
❑ 6 Karl Malone	12.00	5.50
❑ 7 Hakeem Olajuwon	12.00	5.50
❑ 8 Gary Payton	12.00	5.50
❑ 9 David Robinson	12.00	5.50
❑ 10 Damon Stoudamire	12.00	5.50
❑ 11 Juwan Howard	5.00	2.20
❑ 12 Shawn Kemp	8.00	3.60
❑ 13 Kerry Kittles	5.00	2.20
❑ 14 Stephon Marbury	15.00	6.75
❑ 15 Dennis Rodman	10.00	4.50
❑ 16 Joe Smith	5.00	2.20
❑ 17 Jerry Stackhouse	5.00	2.20
❑ 18 John Stockton	5.00	2.20
❑ 19 Antoine Walker	10.00	4.50
❑ 20 Chris Webber	15.00	6.75

1996-97 Metal Metal Edge

	MINT	NRMT
COMPLETE SET (15)	60.00	27.00
COMMON CARD (1-15)	2.00	.90
SEMISTARS	2.50	1.10
UNLISTED STARS	4.00	1.80

SER.1 STATED ODDS 1:36 HOBBY/RETAIL

	MINT	NRMT
❑ 1 Charles Barkley	6.00	2.70
❑ 2 Jamal Mashburn	2.00	.90
❑ 3 Alonzo Mourning	4.00	1.80
❑ 4 Gary Payton	6.00	2.70
❑ 5 Scottie Pippen	12.00	5.50
❑ 6 Steve Smith	2.50	1.10
❑ 7 Latrell Sprewell	8.00	3.60
❑ 8 John Stockton	4.00	1.80
❑ 9 Nick Van Exel	2.50	1.10
❑ 10 Chris Webber	12.00	5.50
❑ 11 Stephon Marbury	10.00	4.50
❑ 12 Shareef Abdur-Rahim	10.00	4.50
❑ 13 Ray Allen	6.00	2.70
❑ 14 Antoine Walker	6.00	2.70
❑ 15 Kobe Bryant	30.00	13.50

1996-97 Metal Minted Metal

	MINT	NRMT
COMP.BRONZE SET (2)	80.00	36.00
COMMON CARD (1-2)	25.00	11.00

*SILVER: 1.5X HI COLUMN
SER.2 STATED ODDS 1:720 HOBBY FOR ANY
PLAYERS LISTED ALPHABETICALLY

	MINT	NRMT
❑ 1 Grant Hill Bronze	60.00	27.00
❑ 2 Jerry Stackhouse Bronze	25.00	11.00
❑ 3 Grant Hill Silver	80.00	36.00
❑ 4 Jerry Stackhouse Silver	40.00	18.00

1996-97 Metal Molten Metal

	MINT	NRMT
COMPLETE SET (30)	450.00	200.00
COMPLETE SERIES 1 (10)	200.00	90.00
COMPLETE SERIES 2 (20)	250.00	110.00
COMMON CARD (1-10)	10.00	4.50
COMMON CARD (11-30)	4.00	1.80
SEMISTARS SER.2	5.00	2.20
UNLISTED STARS SER.2	6.00	2.70

1-10: SER.1 STATED ODDS 1:180 RETAIL

11-30: SER.2 STATED ODDS 1:72 HOBBY

Card	MINT	NRMT
❑ 1 Michael Finley	12.00	5.50
❑ 2 Kevin Garnett	60.00	27.00
❑ 3 Anfernee Hardaway	30.00	13.50
❑ 4 Grant Hill	50.00	22.00
❑ 5 Juwan Howard	10.00	4.50
❑ 6 Jason Kidd	30.00	13.50
❑ 7 Antonio McDyess	15.00	6.75
❑ 8 Joe Smith	10.00	4.50
❑ 9 Jerry Stackhouse	10.00	4.50
❑ 10 Damon Stoudamire	15.00	6.75
❑ 11 Shareef Abdur-Rahim	20.00	9.00
❑ 12 Ray Allen	12.00	5.50
❑ 13 Charles Barkley	10.00	4.50
❑ 14 Terrell Brandon	4.00	1.80
❑ 15 Marcus Camby	10.00	4.50
❑ 16 Tom Gugliotta	5.00	2.20
❑ 17 Allen Iverson	30.00	13.50
❑ 18 Michael Jordan	80.00	36.00
❑ 19 Kerry Kittles	6.00	2.70
❑ 20 Karl Malone	10.00	4.50
❑ 21 Hakeem Olajuwon	10.00	4.50
❑ 22 Shaquille O'Neal	30.00	13.50
❑ 23 Gary Payton	10.00	4.50
❑ 24 Scottie Pippen	20.00	9.00
❑ 25 David Robinson	10.00	4.50
❑ 26 Glenn Robinson	6.00	2.70
❑ 27 Joe Smith	6.00	2.70
❑ 28 Latrell Sprewell	12.00	5.50
❑ 29 Antoine Walker	12.00	5.50
❑ 30 Chris Webber	20.00	9.00

1996-97 Metal Net-Rageous

	MINT	NRMT
COMPLETE SET (10)	150.00	70.00
COMMON CARD (1-10)	5.00	2.20

SER.2 STATED ODDS 1:288 HOBBY/RETAIL

Card	MINT	NRMT
❑ 1 Kevin Garnett	30.00	13.50
❑ 2 Anfernee Hardaway	15.00	6.75
❑ 3 Grant Hill	25.00	11.00
❑ 4 Juwan Howard	5.00	2.20
❑ 5 Michael Jordan	60.00	27.00
❑ 6 Shawn Kemp	8.00	3.60
❑ 7 Shaquille O'Neal	25.00	11.00
❑ 8 Dennis Rodman	10.00	4.50
❑ 9 Jerry Stackhouse	5.00	2.20
❑ 10 Damon Stoudamire	8.00	3.60

1996-97 Metal Platinum Portraits

	MINT	NRMT
COMPLETE SET (10)	120.00	55.00
COMMON CARD (1-10)	6.00	2.70

SER.2 STATED ODDS 1:96 HOBBY/RETAIL

Card	MINT	NRMT
❑ 1 Charles Barkley	6.00	2.70
❑ 2 Kevin Garnett	25.00	11.00
❑ 3 Anfernee Hardaway	12.00	5.50
❑ 4 Grant Hill	20.00	9.00
❑ 5 Michael Jordan	50.00	22.00
❑ 6 Shawn Kemp	6.00	2.70
❑ 7 Karl Malone	6.00	2.70
❑ 8 Shaquille O'Neal	20.00	9.00
❑ 9 Hakeem Olajuwon	6.00	2.70
❑ 10 Damon Stoudamire	6.00	2.70

1996-97 Metal Power Tools

	MINT	NRMT
COMPLETE SET (10)	20.00	9.00
COMMON CARD (1-10)	1.00	.45
SEMISTARS	1.50	.70
UNLISTED STARS	2.50	1.10

SER.1 STATED ODDS 1:18 HOBBY/RETAIL

Card	MINT	NRMT
❑ 1 Vin Baker	1.50	.70
❑ 2 Charles Barkley	4.00	1.80
❑ 3 Horace Grant	1.00	.45
❑ 4 Juwan Howard	1.50	.70
❑ 5 Larry Johnson	1.50	.70
❑ 6 Shawn Kemp	4.00	1.80
❑ 7 Karl Malone	4.00	1.80
❑ 8 Antonio McDyess	4.00	1.80
❑ 9 Dennis Rodman	5.00	2.20
❑ 10 Joe Smith	2.50	1.10

1996-97 Metal Steel Slammin'

	MINT	NRMT
COMPLETE SET (10)	120.00	55.00
COMMON CARD (1-10)	2.00	.90
UNLISTED STARS	5.00	2.20

SER.1 STATED ODDS 1:72 HOBBY/RETAIL

Card	MINT	NRMT
❑ 1 Brent Barry	2.00	.90
❑ 2 Clyde Drexler	5.00	2.20
❑ 3 Michael Finley	6.00	2.70
❑ 4 Kevin Garnett	30.00	13.50
❑ 5 Eddie Jones	10.00	4.50
❑ 6 Michael Jordan	60.00	27.00
❑ 7 Shawn Kemp	8.00	3.60
❑ 8 Shaquille O'Neal	25.00	11.00
❑ 9 Joe Smith	5.00	2.20
❑ 10 Jerry Stackhouse	5.00	2.20

1999-00 Metal

	MINT	NRMT
COMPLETE SET (180)	50.00	22.00
COMMON CARD (1-150)	.10	.05
COMMON RC (151-180)	.50	.23
SEMISTARS	.15	.07
SEMISTARS RC	.60	.25
UNLISTED STARS	.25	.11
UNLISTED STARS RC	.75	.35

RCs: STATED ODDS 1:2

Card	MINT	NRMT
❑ 1 Vince Carter	2.50	1.10
❑ 2 Stephon Marbury	.50	.23
❑ 3 David Robinson	.40	.18
❑ 4 Ray Allen	.25	.11
❑ 5 P.J. Brown	.10	.05
❑ 6 Shawn Kemp	.40	.18
❑ 7 Cedric Ceballos	.10	.05
❑ 8 Dale Davis	.10	.05
❑ 9 Rodney Rogers	.10	.05
❑ 10 Chris Gatling	.10	.05
❑ 11 Bryant Reeves	.10	.05
❑ 12 Al Harrington	.30	.14
❑ 13 Brent Barry	.10	.05
❑ 14 Brevin Knight	.10	.05
❑ 15 Radoslav Nesterovic	.10	.05
❑ 16 Tom Gugliotta	.15	.07
❑ 17 Charles Barkley	.40	.18
❑ 18 Cuttino Mobley	.25	.11
❑ 19 Corliss Williamson	.10	.05
❑ 20 Hersey Hawkins	.15	.07
❑ 21 Mike Bibby	.30	.14
❑ 22 Pat Garrity	.10	.05
❑ 23 Kelvin Cato	.10	.05
❑ 24 Alan Henderson	.10	.05
❑ 25 Alvin Williams	.10	.05
❑ 26 Antonio McDyess	.25	.11
❑ 27 Damon Stoudamire	.25	.11
❑ 28 Kerry Kittles	.15	.07
❑ 29 Michael Olowokandi	.15	.07
❑ 30 Brent Price	.10	.05
❑ 31 Fred Hoiberg	.10	.05
❑ 32 Glenn Robinson	.15	.07
❑ 33 Hakeem Olajuwon	.40	.18
❑ 34 Monty Williams	.10	.05
❑ 35 Terry Porter	.10	.05
❑ 36 Allen Iverson	1.00	.45
❑ 37 Juwan Howard	.15	.07
❑ 38 Mario Elie	.10	.05
❑ 39 Mookie Blaylock	.10	.05
❑ 40 Sam Cassell	.15	.07
❑ 41 Toni Kukoc	.30	.14
❑ 42 Anthony Mason	.15	.07
❑ 43 George Lynch	.10	.05

❑ 44 John Starks	.10	.05
❑ 45 Malik Rose	.10	.05
❑ 46 Rod Strickland	.15	.07
❑ 47 Tim Thomas	.30	.14
❑ 48 Howard Eisley	.10	.05
❑ 49 Kenny Anderson	.15	.07
❑ 50 Kurt Thomas	.10	.05
❑ 51 Lindsey Hunter	.10	.05
❑ 52 Rick Fox	.10	.05
❑ 53 Vlade Divac	.10	.05
❑ 54 Avery Johnson	.10	.05
❑ 55 Dale Ellis	.10	.05
❑ 56 Donyell Marshall	.10	.05
❑ 57 Elden Campbell	.10	.05
❑ 58 Larry Hughes	.60	.25
❑ 59 Mitch Richmond	.25	.11
❑ 60 Chris Mills	.10	.05
❑ 61 David Wesley	.10	.05
❑ 62 Gary Payton	.40	.18
❑ 63 Isaac Austin	.10	.05
❑ 64 Robert Traylor	.10	.05
❑ 65 Theo Ratliff	.10	.05
❑ 66 Antawn Jamison	.50	.23
❑ 67 Eddie Jones	.50	.23
❑ 68 Kevin Garnett	1.50	.70
❑ 69 Matt Geiger	.10	.05
❑ 70 Vernon Maxwell	.10	.05
❑ 71 Antonio Davis	.10	.05
❑ 72 Dirk Nowitzki	.40	.18
❑ 73 Johnny Newman	.10	.05
❑ 74 Maurice Taylor	.25	.11
❑ 75 Steve Smith	.15	.07
❑ 76 Derek Anderson	.25	.11
❑ 77 Doug Christie	.10	.05
❑ 78 Erick Strickland	.10	.05
❑ 79 Keith Van Horn	.50	.23
❑ 80 Luc Longley	.10	.05
❑ 81 Alonzo Mourning	.25	.11
❑ 82 Christian Laettner	.15	.07
❑ 83 Jamal Mashburn	.15	.07
❑ 84 Jon Barry	.10	.05
❑ 85 Patrick Ewing	.25	.11
❑ 86 Shareef Abdur-Rahim	.50	.23
❑ 87 Vitaly Potapenko	.10	.05
❑ 88 Darrell Armstrong	.15	.07
❑ 89 Eric Williams	.10	.05
❑ 90 Jerome Williams	.15	.07
❑ 91 Nick Anderson	.10	.05
❑ 92 Othella Harrington	.10	.05
❑ 93 Tim Hardaway	.25	.11
❑ 94 Eric Piatkowski	.10	.05
❑ 95 Isaiah Rider	.15	.07
❑ 96 Kendall Gill	.15	.07
❑ 97 Rasheed Wallace	.25	.11
❑ 98 Robert Pack	.10	.05
❑ 99 Tracy McGrady	.75	.35
❑ 100 Allan Houston	.25	.11
❑ 101 Brian Grant	.15	.07
❑ 102 Dikembe Mutombo	.15	.07
❑ 103 Karl Malone	.40	.18
❑ 104 Nick Van Exel	.15	.07
❑ 105 Shaquille O'Neal	1.25	.55
❑ 106 Chris Anstey	.10	.05
❑ 107 Michael Dickerson	.25	.11
❑ 108 Shandon Anderson	.10	.05
❑ 109 Tariq Adbul-Wahad	.10	.05
❑ 110 Tim Duncan	1.25	.55
❑ 111 Voshon Lenard	.10	.05
❑ 112 Bimbo Coles	.10	.05
❑ 113 Detlef Schrempf	.15	.07
❑ 114 John Stockton	.25	.11
❑ 115 Kobe Bryant	2.00	.90
❑ 116 Latrell Sprewell	.50	.23
❑ 117 Raef LaFrentz	.25	.11
❑ 118 Antoine Walker	.30	.14
❑ 119 Bryon Russell	.10	.05
❑ 120 Derek Fisher	.15	.07
❑ 121 Jason Williams	.60	.25
❑ 122 Jerry Stackhouse	.15	.07
❑ 123 Larry Johnson	.15	.07
❑ 124 Clifford Robinson	.10	.05
❑ 125 Horace Grant	.15	.07
❑ 126 Malik Sealy	.10	.05
❑ 127 Michael Finley	.25	.11
❑ 128 Rik Smits	.10	.05
❑ 129 Dell Curry	.10	.05
❑ 130 Jim Jackson	.10	.05
❑ 131 Ron Mercer	.30	.14
❑ 132 Scott Burrell	.10	.05
❑ 133 Scottie Pippen	.75	.35
❑ 134 Troy Hudson	.10	.05
❑ 135 Anfernee Hardaway	.75	.35
❑ 136 Anthony Peeler	.10	.05
❑ 137 Jalen Rose	.25	.11
❑ 138 Lamond Murray	.10	.05
❑ 139 Ruben Patterson	.25	.11
❑ 140 Chris Webber	.75	.35
❑ 141 Glen Rice	.15	.07
❑ 142 Grant Hill	1.25	.55
❑ 143 Jeff Hornacek	.15	.07
❑ 144 Marcus Camby	.25	.11
❑ 145 Paul Pierce	.50	.23
❑ 146 Bob Sura	.10	.05
❑ 147 Jason Kidd	.75	.35
❑ 148 Reggie Miller	.25	.11
❑ 149 Terrell Brandon	.15	.07
❑ 150 Vin Baker	.15	.07
❑ 151 Lamar Odom RC	6.00	2.70
❑ 152 Steve Francis RC	10.00	4.50
❑ 153 Elton Brand RC	8.00	3.60
❑ 154 Wally Szczerbiak RC	3.00	1.35
❑ 155 Adrian Griffin RC	1.00	.45
❑ 156 Andre Miller RC	2.50	1.10
❑ 157 Jason Terry RC	1.25	.55
❑ 158 Richard Hamilton RC	2.00	.90
❑ 159 Ron Artest RC	2.00	.90
❑ 160 Shawn Marion RC	2.50	1.10
❑ 161 James Posey RC	1.50	.70
❑ 162 Greg Buckner RC	.50	.23
❑ 163 Chucky Atkins RC	1.00	.45
❑ 164 Corey Maggette RC	3.00	1.35
❑ 165 Todd MacCulloch RC	.75	.35
❑ 166 Baron Davis RC	2.00	.90
❑ 167 Trajan Langdon RC	1.25	.55
❑ 168 Bruno Sundov RC	.50	.23
❑ 169 Scott Padgett RC	.75	.35
❑ 170 Vonteego Cummings RC	1.25	.55
❑ 171 Ryan Bowen RC	.50	.23
❑ 172 Jonathan Bender RC	4.00	1.80
❑ 173 Jermaine Jackson RC	.50	.23
❑ 174 Devean George RC	1.50	.70
❑ 175 Chris Herren RC	.50	.23
❑ 176 Rodney Buford RC	.50	.23
❑ 177 Laron Profit RC	.75	.35
❑ 178 Mirsad Turkcan RC	.50	.23
❑ 179 Eddie Robinson RC	1.25	.55
❑ 180 Anthony Carter RC	2.00	.90

1999-00 Metal Emeralds

	MINT	NRMT
COMPLETE SET (180)	100.00	45.00
COMMON CARD (1-150)	.40	.18
COMMON CARD (151-180)	.60	.25

*STARS: 1.5X TO 4X BASE CARD HI
*RCs: .5X TO 1.25X BASE HI
STARS: STATED ODDS 1:4
RCs: STATED ODDS 1:8

1999-00 Metal Vince Carter Scrapbook

	MINT	NRMT
COMPLETE SET (10)	30.00	13.50
COMMON CARD (VC1-VC10)	4.00	1.80

STATED ODDS 1:8

❑ VC1 Vince Carter	4.00	1.80
❑ VC2 Vince Carter	4.00	1.80
❑ VC3 Vince Carter	4.00	1.80
❑ VC4 Vince Carter	4.00	1.80
❑ VC5 Vince Carter	4.00	1.80
❑ VC6 Vince Carter	4.00	1.80
❑ VC7 Vince Carter	4.00	1.80
❑ VC8 Vince Carter	4.00	1.80
❑ VC9 Vince Carter	4.00	1.80
❑ VC10 Vince Carter	4.00	1.80

1999-00 Metal Genuine Coverage

	MINT	NRMT
COMPLETE SET (6)	300.00	135.00
COMMON CARD	30.00	13.50

STATED ODDS 1:288
NNO CARDS LISTED BELOW ALPHABETICALLY

❑ 1 Vince Carter	150.00	70.00
❑ 2 Karl Malone	40.00	18.00
❑ 3 Shaquille O'Neal	100.00	45.00
❑ 4 Paul Pierce	40.00	18.00
❑ 5 John Stockton	40.00	18.00
❑ 6 Antoine Walker	30.00	13.50

1999-00 Metal Heavy Metal

	MINT	NRMT
COMPLETE SET (10)	20.00	9.00
COMMON CARD (HM1-HM10)	.75	.35
STATED ODDS 1:20		
❑ HM1 Kobe Bryant	6.00	2.70
❑ HM2 Vince Carter	8.00	3.60
❑ HM3 Lamar Odom	3.00	1.35
❑ HM4 Kevin Garnett	5.00	2.20
❑ HM5 Shawn Kemp	1.25	.55
❑ HM6 Shareef Abdur-Rahim	1.50	.70
❑ HM7 Antonio McDyess	.75	.35
❑ HM8 Tim Duncan	4.00	1.80
❑ HM9 Keith Van Horn	1.50	.70
❑ HM10 Shaquille O'Neal	4.00	1.80

1999-00 Metal Platinum Portraits

	MINT	NRMT
COMPLETE SET (15)	12.00	5.50
COMMON CARD (PP1-PP15)	.40	.18
UNLISTED STARS	.60	.25
STATED ODDS 1:4		
❑ PP1 Elton Brand	3.00	1.35
❑ PP2 Lamar Odom	2.50	1.10
❑ PP3 Steve Francis	4.00	1.80
❑ PP4 Richard Hamilton	.75	.35
❑ PP5 Baron Davis	.75	.35
❑ PP6 Vonteego Cummings	.60	.25
❑ PP7 Corey Maggette	1.25	.55
❑ PP8 James Posey	.60	.25
❑ PP9 Shawn Marion	1.00	.45
❑ PP10 Wally Szczerbiak	1.25	.55
❑ PP11 Jason Terry	.60	.25
❑ PP12 Andre Miller	1.00	.45
❑ PP13 Scott Padgett	.40	.18
❑ PP14 Trajan Langdon	.60	.25
❑ PP15 Jonathan Bender	1.50	.70

1999-00 Metal Rivalries

	MINT	NRMT
COMPLETE SET (15)	15.00	6.75
COMMON CARD (R1-R15)	.75	.35
STATED ODDS 1:4		
❑ R1 Allen Iverson Stephon Marbury	2.50	1.10
❑ R2 Jason Kidd Gary Payton	2.00	.90
❑ R3 Mike Bibby Jason Williams	1.50	.70
❑ R4 Patrick Ewing Alonzo Mourning	.75	.35
❑ R5 Tim Duncan Kevin Garnett	3.00	1.35
❑ R6 Anfernee Hardaway Kobe Bryant	4.00	1.80
❑ R7 Charles Barkley Karl Malone	1.25	.55
❑ R8 Antonio McDyess Shareef Abdur-Rahim	1.25	.55
❑ R9 Vince Carter Grant Hill	5.00	2.20
❑ R10 Antoine Walker Keith Van Horn	1.25	.55
❑ R11 Shawn Kemp Elton Brand	2.50	1.10
❑ R12 Shaquille O'Neal David Robinson	3.00	1.35
❑ R13 Raef LaFrentz Dirk Nowitzki	1.00	.45
❑ R14 Steve Francis John Stockton	2.50	1.10
❑ R15 Lamar Odom Scottie Pippen	2.50	1.10

1999-00 Metal Scoring Magnets

	MINT	NRMT
COMPLETE SET (10)	12.00	5.50
COMMON CARD (SM1-SM10)	.50	.23
UNLISTED STARS	.75	.35
STATED ODDS 1:20		
❑ SM1 Grant Hill	4.00	1.80
❑ SM2 Stephon Marbury	1.50	.70
❑ SM3 Allen Iverson	3.00	1.35
❑ SM4 Ray Allen	.75	.35
❑ SM5 Steve Francis	4.00	1.80
❑ SM6 Ron Mercer	1.00	.45
❑ SM7 Paul Pierce	1.50	.70
❑ SM8 Latrell Sprewell	1.50	.70
❑ SM9 Glenn Robinson	.50	.23
❑ SM10 Eddie Jones	1.50	.70

1997-98 Metal Universe

	MINT	NRMT
COMPLETE SET (125)	25.00	11.00
COMMON CARD (1-125)	.15	.07
SEMISTARS	.20	.09
UNLISTED STARS	.40	.18
COMMON REEBOK BRONZE	.20	.09
*REEBOK BRONZE: .25X TO .5X HI COLUMN		
COMMON REEBOK GOLD	.60	.25
*REEBOK GOLD: 1.5X TO 3X HI		
COMMON REEBOK SILVER	.30	.14
*REEBOK SILVERS: .5X TO 1X HI		
REEBOK: ONE PER SER.1 PACK		
❑ 1 Charles Barkley	.60	.25
❑ 2 Dell Curry	.15	.07
❑ 3 Derek Fisher	.15	.07
❑ 4 Derek Harper	.15	.07

	MINT	NRMT
❑ 5 Avery Johnson	.15	.07
❑ 6 Steve Smith	.20	.09
❑ 7 Alonzo Mourning	.40	.18
❑ 8 Rod Strickland	.20	.09
❑ 9 Chris Mullin	.40	.18
❑ 10 Rony Seikaly	.15	.07
❑ 11 Vin Baker	.20	.09
❑ 12 Austin Croshere RC	1.00	.45
❑ 13 Vinny Del Negro	.15	.07
❑ 14 Sherman Douglas	.15	.07
❑ 15 Priest Lauderdale	.15	.07
❑ 16 Cedric Ceballos	.15	.07
❑ 17 LaPhonso Ellis	.15	.07
❑ 18 Luc Longley	.15	.07
❑ 19 Brian Grant	.20	.09
❑ 20 Allen Iverson	2.00	.90
❑ 21 Anthony Mason	.20	.09
❑ 22 Bryant Reeves	.15	.07
❑ 23 Michael Jordan	5.00	2.20
❑ 24 Dale Ellis	.15	.07
❑ 25 Terrell Brandon	.20	.09
❑ 26 Patrick Ewing	.40	.18
❑ 27 Allan Houston	.40	.18
❑ 28 Damon Stoudamire	.50	.23
❑ 29 Loy Vaught	.15	.07
❑ 30 Walt Williams	.15	.07
❑ 31 Shareef Abdur-Rahim	1.25	.55
❑ 32 Mario Elie	.15	.07
❑ 33 Juwan Howard	.20	.09
❑ 34 Tom Gugliotta	.20	.09
❑ 35 Glen Rice	.20	.09
❑ 36 Isaiah Rider	.20	.09
❑ 37 Arvydas Sabonis	.20	.09
❑ 38 Derrick Coleman	.20	.09
❑ 39 Kevin Willis	.15	.07
❑ 40 Kendall Gill	.20	.09
❑ 41 John Wallace	.15	.07
❑ 42 Tracy McGrady RC	4.00	1.80
❑ 43 Travis Best	.15	.07
❑ 44 Malik Rose	.15	.07
❑ 45 Anfernee Hardaway	1.25	.55
❑ 46 Roy Rogers	.15	.07
❑ 47 Kerry Kittles	.40	.18
❑ 48 Matt Maloney	.15	.07
❑ 49 Antonio McDyess	.50	.23
❑ 50 Shaquille O'Neal	2.00	.90
❑ 51 George McCloud	.15	.07
❑ 52 Wesley Person	.15	.07
❑ 53 Shawn Bradley	.15	.07
❑ 54 Antonio Davis	.15	.07
❑ 55 P.J. Brown	.15	.07
❑ 56 Joe Dumars	.40	.18
❑ 57 Horace Grant	.20	.09
❑ 58 Steve Kerr	.15	.07
❑ 59 Hakeem Olajuwon	.60	.25
❑ 60 Tim Hardaway	.40	.18
❑ 61 Toni Kukoc	.50	.23
❑ 62 Ron Mercer RC	1.25	.55
❑ 63 Gary Payton	.60	.25
❑ 64 Grant Hill	2.00	.90
❑ 65 Detlef Schrempf	.20	.09
❑ 66 Tim Duncan RC	5.00	2.20
❑ 67 Shawn Kemp	.60	.25
❑ 68 Voshon Lenard	.15	.07
❑ 69 Othella Harrington	.15	.07
❑ 70 Hersey Hawkins	.20	.09
❑ 71 Lindsey Hunter	.15	.07
❑ 72 Antoine Walker	.75	.35

❑ 73 Jamal Mashburn .20 .09
❑ 74 Kenny Anderson .20 .09
❑ 75 Todd Day .15 .07
❑ 76 Todd Fuller .15 .07
❑ 77 Jermaine O'Neal .20 .09
❑ 78 David Robinson .60 .25
❑ 79 Erick Dampier .15 .07
❑ 80 Keith Van Horn RC 2.00 .90
❑ 81 Kobe Bryant 3.00 1.35
❑ 82 Chris Childs .15 .07
❑ 83 Scottie Pippen 1.25 .55
❑ 84 Marcus Camby .50 .23
❑ 85 Danny Ferry .15 .07
❑ 86 Jeff Hornacek .20 .09
❑ 87 Charles Outlaw .15 .07
❑ 88 Larry Johnson .20 .09
❑ 89 Tony Delk .15 .07
❑ 90 Stephon Marbury 1.25 .55
❑ 91 Robert Pack .15 .07
❑ 92 Chris Webber 1.25 .55
❑ 93 Clyde Drexler .40 .18
❑ 94 Eddie Jones .75 .35
❑ 95 Jerry Stackhouse .20 .09
❑ 96 Tyrone Hill .15 .07
❑ 97 Karl Malone .60 .25
❑ 98 Reggie Miller .40 .18
❑ 99 Bryon Russell .15 .07
❑ 100 Dale Davis .15 .07
❑ 101 Steve Nash .15 .07
❑ 102 Vitaly Potapenko .15 .07
❑ 103 Nick Anderson .15 .07
❑ 104 Ray Allen .60 .25
❑ 105 Sean Elliott .15 .07
❑ 106 Dikembe Mutombo .20 .09
❑ 107 Dennis Rodman .75 .35
❑ 108 Lorenzen Wright .15 .07
❑ 109 Kevin Garnett 2.50 1.10
❑ 110 Christian Laettner .20 .09
❑ 111 Mitch Richmond .40 .18
❑ 112 Joe Smith .20 .09
❑ 113 Jason Kidd 1.25 .55
❑ 114 Glenn Robinson .20 .09
❑ 115 Mark Price .15 .07
❑ 116 Mark Jackson .15 .07
❑ 117 Bobby Phills .15 .07
❑ 118 John Starks .15 .07
❑ 119 John Stockton .40 .18
❑ 120 Mookie Blaylock .15 .07
❑ 121 Dean Garrett .15 .07
❑ 122 Olden Polynice .15 .07
❑ 123 Latrell Sprewell .75 .35
❑ 124 Checklist .15 .07
❑ 125 Checklist .15 .07

1997-98 Metal Universe Precious Metal Gems

	MINT	NRMT
COMMON RED (1-123)	12.00	5.50
SEMISTARS	20.00	9.00
UNLISTED STARS	30.00	13.50

RANDOM INSERTS IN HOBBY PACKS
STATED PRINT RUN 100 SERIAL #'d SETS
COMMON GREEN (1-123) .. 150.00 70.00
*GREEN STARS: 7X TO 12X RED GEMS HI
*GREEN RCs: 5X TO 8X RED
FIRST 10 CARDS OF PRINT RUN ARE GREEN

❑ 1 Charles Barkley 50.00 22.00
❑ 2 Dell Curry 12.00 5.50
❑ 3 Derek Fisher 12.00 5.50
❑ 4 Derek Harper 12.00 5.50
❑ 5 Avery Johnson 12.00 5.50
❑ 6 Steve Smith 20.00 9.00
❑ 7 Alonzo Mourning 30.00 13.50
❑ 8 Rod Strickland 20.00 9.00
❑ 9 Chris Mullin 30.00 13.50
❑ 10 Rony Seikaly 12.00 5.50
❑ 11 Vin Baker 20.00 9.00
❑ 12 Austin Croshere 40.00 18.00
❑ 13 Vinny Del Negro 12.00 5.50
❑ 14 Sherman Douglas 12.00 5.50
❑ 15 Priest Lauderdale 12.00 5.50
❑ 16 Cedric Ceballos 12.00 5.50
❑ 17 LaPhonso Ellis 12.00 5.50
❑ 18 Luc Longley 12.00 5.50
❑ 19 Brian Grant 20.00 9.00
❑ 20 Allen Iverson 150.00 70.00
❑ 21 Anthony Mason 20.00 9.00
❑ 22 Bryant Reeves 12.00 5.50
❑ 23 Michael Jordan 750.00 350.00
❑ 23G M.Jordan Green .. 15000.00 6800.00
❑ 24 Dale Ellis 12.00 5.50
❑ 25 Terrell Brandon 20.00 9.00
❑ 26 Patrick Ewing 30.00 13.50
❑ 27 Allan Houston 30.00 13.50
❑ 28 Damon Stoudamire 40.00 18.00
❑ 29 Loy Vaught 12.00 5.50
❑ 30 Walt Williams 12.00 5.50
❑ 31 Shareef Abdur-Rahim 100.00 45.00
❑ 32 Mario Elie 12.00 5.50
❑ 33 Juwan Howard 20.00 9.00
❑ 34 Tom Gugliotta 20.00 9.00
❑ 35 Glen Rice 20.00 9.00
❑ 36 Isaiah Rider 20.00 9.00
❑ 37 Arvydas Sabonis 20.00 9.00
❑ 38 Derrick Coleman 20.00 9.00
❑ 39 Kevin Willis 12.00 5.50
❑ 40 Kendall Gill 20.00 9.00
❑ 41 John Wallace 12.00 5.50
❑ 42 Tracy McGrady 150.00 70.00
❑ 43 Travis Best 12.00 5.50
❑ 44 Malik Rose 12.00 5.50
❑ 45 Anfernee Hardaway .. 125.00 55.00
❑ 46 Roy Rogers 12.00 5.50
❑ 47 Kerry Kittles 30.00 13.50
❑ 48 Matt Maloney 12.00 5.50
❑ 49 Antonio McDyess 40.00 18.00
❑ 50 Shaquille O'Neal 150.00 70.00
❑ 51 George McCloud 12.00 5.50
❑ 52 Wesley Person 12.00 5.50
❑ 53 Shawn Bradley 12.00 5.50
❑ 54 Antonio Davis 12.00 5.50
❑ 55 P.J. Brown 12.00 5.50
❑ 56 Joe Dumars 30.00 13.50
❑ 57 Horace Grant 20.00 9.00
❑ 58 Steve Kerr 12.00 5.50
❑ 59 Hakeem Olajuwon 50.00 22.00
❑ 60 Tim Hardaway 30.00 13.50
❑ 61 Toni Kukoc 80.00 36.00
❑ 62 Ron Mercer 50.00 22.00
❑ 63 Gary Payton 50.00 22.00
❑ 64 Grant Hill 150.00 70.00
❑ 65 Detlef Schrempf 20.00 9.00
❑ 66 Tim Duncan 150.00 70.00
❑ 67 Shawn Kemp 50.00 22.00
❑ 68 Voshon Lenard 12.00 5.50
❑ 69 Othella Harrington 12.00 5.50
❑ 70 Hersey Hawkins 20.00 9.00
❑ 71 Lindsey Hunter 12.00 5.50
❑ 72 Antoine Walker 60.00 27.00
❑ 73 Jamal Mashburn 20.00 9.00
❑ 74 Kenny Anderson 20.00 9.00
❑ 75 Todd Day 12.00 5.50
❑ 76 Todd Fuller 12.00 5.50
❑ 77 Jermaine O'Neal 20.00 9.00
❑ 78 David Robinson 50.00 22.00
❑ 79 Erick Dampier 12.00 5.50
❑ 80 Keith Van Horn 80.00 36.00
❑ 81 Kobe Bryant 400.00 180.00
❑ 82 Chris Childs 12.00 5.50
❑ 83 Scottie Pippen 125.00 55.00
❑ 84 Marcus Camby 40.00 18.00
❑ 85 Danny Ferry 12.00 5.50
❑ 86 Jeff Hornacek 20.00 9.00
❑ 87 Charles Outlaw 12.00 5.50
❑ 88 Larry Johnson 20.00 9.00
❑ 89 Tony Delk 12.00 5.50
❑ 90 Stephon Marbury 100.00 45.00
❑ 91 Robert Pack 12.00 5.50
❑ 92 Chris Webber 125.00 55.00
❑ 93 Clyde Drexler 30.00 13.50
❑ 94 Eddie Jones 80.00 36.00
❑ 95 Jerry Stackhouse 20.00 9.00
❑ 96 Tyrone Hill 12.00 5.50
❑ 97 Karl Malone 50.00 22.00
❑ 98 Reggie Miller 30.00 13.50
❑ 99 Bryon Russell 12.00 5.50
❑ 100 Dale Davis 12.00 5.50
❑ 101 Steve Nash 12.00 5.50
❑ 102 Vitaly Potapenko 12.00 5.50
❑ 103 Nick Anderson 12.00 5.50
❑ 104 Ray Allen 50.00 22.00
❑ 105 Sean Elliott 12.00 5.50
❑ 106 Dikembe Mutombo 20.00 9.00
❑ 107 Dennis Rodman 80.00 36.00
❑ 108 Lorenzen Wright 12.00 5.50
❑ 109 Kevin Garnett 200.00 90.00
❑ 110 Christian Laettner 20.00 9.00
❑ 111 Mitch Richmond 30.00 13.50
❑ 112 Joe Smith 20.00 9.00
❑ 113 Jason Kidd 125.00 55.00
❑ 114 Glenn Robinson 20.00 9.00
❑ 115 Mark Price 12.00 5.50
❑ 116 Mark Jackson 12.00 5.50
❑ 117 Bobby Phills 12.00 5.50
❑ 118 John Starks 12.00 5.50
❑ 119 John Stockton 30.00 13.50
❑ 120 Mookie Blaylock 12.00 5.50
❑ 121 Dean Garrett 12.00 5.50
❑ 122 Olden Polynice 12.00 5.50
❑ 123 Latrell Sprewell 80.00 36.00

1997-98 Metal Universe Gold Universe

	MINT	NRMT
COMPLETE SET (10)	60.00	27.00
COMMON CARD (1-10)	4.00	1.80
SEMISTARS	5.00	2.20
UNLISTED STARS	8.00	3.60

STATED ODDS 1:120 RETAIL

❑ 1 Damon Stoudamire 10.00 4.50
❑ 2 Shawn Kemp 12.00 5.50
❑ 3 John Stockton 8.00 3.60
❑ 4 Jerry Stackhouse 5.00 2.20
❑ 5 John Wallace 4.00 1.80
❑ 6 Juwan Howard 5.00 2.20
❑ 7 David Robinson 12.00 5.50
❑ 8 Gary Payton 12.00 5.50
❑ 9 Joe Smith 5.00 2.20
❑ 10 Charles Barkley 12.00 5.50

1997-98 Metal Universe Planet Metal

	MINT	NRMT
COMPLETE SET (15)	125.00	55.00
COMMON CARD (1-15)	3.00	1.35

STATED ODDS 1:24 HOBBY/RETAIL

❑ 1 Michael Jordan	30.00	13.50
❑ 2 Allen Iverson	12.00	5.50
❑ 3 Kobe Bryant	20.00	9.00
❑ 4 Shaquille O'Neal	12.00	5.50
❑ 5 Stephon Marbury	8.00	3.60
❑ 6 Marcus Camby	3.00	1.35
❑ 7 Anfernee Hardaway	8.00	3.60
❑ 8 Kevin Garnett	15.00	6.75
❑ 9 Shareef Abdur-Rahim	8.00	3.60
❑ 10 Dennis Rodman	5.00	2.20
❑ 11 Grant Hill	12.00	5.50
❑ 12 Hakeem Olajuwon	4.00	1.80
❑ 13 David Robinson	4.00	1.80
❑ 14 Charles Barkley	4.00	1.80
❑ 15 Gary Payton	4.00	1.80

1997-98 Metal Universe Platinum Portraits

	MINT	NRMT
COMPLETE SET (15)	550.00	250.00
COMMON CARD (1-15)	10.00	4.50

STATED ODDS 1:288 HOBBY/RETAIL

❑ 1 Michael Jordan	120.00	55.00
❑ 2 Allen Iverson	50.00	22.00
❑ 3 Kobe Bryant	80.00	36.00
❑ 4 Shaquille O'Neal	50.00	22.00
❑ 5 Stephon Marbury	30.00	13.50
❑ 6 Marcus Camby	12.00	5.50
❑ 7 Anfernee Hardaway	30.00	13.50
❑ 8 Kevin Garnett	60.00	27.00
❑ 9 Shareef Abdur-Rahim	30.00	13.50
❑ 10 Dennis Rodman	20.00	9.00
❑ 11 Ray Allen	15.00	6.75
❑ 12 Grant Hill	50.00	22.00
❑ 13 Kerry Kittles	10.00	4.50
❑ 14 Antoine Walker	20.00	9.00
❑ 15 Scottie Pippen	30.00	13.50

1997-98 Metal Universe Silver Slams

	MINT	NRMT
COMPLETE SET (20)	15.00	6.75
COMMON CARD (1-20)	.50	.23
SEMISTARS	.75	.35
UNLISTED STARS	1.25	.55

STATED ODDS 1:6 HOBBY/RETAIL

❑ 1 Ray Allen	2.00	.90
❑ 2 Kerry Kittles	1.25	.55
❑ 3 Antoine Walker	2.50	1.10
❑ 4 Scottie Pippen	4.00	1.80
❑ 5 Damon Stoudamire	1.50	.70
❑ 6 Shawn Kemp	2.00	.90
❑ 7 Jerry Stackhouse	.75	.35
❑ 8 John Wallace	.50	.23
❑ 9 Juwan Howard	.75	.35
❑ 10 Gary Payton	2.00	.90
❑ 11 Joe Smith	.75	.35
❑ 12 Terrell Brandon	.75	.35
❑ 13 Hakeem Olajuwon	2.00	.90
❑ 14 Tom Gugliotta	.75	.35
❑ 15 Glen Rice	.75	.35
❑ 16 Charles Barkley	2.00	.90
❑ 17 David Robinson	2.00	.90
❑ 18 Patrick Ewing	1.25	.55
❑ 19 Christian Laettner	.75	.35
❑ 20 Chris Webber	4.00	1.80

1997-98 Metal Universe Titanium

	MINT	NRMT
COMPLETE SET (20)	400.00	180.00
COMMON CARD (1-20)	6.00	2.70

STATED ODDS 1:72 HOBBY

❑ 1 Michael Jordan	80.00	36.00
❑ 2 Allen Iverson	30.00	13.50
❑ 3 Kobe Bryant	50.00	22.00
❑ 4 Shaquille O'Neal	30.00	13.50
❑ 5 Stephon Marbury	20.00	9.00
❑ 6 Marcus Camby	8.00	3.60
❑ 7 Anfernee Hardaway	20.00	9.00
❑ 8 Kevin Garnett	40.00	18.00
❑ 9 Shareef Abdur-Rahim	20.00	9.00
❑ 10 Dennis Rodman	12.00	5.50
❑ 11 Ray Allen	10.00	4.50
❑ 12 Grant Hill	30.00	13.50
❑ 13 Kerry Kittles	6.00	2.70
❑ 14 Antoine Walker	12.00	5.50
❑ 15 Scottie Pippen	20.00	9.00
❑ 16 Damon Stoudamire	8.00	3.60
❑ 17 Shawn Kemp	10.00	4.50
❑ 18 Hakeem Olajuwon	10.00	4.50
❑ 19 Jerry Stackhouse	6.00	2.70
❑ 20 Juwan Howard	6.00	2.70

1998-99 Metal Universe

	MINT	NRMT
COMPLETE SET (125)	25.00	11.00
COMMON CARD (1-125)	.15	.07
SEMISTARS	.20	.09
UNLISTED STARS	.40	.18

UNPRICED GEM MASTERS SERIAL #'d TO 1
GEM MASTERS: RANDOM INS.IN HOB

❑ 1 Michael Jordan	5.00	2.20
❑ 2 Mario Elie	.15	.07
❑ 3 Voshon Lenard	.15	.07
❑ 4 John Starks	.15	.07
❑ 5 Juwan Howard	.20	.09
❑ 6 Michael Finley	.40	.18
❑ 7 Bobby Jackson	.15	.07
❑ 8 Glenn Robinson	.20	.09
❑ 9 Antonio McDyess	.40	.18
❑ 10 Marcus Camby	.40	.18
❑ 11 Zydrunas Ilgauskas	.15	.07
❑ 12 LaPhonso Ellis	.15	.07
❑ 13 Terrell Brandon	.20	.09
❑ 14 Rex Chapman	.15	.07
❑ 15 Rod Strickland	.20	.09
❑ 16 Dennis Rodman	.75	.35
❑ 17 Clarence Weatherspoon	.15	.07
❑ 18 P.J. Brown	.15	.07
❑ 19 Anfernee Hardaway	1.25	.55
❑ 20 Dikembe Mutombo	.20	.09
❑ 21 Gary Trent	.15	.07
❑ 22 Patrick Ewing	.40	.18
❑ 23 Sam Mack	.15	.07
❑ 24 Scottie Pippen	1.25	.55
❑ 25 Shaquille O'Neal	2.00	.90
❑ 26 Donyell Marshall	.15	.07
❑ 27 Bo Outlaw	.15	.07
❑ 28 Isaiah Rider	.20	.09
❑ 29 Detlef Schrempf	.20	.09
❑ 30 Mark Price	.15	.07
❑ 31 Jim Jackson	.15	.07
❑ 32 Eddie Jones	.75	.35
❑ 33 Allen Iverson	1.50	.70
❑ 34 Corliss Williamson	.15	.07
❑ 35 Tim Duncan	2.00	.90
❑ 36 Ron Harper	.20	.09
❑ 37 Tony Delk	.15	.07
❑ 38 Derek Fisher	.20	.09
❑ 39 Kendall Gill	.20	.09
❑ 40 Theo Ratliff	.15	.07
❑ 41 Kelvin Cato	.15	.07
❑ 42 Antoine Walker	.60	.25
❑ 43 Lamond Murray	.15	.07
❑ 44 Avery Johnson	.15	.07
❑ 45 John Stockton	.40	.18
❑ 46 David Wesley	.15	.07
❑ 47 Brian Williams	.15	.07
❑ 48 Elden Campbell	.15	.07
❑ 49 Sam Cassell	.20	.09
❑ 50 Grant Hill	2.00	.90
❑ 51 Tracy McGrady	1.50	.70
❑ 52 Glen Rice	.20	.09
❑ 53 Kobe Bryant	3.00	1.35
❑ 54 Cherokee Parks	.15	.07
❑ 55 John Wallace	.15	.07
❑ 56 Bobby Phills	.15	.07
❑ 57 Jerry Stackhouse	.20	.09
❑ 58 Lorenzen Wright	.15	.07

		MINT	NRMT
❑ 59	Stephon Marbury	1.00	.45
❑ 60	Shandon Anderson	.15	.07
❑ 61	Jeff Hornacek	.20	.09
❑ 62	Joe Dumars	.40	.18
❑ 63	Tom Gugliotta	.20	.09
❑ 64	Johnny Newman	.15	.07
❑ 65	Kevin Garnett	2.50	1.10
❑ 66	Clifford Robinson	.15	.07
❑ 67	Dennis Scott	.15	.07
❑ 68	Anthony Mason	.20	.09
❑ 69	Rodney Rogers	.15	.07
❑ 70	Bryon Russell	.15	.07
❑ 71	Maurice Taylor	.40	.18
❑ 72	Mookie Blaylock	.15	.07
❑ 73	Shawn Bradley	.15	.07
❑ 74	Matt Maloney	.15	.07
❑ 75	Karl Malone	.60	.25
❑ 76	Larry Johnson	.20	.09
❑ 77	Calbert Cheaney	.15	.07
❑ 78	Steve Smith	.20	.09
❑ 79	Toni Kukoc	.50	.23
❑ 80	Reggie Miller	.40	.18
❑ 81	Jayson Williams	.20	.09
❑ 82	Gary Payton	.60	.25
❑ 83	George Lynch	.15	.07
❑ 84	Wesley Person	.15	.07
❑ 85	Charles Barkley	.60	.25
❑ 86	Tim Hardaway	.40	.18
❑ 87	Darrell Armstrong	.20	.09
❑ 88	Rasheed Wallace	.40	.18
❑ 89	Tariq Abdul-Wahad	.15	.07
❑ 90	Kenny Anderson	.20	.09
❑ 91	Chris Mullin	.40	.18
❑ 92	Keith Van Horn	1.00	.45
❑ 93	Hersey Hawkins	.20	.09
❑ 94	Billy Owens	.15	.07
❑ 95	Ron Mercer	.60	.25
❑ 96	Rik Smits	.15	.07
❑ 97	David Robinson	.60	.25
❑ 98	Derek Anderson	.50	.23
❑ 99	Danny Fortson	.20	.09
❑ 100	Jason Kidd	1.25	.55
❑ 101	Sean Elliott	.15	.07
❑ 102	Chauncey Billups	.15	.07
❑ 103	Tyrone Hill	.15	.07
❑ 104	Alan Henderson	.15	.07
❑ 105	Chris Anstey	.15	.07
❑ 106	Hakeem Olajuwon	.60	.25
❑ 107	Allan Houston	.40	.18
❑ 108	Bryant Reeves	.15	.07
❑ 109	Anthony Johnson	.15	.07
❑ 110	Shawn Kemp	.60	.25
❑ 111	Brevin Knight	.15	.07
❑ 112	A.C. Green	.20	.09
❑ 113	Ray Allen	.50	.23
❑ 114	Tim Thomas	.60	.25
❑ 115	Walter McCarty	.15	.07
❑ 116	Jalen Rose	.40	.18
❑ 117	Kerry Kittles	.20	.09
❑ 118	Vin Baker	.20	.09
❑ 119	Shareef Abdur-Rahim	1.00	.45
❑ 120	Alonzo Mourning	.40	.18
❑ 121	Joe Smith	.20	.09
❑ 122	Tracy Murray	.15	.07
❑ 123	Damon Stoudamire	.40	.18
❑ 124	Checklist	.15	.07
❑ 125	Checklist	.15	.07
❑ NNO	Grant Hill SAMPLE	4.00	1.80

1998-99 Metal Universe Precious Metal Gems

	MINT	NRMT
COMMON CARD (1-123)	15.00	6.75

*STARS: 40X TO 100X BASE CARD HI
STATED PRINT RUN 50 SERIAL #'d SETS
RANDOM INSERTS IN HOBBY PACKS

		MINT	NRMT
❑ 1	Michael Jordan	1600.00	700.00

1998-99 Metal Universe Big Ups

	MINT	NRMT
COMPLETE SET (15)	20.00	9.00
COMMON CARD (1-15)	.60	.25
UNLISTED STARS	1.00	.45

STATED ODDS 1:18

		MINT	NRMT
❑ 1	Stephon Marbury	2.50	1.10
❑ 2	Shareef Abdur-Rahim	2.50	1.10
❑ 3	Scottie Pippen	3.00	1.35
❑ 4	Marcus Camby	.60	.25
❑ 5	Ray Allen	1.25	.55
❑ 6	Allen Iverson	4.00	1.80
❑ 7	Kerry Kittles	.60	.25
❑ 8	Dennis Rodman	2.00	.90
❑ 9	Damon Stoudamire	.60	.25
❑ 10	Antoine Walker	1.50	.70
❑ 11	Anfernee Hardaway	3.00	1.35
❑ 12	Shawn Kemp	1.50	.70
❑ 13	Juwan Howard	.60	.25
❑ 14	Gary Payton	1.50	.70
❑ 15	Tim Duncan	5.00	2.20

1998-99 Metal Universe Linchpins

	MINT	NRMT
COMPLETE SET (10)	200.00	90.00
COMMON CARD (1-10)	10.00	4.50

STATED ODDS 1:360

		MINT	NRMT
❑ 1	Shaquille O'Neal	30.00	13.50
❑ 2	Kobe Bryant	50.00	22.00
❑ 3	Kevin Garnett	40.00	18.00
❑ 4	Grant Hill	30.00	13.50
❑ 5	Shawn Kemp	10.00	4.50
❑ 6	Keith Van Horn	15.00	6.75
❑ 7	Antoine Walker	10.00	4.50
❑ 8	Michael Jordan	80.00	36.00
❑ 9	Gary Payton	10.00	4.50
❑ 10	Tim Duncan	30.00	13.50

1998-99 Metal Universe Neophytes

	MINT	NRMT
COMPLETE SET (15)	6.00	2.70
COMMON CARD (1-15)	.30	.14
SEMISTARS	.40	.18
UNLISTED STARS	.60	.25

STATED ODDS 1:6

		MINT	NRMT
❑ 1	Antonio Daniels	.30	.14
❑ 2	Bobby Jackson	.30	.14
❑ 3	Brevin Knight	.30	.14
❑ 4	Chauncey Billups	.30	.14
❑ 5	Danny Fortson	.40	.18
❑ 6	Derek Anderson	.75	.35
❑ 7	Jacque Vaughn	.30	.14
❑ 8	Keith Van Horn	1.50	.70
❑ 9	Maurice Taylor	.60	.25
❑ 10	Michael Stewart	.30	.14
❑ 11	Ron Mercer	1.00	.45
❑ 12	Tim Thomas	1.00	.45
❑ 13	Tim Duncan	3.00	1.35
❑ 14	Tracy McGrady	2.50	1.10
❑ 15	Zydrunas Ilgauskas	.30	.14

1998-99 Metal Universe Planet Metal

	MINT	NRMT
COMPLETE SET (15)	100.00	45.00
COMMON CARD (1-15)	1.50	.70
UNLISTED STARS	2.50	1.10

STATED ODDS 1:36

		MINT	NRMT
❑ 1	Michael Jordan	30.00	13.50
❑ 2	Antoine Walker	4.00	1.80

	MINT	NRMT
❑ 3 Scottie Pippen	8.00	3.60
❑ 4 Grant Hill	12.00	5.50
❑ 5 Dennis Rodman	5.00	2.20
❑ 6 Kobe Bryant	20.00	9.00
❑ 7 Kevin Garnett	15.00	6.75
❑ 8 Shaquille O'Neal	12.00	5.50
❑ 9 Stephon Marbury	6.00	2.70
❑ 10 Kerry Kittles	1.50	.70
❑ 11 Anfernee Hardaway	8.00	3.60
❑ 12 Allen Iverson	10.00	4.50
❑ 13 Damon Stoudamire	1.50	.70
❑ 14 Marcus Camby	1.50	.70
❑ 15 Shareef Abdur-Rahim	6.00	2.70

1998-99 Metal Universe Two for Me, Zero for You

	MINT	NRMT
COMPLETE SET (15)	200.00	90.00
COMMON CARD (1-15)	5.00	2.20
STATED ODDS 1:96		

	MINT	NRMT
❑ 1 Kobe Bryant	40.00	18.00
❑ 2 Anfernee Hardaway	15.00	6.75
❑ 3 Allen Iverson	20.00	9.00
❑ 4 Michael Jordan	60.00	27.00
❑ 5 Stephon Marbury	12.00	5.50
❑ 6 Ron Mercer	8.00	3.60
❑ 7 Shareef Abdur-Rahim	12.00	5.50
❑ 8 Marcus Camby	5.00	2.20
❑ 9 Damon Stoudamire	5.00	2.20
❑ 10 Kevin Garnett	30.00	13.50
❑ 11 Grant Hill	25.00	11.00
❑ 12 Scottie Pippen	15.00	6.75
❑ 13 Keith Van Horn	12.00	5.50
❑ 14 Dennis Rodman	10.00	4.50
❑ 15 Shaquille O'Neal	25.00	11.00

1997-98 Metal Universe Championship

	MINT	NRMT
COMPLETE SET (100)	25.00	11.00
COMMON CARD (1-100)	.15	.07
SEMISTARS	.20	.09
UNLISTED STARS	.40	.18

	MINT	NRMT
❑ 1 Shaquille O'Neal	2.00	.90
❑ 2 Chris Mills	.15	.07
❑ 3 Tariq Abdul-Wahad RC	.20	.09
❑ 4 Adonal Foyle RC	.20	.09
❑ 5 Kendall Gill	.20	.09
❑ 6 Vin Baker	.20	.09
❑ 7 Chauncey Billups RC	.50	.23
❑ 8 Bobby Jackson RC	.20	.09
❑ 9 Keith Van Horn RC	2.00	.90
❑ 10 Avery Johnson	.15	.07
❑ 11 Juwan Howard	.20	.09
❑ 12 Steve Smith	.20	.09
❑ 13 Alonzo Mourning	.40	.18
❑ 14 Anfernee Hardaway	1.25	.55
❑ 15 Sean Elliott	.15	.07
❑ 16 Danny Fortson RC	.40	.18
❑ 17 John Stockton	.40	.18
❑ 18 John Thomas RC	.15	.07
❑ 19 Lorenzen Wright	.15	.07
❑ 20 Mark Price	.15	.07
❑ 21 Rasheed Wallace	.40	.18
❑ 22 Ray Allen	.60	.25
❑ 23 Michael Jordan	5.00	2.20
❑ 24 John Wallace	.15	.07
❑ 25 Bryant Reeves	.15	.07
❑ 26 Allen Iverson	2.00	.90
❑ 27 Antoine Walker	.75	.35
❑ 28 Terrell Brandon	.20	.09
❑ 29 Damon Stoudamire	.50	.23
❑ 30 Antonio Daniels RC	.40	.18
❑ 31 Corey Beck	.15	.07
❑ 32 Tyrone Hill	.15	.07
❑ 33 Grant Hill	2.00	.90
❑ 34 Tim Thomas RC	1.25	.55
❑ 35 Clifford Robinson	.15	.07
❑ 36 Tracy McGrady RC	4.00	1.80
❑ 37 Chris Webber	1.25	.55
❑ 38 Austin Croshere RC	1.00	.45
❑ 39 Reggie Miller	.40	.18
❑ 40 Derek Anderson RC	1.00	.45
❑ 41 Kevin Garnett	2.50	1.10
❑ 42 Kevin Johnson	.20	.09
❑ 43 Antonio McDyess	.50	.23
❑ 44 Brevin Knight RC	.60	.25
❑ 45 Charles Barkley	.60	.25
❑ 46 Tom Gugliotta	.20	.09
❑ 47 Jason Kidd	1.25	.55
❑ 48 Marcus Camby	.50	.23
❑ 49 God Shammgod RC	.15	.07
❑ 50 Wesley Person	.15	.07
❑ 51 Clyde Drexler	.40	.18
❑ 52 Paul Grant RC	.15	.07
❑ 53 Rod Strickland	.20	.09
❑ 54 Tony Delk	.15	.07
❑ 55 Stephon Marbury	1.25	.55
❑ 56 Detlef Schrempf	.20	.09
❑ 57 Joe Smith	.20	.09
❑ 58 Sam Cassell	.20	.09
❑ 59 Gary Payton	.60	.25
❑ 60 Chris Crawford RC	.15	.07
❑ 61 Hakeem Olajuwon	.60	.25
❑ 62 Dennis Rodman	.75	.35
❑ 63 Eddie Jones	.75	.35
❑ 64 Mitch Richmond	.40	.18
❑ 65 David Wesley	.15	.07
❑ 66 Tony Battie RC	.40	.18
❑ 67 Isaac Austin	.15	.07
❑ 68 Isaiah Rider	.20	.09
❑ 69 Jacque Vaughn RC	.20	.09
❑ 70 Tim Hardaway	.40	.18
❑ 71 Darrell Armstrong	.20	.09
❑ 72 Tim Duncan RC	5.00	2.20
❑ 73 Glen Rice	.20	.09
❑ 74 Bubba Wells RC	.15	.07
❑ 75 Maurice Taylor RC	.75	.35
❑ 76 Kelvin Cato RC	.40	.18
❑ 77 Shareef Abdur-Rahim	1.25	.55
❑ 78 Shawn Kemp	.60	.25
❑ 79 Michael Finley	.40	.18
❑ 80 Chris Mullin	.40	.18
❑ 81 Ron Mercer RC	1.25	.55
❑ 82 Brian Williams	.15	.07
❑ 83 Kerry Kittles	.40	.18
❑ 84 David Robinson	.60	.25
❑ 85 Scottie Pippen	1.25	.55
❑ 86 Kobe Bryant	3.00	1.35
❑ 87 Anthony Johnson RC	.15	.07
❑ 88 Karl Malone	.60	.25
❑ 89 Mookie Blaylock	.15	.07
❑ 90 Joe Dumars	.40	.18
❑ 91 Patrick Ewing	.40	.18
❑ 92 Bobby Phills	.15	.07
❑ 93 Dennis Scott	.15	.07
❑ 94 Rodney Rogers	.15	.07
❑ 95 Jim Jackson	.15	.07
❑ 96 Kenny Anderson	.20	.09
❑ 97 Jerry Stackhouse	.20	.09
❑ 98 Larry Johnson	.20	.09
❑ 99 Checklist	.15	.07
❑ 100 Checklist	.15	.07

1997-98 Metal Universe Championship Precious Metal Gems

	MINT	NRMT
COMMON CARD (1-98)	25.00	11.00

*STARS: 75X TO 150X BASE CARD HI
*RCs: 40X TO 80X BASE HI
RANDOM INSERTS IN PACKS
STATED PRINT RUN 50 SERIAL #'d SETS

	MINT	NRMT
❑ 23 Michael Jordan	1600.00	700.00

1997-98 Metal Universe Championship All-Millenium Team

	MINT	NRMT
COMPLETE SET (20)	30.00	13.50
COMMON CARD (1-20)	.75	.35
STATED ODDS 1:6		

	MINT	NRMT
❑ 1 Stephon Marbury	2.50	1.10
❑ 2 Shareef Abdur-Rahim	2.50	1.10
❑ 3 Karl Malone	1.25	.55
❑ 4 Scottie Pippen	2.50	1.10
❑ 5 Michael Jordan	10.00	4.50
❑ 6 Marcus Camby	1.00	.45
❑ 7 Kobe Bryant	6.00	2.70
❑ 8 Allen Iverson	4.00	1.80
❑ 9 Kerry Kittles	.75	.35
❑ 10 Ray Allen	1.25	.55
❑ 11 Dennis Rodman	1.50	.70
❑ 12 Damon Stoudamire	1.00	.45

❑ 13 Antoine Walker .... 1.50 .70
❑ 14 Anfernee Hardaway 2.50 1.10
❑ 15 Hakeem Olajuwon .... 1.25 .55
❑ 16 Shawn Kemp .... 1.25 .55
❑ 17 Antonio Daniels .... .75 .35
❑ 18 Juwan Howard .... .75 .35
❑ 19 Gary Payton .... 1.25 .55
❑ 20 Tim Duncan 4.00 1.80

1997-98 Metal Universe Championship Championship Galaxy

	MINT	NRMT
COMPLETE SET (15)	400.00	180.00
COMMON CARD (1-15)	8.00	3.60
STATED ODDS 1:192		

❑ 1 Michael Jordan 100.00 45.00
❑ 2 Allen Iverson 40.00 18.00
❑ 3 Kobe Bryant 60.00 27.00
UER front Kobe, Bryant
❑ 4 Shaquille O'Neal 40.00 18.00
❑ 5 Stephon Marbury 25.00 11.00
❑ 6 Marcus Camby 10.00 4.50
❑ 7 Anfernee Hardaway 25.00 11.00
❑ 8 Kevin Garnett 50.00 22.00
❑ 9 Shareef Abdur-Rahim 25.00 11.00
❑ 10 Dennis Rodman 15.00 6.75
❑ 11 Grant Hill 40.00 18.00
❑ 12 Kerry Kittles 8.00 3.60
❑ 13 Antoine Walker 15.00 6.75
❑ 14 Scottie Pippen 25.00 11.00
❑ 15 Damon Stoudamire 10.00 4.50

1997-98 Metal Universe Championship Future Champions

	MINT	NRMT
COMPLETE SET (15)	40.00	18.00
COMMON CARD (1-15)	1.25	.55
SEMISTARS	1.50	.70
UNLISTED STARS	2.50	1.10
STATED ODDS 1:18		

❑ 1 Tim Duncan 12.00 5.50
❑ 2 Tony Battie .... 1.25 .55
❑ 3 Keith Van Horn 6.00 2.70
❑ 4 Antonio Daniels .... 1.50 .70
❑ 5 Chauncey Billups .... 1.50 .70
❑ 6 Ron Mercer 4.00 1.80
❑ 7 Tracy McGrady 12.00 5.50
❑ 8 Danny Fortson .... 1.25 .55
❑ 9 Brevin Knight 2.50 1.10
❑ 10 Derek Anderson 3.00 1.35
❑ 11 Bobby Jackson .... 1.25 .55
❑ 12 Jacque Vaughn .... 1.25 .55
❑ 13 Tim Thomas 4.00 1.80
❑ 14 Austin Croshere 3.00 1.35
❑ 15 Kelvin Cato .... 1.25 .55

1997-98 Metal Universe Championship Hardware

	MINT	NRMT
COMPLETE SET (15)	700.00	325.00
COMMON CARD (1-15)	12.00	5.50
STATED ODDS 1:360		

❑ 1 Stephon Marbury 40.00 18.00
❑ 2 Shareef Abdur-Rahim 40.00 18.00
❑ 3 Shaquille O'Neal 60.00 27.00
❑ 4 Scottie Pippen 40.00 18.00
❑ 5 Michael Jordan 150.00 70.00
❑ 6 Marcus Camby 20.00 9.00
❑ 7 Kobe Bryant 100.00 45.00
❑ 8 Kevin Garnett 80.00 36.00
❑ 9 Kerry Kittles 12.00 5.50
❑ 10 Grant Hill 60.00 27.00
❑ 11 Dennis Rodman 25.00 11.00
❑ 12 Tim Duncan 60.00 27.00
❑ 13 Antonio Daniels 12.00 5.50
❑ 14 Anfernee Hardaway 40.00 18.00
❑ 15 Allen Iverson 60.00 27.00

1997-98 Metal Universe Championship Trophy Case

	MINT	NRMT
COMPLETE SET (10)	80.00	36.00
COMMON CARD (1-10)	4.00	1.80
STATED ODDS 1:96		

❑ 1 Kevin Garnett 25.00 11.00
❑ 2 Grant Hill 20.00 9.00
❑ 3 Damon Stoudamire 5.00 2.20
❑ 4 Shaquille O'Neal 20.00 9.00
❑ 5 Ray Allen 6.00 2.70
❑ 6 Gary Payton 6.00 2.70
❑ 7 Shawn Kemp 6.00 2.70
❑ 8 Hakeem Olajuwon 6.00 2.70
❑ 9 John Stockton 4.00 1.80
❑ 10 Antoine Walker 8.00 3.60

1990-91 SkyBox

	MINT	NRMT
COMPLETE SET (423)	20.00	9.00
COMPLETE SERIES 1 (300)	12.00	5.50
COMPLETE SERIES 2 (123)	8.00	3.60
COMMON CARD (1-300)	.05	.02
COMMON CARD (301-423)	.10	.05
COMMON SP	.10	.05
SEMISTARS SER.1	.10	.05
SEMISTARS SER.2	.30	.14
UNLISTED STARS SER.1	.25	.11
UNLISTED STARS SER.2	.60	.25

❑ 1 John Battle .... .05 .02
❑ 2 Duane Ferrell SP RC .... .10 .05
❑ 3 Jon Koncak .... .05 .02
❑ 4 Cliff Levingston SP .... .10 .05
❑ 5 John Long SP .... .10 .05
❑ 6 Moses Malone .... .25 .11
❑ 7 Doc Rivers .... .10 .05
❑ 8 Kenny Smith SP .... .10 .05
❑ 9 Alexander Volkov .... .05 .02
❑ 10 Spud Webb .... .10 .05
❑ 11 Dominique Wilkins .... .25 .11
❑ 12 Kevin Willis .... .10 .05
❑ 13 John Bagley .... .05 .02
❑ 14 Larry Bird .... 1.00 .45
❑ 15 Kevin Gamble .... .05 .02
❑ 16 Dennis Johnson SP .... .05 .02
❑ 17 Joe Kleine .... .05 .02
❑ 18 Reggie Lewis .... .10 .05
❑ 19 Kevin McHale .... .10 .05
❑ 20 Robert Parish .... .10 .05
❑ 21 Jim Paxson SP .... .10 .05
❑ 22 Ed Pinckney .... .05 .02
❑ 23 Brian Shaw .... .25 .11
❑ 24 Michael Smith .... .05 .02
❑ 25 Richard Anderson SP .... .10 .05
❑ 26 Muggsy Bogues .... .10 .05
❑ 27 Rex Chapman .... .25 .11
❑ 28 Dell Curry .... .05 .02
❑ 29 Armon Gilliam .... .05 .02
❑ 30 Michael Holton SP .... .10 .05
❑ 31 Dave Hoppen .... .05 .02
❑ 32 J.R. Reid RC .... .05 .02
❑ 33 Robert Reid SP .... .10 .05
❑ 34 Brian Rowsom SP .... .10 .05
❑ 35 Kelly Tripucka .... .05 .02
❑ 36 Micheal Williams SP .... .10 .05
UER (Misspelled Michael on card)
❑ 37 B.J. Armstrong RC .... .05 .02
❑ 38 Bill Cartwright .... .05 .02
❑ 39 Horace Grant .... .10 .05
❑ 40 Craig Hodges .... .05 .02
❑ 41 Michael Jordan 3.00 1.35
❑ 42 Stacey King RC .... .05 .02
❑ 43 Ed Nealy SP .... .10 .05

❑ 44 John Paxson .10 .05
❑ 45 Will Perdue .05 .02
❑ 46 Scottie Pippen 1.00 .45
❑ 47 Jeff Sanders SP RC .10 .05
❑ 48 Winston Bennett .05 .02
❑ 49 Chucky Brown RC .05 .02
❑ 50 Brad Daugherty .05 .02
❑ 51 Craig Ehlo .05 .02
❑ 52 Steve Kerr .25 .11
❑ 53 Paul Mokeski SP .10 .05
❑ 54 John Morton .05 .02
❑ 55 Larry Nance .05 .02
❑ 56 Mark Price .10 .05
❑ 57 Tree Rollins SP .10 .05
❑ 58 Hot Rod Williams .05 .02
❑ 59 Steve Alford .05 .02
❑ 60 Rolando Blackman .05 .02
❑ 61 Adrian Dantley SP .05 .02
❑ 62 Brad Davis .05 .02
❑ 63 James Donaldson .05 .02
❑ 64 Derek Harper .10 .05
❑ 65 Anthony Jones SP .10 .05
❑ 66 Sam Perkins SP .10 .05
❑ 67 Roy Tarpley .05 .02
❑ 68 Bill Wennington SP .10 .05
❑ 69 Randy White RC .05 .02
❑ 70 Herb Williams .05 .02
❑ 71 Michael Adams .05 .02
❑ 72 Joe Barry Carroll SP .10 .05
❑ 73 Walter Davis .05 .02
❑ 74 Alex English SP .05 .02
❑ 75 Bill Hanzlik .05 .02
❑ 76 Tim Kempton SP .05 .02
❑ 77 Jerome Lane .05 .02
❑ 78 Lafayette Lever SP .10 .05
❑ 79 Todd Lichti RC .05 .02
❑ 80 Blair Rasmussen .05 .02
❑ 81 Dan Schayes SP .10 .05
❑ 82 Mark Aguirre .05 .02
❑ 83 William Bedford RC .05 .02
❑ 84 Joe Dumars .25 .11
❑ 85 James Edwards .05 .02
❑ 86 David Greenwood SP .10 .05
❑ 87 Scott Hastings .05 .02
❑ 88 Gerald Henderson SP .10 .05
❑ 89 Vinnie Johnson .05 .02
❑ 90 Bill Laimbeer .10 .05
❑ 91 Dennis Rodman .60 .25
(SkyBox logo in upper right or left)
❑ 91B Dennis Rodman .30 .23
(SkyBox logo in upper left corner)
❑ 92 John Salley .05 .02
❑ 93 Isiah Thomas .25 .11
❑ 94 Manute Bol SP .10 .05
❑ 95 Tim Hardaway RC 1.50 .70
❑ 96 Rod Higgins .05 .02
❑ 97 Sarunas Marciulionis RC .05 .02
❑ 98 Chris Mullin .25 .11
❑ 99 Jim Petersen .05 .02
❑ 100 Mitch Richmond .30 .14
❑ 101 Mike Smrek .05 .02
❑ 102 Terry Teagle SP .10 .05
❑ 103 Tom Tolbert RC .05 .02
❑ 104 Kelvin Upshaw SP .10 .05
❑ 105 Anthony Bowie SP RC .10 .05
❑ 106 Adrian Caldwell .05 .02
❑ 107 Eric(Sleepy) Floyd .05 .02
❑ 108 Buck Johnson .05 .02
❑ 109 Vernon Maxwell .05 .02
❑ 110 Hakeem Olajuwon .40 .18
❑ 111 Larry Smith .05 .02
❑ 112A Otis Thorpe ERR .50 .23
(Front photo actually Mitchell Wiggins)
❑ 112B Otis Thorpe COR .10 .05
❑ 113A M. Wiggins SP ERR .30 .23
(Front photo actually Otis Thorpe)
❑ 113B M. Wiggins SP COR .10 .05
❑ 114 Vern Fleming .05 .02
❑ 115 Rickey Green SP .10 .05
❑ 116 George McCloud RC .25 .11
❑ 117 Reggie Miller .30 .14
❑ 118A Dyron Nix SP ERR 1.50 .70
(Back photo actually Wayman Tisdale)
❑ 118B Dyron Nix SP COR .10 .05
❑ 119 Chuck Person .10 .05
❑ 120 Mike Sanders .05 .02
❑ 121 Detlef Schrempf .10 .05
❑ 122 Rik Smits .25 .11
❑ 123 LaSalle Thompson .05 .02
❑ 124 Benoit Benjamin .05 .02
❑ 125 Winston Garland .05 .02
❑ 126 Tom Garrick .05 .02
❑ 127 Gary Grant .05 .02
❑ 128 Ron Harper .10 .05
❑ 129 Danny Manning .10 .05
❑ 130 Jeff Martin .05 .02
❑ 131 Ken Norman .05 .02
❑ 132 Charles Smith .05 .02
❑ 133 Joe Wolf SP .10 .05
❑ 134 Michael Cooper SP .10 .05
❑ 135 Vlade Divac RC .50 .23
❑ 136 Larry Drew .05 .02
❑ 137 A.C. Green .10 .05
❑ 138 Magic Johnson .75 .35
❑ 139 Mark McNamara SP .10 .05
❑ 140 Byron Scott .10 .05
❑ 141 Mychal Thompson .05 .02
❑ 142 Orlando Woolridge SP .10 .05
❑ 143 James Worthy .25 .11
❑ 144 Terry Davis RC .05 .02
❑ 145 Sherman Douglas RC .10 .05
❑ 146 Kevin Edwards .05 .02
❑ 147 Tellis Frank SP .10 .05
❑ 148 Scott Haffner SP .10 .05
❑ 149 Grant Long .05 .02
❑ 150 Glen Rice RC 1.00 .45
❑ 151 Rony Seikaly .10 .05
❑ 152 Rory Sparrow SP .10 .05
❑ 153 Jon Sundvold .05 .02
❑ 154 Billy Thompson .05 .02
❑ 155 Greg Anderson .05 .02
❑ 156 Ben Coleman SP .10 .05
❑ 157 Jeff Grayer RC .05 .02
❑ 158 Jay Humphries .05 .02
❑ 159 Frank Kornet .05 .02
❑ 160 Larry Krystkowiak .05 .02
❑ 161 Brad Lohaus .05 .02
❑ 162 Ricky Pierce .05 .02
❑ 163 Paul Pressey SP .10 .05
❑ 164 Fred Roberts .05 .02
❑ 165 Alvin Robertson .05 .02
❑ 166 Jack Sikma .05 .02
❑ 167 Randy Breuer .05 .02
❑ 168 Tony Campbell .05 .02
❑ 169 Tyrone Corbin .05 .02
❑ 170 Sidney Lowe SP .10 .05
❑ 171 Sam Mitchell RC .05 .02
❑ 172 Tod Murphy .05 .02
❑ 173 Pooh Richardson RC .10 .05
❑ 174 Donald Royal SP RC .10 .05
❑ 175 Brad Sellers SP .10 .05
❑ 176 Mookie Blaylock RC .50 .23
❑ 177 Sam Bowie .05 .02
❑ 178 Lester Conner .05 .02
❑ 179 Derrick Gervin .05 .02
❑ 180 Jack Haley RC .05 .02
❑ 181 Roy Hinson .05 .02
❑ 182 Dennis Hopson SP .10 .05
❑ 183 Chris Morris .10 .05
❑ 184 Pete Myers SP RC .10 .05
❑ 185 Purvis Short SP .10 .05
❑ 186 Maurice Cheeks .05 .02
❑ 187 Patrick Ewing .25 .11
❑ 188 Stuart Gray .05 .02
❑ 189 Mark Jackson .10 .05
❑ 190 Johnny Newman SP .10 .05
❑ 191 Charles Oakley .10 .05
❑ 192 Brian Quinnett .05 .02
❑ 193 Trent Tucker .05 .02
❑ 194 Kiki Vandeweghe .05 .02
❑ 195 Kenny Walker .05 .02
❑ 196 Eddie Lee Wilkins .05 .02
❑ 197 Gerald Wilkins .05 .02
❑ 198 Mark Acres .05 .02
❑ 199 Nick Anderson RC .50 .23
❑ 200 Michael Ansley .05 .02
❑ 201 Terry Catledge .05 .02
❑ 202 Dave Corzine SP .10 .05
❑ 203 Sidney Green SP .10 .05
❑ 204 Jerry Reynolds .05 .02
❑ 205 Scott Skiles .05 .02
❑ 206 Otis Smith .05 .02
❑ 207 Reggie Theus SP .10 .05
❑ 208 Jeff Turner .05 .02
❑ 209 Sam Vincent .05 .02
❑ 210 Ron Anderson .05 .02
❑ 211 Charles Barkley .40 .18
❑ 212 Scott Brooks SP .10 .05
❑ 213 Lanard Copeland SP .10 .05
❑ 214 Johnny Dawkins .05 .02
❑ 215 Mike Gminski .05 .02
❑ 216 Hersey Hawkins .10 .05
❑ 217 Rick Mahorn .05 .02
❑ 218 Derek Smith SP .10 .05
❑ 219 Bob Thornton .05 .02
❑ 220 Tom Chambers .05 .02
❑ 221 Greg Grant SP RC .10 .05
❑ 222 Jeff Hornacek .10 .05
❑ 223 Eddie Johnson .10 .05
❑ 224A Kevin Johnson .25 .11
(SkyBox logo in lower right corner)
❑ 224B Kevin Johnson .25 .11
(SkyBox logo in upper right corner)
❑ 225 Andrew Lang RC .25 .11
❑ 226 Dan Majerle .25 .11
❑ 227 Mike McGee SP .10 .05
❑ 228 Tim Perry .05 .02
❑ 229 Kurt Rambis .05 .02
❑ 230 Mark West .05 .02
❑ 231 Mark Bryant .05 .02
❑ 232 Wayne Cooper .05 .02
❑ 233 Clyde Drexler .25 .11
❑ 234 Kevin Duckworth .05 .02
❑ 235 Byron Irvin SP .10 .05
❑ 236 Jerome Kersey .05 .02
❑ 237 Drazen Petrovic RC .30 .14
❑ 238 Terry Porter .05 .02
❑ 239 Clifford Robinson RC .40 .18
❑ 240 Buck Williams .05 .02
❑ 241 Danny Young .05 .02
❑ 242 Danny Ainge SP .10 .05
❑ 243 Randy Allen SP .10 .05
❑ 244A Antoine Carr SP .15 .07
(Wearing Atlanta jersey on back)
❑ 244B Antoine Carr .05 .02
(Wearing Sacramento jersey on back)
❑ 245 Vinny Del Negro SP .10 .05
❑ 246 Pervis Ellison SP RC .10 .05
❑ 247 Greg Kite SP .10 .05
❑ 248 Rodney McCray SP .10 .05
❑ 249 Harold Pressley SP .10 .05
❑ 250 Ralph Sampson .05 .02
❑ 251 Wayman Tisdale .05 .02
❑ 252 Willie Anderson .05 .02
❑ 253 Uwe Blab SP .10 .05
❑ 254 Frank Brickowski SP .10 .05
❑ 255 Terry Cummings .05 .02
❑ 256 Sean Elliott RC .50 .23
❑ 257 Caldwell Jones SP .10 .05
❑ 258 Johnny Moore SP .10 .05
❑ 259 Zarko Paspalj SP .10 .05
❑ 260 David Robinson .75 .35
❑ 261 Rod Strickland .25 .11
❑ 262 David Wingate SP .10 .05
❑ 263 Dana Barros RC .25 .11
❑ 264 Michael Cage .05 .02
❑ 265 Quintin Dailey .05 .02
❑ 266 Dale Ellis .10 .05
❑ 267 Steve Johnson SP .10 .05
❑ 268 Shawn Kemp RC 2.50 1.10
❑ 269 Xavier McDaniel .05 .02
❑ 270 Derrick McKey .05 .02
❑ 271A Nate McMillan SP ERR .20 .09
(Back photo actually Olden Polynice; first series)
❑ 271B Nate McMillan COR .10 .05
(second series)
❑ 272 Olden Polynice .05 .02

❑ 273 Sedale Threatt .05 .02
❑ 274 Thurl Bailey .05 .02
❑ 275 Mike Brown .05 .02
❑ 276 Mark Eaton .05 .02
❑ 277 Blue Edwards RC .05 .02
❑ 278 Darrell Griffith .05 .02
❑ 279 Bobby Hansen SP .10 .05
❑ 280 Eric Johnson .05 .02
❑ 281 Eric Leckner SP .10 .05
❑ 282 Karl Malone .40 .18
❑ 283 Delaney Rudd .05 .02
❑ 284 John Stockton .30 .14
❑ 285 Mark Alarie .05 .02
❑ 286 Steve Colter SP .10 .05
❑ 287 Ledell Eackles SP .10 .05
❑ 288 Harvey Grant .05 .02
❑ 289 Tom Hammonds RC .05 .02
❑ 290 Charles Jones .05 .02
❑ 291 Bernard King .05 .02
❑ 292 Jeff Malone SP .10 .05
❑ 293 Darrell Walker .05 .02
❑ 294 John Williams .05 .02
❑ 295 Checklist 1 SP .10 .05
❑ 296 Checklist 2 SP .10 .05
❑ 297 Checklist 3 SP .10 .05
❑ 298 Checklist 4 SP .10 .05
❑ 299 Checklist 5 SP .10 .05
❑ 300 Danny Ferry SP RC .50 .23
❑ 301 Bob Weiss CO .10 .05
❑ 302 Chris Ford CO .10 .05
❑ 303 Gene Littles CO .10 .05
❑ 304 Phil Jackson CO .30 .14
❑ 305 Lenny Wilkens CO .30 .14
❑ 306 Richie Adubato CO .10 .05
❑ 307 Paul Westhead CO .10 .05
❑ 308 Chuck Daly CO .30 .14
❑ 309 Don Nelson CO .30 .14
❑ 310 Don Chaney CO .10 .05
❑ 311 Dick Versace CO .10 .05
❑ 312 Mike Schuler CO .10 .05
❑ 313 Mike Dunleavy CO .10 .05
❑ 314 Ron Rothstein CO .10 .05
❑ 315 Del Harris CO .10 .05
❑ 316 Bill Musselman CO .10 .05
❑ 317 Bill Fitch CO .10 .05
❑ 318 Stu Jackson CO .10 .05
❑ 319 Matt Guokas CO .10 .05
❑ 320 Jim Lynam CO .10 .05
❑ 321 Cotton Fitzsimmons CO .10 .05
❑ 322 Rick Adelman CO .10 .05
❑ 323 Dick Motta CO .10 .05
❑ 324 Larry Brown CO .10 .05
❑ 325 K.C. Jones CO .30 .14
❑ 326 Jerry Sloan CO .30 .14
❑ 327 Wes Unseld CO .10 .05
❑ 328 Atlanta Hawks TC .10 .05
❑ 329 Boston Celtics TC .10 .05
❑ 330 Charlotte Hornets TC .10 .05
❑ 331 Chicago Bulls TC .30 .14
❑ 332 Cleveland Cavaliers TC .10 .05
❑ 333 Dallas Mavericks TC .10 .05
❑ 334 Denver Nuggets TC .10 .05
❑ 335 Detroit Pistons TC .10 .05
❑ 336 Golden State Warriors TC .10 .05
❑ 337 Houston Rockets TC .10 .05
❑ 338 Indiana Pacers TC .10 .05
❑ 339 Los Angeles Clippers TC .10 .05
❑ 340 Los Angeles Lakers TC .10 .05
❑ 341 Miami Heat TC .10 .05
❑ 342 Milwaukee Bucks TC .10 .05
❑ 343 Minn. Timberwolves TC .10 .05
❑ 344 New Jersey Nets TC .10 .05
❑ 345 New York Knicks TC .10 .05
❑ 346 Orlando Magic TC .10 .05
❑ 347 Philadelphia 76ers TC .10 .05
❑ 348 Phoenix Suns TC .10 .05
❑ 349 Portland Trail Blazers TC .10 .05
❑ 350 Sacramento Kings TC .10 .05
❑ 351 San Antonio Spurs TC .10 .05
❑ 352 Seattle SuperSonics TC .10 .05
❑ 353 Utah Jazz TC .10 .05
❑ 354 Washington Bullets TC .10 .05
❑ 355 Rumeal Robinson RC .10 .05
❑ 356 Kendall Gill RC 1.25 .55
❑ 357 Chris Jackson RC .60 .25
❑ 358 Tyrone Hill RC .50 .23
❑ 359 Bo Kimble RC .10 .05
❑ 360 Willie Burton RC .10 .05
❑ 361 Felton Spencer RC .30 .14
❑ 362 Derrick Coleman RC 1.25 .55
❑ 363 Dennis Scott RC .75 .35
❑ 364 Lionel Simmons RC .30 .14
❑ 365 Gary Payton RC 4.00 1.80
❑ 366 Tim McCormick .10 .05
❑ 367 Sidney Moncrief .10 .05
❑ 368 Kenny Gattison RC .10 .05
❑ 369 Randolph Keys .10 .05
❑ 370 Johnny Newman .10 .05
❑ 371 Dennis Hopson .10 .05
❑ 372 Cliff Levingston .10 .05
❑ 373 Derrick Chievous .10 .05
❑ 374 Danny Ferry .30 .14
❑ 375 Alex English .10 .05
❑ 376 Lafayette Lever .10 .05
❑ 377 Rodney McCray .10 .05
❑ 378 T.R. Dunn .10 .05
❑ 379 Corey Gaines .10 .05
❑ 380 Avery Johnson RC .75 .35
❑ 381 Joe Wolf .10 .05
❑ 382 Orlando Woolridge .10 .05
❑ 383 Tree Rollins .10 .05
❑ 384 Steve Johnson .10 .05
❑ 385 Kenny Smith .10 .05
❑ 386 Mike Woodson .10 .05
❑ 387 Greg Dreiling RC .10 .05
❑ 388 Micheal Williams .30 .14
❑ 389 Randy Wittman .10 .05
❑ 390 Ken Bannister .10 .05
❑ 391 Sam Perkins .30 .14
❑ 392 Terry Teagle .10 .05
❑ 393 Milt Wagner .10 .05
❑ 394 Frank Brickowski .10 .05
❑ 395 Dan Schayes .10 .05
❑ 396 Scott Brooks .10 .05
❑ 397 Doug West RC .30 .14
❑ 398 Chris Dudley RC .10 .05
❑ 399 Reggie Theus .30 .14
❑ 400 Greg Grant .10 .05
❑ 401 Greg Kite .10 .05
❑ 402 Mark McNamara .10 .05
❑ 403 Manute Bol .10 .05
❑ 404 Rickey Green .10 .05
❑ 405 Kenny Battle RC .10 .05
❑ 406 Ed Nealy .10 .05
❑ 407 Danny Ainge .30 .14
❑ 408 Steve Colter .10 .05
❑ 409 Bobby Hansen .10 .05
❑ 410 Eric Leckner .10 .05
❑ 411 Rory Sparrow .10 .05
❑ 412 Bill Wennington .10 .05
❑ 413 Sidney Green .10 .05
❑ 414 David Greenwood .10 .05
❑ 415 Paul Pressey .10 .05
❑ 416 Reggie Williams .10 .05
❑ 417 Dave Corzine .10 .05
❑ 418 Jeff Malone .10 .05
❑ 419 Pervis Ellison .10 .05
❑ 420 Byron Irvin .10 .05
❑ 421 Checklist 1 .10 .05
❑ 422 Checklist 2 .10 .05
❑ 423 Checklist 3 .10 .05
❑ NNO SkyBox Salutes the NBA 5.00 2.20

1991-92 SkyBox

	MINT	NRMT
COMPLETE SET (659)	60.00	27.00
COMPLETE SERIES 1 (350)	20.00	9.00
COMPLETE SERIES 2 (309)	40.00	18.00
COMMON CARD (1-659)	.05	.02
SEMISTARS	.20	.09
UNLISTED STARS	.40	.18

SUBSET CARDS HALF VALUE OF BASE CARDS

❑ 1 John Battle .05 .02
❑ 2 Duane Ferrell .05 .02
❑ 3 Jon Koncak .05 .02
❑ 4 Moses Malone .40 .18
❑ 5 Tim McCormick .05 .02
❑ 6 Sidney Moncrief .05 .02
❑ 7 Doc Rivers .20 .09
❑ 8 Rumeal Robinson UER .05 .02
(Drafted 11th& should say 10th)
❑ 9 Spud Webb .20 .09
❑ 10 Dominique Wilkins .40 .18
❑ 11 Kevin Willis .05 .02
❑ 12 Larry Bird 1.50 .70
❑ 13 Dee Brown .05 .02
❑ 14 Kevin Gamble .05 .02
❑ 15 Joe Kleine .05 .02
❑ 16 Reggie Lewis .20 .09
❑ 17 Kevin McHale .20 .09
❑ 18 Robert Parish .20 .09
❑ 19 Ed Pinckney .05 .02
❑ 20 Brian Shaw .05 .02
❑ 21 Michael Smith .05 .02
❑ 22 Stojko Vrankovic .05 .02
❑ 23 Muggsy Bogues .20 .09
❑ 24 Rex Chapman .20 .09
❑ 25 Dell Curry .05 .02
❑ 26 Kenny Gattison .05 .02
❑ 27 Kendall Gill .20 .09
❑ 28 Mike Gminski .05 .02
❑ 29 Randolph Keys .05 .02
❑ 30 Eric Leckner .05 .02
❑ 31 Johnny Newman .05 .02
❑ 32 J.R. Reid .05 .02
❑ 33 Kelly Tripucka .05 .02
❑ 34 B.J. Armstrong .05 .02
❑ 35 Bill Cartwright .05 .02
❑ 36 Horace Grant .20 .09
❑ 37 Craig Hodges .05 .02
❑ 38 Dennis Hopson .05 .02
❑ 39 Michael Jordan 5.00 2.20
❑ 40 Stacey King .05 .02
❑ 41 Cliff Levingston .05 .02
❑ 42 John Paxson .05 .02
❑ 43 Will Perdue .05 .02
❑ 44 Scottie Pippen 1.25 .55
❑ 45 Winston Bennett .05 .02
❑ 46 Chucky Brown .05 .02
❑ 47 Brad Daugherty .05 .02
❑ 48 Craig Ehlo .05 .02
❑ 49 Danny Ferry .05 .02
❑ 50 Steve Kerr .20 .09
❑ 51 John Morton .05 .02
❑ 52 Larry Nance .20 .09
❑ 53 Mark Price .05 .02
❑ 54 Darnell Valentine .05 .02
❑ 55 John Williams .05 .02
❑ 56 Steve Alford .05 .02
❑ 57 Rolando Blackman .05 .02
❑ 58 Brad Davis .05 .02
❑ 59 James Donaldson .05 .02
❑ 60 Derek Harper .20 .09
❑ 61 Fat Lever .05 .02
❑ 62 Rodney McCray .05 .02
❑ 63 Roy Tarpley .05 .02
❑ 64 Kelvin Upshaw .05 .02
❑ 65 Randy White .05 .02
❑ 66 Herb Williams .05 .02
❑ 67 Michael Adams .05 .02
❑ 68 Greg Anderson .05 .02
❑ 69 Anthony Cook .05 .02
❑ 70 Chris Jackson .05 .02
❑ 71 Jerome Lane .05 .02
❑ 72 Marcus Liberty .05 .02

73	Todd Lichti	.05	.02
74	Blair Rasmussen	.05	.02
75	Reggie Williams	.05	.02
76	Joe Wolf	.05	.02
77	Orlando Woolridge	.05	.02
78	Mark Aguirre	.05	.02
79	William Bedford	.05	.02
80	Lance Blanks	.05	.02
81	Joe Dumars	.40	.18
82	James Edwards	.05	.02
83	Scott Hastings	.05	.02
84	Vinnie Johnson	.05	.02
85	Bill Laimbeer	.20	.09
86	Dennis Rodman	.75	.35
87	John Salley	.05	.02
88	Isiah Thomas	.40	.18
89	Mario Elie RC	.40	.18
90	Tim Hardaway	.60	.25
91	Rod Higgins	.05	.02
92	Tyrone Hill	.20	.09
93	Les Jepsen	.05	.02
94	Alton Lister	.05	.02
95	Sarunas Marciulionis	.05	.02
96	Chris Mullin	.40	.18
97	Jim Petersen	.05	.02
98	Mitch Richmond	.40	.18
99	Tom Tolbert	.05	.02
100	Adrian Caldwell	.05	.02
101	Eric(Sleepy) Floyd	.05	.02
102	Dave Jamerson	.05	.02
103	Buck Johnson	.05	.02
104	Vernon Maxwell	.05	.02
105	Hakeem Olajuwon	.60	.25
106	Kenny Smith	.05	.02
107	Larry Smith	.05	.02
108	Otis Thorpe	.20	.09
109	Kennard Winchester RC	.05	.02
110	David Wood RC	.05	.02
111	Greg Dreiling	.05	.02
112	Vern Fleming	.05	.02
113	George McCloud	.05	.02
114	Reggie Miller	.40	.18
115	Chuck Person	.05	.02
116	Mike Sanders	.05	.02
117	Detlef Schrempf	.20	.09
118	Rik Smits	.20	.09
119	LaSalle Thompson	.05	.02
120	Kenny Williams	.05	.02
121	Micheal Williams	.05	.02
122	Ken Bannister	.05	.02
123	Winston Garland	.05	.02
124	Gary Grant	.05	.02
125	Ron Harper	.20	.09
126	Bo Kimble	.05	.02
127	Danny Manning	.20	.09
128	Jeff Martin	.05	.02
129	Ken Norman	.05	.02
130	Olden Polynice	.05	.02
131	Charles Smith	.05	.02
132	Loy Vaught	.05	.02
133	Elden Campbell	.20	.09
134	Vlade Divac	.20	.09
135	Larry Drew	.05	.02
136	A.C. Green	.20	.09
137	Magic Johnson	1.25	.55
138	Sam Perkins	.20	.09
139	Byron Scott	.20	.09
140	Tony Smith	.05	.02
141	Terry Teagle	.05	.02
142	Mychal Thompson	.05	.02
143	James Worthy	.40	.18
144	Willie Burton	.05	.02
145	Bimbo Coles	.05	.02
146	Terry Davis	.05	.02
147	Sherman Douglas	.05	.02
148	Kevin Edwards	.05	.02
149	Alec Kessler	.05	.02
150	Grant Long	.05	.02
151	Glen Rice	.40	.18
152	Rony Seikaly	.05	.02
153	Jon Sundvold	.05	.02
154	Billy Thompson	.05	.02
155	Frank Brickowski	.05	.02
156	Lester Conner	.05	.02
157	Jeff Grayer	.05	.02
158	Jay Humphries	.05	.02
159	Larry Krystkowiak	.05	.02
160	Brad Lohaus	.05	.02
161	Dale Ellis	.20	.09
162	Fred Roberts	.05	.02
163	Alvin Robertson	.05	.02
164	Danny Schayes	.05	.02
165	Jack Sikma	.05	.02
166	Randy Breuer	.05	.02
167	Scott Brooks	.05	.02
168	Tony Campbell	.05	.02
169	Tyrone Corbin	.05	.02
170	Gerald Glass	.05	.02
171	Sam Mitchell	.05	.02
172	Tod Murphy	.05	.02
173	Pooh Richardson	.05	.02
174	Felton Spencer	.05	.02
175	Bob Thornton	.05	.02
176	Doug West	.05	.02
177	Mookie Blaylock	.20	.09
178	Sam Bowie	.05	.02
179	Jud Buechler	.05	.02
180	Derrick Coleman	.20	.09
181	Chris Dudley	.05	.02
182	Tate George	.05	.02
183	Jack Haley	.05	.02
184	Terry Mills RC	.40	.18
185	Chris Morris	.05	.02
186	Drazen Petrovic	.20	.09
187	Reggie Theus	.20	.09
188	Maurice Cheeks	.05	.02
189	Patrick Ewing	.40	.18
190	Mark Jackson	.20	.09
191	Jerrod Mustaf	.05	.02
192	Charles Oakley	.20	.09
193	Brian Quinnett	.05	.02
194	John Starks RC	.40	.18
195	Trent Tucker	.05	.02
196	Kiki Vandeweghe	.05	.02
197	Kenny Walker	.05	.02
198	Gerald Wilkins	.05	.02
199	Mark Acres	.05	.02
200	Nick Anderson	.20	.09
201	Michael Ansley	.05	.02
202	Terry Catledge	.05	.02
203	Greg Kite	.05	.02
204	Jerry Reynolds	.05	.02
205	Dennis Scott	.20	.09
206	Scott Skiles	.05	.02
207	Otis Smith	.05	.02
208	Jeff Turner	.05	.02
209	Sam Vincent	.05	.02
210	Ron Anderson	.05	.02
211	Charles Barkley	.60	.25
212	Manute Bol	.05	.02
213	Johnny Dawkins	.05	.02
214	Armon Gilliam	.05	.02
215	Rickey Green	.05	.02
216	Hersey Hawkins	.20	.09
217	Rick Mahorn	.05	.02
218	Brian Oliver	.05	.02
219	Andre Turner	.05	.02
220	Jayson Williams	.40	.18
221	Joe Barry Carroll	.05	.02
222	Cedric Ceballos	.20	.09
223	Tom Chambers	.05	.02
224	Jeff Hornacek	.20	.09
225	Kevin Johnson	.40	.18
226	Negele Knight	.05	.02
227	Andrew Lang	.05	.02
228	Dan Majerle	.20	.09
229	Xavier McDaniel	.05	.02
230	Kurt Rambis	.05	.02
231	Mark West	.05	.02
232	Alaa Abdelnaby	.05	.02
233	Danny Ainge	.20	.09
234	Mark Bryant	.05	.02
235	Wayne Cooper	.05	.02
236	Walter Davis	.05	.02
237	Clyde Drexler	.40	.18
238	Kevin Duckworth	.05	.02
239	Jerome Kersey	.05	.02
240	Terry Porter	.05	.02
241	Clifford Robinson	.20	.09
242	Buck Williams	.05	.02
243	Anthony Bonner	.05	.02
244	Antoine Carr	.05	.02
245	Duane Causwell	.05	.02
246	Bobby Hansen	.05	.02
247	Jim Les RC	.05	.02
248	Travis Mays	.05	.02
249	Ralph Sampson	.05	.02
250	Lionel Simmons	.05	.02
251	Rory Sparrow	.05	.02
252	Wayman Tisdale	.05	.02
253	Bill Wennington	.05	.02
254	Willie Anderson	.05	.02
255	Terry Cummings	.05	.02
256	Sean Elliott	.20	.09
257	Sidney Green	.05	.02
258	David Greenwood	.05	.02
259	Avery Johnson	.20	.09
260	Paul Pressey	.05	.02
261	David Robinson	.75	.35
262	Dwayne Schintzius	.05	.02
263	Rod Strickland	.40	.18
264	David Wingate	.05	.02
265	Dana Barros	.05	.02
266	Benoit Benjamin	.05	.02
267	Michael Cage	.05	.02
268	Quintin Dailey	.05	.02
269	Ricky Pierce	.05	.02
270	Eddie Johnson	.20	.09
271	Shawn Kemp	1.00	.45
272	Derrick McKey	.05	.02
273	Nate McMillan	.05	.02
274	Gary Payton	1.00	.45
275	Sedale Threatt	.05	.02
276	Thurl Bailey	.05	.02
277	Mike Brown	.05	.02
278	Tony Brown	.05	.02
279	Mark Eaton	.05	.02
280	Blue Edwards	.05	.02
281	Darrell Griffith	.05	.02
282	Jeff Malone	.05	.02
283	Karl Malone	.60	.25
284	Delaney Rudd	.05	.02
285	John Stockton	.40	.18
286	Andy Toolson	.05	.02
287	Mark Alarie	.05	.02
288	Ledell Eackles	.05	.02
289	Pervis Ellison	.05	.02
290	A.J. English	.05	.02
291	Harvey Grant	.05	.02
292	Tom Hammonds	.05	.02
293	Charles Jones	.05	.02
294	Bernard King	.05	.02
295	Darrell Walker	.05	.02
296	John Williams	.05	.02
297	Haywoode Workman RC	.20	.09
298	Muggsy Bogues Assist-to-Turnover Ratio Leader	.05	.02
299	Lester Conner Steal-to Turnover Ratio Leader	.05	.02
300	Michael Adams Largest One-Year Scoring Improvement	.05	.02
301	Chris Mullin Most Minutes Per Game	.20	.09
302	Otis Thorpe Most Consecutive Games Played	.05	.02
303	Mitch Richmond Chris Mullin Tim Hardaway Highest Scoring Trio	.40	.18
304	Darrell Walker Top Rebounding Guard	.05	.02
305	Jerome Lane Rebounds Per 48 Minutes	.05	.02
306	John Stockton Assists Per 48 Minutes	.20	.09
307	Michael Jordan Points Per 48 Minutes	2.50	1.10
308	Michael Adams Best Single Game Performance: Points	.05	.02
309	Larry Smith Jerome Lane Best Single Game Performance: Rebounds	.05	.02

❑	310	Scott Skiles	.05	.02
		Best Single Game		
		Performance: Assists		
❑	311	Hakeem Olajuwon	.40	.18
		David Robinson		
		Best Single Game		
		Performance: Blocks		
❑	312	Alvin Robertson	.05	.02
		Best Single Game		
		Performance: Steals		
❑	313	Stay In School Jam	.05	.02
❑	314	Craig Hodges	.05	.02
		Three-Point Shootout		
❑	315	Dee Brown	.05	.02
		Slam-Dunk Championship		
❑	316	Charles Barkley	.40	.18
		All-Star Game MVP		
❑	317	Behind the Scenes	.40	.18
		Charles Barkley		
		Joe Dumars		
		Kevin McHale		
❑	318	Derrick Coleman ART	.05	.02
❑	319	Lionel Simmons ART	.05	.02
❑	320	Dennis Scott ART	.05	.02
❑	321	Kendall Gill ART	.05	.02
❑	322	Dee Brown ART	.05	.02
❑	323	Magic Johnson	.60	.25
		GQ All-Star Style Team		
❑	324	Hakeem Olajuwon	.40	.18
		GQ All-Star Style Team		
❑	325	Kevin Willis	.20	.09
		Dominique Wilkins		
		GQ All-Star Style Team		
❑	326	Kevin Willis	.20	.09
		Dominique Wilkins		
		GQ All-Star Style Team		
❑	327	Gerald Wilkins	.05	.02
		GQ All-Star Style Team		
❑	328	1891-1991 Basketball	.05	.02
		Centennial Logo		
❑	329	Old-Fashioned Ball	.05	.02
❑	330	Women Take the Court	.05	.02
❑	331	The Peach Basket	.05	.02
❑	332	James A. Naismith	.20	.09
		Founder of Basketball		
❑	333	Magic Johnson FIN	2.00	.90
		Michael Jordan FIN		
❑	334	Michael Jordan FIN	2.50	1.10
❑	335	Vlade Divac FIN	.05	.02
❑	336	John Paxson FIN	.05	.02
❑	337	Bulls Starting Five	1.25	.55
		Great Moments from		
		the NBA Finals		
❑	338	Language Arts	.05	.02
		Stay in School		
❑	339	Mathematics	.05	.02
		Stay in School		
❑	340	Vocational Education	.05	.02
		Stay in School		
❑	341	Social Studies	.05	.02
		Stay in School		
❑	342	Physical Education	.05	.02
		Stay in School		
❑	343	Art	.05	.02
		Stay in School		
❑	344	Science	.05	.02
		Stay in School		
❑	345	Checklist 1 (1-60)	.05	.02
❑	346	Checklist 2 (61-120)	.05	.02
❑	347	Checklist 3 (121-180)	.05	.02
❑	348	Checklist 4 (181-244)	.05	.02
❑	349	Checklist 5 (245-305)	.05	.02
❑	350	Checklist 6 (306-350)	.05	.02
❑	351	Atlanta Hawks	.05	.02
		Team Logo		
❑	352	Boston Celtics	.05	.02
		Team Logo		
❑	353	Charlotte Hornets	.05	.02
		Team Logo		
❑	354	Chicago Bulls	.05	.02
		Team Logo		
❑	355	Cleveland Cavaliers	.05	.02
		Team Logo		
❑	356	Dallas Mavericks	.05	.02
		Team Logo		
❑	357	Denver Nuggets	.05	.02
		Team Logo		
❑	358	Detroit Pistons	.05	.02
		Team Logo		
❑	359	Golden State Warriors	.05	.02
		Team Logo		
❑	360	Houston Rockets	.05	.02
		Team Logo		
❑	361	Indiana Pacers	.05	.02
		Team Logo		
❑	362	Los Angeles Clippers	.05	.02
		Team Logo		
❑	363	Los Angeles Lakers	.05	.02
		Team Logo		
❑	364	Miami Heat	.05	.02
		Team Logo		
❑	365	Milwaukee Bucks	.05	.02
		Team Logo		
❑	366	Minnesota Timberwolves	.05	.02
		Team Logo		
❑	367	New Jersey Nets	.05	.02
		Team Logo		
❑	368	New York Knicks	.05	.02
		Team Logo		
❑	369	Orlando Magic	.05	.02
		Team Logo		
❑	370	Philadelphia 76ers	.05	.02
		Team Logo		
❑	371	Phoenix Suns	.05	.02
		Team Logo		
❑	372	Portland Trail Blazers	.05	.02
		Team Logo		
❑	373	Sacramento Kings	.05	.02
		Team Logo		
❑	374	San Antonio Spurs	.05	.02
		Team Logo		
❑	375	Seattle Supersonics	.05	.02
		Team Logo		
❑	376	Utah Jazz	.05	.02
		Team Logo		
❑	377	Washington Bullets	.05	.02
		Team Logo		
❑	378	Bob Weiss CO	.05	.02
❑	379	Chris Ford CO	.05	.02
❑	380	Allan Bristow CO	.05	.02
❑	381	Phil Jackson CO	.20	.09
❑	382	Lenny Wilkens CO	.20	.09
❑	383	Richie Adubato CO	.05	.02
❑	384	Paul Westhead CO	.05	.02
❑	385	Chuck Daly CO	.20	.09
❑	386	Don Nelson CO	.20	.09
❑	387	Don Chaney CO	.05	.02
❑	388	Bob Hill CO RC	.05	.02
❑	389	Mike Schuler CO	.05	.02
❑	390	Mike Dunleavy CO	.05	.02
❑	391	Kevin Loughery CO	.05	.02
❑	392	Del Harris CO	.05	.02
❑	393	Jimmy Rodgers CO	.05	.02
❑	394	Bill Fitch CO	.05	.02
❑	395	Pat Riley CO	.20	.09
❑	396	Matt Guokas CO	.05	.02
❑	397	Jim Lynam CO	.05	.02
❑	398	Cotton Fitzsimmons CO	.05	.02
❑	399	Rick Adelman CO	.05	.02
❑	400	Dick Motta CO	.05	.02
❑	401	Larry Brown CO	.05	.02
❑	402	K.C. Jones CO	.20	.09
❑	403	Jerry Sloan CO	.20	.09
❑	404	Wes Unseld CO	.20	.09
❑	405	Mo Cheeks GF	.05	.02
❑	406	Dee Brown GF	.05	.02
❑	407	Rex Chapman GF	.05	.02
❑	408	Michael Jordan GF	2.50	1.10
❑	409	John Williams GF	.05	.02
❑	410	James Donaldson GF	.05	.02
❑	411	Dikembe Mutombo GF	.40	.18
❑	412	Isiah Thomas GF	.20	.09
❑	413	Tim Hardaway GF	.40	.18
❑	414	Hakeem Olajuwon GF	.40	.18
❑	415	Detlef Schrempf GF	.05	.02
❑	416	Danny Manning GF	.05	.02
❑	417	Magic Johnson GF	.60	.25
❑	418	Bimbo Coles GF	.05	.02
❑	419	Alvin Robertson GF	.05	.02
❑	420	Sam Mitchell GF	.05	.02
❑	421	Sam Bowie GF	.05	.02
❑	422	Mark Jackson GF	.05	.02
❑	423	Orlando Magic	.05	.02
		Game Frame		
❑	424	Charles Barkley GF	.40	.18
❑	425	Dan Majerle GF	.05	.02
❑	426	Robert Pack GF	.05	.02
❑	427	Wayman Tisdale GF	.05	.02
❑	428	David Robinson GF	.40	.18
❑	429	Nate McMillan GF	.05	.02
		Seattle Supersonics)		
❑	430	Karl Malone GF	.40	.18
❑	431	Michael Adams GF	.05	.02
❑	432	Duane Ferrell SM	.05	.02
❑	433	Kevin McHale SM	.05	.02
❑	434	Dell Curry SM	.05	.02
❑	435	B.J. Armstrong SM	.05	.02
❑	436	John Williams SM	.05	.02
❑	437	Brad Davis SM	.05	.02
❑	438	Marcus Liberty SM	.05	.02
❑	439	Mark Aguirre SM	.05	.02
❑	440	Rod Higgins SM	.05	.02
❑	441	Eric(Sleepy) Floyd SM	.05	.02
❑	442	Detlef Schrempf SM	.05	.02
❑	443	Loy Vaught SM	.05	.02
❑	444	Terry Teagle SM	.05	.02
❑	445	Kevin Edwards SM	.05	.02
❑	446	Dale Ellis SM	.05	.02
❑	447	Tod Murphy SM	.05	.02
❑	448	Chris Dudley SM	.05	.02
❑	449	Mark Jackson SM	.05	.02
❑	450	Jerry Reynolds SM	.05	.02
❑	451	Ron Anderson SM	.05	.02
❑	452	Dan Majerle SM	.05	.02
❑	453	Danny Ainge SM	.05	.02
❑	454	Jim Les SM	.05	.02
❑	455	Paul Pressey SM	.05	.02
❑	456	Ricky Pierce SM	.05	.02
❑	457	Mike Brown SM	.05	.02
❑	458	Ledell Eackles SM	.05	.02
❑	459	Atlanta Hawks	.20	.09
		Teamwork		
		(Dominique Wilkins		
		and Kevin Willis)		
❑	460	Boston Celtics	.40	.18
		Teamwork		
		(Larry Bird and		
		Robert Parish)		
❑	461	Charlotte Hornets	.05	.02
		Teamwork		
		(Rex Chapman and		
		Kendall Gill)		
❑	462	Chicago Bulls	1.50	.70
		Teamwork		
		(Michael Jordan and		
		Scottie Pippen)		
❑	463	Cleveland Cavaliers	.05	.02
		Teamwork		
		(Craig Ehlo and		
		Mark Price)		
❑	464	Dallas Mavericks	.05	.02
		Teamwork		
		(Derek Harper and		
		Rolando Blackman)		
❑	465	Denver Nuggets	.05	.02
		Teamwork		
		(Reggie Williams and		
		Chris Jackson)		
❑	466	Detroit Pistons	.20	.09
		Teamwork		
		(Isiah Thomas and		
		Bill Laimbeer)		
❑	467	Golden State Warriors	.20	.09
		Teamwork		
		(Tim Hardaway and		
		Chris Mullin)		
❑	468	Houston Rockets	.05	.02
		Teamwork		
		(Vernon Maxwell and		
		Kenny Smith)		
❑	469	Indiana Pacers	.20	.09
		Teamwork		
		(Detlef Schrempf and		
		Reggie Miller)		
❑	470	Los Angeles Clippers	.05	.02
		Teamwork		
		(Charles Smith and		
		Danny Manning)		

❑ 471 Los Angeles Lakers .... .40 .18
Teamwork
(Magic Johnson and
James Worthy)
❑ 472 Miami Heat .... .40 .18
Teamwork
(Glen Rice and
Rony Seikaly)
❑ 473 Milwaukee Bucks .... .05 .02
Teamwork
(Jay Humphries and
Alvin Robertson)
❑ 474 Minnesota Timberwolves .05 .02
Teamwork
(Tony Campbell and
Pooh Richardson)
❑ 475 New Jersey Nets .... .05 .02
Teamwork
(Derrick Coleman and
Sam Bowie)
❑ 476 New York Knicks .... .20 .09
Teamwork
(Patrick Ewing and
Charles Oakley)
❑ 477 Orlando Magic .... .05 .02
Teamwork
(Dennis Scott and
Scott Skiles)
❑ 478 Philadelphia 76ers .... .40 .18
Teamwork
(Charles Barkley and
Hersey Hawkins)
❑ 479 Phoenix Suns .... .20 .09
Teamwork
(Kevin Johnson and
Tom Chambers)
❑ 480 Portland Trail Blazers .... .40 .18
Teamwork
(Clyde Drexler and
Terry Porter)
❑ 481 Sacramento Kings .... .05 .02
Teamwork
(Lionel Simmons and
Wayman Tisdale)
❑ 482 San Antonio Spurs .... .05 .02
Teamwork
(Terry Cummings and
Sean Elliott)
❑ 483 Seattle Supersonics ...... .05 .02
Teamwork
(Eddie Johnson and
Ricky Pierce)
❑ 484 Utah Jazz .... .40 .18
Teamwork
(Karl Malone and
John Stockton)
❑ 485 Washington Bullets .... .05 .02
Teamwork
(Harvey Grant and
Bernard King)
❑ 486 Rumeal Robinson RS .... .05 .02
❑ 487 Dee Brown RS .... .05 .02
❑ 488 Kendall Gill RS .... .05 .02
❑ 489 B.J. Armstrong RS .... .05 .02
❑ 490 Danny Ferry RS .... .05 .02
❑ 491 Randy White RS .... .05 .02
❑ 492 Chris Jackson RS .... .05 .02
❑ 493 Lance Blanks RS .... .05 .02
❑ 494 Tim Hardaway RS .... .40 .18
❑ 495 Vernon Maxwell RS .... .05 .02
❑ 496 Micheal Williams RS ...... .05 .02
❑ 497 Charles Smith RS .... .05 .02
❑ 498 Vlade Divac RS .... .05 .02
❑ 499 Willie Burton RS .... .05 .02
❑ 500 Jeff Grayer RS .... .05 .02
❑ 501 Pooh Richardson RS ...... .05 .02
❑ 502 Derrick Coleman RS ...... .05 .02
❑ 503 John Starks RS .... .20 .09
❑ 504 Dennis Scott RS .... .05 .02
❑ 505 Hersey Hawkins RS ...... .05 .02
❑ 506 Negele Knight RS .... .05 .02
❑ 507 Clifford Robinson RS ...... .05 .02
❑ 508 Lionel Simmons RS .... .05 .02
❑ 509 David Robinson RS .... .40 .18
❑ 510 Gary Payton RS .... .50 .23
❑ 511 Blue Edwards RS .... .05 .02
❑ 512 Harvey Grant RS .... .05 .02
❑ 513 Larry Johnson RC .... 1.50 .70
❑ 514 Kenny Anderson RC ...... .75 .35
❑ 515 Billy Owens RC .... .40 .18
❑ 516 Dikembe Mutombo RC 1.25 .55
❑ 517 Steve Smith RC .... 1.50 .70
❑ 518 Doug Smith RC .... .05 .02
❑ 519 Luc Longley RC .... .40 .18
❑ 520 Mark Macon RC .... .05 .02
❑ 521 Stacey Augmon RC .... .40 .18
❑ 522 Brian Williams RC .... .40 .18
❑ 523 Terrell Brandon RC ...... 1.25 .55
❑ 524 The Ball .... .05 .02
❑ 525 The Basket .... .05 .02
❑ 526 The 24-second Shot ...... .05 .02
Clock
❑ 527 The Game Program ...... .05 .02
❑ 528 The Championship Gift .. .05 .02
❑ 529 Championship Trophy .... .05 .02
❑ 530 Charles Barkley USA .. 1.25 .55
❑ 531 Larry Bird USA 3.00 1.35
❑ 532 Patrick Ewing USA .... .75 .35
❑ 533 Magic Johnson USA 2.50 1.10
❑ 534 Michael Jordan USA .. 10.00 4.50
❑ 535 Karl Malone USA .... 1.25 .55
❑ 536 Chris Mullin USA .... .40 .18
❑ 537 Scottie Pippen USA 2.50 1.10
❑ 538 David Robinson USA .. 1.50 .70
❑ 539 John Stockton USA ...... .75 .35
❑ 540 Chuck Daly CO USA ...... .20 .09
❑ 541 P.J. Carlesimo CO USA .05 .02
❑ 542 M. Krzyzewski CO USA RC .. .60 .25
❑ 543 Lenny Wilkens CO USA .20 .09
❑ 544 Team USA Card 1 .... 2.50 1.10
❑ 545 Team USA Card 2 .... 2.50 1.10
❑ 546 Team USA Card 3 .... 2.50 1.10
❑ 547 Willie Anderson USA ...... .05 .02
❑ 548 Stacey Augmon USA ...... .40 .18
❑ 549 Bimbo Coles USA .... .05 .02
❑ 550 Jeff Grayer USA .... .05 .02
❑ 551 Hersey Hawkins USA .... .05 .02
❑ 552 Dan Majerle USA .... .05 .02
❑ 553 Danny Manning USA ...... .05 .02
❑ 554 J.R. Reid USA .... .05 .02
❑ 555 Mitch Richmond USA .... .75 .35
❑ 556 Charles Smith USA .... .05 .02
❑ 557 Vern Fleming USA .... .05 .02
❑ 558 Joe Kleine USA .... .05 .02
❑ 559 Jon Koncak USA .... .05 .02
❑ 560 Sam Perkins USA .... .05 .02
❑ 561 Alvin Robertson USA .... .05 .02
❑ 562 Wayman Tisdale USA .... .05 .02
❑ 563 Jeff Turner USA .... .05 .02
❑ 564 Tony Campbell .... .05 .02
Magic of SkyBox
❑ 565 Joe Dumars .... .20 .09
Magic of SkyBox
❑ 566 Horace Grant .... .05 .02
Magic of SkyBox
❑ 567 Reggie Lewis .... .05 .02
Magic of SkyBox
❑ 568 Hakeem Olajuwon .... .40 .18
Magic of SkyBox
❑ 569 Sam Perkins .... .05 .02
Magic of SkyBox
❑ 570 Chuck Person .... .05 .02
Magic of SkyBox
❑ 571 Buck Williams .... .05 .02
Magic of SkyBox
❑ 572 Michael Jordan 2.50 1.10
SkyBox Salutes
❑ 573 Bernard King .... .05 .02
NBA All-Star
SkyBox Salutes
❑ 574 Moses Malone .... .20 .09
SkyBox Salutes
❑ 575 Robert Parish .... .05 .02
SkyBox Salutes
❑ 576 Pat Riley CO .... .20 .09
SkyBox Salutes
❑ 577 Dee Brown .... .05 .02
SkyMaster
❑ 578 Rex Chapman .... .05 .02
SkyMaster
❑ 579 Clyde Drexler .... .20 .09
SkyMaster
❑ 580 Blue Edwards .... .05 .02
SkyMaster
❑ 581 Ron Harper .... .05 .02
SkyMaster
❑ 582 Kevin Johnson .... .20 .09
SkyMaster
❑ 583 Michael Jordan 2.50 1.10
SkyMaster
❑ 584 Shawn Kemp .... .75 .35
SkyMaster
❑ 585 Xavier McDaniel .... .05 .02
SkyMaster
❑ 586 Scottie Pippen .... .60 .25
SkyMaster
❑ 587 Kenny Smith .... .05 .02
SkyMaster
❑ 588 Dominique Wilkins .... .20 .09
SkyMaster
❑ 589 Michael Adams .... .05 .02
Shooting Star
❑ 590 Danny Ainge .... .05 .02
Shooting Star
❑ 591 Larry Bird .... .75 .35
Shooting Star
❑ 592 Dale Ellis .... .05 .02
Shooting Star
❑ 593 Hersey Hawkins .... .05 .02
Shooting Star
❑ 594 Jeff Hornacek .... .05 .02
Shooting Star
❑ 595 Jeff Malone .... .05 .02
Shooting Star
❑ 596 Reggie Miller .... .20 .09
Shooting Star
❑ 597 Chris Mullin .... .20 .09
Shooting Star
❑ 598 John Paxson .... .05 .02
Shooting Star
❑ 599 Drazen Petrovic .... .05 .02
Shooting Star
❑ 600 Ricky Pierce .... .05 .02
Shooting Star
❑ 601 Mark Price .... .05 .02
Shooting Star
❑ 602 Dennis Scott .... .05 .02
Shooting Star
❑ 603 Manute Bol .... .05 .02
Small School Sensation
❑ 604 Jerome Kersey .... .05 .02
Small School Sensation
❑ 605 Charles Oakley .... .05 .02
Small School Sensation
❑ 606 Scottie Pippen .... .60 .25
Small School Sensation
❑ 607 Terry Porter .... .05 .02
Small School Sensation
❑ 608 Dennis Rodman .... .40 .18
Small School Sensation
❑ 609 Sedale Threatt .... .05 .02
Small School Sensation
❑ 610 Business .... .05 .02
Stay in School
❑ 611 Engineering .... .05 .02
Stay in School
❑ 612 Law .... .05 .02
Stay in School
❑ 613 Liberal Arts .... .05 .02
Stay in School
❑ 614 Medicine .... .05 .02
Stay in School
❑ 615 Maurice Cheeks .... .05 .02
❑ 616 Travis Mays .... .05 .02
❑ 617 Blair Rasmussen .... .05 .02
❑ 618 Alexander Volkov .... .05 .02
❑ 619 Rickey Green .... .05 .02
❑ 620 Bobby Hansen .... .05 .02
❑ 621 John Battle .... .05 .02
❑ 622 Terry Davis .... .05 .02
❑ 623 Walter Davis .... .05 .02
❑ 624 Winston Garland .... .05 .02
❑ 625 Scott Hastings .... .05 .02
❑ 626 Brad Sellers .... .05 .02
❑ 627 Darrell Walker .... .05 .02
❑ 628 Orlando Woolridge .... .05 .02
❑ 629 Tony Brown .... .05 .02
❑ 630 James Edwards .... .05 .02

Card	MINT	NRMT
❑ 631 Doc Rivers	.20	.09
❑ 632 Jack Haley	.05	.02
❑ 633 Sedale Threatt	.05	.02
❑ 634 Moses Malone	.40	.18
❑ 635 Thurl Bailey	.05	.02
❑ 636 Rafael Addison RC	.05	.02
❑ 637 Tim McCormick	.05	.02
❑ 638 Xavier McDaniel	.05	.02
❑ 639 Charles Shackleford	.05	.02
❑ 640 Mitchell Wiggins	.05	.02
❑ 641 Jerrod Mustaf	.05	.02
❑ 642 Dennis Hopson	.05	.02
❑ 643 Les Jepsen	.05	.02
❑ 644 Mitch Richmond	.40	.18
❑ 645 Dwayne Schintzius	.05	.02
❑ 646 Spud Webb	.20	.09
❑ 647 Jud Buechler	.05	.02
❑ 648 Antoine Carr	.05	.02
❑ 649 Tyrone Corbin	.05	.02
❑ 650 Michael Adams	.05	.02
❑ 651 Ralph Sampson	.05	.02
❑ 652 Andre Turner	.05	.02
❑ 653 David Wingate	.05	.02
❑ 654 Checklist "S" (351-404)	.05	.02
❑ 655 Checklist "K" (405-458)	.05	.02
❑ 656 Checklist "Y" (459-512)	.05	.02
❑ 657 Checklist "B" (513-563)	.05	.02
❑ 658 Checklist "O" (564-614)	.05	.02
❑ 659 Checklist "X" (615-659)	.05	.02
❑ NNO Clyde Drexler USA (Send-away)	75.00	34.00
❑ NNO Team USA Card	12.00	5.50

1991-92 SkyBox Blister Inserts

	MINT	NRMT
COMPLETE SET (6)	2.50	1.10
COMMON CARD (1-4)	.25	.11
COMMON CARD (5-6)	.50	.23

ONE CARD PER BLISTER PACK

Card	MINT	NRMT
❑ 1 USA Basketball (Numbered I)	.25	.11
❑ 2 Stay in School It's Your Best Move (Numbered II)	.25	.11
❑ 3 Orlando All-Star Weekend (Numbered III)	.25	.11
❑ 4 Inside Stuff (Numbered IV)	.25	.11
❑ 5 Magic Johnson and James Worthy Back to Back NBA Finals MVP 1987/1988 (Numbered V)	1.00	.45
❑ 6 Joe Dumars and Isiah Thomas Back to Back NBA Finals MVP 1989/1990 (Numbered VI)	.50	.23

1992-93 SkyBox

	MINT	NRMT
COMPLETE SET (413)	50.00	22.00
COMPLETE SERIES 1 (327)	30.00	13.50
COMPLETE SERIES 2 (86)	20.00	9.00
COMMON CARD (1-413)	.10	.05
SEMISTARS	.25	.11
UNLISTED STARS	.50	.23

SUBSET CARDS HALF VALUE OF BASE CARDS

Card	MINT	NRMT
❑ 1 Stacey Augmon	.25	.11
❑ 2 Maurice Cheeks	.10	.05
❑ 3 Duane Ferrell	.10	.05
❑ 4 Paul Graham	.10	.05
❑ 5 Jon Koncak	.10	.05
❑ 6 Blair Rasmussen	.10	.05
❑ 7 Rumeal Robinson	.10	.05
❑ 8 Dominique Wilkins	.50	.23
❑ 9 Kevin Willis	.10	.05
❑ 10 Larry Bird	2.00	.90
❑ 11 Dee Brown	.10	.05
❑ 12 Sherman Douglas	.10	.05
❑ 13 Rick Fox	.25	.11
❑ 14 Kevin Gamble	.10	.05
❑ 15 Reggie Lewis	.25	.11
❑ 16 Kevin McHale	.50	.23
❑ 17 Robert Parish	.25	.11
❑ 18 Ed Pinckney	.10	.05
❑ 19 Muggsy Bogues	.25	.11
❑ 20 Dell Curry	.10	.05
❑ 21 Kenny Gattison	.10	.05
❑ 22 Kendall Gill	.25	.11
❑ 23 Mike Gminski	.10	.05
❑ 24 Tom Hammonds	.10	.05
❑ 25 Larry Johnson	.60	.25
❑ 26 Johnny Newman	.10	.05
❑ 27 J.R. Reid	.10	.05
❑ 28 B.J. Armstrong	.10	.05
❑ 29 Bill Cartwright	.10	.05
❑ 30 Horace Grant	.25	.11
❑ 31 Michael Jordan	6.00	2.70
❑ 32 Stacey King	.10	.05
❑ 33 John Paxson	.10	.05
❑ 34 Will Perdue	.10	.05
❑ 35 Scottie Pippen	1.50	.70
❑ 36 Scott Williams	.10	.05
❑ 37 John Battle	.10	.05
❑ 38 Terrell Brandon	.50	.23
❑ 39 Brad Daugherty	.10	.05
❑ 40 Craig Ehlo	.10	.05
❑ 41 Danny Ferry	.10	.05
❑ 42 Henry James	.10	.05
❑ 43 Larry Nance	.10	.05
❑ 44 Mark Price	.10	.05
❑ 45 Mike Sanders	.10	.05
❑ 46 Hot Rod Williams	.10	.05
❑ 47 Rolando Blackman	.10	.05
❑ 48 Terry Davis	.10	.05
❑ 49 Derek Harper	.25	.11
❑ 50 Donald Hodge	.10	.05
❑ 51 Mike Iuzzolino	.10	.05
❑ 52 Fat Lever	.10	.05
❑ 53 Rodney McCray	.10	.05
❑ 54 Doug Smith	.10	.05
❑ 55 Randy White	.10	.05
❑ 56 Herb Williams	.10	.05
❑ 57 Greg Anderson	.10	.05
❑ 58 Walter Davis	.10	.05
❑ 59 Winston Garland	.10	.05
❑ 60 Chris Jackson	.10	.05
❑ 61 Marcus Liberty	.10	.05
❑ 62 Todd Lichti	.10	.05
❑ 63 Mark Macon	.10	.05
❑ 64 Dikembe Mutombo	.50	.23
❑ 65 Reggie Williams	.10	.05
❑ 66 Mark Aguirre	.10	.05
❑ 67 William Bedford	.10	.05
❑ 68 Lance Blanks	.10	.05
❑ 69 Joe Dumars	.50	.23
❑ 70 Bill Laimbeer	.25	.11
❑ 71 Dennis Rodman	1.00	.45
❑ 72 John Salley	.10	.05
❑ 73 Isiah Thomas	.50	.23
❑ 74 Darrell Walker	.10	.05
❑ 75 Orlando Woolridge	.10	.05
❑ 76 Victor Alexander	.10	.05
❑ 77 Mario Elie	.25	.11
❑ 78 Chris Gatling	.10	.05
❑ 79 Tim Hardaway	.60	.25
❑ 80 Tyrone Hill	.10	.05
❑ 81 Alton Lister	.10	.05
❑ 82 Sarunas Marciulionis	.10	.05
❑ 83 Chris Mullin	.50	.23
❑ 84 Billy Owens	.25	.11
❑ 85 Matt Bullard	.10	.05
❑ 86 Sleepy Floyd	.10	.05
❑ 87 Avery Johnson	.10	.05
❑ 88 Buck Johnson	.10	.05
❑ 89 Vernon Maxwell	.10	.05
❑ 90 Hakeem Olajuwon	.75	.35
❑ 91 Kenny Smith	.10	.05
❑ 92 Larry Smith	.10	.05
❑ 93 Otis Thorpe	.25	.11
❑ 94 Dale Davis	.10	.05
❑ 95 Vern Fleming	.10	.05
❑ 96 George McCloud	.10	.05
❑ 97 Reggie Miller	.50	.23
❑ 98 Chuck Person	.10	.05
❑ 99 Detlef Schrempf	.25	.11
❑ 100 Rik Smits	.25	.11
❑ 101 LaSalle Thompson	.10	.05
❑ 102 Micheal Williams	.10	.05
❑ 103 James Edwards	.10	.05
❑ 104 Gary Grant	.10	.05
❑ 105 Ron Harper	.25	.11
❑ 106 Bo Kimble	.10	.05
❑ 107 Danny Manning	.25	.11
❑ 108 Ken Norman	.10	.05
❑ 109 Olden Polynice	.10	.05
❑ 110 Doc Rivers	.25	.11
❑ 111 Charles Smith	.10	.05
❑ 112 Loy Vaught	.10	.05
❑ 113 Elden Campbell	.25	.11
❑ 114 Vlade Divac	.25	.11
❑ 115 A.C. Green	.25	.11
❑ 116 Jack Haley	.10	.05
❑ 117 Sam Perkins	.25	.11
❑ 118 Byron Scott	.25	.11
❑ 119 Tony Smith	.10	.05
❑ 120 Sedale Threatt	.10	.05
❑ 121 James Worthy	.50	.23
❑ 122 Keith Askins	.10	.05
❑ 123 Willie Burton	.10	.05
❑ 124 Bimbo Coles	.10	.05
❑ 125 Kevin Edwards	.10	.05
❑ 126 Alec Kessler	.10	.05
❑ 127 Grant Long	.10	.05
❑ 128 Glen Rice	.50	.23
❑ 129 Rony Seikaly	.10	.05
❑ 130 Brian Shaw	.10	.05
❑ 131 Steve Smith	.60	.25
❑ 132 Frank Brickowski	.10	.05
❑ 133 Dale Ellis	.10	.05
❑ 134 Jeff Grayer	.10	.05
❑ 135 Jay Humphries	.10	.05
❑ 136 Larry Krystkowiak	.10	.05
❑ 137 Moses Malone	.50	.23
❑ 138 Fred Roberts	.10	.05
❑ 139 Alvin Robertson	.10	.05
❑ 140 Dan Schayes	.10	.05
❑ 141 Thurl Bailey	.10	.05
❑ 142 Scott Brooks	.10	.05

❑ 143 Tony Campbell .10 .05
❑ 144 Gerald Glass .10 .05
❑ 145 Luc Longley .25 .11
❑ 146 Sam Mitchell .10 .05
❑ 147 Pooh Richardson .10 .05
❑ 148 Felton Spencer .10 .05
❑ 149 Doug West .10 .05
❑ 150 Rafael Addison .10 .05
❑ 151 Kenny Anderson .50 .23
❑ 152 Mookie Blaylock .25 .11
❑ 153 Sam Bowie .10 .05
❑ 154 Derrick Coleman .25 .11
❑ 155 Chris Dudley .10 .05
❑ 156 Tate George .10 .05
❑ 157 Terry Mills .10 .05
❑ 158 Chris Morris .10 .05
❑ 159 Drazen Petrovic .10 .05
❑ 160 Greg Anthony .10 .05
❑ 161 Patrick Ewing .50 .23
❑ 162 Mark Jackson .25 .11
❑ 163 Anthony Mason .50 .23
❑ 164 Tim McCormick .10 .05
❑ 165 Xavier McDaniel .10 .05
❑ 166 Charles Oakley .25 .11
❑ 167 John Starks .25 .11
❑ 168 Gerald Wilkins .10 .05
❑ 169 Nick Anderson .25 .11
❑ 170 Terry Catledge .10 .05
❑ 171 Jerry Reynolds .10 .05
❑ 172 Stanley Roberts .10 .05
❑ 173 Dennis Scott .25 .11
❑ 174 Scott Skiles .10 .05
❑ 175 Jeff Turner .10 .05
❑ 176 Sam Vincent .10 .05
❑ 177 Brian Williams .10 .05
❑ 178 Ron Anderson .10 .05
❑ 179 Charles Barkley .75 .35
❑ 180 Manute Bol .10 .05
❑ 181 Johnny Dawkins .10 .05
❑ 182 Armon Gilliam .10 .05
❑ 183 Greg Grant .10 .05
❑ 184 Hersey Hawkins .25 .11
❑ 185 Brian Oliver .10 .05
❑ 186 Charles Shackleford .10 .05
❑ 187 Jayson Williams .25 .11
❑ 188 Cedric Ceballos .25 .11
❑ 189 Tom Chambers .10 .05
❑ 190 Jeff Hornacek .25 .11
❑ 191 Kevin Johnson .50 .23
❑ 192 Negele Knight .10 .05
❑ 193 Andrew Lang .10 .05
❑ 194 Dan Majerle .25 .11
❑ 195 Jerrod Mustaf .10 .05
❑ 196 Tim Perry .10 .05
❑ 197 Mark West .10 .05
❑ 198 Alaa Abdelnaby .10 .05
❑ 199 Danny Ainge .25 .11
❑ 200 Mark Bryant .10 .05
❑ 201 Clyde Drexler .50 .23
❑ 202 Kevin Duckworth .10 .05
❑ 203 Jerome Kersey .10 .05
❑ 204 Robert Pack .10 .05
❑ 205 Terry Porter .10 .05
❑ 206 Clifford Robinson .25 .11
❑ 207 Buck Williams .25 .11
❑ 208 Anthony Bonner .10 .05
❑ 209 Randy Brown .10 .05
❑ 210 Duane Causwell .10 .05
❑ 211 Pete Chilcutt .10 .05
❑ 212 Dennis Hopson .10 .05
❑ 213 Jim Les .10 .05
❑ 214 Mitch Richmond .50 .23
❑ 215 Lionel Simmons .10 .05
❑ 216 Wayman Tisdale .10 .05
❑ 217 Spud Webb .25 .11
❑ 218 Willie Anderson .10 .05
❑ 219 Antoine Carr .10 .05
❑ 220 Terry Cummings .25 .11
❑ 221 Sean Elliott .25 .11
❑ 222 Sidney Green .10 .05
❑ 223 Vinnie Johnson .10 .05
❑ 224 David Robinson .75 .35
❑ 225 Rod Strickland .50 .23
❑ 226 Greg Sutton .10 .05
❑ 227 Dana Barros .10 .05
❑ 228 Benoit Benjamin .10 .05
❑ 229 Michael Cage .10 .05
❑ 230 Eddie Johnson .10 .05
❑ 231 Shawn Kemp 1.00 .45
❑ 232 Derrick McKey .10 .05
❑ 233 Nate McMillan .10 .05
❑ 234 Gary Payton 1.00 .45
❑ 235 Ricky Pierce .10 .05
❑ 236 David Benoit .10 .05
❑ 237 Mike Brown .10 .05
❑ 238 Tyrone Corbin .10 .05
❑ 239 Mark Eaton .10 .05
❑ 240 Blue Edwards .10 .05
❑ 241 Jeff Malone .10 .05
❑ 242 Karl Malone .75 .35
❑ 243 Eric Murdock .10 .05
❑ 244 John Stockton .50 .23
❑ 245 Michael Adams .10 .05
❑ 246 Rex Chapman .10 .05
❑ 247 Ledell Eackles .10 .05
❑ 248 Pervis Ellison .10 .05
❑ 249 A.J. English .10 .05
❑ 250 Harvey Grant .10 .05
❑ 251 Charles Jones .10 .05
❑ 252 Bernard King .10 .05
❑ 253 LaBradford Smith .10 .05
❑ 254 Larry Stewart .10 .05
❑ 255 Bob Weiss CO .10 .05
❑ 256 Chris Ford CO .10 .05
❑ 257 Allan Bristow CO .10 .05
❑ 258 Phil Jackson CO .25 .11
❑ 259 Lenny Wilkens CO .25 .11
❑ 260 Richie Adubato CO .10 .05
❑ 261 Dan Issel CO .10 .05
❑ 262 Ron Rothstein CO .10 .05
❑ 263 Don Nelson CO .25 .11
❑ 264 Rudy Tomjanovich CO .. .25 .11
❑ 265 Bob Hill CO .10 .05
❑ 266 Larry Brown CO .25 .11
❑ 267 Randy Pfund CO RC .10 .05
❑ 268 Kevin Loughery CO .10 .05
❑ 269 Mike Dunleavy CO .10 .05
❑ 270 Jimmy Rodgers CO .10 .05
❑ 271 Chuck Daly CO .25 .11
❑ 272 Pat Riley CO .25 .11
❑ 273 Matt Guokas CO .10 .05
❑ 274 Doug Moe CO .10 .05
❑ 275 Paul Westphal CO .10 .05
❑ 276 Rick Adelman CO .10 .05
❑ 277 Garry St. Jean CO RC .. .10 .05
❑ 278 Jerry Tarkanian CO RC .. .10 .05
❑ 279 George Karl CO .25 .11
❑ 280 Jerry Sloan CO .25 .11
❑ 281 Wes Unseld CO .25 .11
❑ 282 Dominique Wilkins TT .25 .11
❑ 283 Reggie Lewis TT .10 .05
❑ 284 Kendall Gill TT .10 .05
❑ 285 Horace Grant TT .10 .05
❑ 286 Brad Daugherty TT .10 .05
❑ 287 Derek Harper TT .10 .05
❑ 288 Chris Jackson TT .10 .05
❑ 289 Isiah Thomas TT .25 .11
❑ 290 Chris Mullin TT .25 .11
❑ 291 Kenny Smith TT .10 .05
❑ 292 Reggie Miller TT .25 .11
❑ 293 Ron Harper TT .10 .05
❑ 294 Vlade Divac TT .10 .05
❑ 295 Glen Rice TT .25 .11
❑ 296 Moses Malone TT .25 .11
❑ 297 Doug West TT .10 .05
❑ 298 Derrick Coleman TT .10 .05
❑ 299 Patrick Ewing TT .25 .11
(See also card 305)
❑ 300 Scott Skiles TT .10 .05
❑ 301 Hersey Hawkins TT .10 .05
❑ 302 Kevin Johnson TT .25 .11
❑ 303 Clifford Robinson TT .10 .05
❑ 304 Spud Webb TT .10 .05
❑ 305 David Robinson TT COR .50 .23
❑ 305A David Robinson TT ERR .50 .23
(Card misnumbered as 299)
❑ 306 Shawn Kemp TT .50 .23
❑ 307 John Stockton TT .25 .11
❑ 308 Pervis Ellison TT .10 .05
❑ 309 Craig Hodges AS .10 .05
❑ 310 Magic Johnson A-S MVP .75 .35
❑ 311 Cedric Ceballos .10 .05
Slam Dunk Champ
❑ 312 Karl Malone ASG .50 .23
❑ 313 Dennis Rodman ASG .50 .23
❑ 314 Michael Jordan MVP 3.00 1.35
❑ 315 Clyde Drexler FIN .25 .11
❑ 316 Danny Ainge PO .25 .11
❑ 317 Scottie Pippen PO .75 .35
❑ 318 NBA Champs .10 .05
❑ 319 Larry Johnson ART .25 .11
Dikembe Mutombo
❑ 320 NBA Stay in School .10 .05
❑ 321 Boys and Girls .10 .05
Clubs of America
❑ 322 Checklist 1 .10 .05
❑ 323 Checklist 2 .10 .05
❑ 324 Checklist 3 .10 .05
❑ 325 Checklist 4 .10 .05
❑ 326 Checklist 5 .10 .05
❑ 327 Checklist 6 .10 .05
❑ 328 Adam Keefe RC .10 .05
❑ 329 Sean Rooks RC .10 .05
❑ 330 Xavier McDaniel .10 .05
❑ 331 Kiki Vandeweghe .10 .05
❑ 332 Alonzo Mourning RC 2.50 1.10
❑ 333 Rodney McCray .10 .05
❑ 334 Gerald Wilkins .10 .05
❑ 335 Tony Bennett RC .10 .05
❑ 336 LaPhonso Ellis RC .50 .23
❑ 337 Bryant Stith RC .25 .11
❑ 338 Isaiah Morris RC .10 .05
❑ 339 Olden Polynice .10 .05
❑ 340 Jeff Grayer .10 .05
❑ 341 Byron Houston RC .10 .05
❑ 342 Latrell Sprewell RC 4.00 1.80
❑ 343 Scott Brooks .10 .05
❑ 344 Frank Johnson .10 .05
❑ 345 Robert Horry RC .50 .23
❑ 346 David Wood .10 .05
❑ 347 Sam Mitchell .10 .05
❑ 348 Pooh Richardson .10 .05
❑ 349 Malik Sealy RC .25 .11
❑ 350 Morlon Wiley .10 .05
❑ 351 Mark Jackson .25 .11
❑ 352 Stanley Roberts .10 .05
❑ 353 Elmore Spencer RC .10 .05
❑ 354 John Williams .10 .05
❑ 355 Randy Woods RC .10 .05
❑ 356 James Edwards .10 .05
❑ 357 Jeff Sanders .10 .05
❑ 358 Magic Johnson 1.50 .70
❑ 359 Anthony Peeler RC .25 .11
❑ 360 Harold Miner RC .25 .11
❑ 361 John Salley .10 .05
❑ 362 Alaa Abdelnaby .10 .05
❑ 363 Todd Day RC .25 .11
❑ 364 Blue Edwards .10 .05
❑ 365 Lee Mayberry RC .10 .05
❑ 366 Eric Murdock .10 .05
❑ 367 Mookie Blaylock .25 .11
❑ 368 Anthony Avent RC .10 .05
❑ 369 Christian Laettner RC .. 1.00 .45
❑ 370 Chuck Person .10 .05
❑ 371 Chris Smith RC .10 .05
❑ 372 Micheal Williams .10 .05
❑ 373 Rolando Blackman .10 .05
❑ 374 Tony Campbell UER .10 .05
(Back photo actually
Alvin Robertson)
❑ 375 Hubert Davis RC .25 .11
❑ 376 Travis Mays .10 .05
❑ 377 Doc Rivers .25 .11
❑ 378 Charles Smith .10 .05
❑ 379 Rumeal Robinson .10 .05
❑ 380 Vinny Del Negro .10 .05
❑ 381 Steve Kerr .25 .11
❑ 382 Shaquille O'Neal RC .. 12.00 5.50
❑ 383 Donald Royal .10 .05
❑ 384 Jeff Hornacek .25 .11
❑ 385 Andrew Lang .10 .05
❑ 386 Tim Perry UER .10 .05
(Alvin Robertson pictured on back)
❑ 387 C. Weatherspoon RC .50 .23
❑ 388 Danny Ainge .25 .11
❑ 389 Charles Barkley .75 .35
❑ 390 Tim Kempton .10 .05
❑ 391 Oliver Miller RC .25 .11

❑ 392 Dave Johnson RC .... .10 .05
❑ 393 Tracy Murray RC .... .25 .11
❑ 394 Rod Strickland .... .50 .23
❑ 395 Marty Conlon .... .10 .05
❑ 396 Walt Williams RC .... .50 .23
❑ 397 Lloyd Daniels RC .... .10 .05
❑ 398 Dale Ellis .... .10 .05
❑ 399 Dave Hoppen .... .10 .05
❑ 400 Larry Smith .... .10 .05
❑ 401 Doug Overton .... .10 .05
❑ 402 Isaac Austin RC .... .25 .11
❑ 403 Jay Humphries .... .10 .05
❑ 404 Larry Krystkowiak .... .10 .05
❑ 405 Tom Gugliotta RC .... 1.50 .70
❑ 406 Buck Johnson .... .10 .05
❑ 407 Don MacLean RC .... .10 .05
❑ 408 Marlon Maxey RC .... .10 .05
❑ 409 Corey Williams RC .... .10 .05
❑ 410 Special Olympics .... .25 .11
Dan Majerle
❑ 411 Checklist 1 .... .10 .05
❑ 412 Checklist 2 .... .10 .05
❑ 413 Checklist 3 .... .10 .05
❑ NNO Magic Johnson AU 200.00 90.00
❑ NNO David Robinson 4.00 1.80
The Admiral Comes
Prepared
❑ NNO David Robinson AU 100.00 45.00
❑ NNO Head of the Class 30.00 13.50
LaPhonso Ellis
Tom Gugliotta
Christian Laettner
Alonzo Mourning
Shaquille O'Neal
Walt Williams
❑ NNO Magic Johnson 6.00 2.70
The Magic Never Ends

1992-93 SkyBox Draft Picks

	MINT	NRMT
COMPLETE SET (25)	45.00	20.00
COMPLETE SERIES 1 (6)	10.00	4.50
COMPLETE SERIES 2 (19)	35.00	16.00
COMMON CARD	.50	.23
SEMISTARS	1.25	.55
UNLISTED STARS	2.00	.90

SER.1/2 STATED ODDS 1:8
4/17 ISSUED THE NEXT YEAR

❑ DP1 Shaquille O'Neal 25.00 11.00
❑ DP2 Alonzo Mourning 6.00 2.70
❑ DP3 Christian Laettner 2.50 1.10
❑ DP4 Not issued
..........(Player unsigned)
❑ DP5 LaPhonso Ellis .... 2.00 .90
❑ DP6 Tom Gugliotta 4.00 1.80
❑ DP7 Walt Williams .... 1.25 .55
❑ DP8 Todd Day .... 1.25 .55
❑ DP9 Clarence Weatherspoon 1.25 .55
❑ DP10 Adam Keefe .... .50 .23
❑ DP11 Robert Horry .... 2.00 .90
❑ DP12 Harold Miner .... 1.25 .55
❑ DP13 Bryant Stith .... 1.25 .55
❑ DP14 Malik Sealy .... 1.25 .55
❑ DP15 Anthony Peeler .... 1.25 .55
❑ DP16 Randy Woods .... .50 .23
❑ DP17 Not issued
..........(Player unsigned)
❑ DP18 Tracy Murray .... 1.25 .55
❑ DP19 Don MacLean .... .50 .23
❑ DP20 Hubert Davis .... 1.25 .55
❑ DP21 Jon Barry .... 1.25 .55
❑ DP22 Oliver Miller .... 1.25 .55
❑ DP23 Lee Mayberry .... .50 .23
❑ DP24 Latrell Sprewell 10.00 4.50
❑ DP25 Elmore Spencer .... .50 .23
❑ DP26 Dave Johnson .... .50 .23
❑ DP27 Byron Houston .... .50 .23

1992-93 SkyBox Olympic Team

	MINT	NRMT
COMPLETE SET (12)	50.00	22.00

*SINGLES: 1.5X TO 4X BASE CARD HI
SER.1 STATED ODDS 1:6

❑ USA1 Clyde Drexler .... 2.00 .90
❑ USA2 Chris Mullin .... 2.00 .90
❑ USA3 John Stockton .... 2.00 .90
❑ USA4 Karl Malone 3.00 1.35
❑ USA5 Scottie Pippen 6.00 2.70
❑ USA6 Larry Bird 8.00 3.60
❑ USA7 Charles Barkley 3.00 1.35
❑ USA8 Patrick Ewing .... 2.00 .90
❑ USA9 Christian Laettner 4.00 1.80
❑ USA10 David Robinson 3.00 1.35
❑ USA11 Michael Jordan 25.00 11.00
❑ USA12 Magic Johnson 6.00 2.70

1992-93 SkyBox David Robinson

	MINT	NRMT
COMPLETE SET (10)	4.00	1.80
COMPLETE SERIES 1 (5)	2.00	.90
COMPLETE SERIES 2 (5)	2.00	.90
COMMON D.ROB. (R1-R10)	.50	.23

SER.1/2 STATED ODDS 1:8

❑ R1 David Robinson .... .50 .23
Childhood
❑ R2 David Robinson .... .50 .23
At Ease
❑ R3 David Robinson .... .50 .23
College
❑ R4 David Robinson .... .50 .23
College
❑ R5 David Robinson .... .50 .23
At Ease
❑ R6 David Robinson .... .50 .23
College
❑ R7 David Robinson .... .50 .23
College
❑ R8 David Robinson .... .50 .23
Doug Drotman
Awards
❑ R9 David Robinson .... .50 .23
Awards
❑ R10 David Robinson .... .50 .23
At Ease

1992-93 SkyBox School Ties

	MINT	NRMT
COMPLETE SET (18)	15.00	6.75
COMMON CARD (ST1-ST18)	.25	.11
SEMISTARS	.50	.23

SER.2 STATED ODDS 1:4

❑ ST1 Patrick Ewing 2.50 1.10
Alonzo Mourning
Georgetown
❑ ST2 Dikembe Mutombo .... .50 .23
Eric Floyd
Georgetown
❑ ST3 Reggie Williams .... .25 .11
David Wingate
Georgetown
❑ ST4 Kenny Anderson .... .50 .23
Duane Ferrell
Georgia Tech
❑ ST5 Tom Hammonds .... .25 .11
Jon Barry
Mark Price
Georgia Tech
❑ ST6 John Salley .... .50 .23
Dennis Scott
Georgia Tech
❑ ST7 Rafael Addison .... .25 .11
Dave Johnson
Syracuse
❑ ST8 Billy Owens .... .50 .23
Derrick Coleman
Rony Seikaly
Syracuse
❑ ST9 Sherman Douglas .... .25 .11
Danny Schayes
Syracuse
❑ ST10 Nick Anderson .... .50 .23
Kendall Gill
Illinois
❑ ST11 Derek Harper .... .25 .11
Eddie Johnson
Illinois
❑ ST12 Marcus Liberty .... .25 .11
Ken Norman
Illinois
❑ ST13 Greg Anthony .... .50 .23
Stacey Augmon
Nevada-Las Vegas
❑ ST14 Armon Gilliam .... .50 .23
Larry Johnson

Sidney Green
Nevada-Las Vegas
❑ ST15 Elmore Spencer .25 .11
Gerald Paddio
Nevada-Las Vegas
❑ ST16 James Worthy 12.00 5.50
Michael Jordan
Sam Perkins
North Carolina
❑ ST17 J.R. Reid .25 .11
Pete Chilcutt
Brad Daugherty
Rick Fox
North Carolina
❑ ST18 Hubert Davis .50 .23
Kenny Smith
Scott Williams
North Carolina

1992-93 SkyBox Thunder and Lightning

	MINT	NRMT
COMPLETE SET (9)	40.00	18.00
COMMON PAIR (TL1-TL9)	1.50	.70
SEMISTARS	3.00	1.35
UNLISTED STARS	4.00	1.80

SER.2 STATED ODDS 1:40

❑ TL1 Dikembe Mutombo 4.00 1.80
Mark Macon
❑ TL2 Buck Williams 4.00 1.80
Clyde Drexler
❑ TL3 Charles Barkley 8.00 3.60
Kevin Johnson
❑ TL4 Pervis Ellison 1.50 .70
Michael Adams
❑ TL5 Larry Johnson 3.00 1.35
Tyrone Bogues
❑ TL6 Brad Daugherty 1.50 .70
Mark Price
❑ TL7 Shawn Kemp 15.00 6.75
Gary Payton
❑ TL8 Karl Malone 12.00 5.50
John Stockton
❑ TL9 Billy Owens 5.00 2.20
Tim Hardaway

1993-94 SkyBox Premium

	MINT	NRMT
COMPLETE SET (341)	30.00	13.50
COMPLETE SERIES 1 (191)	15.00	6.75
COMPLETE SERIES 2 (150)	15.00	6.75
COMMON CARD (1-341)	.05	.02
SEMISTARS	.15	.07
UNLISTED STARS	.30	.14

SUBSET CARDS HALF VALUE OF BASE CARDS
DP4/DP17: SER.1 STATED ODDS 1:36
HOC EXCH: SER.1 STATED ODDS 1:360

❑ 1 Checklist .05 .02

❑ 2 Checklist .05 .02
❑ 3 Checklist .05 .02
❑ 4 Larry Johnson PO .15 .07
❑ 5 Alonzo Mourning PO .30 .14
❑ 6 Hakeem Olajuwon PO .30 .14
❑ 7 Brad Daugherty PO .05 .02
❑ 8 Oliver Miller PO .05 .02
❑ 9 David Robinson PO .30 .14
❑ 10 Patrick Ewing PO .15 .07
❑ 11 Ricky Pierce PO .05 .02
❑ 12 Sam Perkins PO .05 .02
❑ 13 John Starks PO .05 .02
❑ 14 Michael Jordan PO 2.00 .90
❑ 15 Dan Majerle PO .05 .02
❑ 16 Scottie Pippen PO .50 .23
❑ 17 Shawn Kemp PO .30 .14
❑ 18 Charles Barkley PO .30 .14
❑ 19 Horace Grant PO .05 .02
❑ 20 Kevin Johnson PO .05 .02
❑ 21 John Paxson PO .05 .02
❑ 22 David Robinson IS .30 .14
❑ 23 NBA On NBC .05 .02
❑ 24 Stacey Augmon .05 .02
❑ 25 Mookie Blaylock .15 .07
❑ 26 Craig Ehlo .05 .02
❑ 27 Adam Keefe .05 .02
❑ 28 Dominique Wilkins .30 .14
❑ 29 Kevin Willis .05 .02
❑ 30 Dee Brown .05 .02
❑ 31 Sherman Douglas .05 .02
❑ 32 Rick Fox .05 .02
❑ 33 Kevin Gamble .05 .02
❑ 34 Xavier McDaniel .05 .02
❑ 35 Robert Parish .15 .07
❑ 36 Muggsy Bogues .15 .07
❑ 37 Dell Curry .05 .02
❑ 38 Kendall Gill .15 .07
❑ 39 Larry Johnson .30 .14
❑ 40 Alonzo Mourning .50 .23
❑ 41 Johnny Newman .05 .02
❑ 42 B.J. Armstrong .05 .02
❑ 43 Bill Cartwright .05 .02
❑ 44 Horace Grant .15 .07
❑ 45 Michael Jordan 4.00 1.80
❑ 46 John Paxson .05 .02
❑ 47 Scottie Pippen 1.00 .45
❑ 48 Scott Williams .05 .02
❑ 49 Terrell Brandon .15 .07
❑ 50 Brad Daugherty .05 .02
❑ 51 Larry Nance .05 .02
❑ 52 Mark Price .05 .02
❑ 53 Gerald Wilkins .05 .02
❑ 54 John Williams .05 .02
❑ 55 Terry Davis .05 .02
❑ 56 Derek Harper .15 .07
❑ 57 Jim Jackson .15 .07
❑ 58 Sean Rooks .05 .02
❑ 59 Doug Smith .05 .02
❑ 60 Mahmoud Abdul-Rauf .05 .02
❑ 61 LaPhonso Ellis .05 .02
❑ 62 Mark Macon .05 .02
❑ 63 Dikembe Mutombo .15 .07
❑ 64 Bryant Stith .05 .02
❑ 65 Reggie Williams .05 .02
❑ 66 Joe Dumars .30 .14
❑ 67 Bill Laimbeer .05 .02
❑ 68 Terry Mills .05 .02
❑ 69 Alvin Robertson .05 .02
❑ 70 Dennis Rodman .60 .25
❑ 71 Isiah Thomas .30 .14
❑ 72 Victor Alexander .05 .02
❑ 73 Tim Hardaway .30 .14
❑ 74 Tyrone Hill .05 .02
❑ 75 Sarunas Marciulionis .05 .02
❑ 76 Chris Mullin .30 .14
❑ 77 Billy Owens .05 .02
❑ 78 Latrell Sprewell .75 .35
❑ 79 Robert Horry .15 .07
❑ 80 Vernon Maxwell .05 .02
❑ 81 Hakeem Olajuwon .50 .23
❑ 82 Kenny Smith .05 .02
❑ 83 Otis Thorpe .15 .07
❑ 84 Dale Davis .05 .02
❑ 85 Reggie Miller .30 .14
❑ 86 Pooh Richardson .05 .02
❑ 87 Detlef Schrempf .15 .07
❑ 88 Malik Sealy .05 .02
❑ 89 Rik Smits .15 .07
❑ 90 Ron Harper .15 .07
❑ 91 Mark Jackson .15 .07
❑ 92 Danny Manning .15 .07
❑ 93 Stanley Roberts .05 .02
❑ 94 Loy Vaught .05 .02
❑ 95 Randy Woods .05 .02
❑ 96 Sam Bowie .05 .02
❑ 97 Doug Christie .05 .02
❑ 98 Vlade Divac .15 .07
❑ 99 Anthony Peeler .05 .02
❑ 100 Sedale Threatt .05 .02
❑ 101 James Worthy .30 .14
❑ 102 Grant Long .05 .02
❑ 103 Harold Miner .05 .02
❑ 104 Glen Rice .15 .07
❑ 105 John Salley .05 .02
❑ 106 Rony Seikaly .05 .02
❑ 107 Steve Smith .30 .14
❑ 108 Anthony Avent .05 .02
❑ 109 Jon Barry .05 .02
❑ 110 Frank Brickowski .05 .02
❑ 111 Blue Edwards .05 .02
❑ 112 Todd Day .05 .02
❑ 113 Lee Mayberry .05 .02
❑ 114 Eric Murdock .05 .02
❑ 115 Thurl Bailey .05 .02
❑ 116 Christian Laettner .15 .07
❑ 117 Chuck Person .05 .02
❑ 118 Doug West .05 .02
❑ 119 Micheal Williams .05 .02
❑ 120 Kenny Anderson .15 .07
❑ 121 Benoit Benjamin .05 .02
❑ 122 Derrick Coleman .15 .07
❑ 123 Chris Morris .05 .02
❑ 124 Rumeal Robinson .05 .02
❑ 125 Rolando Blackman .05 .02
❑ 126 Patrick Ewing .30 .14
❑ 127 Anthony Mason .15 .07
❑ 128 Charles Oakley .15 .07
❑ 129 Doc Rivers .15 .07
❑ 130 Charles Smith .05 .02
❑ 131 John Starks .15 .07
❑ 132 Nick Anderson .15 .07
❑ 133 Shaquille O'Neal 1.50 .70
❑ 134 Donald Royal .05 .02
❑ 135 Dennis Scott .05 .02
❑ 136 Scott Skiles .05 .02
❑ 137 Brian Williams .05 .02
❑ 138 Johnny Dawkins .05 .02
❑ 139 Hersey Hawkins .15 .07
❑ 140 Jeff Hornacek .15 .07
❑ 141 Andrew Lang .05 .02
❑ 142 Tim Perry .05 .02
❑ 143 Clarence Weatherspoon .05 .02
❑ 144 Danny Ainge .15 .07
❑ 145 Charles Barkley .50 .23
❑ 146 Cedric Ceballos .15 .07
❑ 147 Kevin Johnson .15 .07
❑ 148 Oliver Miller .05 .02
❑ 149 Dan Majerle .15 .07
❑ 150 Clyde Drexler .30 .14
❑ 151 Harvey Grant .05 .02
❑ 152 Jerome Kersey .05 .02
❑ 153 Terry Porter .05 .02
❑ 154 Clifford Robinson .15 .07
❑ 155 Rod Strickland .15 .07

❑ 156 Buck Williams .05 .02
❑ 157 Mitch Richmond .30 .14
❑ 158 Lionel Simmons .05 .02
❑ 159 Wayman Tisdale .05 .02
❑ 160 Spud Webb .15 .07
❑ 161 Walt Williams .05 .02
❑ 162 Antoine Carr .05 .02
❑ 163 Lloyd Daniels .05 .02
❑ 164 Sean Elliott .15 .07
❑ 165 Dale Ellis .05 .02
❑ 166 Avery Johnson .05 .02
❑ 167 J.R. Reid .05 .02
❑ 168 David Robinson .50 .23
❑ 169 Shawn Kemp .50 .23
❑ 170 Derrick McKey .05 .02
❑ 171 Nate McMillan .05 .02
❑ 172 Gary Payton .50 .23
❑ 173 Sam Perkins .15 .07
❑ 174 Ricky Pierce .05 .02
❑ 175 Tyrone Corbin .05 .02
❑ 176 Jay Humphries .05 .02
❑ 177 Jeff Malone .05 .02
❑ 178 Karl Malone .50 .23
❑ 179 John Stockton .30 .14
❑ 180 Michael Adams .05 .02
❑ 181 Kevin Duckworth .05 .02
❑ 182 Pervis Ellison .05 .02
❑ 183 Tom Gugliotta .30 .14
❑ 184 Don MacLean .05 .02
❑ 185 Brent Price .05 .02
❑ 186 George Lynch RC .05 .02
❑ 187 Rex Walters RC .05 .02
❑ 188 Shawn Bradley RC .30 .14
❑ 189 Ervin Johnson RC .15 .07
❑ 190 Luther Wright RC .05 .02
❑ 191 Calbert Cheaney RC .15 .07
❑ 192 Craig Ehlo .05 .02
❑ 193 Duane Ferrell .05 .02
❑ 194 Paul Graham .05 .02
❑ 195 Andrew Lang .05 .02
❑ 196 Chris Corchiani .05 .02
❑ 197 Acie Earl RC .05 .02
❑ 198 Dino Radja RC .05 .02
❑ 199 Ed Pinckney .05 .02
❑ 200 Tony Bennett .05 .02
❑ 201 Scott Burrell RC .30 .14
❑ 202 Kenny Gattison .05 .02
❑ 203 Hersey Hawkins .15 .07
❑ 204 Eddie Johnson .05 .02
❑ 205 Corie Blount RC .05 .02
❑ 206 Steve Kerr .15 .07
❑ 207 Toni Kukoc RC 1.25 .55
❑ 208 Pete Myers .05 .02
❑ 209 Danny Ferry .05 .02
❑ 210 Tyrone Hill .05 .02
❑ 211 Gerald Madkins RC .05 .02
❑ 212 Chris Mills RC .30 .14
❑ 213 Lucious Harris RC .05 .02
❑ 214 Popeye Jones RC .05 .02
❑ 215 Jamal Mashburn RC .60 .25
❑ 216 Darnell Mee RC .05 .02
❑ 217 Rodney Rogers RC .30 .14
❑ 218 Brian Williams .05 .02
❑ 219 Greg Anderson .05 .02
❑ 220 Sean Elliott .15 .07
❑ 221 Allan Houston RC 1.25 .55
❑ 222 Lindsey Hunter RC .30 .14
❑ 223 Chris Gatling .05 .02
❑ 224 Josh Grant RC .05 .02
❑ 225 Keith Jennings .05 .02
❑ 226 Avery Johnson .05 .02
❑ 227 Chris Webber RC 3.00 1.35
❑ 228 Sam Cassell RC .75 .35
❑ 229 Mario Elie .05 .02
❑ 230 Richard Petruska RC .05 .02
❑ 231 Eric Riley RC .05 .02
❑ 232 Antonio Davis RC .15 .07
❑ 233 Scott Haskin RC .05 .02
❑ 234 Derrick McKey .05 .02
❑ 235 Mark Aguirre .05 .02
❑ 236 Terry Dehere RC .05 .02
❑ 237 Gary Grant .05 .02
❑ 238 Randy Woods .05 .02
❑ 239 Sam Bowie .05 .02
❑ 240 Elden Campbell .05 .02
❑ 241 Nick Van Exel RC .75 .35
❑ 242 Manute Bol .05 .02
❑ 243 Brian Shaw .05 .02
❑ 244 Vin Baker RC .75 .35
❑ 245 Brad Lohaus .05 .02
❑ 246 Ken Norman .05 .02
❑ 247 Derek Strong RC .05 .02
❑ 248 Dan Schayes .05 .02
❑ 249 Mike Brown .05 .02
❑ 250 Luc Longley .15 .07
❑ 251 Isaiah Rider RC .60 .25
❑ 252 Kevin Edwards .05 .02
❑ 253 Armon Gilliam .05 .02
❑ 254 Greg Anthony .05 .02
❑ 255 Anthony Bonner .05 .02
❑ 256 Tony Campbell .05 .02
❑ 257 Hubert Davis .05 .02
❑ 258 Litterial Green .05 .02
❑ 259 Anfernee Hardaway RC 3.00 1.35
❑ 260 Larry Krystkowiak .05 .02
❑ 261 Todd Lichti .05 .02
❑ 262 Dana Barros .05 .02
❑ 263 Greg Graham RC .05 .02
❑ 264 Warren Kidd RC .05 .02
❑ 265 Moses Malone .30 .14
❑ 266 A.C. Green .15 .07
❑ 267 Joe Kleine .05 .02
❑ 268 Malcolm Mackey RC .05 .02
❑ 269 Mark Bryant .05 .02
❑ 270 Chris Dudley .05 .02
❑ 271 Harvey Grant .05 .02
❑ 272 James Robinson RC .05 .02
❑ 273 Duane Causwell .05 .02
❑ 274 Bobby Hurley RC .15 .07
❑ 275 Jim Les .05 .02
❑ 276 Willie Anderson .05 .02
❑ 277 Terry Cummings .05 .02
❑ 278 Vinny Del Negro .05 .02
❑ 279 Sleepy Floyd .05 .02
❑ 280 Dennis Rodman .60 .25
❑ 281 Vincent Askew .05 .02
❑ 282 Kendall Gill .15 .07
❑ 283 Steve Scheffler .05 .02
❑ 284 Detlef Schrempf .15 .07
❑ 285 David Benoit .05 .02
❑ 286 Tom Chambers .05 .02
❑ 287 Felton Spencer .05 .02
❑ 288 Rex Chapman .05 .02
❑ 289 Kevin Duckworth .05 .02
❑ 290 Gheorghe Muresan RC .30 .14
❑ 291 Kenny Walker .05 .02
❑ 292 Andrew Lang CF .05 .02
Craig Ehlo
❑ 293 Dino Radja CF .05 .02
Acie Earl
❑ 294 Eddie Johnson CF .05 .02
Hersey Hawkins
❑ 295 Toni Kukoc CF .30 .14
Corie Blount
❑ 296 Tyrone Hill CF .05 .02
Chris Mills
❑ 297 Jamal Mashburn CF .30 .14
Popeye Jones
❑ 298 Darnell Mee CF .05 .02
Rodney Rogers
❑ 299 Lindsey Hunter CF .15 .07
Allan Houston
❑ 300 Chris Webber CF .30 .14
Avery Johnson
❑ 301 Sam Cassell CF .30 .14
Mario Elie
❑ 302 Derrick McKey CF .05 .02
Antonio Davis
❑ 303 Terry Dehere CF .05 .02
Mark Aguirre
❑ 304 Nick Van Exel CF .30 .14
George Lynch
❑ 305 Harold Miner CF .05 .02
Steve Smith
❑ 306 Ken Norman CF .15 .07
Vin Baker
❑ 307 Mike Brown CF .15 .07
Isaiah Rider
❑ 308 Kevin Edwards CF .05 .02
Rex Walters
❑ 309 Hubert Davis CF .05 .02
Anthony Bonner
❑ 310 Anfernee Hardaway CF 1.25 .55
Larry Krystkowiak
❑ 311 Moses Malone CF .30 .14
Shawn Bradley
❑ 312 Joe Kleine CF .05 .02
A.C. Green
❑ 313 Harvey Grant CF .05 .02
Chris Dudley
❑ 314 Bobby Hurley CF .30 .14
Mitch Richmond
❑ 315 Sleepy Floyd CF .30 .14
Dennis Rodman
❑ 316 Kendall Gill CF .05 .02
Detlef Schrempf
❑ 317 Felton Spencer CF .05 .02
Luther Wright
❑ 318 Calbert Cheaney CF .05 .02
Kevin Duckworth
❑ 319 Karl Malone PC .30 .14
❑ 320 Alonzo Mourning PC .30 .14
❑ 321 Scottie Pippen PC .50 .23
❑ 322 Mark Price PC .05 .02
❑ 323 LaPhonso Ellis PC .05 .02
❑ 324 Joe Dumars PC .15 .07
❑ 325 Chris Mullin PC .15 .07
❑ 326 Ron Harper PC .05 .02
❑ 327 Glen Rice PC .05 .02
❑ 328 Christian Laettner PC .05 .02
❑ 329 Kenny Anderson PC .05 .02
❑ 330 John Starks PC .05 .02
❑ 331 Shaquille O'Neal PC .60 .25
❑ 332 Charles Barkley PC .30 .14
❑ 333 Clifford Robinson PC .05 .02
❑ 334 Clyde Drexler PC .15 .07
❑ 335 Mitch Richmond PC .15 .07
❑ 336 David Robinson PC .30 .14
❑ 337 Shawn Kemp PC .30 .14
❑ 338 John Stockton PC .15 .07
❑ 339 Checklist 4 .05 .02
❑ 340 Checklist 5 .05 .02
❑ 341 Checklist 6 .05 .02
❑ DP4 Jim Jackson 1.50 .70
❑ DP17 Doug Christie .40 .18
❑ NNO Head of the Class 1.50 .70
Expired Exchange
❑ NNO HOC Card 30.00 13.50
Shawn Bradley
Calbert Cheaney
Anfernee Hardaway
Jamal Mashburn
Isaiah Rider
Chris Webber

1993-94 SkyBox Premium All-Rookies

	MINT	NRMT
COMPLETE SET (5)	15.00	6.75

*SINGLES: 2.5X TO 6X BASE CARD HI
SER.1 STATED ODDS 1:36

❑ AR1 Shaquille O'Neal 10.00 4.50
❑ AR2 Alonzo Mourning 3.00 1.35
❑ AR3 Christian Laettner 1.00 .45
❑ AR4 Tom Gugliotta 2.00 .90
❑ AR5 LaPhonso Ellis .30 .14

1993-94 SkyBox Premium Center Stage

	MINT	NRMT
COMPLETE SET (9)	30.00	13.50

*SINGLES: 2.5X TO 6X BASE CARD HI
SER.1 STATED ODDS 1:12

Card	Player	MINT	NRMT
❑ CS1	Michael Jordan	25.00	11.00
❑ CS2	Shaquille O'Neal	10.00	4.50
❑ CS3	Charles Barkley	3.00	1.35
❑ CS4	John Starks	1.00	.45
❑ CS5	Larry Johnson	2.00	.90
❑ CS6	Hakeem Olajuwon	3.00	1.35
❑ CS7	Kenny Anderson	1.00	.45
❑ CS8	Mahmoud Abdul-Rauf	.30	.14
❑ CS9	Clifford Robinson	1.00	.45

1993-94 SkyBox Premium Draft Picks

	MINT	NRMT
COMPLETE SET (26)	50.00	22.00
COMPLETE SERIES 1 (9)	10.00	4.50
COMPLETE SERIES 2 (17)	40.00	18.00
COMMON CARD (1-26)	.50	.23
SEMISTARS	1.00	.45
UNLISTED STARS	2.50	1.10

NUMBER 26 NEVER ISSUED
SER.1/2 STATED ODDS 1:12

Card	Player	MINT	NRMT
❑ DP1	Chris Webber	15.00	6.75
❑ DP2	Shawn Bradley	2.50	1.10
❑ DP3	Anfernee Hardaway	15.00	6.75
❑ DP4	Jamal Mashburn	3.00	1.35
❑ DP5	Isaiah Rider	3.00	1.35
❑ DP6	Calbert Cheaney	1.00	.45
❑ DP7	Bobby Hurley	1.00	.45
❑ DP8	Vin Baker	4.00	1.80
❑ DP9	Rodney Rogers	1.00	.45
❑ DP10	Lindsey Hunter	1.00	.45
❑ DP11	Allan Houston	6.00	2.70
❑ DP12	George Lynch	.50	.23
❑ DP13	Terry Dehere	.50	.23
❑ DP14	Scott Haskin	.50	.23
❑ DP15	Doug Edwards	.50	.23
❑ DP16	Rex Walters	.50	.23
❑ DP17	Greg Graham	.50	.23
❑ DP18	Luther Wright	.50	.23
❑ DP19	Acie Earl	.50	.23
❑ DP20	Scott Burrell	2.50	1.10
❑ DP21	James Robinson	.50	.23
❑ DP22	Chris Mills	2.50	1.10
❑ DP23	Ervin Johnson	1.00	.45
❑ DP24	Sam Cassell	4.00	1.80
❑ DP25	Corie Blount	.50	.23
❑ DP26	Not Issued		
❑ DP27	Malcolm Mackey	.50	.23

1993-94 SkyBox Premium Dynamic Dunks

	MINT	NRMT
COMPLETE SET (9)	25.00	11.00

*SINGLES: 2X TO 5X BASE CARD HI
SER.2 STATED ODDS 1:36

Card	Player	MINT	NRMT
❑ D1	Nick Anderson	.75	.35
❑ D2	Charles Barkley	2.50	1.10
❑ D3	Robert Horry	.75	.35
❑ D4	Michael Jordan	20.00	9.00
❑ D5	Shawn Kemp	2.50	1.10
❑ D6	Anthony Mason	.75	.35
❑ D7	Alonzo Mourning	2.50	1.10
❑ D8	Hakeem Olajuwon	2.50	1.10
❑ D9	Dominique Wilkins	1.50	.70

1993-94 SkyBox Premium Shaq Talk

	MINT	NRMT
COMPLETE SET (10)	40.00	18.00
COMPLETE SERIES 1 (5)	20.00	9.00
COMPLETE SERIES 2 (5)	20.00	9.00
COMMON SHAQ (1-10)	5.00	2.20

SER.1/2 STATED ODDS 1:36
SHAQ TALK PREFIX ON CARD NUMBER

Card	Player	MINT	NRMT
❑ 1	Shaquille O'Neal The Rebound	5.00	2.20
❑ 2	Shaquille O'Neal The Block (Blocking David Robinson's shot)	5.00	2.20
❑ 3	Shaquille O'Neal The Postup	5.00	2.20
❑ 4	Shaquille O'Neal The Dunk	5.00	2.20
❑ 5	Shaquille O'Neal Defense	5.00	2.20
❑ 6	Shaquille O'Neal Scoring	5.00	2.20
❑ 7	Shaquille O'Neal Passing	5.00	2.20
❑ 8	Shaquille O'Neal Rejections	5.00	2.20
❑ 9	Shaquille O'Neal Confidence	5.00	2.20
❑ 10	Shaquille O'Neal Legends	5.00	2.20

1993-94 SkyBox Premium Showdown Series

	MINT	NRMT
COMPLETE SET (12)	6.00	2.70
COMPLETE SERIES 1 (6)	3.00	1.35
COMPLETE SERIES 2 (6)	3.00	1.35
COMMON PAIR (SS1-SS12)	.25	.11
SEMISTARS	.40	.18
UNLISTED STARS	.50	.23

SER.1/2 STATED ODDS 1:6

		MINT	NRMT
❑ SS1	Alonzo Mourning Patrick Ewing	.40	.18
❑ SS2	Shaquille O'Neal Patrick Ewing	1.25	.55
❑ SS3	Alonzo Mourning Shaquille O'Neal	1.50	.70
❑ SS4	Hakeem Olajuwon Dikembe Mutombo	.50	.23
❑ SS5	David Robinson Hakeem Olajuwon	.60	.25
❑ SS6	David Robinson Dikembe Mutombo	.40	.18
❑ SS7	Shawn Kemp Karl Malone	.60	.25
❑ SS8	Larry Johnson Charles Barkley	.40	.18
❑ SS9	Dominique Wilkins Scottie Pippen	.50	.23
❑ SS10	Joe Dumars Reggie Miller	.25	.11
❑ SS11	Clyde Drexler Michael Jordan	2.00	.90
❑ SS12	Magic Johnson Larry Bird	1.50	.70

1993-94 SkyBox Premium Thunder and Lightning

	MINT	NRMT
COMPLETE SET (9)	15.00	6.75
COMMON PAIR (1-9)	.50	.23
SEMISTARS	.60	.25
UNLISTED STARS	1.00	.45

SER.2 STATED ODDS 1:12

		MINT	NRMT
❑ TL1	Jamal Mashburn Jim Jackson	1.50	.70
❑ TL2	Harold Miner Steve Smith	.50	.23

		MINT	NRMT
❑ TL3	Isaiah Rider Micheal Williams	1.25	.55
❑ TL4	Derrick Coleman Kenny Anderson	.60	.25
❑ TL5	Patrick Ewing John Starks	1.00	.45
❑ TL6	Shaquille O'Neal Anfernee Hardaway	12.00	5.50
❑ TL7	Shawn Bradley Jeff Hornacek	.50	.23
❑ TL8	Walt Williams Bobby Hurley	.60	.25
❑ TL9	Dennis Rodman David Robinson	3.00	1.35

1993-94 SkyBox Premium USA Tip-Off

	MINT	NRMT
COMPLETE SET (14)	25.00	11.00
COMMON CARD (1-13)	.75	.35
SEMISTARS	1.00	.45
UNLISTED STARS	1.25	.55

ONE SET PER EXCHANGE CARD BY MAIL
EXCH.CARD: SER.2 STATED ODDS 1:240

		MINT	NRMT
❑ 1	Steve Smith Magic Johnson	4.00	1.80
❑ 2	Larry Johnson Charles Barkley	2.50	1.10
❑ 3	Patrick Ewing Alonzo Mourning	2.50	1.10
❑ 4	Shawn Kemp Karl Malone	3.00	1.35
❑ 5	Chris Mullin Dan Majerle	.75	.35
❑ 6	John Stockton Mark Price	1.25	.55
❑ 7	Christian Laettner Derrick Coleman	1.00	.45
❑ 8	Dominique Wilkins Clyde Drexler	1.50	.70
❑ 9	Joe Dumars Scottie Pippen	3.00	1.35
❑ 10	David Robinson Shaquille O'Neal	6.00	2.70
❑ 11	Reggie Miller Larry Bird	5.00	2.20
❑ 12	Tim Hardaway	1.25	.55
❑ 13	Isiah Thomas	.75	.35
❑ NNO	Checklist	1.50	.70

1994-95 SkyBox Premium

	MINT	NRMT
COMPLETE SET (350)	30.00	13.50
COMPLETE SERIES 1 (200)	15.00	6.75
COMPLETE SERIES 2 (150)	15.00	6.75
COMMON CARD (1-200)	.10	.05
COMMON CARD (201-350)	.05	.02
SEMISTARS SER.1	.20	.09
SEMISTARS SER.2	.10	.05
UNLISTED STARS SER.1	.40	.18
UNLISTED STARS SER.2	.25	.11

SUBSET CARDS HALF VALUE OF BASE CARDS
GHO: SER.2 STATED ODDS 1:360 RETAIL
OLAJ.GLD: SER.1 STATED ODDS 1:360 RET
DUAL AU: SER.2 STATED ODDS 1:15,000

		MINT	NRMT
❑ 1	Stacey Augmon	.10	.05
❑ 2	Mookie Blaylock	.10	.05
❑ 3	Doug Edwards	.10	.05
❑ 4	Craig Ehlo	.10	.05
❑ 5	Adam Keefe	.10	.05
❑ 6	Danny Manning	.20	.09
❑ 7	Kevin Willis	.10	.05
❑ 8	Dee Brown	.10	.05
❑ 9	Sherman Douglas	.10	.05
❑ 10	Acie Earl	.10	.05
❑ 11	Kevin Gamble	.10	.05
❑ 12	Xavier McDaniel	.10	.05
❑ 13	Dino Radja	.10	.05
❑ 14	Muggsy Bogues	.20	.09
❑ 15	Scott Burrell	.10	.05
❑ 16	Dell Curry	.10	.05
❑ 17	LeRon Ellis	.10	.05
❑ 18	Hersey Hawkins	.20	.09
❑ 19	Larry Johnson	.20	.09
❑ 20	Alonzo Mourning	.50	.23
❑ 21	B.J. Armstrong	.10	.05
❑ 22	Corie Blount	.10	.05
❑ 23	Horace Grant	.20	.09
❑ 24	Toni Kukoc	.60	.25
❑ 25	Luc Longley	.10	.05
❑ 26	Scottie Pippen	1.25	.55
❑ 27	Scott Williams	.10	.05
❑ 28	Terrell Brandon	.20	.09
❑ 29	Brad Daugherty	.10	.05
❑ 30	Tyrone Hill	.10	.05
❑ 31	Chris Mills	.20	.09
❑ 32	Bobby Phills	.10	.05
❑ 33	Mark Price	.10	.05
❑ 34	Gerald Wilkins	.10	.05
❑ 35	Lucious Harris	.10	.05
❑ 36	Jim Jackson	.20	.09
❑ 37	Popeye Jones	.10	.05
❑ 38	Jamal Mashburn	.40	.18
❑ 39	Sean Rooks	.10	.05
❑ 40	Mahmoud Abdul-Rauf	.10	.05
❑ 41	LaPhonso Ellis	.10	.05
❑ 42	Dikembe Mutombo	.20	.09
❑ 43	Robert Pack	.10	.05
❑ 44	Rodney Rogers	.10	.05
❑ 45	Bryant Stith	.10	.05
❑ 46	Reggie Williams	.10	.05
❑ 47	Joe Dumars	.40	.18
❑ 48	Sean Elliott	.20	.09
❑ 49	Allan Houston	.60	.25
❑ 50	Lindsey Hunter	.20	.09
❑ 51	Terry Mills	.10	.05
❑ 52	Victor Alexander	.10	.05
❑ 53	Tim Hardaway	.40	.18
❑ 54	Chris Mullin	.40	.18
❑ 55	Billy Owens	.10	.05
❑ 56	Latrell Sprewell	.75	.35
❑ 57	Chris Webber	1.25	.55
❑ 58	Sam Cassell	.40	.18
❑ 59	Carl Herrera	.10	.05
❑ 60	Robert Horry	.10	.05
❑ 61	Vernon Maxwell	.10	.05
❑ 62	Hakeem Olajuwon	.60	.25
❑ 63	Kenny Smith	.10	.05
❑ 64	Otis Thorpe	.10	.05
❑ 65	Antonio Davis	.10	.05
❑ 66	Dale Davis	.10	.05
❑ 67	Derrick McKey	.10	.05
❑ 68	Reggie Miller	.40	.18
❑ 69	Pooh Richardson	.10	.05
❑ 70	Rik Smits	.10	.05
❑ 71	Haywoode Workman	.10	.05
❑ 72	Terry Dehere	.10	.05
❑ 73	Harold Ellis	.10	.05
❑ 74	Ron Harper	.20	.09
❑ 75	Mark Jackson	.10	.05
❑ 76	Loy Vaught	.10	.05
❑ 77	Dominique Wilkins	.40	.18
❑ 78	Elden Campbell	.10	.05
❑ 79	Doug Christie	.10	.05
❑ 80	Vlade Divac	.10	.05
❑ 81	George Lynch	.10	.05
❑ 82	Anthony Peeler	.10	.05
❑ 83	Sedale Threatt	.10	.05
❑ 84	Nick Van Exel	.40	.18
❑ 85	Harold Miner	.10	.05
❑ 86	Glen Rice	.20	.09
❑ 87	John Salley	.10	.05
❑ 88	Rony Seikaly	.10	.05
❑ 89	Brian Shaw	.10	.05
❑ 90	Steve Smith	.20	.09
❑ 91	Vin Baker	.40	.18
❑ 92	Jon Barry	.10	.05
❑ 93	Todd Day	.10	.05
❑ 94	Blue Edwards	.10	.05
❑ 95	Lee Mayberry	.10	.05
❑ 96	Eric Murdock	.10	.05
❑ 97	Mike Brown	.10	.05
❑ 98	Stacey King	.10	.05
❑ 99	Christian Laettner	.20	.09
❑ 100	Isaiah Rider	.20	.09
❑ 101	Doug West	.10	.05
❑ 102	Micheal Williams	.10	.05
❑ 103	Kenny Anderson	.20	.09
❑ 104	P.J. Brown	.10	.05
❑ 105	Derrick Coleman	.20	.09
❑ 106	Kevin Edwards	.10	.05
❑ 107	Chris Morris	.10	.05
❑ 108	Rex Walters	.10	.05
❑ 109	Hubert Davis	.10	.05
❑ 110	Patrick Ewing	.40	.18
❑ 111	Derek Harper	.10	.05
❑ 112	Anthony Mason	.20	.09
❑ 113	Charles Oakley	.10	.05
❑ 114	Charles Smith	.10	.05
❑ 115	John Starks	.10	.05
❑ 116	Nick Anderson	.10	.05
❑ 117	Anfernee Hardaway	1.25	.55
❑ 118	Shaquille O'Neal	2.00	.90
❑ 119	Donald Royal	.10	.05
❑ 120	Dennis Scott	.10	.05
❑ 121	Scott Skiles	.10	.05
❑ 122	Dana Barros	.10	.05
❑ 123	Shawn Bradley	.10	.05
❑ 124	Johnny Dawkins	.10	.05
❑ 125	Greg Graham	.10	.05
❑ 126	Clarence Weatherspoon	.10	.05
❑ 127	Danny Ainge	.10	.05
❑ 128	Charles Barkley	.60	.25
❑ 129	Cedric Ceballos	.10	.05
❑ 130	A.C. Green	.20	.09
❑ 131	Kevin Johnson	.20	.09
❑ 132	Dan Majerle	.20	.09
❑ 133	Oliver Miller	.10	.05
❑ 134	Clyde Drexler	.40	.18
❑ 135	Harvey Grant	.10	.05

❑ 136 Tracy Murray .10 .05
❑ 137 Terry Porter .10 .05
❑ 138 Clifford Robinson .20 .09
❑ 139 James Robinson .10 .05
❑ 140 Rod Strickland .20 .09
❑ 141 Bobby Hurley .10 .05
❑ 142 Olden Polynice .10 .05
❑ 143 Mitch Richmond .40 .18
❑ 144 Lionel Simmons .10 .05
❑ 145 Wayman Tisdale .10 .05
❑ 146 Spud Webb .10 .05
❑ 147 Walt Williams .10 .05
❑ 148 Willie Anderson .10 .05
❑ 149 Vinny Del Negro .10 .05
❑ 150 Dale Ellis .10 .05
❑ 151 J.R. Reid .10 .05
❑ 152 David Robinson .60 .25
❑ 153 Dennis Rodman .75 .35
❑ 154 Kendall Gill .20 .09
❑ 155 Shawn Kemp .60 .25
❑ 156 Nate McMillan .10 .05
❑ 157 Gary Payton .60 .25
❑ 158 Sam Perkins .20 .09
❑ 159 Ricky Pierce .10 .05
❑ 160 Detlef Schrempf .20 .09
❑ 161 David Benoit .10 .05
❑ 162 Tyrone Corbin .10 .05
❑ 163 Jeff Hornacek .20 .09
❑ 164 Jay Humphries .10 .05
❑ 165 Karl Malone .60 .25
❑ 166 Bryon Russell .10 .05
❑ 167 Felton Spencer .10 .05
❑ 168 John Stockton .40 .18
❑ 169 Michael Adams .10 .05
❑ 170 Rex Chapman .10 .05
❑ 171 Calbert Cheaney .10 .05
❑ 172 Pervis Ellison .10 .05
❑ 173 Tom Gugliotta .20 .09
❑ 174 Don MacLean .10 .05
❑ 175 Gheorghe Muresan .10 .05
❑ 176 Charles Barkley NBC .40 .18
❑ 177 Charles Oakley NBC .10 .05
❑ 178 Hakeem Olajuwon NBC .40 .18
❑ 179 Dikembe Mutombo NBC .10 .05
❑ 180 Scottie Pippen NBC .60 .25
❑ 181 Sam Cassell NBC .20 .09
❑ 182 Karl Malone NBC .40 .18
❑ 183 Reggie Miller PO .20 .09
❑ 184 Patrick Ewing NBC .20 .09
❑ 185 Vernon Maxwell NBC .10 .05
❑ 186 Anfernee Hardaway DD .40 .18
Steve Smith
❑ 187 Chris Webber DD .40 .18
Shaquille O'Neal
❑ 188 Jamal Mashburn DD .10 .05
Rodney Rogers
❑ 189 Toni Kukoc DD .20 .09
Dino Radja
❑ 190 Lindsey Hunter DD .10 .05
Kenny Anderson
❑ 191 Latrell Sprewell DD .20 .09
Jimmy Jackson
❑ 192 Clarence Weatherspoon .10 .05
Vin Baker DD
❑ 193 Calbert Cheaney DD .10 .05
Chris Mills
❑ 194 Isaiah Rider DD .10 .05
Robert Horry
❑ 195 Sam Cassell DD .10 .05
Nick Van Exel
❑ 196 Gheorghe Muresan DD .10 .05
Shawn Bradley
❑ 197 LaPhonso Ellis DD .10 .05
Tom Gugliotta
❑ 198 USA Basketball Card .10 .05
❑ 199 Checklist .10 .05
❑ 200 Checklist .10 .05
❑ 201 Sergei Bazarevich .05 .02
❑ 202 Tyrone Corbin .05 .02
❑ 203 Grant Long .05 .02
❑ 204 Ken Norman .05 .02
❑ 205 Steve Smith .10 .05
❑ 206 Blue Edwards .05 .02
❑ 207 Greg Minor RC .05 .02
❑ 208 Eric Montross RC .05 .02
❑ 209 Dominique Wilkins .25 .11
❑ 210 Michael Adams .05 .02
❑ 211 Kenny Gattison .05 .02
❑ 212 Darrin Hancock .05 .02
❑ 213 Robert Parish .10 .05
❑ 214 Ron Harper .10 .05
❑ 215 Steve Kerr .05 .02
❑ 216 Will Perdue .05 .02
❑ 217 Dickey Simpkins RC .05 .02
❑ 218 John Battle .05 .02
❑ 219 Michael Cage .05 .02
❑ 220 Tony Dumas RC .05 .02
❑ 221 Jason Kidd RC 2.00 .90
❑ 222 Roy Tarpley .05 .02
❑ 223 Dale Ellis .05 .02
❑ 224 Jalen Rose RC 1.00 .45
❑ 225 Bill Curley RC .05 .02
❑ 226 Grant Hill RC 2.50 1.10
❑ 227 Oliver Miller .05 .02
❑ 228 Mark West .05 .02
❑ 229 Tom Gugliotta .10 .05
❑ 230 Ricky Pierce .05 .02
❑ 231 Carlos Rogers RC .05 .02
❑ 232 Clifford Rozier RC .05 .02
❑ 233 Rony Seikaly .05 .02
❑ 234 Tim Breaux .05 .02
❑ 235 Duane Ferrell .05 .02
❑ 236 Mark Jackson .05 .02
❑ 237 Byron Scott .10 .05
❑ 238 John Williams .05 .02
❑ 239 Lamond Murray RC .10 .05
❑ 240 Eric Piatkowski RC .05 .02
❑ 241 Pooh Richardson .05 .02
❑ 242 Malik Sealy .05 .02
❑ 243 Cedric Ceballos .05 .02
❑ 244 Eddie Jones RC 1.50 .70
❑ 245 Anthony Miller RC .05 .02
❑ 246 Tony Smith .05 .02
❑ 247 Kevin Gamble .05 .02
❑ 248 Brad Lohaus .05 .02
❑ 249 Billy Owens .05 .02
❑ 250 Khalid Reeves RC .05 .02
❑ 251 Kevin Willis .05 .02
❑ 252 Eric Mobley RC .05 .02
❑ 253 Johnny Newman .05 .02
❑ 254 Ed Pinckney .05 .02
❑ 255 Glenn Robinson RC .75 .35
❑ 256 Howard Eisley .05 .02
❑ 257 Donyell Marshall RC .25 .11
❑ 258 Yinka Dare RC .05 .02
❑ 259 Sean Higgins .05 .02
❑ 260 Jayson Williams .10 .05
❑ 261 Charlie Ward RC .25 .11
❑ 262 Monty Williams RC .05 .02
❑ 263 Horace Grant .10 .05
❑ 264 Brian Shaw .05 .02
❑ 265 Brooks Thompson RC .05 .02
❑ 266 Derrick Alston RC .05 .02
❑ 267 B.J. Tyler RC .05 .02
❑ 268 Scott Williams .05 .02
❑ 269 Sharone Wright RC .05 .02
❑ 270 Antonio Lang RC .05 .02
❑ 271 Danny Manning .10 .05
❑ 272 Wesley Person RC .25 .11
❑ 273 Trevor Ruffin RC .05 .02
❑ 274 Wayman Tisdale .05 .02
❑ 275 Jerome Kersey .05 .02
❑ 276 Aaron McKie RC .05 .02
❑ 277 Frank Brickowski .05 .02
❑ 278 Brian Grant RC .60 .25
❑ 279 Michael Smith RC .05 .02
❑ 280 Terry Cummings .05 .02
❑ 281 Sean Elliott .10 .05
❑ 282 Avery Johnson .05 .02
❑ 283 Moses Malone .25 .11
❑ 284 Chuck Person .05 .02
❑ 285 Vincent Askew .05 .02
❑ 286 Bill Cartwright .05 .02
❑ 287 Sarunas Marciulionis .05 .02
❑ 288 Dontonio Wingfield RC .05 .02
❑ 289 Jay Humphries .05 .02
❑ 290 Adam Keefe .05 .02
❑ 291 Jamie Watson RC .05 .02
❑ 292 Kevin Duckworth .05 .02
❑ 293 Juwan Howard RC .60 .25
❑ 294 Jim McIlvaine .05 .02
❑ 295 Scott Skiles .05 .02
❑ 296 Anthony Tucker RC .05 .02
❑ 297 Chris Webber .75 .35
❑ 298 Checklist 201-265 .05 .02
❑ 299 Checklist 266-345 .05 .02
❑ 300 Checklist 346-350/Inserts .05 .02
❑ 301 Vin Baker SSL .10 .05
❑ 302 Charles Barkley SSL .25 .11
❑ 303 Derrick Coleman SSL .05 .02
❑ 304 Clyde Drexler SSL .10 .05
❑ 305 LaPhonso Ellis SSL .05 .02
❑ 306 Larry Johnson SSL .05 .02
❑ 307 Shawn Kemp SSL .25 .11
❑ 308 Karl Malone SSL .25 .11
❑ 309 Jamal Mashburn SSL .10 .05
❑ 310 Scottie Pippen SSL .40 .18
❑ 311 Dominique Wilkins SSL .10 .05
❑ 312 Walt Williams SSL .05 .02
❑ 313 Sharone Wright SSL .05 .02
❑ 314 B.J. Armstrong SSH .05 .02
❑ 315 Joe Dumars SSH .10 .05
❑ 316 Tony Dumas SSH .05 .02
❑ 317 Tim Hardaway SSH .10 .05
❑ 318 Toni Kukoc SSH .25 .11
❑ 319 Danny Manning SSH .05 .02
❑ 320 Reggie Miller SSH .10 .05
❑ 321 Chris Mullin SSH .10 .05
❑ 322 Wesley Person SSH .10 .05
❑ 323 John Starks SSH .05 .02
❑ 324 John Stockton SSH .10 .05
❑ 325 C. Weatherspoon SSH .05 .02
❑ 326 Shawn Bradley SSW .05 .02
❑ 327 Vlade Divac SSW .05 .02
❑ 328 Patrick Ewing SSW .10 .05
❑ 329 Christian Laettner SSW .05 .02
❑ 330 Eric Montross SSW .05 .02
❑ 331 Gheorghe Muresan SSW .05 .02
❑ 332 Dikembe Mutombo SSW .05 .02
❑ 333 Hakeem Olajuwon SSW .25 .11
❑ 334 Robert Parish SSW .05 .02
❑ 335 David Robinson SSW .25 .11
❑ 336 Dennis Rodman SSW .25 .11
❑ 337 Rony Seikaly SSW .05 .02
❑ 338 Rik Smits SSW .10 .05
❑ 339 Kenny Anderson SPI .05 .02
❑ 340 Dee Brown SPI .05 .02
❑ 341 Bobby Hurley SPI .05 .02
❑ 342 Kevin Johnson SPI .05 .02
❑ 343 Jason Kidd SPI .75 .35
❑ 344 Gary Payton SPI .25 .11
❑ 345 Mark Price SPI .05 .02
❑ 346 Khalid Reeves SPI .05 .02
❑ 347 Jalen Rose SPI .10 .05
❑ 348 Latrell Sprewell SPI .25 .11
❑ 349 B.J. Tyler SPI .05 .02
❑ 350 Charlie Ward SPI .10 .05
❑ GHO Grant Hill 25.00 11.00
Gold
❑ NNO Grant Hill 10.00 4.50
Slammin' Universe
Jumbo Card
❑ NNO Grant Hill 10.00 4.50
SkyBox Jumbo
❑ NNO Grant Hill 10.00 4.50
Hoops Jumbo
❑ NNO Hakeem Olajuwon 10.00 4.50
Gold
❑ NNO Emotion Sheet A 30.00 13.50
❑ NNO Emotion Sheet B 30.00 13.50
❑ NNO Emotion Exchange A 1.00 .45
Expired
❑ NNO Emotion Exchange B 1.00 .45
Expired
❑ NNO Emotion Exchange C 1.00 .45
Expired
❑ NNO 3rd Prize Game Card .25 .11
Expired
❑ NNO Hakeem Olajuwon 300.00 135.00
David Robinson AU
❑ NNO Magic Johnson 5.00 2.20
Exchange Card
❑ NNO 3 Card Panel Exchange 4.00 1.80
Magic Johnson
Hakeem Olajuwon
David Robinson

1994-95 SkyBox Premium Center Stage

	MINT	NRMT
COMPLETE SET (9)	60.00	27.00

*SINGLES: 4X TO 10X BASE CARD HI
SER.1 STATED ODDS 1:72

	MINT	NRMT
❑ CS1 Hakeem Olajuwon	6.00	2.70
❑ CS2 Shaquille O'Neal	20.00	9.00
❑ CS3 Anfernee Hardaway	12.00	5.50
❑ CS4 Chris Webber	8.00	3.60
❑ CS5 Scottie Pippen	12.00	5.50
❑ CS6 David Robinson	6.00	2.70
❑ CS7 Latrell Sprewell	8.00	3.60
❑ CS8 Charles Barkley	6.00	2.70
❑ CS9 Alonzo Mourning	5.00	2.20

1994-95 SkyBox Premium Draft Picks

	MINT	NRMT
COMPLETE SET (27)	60.00	27.00
COMPLETE SERIES 1 (5)	20.00	9.00
COMPLETE SERIES 2 (22)	40.00	18.00
COMMON CARD (1-27)	1.00	.45
SEMISTARS	2.00	.90

SER.1 STATED ODDS 1:45
SER.2 STATED ODDS 1:18

	MINT	NRMT
❑ DP1 Glenn Robinson	6.00	2.70
❑ DP2 Jason Kidd	15.00	6.75
❑ DP3 Grant Hill	20.00	9.00
❑ DP4 Donyell Marshall	2.00	.90
❑ DP5 Juwan Howard	5.00	2.20
❑ DP6 Sharone Wright	1.00	.45
❑ DP7 Lamond Murray	1.00	.45
❑ DP8 Brian Grant	5.00	2.20
❑ DP9 Eric Montross	1.00	.45
❑ DP10 Eddie Jones	12.00	5.50
❑ DP11 Carlos Rogers	1.00	.45
❑ DP12 Kahlid Reeves	1.00	.45
❑ DP13 Jalen Rose	8.00	3.60
❑ DP14 Yinka Dare	1.00	.45
❑ DP15 Eric Piatkowski	1.00	.45
❑ DP16 Clifford Rozier	1.00	.45
❑ DP17 Aaron McKie	1.00	.45
❑ DP18 Eric Mobley	1.00	.45
❑ DP19 Tony Dumas	1.00	.45
❑ DP20 B.J. Tyler	1.00	.45
❑ DP21 Dickey Simpkins	1.00	.45
❑ DP22 Bill Curley	1.00	.45
❑ DP23 Wesley Person	2.00	.90
❑ DP24 Monty Williams	1.00	.45
❑ DP25 Greg Minor	1.00	.45
❑ DP26 Charlie Ward	2.00	.90
❑ DP27 Brooks Thompson	1.00	.45

1994-95 SkyBox Premium Grant Hill

	MINT	NRMT
COMPLETE SET (5)	40.00	18.00
COMMON HILL (GH1-GH5)	10.00	4.50

SER.2 STATED ODDS 1:36 HOBBY

	MINT	NRMT
❑ GH1 Grant Hill (Two-handed jam; back turned)	10.00	4.50
❑ GH2 Grant Hill (One arm jam)	10.00	4.50
❑ GH3 Grant Hill (Dribbling)	10.00	4.50
❑ GH4 Grant Hill (Driving to hoop at left)	10.00	4.50
❑ GH5 Grant Hill (Two-handed jam)	10.00	4.50

1994-95 SkyBox Premium Head of the Class

	MINT	NRMT
COMPLETE SET (6)	30.00	13.50
COMMON CARD (1-6)	1.50	.70

ONE SET PER HOC EXCHANGE CARD
EXCH.CARD: SER.1 STATED ODDS 1:480

	MINT	NRMT
❑ 1 Grant Hill	20.00	9.00
❑ 2 Juwan Howard	5.00	2.20
❑ 3 Jason Kidd	15.00	6.75
❑ 4 Donyell Marshall	1.50	.70
❑ 5 Glenn Robinson	6.00	2.70
❑ 6 Sharone Wright	1.50	.70
❑ NNO Checklist Card	.25	.11
❑ NNO HOC Exchange Card Expired	2.00	.90

1994-95 SkyBox Premium Ragin' Rookies

	MINT	NRMT
COMPLETE SET (24)	25.00	11.00

*SINGLES: 2.5X TO 6X BASE CARD HI
SER.1 STATED ODDS 1:5

	MINT	NRMT
❑ RR1 Dino Radja	.60	.25
❑ RR2 Corie Blount	.60	.25
❑ RR3 Toni Kukoc	4.00	1.80
❑ RR4 Chris Mills	1.25	.55
❑ RR5 Jamal Mashburn	2.50	1.10
❑ RR6 Rodney Rogers	.60	.25
❑ RR7 Allan Houston	4.00	1.80
❑ RR8 Lindsey Hunter	1.25	.55
❑ RR9 Chris Webber	5.00	2.20
❑ RR10 Sam Cassell	2.50	1.10
❑ RR11 Antonio Davis	.60	.25
❑ RR12 Terry Dehere	.60	.25
❑ RR13 Nick Van Exel	2.50	1.10
❑ RR14 George Lynch	.60	.25
❑ RR15 Vin Baker	2.50	1.10
❑ RR16 Isaiah Rider	1.25	.55
❑ RR17 P.J. Brown	.60	.25
❑ RR18 Anfernee Hardaway	8.00	3.60
❑ RR19 Shawn Bradley	.60	.25
❑ RR20 James Robinson	.60	.25
❑ RR21 Bobby Hurley	.60	.25
❑ RR22 Ervin Johnson	1.25	.55
❑ RR23 Bryon Russell	.60	.25
❑ RR24 Calbert Cheaney	.60	.25

1994-95 SkyBox Premium Revolution

	MINT	NRMT
COMPLETE SET (10)	70.00	32.00

*STARS: 4X TO 10X BASE CARD HI
*RCs: 3X TO 8X BASE HI
SER.2 STATED ODDS 1:72

	MINT	NRMT
❑ R1 Patrick Ewing	4.00	1.80
❑ R2 Grant Hill	20.00	9.00
❑ R3 Jamal Mashburn	4.00	1.80
❑ R4 Alonzo Mourning	5.00	2.20
❑ R5 Dikembe Mutombo	2.00	.90
❑ R6 Shaquille O'Neal	20.00	9.00
❑ R7 Scottie Pippen	12.00	5.50
❑ R8 Glenn Robinson	6.00	2.70

❑ R9 Latrell Sprewell	8.00	3.60
❑ R10 Chris Webber	8.00	3.60

1994-95 SkyBox Premium SkyTech Force

	MINT	NRMT
COMPLETE SET (30)	10.00	4.50

*SINGLES: .6X TO 1.5X BASE CARD HI
SER.2 STATED ODDS 1:2

❑ SF1 Kenny Anderson	.30	.14
❑ SF2 B.J. Armstrong	.15	.07
❑ SF3 Charles Barkley	1.00	.45
❑ SF4 Shawn Bradley	.15	.07
❑ SF5 LaPhonso Ellis	.15	.07
❑ SF6 Anfernee Hardaway	2.00	.90
❑ SF7 Bobby Hurley	.15	.07
❑ SF8 Kevin Johnson	.30	.14
❑ SF9 Larry Johnson	.30	.14
❑ SF10 Shawn Kemp	1.00	.45
❑ SF11 Jason Kidd	4.00	1.80
❑ SF12 Christian Laettner	.30	.14
❑ SF13 Karl Malone	1.00	.45
❑ SF14 Danny Manning	.15	.07
❑ SF15 Chris Mills	.30	.14
❑ SF16 Chris Mullin	.60	.25
❑ SF17 Lamond Murray	.15	.07
❑ SF18 Charles Oakley	.15	.07
❑ SF19 Hakeem Olajuwon	1.00	.45
❑ SF20 Gary Payton	1.00	.45
❑ SF21 Mark Price	.15	.07
❑ SF22 Dino Radja	.15	.07
❑ SF23 Mitch Richmond	.60	.25
❑ SF24 Clifford Robinson	.30	.14
❑ SF25 David Robinson	1.00	.45
❑ SF26 Dennis Rodman	1.25	.55
❑ SF27 Dickey Simpkins	.10	.05
❑ SF28 John Starks	.15	.07
❑ SF29 John Stockton	.60	.25
❑ SF30 Charlie Ward	.40	.18

1994-95 SkyBox Premium Slammin' Universe

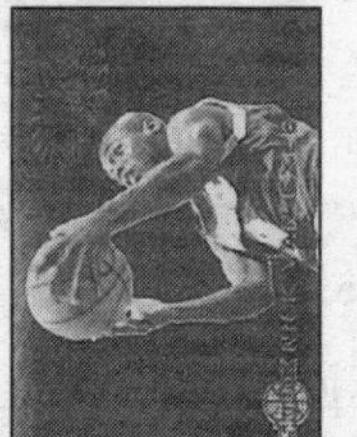

	MINT	NRMT
COMPLETE SET (30)	10.00	4.50

*SINGLES: .6X TO 1.5X BASE CARD HI
SER.2 STATED ODDS 1:2

❑ SU1 Vin Baker	.60	.25
❑ SU2 Dee Brown	.15	.07
❑ SU3 Derrick Coleman	.30	.14
❑ SU4 Clyde Drexler	.60	.25
❑ SU5 Joe Dumars	.60	.25
❑ SU6 Tony Dumas	.10	.05
❑ SU7 Patrick Ewing	.60	.25
❑ SU8 Horace Grant	.15	.07
❑ SU9 Tom Gugliotta	.15	.07
❑ SU10 Grant Hill	5.00	2.20
❑ SU11 Jim Jackson	.30	.14
❑ SU12 Toni Kukoc	1.00	.45
❑ SU13 Donyell Marshall	.40	.18
❑ SU14 Jamal Mashburn	.60	.25
❑ SU15 Reggie Miller	.60	.25
❑ SU16 Eric Montross	.10	.05
❑ SU17 Alonzo Mourning	.75	.35
❑ SU18 Dikembe Mutombo	.30	.14
❑ SU19 Shaquille O'Neal	3.00	1.35
❑ SU20 Glen Rice	.30	.14
❑ SU21 Isaiah Rider	.30	.14
❑ SU22 Glenn Robinson	1.50	.70
❑ SU23 Jalen Rose	2.00	.90
❑ SU24 Detlef Schrempf	.30	.14
❑ SU25 Steve Smith	.30	.14
❑ SU26 Latrell Sprewell	1.25	.55
❑ SU27 Rod Strickland	.30	.14
❑ SU28 B.J. Tyler	.10	.05
❑ SU29 Nick Van Exel	.60	.25
❑ SU30 Dominique Wilkins	.40	.18

1995-96 SkyBox Premium

	MINT	NRMT
COMPLETE SET (301)	35.00	16.00
COMPLETE SERIES 1 (150)	15.00	6.75
COMPLETE SERIES 2 (151)	20.00	9.00
COMMON CARD (1-301)	.10	.05
SEMISTARS	.15	.07
UNLISTED STARS	.30	.14

SUBSET CARDS HALF VALUE OF BASE CARDS

❑ 1 Stacey Augmon	.10	.05
❑ 2 Mookie Blaylock	.10	.05
❑ 3 Grant Long	.10	.05
❑ 4 Steve Smith	.15	.07
❑ 5 Dee Brown	.10	.05
❑ 6 Sherman Douglas	.10	.05
❑ 7 Eric Montross	.10	.05
❑ 8 Dino Radja	.10	.05
❑ 9 Dominique Wilkins	.30	.14
❑ 10 Muggsy Bogues	.10	.05
❑ 11 Scott Burrell	.10	.05
❑ 12 Dell Curry	.10	.05
❑ 13 Larry Johnson	.15	.07
❑ 14 Alonzo Mourning	.30	.14
❑ 15 Michael Jordan UER Career block total is wrong	4.00	1.80
❑ 16 Steve Kerr	.10	.05
❑ 17 Toni Kukoc	.40	.18
❑ 18 Scottie Pippen	1.00	.45
❑ 19 Terrell Brandon	.15	.07
❑ 20 Tyrone Hill	.10	.05
❑ 21 Chris Mills	.10	.05
❑ 22 Mark Price	.10	.05
❑ 23 John Williams	.10	.05
❑ 24 Tony Dumas	.10	.05
❑ 25 Jim Jackson	.10	.05
❑ 26 Popeye Jones	.10	.05
❑ 27 Jason Kidd	1.00	.45
❑ 28 Jamal Mashburn	.15	.07
❑ 29 LaPhonso Ellis	.10	.05
❑ 30 Dikembe Mutombo	.15	.07
❑ 31 Robert Pack	.10	.05
❑ 32 Jalen Rose	.40	.18
❑ 33 Bryant Stith	.10	.05
❑ 34 Joe Dumars	.30	.14
❑ 35 Grant Hill	1.50	.70
❑ 36 Allan Houston	.40	.18
❑ 37 Lindsey Hunter	.10	.05
❑ 38 Chris Gatling	.10	.05
❑ 39 Tim Hardaway	.30	.14
❑ 40 Donyell Marshall	.15	.07
❑ 41 Chris Mullin	.30	.14
❑ 42 Carlos Rogers	.10	.05
❑ 43 Latrell Sprewell	.60	.25
❑ 44 Sam Cassell	.15	.07
❑ 45 Clyde Drexler	.30	.14
❑ 46 Robert Horry	.10	.05
❑ 47 Hakeem Olajuwon	.50	.23
❑ 48 Kenny Smith	.10	.05
❑ 49 Dale Davis	.10	.05
❑ 50 Mark Jackson	.10	.05
❑ 51 Reggie Miller	.30	.14
❑ 52 Rik Smits	.10	.05
❑ 53 Lamond Murray	.10	.05
❑ 54 Eric Piatkowski	.10	.05
❑ 55 Pooh Richardson	.10	.05
❑ 56 Rodney Rogers	.10	.05
❑ 57 Loy Vaught	.10	.05
❑ 58 Elden Campbell	.10	.05
❑ 59 Cedric Ceballos	.10	.05
❑ 60 Vlade Divac	.10	.05
❑ 61 Eddie Jones	.60	.25
❑ 62 Anthony Peeler	.10	.05
❑ 63 Nick Van Exel	.15	.07
❑ 64 Bimbo Coles	.10	.05
❑ 65 Billy Owens	.10	.05
❑ 66 Khalid Reeves	.10	.05
❑ 67 Glen Rice	.15	.07
❑ 68 Kevin Willis	.10	.05
❑ 69 Vin Baker	.30	.14
❑ 70 Todd Day	.10	.05
❑ 71 Eric Murdock	.10	.05
❑ 72 Glenn Robinson	.30	.14
❑ 73 Tom Gugliotta	.15	.07
❑ 74 Christian Laettner	.15	.07
❑ 75 Isaiah Rider	.15	.07
❑ 76 Doug West	.10	.05
❑ 77 Kenny Anderson	.15	.07
❑ 78 P.J. Brown	.10	.05
❑ 79 Derrick Coleman	.15	.07
❑ 80 Armon Gilliam	.10	.05
❑ 81 Patrick Ewing	.30	.14
❑ 82 Derek Harper	.10	.05
❑ 83 Anthony Mason	.15	.07
❑ 84 Charles Oakley	.10	.05
❑ 85 John Starks	.10	.05
❑ 86 Nick Anderson	.10	.05
❑ 87 Horace Grant	.15	.07
❑ 88 Anfernee Hardaway	1.00	.45
❑ 89 Shaquille O'Neal	1.50	.70
❑ 90 Dana Barros	.10	.05
❑ 91 Shawn Bradley	.10	.05
❑ 92 Clarence Weatherspoon	.10	.05
❑ 93 Sharone Wright	.10	.05
❑ 94 Charles Barkley	.50	.23
❑ 95 Kevin Johnson	.15	.07
❑ 96 Dan Majerle	.10	.05
❑ 97 Danny Manning	.15	.07
❑ 98 Wesley Person	.15	.07
❑ 99 Clifford Robinson	.10	.05
❑ 100 Rod Strickland	.15	.07
❑ 101 Otis Thorpe	.10	.05
❑ 102 Buck Williams	.10	.05
❑ 103 Brian Grant	.30	.14
❑ 104 Olden Polynice	.10	.05
❑ 105 Mitch Richmond	.30	.14
❑ 106 Walt Williams	.10	.05
❑ 107 Vinny Del Negro	.10	.05

❑ 108	Sean Elliott	.10	.05
❑ 109	Avery Johnson	.10	.05
❑ 110	David Robinson	.50	.23
❑ 111	Dennis Rodman	.60	.25
❑ 112	Shawn Kemp	.50	.23
❑ 113	Gary Payton	.50	.23
❑ 114	Sam Perkins	.15	.07
❑ 115	Detlef Schrempf	.15	.07
❑ 116	David Benoit	.10	.05
❑ 117	Jeff Hornacek	.15	.07
❑ 118	Karl Malone	.50	.23
❑ 119	John Stockton	.30	.14
❑ 120	Calbert Cheaney	.10	.05
❑ 121	Juwan Howard	.30	.14
❑ 122	Don MacLean	.10	.05
❑ 123	Gheorghe Muresan	.10	.05
❑ 124	Chris Webber	1.00	.45
❑ 125	Robert Horry FC	.10	.05
❑ 126	Mark Jackson FC	.10	.05
❑ 127	Steve Smith FC	.10	.05
❑ 128	Lamond Murray FC	.10	.05
❑ 129	Christian Laettner FC	.10	.05
❑ 130	Kenny Anderson FC	.10	.05
❑ 131	Anthony Mason FC	.10	.05
❑ 132	Kevin Johnson FC	.10	.05
❑ 133	Jeff Hornacek FC	.10	.05
❑ 134	Larry Johnson TP	.10	.05
❑ 135	Popeye Jones TP	.10	.05
❑ 136	Allan Houston TP	.30	.14
❑ 137	Chris Gatling TP	.10	.05
❑ 138	Sam Cassell TP	.10	.05
❑ 139	Anthony Peeler TP	.10	.05
❑ 140	Vin Baker TP	.15	.07
❑ 141	Dana Barros TP	.10	.05
❑ 142	Gheorghe Muresan TP	.10	.05
❑ 143	Toronto Raptors	.10	.05
❑ 144	Vancouver Grizzlies	.10	.05
❑ 145	Glen Rice EXP Muggsy Bogues EXP	.15	.07
❑ 146	Nick Anderson EXP Christian Laettner EXP	.10	.05
❑ 147	John Salley TF	.10	.05
❑ 148	Greg Anthony TF	.10	.05
❑ 149	Checklist #1	.10	.05
❑ 150	Checklist #2	.10	.05
❑ 151	Craig Ehlo	.10	.05
❑ 152	Spud Webb	.10	.05
❑ 153	Dana Barros	.10	.05
❑ 155	Kendall Gill	.15	.07
❑ 156	Khalid Reeves	.10	.05
❑ 157	Glen Rice	.15	.07
❑ 158	Luc Longley	.10	.05
❑ 159	Dennis Rodman	.60	.25
❑ 160	Dickey Simpkins	.10	.05
❑ 161	Danny Ferry	.10	.05
❑ 162	Dan Majerle	.10	.05
❑ 163	Bobby Phills	.10	.05
❑ 164	Lucious Harris	.10	.05
❑ 165	George McCloud	.10	.05
❑ 166	Mahmoud Abdul-Rauf	.10	.05
❑ 167	Don MacLean	.10	.05
❑ 168	Reggie Williams	.10	.05
❑ 169	Terry Mills	.10	.05
❑ 170	Otis Thorpe	.10	.05
❑ 171	B.J. Armstrong	.10	.05
❑ 172	Rony Seikaly	.10	.05
❑ 173	Chucky Brown	.10	.05
❑ 174	Mario Elie	.10	.05
❑ 175	Antonio Davis	.10	.05
❑ 176	Ricky Pierce	.10	.05
❑ 177	Terry Dehere	.10	.05
❑ 178	Rodney Rogers	.10	.05
❑ 179	Malik Sealy	.10	.05
❑ 180	Brian Williams	.10	.05
❑ 181	Sedale Threatt	.10	.05
❑ 182	Alonzo Mourning	.30	.14
❑ 183	Lee Mayberry	.10	.05
❑ 184	Sean Rooks	.10	.05
❑ 185	Shawn Bradley	.10	.05
❑ 186	Kevin Edwards	.10	.05
❑ 187	Hubert Davis	.10	.05
❑ 188	Charles Smith	.10	.05
❑ 189	Charlie Ward	.10	.05
❑ 190	Dennis Scott	.10	.05
❑ 191	Brian Shaw	.10	.05
❑ 192	Derrick Coleman	.15	.07
❑ 193	Richard Dumas	.10	.05
❑ 194	Vernon Maxwell	.10	.05
❑ 195	A.C. Green	.15	.07
❑ 196	Elliot Perry	.10	.05
❑ 197	John Williams	.10	.05
❑ 198	Aaron McKie	.10	.05
❑ 199	Bobby Hurley	.10	.05
❑ 200	Michael Smith	.10	.05
❑ 201	J.R. Reid	.10	.05
❑ 202	Hersey Hawkins	.15	.07
❑ 203	Willie Anderson	.10	.05
❑ 204	Oliver Miller	.10	.05
❑ 205	Tracy Murray	.10	.05
❑ 206	Alvin Robertson	.10	.05
❑ 207	Carlos Rogers UER Card says Rodney Rogers on front with picture	.10	.05
❑ 208	John Salley	.10	.05
❑ 209	Zan Tabak	.10	.05
❑ 210	Adam Keefe	.10	.05
❑ 211	Chris Morris	.10	.05
❑ 212	Greg Anthony	.10	.05
❑ 213	Blue Edwards	.10	.05
❑ 214	Kenny Gattison	.10	.05
❑ 215	Antonio Harvey	.10	.05
❑ 216	Chris King	.10	.05
❑ 217	Byron Scott	.10	.05
❑ 218	Robert Pack	.10	.05
❑ 219	Alan Henderson RC	.30	.14
❑ 220	Eric Williams RC	.15	.07
❑ 221	George Zidek RC	.10	.05
❑ 222	Jason Caffey RC	.15	.07
❑ 223	Bob Sura RC	.15	.07
❑ 224	Cherokee Parks RC	.10	.05
❑ 225	Antonio McDyess RC	1.50	.70
❑ 226	Theo Ratliff RC	.40	.18
❑ 227	Joe Smith RC	1.00	.45
❑ 228	Travis Best RC	.15	.07
❑ 229	Brent Barry RC	.30	.14
❑ 230	Sasha Danilovic RC	.10	.05
❑ 231	Kurt Thomas RC	.15	.07
❑ 232	Shawn Respert RC	.10	.05
❑ 233	Kevin Garnett RC	4.00	1.80
❑ 234	Ed O'Bannon RC	.10	.05
❑ 235	Jerry Stackhouse RC	1.00	.45
❑ 236	Michael Finley RC	1.25	.55
❑ 237	Mario Bennett RC	.10	.05
❑ 238	Randolph Childress RC	.10	.05
❑ 239	Arvydas Sabonis RC	.50	.23
❑ 240	Gary Trent RC	.10	.05
❑ 241	Tyus Edney RC	.10	.05
❑ 242	Corliss Williamson RC	.60	.25
❑ 243	Cory Alexander RC	.10	.05
❑ 244	Damon Stoudamire RC	1.50	.70
❑ 245	Greg Ostertag RC	.10	.05
❑ 246	Lawrence Moten RC	.10	.05
❑ 247	Bryant Reeves RC	.30	.14
❑ 248	Rasheed Wallace RC	1.25	.55
❑ 249	Muggsy Bogues HR	.10	.05
❑ 250	Dell Curry HR	.10	.05
❑ 251	Scottie Pippen HR	.50	.23
❑ 252	Danny Ferry HR	.10	.05
❑ 253	Mahmoud Abdul-Rauf HR	.10	.05
❑ 254	Joe Dumars HR	.15	.07
❑ 255	Tim Hardaway HR	.15	.07
❑ 256	Chris Mullin HR	.15	.07
❑ 257	Hakeem Olajuwon HR	.30	.14
❑ 258	Kenny Smith HR	.10	.05
❑ 259	Reggie Miller HR	.15	.07
❑ 260	Rik Smits HR	.10	.05
❑ 261	Vlade Divac HR	.10	.05
❑ 262	Doug West HR	.10	.05
❑ 263	Patrick Ewing HR	.15	.07
❑ 264	Charles Oakley HR	.10	.05
❑ 265	Nick Anderson HR	.10	.05
❑ 266	Dennis Scott HR	.10	.05
❑ 267	Jeff Turner HR	.10	.05
❑ 268	Charles Barkley HR	.30	.14
❑ 269	Kevin Johnson HR	.10	.05
❑ 270	Clifford Robinson HR	.10	.05
❑ 271	Buck Williams HR	.10	.05
❑ 272	Lionel Simmons HR	.10	.05
❑ 273	David Robinson HR	.30	.14
❑ 274	Gary Payton HR	.30	.14
❑ 275	Karl Malone HR	.30	.14
❑ 276	John Stockton HR	.15	.07
❑ 277	Steve Smith ELE	.10	.05
❑ 278	Michael Jordan ELE	2.00	.90
❑ 279	Jim Jackson ELE	.10	.05
❑ 280	Jason Kidd ELE	.40	.18
❑ 281	Jamal Mashburn ELE	.10	.05
❑ 282	Dikembe Mutombo ELE	.10	.05
❑ 283	Grant Hill ELE	1.00	.45
❑ 284	Tim Hardaway ELE	.15	.07
❑ 285	Clyde Drexler ELE	.15	.07
❑ 286	Cedric Ceballos ELE	.10	.05
❑ 287	Gary Payton ELE	.30	.14
❑ 288	Billy Owens ELE	.10	.05
❑ 289	Vin Baker ELE	.15	.07
❑ 290	Glenn Robinson ELE	.15	.07
❑ 291	Kenny Anderson ELE	.10	.05
❑ 292	Anfernee Hardaway ELE	.60	.25
❑ 293	Shaquille O'Neal ELE	.60	.25
❑ 294	Charles Barkley ELE	.30	.14
❑ 295	Rod Strickland ELE	.10	.05
❑ 296	Mitch Richmond ELE	.15	.07
❑ 297	Juwan Howard ELE	.15	.07
❑ 298	Chris Webber ELE	.40	.18
❑ 299	Checklist #1	.10	.05
❑ 300	Checklist #2	.10	.05
❑ 301	Magic Johnson	1.00	.45
❑ PR	Grant Hill JUMBO	10.00	4.50
❑ NNO	Grant Hill Meltdown Exchange	35.00	16.00
❑ NNO	Jerry Stackhouse Meltdown Exchange	20.00	9.00

1995-96 SkyBox Premium Atomic

	MINT	NRMT
COMPLETE SET (15)	6.00	2.70
COMMON CARD (A1-A15)	.30	.14
SEMISTARS	.50	.23
UNLISTED STARS	.75	.35

SER.1 STATED ODDS 1:4 HOBBY/RETAIL

❑ A1	Eric Montross	.30	.14
❑ A2	Charles Oakley	.30	.14
❑ A3	Rik Smits	.30	.14
❑ A4	Vlade Divac	.30	.14
❑ A5	Buck Williams	.30	.14
❑ A6	Vin Baker	.75	.35
❑ A7	Glenn Robinson	.75	.35
❑ A8	Isaiah Rider	.50	.23
❑ A9	Derrick Coleman	.50	.23
❑ A10	Clarence Weatherspoon	.30	.14
❑ A11	Sharone Wright	.30	.14
❑ A12	Brian Grant	.75	.35
❑ A13	Jim Jackson	.30	.14
❑ A14	Clyde Drexler	.75	.35
❑ A15	Anfernee Hardaway	2.50	1.10

1995-96 SkyBox Premium Close-Ups

	MINT	NRMT
COMPLETE SET (9)	20.00	9.00
COMMON CARD (C1-C9)	2.00	.90

SER.1 STATED ODDS 1:9 RETAIL
ONE PER SPECIAL SER.1 RETAIL PACK

❑ C1	Scottie Pippen	6.00	2.70

Card	MINT	NRMT
❑ C2 Grant Hill	10.00	4.50
❑ C3 Clyde Drexler	2.00	.90
❑ C4 Nick Van Exel	2.00	.90
❑ C5 Tom Gugliotta	2.00	.90
❑ C6 Patrick Ewing	2.00	.90
❑ C7 Charles Barkley	3.00	1.35
❑ C8 Karl Malone	3.00	1.35
❑ C9 Juwan Howard	2.00	.90

1995-96 SkyBox Premium Dynamic

	MINT	NRMT
COMPLETE SET (12)	5.00	2.20
COMMON CARD (D1-D12)	.25	.11
SEMISTARS	.40	.18
UNLISTED STARS	.60	.25

SER.1 STATED ODDS 1:4 HOBBY/RETAIL

Card	MINT	NRMT
❑ D1 Larry Johnson	.40	.18
❑ D2 Alonzo Mourning	.60	.25
❑ D3 Dikembe Mutombo	.40	.18
❑ D4 Jalen Rose	.75	.35
❑ D5 Grant Hill	3.00	1.35
❑ D6 Latrell Sprewell	1.25	.55
❑ D7 Reggie Miller	.60	.25
❑ D8 John Starks	.25	.11
❑ D9 Calbert Cheaney	.25	.11
❑ D10 Dennis Rodman	1.25	.55
❑ D11 Detlef Schrempf	.40	.18
❑ D12 Chris Webber	2.00	.90

1995-96 SkyBox Premium High Hopes

	MINT	NRMT
COMPLETE SET (20)	50.00	22.00
COMMON CARD (HH1-HH20)	.75	.35
SEMISTARS	1.50	.70
UNLISTED STARS	2.50	1.10

SER.2 STATED ODDS 1:18 H/R, 1:12 JUM

Card	MINT	NRMT
❑ HH1 Alan Henderson	1.50	.70
❑ HH2 Eric Williams	.75	.35
❑ HH3 George Zidek	.75	.35
❑ HH4 Bob Sura	1.50	.70
❑ HH5 Cherokee Parks	.75	.35
❑ HH6 Antonio McDyess	6.00	2.70
❑ HH7 Joe Smith	4.00	1.80
❑ HH8 Brent Barry	2.50	1.10

Card	MINT	NRMT
❑ HH9 Shawn Respert	.75	.35
❑ HH10 Kevin Garnett	20.00	9.00
❑ HH11 Ed O'Bannon	.75	.35
❑ HH12 Jerry Stackhouse	4.00	1.80
❑ HH13 Michael Finley	5.00	2.20
❑ HH14 Arvydas Sabonis	2.50	1.10
❑ HH15 Gary Trent	.75	.35
❑ HH16 Tyus Edney	.75	.35
❑ HH17 Damon Stoudamire	6.00	2.70
❑ HH18 Greg Ostertag	.75	.35
❑ HH19 Bryant Reeves	1.50	.70
❑ HH20 Rasheed Wallace	5.00	2.20

1995-96 SkyBox Premium Hot Sparks

	MINT	NRMT
COMPLETE SET (11)	25.00	11.00
COMMON CARD (HS1-HS11)	1.00	.45
SEMISTARS	1.25	.55
UNLISTED STARS	2.00	.90

SER.2 STATED ODDS 1:12 HOBBY

Card	MINT	NRMT
❑ HS1 Mookie Blaylock	1.00	.45
❑ HS2 Jason Kidd	6.00	2.70
❑ HS3 Tim Hardaway	2.00	.90
❑ HS4 Nick Van Exel	1.25	.55
❑ HS5 Kenny Anderson	1.25	.55
❑ HS6 Anfernee Hardaway	6.00	2.70
❑ HS7 Rod Strickland	1.25	.55
❑ HS8 Gary Payton	3.00	1.35
❑ HS9 Damon Stoudamire	5.00	2.20
❑ HS10 John Stockton	2.00	.90
❑ HS11 Magic Johnson	6.00	2.70

1995-96 SkyBox Premium Kinetic

	MINT	NRMT
COMPLETE SET (9)	2.00	.90
COMMON CARD (K1-K9)	.25	.11
SEMISTARS	.40	.18
UNLISTED STARS	.60	.25

SER.1 STATED ODDS 1:4 HOBBY/RETAIL

Card	MINT	NRMT
❑ K1 Mookie Blaylock	.25	.11
❑ K2 Tim Hardaway	.60	.25
❑ K3 Lamond Murray UER Mach is spelled Mock	.25	.11
❑ K4 Stacey Augmon	.25	.11

Card	MINT	NRMT
❑ K5 Nick Van Exel	.40	.18
❑ K6 Khalid Reeves	.25	.11
❑ K7 Kenny Anderson	.40	.18
❑ K8 Rod Strickland	.40	.18
❑ K9 Gary Payton	1.00	.45

1995-96 SkyBox Premium Larger Than Life

	MINT	NRMT
COMPLETE SET (10)	80.00	36.00
COMMON CARD (L1-L10)	3.00	1.35

SER.1 STATED ODDS 1:48 HOBBY/RETAIL

Card	MINT	NRMT
❑ L1 Michael Jordan	40.00	18.00
❑ L2 Jason Kidd	10.00	4.50
❑ L3 Grant Hill	15.00	6.75
❑ L4 Hakeem Olajuwon	5.00	2.20
❑ L5 Glenn Robinson	3.00	1.35
❑ L6 Patrick Ewing	3.00	1.35
❑ L7 Shaquille O'Neal	15.00	6.75
❑ L8 Charles Barkley	5.00	2.20
❑ L9 David Robinson	5.00	2.20
❑ L10 John Stockton	3.00	1.35

1995-96 SkyBox Premium Lottery Exchange

	MINT	NRMT
COMPLETE SET (13)	30.00	13.50
COMMON CARD (1-13)	1.00	.45
SEMISTARS	1.50	.70
UNLISTED STARS	2.00	.90

ONE SET PER THREE EXCH.CARDS BY MAIL
EXCH.CARDS: SER.1 STATED ODDS 1:40

	MINT	NRMT
❑ 1 Joe Smith	3.00	1.35
❑ 2 Antonio McDyess	5.00	2.20
❑ 3 Jerry Stackhouse	3.00	1.35
❑ 4 Rasheed Wallace	4.00	1.80
❑ 5 Kevin Garnett	12.00	5.50
❑ 6 Bryant Reeves	1.50	.70
❑ 7 Damon Stoudamire	5.00	2.20
❑ 8 Shawn Respert	1.00	.45
❑ 9 Ed O'Bannon	1.00	.45
❑ 10 Kurt Thomas	1.00	.45
❑ 11 Gary Trent	1.00	.45
❑ 12 Cherokee Parks	1.00	.45
❑ 13 Corliss Williamson	2.00	.90
❑ NNO Exchange Card 1 Expired	1.00	.45
❑ NNO Exchange Card 2 Expired	1.00	.45
❑ NNO Exchange Card 3 Expired	1.00	.45

1995-96 SkyBox Premium Meltdown

	MINT	NRMT
COMPLETE SET (10)	100.00	45.00
COMMON CARD (M1-M10)	2.00	.90

SER.2 STATED ODDS 1:54 H/R, 1:42 JUM

	MINT	NRMT
❑ M1 Michael Jordan	50.00	22.00
❑ M2 Dan Majerle	2.00	.90
❑ M3 Jason Kidd	12.00	5.50
❑ M4 Antonio McDyess	10.00	4.50
❑ M5 Grant Hill	20.00	9.00
❑ M6 Joe Smith	6.00	2.70
❑ M7 Hakeem Olajuwon	6.00	2.70
❑ M8 Shaquille O'Neal	20.00	9.00
❑ M9 Jerry Stackhouse	6.00	2.70
❑ M10 David Robinson	6.00	2.70

1995-96 SkyBox Premium Rookie Prevue

	MINT	NRMT
COMPLETE SET (20)	60.00	27.00
COMMON CARD (RP1-RP20)	1.00	.45
SEMISTARS	2.50	1.10
UNLISTED STARS	4.00	1.80

SER.1 STATED ODDS 1:9 HOBBY/RETAIL

	MINT	NRMT
❑ RP1 Joe Smith	6.00	2.70
❑ RP2 Antonio McDyess	10.00	4.50
❑ RP3 Jerry Stackhouse	6.00	2.70
❑ RP4 Rasheed Wallace	8.00	3.60
❑ RP5 Bryant Reeves	2.50	1.10
❑ RP6 Damon Stoudamire	10.00	4.50
❑ RP7 Shawn Respert	1.00	.45
❑ RP8 Ed O'Bannon	1.00	.45
❑ RP9 Kurt Thomas	1.00	.45
❑ RP10 Gary Trent	1.00	.45
❑ RP11 Cherokee Parks	1.00	.45
❑ RP12 Corliss Williamson	4.00	1.80
❑ RP13 Eric Williams	1.00	.45
❑ RP14 Brent Barry	4.00	1.80
❑ RP15 Alan Henderson	2.50	1.10
❑ RP16 Bob Sura	2.50	1.10
❑ RP17 Theo Ratliff	4.00	1.80
❑ RP18 Randolph Childress	1.00	.45
❑ RP19 Michael Finley	8.00	3.60
❑ RP20 George Zidek	1.00	.45

1995-96 SkyBox Premium Standouts

	MINT	NRMT
COMPLETE SET (12)	30.00	13.50
COMMON CARD (S1-S12)	1.50	.70
SEMISTARS	2.00	.90
UNLISTED STARS	3.00	1.35

SER.1 STATED ODDS 1:18 H/R, 1:36 JUM

	MINT	NRMT
❑ S1 Alonzo Mourning	3.00	1.35
❑ S2 Scottie Pippen	10.00	4.50
❑ S3 Danny Manning	2.00	.90
❑ S4 Jamal Mashburn	2.00	.90
❑ S5 Latrell Sprewell	6.00	2.70
❑ S6 Reggie Miller	3.00	1.35
❑ S7 Anfernee Hardaway	10.00	4.50
❑ S8 Brian Grant	3.00	1.35
❑ S9 Shawn Kemp	5.00	2.20
❑ S10 Clifford Robinson	1.50	.70
❑ S11 Joe Dumars	3.00	1.35
❑ S12 Chris Webber	10.00	4.50

1995-96 SkyBox Premium Standouts Hobby

	MINT	NRMT
COMPLETE SET (6)	90.00	40.00
COMMON CARD (SH1-SH6)	6.00	2.70

SER.1 STATED ODDS 1:18 HOBBY

	MINT	NRMT
❑ SH1 Michael Jordan	50.00	22.00
❑ SH2 Jason Kidd	12.00	5.50
❑ SH3 Hakeem Olajuwon	6.00	2.70
❑ SH4 Eddie Jones	8.00	3.60
❑ SH5 Shaquille O'Neal	20.00	9.00
❑ SH6 Grant Hill	20.00	9.00

1995-96 SkyBox Premium USA Basketball

	MINT	NRMT
COMPLETE SET (10)	20.00	9.00
COMMON CARD (U1-U10)	1.25	.55

SER.2 STATED ODDS 1:12 RETAIL
ONE PER SPECIAL SER.2 RETAIL PACK

	MINT	NRMT
❑ U1 Anfernee Hardaway	4.00	1.80
❑ U2 Grant Hill	6.00	2.70
❑ U3 Karl Malone	2.00	.90
❑ U4 Reggie Miller	1.25	.55
❑ U5 Scottie Pippen	4.00	1.80
❑ U6 Hakeem Olajuwon	2.00	.90
❑ U7 Shaquille O'Neal	6.00	2.70
❑ U8 David Robinson	2.00	.90
❑ U9 Glenn Robinson	1.25	.55
❑ U10 John Stockton	1.25	.55

1996-97 SkyBox Premium

	MINT	NRMT
COMPLETE SET (281)	40.00	18.00
COMPLETE SERIES 1 (131)	25.00	11.00
COMPLETE SERIES 2 (150)	15.00	6.75
COMMON CARD (1-281)	.10	.05
SEMISTARS	.15	.07
UNLISTED STARS	.30	.14

SUBSET CARDS HALF VALUE OF BASE CARDS

- ❑ 1 Mookie Blaylock .10 .05
- ❑ 2 Alan Henderson .10 .05
- ❑ 3 Christian Laettner .15 .07
- ❑ 4 Dikembe Mutombo .15 .07
- ❑ 5 Steve Smith .15 .07
- ❑ 6 Dana Barros .10 .05
- ❑ 7 Rick Fox .10 .05
- ❑ 8 Dino Radja .10 .05
- ❑ 9 Antoine Walker RC 1.25 .55
- ❑ 10 Eric Williams .10 .05
- ❑ 11 Dell Curry .10 .05
- ❑ 12 Tony Delk RC .15 .07
- ❑ 13 Matt Geiger .10 .05
- ❑ 14 Glen Rice .15 .07
- ❑ 15 Ron Harper .15 .07
- ❑ 16 Michael Jordan 4.00 1.80
- ❑ 17 Toni Kukoc .40 .18
- ❑ 18 Scottie Pippen 1.00 .45
- ❑ 19 Dennis Rodman .60 .25
- ❑ 20 Terrell Brandon .15 .07
- ❑ 21 Danny Ferry .10 .05
- ❑ 22 Chris Mills .10 .05
- ❑ 23 Bobby Phills .10 .05
- ❑ 24 Vitaly Potapenko RC .10 .05
- ❑ 25 Jim Jackson .10 .05
- ❑ 26 Jason Kidd 1.00 .45
- ❑ 27 Jamal Mashburn .15 .07
- ❑ 28 George McCloud .10 .05
- ❑ 29 Samaki Walker RC .10 .05
- ❑ 30 LaPhonso Ellis .10 .05
- ❑ 31 Antonio McDyess .50 .23
- ❑ 32 Bryant Stith .10 .05
- ❑ 33 Joe Dumars .30 .14
- ❑ 34 Grant Hill 1.50 .70
- ❑ 35 Lindsey Hunter .10 .05
- ❑ 36 Theo Ratliff .15 .07
- ❑ 37 Otis Thorpe .10 .05
- ❑ 38 Todd Fuller RC .10 .05
- ❑ 39 Chris Mullin .30 .14
- ❑ 40 Joe Smith .30 .14
- ❑ 41 Latrell Sprewell .60 .25
- ❑ 42 Charles Barkley .50 .23
- ❑ 43 Clyde Drexler .30 .14
- ❑ 44 Mario Elie .10 .05
- ❑ 45 Hakeem Olajuwon .50 .23
- ❑ 46 Erick Dampier RC .15 .07
- ❑ 47 Dale Davis .10 .05
- ❑ 48 Derrick McKey .10 .05
- ❑ 49 Reggie Miller .30 .14
- ❑ 50 Rik Smits .10 .05
- ❑ 51 Brent Barry .10 .05
- ❑ 52 Rodney Rogers .10 .05
- ❑ 53 Loy Vaught .10 .05
- ❑ 54 Lorenzen Wright RC .15 .07
- ❑ 55 Kobe Bryant RC 10.00 4.50
- ❑ 56 Cedric Ceballos .10 .05
- ❑ 57 Eddie Jones .60 .25
- ❑ 58 Shaquille O'Neal 1.50 .70
- ❑ 59 Nick Van Exel .15 .07
- ❑ 60 Tim Hardaway .30 .14
- ❑ 61 Alonzo Mourning .30 .14
- ❑ 62 Kurt Thomas .10 .05
- ❑ 63 Ray Allen RC 1.25 .55
- ❑ 64 Vin Baker .15 .07
- ❑ 65 Shawn Respert .10 .05
- ❑ 66 Glenn Robinson .30 .14
- ❑ 67 Kevin Garnett 2.00 .90
- ❑ 68 Tom Gugliotta .15 .07
- ❑ 69 Stephon Marbury RC 2.00 .90
- ❑ 70 Sam Mitchell .10 .05
- ❑ 71 Shawn Bradley .10 .05
- ❑ 72 Kendall Gill .15 .07
- ❑ 73 Kerry Kittles RC .60 .25
- ❑ 74 Ed O'Bannon .10 .05
- ❑ 75 Patrick Ewing .30 .14
- ❑ 76 Larry Johnson .15 .07
- ❑ 77 Charles Oakley .10 .05
- ❑ 78 John Starks .10 .05
- ❑ 79 John Wallace RC .30 .14
- ❑ 80 Nick Anderson .10 .05
- ❑ 81 Horace Grant .15 .07
- ❑ 82 Anfernee Hardaway 1.00 .45
- ❑ 83 Dennis Scott .10 .05
- ❑ 84 Derrick Coleman .15 .07
- ❑ 85 Allen Iverson RC 3.00 1.35
- ❑ 86 Jerry Stackhouse .30 .14
- ❑ 87 Clarence Weatherspoon .10 .05
- ❑ 88 Michael Finley .40 .18
- ❑ 89 Robert Horry .10 .05
- ❑ 90 Kevin Johnson .15 .07
- ❑ 91 Steve Nash RC .15 .07
- ❑ 92 Wesley Person .10 .05
- ❑ 93 Aaron McKie .10 .05
- ❑ 94 Jermaine O'Neal RC .60 .25
- ❑ 95 Clifford Robinson .10 .05
- ❑ 96 Arvydas Sabonis .15 .07
- ❑ 97 Gary Trent .10 .05
- ❑ 98 Tyus Edney .10 .05
- ❑ 99 Brian Grant .30 .14
- ❑ 100 Mitch Richmond .30 .14
- ❑ 101 Billy Owens .10 .05
- ❑ 102 Corliss Williamson .10 .05
- ❑ 103 Vinny Del Negro .10 .05
- ❑ 104 Sean Elliott .10 .05
- ❑ 105 Avery Johnson .10 .05
- ❑ 106 Chuck Person .10 .05
- ❑ 107 David Robinson .50 .23
- ❑ 108 Hersey Hawkins .15 .07
- ❑ 109 Shawn Kemp .50 .23
- ❑ 110 Gary Payton .50 .23
- ❑ 111 Sam Perkins .15 .07
- ❑ 112 Detlef Schrempf .15 .07
- ❑ 113 Marcus Camby RC 1.00 .45
- ❑ 114 Carlos Rogers .10 .05
- ❑ 115 Damon Stoudamire .50 .23
- ❑ 116 Zan Tabak .10 .05
- ❑ 117 Antoine Carr .10 .05
- ❑ 118 Jeff Hornacek .15 .07
- ❑ 119 Karl Malone .50 .23
- ❑ 120 Chris Morris .10 .05
- ❑ 121 John Stockton .30 .14
- ❑ 122 Shareef Abdur-Rahim RC 2.00 .90
- ❑ 123 Greg Anthony .10 .05
- ❑ 124 Bryant Reeves .10 .05
- ❑ 125 Roy Rogers RC .10 .05
- ❑ 126 Calbert Cheaney .10 .05
- ❑ 127 Juwan Howard .15 .07
- ❑ 128 Gheorghe Muresan .10 .05
- ❑ 129 Chris Webber 1.00 .45
- ❑ 130 Checklist .10 .05
- ❑ 131 Checklist .10 .05
- ❑ 132 Jon Barry .10 .05
- ❑ 133 Christian Laettner .15 .07
- ❑ 134 Dikembe Mutombo .15 .07
- ❑ 135 Dee Brown .10 .05
- ❑ 136 Todd Day .10 .05
- ❑ 137 David Wesley .10 .05
- ❑ 138 Vlade Divac .10 .05
- ❑ 139 Anthony Goldwire .10 .05
- ❑ 140 Anthony Mason .15 .07
- ❑ 141 Jason Caffey .10 .05
- ❑ 142 Luc Longley .10 .05
- ❑ 143 Tyrone Hill .10 .05
- ❑ 144 Antonio Lang .10 .05
- ❑ 145 Sam Cassell .15 .07
- ❑ 146 Chris Gatling .10 .05
- ❑ 147 Eric Montross .10 .05
- ❑ 148 Ervin Johnson .10 .05
- ❑ 149 Sarunas Marciulionis .10 .05
- ❑ 150 Stacey Augmon .10 .05
- ❑ 151 Grant Long .10 .05
- ❑ 152 Terry Mills .10 .05
- ❑ 153 Kenny Smith .10 .05
- ❑ 154 B.J. Armstrong .10 .05
- ❑ 155 Bimbo Coles .10 .05
- ❑ 156 Charles Barkley .50 .23
- ❑ 157 Brent Price .10 .05
- ❑ 158 Duane Ferrell .10 .05
- ❑ 159 Jalen Rose .30 .14
- ❑ 160 Terry Dehere .10 .05
- ❑ 161 Charles Outlaw .10 .05
- ❑ 162 Corie Blount .10 .05
- ❑ 163 Shaquille O'Neal 1.50 .70
- ❑ 164 Rumeal Robinson .10 .05
- ❑ 165 P.J. Brown .10 .05
- ❑ 166 Ronnie Grandison .10 .05
- ❑ 167 Sherman Douglas .10 .05
- ❑ 168 Johnny Newman .10 .05
- ❑ 169 James Robinson .10 .05
- ❑ 170 Doug West .10 .05
- ❑ 171 Robert Pack .10 .05
- ❑ 172 Khalid Reeves .10 .05
- ❑ 173 Chris Childs .10 .05
- ❑ 174 Allan Houston .30 .14
- ❑ 175 Charlie Ward .10 .05
- ❑ 176 Darrell Armstrong RC 2.00 .90
- ❑ 177 Gerald Wilkins .10 .05
- ❑ 178 Lucious Harris .10 .05
- ❑ 179 Robert Horry .10 .05
- ❑ 180 Danny Manning .15 .07
- ❑ 181 Kenny Anderson .15 .07
- ❑ 182 Isaiah Rider .15 .07
- ❑ 183 Rasheed Wallace .40 .18
- ❑ 184 Mahmoud Abdul-Rauf .10 .05
- ❑ 185 Cory Alexander .10 .05
- ❑ 186 Vernon Maxwell .10 .05
- ❑ 187 Dominique Wilkins .30 .14
- ❑ 188 Nate McMillan .10 .05
- ❑ 189 Larry Stewart .10 .05
- ❑ 190 Doug Christie .10 .05
- ❑ 191 Hubert Davis .10 .05
- ❑ 192 Walt Williams .10 .05
- ❑ 193 Adam Keefe .10 .05
- ❑ 194 Greg Ostertag .10 .05
- ❑ 195 John Stockton .30 .14
- ❑ 196 George Lynch .10 .05
- ❑ 197 Lee Mayberry .10 .05
- ❑ 198 Tracy Murray .10 .05
- ❑ 199 Rod Strickland .15 .07
- ❑ 200 S. Abdur-Rahim ROO 1.00 .45
- ❑ 201 Ray Allen ROO .50 .23
- ❑ 202 S. Anderson ROO RC .40 .18
- ❑ 203 Kobe Bryant ROO 4.00 1.80
- ❑ 204 Marcus Camby ROO .40 .18
- ❑ 205 Erick Dampier ROO .10 .05
- ❑ 206 Emanual Davis ROO RC .10 .05
- ❑ 207 Tony Delk ROO .10 .05
- ❑ 208 Brian Evans ROO RC .10 .05
- ❑ 209 Derek Fisher ROO RC .50 .23
- ❑ 210 Todd Fuller ROO .10 .05
- ❑ 211 Dean Garrett ROO RC .10 .05
- ❑ 212 Reggie Geary ROO RC .10 .05
- ❑ 213 Darvin Ham ROO RC .10 .05
- ❑ 214 O. Harrington ROO RC .15 .07
- ❑ 215 Shane Heal ROO RC .10 .05
- ❑ 216 Allen Iverson ROO 1.25 .55
- ❑ 217 Dontae' Jones ROO RC .10 .05
- ❑ 218 Kerry Kittles ROO .30 .14
- ❑ 219 P. Lauderdale ROO RC .10 .05
- ❑ 220 R. Livingston ROO RC .10 .05
- ❑ 221 Matt Maloney ROO RC .10 .05
- ❑ 222 Stephon Marbury ROO 1.50 .70
- ❑ 223 Walter McCarty ROO RC .10 .05
- ❑ 224 Amal McCaskill ROO RC .10 .05
- ❑ 225 Jeff McInnis ROO RC .10 .05
- ❑ 226 M.n Muursepp ROO RC .10 .05
- ❑ 227 Steve Nash ROO .10 .05
- ❑ 228 R.n Nembhard ROO RC .10 .05
- ❑ 229 Jermaine O'Neal ROO .30 .14
- ❑ 230 Vitaly Potapenko ROO .10 .05
- ❑ 231 V. Praskevicius ROO RC .10 .05
- ❑ 232 Roy Rogers ROO .10 .05
- ❑ 233 Malik Rose ROO RC .15 .07
- ❑ 234 Antoine Walker ROO 1.50 .70
- ❑ 235 Samaki Walker ROO .10 .05
- ❑ 236 Ben Wallace ROO RC .10 .05
- ❑ 237 John Wallace ROO .15 .07
- ❑ 238 J. Williams ROO RC .50 .23
- ❑ 239 Lorenzen Wright ROO .10 .05
- ❑ 240 Sam Cassell PM .10 .05
- ❑ 241 Anfernee Hardaway PM .60 .25
- ❑ 242 Tim Hardaway PM .15 .07
- ❑ 243 Grant Hill PM 1.00 .45
- ❑ 244 Allan Houston PM .15 .07
- ❑ 245 Juwan Howard PM .10 .05
- ❑ 246 Kevin Johnson PM .15 .07
- ❑ 247 Michael Jordan PM 2.00 .90
- ❑ 248 Jason Kidd PM .30 .14
- ❑ 249 Karl Malone PM .30 .14
- ❑ 250 Reggie Miller PM .15 .07
- ❑ 251 Gary Payton PM .30 .14
- ❑ 252 Wesley Person PM .10 .05
- ❑ 253 Glen Rice PM .10 .05
- ❑ 254 David Robinson PM .30 .14
- ❑ 255 Steve Smith PM .10 .05

❑ 256 Latrell Sprewell PM .... .30 .14
❑ 257 Jerry Stackhouse PM .... .15 .07
❑ 258 Rod Strickland PM .... .10 .05
❑ 259 Nick Van Exel PM .... .10 .05
❑ 260 Charles Barkley DT .... .30 .14
❑ 261 Dale Davis DT .... .10 .05
❑ 262 Patrick Ewing DT............. .15 .07
❑ 263 Michael Finley DT .... .30 .14
❑ 264 Chris Gatling DT .... .10 .05
❑ 265 Armon Gilliam DT .... .10 .05
❑ 266 Tyrone Hill DT .... .10 .05
❑ 267 Robert Horry DT .... .10 .05
❑ 268 Mark Jackson DT .... .10 .05
❑ 269 Shawn Kemp DT .... .30 .14
❑ 270 Jamal Mashburn DT ...... .10 .05
❑ 271 Anthony Mason DT .... .10 .05
❑ 272 Alonzo Mourning DT ...... .15 .07
❑ 273 Dikembe Mutombo DT .. .10 .05
❑ 274 Shaquille O'Neal DT ...... .60 .25
❑ 275 Isaiah Rider DT .... .10 .05
❑ 276 Dennis Rodman DT......... .30 .14
❑ 277 Damon Stoudamire DT .. .30 .14
❑ 278 Chris Webber DT .... .40 .18
❑ 279 Jayson Williams DT........ .10 .05
❑ 280 Checklist .... .10 .05
(132-239)
❑ 281 Checklist .... .10 .05
(240-281/inserts)
❑ NNO Jerry Stackhouse Promo 3.00 1.35

1996-97 SkyBox Premium Rubies

	MINT	NRMT
COMPLETE SET (279)	1800.00	800.00
COMPLETE SERIES 1 (131)	1200.00	550.00
COMPLETE SERIES 2 (148)	600.00	275.00
COMMON CARD	3.00	1.35

*STARS: 12.5X TO 30X BASE CARD HI
*RCs: 6X TO 15X BASE HI
ONE PER SER.1/2 HOBBY BOX

❑ 55 Kobe Bryant 200.00 90.00

1996-97 SkyBox Premium Autographics Black

	MINT	NRMT
COMP.BLACK AU SET (95)	2000.00	900.00
COMMON BLACK AU CARD....	6.00	2.70
COMMON BLUE AU CARD	12.00	5.50
SEMISTARS BLACK	10.00	4.50
SEMISTARS BLUE	20.00	9.00

STATED ODDS 1:72 FLEER/SKYBOX PROD.
*BLUE INK AU: .75X TO 2X HI COLUMN
BLUES: RANDOM INS.IN SKYBOX PRODUCTS
ALL OLAJUWON CARDS SIGNED IN BLUE
ALL PIPPEN CARDS SIGNED IN BLUE
GARNETT BLUE CARDS: 2:1 VERSUS BLACK
NO JOHN WALLACE BLUE AU's EXIST
SET INCLUDES #'s 22A, 61 AND 68
CARDS LISTED BELOW ALPHABETICALLY
BEWARE COUNTERFEITS

❑ 1 Ray Allen..................... 40.00 18.00
❑ 2 Kenny Anderson 15.00 6.75
❑ 3 Nick Anderson.............. 20.00 9.00
❑ 4 B.J. Armstrong 6.00 2.70
❑ 5 Vincent Askew............... 6.00 2.70
❑ 6 Dana Barros 6.00 2.70
❑ 7 Brent Barry 10.00 4.50
❑ 8 Travis Best 6.00 2.70
❑ 9 Muggsy Bogues 6.00 2.70
❑ 10 P.J. Brown.................... 6.00 2.70
❑ 11 Randy Brown............... 15.00 6.75
❑ 12 Marcus Camby 40.00 18.00
❑ 13 Chris Childs................. 10.00 4.50
❑ 14 Dell Curry 6.00 2.70
❑ 15 Andrew DeClercq 6.00 2.70
❑ 16 Tony Delk 20.00 9.00
❑ 17 Sherman Douglas 6.00 2.70
❑ 18 Clyde Drexler 80.00 36.00
❑ 19 Tyus Edney.................. 6.00 2.70
❑ 20 Michael Finley 25.00 11.00
❑ 21 Rick Fox 6.00 2.70
❑ 22A Kevin Garnett 300.00 135.00
❑ 23 Matt Geiger 6.00 2.70
❑ 24 Kendall Gill 15.00 6.75
❑ 25 Brian Grant 10.00 4.50
❑ 26 Tim Hardaway 20.00 9.00
❑ 27 Grant Hill 120.00 55.00
❑ 28 Tyrone Hill 6.00 2.70
❑ 29 Allan Houston 25.00 11.00
❑ 30 Juwan Howard 120.00 55.00
❑ 31 Zydrunas Ilgauskas 30.00 13.50
❑ 32 Jim Jackson 6.00 2.70
❑ 33 Mark Jackson 10.00 4.50
❑ 34 Eddie Jones 40.00 18.00
❑ 35 Adam Keefe 6.00 2.70
❑ 36 Steve Kerr 15.00 6.75
❑ 37 Kerry Kittles 30.00 13.50
❑ 38 Toni Kukoc 25.00 11.00
❑ 39 Andrew Lang 6.00 2.70
❑ 40 Voshon Lenard 10.00 4.50
❑ 41 Grant Long 6.00 2.70
❑ 42 Luc Longley 20.00 9.00
❑ 43 George Lynch 6.00 2.70
❑ 44 Don MacLean 6.00 2.70
❑ 45 Stephon Marbury.......... 80.00 36.00
❑ 46 Lee Mayberry 6.00 2.70
❑ 47 Walter McCarty 20.00 9.00
❑ 48 George McCloud........... 60.00 27.00
❑ 49 Antonio McDyess 60.00 27.00
❑ 50 Nate McMillan 6.00 2.70
❑ 51 Chris Mills 6.00 2.70
❑ 52 Sam Mitchell 6.00 2.70
❑ 53 Eric Montross 6.00 2.70
❑ 54 Chris Morris................... 6.00 2.70
❑ 55 Lawrence Moten 6.00 2.70
❑ 56 Alonzo Mourning 120.00 55.00
❑ 57 Gheorghe Muresan 6.00 2.70
❑ 58 Steve Nash 100.00 45.00
❑ 59 Ed O'Bannon.................. 6.00 2.70
❑ 60 Charles Oakley 20.00 9.00
❑ 61 Hakeem Olajuwon Blue 120.00 55.00
❑ 62 Greg Ostertag 6.00 2.70
❑ 63 Billy Owens 6.00 2.70
❑ 64 Sam Perkins 10.00 4.50
❑ 65 Chuck Person 6.00 2.70
❑ 66 Wesley Person 6.00 2.70
❑ 67 Bobby Phills 20.00 9.00
❑ 68 Scottie Pippen 150.00 70.00
Blue Ink
❑ 69 Theo Ratliff 10.00 4.50
❑ 70 Glen Rice 15.00 6.75
❑ 71 Rodney Rogers 6.00 2.70
❑ 72 Byron Scott 6.00 2.70
❑ 73 Dennis Scott 6.00 2.70
❑ 74 Joe Smith 25.00 11.00
❑ 75 Kenny Smith 6.00 2.70
❑ 76 Rik Smits........................ 6.00 2.70
❑ 77 Eric Snow 6.00 2.70
❑ 78 Latrell Sprewell 50.00 22.00
❑ 79 Jerry Stackhouse 20.00 9.00
❑ 80 John Starks 20.00 9.00
❑ 81 Bryant Stith 6.00 2.70
❑ 82 Damon Stoudamire 120.00 55.00
❑ 83 Rod Strickland........... 120.00 55.00
❑ 84 Bob Sura 10.00 4.50
❑ 85 Zan Tabak...................... 6.00 2.70
❑ 86 Loy Vaught 6.00 2.70
❑ 87 Antoine Walker 60.00 27.00
❑ 88 Samaki Walker 15.00 6.75
❑ 89 John Wallace............... 20.00 9.00
❑ 90 Bill Wennington 10.00 4.50
❑ 91 David Wesley 6.00 2.70
❑ 92 Doug West 6.00 2.70
❑ 93 Monty Williams 6.00 2.70
❑ 94 Joe Wolf 6.00 2.70
❑ 95 Sharone Wright............. 6.00 2.70

1996-97 SkyBox Premium Close-Ups

	MINT	NRMT
COMPLETE SET (9)	25.00	11.00
COMMON CARD (CU1-CU9)....	2.00	.90

SER.1 STATED ODDS 1:24 HOBBY/RETAIL

❑ CU1 Anfernee Hardaway 6.00 2.70
❑ CU2 Grant Hill 10.00 4.50
❑ CU3 Juwan Howard .... 2.00 .90
❑ CU4 Jason Kidd 6.00 2.70
❑ CU5 Shawn Kemp 3.00 1.35
❑ CU6 Alonzo Mourning .... 2.00 .90
❑ CU7 Hakeem Olajuwon 3.00 1.35
❑ CU8 Jerry Stackhouse .... 2.00 .90
❑ CU9 Damon Stoudamire 3.00 1.35

1996-97 SkyBox Premium Emerald Autographs

	MINT	NRMT
COMPLETE SET (5)	350.00	160.00
COMMON CARD (E1-E5)	25.00	11.00
SER.2 STATED ODDS 1:20 HOBBY BOXES		
❑ E1 Ray Allen	40.00	18.00
❑ E2 Marcus Camby	40.00	18.00
❑ E3 Grant Hill	300.00	135.00
❑ E4 Kerry Kittles	25.00	11.00
❑ E5 Jerry Stackhouse	40.00	18.00
❑ NNO Expired Trade Cards	1.00	.45

1996-97 SkyBox Premium Golden Touch

	MINT	NRMT
COMPLETE SET (10)	200.00	90.00
COMMON CARD (1-10)	4.00	1.80
SEMISTARS	5.00	2.20
UNLISTED STARS	8.00	3.60
SER.2 STATED ODDS 1:240 HOBBY/RETAIL		
❑ 1 Vin Baker	5.00	2.20
❑ 2 Terrell Brandon	4.00	1.80
❑ 3 Allan Houston	8.00	3.60
❑ 4 Allen Iverson	40.00	18.00
❑ 5 Michael Jordan	100.00	45.00
❑ 6 Shawn Kemp	12.00	5.50
❑ 7 Karl Malone	12.00	5.50
❑ 8 Stephon Marbury	25.00	11.00
❑ 9 Latrell Sprewell	15.00	6.75
❑ 10 Damon Stoudamire	12.00	5.50

1996-97 SkyBox Premium Intimidators

	MINT	NRMT
COMPLETE SET (20)	30.00	13.50
COMMON CARD (1-20)	.60	.25
SEMISTARS	1.00	.45
UNLISTED STARS	1.50	.70
SER.2 STATED ODDS 1:8 HOBBY/RETAIL		
❑ 1 Shareef Abdur-Rahim	5.00	2.20
❑ 2 Charles Barkley	2.50	1.10
❑ 3 Marcus Camby	2.50	1.10
❑ 4 Elden Campbell	.60	.25
❑ 5 Derrick Coleman	.60	.25
❑ 6 Patrick Ewing	1.50	.70
❑ 7 Michael Finley	2.00	.90
❑ 8 Kevin Garnett	10.00	4.50
❑ 9 Jim Jackson	.60	.25
❑ 10 Anthony Mason	1.00	.45
❑ 11 Antonio McDyess	2.50	1.10
❑ 12 Alonzo Mourning	1.50	.70
❑ 13 Gheorghe Muresan	.60	.25
❑ 14 Dikembe Mutombo	1.00	.45
❑ 15 Shaquille O'Neal	8.00	3.60
❑ 16 Isaiah Rider	1.00	.45
❑ 17 Clifford Robinson	.60	.25
❑ 18 David Robinson	2.50	1.10
❑ 19 Dennis Rodman	3.00	1.35
❑ 20 Clarence Weatherspoon	.60	.25

1996-97 SkyBox Premium Larger Than Life

	MINT	NRMT
COMPLETE SET (18)	350.00	160.00
COMMON CARD (B1-B18)	4.00	1.80
SEMISTARS	6.00	2.70
UNLISTED STARS	8.00	3.60
SER.1 STATED ODDS 1:180 HOBBY		
❑ B1 Shareef Abdur-Rahim	25.00	11.00
❑ B2 Marcus Camby	12.00	5.50
❑ B3 Kevin Garnett	40.00	18.00
❑ B4 Anfernee Hardaway	20.00	9.00
❑ B5 Grant Hill	30.00	13.50
❑ B6 Allen Iverson	40.00	18.00
❑ B7 Michael Jordan	120.00	55.00
❑ B8 Shawn Kemp	10.00	4.50
❑ B9 Stephon Marbury	25.00	11.00
❑ B10 Jamal Mashburn	6.00	2.70
❑ B11 Antonio McDyess	10.00	4.50
❑ B12 Alonzo Mourning	6.00	2.70
❑ B13 Dikembe Mutombo	4.00	1.80
❑ B14 Hakeem Olajuwon	10.00	4.50
❑ B15 Shaquille O'Neal	30.00	13.50
❑ B16 Dennis Rodman	12.00	5.50
❑ B17 Jerry Stackhouse	8.00	3.60
❑ B18 Damon Stoudamire	10.00	4.50

1996-97 SkyBox Premium Net Set

	MINT	NRMT
COMPLETE SET (20)	200.00	90.00
COMMON CARD (1-20)	5.00	2.20
SER.2 STATED ODDS 1:48 HOBBY		
❑ 1 Vin Baker	5.00	2.20
❑ 2 Clyde Drexler	5.00	2.20
❑ 3 Patrick Ewing	5.00	2.20
❑ 4 Anfernee Hardaway	15.00	6.75
❑ 5 Grant Hill	25.00	11.00
❑ 6 Juwan Howard	5.00	2.20
❑ 7 Allen Iverson	25.00	11.00
❑ 8 Michael Jordan	60.00	27.00
❑ 9 Shawn Kemp	8.00	3.60
❑ 10 Jason Kidd	15.00	6.75
❑ 11 Karl Malone	8.00	3.60
❑ 12 Stephon Marbury	15.00	6.75
❑ 13 Alonzo Mourning	5.00	2.20
❑ 14 Hakeem Olajuwon	8.00	3.60
❑ 15 Shaquille O'Neal	25.00	11.00
❑ 16 Scottie Pippen	15.00	6.75
❑ 17 David Robinson	8.00	3.60
❑ 18 Joe Smith	5.00	2.20
❑ 19 Damon Stoudamire	8.00	3.60
❑ 20 Chris Webber	15.00	6.75

1996-97 SkyBox Premium New Edition

	MINT	NRMT
COMPLETE SET (10)	60.00	27.00
COMMON CARD (1-10)	1.50	.70
SEMISTARS	2.00	.90
UNLISTED STARS	3.00	1.35
SER.2 STATED ODDS 1:36 RETAIL		
❑ 1 Shareef Abdur-Rahim	10.00	4.50
❑ 2 Ray Allen	6.00	2.70
❑ 3 Kobe Bryant	30.00	13.50
❑ 4 Marcus Camby	5.00	2.20
❑ 5 Allen Iverson	15.00	6.75
❑ 6 Kerry Kittles	3.00	1.35
❑ 7 Matt Maloney	1.50	.70
❑ 8 Stephon Marbury	10.00	4.50
❑ 9 Steve Nash	1.50	.70
❑ 10 Samaki Walker	1.50	.70

1996-97 SkyBox Premium Rookie Prevue

	MINT	NRMT
COMPLETE SET (18)	120.00	55.00

COMMON CARD (R1-R18)	1.50	.70
SEMISTARS	3.00	1.35
UNLISTED STARS	5.00	2.20

SER.1 STATED ODDS 1:54 HOBBY/RETAIL

❑ R1 Shareef Abdur-Rahim	15.00	6.75
❑ R2 Ray Allen	10.00	4.50
❑ R3 Kobe Bryant	50.00	22.00
❑ R4 Marcus Camby	8.00	3.60
❑ R5 Erick Dampier	1.50	.70
❑ R6 Tony Delk	1.50	.70
❑ R7 Brian Evans	1.50	.70
❑ R8 Todd Fuller	1.50	.70
❑ R9 Allen Iverson	25.00	11.00
❑ R10 Kerry Kittles	5.00	2.20
❑ R11 Stephon Marbury	15.00	6.75
❑ R12 Steve Nash	1.50	.70
❑ R13 Vitaly Potapenko	1.50	.70
❑ R14 Roy Rogers	1.50	.70
❑ R15 Antoine Walker	10.00	4.50
❑ R16 Samaki Walker	1.50	.70
❑ R17 John Wallace	3.00	1.35
❑ R18 Lorenzen Wright	1.50	.70

1996-97 SkyBox Premium Standouts

	MINT	NRMT
COMPLETE SET (9)	150.00	70.00
COMMON CARD (SO1-SO9)	10.00	4.50

SER.1 STATED ODDS 1:180 RETAIL

❑ SO1 Grant Hill	50.00	22.00
❑ SO2 Juwan Howard	10.00	4.50
❑ SO3 Jason Kidd	30.00	13.50
❑ SO4 Reggie Miller	10.00	4.50
❑ SO5 Shaquille O'Neal	50.00	22.00
❑ SO6 Gary Payton	15.00	6.75
❑ SO7 Scottie Pippen	30.00	13.50
❑ SO8 Mitch Richmond	10.00	4.50
❑ SO9 Joe Smith	10.00	4.50

1996-97 SkyBox Premium Thunder and Lightning

	MINT	NRMT
COMPLETE SET (10)	150.00	70.00
COMMON CARD (1-10)	4.00	1.80

SER.2 STATED ODDS 1:144 HOBBY/RETAIL

❑ 1 Michael Jordan Scottie Pippen	60.00	27.00
❑ 2 Kevin Johnson Danny Manning	4.00	1.80
❑ 3 Grant Hill Joe Dumars	25.00	11.00
❑ 4 Latrell Sprewell Joe Smith	12.00	5.50
❑ 5 Charles Barkley Hakeem Olajuwon	15.00	6.75
❑ 6 Vin Baker Glenn Robinson	4.00	1.80
❑ 7 Patrick Ewing Larry Johnson	10.00	4.50
❑ 8 Shawn Kemp Gary Payton	15.00	6.75
❑ 9 Karl Malone John Stockton	15.00	6.75
❑ 10 Juwan Howard Chris Webber	15.00	6.75

1996-97 SkyBox Premium Triple Threats

	MINT	NRMT
COMPLETE SET (9)	1.50	.70
COMMON CARD (TT1-TT12)	.10	.05
SEMISTARS	.15	.07
UNLISTED STARS	.30	.14

SPs: SER.1 STATED ODDS 1:720 HOB/RET
SPs NOT CONSIDERED PART OF SET
*RUBIES: 12.5X TO 30X HI COLUMN
RUBIES: ONE PER HOBBY BOX
SPs DO NOT HAVE RUBY PARALLEL

❑ TT1 Chris Mullin	.30	.14
❑ TT2 Joe Smith	.30	.14
❑ TT3 Latrell Sprewell	.60	.25
❑ TT4 Avery Johnson	.10	.05
❑ TT5 Sean Elliott	.10	.05
❑ TT6 David Robinson	.50	.23
❑ TT7 John Stockton	.30	.14
❑ TT8 Karl Malone	.50	.23
❑ TT9 Jeff Hornacek	.15	.07
❑ TT10 Dennis Rodman SP	10.00	4.50
❑ TT11 Michael Jordan SP	60.00	27.00
❑ TT12 Scottie Pippen SP	15.00	6.75

1997-98 SkyBox Premium

	MINT	NRMT
COMPLETE SET (250)	90.00	40.00
COMPLETE SERIES 1 (125)	25.00	11.00
COMPLETE SERIES 2 (125)	70.00	32.00
COMMON CARD (1-250)	.15	.07
SEMISTARS	.20	.09
UNLISTED STARS	.40	.18

TS SUBSET 1:4 HOB/RET
TS SUBSET: .75X TO 2X BASE CARD HI

COMMON REEBOK BRONZE	.20	.09

*REEBOK BRONZE: .25X TO .5X HI COLUMN

COMMON REEBOK GOLD	.60	.25

*REEBOK GOLD: 1.5X TO 3X HI

COMMON REEBOK SILVER	.30	.14

*REEBOK SILVER: .5X TO 1X HI
REEBOK: ONE PER SER.1 PACK

❑ 1 Grant Hill	2.00	.90
❑ 2 Matt Maloney	.15	.07
❑ 3 Vinny Del Negro	.15	.07
❑ 4 Kevin Willis	.15	.07
❑ 5 Mark Jackson	.15	.07
❑ 6 Ray Allen	.60	.25
❑ 7 Derrick Coleman	.20	.09
❑ 8 Isaiah Rider	.20	.09
❑ 9 Rod Strickland	.20	.09
❑ 10 Danny Ferry	.15	.07
❑ 11 Antonio Davis	.15	.07
❑ 12 Glenn Robinson	.20	.09
❑ 13 Cedric Ceballos	.15	.07
❑ 14 Sean Elliott	.15	.07
❑ 15 Walt Williams	.15	.07
❑ 16 Glen Rice	.20	.09
❑ 17 Clyde Drexler	.40	.18
❑ 18 Sherman Douglas	.15	.07
❑ 19 Othella Harrington	.15	.07
❑ 20 John Stockton	.40	.18
❑ 21 Priest Lauderdale	.15	.07
❑ 22 Khalid Reeves	.15	.07
❑ 23 Kobe Bryant	3.00	1.35
❑ 24 Vin Baker	.20	.09
❑ 25 Steve Nash	.15	.07
❑ 26 Jeff Hornacek	.20	.09
❑ 27 Tyrone Corbin	.15	.07
❑ 28 Charles Barkley	.60	.25
❑ 29 Michael Jordan	5.00	2.20
❑ 30 Latrell Sprewell	.75	.35
❑ 31 Anfernee Hardaway	1.25	.55
❑ 32 Steve Kerr	.15	.07
❑ 33 Joe Smith	.20	.09
❑ 34 Jermaine O'Neal	.20	.09
❑ 35 Ron Mercer RC	1.25	.55
❑ 36 Antonio McDyess	.50	.23
❑ 37 Patrick Ewing	.40	.18
❑ 38 Avery Johnson	.15	.07
❑ 39 Toni Kukoc	.50	.23
❑ 40 Sam Perkins	.20	.09
❑ 41 Voshon Lenard	.15	.07
❑ 42 Detlef Schrempf	.20	.09
❑ 43 Horace Grant	.20	.09
❑ 44 Luc Longley	.15	.07
❑ 45 Todd Fuller	.15	.07
❑ 46 Tim Hardaway	.40	.18
❑ 47 Nick Anderson	.15	.07
❑ 48 Scottie Pippen	1.25	.55
❑ 49 Lindsey Hunter	.15	.07
❑ 50 Shawn Kemp	.60	.25
❑ 51 Larry Johnson	.20	.09
❑ 52 Shawn Bradley	.15	.07
❑ 53 Martin Muursepp	.15	.07
❑ 54 Jamal Mashburn	.20	.09
❑ 55 John Starks	.15	.07
❑ 56 Rony Seikaly	.15	.07
❑ 57 Gary Payton	.60	.25
❑ 58 Juwan Howard	.20	.09
❑ 59 Vitaly Potapenko	.15	.07
❑ 60 Reggie Miller	.40	.18
❑ 61 Alonzo Mourning	.40	.18
❑ 62 Roy Rogers	.15	.07
❑ 63 Antoine Walker	.75	.35
❑ 64 Joe Dumars	.40	.18
❑ 65 Allan Houston	.40	.18

Card	Player	MINT	NRMT
❑ 66	Hersey Hawkins	.20	.09
❑ 67	Dell Curry	.15	.07
❑ 68	Tony Delk	.15	.07
❑ 69	Mookie Blaylock	.15	.07
❑ 70	Derek Harper	.15	.07
❑ 71	Loy Vaught	.15	.07
❑ 72	Tom Gugliotta	.20	.09
❑ 73	Mitch Richmond	.40	.18
❑ 74	Dikembe Mutombo	.20	.09
❑ 75	Tony Battie RC	.40	.18
❑ 76	Derek Fisher	.15	.07
❑ 77	Jason Kidd	1.25	.55
❑ 78	Shareef Abdur-Rahim	1.25	.55
❑ 79	Tracy McGrady RC	4.00	1.80
❑ 80	Anthony Mason	.20	.09
❑ 81	Mario Elie	.15	.07
❑ 82	Karl Malone	.60	.25
❑ 83	Mark Price	.15	.07
❑ 84	Steve Smith	.20	.09
❑ 85	LaPhonso Ellis	.15	.07
❑ 86	Robert Horry	.15	.07
❑ 87	Wesley Person	.15	.07
❑ 88	Marcus Camby	.50	.23
❑ 89	Antonio Daniels RC	.40	.18
❑ 90	Eddie Jones	.75	.35
❑ 91	Gary Trent	.15	.07
❑ 92	Danny Fortson RC	.40	.18
❑ 93	Chris Childs	.15	.07
❑ 94	David Robinson	.60	.25
❑ 95	Bryant Reeves	.15	.07
❑ 96	Chris Webber	1.25	.55
❑ 97	P.J. Brown	.15	.07
❑ 98	Tyrone Hill	.15	.07
❑ 99	Dale Davis	.15	.07
❑ 100	Allen Iverson	2.00	.90
❑ 101	Jerry Stackhouse	.20	.09
❑ 102	Arvydas Sabonis	.20	.09
❑ 103	Damon Stoudamire	.50	.23
❑ 104	Tim Thomas RC	1.25	.55
❑ 105	Christian Laettner	.20	.09
❑ 106	Robert Pack	.15	.07
❑ 107	Lorenzen Wright	.15	.07
❑ 108	Olden Polynice	.15	.07
❑ 109	Terrell Brandon	.20	.09
❑ 110	Theo Ratliff	.15	.07
❑ 111	Kevin Garnett	2.50	1.10
❑ 112	Tim Duncan RC	5.00	2.20
❑ 113	Bryon Russell	.15	.07
❑ 114	Chauncey Billups RC	.50	.23
❑ 115	Dale Ellis	.15	.07
❑ 116	Shaquille O'Neal	2.00	.90
❑ 117	Keith Van Horn RC	2.00	.90
❑ 118	Kenny Anderson	.20	.09
❑ 119	Dennis Rodman	.75	.35
❑ 120	Hakeem Olajuwon	.60	.25
❑ 121	Stephon Marbury	1.25	.55
❑ 122	Kendall Gill	.20	.09
❑ 123	Kerry Kittles	.40	.18
❑ 124	Checklist	.15	.07
❑ 125	Checklist	.15	.07
❑ 126	Anthony Johnson RC	.15	.07
❑ 127	Chris Anstey RC	.15	.07
❑ 128	Dean Garrett	.15	.07
❑ 129	Rik Smits	.15	.07
❑ 130	Tracy Murray	.15	.07
❑ 131	Charles O'Bannon RC	.15	.07
❑ 132	Eldridge Recasner	.15	.07
❑ 133	Johnny Taylor RC	.15	.07
❑ 134	Priest Lauderdale	.15	.07
❑ 135	Rod Strickland	.20	.09
❑ 136	Alan Henderson	.15	.07
❑ 137	Austin Croshere RC	1.00	.45
❑ 138	Buck Williams	.15	.07
❑ 139	Clifford Robinson	.15	.07
❑ 140	Darrell Armstrong	.20	.09
❑ 141	Dennis Scott	.15	.07
❑ 142	Carl Herrera	.15	.07
❑ 143	Maurice Taylor RC	.75	.35
❑ 144	Chris Gatling	.15	.07
❑ 145	Alvin Williams RC	.15	.07
❑ 146	Antonio McDyess	.50	.23
❑ 147	Chauncey Billups	.15	.07
❑ 148	George McCloud	.15	.07
❑ 149	George Lynch	.15	.07
❑ 150	John Thomas RC	.15	.07
❑ 151	Jayson Williams	.20	.09
❑ 152	Otis Thorpe	.15	.07
❑ 153	Serge Zwikker RC	.15	.07
❑ 154	Chris Crawford RC	.15	.07
❑ 155	Muggsy Bogues	.15	.07
❑ 156	Mark Jackson	.15	.07
❑ 157	Dontonio Wingfield	.15	.07
❑ 158	Rodrick Rhodes RC	.15	.07
❑ 159	Sam Cassell	.20	.09
❑ 160	Hubert Davis	.15	.07
❑ 161	Clarence Weatherspoon	.15	.07
❑ 162	Eddie Johnson	.15	.07
❑ 163	Jacque Vaughn RC	.20	.09
❑ 164	Mark Price	.15	.07
❑ 165	Terry Dehere	.15	.07
❑ 166	Travis Knight	.15	.07
❑ 167	Charles Smith RC	.15	.07
❑ 168	David Wesley	.15	.07
❑ 169	David Wingate	.15	.07
❑ 170	Todd Day	.15	.07
❑ 171	Adonal Foyle RC	.20	.09
❑ 172	Chris Mills	.15	.07
❑ 173	Paul Grant RC	.15	.07
❑ 174	Adam Keefe	.15	.07
❑ 175	Erick Dampier UER back Eric	.15	.07
❑ 176	Ervin Johnson	.15	.07
❑ 177	Lamond Murray	.15	.07
❑ 178	Vlade Divac	.15	.07
❑ 179	Bobby Phills	.15	.07
❑ 180	Brian Williams	.15	.07
❑ 181	Chris Dudley	.15	.07
❑ 182	Tyrone Hill	.15	.07
❑ 183	Donyell Marshall	.15	.07
❑ 184	Kevin Gamble	.15	.07
❑ 185	Scot Pollard RC	.20	.09
❑ 186	Cherokee Parks	.15	.07
❑ 187	Terry Mills	.15	.07
❑ 188	Glen Rice	.20	.09
❑ 189	Shawn Respert	.15	.07
❑ 190	Terrell Brandon	.20	.09
❑ 191	Keith Closs RC	.15	.07
❑ 192	Tariq Abdul-Wahad RC	.20	.09
❑ 193	Wesley Person	.15	.07
❑ 194	Chuck Person	.15	.07
❑ 195	Derek Anderson RC	1.00	.45
❑ 196	Jon Barry	.15	.07
❑ 197	Chris Mullin	.40	.18
❑ 198	Ed Gray RC	.15	.07
❑ 199	Charlie Ward	.15	.07
❑ 200	Kelvin Cato RC	.40	.18
❑ 201	Michael Finley	.40	.18
❑ 202	Rick Fox	.15	.07
❑ 203	Scott Burrell	.15	.07
❑ 204	Vin Baker	.20	.09
❑ 205	Eric Snow	.15	.07
❑ 206	Isaac Austin	.15	.07
❑ 207	Keith Booth RC	.15	.07
❑ 208	Brian Grant	.20	.09
❑ 209	Chris Webber	1.25	.55
❑ 210	Eric Williams	.15	.07
❑ 211	Jim Jackson	.15	.07
❑ 212	Anthony Parker RC	.15	.07
❑ 213	Brevin Knight RC	.60	.25
❑ 214	Cory Alexander	.15	.07
❑ 215	James Robinson	.15	.07
❑ 216	Bobby Jackson RC	.20	.09
❑ 217	Charles Outlaw	.15	.07
❑ 218	God Shammgod RC	.15	.07
❑ 219	James Cotton RC	.15	.07
❑ 220	Jud Buechler	.15	.07
❑ 221	Shandon Anderson	.15	.07
❑ 222	Kevin Johnson	.20	.09
❑ 223	Chris Morris	.15	.07
❑ 224	Shareef Abdur-Rahim TS	2.50	1.10
❑ 225	Ray Allen TS	1.00	.45
❑ 226	Kobe Bryant TS	8.00	3.60
❑ 227	Marcus Camby TS	1.00	.45
❑ 228	Antonio Daniels TS	1.00	.45
❑ 229	Tim Duncan TS	5.00	2.20
❑ 230	Kevin Garnett TS	5.00	2.20
❑ 231	Anfernee Hardaway TS	3.00	1.35
❑ 232	Grant Hill TS	5.00	2.20
❑ 233	Allen Iverson TS	4.00	1.80
❑ 234	Bobby Jackson TS	.75	.35
❑ 235	Michael Jordan TS	10.00	4.50
❑ 236	Shawn Kemp TS	1.50	.70
❑ 237	Karl Malone TS	1.25	.55
❑ 238	Stephon Marbury TS	3.00	1.35
❑ 239	Hakeem Olajuwon TS	1.50	.70
❑ 240	Shaquille O'Neal TS	3.00	1.35
❑ 241	Gary Payton TS	1.25	.55
❑ 242	Scottie Pippen TS	2.50	1.10
❑ 243	David Robinson TS	1.25	.55
❑ 244	Dennis Rodman TS	2.50	1.10
❑ 245	Jerry Stackhouse TS	.75	.35
❑ 246	Damon Stoudamire TS	1.25	.55
❑ 247	Keith Van Horn TS	3.00	1.35
❑ 248	Antoine Walker TS	3.00	1.35
❑ 249	Grant Hill CL	.50	.23
❑ 250	Hakeem Olajuwon CL	.20	.09
❑ NNO	Allen Iverson Ruby Shoe	25.00	11.00
❑ NNO	Allen Iverson Gold Shoe	8.00	3.60
❑ NNO	Allen Iverson Bronze Shoe	2.00	.90
❑ NNO	Allen Iverson Emerald Shoe	60.00	27.00
❑ NNO	Allen Iverson Silver Shoe	4.00	1.80

1997-98 SkyBox Premium Star Rubies

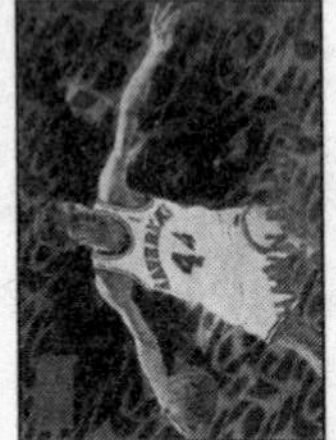

	MINT	NRMT
COMMON CARD (1-250)	40.00	18.00

*STARS: 100X TO 200X BASE CARD HI
*RCs: 50X TO 100X BASE HI
*TS: 30X TO 80X BASE SUBSET HI
*TS RCs: 15X TO 40X BASE SUBSET HI
RANDOM INS.IN BOTH SERIES HOB.PACKS
STATED PRINT RUN 50 SERIAL #'d SETS
SUBSETS ARE NOT SP'S IN PARALLEL SET

Card	Player	MINT	NRMT
❑ 23	Kobe Bryant	750.00	350.00
❑ 29	Michael Jordan	2000.00	900.00
❑ 31	Anfernee Hardaway	400.00	180.00
❑ 39	Toni Kukoc	150.00	70.00
❑ 112	Tim Duncan	400.00	180.00
❑ 226	Kobe Bryant TS	600.00	275.00
❑ 229	Tim Duncan TS	300.00	135.00
❑ 235	Michael Jordan TS	1600.00	700.00
❑ 247	Keith Van Horn TS	150.00	70.00
❑ 249	Grant Hill CL	250.00	110.00
❑ 250	Hakeem Olajuwon CL	80.00	36.00

1997-98 SkyBox Premium And One

	MINT	NRMT
COMPLETE SET (10)	100.00	45.00
COMMON CARD (1-10)	6.00	2.70

SER.1 STATED ODDS 1:96 HOB/RET

Card	Player	MINT	NRMT
❑ 1	Shawn Kemp	8.00	3.60
❑ 2	Hakeem Olajuwon	8.00	3.60
❑ 3	Charles Barkley	8.00	3.60
❑ 4	Antoine Walker	10.00	4.50
❑ 5	Dennis Rodman	10.00	4.50
❑ 6	Tim Duncan	25.00	11.00
❑ 7	Marcus Camby	6.00	2.70
❑ 8	Keith Van Horn	12.00	5.50

		MINT	NRMT
❑ 9	Shareef Abdur-Rahim	15.00	6.75
❑ 10	Michael Jordan	60.00	27.00

1997-98 SkyBox Premium Autographics

	MINT	NRMT
COMPLETE SET (119)	2500.00	1100.00
COMMON AUTOGRAPH	6.00	2.70
SEMISTARS	12.00	5.50
COMMON CENTURY MARK	12.00	5.50

CENTURY MARKS: 1X TO 2X HI COLUMN
C.M: STATED PRT.RUN 100 SERIAL #'d SETS
ALL MCGRADY CARDS ARE CEN.MARKS
ALL R.WALLACE CARDS ARE CEN.MARKS
SET INCLUDES #'s 71 AND 108
STATED ODDS 1:240 HOOPS 1
STATED ODDS 1:144 HOOPS 2
STATED ODDS 1:96 METAL
STATED ODDS 1:72 METAL CHAMP.
STATED ODDS 1:72 SKYBOX 1,2
STATED ODDS 1:60 SKY.E-X2001
STATED ODDS 1:120 Z-FORCE 1,2
CARDS LISTED BELOW ALPHABETICALLY

		MINT	NRMT
❑ 1	Shareef Abdur-Rahim	60.00	27.00
❑ 2	Cory Alexander	6.00	2.70
❑ 3	Kenny Anderson	15.00	6.75
❑ 4	Nick Anderson	12.00	5.50
❑ 5	Stacey Augmon	6.00	2.70
❑ 6	Isaac Austin	6.00	2.70
❑ 7	Vin Baker	15.00	6.75
❑ 8	Charles Barkley	300.00	135.00
❑ 9	Dana Barros	6.00	2.70
❑ 10	Brent Barry	6.00	2.70
❑ 11	Tony Battie	12.00	5.50
❑ 12	Travis Best	6.00	2.70
❑ 13	Corie Blount	6.00	2.70
❑ 14	P.J. Brown	6.00	2.70
❑ 15	Randy Brown	12.00	5.50
❑ 16	Jud Buechler	12.00	5.50
❑ 17	Marcus Camby	25.00	11.00
❑ 18	Elden Campbell	6.00	2.70
❑ 19	Chris Carr	6.00	2.70
❑ 20	Kelvin Cato	20.00	9.00
❑ 21	Duane Causwell	6.00	2.70
❑ 22	Rex Chapman	30.00	13.50
❑ 23	Calbert Cheaney	6.00	2.70
❑ 24	Randolph Childress	6.00	2.70
❑ 25	Derrick Coleman	25.00	11.00
❑ 26	Austin Croshere	30.00	13.50
❑ 27	Dell Curry	6.00	2.70
❑ 28	Ben Davis	6.00	2.70
❑ 29	Mark Davis	6.00	2.70
❑ 30	Andrew DeClercq	6.00	2.70
❑ 31	Tony Delk	12.00	5.50
❑ 32	Vlade Divac	6.00	2.70
❑ 33	Clyde Drexler	80.00	36.00
❑ 34	Joe Dumars	20.00	9.00
❑ 35	Howard Eisley	6.00	2.70
❑ 36	Danny Ferry	6.00	2.70
❑ 37	Michael Finley	25.00	11.00
❑ 38	Derek Fisher	15.00	6.75
❑ 39	Danny Fortson	25.00	11.00
❑ 40	Todd Fuller	6.00	2.70
❑ 41	Chris Gatling	6.00	2.70
❑ 42	Matt Geiger	6.00	2.70
❑ 43	Brian Grant	12.00	5.50
❑ 44	Tom Gugliotta	25.00	11.00
❑ 45	Tim Hardaway	40.00	18.00
❑ 46	Ron Harper	30.00	13.50
❑ 47	Othella Harrington	6.00	2.70
❑ 48	Grant Hill	120.00	55.00
❑ 49	Tyrone Hill	6.00	2.70
❑ 50	Allan Houston	20.00	9.00
❑ 51	Juwan Howard	25.00	11.00
❑ 52	Lindsey Hunter	30.00	13.50
❑ 53	Bobby Hurley	6.00	2.70
❑ 54	Jim Jackson	6.00	2.70
❑ 55	Avery Johnson	6.00	2.70
❑ 56	Eddie Johnson	6.00	2.70
❑ 57	Ervin Johnson	6.00	2.70
❑ 58	Larry Johnson	15.00	6.75
❑ 59	Popeye Jones	6.00	2.70
❑ 60	Adam Keefe	6.00	2.70
❑ 61	Steve Kerr	12.00	5.50
❑ 62	Kerry Kittles	25.00	11.00
❑ 63	Brevin Knight	15.00	6.75
❑ 64	Travis Knight	12.00	5.50
❑ 65	George Lynch	6.00	2.70
❑ 66	Don MacLean	6.00	2.70
❑ 67	Stephon Marbury	80.00	36.00
❑ 68	Donny Marshall	6.00	2.70
❑ 69	Walter McCarty	6.00	2.70
❑ 70	Antonio McDyess	40.00	18.00
❑ 72	Ron Mercer	20.00	9.00
❑ 73	Reggie Miller	200.00	90.00
❑ 74	Chris Mills	6.00	2.70
❑ 75	Sam Mitchell	6.00	2.70
❑ 76	Chris Morris	6.00	2.70
❑ 77	Alonzo Mourning	50.00	22.00
❑ 78	Chris Mullin	40.00	18.00
❑ 79	Dikembe Mutombo	30.00	13.50
❑ 80	Anthony Parker	25.00	11.00
❑ 81	Sam Perkins	12.00	5.50
❑ 82	Elliot Perry	6.00	2.70
❑ 83	Bobby Phills	6.00	2.70
❑ 84	Eric Piatkowski	6.00	2.70
❑ 85	Scottie Pippen	120.00	55.00
❑ 86	Vitaly Potapenko	6.00	2.70
❑ 87	Brent Price	6.00	2.70
❑ 88	Theo Ratliff	6.00	2.70
❑ 89	Glen Rice	20.00	9.00
❑ 90	Glenn Robinson	25.00	11.00
❑ 91	Dennis Rodman	250.00	110.00
❑ 92	Roy Rogers	6.00	2.70
❑ 93	Malik Rose	6.00	2.70
❑ 94	Joe Smith	20.00	9.00
❑ 95	Tony Smith	6.00	2.70
❑ 96	Eric Snow	6.00	2.70
❑ 97	Jerry Stackhouse Pistons Uniform	80.00	36.00
❑ 98	Jerry Stackhouse Sixers Uniform	25.00	11.00
❑ 99	John Starks	20.00	9.00
❑ 100	Bryant Stith	6.00	2.70
❑ 101	Erick Strickland	6.00	2.70
❑ 102	Rod Strickland	40.00	18.00
❑ 103	Nick Van Exel	20.00	9.00
❑ 104	Keith Van Horn	40.00	18.00
❑ 105	David Vaughn	6.00	2.70
❑ 106	Jacque Vaughn	6.00	2.70
❑ 107	Antoine Walker	25.00	11.00
❑ 109	Clarence Weatherspoon	6.00	2.70
❑ 110	David Wesley	6.00	2.70
❑ 111	Dominique Wilkins	30.00	13.50
❑ 112	Gerald Wilkins	6.00	2.70
❑ 113	Eric Williams	6.00	2.70
❑ 114	John Williams	6.00	2.70
❑ 115	Lorenzo Williams	6.00	2.70
❑ 116	Monty Williams	6.00	2.70
❑ 117	Scott Williams	6.00	2.70
❑ 118	Walt Williams	6.00	2.70
❑ 119	Lorenzen Wright	6.00	2.70

1997-98 SkyBox Premium Competitive Advantage

	MINT	NRMT
COMPLETE SET (15)	150.00	70.00
COMMON CARD (CA1-CA15)	3.00	1.35

SER.2 STATED ODDS 1:96 HOB/RET

		MINT	NRMT
❑ CA1	Allen Iverson	15.00	6.75
❑ CA2	Kobe Bryant	25.00	11.00
❑ CA3	Michael Jordan	40.00	18.00
❑ CA4	Shaquille O'Neal	15.00	6.75
❑ CA5	Stephon Marbury	10.00	4.50
❑ CA6	Shareef Abdur-Rahim	10.00	4.50
❑ CA7	Marcus Camby	4.00	1.80
❑ CA8	Kevin Garnett	20.00	9.00
❑ CA9	Dennis Rodman	6.00	2.70
❑ CA10	Anfernee Hardaway	10.00	4.50
❑ CA11	Ray Allen	5.00	2.20
❑ CA12	Scottie Pippen	10.00	4.50
❑ CA13	Shawn Kemp	5.00	2.20
❑ CA14	Hakeem Olajuwon	5.00	2.20
❑ CA15	John Stockton	3.00	1.35

1997-98 SkyBox Premium Golden Touch

	MINT	NRMT
COMPLETE SET (15)	500.00	220.00
COMMON CARD (GT1-GT15)	10.00	4.50

SER.2 STATED ODDS 1:360 HOB/RET

		MINT	NRMT
❑ GT1	Michael Jordan	120.00	55.00
❑ GT2	Allen Iverson	50.00	22.00
❑ GT3	Kobe Bryant	80.00	36.00
❑ GT4	Shaquille O'Neal	50.00	22.00
❑ GT5	Stephon Marbury	30.00	13.50
❑ GT6	Marcus Camby	12.00	5.50
❑ GT7	Anfernee Hardaway	30.00	13.50

		MINT	NRMT
❑ GT8	Kevin Garnett	60.00	27.00
❑ GT9	Shareef Abdur-Rahim	30.00	13.50
❑ GT10	Dennis Rodman	20.00	9.00
❑ GT11	Grant Hill	50.00	22.00
❑ GT12	Kerry Kittles	10.00	4.50
❑ GT13	Antoine Walker	20.00	9.00
❑ GT14	Scottie Pippen	30.00	13.50
❑ GT15	Damon Stoudamire	12.00	5.50

1997-98 SkyBox Premium Jam Pack

	MINT	NRMT
COMPLETE SET (15)	40.00	18.00
COMMON CARD (JP1-JP15)	1.50	.70
SEMISTARS	2.00	.90
UNLISTED STARS	3.00	1.35

SER.2 STATED ODDS 1:18 HOB/RET

		MINT	NRMT
❑ JP1	Ray Allen	5.00	2.20
❑ JP2	Damon Stoudamire	4.00	1.80
❑ JP3	Shawn Kemp	5.00	2.20
❑ JP4	Hakeem Olajuwon	5.00	2.20
❑ JP5	Jerry Stackhouse	2.00	.90
❑ JP6	John Wallace	1.50	.70
❑ JP7	Juwan Howard	2.00	.90
❑ JP8	David Robinson	5.00	2.20
❑ JP9	Gary Payton	5.00	2.20
❑ JP10	Joe Smith	2.00	.90
❑ JP11	Charles Barkley	5.00	2.20
❑ JP12	Terrell Brandon	2.00	.90
❑ JP13	Vin Baker	2.00	.90
❑ JP14	Antonio McDyess	4.00	1.80
❑ JP15	Tim Duncan	15.00	6.75

1997-98 SkyBox Premium Next Game

	MINT	NRMT
COMPLETE SET (15)	15.00	6.75
COMMON CARD (1-15)	.60	.25
SEMISTARS	.75	.35
UNLISTED STARS	1.25	.55

SER.1 STATED ODDS 1:6 HOB/RET

		MINT	NRMT
❑ 1	Derek Anderson	1.50	.70
❑ 2	Tony Battie	.60	.25
❑ 3	Chauncey Billups	.75	.35
❑ 4	Kelvin Cato	.60	.25
❑ 5	Austin Croshere	1.50	.70
❑ 6	Antonio Daniels	.75	.35
❑ 7	Tim Duncan	6.00	2.70
❑ 8	Danny Fortson	.60	.25
❑ 9	Adonal Foyle	.60	.25
❑ 10	Tracy McGrady	6.00	2.70
❑ 11	Ron Mercer	2.00	.90
❑ 12	Olivier Saint-Jean	.60	.25
❑ 13	Maurice Taylor	1.25	.55
❑ 14	Tim Thomas	2.00	.90
❑ 15	Keith Van Horn	3.00	1.35

1997-98 SkyBox Premium Premium Players

	MINT	NRMT
COMPLETE SET (15)	400.00	180.00
COMMON CARD (1-15)	8.00	3.60

SER 1 STATED ODDS 1:192 HOB/RET

		MINT	NRMT
❑ 1	Michael Jordan	100.00	45.00
❑ 2	Allen Iverson	40.00	18.00
❑ 3	Kobe Bryant	60.00	27.00
❑ 4	Shaquille O'Neal	40.00	18.00
❑ 5	Stephon Marbury	25.00	11.00
❑ 6	Marcus Camby	10.00	4.50
❑ 7	Anfernee Hardaway	25.00	11.00
❑ 8	Kevin Garnett	50.00	22.00
❑ 9	Shareef Abdur-Rahim	25.00	11.00
❑ 10	Dennis Rodman	15.00	6.75
❑ 11	Ray Allen	12.00	5.50
❑ 12	Grant Hill	40.00	18.00
❑ 13	Kerry Kittles	8.00	3.60
❑ 14	Karl Malone	12.00	5.50
❑ 15	Scottie Pippen	25.00	11.00

1997-98 SkyBox Premium Rock 'n Fire

	MINT	NRMT
COMPLETE SET (10)	80.00	36.00
COMMON CARD (1-10)	3.00	1.35

SER 1 STATED ODDS 1:18 HOB/RET

		MINT	NRMT
❑ 1	Allen Iverson	12.00	5.50
❑ 2	Kobe Bryant	20.00	9.00
❑ 3	Shaquille O'Neal	12.00	5.50
❑ 4	Stephon Marbury	8.00	3.60
❑ 5	Marcus Camby	3.00	1.35
❑ 6	Anfernee Hardaway	8.00	3.60
❑ 7	Kevin Garnett	15.00	6.75
❑ 8	Shareef Abdur-Rahim	8.00	3.60
❑ 9	Damon Stoudamire	3.00	1.35
❑ 10	Grant Hill	12.00	5.50

1997-98 SkyBox Premium Silky Smooth

	MINT	NRMT
COMPLETE SET (10)	450.00	200.00
COMMON CARD (1-10)	15.00	6.75

SER.1 STATED ODDS 1:360 HOB/RET

		MINT	NRMT
❑ 1	Michael Jordan	120.00	55.00
❑ 2	Allen Iverson	50.00	22.00
❑ 3	Kobe Bryant	80.00	36.00
❑ 4	Shaquille O'Neal	50.00	22.00
❑ 5	Stephon Marbury	30.00	13.50
❑ 6	Gary Payton	15.00	6.75
❑ 7	Anfernee Hardaway	30.00	13.50
❑ 8	Kevin Garnett	60.00	27.00
❑ 9	Scottie Pippen	30.00	13.50
❑ 10	Grant Hill	50.00	22.00

1997-98 SkyBox Premium Star Search

	MINT	NRMT
COMPLETE SET (15)	15.00	6.75
COMMON CARD (SS1-SS15)	.60	.25
SEMISTARS	.75	.35
UNLISTED STARS	1.25	.55

SER.2 STATED ODDS 1:6 HOB/RET

		MINT	NRMT
❑ SS1	Tim Duncan	6.00	2.70
❑ SS2	Tony Battie	.60	.25
❑ SS3	Keith Van Horn	3.00	1.35
❑ SS4	Antonio Daniels	.75	.35
❑ SS5	Chauncey Billups	.75	.35
❑ SS6	Ron Mercer	2.00	.90
❑ SS7	Tracy McGrady	6.00	2.70
❑ SS8	Danny Fortson	.60	.25
❑ SS9	Brevin Knight	1.25	.55
❑ SS10	Derek Anderson	1.50	.70
❑ SS11	Bobby Jackson	.60	.25
❑ SS12	Jacque Vaughn	.60	.25
❑ SS13	Tim Thomas	2.00	.90
❑ SS14	Austin Croshere	1.50	.70
❑ SS15	Kelvin Cato	.60	.25

1997-98 SkyBox Premium Thunder and Lightning

	MINT	NRMT
COMPLETE SET (15)	400.00	180.00
COMMON CARD (TL1-TL15)	8.00	3.60
SER.2 STATED ODDS 1:192 HOB/RET		

Card	MINT	NRMT
❑ TL1 Stephon Marbury	25.00	11.00
❑ TL2 Shareef Abdur-Rahim	25.00	11.00
❑ TL3 Shaquille O'Neal	40.00	18.00
❑ TL4 Scottie Pippen	25.00	11.00
❑ TL5 Michael Jordan	100.00	45.00
❑ TL6 Marcus Camby	8.00	3.60
❑ TL7 Kobe Bryant	60.00	27.00
❑ TL8 Kevin Garnett	50.00	22.00
❑ TL9 Kerry Kittles	8.00	3.60
❑ TL10 Grant Hill	40.00	18.00
❑ TL11 Dennis Rodman	15.00	6.75
❑ TL12 Damon Stoudamire	10.00	4.50
❑ TL13 Antoine Walker	15.00	6.75
❑ TL14 Anfernee Hardaway	25.00	11.00
❑ TL15 Allen Iverson	40.00	18.00

1998-99 SkyBox Premium

	MINT	NRMT
COMPLETE SET (265)	150.00	70.00
COMPLETE SET w/o SP (225)	40.00	18.00
COMPLETE SERIES 1 (125)	25.00	11.00
COMPLETE SERIES 2 (140)	120.00	55.00
COMMON CARD (1-225)	.15	.07
COMMON RC (226-265)	1.25	.55
SEMISTARS	.20	.09
SEMISTARS RC	1.50	.70
UNLISTED STARS	.40	.18
UNLISTED STARS RC	2.50	1.10
RC's: STATED ODDS 1:4 PACKS		
SUBSET CARDS HALF VALUE OF BASE CARDS		

Card	MINT	NRMT
❑ 1 Tim Duncan	2.00	.90
❑ 2 Voshon Lenard	.15	.07
❑ 3 John Starks	.15	.07
❑ 4 Juwan Howard	.20	.09
❑ 5 Michael Finley	.40	.18
❑ 6 Bobby Jackson	.15	.07
❑ 7 Glenn Robinson	.20	.09
❑ 8 Antonio McDyess	.40	.18
❑ 9 Eric Williams	.15	.07
❑ 10 Zydrunas Ilgauskas	.15	.07
❑ 11 Terrell Brandon	.20	.09
❑ 12 Shandon Anderson	.15	.07
❑ 13 Rod Strickland	.20	.09
❑ 14 Dennis Rodman	.75	.35
❑ 15 Clarence Weatherspoon	.15	.07
❑ 16 P.J. Brown	.15	.07
❑ 17 Anfernee Hardaway	1.25	.55
❑ 18 Dikembe Mutombo	.20	.09
❑ 19 Patrick Ewing	.40	.18
❑ 20 Scottie Pippen	1.25	.55
❑ 21 Shaquille O'Neal	2.00	.90
❑ 22 Donyell Marshall	.15	.07
❑ 23 Michael Jordan	5.00	2.20
❑ 24 Mark Price	.15	.07
❑ 25 Jim Jackson	.15	.07
❑ 26 Isaiah Rider	.20	.09
❑ 27 Eddie Jones	.75	.35
❑ 28 Detlef Schrempf	.20	.09
❑ 29 Corliss Williamson	.15	.07
❑ 30 Bo Outlaw	.15	.07
❑ 31 Allen Iverson	1.50	.70
❑ 32 Luc Longley	.15	.07
❑ 33 Theo Ratliff	.15	.07
❑ 34 Antoine Walker	.60	.25
❑ 35 Lamond Murray	.15	.07
❑ 36 Avery Johnson	.15	.07
❑ 37 John Stockton	.40	.18
❑ 38 David Wesley	.15	.07
❑ 39 Elden Campbell	.15	.07
❑ 40 Grant Hill	2.00	.90
❑ 41 Sam Cassell	.20	.09
❑ 42 Tracy McGrady	1.50	.70
❑ 43 Glen Rice	.20	.09
❑ 44 Kobe Bryant	3.00	1.35
❑ 45 John Wallace	.15	.07
❑ 46 Bobby Phills	.15	.07
❑ 47 Jerry Stackhouse	.20	.09
❑ 48 Stephon Marbury	1.00	.45
❑ 49 Jeff Hornacek	.20	.09
❑ 50 Tom Gugliotta	.20	.09
❑ 51 Joe Dumars	.40	.18
❑ 52 Johnny Newman	.15	.07
❑ 53 Kevin Garnett	2.50	1.10
❑ 54 Dennis Scott	.15	.07
❑ 55 Anthony Mason	.20	.09
❑ 56 Rodney Rogers	.15	.07
❑ 57 Bryon Russell	.15	.07
❑ 58 Maurice Taylor	.40	.18
❑ 59 Mookie Blaylock	.15	.07
❑ 60 Shawn Bradley	.15	.07
❑ 61 Matt Maloney	.15	.07
❑ 62 Karl Malone	.60	.25
❑ 63 Larry Johnson	.20	.09
❑ 64 Calbert Cheaney	.15	.07
❑ 65 Steve Smith	.20	.09
❑ 66 Toni Kukoc	.50	.23
❑ 67 Reggie Miller	.40	.18
❑ 68 Jayson Williams	.20	.09
❑ 69 Gary Payton	.60	.25
❑ 70 Sean Elliott	.15	.07
❑ 71 Charles Barkley	.60	.25
❑ 72 Tim Hardaway	.40	.18
❑ 73 Rasheed Wallace	.40	.18
❑ 74 Tariq Abdul-Wahad	.15	.07
❑ 75 Kenny Anderson	.20	.09
❑ 76 Chris Mullin	.40	.18
❑ 77 Keith Van Horn	1.00	.45
❑ 78 Hersey Hawkins	.20	.09
❑ 79 Ron Mercer	.60	.25
❑ 80 Rik Smits	.15	.07
❑ 81 David Robinson	.60	.25
❑ 82 Derek Anderson	.50	.23
❑ 83 Danny Fortson	.20	.09
❑ 84 Jason Kidd	1.25	.55
❑ 85 Chauncey Billups	.15	.07
❑ 86 Chris Anstey	.15	.07
❑ 87 Hakeem Olajuwon	.60	.25
❑ 88 Bryant Reeves	.15	.07
❑ 89 Anthony Johnson	.15	.07
❑ 90 Shawn Kemp	.60	.25
❑ 91 Brevin Knight	.15	.07
❑ 92 Ray Allen	.50	.23
❑ 93 Tim Thomas	.60	.25
❑ 94 Jalen Rose	.40	.18
❑ 95 Kerry Kittles	.20	.09
❑ 96 Vin Baker	.20	.09
❑ 97 Shareef Abdur-Rahim	1.00	.45
❑ 98 Alonzo Mourning	.40	.18
❑ 99 Joe Smith	.20	.09
❑ 100 Damon Stoudamire	.40	.18
❑ 101 Alan Henderson	.15	.07
❑ 102 Walter McCarty	.15	.07
❑ 103 Vlade Divac	.15	.07
❑ 104 Wesley Person	.15	.07
❑ 105 A.C. Green	.20	.09
❑ 106 Malik Sealy	.15	.07
❑ 107 Carl Thomas	.15	.07
❑ 108 Brent Price	.15	.07
❑ 109 Mark Jackson	.15	.07
❑ 110 Lorenzen Wright	.15	.07
❑ 111 Derek Fisher	.20	.09
❑ 112 Michael Smith	.15	.07
❑ 113 Tyrone Hill	.15	.07
❑ 114 Cherokee Parks	.15	.07
❑ 115 Kendall Gill	.20	.09
❑ 116 Darrell Armstrong	.20	.09
❑ 117 Derrick Coleman	.20	.09
❑ 118 Rex Chapman	.15	.07
❑ 119 Arvydas Sabonis	.20	.09
❑ 120 Billy Owens	.15	.07
❑ 121 Sam Perkins	.20	.09
❑ 122 Gary Trent	.15	.07
❑ 123 Sam Mack	.15	.07
❑ 124 Tracy Murray	.15	.07
❑ 125 Allan Houston	.40	.18
❑ 126 Mitch Richmond	.40	.18
❑ 127 Carl Herrera	.15	.07
❑ 128 Ron Harper	.20	.09
❑ 129 Gary Trent	.15	.07
❑ 130 Chris Webber	1.25	.55
❑ 131 Antonio Daniels	.15	.07
❑ 132 Charles Oakley	.15	.07
❑ 133 Marcus Camby	.40	.18
❑ 134 Tony Battie	.20	.09
❑ 135 Otis Thorpe	.15	.07
❑ 136 Dale Davis	.15	.07
❑ 137 Chuck Person	.15	.07
❑ 138 Ervin Johnson	.15	.07
❑ 139 Jamal Mashburn	.20	.09
❑ 140 Brian Grant	.20	.09
❑ 141 Chris Mills	.15	.07
❑ 142 Doug Christie	.15	.07
❑ 143 George McCloud	.15	.07
❑ 144 Todd Fuller	.15	.07
❑ 145 Jerome Williams	.20	.09
❑ 146 Chauncey Billups	.15	.07
❑ 147 Dean Garrett	.15	.07
❑ 148 Robert Pack	.15	.07
❑ 149 Clarence Weatherspoon	.15	.07
❑ 150 Tim Legler	.15	.07
❑ 151 Bob Sura	.15	.07
❑ 152 B.J. Armstrong	.15	.07
❑ 153 Charlie Ward	.15	.07
❑ 154 Rony Seikaly	.15	.07
❑ 155 Chris Carr	.15	.07
❑ 156 Eldridge Recasner	.15	.07
❑ 157 Michael Stewart	.15	.07
❑ 158 Jim McIlvaine	.15	.07
❑ 159 Adam Keefe	.15	.07
❑ 160 Antonio Davis	.15	.07
❑ 161 Lawrence Funderburke	.15	.07
❑ 162 Greg Ostertag	.15	.07
❑ 163 Dan Majerle	.20	.09
❑ 164 Dale Ellis	.15	.07
❑ 165 Greg Anthony	.15	.07
❑ 166 Chris Whitney	.15	.07
❑ 167 Eric Piatkowski	.15	.07
❑ 168 Tom Gugliotta	.20	.09
❑ 169 Luc Longley	.15	.07
❑ 170 Antonio McDyess	.40	.18
❑ 171 George Lynch	.15	.07
❑ 172 Dell Curry	.15	.07
❑ 173 Johnny Newman	.15	.07
❑ 174 Christian Laettner	.20	.09
❑ 175 Steve Kerr	.15	.07
❑ 176 Popeye Jones	.15	.07
❑ 177 Brent Barry	.15	.07
❑ 178 Billy Owens	.15	.07

❑ 179 Cherokee Parks	.15	.07
❑ 180 Derek Harper	.15	.07
❑ 181 Howard Eisley	.15	.07
❑ 182 Matt Geiger	.15	.07
❑ 183 Darrick Martin	.15	.07
❑ 184 Isaac Austin	.15	.07
❑ 185 Dennis Scott	.15	.07
❑ 186 Derrick Coleman	.20	.09
❑ 187 Sam Perkins	.20	.09
❑ 188 Latrell Sprewell	.75	.35
❑ 189 Jud Buechler	.15	.07
❑ 190 Jason Caffey	.15	.07
❑ 191 Vlade Divac	.15	.07
❑ 192 Travis Best	.15	.07
❑ 193 Loy Vaught	.15	.07
❑ 194 Mario Elie	.15	.07
❑ 195 Ed Gray	.15	.07
❑ 196 Joe Smith	.20	.09
❑ 197 John Starks	.15	.07
❑ 198 Anthony Johnson	.15	.07
❑ 199 Kurt Thomas	.15	.07
❑ 200 Chris Dudley	.15	.07
❑ 201 Shareef Abdur-Rahim NF	.40	.18
❑ 202 Ray Allen NF	.40	.18
❑ 203 Vin Baker NF	.15	.07
❑ 204 Charles Barkley NF	.40	.18
❑ 205 Kobe Bryant NF	1.50	.70
❑ 206 Tim Duncan NF	1.25	.55
❑ 207 Anfernee Hardaway NF	.75	.35
❑ 208 Grant Hill NF	1.25	.55
❑ 209 Allen Iverson NF	.75	.35
❑ 210 Jason Kidd NF	.50	.23
❑ 211 Shawn Kemp NF	.40	.18
❑ 212 Shaquille O'Neal NF	.75	.35
❑ 213 Kerry Kittles NF	.15	.07
❑ 214 Karl Malone NF	.40	.18
❑ 215 Stephon Marbury NF	.60	.25
❑ 216 Ron Mercer NF	.40	.18
❑ 217 Reggie Miller NF	.20	.09
❑ 218 Kevin Garnett NF	1.25	.55
❑ 219 Gary Payton NF	.40	.18
❑ 220 Scottie Pippen NF	.60	.25
❑ 221 David Robinson NF	.40	.18
❑ 222 Hakeem Olajuwon NF	.40	.18
❑ 223 Damon Stoudamire NF	.20	.09
❑ 224 Keith Van Horn NF	.40	.18
❑ 225 Antoine Walker NF	.40	.18
❑ 226 Cory Carr RC	1.25	.55
❑ 227 Cuttino Mobley RC	5.00	2.20
❑ 228 Miles Simon RC	1.25	.55
❑ 229 J.R. Henderson RC	1.25	.55
❑ 230 Jason Williams RC	15.00	6.75
❑ 231 Felipe Lopez RC	3.00	1.35
❑ 232 Shammond Williams RC	5.00	2.20
❑ 233 Ricky Davis RC	5.00	2.20
❑ 234 Vince Carter RC	60.00	27.00
❑ 235 Antawn Jamison RC	12.00	5.50
❑ 236 Ryan Stack RC	1.25	.55
❑ 237 Nazr Mohammed RC	1.50	.70
❑ 238 Sam Jacobson RC	1.25	.55
❑ 239 Larry Hughes RC	15.00	6.75
❑ 240 Ruben Patterson RC	5.00	2.20
❑ 241 Al Harrington RC	8.00	3.60
❑ 242 Ansu Sesay RC	1.25	.55
❑ 243 Vladimir Stepania RC	1.25	.55
❑ 244 Matt Harpring RC	2.50	1.10
❑ 245 Andrae Patterson RC	1.25	.55
❑ 246 Pat Garrity RC	1.50	.70
❑ 247 Bonzi Wells RC	10.00	4.50
❑ 248 Bryce Drew RC	2.50	1.10
❑ 249 Toby Bailey RC	1.25	.55
❑ 250 Michael Doleac RC	2.50	1.10
❑ 251 Michael Dickerson RC	5.00	2.20
❑ 252 Predrag Stojakovic RC	4.00	1.80
❑ 253 Robert Traylor RC	2.50	1.10
❑ 254 Tyronn Lue RC	1.50	.70
❑ 255 Dirk Nowitzki RC	10.00	4.50
❑ 256 Raef LaFrentz RC	5.00	2.20
❑ 257 Jelani McCoy RC	1.25	.55
❑ 258 Michael Olowokandi RC	4.00	1.80
❑ 259 Brian Skinner RC	2.50	1.10
❑ 260 Keon Clark RC	2.50	1.10
❑ 261 Roshown McLeod RC	1.50	.70
❑ 262 Mike Bibby RC	8.00	3.60
❑ 263 Paul Pierce RC	12.00	5.50
❑ 264 Tyson Wheeler RC	1.25	.55
❑ 265 Corey Benjamin RC	2.50	1.10

1998-99 SkyBox Premium Star Rubies

	MINT	NRMT
COMMON CARD (1-225)	25.00	11.00
COMMON RC (226-265)	30.00	13.50

*STARS: 50X TO 120X BASE CARD HI
*RCs: 7.5X TO 15X BASE HI
*NF: 40X TO 100X BASE HI
RANDOM INSERTS IN BOTH SERIES HOBBY
VETS: STATED PRINT RUN 50 SERIAL #'d SETS
RC's: STATED PRINT RUN 25 SERIAL #'d SETS

❑ 23 Michael Jordan	2000.00	900.00
❑ 44 Kobe Bryant	500.00	220.00
❑ 66 Toni Kukoc	100.00	45.00
❑ 205 Kobe Bryant NF	400.00	180.00
❑ 234 Vince Carter	1000.00	450.00

1998-99 SkyBox Premium 3D's

	MINT	NRMT
COMPLETE SET (15)	150.00	70.00
COMMON CARD (1-15)	4.00	1.80

SER.1 STATED ODDS 1:96

❑ 1 Kobe Bryant	30.00	13.50
❑ 2 Anfernee Hardaway	12.00	5.50
❑ 3 Allen Iverson	15.00	6.75
❑ 4 Michael Jordan	50.00	22.00
❑ 5 Stephon Marbury	10.00	4.50
❑ 6 Ron Mercer	6.00	2.70
❑ 7 Shareef Abdur-Rahim	10.00	4.50
❑ 8 Tim Duncan	20.00	9.00
❑ 9 Damon Stoudamire	4.00	1.80
❑ 10 Kevin Garnett	25.00	11.00
❑ 11 Grant Hill	20.00	9.00
❑ 12 Scottie Pippen	12.00	5.50
❑ 13 Keith Van Horn	10.00	4.50
❑ 14 Dennis Rodman	8.00	3.60
❑ 15 Shaquille O'Neal	20.00	9.00

1998-99 SkyBox Premium Autographics Black

	MINT	NRMT
COMMON BLACK AU CARD	6.00	2.70
SEMISTARS BLACK	10.00	4.50
COMMON BLUE CEN.MARK	15.00	6.75

*BLUE CENTURY MARKS: 1X TO 2.5X HI
BLUE: PRINT RUN 50 SERIAL #'d SETS
STATED ODDS 1:18 E-X CENTURY
STATED ODDS 1:144 HOOPS
STATED ODDS 1:68 METAL
STATED ODDS 1:24 MOLTEN METAL
STATED ODDS 1:68 SKYBOX PREM.1
STATED ODDS 1:24 SKYBOX PREM.2
STATED ODDS 1:112 THUNDER
IVERSON SIGNED EQUAL BLACK/BLUE

RCs HAVE REGULAR AND TRADE CARDS
TRADE EXPIRATION: 6/1/99
PIERCE DID NOT SIGN FOR TRADE
CARDS LISTED BELOW ALPHABETICALLY

❑ 1 Tariq Abdul-Wahad	25.00	11.00
❑ 2 Shareef Abdur-Rahim	60.00	27.00
❑ 3 Cory Alexander	6.00	2.70
❑ 4 Ray Allen	40.00	18.00
❑ 5 Kenny Anderson	15.00	6.75
❑ 6 Nick Anderson	6.00	2.70
❑ 7 Chris Anstey	6.00	2.70
❑ 8 Isaac Austin	6.00	2.70
❑ 9 Vin Baker	25.00	11.00
❑ 10 Dana Barros	6.00	2.70
❑ 11 Tony Battie	10.00	4.50
❑ 12 Corey Benjamin	10.00	4.50
❑ 13 Travis Best	6.00	2.70
❑ 14 Mike Bibby	30.00	13.50
❑ 15 Chauncey Billups	20.00	9.00
❑ 16 Corie Blount	6.00	2.70
❑ 17 Terrell Brandon	10.00	4.50
❑ 18 P.J. Brown	6.00	2.70
❑ 19 Scott Burrell	6.00	2.70
❑ 20 Jason Caffey	6.00	2.70
❑ 21 Marcus Camby	25.00	11.00
❑ 22 Elden Campbell	6.00	2.70
❑ 23 Chris Carr	6.00	2.70
❑ 24 Cory Carr	6.00	2.70
❑ 25 Vince Carter	350.00	160.00
❑ 26 Kelvin Cato	10.00	4.50
❑ 27 Calbert Cheaney	6.00	2.70
❑ 28 Keith Closs	6.00	2.70
❑ 29 Antonio Daniels	6.00	2.70
❑ 30 Dale Davis	6.00	2.70
❑ 31 Ricky Davis	30.00	13.50
❑ 32 Andrew DeClercq	6.00	2.70
❑ 33 Tony Delk	6.00	2.70
❑ 34 Michael Dickerson	25.00	11.00
❑ 35 Michael Doleac	15.00	6.75
❑ 36 Bryce Drew	15.00	6.75
❑ 37 Tim Duncan	200.00	90.00
❑ 38 Howard Eisley	6.00	2.70
❑ 39 Danny Ferry	6.00	2.70
❑ 40 Derek Fisher	10.00	4.50
❑ 41 Danny Fortson	10.00	4.50
❑ 42 Adonal Foyle	6.00	2.70
❑ 43 Todd Fuller	6.00	2.70
❑ 44 Kevin Garnett	150.00	70.00
❑ 45 Pat Garrity	15.00	6.75
❑ 46 Brian Grant	10.00	4.50
❑ 47 Tom Gugliotta	20.00	9.00
❑ 48 Tom Hammonds	6.00	2.70
❑ 49 Tim Hardaway	50.00	22.00
❑ 50 Matt Harpring	15.00	6.75
❑ 51 Othella Harrington	6.00	2.70
❑ 52 Hersey Hawkins	10.00	4.50
❑ 53 Cedric Henderson	10.00	4.50
❑ 54 Grant Hill	200.00	90.00
❑ 55 Tyrone Hill	6.00	2.70
❑ 56 Allan Houston	25.00	11.00
❑ 57 Juwan Howard	25.00	11.00
❑ 58 Larry Hughes	50.00	22.00
❑ 59 Zydrunas Ilgauskas	6.00	2.70
❑ 60 Allen Iverson Blk/Blu	250.00	110.00
❑ 61 Bobby Jackson	20.00	9.00
❑ 62 Antawn Jamison	50.00	22.00
❑ 63 Anthony Johnson	6.00	2.70

❑ 64 Ervin Johnson	6.00	2.70
❑ 65 Larry Johnson	30.00	13.50
❑ 66 Eddie Jones	50.00	22.00
❑ 67 Adam Keefe	6.00	2.70
❑ 68 Shawn Kemp	60.00	27.00
❑ 69 Steve Kerr	6.00	2.70
❑ 70 Jason Kidd	150.00	70.00
❑ 71 Kerry Kittles	20.00	9.00
❑ 72 Brevin Knight	15.00	6.75
❑ 73 Raef LaFrentz	25.00	11.00
❑ 74 Felipe Lopez	10.00	4.50
❑ 75 George Lynch	6.00	2.70
❑ 76 Karl Malone	200.00	90.00
❑ 77 Danny Manning	20.00	9.00
❑ 78 Stephon Marbury	40.00	18.00
❑ 79 Donyell Marshall	20.00	9.00
❑ 80 Tony Massenburg	6.00	2.70
❑ 81 Walter McCarty	6.00	2.70
❑ 82 Jelani McCoy	20.00	9.00
❑ 83 Antonio McDyess	30.00	13.50
❑ 84 Tracy McGrady	40.00	18.00
❑ 85 Ron Mercer	30.00	13.50
❑ 86 Sam Mitchell	6.00	2.70
❑ 87 Nazr Mohammed	10.00	4.50
❑ 88 Alonzo Mourning	50.00	22.00
❑ 89 Chris Mullin	40.00	18.00
❑ 90 Dikembe Mutombo	25.00	11.00
❑ 91 Hakeem Olajuwon	60.00	27.00
❑ 92 Michael Olowokandi	25.00	11.00
❑ 93 Elliot Perry	6.00	2.70
❑ 94 Bobby Phills	6.00	2.70
❑ 95 Eric Piatkowski	6.00	2.70
❑ 96 Scottie Pippen	100.00	45.00
❑ 97 Scot Pollard	15.00	6.75
❑ 98 Vitaly Potapenko	6.00	2.70
❑ 99 Brent Price	6.00	2.70
❑ 100 Theo Ratliff	6.00	2.70
❑ 101 Eldridge Recasner	6.00	2.70
❑ 102 Bryant Reeves	15.00	6.75
❑ 103 Glen Rice	20.00	9.00
❑ 104 Chris Robinson	6.00	2.70
❑ 105 David Robinson	150.00	70.00
❑ 106 Glenn Robinson	20.00	9.00
❑ 107 Dennis Rodman	250.00	110.00
❑ 108 Bryon Russell	6.00	2.70
❑ 109 Danny Schayes	6.00	2.70
❑ 110 Detlef Schrempf	30.00	13.50
❑ 111 Rony Seikaly	6.00	2.70
❑ 112 Brian Skinner	20.00	9.00
❑ 113 Reggie Slater	6.00	2.70
❑ 114 Joe Smith	15.00	6.75
❑ 115 Steve Smith	20.00	9.00
❑ 116 Rik Smits	6.00	2.70
❑ 117 Jerry Stackhouse	25.00	11.00
❑ 118 John Starks	20.00	9.00
❑ 119 Bryant Stith	6.00	2.70
❑ 120 Damon Stoudamire	30.00	13.50
❑ 121 Mark Strickland	6.00	2.70
❑ 122 Rod Strickland	25.00	11.00
❑ 123 Bob Sura	6.00	2.70
❑ 124 Tim Thomas	15.00	6.75
❑ 125 Robert Traylor	10.00	4.50
❑ 126 Gary Trent	6.00	2.70
❑ 127 Keith Van Horn	25.00	11.00
❑ 128 Jacque Vaughn	6.00	2.70
❑ 129 Antoine Walker	25.00	11.00
❑ 130 Eric Washington	6.00	2.70
❑ 131 Clarence Weatherspoon	6.00	2.70
❑ 132 Bonzi Wells	25.00	11.00
❑ 133 David Wesley	6.00	2.70
❑ 134 Eric Williams	6.00	2.70
❑ 135 Jason Williams	100.00	45.00
❑ 136 Jayson Williams	20.00	9.00
❑ 137 Monty Williams	6.00	2.70
❑ 138 Walt Williams	6.00	2.70
❑ 139 Lorenzen Wright	6.00	2.70

1998-99 SkyBox Premium B.P.O.

	MINT	NRMT
COMPLETE SET (15)	12.00	5.50
COMMON CARD (1-15)	.40	.18
SEMISTARS	.60	.25

SER.2 STATED ODDS 1:6 HOB/RET

❑ 1 Ron Mercer	1.00	.45
❑ 2 Shareef Abdur-Rahim	1.50	.70
❑ 3 Stephon Marbury	1.50	.70
❑ 4 Tim Thomas	1.00	.45
❑ 5 Tim Duncan	3.00	1.35
❑ 6 Mike Bibby	1.00	.45
❑ 7 Ray Allen	.75	.35
❑ 8 Shawn Kemp	1.00	.45
❑ 9 Vince Carter	8.00	3.60
❑ 10 Antoine Walker	1.00	.45
❑ 11 Raef LaFrentz	.60	.25
❑ 12 Damon Stoudamire	.60	.25
❑ 13 Keith Van Horn	1.50	.70
❑ 14 Kerry Kittles	.40	.18
❑ 15 Allen Iverson	2.50	1.10

1998-99 SkyBox Premium Fresh Faces

	MINT	NRMT
COMPLETE SET (10)	40.00	18.00
COMMON CARD (1-10)	1.50	.70
UNLISTED STARS	2.00	.90

SER.2 STATED ODDS 1:36 HOB/RET

❑ 1 Mike Bibby	3.00	1.35
❑ 2 Vince Carter	25.00	11.00
❑ 3 Al Harrington	3.00	1.35
❑ 4 Larry Hughes	6.00	2.70
❑ 5 Antawn Jamison	5.00	2.20
❑ 6 Raef LaFrentz	2.00	.90
❑ 7 Michael Olowokandi	2.00	.90
❑ 8 Paul Pierce	5.00	2.20
❑ 9 Robert Traylor	1.50	.70
❑ 10 Bonzi Wells	4.00	1.80

1998-99 SkyBox Premium Intimidation Nation

	MINT	NRMT
COMPLETE SET (10)	150.00	70.00
COMMON CARD (1-10)	8.00	3.60

SER.1 STATED ODDS 1:360

❑ 1 Shaquille O'Neal	25.00	11.00
❑ 2 Kobe Bryant	40.00	18.00
❑ 3 Kevin Garnett	30.00	13.50

❑ 4 Grant Hill	25.00	11.00
❑ 5 Shawn Kemp	8.00	3.60
❑ 6 Keith Van Horn	12.00	5.50
❑ 7 Antoine Walker	8.00	3.60
❑ 8 Michael Jordan	60.00	27.00
❑ 9 Gary Payton	8.00	3.60
❑ 10 Tim Duncan	25.00	11.00

1998-99 SkyBox Premium Just Cookin'

	MINT	NRMT
COMPLETE SET (10)	6.00	2.70
COMMON CARD (1-10)	.50	.23
UNLISTED STARS	.75	.35

SER.1 STATED ODDS 1:12

❑ 1 Maurice Taylor	.75	.35
❑ 2 Brevin Knight	.50	.23
❑ 3 Tim Thomas	1.25	.55
❑ 4 Chauncey Billups	.50	.23
❑ 5 Chris Anstey	.50	.23
❑ 6 Tracy McGrady	3.00	1.35
❑ 7 Zydrunas Ilgauskas	.50	.23
❑ 8 Antonio Daniels	.50	.23
❑ 9 Bobby Jackson	.50	.23
❑ 10 Derek Anderson	1.00	.45

1998-99 SkyBox Premium Mod Squad

	MINT	NRMT
COMPLETE SET (16)	60.00	27.00
COMMON CARD (1-16)	.75	.35
UNLISTED STARS	1.25	.55
SER.2 STATED ODDS 1:18 HOB/RET		
❑ 1 Tim Thomas	2.00	.90
❑ 2 Shaquille O'Neal	6.00	2.70
❑ 3 Scottie Pippen	4.00	1.80
❑ 4 Kobe Bryant	10.00	4.50
❑ 5 Kevin Garnett	8.00	3.60
❑ 6 Grant Hill	6.00	2.70
❑ 7 Anfernee Hardaway	4.00	1.80
❑ 8 Antoine Walker	2.00	.90
❑ 9 Stephon Marbury	3.00	1.35
❑ 10 Kerry Kittles	.75	.35
❑ 11 Allen Iverson	5.00	2.20
❑ 12 Gary Payton	2.00	.90
❑ 13 Damon Stoudamire	.75	.35
❑ 14 Marcus Camby	.75	.35
❑ 15 Shareef Abdur-Rahim	3.00	1.35
❑ 16 Michael Jordan	15.00	6.75

1998-99 SkyBox Premium Net Set

	MINT	NRMT
COMPLETE SET (15)	50.00	22.00
COMMON CARD (1-15)	2.00	.90
UNLISTED STARS	3.00	1.35
SER.1 STATED ODDS 1:36		
❑ 1 Ron Mercer	5.00	2.20
❑ 2 Shawn Kemp	5.00	2.20
❑ 3 Brevin Knight	2.00	.90
❑ 4 Maurice Taylor	3.00	1.35
❑ 5 Ray Allen	4.00	1.80
❑ 6 Dennis Rodman	6.00	2.70
❑ 7 Kerry Kittles	2.00	.90
❑ 8 Tim Thomas	5.00	2.20
❑ 9 Gary Payton	5.00	2.20
❑ 10 Marcus Camby	3.00	1.35
❑ 11 Karl Malone	5.00	2.20
❑ 12 Juwan Howard	2.00	.90
❑ 13 Zydrunas Ilgauskas	2.00	.90
❑ 14 Scottie Pippen	10.00	4.50
❑ 15 Anfernee Hardaway	10.00	4.50

1998-99 SkyBox Premium Slam Funk

	MINT	NRMT
COMPLETE SET (10)	150.00	70.00
COMMON CARD (1-10)	5.00	2.20
SER.2 STATED ODDS 1:360 HOB/RET		
❑ 1 Kobe Bryant	40.00	18.00
❑ 2 Kevin Garnett	30.00	13.50
❑ 3 Grant Hill	25.00	11.00
❑ 4 Shaquille O'Neal	25.00	11.00
❑ 5 Michael Olowokandi	5.00	2.20
❑ 6 Tim Duncan	25.00	11.00
❑ 7 Antawn Jamison	12.00	5.50
❑ 8 Keith Van Horn	12.00	5.50
❑ 9 Ron Mercer	8.00	3.60
❑ 10 Scottie Pippen	15.00	6.75

1998-99 SkyBox Premium Smooth

	MINT	NRMT
COMPLETE SET (15)	8.00	3.60
COMMON CARD (1-15)	.40	.18
UNLISTED STARS	.60	.25
SER.1 STATED ODDS 1:6		
❑ 1 Stephon Marbury	1.50	.70
❑ 2 Shareef Abdur-Rahim	1.50	.70
❑ 3 Keith Van Horn	1.50	.70
❑ 4 Marcus Camby	.60	.25
❑ 5 Ray Allen	.75	.35
❑ 6 Allen Iverson	2.50	1.10
❑ 7 Kerry Kittles	.40	.18
❑ 8 Tim Thomas	1.00	.45
❑ 9 Damon Stoudamire	.60	.25
❑ 10 Antoine Walker	1.00	.45
❑ 11 Brevin Knight	.40	.18
❑ 12 Zydrunas Ilgauskas	.40	.18
❑ 13 Ron Mercer	1.00	.45
❑ 14 Maurice Taylor	.60	.25
❑ 15 Tim Duncan	3.00	1.35

1998-99 SkyBox Premium Soul of the Game

	MINT	NRMT
COMPLETE SET (15)	50.00	22.00
COMMON CARD (1-15)	.75	.35
UNLISTED STARS	1.25	.55
SER.1 STATED ODDS 1:18		
❑ 1 Michael Jordan	15.00	6.75
❑ 2 Antoine Walker	2.00	.90
❑ 3 Scottie Pippen	4.00	1.80
❑ 4 Grant Hill	6.00	2.70
❑ 5 Dennis Rodman	2.50	1.10
❑ 6 Kobe Bryant	10.00	4.50
❑ 7 Kevin Garnett	8.00	3.60
❑ 8 Shaquille O'Neal	6.00	2.70
❑ 9 Stephon Marbury	3.00	1.35
❑ 10 Kerry Kittles	.75	.35
❑ 11 Anfernee Hardaway	4.00	1.80
❑ 12 Allen Iverson	5.00	2.20
❑ 13 Damon Stoudamire	.75	.35
❑ 14 Marcus Camby	.75	.35
❑ 15 Shareef Abdur-Rahim	3.00	1.35

1998-99 SkyBox Premium That's Jam

	MINT	NRMT
COMPLETE SET (15)	150.00	70.00
COMMON CARD (1-15)	4.00	1.80
SER.2 STATED ODDS 1:96 HOB/RET		
❑ 1 Tim Duncan	20.00	9.00
❑ 2 Stephon Marbury	10.00	4.50
❑ 3 Shareef Abdur-Rahim	10.00	4.50
❑ 4 Shaquille O'Neal	20.00	9.00
❑ 5 Ron Mercer	6.00	2.70
❑ 6 Scottie Pippen	12.00	5.50
❑ 7 Antawn Jamison	10.00	4.50
❑ 8 Anfernee Hardaway	12.00	5.50
❑ 9 Damon Stoudamire	4.00	1.80
❑ 10 Allen Iverson	15.00	6.75
❑ 11 Keith Van Horn	10.00	4.50
❑ 12 Grant Hill	20.00	9.00
❑ 13 Kevin Garnett	25.00	11.00
❑ 14 Kobe Bryant	30.00	13.50
❑ 15 Antoine Walker	6.00	2.70

1999-00 SkyBox Premium

	MINT	NRMT
COMPLETE SET (150)	120.00	55.00
COMPLETE SET w/o SP (125)	50.00	22.00

COMMON CARD (1-100) .15 .07
COMMON RC (101-125) .30 .14
COMMON SP (101-125) 1.25 .55
SEMISTARS .20 .09
SEMISTARS RC .40 .18
UNLISTED STARS .40 .18
UNLISTED STARS RC .50 .23
*SP DRAFT PICKS: 1.5X TO 4X BASE RC
SP DRAFT PICKS FEATURE ACTION PHOTOS
SP DRAFT PICK STATED ODDS 1:8

❑ 1 Vince Carter 4.00 1.80
❑ 2 Nick Anderson .15 .07
❑ 3 Isaiah Rider .20 .09
❑ 4 Mitch Richmond .40 .18
❑ 5 Danny Fortson .15 .07
❑ 6 Kenny Anderson .20 .09
❑ 7 Reggie Miller .40 .18
❑ 8 Tracy McGrady 1.25 .55
❑ 9 Steve Nash .15 .07
❑ 10 Robert Traylor .15 .07
❑ 11 Tom Gugliotta .20 .09
❑ 12 Steve Smith .20 .09
❑ 13 Jalen Rose .40 .18
❑ 14 Kerry Kittles .20 .09
❑ 15 Nick Van Exel .20 .09
❑ 16 Raef LaFrentz .40 .18
❑ 17 Damon Stoudamire .40 .18
❑ 18 Gary Trent .15 .07
❑ 19 Jayson Williams .20 .09
❑ 20 Brian Grant .20 .09
❑ 21 Rod Strickland .20 .09
❑ 22 Larry Hughes 1.00 .45
❑ 23 Derek Anderson .40 .18
❑ 24 Hakeem Olajuwon .60 .25
❑ 25 Ray Allen .40 .18
❑ 26 Gary Payton .60 .25
❑ 27 Michael Finley .40 .18
❑ 28 Keith Van Horn .75 .35
❑ 29 Clifford Robinson .15 .07
❑ 30 Shawn Kemp .60 .25
❑ 31 Glenn Robinson .20 .09
❑ 32 Theo Ratliff .15 .07
❑ 33 Lindsey Hunter .15 .07
❑ 34 Chris Webber 1.25 .55
❑ 35 Grant Hill 2.00 .90
❑ 36 Vlade Divac .15 .07
❑ 37 Paul Pierce .75 .35
❑ 38 Tyrone Nesby RC .15 .07
❑ 39 Larry Johnson .20 .09
❑ 40 Bryon Russell .15 .07
❑ 41 Antoine Walker .50 .23
❑ 42 Michael Olowokandi .20 .09
❑ 43 John Stockton .40 .18
❑ 44 Elden Campbell .15 .07
❑ 45 Christian Laettner .20 .09
❑ 46 Maurice Taylor .40 .18
❑ 47 Shareef Abdur-Rahim .75 .35
❑ 48 Ricky Davis .40 .18
❑ 49 Jerry Stackhouse .20 .09
❑ 50 Kobe Bryant 3.00 1.35
❑ 51 Jason Williams 1.00 .45
❑ 52 Mike Bibby .50 .23
❑ 53 Eddie Jones .75 .35
❑ 54 Antawn Jamison .75 .35
❑ 55 Shaquille O'Neal 2.00 .90
❑ 56 Tim Duncan 2.00 .90
❑ 57 Cherokee Parks .15 .07
❑ 58 Antonio McDyess .40 .18
❑ 59 Rasheed Wallace .40 .18
❑ 60 Anthony Mason .20 .09
❑ 61 Chris Mills .15 .07
❑ 62 Glen Rice .20 .09
❑ 63 Latrell Sprewell .75 .35
❑ 64 Darrell Armstrong .20 .09
❑ 65 Sean Elliott .15 .07
❑ 66 Juwan Howard .20 .09
❑ 67 Brent Barry .15 .07
❑ 68 John Starks .15 .07
❑ 69 Tim Hardaway .40 .18
❑ 70 Marcus Camby .40 .18
❑ 71 Anfernee Hardaway 1.25 .55
❑ 72 Avery Johnson .15 .07
❑ 73 Tariq Abdul-Wahad .15 .07
❑ 74 Charles Barkley .60 .25
❑ 75 Stephon Marbury .75 .35
❑ 76 Jamal Mashburn .20 .09
❑ 77 Matt Harpring .15 .07
❑ 78 David Robinson .60 .25
❑ 79 Cedric Ceballos .15 .07
❑ 80 Terrell Brandon .20 .09
❑ 81 Jason Kidd 1.25 .55
❑ 82 Toni Kukoc .50 .23
❑ 83 Michael Dickerson .40 .18
❑ 84 Alonzo Mourning .40 .18
❑ 85 Kevin Garnett 2.50 1.10
❑ 86 Matt Geiger .15 .07
❑ 87 Vin Baker .20 .09
❑ 88 Dikembe Mutombo .20 .09
❑ 89 Hersey Hawkins .20 .09
❑ 90 Joe Smith .20 .09
❑ 91 Charles Oakley .15 .07
❑ 92 Ron Mercer .50 .23
❑ 93 Rik Smits .15 .07
❑ 94 Patrick Ewing .40 .18
❑ 95 Karl Malone .60 .25
❑ 96 Scottie Pippen 1.25 .55
❑ 97 Zydrunas Ilgauskas .15 .07
❑ 98 Sam Cassell .20 .09
❑ 99 Detlef Schrempf .20 .09
❑ 100 Allen Iverson 1.50 .70
❑ 101 Elton Brand RC 5.00 2.20
❑ 102 Steve Francis RC 6.00 2.70
❑ 103 Baron Davis RC 1.25 .55
❑ 104 Lamar Odom RC 4.00 1.80
❑ 105 Jonathan Bender RC 2.50 1.10
❑ 106 Wally Szczerbiak RC 2.00 .90
❑ 107 Richard Hamilton RC 1.25 .55
❑ 108 Andre Miller RC 1.50 .70
❑ 109 Shawn Marion RC 1.50 .70
❑ 110 Jason Terry RC .75 .35
❑ 111 Trajan Langdon RC .75 .35
❑ 112 Aleksandar Radojevic RC .30 .14
❑ 113 Corey Maggette RC 2.00 .90
❑ 114 William Avery RC .75 .35
❑ 115 Vonteego Cummings RC .75 .35
❑ 116 Ron Artest RC 1.25 .55
❑ 117 Cal Bowdler RC .50 .23
❑ 118 James Posey RC 1.00 .45
❑ 119 Quincy Lewis RC .50 .23
❑ 120 Dion Glover RC .50 .23
❑ 121 Jeff Foster RC .50 .23
❑ 122 Kenny Thomas RC .75 .35
❑ 123 Devean George RC 1.00 .45
❑ 124 Scott Padgett RC .50 .23
❑ 125 Tim James RC .60 .25

1999-00 SkyBox Premium Star Rubies

MINT NRMT
COMMON CARD (1-125) 15.00 6.75
COMMON SP (101-125) 40.00 18.00
SEMISTARS SP 50.00 22.00
UNLISTED STARS SP 60.00 27.00
*STARS: 30X TO 80X HI COLUMN
*RCs: 15X TO 40X HI
*SPs: 12.5X TO 30X HI
RANDOM INSERTS IN HOBBY PACKS
STARS/RC's: PRINT RUN 45 SERIAL #'d SETS
SP's: PRINT RUN 25 SERIAL #'d SETS

❑ 101 Elton Brand 200.00 90.00
❑ 101A Elton Brand SP 300.00 135.00
❑ 102 Steve Francis 250.00 110.00
❑ 102A Steve Francis SP 400.00 180.00
❑ 103 Baron Davis 50.00 22.00
❑ 103A Baron Davis SP 80.00 36.00
❑ 104 Lamar Odom 150.00 70.00
❑ 104A Lamar Odom SP 250.00 110.00
❑ 105 Jonathan Bender 100.00 45.00
❑ 105A Jonathan Bender SP 150.00 70.00
❑ 106 Wally Szczerbiak 80.00 36.00
❑ 106A Wally Szczerbiak SP 120.00 55.00
❑ 107 Richard Hamilton 50.00 22.00
❑ 107A Richard Hamilton SP 80.00 36.00
❑ 108 Andre Miller 60.00 27.00
❑ 108A Andre Miller SP 100.00 45.00
❑ 109 Shawn Marion 60.00 27.00
❑ 109A Shawn Marion SP 100.00 45.00
❑ 113 Corey Maggette 80.00 36.00
❑ 113A Corey Maggette SP 120.00 55.00
❑ 116 Ron Artest 50.00 22.00
❑ 116A Ron Artest SP 80.00 36.00

1999-00 SkyBox Premium Autographics Black

MINT NRMT
COMMON CARD 6.00 2.70
SEMISTARS 10.00 4.50
COMMON BLUE CEN.MARK 12.00 5.50
*BLUE CENTURY MARKS: .75X TO 2X HI
BLUE: PRINT RUN 50 SERIAL #'d SETS
STATED ODDS 1:68/1:144 HOO DECADE
STATED ODDS 1:96 METAL
STATED ODDS 1:288 IMPACT
CARDS LISTED BELOW ALPHABETICALLY

❑ 1 Cory Alexander 6.00 2.70
❑ 2 Ray Allen 40.00 18.00
❑ 3 Darrell Armstrong 10.00 4.50
❑ 4 Ron Artest 20.00 9.00
❑ 5 William Avery 12.00 5.50
❑ 6 Charles Barkley 200.00 90.00
❑ 7 Dana Barros 6.00 2.70
❑ 8 Corey Benjamin 10.00 4.50
❑ 9 Travis Best 6.00 2.70
❑ 10 Mike Bibby 30.00 13.50
❑ 11 Calvin Booth 10.00 4.50
❑ 12 Cal Bowdler 10.00 4.50
❑ 13 Bruce Bowen 6.00 2.70
❑ 14 P.J. Brown 6.00 2.70
❑ 15 Jud Buechler 10.00 4.50
❑ 16 Marcus Camby 20.00 9.00
❑ 17 Elden Campbell 6.00 2.70
❑ 18 Cory Carr 6.00 2.70
❑ 19 Vince Carter 250.00 110.00
❑ 20 John Celestand 6.00 2.70
❑ 21 Dell Curry 6.00 2.70
❑ 22 Baron Davis 25.00 11.00
❑ 23 Andrew DeClercq 6.00 2.70
❑ 24 Tony Delk 6.00 2.70
❑ 25 Michael Dickerson 15.00 6.75
❑ 26 Michael Doleac 6.00 2.70
❑ 27 Bryce Drew 6.00 2.70
❑ 28 Obinna Ekezie 6.00 2.70
❑ 29 Evan Eschmeyer 6.00 2.70
❑ 30 Michael Finley 25.00 11.00
❑ 31 Greg Foster 10.00 4.50
❑ 32 Jeff Foster 10.00 4.50
❑ 33 Steve Francis 100.00 45.00
❑ 34 Todd Fuller 6.00 2.70
❑ 35 Lawrence Funderburke 6.00 2.70
❑ 36 Dean Garrett 6.00 2.70
❑ 37 Pat Garrity 6.00 2.70
❑ 38 Devean George 12.00 5.50
❑ 39 Kendall Gill 10.00 4.50
❑ 40 Dion Glover 10.00 4.50
❑ 41 Brian Grant 15.00 6.75
❑ 42 Paul Grant 6.00 2.70
❑ 43 Tom Gugliotta 20.00 9.00
❑ 44 Richard Hamilton 15.00 6.75
❑ 45 Tim Hardaway 20.00 9.00
❑ 46 Matt Harpring 6.00 2.70
❑ 47 Al Harrington 12.00 5.50
❑ 48 Othella Harrington 6.00 2.70

❑ 49	Troy Hudson	12.00	5.50
❑ 50	Larry Hughes	40.00	18.00
❑ 51	Tim James	10.00	4.50
❑ 52	Antawn Jamison	20.00	9.00
❑ 53	Anthony Johnson	6.00	2.70
❑ 54	Avery Johnson	6.00	2.70
❑ 55	Ervin Johnson	6.00	2.70
❑ 56	Eddie Jones	50.00	22.00
❑ 57	Jumaine Jones	10.00	4.50
❑ 58	Adam Keefe	6.00	2.70
❑ 59	Shawn Kemp	30.00	13.50
❑ 60	Kerry Kittles	15.00	6.75
❑ 61	Raef LaFrentz	15.00	6.75
❑ 62	Trajan Langdon	15.00	6.75
❑ 63	Quincy Lewis	10.00	4.50
❑ 64	Felipe Lopez	6.00	2.70
❑ 65	Tyronn Lue	10.00	4.50
❑ 66	George Lynch	6.00	2.70
❑ 67	Sam Mack	6.00	2.70
❑ 68	Stephon Marbury	25.00	11.00
❑ 69	Shawn Marion	20.00	9.00
❑ 70	Tony Massenburg	6.00	2.70
❑ 71	Jelani McCoy	6.00	2.70
❑ 72	Antonio McDyess	20.00	9.00
❑ 73	Tracy McGrady	40.00	18.00
❑ 74	Roshown McLeod	6.00	2.70
❑ 75	Brad Miller	6.00	2.70
❑ 76	Sam Mitchell	6.00	2.70
❑ 77	Nazr Mohammed	6.00	2.70
❑ 78	Alonzo Mourning	50.00	22.00
❑ 79	Tyrone Nesby	10.00	4.50
❑ 80	Shaquille O'Neal	300.00	135.00
❑ 81	Lamar Odom	100.00	45.00
❑ 82	Hakeem Olajuwon	50.00	22.00
❑ 83	Michael Olowokandi	10.00	4.50
❑ 84	Andrae Patterson	6.00	2.70
❑ 85	Eric Piatkowski	6.00	2.70
❑ 86	Scottie Pippen	120.00	55.00
❑ 87	Scot Pollard	6.00	2.70
❑ 88	James Posey	12.00	5.50
❑ 89	Brent Price	6.00	2.70
❑ 90	Aleksandar Radojevic	6.00	2.70
❑ 91	Theo Ratliff	6.00	2.70
❑ 92	J.R. Reid	6.00	2.70
❑ 93	David Robinson	100.00	45.00
❑ 94	Glenn Robinson	25.00	11.00
❑ 95	Jalen Rose	25.00	11.00
❑ 96	Michael Ruffin	6.00	2.70
❑ 97	Wally Szczerbiak	30.00	13.50
❑ 98	Joe Smith	15.00	6.75
❑ 99	Jerry Stackhouse	20.00	9.00
❑ 100	John Starks	15.00	6.75
❑ 101	Vladimir Stepania	6.00	2.70
❑ 102	Damon Stoudamire	20.00	9.00
❑ 103	Maurice Taylor	12.00	5.50
❑ 104	Jason Terry	12.00	5.50
❑ 105	Kenny Thomas	15.00	6.75
❑ 106	Robert Traylor	6.00	2.70
❑ 107	Gary Trent	6.00	2.70
❑ 108	Antoine Walker	30.00	13.50
❑ 109	Chris Webber	120.00	55.00
❑ 110	David Wesley	6.00	2.70
❑ 111	Aaron Williams	6.00	2.70
❑ 112	Jerome Williams	10.00	4.50
❑ 113	Haywoode Workman	6.00	2.70

1999-00 SkyBox Premium Back for More

	MINT	NRMT
COMPLETE SET (15)	6.00	2.70
COMMON CARD (1-15)	.25	.11
SEMISTARS	.40	.18
UNLISTED STARS	.50	.23

STATED ODDS 1:6 HOB/RET

❑ 1	Mike Bibby	.75	.35
❑ 2	Tyrone Nesby	.25	.11
❑ 3	Ricky Davis	.50	.23
❑ 4	Michael Dickerson	.50	.23
❑ 5	Michael Doleac	.25	.11
❑ 6	Antawn Jamison	1.25	.55
❑ 7	Larry Hughes	1.50	.70
❑ 8	Matt Harpring	.25	.11
❑ 9	Predrag Stojakovic	.40	.18
❑ 10	Raef LaFrentz	.50	.23
❑ 11	Michael Olowokandi	.40	.18
❑ 12	Robert Traylor	.25	.11
❑ 13	Paul Pierce	1.25	.55
❑ 14	Kornel David	.25	.11
❑ 15	Jason Williams	1.50	.70

1999-00 SkyBox Premium Club Vertical

	MINT	NRMT
COMPLETE SET (10)	500.00	220.00
COMMON CARD (1-10)	25.00	11.00

RANDOM INSERTS IN PACKS
STATED PRINT RUN 100 SERIAL #'d SETS

❑ 1	Vince Carter	120.00	55.00
❑ 2	Tim Duncan	60.00	27.00
❑ 3	Shaquille O'Neal	60.00	27.00
❑ 4	Paul Pierce	25.00	11.00
❑ 5	Kobe Bryant	100.00	45.00
❑ 6	Kevin Garnett	80.00	36.00
❑ 7	Keith Van Horn	25.00	11.00
❑ 8	Jason Williams	30.00	13.50
❑ 9	Grant Hill	60.00	27.00
❑ 10	Allen Iverson	50.00	22.00

1999-00 SkyBox Premium Genuine Coverage

	MINT	NRMT
COMPLETE SET (6)	1000.00	450.00
COMMON CARD (1-6)	100.00	45.00

RANDOM INSERTS IN PACKS

❑ 1	Kobe Bryant/340	400.00	180.00
❑ 2	Vince Carter/355	400.00	180.00
❑ 3	Patrick Ewing/450	100.00	45.00
❑ 4	Grant Hill/370	150.00	70.00
❑ 5	Allen Iverson/275	200.00	90.00
❑ 6	Alonzo Mourning/360	100.00	45.00

1999-00 SkyBox Premium Good Stuff

	MINT	NRMT
COMPLETE SET (10)	40.00	18.00
COMMON CARD (1-10)	2.50	1.10

STATED ODDS 1:36 HOB/RET

COMP.PARALLEL SET (10)	400.00	180.00
COMMON PARALLEL (1-10)	25.00	11.00

*PARALLEL: 4X TO 10X HI COLUMN

PARALLEL: RANDOM INS.IN PACKS
PARALLEL: PRINT RUN 99 SERIAL #'d SETS

❑ 1	Kobe Bryant	10.00	4.50
❑ 2	Vince Carter	12.00	5.50
❑ 3	Jason Williams	3.00	1.35
❑ 4	Paul Pierce	2.50	1.10
❑ 5	Tim Duncan	6.00	2.70
❑ 6	Kevin Garnett	8.00	3.60
❑ 7	Grant Hill	6.00	2.70
❑ 8	Keith Van Horn	2.50	1.10
❑ 9	Allen Iverson	5.00	2.20
❑ 10	Shaquille O'Neal	6.00	2.70

1999-00 SkyBox Premium Majestic

	MINT	NRMT
COMPLETE SET (15)	25.00	11.00
COMMON CARD (1-15)	1.00	.45

STATED ODDS 1:12 HOB/RET

❑ 1	Antawn Jamison	1.50	.70
❑ 2	Jason Kidd	2.50	1.10
❑ 3	Ron Mercer	1.00	.45
❑ 4	Shawn Kemp	1.25	.55
❑ 5	Stephon Marbury	1.50	.70
❑ 6	Shaquille O'Neal	4.00	1.80
❑ 7	Larry Hughes	2.00	.90
❑ 8	Kevin Garnett	5.00	2.20
❑ 9	Antoine Walker	1.00	.45
❑ 10	Keith Van Horn	1.50	.70
❑ 11	Anfernee Hardaway	2.50	1.10
❑ 12	Tim Duncan	4.00	1.80
❑ 13	Scottie Pippen	2.50	1.10
❑ 14	Shareef Abdur-Rahim	1.50	.70
❑ 15	Chris Webber	2.50	1.10

1999-00 SkyBox Premium Prime Time Rookies

	MINT	NRMT
COMPLETE SET (15)	100.00	45.00
COMMON CARD (PT1-PT15)	2.50	1.10
UNLISTED STARS	4.00	1.80

STATED ODDS 1:96 HOB/RET

❑ PT1	Elton Brand	25.00	11.00

❑ PT2 Steve Francis	30.00	13.50
❑ PT3 Baron Davis	6.00	2.70
❑ PT4 Lamar Odom	20.00	9.00
❑ PT5 Jonathan Bender	12.00	5.50
❑ PT6 Wally Szczerbiak	10.00	4.50
❑ PT7 Richard Hamilton	6.00	2.70
❑ PT8 Andre Miller	8.00	3.60
❑ PT9 Shawn Marion	8.00	3.60
❑ PT10 Jason Terry	4.00	1.80
❑ PT11 Trajan Langdon	4.00	1.80
❑ PT12 Dion Glover	2.50	1.10
❑ PT13 Corey Maggette	10.00	4.50
❑ PT14 William Avery	4.00	1.80
❑ PT15 Tim James	4.00	1.80

1999-00 SkyBox Premium Prime Time Rookies Autographs

	MINT	NRMT
COMMON CARD (PT1-PT15)		
RANDOM INSERTS IN HOBBY PACKS		
STATED PRINT RUN 25 SERIAL #'d SETS		
❑ PT1 Elton Brand		
❑ PT2 Steve Francis	500.00	220.00
❑ PT3 Baron Davis	150.00	70.00
❑ PT4 Lamar Odom	350.00	160.00
❑ PT5 Jonathan Bender		
❑ PT6 Wally Szczerbiak	200.00	90.00
❑ PT7 Richard Hamilton	120.00	55.00
❑ PT8 Andre Miller		
❑ PT9 Shawn Marion		
❑ PT10 Jason Terry		
❑ PT11 Trajan Langdon		
❑ PT12 Dion Glover		
❑ PT13 Corey Maggette		
❑ PT14 William Avery	80.00	36.00
❑ PT15 Tim James		

1999-00 SkyBox APEX

	MINT	NRMT
COMPLETE SET (163)	80.00	36.00
COMPLETE SET w/o RC (150)	25.00	11.00
COMMON CARD (1-150)	.15	.07
COMMON RC (151-163)	1.00	.45
SEMISTARS	.20	.09
UNLISTED STARS	.40	.18
RC SUBSET: STATED ODDS 1:13		
VAN HORN AU JERSEY RED. #'d TO 50		

❑ 1 Paul Pierce	.75	.35
❑ 2 Stephon Marbury	.75	.35
❑ 3 Chris Webber	1.25	.55
❑ 4 Kobe Bryant	3.00	1.35
❑ 5 David Robinson	.60	.25
❑ 6 Gary Payton	.60	.25
❑ 7 Kornel David RC	.15	.07
❑ 8 Glenn Robinson	.20	.09
❑ 9 Nick Van Exel	.20	.09
❑ 10 Jelani McCoy	.15	.07
❑ 11 Charles Oakley	.15	.07
❑ 12 Michael Finley	.40	.18
❑ 13 Steve Smith	.20	.09
❑ 14 Arvydas Sabonis	.20	.09
❑ 15 Cuttino Mobley	.40	.18
❑ 16 Eric Piatkowski	.15	.07
❑ 17 Bobby Jackson	.15	.07
❑ 18 Keith Van Horn	.75	.35
❑ 19 Shaquille O'Neal	2.00	.90
❑ 20 Karl Malone	.60	.25
❑ 21 Allan Houston	.40	.18
❑ 22 Ron Mercer	.50	.23
❑ 23 Vince Carter	4.00	1.80
❑ 24 Lindsey Hunter	.15	.07
❑ 25 Scottie Pippen	1.25	.55
❑ 26 Wesley Person	.15	.07
❑ 27 Vitaly Potapenko	.15	.07
❑ 28 Glen Rice	.20	.09
❑ 29 Tyrone Nesby RC	.15	.07
❑ 30 Detlef Schrempf	.20	.09
❑ 31 Clifford Robinson	.15	.07
❑ 32 Joe Smith	.20	.09
❑ 33 P.J. Brown	.15	.07
❑ 34 Christian Laettner	.20	.09
❑ 35 Avery Johnson	.15	.07
❑ 36 Kevin Garnett	2.50	1.10
❑ 37 Jason Kidd	1.25	.55
❑ 38 Kenny Anderson	.20	.09
❑ 39 Shawn Kemp	.60	.25
❑ 40 Bison Dele	.15	.07
❑ 41 Rodney Rogers	.15	.07
❑ 42 Jamal Mashburn	.20	.09
❑ 43 Grant Hill	2.00	.90
❑ 44 Larry Johnson	.20	.09
❑ 45 Darrell Armstrong	.20	.09
❑ 46 Shandon Anderson	.15	.07
❑ 47 Kendall Gill	.20	.09
❑ 48 Jason Williams	1.00	.45
❑ 49 Tom Gugliotta	.20	.09
❑ 50 Ray Allen	.40	.18
❑ 51 Sam Mitchell	.15	.07
❑ 52 Brent Barry	.15	.07
❑ 53 Antawn Jamison	.75	.35
❑ 54 Chris Mullin	.40	.18
❑ 55 Alan Henderson	.15	.07
❑ 56 Derek Anderson	.40	.18
❑ 57 Tim Thomas	.50	.23
❑ 58 Anfernee Hardaway	1.25	.55
❑ 59 Pat Garrity	.15	.07
❑ 60 Corliss Williamson	.15	.07
❑ 61 Gary Trent	.15	.07
❑ 62 Greg Ostertag	.15	.07
❑ 63 Vin Baker	.20	.09
❑ 64 LaPhonso Ellis	.15	.07
❑ 65 Brevin Knight	.15	.07
❑ 66 Rick Fox	.15	.07
❑ 67 Bryant Reeves	.15	.07
❑ 68 Mark Jackson	.15	.07
❑ 69 John Starks	.15	.07
❑ 70 Robert Traylor	.15	.07
❑ 71 Maurice Taylor	.40	.18
❑ 72 Hersey Hawkins	.20	.09
❑ 73 Zydrunas Ilgauskas	.15	.07
❑ 74 Charles Barkley	.60	.25
❑ 75 Isaac Austin	.15	.07
❑ 76 Mike Bibby	.50	.23
❑ 77 Michael Olowokandi	.20	.09
❑ 78 Brian Grant	.20	.09
❑ 79 Felipe Lopez	.15	.07
❑ 80 Chris Crawford	.15	.07
❑ 81 Dee Brown	.15	.07
❑ 82 Antoine Walker	.50	.23
❑ 83 Vlade Divac	.15	.07
❑ 84 Rod Strickland	.20	.09
❑ 85 Dickey Simpkins	.15	.07
❑ 86 Donyell Marshall	.15	.07
❑ 87 Larry Hughes	1.00	.45
❑ 88 Rasheed Wallace	.40	.18
❑ 89 Erick Dampier	.15	.07
❑ 90 Kerry Kittles	.20	.09
❑ 91 Mitch Richmond	.40	.18
❑ 92 Isaiah Rider	.20	.09
❑ 93 Bobby Phills	.15	.07
❑ 94 Dirk Nowitzki	.60	.25
❑ 95 Cedric Henderson	.15	.07
❑ 96 Howard Eisley	.15	.07
❑ 97 Toni Kukoc	.50	.23
❑ 98 Jalen Rose	.40	.18
❑ 99 Michael Doleac	.15	.07
❑ 100 Matt Geiger	.15	.07
❑ 101 Bryon Russell	.15	.07
❑ 102 Alvin Williams	.15	.07
❑ 103 Shawn Bradley	.15	.07
❑ 104 Latrell Sprewell	.75	.35
❑ 105 Vernon Maxwell	.15	.07
❑ 106 Tim Hardaway	.40	.18
❑ 107 Predrag Stojakovic	.20	.09
❑ 108 Tracy Murray	.15	.07
❑ 109 Theo Ratliff	.15	.07
❑ 110 Dikembe Mutombo	.20	.09
❑ 111 Alonzo Mourning	.40	.18
❑ 112 Raef LaFrentz	.40	.18
❑ 113 Marcus Camby	.40	.18
❑ 114 Eddie Jones	.75	.35
❑ 115 Chauncey Billups	.15	.07
❑ 116 Jayson Williams	.20	.09
❑ 117 Anthony Mason	.20	.09
❑ 118 Tracy McGrady	1.25	.55
❑ 119 John Stockton	.40	.18
❑ 120 Matt Harpring	.15	.07
❑ 121 Mario Elie	.15	.07
❑ 122 Juwan Howard	.20	.09
❑ 123 Antonio McDyess	.40	.18
❑ 124 Ricky Davis	.40	.18
❑ 125 Reggie Miller	.40	.18
❑ 126 Allen Iverson	1.50	.70
❑ 127 Terrell Brandon	.20	.09
❑ 128 Hakeem Olajuwon	.60	.25
❑ 129 Damon Stoudamire	.40	.18
❑ 130 Randy Brown	.15	.07
❑ 131 Cedric Ceballos	.15	.07
❑ 132 Jerry Stackhouse	.20	.09
❑ 133 Michael Dickerson	.40	.18
❑ 134 Rik Smits	.15	.07
❑ 135 Cherokee Parks	.15	.07
❑ 136 Tim Duncan	2.00	.90
❑ 137 Shareef Abdur-Rahim	.75	.35
❑ 138 Derek Fisher	.20	.09
❑ 139 Charles Outlaw	.15	.07
❑ 140 Eric Snow	.15	.07
❑ 141 Jaren Jackson	.15	.07
❑ 142 Tony Battie	.15	.07
❑ 143 Derrick Coleman	.20	.09
❑ 144 Corey Benjamin	.15	.07
❑ 145 Steve Nash	.15	.07
❑ 146 Mookie Blaylock	.15	.07
❑ 147 Voshon Lenard	.15	.07
❑ 148 Vinny Del Negro	.15	.07
❑ 149 Jeff Hornacek	.20	.09
❑ 150 Patrick Ewing	.40	.18
❑ 151 Elton Brand RC	15.00	6.75
❑ 152 Steve Francis RC	20.00	9.00
❑ 153 Baron Davis RC	4.00	1.80

❑ 154 Lamar Odom RC	12.00	5.50
❑ 155 Jonathan Bender RC	8.00	3.60
❑ 156 Wally Szczerbiak RC	6.00	2.70
❑ 157 Richard Hamilton RC	4.00	1.80
❑ 158 Andre Miller RC	5.00	2.20
❑ 159 Shawn Marion RC	5.00	2.20
❑ 160 Jason Terry RC	2.50	1.10
❑ 161 Trajan Langdon RC	2.50	1.10
❑ 162 Aleksandar Radojevic RC	1.00	.45
❑ 163 Corey Maggette RC	6.00	2.70
❑ P2 S Marbury PROMO	2.00	.90
❑ NNO Keith Van Horn Autographed Jersey Redemption	250.00	110.00

1999-00 SkyBox APEX Xtra

	MINT	NRMT
COMMON CARD (1-150)	15.00	6.75
COMMON CARD (151-163)	15.00	6.75

*STARS: 30X TO 80X BASE CARD HI
*RCs: 5X TO 12X BASE HI
STATED PRINT RUN 50 SERIAL #'d SETS
RANDOM INSERTS IN HOBBY PACKS

1999-00 SkyBox APEX Allies

	MINT	NRMT
COMPLETE SET (15)	15.00	6.75
COMMON CARD (1-15)	.60	.25

STATED ODDS 1:6 HOB/RET

❑ 1 Kobe Bryant / Shaquille O'Neal	6.00	2.70
❑ 2 Keith Van Horn / Stephon Marbury	1.50	.70
❑ 3 John Stockton / Karl Malone	1.00	.45
❑ 4 Mike Bibby / Shareef Abdur-Rahim	1.25	.55
❑ 5 Allen Iverson / Larry Hughes	2.50	1.10
❑ 6 Michael Olowokandi / Maurice Taylor	.60	.25
❑ 7 Vince Carter / Tracy McGrady	5.00	2.20
❑ 8 Grant Hill / Jerry Stackhouse	2.50	1.10
❑ 9 Jason Williams / Chris Webber	2.00	.90
❑ 10 Tim Duncan / David Robinson	2.00	.90
❑ 11 Jason Kidd / Tom Gugliotta	1.50	.70
❑ 12 Vin Baker / Gary Payton	.75	.35
❑ 13 Michael Dickerson / Cuttino Mobley	.75	.35
❑ 14 Shawn Kemp / Brevin Knight	1.00	.45
❑ 15 Antonio McDyess / Raef LaFrentz	.75	.35

1999-00 SkyBox APEX Cutting Edge

	MINT	NRMT
COMPLETE SET (15)	50.00	22.00
COMMON CARD (1-15)	.75	.35
UNLISTED STARS	1.00	.45
STATED ODDS 1:24 HOB/RET		
COMP.PLUS SET (15)	200.00	90.00
COMMON PLUS (1-15)	3.00	1.35
*PLUS: 1.5X TO 4X HI COLUMN		
PLUS: STATED ODDS 1:240 HOB/RET		
COMMON WARP TEK (1-15)	30.00	13.50
*WARP TEK: 15X TO 40X HI		
WARP TEK: PRINT RUN 25 SERIAL #'d SETS		
WARP TEK: RANDOM INS.IN HOB/RET		

❑ 1 Allen Iverson	5.00	2.20
❑ 2 Paul Pierce	2.50	1.10
❑ 3 Vince Carter	12.00	5.50
❑ 4 Jason Williams	3.00	1.35
❑ 5 Kobe Bryant	10.00	4.50
❑ 6 Kevin Garnett	8.00	3.60
❑ 7 Stephon Marbury	2.50	1.10
❑ 8 Jason Kidd	4.00	1.80
❑ 9 Tim Duncan	6.00	2.70
❑ 10 Mike Bibby	1.50	.70
❑ 11 Marcus Camby	.75	.35
❑ 12 Michael Olowokandi	.75	.35
❑ 13 Antawn Jamison	2.50	1.10
❑ 14 Keith Van Horn	2.50	1.10
❑ 15 Raef LaFrentz	.75	.35

1999-00 SkyBox APEX First Impressions

	MINT	NRMT
COMPLETE SET (20)	30.00	13.50
COMMON CARD (1-20)	.50	.23
SEMISTARS	1.00	.45
UNLISTED STARS	1.50	.70

STATED ODDS 1:12 HOB/RET

❑ 1 Jonathan Bender	4.00	1.80
❑ 2 Steve Francis	10.00	4.50
❑ 3 Ron Artest	2.00	.90
❑ 4 Baron Davis	2.00	.90
❑ 5 Shawn Marion	2.50	1.10
❑ 6 Jason Terry	1.50	.70
❑ 7 Elton Brand	8.00	3.60
❑ 8 Kenny Thomas	1.50	.70
❑ 9 Trajan Langdon	1.50	.70
❑ 10 Aleksandar Radojevic	.50	.23
❑ 11 Corey Maggette	3.00	1.35
❑ 12 Jeff Foster	1.00	.45
❑ 13 Scott Padgett	1.00	.45
❑ 14 Lamar Odom	6.00	2.70
❑ 15 William Avery	1.50	.70
❑ 16 Andre Miller	2.50	1.10
❑ 17 Wally Szczerbiak	3.00	1.35
❑ 18 Richard Hamilton	2.00	.90
❑ 19 James Posey	1.50	.70
❑ 20 Jumaine Jones	1.00	.45

1999-00 SkyBox APEX Jam Session

	MINT	NRMT
COMPLETE SET (15)	100.00	45.00
COMMON CARD (1-15)	2.00	.90
UNLISTED STARS	3.00	1.35

STATED ODDS 1:96 HOB/RET

❑ 1 Stephon Marbury	6.00	2.70
❑ 2 Paul Pierce	6.00	2.70
❑ 3 Kobe Bryant	25.00	11.00
❑ 4 Keith Van Horn	6.00	2.70
❑ 5 Shaquille O'Neal	15.00	6.75
❑ 6 Anfernee Hardaway	10.00	4.50
❑ 7 Grant Hill	15.00	6.75
❑ 8 Antonio McDyess	3.00	1.35
❑ 9 Kevin Garnett	20.00	9.00
❑ 10 Tracy McGrady	10.00	4.50
❑ 11 Shareef Abdur-Rahim	6.00	2.70
❑ 12 Shawn Kemp	5.00	2.20
❑ 13 Antoine Walker	4.00	1.80
❑ 14 Eddie Jones	6.00	2.70
❑ 15 Vin Baker	2.00	.90

1999-00 SkyBox APEX Net Shredders

	MINT	NRMT
COMPLETE SET (10)	700.00	325.00
COMMON CARD	30.00	13.50

RANDOM INSERTS IN HOBBY PACKS

❑ 1 Vince Carter	225.00	100.00
❑ 2 Tracy McGrady	80.00	36.00
❑ 3 Allen Iverson	100.00	45.00
❑ 4 Larry Hughes	50.00	22.00
❑ 5 Glenn Robinson	30.00	13.50
❑ 6 Ray Allen	40.00	18.00
❑ 7 Jason Williams	80.00	36.00
❑ 8 Chris Webber	80.00	36.00

❑ 9 Tim Duncan	80.00	36.00
❑ 10 David Robinson	50.00	22.00

1999-00 SkyBox Dominion

	MINT	NRMT
COMPLETE SET (220)	40.00	18.00
COMMON CARD (1-200)	.10	.05
COMMON RC (201-220)	.30	.14
SEMISTARS	.15	.07
SEMISTARS RC	.40	.18
UNLISTED STARS	.25	.11
UNLISTED STARS RC	.50	.23

❑ 1 Jason Williams	.60	.25
❑ 2 Isaiah Rider	.15	.07
❑ 3 Tim Hardaway	.25	.11
❑ 4 Isaac Austin	.10	.05
❑ 5 Joe Smith	.15	.07
❑ 6 Mitch Richmond	.25	.11
❑ 7 Sam Mitchell	.10	.05
❑ 8 Terrell Brandon	.15	.07
❑ 9 Grant Long	.10	.05
❑ 10 Shaquille O'Neal	1.25	.55
❑ 11 Derrick Coleman	.15	.07
❑ 12 Rod Strickland	.15	.07
❑ 13 J.R. Reid	.10	.05
❑ 14 Tyrone Corbin	.10	.05
❑ 15 Jeff Hornacek	.15	.07
❑ 16 Malik Rose	.10	.05
❑ 17 Terry Davis	.10	.05
❑ 18 Theo Ratliff	.10	.05
❑ 19 Kevin Willis	.10	.05
❑ 20 Raef LaFrentz	.25	.11
❑ 21 Othella Harrington	.10	.05
❑ 22 Marcus Camby	.25	.11
❑ 23 Keon Clark	.10	.05
❑ 24 Robert Pack	.10	.05
❑ 25 Sam Mack	.10	.05
❑ 26 Shawn Kemp	.40	.18
❑ 27 Nick Anderson	.10	.05
❑ 28 Bill Wennington	.10	.05
❑ 29 Steve Smith	.15	.07
❑ 30 Kobe Bryant	2.00	.90
❑ 31 Bobby Phills	.10	.05
❑ 32 Cedric Ceballos	.10	.05
❑ 33 Derek Fisher	.15	.07
❑ 34 Doug Christie	.10	.05
❑ 35 Danny Manning	.15	.07
❑ 36 Eric Murdock	.10	.05
❑ 37 Glen Rice	.15	.07
❑ 38 Dikembe Mutombo	.15	.07
❑ 39 Jason Kidd	.75	.35
❑ 40 Cedric Henderson	.10	.05
❑ 41 Rasheed Wallace	.25	.11
❑ 42 Tim Duncan	1.25	.55
❑ 43 John Stockton	.25	.11
❑ 44 Dell Curry	.10	.05
❑ 45 Muggsy Bogues	.10	.05
❑ 46 Danny Fortson	.10	.05
❑ 47 Charles Oakley	.10	.05
❑ 48 Elden Campbell	.10	.05
❑ 49 Tony Massenburg	.10	.05
❑ 50 Kevin Garnett	1.50	.70
❑ 51 Cherokee Parks	.10	.05
❑ 52 LaPhonso Ellis	.10	.05
❑ 53 Sam Cassell	.15	.07
❑ 54 Shawn Bradley	.10	.05
❑ 55 David Robinson	.40	.18
❑ 56 Juwan Howard	.15	.07
❑ 57 Lindsey Hunter	.10	.05
❑ 58 Mark Jackson	.10	.05
❑ 59 Olden Polynice	.10	.05
❑ 60 Tracy McGrady	.75	.35
❑ 61 Michael Finley	.25	.11
❑ 62 Matt Geiger	.10	.05
❑ 63 Maurice Taylor	.25	.11
❑ 64 Rex Chapman	.10	.05
❑ 65 Chris Mullin	.25	.11
❑ 66 Ray Allen	.25	.11
❑ 67 Bison Dele	.10	.05
❑ 68 Dickey Simpkins	.10	.05
❑ 69 Alvin Williams	.10	.05
❑ 70 Grant Hill	1.25	.55
❑ 71 Mark Bryant	.10	.05
❑ 72 Adam Keefe	.10	.05
❑ 73 Alan Henderson	.10	.05
❑ 74 Eric Snow	.10	.05
❑ 75 Matt Harpring	.10	.05
❑ 76 Jalen Rose	.25	.11
❑ 77 Derek Harper	.15	.07
❑ 78 Kerry Kittles	.15	.07
❑ 79 Tony Battie	.10	.05
❑ 80 Larry Hughes	.60	.25
❑ 81 Arvydas Sabonis	.15	.07
❑ 82 Allan Houston	.25	.11
❑ 83 Tom Gugliotta	.15	.07
❑ 84 Reggie Miller	.25	.11
❑ 85 Dejuan Wheat	.10	.05
❑ 86 Pat Garrity	.10	.05
❑ 87 Karl Malone	.40	.18
❑ 88 Sam Perkins	.10	.05
❑ 89 Michael Olowokandi	.15	.07
❑ 90 Anfernee Hardaway	.75	.35
❑ 91 Bryant Reeves	.10	.05
❑ 92 Gary Trent	.10	.05
❑ 93 George Lynch	.10	.05
❑ 94 Scottie Pippen	.75	.35
❑ 95 Jerry Stackhouse	.15	.07
❑ 96 Kendall Gill	.15	.07
❑ 97 Vin Baker	.15	.07
❑ 98 Dale Davis	.10	.05
❑ 99 Charles Barkley	.40	.18
❑ 100 Allen Iverson	1.00	.45
❑ 101 Keith Van Horn	.50	.23
❑ 102 Andrew DeClercq	.10	.05
❑ 103 Michael Doleac	.10	.05
❑ 104 Chauncey Billups	.10	.05
❑ 105 Chris Mills	.10	.05
❑ 106 Lamond Murray	.10	.05
❑ 107 Glenn Robinson	.15	.07
❑ 108 Brian Grant	.15	.07
❑ 109 Christian Laettner	.15	.07
❑ 110 Antawn Jamison	.50	.23
❑ 111 Erick Dampier	.10	.05
❑ 112 Vernon Maxwell	.10	.05
❑ 113 Kenny Anderson	.15	.07
❑ 114 Clarence Weatherspoon	.10	.05
❑ 115 Corliss Williamson	.10	.05
❑ 116 Paul Pierce	.50	.23
❑ 117 Clifford Robinson	.10	.05
❑ 118 Damon Stoudamire	.25	.11
❑ 119 Dana Barros	.10	.05
❑ 120 Stephon Marbury	.50	.23
❑ 121 Latrell Sprewell	.50	.23
❑ 122 Tyronn Lue	.10	.05
❑ 123 Walt Williams	.10	.05
❑ 124 P.J. Brown	.10	.05
❑ 125 Gary Payton	.40	.18
❑ 126 Nick Van Exel	.15	.07
❑ 127 Bryant Stith	.10	.05
❑ 128 Eric Piatkowski	.10	.05
❑ 129 Tyrone Nesby RC	.10	.05
❑ 130 Ron Mercer	.30	.14
❑ 131 Hersey Hawkins	.15	.07
❑ 132 Vlade Divac	.10	.05
❑ 133 Darrick Martin	.10	.05
❑ 134 Avery Johnson	.10	.05
❑ 135 Jaren Jackson	.10	.05
❑ 136 Brevin Knight	.10	.05
❑ 137 Wesley Person	.10	.05
❑ 138 Derek Anderson	.25	.11
❑ 139 Tim Thomas	.30	.14
❑ 140 Antonio McDyess	.25	.11
❑ 141 A.C. Green	.15	.07
❑ 142 Chris Webber	.75	.35
❑ 143 Scott Burrell	.10	.05
❑ 144 John Starks	.10	.05
❑ 145 Howard Eisley	.10	.05
❑ 146 Mike Bibby	.30	.14
❑ 147 Toni Kukoc	.30	.14
❑ 148 Eddie Jones	.50	.23
❑ 149 Otis Thorpe	.10	.05
❑ 150 Shareef Abdur-Rahim	.50	.23
❑ 151 Calbert Cheaney	.10	.05
❑ 152 Cuttino Mobley	.25	.11
❑ 153 Michael Dickerson	.25	.11
❑ 154 Sean Elliott	.10	.05
❑ 155 Terry Porter	.10	.05
❑ 156 Dean Garrett	.10	.05
❑ 157 Charlie Ward	.10	.05
❑ 158 Larry Johnson	.15	.07
❑ 159 Dan Majerle	.15	.07
❑ 160 Jayson Williams	.15	.07
❑ 161 Anthony Peeler	.10	.05
❑ 162 Ron Harper	.15	.07
❑ 163 Darrell Armstrong	.15	.07
❑ 164 Kurt Thomas	.10	.05
❑ 165 Brent Barry	.10	.05
❑ 166 Lawrence Funderburke	.10	.05
❑ 167 Terry Cummings	.10	.05
❑ 168 Jamal Mashburn	.15	.07
❑ 169 Robert Traylor	.10	.05
❑ 170 Greg Ostertag	.10	.05
❑ 171 Brad Miller	.10	.05
❑ 172 Mario Elie	.10	.05
❑ 173 Antoine Walker	.30	.14
❑ 174 Ricky Davis	.25	.11
❑ 175 Vince Carter	2.50	1.10
❑ 176 Hakeem Olajuwon WT	.25	.11
❑ 177 Luc Longley WT	.10	.05
❑ 178 Tim Duncan WT	.60	.25
❑ 179 Rick Fox WT	.10	.05
❑ 180 Zydrunas Ilgauskas WT	.10	.05
❑ 181 Toni Kukoc WT	.25	.11
❑ 182 Felipe Lopez WT	.10	.05
❑ 183 Dikembe Mutombo WT	.10	.05
❑ 184 Steve Nash WT	.10	.05
❑ 185 Dirk Nowitzki WT	.25	.11
❑ 186 Vitaly Potapenko WT	.10	.05
❑ 187 Detlef Schrempf WT	.10	.05
❑ 188 Rik Smits WT	.10	.05
❑ 189 Vladimir Stepania WT	.10	.05
❑ 190 Predrag Stojakovic WT	.10	.05
❑ 191 Donyell Marshall 3FA	.10	.05
❑ 192 S Abdur-Rahim 3FA	.25	.11
❑ 193 Michael Dickerson 3FA	.15	.07
❑ 194 Damon Stoudamire 3FA	.15	.07
❑ 195 Allen Iverson 3FA	.50	.23
❑ 196 Grant Hill 3FA	.60	.25
❑ 197 Scottie Pippen 3FA	.40	.18
❑ 198 Bryon Russell 3FA	.10	.05
❑ 199 Alonzo Mourning 3FA	.15	.07
❑ 200 Patrick Ewing 3FA	.15	.07
❑ 201 Ron Artest RC	1.25	.55
❑ 202 William Avery RC	.75	.35
❑ 203 Lamar Odom RC	4.00	1.80
❑ 204 Baron Davis RC	1.25	.55
❑ 205 John Celestand RC	.50	.23
❑ 206 Jumaine Jones RC	.40	.18
❑ 207 Andre Miller RC	1.50	.70

❑ 208 Elton Brand RC	5.00	2.20
❑ 209 James Posey RC	1.00	.45
❑ 210 Jason Terry RC	.75	.35
❑ 211 Kenny Thomas RC	.75	.35
❑ 212 Steve Francis RC	6.00	2.70
❑ 213 Wally Szczerbiak RC	2.00	.90
❑ 214 Richard Hamilton RC	1.25	.55
❑ 215 Jonathan Bender RC	2.50	1.10
❑ 216 Shawn Marion RC	1.50	.70
❑ 217 Aleksandar Radojevic RC	.30	.14
❑ 218 Tim James RC	.60	.25
❑ 219 Trajan Langdon RC	.75	.35
❑ 220 Corey Maggette RC	2.00	.90

1999-00 SkyBox Dominion 2 Point Play

	MINT	NRMT
COMPLETE SET (10)	15.00	6.75
COMMON CARD (1-10)	1.25	.55
STATED ODDS 1:9		
COMP.PLUS SET (10)	80.00	36.00
COMMON PLUS (1-10)	5.00	2.20
*PLUS: 1.5X TO 4X HI COLUMN		
PLUS: STATED ODDS 1:90		
COMP.WARP TEK SET (10)	600.00	275.00
COMMON WARP TEK (1-10)	40.00	18.00
*WARP TEK: 12.5X TO 30X HI		
WARP TEK: STATED ODDS 1:900		

❑ 1 Keith Van Horn Grant Hill	2.00	.90
❑ 2 Paul Pierce Scottie Pippen	2.00	.90
❑ 3 Tim Duncan Kevin Garnett	3.00	1.35
❑ 4 Kobe Bryant Vince Carter	6.00	2.70
❑ 5 Shaquille O'Neal Michael Olowokandi	2.50	1.10
❑ 6 Chris Webber Shawn Kemp	2.00	.90
❑ 7 Jason Williams Allen Iverson	3.00	1.35
❑ 8 Stephon Marbury Anfernee Hardaway	2.50	1.10
❑ 9 Jason Kidd Mike Bibby	1.50	.70
❑ 10 Shareef Abdur-Rahim Antonio McDyess	1.25	.55

1999-00 SkyBox Dominion Game Day 2K

	MINT	NRMT
COMPLETE SET (20)	12.00	5.50
COMMON CARD (1-20)	.25	.11
UNLISTED STARS	.40	.18
STATED ODDS 1:3		
COMP.PLUS SET (20)	60.00	27.00
COMMON PLUS (1-20)	1.00	.45
*PLUS: 1.5X TO 4X HI COLUMN		
PLUS: STATED ODDS 1:30		
COMP.WARP TEK SET (20)	400.00	180.00
COMMON WARP TEK (1-20)	6.00	2.70
*WARP TEK: 10X TO 25X HI		
WARP TEK: STATED ODDS 1:300		

❑ 1 Vince Carter	4.00	1.80
❑ 2 Kobe Bryant	3.00	1.35
❑ 3 Dirk Nowitzki	.60	.25
❑ 4 Cuttino Mobley	.40	.18
❑ 5 Kevin Garnett	2.50	1.10
❑ 6 Stephon Marbury	.75	.35
❑ 7 Shaquille O'Neal	2.00	.90
❑ 8 Keith Van Horn	.75	.35
❑ 9 Paul Pierce	.75	.35
❑ 10 Jason Williams	1.00	.45
❑ 11 Mike Bibby	.50	.23
❑ 12 Michael Dickerson	.40	.18
❑ 13 Antawn Jamison	.75	.35
❑ 14 Raef LaFrentz	.40	.18
❑ 15 Tyrone Nesby	.25	.11
❑ 16 Ron Mercer	.50	.23
❑ 17 Tracy McGrady	1.25	.55
❑ 18 Larry Hughes	1.00	.45
❑ 19 Robert Traylor	.25	.11
❑ 20 Michael Doleac	.25	.11

1999-00 SkyBox Dominion Hats Off

	MINT	NRMT
COMMON CARD (1-14)	60.00	27.00
RANDOM INSERTS IN PACKS		
PRINT RUNS LISTED BELOW		

❑ 1 Elton Brand/135	250.00	110.00
❑ 2 Steve Francis/170	250.00	110.00
❑ 3 Baron Davis/170	100.00	45.00
❑ 4 Wally Szczerbiak/140	200.00	90.00
❑ 5 Richard Hamilton/150	100.00	45.00
❑ 6 Andre Miller/140	100.00	45.00
❑ 7 Shawn Marion/150	100.00	45.00
❑ 8 Jason Terry/170	80.00	36.00
❑ 9 A.Radojevic/135	60.00	27.00
❑ 10 William Avery/185	80.00	36.00
❑ 11 Ron Artest/140	100.00	45.00
❑ 12 James Posey/170	80.00	36.00
❑ 13 Tim James/140	80.00	36.00
❑ 14 Jumaine Jones/135	80.00	36.00

1999-00 SkyBox Dominion Sky's the Limit

	MINT	NRMT
COMPLETE SET (15)	50.00	22.00
COMMON CARD (1-15)	1.50	.70
STATED ODDS 1:24		
COMP.PLUS SET (15)	200.00	90.00
COMMON PLUS (1-15)	6.00	2.70
*PLUS: 1.5X TO 4X HI COLUMN		
PLUS: STATED ODDS 1:240		
COMMON WARP TEK (1-15)	80.00	36.00
*WARP TEK: 15X TO 40X HI		
WARP TEK: RANDOM INSERTS IN PACKS		
WARP TEK: PRINT RUN 25 SERIAL #'d SETS		

❑ 1 Kevin Garnett	8.00	3.60
❑ 2 Jason Williams	3.00	1.35
❑ 3 Grant Hill	6.00	2.70
❑ 4 Keith Van Horn	2.50	1.10
❑ 5 Allen Iverson	5.00	2.20
❑ 6 Ron Mercer	1.50	.70
❑ 7 Anfernee Hardaway	4.00	1.80
❑ 8 Kobe Bryant	10.00	4.50
❑ 9 Shareef Abdur-Rahim	3.00	1.35
❑ 10 Jason Kidd	4.00	1.80
❑ 11 Shaquille O'Neal	6.00	2.70
❑ 12 Stephon Marbury	2.50	1.10
❑ 13 Paul Pierce	2.50	1.10
❑ 14 Tim Duncan	6.00	2.70
❑ 15 Vince Carter	12.00	5.50

1999-00 SkyBox Impact

	MINT	NRMT
COMPLETE SET (200)	25.00	11.00
COMMON CARD (1-200)	.05	.02
COMMON RC	.20	.09
SEMISTARS	.10	.05
SEMISTARS RC	.25	.11
UNLISTED STARS	.20	.09
UNLISTED STARS RC	.30	.14
V.CARTER COMM: PRINT RUN #'d TO 2000		
V.CARTER AU: PRINT RUN #'d TO 15		
BOTH CARTERS RANDOM INS.IN PACKS		

❑ 1 Tim Duncan	1.00	.45
❑ 2 Doug Christie	.05	.02
❑ 3 Mark Jackson	.05	.02
❑ 4 Paul Pierce	.40	.18
❑ 5 James Posey RC	.60	.25
❑ 6 Steve Smith	.10	.05
❑ 7 Charlie Ward	.05	.02
❑ 8 Elton Brand RC	3.00	1.35

❑ 9 Howard Eisley .05 .02
❑ 10 Grant Hill 1.00 .45
❑ 11 Christian Laettner .10 .05
❑ 12 Corey Maggette RC 1.25 .55
❑ 13 Scot Pollard .05 .02
❑ 14 Robert Traylor .05 .02
❑ 15 Nick Anderson .05 .02
❑ 16 Pat Garrity .05 .02
❑ 17 Hersey Hawkins .10 .05
❑ 18 Troy Hudson .05 .02
❑ 19 Charles Oakley .05 .02
❑ 20 Gary Payton .30 .14
❑ 21 Rik Smits .05 .02
❑ 22 Muggsy Bogues .05 .02
❑ 23 Dale Davis .05 .02
❑ 24 Larry Johnson .10 .05
❑ 25 Antonio McDyess .20 .09
❑ 26 Alonzo Mourning .20 .09
❑ 27 Scottie Pippen .60 .25
❑ 28 Rod Strickland .10 .05
❑ 29 Antoine Walker .25 .11
❑ 30 Allen Iverson .75 .35
❑ 31 Sam Cassell .10 .05
❑ 32 Mookie Blaylock .05 .02
❑ 33 Jim Jackson .05 .02
❑ 34 Brevin Knight .05 .02
❑ 35 Anthony Peeler .05 .02
❑ 36 Bryon Russell .05 .02
❑ 37 Maurice Taylor .20 .09
❑ 38 Elden Campbell .05 .02
❑ 39 Austin Croshere .20 .09
❑ 40 Keith Van Horn .40 .18
❑ 41 Raef LaFrentz .20 .09
❑ 42 Jamal Mashburn .10 .05
❑ 43 Jermaine O'Neal .10 .05
❑ 44 Glenn Robinson .10 .05
❑ 45 Mitch Richmond .20 .09
❑ 46 Keon Clark .05 .02
❑ 47 Derrick Coleman .10 .05
❑ 48 Patrick Ewing .20 .09
❑ 49 Brian Grant .10 .05
❑ 50 Kobe Bryant 1.50 .70
❑ 51 Dan Majerle .10 .05
❑ 52 Ruben Patterson .20 .09
❑ 53 Walt Williams .05 .02
❑ 54 Chris Childs .05 .02
❑ 55 Baron Davis RC .75 .35
❑ 56 Richard Hamilton RC .75 .35
❑ 57 Voshon Lenard .05 .02
❑ 58 Vernon Maxwell .05 .02
❑ 59 Hakeem Olajuwon .30 .14
❑ 60 Jason Williams .50 .23
❑ 61 Gary Trent .05 .02
❑ 62 Kenny Anderson .10 .05
❑ 63 Shawn Bradley .05 .02
❑ 64 Obinna Ekezie RC .25 .11
❑ 65 Tom Gugliotta .10 .05
❑ 66 Ron Harper .10 .05
❑ 67 Corey Benjamin .05 .02
❑ 68 Donyell Marshall .05 .02
❑ 69 David Robinson .30 .14
❑ 70 Stephon Marbury .40 .18
❑ 71 Marcus Camby .20 .09
❑ 72 Horace Grant .10 .05
❑ 73 Tim Hardaway .20 .09
❑ 74 Greg Foster .05 .02
❑ 75 Cuttino Mobley .20 .09
❑ 76 Rodney Buford RC .20 .09
❑ 77 Clifford Robinson .05 .02
❑ 78 Isaac Austin .05 .02
❑ 79 Robert Pack .05 .02
❑ 80 Eddie Jones .40 .18
❑ 81 Shawn Marion RC 1.00 .45
❑ 82 Anthony Mason .10 .05
❑ 83 Oliver Miller .05 .02
❑ 84 Dirk Nowitzki .30 .14
❑ 85 Jayson Williams .10 .05
❑ 86 Brent Barry .05 .02
❑ 87 P.J. Brown .05 .02
❑ 88 Kelvin Cato .05 .02
❑ 89 Jim McIlvaine .05 .02
❑ 90 Steve Francis RC 4.00 1.80
❑ 91 Bryant Reeves .05 .02
❑ 92 Jerry Stackhouse .10 .05
❑ 93 Allan Houston .20 .09
❑ 94 Kevin Garnett 1.25 .55
❑ 95 Karl Malone .30 .14
❑ 96 David Wesley .05 .02
❑ 97 Eddie Robinson RC .50 .23
❑ 98 Ben Wallace .05 .02
❑ 99 Chris Webber .60 .25
❑ 100 Lamar Odom RC 2.50 1.10
❑ 101 Shandon Anderson .05 .02
❑ 102 Terrell Brandon .10 .05
❑ 103 Jeff Hornacek .10 .05
❑ 104 Terry Mills .05 .02
❑ 105 Tyrone Nesby RC .05 .02
❑ 106 Charles Outlaw .05 .02
❑ 107 Predrag Stojakovic .10 .05
❑ 108 Ron Artest RC .75 .35
❑ 109 Tony Battie .05 .02
❑ 110 Cedric Ceballos .05 .02
❑ 111 Anfernee Hardaway .60 .25
❑ 112 Othella Harrington .05 .02
❑ 113 Rick Hughes RC .20 .09
❑ 114 Loy Vaught .05 .02
❑ 115 Malik Rose .05 .02
❑ 116 Vin Baker .10 .05
❑ 117 Charles Barkley .30 .14
❑ 118 Michael Finley .20 .09
❑ 119 Adrian Griffin RC .40 .18
❑ 120 Jason Kidd .60 .25
❑ 121 Gheorghe Muresan .05 .02
❑ 122 Cherokee Parks .05 .02
❑ 123 Glen Rice .10 .05
❑ 124 Bimbo Coles .05 .02
❑ 125 Andrew DeClercq .05 .02
❑ 126 Matt Geiger .05 .02
❑ 127 Bobby Jackson .05 .02
❑ 128 Michael Olowokandi .10 .05
❑ 129 Greg Ostertag .05 .02
❑ 130 Tracy McGrady .60 .25
❑ 131 Rodney Rogers .05 .02
❑ 132 Juwan Howard .10 .05
❑ 133 Terry Cummings .05 .02
❑ 134 Mario Elie .05 .02
❑ 135 Trajan Langdon RC .50 .23
❑ 136 George Lynch .05 .02
❑ 137 Roshown McLeod .05 .02
❑ 138 Joe Smith .10 .05
❑ 139 John Stockton .20 .09
❑ 140 Ray Allen .20 .09
❑ 141 Vince Carter 2.00 .90
❑ 142 Al Harrington .25 .11
❑ 143 Ron Mercer .25 .11
❑ 144 Vitaly Potapenko .05 .02
❑ 145 Arvydas Sabonis .10 .05
❑ 146 Latrell Sprewell .40 .18
❑ 147 Aaron Williams .05 .02
❑ 148 Shareef Abdur-Rahim .40 .18
❑ 149 Vonteego Cummings RC .50 .23
❑ 150 Shaquille O'Neal 1.00 .45
❑ 151 Derek Fisher .10 .05
❑ 152 Todd MacCulloch RC .30 .14
❑ 153 Andre Miller RC 1.00 .45
❑ 154 Dikembe Mutombo .10 .05
❑ 155 Ervin Johnson .05 .02
❑ 156 Michael Dickerson .20 .09
❑ 157 A.C. Green .10 .05
❑ 158 Kevin Willis .05 .02
❑ 159 Kerry Kittles .10 .05
❑ 160 Damon Stoudamire .20 .09
❑ 161 Eric Snow .05 .02
❑ 162 Bob Sura .05 .02
❑ 163 Jason Terry RC .50 .23
❑ 164 Derek Anderson .20 .09
❑ 165 Randy Brown .05 .02
❑ 166 Vlade Divac .05 .02
❑ 167 Chris Gatling .05 .02
❑ 168 Lindsey Hunter .05 .02
❑ 169 Tim Thomas .25 .11
❑ 170 Antawn Jamison .40 .18
❑ 171 Alan Henderson .05 .02
❑ 172 Larry Hughes .50 .23
❑ 173 Shawn Kemp .30 .14
❑ 174 Radoslav Nesterovic .05 .02
❑ 175 Scott Padgett .10 .05
❑ 176 Brian Skinner .05 .02
❑ 177 Jerome Williams .10 .05
❑ 178 Corliss Williamson .05 .02
❑ 179 Sean Elliott .05 .02
❑ 180 Wally Szczerbiak RC 1.25 .55
❑ 181 Toni Kukoc .25 .11
❑ 182 Chucky Atkins RC .40 .18
❑ 183 Jalen Rose .20 .09
❑ 184 Nick Van Exel .10 .05
❑ 185 Rasheed Wallace .20 .09
❑ 186 Avery Johnson .05 .02
❑ 187 Jamie Feick RC .20 .09
❑ 188 Adonal Foyle .05 .02
❑ 189 Devean George RC .60 .25
❑ 190 Mike Bibby .25 .11
❑ 191 Lamond Murray .05 .02
❑ 192 Billy Owens .05 .02
❑ 193 Isaiah Rider .10 .05
❑ 194 Darrell Armstrong .10 .05
❑ 195 Antonio Davis .05 .02
❑ 196 Dale Ellis .05 .02
❑ 197 Tim Young RC .20 .09
❑ 198 Roy Rogers .05 .02
❑ 199 Terry Porter .05 .02
❑ 200 Reggie Miller .20 .09
❑ P141 Vince Carter PROMO 3.00 1.35
❑ NNO Vince Carter 30.00 13.50
Commemorative card
Numbered to 2000
❑ NNO Vince Carter
Commemorative card
Autographed to 15

1999-00 SkyBox Impact Rewind '99

	MINT	NRMT
COMPLETE SET (40)	20.00	9.00
COMMON CARD (RN1-RN40)	.15	.07
SEMISTARS	.20	.09
UNLISTED STARS	.30	.14
ONE PER PACK		

❑ RN1 Tim Duncan 1.50 .70
❑ RN2 David Robinson .50 .23
❑ RN3 Sean Elliott .15 .07
❑ RN4 Mario Elie .15 .07
❑ RN5 Avery Johnson .15 .07
❑ RN6 Malik Rose .15 .07
❑ RN7 Jaren Jackson .15 .07
❑ RN8 Tim Duncan 1.50 .70
❑ RN9 Gerald King .15 .07
❑ RN10 Jerome Kersey .15 .07
❑ RN11 Steve Kerr .15 .07
❑ RN12 Antonio Daniels .15 .07
❑ RN13 Karl Malone .50 .23
❑ RN14 Vince Carter 3.00 1.35
❑ RN15 Karl Malone .50 .23
❑ RN16 Tim Duncan 1.50 .70
❑ RN17 Alonzo Mourning .30 .14
❑ RN18 Allen Iverson 1.25 .55
❑ RN19 Jason Kidd 1.00 .45
❑ RN20 Chris Webber 1.00 .45
❑ RN21 Grant Hill 1.50 .70
❑ RN22 Shaquille O'Neal 1.50 .70
❑ RN23 Gary Payton .50 .23
❑ RN24 Tim Hardaway .30 .14
❑ RN25 Kevin Garnett 2.00 .90
❑ RN26 Antonio McDyess .30 .14
❑ RN27 Hakeem Olajuwon .50 .23
❑ RN28 Kobe Bryant 2.50 1.10
❑ RN29 John Stockton .30 .14
❑ RN30 Vince Carter 3.00 1.35

Card	MINT	NRMT
❑ RN31 Paul Pierce	.60	.25
❑ RN32 Jason Williams	.75	.35
❑ RN33 Mike Bibby	.40	.18
❑ RN34 Matt Harpring	.15	.07
❑ RN35 Michael Dickerson	.30	.14
❑ RN36 Cuttino Mobley	.30	.14
❑ RN37 Michael Doleac	.15	.07
❑ RN38 Michael Olowokandi	.20	.09
❑ RN39 Antawn Jamison	.60	.25
❑ RN40 Vince Carter	3.00	1.35

1998-99 SkyBox Molten Metal

	MINT	NRMT
COMPLETE SET (150)	100.00	45.00
COMMON CARD (1-100)	.10	.05
COMMON CARD (101-130)	.15	.07
COMMON CARD (131-150)	1.25	.55
COMMON RC	.75	.35
SEMISTARS 1-100	.15	.07
SEMISTARS 101-130	.20	.09
SEMISTARS RC	1.00	.45
UNLISTED STARS 1-100	.25	.11
UNLISTED STARS 101-130	.40	.18
UNLISTED STARS RC	1.50	.70

CARDS 1-100 INSERTED 4:1 PACKS
CARDS 101-130 INSERTED 1:1 PACKS
CARDS 131-150 INSERTED 1:2 PACKS

Card	MINT	NRMT
❑ 1 Maurice Taylor	.25	.11
❑ 2 Bison Dele	.10	.05
❑ 3 Anthony Mason	.15	.07
❑ 4 John Starks	.10	.05
❑ 5 Anthony Johnson	.10	.05
❑ 6 Calbert Cheaney	.10	.05
❑ 7 Roshown McLeod RC	.75	.35
❑ 8 Jalen Rose	.25	.11
❑ 9 Kelvin Cato	.10	.05
❑ 10 Walter McCarty	.10	.05
❑ 11 Isaac Austin	.10	.05
❑ 12 Arvydas Sabonis	.15	.07
❑ 13 David Wesley	.10	.05
❑ 14 Jim Jackson	.10	.05
❑ 15 Elden Campbell	.10	.05
❑ 16 Michael Doleac RC	1.50	.70
❑ 17 Chris Webber	.75	.35
❑ 18 Mitch Richmond	.25	.11
❑ 19 Johnny Newman	.10	.05
❑ 20 Jayson Williams	.15	.07
❑ 21 George Lynch	.10	.05
❑ 22 Ron Harper	.15	.07
❑ 23 Donyell Marshall	.10	.05
❑ 24 Derek Fisher	.15	.07
❑ 25 Matt Harpring RC	1.50	.70
❑ 26 Jason Williams RC	10.00	4.50
❑ 27 Toni Kukoc	.30	.14
❑ 28 Clarence Weatherspoon	.10	.05
❑ 29 Eddie Jones	.50	.23
❑ 30 Bo Outlaw	.10	.05
❑ 31 Zydrunas Ilgauskas	.10	.05
❑ 32 Michael Dickerson RC	3.00	1.35
❑ 33 Tyronn Lue RC	1.00	.45
❑ 34 Theo Ratliff	.10	.05
❑ 35 Dirk Nowitzki RC	6.00	2.70
❑ 36 Robert Traylor RC	1.50	.70
❑ 37 Gary Trent	.10	.05
❑ 38 Wesley Person	.10	.05
❑ 39 Bryce Drew RC	1.50	.70
❑ 40 P.J. Brown	.10	.05
❑ 41 Joe Smith	.15	.07
❑ 42 Avery Johnson	.10	.05
❑ 43 Chris Anstey	.10	.05
❑ 44 Mario Elie	.10	.05
❑ 45 Voshon Lenard	.10	.05
❑ 46 Rex Chapman	.10	.05
❑ 47 Hersey Hawkins	.15	.07
❑ 48 Shawn Bradley	.10	.05
❑ 49 Matt Maloney	.10	.05
❑ 50 Dan Majerle	.15	.07
❑ 51 Pat Garrity RC	1.00	.45
❑ 52 Sam Perkins	.15	.07
❑ 53 Mookie Blaylock	.10	.05
❑ 54 Al Harrington RC	5.00	2.20
❑ 55 Clifford Robinson	.10	.05
❑ 56 Alan Henderson	.10	.05
❑ 57 Chris Mullin	.25	.11
❑ 58 Dennis Scott	.10	.05
❑ 59 A.C. Green	.15	.07
❑ 60 Tyrone Hill	.10	.05
❑ 61 Chauncey Billups	.10	.05
❑ 62 Michael Finley	.25	.11
❑ 63 Terrell Brandon	.15	.07
❑ 64 Detlef Schrempf	.15	.07
❑ 65 Bonzi Wells RC	6.00	2.70
❑ 66 Larry Johnson	.15	.07
❑ 67 Bryant Reeves	.10	.05
❑ 68 Raef LaFrentz RC	3.00	1.35
❑ 69 Kendall Gill	.15	.07
❑ 70 Bryon Russell	.10	.05
❑ 71 Bobby Phills	.10	.05
❑ 72 Tony Delk	.10	.05
❑ 73 Lorenzen Wright	.10	.05
❑ 74 Keon Clark RC	1.50	.70
❑ 75 Billy Owens	.10	.05
❑ 76 Tracy Murray	.10	.05
❑ 77 Bobby Jackson	.10	.05
❑ 78 Sam Cassell	.15	.07
❑ 79 Corliss Williamson	.10	.05
❑ 80 Jeff Hornacek	.15	.07
❑ 81 LaPhonso Ellis	.10	.05
❑ 82 Sam Mitchell	.10	.05
❑ 83 Sean Elliott	.10	.05
❑ 84 John Wallace	.10	.05
❑ 85 Dikembe Mutombo	.15	.07
❑ 86 Rik Smits	.10	.05
❑ 87 Isaiah Rider	.15	.07
❑ 88 Joe Dumars	.25	.11
❑ 89 Allan Houston	.25	.11
❑ 90 Sam Mack	.10	.05
❑ 91 Paul Pierce RC	8.00	3.60
❑ 92 Lamond Murray	.10	.05
❑ 93 Rasheed Wallace	.25	.11
❑ 94 Danny Fortson	.15	.07
❑ 95 Cherokee Parks	.10	.05
❑ 96 Antonio Daniels	.10	.05
❑ 97 Shandon Anderson	.10	.05
❑ 98 Ricky Davis RC	3.00	1.35
❑ 99 Rodney Rogers	.10	.05
❑ 100 Tariq Abdul-Wahad	.15	.07
❑ 101 Glenn Robinson	.20	.09
❑ 102 Ron Mercer	.60	.25
❑ 103 Alonzo Mourning	.40	.18
❑ 104 Marcus Camby	.25	.11
❑ 105 Steve Smith	.20	.09
❑ 106 Tim Hardaway	.25	.11
❑ 107 Rod Strickland	.20	.09
❑ 108 Reggie Miller	.40	.18
❑ 109 Juwan Howard	.20	.09
❑ 110 Hakeem Olajuwon	.60	.25
❑ 111 John Stockton	.40	.18
❑ 112 Antonio McDyess	.40	.18
❑ 113 Charles Barkley	.60	.25
❑ 114 Karl Malone	.50	.23
❑ 115 Jerry Stackhouse	.20	.09
❑ 116 Tracy McGrady	1.50	.70
❑ 117 Brevin Knight	.15	.07
❑ 118 Gary Payton	.60	.25
❑ 119 Derek Anderson	.50	.23
❑ 120 Glen Rice	.20	.09
❑ 121 David Robinson	.60	.25
❑ 122 Vin Baker	.20	.09
❑ 123 Tom Gugliotta	.20	.09
❑ 124 Patrick Ewing	.40	.18
❑ 125 Ray Allen	.50	.23
❑ 126 Anfernee Hardaway	1.25	.55
❑ 127 Jason Kidd	1.25	.55
❑ 128 Kenny Anderson	.20	.09
❑ 129 Kerry Kittles	.20	.09
❑ 130 Tim Thomas	.60	.25
❑ 131 Shareef Abdur-Rahim	2.00	.90
❑ 132 Mike Bibby RC	6.00	2.70
❑ 133 Kobe Bryant	6.00	2.70
❑ 134 Vince Carter RC	40.00	18.00
❑ 135 Tim Duncan	4.00	1.80
❑ 136 Kevin Garnett	5.00	2.20
❑ 137 Grant Hill	4.00	1.80
❑ 138 Larry Hughes RC	12.00	5.50
❑ 139 Allen Iverson	3.00	1.35
❑ 140 Antawn Jamison RC	10.00	4.50
❑ 141 Michael Jordan	10.00	4.50
❑ 142 Shawn Kemp	1.25	.55
❑ 143 Stephon Marbury	2.00	.90
❑ 144 Michael Olowokandi RC	3.00	1.35
❑ 145 Shaquille O'Neal	4.00	1.80
❑ 146 Scottie Pippen	2.50	1.10
❑ 147 Dennis Rodman	1.50	.70
❑ 148 Damon Stoudamire	.40	.18
❑ 149 Keith Van Horn	2.00	.90
❑ 150 Antoine Walker	1.25	.55

1998-99 SkyBox Molten Metal Xplosion

	MINT	NRMT
COMPLETE SET (150)	250.00	110.00
COMMON CARD (1-100)	.15	.07
*STARS: .6X TO 1.5X BASE CARD HI		
*RCs: .5X TO 1.25X BASE HI		
STATED ODDS 1:2.5		
COMMON CARD (101-130)	1.25	.55
*STARS: 2X TO 5X BASE HI		
STATED ODDS 1:18		
COMMON CARD (131-150)	6.00	2.70
*STARS: 2X TO 5X BASE HI		
*RCs: .6X TO 1.5X BASE HI		
STATED ODDS 1:60		
❑ 134 Vince Carter	100.00	45.00

1998-99 SkyBox Molten Metal Fusion

	MINT	NRMT
COMMON CARD (1-30)	1.50	.70

	MINT	NRMT
SEMISTARS	2.00	.90
UNLISTED STARS	2.50	1.10
STATED ODDS 1:16		
COMMON CARD (31-50)	15.00	6.75
RANDOM INSERTS IN PACKS		
31-50: PRINT RUN 40 SERIAL #'d SETS		
36/37/39/41-43: PRINT RUN 250 #'d SETS		

Card	MINT	NRMT
❑ 1 Glenn Robinson	2.00	.90
❑ 2 Ron Mercer	4.00	1.80
❑ 3 Alonzo Mourning	2.50	1.10
❑ 4 Marcus Camby	2.50	1.10
❑ 5 Steve Smith	2.00	.90
❑ 6 Tim Hardaway	2.50	1.10
❑ 7 Rod Strickland	2.00	.90
❑ 8 Reggie Miller	2.50	1.10
❑ 9 Juwan Howard	2.00	.90
❑ 10 Hakeem Olajuwon	4.00	1.80
❑ 11 John Stockton	2.50	1.10
❑ 12 Antonio McDyess	2.50	1.10
❑ 13 Charles Barkley	4.00	1.80
❑ 14 Karl Malone	3.00	1.35
❑ 15 Jerry Stackhouse	2.00	.90
❑ 16 Tracy McGrady	10.00	4.50
❑ 17 Brevin Knight	1.50	.70
❑ 18 Gary Payton	4.00	1.80
❑ 19 Derek Anderson	3.00	1.35
❑ 20 Glen Rice	2.00	.90
❑ 21 David Robinson	4.00	1.80
❑ 22 Vin Baker	2.00	.90
❑ 23 Tom Gugliotta	2.00	.90
❑ 24 Patrick Ewing	2.50	1.10
❑ 25 Ray Allen	3.00	1.35
❑ 26 Anfernee Hardaway	8.00	3.60
❑ 27 Jason Kidd	8.00	3.60
❑ 28 Kenny Anderson	2.00	.90
❑ 29 Kerry Kittles	2.00	.90
❑ 30 Tim Thomas	4.00	1.80
❑ 31 Shareef Abdur-Rahim	100.00	45.00
❑ 32 Mike Bibby	60.00	27.00
❑ 33 Kobe Bryant	300.00	135.00
❑ 34 Vince Carter	500.00	220.00
❑ 35 Tim Duncan	200.00	90.00
❑ 36 Kevin Garnett	60.00	27.00
❑ 37 Grant Hill	50.00	22.00
❑ 38 Larry Hughes	120.00	55.00
❑ 39 Allen Iverson	40.00	18.00
❑ 40 Antawn Jamison	100.00	45.00
❑ 41 Michael Jordan	120.00	55.00
❑ 42 Shawn Kemp	15.00	6.75
❑ 43 Stephon Marbury	25.00	11.00
❑ 44 Michael Olowokandi	30.00	13.50
❑ 45 Shaquille O'Neal	200.00	90.00
❑ 46 Scottie Pippen	120.00	55.00
❑ 47 Dennis Rodman	80.00	36.00
❑ 48 Damon Stoudamire	15.00	6.75
❑ 49 Keith Van Horn	100.00	45.00
❑ 50 Antoine Walker	60.00	27.00

1998-99 SkyBox Molten Metal Fusion Titanium

	MINT	NRMT
COMMON CARD (1-30)	4.00	1.80
SEMISTARS	5.00	2.20
UNLISTED STARS	6.00	2.70
STATED ODDS 1:96		
COMMON CARD (31-50)	10.00	4.50
RANDOM INSERTS IN PACKS		
31-50: PRINT RUN 250 SERIAL #'d SETS		
36/37/39/41-43: PRINT RUN 40 #'d SETS		

Card	MINT	NRMT
❑ 1 Glenn Robinson	5.00	2.20
❑ 2 Ron Mercer	10.00	4.50
❑ 3 Alonzo Mourning	6.00	2.70
❑ 4 Marcus Camby	6.00	2.70
❑ 5 Steve Smith	5.00	2.20
❑ 6 Tim Hardaway	6.00	2.70
❑ 7 Rod Strickland	5.00	2.20
❑ 8 Reggie Miller	6.00	2.70
❑ 9 Juwan Howard	5.00	2.20
❑ 10 Hakeem Olajuwon	10.00	4.50
❑ 11 John Stockton	6.00	2.70
❑ 12 Antonio McDyess	6.00	2.70
❑ 13 Charles Barkley	10.00	4.50
❑ 14 Karl Malone	8.00	3.60
❑ 15 Jerry Stackhouse	5.00	2.20
❑ 16 Tracy McGrady	25.00	11.00
❑ 17 Brevin Knight	4.00	1.80
❑ 18 Gary Payton	10.00	4.50
❑ 19 Derek Anderson	8.00	3.60
❑ 20 Glen Rice	5.00	2.20
❑ 21 David Robinson	10.00	4.50
❑ 22 Vin Baker	5.00	2.20
❑ 23 Tom Gugliotta	5.00	2.20
❑ 24 Patrick Ewing	6.00	2.70
❑ 25 Ray Allen	8.00	3.60
❑ 26 Anfernee Hardaway	20.00	9.00
❑ 27 Jason Kidd	20.00	9.00
❑ 28 Kenny Anderson	5.00	2.20
❑ 29 Kerry Kittles	5.00	2.20
❑ 30 Tim Thomas	10.00	4.50
❑ 31 Shareef Abdur-Rahim	25.00	11.00
❑ 32 Mike Bibby	15.00	6.75
❑ 33 Kobe Bryant	80.00	36.00
❑ 34 Vince Carter	120.00	55.00
❑ 35 Tim Duncan	50.00	22.00
❑ 36 Kevin Garnett	250.00	110.00
❑ 37 Grant Hill	200.00	90.00
❑ 38 Larry Hughes	30.00	13.50
❑ 39 Allen Iverson	150.00	70.00
❑ 40 Antawn Jamison	25.00	11.00
❑ 41 Michael Jordan	800.00	350.00
❑ 42 Shawn Kemp	60.00	27.00
❑ 43 Stephon Marbury	100.00	45.00
❑ 44 Michael Olowokandi	10.00	4.50
❑ 45 Shaquille O'Neal	50.00	22.00
❑ 46 Scottie Pippen	30.00	13.50
❑ 47 Dennis Rodman	20.00	9.00
❑ 48 Damon Stoudamire	10.00	4.50
❑ 49 Keith Van Horn	25.00	11.00
❑ 50 Antoine Walker	15.00	6.75

1994-95 SP

	MINT	NRMT
COMPLETE SET (165)	40.00	18.00
COMMON FOIL RC (1-30)	.50	.23
COMMON CARD (31-165)	.15	.07
SEMISTARS	.25	.11
UNLISTED STARS	.50	.23
FOIL RC's CONDITION SENSITIVE!		
MJ1R: STATED ODDS 1:30		
MJ1S: STATED ODDS 1:192		

Card	MINT	NRMT
❑ 1 Glenn Robinson FOIL RC	2.50	1.10
❑ 2 Jason Kidd FOIL RC	6.00	2.70
❑ 3 Grant Hill FOIL RC	10.00	4.50
❑ 4 Donyell Marshall FOIL RC	.75	.35
❑ 5 Juwan Howard FOIL RC	1.50	.70
❑ 6 Sharone Wright FOIL RC	.50	.23
❑ 7 Lamond Murray FOIL RC	.50	.23
❑ 8 Brian Grant FOIL RC	2.00	.90
❑ 9 Eric Montross FOIL RC	.50	.23
❑ 10 Eddie Jones FOIL RC	5.00	2.20
❑ 11 Carlos Rogers FOIL RC	.50	.23
❑ 12 Khalid Reeves FOIL RC	.50	.23
❑ 13 Jalen Rose FOIL RC	3.00	1.35
❑ 14 Eric Piatkowski FOIL RC	.50	.23
❑ 15 Clifford Rozier FOIL RC	.50	.23
❑ 16 Aaron McKie FOIL RC	.50	.23
❑ 17 Eric Mobley FOIL RC	.50	.23
❑ 18 Tony Dumas FOIL RC	.50	.23
❑ 19 B.J. Tyler FOIL RC	.50	.23
❑ 20 Dickey Simpkins FOIL RC	.50	.23
❑ 21 Bill Curley FOIL RC	.50	.23
❑ 22 Wesley Person FOIL RC	.75	.35
❑ 23 Monty Williams FOIL RC	.50	.23
❑ 24 Greg Minor FOIL RC	.50	.23
❑ 25 Charlie Ward FOIL RC	.50	.23
❑ 26 B. Thompson FOIL RC	.50	.23
❑ 27 Trevor Ruffin FOIL RC	.50	.23
❑ 28 Derrick Alston FOIL RC	.50	.23
❑ 29 Michael Smith FOIL RC	.50	.23
❑ 30 D. Wingfield FOIL RC	.50	.23
❑ 31 Stacey Augmon	.15	.07
❑ 32 Steve Smith	.25	.11
❑ 33 Mookie Blaylock	.15	.07
❑ 34 Grant Long	.15	.07
❑ 35 Ken Norman	.15	.07
❑ 36 Dominique Wilkins	.50	.23
❑ 37 Dino Radja	.15	.07
❑ 38 Dee Brown	.15	.07
❑ 39 David Wesley	.15	.07
❑ 40 Rick Fox	.15	.07
❑ 41 Alonzo Mourning	.60	.25
❑ 42 Larry Johnson	.25	.11
❑ 43 Hersey Hawkins	.25	.11
❑ 44 Scott Burrell	.15	.07
❑ 45 Muggsy Bogues	.25	.11
❑ 46 Scottie Pippen	1.50	.70
❑ 47 Toni Kukoc	.75	.35
❑ 48 B.J. Armstrong	.15	.07
❑ 49 Will Perdue	.15	.07
❑ 50 Ron Harper	.25	.11
❑ 51 Mark Price	.15	.07
❑ 52 Tyrone Hill	.15	.07
❑ 53 Chris Mills	.25	.11
❑ 54 John Williams	.15	.07
❑ 55 Bobby Phills	.15	.07
❑ 56 Jim Jackson	.25	.11
❑ 57 Jamal Mashburn	.50	.23
❑ 58 Popeye Jones	.15	.07
❑ 59 Roy Tarpley	.15	.07
❑ 60 Lorenzo Williams	.15	.07
❑ 61 Mahmoud Abdul-Rauf	.15	.07
❑ 62 Rodney Rogers	.15	.07
❑ 63 Bryant Stith	.15	.07
❑ 64 Dikembe Mutombo	.25	.11
❑ 65 Robert Pack	.15	.07
❑ 66 Joe Dumars	.50	.23
❑ 67 Terry Mills	.15	.07
❑ 68 Oliver Miller	.15	.07
❑ 69 Lindsey Hunter	.25	.11
❑ 70 Mark West	.15	.07
❑ 71 Latrell Sprewell	1.00	.45
❑ 72 Tim Hardaway	.50	.23
❑ 73 Ricky Pierce	.15	.07
❑ 74 Rony Seikaly	.15	.07
❑ 75 Tom Gugliotta	.25	.11
❑ 76 Hakeem Olajuwon	.75	.35
❑ 77 Clyde Drexler	.50	.23
❑ 78 Vernon Maxwell	.15	.07
❑ 79 Robert Horry	.15	.07
❑ 80 Sam Cassell	.50	.23
❑ 81 Reggie Miller	.50	.23
❑ 82 Rik Smits	.15	.07
❑ 83 Derrick McKey	.15	.07
❑ 84 Mark Jackson	.15	.07
❑ 85 Dale Davis	.15	.07
❑ 86 Loy Vaught	.15	.07
❑ 87 Terry Dehere	.15	.07
❑ 88 Malik Sealy	.15	.07
❑ 89 Pooh Richardson	.15	.07
❑ 90 Tony Massenburg	.15	.07
❑ 91 Cedric Ceballos	.15	.07
❑ 92 Nick Van Exel	.50	.23
❑ 93 George Lynch	.15	.07
❑ 94 Vlade Divac	.15	.07
❑ 95 Elden Campbell	.15	.07
❑ 96 Glen Rice	.25	.11
❑ 97 Kevin Willis	.15	.07
❑ 98 Billy Owens	.15	.07
❑ 99 Bimbo Coles	.15	.07
❑ 100 Harold Miner	.15	.07
❑ 101 Vin Baker	.50	.23
❑ 102 Todd Day	.15	.07
❑ 103 Marty Conlon	.15	.07
❑ 104 Lee Mayberry	.15	.07
❑ 105 Eric Murdock	.15	.07
❑ 106 Isaiah Rider	.25	.11

❑ 107 Doug West .15 .07
❑ 108 Christian Laettner .25 .11
❑ 109 Sean Rooks .15 .07
❑ 110 Stacey King .15 .07
❑ 111 Derrick Coleman .25 .11
❑ 112 Kenny Anderson .25 .11
❑ 113 Chris Morris .15 .07
❑ 114 Armon Gilliam .15 .07
❑ 115 Benoit Benjamin .15 .07
❑ 116 Patrick Ewing .50 .23
❑ 117 Charles Oakley .15 .07
❑ 118 John Starks .15 .07
❑ 119 Derek Harper .15 .07
❑ 120 Charles Smith .15 .07
❑ 121 Shaquille O'Neal 2.50 1.10
❑ 122 Anfernee Hardaway 1.50 .70
❑ 123 Nick Anderson .15 .07
❑ 124 Horace Grant .25 .11
❑ 125 Donald Royal .15 .07
❑ 126 Clarence Weatherspoon .15 .07
❑ 127 Dana Barros .15 .07
❑ 128 Jeff Malone .15 .07
❑ 129 Willie Burton .15 .07
❑ 130 Shawn Bradley .15 .07
❑ 131 Charles Barkley .75 .35
❑ 132 Kevin Johnson .25 .11
❑ 133 Danny Manning .25 .11
❑ 134 Dan Majerle .25 .11
❑ 135 A.C. Green .25 .11
❑ 136 Otis Thorpe .15 .07
❑ 137 Clifford Robinson .25 .11
❑ 138 Rod Strickland .25 .11
❑ 139 Buck Williams .15 .07
❑ 140 James Robinson .15 .07
❑ 141 Mitch Richmond .50 .23
❑ 142 Walt Williams .15 .07
❑ 143 Olden Polynice .15 .07
❑ 144 Spud Webb .15 .07
❑ 145 Duane Causwell .15 .07
❑ 146 David Robinson .75 .35
❑ 147 Dennis Rodman 1.00 .45
❑ 148 Sean Elliott .25 .11
❑ 149 Avery Johnson .15 .07
❑ 150 J.R. Reid .15 .07
❑ 151 Shawn Kemp .75 .35
❑ 152 Gary Payton .75 .35
❑ 153 Detlef Schrempf .25 .11
❑ 154 Nate McMillan .15 .07
❑ 155 Kendall Gill .25 .11
❑ 156 Karl Malone .75 .35
❑ 157 John Stockton .50 .23
❑ 158 Jeff Hornacek .25 .11
❑ 159 Felton Spencer .15 .07
❑ 160 David Benoit .15 .07
❑ 161 Chris Webber 1.50 .70
❑ 162 Rex Chapman .15 .07
❑ 163 Don MacLean .15 .07
❑ 164 Calbert Cheaney .15 .07
❑ 165 Scott Skiles .15 .07
❑ P23 Michael Jordan Promo 20.00 9.00
❑ MJ1R Michael Jordan Red 5.00 2.20
❑ MJ1S Michael Jordan Silver 20.00 9.00

1994-95 SP Die Cuts

	MINT	NRMT
COMPLETE SET (165)	60.00	27.00
COMMON CARD (1-165)	.30	.14

*STARS: 1.25X TO 2.5X BASE CARD HI
*RCs: .75X TO 1.5X BASE HI
ONE PER PACK

1994-95 SP Holoviews

	MINT	NRMT
COMPLETE SET (36)	75.00	34.00
COMMON CARD (PC1-PC36)	1.00	.45
SEMISTARS	1.50	.70
UNLISTED STARS	3.00	1.35

STATED ODDS 1:5

COMP.DIE CUT SET (36)	300.00	135.00
COMMON DC (DPC1-DPC36)	3.00	1.35

*DIE CUTS: 1.5X TO 3X HI COLUMN
DIE CUTS: STATED ODDS 1:75

❑ PC1 Eric Montross 1.00 .45
❑ PC2 Dominique Wilkins 3.00 1.35
❑ PC3 Larry Johnson 1.50 .70
❑ PC4 Dickey Simpkins 1.00 .45
❑ PC5 Jalen Rose 6.00 2.70
❑ PC6 Latrell Sprewell 6.00 2.70
❑ PC7 Carlos Rogers 1.00 .45
❑ PC8 Lamond Murray 1.00 .45
❑ PC9 Eddie Jones 10.00 4.50
❑ PC10 Cedric Ceballos 1.00 .45
❑ PC11 Khalid Reeves 1.00 .45
❑ PC12 Glenn Robinson 5.00 2.20
❑ PC13 Christian Laettner 1.50 .70
❑ PC14 Derrick Coleman 1.50 .70
❑ PC15 Vin Baker 3.00 1.35
❑ PC16 Donyell Marshall 1.50 .70
❑ PC17 Kenny Anderson 1.50 .70
❑ PC18 Sharone Wright 1.00 .45
❑ PC19 Wesley Person 1.50 .70
❑ PC20 Brian Grant 4.00 1.80
❑ PC21 Mitch Richmond 3.00 1.35
❑ PC22 Shawn Kemp 5.00 2.20
❑ PC23 Gary Payton 5.00 2.20
❑ PC24 Juwan Howard 4.00 1.80
❑ PC25 Stacey Augmon 1.00 .45
❑ PC26 Aaron McKie 1.00 .45
❑ PC27 Clifford Rozier 1.00 .45
❑ PC28 Eric Piatkowski 1.00 .45
❑ PC29 Shaquille O'Neal 15.00 6.75
❑ PC30 Charlie Ward 3.00 1.35
❑ PC31 Monty Williams 1.00 .45
❑ PC32 Jason Kidd 12.00 5.50
❑ PC33 Bill Curley 1.00 .45
❑ PC34 Grant Hill 15.00 6.75
❑ PC35 Jamal Mashburn 3.00 1.35
❑ PC36 Nick Van Exel 3.00 1.35

1995-96 SP

	MINT	NRMT
COMPLETE SET (167)	35.00	16.00
COMMON CARD (1-167)	.15	.07
SEMISTARS	.20	.09
UNLISTED STARS	.40	.18

C1: STATED ODDS 1:359

❑ 1 Stacey Augmon .15 .07
❑ 2 Mookie Blaylock .15 .07
❑ 3 Andrew Lang .15 .07
❑ 4 Steve Smith .20 .09
❑ 5 Spud Webb .15 .07
❑ 6 Dana Barros .15 .07
❑ 7 Dee Brown .15 .07
❑ 8 Todd Day .15 .07
❑ 9 Rick Fox .15 .07
❑ 10 Eric Montross .15 .07
❑ 11 Dino Radja .15 .07
❑ 12 Kenny Anderson .20 .09
❑ 13 Scott Burrell .15 .07
❑ 14 Dell Curry .15 .07
❑ 15 Matt Geiger .15 .07
❑ 16 Larry Johnson .20 .09
❑ 17 Glen Rice .20 .09
❑ 18 Steve Kerr .15 .07
❑ 19 Toni Kukoc .50 .23
❑ 20 Luc Longley .15 .07
❑ 21 Scottie Pippen 1.25 .55
❑ 22 Dennis Rodman .75 .35
❑ 23 Michael Jordan 5.00 2.20
❑ 24 Terrell Brandon .20 .09
❑ 25 Michael Cage .15 .07
❑ 26 Danny Ferry .15 .07
❑ 27 Chris Mills .15 .07
❑ 28 Bobby Phills .15 .07
❑ 29 Tony Dumas .15 .07
❑ 30 Jim Jackson .15 .07
❑ 31 Popeye Jones .15 .07
❑ 32 Jason Kidd 1.25 .55
❑ 33 Jamal Mashburn .20 .09
❑ 34 Mahmoud Abdul-Rauf .15 .07
❑ 35 LaPhonso Ellis .15 .07
❑ 36 Dikembe Mutombo .20 .09
❑ 37 Jalen Rose .50 .23
❑ 38 Bryant Stith .15 .07
❑ 39 Joe Dumars .40 .18
❑ 40 Grant Hill 2.00 .90
❑ 41 Lindsey Hunter .15 .07
❑ 42 Allan Houston .50 .23
❑ 43 Otis Thorpe .15 .07
❑ 44 B.J. Armstrong .15 .07
❑ 45 Tim Hardaway .40 .18
❑ 46 Chris Mullin .40 .18
❑ 47 Latrell Sprewell .75 .35
❑ 48 Rony Seikaly .15 .07
❑ 49 Sam Cassell .20 .09
❑ 50 Clyde Drexler .40 .18
❑ 51 Robert Horry .15 .07
❑ 52 Hakeem Olajuwon .60 .25
❑ 53 Kenny Smith .15 .07
❑ 54 Dale Davis .15 .07
❑ 55 Derrick McKey .15 .07
❑ 56 Reggie Miller .40 .18
❑ 57 Ricky Pierce .15 .07
❑ 58 Rik Smits .15 .07
❑ 59 Lamond Murray .15 .07
❑ 60 Rodney Rogers .15 .07
❑ 61 Malik Sealy .15 .07
❑ 62 Loy Vaught .15 .07
❑ 63 Brian Williams .15 .07
❑ 64 Elden Campbell .15 .07
❑ 65 Cedric Ceballos .15 .07
❑ 66 Magic Johnson 1.25 .55
❑ 67 Eddie Jones .75 .35
❑ 68 Nick Van Exel .20 .09
❑ 69 Bimbo Coles .15 .07
❑ 70 Alonzo Mourning .40 .18
❑ 71 Billy Owens .15 .07
❑ 72 Kevin Willis .15 .07
❑ 73 Vin Baker .40 .18
❑ 74 Benoit Benjamin .15 .07
❑ 75 Sherman Douglas .15 .07
❑ 76 Lee Mayberry .15 .07
❑ 77 Glenn Robinson .40 .18
❑ 78 Tom Gugliotta .20 .09
❑ 79 Christian Laettner .20 .09
❑ 80 Sam Mitchell .15 .07
❑ 81 Terry Porter .15 .07
❑ 82 Isaiah Rider .20 .09
❑ 83 Shawn Bradley .15 .07
❑ 84 P.J. Brown .15 .07
❑ 85 Kendall Gill .20 .09
❑ 86 Armon Gilliam .15 .07
❑ 87 Jayson Williams .20 .09
❑ 88 Patrick Ewing .40 .18
❑ 89 Derek Harper .15 .07
❑ 90 Anthony Mason .20 .09

Card	MINT	NRMT
❑ 91 Charles Oakley	.15	.07
❑ 92 John Starks	.15	.07
❑ 93 Nick Anderson	.15	.07
❑ 94 Horace Grant	.20	.09
❑ 95 Anfernee Hardaway	1.25	.55
❑ 96 Shaquille O'Neal	2.00	.90
❑ 97 Dennis Scott	.15	.07
❑ 98 Derrick Coleman	.20	.09
❑ 99 Vernon Maxwell	.15	.07
❑ 100 Trevor Ruffin	.15	.07
❑ 101 Clarence Weatherspoon	.15	.07
❑ 102 Sharone Wright	.15	.07
❑ 103 Charles Barkley	.60	.25
❑ 104 A.C. Green	.20	.09
❑ 105 Kevin Johnson	.20	.09
❑ 106 Wesley Person	.20	.09
❑ 107 John Williams	.15	.07
❑ 108 Chris Dudley	.15	.07
❑ 109 Harvey Grant	.15	.07
❑ 110 Aaron McKie	.15	.07
❑ 111 Clifford Robinson	.15	.07
❑ 112 Rod Strickland	.20	.09
❑ 113 Brian Grant	.40	.18
❑ 114 Sarunas Marciulionis	.15	.07
❑ 115 Olden Polynice	.15	.07
❑ 116 Mitch Richmond	.40	.18
❑ 117 Walt Williams	.15	.07
❑ 118 Vinny Del Negro	.15	.07
❑ 119 Sean Elliott	.15	.07
❑ 120 Avery Johnson	.15	.07
❑ 121 Chuck Person	.15	.07
❑ 122 David Robinson	.60	.25
❑ 123 Hersey Hawkins	.20	.09
❑ 124 Shawn Kemp	.60	.25
❑ 125 Gary Payton	.60	.25
❑ 126 Sam Perkins	.20	.09
❑ 127 Detlef Schrempf	.20	.09
❑ 128 Oliver Miller	.15	.07
❑ 129 Tracy Murray	.15	.07
❑ 130 Ed Pinckney	.15	.07
❑ 131 Alvin Robertson	.15	.07
❑ 132 Zan Tabak	.15	.07
❑ 133 Jeff Hornacek	.20	.09
❑ 134 Adam Keefe	.15	.07
❑ 135 Karl Malone	.60	.25
❑ 136 Chris Morris	.15	.07
❑ 137 John Stockton	.40	.18
❑ 138 Greg Anthony	.15	.07
❑ 139 Blue Edwards	.15	.07
❑ 140 Kenny Gattison	.15	.07
❑ 141 Chris King	.15	.07
❑ 142 Byron Scott	.15	.07
❑ 143 Calbert Cheaney	.15	.07
❑ 144 Juwan Howard	.40	.18
❑ 145 Gheorghe Muresan	.15	.07
❑ 146 Robert Pack	.15	.07
❑ 147 Chris Webber	1.25	.55
❑ 148 Alan Henderson RC	.40	.18
❑ 149 Eric Williams RC	.20	.09
❑ 150 George Zidek RC	.15	.07
❑ 151 Bob Sura RC	.20	.09
❑ 152 Antonio McDyess RC	2.00	.90
❑ 153 Theo Ratliff RC	.50	.23
❑ 154 Joe Smith RC	1.25	.55
❑ 155 Brent Barry RC	.40	.18
❑ 156 Sasha Danilovic RC	.15	.07
❑ 157 Kurt Thomas RC	.20	.09
❑ 158 Shawn Respert RC	.15	.07
❑ 159 Kevin Garnett RC	20.00	9.00
❑ 160 Ed O'Bannon RC	.15	.07
❑ 161 Jerry Stackhouse RC	1.25	.55
❑ 162 Michael Finley RC	1.50	.70
❑ 163 Arvydas Sabonis RC	.60	.25
❑ 164 Cory Alexander RC	.15	.07
❑ 165 Damon Stoudamire RC	2.00	.90
❑ 166 Bryant Reeves RC	.40	.18
❑ 167 Rasheed Wallace RC	1.50	.70
❑ C1 Hakeem Olajuwon Commemorative	12.00	5.50
❑ P23 Michael Jordan Promo	10.00	4.50

1995-96 SP All-Stars

	MINT	NRMT
COMPLETE SET (30)	60.00	27.00
COMMON CARD (AS1-AS30)	.60	.25
SEMISTARS	.75	.35
UNLISTED STARS	1.25	.55

STATED ODDS 1:5

COMP.GOLD SET (30)	300.00	135.00
COMMON GOLD (AS1-AS30)	4.00	1.80

*GOLD STARS: 2.5X TO 6X HI COLUMN
*GOLD RCs: 2X TO 5X HI
GOLD: STATED ODDS 1:61

Card	MINT	NRMT
❑ AS1 Anfernee Hardaway	4.00	1.80
❑ AS2 Michael Jordan	20.00	9.00
❑ AS3 Grant Hill	6.00	2.70
❑ AS4 Scottie Pippen	4.00	1.80
❑ AS5 Shaquille O'Neal	6.00	2.70
❑ AS6 Vin Baker	1.25	.55
❑ AS7 Terrell Brandon	.75	.35
❑ AS8 Patrick Ewing	1.25	.55
❑ AS9 Juwan Howard	1.25	.55
❑ AS10 Reggie Miller	1.25	.55
❑ AS11 Alonzo Mourning	1.25	.55
❑ AS12 Glen Rice	.75	.35
❑ AS13 Clyde Drexler	1.25	.55
❑ AS14 Jason Kidd	4.00	1.80
❑ AS15 Charles Barkley	2.00	.90
❑ AS16 Shawn Kemp	2.00	.90
❑ AS17 Hakeem Olajuwon	2.00	.90
❑ AS18 Sean Elliott	.60	.25
❑ AS19 Karl Malone	2.00	.90
❑ AS20 Dikembe Mutombo	.75	.35
❑ AS21 Gary Payton	2.00	.90
❑ AS22 Mitch Richmond	1.25	.55
❑ AS23 David Robinson	2.00	.90
❑ AS24 John Stockton	1.25	.55
❑ AS25 Jerry Stackhouse	2.00	.90
❑ AS26 Damon Stoudamire	3.00	1.35
❑ AS27 Rasheed Wallace	2.50	1.10
❑ AS28 Kevin Garnett	10.00	4.50
❑ AS29 Antonio McDyess	3.00	1.35
❑ AS30 Joe Smith	2.00	.90

1995-96 SP Holoviews

	MINT	NRMT
COMPLETE SET (40)	125.00	55.00
COMMON CARD (PC1-PC40)	1.00	.45
SEMISTARS	1.50	.70
UNLISTED STARS	2.50	1.10

STATED ODDS 1:7

COMP.DIE CUT SET (40)	500.00	220.00
COMMON CARD (PC1-PC40)	4.00	1.80

*DIE CUTS: 2X TO 4X HI COLUMN
DIE CUT: STATED ODDS 1:76

Card	MINT	NRMT
❑ PC1 Mookie Blaylock	1.00	.45
❑ PC2 Eric Williams	1.00	.45
❑ PC3 Larry Johnson	1.50	.70
❑ PC4 George Zidek	1.00	.45
❑ PC5 Michael Jordan	30.00	13.50
❑ PC6 Bob Sura	1.50	.70
❑ PC7 Jason Kidd	8.00	3.60
❑ PC8 Cherokee Parks	1.00	.45
❑ PC9 Antonio McDyess	6.00	2.70
❑ PC10 Grant Hill	12.00	5.50
❑ PC11 Theo Ratliff	2.50	1.10
❑ PC12 Joe Smith	4.00	1.80
❑ PC13 Latrell Sprewell	5.00	2.20
❑ PC14 Hakeem Olajuwon	4.00	1.80
❑ PC15 Travis Best	1.50	.70
❑ PC16 Brent Barry	2.50	1.10
❑ PC17 Nick Van Exel	1.50	.70
❑ PC18 Kurt Thomas	1.00	.45
❑ PC19 Shawn Respert	1.00	.45
❑ PC20 Glenn Robinson	2.50	1.10
❑ PC21 Christian Laettner	1.50	.70
❑ PC22 Ed O'Bannon	1.00	.45
❑ PC23 Patrick Ewing	2.50	1.10
❑ PC24 Anfernee Hardaway	8.00	3.60
❑ PC25 Shaquille O'Neal	12.00	5.50
❑ PC26 Jerry Stackhouse	4.00	1.80
❑ PC27 Mario Bennett	1.00	.45
❑ PC28 Michael Finley	5.00	2.20
❑ PC29 Randolph Childress	1.00	.45
❑ PC30 Brian Grant	2.50	1.10
❑ PC31 Mitch Richmond	2.50	1.10
❑ PC32 Cory Alexander	1.00	.45
❑ PC33 David Robinson	4.00	1.80
❑ PC34 Sherrell Ford	1.00	.45
❑ PC35 Shawn Kemp	4.00	1.80
❑ PC36 Damon Stoudamire	6.00	2.70
❑ PC37 Greg Ostertag	1.00	.45
❑ PC38 Bryant Reeves	1.50	.70
❑ PC39 Juwan Howard	2.50	1.10
❑ PC40 Rasheed Wallace	5.00	2.20

1996-97 SP

	MINT	NRMT
COMPLETE SET (146)	50.00	22.00
COMMON CARD (1-126)	.15	.07
COMMON RC (127-146)	.60	.25
SEMISTARS	.20	.09
UNLISTED STARS	.40	.18

RC's CONDITION SENSITIVE

Card	MINT	NRMT
❑ 1 Mookie Blaylock	.15	.07
❑ 2 Christian Laettner	.20	.09
❑ 3 Dikembe Mutombo	.20	.09
❑ 4 Steve Smith	.20	.09
❑ 5 Dana Barros	.15	.07
❑ 6 Rick Fox	.15	.07
❑ 7 Dino Radja	.15	.07
❑ 8 Eric Williams	.15	.07
❑ 9 Dell Curry	.15	.07
❑ 10 Vlade Divac	.15	.07
❑ 11 Anthony Mason	.20	.09
❑ 12 Glen Rice	.20	.09
❑ 13 Scottie Pippen	1.25	.55
❑ 14 Toni Kukoc	.50	.23
❑ 15 Luc Longley	.15	.07

❑ 16 Michael Jordan	5.00	2.20
❑ 17 Dennis Rodman	.75	.35
❑ 18 Terrell Brandon	.20	.09
❑ 19 Tyrone Hill	.15	.07
❑ 20 Bobby Phills	.15	.07
❑ 21 Bob Sura	.15	.07
❑ 22 Chris Gatling	.15	.07
❑ 23 Jim Jackson	.15	.07
❑ 24 Sam Cassell	.20	.09
❑ 25 Jamal Mashburn	.20	.09
❑ 26 Dale Ellis	.15	.07
❑ 27 LaPhonso Ellis	.15	.07
❑ 28 Mark Jackson	.15	.07
❑ 29 Antonio McDyess	.60	.25
❑ 30 Bryant Stith	.15	.07
❑ 31 Joe Dumars	.40	.18
❑ 32 Grant Hill	2.00	.90
❑ 33 Lindsey Hunter	.15	.07
❑ 34 Otis Thorpe	.15	.07
❑ 35 Chris Mullin	.40	.18
❑ 36 Mark Price	.15	.07
❑ 37 Joe Smith	.40	.18
❑ 38 Latrell Sprewell	.75	.35
❑ 39 Charles Barkley	.60	.25
❑ 40 Clyde Drexler	.40	.18
❑ 41 Mario Elie	.15	.07
❑ 42 Hakeem Olajuwon	.60	.25
❑ 43 Travis Best	.15	.07
❑ 44 Dale Davis	.15	.07
❑ 45 Reggie Miller	.40	.18
❑ 46 Rik Smits	.15	.07
❑ 47 Pooh Richardson	.15	.07
❑ 48 Rodney Rogers	.15	.07
❑ 49 Malik Sealy	.15	.07
❑ 50 Loy Vaught	.15	.07
❑ 51 Elden Campbell	.15	.07
❑ 52 Robert Horry	.15	.07
❑ 53 Eddie Jones	.75	.35
❑ 54 Shaquille O'Neal	2.00	.90
❑ 55 Nick Van Exel	.20	.09
❑ 56 Sasha Danilovic	.15	.07
❑ 57 Tim Hardaway	.40	.18
❑ 58 Dan Majerle	.20	.09
❑ 59 Alonzo Mourning	.40	.18
❑ 60 Vin Baker	.20	.09
❑ 61 Sherman Douglas	.15	.07
❑ 62 Armon Gilliam	.15	.07
❑ 63 Glenn Robinson	.40	.18
❑ 64 Kevin Garnett	2.50	1.10
❑ 65 Tom Gugliotta	.20	.09
❑ 66 Terry Porter	.15	.07
❑ 67 Doug West	.15	.07
❑ 68 Shawn Bradley	.15	.07
❑ 69 Kendall Gill	.20	.09
❑ 70 Robert Pack	.15	.07
❑ 71 Jayson Williams	.20	.09
❑ 72 Chris Childs	.15	.07
❑ 73 Patrick Ewing	.40	.18
❑ 74 Allan Houston	.40	.18
❑ 75 Larry Johnson	.20	.09
❑ 76 John Starks	.15	.07
❑ 77 Nick Anderson	.15	.07
❑ 78 Horace Grant	.20	.09
❑ 79 Anfernee Hardaway	1.25	.55
❑ 80 Dennis Scott	.15	.07
❑ 81 Derrick Coleman	.20	.09
❑ 82 Mark Davis	.15	.07
❑ 83 Jerry Stackhouse	.40	.18
❑ 84 Clarence Weatherspoon	.15	.07
❑ 85 Cedric Ceballos	.15	.07
❑ 86 Kevin Johnson	.20	.09
❑ 87 Jason Kidd	1.25	.55
❑ 88 Danny Manning	.20	.09
❑ 89 Wesley Person	.15	.07
❑ 90 Kenny Anderson	.20	.09
❑ 91 Isaiah Rider	.20	.09
❑ 92 Clifford Robinson	.15	.07
❑ 93 Arvydas Sabonis	.20	.09
❑ 94 Rasheed Wallace	.50	.23
❑ 95 Mahmoud Abdul-Rauf	.15	.07
❑ 96 Brian Grant	.40	.18
❑ 97 Olden Polynice	.15	.07
❑ 98 Mitch Richmond	.40	.18
❑ 99 Corliss Williamson	.15	.07
❑ 100 Sean Elliott	.15	.07
❑ 101 Avery Johnson	.15	.07
❑ 102 David Robinson	.60	.25
❑ 103 Dominique Wilkins	.40	.18
❑ 104 Hersey Hawkins	.20	.09
❑ 105 Jim McIlvaine	.15	.07
❑ 106 Shawn Kemp	.60	.25
❑ 107 Gary Payton	.60	.25
❑ 108 Detlef Schrempf	.20	.09
❑ 109 Doug Christie	.15	.07
❑ 110 Popeye Jones	.15	.07
❑ 111 Damon Stoudamire	.60	.25
❑ 112 Walt Williams	.15	.07
❑ 113 Jeff Hornacek	.20	.09
❑ 114 Karl Malone	.60	.25
❑ 115 Greg Ostertag	.15	.07
❑ 116 Bryon Russell	.15	.07
❑ 117 John Stockton	.40	.18
❑ 118 Greg Anthony	.15	.07
❑ 119 Blue Edwards	.15	.07
❑ 120 Anthony Peeler	.15	.07
❑ 121 Bryant Reeves	.15	.07
❑ 122 Calbert Cheaney	.15	.07
❑ 123 Juwan Howard	.20	.09
❑ 124 Gheorghe Muresan	.15	.07
❑ 125 Rod Strickland	.20	.09
❑ 126 Chris Webber	1.25	.55
❑ 127 Antoine Walker RC	3.00	1.35
❑ 128 Tony Delk RC	.60	.25
❑ 129 Vitaly Potapenko RC	.60	.25
❑ 130 Samaki Walker RC	.60	.25
❑ 131 Todd Fuller RC	.60	.25
❑ 132 Erick Dampier RC	.60	.25
❑ 133 Lorenzen Wright RC	.60	.25
❑ 134 Kobe Bryant RC	25.00	11.00
❑ 135 Derek Fisher RC	1.00	.45
❑ 136 Ray Allen RC	3.00	1.35
❑ 137 Stephon Marbury RC	5.00	2.20
❑ 138 Kerry Kittles RC	1.25	.55
❑ 139 Walter McCarty RC	.60	.25
❑ 140 John Wallace RC	.60	.25
❑ 141 Allen Iverson RC	10.00	4.50
❑ 142 Steve Nash RC	.60	.25
❑ 143 Jermaine O'Neal RC	1.25	.55
❑ 144 Marcus Camby RC	2.50	1.10
❑ 145 Shareef Abdur-Rahim RC	4.00	1.80
❑ 146 Roy Rogers RC	.60	.25

1996-97 SP Game Film

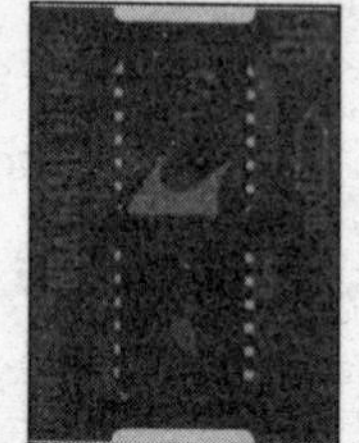

	MINT	NRMT
COMPLETE SET (10)	200.00	90.00
COMMON CARD (GF1-GF10)	4.00	1.80
SEMISTARS	6.00	2.70
STATED ODDS 1:120		

❑ GF1 Michael Jordan	80.00	36.00
❑ GF2 Kevin Garnett	40.00	18.00
❑ GF3 Charles Barkley	10.00	4.50
❑ GF4 Anfernee Hardaway	20.00	9.00
❑ GF5 Shaquille O'Neal	30.00	13.50
❑ GF6 Jim Jackson	4.00	1.80
❑ GF7 Dennis Rodman	12.00	5.50
❑ GF8 Alonzo Mourning	6.00	2.70
❑ GF9 Grant Hill	30.00	13.50
❑ GF10 Shawn Kemp	10.00	4.50

1996-97 SP Holoviews

	MINT	NRMT
COMPLETE SET (40)	150.00	70.00

COMMON CARD (PC1-PC40)	1.25	.55
SEMISTARS	1.50	.70
UNLISTED STARS	2.50	1.10
STATED ODDS 1:10		

❑ PC1 Mookie Blaylock	1.25	.55
❑ PC2 Antoine Walker	6.00	2.70
❑ PC3 Eric Williams	1.25	.55
❑ PC4 Tony Delk	1.25	.55
❑ PC5 Michael Jordan	30.00	13.50
❑ PC6 Dennis Rodman	5.00	2.20
❑ PC7 Vitaly Potapenko	1.25	.55
❑ PC8 Bob Sura	1.25	.55
❑ PC9 Jamal Mashburn	1.50	.70
❑ PC10 Antonio McDyess	4.00	1.80
❑ PC11 Grant Hill	12.00	5.50
❑ PC12 Joe Smith	2.50	1.10
❑ PC13 Latrell Sprewell	5.00	2.20
❑ PC14 Charles Barkley	4.00	1.80
❑ PC15 Hakeem Olajuwon	4.00	1.80
❑ PC16 Erick Dampier	1.25	.55
❑ PC17 Lorenzen Wright	1.25	.55
❑ PC18 Kobe Bryant	30.00	13.50
❑ PC19 Shaquille O'Neal	12.00	5.50
❑ PC20 Alonzo Mourning	2.50	1.10
❑ PC21 Ray Allen	6.00	2.70
❑ PC22 Kevin Garnett	15.00	6.75
❑ PC23 Stephon Marbury	10.00	4.50
❑ PC24 Kerry Kittles	2.50	1.10
❑ PC25 Walter McCarty	1.25	.55
❑ PC26 John Wallace	1.50	.70
❑ PC27 Anfernee Hardaway	8.00	3.60
❑ PC28 Allen Iverson	15.00	6.75
❑ PC29 Jerry Stackhouse	2.50	1.10
❑ PC30 Steve Nash	1.25	.55
❑ PC31 Jermaine O'Neal	2.50	1.10
❑ PC32 Brian Grant	2.50	1.10
❑ PC33 Mitch Richmond	2.50	1.10
❑ PC34 David Robinson	4.00	1.80
❑ PC35 Shawn Kemp	4.00	1.80
❑ PC36 Marcus Camby	5.00	2.20
❑ PC37 Damon Stoudamire	4.00	1.80
❑ PC38 John Stockton	2.50	1.10
❑ PC39 Shareef Abdur-Rahim	10.00	4.50
❑ PC40 Juwan Howard	1.50	.70

1996-97 SP Inside Info

	MINT	NRMT
COMPLETE SET (17)	200.00	90.00
COMMON CARD (IN1-IN16/25K)	2.50	1.10

SEMISTARS	4.00	1.80

ONE PER BOX
*GOLD: 1.5X TO 3X HI COLUMN
GOLD: RANDOM INSERTS IN BOXES

❑ IN1 Charles Barkley	6.00	2.70
❑ IN2 Kevin Garnett	25.00	11.00
❑ IN3 Anfernee Hardaway	12.00	5.50
❑ IN4 Grant Hill	20.00	9.00
❑ IN5 Allen Iverson	20.00	9.00
❑ IN6 Jason Kidd	12.00	5.50
❑ IN7 Shawn Kemp	6.00	2.70
❑ IN8 Antonio McDyess	6.00	2.70
❑ IN9 Dikembe Mutombo	2.50	1.10
❑ IN10 Shaquille O'Neal	20.00	9.00
❑ IN11 Hakeem Olajuwon	6.00	2.70
❑ IN12 Dennis Rodman	8.00	3.60
❑ IN13 Jerry Stackhouse	5.00	2.20
❑ IN14 John Stockton	4.00	1.80
❑ IN15 Damon Stoudamire	6.00	2.70
❑ IN16 Chris Webber	12.00	5.50
❑ IN17 Michael Jordan 25K	60.00	27.00

1996-97 SP SPx Force

	MINT	NRMT
COMPLETE SET (5)	150.00	70.00
COMMON CARD (F1-F5)	20.00	9.00

STATED ODDS 1:360
AUTOGRAPHS NUMBERED TO 100

❑ F1 Michael Jordan	60.00	27.00
Jerry Stackhouse		
Mitch Richmond		
Latrell Sprewell		
❑ F2 Shawn Kemp	25.00	11.00
Dennis Rodman		
Charles Barkley		
Juwan Howard		
❑ F3 Mookie Blaylock	20.00	9.00
Nick Van Exel#(Stephon Marbury		
Damon Stoudamire		
❑ F4 Marcus Camby	40.00	18.00
Erick Dampier		
Anfernee Hardaway		
Antonio McDyess		
❑ F5 Michael Jordan	60.00	27.00
Anfernee Hardaway		
Shawn Kemp		
Damon Stoudamire		
❑ F5A Michael Jordan AU	2500.00	1100.00
Numbered to 100		
❑ F5B Anfernee Hardaway AU	500.00	220.00
Numbered to 100		
❑ F5C Shawn Kemp AU	250.00	110.00
Numbered to 100		
❑ F5D Damon Stoudamire AU	150.00	70.00
Numbered to 100		

1997-98 SP Authentic

	MINT	NRMT
COMPLETE SET (176)	150.00	70.00
COMMON CARD (1-176)	.25	.11
COMMON RC	.75	.35
SEMISTARS	.40	.18
SEMISTARS RC	1.00	.45
UNLISTED STARS	.60	.25
UNLISTED STARS RC	1.50	.70

❑ 1 Steve Smith	.40	.18
❑ 2 Dikembe Mutombo	.40	.18
❑ 3 Christian Laettner	.40	.18
❑ 4 Mookie Blaylock	.25	.11
❑ 5 Alan Henderson	.25	.11
❑ 6 Antoine Walker	1.25	.55
❑ 7 Ron Mercer RC	5.00	2.20
❑ 8 Walter McCarty	.25	.11
❑ 9 Kenny Anderson	.40	.18
❑ 10 Travis Knight	.25	.11
❑ 11 Dana Barros	.25	.11
❑ 12 Glen Rice	.40	.18
❑ 13 Vlade Divac	.25	.11
❑ 14 Dell Curry	.25	.11
❑ 15 David Wesley	.25	.11
❑ 16 Bobby Phills	.25	.11
❑ 17 Anthony Mason	.40	.18
❑ 18 Toni Kukoc	.75	.35
❑ 19 Dennis Rodman	1.25	.55
❑ 20 Ron Harper	.40	.18
❑ 21 Steve Kerr	.25	.11
❑ 22 Scottie Pippen	2.00	.90
❑ 23 Michael Jordan	8.00	3.60
❑ 24 Shawn Kemp	1.00	.45
❑ 25 Wesley Person	.25	.11
❑ 26 Derek Anderson RC	3.00	1.35
❑ 27 Zydrunas Ilgauskas	.25	.11
❑ 28 Brevin Knight RC	2.00	.90
❑ 29 Michael Finley	.60	.25
❑ 30 Shawn Bradley	.25	.11
❑ 31 A.C. Green	.40	.18
❑ 32 Hubert Davis	.25	.11
❑ 33 Dennis Scott	.25	.11
❑ 34 Tony Battie RC	1.50	.70
❑ 35 Bobby Jackson RC	1.00	.45
❑ 36 LaPhonso Ellis	.25	.11
❑ 37 Bryant Stith	.25	.11
❑ 38 Dean Garrett	.25	.11
❑ 39 Danny Fortson RC	1.50	.70
❑ 40 Grant Hill	3.00	1.35
❑ 41 Brian Williams	.25	.11
❑ 42 Lindsey Hunter	.25	.11
❑ 43 Malik Sealy	.25	.11
❑ 44 Jerry Stackhouse	.40	.18
❑ 45 Muggsy Bogues	.25	.11
❑ 46 Joe Smith	.40	.18
❑ 47 Donyell Marshall	.25	.11
❑ 48 Erick Dampier	.25	.11
❑ 49 Bimbo Coles	.25	.11
❑ 50 Charles Barkley	1.00	.45
❑ 51 Hakeem Olajuwon	1.00	.45
❑ 52 Clyde Drexler	.60	.25
❑ 53 Kevin Willis	.25	.11
❑ 54 Mario Elie	.25	.11
❑ 55 Reggie Miller	.60	.25
❑ 56 Rik Smits	.25	.11
❑ 57 Chris Mullin	.60	.25
❑ 58 Antonio Davis	.25	.11
❑ 59 Dale Davis	.25	.11
❑ 60 Mark Jackson	.25	.11
❑ 61 Brent Barry	.25	.11
❑ 62 Loy Vaught	.25	.11
❑ 63 Rodney Rogers	.25	.11
❑ 64 Lamond Murray	.25	.11
❑ 65 Maurice Taylor RC	4.00	1.80
❑ 66 Shaquille O'Neal	3.00	1.35
❑ 67 Eddie Jones	1.25	.55
❑ 68 Kobe Bryant	5.00	2.20
❑ 69 Nick Van Exel	.40	.18
❑ 70 Robert Horry	.25	.11
❑ 71 Tim Hardaway	.60	.25
❑ 72 Jamal Mashburn	.40	.18
❑ 73 Alonzo Mourning	.60	.25
❑ 74 Isaac Austin	.25	.11
❑ 75 P.J. Brown	.25	.11
❑ 76 Ray Allen	1.00	.45
❑ 77 Glenn Robinson	.40	.18
❑ 78 Ervin Johnson	.25	.11
❑ 79 Terrell Brandon	.40	.18
❑ 80 Tyrone Hill	.25	.11
❑ 81 Stephon Marbury	2.00	.90
❑ 82 Kevin Garnett	4.00	1.80
❑ 83 Tom Gugliotta	.40	.18
❑ 84 Chris Carr	.25	.11
❑ 85 Cherokee Parks	.25	.11
❑ 86 Sam Cassell	.40	.18
❑ 87 Chris Gatling	.25	.11
❑ 88 Kendall Gill	.40	.18
❑ 89 Keith Van Horn RC	8.00	3.60
❑ 90 Jayson Williams	.40	.18
❑ 91 Kerry Kittles	.60	.25
❑ 92 Patrick Ewing	.60	.25
❑ 93 Larry Johnson	.40	.18
❑ 94 Chris Childs	.25	.11
❑ 95 John Starks	.25	.11
❑ 96 Charles Oakley	.25	.11
❑ 97 Allan Houston	.60	.25
❑ 98 Mark Price	.25	.11
❑ 99 Anfernee Hardaway	2.00	.90
❑ 100 Rony Seikaly	.25	.11
❑ 101 Horace Grant	.40	.18
❑ 102 Charles Outlaw	.25	.11
❑ 103 Clarence Weatherspoon	.25	.11
❑ 104 Allen Iverson	3.00	1.35
❑ 105 Jim Jackson	.25	.11
❑ 106 Theo Ratliff	.25	.11
❑ 107 Tim Thomas RC	10.00	4.50
❑ 108 Danny Manning	.40	.18
❑ 109 Jason Kidd	2.00	.90
❑ 110 Kevin Johnson	.40	.18
❑ 111 Rex Chapman	.25	.11
❑ 112 Clifford Robinson	.25	.11
❑ 113 Antonio McDyess	.75	.35
❑ 114 Damon Stoudamire	.75	.35
❑ 115 Isaiah Rider	.40	.18
❑ 116 Arvydas Sabonis	.40	.18
❑ 117 Rasheed Wallace	.60	.25
❑ 118 Brian Grant	.40	.18
❑ 119 Gary Trent	.25	.11
❑ 120 Mitch Richmond	.60	.25
❑ 121 Corliss Williamson	.25	.11
❑ 122 L. Funderburke RC	1.00	.45
❑ 123 Olden Polynice	.25	.11
❑ 124 Billy Owens	.25	.11
❑ 125 Avery Johnson	.25	.11
❑ 126 Sean Elliott	.25	.11
❑ 127 David Robinson	1.00	.45
❑ 128 Tim Duncan RC	60.00	27.00
❑ 129 Jaren Jackson	.25	.11
❑ 130 Detlef Schrempf	.40	.18
❑ 131 Gary Payton	1.00	.45
❑ 132 Vin Baker	.40	.18
❑ 133 Hersey Hawkins	.40	.18
❑ 134 Dale Ellis	.25	.11
❑ 135 Sam Perkins	.40	.18
❑ 136 Marcus Camby	.75	.35
❑ 137 John Wallace	.25	.11
❑ 138 Doug Christie	.25	.11
❑ 139 Chauncey Billups RC	1.50	.70
❑ 140 Walt Williams	.25	.11
❑ 141 Karl Malone	1.00	.45
❑ 142 Bryon Russell	.25	.11
❑ 143 Jeff Hornacek	.40	.18
❑ 144 Greg Ostertag	.25	.11
❑ 145 John Stockton	.60	.25
❑ 146 Shandon Anderson	.25	.11
❑ 147 Shareef Abdur-Rahim	2.00	.90
❑ 148 Bryant Reeves	.25	.11
❑ 149 Antonio Daniels RC	1.50	.70
❑ 150 Otis Thorpe	.25	.11
❑ 151 Blue Edwards	.25	.11
❑ 152 Chris Webber	2.00	.90

❑ 153 Juwan Howard	.40	.18
❑ 154 Rod Strickland	.40	.18
❑ 155 Calbert Cheaney	.25	.11
❑ 156 Tracy Murray	.25	.11
❑ 157 Chauncey Billups	.75	.35
❑ 158 Ed Gray RC	.75	.35
❑ 159 Tony Battie FW	1.00	.45
❑ 160 Keith Van Horn FW	3.00	1.35
❑ 161 Cedric Henderson RC	1.00	.45
❑ 162 Kelvin Cato RC	1.50	.70
❑ 163 Tariq Abdul-Wahad RC	1.00	.45
❑ 164 Derek Anderson FW	1.50	.70
❑ 165 Tim Duncan FW	8.00	3.60
❑ 166 Tracy McGrady RC	60.00	27.00
❑ 167 Ron Mercer FW	2.00	.90
❑ 168 Bobby Jackson FW	.75	.35
❑ 169 Antonio Daniels FW	1.00	.45
❑ 170 Zydrunas Ilgauskas FW	.75	.35
❑ 171 Maurice Taylor FW	1.25	.55
❑ 172 Tim Thomas FW	2.00	.90
❑ 173 Brevin Knight FW	1.50	.70
❑ 174 L. Funderburke FW	.75	.35
❑ 175 Jacque Vaughn RC	1.00	.45
❑ 176 Danny Fortson FW	1.00	.45

1997-98 SP Authentic Authentics

	MINT	NRMT
COMMON CARD	40.00	18.00

OVERALL STATED ODDS 1:288
JORDAN GAME NIGHT SERIAL #'d TO 100
FIVE DIFFERENT JORDAN GAME NIGHT CARDS
AUTOGRAPHED ITEMS LABELED WITH AU
CARD PRINT RUNS LISTED IN PARENTHESIS

❑ AH1 Anfernee Hardaway Signed Black Jersey	500.00	220.00
❑ AH2 Anfernee Hardaway Signed Blue Jersey	400.00	180.00
❑ AH3 Anfernee Hardaway Signed Sports Illustrated	80.00	36.00
❑ AH4 Anfernee Hardaway Unsigned 8x10 photo	40.00	18.00
❑ MJ1 Michael Jordan Signed Jersey	2000.00	900.00
❑ MJ2 Michael Jordan Signed 16x20 Photo	700.00	325.00
❑ MJ3 Michael Jordan Unsigned 2-card set	60.00	27.00
❑ MJ4 Michael Jordan Unsigned 8x10 Photo	60.00	27.00
❑ MJ5 Michael Jordan Unsigned Gold Card	40.00	18.00
❑ MJ6 Michael Jordan Unsigned Game Night Card	400.00	180.00
❑ MJ6B Michael Jordan Unsigned Game Night Card	400.00	180.00
❑ MJ6C Michael Jordan Unsigned Game Night Card	400.00	180.00
❑ MJ6D Michael Jordan Unsigned Game Night Card	400.00	180.00
❑ MJ6E Michael Jordan Unsigned Game Night Card	400.00	180.00
❑ MJ7 Michael Jordan Unsigned Blow-up Poster	80.00	36.00
❑ MJ8 Michael Jordan Signed Game Night Card	7000.00	3200.00
❑ SK1 Shawn Kemp Signed Sonics Jersey	500.00	220.00
❑ SK2 Shawn Kemp Signed All-Star Photo	80.00	36.00
❑ SK3 Shawn Kemp Signed Mini-ball	80.00	36.00
❑ NNO SP Uncut Sheet (200)	150.00	70.00

1997-98 SP Authentic BuyBack

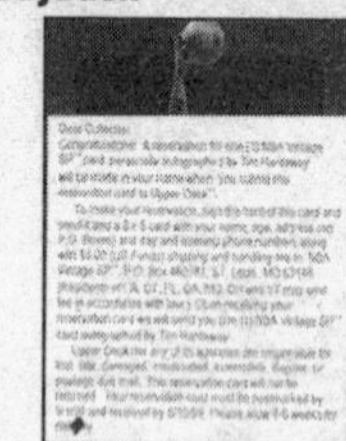

	MINT	NRMT
COMMON CARD	30.00	13.50

STATED ODDS 1:309 PACKS
CARDS NUMBERED BELOW ALPHABETICALLY

❑ 1 Shareef Abdur-Rahim '96/7	60.00	27.00
❑ 2 Vin Baker '94/5	150.00	70.00
❑ 3 Vin Baker '95/6	40.00	18.00
❑ 4 Vin Baker '95/6AS	150.00	70.00
❑ 5 Clyde Drexler '94/5	80.00	36.00
❑ 6 Clyde Drexler '95/6	80.00	36.00
❑ 7 Clyde Drexler '96/7	125.00	55.00
❑ 8 Anfernee Hardaway '94/5	250.00	110.00
❑ 9 Anfernee Hardaway '95/6	200.00	90.00
❑ 10 Anfernee Hardaway '96/7	400.00	180.00
❑ 11 Tim Hardaway '94/5	80.00	36.00
❑ 12 Tim Hardaway '95/6	80.00	36.00
❑ 13 Tim Hardaway '96/7	100.00	45.00
❑ 14 Juwan Howard '94/5	100.00	45.00
❑ 15 Juwan Howard '95/6	30.00	13.50
❑ 16 Juwan Howard '95/6AS	100.00	45.00
❑ 17 Juwan Howard '96/7	125.00	55.00
❑ 18 Eddie Jones '94/5	100.00	45.00
❑ 19 Eddie Jones '95/6	80.00	36.00
❑ 20 Eddie Jones '96/7	200.00	90.00
❑ 21 M. Jordan '94MJ1R	4000.00	1800.00
❑ 22 Jason Kidd '94/5	150.00	70.00
❑ 23 Jason Kidd '95/6	80.00	36.00
❑ 24 Jason Kidd '95/6AS	125.00	55.00
❑ 25 Jason Kidd '96/7	125.00	55.00
❑ 26 Kerry Kittles '96/7	40.00	18.00
❑ 27 Karl Malone '94/5	60.00	27.00
❑ 28 Karl Malone '95/6	200.00	90.00
❑ 29 Glen Rice '95/6AS	50.00	22.00
❑ 30 Glen Rice '96/7	80.00	36.00
❑ 31 Mitch Richmond '94/5	50.00	22.00
❑ 32 Mitch Richmond '95/6	60.00	27.00
❑ 33 Mitch Richmond '96/7	120.00	55.00
❑ 34 Damon Stoudamire '95/6	150.00	70.00
❑ 35 Damon Stoudamire '96/7	150.00	70.00
❑ 36 Antoine Walker '96/7	60.00	27.00

1997-98 SP Authentic Premium Portraits

	MINT	NRMT
COMPLETE SET (7)	800.00	350.00
COMMON CARD	60.00	27.00

STATED ODDS 1:1,528

❑ DP Damon Stoudamire	150.00	70.00
❑ EP Eddie Jones	200.00	90.00
❑ JP Jason Kidd	250.00	110.00
❑ KP Kerry Kittles	60.00	27.00
❑ MP Dikembe Mutombo	60.00	27.00
❑ RP Glen Rice	80.00	36.00
❑ TP Tim Hardaway	120.00	55.00

1997-98 SP Authentic Profiles 1

	MINT	NRMT
COMPLETE SET (40)	60.00	27.00
COMMON CARD (P1-P40)	.40	.18
SEMISTARS	.50	.23
UNLISTED STARS	.75	.35

STATED ODDS 1:3

COMP.PRO.2 SET (40)	200.00	90.00
COMMON PRO.2	1.00	.45

*PRO.2: 1X TO 2.5X HI COLUMN
PRO.2: STATED ODDS 1:12

COMMON PRO.3	12.00	5.50

*PRO.3 STARS: 15X TO 40X HI COLUMN
*PRO.3 RC's: 10X TO 25X HI
PRO.3: RANDOM INSERTS IN PACKS
PRO.3: PRINT RUN 100 SERIAL #'d SETS

❑ P1 Michael Jordan	10.00	4.50
❑ P2 Glen Rice	.50	.23
❑ P3 Brent Barry	.40	.18
❑ P4 LaPhonso Ellis	.40	.18
❑ P5 Allen Iverson	4.00	1.80
❑ P6 Dikembe Mutombo	.50	.23
❑ P7 Charles Barkley	1.25	.55
❑ P8 Antoine Walker	1.50	.70
❑ P9 Karl Malone	1.25	.55
❑ P10 Jason Kidd	2.50	1.10
❑ P11 Gary Payton	1.25	.55
❑ P12 Kevin Garnett	5.00	2.20
❑ P13 Keith Van Horn	3.00	1.35
❑ P14 Glenn Robinson	.50	.23
❑ P15 Michael Finley	.75	.35
❑ P16 Hakeem Olajuwon	1.25	.55
❑ P17 Chris Webber	2.50	1.10
❑ P18 Mitch Richmond	.75	.35
❑ P19 Marcus Camby	1.00	.45
❑ P20 Tim Hardaway	.75	.35
❑ P21 Shawn Kemp	1.25	.55
❑ P22 Reggie Miller	.75	.35
❑ P23 Shaquille O'Neal	4.00	1.80
❑ P24 Chauncey Billups	.50	.23
❑ P25 Grant Hill	4.00	1.80
❑ P26 Shareef Abdur-Rahim	2.50	1.10
❑ P27 David Robinson	1.25	.55

❑ P28 Scottie Pippen	2.50	1.10
❑ P29 Juwan Howard	.50	.23
❑ P30 Anfernee Hardaway	2.50	1.10
❑ P31 Jerry Stackhouse	.50	.23
❑ P32 Kobe Bryant	6.00	2.70
❑ P33 Patrick Ewing	.75	.35
❑ P34 Alonzo Mourning	.75	.35
❑ P35 John Stockton	.75	.35
❑ P36 Kenny Anderson	.50	.23
❑ P37 Tim Duncan	6.00	2.70
❑ P38 Stephon Marbury	2.50	1.10
❑ P39 Dennis Rodman	1.50	.70
❑ P40 Joe Smith	.50	.23

1997-98 SP Authentic Sign of the Times

	MINT	NRMT
COMPLETE SET (23)	250.00	110.00
COMMON CARD	6.00	2.70
SEMISTARS	10.00	4.50
STATED ODDS 1:42		

❑ AH Allan Houston	15.00	6.75
❑ AJ Avery Johnson	6.00	2.70
❑ BB Brent Barry	6.00	2.70
❑ BW Brian Williams	6.00	2.70
❑ CM Chris Mullin	10.00	4.50
❑ DM Dikembe Mutombo	10.00	4.50
❑ DS Damon Stoudamire	15.00	6.75
❑ EJ Eddie Jones	30.00	13.50
❑ GM Gheorghe Muresan	6.00	2.70
❑ GP Gary Payton	60.00	27.00
❑ GR Glen Rice	12.00	5.50
❑ HW Juwan Howard	20.00	9.00
❑ KJ Kevin Johnson	15.00	6.75
❑ KK Kerry Kittles	10.00	4.50
❑ LH Lindsey Hunter	6.00	2.70
❑ MB Mookie Blaylock	6.00	2.70
❑ MR Mitch Richmond	15.00	6.75
❑ SC Sam Cassell	10.00	4.50
❑ SE Sean Elliott	6.00	2.70
❑ TE Terrell Brandon	15.00	6.75
❑ TG Tom Gugliotta	20.00	9.00
❑ TH Tim Hardaway	25.00	11.00
❑ VB Vin Baker	12.00	5.50

1997-98 SP Authentic Sign of the Times Stars and Rookies

	MINT	NRMT
COMMON CARD	12.00	5.50

STATED ODDS 1:113
STOCKTON DID NOT SIGN TRADE CARDS
A.HARDAWAY 8X10 AU REPLACES STOCKTON

❑ AW Antoine Walker	20.00	9.00
❑ CD Clyde Drexler	125.00	55.00
❑ CH Chauncey Billups	12.00	5.50
❑ JK Jason Kidd	100.00	45.00
❑ JS John Stockton TRADE Did not sign	60.00	27.00
❑ KM Karl Malone	60.00	27.00
❑ KV Keith Van Horn	40.00	18.00

❑ MJ Michael Jordan	4500.00	2000.00
❑ RO Ron Mercer	15.00	6.75
❑ SA Shareef Abdur-Rahim	40.00	18.00
❑ TB Tony Battie	12.00	5.50

1998-99 SP Authentic

	MINT	NRMT
COMPLETE SET (120)	1500.00	700.00
COMPLETE SET w/o RC (90)	40.00	18.00
COMMON MJ (1-10)	3.00	1.35
COMMON CARD (11-90)	.25	.11
COMMON RC (91-120)	8.00	3.60
SEMISTARS	.30	.14
SEMISTARS RC	10.00	4.50
UNLISTED STARS	.50	.23
RC's: PRINT RUN 3500 SERIAL #'d SETS		

❑ 1 Michael Jordan	3.00	1.35
❑ 2 Michael Jordan	3.00	1.35
❑ 3 Michael Jordan	3.00	1.35
❑ 4 Michael Jordan	3.00	1.35
❑ 5 Michael Jordan	3.00	1.35
❑ 6 Michael Jordan	3.00	1.35
❑ 7 Michael Jordan	3.00	1.35
❑ 8 Michael Jordan	3.00	1.35
❑ 9 Michael Jordan	3.00	1.35
❑ 10 Michael Jordan	3.00	1.35
❑ 11 Steve Smith	.30	.14
❑ 12 Dikembe Mutombo	.30	.14
❑ 13 Alan Henderson	.25	.11
❑ 14 Antoine Walker	.75	.35
❑ 15 Ron Mercer	.75	.35
❑ 16 Kenny Anderson	.30	.14
❑ 17 Derrick Coleman	.30	.14
❑ 18 David Wesley	.25	.11
❑ 19 Glen Rice	.30	.14
❑ 20 Toni Kukoc	.60	.25
❑ 21 Ron Harper	.30	.14
❑ 22 Brent Barry	.25	.11
❑ 23 Shawn Kemp	.75	.35
❑ 24 Zydrunas Ilgauskas	.25	.11
❑ 25 Brevin Knight	.25	.11
❑ 26 Michael Finley	.50	.23
❑ 27 Steve Nash	.25	.11
❑ 28 Cedric Ceballos	.25	.11
❑ 29 Antonio McDyess	.50	.23
❑ 30 Nick Van Exel	.30	.14
❑ 31 Grant Hill	2.50	1.10
❑ 32 Jerry Stackhouse	.30	.14
❑ 33 Bison Dele	.25	.11
❑ 34 John Starks	.25	.11
❑ 35 Chris Mills	.25	.11
❑ 36 Hakeem Olajuwon	.75	.35
❑ 37 Charles Barkley	.75	.35
❑ 38 Scottie Pippen	1.50	.70
❑ 39 Reggie Miller	.50	.23
❑ 40 Chris Mullin	.50	.23
❑ 41 Rik Smits	.25	.11
❑ 42 Lamond Murray	.25	.11
❑ 43 Maurice Taylor	.50	.23
❑ 44 Kobe Bryant	4.00	1.80
❑ 45 Dennis Rodman	1.00	.45
❑ 46 Shaquille O'Neal	2.50	1.10
❑ 47 Alonzo Mourning	.50	.23
❑ 48 Tim Hardaway	.50	.23
❑ 49 Jamal Mashburn	.30	.14
❑ 50 Ray Allen	.60	.25
❑ 51 Glenn Robinson	.30	.14
❑ 52 Terrell Brandon	.30	.14
❑ 53 Kevin Garnett	3.00	1.35
❑ 54 Stephon Marbury	1.25	.55
❑ 55 Joe Smith	.30	.14
❑ 56 Keith Van Horn	1.25	.55
❑ 57 Kendall Gill	.30	.14
❑ 58 Jayson Williams	.30	.14
❑ 59 Patrick Ewing	.50	.23
❑ 60 Allan Houston	.50	.23
❑ 61 Larry Johnson	.30	.14
❑ 62 Anfernee Hardaway	1.50	.70
❑ 63 Horace Grant	.30	.14
❑ 64 Allen Iverson	2.00	.90
❑ 65 Tim Thomas	.75	.35
❑ 66 Jason Kidd	1.50	.70
❑ 67 Tom Gugliotta	.30	.14
❑ 68 Rex Chapman	.25	.11
❑ 69 Damon Stoudamire	.50	.23
❑ 70 Isaiah Rider	.30	.14
❑ 71 Rasheed Wallace	.50	.23
❑ 72 Chris Webber	1.50	.70
❑ 73 Vlade Divac	.25	.11
❑ 74 Corliss Williamson	.25	.11
❑ 75 Tim Duncan	2.50	1.10
❑ 76 David Robinson	.75	.35
❑ 77 Sean Elliott	.25	.11
❑ 78 Detlef Schrempf	.30	.14
❑ 79 Vin Baker	.30	.14
❑ 80 Gary Payton	.75	.35
❑ 81 Doug Christie	.25	.11
❑ 82 Tracy McGrady	2.00	.90
❑ 83 Karl Malone	.75	.35
❑ 84 John Stockton	.50	.23
❑ 85 Jeff Hornacek	.30	.14
❑ 86 Shareef Abdur-Rahim	1.25	.55
❑ 87 Bryant Reeves	.25	.11
❑ 88 Juwan Howard	.30	.14
❑ 89 Mitch Richmond	.50	.23
❑ 90 Rod Strickland	.30	.14
❑ 91 Michael Olowokandi RC	25.00	11.00
❑ 92 Mike Bibby RC	50.00	22.00
❑ 93 Raef LaFrentz RC	30.00	13.50
❑ 94 Antawn Jamison RC	80.00	36.00
❑ 95 Vince Carter RC	1000.00	450.00
❑ 96 Robert Traylor RC	12.00	5.50
❑ 97 Jason Williams RC	150.00	70.00
❑ 98 Larry Hughes RC	150.00	70.00
❑ 99 Dirk Nowitzki RC	70.00	32.00
❑ 100 Paul Pierce RC	100.00	45.00
❑ 101 Bonzi Wells RC	80.00	36.00
❑ 102 Michael Doleac RC	10.00	4.50
❑ 103 Keon Clark RC	15.00	6.75
❑ 104 Michael Dickerson RC	50.00	22.00
❑ 105 Matt Harpring RC	10.00	4.50
❑ 106 Bryce Drew RC	12.00	5.50
❑ 107 Pat Garrity RC	10.00	4.50
❑ 108 Roshown McLeod RC	12.00	5.50
❑ 109 Ricky Davis RC	40.00	18.00
❑ 110 Brian Skinner RC	10.00	4.50
❑ 111 Tyronn Lue RC	12.00	5.50
❑ 112 Felipe Lopez RC	12.00	5.50
❑ 113 Al Harrington RC	80.00	36.00
❑ 114 Sam Jacobson RC	8.00	3.60
❑ 115 Cory Carr RC	8.00	3.60
❑ 116 Corey Benjamin RC	15.00	6.75
❑ 117 Nazr Mohammed RC	10.00	4.50
❑ 118 Rashard Lewis RC	150.00	70.00
❑ 119 Predrag Stojakovic RC	30.00	13.50
❑ 120 Andrae Patterson RC	8.00	3.60

1998-99 SP Authentic Authentics

	MINT	NRMT
COMMON CARD (T1-T30)	25.00	11.00

STATED ODDS 1:864
T1-T16 ARE ALL AUTOGRAPHED
T18-T27 NOT PRICED DUE TO SCARCITY
CARD PRINT RUNS LISTED IN PARENTHESIS

Card		MINT	NRMT
❑ T1	Larry Bird Autographed NBA Ball	600.00	275.00
❑ T2	Julius Erving Signed SI Cover	250.00	110.00
❑ T3	Anfernee Hardaway Signed SI Cover	60.00	27.00
❑ T4	Anfernee Hardaway Signed 8x10 photo	40.00	18.00
❑ T5	Tim Hardaway Signed Mini-ball	40.00	18.00
❑ T6	Tim Hardaway Signed 8x10 First version	25.00	11.00
❑ T7	Tim Hardaway Signed 8x10 Second version	40.00	18.00
❑ T8	Juwan Howard Signed Mini-ball	25.00	11.00
❑ T9	Eddie Jones Signed Mini-ball	40.00	18.00
❑ T10	Eddie Jones Signed 8x10	30.00	13.50
❑ T11	Michael Jordan Signed black jersey	2000.00	900.00
❑ T12	Michael Jordan Signed white jersey	2000.00	900.00
❑ T13	Shawn Kemp Signed 8x10	40.00	18.00
❑ T14	Shawn Kemp Signed jersey	250.00	110.00
❑ T15	Gary Payton Signed SI Cover	100.00	45.00
❑ T16	Scottie Pippen Signed Ball	250.00	110.00
❑ T17	Forum Floor Pieces (23)	250.00	110.00
❑ T18	Shaquille O'Neal Game Worn Authentics		
❑ T19	Shareef Abdur-Rahim Game worn Authentics		
❑ T20	Karl Malone Game worn Authentics		
❑ T21	Tim Duncan Game worn Authentics		
❑ T22	Gary Payton Game worn Authentics		
❑ T23	Antonie Walker Game worn Authentics		
❑ T24	Hakeem Olajuwon Game worn Authentics		
❑ T25	Charles Barkley Game worn Authentics		
❑ T26	Allen Iverson Game worn Authentics		
❑ T27	Kevin Garnett Game worn Authentics		

1998-99 SP Authentic First Class

	MINT	NRMT
COMPLETE SET (30)	80.00	36.00
COMMON CARD (FC1-30)	.60	.25
UNLISTED STARS	1.00	.45

STATED ODDS 1:7

Card		MINT	NRMT
❑ FC1	Michael Jordan	12.00	5.50
❑ FC2	Dikembe Mutombo	.60	.25
❑ FC3	Antoine Walker	1.50	.70
❑ FC4	Glen Rice	.60	.25
❑ FC5	Toni Kukoc	1.25	.55
❑ FC6	Shawn Kemp	1.50	.70
❑ FC7	Michael Finley	1.00	.45
❑ FC8	Raef LaFrentz	3.00	1.35
❑ FC9	Grant Hill	5.00	2.20
❑ FC10	Antawn Jamison	8.00	3.60
❑ FC11	Scottie Pippen	3.00	1.35
❑ FC12	Reggie Miller	1.00	.45
❑ FC13	Michael Olowokandi	2.50	1.10
❑ FC14	Kobe Bryant	8.00	3.60
❑ FC15	Tim Hardaway	1.00	.45
❑ FC16	Ray Allen	1.25	.55
❑ FC17	Kevin Garnett	6.00	2.70
❑ FC18	Keith Van Horn	2.50	1.10
❑ FC19	Allan Houston	1.00	.45
❑ FC20	Anfernee Hardaway	3.00	1.35
❑ FC21	Allen Iverson	4.00	1.80
❑ FC22	Jason Kidd	3.00	1.35
❑ FC23	Damon Stoudamire	1.00	.45
❑ FC24	Jason Williams	10.00	4.50
❑ FC25	Tim Duncan	5.00	2.20
❑ FC26	Gary Payton	1.50	.70
❑ FC27	Vince Carter	40.00	18.00
❑ FC28	Karl Malone	1.50	.70
❑ FC29	Mike Bibby	5.00	2.20
❑ FC30	Mitch Richmond	1.00	.45

1998-99 SP Authentic MICHAEL

	MINT	NRMT
COMPLETE SET (15)	400.00	180.00
COMMON CARD (M1-15)	30.00	13.50

STATED ODDS 1:144

Card		MINT	NRMT
❑ M1	Michael Jordan	30.00	13.50
❑ M2	Michael Jordan	30.00	13.50
❑ M3	Michael Jordan	30.00	13.50
❑ M4	Michael Jordan	30.00	13.50
❑ M5	Michael Jordan	30.00	13.50
❑ M6	Michael Jordan	30.00	13.50
❑ M7	Michael Jordan	30.00	13.50
❑ M8	Michael Jordan	30.00	13.50
❑ M9	Michael Jordan	30.00	13.50
❑ M10	Michael Jordan	30.00	13.50
❑ M11	Michael Jordan	30.00	13.50
❑ M12	Michael Jordan	30.00	13.50
❑ M13	Michael Jordan	30.00	13.50
❑ M14	Michael Jordan	30.00	13.50
❑ M15	Michael Jordan	30.00	13.50

1998-99 SP Authentic NBA 2K

	MINT	NRMT
COMPLETE SET (20)	100.00	45.00
COMMON CARDS (2K1-20)	2.50	1.10
UNLISTED STARS	4.00	1.80

STATED ODDS 1:23

Card		MINT	NRMT
❑ 2K1	Michael Olowokandi	4.00	1.80
❑ 2K2	Mike Bibby	6.00	2.70
❑ 2K3	Raef LaFrentz	4.00	1.80
❑ 2K4	Antawn Jamison	10.00	4.50
❑ 2K5	Vince Carter	50.00	22.00
❑ 2K6	Robert Traylor	2.50	1.10
❑ 2K7	Jason Williams	12.00	5.50
❑ 2K8	Larry Hughes	12.00	5.50
❑ 2K9	Dirk Nowitzki	8.00	3.60
❑ 2K10	Paul Pierce	10.00	4.50
❑ 2K11	Cuttino Mobley	6.00	2.70
❑ 2K12	Michael Doleac	2.50	1.10
❑ 2K13	Corey Benjamin	2.50	1.10
❑ 2K14	Michael Dickerson	4.00	1.80
❑ 2K15	Allen Iverson	6.00	2.70
❑ 2K16	Kobe Bryant	12.00	5.50
❑ 2K17	Tim Duncan	8.00	3.60
❑ 2K18	Keith Van Horn	4.00	1.80
❑ 2K19	Kevin Garnett	10.00	4.50
❑ 2K20	Grant Hill	8.00	3.60

1998-99 SP Authentic Sign of the Times Bronze

	MINT	NRMT
COMMON CARD	8.00	3.60
SEMISTARS	12.00	5.50

STATED ODDS 1:23

Card		MINT	NRMT
❑ AM	Antonio McDyess	15.00	6.75
❑ AV	Avery Johnson	8.00	3.60
❑ BE	Blue Edwards	8.00	3.60
❑ BG	Brian Grant	15.00	6.75
❑ BK	Brevin Knight	8.00	3.60
❑ BL	Mookie Blaylock	8.00	3.60
❑ BP	Bobby Phills	8.00	3.60
❑ BR	Bryon Russell	8.00	3.60
❑ CB	Chauncey Billups	8.00	3.60
❑ CC	Chris Carr	8.00	3.60

		MINT	NRMT
❑ CH	Calbert Cheaney	8.00	3.60
❑ DA	Derek Anderson	12.00	5.50
❑ DC	Doug Christie	8.00	3.60
❑ DK	Derek Fisher	12.00	5.50
❑ DM	Donyell Marshall	8.00	3.60
❑ DN	Danny Manning	12.00	5.50
❑ DT	Detlef Schrempf	15.00	6.75
❑ DV	David Wesley	8.00	3.60
❑ ED	Erick Dampier	8.00	3.60
❑ EG	Ed Gray	8.00	3.60
❑ GR	Glen Rice	15.00	6.75
❑ HG	Horace Grant	12.00	5.50
❑ HW	Juwan Howard	15.00	6.75
❑ JH	Jeff Hornacek	15.00	6.75
❑ JR	Jalen Rose	15.00	6.75
❑ JW	Jerome Williams	12.00	5.50
❑ JY	Jayson Williams	12.00	5.50
❑ KA	Kenny Anderson	12.00	5.50
❑ LH	Lindsey Hunter	8.00	3.60
❑ LJ	Larry Johnson	12.00	5.50
❑ MG	Tracy McGrady	50.00	22.00
❑ MI	Michael Finley	12.00	5.50
❑ MK	Mark Jackson	8.00	3.60
❑ NA	Nick Anderson	8.00	3.60
❑ OH	Othella Harrington	8.00	3.60
❑ PJ	P.J. Brown	8.00	3.60
❑ RH	Ron Harper	12.00	5.50
❑ RR	Rodrick Rhodes	8.00	3.60
❑ SE	Sean Elliott	12.00	5.50
❑ TB	Terrell Brandon	12.00	5.50
❑ TK	Toni Kukoc	20.00	9.00
❑ TQ	Tariq Abdul-Wahad	8.00	3.60
❑ TR	Theo Ratliff	8.00	3.60
❑ TY	Maurice Taylor	12.00	5.50
❑ WM	Walter McCarty	8.00	3.60

1998-99 SP Authentic Sign of the Times Gold

	MINT	NRMT
COMMON CARD	50.00	22.00
STATED ODDS 1:864		

		MINT	NRMT
❑ AI	Allen Iverson	150.00	70.00
❑ AW	Antoine Walker	60.00	27.00
❑ MJ	Michael Jordan	1200.00	550.00
❑ TH	Tim Hardaway	50.00	22.00

1998-99 SP Authentic Sign of the Times Silver

	MINT	NRMT
COMMON CARD	8.00	3.60
SEMISTARS	12.00	5.50
STATED ODDS 1:115		

		MINT	NRMT
❑ AJ	Antawn Jamison	50.00	22.00
❑ DR	Dennis Rodman	80.00	36.00
❑ HO	Hakeem Olajuwon	30.00	13.50
❑ LR	Larry Hughes	50.00	22.00
❑ MB	Mike Bibby	20.00	9.00
❑ MO	Michael Olowokandi	8.00	3.60
❑ MT	Dikembe Mutombo	12.00	5.50
❑ PN	Anfernee Hardaway	60.00	27.00
❑ RL	Raef LaFrentz	12.00	5.50
❑ RM	Ron Mercer	15.00	6.75
❑ RT	Robert Traylor	8.00	3.60
❑ SH	Shawn Kemp	25.00	11.00
❑ VC	Vince Carter	450.00	200.00

1999-00 SP Authentic

	MINT	NRMT
COMPLETE SET (135)	2000.00	900.00
COMPLETE SET w/o RC (90)	30.00	13.50
COMMON CARD (1-90)	.25	.11
COMMON RC (91-135)	15.00	6.75
SEMISTARS	.30	.14
SEMISTARS RC	20.00	9.00
UNLISTED STARS	.50	.23

RCs: PRINT RUN 1500 SERIAL #'d SETS
RCs: RANDOM INSERTS IN PACKS

		MINT	NRMT
❑ 1	Dikembe Mutombo	.30	.14
❑ 2	Jim Jackson	.25	.11
❑ 3	Alan Henderson	.25	.11
❑ 4	Antoine Walker	.60	.25
❑ 5	Paul Pierce	1.00	.45
❑ 6	Kenny Anderson	.30	.14
❑ 7	Eddie Jones	1.00	.45
❑ 8	Derrick Coleman	.30	.14
❑ 9	Anthony Mason	.30	.14
❑ 10	Chris Carr	.25	.11
❑ 11	Hersey Hawkins	.30	.14
❑ 12	B.J. Armstrong	.25	.11
❑ 13	Shawn Kemp	.75	.35
❑ 14	Bob Sura	.25	.11
❑ 15	Lamond Murray	.25	.11
❑ 16	Michael Finley	.50	.23
❑ 17	Cedric Ceballos	.25	.11
❑ 18	Dirk Nowitzki	.75	.35
❑ 19	Erick Strickland	.25	.11
❑ 20	Antonio McDyess	.50	.23
❑ 21	Nick Van Exel	.30	.14
❑ 22	Grant Hill	2.50	1.10
❑ 23	Jerry Stackhouse	.30	.14
❑ 24	Lindsey Hunter	.25	.11
❑ 25	Christian Laettner	.30	.14
❑ 26	Antawn Jamison	1.00	.45
❑ 27	Chris Mills	.25	.11
❑ 28	Larry Hughes	1.25	.55
❑ 29	Charles Barkley	.75	.35
❑ 30	Hakeem Olajuwon	.75	.35
❑ 31	Cuttino Mobley	.50	.23
❑ 32	Reggie Miller	.50	.23
❑ 33	Jalen Rose	.50	.23
❑ 34	Rik Smits	.25	.11
❑ 35	Maurice Taylor	.50	.23
❑ 36	Derek Anderson	.50	.23
❑ 37	Tyrone Nesby RC	.25	.11
❑ 38	Kobe Bryant	4.00	1.80
❑ 39	Shaquille O'Neal	2.50	1.10
❑ 40	Glen Rice	.30	.14
❑ 41	Tim Hardaway	.50	.23
❑ 42	Alonzo Mourning	.50	.23
❑ 43	Jamal Mashburn	.30	.14
❑ 44	Ray Allen	.50	.23
❑ 45	Sam Cassell	.30	.14
❑ 46	Glenn Robinson	.30	.14
❑ 47	Kevin Garnett	3.00	1.35
❑ 48	Terrell Brandon	.30	.14
❑ 49	Joe Smith	.30	.14
❑ 50	Stephon Marbury	1.00	.45
❑ 51	Keith Van Horn	1.00	.45
❑ 52	Jamie Feick RC	1.00	.45
❑ 53	Kerry Kittles	.30	.14
❑ 54	Allan Houston	.50	.23
❑ 55	Latrell Sprewell	1.00	.45
❑ 56	Patrick Ewing	.50	.23
❑ 57	Darrell Armstrong	.30	.14
❑ 58	Ron Mercer	.60	.25
❑ 59	Michael Doleac	.25	.11
❑ 60	Allen Iverson	2.00	.90
❑ 61	Toni Kukoc	.60	.25
❑ 62	Eric Snow	.25	.11
❑ 63	Anfernee Hardaway	1.50	.70
❑ 64	Jason Kidd	1.50	.70
❑ 65	Tom Gugliotta	.30	.14
❑ 66	Scottie Pippen	1.50	.70
❑ 67	Steve Smith	.30	.14
❑ 68	Damon Stoudamire	.50	.23
❑ 69	Jason Williams	1.25	.55
❑ 70	Predrag Stojakovic	.30	.14
❑ 71	Chris Webber	1.50	.70
❑ 72	Vlade Divac	.25	.11
❑ 73	Tim Duncan	2.50	1.10
❑ 74	David Robinson	.75	.35
❑ 75	Avery Johnson	.25	.11
❑ 76	Gary Payton	.75	.35
❑ 77	Vin Baker	.30	.14
❑ 78	Vernon Maxwell	.25	.11
❑ 79	Vince Carter	5.00	2.20
❑ 80	Tracy McGrady	1.50	.70
❑ 81	Doug Christie	.25	.11
❑ 82	Karl Malone	.75	.35
❑ 83	John Stockton	.50	.23
❑ 84	Jeff Hornacek	.30	.14
❑ 85	Mike Bibby	.60	.25
❑ 86	Shareef Abdur-Rahim	1.00	.45
❑ 87	Othella Harrington	.25	.11
❑ 88	Mitch Richmond	.50	.23
❑ 89	Juwan Howard	.30	.14
❑ 90	Rod Strickland	.30	.14
❑ 91	Elton Brand RC	200.00	90.00
❑ 92	Steve Francis RC	600.00	275.00
❑ 93	Baron Davis RC	60.00	27.00
❑ 94	Lamar Odom RC	200.00	90.00
❑ 95	Jonathan Bender RC	150.00	70.00
❑ 96	Wally Szczerbiak RC	100.00	45.00
❑ 97	Richard Hamilton RC	60.00	27.00
❑ 98	Andre Miller RC	80.00	36.00
❑ 99	Shawn Marion RC	80.00	36.00
❑ 100	Jason Terry RC	40.00	18.00
❑ 101	Trajan Langdon RC	25.00	11.00
❑ 102	Aleksandar Radojevic RC	15.00	6.75
❑ 103	Corey Maggette RC	100.00	45.00
❑ 104	William Avery RC	40.00	18.00
❑ 105	Ron Artest RC	60.00	27.00
❑ 106	James Posey RC	40.00	18.00
❑ 107	Quincy Lewis RC	25.00	11.00
❑ 108	Dion Glover RC	20.00	9.00
❑ 109	Kenny Thomas RC	25.00	11.00
❑ 110	Devean George RC	50.00	22.00
❑ 111	Tim James RC	25.00	11.00
❑ 112	Vonteego Cummings RC	40.00	18.00
❑ 113	Jumaine Jones RC	20.00	9.00
❑ 114	Scott Padgett RC	20.00	9.00
❑ 115	Adrian Griffin RC	25.00	11.00
❑ 116	Anthony Carter RC	50.00	22.00
❑ 117	Todd MacCulloch RC	20.00	9.00
❑ 118	Chucky Atkins RC	20.00	9.00
❑ 119	Obinna Ekezie RC	20.00	9.00
❑ 120	Eddie Robinson RC	40.00	18.00
❑ 121	Michael Ruffin RC	20.00	9.00
❑ 122	Laron Profit RC	20.00	9.00
❑ 123	Cal Bowdler RC	20.00	9.00
❑ 124	Chris Herren RC	15.00	6.75
❑ 125	Milt Palacio RC	15.00	6.75
❑ 126	Jeff Foster RC	20.00	9.00
❑ 127	Ryan Bowen RC	15.00	6.75
❑ 128	Tim Young RC	15.00	6.75
❑ 129	Derrick Dial RC	15.00	6.75
❑ 130	Greg Buckner RC	15.00	6.75
❑ 131	Rodney Buford RC	15.00	6.75
❑ 132	Evan Eschmeyer RC	15.00	6.75
❑ 133	Jermaine Jackson RC	15.00	6.75
❑ 134	John Celestand RC	20.00	9.00
❑ 135	Ryan Robertson RC	20.00	9.00
❑ KG	Kevin Garnett PROMO	3.00	1.35

1999-00 SP Authentic Athletic

	MINT	NRMT
COMPLETE SET (12)	25.00	11.00
COMMON CARD (A1-A12)	.60	.25
STATED ODDS 1:12		

Card	MINT	NRMT
❑ A1 Grant Hill	4.00	1.80
❑ A2 Shareef Abdur-Rahim	1.50	.70
❑ A3 Jason Kidd	2.50	1.10
❑ A4 Vince Carter	8.00	3.60
❑ A5 Steve Francis	5.00	2.20
❑ A6 Scottie Pippen	2.50	1.10
❑ A7 Paul Pierce	1.50	.70
❑ A8 Kobe Bryant	6.00	2.70
❑ A9 Stephon Marbury	1.50	.70
❑ A10 Michael Finley	.60	.25
❑ A11 Eddie Jones	1.50	.70
❑ A12 Kevin Garnett	5.00	2.20

1999-00 SP Authentic BuyBack

	MINT	NRMT
COMMON CARD	10.00	4.50

STATED ODDS 1:288
PRINT RUNS LISTED BELOW
CARDS NUMBERED BELOW ALPHABETICAL-LY
LOWER PRINT RUNS UNPRICED

Card	MINT	NRMT
❑ 1 M.Bibby 98-9SPA/3		
❑ 2 M.Bibby 98-9SPA2K/42	60.00	27.00
❑ 3 K.Bryant 96-7SP/8		
❑ 3A K.Bryant Redemption	600.00	275.00
❑ 4 K.Bryant 96-7SPHo/1		
❑ 5 K.Bryant 97SPx/1		
❑ 6 K.Bryant 97-8SPA/7		
❑ 7 K.Bryant 97-8SPAPro/1		
❑ 8 K.Bryant 98-9SPA/NNO		
❑ 9 K.Garnett 95-6SP/21	650.00	300.00
❑ 10 K.Garnett 95-6SPAS/1		
❑ 11 K.Garnett 96-7SP/21	500.00	220.00
❑ 12 K.Garnett 96-7SPHo/1		
❑ 13 K.Garnett 97-8SPA/10		
❑ 14 K.Garnett 97-8SPAPro/1		
❑ 15 K.Garnett 98-9SPA/NNO	150.00	70.00
❑ 16 K.Garnett 98-9SPAFC/1		
❑ 17 K.Garnett 98-9SPA2K/1		
❑ 18 B.Grant 94-5SP/NNO	50.00	22.00
❑ 19 B.Grant 94-5SPDC/8		
❑ 20 B.Grant 94-5SPHo/9		
❑ 21 B.Grant 94-5SPHoDC/2		
❑ 22 B.Grant 95-6SP/NNO	30.00	13.50
❑ 23 B.Grant 95-6SPHo/1		
❑ 24 B.Grant 95-6SPHoDC/6		
❑ 25 B.Grant 96-7SP/16	100.00	45.00
❑ 26 B.Grant 97-8SPA/16		
❑ 27 T.Gugliotta 94-5SP/24		
❑ 28 T.Gugliotta 94-95SPDC/6		
❑ 29 T.Gugliotta 95-6SP/24		
❑ 30 T.Gugliotta 96-7SP/24	50.00	22.00
❑ 31 T.Gugliotta 97-8SPA/8		
❑ 32 T.Gugliotta 98-9SPA/110	20.00	9.00
❑ 33 A.Hard 94-5SP/30	300.00	135.00
❑ 34 A.Hard 94-5SPDC/1		
❑ 35 A.Hard 95-6SP/30	300.00	135.00
❑ 36 A.Hard 95-6SPAS/1		
❑ 37 A.Hard 96-7SP/1		
❑ 38 A.Hard 96-7SPHo/1		
❑ 39 A.Hard 97-8SPA/1		
❑ 40 A.Hard 98-9SPA/32	300.00	135.00
❑ 41 A.Hard 98-9SPAFC/1		
❑ 42 L.Hughes 98-9SPA/3		
❑ 43 L.Hughes 98-9SPA2K/90	80.00	36.00
❑ 44 M.Jackson 94-5SP/NNO		
❑ 44A M.Jackson Redemption		
❑ 45 M.Jackson 94-5SPDC/3		
❑ 46 M.Jackson 96-7SP/18		
❑ 47 M.Jackson 97-8SPA/8		
❑ 48 A.Jamison 98-9SPAFC/NNO	50.00	22.00
❑ 49 A.Jamison 98-9SPA2K/2		
❑ 50 E.Jones 94-5SP/NNO	80.00	36.00
❑ 51 E.Jones 94-5SPDC/7		
❑ 52 E.Jones 95-6SP/NNO	50.00	22.00
❑ 53 E.Jones 95-6SPHo/5		
❑ 54 E.Jones 96-7SP/NNO	50.00	22.00
❑ 55 E.Jones 97-8SPA/12		
❑ 56 M.Jordan 94-5SP/1		
❑ 57 M.Jordan 95-6SP/1		
❑ 58 M.Jordan 95-6SPAS/1		
❑ 59 B.Knight 97-8SPA/12		
❑ 60 B.Knight 97-8SPA/24		
❑ 61 B.Knight 98-9SPA/NNO	10.00	4.50
❑ 62 R.LaFrentz 98-9SPA/3		
❑ 63 R.LaFrentz 98-9SPAFC/NNO	25.00	11.00
❑ 64 R.LaFrentz 98-9SPA2K/NNO		
❑ 65 K.Malone 94-5SP/NNO	60.00	27.00
❑ 66 K.Malone 94-5SPDC/51		
❑ 67 K.Malone 95-6SP/1		
❑ 68 K.Malone 95-6SPAS/1		
❑ 69 K.Malone 96-7SP/10		
❑ 70 K.Malone 97-8SPA/10		
❑ 71 K.Malone 97-8SPAPro/1		
❑ 72 K.Malone 98-9SPA/6		
❑ 73 K.Malone 98-9SPAFC/1		
❑ 74 J.O'Neal 96-7SP/170	50.00	22.00
❑ 75 J.O'Neal 96-7SPHo/3		
❑ 76 J.O'Neal 97-8SPA/2		
❑ 77 G.Rice 94-5SP/41	50.00	22.00
❑ 78 G.Rice 94-5SPDC/1		
❑ 79 G.Rice 95-6SP/NNO	15.00	6.75
❑ 80 G.Rice 95-6SPASG/1		
❑ 81 G.Rice 95-6SPASS/1		
❑ 82 G.Rice 96-7SP/41	50.00	22.00
❑ 83 G.Rice 97-8SPA/10		
❑ 84 G.Rice 97-8SPAPro/1		
❑ 85 G.Rice 98-9SPA/NNO	15.00	6.75
❑ 86 G.Rice 98-9SPAFC/1		
❑ 87 J.Rose 94-5SP/100	80.00	36.00
❑ 88 J.Rose 95-6SP/120	50.00	22.00
❑ 89 J.Stack 95-6SP/NNO	50.00	22.00
❑ 90 J.Stack 95-6SPAS/1		
❑ 91 J.Stack 95-6SPHo/8		
❑ 92 J.Stack 95-6SPC/1		
❑ 93 J.Stack 95-6SPC/4		
❑ 94 J.Stack 96-7SP/16	120.00	55.00
❑ 95 J.Stack 96-7SPHo/6		
❑ 96 J.Stack 97-8SPA/25	80.00	36.00
❑ 97 J.Stack 98-9SPA/NNO	30.00	13.50
❑ 98 D.Stoud 95-6SP/NNO	50.00	22.00
❑ 99 D.Stoud 95-6SPASG/7		
❑ 100 D.Stoud 95-6SPHo/35	80.00	36.00
❑ 101 D.Stoud 95-6SPHoDC/10		
❑ 102 D.Stoud 96-7SP/31	80.00	36.00
❑ 103 D.Stoud 96-7SPHo/1		
❑ 104 D.Stoud 97-8SPA/11		
❑ 105 D.Stoud 98-9SPA/NNO	30.00	13.50
❑ 106 D.Stoud 98-9SPAFC/3		
❑ 107 M.Taylor 97-8SPA/12		
❑ 108 M.Taylor 97-8SPA/20	80.00	36.00
❑ 109 M.Taylor 98-9SPA/NNO	20.00	9.00
❑ 110 R.Traylor 98-9SPA/6		
❑ 111 R.Traylor 98-9SPA2K/NNO	15.00	6.75
❑ 112 A.Walker 96-7SP/NNO	40.00	18.00
❑ 113 A.Walker 96-7SPHo/1		
❑ 114 A.Walker 97-8SPA/19	120.00	55.00
❑ 115 A.Walker 98-9SPA/NNO	30.00	13.50
❑ 116 A.Walker 98-9SPAFC/1		
❑ 117 Jay.Will 95-6SP/NNO	15.00	6.75
❑ 118 Jay.Will 96-7SP/33		
❑ 119 Jay.Will 97-8SPA/12		
❑ 120 Jay.Will 98-9SPA/NNO	15.00	6.75

1999-00 SP Authentic First Class

	MINT	NRMT
COMPLETE SET (12)	15.00	6.75
COMMON CARD (FC1-FC12)	.75	.35
STATED ODDS 1:12		

Card	MINT	NRMT
❑ FC1 Kevin Garnett	5.00	2.20
❑ FC2 Kobe Bryant	6.00	2.70
❑ FC3 Gary Payton	1.25	.55
❑ FC4 Tim Hardaway	.75	.35
❑ FC5 Antonio McDyess	.75	.35
❑ FC6 Allan Houston	.75	.35
❑ FC7 Jason Kidd	2.50	1.10
❑ FC8 Reggie Miller	.75	.35
❑ FC9 Jason Williams	2.00	.90
❑ FC10 Allen Iverson	3.00	1.35
❑ FC11 David Robinson	1.25	.55
❑ FC12 Shaquille O'Neal	4.00	1.80

1999-00 SP Authentic Maximum Force

	MINT	NRMT
COMPLETE SET (15)	10.00	4.50
COMMON CARD (M1-M15)	.30	.14
UNLISTED STARS	.50	.23
STATED ODDS 1:4		

❑ M1 Karl Malone	.75	.35
❑ M2 Antawn Jamison	1.00	.45
❑ M3 Shareef Abdur-Rahim	1.00	.45
❑ M4 Tim Duncan	2.50	1.10
❑ M5 Allen Iverson	2.00	.90
❑ M6 Michael Finley	.50	.23
❑ M7 Kevin Garnett	3.00	1.35
❑ M8 Kobe Bryant	4.00	1.80
❑ M9 Gary Payton	.75	.35
❑ M10 Keith Van Horn	1.00	.45
❑ M11 Chris Webber	1.50	.70
❑ M12 Glenn Robinson	.30	.14
❑ M13 Alonzo Mourning	.50	.23
❑ M14 Antoine Walker	.60	.25
❑ M15 Antonio McDyess	.50	.23

1999-00 SP Authentic Premier Powers

	MINT	NRMT
COMPLETE SET (9)	80.00	36.00
COMMON CARD (P1-P9)	10.00	4.50
STATED ODDS 1:72		

❑ P1 Kobe Bryant	20.00	9.00
❑ P2 Kevin Garnett	15.00	6.75
❑ P3 Tim Duncan	12.00	5.50
❑ P4 Elton Brand	12.00	5.50
❑ P5 Vince Carter	25.00	11.00
❑ P6 Lamar Odom	10.00	4.50
❑ P7 Grant Hill	12.00	5.50
❑ P8 Shaquille O'Neal	12.00	5.50
❑ P9 Allen Iverson	10.00	4.50

1999-00 SP Authentic Sign of the Times

	MINT	NRMT
COMMON CARD	8.00	3.60
STATED ODDS 1:23		

❑ AC Anthony Carter	25.00	11.00
❑ AD Antonio Davis	8.00	3.60
❑ AG Adrian Griffin	10.00	4.50
❑ AH Al Harrington	15.00	6.75
❑ AJ Antawn Jamison	20.00	9.00
❑ AL Alan Henderson	8.00	3.60
❑ AM Andre Miller	12.00	5.50
❑ AN Anfernee Hardaway	80.00	36.00
❑ AW Antoine Walker	15.00	6.75
❑ BD Baron Davis	12.00	5.50
❑ BG Brian Grant	12.00	5.50
❑ BR Brevin Knight	10.00	4.50
❑ BW Bonzi Wells	20.00	9.00
❑ CA Chucky Atkins	8.00	3.60
❑ CM Corey Maggette	25.00	11.00
❑ CR Austin Croshere	20.00	9.00
❑ CT Cuttino Mobley	12.00	5.50
❑ DA Darrell Armstrong	10.00	4.50
❑ DG Dion Glover	8.00	3.60
❑ DN Dirk Nowitzki	25.00	11.00
❑ DS Damon Stoudamire	20.00	9.00
❑ EJ Eddie Jones	25.00	11.00
❑ GR Glen Rice	15.00	6.75
❑ JB Jonathan Bender	25.00	11.00
❑ JO Jermaine O'Neal	15.00	6.75
❑ JP James Posey	8.00	3.60
❑ JR Jalen Rose	20.00	9.00
❑ JS Jerry Stackhouse	15.00	6.75
❑ JT Jason Terry	8.00	3.60
❑ JY Jayson Williams	8.00	3.60
❑ KB Kobe Bryant	200.00	90.00
❑ KG Kevin Garnett	150.00	70.00
❑ KM Karl Malone	50.00	22.00
❑ LH Larry Hughes	30.00	13.50
❑ LM Lamond Murray	8.00	3.60
❑ MB Mike Bibby	15.00	6.75
❑ MD Antonio McDyess	12.00	5.50
❑ ME Mario Elie	8.00	3.60
❑ MI Michael Dickerson	12.00	5.50
❑ MJ Michael Jordan	1500.00	700.00
❑ MK Mark Jackson	10.00	4.50
❑ MT Maurice Taylor	8.00	3.60
❑ QL Quincy Lewis	8.00	3.60
❑ RA Ron Artest	15.00	6.75
❑ RH Richard Hamilton	10.00	4.50
❑ RL Raef LaFrentz	10.00	4.50
❑ RP Ruben Patterson	10.00	4.50
❑ RT Robert Traylor	8.00	3.60
❑ SF Steve Francis	100.00	45.00
❑ SH Shawn Marion	20.00	9.00
❑ SM Sam Mack	8.00	3.60
❑ SU Bob Sura	8.00	3.60
❑ TG Tom Gugliotta	12.00	5.50
❑ TL Trajan Langdon	12.00	5.50
❑ TN Tyrone Nesby	8.00	3.60
❑ TR Tracy McGrady	40.00	18.00
❑ WA William Avery	8.00	3.60
❑ WS Wally Szczerbiak	25.00	11.00

1999-00 SP Authentic Sign of the Times Gold

	MINT	NRMT
COMMON CARD	30.00	13.50

*GOLD: 1.5X TO 4X BASE AUTO
STATED PRINT RUN 25 SERIAL #'d SETS
RANDOM INSERTS IN PACKS

1999-00 SP Authentic Supremacy

	MINT	NRMT
COMPLETE SET (9)	30.00	13.50
COMMON CARD (S1-S9)	1.50	.70
STATED ODDS 1:24		

❑ S1 Vince Carter	10.00	4.50
❑ S2 Shaquille O'Neal	5.00	2.20
❑ S3 Tim Duncan	5.00	2.20
❑ S4 Kevin Garnett	6.00	2.70
❑ S5 Jason Williams	2.50	1.10
❑ S6 Stephon Marbury	2.00	.90
❑ S7 Gary Payton	1.50	.70
❑ S8 Kobe Bryant	8.00	3.60
❑ S9 Grant Hill	5.00	2.20

1996 SPx

	MINT	NRMT
COMPLETE SET (50)	60.00	27.00
COMMON CARD (1-50)	.75	.35
SEMISTARS	1.00	.45
UNLISTED STARS	1.50	.70
R1: STATED ODDS 1:75		
T1: STATED ODDS 1:95		

❑ 1 Stacey Augmon	.75	.35
❑ 2 Mookie Blaylock	.75	.35
❑ 3 Eric Montross	.75	.35
❑ 4 Eric Williams	.75	.35
❑ 5 Larry Johnson	1.00	.45
❑ 6 George Zidek	.75	.35
❑ 7 Jason Caffey	.75	.35
❑ 8 Michael Jordan	20.00	9.00
❑ 9 Chris Mills	.75	.35
❑ 10 Bob Sura	.75	.35
❑ 11 Jason Kidd	6.00	2.70
❑ 12 Jamal Mashburn	1.00	.45
❑ 13 Antonio McDyess	3.00	1.35
❑ 14 Jalen Rose	1.50	.70
❑ 15 Grant Hill	8.00	3.60
❑ 16 Theo Ratliff	1.00	.45
❑ 17 Joe Smith	2.00	.90
❑ 18 Latrell Sprewell	3.00	1.35
❑ 19 Hakeem Olajuwon	2.50	1.10
❑ 20 Reggie Miller	1.50	.70
❑ 21 Rik Smits	.75	.35
❑ 22 Brent Barry	.75	.35
❑ 23 Lamond Murray	.75	.35
❑ 24 Magic Johnson	5.00	2.20
❑ 25 Eddie Jones	3.00	1.35
❑ 26 Nick Van Exel	1.00	.45
❑ 27 Alonzo Mourning	1.50	.70
❑ 28 Kurt Thomas	.75	.35
❑ 29 Vin Baker	1.00	.45
❑ 30 Glenn Robinson	1.50	.70
❑ 31 Kevin Garnett	10.00	4.50
❑ 32 Ed O'Bannon	.75	.35

	MINT	NRMT
❑ 33 Patrick Ewing	1.50	.70
❑ 34 Anfernee Hardaway	5.00	2.20
❑ 35 Shaquille O'Neal	8.00	3.60
❑ 36 Jerry Stackhouse	2.00	.90
❑ 37 Charles Barkley	2.50	1.10
❑ 38 Michael Finley	2.50	1.10
❑ 39 Randolph Childress	.75	.35
❑ 40 Gary Trent	.75	.35
❑ 41 Brian Grant	1.50	.70
❑ 42 Mitch Richmond	1.50	.70
❑ 43 David Robinson	2.50	1.10
❑ 44 Shawn Kemp	2.50	1.10
❑ 45 Gary Payton	2.50	1.10
❑ 46 Damon Stoudamire	3.00	1.35
❑ 47 Karl Malone	2.50	1.10
❑ 48 John Stockton	1.50	.70
❑ 49 Bryant Reeves	.75	.35
❑ 50 Rasheed Wallace	1.50	.70
❑ R1 Michael Jordan Record Breaker	15.00	6.75
❑ T1 Anfernee Hardaway Tribute	4.00	1.80
❑ NNO Anfernee Hardaway Certified Autograph	100.00	45.00
❑ NNO Anfernee Hardaway Expired Exchange	40.00	18.00
❑ NNO Michael Jordan Certified Autograph	2000.00	900.00
❑ NNO Michael Jordan Expired Exchange	1000.00	450.00

1996 SPx Gold

	MINT	NRMT
COMPLETE SET (50)	200.00	90.00
COMMON CARD (1-50)	1.50	.70

*GOLD: 1X TO 2X BASE CARD HI
STATED ODDS 1:7

1996 SPx Holoview Heroes

	MINT	NRMT
COMPLETE SET (10)	80.00	36.00
COMMON CARD (H1-H10)	3.00	1.35

STATED ODDS 1:24

	MINT	NRMT
❑ H1 Michael Jordan	30.00	13.50
❑ H2 Jason Kidd	10.00	4.50
❑ H3 Grant Hill	12.00	5.50
❑ H4 Joe Smith	3.00	1.35
❑ H5 Magic Johnson	8.00	3.60
❑ H6 Antonio McDyess	5.00	2.20
❑ H7 Anfernee Hardaway	8.00	3.60
❑ H8 Jerry Stackhouse	3.00	1.35
❑ H9 Damon Stoudamire	5.00	2.20
❑ H10 Shaquille O'Neal	12.00	5.50

1997 SPx

	MINT	NRMT
COMPLETE SET (50)	100.00	45.00
COMMON CARD (1-50)	.75	.35
SEMISTARS	1.00	.45
UNLISTED STARS	1.50	.70

SPX PREFIX ON CARDS

	MINT	NRMT
❑ 1 Mookie Blaylock	.75	.35
❑ 2 Antoine Walker	3.00	1.35
❑ 3 Eric Williams	.75	.35
❑ 4 Tony Delk	.75	.35
❑ 5 Michael Jordan	20.00	9.00
❑ 6 Dennis Rodman	3.00	1.35
❑ 7 Vitaly Potapenko	.75	.35
❑ 8 Bob Sura	.75	.35
❑ 9 Jamal Mashburn	1.00	.45
❑ 10 Samaki Walker	.75	.35
❑ 11 Antonio McDyess	2.00	.90
❑ 12 Joe Dumars	1.50	.70
❑ 13 Grant Hill	8.00	3.60
❑ 14 Joe Smith	1.00	.45
❑ 15 Latrell Sprewell	3.00	1.35
❑ 16 Charles Barkley	2.50	1.10
❑ 17 Hakeem Olajuwon	2.50	1.10
❑ 18 Erick Dampier	.75	.35
❑ 19 Reggie Miller	1.50	.70
❑ 20 Brent Barry	.75	.35
❑ 21 Lorenzen Wright	.75	.35
❑ 22 Kobe Bryant	12.00	5.50
❑ 23 Eddie Jones	3.00	1.35
❑ 24 Shaquille O'Neal	8.00	3.60
❑ 25 Alonzo Mourning	1.50	.70
❑ 26 Kurt Thomas	.75	.35
❑ 27 Vin Baker	1.00	.45
❑ 28 Glenn Robinson	1.00	.45
❑ 29 Kevin Garnett	10.00	4.50
❑ 30 Stephon Marbury	5.00	2.20
❑ 31 Kerry Kittles	1.50	.70
❑ 32 Patrick Ewing	1.50	.70
❑ 33 Larry Johnson	1.00	.45
❑ 34 Anfernee Hardaway	5.00	2.20
❑ 35 Allen Iverson	8.00	3.60
❑ 36 Jerry Stackhouse	1.00	.45
❑ 37 Kevin Johnson	1.00	.45
❑ 38 Steve Nash	.75	.35
❑ 39 Jermaine O'Neal	1.00	.45
❑ 40 Mitch Richmond	1.50	.70
❑ 41 David Robinson	2.50	1.10
❑ 42 Shawn Kemp	2.50	1.10
❑ 43 Gary Payton	2.50	1.10
❑ 44 Marcus Camby	2.00	.90
❑ 45 Damon Stoudamire	2.00	.90
❑ 46 Karl Malone	2.50	1.10
❑ 47 John Stockton	1.50	.70
❑ 48 Shareef Abdur-Rahim	5.00	2.20
❑ 49 Bryant Reeves	.75	.35
❑ 50 Juwan Howard	1.00	.45
❑ NNO Michael Jordan Promo	15.00	6.75

1997 SPx Gold

	MINT	NRMT
COMPLETE SET (50)	250.00	110.00
COMMON CARD (1-50)	1.50	.70

*STARS: 1X TO 2X BASE CARD HI
STATED ODDS 1:9

1997 SPx Holoview Heroes

	MINT	NRMT
COMPLETE SET (20)	300.00	135.00
COMMON CARD (H1-H20)	6.00	2.70

STATED ODDS 1:75

	MINT	NRMT
❑ H1 Michael Jordan	80.00	36.00
❑ H2 Grant Hill	30.00	13.50
❑ H3 Reggie Miller	6.00	2.70
❑ H4 Joe Smith	6.00	2.70
❑ H5 Kevin Garnett	40.00	18.00
❑ H6 Mitch Richmond	6.00	2.70
❑ H7 Allen Iverson	30.00	13.50
❑ H8 Patrick Ewing	6.00	2.70
❑ H9 Hakeem Olajuwon	10.00	4.50
❑ H10 David Robinson	10.00	4.50
❑ H11 Anfernee Hardaway	20.00	9.00
❑ H12 Juwan Howard	6.00	2.70
❑ H13 Gary Payton	10.00	4.50
❑ H14 Dennis Rodman	12.00	5.50
❑ H15 Shaquille O'Neal	30.00	13.50
❑ H16 Charles Barkley	10.00	4.50
❑ H17 Damon Stoudamire	8.00	3.60
❑ H18 Shawn Kemp	10.00	4.50
❑ H19 Glenn Robinson	6.00	2.70
❑ H20 John Stockton	6.00	2.70

1997 SPx ProMotion

	MINT	NRMT
COMPLETE SET (5)	150.00	70.00
COMMON CARD (1-5)	12.00	5.50

STATED ODDS 1:430

	MINT	NRMT
❑ 1 Michael Jordan	120.00	55.00
❑ 2 Damon Stoudamire	12.00	5.50
❑ 3 Anfernee Hardaway	30.00	13.50
❑ 4 Shawn Kemp	15.00	6.75
❑ 5 Antonio McDyess	12.00	5.50

1997 SPx ProMotion Autographs

	MINT	NRMT
COMPLETE SET (5)	3000.00	1350.00
COMMON CARD (1-5)	125.00	55.00

RANDOM INSERTS IN PACKS
CARDS NUMBERED TO 100

	MINT	NRMT
❑ 1 Michael Jordan	2500.00	1100.00
❑ 2 Damon Stoudamire	200.00	90.00
❑ 3 Anfernee Hardaway	400.00	180.00
❑ 4 Shawn Kemp	250.00	110.00
❑ 5 Antonio McDyess	125.00	55.00

1997-98 SPx

	MINT	NRMT
COMPLETE SET (50)	75.00	34.00
COMMON CARD (1-50)	.50	.23
SEMISTARS	.60	.25
UNLISTED STARS	1.00	.45

	MINT	NRMT
❑ 1 Mookie Blaylock	.50	.23
❑ 2 Dikembe Mutombo	.60	.25
❑ 3 Chauncey Billups RC	1.25	.55
❑ 4 Antoine Walker	2.00	.90
❑ 5 Glen Rice	.60	.25
❑ 6 Michael Jordan	12.00	5.50
❑ 7 Scottie Pippen	3.00	1.35
❑ 8 Dennis Rodman	2.00	.90
❑ 9 Shawn Kemp	1.50	.70
❑ 10 Michael Finley	1.00	.45
❑ 11 Tony Battie RC	1.00	.45
❑ 12 LaPhonso Ellis	.50	.23
❑ 13 Grant Hill	5.00	2.20
❑ 14 Joe Dumars	1.00	.45
❑ 15 Joe Smith	.60	.25
❑ 16 Clyde Drexler	1.00	.45
❑ 17 Charles Barkley	1.50	.70
❑ 18 Hakeem Olajuwon	1.50	.70
❑ 19 Reggie Miller	1.00	.45
❑ 20 Brent Barry	.50	.23
❑ 21 Kobe Bryant	8.00	3.60
❑ 22 Shaquille O'Neal	5.00	2.20
❑ 23 Alonzo Mourning	1.00	.45
❑ 24 Glenn Robinson	.60	.25
❑ 25 Kevin Garnett	6.00	2.70
❑ 26 Stephon Marbury	3.00	1.35
❑ 27 Keith Van Horn RC	6.00	2.70
❑ 28 Patrick Ewing	1.00	.45
❑ 29 Anfernee Hardaway	3.00	1.35
❑ 30 Allen Iverson	5.00	2.20
❑ 31 Kevin Johnson	.60	.25
❑ 32 Antonio McDyess	1.25	.55
❑ 33 Jason Kidd	3.00	1.35
❑ 34 Kenny Anderson	.60	.25
❑ 35 Rasheed Wallace	1.00	.45
❑ 36 Mitch Richmond	1.00	.45
❑ 37 Tim Duncan RC	15.00	6.75
❑ 38 David Robinson	1.50	.70
❑ 39 Vin Baker	.60	.25
❑ 40 Gary Payton	1.50	.70
❑ 41 Marcus Camby	1.25	.55
❑ 42 Tracy McGrady RC	12.00	5.50
❑ 43 Damon Stoudamire	1.25	.55
❑ 44 Karl Malone	1.50	.70
❑ 45 John Stockton	1.00	.45
❑ 46 Shareef Abdur-Rahim	3.00	1.35
❑ 47 Antonio Daniels RC	1.00	.45
❑ 48 Bryant Reeves	.50	.23
❑ 49 Juwan Howard	.60	.25
❑ 50 Chris Webber	3.00	1.35
❑ T1 Piece of History Trade	200.00	90.00

1997-98 SPx Sky

	MINT	NRMT
COMPLETE SET (50)	100.00	45.00
COMMON CARD (1-50)	.60	.25

*STARS: .5X TO 1.2X BASE CARD HI
*RCs: .4X TO 1X BASE HI
ONE PER PACK

1997-98 SPx Bronze

	MINT	NRMT
COMPLETE SET (50)	150.00	70.00
COMMON CARD (1-50)	1.00	.45

*STARS: .75X TO 2X BASE CARD HI
*RCs: .6X TO 1.5X BASE HI
STATED ODDS 1:3

1997-98 SPx Silver

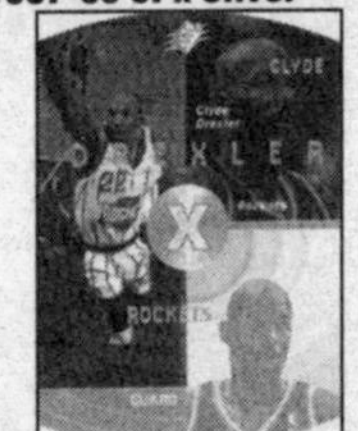

	MINT	NRMT
COMPLETE SET (50)	350.00	160.00
COMMON CARD (1-50)	2.00	.90

*STARS: 1.5X TO 4X BASE CARD HI
*RCs: 1.25X TO 3X BASE HI
STATED ODDS 1:6

1997-98 SPx Gold

	MINT	NRMT
COMPLETE SET (50)	700.00	325.00

COMMON CARD (1-50)	4.00	1.80

*STARS: 3X TO 8X BASE CARD HI
*RCs: 2.5X TO 6X BASE HI
STATED ODDS 1:17

1997-98 SPx Grand Finale

	MINT	NRMT
COMMON CARD (1-50)	30.00	13.50

*STARS: 25X TO 60X BASE CARD HI
*RCs: 12.5X TO 30X BASE HI
RANDOM INSERTS IN PACKS
STATED PRINT RUN 50 SERIAL #'d SETS

❑ 6 Michael Jordan	1200.00	550.00

1997-98 SPx Hardcourt Holoview

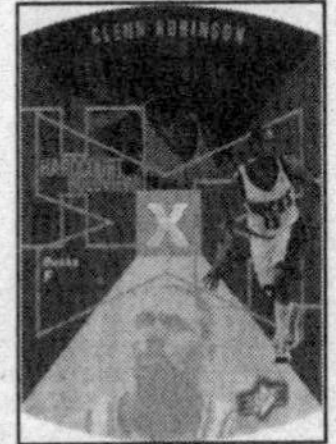

	MINT	NRMT
COMPLETE SET (20)	300.00	135.00
COMMON CARD (HH1-HH20)	3.00	1.35
SEMISTARS	4.00	1.80
UNLISTED STARS	6.00	2.70

STATED ODDS 1:54

	MINT	NRMT
❑ HH1 Michael Jordan	80.00	36.00
❑ HH2 Allen Iverson	30.00	13.50
❑ HH3 Antoine Walker	12.00	5.50
❑ HH4 Chris Webber	20.00	9.00
❑ HH5 Glenn Robinson	4.00	1.80
❑ HH6 Kevin Garnett	40.00	18.00
❑ HH7 Shareef Abdur-Rahim	20.00	9.00
❑ HH8 Keith Van Horn	15.00	6.75
❑ HH9 Kobe Bryant	50.00	22.00
❑ HH10 Glen Rice	4.00	1.80
❑ HH11 Damon Stoudamire	8.00	3.60
❑ HH12 Hakeem Olajuwon	10.00	4.50
❑ HH13 Mookie Blaylock	3.00	1.35
❑ HH14 Shaquille O'Neal	30.00	13.50
❑ HH15 Stephon Marbury	20.00	9.00
❑ HH16 Chauncey Billups	4.00	1.80
❑ HH17 Anfernee Hardaway	20.00	9.00
❑ HH18 Tim Duncan	30.00	13.50
❑ HH19 Mitch Richmond	6.00	2.70
❑ HH20 Grant Hill	30.00	13.50

1997-98 SPx ProMotion

	MINT	NRMT
COMPLETE SET (10)	450.00	200.00

COMMON CARD (PM1-PM10) 15.00 6.75
STATED ODDS 1:252

- ❑ PM1 Michael Jordan 150.00 70.00
- ❑ PM2 Shaquille O'Neal 60.00 27.00
- ❑ PM3 Tim Duncan 60.00 27.00
- ❑ PM4 Shareef Abdur-Rahim 40.00 18.00
- ❑ PM5 Grant Hill 60.00 27.00
- ❑ PM6 Karl Malone 20.00 9.00
- ❑ PM7 Anfernee Hardaway .. 40.00 18.00
- ❑ PM8 Keith Van Horn 30.00 13.50
- ❑ PM9 Kevin Garnett........... 80.00 36.00
- ❑ PM10 Damon Stoudamire 15.00 6.75

1998-99 SPx Finite

	MINT	NRMT
COMPLETE SET (210)	500.00	220.00
COMPLETE SET w/RC (238)	1500.00	700.00
COMP.BASIC SET (90)	100.00	45.00
COMMON CARD (1-90)	.50	.23
SEMISTARS 1-90........................	.75	.35
UNLISTED STARS 1-90...........	1.25	.55
BASE CARD PRINT RUN 10000 SERIAL #'d SETS		
COMP.ST.POWER SET (60)	125.00	55.00
COMMON ST.POWER (91-150)	.75	.35
SEMISTARS 91-150.................	1.25	.55
UNLISTED STARS 91-150........	2.00	.90
SP PRINT RUN 5400 SERIAL #'d SETS		
COMP.SPx 2000 SET (30)....	125.00	55.00
COMMON SPx 2000 (151-180)	1.25	.55
SEMISTARS 151-180................	2.00	.90
UNLISTED STARS 151-180......	3.00	1.35
SPx STATED PRINT RUN 4050 SERIAL #'d SETS		
COMP.TP.FLIGHT SET (20)	100.00	45.00
COMMON TP.FLIGHT (181-200)	1.50	.70
SEMISTARS 181-200...............	2.50	1.10
UNLISTED STARS 181-200......	4.00	1.80
TF STATED PRINT RUN 3390 SERIAL #'d SETS		
COMP.FIN.EXC.SET (10)	125.00	55.00
COMMON FIN.EXC. (201-210)	6.00	2.70
FE STATED PRINT RUN 1770 SERIAL #'d SETS		
COMP.ROOKIE SET (28) ..	1000.00	450.00
COMMON ROOKIE (211-240) ..	6.00	2.70
SEMISTARS 211-240...............	8.00	3.60
RC STATED PRINT RUN 2500 SERIAL #'d SETS		

CARDS 227/228 DO NOT EXIST
UNPRICED EXTREME SERIAL #'d TO 1
EXTREME: RANDOM INS.IN SER.1 PACKS

- ❑ 1 Michael Jordan 15.00 6.75
- ❑ 2 Hakeem Olajuwon........... 2.00 .90
- ❑ 3 Keith Van Horn 3.00 1.35
- ❑ 4 Rasheed Wallace .... 1.25 .55
- ❑ 5 Mookie Blaylock .... .50 .23
- ❑ 6 Bobby Jackson .... .50 .23
- ❑ 7 Detlef Schrempf .... .75 .35
- ❑ 8 Antonio McDyess .... 1.25 .55
- ❑ 9 Lamond Murray.................. .50 .23
- ❑ 10 Chris Mullin .... 1.25 .55
- ❑ 11 Zydrunas Ilgauskas .... .50 .23
- ❑ 12 Tracy Murray..................... .50 .23
- ❑ 13 Jerry Stackhouse .... .75 .35
- ❑ 14 Avery Johnson .... .50 .23
- ❑ 15 Larry Johnson .... .75 .35
- ❑ 16 Alan Henderson .... .50 .23
- ❑ 17 David Wesley .... .50 .23
- ❑ 18 Kevin Willis .... .50 .23
- ❑ 19 Eddie Jones 2.50 1.10
- ❑ 20 Horace Grant...................... .75 .35
- ❑ 21 Ray Allen....................... 1.50 .70
- ❑ 22 Derrick Coleman .... .75 .35
- ❑ 23 Derek Anderson .... 1.50 .70
- ❑ 24 Tim Hardaway .... 1.25 .55
- ❑ 25 Danny Fortson..................... .75 .35
- ❑ 26 Tariq Abdul-Wahad .... .50 .23
- ❑ 27 Charles Barkley.............. 2.00 .90
- ❑ 28 Sam Cassell .... .75 .35
- ❑ 29 Kevin Garnett 8.00 3.60
- ❑ 30 Jeff Hornacek .... .75 .35
- ❑ 31 Isaac Austin........................ .50 .23
- ❑ 32 Allan Houston .... 1.25 .55
- ❑ 33 David Robinson.............. 2.00 .90
- ❑ 34 Tracy McGrady 5.00 2.20
- ❑ 35 LaPhonso Ellis .... .50 .23
- ❑ 36 Shawn Kemp.................. 2.00 .90
- ❑ 37 Glenn Robinson .... .75 .35
- ❑ 38 Shareef Abdur-Rahim 3.00 1.35
- ❑ 39 Vin Baker............................ .75 .35
- ❑ 40 Rik Smits............................ .50 .23
- ❑ 41 Jason Kidd 4.00 1.80
- ❑ 42 Erick Dampier .... .50 .23
- ❑ 43 Shawn Bradley .... .50 .23
- ❑ 44 Anfernee Hardaway 4.00 1.80
- ❑ 45 John Stockton .... 1.25 .55
- ❑ 46 Calbert Cheaney .... .50 .23
- ❑ 47 Terrell Brandon .... .75 .35
- ❑ 48 Hubert Davis .... .50 .23
- ❑ 49 Patrick Ewing .... 1.25 .55
- ❑ 50 Kobe Bryant 10.00 4.50
- ❑ 51 Gary Payton .... 2.00 .90
- ❑ 52 Marcus Camby .... 1.25 .55
- ❑ 53 Bryant Reeves.................... .50 .23
- ❑ 54 Reggie Miller .... 1.25 .55
- ❑ 55 Antoine Walker .... 2.00 .90
- ❑ 56 Scottie Pippen................ 4.00 1.80
- ❑ 57 Hersey Hawkins .... .75 .35
- ❑ 58 John Starks .... .50 .23
- ❑ 59 Dikembe Mutombo .... .75 .35
- ❑ 60 Damon Stoudamire .... 1.25 .55
- ❑ 61 Rodney Rogers .... .50 .23
- ❑ 62 Nick Anderson..................... .50 .23
- ❑ 63 Brian Williams .... .50 .23
- ❑ 64 Ron Mercer .... 2.00 .90
- ❑ 65 Donyell Marshall .... .50 .23
- ❑ 66 Glen Rice .... .75 .35
- ❑ 67 Michael Finley .... 1.25 .55
- ❑ 68 Tim Duncan.................... 6.00 2.70
- ❑ 69 Stephon Marbury............ 3.00 1.35
- ❑ 70 Antonio Daniels.................. .50 .23
- ❑ 71 Chauncey Billups .... .50 .23
- ❑ 72 Kerry Kittles....................... .75 .35
- ❑ 73 Brian Grant .... .75 .35
- ❑ 74 Anthony Mason .... .75 .35
- ❑ 75 Allen Iverson 5.00 2.20
- ❑ 76 Juwan Howard .... .75 .35
- ❑ 77 Grant Hill 6.00 2.70
- ❑ 78 Tony Delk .... .50 .23
- ❑ 79 Olden Polynice .... .50 .23
- ❑ 80 Alonzo Mourning .... 1.25 .55
- ❑ 81 Karl Malone .... 2.00 .90
- ❑ 82 Isaiah Rider........................ .75 .35
- ❑ 83 Shaquille O'Neal 6.00 2.70
- ❑ 84 Steve Smith....................... .75 .35
- ❑ 85 Kenny Anderson .... .75 .35
- ❑ 86 Toni Kukoc .... 1.50 .70
- ❑ 87 Anthony Peeler .... .50 .23
- ❑ 88 Tim Thomas .... 2.00 .90
- ❑ 89 Nick Van Exel .... .75 .35
- ❑ 90 Jamal Mashburn .... .75 .35
- ❑ 91 Reggie Miller SP .... 2.00 .90
- ❑ 92 Juwan Howard SP .... 1.25 .55
- ❑ 93 Glen Rice SP.................. 1.25 .55
- ❑ 94 Grant Hill SP 10.00 4.50
- ❑ 95 Maurice Taylor SP......... 2.00 .90
- ❑ 96 Vin Baker SP................. 1.25 .55
- ❑ 97 Tim Thomas SP 3.00 1.35
- ❑ 98 Bobby Jackson SP .... .75 .35
- ❑ 99 Damon Stoudamire SP .. 2.00 .90
- ❑ 100 Michael Jordan SP 30.00 13.50
- ❑ 101 Eddie Jones SP............ 4.00 1.80
- ❑ 102 Keith Van Horn SP 6.00 2.70
- ❑ 103 Dikembe Mutombo SP 1.25 .55
- ❑ 104 Brevin Knight SP............ .75 .35
- ❑ 105 Shawn Bradley SP .... .75 .35
- ❑ 106 Lamond Murray SP .... .75 .35
- ❑ 107 Tim Duncan SP 10.00 4.50
- ❑ 108 Bryant Reeves SP .... .75 .35
- ❑ 109 Antoine Walker SP 3.00 1.35
- ❑ 110 John Stockton SP .... 2.00 .90
- ❑ 111 Nick Anderson SP .... .75 .35
- ❑ 112 Chris Mullin SP .... 2.00 .90
- ❑ 113 Glenn Robinson SP...... 1.25 .55
- ❑ 114 Kevin Garnett SP 12.00 5.50
- ❑ 115 Michael Stewart SP........ .75 .35
- ❑ 116 Antonio McDyess SP .. 2.00 .90
- ❑ 117 Jim Jackson SP.............. .75 .35
- ❑ 118 Chauncey Billups SP...... .75 .35
- ❑ 119 Sam Cassell SP .... 1.25 .55
- ❑ 120 Dennis Rodman SP...... 4.00 1.80
- ❑ 121 Rasheed Wallace SP .. 2.00 .90
- ❑ 122 Brian Williams SP .... .75 .35
- ❑ 123 Anfernee Hardaway SP 6.00 2.70
- ❑ 124 Scottie Pippen SP 6.00 2.70
- ❑ 125 Terrell Brandon SP ...... 1.25 .55
- ❑ 126 Michael Finley SP .... 2.00 .90
- ❑ 127 Kerry Kittles SP .... 1.25 .55
- ❑ 128 Toni Kukoc SP 2.50 1.10
- ❑ 129 Hakeem Olajuwon SP .. 3.00 1.35
- ❑ 130 Tim Hardaway SP .... 2.00 .90
- ❑ 131 Shareef Abdur-Rahim SP 5.00 2.20
- ❑ 132 Donyell Marshall SP ...... .75 .35
- ❑ 133 David Robinson SP...... 3.00 1.35
- ❑ 134 LaPhonso Ellis SP.......... .75 .35
- ❑ 135 Ray Allen SP 2.50 1.10
- ❑ 136 Nick Van Exel SP .... 1.25 .55
- ❑ 137 Patrick Ewing SP......... 2.00 .90
- ❑ 138 Anthony Mason SP ...... 1.25 .55
- ❑ 139 Shaquille O'Neal SP .. 10.00 4.50
- ❑ 140 Shawn Kemp SP.......... 3.00 1.35
- ❑ 141 Stephon Marbury SP.... 5.00 2.20
- ❑ 142 Karl Malone SP 3.00 1.35
- ❑ 143 Allen Iverson SP 8.00 3.60
- ❑ 144 Kenny Anderson SP .... 1.25 .55
- ❑ 145 Marcus Camby SP ...... 2.00 .90
- ❑ 146 Steve Smith SP............ 1.25 .55
- ❑ 147 Gary Payton SP 3.00 1.35
- ❑ 148 Jason Kidd SP.............. 6.00 2.70
- ❑ 149 Alonzo Mourning SP .... 2.00 .90
- ❑ 150 Charles Barkley SP 3.00 1.35
- ❑ 151 Kobe Bryant SPx........ 25.00 11.00
- ❑ 152 Ron Mercer SPx 5.00 2.20
- ❑ 153 Maurice Taylor SPx...... 3.00 1.35
- ❑ 154 Tim Duncan SPx 15.00 6.75
- ❑ 155 S. Abdur-Rahim SPx.... 8.00 3.60
- ❑ 156 Eddie Jones SPx.......... 6.00 2.70
- ❑ 157 Chauncey Billups SPx.. 1.25 .55
- ❑ 158 Derek Anderson SPx.... 4.00 1.80
- ❑ 159 Bobby Jackson SPx ..... 1.25 .55
- ❑ 160 Stephon Marbury SPx .. 8.00 3.60
- ❑ 161 Anfernee Hardaway SPx 10.00 4.50
- ❑ 162 Zydrunas Ilgauskas SPx 1.25 .55
- ❑ 163 Allen Iverson SPx 12.00 5.50
- ❑ 164 Antoine Walker SPx 5.00 2.20
- ❑ 165 Tracy McGrady SPx .. 12.00 5.50
- ❑ 166 Rasheed Wallace SPx 3.00 1.35
- ❑ 167 Jason Kidd SPx.......... 10.00 4.50
- ❑ 168 Kevin Garnett SPx...... 20.00 9.00

	Card	Player	MINT	NRMT
❑	169	Damon Stoudamire SPx	3.00	1.35
❑	170	Brevin Knight SPx	1.25	.55
❑	171	Tim Thomas SPx	5.00	2.20
❑	172	Danny Fortson SPx	2.00	.90
❑	173	Jermaine O'Neal SPx	2.00	.90
❑	174	Keith Van Horn SPx	8.00	3.60
❑	175	Ray Allen SPx	4.00	1.80
❑	176	Kerry Kittles SPx	2.00	.90
❑	177	Vin Baker SPx	2.00	.90
❑	178	Allan Houston SPx	3.00	1.35
❑	179	Alan Henderson SPx	1.25	.55
❑	180	Bryon Russell SPx	1.25	.55
❑	181	Michael Jordan TF	50.00	22.00
❑	182	Maurice Taylor TF	4.00	1.80
❑	183	Isaiah Rider TF	2.50	1.10
❑	184	Antonio McDyess TF	4.00	1.80
❑	185	Anfernee Hardaway TF	12.00	5.50
❑	186	Glenn Robinson TF	2.50	1.10
❑	187	Dikembe Mutombo TF	2.50	1.10
❑	188	Shawn Kemp TF	6.00	2.70
❑	189	Tracy McGrady TF	15.00	6.75
❑	190	Reggie Miller TF	4.00	1.80
❑	191	Derek Anderson TF	5.00	2.20
❑	192	Allan Houston TF	4.00	1.80
❑	193	Michael Finley TF	4.00	1.80
❑	194	Nick Van Exel TF	2.50	1.10
❑	195	Juwan Howard TF	2.50	1.10
❑	196	LaPhonso Ellis TF	1.50	.70
❑	197	Ron Mercer TF	6.00	2.70
❑	198	Glen Rice TF	2.50	1.10
❑	199	Joe Smith TF	2.50	1.10
❑	200	Kobe Bryant TF	30.00	13.50
❑	201	Michael Jordan FE	80.00	36.00
❑	202	Karl Malone FE	10.00	4.50
❑	203	Hakeem Olajuwon FE	10.00	4.50
❑	204	David Robinson FE	10.00	4.50
❑	205	Shaquille O'Neal FE	30.00	13.50
❑	206	John Stockton FE	6.00	2.70
❑	207	Grant Hill FE	30.00	13.50
❑	208	Tim Hardaway FE	6.00	2.70
❑	209	Scottie Pippen FE	20.00	9.00
❑	210	Gary Payton FE	10.00	4.50
❑	211	Michael Olowokandi RC	12.00	5.50
❑	212	Mike Bibby RC	25.00	11.00
❑	213	Raef LaFrentz RC	20.00	9.00
❑	214	Antawn Jamison RC	40.00	18.00
❑	215	Vince Carter RC	800.00	350.00
❑	216	Robert Traylor RC	8.00	3.60
❑	217	Jason Williams RC	60.00	27.00
❑	218	Larry Hughes RC	80.00	36.00
❑	219	Dirk Nowitzki RC	50.00	22.00
❑	220	Paul Pierce RC	40.00	18.00
❑	221	Bonzi Wells RC	40.00	18.00
❑	222	Michael Doleac RC	8.00	3.60
❑	223	Keon Clark RC	8.00	3.60
❑	224	Michael Dickerson RC	20.00	9.00
❑	225	Matt Harpring RC	8.00	3.60
❑	226	Bryce Drew RC	8.00	3.60
❑	227	Does not exist		
❑	228	Does not exist		
❑	229	Pat Garrity RC	6.00	2.70
❑	230	Roshown McLeod RC	6.00	2.70
❑	231	Ricky Davis RC	12.00	5.50
❑	232	Brian Skinner RC	8.00	3.60
❑	233	Tyronn Lue RC	6.00	2.70
❑	234	Felipe Lopez RC	8.00	3.60
❑	235	Al Harrington RC	30.00	13.50
❑	236	Ruben Patterson RC	12.00	5.50
❑	237	Jelani McCoy RC	6.00	2.70
❑	238	Corey Benjamin RC	8.00	3.60
❑	239	Nazr Mohammed RC	8.00	3.60
❑	240	Rashard Lewis RC	50.00	22.00

1998-99 SPx Finite Radiance

	MINT	NRMT
COMPLETE SET (210)	1100.00	500.00
COMP.BASIC SET (90)	200.00	90.00
COMMON CARD (1-90)	1.00	.45

*BASE STARS: .75X TO 2X BASE CARD HI
BASE CARD PRINT RUN 5000 SERIAL #'d SETS

COMP.ST.POWER SET (60)	250.00	110.00
COMMON ST.POWER (91-150)	1.50	.70

*SP STARS: .75X TO 2X BASE CARD HI
SP PRINT RUN 2700 SERIAL #'d SETS

COMP.SPx 2000 SET (30)	200.00	90.00
COMMON SPx 2000 (151-180)	2.00	.90

*SPx STARS: .75X TO 1.5X BASE CARD HI
SPx STATED PRINT RUN 2025 SERIAL #'d SETS

COMP.TP.FLIGHT SET (20)	250.00	110.00
COMMON TP.FLIGHT (181-200)	4.00	1.80

*TF STARS: 1.25X TO 2.5X BASE CARD HI
TF STATED PRINT RUN 1130 SERIAL #'d SETS

COMP.FIN.EXC.SET (10)	250.00	110.00
COMMON FIN.EXC. (201-210)	12.00	5.50

*FE STARS: 1X TO 2X BASE CARD HI
FE STATED PRINT RUN 590 SERIAL #'d SETS

COMP.ROOKIE SET (28)	700.00	325.00
COMMON ROOKIE (211-240)	2.50	1.10

ROOKIES: .25X TO .6X BASE CARD HI
RC STATED PRINT RUN 1500 SERIAL #'d SETS
CARDS 227/228 DO NOT EXIST
RC SET NOT INCLUDED IN BASE SET PRICE

	Card	Player	MINT	NRMT
❑	1	Michael Jordan	40.00	18.00
❑	100	Michael Jordan SP	60.00	27.00
❑	181	Michael Jordan TF	125.00	55.00
❑	201	Michael Jordan FE	150.00	70.00
❑	212	Mike Bibby	12.00	5.50
❑	214	Antawn Jamison	25.00	11.00
❑	215	Vince Carter	500.00	220.00
❑	217	Jason Williams	40.00	18.00
❑	218	Larry Hughes	40.00	18.00
❑	219	Dirk Nowitzki	25.00	11.00
❑	220	Paul Pierce	25.00	11.00
❑	221	Bonzi Wells	25.00	11.00
❑	235	Al Harrington	20.00	9.00
❑	240	Rashard Lewis	25.00	11.00

1998-99 SPx Finite Spectrum

	MINT	NRMT
COMMON CARD (1-90)	6.00	2.70

*BASE STARS: 5X TO 12X BASE CARD HI
BASE CARD PRINT RUN 350 SERIAL #'d SETS

COMMON ST.POWER (91-150)	8.00	3.60

*SP STARS: 4X TO 10X BASE CARD HI
SP PRINT RUN 250 SERIAL #'d SETS

COMMON SPx 2000 (151-180)	12.00	5.50

*SPx STARS: 4X TO 10X BASE CARD HI
SPx STATED PRINT RUN 75 SERIAL #'d SETS

COMMON TP.FLIGHT (181-200)	20.00	9.00

*TF STARS: 5X TO 12X BASE CARD HI
TF STATED PRINT RUN 50 SERIAL #'d SETS

COMMON FIN.EXC. (201-210)	80.00	36.00

*FE STARS: 5X TO 12X BASE CARD HI
FE STATED PRINT RUN 25 SERIAL #'d SETS

COMMON ROOKIE (211-240)	30.00	13.50

ROOKIES: 3X TO 6X BASE CARD HI
RC STATED PRINT RUN 25 SERIAL #'d SETS
CARDS 227/228 DO NOT EXIST

	Card	Player	MINT	NRMT
❑	1	Michael Jordan	250.00	110.00
❑	100	Michael Jordan SP	350.00	160.00
❑	181	Michael Jordan TF	1000.00	450.00
❑	201	Michael Jordan FE	3000.00	1350.00
❑	212	Mike Bibby	150.00	70.00
❑	214	Antawn Jamison	200.00	90.00
❑	215	Vince Carter	1500.00	700.00
❑	217	Jason Williams	250.00	110.00
❑	218	Larry Hughes	250.00	110.00
❑	219	Dirk Nowitzki	200.00	90.00
❑	220	Paul Pierce	200.00	90.00
❑	221	Bonzi Wells	150.00	70.00
❑	235	Al Harrington	125.00	55.00
❑	240	Rashard Lewis	200.00	90.00

1999-00 SPx

	MINT	NRMT
COMPLETE SET (120)	1800.00	800.00
COMPLETE SET w/o RC (90)	30.00	13.50
COMMON CARD (1-90)	.30	.14
COMMON CARD (91-120)	4.00	1.80
SEMISTARS	.40	.18
SEMISTARS RC	5.00	2.20
UNLISTED STARS	.60	.25
UNLISTED STARS RC	6.00	2.70

UNSIGNED RC's #'d TO 3500
SIGNED RC's #'d TO 2500 UNLESS NOTED
SOME RC AUTOS ISSUED VIA REDEMPTION
MJ FINAL FLOOR PRICED UNDER 99-00 UD
UNPRICED SPECTRUM SERIAL #'d TO 1

	Card	Player	MINT	NRMT
❑	1	Dikembe Mutombo	.40	.18
❑	2	Alan Henderson	.30	.14
❑	3	Antoine Walker	.75	.35
❑	4	Paul Pierce	1.25	.55
❑	5	Kenny Anderson	.40	.18
❑	6	Eddie Jones	1.25	.55
❑	7	David Wesley	.30	.14
❑	8	Elden Campbell	.30	.14
❑	9	Toni Kukoc	.75	.35
❑	10	Dickey Simpkins	.30	.14
❑	11	Shawn Kemp	1.00	.45
❑	12	Brevin Knight	.30	.14
❑	13	Michael Finley	.50	.23
❑	14	Cedric Ceballos	.30	.14
❑	15	Dirk Nowitzki	1.00	.45
❑	16	Antonio McDyess	.60	.25
❑	17	Nick Van Exel	.40	.18
❑	18	Chauncey Billups	.30	.14
❑	19	Grant Hill	3.00	1.35
❑	20	Jerry Stackhouse	.40	.18
❑	21	Bison Dele	.30	.14
❑	22	Lindsey Hunter	.30	.14

❑ 23 Antawn Jamison 1.25 .55
❑ 24 Donyell Marshall .30 .14
❑ 25 John Starks .30 .14
❑ 26 Chris Mills .30 .14
❑ 27 Hakeem Olajuwon 1.00 .45
❑ 28 Scottie Pippen 2.00 .90
❑ 29 Charles Barkley 1.00 .45
❑ 30 Reggie Miller .60 .25
❑ 31 Rik Smits .30 .14
❑ 32 Jalen Rose .60 .25
❑ 33 Chris Mullin .60 .25
❑ 34 Maurice Taylor .60 .25
❑ 35 Michael Olowokandi .40 .18
❑ 36 Shaquille O'Neal 3.00 1.35
❑ 37 Kobe Bryant 5.00 2.20
❑ 38 Glen Rice .40 .18
❑ 39 Tim Hardaway .60 .25
❑ 40 Alonzo Mourning .60 .25
❑ 41 Dan Majerle .40 .18
❑ 42 P.J. Brown .30 .14
❑ 43 Glenn Robinson .40 .18
❑ 44 Ray Allen .60 .25
❑ 45 Sam Cassell .40 .18
❑ 46 Tim Thomas .75 .35
❑ 47 Kevin Garnett 4.00 1.80
❑ 48 Bobby Jackson .30 .14
❑ 49 Joe Smith .40 .18
❑ 50 Stephon Marbury 1.25 .55
❑ 51 Keith Van Horn 1.25 .55
❑ 52 Jayson Williams .40 .18
❑ 53 Patrick Ewing .60 .25
❑ 54 Latrell Sprewell 1.25 .55
❑ 55 Allan Houston .60 .25
❑ 56 Marcus Camby .60 .25
❑ 57 Charles Outlaw .30 .14
❑ 58 Darrell Armstrong .40 .18
❑ 59 Allen Iverson 2.50 1.10
❑ 60 Theo Ratliff .30 .14
❑ 61 Larry Hughes 1.50 .70
❑ 62 Jason Kidd 2.00 .90
❑ 63 Tom Gugliotta .40 .18
❑ 64 Clifford Robinson .30 .14
❑ 65 Brian Grant .40 .18
❑ 66 Jermaine O'Neal .40 .18
❑ 67 Rasheed Wallace .60 .25
❑ 68 Damon Stoudamire .60 .25
❑ 69 Jason Williams 1.50 .70
❑ 70 Chris Webber 2.00 .90
❑ 71 Vlade Divac .30 .14
❑ 72 Avery Johnson .30 .14
❑ 73 Tim Duncan 3.00 1.35
❑ 74 David Robinson 1.00 .45
❑ 75 Sean Elliott .30 .14
❑ 76 Gary Payton 1.00 .45
❑ 77 Vin Baker .40 .18
❑ 78 Jelani McCoy .30 .14
❑ 79 Charles Oakley .30 .14
❑ 80 Vince Carter 6.00 2.70
❑ 81 Tracy McGrady 2.00 .90
❑ 82 Doug Christie .30 .14
❑ 83 Karl Malone 1.00 .45
❑ 84 John Stockton .60 .25
❑ 85 Shareef Abdur-Rahim 1.25 .55
❑ 86 Bryant Reeves .30 .14
❑ 87 Mike Bibby .75 .35
❑ 88 Juwan Howard .40 .18
❑ 89 Mitch Richmond .60 .25
❑ 90 Rod Strickland .40 .18
❑ 91 Elton Brand RC 60.00 27.00
❑ 92 Steve Francis AU RC 850.00 375.00
❑ 93 Baron Davis AU RC 200.00 90.00
❑ 94 Lamar Odom RC 60.00 27.00
❑ 95 Jonathan Bender RC 30.00 13.50
❑ 96 Wally Szczerbiak AU RC 250.00 110.00
❑ 97 Richard Hamilton AU RC 30.00 13.50
❑ 98 Andre Miller AU RC 200.00 90.00
❑ 99 Shawn Marion AU RC 40.00 18.00
❑ 100 Jason Terry AU RC 15.00 6.75
❑ 101 Trajan Langdon AU RC 15.00 6.75
❑ 102 Venson Hamilton RC 4.00 1.80
❑ 103 Corey Maggette AU RC 250.00 110.00
❑ 104 William Avery AU RC 15.00 6.75
❑ 105 Dion Glover RC 5.00 2.20
❑ 106 Ron Artest AU RC 30.00 13.50
❑ 107 Cal Bowdler RC 5.00 2.20
❑ 108 James Posey AU RC 15.00 6.75
❑ 109 Quincy Lewis AU RC 10.00 4.50
❑ 110 Devean George AU RC 30.00 13.50
❑ 111 Tim James AU RC 12.00 5.50
❑ 112 Vonteego Cummings RC 10.00 4.50
❑ 113 Jumaine Jones AU RC 10.00 4.50
❑ 114 Scott Padgett AU RC 10.00 4.50
❑ 115 Kenny Thomas RC 10.00 4.50
❑ 116 Jeff Foster RC 5.00 2.20
❑ 117 Ryan Robertson RC 5.00 2.20
❑ 118 Chris Herren AU RC 12.00 5.50
❑ 119 Evan Eschmeyer AU RC 10.00 4.50
❑ 120 A.J. Bramlett AU RC 10.00 4.50

1999-00 SPx Radiance

	MINT	NRMT
COMMON CARD (1-90)	8.00	3.60
COMMON CARD (91-120)	12.00	5.50
SEMISTARS 91-120	15.00	6.75
UNLISTED STARS 91-120	20.00	9.00

*STARS: 10X TO 25X BASE CARD HI
*RCs: 1.25X TO 3X BASE HI
STATED PRINT RUN 100 SERIAL #'d SETS
RANDOM INSERTS IN PACKS

❑ 91 Elton Brand 150.00 70.00
❑ 92 Steve Francis 200.00 90.00
❑ 93 Baron Davis 40.00 18.00
❑ 94 Lamar Odom 120.00 55.00
❑ 95 Jonathan Bender 80.00 36.00
❑ 96 Wally Szczerbiak 60.00 27.00
❑ 97 Richard Hamilton 40.00 18.00
❑ 98 Andre Miller 50.00 22.00
❑ 99 Shawn Marion 50.00 22.00
❑ 103 Corey Maggette 60.00 27.00
❑ 106 Ron Artest 40.00 18.00

1999-00 SPx Decade of Jordan

	MINT	NRMT
COMPLETE SET (10)	40.00	18.00
COMMON CARD (J1-J10)	5.00	2.20

STATED ODDS 1:9

❑ J1 Michael Jordan 5.00 2.20
❑ J2 Michael Jordan 5.00 2.20
❑ J3 Michael Jordan 5.00 2.20
❑ J4 Michael Jordan 5.00 2.20
❑ J5 Michael Jordan 5.00 2.20
❑ J6 Michael Jordan 5.00 2.20
❑ J7 Michael Jordan 5.00 2.20
❑ J8 Michael Jordan 5.00 2.20
❑ J9 Michael Jordan 5.00 2.20
❑ J10 Michael Jordan 5.00 2.20

1999-00 SPx Masters

	MINT	NRMT
COMPLETE SET (15)	60.00	27.00
COMMON CARD (M1-M15)	1.25	.55

STATED ODDS 1:17

❑ M1 Michael Jordan 15.00 6.75
❑ M2 Vince Carter 12.00 5.50
❑ M3 Tim Duncan 6.00 2.70
❑ M4 Allen Iverson 5.00 2.20
❑ M5 Gary Payton 2.00 .90
❑ M6 Shareef Abdur-Rahim 2.50 1.10
❑ M7 Keith Van Horn 2.50 1.10
❑ M8 Grant Hill 6.00 2.70
❑ M9 Kobe Bryant 10.00 4.50
❑ M10 Kevin Garnett 8.00 3.60
❑ M11 Karl Malone 2.00 .90
❑ M12 Allan Houston 1.25 .55
❑ M13 Jason Kidd 4.00 1.80
❑ M14 Antoine Walker 1.50 .70
❑ M15 Jason Williams 3.00 1.35

1999-00 SPx Prolifics

	MINT	NRMT
COMPLETE SET (15)	25.00	11.00
COMMON CARD (P1-P15)	.75	.35
UNLISTED STARS	1.25	.55

STATED ODDS 1:17

❑ P1 Michael Jordan 15.00 6.75
❑ P2 Karl Malone 2.00 .90
❑ P3 Jason Kidd 4.00 1.80
❑ P4 Reggie Miller 1.25 .55
❑ P5 Glen Rice .75 .35
❑ P6 Hakeem Olajuwon 2.00 .90
❑ P7 Mitch Richmond 1.25 .55
❑ P8 Shawn Kemp 2.00 .90
❑ P9 Patrick Ewing 1.25 .55
❑ P10 Dikembe Mutombo .75 .35
❑ P11 Scottie Pippen 4.00 1.80
❑ P12 John Stockton 1.25 .55
❑ P13 David Robinson 2.00 .90
❑ P14 Tim Hardaway 1.25 .55

		MINT	NRMT
❑ P15	Charles Barkley	2.00	.90

1999-00 SPx Spxcitement

	MINT	NRMT
COMPLETE SET (20)	10.00	4.50
COMMON CARD (S1-S20)	.30	.14
UNLISTED STARS	.50	.23

STATED ODDS 1:3

		MINT	NRMT
❑ S1	Antoine Walker	.60	.25
❑ S2	Antonio McDyess	.50	.23
❑ S3	Antawn Jamison	1.00	.45
❑ S4	Vin Baker	.30	.14
❑ S5	Juwan Howard	.30	.14
❑ S6	Brian Grant	.30	.14
❑ S7	Brevin Knight	.30	.14
❑ S8	Glenn Robinson	.30	.14
❑ S9	Stephon Marbury	1.00	.45
❑ S10	Reggie Miller	.50	.23
❑ S11	Nick Van Exel	.30	.14
❑ S12	Alonzo Mourning	.50	.23
❑ S13	David Robinson	.75	.35
❑ S14	Hakeem Olajuwon	.75	.35
❑ S15	Toni Kukoc	.60	.25
❑ S16	Maurice Taylor	.50	.23
❑ S17	Darrell Armstrong	.30	.14
❑ S18	Latrell Sprewell	1.00	.45
❑ S19	Tom Gugliotta	.30	.14
❑ S20	Michael Jordan	6.00	2.70

1999-00 SPx Spxtreme

	MINT	NRMT
COMPLETE SET (20)	25.00	11.00
COMMON CARD (X1-X20)	.50	.23
UNLISTED STARS	.75	.35

STATED ODDS 1:6

		MINT	NRMT
❑ X1	Michael Jordan	10.00	4.50
❑ X2	Tim Hardaway	.75	.35
❑ X3	Marcus Camby	.75	.35
❑ X4	Jason Williams	2.00	.90
❑ X5	Shareef Abdur-Rahim	1.50	.70
❑ X6	Keith Van Horn	1.50	.70
❑ X7	Glen Rice	.50	.23
❑ X8	Gary Payton	1.25	.55
❑ X9	Grant Hill	4.00	1.80
❑ X10	Allan Houston	.50	.23
❑ X11	Ray Allen	.75	.35
❑ X12	Michael Finley	.75	.35
❑ X13	Shawn Kemp	1.25	.55
❑ X14	Shaquille O'Neal	4.00	1.80
❑ X15	Paul Pierce	1.50	.70
❑ X16	Mike Bibby	1.00	.45
❑ X17	Michael Olowokandi	.50	.23
❑ X18	Damon Stoudamire	.75	.35
❑ X19	Mitch Richmond	.75	.35
❑ X20	Eddie Jones	1.50	.70

1999-00 SPx Starscape

	MINT	NRMT
COMPLETE SET (10)	12.00	5.50
COMMON CARD (ST1-ST10)	.60	.25

STATED ODDS 1:9

		MINT	NRMT
❑ ST1	Michael Jordan	8.00	3.60
❑ ST2	John Stockton	.60	.25
❑ ST3	Antonio McDyess	.60	.25
❑ ST4	Alonzo Mourning	.60	.25
❑ ST5	Shaquille O'Neal	3.00	1.35
❑ ST6	Stephon Marbury	1.25	.55
❑ ST7	Chris Webber	2.00	.90
❑ ST8	Charles Barkley	1.00	.45
❑ ST9	Antawn Jamison	1.25	.55
❑ ST10	Scottie Pippen	2.00	.90

1999-00 SPx Winning Materials

	MINT	NRMT
COMPLETE SET (8)	1800.00	800.00
COMMON CARD (WM1-10)	80.00	36.00

STATED ODDS 1:252
AU CARDS NOT INCLUDED IN SET PRICE
CARDS WM3 AND WM7 DO NOT EXIST

		MINT	NRMT
❑ WM1	Michael Jordan	1000.00	450.00
❑ WM1-A	M. Jordan AU/23	10000.00	4500.00
❑ WM2	Karl Malone	80.00	36.00
❑ WM2-A	Karl Malone AU/32	800.00	350.00
❑ WM3	Does Not Exist		
❑ WM4	Kobe Bryant	350.00	160.00
❑ WM5	Paul Pierce	80.00	36.00
❑ WM6	Kevin Garnett	200.00	90.00
❑ WM7	Does Not Exist		
❑ WM8	Shaquille O'Neal	200.00	90.00
❑ WM9	David Robinson	100.00	45.00
❑ WM10	Charles Barkley	120.00	55.00

1992-93 Stadium Club

	MINT	NRMT
COMPLETE SET (400)	50.00	22.00
COMPLETE SERIES 1 (200)	20.00	9.00
COMPLETE SERIES 2 (200)	30.00	13.50
COMMON CARD (1-400)	.10	.05
SEMISTARS	.30	.14
UNLISTED STARS	.60	.25

SUBSET CARDS HALF VALUE OF BASE CARDS

		MINT	NRMT
❑ 1	Michael Jordan	8.00	3.60
❑ 2	Greg Anthony	.10	.05
❑ 3	Otis Thorpe	.30	.14
❑ 4	Jim Les	.10	.05
❑ 5	Kevin Willis	.10	.05
❑ 6	Derek Harper	.30	.14
❑ 7	Elden Campbell	.30	.14
❑ 8	A.J. English	.10	.05
❑ 9	Kenny Gattison	.10	.05
❑ 10	Drazen Petrovic	.10	.05
❑ 11	Chris Mullin	.60	.25
❑ 12	Mark Price	.10	.05
❑ 13	Karl Malone	1.00	.45
❑ 14	Gerald Glass	.10	.05
❑ 15	Negele Knight	.10	.05
❑ 16	Mark Macon	.10	.05
❑ 17	Michael Cage	.10	.05
❑ 18	Kevin Edwards	.10	.05
❑ 19	Sherman Douglas	.10	.05
❑ 20	Ron Harper	.30	.14
❑ 21	Clifford Robinson	.30	.14
❑ 22	Byron Scott	.30	.14
❑ 23	Antoine Carr	.10	.05
❑ 24	Greg Dreiling	.10	.05
❑ 25	Bill Laimbeer	.30	.14
❑ 26	Hersey Hawkins	.30	.14
❑ 27	Will Perdue	.10	.05
❑ 28	Todd Lichti	.10	.05
❑ 29	Gary Grant	.10	.05
❑ 30	Sam Perkins	.30	.14
❑ 31	Jayson Williams	.30	.14
❑ 32	Magic Johnson	2.00	.90
❑ 33	Larry Bird	2.50	1.10
❑ 34	Chris Morris	.10	.05
❑ 35	Nick Anderson	.30	.14
❑ 36	Scott Hastings	.10	.05
❑ 37	Ledell Eackles	.10	.05
❑ 38	Robert Pack	.10	.05
❑ 39	Dana Barros	.10	.05
❑ 40	Anthony Bonner	.10	.05
❑ 41	J.R. Reid	.10	.05
❑ 42	Tyrone Hill	.10	.05
❑ 43	Rik Smits	.30	.14
❑ 44	Kevin Duckworth	.10	.05
❑ 45	LaSalle Thompson	.10	.05
❑ 46	Brian Williams	.10	.05
❑ 47	Willie Anderson	.10	.05
❑ 48	Ken Norman	.10	.05
❑ 49	Mike Iuzzolino	.10	.05
❑ 50	Isiah Thomas	.60	.25
❑ 51	Alec Kessler	.10	.05
❑ 52	Johnny Dawkins	.10	.05
❑ 53	Avery Johnson	.10	.05
❑ 54	Stacey Augmon	.30	.14

❑ 55 Charles Oakley .30 .14
❑ 56 Rex Chapman .10 .05
❑ 57 Charles Shackleford .10 .05
❑ 58 Jeff Ruland .10 .05
❑ 59 Craig Ehlo .10 .05
❑ 60 Jon Koncak .10 .05
❑ 61 Danny Schayes .10 .05
❑ 62 David Benoit .10 .05
❑ 63 Robert Parish .30 .14
❑ 64 Mookie Blaylock .30 .14
❑ 65 Sean Elliott .30 .14
❑ 66 Mark Aguirre .10 .05
❑ 67 Scott Williams .10 .05
❑ 68 Doug West .10 .05
❑ 69 Kenny Anderson .60 .25
❑ 70 Randy Brown .10 .05
❑ 71 Muggsy Bogues .30 .14
❑ 72 Spud Webb .30 .14
❑ 73 Sedale Threatt .10 .05
❑ 74 Chris Gatling .10 .05
❑ 75 Derrick McKey .10 .05
❑ 76 Sleepy Floyd .10 .05
❑ 77 Chris Jackson .10 .05
❑ 78 Thurl Bailey .10 .05
❑ 79 Steve Smith .75 .35
❑ 80 Jerrod Mustaf .10 .05
❑ 81 Anthony Bowie .10 .05
❑ 82 John Williams .10 .05
❑ 83 Paul Graham .10 .05
❑ 84 Willie Burton .10 .05
❑ 85 Vernon Maxwell .10 .05
❑ 86 Stacey King .10 .05
❑ 87 B.J. Armstrong .10 .05
❑ 88 Kevin Gamble .10 .05
❑ 89 Terry Catledge .10 .05
❑ 90 Jeff Malone .10 .05
❑ 91 Sam Bowie .10 .05
❑ 92 Orlando Woolridge .10 .05
❑ 93 Steve Kerr .30 .14
❑ 94 Eric Leckner .10 .05
❑ 95 Loy Vaught .10 .05
❑ 96 Jud Buechler .10 .05
❑ 97 Doug Smith .10 .05
❑ 98 Sidney Green .10 .05
❑ 99 Jerome Kersey .10 .05
❑ 100 Patrick Ewing .60 .25
❑ 101 Ed Nealy .10 .05
❑ 102 Shawn Kemp 1.25 .55
❑ 103 Luc Longley .30 .14
❑ 104 George McCloud .10 .05
❑ 105 Ron Anderson .10 .05
❑ 106 Moses Malone UER .60 .25
(Rookie Card is 1975-76& not 1976-77)
❑ 107 Tony Smith .10 .05
❑ 108 Terry Porter .10 .05
❑ 109 Blair Rasmussen .10 .05
❑ 110 Bimbo Coles .10 .05
❑ 111 Grant Long .10 .05
❑ 112 John Battle .10 .05
❑ 113 Brian Oliver .10 .05
❑ 114 Tyrone Corbin .10 .05
❑ 115 Benoit Benjamin .10 .05
❑ 116 Rick Fox .30 .14
❑ 117 Rafael Addison .10 .05
❑ 118 Danny Young .10 .05
❑ 119 Fat Lever .10 .05
❑ 120 Terry Cummings .30 .14
❑ 121 Felton Spencer .10 .05
❑ 122 Joe Kleine .10 .05
❑ 123 Johnny Newman .10 .05
❑ 124 Gary Payton 1.25 .55
❑ 125 Kurt Rambis .10 .05
❑ 126 Vlade Divac .30 .14
❑ 127 John Paxson .10 .05
❑ 128 Lionel Simmons .10 .05
❑ 129 Randy Wittman .10 .05
❑ 130 Winston Garland .10 .05
❑ 131 Jerry Reynolds .10 .05
❑ 132 Dell Curry .10 .05
❑ 133 Fred Roberts .10 .05
❑ 134 Michael Adams .10 .05
❑ 135 Charles Jones .10 .05
❑ 136 Frank Brickowski .10 .05
❑ 137 Alton Lister .10 .05
❑ 138 Horace Grant .30 .14
❑ 139 Greg Sutton .10 .05
❑ 140 John Starks .30 .14
❑ 141 Detlef Schrempf .30 .14
❑ 142 Rodney Monroe .10 .05
❑ 143 Pete Chilcutt .10 .05
❑ 144 Mike Brown .10 .05
❑ 145 Rony Seikaly .10 .05
❑ 146 Donald Hodge .10 .05
❑ 147 Kevin McHale .60 .25
❑ 148 Ricky Pierce .10 .05
❑ 149 Brian Shaw .10 .05
❑ 150 Reggie Williams .10 .05
❑ 151 Kendall Gill .30 .14
❑ 152 Tom Chambers .10 .05
❑ 153 Jack Haley .10 .05
❑ 154 Terrell Brandon .60 .25
❑ 155 Dennis Scott .30 .14
❑ 156 Mark Randall .10 .05
❑ 157 Kenny Payne .10 .05
❑ 158 Bernard King .10 .05
❑ 159 Tate George .10 .05
❑ 160 Scott Skiles .10 .05
❑ 161 Pervis Ellison .10 .05
❑ 162 Marcus Liberty .10 .05
❑ 163 Rumeal Robinson .10 .05
❑ 164 Anthony Mason .60 .25
❑ 165 Les Jepsen .10 .05
❑ 166 Kenny Smith .10 .05
❑ 167 Randy White .10 .05
❑ 168 Dee Brown .10 .05
❑ 169 Chris Dudley .10 .05
❑ 170 Armon Gilliam .10 .05
❑ 171 Eddie Johnson .10 .05
❑ 172 A.C. Green .30 .14
❑ 173 Darrell Walker .10 .05
❑ 174 Bill Cartwright .10 .05
❑ 175 Mike Gminski .10 .05
❑ 176 Tom Tolbert .10 .05
❑ 177 Buck Williams .30 .14
❑ 178 Mark Eaton .10 .05
❑ 179 Danny Manning .30 .14
❑ 180 Glen Rice .60 .25
❑ 181 Sarunas Marciulionis .10 .05
❑ 182 Danny Ferry .10 .05
❑ 183 Chris Corchiani .10 .05
❑ 184 Dan Majerle .30 .14
❑ 185 Alvin Robertson .10 .05
❑ 186 Vern Fleming .10 .05
❑ 187 Kevin Lynch .10 .05
❑ 188 John Williams .10 .05
❑ 189 Checklist 1-100 .10 .05
❑ 190 Checklist 101-200 .10 .05
❑ 191 David Robinson MC .60 .25
❑ 192 Larry Johnson MC .60 .25
❑ 193 Derrick Coleman MC .10 .05
❑ 194 Larry Bird MC 1.25 .55
❑ 195 Billy Owens MC .10 .05
❑ 196 Dikembe Mutombo MC .30 .14
❑ 197 Charles Barkley MC .60 .25
❑ 198 Scottie Pippen MC 1.00 .45
❑ 199 Clyde Drexler MC .30 .14
❑ 200 John Stockton MC .30 .14
❑ 201 Shaquille O'Neal MC 4.00 1.80
❑ 202 Chris Mullin MC .30 .14
❑ 203 Glen Rice MC .30 .14
❑ 204 Isiah Thomas MC .30 .14
❑ 205 Karl Malone MC .60 .25
❑ 206 Christian Laettner MC .60 .25
❑ 207 Patrick Ewing MC .30 .14
❑ 208 Dominique Wilkins MC .30 .14
❑ 209 Alonzo Mourning MC 1.00 .45
❑ 210 Michael Jordan MC 4.00 1.80
❑ 211 Tim Hardaway .75 .35
❑ 212 Rodney McCray .10 .05
❑ 213 Larry Johnson .75 .35
❑ 214 Charles Smith .10 .05
❑ 215 Kevin Brooks .10 .05
❑ 216 Kevin Johnson .60 .25
❑ 217 Duane Cooper RC .10 .05
❑ 218 C. Laettner RC UER 1.25 .55
(Missing '92 Draft Pick logo)
❑ 219 Tim Perry .10 .05
❑ 220 Hakeem Olajuwon 1.00 .45
❑ 221 Lee Mayberry RC .10 .05
❑ 222 Mark Bryant .10 .05
❑ 223 Robert Horry RC .60 .25
❑ 224 Tracy Murray RC UER .30 .14
(Missing '92 Draft Pick logo)
❑ 225 Greg Grant .10 .05
❑ 226 Rolando Blackman .10 .05
❑ 227 James Edwards UER .10 .05
(Rookie Card is 1978-79& not 1980-81)
❑ 228 Sean Green .10 .05
❑ 229 Buck Johnson .10 .05
❑ 230 Andrew Lang .10 .05
❑ 231 Tracy Moore RC .10 .05
❑ 232 Adam Keefe RC UER .10 .05
(Missing '92 Draft Pick logo)
❑ 233 Tony Campbell .10 .05
❑ 234 Rod Strickland .60 .25
❑ 235 Terry Mills .10 .05
❑ 236 Billy Owens .30 .14
❑ 237 Bryant Stith RC UER .30 .14
(Missing '92 Draft Pick logo)
❑ 238 Tony Bennett RC UER .10 .05
(Missing '92 Draft Pick logo)
❑ 239 David Wood .10 .05
❑ 240 Jay Humphries .10 .05
❑ 241 Doc Rivers .30 .14
❑ 242 Wayman Tisdale .10 .05
❑ 243 Litterial Green RC .10 .05
❑ 244 Jon Barry .30 .14
❑ 245 Brad Daugherty .10 .05
❑ 246 Nate McMillan .10 .05
❑ 247 Shaquille O'Neal RC 20.00 9.00
❑ 248 Chris Smith RC .10 .05
❑ 249 Duane Ferrell .10 .05
❑ 250 Anthony Peeler RC .30 .14
❑ 251 Gundars Vetra RC .10 .05
❑ 252 Danny Ainge .30 .14
❑ 253 Mitch Richmond .60 .25
❑ 254 Malik Sealy RC .30 .14
❑ 255 Brent Price RC .30 .14
❑ 256 Xavier McDaniel .10 .05
❑ 257 Bobby Phills RC .60 .25
❑ 258 Donald Royal .10 .05
❑ 259 Olden Polynice .10 .05
❑ 260 Dominique Wilkins UER .60 .25
(Scoring 10,000th point& should be 20,000th)
❑ 261 Larry Krystkowiak .10 .05
❑ 262 Duane Causwell .10 .05
❑ 263 Todd Day RC .30 .14
❑ 264 Sam Mack RC .30 .14
❑ 265 John Stockton .60 .25
❑ 266 Eddie Lee Wilkins .10 .05
❑ 267 Gerald Glass .10 .05
❑ 268 Robert Pack .10 .05
❑ 269 Gerald Wilkins .10 .05
❑ 270 Reggie Lewis .30 .14
❑ 271 Scott Brooks .10 .05
❑ 272 Randy Woods RC UER .10 .05
(Missing '92 Draft Pick logo)
❑ 273 Dikembe Mutombo .60 .25
❑ 274 Kiki Vandeweghe .10 .05
❑ 275 Rich King .10 .05
❑ 276 Jeff Turner .10 .05
❑ 277 Vinny Del Negro .10 .05
❑ 278 Marlon Maxey RC .10 .05
❑ 279 Elmore Spencer RC UER .10 .05
(Missing '92 Draft Pick logo)
❑ 280 Cedric Ceballos .30 .14
❑ 281 Alex Blackwell RC .10 .05
❑ 282 Terry Davis .10 .05
❑ 283 Morlon Wiley .10 .05
❑ 284 Trent Tucker .10 .05
❑ 285 Carl Herrera .10 .05
❑ 286 Eric Anderson RC .10 .05
❑ 287 Clyde Drexler .60 .25
❑ 288 Tom Gugliotta RC 2.00 .90
❑ 289 Dale Ellis .10 .05
❑ 290 Lance Blanks .10 .05
❑ 291 Tom Hammonds .10 .05
❑ 292 Eric Murdock .10 .05

❑ 293 Walt Williams RC .60 .25
❑ 294 Gerald Paddio .10 .05
❑ 295 Brian Howard RC .10 .05
❑ 296 Ken Williams .10 .05
❑ 297 Alonzo Mourning RC 3.00 1.35
❑ 298 Larry Nance .10 .05
❑ 299 Jeff Grayer .10 .05
❑ 300 Dave Johnson RC .10 .05
❑ 301 Bob McCann RC .10 .05
❑ 302 Bart Kofoed .10 .05
❑ 303 Anthony Cook .10 .05
❑ 304 Radisav Curcic RC .10 .05
❑ 305 John Crotty RC .10 .05
❑ 306 Brad Sellers .10 .05
❑ 307 Marcus Webb RC .10 .05
❑ 308 Winston Garland .10 .05
❑ 309 Walter Palmer .10 .05
❑ 310 Rod Higgins .10 .05
❑ 311 Travis Mays .10 .05
❑ 312 Alex Stivrins RC .10 .05
❑ 313 Greg Kite .10 .05
❑ 314 Dennis Rodman 1.25 .55
❑ 315 Mike Sanders .10 .05
❑ 316 Ed Pinckney .10 .05
❑ 317 Harold Miner RC .30 .14
❑ 318 Pooh Richardson .10 .05
❑ 319 Oliver Miller RC .30 .14
❑ 320 Latrell Sprewell RC 5.00 2.20
❑ 321 Anthony Pullard RC .10 .05
❑ 322 Mark Randall .10 .05
❑ 323 Jeff Hornacek .30 .14
❑ 324 Rick Mahorn UER .10 .05
(Rookie Card is 1981-82& not 1992-93)
❑ 325 Sean Rooks RC .10 .05
❑ 326 Paul Pressey .10 .05
❑ 327 James Worthy .60 .25
❑ 328 Matt Bullard .10 .05
❑ 329 Reggie Smith RC .10 .05
❑ 330 Don MacLean RC UER .10 .05
(Missing '92 Draft Pick logo)
❑ 331 John Williams UER .10 .05
(Rookie Card erroneously shows Hot Rod)
❑ 332 Frank Johnson .10 .05
❑ 333 Hubert Davis RC UER .30 .14
(Missing '92 Draft Pick logo)
❑ 334 Lloyd Daniels RC .10 .05
❑ 335 Steve Bardo RC .10 .05
❑ 336 Jeff Sanders .10 .05
❑ 337 Tree Rollins .10 .05
❑ 338 Micheal Williams .10 .05
❑ 339 Lorenzo Williams RC .10 .05
❑ 340 Harvey Grant .10 .05
❑ 341 Avery Johnson .10 .05
❑ 342 Bo Kimble .10 .05
❑ 343 LaPhonso Ellis RC UER .60 .25
(Missing '92 Draft Pick logo)
❑ 344 Mookie Blaylock .30 .14
❑ 345 Isaiah Morris RC UER .10 .05
(Missing '92 Draft Pick logo)
❑ 346 C. Weatherspoon RC .60 .25
❑ 347 Manute Bol .10 .05
❑ 348 Victor Alexander .10 .05
❑ 349 Corey Williams RC .10 .05
❑ 350 Byron Houston RC .10 .05
❑ 351 Stanley Roberts .10 .05
❑ 352 Anthony Avent RC .10 .05
❑ 353 Vincent Askew .10 .05
❑ 354 Herb Williams .10 .05
❑ 355 J.R. Reid .10 .05
❑ 356 Brad Lohaus .10 .05
❑ 357 Reggie Miller .60 .25
❑ 358 Blue Edwards .10 .05
❑ 359 Tom Tolbert .10 .05
❑ 360 Charles Barkley 1.00 .45
❑ 361 David Robinson 1.00 .45
❑ 362 Dale Davis .10 .05
❑ 363 Robert Werdann RC UER .10 .05
(Missing '92 Draft Pick logo)
❑ 364 Chuck Person .10 .05
❑ 365 Alaa Abdelnaby .10 .05
❑ 366 Dave Jamerson .10 .05
❑ 367 Scottie Pippen 2.00 .90
❑ 368 Mark Jackson .30 .14
❑ 369 Keith Askins .10 .05
❑ 370 Marty Conlon .10 .05
❑ 371 Chucky Brown .10 .05
❑ 372 LaBradford Smith .10 .05
❑ 373 Tim Kempton .10 .05
❑ 374 Sam Mitchell .10 .05
❑ 375 John Salley .10 .05
❑ 376 Mario Elie .30 .14
❑ 377 Mark West .10 .05
❑ 378 David Wingate .10 .05
❑ 379 Jaren Jackson RC .30 .14
❑ 380 Rumeal Robinson .10 .05
❑ 381 Kennard Winchester .10 .05
❑ 382 Walter Bond RC .10 .05
❑ 383 Isaac Austin RC .30 .14
❑ 384 Derrick Coleman .30 .14
❑ 385 Larry Smith .10 .05
❑ 386 Joe Dumars .60 .25
❑ 387 Matt Geiger RC UER .30 .14
(Missing '92 Draft Pick logo)
❑ 388 Stephen Howard RC .10 .05
❑ 389 William Bedford .10 .05
❑ 390 Jayson Williams .30 .14
❑ 391 Kurt Rambis .10 .05
❑ 392 Keith Jennings RC .10 .05
❑ 393 Steve Kerr UER .30 .14
(The words key stat are repeated on back)
❑ 394 Larry Stewart .10 .05
❑ 395 Danny Young .10 .05
❑ 396 Doug Overton .10 .05
❑ 397 Mark Acres .10 .05
❑ 398 John Bagley .10 .05
❑ 399 Checklist 201-300 .10 .05
❑ 400 Checklist 301-400 .10 .05

1992-93 Stadium Club Beam Team

	MINT	NRMT
COMPLETE SET (21)	200.00	90.00
COMMON CARD (1-21)	2.00	.90
SEMISTARS	2.50	1.10
UNLISTED STARS	5.00	2.20

SER.2 STATED ODDS 1:36

❑ 1 Michael Jordan 60.00 27.00
❑ 2 Dominique Wilkins 5.00 2.20
❑ 3 Shawn Kemp 8.00 3.60
❑ 4 Clyde Drexler 5.00 2.20
❑ 5 Scottie Pippen 15.00 6.75
❑ 6 Chris Mullin 5.00 2.20
❑ 7 Reggie Miller 5.00 2.20
❑ 8 Glen Rice 5.00 2.20
❑ 9 Jeff Hornacek 2.50 1.10
❑ 10 Jeff Malone 2.00 .90
❑ 11 John Stockton 5.00 2.20
❑ 12 Kevin Johnson 5.00 2.20
❑ 13 Mark Price 2.00 .90
❑ 14 Tim Hardaway 6.00 2.70
❑ 15 Charles Barkley 8.00 3.60
❑ 16 Hakeem Olajuwon 8.00 3.60
❑ 17 Karl Malone 8.00 3.60
❑ 18 Patrick Ewing 5.00 2.20
❑ 19 Dennis Rodman 10.00 4.50
❑ 20 David Robinson 8.00 3.60
❑ 21 Shaquille O'Neal 100.00 45.00

1993-94 Stadium Club

	MINT	NRMT
COMPLETE SET (360)	40.00	18.00
COMPLETE SERIES 1 (180)	20.00	9.00
COMPLETE SERIES 2 (180)	20.00	9.00
COMMON CARD (1-180)	.10	.05
COMMON CARD (181-360)	.05	.02
SEMISTARS SER.1	.20	.09
SEMISTARS SER.2	.15	.07
UNLISTED STARS SER.1	.40	.18
UNLISTED STARS SER.2	.30	.14

SUBSET CARDS HALF VALUE OF BASE CARDS
NUMBER 345 NEVER ISSUED
KUKOC AND CORCHIANI NUMBERED 336

❑ 1 Michael Jordan TD 2.50 1.10
❑ 2 Kenny Anderson TD .10 .05
❑ 3 Steve Smith TD .20 .09
❑ 4 Kevin Gamble TD .10 .05
❑ 5 Detlef Schrempf TD .10 .05
❑ 6 Larry Johnson TD .20 .09
❑ 7 Brad Daugherty TD .10 .05
❑ 8 Rumeal Robinson TD .10 .05
❑ 9 Micheal Williams TD .10 .05
❑ 10 David Robinson TD .40 .18
❑ 11 Sam Perkins TD .10 .05
❑ 12 Thurl Bailey .10 .05
❑ 13 Sherman Douglas .10 .05
❑ 14 Larry Stewart .10 .05
❑ 15 Kevin Johnson .20 .09
❑ 16 Bill Cartwright .10 .05
❑ 17 Larry Nance .10 .05
❑ 18 P.J. Brown RC .40 .18
❑ 19 Tony Bennett .10 .05
❑ 20 Robert Parish .20 .09
❑ 21 David Benoit .10 .05
❑ 22 Detlef Schrempf .20 .09
❑ 23 Hubert Davis .10 .05
❑ 24 Donald Hodge .10 .05
❑ 25 Hersey Hawkins .20 .09
❑ 26 Mark Jackson .20 .09
❑ 27 Reggie Williams .10 .05
❑ 28 Lionel Simmons .10 .05
❑ 29 Ron Harper .20 .09
❑ 30 Chris Mills RC .40 .18
❑ 31 Danny Schayes .10 .05
❑ 32 J.R. Reid .10 .05
❑ 33 Willie Burton .10 .05
❑ 34 Greg Anthony .10 .05
❑ 35 Elden Campbell .10 .05
❑ 36 Ervin Johnson RC .20 .09
❑ 37 Scott Brooks .10 .05
❑ 38 Johnny Newman .10 .05
❑ 39 Rex Chapman .10 .05
❑ 40 Chuck Person .10 .05
❑ 41 John Williams .10 .05
❑ 42 Anthony Bowie .10 .05
❑ 43 Negele Knight .10 .05
❑ 44 Tyrone Corbin .10 .05
❑ 45 Jud Buechler .10 .05

❑ 46 Adam Keefe .10 .05
❑ 47 Glen Rice .20 .09
❑ 48 Tracy Murray .10 .05
❑ 49 Rick Mahorn .10 .05
❑ 50 Vlade Divac .20 .09
❑ 51 Eric Murdock .10 .05
❑ 52 Isaiah Morris .10 .05
❑ 53 Bobby Hurley RC .20 .09
❑ 54 Mitch Richmond .40 .18
❑ 55 Danny Ainge .20 .09
❑ 56 Dikembe Mutombo .20 .09
❑ 57 Jeff Hornacek .20 .09
❑ 58 Tony Campbell .10 .05
❑ 59 Vinny Del Negro .10 .05
❑ 60 Xavier McDaniel HC .10 .05
❑ 61 Scottie Pippen HC .60 .25
❑ 62 Larry Nance HC .10 .05
❑ 63 Dikembe Mutombo HC .10 .05
❑ 64 Hakeem Olajuwon HC .40 .18
❑ 65 Dominique Wilkins HC .20 .09
❑ 66 C. Weatherspoon HC .10 .05
❑ 67 Chris Morris HC .10 .05
❑ 68 Patrick Ewing HC .20 .09
❑ 69 Kevin Willis HC .10 .05
❑ 70 Jon Barry .10 .05
❑ 71 Jerry Reynolds .10 .05
❑ 72 Sarunas Marciulionis .10 .05
❑ 73 Mark West .10 .05
❑ 74 B.J. Armstrong .10 .05
❑ 75 Greg Kite .10 .05
❑ 76 LaSalle Thompson .10 .05
❑ 77 Randy White .10 .05
❑ 78 Alaa Abdelnaby .10 .05
❑ 79 Kevin Brooks .10 .05
❑ 80 Vern Fleming .10 .05
❑ 81 Doc Rivers .20 .09
❑ 82 Shawn Bradley RC .40 .18
❑ 83 Wayman Tisdale .10 .05
❑ 84 Olden Polynice .10 .05
❑ 85 Michael Cage .10 .05
❑ 86 Harold Miner .10 .05
❑ 87 Doug Smith .10 .05
❑ 88 Tom Gugliotta .40 .18
❑ 89 Hakeem Olajuwon .60 .25
❑ 90 Loy Vaught .10 .05
❑ 91 James Worthy .40 .18
❑ 92 John Paxson .10 .05
❑ 93 Jon Koncak .10 .05
❑ 94 Lee Mayberry .10 .05
❑ 95 Clarence Weatherspoon .10 .05
❑ 96 Mark Eaton .10 .05
❑ 97 Rex Walters RC .10 .05
❑ 98 Alvin Robertson .10 .05
❑ 99 Dan Majerle .20 .09
❑ 100 Shaquille O'Neal 2.00 .90
❑ 101 Derrick Coleman TD .10 .05
❑ 102 Hersey Hawkins TD .10 .05
❑ 103 Scottie Pippen TD .60 .25
❑ 104 Scott Skiles TD .10 .05
❑ 105 Rod Strickland TD .10 .05
❑ 106 Pooh Richardson TD .10 .05
❑ 107 Tom Gugliotta TD .20 .09
❑ 108 Mark Jackson TD .10 .05
❑ 109 Dikembe Mutombo TD .10 .05
❑ 110 Charles Barkley TD .40 .18
❑ 111 Otis Thorpe TD .10 .05
❑ 112 Malik Sealy .10 .05
❑ 113 Mark Macon .10 .05
❑ 114 Dee Brown .10 .05
❑ 115 Nate McMillan .10 .05
❑ 116 John Starks .20 .09
❑ 117 Clyde Drexler .40 .18
❑ 118 Antoine Carr .10 .05
❑ 119 Doug West .10 .05
❑ 120 Victor Alexander .10 .05
❑ 121 Kenny Gattison .10 .05
❑ 122 Spud Webb .20 .09
❑ 123 Rumeal Robinson .10 .05
❑ 124 Tim Kempton .10 .05
❑ 125 Karl Malone .60 .25
❑ 126 Randy Woods .10 .05
❑ 127 Calbert Cheaney RC .20 .09
❑ 128 Johnny Dawkins .10 .05
❑ 129 Dominique Wilkins .40 .18
❑ 130 Horace Grant .20 .09
❑ 131 Bill Laimbeer .10 .05
❑ 132 Kenny Smith .10 .05
❑ 133 Sedale Threatt .10 .05
❑ 134 Brian Shaw .10 .05
❑ 135 Dennis Scott .10 .05
❑ 136 Mark Bryant .10 .05
❑ 137 Xavier McDaniel .10 .05
❑ 138 David Wood .10 .05
❑ 139 Luther Wright RC .10 .05
❑ 140 Lloyd Daniels .10 .05
❑ 141 Marlon Maxey UER .10 .05
(Name spelled Maxley on the front)
❑ 142 Pooh Richardson .10 .05
❑ 143 Jeff Grayer .10 .05
❑ 144 LaPhonso Ellis .10 .05
❑ 145 Gerald Wilkins .10 .05
❑ 146 Dell Curry .10 .05
❑ 147 Duane Causwell .10 .05
❑ 148 Tim Hardaway .40 .18
❑ 149 Isiah Thomas .40 .18
❑ 150 Doug Edwards RC .10 .05
❑ 151 Anthony Peeler .10 .05
❑ 152 Tate George .10 .05
❑ 153 Terry Davis .10 .05
❑ 154 Sam Perkins .20 .09
❑ 155 John Salley .10 .05
❑ 156 Vernon Maxwell .10 .05
❑ 157 Anthony Avent .10 .05
❑ 158 Clifford Robinson .20 .09
❑ 159 Corie Blount RC .10 .05
❑ 160 Gerald Paddio .10 .05
❑ 161 Blair Rasmussen .10 .05
❑ 162 Carl Herrera .10 .05
❑ 163 Chris Smith .10 .05
❑ 164 Pervis Ellison .10 .05
❑ 165 Rod Strickland .20 .09
❑ 166 Jeff Malone .10 .05
❑ 167 Danny Ferry .10 .05
❑ 168 Kevin Lynch .10 .05
❑ 169 Michael Jordan 5.00 2.20
❑ 170 Derrick Coleman HC .10 .05
❑ 171 Jerome Kersey HC .10 .05
❑ 172 David Robinson HC .40 .18
❑ 173 Shawn Kemp HC .40 .18
❑ 174 Karl Malone HC .40 .18
❑ 175 Shaquille O'Neal HC .75 .35
❑ 176 Alonzo Mourning HC .40 .18
❑ 177 Charles Barkley HC .40 .18
❑ 178 Larry Johnson HC .20 .09
❑ 179 Checklist 1-90 .10 .05
❑ 180 Checklist 91-180 .10 .05
❑ 181 Michael Jordan FF 2.00 .90
❑ 182 Dominique Wilkins FF .15 .07
❑ 183 Dennis Rodman FF .30 .14
❑ 184 Scottie Pippen FF .50 .23
❑ 185 Larry Johnson FF .20 .09
❑ 186 Karl Malone FF .30 .14
❑ 187 C. Weatherspoon FF .05 .02
❑ 188 Charles Barkley FF .30 .14
❑ 189 Patrick Ewing FF .20 .09
❑ 190 Derrick Coleman FF .05 .02
❑ 191 LaBradford Smith .05 .02
❑ 192 Derek Harper .15 .07
❑ 193 Ken Norman .05 .02
❑ 194 Rodney Rogers RC .30 .14
❑ 195 Chris Dudley .05 .02
❑ 196 Gary Payton .50 .23
❑ 197 Andrew Lang .05 .02
❑ 198 Billy Owens .05 .02
❑ 199 Bryon Russell RC .30 .14
❑ 200 Patrick Ewing .30 .14
❑ 201 Stacey King .05 .02
❑ 202 Grant Long .05 .02
❑ 203 Sean Elliott .15 .07
❑ 204 Muggsy Bogues .15 .07
❑ 205 Kevin Edwards .05 .02
❑ 206 Dale Davis .05 .02
❑ 207 Dale Ellis .05 .02
❑ 208 Terrell Brandon .15 .07
❑ 209 Kevin Gamble .05 .02
❑ 210 Robert Horry .15 .07
❑ 211 Moses Malone UER .40 .18
Birthdate on back is 1993
❑ 212 Gary Grant .05 .02
❑ 213 Bobby Hurley .15 .07
❑ 214 Larry Krystkowiak .05 .02
❑ 215 A.C. Green .15 .07
❑ 216 Christian Laettner .15 .07
❑ 217 Orlando Woolridge .05 .02
❑ 218 Craig Ehlo .05 .02
❑ 219 Terry Porter .05 .02
❑ 220 Jamal Mashburn RC .75 .35
❑ 221 Kevin Duckworth .05 .02
❑ 222 Shawn Kemp .50 .23
❑ 223 Frank Brickowski .05 .02
❑ 224 Chris Webber RC 3.00 1.35
❑ 225 Charles Oakley .15 .07
❑ 226 Jay Humphries .05 .02
❑ 227 Steve Kerr .15 .07
❑ 228 Tim Perry .05 .02
❑ 229 Sleepy Floyd .05 .02
❑ 230 Bimbo Coles .05 .02
❑ 231 Eddie Johnson .05 .02
❑ 232 Terry Mills .05 .02
❑ 233 Danny Manning .15 .07
❑ 234 Isaiah Rider RC .75 .35
❑ 235 Darnell Mee RC .05 .02
❑ 236 Haywoode Workman .05 .02
❑ 237 Scott Skiles .05 .02
❑ 238 Otis Thorpe .15 .07
❑ 239 Mike Peplowski RC .05 .02
❑ 240 Eric Leckner .05 .02
❑ 241 Johnny Newman .05 .02
❑ 242 Benoit Benjamin .05 .02
❑ 243 Doug Christie .05 .02
❑ 244 Acie Earl RC .05 .02
❑ 245 Luc Longley .15 .07
❑ 246 Tyrone Hill .05 .02
❑ 247 Allan Houston RC 1.25 .55
❑ 248 Joe Kleine .05 .02
❑ 249 Mookie Blaylock .15 .07
❑ 250 Anthony Bonner .05 .02
❑ 251 Luther Wright .05 .02
❑ 252 Todd Day .05 .02
❑ 253 Kendall Gill .15 .07
❑ 254 Mario Elie .05 .02
❑ 255 Pete Myers UER .05 .02
Card has born in 1993
❑ 256 Jim Les .05 .02
❑ 257 Stanley Roberts .05 .02
❑ 258 Michael Adams .05 .02
❑ 259 Hersey Hawkins .15 .07
❑ 260 Shawn Bradley .20 .09
❑ 261 Scott Haskin RC .05 .02
❑ 262 Corie Blount .05 .02
❑ 263 Charles Smith .05 .02
❑ 264 Armon Gilliam .05 .02
❑ 265 Jamal Mashburn NW .30 .14
❑ 266 Anfernee Hardaway NW 1.50 .70
❑ 267 Shawn Bradley NW .20 .09
❑ 268 Chris Webber NW .75 .35
❑ 269 Bobby Hurley NW .05 .02
❑ 270 Isaiah Rider NW .30 .14
❑ 271 Dino Radja NW .05 .02
❑ 272 Chris Mills NW .15 .07
❑ 273 Nick Van Exel NW .30 .14
❑ 274 Lindsey Hunter NW .20 .09
❑ 275 Toni Kukoc NW .30 .14
❑ 276 Popeye Jones NW .05 .02
❑ 277 Chris Mills .40 .18
❑ 278 Ricky Pierce .05 .02
❑ 279 Negele Knight .05 .02
❑ 280 Kenny Walker .05 .02
❑ 281 Nick Van Exel RC .75 .35
❑ 282 Derrick Coleman UER .15 .07
(Career stats listed under '92-93)
❑ 283 Popeye Jones RC .05 .02
❑ 284 Derrick McKey .05 .02
❑ 285 Rick Fox .05 .02
❑ 286 Jerome Kersey .05 .02
❑ 287 Steve Smith .30 .14
❑ 288 Brian Williams .05 .02
❑ 289 Chris Mullin .30 .14
❑ 290 Terry Cummings .05 .02
❑ 291 Donald Royal .05 .02
❑ 292 Alonzo Mourning .50 .23
❑ 293 Mike Brown .05 .02
❑ 294 Latrell Sprewell .75 .35
❑ 295 Oliver Miller .05 .02
❑ 296 Terry Dehere RC .05 .02
❑ 297 Detlef Schrempf .15 .07
❑ 298 Sam Bowie UER .05 .02
(Last name Bowe on front)

Card	Player	Mint	NrMt
❑ 299	Chris Morris	.05	.02
❑ 300	Scottie Pippen	1.00	.45
❑ 301	Warren Kidd RC	.05	.02
❑ 302	Don MacLean	.05	.02
❑ 303	Sean Rooks	.05	.02
❑ 304	Matt Geiger	.05	.02
❑ 305	Dennis Rodman	.60	.25
❑ 306	Reggie Miller	.30	.14
❑ 307	Vin Baker RC	.75	.35
❑ 308	Anfernee Hardaway RC	3.00	1.35
❑ 309	Lindsey Hunter RC	.30	.14
❑ 310	Stacey Augmon	.05	.02
❑ 311	Randy Brown	.05	.02
❑ 312	Anthony Mason	.15	.07
❑ 313	John Stockton	.30	.14
❑ 314	Sam Cassell RC	.75	.35
❑ 315	Buck Williams	.05	.02
❑ 316	Bryant Stith	.05	.02
❑ 317	Brad Daugherty	.05	.02
❑ 318	Dino Radja RC	.05	.02
❑ 319	Rony Seikaly	.05	.02
❑ 320	Charles Barkley	.60	.25
❑ 321	Avery Johnson	.05	.02
❑ 322	Mahmoud Abdul-Rauf	.05	.02
❑ 323	Larry Johnson	.30	.14
❑ 324	Micheal Williams	.05	.02
❑ 325	Mark Aguirre	.05	.02
❑ 326	Jim Jackson	.15	.07
❑ 327	Antonio Harvey RC	.05	.02
❑ 328	David Robinson	.50	.23
❑ 329	Calbert Cheaney	.10	.05
❑ 330	Kenny Anderson	.20	.09
❑ 331	Walt Williams	.10	.05
❑ 332	Kevin Willis	.05	.02
❑ 333	Nick Anderson	.15	.07
❑ 334	Rik Smits	.15	.07
❑ 335	Joe Dumars	.40	.18
❑ 336	Toni Kukoc RC	1.25	.55
❑ 337	Harvey Grant	.05	.02
❑ 338	Tom Chambers	.05	.02
❑ 339	Blue Edwards	.05	.02
❑ 340	Mark Price	.05	.02
❑ 341	Ervin Johnson	.15	.07
❑ 342	Rolando Blackman	.05	.02
❑ 343	Scott Burrell RC	.30	.14
❑ 344	Gheorghe Muresan RC	.30	.14
❑ 345	Chris Corchiani UER 336	.05	.02
❑ 346	Richard Petruska RC	.05	.02
❑ 347	Dana Barros	.05	.02
❑ 348	Hakeem Olajuwon FF	.30	.14
❑ 349	Dee Brown FF	.05	.02
❑ 350	John Starks FF	.05	.02
❑ 351	Ron Harper FF	.05	.02
❑ 352	Chris Webber FF	.75	.35
❑ 353	Dan Majerle FF	.05	.02
❑ 354	Clyde Drexler FF	.15	.07
❑ 355	Shawn Kemp FF	.30	.14
❑ 356	David Robinson FF	.30	.14
❑ 357	Chris Morris FF	.05	.02
❑ 358	Shaquille O'Neal FF	.60	.25
❑ 359	Checklist	.05	.02
❑ 360	Checklist	.05	.02

1993-94 Stadium Club First Day Issue

	MINT	NRMT
COMPLETE SET (360)	900.00	400.00
COMPLETE SERIES 1 (180)	400.00	180.00
COMPLETE SERIES 2 (180)	500.00	220.00
COMMON CARD (1-360)	1.50	.70

*STARS: 10X TO 20X BASE CARD HI
*RCs: 7.5X TO 15X BASE HI
SER.1/2 STATED ODDS 1:24

1993-94 Stadium Club Beam Team

	MINT	NRMT
COMPLETE SET (27)	60.00	27.00
COMPLETE SERIES 1 (13)	30.00	13.50
COMPLETE SERIES 2 (14)	30.00	13.50
COMMON CARD (1-13)	.50	.23
COMMON CARD (14-27)	.60	.25
SEMISTARS SER.1	1.00	.45
SEMISTARS SER.2	1.00	.45
UNLISTED STARS SER.1	1.25	.55
UNLISTED STARS SER.2	1.50	.70

SER.1/2 STATED ODDS 1:24

Card	Player	Mint	NrMt
❑ 1	Shaquille O'Neal	8.00	3.60
❑ 2	Mark Price	.50	.23
❑ 3	Patrick Ewing	1.25	.55
❑ 4	Michael Jordan	20.00	9.00
❑ 5	Charles Barkley	2.00	.90
❑ 6	Reggie Miller	1.25	.55
❑ 7	Derrick Coleman	1.00	.45
❑ 8	Dominique Wilkins	1.25	.55
❑ 9	Karl Malone	2.00	.90
❑ 10	Alonzo Mourning	2.00	.90
❑ 11	Tim Hardaway	1.25	.55
❑ 12	Hakeem Olajuwon	2.00	.90
❑ 13	David Robinson	2.00	.90
❑ 14	Dan Majerle	1.00	.45
❑ 15	Larry Johnson	1.50	.70
❑ 16	LaPhonso Ellis	.60	.25
❑ 17	Nick Van Exel	2.50	1.10
❑ 18	Scottie Pippen	5.00	2.20
❑ 19	John Stockton	1.50	.70
❑ 20	Bobby Hurley	1.00	.45
❑ 21	Chris Webber	10.00	4.50
❑ 22	Jamal Mashburn	2.00	.90
❑ 23	Anfernee Hardaway	10.00	4.50
❑ 24	Isaiah Rider	2.00	.90
❑ 25	Ken Norman	.60	.25
❑ 26	Danny Manning	1.00	.45
❑ 27	Calbert Cheaney	1.00	.45

1993-94 Stadium Club Big Tips

	MINT	NRMT
COMPLETE SET (27)	5.00	2.20
COMMON CARD (1-27)	.25	.11

SER.2 STATED ODDS 1:6

Card	Team	Mint	NrMt
❑ 1	Atlanta Hawks	.25	.11
❑ 2	Boston Celtics	.25	.11
❑ 3	Charlotte Hornets	.25	.11
❑ 4	Chicago Bulls	.25	.11
❑ 5	Cleveland Cavaliers	.25	.11
❑ 6	Dallas Mavericks	.25	.11
❑ 7	Denver Nuggets	.25	.11
❑ 8	Detroit Pistons	.25	.11
❑ 9	Golden State Warriors	.25	.11
❑ 10	Houston Rockets	.25	.11
❑ 11	Indiana Pacers	.25	.11
❑ 12	Los Angeles Clippers	.25	.11
❑ 13	Los Angeles Lakers	.25	.11
❑ 14	Miami Heat	.25	.11
❑ 15	Milwaukee Bucks	.25	.11
❑ 16	Minnesota Timberwolves	.25	.11
❑ 17	New Jersey Nets	.25	.11
❑ 18	New York Knicks	.25	.11
❑ 19	Orlando Magic	.25	.11
❑ 20	Philadelphia 76ers	.25	.11
❑ 21	Phoenix Suns	.25	.11
❑ 22	Portland Trail Blazers	.25	.11
❑ 23	Sacramento Kings	.25	.11
❑ 24	San Antonio Spurs	.25	.11
❑ 25	Seattle Supersonics	.25	.11
❑ 26	Utah Jazz	.25	.11
❑ 27	Washington Bullets	.25	.11

1993-94 Stadium Club Frequent Flyer Upgrades

	MINT	NRMT
COMPLETE SET (20)	75.00	34.00

*STARS: 5X TO 12X BASE CARD HI
*RCs: 3X TO 8X BASE HI
ONE CARD BY MAIL PER 50 FF POINTS
POINT CARDS: SER.2 STATED ODDS 1:6

Card	Player	Mint	NrMt
❑ 182	Dominique Wilkins	5.00	2.20
❑ 183	Dennis Rodman	8.00	3.60
❑ 184	Scottie Pippen	12.00	5.50
❑ 185	Larry Johnson	4.00	1.80
❑ 186	Karl Malone	8.00	3.60
❑ 187	Clarence Weatherspoon	1.25	.55
❑ 188	Charles Barkley	8.00	3.60
❑ 189	Patrick Ewing	4.00	1.80
❑ 190	Derrick Coleman	2.00	.90
❑ 348	Hakeem Olajuwon	8.00	3.60
❑ 349	Dee Brown	1.25	.55
❑ 350	John Starks	2.50	1.10
❑ 351	Ron Harper	2.50	1.10
❑ 352	Chris Webber	25.00	11.00
❑ 353	Dan Majerle	2.50	1.10
❑ 354	Clyde Drexler	5.00	2.20
❑ 355	Shawn Kemp	6.00	2.70
❑ 356	David Robinson	6.00	2.70
❑ 357	Chris Morris	.60	.25
❑ 358	Shaquille O'Neal	25.00	11.00
❑ NNO	Expired Point Cards	.25	.11

1993-94 Stadium Club Rim Rockers

	MINT	NRMT
COMPLETE SET (6)	6.00	2.70

*SINGLES: .75X TO 2X BASE CARD HI
SER.2 STATED ODDS 1:24

Card	Player	Mint	NrMt
❑ 1	Shaquille O'Neal	4.00	1.80
❑ 2	Harold Miner	.20	.09
❑ 3	Charles Barkley	1.25	.55
❑ 4	Dominique Wilkins	.75	.35
❑ 5	Shawn Kemp	1.00	.45
❑ 6	Robert Horry	.30	.14

1993-94 Stadium Club Super Teams

	MINT	NRMT
COMPLETE SET (27)	15.00	6.75
COMMON CARD (1-27)	.40	.18
SER.1 STATED ODDS 1:24		
COMP.DW BAG HAWKS (11)	6.00	2.70
COMP.DW BAG KNICKS (11)	6.00	2.70
COMP.DW BAG ROCKETS (11)	10.00	4.50
COMP.DW BAG SONICS (11)	10.00	4.50
ONE BAG BY MAIL PER DIV.WIN.SUPER TM.		
COMP.MP BAG KNICKS (11)	10.00	4.50
COMP.MP BAG ROCKETS (11)	15.00	6.75
ONE BAG BY MAIL PER CON.WIN.SUP.TEAM		

	MINT	NRMT
❑ 1 Atlanta Hawks WD (Kevin Willis, Dominique Wilkins)	.40	.18
❑ 2 Boston Celtics (Xavier McDaniel, Robert Parish)	.40	.18
❑ 3 Charlotte Hornets (Larry Johnson, Alonzo Mourning)	2.00	.90
❑ 4 Chicago Bulls (Horace Grant)	.40	.18
❑ 5 Cleveland Cavaliers (Brad Daugherty, John Williams)	.40	.18
❑ 6 Dallas Mavericks (Group photo)	.40	.18
❑ 7 Denver Nuggets (Dikembe Mutombo, Kevin Brooks)	2.00	.90
❑ 8 Detroit Pistons (Group photo)	.40	.18
❑ 9 Golden State Warriors (Group photo)	.40	.18
❑ 10 Houston Rockets WCDF (Group photo)	6.00	2.70
❑ 11 Indiana Pacers (Group photo)	.40	.18
❑ 12 Los Angeles Clippers (Danny Manning, Ron Harper)	.40	.18
❑ 13 Los Angeles Lakers (Group photo)	.40	.18
❑ 14 Miami Heat (John Salley, Willie Burton)	.40	.18
❑ 15 Milwaukee Bucks (Group photo)	.40	.18
❑ 16 Minnesota Timberwolves (Christian Laettner, Felton Spencer)	2.00	.90
❑ 17 New Jersey Nets (Derrick Coleman)	.40	.18
❑ 18 New York Knicks WCD (Patrick Ewing)	2.50	1.10
❑ 19 Orlando Magic (Shaquille O'Neal)	6.00	2.70
❑ 20 Philadelphia 76ers (Clarence Weatherspoon, Jeff Hornacek)	.40	.18
❑ 21 Phoenix Suns (Charles Barkley, Dan Majerle)	1.25	.55
❑ 22 Portland Trail Blazers (Buck Williams)	.40	.18
❑ 23 Sacramento Kings (Lionel Simmons)	.40	.18
❑ 24 San Antonio Spurs (David Robinson)	1.25	.55
❑ 25 Seattle Supersonics WD (Shawn Kemp)	2.00	.90
❑ 26 Utah Jazz (Group photo)	.40	.18
❑ 27 Washington Bullets (Group photo)	.40	.18

1994-95 Stadium Club

	MINT	NRMT
COMPLETE SET (362)	40.00	18.00
COMPLETE SERIES 1 (182)	20.00	9.00
COMPLETE SERIES 2 (180)	20.00	9.00
COMMON CARD (1-362)	.10	.05
SEMISTARS	.15	.07
UNLISTED STARS	.40	.18
SUBSET CARDS HALF VALUE OF BASE CARDS		
R.MILLER AU: ONE PER SPECIAL RETAIL BOX		

	MINT	NRMT
❑ 1 Patrick Ewing	.40	.18
❑ 2 Patrick Ewing TTG	.15	.07
❑ 3 Bimbo Coles	.10	.05
❑ 4 Elden Campbell	.10	.05
❑ 5 Brent Price	.10	.05
❑ 6 Hubert Davis	.10	.05
❑ 7 Donald Royal	.10	.05
❑ 8 Tim Perry	.10	.05
❑ 9 Chris Webber	1.25	.55
❑ 10 Chris Webber TTG	.50	.23
❑ 11 Brad Daugherty	.10	.05
❑ 12 P.J. Brown	.10	.05
❑ 13 Charles Barkley	.60	.25
❑ 14 Mario Elie	.10	.05
❑ 15 Tyrone Hill	.10	.05
❑ 16 Anfernee Hardaway	1.25	.55
❑ 17 Anfernee Hardaway TTG	.75	.35
❑ 18 Toni Kukoc	.60	.25
❑ 19 Chris Morris	.10	.05
❑ 20 Gerald Wilkins	.10	.05
❑ 21 David Benoit	.10	.05
❑ 22 Kevin Duckworth	.10	.05
❑ 23 Derrick Coleman	.15	.07
❑ 24 Adam Keefe	.10	.05
❑ 25 Marlon Maxey	.10	.05
❑ 26 Vern Fleming	.10	.05
❑ 27 Jeff Malone	.10	.05
❑ 28 Rodney Rogers	.10	.05
❑ 29 Terry Mills	.10	.05
❑ 30 Doug West	.10	.05
❑ 31 Doug West TTG	.10	.05
❑ 32 Shaquille O'Neal	2.00	.90
❑ 33 Scottie Pippen	1.25	.55
❑ 34 Lee Mayberry	.10	.05
❑ 35 Dale Ellis	.10	.05
❑ 36 Cedric Ceballos	.10	.05
❑ 37 Lionel Simmons	.10	.05
❑ 38 Kenny Gattison	.10	.05
❑ 39 Popeye Jones	.10	.05
❑ 40 Jerome Kersey	.10	.05
❑ 41 Jerome Kersey TTG	.10	.05
❑ 42 Larry Stewart	.10	.05
❑ 43 Rod Strickland	.15	.07
❑ 44 Chris Mills	.15	.07
❑ 45 Latrell Sprewell	.75	.35
❑ 46 Haywoode Workman	.10	.05
❑ 47 Charles Smith	.10	.05
❑ 48 Detlef Schrempf	.15	.07
❑ 49 Gary Grant	.10	.05
❑ 50 Gary Grant TTG	.10	.05
❑ 51 Tom Chambers	.10	.05
❑ 52 J.R. Reid	.10	.05
❑ 53 Mookie Blaylock	.10	.05
❑ 54 Mookie Blaylock TTG	.10	.05
❑ 55 Rony Seikaly	.10	.05
❑ 56 Isaiah Rider	.15	.07
❑ 57 Isaiah Rider TTG	.10	.05
❑ 58 Nick Anderson	.10	.05
❑ 59 Victor Alexander	.10	.05
❑ 60 Lucious Harris	.10	.05
❑ 61 Mark Macon	.10	.05
❑ 62 Otis Thorpe	.10	.05
❑ 63 Randy Woods	.10	.05
❑ 64 Clyde Drexler	.40	.18
❑ 65 Dikembe Mutombo	.15	.07
❑ 66 Todd Day	.10	.05
❑ 67 Greg Anthony	.10	.05
❑ 68 Sherman Douglas	.10	.05
❑ 69 Chris Mullin	.40	.18
❑ 70 Kevin Johnson	.15	.07
❑ 71 Kendall Gill	.15	.07
❑ 72 Dennis Rodman	.75	.35
❑ 73 Dennis Rodman TG	.40	.18
❑ 74 Jeff Turner	.10	.05
❑ 75 John Stockton	.40	.18
❑ 76 John Stockton TTG	.15	.07
❑ 77 Doug Edwards	.10	.05
❑ 78 Jim Jackson	.15	.07
❑ 79 Hakeem Olajuwon	.60	.25
❑ 80 Glen Rice	.15	.07
❑ 81 Christian Laettner	.15	.07
❑ 82 Terry Porter	.10	.05
❑ 83 Joe Dumars	.40	.18
❑ 84 David Wingate	.10	.05
❑ 85 B.J. Armstrong	.10	.05
❑ 86 Derrick McKey	.10	.05
❑ 87 Elmore Spencer	.10	.05
❑ 88 Walt Williams	.10	.05
❑ 89 Shawn Bradley	.10	.05
❑ 90 Acie Earl	.10	.05
❑ 91 Acie Earl TTG	.10	.05
❑ 92 Randy Brown	.10	.05
❑ 93 Grant Long	.10	.05
❑ 94 Terry Dehere	.10	.05
❑ 95 Spud Webb	.10	.05
❑ 96 Lindsey Hunter	.15	.07
❑ 97 Blair Rasmussen	.10	.05
❑ 98 Tim Hardaway	.40	.18
❑ 99 Kevin Edwards	.10	.05
❑ 100 Patrick Ewing CT, Reggie Williams CT, Georgetown Hoyas	.15	.07
❑ 101 Chuck Person CT, Charles Barkley CT, Auburn Tigers	.40	.18
❑ 102 Mahmoud Abdul-Rauf CT, Shaquille O'Neal CT, LSU Tigers	.40	.18

❑ 103 Rony Seikaly CT .10 .05
Derrick Coleman CT
Syracuse Orangemen
❑ 104 Hakeem Olajuwon CT .40 .18
Clyde Drexler CT
Houston Cougars
❑ 105 Chris Mullin CT .15 .07
Mark Jackson CT
St. John Red Storm
❑ 106 Robert Horry CT .40 .18
Latrell Sprewell CT
Alabama Crimson Tide
❑ 107 Pooh Richardson CT .15 .07
Reggie Miller CT
UCLA Bruins
❑ 108 Dennis Scott CT .10 .05
Kenny Anderson CT
GA Tech Yellow Jackets
❑ 109 Kendall Gill CT .10 .05
Ken Norman CT
Illinois Fightin' Illini
❑ 110 Scott Skiles CT .10 .05
Kevin Willis CT
Michigan State Spartans
❑ 111 Terry Mills CT .15 .07
Glen Rice CT
Michigan Wolverines
❑ 112 Christian Laettner CT .10 .05
Bobby Hurley CT
Duke Blue Devils
❑ 113 Stacey Augmon CT .10 .05
Larry Johnson CT
UNLV Runnin' Rebels
❑ 114 Sam Perkins CT .15 .07
James Worthy CT
North Carolina Tar Heels
❑ 115 Carl Herrera .10 .05
❑ 116 Sam Bowie .10 .05
❑ 117 Gary Payton .60 .25
❑ 118 Danny Ainge .10 .05
❑ 119 Danny Ainge TTG .10 .05
❑ 120 Luc Longley .10 .05
❑ 121 Antonio Davis .10 .05
❑ 122 Terry Cummings .10 .05
❑ 123 Terry Cummings TTG .10 .05
❑ 124 Mark Price .10 .05
❑ 125 Jamal Mashburn .40 .18
❑ 126 Mahmoud Abdul-Rauf .10 .05
❑ 127 Charles Oakley .10 .05
❑ 128 Steve Smith .15 .07
❑ 129 Vin Baker .40 .18
❑ 130 Robert Horry .10 .05
❑ 131 Doug Christie .10 .05
❑ 132 Wayman Tisdale .10 .05
❑ 133 Wayman Tisdale TTG .10 .05
❑ 134 Muggsy Bogues .15 .07
❑ 135 Dino Radja .10 .05
❑ 136 Jeff Hornacek .15 .07
❑ 137 Gheorghe Muresan .10 .05
❑ 138 Loy Vaught .10 .05
❑ 139 Loy Vaught TTG .10 .05
❑ 140 Benoit Benjamin .10 .05
❑ 141 Johnny Dawkins .10 .05
❑ 142 Allan Houston .60 .25
❑ 143 Jon Barry .10 .05
❑ 144 Reggie Miller .40 .18
❑ 145 Kevin Willis .10 .05
❑ 146 James Worthy .40 .18
❑ 147 James Worthy TTG .15 .07
❑ 148 Scott Burrell .10 .05
❑ 149 Tom Gugliotta .15 .07
❑ 150 LaPhonso Ellis .10 .05
❑ 151 Doug Smith .10 .05
❑ 152 A.C. Green .15 .07
❑ 153 A.C. Green TTG .10 .05
❑ 154 George Lynch .10 .05
❑ 155 Sam Perkins .15 .07
❑ 156 Corie Blount .10 .05
❑ 157 Xavier McDaniel .10 .05
❑ 158 Xavier McDaniel TTG .10 .05
❑ 159 Eric Murdock .10 .05
❑ 160 David Robinson .60 .25
❑ 161 Karl Malone .60 .25
❑ 162 Karl Malone TTG .40 .18
❑ 163 Clarence Weatherspoon .10 .05
❑ 164 Calbert Cheaney .10 .05
❑ 165 Tom Hammonds .10 .05
❑ 166 Tom Hammonds TTG .10 .05
❑ 167 Alonzo Mourning .50 .23
❑ 168 Clifford Robinson .15 .07
❑ 169 Micheal Williams .10 .05
❑ 170 Ervin Johnson .10 .05
❑ 171 Mike Gminski .10 .05
❑ 172 Jason Kidd RC 3.00 1.35
❑ 173 Anthony Bonner .10 .05
❑ 174 Stacey King .10 .05
❑ 175 Rex Chapman .10 .05
❑ 176 Greg Graham .10 .05
❑ 177 Stanley Roberts .10 .05
❑ 178 Mitch Richmond .40 .18
❑ 179 Eric Montross RC .10 .05
❑ 180 Eddie Jones RC 2.50 1.10
❑ 181 Grant Hill RC 4.00 1.80
❑ 182 Donyell Marshall RC .40 .18
❑ 183 Glenn Robinson RC 1.25 .55
❑ 184 Dominique Wilkins .40 .18
❑ 185 Mark Price .10 .05
❑ 186 Anthony Mason .15 .07
❑ 187 Tyrone Corbin .10 .05
❑ 188 Dale Davis .10 .05
❑ 189 Nate McMillan .10 .05
❑ 190 Jason Kidd 1.50 .70
❑ 191 John Salley .10 .05
❑ 192 Keith Jennings .10 .05
❑ 193 Mark Bryant .10 .05
❑ 194 Sleepy Floyd .10 .05
❑ 195 Grant Hill 2.00 .90
❑ 196 Joe Kleine .10 .05
❑ 197 Anthony Peeler .10 .05
❑ 198 Malik Sealy .10 .05
❑ 199 Kenny Walker .10 .05
❑ 200 Donyell Marshall .40 .18
❑ 201 Vlade Divac AI .10 .05
❑ 202 Dino Radja AI .10 .05
❑ 203 Carl Herrera AI .10 .05
❑ 204 Olden Polynice AI .10 .05
❑ 205 Patrick Ewing AI .15 .07
❑ 206 Willie Anderson .10 .05
❑ 207 Mitch Richmond .40 .18
❑ 208 John Crotty .10 .05
❑ 209 Tracy Murray .10 .05
❑ 210 Juwan Howard RC 1.00 .45
❑ 211 Robert Parish .15 .07
❑ 212 Steve Kerr .10 .05
❑ 213 Anthony Bowie .10 .05
❑ 214 Tim Breaux .10 .05
❑ 215 Sharone Wright RC .10 .05
❑ 216 Brian Williams .10 .05
❑ 217 Rick Fox .10 .05
❑ 218 Harold Miner .10 .05
❑ 219 Duane Ferrell .10 .05
❑ 220 Lamond Murray RC .15 .07
❑ 221 Blue Edwards .10 .05
❑ 222 Bill Cartwright .10 .05
❑ 223 Sergei Bazarevich .10 .05
❑ 224 Herb Williams .10 .05
❑ 225 Brian Grant RC 1.00 .45
❑ 226 Derek Harper BCT .10 .05
John Starks
❑ 227 Rod Strickland BCT .40 .18
Clyde Drexler
❑ 228 Kevin Johnson BCT .10 .05
Dan Majerle
❑ 229 Lindsey Hunter BCT .10 .05
Joe Dumars
❑ 230 Tim Hardaway BCT .15 .07
Latrell Sprewell
❑ 231 Bill Wennington .10 .05
❑ 232 Brian Shaw .10 .05
❑ 233 Jamie Watson RC .10 .05
❑ 234 Chris Whitney .10 .05
❑ 235 Eric Montross .10 .05
❑ 236 Kenny Smith .10 .05
❑ 237 Andrew Lang .10 .05
❑ 238 Lorenzo Williams .10 .05
❑ 239 Dana Barros .10 .05
❑ 240 Eddie Jones 1.25 .55
❑ 241 Harold Ellis .10 .05
❑ 242 James Edwards .10 .05
❑ 243 Don MacLean .10 .05
❑ 244 Ed Pinckney .10 .05
❑ 245 Carlos Rogers RC .10 .05
❑ 246 Michael Adams .10 .05
❑ 247 Rex Walters .10 .05
❑ 248 John Starks .10 .05
❑ 249 Terrell Brandon .15 .07
❑ 250 Khalid Reeves RC .10 .05
❑ 251 Dominique Wilkins AI .15 .07
❑ 252 Toni Kukoc AI .40 .18
❑ 253 Rick Fox AI .10 .05
❑ 254 Detlef Schrempf AI .10 .05
❑ 255 Rik Smits AI .10 .05
❑ 256 Johnny Dawkins .10 .05
❑ 257 Dan Majerle .15 .07
❑ 258 Mike Brown .10 .05
❑ 259 Byron Scott .15 .07
❑ 260 Jalen Rose RC 1.50 .70
❑ 261 Byron Houston .10 .05
❑ 262 Frank Brickowski .10 .05
❑ 263 Vernon Maxwell .10 .05
❑ 264 Craig Ehlo .10 .05
❑ 265 Yinka Dare RC .10 .05
❑ 266 Dee Brown .10 .05
❑ 267 Felton Spencer .10 .05
❑ 268 Harvey Grant .10 .05
❑ 269 Nick Van Exel .40 .18
❑ 270 Bob Martin .10 .05
❑ 271 Hersey Hawkins .15 .07
❑ 272 Scott Williams .10 .05
❑ 273 Sarunas Marciulionis .10 .05
❑ 274 Kevin Gamble .10 .05
❑ 275 Clifford Rozier RC .10 .05
❑ 276 B.J. Armstrong BCT .10 .05
Ron Harper
❑ 277 John Stockton BCT .15 .07
Jeff Hornacek
❑ 278 Bobby Hurley BCT .15 .07
Mitch Richmond
❑ 279 Anfernee Hardaway BCT .40 .18
Dennis Scott
❑ 280 Jason Kidd BCT .40 .18
Jim Jackson
❑ 281 Ron Harper .15 .07
❑ 282 Chuck Person .10 .05
❑ 283 John Williams .10 .05
❑ 284 Robert Pack .10 .05
❑ 285 Aaron McKie RC .10 .05
❑ 286 Chris Smith .10 .05
❑ 287 Horace Grant .15 .07
❑ 288 Oliver Miller .10 .05
❑ 289 Derek Harper .10 .05
❑ 290 Eric Mobley RC .10 .05
❑ 291 Scott Skiles .10 .05
❑ 292 Olden Polynice .10 .05
❑ 293 Mark Jackson .10 .05
❑ 294 Wayman Tisdale .10 .05
❑ 295 Tony Dumas RC .10 .05
❑ 296 Bryon Russell .10 .05
❑ 297 Vlade Divac .10 .05
❑ 298 David Wesley .10 .05
❑ 299 Askia Jones RC .10 .05
❑ 300 B.J. Tyler RC .10 .05
❑ 301 Hakeem Olajuwon AI .40 .18
❑ 302 Luc Longley AI .10 .05
❑ 303 Rony Seikaly AI .10 .05
❑ 304 Sarunas Marciulionis AI .10 .05
❑ 305 Dikembe Mutombo AI .10 .05
❑ 306 Ken Norman .10 .05
❑ 307 Dell Curry .10 .05
❑ 308 Danny Ferry .10 .05
❑ 309 Shawn Kemp .60 .25
❑ 310 Dickey Simpkins RC .10 .05
❑ 311 Johnny Newman .10 .05
❑ 312 Dwayne Schintzius .10 .05
❑ 313 Sean Elliott .15 .07
❑ 314 Sean Rooks .10 .05
❑ 315 Bill Curley RC .10 .05
❑ 316 Bryant Stith .10 .05
❑ 317 Pooh Richardson .10 .05
❑ 318 Jim McIlvaine .10 .05
❑ 319 Dennis Scott .10 .05
❑ 320 Wesley Person RC .40 .18
❑ 321 Bobby Hurley .10 .05
❑ 322 Armon Gilliam .10 .05
❑ 323 Rik Smits .10 .05
❑ 324 Tony Smith .10 .05
❑ 325 Monty Williams RC .10 .05
❑ 326 Gary Payton BCT .40 .18

Card	MINT	NRMT
Kendall Gill		
❑ 327 Mookie Blaylock BCT	.10	.05
Stacey Augmon		
❑ 328 Mark Jackson BCT	.15	.07
Reggie Miller		
❑ 329 Sam Cassell BCT	.15	.07
Vernon Maxwell		
❑ 330 Harold Miner BCT	.10	.05
Khalid Reeves		
❑ 331 Vinny Del Negro	.10	.05
❑ 332 Billy Owens	.10	.05
❑ 333 Mark West	.10	.05
❑ 334 Matt Geiger	.10	.05
❑ 335 Greg Minor RC	.10	.05
❑ 336 Larry Johnson	.15	.07
❑ 337 Donald Hodge	.10	.05
❑ 338 Aaron Williams RC	.10	.05
❑ 339 Jay Humphries	.10	.05
❑ 340 Charlie Ward RC	.40	.18
❑ 341 Scott Brooks	.10	.05
❑ 342 Stacey Augmon	.10	.05
❑ 343 Will Perdue	.10	.05
❑ 344 Dale Ellis	.10	.05
❑ 345 Brooks Thompson RC	.10	.05
❑ 346 Manute Bol	.10	.05
❑ 347 Kenny Anderson	.15	.07
❑ 348 Willie Burton	.10	.05
❑ 349 Michael Cage	.10	.05
❑ 350 Danny Manning	.15	.07
❑ 351 Ricky Pierce	.10	.05
❑ 352 Sam Cassell	.40	.18
❑ 353 Reggie Miller FG	.15	.07
❑ 354 David Robinson FG	.40	.18
❑ 355 Shaquille O'Neal FG	.75	.35
❑ 356 Scottie Pippen FG	.60	.25
❑ 357 Alonzo Mourning FG	.40	.18
❑ 358 C. Weatherspoon FG	.10	.05
❑ 359 Derrick Coleman FG	.10	.05
❑ 360 Charles Barkley FG	.40	.18
❑ 361 Karl Malone FG	.40	.18
❑ 362 Chris Webber FG	.50	.23

1994-95 Stadium Club First Day Issue

	MINT	NRMT
COMPLETE SET (362)	750.00	350.00
COMPLETE SERIES 1 (182)	500.00	220.00
COMPLETE SERIES 2 (180)	250.00	110.00
COMMON CARD (1-362)	1.25	.55

*STARS: 10X TO 20X BASE CARD HI
*RCs: 6X TO 12X BASE HI
SER.1/2 STATED ODDS 1:24

1994-95 Stadium Club Beam Team

	MINT	NRMT
COMPLETE SET (27)	70.00	32.00

*SINGLES: 2.5X TO 6X BASE CARD HI
SER.2 STATED ODDS 1:24

Card	MINT	NRMT
❑ 1 Mookie Blaylock	.60	.25
❑ 2 Dominique Wilkins	2.50	1.10
❑ 3 Alonzo Mourning	3.00	1.35
❑ 4 Toni Kukoc	4.00	1.80
❑ 5 Mark Price	.60	.25
❑ 6 Jason Kidd	20.00	9.00

Card	MINT	NRMT
❑ 7 Jalen Rose	10.00	4.50
❑ 8 Grant Hill	25.00	11.00
❑ 9 Latrell Sprewell	5.00	2.20
❑ 10 Hakeem Olajuwon	4.00	1.80
❑ 11 Reggie Miller	2.50	1.10
❑ 12 Lamond Murray	1.00	.45
❑ 13 George Lynch	.60	.25
❑ 14 Khalid Reeves	.60	.25
❑ 15 Glenn Robinson	8.00	3.60
❑ 16 Donyell Marshall	2.50	1.10
❑ 17 Derrick Coleman	1.00	.45
❑ 18 Patrick Ewing	2.50	1.10
❑ 19 Shaquille O'Neal	12.00	5.50
❑ 20 Clarence Weatherspoon	.60	.25
❑ 21 Charles Barkley	4.00	1.80
❑ 22 Clifford Robinson	1.00	.45
❑ 23 Bobby Hurley	.60	.25
❑ 24 David Robinson	4.00	1.80
❑ 25 Shawn Kemp	4.00	1.80
❑ 26 Karl Malone	4.00	1.80
❑ 27 Chris Webber	8.00	3.60

1994-95 Stadium Club Clear Cut

	MINT	NRMT
COMPLETE SET (27)	30.00	13.50

*SINGLES: 2.5X TO 6X BASE CARD HI
SER.1 STATED ODDS 1:12

Card	MINT	NRMT
❑ 1 Stacey Augmon	.60	.25
❑ 2 Dino Radja	.60	.25
❑ 3 Alonzo Mourning	3.00	1.35
❑ 4 Scottie Pippen	8.00	3.60
❑ 5 Gerald Wilkins	.60	.25
❑ 6 Jamal Mashburn	2.50	1.10
❑ 7 Dikembe Mutombo	1.00	.45
❑ 8 Lindsey Hunter	1.00	.45
❑ 9 Chris Mullin	2.50	1.10
❑ 10 Hakeem Olajuwon	4.00	1.80
❑ 11 Reggie Miller	2.50	1.10
❑ 12 Gary Grant	.60	.25
❑ 13 Doug Christie	.60	.25
❑ 14 Steve Smith	1.00	.45
❑ 15 Vin Baker	2.50	1.10
❑ 16 Christian Laettner	1.00	.45
❑ 17 Derrick Coleman	1.00	.45
❑ 18 Charles Oakley	.60	.25
❑ 19 Dennis Scott	.60	.25
❑ 20 Clarence Weatherspoon	.60	.25
❑ 21 Charles Barkley	4.00	1.80
❑ 22 Clifford Robinson	1.00	.45
❑ 23 Mitch Richmond	2.50	1.10
❑ 24 David Robinson	4.00	1.80
❑ 25 Shawn Kemp	4.00	1.80
❑ 26 Karl Malone	4.00	1.80
❑ 27 Don MacLean	.60	.25

1994-95 Stadium Club Dynasty and Destiny

	MINT	NRMT
COMPLETE SET (20)	10.00	4.50

*SINGLES: .6X TO 1.5X BASE CARD HI
SER.1 STATED ODDS 1:6
ONE PER SER.1 RACK PACK

Card	MINT	NRMT
❑ 1A Mark Price	.15	.07
❑ 1B Kenny Anderson	.25	.11
❑ 2A Karl Malone	1.00	.45
❑ 2B Derrick Coleman	.25	.11
❑ 3A John Stockton	.60	.25
❑ 3B Anfernee Hardaway	2.00	.90
❑ 4A Mitch Richmond	.60	.25
❑ 4B Jim Jackson	.25	.11
❑ 5A James Worthy	.60	.25
❑ 5B Jamal Mashburn	.60	.25
❑ 6A Patrick Ewing	.60	.25
❑ 6B Alonzo Mourning	.75	.35
❑ 7A Hakeem Olajuwon	1.00	.45
❑ 7B Shaquille O'Neal	3.00	1.35
❑ 8A Clyde Drexler	.60	.25
❑ 8B Isaiah Rider	.25	.11
❑ 9A Scottie Pippen	2.00	.90
❑ 9B Latrell Sprewell	1.25	.55
❑ 10A Charles Barkley	1.00	.45
❑ 10B Chris Webber	2.00	.90

1994-95 Stadium Club Rising Stars

	MINT	NRMT
COMPLETE SET (12)	40.00	18.00
COMMON CARD (1-12)	.60	.25
SEMISTARS	1.25	.55
UNLISTED STARS	3.00	1.35

SER.1 STATED ODDS 1:24

Card	MINT	NRMT
❑ 1 Kenny Anderson	1.25	.55
❑ 2 Latrell Sprewell	6.00	2.70

❑ 3 Jamal Mashburn	3.00	1.35
❑ 4 Alonzo Mourning	4.00	1.80
❑ 5 Shaquille O'Neal	15.00	6.75
❑ 6 LaPhonso Ellis	.60	.25
❑ 7 Chris Webber	10.00	4.50
❑ 8 Isaiah Rider	1.25	.55
❑ 9 Dikembe Mutombo	1.25	.55
❑ 10 Anfernee Hardaway	10.00	4.50
❑ 11 Antonio Davis	.60	.25
❑ 12 Robert Horry	.60	.25

1994-95 Stadium Club Super Skills

	MINT	NRMT
COMPLETE SET (25)	40.00	18.00

*SINGLES: 2X TO 5X BASE CARD HI
SER.2 STATED ODDS 1:24
ONE PER SER.2 RACK PACK

❑ 1 Mark Price	.50	.23
❑ 2 Tim Hardaway	2.00	.90
❑ 3 Kevin Johnson	.75	.35
❑ 4 John Stockton	2.00	.90
❑ 5 Mookie Blaylock	.50	.23
❑ 6 Reggie Miller	2.00	.90
❑ 7 Jeff Hornacek	.75	.35
❑ 8 Latrell Sprewell	4.00	1.80
❑ 9 John Starks	.50	.23
❑ 10 Nate McMillan	.50	.23
❑ 11 Chris Mullin	2.00	.90
❑ 12 Toni Kukoc	3.00	1.35
❑ 13 Anthony Mason	.75	.35
❑ 14 Robert Horry	.50	.23
❑ 15 Scottie Pippen	6.00	2.70
❑ 16 Charles Barkley	3.00	1.35
❑ 17 Dennis Rodman	4.00	1.80
❑ 18 Karl Malone	3.00	1.35
❑ 19 Chris Webber	6.00	2.70
❑ 20 Charles Oakley	.50	.23
❑ 21 Patrick Ewing	2.00	.90
❑ 22 Shaquille O'Neal	10.00	4.50
❑ 23 Dikembe Mutombo	.75	.35
❑ 24 David Robinson	3.00	1.35
❑ 25 Hakeem Olajuwon	3.00	1.35

1994-95 Stadium Club Super Teams

	MINT	NRMT
COMPLETE SET (27)	30.00	13.50
COMMON TEAM (1-27)	1.00	.45
SEMISTARS	1.50	.70
UNLISTED STARS	2.50	1.10

SER.1 STATED ODDS 1:24

COMP.DW BAG MAGIC (11)	12.00	5.50
COMP.DW BAG PACERS (11)	3.00	1.35
COMP.DW BAG SPURS (11)	8.00	3.60
COMP.DW BAG SUNS (11)	6.00	2.70

ONE BAG BY MAIL PER DIV.WIN.SUPER TM.

COMP.MP BAG MAGIC (11)	15.00	6.75
COMP.MP BAG ROCKETS (11)	8.00	3.60

ONE BAG BY MAIL PER CONF.WIN.SUP.TEAM

❑ 1 Atlanta Hawks Kevin Willis	1.00	.45
❑ 2 Boston Celtics Group	1.00	.45
❑ 3 Charlotte Hornets Muggsy Bogues	1.00	.45
❑ 4 Chicago Bulls Group	1.00	.45
❑ 5 Cleveland Cavaliers Danny Ferry	1.00	.45
❑ 6 Dallas Mavericks Jim Jackson	1.50	.70
❑ 7 Denver Nuggets Rodney Rogers	1.00	.45
❑ 8 Detroit Pistons Joe Dumars	1.50	.70
❑ 9 Golden State Warriors Chris Webber	8.00	3.60
❑ 10 Houston Rockets WCF Hakeem Olajuwon	10.00	4.50
❑ 11 Indiana Pacers WD Rik Smits	1.00	.45
❑ 12 LA Clippers Group	1.00	.45
❑ 13 L.A. Lakers Nick Van Exel	2.50	1.10
❑ 14 Miami Heat Glen Rice	2.50	1.10
❑ 15 Milwaukee Bucks Vin Baker	2.50	1.10
❑ 16 Minnesota Timberwolves Christian Laettner	1.50	.70
❑ 17 New Jersey Nets Chris Morris	1.00	.45
❑ 18 New York Knicks Group	1.00	.45
❑ 19 Orlando Magic WCD Shaquille O'Neal	15.00	6.75
❑ 20 Philadelphia 76ers Dana Barros	1.00	.45
❑ 21 Phoenix Suns WD Charles Barkley	5.00	2.20
❑ 22 Portland Trail Blazers Group	1.00	.45
❑ 23 Sacramento Kings Olden Polynice	1.00	.45
❑ 24 San Antonio Spurs WD Group	1.00	.45
❑ 25 Seattle Supersonics Group	1.00	.45
❑ 26 Utah Jazz John Stockton	2.50	1.10
❑ 27 Washington Bullets Group	1.00	.45

1994-95 Stadium Club Team of the Future

	MINT	NRMT
COMPLETE SET (10)	30.00	13.50

*SINGLES: 2X TO 5X BASE CARD HI
SER.2 STATED ODDS 1:24

❑ 1 Anfernee Hardaway	6.00	2.70
❑ 2 Latrell Sprewell	4.00	1.80
❑ 3 Grant Hill	10.00	4.50
❑ 4 Chris Webber	6.00	2.70
❑ 5 Shaquille O'Neal	10.00	4.50
❑ 6 Jason Kidd	8.00	3.60
❑ 7 Jim Jackson	.75	.35
❑ 8 Jamal Mashburn	2.00	.90

❑ 9 Glenn Robinson	3.00	1.35
❑ 10 Alonzo Mourning	2.50	1.10

1995-96 Stadium Club

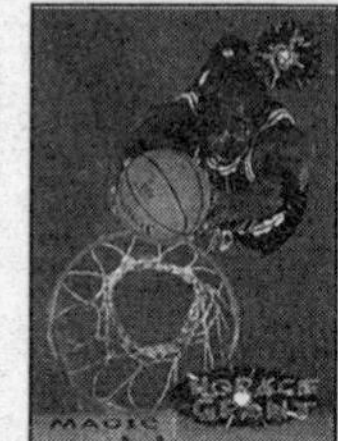

	MINT	NRMT
COMPLETE SET (361)	50.00	22.00
COMPLETE SERIES 1 (180)	25.00	11.00
COMPLETE SERIES 2 (181)	25.00	11.00
COMMON CARD (1-361)	.15	.07
SEMISTARS	.20	.09
UNLISTED STARS	.40	.18

SUBSET CARDS EQUAL VALUE TO BASE CARDS
FOIL VARIATIONS: SAME PRICE

❑ 1 Michael Jordan	5.00	2.20
❑ 2 Glenn Robinson	.40	.18
❑ 3 Jason Kidd	1.25	.55
❑ 4 Clyde Drexler	.40	.18
❑ 5 Horace Grant	.20	.09
❑ 6 Allan Houston	.50	.23
❑ 7 Xavier McDaniel	.15	.07
❑ 8 Jeff Hornacek	.20	.09
❑ 9 Vlade Divac	.15	.07
❑ 10 Juwan Howard	.40	.18
❑ 11 Keith Jennings EXP	.15	.07
❑ 12 Grant Long	.15	.07
❑ 13 Jalen Rose	.50	.23
❑ 14 Malik Sealy	.15	.07
❑ 15 Gary Payton	.60	.25
❑ 16 Danny Ferry	.15	.07
❑ 17 Glen Rice	.20	.09
❑ 18 Randy Brown	.15	.07
❑ 19 Greg Graham	.15	.07
❑ 20 Kenny Anderson UER Name is spelled Kenney	.20	.09
❑ 21 Aaron McKie	.15	.07
❑ 22 John Salley EXP	.15	.07
❑ 23 Darrin Hancock	.15	.07
❑ 24 Carlos Rogers	.15	.07
❑ 25 Vin Baker	.40	.18
❑ 26 Bill Wennington	.15	.07
❑ 27 Kenny Smith	.15	.07
❑ 28 Sherman Douglas	.15	.07
❑ 29 Terry Davis	.15	.07
❑ 30 Grant Hill	2.00	.90
❑ 31 Reggie Miller	.40	.18
❑ 32 Anfernee Hardaway	1.25	.55
❑ 33 Patrick Ewing	.40	.18
❑ 34 Charles Barkley	.60	.25

❑ 35 Eddie Jones .75 .35
❑ 36 Kevin Duckworth .15 .07
❑ 37 Tom Hammonds .15 .07
❑ 38 Craig Ehlo .15 .07
❑ 39 Micheal Williams .15 .07
❑ 40 Alonzo Mourning .40 .18
❑ 41 John Williams .15 .07
❑ 42 Felton Spencer .15 .07
❑ 43 Lamond Murray .15 .07
❑ 44 Dontonio Wingfield EXP .15 .07
❑ 45 Rik Smits .15 .07
❑ 46 Donyell Marshall .20 .09
❑ 47 Clarence Weatherspoon .15 .07
❑ 48 Kevin Edwards .15 .07
❑ 49 Charlie Ward .15 .07
❑ 50 David Robinson .60 .25
❑ 51 James Robinson .15 .07
❑ 52 Bill Cartwright .15 .07
❑ 53 Bobby Hurley .15 .07
❑ 54 Kevin Gamble .15 .07
❑ 55 B.J. Tyler EXP .15 .07
❑ 56 Chris Smith .15 .07
❑ 57 Wesley Person .20 .09
❑ 58 Tim Breaux .15 .07
❑ 59 Mitchell Butler .15 .07
❑ 60 Toni Kukoc .50 .23
❑ 61 Roy Tarpley .15 .07
❑ 62 Todd Day .15 .07
❑ 63 Anthony Peeler .15 .07
❑ 64 Brian Williams .15 .07
❑ 65 Muggsy Bogues .15 .07
❑ 66 Jerome Kersey EXP .15 .07
❑ 67 Eric Piatkowski .15 .07
❑ 68 Tim Perry .15 .07
❑ 69 Chris Gatling .15 .07
❑ 70 Mark Price .15 .07
❑ 71 Terry Mills .15 .07
❑ 72 Anthony Avent .15 .07
❑ 73 Matt Geiger .15 .07
❑ 74 Walt Williams .15 .07
❑ 75 Sean Elliott .15 .07
❑ 76 Ken Norman .15 .07
❑ 77 Kendall Gill TA .20 .09
❑ 78 Byron Houston .15 .07
❑ 79 Rick Fox .15 .07
❑ 80 Derek Harper .15 .07
❑ 81 Rod Strickland .20 .09
❑ 82 Bryon Russell .15 .07
❑ 83 Antonio Davis .15 .07
❑ 84 Isaiah Rider .20 .09
❑ 85 Kevin Johnson .20 .09
❑ 86 Derrick Coleman .20 .09
❑ 87 Doug Overton .15 .07
❑ 88 Hersey Hawkins TA .20 .09
❑ 89 Popeye Jones .15 .07
❑ 90 Dickey Simpkins .15 .07
❑ 91 Rodney Rogers TA .15 .07
❑ 92 Rex Chapman TA .15 .07
❑ 93 Spud Webb TA .15 .07
❑ 94 Lee Mayberry .15 .07
❑ 95 Cedric Ceballos .15 .07
❑ 96 Tyrone Hill .15 .07
❑ 97 Bill Curley .15 .07
❑ 98 Jeff Turner .15 .07
❑ 99 Tyrone Corbin TA .15 .07
❑ 100 John Stockton .40 .18
❑ 101 Mookie Blaylock EC .15 .07
❑ 102 Dino Radja EC .15 .07
❑ 103 Alonzo Mourning EC .40 .18
❑ 104 Scottie Pippen EC 1.25 .55
❑ 105 Terrell Brandon EC .20 .09
❑ 106 Jim Jackson EC .15 .07
❑ 107 Mahmoud Abdul-Rauf EC .15 .07
❑ 108 Grant Hill EC 2.50 1.10
❑ 109 Tim Hardaway EC .40 .18
❑ 110 Hakeem Olajuwon EC .75 .35
❑ 111 Rik Smits EC .15 .07
❑ 112 Loy Vaught EC .15 .07
❑ 113 Vlade Divac EC .15 .07
❑ 114 Kevin Willis EC .15 .07
❑ 115 Glenn Robinson EC .40 .18
❑ 116 Christian Laettner EC .20 .09
❑ 117 Derrick Coleman EC .20 .09
❑ 118 Patrick Ewing EC .40 .18
❑ 119 Shaquille O'Neal EC 2.00 .90
❑ 120 Dana Barros EC .15 .07
❑ 121 Charles Barkley EC .60 .25
❑ 122 Rod Strickland EC .20 .09
❑ 123 Brian Grant EC .40 .18
❑ 124 David Robinson EC .60 .25
❑ 125 Shawn Kemp EC 1.00 .45
❑ 126 Oliver Miller EC .15 .07
❑ 127 Karl Malone EC .60 .25
❑ 128 Benoit Benjamin EC .15 .07
❑ 129 Chris Webber EC 1.00 .45
❑ 130 Dan Majerle .15 .07
❑ 131 Calbert Cheaney .15 .07
❑ 132 Mark Jackson .15 .07
❑ 133 Greg Anthony EXP .15 .07
❑ 134 Scott Burrell .15 .07
❑ 135 Detlef Schrempf .20 .09
❑ 136 Marty Conlon .15 .07
❑ 137 Rony Seikaly .15 .07
❑ 138 Olden Polynice .15 .07
❑ 139 Terry Cummings .15 .07
❑ 140 Stacey Augmon .15 .07
❑ 141 Bryant Stith .15 .07
❑ 142 Sean Higgins .15 .07
❑ 143 Antoine Carr .15 .07
❑ 144 Blue Edwards EXP .15 .07
❑ 145 A.C. Green .20 .09
❑ 146 Bobby Phills .15 .07
❑ 147 Terry Dehere .15 .07
❑ 148 Sharone Wright .15 .07
❑ 149 Nick Anderson .15 .07
❑ 150 Jim Jackson .15 .07
❑ 151 Eric Montross .15 .07
❑ 152 Doug West .15 .07
❑ 153 Charles Smith .15 .07
❑ 154 Will Perdue .15 .07
❑ 155 Gerald Wilkins EXP .15 .07
❑ 156 Robert Horry .15 .07
❑ 157 Robert Parish .20 .09
❑ 158 Lindsey Hunter .15 .07
❑ 159 Harvey Grant .15 .07
❑ 160 Tim Hardaway .40 .18
❑ 161 Sarunas Marciulionis .15 .07
❑ 162 Khalid Reeves .15 .07
❑ 163 Bo Outlaw .15 .07
❑ 164 Dale Davis .15 .07
❑ 165 Nick Van Exel .20 .09
❑ 166 Byron Scott EXP .15 .07
❑ 167 Steve Smith .20 .09
❑ 168 Brian Grant .40 .18
❑ 169 Avery Johnson .15 .07
❑ 170 Dikembe Mutombo .20 .09
❑ 171 Tom Gugliotta .20 .09
❑ 172 Armon Gilliam .15 .07
❑ 173 Shawn Bradley .15 .07
❑ 174 Herb Williams .15 .07
❑ 175 Dino Radja .15 .07
❑ 176 Billy Owens .15 .07
❑ 177 Kenny Gattison EXP .15 .07
❑ 178 J.R. Reid .15 .07
❑ 179 Otis Thorpe .15 .07
❑ 180 Sam Cassell .20 .09
❑ 181 Sam Cassell .20 .09
❑ 182 Pooh Richardson .15 .07
❑ 183 Johnny Newman .15 .07
❑ 184 Dennis Scott .15 .07
❑ 185 Will Perdue .15 .07
❑ 186 Andrew Lang .15 .07
❑ 187 Karl Malone .60 .25
❑ 188 Buck Williams .15 .07
❑ 189 P.J. Brown .15 .07
❑ 190 Khalid Reeves .15 .07
❑ 191 Kevin Willis .15 .07
❑ 192 Robert Pack .15 .07
❑ 193 Joe Dumars .40 .18
❑ 194 Sam Perkins .20 .09
❑ 195 Dan Majerle .15 .07
❑ 196 John Williams .15 .07
❑ 197 Reggie Williams .15 .07
❑ 198 Greg Anthony .15 .07
❑ 199 Steve Kerr .15 .07
❑ 200 Richard Dumas .15 .07
❑ 201 Dee Brown .15 .07
❑ 202 Zan Tabak .15 .07
❑ 203 David Wood .15 .07
❑ 204 Duane Causwell .15 .07
❑ 205 Sedale Threatt .15 .07
❑ 206 Hubert Davis .15 .07
❑ 207 Donald Hodge .15 .07
❑ 208 Duane Ferrell .15 .07
❑ 209 Sam Mitchell .15 .07
❑ 210 Adam Keefe .15 .07
❑ 211 Clifford Robinson .15 .07
❑ 212 Rodney Rogers .15 .07
❑ 213 Jayson Williams .20 .09
❑ 214 Brian Shaw .15 .07
❑ 215 Luc Longley .15 .07
❑ 216 Don MacLean .15 .07
❑ 217 Rex Chapman .15 .07
❑ 218 Wayman Tisdale .15 .07
❑ 219 Shawn Kemp .60 .25
❑ 220 Chris Webber 1.25 .55
❑ 221 Antonio Harvey .15 .07
❑ 222 Sarunas Marciulionis .15 .07
❑ 223 Jeff Malone .15 .07
❑ 224 Chucky Brown .15 .07
❑ 225 Greg Minor .15 .07
❑ 226 Clifford Rozier .15 .07
❑ 227 Derrick McKey .15 .07
❑ 228 Tony Dumas .15 .07
❑ 229 Oliver Miller .15 .07
❑ 230 Charles Oakley .15 .07
❑ 231 Fred Roberts .15 .07
❑ 232 Glen Rice .20 .09
❑ 233 Terry Porter .15 .07
❑ 234 Mark Macon .15 .07
❑ 235 Michael Cage .15 .07
❑ 236 Eric Murdock .15 .07
❑ 237 Vinny Del Negro .15 .07
❑ 238 Spud Webb .15 .07
❑ 239 Mario Elie .15 .07
❑ 240 Blue Edwards .15 .07
❑ 241 Dontonio Wingfield .15 .07
❑ 242 Brooks Thompson .15 .07
❑ 243 Alonzo Mourning .40 .18
❑ 244 Dennis Rodman .75 .35
❑ 245 Lorenzo Williams .15 .07
❑ 246 Haywoode Workman .15 .07
❑ 247 Loy Vaught .15 .07
❑ 248 Vernon Maxwell .15 .07
❑ 249 Lionel Simmons .15 .07
❑ 250 Chris Childs .15 .07
❑ 251 Mahmoud Abdul-Rauf .15 .07
❑ 252 Vincent Askew .15 .07
❑ 253 Chris Morris .15 .07
❑ 254 Elliot Perry .15 .07
❑ 255 Dell Curry .15 .07
❑ 256 Dana Barros .15 .07
❑ 257 Terrell Brandon .20 .09
❑ 258 Monty Williams .15 .07
❑ 259 Corie Blount .15 .07
❑ 260 B.J. Armstrong .15 .07
❑ 261 Jim McIlvaine .15 .07
❑ 262 Otis Thorpe .15 .07
❑ 263 Sean Rooks .15 .07
❑ 264 Tony Massenburg .15 .07
❑ 265 Steve Smith .20 .09
❑ 266 Ron Harper .20 .09
❑ 267 Dale Ellis .15 .07
❑ 268 Clyde Drexler .40 .18
❑ 269 Jamie Watson .15 .07
❑ 270 Doc Rivers .15 .07
❑ 271 Derrick Alston .15 .07
❑ 272 Eric Mobley .15 .07
❑ 273 Ricky Pierce .15 .07
❑ 274 David Wesley .15 .07
❑ 275 John Starks .15 .07
❑ 276 Chris Mullin .40 .18
❑ 277 Ervin Johnson .15 .07
❑ 278 Jamal Mashburn .20 .09
❑ 279 Joe Kleine .15 .07
❑ 280 Mitch Richmond .40 .18
❑ 281 Chris Mills .15 .07
❑ 282 Bimbo Coles .15 .07
❑ 283 Larry Johnson .20 .09
❑ 284 Stanley Roberts .15 .07
❑ 285 Rex Walters .15 .07
❑ 286 Donald Royal .15 .07
❑ 287 Benoit Benjamin .15 .07
❑ 288 Chris Dudley .15 .07
❑ 289 Elden Campbell .15 .07
❑ 290 Mookie Blaylock .15 .07
❑ 291 Hersey Hawkins .20 .09
❑ 292 Anthony Mason .20 .09

❑ 293 Latrell Sprewell	.75	.35
❑ 294 Harold Miner	.15	.07
❑ 295 Scott Williams	.15	.07
❑ 296 David Benoit	.15	.07
❑ 297 Christian Laettner	.20	.09
❑ 298 LaPhonso Ellis	.15	.07
❑ 299 Gheorghe Muresan	.15	.07
❑ 300 Kendall Gill	.20	.09
❑ 301 Eddie Johnson	.15	.07
❑ 302 Terry Cummings	.15	.07
❑ 303 Chuck Person	.15	.07
❑ 304 Michael Smith	.15	.07
❑ 305 Mark West	.15	.07
❑ 306 Willie Anderson	.15	.07
❑ 307 Pervis Ellison	.15	.07
❑ 308 Brian Williams	.15	.07
❑ 309 Danny Manning	.20	.09
❑ 310 Hakeem Olajuwon	.60	.25
❑ 311 Scottie Pippen	1.25	.55
❑ 312 Jon Koncak	.15	.07
❑ 313 Sasha Danilovic RC	.15	.07
❑ 314 Lucious Harris	.15	.07
❑ 315 Yinka Dare	.15	.07
❑ 316 Eric Williams RC	.20	.09
❑ 317 Gary Trent RC	.15	.07
❑ 318 Theo Ratliff RC	.50	.23
❑ 319 Lawrence Moten RC	.15	.07
❑ 320 Jerome Allen RC	.15	.07
❑ 321 Tyus Edney RC	.15	.07
❑ 322 Loren Meyer RC	.15	.07
❑ 323 Michael Finley RC	1.50	.70
❑ 324 Alan Henderson RC	.40	.18
❑ 325 Bob Sura RC	.20	.09
❑ 326 Joe Smith RC	1.25	.55
❑ 327 Damon Stoudamire RC	2.00	.90
❑ 328 Sherrell Ford RC	.15	.07
❑ 329 Jerry Stackhouse RC	1.25	.55
❑ 330 George Zidek RC	.15	.07
❑ 331 Brent Barry RC	.40	.18
❑ 332 Shawn Respert RC	.15	.07
❑ 333 Rasheed Wallace RC	1.50	.70
❑ 334 Antonio McDyess RC	2.00	.90
❑ 335 David Vaughn RC	.15	.07
❑ 336 Cory Alexander RC	.15	.07
❑ 337 Jason Caffey RC	.20	.09
❑ 338 Frankie King RC	.15	.07
❑ 339 Travis Best RC	.20	.09
❑ 340 Greg Ostertag RC	.15	.07
❑ 341 Ed O'Bannon RC	.15	.07
❑ 342 Kurt Thomas RC	.20	.09
❑ 343 Kevin Garnett RC	5.00	2.20
❑ 344 Bryant Reeves RC	.40	.18
❑ 345 Corliss Williamson RC	.75	.35
❑ 346 Cherokee Parks RC	.15	.07
❑ 347 Junior Burrough RC	.15	.07
❑ 348 Randolph Childress RC	.15	.07
❑ 349 Lou Roe RC	.15	.07
❑ 350 Mario Bennett RC	.15	.07
❑ 351 Dikembe Mutombo XP	.15	.07
❑ 352 Larry Johnson XP	.20	.09
❑ 353 Vlade Divac XP	.15	.07
❑ 354 Karl Malone XP	.40	.18
❑ 355 John Stockton XP	.20	.09
❑ 356 Alonzo Mourning TA	.20	.09
❑ 357 Glen Rice TA	.15	.07
❑ 358 Dan Majerle TA	.15	.07
❑ 359 John Williams TA	.15	.07
❑ 360 Mark Price TA	.15	.07
❑ 361 Magic Johnson	1.25	.55

1995-96 Stadium Club Beam Team

	MINT	NRMT
COMPLETE SET (20)	80.00	36.00
COMPLETE SERIES 1 (10)	10.00	4.50
COMPLETE SERIES 2 (10)	70.00	32.00
COMMON CARD (BT1-BT10)	.75	.35
COMMON CARD (BT11-BT20)	2.00	.90
SEMISTARS SER.1	1.00	.45
SEMISTARS SER.2	2.50	1.10
UNLISTED STARS SER.1	1.50	.70
UNLISTED STARS SER.2	4.00	1.80

SER.1 STATED ODDS 1:18 HOB/RET, 1:9 JUM
SER.2 STATED ODDS 1:36 HOB, 1:144 JUM
SER.2 STATED ODDS 1:72 RETAIL

❑ BT1 David Robinson	2.50	1.10
❑ BT2 Juwan Howard	1.50	.70
❑ BT3 Mitch Richmond	1.50	.70
❑ BT4 Reggie Miller	1.50	.70
❑ BT5 Glenn Robinson	1.50	.70
❑ BT6 Shaquille O'Neal	8.00	3.60
❑ BT7 Shawn Kemp	2.50	1.10
❑ BT8 Karl Malone	2.50	1.10
❑ BT9 Jamal Mashburn	.75	.35
❑ BT10 Alonzo Mourning	1.50	.70
❑ BT11 Charles Barkley	6.00	2.70
❑ BT12 Hakeem Olajuwon	6.00	2.70
❑ BT13 Kenny Anderson	2.50	1.10
❑ BT14 Michael Jordan	50.00	22.00
❑ BT15 Dikembe Mutombo	2.50	1.10
❑ BT16 Rod Strickland	2.50	1.10
❑ BT17 Patrick Ewing	4.00	1.80
❑ BT18 Latrell Sprewell	8.00	3.60
❑ BT19 Grant Hill	20.00	9.00
❑ BT20 Cedric Ceballos	2.00	.90

1995-96 Stadium Club Draft Picks

	MINT	NRMT
COMPLETE SET (15)	8.00	3.60
COMMON CARD	.15	.07
SEMISTARS	.25	.11
UNLISTED STARS	.40	.18

RANDOM INSERTS IN ALL SER.1 PACKS
SKIP-NUMBERED SET

❑ 2 Antonio McDyess	2.00	.90
❑ 3 Jerry Stackhouse	1.25	.55
❑ 4 Rasheed Wallace	1.50	.70
❑ 5 Kevin Garnett	5.00	2.20
❑ 6 Bryant Reeves	.40	.18
❑ 8 Shawn Respert	.15	.07
❑ 9 Ed O'Bannon	.15	.07
❑ 11 Gary Trent	.15	.07
❑ 12 Cherokee Parks	.15	.07
❑ 15 Brent Barry	.40	.18
❑ 16 Alan Henderson	.25	.11
❑ 17 Bob Sura	.25	.11
❑ 18 Theo Ratliff	.40	.18
❑ 19 Randolph Childress	.15	.07
❑ 22 George Zidek	.15	.07

1995-96 Stadium Club Nemeses

	MINT	NRMT
COMPLETE SET (10)	80.00	36.00
COMMON CARD (N1-N10)	1.50	.70

SER.1 STATED ODDS 1:18 HOB/RET, 1:9 JUM

❑ N1 Hakeem Olajuwon David Robinson	8.00	3.60
❑ N2 Patrick Ewing Rik Smits	1.50	.70
❑ N3 John Stockton Kevin Johnson	1.50	.70
❑ N4 Shaquille O'Neal Alonzo Mourning	12.00	5.50
❑ N5 Charles Barkley Karl Malone	8.00	3.60
❑ N6 Scottie Pippen Grant Hill	20.00	9.00
❑ N7 Anfernee Hardaway Kenny Anderson	10.00	4.50
❑ N8 Reggie Miller John Starks	1.50	.70
❑ N9 Toni Kukoc Dino Radja	3.00	1.35
❑ N10 Michael Jordan Joe Dumars	30.00	13.50

1995-96 Stadium Club Power Zone

	MINT	NRMT
COMPLETE SET (12)	40.00	18.00
COMPLETE SERIES 1 (6)	20.00	9.00
COMPLETE SERIES 2 (6)	25.00	11.00
COMMON CARD (PZ1-PZ6)	1.50	.70
COMMON CARD (PZ7-PZ12)	4.00	1.80
SEMISTARS SER.1	2.00	.90
UNLISTED STARS SER.1	3.00	1.35

SER.1 STATED ODDS 1:36 H/R, 1:18 JUM
SER.2 STATED ODDS 1:48 HOB/JUM/RET

❑ PZ1 Shaquille O'Neal	15.00	6.75
❑ PZ2 Charles Barkley	5.00	2.20
❑ PZ3 Patrick Ewing	3.00	1.35
❑ PZ4 Karl Malone	5.00	2.20
❑ PZ5 Larry Johnson	2.00	.90
❑ PZ6 Derrick Coleman	1.50	.70
❑ PZ7 Hakeem Olajuwon	6.00	2.70

❑ PZ8 David Robinson	6.00	2.70
❑ PZ9 Shawn Kemp	6.00	2.70
❑ PZ10 Dennis Rodman	8.00	3.60
❑ PZ11 Alonzo Mourning	4.00	1.80
❑ PZ12 Vin Baker	3.00	1.35

1995-96 Stadium Club Reign Men

	MINT	NRMT
COMPLETE SET (10)	80.00	36.00
COMMON CARD (RM1-RM10)	2.00	.90
SEMISTARS	2.50	1.10

SER.2 STATED ODDS 1:48 HOB, 1:96 JUM
SER.2 STATED ODDS 1:24 RETAIL

❑ RM1 Shawn Kemp	6.00	2.70
❑ RM2 Michael Jordan	50.00	22.00
❑ RM3 Larry Johnson	2.50	1.10
❑ RM4 Grant Hill	20.00	9.00
❑ RM5 Isaiah Rider	2.50	1.10
❑ RM6 Sean Elliott	2.00	.90
❑ RM7 Scottie Pippen	12.00	5.50
❑ RM8 Robert Horry	2.00	.90
❑ RM9 Kendall Gill	2.50	1.10
❑ RM10 Jerry Stackhouse	6.00	2.70

1995-96 Stadium Club Spike Says

	MINT	NRMT
COMPLETE SET (10)	20.00	9.00
COMMON CARD (SS1-SS10)	.60	.25
SEMISTARS	.75	.35
UNLISTED STARS	1.25	.55

SER.2 STATED ODDS 1:24 HOB, 1:12 RET

❑ SS1 Michael Jordan	15.00	6.75
❑ SS2 Alonzo Mourning	1.25	.55
❑ SS3 Reggie Miller	1.25	.55
❑ SS4 Patrick Ewing	1.25	.55
❑ SS5 Charles Barkley	2.00	.90
❑ SS6 Kenny Anderson	.75	.35
❑ SS7 Scottie Pippen	4.00	1.80
❑ SS8 Jerry Stackhouse	2.00	.90
❑ SS9 Shaquille O'Neal	6.00	2.70
❑ SS10 John Starks	.60	.25

1995-96 Stadium Club Warp Speed

	MINT	NRMT
COMPLETE SET (12)	90.00	40.00
COMPLETE SERIES 1 (6)	60.00	27.00
COMPLETE SERIES 2 (6)	30.00	13.50
COMMON CARD (WS1-WS12)	2.00	.90
SEMISTARS	4.00	1.80

SER.1 STATED ODDS 1:36 H/R, 1:18 JUM
SER.2 STATED ODDS 1:48 H/R, 1:48 JUM

❑ WS1 Michael Jordan	50.00	22.00
❑ WS2 Kevin Johnson	4.00	1.80
❑ WS3 Gary Payton	6.00	2.70
❑ WS4 Anfernee Hardaway	12.00	5.50
❑ WS5 Mookie Blaylock	2.00	.90
❑ WS6 Tim Hardaway	4.00	1.80
❑ WS7 Scottie Pippen	12.00	5.50
❑ WS8 Jason Kidd	12.00	5.50
❑ WS9 Grant Hill	20.00	9.00
❑ WS10 Nick Van Exel	4.00	1.80
❑ WS11 Kenny Anderson	2.00	.90
❑ WS12 Latrell Sprewell	8.00	3.60

1995-96 Stadium Club Wizards

	MINT	NRMT
COMPLETE SET (10)	30.00	13.50
COMMON CARD (W1-W10)	1.50	.70
SEMISTARS	2.50	1.10
UNLISTED STARS	4.00	1.80

SER.1 STATED ODDS 1:24 HOB, 1:9 JUM

❑ W1 Nick Van Exel	2.50	1.10
❑ W2 Tim Hardaway	4.00	1.80
❑ W3 Mookie Blaylock	1.50	.70
❑ W4 Gary Payton	6.00	2.70
❑ W5 Jason Kidd	12.00	5.50
❑ W6 Kenny Anderson	2.50	1.10
❑ W7 John Stockton	4.00	1.80
❑ W8 Kevin Johnson	2.50	1.10
❑ W9 Muggsy Bogues	1.50	.70
❑ W10 Anfernee Hardaway	12.00	5.50

1995-96 Stadium Club X-2

	MINT	NRMT
COMPLETE SET (10)	25.00	11.00
COMMON CARD (X1-X10)	1.00	.45
SEMISTARS	1.50	.70
UNLISTED STARS	2.50	1.10

SER.2 STATED ODDS 1:24 HOB, 1:96 JUM
SER.2 STATED ODDS 1:48 RETAIL

❑ X1 Hakeem Olajuwon	4.00	1.80
❑ X2 Shaquille O'Neal	12.00	5.50
❑ X3 David Robinson	4.00	1.80
❑ X4 Patrick Ewing	2.50	1.10
❑ X5 Charles Barkley	4.00	1.80
❑ X6 Karl Malone	4.00	1.80
❑ X7 Derrick Coleman	1.50	.70
❑ X8 Shawn Kemp	3.00	1.35
❑ X9 Vin Baker	2.50	1.10
❑ X10 Vlade Divac	1.00	.45

1996-97 Stadium Club

	MINT	NRMT
COMPLETE SET (180)	25.00	11.00
COMPLETE SERIES 1 (90)	10.00	4.50
COMPLETE SERIES 2 (90)	15.00	6.75
COMMON CARD (1-180)	.15	.07
CL (NNO)	.05	.02
SEMISTARS	.20	.09
UNLISTED STARS	.40	.18

❑ 1 Scottie Pippen	1.25	.55
❑ 2 Dale Davis	.15	.07
❑ 3 Horace Grant	.20	.09
❑ 4 Gheorghe Muresan	.15	.07
❑ 5 Elliot Perry	.15	.07
❑ 6 Carlos Rogers	.15	.07
❑ 7 Glenn Robinson	.40	.18
❑ 8 Avery Johnson	.15	.07
❑ 9 Dee Brown	.15	.07
❑ 10 Grant Hill	2.00	.90
❑ 11 Tyus Edney	.15	.07
❑ 12 Patrick Ewing	.40	.18
❑ 13 Jason Kidd	1.25	.55
❑ 14 Clifford Robinson	.15	.07
❑ 15 Robert Horry	.15	.07
❑ 16 Dell Curry	.15	.07
❑ 17 Terry Porter	.15	.07

❑ 18 Shaquille O'Neal 2.00 .90
❑ 19 Bryant Stith .15 .07
❑ 20 Shawn Kemp .60 .25
❑ 21 Kurt Thomas .15 .07
❑ 22 Pooh Richardson .15 .07
❑ 23 Bob Sura .15 .07
❑ 24 Olden Polynice .15 .07
❑ 25 Lawrence Moten .15 .07
❑ 26 Kendall Gill .20 .09
❑ 27 Cedric Ceballos .15 .07
❑ 28 Latrell Sprewell .75 .35
❑ 29 Christian Laettner .20 .09
❑ 30 Jamal Mashburn .20 .09
❑ 31 Jerry Stackhouse .40 .18
❑ 32 John Stockton .40 .18
❑ 33 Arvydas Sabonis .20 .09
❑ 34 Detlef Schrempf .20 .09
❑ 35 Toni Kukoc .50 .23
❑ 36 Sasha Danilovic .15 .07
❑ 37 Dana Barros .15 .07
❑ 38 Loy Vaught .15 .07
❑ 39 John Starks .15 .07
❑ 40 Marty Conlon .15 .07
❑ 41 Antonio McDyess .60 .25
❑ 42 Michael Finley .50 .23
❑ 43 Tom Gugliotta .20 .09
❑ 44 Terrell Brandon .20 .09
❑ 45 Derrick McKey .15 .07
❑ 46 Damon Stoudamire .60 .25
❑ 47 Elden Campbell .15 .07
❑ 48 Luc Longley .15 .07
❑ 49 B.J. Armstrong .15 .07
❑ 50 Lindsey Hunter .15 .07
❑ 51 Glen Rice .20 .09
❑ 52 Shawn Respert .15 .07
❑ 53 Cory Alexander .15 .07
❑ 54 Tim Legler .15 .07
❑ 55 Bryant Reeves .15 .07
❑ 56 Anfernee Hardaway 1.25 .55
❑ 57 Charles Barkley .60 .25
❑ 58 Mookie Blaylock .15 .07
❑ 59 Kevin Garnett 2.50 1.10
❑ 60 Hersey Hawkins .20 .09
❑ 61 Ed O'Bannon .15 .07
❑ 62 George Zidek .15 .07
❑ 63 Mitch Richmond .40 .18
❑ 64 Derrick Coleman .20 .09
❑ 65 Chris Webber 1.25 .55
❑ 66 Bobby Phills .15 .07
❑ 67 Rik Smits .15 .07
❑ 68 Jeff Hornacek .20 .09
❑ 69 Sam Cassell .20 .09
❑ 70 Gary Trent .15 .07
❑ 71 LaPhonso Ellis .15 .07
❑ 72 Oliver Miller .15 .07
❑ 73 Rex Chapman .15 .07
❑ 74 Jim Jackson .15 .07
❑ 75 Eric Williams .15 .07
❑ 76 Brent Barry .15 .07
❑ 77 Nick Anderson .15 .07
❑ 78 David Robinson .60 .25
❑ 79 Calbert Cheaney .15 .07
❑ 80 Joe Smith .40 .18
❑ 81 Steve Kerr .15 .07
❑ 82 Wayman Tisdale .15 .07
❑ 83 Steve Smith .20 .09
❑ 84 Clyde Drexler .40 .18
❑ 85 Theo Ratliff .20 .09
❑ 86 Charlie Ward .15 .07
❑ 87 Karl Malone .60 .25
❑ 88 Clarence Weatherspoon .15 .07
❑ 89 Greg Anthony .15 .07
❑ 90 Shawn Bradley .15 .07
❑ 91 Otis Thorpe .15 .07
❑ 92 Larry Johnson .20 .09
❑ 93 Sharone Wright .15 .07
❑ 94 Charles Barkley .60 .25
❑ 95 Wesley Person .15 .07
❑ 96 Dikembe Mutombo .20 .09
❑ 97 Eddie Jones .75 .35
❑ 98 Juwan Howard .20 .09
❑ 99 Grant Hill 2.00 .90
❑ 100 Chris Carr RC .15 .07
❑ 101 Michael Jordan 5.00 2.20
❑ 102 Vincent Askew .15 .07
❑ 103 Gary Payton .60 .25
❑ 104 Chris Mills .15 .07
❑ 105 Reggie Miller .40 .18
❑ 106 Don MacLean .15 .07
❑ 107 John Stockton .40 .18
❑ 108 Mahmoud Abdul-Rauf .15 .07
❑ 109 P.J. Brown .15 .07
❑ 110 Kenny Anderson .20 .09
❑ 111 Mark Price .15 .07
❑ 112 Derek Harper .15 .07
❑ 113 Dino Radja .15 .07
❑ 114 Terry Dehere .15 .07
❑ 115 Mark Jackson .15 .07
❑ 116 Vin Baker .20 .09
❑ 117 Dennis Scott .15 .07
❑ 118 Sean Elliott .15 .07
❑ 119 Lee Mayberry .15 .07
❑ 120 Vlade Divac .15 .07
❑ 121 Joe Dumars .40 .18
❑ 122 Isaiah Rider .20 .09
❑ 123 Hakeem Olajuwon .60 .25
❑ 124 Robert Pack .15 .07
❑ 125 Jalen Rose .40 .18
❑ 126 Allan Houston .40 .18
❑ 127 Nate McMillan .15 .07
❑ 128 Rod Strickland .20 .09
❑ 129 Sean Rooks .15 .07
❑ 130 Dennis Rodman .75 .35
❑ 131 Alonzo Mourning .40 .18
❑ 132 Danny Ferry .15 .07
❑ 133 Sam Cassell .20 .09
❑ 134 Brian Grant .40 .18
❑ 135 Karl Malone .60 .25
❑ 136 Chris Gatling .15 .07
❑ 137 Tom Gugliotta .20 .09
❑ 138 Hubert Davis .15 .07
❑ 139 Lucious Harris .15 .07
❑ 140 Rony Seikaly .15 .07
❑ 141 Alan Henderson .15 .07
❑ 142 Mario Elie .15 .07
❑ 143 Vinny Del Negro .15 .07
❑ 144 Harvey Grant .15 .07
❑ 145 Muggsy Bogues .15 .07
❑ 146 Rodney Rogers .15 .07
❑ 147 Kevin Johnson .20 .09
❑ 148 Anthony Peeler .15 .07
❑ 149 Jon Koncak .15 .07
❑ 150 Ricky Pierce .15 .07
❑ 151 Todd Day .15 .07
❑ 152 Tyrone Hill .15 .07
❑ 153 Nick Van Exel .20 .09
❑ 154 Rasheed Wallace .50 .23
❑ 155 Jayson Williams .20 .09
❑ 156 Sherman Douglas .15 .07
❑ 157 Bryon Russell .15 .07
❑ 158 Ron Harper .20 .09
❑ 159 Stacey Augmon .15 .07
❑ 160 Antonio Davis .15 .07
❑ 161 Tim Hardaway .40 .18
❑ 162 Charles Oakley .15 .07
❑ 163 Billy Owens .15 .07
❑ 164 Sam Perkins .20 .09
❑ 165 Chris Whitney .15 .07
❑ 166 Matt Geiger .15 .07
❑ 167 Andrew Lang .15 .07
❑ 168 Danny Manning .20 .09
❑ 169 Doug Christie .15 .07
❑ 170 George Lynch .15 .07
❑ 171 Malik Sealy .15 .07
❑ 172 Eric Montross .15 .07
❑ 173 Rick Fox .15 .07
❑ 174 Chris Mullin .40 .18
❑ 175 Ken Norman .15 .07
❑ 176 Sarunas Marciulionis .15 .07
❑ 177 Kevin Garnett 2.50 1.10
❑ 178 Brian Shaw .15 .07
❑ 179 Will Perdue .15 .07
❑ 180 Scott Williams .15 .07

1996-97 Stadium Club Matrix

	MINT	NRMT
COMPLETE SET (90)	250.00	110.00
COMMON CARD (1-90)	2.00	.90

*STARS: 6X TO 12X BASE CARD HI
SER.1 STATED ODDS 1:12 H, 1:10 R

1996-97 Stadium Club Class Acts

	MINT	NRMT
COMPLETE SET (10)	60.00	27.00
COMMON CARD (CA1-CA10)	3.00	1.35

SER.2 STATED ODDS 1:24 HOBBY/RETAIL

COMP.REF.SET (10)	150.00	70.00
COMMON REF. (CA1-CA10)	8.00	3.60

*REF: 1X TO 2.5X HI COLUMN
REF: SER.2 STATED ODDS 1:96 H/R

COMP.ATO.REF.SET (10)	400.00	180.00
COMMON ATO. (CA1-CA10)	15.00	6.75

*ATO.REF: 2X TO 5X HI
ATO.REF: SER.2 STATED ODDS 1:192 H/R

❑ CA1 Michael Jordan / Jerry Stackhouse 20.00 9.00
❑ CA2 Patrick Ewing / Alonzo Mourning 3.00 1.35
❑ CA3 Gary Payton / Brent Barry 3.00 1.35
❑ CA4 Chris Webber / Juwan Howard 5.00 2.20
❑ CA5 Christian Laettner / Grant Hill 8.00 3.60
❑ CA6 Shareef Abdur-Rahim / Jason Kidd 10.00 4.50
❑ CA7 Clyde Drexler / Hakeem Olajuwon 4.00 1.80
❑ CA8 Stephon Marbury / Kenny Anderson 8.00 3.60
❑ CA9 Anfernee Hardaway / Lorenzen Wright 5.00 2.20
❑ CA10 Allen Iverson / Dikembe Mutombo 10.00 4.50

1996-97 Stadium Club Finest Reprints

	MINT	NRMT
COMPLETE SERIES 1 (25)	100.00	45.00
COMMON CARD (1-50)	3.00	1.35

SER.1 STATED ODDS 1:24 HOB, 1:20 RET

COMP.REF.SER.1 (25)	350.00	160.00
COMMON REFRACTOR (1-50)	6.00	2.70

*REF: 1.5X TO 3X HI COLUMN
REF: SER.1 STATED ODDS 1:36 HOB, 1:80 RET

SKIP-NUMBERED SET
SERIES 2 SET LISTED UNDER TOPPS

		MINT	NRMT
❑ 2	Nate Archibald	3.00	1.35
❑ 4	Charles Barkley	8.00	3.60
❑ 5	Rick Barry	3.00	1.35
❑ 6	Elgin Baylor	3.00	1.35
❑ 7	Dave Bing	3.00	1.35
❑ 8	Larry Bird Julius Erving Magic Johnson	15.00	6.75
❑ 10	Bob Cousy	6.00	2.70
❑ 12	Billy Cunningham	3.00	1.35
❑ 13	Dave DeBusschere	3.00	1.35
❑ 15	Julius Erving	6.00	2.70
❑ 17	Walt Frazier	3.00	1.35
❑ 18	George Gervin	3.00	1.35
❑ 19	Hal Greer	3.00	1.35
❑ 24	Michael Jordan	40.00	18.00
❑ 26	Karl Malone	6.00	2.70
❑ 28	Pete Maravich	4.00	1.80
❑ 29	Kevin McHale	3.00	1.35
❑ 34	Robert Parish	3.00	1.35
❑ 35	Bob Pettit	3.00	1.35
❑ 36	Scottie Pippen	8.00	3.60
❑ 41	Dolph Schayes	3.00	1.35
❑ 44	Isiah Thomas	3.00	1.35
❑ 48	Jerry West	6.00	2.70
❑ 49	Lenny Wilkens UER	3.00	1.35
❑ 50	James Worthy	3.00	1.35

1996-97 Stadium Club Fusion

	MINT	NRMT
COMPLETE SET (32)	140.00	65.00
COMPLETE SERIES 1 (16)	100.00	45.00
COMPLETE SERIES 2 (16)	40.00	18.00
COMMON CARD (F1-F32)	1.25	.55
SEMISTARS	2.00	.90
UNLISTED STARS	3.00	1.35

SER.1/2 STATED ODDS 1:24 HOBBY

		MINT	NRMT
❑ F1	Michael Jordan	40.00	18.00
❑ F2	Chris Webber	10.00	4.50
❑ F3	Glenn Robinson	3.00	1.35
❑ F4	Glen Rice	2.00	.90
❑ F5	Gary Payton	5.00	2.20
❑ F6	Rik Smits	1.25	.55
❑ F7	Grant Hill	15.00	6.75
❑ F8	Horace Grant	2.00	.90
❑ F9	Scottie Pippen	10.00	4.50
❑ F10	Gheorghe Muresan	1.25	.55
❑ F11	Vin Baker	2.00	.90
❑ F12	Dell Curry	1.25	.55
❑ F13	Shawn Kemp	5.00	2.20
❑ F14	Reggie Miller	3.00	1.35
❑ F15	Joe Dumars	3.00	1.35
❑ F16	Anfernee Hardaway	10.00	4.50
❑ F17	Charles Barkley	5.00	2.20
❑ F18	Juwan Howard	2.00	.90
❑ F19	Patrick Ewing	3.00	1.35
❑ F20	John Stockton	3.00	1.35
❑ F21	David Robinson	5.00	2.20
❑ F22	Cedric Ceballos	1.25	.55
❑ F23	Alonzo Mourning	3.00	1.35
❑ F24	Mookie Blaylock	1.25	.55
❑ F25	Clyde Drexler	3.00	1.35
❑ F26	Rod Strickland	2.00	.90
❑ F27	Larry Johnson	2.00	.90
❑ F28	Karl Malone	5.00	2.20
❑ F29	Sean Elliott	1.25	.55
❑ F30	Shaquille O'Neal	15.00	6.75
❑ F31	Tim Hardaway	3.00	1.35
❑ F32	Dikembe Mutombo	2.00	.90

1996-97 Stadium Club Gallery Player's Private Issue

	MINT	NRMT
COMPLETE SET (18)	600.00	275.00
COMMON CARD (1-18)	8.00	3.60
SEMISTARS	10.00	4.50
UNLISTED STARS	15.00	6.75

SER.2 STATED ODDS 1:96 HOBBY

		MINT	NRMT
❑ 1	Shaquille O'Neal	80.00	36.00
❑ 2	Shawn Kemp	25.00	11.00
❑ 3	Reggie Miller	15.00	6.75
❑ 4	Mitch Richmond	15.00	6.75
❑ 5	Grant Hill	80.00	36.00
❑ 6	Magic Johnson	40.00	18.00
❑ 7	Vin Baker	10.00	4.50
❑ 8	Charles Barkley	25.00	11.00
❑ 9	Hakeem Olajuwon	25.00	11.00
❑ 10	Michael Jordan	250.00	110.00
❑ 11	Patrick Ewing	15.00	6.75
❑ 12	David Robinson	25.00	11.00
❑ 13	Alonzo Mourning	15.00	6.75
❑ 14	Karl Malone	25.00	11.00
❑ 15	Chris Webber	50.00	22.00
❑ 16	Dikembe Mutombo	8.00	3.60
❑ 17	Larry Johnson	10.00	4.50
❑ 18	Jamal Mashburn	10.00	4.50

1996-97 Stadium Club Golden Moments

	MINT	NRMT
COMPLETE SET (5)	5.00	2.20
COMMON CARD (GM1-GM5)	.15	.07
SEMISTARS	.20	.09
UNLISTED STARS	.40	.18

RANDOM INSERTS IN ALL SER.1 PACKS

		MINT	NRMT
❑ GM1	Robert Parish	.20	.09
❑ GM2	John Stockton	.40	.18
❑ GM3	Michael Jordan Dennis Rodman	4.00	1.80
❑ GM4	Dennis Scott	.15	.07
❑ GM5	Hakeem Olajuwon	.60	.25

1996-97 Stadium Club High Risers

	MINT	NRMT
COMPLETE SET (15)	125.00	55.00
COMMON CARD (HR1-HR15)	1.50	.70
UNLISTED STARS	3.00	1.35

SER.2 STATED ODDS 1:36 HOBBY/RETAIL

		MINT	NRMT
❑ HR1	Scottie Pippen	10.00	4.50
❑ HR2	Anfernee Hardaway	10.00	4.50
❑ HR3	Vin Baker	1.50	.70
❑ HR4	Brent Barry	1.50	.70
❑ HR5	Clyde Drexler	3.00	1.35
❑ HR6	Kevin Garnett	20.00	9.00
❑ HR7	Grant Hill	15.00	6.75
❑ HR8	Michael Finley	4.00	1.80
❑ HR9	Jerry Stackhouse	3.00	1.35
❑ HR10	Isaiah Rider	1.50	.70
❑ HR11	Shaquille O'Neal	15.00	6.75
❑ HR12	Antonio McDyess	5.00	2.20
❑ HR13	Shawn Kemp	5.00	2.20
❑ HR14	Michael Jordan	40.00	18.00
❑ HR15	Juwan Howard	1.50	.70

1996-97 Stadium Club Mega Heroes

	MINT	NRMT
COMPLETE SET (9)	12.00	5.50
COMMON CARD (MH1-MH9)	.75	.35
UNLISTED STARS	1.50	.70

SER.2 STATED ODDS 1:20 RETAIL

		MINT	NRMT
❑ MH1	Dennis Rodman	3.00	1.35
❑ MH2	David Robinson	2.50	1.10
❑ MH3	Karl Malone	2.50	1.10
❑ MH4	Clyde Drexler	1.50	.70
❑ MH5	Anfernee Hardaway	5.00	2.20
❑ MH6	Hakeem Olajuwon	2.50	1.10
❑ MH7	Charles Oakley	.75	.35
❑ MH8	Joe Smith	1.50	.70
❑ MH9	Glenn Robinson	1.50	.70

1996-97 Stadium Club Rookie Showcase

	MINT	NRMT
COMPLETE SET (25)	80.00	36.00
COMMON CARD (RS1-RS25)	1.00	.45
SEMISTARS	2.00	.90
UNLISTED STARS	3.00	1.35

SER.2 STATED ODDS 1:12 HOBBY/RETAIL

	MINT	NRMT
❑ RS1 Marcus Camby	5.00	2.20
❑ RS2 Shareef Abdur-Rahim	10.00	4.50
❑ RS3 Stephon Marbury	10.00	4.50
❑ RS4 Ray Allen	6.00	2.70
❑ RS5 Antoine Walker	6.00	2.70
❑ RS6 Lorenzen Wright	1.00	.45
❑ RS7 Kerry Kittles	3.00	1.35
❑ RS8 Samaki Walker	1.00	.45
❑ RS9 Erick Dampier	1.00	.45
❑ RS10 Todd Fuller	1.00	.45
❑ RS11 Kobe Bryant	30.00	13.50
❑ RS12 Steve Nash	1.00	.45
❑ RS13 Tony Delk	1.00	.45
❑ RS14 Jermaine O'Neal	3.00	1.35
❑ RS15 John Wallace	2.00	.90
❑ RS16 Walter McCarty	1.00	.45
❑ RS17 Dontae' Jones	1.00	.45
❑ RS18 Roy Rogers	1.00	.45
❑ RS19 Derek Fisher	3.00	1.35
❑ RS20 Martin Muursepp	1.00	.45
❑ RS21 Jerome Williams	3.00	1.35
❑ RS22 Brian Evans	1.00	.45
❑ RS23 Priest Lauderdale	1.00	.45
❑ RS24 Travis Knight	1.00	.45
❑ RS25 Allen Iverson	15.00	6.75

1996-97 Stadium Club Rookies 1

	MINT	NRMT
COMPLETE SET (25)	15.00	6.75
COMMON CARD (1-25)	.15	.07
SEMISTARS	.20	.09
UNLISTED STARS	.40	.18

RANDOM INSERTS IN ALL SER.1 PACKS

	MINT	NRMT
❑ R1 Allen Iverson	4.00	1.80
❑ R2 Marcus Camby	1.25	.55
❑ R3 Shareef Abdur-Rahim	2.50	1.10
❑ R4 Stephon Marbury	2.50	1.10
❑ R5 Ray Allen	1.50	.70
❑ R6 Antoine Walker	1.50	.70
❑ R7 Lorenzen Wright	.15	.07
❑ R8 Kerry Kittles	.75	.35
❑ R9 Samaki Walker	.15	.07
❑ R10 Erick Dampier	.20	.09
❑ R11 Todd Fuller	.15	.07
❑ R12 Kobe Bryant	10.00	4.50
❑ R13 Steve Nash	.20	.09
❑ R14 Tony Delk	.20	.09
❑ R15 Jermaine O'Neal	.75	.35
❑ R16 John Wallace	.40	.18
❑ R17 Walter McCarty	.15	.07
❑ R18 Dontae Jones	.15	.07
❑ R19 Roy Rogers	.15	.07
❑ R20 Derek Fisher	.60	.25
❑ R21 Martin Muursepp	.15	.07
❑ R22 Jerome Williams	.60	.25
❑ R23 Brian Evans	.15	.07
❑ R24 Priest Lauderdale	.15	.07
❑ R25 Travis Knight	.15	.07

1996-97 Stadium Club Rookies 2

	MINT	NRMT
COMPLETE SET (20)	15.00	6.75
COMMON CARD (R1-R20)	.15	.07
SEMISTARS	.20	.09
UNLISTED STARS	.40	.18

RANDOM INSERTS IN ALL SER.2 PACKS

	MINT	NRMT
❑ R1 Shareef Abdur-Rahim	2.50	1.10
❑ R2 Tony Delk	.20	.09
❑ R3 Priest Lauderdale	.15	.07
❑ R4 Roy Rogers	.15	.07
❑ R5 Lorenzen Wright	.15	.07
❑ R6 Stephon Marbury	2.50	1.10
❑ R7 Derek Fisher	.60	.25
❑ R8 John Wallace	.40	.18
❑ R9 Kobe Bryant	10.00	4.50
❑ R10 Kerry Kittles	.75	.35
❑ R11 Antoine Walker	1.50	.70
❑ R12 Steve Nash	.20	.09
❑ R13 Erick Dampier	.20	.09
❑ R14 Walter McCarty	.15	.07
❑ R15 Vitaly Potapenko	.15	.07
❑ R16 Allen Iverson	4.00	1.80
❑ R17 Marcus Camby	1.25	.55
❑ R18 Todd Fuller	.15	.07
❑ R19 Ray Allen	1.50	.70
❑ R20 Jermaine O'Neal	.75	.35

1996-97 Stadium Club Shining Moments

	MINT	NRMT
COMPLETE SET (15)	8.00	3.60
COMMON CARD (SM1-SM15)	.15	.07
SEMISTARS	.20	.09
UNLISTED STARS	.40	.18

RANDOM INSERTS IN ALL SER.1 PACKS

	MINT	NRMT
❑ SM1 Charles Barkley	.60	.25
❑ SM2 Michael Jordan	5.00	2.20
❑ SM3 Karl Malone	.60	.25
❑ SM4 Hakeem Olajuwon	.60	.25
❑ SM5 John Stockton	.40	.18
❑ SM6 Patrick Ewing	.40	.18
❑ SM7 Reggie Miller	.40	.18
❑ SM8 David Robinson	.60	.25
❑ SM9 Dennis Rodman	.75	.35
❑ SM10 Damon Stoudamire	.60	.25
❑ SM11 Brent Barry	.15	.07
❑ SM12 Tim Legler	.15	.07
❑ SM13 Jason Kidd	1.25	.55
❑ SM14 Terrell Brandon	.20	.09
❑ SM15 Allen Iverson	4.00	1.80

1996-97 Stadium Club Special Forces

	MINT	NRMT
COMPLETE SET (10)	50.00	22.00
COMMON CARD (SF1-SF10)	2.00	.90

SER.1 STATED ODDS 1:20 RETAIL

	MINT	NRMT
❑ SF1 Anfernee Hardaway	6.00	2.70
❑ SF2 Grant Hill	10.00	4.50
❑ SF3 Shawn Kemp	3.00	1.35
❑ SF4 Michael Jordan	25.00	11.00
❑ SF5 Shaquille O'Neal	10.00	4.50
❑ SF6 Scottie Pippen	6.00	2.70
❑ SF7 Damon Stoudamire	3.00	1.35
❑ SF8 Jerry Stackhouse	2.00	.90
❑ SF9 Gary Payton	3.00	1.35
❑ SF10 Dennis Rodman	4.00	1.80

1996-97 Stadium Club Top Crop

	MINT	NRMT
COMPLETE SET (12)	60.00	27.00
COMMON CARD (TC1-TC12)	3.00	1.35

SER.1 STATED ODDS 1:24 HOB, 1:20 RET

	MINT	NRMT
❑ TC1 Shaquille O'Neal Hakeem Olajuwon	12.00	5.50
❑ TC2 Alonzo Mourning Dikembe Mutombo	3.00	1.35
❑ TC3 Patrick Ewing David Robinson	5.00	2.20
❑ TC4 Grant Hill Sean Elliott	10.00	4.50
❑ TC5 Scottie Pippen Shawn Kemp	6.00	2.70
❑ TC6 Vin Baker	4.00	1.80

Karl Malone		
❑ TC7 Juwan Howard	4.00	1.80
Charles Barkley		
❑ TC8 Glen Rice	3.00	1.35
Clyde Drexler		
❑ TC9 Michael Jordan	30.00	13.50
Gary Payton		
❑ TC10 Terrell Brandon	3.00	1.35
John Stockton		
❑ TC11 Reggie Miller	4.00	1.80
Mitch Richmond		
❑ TC12 Anfernee Hardaway	12.00	5.50
Jason Kidd		

1996-97 Stadium Club Welcome Additions

	MINT	NRMT
COMPLETE SET (25)	3.00	1.35
COMMON CARD (WA1-WA25)	.15	.07
SEMISTARS	.20	.09
UNLISTED STARS	.40	.18
RANDOM INSERTS IN ALL SER.2 PACKS		

❑ WA1 Charles Barkley	.60	.25
❑ WA2 Armon Gilliam	.15	.07
❑ WA3 Larry Johnson	.20	.09
❑ WA4 Felton Spencer	.15	.07
❑ WA5 Isaiah Rider	.20	.09
❑ WA6 Kevin Willis	.15	.07
❑ WA7 Mahmoud Abdul-Rauf	.15	.07
❑ WA8 Chris Childs	.15	.07
❑ WA9 Robert Horry	.15	.07
❑ WA10 Dan Majerle	.20	.09
❑ WA11 Robert Pack	.15	.07
❑ WA12 Rod Strickland	.20	.09
❑ WA13 Tyrone Corbin	.15	.07
❑ WA14 Anthony Mason	.20	.09
❑ WA15 Derek Harper	.15	.07
❑ WA16 Kenny Anderson	.20	.09
❑ WA17 Hubert Davis	.15	.07
❑ WA18 Allan Houston	.40	.18
❑ WA19 Shaquille O'Neal	2.00	.90
❑ WA20 Brent Price	.15	.07
❑ WA21 Ervin Johnson	.15	.07
❑ WA22 Craig Ehlo	.15	.07
❑ WA23 Jalen Rose	.40	.18
❑ WA24 Oliver Miller	.15	.07
❑ WA25 Mark West	.15	.07

1997-98 Stadium Club

	MINT	NRMT
COMPLETE SET (240)	45.00	20.00
COMPLETE SERIES 1 (120)	25.00	11.00
COMPLETE SERIES 2 (120)	20.00	9.00
COMMON CARD (1-240)	.15	.07
SEMISTARS	.20	.09
UNLISTED STARS	.40	.18
UNPRICED PRIN.PLATES PRINT RUN TO 1		
FOUR VERSIONS OF PRIN.PLATES EXIST		
PRIN.PLATES: RANDOM INSERTS IN HTA		

❑ 1 Scottie Pippen	1.25	.55
❑ 2 Bryon Russell	.15	.07
❑ 3 Muggsy Bogues	.15	.07
❑ 4 Gary Payton	.60	.25
❑ 5 Bulls - Team of the 90s	5.00	2.20
Ron Harper		
Michael Jordan		
Scottie Pippen		
Dennis Rodman		
❑ 6 Corliss Williamson	.15	.07
❑ 7 Samaki Walker	.15	.07
❑ 8 Allan Houston	.40	.18
❑ 9 Ray Allen	.60	.25
❑ 10 Nick Van Exel	.20	.09
❑ 11 Chris Mullin	.40	.18
❑ 12 Popeye Jones	.15	.07
❑ 13 Horace Grant	.20	.09
❑ 14 Rik Smits	.15	.07
❑ 15 Wayman Tisdale	.15	.07
❑ 16 Donny Marshall	.15	.07
❑ 17 Rod Strickland	.20	.09
❑ 18 Rod Strickland	.20	.09
❑ 19 Greg Anthony	.15	.07
❑ 20 Lindsey Hunter	.15	.07
❑ 21 Glen Rice	.20	.09
❑ 22 Anthony Goldwire	.15	.07
❑ 23 Mahmoud Abdul-Rauf	.15	.07
❑ 24 Sean Elliott	.15	.07
❑ 25 Cory Alexander	.15	.07
❑ 26 Tyrone Corbin	.15	.07
❑ 27 Sam Perkins	.20	.09
❑ 28 Brian Shaw	.15	.07
❑ 29 Doug Christie	.15	.07
❑ 30 Mark Jackson	.15	.07
❑ 31 Christian Laettner	.20	.09
❑ 32 Damon Stoudamire	.50	.23
❑ 33 Eric Williams	.15	.07
❑ 34 Glenn Robinson	.20	.09
❑ 35 Brooks Thompson	.15	.07
❑ 36 Derrick Coleman	.20	.09
❑ 37 Theo Ratliff	.15	.07
❑ 38 Ron Harper	.20	.09
❑ 39 Hakeem Olajuwon	.60	.25
❑ 40 Mitch Richmond	.40	.18
❑ 41 Reggie Miller	.40	.18
❑ 42 Reggie Miller	.40	.18
❑ 43 Shaquille O'Neal	2.00	.90
❑ 44 Zydrunas Ilgauskas	.15	.07
❑ 45 Jamal Mashburn	.20	.09
❑ 46 Isaiah Rider	.20	.09
❑ 47 Tom Gugliotta	.20	.09
❑ 48 Rex Chapman	.15	.07
❑ 49 Lorenzen Wright	.15	.07
❑ 50 Pooh Richardson	.15	.07
❑ 51 Armon Gilliam	.15	.07
❑ 52 Kevin Johnson	.20	.09
❑ 53 Kerry Kittles	.40	.18
❑ 54 Kerry Kittles	.40	.18
❑ 55 Charles Oakley	.15	.07
❑ 56 Dennis Rodman	.75	.35
❑ 57 Greg Ostertag	.15	.07
❑ 58 Todd Fuller	.15	.07
❑ 59 Mark Davis	.15	.07
❑ 60 Erick Strickland RC	.20	.09
❑ 61 Clifford Robinson	.15	.07
❑ 62 Nate McMillan	.15	.07
❑ 63 Steve Kerr	.15	.07
❑ 64 Bob Sura	.15	.07
❑ 65 Danny Ferry	.15	.07
❑ 66 Loy Vaught	.15	.07
❑ 67 A.C. Green	.20	.09
❑ 68 John Stockton	.40	.18
❑ 69 Terry Mills	.15	.07
❑ 70 Voshon Lenard	.15	.07
❑ 71 Matt Maloney	.15	.07
❑ 72 Charlie Ward	.15	.07
❑ 73 Brent Barry	.15	.07
❑ 74 Chris Webber	1.25	.55
❑ 75 Stephon Marbury	1.25	.55
❑ 76 Bryant Stith	.15	.07
❑ 77 Shareef Abdur-Rahim	1.25	.55
❑ 78 Sean Rooks	.15	.07
❑ 79 Rony Seikaly	.15	.07
❑ 80 Brent Price	.15	.07
❑ 81 Wesley Person	.15	.07
❑ 82 Michael Smith	.15	.07
❑ 83 Gary Trent	.15	.07
❑ 84 Dan Majerle	.20	.09
❑ 85 Rex Walters	.15	.07
❑ 86 Clarence Weatherspoon	.15	.07
❑ 87 Patrick Ewing	.40	.18
❑ 88 B.J. Armstrong	.15	.07
❑ 89 Travis Best	.15	.07
❑ 90 Steve Smith	.20	.09
❑ 91 Vitaly Potapenko	.15	.07
❑ 92 Derek Strong	.15	.07
❑ 93 Michael Finley	.40	.18
❑ 94 Will Perdue	.15	.07
❑ 95 Antoine Walker	.75	.35
❑ 96 Chuck Person	.15	.07
❑ 97 Mookie Blaylock	.15	.07
❑ 98 Eric Snow	.15	.07
❑ 99 Tony Delk	.15	.07
❑ 100 Mario Elie	.15	.07
❑ 101 Terrell Brandon	.20	.09
❑ 102 Shawn Bradley	.15	.07
❑ 103 Latrell Sprewell	.75	.35
❑ 104 Latrell Sprewell	.75	.35
❑ 105 Tim Hardaway	.40	.18
❑ 106 Terry Porter	.15	.07
❑ 107 Darrell Armstrong	.20	.09
❑ 108 Rasheed Wallace	.40	.18
❑ 109 Vinny Del Negro	.15	.07
❑ 110 Tracy Murray	.15	.07
❑ 111 Lawrence Moten	.15	.07
❑ 112 Lamond Murray	.15	.07
❑ 113 Juwan Howard	.20	.09
❑ 114 Juwan Howard	.20	.09
❑ 115 Karl Malone	.60	.25
❑ 116 Aaron McKie	.15	.07
❑ 117 Shawn Respert	.15	.07
❑ 118 Michael Jordan	5.00	2.20
❑ 119 Shawn Kemp	.60	.25
❑ 120 Arvydas Sabonis	.20	.09
❑ 121 Tyus Edney	.15	.07
❑ 122 Bryant Reeves	.15	.07
❑ 123 Jason Kidd	1.25	.55
❑ 124 Dikembe Mutombo	.20	.09
❑ 125 Allen Iverson	2.00	.90
❑ 126 Allen Iverson	2.00	.90
❑ 127 Larry Johnson	.20	.09
❑ 128 Jerry Stackhouse	.20	.09
❑ 129 Kendall Gill	.20	.09
❑ 130 Kendall Gill	.20	.09
❑ 131 Vin Baker	.20	.09
❑ 132 Joe Dumars	.40	.18
❑ 133 Calbert Cheaney	.15	.07
❑ 134 Alonzo Mourning	.40	.18
❑ 135 Isaac Austin	.15	.07
❑ 136 Joe Smith	.20	.09
❑ 137 Elden Campbell	.15	.07

❑ 138 Kevin Garnett 2.50 1.10
❑ 139 Malik Sealy .... .15 .07
❑ 140 John Starks .... .15 .07
❑ 141 Clyde Drexler .... .40 .18
❑ 142 Matt Geiger .... .15 .07
❑ 143 Mark Price .... .15 .07
❑ 144 Buck Williams .... .15 .07
❑ 145 Grant Hill .... 2.00 .90
❑ 146 Kobe Bryant 3.00 1.35
❑ 147 Dale Ellis .... .15 .07
❑ 148 Jason Caffey .... .15 .07
❑ 149 Toni Kukoc .... .50 .23
❑ 150 Avery Johnson .... .15 .07
❑ 151 Alan Henderson .... .15 .07
❑ 152 Walt Williams .... .15 .07
❑ 153 Greg Minor .... .15 .07
❑ 154 Calbert Cheaney .... .15 .07
❑ 155 Vlade Divac .... .15 .07
❑ 156 Greg Foster .... .15 .07
❑ 157 LaPhonso Ellis .... .15 .07
❑ 158 Charles Barkley .... .60 .25
❑ 159 Antonio Davis .... .15 .07
❑ 160 Roy Rogers .... .15 .07
❑ 161 Robert Horry .... .15 .07
❑ 162 Sam Cassell .... .20 .09
❑ 163 Chris Carr .... .15 .07
❑ 164 Robert Pack .... .15 .07
❑ 165 Sam Cassell .... .20 .09
❑ 166 Rodney Rogers .... .15 .07
❑ 167 Chris Childs .... .15 .07
❑ 168 Shandon Anderson .... .15 .07
❑ 169 Kenny Anderson .... .20 .09
❑ 170 Anthony Mason .... .20 .09
❑ 171 Olden Polynice .... .15 .07
❑ 172 David Wingate .... .15 .07
❑ 173 David Robinson .... .60 .25
❑ 174 Billy Owens .... .15 .07
❑ 175 Detlef Schrempf .... .20 .09
❑ 176 Carlos Rogers .... .15 .07
❑ 177 Marcus Camby .... .50 .23
❑ 178 Dana Barros .... .15 .07
❑ 179 Shandon Anderson .... .15 .07
❑ 180 Jayson Williams .... .20 .09
❑ 181 Eldridge Recasner .... .15 .07
❑ 182 Doug West .... .15 .07
❑ 183 Kevin Willis .... .15 .07
❑ 184 Eddie Johnson .... .15 .07
❑ 185 Derek Fisher .... .15 .07
❑ 186 Eddie Jones .... .75 .35
❑ 187 Sherman Douglas .... .15 .07
❑ 188 Anthony Peeler .... .15 .07
❑ 189 Danny Manning .... .20 .09
❑ 190 Stacey Augmon .... .15 .07
❑ 191 Hersey Hawkins .... .20 .09
❑ 192 Micheal Williams .... .15 .07
❑ 193 Jeff Hornacek .... .20 .09
❑ 194 Anfernee Hardaway .... 1.25 .55
❑ 195 Harvey Grant .... .15 .07
❑ 196 Nick Anderson .... .15 .07
❑ 197 Luc Longley .... .15 .07
❑ 198 Andrew Lang .... .15 .07
❑ 199 P.J. Brown .... .15 .07
❑ 200 Cedric Ceballos .... .15 .07
❑ 201 Tim Duncan RC 5.00 2.20
❑ 202 Ervin Johnson TRAN .... .15 .07
❑ 203 Keith Van Horn RC .... 2.00 .90
❑ 204 David Wesley TRAN .... .15 .07
❑ 205 Chauncey Billups RC .... .50 .23
❑ 206 Jim Jackson TRAN .... .15 .07
❑ 207 Antonio Daniels RC .... .40 .18
❑ 208 Travis Knight TRAN .... .15 .07
❑ 209 Tony Battie RC .... .40 .18
❑ 210 Bobby Phills TRAN .... .15 .07
❑ 211 Bobby Jackson RC .... .20 .09
❑ 212 Otis Thorpe TRAN .... .15 .07
❑ 213 Tim Thomas RC .... 1.25 .55
❑ 214 Chris Mullin TRAN .... .20 .09
❑ 215 Adonal Foyle RC .... .20 .09
❑ 216 Brian Williams TRAN .... .15 .07
❑ 217 Tracy McGrady RC 4.00 1.80
❑ 218 Tyus Edney TRAN .... .15 .07
❑ 219 Danny Fortson RC .... .40 .18
❑ 220 Clifford Robinson TRAN .... .15 .07
❑ 221 Olivier Saint-Jean RC .... .15 .07
❑ 222 Vin Baker TRAN .... .15 .07
❑ 223 Austin Croshere RC .... 1.00 .45
❑ 224 John Wallace TRAN .... .15 .07
❑ 225 Derek Anderson RC .... 1.00 .45
❑ 226 Kelvin Cato RC .... .40 .18
❑ 227 Maurice Taylor RC .... .75 .35
❑ 228 Scot Pollard RC .... .20 .09
❑ 229 John Thomas RC .... .15 .07
❑ 230 Dean Garrett TRAN .... .15 .07
❑ 231 Brevin Knight RC .... .60 .25
❑ 232 Ron Mercer RC .... 1.25 .55
❑ 233 Johnny Taylor RC .... .15 .07
❑ 234 Antonio McDyess TRAN .... .40 .18
❑ 235 Ed Gray RC .... .15 .07
❑ 236 Terrell Brandon TRAN .... .15 .07
❑ 237 Anthony Parker RC .... .15 .07
❑ 238 Shawn Kemp TRAN .... .40 .18
❑ 239 Paul Grant RC .... .15 .07
❑ 240 Dennis Scott TRAN .... .15 .07

1997-98 Stadium Club First Day Issue

	MINT	NRMT
COMPLETE SET (240)	1800.00	800.00
COMPLETE SERIES 1 (120)	1000.00	450.00
COMPLETE SERIES 2 (120)	800.00	350.00
COMMON CARD (1-240)	2.00	.90

*STARS: 15X TO 30X BASE CARD HI
*RCs: 7.5X TO 15X BASE HI
SER.1/2 STATED ODDS 1:24 RETAIL
STATED PRINT RUN 200 SETS

1997-98 Stadium Club One Of A Kind

	MINT	NRMT
COMMON CARD (1-240)	10.00	4.50

*STARS: 30X TO 60X BASE CARD HI
*RCs: 15X TO 30X BASE HI
SER.1 STATED ODDS 1:86 HOBBY
SER.2 STATED ODDS 1:69 HOBBY
STATED PRINT RUN 150 SERIAL #'d SETS

❑ 5 Bulls - Team of the 90s 250.00 110.00
Ron Harper
Michael Jordan
Scottie Pippen
Dennis Rodman
❑ 118 Michael Jordan 350.00 160.00

1997-98 Stadium Club Bowman's Best Previews

	MINT	NRMT
COMPLETE SET (20)	40.00	18.00
COMPLETE SERIES 1 (10)	30.00	13.50
COMPLETE SERIES 2 (10)	8.00	3.60
COMMON CARD (BBP1-20)	.75	.35
SEMISTARS	1.00	.45
UNLISTED STARS	1.50	.70
SER.1/2 STATED ODDS 1:24 HOB/RET		
COMP.REF.SET (20)	120.00	55.00
COMP.REF.SER.1 (10)	100.00	45.00
COMP.REF.SER.2 (10)	25.00	11.00
COMMON REF.	2.00	.90
*REF: 1.25X TO 3X HI COLUMN		
REF: SER.1/2 STATED ODDS 1:96 H/R		
COMP.ATO.REF.SET (20)	200.00	90.00
COMP.ATO.REF.SER.1 (10)	150.00	70.00
COMP.ATO.REF.SER.2 (10)	40.00	18.00
COMMON ATO.REF.	4.00	1.80
*ATO.REF: 2X TO 5X HI		
ATO.REF: SER.1/2 STATED ODDS 1:192 H/R		

❑ BBP1 Allen Iverson 8.00 3.60
❑ BBP2 Gary Payton 2.50 1.10
❑ BBP3 Grant Hill 8.00 3.60
❑ BBP4 Anfernee Hardaway 5.00 2.20
❑ BBP5 Karl Malone 2.50 1.10
❑ BBP6 Glen Rice .... 1.00 .45
❑ BBP7 Antoine Walker 3.00 1.35
❑ BBP8 Alonzo Mourning .... 1.50 .70
❑ BBP9 Shareef Abdur-Rahim 5.00 2.20
❑ BBP10 Shaquille O'Neal 8.00 3.60
❑ BBP11 Maurice Taylor .... 1.50 .70
❑ BBP12 Chauncey Billups ...... 1.00 .45
❑ BBP13 Paul Grant .... .75 .35
❑ BBP14 Tony Battie .... .75 .35
❑ BBP15 Austin Croshere .... 2.00 .90
❑ BBP16 Brevin Knight .... 1.50 .70
❑ BBP17 Bobby Jackson .... .75 .35
❑ BBP18 Johnny Taylor .... .75 .35
❑ BBP19 Scot Pollard .... .75 .35
❑ BBP20 Tariq Abdul-Wahad ..... .75 .35

1997-98 Stadium Club Co-Signers

	MINT	NRMT
COMMON CARD (CO1-24)	30.00	13.50

SER.1 STATED ODDS 1:387 HOB
SER.2 STATED ODDS 1:309 HOB

- ❑ CO1 Karl Malone / Kobe Bryant 1200.00 550.00
- ❑ CO2 Juwan Howard / Hakeem Olajuwon 350.00 160.00
- ❑ CO3 John Starks / Joe Smith 250.00 110.00
- ❑ CO4 Clyde Drexler / Tim Hardaway 300.00 135.00
- ❑ CO5 Kobe Bryant / John Starks 400.00 180.00
- ❑ CO6 Hakeem Olajuwon / Clyde Drexler .. 200.00 90.00
- ❑ CO7 Tim Hardaway / Juwan Howard 120.00 55.00
- ❑ CO8 Joe Smith / Karl Malone 125.00 55.00
- ❑ CO9 Juwan Howard / Clyde Drexler 50.00 22.00
- ❑ CO10 Hakeem Olajuwon / Tim Hardaway .. 60.00 27.00
- ❑ CO11 Joe Smith / Kobe Bryant 150.00 70.00
- ❑ CO12 Karl Malone / John Starks 50.00 22.00
- ❑ CO13 Dikembe Mutombo / Chauncey Billups 150.00 70.00
- ❑ CO14 Keith Van Horn / Chris Webber 400.00 180.00
- ❑ CO15 Karl Malone / Kerry Kittles 250.00 110.00
- ❑ CO16 Ron Mercer / Antoine Walker 400.00 180.00
- ❑ CO17 Chris Webber / Karl Malone 150.00 70.00
- ❑ CO18 Antoine Walker / Dikembe Mutombo 125.00 55.00
- ❑ CO19 Kerry Kittles / Keith Van Horn 200.00 90.00
- ❑ CO20 Chauncey Billups / Ron Mercer .. 100.00 45.00
- ❑ CO21 Antoine Walker / Chauncey Billups 30.00 13.50
- ❑ CO22 Dikembe Mutombo / Ron Mercer .. 30.00 13.50
- ❑ CO23 Keith Van Horn / Karl Malone 80.00 36.00
- ❑ CO24 Chris Webber / Kerry Kittles 60.00 27.00

1997-98 Stadium Club Hardcourt Heroics

	MINT	NRMT
COMPLETE SET (10)	25.00	11.00
COMMON CARD (H1-H10)	.60	.25
UNLISTED STARS	1.00	.45

SER.1 STATED ODDS 1:12 HOB/RET

- ❑ H1 Michael Jordan 12.00 5.50
- ❑ H2 Gary Payton .... 1.50 .70
- ❑ H3 Charles Barkley .... 1.50 .70
- ❑ H4 Mitch Richmond .... 1.00 .45
- ❑ H5 Shawn Kemp .... 1.50 .70
- ❑ H6 Anfernee Hardaway 3.00 1.35
- ❑ H7 Vin Baker .... .60 .25
- ❑ H8 Shaquille O'Neal 5.00 2.20
- ❑ H9 Scottie Pippen 3.00 1.35
- ❑ H10 Grant Hill 5.00 2.20

1997-98 Stadium Club Hardwood Hopefuls

	MINT	NRMT
COMPLETE SET (10)	50.00	22.00
COMMON CARD (HH1-HH10)..	2.00	.90
SEMISTARS	2.50	1.10
UNLISTED STARS	4.00	1.80

SER.1 STATED ODDS 1:36 HOB/RET

- ❑ HH1 Brevin Knight 4.00 1.80
- ❑ HH2 Adonal Foyle .... 2.00 .90
- ❑ HH3 Keith Van Horn 10.00 4.50
- ❑ HH4 Tim Duncan 20.00 9.00
- ❑ HH5 Danny Fortson .... 2.00 .90
- ❑ HH6 Tracy McGrady 20.00 9.00
- ❑ HH7 Tony Battie .... 2.00 .90
- ❑ HH8 Chauncey Billups 2.50 1.10
- ❑ HH9 Austin Croshere 5.00 2.20
- ❑ HH10 Antonio Daniels 2.50 1.10

1997-98 Stadium Club Hoop Screams

	MINT	NRMT
COMPLETE SET (10)	30.00	13.50
COMMON CARD (HS1-HS10)	.50	.23
SEMISTARS	.60	.25
UNLISTED STARS	1.00	.45

SER.1 STATED ODDS 1:12 HOB/RET

- ❑ HS1 Shaquille O'Neal 5.00 2.20
- ❑ HS2 Cedric Ceballos .... .50 .23
- ❑ HS3 Kevin Garnett 6.00 2.70
- ❑ HS4 Shawn Kemp .... 1.50 .70
- ❑ HS5 Jerry Stackhouse .... .60 .25
- ❑ HS6 Grant Hill 5.00 2.20
- ❑ HS7 Patrick Ewing .... 1.00 .45
- ❑ HS8 Marcus Camby .... 1.25 .55
- ❑ HS9 Kobe Bryant 8.00 3.60
- ❑ HS10 Michael Jordan 12.00 5.50

1997-98 Stadium Club Never Compromise

	MINT	NRMT
COMPLETE SET (20)	150.00	70.00
COMMON CARD (NC1-NC20)..	1.50	.70
SEMISTARS	2.00	.90
UNLISTED STARS	3.00	1.35

SER.2 STATED ODDS 1:36 HOB/RET

- ❑ NC1 Michael Jordan 40.00 18.00
- ❑ NC2 Karl Malone 5.00 2.20
- ❑ NC3 Hakeem Olajuwon 5.00 2.20
- ❑ NC4 Kevin Garnett 20.00 9.00
- ❑ NC5 Dikembe Mutombo ...... 2.00 .90
- ❑ NC6 Gary Payton 5.00 2.20
- ❑ NC7 Grant Hill 15.00 6.75
- ❑ NC8 Charles Barkley 5.00 2.20
- ❑ NC9 Shaquille O'Neal 15.00 6.75
- ❑ NC10 Anfernee Hardaway 10.00 4.50
- ❑ NC11 Tim Duncan 15.00 6.75
- ❑ NC12 Keith Van Horn 8.00 3.60
- ❑ NC13 Tracy McGrady 15.00 6.75
- ❑ NC14 Tim Thomas 5.00 2.20
- ❑ NC15 Austin Croshere 4.00 1.80
- ❑ NC16 Maurice Taylor 3.00 1.35
- ❑ NC17 Chauncey Billups ...... 2.00 .90
- ❑ NC18 Adonal Foyle .... 1.50 .70
- ❑ NC19 Tony Battie .... 1.50 .70
- ❑ NC20 Bobby Jackson .... 1.50 .70

1997-98 Stadium Club Royal Court

	MINT	NRMT
COMPLETE SET (20)	60.00	27.00
COMMON CARD (RC1-RC20)	.75	.35
SEMISTARS	1.00	.45
UNLISTED STARS	1.50	.70

SER.2 STATED ODDS 1:12 HOB/RET

- ❑ RC1 Scottie Pippen 5.00 2.20
- ❑ RC2 Karl Malone 2.50 1.10
- ❑ RC3 Gary Payton 2.50 1.10
- ❑ RC4 Kobe Bryant 12.00 5.50
- ❑ RC5 Antoine Walker 3.00 1.35
- ❑ RC6 Michael Jordan 20.00 9.00
- ❑ RC7 Shaquille O'Neal 8.00 3.60
- ❑ RC8 Dikembe Mutombo ...... 1.00 .45
- ❑ RC9 Hakeem Olajuwon 2.50 1.10

	Card	Player	Mint	NrMt
❑	RC10	Grant Hill	8.00	3.60
❑	RC11	Tim Duncan	8.00	3.60
❑	RC12	Keith Van Horn	4.00	1.80
❑	RC13	Chauncey Billups	1.00	.45
❑	RC14	Antonio Daniels	1.00	.45
❑	RC15	Tony Battie	.75	.35
❑	RC16	Bobby Jackson	.75	.35
❑	RC17	Tim Thomas	2.50	1.10
❑	RC18	Adonal Foyle	.75	.35
❑	RC19	Tracy McGrady	8.00	3.60
❑	RC20	Danny Fortson	.75	.35

1997-98 Stadium Club Triumvirate

	MINT	NRMT
COMPLETE SET (48)	400.00	180.00
COMPLETE SERIES 1 (24)	150.00	70.00
COMPLETE SERIES 2 (24)	250.00	110.00
COMMON CARD (T1A-T16C)	2.00	.90
SEMISTARS	3.00	1.35
UNLISTED STARS	5.00	2.20
SER.1/2 STATED ODDS 1:48 RETAIL		
COMP.LUM.SET (48)	1200.00	550.00
COMP.LUM.SER.1 (24)	500.00	220.00
COMP.LUM.SER.2 (24)	700.00	325.00
COMMON LUM. (T1A-T16C)	6.00	2.70
*LUM.CARDS: 1.25X TO 3X HI COLUMN		
LUM: SER.1/2 STATED ODDS 1:192 RET		
COMP.ILLUM.SET (48)	2000.00	900.00
COMP.ILLUM.SER.1 (24)	800.00	350.00
COMP.ILLUM.SER.2 (24)	1200.00	550.00
COMMON ILLUM. (T1A-T16C)	10.00	4.50
*ILLUM.CARDS: 2X TO 5X HI		
ILLUM: SER.1/2 STATED ODDS 1:384 RET		

	Card	Player	Mint	NrMt
❑	T1A	Scottie Pippen	15.00	6.75
❑	T1B	Michael Jordan	60.00	27.00
❑	T1C	Dennis Rodman	10.00	4.50
❑	T2A	Ray Allen	8.00	3.60
❑	T2B	Vin Baker	3.00	1.35
❑	T2C	Glenn Robinson	3.00	1.35
❑	T3A	Juwan Howard	3.00	1.35
❑	T3B	Chris Webber	15.00	6.75
❑	T3C	Rod Strickland	3.00	1.35
❑	T4A	Christian Laettner	3.00	1.35
❑	T4B	Dikembe Mutombo	3.00	1.35
❑	T4C	Steve Smith	3.00	1.35
❑	T5A	Tom Gugliotta	3.00	1.35
❑	T5B	Kevin Garnett	30.00	13.50
❑	T5C	Stephon Marbury	15.00	6.75
❑	T6A	Charles Barkley	8.00	3.60
❑	T6B	Hakeem Olajuwon	8.00	3.60
❑	T6C	Clyde Drexler	5.00	2.20
❑	T7A	John Stockton	5.00	2.20
❑	T7B	Karl Malone	8.00	3.60
❑	T7C	Bryon Russell	2.00	.90
❑	T8A	Larry Johnson	3.00	1.35
❑	T8B	Patrick Ewing	5.00	2.20
❑	T8C	Allan Houston	5.00	2.20
❑	T9A	Tim Hardaway	5.00	2.20
❑	T9B	Michael Jordan	60.00	27.00
❑	T9C	Anfernee Hardaway	15.00	6.75
❑	T10A	Glen Rice	3.00	1.35
❑	T10B	Scottie Pippen	15.00	6.75
❑	T10C	Grant Hill	25.00	11.00
❑	T11A	Dikembe Mutombo	3.00	1.35
❑	T11B	Patrick Ewing	5.00	2.20
❑	T11C	Alonzo Mourning	5.00	2.20
❑	T12A	Ron Mercer	8.00	3.60
❑	T12B	Keith Van Horn	12.00	5.50
❑	T12C	Tracy McGrady	25.00	11.00
❑	T13A	Gary Payton	8.00	3.60
❑	T13B	John Stockton	5.00	2.20
❑	T13C	Stephon Marbury	15.00	6.75
❑	T14A	Karl Malone	8.00	3.60
❑	T14B	Charles Barkley	8.00	3.60
❑	T14C	Kevin Garnett	30.00	13.50
❑	T15A	David Robinson	8.00	3.60
❑	T15B	Hakeem Olajuwon	8.00	3.60
❑	T15C	Shaquille O'Neal	25.00	11.00
❑	T16A	Antonio Daniels	3.00	1.35
❑	T16B	Tim Duncan	25.00	11.00
❑	T16C	Adonal Foyle	2.00	.90

1998-99 Stadium Club

	MINT	NRMT
COMPLETE SET (240)	170.00	75.00
COMPLETE SERIES 1 (120)	140.00	65.00
COMP.SERIES 1 w/o RC (100)	15.00	6.75
COMPLETE SERIES 2 (120)	30.00	13.50
COMMON CARD (1-240)	.15	.07
COMMON CARD (101-120)	.75	.35
SEMISTARS	.20	.09
SEMISTARS SER.1 RC	1.00	.45
UNLISTED STARS	.40	.18
UNLISTED STARS SER.1 RC	1.50	.70
SER.1 ROOKIE REDEMPTION ODDS 1:6		
UNPRICED PRIN.PLATES PRINT RUN TO 1		
FOUR VERSIONS OF PRIN.PLATES EXIST		
PRIN.PLATES: RAND.INS.IN BOTH SERIES HTA		
SER.1 RC's AVAILABLE VIA TRADE CARDS		

	Card	Player	Mint	NrMt
❑	1	Eddie Jones	.75	.35
❑	2	Matt Geiger	.15	.07
❑	3	Ray Allen	.50	.23
❑	4	Billy Owens	.15	.07
❑	5	Larry Johnson	.20	.09
❑	6	Jerry Stackhouse	.20	.09
❑	7	Travis Best	.15	.07
❑	8	Sam Cassell	.20	.09
❑	9	Isaiah Rider	.20	.09
❑	10	Walter McCarty	.15	.07
❑	11	Hakeem Olajuwon	.60	.25
❑	12	Detlef Schrempf	.20	.09
❑	13	Chris Garner	.15	.07
❑	14	Voshon Lenard	.15	.07
❑	15	Kevin Garnett	2.50	1.10
❑	16	Doug Christie	.15	.07
❑	17	Dikembe Mutombo	.20	.09
❑	18	Terrell Brandon	.20	.09
❑	19	Brevin Knight	.15	.07
❑	20	Dan Majerle	.20	.09
❑	21	Keith Van Horn	1.00	.45
❑	22	Jim Jackson	.15	.07
❑	23	Theo Ratliff	.15	.07
❑	24	Anthony Peeler	.15	.07
❑	25	Tim Hardaway	.40	.18
❑	26	Charles Outlaw	.15	.07
❑	27	Blue Edwards	.15	.07
❑	28	Khalid Reeves	.15	.07
❑	29	David Wesley	.15	.07
❑	30	Toni Kukoc	.50	.23
❑	31	Jaren Jackson	.15	.07
❑	32	Mario Elie	.15	.07
❑	33	Nick Anderson	.15	.07
❑	34	Derek Anderson	.50	.23
❑	35	Rodney Rogers	.15	.07
❑	36	Jalen Rose	.40	.18
❑	37	Corliss Williamson	.15	.07
❑	38	Tyrone Corbin	.15	.07
❑	39	Antonio Davis	.15	.07
❑	40	Chris Mills	.15	.07
❑	41	Clarence Weatherspoon	.15	.07
❑	42	George Lynch	.15	.07
❑	43	Kelvin Cato	.15	.07
❑	44	Anthony Mason	.20	.09
❑	45	Tracy McGrady	1.50	.70
❑	46	Lamond Murray	.15	.07
❑	47	Mookie Blaylock	.15	.07
❑	48	Tracy Murray	.15	.07
❑	49	Ron Harper	.20	.09
❑	50	Tom Gugliotta	.20	.09
❑	51	Allan Houston	.40	.18
❑	52	Arvydas Sabonis	.20	.09
❑	53	Brian Williams	.15	.07
❑	54	Brian Shaw	.15	.07
❑	55	John Stockton	.40	.18
❑	56	Rick Fox	.15	.07
❑	57	Hersey Hawkins	.20	.09
❑	58	Danny Manning	.20	.09
❑	59	Chris Carr	.15	.07
❑	60	Lindsey Hunter	.15	.07
❑	61	Donyell Marshall	.15	.07
❑	62	Michael Jordan	5.00	2.20
❑	63	Mark Strickland	.15	.07
❑	64	LaPhonso Ellis	.15	.07
❑	65	Rod Strickland	.20	.09
❑	66	David Robinson	.60	.25
❑	67	Cedric Ceballos	.15	.07
❑	68	Christian Laettner	.20	.09
❑	69	Anthony Goldwire	.15	.07
❑	70	Armon Gilliam	.15	.07
❑	71	Shaquille O'Neal	2.00	.90
❑	72	Sherman Douglas	.15	.07
❑	73	Kendall Gill	.20	.09
❑	74	Charlie Ward	.15	.07
❑	75	Allen Iverson	1.50	.70
❑	76	Shawn Kemp	.60	.25
❑	77	Travis Knight	.15	.07
❑	78	Gary Payton	.60	.25
❑	79	Cedric Henderson	.15	.07
❑	80	Matt Bullard	.15	.07
❑	81	Steve Kerr	.15	.07
❑	82	Shawn Bradley	.15	.07
❑	83	Antonio McDyess	.40	.18
❑	84	Robert Horry	.15	.07
❑	85	Darrick Martin	.15	.07
❑	86	Derek Strong	.15	.07
❑	87	Shandon Anderson	.15	.07
❑	88	Lawrence Funderburke	.15	.07
❑	89	Brent Price	.15	.07
❑	90	Reggie Miller	.40	.18
❑	91	Shareef Abdur-Rahim	1.00	.45
❑	92	Jeff Hornacek	.20	.09
❑	93	Antoine Carr	.15	.07
❑	94	Greg Anthony	.15	.07
❑	95	Rex Chapman	.15	.07
❑	96	Antoine Walker	.60	.25
❑	97	Bobby Jackson	.15	.07
❑	98	Calbert Cheaney	.15	.07
❑	99	Avery Johnson	.15	.07
❑	100	Jason Kidd	1.25	.55
❑	101	Michael Olowokandi RC	2.50	1.10
❑	102	Mike Bibby RC	5.00	2.20
❑	103	Raef LaFrentz RC	3.00	1.35
❑	104	Antawn Jamison RC	8.00	3.60
❑	105	Vince Carter RC	120.00	55.00
❑	106	Robert Traylor RC	1.50	.70
❑	107	Jason Williams RC	10.00	4.50
❑	108	Larry Hughes RC	10.00	4.50
❑	109	Dirk Nowitzki RC	6.00	2.70
❑	110	Paul Pierce RC	8.00	3.60
❑	111	Bonzi Wells RC	6.00	2.70
❑	112	Michael Doleac RC	1.50	.70
❑	113	Keon Clark RC	1.50	.70
❑	114	Michael Dickerson RC	3.00	1.35
❑	115	Matt Harpring RC	1.50	.70
❑	116	Bryce Drew RC	1.50	.70
❑	117	Pat Garrity RC	1.00	.45

	Card	MINT	NRMT
❑	118 Roshown McLeod RC	.75	.35
❑	119 Ricky Davis RC	3.00	1.35
❑	120 Brian Skinner RC	1.50	.70
❑	121 Dee Brown	.15	.07
❑	122 Hubert Davis	.15	.07
❑	123 Vitaly Potapenko	.15	.07
❑	124 Ervin Johnson	.15	.07
❑	125 Chris Gatling	.15	.07
❑	126 Darrell Armstrong	.20	.09
❑	127 Glen Rice	.20	.09
❑	128 Ben Wallace	.15	.07
❑	129 Sam Mitchell	.15	.07
❑	130 Joe Dumars	.40	.18
❑	131 Terry Davis	.15	.07
❑	132 A.C. Green	.20	.09
❑	133 Alan Henderson	.15	.07
❑	134 Ron Mercer	.60	.25
❑	135 Brian Grant	.20	.09
❑	136 Chris Childs	.15	.07
❑	137 Rony Seikaly	.15	.07
❑	138 Pete Chilcutt	.15	.07
❑	139 Anfernee Hardaway	1.25	.55
❑	140 Bryon Russell	.15	.07
❑	141 Tim Thomas	.60	.25
❑	142 Erick Dampier	.15	.07
❑	143 Charles Barkley	.60	.25
❑	144 Mark Jackson	.15	.07
❑	145 Bryant Reeves	.15	.07
❑	146 Tyrone Hill	.15	.07
❑	147 Rasheed Wallace	.40	.18
❑	148 Tim Duncan	2.00	.90
❑	149 Steve Smith	.20	.09
❑	150 Alonzo Mourning	.40	.18
❑	151 Danny Fortson	.20	.09
❑	152 Aaron Williams	.15	.07
❑	153 Andrew DeClercq	.15	.07
❑	154 Elden Campbell	.15	.07
❑	155 Don Reid	.15	.07
❑	156 Rik Smits	.15	.07
❑	157 Adonal Foyle	.15	.07
❑	158 Muggsy Bogues	.15	.07
❑	159 Chris Mullin	.40	.18
❑	160 Randy Brown	.15	.07
❑	161 Kenny Anderson	.20	.09
❑	162 Tariq Abdul-Wahad	.15	.07
❑	163 P.J. Brown	.15	.07
❑	164 Jayson Williams	.20	.09
❑	165 Grant Hill	2.00	.90
❑	166 Clifford Robinson	.15	.07
❑	167 Damon Stoudamire	.40	.18
❑	168 Aaron McKie	.15	.07
❑	169 Erick Strickland	.15	.07
❑	170 Kobe Bryant	3.00	1.35
❑	171 Karl Malone	.60	.25
❑	172 Eric Piatkowski	.15	.07
❑	173 Rodrick Rhodes	.15	.07
❑	174 Sean Elliott	.15	.07
❑	175 John Wallace	.15	.07
❑	176 Derek Fisher	.20	.09
❑	177 Maurice Taylor	.40	.18
❑	178 Wesley Person	.15	.07
❑	179 Jamal Mashburn	.20	.09
❑	180 Patrick Ewing	.40	.18
❑	181 Howard Eisley	.15	.07
❑	182 Michael Finley	.40	.18
❑	183 Juwan Howard	.20	.09
❑	184 Matt Maloney	.15	.07
❑	185 Glenn Robinson	.20	.09
❑	186 Zydrunas Ilgauskas	.15	.07
❑	187 Dana Barros	.15	.07
❑	188 Stacey Augmon	.15	.07
❑	189 Bobby Phills	.15	.07
❑	190 Kerry Kittles	.20	.09
❑	191 Vin Baker	.20	.09
❑	192 Stephon Marbury	1.00	.45
❑	193 Predrag Stojakovic RC	.60	.25
❑	194 Michael Olowokandi	.60	.25
❑	195 Mike Bibby	1.25	.55
❑	196 Raef LaFrentz	.75	.35
❑	197 Antawn Jamison	2.00	.90
❑	198 Vince Carter	12.00	5.50
❑	199 Robert Traylor	.15	.07
❑	200 Jason Williams	2.50	1.10
❑	201 Larry Hughes	2.50	1.10
❑	202 Dirk Nowitzki	1.50	.70
❑	203 Paul Pierce	2.00	.90
❑	204 Bonzi Wells	1.50	.70
❑	205 Michael Doleac	.20	.09
❑	206 Keon Clark	.20	.09
❑	207 Michael Dickerson	.75	.35
❑	208 Matt Harpring	.20	.09
❑	209 Bryce Drew	.20	.09
❑	210 Pat Garrity	.15	.07
❑	211 Roshown McLeod	.15	.07
❑	212 Ricky Davis	.75	.35
❑	213 Brian Skinner	.20	.09
❑	214 Tyronn Lue RC	.20	.09
❑	215 Felipe Lopez RC	.50	.23
❑	216 Al Harrington RC	1.25	.55
❑	217 Sam Jacobson RC	.15	.07
❑	218 Vladimir Stepania RC	.15	.07
❑	219 Corey Benjamin RC	.40	.18
❑	220 Nazr Mohammed RC	.20	.09
❑	221 Tom Gugliotta TRAN	.15	.07
❑	222 Derrick Coleman TRAN	.15	.07
❑	223 Mitch Richmond TRAN	.20	.09
❑	224 John Starks TRAN	.15	.07
❑	225 Antonio McDyess TRAN	.20	.09
❑	226 Joe Smith TRAN	.15	.07
❑	227 Bobby Jackson TRAN	.15	.07
❑	228 Luc Longley TRAN	.15	.07
❑	229 Isaac Austin TRAN	.15	.07
❑	230 Chris Webber TRAN	.60	.25
❑	231 Chauncey Billups TRAN	.15	.07
❑	232 Sam Perkins TRAN	.15	.07
❑	233 Loy Vaught TRAN	.15	.07
❑	234 Antonio Daniels TRAN	.15	.07
❑	235 Brent Barry TRAN	.15	.07
❑	236 Latrell Sprewell TRAN	.40	.18
❑	237 Vlade Divac TRAN	.15	.07
❑	238 Marcus Camby TRAN	.20	.09
❑	239 Charles Oakley TRAN	.15	.07
❑	240 Scottie Pippen TRAN	.60	.25

1998-99 Stadium Club First Day Issue

	MINT	NRMT
COMMON CARD (1-240)	5.00	2.20

*STARS: 12.5X TO 30X BASE CARD HI
*SER.1 RCs: 3X TO 8X BASE HI
*SER.2 RCs: 6X TO 15X BASE HI
STATED PRINT RUN 200 SERIAL #'d SETS
SER.1/2 STATED ODDS 1:44 RETAIL

	Card	MINT	NRMT
❑	105 Vince Carter	500.00	220.00

1998-99 Stadium Club One Of A Kind

	MINT	NRMT
COMMON CARD (1-240)	8.00	3.60

*STARS: 20X TO 50X BASE CARD HI
*SER.1 RCs: 4X TO 10X BASE HI
*SER.2 RCs: 8X TO 20X BASE HI
SER.1 STATED ODDS 1:56 HOBBY
SER.2 STATED ODDS 1:55 HOBBY
STATED PRINT RUN 150 SERIAL #'d SETS

	Card	MINT	NRMT
❑	105 Vince Carter	600.00	275.00

1998-99 Stadium Club Chrome

	MINT	NRMT
COMPLETE SET (40)	75.00	34.00
COMPLETE SERIES 1 (20)	25.00	11.00
COMPLETE SERIES 2 (20)	50.00	22.00
COMMON CARD (SCC1-40)	.75	.35
UNLISTED STARS	1.25	.55
SER.1/2 STATED ODDS 1:12 HOB/RET		
COMP.REF.SET (40)	150.00	70.00
COMP.REF.SER.1 (20)	50.00	22.00
COMP.REF.SER.2 (20)	100.00	45.00
COMMON REF. (SCC1-40)	1.50	.70

*REF: .75X TO 2X HI COLUMN
REF: SER.1/2 STATED ODDS 1:48 H/R

	Card	MINT	NRMT
❑	SCC1 Alonzo Mourning	1.25	.55
❑	SCC2 Scottie Pippen	4.00	1.80
❑	SCC3 Patrick Ewing	1.25	.55
❑	SCC4 Vin Baker	.75	.35
❑	SCC5 Glenn Robinson	.75	.35
❑	SCC6 Kobe Bryant	10.00	4.50
❑	SCC7 Charles Barkley	2.00	.90
❑	SCC8 Chris Mullin	1.25	.55
❑	SCC9 Steve Smith	.75	.35
❑	SCC10 Stephon Marbury	3.00	1.35
❑	SCC11 Zydrunas Ilgauskas	.75	.35
❑	SCC12 Jayson Williams	.75	.35
❑	SCC13 Juwan Howard	.75	.35
❑	SCC14 Grant Hill	6.00	2.70
❑	SCC15 Damon Stoudamire	1.25	.55
❑	SCC16 Ron Mercer	2.00	.90
❑	SCC17 Tim Duncan	6.00	2.70
❑	SCC18 Michael Finley	1.25	.55
❑	SCC19 Glen Rice	.75	.35
❑	SCC20 Karl Malone	2.00	.90
❑	SCC21 Eddie Jones	2.50	1.10
❑	SCC22 Dikembe Mutombo	.75	.35
❑	SCC23 Keith Van Horn	3.00	1.35
❑	SCC24 Jason Kidd	4.00	1.80
❑	SCC25 Shaquille O'Neal	6.00	2.70
❑	SCC26 Kevin Garnett	8.00	3.60
❑	SCC27 Allen Iverson	5.00	2.20
❑	SCC28 Shawn Kemp	2.00	.90
❑	SCC29 Gary Payton	2.00	.90
❑	SCC30 Shareef Abdur-Rahim	3.00	1.35
❑	SCC31 Mike Bibby	3.00	1.35
❑	SCC32 Raef LaFrentz	2.00	.90
❑	SCC33 Jason Williams	6.00	2.70
❑	SCC34 Paul Pierce	5.00	2.20
❑	SCC35 Michael Doleac	.75	.35
❑	SCC36 Michael Dickerson	1.25	.55
❑	SCC37 Bryce Drew	.75	.35
❑	SCC38 Roshown McLeod	.75	.35
❑	SCC39 Felipe Lopez	.75	.35
❑	SCC40 Al Harrington	3.00	1.35

1998-99 Stadium Club Co-Signers

	MINT	NRMT
COMMON CARD (CO1-24)	30.00	13.50

SER.1 STATED OVERALL ODDS 1:209 HOB
SER.2 STATED OVERALL ODDS 1:290 HOB

	Card	MINT	NRMT
❑	CO1 Tim Duncan	1000.00	450.00

		MINT	NRMT
	Kobe Bryant		
❑ CO2	Larry Johnson .... / Damon Stoudamire	200.00	90.00
❑ CO3	Antoine Walker ...... / Jason Kidd	300.00	135.00
❑ CO4	Gary Payton............ / Shareef Abdur-Rahim	300.00	135.00
❑ CO5	Kobe Bryant............ / Larry Johnson	300.00	135.00
❑ CO6	Tim Duncan .... / Damon Stoudamire	200.00	90.00
❑ CO7	Shareef Abdur-Rahim / Antoine Walker	120.00	55.00
❑ CO8	Gary Payton............ / Jason Kidd	200.00	90.00
❑ CO9	Damon Stoudamire / Kobe Bryant	150.00	70.00
❑ CO10	Larry Johnson .... / Tim Duncan	60.00	27.00
❑ CO11	Jason Kidd.............. / Shareef Abdur-Rahim	60.00	27.00
❑ CO12	Antoine Walker ...... / Gary Payton	40.00	18.00
❑ CO13	Tim Duncan .... / Eddie Jones	400.00	180.00
❑ CO14	Jayson Williams .... / Vin Baker	120.00	55.00
❑ CO15	Eddie Jones............ / Jayson Williams	60.00	27.00
❑ CO16	Vin Baker .... / Tim Duncan	100.00	45.00
❑ CO17	Eddie Jones............ / Vin Baker	30.00	13.50
❑ CO18	Tim Duncan .... / Jayson Williams	60.00	27.00
❑ CO19	Antawn Jamison .... / Michael Olowokandi	40.00	18.00
❑ CO20	Vince Carter.......... / Mike Bibby	150.00	70.00
❑ CO21	Michael Olowokandi / Vince Carter	250.00	110.00
❑ CO22	Mike Bibby .... / Antawn Jamison	100.00	45.00
❑ CO23	Antawn Jamison .. / Vince Carter	500.00	220.00
❑ CO24	Mike Bibby.............. / Michael Olowokandi	60.00	27.00

1998-99 Stadium Club Never Compromise

	MINT	NRMT
COMPLETE SET (20)	40.00	18.00
COMPLETE SERIES 1 (10)	20.00	9.00
COMPLETE SERIES 2 (10)	20.00	9.00
COMMON CARD (NC1-20)	.75	.35
SEMISTARS..............................	1.25	.55
SER.1/2 STATED ODDS 1:12 HOB/RET		
COMP.JUMBO SET (8)	20.00	9.00
COMMON JUMBO (1-8)............	1.00	.45
*JUMBOS: .5X TO 1.25X HI COLUMN		
JUMBOS: ONE PER SERIES 1 HOBBY BOX		
NO JORDAN OR HILL IN JUMBO SET		

❑ NC1	Michael Jordan..........	10.00	4.50
❑ NC2	Kobe Bryant	6.00	2.70
❑ NC3	Vin Baker	1.25	.55
❑ NC4	Tim Duncan	4.00	1.80
❑ NC5	Eddie Jones	1.50	.70
❑ NC6	Shawn Kemp	1.25	.55
❑ NC7	Grant Hill	4.00	1.80
❑ NC8	Antoine Walker............	1.25	.55
❑ NC9	Karl Malone	1.25	.55
❑ NC10	Scottie Pippen	2.50	1.10
❑ NC11	Michael Olowokandi..	1.25	.55
❑ NC12	Mike Bibby	2.00	.90
❑ NC13	Raef LaFrentz	1.25	.55
❑ NC14	Antawn Jamison........	3.00	1.35
❑ NC15	Vince Carter............	15.00	6.75
❑ NC16	Robert Traylor	.75	.35
❑ NC17	Jason Williams..........	4.00	1.80
❑ NC18	Bryce Drew	1.25	.55
❑ NC19	Paul Pierce................	3.00	1.35
❑ NC20	Felipe Lopez	1.25	.55

1998-99 Stadium Club Prime Rookies

	MINT	NRMT
COMPLETE SET (10)	70.00	32.00
COMMON CARD (P1-P10)	2.00	.90
UNLISTED STARS....................	3.00	1.35
SER.1 STATED ODDS 1:16 HOB/RET		

❑ P1	Michael Olowokandi	3.00	1.35
❑ P2	Mike Bibby	5.00	2.20
❑ P3	Raef LaFrentz..............	3.00	1.35
❑ P4	Antawn Jamison	8.00	3.60
❑ P5	Vince Carter	40.00	18.00
❑ P6	Robert Traylor..............	2.00	.90
❑ P7	Jason Williams	10.00	4.50
❑ P8	Larry Hughes	10.00	4.50
❑ P9	Dirk Nowitzki	6.00	2.70
❑ P10	Paul Pierce	8.00	3.60

1998-99 Stadium Club Royal Court

	MINT	NRMT
COMPLETE SET (15)	50.00	22.00
COMMON CARD (RC1-15)	1.25	.55
UNLISTED STARS....................	1.50	.70
SER.2 STATED ODDS 1:16 HOB/RET		

❑ RC1	Gary Payton..............	2.00	.90
❑ RC2	Kobe Bryant..............	10.00	4.50
❑ RC3	Tim Duncan..............	6.00	2.70
❑ RC4	Scottie Pippen	4.00	1.80
❑ RC5	Allen Iverson	5.00	2.20
❑ RC6	Shaquille O'Neal	6.00	2.70
❑ RC7	Stephon Marbury	3.00	1.35
❑ RC8	Antoine Walker............	2.00	.90
❑ RC9	Michael Jordan..........	15.00	6.75
❑ RC10	Keith Van Horn..........	3.00	1.35
❑ RC11	Michael Olowokandi..	1.50	.70
❑ RC12	Mike Bibby	2.50	1.10
❑ RC13	Antawn Jamison........	4.00	1.80
❑ RC14	Robert Traylor	1.25	.55
❑ RC15	Roshown McLeod	1.25	.55

1998-99 Stadium Club Statliners

	MINT	NRMT
COMPLETE SET (20)	40.00	18.00
COMMON CARD (S1-S20)	.60	.25
UNLISTED STARS....................	1.00	.45
SER.1 STATED ODDS 1:8 HOB/RET		

❑ S1	Karl Malone....................	1.50	.70
❑ S2	Michael Jordan	12.00	5.50
❑ S3	Antoine Walker	1.50	.70
❑ S4	Tim Duncan	5.00	2.20
❑ S5	Grant Hill......................	5.00	2.20
❑ S6	Allen Iverson................	4.00	1.80
❑ S7	Kevin Garnett	6.00	2.70
❑ S8	Gary Payton	1.50	.70
❑ S9	Shareef Abdur-Rahim	2.50	1.10
❑ S10	Shawn Kemp	1.50	.70
❑ S11	Stephon Marbury	2.50	1.10
❑ S12	Vin Baker	1.00	.45
❑ S13	Ray Allen	1.25	.55
❑ S14	Glen Rice	1.00	.45
❑ S15	Dikembe Mutombo	.60	.25
❑ S16	Shaquille O'Neal..........	5.00	2.20
❑ S17	Kobe Bryant	8.00	3.60
❑ S18	Scottie Pippen..............	3.00	1.35
❑ S19	Keith Van Horn	2.50	1.10
❑ S20	David Robinson	1.50	.70

1998-99 Stadium Club Triumvirate

	MINT	NRMT
COMPLETE SET (48)	200.00	90.00
COMPLETE SERIES 1 (24)....	80.00	36.00
COMPLETE SERIES 2 (24) ..	120.00	55.00
COMMON CARD (T1A-T16C) ..	1.00	.45

SEMISTARS	1.50	.70
UNLISTED STARS	2.50	1.10

SER.1/2 STATED ODDS 1:24 HOBBY

COMP.LUM.SET (48)	400.00	180.00
COMP.LUM.SERIES 1 (24)	150.00	70.00
COMP.LUM.SERIES 2 (24)	250.00	110.00
COMMON LUM. (T1A-T16C)	2.00	.90

*LUMINESCENT: .75X TO 2X HI COLUMN
LUM: SER.1/2 STATED ODDS 1:96 HOB

COMP.ILLUM.SET (48)	800.00	350.00
COMP.ILLUM.SERIES 1 (24)	300.00	135.00
COMP.ILLUM.SERIES 2 (24)	500.00	220.00
COMMON ILLUM (T1A-T8C)	4.00	1.80

*ILLUMINATOR: 1.5X TO 4X HI
ILLUM: SER.1/2 STATED ODDS 1:192 HOB

❑ T1A Kenny Anderson	1.50	.70
❑ T1B Antoine Walker	4.00	1.80
❑ T1C Ron Mercer	4.00	1.80
❑ T2A Kobe Bryant	20.00	9.00
❑ T2B Shaquille O'Neal	12.00	5.50
❑ T2C Eddie Jones	5.00	2.20
❑ T3A Stephon Marbury	6.00	2.70
❑ T3B Kevin Garnett	15.00	6.75
❑ T3C Tom Gugliotta	1.50	.70
❑ T4A Jayson Williams	1.50	.70
❑ T4B Keith Van Horn	6.00	2.70
❑ T4C Kerry Kittles	1.50	.70
❑ T5A Kevin Johnson	1.50	.70
❑ T5B Antonio McDyess	2.50	1.10
❑ T5C Jason Kidd	8.00	3.60
❑ T6A Avery Johnson	1.00	.45
❑ T6B David Robinson	4.00	1.80
❑ T6C Tim Duncan	12.00	5.50
❑ T7A Vin Baker	1.50	.70
❑ T7B Gary Payton	4.00	1.80
❑ T7C Detlef Schrempf	1.50	.70
❑ T8A John Stockton	2.50	1.10
❑ T8B Karl Malone	4.00	1.80
❑ T8C Jeff Hornacek	1.50	.70
❑ T9A Shaquille O'Neal	12.00	5.50
❑ T9B David Robinson	4.00	1.80
❑ T9C Hakeem Olajuwon	4.00	1.80
❑ T10A Dikembe Mutombo	1.50	.70
❑ T10B Alonzo Mourning	2.50	1.10
❑ T10C Patrick Ewing	2.50	1.10
❑ T11A Tim Duncan	12.00	5.50
❑ T11B Kevin Garnett	15.00	6.75
❑ T11C Shareef Abdur-Rahim	6.00	2.70
❑ T12A Shawn Kemp	4.00	1.80
❑ T12B Grant Hill	12.00	5.50
❑ T12C Antoine Walker	4.00	1.80
❑ T13A Kobe Bryant	20.00	9.00
❑ T13B Gary Payton	4.00	1.80
❑ T13C Stephon Marbury	6.00	2.70
❑ T14A Ray Allen	3.00	1.35
❑ T14B Allen Iverson	10.00	4.50
❑ T14C Anfernee Hardaway	8.00	3.60
❑ T15A Antawn Jamison	8.00	3.60
❑ T15B Michael Olowokandi	2.50	1.10
❑ T15C Raef LaFrentz	2.50	1.10
❑ T16A Robert Traylor	1.00	.45
❑ T16B Larry Hughes	10.00	4.50
❑ T16C Vince Carter	40.00	18.00

1998-99 Stadium Club Wing Men

	MINT	NRMT
COMPLETE SET (20)	30.00	13.50
COMMON CARD (W1-W20)	.60	.25
UNLISTED STARS	1.00	.45

SER.2 STATED ODDS 1:8 HOB/RET

❑ W1 Kobe Bryant	8.00	3.60
❑ W2 Tim Duncan	5.00	2.20
❑ W3 Michael Finley	1.00	.45
❑ W4 Kevin Garnett	6.00	2.70
❑ W5 Shawn Kemp	1.50	.70
❑ W6 Grant Hill	5.00	2.20
❑ W7 Eddie Jones	2.00	.90
❑ W8 Tim Thomas	1.50	.70
❑ W9 Vin Baker	.60	.25
❑ W10 Antoine Walker	1.50	.70
❑ W11 Steve Smith	.60	.25
❑ W12 Glen Rice	.60	.25
❑ W13 Ron Mercer	1.50	.70
❑ W14 Allen Iverson	4.00	1.80
❑ W15 Ray Allen	1.25	.55
❑ W16 Glenn Robinson	.60	.25
❑ W17 Kerry Kittles	.60	.25
❑ W18 Vince Carter	12.00	5.50
❑ W19 Larry Hughes	3.00	1.35
❑ W20 Paul Pierce	2.50	1.10

1999-00 Stadium Club

	MINT	NRMT
COMPLETE SET (201)	80.00	36.00
COMPLETE SET w/o RC (175)	40.00	18.00
COMMON CARD (1-175)	.10	.05
COMMON RC (176-201)	.60	.25
SEMISTARS	.15	.07
SEMISTARS RC	.75	.35
UNLISTED STARS	.30	.14
UNLISTED STARS RC	1.00	.45

RC SUBSET STATED ODDS 1:3
UNPRICED PRIN.PLATES PRINT RUN TO 1
FOUR VERSIONS OF PRIN.PLATES EXIST
PRIN.PLATES: RAND.INS.IN HTA PACKS

❑ 1 Allen Iverson	1.25	.55
❑ 2 Chris Crawford	.10	.05
❑ 3 Chris Webber	1.00	.45
❑ 4 Antawn Jamison	.60	.25
❑ 5 Karl Malone	.50	.23
❑ 6 Sam Cassell	.15	.07
❑ 7 Kerry Kittles	.15	.07
❑ 8 Tim Thomas	.40	.18
❑ 9 Chauncey Billups	.10	.05
❑ 10 Shawn Bradley	.10	.05
❑ 11 Alan Henderson	.10	.05
❑ 12 David Wesley	.10	.05
❑ 13 Glenn Robinson	.15	.07
❑ 14 Mitch Richmond	.30	.14
❑ 15 Luc Longley	.10	.05
❑ 16 Shareef Abdur-Rahim	.60	.25
❑ 17 Christian Laettner	.15	.07
❑ 18 Anthony Mason	.15	.07
❑ 19 Randy Brown	.10	.05
❑ 20 Charles Barkley	.50	.23
❑ 21 Bob Sura	.10	.05
❑ 22 Bobby Jackson	.10	.05
❑ 23 Arvydas Sabonis	.15	.07
❑ 24 Tracy Murray	.10	.05
❑ 25 Matt Harpring	.10	.05
❑ 26 Shawn Kemp	.50	.23
❑ 27 Travis Best	.10	.05
❑ 28 Ruben Patterson	.30	.14
❑ 29 Mike Bibby	.40	.18
❑ 30 Vlade Divac	.10	.05
❑ 31 Tyrone Hill	.10	.05
❑ 32 David Robinson	.50	.23
❑ 33 Keith Van Horn	.60	.25
❑ 34 Alvin Williams	.10	.05
❑ 35 Juwan Howard	.15	.07
❑ 36 Shaquille O'Neal	1.50	.70
❑ 37 Dale Davis	.10	.05
❑ 38 Alonzo Mourning	.30	.14
❑ 39 Michael Olowokandi	.15	.07
❑ 40 Jason Caffey	.10	.05
❑ 41 Andrew DeClercq	.10	.05
❑ 42 Jud Buechler	.10	.05
❑ 43 Toni Kukoc	.40	.18
❑ 44 Dikembe Mutombo	.15	.07
❑ 45 Steve Nash	.10	.05
❑ 46 Eddie Jones	.60	.25
❑ 47 Reggie Miller	.30	.14
❑ 48 Rick Fox	.10	.05
❑ 49 Larry Hughes	.75	.35
❑ 50 Tim Duncan	1.50	.70
❑ 51 Jerome Williams	.15	.07
❑ 52 Rod Strickland	.15	.07
❑ 53 Anthony Peeler	.10	.05
❑ 54 Greg Ostertag	.10	.05
❑ 55 Patrick Ewing	.30	.14
❑ 56 Grant Hill	1.50	.70
❑ 57 Derrick Coleman	.15	.07
❑ 58 Raef LaFrentz	.30	.14
❑ 59 Mark Bryant	.10	.05
❑ 60 Rik Smits	.10	.05
❑ 61 Latrell Sprewell	.60	.25
❑ 62 John Starks	.10	.05
❑ 63 Brevin Knight	.10	.05
❑ 64 Cuttino Mobley	.30	.14
❑ 65 Clarence Weatherspoon	.10	.05
❑ 66 Marcus Camby	.30	.14
❑ 67 Stephon Marbury	.60	.25
❑ 68 Tom Gugliotta	.15	.07
❑ 69 Vince Carter	3.00	1.35
❑ 70 Vladimir Stepania	.10	.05
❑ 71 Chris Mullin	.30	.14
❑ 72 Tyrone Nesby RC	.10	.05
❑ 73 Kornel David RC	.10	.05
❑ 74 Elden Campbell	.10	.05
❑ 75 Lindsey Hunter	.10	.05
❑ 76 Chris Childs	.10	.05
❑ 77 Ervin Johnson	.10	.05
❑ 78 Rasheed Wallace	.30	.14
❑ 79 Jeff Hornacek	.15	.07
❑ 80 Matt Geiger	.10	.05
❑ 81 Antoine Walker	.40	.18
❑ 82 Jason Williams	.75	.35
❑ 83 Robert Horry	.10	.05
❑ 84 Jaren Jackson	.10	.05
❑ 85 Kendall Gill	.15	.07
❑ 86 Dan Majerle	.15	.07
❑ 87 Bobby Phills	.10	.05
❑ 88 Eric Piatkowski	.10	.05
❑ 89 Robert Traylor	.10	.05
❑ 90 Cory Carr	.10	.05

❑ 91 P.J. Brown .10 .05
❑ 92 Terrell Brandon .15 .07
❑ 93 Corliss Williamson .10 .05
❑ 94 Bryant Reeves .10 .05
❑ 95 Larry Johnson .15 .07
❑ 96 Keith Closs .10 .05
❑ 97 Gary Trent .10 .05
❑ 98 Walter McCarty .10 .05
❑ 99 Wesley Person .10 .05
❑ 100 Chris Mills .10 .05
❑ 101 Glen Rice .15 .07
❑ 102 Predrag Stojakovic .15 .07
❑ 103 Jason Kidd 1.00 .45
❑ 104 Dirk Nowitzki .50 .23
❑ 105 Bryon Russell .10 .05
❑ 106 Vin Baker .15 .07
❑ 107 Darrell Armstrong .15 .07
❑ 108 Eric Snow .10 .05
❑ 109 Hakeem Olajuwon .50 .23
❑ 110 Tracy McGrady 1.00 .45
❑ 111 Kenny Anderson .15 .07
❑ 112 Jalen Rose .30 .14
❑ 113 Greg Anthony .10 .05
❑ 114 Tim Hardaway .30 .14
❑ 115 Doug Christie .10 .05
❑ 116 Allan Houston .30 .14
❑ 117 Kobe Bryant 2.50 1.10
❑ 118 Kevin Garnett 2.00 .90
❑ 119 Vitaly Potapenko .10 .05
❑ 120 Steve Kerr .10 .05
❑ 121 Nick Van Exel .15 .07
❑ 122 Jerry Stackhouse .15 .07
❑ 123 Derek Fisher .15 .07
❑ 124 Donyell Marshall .10 .05
❑ 125 Mark Jackson .10 .05
❑ 126 Ray Allen .30 .14
❑ 127 Avery Johnson .10 .05
❑ 128 Michael Doleac .10 .05
❑ 129 Charles Oakley .10 .05
❑ 130 Gary Payton .50 .23
❑ 131 Theo Ratliff .10 .05
❑ 132 Cedric Ceballos .10 .05
❑ 133 Paul Pierce .60 .25
❑ 134 Michael Finley .30 .14
❑ 135 Malik Sealy .10 .05
❑ 136 Brian Grant .15 .07
❑ 137 John Stockton .30 .14
❑ 138 Chris Whitney .10 .05
❑ 139 Maurice Taylor .30 .14
❑ 140 Antonio McDyess .30 .14
❑ 141 Adrian Griffin RC 1.25 .55
❑ 142 Vernon Maxwell .10 .05
❑ 143 Jamal Mashburn .15 .07
❑ 144 Jayson Williams .15 .07
❑ 145 Joe Smith .15 .07
❑ 146 Clifford Robinson .10 .05
❑ 147 Mario Elie .10 .05
❑ 148 Damon Stoudamire .30 .14
❑ 149 Felipe Lopez .10 .05
❑ 150 Rex Chapman .10 .05
❑ 151 Antonio Davis TRAN .10 .05
❑ 152 Mookie Blaylock TRAN .10 .05
❑ 153 Ron Mercer TRAN .40 .18
❑ 154 Horace Grant TRAN .15 .07
❑ 155 Steve Smith TRAN .15 .07
❑ 156 Isaiah Rider TRAN .15 .07
❑ 157 T. Abdul-Wahad TRAN .10 .05
❑ 158 Michael Dickerson TRAN .30 .14
❑ 159 Nick Anderson TRAN .10 .05
❑ 160 Jim Jackson TRAN .10 .05
❑ 161 Hersey Hawkins TRAN .15 .07
❑ 162 Brent Barry TRAN .10 .05
❑ 163 Shandon Anderson TRAN .10 .05
❑ 164 Scottie Pippen TRAN 1.00 .45
❑ 165 Isaac Austin TRAN .10 .05
❑ 166 A. Hardaway TRAN 1.00 .45
❑ 167 Natalie Williams USA 2.50 1.10
❑ 168 Teresa Edwards USA 2.00 .90
❑ 169 Yolanda Griffith USA 2.50 1.10
❑ 170 Nikki McCray USA 1.25 .55
❑ 171 Katie Smith USA 1.50 .70
❑ 172 C. Holdsclaw USA 8.00 3.60
❑ 173 Dawn Staley USA 2.00 .90
❑ 174 R. Bolton-Holifield USA 1.25 .55
❑ 175 Lisa Leslie USA 2.00 .90
❑ 176 Elton Brand RC 10.00 4.50
❑ 177 Steve Francis RC 12.00 5.50
❑ 178 Baron Davis RC 2.50 1.10
❑ 179 Lamar Odom RC 8.00 3.60
❑ 180 Jonathan Bender RC 5.00 2.20
❑ 181 Wally Szczerbiak RC 4.00 1.80
❑ 182 Richard Hamilton RC 2.50 1.10
❑ 183 Andre Miller RC 3.00 1.35
❑ 184 Shawn Marion RC 3.00 1.35
❑ 185 Jason Terry RC 1.50 .70
❑ 186 Trajan Langdon RC 1.50 .70
❑ 187 Aleksandar Radojevic RC .60 .25
❑ 188 Corey Maggette RC 4.00 1.80
❑ 189 William Avery RC 1.50 .70
❑ 190 DeMarco Johnson RC .75 .35
❑ 191 Ron Artest RC 2.50 1.10
❑ 192 Cal Bowdler RC 1.00 .45
❑ 193 James Posey RC 2.00 .90
❑ 194 Quincy Lewis RC 1.00 .45
❑ 195 Scott Padgett RC 1.00 .45
❑ 196 Jeff Foster RC 1.00 .45
❑ 197 Kenny Thomas RC 1.50 .70
❑ 198 Devean George RC 2.00 .90
❑ 199 Tim James RC 1.25 .55
❑ 200 Vonteego Cummings RC 1.50 .70
❑ 201 Jumaine Jones RC .75 .35

1999-00 Stadium Club First Day Issue

	MINT	NRMT
COMMON CARD (1-175)	2.50	1.10
COMMON RC (176-201)	4.00	1.80

*STARS: 10X TO 25X BASE CARD HI
*RCs: 2.5X TO 6X BASE HI
*USA: 6X TO 15X BASE HI
STATED ODDS 1:26 RETAIL
STATED PRINT RUN 150 SERIAL #'d SETS

1999-00 Stadium Club One of a Kind

	MINT	NRMT
COMMON CARD (1-175)	2.50	1.10
COMMON RC (176-201)	4.00	1.80

*STARS: 10X TO 25X BASE CARD HI
*RCs: 2.5X TO 6X BASE HI
*USA: 6X TO 15X BASE HI
STATED ODDS 1:22 HOBBY, 1:9 HTA
STATED PRINT RUN 150 SERIAL #'d SETS

1999-00 Stadium Club 3x3

	MINT	NRMT
COMPLETE SET (30)	120.00	55.00
COMMON CARD (1A-10C)	1.25	.55
UNLISTED STARS	2.00	.90

STATED ODDS 1:27 H/R, 1:14 HTA

COMP.LUM.SET (30)	250.00	110.00
COMMON LUM (1A-10C)	2.50	1.10

*LUMINESCENT: .75X TO 2X HI COLUMN
LUM: STATED ODDS 1:108 H/R, 1:54 HTA

COMP.ILLUM.SET (30)	500.00	220.00
COMMON ILLUM (1A-10C)	5.00	2.20

ILLUMINATOR: 1.5X TO 4X HI COLUMN
ILLUM: STATED ODDS 1:216 H/R, 1:108 HTA

❑ 1A Vince Carter 20.00 9.00
❑ 1B Shareef Abdur-Rahim 4.00 1.80
❑ 1C Grant Hill 10.00 4.50
❑ 2A Allen Iverson 8.00 3.60
❑ 2B Stephon Marbury 4.00 1.80
❑ 2C Jason Williams 5.00 2.20
❑ 3A Kevin Garnett 12.00 5.50
❑ 3B Antoine Walker 2.50 1.10
❑ 3C Scottie Pippen 6.00 2.70
❑ 4A Kobe Bryant 15.00 6.75
❑ 4B Eddie Jones 4.00 1.80
❑ 4C Michael Finley 2.00 .90
❑ 5A Tim Duncan 10.00 4.50
❑ 5B Keith Van Horn 4.00 1.80
❑ 5C Antonio McDyess 2.00 .90
❑ 6A Shaquille O'Neal 10.00 4.50
❑ 6B Alonzo Mourning 2.00 .90
❑ 6C Dikembe Mutombo 1.25 .55
❑ 7A Karl Malone 3.00 1.35
❑ 7B Chris Webber 6.00 2.70
❑ 7C Shawn Kemp 3.00 1.35
❑ 8A John Stockton 2.00 .90
❑ 8B Gary Payton 3.00 1.35
❑ 8C Jason Kidd 6.00 2.70
❑ 9A Elton Brand 10.00 4.50
❑ 9B Lamar Odom 8.00 3.60
❑ 9C Wally Szczerbiak 4.00 1.80
❑ 10A Steve Francis 12.00 5.50
❑ 10B Baron Davis 2.50 1.10
❑ 10C Jason Terry 2.00 .90

1999-00 Stadium Club Chrome Previews

	MINT	NRMT
COMPLETE SET (20)	60.00	27.00
COMMON CARD (SCC1-SCC20)	1.50	.70

STATED ODDS 1:24 H/R, 1:12 HTA

COMP.REF.SET (20)	200.00	90.00
COMMON REF (SCC1-SCC20)	5.00	2.20

*REF: 1.25X TO 3X HI COLUMN
REF: STATED ODDS 1:120 H/R, 1:60 HTA

COMP.JUMBO SET (20)	60.00	27.00
COMMON JUMBO (1-20)	1.25	.55

*JUMBO: .3X TO .8X HI
JUMBO: ONE PER HOB/HTA BOX

COMP.JUMBO.REF.SET (20)	250.00	110.00
COMMON JUMBO.REF (1-20)	6.00	2.70

*JUMBO.REF: 1.5X TO 4X HI
JUMBO.REF: STATED ODDS 1:12 H, 1:8 HTA

		MINT	NRMT
❑ SCC1	Kevin Garnett	6.00	2.70
❑ SCC2	Grant Hill	5.00	2.20
❑ SCC3	Vince Carter	10.00	4.50
❑ SCC4	Allen Iverson	4.00	1.80
❑ SCC5	Shareef Abdur-Rahim	2.00	.90
❑ SCC6	Stephon Marbury	2.00	.90
❑ SCC7	Kobe Bryant	8.00	3.60
❑ SCC8	Keith Van Horn	2.00	.90
❑ SCC9	Tim Duncan	5.00	2.20
❑ SCC10	Shaquille O'Neal	5.00	2.20
❑ SCC11	Jason Williams	2.50	1.10
❑ SCC12	Scottie Pippen	3.00	1.35
❑ SCC13	Gary Payton	1.50	.70
❑ SCC14	Karl Malone	1.50	.70
❑ SCC15	Elton Brand	8.00	3.60
❑ SCC16	Steve Francis	10.00	4.50
❑ SCC17	Baron Davis	2.00	.90
❑ SCC18	Lamar Odom	6.00	2.70
❑ SCC19	Ron Artest	2.00	.90
❑ SCC20	Corey Maggette	3.00	1.35

1999-00 Stadium Club Co-Signers

	MINT	NRMT
COMMON CARD (CS1-CS26)	40.00	18.00

OVERALL STATED ODDS 1:254 H, 1:102 HTA
CS1-8: STATED ODDS 1:3294 H, 1:1332 HTA
CS9-14: STATED ODDS 1:2202 H, 1:882 HTA
CS15-20: STATED ODDS 1:733 H, 1:294 HTA
CS21-26: STATED ODDS 1:550 H, 1:220 HTA

		MINT	NRMT
❑ CS1	Tim Duncan Tracy McGrady	200.00	90.00
❑ CS2	Tim Duncan Marcus Camby	150.00	70.00
❑ CS3	Tim Duncan Elton Brand	250.00	110.00
❑ CS4	Tim Duncan Steve Francis	300.00	135.00
❑ CS5	Tim Duncan Shawn Marion	150.00	70.00
❑ CS6	Tim Duncan Jonathan Bender	200.00	90.00
❑ CS7	Tim Duncan Wally Szczerbiak	250.00	110.00
❑ CS8	Tim Duncan Corey Maggette	200.00	90.00
❑ CS9	Tracy McGrady Steve Francis	200.00	90.00
❑ CS10	Corey Maggette Shawn Marion	80.00	36.00
❑ CS11	Marcus Camby Gary Payton	60.00	27.00
❑ CS12	Elton Brand Shareef Abdur-Rahim	120.00	55.00
❑ CS13	Paul Pierce Jonathan Bender	80.00	36.00
❑ CS14	Tom Gugliotta Wally Szczerbiak	60.00	27.00
❑ CS15	Tracy McGrady Corey Maggette	80.00	36.00
❑ CS16	Steve Francis Shawn Marion	100.00	45.00
❑ CS17	Gary Payton Jonathan Bender	50.00	22.00
❑ CS18	Paul Pierce Marcus Camby	50.00	22.00
❑ CS19	Elton Brand Tom Gugliotta	60.00	27.00
❑ CS20	Wally Szczerbiak Shareef Abdur-Rahim	80.00	36.00
❑ CS21	Tracy McGrady Shawn Marion	60.00	27.00
❑ CS22	Steve Francis Corey Maggette	150.00	70.00
❑ CS23	Gary Payton Paul Pierce	50.00	22.00
❑ CS24	Jonathan Bender Marcus Camby	40.00	18.00
❑ CS25	Elton Brand Wally Szczerbiak	120.00	55.00
❑ CS26	Tom Gugliotta Shareef Abdur-Rahim	40.00	18.00

1999-00 Stadium Club Lone Star Signatures

	MINT	NRMT
COMMON CARD (LS1-LS13)	25.00	11.00

OVERALL STATED ODDS 1:389 H, 1:156 HTA
LS1: STATED ODDS 1:28620 H/R, 1:12578 HTA
LS2-5: STATED ODDS 1:4871 H/R, 1:1956 HTA
LS6-7: STATED ODDS 1:7269 H/R, 1:2981 HTA
LS8-10: STATED ODDS 1:1024 H/R, 1:409 HTA
LS11-12: STATED ODDS 1:1215 H/R, 1:485 HTA
LS13: STATED ODDS 1:2544 H/R, 1:1010 HTA

		MINT	NRMT
❑ LS1	Tim Duncan	200.00	90.00
❑ LS2	Shawn Marion	40.00	18.00
❑ LS3	Jonathan Bender	60.00	27.00
❑ LS4	Wally Szczerbiak	60.00	27.00
❑ LS5	Corey Maggette	60.00	27.00
❑ LS6	Gary Payton	80.00	36.00
❑ LS7	Tom Gugliotta	40.00	18.00
❑ LS8	Steve Francis	100.00	45.00
❑ LS9	Elton Brand	60.00	27.00
❑ LS10	Tracy McGrady	30.00	13.50
❑ LS11	Paul Pierce	25.00	11.00
❑ LS12	Shareef Abdur-Rahim	25.00	11.00
❑ LS13	Marcus Camby	25.00	11.00

1999-00 Stadium Club Never Compromise

	MINT	NRMT
COMPLETE SET (10)	50.00	22.00
COMMON CARD (NC1-NC30)	.60	.25
UNLISTED STARS	.75	.35

STATED ODDS 1:12 H/R, 1:6 HTA
COMMON GAME-VIEW (NC1-30) 8.00 3.60
*GAME-VIEW: 5X TO 12X HI COLUMN
GAME-VIEW: STATED ODDS 1:220 H, 1:88 HTA
GAME-VIEW: PRINT RUN 100 SERIAL #'d SETS

		MINT	NRMT
❑ NC1	Elton Brand	4.00	1.80
❑ NC2	Steve Francis	5.00	2.20
❑ NC3	Baron Davis	1.00	.45
❑ NC4	Lamar Odom	3.00	1.35
❑ NC5	Jonathan Bender	2.00	.90
❑ NC6	Wally Szczerbiak	1.50	.70
❑ NC7	Richard Hamilton	1.00	.45
❑ NC8	Andre Miller	1.25	.55
❑ NC9	Corey Maggette	1.50	.70
❑ NC10	Jason Terry	.60	.25
❑ NC11	Kevin Garnett	5.00	2.20
❑ NC12	Grant Hill	4.00	1.80
❑ NC13	Vince Carter	8.00	3.60
❑ NC14	Allen Iverson	3.00	1.35
❑ NC15	Shareef Abdur-Rahim	1.50	.70
❑ NC16	Stephon Marbury	1.50	.70
❑ NC17	Kobe Bryant	6.00	2.70
❑ NC18	Keith Van Horn	1.50	.70
❑ NC19	Tim Duncan	4.00	1.80
❑ NC20	Shaquille O'Neal	4.00	1.80
❑ NC21	Karl Malone	1.25	.55
❑ NC22	Scottie Pippen	2.50	1.10
❑ NC23	David Robinson	1.25	.55
❑ NC24	John Stockton	.75	.35
❑ NC25	Charles Barkley	1.25	.55
❑ NC26	Gary Payton	1.25	.55
❑ NC27	Shawn Kemp	1.25	.55
❑ NC28	Alonzo Mourning	.75	.35
❑ NC29	Reggie Miller	.75	.35
❑ NC30	Mitch Richmond	.75	.35

1999-00 Stadium Club Onyx Extreme

	MINT	NRMT
COMPLETE SET (10)	10.00	4.50

COMMON CARD (OE1-OE10) .50 .23
UNLISTED STARS .60 .25
STATED ODDS 1:8 H/R, 1:6 HTA
COMP.DIE CUT SET (10) 25.00 11.00
COMMON DIE CUT (OE1-OE10) 1.25 .55
*DIE CUTS: 1X TO 2.5X HI COLUMN
DIE CUTS: STATED ODDS 1:40 H/R, 1:30 HTA

❑ OE1 Antonio McDyess .60 .25
❑ OE2 Antoine Walker .75 .35
❑ OE3 Jason Williams 1.50 .70
❑ OE4 Chris Webber 2.00 .90
❑ OE5 David Robinson 1.00 .45
❑ OE6 Wally Szczerbiak 1.25 .55
❑ OE7 Jason Kidd 2.00 .90
❑ OE8 Shawn Kemp 1.00 .45
❑ OE9 Aleksandar Radojevic .50 .23
❑ OE10 Tim Duncan 3.00 1.35

1999-00 Stadium Club Picture Ending

	MINT	NRMT
COMPLETE SET (10)	4.00	1.80
COMMON CARD (PE1-PE10)	.40	.18
SEMISTARS	.50	.23
UNLISTED STARS	.75	.35

STATED ODDS 1:12 H/R, 1:6 HTA

❑ PE1 Allan Houston .75 .35
❑ PE2 John Stockton .75 .35
❑ PE3 Sean Elliott .40 .18
❑ PE4 Latrell Sprewell 1.50 .70
❑ PE5 Darrell Armstrong .50 .23
❑ PE6 Marcus Camby .75 .35
❑ PE7 Keith Van Horn 1.50 .70
❑ PE8 Antoine Walker 1.00 .45
❑ PE9 Larry Johnson .50 .23
❑ PE10 Avery Johnson .40 .18

1999-00 Stadium Club Pieces of Patriotism

	MINT	NRMT
COMPLETE SET (9)	400.00	180.00
COMMON CARD (P1-P9)	25.00	11.00

STATED ODDS 1:147 HOB, 1:59 HTA

❑ P1 Allan Houston 50.00 22.00
❑ P2 Kevin Garnett 100.00 45.00
❑ P3 Gary Payton 40.00 18.00
❑ P4 Steve Smith 25.00 11.00
❑ P5 Tim Hardaway 40.00 18.00
❑ P6 Tim Duncan 80.00 36.00
❑ P7 Jason Kidd 80.00 36.00
❑ P8 Tom Gugliotta 25.00 11.00
❑ P9 Vin Baker 25.00 11.00

1999-00 Stadium Club Chrome

	MINT	NRMT
COMPLETE SET (150)	80.00	36.00
COMMON CARD (1-150)	.15	.07
COMMON RC	.75	.35
SEMISTARS	.20	.09
SEMISTARS RC	1.00	.45
UNLISTED STARS	.40	.18
UNLISTED STARS RC	1.25	.55

❑ 1 Allen Iverson 1.50 .70
❑ 2 Chris Webber 1.25 .55
❑ 3 Antawn Jamison .75 .35
❑ 4 Karl Malone .60 .25
❑ 5 Sam Cassell .20 .09
❑ 6 Kerry Kittles .20 .09
❑ 7 Tim Thomas .50 .23
❑ 8 Shawn Bradley .15 .07
❑ 9 David Wesley .15 .07
❑ 10 Glenn Robinson .20 .09
❑ 11 Mitch Richmond .40 .18
❑ 12 Shareef Abdur-Rahim .75 .35
❑ 13 Christian Laettner .20 .09
❑ 14 Anthony Mason .20 .09
❑ 15 Randy Brown .15 .07
❑ 16 Charles Barkley .60 .25
❑ 17 Bobby Jackson .15 .07
❑ 18 Matt Harpring .15 .07
❑ 19 Shawn Kemp .60 .25
❑ 20 Ruben Patterson .40 .18
❑ 21 Mike Bibby .50 .23
❑ 22 Vlade Divac .15 .07
❑ 23 David Robinson .60 .25
❑ 24 Keith Van Horn .75 .35
❑ 25 Juwan Howard .20 .09
❑ 26 Shaquille O'Neal 2.00 .90
❑ 27 Alonzo Mourning .40 .18
❑ 28 Michael Olowokandi .20 .09
❑ 29 Andrew DeClercq .15 .07
❑ 30 Toni Kukoc .50 .23
❑ 31 Dikembe Mutombo .20 .09
❑ 32 Steve Nash .15 .07
❑ 33 Eddie Jones .75 .35
❑ 34 Reggie Miller .40 .18
❑ 35 Larry Hughes 1.00 .45
❑ 36 Tim Duncan 2.00 .90
❑ 37 Jerome Williams .20 .09
❑ 38 Rod Strickland .20 .09
❑ 39 Patrick Ewing .40 .18
❑ 40 Grant Hill 2.00 .90
❑ 41 Derrick Coleman .20 .09
❑ 42 Raef LaFrentz .40 .18
❑ 43 Rik Smits .15 .07
❑ 44 Latrell Sprewell .75 .35
❑ 45 John Starks .15 .07
❑ 46 Cuttino Mobley .40 .18
❑ 47 Marcus Camby .40 .18
❑ 48 Stephon Marbury .75 .35
❑ 49 Tom Gugliotta .20 .09
❑ 50 Vince Carter 4.00 1.80
❑ 51 Chris Mullin .40 .18
❑ 52 Tyrone Nesby RC .15 .07
❑ 53 Elden Campbell .15 .07
❑ 54 Lindsey Hunter .15 .07
❑ 55 Rasheed Wallace .40 .18
❑ 56 Jeff Hornacek .20 .09
❑ 57 Matt Geiger .15 .07
❑ 58 Antoine Walker .50 .23
❑ 59 Jason Williams 1.00 .45
❑ 60 Robert Horry .15 .07
❑ 61 Kendall Gill .20 .09
❑ 62 Dan Majerle .20 .09
❑ 63 Robert Traylor .15 .07
❑ 64 P.J. Brown .15 .07
❑ 65 Terrell Brandon .20 .09
❑ 66 Corliss Williamson .15 .07
❑ 67 Bryant Reeves .15 .07
❑ 68 Larry Johnson .20 .09
❑ 69 Keith Closs .15 .07
❑ 70 Walter McCarty .15 .07
❑ 71 Wesley Person .15 .07
❑ 72 Chris Mills .15 .07
❑ 73 Glen Rice .20 .09
❑ 74 Jason Kidd 1.25 .55
❑ 75 Dirk Nowitzki .60 .25
❑ 76 Bryon Russell .15 .07
❑ 77 Vin Baker .20 .09
❑ 78 Darrell Armstrong .20 .09
❑ 79 Eric Snow .15 .07
❑ 80 Hakeem Olajuwon .60 .25
❑ 81 Tracy McGrady 1.25 .55
❑ 82 Kenny Anderson .20 .09
❑ 83 Jalen Rose .40 .18
❑ 84 Tim Hardaway .40 .18
❑ 85 Doug Christie .15 .07
❑ 86 Allan Houston .40 .18
❑ 87 Kobe Bryant 3.00 1.35
❑ 88 Kevin Garnett 2.50 1.10
❑ 89 Steve Kerr .15 .07
❑ 90 Nick Van Exel .20 .09
❑ 91 Jerry Stackhouse .20 .09
❑ 92 Derek Fisher .20 .09
❑ 93 Donyell Marshall .15 .07
❑ 94 Mark Jackson .15 .07
❑ 95 Ray Allen .40 .18
❑ 96 Avery Johnson .15 .07
❑ 97 Michael Doleac .15 .07
❑ 98 Charles Oakley .15 .07
❑ 99 Gary Payton .60 .25
❑ 100 Theo Ratliff .15 .07
❑ 101 Cedric Ceballos .15 .07
❑ 102 Paul Pierce .75 .35
❑ 103 Michael Finley .40 .18
❑ 104 Brian Grant .20 .09
❑ 105 John Stockton .40 .18
❑ 106 Maurice Taylor .40 .18
❑ 107 Antonio McDyess .40 .18
❑ 108 Adrian Griffin RC 1.50 .70
❑ 109 Jamal Mashburn .20 .09
❑ 110 Jayson Williams .20 .09
❑ 111 Joe Smith .20 .09
❑ 112 Clifford Robinson .15 .07
❑ 113 Mario Elie .15 .07
❑ 114 Damon Stoudamire .40 .18
❑ 115 Felipe Lopez .15 .07
❑ 116 Antonio Davis TRAN .15 .07
❑ 117 Mookie Blaylock TRAN .15 .07
❑ 118 Ron Mercer TRAN .50 .23
❑ 119 Horace Grant TRAN .20 .09
❑ 120 Steve Smith TRAN .20 .09
❑ 121 Isaiah Rider TRAN .20 .09
❑ 122 T.Abdul-Wahad TRAN .15 .07
❑ 123 Michael Dickerson TRAN .40 .18
❑ 124 Nick Anderson TRAN .15 .07
❑ 125 Jim Jackson TRAN .15 .07
❑ 126 Hersey Hawkins TRAN .20 .09
❑ 127 Brent Barry TRAN .15 .07
❑ 128 Shandon Anderson TRAN .15 .07
❑ 129 Scottie Pippen TRAN 1.25 .55
❑ 130 Isaac Austin TRAN .15 .07
❑ 131 A. Hardaway TRAN 1.25 .55
❑ 132 Elton Brand RC 12.00 5.50
❑ 133 Steve Francis RC 15.00 6.75
❑ 134 Baron Davis RC 3.00 1.35

- ❑ 135 Lamar Odom RC 10.00 4.50
- ❑ 136 Jonathan Bender RC.... 6.00 2.70
- ❑ 137 Wally Szczerbiak RC.... 5.00 2.20
- ❑ 138 Richard Hamilton RC .. 3.00 1.35
- ❑ 139 Andre Miller RC........... 4.00 1.80
- ❑ 140 Shawn Marion RC 4.00 1.80
- ❑ 141 Jason Terry RC .... 2.00 .90
- ❑ 142 Trajan Langdon RC...... 2.00 .90
- ❑ 143 Aleksandar Radojevic RC .75 .35
- ❑ 144 Corey Maggette RC 5.00 2.20
- ❑ 145 William Avery RC .... 2.00 .90
- ❑ 146 Ron Artest RC.............. 3.00 1.35
- ❑ 147 Cal Bowdler RC............ 1.25 .55
- ❑ 148 James Posey RC 2.50 1.10
- ❑ 149 Quincy Lewis RC.......... 1.25 .55
- ❑ 150 Scott Padgett RC .... 1.25 .55

1999-00 Stadium Club Chrome First Day Issue

	MINT	NRMT
COMMON CARD (1-150)..........	5.00	2.20
COMMON RC..........................	6.00	2.70

*STARS: 12.5X TO 30X BASE CARD HI
*RCs: 3X TO 8X BASE HI
STATED PRINT RUN 100 SERIAL #'d SETS
STATED ODDS 1:47

1999-00 Stadium Club Chrome First Day Issue Refractors

	MINT	NRMT
COMMON CARD (1-131).......	15.00	6.75
COMMON RC (132-150)	12.00	5.50

*STARS: 40X TO 100X BASE CARD HI
*RCs: 6X TO 15X BASE HI
STATED PRINT RUN 25 SERIAL #'d SETS
STATED ODDS 1:186

1999-00 Stadium Club Chrome Refractors

	MINT	NRMT
COMPLETE SET (150)	500.00	220.00
COMMON CARD (1-150)..........	1.25	.55

*STARS: 3X TO 8X BASE CARD HI
*RCs: 1.5X TO 4X BASE HI
STATED ODDS 1:12

1999-00 Stadium Club Chrome Clear Shots

	MINT	NRMT
COMPLETE SET (10)	15.00	6.75
COMMON CARD (CS1-CS10).....	.75	.35
STATED ODDS 1:16		
COMP.REF.SET (10)..............	40.00	18.00
COMMON REF (CS1-CS10)	2.00	.90

*REF: 1X TO 2.5X HI COLUMN
REF: STATED ODDS 1:80

- ❑ CS1 Lamar Odom 4.00 1.80
- ❑ CS2 Elton Brand 5.00 2.20
- ❑ CS3 Steve Francis 6.00 2.70
- ❑ CS4 Shawn Marion .... 1.50 .70
- ❑ CS5 Wally Szczerbiak .... 2.00 .90
- ❑ CS6 Richard Hamilton .... 1.25 .55
- ❑ CS7 Andre Miller .... 1.50 .70
- ❑ CS8 Jason Terry .... .75 .35
- ❑ CS9 Baron Davis .... 1.25 .55
- ❑ CS10 Jonathan Bender 2.50 1.10

1999-00 Stadium Club Chrome Eyes of the Game

	MINT	NRMT
COMPLETE SET (10)	30.00	13.50
COMMON CARD (EG1-EG10)..	1.25	.55
STATED ODDS 1:24		
COMP.REF.SET (10).............	80.00	36.00
COMMON REF (EG1-EG10)	3.00	1.35

*REF: 1X TO 2.5X HI COLUMN
REF: STATED ODDS 1:120

- ❑ EG1 Jason Kidd 4.00 1.80
- ❑ EG2 Jason Williams 3.00 1.35
- ❑ EG3 Gary Payton .... 2.00 .90
- ❑ EG4 Kevin Garnett 8.00 3.60
- ❑ EG5 Vince Carter 12.00 5.50
- ❑ EG6 Kobe Bryant 10.00 4.50
- ❑ EG7 Stephon Marbury 2.50 1.10
- ❑ EG8 Allen Iverson 5.00 2.20
- ❑ EG9 Alonzo Mourning .... 1.25 .55
- ❑ EG10 John Stockton .... 1.25 .55

1999-00 Stadium Club Chrome True Colors

	MINT	NRMT
COMPLETE SET (10)	12.00	5.50
COMMMON CARD (TC1-TC10)	.50	.23
STATED ODDS 1:8		
COMP.REF.SET (10)..............	30.00	13.50
COMMON REF (TC1-TC10)	1.25	.55

*REF: 1X TO 2.5X HI COLUMN
REF: STATED ODDS 1:40

- ❑ TC1 Gary Payton .... .75 .35
- ❑ TC2 Stephon Marbury .... 1.00 .45
- ❑ TC3 Karl Malone .... .75 .35
- ❑ TC4 Kevin Garnett 3.00 1.35
- ❑ TC5 Allen Iverson............... 2.00 .90
- ❑ TC6 Vince Carter 5.00 2.20
- ❑ TC7 Grant Hill 2.50 1.10
- ❑ TC8 Shaquille O'Neal.......... 2.50 1.10
- ❑ TC9 Reggie Miller .... .50 .23
- ❑ TC10 Tim Duncan 2.50 1.10

1999-00 Stadium Club Chrome Visionaries

	MINT	NRMT
COMPLETE SET (10)	40.00	18.00
COMMON CARD (V1-V10)	2.50	1.10
STATED ODDS 1:32		
COMP.REF.SET (10)...........	100.00	45.00
COMMON REF (V1-V10)	6.00	2.70

*REF: 1X TO 2.5X HI COLUMN
REF: STATED ODDS 1:160

V1 Vince Carter	15.00	6.75
V2 Tim Duncan	8.00	3.60
V3 Jason Williams	4.00	1.80
V4 Lamar Odom	6.00	2.70
V5 Steve Francis	10.00	4.50
V6 Paul Pierce	3.00	1.35
V7 Tracy McGrady	5.00	2.20
V8 Elton Brand	8.00	3.60
V9 Shawn Marion	2.50	1.10
V10 Antawn Jamison	3.00	1.35

1957-58 Topps

	EX-MT	VG-E
COMPLETE SET (80)	5500.00	2500.00
COMMON NON-DP (1-80)	40.00	18.00
DP (9/11/14/20)	25.00	11.00
DP (31/38/46/47/52)	25.00	11.00
DP (55/57/64/65/68/79)	25.00	11.00
DP (6/7/8/18/21/25/34/66)	35.00	16.00

CONDITION SENSITIVE SET
CARDS PRICED IN EX-MT CONDITION

1 Nat Clifton DP RC !	250.00	75.00
2 George Yardley DP RC	70.00	32.00
3 Neil Johnston DP RC	55.00	25.00
4 Carl Braun DP	50.00	22.00
5 Bill Sharman DP RC !	150.00	70.00
6 George King DP RC	35.00	16.00
7 Kenny Sears DP RC	35.00	16.00
8 Dick Ricketts DP RC	35.00	16.00
9 Jack Nichols DP	25.00	11.00
10 Paul Arizin DP RC	110.00	50.00
11 Chuck Noble DP	25.00	11.00
12 Slater Martin DP RC	70.00	32.00
13 Dolph Schayes DP RC	140.00	65.00
14 Dick Atha DP	25.00	11.00
15 Frank Ramsey DP RC	90.00	40.00
16 Dick McGuire DP RC	55.00	25.00
17 Bob Cousy DP RC !	500.00	220.00
18 Larry Foust DP RC	35.00	16.00
19 Tom Heinsohn RC !	300.00	135.00
20 Bill Thieben DP	25.00	11.00
21 Don Meineke DP RC	35.00	16.00
22 Tom Marshall	40.00	18.00
23 Dick Garmaker	40.00	18.00
24 Bob Pettit QP RC !	200.00	90.00
25 Jim Krebs DP RC	35.00	16.00
26 Gene Shue DP RC	60.00	27.00
27 Ed Macauley DP RC	70.00	32.00
28 Vern Mikkelsen RC	100.00	45.00
29 Willie Naulls RC	60.00	27.00
30 Walter Dukes DP RC	45.00	20.00
31 Dave Piontek DP	25.00	11.00
32 John Kerr RC	125.00	55.00
33 Larry Costello DP RC	50.00	22.00
34 Woody Sauldsberry DP RC	35.00	16.00
35 Ray Felix RC	45.00	20.00
36 Ernie Beck	40.00	18.00
37 Cliff Hagan RC	135.00	60.00
38 Guy Sparrow DP	25.00	11.00
39 Jim Loscutoff RC	60.00	27.00
40 Arnie Risen DP	45.00	20.00
41 Joe Graboski	40.00	18.00
42 M. Stokes DP RC ! UER (Text refers to N.F.L. Record)	125.00	55.00
43 Rod Hundley DP RC !	125.00	55.00
44 Tom Gola DP RC	80.00	36.00
45 Med Park RC	45.00	20.00
46 Mel Hutchins DP	25.00	11.00
47 Larry Friend DP	25.00	11.00
48 Lennie Rosenbluth DP RC	55.00	25.00
49 Walt Davis	40.00	18.00
50 Richie Regan RC	45.00	20.00
51 Frank Selvy DP RC	50.00	22.00
52 Art Spoelstra DP	25.00	11.00
53 Bob Hopkins RC	45.00	20.00
54 Earl Lloyd RC	50.00	22.00
55 Phil Jordan DP	25.00	11.00
56 Bob Houbregs DP RC	40.00	18.00
57 Lou Tsioropoulos DP	25.00	11.00
58 Ed Conlin RC	45.00	20.00
59 Al Bianchi RC	80.00	36.00
60 George Dempsey RC	45.00	20.00
61 Chuck Share	40.00	18.00
62 Harry Gallatin DP RC	50.00	22.00
63 Bob Harrison	40.00	18.00
64 Bob Burrow DP	25.00	11.00
65 Win Wilfong DP	25.00	11.00
66 Jack McMahon DP RC	35.00	16.00
67 Jack George	40.00	18.00
68 Charlie Tyra DP	25.00	11.00
69 Ron Sobie	40.00	18.00
70 Jack Coleman	40.00	18.00
71 Jack Twyman DP RC	110.00	50.00
72 Paul Seymour RC	45.00	20.00
73 Jim Paxson DP RC	55.00	25.00
74 Bob Leonard RC	50.00	22.00
75 Andy Phillip	60.00	27.00
76 Joe Holup	40.00	18.00
77 Bill Russell RC !	1200.00	550.00
78 Clyde Lovellette DP RC	120.00	55.00
79 Ed Fleming DP	25.00	11.00
80 Dick Schnittker RC !	120.00	36.00

1969-70 Topps

	NRMT-MT	EXC
COMPLETE SET (99)	1800.00	800.00
COMMON CARD (1-99)	4.00	1.80
CL (99) !	300.00	135.00
SEMISTARS	6.00	2.70
UNLISTED STARS	8.00	3.60

CONDITION SENSITIVE SET

1 Wilt Chamberlain	175.00	52.50
2 Gail Goodrich RC	50.00	22.00
3 Cazzie Russell RC	15.00	6.75
4 Darrall Imhoff RC	6.00	2.70
5 Bailey Howell	8.00	3.60
6 Lucius Allen RC	10.00	4.50
7 Tom Boerwinkle RC	6.00	2.70
8 Jimmy Walker RC	8.00	3.60
9 John Block RC	6.00	2.70
10 Nate Thurmond RC	35.00	16.00
11 Gary Gregor	4.00	1.80
12 Gus Johnson RC	20.00	9.00
13 Luther Rackley	4.00	1.80
14 Jon McGlocklin RC	6.00	2.70
15 Connie Hawkins RC	45.00	20.00
16 Johnny Egan	4.00	1.80
17 Jim Washington	4.00	1.80
18 Dick Barnett RC	8.00	3.60
19 Tom Meschery	8.00	3.60
20 John Havlicek RC !	150.00	70.00
21 Eddie Miles	4.00	1.80
22 Walt Wesley	6.00	2.70
23 Rick Adelman RC	8.00	3.60
24 Al Attles	8.00	3.60
25 Lew Alcindor RC !	400.00	180.00
26 Jack Marin RC	8.00	3.60
27 Walt Hazzard RC	12.00	5.50
28 Connie Dierking	4.00	1.80
29 Keith Erickson RC	12.00	5.50
30 Bob Rule RC	10.00	4.50
31 Dick Van Arsdale RC	10.00	4.50
32 Archie Clark RC	12.00	5.50
33 Terry Dischinger RC	4.00	1.80
34 Henry Finkel RC	4.00	1.80
35 Elgin Baylor	50.00	22.00
36 Ron Williams	4.00	1.80
37 Loy Petersen	4.00	1.80
38 Guy Rodgers	8.00	3.60
39 Toby Kimball	4.00	1.80
40 Billy Cunningham RC	50.00	22.00
41 Joe Caldwell RC	8.00	3.60
42 Leroy Ellis RC	6.00	2.70
43 Bill Bradley RC	125.00	55.00
44 Len Wilkens UER (Misspelled Wilkins on card back)	30.00	13.50
45 Jerry Lucas RC	40.00	18.00
46 Neal Walk RC	6.00	2.70
47 Emmette Bryant RC	6.00	2.70
48 Bob Kauffman RC	4.00	1.80
49 Mel Counts RC	6.00	2.70
50 Oscar Robertson	60.00	27.00
51 Jim Barnett RC	8.00	3.60
52 Don Smith	4.00	1.80
53 Jim Davis	4.00	1.80
54 Wally Jones RC	6.00	2.70
55 Dave Bing RC	35.00	16.00
56 Wes Unseld RC	50.00	22.00
57 Joe Ellis	4.00	1.80
58 John Tresvant	4.00	1.80
59 Larry Siegfried RC	6.00	2.70
60 Willis Reed RC	50.00	22.00
61 Paul Silas RC	20.00	9.00
62 Bob Weiss RC	8.00	3.60
63 Willie McCarter	4.00	1.80
64 Don Kojis RC	4.00	1.80
65 Lou Hudson RC	20.00	9.00
66 Jim King	4.00	1.80
67 Luke Jackson RC	6.00	2.70
68 Len Chappell RC	4.00	1.80
69 Ray Scott	4.00	1.80
70 Jeff Mullins RC	8.00	3.60
71 Howie Komives	4.00	1.80
72 Tom Sanders RC	10.00	4.50
73 Dick Snyder	4.00	1.80
74 Dave Stallworth RC	6.00	2.70
75 Elvin Hayes RC	70.00	32.00
76 Art Harris	4.00	1.80
77 Don Ohl	6.00	2.70
78 Bob Love RC	40.00	18.00
79 Tom Van Arsdale RC	10.00	4.50
80 Earl Monroe RC	40.00	18.00
81 Greg Smith	4.00	1.80
82 Don Nelson RC	35.00	16.00
83 Happy Hairston RC	8.00	3.60
84 Hal Greer	12.00	5.50
85 Dave DeBusschere RC	40.00	18.00
86 Bill Bridges RC	8.00	3.60
87 Herm Gilliam RC	6.00	2.70
88 Jim Fox	4.00	1.80
89 Bob Boozer	6.00	2.70
90 Jerry West	90.00	40.00
91 Chet Walker RC	15.00	6.75
92 Flynn Robinson RC	6.00	2.70
93 Clyde Lee	4.00	1.80
94 Kevin Loughery RC	10.00	4.50
95 Walt Bellamy	10.00	4.50
96 Art Williams	4.00	1.80
97 Adrian Smith RC	6.00	2.70
98 Walt Frazier RC	70.00	32.00
99 Checklist 1-99	300.00	90.00

1970-71 Topps

	NRMT-MT	EXC
COMPLETE SET (175)	1200.00	550.00
COMMON CARD (1-110)	2.50	1.10
COMMON CARD (111-175)	3.00	1.35
SP (32/33/35/78/87/104)	6.00	2.70
SP (31/36/37/49/62/74)	8.00	3.60
CL (24) !	60.00	27.00
CL DP (101A/101B) !	30.00	13.50
LL (1-6)	5.00	2.20
AS (106-110)	8.00	3.60
AS (111-115)	4.00	1.80
PLAYOFFS (168-175)	5.00	2.20
SEMISTARS	4.00	1.80
UNLISTED STARS	6.00	2.70
CONDITION SENSITIVE SET		

Card	NRMT-MT	EXC
❑ 1 NBA Scoring Leaders Lew Alcindor Jerry West Elvin Hayes	35.00	10.50
❑ 2 NBA Scoring SP Average Leaders Jerry West Lew Alcindor Elvin Hayes	35.00	16.00
❑ 3 NBA FG Pct Leaders Johnny Green Darrall Imhoff Lou Hudson	5.00	2.20
❑ 4 NBA FT Pct Leaders SP Flynn Robinson Chet Walker Jeff Mullins	10.00	4.50
❑ 5 NBA Rebound Leaders Elvin Hayes Wes Unseld Lew Alcindor	25.00	11.00
❑ 6 NBA Assist Leaders SP Len Wilkens Walt Frazier Clem Haskins	12.00	5.50
❑ 7 Bill Bradley	50.00	22.00
❑ 8 Ron Williams	2.50	1.10
❑ 9 Otto Moore	2.50	1.10
❑ 10 John Havlicek SP	75.00	34.00
❑ 11 George Wilson RC	2.50	1.10
❑ 12 John Trapp	2.50	1.10
❑ 13 Pat Riley RC	60.00	27.00
❑ 14 Jim Washington	2.50	1.10
❑ 15 Bob Rule	4.00	1.80
❑ 16 Bob Weiss	4.00	1.80
❑ 17 Neil Johnson	2.50	1.10
❑ 18 Walt Bellamy	6.00	2.70
❑ 19 McCoy McLemore	2.50	1.10
❑ 20 Earl Monroe	15.00	6.75
❑ 21 Wally Anderzunas	2.50	1.10
❑ 22 Guy Rodgers	4.00	1.80
❑ 23 Rick Roberson	2.50	1.10
❑ 24 Checklist 1-110	40.00	12.00
❑ 25 Jimmy Walker	4.00	1.80
❑ 26 Mike Riordan RC	6.00	2.70
❑ 27 Henry Finkel	2.50	1.10
❑ 28 Joe Ellis	2.50	1.10
❑ 29 Mike Davis	2.50	1.10
❑ 30 Lou Hudson	6.00	2.70
❑ 31 Lucius Allen SP	8.00	3.60
❑ 32 Toby Kimball SP	6.00	2.70
❑ 33 Luke Jackson SP	6.00	2.70
❑ 34 Johnny Egan	2.50	1.10
❑ 35 Leroy Ellis SP	6.00	2.70
❑ 36 Jack Marin SP	8.00	3.60
❑ 37 Joe Caldwell SP	8.00	3.60
❑ 38 Keith Erickson	6.00	2.70
❑ 39 Don Smith	2.50	1.10
❑ 40 Flynn Robinson	4.00	1.80
❑ 41 Bob Boozer	2.50	1.10
❑ 42 Howie Komives	2.50	1.10
❑ 43 Dick Barnett	4.00	1.80
❑ 44 Stu Lantz RC	3.00	1.35
❑ 45 Dick Van Arsdale	6.00	2.70
❑ 46 Jerry Lucas	10.00	4.50
❑ 47 Don Chaney RC	10.00	4.50
❑ 48 Ray Scott	2.50	1.10
❑ 49 Dick Cunningham SP	8.00	3.60
❑ 50 Wilt Chamberlain	80.00	36.00
❑ 51 Kevin Loughery	4.00	1.80
❑ 52 Stan McKenzie	2.50	1.10
❑ 53 Fred Foster	2.50	1.10
❑ 54 Jim Davis	2.50	1.10
❑ 55 Walt Wesley	2.50	1.10
❑ 56 Bill Hewitt	2.50	1.10
❑ 57 Darrall Imhoff	2.50	1.10
❑ 58 John Block	2.50	1.10
❑ 59 Al Attles SP	8.00	3.60
❑ 60 Chet Walker	6.00	2.70
❑ 61 Luther Rackley	2.50	1.10
❑ 62 Jerry Chambers SP RC	8.00	3.60
❑ 63 Bob Dandridge RC	8.00	3.60
❑ 64 Dick Snyder	2.50	1.10
❑ 65 Elgin Baylor	30.00	13.50
❑ 66 Connie Dierking	2.50	1.10
❑ 67 Steve Kuberski RC	2.50	1.10
❑ 68 Tom Boerwinkle	2.50	1.10
❑ 69 Paul Silas	6.00	2.70
❑ 70 Elvin Hayes	30.00	13.50
❑ 71 Bill Bridges	4.00	1.80
❑ 72 Wes Unseld	15.00	6.75
❑ 73 Herm Gilliam	2.50	1.10
❑ 74 Bobby Smith SP RC	8.00	3.60
❑ 75 Lew Alcindor	100.00	45.00
❑ 76 Jeff Mullins	4.00	1.80
❑ 77 Happy Hairston	4.00	1.80
❑ 78 Dave Stallworth SP	6.00	2.70
❑ 79 Fred Hetzel	2.50	1.10
❑ 80 Len Wilkens SP	20.00	9.00
❑ 81 Johnny Green RC	6.00	2.70
❑ 82 Erwin Mueller	2.50	1.10
❑ 83 Wally Jones	4.00	1.80
❑ 84 Bob Love	8.00	3.60
❑ 85 Dick Garrett RC	2.50	1.10
❑ 86 Don Nelson SP	20.00	9.00
❑ 87 Neal Walk SP	6.00	2.70
❑ 88 Larry Siegfried	2.50	1.10
❑ 89 Gary Gregor	2.50	1.10
❑ 90 Nate Thurmond	8.00	3.60
❑ 91 John Warren	2.50	1.10
❑ 92 Gus Johnson	6.00	2.70
❑ 93 Gail Goodrich	15.00	6.75
❑ 94 Dorie Murrey	2.50	1.10
❑ 95 Cazzie Russell SP	10.00	4.50
❑ 96 Terry Dischinger	2.50	1.10
❑ 97 Norm Van Lier SP RC	15.00	6.75
❑ 98 Jim Fox	2.50	1.10
❑ 99 Tom Meschery	2.50	1.10
❑ 100 Oscar Robertson	35.00	16.00
❑ 101A Checklist 111-175 (1970-71 in black)	30.00	9.00
❑ 101B Checklist 111-175 (1970-71 in white)	30.00	9.00
❑ 102 Rich Johnson	2.50	1.10
❑ 103 Mel Counts	4.00	1.80
❑ 104 Bill Hosket SP RC	6.00	2.70
❑ 105 Archie Clark	4.00	1.80
❑ 106 Walt Frazier AS	10.00	4.50
❑ 107 Jerry West AS	25.00	11.00
❑ 108 Bill Cunningham AS	10.00	4.50
❑ 109 Connie Hawkins AS	8.00	3.60
❑ 110 Willis Reed AS	8.00	3.60
❑ 111 Nate Thurmond AS	4.00	1.80
❑ 112 John Havlicek AS	30.00	13.50
❑ 113 Elgin Baylor AS	18.00	8.00
❑ 114 Oscar Robertson AS	20.00	9.00
❑ 115 Lou Hudson AS	4.00	1.80
❑ 116 Emmette Bryant	3.00	1.35
❑ 117 Greg Howard	3.00	1.35
❑ 118 Rick Adelman	5.00	2.20
❑ 119 Barry Clemens	3.00	1.35
❑ 120 Walt Frazier	30.00	13.50
❑ 121 Jim Barnes RC	3.00	1.35
❑ 122 Bernie Williams	3.00	1.35
❑ 123 Pete Maravich RC !	250.00	110.00
❑ 124 Matt Guokas RC	8.00	3.60
❑ 125 Dave Bing	12.00	5.50
❑ 126 John Tresvant	3.00	1.35
❑ 127 Shaler Halimon	3.00	1.35
❑ 128 Don Ohl	3.00	1.35
❑ 129 Fred Carter RC	6.00	2.70
❑ 130 Connie Hawkins	18.00	8.00
❑ 131 Jim King	3.00	1.35
❑ 132 Ed Manning RC	6.00	2.70
❑ 133 Adrian Smith	3.00	1.35
❑ 134 Walt Hazzard	6.00	2.70
❑ 135 Dave DeBusschere	15.00	6.75
❑ 136 Don Kojis	3.00	1.35
❑ 137 Calvin Murphy RC	30.00	13.50
❑ 138 Nate Bowman	3.00	1.35
❑ 139 Jon McGlocklin	5.00	2.20
❑ 140 Billy Cunningham	18.00	8.00
❑ 141 Willie McCarter	3.00	1.35
❑ 142 Jim Barnett	3.00	1.35
❑ 143 JoJo White RC	20.00	9.00
❑ 144 Clyde Lee	3.00	1.35
❑ 145 Tom Van Arsdale	6.00	2.70
❑ 146 Len Chappell	3.00	1.35
❑ 147 Lee Winfield	3.00	1.35
❑ 148 Jerry Sloan RC	20.00	9.00
❑ 149 Art Harris	3.00	1.35
❑ 150 Willis Reed	18.00	8.00
❑ 151 Art Williams	3.00	1.35
❑ 152 Don May	3.00	1.35
❑ 153 Loy Petersen	3.00	1.35
❑ 154 Dave Gambee	3.00	1.35
❑ 155 Hal Greer	6.00	2.70
❑ 156 Dave Newmark	3.00	1.35
❑ 157 Jimmy Collins	3.00	1.35
❑ 158 Bill Turner	3.00	1.35
❑ 159 Eddie Miles	3.00	1.35
❑ 160 Jerry West	50.00	22.00
❑ 161 Bob Quick	3.00	1.35
❑ 162 Fred Crawford	3.00	1.35
❑ 163 Tom Sanders	6.00	2.70
❑ 164 Dale Schlueter	3.00	1.35
❑ 165 Clem Haskins RC	12.00	5.50
❑ 166 Greg Smith	3.00	1.35
❑ 167 Rod Thorn RC	8.00	3.60
❑ 168 Willis Reed PO	10.00	4.50
❑ 169 Dick Garrett PO	5.00	2.20
❑ 170 Dave DeBusschere PO	10.00	4.50
❑ 171 Jerry West PO	18.00	8.00
❑ 172 Bill Bradley PO	18.00	8.00
❑ 173 Wilt Chamberlain PO	18.00	8.00
❑ 174 Walt Frazier PO	12.00	5.50
❑ 175 Knicks Celebrate (New York Knicks& World Champs)	20.00	6.00

1971-72 Topps

	NRMT-MT	EXC
COMPLETE SET (233)	750.00	350.00
COM. NBA CARD (1-144)	1.50	.70

COM. ABA CARD (145-233) 2.00 .90
NBA PLAYOFFS (134/135) 3.00 1.35
CL (144A/144B/145) 18.00 8.00
ABA LL (148/150/151) 4.00 1.80
NBA SEMISTARS 2.00 .90
ABA SEMISTARS 2.50 1.10
UNLISTED STARS 4.00 1.80

❑ 1 Oscar Robertson 40.00 12.00
❑ 2 Bill Bradley 30.00 13.50
❑ 3 Jim Fox 1.50 .70
❑ 4 John Johnson RC 2.00 .90
❑ 5 Luke Jackson 2.00 .90
❑ 6 Don May DP 1.50 .70
❑ 7 Kevin Loughery 2.00 .90
❑ 8 Terry Dischinger 1.50 .70
❑ 9 Neal Walk 2.00 .90
❑ 10 Elgin Baylor 25.00 11.00
❑ 11 Rick Adelman 2.00 .90
❑ 12 Clyde Lee 1.50 .70
❑ 13 Jerry Chambers 1.50 .70
❑ 14 Fred Carter 2.00 .90
❑ 15 Tom Boerwinkle DP 1.50 .70
❑ 16 John Block 1.50 .70
❑ 17 Dick Barnett 2.00 .90
❑ 18 Henry Finkel 1.50 .70
❑ 19 Norm Van Lier 4.00 1.80
❑ 20 Spencer Haywood RC 15.00 6.75
❑ 21 George Johnson 1.50 .70
❑ 22 Bobby Lewis 1.50 .70
❑ 23 Bill Hewitt 1.50 .70
❑ 24 Walt Hazzard DP 4.00 1.80
❑ 25 Happy Hairston 2.00 .90
❑ 26 George Wilson 1.50 .70
❑ 27 Lucius Allen 2.00 .90
❑ 28 Jim Washington 1.50 .70
❑ 29 Nate Archibald RC ! 25.00 11.00
❑ 30 Willis Reed 10.00 4.50
❑ 31 Erwin Mueller 1.50 .70
❑ 32 Art Harris 1.50 .70
❑ 33 Pete Cross 1.50 .70
❑ 34 Geoff Petrie RC 4.00 1.80
❑ 35 John Havlicek 30.00 13.50
❑ 36 Larry Siegfried 1.50 .70
❑ 37 John Tresvant DP 1.50 .70
❑ 38 Ron Williams 1.50 .70
❑ 39 Lamar Green DP 1.50 .70
❑ 40 Bob Rule DP 2.00 .90
❑ 41 Jim McMillian RC 2.00 .90
❑ 42 Wally Jones 2.00 .90
❑ 43 Bob Boozer 1.50 .70
❑ 44 Eddie Miles 1.50 .70
❑ 45 Bob Love DP 5.00 2.20
❑ 46 Claude English 1.50 .70
❑ 47 Dave Cowens RC 40.00 18.00
❑ 48 Emmette Bryant 1.50 .70
❑ 49 Dave Stallworth 2.00 .90
❑ 50 Jerry West 40.00 18.00
❑ 51 Joe Ellis 1.50 .70
❑ 52 Walt Wesley DP 1.50 .70
❑ 53 Howie Komives 1.50 .70
❑ 54 Paul Silas 4.00 1.80
❑ 55 Pete Maravich DP 40.00 18.00
❑ 56 Gary Gregor 1.50 .70
❑ 57 Sam Lacey RC 4.00 1.80
❑ 58 Calvin Murphy DP 6.00 2.70
❑ 59 Bob Dandridge 2.00 .90
❑ 60 Hal Greer 4.00 1.80
❑ 61 Keith Erickson 4.00 1.80
❑ 62 Joe Cooke 1.50 .70
❑ 63 Bob Lanier RC 40.00 18.00
❑ 64 Don Kojis 1.50 .70
❑ 65 Walt Frazier 18.00 8.00
❑ 66 Chet Walker DP 4.00 1.80
❑ 67 Dick Garrett 1.50 .70
❑ 68 John Trapp 2.00 .90
❑ 69 JoJo White 8.00 3.60
❑ 70 Wilt Chamberlain 50.00 22.00
❑ 71 Dave Sorenson 1.50 .70
❑ 72 Jim King 1.50 .70
❑ 73 Cazzie Russell 4.00 1.80
❑ 74 Jon McGlocklin 2.00 .90
❑ 75 Tom Van Arsdale 2.00 .90
❑ 76 Dale Schlueter 1.50 .70
❑ 77 Gus Johnson DP 4.00 1.80
❑ 78 Dave Bing 8.00 3.60
❑ 79 Billy Cunningham 10.00 4.50
❑ 80 Len Wilkens 10.00 4.50
❑ 81 Jerry Lucas DP 5.00 2.20
❑ 82 Don Chaney 4.00 1.80
❑ 83 McCoy McLemore 1.50 .70
❑ 84 Bob Kauffman DP 1.50 .70
❑ 85 Dick Van Arsdale 4.00 1.80
❑ 86 Johnny Green 2.00 .90
❑ 87 Jerry Sloan 5.00 2.20
❑ 88 Luther Rackley DP 1.50 .70
❑ 89 Shaler Halimon 1.50 .70
❑ 90 Jimmy Walker 2.00 .90
❑ 91 Rudy Tomjanovich RC 25.00 11.00
❑ 92 Levi Fontaine 1.50 .70
❑ 93 Bobby Smith 2.00 .90
❑ 94 Bob Arnzen 1.50 .70
❑ 95 Wes Unseld DP 6.00 2.70
❑ 96 Clem Haskins DP 4.00 1.80
❑ 97 Jim Davis 1.50 .70
❑ 98 Steve Kuberski 1.50 .70
❑ 99 Mike Davis DP 1.50 .70
❑ 100 Lew Alcindor 50.00 22.00
❑ 101 Willie McCarter 1.50 .70
❑ 102 Charlie Paulk 1.50 .70
❑ 103 Lee Winfield 1.50 .70
❑ 104 Jim Barnett 1.50 .70
❑ 105 Connie Hawkins DP 8.00 3.60
❑ 106 Archie Clark DP 2.00 .90
❑ 107 Dave DeBusschere 8.00 3.60
❑ 108 Stu Lantz DP 2.00 .90
❑ 109 Don Smith 1.50 .70
❑ 110 Lou Hudson 4.00 1.80
❑ 111 Leroy Ellis 1.50 .70
❑ 112 Jack Marin 2.00 .90
❑ 113 Matt Guokas 2.00 .90
❑ 114 Don Nelson 6.00 2.70
❑ 115 Jeff Mullins DP 2.00 .90
❑ 116 Walt Bellamy 6.00 2.70
❑ 117 Bob Quick 1.50 .70
❑ 118 John Warren 1.50 .70
❑ 119 Barry Clemens 1.50 .70
❑ 120 Elvin Hayes DP 10.00 4.50
❑ 121 Gail Goodrich 8.00 3.60
❑ 122 Ed Manning 2.00 .90
❑ 123 Herm Gilliam DP 1.50 .70
❑ 124 Dennis Awtrey RC 2.00 .90
❑ 125 John Hummer DP 1.50 .70
❑ 126 Mike Riordan 2.00 .90
❑ 127 Mel Counts 2.00 .90
❑ 128 Bob Weiss DP 1.50 .70
❑ 129 Greg Smith DP 1.50 .70
❑ 130 Earl Monroe 10.00 4.50
❑ 131 Nate Thurmond DP 4.00 1.80
❑ 132 Bill Bridges DP 2.00 .90
❑ 133 Lew Alcindor PO 12.00 5.50
❑ 134 NBA Playoffs G2 3.00 1.35
Bucks make it
Two Straight
❑ 135 Bob Dandridge PO 3.00 1.35
❑ 136 Oscar Robertsen PO 8.00 3.60
❑ 137 NBA Champs Celeb./Oscar 15.00 6.75
Bucks sweep Bullets
❑ 138 NBA Scoring Leaders 20.00 9.00
Lew Alcindor
Elvin Hayes
John Havlicek
❑ 139 NBA Scoring Average 20.00 9.00
Leaders
Lew Alcindor
John Havlicek
Elvin Hayes
❑ 140 NBA FG Pct Leaders 15.00 6.75
Johnny Green
Lew Alcindor
Wilt Chamberlain
❑ 141 NBA FT Pct Leaders 5.00 2.20
Chet Walker
Oscar Robertson
Ron Williams
❑ 142 NBA Rebound Leaders 25.00 11.00
Wilt Chamberlain
Elvin Hayes
Lew Alcindor
❑ 143 NBA Assist Leaders 12.00 5.50
Norm Van Lier
Oscar Robertson
Jerry West
❑ 144A NBA Checklist 1-144 18.00 5.50
(Copyright notation
extends up to
card 110)
❑ 144B NBA Checklist 1-144 18.00 5.50
(Copyright notation
extends up to
card 108)
❑ 145 ABA Checklist 145-233 18.00 5.50
❑ 146 ABA Scoring Leaders 8.00 3.60
Dan Issel
John Brisker
Charlie Scott
❑ 147 ABA Scoring Average 12.00 5.50
Leaders
Dan Issel
Rick Barry
John Brisker
❑ 148 ABA 2pt FG Pct Leaders 4.00 1.80
Zelmo Beaty
Bill Paultz
Roger Brown
❑ 149 ABA FT Pct Leaders 10.00 4.50
Rick Barry
Darrell Carrier
Billy Keller
❑ 150 ABA Rebound Leaders 4.00 1.80
Mel Daniels
Julius Keye
Mike Lewis
❑ 151 ABA Assist Leaders 4.00 1.80
Bill Melchionni
Mack Calvin
Charlie Scott
❑ 152 Larry Brown RC 20.00 9.00
❑ 153 Bob Bedell 2.00 .90
❑ 154 Merv Jackson 2.00 .90
❑ 155 Joe Caldwell 2.50 1.10
❑ 156 Billy Paultz RC 5.00 2.20
❑ 157 Les Hunter 2.50 1.10
❑ 158 Charlie Williams 2.00 .90
❑ 159 Stew Johnson 2.00 .90
❑ 160 Mack Calvin RC 5.00 2.20
❑ 161 Don Sidle 2.00 .90
❑ 162 Mike Barrett 2.00 .90
❑ 163 Tom Workman 2.00 .90
❑ 164 Joe Hamilton 2.50 1.10
❑ 165 Zelmo Beaty RC 8.00 3.60
❑ 166 Dan Hester 2.00 .90
❑ 167 Bob Verga 2.00 .90
❑ 168 Wilbert Jones 2.00 .90
❑ 169 Skeeter Swift 2.00 .90
❑ 170 Rick Barry RC 50.00 22.00
❑ 171 Billy Keller RC 4.00 1.80
❑ 172 Ron Franz 2.00 .90
❑ 173 Roland Taylor RC 2.50 1.10
❑ 174 Julian Hammond 2.00 .90
❑ 175 Steve Jones RC 6.00 2.70
❑ 176 Gerald Govan 2.50 1.10
❑ 177 Darrell Carrier RC 2.50 1.10
❑ 178 Ron Boone RC 5.00 2.20
❑ 179 George Peeples 2.00 .90
❑ 180 John Brisker 2.50 1.10
❑ 181 Doug Moe RC 6.00 2.70
❑ 182 Ollie Taylor 2.00 .90
❑ 183 Bob Netolicky RC 2.50 1.10
❑ 184 Sam Robinson 2.00 .90
❑ 185 James Jones 2.50 1.10
❑ 186 Julius Keye 2.50 1.10
❑ 187 Wayne Hightower 2.00 .90
❑ 188 Warren Armstrong RC 2.50 1.10
❑ 189 Mike Lewis 2.00 .90
❑ 190 Charlie Scott RC 8.00 3.60
❑ 191 Jim Ard 2.00 .90
❑ 192 George Lehmann 2.00 .90
❑ 193 Ira Harge 2.00 .90
❑ 194 Willie Wise RC 5.00 2.20
❑ 195 Mel Daniels RC 8.00 3.60
❑ 196 Larry Cannon 2.00 .90
❑ 197 Jim Eakins 2.50 1.10
❑ 198 Rich Jones 2.50 1.10
❑ 199 Bill Melchionni RC 4.00 1.80
❑ 200 Dan Issel RC 30.00 13.50
❑ 201 George Stone 2.00 .90
❑ 202 George Thompson 2.00 .90

	NRMT-MT	EXC
❑ 203 Craig Raymond	2.00	.90
❑ 204 Freddie Lewis RC	2.50	1.10
❑ 205 George Carter	2.50	1.10
❑ 206 Lonnie Wright	2.00	.90
❑ 207 Cincy Powell	2.50	1.10
❑ 208 Larry Miller	2.50	1.10
❑ 209 Sonny Dove	2.00	.90
❑ 210 Byron Beck RC	2.50	1.10
❑ 211 John Beasley	2.00	.90
❑ 212 Lee Davis	2.00	.90
❑ 213 Rick Mount RC	6.00	2.70
❑ 214 Walt Simon	2.00	.90
❑ 215 Glen Combs	2.00	.90
❑ 216 Neil Johnson	2.00	.90
❑ 217 Manny Leaks	2.00	.90
❑ 218 Chuck Williams	2.50	1.10
❑ 219 Warren Davis	2.00	.90
❑ 220 Donnie Freeman RC	2.50	1.10
❑ 221 Randy Mahaffey	2.00	.90
❑ 222 John Barnhill	2.00	.90
❑ 223 Al Cueto	2.00	.90
❑ 224 Louie Dampier RC	8.00	3.60
❑ 225 Roger Brown RC	5.00	2.20
❑ 226 Joe DePre	2.00	.90
❑ 227 Ray Scott	2.00	.90
❑ 228 Arvesta Kelly	2.00	.90
❑ 229 Vann Williford	2.00	.90
❑ 230 Larry Jones	2.50	1.10
❑ 231 Gene Moore	2.00	.90
❑ 232 Ralph Simpson RC	2.50	1.10
❑ 233 Red Robbins RC !	5.00	1.50

1972-73 Topps

	NRMT-MT	EXC
COMPLETE SET (264)	800.00	350.00
COM. NBA CARD (1-176)	1.00	.45
COM. ABA CARD (177-264)	1.50	.70
NBA PLAYOFFS (155-157)	2.50	1.10
NBA AS (162/166/170)	2.00	.90
ABA PLAYOFFS (241/245-247)	2.50	1.10
ABA AS (252-254/256-258)	2.00	.90
ABA LL (261/265)	2.50	1.10
CL (160/248)	16.00	7.25
NBA SEMISTARS	1.50	.70
ABA SEMISTARS	2.00	.90
UNLISTED STARS	3.00	1.35

	NRMT-MT	EXC
❑ 1 Wilt Chamberlain	60.00	18.00
❑ 2 Stan Love	1.00	.45
❑ 3 Geoff Petrie	1.50	.70
❑ 4 Curtis Perry RC	1.00	.45
❑ 5 Pete Maravich	35.00	16.00
❑ 6 Gus Johnson	3.00	1.35
❑ 7 Dave Cowens	15.00	6.75
❑ 8 Randy Smith RC	4.00	1.80
❑ 9 Matt Guokas	1.50	.70
❑ 10 Spencer Haywood	4.00	1.80
❑ 11 Jerry Sloan	3.00	1.35
❑ 12 Dave Sorenson	1.00	.45
❑ 13 Howie Komives	1.00	.45
❑ 14 Joe Ellis	1.00	.45
❑ 15 Jerry Lucas	5.00	2.20
❑ 16 Stu Lantz	1.50	.70
❑ 17 Bill Bridges	1.50	.70
❑ 18 Leroy Ellis	1.00	.45
❑ 19 Art Williams	1.00	.45
❑ 20 Sidney Wicks RC	8.00	3.60
❑ 21 Wes Unseld	6.00	2.70
❑ 22 Jim Washington	1.00	.45
❑ 23 Fred Hilton	1.00	.45
❑ 24 Curtis Rowe RC	1.50	.70
❑ 25 Oscar Robertson	20.00	9.00
❑ 26 Larry Steele RC	1.50	.70
❑ 27 Charlie Davis	1.00	.45
❑ 28 Nate Thurmond	5.00	2.20
❑ 29 Fred Carter	1.50	.70
❑ 30 Connie Hawkins	7.00	3.10
❑ 31 Calvin Murphy	5.00	2.20
❑ 32 Phil Jackson RC	40.00	18.00
❑ 33 Lee Winfield	1.00	.45
❑ 34 Jim Fox	1.00	.45
❑ 35 Dave Bing	6.00	2.70
❑ 36 Gary Gregor	1.00	.45
❑ 37 Mike Riordan	1.50	.70
❑ 38 George Trapp	1.00	.45
❑ 39 Mike Davis	1.00	.45
❑ 40 Bob Rule	1.50	.70
❑ 41 John Block	1.00	.45
❑ 42 Bob Dandridge	1.50	.70
❑ 43 John Johnson	1.50	.70
❑ 44 Rick Barry	18.00	8.00
❑ 45 JoJo White	4.00	1.80
❑ 46 Cliff Meely	1.00	.45
❑ 47 Charlie Scott	3.00	1.35
❑ 48 Johnny Green	1.50	.70
❑ 49 Pete Cross	1.00	.45
❑ 50 Gail Goodrich	6.00	2.70
❑ 51 Jim Davis	1.00	.45
❑ 52 Dick Barnett	1.50	.70
❑ 53 Bob Christian	1.00	.45
❑ 54 Jon McGlocklin	1.50	.70
❑ 55 Paul Silas	3.00	1.35
❑ 56 Hal Greer	3.00	1.35
❑ 57 Barry Clemens	1.00	.45
❑ 58 Nick Jones	1.00	.45
❑ 59 Cornell Warner	1.00	.45
❑ 60 Walt Frazier	10.00	4.50
❑ 61 Dorie Murrey	1.00	.45
❑ 62 Dick Cunningham	1.00	.45
❑ 63 Sam Lacey	1.50	.70
❑ 64 John Warren	1.00	.45
❑ 65 Tom Boerwinkle	1.00	.45
❑ 66 Fred Foster	1.00	.45
❑ 67 Mel Counts	1.00	.45
❑ 68 Toby Kimball	1.00	.45
❑ 69 Dale Schlueter	1.00	.45
❑ 70 Jack Marin	1.50	.70
❑ 71 Jim Barnett	1.00	.45
❑ 72 Clem Haskins	3.00	1.35
❑ 73 Earl Monroe	6.00	2.70
❑ 74 Tom Sanders	1.50	.70
❑ 75 Jerry West	25.00	11.00
❑ 76 Elmore Smith RC	1.50	.70
❑ 77 Don Adams	1.00	.45
❑ 78 Wally Jones	1.50	.70
❑ 79 Tom Van Arsdale	1.50	.70
❑ 80 Bob Lanier	18.00	8.00
❑ 81 Len Wilkens	8.00	3.60
❑ 82 Neal Walk	1.50	.70
❑ 83 Kevin Loughery	1.50	.70
❑ 84 Stan McKenzie	1.00	.45
❑ 85 Jeff Mullins	1.50	.70
❑ 86 Otto Moore	1.00	.45
❑ 87 John Tresvant	1.00	.45
❑ 88 Dean Meminger RC	1.00	.45
❑ 89 Jim McMillian	1.50	.70
❑ 90 Austin Carr RC	7.00	3.10
❑ 91 Clifford Ray RC	1.50	.70
❑ 92 Don Nelson	4.00	1.80
❑ 93 Mahdi Abdul-Rahman (formerly Walt Hazzard)	1.50	.70
❑ 94 Willie Norwood	1.00	.45
❑ 95 Dick Van Arsdale	1.50	.70
❑ 96 Don May	1.00	.45
❑ 97 Walt Bellamy	4.00	1.80
❑ 98 Garfield Heard RC	4.00	1.80
❑ 99 Dave Wohl	1.00	.45
❑ 100 Kareem Abdul-Jabbar	30.00	13.50
❑ 101 Ron Knight	1.00	.45
❑ 102 Phil Chenier RC	4.00	1.80
❑ 103 Rudy Tomjanovich	8.00	3.60
❑ 104 Flynn Robinson	1.00	.45
❑ 105 Dave DeBusschere	6.00	2.70
❑ 106 Dennis Layton	1.00	.45
❑ 107 Bill Hewitt	1.00	.45
❑ 108 Dick Garrett	1.00	.45
❑ 109 Walt Wesley	1.00	.45
❑ 110 John Havlicek	25.00	11.00
❑ 111 Norm Van Lier	1.50	.70
❑ 112 Cazzie Russell	3.00	1.35
❑ 113 Herm Gilliam	1.00	.45
❑ 114 Greg Smith	1.00	.45
❑ 115 Nate Archibald	6.00	2.70
❑ 116 Don Kojis	1.00	.45
❑ 117 Rick Adelman	1.50	.70
❑ 118 Luke Jackson	1.50	.70
❑ 119 Lamar Green	1.00	.45
❑ 120 Archie Clark	1.50	.70
❑ 121 Happy Hairston	1.50	.70
❑ 122 Bill Bradley	20.00	9.00
❑ 123 Ron Williams	1.00	.45
❑ 124 Jimmy Walker	1.50	.70
❑ 125 Bob Kauffman	1.00	.45
❑ 126 Rick Roberson	1.00	.45
❑ 127 Howard Porter RC	1.50	.70
❑ 128 Mike Newlin RC	1.50	.70
❑ 129 Willis Reed	8.00	3.60
❑ 130 Lou Hudson	3.00	1.35
❑ 131 Don Chaney	3.00	1.35
❑ 132 Dave Stallworth	1.00	.45
❑ 133 Charlie Yelverton	1.00	.45
❑ 134 Ken Durrett	1.00	.45
❑ 135 John Brisker	1.50	.70
❑ 136 Dick Snyder	1.00	.45
❑ 137 Jim McDaniels	1.00	.45
❑ 138 Clyde Lee	1.00	.45
❑ 139 Dennis Awtrey UER (Misspelled Awtry on card front)	1.50	.70
❑ 140 Keith Erickson	1.50	.70
❑ 141 Bob Weiss	1.50	.70
❑ 142 Butch Beard RC	3.00	1.35
❑ 143 Terry Dischinger	1.00	.45
❑ 144 Pat Riley	18.00	8.00
❑ 145 Lucius Allen	1.50	.70
❑ 146 John Mengelt RC	1.00	.45
❑ 147 John Hummer	1.00	.45
❑ 148 Bob Love	5.00	2.20
❑ 149 Bobby Smith	1.50	.70
❑ 150 Elvin Hayes	10.00	4.50
❑ 151 Nate Williams	1.00	.45
❑ 152 Chet Walker	3.00	1.35
❑ 153 Steve Kuberski	1.00	.45
❑ 154 Earl Monroe PO	3.00	1.35
❑ 155 NBA Playoffs G2 Lakers Come Back (under the basket)	2.50	1.10
❑ 156 NBA Playoffs G3 Two in a Row (under the basket)	2.50	1.10
❑ 157 Leroy Ellis PO	2.50	1.10
❑ 158 Jerry West PO	8.00	3.60
❑ 159 Wilt Chamberlain PO	10.00	4.50
❑ 160 NBA Checklist 1-176 UER (135 Jim King)	16.00	4.80
❑ 161 John Havlicek AS	10.00	4.50
❑ 162 Spencer Haywood AS	2.00	.90
❑ 163 Kareem Abdul-Jabbar AS	25.00	11.00
❑ 164 Jerry West AS	18.00	8.00
❑ 165 Walt Frazier AS	5.00	2.20
❑ 166 Bob Love AS	2.00	.90
❑ 167 Billy Cunningham AS	4.00	1.80
❑ 168 Wilt Chamberlain AS	20.00	9.00
❑ 169 Nate Archibald AS	4.00	1.80
❑ 170 Archie Clark AS	2.00	.90
❑ 171 NBA Scoring Leaders Kareem Abdul-Jabbar John Havlicek Nate Archibald	14.00	6.25
❑ 172 NBA Scoring Average Leaders Kareem Abdul-Jabbar Nate Archibald John Havlicek	14.00	6.25
❑ 173 NBA FG Pct Leaders Wilt Chamberlain Kareem Abdul-Jabbar Walt Bellamy	16.00	7.25
❑ 174 NBA FT Pct Leaders	3.00	1.35

Jack Marin
Calvin Murphy
Gail Goodrich
❑ 175 NBA Rebound Leaders 16.00 7.25
Wilt Chamberlain
Kareem Abdul-Jabbar
Wes Unseld
❑ 176 NBA Assist Leaders .. 12.00 5.50
Len Wilkens
Jerry West
Nate Archibald
❑ 177 Roland Taylor .... 1.50 .70
❑ 178 Art Becker .... 1.50 .70
❑ 179 Mack Calvin.................. 2.00 .90
❑ 180 Artis Gilmore RC 20.00 9.00
❑ 181 Collis Jones................. 1.50 .70
❑ 182 John Roche RC............ 2.00 .90
❑ 183 George McGinnis RC 14.00 6.25
❑ 184 Johnny Neumann .... 2.00 .90
❑ 185 Willie Wise.................. 2.00 .90
❑ 186 Bernie Williams .... 1.50 .70
❑ 187 Byron Beck .... 2.00 .90
❑ 188 Larry Miller .... 2.00 .90
❑ 189 Cincy Powell .... 1.50 .70
❑ 190 Donnie Freeman .... 2.00 .90
❑ 191 John Baum .... 1.50 .70
❑ 192 Billy Keller .... 2.00 .90
❑ 193 Wilbert Jones .... 1.50 .70
❑ 194 Glen Combs .... 1.50 .70
❑ 195 Julius Erving RC...... 200.00 90.00
(Forward on front&
but Center on back)
❑ 196 Al Smith........................ 1.50 .70
❑ 197 George Carter .... 1.50 .70
❑ 198 Louie Dampier.............. 3.00 1.35
❑ 199 Rich Jones .... 1.50 .70
❑ 200 Mel Daniels 3.00 1.35
❑ 201 Gene Moore .... 1.50 .70
❑ 202 Randy Denton .... 1.50 .70
❑ 203 Larry Jones .... 1.50 .70
❑ 204 Jim Ligon...................... 2.00 .90
❑ 205 Warren Jabali .... 2.00 .90
❑ 206 Joe Caldwell .... 2.00 .90
❑ 207 Darrell Carrier .... 2.00 .90
❑ 208 Gene Kennedy .... 1.50 .70
❑ 209 Ollie Taylor .... 1.50 .70
❑ 210 Roger Brown .... 2.00 .90
❑ 211 George Lehmann .... 1.50 .70
❑ 212 Red Robbins .... 2.00 .90
❑ 213 Jim Eakins.................... 2.00 .90
❑ 214 Willie Long................... 1.50 .70
❑ 215 Billy Cunningham 8.00 3.60
❑ 216 Steve Jones .... 2.00 .90
❑ 217 Les Hunter.................... 1.50 .70
❑ 218 Billy Paultz................... 2.00 .90
❑ 219 Freddie Lewis .... 2.00 .90
❑ 220 Zelmo Beaty .... 2.00 .90
❑ 221 George Thompson ...... 1.50 .70
❑ 222 Neil Johnson .... 1.50 .70
❑ 223 Dave Robisch RC .... 2.00 .90
❑ 224 Walt Simon .... 1.50 .70
❑ 225 Bill Melchionni .... 2.00 .90
❑ 226 Wendell Ladner RC...... 2.00 .90
❑ 227 Joe Hamilton .... 1.50 .70
❑ 228 Bob Netolicky .... 2.00 .90
❑ 229 James Jones................ 2.00 .90
❑ 230 Dan Issel 10.00 4.50
❑ 231 Charlie Williams .... 1.50 .70
❑ 232 Willie Sojourner........... 1.50 .70
❑ 233 Merv Jackson .... 1.50 .70
❑ 234 Mike Lewis .... 1.50 .70
❑ 235 Ralph Simpson .... 2.00 .90
❑ 236 Darnell Hillman .... 2.00 .90
❑ 237 Rick Mount 3.00 1.35
❑ 238 Gerald Govan .... 1.50 .70
❑ 239 Ron Boone .... 2.00 .90
❑ 240 Tom Washington.......... 1.50 .70
❑ 241 ABA Playoffs G1 .... 2.50 1.10
Pacers take lead
(under the basket)
❑ 242 Rick Barry PO 5.00 2.20
❑ 243 George McGinnis PO .. 4.00 1.80
❑ 244 Rick Barry PO 5.00 2.20
❑ 245 Billy Keller PO 2.50 1.10
❑ 246 ABA Playoffs G6 .... 2.50 1.10
Tight Defense
❑ 247 ABA Champs: Pacers 3.00 1.35
❑ 248 ABA Checklist 177-264 16.00 4.80
UER (236 John Brisker)
❑ 249 Dan Issel AS 6.00 2.70
❑ 250 Rick Barry AS 8.00 3.60
❑ 251 Artis Gilmore AS 6.00 2.70
❑ 252 Donnie Freeman AS .... 2.00 .90
❑ 253 Bill Melchionni AS .... 2.00 .90
❑ 254 Willie Wise AS 2.00 1.10
❑ 255 Julius Erving AS 50.00 22.00
❑ 256 Zelmo Beaty AS 2.50 1.10
❑ 257 Ralph Simpson AS 2.50 1.10
❑ 258 Charlie Scott AS........... 2.50 1.10
❑ 259 ABA Scoring Average .. 8.00 3.60
Leaders
Charlie Scott
Rick Barry
Dan Issel
❑ 260 ABA 2pt FG Pct. 4.00 1.80
Leaders
Artis Gilmore
Tom Washington
Larry Jones
❑ 261 ABA 3pt FG Pct. 2.50 1.10
Leaders
Glen Combs
Louie Dampier
Warren Jabali
❑ 262 ABA FT Pct Leaders 4.00 1.80
Rick Barry
Mack Calvin
Steve Jones
❑ 263 ABA Rebound Leaders 20.00 9.00
Artis Gilmore
Julius Erving
Mel Daniels
❑ 264 ABA Assist Leaders 6.00 1.80
Bill Melchionni
Larry Brown
Louie Dampier

1973-74 Topps

	NRMT-MT	EXC
COMPLETE SET (264)	325.00	145.00
COM. NBA CARD (1-176)	.50	.23
COM. ABA CARD (177-264)	1.00	.45
NBA PLAYOFFS (62/63/65/67)	1.00	.45
CL (121/242)	12.00	5.50
ABA PLAYOFFS (202-208)	2.00	.90
ABA LL (235-239)	2.00	.90
NBA SEMISTARS	1.00	.45
ABA SEMISTARS	1.50	.70
UNLISTED STARS	3.00	1.35
CONDITION SENSITIVE SET		

❑ 1 Nate Archibald AS1........ 10.00 3.00
❑ 2 Steve Kuberski .... .50 .23
❑ 3 John Mengelt.................... .50 .23
❑ 4 Jim McMillian................... 1.00 .45
❑ 5 Nate Thurmond 4.00 1.80
❑ 6 Dave Wohl........................ .50 .23
❑ 7 John Brisker .... .50 .23
❑ 8 Charlie Davis.................... .50 .23
❑ 9 Lamar Green.................... .50 .23
❑ 10 Walt Frazier AS2............ 6.00 2.70
❑ 11 Bob Christian.................. .50 .23
❑ 12 Cornell Warner .... .50 .23
❑ 13 Calvin Murphy 4.00 1.80
❑ 14 Dave Sorenson .... .50 .23
❑ 15 Archie Clark.................... 1.00 .45
❑ 16 Clifford Ray .... 1.00 .45
❑ 17 Terry Driscoll .... .50 .23
❑ 18 Matt Guokas .... 1.00 .45
❑ 19 Elmore Smith.................. 1.00 .45
❑ 20 John Havlicek AS1 ...... 15.00 6.75
❑ 21 Pat Riley 8.00 3.60
❑ 22 George Trapp .... .50 .23
❑ 23 Ron Williams .... .50 .23
❑ 24 Jim Fox .... .50 .23
❑ 25 Dick Van Arsdale............ 1.00 .45
❑ 26 John Tresvant .... .50 .23
❑ 27 Rick Adelman .... 1.00 .45
❑ 28 Eddie Mast .... .50 .23
❑ 29 Jim Cleamons .... 1.00 .45
❑ 30 Dave DeBusschere AS2 5.00 2.20
❑ 31 Norm Van Lier .... 1.00 .45
❑ 32 Stan McKenzie .... .50 .23
❑ 33 Bob Dandridge .... 1.00 .45
❑ 34 Leroy Ellis .... 1.00 .45
❑ 35 Mike Riordan .... 1.00 .45
❑ 36 Fred Hilton........................ .50 .23
❑ 37 Toby Kimball .... .50 .23
❑ 38 Jim Price .... .50 .23
❑ 39 Willie Norwood .... .50 .23
❑ 40 Dave Cowens AS2 ...... 10.00 4.50
❑ 41 Cazzie Russell .... 1.00 .45
❑ 42 Lee Winfield .... .50 .23
❑ 43 Connie Hawkins 5.00 2.20
❑ 44 Mike Newlin.................... 1.00 .45
❑ 45 Chet Walker .... 1.00 .45
❑ 46 Walt Bellamy 4.00 1.80
❑ 47 John Johnson .... 1.00 .45
❑ 48 Henry Bibby RC 5.00 2.20
❑ 49 Bobby Smith .... 1.00 .45
❑ 50 K.Abdul-Jabbar AS1 .... 25.00 11.00
❑ 51 Mike Price .... .50 .23
❑ 52 John Hummer .... .50 .23
❑ 53 Kevin Porter RC 5.00 2.20
❑ 54 Nate Williams .... .50 .23
❑ 55 Gail Goodrich 4.00 1.80
❑ 56 Fred Foster .... .50 .23
❑ 57 Don Chaney .... 1.00 .45
❑ 58 Bud Stallworth .... .50 .23
❑ 59 Clem Haskins .... 1.00 .45
❑ 60 Bob Love AS2 .... 3.00 1.35
❑ 61 Jimmy Walker .... 1.00 .45
❑ 62 NBA Eastern Semis ...... 1.00 .45
Knicks shoot down
Bullets in 5
❑ 63 NBA Eastern Semis ...... 1.00 .45
Celts oust Hawks
2nd Straight Year
❑ 64 Wilt Chamberlain PO...... 8.00 3.60
❑ 65 NBA Western Semis ...... 1.00 .45
Warriors over-
whelm Milwaukee
❑ 66 Willis Reed PO 3.00 1.35
Henry Finkel
❑ 67 NBA Western Finals ...... 1.00 .45
Lakers Breeze Past
Golden State
❑ 68 NBA Championship........ 4.00 1.80
Knicks Do It&
Repeat '70 Miracle
(W.Frazier/Erickson)
❑ 69 Larry Steele.................... 1.00 .45
❑ 70 Oscar Robertson 15.00 6.75
❑ 71 Phil Jackson 15.00 6.75
❑ 72 John Wetzel .... .50 .23
❑ 73 Steve Patterson RC ...... 1.00 .45
❑ 74 Manny Leaks.................... .50 .23
❑ 75 Jeff Mullins .... 1.00 .45
❑ 76 Stan Love .... .50 .23
❑ 77 Dick Garrett .... .50 .23
❑ 78 Don Nelson 4.00 1.80
❑ 79 Chris Ford RC 3.00 1.35
❑ 80 Wilt Chamberlain 25.00 11.00
❑ 81 Dennis Layton .... .50 .23
❑ 82 Bill Bradley 15.00 6.75
❑ 83 Jerry Sloan .... 1.00 .45
❑ 84 Cliff Meely .... .50 .23
❑ 85 Sam Lacey .... .50 .23
❑ 86 Dick Snyder .... .50 .23

Card	NRMT-MT	EXC
❑ 87 Jim Washington	.50	.23
❑ 88 Lucius Allen	1.00	.45
❑ 89 LaRue Martin	.50	.23
❑ 90 Rick Barry	8.00	3.60
❑ 91 Fred Boyd	.50	.23
❑ 92 Barry Clemens	.50	.23
❑ 93 Dean Meminger	.50	.23
❑ 94 Henry Finkel	.50	.23
❑ 95 Elvin Hayes	6.00	2.70
❑ 96 Stu Lantz	1.00	.45
❑ 97 Bill Hewitt	.50	.23
❑ 98 Neal Walk	.50	.23
❑ 99 Garfield Heard	1.00	.45
❑ 100 Jerry West AS1	20.00	9.00
❑ 101 Otto Moore	.50	.23
❑ 102 Don Kojis	.50	.23
❑ 103 Fred Brown RC	6.00	2.70
❑ 104 Dwight Davis	.50	.23
❑ 105 Willis Reed	6.00	2.70
❑ 106 Herm Gilliam	.50	.23
❑ 107 Mickey Davis	.50	.23
❑ 108 Jim Barnett	.50	.23
❑ 109 Ollie Johnson	.50	.23
❑ 110 Bob Lanier	6.00	2.70
❑ 111 Fred Carter	1.00	.45
❑ 112 Paul Silas	3.00	1.35
❑ 113 Phil Chenier	1.00	.45
❑ 114 Dennis Awtrey	.50	.23
❑ 115 Austin Carr	1.00	.45
❑ 116 Bob Kauffman	.50	.23
❑ 117 Keith Erickson	1.00	.45
❑ 118 Walt Wesley	.50	.23
❑ 119 Steve Bracey	.50	.23
❑ 120 Spencer Haywood AS1	3.00	1.35
❑ 121 NBA Checklist 1-176	12.00	3.60
❑ 122 Jack Marin	1.00	.45
❑ 123 Jon McGlocklin	.50	.23
❑ 124 Johnny Green	1.00	.45
❑ 125 Jerry Lucas	3.00	1.35
❑ 126 Paul Westphal RC	20.00	9.00
❑ 127 Curtis Rowe	1.00	.45
❑ 128 Mahdi Abdul-Rahman	1.00	.45
(formerly Walt Hazzard)		
❑ 129 Lloyd Neal RC	.50	.23
❑ 130 Pete Maravich AS1	30.00	13.50
❑ 131 Don May	.50	.23
❑ 132 Bob Weiss	1.00	.45
❑ 133 Dave Stallworth	.50	.23
❑ 134 Dick Cunningham	.50	.23
❑ 135 Bob McAdoo RC !	20.00	9.00
❑ 136 Butch Beard	1.00	.45
❑ 137 Happy Hairston	1.00	.45
❑ 138 Bob Rule	1.00	.45
❑ 139 Don Adams	.50	.23
❑ 140 Charlie Scott	1.00	.45
❑ 141 Ron Riley	.50	.23
❑ 142 Earl Monroe	4.00	1.80
❑ 143 Clyde Lee	.50	.23
❑ 144 Rick Roberson	.50	.23
❑ 145 Rudy Tomjanovich	6.00	2.70
(Printed without		
Houston on basket)		
❑ 146 Tom Van Arsdale	1.00	.45
❑ 147 Art Williams	.50	.23
❑ 148 Curtis Perry	.50	.23
❑ 149 Rich Rinaldi	.50	.23
❑ 150 Lou Hudson	1.00	.45
❑ 151 Mel Counts	.50	.23
❑ 152 Jim McDaniels	.50	.23
❑ 153 NBA Scoring Leaders	8.00	3.60
Nate Archibald		
Kareem Abdul-Jabbar		
Spencer Haywood		
❑ 154 NBA Scoring Average	8.00	3.60
Leaders		
Nate Archibald		
Kareem Abdul-Jabbar		
Spencer Haywood		
❑ 155 NBA FG Pct Leaders	12.00	5.50
Wilt Chamberlain		
Matt Guokas		
Kareem Abdul-Jabbar		
❑ 156 NBA FT Pct Leaders	4.00	1.80
Rick Barry		
Calvin Murphy		
Mike Newlin		
❑ 157 NBA Rebound Leaders	8.00	3.60
Wilt Chamberlain		
Nate Thurmond		
Dave Cowens		
❑ 158 NBA Assist Leaders	4.00	1.80
Nate Archibald		
Len Wilkens		
Dave Bing		
❑ 159 Don Smith	.50	.23
❑ 160 Sidney Wicks	3.00	1.35
❑ 161 Howie Komives	.50	.23
❑ 162 John Gianelli	.50	.23
❑ 163 Jeff Halliburton	.50	.23
❑ 164 Kennedy McIntosh	.50	.23
❑ 165 Len Wilkens	6.00	2.70
❑ 166 Corky Calhoun	.50	.23
❑ 167 Howard Porter	1.00	.45
❑ 168 JoJo White	3.00	1.35
❑ 169 John Block	.50	.23
❑ 170 Dave Bing	4.00	1.80
❑ 171 Joe Ellis	.50	.23
❑ 172 Chuck Terry	.50	.23
❑ 173 Randy Smith	1.00	.45
❑ 174 Bill Bridges	1.00	.45
❑ 175 Geoff Petrie	1.00	.45
❑ 176 Wes Unseld	4.00	1.80
❑ 177 Skeeter Swift	1.00	.45
❑ 178 Jim Eakins	1.50	.70
❑ 179 Steve Jones	1.50	.70
❑ 180 George McGinnis AS1	3.00	1.35
❑ 181 Al Smith	1.00	.45
❑ 182 Tom Washington	1.00	.45
❑ 183 Louie Dampier	1.50	.70
❑ 184 Simmie Hill	1.00	.45
❑ 185 George Thompson	1.00	.45
❑ 186 Cincy Powell	1.50	.70
❑ 187 Larry Jones	1.00	.45
❑ 188 Neil Johnson	1.00	.45
❑ 189 Tom Owens	1.00	.45
❑ 190 Ralph Simpson AS2	1.50	.70
❑ 191 George Carter	1.50	.70
❑ 192 Rick Mount	1.50	.70
❑ 193 Red Robbins	1.50	.70
❑ 194 George Lehmann	1.00	.45
❑ 195 Mel Daniels AS2	1.50	.70
❑ 196 Bob Warren	1.00	.45
❑ 197 Gene Kennedy	1.00	.45
❑ 198 Mike Barr	1.00	.45
❑ 199 Dave Robisch	1.00	.45
❑ 200 Billy Cunningham AS1	5.00	2.20
❑ 201 John Roche	1.50	.70
❑ 202 ABA Western Semis	2.00	.90
Pacers Oust		
Injured Rockets		
❑ 203 ABA Western Semis	2.00	.90
Stars sweep Q's		
in Four Straight		
❑ 204 Dan Issel PO	2.00	.90
❑ 205 ABA Eastern Semis	2.00	.90
Cougars in strong		
finish over Nets		
❑ 206 ABA Western Finals	2.00	.90
Pacers nip bitter		
rival& Stars		
❑ 207 Artis Gilmore PO	3.00	1.35
❑ 208 George McGinnis PO	2.00	.90
❑ 209 Glen Combs	1.00	.45
❑ 210 Dan Issel AS2	6.00	2.70
❑ 211 Randy Denton	1.00	.45
❑ 212 Freddie Lewis	1.50	.70
❑ 213 Stew Johnson	1.00	.45
❑ 214 Roland Taylor	1.00	.45
❑ 215 Rich Jones	1.00	.45
❑ 216 Billy Paultz	1.50	.70
❑ 217 Ron Boone	1.50	.70
❑ 218 Walt Simon	1.00	.45
❑ 219 Mike Lewis	1.00	.45
❑ 220 Warren Jabali AS1	1.50	.70
❑ 221 Wilbert Jones	1.00	.45
❑ 222 Don Buse RC	1.50	.70
❑ 223 Gene Moore	1.00	.45
❑ 224 Joe Hamilton	1.50	.70
❑ 225 Zelmo Beaty	1.50	.70
❑ 226 Brian Taylor RC	1.50	.70
❑ 227 Julius Keye	1.00	.45
❑ 228 Mike Gale RC	1.50	.70
❑ 229 Warren Davis	1.00	.45
❑ 230 Mack Calvin AS2	1.50	.70
❑ 231 Roger Brown	1.50	.70
❑ 232 Chuck Williams	1.50	.70
❑ 233 Gerald Govan	1.50	.70
❑ 234 ABA Scoring Average	10.00	4.50
Leaders		
Julius Erving		
George McGinnis		
Dan Issel		
❑ 235 ABA 2 Pt. Pct.	2.00	1.10
Leaders		
Artis Gilmore		
Gene Kennedy		
Tom Owens		
❑ 236 ABA 3 Pt. Pct.	2.00	.90
Leaders		
Glen Combs		
Roger Brown		
Louie Dampier		
❑ 237 ABA F.T. Pct. Leaders	2.00	.90
Billy Keller		
Ron Boone		
Bob Warren		
❑ 238 ABA Rebound Leaders	3.00	1.35
Artis Gilmore		
Mel Daniels		
Bill Paultz		
❑ 239 ABA Assist Leaders	2.00	.90
Bill Melchionni		
Chuck Williams		
Warren Jabali		
❑ 240 Julius Erving AS2	50.00	22.00
❑ 241 Jimmy O'Brien	1.00	.45
❑ 242 ABA Checklist 177-264	12.00	3.60
❑ 243 Johnny Neumann	1.00	.45
❑ 244 Darnell Hillman	1.50	.70
❑ 245 Willie Wise	1.50	.70
❑ 246 Collis Jones	1.00	.45
❑ 247 Ted McClain	1.00	.45
❑ 248 George Irvine RC	1.00	.45
❑ 249 Bill Melchionni	1.50	.70
❑ 250 Artis Gilmore AS1	6.00	2.70
❑ 251 Willie Long	1.00	.45
❑ 252 Larry Miller	1.00	.45
❑ 253 Lee Davis	1.00	.45
❑ 254 Donnie Freeman	1.50	.70
❑ 255 Joe Caldwell	1.50	.70
❑ 256 Bob Netolicky	1.50	.70
❑ 257 Bernie Williams	1.00	.45
❑ 258 Byron Beck	1.50	.70
❑ 259 Jim Chones RC	3.00	1.35
❑ 260 James Jones AS1	1.50	.70
❑ 261 Wendell Ladner	1.00	.45
❑ 262 Ollie Taylor	1.00	.45
❑ 263 Les Hunter	1.00	.45
❑ 264 Billy Keller	3.00	.90

1974-75 Topps

	NRMT-MT	EXC
COMPLETE SET (264)	325.00	145.00
COM. NBA CARD (1-176)	.50	.23
COM. ABA CARD (177-264)	1.00	.45
NBA TL (83/85/86/88-90)	1.00	.45
NBA TL (92/94-98)	1.00	.45
NBA TL (84/87)	3.00	1.35
CL (141/203)	10.00	4.50

NBA LL (147/149)	1.00	.45
NBA PLAYOFFS (161-164)	1.00	.45
ABA LL (208-212)	2.00	.90
ABA TL (221-225/228-230)	2.00	.90
ABA PLAYOFFS (246-248)	2.00	.90
NBA SEMISTARS	1.00	.45
ABA SEMISTARS	1.50	.70
UNLISTED STARS	3.00	1.35

❑	1 K.Abdul-Jabbar AS1	30.00	9.00
❑	2 Don May	.50	.23
❑	3 Bernie Fryer RC	1.00	.45
❑	4 Don Adams	.50	.23
❑	5 Herm Gilliam	.50	.23
❑	6 Jim Chones	1.00	.45
❑	7 Rick Adelman	1.00	.45
❑	8 Randy Smith	1.00	.45
❑	9 Paul Silas	3.00	1.35
❑	10 Pete Maravich	25.00	11.00
❑	11 Ron Behagen	.50	.23
❑	12 Kevin Porter	1.00	.45
❑	13 Bill Bridges	1.00	.45
	(On back team shown as Los And.& should be Los Ang.)		
❑	14 Charles Johnson RC	.50	.23
❑	15 Bob Love	1.00	.45
❑	16 Henry Bibby	1.00	.45
❑	17 Neal Walk	.50	.23
❑	18 John Brisker	.50	.23
❑	19 Lucius Allen	.50	.23
❑	20 Tom Van Arsdale	1.00	.45
❑	21 Larry Steele	.50	.23
❑	22 Curtis Rowe	1.00	.45
❑	23 Dean Meminger	.50	.23
❑	24 Steve Patterson	.50	.23
❑	25 Earl Monroe	3.00	1.35
❑	26 Jack Marin	.50	.23
❑	27 JoJo White	3.00	1.35
❑	28 Rudy Tomjanovich	6.00	2.70
❑	29 Otto Moore	.50	.23
❑	30 Elvin Hayes AS2	5.00	2.20
❑	31 Pat Riley	8.00	3.60
❑	32 Clyde Lee	.50	.23
❑	33 Bob Weiss	.50	.23
❑	34 Jim Fox	.50	.23
❑	35 Charlie Scott	1.00	.45
❑	36 Cliff Meely	.50	.23
❑	37 Jon McGlocklin	.50	.23
❑	38 Jim McMillian	1.00	.45
❑	39 Bill Walton RC	50.00	22.00
❑	40 Dave Bing AS2	3.00	1.35
❑	41 Jim Washington	.50	.23
❑	42 Jim Cleamons	1.00	.45
❑	43 Mel Davis	.50	.23
❑	44 Garfield Heard	1.00	.45
❑	45 Jimmy Walker	1.00	.45
❑	46 Don Nelson	1.00	.45
❑	47 Jim Barnett	.50	.23
❑	48 Manny Leaks	.50	.23
❑	49 Elmore Smith	1.00	.45
❑	50 Rick Barry AS1	6.00	2.70
❑	51 Jerry Sloan	1.00	.45
❑	52 John Hummer	.50	.23
❑	53 Keith Erickson	1.00	.45
❑	54 George E. Johnson	.50	.23
❑	55 Oscar Robertson	12.00	5.50
❑	56 Steve Mix RC	1.00	.45
❑	57 Rick Roberson	.50	.23
❑	58 John Mengelt	.50	.23
❑	59 Dwight Jones RC	1.00	.45
❑	60 Austin Carr	1.00	.45
❑	61 Nick Weatherspoon RC	1.00	.45
❑	62 Clem Haskins	1.00	.45
❑	63 Don Kojis	.50	.23
❑	64 Paul Westphal	3.00	1.35
❑	65 Walt Bellamy	4.00	1.80
❑	66 John Johnson	1.00	.45
❑	67 Butch Beard	1.00	.45
❑	68 Happy Hairston	1.00	.45
❑	69 Tom Boerwinkle	.50	.23
❑	70 Spencer Haywood AS2	3.00	1.35
❑	71 Gary Melchionni	.50	.23
❑	72 Ed Ratleff RC	1.00	.45
❑	73 Mickey Davis	.50	.23
❑	74 Dennis Awtrey	.50	.23
❑	75 Fred Carter	1.00	.45
❑	76 George Trapp	.50	.23
❑	77 John Wetzel	.50	.23
❑	78 Bobby Smith	1.00	.45
❑	79 John Gianelli	.50	.23
❑	80 Bob McAdoo AS2	6.00	2.70
❑	81 Atlanta Hawks TL	6.00	2.70
	Pete Maravich		
	Lou Hudson		
	Walt Bellamy		
	Pete Maravich		
❑	82 Boston Celtics TL	5.00	2.20
	John Havlicek		
	JoJo White		
	Dave Cowens		
	JoJo White		
❑	83 Buffalo Braves TL	1.00	.45
	Bob McAdoo		
	Ernie DiGregorio		
	Bob McAdoo		
	Ernie DiGregorio		
❑	84 Chicago Bulls TL	3.00	1.35
	Bob Love		
	Chet Walker		
	Clifford Ray		
	Norm Van Lier		
❑	85 Cleveland Cavs TL	1.00	.45
	Austin Carr		
	Austin Carr		
	Dwight Davis		
	Len Wilkens		
❑	86 Detroit Pistons TL	1.00	.45
	Bob Lanier		
	Stu Lantz		
	Bob Lanier		
	Dave Bing		
❑	87 Golden State Warriors TL	3.00	1.35
	Rick Barry		
	Rick Barry		
	Nate Thurmond		
	Rick Barry		
❑	88 Houston Rockets TL	1.00	.45
	Rudy Tomjanovich		
	Calvin Murphy		
	Don Smith		
	Calvin Murphy		
❑	89 Kansas City Omaha TL	1.00	.45
	Jimmy Walker		
	Jimmy Walker		
	Sam Lacey		
	Jimmy Walker		
❑	90 Los Angeles Lakers TL	1.00	.45
	Gail Goodrich		
	Gail Goodrich		
	Happy Hairston		
	Gail Goodrich		
❑	91 Milwaukee Bucks TL	12.00	5.50
	Kareem Abdul-Jabbar		
	Oscar Robertson		
	Kareem Abdul-Jabbar		
	Oscar Robertson		
❑	92 New Orleans Jazz	1.00	.45
	Emblem; Expansion Draft Picks on Back		
❑	93 New York Knicks TL	5.00	2.20
	Walt Frazier		
	Bill Bradley		
	Dave DeBusschere		
	Walt Frazier		
❑	94 Philadelphia 76ers TL	1.00	.45
	Fred Carter		
	Tom Van Arsdale		
	Leroy Ellis		
	Fred Carter		
❑	95 Phoenix Suns TL	1.00	.45
	Charlie Scott		
	Dick Van Arsdale		
	Neal Walk		
	Neal Walk		
❑	96 Portland Trail Blazers TL	1.00	.45
	Geoff Petrie		
	Geoff Petrie		
	Rick Roberson		
	Sidney Wicks		
❑	97 Seattle Supersonics TL	1.00	.45
	Spencer Haywood		
	Dick Snyder		
	Spencer Haywood		
	Fred Brown		
❑	98 Capitol Bullets TL	1.00	.45
	Phil Chenier		
	Phil Chenier		
	Elvin Hayes		
	Kevin Porter		
❑	99 Sam Lacey	.50	.23
❑	100 John Havlicek AS1	10.00	4.50
❑	101 Stu Lantz	1.00	.45
❑	102 Mike Riordan	.50	.23
❑	103 Larry Jones	.50	.23
❑	104 Connie Hawkins	4.00	1.80
❑	105 Nate Thurmond	3.00	1.35
❑	106 Dick Gibbs	.50	.23
❑	107 Corky Calhoun	.50	.23
❑	108 Dave Wohl	.50	.23
❑	109 Cornell Warner	.50	.23
❑	110 Geoff Petrie UER	1.00	.45
	(Misspelled Patrie on card front)		
❑	111 Leroy Ellis	1.00	.45
❑	112 Chris Ford	1.00	.45
❑	113 Bill Bradley	10.00	4.50
❑	114 Clifford Ray	1.00	.45
❑	115 Dick Snyder	.50	.23
❑	116 Nate Williams	.50	.23
❑	117 Matt Guokas	1.00	.45
❑	118 Henry Finkel	.50	.23
❑	119 Curtis Perry	.50	.23
❑	120 Gail Goodrich AS1	3.00	1.35
❑	121 Wes Unseld	3.00	1.35
❑	122 Howard Porter	1.00	.45
❑	123 Jeff Mullins	.50	.23
❑	124 Mike Bantom RC	1.00	.45
❑	125 Fred Brown	1.00	.45
❑	126 Bob Dandridge	1.00	.45
❑	127 Mike Newlin	1.00	.45
❑	128 Greg Smith	.50	.23
❑	129 Doug Collins RC	16.00	7.25
❑	130 Lou Hudson	1.00	.45
❑	131 Bob Lanier	5.00	2.20
❑	132 Phil Jackson	10.00	4.50
❑	133 Don Chaney	1.00	.45
❑	134 Jim Brewer RC	1.00	.45
❑	135 Ernie DiGregorio RC	3.00	1.35
❑	136 Steve Kuberski	.50	.23
❑	137 Jim Price	.50	.23
❑	138 Mike D'Antoni	.50	.23
❑	139 John Brown	.50	.23
❑	140 Norm Van Lier AS2	1.00	.45
❑	141 NBA Checklist 1-176	10.00	3.00
❑	142 Don Slick Watts RC	1.00	.45
❑	143 Walt Wesley	.50	.23
❑	144 NBA Scoring Leaders	12.00	5.50
	Bob McAdoo		
	Kareem Abdul-Jabbar		
	Pete Maravich		
❑	145 NBA Scoring Average Leaders	12.00	5.50
	Bob McAdoo		
	Pete Maravich		
	Kareem Abdul-Jabbar		
❑	146 NBA F.G. Pct. Leaders	10.00	4.50
	Bob McAdoo		
	Kareem Abdul-Jabbar		
	Rudy Tomjanovich		
❑	147 NBA F.T. Pct. Leaders	1.00	.45
	Ernie DiGregorio		
	Rick Barry		
	Jeff Mullins		
❑	148 NBA Rebound Leaders	4.00	1.80
	Elvin Hayes		
	Dave Cowens		
	Bob McAdoo		
❑	149 NBA Assist Leaders	1.00	.45
	Ernie DiGregorio		
	Calvin Murphy		
	Len Wilkens		
❑	150 Walt Frazier AS1	5.00	2.20
❑	151 Cazzie Russell	1.00	.45
❑	152 Calvin Murphy	3.00	1.35
❑	153 Bob Kauffman	.50	.23

❑ 154 Fred Boyd .50 .23
❑ 155 Dave Cowens 6.00 2.70
❑ 156 Willie Norwood .50 .23
❑ 157 Lee Winfield .50 .23
❑ 158 Dwight Davis .50 .23
❑ 159 George T. Johnson .50 .23
❑ 160 Dick Van Arsdale 1.00 .45
❑ 161 NBA Eastern Semis 1.00 .45
Celts over Braves
Knicks edge Bullets
❑ 162 NBA Western Semis 1.00 .45
Bucks over Lakers
Bulls edge Pistons
❑ 163 NBA Div. Finals 1.00 .45
Celts over Knicks
Bucks sweep Bulls
❑ 164 NBA Championship 1.50 .70
Celtics over Bucks
❑ 165 Phil Chenier 1.00 .45
❑ 166 Kermit Washington RC 1.00 .45
❑ 167 Dale Schlueter .50 .23
❑ 168 John Block .50 .23
❑ 169 Don Smith .50 .23
❑ 170 Nate Archibald 4.00 1.80
❑ 171 Chet Walker 1.00 .45
❑ 172 Archie Clark 1.00 .45
❑ 173 Kennedy McIntosh .50 .23
❑ 174 George Thompson .50 .23
❑ 175 Sidney Wicks 3.00 1.35
❑ 176 Jerry West 20.00 9.00
❑ 177 Dwight Lamar 1.00 .45
❑ 178 George Carter 1.50 .70
❑ 179 Wil Robinson 1.00 .45
❑ 180 Artis Gilmore AS1 4.00 1.80
❑ 181 Brian Taylor 1.50 .70
❑ 182 Darnell Hillman 1.50 .70
❑ 183 Dave Robisch 1.50 .70
❑ 184 Gene Littles RC 1.50 .70
❑ 185 Willie Wise AS2 1.50 .70
❑ 186 James Silas RC 3.00 1.35
❑ 187 Caldwell Jones RC 3.00 1.35
❑ 188 Roland Taylor 1.00 .45
❑ 189 Randy Denton 1.00 .45
❑ 190 Dan Issel AS2 5.00 2.20
❑ 191 Mike Gale 1.00 .45
❑ 192 Mel Daniels 1.50 .70
❑ 193 Steve Jones 1.50 .70
❑ 194 Marv Roberts 1.00 .45
❑ 195 Ron Boone AS2 1.50 .70
❑ 196 George Gervin RC ! 40.00 18.00
❑ 197 Flynn Robinson 1.00 .45
❑ 198 Cincy Powell 1.50 .70
❑ 199 Glen Combs 1.00 .45
❑ 200 Julius Erving AS1 UER 40.00 18.00
(Misspelled Irving
on card back)
❑ 201 Billy Keller 1.50 .70
❑ 202 Willie Long 1.00 .45
❑ 203 ABA Checklist 177-264 10.00 3.00
❑ 204 Joe Caldwell 1.50 .70
❑ 205 Swen Nater AS2 RC 1.50 .70
❑ 206 Rick Mount 1.50 .70
❑ 207 ABA Scoring 10.00 4.50
Avg. Leaders
Julius Erving
George McGinnis
Dan Issel
❑ 208 ABA Two-Point Field 2.00 .90
Goal Percent Leaders
Swen Nater
James Jones
Tom Owens
❑ 209 ABA Three-Point Field 2.00 .90
Goal Percent Leaders
Louie Dampier
Billy Keller
Roger Brown
❑ 210 ABA Free Throw 2.00 .90
Percent Leaders
James Jones
Mack Calvin
Ron Boone
❑ 211 ABA Rebound Leaders 2.50 1.10
Artis Gilmore
George McGinnis
Caldwell Jones
❑ 212 ABA Assist Leaders 2.00 .90
Al Smith
Chuck Williams
Louie Dampier
❑ 213 Larry Miller 1.00 .45
❑ 214 Stew Johnson 1.00 .45
❑ 215 Larry Finch RC 1.50 .70
❑ 216 Larry Kenon RC 3.00 1.35
❑ 217 Joe Hamilton 1.50 .70
❑ 218 Gerald Govan 1.50 .70
❑ 219 Ralph Simpson 1.50 .70
❑ 220 George McGinnis AS1 3.00 1.35
❑ 221 Carolina Cougars TL 2.50 1.10
Billy Cunningham
Mack Calvin
Tom Owens
Joe Caldwell
❑ 222 Denver Nuggets TL 2.50 1.10
Ralph Simpson
Byron Beck
Dave Robisch
Al Smith
❑ 223 Indiana Pacers TL 2.50 1.10
George McGinnis
Billy Keller
George McGinnis
Freddie Lewis
❑ 224 Kentucky Colonels TL 3.00 1.35
Dan Issel
Louie Dampier
Artis Gilmore
Louie Dampier
❑ 225 Memphis Sounds TL 2.00 .90
George Thompson
Larry Finch
Randy Denton
George Thompson
❑ 226 New York Nets TL 10.00 4.50
Julius Erving
John Roche
Larry Kenon
Julius Erving
❑ 227 San Antonio Spurs TL 6.00 2.70
George Gervin
George Gervin
Swen Nater
James Silas
❑ 228 San Diego Conq. TL 2.00 .90
Dwight Lamar
Stew Johnson
Caldwell Jones
Chuck Williams
❑ 229 Utah Stars TL 2.50 1.10
Willie Wise
James Jones
Gerald Govan
James Jones
❑ 230 Virginia Squires TL 2.00 .90
George Carter
George Irvine
Jim Eakins
Roland Taylor
❑ 231 Bird Averitt 1.00 .45
❑ 232 John Roche 1.00 .45
❑ 233 George Irvine 1.00 .45
❑ 234 John Williamson RC 1.50 .70
❑ 235 Billy Cunningham 4.00 1.80
❑ 236 Jimmy O'Brien 1.00 .45
❑ 237 Wilbert Jones 1.00 .45
❑ 238 Johnny Neumann 1.00 .45
❑ 239 Al Smith 1.00 .45
❑ 240 Roger Brown 1.50 .70
❑ 241 Chuck Williams 1.50 .70
❑ 242 Rich Jones 1.00 .45
❑ 243 Dave Twardzik RC 1.50 .70
❑ 244 Wendell Ladner 1.50 .70
❑ 245 Mack Calvin AS1 1.50 .70
❑ 246 ABA Eastern Semis 2.00 .90
Nets over Squires
Colonels sweep Cougars
❑ 247 ABA Western Semis 2.00 .90
Stars over Conquistadors
Pacers over Spurs
❑ 248 ABA Div. Finals 2.00 .90
Nets sweep Colonels
Stars edge Pacers
❑ 249 Julius Erving PO 12.00 5.50
❑ 250 Wilt Chamberlain CO 35.00 16.00
❑ 251 Ron Robinson 1.00 .45
❑ 252 Zelmo Beaty 1.50 .70
❑ 253 Donnie Freeman 1.50 .70
❑ 254 Mike Green 1.00 .45
❑ 255 Louie Dampier AS2 1.50 .70
❑ 256 Tom Owens 1.00 .45
❑ 257 George Karl RC 10.00 4.50
❑ 258 Jim Eakins 1.50 .70
❑ 259 Travis Grant 1.50 .70
❑ 260 James Jones AS1 1.50 .70
❑ 261 Mike Jackson 1.00 .45
❑ 262 Billy Paultz 1.50 .70
❑ 263 Freddie Lewis 1.50 .70
❑ 264 Byron Beck 3.00 .90
(Back refers to ANA&
should be ABA)

1975-76 Topps

	NRMT-MT	EXC
COMPLETE SET (330)	450.00	200.00
COM. NBA CARD (1-220)	.75	.35
COM. ABA CARD (221-330)	1.50	.70
NBA LL (4/5)	1.50	.70
COMMON NBA TL (116-133)	1.50	.70
NBA TL (117/119/121)	3.00	1.35
NBA TL (122/128/133)	3.00	1.35
NBA PLAYOFFS (188-189)	1.50	.70
NBA TC (203/205-218/220)	1.50	.70
ABA LL (223-226)	2.00	.90
ABA TL (278/281/285/287)	2.00	.90
ABA TL (279/280/283)	2.50	1.10
ABA PLAYOFFS (309-310)	2.00	.90
ABA TC (321-329)	2.00	.90
CL (61/181/257)	8.00	3.60
NBA SEMISTARS	1.25	.55
ABA SEMISTARS	2.00	.90
UNLISTED STARS	3.00	1.35

❑ 1 NBA Scoring Average 12.00 3.60
Leaders
Bob McAdoo
Rick Barry
Kareem Abdul-Jabbar
❑ 2 NBA Field Goal 4.00 1.80
Percentage Leaders
Don Nelson
Butch Beard
Rudy Tomjanovich
❑ 3 NBA Free Throw 5.00 2.20
Percentage Leaders
Rick Barry
Calvin Murphy
Bill Bradley
❑ 4 NBA Rebounds Leaders 1.50 .70
Wes Unseld
Dave Cowens
Sam Lacey
❑ 5 NBA Assists Leaders 1.50 .70
Kevin Porter
Dave Bing
Nate Archibald
❑ 6 NBA Steals Leaders 4.00 1.80
Rick Barry
Walt Frazier
Larry Steele

❑ 7 Tom Van Arsdale 1.25 .55
❑ 8 Paul Silas 1.25 .55
❑ 9 Jerry Sloan 1.25 .55
❑ 10 Bob McAdoo AS1 6.00 2.70
❑ 11 Dwight Davis .75 .35
❑ 12 John Mengelt .75 .35
❑ 13 George Johnson .75 .35
❑ 14 Ed Ratleff .75 .35
❑ 15 Nate Archibald AS1 4.00 1.80
❑ 16 Elmore Smith .75 .35
❑ 17 Bob Dandridge 1.25 .55
❑ 18 Louie Nelson RC .75 .35
❑ 19 Neal Walk .75 .35
❑ 20 Billy Cunningham 4.00 1.80
❑ 21 Gary Melchionni .75 .35
❑ 22 Barry Clemens .75 .35
❑ 23 Jimmy Jones .75 .35
❑ 24 Tom Burleson RC 1.25 .55
❑ 25 Lou Hudson 1.25 .55
❑ 26 Henry Finkel .75 .35
❑ 27 Jim McMillian 1.25 .55
❑ 28 Matt Guokas 1.25 .55
❑ 29 Fred Foster DP .75 .35
❑ 30 Bob Lanier 5.00 2.20
❑ 31 Jimmy Walker 1.25 .55
❑ 32 Cliff Meely .75 .35
❑ 33 Butch Beard 1.25 .55
❑ 34 Cazzie Russell 1.25 .55
❑ 35 Jon McGlocklin .75 .35
❑ 36 Bernie Fryer .75 .35
❑ 37 Bill Bradley 10.00 4.50
❑ 38 Fred Carter 1.25 .55
❑ 39 Dennis Awtrey DP .75 .35
❑ 40 Sidney Wicks 1.25 .55
❑ 41 Fred Brown 1.25 .55
❑ 42 Rowland Garrett .75 .35
❑ 43 Herm Gilliam .75 .35
❑ 44 Don Nelson 1.25 .55
❑ 45 Ernie DiGregorio 1.25 .55
❑ 46 Jim Brewer .75 .35
❑ 47 Chris Ford 1.25 .55
❑ 48 Nick Weatherspoon .75 .35
❑ 49 Zaid Abdul-Aziz .75 .35
(formerly Don Smith)
❑ 50 Keith Wilkes RC 10.00 4.50
❑ 51 Ollie Johnson DP .75 .35
❑ 52 Lucius Allen 1.25 .55
❑ 53 Mickey Davis .75 .35
❑ 54 Otto Moore .75 .35
❑ 55 Walt Frazier AS1 5.00 2.20
❑ 56 Steve Mix 1.25 .55
❑ 57 Nate Hawthorne .75 .35
❑ 58 Lloyd Neal .75 .35
❑ 59 Don Slick Watts 1.25 .55
❑ 60 Elvin Hayes 5.00 2.20
❑ 61 Checklist 1-110 8.00 2.40
❑ 62 Mike Sojourner .75 .35
❑ 63 Randy Smith 1.25 .55
❑ 64 John Block DP .75 .35
❑ 65 Charlie Scott 1.25 .55
❑ 66 Jim Chones 1.25 .55
❑ 67 Rick Adelman 1.25 .55
❑ 68 Curtis Rowe .75 .35
❑ 69 Derrek Dickey RC 1.25 .55
❑ 70 Rudy Tomjanovich 5.00 2.20
❑ 71 Pat Riley 6.00 2.70
❑ 72 Cornell Warner .75 .35
❑ 73 Earl Monroe 3.00 1.35
❑ 74 Allan Bristow RC 3.00 1.35
❑ 75 Pete Maravich DP 20.00 9.00
❑ 76 Curtis Perry .75 .35
❑ 77 Bill Walton 20.00 9.00
❑ 78 Leonard Gray .75 .35
❑ 79 Kevin Porter 1.25 .55
❑ 80 John Havlicek AS2 10.00 4.50
❑ 81 Dwight Jones .75 .35
❑ 82 Jack Marin .75 .35
❑ 83 Dick Snyder .75 .35
❑ 84 George Trapp .75 .35
❑ 85 Nate Thurmond 3.00 1.35
❑ 86 Charles Johnson .75 .35
❑ 87 Ron Riley .75 .35
❑ 88 Stu Lantz 1.25 .55
❑ 89 Scott Wedman RC 1.25 .55
❑ 90 Kareem Abdul-Jabbar 20.00 9.00
❑ 91 Aaron James .75 .35
❑ 92 Jim Barnett .75 .35
❑ 93 Clyde Lee .75 .35
❑ 94 Larry Steele 1.25 .55
❑ 95 Mike Riordan .75 .35
❑ 96 Archie Clark 1.25 .55
❑ 97 Mike Bantom .75 .35
❑ 98 Bob Kauffman .75 .35
❑ 99 Kevin Stacom RC .75 .35
❑ 100 Rick Barry AS1 6.00 2.70
❑ 101 Ken Charles .75 .35
❑ 102 Tom Boerwinkle .75 .35
❑ 103 Mike Newlin 1.25 .55
❑ 104 Leroy Ellis 1.25 .55
❑ 105 Austin Carr 1.25 .55
❑ 106 Ron Behagen .75 .35
❑ 107 Jim Price .75 .35
❑ 108 Bud Stallworth .75 .35
❑ 109 Earl Williams .75 .35
❑ 110 Gail Goodrich 3.00 1.35
❑ 111 Phil Jackson 7.00 3.10
❑ 112 Rod Derline .75 .35
❑ 113 Keith Erickson .75 .35
❑ 114 Phil Lumpkin .75 .35
❑ 115 Wes Unseld 3.00 1.35
❑ 116 Atlanta Hawks TL 1.50 .70
Lou Hudson
Lou Hudson
John Drew
Dean Meminger
❑ 117 Boston Celtics TL 3.00 1.35
Dave Cowens
Kevin Stacom
Paul Silas
JoJo White
❑ 118 Buffalo Braves TL 3.00 1.35
Bob McAdoo
Jack Marin
Bob McAdoo
Randy Smith
❑ 119 Chicago Bulls TL 3.00 1.35
Bob Love
Chet Walker
Nate Thurmond
Norm Van Lier
❑ 120 Cleveland Cavs TL 1.50 .70
Bobby Smith
Dick Snyder
Jim Chones
Jim Cleamons
❑ 121 Detroit Pistons TL 3.00 1.35
Bob Lanier
John Mengelt
Bob Lanier
Dave Bing
❑ 122 Golden State TL 3.00 1.35
Rick Barry
Rick Barry
Clifford Ray
Rick Barry
❑ 123 Houston Rockets TL 2.00 .90
Rudy Tomjanovich
Calvin Murphy
Kevin Kunnert
Mike Newlin
❑ 124 Kansas City Kings TL 2.00 .90
Nate Archibald
Ollie Johnson
Sam Lacey UER
(Lacy on front)
Nate Archibald
❑ 125 Los Angeles Lakers TL 1.50 .70
Gail Goodrich
Cazzie Russell
Happy Hairston
Gail Goodrich
❑ 126 Milwaukee Bucks TL 8.00 3.60
Kareem Abdul-Jabbar
Mickey Davis
Kareem Abdul-Jabbar
Kareem Abdul-Jabbar
❑ 127 New Orleans Jazz TL 10.00 4.50
Pete Maravich
Stu Lantz
E.C. Coleman
Pete Maravich
❑ 128 New York Knicks TL DP 3.00 1.35
Walt Frazier
Bill Bradley
John Gianelli
Walt Frazier
❑ 129 Phila. 76ers TL DP 2.00 .90
Fred Carter
Doug Collins
Billy Cunningham
Billy Cunningham
❑ 130 Phoenix Suns TL DP 1.50 .70
Charlie Scott
Keith Erickson
Curtis Perry
Dennis Awtrey
❑ 131 Portland Blazers TL DP 1.50 .70
Sidney Wicks
Geoff Petrie
Sidney Wicks
Geoff Petrie
❑ 132 Seattle Sonics TL 2.00 .90
Spencer Haywood
Archie Clark
Spencer Haywood
Don Watts
❑ 133 Washington Bullets TL 3.00 1.35
Elvin Hayes
Clem Haskins
Wes Unseld
Kevin Porter
❑ 134 John Drew RC 1.25 .55
❑ 135 JoJo White AS2 2.00 .90
❑ 136 Garfield Heard 1.25 .55
❑ 137 Jim Cleamons .75 .35
❑ 138 Howard Porter 1.25 .55
❑ 139 Phil Smith RC 1.25 .55
❑ 140 Bob Love 1.25 .55
❑ 141 John Gianelli DP .75 .35
❑ 142 Larry McNeill RC .75 .35
❑ 143 Brian Winters RC 3.00 1.35
❑ 144 George Thompson .75 .35
❑ 145 Kevin Kunnert .75 .35
❑ 146 Henry Bibby 1.25 .55
❑ 147 John Johnson .75 .35
❑ 148 Doug Collins 4.00 1.80
❑ 149 John Brisker .75 .35
❑ 150 Dick Van Arsdale 1.25 .55
❑ 151 Leonard Robinson RC 3.00 1.35
❑ 152 Dean Meminger .75 .35
❑ 153 Phil Hankinson .75 .35
❑ 154 Dale Schlueter .75 .35
❑ 155 Norm Van Lier 1.25 .55
❑ 156 Campy Russell RC 3.00 1.35
❑ 157 Jeff Mullins 1.25 .55
❑ 158 Sam Lacey .75 .35
❑ 159 Happy Hairston 1.25 .55
❑ 160 Dave Bing DP 3.00 1.35
❑ 161 Kevin Restani RC .75 .35
❑ 162 Dave Wohl .75 .35
❑ 163 E.C. Coleman .75 .35
❑ 164 Jim Fox .75 .35
❑ 165 Geoff Petrie 1.25 .55
❑ 166 H. Wingo DP UER .75 .35
(Misspelled Harthorne
on card front)
❑ 167 Fred Boyd .75 .35
❑ 168 Willie Norwood .75 .35
❑ 169 Bob Wilson .75 .35
❑ 170 Dave Cowens 6.00 2.70
❑ 171 Tom Henderson RC .75 .35
❑ 172 Jim Washington .75 .35
❑ 173 Clem Haskins 1.25 .55
❑ 174 Jim Davis .75 .35
❑ 175 Bobby Smith DP .75 .35
❑ 176 Mike D'Antoni .75 .35
❑ 177 Zelmo Beaty 1.25 .55
❑ 178 Gary Brokaw RC .75 .35
❑ 179 Mel Davis .75 .35
❑ 180 Calvin Murphy 3.00 1.35
❑ 181 Checklist 111-220 DP 8.00 2.40
❑ 182 Nate Williams .75 .35
❑ 183 LaRue Martin .75 .35
❑ 184 George McGinnis 3.00 1.35
❑ 185 Clifford Ray .75 .35
❑ 186 Paul Westphal 4.00 1.80
❑ 187 Talvin Skinner .75 .35
❑ 188 NBA Playoff Semis DP 1.50 .70

Warriors edge Bulls
Bullets over Celts
❑ 189 Clifford Ray PO .... 1.50 .70
❑ 190 Phil Chenier AS2 DP.... 1.25 .55
❑ 191 John Brown .... .75 .35
❑ 192 Lee Winfield .... .75 .35
❑ 193 Steve Patterson............ .75 .35
❑ 194 Charles Dudley .... .75 .35
❑ 195 Connie Hawkins DP 3.00 1.35
❑ 196 Leon Benbow .... .75 .35
❑ 197 Don Kojis...................... .75 .35
❑ 198 Ron Williams .... .75 .35
❑ 199 Mel Counts .... .75 .35
❑ 200 Spencer Haywood AS2 3.00 1.35
❑ 201 Greg Jackson .... .75 .35
❑ 202 Tom Kozelko DP .... .75 .35
❑ 203 Atlanta Hawks .... 1.50 .70
Checklist
❑ 204 Boston Celtics 3.00 1.35
Checklist
❑ 205 Buffalo Braves............. 1.50 .70
Checklist
❑ 206 Chicago Bulls 3.00 1.35
Checklist
❑ 207 Cleveland Cavs........... 1.50 .70
Checklist
❑ 208 Detroit Pistons............ 1.50 .70
Checklist
❑ 209 Golden State .... 1.50 .70
Checklist
❑ 210 Houston Rockets.......... 1.50 .70
Checklist
❑ 211 Kansas City Kings DP.. 1.50 .70
Checklist
❑ 212 Los Angeles Lakers DP 1.50 .70
Checklist
❑ 213 Milwaukee Bucks .... 1.50 .70
Checklist
❑ 214 New Orleans Jazz .... 1.50 .70
Checklist
❑ 215 New York Knicks .... 1.50 .70
Checklist
❑ 216 Philadelphia 76ers........ 1.50 .70
Checklist
❑ 217 Phoenix Suns DP .... 1.50 .70
Checklist
❑ 218 Portland Blazers .... 1.50 .70
Checklist
❑ 219 Seattle Sonics DP 10.00 4.50
Checklist
❑ 220 Washington Bullets ...... 1.50 .70
Checklist
❑ 221 ABA Scoring 8.00 3.60
Average Leaders
George McGinnis
Julius Erving
Ron Boone
❑ 222 ABA 2 Pt. Field Goal 8.00 3.60
Percentage Leaders
Bobby Jones
Artis Gilmore
Moses Malone
❑ 223 ABA 3 Pt. Field Goal .... 2.00 .90
Percentage Leaders
Billy Shepherd
Louie Dampier
Al Smith
❑ 224 ABA Free Throw .... 2.00 .90
Percentage Leaders
Mack Calvin
James Silas
Dave Robisch
❑ 225 ABA Rebounds Leaders 2.00 .90
Swen Nater
Artis Gilmore
Marvin Barnes
❑ 226 ABA Assists Leaders.... 2.00 .90
Mack Calvin
Chuck Williams
George McGinnis
❑ 227 Mack Calvin AS1 .... 2.00 .90
❑ 228 Billy Knight AS1 RC 3.00 1.35
❑ 229 Bird Averitt.................. 1.50 .70
❑ 230 George Carter .... 1.50 .70
❑ 231 Swen Nater AS2 .... 2.00 .90
❑ 232 Steve Jones .... 2.00 .90
❑ 233 George Gervin............ 18.00 8.00
❑ 234 Lee Davis .... 1.50 .70
❑ 235 Ron Boone AS1 .... 2.00 .90
❑ 236 Mike Jackson .... 1.50 .70
❑ 237 Kevin Joyce RC........... 1.50 .70
❑ 238 Marv Roberts............... 1.50 .70
❑ 239 Tom Owens.................. 1.50 .70
❑ 240 Ralph Simpson .... 2.00 .90
❑ 241 Gus Gerard .... 1.50 .70
❑ 242 Brian Taylor AS2......... 2.00 .90
❑ 243 Rich Jones .... 1.50 .70
❑ 244 John Roche.................. 1.50 .70
❑ 245 Travis Grant .... 2.00 .90
❑ 246 Dave Twardzik .... 2.00 .90
❑ 247 Mike Green .... 1.50 .70
❑ 248 Billy Keller .... 2.00 .90
❑ 249 Stew Johnson .... 1.50 .70
❑ 250 Artis Gilmore AS1 .... 4.00 1.80
❑ 251 John Williamson .... 2.00 .90
❑ 252 Marvin Barnes AS2 RC 4.00 1.80
❑ 253 James Silas AS2.......... 2.00 .90
❑ 254 Moses Malone RC !.... 35.00 16.00
❑ 255 Willie Wise.................. 2.00 .90
❑ 256 Dwight Lamar .... 1.50 .70
❑ 257 Checklist 221-330 .... 8.00 2.40
❑ 258 Byron Beck .... 2.00 .90
❑ 259 Len Elmore RC 3.00 1.35
❑ 260 Dan Issel...................... 5.00 2.20
❑ 261 Rick Mount .... 1.50 .70
❑ 262 Billy Paultz.................. 2.00 .90
❑ 263 Donnie Freeman .... 1.50 .70
❑ 264 George Adams .... 1.50 .70
❑ 265 Don Chaney .... 2.00 .90
❑ 266 Randy Denton .... 1.50 .70
❑ 267 Don Washington .... 1.50 .70
❑ 268 Roland Taylor .... 1.50 .70
❑ 269 Charlie Edge .... 1.50 .70
❑ 270 Louie Dampier............. 2.00 .90
❑ 271 Collis Jones................. 1.50 .70
❑ 272 Al Skinner RC .... 1.50 .70
❑ 273 Coby Dietrick............... 1.50 .70
❑ 274 Tim Bassett.................. 1.50 .70
❑ 275 Freddie Lewis .... 2.00 .90
❑ 276 Gerald Govan .... 1.50 .70
❑ 277 Ron Thomas .... 1.50 .70
❑ 278 Denver Nuggets TL...... 2.00 .90
Ralph Simpson
Mack Calvin
Mike Green
Mack Calvin
❑ 279 Indiana Pacers TL........ 2.50 1.10
George McGinnis
Billy Keller
George McGinnis
George McGinnis
❑ 280 Kentucky Colonels TL .. 2.50 1.10
Artis Gilmore
Louie Dampier
Artis Gilmore
Louie Dampier
❑ 281 Memphis Sounds TL .... 2.00 .90
George Carter
Larry Finch
Tom Owens
Chuck Williams
❑ 282 New York Nets TL...... 15.00 6.75
Julius Erving
John Williamson
Julius Erving
Julius Erving
❑ 283 St. Louis Spirits TL 2.50 1.10
Marvin Barnes
Freddie Lewis
Marvin Barnes
Freddie Lewis
❑ 284 San Antonio Spurs TL .. 5.00 2.20
George Gervin
James Silas
Swen Nater
James Silas
❑ 285 San Diego Sails TL ...... 2.00 .90
Travis Grant
Jimmy O'Brien
Caldwell Jones
Jimmy O'Brien
❑ 286 Utah Stars TL 8.00 3.60
Ron Boone
Ron Boone
Moses Malone
Al Smith
❑ 287 Virginia Squires TL ...... 2.00 .90
Willie Wise
Red Robbins
Dave Vaughn
Dave Twardzik
❑ 288 Claude Terry .... 1.50 .70
❑ 289 Wilbert Jones .... 1.50 .70
❑ 290 Darnell Hillman .... 2.00 .90
❑ 291 Bill Melchionni .... 2.00 .90
❑ 292 Mel Daniels .... 2.00 .90
❑ 293 Fly Williams RC........... 2.00 .90
❑ 294 Larry Kenon................. 2.00 .90
❑ 295 Red Robbins .... 2.00 .90
❑ 296 Warren Jabali .... 2.00 .90
❑ 297 Jim Eakins.................... 2.00 .90
❑ 298 Bobby Jones RC 12.00 5.50
❑ 299 Don Buse .... 2.00 .90
❑ 300 Julius Erving AS1 ...... 35.00 16.00
❑ 301 Billy Shepherd .... 1.50 .70
❑ 302 Maurice Lucas RC........ 6.00 2.70
❑ 303 George Karl................. 5.00 2.20
❑ 304 Jim Bradley .... 1.50 .70
❑ 305 Caldwell Jones .... 2.00 .90
❑ 306 Al Smith .... 1.50 .70
❑ 307 Jan Van Breda Kolff RC 2.00 .90
❑ 308 Darrell Elston............... 1.50 .70
❑ 309 ABA Playoff Semifinals 2.00 .90
Colonels over Spirits;
Pacers edge Nuggets
❑ 310 Artis Gilmore PO 2.50 1.10
❑ 311 Ted McClain .... 1.50 .70
❑ 312 Willie Sojourner........... 1.50 .70
❑ 313 Bob Warren.................. 1.50 .70
❑ 314 Bob Netolicky .... 2.00 .90
❑ 315 Chuck Williams .... 1.50 .70
❑ 316 Gene Kennedy .... 1.50 .70
❑ 317 Jimmy O'Brien............. 1.50 .70
❑ 318 Dave Robisch .... 1.50 .70
❑ 319 Wali Jones................... 1.50 .70
❑ 320 George Irvine .... 1.50 .70
❑ 321 Denver Nuggets .... 2.00 .90
Checklist
❑ 322 Indiana Pacers .... 2.00 .90
Checklist
❑ 323 Kentucky Colonels ...... 2.00 .90
Checklist
❑ 324 Memphis Sounds .... 2.00 .90
Checklist
❑ 325 New York Nets .... 2.00 .90
Checklist
❑ 326 St. Louis Spirits .... 2.00 .90
Checklist
(Spirits of St. Louis
on card back)
❑ 327 San Antonio Spurs ...... 2.00 .90
Checklist
❑ 328 San Diego Sails........... 2.00 .90
Checklist
❑ 329 Utah Stars .... 2.00 .90
Checklist
❑ 330 Virginia Squires........... 4.00 1.20
Checklist

1976-77 Topps

	NRMT-MT	EXC
COMPLETE SET (144)	375.00	170.00
COMMON CARD (1-144)	1.75	.80
AS (126-135)	2.00	.90
CL (48)	30.00	13.50
SEMISTARS	2.50	1.10
UNLISTED STARS	5.00	2.20
CONDITION SENSITIVE SET		

❑ 1 Julius Erving 60.00 18.00
❑ 2 Dick Snyder.................. 1.75 .80
❑ 3 Paul Silas 2.50 1.10
❑ 4 Keith Erickson .... 1.75 .80
❑ 5 Wes Unseld.................. 5.00 2.20
❑ 6 Butch Beard 2.50 1.10
❑ 7 Lloyd Neal .... 1.75 .80

❑ 8 Tom Henderson 1.75 .80
❑ 9 Jim McMillian 2.50 1.10
❑ 10 Bob Lanier 6.00 2.70
❑ 11 Junior Bridgeman RC 2.50 1.10
❑ 12 Corky Calhoun 1.75 .80
❑ 13 Billy Keller 2.50 1.10
❑ 14 Mickey Johnson RC 1.75 .80
❑ 15 Fred Brown 2.50 1.10
❑ 16 Jamaal Wilkes 2.50 1.10
❑ 17 Louie Nelson 1.75 .80
❑ 18 Ed Ratleff 1.75 .80
❑ 19 Billy Paultz 2.50 1.10
❑ 20 Nate Archibald 5.00 2.20
❑ 21 Steve Mix 2.50 1.10
❑ 22 Ralph Simpson 1.75 .80
❑ 23 Campy Russell 2.50 1.10
❑ 24 Charlie Scott 2.50 1.10
❑ 25 Artis Gilmore 5.00 2.20
❑ 26 Dick Van Arsdale 2.50 1.10
❑ 27 Phil Chenier 2.50 1.10
❑ 28 Spencer Haywood 5.00 2.20
❑ 29 Chris Ford 2.50 1.10
❑ 30 Dave Cowens 10.00 4.50
❑ 31 Sidney Wicks 2.50 1.10
❑ 32 Jim Price 1.75 .80
❑ 33 Dwight Jones 1.75 .80
❑ 34 Lucius Allen 1.75 .80
❑ 35 Marvin Barnes 2.50 1.10
❑ 36 Henry Bibby 2.50 1.10
❑ 37 Joe Meriweather RC 1.75 .80
❑ 38 Doug Collins 6.00 2.70
❑ 39 Garfield Heard 2.50 1.10
❑ 40 Randy Smith 2.50 1.10
❑ 41 Tom Burleson 2.50 1.10
❑ 42 Dave Twardzik 2.50 1.10
❑ 43 Bill Bradley 12.00 5.50
❑ 44 Calvin Murphy 5.00 2.20
❑ 45 Bob Love 2.50 1.10
❑ 46 Brian Winters 2.50 1.10
❑ 47 Glenn McDonald 1.75 .80
❑ 48 Checklist 1-144 30.00 9.00
❑ 49 Bird Averitt 1.75 .80
❑ 50 Rick Barry 10.00 4.50
❑ 51 Ticky Burden 1.75 .80
❑ 52 Rich Jones 1.75 .80
❑ 53 Austin Carr 2.50 1.10
❑ 54 Steve Kuberski 1.75 .80
❑ 55 Paul Westphal 2.50 1.10
❑ 56 Mike Riordan 1.75 .80
❑ 57 Bill Walton 25.00 11.00
❑ 58 Eric Money RC 1.75 .80
❑ 59 John Drew 2.50 1.10
❑ 60 Pete Maravich 45.00 20.00
❑ 61 John Shumate RC 2.50 1.10
❑ 62 Mack Calvin 2.50 1.10
❑ 63 Bruce Seals 1.75 .80
❑ 64 Walt Frazier 6.00 2.70
❑ 65 Elmore Smith 1.75 .80
❑ 66 Rudy Tomjanovich 6.00 2.70
❑ 67 Sam Lacey 1.75 .80
❑ 68 George Gervin 25.00 11.00
❑ 69 Gus Williams RC 5.00 2.20
❑ 70 George McGinnis 2.50 1.10
❑ 71 Len Elmore 1.75 .80
❑ 72 Jack Marin 1.75 .80
❑ 73 Brian Taylor 1.75 .80
❑ 74 Jim Brewer 1.75 .80
❑ 75 Alvan Adams RC 6.00 2.70
❑ 76 Dave Bing 5.00 2.20
❑ 77 Phil Jackson 10.00 4.50
❑ 78 Geoff Petrie 2.50 1.10
❑ 79 Mike Sojourner 1.75 .80
❑ 80 James Silas 2.50 1.10
❑ 81 Bob Dandridge 2.50 1.10
❑ 82 Ernie DiGregorio 2.50 1.10
❑ 83 Cazzie Russell 2.50 1.10
❑ 84 Kevin Porter 2.50 1.10
❑ 85 Tom Boerwinkle 1.75 .80
❑ 86 Darnell Hillman 2.50 1.10
❑ 87 Herm Gilliam 1.75 .80
❑ 88 Nate Williams 1.75 .80
❑ 89 Phil Smith 2.50 1.10
❑ 90 John Havlicek 15.00 6.75
❑ 91 Kevin Kunnert 1.75 .80
❑ 92 Jimmy Walker 2.50 1.10
❑ 93 Billy Cunningham 5.00 2.20
❑ 94 Dan Issel 6.00 2.70
❑ 95 Ron Boone 2.50 1.10
❑ 96 Lou Hudson 2.50 1.10
❑ 97 Jim Chones 2.50 1.10
❑ 98 Earl Monroe 5.00 2.20
❑ 99 Tom Van Arsdale 2.50 1.10
❑ 100 Kareem Abdul-Jabbar 40.00 18.00
❑ 101 Moses Malone 25.00 11.00
❑ 102 Ricky Sobers RC 1.75 .80
❑ 103 Swen Nater 2.50 1.10
❑ 104 Leonard Robinson 2.50 1.10
❑ 105 Don Slick Watts 2.50 1.10
❑ 106 Otto Moore 1.75 .80
❑ 107 Maurice Lucas 2.50 1.10
❑ 108 Norm Van Lier 2.50 1.10
❑ 109 Clifford Ray 1.75 .80
❑ 110 David Thompson RC 40.00 18.00
❑ 111 Fred Carter 2.50 1.10
❑ 112 Caldwell Jones 2.50 1.10
❑ 113 John Williamson 2.50 1.10
❑ 114 Bobby Smith 2.50 1.10
❑ 115 JoJo White 2.50 1.10
❑ 116 Curtis Perry 1.75 .80
❑ 117 John Gianelli 1.75 .80
❑ 118 Curtis Rowe 1.75 .80
❑ 119 Lionel Hollins RC 2.50 1.10
❑ 120 Elvin Hayes 6.00 2.70
❑ 121 Ken Charles 1.75 .80
❑ 122 Dave Meyers RC 2.50 1.10
❑ 123 Jerry Sloan 2.50 1.10
❑ 124 Billy Knight 2.50 1.10
❑ 125 Gail Goodrich 2.50 1.10
❑ 126 Kareem Abdul-Jabbar AS 20.00 9.00
❑ 127 Julius Erving AS 25.00 11.00
❑ 128 George McGinnis AS 2.50 1.10
❑ 129 Nate Archibald AS 2.50 1.10
❑ 130 Pete Maravich AS 25.00 11.00
❑ 131 Dave Cowens AS 5.00 2.20
❑ 132 Rick Barry AS 5.00 2.20
❑ 133 Elvin Hayes AS 5.00 2.20
❑ 134 James Silas AS 2.00 .90
❑ 135 Randy Smith AS 2.00 .90
❑ 136 Leonard Gray 1.75 .80
❑ 137 Charles Johnson 1.75 .80
❑ 138 Ron Behagen 1.75 .80
❑ 139 Mike Newlin 2.50 1.10
❑ 140 Bob McAdoo 6.00 2.70
❑ 141 Mike Gale 1.75 .80
❑ 142 Scott Wedman 2.50 1.10
❑ 143 Lloyd Free RC 6.00 2.70
❑ 144 Bobby Jones 8.00 2.40

1977-78 Topps

	NRMT-MT	EXC
COMPLETE SET (132)	90.00	40.00
COMMON CARD (1-132)	.30	.14
CL (29)	3.00	1.35
SEMISTARS	.60	.25

*GRAY AND WHITE BACKS: EQUAL VALUE
1977-78 THRU 1988-89 PRICED IN NM-MT

❑ 1 Kareem Abdul-Jabbar 15.00 4.50
❑ 2 Henry Bibby .40 .18
❑ 3 Curtis Rowe .30 .14
❑ 4 Norm Van Lier .40 .18
❑ 5 Darnell Hillman .40 .18
❑ 6 Earl Monroe 1.50 .70

❑ 7 Leonard Gray .30 .14
❑ 8 Bird Averitt .30 .14
❑ 9 Jim Brewer .30 .14
❑ 10 Paul Westphal 1.00 .45
❑ 11 Bob Gross RC .40 .18
❑ 12 Phil Smith .30 .14
❑ 13 Dan Roundfield RC .60 .25
❑ 14 Brian Taylor .30 .14
❑ 15 Rudy Tomjanovich 2.00 .90
❑ 16 Kevin Porter .40 .18
❑ 17 Scott Wedman .40 .18
❑ 18 Lloyd Free .60 .25
❑ 19 Tom Boswell RC .30 .14
❑ 20 Pete Maravich 15.00 6.75
❑ 21 Cliff Poindexter .30 .14
❑ 22 Bubbles Hawkins .40 .18
❑ 23 Kevin Grevey RC 1.25 .55
❑ 24 Ken Charles .30 .14
❑ 25 Bob Dandridge .40 .18
❑ 26 Lonnie Shelton RC .40 .18
❑ 27 Don Chaney .40 .18
❑ 28 Larry Kenon .40 .18
❑ 29 Checklist 1-132 3.00 .90
❑ 30 Fred Brown .40 .18
❑ 31 John Gianelli UER .30 .14
(Listed as Cavaliers&
should be Buffalo Braves)
❑ 32 Austin Carr .40 .18
❑ 33 Jamaal Wilkes .60 .25
❑ 34 Caldwell Jones .40 .18
❑ 35 JoJo White .60 .25
❑ 36 Scott May RC 1.25 .55
❑ 37 Mike Newlin .30 .14
❑ 38 Mel Davis .30 .14
❑ 39 Lionel Hollins .60 .25
❑ 40 Elvin Hayes 2.50 1.10
❑ 41 Dan Issel 2.00 .90
❑ 42 Ricky Sobers .30 .14
❑ 43 Don Ford .30 .14
❑ 44 John Williamson .30 .14
❑ 45 Bob McAdoo 2.00 .90
❑ 46 Geoff Petrie .40 .18
❑ 47 M.L. Carr RC 2.00 .90
❑ 48 Brian Winters .60 .25
❑ 49 Sam Lacey .30 .14
❑ 50 George McGinnis .60 .25
❑ 51 Don Slick Watts .40 .18
❑ 52 Sidney Wicks .60 .25
❑ 53 Wilbur Holland .30 .14
❑ 54 Tim Bassett .30 .14
❑ 55 Phil Chenier .40 .18
❑ 56 Adrian Dantley RC 8.00 3.60
❑ 57 Jim Chones .40 .18
❑ 58 John Lucas RC 2.50 1.10
❑ 59 Cazzie Russell .40 .18
❑ 60 David Thompson 5.00 2.20
❑ 61 Bob Lanier 2.00 .90
❑ 62 Dave Twardzik .40 .18
❑ 63 Wilbert Jones .30 .14
❑ 64 Clifford Ray .30 .14
❑ 65 Doug Collins 1.50 .70
❑ 66 Tom McMillen RC 2.50 1.10
❑ 67 Rich Kelley RC .30 .14
❑ 68 Mike Bantom .30 .14
❑ 69 Tom Boerwinkle .30 .14
❑ 70 John Havlicek 6.00 2.70
❑ 71 Marvin Webster RC .40 .18
❑ 72 Curtis Perry .30 .14

Card	NRMT-MT	EXC
❑ 73 George Gervin	8.00	3.60
❑ 74 Leonard Robinson	.60	.25
❑ 75 Wes Unseld	1.50	.70
❑ 76 Dave Meyers	.40	.18
❑ 77 Gail Goodrich	.60	.25
❑ 78 Richard Washington RC	.60	.25
❑ 79 Mike Gale	.30	.14
❑ 80 Maurice Lucas	.60	.25
❑ 81 Harvey Catchings RC	.40	.18
❑ 82 Randy Smith	.30	.14
❑ 83 Campy Russell	.40	.18
❑ 84 Kevin Kunnert	.30	.14
❑ 85 Lou Hudson	.40	.18
❑ 86 Mickey Johnson	.30	.14
❑ 87 Lucius Allen	.30	.14
❑ 88 Spencer Haywood	1.00	.45
❑ 89 Gus Williams	.60	.25
❑ 90 Dave Cowens	3.00	1.35
❑ 91 Al Skinner	.30	.14
❑ 92 Swen Nater	.30	.14
❑ 93 Tom Henderson	.30	.14
❑ 94 Don Buse	.40	.18
❑ 95 Alvan Adams	.60	.25
❑ 96 Mack Calvin	.40	.18
❑ 97 Tom Burleson	.30	.14
❑ 98 John Drew	.40	.18
❑ 99 Mike Green	.30	.14
❑ 100 Julius Erving	15.00	6.75
❑ 101 John Mengelt	.30	.14
❑ 102 Howard Porter	.40	.18
❑ 103 Billy Paultz	.40	.18
❑ 104 John Shumate	.40	.18
❑ 105 Calvin Murphy	1.50	.70
❑ 106 Elmore Smith	.30	.14
❑ 107 Jim McMillian	.30	.14
❑ 108 Kevin Stacom	.30	.14
❑ 109 Jan Van Breda Kolff	.30	.14
❑ 110 Billy Knight	.40	.18
❑ 111 Robert Parish RC !	30.00	13.50
❑ 112 Larry Wright	.30	.14
❑ 113 Bruce Seals	.30	.14
❑ 114 Junior Bridgeman	.40	.18
❑ 115 Artis Gilmore	1.50	.70
❑ 116 Steve Mix	.40	.18
❑ 117 Ron Lee	.30	.14
❑ 118 Bobby Jones	.60	.25
❑ 119 Ron Boone	.40	.18
❑ 120 Bill Walton	8.00	3.60
❑ 121 Chris Ford	.40	.18
❑ 122 Earl Tatum	.30	.14
❑ 123 E.C. Coleman	.30	.14
❑ 124 Moses Malone	6.00	2.70
❑ 125 Charlie Scott	.40	.18
❑ 126 Bobby Smith	.30	.14
❑ 127 Nate Archibald	1.50	.70
❑ 128 Mitch Kupchak RC	1.25	.55
❑ 129 Walt Frazier	2.50	1.10
❑ 130 Rick Barry	3.00	1.35
❑ 131 Ernie DiGregorio	.40	.18
❑ 132 Darryl Dawkins RC !	12.00	3.60

1978-79 Topps

	NRMT-MT	EXC
COMPLETE SET (132)	70.00	32.00
COMMON CARD (1-132)	.30	.14
CL (67)	2.00	.90
UNLISTED STARS	.75	.35

Card	NRMT-MT	EXC
❑ 1 Bill Walton	10.00	3.00
❑ 2 Doug Collins	1.50	.70
❑ 3 Jamaal Wilkes	.75	.35
❑ 4 Wilbur Holland	.30	.14
❑ 5 Bob McAdoo	1.25	.55
❑ 6 Lucius Allen	.30	.14
❑ 7 Wes Unseld	1.25	.55
❑ 8 Dave Meyers	.50	.23
❑ 9 Austin Carr	.50	.23
❑ 10 Walter Davis RC	7.00	3.10
❑ 11 John Williamson	.30	.14
❑ 12 E.C. Coleman	.30	.14
❑ 13 Calvin Murphy	1.00	.45
❑ 14 Bobby Jones	.75	.35
❑ 15 Chris Ford	.50	.23
❑ 16 Kermit Washington	.50	.23
❑ 17 Butch Beard	.50	.23
❑ 18 Steve Mix	.30	.14
❑ 19 Marvin Webster	.50	.23
❑ 20 George Gervin	6.00	2.70
❑ 21 Steve Hawes	.30	.14
❑ 22 Johnny Davis RC	.50	.23
❑ 23 Swen Nater	.30	.14
❑ 24 Lou Hudson	.50	.23
❑ 25 Elvin Hayes	1.50	.70
❑ 26 Nate Archibald	1.00	.45
❑ 27 James Edwards RC	3.00	1.35
❑ 28 Howard Porter	.50	.23
❑ 29 Quinn Buckner RC	1.25	.55
❑ 30 Leonard Robinson	.50	.23
❑ 31 Jim Cleamons	.30	.14
❑ 32 Campy Russell	.50	.23
❑ 33 Phil Smith	.30	.14
❑ 34 Darryl Dawkins	2.00	.90
❑ 35 Don Buse	.50	.23
❑ 36 Mickey Johnson	.30	.14
❑ 37 Mike Gale	.30	.14
❑ 38 Moses Malone	4.00	1.80
❑ 39 Gus Williams	.75	.35
❑ 40 Dave Cowens	2.00	.90
❑ 41 Bobby Wilkerson RC	.50	.23
❑ 42 Wilbert Jones	.30	.14
❑ 43 Charlie Scott	.50	.23
❑ 44 John Drew	.50	.23
❑ 45 Earl Monroe	1.25	.55
❑ 46 John Shumate	.50	.23
❑ 47 Earl Tatum	.30	.14
❑ 48 Mitch Kupchak	.50	.23
❑ 49 Ron Boone	.50	.23
❑ 50 Maurice Lucas	.75	.35
❑ 51 Louie Dampier	.50	.23
❑ 52 Aaron James	.30	.14
❑ 53 John Mengelt	.30	.14
❑ 54 Garfield Heard	.50	.23
❑ 55 George Johnson	.30	.14
❑ 56 Junior Bridgeman	.30	.14
❑ 57 Elmore Smith	.30	.14
❑ 58 Rudy Tomjanovich	1.50	.70
❑ 59 Fred Brown	.50	.23
❑ 60 Rick Barry UER (reversed negative)	2.00	.90
❑ 61 Dave Bing	1.25	.55
❑ 62 Anthony Roberts	.30	.14
❑ 63 Norm Nixon RC	2.00	.90
❑ 64 Leon Douglas RC	.50	.23
❑ 65 Henry Bibby	.50	.23
❑ 66 Lonnie Shelton	.30	.14
❑ 67 Checklist 1-132	2.00	.60
❑ 68 Tom Henderson	.30	.14
❑ 69 Dan Roundfield	.50	.23
❑ 70 Armond Hill RC	.50	.23
❑ 71 Larry Kenon	.50	.23
❑ 72 Billy Knight	.50	.23
❑ 73 Artis Gilmore	1.00	.45
❑ 74 Lionel Hollins	.50	.23
❑ 75 Bernard King RC	7.00	3.10
❑ 76 Brian Winters	.75	.35
❑ 77 Alvan Adams	.75	.35
❑ 78 Dennis Johnson RC	8.00	3.60
❑ 79 Scott Wedman	.30	.14
❑ 80 Pete Maravich	10.00	4.50
❑ 81 Dan Issel	1.50	.70
❑ 82 M.L. Carr	.75	.35
❑ 83 Walt Frazier	1.50	.70
❑ 84 Dwight Jones	.30	.14
❑ 85 JoJo White	.75	.35
❑ 86 Robert Parish	5.00	2.20
❑ 87 Charlie Criss RC	.50	.23
❑ 88 Jim McMillian	.30	.14
❑ 89 Chuck Williams	.30	.14
❑ 90 George McGinnis	.75	.35
❑ 91 Billy Paultz	.50	.23
❑ 92 Bob Dandridge	.50	.23
❑ 93 Ricky Sobers	.30	.14
❑ 94 Paul Silas	.50	.23
❑ 95 Gail Goodrich	.75	.35
❑ 96 Tim Bassett	.30	.14
❑ 97 Ron Lee	.30	.14
❑ 98 Bob Gross	.50	.23
❑ 99 Sam Lacey	.30	.14
❑ 100 David Thompson (College North Carolina& should be NC State)	3.00	1.35
❑ 101 John Gianelli	.30	.14
❑ 102 Norm Van Lier	.50	.23
❑ 103 Caldwell Jones	.50	.23
❑ 104 Eric Money	.30	.14
❑ 105 Jim Chones	.50	.23
❑ 106 John Lucas	1.00	.45
❑ 107 Spencer Haywood	.75	.35
❑ 108 Eddie Johnson RC	.30	.14
❑ 109 Sidney Wicks	.75	.35
❑ 110 Kareem Abdul-Jabbar	8.00	3.60
❑ 111 Sonny Parker RC	.50	.23
❑ 112 Randy Smith	.30	.14
❑ 113 Kevin Grevey	.50	.23
❑ 114 Rich Kelley	.30	.14
❑ 115 Scott May	.50	.23
❑ 116 Lloyd Free	.75	.35
❑ 117 Jack Sikma RC	2.00	.90
❑ 118 Kevin Porter	.50	.23
❑ 119 Darnell Hillman	.50	.23
❑ 120 Paul Westphal	1.00	.45
❑ 121 Richard Washington	.30	.14
❑ 122 Dave Twardzik		.23
❑ 123 Mike Bantom	.30	.14
❑ 124 Mike Newlin	.30	.14
❑ 125 Bob Lanier	1.50	.70
❑ 126 Marques Johnson RC	4.00	1.80
❑ 127 Foots Walker RC	.50	.23
❑ 128 Cedric Maxwell RC	1.25	.55
❑ 129 Ray Williams RC	.50	.23
❑ 130 Julius Erving	10.00	4.50
❑ 131 Clifford Ray	.30	.14
❑ 132 Adrian Dantley	3.00	.90

1979-80 Topps

	NRMT-MT	EXC
COMPLETE SET (132)	70.00	32.00
COMMON CARD (1-132)	.30	.14
CL (101)	2.00	.90
SEMISTARS	.60	.25

Card	NRMT-MT	EXC
❑ 1 George Gervin	6.00	2.70
❑ 2 Mitch Kupchak	.40	.18
❑ 3 Henry Bibby	.40	.18
❑ 4 Bob Gross	.40	.18
❑ 5 Dave Cowens	2.00	.90
❑ 6 Dennis Johnson	1.50	.70
❑ 7 Scott Wedman	.30	.14
❑ 8 Earl Monroe	1.25	.55
❑ 9 Mike Bantom	.30	.14

❑ 10 Kareem Abdul-Jabbar AS 8.00 3.60
❑ 11 JoJo White .60 .25
❑ 12 Spencer Haywood .60 .25
❑ 13 Kevin Porter .40 .18
❑ 14 Bernard King 1.50 .70
❑ 15 Mike Newlin .30 .14
❑ 16 Sidney Wicks .60 .25
❑ 17 Dan Issel 1.25 .55
❑ 18 Tom Henderson .30 .14
❑ 19 Jim Chones .40 .18
❑ 20 Julius Erving 10.00 4.50
❑ 21 Brian Winters .60 .25
❑ 22 Billy Paultz .40 .18
❑ 23 Cedric Maxwell .40 .18
❑ 24 Eddie Johnson .30 .14
❑ 25 Artis Gilmore .75 .35
❑ 26 Maurice Lucas .60 .25
❑ 27 Gus Williams .60 .25
❑ 28 Sam Lacey .30 .14
❑ 29 Toby Knight .30 .14
❑ 30 Paul Westphal AS1 .60 .25
❑ 31 Alex English RC 8.00 3.60
❑ 32 Gail Goodrich .60 .25
❑ 33 Caldwell Jones .40 .18
❑ 34 Kevin Grevey .40 .18
❑ 35 Jamaal Wilkes .60 .25
❑ 36 Sonny Parker .30 .14
❑ 37 John Gianelli .30 .14
❑ 38 John Long RC .18
❑ 39 George Johnson .30 .14
❑ 40 Lloyd Free AS2 .60 .25
❑ 41 Rudy Tomjanovich 1.25 .55
❑ 42 Foots Walker .40 .18
❑ 43 Dan Roundfield .40 .18
❑ 44 Reggie Theus RC 3.00 1.35
❑ 45 Bill Walton 3.00 1.35
❑ 46 Fred Brown .40 .18
❑ 47 Darnell Hillman .40 .18
❑ 48 Ray Williams .30 .14
❑ 49 Larry Kenon .40 .18
❑ 50 David Thompson 2.00 .90
❑ 51 Billy Knight .40 .18
❑ 52 Alvan Adams .60 .25
❑ 53 Phil Smith .30 .14
❑ 54 Adrian Dantley 1.25 .55
❑ 55 John Williamson .30 .14
❑ 56 Campy Russell .40 .18
❑ 57 Armond Hill .40 .18
❑ 58 Bob Lanier 1.25 .55
❑ 59 Mickey Johnson .30 .14
❑ 60 Pete Maravich 10.00 4.50
❑ 61 Nick Weatherspoon .30 .14
❑ 62 Robert Reid RC .60 .25
❑ 63 Mychal Thompson RC 1.50 .70
❑ 64 Doug Collins 1.00 .45
❑ 65 Wes Unseld 1.25 .55
❑ 66 Jack Sikma .60 .25
❑ 67 Bobby Wilkerson .30 .14
❑ 68 Bill Robinzine .30 .14
❑ 69 Joe Meriweather .30 .14
❑ 70 Marques Johnson AS1 .40 .18
❑ 71 Ricky Sobers .30 .14
❑ 72 Clifford Ray .30 .14
❑ 73 Tim Bassett .30 .14
❑ 74 James Silas .40 .18
❑ 75 Bob McAdoo .75 .35
❑ 76 Austin Carr .40 .18
❑ 77 Don Ford .30 .14
❑ 78 Steve Hawes .30 .14
❑ 79 Ron Brewer RC .30 .14
❑ 80 Walter Davis 1.00 .45
❑ 81 Calvin Murphy .75 .35
❑ 82 Tom Boswell .30 .14
❑ 83 Lonnie Shelton .30 .14
❑ 84 Terry Tyler RC .40 .18
❑ 85 Randy Smith .30 .14
❑ 86 Rich Kelley .30 .14
❑ 87 Otis Birdsong RC .60 .25
❑ 88 Marvin Webster .30 .14
❑ 89 Eric Money .30 .14
❑ 90 Elvin Hayes AS1 1.50 .70
❑ 91 Junior Bridgeman .30 .14
❑ 92 Johnny Davis .30 .14
❑ 93 Robert Parish 3.00 1.35
❑ 94 Eddie Jordan .40 .18
❑ 95 Leonard Robinson .40 .18
❑ 96 Rick Robey RC .40 .18
❑ 97 Norm Nixon .60 .25
❑ 98 Mark Olberding .30 .14
❑ 99 Wilbur Holland .30 .14
❑ 100 Moses Malone AS1 3.00 1.35
❑ 101 Checklist 1-132 2.00 .60
❑ 102 Tom Owens .30 .14
❑ 103 Phil Chenier .40 .18
❑ 104 John Johnson .30 .14
❑ 105 Darryl Dawkins 1.00 .45
❑ 106 Charlie Scott .40 .18
❑ 107 M.L. Carr .60 .25
❑ 108 Phil Ford RC 2.50 1.10
❑ 109 Swen Nater .30 .14
❑ 110 Nate Archibald 1.25 .55
❑ 111 Aaron James .30 .14
❑ 112 Jim Cleamons .30 .14
❑ 113 James Edwards .60 .25
❑ 114 Don Buse .40 .18
❑ 115 Steve Mix .30 .14
❑ 116 Charles Johnson .30 .14
❑ 117 Elmore Smith .30 .14
❑ 118 John Drew .30 .14
❑ 119 Lou Hudson .40 .18
❑ 120 Rick Barry 2.00 .90
❑ 121 Kent Benson RC .40 .18
❑ 122 Mike Gale .30 .14
❑ 123 Jan Van Breda Kolff .30 .14
❑ 124 Chris Ford .40 .18
❑ 125 George McGinnis .60 .25
❑ 126 Leon Douglas .30 .14
❑ 127 John Lucas .60 .25
❑ 128 Kermit Washington .40 .18
❑ 129 Lionel Hollins .40 .18
❑ 130 Bob Dandridge AS2 .40 .18
❑ 131 James McElroy .30 .14
❑ 132 Bobby Jones 1.50 .70

1980-81 Topps

	NRMT-MT	EXC
COMPLETE SET (176)	500.00	220.00
COMMON PANEL (1-176)	.30	.14
SEMISTARS	.60	.25
UNLISTED STARS	1.00	.45
CONDITION SENSITIVE SET		

❑ 1 3 Dan Roundfield AS 5.00 2.20
181 Julius Erving
258 Ron Brewer SD
❑ 2 7 Moses Malone AS 1.50 .70
185 Steve Mix
92 Robert Parish TL
❑ 3 12 Gus Williams AS .60 .25
67 Geoff Huston
5 John Drew AS
❑ 4 24 Steve Hawes 1.00 .45
32 Nate Archibald TL
248 Elvin Hayes
❑ 5 29 Dan Roundfield .60 .25
73 Dan Issel TL
152 Brian Winters
❑ 6 34 Larry Bird 350.00 160.00
174 Julius Erving TL
139 Magic Johnson
❑ 7 36 Dave Cowens 1.00 .45
186 Paul Westphal TL
142 Jamaal Wilkes
❑ 8 38 Pete Maravich 6.00 2.70
264 Lloyd Free SD
194 Dennis Johnson
❑ 9 40 Rick Robey .60 .25
234 Ad.Dantley TL
26 Eddie Johnson
❑ 10 47 Scott May .30 .14
196 K.Washington TL
177 Henry Bibby
❑ 11 55 Don Ford .30 .14
145 Quinn Buckner TL
138 Brad Holland
❑ 12 58 Campy Russell .30 .14
247 Kevin Grevey
52 Dave Robisch TL
❑ 13 60 Foots Walker .30 .14
113 Mick.Johnson TL
130 Bill Robinzine
❑ 14 61 Austin Carr 3.00 1.35
8 Kareem Abdul-Jabbar AS
200 Calvin Natt
❑ 15 63 Jim Cleamons .30 .14
256 Robert Reid SD
22 Charlie Criss
❑ 16 69 Tom LaGarde .30 .14
215 Swen Nater TL
213 James Silas
❑ 17 71 Jerome Whitehead .60 .25
259 Artis Gilmore SD
184 Caldwell Jones
❑ 18 74 John Roche TL .30 .14
99 Clifford Ray
235 Ben Poquette TL
❑ 19 75 Alex English 1.25 .55
2 Marques Johnson AS
68 Jeff Judkins
❑ 20 82 Terry Tyler TL .30 .14
21 Armond Hill TL
171 M.R. Richardson
❑ 21 84 Kent Benson .60 .25
212 John Shumate
229 Paul Westphal
❑ 22 86 Phil Hubbard 1.50 .70
93 Robert Parish TL
126 Tom Burleson
❑ 23 88 John Long 3.00 1.35
1 Julius Erving AS
49 Ricky Sobers
❑ 24 90 Eric Money .30 .14
57 Dave Robisch
254 Rick Robey SD
❑ 25 95 Wayne Cooper .30 .14
226 John Johnson TL
45 David Greenwood
❑ 26 97 Robert Parish 2.00 .90
187 Leon.Robinson TL
46 Dwight Jones
❑ 27 98 Sonny Parker .30 .14
197 Dave Twardzik TL
39 Cedric Maxwell
❑ 28 105 Rick Barry 1.00 .45
122 Otis Birdsong TL
48 John Mengelt
❑ 29 106 Allen Leavell .30 .14
53 Foots Walker TL
223 Freeman Williams
❑ 30 108 Calvin Murphy .60 .25
176 Maur.Cheeks TL
87 Greg Kelser
❑ 31 110 Robert Reid .60 .25
243 Wes Unseld TL
50 Reggie Theus
❑ 32 111 Rudy Tomjanovich .60 .25
13 Eddie Johnson AS
179 Doug Collins
❑ 33 112 Mickey Johnson TL .30 .14
28 Wayne Rollins
15 M.R.Richardson AS
❑ 34 115 Mike Bantom .60 .25
6 Adrian Dantley AS
227 James Bailey
❑ 35 116 Dudley Bradley .30 .14
155 Eddie Jordan TL
239 Allan Bristow
❑ 36 118 James Edwards .30 .14

153 Mike Newlin TL
182 Lionel Hollins
❑ 37 119 Mickey Johnson .... .30 .14
154 Geo.Johnson TL
193 Leonard Robinson
❑ 38 120 Billy Knight .... .60 .25
16 Paul Westphal AS
59 Randy Smith
❑ 39 121 George McGinnis ...... .60 .25
83 Eric Money TL
65 Mike Bratz
❑ 40 124 Phil Ford TL .... .30 .14
101 Phil Smith
224 Gus Williams TL
❑ 41 127 Phil Ford .... .30 .14
19 John Drew TL
209 Larry Kenon
❑ 42 131 Scott Wedman .... .60 .25
164 B.Cartwright TL
23 John Drew
❑ 43 132 K.Abdul-Jabbar TL .. 3.00 1.35
56 Mike Mitchell
81 Terry Tyler TL
❑ 44 135 K.Abdul-Jabbar 5.00 2.20
79 David Thompson
216 Brian Taylor TL
❑ 45 137 Michael Cooper ...... 1.50 .70
103 Moses Malone TL
148 George Johnson
❑ 46 140 Mark Landsberger .. 1.50 .70
10 Bob Lanier AS
222 Bill Walton
❑ 47 141 Norm Nixon .... .60 .25
123 Sam Lacey TL
54 Kenny Carr
❑ 48 143 Marq.Johnson TL .. 15.00 6.75
30 Larry Bird TL
232 Jack Sikma
❑ 49 146 Junior Bridgeman .. 15.00 6.75
31 Larry Bird TL
198 Ron Brewer
❑ 50 147 Quinn Buckner 3.00 1.35
133 K.Abdul-Jabbar TL
207 Mike Gale
❑ 51 149 Marques Johnson.... 3.00 1.35
262 Julius Erving SD
62 Abdul Jeelani
❑ 52 151 Sidney Moncrief 3.00 1.35
260 Lonnie Shelton SD
220 Paul Silas
❑ 53 156 George Johnson........ .60 .25
9 Bill Cartwright AS
199 Bob Gross
❑ 54 158 Maurice Lucas .... .60 .25
261 James Edwards SD
157 Eddie Jordan
❑ 55 159 Mike Newlin .... .30 .14
134 Norm Nixon TL
180 Darryl Dawkins
❑ 56 160 Roger Phegley .... .30 .14
206 James Silas TL
91 Terry Tyler UER
(First name spelled Jams)
❑ 57 161 Cliff Robinson............ .30 .14
51 Mike Mitchell TL
80 Bobby Wilkerson
❑ 58 162 Jan V.Breda Kolff ...... .60 .25
204 George Gervin TL
117 Johnny Davis
❑ 59 165 M.R.Richardson TL .. .30 .14
214 Lloyd Free TL
44 Artis Gilmore
❑ 60 166 Bill Cartwright.......... 1.50 .70
244 Kevin Porter TL
25 Armond Hill
❑ 61 168 Toby Knight .... .30 .14
14 Lloyd Free AS
240 Adrian Dantley
❑ 62 169 Joe Meriweather........ .60 .25
218 Lloyd Free
42 D.Greenwood TL
❑ 63 170 Earl Monroe .... .60 .25
27 James McElroy
85 Leon Douglas
❑ 64 172 Marvin Webster .... .60 .25
175 Caldwell Jones TL

129 Sam Lacey
❑ 65 173 Ray Williams .... .30 .14
94 John Lucas TL
202 Dave Twardzik
❑ 66 178 Maurice Cheeks 12.00 5.50
18 Magic Johnson AS
237 Ron Boone
❑ 67 183 Bobby Jones .... 1.00 .45
37 Chris Ford
66 Joe Hassett
❑ 68 189 Alvan Adams .... 1.00 .45
163 B.Cartwright TL
76 Dan Issel
❑ 69 190 Don Buse .... .60 .25
242 Elvin Hayes TL
35 M.L. Carr
❑ 70 191 Walter Davis............ 1.00 .45
11 George Gervin AS
136 Jim Chones
❑ 71 192 Rich Kelley .... 1.00 .45
102 Moses Malone TL
64 Winford Boynes
❑ 72 201 Tom Owens .... .30 .14
225 Jack Sikma TL
100 Purvis Short
❑ 73 208 George Gervin .... 1.50 .70
72 Dan Issel TL
249 Mitch Kupchak
❑ 74 217 Joe Bryant .... 1.50 .70
263 Bobby Jones SD
107 Moses Malone
❑ 75 219 Swen Nater .... .60 .25
17 Calvin Murphy AS
70 Rich.Washington
❑ 76 221 Brian Taylor .... .30 .14
253 John Shumate SD
167 Larry Demic
❑ 77 228 Fred Brown................ .30 .14
205 Larry Kenon TL
203 Kerm.Washington
❑ 78 230 John Johnson.......... 1.00 .45
4 Walter Davis AS
33 Nate Archibald
❑ 79 231 Lonnie Shelton .... .60 .25
104 Allen Leavell TL
96 John Lucas
❑ 80 233 Gus Williams .... .30 .14
20 Dan Roundfield TL
211 Kevin Restani
❑ 81 236 Allan Bristow TL .... .30 .14
210 Mark Olberding
255 James Bailey SD
❑ 82 238 Tom Boswell............ 1.00 .45
109 Billy Paultz
150 Bob Lanier
❑ 83 241 Ben Poquette .... 1.00 .45
188 Paul Westphal TL
77 Charlie Scott
❑ 84 245 Greg Ballard.............. .30 .14
43 Reggie Theus TL
252 John Williamson
❑ 85 246 Bob Dandridge .... .60 .25
41 Reggie Theus TL
128 Reggie King
❑ 86 250 Kevin Porter .... .30 .14
114 Johnny Davis TL
125 Otis Birdsong
❑ 87 251 Wes Unseld .... .60 .25
195 Tom Owens TL
78 John Roche
❑ 88 257 Elvin Hayes SD .... .60 .25
144 Marq.Johnson TL
89 Bob McAdoo
❑ 89 3 Dan Roundfield .... .60 .25
218 Lloyd Free
42 D.Greenwood TL
❑ 90 7 Moses Malone .... 1.00 .45
247 Kevin Grevey
52 Dave Robisch TL
❑ 91 12 Gus Williams .... .30 .14
210 Mark Olberding
255 James Bailey SD
❑ 92 24 Steve Hawes .... .30 .14
226 John Johnson TL
45 David Greenwood
❑ 93 29 Dan Roundfield .... .30 .14

113 Mick.Johnson TL
130 Bill Robinzine
❑ 94 34 Larry Bird 40.00 18.00
164 B.Cartwright TL
23 John Drew
❑ 95 36 Dave Cowens............ 1.00 .45
16 Paul Westphal AS
59 Randy Smith
❑ 96 38 Pete Maravich 5.00 2.20
187 Leon.Robinson TL
46 Dwight Jones
❑ 97 40 Rick Robey.................. .60 .25
37 Chris Ford
66 Joe Hassett
❑ 98 47 Scott May 15.00 6.75
30 Larry Bird TL
232 Jack Sikma
❑ 99 55 Don Ford .... 1.00 .45
144 Marq.Johnson TL
89 Bob McAdoo
❑ 100 58 Campy Russell.......... .60 .25
21 Armond Hill TL
171 M.R.Richardson
❑ 101 60 Foots Walker .... .30 .14
122 Otis Birdsong TL
48 John Mengelt
❑ 102 61 Austin Carr .... .30 .14
56 Mike Mitchell
81 Terry Tyler TL
❑ 103 63 Jim Cleamons .... .30 .14
261 James Edwards SD
157 Eddie Jordan
❑ 104 69 Tom LaGarde.......... 1.00 .45
109 Billy Paultz
150 Bob Lanier
❑ 105 71 Jerome Whitehead .... .60 .25
17 Calvin Murphy AS
70 Rich.Washington
❑ 106 74 John Roche TL.......... .30 .14
28 Wayne Rollins
15 M.R.Richardson AS
❑ 107 75 Alex English .... 1.50 .70
102 Moses Malone TL
64 Winford Boynes
❑ 108 82 Terry Tyler TL............ .30 .14
79 David Thompson
216 Brian Taylor TL
❑ 109 84 Kent Benson.............. .60 .25
259 Artis Gilmore SD
184 Caldwell Jones
❑ 110 86 Phil Hubbard .... .30 .14
195 Tom Owens TL
78 John Roche
❑ 111 88 John Long 10.00 4.50
18 Magic Johnson AS
237 Ron Boone
❑ 112 90 Eric Money .... .30 .14
215 Swen Nater TL
213 James Silas
❑ 113 95 Wayne Cooper .... .30 .14
154 Geo.Johnson TL
193 Leon.Robinson
❑ 114 97 Robert Parish .... 2.00 .90
103 Moses Malone TL
148 George Johnson
❑ 115 98 Sonny Parker .... .60 .25
94 John Lucas TL
202 Dave Twardzik
❑ 116 105 Rick Barry.............. 1.00 .45
123 Sam Lacey TL
54 Kenny Carr
❑ 117 106 Allen Leavell............ .30 .14
197 Dave Twardzik TL
39 Cedric Maxwell
❑ 118 108 Calvin Murphy .... .60 .25
51 Mike Mitchell TL
80 Bobby Wilkerson
❑ 119 110 Robert Reid .... .60 .25
153 Mike Newlin TL
182 Lionel Hollins
❑ 120 111 Rudy Tomjanovich 1.00 .45
73 Dan Issel TL
152 Brian Winters
❑ 121 112 Mick.Johnson TL .. 1.00 .45
264 Lloyd Free SD
194 Dennis Johnson

❑ 122 115 Mike Bantom .... .60 .25
204 George Gervin TL
117 Johnny Davis
❑ 123 116 Dudley Bradley...... 1.00 .45
186 Paul Westphal TL
142 Jamaal Wilkes
❑ 124 118 James Edwards .... 1.25 .55
32 Nate Archibald TL
248 Elvin Hayes
❑ 125 119 Mickey Johnson .... 1.00 .45
72 Dan Issel TL
249 Mitch Kupchak
❑ 126 120 Billy Knight .... .30 .14
104 Allen Leavell TL
96 John Lucas
❑ 127 121 George McGinnis .. 1.50 .70
10 Bob Lanier AS
222 Bill Walton
❑ 128 124 Phil Ford TL .... .60 .25
234 Adr.Dantley TL
26 Eddie Johnson
❑ 129 127 Phil Ford.................. .60 .25
43 Reggie Theus TL
252 John Williamson
❑ 130 131 Scott Wedman .... .30 .14
244 Kevin Porter TL
25 Armond Hill
❑ 131 132 K.Abdul-Jabbar TL 4.00 1.80
93 Robert Parish TL
126 Tom Burleson
❑ 132 135 K.Abdul-Jabbar 5.00 2.20
253 John Shumate SD
167 Larry Demic
❑ 133 137 Michael Cooper .... 1.00 .45
212 John Shumate
229 Paul Westphal
❑ 134 140 Mark Landsberger .. .60 .25
214 Lloyd Free TL
44 Artis Gilmore
❑ 135 141 Norm Nixon .... .60 .25
242 Elvin Hayes TL
35 M.L. Carr
❑ 136 143 Marq.Johnson TL .... .30 .14
57 Dave Robisch
254 Rick Robey SD
❑ 137 146 Junior Bridgeman .. 3.00 1.35
1 Julius Erving AS
49 Ricky Sobers
❑ 138 147 Quinn Buckner .... .60 .25
2 Marques Johnson AS
68 Jeff Judkins
❑ 139 149 Marques Johnson.... .30 .14
83 Eric Money TL
65 Mike Bratz
❑ 140 151 Sidney Moncrief 4.00 1.80
133 K.Abdul-Jabbar TL
207 Mike Gale
❑ 141 156 George Johnson...... .30 .14
175 Caldw.Jones TL
129 Sam Lacey
❑ 142 158 Maurice Lucas 3.00 1.35
262 Julius Erving SD
62 Abdul Jeelani
❑ 143 159 Mike Newlin .... .60 .25
243 Wes Unseld TL
50 Reggie Theus
❑ 144 160 Roger Phegley .... .30 .14
145 Quinn Buckner TL
138 Brad Holland
❑ 145 161 Cliff Robinson.......... .30 .14
114 Johnny Davis TL
125 Otis Birdsong
❑ 146 162 Jan V.Breda Kolff 35.00 16.00
174 Julius Erving TL
139 Magic Johnson
❑ 147 165 M.R.Richardson TL 1.00 .45
185 Steve Mix
92 Robert Parish TL
❑ 148 166 Bill Cartwright........ 1.00 .45
13 Eddie Johnson AS
179 Doug Collins
❑ 149 168 Toby Knight .... .60 .25
188 Paul Westphal TL
77 Charlie Scott
❑ 150 169 Joe Meriweather...... .30 .14
196 K.Washington TL
177 Henry Bibby
❑ 151 170 Earl Monroe .... .30 .14
206 James Silas TL
91 Terry Tyler
❑ 152 172 Marvin Webster ...... .60 .25
155 Eddie Jordan TL
239 Allan Bristow
❑ 153 173 Ray Williams .... .30 .14
225 Jack Sikma TL
100 Purvis Short
❑ 154 178 Maurice Cheeks 4.00 1.80
11 George Gervin AS
136 Jim Chones
❑ 155 183 Bobby Jones .... .60 .25
99 Clifford Ray
235 Ben Poquette TL
❑ 156 189 Alvan Adams .... .60 .25
14 Lloyd Free AS
240 Adrian Dantley
❑ 157 190 Don Buse .... .60 .25
6 Adrian Dantley AS
227 James Bailey
❑ 158 191 Walter Davis............ .60 .25
9 Bill Cartwright AS
199 Bob Gross
❑ 159 192 Rich Kelley .... 1.50 .70
263 Bobby Jones SD
107 Moses Malone
❑ 160 201 Tom Owens .... .60 .25
134 Norm Nixon TL
180 Darryl Dawkins
❑ 161 208 George Gervin ...... 1.50 .70
53 Foots Walker TL
223 Freeman Williams
❑ 162 217 Joe Bryant 3.00 1.35
8 K.Abdul-Jabbar AS
200 Calvin Natt
❑ 163 219 Swen Nater .... .30 .14
101 Phil Smith
224 Gus Williams TL
❑ 164 221 Brian Taylor .... .30 .14
256 Robert Reid SD
22 Charlie Criss
❑ 165 228 Fred Brown.......... 15.00 6.75
31 Larry Bird TL
198 Ron Brewer
❑ 166 230 John Johnson........ 1.00 .45
163 B.Cartwright TL
76 Dan Issel
❑ 167 231 Lonnie Shelton .... .30 .14
205 Larry Kenon TL
203 Kermit Washington
❑ 168 233 Gus Williams .... .60 .25
41 Reggie Theus TL
128 Reggie King
❑ 169 236 Allan Bristow TL ...... .30 .14
260 Lonnie Shelton SD
220 Paul Silas
❑ 170 238 Tom Boswell............ .30 .14
27 James McElroy
85 Leon Douglas
❑ 171 241 Ben Poquette .... 1.00 .45
176 Maurice Cheeks TL
87 Greg Kelser
❑ 172 245 Greg Ballard.......... 1.00 .45
4 Walter Davis AS
33 Nate Archibald
❑ 173 246 Bob Dandridge........ .30 .14
19 John Drew TL
209 Larry Kenon
❑ 174 250 Kevin Porter .... .30 .14
20 Dan Roundfield TL
211 Kevin Restani
❑ 175 251 Wes Unseld .... 1.00 .45
67 Geoff Huston
5 John Drew AS
❑ 176 257 Elvin Hayes SD 5.00 2.20
181 Julius Erving
258 Ron Brewer SD

1981-82 Topps

	NRMT-MT	EXC
COMPLETE SET (198)	80.00	36.00
COMMON CARD (1-66)	.10	.05
COMMON CARD (E67-E110)	.15	.07
COMMON CARD (MW67-MW110)	.15	.07
COMMON CARD (W67-W110) ..	.15	.07
TL (44-66)............................	.15	.07
CL (E93B/MW76/W97)............	1.00	.45
CL ERR (E93A)	2.00	.90
SEMISTARS............................	.25	.11

ALL CARDS 1-66 ARE DP
CONDITION SENSITIVE SET

❑ 1 John Drew........................ .20 .09
❑ 2 Dan Roundfield .... .20 .09
❑ 3 Nate Archibald.................. .60 .25
❑ 4 Larry Bird.................... 20.00 9.00
❑ 5 Cedric Maxwell .... .20 .09
❑ 6 Robert Parish .... 1.50 .70
❑ 7 Artis Gilmore .... .60 .25
❑ 8 Ricky Sobers.................... .10 .05
❑ 9 Mike Mitchell .... .20 .09
❑ 10 Tom LaGarde .... .10 .05
❑ 11 Dan Issel .... .75 .35
❑ 12 David Thompson .... .75 .35
❑ 13 Lloyd Free...................... .25 .11
❑ 14 Moses Malone.............. 1.50 .70
❑ 15 Calvin Murphy .... .25 .11
❑ 16 Johnny Davis.................. .10 .05
❑ 17 Otis Birdsong.................. .25 .11
❑ 18 Phil Ford .... .20 .09
❑ 19 Scott Wedman................ .10 .05
❑ 20 Kareem Abdul-Jabbar 4.00 1.80
❑ 21 Magic Johnson 15.00 6.75
❑ 22 Norm Nixon .... .25 .11
❑ 23 Jamaal Wilkes................ .25 .11
❑ 24 Marques Johnson .... .25 .11
❑ 25 Bob Lanier...................... .75 .35
❑ 26 Bill Cartwright .... .50 .23
❑ 27 Michael Ray Richardson .. .20 .09
❑ 28 Ray Williams .... .20 .09
❑ 29 Darryl Dawkins .... .25 .11
❑ 30 Julius Erving 4.00 1.80
❑ 31 Lionel Hollins.................. .10 .05
❑ 32 Bobby Jones .... .25 .11
❑ 33 Walter Davis .... .50 .23
❑ 34 Dennis Johnson .... .50 .23
❑ 35 Leonard Robinson............ .25 .11
❑ 36 Mychal Thompson............ .25 .11
❑ 37 George Gervin.............. 2.00 .90
❑ 38 Swen Nater .... .10 .05
❑ 39 Jack Sikma...................... .25 .11
❑ 40 Adrian Dantley................ .60 .25
❑ 41 Darrell Griffith RC .... 1.00 .45
❑ 42 Elvin Hayes...................... .75 .35
❑ 43 Fred Brown...................... .25 .11
❑ 44 Atlanta Hawks TL .... .15 .07
John Drew
Dan Roundfield
Eddie Johnson
❑ 45 Boston Celtics TL .... 2.00 .90
Larry Bird
Larry Bird
Nate Archibald
❑ 46 Chicago Bulls TL.............. .25 .11
Reggie Theus
Artis Gilmore
Reggie Theus
❑ 47 Cleveland Cavs TL .... .15 .07
Mike Mitchell
Kenny Carr

Mike Bratz
❑ 48 Dallas Mavericks TL ... .15 .07
Jim Spanarkel
Tom LaGarde
Brad Davis
❑ 49 Denver Nuggets TL ... .25 .11
David Thompson
Dan Issel
Kenny Higgs
❑ 50 Detroit Pistons TL ... .15 .07
John Long
Phil Hubbard
Ron Lee
❑ 51 Golden State TL ... .25 .11
Lloyd Free
Larry Smith
John Lucas
❑ 52 Houston Rockets TL ... .40 .18
Moses Malone
Moses Malone
Allen Leavell
❑ 53 Indiana Pacers TL ... .25 .11
Billy Knight
James Edwards
Johnny Davis
❑ 54 Kansas City Kings TL ... .15 .07
Otis Birdsong
Reggie King
Phil Ford
❑ 55 Los Angeles Lakers TL .. 1.25 .55
Kareem Abdul-Jabbar
Kareem Abdul-Jabbar
Norm Nixon
❑ 56 Milwaukee Bucks TL ... .25 .11
Marques Johnson
Mickey Johnson
Quinn Buckner
❑ 57 New Jersey Nets TL ... .15 .07
Mike Newlin
Maurice Lucas
Mike Newlin
❑ 58 New York Knicks TL ... .25 .11
Bill Cartwright
Bill Cartwright
M.R. Richardson
❑ 59 Philadelphia 76ers TL ... 1.25 .55
Julius Erving
Caldwell Jones
Maurice Cheeks
❑ 60 Phoenix Suns TL ... .25 .11
Truck Robinson
Truck Robinson
Alvan Adams
❑ 61 Portland Blazers TL ... .15 .07
Jim Paxson
Mychal Thompson
Kermit Washington
Kelvin Ransey
❑ 62 San Antonio Spurs TL ... .25 .11
George Gervin
Dave Corzine
Johnny Moore
❑ 63 San Diego Clippers TL ... .15 .07
Freeman Williams
Swen Nater
Brian Taylor
❑ 64 Seattle Sonics TL ... .25 .11
Jack Sikma
Jack Sikma
Vinnie Johnson
❑ 65 Utah Jazz TL ... .25 .11
Adrian Dantley
Ben Poquette
Allan Bristow
❑ 66 Washington Bullets TL ... .25 .11
Elvin Hayes
Elvin Hayes
Kevin Porter
❑ E67 Charlie Criss ... .25 .11
❑ E68 Eddie Johnson ... .15 .07
❑ E69 Wes Matthews ... .15 .07
❑ E70 Tom McMillen ... .40 .18
❑ E71 Tree Rollins ... .40 .18
❑ E72 M.L. Carr ... .25 .11
❑ E73 Chris Ford ... .25 .11
❑ E74 Gerald Henderson RC .. .40 .18
❑ E75 Kevin McHale RC ! ... 20.00 9.00
❑ E76 Rick Robey ... .25 .11
❑ E77 Darwin Cook RC ... .15 .07
❑ E78 Mike Gminski RC ... .75 .35
❑ E79 Maurice Lucas ... .25 .11
❑ E80 Mike Newlin ... .25 .11
❑ E81 Mike O'Koren RC ... .25 .11
❑ E82 Steve Hawes ... .15 .07
❑ E83 Foots Walker ... .25 .11
❑ E84 Campy Russell ... .25 .11
❑ E85 DeWayne Scales ... .15 .07
❑ E86 Randy Smith ... .25 .11
❑ E87 Marvin Webster ... .25 .11
❑ E88 Sly Williams ... .15 .07
❑ E89 Mike Woodson RC ... .25 .11
❑ E90 Maurice Cheeks ... 1.50 .70
❑ E91 Caldwell Jones ... .25 .11
❑ E92 Steve Mix ... .25 .11
❑ E93A Checklist 1-110 ERR 2.00 .60
(WEST above card number)
❑ E93B Checklist 1-110 COR 1.00 .30
❑ E94 Greg Ballard ... .15 .07
❑ E95 Don Collins ... .15 .07
❑ E96 Kevin Grevey ... .25 .11
❑ E97 Mitch Kupchak ... .25 .11
❑ E98 Rick Mahorn RC ... .75 .35
❑ E99 Kevin Porter ... .25 .11
❑ E100 Nate Archibald SA ... .25 .11
❑ E101 Larry Bird SA ... 12.00 5.50
❑ E102 Bill Cartwright SA ... .15 .07
❑ E103 Darryl Dawkins SA ... .25 .11
❑ E104 Julius Erving SA ... 2.00 .90
❑ E105 Kevin Porter SA ... .25 .11
❑ E106 Bobby Jones SA ... .25 .11
❑ E107 Cedric Maxwell SA ... .25 .11
❑ E108 Robert Parish SA ... 1.00 .45
❑ E109 M.R.Richardson SA ... .25 .11
❑ E110 Dan Roundfield SA ... .25 .11
❑ W67 T.R. Dunn RC ... .15 .07
❑ W68 Alex English ... 1.50 .70
❑ W69 Billy McKinney RC ... .25 .11
❑ W70 Dave Robisch ... .25 .11
❑ W71 Joe Barry Carroll RC ... .40 .18
❑ W72 Bernard King ... 1.00 .45
❑ W73 Sonny Parker ... .15 .07
❑ W74 Purvis Short ... .25 .11
❑ W75 Larry Smith RC ... .40 .18
❑ W76 Jim Chones ... .25 .11
❑ W77 Michael Cooper ... .75 .35
❑ W78 Mark Landsberger ... .15 .07
❑ W79 Alvan Adams ... .25 .11
❑ W80 Jeff Cook ... .15 .07
❑ W81 Rich Kelley ... .15 .07
❑ W82 Kyle Macy RC ... .40 .18
❑ W83 Billy Ray Bates RC ... .40 .18
❑ W84 Bob Gross ... .25 .11
❑ W85 Calvin Natt ... .25 .11
❑ W86 Lonnie Shelton ... .25 .11
❑ W87 Jim Paxson RC ... .75 .35
❑ W88 Kelvin Ransey ... .15 .07
❑ W89 Kermit Washington ... .25 .11
❑ W90 Henry Bibby ... .25 .11
❑ W91 Michael Brooks RC ... .15 .07
❑ W92 Joe Bryant ... .15 .07
❑ W93 Phil Smith ... .15 .07
❑ W94 Brian Taylor ... .15 .07
❑ W95 Freeman Williams ... .25 .11
❑ W96 James Bailey ... .15 .07
❑ W97 Checklist 1-110 ... 1.00 .30
❑ W98 John Johnson ... .15 .07
❑ W99 Vinnie Johnson RC ... 1.50 .70
❑ W100 Wally Walker RC ... .25 .11
❑ W101 Paul Westphal ... .25 .11
❑ W102 Allan Bristow ... .25 .11
❑ W103 Wayne Cooper ... .15 .07
❑ W104 Carl Nicks ... .15 .07
❑ W105 Ben Poquette ... .15 .07
❑ W106 K. Abdul-Jabbar SA .. 2.00 .90
❑ W107 Dan Issel SA ... .50 .23
❑ W108 Dennis Johnson SA ... .25 .11
❑ W109 Magic Johnson SA ... 8.00 3.60
❑ W110 Jack Sikma SA ... .25 .11
❑ MW67 David Greenwood ... .25 .11
❑ MW68 Dwight Jones ... .15 .07
❑ MW69 Reggie Theus ... .25 .11
❑ MW70 Bobby Wilkerson ... .15 .07
❑ MW71 Mike Bratz ... .15 .07
❑ MW72 Kenny Carr ... .15 .07
❑ MW73 Geoff Huston ... .15 .07
❑ MW74 Bill Laimbeer RC ... 3.00 1.35
❑ MW75 Roger Phegley ... .15 .07
❑ MW76 Checklist 1-110 ... 1.00 .30
❑ MW77 Abdul Jeelani ... .15 .07
❑ MW78 Bill Robinzine ... .15 .07
❑ MW79 Jim Spanarkel ... .15 .07
❑ MW80 Kent Benson ... .25 .11
❑ MW81 Keith Herron ... .15 .07
❑ MW82 Phil Hubbard ... .15 .07
❑ MW83 John Long ... .15 .07
❑ MW84 Terry Tyler ... .15 .07
❑ MW85 Mike Dunleavy RC ... .75 .35
❑ MW86 Tom Henderson ... .15 .07
❑ MW87 Billy Paultz ... .25 .11
❑ MW88 Robert Reid ... .15 .07
❑ MW89 Mike Bantom ... .15 .07
❑ MW90 James Edwards ... .25 .11
❑ MW91 Billy Knight ... .25 .11
❑ MW92 George McGinnis ... .25 .11
❑ MW93 Louis Orr ... .15 .07
❑ MW94 Ernie Grunfeld RC ... .40 .18
❑ MW95 Reggie King ... .15 .07
❑ MW96 Sam Lacey ... .15 .07
❑ MW97 Junior Bridgeman ... .25 .11
❑ MW98 Mickey Johnson ... .25 .11
❑ MW99 Sidney Moncrief ... .75 .35
❑ MW100 Brian Winters ... .25 .11
❑ MW101 Dave Corzine RC ... .15 .07
❑ MW102 Paul Griffin ... .15 .07
❑ MW103 Johnny Moore RC ... .25 .11
❑ MW104 Mark Olberding ... .15 .07
❑ MW105 James Silas ... .25 .11
❑ MW106 George Gervin SA .. .75 .35
❑ MW107 Artis Gilmore SA ... .25 .11
❑ MW108 Marques Johnson SA .25 .11
❑ MW109 Bob Lanier SA ... .50 .23
❑ MW110 Moses Malone SA .. 1.00 .45

1992-93 Topps

	MINT	NRMT
COMPLETE SET (396)	12.00	5.50
COMPLETE FACT. SET (408)	15.00	6.75
COMPLETE SERIES 1 (198)	4.00	1.80
COMPLETE SERIES 2 (198)	8.00	3.60
COMMON CARD (1-396)	.05	.02
SEMISTARS	.08	.04
UNLISTED STARS	.15	.07

SUBSET CARDS HALF VALUE OF BASE CARDS

❑ 1 Larry Bird ... .60 .25
❑ 2 Magic Johnson HL ... .25 .11
Earvin's Magical
Moment 2/9/92
❑ 3 Michael Jordan HL ... 1.00 .45
Michael Lights It
Up 6/3/92
❑ 4 David Robinson HL ... .15 .07
Admiral Ranks High
In Five 4/19/92
❑ 5 Johnny Newman ... .05 .02
❑ 6 Mike Iuzzolino ... .05 .02
❑ 7 Ken Norman ... .05 .02

❑ 8 Chris Jackson .05 .02
❑ 9 Duane Ferrell .05 .02
❑ 10 Sean Elliott .08 .04
❑ 11 Bernard King .05 .02
❑ 12 Armon Gilliam .05 .02
❑ 13 Reggie Williams .05 .02
❑ 14 Steve Kerr .08 .04
❑ 15 Anthony Bowie .05 .02
❑ 16 Alton Lister .05 .02
❑ 17 Dee Brown .05 .02
❑ 18 Tom Chambers .05 .02
❑ 19 Otis Thorpe .08 .04
❑ 20 Karl Malone .25 .11
❑ 21 Kenny Gattison .05 .02
❑ 22 Lionel Simmons UER .05 .02
(Misspelled Lionell
on card front)
❑ 23 Vern Fleming .05 .02
❑ 24 John Paxson .05 .02
❑ 25 Mitch Richmond .15 .07
❑ 26 Danny Schayes .05 .02
❑ 27 Derrick McKey .05 .02
❑ 28 Mark Randall .05 .02
❑ 29 Bill Laimbeer .08 .04
❑ 30 Chris Morris .05 .02
❑ 31 Alec Kessler .05 .02
❑ 32 Vlade Divac .08 .04
❑ 33 Rick Fox .08 .04
❑ 34 Charles Shackleford .05 .02
❑ 35 Dominique Wilkins .15 .07
❑ 36 Sleepy Floyd .05 .02
❑ 37 Doug West .05 .02
❑ 38 Pete Chilcutt .05 .02
❑ 39 Orlando Woolridge .05 .02
❑ 40 Eric Leckner .05 .02
❑ 41 Joe Kleine .05 .02
❑ 42 Scott Skiles .05 .02
❑ 43 Jerrod Mustaf .05 .02
❑ 44 John Starks .08 .04
❑ 45 Sedale Threatt .05 .02
❑ 46 Doug Smith .05 .02
❑ 47 Byron Scott .08 .04
❑ 48 Willie Anderson .05 .02
❑ 49 David Benoit .05 .02
❑ 50 Scott Hastings .05 .02
❑ 51 Terry Porter .05 .02
❑ 52 Sidney Green .05 .02
❑ 53 Danny Young .05 .02
❑ 54 Magic Johnson .50 .23
❑ 55 Brian Williams .05 .02
❑ 56 Randy Wittman .05 .02
❑ 57 Kevin McHale .15 .07
❑ 58 Dana Barros .05 .02
❑ 59 Thurl Bailey .05 .02
❑ 60 Kevin Duckworth .05 .02
❑ 61 John Williams .05 .02
❑ 62 Willie Burton .05 .02
❑ 63 Spud Webb .08 .04
❑ 64 Detlef Schrempf .08 .04
❑ 65 Sherman Douglas .05 .02
❑ 66 Patrick Ewing .15 .07
❑ 67 Michael Adams .05 .02
❑ 68 Vernon Maxwell .05 .02
❑ 69 Terrell Brandon .15 .07
❑ 70 Terry Catledge .05 .02
❑ 71 Mark Eaton .05 .02
❑ 72 Tony Smith .05 .02
❑ 73 B.J. Armstrong .05 .02
❑ 74 Moses Malone .15 .07
❑ 75 Anthony Bonner .05 .02
❑ 76 George McCloud .05 .02
❑ 77 Glen Rice .15 .07
❑ 78 Jon Koncak .05 .02
❑ 79 Michael Cage .05 .02
❑ 80 Ron Harper .08 .04
❑ 81 Tom Tolbert .05 .02
❑ 82 Brad Sellers .05 .02
❑ 83 Winston Garland .05 .02
❑ 84 Negele Knight .05 .02
❑ 85 Ricky Pierce .05 .02
❑ 86 Mark Aguirre .05 .02
❑ 87 Ron Anderson .05 .02
❑ 88 Loy Vaught .05 .02
❑ 89 Luc Longley .08 .04
❑ 90 Jerry Reynolds .05 .02
❑ 91 Terry Cummings .08 .04
❑ 92 Rony Seikaly .05 .02
❑ 93 Derek Harper .08 .04
❑ 94 Clifford Robinson .08 .04
❑ 95 Kenny Anderson .15 .07
❑ 96 Chris Gatling .05 .02
❑ 97 Stacey Augmon .08 .04
❑ 98 Chris Corchiani .05 .02
❑ 99 Pervis Ellison .05 .02
❑ 100 Larry Bird AS .30 .14
❑ 101 John Stockton AS UER .08 .04
(Listed as Center
on card back)
❑ 102 Clyde Drexler AS .08 .04
❑ 103 Scottie Pippen AS .25 .11
❑ 104 Reggie Lewis AS .05 .02
❑ 105 Hakeem Olajuwon AS .15 .07
❑ 106 David Robinson AS .15 .07
❑ 107 Charles Barkley AS .15 .07
❑ 108 James Worthy AS .08 .04
❑ 109 Kevin Willis AS .05 .02
❑ 110 Dikembe Mutombo AS .08 .04
❑ 111 Joe Dumars AS .08 .04
❑ 112 Jeff Hornacek AS UER .05 .02
(5 or 7 shots should
be 5 of 7 shots)
❑ 113 Mark Price AS .05 .02
❑ 114 Michael Adams AS .05 .02
❑ 115 Michael Jordan AS 1.00 .45
❑ 116 Brad Daugherty AS .05 .02
❑ 117 Dennis Rodman AS .15 .07
❑ 118 Isiah Thomas AS .08 .04
❑ 119 Tim Hardaway AS .15 .07
❑ 120 Chris Mullin AS .08 .04
❑ 121 Patrick Ewing AS .08 .04
❑ 122 Dan Majerle AS .05 .02
❑ 123 Karl Malone AS .15 .07
❑ 124 Otis Thorpe AS .05 .02
❑ 125 Dominique Wilkins AS .08 .04
❑ 126 Magic Johnson AS .25 .11
❑ 127 Charles Oakley .08 .04
❑ 128 Robert Pack .05 .02
❑ 129 Billy Owens .08 .04
❑ 130 Jeff Malone .05 .02
❑ 131 Danny Ferry .05 .02
❑ 132 Sam Bowie .05 .02
❑ 133 Avery Johnson .05 .02
❑ 134 Jayson Williams .08 .04
❑ 135 Fred Roberts .05 .02
❑ 136 Greg Sutton .05 .02
❑ 137 Dennis Rodman .30 .14
❑ 138 John Williams .05 .02
❑ 139 Greg Dreiling .05 .02
❑ 140 Rik Smits .08 .04
❑ 141 Michael Jordan 2.00 .90
❑ 142 Nick Anderson .08 .04
❑ 143 Jerome Kersey .05 .02
❑ 144 Fat Lever .05 .02
❑ 145 Tyrone Corbin .05 .02
❑ 146 Robert Parish .08 .04
❑ 147 Steve Smith .20 .09
❑ 148 Chris Dudley .05 .02
❑ 149 Antoine Carr .05 .02
❑ 150 Elden Campbell .08 .04
❑ 151 Randy White .05 .02
❑ 152 Felton Spencer .05 .02
❑ 153 Cedric Ceballos .08 .04
❑ 154 Mark Macon .05 .02
❑ 155 Jack Haley .05 .02
❑ 156 Bimbo Coles .05 .02
❑ 157 A.J. English .05 .02
❑ 158 Kendall Gill .08 .04
❑ 159 A.C. Green .08 .04
❑ 160 Mark West .05 .02
❑ 161 Benoit Benjamin .05 .02
❑ 162 Tyrone Hill .05 .02
❑ 163 Larry Nance .05 .02
❑ 164 Gary Grant .05 .02
❑ 165 Bill Cartwright .05 .02
❑ 166 Greg Anthony .05 .02
❑ 167 Jim Les .05 .02
❑ 168 Johnny Dawkins .05 .02
❑ 169 Alvin Robertson .05 .02
❑ 170 Kenny Smith .05 .02
❑ 171 Gerald Glass .05 .02
❑ 172 Harvey Grant .05 .02
❑ 173 Paul Graham .05 .02
❑ 174 Sam Perkins .08 .04
❑ 175 Manute Bol .05 .02
❑ 176 Muggsy Bogues .08 .04
❑ 177 Mike Brown .05 .02
❑ 178 Donald Hodge .05 .02
❑ 179 Dave Jamerson .05 .02
❑ 180 Mookie Blaylock .08 .04
❑ 181 Randy Brown .05 .02
❑ 182 Todd Lichti .05 .02
❑ 183 Kevin Gamble .05 .02
❑ 184 Gary Payton .30 .14
❑ 185 Brian Shaw .05 .02
❑ 186 Grant Long .05 .02
❑ 187 Frank Brickowski .05 .02
❑ 188 Tim Hardaway .20 .09
❑ 189 Danny Manning .08 .04
❑ 190 Kevin Johnson .15 .07
❑ 191 Craig Ehlo .05 .02
❑ 192 Dennis Scott .08 .04
❑ 193 Reggie Miller .15 .07
❑ 194 Darrell Walker .05 .02
❑ 195 Anthony Mason .15 .07
❑ 196 Buck Williams .08 .04
❑ 197 Checklist 1-99 .05 .02
❑ 198 Checklist 100-198 .05 .02
❑ 199 Karl Malone 50P .15 .07
❑ 200 Dominique Wilkins 50P .08 .04
❑ 201 Tom Chambers 50P .05 .02
❑ 202 Bernard King 50P .05 .02
❑ 203 Kiki Vandeweghe 50P .05 .02
❑ 204 Dale Ellis 50P .05 .02
❑ 205 Michael Jordan 50P 1.00 .45
❑ 206 Michael Adams 50P .05 .02
❑ 207 Charles Smith 50P .05 .02
❑ 208 Moses Malone 50P .08 .04
❑ 209 Terry Cummings 50P .05 .02
❑ 210 Vernon Maxwell 50P .05 .02
❑ 211 Patrick Ewing 50P .08 .04
❑ 212 Clyde Drexler 50P .08 .04
❑ 213 Kevin McHale 50P .08 .04
❑ 214 Hakeem Olajuwon 50P .15 .07
❑ 215 Reggie Miller 50P .08 .04
❑ 216 Gary Grant 20A .05 .02
❑ 217 Doc Rivers 20A .05 .02
❑ 218 Mark Price 20A .05 .02
❑ 219 Isiah Thomas 20A .08 .04
❑ 220 Nate McMillan 20A .05 .02
❑ 221 Fat Lever 20A .05 .02
❑ 222 Kevin Johnson 20A .08 .04
❑ 223 John Stockton 20A .08 .04
❑ 224 Scott Skiles 20A .05 .02
❑ 225 Kevin Brooks .05 .02
❑ 226 Bobby Phills RC .15 .07
❑ 227 Oliver Miller RC .08 .04
❑ 228 John Williams .05 .02
❑ 229 Brad Lohaus .05 .02
❑ 230 Derrick Coleman .08 .04
❑ 231 Ed Pinckney .05 .02
❑ 232 Trent Tucker .05 .02
❑ 233 Lance Blanks .05 .02
❑ 234 Drazen Petrovic .05 .02
❑ 235 Mark Bryant .05 .02
❑ 236 Lloyd Daniels RC .05 .02
❑ 237 Dale Davis .05 .02
❑ 238 Jayson Williams .08 .04
❑ 239 Mike Sanders .05 .02
❑ 240 Mike Gminski .05 .02
❑ 241 William Bedford .05 .02
❑ 242 Dell Curry .05 .02
❑ 243 Gerald Paddio .05 .02
❑ 244 Chris Smith RC .05 .02
❑ 245 Jud Buechler .05 .02
❑ 246 Walter Palmer .05 .02
❑ 247 Larry Krystkowiak .05 .02
❑ 248 Marcus Liberty .05 .02
❑ 249 Sam Mitchell .05 .02
❑ 250 Kiki Vandeweghe .05 .02
❑ 251 Vincent Askew .05 .02
❑ 252 Travis Mays .05 .02
❑ 253 Charles Smith .05 .02
❑ 254 John Bagley .05 .02
❑ 255 James Worthy .15 .07
❑ 256 Paul Pressey P/CO .05 .02
❑ 257 Rumeal Robinson .05 .02
❑ 258 Tom Gugliotta RC .50 .23
❑ 259 Eric Anderson RC .05 .02

❑ 260 Hersey Hawkins .08 .04
❑ 261 Terry Davis .05 .02
❑ 262 Rex Chapman .05 .02
❑ 263 Chucky Brown .05 .02
❑ 264 Danny Young .05 .02
❑ 265 Olden Polynice .05 .02
❑ 266 Kevin Willis .05 .02
❑ 267 Shawn Kemp .30 .14
❑ 268 Mookie Blaylock .08 .04
❑ 269 Malik Sealy RC .08 .04
❑ 270 Charles Barkley .25 .11
❑ 271 Corey Williams RC .05 .02
❑ 272 Stephen Howard RC .05 .02
(See also card 286)
❑ 273 Keith Askins .05 .02
❑ 274 Matt Bullard .05 .02
❑ 275 John Battle .05 .02
❑ 276 Andrew Lang .05 .02
❑ 277 David Robinson .25 .11
❑ 278 Harold Miner RC .08 .04
❑ 279 Tracy Murray RC .08 .04
❑ 280 Pooh Richardson .05 .02
❑ 281 Dikembe Mutombo .15 .07
❑ 282 Wayman Tisdale .05 .02
❑ 283 Larry Johnson .20 .09
❑ 284 Todd Day RC .08 .04
❑ 285 Stanley Roberts .05 .02
❑ 286 Randy Woods RC UER .05 .02
(Card misnumbered 272;
run he show should
be run the show)
❑ 287 Avery Johnson .05 .02
❑ 288 Anthony Peeler RC .08 .04
❑ 289 Mario Elie .08 .04
❑ 290 Doc Rivers .08 .04
❑ 291 Blue Edwards .05 .02
❑ 292 Sean Rooks RC .05 .02
❑ 293 Xavier McDaniel .05 .02
❑ 294 C. Weatherspoon RC .15 .07
❑ 295 Morlon Wiley .05 .02
❑ 296 LaBradford Smith .05 .02
❑ 297 Reggie Lewis .08 .04
❑ 298 Chris Mullin .15 .07
❑ 299 Litterial Green RC .05 .02
❑ 300 Elmore Spencer RC .05 .02
❑ 301 John Stockton .15 .07
❑ 302 Walt Williams RC .15 .07
❑ 303 Anthony Pullard RC .05 .02
❑ 304 Gundars Vetra RC .05 .02
❑ 305 LaSalle Thompson .05 .02
❑ 306 Nate McMillan .05 .02
❑ 307 Steve Bardo RC .05 .02
❑ 308 Robert Horry RC .15 .07
❑ 309 Scott Williams .05 .02
❑ 310 Bo Kimble .05 .02
❑ 311 Tree Rollins .05 .02
❑ 312 Tim Perry .05 .02
❑ 313 Isaac Austin RC .08 .04
❑ 314 Tate George .05 .02
❑ 315 Kevin Lynch .05 .02
❑ 316 Victor Alexander .05 .02
❑ 317 Doug Overton .05 .02
❑ 318 Tom Hammonds .05 .02
❑ 319 LaPhonso Ellis RC .15 .07
❑ 320 Scott Brooks .05 .02
❑ 321 Anthony Avent RC UER .05 .02
(Front photo actually Blue Edwards)
❑ 322 Matt Geiger RC .08 .04
❑ 323 Duane Causwell .05 .02
❑ 324 Horace Grant .08 .04
❑ 325 Mark Jackson .08 .04
❑ 326 Dan Majerle .08 .04
❑ 327 Chuck Person .05 .02
❑ 328 Buck Johnson .05 .02
❑ 329 Duane Cooper RC .05 .02
❑ 330 Rod Strickland .15 .07
❑ 331 Isiah Thomas .15 .07
❑ 332 Greg Kite .05 .02
(See also card 387)
❑ 333 Don MacLean RC .05 .02
❑ 334 Christian Laettner RC .30 .14
❑ 335 John Crotty RC .05 .02
❑ 336 Tracy Moore RC .05 .02
❑ 337 Hakeem Olajuwon .25 .11
❑ 338 Byron Houston RC .05 .02
❑ 339 Walter Bond RC .05 .02
❑ 340 Brent Price RC .08 .04
❑ 341 Bryant Stith RC .08 .04
❑ 342 Will Perdue .05 .02
❑ 343 Jeff Hornacek .08 .04
❑ 344 Adam Keefe RC .05 .02
❑ 345 Rafael Addison .05 .02
❑ 346 Marlon Maxey RC .05 .02
❑ 347 Joe Dumars .15 .07
❑ 348 Jon Barry RC .08 .04
❑ 349 Marty Conlon .05 .02
❑ 350 Alaa Abdelnaby .05 .02
❑ 351 Micheal Williams .05 .02
❑ 352 Brad Daugherty .05 .02
❑ 353 Tony Bennett RC .05 .02
❑ 354 Clyde Drexler .15 .07
❑ 355 Rolando Blackman .05 .02
❑ 356 Tom Tolbert .05 .02
❑ 357 Sarunas Marciulionis .05 .02
❑ 358 Jaren Jackson RC .08 .04
❑ 359 Stacey King .05 .02
❑ 360 Danny Ainge .08 .04
❑ 361 Dale Ellis .05 .02
❑ 362 Shaquille O'Neal RC 5.00 2.20
❑ 363 Bob McCann RC .05 .02
❑ 364 Reggie Smith RC .05 .02
❑ 365 Vinny Del Negro .05 .02
❑ 366 Robert Pack .05 .02
❑ 367 David Wood .05 .02
❑ 368 Rodney McCray .05 .02
❑ 369 Terry Mills .05 .02
❑ 370 Eric Murdock UER .05 .02
(Jazz on back spelled Jass)
❑ 371 Alex Blackwell RC .05 .02
❑ 372 Jay Humphries .05 .02
❑ 373 Eddie Lee Wilkins .05 .02
❑ 374 James Edwards .05 .02
❑ 375 Tim Kempton .05 .02
❑ 376 J.R. Reid .05 .02
❑ 377 Sam Mack RC .08 .04
❑ 378 Donald Royal .05 .02
❑ 379 Mark Price .05 .02
❑ 380 Mark Acres .05 .02
❑ 381 Hubert Davis RC .08 .04
❑ 382 Dave Johnson RC .05 .02
❑ 383 John Salley .05 .02
❑ 384 Eddie Johnson .05 .02
❑ 385 Brian Howard RC .05 .02
❑ 386 Isaiah Morris RC .05 .02
❑ 387 Frank Johnson .05 .02
(Card misnumbered 332)
❑ 388 Rick Mahorn .05 .02
❑ 389 Scottie Pippen .50 .23
❑ 390 Lee Mayberry RC .05 .02
❑ 391 Tony Campbell .05 .02
❑ 392 Latrell Sprewell RC 1.25 .55
❑ 393 Alonzo Mourning RC .75 .35
❑ 394 Robert Werdann RC .05 .02
❑ 395 Checklist 199-297 UER .05 .02
(286 Kennard Winchester;
should be Randy Woods)
❑ 396 Checklist 298-396 .05 .02

1992-93 Topps Gold

	MINT	NRMT
COMPLETE SET (396)	70.00	32.00
COMPLETE FACT.SET (403)	75.00	34.00
COMPLETE SERIES 1 (198)	20.00	9.00
COMPLETE SERIES 2 (198)	50.00	22.00
COMMON CARD (1G-396G)	.10	.05
CL REPLACEMENT (197G/198G)	.50	.23
CL REPLACEMENT (395G/396G)	.50	.23

*STARS: 2.5X TO 5X BASE CARD HI
*RCs: 1.5X TO 3X BASE HI
ONE PER PACK
TWELVE PER FACTORY SET

❑ 197G Jeff Sanders .50 .23
❑ 198G Elliott Perry UER .50 .23
(Misspelled Elliot
on front)
❑ 362G Shaquille O'Neal 40.00 18.00
❑ 395G David Wingate .50 .23
❑ 396G Carl Herrera .50 .23

1992-93 Topps Beam Team

	MINT	NRMT
COMPLETE SET (7)	10.00	4.50
COMMON TRIO (1-7)	.75	.35

SER.2 STATED ODDS 1:18
COMP.GOLD BEAM TEAM (7) 25.00 11.00
*GOLD: 1.5X TO 3X HI COLUMN
ONE GOLD BT SET PER GOLD FACTORY SET

❑ 1 Reggie Miller 1.00 .45
Charles Barkley
Clyde Drexler
❑ 2 Patrick Ewing .75 .35
Tim Hardaway
Jeff Hornacek
❑ 3 Kevin Johnson 5.00 2.20
Michael Jordan
Dennis Rodman
❑ 4 Dominique Wilkins .75 .35
John Stockton
Karl Malone
❑ 5 Hakeem Olajuwon 1.25 .55
Mark Price
Shawn Kemp
❑ 6 Scottie Pippen 1.00 .45
David Robinson
Jeff Malone
❑ 7 Chris Mullin 5.00 2.20
Shaquille O'Neal
Glen Rice

1993-94 Topps

	MINT	NRMT
COMPLETE SET (396)	20.00	9.00
COMPLETE FACT.SET (410)	25.00	11.00
COMPLETE SERIES 1 (198)	10.00	4.50
COMPLETE SERIES 2 (198)	10.00	4.50
COMMON CARD (1-396)	.05	.02
SEMISTARS	.10	.05
UNLISTED STARS	.25	.11

SUBSET CARDS HALF VALUE OF BASE CARDS

❑ 1 Charles Barkley HL .25 .11
❑ 2 Hakeem Olajuwon HL .25 .11

❑ 3 Shaquille O'Neal HL .50 .23
❑ 4 Chris Jackson HL .05 .02
❑ 5 Clifford Robinson HL .05 .02
❑ 6 Donald Hodge .05 .02
❑ 7 Victor Alexander .05 .02
❑ 8 Chris Morris .05 .02
❑ 9 Muggsy Bogues .10 .05
❑ 10 Steve Smith UER .25 .11
(Listed with Kings in '90-91; was not in NBA that year)
❑ 11 Dave Johnson .05 .02
❑ 12 Tom Gugliotta .25 .11
❑ 13 Doug Edwards RC .05 .02
❑ 14 Vlade Divac .10 .05
❑ 15 Corie Blount RC .05 .02
❑ 16 Derek Harper .10 .05
❑ 17 Matt Bullard .05 .02
❑ 18 Terry Catledge .05 .02
❑ 19 Mark Eaton .05 .02
❑ 20 Mark Jackson .10 .05
❑ 21 Terry Mills .05 .02
❑ 22 Johnny Dawkins .05 .02
❑ 23 Michael Jordan UER 3.00 1.35
(Listed as a forward with birthdate of 1968; he is a guard with bithdate of 1963)
❑ 24 Rick Fox UER .05 .02
(Listed with Kings in '91-92)
❑ 25 Charles Oakley .10 .05
❑ 26 Derrick McKey .05 .02
❑ 27 Christian Laettner .10 .05
❑ 28 Todd Day .05 .02
❑ 29 Danny Ferry .05 .02
❑ 30 Kevin Johnson .10 .05
❑ 31 Vinny Del Negro .05 .02
❑ 32 Kevin Brooks .05 .02
❑ 33 Pete Chilcutt .05 .02
❑ 34 Larry Stewart .05 .02
❑ 35 Dave Jamerson .05 .02
❑ 36 Sidney Green .05 .02
❑ 37 J.R. Reid .05 .02
❑ 38 Jim Jackson .10 .05
❑ 39 Micheal Williams UER .05 .02
(350.2 minutes per game)
❑ 40 Rex Walters RC .05 .02
❑ 41 Shawn Bradley RC .25 .11
❑ 42 Jon Koncak .05 .02
❑ 43 Byron Houston .05 .02
❑ 44 Brian Shaw .05 .02
❑ 45 Bill Cartwright .05 .02
❑ 46 Jerome Kersey .05 .02
❑ 47 Danny Schayes .05 .02
❑ 48 Olden Polynice .05 .02
❑ 49 Anthony Peeler .05 .02
❑ 50 Nick Anderson 50 .05 .02
❑ 51 David Benoit .05 .02
❑ 52 David Robinson .25 .11
❑ 53 Greg Kite .05 .02
❑ 54 Gerald Paddio .05 .02
❑ 55 Don MacLean .05 .02
❑ 56 Randy Woods .05 .02
❑ 57 Reggie Miller 50 .10 .05
❑ 58 Kevin Gamble .05 .02
❑ 59 Sean Green .05 .02
❑ 60 Jeff Hornacek .10 .05
❑ 61 John Starks .10 .05
❑ 62 Gerald Wilkins .05 .02
❑ 63 Jim Les .05 .02
❑ 64 Michael Jordan 50 1.50 .70
❑ 65 Alvin Robertson .05 .02
❑ 66 Tim Kempton .05 .02
❑ 67 Bryant Stith .05 .02
❑ 68 Jeff Turner .05 .02
❑ 69 Malik Sealy .05 .02
❑ 70 Dell Curry .05 .02
❑ 71 Brent Price .05 .02
❑ 72 Kevin Lynch .05 .02
❑ 73 Bimbo Coles .05 .02
❑ 74 Larry Nance .05 .02
❑ 75 Luther Wright RC .05 .02
❑ 76 Willie Anderson .05 .02
❑ 77 Dennis Rodman .50 .23
❑ 78 Anthony Mason .10 .05
❑ 79 Chris Gatling .05 .02
❑ 80 Antoine Carr .05 .02
❑ 81 Kevin Willis .05 .02
❑ 82 Thurl Bailey .05 .02
❑ 83 Reggie Williams .05 .02
❑ 84 Rod Strickland .10 .05
❑ 85 Rolando Blackman .05 .02
❑ 86 Bobby Hurley RC .10 .05
❑ 87 Jeff Malone .05 .02
❑ 88 James Worthy .25 .11
❑ 89 Alaa Abdelnaby .05 .02
❑ 90 Duane Ferrell .05 .02
❑ 91 Anthony Avent .05 .02
❑ 92 Scottie Pippen .75 .35
❑ 93 Ricky Pierce .05 .02
❑ 94 P.J. Brown RC .25 .11
❑ 95 Jeff Grayer .05 .02
❑ 96 Jerrod Mustaf .05 .02
❑ 97 Elmore Spencer .05 .02
❑ 98 Walt Williams .05 .02
❑ 99 Otis Thorpe .10 .05
❑ 100 Patrick Ewing AS .10 .05
❑ 101 Michael Jordan AS 1.50 .70
❑ 102 John Stockton AS .10 .05
❑ 103 Dominique Wilkins AS .10 .05
❑ 104 Charles Barkley AS .25 .11
❑ 105 Lee Mayberry .05 .02
❑ 106 James Edwards .05 .02
❑ 107 Scott Brooks .05 .02
❑ 108 John Battle .05 .02
❑ 109 Kenny Gattison .05 .02
❑ 110 Pooh Richardson .05 .02
❑ 111 Rony Seikaly .05 .02
❑ 112 Mahmoud Abdul-Rauf .05 .02
❑ 113 Nick Anderson .10 .05
❑ 114 Gundars Vetra .05 .02
❑ 115 Joe Dumars AS .10 .05
❑ 116 Hakeem Olajuwon AS .25 .11
❑ 117 Scottie Pippen AS .40 .18
❑ 118 Mark Price AS .05 .02
❑ 119 Karl Malone AS .25 .11
❑ 120 Michael Cage .05 .02
❑ 121 Ed Pinckney .05 .02
❑ 122 Jay Humphries .05 .02
❑ 123 Dale Davis .05 .02
❑ 124 Sean Rooks .05 .02
❑ 125 Mookie Blaylock .10 .05
❑ 126 Buck Williams .05 .02
❑ 127 John Williams .05 .02
❑ 128 Stacey King .05 .02
❑ 129 Tim Perry .05 .02
❑ 130 Tim Hardaway AS .10 .05
❑ 131 Larry Johnson AS .10 .05
❑ 132 Detlef Schrempf AS .05 .02
❑ 133 Reggie Miller AS .10 .05
❑ 134 Shaquille O'Neal .50 .23
❑ 135 Dale Ellis .05 .02
❑ 136 Duane Causwell .05 .02
❑ 137 Rumeal Robinson .05 .02
❑ 138 Billy Owens .05 .02
❑ 139 Malcolm Mackey RC .05 .02
❑ 140 Vernon Maxwell .05 .02
❑ 141 LaPhonso Ellis .05 .02
❑ 142 Robert Parish .10 .05
❑ 143 LaBradford Smith .05 .02
❑ 144 Charles Smith .05 .02
❑ 145 Terry Porter .05 .02
❑ 146 Elden Campbell .05 .02
❑ 147 Bill Laimbeer .05 .02
❑ 148 Chris Mills RC .25 .11
❑ 149 Brad Lohaus .05 .02
❑ 150 Jimmy Jackson ART .05 .02
❑ 151 Tom Gugliotta ART .10 .05
❑ 152 Shaquille O'Neal ART .50 .23
❑ 153 Latrell Sprewell ART .25 .11
❑ 154 Walt Williams ART .05 .02
❑ 155 Gary Payton .40 .18
❑ 156 Orlando Woolridge .05 .02
❑ 157 Adam Keefe .05 .02
❑ 158 Calbert Cheaney RC .10 .05
❑ 159 Rick Mahorn .05 .02
❑ 160 Robert Horry .10 .05
❑ 161 John Salley .05 .02
❑ 162 Sam Mitchell .05 .02
❑ 163 Stanley Roberts .05 .02
❑ 164 Clarence Weatherspoon .05 .02
❑ 165 Anthony Bowie .05 .02
❑ 166 Derrick Coleman .10 .05
❑ 167 Negele Knight .05 .02
❑ 168 Marlon Maxey .05 .02
❑ 169 Spud Webb UER .10 .05
(Listed as center instead of guard)
❑ 170 Alonzo Mourning .40 .18
❑ 171 Ervin Johnson RC .10 .05
❑ 172 Sedale Threatt .05 .02
❑ 173 Mark Macon .05 .02
❑ 174 B.J. Armstrong .05 .02
❑ 175 Harold Miner ART .05 .02
❑ 176 Anthony Peeler ART .05 .02
❑ 177 Alonzo Mourning ART .25 .11
❑ 178 Christian Laettner ART .05 .02
❑ 179 Clarence Weatherspoon ART .05
.02
❑ 180 Dee Brown .05 .02
❑ 181 Shaquille O'Neal 1.25 .55
❑ 182 Loy Vaught .05 .02
❑ 183 Terrell Brandon .10 .05
❑ 184 Lionel Simmons .05 .02
❑ 185 Mark Aguirre .05 .02
❑ 186 Danny Ainge .10 .05
❑ 187 Reggie Miller .25 .11
❑ 188 Terry Davis .05 .02
❑ 189 Mark Bryant .05 .02
❑ 190 Tyrone Corbin .05 .02
❑ 191 Chris Mullin .25 .11
❑ 192 Johnny Newman .05 .02
❑ 193 Doug West .05 .02
❑ 194 Keith Askins .05 .02
❑ 195 Bo Kimble .05 .02
❑ 196 Sean Elliott .10 .05
❑ 197 Checklist 1-99 UER .05 .02
(No. 18 listed as Terry Mills instead of Terry Cummings and No. 23 listed as Sam Mitchell instead of Michael Jordan)
❑ 198 Checklist 100-198 .05 .02
❑ 199 Michael Jordan FPM 1.50 .70
❑ 200 Patrick Ewing FPM .10 .05
❑ 201 John Stockton FPM .10 .05
❑ 202 Shawn Kemp FPM .25 .11
❑ 203 Mark Price FPM .05 .02
❑ 204 Charles Barkley FPM .25 .11
❑ 205 Hakeem Olajuwon FPM .25 .11
❑ 206 Clyde Drexler FPM .10 .05
❑ 207 Kevin Johnson FPM .05 .02
❑ 208 John Starks FPM .05 .02
❑ 209 Chris Mullin FPM .10 .05
❑ 210 Doc Rivers .10 .05
❑ 211 Kenny Walker .05 .02
❑ 212 Doug Christie .05 .02
❑ 213 James Robinson RC .05 .02
❑ 214 Larry Krystkowiak .05 .02
❑ 215 Manute Bol .05 .02
❑ 216 Carl Herrera .05 .02
❑ 217 Paul Graham .05 .02
❑ 218 Jud Buechler .05 .02
❑ 219 Mike Brown .05 .02
❑ 220 Tom Chambers .05 .02
❑ 221 Kendall Gill .10 .05
❑ 222 Kenny Anderson .10 .05
❑ 223 Larry Johnson .25 .11
❑ 224 Chris Webber RC 2.50 1.10
❑ 225 Randy White .05 .02
❑ 226 Rik Smits .10 .05
❑ 227 A.C. Green .10 .05
❑ 228 David Robinson .40 .18
❑ 229 Sean Elliott .10 .05

❑ 230 Gary Grant	.05	.02
❑ 231 Dana Barros	.05	.02
❑ 232 Bobby Hurley	.10	.05
❑ 233 Blue Edwards	.05	.02
❑ 234 Tom Hammonds	.05	.02
❑ 235 Pete Myers UER	.05	.02
Card says born in 1993		
❑ 236 Acie Earl RC	.05	.02
❑ 237 Tony Smith	.05	.02
❑ 238 Bill Wennington	.05	.02
❑ 239 Andrew Lang	.05	.02
❑ 240 Ervin Johnson	.10	.05
❑ 241 Byron Scott	.10	.05
❑ 242 Eddie Johnson	.05	.02
❑ 243 Anthony Bonner	.05	.02
❑ 244 Luther Wright	.05	.02
❑ 245 LaSalle Thompson	.05	.02
❑ 246 Harold Miner	.05	.02
❑ 247 Chris Smith	.05	.02
❑ 248 John Williams	.05	.02
❑ 249 Clyde Drexler	.25	.11
❑ 250 Calbert Cheaney	.10	.05
❑ 251 Avery Johnson	.05	.02
❑ 252 Steve Kerr	.10	.05
❑ 253 Warren Kidd RC	.05	.02
❑ 254 Wayman Tisdale	.05	.02
❑ 255 Bob Martin RC	.05	.02
❑ 256 Popeye Jones RC	.05	.02
❑ 257 Jimmy Oliver	.05	.02
❑ 258 Kevin Edwards	.05	.02
❑ 259 Dan Majerle	.10	.05
❑ 260 Jon Barry	.05	.02
❑ 261 Allan Houston RC	1.00	.45
❑ 262 Dikembe Mutombo	.10	.05
❑ 263 Sleepy Floyd	.05	.02
❑ 264 George Lynch RC	.05	.02
❑ 265 Stacey Augmon UER	.05	.02
(Listed with Heat in stats)		
❑ 266 Hakeem Olajuwon	.40	.18
❑ 267 Scott Skiles	.05	.02
❑ 268 Detlef Schrempf	.10	.05
❑ 269 Brian Davis RC	.05	.02
❑ 270 Tracy Murray	.05	.02
❑ 271 Gheorghe Muresan RC	.25	.11
❑ 272 Terry Dehere RC	.05	.02
❑ 273 Terry Cummings	.05	.02
❑ 274 Keith Jennings	.05	.02
❑ 275 Tyrone Hill	.05	.02
❑ 276 Hersey Hawkins	.10	.05
❑ 277 Grant Long	.05	.02
❑ 278 Herb Williams	.05	.02
❑ 279 Karl Malone	.40	.18
❑ 280 Mitch Richmond	.25	.11
❑ 281 Derek Strong RC	.05	.02
❑ 282 Dino Radja RC	.05	.02
❑ 283 Jack Haley	.05	.02
❑ 284 Derek Harper	.10	.05
❑ 285 Dwayne Schintzius	.05	.02
❑ 286 Michael Curry RC	.05	.02
❑ 287 Rodney Rogers RC	.25	.11
❑ 288 Horace Grant	.10	.05
❑ 289 Oliver Miller	.05	.02
❑ 290 Luc Longley	.10	.05
❑ 291 Walter Bond	.05	.02
❑ 292 Dominique Wilkins	.25	.11
❑ 293 Vern Fleming	.05	.02
❑ 294 Mark Price	.05	.02
❑ 295 Mark Aguirre	.05	.02
❑ 296 Shawn Kemp	.40	.18
❑ 297 Pervis Ellison	.05	.02
❑ 298 Josh Grant RC	.05	.02
❑ 299 Scott Burrell RC	.25	.11
❑ 300 Patrick Ewing	.25	.11
❑ 301 Sam Cassell RC	.60	.25
❑ 302 Nick Van Exel RC	.60	.25
❑ 303 Clifford Robinson	.10	.05
❑ 304 Frank Johnson	.05	.02
❑ 305 Matt Geiger	.05	.02
❑ 306 Vin Baker RC	.60	.25
❑ 307 Benoit Benjamin	.05	.02
❑ 308 Shawn Bradley	.25	.11
❑ 309 Chris Whitney RC	.05	.02
❑ 310 Eric Riley RC	.05	.02
❑ 311 Isiah Thomas	.25	.11
❑ 312 Jamal Mashburn RC	.50	.23
❑ 313 Xavier McDaniel	.05	.02
❑ 314 Mike Peplowski RC	.05	.02
❑ 315 Darnell Mee RC	.05	.02
❑ 316 Toni Kukoc RC	1.00	.45
❑ 317 Felton Spencer	.05	.02
❑ 318 Sam Bowie	.05	.02
❑ 319 Mario Elie	.05	.02
❑ 320 Tim Hardaway	.25	.11
❑ 321 Ken Norman	.05	.02
❑ 322 Isaiah Rider RC	.50	.23
❑ 323 Rex Chapman	.05	.02
❑ 324 Dennis Rodman	.50	.23
❑ 325 Derrick McKey	.05	.02
❑ 326 Corie Blount	.05	.02
❑ 327 Fat Lever	.05	.02
❑ 328 Ron Harper	.10	.05
❑ 329 Eric Anderson	.05	.02
❑ 330 Armon Gilliam	.05	.02
❑ 331 Lindsey Hunter RC	.25	.11
❑ 332 Eric Leckner	.05	.02
❑ 333 Chris Corchiani	.05	.02
❑ 334 Anfernee Hardaway RC	2.50	1.10
❑ 335 Randy Brown	.05	.02
❑ 336 Sam Perkins	.10	.05
❑ 337 Glen Rice	.10	.05
❑ 338 Orlando Woolridge	.05	.02
❑ 339 Mike Gminski	.05	.02
❑ 340 Latrell Sprewell	.60	.25
❑ 341 Harvey Grant	.05	.02
❑ 342 Doug Smith	.05	.02
❑ 343 Kevin Duckworth	.05	.02
❑ 344 Cedric Ceballos	.10	.05
❑ 345 Chuck Person	.05	.02
❑ 346 Scott Haskin RC	.05	.02
❑ 347 Frank Brickowski	.05	.02
❑ 348 Scott Williams	.05	.02
❑ 349 Brad Daugherty	.05	.02
❑ 350 Willie Burton	.05	.02
❑ 351 Joe Dumars	.25	.11
❑ 352 Craig Ehlo	.05	.02
❑ 353 Lucious Harris RC	.05	.02
❑ 354 Danny Manning	.10	.05
❑ 355 Litterial Green	.05	.02
❑ 356 John Stockton	.25	.11
❑ 357 Nate McMillan	.05	.02
❑ 358 Greg Graham RC	.05	.02
❑ 359 Rex Walters	.05	.02
❑ 360 Lloyd Daniels	.05	.02
❑ 361 Antonio Harvey RC	.05	.02
❑ 362 Brian Williams	.05	.02
❑ 363 LeRon Ellis	.05	.02
❑ 364 Chris Dudley	.05	.02
❑ 365 Hubert Davis	.05	.02
❑ 366 Evers Burns RC	.05	.02
❑ 367 Sherman Douglas	.05	.02
❑ 368 Sarunas Marciulionis	.05	.02
❑ 369 Tom Tolbert	.05	.02
❑ 370 Robert Pack	.05	.02
❑ 371 Michael Adams	.05	.02
❑ 372 Negele Knight	.05	.02
❑ 373 Charles Barkley	.40	.18
❑ 374 Bryon Russell RC	.25	.11
❑ 375 Greg Anthony	.05	.02
❑ 376 Ken Williams	.05	.02
❑ 377 John Paxson	.05	.02
❑ 378 Corey Gaines	.05	.02
❑ 379 Eric Murdock	.05	.02
❑ 380 Kevin Thompson RC	.05	.02
❑ 381 Moses Malone	.25	.11
❑ 382 Kenny Smith	.05	.02
❑ 383 Dennis Scott	.05	.02
❑ 384 Michael Jordan FSL	1.50	.70
❑ 385 Hakeem Olajuwon FSL	.25	.11
❑ 386 Shaquille O'Neal FSL	.50	.23
❑ 387 David Robinson FSL	.25	.11
❑ 388 Derrick Coleman FSL	.05	.02
❑ 389 Karl Malone FSL	.25	.11
❑ 390 Patrick Ewing FSL	.10	.05
❑ 391 Scottie Pippen FSL	.40	.18
❑ 392 Dominique Wilkins FSL	.10	.05
❑ 393 Charles Barkley FSL	.25	.11
❑ 394 Larry Johnson FSL	.10	.05
❑ 395 Checklist	.05	.02
❑ 396 Checklist	.05	.02
❑ NNO Expired Finest Redemption Card	1.00	.45

1993-94 Topps Gold

	MINT	NRMT
COMPLETE SET (396)	70.00	32.00
COMPLETE SERIES 1 (198)	30.00	13.50
COMPLETE SERIES 2 (198)	40.00	18.00
COMMON CARD (1G-396G)	.10	.05
CL REPLACEMENT (197G/198G)	.50	.23
CL REPLACEMENT (395G/396G)	.50	.23

*STARS: 2X TO 4X BASE CARD HI
*RCs: 1.25X TO 2.5X BASE HI
ONE PER PACK
TEN PER FACTORY SET

❑ 197G Frank Johnson	.50	.23
❑ 198G David Wingate	.50	.23
❑ 395G Will Perdue	.50	.23
❑ 396G Mark West	.50	.23

1993-94 Topps Black Gold

	MINT	NRMT
COMPLETE SET (25)	25.00	11.00
COMPLETE SERIES 1 (13)	5.00	2.20
COMPLETE SERIES 2 (12)	20.00	9.00

*STARS: 1.5X TO 4X BASE CARD HI
*RCs: 1.25X TO 3X BASE CARD HI
SER.1/2 STATED ODDS 1:72 HOB/RET
SER.1/2 STATED ODDS 1:18 JUM/RACK
THREE PER FACTORY SET

❑ 1 Sean Elliott	.40	.18
❑ 2 Dennis Scott	.20	.09
❑ 3 Kenny Anderson	.40	.18
❑ 4 Alonzo Mourning	1.50	.70
❑ 5 Glen Rice	.40	.18
❑ 6 Billy Owens	.20	.09
❑ 7 Jim Jackson	.40	.18
❑ 8 Derrick Coleman	.40	.18
❑ 9 Larry Johnson	1.00	.45
❑ 10 Gary Payton	1.50	.70
❑ 11 Christian Laettner	.40	.18
❑ 12 Dikembe Mutombo	.40	.18
❑ 13 Mahmoud Abdul-Rauf	.20	.09
❑ 14 Isaiah Rider	1.50	.70
❑ 15 Steve Smith	1.00	.45
❑ 16 LaPhonso Ellis	.20	.09
❑ 17 Danny Ferry	.20	.09
❑ 18 Shaquille O'Neal	5.00	2.20
❑ 19 Anfernee Hardaway	8.00	3.60
❑ 20 J.R. Reid	.20	.09
❑ 21 Shawn Bradley	1.00	.45
❑ 22 Pervis Ellison	.20	.09
❑ 23 Chris Webber	8.00	3.60
❑ 24 Jamal Mashburn	1.50	.70
❑ 25 Kendall Gill	.40	.18
❑ A Expired Winner A	.75	.35
❑ B Expired Winner B	.75	.35
❑ AX Redeemed Winner A	.25	.11
❑ BX Redeemed Winner B	.25	.11
❑ AB Expired Winner A/B	1.50	.70

1994-95 Topps

	MINT	NRMT
COMPLETE SET (396)	25.00	11.00

COMPLETE SERIES 1 (198) .. 10.00 4.50
COMPLETE SERIES 2 (198) .. 15.00 6.75
COMMON CARD (1-396) .... .05 .02
SEMISTARS .... .10 .05
UNLISTED STARS .... .25 .11
SUBSET CARDS HALF VALUE OF BASE CARDS

- ❑ 1 Patrick Ewing AS .... .10 .05
- ❑ 2 Mookie Blaylock AS .... .05 .02
- ❑ 3 Charles Oakley AS .... .05 .02
- ❑ 4 Mark Price AS .... .05 .02
- ❑ 5 John Starks AS .... .05 .02
- ❑ 6 Dominique Wilkins AS .... .10 .05
- ❑ 7 Horace Grant AS .... .05 .02
- ❑ 8 Alonzo Mourning AS .... .25 .11
- ❑ 9 B.J. Armstrong AS .... .05 .02
- ❑ 10 Kenny Anderson AS .... .05 .02
- ❑ 11 Scottie Pippen AS .... .40 .18
- ❑ 12 Derrick Coleman AS .... .05 .02
- ❑ 13 Shaquille O'Neal AS .... .50 .23
- ❑ 14 Anfernee Hardaway SPEC .50 .23
- ❑ 15 Isaiah Rider SPEC .... .05 .02
- ❑ 16 John Williams .... .05 .02
- ❑ 17 Todd Day .... .05 .02
- ❑ 18 Dale Davis .... .05 .02
- ❑ 19 Sean Rooks .... .05 .02
- ❑ 20 George Lynch .... .05 .02
- ❑ 21 Mitchell Butler .... .05 .02
- ❑ 22 Stacey King .... .05 .02
- ❑ 23 Sherman Douglas .... .05 .02
- ❑ 24 Derrick McKey .... .05 .02
- ❑ 25 Joe Dumars .... .25 .11
- ❑ 26 Scott Brooks .... .05 .02
- ❑ 27 Clarence Weatherspoon .. .05 .02
- ❑ 28 Jayson Williams .... .10 .05
- ❑ 29 Scottie Pippen .... .75 .35
- ❑ 30 John Starks .... .05 .02
- ❑ 31 Robert Pack .... .05 .02
- ❑ 32 Donald Royal .... .05 .02
- ❑ 33 Haywoode Workman .... .05 .02
- ❑ 34 Greg Graham .... .05 .02
- ❑ 35 Terry Cummings .... .05 .02
- ❑ 36 Andrew Lang .... .05 .02
- ❑ 37 Jason Kidd RC .... 2.00 .90
- ❑ 38 Terry Mills .... .05 .02
- ❑ 39 Alonzo Mourning .... .30 .14
- ❑ 40 Shawn Kemp .... .40 .18
- ❑ 41 Kevin Willis FTR .... .05 .02
- ❑ 42 Kevin Willis .... .05 .02
- ❑ 43 Armon Gilliam .... .05 .02
- ❑ 44 Bobby Hurley .... .05 .02
- ❑ 45 Jerome Kersey .... .05 .02
- ❑ 46 Xavier McDaniel .... .05 .02
- ❑ 47 Chris Webber .... .75 .35
- ❑ 48 Chris Webber FTR .... .30 .14
- ❑ 49 Jeff Malone .... .05 .02
- ❑ 50 Dikembe Mutombo SPEC .05 .02
- ❑ 51 Dan Majerle SPEC .... .05 .02
- ❑ 52 Dee Brown SPEC .... .05 .02
- ❑ 53 John Stockton SPEC .... .10 .05
- ❑ 54 Dennis Rodman SPEC .... .25 .11
- ❑ 55 Eric Murdock SPEC .... .05 .02
- ❑ 56 Glen Rice .... .10 .05
- ❑ 57 Glen Rice FTR .... .05 .02
- ❑ 58 Dino Radja .... .05 .02
- ❑ 59 Billy Owens .... .05 .02
- ❑ 60 Doc Rivers .... .10 .05
- ❑ 61 Don MacLean .... .05 .02
- ❑ 62 Lindsey Hunter .... .10 .05
- ❑ 63 Sam Cassell .... .25 .11
- ❑ 64 James Worthy .... .25 .11
- ❑ 65 Christian Laettner .... .10 .05
- ❑ 66 Wesley Person RC .... .25 .11
- ❑ 67 Rich King .... .05 .02
- ❑ 68 Jon Koncak .... .05 .02
- ❑ 69 Muggsy Bogues .... .10 .05
- ❑ 70 Jamal Mashburn .... .25 .11
- ❑ 71 Gary Grant .... .05 .02
- ❑ 72 Eric Murdock .... .05 .02
- ❑ 73 Scott Burrell .... .05 .02
- ❑ 74 Scott Burrell FTR .... .05 .02
- ❑ 75 Anfernee Hardaway .... .75 .35
- ❑ 76 Anfernee Hardaway FTR .50 .23
- ❑ 77 Yinka Dare RC .... .05 .02
- ❑ 78 Anthony Avent .... .05 .02
- ❑ 79 Jon Barry .... .05 .02
- ❑ 80 Rodney Rogers .... .05 .02
- ❑ 81 Chris Mills .... .10 .05
- ❑ 82 Antonio Davis .... .05 .02
- ❑ 83 Steve Smith .... .10 .05
- ❑ 84 Buck Williams .... .05 .02
- ❑ 85 Spud Webb .... .05 .02
- ❑ 86 Stacey Augmon .... .05 .02
- ❑ 87 Allan Houston .... .40 .18
- ❑ 88 Will Perdue .... .05 .02
- ❑ 89 Chris Gatling .... .05 .02
- ❑ 90 Danny Ainge .... .05 .02
- ❑ 91 Rick Mahorn .... .05 .02
- ❑ 92 Elmore Spencer .... .05 .02
- ❑ 93 Vin Baker .... .25 .11
- ❑ 94 Rex Chapman .... .05 .02
- ❑ 95 Dale Ellis .... .05 .02
- ❑ 96 Doug Smith .... .05 .02
- ❑ 97 Tim Perry .... .05 .02
- ❑ 98 Toni Kukoc .... .40 .18
- ❑ 99 Terry Dehere .... .05 .02
- ❑ 100 Shaquille O'Neal PP .... .50 .23
- ❑ 101 Shawn Kemp PP .... .25 .11
- ❑ 102 Hakeem Olajuwon PP .... .25 .11
- ❑ 103 Derrick Coleman PP .... .05 .02
- ❑ 104 Alonzo Mourning PP .... .25 .11
- ❑ 105 Dikembe Mutombo PP .. .05 .02
- ❑ 106 Chris Webber PP .... .30 .14
- ❑ 107 Dennis Rodman PP .... .25 .11
- ❑ 108 David Robinson PP .... .25 .11
- ❑ 109 Charles Barkley PP .... .25 .11
- ❑ 110 Brad Daugherty .... .05 .02
- ❑ 111 Derek Harper .... .05 .02
- ❑ 112 Detlef Schrempf .... .10 .05
- ❑ 113 Harvey Grant .... .05 .02
- ❑ 114 Vlade Divac .... .05 .02
- ❑ 115 Isaiah Rider .... .10 .05
- ❑ 116 Mitch Richmond .... .25 .11
- ❑ 117 Tom Chambers .... .05 .02
- ❑ 118 Kenny Gattison .... .05 .02
- ❑ 119 Kenny Gattison FTR .... .05 .02
- ❑ 120 Vernon Maxwell .... .05 .02
- ❑ 121 Reggie Williams .... .05 .02
- ❑ 122 Chris Mullin .... .25 .11
- ❑ 123 Harold Miner .... .05 .02
- ❑ 124 Harold Miner FTR .... .05 .02
- ❑ 125 Calbert Cheaney .... .05 .02
- ❑ 126 Randy Woods .... .05 .02
- ❑ 127 Mike Gminski .... .05 .02
- ❑ 128 Willie Anderson .... .05 .02
- ❑ 129 Mark Macon .... .05 .02
- ❑ 130 Avery Johnson .... .05 .02
- ❑ 131 Bimbo Coles .... .05 .02
- ❑ 132 Kenny Smith .... .05 .02
- ❑ 133 Dennis Scott .... .05 .02
- ❑ 134 Lionel Simmons .... .05 .02
- ❑ 135 Nate McMillan .... .05 .02
- ❑ 136 Eric Montross RC .... .05 .02
- ❑ 137 Sedale Threatt .... .05 .02
- ❑ 138 Kenny Anderson .... .10 .05
- ❑ 139 Micheal Williams .... .05 .02
- ❑ 140 Grant Long .... .05 .02
- ❑ 141 Grant Long FTR .... .05 .02
- ❑ 142 Tyrone Corbin .... .05 .02
- ❑ 143 Craig Ehlo .... .05 .02
- ❑ 144 Gerald Wilkins .... .05 .02
- ❑ 145 LaPhonso Ellis .... .05 .02
- ❑ 146 Reggie Miller .... .25 .11
- ❑ 147 Tracy Murray .... .05 .02
- ❑ 148 Victor Alexander .... .05 .02
- ❑ 149 Victor Alexander FTR .... .05 .02
- ❑ 150 Clifford Robinson .... .10 .05
- ❑ 151 Anthony Mason FTR .... .05 .02
- ❑ 152 Anthony Mason .... .10 .05
- ❑ 153 Jim Jackson .... .10 .05
- ❑ 154 Jeff Hornacek .... .10 .05
- ❑ 155 Nick Anderson .... .05 .02
- ❑ 156 Mike Brown .... .05 .02
- ❑ 157 Kevin Johnson .... .10 .05
- ❑ 158 John Paxson .... .05 .02
- ❑ 159 Loy Vaught .... .05 .02
- ❑ 160 Carl Herrera .... .05 .02
- ❑ 161 Shawn Bradley .... .05 .02
- ❑ 162 Hubert Davis .... .05 .02
- ❑ 163 David Benoit .... .05 .02
- ❑ 164 Dell Curry .... .05 .02
- ❑ 165 Dee Brown .... .05 .02
- ❑ 166 LaSalle Thompson .... .05 .02
- ❑ 167 Eddie Jones RC .... 1.50 .70
- ❑ 168 Walt Williams .... .05 .02
- ❑ 169 A.C. Green .... .10 .05
- ❑ 170 Kendall Gill .... .10 .05
- ❑ 171 Kendall Gill FTR .... .05 .02
- ❑ 172 Danny Ferry .... .05 .02
- ❑ 173 Bryant Stith .... .05 .02
- ❑ 174 John Salley .... .05 .02
- ❑ 175 Cedric Ceballos .... .05 .02
- ❑ 176 Derrick Coleman .... .10 .05
- ❑ 177 Tony Bennett .... .05 .02
- ❑ 178 Kevin Duckworth .... .05 .02
- ❑ 179 Jay Humphries .... .05 .02
- ❑ 180 Sean Elliott .... .10 .05
- ❑ 181 Sam Perkins .... .10 .05
- ❑ 182 Luc Longley .... .05 .02
- ❑ 183 Mitch Richmond AS .... .10 .05
- ❑ 184 Clyde Drexler AS .... .10 .05
- ❑ 185 Karl Malone AS .... .25 .11
- ❑ 186 Shawn Kemp AS .... .25 .11
- ❑ 187 Hakeem Olajuwon AS .... .25 .11
- ❑ 188 Danny Manning AS .... .05 .02
- ❑ 189 Kevin Johnson AS .... .05 .02
- ❑ 190 John Stockton AS .... .10 .05
- ❑ 191 Latrell Sprewell AS .... .25 .11
- ❑ 192 Gary Payton AS .... .25 .11
- ❑ 193 Clifford Robinson AS .... .05 .02
- ❑ 194 David Robinson AS .... .25 .11
- ❑ 195 Charles Barkley AS .... .25 .11
- ❑ 196 Mark Price SPEC .... .05 .02
- ❑ 197 Checklist 1-99 .... .05 .02
- ❑ 198 Checklist 100-198 .... .05 .02
- ❑ 199 Patrick Ewing .... .25 .11
- ❑ 200 Patrick Ewing FTR .... .10 .05
- ❑ 201 Tracy Murray PP .... .05 .02
- ❑ 202 Craig Ehlo PP .... .05 .02
- ❑ 203 Nick Anderson PP .... .05 .02
- ❑ 204 John Starks PP .... .05 .02
- ❑ 205 Rex Chapman PP .... .05 .02
- ❑ 206 Hersey Hawkins PP .... .05 .02
- ❑ 207 Glen Rice PP .... .05 .02
- ❑ 208 Jeff Malone PP .... .05 .02
- ❑ 209 Dan Majerle PP .... .05 .02
- ❑ 210 Chris Mullin PP .... .10 .05
- ❑ 211 Grant Hill RC 2.50 1.10
- ❑ 212 Bobby Phills .... .05 .02
- ❑ 213 Dennis Rodman .... .50 .23
- ❑ 214 Doug West .... .05 .02
- ❑ 215 Harold Ellis .... .05 .02
- ❑ 216 Kevin Edwards .... .05 .02
- ❑ 217 Lorenzo Williams .... .05 .02
- ❑ 218 Rick Fox .... .05 .02
- ❑ 219 Mookie Blaylock .... .05 .02
- ❑ 220 Mookie Blaylock FTR .... .05 .02
- ❑ 221 John Williams .... .05 .02
- ❑ 222 Keith Jennings .... .05 .02
- ❑ 223 Nick Van Exel .... .25 .11
- ❑ 224 Gary Payton .... .40 .18
- ❑ 225 John Stockton .... .25 .11
- ❑ 226 Ron Harper .... .10 .05
- ❑ 227 Monty Williams RC .... .05 .02
- ❑ 228 Marty Conlon .... .05 .02
- ❑ 229 Hersey Hawkins .... .10 .05
- ❑ 230 Rik Smits .... .05 .02
- ❑ 231 James Robinson .... .05 .02
- ❑ 232 Malik Sealy .... .05 .02

❑ 233 Sergei Bazarevich	.05	.02
❑ 234 Brad Lohaus	.05	.02
❑ 235 Olden Polynice	.05	.02
❑ 236 Brian Williams	.05	.02
❑ 237 Tyrone Hill	.05	.02
❑ 238 Jim McIlvaine RC	.05	.02
❑ 239 Latrell Sprewell	.50	.23
❑ 240 Latrell Sprewell FTR	.25	.11
❑ 241 Popeye Jones	.05	.02
❑ 242 Scott Williams	.05	.02
❑ 243 Eddie Jones	.75	.35
❑ 244 Moses Malone	.25	.11
❑ 245 B.J. Armstrong	.05	.02
❑ 246 Jim Les	.05	.02
❑ 247 Greg Grant	.05	.02
❑ 248 Lee Mayberry	.05	.02
❑ 249 Mark Jackson	.05	.02
❑ 250 Larry Johnson	.10	.05
❑ 251 Terrell Brandon	.10	.05
❑ 252 Ledell Eackles	.05	.02
❑ 253 Yinka Dare	.05	.02
❑ 254 Dontonio Wingfield RC	.05	.02
❑ 255 Clyde Drexler	.25	.11
❑ 256 Andres Guibert	.05	.02
❑ 257 Gheorghe Muresan	.05	.02
❑ 258 Tom Hammonds	.05	.02
❑ 259 Charles Barkley	.40	.18
❑ 260 Charles Barkley FTR	.25	.11
❑ 261 Acie Earl	.05	.02
❑ 262 Lamond Murray RC	.10	.05
❑ 263 Dana Barros	.05	.02
❑ 264 Greg Anthony	.05	.02
❑ 265 Dan Majerle	.10	.05
❑ 266 Zan Tabak	.05	.02
❑ 267 Ricky Pierce	.05	.02
❑ 268 Eric Leckner	.05	.02
❑ 269 Duane Ferrell	.05	.02
❑ 270 Mark Price	.05	.02
❑ 271 Anthony Peeler	.05	.02
❑ 272 Adam Keefe	.05	.02
❑ 273 Rex Walters	.05	.02
❑ 274 Scott Skiles	.05	.02
❑ 275 Glenn Robinson RC	.75	.35
❑ 276 Tony Dumas RC	.05	.02
❑ 277 Elliot Perry	.05	.02
❑ 278 Charles Outlaw RC	.05	.02
❑ 279 Karl Malone	.40	.18
❑ 280 Karl Malone FTR	.25	.11
❑ 281 Herb Williams	.05	.02
❑ 282 Vincent Askew	.05	.02
❑ 283 Askia Jones RC	.05	.02
❑ 284 Shawn Bradley	.05	.02
❑ 285 Tim Hardaway	.25	.11
❑ 286 Mark West	.05	.02
❑ 287 Chuck Person	.05	.02
❑ 288 James Edwards	.05	.02
❑ 289 Antonio Lang RC	.05	.02
❑ 290 Dominique Wilkins	.25	.11
❑ 291 Khalid Reeves RC	.05	.02
❑ 292 Jamie Watson RC	.05	.02
❑ 293 Darnell Mee	.05	.02
❑ 294 Brian Grant RC	.60	.25
❑ 295 Hakeem Olajuwon	.40	.18
❑ 296 Dickey Simpkins RC	.05	.02
❑ 297 Tyrone Corbin	.05	.02
❑ 298 David Wingate	.05	.02
❑ 299 Shaquille O'Neal	1.25	.55
❑ 300 Shaquille O'Neal FR	.50	.23
❑ 301 B.J. Armstrong PP	.05	.02
❑ 302 Mitch Richmond PP	.10	.05
❑ 303 Jim Jackson PP	.05	.02
❑ 304 Jeff Hornacek PP	.05	.02
❑ 305 Mark Price PP	.05	.02
❑ 306 Kendall Gill PP	.05	.02
❑ 307 Dale Ellis PP	.05	.02
❑ 308 Vernon Maxwell PP	.05	.02
❑ 309 Joe Dumars PP	.10	.05
❑ 310 Reggie Miller PP	.10	.05
❑ 311 Geert Hammink	.05	.02
❑ 312 Charles Smith	.05	.02
❑ 313 Bill Cartwright	.05	.02
❑ 314 Aaron McKie RC	.05	.02
❑ 315 Tom Gugliotta	.10	.05
❑ 316 P.J. Brown	.05	.02
❑ 317 David Wesley	.05	.02
❑ 318 Felton Spencer	.05	.02
❑ 319 Robert Horry	.05	.02
❑ 320 Robert Horry FR	.05	.02
❑ 321 Larry Krystkowiak	.05	.02
❑ 322 Eric Piatkowski RC	.05	.02
❑ 323 Anthony Bonner	.05	.02
❑ 324 Keith Askins	.05	.02
❑ 325 Mahmoud Abdul-Rauf	.05	.02
❑ 326 Darrin Hancock RC	.05	.02
❑ 327 Vern Fleming	.05	.02
❑ 328 Wayman Tisdale	.05	.02
❑ 329 Sam Bowie	.05	.02
❑ 330 Billy Owens	.05	.02
❑ 331 Donald Hodge	.05	.02
❑ 332 Derrick Alston RC	.05	.02
❑ 333 Doug Edwards	.05	.02
❑ 334 Johnny Newman	.05	.02
❑ 335 Otis Thorpe	.05	.02
❑ 336 Bill Curley RC	.05	.02
❑ 337 Michael Cage	.05	.02
❑ 338 Chris Smith	.05	.02
❑ 339 Dikembe Mutombo	.10	.05
❑ 340 Dikembe Mutombo FTR	.05	.02
❑ 341 Duane Causwell	.05	.02
❑ 342 Sean Higgins	.05	.02
❑ 343 Steve Kerr	.05	.02
❑ 344 Eric Montross	.05	.02
❑ 345 Charles Oakley	.05	.02
❑ 346 Brooks Thompson RC	.05	.02
❑ 347 Rony Seikaly	.05	.02
❑ 348 Chris Dudley	.05	.02
❑ 349 Sharone Wright RC	.05	.02
❑ 350 Sarunas Marciulionis	.05	.02
❑ 351 Anthony Miller RC	.05	.02
❑ 352 Pooh Richardson	.05	.02
❑ 353 Byron Scott	.10	.05
❑ 354 Michael Adams	.05	.02
❑ 355 Ken Norman	.05	.02
❑ 356 Clifford Rozier RC	.05	.02
❑ 357 Tim Breaux	.05	.02
❑ 358 Derek Strong	.05	.02
❑ 359 David Robinson	.40	.18
❑ 360 David Robinson FR	.25	.11
❑ 361 Benoit Benjamin	.05	.02
❑ 362 Terry Porter	.05	.02
❑ 363 Ervin Johnson	.05	.02
❑ 364 Alaa Abdelnaby	.05	.02
❑ 365 Robert Parish	.10	.05
❑ 366 Mario Elie	.05	.02
❑ 367 Antonio Harvey	.05	.02
❑ 368 Charlie Ward RC	.25	.11
❑ 369 Kevin Gamble	.05	.02
❑ 370 Rod Strickland	.10	.05
❑ 371 Jason Kidd	1.00	.45
❑ 372 Oliver Miller	.05	.02
❑ 373 Eric Mobley RC	.05	.02
❑ 374 Brian Shaw	.05	.02
❑ 375 Horace Grant	.10	.05
❑ 376 Corie Blount	.05	.02
❑ 377 Sam Mitchell	.05	.02
❑ 378 Jalen Rose RC	1.00	.45
❑ 379 Elden Campbell	.05	.02
❑ 380 Elden Campbell FTR	.05	.02
❑ 381 Donyell Marshall RC	.25	.11
❑ 382 Frank Brickowski	.05	.02
❑ 383 B.J. Tyler RC	.05	.02
❑ 384 Bryon Russell	.05	.02
❑ 385 Danny Manning	.10	.05
❑ 386 Manute Bol	.05	.02
❑ 387 Brent Price	.05	.02
❑ 388 J.R. Reid	.05	.02
❑ 389 Byron Houston	.05	.02
❑ 390 Blue Edwards	.05	.02
❑ 391 Adrian Caldwell	.05	.02
❑ 392 Wesley Person	.10	.05
❑ 393 Juwan Howard RC	.60	.25
❑ 394 Chris Morris	.05	.02
❑ 395 Checklist 199-296	.05	.02
❑ 396 Checklist 297-396	.05	.02

1994-95 Topps Spectralight

	MINT	NRMT
COMPLETE SET (396)	300.00	135.00
COMPLETE SERIES 1 (198)	125.00	55.00
COMPLETE SERIES 2 (198)	175.00	80.00
COMMON CARD (1-396)	.25	.11
CL REPLACEMENT (197-198)	.50	.23

*STARS: 5X TO 10X BASE CARD HI
*RCs: 4X TO 8X BASE HI
SER.1/2 STATED ODDS 1:4

❑ 197 Keith Jennings	.50	.23
❑ 198 Mark Price	.50	.23
❑ 395 Chris Webber	80.00	36.00
❑ 396 Mitch Richmond	25.00	11.00

1994-95 Topps Franchise/Futures

	MINT	NRMT
COMPLETE SET (20)	50.00	22.00

*SINGLES: 5X TO 12X BASE CARD HI
SER.2 STATED ODDS 1:18

❑ 1 Mookie Blaylock	.60	.25
❑ 2 Stacey Augmon	.60	.25
❑ 3 Dominique Wilkins	3.00	1.35
❑ 4 Eric Montross	.60	.25
❑ 5 Dikembe Mutombo	1.25	.55
❑ 6 Jalen Rose	6.00	2.70
❑ 7 Joe Dumars	3.00	1.35
❑ 8 Grant Hill	15.00	6.75
❑ 9 Chris Mullin	3.00	1.35
❑ 10 Latrell Sprewell	6.00	2.70
❑ 11 Glen Rice	1.25	.55
❑ 12 Khalid Reeves	.60	.25
❑ 13 Derrick Coleman	1.25	.55
❑ 14 Yinka Dare	.60	.25
❑ 15 Patrick Ewing	3.00	1.35
❑ 16 Monty Williams	.60	.25
❑ 17 Shaquille O'Neal	15.00	6.75
❑ 18 Anfernee Hardaway	10.00	4.50
❑ 19 Charles Barkley	5.00	2.20
❑ 20 Wesley Person	3.00	1.35

1994-95 Topps Own the Game

	MINT	NRMT
COMPLETE SET (50)	20.00	9.00

*SINGLES: 1X TO 2.5X BASE CARD HI
SER.1 STATED ODDS 1:18

COMP.EXCHANGE SET (10)	10.00	4.50

*EXCHANGE CARDS: 1X HI COLUMN

ONE EXCHANGE SET PER "W" CARD BY MAIL
NNO CARDS LISTED ALPHABETICALLY

❑ 1 Kenny Anderson PASS	.25	.11
❑ 2 Charles Barkley SCORE	1.00	.45
❑ 3 Mookie Blaylock PASS	.15	.07
❑ 4 Mookie Blaylock STEAL	.15	.07
❑ 5 Muggsy Bogues PASS	.25	.11
❑ 6 Shawn Bradley SWAT	.15	.07
❑ 7 Derrick Coleman REB	.25	.11
❑ 8 Sherman Douglas PASS	.15	.07
❑ 9 Patrick Ewing REB	.60	.25
❑ 10 Patrick Ewing SCORE	.60	.25
❑ 11 Patrick Ewing SWAT	.60	.25
❑ 12 Tom Gugliotta STEAL	.25	.11
❑ 13 A.Hardaway STEAL	2.00	.90
❑ 14 Mark Jackson PASS	.15	.07
❑ 15 Kevin Johnson PASS	.25	.11
❑ 16 Karl Malone REB	1.00	.45
❑ 17 Karl Malone SCORE	1.00	.45
❑ 18 Nate McMillan STEAL	.15	.07
❑ 19 Oliver Miller SWAT	.15	.07
❑ 20 Alonzo Mourning SWAT	.75	.35
❑ 21 Eric Murdock STEAL	.15	.07
❑ 22 D.Mutombo REB	.25	.11
❑ 23 D.Mutombo SWAT	.25	.11
❑ 24 Charles Oakley REB	.15	.07
❑ 25 H.Olajuwon REB	1.00	.45
❑ 26 H.Olajuwon SCORE	1.00	.45
❑ 27 H.Olajuwon SWAT	1.00	.45
❑ 28 Shaquille O'Neal REB	3.00	1.35
❑ 29 S. O'Neal SCORE W	3.00	1.35
❑ 30 Shaquille O'Neal SWAT	3.00	1.35
❑ 31 Gary Payton STEAL	1.00	.45
❑ 32 Scottie Pippen SCORE	2.00	.90
❑ 33 Scottie Pippen STEAL W	2.00	.90
❑ 34 Mark Price PASS	.15	.07
❑ 35 Mitch Richmond SCORE	.60	.25
❑ 36 David Robinson SCORE	1.00	.45
❑ 37 David Robinson SWAT	1.00	.45
❑ 38 Dennis Rodman REB W	1.25	.55
❑ 39 Latrell Sprewell STEAL	1.25	.55
❑ 40 John Stockton PASS W	.60	.25
❑ 41 John Stockton STEAL	.60	.25
❑ 42 Rod Strickland PASS	.25	.11
❑ 43 Chris Webber SWAT	2.00	.90
❑ 44 Kevin Willis REB	.15	.07
❑ 45 D.Wilkins SCORE	.60	.25
❑ 46 Passers Field Card	.15	.07
❑ 47 Rebounders Field Card	.15	.07
❑ 48 Scorers Field Card	.15	.07
❑ 49 Stealers Field Card	.15	.07
❑ 50 Swatters Field Card	.15	.07

1994-95 Topps Super Sophomores

	MINT	NRMT
COMPLETE SET (10)	40.00	18.00
COMMON CARD (1-10)	1.50	.70
SEMISTARS	2.50	1.10
UNLISTED STARS	5.00	2.20

SER.2 STATED ODDS 1:36

❑ 1 Chris Webber	15.00	6.75
❑ 2 Anfernee Hardaway	15.00	6.75
❑ 3 Vin Baker	5.00	2.20
❑ 4 Sam Cassell	5.00	2.20
❑ 5 Jamal Mashburn	5.00	2.20
❑ 6 Isaiah Rider	2.50	1.10
❑ 7 Chris Mills	2.50	1.10
❑ 8 Antonio Davis	1.50	.70
❑ 9 Nick Van Exel	5.00	2.20
❑ 10 Lindsey Hunter	2.50	1.10

1995-96 Topps

	MINT	NRMT
COMPLETE SET (291)	30.00	13.50
COMPLETE SERIES 1 (181)	15.00	6.75
COMPLETE SERIES 2 (110)	15.00	6.75
COMMON CARD (1-291)	.10	.05
SEMISTARS	.15	.07
UNLISTED STARS	.25	.11

SUBSET CARDS HALF VALUE OF BASE CARDS

❑ 1 Michael Jordan AL	1.50	.70
❑ 2 Dennis Rodman AL	.25	.11
❑ 3 John Stockton AL	.15	.07
❑ 4 Michael Jordan AL	1.50	.70
❑ 5 David Robinson AL	.25	.11
❑ 6 Shaquille O'Neal LL	.50	.23
❑ 7 Hakeem Olajuwon LL	.25	.11
❑ 8 David Robinson LL	.25	.11
❑ 9 Karl Malone LL	.25	.11
❑ 10 Jamal Mashburn LL	.10	.05
❑ 11 Dennis Rodman LL	.25	.11
❑ 12 Dikembe Mutombo LL	.10	.05
❑ 13 Shaquille O'Neal LL	.50	.23
❑ 14 Patrick Ewing LL	.15	.07
❑ 15 Tyrone Hill LL	.10	.05
❑ 16 John Stockton LL	.15	.07
❑ 17 Kenny Anderson LL	.10	.05
❑ 18 Tim Hardaway LL	.15	.07
❑ 19 Rod Strickland LL	.10	.05
❑ 20 Muggsy Bogues LL	.10	.05
❑ 21 Scottie Pippen LL	.40	.18
❑ 22 Mookie Blaylock LL	.10	.05
❑ 23 Gary Payton LL	.25	.11
❑ 24 John Stockton LL	.15	.07
❑ 25 Nate McMillan LL	.10	.05
❑ 26 Dikembe Mutombo LL	.10	.05
❑ 27 Hakeem Olajuwon LL	.25	.11
❑ 28 Shawn Bradley LL	.10	.05
❑ 29 David Robinson LL	.25	.11
❑ 30 Alonzo Mourning LL	.15	.07
❑ 31 Reggie Miller	.25	.11
❑ 32 Karl Malone	.40	.18
❑ 33 Grant Hill	1.25	.55
❑ 34 Charles Barkley	.40	.18
❑ 35 Cedric Ceballos	.10	.05
❑ 36 Gheorghe Muresan	.10	.05
❑ 37 Doug West	.10	.05
❑ 38 Tony Dumas	.10	.05
❑ 39 Kenny Gattison	.10	.05
❑ 40 Chris Mullin	.25	.11
❑ 41 Pervis Ellison	.10	.05
❑ 42 Vinny Del Negro	.10	.05
❑ 43 Mario Elie	.10	.05
❑ 44 Todd Day	.10	.05
❑ 45 Scottie Pippen	.75	.35
❑ 46 Buck Williams	.10	.05
❑ 47 P.J. Brown	.10	.05
❑ 48 Bimbo Coles	.10	.05
❑ 49 Terrell Brandon	.15	.07
❑ 50 Charles Oakley	.10	.05
❑ 51 Sam Perkins	.15	.07
❑ 52 Dale Ellis	.10	.05
❑ 53 Andrew Lang	.10	.05
❑ 54 Harold Ellis	.10	.05
❑ 55 Clarence Weatherspoon	.10	.05
❑ 56 Bill Curley	.10	.05
❑ 57 Robert Parish	.15	.07
❑ 58 David Benoit	.10	.05
❑ 59 Anthony Avent	.10	.05
❑ 60 Jamal Mashburn	.15	.07
❑ 61 Duane Ferrell	.10	.05
❑ 62 Elden Campbell	.10	.05
❑ 63 Rex Chapman	.10	.05
❑ 64 Wesley Person	.15	.07
❑ 65 Mitch Richmond	.25	.11
❑ 66 Micheal Williams	.10	.05
❑ 67 Clifford Rozier	.10	.05
❑ 68 Eric Montross	.10	.05
❑ 69 Dennis Rodman	.50	.23
❑ 70 Vin Baker	.25	.11
❑ 71 Tyrone Hill	.10	.05
❑ 72 Tyrone Corbin	.10	.05
❑ 73 Chris Dudley	.10	.05
❑ 74 Nate McMillan	.10	.05
❑ 75 Kenny Anderson	.15	.07
❑ 76 Monty Williams	.10	.05
❑ 77 Kenny Smith	.10	.05
❑ 78 Rodney Rogers	.10	.05
❑ 79 Corie Blount	.10	.05
❑ 80 Glen Rice	.15	.07
❑ 81 Walt Williams	.10	.05
❑ 82 Scott Williams	.10	.05
❑ 83 Michael Adams	.10	.05
❑ 84 Terry Mills	.10	.05
❑ 85 Horace Grant	.15	.07
❑ 86 Chuck Person	.10	.05
❑ 87 Adam Keefe	.10	.05
❑ 88 Scott Brooks	.10	.05
❑ 89 George Lynch	.10	.05
❑ 90 Kevin Johnson	.15	.07
❑ 91 Armon Gilliam	.10	.05
❑ 92 Greg Minor	.10	.05
❑ 93 Derrick McKey	.10	.05
❑ 94 Victor Alexander	.10	.05
❑ 95 B.J. Armstrong	.10	.05
❑ 96 Terry Dehere	.10	.05
❑ 97 Christian Laettner	.15	.07
❑ 98 Hubert Davis	.10	.05
❑ 99 Aaron McKie	.10	.05
❑ 100 Hakeem Olajuwon	.40	.18
❑ 101 Michael Cage	.10	.05
❑ 102 Grant Long	.10	.05
❑ 103 Calbert Cheaney	.10	.05
❑ 104 Olden Polynice	.10	.05
❑ 105 Sharone Wright	.10	.05
❑ 106 Lee Mayberry	.10	.05
❑ 107 Robert Pack	.10	.05
❑ 108 Loy Vaught	.10	.05
❑ 109 Khalid Reeves	.10	.05
❑ 110 Shawn Kemp	.40	.18
❑ 111 Lindsey Hunter	.10	.05
❑ 112 Dell Curry	.10	.05
❑ 113 Dan Majerle	.10	.05
❑ 114 Bryon Russell	.10	.05
❑ 115 John Starks	.10	.05
❑ 116 Roy Tarpley	.10	.05
❑ 117 Dale Davis	.10	.05
❑ 118 Nick Anderson	.10	.05
❑ 119 Rex Walters	.10	.05
❑ 120 Dominique Wilkins	.25	.11
❑ 121 Sam Cassell	.15	.07
❑ 122 Sean Elliott	.10	.05
❑ 123 B.J. Tyler	.10	.05
❑ 124 Eric Mobley	.10	.05
❑ 125 Toni Kukoc	.30	.14
❑ 126 Pooh Richardson	.10	.05
❑ 127 Isaiah Rider	.15	.07
❑ 128 Steve Smith	.15	.07
❑ 129 Chris Mills	.10	.05
❑ 130 Detlef Schrempf	.15	.07
❑ 131 Donyell Marshall	.15	.07
❑ 132 Eddie Jones	.50	.23
❑ 133 Otis Thorpe	.10	.05
❑ 134 Lionel Simmons	.10	.05

❑ 135	Jeff Hornacek	.15	.07
❑ 136	Jalen Rose	.30	.14
❑ 137	Kevin Willis	.10	.05
❑ 138	Don MacLean	.10	.05
❑ 139	Dee Brown	.10	.05
❑ 140	Glenn Robinson	.25	.11
❑ 141	Joe Kleine	.10	.05
❑ 142	Ron Harper	.15	.07
❑ 143	Antonio Davis	.10	.05
❑ 144	Jeff Malone	.10	.05
❑ 145	Joe Dumars	.25	.11
❑ 146	Jason Kidd	.75	.35
❑ 147	J.R. Reid	.10	.05
❑ 148	Lamond Murray	.10	.05
❑ 149	Derrick Coleman	.15	.07
❑ 150	Alonzo Mourning	.25	.11
❑ 151	Clifford Robinson	.10	.05
❑ 152	Kendall Gill	.15	.07
❑ 153	Doug Christie	.10	.05
❑ 154	Stacey Augmon	.10	.05
❑ 155	Anfernee Hardaway	.75	.35
❑ 156	Mahmoud Abdul-Rauf	.10	.05
❑ 157	Latrell Sprewell	.50	.23
❑ 158	Mark Price	.10	.05
❑ 159	Brian Grant	.25	.11
❑ 160	Clyde Drexler	.25	.11
❑ 161	Juwan Howard	.25	.11
❑ 162	Tom Gugliotta	.15	.07
❑ 163	Nick Van Exel	.15	.07
❑ 164	Billy Owens	.10	.05
❑ 165	Brooks Thompson	.10	.05
❑ 166	Acie Earl	.10	.05
❑ 167	Ed Pinckney	.10	.05
❑ 168	Oliver Miller	.10	.05
❑ 169	John Salley	.10	.05
❑ 170	Jerome Kersey	.10	.05
❑ 171	Willie Anderson	.10	.05
❑ 172	Keith Jennings	.10	.05
❑ 173	Doug Smith	.10	.05
❑ 174	Gerald Wilkins	.10	.05
❑ 175	Byron Scott	.10	.05
❑ 176	Benoit Benjamin	.10	.05
❑ 177	Blue Edwards	.10	.05
❑ 178	Greg Anthony	.10	.05
❑ 179	Trevor Ruffin	.10	.05
❑ 180	Kenny Gattison	.10	.05
❑ 181	Checklist 1-181	.10	.05
❑ 182	Cherokee Parks RC	.10	.05
❑ 183	Kurt Thomas RC	.15	.07
❑ 184	Ervin Johnson	.10	.05
❑ 185	Chucky Brown	.10	.05
❑ 186	Luc Longley	.10	.05
❑ 187	Anthony Miller	.10	.05
❑ 188	Ed O'Bannon RC	.10	.05
❑ 189	Bobby Hurley	.10	.05
❑ 190	Dikembe Mutombo	.15	.07
❑ 191	Robert Horry	.10	.05
❑ 192	George Zidek RC	.10	.05
❑ 193	Rasheed Wallace RC	1.00	.45
❑ 194	Marty Conlon	.10	.05
❑ 195	A.C. Green	.15	.07
❑ 196	Mike Brown	.10	.05
❑ 197	Oliver Miller	.10	.05
❑ 198	Charles Smith	.10	.05
❑ 199	Eric Williams RC	.15	.07
❑ 200	Rik Smits	.10	.05
❑ 201	Donald Royal	.10	.05
❑ 202	Bryant Reeves RC	.25	.11
❑ 203	Danny Ferry	.10	.05
❑ 204	Brian Williams	.10	.05
❑ 205	Joe Smith RC	.75	.35
❑ 206	Gary Trent RC	.10	.05
❑ 207	Greg Ostertag RC	.10	.05
❑ 208	Ken Norman	.10	.05
❑ 209	Avery Johnson	.10	.05
❑ 210	Theo Ratliff RC UER Card has no draft pick logo	.30	.14
❑ 211	Corie Blount	.10	.05
❑ 212	Hersey Hawkins	.15	.07
❑ 213	Loren Meyer RC	.10	.05
❑ 214	Mario Bennett RC	.10	.05
❑ 215	Randolph Childress RC	.10	.05
❑ 216	Spud Webb	.10	.05
❑ 217	Popeye Jones	.10	.05
❑ 218	Shawn Respert RC	.10	.05
❑ 219	Malik Sealy	.10	.05
❑ 220	Dino Radja	.10	.05
❑ 221	James Robinson	.10	.05
❑ 222	David Vaughn	.10	.05
❑ 223	Michael Smith	.10	.05
❑ 224	Jamie Watson	.10	.05
❑ 225	LaPhonso Ellis	.10	.05
❑ 226	Kevin Gamble	.10	.05
❑ 227	Dennis Rodman	.50	.23
❑ 228	B.J. Armstrong	.10	.05
❑ 229	Jerry Stackhouse RC	.75	.35
❑ 230	Muggsy Bogues	.10	.05
❑ 231	Lawrence Moten RC	.10	.05
❑ 232	Cory Alexander RC	.10	.05
❑ 233	Carlos Rogers	.10	.05
❑ 234	Tyus Edney RC	.10	.05
❑ 235	Doc Rivers	.10	.05
❑ 236	Antonio Harvey	.10	.05
❑ 237	Kevin Garnett RC	3.00	1.35
❑ 238	Derek Harper	.10	.05
❑ 239	Kevin Edwards	.10	.05
❑ 240	Chris Smith	.10	.05
❑ 241	Haywoode Workman	.10	.05
❑ 242	Bobby Phills	.10	.05
❑ 243	Sherrell Ford RC	.10	.05
❑ 244	Corliss Williamson RC	.50	.23
❑ 245	Shawn Bradley	.10	.05
❑ 246	Jason Caffey RC	.15	.07
❑ 247	Bryant Stith	.10	.05
❑ 248	Mark West	.10	.05
❑ 249	Dennis Scott	.10	.05
❑ 250	Jim Jackson	.10	.05
❑ 251	Travis Best RC	.15	.07
❑ 252	Sean Rooks	.10	.05
❑ 253	Yinka Dare	.10	.05
❑ 254	Felton Spencer	.10	.05
❑ 255	Vlade Divac	.10	.05
❑ 256	Michael Finley RC	1.00	.45
❑ 257	Damon Stoudamire RC	1.25	.55
❑ 258	Mark Bryant	.10	.05
❑ 259	Brent Barry RC	.25	.11
❑ 260	Rony Seikaly	.10	.05
❑ 261	Alan Henderson RC	.25	.11
❑ 262	Kendall Gill	.15	.07
❑ 263	Rex Chapman	.10	.05
❑ 264	Eric Murdock	.10	.05
❑ 265	Rodney Rogers	.10	.05
❑ 266	Greg Graham	.10	.05
❑ 267	Jayson Williams	.15	.07
❑ 268	Antonio McDyess RC	1.25	.55
❑ 269	Sedale Threatt	.10	.05
❑ 270	Danny Manning	.15	.07
❑ 271	Pete Chilcutt	.10	.05
❑ 272	Bob Sura RC	.15	.07
❑ 273	Dana Barros	.10	.05
❑ 274	Allan Houston	.30	.14
❑ 275	Tracy Murray	.10	.05
❑ 276	Anthony Mason	.15	.07
❑ 277	Michael Jordan	3.00	1.35
❑ 278	Patrick Ewing	.25	.11
❑ 279	Shaquille O'Neal	1.25	.55
❑ 280	Larry Johnson	.15	.07
❑ 281	Mark Jackson	.10	.05
❑ 282	Chris Webber	.75	.35
❑ 283	David Robinson	.40	.18
❑ 284	John Stockton	.25	.11
❑ 285	Mookie Blaylock	.10	.05
❑ 286	Mark Price	.10	.05
❑ 287	Tim Hardaway	.25	.11
❑ 288	Rod Strickland	.15	.07
❑ 289	Sherman Douglas	.10	.05
❑ 290	Gary Payton	.40	.18
❑ 291	Checklist (182-291)	.10	.05

1995-96 Topps Draft Redemption

	MINT	NRMT
COMPLETE SET (29)	80.00	36.00
COMMON CARD (1-29)	1.50	.70
SEMISTARS	2.50	1.10
UNLISTED STARS	4.00	1.80

ONE CARD PER EXCHANGE CARD BY MAIL
EXCH.CARDS: SER.1 STATED ODDS 1:18

❑ 1	Joe Smith	6.00	2.70
❑ 2	Antonio McDyess	10.00	4.50
❑ 3	Jerry Stackhouse	6.00	2.70
❑ 4	Rasheed Wallace	8.00	3.60
❑ 5	Kevin Garnett	30.00	13.50
❑ 6	Bryant Reeves	2.50	1.10
❑ 7	Damon Stoudamire	10.00	4.50
❑ 8	Shawn Respert	1.50	.70
❑ 9	Ed O'Bannon	1.50	.70
❑ 10	Kurt Thomas	1.50	.70
❑ 11	Gary Trent	1.50	.70
❑ 12	Cherokee Parks	1.50	.70
❑ 13	Corliss Williamson	4.00	1.80
❑ 14	Eric Williams	1.50	.70
❑ 15	Brent Barry	4.00	1.80
❑ 16	Alan Henderson	2.50	1.10
❑ 17	Bob Sura	2.50	1.10
❑ 18	Theo Ratliff	4.00	1.80
❑ 19	Randolph Childress	1.50	.70
❑ 20	Jason Caffey	1.50	.70
❑ 21	Michael Finley	8.00	3.60
❑ 22	George Zidek	1.50	.70
❑ 23	Travis Best	2.50	1.10
❑ 24	Loren Meyer	1.50	.70
❑ 25	David Vaughn	1.50	.70
❑ 26	Sherrell Ford	1.50	.70
❑ 27	Mario Bennett	1.50	.70
❑ 28	Greg Ostertag	1.50	.70
❑ 29	Cory Alexander	1.50	.70
❑ NNO	Expired Trade Cards	1.00	.45

1995-96 Topps Mystery Finest

	MINT	NRMT
COMPLETE SET (22)	120.00	55.00
COMMON CARD (M1-M22)	2.00	.90
SEMISTARS	2.50	1.10
UNLISTED STARS	4.00	1.80

SER.2 STATED ODDS 1:36 HOBBY/RETAIL

COMP.REF.SET (22)	800.00	350.00
COMMON REF. (M1-M22)	12.00	5.50

*REFRACTORS: 3X TO 6X HI COLUMN
SER.2 STATED ODDS 1:36 HOB, 1:216 RET
CONDITION SENSITIVE SET

❑ M1	Michael Jordan	50.00	22.00
❑ M2	Anfernee Hardaway	12.00	5.50
❑ M3	Clyde Drexler	4.00	1.80
❑ M4	Mark Price	2.00	.90
❑ M5	Steve Smith	2.50	1.10

❑ M6 Jim Jackson	2.00	.90
❑ M7 Nick Anderson	2.00	.90
❑ M8 Kenny Anderson	2.50	1.10
❑ M9 Mookie Blaylock	2.00	.90
❑ M10 Jason Kidd	12.00	5.50
❑ M11 Tim Hardaway	4.00	1.80
❑ M12 Kevin Johnson	2.50	1.10
❑ M13 Gary Payton	6.00	2.70
❑ M14 John Stockton	4.00	1.80
❑ M15 Rod Strickland	2.50	1.10
❑ M16 Jamal Mashburn	2.50	1.10
❑ M17 Danny Manning	2.50	1.10
❑ M18 Billy Owens	2.00	.90
❑ M19 Grant Hill	20.00	9.00
❑ M20 Scottie Pippen	12.00	5.50
❑ M21 Isaiah Rider	2.50	1.10
❑ M22 Latrell Sprewell	8.00	3.60

1995-96 Topps Pan For Gold

	MINT	NRMT
COMPLETE SET (15)	40.00	18.00
COMMON CARD (1-15)	1.00	.45
SEMISTARS	2.50	1.10
UNLISTED STARS	4.00	1.80

SER.1 STATED ODDS 1:4 JUM, 1:8 RET
PFG PREFIX ON CARD NUMBERS

❑ 1 Vin Baker	4.00	1.80
❑ 2 John Stockton	4.00	1.80
❑ 3 Dan Majerle	1.00	.45
❑ 4 Joe Dumars	4.00	1.80
❑ 5 Rik Smits	1.00	.45
❑ 6 Tim Hardaway	4.00	1.80
❑ 7 Charles Oakley	1.00	.45
❑ 8 Cedric Ceballos	1.00	.45
❑ 9 Karl Malone	6.00	2.70
❑ 10 Scottie Pippen	12.00	5.50
❑ 11 David Robinson	6.00	2.70
❑ 12 Gary Payton	6.00	2.70
❑ 13 Mitch Richmond	4.00	1.80
❑ 14 Antonio Davis	1.00	.45
❑ 15 Dennis Rodman	8.00	3.60

1995-96 Topps Power Boosters

	MINT	NRMT
COMPLETE SET (45)	260.00	115.00
COMPLETE SERIES 1 (30)	200.00	90.00
COMPLETE SERIES 2 (15)	60.00	27.00
COMMON CARD (1-30)	1.50	.70
COMMON CARD (276-290)	1.25	.55
SEMISTARS SER.1	2.50	1.10
SEMISTARS SER.2	2.00	.90
UNLISTED STARS SER.1	4.00	1.80
UNLISTED STARS SER.2	3.00	1.35

SER.1/2 STATED ODDS 1:36 HOBBY/RETAIL

❑ 1 Michael Jordan	50.00	22.00
❑ 2 Dennis Rodman	8.00	3.60
❑ 3 John Stockton	4.00	1.80
❑ 4 Michael Jordan	50.00	22.00
❑ 5 David Robinson	6.00	2.70
❑ 6 Shaquille O'Neal	20.00	9.00
❑ 7 Hakeem Olajuwon	6.00	2.70
❑ 8 David Robinson	6.00	2.70
❑ 9 Karl Malone	6.00	2.70
❑ 10 Jamal Mashburn	2.50	1.10
❑ 11 Dennis Rodman	8.00	3.60
❑ 12 Dikembe Mutombo	2.50	1.10
❑ 13 Shaquille O'Neal	20.00	9.00
❑ 14 Patrick Ewing	4.00	1.80
❑ 15 Tyrone Hill	1.50	.70
❑ 16 John Stockton	4.00	1.80
❑ 17 Kenny Anderson	2.50	1.10
❑ 18 Tim Hardaway	4.00	1.80
❑ 19 Rod Strickland	2.50	1.10
❑ 20 Muggsy Bogues	1.50	.70
❑ 21 Scottie Pippen	12.00	5.50
❑ 22 Mookie Blaylock	1.50	.70
❑ 23 Gary Payton	6.00	2.70
❑ 24 John Stockton	4.00	1.80
❑ 25 Nate McMillan	1.50	.70
❑ 26 Dikembe Mutombo	2.50	1.10
❑ 27 Hakeem Olajuwon	6.00	2.70
❑ 28 Shawn Bradley	1.50	.70
❑ 29 David Robinson	6.00	2.70
❑ 30 Alonzo Mourning	4.00	1.80
❑ 276 Anthony Mason	1.25	.55
❑ 277 Michael Jordan	40.00	18.00
❑ 278 Patrick Ewing	3.00	1.35
❑ 279 Shaquille O'Neal	15.00	6.75
❑ 280 Larry Johnson	2.00	.90
❑ 281 Mark Jackson	1.25	.55
❑ 282 Chris Webber	10.00	4.50
❑ 283 David Robinson	5.00	2.20
❑ 284 John Stockton	3.00	1.35
❑ 285 Mookie Blaylock	1.25	.55
❑ 286 Mark Price	1.25	.55
❑ 287 Tim Hardaway	3.00	1.35
❑ 288 Rod Strickland	2.00	.90
❑ 289 Sherman Douglas	1.25	.55
❑ 290 Gary Payton	5.00	2.20

1995-96 Topps Rattle and Roll

	MINT	NRMT
COMPLETE SET (10)	12.00	5.50
COMMON CARD (R1-R10)	.75	.35
SEMISTARS	1.00	.45
UNLISTED STARS	1.50	.70

SER.2 STATED ODDS 1:12 RETAIL

❑ R1 Juwan Howard	1.50	.70
❑ R2 Glenn Robinson	1.50	.70
❑ R3 Grant Hill	8.00	3.60
❑ R4 Sharone Wright	.75	.35
❑ R5 Brian Grant	1.50	.70
❑ R6 Antonio McDyess	4.00	1.80
❑ R7 Bryant Reeves	1.00	.45
❑ R8 Gary Trent	.75	.35
❑ R9 Jerry Stackhouse	2.50	1.10
❑ R10 Joe Smith	2.50	1.10

1995-96 Topps Show Stoppers

	MINT	NRMT
COMPLETE SET (10)	90.00	40.00
COMMON CARD (1-10)	3.00	1.35

SER.1 STATED ODDS 1:24 HOBBY

❑ SS1 Michael Jordan	40.00	18.00
❑ SS2 Grant Hill	15.00	6.75
❑ SS3 Glenn Robinson	3.00	1.35
❑ SS4 Anfernee Hardaway	10.00	4.50
❑ SS5 Charles Barkley	5.00	2.20
❑ SS6 Patrick Ewing	3.00	1.35
❑ SS7 Shaquille O'Neal	15.00	6.75
❑ SS8 Jason Kidd	10.00	4.50
❑ SS9 Glen Rice	3.00	1.35
❑ SS10 Karl Malone	5.00	2.20

1995-96 Topps Spark Plugs

	MINT	NRMT
COMPLETE SET (10)	30.00	13.50
COMMON CARD (SP1-SP10)	1.25	.55

SER.2 STATED ODDS 1:8 HOBBY/RETAIL

❑ SP1 Shaquille O'Neal	6.00	2.70
❑ SP2 Michael Jordan	15.00	6.75
❑ SP3 Reggie Miller	1.25	.55
❑ SP4 Anfernee Hardaway	4.00	1.80
❑ SP5 John Stockton	1.25	.55
❑ SP6 David Robinson	2.00	.90
❑ SP7 Hakeem Olajuwon	2.00	.90
❑ SP8 Tim Hardaway	1.25	.55
❑ SP9 Grant Hill	6.00	2.70
❑ SP10 Scottie Pippen	4.00	1.80

1995-96 Topps Sudden Impact

	MINT	NRMT
COMPLETE SET (10)	60.00	27.00
COMMON CARD (S1-S10)	3.00	1.35
SEMISTARS	4.00	1.80
UNLISTED STARS	6.00	2.70

SER.2 STATED ODDS 1:72 HOBBY

	MINT	NRMT
❑ S1 Damon Stoudamire	15.00	6.75
❑ S2 Cherokee Parks	3.00	1.35
❑ S3 Kurt Thomas	3.00	1.35
❑ S4 Gary Trent	3.00	1.35
❑ S5 Bryant Reeves	4.00	1.80
❑ S6 Ed O'Bannon	3.00	1.35
❑ S7 Shawn Respert	3.00	1.35
❑ S8 Antonio McDyess	15.00	6.75
❑ S9 Joe Smith	10.00	4.50
❑ S10 Jerry Stackhouse	10.00	4.50

1995-96 Topps Top Flight

	MINT	NRMT
COMPLETE SET (20)	70.00	32.00
COMMON CARD (TF1-TF20)	1.00	.45
SEMISTARS	1.50	.70
UNLISTED STARS	2.50	1.10

ONE PER SPECIAL SER.1 RETAIL PACK

	MINT	NRMT
❑ TF1 Michael Jordan	30.00	13.50
❑ TF2 Isaiah Rider	1.50	.70
❑ TF3 Harold Miner	1.00	.45
❑ TF4 Dominique Wilkins	2.50	1.10
❑ TF5 Clyde Drexler	2.50	1.10
❑ TF6 Scottie Pippen	8.00	3.60
❑ TF7 Shawn Kemp	4.00	1.80
❑ TF8 Chris Webber	8.00	3.60
❑ TF9 Anfernee Hardaway	8.00	3.60
❑ TF10 Grant Hill	12.00	5.50
❑ TF11 Kevin Johnson	1.50	.70
❑ TF12 John Starks	1.00	.45
❑ TF13 Dan Majerle	1.00	.45
❑ TF14 Latrell Sprewell	5.00	2.20
❑ TF15 Dee Brown	1.00	.45
❑ TF16 Stacey Augmon	1.00	.45
❑ TF17 David Benoit	1.00	.45
❑ TF18 Sean Elliott	1.00	.45
❑ TF19 Cedric Ceballos	1.00	.45
❑ TF20 Robert Horry	1.00	.45

1995-96 Topps Whiz Kids

	MINT	NRMT
COMPLETE SET (12)	40.00	18.00
COMMON CARD (WK1-WK12)	1.00	.45
SEMISTARS	2.00	.90
UNLISTED STARS	3.00	1.35

SER.1 STATED ODDS 1:24 HOBBY/RETAIL

	MINT	NRMT
❑ WK1 Grant Hill	15.00	6.75
❑ WK2 Nick Van Exel	2.00	.90
❑ WK3 Juwan Howard	3.00	1.35
❑ WK4 Chris Webber	10.00	4.50
❑ WK5 Brian Grant	3.00	1.35
❑ WK6 Glenn Robinson	3.00	1.35
❑ WK7 Donyell Marshall	1.00	.45
❑ WK8 Jason Kidd	10.00	4.50
❑ WK9 Anfernee Hardaway	10.00	4.50
❑ WK10 Jamal Mashburn	2.00	.90
❑ WK11 Vin Baker	3.00	1.35
❑ WK12 Eddie Jones	6.00	2.70

1996-97 Topps

	MINT	NRMT
COMPLETE SET (221)	30.00	13.50
COMP.FACT.HOB.SET (227)	35.00	16.00
COMPLETE SERIES 1 (110)	12.00	5.50
COMPLETE SERIES 2 (111)	20.00	9.00
COMMON CARD (1-221)	.10	.05
CL (111) SP	2.50	1.10
SEMISTARS	.15	.07
UNLISTED STARS	.25	.11

SERIES 1 CL NOT CONSIDERED PART OF SET

	MINT	NRMT
❑ 1 Patrick Ewing	.25	.11
❑ 2 Christian Laettner	.15	.07
❑ 3 Mahmoud Abdul-Rauf	.10	.05
❑ 4 Chris Webber	.75	.35
❑ 5 Jason Kidd	.75	.35
❑ 6 Clifford Rozier	.10	.05
❑ 7 Elden Campbell	.10	.05
❑ 8 Chuck Person	.10	.05
❑ 9 Jeff Hornacek	.15	.07
❑ 10 Rik Smits	.10	.05
❑ 11 Kurt Thomas	.10	.05
❑ 12 Rod Strickland	.15	.07
❑ 13 Kendall Gill	.15	.07
❑ 14 Brian Williams	.10	.05
❑ 15 Tom Gugliotta	.15	.07
❑ 16 Ron Harper	.15	.07
❑ 17 Eric Williams	.10	.05
❑ 18 A.C. Green	.15	.07
❑ 19 Scott Williams	.10	.05
❑ 20 Damon Stoudamire	.40	.18
❑ 21 Bryant Reeves	.10	.05
❑ 22 Bob Sura	.10	.05
❑ 23 Mitch Richmond	.25	.11
❑ 24 Larry Johnson	.15	.07
❑ 25 Vin Baker	.15	.07
❑ 26 Mark Bryant	.10	.05
❑ 27 Horace Grant	.15	.07
❑ 28 Allan Houston	.25	.11
❑ 29 Sam Perkins	.15	.07
❑ 30 Antonio McDyess	.40	.18
❑ 31 Rasheed Wallace	.30	.14
❑ 32 Malik Sealy	.10	.05
❑ 33 Scottie Pippen	.75	.35
❑ 34 Charles Barkley	.40	.18
❑ 35 Hakeem Olajuwon	.40	.18
❑ 36 John Starks	.10	.05
❑ 37 Byron Scott	.10	.05
❑ 38 Arvydas Sabonis	.15	.07
❑ 39 Vlade Divac	.10	.05
❑ 40 Joe Dumars	.25	.11
❑ 41 Danny Ferry	.10	.05
❑ 42 Jerry Stackhouse	.25	.11
❑ 43 B.J. Armstrong	.10	.05
❑ 44 Shawn Bradley	.10	.05
❑ 45 Kevin Garnett	1.50	.70
❑ 46 Dee Brown	.10	.05
❑ 47 Michael Smith	.10	.05
❑ 48 Doug Christie	.10	.05
❑ 49 Mark Jackson	.10	.05
❑ 50 Shawn Kemp	.40	.18
❑ 51 Sasha Danilovic	.10	.05
❑ 52 Nick Anderson	.10	.05
❑ 53 Matt Geiger	.10	.05
❑ 54 Charles Smith	.10	.05
❑ 55 Mookie Blaylock	.10	.05
❑ 56 Johnny Newman	.10	.05
❑ 57 George McCloud	.10	.05
❑ 58 Greg Ostertag	.10	.05
❑ 59 Reggie Williams	.10	.05
❑ 60 Brent Barry	.10	.05
❑ 61 Doug West	.10	.05
❑ 62 Donald Royal	.10	.05
❑ 63 Randy Brown	.10	.05
❑ 64 Vincent Askew	.10	.05
❑ 65 John Stockton	.25	.11
❑ 66 Joe Kleine	.10	.05
❑ 67 Keith Askins	.10	.05
❑ 68 Bobby Phills	.10	.05
❑ 69 Chris Mullin	.25	.11
❑ 70 Nick Van Exel	.15	.07
❑ 71 Rick Fox	.10	.05
❑ 72 Chicago Bulls - 72 Wins	1.50	.70
❑ 73 Shawn Respert	.10	.05
❑ 74 Hubert Davis	.10	.05
❑ 75 Jim Jackson	.10	.05
❑ 76 Olden Polynice	.10	.05
❑ 77 Gheorghe Muresan	.10	.05
❑ 78 Theo Ratliff	.15	.07
❑ 79 Khalid Reeves	.10	.05
❑ 80 David Robinson	.40	.18
❑ 81 Lawrence Moten	.10	.05
❑ 82 Sam Cassell	.15	.07
❑ 83 George Zidek	.10	.05
❑ 84 Sharone Wright	.10	.05
❑ 85 Clarence Weatherspoon	.10	.05
❑ 86 Alan Henderson	.10	.05
❑ 87 Chris Dudley	.10	.05
❑ 88 Ed O'Bannon	.10	.05
❑ 89 Calbert Cheaney	.10	.05
❑ 90 Cedric Ceballos	.10	.05
❑ 91 Michael Cage	.10	.05
❑ 92 Ervin Johnson	.10	.05
❑ 93 Gary Trent	.10	.05
❑ 94 Sherman Douglas	.10	.05
❑ 95 Joe Smith	.25	.11
❑ 96 Dale Davis	.10	.05
❑ 97 Tony Dumas	.10	.05
❑ 98 Muggsy Bogues	.10	.05
❑ 99 Toni Kukoc	.30	.14

❑ 100 Grant Hill	1.25	.55
❑ 101 Michael Finley	.30	.14
❑ 102 Isaiah Rider	.15	.07
❑ 103 Bryant Stith	.10	.05
❑ 104 Pooh Richardson	.10	.05
❑ 105 Karl Malone	.40	.18
❑ 106 Brian Grant	.25	.11
❑ 107 Sean Elliott	.10	.05
❑ 108 Charles Oakley	.10	.05
❑ 109 Pervis Ellison	.10	.05
❑ 110 Anfernee Hardaway	.75	.35
❑ 111 Checklist	2.50	1.10
❑ 112 Dikembe Mutombo	.15	.07
❑ 113 Alonzo Mourning	.25	.11
❑ 114 Hubert Davis	.10	.05
❑ 115 Rony Seikaly	.10	.05
❑ 116 Danny Manning	.15	.07
❑ 117 Donyell Marshall	.10	.05
❑ 118 Gerald Wilkins	.10	.05
❑ 119 Ervin Johnson	.10	.05
❑ 120 Jalen Rose	.25	.11
❑ 121 Dino Radja	.10	.05
❑ 122 Glenn Robinson	.25	.11
❑ 123 John Stockton	.25	.11
❑ 124 Matt Maloney RC	.15	.07
❑ 125 Clifford Robinson	.10	.05
❑ 126 Steve Kerr	.10	.05
❑ 127 Nate McMillan	.10	.05
❑ 128 Shareef Abdur-Rahim RC	1.50	.70
❑ 129 Loy Vaught	.10	.05
❑ 130 Anthony Mason	.15	.07
❑ 131 Kevin Garnett	1.50	.70
❑ 132 Roy Rogers RC	.10	.05
❑ 133 Erick Dampier RC	.15	.07
❑ 134 Tyus Edney	.10	.05
❑ 135 Chris Mills	.10	.05
❑ 136 Cory Alexander	.10	.05
❑ 137 Juwan Howard	.15	.07
❑ 138 Kobe Bryant RC	12.00	5.50
❑ 139 Michael Jordan	3.00	1.35
❑ 140 Jayson Williams	.15	.07
❑ 141 Rod Strickland	.15	.07
❑ 142 Lorenzen Wright RC	.15	.07
❑ 143 Will Perdue	.10	.05
❑ 144 Derek Harper	.10	.05
❑ 145 Billy Owens	.10	.05
❑ 146 Antoine Walker RC	1.00	.45
❑ 147 P.J. Brown	.10	.05
❑ 148 Terrell Brandon	.15	.07
❑ 149 Larry Johnson	.15	.07
❑ 150 Steve Smith	.15	.07
❑ 151 Eddie Jones	.50	.23
❑ 152 Detlef Schrempf	.15	.07
❑ 153 Dale Ellis	.10	.05
❑ 154 Isaiah Rider	.15	.07
❑ 155 Tony Delk RC	.15	.07
❑ 156 Adrian Caldwell	.10	.05
❑ 157 Jamal Mashburn	.15	.07
❑ 158 Dennis Scott	.10	.05
❑ 159 Dana Barros	.10	.05
❑ 160 Martin Muursepp RC	.10	.05
❑ 161 Marcus Camby RC	.75	.35
❑ 162 Jerome Williams RC	.40	.18
❑ 163 Wesley Person	.10	.05
❑ 164 Luc Longley	.10	.05
❑ 165 Charlie Ward	.10	.05
❑ 166 Mark Jackson	.10	.05
❑ 167 Derrick Coleman	.15	.07
❑ 168 Dell Curry	.10	.05
❑ 169 Armon Gilliam	.10	.05
❑ 170 Vlade Divac	.10	.05
❑ 171 Allen Iverson RC	2.50	1.10
❑ 172 Vitaly Potapenko RC	.10	.05
❑ 173 Jon Koncak	.10	.05
❑ 174 Lindsey Hunter	.10	.05
❑ 175 Kevin Johnson	.15	.07
❑ 176 Dennis Rodman	.50	.23
❑ 177 Stephon Marbury RC	1.50	.70
❑ 178 Karl Malone	.40	.18
❑ 179 Charles Barkley	.40	.18
❑ 180 Popeye Jones	.10	.05
❑ 181 Samaki Walker RC	.10	.05
❑ 182 Steve Nash RC	.15	.07
❑ 183 Latrell Sprewell	.50	.23
❑ 184 Kenny Anderson	.15	.07
❑ 185 Tyrone Hill	.10	.05
❑ 186 Robert Pack	.10	.05
❑ 187 Greg Anthony	.10	.05
❑ 188 Derrick McKey	.10	.05
❑ 189 John Wallace RC	.25	.11
❑ 190 Bryon Russell	.10	.05
❑ 191 Jermaine O'Neal RC	.50	.23
❑ 192 Clyde Drexler	.25	.11
❑ 193 Mahmoud Abdul-Rauf	.10	.05
❑ 194 Eric Montross	.10	.05
❑ 195 Allan Houston	.25	.11
❑ 196 Harvey Grant	.10	.05
❑ 197 Rodney Rogers	.10	.05
❑ 198 Kerry Kittles RC	.50	.23
❑ 199 Grant Hill	1.25	.55
❑ 200 Lionel Simmons	.10	.05
❑ 201 Reggie Miller	.25	.11
❑ 202 Avery Johnson	.10	.05
❑ 203 LaPhonso Ellis	.10	.05
❑ 204 Brian Shaw	.10	.05
❑ 205 Priest Lauderdale RC	.10	.05
❑ 206 Derek Fisher RC	.40	.18
❑ 207 Terry Porter	.10	.05
❑ 208 Todd Fuller RC	.10	.05
❑ 209 Hersey Hawkins	.15	.07
❑ 210 Tim Legler	.10	.05
❑ 211 Terry Dehere	.10	.05
❑ 212 Gary Payton	.40	.18
❑ 213 Joe Dumars	.25	.11
❑ 214 Don MacLean	.10	.05
❑ 215 Greg Minor	.10	.05
❑ 216 Tim Hardaway	.25	.11
❑ 217 Ray Allen RC	1.00	.45
❑ 218 Mario Elie	.10	.05
❑ 219 Brooks Thompson	.10	.05
❑ 220 Shaquille O'Neal	1.25	.55

1996-97 Topps NBA at 50

	MINT	NRMT
COMPLETE SET (220)	200.00	90.00
COMPLETE SERIES 1 (110)	70.00	32.00
COMPLETE SERIES 2 (110)	130.00	57.50
COMMON CARD (1-220)	.25	.11

*STARS: 3X TO 6X BASE CARD HI
*RCs: 2.5X TO 5X BASE HI
SER.1/2 STATED ODDS 1:3 HOB/RET
ONE PER FACTORY SET

1996-97 Topps Draft Redemption

	MINT	NRMT
COMPLETE SET (27)	120.00	55.00
COMMON CARD (1-27)	2.00	.90
SEMISTARS	2.50	1.10
UNLISTED STARS	4.00	1.80

ONE CARD PER EXCHANGE CARD BY MAIL
EXCH.CARDS: SER.1 STATED ODDS 1:18 H/R

Card		
❑ 1 Allen Iverson	20.00	9.00
❑ 2 Marcus Camby	6.00	2.70
❑ 3 Shareef Abdur-Rahim	12.00	5.50
❑ 4 Stephon Marbury	12.00	5.50
❑ 5 Ray Allen	8.00	3.60
❑ 6 Antoine Walker	8.00	3.60
❑ 7 Lorenzen Wright	2.00	.90
❑ 8 Kerry Kittles	4.00	1.80
❑ 9 Samaki Walker	2.00	.90
❑ 10 Erick Dampier	2.00	.90
❑ 11 Todd Fuller	2.00	.90
❑ 12 Vitaly Potapenko	2.00	.90
❑ 13 Kobe Bryant	60.00	27.00
❑ 14 Not Issued	2.00	.90
❑ 15 Steve Nash	2.00	.90
❑ 16 Tony Delk	2.00	.90
❑ 17 Jermaine O'Neal	4.00	1.80
❑ 18 John Wallace	2.50	1.10
❑ 19 Walter McCarty	2.00	.90
❑ 20 Zydrunas Ilgauskas	2.50	1.10
❑ 21 Dontae' Jones	2.00	.90
❑ 22 Roy Rogers	2.00	.90
❑ 23 Not Issued	2.00	.90
❑ 24 Derek Fisher	4.00	1.80
❑ 25 Martin Muursepp	2.00	.90
❑ 26 Jerome Williams	4.00	1.80
❑ 27 Brian Evans	2.00	.90
❑ 28 Priest Lauderdale	2.00	.90
❑ 29 Travis Knight	2.00	.90
❑ NNO Expired Trade Cards	.50	.23

1996-97 Topps Finest Reprints

	MINT	NRMT
COMPLETE SERIES 2 (25)	120.00	55.00
COMMON CARD (1-50)	4.00	1.80

SER.2 STATED ODDS 1:36 HOBBY/RETAIL

COMP.REF.SER.2 (25)	400.00	180.00
COMMON REFRACTOR (1-50)	8.00	3.60

*REF: 1.5X TO 3X HI COLUMN
REF: SER.2 STATED ODDS 1:144 HOB/RET
SKIP-NUMBERED SET
SER.1 SET LISTED UNDER STADIUM CLUB

❑ 1 Lew Alcindor	12.00	5.50
❑ 3 Paul Arizin	4.00	1.80
❑ 9 Wilt Chamberlain	12.00	5.50
❑ 11 Dave Cowens	4.00	1.80
❑ 14 Clyde Drexler	8.00	3.60
❑ 16 Patrick Ewing	8.00	3.60
❑ 20 John Havlicek	10.00	4.50
❑ 21 Elvin Hayes	4.00	1.80
❑ 22 Larry Bird Julius Erving Magic Johnson	15.00	6.75
❑ 23 Sam Jones	4.00	1.80
❑ 25 Jerry Lucas	4.00	1.80
❑ 27 Moses Malone	4.00	1.80
❑ 30 George Mikan	10.00	4.50
❑ 31 Earl Monroe	8.00	3.60
❑ 32 Shaquille O'Neal	12.00	5.50
❑ 33 Hakeem Olajuwon	8.00	3.60
❑ 37 Willis Reed	4.00	1.80
❑ 38 Oscar Robertson	8.00	3.60
❑ 39 David Robinson	8.00	3.60
❑ 40 Bill Russell	12.00	5.50
❑ 42 Bill Sharman	4.00	1.80
❑ 43 John Stockton	8.00	3.60
❑ 45 Nate Thurmond	4.00	1.80
❑ 46 Wes Unseld	4.00	1.80
❑ 47 Bill Walton		

1996-97 Topps Hobby Masters

	MINT	NRMT
COMPLETE SET (20)	140.00	65.00
COMPLETE SERIES 1 (10)	80.00	36.00
COMPLETE SERIES 2 (10)	60.00	27.00
COMMON CARD (HM11-HM30)	3.00	1.35
SEMISTARS	5.00	2.20

SER.1/2 STATED ODDS 1:36 HOBBY

	MINT	NRMT
❑ HM11 Shaquille O'Neal	25.00	11.00
❑ HM12 Jerry Stackhouse	5.00	2.20
❑ HM13 Dennis Rodman	10.00	4.50
❑ HM14 Joe Smith	5.00	2.20
❑ HM15 Damon Stoudamire	8.00	3.60
❑ HM16 Gary Payton	8.00	3.60
❑ HM17 Mitch Richmond	5.00	2.20
❑ HM18 Reggie Miller	5.00	2.20
❑ HM19 Chris Webber	15.00	6.75
❑ HM20 Vin Baker	5.00	2.20
❑ HM21 Grant Hill	25.00	11.00
❑ HM22 Scottie Pippen	15.00	6.75
❑ HM23 Karl Malone	8.00	3.60
❑ HM24 Patrick Ewing	5.00	2.20
❑ HM25 Shawn Kemp	8.00	3.60
❑ HM26 Anfernee Hardaway	15.00	6.75
❑ HM27 Charles Barkley	8.00	3.60
❑ HM28 Jason Kidd	15.00	6.75
❑ HM29 Hakeem Olajuwon	8.00	3.60
❑ HM30 Larry Johnson	3.00	1.35

1996-97 Topps Holding Court

	MINT	NRMT
COMPLETE SET (15)	60.00	27.00
COMMON CARD (HC1-HC15)	1.25	.55
SEMISTARS	1.50	.70
UNLISTED STARS	2.50	1.10

SER.1 STATED ODDS 1:36 H/R, 1:24 JUM

	MINT	NRMT
COMP.REF.SET (15)	120.00	55.00
COMMON REF. (HC1-HC15)	2.50	1.10

*REF: 1X TO 2X HI COLUMN
REF: SER.1 STATED ODDS 1:108 H/R, 1:72 J

	MINT	NRMT
❑ HC1 Larry Johnson	1.50	.70
❑ HC2 Michael Jordan	30.00	13.50
❑ HC3 Cedric Ceballos	1.25	.55
❑ HC4 Grant Hill	12.00	5.50
❑ HC5 Anfernee Hardaway	8.00	3.60
❑ HC6 Reggie Miller	2.50	1.10
❑ HC7 Glenn Robinson	2.50	1.10
❑ HC8 Patrick Ewing	2.50	1.10
❑ HC9 Chris Webber	8.00	3.60
❑ HC10 Shaquille O'Neal	12.00	5.50
❑ HC11 John Stockton	2.50	1.10
❑ HC12 Mitch Richmond	2.50	1.10
❑ HC13 David Robinson	4.00	1.80
❑ HC14 Gary Payton	4.00	1.80
❑ HC15 Karl Malone	4.00	1.80

1996-97 Topps Mystery Finest

	MINT	NRMT
COMPLETE SET (22)	100.00	45.00
COMMON CARD (M1-M22)	1.50	.70
SEMISTARS	2.00	.90
UNLISTED STARS	3.00	1.35

SER.2 STATED ODDS 1:36 HOBBY/RETAIL

	MINT	NRMT
COMP.MYS.BDLS.SET (22)	200.00	90.00
COMMON BDLS. (M1-22)	2.50	1.10

*BORDERLESS: .75X TO 1.5X HI COLUMN
BDLS: SER.2 STATED ODDS 1:72 HOB/RET

	MINT	NRMT
COMP.BDLS.REF.SET (22)	500.00	220.00
COMMON BDLS.REF. (M1-22)	6.00	2.70

*BDLS.REF: 2X TO 4X HI
BDLS.REF: SER.2 STATED ODDS 1:216 H/R

	MINT	NRMT
COMP.DW BDRD.ATLANTIC (5)	6.00	2.70
COMP.DW BDRD.CENTRAL (6)	8.00	3.60
COMP.DW BDRD.MIDWEST (6)	6.00	2.70
COMP.DW BDRD.PACIFIC (5)	6.00	2.70

*SUP.DW.CARDS: .1X TO .2X HI
ONE DW SET BY MAIL PER DW SUPER TM.

	MINT	NRMT
COMP.CON.BDLS.EAST (11)	25.00	11.00
COMP.CON.BDLS.WEST (11)	8.00	3.60

*SUP.CON.CARDS: .1X TO .2X HI
ONE CON.SET BY MAIL PER CON.WIN.SUP.TM.

	MINT	NRMT
❑ M1 Scottie Pippen	10.00	4.50
❑ M2 Jason Kidd	10.00	4.50
❑ M3 Anfernee Hardaway	10.00	4.50
❑ M4 Gary Payton	5.00	2.20
❑ M5 Juwan Howard	2.00	.90
❑ M6 Sean Elliott	1.50	.70
❑ M7 Dennis Rodman	6.00	2.70
❑ M8 Shawn Kemp	5.00	2.20
❑ M9 David Robinson	5.00	2.20
❑ M10 Alonzo Mourning	3.00	1.35
❑ M11 Dikembe Mutombo	2.00	.90
❑ M12 Shaquille O'Neal	15.00	6.75
❑ M13 Clyde Drexler	3.00	1.35
❑ M14 Michael Jordan	40.00	18.00
❑ M15 Damon Stoudamire	5.00	2.20
❑ M16 Mitch Richmond	3.00	1.35
❑ M17 Patrick Ewing	3.00	1.35
❑ M18 Vin Baker	2.00	.90
❑ M19 Hakeem Olajuwon	5.00	2.20
❑ M20 Joe Smith	3.00	1.35
❑ M21 Charles Barkley	5.00	2.20
❑ M22 Reggie Miller	3.00	1.35

1996-97 Topps Mystery Finest Bordered Refractors

	MINT	NRMT
COMPLETE SET (22)	800.00	350.00
COMMON CARD (M1-M22)	10.00	4.50
SEMISTARS	12.00	5.50
UNLISTED STARS	20.00	9.00

SER.2 STATED ODDS 1:66 HOBBY JUMBO

	MINT	NRMT
COMP.SUP.TM.FIN.SET (22)	125.00	55.00

*SUP.TM.CARDS: .1X TO .15X HI COLUMN
ONE BDRD.REF.ST.SET BY MAIL PER BULLS
ONE BDRD.REF.ST.SET BY MAIL PER SPURS

	MINT	NRMT
❑ M1 Scottie Pippen	60.00	27.00
❑ M2 Jason Kidd	60.00	27.00
❑ M3 Anfernee Hardaway	60.00	27.00
❑ M4 Gary Payton	30.00	13.50
❑ M5 Juwan Howard	12.00	5.50
❑ M6 Sean Elliott	10.00	4.50
❑ M7 Dennis Rodman	40.00	18.00
❑ M8 Shawn Kemp	30.00	13.50
❑ M9 David Robinson	30.00	13.50
❑ M10 Alonzo Mourning	20.00	9.00
❑ M11 Dikembe Mutombo	12.00	5.50
❑ M12 Shaquille O'Neal	100.00	45.00
❑ M13 Clyde Drexler	20.00	9.00
❑ M14 Michael Jordan	300.00	135.00
❑ M15 Damon Stoudamire	30.00	13.50
❑ M16 Mitch Richmond	20.00	9.00
❑ M17 Patrick Ewing	20.00	9.00
❑ M18 Vin Baker	12.00	5.50
❑ M19 Hakeem Olajuwon	30.00	13.50
❑ M20 Joe Smith	20.00	9.00
❑ M21 Charles Barkley	30.00	13.50
❑ M22 Reggie Miller	20.00	9.00

1996-97 Topps Pro Files

	MINT	NRMT
COMPLETE SET (20)	30.00	13.50
COMPLETE SERIES 1 (10)	20.00	9.00
COMPLETE SERIES 2 (10)	10.00	4.50
COMMON CARD (PF1-PF20)	.40	.18
SEMISTARS	.75	.35

SER.1/2 STATED ODDS 1:12 H/R, 1:6 JUM
TWO PER FACTORY SET

	MINT	NRMT
❑ PF1 Grant Hill	4.00	1.80
❑ PF2 Shawn Kemp	1.25	.55
❑ PF3 Michael Jordan	10.00	4.50
❑ PF4 Vin Baker	.75	.35
❑ PF5 Chris Webber	2.50	1.10
❑ PF6 Joe Smith	.75	.35
❑ PF7 Shaquille O'Neal	4.00	1.80
❑ PF8 Patrick Ewing	.75	.35
❑ PF9 Scottie Pippen	2.50	1.10
❑ PF10 Damon Stoudamire	1.25	.55
❑ PF11 Anfernee Hardaway	2.50	1.10
❑ PF12 Juwan Howard	.75	.35
❑ PF13 Dikembe Mutombo	.40	.18
❑ PF14 Dennis Rodman	1.50	.70
❑ PF15 Kevin Garnett	5.00	2.20
❑ PF16 Jerry Stackhouse	.75	.35
❑ PF17 Alonzo Mourning	.75	.35
❑ PF18 Karl Malone	1.25	.55

❑ PF19 Hakeem Olajuwon	1.25	.55
❑ PF20 Gary Payton	1.25	.55

1996-97 Topps Season's Best

	MINT	NRMT
COMPLETE SET (25)	40.00	18.00
COMMON CARD (SB1-SB25)	.40	.18
SEMISTARS	.75	.35
UNLISTED STARS	1.25	.55

SER.1 STATED ODDS 1:8 HOB/RET, 1:4 JUM
TWO PER FACTORY SET

❑ SB1 Michael Jordan	15.00	6.75
❑ SB2 Hakeem Olajuwon	2.00	.90
❑ SB3 Shaquille O'Neal	6.00	2.70
❑ SB4 Karl Malone	2.00	.90
❑ SB5 David Robinson	2.00	.90
❑ SB6 Dennis Rodman	2.50	1.10
❑ SB7 David Robinson	2.00	.90
❑ SB8 Dikembe Mutombo	.75	.35
❑ SB9 Charles Barkley	2.00	.90
❑ SB10 Shawn Kemp	2.00	.90
❑ SB11 John Stockton	1.25	.55
❑ SB12 Jason Kidd	4.00	1.80
❑ SB13 Avery Johnson	.40	.18
❑ SB14 Rod Strickland	.75	.35
❑ SB15 Damon Stoudamire	2.00	.90
❑ SB16 Gary Payton	2.00	.90
❑ SB17 Mookie Blaylock	.40	.18
❑ SB18 Michael Jordan	15.00	6.75
❑ SB19 Jason Kidd	4.00	1.80
❑ SB20 Alvin Robertson	.40	.18
❑ SB21 Dikembe Mutombo	.75	.35
❑ SB22 Shawn Bradley	.40	.18
❑ SB23 David Robinson	2.00	.90
❑ SB24 Hakeem Olajuwon	2.00	.90
❑ SB25 Alonzo Mourning	1.25	.55

1996-97 Topps Super Teams

	MINT	NRMT
COMPLETE SET (29)	60.00	27.00
COMMON CARD (ST1-ST29)	2.00	.90

SER.1 STATED ODDS 1:36 HOBBY/RETAIL
RED.SETS LISTED UNDER MYSTERY FINEST

❑ ST1 Atlanta Hawks ... 2.00 .90
Stacy Augmon
Grant Long
Ken Norman

❑ ST2 Boston Celtics ... 2.00 .90
Dino Radja
Dana Barros
Eric Williams

❑ ST3 Charlotte Hornets ... 2.00 .90
Robert Parish
Glen Rice
Kenny Anderson
Larry Johnson
Dell Curry
Muggsy Bogues

❑ ST4 Chicago Bulls ... 25.00 11.00
Michael Jordan
Scottie Pippen
Dennis Rodman
Luc Longley
Ron Harper

❑ ST5 Cleveland Cavaliers ... 2.00 .90
Bob Sura
Dan Majerle
Donny Marshall

❑ ST6 Dallas Mavericks ... 2.00 .90
Jason Kidd
Jamal Mashburn
Jim Jackson
Popeye Jones

❑ ST7 Denver Nuggets ... 2.00 .90
Dikembe Mutombo
Bryant Stith
Don MacLean

❑ ST8 Detroit Pistons ... 2.00 .90
Mark West
Theo Ratliff
Lindsey Hunter
Joe Dumars
Terry Cummings
Grant Hill
Lou Roe

❑ ST9 Golden State Warriors 2.00 .90
B.J. Armstrong
Latrell Sprewell
Joe Smith

❑ ST10 Houston Rockets ... 2.50 1.10
Hakeem Olajuwon
Robert Horry
Chucky Brown
Eldridge Recasner
Clyde Drexler

❑ ST11 Indiana Pacers ... 2.00 .90
Rik Smits
Reggie Miller
Dale Davis
Mark Jackson

❑ ST12 Los Angeles Clippers 2.00 .90
Malik Sealy
Terry Dehere

❑ ST13 Los Angeles Lakers .. 4.00 1.80
Elden Campbell
Sedale Threatt
Vlade Divac
Anthony Peeler
Eddie Jones
Derek Strong
Frankie King

❑ ST14 Miami Heat ... 4.00 1.80
Voshon Lenard
Alonzo Mourning
Rex Chapman
Keith Askins
Dan Schayes
Jeff Malone
Tony Smith

❑ ST15 Milwaukee Bucks ... 2.00 .90
Glenn Robinson
Vin Baker
Benoit Benjamin
Lee Mayberry
Johnny Newman

❑ ST16 Minnesota T'wolves .. 2.00 .90
Doug West
Tom Gugliotta
Kevin Garnett
Sam Mitchell

❑ ST17 New Jersey Nets ... 2.00 .90
P.J. Brown
Armon Gilliam
Ed O'Bannon
Chris Childs
Vern Fleming

❑ ST18 New York Knicks ... 2.50 1.10
J.R. Reid
Anthony Mason
Hubert Davis

❑ ST19 Orlando Magic ... 2.00 .90
Anfernee Hardaway
Shaquille O'Neal
Dennis Scott

❑ ST20 Philadelphia 76ers ... 2.00 .90
Trevor Ruffin
Derrick Alston
LaSalle Thompson

❑ ST21 Phoenix Suns ... 2.00 .90
Joe Kleine
Charles Barkley
Wayman Tisdale
Michael Finley
Elliot Perry

❑ ST22 Portland Trail Blazers 2.00 .90
Arvydas Sabonis
Chris Dudley
Clifford Robinson
James Robinson
Gary Trent
Aaron McKie

❑ ST23 Sacramento Kings ... 2.00 .90
Bobby Hurley
Sarunas Marciulionis
Mitch Richmond
Olden Polynice
Brian Grant

❑ ST24 San Antonio Spurs .. 10.00 4.50
Vinny Del Negro
David Robinson
Doc Rivers
Dell Demps

❑ ST25 Seattle Supersonics .. 2.50 1.10
Ervin Johnson
Gary Payton
Shawn Kemp

❑ ST26 Toronto Raptors ... 2.00 .90
Acie Earl
Carlos Rogers
Alvin Robertson
B.J. Tyler

❑ ST27 Utah Jazz ... 5.00 2.20
John Stockton
Karl Malone
David Benoit
Felton Spencer

❑ ST28 Vancouver Grizzlies .. 2.00 .90
Eric Murdock
Eric Mobley
Lawrence Moten
Blue Edwards
Doug Edwards
Ashraf Amaya
Literrial Green

❑ ST29 Washington Bullets ... 2.00 .90
Juwan Howard
Gheorghe Muresan
Chris Webber
Ledell Eackles

1996-97 Topps Youthquake

	MINT	NRMT
COMPLETE SET (15)	80.00	36.00
COMMON CARD (YQ1-YQ15)	1.25	.55
SEMISTARS	2.00	.90
UNLISTED STARS	3.00	1.35

SER.2 STATED ODDS 1:36 RETAIL

❑ YQ1 Allen Iverson	15.00	6.75
❑ YQ2 Samaki Walker	1.25	.55
❑ YQ3 Stephon Marbury	10.00	4.50
❑ YQ4 Damon Stoudamire	5.00	2.20
❑ YQ5 John Wallace	2.00	.90

Card	Mint	Nrmt
❑ YQ6 Michael Finley	3.00	1.35
❑ YQ7 Marcus Camby	5.00	2.20
❑ YQ8 Kerry Kittles	3.00	1.35
❑ YQ9 Ray Allen	6.00	2.70
❑ YQ10 Jerry Stackhouse	3.00	1.35
❑ YQ11 Shareef Abdur-Rahim	10.00	4.50
❑ YQ12 Antonio McDyess	5.00	2.20
❑ YQ13 Joe Smith	3.00	1.35
❑ YQ14 Brent Barry	1.25	.55
❑ YQ15 Kobe Bryant	30.00	13.50

1997-98 Topps

	MINT	NRMT
COMPLETE SET (220)	30.00	13.50
COMPLETE SERIES 1 (110)	10.00	4.50
COMPLETE SERIES 2 (110)	20.00	9.00
COMMON CARD (1-220)	.10	.05
SEMISTARS	.15	.07
UNLISTED STARS	.25	.11

Card	Mint	Nrmt
❑ 1 Scottie Pippen	.75	.35
❑ 2 Nate McMillan	.10	.05
❑ 3 Byron Scott	.10	.05
❑ 4 Mark Davis	.10	.05
❑ 5 Rod Strickland	.15	.07
❑ 6 Brian Grant	.15	.07
❑ 7 Damon Stoudamire	.30	.14
❑ 8 John Stockton	.25	.11
❑ 9 Grant Long	.10	.05
❑ 10 Darrell Armstrong	.15	.07
❑ 11 Anthony Mason	.15	.07
❑ 12 Travis Best	.10	.05
❑ 13 Stephon Marbury	.75	.35
❑ 14 Jamal Mashburn	.15	.07
❑ 15 Detlef Schrempf	.15	.07
❑ 16 Terrell Brandon	.15	.07
❑ 17 Charles Barkley	.40	.18
❑ 18 Vin Baker	.15	.07
❑ 19 Gary Trent	.10	.05
❑ 20 Vinny Del Negro	.10	.05
❑ 21 Todd Day	.10	.05
❑ 22 Malik Sealy	.10	.05
❑ 23 Wesley Person	.10	.05
❑ 24 Reggie Miller	.25	.11
❑ 25 Dan Majerle	.15	.07
❑ 26 Todd Fuller	.10	.05
❑ 27 Juwan Howard	.15	.07
❑ 28 Clarence Weatherspoon	.10	.05
❑ 29 Grant Hill	1.25	.55
❑ 30 John Williams	.15	.07
❑ 31 Ken Norman	.10	.05
❑ 32 Patrick Ewing	.25	.11
❑ 33 Bryon Russell	.10	.05
❑ 34 Tony Smith	.10	.05
❑ 35 Andrew Lang	.10	.05
❑ 36 Rony Seikaly	.10	.05
❑ 37 Billy Owens	.10	.05
❑ 38 Dino Radja	.10	.05
❑ 39 Chris Gatling	.10	.05
❑ 40 Dale Davis	.10	.05
❑ 41 Arvydas Sabonis	.15	.07
❑ 42 Chris Mills	.10	.05
❑ 43 A.C. Green	.15	.07
❑ 44 Tyrone Hill	.10	.05
❑ 45 Tracy Murray	.10	.05
❑ 46 David Robinson	.40	.18
❑ 47 Lee Mayberry	.10	.05
❑ 48 Jayson Williams	.15	.07
❑ 49 Jason Kidd	.75	.35
❑ 50 Bryant Stith	.10	.05
❑ 51 Latrell Sprewell	.50	.23
❑ 52 Brent Barry	.10	.05
❑ 53 Henry James	.10	.05
❑ 54 Allen Iverson	1.25	.55
❑ 55 Shandon Anderson	.10	.05
❑ 56 Mitch Richmond	.25	.11
❑ 57 Allan Houston	.25	.11
❑ 58 Ron Harper	.15	.07
❑ 59 Gheorghe Muresan	.10	.05
❑ 60 Vincent Askew	.10	.05
❑ 61 Ray Allen	.40	.18
❑ 62 Kenny Anderson	.15	.07
❑ 63 Dikembe Mutombo	.15	.07
❑ 64 Sam Perkins	.15	.07
❑ 65 Walt Williams	.10	.05
❑ 66 Chris Carr	.10	.05
❑ 67 Vlade Divac	.10	.05
❑ 68 LaPhonso Ellis	.10	.05
❑ 69 B.J. Armstrong	.10	.05
❑ 70 Jim Jackson	.10	.05
❑ 71 Clyde Drexler	.25	.11
❑ 72 Lindsey Hunter	.10	.05
❑ 73 Sasha Danilovic	.10	.05
❑ 74 Elden Campbell	.10	.05
❑ 75 Robert Pack	.10	.05
❑ 76 Dennis Scott	.10	.05
❑ 77 Will Perdue	.10	.05
❑ 78 Anthony Peeler	.10	.05
❑ 79 Steve Smith	.15	.07
❑ 80 Steve Kerr	.10	.05
❑ 81 Buck Williams	.10	.05
❑ 82 Terry Mills	.10	.05
❑ 83 Michael Smith	.10	.05
❑ 84 Adam Keefe	.10	.05
❑ 85 Kevin Willis	.10	.05
❑ 86 David Wesley	.10	.05
❑ 87 Muggsy Bogues	.10	.05
❑ 88 Bimbo Coles	.10	.05
❑ 89 Tom Gugliotta	.15	.07
❑ 90 Jermaine O'Neal	.15	.07
❑ 91 Cedric Ceballos	.10	.05
❑ 92 Shawn Kemp	.40	.18
❑ 93 Horace Grant	.15	.07
❑ 94 Shareef Abdur-Rahim	.75	.35
❑ 95 Robert Horry	.10	.05
❑ 96 Vitaly Potapenko	.10	.05
❑ 97 Pooh Richardson	.10	.05
❑ 98 Doug Christie	.10	.05
❑ 99 Voshon Lenard	.10	.05
❑ 100 Dominique Wilkins	.25	.11
❑ 101 Alonzo Mourning	.25	.11
❑ 102 Sam Cassell	.15	.07
❑ 103 Sherman Douglas	.10	.05
❑ 104 Shawn Bradley	.10	.05
❑ 105 Mark Jackson	.10	.05
❑ 106 Dennis Rodman	.50	.23
❑ 107 Charles Oakley	.10	.05
❑ 108 Matt Maloney	.10	.05
❑ 109 Shaquille O'Neal	1.25	.55
❑ 110 Checklist	.10	.05
❑ 111 Antonio McDyess	.30	.14
❑ 112 Bob Sura	.10	.05
❑ 113 Terrell Brandon	.15	.07
❑ 114 Tim Thomas RC	.75	.35
❑ 115 Tim Duncan RC	3.00	1.35
❑ 116 Antonio Daniels RC	.25	.11
❑ 117 Bryant Reeves	.10	.05
❑ 118 Keith Van Horn RC	1.25	.55
❑ 119 Loy Vaught	.10	.05
❑ 120 Rasheed Wallace	.25	.11
❑ 121 Bobby Jackson RC	.15	.07
❑ 122 Kevin Johnson	.15	.07
❑ 123 Michael Jordan	3.00	1.35
❑ 124 Ron Mercer RC	.75	.35
❑ 125 Tracy McGrady RC	2.50	1.10
❑ 126 Antoine Walker	.50	.23
❑ 127 Carlos Rogers	.10	.05
❑ 128 Isaac Austin	.10	.05
❑ 129 Mookie Blaylock	.10	.05
❑ 130 Rodrick Rhodes RC	.10	.05
❑ 131 Dennis Scott	.10	.05
❑ 132 Chris Mullin	.25	.11
❑ 133 P.J. Brown	.10	.05
❑ 134 Rex Chapman	.10	.05
❑ 135 Sean Elliott	.10	.05
❑ 136 Alan Henderson	.10	.05
❑ 137 Austin Croshere RC	.60	.25
❑ 138 Nick Van Exel	.15	.07
❑ 139 Derek Strong	.10	.05
❑ 140 Glenn Robinson	.15	.07
❑ 141 Avery Johnson	.10	.05
❑ 142 Calbert Cheaney	.10	.05
❑ 143 Mahmoud Abdul-Rauf	.10	.05
❑ 144 Stojko Vrankovic	.10	.05
❑ 145 Chris Childs	.10	.05
❑ 146 Danny Manning	.15	.07
❑ 147 Jeff Hornacek	.15	.07
❑ 148 Kevin Garnett	1.50	.70
❑ 149 Joe Dumars	.25	.11
❑ 150 Johnny Taylor RC	.10	.05
❑ 151 Mark Price	.10	.05
❑ 152 Toni Kukoc	.30	.14
❑ 153 Erick Dampier	.10	.05
❑ 154 Lorenzen Wright	.10	.05
❑ 155 Matt Geiger	.10	.05
❑ 156 Tim Hardaway	.25	.11
❑ 157 Charles Smith RC	.10	.05
❑ 158 Hersey Hawkins	.15	.07
❑ 159 Michael Finley	.25	.11
❑ 160 Tyus Edney	.10	.05
❑ 161 Christian Laettner	.15	.07
❑ 162 Doug West	.10	.05
❑ 163 Jim Jackson	.10	.05
❑ 164 Larry Johnson	.15	.07
❑ 165 Vin Baker	.15	.07
❑ 166 Karl Malone	.40	.18
❑ 167 Kelvin Cato RC	.25	.11
❑ 168 Luc Longley	.10	.05
❑ 169 Dale Davis	.10	.05
❑ 170 Joe Smith	.15	.07
❑ 171 Kobe Bryant	2.00	.90
❑ 172 Scot Pollard RC	.15	.07
❑ 173 Derek Anderson RC	.60	.25
❑ 174 Erick Strickland RC	.15	.07
❑ 175 Olden Polynice	.10	.05
❑ 176 Chris Whitney	.10	.05
❑ 177 Anthony Parker RC	.10	.05
❑ 178 Armon Gilliam	.10	.05
❑ 179 Gary Payton	.40	.18
❑ 180 Glen Rice	.15	.07
❑ 181 Chauncey Billups RC	.30	.14
❑ 182 Derek Fisher	.10	.05
❑ 183 John Starks	.10	.05
❑ 184 Mario Elie	.10	.05
❑ 185 Chris Webber	.75	.35
❑ 186 Shawn Kemp	.40	.18
❑ 187 Greg Ostertag	.10	.05
❑ 188 Olivier Saint-Jean RC	.10	.05
❑ 189 Eric Snow	.10	.05
❑ 190 Isaiah Rider	.15	.07
❑ 191 Paul Grant RC	.10	.05
❑ 192 Samaki Walker	.10	.05
❑ 193 Cory Alexander	.10	.05
❑ 194 Eddie Jones	.50	.23
❑ 195 John Thomas RC	.10	.05
❑ 196 Otis Thorpe	.10	.05
❑ 197 Rod Strickland	.15	.07
❑ 198 David Wesley	.10	.05
❑ 199 Jacque Vaughn RC	.15	.07
❑ 200 Rik Smits	.10	.05
❑ 201 Brevin Knight RC	.40	.18
❑ 202 Clifford Robinson	.10	.05

❑ 203 Hakeem Olajuwon	.40	.18
❑ 204 Jerry Stackhouse	.15	.07
❑ 205 Tyrone Hill	.10	.05
❑ 206 Kendall Gill	.15	.07
❑ 207 Marcus Camby	.30	.14
❑ 208 Tony Battie RC	.25	.11
❑ 209 Brent Price	.10	.05
❑ 210 Danny Fortson RC	.25	.11
❑ 211 Jerome Williams	.15	.07
❑ 212 Maurice Taylor RC	.50	.23
❑ 213 Brian Williams	.10	.05
❑ 214 Keith Booth RC	.10	.05
❑ 215 Nick Anderson	.10	.05
❑ 216 Travis Knight	.10	.05
❑ 217 Adonal Foyle RC	.15	.07
❑ 218 Anfernee Hardaway	.75	.35
❑ 219 Kerry Kittles	.25	.11
❑ 220 Checklist	.10	.05

1997-98 Topps Minted in Springfield

	MINT	NRMT
COMPLETE SET (220)	200.00	90.00
COMPLETE SERIES 1 (110)	80.00	36.00
COMPLETE SERIES 2 (110)	120.00	55.00
COMMON CARD (1-220)	.50	.23

*STARS: 2X TO 5X BASE CARD HI
*RCs: 2X TO 4X BASE HI
SER.1 STATED ODDS 1:6 HOBBY/RETAIL
SER.2 STATED ODDS 1:9 HOBBY/RETAIL

1997-98 Topps Autographs

	MINT	NRMT
COMPLETE SET (8)	100.00	45.00
COMMON CARD (1-8)	12.00	5.50

SER.1 STATED ODDS 1:212 HOBBY

❑ 1 John Starks	12.00	5.50
❑ 2 Juwan Howard	12.00	5.50
❑ 3 Mitch Richmond	20.00	9.00
❑ 4 Hakeem Olajuwon	40.00	18.00
❑ 5 Glenn Robinson	12.00	5.50
❑ 6 Steve Smith	12.00	5.50
❑ 7 Antoine Walker	20.00	9.00
❑ 8 Clyde Drexler	40.00	18.00

1997-98 Topps Bound for Glory

	MINT	NRMT
COMPLETE SET (15)	60.00	27.00
COMMON CARD (BG1-BG15)	1.25	.55
SEMISTARS	1.50	.70
UNLISTED STARS	2.50	1.10

SER.1 STATED ODDS 1:36 HOBBY

❑ BG1 Robert Parish	1.25	.55
❑ BG2 Grant Hill	12.00	5.50
❑ BG3 Chris Mullin	1.25	.55
❑ BG4 Hakeem Olajuwon	4.00	1.80
❑ BG5 Dennis Rodman	5.00	2.20
❑ BG6 Patrick Ewing	2.50	1.10
❑ BG7 Karl Malone	4.00	1.80
❑ BG8 Charles Barkley	4.00	1.80
❑ BG9 David Robinson	4.00	1.80
❑ BG10 Michael Jordan	30.00	13.50
❑ BG11 Dominique Wilkins	2.50	1.10
❑ BG12 Shaquille O'Neal	12.00	5.50
❑ BG13 Clyde Drexler	2.50	1.10
❑ BG14 John Stockton	2.50	1.10
❑ BG15 Scottie Pippen	8.00	3.60

1997-98 Topps Clutch Time

	MINT	NRMT
COMPLETE SET (20)	80.00	36.00
COMMON CARD (CT1-CT20)	1.25	.55
SEMISTARS	1.50	.70
UNLISTED STARS	2.50	1.10

SER.2 STATED ODDS 1:36 HOBBY

❑ CT1 Michael Jordan	30.00	13.50
❑ CT2 Christian Laettner	1.25	.55
❑ CT3 Patrick Ewing	2.50	1.10
❑ CT4 Glen Rice	1.50	.70
❑ CT5 Stephon Marbury	8.00	3.60
❑ CT6 Tim Hardaway	2.50	1.10
❑ CT7 Reggie Miller	2.50	1.10
❑ CT8 Gary Payton	4.00	1.80
❑ CT9 Charles Barkley	4.00	1.80
❑ CT10 Grant Hill	12.00	5.50
❑ CT11 Karl Malone	4.00	1.80
❑ CT12 Dikembe Mutombo	1.25	.55
❑ CT13 Hakeem Olajuwon	4.00	1.80
❑ CT14 Shawn Kemp	4.00	1.80
❑ CT15 John Stockton	2.50	1.10
❑ CT16 Anfernee Hardaway	8.00	3.60
❑ CT17 Glenn Robinson	1.50	.70
❑ CT18 Chris Webber	8.00	3.60
❑ CT19 Allen Iverson	12.00	5.50
❑ CT20 Scottie Pippen	8.00	3.60

1997-98 Topps Destiny

	MINT	NRMT
COMPLETE SET (15)	60.00	27.00
COMMON CARD (D1-D15)	1.50	.70

SER.2 STATED ODDS 1:18 RETAIL

❑ D1 Grant Hill	8.00	3.60
❑ D2 Kevin Garnett	10.00	4.50
❑ D3 Vin Baker	1.50	.70
❑ D4 Antoine Walker	3.00	1.35
❑ D5 Kobe Bryant	12.00	5.50
❑ D6 Tracy McGrady	8.00	3.60
❑ D7 Keith Van Horn	4.00	1.80
❑ D8 Tim Duncan	8.00	3.60
❑ D9 Eddie Jones	3.00	1.35
❑ D10 Stephon Marbury	5.00	2.20
❑ D11 Marcus Camby	2.00	.90
❑ D12 Antonio McDyess	2.00	.90
❑ D13 Shareef Abdur-Rahim	5.00	2.20
❑ D14 Allen Iverson	8.00	3.60
❑ D15 Shaquille O'Neal	8.00	3.60

1997-98 Topps Draft Redemption

	MINT	NRMT
COMPLETE SET (29)	60.00	27.00
COMMON CARD (1-29)	1.50	.70
SEMISTARS	2.00	.90
UNLISTED STARS	3.00	1.35

*TRADE CARDS: .25X TO .5X HI COLUMN
SER.1 STATED ODDS 1:12 HOB, 1:18 RET

❑ 1 Tim Duncan	15.00	6.75
❑ 2 Keith Van Horn	8.00	3.60
❑ 3 Chauncey Billups	2.00	.90
❑ 4 Antonio Daniels	2.00	.90
❑ 5 Tony Battie	1.50	.70
❑ 6 Ron Mercer	5.00	2.20
❑ 7 Tim Thomas	5.00	2.20
❑ 8 Adonal Foyle	3.00	1.35
❑ 9 Tracy McGrady	15.00	6.75

❑ 10 Danny Fortson	1.50	.70
❑ 11 Olivier Saint-Jean	1.50	.70
❑ 12 Austin Croshere	4.00	1.80
❑ 13 Derek Anderson	4.00	1.80
❑ 14 Maurice Taylor	3.00	1.35
❑ 15 Kelvin Cato	1.50	.70
❑ 16 Brevin Knight	3.00	1.35
❑ 17 Johnny Taylor	1.50	.70
❑ 18 Chris Anstey	1.50	.70
❑ 19 Scot Pollard	1.50	.70
❑ 20 Paul Grant	1.50	.70
❑ 21 Anthony Parker	1.50	.70
❑ 22 Ed Gray	3.00	1.35
❑ 23 Bobby Jackson	1.50	.70
❑ 24 Rodrick Rhodes	1.50	.70
❑ 25 John Thomas	1.50	.70
❑ 26 Charles Smith	1.50	.70
❑ 27 Jacque Vaughn	1.50	.70
❑ 28 Keith Booth	1.50	.70
❑ 29 Serge Zwikker	1.50	.70

1997-98 Topps Fantastic 15

	MINT	NRMT
COMPLETE SET (15)	80.00	36.00
COMMON CARD (F1-F15)	1.50	.70
SEMISTARS	2.00	.90
UNLISTED STARS	3.00	1.35
SER.1 STATED ODDS 1:36 RETAIL		
❑ F1 Antoine Walker	6.00	2.70
❑ F2 Damon Stoudamire	4.00	1.80
❑ F3 Brent Barry	1.50	.70
❑ F4 Michael Finley	3.00	1.35
❑ F5 Ray Allen	5.00	2.20
❑ F6 Allen Iverson	15.00	6.75
❑ F7 Stephon Marbury	10.00	4.50
❑ F8 Kerry Kittles	3.00	1.35
❑ F9 John Wallace	1.50	.70
❑ F10 Kevin Garnett	20.00	9.00
❑ F11 Jerry Stackhouse	2.00	.90
❑ F12 Kobe Bryant	25.00	11.00
❑ F13 Marcus Camby	4.00	1.80
❑ F14 Joe Smith	2.00	.90
❑ F15 Shareef Abdur-Rahim	10.00	4.50

1997-98 Topps Generations

	MINT	NRMT
COMPLETE SET (30)	200.00	90.00
COMMON CARD (G1-G30)	1.50	.70
SEMISTARS	2.00	.90
UNLISTED STARS	3.00	1.35
SER.2 STATED ODDS 1:36 HOBBY/RETAIL		
COMP.REF.SET (30)	600.00	275.00
COMMON REF. (G1-G30)	5.00	2.20
*REF: 1.25X TO 3X HI COLUMN		
REF: SER.2 STATED ODDS 1:144 HOB/RET		
❑ G1 Clyde Drexler	3.00	1.35
❑ G2 Michael Jordan	40.00	18.00
❑ G3 Charles Barkley	5.00	2.20
❑ G4 Hakeem Olajuwon	5.00	2.20
❑ G5 John Stockton	3.00	1.35
❑ G6 Patrick Ewing	3.00	1.35
❑ G7 Karl Malone	5.00	2.20
❑ G8 Dennis Rodman	6.00	2.70
❑ G9 Scottie Pippen	10.00	4.50
❑ G10 David Robinson	5.00	2.20
❑ G11 Mitch Richmond	3.00	1.35
❑ G12 Glen Rice	2.00	.90
❑ G13 Shawn Kemp	5.00	2.20
❑ G14 Gary Payton	5.00	2.20
❑ G15 Dikembe Mutombo	1.50	.70
❑ G16 Steve Smith	1.50	.70
❑ G17 Christian Laettner	1.50	.70
❑ G18 Shaquille O'Neal	15.00	6.75
❑ G19 Alonzo Mourning	3.00	1.35
❑ G20 Tom Gugliotta	2.00	.90
❑ G21 Anfernee Hardaway	10.00	4.50
❑ G22 Grant Hill	15.00	6.75
❑ G23 Kevin Garnett	20.00	9.00
❑ G24 Kobe Bryant	25.00	11.00
❑ G25 Stephon Marbury	10.00	4.50
❑ G26 Antoine Walker	6.00	2.70
❑ G27 Shareef Abdur-Rahim	10.00	4.50
❑ G28 Tim Duncan	15.00	6.75
❑ G29 Keith Van Horn	8.00	3.60
❑ G30 Tracy McGrady	15.00	6.75

1997-98 Topps Inside Stuff

	MINT	NRMT
COMPLETE SET (10)	40.00	18.00
COMMON CARD (IS1-IS10)	.75	.35
SEMISTARS	1.00	.45
UNLISTED STARS	1.50	.70
SER.2 STATED ODDS 1:36 HOBBY/RETAIL		
❑ IS1 Michael Jordan	20.00	9.00
❑ IS2 Eddie Johnson	.75	.35
❑ IS3 John Stockton	1.50	.70
❑ IS4 Patrick Ewing	1.50	.70
❑ IS5 Shaquille O'Neal	8.00	3.60
❑ IS6 Rex Chapman	.75	.35
❑ IS7 Shawn Kemp	2.50	1.10
❑ IS8 Scottie Pippen	5.00	2.20
❑ IS9 Kobe Bryant	12.00	5.50
❑ IS10 Anfernee Hardaway	5.00	2.20

1997-98 Topps New School

	MINT	NRMT
COMPLETE SET (15)	60.00	27.00
COMMON CARD (NS1-NS15)	1.50	.70

SEMISTARS	2.00	.90
UNLISTED STARS	3.00	1.35
SER.2 STATED ODDS 1:36 HOBBY/RETAIL		
❑ NS1 Austin Croshere	4.00	1.80
❑ NS2 Antonio Daniels	2.00	.90
❑ NS3 Tim Thomas	5.00	2.20
❑ NS4 Keith Van Horn	8.00	3.60
❑ NS5 Bobby Jackson	1.50	.70
❑ NS6 Derek Anderson	4.00	1.80
❑ NS7 Adonal Foyle	1.50	.70
❑ NS8 Johnny Taylor	1.50	.70
❑ NS9 Jacque Vaughn	1.50	.70
❑ NS10 Chauncey Billups	2.00	.90
❑ NS11 Brevin Knight	3.00	1.35
❑ NS12 Tracy McGrady	15.00	6.75
❑ NS13 Tony Battie	1.50	.70
❑ NS14 Scot Pollard	1.50	.70
❑ NS15 Tim Duncan	15.00	6.75

1997-98 Topps Rock Stars

	MINT	NRMT
COMPLETE SET (20)	120.00	55.00
COMMON CARD (RS1-RS20)	1.50	.70
SEMISTARS	2.00	.90
UNLISTED STARS	3.00	1.35
SER.1 STATED ODDS 1:36 HOBBY/RETAIL		
COMP.REF.SET (20)	400.00	180.00
COMMON REF (RS1-RS20)	5.00	2.20
*REF: 1.25X TO 3X HI COLUMN		
REF: SER.1 STATED ODDS 1:144 H/R		
❑ RS1 Michael Jordan	40.00	18.00
❑ RS2 Jerry Stackhouse	2.00	.90
❑ RS3 Chris Webber	10.00	4.50
❑ RS4 Charles Barkley	5.00	2.20
❑ RS5 Dennis Rodman	6.00	2.70
❑ RS6 Anfernee Hardaway	10.00	4.50
❑ RS7 Juwan Howard	2.00	.90
❑ RS8 Tim Hardaway	3.00	1.35
❑ RS9 Gary Payton	5.00	2.20
❑ RS10 Dikembe Mutombo	1.50	.70
❑ RS11 Tom Gugliotta	2.00	.90
❑ RS12 Kevin Garnett	20.00	9.00
❑ RS13 Shaquille O'Neal	15.00	6.75
❑ RS14 Hakeem Olajuwon	5.00	2.20
❑ RS15 Grant Hill	15.00	6.75
❑ RS16 Karl Malone	5.00	2.20

		MINT	NRMT
❑ RS17	Damon Stoudamire	4.00	1.80
❑ RS18	Shawn Kemp	5.00	2.20
❑ RS19	Alonzo Mourning	3.00	1.35
❑ RS20	Scottie Pippen	10.00	4.50

1997-98 Topps Season's Best

	MINT	NRMT
COMPLETE SET (30)	60.00	27.00
COMMON CARD (SB1-SB30)	.75	.35
SEMISTARS	1.00	.45
UNLISTED STARS	1.50	.70

SER.1 STATED ODDS 1:16 HOBBY/RETAIL

		MINT	NRMT
❑ SB1	Gary Payton	2.50	1.10
❑ SB2	Kevin Johnson	.75	.35
❑ SB3	Tim Hardaway	1.50	.70
❑ SB4	John Stockton	1.50	.70
❑ SB5	Damon Stoudamire	2.00	.90
❑ SB6	Michael Jordan	20.00	9.00
❑ SB7	Mitch Richmond	1.50	.70
❑ SB8	Latrell Sprewell	3.00	1.35
❑ SB9	Reggie Miller	1.50	.70
❑ SB10	Clyde Drexler	1.50	.70
❑ SB11	Grant Hill	8.00	3.60
❑ SB12	Scottie Pippen	5.00	2.20
❑ SB13	Kendall Gill	.75	.35
❑ SB14	Glen Rice	1.00	.45
❑ SB15	LaPhonso Ellis	.75	.35
❑ SB16	Karl Malone	2.50	1.10
❑ SB17	Charles Barkley	2.50	1.10
❑ SB18	Vin Baker	1.00	.45
❑ SB19	Chris Webber	5.00	2.20
❑ SB20	Tom Gugliotta	1.00	.45
❑ SB21	Shaquille O'Neal	8.00	3.60
❑ SB22	Patrick Ewing	1.50	.70
❑ SB23	Hakeem Olajuwon	2.50	1.10
❑ SB24	Alonzo Mourning	1.50	.70
❑ SB25	Dikembe Mutombo	.75	.35
❑ SB26	Allen Iverson	8.00	3.60
❑ SB27	Antoine Walker	3.00	1.35
❑ SB28	Shareef Abdur-Rahim	5.00	2.20
❑ SB29	Stephon Marbury	5.00	2.20
❑ SB30	Kerry Kittles	1.50	.70

1997-98 Topps Topps 40

	MINT	NRMT
COMPLETE SET (40)	80.00	36.00
COMPLETE SERIES 1 (20)	40.00	18.00
COMPLETE SERIES 2 (20)	40.00	18.00
COMMON CARD (T1-T40)	.75	.35
SEMISTARS	1.00	.45
UNLISTED STARS	1.50	.70

BOTH SERIES STATED ODDS 1:12 H/R
T-40 PREFIX ON CARD NUMBERS

		MINT	NRMT
❑ T1	Glen Rice	1.00	.45
❑ T2	Patrick Ewing	1.50	.70
❑ T3	Terrell Brandon	.75	.35
❑ T4	Jerry Stackhouse	1.00	.45
❑ T5	Michael Jordan	20.00	9.00
❑ T6	Christian Laettner	.75	.35
❑ T7	Latrell Sprewell	3.00	1.35
❑ T8	Reggie Miller	1.50	.70
❑ T9	Gary Payton	2.50	1.10
❑ T10	Detlef Schrempf	.75	.35
❑ T11	Kevin Garnett	10.00	4.50
❑ T12	Eddie Jones	3.00	1.35
❑ T13	Clyde Drexler	1.50	.70
❑ T14	Anfernee Hardaway	5.00	2.20
❑ T15	Chris Webber	5.00	2.20
❑ T16	Jayson Williams	.75	.35
❑ T17	Joe Smith	1.00	.45
❑ T18	Karl Malone	2.50	1.10
❑ T19	Tim Hardaway	1.50	.70
❑ T20	Vin Baker	1.00	.45
❑ T21	Tom Gugliotta	1.00	.45
❑ T22	Allen Iverson	8.00	3.60
❑ T23	David Robinson	2.50	1.10
❑ T24	Dikembe Mutombo	1.00	.45
❑ T25	John Stockton	1.50	.70
❑ T26	Charles Barkley	2.50	1.10
❑ T27	Mitch Richmond	1.50	.70
❑ T28	Damon Stoudamire	2.00	.90
❑ T29	Anthony Mason	1.00	.45
❑ T30	Shaquille O'Neal	8.00	3.60
❑ T31	Glenn Robinson	1.00	.45
❑ T32	Juwan Howard	1.00	.45
❑ T33	Shawn Kemp	2.50	1.10
❑ T34	Dennis Rodman	3.00	1.35
❑ T35	Grant Hill	8.00	3.60
❑ T36	Kevin Johnson	1.00	.45
❑ T37	Alonzo Mourning	1.50	.70
❑ T38	Hakeem Olajuwon	2.50	1.10
❑ T39	Joe Dumars	1.50	.70
❑ T40	Scottie Pippen	5.00	2.20

1998-99 Topps

	MINT	NRMT
COMPLETE SET (220)	35.00	16.00
COMPLETE SERIES 1 (110)	10.00	4.50
COMPLETE SERIES 2 (110)	25.00	11.00
COMMON CARD (1-220)	.10	.05
COMMON RC	.15	.07
SEMISTARS	.15	.07
SEMISTARS RC	.20	.09
UNLISTED STARS	.25	.11
UNLISTED STARS RC	.30	.14

		MINT	NRMT
❑ 1	Scottie Pippen	.75	.35
❑ 2	Shareef Abdur-Rahim	.60	.25
❑ 3	Rod Strickland	.15	.07
❑ 4	Keith Van Horn	.60	.25
❑ 5	Ray Allen	.30	.14
❑ 6	Chris Mullin	.25	.11
❑ 7	Anthony Parker	.10	.05
❑ 8	Lindsey Hunter	.10	.05
❑ 9	Mario Elie	.10	.05
❑ 10	Jerry Stackhouse	.15	.07
❑ 11	Eldridge Recasner	.10	.05
❑ 12	Jeff Hornacek	.15	.07
❑ 13	Chris Webber	.75	.35
❑ 14	Lee Mayberry	.10	.05
❑ 15	Erick Strickland	.10	.05
❑ 16	Arvydas Sabonis	.15	.07
❑ 17	Tim Thomas	.40	.18
❑ 18	Luc Longley	.10	.05
❑ 19	Detlef Schrempf	.15	.07
❑ 20	Alonzo Mourning	.25	.11
❑ 21	Adonal Foyle	.10	.05
❑ 22	Tony Battie	.15	.07
❑ 23	Robert Horry	.10	.05
❑ 24	Derek Harper	.10	.05
❑ 25	Jamal Mashburn	.15	.07
❑ 26	Elliot Perry	.10	.05
❑ 27	Jalen Rose	.25	.11
❑ 28	Joe Smith	.15	.07
❑ 29	Henry James	.10	.05
❑ 30	Travis Knight	.10	.05
❑ 31	Tom Gugliotta	.15	.07
❑ 32	Chris Anstey	.10	.05
❑ 33	Antonio Daniels	.10	.05
❑ 34	Elden Campbell	.10	.05
❑ 35	Charlie Ward	.10	.05
❑ 36	Eddie Johnson	.10	.05
❑ 37	John Wallace	.10	.05
❑ 38	Antonio Davis	.10	.05
❑ 39	Antoine Walker	.40	.18
❑ 40	Patrick Ewing	.25	.11
❑ 41	Doug Christie	.10	.05
❑ 42	Andrew Lang	.10	.05
❑ 43	Joe Dumars	.25	.11
❑ 44	Jaren Jackson	.10	.05
❑ 45	Loy Vaught	.10	.05
❑ 46	Allan Houston	.25	.11
❑ 47	Mark Jackson	.10	.05
❑ 48	Tracy Murray	.10	.05
❑ 49	Tim Duncan	1.25	.55
❑ 50	Micheal Williams	.10	.05
❑ 51	Steve Nash	.10	.05
❑ 52	Matt Maloney	.10	.05
❑ 53	Sam Cassell	.15	.07
❑ 54	Voshon Lenard	.10	.05
❑ 55	Dikembe Mutombo	.15	.07
❑ 56	Malik Sealy	.10	.05
❑ 57	Dell Curry	.10	.05
❑ 58	Stephon Marbury	.60	.25
❑ 59	Tariq Abdul-Wahad	.10	.05
❑ 60	Isaiah Rider	.15	.07
❑ 61	Kelvin Cato	.10	.05
❑ 62	LaPhonso Ellis	.10	.05
❑ 63	Jim Jackson	.10	.05
❑ 64	Greg Ostertag	.10	.05
❑ 65	Glenn Robinson	.15	.07
❑ 66	Chris Carr	.10	.05
❑ 67	Marcus Camby	.25	.11
❑ 68	Kobe Bryant	2.00	.90
❑ 69	Bobby Jackson	.10	.05
❑ 70	B.J. Armstrong	.10	.05
❑ 71	Alan Henderson	.10	.05
❑ 72	Terry Davis	.10	.05
❑ 73	John Stockton	.25	.11
❑ 74	Lamond Murray	.10	.05
❑ 75	Mark Price	.10	.05
❑ 76	Rex Chapman	.10	.05
❑ 77	Michael Jordan	3.00	1.35
❑ 78	Terry Cummings	.10	.05
❑ 79	Dan Majerle	.15	.07
❑ 80	Charles Outlaw	.10	.05
❑ 81	Michael Finley	.25	.11
❑ 82	Vin Baker	.15	.07
❑ 83	Clifford Robinson	.10	.05
❑ 84	Greg Anthony	.10	.05
❑ 85	Brevin Knight	.10	.05
❑ 86	Jacque Vaughn	.10	.05
❑ 87	Bobby Phills	.10	.05
❑ 88	Sherman Douglas	.10	.05
❑ 89	Kevin Johnson	.15	.07
❑ 90	Mahmoud Abdul-Rauf	.10	.05
❑ 91	Lorenzen Wright	.10	.05
❑ 92	Eric Williams	.10	.05

Card	MINT	NRMT
❑ 93 Will Perdue	.10	.05
❑ 94 Charles Barkley	.40	.18
❑ 95 Kendall Gill	.15	.07
❑ 96 Wesley Person	.10	.05
❑ 97 Buck Williams	.10	.05
❑ 98 Erick Dampier	.10	.05
❑ 99 Nate McMillan	.10	.05
❑ 100 Sean Elliott	.10	.05
❑ 101 Rasheed Wallace	.25	.11
❑ 102 Zydrunas Ilgauskas	.10	.05
❑ 103 Eddie Jones	.50	.23
❑ 104 Ron Mercer	.40	.18
❑ 105 Horace Grant	.15	.07
❑ 106 Corliss Williamson	.10	.05
❑ 107 Anthony Mason	.15	.07
❑ 108 Mookie Blaylock	.10	.05
❑ 109 Dennis Rodman	.50	.23
❑ 110 Checklist	.10	.05
❑ 111 Steve Smith	.15	.07
❑ 112 Cedric Henderson	.10	.05
❑ 113 Raef LaFrentz RC	.60	.25
❑ 114 Calbert Cheaney	.10	.05
❑ 115 Rik Smits	.10	.05
❑ 116 Rony Seikaly	.10	.05
❑ 117 Lawrence Funderburke	.10	.05
❑ 118 Ricky Davis RC	.60	.25
❑ 119 Howard Eisley	.10	.05
❑ 120 Kenny Anderson	.15	.07
❑ 121 Corey Benjamin RC	.30	.14
❑ 122 Maurice Taylor	.25	.11
❑ 123 Eric Murdock	.10	.05
❑ 124 Derek Fisher	.15	.07
❑ 125 Kevin Garnett	1.50	.70
❑ 126 Walt Williams	.10	.05
❑ 127 Bryce Drew RC	.30	.14
❑ 128 A.C. Green	.15	.07
❑ 129 Ervin Johnson	.10	.05
❑ 130 Christian Laettner	.15	.07
❑ 131 Chauncey Billups	.10	.05
❑ 132 Hakeem Olajuwon	.40	.18
❑ 133 Al Harrington RC	1.00	.45
❑ 134 Danny Manning	.15	.07
❑ 135 Paul Pierce RC	1.50	.70
❑ 136 Terrell Brandon	.15	.07
❑ 137 Bob Sura	.10	.05
❑ 138 Chris Gatling	.10	.05
❑ 139 Donyell Marshall	.10	.05
❑ 140 Marcus Camby	.25	.11
❑ 141 Brian Skinner RC	.30	.14
❑ 142 Charles Oakley	.10	.05
❑ 143 Antawn Jamison RC	1.50	.70
❑ 144 Nazr Mohammed RC	.20	.09
❑ 145 Karl Malone	.30	.14
❑ 146 Chris Mills	.10	.05
❑ 147 Bison Dele	.10	.05
❑ 148 Gary Payton	.40	.18
❑ 149 Terry Porter	.10	.05
❑ 150 Tim Hardaway	.25	.11
❑ 151 Larry Hughes RC	2.00	.90
❑ 152 Derek Anderson	.30	.14
❑ 153 Jason Williams RC	2.00	.90
❑ 154 Dirk Nowitzki RC	1.25	.55
❑ 155 Juwan Howard	.15	.07
❑ 156 Avery Johnson	.10	.05
❑ 157 Matt Harpring RC	.30	.14
❑ 158 Reggie Miller	.25	.11
❑ 159 Walter McCarty	.10	.05
❑ 160 Allen Iverson	1.00	.45
❑ 161 Felipe Lopez RC	.40	.18
❑ 162 Tracy McGrady	1.00	.45
❑ 163 Damon Stoudamire	.25	.11
❑ 164 Antonio McDyess	.25	.11
❑ 165 Grant Hill	1.25	.55
❑ 166 Tyronn Lue RC	.20	.09
❑ 167 P.J. Brown	.10	.05
❑ 168 Antonio Daniels	.10	.05
❑ 169 Mitch Richmond	.25	.11
❑ 170 David Robinson	.40	.18
❑ 171 Shawn Bradley	.10	.05
❑ 172 Shandon Anderson	.10	.05
❑ 173 Chris Childs	.10	.05
❑ 174 Shawn Kemp	.40	.18
❑ 175 Shaquille O'Neal	1.25	.55
❑ 176 John Starks	.10	.05
❑ 177 Tyrone Hill	.10	.05
❑ 178 Jayson Williams	.15	.07
❑ 179 Anfernee Hardaway	.75	.35
❑ 180 Chris Webber	.75	.35
❑ 181 Don Reid	.10	.05
❑ 182 Stacey Augmon	.10	.05
❑ 183 Hersey Hawkins	.15	.07
❑ 184 Sam Mitchell	.10	.05
❑ 185 Jason Kidd	.75	.35
❑ 186 Nick Van Exel	.15	.07
❑ 187 Larry Johnson	.15	.07
❑ 188 Bryant Reeves	.10	.05
❑ 189 Glen Rice	.15	.07
❑ 190 Kerry Kittles	.15	.07
❑ 191 Toni Kukoc	.30	.14
❑ 192 Ron Harper	.15	.07
❑ 193 Bryon Russell	.10	.05
❑ 194 Vladimir Stepania RC	.15	.07
❑ 195 Michael Olowokandi RC	.50	.23
❑ 196 Mike Bibby RC	1.00	.45
❑ 197 Dale Ellis	.10	.05
❑ 198 Muggsy Bogues	.10	.05
❑ 199 Vince Carter RC	15.00	6.75
❑ 200 Robert Traylor RC	.30	.14
❑ 201 Predrag Stojakovic RC	.50	.23
❑ 202 Aaron McKie	.10	.05
❑ 203 Hubert Davis	.10	.05
❑ 204 Dana Barros	.10	.05
❑ 205 Bonzi Wells RC	1.25	.55
❑ 206 Michael Doleac RC	.30	.14
❑ 207 Keon Clark RC	.30	.14
❑ 208 Michael Dickerson RC	.60	.25
❑ 209 Nick Anderson	.10	.05
❑ 210 Brent Price	.10	.05
❑ 211 Cherokee Parks	.10	.05
❑ 212 Sam Jacobson RC	.15	.07
❑ 213 Pat Garrity RC	.20	.09
❑ 214 Tyrone Corbin	.10	.05
❑ 215 David Wesley	.10	.05
❑ 216 Rodney Rogers	.10	.05
❑ 217 Dean Garrett	.10	.05
❑ 218 Roshown McLeod RC	.20	.09
❑ 219 Dale Davis	.10	.05
❑ 220 Checklist	.10	.05

1998-99 Topps Apparitions

	MINT	NRMT
COMPLETE SET (15)	100.00	45.00
COMMON CARD (A1-A15)	1.50	.70
UNLISTED STARS	2.50	1.10

SER.1 STATED ODDS 1:36 RETAIL

Card	MINT	NRMT
❑ A1 Kobe Bryant	20.00	9.00
❑ A2 Stephon Marbury	8.00	3.60
❑ A3 Brent Barry	1.50	.70
❑ A4 Karl Malone	4.00	1.80
❑ A5 Shaquille O'Neal	12.00	5.50
❑ A6 Chris Webber	8.00	3.60
❑ A7 Shawn Kemp	4.00	1.80
❑ A8 Hakeem Olajuwon	4.00	1.80
❑ A9 Anfernee Hardaway	8.00	3.60
❑ A10 Michael Finley	2.50	1.10
❑ A11 Keith Van Horn	6.00	2.70
❑ A12 Kevin Garnett	15.00	6.75
❑ A13 Vin Baker	1.50	.70
❑ A14 Tim Duncan	12.00	5.50
❑ A15 Michael Jordan	40.00	18.00

1998-99 Topps Autographs

	MINT	NRMT
COMPLETE SET (16)	550.00	250.00
COMPLETE SERIES 1 (8)	250.00	110.00
COMPLETE SERIES 2 (10)	300.00	135.00
COMMON CARD (AG1-AG18)	12.00	5.50

SER.1 STATED ODDS 1:329 HOBBY
SER.2 STATED ODDS 1:378 HOBBY

Card	MINT	NRMT
❑ AG1 Joe Smith	15.00	6.75
❑ AG2 Kobe Bryant	150.00	70.00
❑ AG3 Stephon Marbury	30.00	13.50
❑ AG4 Dikembe Mutombo	12.00	5.50
❑ AG5 Shareef Abdur-Rahim	30.00	13.50
❑ AG6 Eddie Jones	25.00	11.00
❑ AG7 Keith Van Horn	25.00	11.00
❑ AG8 Glen Rice	15.00	6.75
❑ AG9 Kobe Bryant	150.00	70.00
❑ AG10 Ron Mercer	20.00	9.00
❑ AG11 Glen Rice	15.00	6.75
❑ AG12 Stephon Marbury	30.00	13.50
❑ AG13 Kerry Kittles	12.00	5.50
❑ AG14 Michael Olowokandi	20.00	9.00
❑ AG15 Antawn Jamison	30.00	13.50
❑ AG16 Mike Bibby	30.00	13.50
❑ AG17 Robert Traylor	12.00	5.50
❑ AG18 Paul Pierce	50.00	22.00

1998-99 Topps Chrome Preview

	MINT	NRMT
COMPLETE SET (10)	80.00	36.00
COMMON CARD	5.00	2.20
UNLISTED STARS	10.00	4.50
SER.2 STATED ODDS 1:36 HOB/RET		
COMP.REF.SET (10)	400.00	180.00
COMMON REF.	25.00	11.00

*REF: 2X TO 5X HI COLUMN
REF: SER.2 STATED ODDS 1:40 HCP
SKIP-NUMBERED SET

Card	MINT	NRMT
❑ 6 Chris Mullin	10.00	4.50
❑ 10 Jerry Stackhouse	10.00	4.50
❑ 19 Detlef Schrempf	5.00	2.20
❑ 40 Patrick Ewing	10.00	4.50
❑ 43 Joe Dumars	10.00	4.50
❑ 60 Isaiah Rider	10.00	4.50

		MINT	NRMT
❑ 73	John Stockton	10.00	4.50
❑ 77	Michael Jordan	25.00	11.00
❑ 81	Michael Finley	10.00	4.50
❑ 100	Sean Elliott	5.00	2.20

1998-99 Topps Classic Collection

	MINT	NRMT
COMPLETE SET (10)	10.00	4.50
COMMON CARD (CL1-CL10)	1.00	.45
UNLISTED STARS	2.00	.90

SER.2 STATED ODDS 1:12 HOB/RET

		MINT	NRMT
❑ CL1	Larry Bird	3.00	1.35
❑ CL2	Magic Johnson	2.50	1.10
❑ CL3	Kareem Abdul-Jabbar	2.50	1.10
❑ CL4	Julius Erving	2.50	1.10
❑ CL5	Bill Russell	2.00	.90
❑ CL6	Wilt Chamberlain	2.00	.90
❑ CL7	Oscar Robertson	2.00	.90
❑ CL8	Jerry West	2.00	.90
❑ CL9	Elgin Baylor	1.00	.45
❑ CL10	Bob Cousy	2.00	.90

1998-99 Topps Coast to Coast

	MINT	NRMT
COMPLETE SET (15)	60.00	27.00
COMMON CARD (CC1-CC15)	1.50	.70
UNLISTED STARS	2.50	1.10

SER.2 STATED ODDS 1:36 RETAIL

		MINT	NRMT
❑ CC1	Kobe Bryant	20.00	9.00
❑ CC2	Scottie Pippen	8.00	3.60
❑ CC3	Eddie Jones	5.00	2.20
❑ CC4	Grant Hill	12.00	5.50
❑ CC5	Jason Kidd	8.00	3.60
❑ CC6	Antoine Walker	4.00	1.80
❑ CC7	Michael Finley	2.50	1.10
❑ CC8	Kevin Garnett	15.00	6.75
❑ CC9	Allen Iverson	12.00	5.50
❑ CC10	Shawn Kemp	4.00	1.80
❑ CC11	Glenn Robinson	1.50	.70
❑ CC12	Anfernee Hardaway	8.00	3.60
❑ CC13	Tim Hardaway	2.50	1.10
❑ CC14	Ron Mercer	4.00	1.80
❑ CC15	Kerry Kittles	1.50	.70

1998-99 Topps Cornerstones

	MINT	NRMT
COMPLETE SET (15)	60.00	27.00
COMMON CARD (C1-C15)	1.25	.55
UNLISTED STARS	2.00	.90

SER.1 STATED ODDS 1:36 HOBBY

		MINT	NRMT
❑ C1	Keith Van Horn	5.00	2.20
❑ C2	Kevin Garnett	12.00	5.50
❑ C3	Shareef Abdur-Rahim	5.00	2.20
❑ C4	Antoine Walker	3.00	1.35
❑ C5	Allen Iverson	8.00	3.60
❑ C6	Grant Hill	10.00	4.50
❑ C7	Marcus Camby	2.00	.90
❑ C8	Stephon Marbury	5.00	2.20
❑ C9	Kobe Bryant	15.00	6.75
❑ C10	Bobby Jackson	1.25	.55
❑ C11	Kerry Kittles	1.25	.55
❑ C12	Ron Mercer	3.00	1.35
❑ C13	Eddie Jones	4.00	1.80
❑ C14	Tim Thomas	3.00	1.35
❑ C15	Tim Duncan	10.00	4.50

1998-99 Topps Draft Redemption

	MINT	NRMT
COMPLETE SET (27)	100.00	45.00
COMMON CARD (1-27)	1.25	.55
SEMISTARS	2.00	.90
UNLISTED STARS	3.00	1.35

SER.1 STATED ODDS 1:18 HOB/RET
EXPIRATION: 4/1/99
RED.CARDS NOT AVAILABLE FOR 17/18

		MINT	NRMT
❑ 1	Michael Olowokandi	3.00	1.35
❑ 2	Mike Bibby	5.00	2.20
❑ 3	Raef LaFrentz	3.00	1.35
❑ 4	Antawn Jamison	8.00	3.60
❑ 5	Vince Carter	50.00	22.00
❑ 6	Robert Traylor	1.25	.55
❑ 7	Jason Williams	10.00	4.50
❑ 8	Larry Hughes	10.00	4.50
❑ 9	Dirk Nowitzki	6.00	2.70
❑ 10	Paul Pierce	8.00	3.60
❑ 11	Bonzi Wells	6.00	2.70
❑ 12	Michael Doleac	2.00	.90
❑ 13	Keon Clark	2.00	.90
❑ 14	Michael Dickerson	3.00	1.35
❑ 15	Matt Harpring	2.00	.90
❑ 16	Bryce Drew	2.00	.90
❑ 19	Pat Garrity	1.25	.55
❑ 20	Roshown McLeod	1.25	.55
❑ 21	Ricky Davis	3.00	1.35
❑ 22	Brian Skinner	2.00	.90
❑ 23	Tyronn Lue	1.25	.55
❑ 24	Felipe Lopez	2.00	.90
❑ 25	Al Harrington	5.00	2.20
❑ 26	Sam Jacobson	1.25	.55
❑ 27	Vladimir Stepania	1.25	.55
❑ 28	Corey Benjamin	2.00	.90
❑ 29	Nazr Mohammed	1.25	.55

1998-99 Topps East/West

	MINT	NRMT
COMPLETE SET (20)	100.00	45.00
COMMON CARD (EW1-EW20)	2.50	1.10
SER.2 STATED ODDS 1:36 HOB/RET		
COMP.REF.SET (20)	250.00	110.00
COMMON REF (EW1-EW20)	6.00	2.70

*REF: 1X TO 2.5X HI COLUMN
REF: SER.2 STATED ODDS 1:144 H/R

		MINT	NRMT
❑ EW1	Antoine Walker Shareef Abdur-Rahim	8.00	3.60
❑ EW2	Alonzo Mourning Shaquille O'Neal	12.00	5.50
❑ EW3	Tim Hardaway John Stockton	3.00	1.35
❑ EW4	Scottie Pippen Kevin Garnett	15.00	6.75
❑ EW5	Michael Jordan Kobe Bryant	30.00	13.50
❑ EW6	Grant Hill Michael Finley	10.00	4.50
❑ EW7	Dikembe Mutombo Hakeem Olajuwon	4.00	1.80
❑ EW8	Keith Van Horn Tim Duncan	10.00	4.50
❑ EW9	Allen Iverson Gary Payton	10.00	4.50
❑ EW10	Patrick Ewing David Robinson	5.00	2.20
❑ EW11	Juwan Howard Chris Webber	6.00	2.70
❑ EW12	Brevin Knight Stephon Marbury	6.00	2.70
❑ EW13	Shawn Kemp Vin Baker	3.00	1.35
❑ EW14	Anthony Mason Tom Gugliotta	2.50	1.10
❑ EW15	Anfernee Hardaway Damon Stoudamire	6.00	2.70
❑ EW16	Ron Mercer Eddie Jones	4.00	1.80
❑ EW17	Rod Strickland Jason Kidd	6.00	2.70
❑ EW18	Tim Thomas Antonio McDyess	3.00	1.35
❑ EW19	Jayson Williams Karl Malone	4.00	1.80
❑ EW20	Reggie Miller Jim Jackson	2.50	1.10

1998-99 Topps Emissaries

	MINT	NRMT
COMPLETE SET (20)	50.00	22.00
COMMON CARD (E1-E20)	1.00	.45
SEMISTARS	1.25	.55
UNLISTED STARS	2.00	.90
SER.1 STATED ODDS 1:24 HOB/RET		

	MINT	NRMT
❑ E1 Scottie Pippen	6.00	2.70
❑ E2 Karl Malone	3.00	1.35
❑ E3 Chris Webber	6.00	2.70
❑ E4 Anfernee Hardaway	6.00	2.70
❑ E5 Detlef Schrempf	1.25	.55
❑ E6 Mitch Richmond	2.00	.90
❑ E7 Vlade Divac	1.00	.45
❑ E8 Shaquille O'Neal	10.00	4.50
❑ E9 Luc Longley	1.00	.45
❑ E10 Grant Hill	10.00	4.50
❑ E11 Christian Laettner	1.25	.55
❑ E12 Gary Payton	3.00	1.35
❑ E13 Patrick Ewing	2.00	.90
❑ E14 Shawn Kemp	3.00	1.35
❑ E15 Toni Kukoc	2.50	1.10
❑ E16 David Robinson	3.00	1.35
❑ E17 Hakeem Olajuwon	3.00	1.35
❑ E18 Charles Barkley	3.00	1.35
❑ E19 John Stockton	2.00	.90
❑ E20 Arvydas Sabonis	1.25	.55

1998-99 Topps Gold Label

	MINT	NRMT
COMPLETE SET (10)	40.00	18.00
COMMON CARD (GL1-GL10)	2.00	.90
SER.2 STATED ODDS 1:12 HOB/RET		
COMP.BLACK SET (10)	100.00	45.00
COMMON BLACK (GL1-GL10)	5.00	2.20
*BLACK LABEL: 1X TO 2.5X HI COLUMN		
BLACK: SER.2 STATED ODDS 1:96 H/R		
COMP.RED SET (10)	700.00	325.00
COMMON RED (GL1-GL10)	30.00	13.50
*RED: 7.5X TO 15X HI		
RED: RANDOM INS.IN SER.2 PACKS		
STATED PRINT RUN 100 SERIAL #'d SETS		

	MINT	NRMT
❑ GL1 Michael Jordan	15.00	6.75
❑ GL2 Shaquille O'Neal	6.00	2.70
❑ GL3 Kobe Bryant	10.00	4.50
❑ GL4 Antoine Walker	2.00	.90
❑ GL5 Charles Barkley	2.00	.90
❑ GL6 Keith Van Horn	3.00	1.35
❑ GL7 Tim Duncan	6.00	2.70
❑ GL8 Stephon Marbury	3.00	1.35
❑ GL9 Shareef Abdur-Rahim	3.00	1.35
❑ GL10 Gary Payton	2.00	.90

1998-99 Topps Kick Start

	MINT	NRMT
COMPLETE SET (15)	30.00	13.50
COMMON CARD (KS1-KS15)	.60	.25
SER.2 STATED ODDS 1:12 HOB/RET		

	MINT	NRMT
❑ KS1 Tim Duncan	5.00	2.20
❑ KS2 Kobe Bryant	8.00	3.60
❑ KS3 Antoine Walker	1.50	.70
❑ KS4 Stephon Marbury	2.50	1.10
❑ KS5 Allen Iverson	4.00	1.80
❑ KS6 Shareef Abdur-Rahim	2.50	1.10
❑ KS7 Keith Van Horn	2.50	1.10
❑ KS8 Ray Allen	1.25	.55
❑ KS9 Vince Carter	12.00	5.50
❑ KS10 Kevin Garnett	6.00	2.70
❑ KS11 Kerry Kittles	.60	.25
❑ KS12 Tim Thomas	1.50	.70
❑ KS13 Ron Mercer	1.50	.70
❑ KS14 Antawn Jamison	2.50	1.10
❑ KS15 Mike Bibby	1.50	.70

1998-99 Topps Legacies

	MINT	NRMT
COMPLETE SET (15)	60.00	27.00
COMMON CARD (L1-L15)	1.25	.55
UNLISTED STARS	2.00	.90
SER.2 STATED ODDS 1:36 HOBBY		

	MINT	NRMT
❑ L1 Scottie Pippen	6.00	2.70
❑ L2 Grant Hill	10.00	4.50
❑ L3 Hakeem Olajuwon	3.00	1.35
❑ L4 Alonzo Mourning	2.00	.90
❑ L5 Shaquille O'Neal	10.00	4.50
❑ L6 Shawn Kemp	3.00	1.35
❑ L7 Gary Payton	3.00	1.35
❑ L8 Karl Malone	2.50	1.10
❑ L9 Patrick Ewing	2.00	.90
❑ L10 Tim Hardaway	2.00	.90
❑ L11 Reggie Miller	2.00	.90
❑ L12 Glen Rice	1.25	.55
❑ L13 Dikembe Mutombo	1.25	.55
❑ L14 John Stockton	2.00	.90
❑ L15 Michael Jordan	25.00	11.00

1998-99 Topps Roundball Royalty

	MINT	NRMT
COMPLETE SET (20)	125.00	55.00
COMMON CARD (R1-R20)	1.50	.70
UNLISTED STARS	2.50	1.10
SER.1 STATED ODDS 1:36 HOB/RET		
COMP.REF.SET (20)	250.00	110.00
COMMON REF (R1-R20)	3.00	1.35
*REF: .75X TO 2X HI COLUMN		
REF: SER.1 STATED ODDS 1:144 HOB/RET		

	MINT	NRMT
❑ R1 Michael Jordan	30.00	13.50
❑ R2 Kevin Garnett	15.00	6.75
❑ R3 David Robinson	4.00	1.80
❑ R4 Allen Iverson	10.00	4.50
❑ R5 Hakeem Olajuwon	4.00	1.80
❑ R6 Anfernee Hardaway	8.00	3.60
❑ R7 Gary Payton	4.00	1.80
❑ R8 Scottie Pippen	8.00	3.60
❑ R9 Shaquille O'Neal	12.00	5.50
❑ R10 Mitch Richmond	2.50	1.10
❑ R11 John Stockton	2.50	1.10
❑ R12 Grant Hill	12.00	5.50
❑ R13 Charles Barkley	4.00	1.80
❑ R14 Dikembe Mutombo	1.50	.70
❑ R15 Karl Malone	4.00	1.80
❑ R16 Shawn Kemp	4.00	1.80
❑ R17 Patrick Ewing	2.50	1.10
❑ R18 Kobe Bryant	20.00	9.00
❑ R19 Terrell Brandon	1.50	.70
❑ R20 Vin Baker	2.20	1.10

1998-99 Topps Season's Best

	MINT	NRMT
COMPLETE SET (30)	60.00	27.00
COMMON CARD (SB1-SB30)	.75	.35
SEMISTARS	1.00	.45
UNLISTED STARS	1.50	.70
SER.1 STATED ODDS 1:12 HOB/RET		

Card	Player	Mint	NRMT
SB1	Rod Strickland	1.00	.45
SB2	Gary Payton	2.50	1.10
SB3	Tim Hardaway	1.50	.70
SB4	Stephon Marbury	4.00	1.80
SB5	Sam Cassell	1.00	.45
SB6	Michael Jordan	20.00	9.00
SB7	Mitch Richmond	1.50	.70
SB8	Steve Smith	1.00	.45
SB9	Ray Allen	2.00	.90
SB10	Isaiah Rider	1.00	.45
SB11	Grant Hill	8.00	3.60
SB12	Kevin Garnett	10.00	4.50
SB13	Shareef Abdur-Rahim	4.00	1.80
SB14	Glenn Robinson	1.00	.45
SB15	Michael Finley	1.50	.70
SB16	Karl Malone	2.50	1.10
SB17	Tim Duncan	8.00	3.60
SB18	Antoine Walker	2.50	1.10
SB19	Chris Webber	5.00	2.20
SB20	Vin Baker	1.00	.45
SB21	Shaquille O'Neal	8.00	3.60
SB22	David Robinson	2.50	1.10
SB23	Alonzo Mourning	1.50	.70
SB24	Dikembe Mutombo	1.00	.45
SB25	Hakeem Olajuwon	2.50	1.10
SB26	Tim Duncan	8.00	3.60
SB27	Keith Van Horn	4.00	1.80
SB28	Zydrunas Ilgauskas	.75	.35
SB29	Brevin Knight	.75	.35
SB30	Bobby Jackson	.75	.35

1999-00 Topps

	MINT	NRMT
COMPLETE SET (257)	70.00	32.00
COMPLETE SERIES 1 (120)	30.00	13.50
COMPLETE SERIES 2 (137)	40.00	18.00
COMP.SERIES 1 w/o SP (110)	12.00	5.50
COMP.SERIES 2 w/o SP (110)	10.00	4.50
COMMON CARD (1-257)	.10	.05
COMMON RC (111-120/231-248)	.60	.25
COMMON USA (249-257)	.30	.14
SEMISTARS	.15	.07
SEMISTARS RC	.75	.35
UNLISTED STARS	.25	.11
UNLISTED STARS RC	1.00	.45

SER.1/2 RC STATED ODDS 1:5 HOB/RET
USA STATED ODDS 1:5 HOB/RET

Card	Player	Mint	NRMT
1	Steve Smith	.15	.07
2	Ron Harper	.15	.07
3	Michael Dickerson	.25	.11
4	LaPhonso Ellis	.10	.05
5	Chris Webber	.75	.35
6	Jason Caffey	.10	.05
7	Bryon Russell	.10	.05
8	Bison Dele	.10	.05
9	Isaiah Rider	.15	.07
10	Dean Garrett	.10	.05
11	Eric Murdock	.10	.05
12	Juwan Howard	.15	.07
13	Latrell Sprewell	.50	.23
14	Jalen Rose	.25	.11
15	Larry Johnson	.15	.07
16	Eric Williams	.10	.05
17	Bryant Reeves	.10	.05
18	Tony Battie	.10	.05
19	Luc Longley	.10	.05
20	Gary Payton	.40	.18
21	Tariq Abdul-Wahad	.10	.05
22	Armen Gilliam UER should be Armon	.10	.05
23	Shaquille O'Neal	1.25	.55
24	Gary Trent	.10	.05
25	John Stockton	.25	.11
26	Mark Jackson	.10	.05
27	Cherokee Parks	.10	.05
28	Michael Olowokandi	.15	.07
29	Raef LaFrentz	.25	.11
30	Dell Curry	.10	.05
31	Travis Best	.10	.05
32	Shawn Kemp	.40	.18
33	Voshon Lenard	.10	.05
34	Brian Grant	.15	.07
35	Alvin Williams	.10	.05
36	Derek Fisher	.15	.07
37	Allan Houston	.25	.11
38	Arvydas Sabonis	.15	.07
39	Terry Cummings	.10	.05
40	Dale Ellis	.10	.05
41	Maurice Taylor	.25	.11
42	Grant Hill	1.25	.55
43	Anthony Mason	.15	.07
44	John Wallace	.10	.05
45	David Wesley	.10	.05
46	Nick Van Exel	.15	.07
47	Cuttino Mobley	.25	.11
48	Anfernee Hardaway	.75	.35
49	Terry Porter	.10	.05
50	Brent Barry	.10	.05
51	Derek Harper	.15	.07
52	Antoine Walker	.30	.14
53	Karl Malone	.40	.18
54	Ben Wallace	.10	.05
55	Vlade Divac	.10	.05
56	Sam Mitchell	.10	.05
57	Joe Smith	.15	.07
58	Shawn Bradley	.10	.05
59	Darrell Armstrong	.15	.07
60	Kenny Anderson	.15	.07
61	Jason Williams	.60	.25
62	Alonzo Mourning	.25	.11
63	Matt Harpring	.10	.05
64	Antonio Davis	.10	.05
65	Lindsey Hunter	.10	.05
66	Allen Iverson	1.00	.45
67	Mookie Blaylock	.10	.05
68	Wesley Person	.10	.05
69	Bobby Phills	.10	.05
70	Theo Ratliff	.10	.05
71	Antonio Daniels	.10	.05
72	P.J. Brown	.10	.05
73	David Robinson	.40	.18
74	Sean Elliott	.10	.05
75	Zydrunas Ilgauskas	.10	.05
76	Kerry Kittles	.15	.07
77	Otis Thorpe	.10	.05
78	John Starks	.10	.05
79	Jaren Jackson	.10	.05
80	Hersey Hawkins	.15	.07
81	Glenn Robinson	.15	.07
82	Paul Pierce	.50	.23
83	Glen Rice	.15	.07
84	Charlie Ward	.10	.05
85	Dee Brown	.10	.05
86	Danny Fortson	.10	.05
87	Billy Owens	.10	.05
88	Jason Kidd	.75	.35
89	Brent Price	.10	.05
90	Don Reid	.10	.05
91	Mark Bryant	.10	.05
92	Vinny Del Negro	.10	.05
93	Stephon Marbury	.50	.23
94	Donyell Marshall	.10	.05
95	Jim Jackson	.10	.05
96	Horace Grant	.15	.07
97	Calbert Cheaney	.10	.05
98	Vince Carter	2.50	1.10
99	Bobby Jackson	.10	.05
100	Alan Henderson	.10	.05
101	Mike Bibby	.30	.14
102	Cedric Henderson	.10	.05
103	Lamond Murray	.10	.05
104	A.C. Green	.15	.07
105	Hakeem Olajuwon	.40	.18
106	George Lynch	.10	.05
107	Kendall Gill	.15	.07
108	Rex Chapman	.10	.05
109	Eddie Jones	.50	.23
110	Kornel David RC	.10	.05
111	Jason Terry RC	1.50	.70
112	Corey Maggette RC	4.00	1.80
113	Ron Artest RC	2.50	1.10
114	Richard Hamilton RC	2.50	1.10
115	Elton Brand RC	10.00	4.50
116	Baron Davis RC	2.50	1.10
117	Wally Szczerbiak RC	4.00	1.80
118	Steve Francis RC	12.00	5.50
119	James Posey RC	2.00	.90
120	Shawn Marion RC	3.00	1.35
121	Tim Duncan	1.25	.55
122	Danny Manning	.15	.07
123	Chris Mullin	.25	.11
124	Antawn Jamison	.50	.23
125	Kobe Bryant	2.00	.90
126	Matt Geiger	.10	.05
127	Rod Strickland	.15	.07
128	Howard Eisley	.10	.05
129	Steve Nash	.10	.05
130	Felipe Lopez	.10	.05
131	Ron Mercer	.30	.14
132	Ruben Patterson	.25	.11
133	Dana Barros	.10	.05
134	Dale Davis	.10	.05
135	Charles Outlaw	.10	.05
136	Shandon Anderson	.10	.05
137	Mitch Richmond	.25	.11
138	Doug Christie	.10	.05
139	Rasheed Wallace	.25	.11
140	Chris Childs	.10	.05
141	Jamal Mashburn	.15	.07
142	Terrell Brandon	.15	.07
143	Jamie Feick RC	.60	.25
144	Robert Traylor	.10	.05
145	Rick Fox	.10	.05
146	Charles Barkley	.40	.18
147	Tyrone Nesby RC	.10	.05
148	Jerry Stackhouse	.15	.07
149	Cedric Ceballos	.10	.05
150	Dikembe Mutombo	.15	.07
151	Anthony Peeler	.10	.05
152	Larry Hughes	.60	.25
153	Clifford Robinson	.10	.05
154	Corliss Williamson	.10	.05
155	Olden Polynice	.10	.05
156	Avery Johnson	.10	.05
157	Tracy Murray	.10	.05
158	Tom Gugliotta	.15	.07
159	Tim Thomas	.30	.14
160	Reggie Miller	.25	.11
161	Tim Hardaway	.25	.11
162	Dan Majerle	.15	.07
163	Will Perdue	.10	.05
164	Brevin Knight	.10	.05
165	Elden Campbell	.10	.05
166	Chris Gatling	.10	.05
167	Walter McCarty	.10	.05
168	Chauncey Billups	.10	.05
169	Chris Mills	.10	.05
170	Christian Laettner	.15	.07
171	Robert Pack	.10	.05
172	Rik Smits	.10	.05
173	Tyrone Hill	.10	.05
174	Damon Stoudamire	.25	.11
175	Nick Anderson	.10	.05
176	Predrag Stojakovic	.15	.07
177	Vladimir Stepania	.10	.05
178	Tracy McGrady	.75	.35
179	Adam Keefe	.10	.05
180	Shareef Abdur-Rahim	.50	.23
181	Isaac Austin	.10	.05
182	Mario Elie	.10	.05
183	Rashard Lewis	.40	.18
184	Scott Burrell	.10	.05
185	Othella Harrington	.10	.05
186	Eric Piatkowski	.10	.05
187	Bryant Stith	.10	.05
188	Michael Finley	.25	.11
189	Chris Crawford	.10	.05

❑ 190 Toni Kukoc .30 .14
❑ 191 Danny Ferry .10 .05
❑ 192 Erick Dampier .10 .05
❑ 193 Clarence Weatherspoon .10 .05
❑ 194 Bob Sura .10 .05
❑ 195 Jayson Williams .15 .07
❑ 196 Kurt Thomas .10 .05
❑ 197 Greg Anthony .10 .05
❑ 198 Rodney Rogers .10 .05
❑ 199 Detlef Schrempf .15 .07
❑ 200 Keith Van Horn .50 .23
❑ 201 Robert Horry .10 .05
❑ 202 Sam Cassell .15 .07
❑ 203 Malik Sealy .10 .05
❑ 204 Kelvin Cato .10 .05
❑ 205 Antonio McDyess .25 .11
❑ 206 Andrew DeClercq .10 .05
❑ 207 Ricky Davis .25 .11
❑ 208 Vitaly Potapenko .10 .05
❑ 209 Loy Vaught .10 .05
❑ 210 Kevin Garnett 1.50 .70
❑ 211 Eric Snow .10 .05
❑ 212 Anfernee Hardaway .75 .35
❑ 213 Vin Baker .15 .07
❑ 214 Lawrence Funderburke .10 .05
❑ 215 Jeff Hornacek .15 .07
❑ 216 Doug West .10 .05
❑ 217 Michael Doleac .10 .05
❑ 218 Ray Allen .25 .11
❑ 219 Derek Anderson .25 .11
❑ 220 Jerome Williams .15 .07
❑ 221 Derrick Coleman .15 .07
❑ 222 Randy Brown .10 .05
❑ 223 Patrick Ewing .25 .11
❑ 224 Walt Williams .10 .05
❑ 225 Charles Oakley .10 .05
❑ 226 Steve Kerr .10 .05
❑ 227 Muggsy Bogues .10 .05
❑ 228 Kevin Willis .10 .05
❑ 229 Marcus Camby .25 .11
❑ 230 Scottie Pippen .75 .35
❑ 231 Lamar Odom RC 8.00 3.60
❑ 232 Jonathan Bender RC 5.00 2.20
❑ 233 Andre Miller RC 3.00 1.35
❑ 234 Trajan Langdon RC 1.50 .70
❑ 235 Aleksandar Radojevic RC .60 .25
❑ 236 William Avery RC 1.50 .70
❑ 237 Cal Bowdler RC 1.00 .45
❑ 238 Quincy Lewis RC 1.00 .45
❑ 239 Dion Glover RC 1.00 .45
❑ 240 Jeff Foster RC 1.00 .45
❑ 241 Kenny Thomas RC 1.50 .70
❑ 242 Devean George RC 2.00 .90
❑ 243 Tim James RC 1.25 .55
❑ 244 Vonteego Cummings RC 1.50 .70
❑ 245 Jumaine Jones RC .60 .25
❑ 246 Scott Padgett RC 1.00 .45
❑ 247 Adrian Griffin RC 1.25 .55
❑ 248 Chris Herren RC .60 .25
❑ 249 Allan Houston USA .50 .23
❑ 250 Kevin Garnett USA 3.00 1.35
❑ 251 Gary Payton USA .75 .35
❑ 252 Steve Smith USA .30 .14
❑ 253 Tim Hardaway USA .50 .23
❑ 254 Tim Duncan USA 2.50 1.10
❑ 255 Jason Kidd USA 1.50 .70
❑ 256 Tom Gugliotta USA .30 .14
❑ 257 Vin Baker USA .30 .14

1999-00 Topps MVP Promotion

	MINT	NRMT
COMMON CARD (1-248)	5.00	2.20

*MVP STARS: 20X TO 50X BASE CARD HI
*MVP RCs: 2X TO 5X BASE HI
SER.1 STATED ODDS 1:336
SER.2 STATED ODDS 1:172
STATED PRINT RUN 100 SETS

❑ 5 Chris Webber W 60.00 27.00
❑ 23 Shaquille O'Neal W 60.00 27.00
❑ 42 Grant Hill W 60.00 27.00
❑ 43 Anthony Mason W 60.00 27.00
❑ 53 Karl Malone W 60.00 27.00

❑ 62 Alonzo Mourning W 60.00 27.00
❑ 66 Allen Iverson W 60.00 27.00
❑ 88 Jason Kidd W 60.00 27.00
❑ 93 Stephon Marbury W 60.00 27.00
❑ 98 Vince Carter W 80.00 36.00
❑ 109 Eddie Jones W 60.00 27.00
❑ 118 Steve Francis W 60.00 27.00
❑ 121 Tim Duncan W 60.00 27.00
❑ 125 Kobe Bryant W 60.00 27.00
❑ 142 Terrell Brandon W 60.00 27.00
❑ 188 Michael Finley W 60.00 27.00
❑ 202 Sam Cassell W 60.00 27.00
❑ 210 Kevin Garnett W 60.00 27.00

1999-00 Topps MVP Promotion Exchange

	MINT	NRMT
COMPLETE SET (22)	60.00	27.00
COMMON CARD (MVP1-22)	.75	.35

ONE SET VIA MAIL PER MVP WINNER

❑ MVP1 Allen Iverson 5.00 2.20
❑ MVP2 Alonzo Mourning 1.25 .55
❑ MVP3 Anthony Mason .75 .35
❑ MVP4 Chris Webber 4.00 1.80
❑ MVP5 Eddie Jones 2.50 1.10
❑ MVP6 Grant Hill 6.00 2.70
❑ MVP7 Jason Kidd 4.00 1.80
❑ MVP8 Karl Malone 2.00 .90
❑ MVP9 Kevin Garnett 8.00 3.60
❑ MVP10 Kobe Bryant 10.00 4.50
❑ MVP11 Michael Finley 1.00 .45
❑ MVP12 Sam Cassell .75 .35
❑ MVP13 Shaquille O'Neal 6.00 2.70
❑ MVP14 Stephon Marbury 2.50 1.10
❑ MVP15 Terrell Brandon .75 .35
❑ MVP16 Tim Duncan 6.00 2.70
❑ MVP17 Vince Carter 12.00 5.50
❑ MVP18 Steve Francis 8.00 3.60
❑ MVP19 Elton Brand 6.00 2.70
Steve Francis
❑ MVP20 Shaquille O'Neal 6.00 2.70
❑ MVP21 Reggie Miller 1.25 .55
❑ MVP22 Shaquille O'Neal 6.00 2.70

1999-00 Topps 21st Century Topps

	MINT	NRMT
COMPLETE SET (16)	30.00	13.50
COMMON CARD (C1-C16)	.75	.35
UNLISTED STARS	1.50	.70

SER.2 STATED ODDS 1:27 HOB/RET

❑ C1 Jason Terry 1.50 .70
❑ C2 Baron Davis 2.00 .90
❑ C3 Lamar Odom 6.00 2.70
❑ C4 Jonathan Bender 4.00 1.80
❑ C5 Ron Artest 2.00 .90
❑ C6 Richard Hamilton 2.00 .90
❑ C7 Andre Miller 2.50 1.10
❑ C8 Shawn Marion 2.50 1.10
❑ C9 Steve Francis 10.00 4.50
❑ C10 Elton Brand 8.00 3.60
❑ C11 Wally Szczerbiak 3.00 1.35
❑ C12 Corey Maggette 3.00 1.35
❑ C13 James Posey 1.50 .70
❑ C14 Trajan Langdon 1.50 .70
❑ C15 Tim James 1.50 .70
❑ C16 Cal Bowdler .75 .35

1999-00 Topps All-Matrix

	MINT	NRMT
COMPLETE SET (30)	100.00	45.00
COMMON CARD (AM1-AM30)	1.25	.55
UNLISTED STARS	1.50	.70

SER.2 STATED ODDS 1:15 HOB/RET

❑ AM1 Karl Malone 2.50 1.10
❑ AM2 Scottie Pippen 5.00 2.20
❑ AM3 Grant Hill 8.00 3.60
❑ AM4 Shawn Kemp 2.50 1.10
❑ AM5 Shaquille O'Neal 8.00 3.60
❑ AM6 Anfernee Hardaway 5.00 2.20
❑ AM7 Chris Webber 5.00 2.20
❑ AM8 Gary Payton 2.50 1.10
❑ AM9 Jason Kidd 5.00 2.20
❑ AM10 John Stockton 1.50 .70
❑ AM11 Kevin Garnett 10.00 4.50
❑ AM12 Vince Carter 15.00 6.75
❑ AM13 Shareef Abdur-Rahim 3.00 1.35
❑ AM14 Antoine Walker 2.00 .90
❑ AM15 Kobe Bryant 12.00 5.50

		MINT	NRMT
❑ AM16	Tim Duncan	8.00	3.60
❑ AM17	Keith Van Horn	3.00	1.35
❑ AM18	Allen Iverson	6.00	2.70
❑ AM19	Jason Williams	4.00	1.80
❑ AM20	Stephon Marbury	3.00	1.35
❑ AM21	Elton Brand	8.00	3.60
❑ AM22	Jason Terry	1.25	.55
❑ AM23	Steve Francis	10.00	4.50
❑ AM24	Corey Maggette	3.00	1.35
❑ AM25	Lamar Odom	6.00	2.70
❑ AM26	Ron Artest	2.00	.90
❑ AM27	Baron Davis	2.00	.90
❑ AM28	Andre Miller	2.50	1.10
❑ AM29	Shawn Marion	2.50	1.10
❑ AM30	Wally Szczerbiak	3.00	1.35

1999-00 Topps Autographs

	MINT	NRMT
COMPLETE SET (21)	350.00	160.00
COMPLETE SERIES 1 (9)	150.00	70.00
COMPLETE SERIES 2 (12)	200.00	90.00
COMMON CARD	6.00	2.70
SEMISTARS	10.00	4.50

SER.1 STATED ODDS 1:877 (A) HOB
SER.1 STATED ODDS 1:351 (B) HOB
SER.2 STATED ODDS 1:196 (A/B) HOB
SER.2 OVERALL STATED ODDS 1:98 H

		MINT	NRMT
❑ AM	Antonio McDyess A	12.00	5.50
❑ AM2	Antonio McDyess B	12.00	5.50
❑ AW	Antoine Walker A	20.00	9.00
❑ BD	Baron Davis A	15.00	6.75
❑ CM	Corey Maggette A	25.00	11.00
❑ DS	Damon Stoudamire A	15.00	6.75
❑ EB	Elton Brand B	50.00	22.00
❑ GP	Gary Payton B	25.00	11.00
❑ GP2	Gary Payton A	25.00	11.00
❑ JJ	Jumaine Jones A	6.00	2.70
❑ JK	Jason Kidd A	60.00	27.00
❑ MR	Mitch Richmond A	12.00	5.50
❑ PP	Paul Pierce B	30.00	13.50
❑ SF	Steve Francis B	60.00	27.00
❑ SP	Scottie Pippen B	80.00	36.00
❑ SS	Steve Smith B	12.00	5.50
❑ TD	Tim Duncan A	80.00	36.00
❑ TG	Tom Gugliotta B	6.00	2.70
❑ WA	William Avery A	6.00	2.70
❑ WS	Wally Szczerbiak A	25.00	11.00
❑ SAR	Shareef Abdur-Rahim B	25.00	11.00

1999-00 Topps Highlight Reels

	MINT	NRMT
COMPLETE SET (15)	30.00	13.50
COMMON CARD (HR1-HR15)	1.00	.45

SER.1 STATED ODDS 1:14 RETAIL

		MINT	NRMT
❑ HR1	Stephon Marbury	2.00	.90
❑ HR2	Vince Carter	10.00	4.50
❑ HR3	Kevin Garnett	6.00	2.70
❑ HR4	Kobe Bryant	8.00	3.60
❑ HR5	Chris Webber	3.00	1.35
❑ HR6	Allen Iverson	4.00	1.80
❑ HR7	Grant Hill	5.00	2.20

		MINT	NRMT
❑ HR8	Antoine Walker	1.25	.55
❑ HR9	Jason Williams	2.50	1.10
❑ HR10	Tim Duncan	5.00	2.20
❑ HR11	Shareef Abdur-Rahim	2.00	.90
❑ HR12	Keith Van Horn	2.00	.90
❑ HR13	Antonio McDyess	1.00	.45
❑ HR14	Jason Kidd	3.00	1.35
❑ HR15	Ron Mercer	1.25	.55

1999-00 Topps Impact

	MINT	NRMT
COMPLETE SET (20)	80.00	36.00
COMMON CARD (I1-I20)	1.25	.55

SER.2 STATED ODDS 1:24 HOB/RET

	MINT	NRMT
COMP.REF.SET (20)	200.00	90.00
COMMON REF (I1-I20)	3.00	1.35

*REF: 1X TO 2.5X HI COLUMN
REF: SER.2 STATED ODDS 1:120 H/R

		MINT	NRMT
❑ I1	Elton Brand	8.00	3.60
❑ I2	Lamar Odom	6.00	2.70
❑ I3	Wally Szczerbiak	3.00	1.35
❑ I4	Jason Terry	1.25	.55
❑ I5	Baron Davis	2.00	.90
❑ I6	Ron Artest	2.00	.90
❑ I7	Steve Francis	10.00	4.50
❑ I8	Andre Miller	2.50	1.10
❑ I9	Allen Iverson	6.00	2.70
❑ I10	Jason Williams	4.00	1.80
❑ I11	Keith Van Horn	3.00	1.35
❑ I12	Vince Carter	15.00	6.75
❑ I13	Kobe Bryant	12.00	5.50
❑ I14	Tim Duncan	8.00	3.60
❑ I15	Scottie Pippen	5.00	2.20
❑ I16	Kevin Garnett	10.00	4.50
❑ I17	Shaquille O'Neal	8.00	3.60
❑ I18	Gary Payton	2.50	1.10
❑ I19	Karl Malone	2.50	1.10
❑ I20	Grant Hill	8.00	3.60

1999-00 Topps Jumbos

	MINT	NRMT
COMPLETE SET (8)	10.00	4.50
COMMON CARD (1-8)	.60	.25

ONE PER SER.1 HOBBY BOX

		MINT	NRMT
❑ 1	Gary Payton	1.00	.45
❑ 2	Shaquille O'Neal	3.00	1.35
❑ 3	Antoine Walker	.75	.35

		MINT	NRMT
❑ 4	Jason Williams	1.50	.70
❑ 5	Alonzo Mourning	.60	.25
❑ 6	Allen Iverson	2.50	1.10
❑ 7	Stephon Marbury	1.25	.55
❑ 8	Vince Carter	6.00	2.70

1999-00 Topps Own the Game

	MINT	NRMT
COMPLETE SET (10)	30.00	13.50
COMMON CARD (OTG1-10)	.50	.23
SEMISTARS	1.00	.45

SER.2 STATED ODDS 1:44 HOB/RET

		MINT	NRMT
❑ OTG1	Allen Iverson	6.00	2.70
❑ OTG2	Shaquille O'Neal	8.00	3.60
❑ OTG3	Jason Kidd	5.00	2.20
❑ OTG4	Stephon Marbury	3.00	1.35
❑ OTG5	Dikembe Mutombo	1.00	.45
❑ OTG6	Tim Duncan	8.00	3.60
❑ OTG7	Wally Szczerbiak	3.00	1.35
❑ OTG8	Quincy Lewis	1.00	.45
❑ OTG9	Elton Brand	8.00	3.60
❑ OTG10	Aleksandar Radojevic	.50	.23

1999-00 Topps Patriarchs

	MINT	NRMT
COMPLETE SET (15)	25.00	11.00
COMMON CARD (P1-P15)	.75	.35

UNLISTED STARS	1.25	.55
SER.1 STATED ODDS 1:22 HOB/RET		

❑ P1 Patrick Ewing	1.25	.55
❑ P2 Reggie Miller	1.25	.55
❑ P3 Hakeem Olajuwon	2.00	.90
❑ P4 Scottie Pippen	4.00	1.80
❑ P5 Grant Hill	6.00	2.70
❑ P6 Shaquille O'Neal	6.00	2.70
❑ P7 Mitch Richmond	1.25	.55
❑ P8 Glen Rice	.75	.35
❑ P9 Charles Barkley	2.00	.90
❑ P10 Karl Malone	2.00	.90
❑ P11 John Stockton	1.25	.55
❑ P12 Gary Payton	2.00	.90
❑ P13 David Robinson	2.00	.90
❑ P14 Tim Hardaway	1.25	.55
❑ P15 Joe Dumars	.75	.35

1999-00 Topps Picture Perfect

	MINT	NRMT
COMPLETE SET (10)	5.00	2.20
COMMON CARD (PIC1-10)	.25	.11
UNLISTED STARS	.40	.18
SER.1 STATED ODDS 1:8 HOB/RET		

❑ PIC1 Shaquille O'Neal	2.00	.90
❑ PIC2 Alonzo Mourning	.40	.18
❑ PIC3 Shareef Abdur-Rahim	.75	.35
❑ PIC4 Juwan Howard	.25	.11
❑ PIC5 Keith Van Horn	.75	.35
❑ PIC6 Ron Mercer	.50	.23
❑ PIC7 Tim Hardaway	.40	.18
❑ PIC8 Kevin Garnett	2.50	1.10
❑ PIC9 David Robinson	.60	.25
❑ PIC10 Kerry Kittles	.25	.11

1999-00 Topps Prodigy

	MINT	NRMT
COMPLETE SET (20)	80.00	36.00
COMMON CARD (PR1-PR20)	1.50	.70
UNLISTED STARS	2.50	1.10
SER.1 STATED ODDS 1:36 HOB/RET		
COMP.REF.SET (20)	150.00	70.00
COMMON REF (PR1-PR20)	3.00	1.35
*REF: .75X TO 2X HI COLUMN		
REF: SER.1 STATED ODDS 1:144 H/R		

❑ PR1 Stephon Marbury	5.00	2.20
❑ PR2 Jason Kidd	8.00	3.60
❑ PR3 Kevin Garnett	15.00	6.75
❑ PR4 Kobe Bryant	20.00	9.00
❑ PR5 Antoine Walker	3.00	1.35
❑ PR6 Ron Mercer	3.00	1.35
❑ PR7 Shareef Abdur-Rahim	5.00	2.20
❑ PR8 Tim Duncan	12.00	5.50
❑ PR9 Keith Van Horn	5.00	2.20
❑ PR10 Ray Allen	2.50	1.10
❑ PR11 Michael Doleac	1.50	.70
❑ PR12 Jason Williams	6.00	2.70
❑ PR13 Michael Dickerson	2.50	1.10
❑ PR14 Mike Bibby	3.00	1.35
❑ PR15 Paul Pierce	5.00	2.20
❑ PR16 Michael Olowokandi	1.50	.70
❑ PR17 Vince Carter	25.00	11.00
❑ PR18 Antawn Jamison	5.00	2.20
❑ PR19 Felipe Lopez	1.50	.70
❑ PR20 Matt Harpring	1.50	.70

1999-00 Topps Record Numbers

	MINT	NRMT
COMPLETE SET (10)	10.00	4.50
COMMON CARD (RN1-RN10)	.40	.18
UNLISTED STARS	.60	.25
SER.1 STATED ODDS 1:12 HOB/RET		

❑ RN1 Karl Malone	1.00	.45
❑ RN2 Kerry Kittles	.40	.18
❑ RN3 Reggie Miller	.60	.25
❑ RN4 Hakeem Olajuwon	1.00	.45
❑ RN5 John Stockton	.60	.25
❑ RN6 Dikembe Mutombo	.40	.18
❑ RN7 Kobe Bryant	5.00	2.20
❑ RN8 Tim Duncan	3.00	1.35
❑ RN9 Allen Iverson	2.50	1.10
❑ RN10 Patrick Ewing	.60	.25

1999-00 Topps Season's Best

	MINT	NRMT
COMPLETE SET (30)	60.00	27.00
COMMON CARD (SB1-SB30)	.60	.25
UNLISTED STARS	1.00	.45
SER.1 STATED ODDS 1:12 HOB/RET		

❑ SB1 David Robinson	1.50	.70
❑ SB2 Shaquille O'Neal	5.00	2.20
❑ SB3 Patrick Ewing	1.00	.45
❑ SB4 Hakeem Olajuwon	1.50	.70
❑ SB5 Alonzo Mourning	1.00	.45
❑ SB6 Antonio McDyess	1.00	.45
❑ SB7 Tim Duncan	5.00	2.20
❑ SB8 Keith Van Horn	2.00	.90
❑ SB9 Karl Malone	1.50	.70
❑ SB10 Chris Webber	3.00	1.35
❑ SB11 Kevin Garnett	6.00	2.70
❑ SB12 Juwan Howard	.60	.25
❑ SB13 Shareef Abdur-Rahim	2.00	.90
❑ SB14 Glenn Robinson	1.00	.45
❑ SB15 Grant Hill	5.00	2.20
❑ SB16 Michael Finley	1.00	.45
❑ SB17 Steve Smith	.60	.25
❑ SB18 Mitch Richmond	1.00	.45
❑ SB19 Kobe Bryant	8.00	3.60
❑ SB20 Ray Allen	1.00	.45
❑ SB21 Allen Iverson	4.00	1.80
❑ SB22 Gary Payton	1.50	.70
❑ SB23 Stephon Marbury	2.00	.90
❑ SB24 Jason Kidd	3.00	1.35
❑ SB25 Tim Hardaway	1.00	.45
❑ SB26 Jason Williams	2.50	1.10
❑ SB27 Vince Carter	10.00	4.50
❑ SB28 Paul Pierce	2.00	.90
❑ SB29 Mike Bibby	1.25	.55
❑ SB30 Michael Dickerson	1.00	.45

1999-00 Topps Team Topps

	MINT	NRMT
COMPLETE SET (24)	60.00	27.00
COMMON CARD (TT1-TT24)	1.00	.45
UNLISTED STARS	1.50	.70
SER.2 STATED ODDS 1:18 HOB/RET		

❑ TT1 Gary Payton	2.50	1.10
❑ TT2 Jason Kidd	5.00	2.20
❑ TT3 Kobe Bryant	12.00	5.50
❑ TT4 Anfernee Hardaway	5.00	2.20
❑ TT5 Kevin Garnett	10.00	4.50
❑ TT6 Patrick Ewing	1.50	.70
❑ TT7 Tim Duncan	8.00	3.60
❑ TT8 Karl Malone	2.50	1.10
❑ TT9 Shaquille O'Neal	8.00	3.60
❑ TT10 Charles Barkley	2.50	1.10
❑ TT11 John Stockton	1.50	.70
❑ TT12 Tim Hardaway	1.50	.70
❑ TT13 Hakeem Olajuwon	2.50	1.10
❑ TT14 Jayson Williams	1.00	.45
❑ TT15 Reggie Miller	1.50	.70
❑ TT16 David Robinson	2.50	1.10
❑ TT17 Grant Hill	8.00	3.60
❑ TT18 Scottie Pippen	5.00	2.20
❑ TT19 Chris Webber	5.00	2.20
❑ TT20 Shawn Kemp	2.50	1.10
❑ TT21 Alonzo Mourning	1.50	.70
❑ TT22 Mitch Richmond	1.50	.70
❑ TT23 Antoine Walker	2.00	.90
❑ TT24 Tom Gugliotta	1.00	.45

1996-97 Topps Chrome

	MINT	NRMT
COMPLETE SET (220)	700.00	325.00
COMMON CARD (1-220)	.40	.18
COMMON RC	2.50	1.10
SEMISTARS	.50	.23
SEMISTARS RC	3.00	1.35
UNLISTED STARS	.75	.35
UNLISTED STARS RC	5.00	2.20

CONDITION SENSITIVE SET
BEWARE KOBE COUNTERFEITS

Card	MINT	NRMT
❑ 1 Patrick Ewing	.75	.35
❑ 2 Christian Laettner	.50	.23
❑ 3 Mahmoud Abdul-Rauf	.40	.18
❑ 4 Chris Webber	2.50	1.10
❑ 5 Jason Kidd	2.50	1.10
❑ 6 Clifford Rozier	.40	.18
❑ 7 Elden Campbell	.40	.18
❑ 8 Chuck Person	.40	.18
❑ 9 Jeff Hornacek	.50	.23
❑ 10 Rik Smits	.40	.18
❑ 11 Kurt Thomas	.40	.18
❑ 12 Rod Strickland	.50	.23
❑ 13 Kendall Gill	.50	.23
❑ 14 Brian Williams	.40	.18
❑ 15 Tom Gugliotta	.50	.23
❑ 16 Ron Harper	.50	.23
❑ 17 Eric Williams	.40	.18
❑ 18 A.C. Green	.50	.23
❑ 19 Scott Williams	.40	.18
❑ 20 Damon Stoudamire	1.25	.55
❑ 21 Bryant Reeves	.40	.18
❑ 22 Bob Sura	.40	.18
❑ 23 Mitch Richmond	.75	.35
❑ 24 Larry Johnson	.50	.23
❑ 25 Vin Baker	.50	.23
❑ 26 Mark Bryant	.40	.18
❑ 27 Horace Grant	.50	.23
❑ 28 Allan Houston	.75	.35
❑ 29 Sam Perkins	.50	.23
❑ 30 Antonio McDyess	1.25	.55
❑ 31 Rasheed Wallace	1.00	.45
❑ 32 Malik Sealy	.40	.18
❑ 33 Scottie Pippen	2.50	1.10
❑ 34 Charles Barkley	1.25	.55
❑ 35 Hakeem Olajuwon	1.25	.55
❑ 36 John Starks	.40	.18
❑ 37 Byron Scott	.40	.18
❑ 38 Arvydas Sabonis	.50	.23
❑ 39 Vlade Divac	.40	.18
❑ 40 Joe Dumars	.75	.35
❑ 41 Danny Ferry	.40	.18
❑ 42 Jerry Stackhouse	.75	.35
❑ 43 B.J. Armstrong	.40	.18
❑ 44 Shawn Bradley	.40	.18
❑ 45 Kevin Garnett	6.00	2.70
❑ 46 Dee Brown	.40	.18
❑ 47 Michael Smith	.40	.18
❑ 48 Doug Christie	.40	.18
❑ 49 Mark Jackson	.40	.18
❑ 50 Shawn Kemp	1.25	.55
❑ 51 Sasha Danilovic	.40	.18
❑ 52 Nick Anderson	.40	.18
❑ 53 Matt Geiger	.40	.18
❑ 54 Charles Smith	.40	.18
❑ 55 Mookie Blaylock	.40	.18
❑ 56 Johnny Newman	.40	.18
❑ 57 George McCloud	.40	.18
❑ 58 Greg Ostertag	.40	.18
❑ 59 Reggie Williams	.40	.18
❑ 60 Brent Barry	.40	.18
❑ 61 Doug West	.40	.18
❑ 62 Donald Royal	.40	.18
❑ 63 Randy Brown	.40	.18
❑ 64 Vincent Askew	.40	.18
❑ 65 John Stockton	.75	.35
❑ 66 Joe Kleine	.40	.18
❑ 67 Keith Askins	.40	.18
❑ 68 Bobby Phills	.40	.18
❑ 69 Chris Mullin	.75	.35
❑ 70 Nick Van Exel	.50	.23
❑ 71 Rick Fox	.40	.18
❑ 72 Chicago Bulls - 72 Wins	4.00	1.80
❑ 73 Shawn Respert	.40	.18
❑ 74 Hubert Davis	.40	.18
❑ 75 Jim Jackson	.40	.18
❑ 76 Olden Polynice	.40	.18
❑ 77 Gheorghe Muresan	.40	.18
❑ 78 Theo Ratliff	.50	.23
❑ 79 Khalid Reeves	.40	.18
❑ 80 David Robinson	1.25	.55
❑ 81 Lawrence Moten	.40	.18
❑ 82 Sam Cassell	.50	.23
❑ 83 George Zidek	.40	.18
❑ 84 Sharone Wright	.40	.18
❑ 85 Clarence Weatherspoon	.40	.18
❑ 86 Alan Henderson	.40	.18
❑ 87 Chris Dudley	.40	.18
❑ 88 Ed O'Bannon	.40	.18
❑ 89 Calbert Cheaney	.40	.18
❑ 90 Cedric Ceballos	.40	.18
❑ 91 Michael Cage	.40	.18
❑ 92 Ervin Johnson	.40	.18
❑ 93 Gary Trent	.40	.18
❑ 94 Sherman Douglas	.40	.18
❑ 95 Joe Smith	.75	.35
❑ 96 Dale Davis	.40	.18
❑ 97 Tony Dumas	.40	.18
❑ 98 Muggsy Bogues	.40	.18
❑ 99 Toni Kukoc	1.00	.45
❑ 100 Grant Hill	4.00	1.80
❑ 101 Michael Finley	1.00	.45
❑ 102 Isaiah Rider	.50	.23
❑ 103 Bryant Stith	.40	.18
❑ 104 Pooh Richardson	.40	.18
❑ 105 Karl Malone	1.25	.55
❑ 106 Brian Grant	.75	.35
❑ 107 Sean Elliott	.40	.18
❑ 108 Charles Oakley	.40	.18
❑ 109 Pervis Ellison	.40	.18
❑ 110 Anfernee Hardaway	2.50	1.10
❑ 111 Checklist (1-220)	.40	.18
❑ 112 Dikembe Mutombo	.50	.23
❑ 113 Alonzo Mourning	.75	.35
❑ 114 Hubert Davis	.40	.18
❑ 115 Rony Seikaly	.40	.18
❑ 116 Danny Manning	.50	.23
❑ 117 Donyell Marshall	.40	.18
❑ 118 Gerald Wilkins	.40	.18
❑ 119 Ervin Johnson	.40	.18
❑ 120 Jalen Rose	.75	.35
❑ 121 Dino Radja	.40	.18
❑ 122 Glenn Robinson	.75	.35
❑ 123 John Stockton	.75	.35
❑ 124 Matt Maloney RC	2.50	1.10
❑ 125 Clifford Robinson	.40	.18
❑ 126 Steve Kerr	.40	.18
❑ 127 Nate McMillan	.40	.18
❑ 128 Shareef Abdur-Rahim RC	50.00	22.00
❑ 129 Loy Vaught	.40	.18
❑ 130 Anthony Mason	.50	.23
❑ 131 Kevin Garnett	6.00	2.70
❑ 132 Roy Rogers RC	2.50	1.10
❑ 133 Erick Dampier RC	3.00	1.35
❑ 134 Tyus Edney	.40	.18
❑ 135 Chris Mills	.40	.18
❑ 136 Cory Alexander	.40	.18
❑ 137 Juwan Howard	.50	.23
❑ 138 Kobe Bryant RC	400.00	180.00
❑ 139 Michael Jordan	25.00	11.00
❑ 140 Jayson Williams	.50	.23
❑ 141 Rod Strickland	.50	.23
❑ 142 Lorenzen Wright RC	3.00	1.35
❑ 143 Will Perdue	.40	.18
❑ 144 Derek Harper	.40	.18
❑ 145 Billy Owens	.40	.18
❑ 146 Antoine Walker RC	40.00	18.00
❑ 147 P.J. Brown	.40	.18
❑ 148 Terrell Brandon	.50	.23
❑ 149 Larry Johnson	.50	.23
❑ 150 Steve Smith	.50	.23
❑ 151 Eddie Jones	1.50	.70
❑ 152 Detlef Schrempf	.50	.23
❑ 153 Dale Ellis	.40	.18
❑ 154 Isaiah Rider	.50	.23
❑ 155 Tony Delk RC	3.00	1.35
❑ 156 Adrian Caldwell	.40	.18
❑ 157 Jamal Mashburn	.50	.23
❑ 158 Dennis Scott	.40	.18
❑ 159 Dana Barros	.40	.18
❑ 160 Martin Muursepp RC	2.50	1.10
❑ 161 Marcus Camby RC	15.00	6.75
❑ 162 Jerome Williams RC	10.00	4.50
❑ 163 Wesley Person	.40	.18
❑ 164 Luc Longley	.40	.18
❑ 165 Charlie Ward	.40	.18
❑ 166 Mark Jackson	.40	.18
❑ 167 Derrick Coleman	.50	.23
❑ 168 Dell Curry	.40	.18
❑ 169 Armon Gilliam	.40	.18
❑ 170 Vlade Divac	.40	.18
❑ 171 Allen Iverson RC	120.00	55.00
❑ 172 Vitaly Potapenko RC	2.50	1.10
❑ 173 Jon Koncak	.40	.18
❑ 174 Lindsey Hunter	.40	.18
❑ 175 Kevin Johnson	.50	.23
❑ 176 Dennis Rodman	1.50	.70
❑ 177 Stephon Marbury RC	50.00	22.00
❑ 178 Karl Malone	1.25	.55
❑ 179 Charles Barkley	1.25	.55
❑ 180 Popeye Jones	.40	.18
❑ 181 Samaki Walker RC	2.50	1.10
❑ 182 Steve Nash RC	3.00	1.35
❑ 183 Latrell Sprewell	1.50	.70
❑ 184 Kenny Anderson	.50	.23
❑ 185 Tyrone Hill	.40	.18
❑ 186 Robert Pack	.40	.18
❑ 187 Greg Anthony	.40	.18
❑ 188 Derrick McKey	.40	.18
❑ 189 John Wallace RC	5.00	2.20
❑ 190 Bryon Russell	.40	.18
❑ 191 Jermaine O'Neal RC	15.00	6.75
❑ 192 Clyde Drexler	.75	.35
❑ 193 Mahmoud Abdul-Rauf	.40	.18
❑ 194 Eric Montross	.40	.18
❑ 195 Allan Houston	.75	.35
❑ 196 Harvey Grant	.40	.18
❑ 197 Rodney Rogers	.40	.18
❑ 198 Kerry Kittles RC	8.00	3.60
❑ 199 Grant Hill	4.00	1.80
❑ 200 Lionel Simmons	.40	.18
❑ 201 Reggie Miller	.75	.35
❑ 202 Avery Johnson	.40	.18
❑ 203 LaPhonso Ellis	.40	.18
❑ 204 Brian Shaw	.40	.18
❑ 205 Priest Lauderdale RC	2.50	1.10
❑ 206 Derek Fisher RC	8.00	3.60
❑ 207 Terry Porter	.40	.18
❑ 208 Todd Fuller RC	2.50	1.10
❑ 209 Hersey Hawkins	.50	.23
❑ 210 Tim Legler	.40	.18
❑ 211 Terry Dehere	.40	.18
❑ 212 Gary Payton	1.25	.55
❑ 213 Joe Dumars	.75	.35
❑ 214 Don MacLean	.40	.18
❑ 215 Greg Minor	.40	.18
❑ 216 Tim Hardaway	.75	.35
❑ 217 Ray Allen RC	40.00	18.00
❑ 218 Mario Elie	.40	.18
❑ 219 Brooks Thompson	.40	.18
❑ 220 Shaquille O'Neal	4.00	1.80

1996-97 Topps Chrome Refractors

	MINT	NRMT
COMPLETE SET (220)	4000.00	1800.00

COMMON CARD (1-220) 8.00 3.60
CONDITION SENSITIVE SET
*STARS: 8X TO 20X HI COLUMN
*RCs: 2X TO 5X HI
STATED ODDS 1:12

	MINT	NRMT
❑ 128 Shareef Abdur-Rahim	200.00	90.00
❑ 138 Kobe Bryant	1500.00	700.00
❑ 139 Michael Jordan	300.00	135.00
❑ 146 Antoine Walker	120.00	55.00
❑ 161 Marcus Camby	100.00	45.00
❑ 171 Allen Iverson	400.00	180.00
❑ 177 Stephon Marbury	200.00	90.00
❑ 217 Ray Allen	150.00	70.00

1996-97 Topps Chrome Pro Files

	MINT	NRMT
COMPLETE SET (20)	40.00	18.00
COMMON CARD (PF1-PF20)	.75	.35
SEMISTARS	1.25	.55

STATED ODDS 1:8

	MINT	NRMT
❑ PF1 Grant Hill	6.00	2.70
❑ PF2 Shawn Kemp	2.00	.90
❑ PF3 Michael Jordan	15.00	6.75
❑ PF4 Vin Baker	1.25	.55
❑ PF5 Chris Webber	4.00	1.80
❑ PF6 Joe Smith	1.25	.55
❑ PF7 Shaquille O'Neal	6.00	2.70
❑ PF8 Patrick Ewing	1.25	.55
❑ PF9 Scottie Pippen	4.00	1.80
❑ PF10 Damon Stoudamire	2.00	.90
❑ PF11 Anfernee Hardaway	4.00	1.80
❑ PF12 Juwan Howard	1.25	.55
❑ PF13 Dikembe Mutombo	.75	.35
❑ PF14 Dennis Rodman	2.50	1.10
❑ PF15 Kevin Garnett	8.00	3.60
❑ PF16 Jerry Stackhouse	1.25	.55
❑ PF17 Alonzo Mourning	1.25	.55
❑ PF18 Karl Malone	2.00	.90
❑ PF19 Hakeem Olajuwon	2.00	.90
❑ PF20 Gary Payton	2.00	.90

1996-97 Topps Chrome Season's Best

	MINT	NRMT
COMPLETE SET (25)	40.00	18.00
COMMON CARD (SB1-SB25)	.40	.18
SEMISTARS	.75	.35
UNLISTED STARS	1.25	.55

STATED ODDS 1:6

	MINT	NRMT
❑ SB1 Michael Jordan	15.00	6.75
❑ SB2 Hakeem Olajuwon	2.00	.90
❑ SB3 Shaquille O'Neal	6.00	2.70
❑ SB4 Karl Malone	2.00	.90
❑ SB5 David Robinson	2.00	.90
❑ SB6 Dennis Rodman	2.50	1.10
❑ SB7 David Robinson	2.00	.90
❑ SB8 Dikembe Mutombo	.75	.35
❑ SB9 Charles Barkley	2.00	.90
❑ SB10 Shawn Kemp	2.00	.90
❑ SB11 John Stockton	1.25	.55
❑ SB12 Jason Kidd	4.00	1.80
❑ SB13 Avery Johnson	.40	.18
❑ SB14 Rod Strickland	.75	.35
❑ SB15 Damon Stoudamire	2.00	.90
❑ SB16 Gary Payton	2.00	.90
❑ SB17 Mookie Blaylock	.40	.18
❑ SB18 Michael Jordan	15.00	6.75
❑ SB19 Jason Kidd	4.00	1.80
❑ SB20 Alvin Robertson	.40	.18
❑ SB21 Dikembe Mutombo	.75	.35
❑ SB22 Shawn Bradley	.40	.18
❑ SB23 David Robinson	2.00	.90
❑ SB24 Hakeem Olajuwon	2.00	.90
❑ SB25 Alonzo Mourning	1.25	.55

1996-97 Topps Chrome Youthquake

	MINT	NRMT
COMPLETE SET (15)	100.00	45.00
COMMON CARD (YQ1-YQ15)	1.25	.55
SEMISTARS	2.00	.90
UNLISTED STARS	3.00	1.35

STATED ODDS 1:12

	MINT	NRMT
❑ YQ1 Allen Iverson	20.00	9.00
❑ YQ2 Samaki Walker	1.25	.55
❑ YQ3 Stephon Marbury	10.00	4.50
❑ YQ4 Damon Stoudamire	5.00	2.20
❑ YQ5 John Wallace	2.00	.90
❑ YQ6 Michael Finley	4.00	1.80
❑ YQ7 Marcus Camby	5.00	2.20
❑ YQ8 Kerry Kittles	3.00	1.35
❑ YQ9 Ray Allen	6.00	2.70
❑ YQ10 Jerry Stackhouse	3.00	1.35
❑ YQ11 Shareef Abdur-Rahim	10.00	4.50
❑ YQ12 Antonio McDyess	5.00	2.20
❑ YQ13 Joe Smith	3.00	1.35
❑ YQ14 Brent Barry	1.25	.55
❑ YQ15 Kobe Bryant	70.00	32.00

1997-98 Topps Chrome

	MINT	NRMT
COMPLETE SET (220)	150.00	70.00
COMMON CARD (1-220)	.30	.14
COMMON RC	1.50	.70
SEMISTARS	.40	.18
SEMISTARS RC	2.00	.90
UNLISTED STARS	.75	.35

	MINT	NRMT
❑ 1 Scottie Pippen	2.50	1.10
❑ 2 Nate McMillan	.30	.14
❑ 3 Byron Scott	.30	.14
❑ 4 Mark Davis	.30	.14
❑ 5 Rod Strickland	.40	.18
❑ 6 Brian Grant	.40	.18
❑ 7 Damon Stoudamire	1.00	.45
❑ 8 John Stockton	.75	.35
❑ 9 Grant Long	.30	.14
❑ 10 Darrell Armstrong	.40	.18
❑ 11 Anthony Mason	.40	.18
❑ 12 Travis Best	.30	.14
❑ 13 Stephon Marbury	2.50	1.10
❑ 14 Jamal Mashburn	.40	.18
❑ 15 Detlef Schrempf	.40	.18
❑ 16 Terrell Brandon	.40	.18
❑ 17 Charles Barkley	1.25	.55
❑ 18 Vin Baker	.40	.18
❑ 19 Gary Trent	.30	.14
❑ 20 Vinny Del Negro	.30	.14
❑ 21 Todd Day	.30	.14
❑ 22 Malik Sealy	.30	.14
❑ 23 Wesley Person	.30	.14
❑ 24 Reggie Miller	.75	.35
❑ 25 Dan Majerle	.40	.18
❑ 26 Todd Fuller	.30	.14
❑ 27 Juwan Howard	.40	.18
❑ 28 Clarence Weatherspoon	.30	.14
❑ 29 Grant Hill	4.00	1.80
❑ 30 John Williams	.30	.14
❑ 31 Ken Norman	.30	.14
❑ 32 Patrick Ewing	.75	.35
❑ 33 Bryon Russell	.30	.14
❑ 34 Tony Smith	.30	.14
❑ 35 Andrew Lang	.30	.14
❑ 36 Rony Seikaly	.30	.14
❑ 37 Billy Owens	.30	.14
❑ 38 Dino Radja	.30	.14
❑ 39 Chris Gatling	.30	.14
❑ 40 Dale Davis	.30	.14
❑ 41 Arvydas Sabonis	.40	.18
❑ 42 Chris Mills	.30	.14
❑ 43 A.C. Green	.40	.18
❑ 44 Tyrone Hill	.30	.14
❑ 45 Tracy Murray	.30	.14
❑ 46 David Robinson	1.25	.55
❑ 47 Lee Mayberry	.30	.14
❑ 48 Jayson Williams	.40	.18
❑ 49 Jason Kidd	2.50	1.10
❑ 50 Bryant Stith	.30	.14
❑ 51 Checklist Bulls - Team of the 90s Michael Jordan Scottie Pippen Dennis Rodman Ron Harper	4.00	1.80
❑ 52 Brent Barry	.30	.14
❑ 53 Henry James	.30	.14
❑ 54 Allen Iverson	4.00	1.80
❑ 55 Shandon Anderson	.30	.14
❑ 56 Mitch Richmond	.75	.35
❑ 57 Allan Houston	.75	.35
❑ 58 Ron Harper	.40	.18
❑ 59 Gheorghe Muresan	.30	.14
❑ 60 Vincent Askew	.30	.14
❑ 61 Ray Allen	1.25	.55
❑ 62 Kenny Anderson	.40	.18
❑ 63 Dikembe Mutombo	.40	.18
❑ 64 Sam Perkins	.40	.18

- ❑ 65 Walt Williams .30 .14
- ❑ 66 Chris Carr .30 .14
- ❑ 67 Vlade Divac .30 .14
- ❑ 68 LaPhonso Ellis .30 .14
- ❑ 69 B.J. Armstrong .30 .14
- ❑ 70 Jim Jackson .30 .14
- ❑ 71 Clyde Drexler .75 .35
- ❑ 72 Lindsey Hunter .30 .14
- ❑ 73 Sasha Danilovic .30 .14
- ❑ 74 Elden Campbell .30 .14
- ❑ 75 Robert Pack .30 .14
- ❑ 76 Dennis Scott .30 .14
- ❑ 77 Will Perdue .30 .14
- ❑ 78 Anthony Peeler .30 .14
- ❑ 79 Steve Smith .40 .18
- ❑ 80 Steve Kerr .30 .14
- ❑ 81 Buck Williams .30 .14
- ❑ 82 Terry Mills .30 .14
- ❑ 83 Michael Smith .30 .14
- ❑ 84 Adam Keefe .30 .14
- ❑ 85 Kevin Willis .30 .14
- ❑ 86 David Wesley .30 .14
- ❑ 87 Muggsy Bogues .30 .14
- ❑ 88 Bimbo Coles .30 .14
- ❑ 89 Tom Gugliotta .40 .18
- ❑ 90 Jermaine O'Neal .40 .18
- ❑ 91 Cedric Ceballos .30 .14
- ❑ 92 Shawn Kemp 1.25 .55
- ❑ 93 Horace Grant .40 .18
- ❑ 94 Shareef Abdur-Rahim 2.50 1.10
- ❑ 95 Robert Horry .30 .14
- ❑ 96 Vitaly Potapenko .30 .14
- ❑ 97 Pooh Richardson .30 .14
- ❑ 98 Doug Christie .30 .14
- ❑ 99 Voshon Lenard .30 .14
- ❑ 100 Dominique Wilkins .75 .35
- ❑ 101 Alonzo Mourning .75 .35
- ❑ 102 Sam Cassell .40 .18
- ❑ 103 Sherman Douglas .30 .14
- ❑ 104 Shawn Bradley .30 .14
- ❑ 105 Mark Jackson .30 .14
- ❑ 106 Dennis Rodman 1.50 .70
- ❑ 107 Charles Oakley .30 .14
- ❑ 108 Matt Maloney .30 .14
- ❑ 109 Shaquille O'Neal 4.00 1.80
- ❑ 110 Checklist .75 .35
  Karl Malone MVP
- ❑ 111 Antonio McDyess 1.00 .45
- ❑ 112 Bob Sura .30 .14
- ❑ 113 Terrell Brandon .40 .18
- ❑ 114 Tim Thomas RC 10.00 4.50
- ❑ 115 Tim Duncan RC 70.00 32.00
- ❑ 116 Antonio Daniels RC 2.00 .90
- ❑ 117 Bryant Reeves .30 .14
- ❑ 118 Keith Van Horn RC 12.00 5.50
- ❑ 119 Loy Vaught .30 .14
- ❑ 120 Rasheed Wallace .75 .35
- ❑ 121 Bobby Jackson RC 2.00 .90
- ❑ 122 Kevin Johnson .40 .18
- ❑ 123 Michael Jordan 15.00 6.75
- ❑ 124 Ron Mercer RC 6.00 2.70
- ❑ 125 Tracy McGrady RC 60.00 27.00
- ❑ 126 Antoine Walker 1.50 .70
- ❑ 127 Carlos Rogers .30 .14
- ❑ 128 Isaac Austin .30 .14
- ❑ 129 Mookie Blaylock .30 .14
- ❑ 130 Rodrick Rhodes RC 1.50 .70
- ❑ 131 Dennis Scott .30 .14
- ❑ 132 Chris Mullin .75 .35
- ❑ 133 P.J. Brown .30 .14
- ❑ 134 Rex Chapman .30 .14
- ❑ 135 Sean Elliott .30 .14
- ❑ 136 Alan Henderson .30 .14
- ❑ 137 Austin Croshere RC 8.00 3.60
- ❑ 138 Nick Van Exel .40 .18
- ❑ 139 Derek Strong .30 .14
- ❑ 140 Glenn Robinson .40 .18
- ❑ 141 Avery Johnson .30 .14
- ❑ 142 Calbert Cheaney .30 .14
- ❑ 143 Mahmoud Abdul-Rauf .30 .14
- ❑ 144 Stojko Vrankovic .30 .14
- ❑ 145 Chris Childs .30 .14
- ❑ 146 Danny Manning .40 .18
- ❑ 147 Jeff Hornacek .40 .18
- ❑ 148 Kevin Garnett 5.00 2.20
- ❑ 149 Joe Dumars .75 .35
- ❑ 150 Johnny Taylor RC 1.50 .70
- ❑ 151 Mark Price .30 .14
- ❑ 152 Toni Kukoc 1.00 .45
- ❑ 153 Erick Dampier .30 .14
- ❑ 154 Lorenzen Wright .30 .14
- ❑ 155 Matt Geiger .30 .14
- ❑ 156 Tim Hardaway .75 .35
- ❑ 157 Charles Smith RC 1.50 .70
- ❑ 158 Hersey Hawkins .40 .18
- ❑ 159 Michael Finley .75 .35
- ❑ 160 Tyus Edney .30 .14
- ❑ 161 Christian Laettner .40 .18
- ❑ 162 Doug West .30 .14
- ❑ 163 Jim Jackson .30 .14
- ❑ 164 Larry Johnson .40 .18
- ❑ 165 Vin Baker .40 .18
- ❑ 166 Karl Malone 1.25 .55
- ❑ 167 Kelvin Cato RC 2.00 .90
- ❑ 168 Luc Longley .30 .14
- ❑ 169 Dale Davis .30 .14
- ❑ 170 Joe Smith .40 .18
- ❑ 171 Kobe Bryant 10.00 4.50
- ❑ 172 Scot Pollard RC 2.00 .90
- ❑ 173 Derek Anderson RC 5.00 2.20
- ❑ 174 Erick Strickland RC 2.00 .90
- ❑ 175 Olden Polynice .30 .14
- ❑ 176 Chris Whitney .30 .14
- ❑ 177 Anthony Parker RC 1.50 .70
- ❑ 178 Armon Gilliam .30 .14
- ❑ 179 Gary Payton 1.25 .55
- ❑ 180 Glen Rice .40 .18
- ❑ 181 Chauncey Billups RC 2.50 1.10
- ❑ 182 Derek Fisher .30 .14
- ❑ 183 John Starks .30 .14
- ❑ 184 Mario Elie .30 .14
- ❑ 185 Chris Webber 2.50 1.10
- ❑ 186 Shawn Kemp 1.25 .55
- ❑ 187 Greg Ostertag .30 .14
- ❑ 188 Olivier Saint-Jean RC 1.50 .70
- ❑ 189 Eric Snow .30 .14
- ❑ 190 Isaiah Rider .40 .18
- ❑ 191 Paul Grant RC 1.50 .70
- ❑ 192 Samaki Walker .30 .14
- ❑ 193 Cory Alexander .30 .14
- ❑ 194 Eddie Jones 1.50 .70
- ❑ 195 John Thomas RC 1.50 .70
- ❑ 196 Otis Thorpe .30 .14
- ❑ 197 Rod Strickland .40 .18
- ❑ 198 David Wesley .30 .14
- ❑ 199 Jacque Vaughn RC 2.00 .90
- ❑ 200 Rik Smits .30 .14
- ❑ 201 Brevin Knight RC 3.00 1.35
- ❑ 202 Clifford Robinson .30 .14
- ❑ 203 Hakeem Olajuwon 1.25 .55
- ❑ 204 Jerry Stackhouse .40 .18
- ❑ 205 Tyrone Hill .30 .14
- ❑ 206 Kendall Gill .40 .18
- ❑ 207 Marcus Camby 1.00 .45
- ❑ 208 Tony Battie RC 2.00 .90
- ❑ 209 Brent Price .30 .14
- ❑ 210 Danny Fortson RC 2.00 .90
- ❑ 211 Jerome Williams .40 .18
- ❑ 212 Maurice Taylor RC 6.00 2.70
- ❑ 213 Brian Williams .30 .14
- ❑ 214 Keith Booth RC 1.50 .70
- ❑ 215 Nick Anderson .30 .14
- ❑ 216 Travis Knight .30 .14
- ❑ 217 Adonal Foyle RC 2.00 .90
- ❑ 218 Anfernee Hardaway 2.50 1.10
- ❑ 219 Kerry Kittles .75 .35
- ❑ 220 Checklist .30 .14
  Dikembe Mutombo
  Defensive POY

1997-98 Topps Chrome Refractors

	MINT	NRMT
COMPLETE SET (220)	1600.00	700.00
COMMON CARD (1-220)	2.00	.90
COMMON RC	8.00	3.60
SEMISTARS RC	10.00	4.50

*STARS: 3X TO 8X BASE CARD HI
*RCs: 1.5X TO 4X BASE HI
STATED ODDS 1:12

- ❑ 114 Tim Thomas 50.00 22.00
- ❑ 115 Tim Duncan 150.00 70.00
- ❑ 118 Keith Van Horn 50.00 22.00
- ❑ 124 Ron Mercer 30.00 13.50
- ❑ 125 Tracy McGrady 200.00 90.00
- ❑ 137 Austin Croshere 40.00 18.00
- ❑ 173 Derek Anderson 25.00 11.00
- ❑ 212 Maurice Taylor 25.00 11.00

1997-98 Topps Chrome Destiny

	MINT	NRMT
COMPLETE SET (15)	60.00	27.00
COMMON CARD (D1-D15)	1.25	.55
STATED ODDS 1:12		
COMP.REF.SET (15)	200.00	90.00
COMMON REF. (D1-D15)	3.00	1.35

*REF: 1X TO 2.5X HI COLUMN
REF: STATED ODDS 1:48

- ❑ D1 Grant Hill 6.00 2.70
- ❑ D2 Kevin Garnett 8.00 3.60
- ❑ D3 Vin Baker 1.25 .55
- ❑ D4 Antoine Walker 2.50 1.10
- ❑ D5 Kobe Bryant 10.00 4.50
- ❑ D6 Tracy McGrady 10.00 4.50
- ❑ D7 Keith Van Horn 5.00 2.20
- ❑ D8 Tim Duncan 10.00 4.50
- ❑ D9 Eddie Jones 2.50 1.10
- ❑ D10 Stephon Marbury 4.00 1.80
- ❑ D11 Marcus Camby 1.50 .70
- ❑ D12 Antonio McDyess 1.50 .70
- ❑ D13 Shareef Abdur-Rahim 4.00 1.80
- ❑ D14 Allen Iverson 6.00 2.70
- ❑ D15 Shaquille O'Neal 6.00 2.70

1997-98 Topps Chrome Season's Best

	MINT	NRMT
COMPLETE SET (29)	60.00	27.00
COMMON CARD (SB1-SB30)	.60	.25
SEMISTARS	.75	.35
UNLISTED STARS	1.25	.55
STATED ODDS 1:8		
COMP.REF.SET (29)	200.00	90.00
COMMON REF. (SB1-SB30)	2.00	.90

*REF: 1.25X TO 3X HI COLUMN

REF: STATED ODDS 1:24
CARD SB8 DOES NOT EXIST

Card	Player	Mint	Nrmt
❑ SB1	Gary Payton	2.00	.90
❑ SB2	Kevin Johnson	.75	.35
❑ SB3	Tim Hardaway	1.25	.55
❑ SB4	John Stockton	1.25	.55
❑ SB5	Damon Stoudamire	1.50	.70
❑ SB6	Michael Jordan	15.00	6.75
❑ SB7	Mitch Richmond	1.25	.55
❑ SB9	Reggie Miller	1.25	.55
❑ SB10	Clyde Drexler	1.25	.55
❑ SB11	Grant Hill	6.00	2.70
❑ SB12	Scottie Pippen	4.00	1.80
❑ SB13	Kendall Gill	.75	.35
❑ SB14	Glen Rice	.75	.35
❑ SB15	LaPhonso Ellis	.60	.25
❑ SB16	Karl Malone	2.00	.90
❑ SB17	Charles Barkley	2.00	.90
❑ SB18	Vin Baker	.75	.35
❑ SB19	Chris Webber	4.00	1.80
❑ SB20	Tom Gugliotta	.75	.35
❑ SB21	Shaquille O'Neal	6.00	2.70
❑ SB22	Patrick Ewing	1.25	.55
❑ SB23	Hakeem Olajuwon	2.00	.90
❑ SB24	Alonzo Mourning	1.25	.55
❑ SB25	Dikembe Mutombo	.75	.35
❑ SB26	Allen Iverson	6.00	2.70
❑ SB27	Antoine Walker	2.50	1.10
❑ SB28	Shareef Abdur-Rahim	4.00	1.80
❑ SB29	Stephon Marbury	4.00	1.80
❑ SB30	Kerry Kittles	1.25	.55

1997-98 Topps Chrome Topps 40

	MINT	NRMT
COMPLETE SET (39)	60.00	27.00
COMMON CARD (T1-T40)	.60	.25
SEMISTARS	.75	.35
UNLISTED STARS	1.25	.55
STATED ODDS 1:6		
COMP.REF.SET (39)	200.00	90.00
COMMON REF. (T1-T40)	2.00	.90

*REF: 1.25X TO 3X HI COLUMN
REF: STATED ODDS 1:18
T-40 PREFIX ON CARD NUMBERS
CARD T-40 7 DOES NOT EXIST

Card	Player	Mint	Nrmt
❑ T1	Glen Rice	.75	.35
❑ T2	Patrick Ewing	1.25	.55
❑ T3	Terrell Brandon	.75	.35
❑ T4	Jerry Stackhouse	.75	.35
❑ T5	Michael Jordan	15.00	6.75
❑ T6	Christian Laettner	.75	.35
❑ T8	Reggie Miller	1.25	.55
❑ T9	Gary Payton	2.00	.90
❑ T10	Detlef Schrempf	.75	.35
❑ T11	Kevin Garnett	8.00	3.60
❑ T12	Eddie Jones	2.50	1.10
❑ T13	Clyde Drexler	1.25	.55
❑ T14	Anfernee Hardaway	4.00	1.80
❑ T15	Chris Webber	4.00	1.80
❑ T16	Jayson Williams	.75	.35
❑ T17	Joe Smith	.75	.35
❑ T18	Karl Malone	2.00	.90
❑ T19	Tim Hardaway	1.25	.55
❑ T20	Vin Baker	.75	.35
❑ T21	Tom Gugliotta	.75	.35
❑ T22	Allen Iverson	6.00	2.70
❑ T23	David Robinson	2.00	.90
❑ T24	Dikembe Mutombo	.75	.35
❑ T25	John Stockton	1.25	.55
❑ T26	Charles Barkley	2.00	.90
❑ T27	Mitch Richmond	1.25	.55
❑ T28	Damon Stoudamire	1.50	.70
❑ T29	Anthony Mason	.75	.35
❑ T30	Shaquille O'Neal	6.00	2.70
❑ T31	Glenn Robinson	.75	.35
❑ T32	Juwan Howard	.75	.35
❑ T33	Shawn Kemp	2.00	.90
❑ T34	Dennis Rodman	2.50	1.10
❑ T35	Grant Hill	6.00	2.70
❑ T36	Kevin Johnson	.60	.25
❑ T37	Alonzo Mourning	1.25	.55
❑ T38	Hakeem Olajuwon	2.00	.90
❑ T39	Joe Dumars	1.25	.55
❑ T40	Scottie Pippen	4.00	1.80

1998-99 Topps Chrome

	MINT	NRMT
COMPLETE SET (220)	175.00	80.00
COMP.SET W/PREV (230)	225.00	100.00
COMMON CARD (1-235)	.25	.11
COMMON RC	1.25	.55
SEMISTARS	.40	.18
SEMISTARS RC	1.50	.70
UNLISTED STARS	.60	.25
UNLISTED STARS RC	2.50	1.10

THE FOLLOWING CARDS DO NOT EXIST: 75/89/90/97/99
THE FOLLOWING CARDS ARE IN PREVIEW: 6/10/19/40/43/60/73/77/81/100
PREV.SET: INSERTED IN TOPPS 2 PACKS
SUBSET CARDS HALF VALUE OF BASE CARDS

Card	Player	Mint	Nrmt
❑ 1	Scottie Pippen	2.00	.90
❑ 2	Shareef Abdur-Rahim	1.50	.70
❑ 3	Rod Strickland	.40	.18
❑ 4	Keith Van Horn	1.50	.70
❑ 5	Ray Allen	.75	.35
❑ 6	Does not exist		
❑ 7	Anthony Parker	.25	.11
❑ 8	Lindsey Hunter	.25	.11
❑ 9	Mario Elie	.25	.11
❑ 10	Does not exist		
❑ 11	Eldridge Recasner	.25	.11
❑ 12	Jeff Hornacek	.40	.18
❑ 13	Chris Webber	2.00	.90
❑ 14	Lee Mayberry	.25	.11
❑ 15	Erick Strickland	.25	.11
❑ 16	Arvydas Sabonis	.40	.18
❑ 17	Tim Thomas	1.00	.45
❑ 18	Luc Longley	.25	.11
❑ 19	Does not exist		
❑ 20	Alonzo Mourning	.60	.25
❑ 21	Adonal Foyle	.25	.11
❑ 22	Tony Battie	.40	.18
❑ 23	Robert Horry	.25	.11
❑ 24	Derek Harper	.25	.11
❑ 25	Jamal Mashburn	.40	.18
❑ 26	Elliott Perry	.25	.11
❑ 27	Jalen Rose	.60	.25
❑ 28	Joe Smith	.40	.18
❑ 29	Henry James	.25	.11
❑ 30	Travis Knight	.25	.11
❑ 31	Tom Gugliotta	.40	.18
❑ 32	Chris Anstey	.25	.11
❑ 33	Antonio Daniels	.25	.11
❑ 34	Elden Campbell	.25	.11
❑ 35	Charlie Ward	.25	.11
❑ 36	Eddie Johnson	.25	.11
❑ 37	John Wallace	.25	.11
❑ 38	Antonio Davis	.25	.11
❑ 39	Antoine Walker	1.00	.45
❑ 40	Does not exist		
❑ 41	Doug Christie	.25	.11
❑ 42	Andrew Lang	.25	.11
❑ 43	Does not exist		
❑ 44	Jaren Jackson	.25	.11
❑ 45	Loy Vaught	.25	.11
❑ 46	Allan Houston	.60	.25
❑ 47	Mark Jackson	.25	.11
❑ 48	Tracy Murray	.25	.11
❑ 49	Tim Duncan	3.00	1.35
❑ 50	Micheal Williams	.25	.11
❑ 51	Steve Nash	.25	.11
❑ 52	Matt Maloney	.25	.11
❑ 53	Sam Cassell	.40	.18
❑ 54	Voshon Lenard	.25	.11
❑ 55	Dikembe Mutombo	.40	.18
❑ 56	Malik Sealy	.25	.11
❑ 57	Dell Curry	.25	.11
❑ 58	Stephon Marbury	1.50	.70
❑ 59	Tariq Abdul-Wahad	.25	.11
❑ 60	Does not exist		
❑ 61	Kelvin Cato	.25	.11
❑ 62	LaPhonso Ellis	.25	.11
❑ 63	Jim Jackson	.25	.11
❑ 64	Greg Ostertag	.25	.11
❑ 65	Glenn Robinson	.40	.18
❑ 66	Chris Carr	.25	.11
❑ 67	Marcus Camby	.60	.25
❑ 68	Kobe Bryant	5.00	2.20
❑ 69	Bobby Jackson	.25	.11
❑ 70	B.J. Armstrong	.25	.11
❑ 71	Alan Henderson	.25	.11
❑ 72	Terry Davis	.25	.11
❑ 73	Does not exist		
❑ 74	Lamond Murray	.25	.11
❑ 75	Does not exist		
❑ 76	Rex Chapman	.25	.11
❑ 77	Does not exist		
❑ 78	Terry Cummings	.25	.11
❑ 79	Dan Majerle	.40	.18
❑ 80	Charles Outlaw	.25	.11
❑ 81	Does not exist		
❑ 82	Vin Baker	.40	.18
❑ 83	Clifford Robinson	.25	.11
❑ 84	Greg Anthony	.25	.11
❑ 85	Brevin Knight	.25	.11
❑ 86	Jacque Vaughn	.25	.11
❑ 87	Bobby Phills	.25	.11
❑ 88	Sherman Douglas	.25	.11
❑ 89	Does not exist		
❑ 90	Does not exist		
❑ 91	Lorenzen Wright	.25	.11
❑ 92	Eric Williams	.25	.11
❑ 93	Will Perdue	.25	.11
❑ 94	Charles Barkley	1.00	.45
❑ 95	Kendall Gill	.40	.18
❑ 96	Wesley Person	.25	.11

Card	MINT	NRMT
❑ 97 Does not exist		
❑ 98 Erick Dampier	.25	.11
❑ 99 Does not exist		
❑ 100 Does not exist		
❑ 101 Rasheed Wallace	.60	.25
❑ 102 Zydrunas Ilgauskas	.25	.11
❑ 103 Eddie Jones	1.25	.55
❑ 104 Ron Mercer	1.00	.45
❑ 105 Horace Grant	.40	.18
❑ 106 Corliss Williamson	.25	.11
❑ 107 Anthony Mason	.40	.18
❑ 108 Mookie Blaylock	.25	.11
❑ 109 Dennis Rodman	1.25	.55
❑ 110 Checklist	.25	.11
❑ 111 Steve Smith	.40	.18
❑ 112 Cedric Henderson	.25	.11
❑ 113 Raef LaFrentz RC	5.00	2.20
❑ 114 Calbert Cheaney	.25	.11
❑ 115 Rik Smits	.25	.11
❑ 116 Rony Seikaly	.25	.11
❑ 117 Lawrence Funderburke	.25	.11
❑ 118 Ricky Davis RC	5.00	2.20
❑ 119 Howard Eisley	.25	.11
❑ 120 Kenny Anderson	.40	.18
❑ 121 Corey Benjamin RC	2.50	1.10
❑ 122 Maurice Taylor	.60	.25
❑ 123 Eric Murdock	.25	.11
❑ 124 Derek Fisher	.40	.18
❑ 125 Kevin Garnett	4.00	1.80
❑ 126 Walt Williams	.25	.11
❑ 127 Bryce Drew RC	2.50	1.10
❑ 128 A.C. Green	.40	.18
❑ 129 Ervin Johnson	.25	.11
❑ 130 Christian Laettner	.40	.18
❑ 131 Chauncey Billups	.25	.11
❑ 132 Hakeem Olajuwon	1.00	.45
❑ 133 Al Harrington RC	10.00	4.50
❑ 134 Danny Manning	.40	.18
❑ 135 Paul Pierce RC	12.00	5.50
❑ 136 Terrell Brandon	.40	.18
❑ 137 Bob Sura	.25	.11
❑ 138 Chris Gatling	.25	.11
❑ 139 Donyell Marshall	.25	.11
❑ 140 Marcus Camby	.60	.25
❑ 141 Brian Skinner RC	2.50	1.10
❑ 142 Charles Oakley	.25	.11
❑ 143 Antawn Jamison RC	12.00	5.50
❑ 144 Nazr Mohammed RC	1.25	.55
❑ 145 Karl Malone	1.00	.45
❑ 146 Chris Mills	.25	.11
❑ 147 Bison Dele	.25	.11
❑ 148 Gary Payton	1.00	.45
❑ 149 Terry Porter	.25	.11
❑ 150 Tim Hardaway	.60	.25
❑ 151 Larry Hughes RC	15.00	6.75
❑ 152 Derek Anderson	.75	.35
❑ 153 Jason Williams RC	15.00	6.75
❑ 154 Dirk Nowitzki RC	10.00	4.50
❑ 155 Juwan Howard	.40	.18
❑ 156 Avery Johnson	.25	.11
❑ 157 Matt Harpring RC	2.50	1.10
❑ 158 Reggie Miller	.60	.25
❑ 159 Walter McCarty	.25	.11
❑ 160 Allen Iverson	2.50	1.10
❑ 161 Felipe Lopez RC	3.00	1.35
❑ 162 Tracy McGrady	2.50	1.10
❑ 163 Damon Stoudamire	.60	.25
❑ 164 Antonio McDyess	.60	.25
❑ 165 Grant Hill	3.00	1.35
❑ 166 Tyronn Lue RC	1.50	.70
❑ 167 P.J. Brown	.25	.11
❑ 168 Antonio Daniels	.25	.11
❑ 169 Mitch Richmond	.60	.25
❑ 170 David Robinson	1.00	.45
❑ 171 Shawn Bradley	.25	.11
❑ 172 Shandon Anderson	.25	.11
❑ 173 Chris Childs	.25	.11
❑ 174 Shawn Kemp	1.00	.45
❑ 175 Shaquille O'Neal	3.00	1.35
❑ 176 John Starks	.25	.11
❑ 177 Tyrone Hill	.25	.11
❑ 178 Jayson Williams	.40	.18
❑ 179 Anfernee Hardaway	2.00	.90
❑ 180 Chris Webber	2.00	.90
❑ 181 Don Reid	.25	.11
❑ 182 Stacey Augmon	.25	.11
❑ 183 Hersey Hawkins	.40	.18
❑ 184 Sam Mitchell	.25	.11
❑ 185 Jason Kidd	2.00	.90
❑ 186 Nick Van Exel	.40	.18
❑ 187 Larry Johnson	.40	.18
❑ 188 Bryant Reeves	.25	.11
❑ 189 Glen Rice	.40	.18
❑ 190 Kerry Kittles	.40	.18
❑ 191 Toni Kukoc	.75	.35
❑ 192 Ron Harper	.40	.18
❑ 193 Bryon Russell	.25	.11
❑ 194 Vladimir Stepania RC	1.25	.55
❑ 195 Michael Olowokandi RC	4.00	1.80
❑ 196 Mike Bibby RC	8.00	3.60
❑ 197 Dale Ellis	.25	.11
❑ 198 Muggsy Bogues	.25	.11
❑ 199 Vince Carter RC	100.00	45.00
❑ 200 Robert Traylor RC	2.50	1.10
❑ 201 Predrag Stojakovic RC	4.00	1.80
❑ 202 Aaron McKie	.25	.11
❑ 203 Hubert Davis	.25	.11
❑ 204 Dana Barros	.25	.11
❑ 205 Bonzi Wells RC	10.00	4.50
❑ 206 Michael Doleac RC	2.50	1.10
❑ 207 Keon Clark RC	2.50	1.10
❑ 208 Michael Dickerson RC	5.00	2.20
❑ 209 Nick Anderson	.25	.11
❑ 210 Brent Price	.25	.11
❑ 211 Cherokee Parks	.25	.11
❑ 212 Sam Jacobson RC	1.25	.55
❑ 213 Pat Garrity RC	1.50	.70
❑ 214 Tyrone Corbin	.25	.11
❑ 215 David Wesley	.25	.11
❑ 216 Rodney Rogers	.25	.11
❑ 217 Dean Garrett	.25	.11
❑ 218 Roshown McLeod RC	1.50	.70
❑ 219 Dale Davis	.25	.11
❑ 220 Checklist	.25	.11
❑ 221 Scottie Pippen MO	1.00	.45
❑ 222 Antonio McDyess MO	.40	.18
❑ 223 Stephon Marbury MO	1.00	.45
❑ 224 Tom Gugliotta MO	.25	.11
❑ 225 Chris Webber MO	.75	.35
❑ 226 Latrell Sprewell MO	.60	.25
❑ 227 Mitch Richmond MO	.40	.18
❑ 228 Joe Smith MO	.25	.11
❑ 229 John Starks MO	.25	.11
❑ 230 Charles Oakley MO	.25	.11
❑ 231 Dennis Rodman MO	.60	.25
❑ 232 Eddie Jones MO	.60	.25
❑ 233 Nick Van Exel MO	.25	.11
❑ 234 Bobby Jackson MO	.25	.11
❑ 235 Glen Rice MO	.25	.11

1998-99 Topps Chrome Refractors

	MINT	NRMT
COMPLETE SET (220)	2000.00	900.00
COMP.SET W/PREV (230)	2400.00	1100.00
COMMON CARD (1-235)	3.00	1.35
COMMON RC	5.00	2.20

*STARS: 5X TO 12X HI COLUMN
*RCs: 1.5X TO 4X HI
STATED ODDS 1:12
THE FOLLOWING CARDS DO NOT EXIST: 75/89/90/97/99
THE FOLLOWING CARDS ARE IN PREVIEW: 6/10/19/40/43/60/73/77/81/100
PREV.SET: INSERTED IN TOPPS 2 HCP

Card	MINT	NRMT
❑ 133 Al Harrington	30.00	13.50
❑ 135 Paul Pierce	50.00	22.00
❑ 143 Antawn Jamison	50.00	22.00
❑ 151 Larry Hughes	60.00	27.00
❑ 153 Jason Williams	80.00	36.00
❑ 154 Dirk Nowitzki	40.00	18.00
❑ 196 Mike Bibby	30.00	13.50
❑ 199 Vince Carter	650.00	300.00
❑ 205 Bonzi Wells	40.00	18.00

1998-99 Topps Chrome Apparitions

	MINT	NRMT
COMPLETE SET (14)	50.00	22.00
COMMON CARD (A1-A14)	1.00	.45
UNLISTED STARS	1.50	.70
STATED ODDS 1:24		
COMP.REF.SET (14)	400.00	180.00
COMMON REF.(A1-A14)	8.00	3.60

*REF: 3X TO 8X HI COLUMN
REF: STATED ODDS 1:1,015
REF: PRINT RUN 100 SERIAL #'d SETS

Card	MINT	NRMT
❑ A1 Kobe Bryant	12.00	5.50
❑ A2 Stephon Marbury	4.00	1.80
❑ A3 Brent Barry	1.00	.45
❑ A4 Karl Malone	2.50	1.10
❑ A5 Shaquille O'Neal	8.00	3.60
❑ A6 Chris Webber	5.00	2.20
❑ A7 Shawn Kemp	2.50	1.10
❑ A8 Hakeem Olajuwon	2.50	1.10
❑ A9 Anfernee Hardaway	5.00	2.20
❑ A10 Michael Finley	1.50	.70
❑ A11 Keith Van Horn	4.00	1.80
❑ A12 Kevin Garnett	10.00	4.50
❑ A13 Vin Baker	1.00	.45
❑ A14 Tim Duncan	8.00	3.60

1998-99 Topps Chrome Back 2 Back

	MINT	NRMT
COMPLETE SET (7)	15.00	6.75
COMMON CARD (B1-B7)	.60	.25
UNLISTED STARS	1.00	.45

STATED ODDS 1:12

	MINT	NRMT
❑ B1 Michael Jordan	12.00	5.50
❑ B2 Scottie Pippen	3.00	1.35
❑ B3 Dennis Rodman	2.00	.90
❑ B4 Hakeem Olajuwon	1.50	.70
❑ B5 John Stockton	1.00	.45
❑ B6 Dikembe Mutombo	.60	.25
❑ B7 Grant Hill	5.00	2.20

1998-99 Topps Chrome Champion Spirit

	MINT	NRMT
COMPLETE SET (7)	15.00	6.75
COMMON CARD (CS1-CS7)	1.00	.45
STATED ODDS 1:12		
❑ CS1 Michael Jordan	12.00	5.50
❑ CS2 Grant Hill	5.00	2.20
❑ CS3 Ron Mercer	1.50	.70
❑ CS4 Mike Bibby	1.50	.70
❑ CS5 Michael Dickerson	1.00	.45
❑ CS6 Patrick Ewing	1.00	.45
❑ CS7 Scottie Pippen	3.00	1.35

1998-99 Topps Chrome Coast to Coast

	MINT	NRMT
COMPLETE SET (15)	40.00	18.00
COMMON CARD (CC1-CC15)	1.00	.45
UNLISTED STARS	1.50	.70
STATED ODDS 1:24		
COMP.REF.SET (15)	120.00	55.00
COMMON REF. (CC1-CC15)	3.00	1.35
*REF: 1.25X TO 3X HI COLUMN		
REF: STATED ODDS 1:96		
❑ CC1 Kobe Bryant	12.00	5.50
❑ CC2 Scottie Pippen	5.00	2.20
❑ CC3 Eddie Jones	4.00	1.80
❑ CC4 Grant Hill	8.00	3.60
❑ CC5 Jason Kidd	5.00	2.20
❑ CC6 Antoine Walker	2.50	1.10
❑ CC7 Michael Finley	1.50	.70
❑ CC8 Kevin Garnett	10.00	4.50
❑ CC9 Allen Iverson	6.00	2.70
❑ CC10 Shawn Kemp	2.50	1.10
❑ CC11 Glenn Robinson	1.00	.45
❑ CC12 Anfernee Hardaway	5.00	2.20
❑ CC13 Tim Hardaway	1.50	.70
❑ CC14 Ron Mercer	2.50	1.10
❑ CC15 Kerry Kittles	1.00	.45

1998-99 Topps Chrome Instant Impact

	MINT	NRMT
COMPLETE SET (10)	60.00	27.00
COMMON CARD (I1-I10)	2.50	1.10
STATED ODDS 1:36		
COMP.REF.SET (10)	200.00	90.00
COMMON REF. (I1-I10)	8.00	3.60
*REF: 1.25X TO 3X HI COLUMN		
REF: STATED ODDS 1:144		
❑ I1 Tim Duncan	10.00	4.50
❑ I2 Keith Van Horn	5.00	2.20
❑ I3 Stephon Marbury	5.00	2.20
❑ I4 Hakeem Olajuwon	3.00	1.35
❑ I5 Shaquille O'Neal	10.00	4.50
❑ I6 Michael Olowokandi	2.50	1.10
❑ I7 Raef LaFrentz	2.50	1.10
❑ I8 Vince Carter	30.00	13.50
❑ I9 Jason Williams	8.00	3.60
❑ I10 Paul Pierce	6.00	2.70

1998-99 Topps Chrome Season's Best

	MINT	NRMT
COMPLETE SET (29)	15.00	6.75
COMMON CARD (SB1-SB30)	.40	.18
SEMISTARS	.50	.23
UNLISTED STARS	.60	.25
STATED ODDS 1:6		
CARD SB6 DOES NOT EXIST		
COMP.REF.SET (29)	50.00	22.00
COMMON REF. (SB1-SB30)	1.25	.55
*REF: 1.25X TO 3X HI COLUMN		
REF: STATED ODDS 1:24		
❑ SB1 Rod Strickland	.50	.23
❑ SB2 Gary Payton	1.00	.45
❑ SB3 Tim Hardaway	.60	.25
❑ SB4 Stephon Marbury	1.50	.70
❑ SB5 Sam Cassell	.50	.23
❑ SB6 Does not exist		
❑ SB7 Mitch Richmond	.60	.25
❑ SB8 Steve Smith	.50	.23
❑ SB9 Ray Allen	.75	.35
❑ SB10 Isaiah Rider	.50	.23
❑ SB11 Grant Hill	3.00	1.35
❑ SB12 Kevin Garnett	4.00	1.80
❑ SB13 Shareef Abdur-Rahim	1.50	.70
❑ SB14 Glenn Robinson	.50	.23
❑ SB15 Michael Finley	.60	.25
❑ SB16 Karl Malone	1.00	.45
❑ SB17 Tim Duncan	3.00	1.35
❑ SB18 Antoine Walker	1.00	.45
❑ SB19 Chris Webber	2.00	.90
❑ SB20 Vin Baker	.50	.23
❑ SB21 Shaquille O'Neal	3.00	1.35
❑ SB22 David Robinson	1.00	.45
❑ SB23 Alonzo Mourning	.60	.25
❑ SB24 Dikembe Mutombo	.50	.23
❑ SB25 Hakeem Olajuwon	1.00	.45
❑ SB26 Tim Duncan	3.00	1.35
❑ SB27 Keith Van Horn	1.50	.70
❑ SB28 Zydrunas Ilgauskas	.40	.18
❑ SB29 Brevin Knight	.40	.18
❑ SB30 Bobby Jackson	.40	.18

1999-00 Topps Chrome

	MINT	NRMT
COMPLETE SET (257)	150.00	70.00
COMMON CARD (1-257)	.25	.11
COMMON RC	1.50	.70
COMMON USA (249-257)	.50	.23
SEMISTARS	.30	.14
SEMISTARS RC	2.00	.90
UNLISTED STARS	.50	.23
UNLISTED STARS RC	2.50	1.10
❑ 1 Steve Smith	.30	.14
❑ 2 Ron Harper	.30	.14
❑ 3 Michael Dickerson	.50	.23
❑ 4 LaPhonso Ellis	.25	.11
❑ 5 Chris Webber	1.50	.70
❑ 6 Jason Caffey	.25	.11
❑ 7 Bryon Russell	.25	.11
❑ 8 Bison Dele	.25	.11
❑ 9 Isaiah Rider	.30	.14
❑ 10 Dean Garrett	.25	.11
❑ 11 Eric Murdock	.25	.11
❑ 12 Juwan Howard	.30	.14
❑ 13 Latrell Sprewell	1.00	.45
❑ 14 Jalen Rose	.50	.23
❑ 15 Larry Johnson	.30	.14
❑ 16 Eric Williams	.25	.11
❑ 17 Bryant Reeves	.25	.11
❑ 18 Tony Battie	.25	.11
❑ 19 Luc Longley	.25	.11
❑ 20 Gary Payton	.75	.35
❑ 21 Tariq Abdul-Wahad	.25	.11
❑ 22 Armon Gilliam UER mispelled Armen	.25	.11
❑ 23 Shaquille O'Neal	2.50	1.10
❑ 24 Gary Trent	.25	.11
❑ 25 John Stockton	.50	.23
❑ 26 Mark Jackson	.25	.11
❑ 27 Cherokee Parks	.25	.11
❑ 28 Michael Olowokandi	.30	.14
❑ 29 Raef LaFrentz	.50	.23
❑ 30 Dell Curry	.25	.11
❑ 31 Travis Best	.25	.11
❑ 32 Shawn Kemp	.75	.35
❑ 33 Voshon Lenard	.25	.11

Card	Mint	Nrmt
❑ 34 Brian Grant	.30	.14
❑ 35 Alvin Williams	.25	.11
❑ 36 Derek Fisher	.30	.14
❑ 37 Allan Houston	.50	.23
❑ 38 Arvydas Sabonis	.30	.14
❑ 39 Terry Cummings	.25	.11
❑ 40 Dale Ellis	.25	.11
❑ 41 Maurice Taylor	.50	.23
❑ 42 Grant Hill	2.50	1.10
❑ 43 Anthony Mason	.30	.14
❑ 44 John Wallace	.25	.11
❑ 45 David Wesley	.25	.11
❑ 46 Nick Van Exel	.30	.14
❑ 47 Cuttino Mobley	.50	.23
❑ 48 Anfernee Hardaway	1.50	.70
❑ 49 Terry Porter	.25	.11
❑ 50 Brent Barry	.25	.11
❑ 51 Derek Harper	.30	.14
❑ 52 Antoine Walker	.60	.25
❑ 53 Karl Malone	.75	.35
❑ 54 Ben Wallace	.25	.11
❑ 55 Vlade Divac	.25	.11
❑ 56 Sam Mitchell	.25	.11
❑ 57 Joe Smith	.30	.14
❑ 58 Shawn Bradley	.25	.11
❑ 59 Darrell Armstrong	.30	.14
❑ 60 Kenny Anderson	.30	.14
❑ 61 Jason Williams	1.25	.55
❑ 62 Alonzo Mourning	.50	.23
❑ 63 Matt Harpring	.25	.11
❑ 64 Antonio Davis	.25	.11
❑ 65 Lindsey Hunter	.25	.11
❑ 66 Allen Iverson	2.00	.90
❑ 67 Mookie Blaylock	.25	.11
❑ 68 Wesley Person	.25	.11
❑ 69 Bobby Phills	.25	.11
❑ 70 Theo Ratliff	.25	.11
❑ 71 Antonio Daniels	.25	.11
❑ 72 P.J. Brown	.25	.11
❑ 73 David Robinson	.75	.35
❑ 74 Sean Elliott	.25	.11
❑ 75 Zydrunas Ilgauskas	.25	.11
❑ 76 Kerry Kittles	.30	.14
❑ 77 Otis Thorpe	.25	.11
❑ 78 John Starks	.25	.11
❑ 79 Jaren Jackson	.25	.11
❑ 80 Hersey Hawkins	.30	.14
❑ 81 Glenn Robinson	.30	.14
❑ 82 Paul Pierce	1.00	.45
❑ 83 Glen Rice	.30	.14
❑ 84 Charlie Ward	.25	.11
❑ 85 Dee Brown	.25	.11
❑ 86 Danny Fortson	.25	.11
❑ 87 Billy Owens	.25	.11
❑ 88 Jason Kidd	1.50	.70
❑ 89 Brent Price	.25	.11
❑ 90 Don Reid	.25	.11
❑ 91 Mark Bryant	.25	.11
❑ 92 Vinny Del Negro	.25	.11
❑ 93 Stephon Marbury	1.00	.45
❑ 94 Donyell Marshall	.25	.11
❑ 95 Jim Jackson	.25	.11
❑ 96 Horace Grant	.30	.14
❑ 97 Calbert Cheaney	.25	.11
❑ 98 Vince Carter	5.00	2.20
❑ 99 Bobby Jackson	.25	.11
❑ 100 Alan Henderson	.25	.11
❑ 101 Mike Bibby	.60	.25
❑ 102 Cedric Henderson	.25	.11
❑ 103 Lamond Murray	.25	.11
❑ 104 A.C. Green	.30	.14
❑ 105 Hakeem Olajuwon	.75	.35
❑ 106 George Lynch	.25	.11
❑ 107 Kendall Gill	.30	.14
❑ 108 Rex Chapman	.25	.11
❑ 109 Eddie Jones	1.00	.45
❑ 110 Kornel David RC	.25	.11
❑ 111 Jason Terry RC	4.00	1.80
❑ 112 Corey Maggette RC	10.00	4.50
❑ 113 Ron Artest RC	6.00	2.70
❑ 114 Richard Hamilton RC	6.00	2.70
❑ 115 Elton Brand RC	25.00	11.00
❑ 116 Baron Davis RC	6.00	2.70
❑ 117 Wally Szczerbiak RC	10.00	4.50
❑ 118 Steve Francis RC	30.00	13.50
❑ 119 James Posey RC	5.00	2.20
❑ 120 Shawn Marion RC	8.00	3.60
❑ 121 Tim Duncan	2.50	1.10
❑ 122 Danny Manning	.30	.14
❑ 123 Chris Mullin	.50	.23
❑ 124 Antawn Jamison	1.00	.45
❑ 125 Kobe Bryant	4.00	1.80
❑ 126 Matt Geiger	.25	.11
❑ 127 Rod Strickland	.30	.14
❑ 128 Howard Eisley	.25	.11
❑ 129 Steve Nash	.25	.11
❑ 130 Felipe Lopez	.25	.11
❑ 131 Ron Mercer	.60	.25
❑ 132 Ruben Patterson	.50	.23
❑ 133 Dana Barros	.25	.11
❑ 134 Dale Davis	.25	.11
❑ 135 Charles Outlaw	.25	.11
❑ 136 Shandon Anderson	.25	.11
❑ 137 Mitch Richmond	.50	.23
❑ 138 Doug Christie	.25	.11
❑ 139 Rasheed Wallace	.50	.23
❑ 140 Chris Childs	.25	.11
❑ 141 Jamal Mashburn	.30	.14
❑ 142 Terrell Brandon	.30	.14
❑ 143 Jamie Feick RC	1.50	.70
❑ 144 Robert Traylor	.25	.11
❑ 145 Rick Fox	.25	.11
❑ 146 Charles Barkley	.75	.35
❑ 147 Tyrone Nesby RC	1.50	.70
❑ 148 Jerry Stackhouse	.30	.14
❑ 149 Cedric Ceballos	.25	.11
❑ 150 Dikembe Mutombo	.30	.14
❑ 151 Anthony Peeler	.25	.11
❑ 152 Larry Hughes	1.25	.55
❑ 153 Clifford Robinson	.25	.11
❑ 154 Corliss Williamson	.25	.11
❑ 155 Olden Polynice	.25	.11
❑ 156 Avery Johnson	.25	.11
❑ 157 Tracy Murray	.25	.11
❑ 158 Tom Gugliotta	.30	.14
❑ 159 Tim Thomas	.60	.25
❑ 160 Reggie Miller	.50	.23
❑ 161 Tim Hardaway	.50	.23
❑ 162 Dan Majerle	.30	.14
❑ 163 Will Perdue	.25	.11
❑ 164 Brevin Knight	.25	.11
❑ 165 Elden Campbell	.25	.11
❑ 166 Chris Gatling	.25	.11
❑ 167 Walter McCarty	.25	.11
❑ 168 Chauncey Billups	.25	.11
❑ 169 Chris Mills	.25	.11
❑ 170 Christian Laettner	.30	.14
❑ 171 Robert Pack	.25	.11
❑ 172 Rik Smits	.25	.11
❑ 173 Tyrone Hill	.25	.11
❑ 174 Damon Stoudamire	.50	.23
❑ 175 Nick Anderson	.25	.11
❑ 176 Predrag Stojakovic	.30	.14
❑ 177 Vladimir Stepania	.25	.11
❑ 178 Tracy McGrady	1.50	.70
❑ 179 Adam Keefe	.25	.11
❑ 180 Shareef Abdur-Rahim	1.00	.45
❑ 181 Isaac Austin	.25	.11
❑ 182 Mario Elie	.25	.11
❑ 183 Rashard Lewis	.75	.35
❑ 184 Scott Burrell	.25	.11
❑ 185 Othella Harrington	.25	.11
❑ 186 Eric Piatkowski	.25	.11
❑ 187 Bryant Stith	.25	.11
❑ 188 Michael Finley	.50	.23
❑ 189 Chris Crawford	.25	.11
❑ 190 Toni Kukoc	.60	.25
❑ 191 Danny Ferry	.25	.11
❑ 192 Erick Dampier	.25	.11
❑ 193 Clarence Weatherspoon	.25	.11
❑ 194 Bob Sura	.25	.11
❑ 195 Jayson Williams	.30	.14
❑ 196 Kurt Thomas	.25	.11
❑ 197 Greg Anthony	.25	.11
❑ 198 Rodney Rogers	.25	.11
❑ 199 Detlef Schrempf	.30	.14
❑ 200 Keith Van Horn	1.00	.45
❑ 201 Robert Horry	.25	.11
❑ 202 Sam Cassell	.30	.14
❑ 203 Malik Sealy	.25	.11
❑ 204 Kelvin Cato	.25	.11
❑ 205 Antonio McDyess	.50	.23
❑ 206 Andrew DeClercq	.25	.11
❑ 207 Ricky Davis	.50	.23
❑ 208 Vitaly Potapenko	.25	.11
❑ 209 Loy Vaught	.25	.11
❑ 210 Kevin Garnett	3.00	1.35
❑ 211 Eric Snow	.25	.11
❑ 212 Anfernee Hardaway	1.50	.70
❑ 213 Vin Baker	.30	.14
❑ 214 Lawrence Funderburke	.25	.11
❑ 215 Jeff Hornacek	.30	.14
❑ 216 Doug West	.25	.11
❑ 217 Michael Doleac	.25	.11
❑ 218 Ray Allen	.50	.23
❑ 219 Derek Anderson	.50	.23
❑ 220 Jerome Williams	.30	.14
❑ 221 Derrick Coleman	.30	.14
❑ 222 Randy Brown	.25	.11
❑ 223 Patrick Ewing	.50	.23
❑ 224 Walt Williams	.25	.11
❑ 225 Charles Oakley	.25	.11
❑ 226 Steve Kerr	.25	.11
❑ 227 Muggsy Bogues	.25	.11
❑ 228 Kevin Willis	.25	.11
❑ 229 Marcus Camby	.50	.23
❑ 230 Scottie Pippen	1.50	.70
❑ 231 Lamar Odom RC	20.00	9.00
❑ 232 Jonathan Bender RC	12.00	5.50
❑ 233 Andre Miller RC	8.00	3.60
❑ 234 Trajan Langdon RC	4.00	1.80
❑ 235 Aleksandar Radojevic RC	1.50	.70
❑ 236 William Avery RC	4.00	1.80
❑ 237 Cal Bowdler RC	2.50	1.10
❑ 238 Quincy Lewis RC	2.50	1.10
❑ 239 Dion Glover RC	2.50	1.10
❑ 240 Jeff Foster RC	2.50	1.10
❑ 241 Kenny Thomas RC	4.00	1.80
❑ 242 Devean George RC	5.00	2.20
❑ 243 Tim James RC	3.00	1.35
❑ 244 Vonteego Cummings RC	4.00	1.80
❑ 245 Jumaine Jones RC	2.00	.90
❑ 246 Scott Padgett RC	2.50	1.10
❑ 247 Adrian Griffin RC	3.00	1.35
❑ 248 Chris Herren RC	1.50	.70
❑ 249 Allan Houston USA	.75	.35
❑ 250 Kevin Garnett USA	5.00	2.20
❑ 251 Gary Payton USA	1.25	.55
❑ 252 Steve Smith USA	.50	.23
❑ 253 Tim Hardaway USA	.75	.35
❑ 254 Tim Duncan USA	4.00	1.80
❑ 255 Jason Kidd USA	2.50	1.10
❑ 256 Tom Gugliotta USA	.50	.23
❑ 257 Vin Baker USA	.50	.23

1999-00 Topps Chrome Refractors

	MINT	NRMT
COMPLETE SET (257)	1000.00	450.00
COMMON CARD (1-257)	2.00	.90
COMMON RC	8.00	3.60

*STARS: 3X TO 8X BASE CARD HI
*RCs: 2X TO 5X BASE HI
*USA: 2X TO 5X BASE HI
STATED ODDS 1:12

Card	Mint	Nrmt
❑ 112 Corey Maggette	50.00	22.00
❑ 113 Ron Artest	30.00	13.50
❑ 114 Richard Hamilton	30.00	13.50

❑ 115 Elton Brand 120.00 55.00
❑ 116 Baron Davis............ 30.00 13.50
❑ 117 Wally Szczerbiak....... 50.00 22.00
❑ 118 Steve Francis 250.00 110.00
❑ 120 Shawn Marion 40.00 18.00
❑ 231 Lamar Odom 100.00 45.00
❑ 232 Jonathan Bender........ 60.00 27.00
❑ 233 Andre Miller............. 40.00 18.00

1999-00 Topps Chrome All-Etch

	MINT	NRMT
COMPLETE SET (30)	80.00	36.00
COMMON CARD (AE1-AE30)	1.00	.45
UNLISTED STARS	1.25	.55
STATED ODDS 1:10		
COMP.REF.SET (30)	350.00	160.00
COMMON REF (AE1-AE30)	5.00	2.20

*REF.STARS: 1.5X TO 4X HI COLUMN
*REF.RCs: 2X TO 5X HI
REF: STATED ODDS 1:100

❑ AE1 Karl Malone .... 2.00 .90
❑ AE2 Scottie Pippen 4.00 1.80
❑ AE3 Grant Hill 6.00 2.70
❑ AE4 Shawn Kemp .... 2.00 .90
❑ AE5 Shaquille O'Neal......... 6.00 2.70
❑ AE6 Anfernee Hardaway 4.00 1.80
❑ AE7 Chris Webber 4.00 1.80
❑ AE8 Gary Payton .... 2.00 .90
❑ AE9 Jason Kidd 4.00 1.80
❑ AE10 John Stockton........... 1.25 .55
❑ AE11 Kevin Garnett 8.00 3.60
❑ AE12 Vince Carter 12.00 5.50
❑ AE13 Shareef Abdur-Rahim 2.50 1.10
❑ AE14 Antoine Walker......... 1.50 .70
❑ AE15 Kobe Bryant 10.00 4.50
❑ AE16 Tim Duncan 6.00 2.70
❑ AE17 Keith Van Horn......... 2.50 1.10
❑ AE18 Allen Iverson............ 5.00 2.20
❑ AE19 Jason Williams 3.00 1.35
❑ AE20 Stephon Marbury 2.50 1.10
❑ AE21 Elton Brand.............. 6.00 2.70
❑ AE22 Jason Terry .... 1.00 .45
❑ AE23 Steve Francis 8.00 3.60
❑ AE24 Corey Maggette 2.50 1.10
❑ AE25 Lamar Odom 5.00 2.20
❑ AE26 Ron Artest .... 1.50 .70
❑ AE27 Baron Davis .... 1.50 .70
❑ AE28 Andre Miller .... 2.00 .90
❑ AE29 Shawn Marion .... 2.00 .90
❑ AE30 Wally Szczerbiak 2.50 1.10

1999-00 Topps Chrome All-Stars

	MINT	NRMT
COMPLETE SET (10)	15.00	6.75
COMMON CARD (AS1-AS10)	1.25	.55
STATED ODDS 1:30		
COMP.REF.SET (10)	60.00	27.00
COMMON REF (AS1-AS10)	5.00	2.20

*REF: 1.5X TO 4X HI COLUMN
REF: STATED ODDS 1:300

❑ AS1 Patrick Ewing .... 1.25 .55

❑ AS2 Karl Malone .... 2.00 .90
❑ AS3 Hakeem Olajuwon ...... 2.00 .90
❑ AS4 Scottie Pippen 4.00 1.80
❑ AS5 Gary Payton .... 2.00 .90
❑ AS6 John Stockton............ 1.25 .55
❑ AS7 Shaquille O'Neal......... 6.00 2.70
❑ AS8 Charles Barkley .... 2.00 .90
❑ AS9 David Robinson .... 2.00 .90
❑ AS10 Grant Hill 6.00 2.70

1999-00 Topps Chrome Highlight Reels

	MINT	NRMT
COMPLETE SET (15)	30.00	13.50
COMMON CARD (HR1-HR15)	.75	.35
STATED ODDS 1:10		
COMP.REF.SET (15)	120.00	55.00
COMMON REF (HR1-HR15)	3.00	1.35

*REF: 1.5X TO 4X HI COLUMN
REF: STATED ODDS 1:100

❑ HR1 Stephon Marbury .... 1.50 .70
❑ HR2 Vince Carter.............. 8.00 3.60
❑ HR3 Kevin Garnett............ 5.00 2.20
❑ HR4 Kobe Bryant.............. 6.00 2.70
❑ HR5 Chris Webber............ 2.50 1.10
❑ HR6 Allen Iverson 3.00 1.35
❑ HR7 Grant Hill 4.00 1.80
❑ HR8 Antoine Walker.......... 1.00 .45
❑ HR9 Jason Williams .... 2.00 .90
❑ HR10 Tim Duncan 4.00 1.80
❑ HR11 Shareef Abdur-Rahim 1.50 .70
❑ HR12 Keith Van Horn......... 1.50 .70
❑ HR13 Antonio McDyess .... .75 .35
❑ HR14 Jason Kidd 2.50 1.10
❑ HR15 Ron Mercer .... 1.00 .45

1999-00 Topps Chrome Instant Impact

	MINT	NRMT
COMPLETE SET (10)	5.00	2.20
COMMON CARD (II1-II10)	.40	.18
SEMISTARS	.50	.23
UNLISTED STARS	.75	.35
STATED ODDS 1:15		
COMP.REF.SET (10)	20.00	9.00
COMMON REF (II1-II10)	1.50	.70

*REF: 1.5X TO 4X HI COLUMN

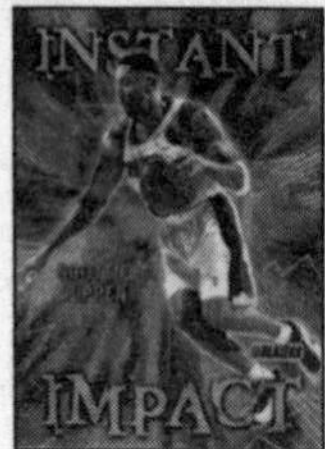

REF: STATED ODDS 1:150

❑ II1 Scottie Pippen.............. 2.50 1.10
❑ II2 Nick Anderson............... .40 .18
❑ II3 Isaiah Rider.................. .50 .23
❑ II4 Antonio Davis .... .40 .18
❑ II5 Ron Mercer .... 1.25 .55
❑ II6 Anfernee Hardaway 2.50 1.10
❑ II7 Isaac Austin.................. .40 .18
❑ II8 Steve Smith.................. .50 .23
❑ II9 Michael Dickerson.......... .75 .35
❑ II10 Horace Grant................ .50 .23

1999-00 Topps Chrome Keepers

	MINT	NRMT
COMPLETE SET (10)	25.00	11.00
COMMON CARD (K1-K10)	1.00	.45
STATED ODDS 1:30		
COMP.REF.SET (10)	120.00	55.00
COMMON REF (K1-K10)	5.00	2.20

*REF: 2X TO 5X HI COLUMN
REF: STATED ODDS 1:300

❑ K1 Elton Brand.................. 6.00 2.70
❑ K2 Lamar Odom................. 5.00 2.20
❑ K3 Steve Francis................ 8.00 3.60
❑ K4 Shawn Marion............... 2.00 .90
❑ K5 Wally Szczerbiak 2.50 1.10
❑ K6 Baron Davis .... 1.50 .70
❑ K7 Andre Miller.................. 2.00 .90
❑ K8 Corey Maggette 2.50 1.10
❑ K9 Jason Terry.................. 1.00 .45
❑ K10 Richard Hamilton .... 1.50 .70

1995-96 Topps Gallery

	MINT	NRMT
COMPLETE SET (144)	30.00	13.50
COMMON CARD (1-144)	.15	.07
SEMISTARS	.20	.09
UNLISTED STARS	.40	.18

❑ 1 Shaquille O'Neal .... 2.00 .90
❑ 2 Shawn Kemp.................... .60 .25
❑ 3 Reggie Miller.................... .40 .18
❑ 4 Mitch Richmond .... .40 .18
❑ 5 Grant Hill .... 2.00 .90
❑ 6 Magic Johnson .... 1.25 .55

❑ 7 Vin Baker .40 .18
❑ 8 Charles Barkley .60 .25
❑ 9 Hakeem Olajuwon .60 .25
❑ 10 Michael Jordan 6.00 2.70
❑ 11 Patrick Ewing .40 .18
❑ 12 David Robinson .60 .25
❑ 13 Alonzo Mourning .40 .18
❑ 14 Karl Malone .60 .25
❑ 15 Chris Webber 1.25 .55
❑ 16 Dikembe Mutombo .20 .09
❑ 17 Larry Johnson .20 .09
❑ 18 Jamal Mashburn .20 .09
❑ 19 Anfernee Hardaway 1.25 .55
❑ 20 Bryant Stith .15 .07
❑ 21 Juwan Howard .40 .18
❑ 22 Jason Kidd 1.25 .55
❑ 23 Sharone Wright .15 .07
❑ 24 Tom Gugliotta .20 .09
❑ 25 Eric Montross .15 .07
❑ 26 Allan Houston .50 .23
❑ 27 Antonio Davis .15 .07
❑ 28 Brian Grant .40 .18
❑ 29 Terrell Brandon .20 .09
❑ 30 Eddie Jones .75 .35
❑ 31 James Robinson .15 .07
❑ 32 Wesley Person .20 .09
❑ 33 Glenn Robinson .40 .18
❑ 34 Donyell Marshall .20 .09
❑ 35 Sam Cassell .20 .09
❑ 36 Lamond Murray .15 .07
❑ 37 Damon Stoudamire RC 2.00 .90
❑ 38 Tyus Edney RC .15 .07
❑ 39 Jerry Stackhouse RC 1.25 .55
❑ 40 Arvydas Sabonis RC .60 .25
❑ 41 Kevin Garnett RC 5.00 2.20
❑ 42 Brent Barry RC .40 .18
❑ 43 Alan Henderson RC .40 .18
❑ 44 Bryant Reeves RC .40 .18
❑ 45 Shawn Respert RC .15 .07
❑ 46 Michael Finley RC 1.50 .70
❑ 47 Gary Trent RC .15 .07
❑ 48 Antonio McDyess RC 2.00 .90
❑ 49 George Zidek RC .15 .07
❑ 50 Joe Smith RC 1.25 .55
❑ 51 Ed O'Bannon RC .15 .07
❑ 52 Rasheed Wallace RC 1.50 .70
❑ 53 Eric Williams RC .20 .09
❑ 54 Kurt Thomas RC .20 .09
❑ 55 Mookie Blaylock .15 .07
❑ 56 Robert Pack .15 .07
❑ 57 Dana Barros .15 .07
❑ 58 Eric Murdock .15 .07
❑ 59 Glen Rice .20 .09
❑ 60 John Stockton .40 .18
❑ 61 Scottie Pippen 1.25 .55
❑ 62 Oliver Miller .15 .07
❑ 63 Tyrone Hill .15 .07
❑ 64 Gary Payton .60 .25
❑ 65 Jim Jackson .15 .07
❑ 66 Avery Johnson .15 .07
❑ 67 Mahmoud Abdul-Rauf .15 .07
❑ 68 Olden Polynice .15 .07
❑ 69 Joe Dumars .40 .18
❑ 70 Rod Strickland .20 .09
❑ 71 Chris Mullin .40 .18
❑ 72 Kevin Johnson .20 .09
❑ 73 Derrick Coleman .20 .09
❑ 74 Clyde Drexler .40 .18
❑ 75 Dale Davis .15 .07
❑ 76 Horace Grant .20 .09
❑ 77 Loy Vaught .15 .07
❑ 78 Armon Gilliam .15 .07
❑ 79 Nick Van Exel .20 .09
❑ 80 Charles Oakley .15 .07
❑ 81 Kevin Willis .15 .07
❑ 82 Sherman Douglas .15 .07
❑ 83 Isaiah Rider .20 .09
❑ 84 Steve Smith .20 .09
❑ 85 Dee Brown .15 .07
❑ 86 Dell Curry .15 .07
❑ 87 Calbert Cheaney .15 .07
❑ 88 Greg Anthony .15 .07
❑ 89 Jeff Hornacek .20 .09
❑ 90 Dennis Rodman .75 .35
❑ 91 Willie Anderson .15 .07
❑ 92 Chris Mills .15 .07
❑ 93 Hersey Hawkins .20 .09
❑ 94 Popeye Jones .15 .07
❑ 95 Chuck Person .15 .07
❑ 96 Reggie Williams .15 .07
❑ 97 A.C. Green .20 .09
❑ 98 Otis Thorpe .15 .07
❑ 99 Walt Williams .15 .07
❑ 100 Latrell Sprewell .75 .35
❑ 101 Buck Williams .15 .07
❑ 102 Robert Horry .15 .07
❑ 103 Clarence Weatherspoon .15 .07
❑ 104 Dennis Scott .15 .07
❑ 105 Rik Smits .15 .07
❑ 106 Jayson Williams .20 .09
❑ 107 Pooh Richardson .15 .07
❑ 108 Anthony Mason .20 .09
❑ 109 Cedric Ceballos .15 .07
❑ 110 Billy Owens .15 .07
❑ 111 Johnny Newman .15 .07
❑ 112 Christian Laettner .20 .09
❑ 113 Stacey Augmon .15 .07
❑ 114 Chris Morris .15 .07
❑ 115 Detlef Schrempf .20 .09
❑ 116 Dino Radja .15 .07
❑ 117 Sean Elliott .15 .07
❑ 118 Muggsy Bogues .15 .07
❑ 119 Toni Kukoc .50 .23
❑ 120 Clifford Robinson .15 .07
❑ 121 Bobby Hurley .15 .07
❑ 122 Lorenzo Williams .15 .07
❑ 123 Wayman Tisdale .15 .07
❑ 124 Bobby Phills .15 .07
❑ 125 Nick Anderson .15 .07
❑ 126 LaPhonso Ellis .15 .07
❑ 127 Scott Williams .15 .07
❑ 128 Mark West .15 .07
❑ 129 P.J. Brown .15 .07
❑ 130 Tim Hardaway .40 .18
❑ 131 Derek Harper .15 .07
❑ 132 Mario Elie .15 .07
❑ 133 Benoit Benjamin .15 .07
❑ 134 Terry Porter .15 .07
❑ 135 Derrick McKey .15 .07
❑ 136 Bimbo Coles .15 .07
❑ 137 John Salley .15 .07
❑ 138 Malik Sealy .15 .07
❑ 139 Byron Scott .15 .07
❑ 140 Vlade Divac .15 .07
❑ 141 Mark Price .15 .07
❑ 142 Rony Seikaly .15 .07
❑ 143 Mark Jackson .15 .07
❑ 144 John Starks .15 .07

1995-96 Topps Gallery Player's Private Issue

	MINT	NRMT
COMPLETE SET (126)	1200.00	550.00
COMMON CARD (19-144)	5.00	2.20

*STARS: 25X TO 50X BASE CARD HI
*RCs: 10X TO 20X BASE HI
STATED ODDS 1:12
1-18 ISSUED IN 96/7 ST.CLUB 2 HOB.PACKS

1995-96 Topps Gallery Expressionists

	MINT	NRMT
COMPLETE SET (15)	100.00	45.00
COMMON CARD (EX1-EX15)	1.00	.45
SEMISTARS	2.00	.90
UNLISTED STARS	3.00	1.35

STATED ODDS 1:24

❑ EX1 Shawn Kemp 5.00 2.20
❑ EX2 Michael Jordan 50.00 22.00
❑ EX3 Reggie Miller 3.00 1.35
❑ EX4 Kevin Willis 1.00 .45
❑ EX5 Jason Kidd 10.00 4.50
❑ EX6 Larry Johnson 2.00 .90
❑ EX7 Patrick Ewing 3.00 1.35
❑ EX8 Rasheed Wallace 6.00 2.70
❑ EX9 Karl Malone 5.00 2.20
❑ EX10 Shaquille O'Neal 15.00 6.75
❑ EX11 Joe Smith 5.00 2.20
❑ EX12 Jerry Stackhouse 5.00 2.20
❑ EX13 Glen Rice 2.00 .90
❑ EX14 Clyde Drexler 3.00 1.35
❑ EX15 Grant Hill 15.00 6.75

1995-96 Topps Gallery Photo Gallery

	MINT	NRMT
COMPLETE SET (17)	100.00	45.00
COMMON CARD (PG1-PG17)	2.50	1.10
SEMISTARS	3.00	1.35
UNLISTED STARS	5.00	2.20

STATED ODDS 1:30

❑ PG1 Vin Baker 5.00 2.20
❑ PG2 Brian Grant 5.00 2.20
❑ PG3 George Zidek 2.50 1.10
❑ PG4 Hakeem Olajuwon 8.00 3.60
❑ PG5 Stacey Augmon 2.50 1.10
❑ PG6 Oliver Miller 2.50 1.10
❑ PG7 Kenny Gattison 2.50 1.10
❑ PG8 Dikembe Mutombo 3.00 1.35
❑ PG9 Rony Seikaly 2.50 1.10
❑ PG10 Tom Gugliotta 3.00 1.35
❑ PG11 Scottie Pippen 15.00 6.75
❑ PG12 David Robinson 8.00 3.60
❑ PG13 Anfernee Hardaway 15.00 6.75
❑ PG14 Dennis Rodman 10.00 4.50

Card	MINT	NRMT
❑ PG15 Kevin Garnett	30.00	13.50
❑ PG16 Damon Stoudamire	12.00	5.50
❑ PG17 Charles Barkley	8.00	3.60

1999-00 Topps Gallery

	MINT	NRMT
COMPLETE SET (150)	60.00	27.00
COMMON CARD (1-124)	.15	.07
COMMON RC (125-150)	.50	.23
SEMISTARS	.20	.09
SEMISTARS RC	.60	.25
UNLISTED STARS	.40	.18
UNLISTED STARS RC	.75	.35

UNPRICED PRIN.PLATES PRINT RUN TO 1
FOUR VERSIONS OF PRIN.PLATES EXIST
PRIN.PLATES: STATED ODDS 1:1028

Card	MINT	NRMT
❑ 1 Gary Payton	.60	.25
❑ 2 Derek Anderson	.40	.18
❑ 3 Jalen Rose	.40	.18
❑ 4 Tim Hardaway	.40	.18
❑ 5 Jerry Stackhouse	.20	.09
❑ 6 Antonio McDyess	.40	.18
❑ 7 Paul Pierce	.75	.35
❑ 8 Reggie Miller	.40	.18
❑ 9 Maurice Taylor	.40	.18
❑ 10 Stephon Marbury	.75	.35
❑ 11 Terrell Brandon	.20	.09
❑ 12 Marcus Camby	.40	.18
❑ 13 Michael Doleac	.15	.07
❑ 14 Doug Christie	.15	.07
❑ 15 Brent Barry	.15	.07
❑ 16 John Stockton	.40	.18
❑ 17 Rod Strickland	.20	.09
❑ 18 Shareef Abdur-Rahim	.75	.35
❑ 19 Vin Baker	.20	.09
❑ 20 Jason Kidd	1.25	.55
❑ 21 Nick Anderson	.15	.07
❑ 22 Brian Grant	.20	.09
❑ 23 Chris Webber	1.25	.55
❑ 24 Tariq Abdul-Wahad	.15	.07
❑ 25 Jason Williams	1.00	.45
❑ 26 Joe Smith	.20	.09
❑ 27 Ray Allen	.40	.18
❑ 28 Glenn Robinson	.20	.09
❑ 29 Alonzo Mourning	.40	.18
❑ 30 Scottie Pippen	1.25	.55
❑ 31 Mookie Blaylock	.15	.07
❑ 32 Christian Laettner	.20	.09
❑ 33 Mark Jackson	.15	.07
❑ 34 Shawn Kemp	.60	.25
❑ 35 Anfernee Hardaway	1.25	.55
❑ 36 Chris Mullin	.40	.18
❑ 37 Dennis Rodman	2.50	1.10
❑ 38 Lamond Murray	.15	.07
❑ 39 Jim Jackson	.15	.07
❑ 40 Shaquille O'Neal	2.00	.90
❑ 41 Randy Brown	.15	.07
❑ 42 Nick Van Exel	.20	.09
❑ 43 Robert Traylor	.15	.07
❑ 44 Vlade Divac	.15	.07
❑ 45 Karl Malone	.60	.25
❑ 46 Avery Johnson	.15	.07
❑ 47 Jayson Williams	.20	.09
❑ 48 Darrell Armstrong	.20	.09
❑ 49 Michael Olowokandi	.20	.09
❑ 50 Kevin Garnett	2.50	1.10
❑ 51 Dirk Nowitzki	.60	.25
❑ 52 Antawn Jamison	.75	.35
❑ 53 Latrell Sprewell	.75	.35
❑ 54 Ruben Patterson	.40	.18
❑ 55 Vince Carter	4.00	1.80
❑ 56 Michael Dickerson	.40	.18
❑ 57 Raef LaFrentz	.40	.18
❑ 58 Keith Van Horn	.75	.35
❑ 59 Tom Gugliotta	.20	.09
❑ 60 Allen Iverson	1.50	.70
❑ 61 Eric Snow	.15	.07
❑ 62 Kerry Kittles	.20	.09
❑ 63 Sam Cassell	.20	.09
❑ 64 Rik Smits	.15	.07
❑ 65 Isaiah Rider	.20	.09
❑ 66 Anthony Mason	.20	.09
❑ 67 Hersey Hawkins	.20	.09
❑ 68 Cuttino Mobley	.40	.18
❑ 69 Allan Houston	.40	.18
❑ 70 Kobe Bryant	3.00	1.35
❑ 71 Damon Stoudamire	.40	.18
❑ 72 Charles Oakley	.15	.07
❑ 73 Mike Bibby	.50	.23
❑ 74 David Robinson	.60	.25
❑ 75 Eddie Jones	.75	.35
❑ 76 Juwan Howard	.20	.09
❑ 77 Antoine Walker	.50	.23
❑ 78 Michael Finley	.40	.18
❑ 79 Larry Hughes	1.00	.45
❑ 80 Charles Barkley	.60	.25
❑ 81 Tracy McGrady	1.25	.55
❑ 82 Dikembe Mutombo	.20	.09
❑ 83 Rasheed Wallace	.40	.18
❑ 84 Jeff Hornacek	.20	.09
❑ 85 Patrick Ewing	.40	.18
❑ 86 P.J. Brown	.15	.07
❑ 87 Brevin Knight	.15	.07
❑ 88 Elden Campbell	.15	.07
❑ 89 Kenny Anderson	.20	.09
❑ 90 Grant Hill	2.00	.90
❑ 91 Mitch Richmond	.40	.18
❑ 92 Steve Smith	.20	.09
❑ 93 Jamal Mashburn	.20	.09
❑ 94 Toni Kukoc	.50	.23
❑ 95 Hakeem Olajuwon	.60	.25
❑ 96 Ron Mercer	.50	.23
❑ 97 John Starks	.15	.07
❑ 98 Glen Rice	.20	.09
❑ 99 Cedric Ceballos	.15	.07
❑ 100 Tim Duncan	2.00	.90
❑ 101 Karl Malone MAS	.40	.18
❑ 102 Alonzo Mourning MAS	.20	.09
❑ 103 Gary Payton MAS	.40	.18
❑ 104 Scottie Pippen MAS	.60	.25
❑ 105 Shaquille O'Neal MAS	1.00	.45
❑ 106 Charles Barkley MAS	.40	.18
❑ 107 Grant Hill MAS	1.00	.45
❑ 108 John Stockton MAS	.20	.09
❑ 109 Jason Kidd MAS	.60	.25
❑ 110 Reggie Miller MAS	.20	.09
❑ 111 Shawn Kemp MAS	.40	.18
❑ 112 Patrick Ewing MAS	.20	.09
❑ 113 Kevin Garnett ART	1.25	.55
❑ 114 Vince Carter ART	2.00	.90
❑ 115 Kobe Bryant ART	1.50	.70
❑ 116 Chris Webber ART	.60	.25
❑ 117 Tracy McGrady ART	.60	.25
❑ 118 S. Abdur-Rahim ART	.40	.18
❑ 119 Paul Pierce ART	.40	.18
❑ 120 Jason Williams ART	.50	.23
❑ 121 Tim Duncan ART	1.00	.45
❑ 122 Eddie Jones ART	.40	.18
❑ 123 Allen Iverson ART	.75	.35
❑ 124 Stephon Marbury ART	.40	.18
❑ 125 Elton Brand RC	8.00	3.60
❑ 126 Lamar Odom RC	6.00	2.70
❑ 127 Steve Francis RC	10.00	4.50
❑ 128 Adrian Griffin RC	1.00	.45
❑ 129 Wally Szczerbiak RC	3.00	1.35
❑ 130 Baron Davis RC	2.00	.90
❑ 131 Richard Hamilton RC	2.00	.90
❑ 132 Jonathan Bender RC	4.00	1.80
❑ 133 Andre Miller RC	2.50	1.10
❑ 134 Shawn Marion RC	2.50	1.10
❑ 135 Jason Terry RC	1.25	.55
❑ 136 Trajan Langdon RC	1.25	.55
❑ 137 Corey Maggette RC	3.00	1.35
❑ 138 William Avery RC	1.25	.55
❑ 139 Ron Artest RC	2.00	.90
❑ 140 Cal Bowdler RC	.75	.35
❑ 141 James Posey RC	1.50	.70
❑ 142 Quincy Lewis RC	.75	.35
❑ 143 Kenny Thomas RC	1.25	.55
❑ 144 Vonteego Cummings RC	1.25	.55
❑ 145 Todd MacCulloch RC	.75	.35
❑ 146 Anthony Carter RC	2.00	.90
❑ 147 Aleksandar Radojevic RC	.50	.23
❑ 148 Devean George RC	1.50	.70
❑ 149 Scott Padgett RC	.75	.35
❑ 150 Jumaine Jones RC	.60	.25

1999-00 Topps Gallery Player's Private Issue

	MINT	NRMT
COMMON CARD (1-124)	2.00	.90
COMMON RC (125-150)	3.00	1.35

*STARS: 5X TO 12X BASE CARD HI
*RCs: 2.5X TO 6X BASE HI
*SUBSETS: 10X TO 25X BASE HI
STATED PRINT RUN 250 SERIAL #'d SETS
STATED ODDS 1:17

1999-00 Topps Gallery Autographs

	MINT	NRMT
COMPLETE SET (4)	150.00	70.00
COMMON CARD	25.00	11.00

OVERALL STATED ODDS 1:375
GROUP A: STATED ODDS 1:437
GROUP B: STATED ODDS 1:2637

Card	MINT	NRMT
❑ CM Corey Maggette A	25.00	11.00
❑ EB Elton Brand B	60.00	27.00
❑ TD Tim Duncan B	100.00	45.00
❑ WS Wally Szczerbiak A	25.00	11.00

1999-00 Topps Gallery Exhibits

	MINT	NRMT
COMPLETE SET (30)	100.00	45.00
COMMON CARD (GE1-GE30)	1.25	.55
UNLISTED STARS	2.00	.90

STATED ODDS 1:24

❑ GE1	Shaquille O'Neal	10.00	4.50
❑ GE2	Chris Webber	6.00	2.70
❑ GE3	Karl Malone	3.00	1.35
❑ GE4	Hakeem Olajuwon	3.00	1.35
❑ GE5	Scottie Pippen	6.00	2.70
❑ GE6	Patrick Ewing	2.00	.90
❑ GE7	John Stockton	2.00	.90
❑ GE8	Tim Duncan	10.00	4.50
❑ GE9	Grant Hill	10.00	4.50
❑ GE10	Dennis Rodman	4.00	1.80
❑ GE11	Reggie Miller	2.00	.90
❑ GE12	Brian Grant	1.25	.55
❑ GE13	Antoine Walker	2.50	1.10
❑ GE14	Damon Stoudamire	2.00	.90
❑ GE15	Tracy McGrady	6.00	2.70
❑ GE16	Alonzo Mourning	2.00	.90
❑ GE17	Shawn Kemp	3.00	1.35
❑ GE18	Isaiah Rider	1.25	.55
❑ GE19	Vince Carter	20.00	9.00
❑ GE20	Antonio McDyess	2.00	.90
❑ GE21	Jason Kidd	6.00	2.70
❑ GE22	Kobe Bryant	15.00	6.75
❑ GE23	Kevin Garnett	12.00	5.50
❑ GE24	Latrell Sprewell	4.00	1.80
❑ GE25	Michael Finley	2.00	.90
❑ GE26	Nick Van Exel	1.25	.55
❑ GE27	Anfernee Hardaway	6.00	2.70
❑ GE28	Elton Brand	10.00	4.50
❑ GE29	Lamar Odom	8.00	3.60
❑ GE30	Baron Davis	2.50	1.10

1999-00 Topps Gallery Gallery of Heroes

	MINT	NRMT
COMPLETE SET (10)	25.00	11.00
COMMON CARD (GH1-GH10)	1.00	.45
STATED ODDS 1:24		

❑ GH1	Kevin Garnett	6.00	2.70
❑ GH2	Stephon Marbury	2.00	.90
❑ GH3	Kobe Bryant	8.00	3.60
❑ GH4	Vince Carter	10.00	4.50
❑ GH5	Tim Duncan	5.00	2.20
❑ GH6	Gary Payton	1.50	.70
❑ GH7	Antoine Walker	1.25	.55
❑ GH8	Chris Webber	3.00	1.35
❑ GH9	Alonzo Mourning	1.00	.45
❑ GH10	Karl Malone	1.50	.70

1999-00 Topps Gallery Heritage

	MINT	NRMT
COMPLETE SET (10)	20.00	9.00
COMMON CARD (TGH1-10)	1.00	.45
STATED ODDS 1:12		
COMP.PROOF SET (10)	40.00	18.00
COMMON PROOF (TGH1-10)	2.00	.90
*PROOF: .75X TO 2X HI COLUMN		
PROOF: STATED ODDS 1:36		

❑ TGH1	Tim Duncan	5.00	2.20
❑ TGH2	Elton Brand	5.00	2.20
❑ TGH3	Shaquille O'Neal	5.00	2.20
❑ TGH4	Stephon Marbury	2.00	.90
❑ TGH5	Allen Iverson	4.00	1.80
❑ TGH6	Grant Hill	5.00	2.20
❑ TGH7	Charles Barkley	1.50	.70
❑ TGH8	Jason Williams	2.50	1.10
❑ TGH9	Scottie Pippen	3.00	1.35
❑ TGH10	Allan Houston	1.00	.45

1999-00 Topps Gallery Originals

	MINT	NRMT
COMPLETE SET (10)	250.00	110.00
COMMON CARD (GO1-GO10)	20.00	9.00
STATED ODDS 1:87		

❑ GO1	Elton Brand	60.00	27.00
❑ GO2	Shawn Marion	30.00	13.50
❑ GO3	Corey Maggette	30.00	13.50
❑ GO4	Steve Francis	80.00	36.00
❑ GO5	Wally Szczerbiak	30.00	13.50
❑ GO6	Baron Davis	20.00	9.00
❑ GO7	Jonathan Bender	50.00	22.00
❑ GO8	Jason Terry	20.00	9.00
❑ GO9	Richard Hamilton	25.00	11.00
❑ GO10	Andre Miller	30.00	13.50

1999-00 Topps Gallery Photo Gallery

	MINT	NRMT
COMPLETE SET (10)	12.00	5.50
COMMON CARD (PG1-PG10)	1.00	.45
STATED ODDS 1:12		

❑ PG1	Tim Duncan	3.00	1.35
❑ PG2	Allen Iverson	2.50	1.10
❑ PG3	Gary Payton	1.00	.45
❑ PG4	Elton Brand	3.00	1.35
❑ PG5	Steve Francis	4.00	1.80
❑ PG6	Latrell Sprewell	1.25	.55
❑ PG7	Jason Kidd	2.00	.90
❑ PG8	Shawn Marion	1.00	.45
❑ PG9	Shareef Abdur-Rahim	1.25	.55
❑ PG10	Jason Williams	1.50	.70

1999-00 Topps Gold Label Class 1

	MINT	NRMT
COMPLETE SET (100)	60.00	27.00
COMMON CARD (1-85)	.25	.11
COMMON RC (86-100)	.60	.25
SEMISTARS	.30	.14
SEMISTARS RC	.75	.35
UNLISTED STARS	.50	.23
UNLISTED STARS RC	1.00	.45
COMP.BLACK SET (100)	120.00	55.00
COMMON BLACK (1-85)	1.00	.45
COMMON BLACK (86-100)	.75	.35
*BLACK STARS: 1.5X TO 4X HI COLUMN		
*BLACK RCs: .5X TO 1.25X HI		
BLACK: STATED ODDS 1:8		
COMMON RED (1-85)	6.00	2.70
COMMON RED (86-100)	8.00	3.60
*RED STARS: 10X TO 25X HI		
*RED RCs: 5X TO 12X HI		
RED: STATED ODDS 1:63		
RED: PRINT RUN 100 SERIAL #'d SETS		
EVERY SET/INSERT HAS A ONE TO ONE		
ONE TO ONE STATED ODDS 1:629		

❑ 1	Tim Duncan	2.50	1.10
❑ 2	Steve Smith	.30	.14
❑ 3	Jeff Hornacek	.30	.14
❑ 4	Kevin Garnett	3.00	1.35
❑ 5	Paul Pierce	1.00	.45
❑ 6	Doug Christie	.25	.11
❑ 7	Charles Barkley	.75	.35
❑ 8	Nick Van Exel	.30	.14
❑ 9	Shareef Abdur-Rahim	1.00	.45
❑ 10	Rod Strickland	.30	.14
❑ 11	Keith Van Horn	1.00	.45
❑ 12	Matt Harpring	.25	.11

		MINT	NRMT
❑ 13	Randy Brown	.25	.11
❑ 14	Vin Baker	.30	.14
❑ 15	Mark Jackson	.25	.11
❑ 16	Latrell Sprewell	1.00	.45
❑ 17	Anthony Mason	.30	.14
❑ 18	Brian Grant	.30	.14
❑ 19	Brevin Knight	.25	.11
❑ 20	Elden Campbell	.25	.11
❑ 21	Allen Iverson	2.00	.90
❑ 22	Kobe Bryant	4.00	1.80
❑ 23	Antawn Jamison	1.00	.45
❑ 24	Lindsey Hunter	.25	.11
❑ 25	Eddie Jones	1.00	.45
❑ 26	Michael Finley	.50	.23
❑ 27	Juwan Howard	.30	.14
❑ 28	Antonio McDyess	.50	.23
❑ 29	David Robinson	.75	.35
❑ 30	Karl Malone	.75	.35
❑ 31	Jason Kidd	1.50	.70
❑ 32	Zydrunas Ilgauskas	.25	.11
❑ 33	Vince Carter	5.00	2.20
❑ 34	Maurice Taylor	.50	.23
❑ 35	Alonzo Mourning	.50	.23
❑ 36	Tim Thomas	.60	.25
❑ 37	Dikembe Mutombo	.30	.14
❑ 38	Grant Hill	2.50	1.10
❑ 39	Jason Williams	1.25	.55
❑ 40	Scottie Pippen	1.50	.70
❑ 41	Stephon Marbury	1.00	.45
❑ 42	Reggie Miller	.50	.23
❑ 43	Tyrone Nesby RC	.25	.11
❑ 44	Ron Mercer	.60	.25
❑ 45	Terrell Brandon	.30	.14
❑ 46	Darrell Armstrong	.30	.14
❑ 47	Larry Hughes	1.25	.55
❑ 48	Alan Henderson	.25	.11
❑ 49	Ray Allen	.50	.23
❑ 50	Rasheed Wallace	.50	.23
❑ 51	Toni Kukoc	.60	.25
❑ 52	Patrick Ewing	.50	.23
❑ 53	Tom Gugliotta	.30	.14
❑ 54	Chris Mills	.25	.11
❑ 55	Gary Payton	.75	.35
❑ 56	Michael Olowokandi	.30	.14
❑ 57	Chris Mullin	.50	.23
❑ 58	Shawn Kemp	.75	.35
❑ 59	Joe Smith	.30	.14
❑ 60	Steve Nash	.25	.11
❑ 61	Gary Trent	.25	.11
❑ 62	Shaquille O'Neal	2.50	1.10
❑ 63	Kerry Kittles	.30	.14
❑ 64	Tim Hardaway	.50	.23
❑ 65	Glenn Robinson	.30	.14
❑ 66	Damon Stoudamire	.50	.23
❑ 67	Anfernee Hardaway	1.50	.70
❑ 68	Vlade Divac	.25	.11
❑ 69	John Starks	.25	.11
❑ 70	Allan Houston	.50	.23
❑ 71	Jerry Stackhouse	.30	.14
❑ 72	Avery Johnson	.25	.11
❑ 73	Glen Rice	.30	.14
❑ 74	Felipe Lopez	.25	.11
❑ 75	Clifford Robinson	.25	.11
❑ 76	Jamal Mashburn	.30	.14
❑ 77	Hakeem Olajuwon	.75	.35
❑ 78	Matt Geiger	.25	.11
❑ 79	John Stockton	.50	.23
❑ 80	Chauncey Billups	.25	.11
❑ 81	Chris Webber	1.50	.70
❑ 82	Antoine Walker	.60	.25
❑ 83	Mike Bibby	.60	.25
❑ 84	Tracy McGrady	1.50	.70
❑ 85	Mitch Richmond	.50	.23
❑ 86	Elton Brand RC	10.00	4.50
❑ 87	Steve Francis RC	12.00	5.50
❑ 88	Baron Davis RC	2.50	1.10
❑ 89	Lamar Odom RC	8.00	3.60
❑ 90	Jonathan Bender RC	5.00	2.20
❑ 91	Wally Szczerbiak RC	4.00	1.80
❑ 92	Richard Hamilton RC	2.50	1.10
❑ 93	Andre Miller RC	3.00	1.35
❑ 94	Shawn Marion RC	3.00	1.35
❑ 95	Jason Terry RC	1.50	.70
❑ 96	Trajan Langdon RC	1.50	.70
❑ 97	Aleksandar Radojevic RC	.60	.25
❑ 98	Corey Maggette RC	4.00	1.80
❑ 99	William Avery RC	1.50	.70
❑ 100	Cal Bowdler RC	1.00	.45

1999-00 Topps Gold Label Class 2

	MINT	NRMT
COMPLETE SET (100)	100.00	45.00
COMMON CARD (1-85)	.50	.23
COMMON CARD (86-100)	.60	.25
*STARS: .75X TO 2X CLASS 1 BASE		
*RCs: .4X TO 1X CLASS 1		
STATED ODDS 1:2		
COMP.BLACK SET (100)	250.00	110.00
COMMON BLACK (1-85)	2.00	.90
COMMON BLACK (86-100)	1.50	.70
*BLACK STARS: 3X TO 8X CLASS 1 BASE		
*BLACK RCs: 1X TO 2.5X CLASS 1		
BLACK: STATED ODDS 1:16		
COMMON RED (1-85)	15.00	6.75
COMMON RED (86-100)	12.00	5.50
*RED STARS: 25X TO 60X CLASS 1 BASE		
*RED RCs: 8X TO 20X CLASS 1		
RED: STATED ODDS 1:126		
RED: PRINT RUN 50 SERIAL #'d SETS		

1999-00 Topps Gold Label Class 3

	MINT	NRMT
COMPLETE SET (100)	150.00	70.00
COMMON CARD (1-100)	.75	.35
*STARS: 1.25X TO 3X CLASS 1 BASE		
*RCs: .5X TO 1.25X CLASS 1		
STATED ODDS 1:4		
COMP.BLACK SET (100)	500.00	220.00
COMMON BLACK (1-85)	3.00	1.35
COMMON BLACK (86-100)	2.50	1.10
*BLACK STARS: 5X TO 12X CLASS 1 BASE		
*BLACK RCs: 1.5X TO 4X HI CLASS 1		
BLACK: STATED ODDS 1:32		
COMMON RED (1-85)	30.00	13.50
COMMON RED (86-100)	20.00	9.00
*RED STARS: 50X TO 120X CLASS 1 BASE		
*RED RCs: 12.5X TO 30X CLASS 1		
RED: STATED ODDS 1:253		
RED: PRINT RUN 25 SERIAL #'d SETS		

1999-00 Topps Gold Label New Standard

	MINT	NRMT
COMPLETE SET (15)	60.00	27.00
COMMON CARD (NS1-15)	1.25	.55
STATED ODDS 1:12		
COMP.BLACK SET (15)	150.00	70.00
COMMON BLACK (NS1-15)	5.00	2.20
*BLACK: 1X TO 2.5X HI COLUMN		
BLACK: STATED ODDS 1:60		
COMMON RED (NS1-15)	100.00	45.00
*RED STARS: 25X TO 60X HI		
*RED RCs: 20X TO 50X HI		
RED: STATED ODDS 1:1692		
RED: PRINT RUN 25 SERIAL #'d SETS		

❑ NS1	Vince Carter	10.00	4.50
❑ NS2	Kevin Garnett	6.00	2.70
❑ NS3	Tim Duncan	5.00	2.20
❑ NS4	Kobe Bryant	8.00	3.60
❑ NS5	Allen Iverson	4.00	1.80
❑ NS6	Jason Williams	2.50	1.10
❑ NS7	Keith Van Horn	2.00	.90
❑ NS8	Elton Brand	8.00	3.60
❑ NS9	Steve Francis	10.00	4.50
❑ NS10	Baron Davis	2.00	.90
❑ NS11	Lamar Odom	6.00	2.70
❑ NS12	Jonathan Bender	4.00	1.80
❑ NS13	Wally Szczerbiak	3.00	1.35
❑ NS14	Jason Terry	1.25	.55
❑ NS15	Corey Maggette	3.00	1.35

1999-00 Topps Gold Label Prime Gold

	MINT	NRMT
COMPLETE SET (11)	15.00	6.75
COMMON CARD (PG1-11)	1.00	.45
STATED ODDS 1:18		
COMP.BLACK SET (11)	40.00	18.00
COMMON BLACK (PG1-11)	2.50	1.10
*BLACK: 1X TO 2.5X HI COLUMN		
BLACK: STATED ODDS 1:90		
COMMON RED (PG1-11)	60.00	27.00
*RED: 25X TO 60X HI		
RED: STATED ODDS 1:2312		
RED: PRINT RUN 25 SERIAL #'d SETS		

❑ PG1	John Stockton	1.00	.45

	Card	Player	MINT	NRMT
❑	PG2	Hakeem Olajuwon	1.50	.70
❑	PG3	Charles Barkley	1.50	.70
❑	PG4	Shaquille O'Neal	5.00	2.20
❑	PG5	Alonzo Mourning	1.00	.45
❑	PG6	Scottie Pippen	3.00	1.35
❑	PG7	Jason Kidd	3.00	1.35
❑	PG8	David Robinson	1.50	.70
❑	PG9	Gary Payton	1.50	.70
❑	PG10	Karl Malone	1.50	.70
❑	PG11	Grant Hill	5.00	2.20

1999-00 Topps Gold Label Quest for the Gold

	MINT	NRMT
COMPLETE SET (9)	6.00	2.70
COMMON CARD (Q1-Q9)	.30	.14
UNLISTED STARS	.50	.23
STATED ODDS 1:9		
COMP.BLACK SET (9)	15.00	6.75
COMMON BLACK (Q1-Q9)	.75	.35
*BLACK: 1X TO 2.5X HI COLUMN		
BLACK: STATED ODDS 1:45		
COMMON RED (Q1-Q9)	40.00	18.00
*RED: 60X TO 120X HI		
RED: STATED ODDS 1:2813		
RED: PRINT RUN 25 SERIAL #'d SETS		

	Card	Player	MINT	NRMT
❑	Q1	Allan Houston	.50	.23
❑	Q2	Kevin Garnett	3.00	1.35
❑	Q3	Gary Payton	.75	.35
❑	Q4	Steve Smith	.30	.14
❑	Q5	Tim Hardaway	.50	.23
❑	Q6	Tim Duncan	2.50	1.10
❑	Q7	Jason Kidd	1.50	.70
❑	Q8	Tom Gugliotta	.30	.14
❑	Q9	Vin Baker	.30	.14

2000 Topps Team USA

	MINT	NRMT
COMPLETE SET (96)	30.00	13.50
COMMON CARD (1-96)	.15	.07
UNLISTED STARS	.25	.11
EACH SUBSET CARD VALUED EQUALLY		
PRICES BELOW FOR INDIVIDUAL CARDS		
CARD NUMBER 16 DOES NOT EXIST		
TWO CARDS NUMBERED 40 WERE PRODUCED		

	Card	Player	MINT	NRMT
❑	1	Tim Duncan ACH	1.25	.55
❑	2	Jason Kidd ACH	.75	.35
❑	3	Vin Baker ACH	.15	.07
❑	4	Steve Smith ACH	.15	.07
❑	5	Grant Hill ACH	1.25	.55
❑	6	Gary Payton ACH	.40	.18
❑	7	Vince Carter ACH	2.50	1.10
❑	8	Ray Allen ACH	.25	.11
❑	9	Kevin Garnett ACH	1.50	.70
❑	10	Tim Hardaway ACH	.25	.11
❑	11	Allan Houston ACH	.25	.11
❑	12	Alonzo Mourning ACH	.25	.11
❑	13	Lisa Leslie ACH	2.00	.90
❑	14	Dawn Staley ACH	1.00	.45
❑	15	Katie Smith ACH	1.00	.45
❑	16	Nikki McCray ACH UER numbered as 40	1.00	.45
❑	17	R.Bolton-Holifield ACH	1.00	.45
❑	18	Chamique Holdsclaw ACH	2.50	1.10
❑	19	Yolanda Griffith ACH	1.25	.55
❑	20	Teresa Edwards ACH	.75	.35
❑	21	Natalie Williams ACH	1.25	.55
❑	22	Delisha Milton ACH	.40	.18
❑	23	Kara Wolters ACH	.60	.25
❑	24	Gary Payton ST	.40	.18
❑	25	Kevin Garnett ST	1.50	.70
❑	26	Tim Hardaway ST	.25	.11
❑	27	Steve Smith ST	.15	.07
❑	28	Ray Allen ST	.25	.11
❑	29	Alonzo Mourning ST	.25	.11
❑	30	Allan Houston ST	.25	.11
❑	31	Vince Carter ST	2.50	1.10
❑	32	Grant Hill ST	1.25	.55
❑	33	Tim Duncan ST	1.25	.55
❑	34	Jason Kidd ST	.75	.35
❑	35	Vin Baker ST	.15	.07
❑	36	R.Bolton-Holifield ST	1.00	.45
❑	37	Natalie Williams ST	1.25	.55
❑	38	Lisa Leslie ST	2.00	.90
❑	39	Chamique Holdsclaw ST	2.50	1.10
❑	40	Nikki McCray ST	1.00	.45
❑	41	Dawn Staley ST	1.00	.45
❑	42	Teresa Edwards ST	.75	.35
❑	43	Yolanda Griffith ST	1.25	.55
❑	44	Katie Smith ST	1.00	.45
❑	45	Delisha Milton ST	1.25	.55
❑	46	Kara Wolters ST	1.00	.45
❑	47	Vin Baker PAI	.15	.07
❑	48	Jason Kidd PAI	.75	.35
❑	49	Allan Houston PAI	.25	.11
❑	50	Ray Allen PAI	.25	.11
❑	51	Alonzo Mourning PAI	.25	.11
❑	52	Kevin Garnett PAI	1.50	.70
❑	53	Gary Payton PAI	.40	.18
❑	54	Steve Smith PAI	.15	.07
❑	55	Vince Carter PAI	2.50	1.10
❑	56	Grant Hill PAI	1.25	.55
❑	57	Tim Duncan PAI	1.25	.55
❑	58	Tim Hardaway PAI	.25	.11
❑	59	Chamique Holdsclaw PAI	2.50	1.10
❑	60	Katie Smith PAI	1.00	.45
❑	61	Yolanda Griffith PAI	1.25	.55
❑	62	Nikki McCray PAI	1.00	.45
❑	63	Lisa Leslie PAI	2.00	.90
❑	64	Teresa Edwards PAI	.75	.35
❑	65	Dawn Staley PAI	1.00	.45
❑	66	R.Bolton-Holifield PAI	1.00	.45
❑	67	Natalie Williams PAI	1.25	.55
❑	68	Delisha Milton PAI	.40	.18
❑	69	Kara Wolters PAI	.60	.25
❑	70	Allan Houston QU	.25	.11
❑	71	Kevin Garnett QU	1.50	.70
❑	72	Tim Duncan QU	1.25	.55
❑	73	Tim Hardaway QU	.25	.11
❑	74	Gary Payton QU	.40	.18
❑	75	Ray Allen QU	.25	.11
❑	76	Vince Carter QU	2.50	1.10
❑	77	Grant Hill QU	1.25	.55
❑	78	Vin Baker QU	.15	.07
❑	79	Alonzo Mourning QU	.25	.11
❑	80	Steve Smith QU	.15	.07
❑	81	Jason Kidd QU	.75	.35
❑	82	Chamique Holdsclaw QU	2.50	1.10
❑	83	Lisa Leslie QU	2.00	.90
❑	84	Dawn Staley QU	1.00	.45
❑	85	Natalie Williams QU	1.25	.55
❑	86	Nikki McCray QU	1.00	.45
❑	87	Katie Smith QU	1.00	.45
❑	88	Teresa Edwards QU	.75	.35
❑	89	Yolanda Griffith QU	1.25	.55
❑	90	R.Bolton-Holifield QU	1.00	.45
❑	91	Delisha Milton QU	.40	.18
❑	92	Kara Wolters QU	.60	.25
❑	93	Team USA Men's	1.00	.45
❑	94	Team USA Women's	1.00	.45
❑	95	Group Shot	1.50	.70
❑	96	Checklist	.15	.07

2000 Topps Team USA Gold

	MINT	NRMT
COMPLETE SET (95)	150.00	70.00

	MINT	NRMT
COMMON CARD (1-95)	.50	.23
*GOLD: 1.25X TO 3X BASE CARD HI		
ONE PER PACK		
CARD NUMBER 16 DOES NOT EXIST		
TWO CARDS NUMBERED 40 WERE PRODUCED		

2000 Topps Team USA Autographs

	MINT	NRMT
COMPLETE SET (10)	700.00	325.00
COMMON CARD	50.00	22.00
STATED ODDS 1:291		

	Card	Player	MINT	NRMT
❑	CH	Chamique Holdsclaw	200.00	90.00
❑	DM	Delisha Milton	50.00	22.00
❑	DS	Dawn Staley	60.00	27.00
❑	KS	Katie Smith	80.00	36.00
❑	LL	Lisa Leslie	100.00	45.00
❑	NM	Nikki McCray	80.00	36.00
❑	NW	Natalie Williams	60.00	27.00
❑	RH	Ruthie Bolton-Holifield	60.00	27.00
❑	TE	Teresa Edwards	80.00	36.00
❑	YG	Yolanda Griffith	80.00	36.00

2000 Topps Team USA National Spirit

	MINT	NRMT
COMPLETE SET (23)	40.00	18.00
COMMON CARD (NS1-NS23)	.50	.23
UNLISTED STARS	.75	.35

STATED ODDS 1:8

Card	Player	MINT	NRMT
❑ NS1	Steve Smith	.50	.23
❑ NS2	Ray Allen	.75	.35
❑ NS3	Grant Hill	4.00	1.80
❑ NS4	Vince Carter	8.00	3.60
❑ NS5	Tim Hardaway	.75	.35
❑ NS6	Jason Kidd	2.50	1.10
❑ NS7	Vin Baker	.50	.23
❑ NS8	Alonzo Mourning	.75	.35
❑ NS9	Tim Duncan	4.00	1.80
❑ NS10	Gary Payton	1.25	.55
❑ NS11	Allan Houston	.75	.35
❑ NS12	Kevin Garnett	5.00	2.20
❑ NS13	Nikki McCray	3.00	1.35
❑ NS14	Dawn Staley	3.00	1.35
❑ NS15	Lisa Leslie	6.00	2.70
❑ NS16	Teresa Edwards	2.00	.90
❑ NS17	Yolanda Griffith	4.00	1.80
❑ NS18	Chamique Holdsclaw	8.00	3.60
❑ NS19	Katie Smith	3.00	1.35
❑ NS20	Ruthie Bolton-Holifield	3.00	1.35
❑ NS21	Natalie Williams	4.00	1.80
❑ NS22	Delisha Milton	1.25	.55
❑ NS23	Kara Wolters	2.00	.90

2000 Topps Team USA Side by Side

	MINT	NRMT
COMPLETE SET (12)	40.00	18.00
COMMON CARD (SS1-SS12)	2.00	.90

STATED ODDS 1:12
RIGHT/LEFT VARIATIONS EQUAL VALUE
*DUAL REF: .75X TO 2X HI COLUMN
DUAL REF: STATED ODDS 1:36

Card	Players	MINT	NRMT
❑ SS1	Tim Duncan / Lisa Leslie	8.00	3.60
❑ SS2	Allan Houston / Ruthie Bolton-Holifield	4.00	1.80
❑ SS3	Kevin Garnett / Chamique Holdsclaw	10.00	4.50
❑ SS4	Jason Kidd / Katie Smith	4.00	1.80
❑ SS5	Vin Baker / Natalie Williams	3.00	1.35
❑ SS6	Gary Payton / Dawn Staley	3.00	1.35
❑ SS7	Vince Carter / Theresa Edwards	6.00	2.70
❑ SS8	Tim Hardaway / Dawn Staley	2.50	1.10
❑ SS9	Steve Smith / Kara Wolters	2.50	1.10
❑ SS10	Alonzo Mourning / Yolanda Griffith	3.00	1.35
❑ SS11	Ray Allen / Delisha Milton	2.00	.90
❑ SS12	Grant Hill / Nikki McCray	5.00	2.20

2000 Topps Team USA USArchival

	MINT	NRMT
COMPLETE SET (9)	450.00	200.00

	MINT	NRMT
COMMON CARD (US1-US9)	25.00	11.00

STATED ODDS 1:323
STATED PRINT RUN 250 SETS

Card	Player	MINT	NRMT
❑ US1	Gary Payton	60.00	27.00
❑ US2	Jason Kidd	80.00	36.00
❑ US3	Vin Baker	30.00	13.50
❑ US4	Tim Duncan	100.00	45.00
❑ US5	Kevin Garnett	100.00	45.00
❑ US6	Allan Houston	50.00	22.00
❑ US7	Steve Smith	30.00	13.50
❑ US8	Tim Hardaway	50.00	22.00
❑ US9	Tom Gugliotta	25.00	11.00

1999-00 Topps Tip-Off

	MINT	NRMT
COMPLETE SET (132)	30.00	13.50
COMMON CARD (1-132)	.10	.05
COMMON RC	1.25	.55
SEMISTARS	.15	.07
UNLISTED STARS	.25	.11

Card	Player	MINT	NRMT
❑ 1	Steve Smith	.15	.07
❑ 2	Ron Harper	.15	.07
❑ 3	Michael Dickerson	.25	.11
❑ 4	LaPhonso Ellis	.10	.05
❑ 5	Chris Webber	.75	.35
❑ 6	Jason Caffey	.10	.05
❑ 7	Bryon Russell	.10	.05
❑ 8	Bison Dele	.10	.05
❑ 9	Isaiah Rider	.15	.07
❑ 10	Dean Garrett	.10	.05
❑ 11	Eric Murdock	.10	.05
❑ 12	Juwan Howard	.15	.07
❑ 13	Latrell Sprewell	.50	.23
❑ 14	Jalen Rose	.25	.11
❑ 15	Larry Johnson	.15	.07
❑ 16	Eric Williams	.10	.05
❑ 17	Bryant Reeves	.10	.05
❑ 18	Tony Battie	.10	.05
❑ 19	Luc Longley	.10	.05
❑ 20	Gary Payton	.40	.18
❑ 21	Tariq Abdul-Wahad	.10	.05
❑ 22	Armen Gilliam	.10	.05
❑ 23	Shaquille O'Neal	1.25	.55
❑ 24	Gary Trent	.10	.05
❑ 25	John Stockton	.25	.11
❑ 26	Mark Jackson	.10	.05
❑ 27	Cherokee Parks	.10	.05
❑ 28	Michael Olowokandi	.15	.07
❑ 29	Raef LaFrentz	.25	.11
❑ 30	Dell Curry	.10	.05
❑ 31	Travis Best	.10	.05
❑ 32	Shawn Kemp	.40	.18
❑ 33	Voshon Lenard	.10	.05
❑ 34	Brian Grant	.15	.07
❑ 35	Alvin Williams	.10	.05
❑ 36	Derek Fisher	.15	.07
❑ 37	Allan Houston	.25	.11
❑ 38	Arvydas Sabonis	.15	.07
❑ 39	Terry Cummings	.10	.05
❑ 40	Dale Ellis	.10	.05
❑ 41	Maurice Taylor	.25	.11
❑ 42	Grant Hill	1.25	.55
❑ 43	Anthony Mason	.15	.07
❑ 44	John Wallace	.10	.05
❑ 45	David Wesley	.10	.05
❑ 46	Nick Van Exel	.15	.07
❑ 47	Cuttino Mobley	.25	.11
❑ 48	Anfernee Hardaway	.75	.35
❑ 49	Terry Porter	.10	.05
❑ 50	Brent Barry	.10	.05
❑ 51	Derek Harper	.15	.07
❑ 52	Antoine Walker	.30	.14
❑ 53	Karl Malone	.40	.18
❑ 54	Ben Wallace	.10	.05
❑ 55	Vlade Divac	.10	.05
❑ 56	Sam Mitchell	.10	.05
❑ 57	Joe Smith	.15	.07
❑ 58	Shawn Bradley	.10	.05
❑ 59	Darrell Armstrong	.15	.07
❑ 60	Kenny Anderson	.15	.07
❑ 61	Jason Williams	.60	.25
❑ 62	Alonzo Mourning	.25	.11
❑ 63	Matt Harpring	.10	.05
❑ 64	Antonio Davis	.10	.05
❑ 65	Lindsey Hunter	.10	.05
❑ 66	Allen Iverson	1.00	.45
❑ 67	Mookie Blaylock	.10	.05
❑ 68	Wesley Person	.10	.05
❑ 69	Bobby Phills	.10	.05
❑ 70	Theo Ratliff	.10	.05
❑ 71	Antonio Daniels	.10	.05
❑ 72	P.J. Brown	.10	.05
❑ 73	David Robinson	.40	.18
❑ 74	Sean Elliott	.10	.05
❑ 75	Zydrunas Ilgauskas	.10	.05
❑ 76	Kerry Kittles	.15	.07
❑ 77	Otis Thorpe	.10	.05
❑ 78	John Starks	.10	.05
❑ 79	Jaren Jackson	.10	.05
❑ 80	Hersey Hawkins	.15	.07
❑ 81	Glenn Robinson	.15	.07
❑ 82	Paul Pierce	.50	.23
❑ 83	Glen Rice	.15	.07
❑ 84	Charlie Ward	.10	.05
❑ 85	Dee Brown	.10	.05
❑ 86	Danny Fortson	.10	.05
❑ 87	Billy Owens	.10	.05
❑ 88	Jason Kidd	.75	.35
❑ 89	Brent Price	.10	.05
❑ 90	Don Reid	.10	.05
❑ 91	Mark Bryant	.10	.05
❑ 92	Vinny Del Negro	.10	.05
❑ 93	Stephon Marbury	.50	.23
❑ 94	Donyell Marshall	.10	.05
❑ 95	Jim Jackson	.10	.05
❑ 96	Horace Grant	.15	.07
❑ 97	Calbert Cheaney	.10	.05
❑ 98	Vince Carter	2.50	1.10
❑ 99	Bobby Jackson	.10	.05
❑ 100	Alan Henderson	.10	.05
❑ 101	Mike Bibby	.30	.14
❑ 102	Cedric Henderson	.10	.05
❑ 103	Lamond Murray	.10	.05
❑ 104	A.C. Green	.15	.07
❑ 105	Hakeem Olajuwon	.40	.18
❑ 106	George Lynch	.10	.05
❑ 107	Kendall Gill	.15	.07
❑ 108	Rex Chapman	.10	.05
❑ 109	Eddie Jones	.50	.23
❑ 110	Kornel David RC	.10	.05
❑ 111	Jason Terry RC	1.25	.55
❑ 112	Corey Maggette RC	3.00	1.35
❑ 113	Ron Artest RC	2.00	.90
❑ 114	Richard Hamilton RC	2.00	.90

❑ 115 Elton Brand RC	8.00	3.60
❑ 116 Baron Davis RC	2.00	.90
❑ 117 Wally Szczerbiak RC	3.00	1.35
❑ 118 Steve Francis RC	10.00	4.50
❑ 119 James Posey RC	1.50	.70
❑ 120 Shawn Marion RC	2.50	1.10
❑ 121 Tim Duncan	1.25	.55
❑ 122 Danny Manning	.15	.07
❑ 123 Chris Mullin	.25	.11
❑ 124 Antawn Jamison	.50	.23
❑ 125 Kobe Bryant	2.00	.90
❑ 126 Matt Geiger	.10	.05
❑ 127 Rod Strickland	.15	.07
❑ 128 Howard Eisley	.10	.05
❑ 129 Steve Nash	.10	.05
❑ 130 Felipe Lopez	.10	.05
❑ 131 Ron Mercer	.30	.14
❑ 132 Checklist	.10	.05

1999-00 Topps Tip-Off Autographs

	MINT	NRMT
COMPLETE SET (2)	400.00	180.00
COMMON CARD (AG1/AG3)	200.00	90.00
AG1 STATED ODDS 1:12,910		
AG2 STATED ODDS 1:4,303		
AG3 STATED ODDS 1:6,455		
CARTER DID NOT SIGN EXCH.CARDS		
❑ AG1 Tim Duncan	300.00	135.00
❑ AG2 Vince Carter	100.00	45.00
Redemption card only		
❑ AG3 Allen Iverson	200.00	90.00

1998-99 UD Choice

	MINT	NRMT
COMPLETE SET (200)	15.00	6.75
COMMON CARD (1-200)	.05	.02
SEMISTARS	.10	.05
UNLISTED STARS	.20	.09

❑ 1 Dikembe Mutombo	.10	.05
❑ 2 Alan Henderson	.05	.02
❑ 3 Mookie Blaylock	.05	.02
❑ 4 Ed Gray	.05	.02
❑ 5 Eldridge Recasner	.05	.02
❑ 6 Kenny Anderson	.10	.05
❑ 7 Ron Mercer	.30	.14
❑ 8 Dana Barros	.05	.02
❑ 9 Walter McCarty	.05	.02
❑ 10 Travis Knight	.05	.02
❑ 11 Andrew DeClercq	.05	.02
❑ 12 David Wesley	.05	.02
❑ 13 Anthony Mason	.10	.05
❑ 14 Glen Rice	.10	.05
❑ 15 J.R. Reid	.05	.02
❑ 16 Bobby Phills	.05	.02
❑ 17 Dell Curry	.05	.02
❑ 18 Toni Kukoc	.25	.11
❑ 19 Randy Brown	.05	.02
❑ 20 Ron Harper	.10	.05
❑ 21 Keith Booth	.05	.02
❑ 22 Scott Burrell	.05	.02
❑ 23 Michael Jordan	2.50	1.10
❑ 24 Derek Anderson	.25	.11
❑ 25 Brevin Knight	.05	.02
❑ 26 Zydrunas Ilgauskas	.05	.02
❑ 27 Cedric Henderson	.05	.02
❑ 28 Vitaly Potapenko	.05	.02
❑ 29 Michael Finley	.20	.09
❑ 30 Erick Strickland	.05	.02
❑ 31 Shawn Bradley	.05	.02
❑ 32 Hubert Davis	.05	.02
❑ 33 Khalid Reeves	.05	.02
❑ 34 Bobby Jackson	.05	.02
❑ 35 Tony Battie	.10	.05
❑ 36 Bryant Stith	.05	.02
❑ 37 Danny Fortson	.10	.05
❑ 38 Dean Garrett	.05	.02
❑ 39 Eric Williams	.05	.02
❑ 40 Brian Williams	.05	.02
❑ 41 Grant Hill	1.00	.45
❑ 42 Lindsey Hunter	.05	.02
❑ 43 Jerome Williams	.10	.05
❑ 44 Eric Montross	.05	.02
❑ 45 Erick Dampier	.05	.02
❑ 46 Muggsy Bogues	.05	.02
❑ 47 Tony Delk	.05	.02
❑ 48 Donyell Marshall	.05	.02
❑ 49 Bimbo Coles	.05	.02
❑ 50 Charles Barkley	.30	.14
❑ 51 Hakeem Olajuwon	.30	.14
❑ 52 Brent Price	.05	.02
❑ 53 Mario Elie	.05	.02
❑ 54 Rodrick Rhodes	.05	.02
❑ 55 Kevin Willis	.05	.02
❑ 56 Reggie Miller	.20	.09
❑ 57 Jalen Rose	.20	.09
❑ 58 Mark Jackson	.05	.02
❑ 59 Dale Davis	.05	.02
❑ 60 Chris Mullin	.20	.09
❑ 61 Derrick McKey	.05	.02
❑ 62 Lorenzen Wright	.05	.02
❑ 63 Rodney Rogers	.05	.02
❑ 64 Eric Piatkowski	.05	.02
❑ 65 Maurice Taylor	.20	.09
❑ 66 Isaac Austin	.05	.02
❑ 67 Corie Blount	.05	.02
❑ 68 Shaquille O'Neal	1.00	.45
❑ 69 Kobe Bryant	1.50	.70
❑ 70 Robert Horry	.05	.02
❑ 71 Sean Rooks	.05	.02
❑ 72 Derek Fisher	.10	.05
❑ 73 P.J. Brown	.05	.02
❑ 74 Alonzo Mourning	.20	.09
❑ 75 Tim Hardaway	.20	.09
❑ 76 Voshon Lenard	.05	.02
❑ 77 Dan Majerle	.10	.05
❑ 78 Ervin Johnson	.05	.02
❑ 79 Ray Allen	.25	.11
❑ 80 Terrell Brandon	.10	.05
❑ 81 Tyrone Hill	.05	.02
❑ 82 Elliot Perry	.05	.02
❑ 83 Anthony Peeler	.05	.02
❑ 84 Stephon Marbury	.50	.23
❑ 85 Kevin Garnett	1.25	.55
❑ 86 Paul Grant	.05	.02
❑ 87 Chris Carr	.05	.02
❑ 88 Micheal Williams UER	.05	.02
spelled Michael		
❑ 89 Keith Van Horn	.50	.23
❑ 90 Sam Cassell	.10	.05
❑ 91 Kendall Gill	.10	.05
❑ 92 Chris Gatling	.05	.02
❑ 93 Kerry Kittles	.10	.05
❑ 94 Allan Houston	.20	.09
❑ 95 Patrick Ewing UER	.05	.02
back Ewing Ewing		
❑ 96 Charles Oakley	.05	.02
❑ 97 John Starks	.05	.02
❑ 98 Charlie Ward	.05	.02
❑ 99 Chris Mills	.05	.02
❑ 100 Anfernee Hardaway	.60	.25
❑ 101 Nick Anderson	.05	.02
❑ 102 Mark Price	.05	.02
❑ 103 Horace Grant	.10	.05
❑ 104 David Benoit	.05	.02
❑ 105 Allen Iverson	.75	.35
❑ 106 Joe Smith	.10	.05
❑ 107 Tim Thomas	.30	.14
❑ 108 Brian Shaw	.05	.02
❑ 109 Aaron McKie	.05	.02
❑ 110 Jason Kidd	.60	.25
❑ 111 Danny Manning	.10	.05
❑ 112 Steve Nash	.05	.02
❑ 113 Rex Chapman	.05	.02
❑ 114 Dennis Scott	.05	.02
❑ 115 Antonio McDyess	.20	.09
❑ 116 Damon Stoudamire	.20	.09
❑ 117 Isaiah Rider	.10	.05
❑ 118 Rasheed Wallace	.20	.09
❑ 119 Kelvin Cato	.05	.02
❑ 120 Jermaine O'Neal	.10	.05
❑ 121 Corliss Williamson	.05	.02
❑ 122 Olden Polynice	.05	.02
❑ 123 Billy Owens	.05	.02
❑ 124 Lawrence Funderburke	.05	.02
❑ 125 Anthony Johnson	.05	.02
❑ 126 Tim Duncan	1.00	.45
❑ 127 Sean Elliott	.05	.02
❑ 128 Avery Johnson	.05	.02
❑ 129 Vinny Del Negro	.05	.02
❑ 130 Monty Williams	.05	.02
❑ 131 Vin Baker	.10	.05
❑ 132 Hersey Hawkins	.10	.05
❑ 133 Nate McMillan	.05	.02
❑ 134 Detlef Schrempf	.10	.05
❑ 135 Gary Payton	.30	.14
❑ 136 Jim McIlvaine	.05	.02
❑ 137 Chauncey Billups	.05	.02
❑ 138 Doug Christie	.05	.02
❑ 139 John Wallace	.05	.02
❑ 140 Tracy McGrady	.75	.35
❑ 141 Dee Brown	.05	.02
❑ 142 John Stockton	.20	.09
❑ 143 Karl Malone	.30	.14
❑ 144 Shandon Anderson	.05	.02
❑ 145 Jacque Vaughn	.05	.02
❑ 146 Bryon Russell	.05	.02
❑ 147 Lee Mayberry	.05	.02
❑ 148 Bryant Reeves	.05	.02
❑ 149 Shareef Abdur-Rahim	.50	.23
❑ 150 Michael Smith	.05	.02
❑ 151 Pete Chilcutt	.05	.02
❑ 152 Harvey Grant	.05	.02
❑ 153 Juwan Howard	.10	.05
❑ 154 Calbert Cheaney	.05	.02
❑ 155 Tracy Murray	.05	.02
❑ 156 Dikembe Mutombo FS	.05	.02
❑ 157 Antoine Walker FS	.20	.09
❑ 158 Glen Rice FS	.05	.02
❑ 159 Michael Jordan FS	1.25	.55
❑ 160 Wesley Person FS	.05	.02
❑ 161 Shawn Bradley FS	.05	.02
❑ 162 Dean Garrett FS	.05	.02
❑ 163 Jerry Stackhouse FS	.05	.02
❑ 164 Donyell Marshall FS	.05	.02
❑ 165 Hakeem Olajuwon FS	.20	.09
❑ 166 Chris Mullin FS	.10	.05
❑ 167 Isaac Austin FS	.05	.02
❑ 168 Shaquille O'Neal FS	.50	.23
❑ 169 Tim Hardaway FS	.10	.05
❑ 170 Glenn Robinson FS	.05	.02
❑ 171 Kevin Garnett FS	.60	.25
❑ 172 Keith Van Horn FS	.25	.11
❑ 173 Larry Johnson FS	.05	.02
❑ 174 Horace Grant FS	.05	.02
❑ 175 Derrick Coleman FS	.05	.02
❑ 176 Steve Nash FS	.05	.02
❑ 177 Arvydas Sabonis FS UER	.05	.02
spelled Arvadas		
❑ 178 Corliss Williamson FS	.05	.02
❑ 179 David Robinson FS	.20	.09
❑ 180 Vin Baker FS	.05	.02
❑ 181 Marcus Camby FS	.10	.05
❑ 182 John Stockton FS	.10	.05
❑ 183 Antonio Daniels FS	.05	.02
❑ 184 Rod Strickland FS	.05	.02
❑ 185 Michael Jordan FS	1.25	.55
❑ 186 Kobe Bryant YIR	.75	.35
❑ 187 Clyde Drexler YIR	.10	.05
❑ 188 Gary Payton YIR	.20	.09
❑ 189 Michael Jordan YIR	1.25	.55
❑ 190 David Robinson	.50	.23
Tim Duncan YIR		
❑ 191 Attendance Record YIR	.05	.02
❑ 192 Karl Malone YIR	.20	.09

❑ 193 Dikembe Mutombo YIR .. .05 .02
❑ 194 New Jersey Nets YIR .... .20 .09
Keith Van Horn
Kerry Kittles
Jayson Williams
Kendall Gill
Sam Cassell
❑ 195 Ray Allen YIR .... .20 .09
❑ 196 Michael Jordan YIR...... 1.25 .55
❑ 197 Los Angeles Lakers YIR .75 .35
Kobe Bryant
Eddie Jones
Shaquille O'Neal
Nick Van Exel
❑ 198 Michael Jordan YIR...... 1.25 .55
❑ 199 Michael Jordan CL .... .60 .25
❑ 200 Michael Jordan CL .... .60 .25

1998-99 UD Choice Reserve

	MINT	NRMT
COMPLETE SET (200)	100.00	45.00
COMMON CARD (1-200)............	.25	.11

*STARS: 2X TO 5X BASE CARD HI
STATED ODDS 1:6 HOB/RET

1998-99 UD Choice Premium Choice Reserve

	MINT	NRMT
COMMON CARD (1-200)..........	6.00	2.70

*STARS: 30X TO 80X BASE CARD HI
*SUBSET CARDS: 50X TO 120X BASE HI
RANDOM INSERTS IN HOB/RET
STATED PRINT RUN 100 SERIAL #'d SETS

❑ 23 Michael Jordan 350.00 160.00

1998-99 UD Choice Mini Bobbing Heads

	MINT	NRMT
COMPLETE SET (30)	10.00	4.50
COMMON CARD (1-30).............	.10	.05
SEMISTARS................................	.15	.07
UNLISTED STARS........................	.25	.11

STATED ODDS 1:4 HOB/RET

❑ 1 Dikembe Mutombo .... .15 .07

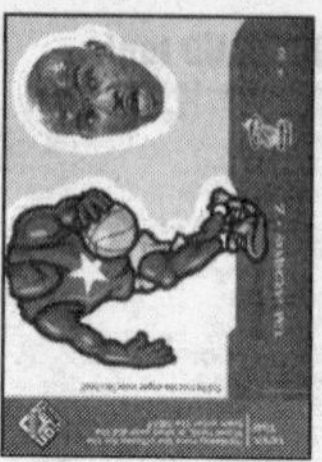

❑ 2 Antoine Walker .... .40 .18
❑ 3 Anthony Mason .... .15 .07
❑ 4 Toni Kukoc .... .30 .14
❑ 5 Shawn Kemp .... .40 .18
❑ 6 Shawn Bradley .... .10 .05
❑ 7 Danny Fortson.................... .15 .07
❑ 8 Brian Williams .... .10 .05
❑ 9 Muggsy Bogues .... .10 .05
❑ 10 Charles Barkley .... .40 .18
❑ 11 Mark Jackson .... .10 .05
❑ 12 Rodney Rogers .... .10 .05
❑ 13 Kobe Bryant .... 2.00 .90
❑ 14 Tim Hardaway .... .25 .11
❑ 15 Ray Allen.......................... .30 .14
❑ 16 Kevin Garnett .... 1.50 .70
❑ 17 Sam Cassell .... .15 .07
❑ 18 John Starks .... .10 .05
❑ 19 Anfernee Hardaway .... .75 .35
❑ 20 Allen Iverson .... 1.00 .45
❑ 21 Danny Manning................. .15 .07
❑ 22 Rasheed Wallace .... .25 .11
❑ 23 Chris Webber .... .75 .35
❑ 24 David Robinson................. .40 .18
❑ 25 Gary Payton .... .40 .18
❑ 26 Marcus Camby .... .25 .11
❑ 27 John Stockton.................... .25 .11
❑ 28 Bryant Reeves................... .10 .05
❑ 29 Juwan Howard .... .15 .07
❑ 30 Michael Jordan 3.00 1.35

1998-99 UD Choice StarQuest Blue

	MINT	NRMT
COMPLETE SET (30)	10.00	4.50
COMMON CARD (SQ1-SQ30).....	.15	.07
SEMISTARS..................................	.20	.09
UNLISTED STARS........................	.30	.14
STATED ODDS 1:1 HOB/RET		
COMPLETE GREEN SET (30)	30.00	13.50
COMMON GREEN (SQ1-SQ30)	.50	.23
*GREEN STARS: 1.25X TO 3X HI COLUMN		
GREEN: STATED ODDS 1:8 H/R		
COMPLETE RED SET (30)	80.00	36.00
COMMON RED (SQ1-SQ30)	1.25	.55
*RED STARS: 4X TO 8X HI COLUMN		
RED: STATED ODDS 1:23 H/R		

❑ SQ1 Steve Smith .... .20 .09
❑ SQ2 Kenny Anderson .... .20 .09
❑ SQ3 Glen Rice .... .20 .09
❑ SQ4 Toni Kukoc.................... .40 .18
❑ SQ5 Shawn Kemp .... .50 .23
❑ SQ6 Michael Finley .... .30 .14
❑ SQ7 Bobby Jackson............. .15 .07
❑ SQ8 Grant Hill .... 1.50 .70
❑ SQ9 Donyell Marshall .... .15 .07
❑ SQ10 Hakeem Olajuwon ...... .50 .23
❑ SQ11 Reggie Miller .... .30 .14
❑ SQ12 Maurice Taylor .... .30 .14
❑ SQ13 Kobe Bryant 2.50 1.10
❑ SQ14 Alonzo Mourning .... .30 .14
❑ SQ15 Terrell Brandon .... .20 .09
❑ SQ16 Stephon Marbury .... .75 .35
❑ SQ17 Keith Van Horn............ .75 .35
❑ SQ18 Patrick Ewing.............. .30 .14
❑ SQ19 Anfernee Hardaway .. 1.00 .45
❑ SQ20 Allen Iverson .... 1.25 .55
❑ SQ21 Jason Kidd .... 1.00 .45
❑ SQ22 Damon Stoudamire .... .30 .14
❑ SQ23 Corliss Williamson ...... .15 .07
❑ SQ24 Tim Duncan .... 1.50 .70
❑ SQ25 Gary Payton .... .50 .23
❑ SQ26 Chauncey Billups .... .15 .07
❑ SQ27 Karl Malone .... .50 .23
❑ SQ28 Shareef Abdur-Rahim .75 .35
❑ SQ29 Juwan Howard .... .20 .09
❑ SQ30 Michael Jordan......... 4.00 1.80

1998-99 UD Choice StarQuest Gold

	MINT	NRMT
COMMON CARD (SQ1-SQ30)..	8.00	3.60
SEMISTARS..............................	12.00	5.50
UNLISTED STARS................	20.00	9.00

*STARS: 25X TO 60X BASE INSERT
RANDOM INSERTS IN HOB/RET
STATED PRINT RUN 100 SERIAL #'d SETS

❑ SQ30 Michael Jordan...... 400.00 180.00

1998-99 UD Ionix

	MINT	NRMT
COMPLETE SET (80)	100.00	45.00
COMPLETE SET w/o RC (60)	30.00	13.50
COMMON MJ (1-6/13)	4.00	1.80
COMMON CARD (7-60)..............	.15	.07
COMMON CARD (61-80)..........	2.00	.90

SEMISTARS	.20	.09
UNLISTED STARS	.40	.18

ELECTRIX RC SUBSET STATED ODDS 1:4

	MINT	NRMT
❑ 1 Michael Jordan	4.00	1.80
❑ 2 Michael Jordan	4.00	1.80
❑ 3 Michael Jordan	4.00	1.80
❑ 4 Michael Jordan	4.00	1.80
❑ 5 Michael Jordan	4.00	1.80
❑ 6 Michael Jordan	4.00	1.80
❑ 7 Steve Smith	.20	.09
❑ 8 Dikembe Mutombo	.20	.09
❑ 9 Ron Mercer	.60	.25
❑ 10 Antoine Walker	.60	.25
❑ 11 Derrick Coleman	.20	.09
❑ 12 Glen Rice	.20	.09
❑ 13 Michael Jordan	4.00	1.80
❑ 14 Toni Kukoc	.50	.23
❑ 15 Derek Anderson	.50	.23
❑ 16 Shawn Kemp	.60	.25
❑ 17 Michael Finley	.40	.18
❑ 18 Steve Nash	.15	.07
❑ 19 Antonio McDyess	.40	.18
❑ 20 Nick Van Exel	.20	.09
❑ 21 Grant Hill	2.00	.90
❑ 22 Jerry Stackhouse	.20	.09
❑ 23 Donyell Marshall	.15	.07
❑ 24 John Starks	.15	.07
❑ 25 Charles Barkley	.60	.25
❑ 26 Hakeem Olajuwon	.60	.25
❑ 27 Scottie Pippen	1.25	.55
❑ 28 Reggie Miller	.40	.18
❑ 29 Rik Smits	.15	.07
❑ 30 Maurice Taylor	.40	.18
❑ 31 Kobe Bryant	3.00	1.35
❑ 32 Shaquille O'Neal	2.00	.90
❑ 33 Tim Hardaway	.40	.18
❑ 34 Alonzo Mourning	.40	.18
❑ 35 Ray Allen	.50	.23
❑ 36 Glenn Robinson	.20	.09
❑ 37 Stephon Marbury	1.00	.45
❑ 38 Kevin Garnett	2.50	1.10
❑ 39 Jayson Williams	.20	.09
❑ 40 Keith Van Horn	1.00	.45
❑ 41 Patrick Ewing	.40	.18
❑ 42 Allan Houston	.40	.18
❑ 43 Anfernee Hardaway	1.25	.55
❑ 44 Isaac Austin	.15	.07
❑ 45 Tim Thomas	.60	.25
❑ 46 Allen Iverson	1.50	.70
❑ 47 Tom Gugliotta	.20	.09
❑ 48 Jason Kidd	1.25	.55
❑ 49 Damon Stoudamire	.40	.18
❑ 50 Chris Webber	1.25	.55
❑ 51 Tim Duncan	2.00	.90
❑ 52 David Robinson	.60	.25
❑ 53 Gary Payton	.60	.25
❑ 54 Vin Baker	.20	.09
❑ 55 Tracy McGrady	1.50	.70
❑ 56 John Stockton	.40	.18
❑ 57 Karl Malone	.60	.25
❑ 58 Shareef Abdur-Rahim	1.00	.45
❑ 59 Juwan Howard	.20	.09
❑ 60 Mitch Richmond	.40	.18
❑ 61 Michael Olowokandi RC	3.00	1.35
❑ 62 Mike Bibby RC	6.00	2.70
❑ 63 Raef LaFrentz RC	4.00	1.80
❑ 64 Antawn Jamison RC	10.00	4.50
❑ 65 Vince Carter RC	50.00	22.00
❑ 66 Robert Traylor RC	2.00	.90
❑ 67 Jason Williams RC	12.00	5.50
❑ 68 Larry Hughes RC	12.00	5.50
❑ 69 Dirk Nowitzki RC	8.00	3.60
❑ 70 Paul Pierce RC	10.00	4.50
❑ 71 Cuttino Mobley RC	4.00	1.80
❑ 72 Corey Benjamin RC	2.00	.90
❑ 73 Predrag Stojakovic RC	3.00	1.35
❑ 74 Michael Dickerson RC	4.00	1.80
❑ 75 Matt Harpring RC	2.00	.90
❑ 76 Rashard Lewis RC	8.00	3.60
❑ 77 Pat Garrity RC	2.00	.90
❑ 78 Roshown McLeod RC	2.00	.90
❑ 79 Ricky Davis RC	4.00	1.80
❑ 80 Felipe Lopez RC	2.50	1.10
❑ J1A Michael Jordan AU	6000.00	2700.00

1998-99 UD Ionix Reciprocal

	MINT	NRMT
COMMON MJ (1-6/13)	50.00	22.00
COMMON CARD (7-60)	2.50	1.10
COMMON CARD (61-80)	25.00	11.00

*STARS: 6X TO 15X BASE CARD HI
*RCs: 5X TO 12X BASE HI
STARS: PRINT RUN 750 SERIAL #'d SETS
RCs: PRINT RUN 100 SERIAL #'d SETS
RANDOM INSERTS IN PACKS

1998-99 UD Ionix Area 23

	MINT	NRMT
COMPLETE SET (10)	125.00	55.00
COMMON CARD (A1-A10)	15.00	6.75

STATED ODDS 1:18

❑ A1 Michael Jordan	15.00	6.75
❑ A2 Michael Jordan	15.00	6.75
❑ A3 Michael Jordan	15.00	6.75
❑ A4 Michael Jordan	15.00	6.75
❑ A5 Michael Jordan	15.00	6.75
❑ A6 Michael Jordan	15.00	6.75
❑ A7 Michael Jordan	15.00	6.75
❑ A8 Michael Jordan	15.00	6.75
❑ A9 Michael Jordan	15.00	6.75
❑ A10 Michael Jordan	15.00	6.75

1998-99 UD Ionix Kinetix

	MINT	NRMT
COMPLETE SET (20)	80.00	36.00
COMMON CARD (K1-K20)	1.25	.55
UNLISTED STARS	2.00	.90

STATED ODDS 1:9

❑ K1 Michael Jordan	15.00	6.75
❑ K2 Michael Olowokandi	2.50	1.10
❑ K3 Keith Van Horn	3.00	1.35
❑ K4 Grant Hill	6.00	2.70
❑ K5 Stephon Marbury	3.00	1.35
❑ K6 Larry Hughes	8.00	3.60
❑ K7 Vince Carter	30.00	13.50
❑ K8 Jason Kidd	4.00	1.80
❑ K9 Robert Traylor	1.25	.55
❑ K10 Ron Mercer	2.00	.90
❑ K11 Dirk Nowitzki	5.00	2.20
❑ K12 Antawn Jamison	6.00	2.70
❑ K13 Kobe Bryant	10.00	4.50
❑ K14 Jason Williams	8.00	3.60
❑ K15 Raef LaFrentz	2.00	.90
❑ K16 Gary Payton	2.00	.90
❑ K17 Tim Duncan	6.00	2.70
❑ K18 Paul Pierce	6.00	2.70
❑ K19 Mike Bibby	4.00	1.80
❑ K20 Scottie Pippen	4.00	1.80

1998-99 UD Ionix MJ HoloGrFX

	MINT	NRMT
COMPLETE SET (10)	2000.00	900.00
COMMON CARD (MJ1-10)	250.00	110.00

STATED ODDS 1:1500

❑ MJ1 Michael Jordan	250.00	110.00
❑ MJ2 Michael Jordan	250.00	110.00
❑ MJ3 Michael Jordan	250.00	110.00
❑ MJ4 Michael Jordan	250.00	110.00
❑ MJ5 Michael Jordan	250.00	110.00
❑ MJ6 Michael Jordan	250.00	110.00
❑ MJ7 Michael Jordan	250.00	110.00
❑ MJ8 Michael Jordan	250.00	110.00
❑ MJ9 Michael Jordan	250.00	110.00
❑ MJ10 Michael Jordan	250.00	110.00

1998-99 UD Ionix Skyonix

	MINT	NRMT
COMPLETE SET (25)	250.00	110.00
COMMON CARD (S1-S25)	5.00	2.20

STATED ODDS 1:53

❑ S1 Michael Jordan	80.00	36.00
❑ S2 Scottie Pippen	15.00	6.75
❑ S3 Derek Anderson	6.00	2.70
❑ S4 Jason Kidd	15.00	6.75
❑ S5 Damon Stoudamire	5.00	2.20
❑ S6 Antoine Walker	8.00	3.60
❑ S7 Shaquille O'Neal	25.00	11.00
❑ S8 Tim Thomas	8.00	3.60
❑ S9 Reggie Miller	5.00	2.20
❑ S10 Allen Iverson	20.00	9.00
❑ S11 Antonio McDyess	5.00	2.20

	MINT	NRMT
❑ S12 Michael Finley	5.00	2.20
❑ S13 Charles Barkley	8.00	3.60
❑ S14 Shareef Abdur-Rahim	12.00	5.50
❑ S15 Gary Payton	8.00	3.60
❑ S16 David Robinson	8.00	3.60
❑ S17 Anfernee Hardaway	15.00	6.75
❑ S18 Ray Allen	8.00	3.60
❑ S19 Ron Mercer	8.00	3.60
❑ S20 Tim Hardaway	5.00	2.20
❑ S21 Chris Webber	15.00	6.75
❑ S22 Kevin Garnett	30.00	13.50
❑ S23 Juwan Howard	5.00	2.20
❑ S24 Karl Malone	8.00	3.60
❑ S25 Keith Van Horn	12.00	5.50

1998-99 UD Ionix UD Authentics

	MINT	NRMT
COMPLETE SET (5)	175.00	80.00
COMMON CARD	20.00	9.00

RANDOM INSERTS IN PACKS
STATED PRINT RUN 475 SETS

❑ CB Corey Benjamin	20.00	9.00
❑ DO Michael Doleac	20.00	9.00
❑ JW Jason Williams	150.00	70.00
❑ RL Raef LaFrentz	25.00	11.00
❑ RM Roshown McLeod	20.00	9.00

1998-99 UD Ionix Warp Zone

	MINT	NRMT
COMPLETE SET (15)	500.00	220.00
COMMON CARD (Z1-Z15)	5.00	2.20
UNLISTED STARS	10.00	4.50

STATED ODDS 1:216

❑ Z1 Michael Jordan	120.00	55.00
❑ Z2 Tim Duncan	50.00	22.00
❑ Z3 Robert Traylor	5.00	2.20
❑ Z4 Michael Olowokandi	10.00	4.50
❑ Z5 Vince Carter	120.00	55.00
❑ Z6 Dirk Nowitzki	20.00	9.00
❑ Z7 Antawn Jamison	25.00	11.00
❑ Z8 Jason Williams	30.00	13.50
❑ Z9 Larry Hughes	30.00	13.50
❑ Z10 Raef LaFrentz	10.00	4.50
❑ Z11 Allen Iverson	40.00	18.00
❑ Z12 Kobe Bryant	80.00	36.00
❑ Z13 Grant Hill	50.00	22.00
❑ Z14 Mike Bibby	15.00	6.75
❑ Z15 Paul Pierce	25.00	11.00

1999-00 UD Ionix

	MINT	NRMT
COMPLETE SET (90)	150.00	70.00
COMPLETE SET w/o SP (60)	20.00	9.00
COMMON CARD (1-60)	.15	.07
COMMON RC (61-90)	2.00	.90
SEMISTARS	.20	.09
SEMISTARS RC	2.50	1.10
UNLISTED STARS	.40	.18
UNLISTED STARS RC	3.00	1.35

RCs: PRINT RUN 3500 SERIAL #'d SETS
RCs: RANDOM INSERTS IN PACKS
MJ FINAL FLOOR LISTED UNDER 99-00 UD

❑ 1 Dikembe Mutombo	.20	.09
❑ 2 Isaiah Rider	.20	.09
❑ 3 Antoine Walker	.50	.23
❑ 4 Paul Pierce	.75	.35
❑ 5 Eddie Jones	.75	.35
❑ 6 Anthony Mason	.20	.09
❑ 7 Toni Kukoc	.50	.23
❑ 8 Hersey Hawkins	.20	.09
❑ 9 Shawn Kemp	.60	.25
❑ 10 Lamond Murray	.15	.07
❑ 11 Michael Finley	.40	.18
❑ 12 Cedric Ceballos	.15	.07
❑ 13 Antonio McDyess	.40	.18
❑ 14 Ron Mercer	.50	.23
❑ 15 Grant Hill	2.00	.90
❑ 16 Jerry Stackhouse	.20	.09
❑ 17 Antawn Jamison	.75	.35
❑ 18 Mookie Blaylock	.15	.07
❑ 19 Charles Barkley	.60	.25
❑ 20 Hakeem Olajuwon	.60	.25
❑ 21 Reggie Miller	.40	.18
❑ 22 Rik Smits	.15	.07
❑ 23 Maurice Taylor	.40	.18
❑ 24 Derek Anderson	.40	.18
❑ 25 Kobe Bryant	3.00	1.35
❑ 26 Shaquille O'Neal	2.00	.90
❑ 27 Tim Hardaway	.40	.18
❑ 28 Alonzo Mourning	.40	.18
❑ 29 Ray Allen	.40	.18
❑ 30 Glenn Robinson	.20	.09
❑ 31 Kevin Garnett	2.50	1.10
❑ 32 Terrell Brandon	.20	.09
❑ 33 Stephon Marbury	.75	.35
❑ 34 Keith Van Horn	.75	.35
❑ 35 Allan Houston	.40	.18
❑ 36 Latrell Sprewell	.75	.35
❑ 37 Darrell Armstrong	.20	.09
❑ 38 Tariq Abdul-Wahad	.15	.07
❑ 39 Allen Iverson	1.50	.70
❑ 40 Larry Hughes	1.00	.45
❑ 41 Anfernee Hardaway	1.25	.55
❑ 42 Jason Kidd	1.25	.55
❑ 43 Tom Gugliotta	.20	.09
❑ 44 Scottie Pippen	1.25	.55
❑ 45 Damon Stoudamire	.40	.18
❑ 46 Rasheed Wallace	.40	.18
❑ 47 Jason Williams	1.00	.45
❑ 48 Chris Webber	1.25	.55
❑ 49 Tim Duncan	2.00	.90
❑ 50 David Robinson	.60	.25
❑ 51 Gary Payton	.60	.25
❑ 52 Vin Baker	.20	.09
❑ 53 Vince Carter	4.00	1.80
❑ 54 Tracy McGrady	1.25	.55
❑ 55 Karl Malone	.60	.25
❑ 56 John Stockton	.40	.18
❑ 57 Mike Bibby	.50	.23
❑ 58 Shareef Abdur-Rahim	.75	.35
❑ 59 Mitch Richmond	.40	.18
❑ 60 Juwan Howard	.20	.09
❑ 61 Elton Brand RC	30.00	13.50
❑ 62 Steve Francis RC	40.00	18.00
❑ 63 Baron Davis RC	8.00	3.60
❑ 64 Lamar Odom RC	25.00	11.00
❑ 65 Jonathan Bender RC	15.00	6.75
❑ 66 Wally Szczerbiak RC	12.00	5.50
❑ 67 Richard Hamilton RC	8.00	3.60
❑ 68 Andre Miller RC	10.00	4.50
❑ 69 Shawn Marion RC	10.00	4.50
❑ 70 Jason Terry RC	5.00	2.20
❑ 71 Trajan Langdon RC	5.00	2.20
❑ 72 Aleksandar Radojevic RC	2.00	.90
❑ 73 Corey Maggette RC	12.00	5.50
❑ 74 William Avery RC	5.00	2.20
❑ 75 Ron Artest RC	8.00	3.60
❑ 76 Cal Bowdler RC	3.00	1.35
❑ 77 James Posey RC	6.00	2.70
❑ 78 Quincy Lewis RC	3.00	1.35
❑ 79 Dion Glover RC	3.00	1.35
❑ 80 Jeff Foster RC	3.00	1.35
❑ 81 Kenny Thomas RC	5.00	2.20
❑ 82 Devean George RC	6.00	2.70
❑ 83 Tim James RC	4.00	1.80
❑ 84 Vonteego Cummings RC	5.00	2.20
❑ 85 Jumaine Jones RC	2.50	1.10
❑ 86 Scott Padgett RC	3.00	1.35
❑ 87 Chucky Atkins RC	4.00	1.80
❑ 88 Adrian Griffin RC	4.00	1.80
❑ 89 Todd MacCulloch RC	3.00	1.35
❑ 90 Anthony Carter RC	8.00	3.60

1999-00 UD Ionix Reciprocal

	MINT	NRMT
COMMON CARD (1-60)	1.00	.45
COMMON CARD (61-90)	6.00	2.70

*STARS: 2X TO 5X BASE CARD HI
*RCs: 1.25X TO 3X BASE HI
STARS: STATED ODDS 1:4
RCs: PRINT RUN 100 SERIAL #'d SETS
RCs: RANDOM INSERTS IN PACKS

1999-00 UD Ionix Awesome Powers

	MINT	NRMT
COMPLETE SET (15)	30.00	13.50
COMMON CARD (AP1-AP15)	1.25	.55
UNLISTED STARS	1.50	.70

STATED ODDS 1:23

❑ AP1 Elton Brand	8.00	3.60
❑ AP2 Corey Maggette	3.00	1.35
❑ AP3 Wally Szczerbiak	3.00	1.35
❑ AP4 Charles Barkley	2.50	1.10

	MINT	NRMT
❑ AP5 Shawn Marion	2.50	1.10
❑ AP6 Jason Terry	1.25	.55
❑ AP7 Keith Van Horn	3.00	1.35
❑ AP8 Steve Francis	10.00	4.50
❑ AP9 Trajan Langdon	1.50	.70
❑ AP10 Reggie Miller	1.50	.70
❑ AP11 Richard Hamilton	2.00	.90
❑ AP12 Jonathan Bender	4.00	1.80
❑ AP13 Baron Davis	2.00	.90
❑ AP14 Paul Pierce	3.00	1.35
❑ AP15 Andre Miller	2.50	1.10

1999-00 UD Ionix BIOrhythm

	MINT	NRMT
COMPLETE SET (15)	15.00	6.75
COMMON CARD (B1-B15)	.60	.25
UNLISTED STARS	.75	.35
STATED ODDS 1:7		
❑ B1 Grant Hill	4.00	1.80
❑ B2 Antawn Jamison	1.50	.70
❑ B3 Shaquille O'Neal	4.00	1.80
❑ B4 Stephon Marbury	1.50	.70
❑ B5 Michael Finley	.60	.25
❑ B6 Hakeem Olajuwon	1.25	.55
❑ B7 Ron Mercer	1.00	.45
❑ B8 Tim Hardaway	.75	.35
❑ B9 Jason Kidd	2.50	1.10
❑ B10 Allan Houston	.75	.35
❑ B11 Ray Allen	.75	.35
❑ B12 Shawn Kemp	1.25	.55
❑ B13 Alonzo Mourning	.75	.35
❑ B14 Tim Duncan	4.00	1.80
❑ B15 Eddie Jones	1.50	.70

1999-00 UD Ionix Pyrotechnics

	MINT	NRMT
COMPLETE SET (15)	120.00	55.00
COMMON CARD (P1-P15)	3.00	1.35
STATED ODDS 1:72		
❑ P1 Kevin Garnett	20.00	9.00
❑ P2 Shareef Abdur-Rahim	6.00	2.70
❑ P3 Jason Kidd	10.00	4.50
❑ P4 Antonio McDyess	3.00	1.35
❑ P5 Karl Malone	5.00	2.20

	MINT	NRMT
❑ P6 Eddie Jones	6.00	2.70
❑ P7 Antoine Walker	4.00	1.80
❑ P8 Kobe Bryant	25.00	11.00
❑ P9 Anfernee Hardaway	10.00	4.50
❑ P10 Antawn Jamison	6.00	2.70
❑ P11 Keith Van Horn	6.00	2.70
❑ P12 Grant Hill	15.00	6.75
❑ P13 Gary Payton	5.00	2.20
❑ P14 Allen Iverson	12.00	5.50
❑ P15 Vince Carter	30.00	13.50

1999-00 UD Ionix UD Authentics

	MINT	NRMT
COMMON CARD	5.00	2.20
STATED ODDS 1:144		
❑ AH Anfernee Hardaway	100.00	45.00
❑ AJ Antawn Jamison	20.00	9.00
❑ AM Andre Miller	15.00	6.75
❑ BD Baron Davis	15.00	6.75
❑ BG Brian Grant	15.00	6.75
❑ CM Corey Maggette	25.00	11.00
❑ JB Jonathan Bender	25.00	11.00
❑ JP James Posey	12.00	5.50
❑ JT Jason Terry	10.00	4.50
❑ KB Kobe Bryant	250.00	110.00
❑ KG Kevin Garnett		
❑ MJ Michael Jordan		
❑ MT Maurice Taylor	8.00	3.60
❑ RA Ron Artest	15.00	6.75
❑ RH Richard Hamilton	15.00	6.75
❑ RT Robert Traylor	5.00	2.20
❑ SF Steve Francis	100.00	45.00
❑ SM Shawn Marion	15.00	6.75
❑ TG Tom Gugliotta	12.00	5.50
❑ TL Trajan Langdon	10.00	4.50
❑ WA William Avery	8.00	3.60
❑ WS Wally Szczerbiak	20.00	9.00

1999-00 UD Ionix Warp Zone

	MINT	NRMT
COMPLETE SET (15)	400.00	180.00
COMMON CARD (WZ1-WZ10)	10.00	4.50
STATED ODDS 1:144		
❑ WZ1 Kobe Bryant	60.00	27.00
❑ WZ2 Kevin Garnett	50.00	22.00
❑ WZ3 Tim Duncan	40.00	18.00
❑ WZ4 Elton Brand	40.00	18.00
❑ WZ5 Wally Szczerbiak	15.00	6.75
❑ WZ6 Stephon Marbury	15.00	6.75
❑ WZ7 Allen Iverson	30.00	13.50
❑ WZ8 Anfernee Hardaway	25.00	11.00
❑ WZ9 Shaquille O'Neal	40.00	18.00
❑ WZ10 Baron Davis	10.00	4.50
❑ WZ11 Scottie Pippen	25.00	11.00
❑ WZ12 Jason Williams	20.00	9.00
❑ WZ13 Steve Francis	50.00	22.00
❑ WZ14 Vince Carter	80.00	36.00
❑ WZ15 Lamar Odom	30.00	13.50

1992-93 Ultra

	MINT	NRMT
COMPLETE SET (375)	30.00	13.50
COMPLETE SERIES 1 (200)	15.00	6.75
COMPLETE SERIES 2 (175)	15.00	6.75
COMMON CARD (1-200)	.10	.05
COMMON CARD (201-375)	.05	.02
SEMISTARS SER.1	.25	.11
SEMISTARS SER.2	.15	.07
UNLISTED STARS SER.1	.50	.23
UNLISTED STARS SER.2	.30	.14
SUBSET CARDS HALF VALUE OF BASE CARDS		
❑ 1 Stacey Augmon	.25	.11
❑ 2 Duane Ferrell	.10	.05
❑ 3 Paul Graham	.10	.05
❑ 4 Blair Rasmussen	.10	.05
❑ 5 Rumeal Robinson	.10	.05
❑ 6 Dominique Wilkins	.50	.23
❑ 7 Kevin Willis	.10	.05
❑ 8 John Bagley	.10	.05
❑ 9 Dee Brown	.10	.05
❑ 10 Rick Fox	.25	.11
❑ 11 Kevin Gamble	.10	.05
❑ 12 Joe Kleine	.10	.05
❑ 13 Reggie Lewis	.25	.11
❑ 14 Kevin McHale	.50	.23
❑ 15 Robert Parish	.25	.11
❑ 16 Ed Pinckney	.10	.05
❑ 17 Muggsy Bogues	.25	.11
❑ 18 Dell Curry	.10	.05
❑ 19 Kenny Gattison	.10	.05
❑ 20 Kendall Gill	.25	.11
❑ 21 Larry Johnson	.60	.25

❑ 22 Johnny Newman .10 .05
❑ 23 J.R. Reid .10 .05
❑ 24 B.J. Armstrong .10 .05
❑ 25 Bill Cartwright .10 .05
❑ 26 Horace Grant .25 .11
❑ 27 Michael Jordan 6.00 2.70
❑ 28 Stacey King .10 .05
❑ 29 John Paxson .10 .05
❑ 30 Will Perdue .10 .05
❑ 31 Scottie Pippen 1.50 .70
❑ 32 Scott Williams .10 .05
❑ 33 John Battle .10 .05
❑ 34 Terrell Brandon .50 .23
❑ 35 Brad Daugherty .10 .05
❑ 36 Craig Ehlo .10 .05
❑ 37 Larry Nance .10 .05
❑ 38 Mark Price .10 .05
❑ 39 Mike Sanders .10 .05
❑ 40 John Williams .10 .05
❑ 41 Terry Davis .10 .05
❑ 42 Derek Harper .25 .11
❑ 43 Donald Hodge .10 .05
❑ 44 Mike Iuzzolino .10 .05
❑ 45 Fat Lever .10 .05
❑ 46 Doug Smith .10 .05
❑ 47 Randy White .10 .05
❑ 48 Winston Garland .10 .05
❑ 49 Chris Jackson .10 .05
❑ 50 Marcus Liberty .10 .05
❑ 51 Todd Lichti .10 .05
❑ 52 Mark Macon .10 .05
❑ 53 Dikembe Mutombo .50 .23
❑ 54 Reggie Williams .10 .05
❑ 55 Mark Aguirre .10 .05
❑ 56 Joe Dumars .50 .23
❑ 57 Bill Laimbeer .25 .11
❑ 58 Dennis Rodman 1.00 .45
❑ 59 Isiah Thomas .50 .23
❑ 60 Darrell Walker .10 .05
❑ 61 Orlando Woolridge .10 .05
❑ 62 Victor Alexander .10 .05
❑ 63 Chris Gatling .10 .05
❑ 64 Tim Hardaway .60 .25
❑ 65 Tyrone Hill .10 .05
❑ 66 Sarunas Marciulionis .10 .05
❑ 67 Chris Mullin .50 .23
❑ 68 Billy Owens .25 .11
❑ 69 Sleepy Floyd .10 .05
❑ 70 Avery Johnson .10 .05
❑ 71 Vernon Maxwell .10 .05
❑ 72 Hakeem Olajuwon .75 .35
❑ 73 Kenny Smith .10 .05
❑ 74 Otis Thorpe .25 .11
❑ 75 Dale Davis .10 .05
❑ 76 Vern Fleming .10 .05
❑ 77 George McCloud .10 .05
❑ 78 Reggie Miller .50 .23
❑ 79 Detlef Schrempf .25 .11
❑ 80 Rik Smits .25 .11
❑ 81 LaSalle Thompson .10 .05
❑ 82 Gary Grant .10 .05
❑ 83 Ron Harper .25 .11
❑ 84 Mark Jackson .25 .11
❑ 85 Danny Manning .25 .11
❑ 86 Ken Norman .10 .05
❑ 87 Stanley Roberts .10 .05
❑ 88 Loy Vaught .10 .05
❑ 89 Elden Campbell .25 .11
❑ 90 Vlade Divac .25 .11
❑ 91 A.C. Green .25 .11
❑ 92 Sam Perkins .25 .11
❑ 93 Byron Scott .25 .11
❑ 94 Tony Smith .10 .05
❑ 95 Sedale Threatt .10 .05
❑ 96 James Worthy .50 .23
❑ 97 Willie Burton .10 .05
❑ 98 Bimbo Coles .10 .05
❑ 99 Kevin Edwards .10 .05
❑ 100 Grant Long .10 .05
❑ 101 Glen Rice .50 .23
❑ 102 Rony Seikaly .10 .05
❑ 103 Brian Shaw .10 .05
❑ 104 Steve Smith .60 .25
❑ 105 Frank Brickowski .10 .05
❑ 106 Moses Malone .50 .23
❑ 107 Fred Roberts .10 .05
❑ 108 Alvin Robertson .10 .05
❑ 109 Thurl Bailey .10 .05
❑ 110 Gerald Glass .10 .05
❑ 111 Luc Longley .25 .11
❑ 112 Felton Spencer .10 .05
❑ 113 Doug West .10 .05
❑ 114 Kenny Anderson .50 .23
❑ 115 Mookie Blaylock .25 .11
❑ 116 Sam Bowie .10 .05
❑ 117 Derrick Coleman .25 .11
❑ 118 Chris Dudley .10 .05
❑ 119 Chris Morris .10 .05
❑ 120 Drazen Petrovic .10 .05
❑ 121 Greg Anthony .10 .05
❑ 122 Patrick Ewing .50 .23
❑ 123 Anthony Mason .50 .23
❑ 124 Charles Oakley .25 .11
❑ 125 Doc Rivers .25 .11
❑ 126 Charles Smith .10 .05
❑ 127 John Starks .25 .11
❑ 128 Nick Anderson .25 .11
❑ 129 Anthony Bowie .10 .05
❑ 130 Terry Catledge .10 .05
❑ 131 Jerry Reynolds .10 .05
❑ 132 Dennis Scott .25 .11
❑ 133 Scott Skiles .10 .05
❑ 134 Brian Williams .10 .05
❑ 135 Ron Anderson .10 .05
❑ 136 Manute Bol .10 .05
❑ 137 Johnny Dawkins .10 .05
❑ 138 Armon Gilliam .10 .05
❑ 139 Hersey Hawkins .25 .11
❑ 140 Jeff Ruland .10 .05
❑ 141 Charles Shackleford .10 .05
❑ 142 Cedric Ceballos .25 .11
❑ 143 Tom Chambers .10 .05
❑ 144 Kevin Johnson .50 .23
❑ 145 Negele Knight .10 .05
❑ 146 Dan Majerle .25 .11
❑ 147 Mark West .10 .05
❑ 148 Mark Bryant .10 .05
❑ 149 Clyde Drexler .50 .23
❑ 150 Kevin Duckworth .10 .05
❑ 151 Jerome Kersey .10 .05
❑ 152 Robert Pack .10 .05
❑ 153 Terry Porter .10 .05
❑ 154 Clifford Robinson .25 .11
❑ 155 Buck Williams .25 .11
❑ 156 Anthony Bonner .10 .05
❑ 157 Duane Causwell .10 .05
❑ 158 Mitch Richmond .50 .23
❑ 159 Lionel Simmons .10 .05
❑ 160 Wayman Tisdale .10 .05
❑ 161 Spud Webb .25 .11
❑ 162 Willie Anderson .10 .05
❑ 163 Antoine Carr .10 .05
❑ 164 Terry Cummings .25 .11
❑ 165 Sean Elliott .25 .11
❑ 166 Sidney Green .10 .05
❑ 167 David Robinson .75 .35
❑ 168 Dana Barros .10 .05
❑ 169 Benoit Benjamin .10 .05
❑ 170 Michael Cage .10 .05
❑ 171 Eddie Johnson .10 .05
❑ 172 Shawn Kemp 1.00 .45
❑ 173 Derrick McKey .10 .05
❑ 174 Nate McMillan .10 .05
❑ 175 Gary Payton 1.00 .45
❑ 176 Ricky Pierce .10 .05
❑ 177 David Benoit .10 .05
❑ 178 Mike Brown .10 .05
❑ 179 Tyrone Corbin .10 .05
❑ 180 Mark Eaton .10 .05
❑ 181 Jeff Malone .10 .05
❑ 182 Karl Malone .75 .35
❑ 183 John Stockton .50 .23
❑ 184 Michael Adams .10 .05
❑ 185 Ledell Eackles .10 .05
❑ 186 Pervis Ellison .10 .05
❑ 187 A.J. English .10 .05
❑ 188 Harvey Grant .10 .05
❑ 189 Buck Johnson .10 .05
❑ 190 LaBradford Smith .10 .05
❑ 191 Larry Stewart .10 .05
❑ 192 David Wingate .10 .05
❑ 193 Alonzo Mourning RC 1.50 .70
❑ 194 Adam Keefe RC .10 .05
❑ 195 Robert Horry RC .50 .23
❑ 196 Anthony Peeler RC .25 .11
❑ 197 Tracy Murray RC .25 .11
❑ 198 Dave Johnson RC .10 .05
❑ 199 Checklist 1-104 .10 .05
❑ 200 Checklist 105-200 .10 .05
❑ 201 David Robinson JS .30 .14
❑ 202 Dikembe Mutombo JS .15 .07
❑ 203 Otis Thorpe JS .05 .02
❑ 204 Hakeem Olajuwon JS .30 .14
❑ 205 Shawn Kemp JS .50 .23
❑ 206 Charles Barkley JS .30 .14
❑ 207 Pervis Ellison JS .05 .02
❑ 208 Chris Morris JS .05 .02
❑ 209 Brad Daugherty JS .05 .02
❑ 210 Derrick Coleman JS .05 .02
❑ 211 Tim Perry JS .05 .02
❑ 212 Duane Causwell JS .05 .02
❑ 213 Scottie Pippen JS .50 .23
❑ 214 Robert Parish JS .05 .02
❑ 215 Stacey Augmon JS .05 .02
❑ 216 Michael Jordan JS 2.00 .90
❑ 217 Karl Malone JS .30 .14
❑ 218 John Williams JS .05 .02
❑ 219 Horace Grant JS .05 .02
❑ 220 Orlando Woolridge JS .05 .02
❑ 221 Mookie Blaylock .15 .07
❑ 222 Greg Foster .05 .02
❑ 223 Steve Henson .05 .02
❑ 224 Adam Keefe .05 .02
❑ 225 Jon Koncak .05 .02
❑ 226 Travis Mays .05 .02
❑ 227 Alaa Abdelnaby .05 .02
❑ 228 Sherman Douglas .05 .02
❑ 229 Xavier McDaniel .05 .02
❑ 230 Marcus Webb RC .05 .02
❑ 231 Tony Bennett RC .05 .02
❑ 232 Mike Gminski .05 .02
❑ 233 Kevin Lynch .05 .02
❑ 234 Alonzo Mourning .75 .35
❑ 235 David Wingate .05 .02
❑ 236 Rodney McCray .05 .02
❑ 237 Trent Tucker .05 .02
❑ 238 Corey Williams RC .05 .02
❑ 239 Danny Ferry .05 .02
❑ 240 Jay Guidinger RC .05 .02
❑ 241 Jerome Lane .05 .02
❑ 242 Bobby Phills RC .30 .14
❑ 243 Gerald Wilkins .05 .02
❑ 244 Walter Bond RC .05 .02
❑ 245 Dexter Cambridge RC .05 .02
❑ 246 Radisav Curcic RC UER .05 .02
(Misspelled Radislav
on card front)
❑ 247 Brian Howard RC .05 .02
❑ 248 Tracy Moore RC .05 .02
❑ 249 Sean Rooks RC .05 .02
❑ 250 Kevin Brooks .05 .02
❑ 251 LaPhonso Ellis RC .30 .14
❑ 252 Scott Hastings .05 .02
❑ 253 Robert Pack .05 .02
❑ 254 Gary Plummer RC .05 .02
❑ 255 Bryant Stith RC .15 .07
❑ 256 Robert Werdann RC .05 .02
❑ 257 Gerald Glass .05 .02
❑ 258 Terry Mills .05 .02
❑ 259 Olden Polynice .05 .02
❑ 260 Danny Young .05 .02
❑ 261 Jud Buechler .05 .02
❑ 262 Jeff Grayer .05 .02
❑ 263 Bryon Houston RC .05 .02
❑ 264 Keith Jennings RC .05 .02
❑ 265 Ed Nealy .05 .02
❑ 266 Latrell Sprewell RC 2.50 1.10
❑ 267 Scott Brooks .05 .02
❑ 268 Matt Bullard .05 .02
❑ 269 Winston Garland .05 .02
❑ 270 Carl Herrera .05 .02
❑ 271 Robert Horry .30 .14
❑ 272 Tree Rollins .05 .02
❑ 273 Greg Dreiling .05 .02
❑ 274 Sean Green .05 .02
❑ 275 Sam Mitchell .05 .02
❑ 276 Pooh Richardson .05 .02
❑ 277 Malik Sealy RC .15 .07

278 Kenny Williams	.05	.02
279 Mark Jackson	.15	.07
280 Stanley Roberts	.05	.02
281 Elmore Spencer RC	.05	.02
282 Kiki Vandeweghe	.05	.02
283 John S. Williams	.05	.02
284 Randy Woods RC	.05	.02
285 Alex Blackwell RC	.05	.02
286 Duane Cooper RC	.05	.02
287 James Edwards	.05	.02
288 Jack Haley	.05	.02
289 Anthony Peeler	.15	.07
290 Keith Askins	.05	.02
291 Matt Geiger RC	.15	.07
292 Alec Kessler	.05	.02
293 Harold Miner RC	.15	.07
294 John Salley	.05	.02
295 Anthony Avent RC	.05	.02
296 Jon Barry RC	.15	.07
297 Todd Day RC	.15	.07
298 Blue Edwards	.05	.02
299 Brad Lohaus	.05	.02
300 Lee Mayberry RC	.05	.02
301 Eric Murdock	.05	.02
302 Dan Schayes	.05	.02
303 Lance Blanks	.05	.02
304 Christian Laettner RC	.60	.25
305 Marlon Maxey RC	.05	.02
306 Bob McCann RC	.05	.02
307 Chuck Person	.05	.02
308 Brad Sellers	.05	.02
309 Chris Smith RC	.05	.02
310 Gundars Vetra RC	.05	.02
311 Micheal Williams	.05	.02
312 Rafael Addison	.05	.02
313 Chucky Brown	.05	.02
314 Maurice Cheeks	.05	.02
315 Tate George	.05	.02
316 Rick Mahorn	.05	.02
317 Rumeal Robinson	.05	.02
318 Eric Anderson RC	.05	.02
319 Rolando Blackman	.05	.02
320 Tony Campbell	.05	.02
321 Hubert Davis RC	.15	.07
322 Doc Rivers	.15	.07
323 Charles Smith	.05	.02
324 Herb Williams	.05	.02
325 Litterial Green RC	.05	.02
326 Steve Kerr	.15	.07
327 Greg Kite	.05	.02
328 Shaquille O'Neal RC	6.00	2.70
329 Tom Tolbert	.05	.02
330 Jeff Turner	.05	.02
331 Greg Grant	.05	.02
332 Jeff Hornacek	.15	.07
333 Andrew Lang	.05	.02
334 Tim Perry	.05	.02
335 C. Weatherspoon RC	.30	.14
336 Danny Ainge	.15	.07
337 Charles Barkley	.50	.23
338 Richard Dumas RC	.05	.02
339 Frank Johnson	.05	.02
340 Tim Kempton	.05	.02
341 Oliver Miller RC	.15	.07
342 Jerrod Mustaf	.05	.02
343 Mario Elie	.15	.07
344 Dave Johnson	.05	.02
345 Tracy Murray	.15	.07
346 Rod Strickland	.30	.14
347 Randy Brown	.05	.02
348 Pete Chilcutt	.05	.02
349 Marty Conlon	.05	.02
350 Jim Les	.05	.02
351 Kurt Rambis	.05	.02
352 Walt Williams RC	.30	.14
353 Lloyd Daniels RC	.05	.02
354 Vinny Del Negro	.05	.02
355 Dale Ellis	.05	.02
356 Avery Johnson	.05	.02
357 Sam Mack RC	.15	.07
358 J.R. Reid	.05	.02
359 David Wood	.05	.02
360 Vincent Askew	.05	.02
361 Isaac Austin RC	.15	.07
362 John Crotty RC	.05	.02
363 Stephen Howard RC	.05	.02
364 Jay Humphries	.05	.02
365 Larry Krystkowiak	.05	.02
366 Rex Chapman	.05	.02
367 Tom Gugliotta RC	1.00	.45
368 Buck Johnson	.05	.02
369 Charles Jones	.05	.02
370 Don MacLean RC	.05	.02
371 Doug Overton	.05	.02
372 Brent Price RC	.15	.07
373 Checklist 201-266	.05	.02
374 Checklist 267-330	.05	.02
375 Checklist 331-375	.05	.02
JS207 Pervis Ellison AU (Certified Autograph)	20.00	9.00
JS212 Duane Causwell AU (Certified Autograph)	15.00	6.75
JS215 Stacey Augmon AU (Certified Autograph)	30.00	13.50
NNO Jam Session Rank 1-10	2.50	1.10
David Robinson		
Dikembe Mutombo		
Otis Thorpe		
Hakeem Olajuwon		
Shawn Kemp		
Charles Barkley		
Pervis Ellison		
Chris Morris		
Brad Daugherty		
Derrick Coleman		
NNO Jam Session 11-20	2.50	1.10
Tim Perry		
Duane Causwell		
Scottie Pippen		
Robert Parish		
Stacey Augmon		
Michael Jordan		
Karl Malone		
John Williams		
Horace Grant		
Orlando Woolridge		

1992-93 Ultra All-NBA

	MINT	NRMT
COMPLETE SET (15)	40.00	18.00

*SINGLES: 1.5X TO 4X BASE CARD HI
SER.1 STATED ODDS 1:14

Card	MINT	NRMT
1 Karl Malone	3.00	1.35
2 Chris Mullin	2.00	.90
3 David Robinson	3.00	1.35
4 Michael Jordan	25.00	11.00
5 Clyde Drexler	2.00	.90
6 Scottie Pippen	6.00	2.70
7 Charles Barkley	2.00	.90
8 Patrick Ewing	2.00	.90
9 Tim Hardaway	2.50	1.10
10 John Stockton	2.00	.90
11 Dennis Rodman	4.00	1.80
12 Kevin Willis	.40	.18
13 Brad Daugherty	.40	.18
14 Mark Price	.40	.18
15 Kevin Johnson	2.00	.90

1992-93 Ultra All-Rookies

	MINT	NRMT
COMPLETE SET (10)	20.00	9.00

*SINGLES: 1X TO 2.5X BASE CARD HI
SER.2 STATED ODDS 1:13

Card	MINT	NRMT
1 LaPhonso Ellis	.75	.35
2 Tom Gugliotta	2.50	1.10
3 Robert Horry	1.25	.55
4 Christian Laettner	1.50	.70
5 Harold Miner	.40	.18
6 Alonzo Mourning	4.00	1.80
7 Shaquille O'Neal	15.00	6.75
8 Latrell Sprewell	6.00	2.70
9 Clarence Weatherspoon	.75	.35
10 Walt Williams	.75	.35

1992-93 Ultra Award Winners

	MINT	NRMT
COMPLETE SET (5)	25.00	11.00

*SINGLES: 1.5X TO 4X BASE CARD HI
SER.1 STATED ODDS 1:42

Card	MINT	NRMT
1 Michael Jordan	25.00	11.00
2 David Robinson	3.00	1.35
3 Larry Johnson	2.50	1.10
4 Detlef Schrempf	1.00	.45
5 Pervis Ellison	.40	.18

1992-93 Ultra Scottie Pippen

	MINT	NRMT
COMPLETE SET (10)	15.00	6.75
COMMON PIPPEN (1-10)	1.50	.70

SER.1 STATED ODDS 1:21

CERTIFIED AUTOGRAPH (AU)	150.00	70.00

PIPPEN AU: SER.1 STATED ODDS 1:9,000

COMMON SEND-OFF (11-12)	1.50	.70

TWO CARDS PER 10 SER.1 WRAPPERS

Card	MINT	NRMT
1 Scottie Pippen (Dribbling, right index finger pointing down)	1.50	.70
2 Scottie Pippen	1.50	.70

(Dribbling, Magnavox ad in background)

	MINT	NRMT
❑ 3 Scottie Pippen (Preparing to dunk)	1.50	.70
❑ 4 Scottie Pippen (Dribbling, defender's hand reaching in)	1.50	.70
❑ 5 Scottie Pippen (In air, ball in both hands, vs. Bucks)	1.50	.70
❑ 6 Scottie Pippen (Driving toward basket& vs. Nuggets)	1.50	.70
❑ 7 Scottie Pippen (Shooting over McDaniel of the Knicks)	1.50	.70
❑ 8 Scottie Pippen (Dribbling, Laker cheer-leader in background)	1.50	.70
❑ 9 Scottie Pippen (Defending against McDaniel of the Knicks)	1.50	.70
❑ 10 Scottie Pippen (Driving toward basket& vs. Nets)	1.50	.70
❑ 11 Scottie Pippen (Defended by Rodman; ball in left hand)	1.50	.70
❑ 12 Scottie Pippen (Dunking over Nugget player)	1.50	.70

1992-93 Ultra Playmakers

	MINT	NRMT
COMPLETE SET (10)	4.00	1.80

*SINGLES: 1.25X TO 3X BASE CARD HI
SER.2 STATED ODDS 1:13

	MINT	NRMT
❑ 1 Kenny Anderson	1.50	.70
❑ 2 Muggsy Bogues	.75	.35
❑ 3 Tim Hardaway	2.00	.90
❑ 4 Mark Jackson	.75	.35
❑ 5 Kevin Johnson	1.50	.70
❑ 6 Mark Price	.30	.14
❑ 7 Terry Porter	.30	.14
❑ 8 Scott Skiles	.30	.14
❑ 9 John Stockton	1.50	.70
❑ 10 Isiah Thomas	1.50	.70

1992-93 Ultra Rejectors

	MINT	NRMT
COMPLETE SET (5)	10.00	4.50

*SINGLES: .6X TO 1.5X BASE CARD HI
SER.2 STATED ODDS 1:26

	MINT	NRMT
❑ 1 Alonzo Mourning	1.25	.55
❑ 2 Dikembe Mutombo	.75	.35
❑ 3 Hakeem Olajuwon	1.25	.55
❑ 4 Shaquille O'Neal	8.00	3.60
❑ 5 David Robinson	1.25	.55

1993-94 Ultra

	MINT	NRMT
COMPLETE SET (375)	30.00	13.50
COMPLETE SERIES 1 (200)	15.00	6.75
COMPLETE SERIES 2 (175)	15.00	6.75
COMMON CARD (1-375)	.05	.02
SEMISTARS	.15	.07
UNLISTED STARS	.30	.14

SUBSET CARDS HALF VALUE OF BASE CARDS

	MINT	NRMT
❑ 1 Stacey Augmon	.05	.02
❑ 2 Mookie Blaylock	.15	.07
❑ 3 Doug Edwards RC	.05	.02
❑ 4 Duane Ferrell	.05	.02
❑ 5 Paul Graham	.05	.02
❑ 6 Adam Keefe	.05	.02
❑ 7 Dominique Wilkins	.30	.14
❑ 8 Kevin Willis	.05	.02
❑ 9 Alaa Abdelnaby	.05	.02
❑ 10 Dee Brown	.05	.02
❑ 11 Sherman Douglas	.05	.02
❑ 12 Rick Fox	.05	.02
❑ 13 Kevin Gamble	.05	.02
❑ 14 Xavier McDaniel	.05	.02
❑ 15 Robert Parish	.15	.07
❑ 16 Muggsy Bogues	.15	.07
❑ 17 Scott Burrell RC	.30	.14
❑ 18 Dell Curry	.05	.02
❑ 19 Kenny Gattison	.05	.02
❑ 20 Hersey Hawkins	.15	.07
❑ 21 Eddie Johnson	.05	.02
❑ 22 Larry Johnson	.30	.14
❑ 23 Alonzo Mourning	.50	.23
❑ 24 Johnny Newman	.05	.02
❑ 25 David Wingate	.05	.02
❑ 26 B.J. Armstrong	.05	.02
❑ 27 Corie Blount RC	.05	.02
❑ 28 Bill Cartwright	.05	.02
❑ 29 Horace Grant	.15	.07
❑ 30 Michael Jordan	4.00	1.80
❑ 31 Stacey King	.05	.02
❑ 32 John Paxson	.05	.02
❑ 33 Will Perdue	.05	.02
❑ 34 Scottie Pippen	1.00	.45
❑ 35 Terrell Brandon	.15	.07
❑ 36 Brad Daugherty	.05	.02
❑ 37 Danny Ferry	.05	.02
❑ 38 Chris Mills RC	.30	.14
❑ 39 Larry Nance	.05	.02
❑ 40 Mark Price	.05	.02
❑ 41 Gerald Wilkins	.05	.02
❑ 42 John Williams	.05	.02
❑ 43 Terry Davis	.05	.02
❑ 44 Derek Harper	.15	.07
❑ 45 Donald Hodge	.05	.02
❑ 46 Jim Jackson	.15	.07
❑ 47 Sean Rooks	.05	.02
❑ 48 Doug Smith	.05	.02
❑ 49 Mahmoud Abdul-Rauf	.05	.02
❑ 50 LaPhonso Ellis	.05	.02
❑ 51 Mark Macon	.05	.02
❑ 52 Dikembe Mutombo	.15	.07
❑ 53 Bryant Stith	.05	.02
❑ 54 Reggie Williams	.05	.02
❑ 55 Mark Aguirre	.05	.02
❑ 56 Joe Dumars	.30	.14
❑ 57 Bill Laimbeer	.05	.02
❑ 58 Terry Mills	.05	.02
❑ 59 Olden Polynice	.05	.02
❑ 60 Alvin Robertson	.05	.02
❑ 61 Sean Elliott	.15	.07
❑ 62 Isiah Thomas	.30	.14
❑ 63 Victor Alexander	.05	.02
❑ 64 Chris Gatling	.05	.02
❑ 65 Tim Hardaway	.30	.14
❑ 66 Byron Houston	.05	.02
❑ 67 Sarunas Marciulionis	.05	.02
❑ 68 Chris Mullin	.30	.14
❑ 69 Billy Owens	.05	.02
❑ 70 Latrell Sprewell	.75	.35
❑ 71 Matt Bullard	.05	.02
❑ 72 Sam Cassell RC	.75	.35
❑ 73 Carl Herrera	.05	.02
❑ 74 Robert Horry	.15	.07
❑ 75 Vernon Maxwell	.05	.02
❑ 76 Hakeem Olajuwon	.50	.23
❑ 77 Kenny Smith	.05	.02
❑ 78 Otis Thorpe	.15	.07
❑ 79 Dale Davis	.05	.02
❑ 80 Vern Fleming	.05	.02
❑ 81 Reggie Miller	.30	.14
❑ 82 Sam Mitchell	.05	.02
❑ 83 Pooh Richardson	.05	.02
❑ 84 Detlef Schrempf	.15	.07
❑ 85 Rik Smits	.15	.07
❑ 86 Ron Harper	.15	.07
❑ 87 Mark Jackson	.15	.07
❑ 88 Danny Manning	.15	.07
❑ 89 Stanley Roberts	.05	.02
❑ 90 Loy Vaught	.05	.02
❑ 91 John Williams	.05	.02
❑ 92 Sam Bowie	.05	.02
❑ 93 Doug Christie	.05	.02
❑ 94 Vlade Divac	.15	.07
❑ 95 George Lynch RC	.05	.02
❑ 96 Anthony Peeler	.05	.02
❑ 97 James Worthy	.30	.14
❑ 98 Bimbo Coles	.05	.02
❑ 99 Grant Long	.05	.02
❑ 100 Harold Miner	.05	.02
❑ 101 Glen Rice	.15	.07
❑ 102 Rony Seikaly	.05	.02
❑ 103 Brian Shaw	.05	.02
❑ 104 Steve Smith	.30	.14
❑ 105 Anthony Avent	.05	.02
❑ 106 Vin Baker RC	.75	.35
❑ 107 Frank Brickowski	.05	.02
❑ 108 Todd Day	.05	.02
❑ 109 Blue Edwards	.05	.02
❑ 110 Lee Mayberry	.05	.02
❑ 111 Eric Murdock	.05	.02
❑ 112 Orlando Woolridge	.05	.02

❑ 113 Thurl Bailey .05 .02
❑ 114 Christian Laettner .15 .07
❑ 115 Chuck Person .05 .02
❑ 116 Doug West .05 .02
❑ 117 Micheal Williams .05 .02
❑ 118 Kenny Anderson .15 .07
❑ 119 Derrick Coleman .15 .07
❑ 120 Rick Mahorn .05 .02
❑ 121 Chris Morris .05 .02
❑ 122 Rumeal Robinson .05 .02
❑ 123 Rex Walters RC .05 .02
❑ 124 Greg Anthony .05 .02
❑ 125 Rolando Blackman .05 .02
❑ 126 Hubert Davis .05 .02
❑ 127 Patrick Ewing .30 .14
❑ 128 Anthony Mason .15 .07
❑ 129 Charles Oakley .15 .07
❑ 130 Doc Rivers .15 .07
❑ 131 Charles Smith .05 .02
❑ 132 John Starks .15 .07
❑ 133 Nick Anderson .15 .07
❑ 134 Anthony Bowie .05 .02
❑ 135 Shaquille O'Neal 1.50 .70
❑ 136 Dennis Scott .05 .02
❑ 137 Scott Skiles .05 .02
❑ 138 Jeff Turner .05 .02
❑ 139 Shawn Bradley RC .30 .14
❑ 140 Johnny Dawkins .05 .02
❑ 141 Jeff Hornacek .15 .07
❑ 142 Tim Perry .05 .02
❑ 143 Clarence Weatherspoon .05 .02
❑ 144 Danny Ainge .15 .07
❑ 145 Charles Barkley .50 .23
❑ 146 Cedric Ceballos .15 .07
❑ 147 Kevin Johnson .15 .07
❑ 148 Negele Knight .05 .02
❑ 149 Malcolm Mackey RC .05 .02
❑ 150 Dan Majerle .15 .07
❑ 151 Oliver Miller .05 .02
❑ 152 Mark West .05 .02
❑ 153 Mark Bryant .05 .02
❑ 154 Clyde Drexler .30 .14
❑ 155 Jerome Kersey .05 .02
❑ 156 Terry Porter .05 .02
❑ 157 Clifford Robinson .15 .07
❑ 158 Rod Strickland .15 .07
❑ 159 Buck Williams .05 .02
❑ 160 Duane Causwell .05 .02
❑ 161 Bobby Hurley RC .15 .07
❑ 162 Mitch Richmond .30 .14
❑ 163 Lionel Simmons .05 .02
❑ 164 Wayman Tisdale .05 .02
❑ 165 Spud Webb .15 .07
❑ 166 Walt Williams .05 .02
❑ 167 Willie Anderson .05 .02
❑ 168 Antoine Carr .05 .02
❑ 169 Lloyd Daniels .05 .02
❑ 170 Dennis Rodman .60 .25
❑ 171 Dale Ellis .05 .02
❑ 172 Avery Johnson .05 .02
❑ 173 J.R. Reid .05 .02
❑ 174 David Robinson .50 .23
❑ 175 Michael Cage .05 .02
❑ 176 Kendall Gill .15 .07
❑ 177 Ervin Johnson RC .15 .07
❑ 178 Shawn Kemp .50 .23
❑ 179 Derrick McKey .05 .02
❑ 180 Nate McMillan .05 .02
❑ 181 Gary Payton .50 .23
❑ 182 Sam Perkins .15 .07
❑ 183 Ricky Pierce .05 .02
❑ 184 David Benoit .05 .02
❑ 185 Tyrone Corbin .05 .02
❑ 186 Mark Eaton .05 .02
❑ 187 Jay Humphries .05 .02
❑ 188 Jeff Malone .05 .02
❑ 189 Karl Malone .50 .23
❑ 190 John Stockton .30 .14
❑ 191 Luther Wright RC .05 .02
❑ 192 Michael Adams .05 .02
❑ 193 Calbert Cheaney RC .15 .07
❑ 194 Pervis Ellison .05 .02
❑ 195 Tom Gugliotta .30 .14
❑ 196 Buck Johnson .05 .02
❑ 197 LaBradford Smith .05 .02
❑ 198 Larry Stewart .05 .02
❑ 199 Checklist .05 .02
❑ 200 Checklist .05 .02
❑ 201 Doug Edwards .05 .02
❑ 202 Craig Ehlo .05 .02
❑ 203 Jon Koncak .05 .02
❑ 204 Andrew Lang .05 .02
❑ 205 Ennis Whatley .05 .02
❑ 206 Chris Corchiani .05 .02
❑ 207 Acie Earl RC .05 .02
❑ 208 Jimmy Oliver .05 .02
❑ 209 Ed Pinckney .05 .02
❑ 210 Dino Radja RC .05 .02
❑ 211 Matt Wenstrom RC .05 .02
❑ 212 Tony Bennett .05 .02
❑ 213 Scott Burrell .30 .14
❑ 214 LeRon Ellis .05 .02
❑ 215 Hersey Hawkins .15 .07
❑ 216 Eddie Johnson .05 .02
❑ 217 Rumeal Robinson .05 .02
❑ 218 Corie Blount .05 .02
❑ 219 Dave Johnson .05 .02
❑ 220 Steve Kerr .15 .07
❑ 221 Toni Kukoc RC 1.25 .55
❑ 222 Pete Myers .05 .02
❑ 223 Bill Wennington .05 .02
❑ 224 Scott Williams .05 .02
❑ 225 John Battle .05 .02
❑ 226 Tyrone Hill .05 .02
❑ 227 Gerald Madkins RC .05 .02
❑ 228 Chris Mills .30 .14
❑ 229 Bobby Phills .05 .02
❑ 230 Greg Dreiling .05 .02
❑ 231 Lucious Harris RC .05 .02
❑ 232 Popeye Jones RC .05 .02
❑ 233 Tim Legler RC .05 .02
❑ 234 Fat Lever .05 .02
❑ 235 Jamal Mashburn RC .60 .25
❑ 236 Tom Hammonds .05 .02
❑ 237 Darnell Mee RC .05 .02
❑ 238 Robert Pack .05 .02
❑ 239 Rodney Rogers RC .30 .14
❑ 240 Brian Williams .05 .02
❑ 241 Greg Anderson .05 .02
❑ 242 Sean Elliott .15 .07
❑ 243 Allan Houston RC 1.25 .55
❑ 244 Lindsey Hunter RC .30 .14
❑ 245 Mark Macon .05 .02
❑ 246 David Wood .05 .02
❑ 247 Jud Buechler .05 .02
❑ 248 Josh Grant RC .05 .02
❑ 249 Jeff Grayer .05 .02
❑ 250 Keith Jennings .05 .02
❑ 251 Avery Johnson .05 .02
❑ 252 Chris Webber RC 3.00 1.35
❑ 253 Scott Brooks .05 .02
❑ 254 Sam Cassell .30 .14
❑ 255 Mario Elie .05 .02
❑ 256 Richard Petruska RC .05 .02
❑ 257 Eric Riley RC .05 .02
❑ 258 Antonio Davis RC .15 .07
❑ 259 Scott Haskin RC .05 .02
❑ 260 Derrick McKey .05 .02
❑ 261 Byron Scott .15 .07
❑ 262 Malik Sealy .05 .02
❑ 263 Kenny Williams .05 .02
❑ 264 Haywoode Workman .05 .02
❑ 265 Mark Aguirre .05 .02
❑ 266 Terry Dehere RC .05 .02
❑ 267 Harold Ellis RC .05 .02
❑ 268 Gary Grant .05 .02
❑ 269 Bob Martin RC .05 .02
❑ 270 Elmore Spencer .05 .02
❑ 271 Tom Tolbert .05 .02
❑ 272 Sam Bowie .05 .02
❑ 273 Elden Campbell .05 .02
❑ 274 Antonio Harvey RC .05 .02
❑ 275 George Lynch .05 .02
❑ 276 Tony Smith .05 .02
❑ 277 Sedale Threatt .05 .02
❑ 278 Nick Van Exel RC .75 .35
❑ 279 Willie Burton .05 .02
❑ 280 Matt Geiger .05 .02
❑ 281 John Salley .05 .02
❑ 282 Vin Baker .40 .18
❑ 283 Jon Barry .05 .02
❑ 284 Brad Lohaus .05 .02
❑ 285 Ken Norman .05 .02
❑ 286 Derek Strong RC .05 .02
❑ 287 Mike Brown .05 .02
❑ 288 Brian Davis RC .05 .02
❑ 289 Tellis Frank .05 .02
❑ 290 Luc Longley .15 .07
❑ 291 Marlon Maxey .05 .02
❑ 292 Isaiah Rider RC .60 .25
❑ 293 Chris Smith .05 .02
❑ 294 P.J. Brown RC .30 .14
❑ 295 Kevin Edwards .05 .02
❑ 296 Armon Gilliam .05 .02
❑ 297 Johnny Newman .05 .02
❑ 298 Rex Walters .05 .02
❑ 299 David Wesley RC .30 .14
❑ 300 Jayson Williams .15 .07
❑ 301 Anthony Bonner .05 .02
❑ 302 Derek Harper .15 .07
❑ 303 Herb Williams .05 .02
❑ 304 Litterial Green .05 .02
❑ 305 Anfernee Hardaway RC 3.00 1.35
❑ 306 Greg Kite .05 .02
❑ 307 Larry Krystkowiak .05 .02
❑ 308 Keith Tower RC .05 .02
❑ 309 Dana Barros .05 .02
❑ 310 Shawn Bradley .30 .14
❑ 311 Greg Graham RC .05 .02
❑ 312 Sean Green .05 .02
❑ 313 Warren Kidd RC .05 .02
❑ 314 Eric Leckner .05 .02
❑ 315 Moses Malone .30 .14
❑ 316 Orlando Woolridge .05 .02
❑ 317 Duane Cooper .05 .02
❑ 318 Joe Courtney RC .05 .02
❑ 319 A.C. Green .15 .07
❑ 320 Frank Johnson .05 .02
❑ 321 Joe Kleine .05 .02
❑ 322 Chris Dudley .05 .02
❑ 323 Harvey Grant .05 .02
❑ 324 Jaren Jackson .05 .02
❑ 325 Tracy Murray .05 .02
❑ 326 James Robinson RC .05 .02
❑ 327 Reggie Smith .05 .02
❑ 328 Kevin Thompson RC .05 .02
❑ 329 Randy Brown .05 .02
❑ 330 Evers Burns RC .05 .02
❑ 331 Pete Chilcutt .05 .02
❑ 332 Bobby Hurley .15 .07
❑ 333 Mike Peplowski RC .05 .02
❑ 334 LaBradford Smith .05 .02
❑ 335 Trevor Wilson .05 .02
❑ 336 Terry Cummings .05 .02
❑ 337 Vinny Del Negro .05 .02
❑ 338 Sleepy Floyd .05 .02
❑ 339 Negele Knight .05 .02
❑ 340 Dennis Rodman .60 .25
❑ 341 Chris Whitney RC .05 .02
❑ 342 Vincent Askew .05 .02
❑ 343 Kendall Gill .15 .07
❑ 344 Ervin Johnson .15 .07
❑ 345 Chris King RC .05 .02
❑ 346 Detlef Schrempf .15 .07
❑ 347 Walter Bond .05 .02
❑ 348 Tom Chambers .05 .02
❑ 349 John Crotty .05 .02
❑ 350 Bryon Russell RC .30 .14
❑ 351 Felton Spencer .05 .02
❑ 352 Mitchell Butler RC .05 .02
❑ 353 Rex Chapman .05 .02
❑ 354 Calbert Cheaney .15 .07
❑ 355 Kevin Duckworth .05 .02
❑ 356 Don MacLean .05 .02
❑ 357 Gheorghe Muresan RC .30 .14
❑ 358 Doug Overton .05 .02
❑ 359 Brent Price .05 .02
❑ 360 Kenny Walker .05 .02
❑ 361 Derrick Coleman USA .05 .02
❑ 362 Joe Dumars USA .15 .07
❑ 363 Tim Hardaway USA .15 .07
❑ 364 Larry Johnson USA .15 .07
❑ 365 Shawn Kemp USA .40 .18
❑ 366 Dan Majerle USA .05 .02
❑ 367 Alonzo Mourning USA .30 .14
❑ 368 Mark Price USA .05 .02
❑ 369 Steve Smith USA .15 .07
❑ 370 Isiah Thomas USA .15 .07

Card	MINT	NRMT
❑ 371 Dominique Wilkins USA	.15	.07
❑ 372 Don Nelson / Don Chaney	.15	.07
❑ 373 Jamal Mashburn CL	.30	.14
❑ 374 Checklist	.05	.02
❑ 375 Checklist	.05	.02
❑ M1 Reggie Miller USA	.75	.35
❑ M2 Shaquille O'Neal USA	6.00	2.70
❑ M3 Team Checklist USA	2.00	.90

1993-94 Ultra All-Defensive

	MINT	NRMT
COMPLETE SET (10)	120.00	55.00
COMMON CARD (1-10)	2.00	.90
SEMISTARS	3.00	1.35

SER.1 STATED ODDS 1:24 JUMBO

Card	MINT	NRMT
❑ 1 Joe Dumars	3.00	1.35
❑ 2 Michael Jordan	80.00	36.00
❑ 3 Hakeem Olajuwon	10.00	4.50
❑ 4 Scottie Pippen	20.00	9.00
❑ 5 Dennis Rodman	12.00	5.50
❑ 6 Horace Grant	3.00	1.35
❑ 7 Dan Majerle	3.00	1.35
❑ 8 Larry Nance	2.00	.90
❑ 9 David Robinson	10.00	4.50
❑ 10 John Starks	3.00	1.35

1993-94 Ultra All-NBA

	MINT	NRMT
COMPLETE SET (14)	50.00	22.00

*SINGLES: 3X TO 8X BASE CARD HI
SER.1 STATED ODDS 1:16

Card	MINT	NRMT
❑ 1 Charles Barkley	4.00	1.80
❑ 2 Michael Jordan	30.00	13.50
❑ 3 Karl Malone	4.00	1.80
❑ 4 Hakeem Olajuwon	4.00	1.80
❑ 5 Mark Price	.40	.18
❑ 6 Joe Dumars	2.50	1.10
❑ 7 Patrick Ewing	2.50	1.10
❑ 8 Larry Johnson	2.50	1.10
❑ 9 John Stockton	2.50	1.10
❑ 10 Dominique Wilkins	2.50	1.10
❑ 11 Derrick Coleman	1.25	.55
❑ 12 Tim Hardaway	2.50	1.10
❑ 13 Scottie Pippen	8.00	3.60
❑ 14 David Robinson	4.00	1.80

1993-94 Ultra All-Rookie Series

	MINT	NRMT
COMPLETE SET (15)	40.00	18.00

*SINGLES: 1.5X TO 4X BASE CARD HI
SER.2 STATED ODDS 1:7

Card	MINT	NRMT
❑ 1 Vin Baker	3.00	1.35
❑ 2 Shawn Bradley	1.25	.55
❑ 3 Calbert Cheaney	.60	.25
❑ 4 Anfernee Hardaway	12.00	5.50
❑ 5 Lindsey Hunter	1.25	.55
❑ 6 Bobby Hurley	.60	.25
❑ 7 Popeye Jones	.20	.09
❑ 8 Toni Kukoc	5.00	2.20
❑ 9 Jamal Mashburn	2.50	1.10
❑ 10 Chris Mills	1.25	.55
❑ 11 Dino Radja	.20	.09
❑ 12 Isaiah Rider	2.50	1.10
❑ 13 Rodney Rogers	1.25	.55
❑ 14 Nick Van Exel	3.00	1.35
❑ 15 Chris Webber	12.00	5.50

1993-94 Ultra All-Rookie Team

	MINT	NRMT
COMPLETE SET (5)	10.00	4.50

*SINGLES: 2X TO 5X BASE CARD HI
SER.1 STATED ODDS 1:24

Card	MINT	NRMT
❑ 1 LaPhonso Ellis	.25	.11
❑ 2 Tom Gugliotta (with Michael Jordan)	1.50	.70
❑ 3 Christian Laettner	.75	.35
❑ 4 Alonzo Mourning	2.50	1.10
❑ 5 Shaquille O'Neal	8.00	3.60

1993-94 Ultra Award Winners

	MINT	NRMT
COMPLETE SET (5)	15.00	6.75

*SINGLES: 3X TO 8X BASE CARD HI
SER.1 STATED ODDS 1:36 JUMBO

Card	MINT	NRMT
❑ 1 Mahmoud Abdul-Rauf	.40	.18
❑ 2 Charles Barkley	4.00	1.80

Card	MINT	NRMT
❑ 3 Hakeem Olajuwon	4.00	1.80
❑ 4 Shaquille O'Neal	12.00	5.50
❑ 5 Clifford Robinson	1.25	.55

1993-94 Ultra Famous Nicknames

	MINT	NRMT
COMPLETE SET (15)	60.00	27.00

*SINGLES: 2.5X TO 6X BASE CARD HI
SER.2 STATED ODDS 1:5

Card	MINT	NRMT
❑ 1 Charles Barkley / Sir Charles	3.00	1.35
❑ 2 Tyrone Bogues / Muggsy	1.00	.45
❑ 3 Derrick Coleman / D.C.	1.00	.45
❑ 4 Clyde Drexler / The Glide	2.00	.90
❑ 5 Anfernee Hardaway / Penny	20.00	9.00
❑ 6 Larry Johnson / L.J.	2.00	.90
❑ 7 Michael Jordan / Air	25.00	11.00
❑ 8 Toni Kukoc / The Pink Panther	8.00	3.60
❑ 9 Karl Malone / The Mailman	3.00	1.35
❑ 10 Harold Miner / Baby Jordan	.30	.14
❑ 11 Alonzo Mourning / Zo	3.00	1.35
❑ 12 Hakeem Olajuwon / The Dream	3.00	1.35
❑ 13 Shaquille O'Neal / Shaq	10.00	4.50
❑ 14 David Robinson / The Admiral	3.00	1.35
❑ 15 Dominique Wilkins / Human Highlight Film	2.00	.90

1993-94 Ultra Inside/Outside

	MINT	NRMT
COMPLETE SET (10)	10.00	4.50

*SINGLES: .75X TO 2X BASE CARD HI
RANDOM INSERTS IN ALL SER.2 PACKS

		MINT	NRMT
❑ 1	Patrick Ewing	.60	.25
❑ 2	Jim Jackson	.30	.14
❑ 3	Larry Johnson	.60	.25
❑ 4	Michael Jordan	8.00	3.60
❑ 5	Dan Majerle	.30	.14
❑ 6	Hakeem Olajuwon	1.00	.45
❑ 7	Scottie Pippen	2.00	.90
❑ 8	Latrell Sprewell	1.50	.70
❑ 9	John Starks	.30	.14
❑ 10	Walt Williams	.10	.05

1993-94 Ultra Jam City

	MINT	NRMT
COMPLETE SET (9)	60.00	27.00

*SINGLES: 6X TO 15X BASE CARD HI
SER.2 STATED ODDS 1:37 JUMBO

		MINT	NRMT
❑ 1	Charles Barkley	8.00	3.60
❑ 2	Derrick Coleman	2.50	1.10
❑ 3	Clyde Drexler	5.00	2.20
❑ 4	Patrick Ewing	5.00	2.20
❑ 5	Shawn Kemp	8.00	3.60
❑ 6	Harold Miner	.75	.35
❑ 7	Shaquille O'Neal	25.00	11.00
❑ 8	David Robinson	8.00	3.60
❑ 9	Dominique Wilkins	5.00	2.20

1993-94 Ultra Karl Malone

	MINT	NRMT
COMPLETE SET (10)	10.00	4.50
COMMON MALONE (1-10)	1.25	.55

SER.1 STATED ODDS 1:16

	MINT	NRMT
CERTIFIED AUTOGRAPH (AU)	100.00	45.00
COMMON SEND-OFF (11-12)	2.00	.90

TWO CARDS PER 10 SER.1 WRAPPERS

		MINT	NRMT
❑ 1	Karl Malone Power Rig	1.25	.55
❑ 2	Karl Malone Summerfield	1.25	.55
❑ 3	Karl Malone Mailman-Born	1.25	.55
❑ 4	Karl Malone Luck of the Draw	1.25	.55
❑ 5	Karl Malone Double-Double	1.25	.55
❑ 6	Karl Malone Dynamic Duo	1.25	.55
❑ 7	Karl Malone Mt. Malone	1.25	.55
❑ 8	Karl Malone Salt Lake Slammer	1.25	.55
❑ 9	Karl Malone Overhead Delivery	1.25	.55
❑ 10	Karl Malone Truckin'	1.25	.55
❑ 11	Karl Malone Role Player	2.00	.90
❑ 12	Karl Malone Rigged	2.00	.90

1993-94 Ultra Power In The Key

	MINT	NRMT
COMPLETE SET (9)	50.00	22.00

*SINGLES: 3X TO 8X BASE CARD HI
SER.2 STATED ODDS 1:37 HOBBY

		MINT	NRMT
❑ 1	Larry Johnson	2.50	1.10
❑ 2	Michael Jordan	30.00	13.50
❑ 3	Karl Malone	4.00	1.80
❑ 4	Oliver Miller	.40	.18
❑ 5	Alonzo Mourning	4.00	1.80
❑ 6	Hakeem Olajuwon	4.00	1.80
❑ 7	Shaquille O'Neal	12.00	5.50
❑ 8	Otis Thorpe	1.25	.55
❑ 9	Chris Webber	25.00	11.00

1993-94 Ultra Rebound Kings

	MINT	NRMT
COMPLETE SET (10)	6.00	2.70

*SINGLES: .75X TO 2X BASE CARD HI
SER.2 STATED ODDS 1:4

		MINT	NRMT
❑ 1	Charles Barkley	1.00	.45
❑ 2	Derrick Coleman	.30	.14
❑ 3	Shawn Kemp	1.00	.45
❑ 4	Karl Malone	1.00	.45
❑ 5	Alonzo Mourning	1.00	.45
❑ 6	Dikembe Mutombo	.30	.14
❑ 7	Charles Oakley	.30	.14
❑ 8	Hakeem Olajuwon	1.00	.45
❑ 9	Shaquille O'Neal	3.00	1.35
❑ 10	Dennis Rodman	1.25	.55

1993-94 Ultra Scoring Kings

	MINT	NRMT
COMPLETE SET (10)	100.00	45.00
COMMON CARD (1-10)	2.00	.90
SEMISTARS	3.00	1.35
UNLISTED STARS	5.00	2.20

SER.1 STATED ODDS 1:36 HOBBY

		MINT	NRMT
❑ 1	Charles Barkley	8.00	3.60
❑ 2	Joe Dumars	3.00	1.35
❑ 3	Patrick Ewing	5.00	2.20
❑ 4	Larry Johnson	2.00	.90
❑ 5	Michael Jordan	60.00	27.00
❑ 6	Karl Malone	8.00	3.60
❑ 7	Alonzo Mourning	8.00	3.60
❑ 8	Shaquille O'Neal	25.00	11.00
❑ 9	David Robinson	8.00	3.60
❑ 10	Dominique Wilkins	3.00	1.35

1994-95 Ultra

	MINT	NRMT
COMPLETE SET (350)	35.00	16.00
COMPLETE SERIES 1 (200)	20.00	9.00
COMPLETE SERIES 2 (150)	15.00	6.75
COMMON CARD (1-350)	.10	.05
SEMISTARS	.15	.07
UNLISTED STARS	.40	.18

		MINT	NRMT
❑ 1	Stacey Augmon	.10	.05

❑ 2 Mookie Blaylock .10 .05
❑ 3 Craig Ehlo .10 .05
❑ 4 Adam Keefe .10 .05
❑ 5 Andrew Lang .10 .05
❑ 6 Ken Norman .10 .05
❑ 7 Kevin Willis .10 .05
❑ 8 Dee Brown .10 .05
❑ 9 Sherman Douglas .10 .05
❑ 10 Acie Earl .10 .05
❑ 11 Pervis Ellison .10 .05
❑ 12 Rick Fox .10 .05
❑ 13 Xavier McDaniel .10 .05
❑ 14 Eric Montross RC .10 .05
❑ 15 Dino Radja .10 .05
❑ 16 Dominique Wilkins .40 .18
❑ 17 Michael Adams .10 .05
❑ 18 Muggsy Bogues .15 .07
❑ 19 Dell Curry .10 .05
❑ 20 Kenny Gattison .10 .05
❑ 21 Hersey Hawkins .15 .07
❑ 22 Larry Johnson .15 .07
❑ 23 Alonzo Mourning .50 .23
❑ 24 Robert Parish .15 .07
❑ 25 B.J. Armstrong .10 .05
❑ 26 Steve Kerr .10 .05
❑ 27 Toni Kukoc .60 .25
❑ 28 Luc Longley .10 .05
❑ 29 Pete Myers .10 .05
❑ 30 Will Perdue .10 .05
❑ 31 Scottie Pippen 1.25 .55
❑ 32 Terrell Brandon .15 .07
❑ 33 Brad Daugherty .10 .05
❑ 34 Tyrone Hill .10 .05
❑ 35 Chris Mills .15 .07
❑ 36 Bobby Phills .10 .05
❑ 37 Mark Price .10 .05
❑ 38 Gerald Wilkins .10 .05
❑ 39 John Williams .10 .05
❑ 40 Terry Davis .10 .05
❑ 41 Jim Jackson .15 .07
❑ 42 Popeye Jones .10 .05
❑ 43 Jason Kidd RC 3.00 1.35
❑ 44 Jamal Mashburn .40 .18
❑ 45 Sean Rooks .10 .05
❑ 46 Doug Smith .10 .05
❑ 47 Mahmoud Abdul-Rauf .10 .05
❑ 48 LaPhonso Ellis .10 .05
❑ 49 Dikembe Mutombo .15 .07
❑ 50 Robert Pack .10 .05
❑ 51 Rodney Rogers .10 .05
❑ 52 Bryant Stith .10 .05
❑ 53 Brian Williams .10 .05
❑ 54 Reggie Williams .10 .05
❑ 55 Greg Anderson .10 .05
❑ 56 Joe Dumars .40 .18
❑ 57 Allan Houston .60 .25
❑ 58 Lindsey Hunter .15 .07
❑ 59 Terry Mills .10 .05
❑ 60 Tim Hardaway .40 .18
❑ 61 Chris Mullin .40 .18
❑ 62 Billy Owens .10 .05
❑ 63 Latrell Sprewell .75 .35
❑ 64 Chris Webber 1.25 .55
❑ 65 Sam Cassell .40 .18
❑ 66 Carl Herrera .10 .05
❑ 67 Robert Horry .10 .05
❑ 68 Vernon Maxwell .10 .05
❑ 69 Hakeem Olajuwon .60 .25
❑ 70 Kenny Smith .10 .05
❑ 71 Otis Thorpe .10 .05
❑ 72 Antonio Davis .10 .05
❑ 73 Dale Davis .10 .05
❑ 74 Mark Jackson .10 .05
❑ 75 Derrick McKey .10 .05
❑ 76 Reggie Miller .40 .18
❑ 77 Byron Scott .15 .07
❑ 78 Rik Smits .10 .05
❑ 79 Haywoode Workman .10 .05
❑ 80 Gary Grant .10 .05
❑ 81 Ron Harper .15 .07
❑ 82 Elmore Spencer .10 .05
❑ 83 Loy Vaught .10 .05
❑ 84 Elden Campbell .10 .05
❑ 85 Doug Christie .10 .05
❑ 86 Vlade Divac .10 .05
❑ 87 Eddie Jones RC 2.50 1.10
❑ 88 George Lynch .10 .05
❑ 89 Anthony Peeler .10 .05
❑ 90 Sedale Threatt .10 .05
❑ 91 Nick Van Exel .40 .18
❑ 92 James Worthy .40 .18
❑ 93 Bimbo Coles .10 .05
❑ 94 Matt Geiger .10 .05
❑ 95 Grant Long .10 .05
❑ 96 Harold Miner .10 .05
❑ 97 Glen Rice .15 .07
❑ 98 John Salley .10 .05
❑ 99 Rony Seikaly .10 .05
❑ 100 Brian Shaw .10 .05
❑ 101 Steve Smith .15 .07
❑ 102 Vin Baker .40 .18
❑ 103 Jon Barry .10 .05
❑ 104 Todd Day .10 .05
❑ 105 Lee Mayberry .10 .05
❑ 106 Eric Murdock .10 .05
❑ 107 Thurl Bailey .10 .05
❑ 108 Stacey King .10 .05
❑ 109 Christian Laettner .15 .07
❑ 110 Isaiah Rider .15 .07
❑ 111 Chris Smith .10 .05
❑ 112 Doug West .10 .05
❑ 113 Micheal Williams .10 .05
❑ 114 Kenny Anderson .15 .07
❑ 115 Benoit Benjamin .10 .05
❑ 116 P.J. Brown .10 .05
❑ 117 Derrick Coleman .15 .07
❑ 118 Yinka Dare RC .10 .05
❑ 119 Kevin Edwards .10 .05
❑ 120 Armon Gilliam .10 .05
❑ 121 Chris Morris .10 .05
❑ 122 Greg Anthony .10 .05
❑ 123 Anthony Bonner .10 .05
❑ 124 Hubert Davis .10 .05
❑ 125 Patrick Ewing .40 .18
❑ 126 Derek Harper .10 .05
❑ 127 Anthony Mason .15 .07
❑ 128 Charles Oakley .10 .05
❑ 129 Doc Rivers .15 .07
❑ 130 John Starks .10 .05
❑ 131 Nick Anderson .10 .05
❑ 132 Anthony Avent .10 .05
❑ 133 Anthony Bowie .10 .05
❑ 134 Anfernee Hardaway 1.25 .55
❑ 135 Shaquille O'Neal 2.00 .90
❑ 136 Dennis Scott .10 .05
❑ 137 Jeff Turner .10 .05
❑ 138 Dana Barros .10 .05
❑ 139 Shawn Bradley .10 .05
❑ 140 Greg Graham .10 .05
❑ 141 Jeff Malone .10 .05
❑ 142 Tim Perry .10 .05
❑ 143 Clarence Weatherspoon .10 .05
❑ 144 Scott Williams .10 .05
❑ 145 Danny Ainge .10 .05
❑ 146 Charles Barkley .60 .25
❑ 147 Cedric Ceballos .10 .05
❑ 148 A.C. Green .15 .07
❑ 149 Frank Johnson .10 .05
❑ 150 Kevin Johnson .15 .07
❑ 151 Dan Majerle .15 .07
❑ 152 Oliver Miller .10 .05
❑ 153 Wesley Person RC .40 .18
❑ 154 Mark Bryant .10 .05
❑ 155 Clyde Drexler .40 .18
❑ 156 Harvey Grant .10 .05
❑ 157 Jerome Kersey .10 .05
❑ 158 Tracy Murray .10 .05
❑ 159 Terry Porter .10 .05
❑ 160 Clifford Robinson .15 .07
❑ 161 James Robinson .10 .05
❑ 162 Rod Strickland .15 .07
❑ 163 Buck Williams .10 .05
❑ 164 Duane Causwell .10 .05
❑ 165 Olden Polynice .10 .05
❑ 166 Mitch Richmond .40 .18
❑ 167 Lionel Simmons .10 .05
❑ 168 Walt Williams .10 .05
❑ 169 Willie Anderson .10 .05
❑ 170 Terry Cummings .10 .05
❑ 171 Sean Elliott .15 .07
❑ 172 Avery Johnson .10 .05
❑ 173 J.R. Reid .10 .05
❑ 174 David Robinson .60 .25
❑ 175 Dennis Rodman .75 .35
❑ 176 Kendall Gill .15 .07
❑ 177 Shawn Kemp .60 .25
❑ 178 Nate McMillan .10 .05
❑ 179 Gary Payton .60 .25
❑ 180 Sam Perkins .15 .07
❑ 181 Detlef Schrempf .15 .07
❑ 182 David Benoit .10 .05
❑ 183 Tyrone Corbin .10 .05
❑ 184 Jeff Hornacek .15 .07
❑ 185 Jay Humphries .10 .05
❑ 186 Karl Malone .60 .25
❑ 187 Bryon Russell .10 .05
❑ 188 Felton Spencer .10 .05
❑ 189 John Stockton .40 .18
❑ 190 Mitchell Butler .10 .05
❑ 191 Rex Chapman .10 .05
❑ 192 Calbert Cheaney .10 .05
❑ 193 Kevin Duckworth .10 .05
❑ 194 Tom Gugliotta .15 .07
❑ 195 Don MacLean .10 .05
❑ 196 Gheorghe Muresan .10 .05
❑ 197 Scott Skiles .10 .05
❑ 198 Checklist .10 .05
❑ 199 Checklist .10 .05
❑ 200 Checklist .10 .05
❑ 201 Tyrone Corbin .10 .05
❑ 202 Doug Edwards .10 .05
❑ 203 Jim Les .10 .05
❑ 204 Grant Long .10 .05
❑ 205 Ken Norman .10 .05
❑ 206 Steve Smith .15 .07
❑ 207 Blue Edwards .10 .05
❑ 208 Greg Minor RC .10 .05
❑ 209 Eric Montross .10 .05
❑ 210 Derek Strong .10 .05
❑ 211 David Wesley .10 .05
❑ 212 Tony Bennett .10 .05
❑ 213 Scott Burrell .10 .05
❑ 214 Darrin Hancock .10 .05
❑ 215 Greg Sutton .10 .05
❑ 216 Corie Blount .10 .05
❑ 217 Jud Buechler .10 .05
❑ 218 Ron Harper .15 .07
❑ 219 Larry Krystkowiak .10 .05
❑ 220 Dickey Simpkins RC .10 .05
❑ 221 Bill Wennington .10 .05
❑ 222 Michael Cage .10 .05
❑ 223 Tony Campbell .10 .05
❑ 224 Steve Colter .10 .05
❑ 225 Greg Dreiling .10 .05
❑ 226 Danny Ferry .10 .05
❑ 227 Tony Dumas RC .10 .05
❑ 228 Lucious Harris .10 .05
❑ 229 Donald Hodge .10 .05
❑ 230 Jason Kidd 1.50 .70
❑ 231 Lorenzo Williams .10 .05
❑ 232 Dale Ellis .10 .05
❑ 233 Tom Hammonds .10 .05
❑ 234 Jalen Rose RC 1.50 .70
❑ 235 Reggie Slater .10 .05
❑ 236 Rafael Addison .10 .05
❑ 237 Bill Curley RC .10 .05
❑ 238 Johnny Dawkins .10 .05
❑ 239 Grant Hill RC 4.00 1.80
❑ 240 Eric Leckner .10 .05
❑ 241 Mark Macon .10 .05
❑ 242 Oliver Miller .10 .05
❑ 243 Mark West .10 .05
❑ 244 Victor Alexander .10 .05
❑ 245 Chris Gatling .10 .05
❑ 246 Tom Gugliotta .15 .07
❑ 247 Keith Jennings .10 .05
❑ 248 Ricky Pierce .10 .05
❑ 249 Carlos Rogers RC .10 .05
❑ 250 Clifford Rozier RC .10 .05
❑ 251 Rony Seikaly .10 .05
❑ 252 David Wood .10 .05
❑ 253 Tim Breaux .10 .05
❑ 254 Scott Brooks .10 .05
❑ 255 Zan Tabak .10 .05
❑ 256 Duane Ferrell .10 .05
❑ 257 Mark Jackson .10 .05
❑ 258 Sam Mitchell .10 .05
❑ 259 John Williams .10 .05

	MINT	NRMT
❑ 260 Terry Dehere	.10	.05
❑ 261 Harold Ellis	.10	.05
❑ 262 Matt Fish	.10	.05
❑ 263 Tony Massenburg	.10	.05
❑ 264 Lamond Murray RC	.15	.07
❑ 265 Charles Outlaw RC	.10	.05
❑ 266 Eric Piatkowski RC	.10	.05
❑ 267 Pooh Richardson	.10	.05
❑ 268 Malik Sealy	.10	.05
❑ 269 Randy Woods	.10	.05
❑ 270 Sam Bowie	.10	.05
❑ 271 Cedric Ceballos	.10	.05
❑ 272 Antonio Harvey	.10	.05
❑ 273 Eddie Jones	1.25	.55
❑ 274 Anthony Miller RC	.10	.05
❑ 275 Tony Smith	.10	.05
❑ 276 Ledell Eackles	.10	.05
❑ 277 Kevin Gamble	.10	.05
❑ 278 Brad Lohaus	.10	.05
❑ 279 Billy Owens	.10	.05
❑ 280 Khalid Reeves RC	.10	.05
❑ 281 Kevin Willis	.10	.05
❑ 282 Marty Conlon	.10	.05
❑ 283 Alton Lister	.10	.05
❑ 284 Eric Mobley RC	.10	.05
❑ 285 Johnny Newman	.10	.05
❑ 286 Ed Pinckney	.10	.05
❑ 287 Glenn Robinson RC	1.25	.55
❑ 288 Howard Eisley	.10	.05
❑ 289 Winston Garland	.10	.05
❑ 290 Andres Guibert	.10	.05
❑ 291 Donyell Marshall RC	.40	.18
❑ 292 Sean Rooks	.10	.05
❑ 293 Yinka Dare	.10	.05
❑ 294 Sleepy Floyd	.10	.05
❑ 295 Sean Higgins	.10	.05
❑ 296 Rex Walters	.10	.05
❑ 297 Jayson Williams	.15	.07
❑ 298 Charles Smith	.10	.05
❑ 299 Charlie Ward RC	.40	.18
❑ 300 Herb Williams	.10	.05
❑ 301 Monty Williams RC	.10	.05
❑ 302 Horace Grant	.15	.07
❑ 303 Geert Hammink	.10	.05
❑ 304 Tree Rollins	.10	.05
❑ 305 Donald Royal	.10	.05
❑ 306 Brian Shaw	.10	.05
❑ 307 Brooks Thompson RC	.10	.05
❑ 308 Derrick Alston RC	.10	.05
❑ 309 Willie Burton	.10	.05
❑ 310 Jaren Jackson	.10	.05
❑ 311 B.J. Tyler RC	.10	.05
❑ 312 Scott Williams	.10	.05
❑ 313 Sharone Wright RC	.10	.05
❑ 314 Joe Kleine	.10	.05
❑ 315 Danny Manning	.15	.07
❑ 316 Elliot Perry	.10	.05
❑ 317 Wesley Person	.15	.07
❑ 318 Trevor Ruffin RC	.10	.05
❑ 319 Dan Schayes	.10	.05
❑ 320 Wayman Tisdale	.10	.05
❑ 321 Chris Dudley	.10	.05
❑ 322 James Edwards	.10	.05
❑ 323 Alaa Abdelnaby	.10	.05
❑ 324 Randy Brown	.10	.05
❑ 325 Brian Grant RC	1.00	.45
❑ 326 Bobby Hurley	.10	.05
❑ 327 Michael Smith RC	.10	.05
❑ 328 Henry Turner	.10	.05
❑ 329 Trevor Wilson	.10	.05
❑ 330 Vinny Del Negro	.10	.05
❑ 331 Moses Malone	.40	.18
❑ 332 Julius Nwosu	.10	.05
❑ 333 Chuck Person	.10	.05
❑ 334 Chris Whitney	.10	.05
❑ 335 Vincent Askew	.10	.05
❑ 336 Bill Cartwright	.10	.05
❑ 337 Ervin Johnson	.10	.05
❑ 338 Sarunas Marciulionis	.10	.05
❑ 339 Antoine Carr	.10	.05
❑ 340 Tom Chambers	.10	.05
❑ 341 John Crotty	.10	.05
❑ 342 Jamie Watson RC	.10	.05
❑ 343 Juwan Howard RC	1.00	.45
❑ 344 Jim McIlvaine	.10	.05
❑ 345 Doug Overton	.10	.05
❑ 346 Scott Skiles	.10	.05
❑ 347 Anthony Tucker RC	.10	.05
❑ 348 Chris Webber	1.25	.55
❑ 349 Checklist	.10	.05
❑ 350 Checklist	.10	.05

1994-95 Ultra All-NBA

	MINT	NRMT
COMPLETE SET (15)	12.00	5.50

*SINGLES: 1X TO 2.5X BASE CARD HI
SER.1 STATED ODDS 1:3 HOBBY/RETAIL

❑ 1 Karl Malone	1.50	.70
❑ 2 Hakeem Olajuwon	1.50	.70
❑ 3 Scottie Pippen	3.00	1.35
❑ 4 Latrell Sprewell	2.00	.90
❑ 5 John Stockton	1.00	.45
❑ 6 Charles Barkley	1.50	.70
❑ 7 Kevin Johnson	.40	.18
❑ 8 Shawn Kemp	1.50	.70
❑ 9 Mitch Richmond	1.00	.45
❑ 10 David Robinson	1.50	.70
❑ 11 Derrick Coleman	.40	.18
❑ 12 Shaquille O'Neal	5.00	2.20
❑ 13 Gary Payton	1.50	.70
❑ 14 Mark Price	.25	.11
❑ 15 Dominique Wilkins	1.00	.45

1994-95 Ultra All-Rookie Team

	MINT	NRMT
COMPLETE SET (10)	100.00	45.00
COMMON CARD (1-10)	2.50	1.10
SEMISTARS	5.00	2.20
UNLISTED STARS	12.00	5.50

SER.1 STATED ODDS 1:36 JUMBO

❑ 1 Vin Baker	12.00	5.50
❑ 2 Anfernee Hardaway	40.00	18.00
❑ 3 Jamal Mashburn	12.00	5.50
❑ 4 Isaiah Rider	5.00	2.20
❑ 5 Chris Webber	40.00	18.00
❑ 6 Shawn Bradley	2.50	1.10
❑ 7 Lindsey Hunter	5.00	2.20
❑ 8 Toni Kukoc	20.00	9.00
❑ 9 Dino Radja	2.50	1.10
❑ 10 Nick Van Exel	12.00	5.50

1994-95 Ultra All-Rookies

	MINT	NRMT
COMPLETE SET (15)	20.00	9.00

*SINGLES: .75X TO 2X BASE CARD HI
SER.2 STATED ODDS 1:5 HOBBY/RETAIL

❑ 1 Brian Grant	2.00	.90
❑ 2 Grant Hill	8.00	3.60
❑ 3 Juwan Howard	2.00	.90
❑ 4 Eddie Jones	5.00	2.20
❑ 5 Jason Kidd	6.00	2.70
❑ 6 Donyell Marshall	.75	.35
❑ 7 Eric Montross	.20	.09
❑ 8 Lamond Murray	.30	.14
❑ 9 Wesley Person	.75	.35
❑ 10 Khalid Reeves	.20	.09
❑ 11 Glenn Robinson	2.50	1.10
❑ 12 Carlos Rogers	.20	.09
❑ 13 Jalen Rose	3.00	1.35
❑ 14 B.J. Tyler	.20	.09
❑ 15 Sharone Wright	.20	.09

1994-95 Ultra Award Winners

	MINT	NRMT
COMPLETE SET (4)	3.00	1.35

*SINGLES: 1X TO 2.5X BASE CARD HI
SER.1 STATED ODDS 1:4 HOBBY/RETAIL

❑ 1 Dell Curry	.25	.11
❑ 2 Don MacLean	.25	.11
❑ 3 Hakeem Olajuwon	1.50	.70
❑ 4 Chris Webber	3.00	1.35

1994-95 Ultra Defensive Gems

	MINT	NRMT
COMPLETE SET (6)	30.00	13.50
COMMON CARD (1-6)	2.00	.90

SER.2 STATED ODDS 1:37 HOBBY/RETAIL

❑ 1 Mookie Blaylock	2.00	.90
❑ 2 Hakeem Olajuwon	8.00	3.60
❑ 3 Gary Payton	8.00	3.60
❑ 4 Scottie Pippen	15.00	6.75

❑ 5 David Robinson	8.00	3.60
❑ 6 Latrell Sprewell	10.00	4.50

1994-95 Ultra Double Trouble

	MINT	NRMT
COMPLETE SET (10)	10.00	4.50

*SINGLES: 1X TO 2.5X BASE CARD HI
SER.1 STATED ODDS 1:5 HOBBY/RETAIL

❑ 1 Derrick Coleman	.40	.18
❑ 2 Patrick Ewing	1.00	.45
❑ 3 Anfernee Hardaway	3.00	1.35
❑ 4 Jamal Mashburn	1.00	.45
❑ 5 Reggie Miller	1.00	.45
❑ 6 Alonzo Mourning	1.25	.55
❑ 7 Scottie Pippen	3.00	1.35
❑ 8 David Robinson	1.50	.70
❑ 9 Latrell Sprewell	2.00	.90
❑ 10 John Stockton	1.00	.45

1994-95 Ultra Inside/Outside

	MINT	NRMT
COMPLETE SET (10)	10.00	4.50

*SINGLES: 1.25X TO 3X BASE CARD HI
SER.2 STATED ODDS 1:7 HOBBY

❑ 1 Sam Cassell	1.25	.55
❑ 2 Cedric Ceballos	.30	.14
❑ 3 Calbert Cheaney	.30	.14
❑ 4 Anfernee Hardaway	4.00	1.80
❑ 5 Jim Jackson	.50	.23
❑ 6 Dan Majerle	.50	.23
❑ 7 Robert Pack	.30	.14
❑ 8 Scottie Pippen	4.00	1.80
❑ 9 Mitch Richmond	1.25	.55
❑ 10 Latrell Sprewell	2.50	1.10

1994-95 Ultra Jam City

	MINT	NRMT
COMPLETE SET (10)	50.00	22.00
COMMON CARD (1-10)	1.50	.70
SEMISTARS	2.00	.90
UNLISTED STARS	4.00	1.80

SER.2 STATED ODDS 1:7 JUMBO

❑ 1 Vin Baker	4.00	1.80
❑ 2 Grant Hill	20.00	9.00
❑ 3 Robert Horry	1.50	.70
❑ 4 Shawn Kemp	6.00	2.70
❑ 5 Jamal Mashburn	2.00	.90
❑ 6 Alonzo Mourning	5.00	2.20
❑ 7 Dikembe Mutombo	2.00	.90
❑ 8 Shaquille O'Neal	20.00	9.00
❑ 9 Glenn Robinson	6.00	2.70
❑ 10 Dominique Wilkins	4.00	1.80

1994-95 Ultra Power

	MINT	NRMT
COMPLETE SET (10)	6.00	2.70

*SINGLES: .75X TO 2X BASE CARD HI
SER.1 STATED ODDS 1:3 HOBBY/RETAIL

❑ 1 Charles Barkley	1.25	.55
❑ 2 Derrick Coleman	.30	.14
❑ 3 Larry Johnson	.30	.14
❑ 4 Shawn Kemp	1.25	.55
❑ 5 Karl Malone	1.25	.55
❑ 6 Dikembe Mutombo	.30	.14
❑ 7 Charles Oakley	.20	.09
❑ 8 Shaquille O'Neal	4.00	1.80
❑ 9 Dennis Rodman	1.50	.70
❑ 10 Chris Webber	2.50	1.10

1994-95 Ultra Power In The Key

	MINT	NRMT
COMPLETE SET (10)	20.00	9.00

*SINGLES: 2X TO 5X BASE CARD HI
SER.2 STATED ODDS 1:7 RETAIL

❑ 1 Charles Barkley	3.00	1.35
❑ 2 Patrick Ewing	2.00	.90
❑ 3 Horace Grant	.75	.35
❑ 4 Larry Johnson	.75	.35
❑ 5 Karl Malone	3.00	1.35
❑ 6 Hakeem Olajuwon	3.00	1.35
❑ 7 Shaquille O'Neal	10.00	4.50
❑ 8 David Robinson	3.00	1.35
❑ 9 Chris Webber	6.00	2.70
❑ 10 Kevin Willis	.50	.23

1994-95 Ultra Rebound Kings

	MINT	NRMT
COMPLETE SET (10)	3.00	1.35

*SINGLES: .4X TO 1X BASE CARD HI
SER.2 STATED ODDS 1:2 HOBBY/RETAIL

❑ 1 Derrick Coleman	.15	.07
❑ 2 A.C. Green	.15	.07
❑ 3 Alonzo Mourning	.50	.23
❑ 4 Dikembe Mutombo	.15	.07
❑ 5 Charles Oakley	.10	.05
❑ 6 Hakeem Olajuwon	.60	.25
❑ 7 Shaquille O'Neal	2.00	.90
❑ 8 David Robinson	.60	.25
❑ 9 Chris Webber	1.25	.55
❑ 10 Kevin Willis	.10	.05

1994-95 Ultra Scoring Kings

	MINT	NRMT
COMPLETE SET (10)	80.00	36.00
COMMON CARD (1-10)	3.00	1.35
SEMISTARS	6.00	2.70

SER.1 STATED ODDS 1:37 HOBBY

❑ 1 Charles Barkley	10.00	4.50
❑ 2 Patrick Ewing	6.00	2.70
❑ 3 Karl Malone	10.00	4.50
❑ 4 Hakeem Olajuwon	10.00	4.50
❑ 5 Shaquille O'Neal	30.00	13.50
❑ 6 Scottie Pippen	20.00	9.00
❑ 7 Mitch Richmond	6.00	2.70
❑ 8 David Robinson	10.00	4.50
❑ 9 Latrell Sprewell	12.00	5.50
❑ 10 Dominique Wilkins	3.00	1.35

1995-96 Ultra

	MINT	NRMT
COMPLETE SET (350)	40.00	18.00
COMPLETE SERIES 1 (200)	20.00	9.00
COMPLETE SERIES 2 (150)	20.00	9.00
COMMON CARD (1-350)	.15	.07
SEMISTARS	.20	.09
UNLISTED STARS	.40	.18

SUBSET CARDS HALF VALUE OF BASE CARDS

❑ 1 Stacey Augmon	.15	.07
❑ 2 Mookie Blaylock	.15	.07
❑ 3 Craig Ehlo	.15	.07
❑ 4 Andrew Lang	.15	.07
❑ 5 Grant Long	.15	.07
❑ 6 Ken Norman	.15	.07
❑ 7 Steve Smith	.20	.09
❑ 8 Spud Webb	.15	.07
❑ 9 Dee Brown	.15	.07
❑ 10 Sherman Douglas	.15	.07
❑ 11 Pervis Ellison	.15	.07
❑ 12 Rick Fox	.15	.07
❑ 13 Eric Montross	.15	.07
❑ 14 Dino Radja	.15	.07
❑ 15 David Wesley	.15	.07
❑ 16 Dominique Wilkins	.40	.18
❑ 17 Muggsy Bogues	.15	.07
❑ 18 Scott Burrell	.15	.07
❑ 19 Dell Curry	.15	.07
❑ 20 Kendall Gill	.20	.09
❑ 21 Larry Johnson	.20	.09
❑ 22 Alonzo Mourning	.40	.18
❑ 23 Robert Parish	.20	.09
❑ 24 Ron Harper	.20	.09
❑ 25 Michael Jordan	5.00	2.20
❑ 26 Toni Kukoc	.50	.23
❑ 27 Will Perdue	.15	.07
❑ 28 Scottie Pippen	1.25	.55
❑ 29 Terrell Brandon	.20	.09
❑ 30 Michael Cage	.15	.07
❑ 31 Tyrone Hill	.15	.07
❑ 32 Chris Mills	.15	.07
❑ 33 Bobby Phills	.15	.07
❑ 34 Mark Price	.15	.07
❑ 35 John Williams	.15	.07
❑ 36 Lucious Harris	.15	.07
❑ 37 Jim Jackson	.15	.07
❑ 38 Popeye Jones	.15	.07
❑ 39 Jason Kidd	1.25	.55
❑ 40 Jamal Mashburn	.20	.09
❑ 41 George McCloud	.15	.07
❑ 42 Roy Tarpley	.15	.07
❑ 43 Lorenzo Williams	.15	.07
❑ 44 Mahmoud Abdul-Rauf	.15	.07
❑ 45 Dikembe Mutombo	.20	.09
❑ 46 Robert Pack	.15	.07
❑ 47 Jalen Rose	.50	.23
❑ 48 Bryant Stith	.15	.07
❑ 49 Brian Williams	.15	.07
❑ 50 Reggie Williams	.15	.07
❑ 51 Joe Dumars	.40	.18
❑ 52 Grant Hill	2.00	.90
❑ 53 Allan Houston	.50	.23
❑ 54 Lindsey Hunter	.15	.07
❑ 55 Terry Mills	.15	.07
❑ 56 Mark West	.15	.07
❑ 57 Chris Gatling	.15	.07
❑ 58 Tim Hardaway	.40	.18
❑ 59 Donyell Marshall	.20	.09
❑ 60 Chris Mullin	.40	.18
❑ 61 Carlos Rogers	.15	.07
❑ 62 Clifford Rozier	.15	.07
❑ 63 Rony Seikaly	.15	.07
❑ 64 Latrell Sprewell	.75	.35
❑ 65 Sam Cassell	.20	.09
❑ 66 Clyde Drexler	.40	.18
❑ 67 Mario Elie	.15	.07
❑ 68 Carl Herrera	.15	.07
❑ 69 Robert Horry	.15	.07
❑ 70 Hakeem Olajuwon	.60	.25
❑ 71 Kenny Smith	.15	.07
❑ 72 Antonio Davis	.15	.07
❑ 73 Dale Davis	.15	.07
❑ 74 Mark Jackson	.15	.07
❑ 75 Derrick McKey	.15	.07
❑ 76 Reggie Miller	.40	.18
❑ 77 Rik Smits	.15	.07
❑ 78 Terry Dehere	.15	.07
❑ 79 Lamond Murray	.15	.07
❑ 80 Charles Outlaw	.15	.07
❑ 81 Pooh Richardson	.15	.07
❑ 82 Rodney Rogers	.15	.07
❑ 83 Malik Sealy	.15	.07
❑ 84 Loy Vaught	.15	.07
❑ 85 Sam Bowie	.15	.07
❑ 86 Elden Campbell	.15	.07
❑ 87 Cedric Ceballos	.15	.07
❑ 88 Vlade Divac	.15	.07
❑ 89 Eddie Jones	.75	.35
❑ 90 Anthony Peeler	.15	.07
❑ 91 Sedale Threatt	.15	.07
❑ 92 Nick Van Exel	.20	.09
❑ 93 Rex Chapman	.15	.07
❑ 94 Bimbo Coles	.15	.07
❑ 95 Matt Geiger	.15	.07
❑ 96 Billy Owens	.15	.07
❑ 97 Khalid Reeves	.15	.07
❑ 98 Glen Rice	.20	.09
❑ 99 Kevin Willis	.15	.07
❑ 100 Vin Baker	.40	.18
❑ 101 Marty Conlon	.15	.07
❑ 102 Todd Day	.15	.07
❑ 103 Eric Murdock	.15	.07
❑ 104 Glenn Robinson	.40	.18
❑ 105 Winston Garland	.15	.07
❑ 106 Tom Gugliotta	.20	.09
❑ 107 Christian Laettner	.20	.09
❑ 108 Isaiah Rider	.20	.09
❑ 109 Sean Rooks	.15	.07
❑ 110 Doug West	.15	.07
❑ 111 Kenny Anderson	.20	.09
❑ 112 P.J. Brown	.15	.07
❑ 113 Derrick Coleman	.20	.09
❑ 114 Armon Gilliam	.15	.07
❑ 115 Chris Morris	.15	.07
❑ 116 Anthony Bonner	.15	.07
❑ 117 Patrick Ewing	.40	.18
❑ 118 Derek Harper	.15	.07
❑ 119 Anthony Mason	.20	.09
❑ 120 Charles Oakley	.15	.07
❑ 121 Charles Smith	.15	.07
❑ 122 John Starks	.15	.07
❑ 123 Nick Anderson	.15	.07
❑ 124 Horace Grant	.20	.09
❑ 125 Anfernee Hardaway	1.25	.55
❑ 126 Shaquille O'Neal	2.00	.90
❑ 127 Donald Royal	.15	.07
❑ 128 Dennis Scott	.15	.07
❑ 129 Brian Shaw	.15	.07
❑ 130 Derrick Alston	.15	.07
❑ 131 Dana Barros	.15	.07
❑ 132 Shawn Bradley	.15	.07
❑ 133 Willie Burton	.15	.07
❑ 134 Jeff Malone	.15	.07
❑ 135 Clarence Weatherspoon	.15	.07
❑ 136 Scott Williams	.15	.07
❑ 137 Sharone Wright	.15	.07
❑ 138 Danny Ainge	.15	.07
❑ 139 Charles Barkley	.60	.25
❑ 140 A.C. Green	.20	.09
❑ 141 Kevin Johnson	.20	.09
❑ 142 Dan Majerle	.15	.07
❑ 143 Danny Manning	.20	.09
❑ 144 Elliot Perry	.15	.07
❑ 145 Wesley Person	.20	.09
❑ 146 Wayman Tisdale	.15	.07
❑ 147 Chris Dudley	.15	.07
❑ 148 Harvey Grant	.15	.07
❑ 149 Aaron McKie	.15	.07
❑ 150 Terry Porter	.15	.07
❑ 151 Clifford Robinson	.15	.07
❑ 152 Rod Strickland	.20	.09
❑ 153 Otis Thorpe	.15	.07
❑ 154 Buck Williams	.15	.07
❑ 155 Brian Grant	.40	.18
❑ 156 Bobby Hurley	.15	.07
❑ 157 Olden Polynice	.15	.07
❑ 158 Mitch Richmond	.40	.18
❑ 159 Michael Smith	.15	.07
❑ 160 Walt Williams	.15	.07
❑ 161 Vinny Del Negro	.15	.07
❑ 162 Sean Elliott	.15	.07
❑ 163 Avery Johnson	.15	.07
❑ 164 Chuck Person	.15	.07
❑ 165 J.R. Reid	.15	.07
❑ 166 Doc Rivers	.15	.07
❑ 167 David Robinson	.60	.25
❑ 168 Dennis Rodman	.75	.35
❑ 169 Vincent Askew	.15	.07
❑ 170 Hersey Hawkins	.20	.09
❑ 171 Shawn Kemp	.60	.25
❑ 172 Sarunas Marciulionis	.15	.07
❑ 173 Nate McMillan	.15	.07
❑ 174 Gary Payton	.60	.25
❑ 175 Sam Perkins	.20	.09
❑ 176 Detlef Schrempf	.20	.09
❑ 177 B.J. Armstrong	.15	.07
❑ 178 Jerome Kersey	.15	.07
❑ 179 Tony Massenburg	.15	.07
❑ 180 Oliver Miller	.15	.07
❑ 181 John Salley	.15	.07
❑ 182 David Benoit	.15	.07
❑ 183 Antoine Carr	.15	.07
❑ 184 Jeff Hornacek	.20	.09
❑ 185 Karl Malone	.60	.25
❑ 186 Felton Spencer	.15	.07
❑ 187 John Stockton	.40	.18
❑ 188 Greg Anthony	.15	.07
❑ 189 Benoit Benjamin	.15	.07
❑ 190 Byron Scott	.15	.07
❑ 191 Calbert Cheaney	.15	.07
❑ 192 Juwan Howard	.40	.18
❑ 193 Don MacLean	.15	.07
❑ 194 Gheorghe Muresan	.15	.07
❑ 195 Doug Overton	.15	.07
❑ 196 Scott Skiles	.15	.07
❑ 197 Chris Webber	1.25	.55
❑ 198 Checklist (1-94)	.15	.07
❑ 199 Checklist (95-190)	.15	.07
❑ 200 Checklist (191-200)	.15	.07
❑ 201 Stacey Augmon	.15	.07
❑ 202 Mookie Blaylock	.15	.07
❑ 203 Grant Long	.15	.07
❑ 204 Steve Smith	.20	.09
❑ 205 Dana Barros	.15	.07
❑ 206 Kendall Gill	.20	.09
❑ 207 Khalid Reeves	.15	.07
❑ 208 Glen Rice	.20	.09
❑ 209 Luc Longley	.15	.07
❑ 210 Dennis Rodman	.75	.35

❑ 211	Dan Majerle	.15	.07
❑ 212	Tony Dumas	.15	.07
❑ 213	Elmore Spencer	.15	.07
❑ 214	Otis Thorpe	.15	.07
❑ 215	B.J. Armstrong	.15	.07
❑ 216	Sam Cassell	.20	.09
❑ 217	Clyde Drexler	.40	.18
❑ 218	Robert Horry	.15	.07
❑ 219	Hakeem Olajuwon	.60	.25
❑ 220	Eddie Johnson	.15	.07
❑ 221	Ricky Pierce	.15	.07
❑ 222	Eric Piatkowski	.15	.07
❑ 223	Rodney Rogers	.15	.07
❑ 224	Brian Williams	.15	.07
❑ 225	George Lynch	.15	.07
❑ 226	Alonzo Mourning	.40	.18
❑ 227	Benoit Benjamin	.15	.07
❑ 228	Terry Porter	.15	.07
❑ 229	Shawn Bradley	.15	.07
❑ 230	Kevin Edwards	.15	.07
❑ 231	Jayson Williams	.20	.09
❑ 232	Charlie Ward	.15	.07
❑ 233	Jon Koncak	.15	.07
❑ 234	Derrick Coleman	.20	.09
❑ 235	Richard Dumas	.15	.07
❑ 236	Vernon Maxwell	.15	.07
❑ 237	John Williams	.15	.07
❑ 238	Dontonio Wingfield	.15	.07
❑ 239	Tyrone Corbin	.15	.07
❑ 240	Will Perdue	.15	.07
❑ 241	Shawn Kemp	.60	.25
❑ 242	Gary Payton	.60	.25
❑ 243	Sam Perkins	.20	.09
❑ 244	Detlef Schrempf	.20	.09
❑ 245	Chris Morris	.15	.07
❑ 246	Robert Pack	.15	.07
❑ 247	Willie Anderson EXP	.15	.07
❑ 248	Oliver Miller EXP	.15	.07
❑ 249	Tracy Murray EXP	.15	.07
❑ 250	Alvin Robertson EXP	.15	.07
❑ 251	Carlos Rogers EXP	.15	.07
❑ 252	John Salley EXP	.15	.07
❑ 253	Damon Stoudamire EXP	1.25	.55
❑ 254	Zan Tabak EXP	.15	.07
❑ 255	Greg Anthony EXP	.15	.07
❑ 256	Blue Edwards EXP	.15	.07
❑ 257	Kenny Gattison EXP	.15	.07
❑ 258	Chris King EXP	.15	.07
❑ 259	Lawrence Moten EXP	.15	.07
❑ 260	Eric Murdock EXP	.15	.07
❑ 261	Bryant Reeves EXP	.20	.09
❑ 262	Byron Scott EXP	.15	.07
❑ 263	Cory Alexander RC	.15	.07
❑ 264	Brent Barry RC	.40	.18
❑ 265	Mario Bennett RC	.15	.07
❑ 266	Travis Best RC	.20	.09
❑ 267	Junior Burrough RC	.15	.07
❑ 268	Jason Caffey RC	.20	.09
❑ 269	Randolph Childress RC	.15	.07
❑ 270	Sasha Danilovic RC	.15	.07
❑ 271	Tyus Edney RC	.15	.07
❑ 272	Michael Finley RC	1.50	.70
❑ 273	Sherrell Ford RC	.15	.07
❑ 274	Kevin Garnett RC	5.00	2.20
❑ 275	Alan Henderson RC	.40	.18
❑ 276	Donny Marshall RC	.15	.07
❑ 277	Antonio McDyess RC	2.00	.90
❑ 278	Loren Meyer RC	.15	.07
❑ 279	Lawrence Moten RC	.15	.07
❑ 280	Ed O'Bannon RC	.15	.07
❑ 281	Greg Ostertag RC	.15	.07
❑ 282	Cherokee Parks RC	.15	.07
❑ 283	Theo Ratliff RC	.50	.23
❑ 284	Bryant Reeves RC	.40	.18
❑ 285	Shawn Respert RC	.15	.07
❑ 286	Lou Roe RC	.15	.07
❑ 287	Arvydas Sabonis RC	.60	.25
❑ 288	Joe Smith RC	1.25	.55
❑ 289	Jerry Stackhouse RC	1.25	.55
❑ 290	Damon Stoudamire RC	2.00	.90
❑ 291	Bob Sura RC	.20	.09
❑ 292	Kurt Thomas RC	.20	.09
❑ 293	Gary Trent RC	.15	.07
❑ 294	David Vaughn RC	.15	.07
❑ 295	Rasheed Wallace RC	1.50	.70
❑ 296	Eric Williams RC	.20	.09
❑ 297	Corliss Williamson RC	.75	.35
❑ 298	George Zidek RC	.15	.07
❑ 299	M. Abdul-Rauf ENC	.15	.07
❑ 300	Kenny Anderson ENC	.15	.07
❑ 301	Vin Baker ENC	.20	.09
❑ 302	Charles Barkley ENC	.40	.18
❑ 303	Mookie Blaylock ENC	.15	.07
❑ 304	Cedric Ceballos ENC	.15	.07
❑ 305	Vlade Divac ENC	.15	.07
❑ 306	Clyde Drexler ENC	.20	.09
❑ 307	Joe Dumars ENC	.20	.09
❑ 308	Sean Elliott ENC	.15	.07
❑ 309	Patrick Ewing ENC	.20	.09
❑ 310	Anfernee Hardaway ENC	.75	.35
❑ 311	Tim Hardaway ENC	.20	.09
❑ 312	Grant Hill ENC	1.25	.55
❑ 313	Tyrone Hill ENC	.15	.07
❑ 314	Robert Horry ENC	.15	.07
❑ 315	Juwan Howard ENC	.20	.09
❑ 316	Jim Jackson ENC	.15	.07
❑ 317	Kevin Johnson ENC	.15	.07
❑ 318	Larry Johnson ENC	.15	.07
❑ 319	Eddie Jones ENC	.40	.18
❑ 320	Shawn Kemp ENC	.40	.18
❑ 321	Jason Kidd ENC	.50	.23
❑ 322	Christian Laettner ENC	.15	.07
❑ 323	Karl Malone ENC	.40	.18
❑ 324	Jamal Mashburn ENC	.15	.07
❑ 325	Reggie Miller ENC	.20	.09
❑ 326	Alonzo Mourning ENC	.20	.09
❑ 327	Dikembe Mutombo ENC	.15	.07
❑ 328	Hakeem Olajuwon ENC	.40	.18
❑ 329	Gary Payton ENC	.40	.18
❑ 330	Scottie Pippen ENC	.60	.25
❑ 331	Dino Radja ENC	.15	.07
❑ 332	Glen Rice ENC	.15	.07
❑ 333	Mitch Richmond ENC	.20	.09
❑ 334	Clifford Robinson ENC	.15	.07
❑ 335	David Robinson ENC	.40	.18
❑ 336	Glenn Robinson ENC	.20	.09
❑ 337	Dennis Rodman ENC	.40	.18
❑ 338	Carlos Rogers ENC	.15	.07
❑ 339	Detlef Schrempf ENC	.15	.07
❑ 340	Byron Scott ENC	.15	.07
❑ 341	Rik Smits ENC	.15	.07
❑ 342	Latrell Sprewell ENC	.40	.18
❑ 343	John Stockton ENC	.20	.09
❑ 344	Nick Van Exel ENC	.15	.07
❑ 345	Loy Vaught ENC	.15	.07
❑ 346	C. Weatherspoon ENC	.15	.07
❑ 347	Chris Webber ENC	.50	.23
❑ 348	Kevin Willis ENC	.15	.07
❑ 349	Checklist (201-298)	.15	.07
❑ 350	Checklist (299-350 ins)	.15	.07

1995-96 Ultra Gold Medallion

	MINT	NRMT
COMPLETE SET (200)	120.00	55.00
COMMON CARD (1-200)	.30	.14

*STARS: 3X TO 6X BASE CARD HI
ONE PER SERIES 1 PACK

1995-96 Ultra All-NBA

	MINT	NRMT
COMPLETE SET (15)	15.00	6.75
COMMON CARD (1-15)	.40	.18
SEMISTARS	.60	.25
UNLISTED STARS	1.00	.45

SER.1 STATED ODDS 1:5 HOBBY/RETAIL
*GOLD MEDALLION: 1.5X TO 3X HI COLUMN
GOLD: SER.1 STATED ODDS 1:50 HOB/RET

❑ 1	Anfernee Hardaway	3.00	1.35
❑ 2	Karl Malone	1.50	.70
❑ 3	Scottie Pippen	3.00	1.35
❑ 4	David Robinson	1.50	.70
❑ 5	John Stockton	1.00	.45
❑ 6	Charles Barkley	1.50	.70
❑ 7	Shawn Kemp	1.50	.70
❑ 8	Shaquille O'Neal	5.00	2.20
❑ 9	Gary Payton	1.50	.70
❑ 10	Mitch Richmond	1.00	.45
❑ 11	Clyde Drexler	1.00	.45
❑ 12	Reggie Miller	1.00	.45
❑ 13	Hakeem Olajuwon	1.50	.70
❑ 14	Dennis Rodman	2.00	.90
❑ 15	Detlef Schrempf	.40	.18

1995-96 Ultra All-Rookie Team

	MINT	NRMT
COMPLETE SET (10)	30.00	13.50
COMMON CARD (1-10)	1.00	.45
SEMISTARS	2.00	.90
UNLISTED STARS	3.00	1.35

SER.1 STATED ODDS 1:7 RETAIL
*GOLD MEDALLION: 1.5X TO 3X HI COLUMN
GOLD: SER.1 STATED ODDS 1:70 RETAIL

❑ 1	Brian Grant	3.00	1.35
❑ 2	Grant Hill	15.00	6.75
❑ 3	Eddie Jones	6.00	2.70
❑ 4	Jason Kidd	10.00	4.50
❑ 5	Glenn Robinson	3.00	1.35
❑ 6	Juwan Howard	3.00	1.35
❑ 7	Donyell Marshall Sharone Wright	1.00	.45
❑ 8	Eric Montross	1.00	.45
❑ 9	Wesley Person	2.00	.90
❑ 10	Jalen Rose	4.00	1.80

1995-96 Ultra All-Rookies

	MINT	NRMT
COMPLETE SET (10)	50.00	22.00

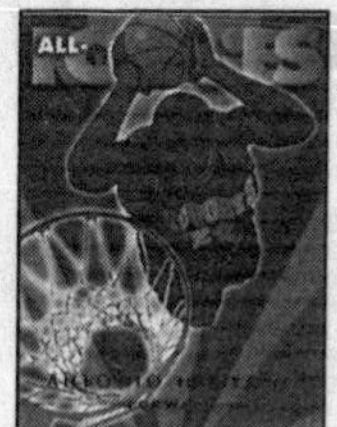

COMMON CARD (1-10)	1.50	.70
SEMISTARS	2.50	1.10

SER.2 STATED ODDS 1:30 HOBBY/RETAIL

❑ 1 Tyus Edney	1.50	.70
❑ 2 Michael Finley	8.00	3.60
❑ 3 Kevin Garnett	25.00	11.00
❑ 4 Antonio McDyess DP	5.00	2.20
❑ 5 Ed O'Bannon	1.50	.70
❑ 6 Joe Smith	6.00	2.70
❑ 7 Jerry Stackhouse	6.00	2.70
❑ 8 Damon Stoudamire DP	5.00	2.20
❑ 9 Rasheed Wallace	8.00	3.60
❑ 10 Eric Williams	1.50	.70

1995-96 Ultra Double Trouble

	MINT	NRMT
COMPLETE SET (10)	12.00	5.50
COMMON CARD (1-10)	.50	.23

SER.1 STATED ODDS 1:5 HOBBY/RETAIL
*GOLD MEDALLION: 1.5X TO 3X HI COLUMN
GOLD: SER.1 STATED ODDS 1:50 HOB/RET

❑ 1 Charles Barkley	1.00	.45
❑ 2 Anfernee Hardaway	2.00	.90
❑ 3 Michael Jordan	8.00	3.60
❑ 4 Alonzo Mourning	.50	.23
❑ 5 Hakeem Olajuwon	1.00	.45
❑ 6 Shaquille O'Neal	3.00	1.35
❑ 7 Gary Payton	1.00	.45
❑ 8 Scottie Pippen	2.00	.90
❑ 9 David Robinson	1.00	.45
❑ 10 John Stockton	.50	.23

1995-96 Ultra Fabulous Fifties

	MINT	NRMT
COMPLETE SET (7)	18.00	8.00
COMMON CARD (1-7)	.50	.23
SEMISTARS	.75	.35
UNLISTED STARS	1.25	.55

SER.1 STATED ODDS 1:12 HOBBY
*GOLD MEDALLION: 1.5X TO 3X HI COLUMN
GOLD: SER.1 STATED ODDS 1:120 HOBBY

❑ 1 Dana Barros	.50	.23
❑ 2 Willie Burton	.50	.23
❑ 3 Cedric Ceballos	.50	.23
❑ 4 Jim Jackson	.50	.23
❑ 5 Michael Jordan	15.00	6.75
❑ 6 Jamal Mashburn	.75	.35
❑ 7 Glen Rice	.75	.35

1995-96 Ultra Jam City

	MINT	NRMT
COMPLETE SET (12)	60.00	27.00
COMMON CARD (1-12)	1.00	.45
SEMISTARS	1.50	.70
UNLISTED STARS	2.50	1.10

SER.2 STATED ODDS 1:12 RETAIL
COMP.HOT PACK SET (12) .. 20.00 9.00
HP CARDS: .1X TO .3X HI COLUMN
HP: SER.2 STATED ODDS 1:72 RETAIL

❑ 1 Grant Hill	12.00	5.50
❑ 2 Robert Horry	1.00	.45
❑ 3 Michael Jordan	30.00	13.50
❑ 4 Shawn Kemp	4.00	1.80
❑ 5 Jamal Mashburn	1.50	.70
❑ 6 Antonio McDyess	6.00	2.70
❑ 7 Alonzo Mourning	2.50	1.10
❑ 8 Hakeem Olajuwon	4.00	1.80
❑ 9 Shaquille O'Neal	12.00	5.50
❑ 10 David Robinson	4.00	1.80
❑ 11 Joe Smith	4.00	1.80
❑ 12 Jerry Stackhouse	4.00	1.80

1995-96 Ultra Power

	MINT	NRMT
COMPLETE SET (10)	5.00	2.20
COMMON CARD (1-10)	.40	.18
UNLISTED STARS	.60	.25

SER.1 STATED ODDS 1:4 HOBBY/RETAIL
*GOLD MEDALLION: 1.5X TO 3X HI COLUMN
GOLD: SER.1 STATED ODDS 1:40 HOB/RET

❑ 1 Charles Barkley	1.00	.45
❑ 2 Patrick Ewing	.60	.25
❑ 3 Larry Johnson	.40	.18
❑ 4 Shawn Kemp	1.00	.45
❑ 5 Karl Malone	1.00	.45
❑ 6 Alonzo Mourning	.60	.25
❑ 7 Dikembe Mutombo	.40	.18
❑ 8 Hakeem Olajuwon	1.00	.45
❑ 9 Shaquille O'Neal	3.00	1.35
❑ 10 David Robinson	1.00	.45

1995-96 Ultra Rising Stars

	MINT	NRMT
COMPLETE SET (9)	80.00	36.00
COMMON CARD (1-9)	3.00	1.35
SEMISTARS	5.00	2.20

SER.1 STATED ODDS 1:37 HOBBY/RETAIL
*GOLD MEDALLION: 2X TO 4X HI COLUMN
GOLD: SER.1 STATED ODDS 1:370 HOB/RET

❑ 1 Vin Baker	5.00	2.20
❑ 2 Anfernee Hardaway	15.00	6.75
❑ 3 Grant Hill	25.00	11.00
❑ 4 Jason Kidd	15.00	6.75
❑ 5 Jamal Mashburn	3.00	1.35
❑ 6 Shaquille O'Neal	25.00	11.00
❑ 7 Glenn Robinson	5.00	2.20
❑ 8 Nick Van Exel	3.00	1.35
❑ 9 Chris Webber	15.00	6.75

1995-96 Ultra Scoring Kings

	MINT	NRMT
COMPLETE SET (12)	125.00	55.00
COMMON CARD (1-12)	2.00	.90
SEMISTARS	2.50	1.10
UNLISTED STARS	4.00	1.80

SER.2 STATED ODDS 1:24 HOBBY
COMP.HOT PACK SET (12) .. 30.00 13.50
HP CARDS: .1X TO .25X HI COLUMN
HP: SER.2 STATED ODDS 1:72 HOBBY

Card	MINT	NRMT
❑ 1 Patrick Ewing	4.00	1.80
❑ 2 Grant Hill	20.00	9.00
❑ 3 Jim Jackson	2.00	.90
❑ 4 Michael Jordan	50.00	22.00
❑ 5 Karl Malone	6.00	2.70
❑ 6 Reggie Miller	4.00	1.80
❑ 7 Hakeem Olajuwon	6.00	2.70
❑ 8 Shaquille O'Neal	20.00	9.00
❑ 9 Scottie Pippen	12.00	5.50
❑ 10 David Robinson	6.00	2.70
❑ 11 Glenn Robinson	4.00	1.80
❑ 12 Jerry Stackhouse	6.00	2.70

1995-96 Ultra USA Basketball

	MINT	NRMT
COMPLETE SET (10)	150.00	70.00
COMMON CARD (1-10)	8.00	3.60

SER.2 STATED ODDS 1:54 HOBBY/RETAIL

Card	MINT	NRMT
❑ 1 Anfernee Hardaway	25.00	11.00
❑ 2 Grant Hill	40.00	18.00
❑ 3 Karl Malone	12.00	5.50
❑ 4 Reggie Miller	8.00	3.60
❑ 5 Hakeem Olajuwon	12.00	5.50
❑ 6 Shaquille O'Neal	40.00	18.00
❑ 7 Scottie Pippen	25.00	11.00
❑ 8 David Robinson	12.00	5.50
❑ 9 Glenn Robinson	8.00	3.60
❑ 10 John Stockton	8.00	3.60

1996-97 Ultra

	MINT	NRMT
COMPLETE SET (300)	55.00	25.00
COMPLETE SERIES 1 (150)	40.00	18.00
COMPLETE SERIES 2 (150)	15.00	6.75
COMMON CARD (1-300)	.15	.07
SEMISTARS	.20	.09
UNLISTED STARS	.40	.18

SUBSET CARDS HALF VALUE OF BASE CARDS

Card	MINT	NRMT
❑ 1 Mookie Blaylock	.15	.07
❑ 2 Alan Henderson	.15	.07
❑ 3 Christian Laettner	.20	.09
❑ 4 Dikembe Mutombo	.20	.09
❑ 5 Steve Smith	.20	.09
❑ 6 Dana Barros	.15	.07
❑ 7 Rick Fox	.15	.07
❑ 8 Dino Radja	.15	.07
❑ 9 Antoine Walker RC	1.50	.70
❑ 10 Eric Williams	.15	.07
❑ 11 Dell Curry	.15	.07
❑ 12 Tony Delk RC	.20	.09
❑ 13 Matt Geiger	.15	.07
❑ 14 Glen Rice	.20	.09
❑ 15 Ron Harper	.20	.09
❑ 16 Michael Jordan	5.00	2.20
❑ 17 Toni Kukoc	.50	.23
❑ 18 Scottie Pippen	1.25	.55
❑ 19 Dennis Rodman	.75	.35
❑ 20 Terrell Brandon	.20	.09
❑ 21 Chris Mills	.15	.07
❑ 22 Bobby Phills	.15	.07
❑ 23 Bob Sura	.15	.07
❑ 24 Jim Jackson	.15	.07
❑ 25 Jason Kidd	1.25	.55
❑ 26 Jamal Mashburn	.20	.09
❑ 27 George McCloud	.15	.07
❑ 28 Samaki Walker RC	.15	.07
❑ 29 LaPhonso Ellis	.15	.07
❑ 30 Antonio McDyess	.60	.25
❑ 31 Bryant Stith	.15	.07
❑ 32 Joe Dumars	.40	.18
❑ 33 Grant Hill	2.00	.90
❑ 34 Theo Ratliff	.20	.09
❑ 35 Otis Thorpe	.15	.07
❑ 36 Chris Mullin	.40	.18
❑ 37 Joe Smith	.40	.18
❑ 38 Latrell Sprewell	.75	.35
❑ 39 Charles Barkley	.60	.25
❑ 40 Clyde Drexler	.40	.18
❑ 41 Mario Elie	.15	.07
❑ 42 Hakeem Olajuwon	.60	.25
❑ 43 Erick Dampier RC	.20	.09
❑ 44 Dale Davis	.15	.07
❑ 45 Derrick McKey	.15	.07
❑ 46 Reggie Miller	.40	.18
❑ 47 Rik Smits	.15	.07
❑ 48 Brent Barry	.15	.07
❑ 49 Malik Sealy	.15	.07
❑ 50 Loy Vaught	.15	.07
❑ 51 Lorenzen Wright RC	.20	.09
❑ 52 Kobe Bryant RC	25.00	11.00
❑ 53 Cedric Ceballos	.15	.07
❑ 54 Eddie Jones	.75	.35
❑ 55 Shaquille O'Neal	2.00	.90
❑ 56 Nick Van Exel	.20	.09
❑ 57 Tim Hardaway	.40	.18
❑ 58 Alonzo Mourning	.40	.18
❑ 59 Kurt Thomas	.15	.07
❑ 60 Ray Allen RC	1.50	.70
❑ 61 Vin Baker	.20	.09
❑ 62 Sherman Douglas	.15	.07
❑ 63 Glenn Robinson	.40	.18
❑ 64 Kevin Garnett	2.50	1.10
❑ 65 Tom Gugliotta	.20	.09
❑ 66 Stephon Marbury RC	2.50	1.10
❑ 67 Doug West	.15	.07
❑ 68 Shawn Bradley	.15	.07
❑ 69 Kendall Gill	.20	.09
❑ 70 Kerry Kittles RC	.75	.35
❑ 71 Ed O'Bannon	.15	.07
❑ 72 Patrick Ewing	.40	.18
❑ 73 Larry Johnson	.20	.09
❑ 74 Charles Oakley	.15	.07
❑ 75 John Starks	.15	.07
❑ 76 John Wallace RC	.40	.18
❑ 77 Nick Anderson	.15	.07
❑ 78 Horace Grant	.20	.09
❑ 79 Anfernee Hardaway	1.25	.55
❑ 80 Dennis Scott	.15	.07
❑ 81 Derrick Coleman	.20	.09
❑ 82 Allen Iverson RC	4.00	1.80
❑ 83 Jerry Stackhouse	.40	.18
❑ 84 Clarence Weatherspoon	.15	.07
❑ 85 Michael Finley	.50	.23
❑ 86 Kevin Johnson	.20	.09
❑ 87 Steve Nash RC	.20	.09
❑ 88 Wesley Person	.15	.07
❑ 89 Jermaine O'Neal RC	.75	.35
❑ 90 Clifford Robinson	.15	.07
❑ 91 Arvydas Sabonis	.20	.09
❑ 92 Gary Trent	.15	.07
❑ 93 Tyus Edney	.15	.07
❑ 94 Brian Grant	.40	.18
❑ 95 Olden Polynice	.15	.07
❑ 96 Mitch Richmond	.40	.18
❑ 97 Corliss Williamson	.15	.07
❑ 98 Vinny Del Negro	.15	.07
❑ 99 Sean Elliott	.15	.07
❑ 100 Avery Johnson	.15	.07
❑ 101 David Robinson	.60	.25
❑ 102 Hersey Hawkins	.20	.09
❑ 103 Shawn Kemp	.60	.25
❑ 104 Gary Payton	.60	.25
❑ 105 Sam Perkins	.20	.09
❑ 106 Detlef Schrempf	.20	.09
❑ 107 Marcus Camby RC	1.25	.55
❑ 108 Doug Christie	.15	.07
❑ 109 Damon Stoudamire	.60	.25
❑ 110 Sharone Wright	.15	.07
❑ 111 Jeff Hornacek	.20	.09
❑ 112 Karl Malone	.60	.25
❑ 113 Chris Morris	.15	.07
❑ 114 Bryon Russell	.15	.07
❑ 115 John Stockton	.40	.18
❑ 116 Shareef Abdur-Rahim RC	2.50	1.10
❑ 117 Greg Anthony	.15	.07
❑ 118 Blue Edwards	.15	.07
❑ 119 Bryant Reeves	.15	.07
❑ 120 Calbert Cheaney	.15	.07
❑ 121 Juwan Howard	.20	.09
❑ 122 Gheorghe Muresan	.15	.07
❑ 123 Chris Webber	1.25	.55
❑ 124 Vin Baker OTB	.15	.07
❑ 125 Charles Barkley OTB	.40	.18
❑ 126 Kevin Garnett OTB	1.25	.55
❑ 127 Juwan Howard OTB	.15	.07
❑ 128 Larry Johnson OTB	.15	.07
❑ 129 Shawn Kemp OTB	.40	.18
❑ 130 Karl Malone OTB	.40	.18
❑ 131 Anthony Mason OTB	.15	.07
❑ 132 Antonio McDyess OTB	.40	.18
❑ 133 Alonzo Mourning OTB	.20	.09
❑ 134 Hakeem Olajuwon OTB	.40	.18
❑ 135 Shaquille O'Neal OTB	.75	.35
❑ 136 David Robinson OTB	.40	.18
❑ 137 Dennis Rodman OTB	.40	.18
❑ 138 Joe Smith OTB	.20	.09
❑ 139 Mookie Blaylock UE	.15	.07
❑ 140 Terrell Brandon UE	.15	.07
❑ 141 Anfernee Hardaway UE	.75	.35
❑ 142 Grant Hill UE	1.25	.55
❑ 143 Michael Jordan UE	2.50	1.10
❑ 144 Jason Kidd UE	.40	.18
❑ 145 Gary Payton UE	.40	.18
❑ 146 Jerry Stackhouse UE	.20	.09
❑ 147 Damon Stoudamire UE	.40	.18
❑ 148 Hakeem Olajuwon David Robinson Robert Horry Oliver Miller Clarence Weatherspoon	.40	.18
❑ 149 Checklist	.15	.07
❑ 150 Checklist	.15	.07
❑ 151 Tyrone Corbin	.15	.07
❑ 152 Priest Lauderdale RC	.15	.07
❑ 153 Dikembe Mutombo	.20	.09
❑ 154 Eldridge Recasner RC	.15	.07
❑ 155 Todd Day	.15	.07
❑ 156 Greg Minor	.15	.07
❑ 157 David Wesley	.15	.07
❑ 158 Vlade Divac	.15	.07
❑ 159 Anthony Mason	.20	.09
❑ 160 Malik Rose RC	.20	.09
❑ 161 Jason Caffey	.15	.07
❑ 162 Steve Kerr	.15	.07
❑ 163 Luc Longley	.15	.07
❑ 164 Danny Ferry	.15	.07
❑ 165 Tyrone Hill	.15	.07
❑ 166 Vitaly Potapenko RC	.15	.07
❑ 167 Sam Cassell	.20	.09
❑ 168 Michael Finley	.50	.23
❑ 169 Chris Gatling	.15	.07
❑ 170 A.C. Green	.20	.09
❑ 171 Oliver Miller	.15	.07
❑ 172 Eric Montross	.15	.07
❑ 173 Dale Ellis	.15	.07
❑ 174 Mark Jackson	.15	.07

❑ 175	Ervin Johnson	.15	.07
❑ 176	Sarunas Marciulionis	.15	.07
❑ 177	Stacey Augmon	.15	.07
❑ 178	Joe Dumars	.40	.18
❑ 179	Grant Hill	2.00	.90
❑ 180	Lindsey Hunter	.15	.07
❑ 181	Grant Long	.15	.07
❑ 182	Terry Mills	.15	.07
❑ 183	Otis Thorpe	.15	.07
❑ 184	Jerome Williams RC	.60	.25
❑ 185	Todd Fuller RC	.15	.07
❑ 186	Ray Owes RC	.15	.07
❑ 187	Mark Price	.15	.07
❑ 188	Felton Spencer	.15	.07
❑ 189	Charles Barkley	.60	.25
❑ 190	Emanual Davis RC	.15	.07
❑ 191	Othella Harrington RC	.40	.18
❑ 192	Matt Maloney RC	.20	.09
❑ 193	Brent Price	.15	.07
❑ 194	Kevin Willis	.15	.07
❑ 195	Travis Best	.15	.07
❑ 196	Antonio Davis	.15	.07
❑ 197	Jalen Rose	.40	.18
❑ 198	Pooh Richardson	.15	.07
❑ 199	Stanley Roberts	.15	.07
❑ 200	Rodney Rogers	.15	.07
❑ 201	Elden Campbell	.15	.07
❑ 202	Derek Fisher RC	.60	.25
❑ 203	Travis Knight RC	.15	.07
❑ 204	Shaquille O'Neal	2.00	.90
❑ 205	Byron Scott	.15	.07
❑ 206	Sasha Danilovic	.15	.07
❑ 207	Dan Majerle	.20	.09
❑ 208	Martin Muursepp RC	.15	.07
❑ 209	Armon Gilliam	.15	.07
❑ 210	Andrew Lang	.15	.07
❑ 211	Johnny Newman	.15	.07
❑ 212	Kevin Garnett	2.50	1.10
❑ 213	Tom Gugliotta	.20	.09
❑ 214	Shane Heal RC	.15	.07
❑ 215	Stojko Vrankovic	.15	.07
❑ 216	Robert Pack	.15	.07
❑ 217	Khalid Reeves	.15	.07
❑ 218	Jayson Williams	.20	.09
❑ 219	Chris Childs	.15	.07
❑ 220	Allan Houston	.40	.18
❑ 221	Larry Johnson	.20	.09
❑ 222	Walter McCarty RC	.15	.07
❑ 223	Charlie Ward	.15	.07
❑ 224	Brian Evans RC	.15	.07
❑ 225	Amal McCaskill RC	.15	.07
❑ 226	Rony Seikaly	.15	.07
❑ 227	Gerald Wilkins	.15	.07
❑ 228	Mark Davis	.15	.07
❑ 229	Lucious Harris	.15	.07
❑ 230	Don MacLean	.15	.07
❑ 231	Cedric Ceballos	.15	.07
❑ 232	Rex Chapman	.15	.07
❑ 233	Jason Kidd	1.25	.55
❑ 234	Danny Manning	.20	.09
❑ 235	Kenny Anderson	.20	.09
❑ 236	Aaron McKie	.15	.07
❑ 237	Isaiah Rider	.20	.09
❑ 238	Rasheed Wallace	.50	.23
❑ 239	Mahmoud Abdul-Rauf	.15	.07
❑ 240	Billy Owens	.15	.07
❑ 241	Michael Smith	.15	.07
❑ 242	Vernon Maxwell	.15	.07
❑ 243	Charles Smith	.15	.07
❑ 244	Dominique Wilkins	.40	.18
❑ 245	Craig Ehlo	.15	.07
❑ 246	Jim McIlvaine	.15	.07
❑ 247	Nate McMillan	.15	.07
❑ 248	Hubert Davis	.15	.07
❑ 249	Carlos Rogers	.15	.07
❑ 250	Zan Tabak	.15	.07
❑ 251	Walt Williams	.15	.07
❑ 252	Jeff Hornacek	.20	.09
❑ 253	Karl Malone	.60	.25
❑ 254	Greg Ostertag	.15	.07
❑ 255	Bryon Russell	.15	.07
❑ 256	John Stockton	.40	.18
❑ 257	George Lynch	.15	.07
❑ 258	Lawrence Moten	.15	.07
❑ 259	Anthony Peeler	.15	.07
❑ 260	Roy Rogers RC	.15	.07
❑ 261	Tracy Murray	.15	.07
❑ 262	Rod Strickland	.20	.09
❑ 263	Ben Wallace RC	.15	.07
❑ 264	Shareef Abdur-Rahim RE	1.25	.55
❑ 265	Ray Allen RE	.60	.25
❑ 266	Kobe Bryant RE	8.00	3.60
❑ 267	Marcus Camby RE	.50	.23
❑ 268	Erick Dampier RE	.15	.07
❑ 269	Tony Delk RE	.15	.07
❑ 270	Allen Iverson RE	1.50	.70
❑ 271	Kerry Kittles RE	.40	.18
❑ 272	Stephon Marbury RE	2.00	.90
❑ 273	Steve Nash RE	.15	.07
❑ 274	Jermaine O'Neal RE	.40	.18
❑ 275	Antoine Walker RE	2.00	.90
❑ 276	Samaki Walker RE	.15	.07
❑ 277	John Wallace RE	.20	.09
❑ 278	Lorenzen Wright RE	.15	.07
❑ 279	Anfernee Hardaway SU	.75	.35
❑ 280	Michael Jordan SU	2.50	1.10
❑ 281	Jason Kidd SU	.40	.18
❑ 282	Hakeem Olajuwon SU	.40	.18
❑ 283	Gary Payton SU	.40	.18
❑ 284	Mitch Richmond SU	.20	.09
❑ 285	David Robinson SU	.40	.18
❑ 286	John Stockton SU	.20	.09
❑ 287	Damon Stoudamire SU	.40	.18
❑ 288	Chris Webber SU	.50	.23
❑ 289	Clyde Drexler PG	.20	.09
❑ 290	Kevin Garnett PG	1.25	.55
❑ 291	Grant Hill PG	1.25	.55
❑ 292	Shawn Kemp PG	.40	.18
❑ 293	Karl Malone PG	.40	.18
❑ 294	Antonio McDyess PG	.40	.18
❑ 295	Alonzo Mourning PG	.20	.09
❑ 296	Shaquille O'Neal PG	.75	.35
❑ 297	Scottie Pippen PG	.60	.25
❑ 298	Jerry Stackhouse PG	.20	.09
❑ 299	Checklist (151-263)	.15	.07
❑ 300	Checklist 264-300/inserts	.15	.07
❑ NNO	Jerry Stackhouse Promo	3.00	1.35

1996-97 Ultra Gold Medallion

	MINT	NRMT
COMPLETE SET (296)	500.00	220.00
COMPLETE SERIES 1 (148)	400.00	180.00
COMPLETE SERIES 2 (148)	80.00	36.00
COMMON CARD (G1-G123)	1.25	.55
COMMON CARD (124-148)	1.25	.55
COMMON CARD (G151-G298)	.20	.09

*SER.1 STARS: 3X TO 8X BASE CARD HI
*SER.1 RCs: 2.5X TO 6X BASE HI
*SER.2 STARS: .75X TO 2X BASE HI
*SER.2 RCs: .6X TO 1.5X BASE HI
SER.1 STATED ODDS 1:12 H/R
SER.2 STATED ODDS ONE PER PACK
SER.1 SUB.CARDS HAVE NO "G" PREFIX

❑ G52	Kobe Bryant	80.00	36.00
❑ G266	Kobe Bryant RE	20.00	9.00

1996-97 Ultra Platinum Medallion

	MINT	NRMT
COMPLETE SET (296)	4500.00	2000.00
COMPLETE SERIES 1 (148)	3000.00	1350.00
COMPLETE SERIES 2 (148)	1500.00	700.00
COMMON CARD	5.00	2.20

*STARS: 15X TO 40X BASE CARD HI
*RCs: 8X TO 20X BASE HI
SER.1 STATED ODDS 1:180 HOB/RET
SER.2 STATED ODDS 1:100 HOB/RET
STATED PRINT RUN LESS THAN 250 SETS

❑ P52	Kobe Bryant	400.00	180.00
❑ P266	Kobe Bryant RE	200.00	90.00

1996-97 Ultra All-Rookies

	MINT	NRMT
COMPLETE SET (15)	40.00	18.00
COMMON CARD (1-15)	.75	.35
SEMISTARS	1.00	.45
UNLISTED STARS	1.50	.70

SER.2 STATED ODDS 1:4 HOBBY/RETAIL

❑ 1	Shareef Abdur-Rahim	5.00	2.20
❑ 2	Ray Allen	3.00	1.35
❑ 3	Kobe Bryant	15.00	6.75
❑ 4	Marcus Camby	2.50	1.10
❑ 5	Tony Delk	.75	.35
❑ 6	Derek Fisher	1.50	.70
❑ 7	Allen Iverson	8.00	3.60
❑ 8	Kerry Kittles	1.50	.70
❑ 9	Matt Maloney	.75	.35
❑ 10	Stephon Marbury	5.00	2.20
❑ 11	Vitaly Potapenko	.75	.35
❑ 12	Roy Rogers	.75	.35
❑ 13	Antoine Walker	3.00	1.35
❑ 14	Samaki Walker	.75	.35
❑ 15	John Wallace	1.00	.45

1996-97 Ultra Board Game

	MINT	NRMT
COMPLETE SET (20)	50.00	22.00
COMMON CARD (1-20)	.75	.35
SEMISTARS	1.00	.45
UNLISTED STARS	1.50	.70

SER.2 STATED ODDS 1:9 HOBBY/RETAIL

❑ 1	Vin Baker	1.00	.45
❑ 2	Charles Barkley	2.50	1.10
❑ 3	Dale Davis	.75	.35
❑ 4	Clyde Drexler	1.50	.70
❑ 5	Patrick Ewing	1.50	.70
❑ 6	Grant Hill	8.00	3.60
❑ 7	Michael Jordan	20.00	9.00
❑ 8	Shawn Kemp	2.50	1.10
❑ 9	Jason Kidd	5.00	2.20
❑ 10	Karl Malone	2.50	1.10
❑ 11	Alonzo Mourning	1.50	.70
❑ 12	Dikembe Mutombo	1.00	.45
❑ 13	Hakeem Olajuwon	2.50	1.10
❑ 14	Shaquille O'Neal	8.00	3.60

		MINT	NRMT
❑ 15	Scottie Pippen	5.00	2.20
❑ 16	David Robinson	2.50	1.10
❑ 17	Dennis Rodman	3.00	1.35
❑ 18	Loy Vaught	.75	.35
❑ 19	Chris Webber	5.00	2.20
❑ 20	Jayson Williams	1.00	.45

1996-97 Ultra Court Masters

	MINT	NRMT
COMPLETE SET (15)	450.00	200.00
COMMON CARD (1-15)	12.00	5.50
SER.1 STATED ODDS 1:180 RETAIL		

		MINT	NRMT
❑ 1	Anfernee Hardaway	40.00	18.00
❑ 2	Michael Jordan	150.00	70.00
❑ 3	Karl Malone	20.00	9.00
❑ 4	Scottie Pippen	40.00	18.00
❑ 5	David Robinson	20.00	9.00
❑ 6	Grant Hill	60.00	27.00
❑ 7	Shawn Kemp	20.00	9.00
❑ 8	Hakeem Olajuwon	20.00	9.00
❑ 9	Gary Payton	20.00	9.00
❑ 10	John Stockton	12.00	5.50
❑ 11	Charles Barkley	20.00	9.00
❑ 12	Juwan Howard	12.00	5.50
❑ 13	Reggie Miller	12.00	5.50
❑ 14	Shaquille O'Neal	60.00	27.00
❑ 15	Mitch Richmond	12.00	5.50

1996-97 Ultra Decade of Excellence

	MINT	NRMT
COMPLETE SET (20)	75.00	34.00
COMPLETE SERIES 1 (10)	50.00	22.00
COMPLETE SERIES 2 (10)	25.00	11.00
COMMON CARD (U1-U20)	2.50	1.10
SEMISTARS	5.00	2.20
SER.1/2 STATED ODDS 1:100 HOBBY/RETAIL		

		MINT	NRMT
❑ U1	Clyde Drexler	5.00	2.20
❑ U2	Joe Dumars	5.00	2.20
❑ U3	Derek Harper	2.50	1.10
❑ U4	Michael Jordan	40.00	18.00
❑ U5	Karl Malone	5.00	2.20
❑ U6	Chris Mullin	5.00	2.20
❑ U7	Charles Oakley	2.50	1.10
❑ U8	Sam Perkins	2.50	1.10
❑ U9	Ricky Pierce	2.50	1.10
❑ U10	Buck Williams	2.50	1.10
❑ U11	Charles Barkley	8.00	3.60
❑ U12	Patrick Ewing	5.00	2.20
❑ U13	Eddie Johnson	2.50	1.10
❑ U14	Hakeem Olajuwon	8.00	3.60
❑ U15	Robert Parish	2.50	1.10
❑ U16	Byron Scott	2.50	1.10
❑ U17	Wayman Tisdale	2.50	1.10
❑ U18	Gerald Wilkins	2.50	1.10
❑ U19	Herb Williams	2.50	1.10
❑ U20	Kevin Willis	2.50	1.10

1996-97 Ultra Fresh Faces

	MINT	NRMT
COMPLETE SET (9)	80.00	36.00
COMMON CARD (1-9)	3.00	1.35
SEMISTARS	4.00	1.80
SER.1 STATED ODDS 1:72 HOBBY/RETAIL		

		MINT	NRMT
❑ 1	Shareef Abdur-Rahim	12.00	5.50
❑ 2	Ray Allen	8.00	3.60
❑ 3	Kobe Bryant	40.00	18.00
❑ 4	Marcus Camby	6.00	2.70
❑ 5	Allen Iverson	15.00	6.75
❑ 6	Kerry Kittles	4.00	1.80
❑ 7	Stephon Marbury	12.00	5.50
❑ 8	Steve Nash	3.00	1.35
❑ 9	Antoine Walker	8.00	3.60

1996-97 Ultra Full Court Trap

	MINT	NRMT
COMPLETE SET (10)	25.00	11.00
COMMON CARD (1-10)	1.00	.45
SER.1 STATED ODDS 1:15 HOBBY/RETAIL		
COMP.GOLD SET (10)	120.00	55.00
COMMON GOLD (1-10)	5.00	2.20
*GOLD STARS: 2.5X TO 5X HI COLUMN		
GOLD: SER.1 STATED ODDS 1:180 HOB/RET		

		MINT	NRMT
❑ 1	Michael Jordan	20.00	9.00
❑ 2	Gary Payton	2.50	1.10
❑ 3	Scottie Pippen	5.00	2.20
❑ 4	David Robinson	2.50	1.10
❑ 5	Dennis Rodman	3.00	1.35
❑ 6	Mookie Blaylock	1.00	.45
❑ 7	Horace Grant	1.00	.45
❑ 8	Derrick McKey	1.00	.45
❑ 9	Hakeem Olajuwon	2.50	1.10
❑ 10	Bobby Phills	1.00	.45

1996-97 Ultra Give and Take

	MINT	NRMT
COMPLETE SET (10)	50.00	22.00
COMMON CARD (1-10)	1.50	.70
SEMISTARS	2.00	.90
SER.2 STATED ODDS 1:18 RETAIL		

		MINT	NRMT
❑ 1	Mookie Blaylock	1.50	.70
❑ 2	Anfernee Hardaway	6.00	2.70
❑ 3	Tim Hardaway	2.00	.90
❑ 4	Allen Iverson	10.00	4.50
❑ 5	Michael Jordan	30.00	13.50
❑ 6	Jason Kidd	6.00	2.70
❑ 7	Gary Payton	3.00	1.35
❑ 8	Scottie Pippen	6.00	2.70
❑ 9	John Stockton	2.00	.90
❑ 10	Damon Stoudamire	3.00	1.35

1996-97 Ultra Rising Stars

	MINT	NRMT
COMPLETE SET (10)	80.00	36.00
COMMON CARD (1-10)	3.00	1.35
SER.1 STATED ODDS 1:180 HOBBY		

		MINT	NRMT
❑ 1	Shareef Abdur-Rahim	10.00	4.50
❑ 2	Kobe Bryant	30.00	13.50
❑ 3	Anfernee Hardaway	10.00	4.50
❑ 4	Grant Hill	15.00	6.75
❑ 5	Juwan Howard	3.00	1.35
❑ 6	Allen Iverson	15.00	6.75
❑ 7	Jason Kidd	10.00	4.50
❑ 8	Stephon Marbury	10.00	4.50
❑ 9	Joe Smith	3.00	1.35
❑ 10	Damon Stoudamire	5.00	2.20

1996-97 Ultra Rookie Flashback

	MINT	NRMT
COMPLETE SET (11)	40.00	18.00
COMMON CARD (1-11)	2.00	.90
SEMISTARS	2.50	1.10

	MINT	NRMT
UNLISTED STARS	4.00	1.80

SER.1 STATED ODDS 1:45 HOBBY/RETAIL

❑ 1 Michael Finley	5.00	2.20
❑ 2 Antonio McDyess	6.00	2.70
❑ 3 Arvydas Sabonis	2.50	1.10
❑ 4 Joe Smith	4.00	1.80
❑ 5 Jerry Stackhouse	4.00	1.80
❑ 6 Damon Stoudamire	6.00	2.70
❑ 7 Brent Barry	2.00	.90
❑ 8 Tyus Edney	2.00	.90
❑ 9 Kevin Garnett	25.00	11.00
❑ 10 Bryant Reeves	2.00	.90
❑ 11 Rasheed Wallace	5.00	2.20

1996-97 Ultra Scoring Kings

	MINT	NRMT
COMPLETE SET (29)	250.00	110.00
COMMON CARD (1-29)	2.50	1.10
SEMISTARS	3.00	1.35
UNLISTED STARS	5.00	2.20
SER.2 STATED ODDS 1:24 HOBBY		
COMP.PLUS SET (29)	650.00	300.00
COMMON PLUS (1-29)	6.00	2.70
*PLUS STARS: 1.25X TO 2.5X HI COLUMN		
PLUS: SER.2 STATED ODDS 1:96 HOBBY		

❑ 1 Steve Smith	3.00	1.35
❑ 2 Dino Radja	2.50	1.10
❑ 3 Glen Rice	3.00	1.35
❑ 4 Michael Jordan	60.00	27.00
❑ 5 Terrell Brandon	3.00	1.35
❑ 6 Jim Jackson	2.50	1.10
❑ 7 Antonio McDyess	8.00	3.60
❑ 8 Grant Hill	25.00	11.00
❑ 9 Latrell Sprewell	10.00	4.50
❑ 10 Hakeem Olajuwon	8.00	3.60
❑ 11 Reggie Miller	5.00	2.20
❑ 12 Loy Vaught	2.50	1.10
❑ 13 Shaquille O'Neal	25.00	11.00
❑ 14 Alonzo Mourning	5.00	2.20
❑ 15 Vin Baker	3.00	1.35
❑ 16 Tom Gugliotta	3.00	1.35
❑ 17 Kendall Gill	3.00	1.35
❑ 18 Patrick Ewing	5.00	2.20
❑ 19 Anfernee Hardaway	15.00	6.75
❑ 20 Allen Iverson	25.00	11.00
❑ 21 Danny Manning	3.00	1.35
❑ 22 Kenny Anderson	3.00	1.35
❑ 23 Mitch Richmond	5.00	2.20
❑ 24 David Robinson	8.00	3.60
❑ 25 Shawn Kemp	8.00	3.60
❑ 26 Damon Stoudamire	8.00	3.60
❑ 27 Karl Malone	8.00	3.60
❑ 28 Shareef Abdur-Rahim	15.00	6.75
❑ 29 Chris Webber	15.00	6.75

1996-97 Ultra Starring Role

	MINT	NRMT
COMPLETE SET (10)	250.00	110.00
COMMON CARD (1-10)	12.00	5.50
SER.2 STATED ODDS 1:288 HOBBY/RETAIL		

❑ 1 Kevin Garnett	50.00	22.00
❑ 2 Anfernee Hardaway	25.00	11.00
❑ 3 Grant Hill	40.00	18.00
❑ 4 Michael Jordan	100.00	45.00
❑ 5 Shawn Kemp	12.00	5.50
❑ 6 Karl Malone	12.00	5.50
❑ 7 Hakeem Olajuwon	12.00	5.50
❑ 8 Shaquille O'Neal	40.00	18.00
❑ 9 David Robinson	12.00	5.50
❑ 10 Damon Stoudamire	12.00	5.50

1997-98 Ultra

	MINT	NRMT
COMPLETE SET (275)	130.00	57.50
COMPLETE SERIES 1 (150)	80.00	36.00
COMPLETE SERIES 2 (125)	50.00	22.00
COMMON CARD (1-123)	.15	.07
COMMON CARD (124-148)	1.00	.45
COMMON CARD (149-275)	.15	.07
SEMISTARS	.20	.09
SEMISTARS RC	1.50	.70
UNLISTED STARS	.40	.18
UNLISTED STARS RC	2.00	.90

SER.1 ROOKIE SUBSET ODDS 1:4 H/R
GRE SUBSET ODDS 1:4 H/R
GRE SUBSET: .75X TO 2X BASE CARD HI
UNPRICED MASTERPIECES SERIAL #'d TO 1
MASTERPIECES: RANDOM INS.IN PACKS
RC's CONDITION SENSITIVE !

❑ 1 Kobe Bryant	3.00	1.35
❑ 2 Charles Barkley	.60	.25
❑ 3 Joe Dumars	.40	.18
❑ 4 Wesley Person	.15	.07
❑ 5 Walt Williams	.15	.07
❑ 6 Vlade Divac	.15	.07
❑ 7 Mookie Blaylock	.15	.07
❑ 8 Jason Kidd	1.25	.55
❑ 9 Ron Harper	.20	.09
❑ 10 Sherman Douglas	.15	.07
❑ 11 Cedric Ceballos	.15	.07
❑ 12 Karl Malone	.60	.25
❑ 13 Antonio McDyess	.50	.23
❑ 14 Steve Kerr	.15	.07
❑ 15 Matt Maloney	.15	.07
❑ 16 Glenn Robinson	.20	.09
❑ 17 Rony Seikaly	.15	.07
❑ 18 Derrick Coleman	.20	.09
❑ 19 Jermaine O'Neal	.20	.09
❑ 20 Scott Burrell	.15	.07
❑ 21 Glen Rice	.20	.09
❑ 22 Dale Ellis	.15	.07
❑ 23 Michael Jordan	5.00	2.20
❑ 24 Anfernee Hardaway	1.25	.55
❑ 25 Bryon Russell	.15	.07
❑ 26 Toni Kukoc	.50	.23
❑ 27 Theo Ratliff	.15	.07
❑ 28 Tom Gugliotta	.20	.09
❑ 29 Dennis Rodman	.75	.35
❑ 30 John Stockton	.40	.18
❑ 31 Priest Lauderdale	.15	.07
❑ 32 Luc Longley	.15	.07
❑ 33 Grant Hill	2.00	.90
❑ 34 Antonio Davis	.15	.07
❑ 35 Eddie Jones	.75	.35
❑ 36 Nick Anderson	.15	.07
❑ 37 Shareef Abdur-Rahim	1.25	.55
❑ 38 Stephon Marbury	1.25	.55
❑ 39 Todd Day	.15	.07
❑ 40 Tim Hardaway	.40	.18
❑ 41 Larry Johnson	.20	.09
❑ 42 Sam Perkins	.20	.09
❑ 43 Dikembe Mutombo	.20	.09
❑ 44 Charles Outlaw	.15	.07
❑ 45 Mitch Richmond	.40	.18
❑ 46 Bryant Reeves	.15	.07
❑ 47 P.J. Brown	.15	.07
❑ 48 Steve Smith	.20	.09
❑ 49 Martin Muursepp	.15	.07
❑ 50 Jamal Mashburn	.20	.09
❑ 51 Kendall Gill	.20	.09
❑ 52 Vinny Del Negro	.15	.07
❑ 53 Roy Rogers	.15	.07
❑ 54 Khalid Reeves	.15	.07
❑ 55 Scottie Pippen	1.25	.55
❑ 56 Joe Smith	.20	.09
❑ 57 Mark Jackson	.15	.07
❑ 58 Voshon Lenard	.15	.07
❑ 59 Dan Majerle	.20	.09
❑ 60 Alonzo Mourning	.40	.18
❑ 61 Kerry Kittles	.40	.18
❑ 62 Chris Childs	.15	.07
❑ 63 Patrick Ewing	.40	.18
❑ 64 Allan Houston	.40	.18
❑ 65 Marcus Camby	.50	.23
❑ 66 Christian Laettner	.20	.09
❑ 67 Loy Vaught	.15	.07
❑ 68 Jayson Williams	.20	.09
❑ 69 Avery Johnson	.15	.07
❑ 70 Damon Stoudamire	.50	.23
❑ 71 Kevin Johnson	.20	.09
❑ 72 Gheorghe Muresan	.15	.07
❑ 73 Reggie Miller	.40	.18
❑ 74 John Wallace	.15	.07
❑ 75 Terrell Brandon	.20	.09
❑ 76 Dale Davis	.15	.07
❑ 77 Latrell Sprewell	.75	.35
❑ 78 Lorenzen Wright	.15	.07
❑ 79 Rod Strickland	.20	.09
❑ 80 Kenny Anderson	.20	.09
❑ 81 Anthony Mason	.20	.09
❑ 82 Hakeem Olajuwon	.60	.25
❑ 83 Kevin Garnett	2.50	1.10
❑ 84 Isaiah Rider	.20	.09
❑ 85 Mark Price	.15	.07
❑ 86 Shawn Bradley	.15	.07
❑ 87 Vin Baker	.20	.09
❑ 88 Steve Nash	.15	.07

❑ 89 Jeff Hornacek .20 .09
❑ 90 Tony Delk .15 .07
❑ 91 Horace Grant .20 .09
❑ 92 Othella Harrington .15 .07
❑ 93 Arvydas Sabonis .20 .09
❑ 94 Antoine Walker .75 .35
❑ 95 Todd Fuller .15 .07
❑ 96 John Starks .15 .07
❑ 97 Olden Polynice .15 .07
❑ 98 Sean Elliott .15 .07
❑ 99 Travis Best .15 .07
❑ 100 Chris Gatling .15 .07
❑ 101 Derek Harper .15 .07
❑ 102 LaPhonso Ellis .15 .07
❑ 103 Dean Garrett .15 .07
❑ 104 Hersey Hawkins .20 .09
❑ 105 Jerry Stackhouse .20 .09
❑ 106 Ray Allen .60 .25
❑ 107 Allen Iverson 2.00 .90
❑ 108 Chris Webber 1.25 .55
❑ 109 Robert Pack .15 .07
❑ 110 Gary Payton .60 .25
❑ 111 Mario Elie .15 .07
❑ 112 Dell Curry .15 .07
❑ 113 Lindsey Hunter .15 .07
❑ 114 Robert Horry .15 .07
❑ 115 David Robinson .60 .25
❑ 116 Kevin Willis .15 .07
❑ 117 Tyrone Hill .15 .07
❑ 118 Vitaly Potapenko .15 .07
❑ 119 Clyde Drexler .40 .18
❑ 120 Derek Fisher .15 .07
❑ 121 Detlef Schrempf .20 .09
❑ 122 Gary Trent .15 .07
❑ 123 Danny Ferry .15 .07
❑ 124 Derek Anderson RC 5.00 2.20
❑ 125 Chris Anstey RC 1.00 .45
❑ 126 Tony Battie RC 2.00 .90
❑ 127 Chauncey Billups RC 2.50 1.10
❑ 128 Kelvin Cato RC 2.00 .90
❑ 129 Austin Croshere RC 5.00 2.20
❑ 130 Antonio Daniels RC 2.00 .90
❑ 131 Tim Duncan RC ! 40.00 18.00
❑ 132 Danny Fortson RC 1.50 .70
❑ 133 Adonal Foyle RC 1.50 .70
❑ 134 Paul Grant RC 1.00 .45
❑ 135 Ed Gray RC 1.00 .45
❑ 136 Bobby Jackson RC 1.50 .70
❑ 137 Brevin Knight RC 3.00 1.35
❑ 138 Tracy McGrady RC 25.00 11.00
❑ 139 Ron Mercer RC 6.00 2.70
❑ 140 Anthony Parker RC 1.00 .45
❑ 141 Scot Pollard RC 1.50 .70
❑ 142 Rodrick Rhodes RC 1.00 .45
❑ 143 Olivier Saint-Jean RC 1.00 .45
❑ 144 Maurice Taylor RC 4.00 1.80
❑ 145 Johnny Taylor RC 1.00 .45
❑ 146 Tim Thomas RC 6.00 2.70
❑ 147 Keith Van Horn RC 10.00 4.50
❑ 148 Jacque Vaughn RC 1.50 .70
❑ 149 Checklist .15 .07
❑ 150 Checklist .15 .07
❑ 151 Scott Burrell .15 .07
❑ 152 Brian Williams .15 .07
❑ 153 Terry Mills .15 .07
❑ 154 Jim Jackson .15 .07
❑ 155 Michael Finley .40 .18
❑ 156 Jeff Nordgaard RC .15 .07
❑ 157 Carl Herrera .15 .07
❑ 158 Otis Thorpe .15 .07
❑ 159 Wesley Person .15 .07
❑ 160 Tyrone Hill .15 .07
❑ 161 Charles O'Bannon RC .15 .07
❑ 162 Greg Anthony .15 .07
❑ 163 Rusty LaRue RC .15 .07
❑ 164 David Wesley .15 .07
❑ 165 Chris Garner RC .15 .07
❑ 166 George McCloud .15 .07
❑ 167 Mark Price .15 .07
❑ 168 God Shammgod RC .15 .07
❑ 169 Isaac Austin .15 .07
❑ 170 Alan Henderson .15 .07
❑ 171 Eric Washington RC .40 .18
❑ 172 Darrell Armstrong .20 .09
❑ 173 Calbert Cheaney .15 .07
❑ 174 Cedric Henderson RC .15 .07
❑ 175 Bryant Stith .15 .07
❑ 176 Sean Rooks .15 .07
❑ 177 Chris Mills .15 .07
❑ 178 Eldridge Recasner .15 .07
❑ 179 Priest Lauderdale .15 .07
❑ 180 Rick Fox .15 .07
❑ 181 Keith Closs RC .15 .07
❑ 182 Chris Dudley .15 .07
❑ 183 L. Funderburke RC .20 .09
❑ 184 Michael Stewart RC .15 .07
❑ 185 Alvin Williams RC .15 .07
❑ 186 Adam Keefe .15 .07
❑ 187 Chauncey Billups .15 .07
❑ 188 Jon Barry .15 .07
❑ 189 Bobby Jackson .15 .07
❑ 190 Sam Cassell .20 .09
❑ 191 Dee Brown .15 .07
❑ 192 Travis Knight .15 .07
❑ 193 Dean Garrett .15 .07
❑ 194 David Benoit .15 .07
❑ 195 Chris Morris .15 .07
❑ 196 Bubba Wells RC .15 .07
❑ 197 James Robinson .15 .07
❑ 198 Anthony Johnson RC .15 .07
❑ 199 Dennis Scott .15 .07
❑ 200 DeJuan Wheat RC .15 .07
❑ 201 Rodney Rogers .15 .07
❑ 202 Tariq Abdul-Wahad .15 .07
❑ 203 Cherokee Parks .15 .07
❑ 204 Jacque Vaughn .15 .07
❑ 205 Cory Alexander .15 .07
❑ 206 Kevin Ollie RC .15 .07
❑ 207 George Lynch .15 .07
❑ 208 Lamond Murray .15 .07
❑ 209 Jud Buechler .15 .07
❑ 210 Erick Dampier .15 .07
❑ 211 Malcolm Huckaby RC .15 .07
❑ 212 Chris Webber 1.25 .55
❑ 213 Chris Crawford RC .15 .07
❑ 214 J.R. Reid .15 .07
❑ 215 Eddie Johnson .15 .07
❑ 216 Nick Van Exel .20 .09
❑ 217 Antonio McDyess .50 .23
❑ 218 David Wingate .15 .07
❑ 219 Malik Sealy .15 .07
❑ 220 Charles Outlaw .15 .07
❑ 221 Serge Zwikker RC .15 .07
❑ 222 Bobby Phills .15 .07
❑ 223 Shea Seals RC .15 .07
❑ 224 Clifford Robinson .15 .07
❑ 225 Zydrunas Ilgauskas .15 .07
❑ 226 John Thomas RC .15 .07
❑ 227 Rik Smits .15 .07
❑ 228 Rasheed Wallace .40 .18
❑ 229 John Wallace .15 .07
❑ 230 Bob Sura .15 .07
❑ 231 Ervin Johnson .15 .07
❑ 232 Keith Booth RC .15 .07
❑ 233 Chuck Person .15 .07
❑ 234 Brian Shaw .15 .07
❑ 235 Todd Day .15 .07
❑ 236 Clarence Weatherspoon .15 .07
❑ 237 Charlie Ward .15 .07
❑ 238 Rod Strickland .20 .09
❑ 239 Shawn Kemp .60 .25
❑ 240 Terrell Brandon .20 .09
❑ 241 Corey Beck RC .15 .07
❑ 242 Vin Baker .20 .09
❑ 243 Fred Hoiberg .15 .07
❑ 244 Chris Mullin .40 .18
❑ 245 Brian Grant .20 .09
❑ 246 Derek Anderson .40 .18
❑ 247 Zan Tabak .15 .07
❑ 248 Charles Smith RC .15 .07
❑ 249 S. Abdur-Rahim GRE 2.50 1.10
❑ 250 Ray Allen GRE 1.00 .45
❑ 251 Charles Barkley GRE 1.25 .55
❑ 252 Kobe Bryant GRE 6.00 2.70
❑ 253 Marcus Camby GRE 1.00 .45
❑ 254 Kevin Garnett GRE 5.00 2.20
❑ 255 Anfernee Hardaway GRE 3.00 1.35
❑ 256 Grant Hill GRE 5.00 2.20
❑ 257 Juwan Howard GRE .40 .18
❑ 258 Allen Iverson GRE 4.00 1.80
❑ 259 Michael Jordan GRE 10.00 4.50
❑ 260 Shawn Kemp GRE 1.50 .70
❑ 261 Kerry Kittles GRE .40 .18
❑ 262 Karl Malone GRE 1.25 .55
❑ 263 Stephon Marbury GRE 3.00 1.35
❑ 264 Hakeem Olajuwon GRE 1.50 .70
❑ 265 Shaquille O'Neal GRE 3.00 1.35
❑ 266 Gary Payton GRE 1.25 .55
❑ 267 Scottie Pippen GRE 2.50 1.10
❑ 268 David Robinson GRE 1.25 .55
❑ 269 Dennis Rodman GRE 2.50 1.10
❑ 270 Joe Smith GRE .40 .18
❑ 271 Jerry Stackhouse GRE .40 .18
❑ 272 Damon Stoudamire GRE 1.25 .55
❑ 273 Antoine Walker GRE 3.00 1.35
❑ 274 Checklist .15 .07
❑ 275 Checklist .15 .07
❑ NNO J. Stackhouse Promo 2.00 .90

1997-98 Ultra Gold Medallion

	MINT	NRMT
COMPLETE SET (271)	250.00	110.00
COMPLETE SERIES 1 (148)	150.00	70.00
COMPLETE SERIES 2 (123)	100.00	45.00
COMMON CARD	.40	.18

*SER.1 STARS: 1.25X TO 2.5X BASE CARD HI
*SER.1 RCs: .25X TO .5X BASE HI
*SER.2 STARS/RCs: 1.25X TO 2.5X BASE HI
*SER.2 98 GREATS: .75X TO 1.25X BASE HI
SUBSETS ARE NOT SP's

1997-98 Ultra Platinum Medallion

	MINT	NRMT
COMMON CARD (1-273)	15.00	6.75
SEMISTARS	20.00	9.00
UNLISTED STARS	30.00	13.50

*STARS: 30X TO 80X BASE CARD HI
*RCs: 3X TO 8X BASE HI
*GREATS: 12.5X TO 30X BASE SUBSET HI
RANDOM INSERTS SER.1/2 HOBBY PACKS
STATED PRINT RUN 100 SERIAL #'d SETS

❑ 1 Kobe Bryant 300.00 135.00
❑ 23 Michael Jordan 650.00 300.00
❑ 124 Derek Anderson 40.00 18.00
❑ 129 Austin Croshere 40.00 18.00
❑ 131 Tim Duncan 150.00 70.00
❑ 138 Tracy McGrady 150.00 70.00
❑ 139 Ron Mercer 50.00 22.00

	MINT	NRMT
❑ 146 Tim Thomas	50.00	22.00
❑ 147 Keith Van Horn	80.00	36.00
❑ 252 Kobe Bryant GRE	250.00	110.00
❑ 259 Michael Jordan GRE	500.00	220.00

1997-98 Ultra All-Rookies

	MINT	NRMT
COMPLETE SET (15)	15.00	6.75
COMMON CARD (AR1-AR15)	.75	.35
UNLISTED STARS	1.25	.55
SER.2 STATED ODDS 1:4 HOB/RET		
❑ AR1 Tim Duncan	6.00	2.70
❑ AR2 Tony Battie	.75	.35
❑ AR3 Keith Van Horn	3.00	1.35
❑ AR4 Antonio Daniels	1.25	.55
❑ AR5 Chauncey Billups	1.25	.55
❑ AR6 Ron Mercer	2.00	.90
❑ AR7 Tracy McGrady	6.00	2.70
❑ AR8 Danny Fortson	.75	.35
❑ AR9 Brevin Knight	1.25	.55
❑ AR10 Derek Anderson	1.50	.70
❑ AR11 Cedric Henderson	.75	.35
❑ AR12 Jacque Vaughn	.75	.35
❑ AR13 Tim Thomas	2.00	.90
❑ AR14 Austin Croshere	1.50	.70
❑ AR15 Kelvin Cato	.75	.35

1997-98 Ultra Big Shots

	MINT	NRMT
COMPLETE SET (15)	15.00	6.75
COMMON CARD (1-15)	.60	.25
SER.1 STATED ODDS 1:4 HOB/RET		
❑ 1 Michael Jordan	8.00	3.60
❑ 2 Allen Iverson	3.00	1.35
❑ 3 Shaquille O'Neal	3.00	1.35
❑ 4 Anfernee Hardaway	2.00	.90
❑ 5 Dennis Rodman	1.25	.55
❑ 6 Grant Hill	3.00	1.35
❑ 7 Juwan Howard	.60	.25
❑ 8 David Robinson	1.00	.45
❑ 9 Gary Payton	1.00	.45
❑ 10 Joe Smith	.60	.25
❑ 11 Charles Barkley	1.00	.45
❑ 12 Terrell Brandon	.60	.25
❑ 13 John Stockton	.60	.25
❑ 14 Mitch Richmond	.60	.25
❑ 15 Vin Baker	.60	.25

1997-98 Ultra Court Masters

	MINT	NRMT
COMPLETE SET (20)	450.00	200.00
COMMON CARD (CM1-CM20)	8.00	3.60
SER.2 STATED ODDS 1:144 HOB/RET		
❑ CM1 Michael Jordan	100.00	45.00
❑ CM2 Allen Iverson	40.00	18.00
❑ CM3 Kobe Bryant	60.00	27.00
❑ CM4 Shaquille O'Neal	40.00	18.00
❑ CM5 Stephon Marbury	25.00	11.00
❑ CM6 Shawn Kemp	12.00	5.50
❑ CM7 Anfernee Hardaway	25.00	11.00
❑ CM8 Kevin Garnett	50.00	22.00
❑ CM9 Shareef Abdur-Rahim	25.00	11.00
❑ CM10 Dennis Rodman	15.00	6.75
❑ CM11 Grant Hill	40.00	18.00
❑ CM12 Kerry Kittles	8.00	3.60
❑ CM13 Antoine Walker	15.00	6.75
❑ CM14 Scottie Pippen	25.00	11.00
❑ CM15 Damon Stoudamire	10.00	4.50
❑ CM16 Marcus Camby	10.00	4.50
❑ CM17 Hakeem Olajuwon	12.00	5.50
❑ CM18 Tim Duncan	40.00	18.00
❑ CM19 Keith Van Horn	20.00	9.00
❑ CM20 Chauncey Billups	8.00	3.60

1997-98 Ultra Heir to the Throne

	MINT	NRMT
COMPLETE SET (15)	40.00	18.00
COMMON CARD (1-15)	1.50	.70
SEMISTARS	2.00	.90
UNLISTED STARS	3.00	1.35
SER.1 STATED ODDS 1:18 HOB/RET		
❑ 1 Derek Anderson	4.00	1.80
❑ 2 Tony Battie	1.50	.70
❑ 3 Chauncey Billups	2.00	.90
❑ 4 Kelvin Cato	1.50	.70
❑ 5 Austin Croshere	4.00	1.80
❑ 6 Antonio Daniels	2.00	.90
❑ 7 Tim Duncan	15.00	6.75
❑ 8 Danny Fortson	1.50	.70
❑ 9 Jacque Vaughn	1.50	.70
❑ 10 Tracy McGrady	15.00	6.75
❑ 11 Ron Mercer	5.00	2.20
❑ 12 Olivier Saint-Jean	1.50	.70
❑ 13 Maurice Taylor	3.00	1.35
❑ 14 Tim Thomas	5.00	2.20
❑ 15 Keith Van Horn	8.00	3.60

1997-98 Ultra Inside/Outside

	MINT	NRMT
COMPLETE SET (15)	8.00	3.60
COMMON CARD (1-15)	.60	.25
SER.1 STATED ODDS 1:6 HOB/RET		
❑ 1 Shareef Abdur-Rahim	2.00	.90
❑ 2 Juwan Howard	.60	.25
❑ 3 David Robinson	1.00	.45
❑ 4 Joe Smith	.60	.25
❑ 5 Charles Barkley	1.00	.45
❑ 6 Tom Gugliotta	.60	.25
❑ 7 Glenn Robinson	.60	.25
❑ 8 Patrick Ewing	.60	.25
❑ 9 Chris Webber	2.00	.90
❑ 10 Glen Rice	.60	.25
❑ 11 Shawn Kemp	1.00	.45
❑ 12 Antonio McDyess	.75	.35
❑ 13 Clyde Drexler	.60	.25
❑ 14 Eddie Jones	1.25	.55
❑ 15 Jason Kidd	2.00	.90

1997-98 Ultra Jam City

	MINT	NRMT
COMPLETE SET (18)	20.00	9.00
COMMON CARD (1-18)	.50	.23
SEMISTARS	.60	.25
UNLISTED STARS	1.00	.45
SER.1 STATED ODDS 1:8 HOB/RET		
❑ 1 Kevin Garnett	6.00	2.70
❑ 2 Antoine Walker	2.00	.90
❑ 3 Scottie Pippen	3.00	1.35
❑ 4 Shawn Kemp	1.50	.70
❑ 5 Hakeem Olajuwon	1.50	.70
❑ 6 Jerry Stackhouse	.60	.25
❑ 7 Karl Malone	1.50	.70
❑ 8 Shaquille O'Neal	5.00	2.20
❑ 9 John Wallace	.50	.23

❑ 10 Marcus Camby	1.25	.55
❑ 11 Juwan Howard	.60	.25
❑ 12 David Robinson	1.50	.70
❑ 13 Gary Payton	1.50	.70
❑ 14 Dennis Rodman	2.00	.90
❑ 15 Joe Smith	.60	.25
❑ 16 Charles Barkley	1.50	.70
❑ 17 Terrell Brandon	.60	.25
❑ 18 Kobe Bryant	8.00	3.60

1997-98 Ultra Neat Feats

	MINT	NRMT
COMPLETE SET (18)	12.00	5.50
COMMON CARD (NF1-NF18)	.50	.23
SEMISTARS	.60	.25
UNLISTED STARS	1.00	.45

SER.2 STATED ODDS 1:8 HOB/RET

❑ NF1 Michael Finley	1.00	.45
❑ NF2 Jason Kidd	3.00	1.35
❑ NF3 Rasheed Wallace	1.00	.45
❑ NF4 Shaquille O'Neal	5.00	2.20
❑ NF5 Tom Gugliotta	.60	.25
❑ NF6 Marcus Camby	1.25	.55
❑ NF7 Jerry Stackhouse	.60	.25
❑ NF8 John Wallace	.50	.23
❑ NF9 Juwan Howard	.60	.25
❑ NF10 David Robinson	1.50	.70
❑ NF11 Gary Payton	1.50	.70
❑ NF12 Joe Smith	.60	.25
❑ NF13 Charles Barkley	1.50	.70
❑ NF14 Terrell Brandon	.60	.25
❑ NF15 John Stockton	1.00	.45
❑ NF16 Vin Baker	.60	.25
❑ NF17 Antonio McDyess	1.25	.55
❑ NF18 Antonio Daniels	.60	.25

1997-98 Ultra Quick Picks

	MINT	NRMT
COMPLETE SET (12)	5.00	2.20
COMMON CARD (1-12)	.30	.14
SEMISTARS	.40	.18
UNLISTED STARS	.60	.25

SER.1 STATED ODDS 1:8 HOB/RET

❑ 1 Stephon Marbury	2.00	.90
❑ 2 Ray Allen	1.00	.45
❑ 3 Damon Stoudamire	.75	.35
❑ 4 Kerry Kittles	.60	.25
❑ 5 Gary Payton	1.00	.45
❑ 6 Terrell Brandon	.40	.18
❑ 7 John Stockton	.60	.25
❑ 8 Mookie Blaylock	.30	.14
❑ 9 Eddie Jones	1.25	.55
❑ 10 Nick Van Exel	.40	.18
❑ 11 Kenny Anderson	.40	.18
❑ 12 Tim Hardaway	.60	.25

1997-98 Ultra Rim Rocker

	MINT	NRMT
COMPLETE SET (12)	5.00	2.20
COMMON CARD (RR1-RR12)	.40	.18

SER.2 STATED ODDS 1:8 HOB/RET

Card		
❑ RR1 Ron Mercer	1.00	.45
❑ RR2 Juwan Howard	.40	.18
❑ RR3 David Robinson	1.00	.45
❑ RR4 Gary Payton	1.00	.45
❑ RR5 Joe Smith	.40	.18
❑ RR6 Charles Barkley	1.00	.45
❑ RR7 Terrell Brandon	.40	.18
❑ RR8 John Stockton	.60	.25
❑ RR9 Adonal Foyle	.60	.25
❑ RR10 Tim Thomas	1.00	.45
❑ RR11 Tony Battie	.60	.25
❑ RR12 Antonio McDyess	1.25	.55

1997-98 Ultra Star Power

	MINT	NRMT
COMPLETE SET (20)	30.00	13.50
COMMON CARD (SP1-SP20)	.60	.25
SER.2 STATED ODDS 1:4 HOB/RET		
COMP.PLUS SET (20)	200.00	90.00
COMMON PLUS	3.00	1.35
*PLUS: 2X TO 5X HI COLUMN		
PLUS: SER.2 STATED ODDS 1:36 H/R		
COMP.SUPREME SET (20)	1000.00	450.00
COMMON SUPREME	12.00	5.50
*SUPREME: 10X TO 25X HI		
SUPREME: SER.2 STATED ODDS 1:288 H/R		

❑ SP1 Michael Jordan	8.00	3.60
❑ SP2 Allen Iverson	3.00	1.35
❑ SP3 Kobe Bryant	5.00	2.20
❑ SP4 Shaquille O'Neal	3.00	1.35
❑ SP5 Stephon Marbury	2.00	.90
❑ SP6 Shawn Kemp	1.00	.45
❑ SP7 Anfernee Hardaway	2.00	.90
❑ SP8 Kevin Garnett	4.00	1.80
❑ SP9 Shareef Abdur-Rahim	2.00	.90
❑ SP10 Dennis Rodman	1.25	.55
❑ SP11 Grant Hill	3.00	1.35
❑ SP12 Gary Payton	1.00	.45
❑ SP13 Antoine Walker	1.25	.55
❑ SP14 Scottie Pippen	2.00	.90
❑ SP15 Damon Stoudamire	.75	.35
❑ SP16 Marcus Camby	.75	.35
❑ SP17 Hakeem Olajuwon	1.00	.45
❑ SP18 Tim Duncan	3.00	1.35
❑ SP19 Keith Van Horn	1.50	.70
❑ SP20 Jerry Stackhouse		.25

1997-98 Ultra Stars

	MINT	NRMT
COMPLETE SET (20)	450.00	200.00
COMMON CARD (1-20)	5.00	2.20
UNLISTED STARS	8.00	3.60

SER.1 STATED ODDS 1:144 HOB/RET
*GOLD: 1.5X TO 3X HI COLUMN
GOLD: RANDOM INSERTS IN PACKS
TEN PERCENT OF PRINT RUN IS GOLD

❑ 1 Michael Jordan	100.00	45.00
❑ 2 Allen Iverson	40.00	18.00
❑ 3 Kobe Bryant	60.00	27.00
❑ 4 Shaquille O'Neal	40.00	18.00
❑ 5 Stephon Marbury	25.00	11.00
❑ 6 Marcus Camby	10.00	4.50
❑ 7 Anfernee Hardaway	25.00	11.00
❑ 8 Kevin Garnett	50.00	22.00
❑ 9 Shareef Abdur-Rahim	25.00	11.00
❑ 10 Dennis Rodman	15.00	6.75
❑ 11 Ray Allen	12.00	5.50
❑ 12 Grant Hill	40.00	18.00
❑ 13 Kerry Kittles	8.00	3.60
❑ 14 Antoine Walker	15.00	6.75
❑ 15 Scottie Pippen	25.00	11.00
❑ 16 Damon Stoudamire	10.00	4.50
❑ 17 Shawn Kemp	12.00	5.50
❑ 18 Hakeem Olajuwon	12.00	5.50
❑ 19 Jerry Stackhouse	8.00	3.60
❑ 20 John Wallace	5.00	2.20

1997-98 Ultra Sweet Deal

	MINT	NRMT
COMPLETE SET (12)	4.00	1.80
COMMON CARD (SD1-SD12)	.30	.14
SEMISTARS	.40	.18
UNLISTED STARS	.60	.25

SER.2 STATED ODDS 1:6 HOB/RET

❑ SD1 Ray Allen	1.00	.45
❑ SD2 Chauncey Billups	.40	.18
❑ SD3 Ron Mercer	1.00	.45
❑ SD4 Hakeem Olajuwon	1.00	.45
❑ SD5 Jerry Stackhouse	.40	.18
❑ SD6 John Wallace	.30	.14

❑ SD7 Juwan Howard	.40	.18
❑ SD8 David Robinson	1.00	.45
❑ SD9 Bobby Jackson	.30	.14
❑ SD10 Joe Smith	.40	.18
❑ SD11 Charles Barkley	1.00	.45
❑ SD12 Terrell Brandon	.40	.18

1997-98 Ultra Ultrabilities

	MINT	NRMT
COMPLETE SET (20)	30.00	13.50
COMMON CARD (1-20)	.60	.25
SER.1 STATED ODDS 1:4 HOB/RET		
COMP.ALL-STAR SET (20)	200.00	90.00
COMMON ALL-STAR	3.00	1.35
*ALL-STAR: 2X TO 5X HI COLUMN		
ALL-STAR: SER.1 STATED ODDS 1:36 H/R		
COMP.SUPERSTAR SET (20)	1000.00	450.00
COMMON SUPERSTAR	12.00	5.50
*SUPERSTAR: 10X TO 25X HI		
SUPERSTAR: SER.1 STATED ODDS 1:288 H/R		

❑ 1 Michael Jordan	8.00	3.60
❑ 2 Allen Iverson	3.00	1.35
❑ 3 Kobe Bryant	5.00	2.20
❑ 4 Shaquille O'Neal	3.00	1.35
❑ 5 Stephon Marbury	2.00	.90
❑ 6 Gary Payton	1.00	.45
❑ 7 Anfernee Hardaway	2.00	.90
❑ 8 Kevin Garnett	4.00	1.80
❑ 9 Scottie Pippen	2.00	.90
❑ 10 Grant Hill	3.00	1.35
❑ 11 Marcus Camby	.75	.35
❑ 12 Ray Allen	1.00	.45
❑ 13 Kerry Kittles	.60	.25
❑ 14 Antoine Walker	1.25	.55
❑ 15 Shareef Abdur-Rahim	2.00	.90
❑ 16 Damon Stoudamire	.75	.35
❑ 17 Shawn Kemp	1.00	.45
❑ 18 Hakeem Olajuwon	1.00	.45
❑ 19 Jerry Stackhouse	.60	.25
❑ 20 Juwan Howard	.60	.25

1997-98 Ultra View to a Thrill

	MINT	NRMT
COMPLETE SET (15)	80.00	36.00
COMMON CARD (VT1-VT15)	1.25	.55
SER.2 STATED ODDS 1:18 HOB/RET		

❑ VT1 Michael Jordan	20.00	9.00
❑ VT2 Allen Iverson	8.00	3.60
❑ VT3 Kobe Bryant	12.00	5.50
❑ VT4 Tracy McGrady	8.00	3.60
❑ VT5 Stephon Marbury	5.00	2.20
❑ VT6 Shawn Kemp	2.50	1.10
❑ VT7 Anfernee Hardaway	5.00	2.20
❑ VT8 Kevin Garnett	10.00	4.50
❑ VT9 Shareef Abdur-Rahim	5.00	2.20
❑ VT10 Dennis Rodman	3.00	1.35
❑ VT11 Grant Hill	8.00	3.60
❑ VT12 Kerry Kittles	1.25	.55
❑ VT13 Antoine Walker	3.00	1.35
❑ VT14 Scottie Pippen	5.00	2.20
❑ VT15 Damon Stoudamire	2.00	.90

1998-99 Ultra

	MINT	NRMT
COMPLETE SET (125)	120.00	55.00
COMPLETE SET w/o SP (100)	25.00	11.00
COMMON CARD (1-100)	.15	.07
COMMON CARD (101-125)	1.00	.45
SEMISTARS	.20	.09
SEMISTARS RC	1.25	.55
UNLISTED STARS	.40	.18
UNLISTED STARS RC	2.50	1.10
ROOKIE SUBSET ODDS 1:4 H/R		
UNPRICED MASTERPIECES SERIAL #'d TO 1		
MASTERPIECES: RANDOM INS.IN PACKS		

❑ 1 Keith Van Horn	1.00	.45
❑ 2 Antonio Daniels	.15	.07
❑ 3 Patrick Ewing	.40	.18
❑ 4 Alonzo Mourning	.40	.18
❑ 5 Isaac Austin	.15	.07
❑ 6 Bryant Reeves	.15	.07
❑ 7 Dennis Scott	.15	.07
❑ 8 Damon Stoudamire	.40	.18
❑ 9 Kenny Anderson	.20	.09
❑ 10 Mookie Blaylock	.15	.07
❑ 11 Mitch Richmond	.40	.18
❑ 12 Jalen Rose	.40	.18
❑ 13 Vin Baker	.20	.09
❑ 14 Donyell Marshall	.15	.07
❑ 15 Bryon Russell	.15	.07
❑ 16 Rasheed Wallace	.40	.18
❑ 17 Allan Houston	.40	.18
❑ 18 Shawn Kemp	.60	.25
❑ 19 Nick Van Exel	.20	.09
❑ 20 Theo Ratliff	.15	.07
❑ 21 Jayson Williams	.20	.09
❑ 22 Chauncey Billups	.15	.07
❑ 23 Brent Barry	.15	.07
❑ 24 David Wesley	.15	.07
❑ 25 Joe Dumars	.40	.18
❑ 26 Marcus Camby	.40	.18
❑ 27 Juwan Howard	.20	.09
❑ 28 Brevin Knight	.15	.07
❑ 29 Reggie Miller	.40	.18
❑ 30 Ray Allen	.50	.23
❑ 31 Michael Finley	.40	.18
❑ 32 Tom Gugliotta	.20	.09
❑ 33 Allen Iverson	1.50	.70
❑ 34 Toni Kukoc	.50	.23
❑ 35 Tim Thomas	.60	.25
❑ 36 Jeff Hornacek	.20	.09
❑ 37 Bobby Jackson	.15	.07
❑ 38 Bo Outlaw	.15	.07
❑ 39 Steve Smith	.20	.09
❑ 40 Terrell Brandon	.20	.09
❑ 41 Glen Rice	.20	.09
❑ 42 Rik Smits	.15	.07
❑ 43 Calbert Cheaney	.15	.07
❑ 44 Stephon Marbury	1.00	.45
❑ 45 Glenn Robinson	.20	.09
❑ 46 Corliss Williamson	.15	.07
❑ 47 Larry Johnson	.20	.09
❑ 48 Antonio McDyess	.40	.18
❑ 49 Detlef Schrempf	.20	.09
❑ 50 Jerry Stackhouse	.20	.09
❑ 51 Doug Christie	.15	.07
❑ 52 Eddie Jones	.75	.35
❑ 53 Karl Malone	.60	.25
❑ 54 Anthony Mason	.20	.09
❑ 55 Tim Duncan	2.00	.90
❑ 56 Christian Laettner	.20	.09
❑ 57 Isaiah Rider	.20	.09
❑ 58 Shawn Bradley	.15	.07
❑ 59 Jim Jackson	.15	.07
❑ 60 Mark Jackson	.15	.07
❑ 61 Kobe Bryant	3.00	1.35
❑ 62 Zydrunas Ilgauskas	.15	.07
❑ 63 Ron Mercer	.60	.25
❑ 64 Hersey Hawkins	.20	.09
❑ 65 John Wallace	.15	.07
❑ 66 Avery Johnson	.15	.07
❑ 67 Dikembe Mutombo	.20	.09
❑ 68 Hakeem Olajuwon	.60	.25
❑ 69 Tony Battie	.20	.09
❑ 70 Jason Kidd	1.25	.55
❑ 71 Latrell Sprewell	.75	.35
❑ 72 Kevin Garnett	2.50	1.10
❑ 73 Voshon Lenard	.15	.07
❑ 74 Gary Payton	.60	.25
❑ 75 Cherokee Parks	.15	.07
❑ 76 Antoine Walker	.60	.25
❑ 77 Anthony Johnson	.15	.07
❑ 78 Danny Fortson	.20	.09
❑ 79 Grant Hill	2.00	.90
❑ 80 Dennis Rodman	.75	.35
❑ 81 Arvydas Sabonis	.20	.09
❑ 82 Tracy McGrady	1.50	.70
❑ 83 David Robinson	.60	.25
❑ 84 Tariq Abdul-Wahad	.15	.07
❑ 85 Michael Jordan	5.00	2.20
❑ 86 Kerry Kittles	.20	.09
❑ 87 Maurice Taylor	.40	.18
❑ 88 Cedric Ceballos	.15	.07
❑ 89 Anfernee Hardaway	1.25	.55
❑ 90 John Stockton	.40	.18
❑ 91 Shareef Abdur-Rahim	1.00	.45
❑ 92 Tim Hardaway	.40	.18
❑ 93 Shaquille O'Neal	2.00	.90
❑ 94 Rodney Rogers	.15	.07
❑ 95 Derek Anderson	.50	.23
❑ 96 Kendall Gill	.20	.09
❑ 97 Rod Strickland	.20	.09
❑ 98 Charles Barkley	.60	.25
❑ 99 Chris Webber	1.25	.55
❑ 100 Scottie Pippen	1.25	.55
❑ 101 Raef LaFrentz RC	5.00	2.20
❑ 102 Ricky Davis RC	5.00	2.20
❑ 103 Robert Traylor RC	2.50	1.10
❑ 104 Roshown McLeod RC	1.25	.55
❑ 105 Tyronn Lue RC	1.25	.55
❑ 106 Vince Carter RC	60.00	27.00

❑ 107 Miles Simon RC	1.00	.45
❑ 108 Paul Pierce RC	12.00	5.50
❑ 109 Pat Garrity RC	1.25	.55
❑ 110 Nazr Mohammed RC	1.25	.55
❑ 111 Mike Bibby RC	8.00	3.60
❑ 112 Michael Dickerson RC	5.00	2.20
❑ 113 Michael Doleac RC	2.50	1.10
❑ 114 Matt Harpring RC	2.50	1.10
❑ 115 Larry Hughes RC	15.00	6.75
❑ 116 Keon Clark RC	2.50	1.10
❑ 117 Felipe Lopez RC	3.00	1.35
❑ 118 Dirk Nowitzki RC	10.00	4.50
❑ 119 Corey Benjamin RC	2.50	1.10
❑ 120 Bryce Drew RC	2.50	1.10
❑ 121 Brian Skinner RC	2.50	1.10
❑ 122 Bonzi Wells RC	10.00	4.50
❑ 123 Antawn Jamison RC	12.00	5.50
❑ 124 Al Harrington RC	8.00	3.60
❑ 125 Michael Olowokandi RC	4.00	1.80

1998-99 Ultra Gold Medallion

	MINT	NRMT
COMPLETE SET (125)	250.00	110.00
COMMON CARD (1-100)	.40	.18
COMMON CARD (101-125)	1.50	.70

*STARS: 1.25X TO 2.5X BASE CARD HI
*RCs: .6X TO 1.5X BASE HI
STARS: ONE PER HOBBY PACK
RCs: STATED ODDS 1:35 HOBBY

1998-99 Ultra Platinum Medallion

	MINT	NRMT
COMMON CARD (1-125)	8.00	3.60

*STARS: 20X TO 50X BASE CARD HI
*RCs: 3X TO 8X HI
RANDOM INSERTS IN HOBBY PACKS
STARS: STD.PRINT RUN 99 SERIAL #'d SETS
RCs: STATED PRINT RUN 66 SERIAL #'d SETS

❑ 85 Michael Jordan	400.00	180.00
❑ 106 Vince Carter	600.00	275.00
❑ 108 Paul Pierce	100.00	45.00
❑ 111 Mike Bibby	60.00	27.00
❑ 115 Larry Hughes	120.00	55.00
❑ 118 Dirk Nowitzki	80.00	36.00
❑ 122 Bonzi Wells	80.00	36.00
❑ 123 Antawn Jamison	100.00	45.00
❑ 124 Al Harrington	60.00	27.00

1998-99 Ultra Exclamation Points

	MINT	NRMT
COMPLETE SET (15)	300.00	135.00
COMMON CARD (1-15)	6.00	2.70

STATED ODDS 1:288 HOB/RET

❑ 1 Vince Carter	80.00	36.00
❑ 2 Tim Duncan	30.00	13.50
❑ 3 Shawn Kemp	10.00	4.50
❑ 4 Shaquille O'Neal	30.00	13.50
❑ 5 Mike Bibby	10.00	4.50
❑ 6 Michael Jordan	80.00	36.00
❑ 7 Michael Olowokandi	6.00	2.70
❑ 8 Larry Hughes	20.00	9.00
❑ 9 Kobe Bryant	50.00	22.00
❑ 10 Kevin Garnett	40.00	18.00
❑ 11 Keith Van Horn	15.00	6.75
❑ 12 Grant Hill	30.00	13.50
❑ 13 Gary Payton	10.00	4.50
❑ 14 Antoine Walker	10.00	4.50
❑ 15 Antawn Jamison	15.00	6.75

1998-99 Ultra Give and Take

	MINT	NRMT
COMPLETE SET (10)	15.00	6.75
COMMON CARD (1-10)	1.00	.45
UNLISTED STARS	1.50	.70

STATED ODDS 1:18 RETAIL

❑ 1 Gary Payton	2.50	1.10
❑ 2 Shawn Kemp	2.50	1.10
❑ 3 Kerry Kittles	1.00	.45
❑ 4 Ron Mercer	2.50	1.10
❑ 5 Scottie Pippen	5.00	2.20
❑ 6 Ray Allen	2.00	.90
❑ 7 Anfernee Hardaway	5.00	2.20
❑ 8 Maurice Taylor	1.50	.70
❑ 9 Brevin Knight	1.00	.45
❑ 10 Karl Malone	2.00	.90

1998-99 Ultra Leading Performers

	MINT	NRMT
COMPLETE SET (15)	150.00	70.00
COMMON CARD (1-15)	3.00	1.35

STATED ODDS 1:72 HOB/RET

❑ 1 Allen Iverson	12.00	5.50
❑ 2 Anfernee Hardaway	10.00	4.50
❑ 3 Kobe Bryant	25.00	11.00
❑ 4 Michael Jordan	40.00	18.00
❑ 5 Ron Mercer	5.00	2.20
❑ 6 Stephon Marbury	8.00	3.60
❑ 7 Tim Duncan	15.00	6.75
❑ 8 Shareef Abdur-Rahim	8.00	3.60
❑ 9 Kevin Garnett	20.00	9.00
❑ 10 Grant Hill	15.00	6.75
❑ 11 Damon Stoudamire	3.00	1.35
❑ 12 Dennis Rodman	6.00	2.70
❑ 13 Keith Van Horn	8.00	3.60
❑ 14 Scottie Pippen	10.00	4.50
❑ 15 Shaquille O'Neal	15.00	6.75

1998-99 Ultra NBAttitude

	MINT	NRMT
COMPLETE SET (20)	8.00	3.60
COMMON CARD (1-20)	.30	.14
SEMISTARS	.40	.18
UNLISTED STARS	.60	.25

STATED ODDS 1:6 HOB/RET

❑ 1 Allen Iverson	2.50	1.10
❑ 2 Chauncey Billups	.30	.14
❑ 3 Keith Van Horn	1.50	.70
❑ 4 Ray Allen	.75	.35
❑ 5 Shareef Abdur-Rahim	1.50	.70
❑ 6 Stephon Marbury	1.50	.70
❑ 7 Kerry Kittles	.40	.18
❑ 8 Tim Thomas	1.00	.45
❑ 9 Damon Stoudamire	.60	.25
❑ 10 Antoine Walker	1.00	.45
❑ 11 Brevin Knight	.30	.14
❑ 12 Maurice Taylor	.60	.25
❑ 13 Ron Mercer	1.00	.45
❑ 14 Tim Duncan	3.00	1.35
❑ 15 Zydrunas Ilgauskas	.30	.14
❑ 16 Michael Finley	.60	.25

	MINT	NRMT
❑ 17 Bobby Jackson	.30	.14
❑ 18 Tim Hardaway	.60	.25
❑ 19 David Robinson	1.00	.45
❑ 20 Vin Baker	.40	.18

1998-99 Ultra Unstoppable

	MINT	NRMT
COMPLETE SET (15)	100.00	45.00
COMMON CARD (1-15)	1.50	.70
UNLISTED STARS	2.50	1.10

STATED ODDS 1:36 HOB/RET

	MINT	NRMT
❑ 1 Michael Jordan	30.00	13.50
❑ 2 Scottie Pippen	8.00	3.60
❑ 3 Grant Hill	12.00	5.50
❑ 4 Dennis Rodman	5.00	2.20
❑ 5 Stephon Marbury	6.00	2.70
❑ 6 Antoine Walker	4.00	1.80
❑ 7 Shareef Abdur-Rahim	6.00	2.70
❑ 8 Shaquille O'Neal	12.00	5.50
❑ 9 Damon Stoudamire	2.50	1.10
❑ 10 Kerry Kittles	1.50	.70
❑ 11 Maurice Taylor	2.50	1.10
❑ 12 Kobe Bryant	20.00	9.00
❑ 13 Kevin Garnett	15.00	6.75
❑ 14 Anfernee Hardaway	8.00	3.60
❑ 15 Allen Iverson	10.00	4.50

1998-99 Ultra World Premiere

	MINT	NRMT
COMPLETE SET (15)	40.00	18.00
COMMON CARD (1-15)	1.25	.55
UNLISTED STARS	2.00	.90

STATED ODDS 1:20 HOB/RET

	MINT	NRMT
❑ 1 Robert Traylor	1.25	.55
❑ 2 Paul Pierce	5.00	2.20
❑ 3 Michael Olowokandi	2.00	.90
❑ 4 Felipe Lopez	1.25	.55
❑ 5 Raef LaFrentz	2.00	.90
❑ 6 Antawn Jamison	5.00	2.20
❑ 7 Larry Hughes	6.00	2.70
❑ 8 Al Harrington	3.00	1.35
❑ 9 Pat Garrity	1.25	.55
❑ 10 Bryce Drew	1.25	.55
❑ 11 Michael Doleac	1.25	.55
❑ 12 Michael Dickerson	2.00	.90
❑ 13 Keon Clark	1.25	.55
❑ 14 Vince Carter	25.00	11.00
❑ 15 Mike Bibby	3.00	1.35

1999-00 Ultra

	MINT	NRMT
COMPLETE SET (150)	120.00	55.00
COMPLETE SET w/o RC (125)	25.00	11.00
COMMON CARD (1-125)	.15	.07
COMMON RC (126-150)	1.25	.55
SEMISTARS	.20	.09
SEMISTARS RC	1.50	.70
UNLISTED STARS	.40	.18
UNLISTED STARS RC	2.00	.90

ROOKIE SUBSET ODDS 1:4 HOB/RET
UNPRICED MASTERPIECES SERIAL #'d TO 1
MASTERPIECES: RANDOM INS.IN PACKS

	MINT	NRMT
❑ 1 Vince Carter	4.00	1.80
❑ 2 Randell Jackson	.15	.07
❑ 3 Ray Allen	.40	.18
❑ 4 Corliss Williamson	.15	.07
❑ 5 Darrell Armstrong	.20	.09
❑ 6 Charles Oakley	.15	.07
❑ 7 Tyrone Nesby RC	.15	.07
❑ 8 Eddie Jones	.75	.35
❑ 9 Kerry Kittles	.20	.09
❑ 10 Jason Williams	1.00	.45
❑ 11 Elden Campbell	.15	.07
❑ 12 Mookie Blaylock	.15	.07
❑ 13 Brent Barry	.15	.07
❑ 14 Mark Jackson	.15	.07
❑ 15 Tim Hardaway	.40	.18
❑ 16 Kendall Gill	.20	.09
❑ 17 Larry Johnson	.20	.09
❑ 18 Eric Snow	.15	.07
❑ 19 Raef LaFrentz	.40	.18
❑ 20 Allen Iverson	1.50	.70
❑ 21 Kenny Anderson	.20	.09
❑ 22 John Starks	.15	.07
❑ 23 Isaiah Rider	.20	.09
❑ 24 Tariq Abdul-Wahad	.15	.07
❑ 25 Vitaly Potapenko	.15	.07
❑ 26 Patrick Ewing	.40	.18
❑ 27 Mitch Richmond	.40	.18
❑ 28 Steve Nash	.15	.07
❑ 29 Dickey Simpkins	.15	.07
❑ 30 Grant Hill	2.00	.90
❑ 31 Matt Geiger	.15	.07
❑ 32 John Stockton	.40	.18
❑ 33 Jayson Williams	.20	.09
❑ 34 Reggie Miller	.40	.18
❑ 35 Eric Piatkowski	.15	.07
❑ 36 Jason Kidd	1.25	.55
❑ 37 Allan Houston	.40	.18
❑ 38 Christian Laettner	.20	.09
❑ 39 Marcus Camby	.40	.18
❑ 40 Shaquille O'Neal	2.00	.90
❑ 41 Derek Anderson	.40	.18
❑ 42 Gary Trent	.15	.07
❑ 43 Vin Baker	.20	.09
❑ 44 Alonzo Mourning	.40	.18
❑ 45 Latrell Sprewell	.75	.35
❑ 46 Rod Strickland	.20	.09
❑ 47 Bobby Jackson	.15	.07
❑ 48 Karl Malone	.60	.25
❑ 49 Mario Elie	.15	.07
❑ 50 Kobe Bryant	3.00	1.35
❑ 51 Clifford Robinson	.15	.07
❑ 52 Jamal Mashburn	.20	.09
❑ 53 Dirk Nowitzki	.60	.25
❑ 54 Rik Smits	.15	.07
❑ 55 Doug Christie	.15	.07
❑ 56 Ricky Davis	.40	.18
❑ 57 Jalen Rose	.40	.18
❑ 58 Michael Olowokandi	.20	.09
❑ 59 Cedric Ceballos	.15	.07
❑ 60 Ron Mercer	.50	.23
❑ 61 Brevin Knight	.15	.07
❑ 62 Rashard Lewis	.60	.25
❑ 63 Detlef Schrempf	.20	.09
❑ 64 Keith Van Horn	.75	.35
❑ 65 Nick Anderson	.15	.07
❑ 66 Larry Hughes	1.00	.45
❑ 67 Antonio McDyess	.40	.18
❑ 68 Terrell Brandon	.20	.09
❑ 69 Felipe Lopez	.15	.07
❑ 70 Scottie Pippen	1.25	.55
❑ 71 Erick Dampier	.15	.07
❑ 72 Arvydas Sabonis	.20	.09
❑ 73 Brian Grant	.20	.09
❑ 74 Nick Van Exel	.20	.09
❑ 75 Bryon Russell	.15	.07
❑ 76 Danny Fortson	.15	.07
❑ 77 Avery Johnson	.15	.07
❑ 78 Jerry Stackhouse	.20	.09
❑ 79 Robert Traylor	.15	.07
❑ 80 Tim Duncan	2.00	.90
❑ 81 Lindsey Hunter	.15	.07
❑ 82 Tyronn Lue	.15	.07
❑ 83 Michael Finley	.40	.18
❑ 84 Dikembe Mutombo	.20	.09
❑ 85 Zydrunas Ilgauskas	.15	.07
❑ 86 Pat Garrity	.15	.07
❑ 87 Damon Stoudamire	.40	.18
❑ 88 Shareef Abdur-Rahim	.75	.35
❑ 89 Matt Harpring	.15	.07
❑ 90 Michael Dickerson	.40	.18
❑ 91 Steve Smith	.20	.09
❑ 92 Bison Dele	.15	.07
❑ 93 Glenn Robinson	.20	.09
❑ 94 Antawn Jamison	.75	.35
❑ 95 Glen Rice	.20	.09
❑ 96 Vlade Divac	.15	.07
❑ 97 Vladimir Stepania	.15	.07
❑ 98 Kornel David RC	.15	.07
❑ 99 Shawn Kemp	.60	.25
❑ 100 Kevin Garnett	2.50	1.10
❑ 101 Tim Thomas	.50	.23
❑ 102 Mike Bibby	.50	.23
❑ 103 Maurice Taylor	.40	.18
❑ 104 Gary Payton	.60	.25
❑ 105 Voshon Lenard	.15	.07
❑ 106 Theo Ratliff	.15	.07
❑ 107 Hakeem Olajuwon	.60	.25
❑ 108 Joe Smith	.20	.09
❑ 109 Toni Kukoc	.50	.23
❑ 110 Stephon Marbury	.75	.35
❑ 111 Anthony Mason	.20	.09
❑ 112 Anfernee Hardaway	1.25	.55
❑ 113 Juwan Howard	.20	.09
❑ 114 Charles Barkley	.60	.25
❑ 115 Antoine Walker	.50	.23
❑ 116 Donyell Marshall	.15	.07
❑ 117 Tom Gugliotta	.20	.09
❑ 118 Rasheed Wallace	.40	.18
❑ 119 Tracy McGrady	1.25	.55
❑ 120 Paul Pierce	.75	.35
❑ 121 Sean Elliott	.15	.07
❑ 122 Bryant Reeves	.15	.07
❑ 123 Michael Doleac	.15	.07
❑ 124 Chris Webber	1.25	.55
❑ 125 David Robinson	.60	.25
❑ 126 Steve Francis RC	25.00	11.00
❑ 127 Elton Brand RC	20.00	9.00
❑ 128 Wally Szczerbiak RC	8.00	3.60
❑ 129 Richard Hamilton RC	5.00	2.20
❑ 130 Shawn Marion RC	6.00	2.70
❑ 131 Trajan Langdon RC	3.00	1.35
❑ 132 Corey Maggette RC	8.00	3.60
❑ 133 Dion Glover RC	2.00	.90
❑ 134 James Posey RC	4.00	1.80

Card	MINT	NRMT
❑ 135 Lamar Odom RC	15.00	6.75
❑ 136 Aleksandar Radojevic RC	1.25	.55
❑ 137 Cal Bowdler RC	2.00	.90
❑ 138 Scott Padgett RC	2.00	.90
❑ 139 Jumaine Jones RC	1.50	.70
❑ 140 Jonathan Bender RC	10.00	4.50
❑ 141 Tim James RC	2.50	1.10
❑ 142 Jason Terry RC	3.00	1.35
❑ 143 Quincy Lewis RC	2.00	.90
❑ 144 William Avery RC	3.00	1.35
❑ 145 Galen Young RC	1.25	.55
❑ 146 Ron Artest RC	5.00	2.20
❑ 147 Kenny Thomas RC	3.00	1.35
❑ 148 Devean George RC	4.00	1.80
❑ 149 Andre Miller RC	6.00	2.70
❑ 150 Baron Davis RC	5.00	2.20

1999-00 Ultra Gold Medallion

	MINT	NRMT
COMPLETE SET (150)	200.00	90.00
COMMON CARD (1-125)	.30	.14
COMMON CARD (126-150)	2.00	.90

*STARS: .75X TO 2X BASE CARD HI
*RCs: .6X TO 1.5X BASE HI
STARS: ONE PER HOBBY PACK
RCs: STATED ODDS 1:35 HOBBY

1999-00 Ultra Platinum Medallion

	MINT	NRMT
COMMON CARD (1-125)	20.00	9.00
COMMON CARD (126-150)	20.00	9.00
SEMISTARS RC	30.00	13.50
UNLISTED STARS RC	50.00	22.00

*STARS: 40X TO 100X BASE CARD HI
RANDOM INSERTS IN HOBBY PACKS
STARS: PRINT RUN 50 SERIAL #'d SETS
RCs: PRINT RUN 25 SERIAL #'d SETS

Card	MINT	NRMT
❑ 126 Steve Francis	300.00	135.00
❑ 127 Elton Brand	250.00	110.00
❑ 128 Wally Szczerbiak	100.00	45.00
❑ 129 Richard Hamilton	60.00	27.00
❑ 130 Shawn Marion	80.00	36.00
❑ 132 Corey Maggette	100.00	45.00
❑ 135 Lamar Odom	200.00	90.00
❑ 140 Jonathan Bender	120.00	55.00
❑ 146 Ron Artest	60.00	27.00
❑ 149 Andre Miller	80.00	36.00
❑ 150 Baron Davis	60.00	27.00

1999-00 Ultra Feel the Game

	MINT	NRMT
COMPLETE SET (15)	500.00	220.00
COMMON CARD (1-15)	20.00	9.00
SEMISTARS	25.00	11.00

RANDOM INSERTS IN HOB/RET PACKS

Card	MINT	NRMT
❑ 1 Steve Francis	120.00	55.00
❑ 2 Richard Hamilton	40.00	18.00
❑ 3 Jonathan Bender	50.00	22.00
❑ 4 Baron Davis	40.00	18.00
❑ 5 Wally Szczerbiak	50.00	22.00
❑ 6 Lamar Odom	80.00	36.00
❑ 7 Andre Miller	30.00	13.50
❑ 8 Jason Terry	20.00	9.00
❑ 9 Trajan Langdon	25.00	11.00
❑ 10 Corey Maggette	40.00	18.00
❑ 11 Cal Bowdler	20.00	9.00
❑ 12 James Posey	20.00	9.00
❑ 13 Tim James	25.00	11.00
❑ 14 Scott Padgett	20.00	9.00
❑ 15 Jumaine Jones	20.00	9.00

1999-00 Ultra Fresh Ink

	MINT	NRMT
COMMON CARD	6.00	2.70
SEMISTARS	10.00	4.50

PRINT RUNS LISTED BELOW
RANDOM INSERTS IN PACKS
SOME CARDS AVAILABLE VIA REDEMPTION

Card	MINT	NRMT
❑ 1 Ray Allen/250	40.00	18.00
❑ 2 Ron Artest/1000	15.00	6.75
❑ 3 William Avery/1000	15.00	6.75
❑ 4 Jonathan Bender/500	40.00	18.00
❑ 5 Mike Bibby/550	12.00	5.50
❑ 6 Calvin Booth/975	6.00	2.70
❑ 7 Cal Bowdler/1000	6.00	2.70
❑ 8 Bruce Bowen/1000	6.00	2.70
❑ 9 Marcus Camby/750	25.00	11.00
❑ 10 John Celestand/1000	6.00	2.70
❑ 11 Baron Davis/475	25.00	11.00
❑ 12 Michael Dickerson/975	12.00	5.50
❑ 13 Michael Doleac/1000	6.00	2.70
❑ 14 Bryce Drew/1000	10.00	4.50
❑ 15 E.Eschmeyer/1000	6.00	2.70
❑ 16 Steve Francis/500	100.00	45.00
❑ 17 Pat Garrity/600	6.00	2.70
❑ 18 Devean George/1000	12.00	5.50
❑ 19 Dion Glover/875	6.00	2.70
❑ 20 Brian Grant/500	15.00	6.75
❑ 21 Richard Hamilton/750	12.00	5.50
❑ 22 Juwan Howard/225	25.00	11.00
❑ 23 Larry Hughes/750	30.00	13.50
❑ 24 Jumaine Jones/1000	6.00	2.70
❑ 25 Eddie Jones/250	60.00	27.00
❑ 26 Raef LaFrentz/500	15.00	6.75
❑ 27 Quincy Lewis/1000	10.00	4.50
❑ 28 Felipe Lopez/1000	6.00	2.70
❑ 29 Corey Maggette/250	50.00	22.00
❑ 30 Stephon Marbury/400	30.00	13.50
❑ 31 Shawn Marion/1000	15.00	6.75
❑ 32 Lamar Odom/500	60.00	27.00
❑ 33 Shaquille O'Neal/200	250.00	110.00
❑ 34 Scottie Pippen/130	175.00	80.00
❑ 35 James Posey/1000	12.00	5.50
❑ 36 A.Radojevic/1000	6.00	2.70
❑ 37 David Robinson/155	125.00	55.00
❑ 38 Jalen Rose/500	25.00	11.00
❑ 39 W.Szczerbiak/500	30.00	13.50
❑ 40 J.Stackhouse/650	15.00	6.75
❑ 41 Maurice Taylor/400	12.00	5.50
❑ 42 Jason Terry/1000	15.00	6.75
❑ 43 Robert Traylor/1000	6.00	2.70
❑ 44 Keith Van Horn/500	25.00	11.00
❑ 45 Antoine Walker/245	25.00	11.00
❑ 46 Chris Webber/200	150.00	70.00

1999-00 Ultra Good Looks

	MINT	NRMT
COMPLETE SET (15)	20.00	9.00
COMMON CARD (1-15)	.75	.35

STATED ODDS 1:6 HOB/RET

Card	MINT	NRMT
❑ 1 Grant Hill	3.00	1.35
❑ 2 Kevin Garnett	4.00	1.80
❑ 3 Richard Hamilton	.75	.35
❑ 4 Larry Hughes	1.50	.70
❑ 5 Shaquille O'Neal	3.00	1.35
❑ 6 Kobe Bryant	5.00	2.20
❑ 7 Antoine Walker	.75	.35
❑ 8 Lamar Odom	2.50	1.10
❑ 9 Allen Iverson	2.50	1.10
❑ 10 Scottie Pippen	2.00	.90
❑ 11 Ron Mercer	.75	.35
❑ 12 Anfernee Hardaway	2.00	.90
❑ 13 Chris Webber	2.00	.90
❑ 14 Jason Williams	1.50	.70
❑ 15 Baron Davis	.75	.35

1999-00 Ultra Heir to the Throne

	MINT	NRMT
COMPLETE SET (10)	25.00	11.00
COMMON CARD (1-10)	1.25	.55

STATED ODDS 1:24 HOB/RET

Card	MINT	NRMT
❑ 1 Allen Iverson	4.00	1.80

❑ 2 Keith Van Horn	2.00	.90
❑ 3 Paul Pierce	2.00	.90
❑ 4 Stephon Marbury	2.00	.90
❑ 5 Vince Carter	10.00	4.50
❑ 6 Tim Duncan	5.00	2.20
❑ 7 Ron Mercer	1.25	.55
❑ 8 Antawn Jamison	2.00	.90
❑ 9 Shaquille O'Neal	5.00	2.20
❑ 10 Grant Hill	5.00	2.20

1999-00 Ultra Millennium Men

	MINT	NRMT
COMPLETE SET (15)	800.00	350.00
COMMON CARD (1-15)	20.00	9.00

STATED PRINT RUN 100 SERIAL #'d SETS
RANDOM INSERTS IN HOBBY PACKS

❑ 1 Allen Iverson	60.00	27.00
❑ 2 Paul Pierce	30.00	13.50
❑ 3 Steve Francis	120.00	55.00
❑ 4 Kobe Bryant	120.00	55.00
❑ 5 Vince Carter	150.00	70.00
❑ 6 Ron Mercer	20.00	9.00
❑ 7 Jason Williams	40.00	18.00
❑ 8 Elton Brand	100.00	45.00
❑ 9 Grant Hill	80.00	36.00
❑ 10 Tim Duncan	80.00	36.00
❑ 11 Stephon Marbury	30.00	13.50
❑ 12 Keith Van Horn	30.00	13.50
❑ 13 Kevin Garnett	100.00	45.00
❑ 14 Antawn Jamison	30.00	13.50
❑ 15 Antoine Walker	20.00	9.00

1999-00 Ultra Parquet Players

	MINT	NRMT
COMPLETE SET (15)	150.00	70.00
COMMON CARD (1-15)	4.00	1.80

STATED ODDS 1:72 HOB/RET

❑ 1 Kobe Bryant	25.00	11.00
❑ 2 Keith Van Horn	6.00	2.70
❑ 3 Tim Duncan	15.00	6.75
❑ 4 Shaquille O'Neal	15.00	6.75
❑ 5 Kevin Garnett	20.00	9.00
❑ 6 Jason Williams	8.00	3.60
❑ 7 Vince Carter	30.00	13.50
❑ 8 Stephon Marbury	6.00	2.70
❑ 9 Paul Pierce	6.00	2.70
❑ 10 Scottie Pippen	10.00	4.50
❑ 11 Baron Davis	4.00	1.80
❑ 12 Antoine Walker	4.00	1.80
❑ 13 Larry Hughes	8.00	3.60
❑ 14 Antawn Jamison	6.00	2.70
❑ 15 Elton Brand	15.00	6.75

1999-00 Ultra World Premiere

	MINT	NRMT
COMPLETE SET (10)	25.00	11.00
COMMON CARD (1-10)	1.00	.45

STATED ODDS 1:12 HOB/RET

❑ 1 Elton Brand	6.00	2.70
❑ 2 Andre Miller	2.00	.90
❑ 3 Baron Davis	1.50	.70
❑ 4 Steve Francis	8.00	3.60
❑ 5 Richard Hamilton	1.50	.70
❑ 6 Jason Terry	1.00	.45
❑ 7 Jonathan Bender	3.00	1.35
❑ 8 Trajan Langdon	1.00	.45
❑ 9 Wally Szczerbiak	2.50	1.10
❑ 10 Lamar Odom	5.00	2.20

1991-92 Upper Deck

	MINT	NRMT
COMPLETE SET (500)	20.00	9.00
COMPLETE FACT.SET (500)	20.00	9.00
COMPLETE SERIES 1 (400)	12.00	5.50
COMPLETE SERIES 2 (100)	8.00	3.60
COMMON CARD (1-400)	.05	.02
COMMON CARD (401-500)	.10	.05
SEMISTARS SER.1	.10	.05
SEMISTARS SER.2	.25	.11
UNLISTED STARS SER.1	.25	.11
UNLISTED STARS SER.2	.50	.23

SUBSET CARDS HALF VALUE OF BASE CARDS

❑ 1 Stacey Augmon CL Rodney Monroe	.05	.02
❑ 2 Larry Johnson RC UER (Career FG Percentage is .643 not .648)	1.00	.45
❑ 3 Dikembe Mutombo RC	.75	.35
❑ 4 Steve Smith RC	1.00	.45
❑ 5 Stacey Augmon RC	.25	.11
❑ 6 Terrell Brandon RC	.75	.35
❑ 7 Greg Anthony RC	.25	.11
❑ 8 Rich King RC	.05	.02
❑ 9 Chris Gatling RC	.25	.11
❑ 10 Victor Alexander RC	.05	.02
❑ 11 John Turner	.05	.02
❑ 12 Eric Murdock RC	.05	.02
❑ 13 Mark Randall RC	.05	.02
❑ 14 Rodney Monroe RC	.05	.02
❑ 15 Myron Brown	.05	.02
❑ 16 Mike Iuzzolino RC	.05	.02
❑ 17 Chris Corchiani RC	.05	.02
❑ 18 Elliot Perry RC	.10	.05
❑ 19 Jimmy Oliver RC	.05	.02
❑ 20 Doug Overton RC	.05	.02
❑ 21 Steve Hood UER (Card has NBA record& but he's a rookie)	.05	.02
❑ 22 Michael Jordan Stay In School	.75	.35
❑ 23 Kevin Johnson Stay In School	.10	.05
❑ 24 Kurk Lee	.05	.02
❑ 25 Sean Higgins RC	.05	.02
❑ 26 Morlon Wiley	.05	.02
❑ 27 Derek Smith	.05	.02
❑ 28 Kenny Payne	.05	.02
❑ 29 Magic Johnson Assist Record	.40	.18
❑ 30 Larry Bird CC and Chuck Person	.25	.11
❑ 31 Karl Malone CC and Charles Barkley	.25	.11
❑ 32 Kevin Johnson CC and John Stockton	.10	.05
❑ 33 Hakeem Olajuwon CC and Patrick Ewing	.25	.11
❑ 34 Magic Johnson CC and Michael Jordan	1.00	.45
❑ 35 Derrick Coleman ART	.05	.02
❑ 36 Lionel Simmons ART	.05	.02
❑ 37 Dee Brown ART	.05	.02
❑ 38 Dennis Scott ART	.05	.02
❑ 39 Kendall Gill ART	.05	.02
❑ 40 Winston Garland	.05	.02
❑ 41 Danny Young	.05	.02
❑ 42 Rick Mahorn	.05	.02
❑ 43 Michael Adams	.05	.02
❑ 44 Michael Jordan	3.00	1.35
❑ 45 Magic Johnson	.75	.35
❑ 46 Doc Rivers	.10	.05
❑ 47 Moses Malone	.25	.11
❑ 48 Michael Jordan AS CL	1.50	.70
❑ 49 James Worthy AS	.10	.05
❑ 50 Tim Hardaway AS	.25	.11
❑ 51 Karl Malone AS	.25	.11
❑ 52 John Stockton AS	.10	.05
❑ 53 Clyde Drexler AS	.10	.05
❑ 54 Terry Porter AS	.05	.02
❑ 55 Kevin Duckworth AS	.05	.02
❑ 56 Tom Chambers AS	.05	.02
❑ 57 Magic Johnson AS	.40	.18
❑ 58 David Robinson AS	.25	.11
❑ 59 Kevin Johnson AS	.10	.05
❑ 60 Chris Mullin AS	.10	.05
❑ 61 Joe Dumars AS	.10	.05
❑ 62 Kevin McHale AS	.05	.02

❑ 63 Brad Daugherty AS .05 .02
❑ 64 Alvin Robertson AS .05 .02
❑ 65 Bernard King AS .05 .02
❑ 66 Dominique Wilkins AS .10 .05
❑ 67 Ricky Pierce AS .05 .02
❑ 68 Patrick Ewing AS .10 .05
❑ 69 Michael Jordan AS 1.50 .70
❑ 70 Charles Barkley AS .25 .11
❑ 71 Hersey Hawkins AS .05 .02
❑ 72 Robert Parish AS .05 .02
❑ 73 Alvin Robertson TC .05 .02
❑ 74 Bernard King TC .05 .02
❑ 75 Michael Jordan TC 1.50 .70
❑ 76 Brad Daugherty TC .05 .02
❑ 77 Larry Bird TC .50 .23
❑ 78 Ron Harper TC .05 .02
❑ 79 Dominique Wilkins TC .10 .05
❑ 80 Rony Seikaly TC .05 .02
❑ 81 Rex Chapman TC .05 .02
❑ 82 Mark Eaton TC .05 .02
❑ 83 Lionel Simmons TC .05 .02
❑ 84 Gerald Wilkins TC .05 .02
❑ 85 James Worthy TC .10 .05
❑ 86 Scott Skiles TC .05 .02
❑ 87 Rolando Blackman TC .05 .02
❑ 88 Derrick Coleman TC .05 .02
❑ 89 Chris Jackson TC .05 .02
❑ 90 Reggie Miller TC .10 .05
❑ 91 Isiah Thomas TC .10 .05
❑ 92 Hakeem Olajuwon TC .25 .11
❑ 93 Hersey Hawkins TC .05 .02
❑ 94 David Robinson TC .25 .11
❑ 95 Tom Chambers TC .05 .02
❑ 96 Shawn Kemp TC .25 .11
❑ 97 Pooh Richardson TC .05 .02
❑ 98 Clyde Drexler TC .10 .05
❑ 99 Chris Mullin TC .10 .05
❑ 100 Checklist 1-100 .05 .02
❑ 101 John Shasky .05 .02
❑ 102 Dana Barros .05 .02
❑ 103 Stojko Vrankovic .05 .02
❑ 104 Larry Drew .05 .02
❑ 105 Randy White .05 .02
❑ 106 Dave Corzine .05 .02
❑ 107 Joe Kleine .05 .02
❑ 108 Lance Blanks .05 .02
❑ 109 Rodney McCray .05 .02
❑ 110 Sedale Threatt .05 .02
❑ 111 Ken Norman .05 .02
❑ 112 Rickey Green .05 .02
❑ 113 Andy Toolson .05 .02
❑ 114 Bo Kimble .05 .02
❑ 115 Mark West .05 .02
❑ 116 Mark Eaton .05 .02
❑ 117 John Paxson .05 .02
❑ 118 Mike Brown .05 .02
❑ 119 Brian Oliver .05 .02
❑ 120 Will Perdue .05 .02
❑ 121 Michael Smith .05 .02
❑ 122 Sherman Douglas .05 .02
❑ 123 Reggie Lewis .10 .05
❑ 124 James Donaldson .05 .02
❑ 125 Scottie Pippen .75 .35
❑ 126 Elden Campbell .10 .05
❑ 127 Michael Cage .05 .02
❑ 128 Tony Smith .05 .02
❑ 129 Ed Pinckney .05 .02
❑ 130 Keith Askins RC .05 .02
❑ 131 Darrell Griffith .05 .02
❑ 132 Vinnie Johnson .05 .02
❑ 133 Ron Harper .10 .05
❑ 134 Andre Turner .05 .02
❑ 135 Jeff Hornacek .10 .05
❑ 136 John Stockton .25 .11
❑ 137 Derek Harper .10 .05
❑ 138 Loy Vaught .05 .02
❑ 139 Thurl Bailey .05 .02
❑ 140 Olden Polynice .05 .02
❑ 141 Kevin Edwards .05 .02
❑ 142 Byron Scott .10 .05
❑ 143 Dee Brown .05 .02
❑ 144 Sam Perkins .10 .05
❑ 145 Rony Seikaly .05 .02
❑ 146 James Worthy .25 .11
❑ 147 Glen Rice .25 .11
❑ 148 Craig Hodges .05 .02
❑ 149 Bimbo Coles .05 .02
❑ 150 Mychal Thompson .05 .02
❑ 151 Xavier McDaniel .05 .02
❑ 152 Roy Tarpley .05 .02
❑ 153 Gary Payton .60 .25
❑ 154 Rolando Blackman .05 .02
❑ 155 Hersey Hawkins .10 .05
❑ 156 Ricky Pierce .05 .02
❑ 157 Fat Lever .05 .02
❑ 158 Andrew Lang .05 .02
❑ 159 Benoit Benjamin .05 .02
❑ 160 Cedric Ceballos .10 .05
❑ 161 Charles Smith .05 .02
❑ 162 Jeff Martin .05 .02
❑ 163 Robert Parish .10 .05
❑ 164 Danny Manning .10 .05
❑ 165 Mark Aguirre .05 .02
❑ 166 Jeff Malone .05 .02
❑ 167 Bill Laimbeer .10 .05
❑ 168 Willie Burton .05 .02
❑ 169 Dennis Hopson .05 .02
❑ 170 Kevin Gamble .05 .02
❑ 171 Terry Teagle .05 .02
❑ 172 Dan Majerle .10 .05
❑ 173 Shawn Kemp .60 .25
❑ 174 Tom Chambers .05 .02
❑ 175 Vlade Divac .10 .05
❑ 176 Johnny Dawkins .05 .02
❑ 177 A.C. Green .10 .05
❑ 178 Manute Bol .05 .02
❑ 179 Terry Davis .05 .02
❑ 180 Ron Anderson .05 .02
❑ 181 Horace Grant .10 .05
❑ 182 Stacey King .05 .02
❑ 183 William Bedford .05 .02
❑ 184 B.J. Armstrong .05 .02
❑ 185 Dennis Rodman .50 .23
❑ 186 Nate McMillan .05 .02
❑ 187 Cliff Levingston .05 .02
❑ 188 Quintin Dailey .05 .02
❑ 189 Bill Cartwright .05 .02
❑ 190 John Salley .05 .02
❑ 191 Jayson Williams .25 .11
❑ 192 Grant Long .05 .02
❑ 193 Negele Knight .05 .02
❑ 194 Alec Kessler .05 .02
❑ 195 Gary Grant .05 .02
❑ 196 Billy Thompson .05 .02
❑ 197 Delaney Rudd .05 .02
❑ 198 Alan Ogg .05 .02
❑ 199 Blue Edwards .05 .02
❑ 200 Checklist 101-200 .05 .02
❑ 201 Mark Acres .05 .02
❑ 202 Craig Ehlo .05 .02
❑ 203 Anthony Cook .05 .02
❑ 204 Eric Leckner .05 .02
❑ 205 Terry Catledge .05 .02
❑ 206 Reggie Williams .05 .02
❑ 207 Greg Kite .05 .02
❑ 208 Steve Kerr .10 .05
❑ 209 Kenny Battle .05 .02
❑ 210 John Morton .05 .02
❑ 211 Kenny Williams .05 .02
❑ 212 Mark Jackson .10 .05
❑ 213 Alaa Abdelnaby .05 .02
❑ 214 Rod Strickland .25 .11
❑ 215 Micheal Williams .05 .02
❑ 216 Kevin Duckworth .05 .02
❑ 217 David Wingate .05 .02
❑ 218 LaSalle Thompson .05 .02
❑ 219 John Starks RC .25 .11
❑ 220 Clifford Robinson .10 .05
❑ 221 Jeff Grayer .05 .02
❑ 222 Marcus Liberty .05 .02
❑ 223 Larry Nance .10 .05
❑ 224 Michael Ansley .05 .02
❑ 225 Kevin McHale .10 .05
❑ 226 Scott Skiles .05 .02
❑ 227 Darnell Valentine .05 .02
❑ 228 Nick Anderson .10 .05
❑ 229 Brad Davis .05 .02
❑ 230 Gerald Paddio .05 .02
❑ 231 Sam Bowie .05 .02
❑ 232 Sam Vincent .05 .02
❑ 233 George McCloud .05 .02
❑ 234 Gerald Wilkins .05 .02
❑ 235 Mookie Blaylock .10 .05
❑ 236 Jon Koncak .05 .02
❑ 237 Danny Ferry .05 .02
❑ 238 Vern Fleming .05 .02
❑ 239 Mark Price .05 .02
❑ 240 Sidney Moncrief .05 .02
❑ 241 Jay Humphries .05 .02
❑ 242 Muggsy Bogues .10 .05
❑ 243 Tim Hardaway .40 .18
❑ 244 Alvin Robertson .05 .02
❑ 245 Chris Mullin .25 .11
❑ 246 Pooh Richardson .05 .02
❑ 247 Winston Bennett .05 .02
❑ 248 Kelvin Upshaw .05 .02
❑ 249 John Williams .05 .02
❑ 250 Steve Alford .05 .02
❑ 251 Spud Webb .10 .05
❑ 252 Sleepy Floyd .05 .02
❑ 253 Chuck Person .05 .02
❑ 254 Hakeem Olajuwon .40 .18
❑ 255 Dominique Wilkins .25 .11
❑ 256 Reggie Miller .25 .11
❑ 257 Dennis Scott .10 .05
❑ 258 Charles Oakley .10 .05
❑ 259 Sidney Green .05 .02
❑ 260 Detlef Schrempf .10 .05
❑ 261 Rod Higgins .05 .02
❑ 262 J.R. Reid .05 .02
❑ 263 Tyrone Hill .10 .05
❑ 264 Reggie Theus .10 .05
❑ 265 Mitch Richmond .25 .11
❑ 266 Dale Ellis .10 .05
❑ 267 Terry Cummings .05 .02
❑ 268 Johnny Newman .05 .02
❑ 269 Doug West .05 .02
❑ 270 Jim Petersen .05 .02
❑ 271 Otis Thorpe .10 .05
❑ 272 John Williams .05 .02
❑ 273 Kennard Winchester RC .05 .02
❑ 274 Duane Ferrell .05 .02
❑ 275 Vernon Maxwell .05 .02
❑ 276 Kenny Smith .05 .02
❑ 277 Jerome Kersey .05 .02
❑ 278 Kevin Willis .05 .02
❑ 279 Danny Ainge .10 .05
❑ 280 Larry Smith .05 .02
❑ 281 Maurice Cheeks .05 .02
❑ 282 Willie Anderson .05 .02
❑ 283 Tom Tolbert .05 .02
❑ 284 Jerrod Mustaf .05 .02
❑ 285 Randolph Keys .05 .02
❑ 286 Jerry Reynolds .05 .02
❑ 287 Sean Elliott .10 .05
❑ 288 Otis Smith .05 .02
❑ 289 Terry Mills RC .25 .11
❑ 290 Kelly Tripucka .05 .02
❑ 291 Jon Sundvold .05 .02
❑ 292 Rumeal Robinson .05 .02
❑ 293 Fred Roberts .05 .02
❑ 294 Rik Smits .10 .05
❑ 295 Jerome Lane .05 .02
❑ 296 Dave Jamerson .05 .02
❑ 297 Joe Wolf .05 .02
❑ 298 David Wood RC .05 .02
❑ 299 Todd Lichti .05 .02
❑ 300 Checklist 201-300 .05 .02
❑ 301 Randy Breuer .05 .02
❑ 302 Buck Johnson .05 .02
❑ 303 Scott Brooks .05 .02
❑ 304 Jeff Turner .05 .02
❑ 305 Felton Spencer .05 .02
❑ 306 Greg Dreiling .05 .02
❑ 307 Gerald Glass .05 .02
❑ 308 Tony Brown .05 .02
❑ 309 Sam Mitchell .05 .02
❑ 310 Adrian Caldwell .05 .02
❑ 311 Chris Dudley .05 .02
❑ 312 Blair Rasmussen .05 .02
❑ 313 Antoine Carr .05 .02
❑ 314 Greg Anderson .05 .02
❑ 315 Drazen Petrovic .10 .05
❑ 316 Alton Lister .05 .02
❑ 317 Jack Haley .05 .02
❑ 318 Bobby Hansen .05 .02
❑ 319 Chris Jackson .05 .02
❑ 320 Herb Williams .05 .02

❑ 321 Kendall Gill .10 .05
❑ 322 Tyrone Corbin .05 .02
❑ 323 Kiki Vandeweghe .05 .02
❑ 324 David Robinson .50 .23
❑ 325 Rex Chapman .10 .05
❑ 326 Tony Campbell .05 .02
❑ 327 Dell Curry .05 .02
❑ 328 Charles Jones .05 .02
❑ 329 Kenny Gattison .05 .02
❑ 330 Haywoode Workman RC .10 .05
❑ 331 Travis Mays .05 .02
❑ 332 Derrick Coleman .10 .05
❑ 333 Isiah Thomas .25 .11
❑ 334 Jud Buechler .05 .02
❑ 335 Joe Dumars .25 .11
❑ 336 Tate George .05 .02
❑ 337 Mike Sanders .05 .02
❑ 338 James Edwards .05 .02
❑ 339 Chris Morris .05 .02
❑ 340 Scott Hastings .05 .02
❑ 341 Trent Tucker .05 .02
❑ 342 Harvey Grant .05 .02
❑ 343 Patrick Ewing .25 .11
❑ 344 Larry Bird 1.00 .45
❑ 345 Charles Barkley .40 .18
❑ 346 Brian Shaw .05 .02
❑ 347 Kenny Walker .05 .02
❑ 348 Danny Schayes .05 .02
❑ 349 Tom Hammonds .05 .02
❑ 350 Frank Brickowski .05 .02
❑ 351 Terry Porter .05 .02
❑ 352 Orlando Woolridge .05 .02
❑ 353 Buck Williams .05 .02
❑ 354 Sarunas Marciulionis .05 .02
❑ 355 Karl Malone .40 .18
❑ 356 Kevin Johnson .25 .11
❑ 357 Clyde Drexler .25 .11
❑ 358 Duane Causwell .05 .02
❑ 359 Paul Pressey .05 .02
❑ 360 Jim Les RC .05 .02
❑ 361 Derrick McKey .05 .02
❑ 362 Scott Williams RC .05 .02
❑ 363 Mark Alarie .05 .02
❑ 364 Brad Daugherty .05 .02
❑ 365 Bernard King .05 .02
❑ 366 Steve Henson .05 .02
❑ 367 Darrell Walker .05 .02
❑ 368 Larry Krystkowiak .05 .02
❑ 369 Henry James UER .05 .02
(Scored 20 points vs. Pistons& not Jazz)
❑ 370 Jack Sikma .05 .02
❑ 371 Eddie Johnson .10 .05
❑ 372 Wayman Tisdale .05 .02
❑ 373 Joe Barry Carroll .05 .02
❑ 374 David Greenwood .05 .02
❑ 375 Lionel Simmons .05 .02
❑ 376 Dwayne Schintzius .05 .02
❑ 377 Tod Murphy .05 .02
❑ 378 Wayne Cooper .05 .02
❑ 379 Anthony Bonner .05 .02
❑ 380 Walter Davis .05 .02
❑ 381 Lester Conner .05 .02
❑ 382 Ledell Eackles .05 .02
❑ 383 Brad Lohaus .05 .02
❑ 384 Derrick Gervin .05 .02
❑ 385 Pervis Ellison .05 .02
❑ 386 Tim McCormick .05 .02
❑ 387 A.J. English .05 .02
❑ 388 John Battle .05 .02
❑ 389 Roy Hinson .05 .02
❑ 390 Armon Gilliam .05 .02
❑ 391 Kurt Rambis .05 .02
❑ 392 Mark Bryant .05 .02
❑ 393 Chucky Brown .05 .02
❑ 394 Avery Johnson .10 .05
❑ 395 Rory Sparrow .05 .02
❑ 396 Mario Elie RC .25 .11
❑ 397 Ralph Sampson .05 .02
❑ 398 Mike Gminski .05 .02
❑ 399 Bill Wennington .05 .02
❑ 400 Checklist 301-400 .05 .02
❑ 401 David Wingate .10 .05
❑ 402 Moses Malone .50 .23
❑ 403 Darrell Walker .10 .05
❑ 404 Antoine Carr .10 .05
❑ 405 Charles Shackleford .10 .05
❑ 406 Orlando Woolridge .10 .05
❑ 407 Robert Pack RC .25 .11
❑ 408 Bobby Hansen .10 .05
❑ 409 Dale Davis RC .50 .23
❑ 410 Vincent Askew RC .10 .05
❑ 411 Alexander Volkov .10 .05
❑ 412 Dwayne Schintzius .10 .05
❑ 413 Tim Perry .10 .05
❑ 414 Tyrone Corbin .10 .05
❑ 415 Pete Chilcutt RC .10 .05
❑ 416 James Edwards .10 .05
❑ 417 Jerrod Mustaf .10 .05
❑ 418 Thurl Bailey .10 .05
❑ 419 Spud Webb .25 .11
❑ 420 Doc Rivers .25 .11
❑ 421 Sean Green RC .10 .05
❑ 422 Walter Davis .10 .05
❑ 423 Terry Davis .10 .05
❑ 424 John Battle .10 .05
❑ 425 Vinnie Johnson .10 .05
❑ 426 Sherman Douglas .10 .05
❑ 427 Kevin Brooks RC .10 .05
❑ 428 Greg Sutton .10 .05
❑ 429 Rafael Addison RC .10 .05
❑ 430 Anthony Mason RC 1.00 .45
❑ 431 Paul Graham RC .10 .05
❑ 432 Anthony Frederick RC .10 .05
❑ 433 Dennis Hopson .10 .05
❑ 434 Rory Sparrow .10 .05
❑ 435 Michael Adams .10 .05
❑ 436 Kevin Lynch RC .10 .05
❑ 437 Randy Brown RC .10 .05
❑ 438 Larry Johnson CL .25 .11
Billy Owens
❑ 439 Stacey Augmon TP .10 .05
❑ 440 Larry Stewart TP RC .10 .05
❑ 441 Terrell Brandon TP .50 .23
❑ 442 Billy Owens TP RC .10 .05
❑ 443 Rick Fox TP RC .25 .11
❑ 444 Kenny Anderson TP RC 1.00 .45
❑ 445 Larry Johnson TP .50 .23
❑ 446 Dikembe Mutombo TP .50 .23
❑ 447 Steve Smith TP .50 .23
❑ 448 Greg Anthony TP .25 .11
❑ 449 East All-Star .25 .11
Checklist
❑ 450 West All-Star .25 .11
Checklist
❑ 451 Isiah Thomas AS .50 .23
(Magic Johnson also shown)
❑ 452 Michael Jordan AS 3.00 1.35
❑ 453 Scottie Pippen AS .75 .35
❑ 454 Charles Barkley AS .50 .23
❑ 455 Patrick Ewing AS .25 .11
❑ 456 Michael Adams AS .10 .05
❑ 457 Dennis Rodman AS .50 .23
❑ 458 Reggie Lewis AS .10 .05
❑ 459 Joe Dumars AS .25 .11
❑ 460 Mark Price AS .10 .05
❑ 461 Brad Daugherty AS .10 .05
❑ 462 Kevin Willis AS .10 .05
❑ 463 Clyde Drexler AS .25 .11
❑ 464 Magic Johnson AS .75 .35
❑ 465 Chris Mullin AS .25 .11
❑ 466 Karl Malone AS .50 .23
❑ 467 David Robinson AS .50 .23
❑ 468 Tim Hardaway AS .50 .23
❑ 469 Jeff Hornacek AS .10 .05
❑ 470 John Stockton AS .25 .11
❑ 471 D. Mutombo AS UER .25 .11
Drafted in 1992 should be 1991
❑ 472 Hakeem Olajuwon AS .50 .23
❑ 473 James Worthy AS .25 .11
❑ 474 Otis Thorpe AS .10 .05
❑ 475 Dan Majerle AS .10 .05
❑ 476 Cedric Ceballos CL .10 .05
All-Star Skills
❑ 477 Nick Anderson SD .10 .05
❑ 478 Stacey Augmon SD .25 .11
❑ 479 Cedric Ceballos SD .10 .05
❑ 480 Larry Johnson SD .50 .23
❑ 481 Shawn Kemp SD .60 .25
❑ 482 John Starks SD .25 .11
❑ 483 Doug West SD .10 .05
❑ 484 Craig Hodges .10 .05
Long Distance Shoot Out
❑ 485 LaBradford Smith RC .10 .05
❑ 486 Winston Garland .10 .05
❑ 487 David Benoit RC .25 .11
❑ 488 John Bagley .10 .05
❑ 489 Mark Macon RC .10 .05
❑ 490 Mitch Richmond .25 .11
❑ 491 Luc Longley RC .25 .11
❑ 492 Sedale Threatt .10 .05
❑ 493 Doug Smith RC .10 .05
❑ 494 Travis Mays .10 .05
❑ 495 Xavier McDaniel .10 .05
❑ 496 Brian Shaw .10 .05
❑ 497 Stanley Roberts RC .10 .05
❑ 498 Blair Rasmussen .10 .05
❑ 499 Brian Williams RC .50 .23
❑ 500 Checklist Card .10 .05

1991-92 Upper Deck Award Winner Holograms

	MINT	NRMT
COMPLETE SET (9)	20.00	9.00

*SINGLES: 1.5X TO 4X BASE CARD HI
RANDOM INSERTS IN BOTH SERIES PACKS

❑ AW1 Michael Jordan 12.00 5.50
Scoring Leader
❑ AW2 Alvin Robertson .20 .09
Steals Leader
❑ AW3 John Stockton 1.00 .45
Assists Leader
❑ AW4 Michael Jordan 12.00 5.50
MVP
❑ AW5 Detlef Schrempf .40 .18
Sixth Man
❑ AW6 David Robinson 2.00 .90
Rebounds Leader
❑ AW7 Derrick Coleman .40 .18
Rookie of the Year
❑ AW8 Hakeem Olajuwon 1.50 .70
Blocked Shots Leader
❑ AW9 Dennis Rodman 2.00 .90
Defensive POY

1991-92 Upper Deck Rookie Standouts

	MINT	NRMT
COMPLETE SET (40)	15.00	6.75
COMPLETE SERIES 1 (20)	5.00	2.20
COMPLETE SERIES 2 (20)	10.00	4.50
COMMON CARD (R1-R40)	.25	.11
SEMISTARS	.40	.18
UNLISTED STARS	.60	.25

ONE PER LO OR HI JUMBO OR LOCKER PACK

❑ R1 Gary Payton 2.50 1.10
❑ R2 Dennis Scott .40 .18
❑ R3 Kendall Gill .60 .25
❑ R4 Felton Spencer .25 .11
❑ R5 Bo Kimble .25 .11

❑ R6 Willie Burton .25 .11
❑ R7 Tyrone Hill .40 .18
❑ R8 Loy Vaught .40 .18
❑ R9 Travis Mays .25 .11
❑ R10 Derrick Coleman .60 .25
❑ R11 Duane Causwell .25 .11
❑ R12 Dee Brown .25 .11
❑ R13 Gerald Glass .25 .11
❑ R14 Jayson Williams .60 .25
❑ R15 Elden Campbell .40 .18
❑ R16 Negele Knight .25 .11
❑ R17 Chris Jackson .25 .11
❑ R18 Danny Ferry .25 .11
❑ R19 Tony Smith .25 .11
❑ R20 Cedric Ceballos .60 .25
❑ R21 Victor Alexander .25 .11
❑ R22 Terrell Brandon 2.00 .90
❑ R23 Rick Fox .60 .25
❑ R24 Stacey Augmon .60 .25
❑ R25 Mark Macon .25 .11
❑ R26 Larry Johnson 2.50 1.10
❑ R27 Paul Graham .25 .11
❑ R28 Stanley Roberts UER .25 .11
(Not the Magic's 1st pick in 1991)
❑ R29 Dikembe Mutombo 2.00 .90
❑ R30 Robert Pack .25 .11
❑ R31 Doug Smith .25 .11
❑ R32 Steve Smith 2.50 1.10
❑ R33 Billy Owens .60 .25
❑ R34 David Benoit .40 .18
❑ R35 Brian Williams .60 .25
❑ R36 Kenny Anderson 1.25 .55
❑ R37 Greg Anthony .60 .25
❑ R38 Dale Davis .60 .25
❑ R39 Larry Stewart .25 .11
❑ R40 Mike Iuzzolino .25 .11

1991-92 Upper Deck Jerry West Heroes

	MINT	NRMT
COMPLETE SET (10)	6.00	2.70
COMMON WEST (1-9)	1.00	.45
WEST HEROES HEADER (NNO)	1.50	.70
CERTIFIED AUTOGRAPH/2500	100.00	45.00

RANDOM INSERTS IN HI SERIES PACKS

❑ 1 Jerry West 1.00 .45
1959 NCAA Tournament MVP
❑ 2 Jerry West 1.00 .45
1960 U.S. Team
❑ 3 Jerry West 1.00 .45
1968-69 NBA Playoff MVP
❑ 4 Jerry West 1.00 .45
1969-70 NBA Scoring Leader
❑ 5 Jerry West 1.00 .45
1972 NBA World Championship
❑ 6 Jerry West 1.00 .45
1973-74 25,000 Points
❑ 7 Jerry West 1.00 .45
1979 Basketball Hall of Fame
❑ 8 Jerry West 1.00 .45
1982 to the present Front Office Success
❑ 9 Jerry West 1.00 .45
Portrait Card

1992-93 Upper Deck

	MINT	NRMT
COMPLETE SET (514)	90.00	40.00
COMPLETE LO SERIES (311)	20.00	9.00
COMPLETE HI SERIES (203)	70.00	32.00
COMMON CARD (1-510)	.05	.02
ERR (100A)	1.00	.45
ERR (110A)	4.00	1.80
SEMISTARS	.15	.07
UNLISTED STARS	.30	.14

LO SERIES SET INCLUDES 1AX/1B/32A/33A
HI SERIES SET INCLUDES 1/32/33
SUBSET CARDS HALF VALUE OF BASE CARDS
SP1: SER.1 STATED ODDS 1:72
SP2: SER.2 STATED ODDS 1:72

❑ 1 Shaquille O'Neal RC ! SP 60.00 27.00
NBA First Draft Pick
❑ 1A 1992 NBA Draft Trade .30 .14
Card SP
❑ 1B Shaquille O'Neal TRADE 12.00 5.50
❑ 1AX 1992 NBA Draft Trade .30 .14
Card (Stamped)
❑ 2 Alonzo Mourning RC 1.50 .70
❑ 3 Christian Laettner RC .60 .25
❑ 4 LaPhonso Ellis RC .30 .14
❑ 5 Clarence Weatherspoon RC .30 .14
❑ 6 Adam Keefe RC .05 .02
❑ 7 Robert Horry RC .30 .14
❑ 8 Harold Miner RC .15 .07
❑ 9 Bryant Stith RC .15 .07
❑ 10 Malik Sealy RC .15 .07
❑ 11 Anthony Peeler RC .15 .07
❑ 12 Randy Woods RC .05 .02
❑ 13 Tracy Murray RC .15 .07
❑ 14 Tom Gugliotta RC 1.00 .45
❑ 15 Hubert Davis RC .15 .07
❑ 16 Don MacLean RC .05 .02
❑ 17 Lee Mayberry RC .05 .02
❑ 18 Corey Williams RC .05 .02
❑ 19 Sean Rooks RC .05 .02
❑ 20 Todd Day RC .15 .07
❑ 21 Bryant Stith CL .30 .14
LaPhonso Ellis
❑ 22 Jeff Hornacek .15 .07
❑ 23 Michael Jordan 4.00 1.80
❑ 24 John Salley .05 .02
❑ 25 Andre Turner .05 .02
❑ 26 Charles Barkley .50 .23
❑ 27 Anthony Frederick .05 .02
❑ 28 Mario Elie .15 .07
❑ 29 Olden Polynice .05 .02
❑ 30 Rodney Monroe .05 .02
❑ 31 Tim Perry .05 .02
❑ 32 Doug Christie SP RC 1.00 .45
❑ 32A Magic Johnson SP 2.00 .90
❑ 33 Jim Jackson SP RC 2.50 1.10
❑ 33A Larry Bird SP 2.50 1.10
❑ 34 Randy White .05 .02
❑ 35 Frank Brickowski TC .05 .02
❑ 36 Michael Adams TC .05 .02
❑ 37 Scottie Pippen TC .50 .23
❑ 38 Mark Price TC .05 .02
❑ 39 Robert Parish TC .05 .02
❑ 40 Danny Manning TC .05 .02
❑ 41 Kevin Willis TC .05 .02
❑ 42 Glen Rice TC .15 .07
❑ 43 Kendall Gill TC .05 .02
❑ 44 Karl Malone TC .30 .14
❑ 45 Mitch Richmond TC .30 .14
❑ 46 Patrick Ewing TC .30 .14
❑ 47 Sam Perkins TC .05 .02
❑ 48 Dennis Scott TC .05 .02
❑ 49 Derek Harper TC .05 .02
❑ 50 Drazen Petrovic TC .05 .02
❑ 51 Reggie Williams TC .05 .02
❑ 52 Rik Smits TC .05 .02
❑ 53 Joe Dumars TC .15 .07
❑ 54 Otis Thorpe TC .05 .02
❑ 55 Johnny Dawkins TC .05 .02
❑ 56 Sean Elliott TC .05 .02
❑ 57 Kevin Johnson TC .15 .07
❑ 58 Ricky Pierce TC .05 .02
❑ 59 Doug West TC .05 .02
❑ 60 Terry Porter TC .05 .02
❑ 61 Tim Hardaway TC .30 .14
❑ 62 Michael Jordan ST 1.00 .45
Scottie Pippen
❑ 63 Kendall Gill ST .30 .14
Larry Johnson
❑ 64 Tom Chambers ST .15 .07
Kevin Johnson
❑ 65 Tim Hardaway ST .15 .07
Chris Mullin
❑ 66 Karl Malone ST .30 .14
John Stockton
❑ 67 Michael Jordan MVP 2.00 .90
❑ 68 Stacey Augmon .05 .02
Six Million Point Man
❑ 69 Bob Lanier .15 .07
Stay in School
❑ 70 Alaa Abdelnaby .05 .02
❑ 71 Andrew Lang .05 .02
❑ 72 Larry Krystkowiak .05 .02
❑ 73 Gerald Wilkins .05 .02
❑ 74 Rod Strickland .30 .14
❑ 75 Danny Ainge .15 .07
❑ 76 Chris Corchiani .05 .02
❑ 77 Jeff Grayer .05 .02
❑ 78 Eric Murdock .05 .02
❑ 79 Rex Chapman .05 .02
❑ 80 LaBradford Smith .05 .02
❑ 81 Jay Humphries .05 .02
❑ 82 David Robinson .50 .23
❑ 83 William Bedford .05 .02
❑ 84 James Edwards .05 .02
❑ 85 Dan Schayes .05 .02
❑ 86 Lloyd Daniels RC .05 .02
❑ 87 Blue Edwards .05 .02
❑ 88 Dale Ellis .05 .02
❑ 89 Rolando Blackman .05 .02
❑ 90 Michael Jordan CL .30 .14
❑ 91 Rik Smits .15 .07
❑ 92 Terry Davis .05 .02
❑ 93 Bill Cartwright .05 .02
❑ 94 Avery Johnson .05 .02
❑ 95 Micheal Williams .05 .02
❑ 96 Spud Webb .15 .07
❑ 97 Benoit Benjamin .05 .02

❑	98	Derek Harper	.15	.07
❑	99	Matt Bullard	.05	.02
❑	100A	Tyrone Corbin ERR (Heat on front)	1.00	.45
❑	100B	Tyrone Corbin COR	.05	.02
❑	101	Doc Rivers	.15	.07
❑	102	Tony Smith	.05	.02
❑	103	Doug West	.05	.02
❑	104	Kevin Duckworth	.05	.02
❑	105	Luc Longley	.15	.07
❑	106	Antoine Carr	.05	.02
❑	107	Clifford Robinson	.15	.07
❑	108	Grant Long	.05	.02
❑	109	Terry Porter	.05	.02
❑	110A	Steve Smith ERR (Jazz on front)	1.00	1.80
❑	110B	Steve Smith COR	.40	.18
❑	111	Brian Williams	.05	.02
❑	112	Karl Malone	.50	.23
❑	113	Reggie Williams	.05	.02
❑	114	Tom Chambers	.05	.02
❑	115	Winston Garland	.05	.02
❑	116	John Stockton	.30	.14
❑	117	Chris Jackson	.05	.02
❑	118	Mike Brown	.05	.02
❑	119	Kevin Johnson	.30	.14
❑	120	Reggie Lewis	.15	.07
❑	121	Bimbo Coles	.05	.02
❑	122	Drazen Petrovic	.05	.02
❑	123	Reggie Miller	.30	.14
❑	124	Derrick Coleman	.15	.07
❑	125	Chuck Person	.05	.02
❑	126	Glen Rice	.30	.14
❑	127	Kenny Anderson	.30	.14
❑	128	Willie Burton	.05	.02
❑	129	Chris Morris	.05	.02
❑	130	Patrick Ewing	.30	.14
❑	131	Sean Elliott	.15	.07
❑	132	Clyde Drexler	.30	.14
❑	133	Scottie Pippen	1.00	.45
❑	134	Pooh Richardson	.05	.02
❑	135	Horace Grant	.15	.07
❑	136	Hakeem Olajuwon	.50	.23
❑	137	John Paxson	.05	.02
❑	138	Kendall Gill	.15	.07
❑	139	Michael Adams	.05	.02
❑	140	Otis Thorpe	.15	.07
❑	141	Dennis Scott	.15	.07
❑	142	Stacey Augmon	.15	.07
❑	143	Robert Pack	.05	.02
❑	144	Kevin Willis	.05	.02
❑	145	Jerome Kersey	.05	.02
❑	146	Paul Graham	.05	.02
❑	147	Stanley Roberts	.05	.02
❑	148	Dominique Wilkins	.30	.14
❑	149	Scott Skiles	.05	.02
❑	150	Rumeal Robinson	.05	.02
❑	151	Mookie Blaylock	.15	.07
❑	152	Elden Campbell	.15	.07
❑	153	Chris Dudley	.05	.02
❑	154	Sedale Threatt	.05	.02
❑	155	Tate George	.05	.02
❑	156	James Worthy	.30	.14
❑	157	B.J. Armstrong	.05	.02
❑	158	Gary Payton	.60	.25
❑	159	Ledell Eackles	.05	.02
❑	160	Sam Perkins	.15	.07
❑	161	Nick Anderson	.15	.07
❑	162	Mitch Richmond	.30	.14
❑	163	Buck Williams	.15	.07
❑	164	Blair Rasmussen	.05	.02
❑	165	Vern Fleming	.05	.02
❑	166	Duane Ferrell	.05	.02
❑	167	George McCloud	.05	.02
❑	168	Terry Cummings	.15	.07
❑	169	Detlef Schrempf	.15	.07
❑	170	Willie Anderson	.05	.02
❑	171	Scott Williams	.05	.02
❑	172	Vernon Maxwell	.05	.02
❑	173	Todd Lichti	.05	.02
❑	174	David Benoit	.05	.02
❑	175	Marcus Liberty	.05	.02
❑	176	Kenny Smith	.05	.02
❑	177	Dan Majerle	.15	.07
❑	178	Jeff Malone	.05	.02
❑	179	Robert Parish	.15	.07
❑	180	Mark Eaton	.05	.02
❑	181	Rony Seikaly	.05	.02
❑	182	Tony Campbell	.05	.02
❑	183	Kevin McHale	.30	.14
❑	184	Thurl Bailey	.05	.02
❑	185	Kevin Edwards	.05	.02
❑	186	Gerald Glass	.05	.02
❑	187	Hersey Hawkins	.15	.07
❑	188	Sam Mitchell	.05	.02
❑	189	Brian Shaw	.05	.02
❑	190	Felton Spencer	.05	.02
❑	191	Mark Macon	.05	.02
❑	192	Jerry Reynolds	.05	.02
❑	193	Dale Davis	.05	.02
❑	194	Sleepy Floyd	.05	.02
❑	195	A.C. Green	.15	.07
❑	196	Terry Catledge	.05	.02
❑	197	Byron Scott	.15	.07
❑	198	Sam Bowie	.05	.02
❑	199	Vlade Divac	.15	.07
❑	200	Michael Jordan CL	.30	.14
❑	201	Brad Lohaus	.05	.02
❑	202	Johnny Newman	.05	.02
❑	203	Gary Grant	.05	.02
❑	204	Sidney Green	.05	.02
❑	205	Frank Brickowski	.05	.02
❑	206	Anthony Bowie	.05	.02
❑	207	Duane Causwell	.05	.02
❑	208	A.J. English	.05	.02
❑	209	Mark Aguirre	.05	.02
❑	210	Jon Koncak	.05	.02
❑	211	Kevin Gamble	.05	.02
❑	212	Craig Ehlo	.05	.02
❑	213	Herb Williams	.15	.07
❑	214	Cedric Ceballos	.15	.07
❑	215	Mark Jackson	.15	.07
❑	216	John Bagley	.05	.02
❑	217	Ron Anderson	.05	.02
❑	218	John Battle	.05	.02
❑	219	Kevin Lynch	.05	.02
❑	220	Donald Hodge	.05	.02
❑	221	Chris Gatling	.05	.02
❑	222	Muggsy Bogues	.15	.07
❑	223	Bill Laimbeer	.15	.07
❑	224	Anthony Bonner	.05	.02
❑	225	Fred Roberts	.05	.02
❑	226	Larry Stewart	.05	.02
❑	227	Darrell Walker	.05	.02
❑	228	Larry Smith	.05	.02
❑	229	Billy Owens	.15	.07
❑	230	Vinnie Johnson	.05	.02
❑	231	Johnny Dawkins	.05	.02
❑	232	Rick Fox	.15	.07
❑	233	Travis Mays	.05	.02
❑	234	Mark Price	.05	.02
❑	235	Derrick McKey	.05	.02
❑	236	Greg Anthony	.05	.02
❑	237	Doug Smith	.05	.02
❑	238	Alec Kessler	.05	.02
❑	239	Anthony Mason	.30	.14
❑	240	Shawn Kemp	.60	.25
❑	241	Jim Les	.05	.02
❑	242	Dennis Rodman	.60	.25
❑	243	Lionel Simmons	.05	.02
❑	244	Pervis Ellison	.05	.02
❑	245	Terrell Brandon	.30	.14
❑	246	Mark Bryant	.05	.02
❑	247	Brad Daugherty	.05	.02
❑	248	Scott Brooks	.05	.02
❑	249	Sarunas Marciulionis	.05	.02
❑	250	Danny Ferry	.05	.02
❑	251	Loy Vaught	.05	.02
❑	252	Dee Brown	.05	.02
❑	253	Alvin Robertson	.05	.02
❑	254	Charles Smith	.05	.02
❑	255	Dikembe Mutombo	.30	.14
❑	256	Greg Kite	.05	.02
❑	257	Ed Pinckney	.05	.02
❑	258	Ron Harper	.15	.07
❑	259	Elliot Perry	.05	.02
❑	260	Rafael Addison	.05	.02
❑	261	Tim Hardaway	.40	.18
❑	262	Randy Brown	.05	.02
❑	263	Isiah Thomas	.30	.14
❑	264	Victor Alexander	.05	.02
❑	265	Wayman Tisdale	.05	.02
❑	266	Harvey Grant	.05	.02
❑	267	Mike Iuzzolino	.05	.02
❑	268	Joe Dumars	.30	.14
❑	269	Xavier McDaniel	.05	.02
❑	270	Jeff Sanders	.05	.02
❑	271	Danny Manning	.15	.07
❑	272	Jayson Williams	.15	.07
❑	273	Ricky Pierce	.05	.02
❑	274	Will Perdue	.05	.02
❑	275	Dana Barros	.05	.02
❑	276	Randy Breuer	.05	.02
❑	277	Manute Bol	.05	.02
❑	278	Negele Knight	.05	.02
❑	279	Rodney McCray	.05	.02
❑	280	Greg Sutton	.05	.02
❑	281	Larry Nance	.05	.02
❑	282	John Starks	.15	.07
❑	283	Pete Chilcutt	.05	.02
❑	284	Kenny Gattison	.05	.02
❑	285	Stacey King	.05	.02
❑	286	Bernard King	.05	.02
❑	287	Larry Johnson	.40	.18
❑	288	John Williams	.05	.02
❑	289	Dell Curry	.05	.02
❑	290	Orlando Woolridge	.05	.02
❑	291	Nate McMillan	.05	.02
❑	292	Terry Mills	.05	.02
❑	293	Sherman Douglas	.05	.02
❑	294	Charles Shackleford	.05	.02
❑	295	Ken Norman	.05	.02
❑	296	LaSalle Thompson	.05	.02
❑	297	Chris Mullin	.30	.14
❑	298	Eddie Johnson	.05	.02
❑	299	Armon Gilliam	.05	.02
❑	300	Michael Cage	.05	.02
❑	301	Moses Malone	.30	.14
❑	302	Charles Oakley	.15	.07
❑	303	David Wingate	.05	.02
❑	304	Steve Kerr	.15	.07
❑	305	Tyrone Hill	.05	.02
❑	306	Mark West	.05	.02
❑	307	Fat Lever	.05	.02
❑	308	J.R. Reid	.05	.02
❑	309	Ed Nealy	.05	.02
❑	310	Michael Jordan CL	.30	.14
❑	311	Alaa Abdelnaby	.05	.02
❑	312	Stacey Augmon	.15	.07
❑	313	Anthony Avent RC	.05	.02
❑	314	Walter Bond RC	.05	.02
❑	315	Byron Houston RC	.05	.02
❑	316	Rick Mahorn	.05	.02
❑	317	Sam Mitchell	.05	.02
❑	318	Mookie Blaylock	.15	.07
❑	319	Lance Blanks	.05	.02
❑	320	John Williams	.05	.02
❑	321	Rolando Blackman	.05	.02
❑	322	Danny Ainge	.15	.07
❑	323	Gerald Glass	.05	.02
❑	324	Robert Pack	.05	.02
❑	325	Oliver Miller RC	.15	.07
❑	326	Charles Smith	.05	.02
❑	327	Duane Ferrell	.05	.02
❑	328	Pooh Richardson	.05	.02
❑	329	Scott Brooks	.05	.02
❑	330	Walt Williams RC	.30	.14
❑	331	Andrew Lang	.05	.02
❑	332	Eric Murdock	.05	.02
❑	333	Vinny Del Negro	.05	.02
❑	334	Charles Barkley	.50	.23
❑	335	James Edwards	.05	.02
❑	336	Xavier McDaniel	.05	.02
❑	337	Paul Graham	.05	.02
❑	338	David Wingate	.05	.02
❑	339	Richard Dumas RC	.05	.02
❑	340	Jay Humphries	.05	.02
❑	341	Mark Jackson	.15	.07
❑	342	John Salley	.05	.02
❑	343	Jon Koncak	.05	.02
❑	344	Rodney McCray	.05	.02
❑	345	Chuck Person	.05	.02
❑	346	Mario Elie	.15	.07
❑	347	Frank Johnson	.05	.02
❑	348	Rumeal Robinson	.05	.02
❑	349	Terry Mills	.05	.02
❑	350	Kevin Willis TFC	.05	.02
❑	351	Dee Brown TFC	.05	.02

- ❑ 352 Muggsy Bogues TFC .05 .02
- ❑ 353 B.J. Armstrong TFC .05 .02
- ❑ 354 Larry Nance TFC .05 .02
- ❑ 355 Doug Smith TFC .05 .02
- ❑ 356 Robert Pack TFC .05 .02
- ❑ 357 Joe Dumars TFC .15 .07
- ❑ 358 Sarunas Marciulionis TFC .05 .02
- ❑ 359 Kenny Smith TFC .05 .02
- ❑ 360 Pooh Richardson TFC .05 .02
- ❑ 361 Mark Jackson TFC .05 .02
- ❑ 362 Sedale Threatt TFC .05 .02
- ❑ 363 Grant Long TFC .05 .02
- ❑ 364 Eric Murdock TFC .05 .02
- ❑ 365 Doug West TFC .05 .02
- ❑ 366 Kenny Anderson TFC .15 .07
- ❑ 367 Anthony Mason TFC .15 .07
- ❑ 368 Nick Anderson TFC .05 .02
- ❑ 369 Jeff Hornacek TFC .05 .02
- ❑ 370 Dan Majerle TFC .05 .02
- ❑ 371 Clifford Robinson TFC .05 .02
- ❑ 372 Lionel Simmons TFC .05 .02
- ❑ 373 Dale Ellis TFC .05 .02
- ❑ 374 Gary Payton TFC .30 .14
- ❑ 375 David Benoit TFC .05 .02
- ❑ 376 Harvey Grant TFC .05 .02
- ❑ 377 Buck Johnson .05 .02
- ❑ 378 Brian Howard RC .05 .02
- ❑ 379 Travis Mays .05 .02
- ❑ 380 Jud Buechler .05 .02
- ❑ 381 Matt Geiger RC .15 .07
- ❑ 382 Bob McCann RC .05 .02
- ❑ 383 Cedric Ceballos .15 .07
- ❑ 384 Rod Strickland .30 .14
- ❑ 385 Kiki Vandeweghe .05 .02
- ❑ 386 Latrell Sprewell RC 2.50 1.10
- ❑ 387 Larry Krystkowiak .05 .02
- ❑ 388 Dale Ellis .05 .02
- ❑ 389 Trent Tucker .05 .02
- ❑ 390 Negele Knight .05 .02
- ❑ 391 Stanley Roberts .05 .02
- ❑ 392 Tony Campbell .05 .02
- ❑ 393 Tim Perry .05 .02
- ❑ 394 Doug Overton .05 .02
- ❑ 395 Dan Majerle .15 .07
- ❑ 396 Duane Cooper RC .05 .02
- ❑ 397 Kevin Willis .05 .02
- ❑ 398 Micheal Williams .05 .02
- ❑ 399 Avery Johnson .05 .02
- ❑ 400 Dominique Wilkins .30 .14
- ❑ 401 Chris Smith RC .05 .02
- ❑ 402 Blair Rasmussen .05 .02
- ❑ 403 Jeff Hornacek .15 .07
- ❑ 404 Blue Edwards .05 .02
- ❑ 405 Olden Polynice .05 .02
- ❑ 406 Jeff Grayer .05 .02
- ❑ 407 Tony Bennett RC .05 .02
- ❑ 408 Don MacLean .05 .02
- ❑ 409 Tom Chambers .05 .02
- ❑ 410 Keith Jennings RC .05 .02
- ❑ 411 Gerald Wilkins .05 .02
- ❑ 412 Kennard Winchester .05 .02
- ❑ 413 Doc Rivers .15 .07
- ❑ 414 Brent Price RC .15 .07
- ❑ 415 Mark West .05 .02
- ❑ 416 J.R. Reid .05 .02
- ❑ 417 Jon Barry RC .15 .07
- ❑ 418 Kevin Johnson .30 .14
- ❑ 419 Michael Jordan CL .30 .14
- ❑ 420 Michael Jordan CL .30 .14
- ❑ 421 Brad Daugherty CL .05 .02
  Mark Price
  Larry Nance
- ❑ 422 Scottie Pippen AS .50 .23
- ❑ 423 Larry Johnson AS .30 .14
- ❑ 424 Shaquille O'Neal AS 2.50 1.10
- ❑ 425 Michael Jordan AS 2.00 .90
- ❑ 426 Isiah Thomas AS .15 .07
- ❑ 427 Brad Daugherty AS .05 .02
- ❑ 428 Joe Dumars AS .15 .07
- ❑ 429 Patrick Ewing AS .15 .07
- ❑ 430 Larry Nance AS .05 .02
- ❑ 431 Mark Price AS .05 .02
- ❑ 432 Detlef Schrempf AS .05 .02
- ❑ 433 Dominique Wilkins AS .15 .07
- ❑ 434 Karl Malone AS .30 .14
- ❑ 435 Charles Barkley AS .30 .14
- ❑ 436 David Robinson AS .30 .14
- ❑ 437 John Stockton AS .15 .07
- ❑ 438 Clyde Drexler AS .15 .07
- ❑ 439 Sean Elliott AS .05 .02
- ❑ 440 Tim Hardaway AS .30 .14
- ❑ 441 Shawn Kemp AS .30 .14
- ❑ 442 Dan Majerle AS .05 .02
- ❑ 443 Danny Manning AS .05 .02
- ❑ 444 Hakeem Olajuwon AS .30 .14
- ❑ 445 Terry Porter AS .05 .02
- ❑ 446 Harold Miner FACE .15 .07
- ❑ 447 David Benoit FACE .05 .02
- ❑ 448 Cedric Ceballos FACE .05 .02
- ❑ 449 Chris Jackson FACE .05 .02
- ❑ 450 Tim Perry FACE .05 .02
- ❑ 451 Kenny Smith FACE .05 .02
- ❑ 452 Clarence Weatherspoon .30 .14
  FACE
- ❑ 453A Michael Jordan 20.00 9.00
  FACE ERR (Slam Dunk Champ
  in 1985 and 1990)
- ❑ 453B Michael Jordan 2.00 .90
  FACE COR (Slam Dunk Champ
  in 1987 and 1988)
- ❑ 454A Dominique Wilkins 2.00 .90
  FACE ERR (Slam Dunk Champ
  in 1987 and 1988)
- ❑ 454B Dominique Wilkins .30 .14
  FACE COR (Slam Dunk Champ
  in 1985 and 1990)
- ❑ 455 Anthony Peeler .05 .02
  Duane Cooper CL
- ❑ 456 Adam Keefe TP .05 .02
- ❑ 457 Alonzo Mourning TP .50 .23
- ❑ 458 Jim Jackson TP .30 .14
- ❑ 459 Sean Rooks TP .05 .02
- ❑ 460 LaPhonso Ellis TP .15 .07
- ❑ 461 Bryant Stith TP .05 .02
- ❑ 462 Byron Houston TP .05 .02
- ❑ 463 Latrell Sprewell TP .30 .14
- ❑ 464 Robert Horry TP .15 .07
- ❑ 465 Malik Sealy TP .05 .02
- ❑ 466 Doug Christie TP .30 .14
- ❑ 467 Duane Cooper TP .05 .02
- ❑ 468 Anthony Peeler TP .05 .02
- ❑ 469 Harold Miner TP .05 .02
- ❑ 470 Todd Day TP .05 .02
- ❑ 471 Lee Mayberry TP .05 .02
- ❑ 472 Christian Laettner TP .30 .14
- ❑ 473 Hubert Davis TP .05 .02
- ❑ 474 Shaquille O'Neal TP 2.50 1.10
- ❑ 475 C. Weatherspoon TP .30 .14
- ❑ 476 Richard Dumas TP .05 .02
- ❑ 477 Oliver Miller TP .05 .02
- ❑ 478 Tracy Murray TP .05 .02
- ❑ 479 Walt Williams TP .15 .07
- ❑ 480 Lloyd Daniels TP .05 .02
- ❑ 481 Tom Gugliotta TP .30 .14
- ❑ 482 Brent Price TP .05 .02
- ❑ 483 Mark Aguirre GF .05 .02
- ❑ 484 Frank Brickowski GF .05 .02
- ❑ 485 Derrick Coleman GF .05 .02
- ❑ 486 Clyde Drexler GF .15 .07
- ❑ 487 Harvey Grant GF .05 .02
- ❑ 488 Michael Jordan GF 2.00 .90
- ❑ 489 Karl Malone GF .30 .14
- ❑ 490 Xavier McDaniel GF .05 .02
- ❑ 491 Drazen Petrovic GF .05 .02
- ❑ 492 John Starks GF .05 .02
- ❑ 493 Robert Parish GF .05 .02
- ❑ 494 Christian Laettner GF .30 .14
- ❑ 495 Ron Harper GF .05 .02
- ❑ 496 David Robinson GF .30 .14
- ❑ 497 John Salley GF .05 .02
- ❑ 498 Brad Daugherty ST .05 .02
  Mark Price
- ❑ 499 Dikembe Mutombo ST .15 .07
  Chris Jackson
- ❑ 500 Isiah Thomas ST .30 .14
  Joe Dumars
- ❑ 501 Hakeem Olajuwon .30 .14
  Otis Thorpe ST
- ❑ 502 Derrick Coleman ST .15 .07
  Drazen Petrovic
- ❑ 503 Terry Porter ST .30 .14
  Clyde Drexler
- ❑ 504 Lionel Simmons ST .15 .07
  Mitch Richmond
- ❑ 505 David Robinson ST .30 .14
  Sean Elliott
- ❑ 506 Michael Jordan FAN 2.00 .90
- ❑ 507 Larry Bird FAN .60 .25
- ❑ 508 Karl Malone FAN .30 .14
- ❑ 509 Dikembe Mutombo FAN .15 .07
- ❑ 510 Larry Bird FAN 1.00 .45
  Michael Jordan
- ❑ SP1 Larry Bird 3.00 1.35
  Magic Johnson
  Retirement
- ❑ SP2 20,000 Points 8.00 3.60
  Dominique Wilkins
  Nov. 6, 1992
  Michael Jordan
  Jan. 8, 1993

1992-93 Upper Deck All-Division

	MINT	NRMT
COMPLETE SET (20)	20.00	9.00

*SINGLES: 1X TO 2.5X BASE CARD HI
ONE PER HI SERIES JUMBO PACK

- ❑ AD1 Shaquille O'Neal 8.00 3.60
- ❑ AD2 Derrick Coleman .40 .18
- ❑ AD3 Glen Rice .75 .35
- ❑ AD4 Reggie Lewis .40 .18
- ❑ AD5 Kenny Anderson .75 .35
- ❑ AD6 Brad Daugherty .15 .07
- ❑ AD7 Dominique Wilkins .75 .35
- ❑ AD8 Larry Johnson 1.00 .45
- ❑ AD9 Michael Jordan 10.00 4.50
- ❑ AD10 Mark Price .15 .07
- ❑ AD11 David Robinson 1.25 .55
- ❑ AD12 Karl Malone 1.25 .55
- ❑ AD13 Sean Elliott .40 .18
- ❑ AD14 John Stockton .75 .35
- ❑ AD15 Derek Harper .40 .18
- ❑ AD16 Kevin Duckworth .15 .07
- ❑ AD17 Chris Mullin .75 .35
- ❑ AD18 Charles Barkley 1.25 .55
- ❑ AD19 Tim Hardaway 1.00 .45
- ❑ AD20 Clyde Drexler .75 .35

1992-93 Upper Deck All-NBA

	MINT	NRMT
COMPLETE SET (10)	50.00	22.00

*SINGLES: 3X TO 8X BASE CARD HI
ONE PER LO SERIES LOCKER PACK
CONDITION SENSITIVE SET

- ❑ AN1 Michael Jordan 30.00 13.50
- ❑ AN2 Clyde Drexler 2.50 1.10
- ❑ AN3 David Robinson 4.00 1.80
- ❑ AN4 Karl Malone 4.00 1.80
- ❑ AN5 Chris Mullin 2.50 1.10
- ❑ AN6 John Stockton 2.50 1.10
- ❑ AN7 Tim Hardaway 3.00 1.35
- ❑ AN8 Patrick Ewing 2.50 1.10
- ❑ AN9 Scottie Pippen 8.00 3.60
- ❑ AN10 Charles Barkley 4.00 1.80

1992-93 Upper Deck All-Rookies

	MINT	NRMT
COMPLETE SET (10)	10.00	4.50

*SINGLES: 2.5X TO 6X BASE CARD HI
LO SERIES STATED ODDS 1:12 RETAIL

Card	Player	MINT	NRMT
❑ AR1	Larry Johnson	2.50	1.10
❑ AR2	Dikembe Mutombo	2.00	.90
❑ AR3	Billy Owens	1.00	.45
❑ AR4	Steve Smith	2.50	1.10
❑ AR5	Stacey Augmon	1.00	.45
❑ AR6	Rick Fox	1.00	.45
❑ AR7	Terrell Brandon	2.00	.90
❑ AR8	Larry Stewart	.30	.14
❑ AR9	Stanley Roberts	.30	.14
❑ AR10	Mark Macon	.30	.14

1992-93 Upper Deck Award Winner Holograms

	MINT	NRMT
COMPLETE SET (9)	30.00	13.50
COMPLETE LO SERIES (6)	15.00	6.75
COMPLETE HI SERIES (3)	15.00	6.75

*SINGLES: 1.25X TO 3X BASE CARD HI
LO/HI SERIES STATED ODDS 1:18 HOB/RET

Card	Player	MINT	NRMT
❑ AW1	Michael Jordan	12.00	5.50
	Scoring		
❑ AW2	John Stockton	1.00	.45
	Steals		
❑ AW3	Dennis Rodman	2.00	.90
	Rebounds		
❑ AW4	Detlef Schrempf	.50	.23
	Sixth Man		
❑ AW5	Larry Johnson	1.25	.55
	Rookie of the Year		
❑ AW6	David Robinson	1.50	.70
	Blocked Shots		
❑ AW7	David Robinson	1.50	.70
	Def. Player of Year		
❑ AW8	John Stockton	1.00	.45
	Assists		
❑ AW9	Michael Jordan	12.00	5.50
	Most Valuable Player		

1992-93 Upper Deck Larry Bird Heroes

	MINT	NRMT
COMPLETE SET (10)	10.00	4.50
COMMON BIRD (19-27)	1.00	.45
BIRD HEADER (NNO)	2.00	.90

HI SERIES STATED ODDS 1:9

Card	Player	MINT	NRMT
❑ 19	Larry Bird	1.00	.45
	1979 College Player of the Year		
❑ 20	Larry Bird	1.00	.45
	1979-80 Rookie of the Year		
❑ 21	Larry Bird	1.00	.45
	1980-92 12-Time NBA All-Star		
❑ 22	Larry Bird	1.00	.45
	1981-86 Three NBA Championships		
❑ 23	Larry Bird	1.00	.45
	1984-86 3-Time NBA MVP		
❑ 24	Larry Bird	1.00	.45
	1986-88 3-Point King		
❑ 25	Larry Bird	1.00	.45
	1990 20,000 Points		
❑ 26	Larry Bird	1.00	.45
	Larry Legend		
❑ 27	Larry Bird	1.00	.45
	(Portrait by Alan Studt)		
❑ NNO	Larry Bird	2.00	.90
	Title/Header Card		

1992-93 Upper Deck Wilt Chamberlain Heroes

	MINT	NRMT
COMPLETE SET (10)	5.00	2.20
COMMON CHAMBER. (10-18)	.50	.23
CHAMBERLAIN HEADER (NNO)	1.00	.45

LO SERIES STATED ODDS 1:9

Card	Player	MINT	NRMT
❑ 10	Wilt Chamberlain	.50	.23
	1956-58 College Star		
❑ 11	Wilt Chamberlain	.50	.23

Card	Player	MINT	NRMT
	1958-59 Harlem Globetrotter		
❑ 12	Wilt Chamberlain	.50	.23
	1960 NBA ROY		
❑ 13	Wilt Chamberlain	.50	.23
	1962 100-Point Game		
❑ 14	Wilt Chamberlain	.50	.23
	1960-68 Four-time NBA MVP		
❑ 15	Wilt Chamberlain	.50	.23
	1960-66 Seven consecutive scoring titles		
❑ 16	Wilt Chamberlain	.50	.23
	1971-72 30,000-Point Plateau		
❑ 17	Wilt Chamberlain	.50	.23
	1978 Basketball HOF		
❑ 18	Wilt Chamberlain	.50	.23
	Basketball Heroes CL		
❑ NNO	Basketball Heroes	1.00	.45
	(Header card)		

1992-93 Upper Deck 15000 Point Club

	MINT	NRMT
COMPLETE SET (20)	50.00	22.00

*SINGLES: 3X TO 8X BASE CARD HI
HI SERIES STATED ODDS 1:9 HOBBY

Card	Player	MINT	NRMT
❑ PC1	Dominique Wilkins	2.50	1.10
❑ PC2	Kevin McHale	2.50	1.10
❑ PC3	Robert Parish	1.25	.55
❑ PC4	Michael Jordan	30.00	13.50
❑ PC5	Isiah Thomas	2.50	1.10
❑ PC6	Mark Aguirre	.40	.18
❑ PC7	Kiki Vandeweghe	.40	.18
❑ PC8	James Worthy	2.50	1.10
❑ PC9	Rolando Blackman	.40	.18
❑ PC10	Moses Malone	2.50	1.10
❑ PC11	Charles Barkley	4.00	1.80
❑ PC12	Tom Chambers	.40	.18
❑ PC13	Clyde Drexler	2.50	1.10
❑ PC14	Terry Cummings	1.25	.55
❑ PC15	Eddie Johnson	.40	.18
❑ PC16	Karl Malone	4.00	1.80
❑ PC17	Bernard King	.40	.18
❑ PC18	Larry Nance	.40	.18
❑ PC19	Jeff Malone	.40	.18
❑ PC20	Hakeem Olajuwon	4.00	1.80

1992-93 Upper Deck Foreign Exchange

	MINT	NRMT
COMPLETE SET (10)	15.00	6.75

*SINGLES: 5X TO 12X BASE CARD HI
ONE PER HI SERIES LOCKER PACK

	MINT	NRMT
❑ FE1 Manute Bol	.60	.25
❑ FE2 Vlade Divac	2.00	.90
❑ FE3 Patrick Ewing	4.00	1.80
❑ FE4 Sarunas Marciulionis	.60	.25
❑ FE5 Dikembe Mutombo	4.00	1.80
❑ FE6 Hakeem Olajuwon	6.00	2.70
❑ FE7 Drazen Petrovic	.60	.25
❑ FE8 Detlef Schrempf	2.00	.90
❑ FE9 Rik Smits	2.00	.90
❑ FE10 Dominique Wilkins	4.00	1.80

1992-93 Upper Deck Rookie Standouts

	MINT	NRMT
COMPLETE SET (20)	25.00	11.00

*SINGLES: 1X TO 2.5X BASE CARD HI
HI SERIES STATED ODDS 1:9 RET/JUM

	MINT	NRMT
❑ RS1 Adam Keefe	.15	.07
❑ RS2 Alonzo Mourning	4.00	1.80
❑ RS3 Sean Rooks	.15	.07
❑ RS4 LaPhonso Ellis	.75	.35
❑ RS5 Latrell Sprewell	6.00	2.70
❑ RS6 Robert Horry	.75	.35
❑ RS7 Malik Sealy	.40	.18
❑ RS8 Anthony Peeler	.40	.18
❑ RS9 Harold Miner	.40	.18
❑ RS10 Anthony Avent	.15	.07
❑ RS11 Todd Day	.40	.18
❑ RS12 Lee Mayberry	.15	.07
❑ RS13 Christian Laettner	1.50	.70
❑ RS14 Hubert Davis	.40	.18
❑ RS15 Shaquille O'Neal	15.00	6.75
❑ RS16 C. Weatherspoon	.75	.35
❑ RS17 Richard Dumas	.15	.07
❑ RS18 Walt Williams	.75	.35
❑ RS19 Lloyd Daniels	.15	.07
❑ RS20 Tom Gugliotta	2.50	1.10

1992-93 Upper Deck Team MVPs

	MINT	NRMT
COMPLETE SET (28)	60.00	27.00

*SINGLES: 2.5X TO 6X BASE CARD HI
ONE PER LO SERIES JUMBO PACK

	MINT	NRMT
❑ TM1 Michael Jordan CL	25.00	11.00
❑ TM2 Dominique Wilkins	2.00	.90
❑ TM3 Reggie Lewis	1.00	.45
❑ TM4 Kendall Gill	1.00	.45
❑ TM5 Michael Jordan	25.00	11.00
❑ TM6 Brad Daugherty	.30	.14
❑ TM7 Derek Harper	1.00	.45
❑ TM8 Dikembe Mutombo	2.00	.90
❑ TM9 Isiah Thomas	2.00	.90
❑ TM10 Chris Mullin	2.00	.90
❑ TM11 Hakeem Olajuwon	3.00	1.35
❑ TM12 Reggie Miller	2.00	.90
❑ TM13 Ron Harper	1.00	.45
❑ TM14 James Worthy	2.00	.90
❑ TM15 Rony Seikaly	.30	.14
❑ TM16 Alvin Robertson	.30	.14
❑ TM17 Pooh Richardson	.30	.14
❑ TM18 Derrick Coleman	1.00	.45
❑ TM19 Patrick Ewing	2.00	.90
❑ TM20 Scott Skiles	.30	.14
❑ TM21 Hersey Hawkins	1.00	.45
❑ TM22 Kevin Johnson	2.00	.90
❑ TM23 Clyde Drexler	2.00	.90
❑ TM24 Mitch Richmond	2.00	.90
❑ TM25 David Robinson	3.00	1.35
❑ TM26 Ricky Pierce	.30	.14
❑ TM27 John Stockton	2.00	.90
❑ TM28 Pervis Ellison	.30	.14

1992-93 Upper Deck Jerry West Selects

	MINT	NRMT
COMPLETE SET (20)	80.00	36.00

*SINGLES: 2.5X TO 6X BASE CARD HI
LO SERIES STATED ODDS 1:9 HOBBY

	MINT	NRMT
❑ JW1 Michael Jordan Best Shooter	25.00	11.00
❑ JW2 Dennis Rodman Best Rebounder	4.00	1.80
❑ JW3 David Robinson Best Shot Blocker	3.00	1.35
❑ JW4 Michael Jordan Best Defender	25.00	11.00
❑ JW5 Magic Johnson Best Point Guard	12.00	5.50
❑ JW6 Detlef Schrempf Best Sixth Man	1.00	.45
❑ JW7 Magic Johnson Most Inspirational Player	12.00	5.50
❑ JW8 Michael Jordan Best All-Around Player	25.00	11.00
❑ JW9 Michael Jordan Best Clutch Player	25.00	11.00
❑ JW10 Magic Johnson Best Court Leader	12.00	5.50
❑ JW11 Glen Rice Best Shooter	2.00	.90
❑ JW12 Dikembe Mutombo Best Rebounder	2.00	.90
❑ JW13 Dikembe Mutombo Best Shot Blocker	2.00	.90
❑ JW14 Stacey Augmon Best Defender	1.00	.45
❑ JW15 Tim Hardaway Best Point Guard	2.50	1.10
❑ JW16 Shawn Kemp Best Sixth Man	4.00	1.80
❑ JW17 Danny Manning Most Inspirational Player	1.00	.45
❑ JW18 Larry Johnson Best All-Around Player	2.50	1.10
❑ JW19 Reggie Lewis Best Clutch Player	1.00	.45
❑ JW20 Tim Hardaway Best Court Leader	2.50	1.10

1993-94 Upper Deck

	MINT	NRMT
COMPLETE SET (510)	30.00	13.50
COMPLETE SERIES 1 (255)	15.00	6.75
COMPLETE SERIES 2 (255)	15.00	6.75
COMMON CARD (1-510)	.05	.02
SEMISTARS	.15	.07
UNLISTED STARS	.30	.14

SUBSET CARDS HALF VALUE OF BASE CARDS
SP3: SER.1 STATED ODDS 1:72
SP4: SER.2 STATED ODDS 1:72

	MINT	NRMT
❑ 1 Muggsy Bogues	.15	.07
❑ 2 Kenny Anderson	.15	.07
❑ 3 Dell Curry	.05	.02
❑ 4 Charles Smith	.05	.02
❑ 5 Chuck Person	.05	.02
❑ 6 Chucky Brown	.05	.02
❑ 7 Kevin Johnson	.15	.07
❑ 8 Winston Garland	.05	.02
❑ 9 John Salley	.05	.02
❑ 10 Dale Ellis	.05	.02
❑ 11 Otis Thorpe	.15	.07
❑ 12 John Stockton	.30	.14
❑ 13 Kendall Gill	.15	.07
❑ 14 Randy White	.05	.02
❑ 15 Mark Jackson	.15	.07
❑ 16 Vlade Divac	.15	.07

❑ 17 Scott Skiles .05 .02
❑ 18 Xavier McDaniel .05 .02
❑ 19 Jeff Hornacek .15 .07
❑ 20 Stanley Roberts .05 .02
❑ 21 Harold Miner .05 .02
❑ 22 Terrell Brandon .15 .07
❑ 23 Michael Jordan 4.00 1.80
❑ 24 Jim Jackson .15 .07
❑ 25 Keith Askins .05 .02
❑ 26 Corey Williams .05 .02
❑ 27 David Benoit .05 .02
❑ 28 Charles Oakley .15 .07
❑ 29 Michael Adams .05 .02
❑ 30 Clarence Weatherspoon .05 .02
❑ 31 Jon Koncak .05 .02
❑ 32 Gerald Wilkins .05 .02
❑ 33 Anthony Bowie .05 .02
❑ 34 Willie Burton .05 .02
❑ 35 Stacey Augmon .05 .02
❑ 36 Doc Rivers .15 .07
❑ 37 Luc Longley .15 .07
❑ 38 Dee Brown .05 .02
❑ 39 Litterial Green .05 .02
❑ 40 Dan Majerle .15 .07
❑ 41 Doug West .05 .02
❑ 42 Joe Dumars .30 .14
❑ 43 Dennis Scott .05 .02
❑ 44 Mahmoud Abdul-Rauf .05 .02
❑ 45 Mark Eaton .05 .02
❑ 46 Danny Ferry .05 .02
❑ 47 Kenny Smith .05 .02
❑ 48 Ron Harper .15 .07
❑ 49 Adam Keefe .05 .02
❑ 50 David Robinson .50 .23
❑ 51 John Starks .15 .07
❑ 52 Jeff Malone .05 .02
❑ 53 Vern Fleming .05 .02
❑ 54 Olden Polynice .05 .02
❑ 55 Dikembe Mutombo .15 .07
❑ 56 Chris Morris .05 .02
❑ 57 Paul Graham .05 .02
❑ 58 Richard Dumas .05 .02
❑ 59 J.R. Reid .05 .02
❑ 60 Brad Daugherty .05 .02
❑ 61 Blue Edwards .05 .02
❑ 62 Mark Macon .05 .02
❑ 63 Latrell Sprewell .75 .35
❑ 64 Mitch Richmond .30 .14
❑ 65 David Wingate .05 .02
❑ 66 LaSalle Thompson .05 .02
❑ 67 Sedale Threatt .05 .02
❑ 68 Larry Krystkowiak .05 .02
❑ 69 John Paxson .05 .02
❑ 70 Frank Brickowski .05 .02
❑ 71 Duane Causwell .05 .02
❑ 72 Fred Roberts .05 .02
❑ 73 Rod Strickland .15 .07
❑ 74 Willie Anderson .05 .02
❑ 75 Thurl Bailey .05 .02
❑ 76 Ricky Pierce .05 .02
❑ 77 Todd Day .05 .02
❑ 78 Hot Rod Williams .05 .02
❑ 79 Danny Ainge .15 .07
❑ 80 Mark West .05 .02
❑ 81 Marcus Liberty .05 .02
❑ 82 Keith Jennings .05 .02
❑ 83 Derrick Coleman .15 .07
❑ 84 Larry Stewart .05 .02
❑ 85 Tracy Murray .05 .02
❑ 86 Robert Horry .15 .07
❑ 87 Derek Harper .15 .07
❑ 88 Scott Hastings .05 .02
❑ 89 Sam Perkins .15 .07
❑ 90 Clyde Drexler .30 .14
❑ 91 Brent Price .05 .02
❑ 92 Chris Mullin .30 .14
❑ 93 Rafael Addison .05 .02
❑ 94 Tyrone Corbin .05 .02
❑ 95 Sarunas Marciulionis .05 .02
❑ 96 Antoine Carr .05 .02
❑ 97 Tony Bennett .05 .02
❑ 98 Sam Mitchell .05 .02
❑ 99 Lionel Simmons .05 .02
❑ 100 Tim Perry .05 .02
❑ 101 Horace Grant .15 .07
❑ 102 Tom Hammonds .05 .02
❑ 103 Walter Bond .05 .02
❑ 104 Detlef Schrempf .15 .07
❑ 105 Terry Porter .05 .02
❑ 106 Dan Schayes .05 .02
❑ 107 Rumeal Robinson .05 .02
❑ 108 Gerald Glass .05 .02
❑ 109 Mike Gminski .05 .02
❑ 110 Terry Mills .05 .02
❑ 111 Loy Vaught .05 .02
❑ 112 Jim Les .05 .02
❑ 113 Byron Houston .05 .02
❑ 114 Randy Brown .05 .02
❑ 115 Anthony Avent .05 .02
❑ 116 Donald Hodge .05 .02
❑ 117 Kevin Willis .05 .02
❑ 118 Robert Pack .05 .02
❑ 119 Dale Davis .05 .02
❑ 120 Grant Long .05 .02
❑ 121 Anthony Bonner .05 .02
❑ 122 Chris Smith .05 .02
❑ 123 Elden Campbell .05 .02
❑ 124 Clifford Robinson .15 .07
❑ 125 Sherman Douglas .05 .02
❑ 126 Alvin Robertson .05 .02
❑ 127 Rolando Blackman .05 .02
❑ 128 Malik Sealy .05 .02
❑ 129 Ed Pinckney .05 .02
❑ 130 Anthony Peeler .05 .02
❑ 131 Scott Brooks .05 .02
❑ 132 Rik Smits .15 .07
❑ 133 Derrick McKey .05 .02
❑ 134 Alaa Abdelnaby .05 .02
❑ 135 Rex Chapman .05 .02
❑ 136 Tony Campbell .05 .02
❑ 137 John Williams .05 .02
❑ 138 Vincent Askew .05 .02
❑ 139 LaBradford Smith .05 .02
❑ 140 Vinny Del Negro .05 .02
❑ 141 Darrell Walker .05 .02
❑ 142 James Worthy .30 .14
❑ 143 Jeff Turner .05 .02
❑ 144 Duane Ferrell .05 .02
❑ 145 Larry Smith .05 .02
❑ 146 Eddie Johnson .05 .02
❑ 147 Chris Gatling .05 .02
❑ 148 Buck Williams .05 .02
❑ 149 Donald Royal .05 .02
❑ 150 Dino Radja RC .05 .02
❑ 151 Johnny Dawkins .05 .02
❑ 152 Tim Legler RC .05 .02
❑ 153 Bill Laimbeer .05 .02
❑ 154 Glen Rice .15 .07
❑ 155 Bill Cartwright .05 .02
❑ 156 Luther Wright RC .05 .02
❑ 157 Rex Walters RC .05 .02
❑ 158 Doug Edwards RC .05 .02
❑ 159 George Lynch RC .05 .02
❑ 160 Chris Mills RC .30 .14
❑ 161 Sam Cassell RC .75 .35
❑ 162 Nick Van Exel RC .75 .35
❑ 163 Shawn Bradley RC .30 .14
❑ 164 Calbert Cheaney RC .15 .07
❑ 165 Corie Blount RC .05 .02
❑ 166 Michael Jordan SL 2.00 .90
Scoring
❑ 167 Dennis Rodman SL .30 .14
Rebounds
❑ 168 John Stockton SL .15 .07
Assists
❑ 169 B.J. Armstrong SL .05 .02
3-pt. field goals
❑ 170 Hakeem Olajuwon SL .30 .14
Blocked shots
❑ 171 Michael Jordan SL 2.00 .90
Steals
❑ 172 Cedric Ceballos SL .05 .02
Field goal percentage
❑ 173 Mark Price SL .05 .02
Free-throw percentage
❑ 174 Charles Barkley SL .30 .14
MVP
❑ 175 Clifford Robinson SL .05 .02
Sixth man
❑ 176 Hakeem Olajuwon SL .30 .14
Defensive player
❑ 177 Shaquille O'Neal SL .60 .25
ROY
❑ 178 Reggie Miller .15 .07
Charles Oakley PO
❑ 179 Rick Fox .05 .02
Kenny Gattison PO
❑ 180 Michael Jordan 1.00 .45
Stackey Augmon PO
❑ 181 Brad Daugherty PO .05 .02
❑ 182 Oliver Miller .05 .02
Byron Scott PO
❑ 183 David Robinson .30 .14
Sean Elliott PO
❑ 184 Kenny Smith .05 .02
Mark Jackson PO
❑ 185 Eddie Johnson PO .05 .02
❑ 186 Anthony Mason .30 .14
Patrick Ewing
A Mourning PO
❑ 187 Michael Jordan 1.00 .45
Gerald Wilkins PO
❑ 188 Oliver Miller PO .05 .02
❑ 189 Sam Perkins .30 .14
Hakeem Olajuwon PO
❑ 190 Bill Cartwright PO .05 .02
❑ 191 Kevin Johnson PO .15 .07
❑ 192 Dan Majerle PO .05 .02
❑ 193 Michael Jordan PO 2.00 .90
❑ 194 Larry Johnson .05 .02
Muggsy Bogues PO
❑ 195 Reggie Miller PO .15 .07
❑ 196 John Starks .30 .14
Scottie Pippen PO
❑ 197 Charles Barkley PO .30 .14
❑ 198 Michael Jordan FIN 2.00 .90
❑ 199 Scottie Pippen FIN .50 .23
❑ 200 Kevin Johnson FIN .05 .02
❑ 201 Michael Jordan FIN 2.00 .90
❑ 202 Richard Dumas FIN .05 .02
❑ 203 Horace Grant FIN .05 .02
❑ 204 Michael Jordan FIN 2.00 .90
1993 Finals MVP
❑ 205 Scottie Pippen FIN .30 .14
Charles Barkley
❑ 206 John Paxson FIN .05 .02
Hits 3 for title
❑ 207 B.J. Armstrong FIN .05 .02
Finals records
❑ 208 1992-93 Bulls FIN .05 .02
Road to 1993 Finals
❑ 209 1992-93 Suns FIN .05 .02
Road to 1993 Finals
❑ 210 Atlanta Hawks Sked .05 .02
Kevin Willis
❑ 211 Boston Celtics Sked .05 .02
Brian Shaw
❑ 212 Charlotte Hornets Sked .05 .02
❑ 213 Chicago Bulls Sked 1.00 .45
Michael Jordan
❑ 214 Cleveland Cavaliers .05 .02
Sked (Mark Price)
❑ 215 Dallas Mavericks Sked .05 .02
(Jim Jackson
Sean Rooks)
❑ 216 Denver Nuggets Sked .15 .07
Dikembe Mutombo
❑ 217 Detroit Pistons Sked .15 .07
Isiah Thomas
Bill Laimbeer
Terry Mills
❑ 218 Golden State Warriors .05 .02
Sked
❑ 219 Houston Rockets Sked .30 .14
(Hakeem Olajuwon)
❑ 220 Indiana Pacers Sked .05 .02
Rik Smits
Detlef Schrempf
❑ 221 L.A. Clippers Sked .05 .02
Ron Harper
Danny Manning
Mark Jackson
❑ 222 L.A. Lakers Sked .05 .02
❑ 223 Miami Heat Sked .15 .07
Steve Smith
Harold Miner
Rony Seikaly
❑ 224 Milwaukee Bucks Sked .05 .02

❑ 225	Minnesota Timberwolves Sked	.05	.02
❑ 226	New Jersey Nets Sked .. Kenny Anderson	.05	.02
❑ 227	New York Knicks Sked .. Rolando Blackmon	.05	.02
❑ 228	Orlando Magic Sked ...... (Shaquille O'Neal)	.40	.18
❑ 229	Philadelphia 76ers.......... Sked Hersey Hawkins Jeff Hornacek	.05	.02
❑ 230	Phoenix Suns Sked........ (Charles Barkley)	.30	.14
❑ 231	Portland Trail Blazers .... Sked Buck Williams Jerome Kersey Terry Porter)	.05	.02
❑ 232	Sacramento Kings Sked	.05	.02
❑ 233	San Antonio Spurs Sked David Robinson Avery Johnson Sean Elliott	.30	.14
❑ 234	Seattle Supersonics Sked Gary Payton Shawn Kemp	.15	.07
❑ 235	Utah Jazz Sked..............	.05	.02
❑ 236	Washington Bullets .... Sked Tom Gugliotta Michael Adams	.15	.07
❑ 237	Michael Jordan SM	2.00	.90
❑ 238	Clyde Drexler SM	.15	.07
❑ 239	Tim Hardaway SM..........	.15	.07
❑ 240	Dominique Wilkins SM ..	.15	.07
❑ 241	Brad Daugherty SM........	.05	.02
❑ 242	Chris Mullin SM............	.15	.07
❑ 243	Kenny Anderson SM	.05	.02
❑ 244	Patrick Ewing SM	.15	.07
❑ 245	Isiah Thomas SM	.15	.07
❑ 246	Dikembe Mutombo SM ..	.05	.02
❑ 247	Danny Manning SM.........	.05	.02
❑ 248	David Robinson SM	.30	.14
❑ 249	Karl Malone SM..............	.30	.14
❑ 250	James Worthy SM..........	.15	.07
❑ 251	Shawn Kemp SM	.30	.14
❑ 252	Checklist 1-64	.05	.02
❑ 253	Checklist 65-128	.05	.02
❑ 254	Checklist 129-192	.05	.02
❑ 255	Checklist 193-255	.05	.02
❑ 256	Patrick Ewing	.30	.14
❑ 257	B.J. Armstrong	.05	.02
❑ 258	Oliver Miller	.05	.02
❑ 259	Jud Buechler	.05	.02
❑ 260	Pooh Richardson............	.05	.02
❑ 261	Victor Alexander	.05	.02
❑ 262	Kevin Gamble	.05	.02
❑ 263	Doug Smith	.05	.02
❑ 264	Isiah Thomas..................	.30	.14
❑ 265	Doug Christie	.05	.02
❑ 266	Mark Bryant....................	.05	.02
❑ 267	Lloyd Daniels..................	.05	.02
❑ 268	Micheal Williams	.05	.02
❑ 269	Nick Anderson................	.15	.07
❑ 270	Tom Gugliotta	.30	.14
❑ 271	Kenny Gattison	.05	.02
❑ 272	Vernon Maxwell..............	.05	.02
❑ 273	Terry Cummings	.05	.02
❑ 274	Karl Malone	.50	.23
❑ 275	Rick Fox	.05	.02
❑ 276	Matt Bullard....................	.05	.02
❑ 277	Johnny Newman	.05	.02
❑ 278	Mark Price	.05	.02
❑ 279	Mookie Blaylock	.15	.07
❑ 280	Charles Barkley..............	.50	.23
❑ 281	Larry Nance....................	.05	.02
❑ 282	Walt Williams..................	.05	.02
❑ 283	Brian Shaw	.05	.02
❑ 284	Robert Parish	.15	.07
❑ 285	Pervis Ellison..................	.05	.02
❑ 286	Spud Webb	.15	.07
❑ 287	Hakeem Olajuwon..........	.50	.23
❑ 288	Jerome Kersey	.05	.02
❑ 289	Carl Herrera	.05	.02
❑ 290	Dominique Wilkins..........	.30	.14
❑ 291	Billy Owens	.05	.02
❑ 292	Greg Anthony	.05	.02
❑ 293	Nate McMillan	.05	.02
❑ 294	Christian Laettner	.15	.07
❑ 295	Gary Payton	.50	.23
❑ 296	Steve Smith....................	.30	.14
❑ 297	Anthony Mason	.15	.07
❑ 298	Sean Rooks....................	.05	.02
❑ 299	Toni Kukoc RC	1.25	.55
❑ 300	Shaquille O'Neal	1.50	.70
❑ 301	Jay Humphries	.05	.02
❑ 302	Sleepy Floyd	.05	.02
❑ 303	Bimbo Coles	.05	.02
❑ 304	John Battle	.05	.02
❑ 305	Shawn Kemp..................	.50	.23
❑ 306	Scott Williams	.05	.02
❑ 307	Wayman Tisdale	.05	.02
❑ 308	Rony Seikaly	.05	.02
❑ 309	Reggie Miller	.30	.14
❑ 310	Scottie Pippen	1.00	.45
❑ 311	Chris Webber RC	3.00	1.35
❑ 312	Trevor Wilson	.05	.02
❑ 313	Derek Strong RC............	.05	.02
❑ 314	Bobby Hurley RC	.15	.07
❑ 315	Herb Williams	.05	.02
❑ 316	Rex Walters....................	.05	.02
❑ 317	Doug Edwards................	.05	.02
❑ 318	Ken Williams	.05	.02
❑ 319	Jon Barry........................	.05	.02
❑ 320	Joe Courtney RC............	.05	.02
❑ 321	Ervin Johnson RC..........	.15	.07
❑ 322	Sam Cassell	.30	.14
❑ 323	Tim Hardaway	.30	.14
❑ 324	Ed Stokes	.05	.02
❑ 325	Steve Kerr......................	.15	.07
❑ 326	Doug Overton	.05	.02
❑ 327	Reggie Williams	.05	.02
❑ 328	Avery Johnson	.05	.02
❑ 329	Stacey King....................	.05	.02
❑ 330	Vin Baker RC	.75	.35
❑ 331	Greg Kite........................	.05	.02
❑ 332	Michael Cage	.05	.02
❑ 333	Alonzo Mourning	.50	.23
❑ 334	Acie Earl RC	.05	.02
❑ 335	Terry Dehere RC............	.05	.02
❑ 336	Negele Knight	.05	.02
❑ 337	Gerald Madkins RC........	.05	.02
❑ 338	Lindsey Hunter RC	.30	.14
❑ 339	Luther Wright..................	.05	.02
❑ 340	Mike Peplowski RC........	.05	.02
❑ 341	Dino Radja	.05	.02
❑ 342	Danny Manning..............	.15	.07
❑ 343	Chris Mills	.30	.14
❑ 344	Kevin Lynch....................	.05	.02
❑ 345	Shawn Bradley	.30	.14
❑ 346	Evers Burns RC	.05	.02
❑ 347	Rodney Rogers RC........	.30	.14
❑ 348	Cedric Ceballos..............	.15	.07
❑ 349	Warren Kidd RC	.05	.02
❑ 350	Darnell Mee RC..............	.05	.02
❑ 351	Matt Geiger	.05	.02
❑ 352	Jamal Mashburn RC	.60	.25
❑ 353	Antonio Davis RC	.15	.07
❑ 354	Calbert Cheaney	.15	.07
❑ 355	George Lynch	.05	.02
❑ 356	Derrick McKey................	.05	.02
❑ 357	Jerry Reynolds	.05	.02
❑ 358	Don MacLean	.05	.02
❑ 359	Scott Haskin RC	.05	.02
❑ 360	Malcolm Mackey RC	.05	.02
❑ 361	Isaiah Rider RC..............	.60	.25
❑ 362	Detlef Schrempf	.15	.07
❑ 363	Josh Grant RC	.05	.02
❑ 364	Richard Petruska............	.05	.02
❑ 365	Larry Johnson	.30	.14
❑ 366	Felton Spencer RC	.05	.02
❑ 367	Ken Norman	.05	.02
❑ 368	Anthony Cook	.05	.02
❑ 369	James Robinson RC	.05	.02
❑ 370	Kevin Duckworth	.05	.02
❑ 371	Chris Whitney RC	.05	.02
❑ 372	Moses Malone	.30	.14
❑ 373	Nick Van Exel	.40	.18
❑ 374	Scott Burrell RC	.30	.14
❑ 375	Harvey Grant..................	.05	.02
❑ 376	Benoit Benjamin	.05	.02
❑ 377	Henry James..................	.05	.02
❑ 378	Craig Ehlo	.05	.02
❑ 379	Ennis Whatley	.05	.02
❑ 380	Sean Green....................	.05	.02
❑ 381	Eric Murdock..................	.05	.02
❑ 382	Anfernee Hardaway RC	3.00	1.35
❑ 383	Gheorghe Muresan RC ..	.30	.14
❑ 384	Kendall Gill	.15	.07
❑ 385	David Wood....................	.05	.02
❑ 386	Mario Elie	.05	.02
❑ 387	Chris Corchiani	.05	.02
❑ 388	Greg Graham RC	.05	.02
❑ 389	Hersey Hawkins	.15	.07
❑ 390	Mark Aguirre	.05	.02
❑ 391	LaPhonso Ellis	.05	.02
❑ 392	Anthony Bonner	.05	.02
❑ 393	Lucious Harris RC..........	.05	.02
❑ 394	Andrew Lang..................	.05	.02
❑ 395	Chris Dudley	.05	.02
❑ 396	Dennis Rodman	.60	.25
❑ 397	Larry Krystkowiak	.05	.02
❑ 398	A.C. Green	.15	.07
❑ 399	Eddie Johnson	.05	.02
❑ 400	Kevin Edwards	.05	.02
❑ 401	Tyrone Hill......................	.05	.02
❑ 402	Greg Anderson	.05	.02
❑ 403	P.J. Brown RC................	.30	.14
❑ 404	Dana Barros	.05	.02
❑ 405	Allan Houston RC	1.25	.55
❑ 406	Mike Brown	.05	.02
❑ 407	Lee Mayberry	.05	.02
❑ 408	Fat Lever........................	.05	.02
❑ 409	Tony Smith	.05	.02
❑ 410	Tom Chambers	.05	.02
❑ 411	Manute Bol	.05	.02
❑ 412	Joe Kleine	.05	.02
❑ 413	Bryant Stith	.05	.02
❑ 414	Eric Riley RC..................	.05	.02
❑ 415	Jo Jo English RC............	.05	.02
❑ 416	Sean Elliott	.15	.07
❑ 417	Sam Bowie	.05	.02
❑ 418	Armon Gilliam	.05	.02
❑ 419	Brian Williams	.05	.02
❑ 420	Popeye Jones RC	.05	.02
❑ 421	Dennis Rodman EB........	.30	.14
❑ 422	Karl Malone EB	.30	.14
❑ 423	Tom Gugliotta EB	.15	.07
❑ 424	Kevin Willis EB	.05	.02
❑ 425	Hakeem Olajuwon EB	.30	.14
❑ 426	Charles Oakley EB	.05	.02
❑ 427	C. Weatherspoon EB	.05	.02
❑ 428	Derrick Coleman EB	.05	.02
❑ 429	Buck Williams EB	.05	.02
❑ 430	Christian Laettner EB	.05	.02
❑ 431	Dikembe Mutombo EB ..	.05	.02
❑ 432	Rony Seikaly EB	.05	.02
❑ 433	Brad Daugherty EB	.05	.02
❑ 434	Horace Grant EB............	.05	.02
❑ 435	Larry Johnson EB	.15	.07
❑ 436	Dee Brown BT................	.05	.02
❑ 437	Muggsy Bogues BT........	.05	.02
❑ 438	Michael Jordan BT	2.00	.90
❑ 439	Tim Hardaway BT	.15	.07
❑ 440	Micheal Williams BT	.05	.02
❑ 441	Gary Payton BT..............	.30	.14
❑ 442	Mookie Blaylock BT........	.05	.02
❑ 443	Doc Rivers BT................	.05	.02
❑ 444	Kenny Smith BT	.05	.02
❑ 445	John Stockton BT	.15	.07
❑ 446	Alvin Robertson BT	.05	.02
❑ 447	Mark Jackson BT	.05	.02
❑ 448	Kenny Anderson BT	.05	.02
❑ 449	Scottie Pippen BT	.50	.23
❑ 450	Isiah Thomas BT............	.15	.07
❑ 451	Mark Price BT	.05	.02
❑ 452	Latrell Sprewell BT	.30	.14
❑ 453	Sedale Threatt BT..........	.05	.02
❑ 454	Nick Anderson BT..........	.05	.02
❑ 455	Rod Strickland BT..........	.05	.02
❑ 456	Oliver Miller GI	.05	.02
❑ 457	James Worthy.............. Vlade Divac GI	.05	.02
❑ 458	Robert Horry GI..............	.05	.02
❑ 459	Rockets Shoot-Around GI	.05	.02
❑ 460	Sean Rooks.................... Jim Jackson	.05	.02

Tim Legler GI
❑ 461 Mitch Richmond GI .15 .07
❑ 462 Chris Morris GI .05 .02
❑ 463 Mark Jackson .05 .02
Gary Grant GI
❑ 464 David Robinson GI .30 .14
❑ 465 Danny Ainge GI .05 .02
❑ 466 Michael Jordan SL 2.00 .90
❑ 467 Dominique Wilkins SL .15 .07
❑ 468 Alonzo Mourning SL .30 .14
❑ 469 Shaquille O'Neal SL .60 .25
❑ 470 Tim Hardaway SL .15 .07
❑ 471 Patrick Ewing SL .15 .07
❑ 472 Kevin Johnson SL .05 .02
❑ 473 Clyde Drexler SL .15 .07
❑ 474 David Robinson SL .30 .14
❑ 475 Shawn Kemp SL .30 .14
❑ 476 Dee Brown SL .05 .02
❑ 477 Jim Jackson SL .05 .02
❑ 478 John Stockton SL .15 .07
❑ 479 Robert Horry SL .05 .02
❑ 480 Glen Rice SL .05 .02
❑ 481 Micheal Williams SIS .05 .02
❑ 482 George Lynch .05 .02
Terry Dehere CL
❑ 483 Chris Webber TP .75 .35
❑ 484 Anfernee Hardaway TP 1.50 .70
❑ 485 Shawn Bradley TP .15 .07
❑ 486 Jamal Mashburn TP .30 .14
❑ 487 Calbert Cheaney TP .05 .02
❑ 488 Isaiah Rider TP .30 .14
❑ 489 Bobby Hurley TP .05 .02
❑ 490 Vin Baker TP .30 .14
❑ 491 Rodney Rogers TP .15 .07
❑ 492 Lindsey Hunter TP .15 .07
❑ 493 Allan Houston TP .30 .14
❑ 494 Terry Dehere TP .05 .02
❑ 495 George Lynch TP .05 .02
❑ 496 Toni Kukoc TP .30 .14
❑ 497 Nick Van Exel TP .30 .14
❑ 498 Charles Barkley MO .30 .14
❑ 499 A.C. Green MO .05 .02
❑ 500 Dan Majerle MO .05 .02
❑ 501 Jerrod Mustaf MO .05 .02
❑ 502 Kevin Johnson MO .05 .02
❑ 503 Negele Knight MO .05 .02
❑ 504 Danny Ainge MO .05 .02
❑ 505 Oliver Miller MO .05 .02
❑ 506 Joe Courtney MO .05 .02
❑ 507 Checklist .05 .02
❑ 508 Checklist .05 .02
❑ 509 Checklist .05 .02
❑ 510 Checklist .05 .02
❑ SP3 Michael Jordan 8.00 3.60
Wilt Chamberlain
❑ SP4 Chicago Bulls' Third 8.00 3.60
NBA Championship

1993-94 Upper Deck All-NBA

	MINT	NRMT
COMPLETE SET (15)	12.00	5.50

*SINGLES: .75X TO 2X BASE CARD HI
ONE PER SER.1 RETAIL/GREEN JUMBO PACK

❑ AN1 Charles Barkley 1.00 .45
❑ AN2 Karl Malone 1.00 .45
❑ AN3 Hakeem Olajuwon 1.00 .45
❑ AN4 Michael Jordan 8.00 3.60
❑ AN5 Mark Price .10 .05
❑ AN6 Dominique Wilkins .60 .25
❑ AN7 Larry Johnson .60 .25
❑ AN8 Patrick Ewing .60 .25
❑ AN9 John Stockton .60 .25
❑ AN10 Joe Dumars .60 .25
❑ AN11 Scottie Pippen 2.00 .90
❑ AN12 Derrick Coleman .30 .14
❑ AN13 David Robinson 1.00 .45
❑ AN14 Tim Hardaway .60 .25
❑ AN15 Michael Jordan CL 8.00 3.60

1993-94 Upper Deck All-Rookies

	MINT	NRMT
COMPLETE SET (10)	15.00	6.75

*SINGLES: 2.5X TO 6X BASE CARD HI
SER.1 STATED ODDS 1:30 RETAIL

❑ AR1 Shaquille O'Neal 10.00 4.50
❑ AR2 Alonzo Mourning 3.00 1.35
❑ AR3 Christian Laettner 1.00 .45
❑ AR4 Tom Gugliotta 2.00 .90
❑ AR5 LaPhonso Ellis .30 .14
❑ AR6 Walt Williams .30 .14
❑ AR7 Robert Horry 1.00 .45
❑ AR8 Latrell Sprewell 5.00 2.20
❑ AR9 Clarence Weatherspoon .30 .14
❑ AR10 Richard Dumas .30 .14

1993-94 Upper Deck Flight Team

	MINT	NRMT
COMPLETE SET (20)	90.00	40.00
COMMON CARD (FT1-FT20)	1.50	.70
SEMISTARS	3.00	1.35
UNLISTED STARS	6.00	2.70

SER.1 STATED ODDS 1:30 HOBBY

❑ FT1 Stacey Augmon 1.50 .70
❑ FT2 Charles Barkley 10.00 4.50
❑ FT3 David Benoit 1.50 .70
❑ FT4 Dee Brown 1.50 .70
❑ FT5 Cedric Ceballos 3.00 1.35
❑ FT6 Derrick Coleman 3.00 1.35
❑ FT7 Clyde Drexler 6.00 2.70
❑ FT8 Sean Elliott 3.00 1.35
❑ FT9 LaPhonso Ellis 1.50 .70
❑ FT10 Kendall Gill 3.00 1.35
❑ FT11 Larry Johnson 6.00 2.70
❑ FT12 Shawn Kemp 10.00 4.50
❑ FT13 Karl Malone 10.00 4.50
❑ FT14 Harold Miner 1.50 .70
❑ FT15 Alonzo Mourning 10.00 4.50
❑ FT16 Shaquille O'Neal 30.00 13.50
❑ FT17 Scottie Pippen 20.00 9.00
❑ FT18 Clarence Weatherspoon 1.50 .70
❑ FT19 Spud Webb 3.00 1.35
❑ FT20 Dominique Wilkins 6.00 2.70

1993-94 Upper Deck Future Heroes

	MINT	NRMT
COMPLETE SET (10)	20.00	9.00

*SINGLES: 3X TO 8X BASE CARD HI
ONE PER SER.1 LOCKER PACK

❑ 28 Derrick Coleman 1.25 .55
❑ 29 LaPhonso Ellis .40 .18
❑ 30 Jim Jackson 1.25 .55
❑ 31 Larry Johnson 2.50 1.10
❑ 32 Shawn Kemp 4.00 1.80
❑ 33 Christian Laettner 1.25 .55
❑ 34 Alonzo Mourning 4.00 1.80
❑ 35 Shaquille O'Neal 12.00 5.50
❑ 36 Walt Williams .40 .18
❑ NNO LaPhonso Ellis CL 1.25 .55
Christian Laettner

1993-94 Upper Deck Locker Talk

	MINT	NRMT
COMPLETE SET (15)	70.00	32.00

*SINGLES: 4X TO 10X BASE CARD HI
ONE PER SER.2 LOCKER PACK
CONDITION SENSITIVE SET

❑ LT1 Michael Jordan 40.00 18.00
❑ LT2 Stacey Augmon .50 .23
❑ LT3 Shaquille O'Neal 15.00 6.75
❑ LT4 Alonzo Mourning 5.00 2.20
❑ LT5 Harold Miner .50 .23
❑ LT6 Clarence Weatherspoon .50 .23

❑ LT7 Derrick Coleman	1.50	.70
❑ LT8 Charles Barkley	5.00	2.20
❑ LT9 David Robinson	5.00	2.20
❑ LT10 Chuck Person	.50	.23
❑ LT11 Karl Malone	5.00	2.20
❑ LT12 Muggsy Bogues	1.50	.70
❑ LT13 Latrell Sprewell	8.00	3.60
❑ LT14 John Starks	1.50	.70
❑ LT15 Jim Jackson	1.50	.70

1993-94 Upper Deck Mr. June

	MINT	NRMT
COMPLETE SET (10)	125.00	55.00
COMMON JORDAN (1-10)	15.00	6.75
SER.2 STATED ODDS 1:30 HOBBY		

❑ MJ1 Michael Jordan Jordan's a Steal	15.00	6.75
❑ MJ2 Michael Jordan M.J.'s High Five	15.00	6.75
❑ MJ3 Michael Jordan 1991 NBA Finals MVP	15.00	6.75
❑ MJ4 Michael Jordan 35 Points in One Half	15.00	6.75
❑ MJ5 Michael Jordan Three-Points King	15.00	6.75
❑ MJ6 Michael Jordan Back-To-Back Finals MVP	15.00	6.75
❑ MJ7 Michael Jordan 55-Point Game	15.00	6.75
❑ MJ8 Michael Jordan Record Scoring Average	15.00	6.75
❑ MJ9 Michael Jordan Jordan's Three-Peat	15.00	6.75
❑ MJ10 Michael Jordan Checklist	15.00	6.75

1993-94 Upper Deck Rookie Exchange

	MINT	NRMT
COMPLETE SILVER SET (10)	8.00	3.60
*SINGLES: .4X TO 1X BASE CARD HI		
COMPLETE GOLD SET (10)	15.00	6.75
*GOLD CARDS: 1X TO 2X HI COLUMN		
ONE SET PER EXCHANGE CARD BY MAIL		
SIL.EXCH: SER.1 STATED ODDS 1:72		
GOLD EXCH: SER.1 STATED ODDS 1:288		

❑ RE1 Chris Webber	3.00	1.35
❑ RE2 Shawn Bradley	.30	.14
❑ RE3 Anfernee Hardaway	3.00	1.35
❑ RE4 Jamal Mashburn	.60	.25
❑ RE5 Isaiah Rider	.60	.25
❑ RE6 Calbert Cheaney	.15	.07
❑ RE7 Bobby Hurley	.15	.07
❑ RE8 Vin Baker	.75	.35
❑ RE9 Rodney Rogers	.30	.14
❑ RE10 Lindsey Hunter	.30	.14
❑ TC2 Redeemed Silver Trade	.25	.11
❑ TC2 Unred ed Silver Trade	.10	.05

1993-94 Upper Deck Rookie Standouts

	MINT	NRMT
COMPLETE SET (20)	40.00	18.00
*SINGLES: 1.5X TO 4X BASE CARD HI		
SER.2 STATED ODDS 1:30 RETAIL		
ONE PER SER.2 PURPLE JUMBO PACK		

❑ RS1 Chris Webber	12.00	5.50
❑ RS2 Bobby Hurley	.60	.25
❑ RS3 Isaiah Rider	2.50	1.10
❑ RS4 Terry Dehere	.20	.09
❑ RS5 Toni Kukoc	5.00	2.20
❑ RS6 Shawn Bradley	1.25	.55
❑ RS7 Allan Houston	5.00	2.20
❑ RS8 Chris Mills	1.25	.55
❑ RS9 Jamal Mashburn	2.50	1.10
❑ RS10 Acie Earl	.20	.09
❑ RS11 George Lynch	.20	.09
❑ RS12 Scott Burrell	1.25	.55
❑ RS13 Calbert Cheaney	.60	.25
❑ RS14 Lindsey Hunter	1.25	.55
❑ RS15 Nick Van Exel	3.00	1.35
❑ RS16 Rex Walters	.20	.09
❑ RS17 Anfernee Hardaway	12.00	5.50
❑ RS18 Sam Cassell	3.00	1.35
❑ RS19 Vin Baker	3.00	1.35
❑ RS20 Rodney Rogers	1.25	.55

1993-94 Upper Deck Team MVPs

	MINT	NRMT
COMPLETE SET (27)	12.00	5.50
*SINGLES: 1X TO 2.5X BASE CARD HI		
ONE PER SER.2 RETAIL/PURPLE JUM.PACK		

❑ TM1 Dominique Wilkins	.75	.35
❑ TM2 Robert Parish	.40	.18
❑ TM3 Larry Johnson	.75	.35
❑ TM4 Scottie Pippen	2.50	1.10
❑ TM5 Mark Price	.15	.07
❑ TM6 Jim Jackson	.40	.18
❑ TM7 Mahmoud Abdul-Rauf	.15	.07
❑ TM8 Joe Dumars	.75	.35
❑ TM9 Chris Mullin	.75	.35
❑ TM10 Hakeem Olajuwon	1.25	.55
❑ TM11 Reggie Miller	.75	.35
❑ TM12 Danny Manning	.40	.18
❑ TM13 James Worthy	.75	.35
❑ TM14 Glen Rice	.40	.18
❑ TM15 Blue Edwards	.15	.07
❑ TM16 Christian Laettner	.40	.18
❑ TM17 Derrick Coleman	.40	.18
❑ TM18 Patrick Ewing	.75	.35
❑ TM19 Shaquille O'Neal	4.00	1.80
❑ TM20 C. Weatherspoon	.15	.07
❑ TM21 Charles Barkley	1.25	.55
❑ TM22 Clyde Drexler	.75	.35
❑ TM23 Mitch Richmond	.75	.35
❑ TM24 David Robinson	1.25	.55
❑ TM25 Shawn Kemp	1.25	.55
❑ TM26 John Stockton	.75	.35
❑ TM27 Tom Gugliotta	.75	.35

1993-94 Upper Deck Triple Double

	MINT	NRMT
COMPLETE SET (10)	20.00	9.00
*SINGLES: 1.5X TO 4X BASE CARD HI		
SER.1 STATED ODDS 1:20		
ONE PER SER.1 GREEN JUMBO PACK		

❑ TD1 Charles Barkley	2.00	.90
❑ TD2 Michael Jordan	15.00	6.75
❑ TD3 Scottie Pippen	4.00	1.80
❑ TD4 Detlef Schrempf	.60	.25
❑ TD5 Mark Jackson	.60	.25
❑ TD6 Kenny Anderson	.60	.25
❑ TD7 Larry Johnson	1.25	.55
❑ TD8 Dikembe Mutombo	.60	.25
❑ TD9 Rumeal Robinson	.20	.09
❑ TD10 Micheal Williams	.20	.09

1994-95 Upper Deck

	MINT	NRMT
COMPLETE SET (360)	45.00	20.00
COMPLETE SERIES 1 (180)	25.00	11.00
COMPLETE SERIES 2 (180)	20.00	9.00
COMMON CARD (1-360)	.10	.05
SEMISTARS	.15	.07
UNLISTED STARS	.40	.18
SUBSET CARDS HALF VALUE OF BASE CARDS		

❑ 1 Chris Webber ART	.50	.23
❑ 2 Anfernee Hardaway ART	.75	.35
❑ 3 Vin Baker ART	.15	.07
❑ 4 Jamal Mashburn ART	.15	.07
❑ 5 Isaiah Rider ART	.10	.05
❑ 6 Dino Radja ART	.10	.05
❑ 7 Nick Van Exel ART	.15	.07

❑ 8	Shawn Bradley ART	.10	.05
❑ 9	Toni Kukoc ART	.40	.18
❑ 10	Lindsey Hunter ART	.10	.05
❑ 11	Scottie Pippen AN	.60	.25
❑ 12	Karl Malone AN	.40	.18
❑ 13	Hakeem Olajuwon AN	.40	.18
❑ 14	John Stockton AN	.15	.07
❑ 15	Latrell Sprewell AN	.40	.18
❑ 16	Shawn Kemp AN	.40	.18
❑ 17	Charles Barkley AN	.40	.18
❑ 18	David Robinson AN	.40	.18
❑ 19	Mitch Richmond AN	.15	.07
❑ 20	Kevin Johnson AN	.10	.05
❑ 21	Derrick Coleman AN	.10	.05
❑ 22	Dominique Wilkins AN	.15	.07
❑ 23	Shaquille O'Neal AN	.75	.35
❑ 24	Mark Price AN	.10	.05
❑ 25	Gary Payton AN	.40	.18
❑ 26	Dan Majerle	.15	.07
❑ 27	Vernon Maxwell	.10	.05
❑ 28	Matt Geiger	.10	.05
❑ 29	Jeff Turner	.10	.05
❑ 30	Vinny Del Negro	.10	.05
❑ 31	B.J. Armstrong	.10	.05
❑ 32	Chris Gatling	.10	.05
❑ 33	Tony Smith	.10	.05
❑ 34	Doug West	.10	.05
❑ 35	Clyde Drexler	.40	.18
❑ 36	Keith Jennings	.10	.05
❑ 37	Steve Smith	.15	.07
❑ 38	Kendall Gill	.15	.07
❑ 39	Bob Martin	.10	.05
❑ 40	Calbert Cheaney	.10	.05
❑ 41	Terrell Brandon	.15	.07
❑ 42	Pete Chilcutt	.10	.05
❑ 43	Avery Johnson	.10	.05
❑ 44	Tom Gugliotta	.15	.07
❑ 45	LaBradford Smith	.10	.05
❑ 46	Sedale Threatt	.10	.05
❑ 47	Chris Smith	.10	.05
❑ 48	Kevin Edwards	.10	.05
❑ 49	Lucious Harris	.10	.05
❑ 50	Tim Perry	.10	.05
❑ 51	Lloyd Daniels	.10	.05
❑ 52	Dee Brown	.10	.05
❑ 53	Sean Elliott	.15	.07
❑ 54	Tim Hardaway	.40	.18
❑ 55	Christian Laettner	.15	.07
❑ 56	Charles Outlaw RC	.10	.05
❑ 57	Kevin Johnson	.15	.07
❑ 58	Duane Ferrell	.10	.05
❑ 59	Jo Jo English	.10	.05
❑ 60	Stanley Roberts	.10	.05
❑ 61	Kevin Willis	.10	.05
❑ 62	Dana Barros	.10	.05
❑ 63	Gheorghe Muresan	.10	.05
❑ 64	Vern Fleming	.10	.05
❑ 65	Anthony Peeler	.10	.05
❑ 66	Negele Knight	.10	.05
❑ 67	Harold Ellis	.10	.05
❑ 68	Vincent Askew	.10	.05
❑ 69	Ennis Whatley	.10	.05
❑ 70	Elden Campbell	.10	.05
❑ 71	Sherman Douglas	.10	.05
❑ 72	Luc Longley	.10	.05
❑ 73	Lorenzo Williams	.10	.05
❑ 74	Jay Humphries	.10	.05
❑ 75	Chris King	.10	.05
❑ 76	Tyrone Corbin	.10	.05
❑ 77	Bobby Hurley	.10	.05
❑ 78	Dell Curry	.10	.05
❑ 79	Dino Radja	.10	.05
❑ 80	A.C. Green	.15	.07
❑ 81	Craig Ehlo	.10	.05
❑ 82	Gary Payton	.60	.25
❑ 83	Sleepy Floyd	.10	.05
❑ 84	Rodney Rogers	.10	.05
❑ 85	Brian Shaw	.10	.05
❑ 86	Kevin Gamble	.10	.05
❑ 87	John Stockton	.40	.18
❑ 88	Hersey Hawkins	.15	.07
❑ 89	Johnny Newman	.10	.05
❑ 90	Larry Johnson	.15	.07
❑ 91	Robert Pack	.10	.05
❑ 92	Willie Burton	.10	.05
❑ 93	Bobby Phills	.10	.05
❑ 94	David Benoit	.10	.05
❑ 95	Harold Miner	.10	.05
❑ 96	David Robinson	.60	.25
❑ 97	Nate McMillan	.10	.05
❑ 98	Chris Mills	.15	.07
❑ 99	Hubert Davis	.10	.05
❑ 100	Shaquille O'Neal	2.00	.90
❑ 101	Loy Vaught	.10	.05
❑ 102	Kenny Smith	.10	.05
❑ 103	Terry Dehere	.10	.05
❑ 104	Carl Herrera	.10	.05
❑ 105	LaPhonso Ellis	.10	.05
❑ 106	Armon Gilliam	.10	.05
❑ 107	Greg Graham	.10	.05
❑ 108	Eric Murdock	.10	.05
❑ 109	Ron Harper	.15	.07
❑ 110	Andrew Lang	.10	.05
❑ 111	Johnny Dawkins	.10	.05
❑ 112	David Wingate	.10	.05
❑ 113	Tom Hammonds	.10	.05
❑ 114	Brad Daugherty	.10	.05
❑ 115	Charles Smith	.10	.05
❑ 116	Dale Ellis	.10	.05
❑ 117	Bryant Stith	.10	.05
❑ 118	Lindsey Hunter	.15	.07
❑ 119	Patrick Ewing	.40	.18
❑ 120	Kenny Anderson	.15	.07
❑ 121	Charles Barkley	.60	.25
❑ 122	Harvey Grant	.10	.05
❑ 123	Anthony Bowie	.10	.05
❑ 124	Shawn Kemp	.60	.25
❑ 125	Lee Mayberry	.10	.05
❑ 126	Reggie Miller	.40	.18
❑ 127	Scottie Pippen	1.25	.55
❑ 128	Spud Webb	.10	.05
❑ 129	Antonio Davis	.10	.05
❑ 130	Greg Anderson	.10	.05
❑ 131	Jim Jackson	.15	.07
❑ 132	Dikembe Mutombo	.15	.07
❑ 133	Terry Porter	.10	.05
❑ 134	Mario Elie	.10	.05
❑ 135	Vlade Divac	.10	.05
❑ 136	Robert Horry	.10	.05
❑ 137	Popeye Jones	.10	.05
❑ 138	Brad Lohaus	.10	.05
❑ 139	Anthony Bonner	.10	.05
❑ 140	Doug Christie	.10	.05
❑ 141	Rony Seikaly	.10	.05
❑ 142	Allan Houston	.60	.25
❑ 143	Tyrone Hill	.10	.05
❑ 144	Latrell Sprewell	.75	.35
❑ 145	Andres Guibert	.10	.05
❑ 146	Dominique Wilkins	.40	.18
❑ 147	Jon Barry	.10	.05
❑ 148	Tracy Murray	.10	.05
❑ 149	Mike Peplowski	.10	.05
❑ 150	Mike Brown	.10	.05
❑ 151	Cedric Ceballos	.10	.05
❑ 152	Stacey King	.10	.05
❑ 153	Trevor Wilson	.10	.05
❑ 154	Anthony Avent	.10	.05
❑ 155	Horace Grant	.15	.07
❑ 156	Bill Curley RC	.10	.05
❑ 157	Grant Hill RC	4.00	1.80
❑ 158	Charlie Ward RC	.40	.18
❑ 159	Jalen Rose RC	1.50	.70
❑ 160	Jason Kidd RC	3.00	1.35
❑ 161	Yinka Dare RC	.10	.05
❑ 162	Eric Montross RC	.10	.05
❑ 163	Donyell Marshall RC	.40	.18
❑ 164	Tony Dumas RC	.10	.05
❑ 165	Wesley Person RC	.40	.18
❑ 166	Eddie Jones RC	2.50	1.10
❑ 167	Tim Hardaway USA	.15	.07
❑ 168	Isiah Thomas USA	.15	.07
❑ 169	Joe Dumars USA	.15	.07
❑ 170	Mark Price USA	.10	.05
❑ 171	Derrick Coleman USA	.10	.05
❑ 172	Shawn Kemp USA	.40	.18
❑ 173	Steve Smith USA	.10	.05
❑ 174	Dan Majerle USA	.10	.05
❑ 175	Reggie Miller USA	.15	.07
❑ 176	Kevin Johnson USA	.10	.05
❑ 177	Dominique Wilkins USA	.15	.07
❑ 178	Shaquille O'Neal USA	.75	.35
❑ 179	Alonzo Mourning USA	.40	.18
❑ 180	Larry Johnson USA	.10	.05
❑ 181	Brian Grant DA	.15	.07
❑ 182	Darrin Hancock DA	.10	.05
❑ 183	Grant Hill DA	2.00	.90
❑ 184	Jalen Rose DA	.15	.07
❑ 185	Lamond Murray DA	.10	.05
❑ 186	Jason Kidd DA	1.25	.55
❑ 187	Donyell Marshall DA	.15	.07
❑ 188	Eddie Jones DA	1.25	.55
❑ 189	Eric Montross DA	.10	.05
❑ 190	Khalid Reeves DA	.10	.05
❑ 191	Sharone Wright DA	.10	.05
❑ 192	Wesley Person DA	.15	.07
❑ 193	Glenn Robinson DA	.60	.25
❑ 194	Carlos Rogers DA	.10	.05
❑ 195	Aaron McKie DA	.10	.05
❑ 196	Juwan Howard DA	.75	.35
❑ 197	Charlie Ward DA	.15	.07
❑ 198	Brooks Thompson DA	.10	.05
❑ 199	Tony Massenburg	.10	.05
❑ 200	James Robinson	.10	.05
❑ 201	Dickey Simpkins RC	.10	.05
❑ 202	Johnny Dawkins	.10	.05
❑ 203	Joe Kleine	.10	.05
❑ 204	Bill Wennington	.10	.05
❑ 205	Sean Higgins	.10	.05
❑ 206	Larry Krystkowiak	.10	.05
❑ 207	Winston Garland	.10	.05
❑ 208	Muggsy Bogues	.15	.07
❑ 209	Charles Oakley	.10	.05
❑ 210	Vin Baker	.40	.18
❑ 211	Malik Sealy	.10	.05
❑ 212	Willie Anderson	.10	.05
❑ 213	Dale Davis	.10	.05
❑ 214	Grant Long	.10	.05
❑ 215	Danny Ainge	.10	.05
❑ 216	Toni Kukoc	.60	.25
❑ 217	Doug Smith	.10	.05
❑ 218	Danny Manning	.15	.07
❑ 219	Otis Thorpe	.10	.05
❑ 220	Mark Price	.10	.05
❑ 221	Victor Alexander	.10	.05
❑ 222	Brent Price	.10	.05
❑ 223	Howard Eisley RC	.10	.05
❑ 224	Chris Mullin	.40	.18
❑ 225	Nick Van Exel	.40	.18
❑ 226	Xavier McDaniel	.10	.05
❑ 227	Khalid Reeves RC	.10	.05
❑ 228	Anfernee Hardaway	1.25	.55
❑ 229	B.J. Tyler RC	.10	.05
❑ 230	Elmore Spencer	.10	.05
❑ 231	Rick Fox	.10	.05
❑ 232	Alonzo Mourning	.50	.23
❑ 233	Hakeem Olajuwon	.60	.25
❑ 234	Blue Edwards	.10	.05
❑ 235	P.J. Brown	.10	.05
❑ 236	Ron Harper	.15	.07
❑ 237	Isaiah Rider	.15	.07
❑ 238	Eric Mobley RC	.10	.05
❑ 239	Brian Williams	.10	.05
❑ 240	Eric Piatkowski RC	.10	.05
❑ 241	Karl Malone	.60	.25
❑ 242	Wayman Tisdale	.10	.05
❑ 243	Sarunas Marciulionis	.10	.05
❑ 244	Sean Rooks	.10	.05
❑ 245	Ricky Pierce	.10	.05
❑ 246	Don MacLean	.10	.05
❑ 247	Aaron McKie RC	.10	.05

❑ 248	Kenny Gattison	.10	.05
❑ 249	Derek Harper	.10	.05
❑ 250	Michael Smith RC	.10	.05
❑ 251	John Williams	.10	.05
❑ 252	Pooh Richardson	.10	.05
❑ 253	Sergei Bazarevich	.10	.05
❑ 254	Brian Grant RC	1.00	.45
❑ 255	Ed Pinckney	.10	.05
❑ 256	Ken Norman	.10	.05
❑ 257	Marty Conlon	.10	.05
❑ 258	Matt Fish	.10	.05
❑ 259	Darrin Hancock RC	.10	.05
❑ 260	Mahmoud Abdul-Rauf	.10	.05
❑ 261	Roy Tarpley	.10	.05
❑ 262	Chris Morris	.10	.05
❑ 263	Sharone Wright RC	.10	.05
❑ 264	Jamal Mashburn	.40	.18
❑ 265	John Starks	.10	.05
❑ 266	Rod Strickland	.15	.07
❑ 267	Adam Keefe	.10	.05
❑ 268	Scott Burrell	.10	.05
❑ 269	Eric Riley	.10	.05
❑ 270	Sam Perkins	.15	.07
❑ 271	Stacey Augmon	.10	.05
❑ 272	Kevin Willis	.10	.05
❑ 273	Lamond Murray RC	.15	.07
❑ 274	Derrick Coleman	.15	.07
❑ 275	Scott Skiles	.10	.05
❑ 276	Buck Williams	.10	.05
❑ 277	Sam Cassell	.40	.18
❑ 278	Rik Smits	.10	.05
❑ 279	Dennis Rodman	.75	.35
❑ 280	Olden Polynice	.10	.05
❑ 281	Glenn Robinson RC	1.25	.55
❑ 282	Clarence Weatherspoon	.10	.05
❑ 283	Monty Williams RC	.10	.05
❑ 284	Terry Mills	.10	.05
❑ 285	Oliver Miller	.10	.05
❑ 286	Dennis Scott	.10	.05
❑ 287	Micheal Williams	.10	.05
❑ 288	Moses Malone	.40	.18
❑ 289	Donald Royal	.10	.05
❑ 290	Mark Jackson	.10	.05
❑ 291	Walt Williams	.10	.05
❑ 292	Bimbo Coles	.10	.05
❑ 293	Derrick Alston RC	.10	.05
❑ 294	Scott Williams	.10	.05
❑ 295	Acie Earl	.10	.05
❑ 296	Jeff Hornacek	.15	.07
❑ 297	Kevin Duckworth	.10	.05
❑ 298	Dontonio Wingfield RC	.10	.05
❑ 299	Danny Ferry	.10	.05
❑ 300	Mark West	.10	.05
❑ 301	Jayson Williams	.15	.07
❑ 302	David Wesley	.10	.05
❑ 303	Jim McIlvaine RC	.10	.05
❑ 304	Michael Adams	.10	.05
❑ 305	Greg Minor RC	.10	.05
❑ 306	Jeff Malone	.10	.05
❑ 307	Pervis Ellison	.10	.05
❑ 308	Clifford Rozier RC	.10	.05
❑ 309	Billy Owens	.10	.05
❑ 310	Duane Causwell	.10	.05
❑ 311	Rex Chapman	.10	.05
❑ 312	Detlef Schrempf	.15	.07
❑ 313	Mitch Richmond	.40	.18
❑ 314	Carlos Rogers RC	.10	.05
❑ 315	Byron Scott	.15	.07
❑ 316	Dwayne Morton	.10	.05
❑ 317	Bill Cartwright	.10	.05
❑ 318	J.R. Reid	.10	.05
❑ 319	Derrick McKey	.10	.05
❑ 320	Jamie Watson RC	.10	.05
❑ 321	Mookie Blaylock	.10	.05
❑ 322	Chris Webber	1.25	.55
❑ 323	Joe Dumars	.40	.18
❑ 324	Shawn Bradley	.10	.05
❑ 325	Chuck Person	.10	.05
❑ 326	Haywoode Workman	.10	.05
❑ 327	Benoit Benjamin	.10	.05
❑ 328	Will Perdue	.10	.05
❑ 329	Sam Mitchell	.10	.05
❑ 330	George Lynch	.10	.05
❑ 331	Juwan Howard RC	1.00	.45
❑ 332	Robert Parish	.15	.07
❑ 333	Glen Rice	.15	.07
❑ 334	Michael Cage	.10	.05
❑ 335	Brooks Thompson RC	.10	.05
❑ 336	Rony Seikaly	.10	.05
❑ 337	Steve Kerr	.10	.05
❑ 338	Anthony Miller RC	.10	.05
❑ 339	Nick Anderson	.10	.05
❑ 340	Clifford Robinson	.15	.07
❑ 341	Todd Day	.10	.05
❑ 342	Jon Koncak	.10	.05
❑ 343	Felton Spencer	.10	.05
❑ 344	Willie Burton	.10	.05
❑ 345	Ledell Eackles	.10	.05
❑ 346	Anthony Mason	.15	.07
❑ 347	Derek Strong	.10	.05
❑ 348	Reggie Williams	.10	.05
❑ 349	Johnny Newman	.10	.05
❑ 350	Terry Cummings	.10	.05
❑ 351	Anthony Tucker RC	.10	.05
❑ 352	Junior Bridgeman TN	.10	.05
❑ 353	Jerry West TN	.40	.18
❑ 354	Harvey Catchings TN	.10	.05
❑ 355	John Lucas TN	.15	.07
❑ 356	Bill Bradley TN	.15	.07
❑ 357	Bill Walton TN	.15	.07
❑ 358	Don Nelson TN	.15	.07
❑ 359	Michael Jordan TN	2.50	1.10
❑ 360	Tom(Satch) Sanders TN	.10	.05

1994-95 Upper Deck Draft Trade

	MINT	NRMT
COMPLETE SET (10)	20.00	9.00

*SINGLES: .75X TO 2X BASE CARD HI
ONE SET PER DRAFT TRADE CARD BY MAIL
TRADE: SER.1 STATED ODDS 1:240

❑ D1	Glenn Robinson	2.50	1.10
❑ D2	Jason Kidd	6.00	2.70
❑ D3	Grant Hill	8.00	3.60
❑ D4	Donyell Marshall	.75	.35
❑ D5	Juwan Howard	2.00	.90
❑ D6	Sharone Wright	.20	.09
❑ D7	Lamond Murray	.30	.14
❑ D8	Brian Grant	2.00	.90
❑ D9	Eric Montross	.20	.09
❑ D10	Eddie Jones	5.00	2.20
❑ NNO	Draft Trade Card	.40	.18

1994-95 Upper Deck Jordan He's Back Reprints

	MINT	NRMT
COMPLETE SET (9)	12.00	5.50
COMMON CARD (1-9)	1.50	.70

ONE PER SER.2 RETAIL RACK PACK

❑ 23A	Michael Jordan (92-93 Upper Deck)	1.50	.70
❑ 23B	Michael Jordan (93-94 Upper Deck)	1.50	.70
❑ 41	Michael Jordan (94-95 SP Championship)	1.50	.70
❑ 44	Michael Jordan (91-92 Upper Deck)	1.50	.70
❑ 204	Michael Jordan (93-94 Upper Deck)	1.50	.70
❑ 237	Michael Jordan (93-94 Upper Deck)	1.50	.70
❑ 402	Michael Jordan (94-95 Collector's Choice)	1.50	.70
❑ 425	Michael Jordan (92-93 Upper Deck)	1.50	.70
❑ 453	Michael Jordan (92-93 Upper Deck)	1.50	.70
❑ J1	Michael Jordan (Team logo upper left)	5.00	2.20
❑ J2	Michael Jordan (Team logo lower left)	5.00	2.20
❑ J3	Michael Jordan (Team logo upper right)	5.00	2.20

1994-95 Upper Deck Jordan Heroes

	MINT	NRMT
COMPLETE SET (10)	80.00	36.00
COMMON JORDAN (37-45/HDR)	10.00	4.50

SER.1 STATED ODDS 1:30 HOB/RET

❑ 37	Michael Jordan (1985 NBA Rookie of the Year)	10.00	4.50
❑ 38	Michael Jordan (1986 63-Point Game)	10.00	4.50
❑ 39	Michael Jordan (1987-88 Air Raid)	10.00	4.50
❑ 40	Michael Jordan (1988)	10.00	4.50
❑ 41	Michael Jordan (1985-93 9-Time NBA All-Star)	10.00	4.50
❑ 42	Michael Jordan (1984)	10.00	4.50
❑ 43	Michael Jordan (1991-93 MJOs Highlight Zone)	10.00	4.50
❑ 44	Michael Jordan (1984-93 Rare Air)	10.00	4.50
❑ 45	Checklist	10.00	4.50
❑ NNO	Header Card	10.00	4.50

1994-95 Upper Deck Predictor Award Winners

	MINT	NRMT
COMPLETE SET (40)	125.00	55.00

COMPLETE SERIES 1 (20)	50.00	22.00
COMPLETE SERIES 2 (20)	75.00	34.00
*SINGLES: 2X TO 5X BASE CARD HI		
SER.1 STATED ODDS 1:25 HOBBY		
SER.2 STATED ODDS 1:30 HOBBY		
COMP.AS MVP RED.SET (10)	15.00	6.75
COMP.DEF.POY RED.SET (10)	10.00	4.50
COMP.MVP RED.SET (10)	15.00	6.75
COMP.ROY RED.SET (10)	15.00	6.75
*RED.CARDS: .2X TO .5X HI COLUMN		
TWO RED.SETS PER "W1" CARD BY MAIL		
ONE RED.SET PER "W2" CARD BY MAIL		

❑ H1 Charles Barkley	3.00	1.35
❑ H2 Hakeem Olajuwon	3.00	1.35
❑ H3 Shaquille O'Neal	10.00	4.50
❑ H4 Scottie Pippen	6.00	2.70
❑ H5 David Robinson	3.00	1.35
❑ H6 Shawn Kemp W2	3.00	1.35
❑ H7 Alonzo Mourning	2.50	1.10
❑ H8 Larry Johnson	.75	.35
❑ H9 Patrick Ewing	2.00	.90
❑ H10 AS-MVP Wild Card W1	.75	.35
❑ H11 Hakeem Olajuwon	3.00	1.35
❑ H12 Dikembe Mutombo W1	.75	.35
❑ H13 Nate McMillan	.50	.23
❑ H14 Dennis Rodman	4.00	1.80
❑ H15 Alonzo Mourning	2.50	1.10
❑ H16 Patrick Ewing	2.00	.90
❑ H17 Charles Barkley	3.00	1.35
❑ H18 David Robinson	3.00	1.35
❑ H19 John Stockton	2.00	.90
❑ H20 DEF-POY Wild Card W2	.75	.35
❑ H21 Shaquille O'Neal W2	10.00	4.50
❑ H22 Hakeem Olajuwon	3.00	1.35
❑ H23 David Robinson W1	3.00	1.35
❑ H24 Scottie Pippen	6.00	2.70
❑ H25 Alonzo Mourning	2.50	1.10
❑ H26 Shawn Kemp	3.00	1.35
❑ H27 Charles Barkley	3.00	1.35
❑ H28 Patrick Ewing	2.00	.90
❑ H29 Larry Johnson	.75	.35
❑ H30 MVP Wild Card	.75	.35
❑ H31 Jason Kidd W1	8.00	3.60
❑ H32 Grant Hill W1	10.00	4.50
❑ H33 Glenn Robinson	3.00	1.35
❑ H34 Eddie Jones	6.00	2.70
❑ H35 Donyell Marshall	2.00	.90
❑ H36 Eric Montross	.50	.23
❑ H37 Sharone Wright	.50	.23
❑ H38 Juwan Howard	2.50	1.10
❑ H39 Carlos Rogers	.50	.23
❑ H40 ROY Wild Card W1	.75	.35

1994-95 Upper Deck Predictor League Leaders

	MINT	NRMT
COMPLETE SET (40)	100.00	45.00
COMPLETE SERIES 1 (20)	50.00	22.00
COMPLETE SERIES 2 (20)	50.00	22.00
*SINGLES: 2X TO 5X BASE CARD HI		
SER.1 STATED ODDS 1:25 RETAIL		
SER.2 STATED ODDS 1:30 RETAIL		
COMP.SCORE.RED.SET (10)	12.00	5.50
COMP.AST.RED.SET (10)	6.00	2.70
COMP.REB.RED.SET (10)	10.00	4.50
COMP.BLK.RED.SET (10)	12.00	5.50
*RED.CARDS: .2X TO .5X HI COLUMN		
TWO RED.SETS PER "W1" CARD BY MAIL		
ONE EXCH.SET PER "W2" CARD BY MAIL		

❑ R1 David Robinson	3.00	1.35
❑ R2 Shaquille O'Neal W1	10.00	4.50
❑ R3 Hakeem Olajuwon W2	3.00	1.35
❑ R4 Scottie Pippen	6.00	2.70
❑ R5 Chris Webber	6.00	2.70
❑ R6 Karl Malone	3.00	1.35
❑ R7 Patrick Ewing	2.00	.90
❑ R8 Mitch Richmond	2.00	.90
❑ R9 Charles Barkley	3.00	1.35
❑ R10 Scorers Wild Card	.75	.35
❑ R11 John Stockton W1	2.00	.90
❑ R12 Mookie Blaylock	.50	.23
❑ R13 Kenny Anderson W2	.75	.35
❑ R14 Kevin Johnson	.75	.35
❑ R15 Muggsy Bogues	.75	.35
❑ R16 Tim Hardaway	2.00	.90
❑ R17 Anfernee Hardaway	6.00	2.70
❑ R18 Rod Strickland	.75	.35
❑ R19 Sherman Douglas	.50	.23
❑ R20 Assists Wild Card	.75	.35
❑ R21 Shaquille O'Neal	10.00	4.50
❑ R22 Hakeem Olajuwon	3.00	1.35
❑ R23 Dennis Rodman W1	4.00	1.80
❑ R24 Dikembe Mutombo W2	.75	.35
❑ R25 Karl Malone	3.00	1.35
❑ R26 Kevin Willis	.50	.23
❑ R27 Chris Webber	6.00	2.70
❑ R28 Alonzo Mourning	2.50	1.10
❑ R29 Derrick Coleman	.75	.35
❑ R30 Rebounds Wild Card	.75	.35
❑ R31 Dikembe Mutombo W1	.75	.35
❑ R32 Hakeem Olajuwon W2	3.00	1.35
❑ R33 David Robinson	3.00	1.35
❑ R34 Shawn Bradley	.50	.23
❑ R35 Shaquille O'Neal	10.00	4.50
❑ R36 Patrick Ewing	2.00	.90
❑ R37 Alonzo Mourning	2.50	1.10
❑ R38 Shawn Kemp	3.00	1.35
❑ R39 Derrick Coleman	.75	.35
❑ R40 Blocks Wild Card	.75	.35

1994-95 Upper Deck Rookie Standouts

	MINT	NRMT
COMPLETE SET (20)	80.00	36.00
COMMON CARD (RS1-RS20)	1.00	.45
SEMISTARS	2.50	1.10
SER.2 STATED ODDS 1:30 HOBBY/RETAIL		

❑ RS1 Glenn Robinson	8.00	3.60
❑ RS2 Jason Kidd	20.00	9.00
❑ RS3 Grant Hill	25.00	11.00
❑ RS4 Donyell Marshall	2.50	1.10
❑ RS5 Juwan Howard	6.00	2.70
❑ RS6 Sharone Wright	1.00	.45
❑ RS7 Lamond Murray	1.00	.45
❑ RS8 Brian Grant	6.00	2.70
❑ RS9 Eric Montross	1.00	.45
❑ RS10 Eddie Jones	15.00	6.75
❑ RS11 Carlos Rogers	1.00	.45
❑ RS12 Khalid Reeves	1.00	.45
❑ RS13 Jalen Rose	10.00	4.50
❑ RS14 Michael Smith	1.00	.45
❑ RS15 Eric Piatkowski	1.00	.45
❑ RS16 Clifford Rozier	1.00	.45
❑ RS17 Aaron McKie	1.00	.45
❑ RS18 Eric Mobley	1.00	.45
❑ RS19 Bill Curley	1.00	.45
❑ RS20 Wesley Person	2.50	1.10

1994-95 Upper Deck Slam Dunk Stars

	MINT	NRMT
COMPLETE SET (20)	120.00	55.00
COMMON CARD (S1-S20)	1.50	.70
SEMISTARS	3.00	1.35
UNLISTED STARS	6.00	2.70
SER.2 STATED ODDS 1:30 HOBBY/RETAIL		

❑ S1 Vin Baker	6.00	2.70
❑ S2 Charles Barkley	10.00	4.50
❑ S3 Derrick Coleman	3.00	1.35
❑ S4 Clyde Drexler	6.00	2.70
❑ S5 LaPhonso Ellis	1.50	.70
❑ S6 Larry Johnson	3.00	1.35
❑ S7 Shawn Kemp	10.00	4.50
❑ S8 Donyell Marshall	3.00	1.35
❑ S9 Jamal Mashburn	6.00	2.70
❑ S10 Gheorghe Muresan	1.50	.70
❑ S11 Alonzo Mourning	8.00	3.60
❑ S12 Shaquille O'Neal	30.00	13.50
❑ S13 Hakeem Olajuwon	10.00	4.50
❑ S14 Scottie Pippen	20.00	9.00
❑ S15 Isaiah Rider	3.00	1.35
❑ S16 David Robinson	10.00	4.50
❑ S17 Clarence Weatherspoon	1.50	.70
❑ S18 Chris Webber	20.00	9.00
❑ S19 Dominique Wilkins	6.00	2.70
❑ S20 Rik Smits	1.50	.70

1994-95 Upper Deck Special Edition

	MINT	NRMT
COMPLETE SET (180)	40.00	18.00
COMPLETE SERIES 1 (90)	15.00	6.75
COMPLETE SERIES 2 (90)	30.00	13.50
*SINGLES: .75X TO 2X BASE CARD HI		
ONE PER PACK		
COMP.GOLD SET (180)	450.00	200.00

COMP.GOLD SER.1 (90) 150.00 70.00
COMP.GOLD SER.2 (90) 300.00 135.00
COMMON GOLD (SE1-SE180) 1.00 .45
*GOLD STARS: 4X TO 8X HI COLUMN
*GOLD RCs: 3X TO 6X HI
GOLD: SER.1/2 STATED ODDS 1:35 HOB/RET
SE PREFIX ON CARD NUMBERS

Card	MINT	NRMT
❑ 1 Stacey Augmon	.20	.09
❑ 2 Kevin Willis	.20	.09
❑ 3 Mookie Blaylock	.20	.09
❑ 4 Rick Fox	.20	.09
❑ 5 Xavier McDaniel	.20	.09
❑ 6 Dee Brown	.20	.09
❑ 7 Muggsy Bogues	.30	.14
❑ 8 Kenny Gattison	.20	.09
❑ 9 Alonzo Mourning	1.00	.45
❑ 10 B.J. Armstrong	.20	.09
❑ 11 Bill Cartwright	.20	.09
❑ 12 Toni Kukoc	1.25	.55
❑ 13 Mark Price	.20	.09
❑ 14 Gerald Wilkins	.20	.09
❑ 15 John Williams	.20	.09
❑ 16 Jamal Mashburn	.75	.35
❑ 17 Sean Rooks	.20	.09
❑ 18 Doug Smith	.20	.09
❑ 19 Jim Jackson	.30	.14
❑ 20 Mahmoud Abdul-Rauf	.20	.09
❑ 21 Rodney Rogers	.20	.09
❑ 22 Reggie Williams	.20	.09
❑ 23 LaPhonso Ellis	.20	.09
❑ 24 Allan Houston	1.25	.55
❑ 25 Terry Mills	.20	.09
❑ 26 Joe Dumars	.75	.35
❑ 27 Chris Mullin	.75	.35
❑ 28 Billy Owens	.20	.09
❑ 29 Latrell Sprewell	1.50	.70
❑ 30 Chris Webber	2.50	1.10
❑ 31 Sam Cassell	.75	.35
❑ 32 Vernon Maxwell	.20	.09
❑ 33 Hakeem Olajuwon	1.25	.55
❑ 34 Otis Thorpe	.20	.09
❑ 35 Rik Smits	.20	.09
❑ 36 Derrick McKey	.20	.09
❑ 37 Haywoode Workman	.20	.09
❑ 38 Charles Outlaw	.20	.09
❑ 39 Elmore Spencer	.20	.09
❑ 40 Loy Vaught	.20	.09
❑ 41 George Lynch	.20	.09
❑ 42 Nick Van Exel	.75	.35
❑ 43 James Worthy	.75	.35
❑ 44 Elden Campbell	.20	.09
❑ 45 Grant Long	.20	.09
❑ 46 Harold Miner	.20	.09
❑ 47 Glen Rice	.30	.14
❑ 48 Steve Smith	.30	.14
❑ 49 Todd Day	.20	.09
❑ 50 Eric Murdock	.20	.09
❑ 51 Vin Baker	.75	.35
❑ 52 Christian Laettner	.30	.14
❑ 53 Isaiah Rider	.30	.14
❑ 54 Micheal Williams	.20	.09
❑ 55 Benoit Benjamin	.20	.09
❑ 56 Derrick Coleman	.30	.14
❑ 57 Chris Morris	.20	.09
❑ 58 Charles Smith	.20	.09
❑ 59 Greg Anthony	.20	.09
❑ 60 Doc Rivers	.20	.09
❑ 61 Derek Harper	.20	.09
❑ 62 John Starks	.20	.09
❑ 63 Anfernee Hardaway	2.50	1.10
❑ 64 Dennis Scott	.20	.09
❑ 65 Nick Anderson	.20	.09
❑ 66 Shawn Bradley	.20	.09
❑ 67 Clarence Weatherspoon	.20	.09
❑ 68 Jeff Malone	.20	.09
❑ 69 Cedric Ceballos	.20	.09
❑ 70 Kevin Johnson	.30	.14
❑ 71 Oliver Miller	.20	.09
❑ 72 Clifford Robinson	.30	.14
❑ 73 Rod Strickland	.30	.14
❑ 74 Buck Williams	.20	.09
❑ 75 Mitch Richmond	.75	.35
❑ 76 Walt Williams	.20	.09
❑ 77 Lionel Simmons	.20	.09
❑ 78 Willie Anderson	.20	.09
❑ 79 Terry Cummings	.20	.09
❑ 80 J.R. Reid	.20	.09
❑ 81 Dennis Rodman	1.50	.70
❑ 82 Kendall Gill	.30	.14
❑ 83 Sam Perkins	.30	.14
❑ 84 Detlef Schrempf	.30	.14
❑ 85 Jeff Hornacek	.30	.14
❑ 86 Karl Malone	1.25	.55
❑ 87 Felton Spencer	.20	.09
❑ 88 Calbert Cheaney	.20	.09
❑ 89 Don MacLean	.20	.09
❑ 90 Brent Price	.20	.09
❑ 91 Tyrone Corbin	.20	.09
❑ 92 Rex Chapman	.20	.09
❑ 93 Ken Norman	.20	.09
❑ 94 Steve Smith	.30	.14
❑ 95 Eric Montross	.20	.09
❑ 96 Dino Radja	.20	.09
❑ 97 Dominique Wilkins	.75	.35
❑ 98 Scott Burrell	.20	.09
❑ 99 Hersey Hawkins	.30	.14
❑ 100 Larry Johnson	.30	.14
❑ 101 Ron Harper	.30	.14
❑ 102 Scottie Pippen	2.50	1.10
❑ 103 Dickey Simpkins	.20	.09
❑ 104 Tyrone Hill	.20	.09
❑ 105 Chris Mills	.30	.14
❑ 106 Bobby Phills	.20	.09
❑ 107 Lorenzo Williams	.20	.09
❑ 108 Popeye Jones	.20	.09
❑ 109 Jason Kidd	5.00	2.20
❑ 110 Dikembe Mutombo	.30	.14
❑ 111 Robert Pack	.20	.09
❑ 112 Jalen Rose	2.50	1.10
❑ 113 Bill Curley	.20	.09
❑ 114 Grant Hill	6.00	2.70
❑ 115 Lindsey Hunter	.30	.14
❑ 116 Roy Tarpley	.20	.09
❑ 117 Tim Hardaway	.75	.35
❑ 118 Ricky Pierce	.20	.09
❑ 119 Carlos Rogers	.20	.09
❑ 120 Clifford Rozier	.20	.09
❑ 121 Rony Seikaly	.20	.09
❑ 122 Mario Elie	.20	.09
❑ 123 Robert Horry	.20	.09
❑ 124 Kenny Smith	.20	.09
❑ 125 Antonio Davis	.20	.09
❑ 126 Dale Davis	.20	.09
❑ 127 Reggie Miller	.75	.35
❑ 128 Lamond Murray	.30	.14
❑ 129 Eric Piatkowski	.20	.09
❑ 130 Pooh Richardson	.20	.09
❑ 131 Cedric Ceballos	.20	.09
❑ 132 Vlade Divac	.20	.09
❑ 133 Eddie Jones	4.00	1.80
❑ 134 Mark Jackson	.20	.09
❑ 135 Matt Geiger	.20	.09
❑ 136 Khalid Reeves	.20	.09
❑ 137 Kevin Willis	.20	.09
❑ 138 Lee Mayberry	.20	.09
❑ 139 Eric Mobley	.20	.09
❑ 140 Glenn Robinson	2.00	.90
❑ 141 Doug West	.20	.09
❑ 142 Donyell Marshall	.75	.35
❑ 143 Chris Smith	.20	.09
❑ 144 Kenny Anderson	.30	.14
❑ 145 Chris Morris	.20	.09
❑ 146 Armon Gilliam	.20	.09
❑ 147 Dana Barros	.20	.09
❑ 148 Patrick Ewing	.75	.35
❑ 149 Charles Oakley	.20	.09
❑ 150 Charlie Ward	.75	.35
❑ 151 Horace Grant	.30	.14
❑ 152 Shaquille O'Neal	4.00	1.80
❑ 153 Brian Shaw	.20	.09
❑ 154 Brooks Thompson	.20	.09
❑ 155 B.J. Tyler	.20	.09
❑ 156 Scott Williams	.20	.09
❑ 157 Sharone Wright	.20	.09
❑ 158 Charles Barkley	1.25	.55
❑ 159 Dan Majerle	.30	.14
❑ 160 Danny Manning	.30	.14
❑ 161 Wesley Person	.75	.35
❑ 162 Clyde Drexler	.75	.35
❑ 163 Harvey Grant	.20	.09
❑ 164 Terry Porter	.20	.09
❑ 165 Brian Grant	1.50	.70
❑ 166 Bobby Hurley	.20	.09
❑ 167 Olden Polynice	.20	.09
❑ 168 Sean Elliott	.30	.14
❑ 169 Chuck Person	.20	.09
❑ 170 David Robinson	1.25	.55
❑ 171 Shawn Kemp	1.25	.55
❑ 172 Nate McMillan	.20	.09
❑ 173 Gary Payton	1.25	.55
❑ 174 Michael Smith	.20	.09
❑ 175 David Benoit	.20	.09
❑ 176 Jay Humphries	.20	.09
❑ 177 John Stockton	.75	.35
❑ 178 Juwan Howard	1.50	.70
❑ 179 Chris Webber	2.50	1.10
❑ 180 Scott Skiles	.20	.09

1995-96 Upper Deck

	MINT	NRMT
COMPLETE SET (360)	50.00	22.00
COMPLETE SERIES 1 (180)	20.00	9.00
COMPLETE SERIES 2 (180)	30.00	13.50
COMMON CARD (1-360)	.15	.07
SEMISTARS	.20	.09
UNLISTED STARS	.40	.18

SUBSET CARDS HALF VALUE OF BASE CARDS

Card	MINT	NRMT
❑ 1 Eddie Jones	.75	.35
❑ 2 Hubert Davis	.15	.07
❑ 3 Latrell Sprewell	.75	.35
❑ 4 Stacey Augmon	.15	.07
❑ 5 Mario Elie	.15	.07
❑ 6 Tyrone Hill	.15	.07
❑ 7 Dikembe Mutombo	.20	.09
❑ 8 Antonio Davis	.15	.07
❑ 9 Horace Grant	.20	.09
❑ 10 Ken Norman	.15	.07
❑ 11 Aaron McKie	.15	.07
❑ 12 Vinny Del Negro	.15	.07
❑ 13 Glenn Robinson	.40	.18
❑ 14 Allan Houston	.50	.23
❑ 15 Bryon Russell	.15	.07
❑ 16 Tony Dumas	.15	.07
❑ 17 Gary Payton	.60	.25
❑ 18 Rik Smits	.15	.07
❑ 19 Dino Radja	.15	.07
❑ 20 Robert Pack	.15	.07
❑ 21 Calbert Cheaney	.15	.07
❑ 22 Clarence Weatherspoon	.15	.07
❑ 23 Michael Jordan	5.00	2.20
❑ 24 Felton Spencer	.15	.07
❑ 25 J.R. Reid	.15	.07
❑ 26 Cedric Ceballos	.15	.07
❑ 27 Dan Majerle	.15	.07
❑ 28 Donald Hodge	.15	.07
❑ 29 Nate McMillan	.15	.07
❑ 30 Bimbo Coles	.15	.07
❑ 31 Mitch Richmond	.40	.18
❑ 32 Scott Brooks	.15	.07
❑ 33 Patrick Ewing	.40	.18
❑ 34 Carl Herrera	.15	.07
❑ 35 Rick Fox	.15	.07
❑ 36 James Robinson	.15	.07
❑ 37 Donald Royal	.15	.07
❑ 38 Joe Dumars	.40	.18
❑ 39 Rony Seikaly	.15	.07

❑ 40 Dennis Rodman .75 .35
❑ 41 Muggsy Bogues .15 .07
❑ 42 Gheorghe Muresan .15 .07
❑ 43 Ervin Johnson .15 .07
❑ 44 Todd Day .15 .07
❑ 45 Rex Walters .15 .07
❑ 46 Terrell Brandon .20 .09
❑ 47 Wesley Person .20 .09
❑ 48 Terry Dehere .15 .07
❑ 49 Steve Smith .20 .09
❑ 50 Brian Grant .40 .18
❑ 51 Eric Piatkowski .15 .07
❑ 52 Lindsey Hunter .15 .07
❑ 53 Chris Webber 1.25 .55
❑ 54 Antoine Carr .15 .07
❑ 55 Chris Dudley .15 .07
❑ 56 Clyde Drexler .40 .18
❑ 57 P.J. Brown .15 .07
❑ 58 Kevin Willis .15 .07
❑ 59 Jeff Turner .15 .07
❑ 60 Sean Elliott .15 .07
❑ 61 Kevin Johnson .20 .09
❑ 62 Scott Skiles .15 .07
❑ 63 Charles Smith .15 .07
❑ 64 Derrick McKey .15 .07
❑ 65 Danny Ferry .15 .07
❑ 66 Detlef Schrempf .20 .09
❑ 67 Shawn Bradley .15 .07
❑ 68 Isaiah Rider .20 .09
❑ 69 Karl Malone .60 .25
❑ 70 Will Perdue .15 .07
❑ 71 Terry Mills .15 .07
❑ 72 Glen Rice .20 .09
❑ 73 Tim Breaux .15 .07
❑ 74 Malik Sealy .15 .07
❑ 75 Walt Williams .15 .07
❑ 76 Bobby Phills .15 .07
❑ 77 Anthony Avent .15 .07
❑ 78 Jamal Mashburn UER .20 .09
Career FG percentage is wrong
❑ 79 Vlade Divac .15 .07
❑ 80 Reggie Williams .15 .07
❑ 81 Xavier McDaniel .15 .07
❑ 82 Avery Johnson .15 .07
❑ 83 Derek Harper .15 .07
❑ 84 Don MacLean .15 .07
❑ 85 Tom Gugliotta .20 .09
❑ 86 Craig Ehlo .15 .07
❑ 87 Robert Horry .15 .07
❑ 88 Kevin Edwards .15 .07
❑ 89 Chuck Person .15 .07
❑ 90 Sharone Wright .15 .07
❑ 91 Steve Kerr .15 .07
❑ 92 Marty Conlon .15 .07
❑ 93 Jalen Rose .50 .23
❑ 94 Bryant Reeves RC .40 .18
❑ 95 Shaquille O'Neal 2.00 .90
❑ 96 David Wesley .15 .07
❑ 97 Chris Mills .15 .07
❑ 98 Rod Strickland .20 .09
❑ 99 Pooh Richardson .15 .07
❑ 100 Sam Perkins .20 .09
❑ 101 Dell Curry .15 .07
❑ 102 David Benoit .15 .07
❑ 103 Christian Laettner .20 .09
❑ 104 Duane Causwell .15 .07
❑ 105 Jason Kidd 1.25 .55
❑ 106 Mark West .15 .07
❑ 107 Lee Mayberry .15 .07
❑ 108 John Salley .15 .07
❑ 109 Jeff Malone .15 .07
❑ 110 George Zidek RC .15 .07
❑ 111 Kenny Smith .15 .07
❑ 112 George Lynch .15 .07
❑ 113 Toni Kukoc .50 .23
❑ 114 A.C. Green .20 .09
❑ 115 Kenny Anderson .20 .09
❑ 116 Robert Parish .20 .09
❑ 117 Chris Mullin .40 .18
❑ 118 Loy Vaught .15 .07
❑ 119 Olden Polynice .15 .07
❑ 120 Clifford Robinson .15 .07
❑ 121 Eric Mobley .15 .07
❑ 122 Doug West .15 .07
❑ 123 Sam Cassell .20 .09
❑ 124 Nick Anderson .15 .07
❑ 125 Matt Geiger .15 .07
❑ 126 Elden Campbell .15 .07
❑ 127 Alonzo Mourning .40 .18
❑ 128 Bryant Stith .15 .07
❑ 129 Mark Jackson .15 .07
❑ 130 Cherokee Parks RC .15 .07
❑ 131 Shawn Respert RC .15 .07
❑ 132 Alan Henderson RC .40 .18
❑ 133 Jerry Stackhouse RC 1.25 .55
❑ 134 Rasheed Wallace RC 1.50 .70
❑ 135 Antonio McDyess RC 2.00 .90
❑ 136 Charles Barkley ROO .40 .18
❑ 137 Michael Jordan ROO 2.50 1.10
❑ 138 Hakeem Olajuwon ROO .40 .18
❑ 139 Joe Dumars ROO .20 .09
❑ 140 Patrick Ewing ROO .20 .09
❑ 141 A.C. Green ROO .15 .07
❑ 142 Karl Malone ROO .40 .18
❑ 143 Detlef Schrempf ROO .15 .07
❑ 144 Chuck Person ROO .15 .07
❑ 145 Muggsy Bogues ROO .15 .07
❑ 146 Horace Grant ROO .15 .07
❑ 147 Mark Jackson ROO .15 .07
❑ 148 Kevin Johnson ROO .15 .07
❑ 149 Mitch Richmond ROO .20 .09
❑ 150 Rik Smits ROO .15 .07
❑ 151 Nick Anderson ROO .15 .07
❑ 152 Tim Hardaway ROO .20 .09
❑ 153 Shawn Kemp ROO .40 .18
❑ 154 David Robinson ROO .40 .18
❑ 155 Jason Kidd ART .50 .23
❑ 156 Grant Hill ART 1.25 .55
❑ 157 Glenn Robinson ART .20 .09
❑ 158 Eddie Jones ART .40 .18
❑ 159 Brian Grant ART .20 .09
❑ 160 Juwan Howard ART .20 .09
❑ 161 Eric Montross ART .15 .07
❑ 162 Wesley Person ART .15 .07
❑ 163 Jalen Rose ART .40 .18
❑ 164 Donyell Marshall ART .15 .07
❑ 165 Sharone Wright ART .15 .07
❑ 166 Karl Malone AN .40 .18
❑ 167 Scottie Pippen AN .60 .25
❑ 168 David Robinson AN .40 .18
❑ 169 John Stockton AN .20 .09
❑ 170 Anfernee Hardaway AN .75 .35
❑ 171 Charles Barkley AN .40 .18
❑ 172 Shawn Kemp AN .40 .18
❑ 173 Shaquille O'Neal AN .75 .35
❑ 174 Gary Payton AN .40 .18
❑ 175 Mitch Richmond AN .20 .09
❑ 176 Dennis Rodman AN .40 .18
❑ 177 Detlef Schrempf AN .15 .07
❑ 178 Hakeem Olajuwon AN .40 .18
❑ 179 Reggie Miller AN .20 .09
❑ 180 Clyde Drexler AN .20 .09
❑ 181 Hakeem Olajuwon .60 .25
❑ 182 Vin Baker .40 .18
❑ 183 Jeff Hornacek .20 .09
❑ 184 Popeye Jones .15 .07
❑ 185 Sedale Threatt .15 .07
❑ 186 Scottie Pippen 1.25 .55
❑ 187 Terry Porter .15 .07
❑ 188 Dan Majerle .15 .07
❑ 189 Clifford Rozier .15 .07
❑ 190 Greg Minor .15 .07
❑ 191 Dennis Scott .15 .07
❑ 192 Hersey Hawkins .20 .09
❑ 193 Chris Gatling .15 .07
❑ 194 Charles Oakley .15 .07
❑ 195 Dale Davis .15 .07
❑ 196 Robert Pack .15 .07
❑ 197 Lamond Murray .15 .07
❑ 198 Mookie Blaylock .15 .07
❑ 199 Dickey Simpkins .15 .07
❑ 200 Kevin Gamble .15 .07
❑ 201 Lorenzo Williams .15 .07
❑ 202 Scott Burrell .15 .07
❑ 203 Armon Gilliam .15 .07
❑ 204 Doc Rivers .15 .07
❑ 205 Blue Edwards .15 .07
❑ 206 Billy Owens .15 .07
❑ 207 Juwan Howard .40 .18
❑ 208 Harvey Grant .15 .07
❑ 209 Richard Dumas .15 .07
❑ 210 Anthony Peeler .15 .07
❑ 211 Matt Geiger .15 .07
❑ 212 Lucious Harris .15 .07
❑ 213 Grant Long .15 .07
❑ 214 Sasha Danilovic RC .15 .07
❑ 215 Chris Morris .15 .07
❑ 216 Donyell Marshall .20 .09
❑ 217 Alonzo Mourning .40 .18
❑ 218 John Stockton .40 .18
❑ 219 Khalid Reeves .15 .07
❑ 220 Mahmoud Abdul-Rauf .15 .07
❑ 221 Sean Rooks .15 .07
❑ 222 Shawn Kemp .60 .25
❑ 223 John Williams .15 .07
❑ 224 Dee Brown .15 .07
❑ 225 Jim Jackson .15 .07
❑ 226 Harold Miner .15 .07
❑ 227 B.J. Armstrong .15 .07
❑ 228 Elliot Perry .15 .07
❑ 229 Anthony Miller .15 .07
❑ 230 Donny Marshall RC .15 .07
❑ 231 Tyrone Corbin .15 .07
❑ 232 Anthony Mason .20 .09
❑ 233 Grant Hill 2.00 .90
❑ 234 Buck Williams .15 .07
❑ 235 Brian Shaw .15 .07
❑ 236 Dale Ellis .15 .07
❑ 237 Magic Johnson 1.25 .55
❑ 238 Eric Montross .15 .07
❑ 239 Rex Chapman .15 .07
❑ 240 Otis Thorpe .15 .07
❑ 241 Tracy Murray .15 .07
❑ 242 Sarunas Marciulionis .15 .07
❑ 243 Luc Longley .15 .07
❑ 244 Elmore Spencer .15 .07
❑ 245 Terry Cummings .15 .07
❑ 246 Sam Mitchell .15 .07
❑ 247 Terrence Rencher RC .15 .07
❑ 248 Byron Houston .15 .07
❑ 249 Pervis Ellison .15 .07
❑ 250 Carlos Rogers .15 .07
❑ 251 Kendall Gill .20 .09
❑ 252 Sherrell Ford RC .15 .07
❑ 253 Michael Finley RC 1.50 .70
❑ 254 Kurt Thomas RC .20 .09
❑ 255 Joe Smith RC 1.25 .55
❑ 256 Bobby Hurley .15 .07
❑ 257 Greg Anthony .15 .07
❑ 258 Willie Anderson .15 .07
❑ 259 Theo Ratliff RC .50 .23
❑ 260 Duane Ferrell .15 .07
❑ 261 Antonio Harvey .15 .07
❑ 262 Gary Grant .15 .07
❑ 263 Brian Williams .15 .07
❑ 264 Danny Manning .20 .09
❑ 265 Micheal Williams .15 .07
❑ 266 Dennis Rodman .75 .35
❑ 267 Arvydas Sabonis RC .60 .25
❑ 268 Don MacLean .15 .07
❑ 269 Keith Askins .15 .07
❑ 270 Reggie Miller .40 .18
❑ 271 Ed Pinckney .15 .07
❑ 272 Bob Sura RC .20 .09
❑ 273 Kevin Garnett RC 5.00 2.20
❑ 274 Byron Scott .15 .07
❑ 275 Mario Bennett RC .15 .07
❑ 276 Junior Burrough RC .15 .07
❑ 277 Anfernee Hardaway 1.25 .55
❑ 278 George McCloud .15 .07
❑ 279 Loren Meyer RC .15 .07
❑ 280 Ed O'Bannon RC .15 .07
❑ 281 Lawrence Moten RC .15 .07
❑ 282 Dana Barros .15 .07
❑ 283 Damon Stoudamire RC 2.00 .90
❑ 284 Eric Williams RC .20 .09
❑ 285 Wayman Tisdale .15 .07
❑ 286 Rodney Rogers .15 .07
❑ 287 Sherman Douglas .15 .07
❑ 288 Greg Ostertag RC .15 .07
❑ 289 Alvin Robertson .15 .07
❑ 290 Tim Legler .15 .07
❑ 291 Zan Tabak .15 .07
❑ 292 Gary Trent RC .15 .07
❑ 293 Haywoode Workman .15 .07
❑ 294 Charles Barkley .60 .25
❑ 295 Derrick Coleman .20 .09
❑ 296 Ricky Pierce .15 .07

	Card	Player	Mint	Nrmt
❑	297	Benoit Benjamin	.15	.07
❑	298	Larry Johnson	.20	.09
❑	299	Travis Best RC	.20	.09
❑	300	Jason Caffey RC	.20	.09
❑	301	Cory Alexander RC	.15	.07
❑	302	Nick Van Exel	.20	.09
❑	303	Corliss Williamson RC	.75	.35
❑	304	Eric Murdock	.15	.07
❑	305	Tyus Edney RC	.15	.07
❑	306	Lou Roe RC	.15	.07
❑	307	John Salley	.15	.07
❑	308	Spud Webb	.15	.07
❑	309	Brent Barry RC	.40	.18
❑	310	David Robinson	.60	.25
❑	311	Glen Rice	.20	.09
❑	312	Chris King	.15	.07
❑	313	David Vaughn RC	.15	.07
❑	314	Kenny Gattison	.15	.07
❑	315	Randolph Childress RC	.15	.07
❑	316	Anfernee Hardaway USA	.75	.35
❑	317	Grant Hill USA	1.25	.55
❑	318	Karl Malone USA	.40	.18
❑	319	Reggie Miller USA	.20	.09
❑	320	Hakeem Olajuwon USA	.40	.18
❑	321	Shaquille O'Neal USA	.75	.35
❑	322	Scottie Pippen USA	.60	.25
❑	323	David Robinson USA	.40	.18
❑	324	Glenn Robinson USA	.20	.09
❑	325	John Stockton USA	.20	.09
❑	326	Cedric Ceballos I95	.15	.07
❑	327	Shaquille O'Neal I95	.75	.35
❑	328	Glenn Robinson I95	.20	.09
❑	329	Shawn Kemp I95	.40	.18
❑	330	Nick Anderson I95	.15	.07
❑	331	Shawn Bradley I95	.15	.07
❑	332	Horace Grant I95 Brooks Thompson	.15	.07
❑	333	Robert Horry I95	.15	.07
❑	334	NBA Expansion I95 Grizzlies/Raptors	.15	.07
❑	335	Michael Jordan I95	2.50	1.10
❑	336	Nick Van Exel Dyan Cannon MA	.20	.09
❑	337	Michael Jordan David Hanson MA	1.25	.55
❑	338	Scottie Pippen Jenna Von Oy MA	.40	.18
❑	339	Michael Jordan Charlie Sheen MA	1.25	.55
❑	340	Jason Kidd Christopher "Kid" Reid MA	.40	.18
❑	341	Michael Jordan Queen Latifah MA	1.25	.55
❑	342	Charles Barkley Don Johnson MA	.40	.18
❑	343	Hakeem Olajuwon Corbin Bernsen MA	.40	.18
❑	344	Ahmad Rashad MA	.15	.07
❑	345	Willow Bay MA	.15	.07
❑	346	Gary Payton Mark Curry MA	.40	.18
❑	347	Horace Grant SJ	.15	.07
❑	348	Juwan Howard SJ	.20	.09
❑	349	David Robinson SJ	.40	.18
❑	350	Reggie Miller SJ	.20	.09
❑	351	Brian Grant SJ	.20	.09
❑	352	Michael Jordan SJ	2.50	1.10
❑	353	Cedric Ceballos SJ	.15	.07
❑	354	Blue Edwards SJ	.15	.07
❑	355	Acie Earl SJ	.15	.07
❑	356	Dennis Rodman SJ	.40	.18
❑	357	Shawn Kemp SJ	.40	.18
❑	358	Jerry Stackhouse SJ	.60	.25
❑	359	Jamal Mashburn SJ	.15	.07
❑	360	Antonio McDyess SJ	.75	.35

1995-96 Upper Deck Electric Court

	MINT	NRMT
COMPLETE SET (360)	100.00	45.00
COMPLETE SERIES 1 (180)	50.00	22.00
COMPLETE SERIES 2 (180)	50.00	22.00
COMMON CARD (1-360)	.30	.14

*STARS: 1.25X TO 2.5X BASE CARD HI
*RCs: 1X TO 2X BASE HI
ONE PER RETAIL PACK

1995-96 Upper Deck Electric Court Gold

	MINT	NRMT
COMPLETE SET (360)	1000.00	450.00
COMPLETE SERIES 1 (180)	500.00	220.00
COMPLETE SERIES 2 (180)	500.00	220.00
COMMON CARD (1-360)	1.50	.70

*STARS: 10X TO 20X BASE CARD HI
*RCs: 6X TO 12X BASE HI
SER.1/2 STATED ODDS 1:35 RETAIL

1995-96 Upper Deck All-Star Class

	MINT	NRMT
COMPLETE SET (25)	120.00	55.00
COMMON CARD (AS1-AS25)	2.00	.90
SEMISTARS	3.00	1.35
UNLISTED STARS	5.00	2.20

SER.1 STATED ODDS 1:17 HOBBY/RETAIL

	Card	Player	Mint	Nrmt
❑	AS1	Anfernee Hardaway	15.00	6.75
❑	AS2	Reggie Miller	5.00	2.20
❑	AS3	Grant Hill	25.00	11.00
❑	AS4	Scottie Pippen	15.00	6.75
❑	AS5	Shaquille O'Neal	25.00	11.00
❑	AS6	Larry Johnson	3.00	1.35
❑	AS7	Dana Barros	2.00	.90
❑	AS8	Vin Baker	5.00	2.20
❑	AS9	Alonzo Mourning	5.00	2.20
❑	AS10	Joe Dumars	5.00	2.20
❑	AS11	Patrick Ewing	5.00	2.20
❑	AS12	Tyrone Hill	2.00	.90
❑	AS13	Latrell Sprewell	10.00	4.50
❑	AS14	Dan Majerle	2.00	.90
❑	AS15	Shawn Kemp	8.00	3.60
❑	AS16	Karl Malone	8.00	3.60
❑	AS17	Hakeem Olajuwon	8.00	3.60
❑	AS18	Gary Payton	8.00	3.60
❑	AS19	Mitch Richmond	5.00	2.20
❑	AS20	David Robinson	8.00	3.60
❑	AS21	Detlef Schrempf	3.00	1.35
❑	AS22	Cedric Ceballos	2.00	.90
❑	AS23	John Stockton	5.00	2.20
❑	AS24	Dikembe Mutombo	3.00	1.35
❑	AS25	Charles Barkley	8.00	3.60

1995-96 Upper Deck Jordan Collection

	MINT	NRMT
COMPLETE SET (24)	125.00	55.00
COMP.COLC SER.1 (4)	10.00	4.50
COMP.UD SER.1 (4)	30.00	13.50
COMP.COLC SER.2 (4)	10.00	4.50
COMP.UD SER.2 (4)	30.00	13.50
COMP.SP SET (4)	40.00	18.00
COMP.SPC SET (4)	40.00	18.00
COMMON COLC 1 (JC1-JC4)	3.00	1.35
COMMON UD 1 (JC5-JC8)	10.00	4.50
COMMON COLC 2 (JC9-JC12)	3.00	1.35
COMMON UD 2 (JC13-JC16)	10.00	4.50
COMMON SP (JC17-JC20)	12.00	5.50
COMMON SPC (JC21-JC24)	12.00	5.50

SER.1/2 COLC STATED ODDS 1:11 HOB/RET

SER.1/2 UD STATED ODDS 1:29 HOB/RET
SP/SPC STATED ODDS 1:29
FOUR COLC PER COLC FACTORY SET

	Card	Player	Mint	Nrmt
❑	JC5	Michael Jordan Slam Dunk Champion 1987	10.00	4.50
❑	JC6	Michael Jordan Slam Dunk Champion 1988	10.00	4.50
❑	JC7	Michael Jordan Rising To The Occasion	10.00	4.50
❑	JC8	Michael Jordan Walking On Air	10.00	4.50
❑	JC13	Michael Jordan 1986 Garden Party	10.00	4.50
❑	JC14	Michael Jordan 1990 69-point Game	10.00	4.50
❑	JC15	Michael Jordan 1995 "He's Back"	10.00	4.50
❑	JC16	Michael Jordan Amazing Performances	10.00	4.50

1995-96 Upper Deck Predictor MVP

	MINT	NRMT
COMPLETE SET (10)	30.00	13.50
COMMON CARD (R1-R10)	.75	.35
SER.2 STATED ODDS 1:30 RETAIL		
COMP.MVP RED.SET (10)	15.00	6.75

*RED.CARDS: .2X TO .5X HI COLUMN
ONE RED.SET PER "W" CARD BY MAIL

	Card	Player	Mint	Nrmt
❑	R1	Michael Jordan MVP W	8.00	3.60
❑	R2	Michael Jordan All-NBA W	8.00	3.60
❑	R3	Michael Jordan Defensive POY L	8.00	3.60
❑	R4	Michael Jordan All-Defensive W	8.00	3.60
❑	R5	Michael Jordan Finals MVP W	8.00	3.60
❑	R6	Hakeem Olajuwon L	2.00	.90
❑	R7	Charles Barkley L	2.00	.90
❑	R8	Karl Malone L	2.00	.90
❑	R9	Anfernee Hardaway L	4.00	1.80
❑	R10	Long Shot Card L	.75	.35

1995-96 Upper Deck Predictor Player of the Month

	MINT	NRMT
COMPLETE SET (10)	30.00	13.50
COMMON CARD (R1-R10)	.75	.35
SEMISTARS	1.25	.55
SER.1 STATED ODDS 1:30 RETAIL		
COMP.POM RED.SET (10)	15.00	6.75
*RED.CARDS: .2X TO .5X HI COLUMN		
ONE RED.SET PER "W" CARD BY MAIL		

Card	MINT	NRMT
❑ R1 Michael Jordan Nov./Dec. L	8.00	3.60
❑ R2 Michael Jordan Jan. W	8.00	3.60
❑ R3 Michael Jordan Feb. L	8.00	3.60
❑ R4 Michael Jordan Mar. L	8.00	3.60
❑ R5 Michael Jordan Apr. L	8.00	3.60
❑ R6 Jamal Mashburn L	1.25	.55
❑ R7 David Robinson W	2.00	.90
❑ R8 Latrell Sprewell L	2.50	1.10
❑ R9 Chris Webber L	4.00	1.80
❑ R10 Long Shot Card W	.75	.35

1995-96 Upper Deck Predictor Player of the Week

	MINT	NRMT
COMPLETE SET (10)	30.00	13.50
COMMON CARD (H1-H10)	.75	.35
SER.1 STATED ODDS 1:30 HOBBY		
COMP.POW RED.SET (10)	15.00	6.75
*RED.CARDS: .2X TO .5X HI COLUMN		
ONE RED.SET PER "W" CARD BY MAIL		

Card	MINT	NRMT
❑ H1 Michael Jordan Nov./Dec. W	8.00	3.60
❑ H2 Michael Jordan Jan. W	8.00	3.60
❑ H3 Michael Jordan Feb. L	8.00	3.60
❑ H4 Michael Jordan Mar. L	8.00	3.60
❑ H5 Michael Jordan Apr. L	8.00	3.60
❑ H6 Anfernee Hardaway W	4.00	1.80
❑ H7 Hakeem Olajuwon W	2.00	.90
❑ H8 Scottie Pippen W	4.00	1.80
❑ H9 Glenn Robinson L	.75	.35
❑ H10 Long Shot Card W	.75	.35

1995-96 Upper Deck Predictor Scoring

	MINT	NRMT
COMPLETE SET (10)	30.00	13.50
COMMON CARD (H1-H10)	.75	.35
SER.2 STATED ODDS 1:30 HOBBY		
COMP.SCORE.RED.SET (10)	15.00	6.75
*RED.CARDS: .2X TO .5X HI COLUMN		
ONE RED.SET PER "W" CARD BY MAIL		

Card	MINT	NRMT
❑ H1 Michael Jordan Scoring W	8.00	3.60
❑ H2 Michael Jordan Assists L	8.00	3.60
❑ H3 Michael Jordan Steals L	8.00	3.60
❑ H4 Michael Jordan 3-pt. L	8.00	3.60
❑ H5 Michael Jordan Playoff W	8.00	3.60
❑ H6 David Robinson L	2.00	.90
❑ H7 Scottie Pippen L	4.00	1.80
❑ H8 Jerry Stackhouse L	2.00	.90
❑ H9 Glenn Robinson L	.75	.35
❑ H10 Long Shot Card L	.75	.35

1995-96 Upper Deck Special Edition

	MINT	NRMT
COMPLETE SET (180)	90.00	40.00
COMPLETE SERIES 1 (90)	30.00	13.50
COMPLETE SERIES 2 (90)	60.00	27.00
COMMON CARD (1-180)	.25	.11
SEMISTARS SER.1	.75	.35
SEMISTARS SER.2	.60	.25
UNLISTED STARS SER.1	1.25	.55
UNLISTED STARS SER.2	1.00	.45
ONE PER BOTH SERIES HOBBY PACK		
COMP.GOLD SET (180)	450.00	200.00
COMP.GOLD SER.1 (90)	150.00	70.00
COMP.GOLD SER.2 (90)	300.00	135.00
COMMON GOLD (SE1-SE180)	1.25	.55
*GOLD STARS: 3X TO 6X HI COLUMN		
*GOLD RCs: 2X TO 4X HI		
GOLD: SER.1/2 STATED ODDS 1:35 HOBBY		
SE PREFIX ON CARD NUMBERS		

Card	MINT	NRMT
❑ 1 Mookie Blaylock	.25	.11
❑ 2 Tyrone Corbin	.25	.11
❑ 3 Grant Long	.25	.11
❑ 4 Dee Brown	.25	.11
❑ 5 Sherman Douglas	.25	.11
❑ 6 Eric Montross	.25	.11
❑ 7 Scott Burrell	.25	.11
❑ 8 Dell Curry	.25	.11
❑ 9 Larry Johnson	.75	.35
❑ 10 Will Perdue	.25	.11
❑ 11 Scottie Pippen	4.00	1.80
❑ 12 Dickey Simpkins	.25	.11
❑ 13 Michael Cage	.25	.11
❑ 14 Mark Price	.25	.11
❑ 15 John Williams	.25	.11
❑ 16 Lucious Harris	.25	.11
❑ 17 Jim Jackson	.25	.11
❑ 18 Popeye Jones	.25	.11
❑ 19 Mahmoud Abdul-Rauf	.25	.11
❑ 20 LaPhonso Ellis	.25	.11
❑ 21 Robert Pack	.25	.11
❑ 22 Bill Curley	.25	.11
❑ 23 Grant Hill	6.00	2.70
❑ 24 Allan Houston	1.50	.70
❑ 25 Chris Gatling	.25	.11
❑ 26 Tim Hardaway	1.25	.55
❑ 27 Donyell Marshall	.75	.35
❑ 28 Clifford Rozier	.25	.11
❑ 29 Mario Elie	.25	.11
❑ 30 Robert Horry	.25	.11
❑ 31 Hakeem Olajuwon	2.00	.90
❑ 32 Kenny Smith	.25	.11
❑ 33 Dale Davis	.25	.11
❑ 34 Duane Ferrell	.25	.11
❑ 35 Derrick McKey	.25	.11
❑ 36 Reggie Miller	1.25	.55
❑ 37 Lamond Murray	.25	.11
❑ 38 Charles Outlaw	.25	.11
❑ 39 Eric Piatkowski	.25	.11
❑ 40 Anthony Peeler	.25	.11
❑ 41 Sedale Threatt	.25	.11
❑ 42 Nick Van Exel	.75	.35
❑ 43 Kevin Gamble	.25	.11
❑ 44 Matt Geiger	.25	.11
❑ 45 Billy Owens	.25	.11
❑ 46 Khalid Reeves	.25	.11
❑ 47 Vin Baker	1.25	.55
❑ 48 Lee Mayberry	.25	.11
❑ 49 Eric Murdock	.25	.11
❑ 50 Christian Laettner	.75	.35
❑ 51 Sean Rooks	.25	.11
❑ 52 Doug West	.25	.11
❑ 53 P.J. Brown	.25	.11
❑ 54 Derrick Coleman	.75	.35
❑ 55 Armon Gilliam	.25	.11
❑ 56 Hubert Davis	.25	.11
❑ 57 Charles Oakley	.25	.11
❑ 58 John Starks	.25	.11
❑ 59 Monty Williams	.25	.11
❑ 60 Anfernee Hardaway	4.00	1.80
❑ 61 Donald Royal	.25	.11
❑ 62 Dennis Scott	.25	.11
❑ 63 Jeff Turner	.25	.11
❑ 64 Clarence Weatherspoon	.25	.11
❑ 65 Jeff Malone	.25	.11
❑ 66 Scott Williams	.25	.11
❑ 67 A.C. Green	.75	.35
❑ 68 Kevin Johnson	.75	.35
❑ 69 Elliot Perry	.25	.11
❑ 70 Wesley Person	.75	.35
❑ 71 Harvey Grant	.25	.11
❑ 72 Aaron McKie	.25	.11
❑ 73 Rod Strickland	.75	.35
❑ 74 Buck Williams	.25	.11
❑ 75 Randy Brown	.25	.11
❑ 76 Bobby Hurley	.25	.11
❑ 77 Lionel Simmons	.25	.11
❑ 78 Terry Cummings	.25	.11

	No.	Player	Mint	NrMt
❑	79	Vinny Del Negro	.25	.11
❑	80	Avery Johnson	.25	.11
❑	81	David Robinson	2.00	.90
❑	82	Vincent Askew	.25	.11
❑	83	Shawn Kemp	2.00	.90
❑	84	Nate McMillan	.25	.11
❑	85	David Benoit	.25	.11
❑	86	Jeff Hornacek	.75	.35
❑	87	John Stockton	1.25	.55
❑	88	Juwan Howard	1.25	.55
❑	89	Gheorghe Muresan	.25	.11
❑	90	Doug Overton	.25	.11
❑	91	Stacey Augmon	.25	.11
❑	92	Alan Henderson	.60	.25
❑	93	Steve Smith	.60	.25
❑	94	Rick Fox	.25	.11
❑	95	Dino Radja	.25	.11
❑	96	Eric Williams	.25	.11
❑	97	Muggsy Bogues	.25	.11
❑	98	Kendall Gill	.60	.25
❑	99	Glen Rice	.60	.25
❑	100	Michael Jordan	12.00	5.50
❑	101	Toni Kukoc	1.25	.55
❑	102	Dennis Rodman	2.50	1.10
❑	103	Terrell Brandon	.60	.25
❑	104	Tyrone Hill	.25	.11
❑	105	Dan Majerle	.25	.11
❑	106	Jason Kidd	3.00	1.35
❑	107	Jamal Mashburn	.60	.25
❑	108	Cherokee Parks	.25	.11
❑	109	Antonio McDyess	4.00	1.80
❑	110	Dikembe Mutombo	.60	.25
❑	111	Reggie Williams	.25	.11
❑	112	Joe Dumars	1.00	.45
❑	113	Lindsey Hunter	.25	.11
❑	114	Otis Thorpe	.25	.11
❑	115	Chris Mullin	1.00	.45
❑	116	Joe Smith	2.50	1.10
❑	117	Latrell Sprewell	2.00	.90
❑	118	Chucky Brown	.25	.11
❑	119	Sam Cassell	.60	.25
❑	120	Clyde Drexler	1.00	.45
❑	121	Travis Best	.60	.25
❑	122	Mark Jackson	.25	.11
❑	123	Rik Smits	.25	.11
❑	124	Brent Barry	1.00	.45
❑	125	Rodney Rogers	.25	.11
❑	126	Loy Vaught	.25	.11
❑	127	Cedric Ceballos	.25	.11
❑	128	Magic Johnson	3.00	1.35
❑	129	Eddie Jones	2.00	.90
❑	130	Alonzo Mourning	1.00	.45
❑	131	Kurt Thomas	.25	.11
❑	132	Kevin Willis	.25	.11
❑	133	Sherman Douglas	.25	.11
❑	134	Shawn Respert	.25	.11
❑	135	Glenn Robinson	1.00	.45
❑	136	Kevin Garnett	10.00	4.50
❑	137	Tom Gugliotta	.60	.25
❑	138	Isaiah Rider	.60	.25
❑	139	Kenny Anderson	.60	.25
❑	140	Ed O'Bannon	.25	.11
❑	141	Jayson Williams	.60	.25
❑	142	Patrick Ewing	1.00	.45
❑	143	Derek Harper	.25	.11
❑	144	Charles Smith	.25	.11
❑	145	Nick Anderson	.25	.11
❑	146	Horace Grant	.60	.25
❑	147	Shaquille O'Neal	5.00	2.20
❑	148	Vernon Maxwell	.25	.11
❑	149	Jerry Stackhouse	2.50	1.10
❑	150	Sharone Wright	.25	.11
❑	151	Charles Barkley	1.50	.70
❑	152	Michael Finley	3.00	1.35
❑	153	Danny Manning	.60	.25
❑	154	John Williams	.25	.11
❑	155	Clifford Robinson	.25	.11
❑	156	Arvydas Sabonis	1.00	.45
❑	157	Gary Trent	.25	.11
❑	158	Brian Grant	1.00	.45
❑	159	Mitch Richmond	1.00	.45
❑	160	Corliss Williamson	1.00	.45
❑	161	Sean Elliott	.25	.11
❑	162	Will Perdue	.25	.11
❑	163	Doc Rivers	.25	.11
❑	164	Gary Payton	1.50	.70
❑	165	Sam Perkins	.60	.25
❑	166	Detlef Schrempf	.60	.25
❑	167	Tracy Murray	.25	.11
❑	168	Ed Pinckney	.25	.11
❑	169	Carlos Rogers	.25	.11
❑	170	Damon Stoudamire	4.00	1.80
❑	171	Karl Malone	1.50	.70
❑	172	Chris Morris	.25	.11
❑	173	Greg Ostertag	.25	.11
❑	174	Greg Anthony	.25	.11
❑	175	Lawrence Moten	.25	.11
❑	176	Bryant Reeves	.60	.25
❑	177	Byron Scott	.25	.11
❑	178	Calbert Cheaney	.25	.11
❑	179	Rasheed Wallace	3.00	1.35
❑	180	Chris Webber	3.00	1.35

1996-97 Upper Deck

	MINT	NRMT
COMPLETE SET (360)	50.00	22.00
COMPLETE SERIES 1 (180)	30.00	13.50
COMPLETE SERIES 2 (180)	20.00	9.00
COMMON CARD (1-360)	.15	.07
SEMISTARS	.20	.09
UNLISTED STARS	.40	.18

SUBSET CARDS HALF VALUE OF BASE CARDS

	No.	Player	Mint	NrMt
❑	1	Mookie Blaylock	.15	.07
❑	2	Alan Henderson	.15	.07
❑	3	Christian Laettner	.20	.09
❑	4	Ken Norman	.15	.07
❑	5	Dee Brown	.15	.07
❑	6	Todd Day	.15	.07
❑	7	Rick Fox	.15	.07
❑	8	Dino Radja	.15	.07
❑	9	Dana Barros	.15	.07
❑	10	Eric Williams	.15	.07
❑	11	Scott Burrell	.15	.07
❑	12	Dell Curry	.15	.07
❑	13	Matt Geiger	.15	.07
❑	14	Glen Rice	.20	.09
❑	15	Ron Harper	.20	.09
❑	16	Michael Jordan	5.00	2.20
❑	17	Luc Longley	.15	.07
❑	18	Toni Kukoc	.50	.23
❑	19	Dennis Rodman	.75	.35
❑	20	Danny Ferry	.15	.07
❑	21	Tyrone Hill	.15	.07
❑	22	Bobby Phills	.15	.07
❑	23	Bob Sura	.15	.07
❑	24	Tony Dumas	.15	.07
❑	25	George McCloud	.15	.07
❑	26	Jim Jackson	.15	.07
❑	27	Jamal Mashburn	.20	.09
❑	28	Loren Meyer	.15	.07
❑	29	Dale Ellis	.15	.07
❑	30	LaPhonso Ellis	.15	.07
❑	31	Tom Hammonds	.15	.07
❑	32	Antonio McDyess	.60	.25
❑	33	Joe Dumars	.40	.18
❑	34	Grant Hill	2.00	.90
❑	35	Lindsey Hunter	.15	.07
❑	36	Terry Mills	.15	.07
❑	37	Theo Ratliff	.20	.09
❑	38	B.J. Armstrong	.15	.07
❑	39	Donyell Marshall	.15	.07
❑	40	Chris Mullin	.40	.18
❑	41	Rony Seikaly	.15	.07
❑	42	Joe Smith	.40	.18
❑	43	Sam Cassell	.20	.09
❑	44	Clyde Drexler	.40	.18
❑	45	Mario Elie	.15	.07
❑	46	Robert Horry	.15	.07
❑	47	Travis Best	.15	.07
❑	48	Antonio Davis	.15	.07
❑	49	Dale Davis	.15	.07
❑	50	Eddie Johnson	.15	.07
❑	51	Derrick McKey	.15	.07
❑	52	Reggie Miller	.40	.18
❑	53	Brent Barry	.15	.07
❑	54	Lamond Murray	.15	.07
❑	55	Eric Piatkowski	.15	.07
❑	56	Rodney Rogers	.15	.07
❑	57	Loy Vaught	.15	.07
❑	58	Kobe Bryant RC	15.00	6.75
❑	59	Eddie Jones	.75	.35
❑	60	Elden Campbell	.15	.07
❑	61	Shaquille O'Neal	2.00	.90
❑	62	Nick Van Exel	.20	.09
❑	63	Keith Askins	.15	.07
❑	64	Rex Chapman	.15	.07
❑	65	Sasha Danilovic	.15	.07
❑	66	Alonzo Mourning	.40	.18
❑	67	Kurt Thomas	.15	.07
❑	68	Tim Hardaway	.40	.18
❑	69	Ray Allen RC	1.50	.70
❑	70	Johnny Newman	.15	.07
❑	71	Shawn Respert	.15	.07
❑	72	Glenn Robinson	.40	.18
❑	73	Tom Gugliotta	.20	.09
❑	74	Stephon Marbury RC	2.50	1.10
❑	75	Terry Porter	.15	.07
❑	76	Doug West	.15	.07
❑	77	Shawn Bradley	.15	.07
❑	78	Kevin Edwards	.15	.07
❑	79	Vern Fleming	.15	.07
❑	80	Ed O'Bannon	.15	.07
❑	81	Jayson Williams	.20	.09
❑	82	John Starks	.15	.07
❑	83	Patrick Ewing	.40	.18
❑	84	Charlie Ward	.15	.07
❑	85	Nick Anderson	.15	.07
❑	86	Anfernee Hardaway	1.25	.55
❑	87	Jon Koncak	.15	.07
❑	88	Donald Royal	.15	.07
❑	89	Brian Shaw	.15	.07
❑	90	Derrick Coleman	.20	.09
❑	91	Allen Iverson RC	4.00	1.80
❑	92	Jerry Stackhouse	.40	.18
❑	93	Clarence Weatherspoon	.15	.07
❑	94	Charles Barkley	.60	.25
❑	95	Kevin Johnson	.20	.09
❑	96	Danny Manning	.20	.09
❑	97	Elliot Perry	.15	.07
❑	98	Wayman Tisdale	.15	.07
❑	99	Randolph Childress	.15	.07
❑	100	Aaron McKie	.15	.07
❑	101	Arvydas Sabonis	.20	.09
❑	102	Gary Trent	.15	.07
❑	103	Chris Dudley	.15	.07
❑	104	Tyus Edney	.15	.07
❑	105	Brian Grant	.40	.18
❑	106	Bobby Hurley	.15	.07
❑	107	Olden Polynice	.15	.07
❑	108	Corliss Williamson	.15	.07
❑	109	Vinny Del Negro	.15	.07
❑	110	Avery Johnson	.15	.07
❑	111	Will Perdue	.15	.07
❑	112	David Robinson	.60	.25
❑	113	Hersey Hawkins	.20	.09
❑	114	Shawn Kemp	.60	.25
❑	115	Nate McMillan	.15	.07
❑	116	Detlef Schrempf	.20	.09
❑	117	Gary Payton	.60	.25
❑	118	Marcus Camby RC	.75	.35
❑	119	Zan Tabak	.15	.07
❑	120	Damon Stoudamire	.60	.25
❑	121	Carlos Rogers	.15	.07
❑	122	Sharone Wright	.15	.07
❑	123	Antoine Carr	.15	.07
❑	124	Jeff Hornacek	.20	.09
❑	125	Adam Keefe	.15	.07

❑ 126 Chris Morris .15 .07
❑ 127 John Stockton .40 .18
❑ 128 Blue Edwards .15 .07
❑ 129 Shareef Abdur-Rahim RC 2.50 1.10
❑ 130 Bryant Reeves .15 .07
❑ 131 Roy Rogers RC .15 .07
❑ 132 Calbert Cheaney .15 .07
❑ 133 Tim Legler .15 .07
❑ 134 Gheorghe Muresan .15 .07
❑ 135 Chris Webber 1.25 .55
❑ 136 Dikembe Mutombo .40 .18
Mookie Blaylock
Steve Smith
Christian Laettner
Alan Henderson
BW- Atlanta Hawks
❑ 137 Dana Barros .15 .07
Dino Radja
Eric Williams
Dee Brown
Pervis Ellison
BW - Boston Celtics
❑ 138 Glen Rice .40 .18
Matt Geiger
Vlade Divac
Scott Burrell
George Zidek
BW - Charlotte Hornets
❑ 139 Michael Jordan 2.00 .90
Scottie Pippen
Dennis Rodman
Toni Kukoc
Ron Harper
BW - Chicago Bulls
❑ 140 Terrell Brandon .20 .09
Danny Ferry
Tyrone Hill
Bobby Phills
Bobby Sura
BW - Cleveland Cavaliers
❑ 141 Jason Kidd .20 .09
Jamal Mashburn
Jim Jackson
Tony Dumas
Loren Meyer
BW - Dallas Mavericks
❑ 142 LaPhonso Ellis .15 .07
Antonio McDyess
Mark Jackson
Dale Ellis
Bryant Stith
BW - Denver Nuggets
❑ 143 Joe Dumars .75 .35
Grant Hill
Stacey Augmon
Lindsey Hunter
Theo Ratliff
BW - Detroit Pistons
❑ 144 Joe Smith .40 .18
Latrell Sprewell
Chris Mullin
Rony Seikaly
BJ Armstrong
BW - Golden State Warriors
❑ 145 Hakeem Olajuwon .40 .18
Clyde Drexler
Charles Barkley
Brent Price
Mario Elie
BW - Houston Rockets
❑ 146 Reggie Miller .20 .09
Travis Best
Rik Smits
Dale Davis
Antonio Davis
BW - Indiana Pacers
❑ 147 Brent Barry .15 .07
Lamond Murray
Rodney Rogers
Terry Dehere
Eric Piatkowski
BW - Los Angeles Clippers
❑ 148 Shaquille O'Neal 2.00 .90
Eddie Jones
Kobe Bryant
Cedric Ceballos
Nick Van Exel
BW - Los Angeles Lakers
❑ 149 Alonzo Mourning .40 .18
Tim Hardaway
Sasha Danilovic
Kurt Thomas
Keith Askins
BW - Miami Heat
❑ 150 Vin Baker .40 .18
Glenn Robinson
Sherman Douglas
Shawn Respert
Johnnie Newman
BW - Milwaukee Bucks
❑ 151 Kevin Garnett 1.00 .45
Tom Gugliotta
Cherokee Parks
Terry Porter
Doug West
BW - Minnesota Timberwolves
❑ 152 Shawn Bradley .20 .09
Kendall Gill
Ed O'Bannon
Jayson Williams
Robert Pack
BW - New Jersey Nets
❑ 153 Patrick Ewing .40 .18
Allan Houston
Larry Johnson
Charles Oakley
John Starks
BW - New York Knicks
❑ 154 Anfernee Hardaway .60 .25
Dennis Scott
Horace Grant
Nick Anderson
Brian Shaw
BW - Orlando Magic
❑ 155 Jerry Stackhouse .20 .09
Clarence Weatherspoon
Derrick Coleman
Scott Williams
Rex Walters
BW - Philadelphia 76'ers
❑ 156 Kevin Johnson .15 .07
Danny Manning
Michael Finley
Wesley Person
AC Green
BW - Phoenix Suns
❑ 157 Clifford Robinson .20 .09
Isaiah Rider
Arvydas Sabonis
Rasheed Wallace
Kenny Anderson
BW - Portland Trail Blazers
❑ 158 Mitch Richmond .20 .09
Brian Grant
Billy Owens
Tyus Edney
Michael Smith
BW - Sacramento Kings
❑ 159 David Robinson .40 .18
Sean Elliott
Avery Johnson
Vinny Del Negro
Chuck Person
BW - San Antonio Spurs
❑ 160 Shawn Kemp .50 .23
Gary Payton
Detlef Schrempf
Hersey Hawkins
Sam Perkins
BW - Seattle Supersonics
❑ 161 Damon Stoudamire .40 .18
Zan Tabak
Sharone Wright
Doug Christie
Carlos Rogers
BW - Toronto Raptors
❑ 162 John Stockton .40 .18
Karl Malone
Jeff Hornacek
Bryon Russell
Antoine Carr
BW - Utah Jazz
❑ 163 Bryant Reeves .40 .18
Shareef Abdur-Rahim
Greg Anthony
Blue Edwards
Lawrence Moten
BW - Vancouver Grizzlies
❑ 164 Juwan Howard .40 .18
Gheorge Muresan
Chris Webber
Calbert Cheaney
Tim Legler
BW - Washington Bullets
❑ 165 Michael Jordan GP 2.50 1.10
❑ 166 Corliss Williamson GP .15 .07
❑ 167 Dell Curry GP .15 .07
❑ 168 John Starks GP .15 .07
❑ 169 Dennis Rodman GP .40 .18
❑ 170 Chris Webber .40 .18
Latrell Sprewell
❑ 171 Cedric Ceballos GP .15 .07
❑ 172 Theo Ratliff GP .15 .07
❑ 173 Anfernee Hardaway GP .75 .35
❑ 174 Grant Hill GP 1.25 .55
❑ 175 Alonzo Mourning GP .20 .09
❑ 176 Shawn Kemp GP .40 .18
❑ 177 Jason Kidd GP .40 .18
❑ 178 Avery Johnson GP .15 .07
❑ 179 Gary Payton GP .40 .18
❑ 180 Checklist .15 .07
❑ 181 Priest Lauderdale RC .15 .07
❑ 182 Dikembe Mutombo .20 .09
❑ 183 Eldridge Recasner RC .15 .07
❑ 184 Steve Smith .20 .09
❑ 185 Pervis Ellison .15 .07
❑ 186 Greg Minor .15 .07
❑ 187 Antoine Walker RC 1.50 .70
❑ 188 David Wesley .15 .07
❑ 189 Muggsy Bogues .15 .07
❑ 190 Tony Delk RC .20 .09
❑ 191 Vlade Divac .15 .07
❑ 192 Anthony Mason .20 .09
❑ 193 George Zidek .15 .07
❑ 194 Jason Caffey .15 .07
❑ 195 Steve Kerr .15 .07
❑ 196 Robert Parish .20 .09
❑ 197 Scottie Pippen 1.25 .55
❑ 198 Terrell Brandon .20 .09
❑ 199 Antonio Lang .15 .07
❑ 200 Chris Mills .15 .07
❑ 201 Vitaly Potapenko RC .15 .07
❑ 202 Mark West .15 .07
❑ 203 Chris Gatling .15 .07
❑ 204 Derek Harper .15 .07
❑ 205 Sam Cassell .20 .09
❑ 206 Eric Montross .15 .07
❑ 207 Samaki Walker RC .15 .07
❑ 208 Mark Jackson .15 .07
❑ 209 Ervin Johnson .15 .07
❑ 210 Sarunas Marciulionis .15 .07
❑ 211 Ricky Pierce .15 .07
❑ 212 Bryant Stith .15 .07
❑ 213 Stacey Augmon .15 .07
❑ 214 Grant Long .15 .07
❑ 215 Rick Mahorn .15 .07
❑ 216 Otis Thorpe .15 .07
❑ 217 Jerome Williams RC .60 .25
❑ 218 Bimbo Coles .15 .07
❑ 219 Todd Fuller RC .15 .07
❑ 220 Mark Price .15 .07
❑ 221 Felton Spencer .15 .07
❑ 222 Latrell Sprewell .75 .35
❑ 223 Charles Barkley .60 .25
❑ 224 Othella Harrington RC .40 .18
❑ 225 Hakeem Olajuwon .60 .25
❑ 226 Matt Maloney RC .20 .09
❑ 227 Kevin Willis .15 .07
❑ 228 Erick Dampier RC .20 .09
❑ 229 Duane Ferrell .15 .07
❑ 230 Jalen Rose .40 .18
❑ 231 Rik Smits .15 .07
❑ 232 Terry Dehere .15 .07
❑ 233 Charles Outlaw .15 .07
❑ 234 Pooh Richardson .15 .07
❑ 235 Malik Sealy .15 .07
❑ 236 Lorenzen Wright RC .20 .09
❑ 237 Cedric Ceballos .15 .07

❑ 238 Derek Fisher RC	.60	.25
❑ 239 Travis Knight RC	.15	.07
❑ 240 Sean Rooks	.15	.07
❑ 241 Byron Scott	.15	.07
❑ 242 P.J. Brown	.15	.07
❑ 243 Voshon Lenard RC	.20	.09
❑ 244 Dan Majerle	.20	.09
❑ 245 Martin Muursepp RC	.15	.07
❑ 246 Gary Grant	.15	.07
❑ 247 Vin Baker	.20	.09
❑ 248 Armon Gilliam	.15	.07
❑ 249 Andrew Lang	.15	.07
❑ 250 Elliot Perry	.15	.07
❑ 251 Kevin Garnett	2.50	1.10
❑ 252 Shane Heal RC	.15	.07
❑ 253 Cherokee Parks	.15	.07
❑ 254 Stojko Vrankovic	.15	.07
❑ 255 Kendall Gill	.20	.09
❑ 256 Kerry Kittles RC	.75	.35
❑ 257 Xavier McDaniel	.15	.07
❑ 258 Robert Pack	.15	.07
❑ 259 Chris Childs	.15	.07
❑ 260 Allan Houston	.40	.18
❑ 261 Larry Johnson	.20	.09
❑ 262 Dontae' Jones RC	.15	.07
❑ 263 Walter McCarty RC	.15	.07
❑ 264 Charles Oakley	.15	.07
❑ 265 John Wallace RC	.40	.18
❑ 266 Buck Williams	.15	.07
❑ 267 Brian Evans RC	.15	.07
❑ 268 Horace Grant	.20	.09
❑ 269 Dennis Scott	.15	.07
❑ 270 Rony Seikaly	.15	.07
❑ 271 David Vaughn	.15	.07
❑ 272 Michael Cage	.15	.07
❑ 273 Lucious Harris	.15	.07
❑ 274 Don MacLean	.15	.07
❑ 275 Mark Davis	.15	.07
❑ 276 Jason Kidd	1.25	.55
❑ 277 Michael Finley	.50	.23
❑ 278 A.C. Green	.20	.09
❑ 279 Robert Horry	.15	.07
❑ 280 Steve Nash RC	.20	.09
❑ 281 Wesley Person	.15	.07
❑ 282 Kenny Anderson	.20	.09
❑ 283 Aleksandar Djordjevic RC	.15	.07
❑ 284 Jermaine O'Neal RC	.75	.35
❑ 285 Isaiah Rider	.20	.09
❑ 286 Clifford Robinson	.15	.07
❑ 287 Rasheed Wallace	.50	.23
❑ 288 Mahmoud Abdul-Rauf	.15	.07
❑ 289 Billy Owens	.15	.07
❑ 290 Mitch Richmond	.40	.18
❑ 291 Michael Smith	.15	.07
❑ 292 Cory Alexander	.15	.07
❑ 293 Sean Elliott	.15	.07
❑ 294 Vernon Maxwell	.15	.07
❑ 295 Dominique Wilkins	.40	.18
❑ 296 Craig Ehlo	.15	.07
❑ 297 Jim McIlvaine	.15	.07
❑ 298 Sam Perkins	.20	.09
❑ 299 Steve Scheffler RC	.15	.07
❑ 300 Hubert Davis	.15	.07
❑ 301 Popeye Jones	.15	.07
❑ 302 Donald Whiteside RC	.15	.07
❑ 303 Walt Williams	.15	.07
❑ 304 Karl Malone	.60	.25
❑ 305 Greg Ostertag	.15	.07
❑ 306 Bryon Russell	.15	.07
❑ 307 Jamie Watson	.15	.07
❑ 308 Greg Anthony	.15	.07
❑ 309 George Lynch	.15	.07
❑ 310 Lawrence Moten	.15	.07
❑ 311 Anthony Peeler	.15	.07
❑ 312 Juwan Howard	.20	.09
❑ 313 Tracy Murray	.15	.07
❑ 314 Rod Strickland	.20	.09
❑ 315 Harvey Grant	.15	.07
❑ 316 Charles Barkley DN	.40	.18
❑ 317 Clyde Drexler DN	.20	.09
❑ 318 Dikembe Mutombo DN	.15	.07
❑ 319 Larry Johnson DN	.15	.07
❑ 320 Shaquille O'Neal DN	.75	.35
❑ 321 Mookie Blaylock DN	.15	.07
❑ 322 Tim Hardaway DN	.20	.09
❑ 323 Dennis Rodman DN	.40	.18
❑ 324 Dan Majerle DN	.15	.07
❑ 325 Stacey Augmon DN	.15	.07
❑ 326 Anthony Mason DN	.15	.07
❑ 327 Kenny Anderson DN	.15	.07
❑ 328 Mahmoud Abdul-Rauf DN	.15	.07
❑ 329 Chris Webber DN	.50	.23
❑ 330 Dominique Wilkins DN	.20	.09
❑ 331 Dikembe Mutombo WD	.15	.07
❑ 332 Dana Barros WD	.15	.07
❑ 333 Glen Rice WD	.15	.07
❑ 334 Dennis Rodman WD	.40	.18
❑ 335 Terrell Brandon WD	.15	.07
❑ 336 Jason Kidd WD	.40	.18
❑ 337 Antonio McDyess WD	.40	.18
❑ 338 Grant Hill WD	1.25	.55
❑ 339 Joe Smith WD	.20	.09
❑ 340 Charles Barkley WD	.40	.18
❑ 341 Reggie Miller WD	.20	.09
❑ 342 Brent Barry WD	.15	.07
❑ 343 Shaquille O'Neal WD	.75	.35
❑ 344 Alonzo Mourning WD	.20	.09
❑ 345 Glenn Robinson WD	.20	.09
❑ 346 Stephon Marbury WD	2.00	.90
❑ 347 Kerry Kittles WD	.40	.18
❑ 348 Patrick Ewing WD	.20	.09
❑ 349 Anfernee Hardaway WD	.75	.35
❑ 350 Allen Iverson WD	1.50	.70
❑ 351 Danny Manning WD	.15	.07
❑ 352 Arvydas Sabonis WD	.15	.07
❑ 353 Mitch Richmond WD	.20	.09
❑ 354 David Robinson WD	.40	.18
❑ 355 Shawn Kemp WD	.40	.18
❑ 356 Marcus Camby WD	.40	.18
❑ 357 Karl Malone WD	.40	.18
❑ 358 S.Abdur-Rahim WD	1.25	.55
❑ 359 Gheorghe Muresan WD	.15	.07
❑ 360 Checklist 181-360	.15	.07

1996-97 Upper Deck Autographs

	MINT	NRMT
COMPLETE SET (4)	400.00	180.00
COMMON CARD (A1-A4)	60.00	27.00
HAND NUMBERED TO 500		
RANDOM INSERTS IN SER.2 PACKS		
❑ A1 Anfernee Hardaway	200.00	90.00
❑ A2 Shawn Kemp	120.00	55.00
❑ A3 Antonio McDyess	80.00	36.00
❑ A4 Damon Stoudamire	60.00	27.00

1996-97 Upper Deck Fast Break Connections

	MINT	NRMT
COMPLETE SET (30)	80.00	36.00
COMMON CARD (FB1-FB30)	1.00	.45
SEMISTARS	1.50	.70
UNLISTED STARS	2.50	1.10
SER.1 STATED ODDS 1:8		
❑ FB1 Jim Jackson	1.00	.45
❑ FB2 Jason Kidd	8.00	3.60
❑ FB3 Jamal Mashburn	1.50	.70
❑ FB4 Mario Elie	1.00	.45
❑ FB5 Hakeem Olajuwon	4.00	1.80
❑ FB6 Clyde Drexler	2.50	1.10
❑ FB7 Cedric Ceballos	1.00	.45
❑ FB8 Nick Van Exel	1.50	.70
❑ FB9 Eddie Jones	5.00	2.20
❑ FB10 Danny Manning	1.50	.70
❑ FB11 Michael Finley	3.00	1.35
❑ FB12 Kevin Johnson	1.50	.70
❑ FB13 Tyus Edney	1.00	.45
❑ FB14 Brian Grant	2.50	1.10
❑ FB15 Mitch Richmond	2.50	1.10
❑ FB16 Sean Elliott	1.00	.45
❑ FB17 David Robinson	4.00	1.80
❑ FB18 Avery Johnson	1.00	.45
❑ FB19 Shawn Kemp	4.00	1.80
❑ FB20 Gary Payton	4.00	1.80
❑ FB21 Detlef Schrempf	1.50	.70
❑ FB22 Scottie Pippen	8.00	3.60
❑ FB23 Michael Jordan	30.00	13.50
❑ FB24 Toni Kukoc	3.00	1.35
❑ FB25 Sherman Douglas	1.00	.45
❑ FB26 Glenn Robinson	2.50	1.10
❑ FB27 Vin Baker	1.50	.70
❑ FB28 Jeff Hornacek	1.50	.70
❑ FB29 John Stockton	2.50	1.10
❑ FB30 Karl Malone	4.00	1.80

1996-97 Upper Deck Generation Excitement

	MINT	NRMT
COMPLETE SET (20)	120.00	55.00
COMMON CARD (G1-G20)	2.50	1.10
SEMISTARS	5.00	2.20
SER.1 STATED ODDS 1:33		
❑ G1 Steve Smith	5.00	2.20
❑ G2 Eric Williams	2.50	1.10
❑ G3 Jason Kidd	15.00	6.75
❑ G4 Antonio McDyess	8.00	3.60
❑ G5 Grant Hill	25.00	11.00
❑ G6 Joe Smith	5.00	2.20
❑ G7 Brent Barry	2.50	1.10
❑ G8 Eddie Jones	10.00	4.50
❑ G9 Vin Baker	5.00	2.20
❑ G10 Kevin Garnett	30.00	13.50
❑ G11 Ed O'Bannon	2.50	1.10
❑ G12 Anfernee Hardaway	15.00	6.75
❑ G13 Jerry Stackhouse	5.00	2.20
❑ G14 Michael Finley	6.00	2.70
❑ G15 Gary Trent	2.50	1.10
❑ G16 Tyus Edney	2.50	1.10
❑ G17 Sean Elliott	2.50	1.10
❑ G18 Shawn Kemp	8.00	3.60
❑ G19 Damon Stoudamire	8.00	3.60
❑ G20 Gheorghe Muresan	2.50	1.10

1996-97 Upper Deck Jordan Greater Heights

	MINT	NRMT
COMPLETE SET (10)	200.00	90.00
COMMON JORDAN (GH1-GH10)	25.00	11.00
SER.1 STATED ODDS 1:66 HOB/RET		
❑ GH1 Michael Jordan Dunking	25.00	11.00

		MINT	NRMT
❑ GH2	Michael Jordan Shooting	25.00	11.00
❑ GH3	Michael Jordan Rebounding	25.00	11.00
❑ GH4	Michael Jordan Defending	25.00	11.00
❑ GH5	Michael Jordan Breakaways	25.00	11.00
❑ GH6	Michael Jordan Put backs	25.00	11.00
❑ GH7	Michael Jordan Passing	25.00	11.00
❑ GH8	Michael Jordan Mid-air magic	25.00	11.00
❑ GH9	Michael Jordan Excitement	25.00	11.00
❑ GH10	Michael Jordan The Future	25.00	11.00

1996-97 Upper Deck Jordan's Viewpoints

	MINT	NRMT
COMPLETE SET (10)	125.00	55.00
COMMON JORDAN (VP1-VP10)	15.00	6.75

SER.2 STATED ODDS 1:34 HOB/RET

		MINT	NRMT
❑ VP1	Michael Jordan MJ on practice	15.00	6.75
❑ VP2	Michael Jordan MJ on entering the arena	15.00	6.75
❑ VP3	Michael Jordan MJ on shooting	15.00	6.75
❑ VP4	Michael Jordan MJ on pressure	15.00	6.75
❑ VP5	Michael Jordan MJ on free throws	15.00	6.75
❑ VP6	Michael Jordan MJ on halftime	15.00	6.75
❑ VP7	Michael Jordan MJ on shooting three-pointers	15.00	6.75
❑ VP8	Michael Jordan MJ on playing defense	15.00	6.75
❑ VP9	Michael Jordan MJ on talking to the media	15.00	6.75
❑ VP10	Michael Jordan MJ on winning	15.00	6.75

1996-97 Upper Deck Predictor Scoring 1

	MINT	NRMT
COMPLETE SET (20)	50.00	22.00
COMMON CARD (P1-P20)	1.00	.45
SEMISTARS	1.25	.55
UNLISTED STARS	2.00	.90

SER.1 STATED ODDS 1:23
*TV CEL RED.CARDS: 1X TO 2X HI COL.

		MINT	NRMT
❑ P1	Mookie Blaylock 30 PTS. W	1.00	.45
❑ P2	Dino Radja 35 PTS. L	1.00	.45
❑ P3	Michael Jordan 35 PTS. W	25.00	11.00
❑ P4	Terrell Brandon 35 PTS. L	1.25	.55
❑ P5	Jason Kidd 30 PTS. W	6.00	2.70
❑ P6	Joe Dumars 25 PTS. W	2.00	.90
❑ P7	Joe Smith 30 PTS. W	2.00	.90
❑ P8	Hakeem Olajuwon 35 PTS. W	3.00	1.35
❑ P9	Rik Smits 35 PTS. W	1.00	.45
❑ P10	Brent Barry 25 PTS. L	1.00	.45
❑ P11	Kurt Thomas 25 PTS. L	1.00	.45
❑ P12	Anfernee Hardaway 35 PTS. W	6.00	2.70
❑ P13	Clarence Weatherspoon 35 PTS. L	1.00	.45
❑ P14	Clifford Robinson 35 PTS. L	1.25	.55
❑ P15	Mitch Richmond 35 PTS. W	2.00	.90
❑ P16	David Robinson 35 PTS. L	3.00	1.35
❑ P17	Shawn Kemp 35 PTS. L	3.00	1.35
❑ P18	Damon Stoudamire 35 PTS. W	3.00	1.35
❑ P19	Karl Malone 35 PTS. W	3.00	1.35
❑ P20	Bryant Reeves 30 PTS. W	1.00	.45

1996-97 Upper Deck Predictor Scoring 2

	MINT	NRMT
COMPLETE SET (20)	60.00	27.00
COMMON CARD (P1-P20)	1.00	.45
SEMISTARS	1.25	.55
UNLISTED STARS	2.00	.90

SER.2 STATED ODDS 1:23
*TV CEL RED.CARDS: 1X TO 2X HI COL.

		MINT	NRMT
❑ P1	Glen Rice 35 PTS. W	1.25	.55
❑ P2	Michael Jordan 35 PTS. W	25.00	11.00
❑ P3	Jamal Mashburn 30 PTS. L	1.25	.55
❑ P4	Antonio McDyess 30 PTS. W	3.00	1.35
❑ P5	Charles Barkley 35 PTS. W	3.00	1.35
❑ P6	Reggie Miller 35 PTS. W	2.00	.90
❑ P7	Shaquille O'Neal 35 PTS. W	10.00	4.50
❑ P8	Alonzo Mourning 35 PTS. W	2.00	.90
❑ P9	Vin Baker 30 PTS. W	1.25	.55
❑ P10	Kevin Garnett 30 PTS. W	12.00	5.50
❑ P11	Kerry Kittles 25 PTS. W	2.00	.90
❑ P12	Patrick Ewing 30 PTS. W	2.00	.90
❑ P13	Anfernee Hardaway 35 PTS. W	6.00	2.70
❑ P14	Allen Iverson 25 PTS. W	10.00	4.50
❑ P15	Robert Horry 30 PTS. L	1.00	.45
❑ P16	Shawn Kemp 35 PTS. L	3.00	1.35
❑ P17	Marcus Camby 25 PTS. W	3.00	1.35
❑ P18	John Stockton 25 PTS. W	2.00	.90
❑ P19	Shareef Abdur-Rahim 25 PTS. W	6.00	2.70
❑ P20	Juwan Howard 30 PTS. W	1.25	.55

1996-97 Upper Deck Rookie Exclusives

	MINT	NRMT
COMPLETE SET (20)	40.00	18.00
COMMON CARD (R1-R20)	.50	.23
SEMISTARS	1.00	.45
UNLISTED STARS	1.50	.70

SER.2 STATED ODDS 1:4 HOB/RET, 1:2 JUM

		MINT	NRMT
❑ R1	Allen Iverson	8.00	3.60
❑ R2	John Wallace	1.00	.45
❑ R3	Kerry Kittles	1.50	.70
❑ R4	Roy Rogers	.50	.23
❑ R5	Marcus Camby	2.50	1.10
❑ R6	Antoine Walker	3.00	1.35
❑ R7	Ray Allen	3.00	1.35
❑ R8	Samaki Walker	.50	.23
❑ R9	Walter McCarty	.50	.23
❑ R10	Kobe Bryant	15.00	6.75
❑ R11	Shareef Abdur-Rahim	5.00	2.20
❑ R12	Dontae' Jones	.50	.23
❑ R13	Todd Fuller	.50	.23
❑ R14	Lorenzen Wright	.50	.23
❑ R15	Stephon Marbury	5.00	2.20
❑ R16	Vitaly Potapenko	.50	.23
❑ R17	Tony Delk	.50	.23
❑ R18	Steve Nash	.50	.23
❑ R19	Jermaine O'Neal	1.50	.70
❑ R20	Erick Dampier	.50	.23

1996-97 Upper Deck Rookie of the Year Collection

	MINT	NRMT
COMPLETE SET (14)	200.00	90.00
COMMON CARD (RC1-RC14)	3.00	1.35
SEMISTARS	4.00	1.80
UNLISTED STARS	6.00	2.70

SER.2 STATED ODDS 1:138

		MINT	NRMT
❑ RC1	Damon Stoudamire	10.00	4.50
❑ RC2	Grant Hill	30.00	13.50
❑ RC3	Jason Kidd	20.00	9.00
❑ RC4	Chris Webber	20.00	9.00
❑ RC5	Shaquille O'Neal	30.00	13.50
❑ RC6	Larry Johnson	4.00	1.80
❑ RC7	Derrick Coleman	4.00	1.80
❑ RC8	David Robinson	10.00	4.50
❑ RC9	Mitch Richmond	6.00	2.70

❑ RC10 Mark Jackson	3.00	1.35
❑ RC11 Chuck Person	3.00	1.35
❑ RC12 Patrick Ewing	6.00	2.70
❑ RC13 Michael Jordan	100.00	45.00
❑ RC14 Buck Williams	3.00	1.35

1996-97 Upper Deck Smooth Grooves

	MINT	NRMT
COMPLETE SET (15)	200.00	90.00
COMMON CARD (SG1-SG15)	5.00	2.20
SER.2 STATED ODDS 1:72		
❑ SG1 Dennis Rodman	10.00	4.50
❑ SG2 Jason Kidd	15.00	6.75
❑ SG3 Grant Hill	25.00	11.00
❑ SG4 Damon Stoudamire	8.00	3.60
❑ SG5 Shaquille O'Neal	25.00	11.00
❑ SG6 Clyde Drexler	5.00	2.20
❑ SG7 Shareef Abdur-Rahim	15.00	6.75
❑ SG8 Michael Jordan	60.00	27.00
❑ SG9 Alonzo Mourning	5.00	2.20
❑ SG10 Allen Iverson	25.00	11.00
❑ SG11 Vin Baker	5.00	2.20
❑ SG12 Kevin Garnett	30.00	13.50
❑ SG13 Anfernee Hardaway	15.00	6.75
❑ SG14 Jerry Stackhouse	5.00	2.20
❑ SG15 Shawn Kemp	8.00	3.60

1997-98 Upper Deck

	MINT	NRMT
COMPLETE SET (360)	50.00	22.00
COMPLETE SERIES 1 (180)	25.00	11.00
COMPLETE SERIES 2 (180)	25.00	11.00
COMMON CARD (1-360)	.15	.07
SEMISTARS	.20	.09
UNLISTED STARS	.40	.18

SUBSET CARDS HALF VALUE OF BASE CARDS
BLACK POWER AUDIO 1:23 HOBBY
RED POWER AUDIO 1:72 HOBBY
UNPRICED WHITE POW.AUD. SERIAL #'d TO 1

❑ 1 Steve Smith	.20	.09
❑ 2 Christian Laettner	.20	.09
❑ 3 Alan Henderson	.15	.07
❑ 4 Dikembe Mutombo	.20	.09
❑ 5 Dana Barros	.15	.07
❑ 6 Antoine Walker	.75	.35
❑ 7 Dee Brown	.15	.07
❑ 8 Eric Williams	.15	.07
❑ 9 Muggsy Bogues	.15	.07
❑ 10 Dell Curry	.15	.07
❑ 11 Vlade Divac	.15	.07
❑ 12 Anthony Mason	.20	.09
❑ 13 Glen Rice	.20	.09
❑ 14 Jason Caffey	.15	.07
❑ 15 Steve Kerr	.15	.07
❑ 16 Toni Kukoc	.50	.23
❑ 17 Luc Longley	.15	.07
❑ 18 Michael Jordan	5.00	2.20
❑ 19 Terrell Brandon	.20	.09
❑ 20 Danny Ferry	.15	.07
❑ 21 Tyrone Hill	.15	.07
❑ 22 Derek Anderson RC	1.00	.45
❑ 23 Bob Sura	.15	.07
❑ 24 Eric Williams	.15	.07
❑ 25 Michael Finley	.40	.18
❑ 26 Ed O'Bannon	.15	.07
❑ 27 Robert Pack	.15	.07
❑ 28 Samaki Walker	.15	.07
❑ 29 LaPhonso Ellis	.15	.07
❑ 30 Tony Battie RC	.40	.18
❑ 31 Antonio McDyess	.50	.23
❑ 32 Bryant Stith	.15	.07
❑ 33 Randolph Childress	.15	.07
❑ 34 Grant Hill	2.00	.90
❑ 35 Lindsey Hunter	.15	.07
❑ 36 Grant Long	.15	.07
❑ 37 Theo Ratliff	.15	.07
❑ 38 B.J. Armstrong	.15	.07
❑ 39 Adonal Foyle RC	.20	.09
❑ 40 Mark Price	.15	.07
❑ 41 Felton Spencer	.15	.07
❑ 42 Latrell Sprewell	.75	.35
❑ 43 Clyde Drexler	.40	.18
❑ 44 Mario Elie	.15	.07
❑ 45 Hakeem Olajuwon	.60	.25
❑ 46 Brent Price	.15	.07
❑ 47 Kevin Willis	.15	.07
❑ 48 Erick Dampier	.15	.07
❑ 49 Antonio Davis	.15	.07
❑ 50 Dale Davis	.15	.07
❑ 51 Mark Jackson	.15	.07
❑ 52 Rik Smits	.15	.07
❑ 53 Brent Barry	.15	.07
❑ 54 Lamond Murray	.15	.07
❑ 55 Eric Piatkowski	.15	.07
❑ 56 Loy Vaught	.15	.07
❑ 57 Lorenzen Wright	.15	.07
❑ 58 Kobe Bryant	3.00	1.35
❑ 59 Elden Campbell	.15	.07
❑ 60 Derek Fisher	.15	.07
❑ 61 Eddie Jones	.75	.35
❑ 62 Nick Van Exel	.20	.09
❑ 63 Keith Askins	.15	.07
❑ 64 Isaac Austin	.15	.07
❑ 65 P.J. Brown	.15	.07
❑ 66 Tim Hardaway	.40	.18
❑ 67 Alonzo Mourning	.40	.18
❑ 68 Ray Allen	.60	.25
❑ 69 Vin Baker	.20	.09
❑ 70 Sherman Douglas	.15	.07
❑ 71 Armon Gilliam	.15	.07
❑ 72 Elliot Perry	.15	.07
❑ 73 Chris Carr	.15	.07
❑ 74 Tom Gugliotta	.20	.09
❑ 75 Kevin Garnett	2.50	1.10
❑ 76 Doug West	.15	.07
❑ 77 Keith Van Horn RC	2.00	.90
❑ 78 Chris Gatling	.15	.07
❑ 79 Kendall Gill	.20	.09
❑ 80 Kerry Kittles	.40	.18
❑ 81 Jayson Williams	.20	.09
❑ 82 Chris Childs	.15	.07
❑ 83 Allan Houston	.40	.18
❑ 84 Larry Johnson	.20	.09
❑ 85 Charles Oakley	.15	.07
❑ 86 John Starks	.15	.07
❑ 87 Horace Grant	.20	.09
❑ 88 Anfernee Hardaway	1.25	.55
❑ 89 Dennis Scott	.15	.07
❑ 90 Rony Seikaly	.15	.07
❑ 91 Brian Shaw	.15	.07
❑ 92 Derrick Coleman	.20	.09
❑ 93 Allen Iverson	2.00	.90
❑ 94 Tim Thomas RC	1.25	.55
❑ 95 Scott Williams	.15	.07
❑ 96 Cedric Ceballos	.15	.07
❑ 97 Kevin Johnson	.20	.09
❑ 98 Loren Meyer	.15	.07
❑ 99 Steve Nash	.15	.07
❑ 100 Wesley Person	.15	.07
❑ 101 Kenny Anderson	.20	.09
❑ 102 Jermaine O'Neal	.20	.09
❑ 103 Isaiah Rider	.20	.09
❑ 104 Arvydas Sabonis	.20	.09
❑ 105 Gary Trent	.15	.07
❑ 106 Mahmoud Abdul-Rauf	.15	.07
❑ 107 Billy Owens	.15	.07
❑ 108 Olden Polynice	.15	.07
❑ 109 Mitch Richmond	.40	.18
❑ 110 Michael Smith	.15	.07
❑ 111 Cory Alexander	.15	.07
❑ 112 Vinny Del Negro	.15	.07
❑ 113 Carl Herrera	.15	.07
❑ 114 Tim Duncan RC	5.00	2.20
❑ 115 Hersey Hawkins	.20	.09
❑ 116 Shawn Kemp	.60	.25
❑ 117 Nate McMillan	.15	.07
❑ 118 Sam Perkins	.20	.09
❑ 119 Detlef Schrempf	.20	.09
❑ 120 Doug Christie	.15	.07
❑ 121 Popeye Jones	.15	.07
❑ 122 Carlos Rogers	.15	.07
❑ 123 Damon Stoudamire	.50	.23
❑ 124 Adam Keefe	.15	.07
❑ 125 Chris Morris	.15	.07
❑ 126 Greg Ostertag	.15	.07
❑ 127 John Stockton	.40	.18
❑ 128 Shareef Abdur-Rahim	1.25	.55
❑ 129 George Lynch	.15	.07
❑ 130 Lee Mayberry	.15	.07
❑ 131 Anthony Peeler	.15	.07
❑ 132 Calbert Cheaney	.15	.07
❑ 133 Tracy Murray	.15	.07
❑ 134 Rod Strickland	.20	.09
❑ 135 Chris Webber	1.25	.55
❑ 136 Christian Laettner JAM	.15	.07
❑ 137 Eric Williams JAM	.15	.07
❑ 138 Vlade Divac JAM	.15	.07
❑ 139 Michael Jordan JAM	2.50	1.10
❑ 140 Tyrone Hill JAM	.15	.07
❑ 141 Michael Finley JAM	.20	.09
❑ 142 Tom Hammonds JAM	.15	.07
❑ 143 Theo Ratliff JAM	.15	.07
❑ 144 Latrell Sprewell JAM	.40	.18
❑ 145 Hakeem Olajuwon JAM	.40	.18
❑ 146 Reggie Miller JAM	.20	.09
❑ 147 Rodney Rogers JAM	.15	.07
❑ 148 Eddie Jones JAM	.40	.18
❑ 149 Jamal Mashburn JAM	.20	.09
❑ 150 Glenn Robinson JAM	.15	.07
❑ 151 Chris Carr JAM	.15	.07
❑ 152 Kendall Gill JAM	.15	.07
❑ 153 John Starks JAM	.15	.07
❑ 154 Anfernee Hardaway JAM	.75	.35
❑ 155 Derrick Coleman JAM	.15	.07
❑ 156 Cedric Ceballos JAM	.15	.07
❑ 157 Rasheed Wallace JAM	.20	.09
❑ 158 Corliss Williamson JAM	.15	.07
❑ 159 Sean Elliott JAM	.15	.07
❑ 160 Shawn Kemp JAM	.40	.18

❑ 161 Doug Christie JAM .15 .07
❑ 162 Karl Malone JAM .40 .18
❑ 163 Bryant Reeves JAM .15 .07
❑ 164 Gheorghe Muresan JAM .15 .07
❑ 165 Michael Jordan CP 2.50 1.10
❑ 166 Dikembe Mutombo CP .15 .07
❑ 167 Glen Rice CP .15 .07
❑ 168 Mitch Richmond CP .20 .09
❑ 169 Juwan Howard CP .15 .07
❑ 170 Clyde Drexler CP .20 .09
❑ 171 Terrell Brandon CP .15 .07
❑ 172 Jerry Stackhouse CP .15 .07
❑ 173 Damon Stoudamire CP .40 .18
❑ 174 Jayson Williams CP .15 .07
❑ 175 P.J. Brown CP .15 .07
❑ 176 Anfernee Hardaway CP .75 .35
❑ 177 Vin Baker CP .15 .07
❑ 178 LaPhonso Ellis CP .15 .07
❑ 179 Shawn Kemp CP .40 .18
❑ 180 Checklist .15 .07
❑ 181 Mookie Blaylock .15 .07
❑ 182 Tyrone Corbin .15 .07
❑ 183 Chucky Brown .15 .07
❑ 184 Ed Gray RC .15 .07
❑ 185 Chauncey Billups RC .50 .23
❑ 186 Tyus Edney .15 .07
❑ 187 Travis Knight .15 .07
❑ 188 Ron Mercer RC 1.25 .55
❑ 189 Walter McCarty .15 .07
❑ 190 B.J. Armstrong .15 .07
❑ 191 Matt Geiger .15 .07
❑ 192 Bobby Phills .15 .07
❑ 193 David Wesley .15 .07
❑ 194 Keith Booth RC .15 .07
❑ 195 Randy Brown .15 .07
❑ 196 Ron Harper .20 .09
❑ 197 Scottie Pippen 1.25 .55
❑ 198 Dennis Rodman .75 .35
❑ 199 Zydrunas Ilgauskas .15 .07
❑ 200 Brevin Knight RC .60 .25
❑ 201 Shawn Kemp .60 .25
❑ 202 Vitaly Potapenko .15 .07
❑ 203 Wesley Person .15 .07
❑ 204 Erick Strickland RC .20 .09
❑ 205 A.C. Green .20 .09
❑ 206 Khalid Reeves .15 .07
❑ 207 Hubert Davis .15 .07
❑ 208 Dennis Scott .15 .07
❑ 209 Danny Fortson RC .40 .18
❑ 210 Bobby Jackson RC .20 .09
❑ 211 Eric Williams .15 .07
❑ 212 Dean Garrett .15 .07
❑ 213 Priest Lauderdale .15 .07
❑ 214 Joe Dumars .40 .18
❑ 215 Aaron McKie .15 .07
❑ 216 Scot Pollard RC .20 .09
❑ 217 Brian Williams .15 .07
❑ 218 Malik Sealy .15 .07
❑ 219 Duane Ferrell .15 .07
❑ 220 Erick Dampier .15 .07
❑ 221 Todd Fuller .15 .07
❑ 222 Donyell Marshall .15 .07
❑ 223 Joe Smith .20 .09
❑ 224 Charles Barkley .60 .25
❑ 225 Matt Bullard .15 .07
❑ 226 Othella Harrington .15 .07
❑ 227 Rodrick Rhodes RC .15 .07
❑ 228 Eddie Johnson .15 .07
❑ 229 Matt Maloney .15 .07
❑ 230 Travis Best .15 .07
❑ 231 Reggie Miller .40 .18
❑ 232 Chris Mullin .40 .18
❑ 233 Fred Hoiberg .15 .07
❑ 234 Austin Croshere RC 1.00 .45
❑ 235 Keith Closs RC .15 .07
❑ 236 Darrick Martin .15 .07
❑ 237 Pooh Richardson .15 .07
❑ 238 Rodney Rogers .15 .07
❑ 239 Maurice Taylor RC .75 .35
❑ 240 Robert Horry .15 .07
❑ 241 Rick Fox .15 .07
❑ 242 Shaquille O'Neal 2.00 .90
❑ 243 Corie Blount .15 .07
❑ 244 Charles Smith RC .15 .07
❑ 245 Voshon Lenard .15 .07
❑ 246 Eric Murdock .15 .07
❑ 247 Dan Majerle .20 .09
❑ 248 Terry Mills .15 .07
❑ 249 Terrell Brandon .20 .09
❑ 250 Tyrone Hill .15 .07
❑ 251 Ervin Johnson .15 .07
❑ 252 Glenn Robinson .20 .09
❑ 253 Terry Porter .15 .07
❑ 254 Paul Grant RC .15 .07
❑ 255 Stephon Marbury 1.25 .55
❑ 256 Sam Mitchell .15 .07
❑ 257 Cherokee Parks .15 .07
❑ 258 Sam Cassell .20 .09
❑ 259 David Benoit .15 .07
❑ 260 Kevin Edwards .15 .07
❑ 261 Don MacLean .15 .07
❑ 262 Patrick Ewing .40 .18
❑ 263 Herb Williams .15 .07
❑ 264 John Starks .15 .07
❑ 265 Chris Mills .15 .07
❑ 266 Chris Dudley .15 .07
❑ 267 Darrell Armstrong .20 .09
❑ 268 Nick Anderson .15 .07
❑ 269 Derek Harper .15 .07
❑ 270 Johnny Taylor RC .15 .07
❑ 271 Mark Price .15 .07
❑ 272 Clarence Weatherspoon .15 .07
❑ 273 Jerry Stackhouse .20 .09
❑ 274 Eric Montross .15 .07
❑ 275 Anthony Parker RC .15 .07
❑ 276 Antonio McDyess .50 .23
❑ 277 Clifford Robinson .15 .07
❑ 278 Jason Kidd 1.25 .55
❑ 279 Danny Manning .20 .09
❑ 280 Rex Chapman .15 .07
❑ 281 Stacey Augmon .15 .07
❑ 282 Kelvin Cato RC .40 .18
❑ 283 Brian Grant .20 .09
❑ 284 Rasheed Wallace .40 .18
❑ 285 L. Funderburke RC .20 .09
❑ 286 Anthony Johnson .15 .07
❑ 287 Tariq Abdul-Wahad RC .20 .09
❑ 288 Corliss Williamson .15 .07
❑ 289 Sean Elliott .15 .07
❑ 290 Avery Johnson .15 .07
❑ 291 David Robinson .60 .25
❑ 292 Will Perdue .15 .07
❑ 293 Greg Anthony .15 .07
❑ 294 Jim McIlvaine .15 .07
❑ 295 Dale Ellis .15 .07
❑ 296 Gary Payton .60 .25
❑ 297 Aaron Williams .15 .07
❑ 298 Marcus Camby .50 .23
❑ 299 John Wallace .15 .07
❑ 300 Tracy McGrady RC 5.00 2.20
❑ 301 Walt Williams .15 .07
❑ 302 Shandon Anderson .15 .07
❑ 303 Antoine Carr .15 .07
❑ 304 Jeff Hornacek .20 .09
❑ 305 Karl Malone .60 .25
❑ 306 Bryon Russell .15 .07
❑ 307 Jacque Vaughn RC .20 .09
❑ 308 Antonio Daniels RC .40 .18
❑ 309 Blue Edwards .15 .07
❑ 310 Bryant Reeves .15 .07
❑ 311 Otis Thorpe .15 .07
❑ 312 Harvey Grant .15 .07
❑ 313 Terry Davis .15 .07
❑ 314 Juwan Howard .20 .09
❑ 315 Gheorghe Muresan .15 .07
❑ 316 Michael Jordan OT 2.50 1.10
❑ 317 Allen Iverson OT .75 .35
❑ 318 Karl Malone OT .40 .18
❑ 319 Glen Rice OT .15 .07
❑ 320 Dikembe Mutombo OT .15 .07
❑ 321 Grant Hill OT 1.25 .55
❑ 322 Hakeem Olajuwon OT .40 .18
❑ 323 Stephon Marbury OT 1.00 .45
❑ 324 Anfernee Hardaway OT .75 .35
❑ 325 Eddie Jones OT .40 .18
❑ 326 Mitch Richmond OT .20 .09
❑ 327 Kevin Johnson OT .15 .07
❑ 328 Kevin Garnett OT 1.25 .55
❑ 329 Shareef Abdur-Rahim OT .60 .25
❑ 330 Damon Stoudamire OT .40 .18
❑ 331 Atlanta Hawks DM .15 .07
Dikembe Mutombo
Christian Laettner
Mookie Blaylock
Steve Smith
❑ 332 Boston Celtics DM .40 .18
Antoine Walker
Ron Mercer
Chauncey Billups
Dana Barros
❑ 333 Charlotte Hornets DM .20 .09
Glen Rice
Larry Johnson
Alonzo Mourning
Vlade Divac
Anthony Mason
❑ 334 Chicago Bulls DM 1.00 .45
Michael Jordan
Scottie Pippen
Dennis Rodman
Toni Kukoc
❑ 335 Cleveland Cavaliers DM .40 .18
Shawn Kemp
Brevin Knight
Terrell Brandon
Mark Price
❑ 336 Dallas Mavericks DM .15 .07
A.C. Green
Michael Finley
Derek Harper
Detlef Schrempf
❑ 337 Denver Nuggets DM .40 .18
Bobby Jackson
Tony Battie
Dikembe Mutombo
LaPhonso Ellis
❑ 338 Detroit Pistons DM .40 .18
Joe Dumars
Grant Hill
Dennis Rodman
Lindsey Hunter
❑ 339 Golden St. Warriors DM .40 .18
Joe Smith
Chris Mullin
Chris Webber
Tim Hardaway
❑ 340 Houston Rockets DM .40 .18
Hakeem Olajuwon
Charles Barkley
Clyde Drexler
Sam Cassell
Otis Thorpe
❑ 341 Indiana Pacers DM .20 .09
Chris Mullin
Reggie Miller
Antonio Davis
Dale Davis
Rik Smits
❑ 342 Los Angeles Clippers DM .15 .07
Brent Barry
Loy Vaught
Danny Manning
Ron Harper
❑ 343 Los Angeles Lakers DM .60 .25
Shaquille O'Neal
Kobe Bryant
Eddie Jones
Nick Van Exel
❑ 344 Miami Heat DM .40 .18
Tim Hardaway
Alonzo Mourning
P.J. Brown
Rony Seikaly
Glen Rice
❑ 345 Milwaukee Bucks DM .20 .09
Terrell Brandon
Glenn Robinson
Vin Baker
Terry Cummings
❑ 346 Minnesota Timberwolves DM .50 .23
Kevin Garnett
Stephon Marbury
Tom Gugliotta
Sam Mitchell
Isaiah Rider
❑ 347 New Jersey Nets DM .40 .18
Keith Van Horn

Jayson Williams
Buck Williams
Kenny Anderson

❑ 348 New York Knicks DM .... .20 .09
Patrick Ewing
Larry Johnson
John Starks
Charles Oakley

❑ 349 Orlando Magic DM .... .40 .18
Anfernee Hardaway
Rony Seikaly
Shaquille O'Neal
Nick Anderson

❑ 350 Philadelphia 76ers DM .. .40 .18
Allen Iverson
Jerry Stackhouse
Charles Barkley
Clarence Weatherspoon

❑ 351 Phoenix Suns DM .... .40 .18
Antonio McDyess
Jason Kidd
Charles Barkley
Kevin Johnson

❑ 352 Portland Trail Blazers DM .15 .07
Kenny Anderson
Isaiah Rider
Clyde Drexler
Terry Porter

❑ 353 Sacramento Kings DM .. .20 .09
Mitch Richmond
Corliss Williamson
Lionel Simmons
Billy Owens

❑ 354 San Antonio Spurs DM .. .50 .23
Tim Duncan
David Robinson
Sean Elliott
Dennis Rodman

❑ 355 Seattle Sonics DM.......... .40 .18
Gary Payton
Vin Baker
Nate McMillan
Shawn Kemp

❑ 356 Toronto Raptors DM ...... .40 .18
Damon Stoudamire
Tracy McGrady
Marcus Camby
Walt Williams

❑ 357 Utah Jazz DM .... .20 .09
John Stockton
Karl Malone
Jeff Hornacek

❑ 358 Vancouver Grizzlies DM .15 .07
Bryant Reeves
Shareef Abdur-Rahim
Antonio Daniels
Greg Anthony

❑ 359 Washington Wizards DM .40 .18
Chris Webber
Juwan Howard
Gheorghe Muresan
Rod Strickland

❑ 360 Checklist .... .15 .07
❑ NNO M.Jordan Black Audio 12.00 5.50
❑ NNO M.Jordan Red Audio 30.00 13.50

1997-98 Upper Deck Game Dated Memorable Moments

	MINT	NRMT
COMPLETE SET (30)	800.00	350.00
COMMON CARD	5.00	2.20

*STARS: 12.5X TO 30X BASE CARD HI
SKIP NUMBERED SET
SER.1 STATED ODDS 1:1500

❑ 4 Dikembe Mutombo	6.00	2.70
❑ 6 Antoine Walker	25.00	11.00
❑ 13 Glen Rice	6.00	2.70
❑ 18 Michael Jordan	150.00	70.00
❑ 23 Bob Sura	5.00	2.20
❑ 25 Michael Finley	12.00	5.50
❑ 31 Antonio McDyess	15.00	6.75

❑ 34 Grant Hill	60.00	27.00
❑ 42 Latrell Sprewell	25.00	11.00
❑ 43 Clyde Drexler	12.00	5.50
❑ 45 Hakeem Olajuwon.........	20.00	9.00
❑ 49 Antonio Davis	5.00	2.20
❑ 56 Loy Vaught	5.00	2.20
❑ 61 Eddie Jones	25.00	11.00
❑ 66 Tim Hardaway..............	12.00	5.50
❑ 69 Vin Baker.......................	6.00	2.70
❑ 75 Kevin Garnett	80.00	36.00
❑ 79 Kendall Gill	6.00	2.70
❑ 83 Allan Houston	12.00	5.50
❑ 88 Anfernee Hardaway	40.00	18.00
❑ 93 Allen Iverson	60.00	27.00
❑ 97 Kevin Johnson..............	6.00	2.70
❑ 103 Isaiah Rider..................	6.00	2.70
❑ 109 Mitch Richmond	12.00	5.50
❑ 112 Vinny Del Negro	5.00	2.20
❑ 116 Shawn Kemp.............	20.00	9.00
❑ 123 Damon Stoudamire	15.00	6.75
❑ 127 John Stockton	12.00	5.50
❑ 128 Shareef Abdur-Rahim	40.00	18.00
❑ 135 Chris Webber	40.00	18.00

1997-98 Upper Deck AIRlines

	MINT	NRMT
COMPLETE SET (12)	700.00	325.00
COMMON JORDAN (AL1-12)	60.00	27.00

SER.2 STATED ODDS 1:230 HOB/RET

❑ AL1 Michael Jordan	60.00	27.00
❑ AL2 Michael Jordan	60.00	27.00
❑ AL3 Michael Jordan	60.00	27.00
❑ AL4 Michael Jordan	60.00	27.00
❑ AL5 Michael Jordan	60.00	27.00
❑ AL6 Michael Jordan	60.00	27.00
❑ AL7 Michael Jordan	60.00	27.00
❑ AL8 Michael Jordan	60.00	27.00
❑ AL9 Michael Jordan	60.00	27.00
❑ AL10 Michael Jordan	60.00	27.00
❑ AL11 Michael Jordan	60.00	27.00
❑ AL12 Michael Jordan	60.00	27.00

1997-98 Upper Deck Diamond Dimensions

	MINT	NRMT
COMMON CARD (D1-D30)	20.00	9.00

SEMISTARS..........................	30.00	13.50
UNLISTED STARS.................	40.00	18.00

STATED PRINT RUN 100 SERIAL #'d SETS
RANDOM INSERTS IN SER.1 PACKS

❑ D1 Anfernee Hardaway ..	200.00	90.00
❑ D2 Gary Payton	80.00	36.00
❑ D3 Marcus Camby	60.00	27.00
❑ D4 Charles Barkley	80.00	36.00
❑ D5 Jason Kidd	150.00	70.00
❑ D6 Alonzo Mourning.........	50.00	22.00
❑ D7 Kenny Anderson..........	30.00	13.50
❑ D8 Kobe Bryant	400.00	180.00
❑ D9 Dennis Rodman	100.00	45.00
❑ D10 Kerry Kittles	40.00	18.00
❑ D11 Dikembe Mutombo	30.00	13.50
❑ D12 Shaquille O'Neal......	250.00	110.00
❑ D13 Glenn Robinson	30.00	13.50
❑ D14 Tony Delk	20.00	9.00
❑ D15 Larry Johnson...........	30.00	13.50
❑ D16 Brent Barry	20.00	9.00
❑ D17 Scottie Pippen	150.00	70.00
❑ D18 Shareef Abdur-Rahim	150.00	70.00
❑ D19 Sean Elliott	20.00	9.00
❑ D20 Damon Stoudamire....	60.00	27.00
❑ D21 Kevin Garnett	300.00	135.00
❑ D22 Bob Sura...................	20.00	9.00
❑ D23 Michael Jordan	750.00	350.00
❑ D24 Latrell Sprewell	100.00	45.00
❑ D25 Karl Malone	80.00	36.00
❑ D26 Antonio McDyess	60.00	27.00
❑ D27 Allen Iverson............	250.00	110.00
❑ D28 Dale Davis	20.00	9.00
❑ D29 Antoine Walker	100.00	45.00
❑ D30 Chris Webber	150.00	70.00

1997-98 Upper Deck Game Jerseys

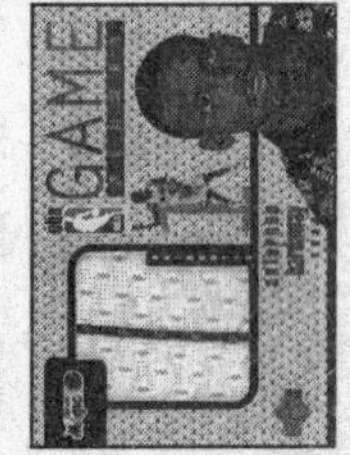

	MINT	NRMT
COMPLETE SET (22)	7000.00	3200.00
COMPLETE SERIES 1 (12)	3200.00	1450.00
COMPLETE SERIES 2 (10)	3800.00	1700.00
COMMON CARD (GJ1-GJ22)	100.00	45.00

SER.1/2 STATED ODDS 1:2500
JORDAN AU SERIAL #'d TO 23
JORDAN AU NOT IN SET PRICE
JORDAN AU: RANDOM INS.IN SER.2 HOB
MULTI-COLOR SWATCHES CARRY PREMIUMS

❑ GJ1 Charles Barkley	350.00	160.00
❑ GJ2 Clyde Drexler	275.00	125.00
❑ GJ3 Kevin Garnett	500.00	220.00
❑ GJ4 Anfernee Hardaway Home Jersey	400.00	180.00
❑ GJ5 Grant Hill Home Jersey	500.00	220.00
❑ GJ6 Allen Iverson	400.00	180.00
❑ GJ7 Kerry Kittles	100.00	45.00
❑ GJ8 Toni Kukoc	300.00	135.00
❑ GJ9 Reggie Miller	300.00	135.00
❑ GJ10 Hakeem Olajuwon	150.00	70.00
❑ GJ11 Glen Rice	150.00	70.00
❑ GJ12 David Robinson	200.00	90.00
❑ GJ13 Michael Jordan	1800.00	800.00
❑ GJ13S Michael Jordan Autographed Game Jersey	15000.00	6800.00
❑ GJ14 Alonzo Mourning	250.00	110.00
❑ GJ15 Tim Hardaway	250.00	110.00
❑ GJ16 Marcus Camby	250.00	110.00
❑ GJ17 Antoine Walker	200.00	90.00
❑ GJ18 Kevin Johnson	120.00	55.00
❑ GJ19 Glenn Robinson	150.00	70.00
❑ GJ20 Patrick Ewing	275.00	125.00
❑ GJ21 Anfernee Hardaway Away Jersey	400.00	180.00
❑ GJ22 Grant Hill Away Jersey	500.00	220.00

1997-98 Upper Deck Great Eight

	MINT	NRMT
COMPLETE SET (8)	275.00	125.00
COMMON CARD (G1-G8)	10.00	4.50
UNLISTED STARS	15.00	6.75

STATED PRINT RUN 800 SERIAL #'d SETS
RANDOM INSERTS IN SER.2 PACKS

❑ G1 Charles Barkley	25.00	11.00
❑ G2 Clyde Drexler	15.00	6.75
❑ G3 Joe Dumars	10.00	4.50
❑ G4 Patrick Ewing	15.00	6.75
❑ G5 Michael Jordan	200.00	90.00
❑ G6 Karl Malone	25.00	11.00
❑ G7 Hakeem Olajuwon	25.00	11.00
❑ G8 John Stockton	15.00	6.75

1997-98 Upper Deck High Dimensions

	MINT	NRMT
COMPLETE SET (30)	500.00	220.00
COMMON CARD (D1-D30)	3.00	1.35
SEMISTARS	5.00	2.20
UNLISTED STARS	8.00	3.60

STATED PRINT RUN 2000 SERIAL #'d SETS
RANDOM INSERTS IN SER.1 PACKS

❑ D1 Anfernee Hardaway	25.00	11.00
❑ D2 Gary Payton	12.00	5.50
❑ D3 Marcus Camby	10.00	4.50
❑ D4 Charles Barkley	12.00	5.50
❑ D5 Jason Kidd	25.00	11.00
❑ D6 Alonzo Mourning	8.00	3.60
❑ D7 Kenny Anderson	5.00	2.20
❑ D8 Kobe Bryant	75.00	34.00
❑ D9 Dennis Rodman	15.00	6.75
❑ D10 Kerry Kittles	8.00	3.60
❑ D11 Dikembe Mutombo	5.00	2.20
❑ D12 Shaquille O'Neal	40.00	18.00
❑ D13 Glenn Robinson	5.00	2.20
❑ D14 Tony Delk	3.00	1.35
❑ D15 Larry Johnson	5.00	2.20
❑ D16 Brent Barry	3.00	1.35
❑ D17 Scottie Pippen	25.00	11.00
❑ D18 Shareef Abdur-Rahim	25.00	11.00
❑ D19 Sean Elliott	3.00	1.35
❑ D20 Damon Stoudamire	10.00	4.50
❑ D21 Kevin Garnett	50.00	22.00
❑ D22 Bob Sura	3.00	1.35
❑ D23 Michael Jordan	100.00	45.00
❑ D24 Latrell Sprewell	15.00	6.75
❑ D25 Karl Malone	12.00	5.50
❑ D26 Antonio McDyess	10.00	4.50
❑ D27 Allen Iverson	40.00	18.00
❑ D28 Dale Davis	3.00	1.35
❑ D29 Antoine Walker	15.00	6.75
❑ D30 Chris Webber	25.00	11.00

1997-98 Upper Deck Jordan Air Time

	MINT	NRMT
COMPLETE SET (10)	160.00	70.00
COMMON JORDAN (AT1-9)	10.00	4.50
COMMON JORDAN (AT10)	100.00	45.00

SER.1 STATED ODDS 1:12

❑ AT1 Michael Jordan	10.00	4.50
❑ AT2 Michael Jordan	10.00	4.50
❑ AT3 Michael Jordan	10.00	4.50
❑ AT4 Michael Jordan	10.00	4.50
❑ AT5 Michael Jordan	10.00	4.50
❑ AT6 Michael Jordan	10.00	4.50
❑ AT7 Michael Jordan	10.00	4.50
❑ AT8 Michael Jordan	10.00	4.50
❑ AT9 Michael Jordan	10.00	4.50
❑ AT10 Michael Jordan	100.00	45.00

1997-98 Upper Deck Records Collection

	MINT	NRMT
COMPLETE SET (30)	120.00	55.00
COMMON CARD (RC1-RC30)	1.50	.70
SEMISTARS	2.00	.90
UNLISTED STARS	3.00	1.35

SER.2 STATED ODDS 1:23

❑ RC1 Dikembe Mutombo	2.00	.90
❑ RC2 Dana Barros	1.50	.70
❑ RC3 Glen Rice	2.00	.90
❑ RC4 Dennis Rodman	6.00	2.70
❑ RC5 Shawn Kemp	5.00	2.20
❑ RC6 A.C. Green	2.00	.90
❑ RC7 LaPhonso Ellis	1.50	.70
❑ RC8 Grant Hill	15.00	6.75
❑ RC9 Joe Smith	2.00	.90
❑ RC10 Charles Barkley	5.00	2.20
❑ RC11 Reggie Miller	3.00	1.35
❑ RC12 Loy Vaught	1.50	.70
❑ RC13 Shaquille O'Neal	15.00	6.75
❑ RC14 Tim Hardaway	3.00	1.35
❑ RC15 Glenn Robinson	2.00	.90
❑ RC16 Stephon Marbury	10.00	4.50
❑ RC17 Sam Cassell	2.00	.90
❑ RC18 Patrick Ewing	3.00	1.35
❑ RC19 Anfernee Hardaway	10.00	4.50
❑ RC20 Allen Iverson	15.00	6.75
❑ RC21 Kevin Johnson	2.00	.90
❑ RC22 Kenny Anderson	2.00	.90
❑ RC23 Mitch Richmond	3.00	1.35
❑ RC24 David Robinson	5.00	2.20
❑ RC25 Gary Payton	5.00	2.20
❑ RC26 Damon Stoudamire	4.00	1.80
❑ RC27 John Stockton	3.00	1.35
❑ RC28 Bryant Reeves	1.50	.70
❑ RC29 Chris Webber	10.00	4.50
❑ RC30 Michael Jordan	40.00	18.00

1997-98 Upper Deck Rookie Discovery 1

	MINT	NRMT
COMPLETE SET (15)	15.00	6.75
COMMON CARD (R1-R15)	.60	.25
SEMISTARS	.75	.35
UNLISTED STARS	1.25	.55

SER.2 STATED ODDS 1:4

COMP.RD2 SET (15)	120.00	55.00
COMMON RD2 (D1-D15)	5.00	2.20

*RD2: 3X TO 8X HI COLUMN
RD2: SER.2 STATED ODDS 1:108

❑ R1 Tim Duncan	6.00	2.70

❑ R2 Keith Van Horn	3.00	1.35
❑ R3 Chauncey Billups	.75	.35
❑ R4 Antonio Daniels	.75	.35
❑ R5 Tony Battie	.60	.25
❑ R6 Ron Mercer	2.00	.90
❑ R7 Tim Thomas	2.00	.90
❑ R8 Adonal Foyle	.60	.25
❑ R9 Tracy McGrady	6.00	2.70
❑ R10 Danny Fortson	.60	.25
❑ R11 Tariq Abdul-Wahad	.60	.25
❑ R12 Austin Croshere	1.50	.70
❑ R13 Derek Anderson	1.50	.70
❑ R14 Maurice Taylor	1.25	.55
❑ R15 Kelvin Cato	.60	.25

1997-98 Upper Deck Teammates

	MINT	NRMT
COMPLETE SET (60)	60.00	27.00
COMMON CARD (T1-T60)	.50	.23
SEMISTARS	.60	.25
UNLISTED STARS	1.00	.45
SER.1 STATED ODDS 1:4		

❑ T1 Mookie Blaylock	.50	.23
❑ T2 Steve Smith	.60	.25
❑ T3 Antoine Walker	2.00	.90
❑ T4 Dana Barros	.50	.23
❑ T5 Anthony Mason	.60	.25
❑ T6 Glen Rice	.60	.25
❑ T7 Michael Jordan	12.00	5.50
❑ T8 Scottie Pippen	3.00	1.35
❑ T9 Terrell Brandon	.60	.25
❑ T10 Tyrone Hill	.50	.23
❑ T11 Shawn Bradley	.50	.23
❑ T12 Robert Pack	.50	.23
❑ T13 LaPhonso Ellis	.50	.23
❑ T14 Antonio McDyess	1.25	.55
❑ T15 Grant Hill	5.00	2.20
❑ T16 Lindsey Hunter	.50	.23
❑ T17 Latrell Sprewell	2.00	.90
❑ T18 Joe Smith	.60	.25
❑ T19 Hakeem Olajuwon	1.50	.70
❑ T20 Charles Barkley	1.50	.70
❑ T21 Mark Jackson	.50	.23
❑ T22 Reggie Miller	1.00	.45
❑ T23 Brent Barry	.50	.23
❑ T24 Loy Vaught	.50	.23
❑ T25 Shaquille O'Neal	5.00	2.20
❑ T26 Nick Van Exel	.60	.25
❑ T27 Tim Hardaway	1.00	.45
❑ T28 Alonzo Mourning	1.00	.45
❑ T29 Vin Baker	.60	.25
❑ T30 Glenn Robinson	.60	.25
❑ T31 Kevin Garnett	6.00	2.70
❑ T32 Stephon Marbury	3.00	1.35
❑ T33 Kendall Gill	.60	.25
❑ T34 Kerry Kittles	1.00	.45
❑ T35 Patrick Ewing	1.00	.45
❑ T36 John Starks	.50	.23
❑ T37 Horace Grant	.60	.25
❑ T38 Anfernee Hardaway	3.00	1.35
❑ T39 Allen Iverson	5.00	2.20
❑ T40 Jerry Stackhouse	.60	.25
❑ T41 Jason Kidd	3.00	1.35
❑ T42 Kevin Johnson	.60	.25
❑ T43 Kenny Anderson	.60	.25
❑ T44 Isaiah Rider	.60	.25
❑ T45 Billy Owens	.50	.23
❑ T46 Mitch Richmond	1.00	.45
❑ T47 Sean Elliott	.50	.23
❑ T48 David Robinson	1.50	.70
❑ T49 Gary Payton	1.50	.70
❑ T50 Shawn Kemp	1.50	.70
❑ T51 Marcus Camby	1.25	.55
❑ T52 Damon Stoudamire	1.25	.55
❑ T53 John Stockton	1.00	.45
❑ T54 Karl Malone	1.50	.70
❑ T55 Shareef Abdur-Rahim	3.00	1.35
❑ T56 Bryant Reeves	.50	.23
❑ T57 Juwan Howard	.60	.25
❑ T58 Chris Webber	3.00	1.35
❑ T59 Michael Jordan	12.00	5.50
❑ T60 Anfernee Hardaway	3.00	1.35

1997-98 Upper Deck Ultimates

	MINT	NRMT
COMPLETE SET (30)	100.00	45.00
COMMON CARD (U1-U30)	1.50	.70
SEMISTARS	2.00	.90
UNLISTED STARS	3.00	1.35
SER.1 STATED ODDS 1:23		

❑ U1 Michael Jordan	40.00	18.00
❑ U2 Grant Hill	15.00	6.75
❑ U3 Charles Barkley	5.00	2.20
❑ U4 Tom Gugliotta	2.00	.90
❑ U5 Dennis Rodman	6.00	2.70
❑ U6 Reggie Miller	3.00	1.35
❑ U7 Jason Kidd	10.00	4.50
❑ U8 Loy Vaught	1.50	.70
❑ U9 Mookie Blaylock	1.50	.70
❑ U10 Tim Hardaway	3.00	1.35
❑ U11 Juwan Howard	2.00	.90
❑ U12 Shawn Kemp	5.00	2.20
❑ U13 Mitch Richmond	3.00	1.35
❑ U14 Patrick Ewing	3.00	1.35
❑ U15 Marcus Camby	4.00	1.80
❑ U16 Bryant Stith	1.50	.70
❑ U17 Bryant Reeves	1.50	.70
❑ U18 Joe Smith	2.00	.90
❑ U19 Jerry Stackhouse	2.00	.90
❑ U20 Arvydas Sabonis	2.00	.90
❑ U21 John Stockton	3.00	1.35
❑ U22 Eddie Jones	6.00	2.70
❑ U23 Anfernee Hardaway	10.00	4.50
❑ U24 Ray Allen	5.00	2.20
❑ U25 Terrell Brandon	2.00	.90
❑ U26 David Robinson	5.00	2.20
❑ U27 Anthony Mason	2.00	.90
❑ U28 Robert Pack	1.50	.70
❑ U29 Dana Barros	1.50	.70
❑ U30 Kendall Gill	2.00	.90

1998-99 Upper Deck

	MINT	NRMT
COMPLETE SET (355)	200.00	90.00
COMPLETE SERIES 1 (175)	100.00	45.00
COMPLETE SERIES 2 (180)	100.00	45.00
COMMON CARD (1-311)	.15	.07
COMMON ROOKIE (312-333)	1.00	.45
COMMON JORDAN (230A-W)	3.00	1.35

COMMON HS SUBSET	.75	.35
COMMON TN SUBSET	1.00	.45
SEMISTARS	.20	.09
SEMISTARS RC	1.25	.55
UNLISTED STARS	.40	.18
UNLISTED STARS RC	2.50	1.10

HS SUBSET STATED ODDS 1:4 HOB, 1:2 RET
JORDAN SUBSET STATED ODDS 1:4 H/R
ROOKIE SUBSET STATED ODDS 1:4 H/R
TO THE NET SUBSET STATED ODDS 1:9 H/R
UNPRICED GOLD PARALLEL SERIAL #'d TO 1

❑ 1 Mookie Blaylock	.15	.07
❑ 2 Ed Gray	.15	.07
❑ 3 Dikembe Mutombo	.20	.09
❑ 4 Steve Smith	.20	.09
❑ 5 Dikembe Mutombo Steve Smith HS	.75	.35
❑ 6 Kenny Anderson	.20	.09
❑ 7 Dana Barros	.15	.07
❑ 8 Travis Knight	.15	.07
❑ 9 Walter McCarty	.15	.07
❑ 10 Ron Mercer	.60	.25
❑ 11 Greg Minor	.15	.07
❑ 12 Antoine Walker Ron Mercer HS	1.00	.45
❑ 13 B.J. Armstrong	.15	.07
❑ 14 David Wesley	.15	.07
❑ 15 Anthony Mason	.20	.09
❑ 16 Glen Rice	.20	.09
❑ 17 J.R. Reid	.15	.07
❑ 18 Bobby Phills	.15	.07
❑ 19 Glen Rice Anthony Mason HS	.75	.35
❑ 20 Ron Harper	.20	.09
❑ 21 Toni Kukoc	.50	.23
❑ 22 Scottie Pippen	1.25	.55
❑ 23 Michael Jordan	5.00	2.20
❑ 24 Dennis Rodman	.75	.35
❑ 25 Michael Jordan Scottie Pippen HS	10.00	4.50
❑ 26 Michael Jordan Michael Jordan HS	12.00	5.50
❑ 27 Shawn Kemp	.60	.25
❑ 28 Zydrunas Ilgauskas	.15	.07
❑ 29 Cedric Henderson	.15	.07
❑ 30 Vitaly Potapenko	.15	.07
❑ 31 Derek Anderson	.50	.23
❑ 32 Shawn Kemp Zydrunas Ilgauskas HS	1.25	.55
❑ 33 Shawn Bradley	.15	.07
❑ 34 Khalid Reeves	.15	.07
❑ 35 Robert Pack	.15	.07
❑ 36 Michael Finley	.40	.18
❑ 37 Erick Strickland	.15	.07
❑ 38 Michael Finley Shawn Bradley HS	1.00	.45
❑ 39 Bryant Stith	.15	.07
❑ 40 Dean Garrett	.15	.07
❑ 41 Eric Williams	.15	.07
❑ 42 Bobby Jackson	.15	.07
❑ 43 Danny Fortson	.20	.09
❑ 44 LaPhonso Ellis Bryant Stith HS	.75	.35
❑ 45 Grant Hill	2.00	.90
❑ 46 Lindsey Hunter	.15	.07
❑ 47 Brian Williams	.15	.07
❑ 48 Scot Pollard	.15	.07

❑ 49	Grant Hill	3.00	1.35
	Brian Williams HS		
❑ 50	Donyell Marshall	.15	.07
❑ 51	Tony Delk	.15	.07
❑ 52	Erick Dampier	.15	.07
❑ 53	Felton Spencer	.15	.07
❑ 54	Bimbo Coles	.15	.07
❑ 55	Muggsy Bogues	.15	.07
❑ 56	Donyell Marshall	.75	.35
	Muggsy Bogues HS		
❑ 57	Charles Barkley	.60	.25
❑ 58	Brent Price	.15	.07
❑ 59	Hakeem Olajuwon	.60	.25
❑ 60	Rodrick Rhodes	.15	.07
❑ 61	Charles Barkley	2.00	.90
	Hakeem Olajuwon HS		
❑ 62	Dale Davis	.15	.07
❑ 63	Antonio Davis	.15	.07
❑ 64	Chris Mullin	.40	.18
❑ 65	Jalen Rose	.40	.18
❑ 66	Reggie Miller	.40	.18
❑ 67	Mark Jackson	.15	.07
❑ 68	Reggie Miller	1.25	.55
	Mark Jackson HS		
❑ 69	Rodney Rogers	.15	.07
❑ 70	Lamond Murray	.15	.07
❑ 71	Eric Piatkowski	.15	.07
❑ 72	Lorenzen Wright	.15	.07
❑ 73	Maurice Taylor	.40	.18
❑ 74	Maurice Taylor	.75	.35
	Lamond Murray HS		
❑ 75	Kobe Bryant	3.00	1.35
❑ 76	Shaquille O'Neal	2.00	.90
❑ 77	Derek Fisher	.20	.09
❑ 78	Elden Campbell	.15	.07
❑ 79	Corie Blount	.15	.07
❑ 80	Shaquille O'Neal	10.00	4.50
	Kobe Bryant HS		
❑ 81	Jamal Mashburn	.20	.09
❑ 82	Alonzo Mourning	.40	.18
❑ 83	Tim Hardaway	.40	.18
❑ 84	Voshon Lenard	.15	.07
❑ 85	Alonzo Mourning	1.25	.55
	Tim Hardaway HS		
❑ 86	Ray Allen	.50	.23
❑ 87	Terrell Brandon	.20	.09
❑ 88	Elliot Perry	.15	.07
❑ 89	Ervin Johnson	.15	.07
❑ 90	Ray Allen	1.25	.55
	Glenn Robinson HS		
❑ 91	Micheal Williams	.15	.07
❑ 92	Anthony Peeler	.15	.07
❑ 93	Chris Carr	.15	.07
❑ 94	Kevin Garnett	2.50	1.10
❑ 95	Kevin Garnett	5.00	2.20
	Stephon Marbury HS		
❑ 96	Keith Van Horn	1.00	.45
❑ 97	Kerry Kittles	.20	.09
❑ 98	Kendall Gill	.20	.09
❑ 99	Sam Cassell	.20	.09
❑ 100	Chris Gatling	.15	.07
❑ 101	Keith Van Horn	1.50	.70
	Sam Cassell HS		
❑ 102	Patrick Ewing	.40	.18
❑ 103	John Starks	.15	.07
❑ 104	Allan Houston	.40	.18
❑ 105	Chris Mills	.15	.07
❑ 106	Chris Childs	.15	.07
❑ 107	Charlie Ward	.15	.07
❑ 108	Patrick Ewing	1.25	.55
	John Starks HS		
❑ 109	Anfernee Hardaway	1.25	.55
❑ 110	Horace Grant	.20	.09
❑ 111	Nick Anderson	.15	.07
❑ 112	Johnny Taylor	.15	.07
❑ 113	Anfernee Hardaway	2.50	1.10
	Horace Grant HS		
❑ 114	Allen Iverson	1.50	.70
❑ 115	Scott Williams	.15	.07
❑ 116	Tim Thomas	.60	.25
❑ 117	Brian Shaw	.15	.07
❑ 118	Anthony Parker	.15	.07
❑ 119	Allen Iverson	2.50	1.10
	Tim Thomas HS		
❑ 120	Jason Kidd	1.25	.55
❑ 121	Rex Chapman	.15	.07
❑ 122	Danny Manning	.20	.09
❑ 123	Jason Kidd	2.50	1.10
	Danny Manning HS		
❑ 124	Rasheed Wallace	.40	.18
❑ 125	Walt Williams	.15	.07
❑ 126	Kelvin Cato	.15	.07
❑ 127	Arvydas Sabonis	.20	.09
❑ 128	Brian Grant	.20	.09
❑ 129	Rasheed Wallace	.75	.35
	Isaiah Rider HS		
❑ 130	Tariq Abdul-Wahad	.15	.07
❑ 131	Corliss Williamson	.15	.07
❑ 132	Olden Polynice	.15	.07
❑ 133	Chris Robinson	.15	.07
❑ 134	Tariq Abdul-Wahad	.75	.35
	Olden Polynice HS		
❑ 135	Tim Duncan	2.00	.90
❑ 136	Avery Johnson	.15	.07
❑ 137	David Robinson	.60	.25
❑ 138	Monty Williams	.15	.07
❑ 139	Tim Duncan	4.00	1.80
	David Robinson HS		
❑ 140	Vin Baker	.20	.09
❑ 141	Hersey Hawkins	.20	.09
❑ 142	Detlef Schrempf	.20	.09
❑ 143	Jim McIlvaine	.15	.07
❑ 144	Gary Payton	1.00	.45
	Vin Baker HS		
❑ 145	Chauncey Billups	.15	.07
❑ 146	Tracy McGrady	1.50	.70
❑ 147	John Wallace	.15	.07
❑ 148	Doug Christie	.15	.07
❑ 149	Dee Brown	.15	.07
❑ 150	Tracy McGrady	1.25	.55
	Chauncey Billups HS		
❑ 151	Karl Malone	.60	.25
❑ 152	John Stockton	.40	.18
❑ 153	Adam Keefe	.15	.07
❑ 154	Howard Eisley	.15	.07
❑ 155	Karl Malone	2.00	.90
	John Stockton HS		
❑ 156	Bryant Reeves	.15	.07
❑ 157	Lee Mayberry	.15	.07
❑ 158	Michael Smith	.15	.07
❑ 159	Shareef Abdur-Rahim	2.00	.90
	Bryant Reeves HS		
❑ 160	Juwan Howard	.20	.09
❑ 161	Calbert Cheaney	.15	.07
❑ 162	Tracy Murray	.15	.07
❑ 163	Juwan Howard	.75	.35
	Calbert Cheaney HS		
❑ 164	Shaquille O'Neal TN	4.00	1.80
❑ 165	Maurice Taylor TN	1.00	.45
❑ 166	Stephon Marbury TN	2.00	.90
❑ 167	Tracy McGrady TN	3.00	1.35
❑ 168	Antoine Walker TN	1.25	.55
❑ 169	Michael Jordan TN	10.00	4.50
❑ 170	Keith Van Horn TN	2.00	.90
❑ 171	Shareef Abdur-Rahim TN	2.00	.90
❑ 172	Kobe Bryant TN	6.00	2.70
❑ 173	Gary Payton TN	1.25	.55
❑ 174	Michael Jordan CL	1.00	.45
❑ 175	Michael Jordan CL	1.00	.45
❑ 176	Kevin Johnson	.20	.09
❑ 177	Glenn Robinson	.20	.09
❑ 178	Antoine Walker	.60	.25
❑ 179	Jerry Stackhouse	.20	.09
❑ 180	Mark Price	.15	.07
❑ 181	Stephon Marbury	1.00	.45
❑ 182	Shareef Abdur-Rahim	1.00	.45
❑ 183	Wesley Person	.15	.07
❑ 184	Keith Booth	.15	.07
❑ 185	Sean Elliott	.15	.07
❑ 186	Alan Henderson	.15	.07
❑ 187	Bryon Russell	.15	.07
❑ 188	Jermaine O'Neal	.20	.09
❑ 189	Steve Nash	.15	.07
❑ 190	Eldridge Recasner	.15	.07
❑ 191	Damon Stoudamire	.40	.18
❑ 192	Dell Curry	.15	.07
❑ 193	Michael Stewart	.15	.07
❑ 194	Bruce Bowen	.15	.07
❑ 195	Steve Kerr	.15	.07
❑ 196	Dale Ellis	.15	.07
❑ 197	Shandon Anderson	.15	.07
❑ 198	Larry Johnson	.20	.09
❑ 199	Chris Webber	1.25	.55
❑ 200	Matt Geiger	.15	.07
❑ 201	Chris Anstey	.15	.07
❑ 202	Loy Vaught	.15	.07
❑ 203	Aaron McKie	.15	.07
❑ 204	A.C. Green	.20	.09
❑ 205	Bo Outlaw	.15	.07
❑ 206	Antonio McDyess	.40	.18
❑ 207	Priest Lauderdale	.15	.07
❑ 208	Greg Ostertag	.15	.07
❑ 209	Dan Majerle	.20	.09
❑ 210	Johnny Newman	.15	.07
❑ 211	Tyrone Corbin	.15	.07
❑ 212	Pervis Ellison	.15	.07
❑ 213	Shawnelle Scott	.15	.07
❑ 214	Travis Best	.15	.07
❑ 215	Stacey Augmon	.15	.07
❑ 216	Brevin Knight	.15	.07
❑ 217	Jerome Williams	.20	.09
❑ 218	Terry Mills	.15	.07
❑ 219	Matt Maloney	.15	.07
❑ 220	Dennis Scott	.15	.07
❑ 221	John Thomas	.15	.07
❑ 222	Nick Van Exel	.20	.09
❑ 223	Duane Ferrell	.15	.07
❑ 224	Chris Whitney	.15	.07
❑ 225	Luc Longley	.15	.07
❑ 226	Robert Horry	.15	.07
❑ 227	Clifford Robinson	.15	.07
❑ 228	Samaki Walker	.15	.07
❑ 229	Derrick McKey	.15	.07
❑ 230A	Michael Jordan	3.00	1.35
❑ 230B	Michael Jordan	3.00	1.35
❑ 230C	Michael Jordan	3.00	1.35
❑ 230D	Michael Jordan	3.00	1.35
❑ 230E	Michael Jordan	3.00	1.35
❑ 230F	Michael Jordan	3.00	1.35
❑ 230G	Michael Jordan	3.00	1.35
❑ 230H	Michael Jordan	3.00	1.35
❑ 230I	Michael Jordan	3.00	1.35
❑ 230J	Michael Jordan	3.00	1.35
❑ 230K	Michael Jordan	3.00	1.35
❑ 230L	Michael Jordan	3.00	1.35
❑ 230M	Michael Jordan	3.00	1.35
❑ 230N	Michael Jordan	3.00	1.35
❑ 230O	Michael Jordan	3.00	1.35
❑ 230P	Michael Jordan	3.00	1.35
❑ 230Q	Michael Jordan	3.00	1.35
❑ 230R	Michael Jordan	3.00	1.35
❑ 230S	Michael Jordan	3.00	1.35
❑ 230T	Michael Jordan	3.00	1.35
❑ 230U	Michael Jordan	3.00	1.35
❑ 230V	Michael Jordan	3.00	1.35
❑ 230W	Michael Jordan	3.00	1.35
❑ 231	Armon Gilliam	.15	.07
❑ 232	Andrew DeClercq	.15	.07
❑ 233	Stojko Vrankovic	.15	.07
❑ 234	Jayson Williams	.20	.09
❑ 235	Vinny Del Negro	.15	.07
❑ 236	Theo Ratliff	.15	.07
❑ 237	Othella Harrington	.15	.07
❑ 238	Mitch Richmond	.40	.18
❑ 239	Vlade Divac	.15	.07
❑ 240	Duane Causwell	.15	.07
❑ 241	Todd Fuller	.15	.07
❑ 242	Tom Gugliotta	.20	.09
❑ 243	LaPhonso Ellis	.15	.07
❑ 244	Brian Evans	.15	.07
❑ 245	Jason Caffey	.15	.07
❑ 246	Pooh Richardson	.15	.07
❑ 247	George Lynch	.15	.07
❑ 248	Bill Wennington	.15	.07
❑ 249	Rik Smits	.15	.07
❑ 250	Kevin Willis	.15	.07
❑ 251	Mario Elie	.15	.07
❑ 252	Austin Croshere	.50	.23
❑ 253	Sharone Wright	.15	.07
❑ 254	Danny Ferry	.15	.07
❑ 255	Jacque Vaughn	.15	.07
❑ 256	Adonal Foyle	.15	.07
❑ 257	Billy Owens	.15	.07
❑ 258	Randy Brown	.15	.07
❑ 259	Joe Smith	.20	.09
❑ 260	Joe Dumars	.40	.18
❑ 261	Sean Rooks	.15	.07
❑ 262	Eric Montross	.15	.07

❑ 263 Hubert Davis .15 .07
❑ 264 Gary Payton .50 .23
❑ 265 Tyrone Hill .15 .07
❑ 266 John Crotty .15 .07
❑ 267 P.J. Brown .15 .07
❑ 268 Michael Cage .15 .07
❑ 269 Scott Burrell .15 .07
❑ 270 Marcus Camby .40 .18
❑ 271 Rod Strickland .20 .09
❑ 272 Jim Jackson .15 .07
❑ 273 Corey Beck .15 .07
❑ 274 James Robinson .15 .07
❑ 275 Cedric Ceballos .15 .07
❑ 276 Charles Oakley .15 .07
❑ 277 Anthony Johnson .15 .07
❑ 278 Bob Sura .15 .07
❑ 279 Isaiah Rider .20 .09
❑ 280 Jeff Hornacek .20 .09
❑ 281 Rony Seikaly .15 .07
❑ 282 Charles Smith .15 .07
❑ 283 Eddie Jones .75 .35
❑ 284 Lucious Harris .15 .07
❑ 285 Andrew Lang .15 .07
❑ 286 Terry Cummings .15 .07
❑ 287 Keith Closs .15 .07
❑ 288 Chris Anstey .15 .07
❑ 289 Clarence Weatherspoon .15 .07
❑ 290 Michael Jordan H99 2.50 1.10
❑ 291 Shawn Kemp H99 .40 .18
❑ 292 Tracy McGrady H99 .75 .35
❑ 293 Glen Rice H99 .15 .07
❑ 294 David Robinson H99 .40 .18
❑ 295 Antonio McDyess H99 .20 .09
❑ 296 Vin Baker H99 .15 .07
❑ 297 Juwan Howard H99 .15 .07
❑ 298 Ron Mercer H99 .40 .18
❑ 299 Michael Finley H99 .20 .09
❑ 300 Scottie Pippen H99 .60 .25
❑ 301 Tim Thomas H99 .40 .18
❑ 302 Rasheed Wallace H99 .20 .09
❑ 303 Alonzo Mourning H99 .20 .09
❑ 304 Dikembe Mutombo H99 .15 .07
❑ 305 Derek Anderson H99 .40 .18
❑ 306 Ray Allen H99 .40 .18
❑ 307 Patrick Ewing H99 .20 .09
❑ 308 Sean Elliott H99 .15 .07
❑ 309 Shaquille O'Neal H99 1.00 .45
❑ 310 Michael Jordan Checklist 1.00 .45
❑ 311 Michael Jordan Checklist 1.00 .45
❑ 312 Michael Olowokandi RC 4.00 1.80
❑ 313 Mike Bibby RC 8.00 3.60
❑ 314 Raef LaFrentz RC 5.00 2.20
❑ 315 Antawn Jamison RC 12.00 5.50
❑ 316 Vince Carter RC 60.00 27.00
❑ 317 Robert Traylor RC 2.50 1.10
❑ 318 Jason Williams RC 15.00 6.75
❑ 319 Larry Hughes RC 15.00 6.75
❑ 320 Dirk Nowitzki RC 10.00 4.50
❑ 321 Paul Pierce RC 12.00 5.50
❑ 322 Bonzi Wells RC 10.00 4.50
❑ 323 Michael Doleac RC 2.50 1.10
❑ 324 Keon Clark RC 2.50 1.10
❑ 325 Michael Dickerson RC 5.00 2.20
❑ 326 Matt Harpring RC 2.50 1.10
❑ 327 Bryce Drew RC 2.50 1.10
❑ 328 Pat Garrity RC 1.25 .55
❑ 329 Roshown McLeod RC 1.00 .45
❑ 330 Ricky Davis RC 5.00 2.20
❑ 331 Predrag Stojakovic RC 4.00 1.80
❑ 332 Felipe Lopez RC 3.00 1.35
❑ 333 Al Harrington RC 8.00 3.60
❑ UDX Michael Jordan Retires 4.00 1.80

1998-99 Upper Deck Bronze

	MINT	NRMT
COMMON CARD (1-311)	6.00	2.70
COMMON CARD (312-333)	5.00	2.20

*STARS: 15X TO 40X BASE CARD HI
*SUBSETS: 6X TO 15X BASE HI
*RCs: 2X TO 5X BASE HI
RANDOM INSERTS IN BOTH SERIES HOBBY
STATED PRINT RUN 100 SERIAL #'d SETS
NUMBER 230 HAS 23 DIFFERENT CARDS

❑ 230A Michael Jordan 50.00 22.00
❑ 316 Vince Carter 400.00 180.00

1998-99 Upper Deck AeroDynamics

	MINT	NRMT
COMPLETE SET (30)	60.00	27.00
COMMON CARD (A1-A30)	.50	.23
SEMISTARS	.75	.35
UNLISTED STARS	1.25	.55

SER.1 STATED ODDS 1:7 HOB/RET
COMMON BRONZE (A1-A30) .. 1.25 .55
*BRONZE: 1X TO 2.5X HI COLUMN
BRONZE: RANDOM INS.IN SER.1 PACKS
STATED PRINT RUN 2000 SERIAL #'d SETS
COMMON SILVER (A1-A30) 8.00 3.60
*SILVER: 6X TO 15X HI
SILVER: RANDOM INS.IN SER.1 PACKS
STATED PRINT RUN 100 SERIAL #'d SETS

❑ A1 Michael Jordan 15.00 6.75
❑ A2 Shawn Kemp 2.00 .90
❑ A3 Anfernee Hardaway 4.00 1.80
❑ A4 Tracy McGrady 5.00 2.20
❑ A5 Glen Rice .75 .35
❑ A6 Maurice Taylor 1.25 .55
❑ A7 Kevin Garnett 8.00 3.60
❑ A8 Jason Kidd 4.00 1.80
❑ A9 Grant Hill 6.00 2.70
❑ A10 Kendall Gill .75 .35
❑ A11 Hakeem Olajuwon 2.00 .90
❑ A12 Mookie Blaylock .50 .23
❑ A13 Toni Kukoc 1.50 .70
❑ A14 Kobe Bryant 10.00 4.50
❑ A15 Corliss Williamson .50 .23
❑ A16 Ray Allen 1.50 .70
❑ A17 Vin Baker .75 .35
❑ A18 Reggie Miller 1.25 .55
❑ A19 Allan Houston 1.25 .55
❑ A20 Shareef Abdur-Rahim 3.00 1.35
❑ A21 Tim Duncan 6.00 2.70
❑ A22 Michael Finley 1.25 .55
❑ A23 Damon Stoudamire 1.25 .55
❑ A24 Juwan Howard .75 .35
❑ A25 Antoine Walker 2.00 .90
❑ A26 Donyell Marshall .50 .23
❑ A27 Allen Iverson 5.00 2.20
❑ A28 Karl Malone 2.00 .90
❑ A29 Bobby Jackson .50 .23
❑ A30 Tim Hardaway 1.25 .55

1998-99 Upper Deck AeroDynamics Gold

	MINT	NRMT
COMMON CARD (A1-A30)	30.00	13.50

*STARS: 25X TO 60X BASE INSERT
RANDOM INSERTS IN SER.1 PACKS
STATED PRINT RUN 25 SERIAL #'d SETS

❑ A1 Michael Jordan 2200.00 1000.00
❑ A13 Toni Kukoc 150.00 70.00

1998-99 Upper Deck Forces

	MINT	NRMT
COMPLETE SET (30)	120.00	55.00
COMMON CARD (F1-F30)	1.00	.45
SEMISTARS	1.50	.70
UNLISTED STARS	2.50	1.10

SER.1 STATED ODDS 1:23 HOB/RET
COMMON BRONZE (F1-F30) .. 2.50 1.10
*BRONZE: 1X TO 2.5X HI COLUMN
BRONZE: RANDOM INS.IN SER.1 PACKS
STATED PRINT RUN 1000 SERIAL #'d SETS
COMMON SILVER (F1-F30) .. 15.00 6.75
*SILVER: 6X TO 15X HI
SILVER: RANDOM INS.IN SER.1 PACKS
STATED PRINT RUN 50 SERIAL #'d SETS

❑ F1 Michael Jordan 30.00 13.50
❑ F2 Shareef Abdur-Rahim 6.00 2.70
❑ F3 Shaquille O'Neal 12.00 5.50
❑ F4 Gary Payton 4.00 1.80
❑ F5 Allen Iverson 10.00 4.50
❑ F6 Allan Houston 2.50 1.10
❑ F7 LaPhonso Ellis 1.00 .45
❑ F8 Kevin Garnett 15.00 6.75
❑ F9 Chauncey Billups 1.00 .45
❑ F10 Tim Hardaway 2.50 1.10
❑ F11 Reggie Miller 2.50 1.10
❑ F12 Glen Rice 1.50 .70
❑ F13 Damon Stoudamire 2.50 1.10
❑ F14 Lamond Murray 1.00 .45
❑ F15 Shawn Kemp 4.00 1.80
❑ F16 Steve Smith 1.50 .70
❑ F17 Tim Duncan 12.00 5.50
❑ F18 Hakeem Olajuwon 4.00 1.80
❑ F19 Karl Malone 4.00 1.80
❑ F20 Donyell Marshall 1.00 .45
❑ F21 Anfernee Hardaway 8.00 3.60
❑ F22 Grant Hill 12.00 5.50
❑ F23 Antoine Walker 4.00 1.80
❑ F24 Toni Kukoc 3.00 1.35
❑ F25 Corliss Williamson 1.00 .45
❑ F26 Glenn Robinson 1.50 .70
❑ F27 Keith Van Horn 6.00 2.70
❑ F28 Jason Kidd 8.00 3.60
❑ F29 Juwan Howard 1.50 .70
❑ F30 Michael Finley 2.50 1.10

1998-99 Upper Deck Forces Gold

	MINT	NRMT
COMMON CARD (F1-F30)	30.00	13.50

*STARS: 12.5X TO 30X BASE INSERT
RANDOM INSERTS IN SER.1 PACKS
STATED PRINT RUN 25 SERIAL #'d SETS

❑ F1 Michael Jordan 2200.00 1000.00
❑ F24 Toni Kukoc 150.00 70.00

1998-99 Upper Deck Game Jerseys

	MINT	NRMT
COMPLETE SET (49)	11000.00	5000.00
COMPLETE SERIES 1 (20)	5000.00	2200.00

COMPLETE SERIES 2 (29) 6000.00 2700.00
COMMON CARD (GJ1-GJ49) 50.00 22.00
1-10/21-30/41-50: STATED ODDS 1:2500
11-20/31-40: STATED ODDS 1:288 HOBBY
GJ38 DOES NOT EXIST
MULTI-COLOR SWATCHES CARRY PREMIUMS

Card	Player	MINT	NRMT
❑ GJ1	Glen Rice	150.00	70.00
❑ GJ2	Shawn Kemp	250.00	110.00
❑ GJ3	Reggie Miller	300.00	135.00
❑ GJ4	Shaquille O'Neal	400.00	180.00
❑ GJ5	Ray Allen	250.00	110.00
❑ GJ6	Keith Van Horn	200.00	90.00
❑ GJ7	Allen Iverson	400.00	180.00
❑ GJ8	David Robinson	250.00	110.00
❑ GJ9	Karl Malone	250.00	110.00
❑ GJ10	Shareef Abdur-Rahim	250.00	110.00
❑ GJ11	Grant Hill	150.00	70.00
❑ GJ12	Hakeem Olajuwon	100.00	45.00
❑ GJ13	Kevin Garnett	200.00	90.00
❑ GJ14	Jayson Williams	60.00	27.00
❑ GJ15	Tim Duncan	200.00	90.00
❑ GJ16	Gary Payton	120.00	55.00
❑ GJ17	John Stockton	150.00	70.00
❑ GJ18	Bryant Reeves	50.00	22.00
❑ GJ19	Kobe Bryant	600.00	275.00
❑ GJ20	Michael Jordan	1500.00	700.00
❑ GJ21	Kobe Bryant	650.00	300.00
❑ GJ22	Grant Hill	400.00	180.00
❑ GJ23	Anfernee Hardaway	400.00	180.00
❑ GJ24	Tim Thomas	150.00	70.00
❑ GJ25	Hakeem Olajuwon	120.00	55.00
❑ GJ26	Damon Stoudamire	250.00	110.00
❑ GJ27	Gary Payton	200.00	90.00
❑ GJ28	Jason Kidd	350.00	160.00
❑ GJ29	Reggie Miller	300.00	135.00
❑ GJ30	Kevin Garnett	400.00	180.00
❑ GJ31	Tim Duncan	200.00	90.00
❑ GJ32	Keith Van Horn	80.00	36.00
❑ GJ33	Stephon Marbury	120.00	55.00
❑ GJ34	Shaquille O'Neal	150.00	70.00
❑ GJ35	Allen Iverson	200.00	90.00
❑ GJ36	Antoine Walker	60.00	27.00
❑ GJ37	Karl Malone	100.00	45.00
❑ GJ38	Does not exist		
❑ GJ39	Shareef Abdur-Rahim	120.00	55.00
❑ GJ40	David Robinson	120.00	55.00
❑ GJ41	Corey Benjamin	80.00	36.00
❑ GJ42	Mike Bibby	250.00	110.00
❑ GJ43	Vince Carter	2000.00	900.00
❑ GJ44	Michael Doleac	100.00	45.00
❑ GJ45	Larry Hughes	400.00	180.00
❑ GJ46	Antawn Jamison	300.00	135.00
❑ GJ47	Raef LaFrentz	150.00	70.00
❑ GJ48	Robert Traylor	100.00	45.00
❑ GJ49	Bonzi Wells	150.00	70.00
❑ GJ50	Jason Williams	550.00	250.00

1998-99 Upper Deck Intensity

	MINT	NRMT
COMPLETE SET (30)	40.00	18.00
COMMON CARD (I1-I30)	.60	.25
SEMISTARS	1.00	.45
UNLISTED STARS	1.50	.70

SER.1 STATED ODDS 1:12 HOB/RET

COMMON BRONZE (I1-I30) .... 1.50 .70
*BRONZE: 1X TO 2.5X HI COLUMN
BRONZE: RANDOM INS.IN SER.1 PACKS
STATED PRINT RUN 1500 SERIAL #'d SETS
COMMON SILVER (I1-I30) 10.00 4.50
*SILVER: 6X TO 15X HI
SILVER: RANDOM INS.IN SER.1 PACKS
STATED PRINT RUN 75 SERIAL #'d SETS

Card	Player	MINT	NRMT
❑ I1	Michael Jordan	20.00	9.00
❑ I2	Tracy Murray	.60	.25
❑ I3	Ron Mercer	2.50	1.10
❑ I4	Terrell Brandon	1.00	.45
❑ I5	Brevin Knight	.60	.25
❑ I6	Rasheed Wallace	1.50	.70
❑ I7	Sam Cassell	1.00	.45
❑ I8	Erick Dampier	.60	.25
❑ I9	LaPhonso Ellis	.60	.25
❑ I10	Tim Thomas	2.50	1.10
❑ I11	Anfernee Hardaway	5.00	2.20
❑ I12	Tariq Abdul-Wahad	.60	.25
❑ I13	Lorenzen Wright	.60	.25
❑ I14	Bryant Reeves	.60	.25
❑ I15	Charles Barkley	2.50	1.10
❑ I16	Chauncey Billups	.60	.25
❑ I17	John Starks	.60	.25
❑ I18	Jerry Stackhouse	1.00	.45
❑ I19	Vlade Divac	.60	.25
❑ I20	Detlef Schrempf	1.00	.45
❑ I21	John Stockton	1.50	.70
❑ I22	Nick Anderson	.60	.25
❑ I23	Alonzo Mourning	1.50	.70
❑ I24	Dikembe Mutombo	1.00	.45
❑ I25	Jalen Rose	1.50	.70
❑ I26	Robert Pack	.60	.25
❑ I27	Antonio McDyess	1.50	.70
❑ I28	Eddie Jones	3.00	1.35
❑ I29	Stephon Marbury	4.00	1.80
❑ I30	David Robinson	2.50	1.10

1998-99 Upper Deck Intensity Gold

	MINT	NRMT
COMMON CARD (I1-I30)	30.00	13.50

*STARS: 20X TO 50X BASE INSERT
RANDOM INSERTS IN SER.1 PACKS
STATED PRINT RUN 25 SERIAL #'d SETS

Card	Player	MINT	NRMT
❑ I1	Michael Jordan	2200.00	1000.00

1998-99 Upper Deck MJ23

	MINT	NRMT
COMPLETE SET (30)	250.00	110.00
COMMON CARD (M1-M30)	10.00	4.50

SER.2 STATED ODDS 1:23 HOB/RET
COMMON BRONZE (M1-M23) 20.00 9.00
BRONZE: RANDOM INS.IN SER.2 PACKS
STATED PRINT RUN 2300 SERIAL #'d SETS
COMMON SILVER (M1-M23) 500.00 220.00
SILVER: RANDOM INS.IN SER.2 PACKS
STATED PRINT RUN 23 SERIAL #'d SETS
UNPRICED GOLD PARALLEL SERIAL #'d TO 1

Card	Player	MINT	NRMT
❑ M1	Michael Jordan	10.00	4.50
❑ M2	Michael Jordan	10.00	4.50
❑ M3	Michael Jordan	10.00	4.50
❑ M4	Michael Jordan	10.00	4.50
❑ M5	Michael Jordan	10.00	4.50
❑ M6	Michael Jordan	10.00	4.50
❑ M7	Michael Jordan	10.00	4.50
❑ M8	Michael Jordan	10.00	4.50
❑ M9	Michael Jordan	10.00	4.50
❑ M10	Michael Jordan	10.00	4.50
❑ M11	Michael Jordan	10.00	4.50
❑ M12	Michael Jordan	10.00	4.50
❑ M13	Michael Jordan	10.00	4.50
❑ M14	Michael Jordan	10.00	4.50
❑ M15	Michael Jordan	10.00	4.50
❑ M16	Michael Jordan	10.00	4.50
❑ M17	Michael Jordan	10.00	4.50
❑ M18	Michael Jordan	10.00	4.50
❑ M19	Michael Jordan	10.00	4.50
❑ M20	Michael Jordan	10.00	4.50
❑ M21	Michael Jordan	10.00	4.50
❑ M22	Michael Jordan	10.00	4.50
❑ M23	Michael Jordan	10.00	4.50
❑ M24	Michael Jordan	10.00	4.50
❑ M25	Michael Jordan	10.00	4.50
❑ M26	Michael Jordan	10.00	4.50
❑ M27	Michael Jordan	10.00	4.50
❑ M28	Michael Jordan	10.00	4.50
❑ M29	Michael Jordan	10.00	4.50
❑ M30	Michael Jordan	10.00	4.50

1998-99 Upper Deck Michael Jordan Game Jersey Autographs

	MINT	NRMT
COMMON CARD	11000.00	5000.00

EACH CARD NUMBERED OUT OF 23
EACH PRODUCT HAS 23 CARDS
RANDOM INSERTS IN MJ LIV.LEG.
RANDOM INSERTS IN MJx
RANDOM INSERTS IN OVATION
RANDOM INSERTS IN SER.1 SPx FINITE
RANDOM INSERTS IN SER.1 UD
RANDOM INSERTS IN SER.2 UD

1998-99 Upper Deck Next Wave

	MINT	NRMT
COMPLETE SET (30)	50.00	22.00

COMMON CARD (NW1-NW30) .. .75 .35
SEMISTARS 1.00 .45
UNLISTED STARS 1.50 .70
SER.2 STATED ODDS 1:11 HOB/RET
COMMON BRONZE (NW1-NW30) 2.00 .90
*BRONZE: 1.25X TO 3X HI COLUMN
BRONZE: RANDOM INS.IN SER.2 PACKS
STATED PRINT RUN 1500 SERIAL #'d SETS
COMMON SILVER (NW1-NW30) 6.00 2.70
*SILVER: 3X TO 8X HI
SILVER: RANDOM INS.IN SER.2 PACKS
STATED PRINT RUN 200 SERIAL #'d SETS
COMMON GOLD (NW1-NW30) 12.00 5.50
*GOLD: 6X TO 15X HI
GOLD: RANDOM INS.IN SER.2 PACKS
STATED PRINT RUN 75 SERIAL #'d SETS

❑ NW1 Kobe Bryant 12.00 5.50
❑ NW2 John Wallace .75 .35
❑ NW3 Kerry Kittles 1.00 .45
❑ NW4 Tim Thomas 2.50 1.10
❑ NW5 Maurice Taylor 1.50 .70
❑ NW6 Antonio McDyess 1.50 .70
❑ NW7 Jermaine O'Neal 1.00 .45
❑ NW8 Zydrunas Ilgauskas .75 .35
❑ NW9 Danny Fortson 1.00 .45
❑ NW10 Tim Duncan 8.00 3.60
❑ NW11 Derek Anderson 2.00 .90
❑ NW12 Ron Mercer 2.50 1.10
❑ NW13 Joe Smith 1.00 .45
❑ NW14 Eddie Jones 3.00 1.35
❑ NW15 Rodrick Rhodes .75 .35
❑ NW16 Kevin Garnett 10.00 4.50
❑ NW17 Ed Gray .75 .35
❑ NW18 Bobby Jackson .75 .35
❑ NW19 Allan Houston 1.50 .70
❑ NW20 Chauncey Billups .75 .35
❑ NW21 Keith Booth .75 .35
❑ NW22 Brevin Knight .75 .35
❑ NW23 Othella Harrington .75 .35
❑ NW24 Keith Van Horn 4.00 1.80
❑ NW25 Michael Finley 1.50 .70
❑ NW26 Tracy McGrady 6.00 2.70
❑ NW27 Derek Fisher 1.00 .45
❑ NW28 Ray Allen 2.00 .90
❑ NW29 Anthony Johnson .75 .35
❑ NW30 Vin Baker 1.00 .45

1998-99 Upper Deck Super Powers

	MINT	NRMT
COMPLETE SET (30)	50.00	22.00
COMMON CARD (PS1-PS30)	.75	.35
UNLISTED STARS	1.25	.55

SER.2 STATED ODDS 1:5 HOB/RET
COMMON BRONZE (PS1-PS30) 2.00 .90
*BRONZE: 1.25X TO 3X HI COLUMN
BRONZE: RANDOM INS.IN SER.2 PACKS
STATED PRINT RUN 1000 SERIAL #'d SETS
COMMON SILVER (PS1-PS30) 12.00 5.50
*SILVER: 6X TO 15X HI
SILVER: RANDOM INS.IN SER.2 PACKS
STATED PRINT RUN 100 SERIAL #'d SETS
COMMON GOLD (PS1-PS30) 25.00 11.00
*GOLD: 15X TO 30X HI
GOLD: RANDOM INS.IN SER.2 PACKS
STATED PRINT RUN 50 SERIAL #'d SETS

❑ PS1 Dikembe Mutombo .75 .35
❑ PS2 Ron Mercer 2.00 .90
❑ PS3 Glen Rice 1.25 .55
❑ PS4 Scottie Pippen 4.00 1.80
❑ PS5 Shawn Kemp 2.00 .90
❑ PS6 Michael Finley 1.25 .55
❑ PS7 Bobby Jackson .75 .35
❑ PS8 Grant Hill 6.00 2.70
❑ PS9 Jim Jackson .75 .35
❑ PS10 Hakeem Olajuwon 2.00 .90
❑ PS11 Reggie Miller 1.25 .55
❑ PS12 Maurice Taylor 1.25 .55
❑ PS13 Kobe Bryant 10.00 4.50
❑ PS14 Tim Hardaway 1.25 .55
❑ PS15 Ray Allen 1.50 .70
❑ PS16 Stephon Marbury 3.00 1.35
❑ PS17 Keith Van Horn 3.00 1.35
❑ PS18 Allan Houston .75 .35
❑ PS19 Anfernee Hardaway 4.00 1.80
❑ PS20 Allen Iverson 5.00 2.20
❑ PS21 Jason Kidd 4.00 1.80
❑ PS22 Damon Stoudamire 1.25 .55
❑ PS23 Corliss Williamson .75 .35
❑ PS24 Tim Duncan 6.00 2.70
❑ PS25 Gary Payton 2.00 .90
❑ PS26 Tracy McGrady 5.00 2.20
❑ PS27 Karl Malone 1.50 .70
❑ PS28 Shareef Abdur-Rahim 3.00 1.35
❑ PS29 Juwan Howard .75 .35
❑ PS30 Michael Jordan 15.00 6.75

1999-00 Upper Deck

	MINT	NRMT
COMPLETE SET (360)	225.00	100.00
COMPLETE SERIES 1 (180)	150.00	70.00
COMPLETE SERIES 2 (180)	75.00	34.00
COMP.SERIES 1 w/o RC (155)	50.00	22.00
COMP.SERIES 2 w/o SP (133)	10.00	4.50
COMMON CARD (1-133/181-315)	.15	.07
COMMON MJ (134-153)	2.50	1.10
COMMON RC (156-180/316-360)	1.25	.55
SEMISTARS	.20	.09
SEMISTARS RC	1.50	.70
UNLISTED STARS	.40	.18
UNLISTED STARS RC	2.00	.90

MJ SUBSET STATED ODDS 1:4 H/R
ROOKIE SUBSET STATED ODDS 1:4 H/R
UNPRICED GOLD PARALLEL SERIAL #'d TO 1

❑ 1 Roshown McLeod .15 .07
❑ 2 Dikembe Mutombo .20 .09
❑ 3 Alan Henderson .15 .07
❑ 4 LaPhonso Ellis .15 .07
❑ 5 Chris Crawford .15 .07
❑ 6 Kenny Anderson .20 .09
❑ 7 Antoine Walker .50 .23
❑ 8 Paul Pierce .75 .35
❑ 9 Vitaly Potapenko .15 .07
❑ 10 Dana Barros .15 .07
❑ 11 Elden Campbell .15 .07
❑ 12 Eddie Jones .75 .35
❑ 13 David Wesley .15 .07
❑ 14 Derrick Coleman .20 .09
❑ 15 Ricky Davis .40 .18
❑ 16 Corey Benjamin .15 .07
❑ 17 Randy Brown .15 .07
❑ 18 Kornel David RC .15 .07
❑ 19 Toni Kukoc .50 .23
❑ 20 Keith Booth .15 .07
❑ 21 Shawn Kemp .60 .25
❑ 22 Wesley Person .15 .07
❑ 23 Brevin Knight .15 .07
❑ 24 Bob Sura .15 .07
❑ 25 Zydrunas Ilgauskas .15 .07
❑ 26 Michael Finley .40 .18
❑ 27 Shawn Bradley .15 .07
❑ 28 Dirk Nowitzki .60 .25
❑ 29 Steve Nash .15 .07
❑ 30 Antonio McDyess .40 .18
❑ 31 Nick Van Exel .20 .09
❑ 32 Chauncey Billups .15 .07
❑ 33 Bryant Stith .15 .07
❑ 34 Raef LaFrentz .40 .18
❑ 35 Grant Hill 2.00 .90
❑ 36 Lindsey Hunter .15 .07
❑ 37 Bison Dele .15 .07
❑ 38 Jerry Stackhouse .20 .09
❑ 39 John Starks .15 .07
❑ 40 Antawn Jamison .75 .35
❑ 41 Erick Dampier .15 .07
❑ 42 Jason Caffey .15 .07
❑ 43 Hakeem Olajuwon .60 .25
❑ 44 Scottie Pippen 1.25 .55
❑ 45 Cuttino Mobley .40 .18
❑ 46 Charles Barkley .60 .25
❑ 47 Bryce Drew .15 .07
❑ 48 Reggie Miller .40 .18
❑ 49 Jalen Rose .40 .18
❑ 50 Mark Jackson .15 .07
❑ 51 Dale Davis .15 .07
❑ 52 Chris Mullin .40 .18
❑ 53 Maurice Taylor .40 .18
❑ 54 Tyrone Nesby RC .15 .07
❑ 55 Michael Olowokandi .20 .09
❑ 56 Eric Piatkowski .15 .07
❑ 57 Troy Hudson RC .15 .07
❑ 58 Kobe Bryant 3.00 1.35
❑ 59 Shaquille O'Neal 2.00 .90
❑ 60 Glen Rice .20 .09
❑ 61 Robert Horry .15 .07
❑ 62 Tim Hardaway .40 .18
❑ 63 Alonzo Mourning .40 .18
❑ 64 P.J. Brown .15 .07
❑ 65 Dan Majerle .20 .09
❑ 66 Ray Allen .40 .18
❑ 67 Glenn Robinson .20 .09
❑ 68 Sam Cassell .20 .09
❑ 69 Robert Traylor .15 .07
❑ 70 Kevin Garnett 2.50 1.10
❑ 71 Sam Mitchell .15 .07
❑ 72 Dean Garrett .15 .07
❑ 73 Bobby Jackson .15 .07
❑ 74 Radoslav Nesterovic .15 .07
❑ 75 Keith Van Horn .75 .35
❑ 76 Stephon Marbury .75 .35
❑ 77 Kendall Gill .20 .09
❑ 78 Scott Burrell .15 .07
❑ 79 Patrick Ewing .40 .18
❑ 80 Allan Houston .40 .18
❑ 81 Latrell Sprewell .75 .35
❑ 82 Larry Johnson .20 .09
❑ 83 Marcus Camby .40 .18
❑ 84 Darrell Armstrong .20 .09
❑ 85 Derek Strong .15 .07
❑ 86 Matt Harpring .15 .07
❑ 87 Michael Doleac .15 .07
❑ 88 Charles Outlaw .15 .07
❑ 89 Allen Iverson 1.50 .70
❑ 90 Theo Ratliff .15 .07
❑ 91 Larry Hughes 1.00 .45
❑ 92 Eric Snow .15 .07
❑ 93 Jason Kidd 1.25 .55
❑ 94 Clifford Robinson .15 .07
❑ 95 Tom Gugliotta .20 .09
❑ 96 Luc Longley .15 .07
❑ 97 Rasheed Wallace .40 .18
❑ 98 Arvydas Sabonis .20 .09
❑ 99 Damon Stoudamire .40 .18
❑ 100 Brian Grant .20 .09
❑ 101 Jason Williams 1.00 .45
❑ 102 Vlade Divac .15 .07
❑ 103 Predrag Stojakovic .20 .09
❑ 104 Lawrence Funderburke .15 .07

❑	105	Tim Duncan	2.00	.90
❑	106	Sean Elliott	.15	.07
❑	107	David Robinson	.60	.25
❑	108	Mario Elie	.15	.07
❑	109	Avery Johnson	.15	.07
❑	110	Gary Payton	.60	.25
❑	111	Vin Baker	.20	.09
❑	112	Rashard Lewis	.60	.25
❑	113	Jelani McCoy	.15	.07
❑	114	Vladimir Stepania	.15	.07
❑	115	Vince Carter	4.00	1.80
❑	116	Doug Christie	.15	.07
❑	117	Kevin Willis	.15	.07
❑	118	Dee Brown	.15	.07
❑	119	John Thomas	.15	.07
❑	120	Karl Malone	.60	.25
❑	121	John Stockton	.40	.18
❑	122	Howard Eisley	.15	.07
❑	123	Bryon Russell	.15	.07
❑	124	Greg Ostertag	.15	.07
❑	125	Shareef Abdur-Rahim	.75	.35
❑	126	Mike Bibby	.50	.23
❑	127	Felipe Lopez	.15	.07
❑	128	Cherokee Parks	.15	.07
❑	129	Juwan Howard	.20	.09
❑	130	Rod Strickland	.20	.09
❑	131	Chris Whitney	.15	.07
❑	132	Tracy Murray	.15	.07
❑	133	Jahidi White	.15	.07
❑	134	Michael Jordan AIR	2.50	1.10
❑	135	Michael Jordan AIR	2.50	1.10
❑	136	Michael Jordan AIR	2.50	1.10
❑	137	Michael Jordan AIR	2.50	1.10
❑	138	Michael Jordan AIR	2.50	1.10
❑	139	Michael Jordan AIR	2.50	1.10
❑	140	Michael Jordan AIR	2.50	1.10
❑	141	Michael Jordan AIR	2.50	1.10
❑	142	Michael Jordan AIR	2.50	1.10
❑	143	Michael Jordan AIR	2.50	1.10
❑	144	Michael Jordan AIR	2.50	1.10
❑	145	Michael Jordan AIR	2.50	1.10
❑	146	Michael Jordan AIR	2.50	1.10
❑	147	Michael Jordan AIR	2.50	1.10
❑	148	Michael Jordan AIR	2.50	1.10
❑	149	Michael Jordan AIR	2.50	1.10
❑	150	Michael Jordan AIR	2.50	1.10
❑	151	Michael Jordan AIR	2.50	1.10
❑	152	Michael Jordan AIR	2.50	1.10
❑	153	Michael Jordan AIR	2.50	1.10
❑	154	Michael Jordan CL	1.00	.45
❑	155	Michael Jordan CL	1.00	.45
❑	156	Elton Brand RC	20.00	9.00
❑	157	Steve Francis RC	25.00	11.00
❑	158	Baron Davis RC	5.00	2.20
❑	159	Lamar Odom RC	15.00	6.75
❑	160	Jonathan Bender RC	10.00	4.50
❑	161	Wally Szczerbiak RC	8.00	3.60
❑	162	Richard Hamilton RC	5.00	2.20
❑	163	Andre Miller RC	6.00	2.70
❑	164	Shawn Marion RC	6.00	2.70
❑	165	Jason Terry RC	3.00	1.35
❑	166	Trajan Langdon RC	3.00	1.35
❑	167	Kenny Thomas RC	3.00	1.35
❑	168	Corey Maggette RC	8.00	3.60
❑	169	William Avery RC	3.00	1.35
❑	170	Jumaine Jones RC	1.50	.70
❑	171	Ron Artest RC	5.00	2.20
❑	172	Cal Bowdler RC	2.00	.90
❑	173	James Posey RC	4.00	1.80
❑	174	Quincy Lewis RC	2.00	.90
❑	175	Vonteego Cummings RC	3.00	1.35
❑	176	Jeff Foster RC	2.00	.90
❑	177	Dion Glover RC	2.00	.90
❑	178	Devean George RC	4.00	1.80
❑	179	Evan Eschmeyer RC	1.25	.55
❑	180	Tim James RC	2.50	1.10
❑	181	Jim Jackson	.15	.07
❑	182	Isaiah Rider	.20	.09
❑	183	Lorenzen Wright	.15	.07
❑	184	Bimbo Coles	.15	.07
❑	185	Anthony Johnson	.15	.07
❑	186	Calbert Cheaney	.15	.07
❑	187	Pervis Ellison	.15	.07
❑	188	Walter McCarty	.15	.07
❑	189	Eric Williams	.15	.07
❑	190	Tony Battie	.15	.07
❑	191	Anthony Mason	.20	.09
❑	192	Bobby Phills	.15	.07
❑	193	Todd Fuller	.15	.07
❑	194	Brad Miller	.15	.07
❑	195	Eldridge Recasner	.15	.07
❑	196	Chris Anstey	.15	.07
❑	197	Fred Hoiberg	.15	.07
❑	198	Hersey Hawkins	.20	.09
❑	199	Will Perdue	.15	.07
❑	200	Mark Bryant	.15	.07
❑	201	Lamond Murray	.15	.07
❑	202	Cedric Henderson	.15	.07
❑	203	Andrew DeClercq	.15	.07
❑	204	Danny Ferry	.15	.07
❑	205	Erick Strickland	.15	.07
❑	206	Cedric Ceballos	.15	.07
❑	207	Hubert Davis	.15	.07
❑	208	Robert Pack	.15	.07
❑	209	Gary Trent	.15	.07
❑	210	Ron Mercer	.50	.23
❑	211	George McCloud	.15	.07
❑	212	Roy Rogers	.15	.07
❑	213	Keon Clark	.15	.07
❑	214	Terry Mills	.15	.07
❑	215	Michael Curry	.15	.07
❑	216	Christian Laettner	.20	.09
❑	217	Jerome Williams	.20	.09
❑	218	Loy Vaught	.15	.07
❑	219	Jud Buechler	.15	.07
❑	220	Mookie Blaylock	.15	.07
❑	221	Terry Cummings	.15	.07
❑	222	Donyell Marshall	.15	.07
❑	223	Chris Mills	.15	.07
❑	224	Adonal Foyle	.15	.07
❑	225	Shandon Anderson	.15	.07
❑	226	Kelvin Cato	.15	.07
❑	227	Walt Williams	.15	.07
❑	228	Al Harrington	.50	.23
❑	229	Rik Smits	.15	.07
❑	230	Derrick McKey	.15	.07
❑	231	Sam Perkins	.15	.07
❑	232	Austin Croshere	.40	.18
❑	233	Derek Anderson	.40	.18
❑	234	Keith Closs	.15	.07
❑	235	Eric Murdock	.15	.07
❑	236	Brian Skinner	.15	.07
❑	237	Charles Jones	.15	.07
❑	238	Ron Harper	.20	.09
❑	239	Derek Fisher	.20	.09
❑	240	Rick Fox	.15	.07
❑	241	A.C. Green	.20	.09
❑	242	Jamal Mashburn	.20	.09
❑	243	Mark Strickland	.15	.07
❑	244	Rex Walters	.15	.07
❑	245	Clarence Weatherspoon	.15	.07
❑	246	Ervin Johnson	.15	.07
❑	247	J.R. Reid	.15	.07
❑	248	Dale Ellis	.15	.07
❑	249	Danny Manning	.20	.09
❑	250	Tim Thomas	.50	.23
❑	251	Terrell Brandon	.20	.09
❑	252	Malik Sealy	.15	.07
❑	253	Joe Smith	.20	.09
❑	254	Anthony Peeler	.15	.07
❑	255	Jayson Williams	.20	.09
❑	256	Jamie Feick RC	1.25	.55
❑	257	Kerry Kittles	.20	.09
❑	258	Johnny Newman	.15	.07
❑	259	Chris Childs	.15	.07
❑	260	Kurt Thomas	.15	.07
❑	261	Charlie Ward	.15	.07
❑	262	Chris Dudley	.15	.07
❑	263	John Wallace	.15	.07
❑	264	Tariq Abdul-Wahad	.15	.07
❑	265	John Amaechi RC	1.25	.55
❑	266	Chris Gatling	.15	.07
❑	267	Monty Williams	.15	.07
❑	268	Ben Wallace	.15	.07
❑	269	George Lynch	.15	.07
❑	270	Tyrone Hill	.15	.07
❑	271	Billy Owens	.15	.07
❑	272	Anfernee Hardaway	1.25	.55
❑	273	Rex Chapman	.15	.07
❑	274	Oliver Miller	.15	.07
❑	275	Rodney Rogers	.15	.07
❑	276	Randy Livingston	.15	.07
❑	277	Scottie Pippen	1.25	.55
❑	278	Detlef Schrempf	.20	.09
❑	279	Steve Smith	.20	.09
❑	280	Jermaine O'Neal	.20	.09
❑	281	Bonzi Wells	.60	.25
❑	282	Chris Webber	1.25	.55
❑	283	Nick Anderson	.15	.07
❑	284	Darrick Martin	.15	.07
❑	285	Corliss Williamson	.15	.07
❑	286	Samaki Walker	.15	.07
❑	287	Terry Porter	.15	.07
❑	288	Malik Rose	.15	.07
❑	289	Jaren Jackson	.15	.07
❑	290	Antonio Daniels	.15	.07
❑	291	Steve Kerr	.15	.07
❑	292	Brent Barry	.15	.07
❑	293	Horace Grant	.20	.09
❑	294	Vernon Maxwell	.15	.07
❑	295	Ruben Patterson	.40	.18
❑	296	Shammond Williams	.15	.07
❑	297	Antonio Davis	.15	.07
❑	298	Tracy McGrady	1.25	.55
❑	299	Dell Curry	.15	.07
❑	300	Charles Oakley	.15	.07
❑	301	Muggsy Bogues	.15	.07
❑	302	Jeff Hornacek	.20	.09
❑	303	Adam Keefe	.15	.07
❑	304	Olden Polynice	.15	.07
❑	305	Doug West	.15	.07
❑	306	Michael Dickerson	.40	.18
❑	307	Othella Harrington	.15	.07
❑	308	Bryant Reeves	.15	.07
❑	309	Brent Price	.15	.07
❑	310	Mitch Richmond	.40	.18
❑	311	Aaron Williams	.15	.07
❑	312	Isaac Austin	.15	.07
❑	313	Michael Smith	.15	.07
❑	314	Michael Jordan CL	1.00	.45
❑	315	Kevin Garnett CL	.50	.23
❑	316	Elton Brand	10.00	4.50
❑	317	Steve Francis	12.00	5.50
❑	318	Baron Davis	2.50	1.10
❑	319	Lamar Odom	8.00	3.60
❑	320	Jonathan Bender	5.00	2.20
❑	321	Wally Szczerbiak	4.00	1.80
❑	322	Richard Hamilton	2.50	1.10
❑	323	Andre Miller	3.00	1.35
❑	324	Shawn Marion	3.00	1.35
❑	325	Jason Terry	1.50	.70
❑	326	Trajan Langdon	1.50	.70
❑	327	Aleksandar Radojevic RC	1.25	.55
❑	328	Corey Maggette	4.00	1.80
❑	329	William Avery	1.50	.70
❑	330	Ron Artest	2.50	1.10
❑	331	Cal Bowdler	1.50	.70
❑	332	James Posey	1.50	.70
❑	333	Quincy Lewis	1.50	.70
❑	334	Dion Glover	1.50	.70
❑	335	Jeff Foster	1.25	.55
❑	336	Kenny Thomas	1.50	.70
❑	337	Devean George	.40	.18
❑	338	Tim James	1.50	.70
❑	339	Vonteego Cummings	1.50	.70
❑	340	Jumaine Jones	1.25	.55
❑	341	Scott Padgett RC	2.00	.90
❑	342	John Celestand RC	2.00	.90
❑	343	Adrian Griffin RC	2.50	1.10
❑	344	Michael Ruffin RC	1.50	.70
❑	345	Chris Herren RC	1.25	.55
❑	346	Evan Eschmeyer	.40	.18
❑	347	Eddie Robinson RC	3.00	1.35
❑	348	Obinna Ekezie RC	1.50	.70
❑	349	Laron Profit RC	2.00	.90
❑	350	Jermaine Jackson RC	1.25	.55
❑	351	Lazaro Borrell RC	1.25	.55
❑	352	Chucky Atkins RC	2.50	1.10
❑	353	Ryan Robertson RC	1.50	.70
❑	354	Todd MacCulloch RC	2.00	.90
❑	355	Rafer Alston RC	2.50	1.10
❑	356	Mirsad Turkcan RC	1.25	.55
❑	357	Anthony Carter RC	5.00	2.20
❑	358	Ryan Bowen RC	1.25	.55
❑	359	Rodney Buford RC	1.25	.55
❑	360	Tim Young RC	1.25	.55

1999-00 Upper Deck Bronze

	MINT	NRMT
COMMON CARD (1-360)	5.00	2.20
COMMON MJ (134-153)	60.00	27.00
COMMON ROOKIE	12.00	5.50

*STARS: 12.5X TO 30X BASE CARD HI
*RCs: 2.5X TO 6X BASE HI
*SER.2 DRAFT PICKS: 4X TO 10X BASE HI
RANDOM INSERTS IN HOBBY PACKS
STATED PRINT RUN 100 SERIAL #'d SETS

1999-00 Upper Deck BioGraphics

	MINT	NRMT
COMPLETE SET (30)	30.00	13.50
COMMON CARD (B1-B30)	.50	.23
UNLISTED STARS	.75	.35

SER.2 STATED ODDS 1:4 HOB/RET
COMMON LEVEL 1 (B1-B30) .. 8.00 3.60
*LEVEL 1: 6X TO 15X HI COLUMN
LEVEL 1: RANDOM INS.IN SER.2 PACKS
LEVEL 1: PRINT RUN 100 SERIAL #'d SETS
COMMON LEVEL 2 (B1-B30) 30.00 13.50
*LEVEL 2: 25X TO 60X HI
LEVEL 2: RANDOM INS.IN SER.2 PACKS
LEVEL 2: PRINT RUN 25 SERIAL #'d SETS

Card	Player	MINT	NRMT
❑ B1	Antawn Jamison	1.50	.70
❑ B2	Mike Bibby	1.00	.45
❑ B3	Antoine Walker	1.00	.45
❑ B4	Ray Allen	.75	.35
❑ B5	Anfernee Hardaway	2.50	1.10
❑ B6	Hakeem Olajuwon	1.25	.55
❑ B7	Jason Williams	2.00	.90
❑ B8	Keith Van Horn	1.50	.70
❑ B9	Jason Kidd	2.50	1.10
❑ B10	Reggie Miller	.75	.35
❑ B11	Eddie Jones	1.50	.70
❑ B12	Jim Jackson	.50	.23
❑ B13	Jerry Stackhouse	.50	.23
❑ B14	Tim Duncan	4.00	1.80
❑ B15	Kevin Garnett	5.00	2.20
❑ B16	Mitch Richmond	.75	.35
❑ B17	Steve Smith	.50	.23
❑ B18	Charles Barkley	1.25	.55
❑ B19	Glen Rice	.50	.23
❑ B20	Paul Pierce	1.50	.70
❑ B21	Alonzo Mourning	.75	.35
❑ B22	Karl Malone	1.25	.55
❑ B23	Stephon Marbury	1.50	.70
❑ B24	Chris Webber	2.50	1.10
❑ B25	Michael Finley	.75	.35
❑ B26	Shawn Kemp	1.25	.55
❑ B27	John Stockton	.75	.35
❑ B28	Ron Mercer	1.00	.45
❑ B29	Tim Hardaway	.75	.35
❑ B30	Allan Houston	.75	.35

1999-00 Upper Deck Cool Air

	MINT	NRMT
COMPLETE SET (8)	70.00	32.00
COMMON CARD (MJ1-MJ8)	10.00	4.50

SER.2 STATED ODDS 1:72 HOB/RET
COMMON LEVEL 1 (MJ1-MJ8) 50.00 22.00
LEVEL 1: RANDOM INS.IN SER.2 HOBBY
LEVEL 1: PRINT RUN 100 SERIAL #'d SETS
UNPRICED LEVEL 2 SERIAL #'d TO 1

Card	Player	MINT	NRMT
❑ MJ1	Michael Jordan	10.00	4.50
❑ MJ2	Michael Jordan	10.00	4.50
❑ MJ3	Michael Jordan	10.00	4.50
❑ MJ4	Michael Jordan	10.00	4.50
❑ MJ5	Michael Jordan	10.00	4.50
❑ MJ6	Michael Jordan	10.00	4.50
❑ MJ7	Michael Jordan	10.00	4.50
❑ MJ8	Michael Jordan	10.00	4.50

1999-00 Upper Deck Julius Erving Heroes

	MINT	NRMT
COMPLETE SET (10)	40.00	18.00
COMMON CARD (H46-H55)	5.00	2.20

SER.1 STATED ODDS 1:23
COMMON LEVEL 1 (H46-55) 20.00 9.00
LEVEL 1: RANDOM INS.IN SER.1 HOBBY
LEVEL 1: PRINT RUN 100 SERIAL #'d SETS
UNPRICED LEVEL 2 SERIAL #'d TO 1

Card	Player	MINT	NRMT
❑ H46	Julius Erving	5.00	2.20
❑ H47	Julius Erving	5.00	2.20
❑ H48	Julius Erving	5.00	2.20
❑ H49	Julius Erving	5.00	2.20
❑ H50	Julius Erving	5.00	2.20
❑ H51	Julius Erving	5.00	2.20
❑ H52	Julius Erving	5.00	2.20
❑ H53	Julius Erving	5.00	2.20
❑ H54	Julius Erving	5.00	2.20
❑ H55	Julius Erving	5.00	2.20

1999-00 Upper Deck Future Charge

	MINT	NRMT
COMPLETE SET (15)	10.00	4.50
COMMON CARD (FC1-FC15)	.50	.23
UNLISTED STARS	.75	.35

SER.1 STATED ODDS 1:8 HOB/RET
COMMON LEVEL 1 (FC1-15) .. 8.00 3.60
*LEVEL 1: 6X TO 15X HI COLUMN
LEVEL 1: RANDOM INS.IN SER.1 PACKS
LEVEL 1: PRINT RUN 100 SERIAL #'d SETS
COMMON LEVEL 2 (FC1-15) 30.00 13.50
*LEVEL 2: 25X TO 60X HI
LEVEL 2: RANDOM INS.IN SER.1 PACKS
LEVEL 2: PRINT RUN 25 SERIAL #'d SETS

Card	Player	MINT	NRMT
❑ FC1	Antawn Jamison	1.50	.70
❑ FC2	Mike Bibby	1.00	.45
❑ FC3	Antoine Walker	1.00	.45
❑ FC4	Baron Davis	1.00	.45
❑ FC5	Jason Terry	.75	.35
❑ FC6	Andre Miller	1.25	.55
❑ FC7	Ray Allen	.75	.35
❑ FC8	Wally Szczerbiak	1.50	.70
❑ FC9	Raef LaFrentz	.75	.35
❑ FC10	William Avery	.75	.35
❑ FC11	Jason Williams	2.00	.90
❑ FC12	Michael Olowokandi	.50	.23
❑ FC13	Stephon Marbury	1.50	.70
❑ FC14	Quincy Lewis	.50	.23
❑ FC15	Shawn Marion	1.25	.55

1999-00 Upper Deck Game Jerseys

	MINT	NRMT
COMPLETE SET (65)	7500.00	3400.00
COMPLETE SERIES 1 (20)	4500.00	2000.00
COMPLETE SERIES 2 (44)	3000.00	1350.00
COMMON CARD (GJ1-GJ64)	40.00	18.00

GJ1-GJ10 STATED ODDS 1:2500 HOB/RET
GJ21-GJ42 STATED ODDS 1:288 H/1:2500 R
GJ11-GJ20 STATED ODDS 1:287 HOBBY
GJ43-GJ64 STATED ODDS 1:288 HOBBY
MULTI-COLOR SWATCHES CARRY PREMI-

UMS
AUTOS NOT INCLUDED IN SET PRICE
GJ4A/GJ56A UNPRICED DUE TO SCARCITY
*CENT.CLUB: .4X TO 1X HI COLUMN
CENT.CLUB: ONLY FOR CARDS GJ43-GJ64
CENT.CLUB: PRINT RUN 100 SERIAL #'d SETS
CENT.CLUB: RANDOM INS.IN SER.2 HOB.

Card	Player	MINT	NRMT
❑ GJ1	Jason Kidd	200.00	90.00
❑ GJ2	Shaquille O'Neal	250.00	110.00
❑ GJ3	Tim Duncan	250.00	110.00
❑ GJ4	Charles Barkley	250.00	110.00
❑ GJ4A	Charles Barkley AU/4		
❑ GJ5	Kevin Garnett	200.00	90.00
❑ GJ5A	Kevin Garnett AU/21	1200.00	550.00
❑ GJ6	John Stockton	150.00	70.00
❑ GJ7	Keith Van Horn	80.00	36.00
❑ GJ8	Hakeem Olajuwon	80.00	36.00
❑ GJ9	Paul Pierce	120.00	55.00
❑ GJ10	Michael Jordan	1500.00	700.00
❑ GJ10A	M.I Jordan AU/23	11000.00	5000.00
❑ GJ11	Kobe Bryant	400.00	180.00
❑ GJ12	Scottie Pippen	150.00	70.00
❑ GJ13	Grant Hill	120.00	55.00
❑ GJ14	Gary Payton	100.00	45.00
❑ GJ15	Vince Carter	600.00	275.00
❑ GJ16	Reggie Miller	150.00	70.00
❑ GJ17	Allen Iverson	150.00	70.00
❑ GJ18	David Robinson	100.00	45.00
❑ GJ19	Antoine Walker	60.00	27.00
❑ GJ20	Karl Malone	80.00	36.00
❑ GJ20A	Karl Malone AU/32	600.00	275.00
❑ GJ21	Kobe Bryant	400.00	180.00
❑ GJ21A	Kobe Bryant AU/8		
❑ GJ22	Wally Szczerbiak	150.00	70.00
❑ GJ23	Richard Hamilton	80.00	36.00
❑ GJ24	Shawn Marion	120.00	55.00
❑ GJ25	Trajan Langdon	80.00	36.00
❑ GJ26	Aleksandar Radojevic	40.00	18.00
❑ GJ27	Corey Maggette	120.00	55.00
❑ GJ28	William Avery	40.00	18.00
❑ GJ29	Quincy Lewis	50.00	22.00
❑ GJ30	Dion Glover	40.00	18.00
❑ GJ31	Jeff Foster	40.00	18.00
❑ GJ32	Devean George	80.00	36.00
❑ GJ33	Shareef Abdur-Rahim	120.00	55.00
❑ GJ34	John Stockton	120.00	55.00
❑ GJ35	Allen Iverson	150.00	70.00
❑ GJ36	Kevin Garnett	150.00	70.00
❑ GJ36A	Kevin Garnett AU/21	1200.00	550.00
❑ GJ37	Grant Hill	120.00	55.00
❑ GJ38	Vin Baker	40.00	18.00
❑ GJ39	Keith Van Horn	80.00	36.00
❑ GJ40	Reggie Miller	150.00	70.00
❑ GJ41	Tim Hardaway	80.00	36.00
❑ GJ42	Hakeem Olajuwon	80.00	36.00
❑ GJ43	Steve Francis	400.00	180.00
❑ GJ44	Jonathan Bender	150.00	70.00
❑ GJ45	Andre Miller	80.00	36.00
❑ GJ46	Jason Terry	60.00	27.00
❑ GJ47	Alonzo Mourning	100.00	45.00
❑ GJ48	Cal Bowdler	40.00	18.00
❑ GJ49	James Posey	40.00	18.00
❑ GJ50	Kenny Thomas	50.00	22.00
❑ GJ51	Tim James	40.00	18.00
❑ GJ52	Vonteego Cummings	50.00	22.00
❑ GJ53	Jumaine Jones	40.00	18.00
❑ GJ54	Scott Padgett	40.00	18.00
❑ GJ55	Baron Davis	80.00	36.00
❑ GJ55A	Baron Davis AU/1		
❑ GJ56	Karl Malone	80.00	36.00
❑ GJ56A	Karl Malone AU/32	600.00	275.00
❑ GJ57	Gary Payton	80.00	36.00
❑ GJ58	Michael Finley	80.00	36.00
❑ GJ59	Bryon Russell	60.00	27.00
❑ GJ60	Antoine Walker	60.00	27.00
❑ GJ61	Shaquille O'Neal	200.00	90.00
❑ GJ62	Jason Kidd	150.00	70.00
❑ GJ63	Jason Williams	150.00	70.00
❑ GJ64	Antonio McDyess	60.00	27.00
❑ MJ	Michael Jordan/23	5000.00	2200.00

1999-00 Upper Deck Game Jerseys Patch

	MINT	NRMT
COMMON CARD (GJP1-30)	400.00	180.00

SER.1/2 STATED ODDS 1:7500 HOB/RET

Card	Player	MINT	NRMT
❑ GJP1	Jason Kidd	600.00	275.00
❑ GJP2	Shaquille O'Neal	600.00	275.00
❑ GJP3	Tim Duncan	700.00	325.00
❑ GJP4	Charles Barkley	600.00	275.00
❑ GJP5	Kevin Garnett	1000.00	450.00
❑ GJP6	John Stockton	550.00	250.00
❑ GJP7	Keith Van Horn	400.00	180.00
❑ GJP8	Hakeem Olajuwon	400.00	180.00
❑ GJP9	Paul Pierce	400.00	180.00
❑ GJP10	Michael Jordan	3000.00	1350.00
❑ GJP11	Kobe Bryant	1500.00	700.00
❑ GJP12	Scottie Pippen	500.00	220.00
❑ GJP13	Grant Hill	800.00	350.00
❑ GJP14	Gary Payton	550.00	250.00
❑ GJP15	Vince Carter	1800.00	800.00
❑ GJP16	Reggie Miller	600.00	275.00
❑ GJP17	Allen Iverson	800.00	350.00
❑ GJP18	David Robinson	500.00	220.00
❑ GJP19	Antoine Walker	400.00	180.00
❑ GJP20	Karl Malone	500.00	220.00
❑ GJP21	Baron Davis	400.00	180.00
❑ GJP22	Shaquille O'Neal	600.00	275.00
❑ GJP23	Grant Hill	800.00	350.00
❑ GJP24	Allen Iverson	800.00	350.00
❑ GJP25	Steve Francis	1000.00	450.00
❑ GJP26	Jonathan Bender	500.00	220.00
❑ GJP27	Kobe Bryant	1500.00	700.00
❑ GJP28	Kevin Garnett	1000.00	450.00
❑ GJP29	Jason Williams	800.00	350.00
❑ GJP30	Jason Kidd	600.00	275.00

1999-00 Upper Deck Game Jerseys Patch Super

	MINT	NRMT
COMMON CARD	500.00	220.00

RANDOM INSERTS IN SER.1/2 PACKS
STATED PRINT RUN 25 SERIAL #'d SETS

Card	Player	MINT	NRMT
❑ AI	Allen Iverson 1	1000.00	450.00
❑ AI	Allen Iverson 2	1000.00	450.00
❑ AW	Antoine Walker	500.00	220.00
❑ BD	Baron Davis	500.00	220.00
❑ GH	Grant Hill 1	800.00	350.00
❑ GH	Grant Hill 2	800.00	350.00
❑ JB	Jonathan Bender	600.00	275.00
❑ JK	Jason Kidd	800.00	350.00
❑ JW	Jason Williams	1000.00	450.00
❑ KB	Kobe Bryant 1	1500.00	700.00
❑ KB	Kobe Bryant 2	1500.00	700.00
❑ KG	Kevin Garnett 1	1000.00	450.00
❑ KG	Kevin Garnett 2	1000.00	450.00
❑ KV	Keith Van Horn	500.00	220.00
❑ MJ	Michael Jordan	6000.00	2700.00
❑ SF	Steve Francis	1300.00	575.00
❑ SO	Shaquille O'Neal 1	1000.00	450.00
❑ SO	Shaquille O'Neal 2	1000.00	450.00
❑ TD	Tim Duncan	800.00	350.00
❑ VC	Vince Carter	2200.00	1000.00

1999-00 Upper Deck High Definition

	MINT	NRMT
COMPLETE SET (20)	50.00	22.00
COMMON CARD (HD1-HD20)	.75	.35
UNLISTED STARS	1.25	.55
SER.2 STATED ODDS 1:11 HOB/RET		
COMMON LEVEL 1 (HD1-HD20)	8.00	3.60
*LEVEL 1: 4X TO 10X HI COLUMN		
LEVEL 1: RANDOM INS.IN SER.2 PACKS		
LEVEL 1: PRINT RUN 100 SERIAL #'d SETS		
COMMON LEVEL 2 (HD1-HD20)	30.00	13.50
*LEVEL 2: 15X TO 40X HI		
LEVEL 2: RANDOM INS.IN SER.2 PACKS		
LEVEL 2: PRINT RUN 25 SERIAL #'d SETS		

Card	Player	MINT	NRMT
❑ HD1	Antonio McDyess	1.25	.55
❑ HD2	Kevin Garnett	8.00	3.60
❑ HD3	Vince Carter	12.00	5.50
❑ HD4	Shareef Abdur-Rahim	2.50	1.10
❑ HD5	Patrick Ewing	1.25	.55
❑ HD6	Gary Payton	2.00	.90
❑ HD7	Glenn Robinson	.75	.35
❑ HD8	Kobe Bryant	10.00	4.50
❑ HD9	Antawn Jamison	2.50	1.10
❑ HD10	Chris Webber	4.00	1.80
❑ HD11	Corey Maggette	2.50	1.10
❑ HD12	Shawn Kemp	2.00	.90
❑ HD13	Derek Anderson	1.25	.55
❑ HD14	Michael Finley	1.25	.55
❑ HD15	Allan Houston	1.25	.55
❑ HD16	Anfernee Hardaway	4.00	1.80
❑ HD17	Grant Hill	6.00	2.70
❑ HD18	Shaquille O'Neal	6.00	2.70
❑ HD19	Paul Pierce	2.50	1.10
❑ HD20	Scottie Pippen	4.00	1.80

1999-00 Upper Deck History Class

	MINT	NRMT
COMPLETE SET (20)	30.00	13.50
COMMON CARD (HC1-HC20)	.75	.35
SEMISTARS	1.00	.45
UNLISTED STARS	1.25	.55
SER.1 STATED ODDS 1:11 HOB/RET		
COMMON LEVEL 1 (HC1-HC20)	8.00	3.60

*LEVEL 1: 5X TO 12X HI COLUMN
LEVEL 1: RANDOM INS.IN SER.1 HOBBY
LEVEL 1: PRINT RUN 100 SERIAL #'d SETS

Card	Player	MINT	NRMT
❑ HC1	Michael Jordan	15.00	6.75
❑ HC2	Julius Erving	4.00	1.80
❑ HC3	Jamaal Wilkes	.75	.35
❑ HC4	John Havlicek	3.00	1.35
❑ HC5	Moses Malone	1.25	.55
❑ HC6	Nate Archibald	1.00	.45
❑ HC7	Jerry West	2.00	.90
❑ HC8	Dave DeBusschere	.75	.35
❑ HC9	Bob Cousy	1.50	.70
❑ HC10	Kevin McHale	1.25	.55
❑ HC11	Dave Bing	.75	.35
❑ HC12	Walt Frazier	1.00	.45
❑ HC13	Bob Lanier	.75	.35
❑ HC14	George Gervin	1.25	.55
❑ HC15	Hal Greer	.75	.35
❑ HC16	Earl Monroe	1.00	.45
❑ HC17	David Thompson	.75	.35
❑ HC18	Wes Unseld	.75	.35
❑ HC19	Bill Walton	1.00	.45
❑ HC20	Larry Bird	10.00	4.50

1999-00 Upper Deck History Class Level 2

	MINT	NRMT
COMMON CARD (HC1-HC20)	25.00	11.00

*LEVEL 2: 12.5X TO 30X VALUE
RANDOM INSERTS IN SER.1 HOBBY
STATED PRINT RUN 25 SERIAL #'d SETS

Card	Player	MINT	NRMT
❑ HC1	Michael Jordan	600.00	275.00
❑ HC20	Larry Bird	600.00	275.00

1999-00 Upper Deck Jamboree

	MINT	NRMT
COMPLETE SET (15)	30.00	13.50
COMMON CARD (J1-J15)	.50	.23
UNLISTED STARS	.75	.35
SER.1 STATED ODDS 1:11 HOB/RET		
COMMON LEVEL 1 (J1-J15)	8.00	3.60
*LEVEL 1: 6X TO 15X HI COLUMN		
LEVEL 1: RANDOM INS.IN SER.1 PACKS		
LEVEL 1: PRINT RUN 100 SERIAL #'d SETS		
COMMON LEVEL 2 (J1-J15)	40.00	18.00

*LEVEL 2: 25X TO 60X HI
LEVEL 2: RANDOM INS.IN SER.1 PACKS
LEVEL 2: PRINT RUN 25 SERIAL #'d SETS

Card	Player	MINT	NRMT
❑ J1	Michael Jordan	10.00	4.50
❑ J2	Karl Malone	1.25	.55
❑ J3	Kevin Garnett	5.00	2.20
❑ J4	Antonio McDyess	.75	.35
❑ J5	Shareef Abdur-Rahim	1.50	.70
❑ J6	David Robinson	1.25	.55
❑ J7	Marcus Camby	.75	.35
❑ J8	Kobe Bryant	6.00	2.70
❑ J9	Jason Kidd	2.50	1.10
❑ J10	Scottie Pippen	2.50	1.10
❑ J11	Keith Van Horn	1.50	.70
❑ J12	Glenn Robinson	.50	.23
❑ J13	Grant Hill	4.00	1.80
❑ J14	Michael Finley	.75	.35
❑ J15	Alonzo Mourning	.75	.35

1999-00 Upper Deck MJ - A Higher Power

	MINT	NRMT
COMPLETE SET (12)	60.00	27.00
COMMON CARD (MJ1-MJ12)	6.00	2.70
SER.1 STATED ODDS 1:23 HOB/RET		
COMMON LEVEL 1 (MJ1-MJ12)	50.00	22.00

LEVEL 1: RANDOM INS.IN SER.1 HOBBY
LEVEL 1: PRINT RUN 100 SERIAL #'d SETS
UNPRICED LEVEL 2 SERIAL #'d TO 1

Card	Player	MINT	NRMT
❑ MJ1	Michael Jordan	6.00	2.70
❑ MJ2	Michael Jordan	6.00	2.70
❑ MJ3	Michael Jordan	6.00	2.70
❑ MJ4	Michael Jordan	6.00	2.70
❑ MJ5	Michael Jordan	6.00	2.70
❑ MJ6	Michael Jordan	6.00	2.70
❑ MJ7	Michael Jordan	6.00	2.70
❑ MJ8	Michael Jordan	6.00	2.70
❑ MJ9	Michael Jordan	6.00	2.70
❑ MJ10	Michael Jordan	6.00	2.70
❑ MJ11	Michael Jordan	6.00	2.70
❑ MJ12	Michael Jordan	6.00	2.70

1999-00 Upper Deck MJ Final Floor

	MINT	NRMT
COMMON CARD (FF1-FF12)	150.00	70.00
COMMON AU (FF1A-FF12A)	3500.00	1600.00

STATED ODDS 1:2500 IN EACH RELEASE
AU PRINT RUN 23 SERIAL #'d SETS
EACH PRODUCT HAS 23 AUTOS
RANDOM INSERTS IN BLACK DIAMOND
RANDOM INSERTS IN 2000 CEN.LEGENDS
RANDOM INSERTS IN 99/00 HARDCOURT
RANDOM INSERTS IN 00/01 HARDCOURT
RANDOM INSERTS IN 00/01 MVP
RANDOM INSERTS IN OVATION
RANDOM INSERTS IN SP AUTH
RANDOM INSERTS IN SPx
RANDOM INSERTS IN UD ENCORE
RANDOM INSERTS IN UD HOLO
RANDOM INSERTS IN UD IONIX
RANDOM INSERTS IN UD2
RANDOM INSERTS IN ULT.VICTORY
UNPRICED WOOD SERIAL NUMBERED TO 1

1999-00 Upper Deck Now Showing

	MINT	NRMT
COMPLETE SET (30)	50.00	22.00
COMMON CARD (NS1-NS30)	.50	.23
UNLISTED STARS	.75	.35
SER.1 STATED ODDS 1:4 HOB/RET		
COMMON LEVEL 1 (NS1-NS30)	8.00	3.60
*LEVEL 1: 6X TO 15X HI COLUMN		
LEVEL 1: RANDOM INS.IN SER.1 RETAIL		
LEVEL 1: PRINT RUN 100 SERIAL #'d SETS		
COMMON LEVEL 2 (NS1-30)	30.00	13.50

*LEVEL 2: 25X TO 60X HI
LEVEL 2: RANDOM INS.IN SER.1 RETAIL
LEVEL 2: PRINT RUN 25 SERIAL #'d SETS

Card	Player	MINT	NRMT
❑ NS1	Dikembe Mutombo	.50	.23
❑ NS2	Antoine Walker	1.00	.45
❑ NS3	Eddie Jones	1.50	.70
❑ NS4	Toni Kukoc	1.00	.45
❑ NS5	Shawn Kemp	1.25	.55
❑ NS6	Michael Finley	.75	.35
❑ NS7	Antonio McDyess	.75	.35
❑ NS8	Grant Hill	4.00	1.80
❑ NS9	Antawn Jamison	1.50	.70
❑ NS10	Scottie Pippen	2.50	1.10
❑ NS11	Reggie Miller	.75	.35
❑ NS12	Maurice Taylor	.75	.35
❑ NS13	Shaquille O'Neal	4.00	1.80
❑ NS14	Tim Hardaway	.75	.35
❑ NS15	Ray Allen	.75	.35
❑ NS16	Kevin Garnett	5.00	2.20
❑ NS17	Stephon Marbury	1.50	.70
❑ NS18	Marcus Camby	.75	.35
❑ NS19	Darrell Armstrong	.50	.23
❑ NS20	Allen Iverson	3.00	1.35
❑ NS21	Jason Kidd	2.50	1.10
❑ NS22	Damon Stoudamire	.75	.35
❑ NS23	Jason Williams	2.00	.90
❑ NS24	Tim Duncan	4.00	1.80
❑ NS25	Gary Payton	1.25	.55
❑ NS26	Vince Carter	8.00	3.60
❑ NS27	Karl Malone	1.25	.55
❑ NS28	Shareef Abdur-Rahim	1.50	.70
❑ NS29	Juwan Howard	.50	.23
❑ NS30	Michael Jordan	10.00	4.50

1999-00 Upper Deck PowerDeck

	MINT	NRMT
COMPLETE SET (14)	100.00	45.00
COMPLETE SERIES 1 (7)	50.00	22.00
COMPLETE SERIES 2 (7)	50.00	22.00
COMMON CARD (PD1-PD14)	4.00	1.80

SER.1 STATED ODDS 1:23 HOBBY
SER.2 STATED ODDS 1:72 HOBBY
MJPD1/2: SER.1 STATED ODDS 1:288 HOB
PDX1/2: SER.2 STATED ODDS 1:2500 HOB
NON-PD CARDS NOT INCLUDED IN SET PRICE
3 UNPRICED MJ CARDS SERIAL #'d TO 1

❑ PD1 Michael Jordan	20.00	9.00
❑ PD2 Kobe Bryant	12.00	5.50
❑ PD3 Tim Duncan	8.00	3.60
❑ PD4 Allen Iverson	6.00	2.70
❑ PD5 Vince Carter	15.00	6.75
❑ PD6 Jason Kidd	5.00	2.20
❑ PD7 Scottie Pippen	5.00	2.20
❑ PD8 Elton Brand	15.00	6.75
❑ PD9 Steve Francis	20.00	9.00
❑ PD10 Baron Davis	4.00	1.80
❑ PD11 Lamar Odom	12.00	5.50
❑ PD12 Wally Szczerbiak	6.00	2.70
❑ PD13 Richard Hamilton	4.00	1.80
❑ PD14 Shawn Marion	5.00	2.20
❑ PDX1 Michael Jordan	100.00	45.00
❑ PDX2 Kevin Garnett	40.00	18.00
❑ MJPD1 Michael Jordan	25.00	11.00
❑ MJPD2 Michael Jordan	25.00	11.00

1999-00 Upper Deck Rookies Illustrated

	MINT	NRMT
COMPLETE SET (10)	15.00	6.75
COMMON CARD (RI1-RI10)	.60	.25
UNLISTED STARS	.75	.35
SER.2 STATED ODDS 1:11 HOB/RET		
COMMON LEVEL 1 (RI1-RI10)	8.00	3.60

*LEVEL 1: 5X TO 12X HI COLUMN
LEVEL 1: RANDOM INS.IN SER.2 RETAIL
LEVEL 1: PRINT RUN 100 SERIAL #'d SETS

COMMON LEVEL 2 (RI1-RI10)	30.00	13.50

*LEVEL 2: 20X TO 50X HI
LEVEL 2: RANDOM INS.IN SER.2 RETAIL
LEVEL 2: PRINT RUN 25 SERIAL #'d SETS

❑ RI1 Elton Brand	5.00	2.20
❑ RI2 Shawn Marion	1.50	.70
❑ RI3 Trajan Langdon	.75	.35
❑ RI4 Adrian Griffin	.60	.25
❑ RI5 Baron Davis	1.25	.55
❑ RI6 Richard Hamilton	1.25	.55
❑ RI7 Lamar Odom	4.00	1.80
❑ RI8 Corey Maggette	2.00	.90
❑ RI9 Steve Francis	6.00	2.70
❑ RI10 Wally Szczerbiak	2.00	.90

1999-00 Upper Deck Star Surge

	MINT	NRMT
COMPLETE SET (15)	75.00	34.00
COMMON CARD (S1-S15)	1.50	.70
SER.2 STATED ODDS 1:23 HOB/RET		
COMMON LEVEL 1 (S1-S15)	12.00	5.50

*LEVEL 1: 3X TO 8X HI COLUMN
LEVEL 1: RANDOM INS.IN SER.2 HOBBY
LEVEL 1: PRINT RUN 100 SERIAL #'d SETS

COMMON LEVEL 2 (S1-S15)	50.00	22.00

*LEVEL 2: 12.5X TO 30X HI
LEVEL 2: RANDOM INS.IN SER.2 HOBBY
LEVEL 2: PRINT RUN 25 SERIAL #'d SETS

❑ S1 Michael Jordan	20.00	9.00
❑ S2 Kevin Garnett	10.00	4.50
❑ S3 Allen Iverson	6.00	2.70
❑ S4 Vince Carter	15.00	6.75
❑ S5 Karl Malone	2.50	1.10
❑ S6 Tim Duncan	8.00	3.60
❑ S7 Grant Hill	8.00	3.60
❑ S8 Scottie Pippen	5.00	2.20
❑ S9 Shaquille O'Neal	8.00	3.60
❑ S10 Antoine Walker	2.00	.90
❑ S11 Shareef Abdur-Rahim	3.00	1.35
❑ S12 Keith Van Horn	3.00	1.35
❑ S13 Gary Payton	2.50	1.10
❑ S14 John Stockton	1.50	.70
❑ S15 Stephon Marbury	3.00	1.35

1999-00 Upper Deck Wild!

	MINT	NRMT
COMPLETE SET (19)	80.00	36.00
COMMON CARD (W1-W19)	1.25	.55
UNLISTED STARS	1.50	.70
SER.2 STATED ODDS 1:23 HOB/RET		
COMMON LEVEL 1 (W1-W19)	10.00	4.50

*LEVEL 1: 3X TO 8X HI COLUMN
LEVEL 1: RANDOM INS.IN SER.2 HOBBY
LEVEL 1: PRINT RUN 100 SERIAL #'d SETS

COMMON LEVEL 2 (W1-W19)	40.00	18.00

*LEVEL 2: 12.5X TO 30X HI
LEVEL 2: RANDOM INS.IN SER.2 HOBBY
LEVEL 2: PRINT RUN 25 SERIAL #'d SETS

❑ W1 Kobe Bryant	12.00	5.50
❑ W2 Kevin Garnett	10.00	4.50
❑ W3 Shareef Abdur-Rahim	3.00	1.35
❑ W4 Tim Hardaway	1.50	.70
❑ W5 Jason Williams	4.00	1.80
❑ W6 Grant Hill	8.00	3.60
❑ W7 Vince Carter	15.00	6.75
❑ W8 Ron Mercer	2.00	.90
❑ W9 Charles Barkley	2.50	1.10
❑ W10 Eddie Jones	3.00	1.35
❑ W11 Tim Duncan	8.00	3.60
❑ W12 Antonio McDyess	1.50	.70
❑ W13 Allen Iverson	6.00	2.70
❑ W14 Anfernee Hardaway	5.00	2.20
❑ W15 Michael Jordan	20.00	9.00
❑ W16 Stephon Marbury	3.00	1.35
❑ W17 Paul Pierce	3.00	1.35
❑ W18 Elton Brand	8.00	3.60
❑ W19 Jason Terry	1.25	.55

1999 Upper Deck Century Legends

	MINT	NRMT
COMPLETE SET (89)	40.00	18.00
COMMON CARD (1-80)	.10	.05
COMMON MJ (81-90)	2.00	.90
SEMISTARS	.15	.07
UNLISTED STARS	.30	.14

CARD NUMBER 6 DOES NOT EXIST

❑ 1 Michael Jordan	4.00	1.80
❑ 2 Bill Russell	1.00	.45
❑ 3 Wilt Chamberlain	1.00	.45
❑ 4 George Mikan	1.00	.45
❑ 5 Oscar Robertson	.75	.35
❑ 6 Does not exist		
❑ 7 Larry Bird	2.50	1.10
❑ 8 Karl Malone	.50	.23
❑ 9 Elgin Baylor	.40	.18
❑ 10 Kareem Abdul-Jabbar	1.00	.45
❑ 11 Jerry West	.50	.23
❑ 12 Bob Cousy	.40	.18
❑ 13 Julius Erving	1.00	.45
❑ 14 Hakeem Olajuwon	.50	.23
❑ 15 John Havlicek	.75	.35
❑ 16 John Stockton	.30	.14
❑ 17 Rick Barry	.15	.07
❑ 18 Moses Malone	.30	.14
❑ 19 Nate Thurmond	.10	.05
❑ 20 Bob Pettit	.15	.07
❑ 21 Pete Maravich	.75	.35
❑ 22 Willis Reed	.15	.07
❑ 23 Isiah Thomas	.30	.14
❑ 24 Dolph Schayes	.15	.07
❑ 25 Walt Frazier	.30	.14

Card	Player	Mint	NrMt
❑ 26	Wes Unseld	.10	.05
❑ 27	Bill Sharman	.10	.05
❑ 28	George Gervin	.30	.14
❑ 29	Hal Greer	.10	.05
❑ 30	Dave DeBusschere	.10	.05
❑ 31	Earl Monroe	.30	.14
❑ 32	Kevin McHale	.30	.14
❑ 33	Charles Barkley	.50	.23
❑ 34	Elvin Hayes	.15	.07
❑ 35	Scottie Pippen	1.00	.45
❑ 36	Jerry Lucas	.10	.05
❑ 37	Dave Bing	.10	.05
❑ 38	Lenny Wilkens	.30	.14
❑ 39	Paul Arizin	.10	.05
❑ 40	Nate Archibald	.30	.14
❑ 41	James Worthy	.30	.14
❑ 42	Patrick Ewing	.30	.14
❑ 43	Billy Cunningham	.10	.05
❑ 44	Sam Jones	.10	.05
❑ 45	Dave Cowens	.15	.07
❑ 46	Robert Parish	.30	.14
❑ 47	Bill Walton	.30	.14
❑ 48	Shaquille O'Neal	1.50	.70
❑ 49	David Robinson	.50	.23
❑ 50	Dominique Wilkins	.30	.14
❑ 51	Kobe Bryant	2.50	1.10
❑ 52	Vince Carter	3.00	1.35
❑ 53	Paul Pierce	.60	.25
❑ 54	Allen Iverson	1.25	.55
❑ 55	Stephon Marbury	.60	.25
❑ 56	Mike Bibby	.40	.18
❑ 57	Jason Williams	.75	.35
❑ 58	Kevin Garnett	2.00	.90
❑ 59	Tim Duncan	1.50	.70
❑ 60	Antawn Jamison	.60	.25
❑ 61	Antoine Walker	.40	.18
❑ 62	Shareef Abdur-Rahim	.60	.25
❑ 63	Michael Olowokandi	.15	.07
❑ 64	Robert Traylor	.10	.05
❑ 65	Keith Van Horn	.60	.25
❑ 66	Shaquille O'Neal	1.50	.70
❑ 67	Ray Allen	.30	.14
❑ 68	Gary Payton	.50	.23
❑ 69	Raef LaFrentz	.30	.14
❑ 70	Grant Hill	1.50	.70
❑ 71	Anfernee Hardaway	1.00	.45
❑ 72	Maurice Taylor	.30	.14
❑ 73	Ron Mercer	.40	.18
❑ 74	Michael Finley	.30	.14
❑ 75	Jason Kidd	1.00	.45
❑ 76	Allan Houston	.30	.14
❑ 77	Damon Stoudamire	.30	.14
❑ 78	Antonio McDyess	.30	.14
❑ 79	Eddie Jones	.60	.25
❑ 80	Michael Dickerson	.30	.14
❑ 81	Michael Jordan	2.00	.90
❑ 82	Michael Jordan	2.00	.90
❑ 83	Michael Jordan	2.00	.90
❑ 84	Michael Jordan	2.00	.90
❑ 85	Michael Jordan	2.00	.90
❑ 86	Michael Jordan	2.00	.90
❑ 87	Michael Jordan	2.00	.90
❑ 88	Michael Jordan	2.00	.90
❑ 89	Michael Jordan	2.00	.90
❑ 90	Michael Jordan	2.00	.90

1999 Upper Deck Century Legends Century Collection

	MINT	NRMT
COMMON CARD (1-80)	6.00	2.70
COMMON CARD (81-90)	80.00	36.00

*STARS: 20X TO 50X BASE CARD HI
*VINTAGE PLAYERS: 25X TO 60X BASE HI
STATED PRINT RUN 100 SERIAL #'d SETS
RANDOM INSERTS IN PACKS
CARD NUMBER 6 DOES NOT EXIST

1999 Upper Deck Century Legends All-Century Team

	MINT	NRMT
COMPLETE SET (12)	30.00	13.50
COMMON CARD (A1-A12)	1.25	.55

STATED ODDS 1:11

Card	Player	Mint	NrMt
❑ A1	Michael Jordan	15.00	6.75
❑ A2	Oscar Robertson	3.00	1.35
❑ A3	Wilt Chamberlain	4.00	1.80
❑ A4	Larry Bird	10.00	4.50
❑ A5	Julius Erving	4.00	1.80
❑ A6	Jerry West	2.00	.90
❑ A7	Charles Barkley	2.00	.90
❑ A8	John Stockton	1.25	.55
❑ A9	Hakeem Olajuwon	2.00	.90
❑ A10	Karl Malone	2.00	.90
❑ A11	Scottie Pippen	4.00	1.80
❑ A12	David Robinson	2.00	.90

1999 Upper Deck Century Legends Epic Milestones

	MINT	NRMT
COMPLETE SET (12)	30.00	13.50
COMMON CARD (EM1-EM12)	1.00	.45
UNLISTED STARS	1.25	.55

STATED ODDS 1:11

Card	Player	Mint	NrMt
❑ EM1	Michael Jordan	15.00	6.75
❑ EM2	Jerry West	2.00	.90
❑ EM3	John Stockton	1.25	.55
❑ EM4	Wilt Chamberlain	4.00	1.80
❑ EM5	Julius Erving	4.00	1.80
❑ EM6	Reggie Miller	1.25	.55
❑ EM7	Hakeem Olajuwon	2.00	.90
❑ EM8	Robert Parish	1.25	.55
❑ EM9	Kobe Bryant	10.00	4.50
❑ EM10	Rick Barry	1.00	.45
❑ EM11	Patrick Ewing	1.25	.55
❑ EM12	Charles Barkley	2.00	.90

1999 Upper Deck Century Legends Epic Signatures

	MINT	NRMT
COMMON CARD	15.00	6.75
SEMISTARS	25.00	11.00

STATED ODDS 1:23
OLAJUWON DID NOT SIGN TRADE CARDS
IVERSON AU REPLACES OLAJUWON

Card	Player	Mint	NrMt
❑ AE	Alex English	15.00	6.75
❑ AI	Allen Iverson	100.00	45.00
❑ BC	Bob Cousy	30.00	13.50
❑ BL	Bob Lanier	15.00	6.75
❑ BP	Bob Pettit	25.00	11.00
❑ BR	Bill Russell	600.00	275.00
❑ BS	Bill Sharman	15.00	6.75
❑ BW	Bill Walton	30.00	13.50
❑ CD	Clyde Drexler	30.00	13.50
❑ DC	Dave Cowens	25.00	11.00
❑ DR	Julius Erving	600.00	275.00
❑ DT	David Thompson	15.00	6.75
❑ EB	Elgin Baylor	40.00	18.00
❑ EH	Elvin Hayes	25.00	11.00
❑ EM	Earl Monroe	30.00	13.50
❑ GG	George Gervin	25.00	11.00
❑ HK	Hakeem Olajuwon Did not sign	100.00	45.00
❑ JH	John Havlicek	30.00	13.50
❑ JL	Jerry Lucas	15.00	6.75
❑ JW	Jerry West	40.00	18.00
❑ KA	Kareem Abdul-Jabbar	200.00	90.00
❑ LB	Larry Bird	650.00	300.00
❑ MB	Mike Bibby	25.00	11.00
❑ MM	Moses Malone	25.00	11.00
❑ MO	Michael Olowokandi	25.00	11.00
❑ NA	Nate Archibald	25.00	11.00
❑ OR	Oscar Robertson	40.00	18.00
❑ TH	Tim Hardaway	40.00	18.00
❑ WC	Wilt Chamberlain	400.00	180.00
❑ WF	Walt Frazier	40.00	18.00
❑ WR	Willis Reed	25.00	11.00
❑ WU	Wes Unseld	15.00	6.75

1999 Upper Deck Century Legends Epic Signatures Century

	MINT	NRMT
COMMON CARD	30.00	13.50

*CENTURY: 1X TO 2X HI COLUMN
STATED PRINT RUN 100 SERIAL #'d SETS

EXCEPTIONS NOTED BELOW
RANDOM INSERTS IN PACKS
BR AND DR NOT PRICED DUE TO SCARCITY
OLAJUWON DID NOT SIGN TRADE CARDS
IVERSON AU REPLACES OLAJUWON

❑ BR Bill Russell ....Autographed to 6		
❑ DR Julius Erving ....Autographed to 6		
❑ KA Kareem Abdul-Jabbar	250.00	110.00
❑ LB Larry Bird	1000.00	450.00
❑ MJ Michael Jordan	7000.00	3200.00
❑ WC Wilt Chamberlain	550.00	250.00

1999 Upper Deck Century Legends Generations

	MINT	NRMT
COMPLETE SET (12)	30.00	13.50
COMMON CARD (G1-G12)	2.00	.90
STATED ODDS 1:4		

❑ G1 Michael Jordan / Julius Erving	10.00	4.50
❑ G2 Kobe Bryant / Michael Jordan	8.00	3.60
❑ G3 Shaquille O'Neal / Wilt Chamberlain	6.00	2.70
❑ G4 Jason Williams / Pete Maravich	5.00	2.20
❑ G5 Stephon Marbury / Nate Archibald	2.00	.90
❑ G6 Antoine Walker / Karl Malone	2.00	.90
❑ G7 Grant Hill / George Gervin	2.50	1.10
❑ G8 Gary Payton / Isiah Thomas	2.00	.90
❑ G9 Kevin Garnett / Dominique Wilkins	2.50	1.10
❑ G10 Hakeem Olajuwon / Moses Malone	2.00	.90
❑ G11 Keith Van Horn / Larry Bird	4.00	1.80
❑ G12 Vince Carter / Oscar Robertson	5.00	2.20

1999 Upper Deck Century Legends Jerseys of the Century

	MINT	NRMT
COMPLETE SET (8)	2800.00	1250.00
COMMON CARD (1-8)	80.00	36.00
STATED ODDS 1:475		
AU's NOT INCLUDED IN SET PRICE		
ERVING AU NOT PRICED DUE TO SCARCITY		

❑ CD Clyde Drexler	80.00	36.00
❑ DR Julius Erving	300.00	135.00
❑ JS John Stockton	100.00	45.00
❑ KA Kareem Abdul-Jabbar	250.00	110.00
❑ KM Karl Malone	80.00	36.00
❑ LB Larry Bird	300.00	135.00
❑ MJ Michael Jordan	2000.00	900.00
❑ SO Shaquille O'Neal	150.00	70.00
❑ DR-A Julius Erving ....Autographed to six		
❑ KA-A Kareem Abdul-Jabbar Autographed to 33	800.00	350.00

1999 Upper Deck Century Legends MJ's Most Memorable Shots

	MINT	NRMT
COMPLETE SET (6)	50.00	22.00
COMMON CARD (MJ1-MJ6)	10.00	4.50
STATED ODDS 1:23		

❑ MJ1 Michael Jordan	10.00	4.50
❑ MJ2 Michael Jordan	10.00	4.50
❑ MJ3 Michael Jordan	10.00	4.50
❑ MJ4 Michael Jordan	10.00	4.50
❑ MJ5 Michael Jordan	10.00	4.50
❑ MJ6 Michael Jordan	10.00	4.50

2000 Upper Deck Century Legends

	MINT	NRMT
COMPLETE SET (90)	25.00	11.00
COMMON CARD (1-90)	.10	.05
COMMON MJ (66-71/81-90)	1.50	.70
SEMISTARS	.15	.07
UNLISTED STARS	.30	.14
UNPRICED GOLD PARALLEL #'d TO 1		

❑ 1 Michael Jordan	4.00	1.80
❑ 2 Magic Johnson	2.00	.90
❑ 3 Larry Bird	2.50	1.10
❑ 4 Bob Cousy	.40	.18
❑ 5 Bill Russell	1.00	.45
❑ 6 Julius Erving	1.00	.45
❑ 7 Nate Archibald	.30	.14
❑ 8 Oscar Robertson	.75	.35
❑ 9 Elgin Baylor	.40	.18
❑ 10 Jo Jo White	.10	.05
❑ 11 Hal Greer	.10	.05
❑ 12 Clyde Drexler	.30	.14
❑ 13 Wilt Chamberlain	1.00	.45
❑ 14 Walt Bellamy	.10	.05
❑ 15 Walt Frazier	.30	.14
❑ 16 Earl Monroe	.30	.14
❑ 17 John Havlicek	.75	.35
❑ 18 George Mikan	1.00	.45
❑ 19 George Karl	.15	.07
❑ 20 Tom Heinsohn	.10	.05
❑ 21 Kareem Abdul-Jabbar	1.00	.45
❑ 22 Bill Sharman	.10	.05
❑ 23 Elvin Hayes	.15	.07
❑ 24 Rick Barry	.30	.14
❑ 25 Paul Silas	.15	.07
❑ 26 Mitch Kupchak	.10	.05
❑ 27 Dave Cowens	.15	.07
❑ 28 Nate Thurmond	.10	.05
❑ 29 Dave DeBusschere	.10	.05
❑ 30 Jerry Lucas	.10	.05
❑ 31 Bill Walton	.30	.14
❑ 32 Jerry West	.50	.23
❑ 33 David Thompson	.10	.05
❑ 34 Spencer Haywood	.10	.05
❑ 35 Moses Malone	.30	.14
❑ 36 Alex English	.10	.05
❑ 37 Willis Reed	.15	.07
❑ 38 George Gervin	.30	.14
❑ 39 Dolph Schayes	.15	.07
❑ 40 Wes Unseld	.10	.05
❑ 41 Bob Lanier	.10	.05
❑ 42 James Worthy	.30	.14
❑ 43 Maurice Lucas	.10	.05
❑ 44 Pete Maravich	.75	.35
❑ 45 Isiah Thomas	.30	.14
❑ 46 Robert Parish	.30	.14
❑ 47 Dominique Wilkins	.30	.14
❑ 48 Walter Davis	.10	.05
❑ 49 Bob Pettit	.15	.07
❑ 50 Kevin McHale	.30	.14
❑ 51 Julius Erving HD	.50	.23
❑ 52 Dominique Wilkins HD	.15	.07
❑ 53 George Gervin HD	.15	.07
❑ 54 Kareem Abdul-Jabbar HD	.50	.23
❑ 55 Clyde Drexler HD	.15	.07
❑ 56 David Thompson HD	.10	.05
❑ 57 Walter Davis HD	.10	.05
❑ 58 James Worthy HD	.15	.07
❑ 59 Moses Malone HD	.15	.07
❑ 60 Bob Lanier HD	.10	.05
❑ 61 Robert Parish HD	.15	.07
❑ 62 Maurice Lucas HD	.10	.05
❑ 63 Wes Unseld HD	.10	.05
❑ 64 Ron Boone HD	.10	.05
❑ 65 Larry Nance HD	.10	.05

❑ 66 Michael Jordan HD	1.50	.70
❑ 67 Michael Jordan HD	1.50	.70
❑ 68 Michael Jordan HD	1.50	.70
❑ 69 Michael Jordan HD	1.50	.70
❑ 70 Michael Jordan HD	1.50	.70
❑ 71 Michael Jordan UDT	1.50	.70
❑ 72 Wilt Chamberlain UDT	.50	.23
❑ 73 Magic Johnson UDT	1.00	.45
❑ 74 Julius Erving UDT	.50	.23
❑ 75 Larry Bird UDT	1.25	.55
❑ 76 Bill Russell UDT	.50	.23
❑ 77 Jerry West UDT	.30	.14
❑ 78 Oscar Robertson UDT	.40	.18
❑ 79 John Havlicek UDT	.40	.18
❑ 80 Elgin Baylor UDT	.15	.07
❑ 81 Michael Jordan TB	1.50	.70
❑ 82 Michael Jordan TB	1.50	.70
❑ 83 Michael Jordan TB	1.50	.70
❑ 84 Michael Jordan TB	1.50	.70
❑ 85 Michael Jordan TB	1.50	.70
❑ 86 Michael Jordan TB	1.50	.70
❑ 87 Michael Jordan TB	1.50	.70
❑ 88 Michael Jordan TB	1.50	.70
❑ 89 Michael Jordan TB	1.50	.70
❑ 90 Michael Jordan TB	1.50	.70

2000 Upper Deck Century Legends Commemorative Collection

	MINT	NRMT
COMMON CARD (1-90)	8.00	3.60
COMMON MJ (66-71/81-90)	80.00	36.00

*STARS: 30X TO 80X BASE CARD HI
STATED PRINT RUN 50 SERIAL #'d SETS
RANDOM INSERTS IN PACKS

2000 Upper Deck Century Legends History's Heroes

	MINT	NRMT
COMPLETE SET (9)	15.00	6.75
COMMON CARD (HH1-HH9)	1.00	.45
UNLISTED STARS	1.25	.55

STATED ODDS 1:12

❑ HH1 Michael Jordan	12.00	5.50
❑ HH2 Julius Erving	3.00	1.35
❑ HH3 Larry Bird	8.00	3.60
❑ HH4 Clyde Drexler	1.25	.55
❑ HH5 Elgin Baylor	1.25	.55
❑ HH6 George Gervin	1.25	.55
❑ HH7 Oscar Robertson	2.50	1.10
❑ HH8 Jerry West	2.00	.90
❑ HH9 Alex English	1.00	.45

2000 Upper Deck Century Legends Legendary Jerseys

	MINT	NRMT
COMPLETE SET (10)	1300.00	575.00
COMMON CARD	50.00	22.00

STATED ODDS 1:288
AU's NOT INCLUDED IN SET PRICE

❑ BC-J Bob Cousy	80.00	36.00
❑ CD-J Clyde Drexler	80.00	36.00
❑ DR-J Julius Erving	150.00	70.00
❑ DW-J Dominique Wilkins	50.00	22.00
❑ IT-J Isiah Thomas	100.00	45.00
❑ KA-J Kareem Abdul-Jabbar	150.00	70.00
❑ LB-A Larry Bird Autographed to 33	2200.00	1000.00
❑ LB-J Larry Bird	200.00	90.00
❑ MJ-A Michael Jordan Autographed to 23	8000.00	3600.00
❑ MJ-J Michael Jordan	700.00	325.00
❑ MM-J Moses Malone	50.00	22.00
❑ WC-J Wilt Chamberlain	150.00	70.00

2000 Upper Deck Century Legends Legendary Jerseys Gold

	MINT	NRMT
COMMON CARD (1-6)	200.00	90.00

RANDOM INSERTS IN PACKS
STATED PRINT RUN 25 SERIAL #'d SETS

❑ DR-G Julius Erving	300.00	135.00
❑ IT-G Isiah Thomas	200.00	90.00
❑ KA-G Kareem Abdul-Jabbar	350.00	160.00
❑ LB-G Larry Bird	800.00	350.00
❑ MJ-G Michael Jordan	3000.00	1350.00
❑ WC-G Wilt Chamberlain	350.00	160.00

2000 Upper Deck Century Legends Legendary Signatures

	MINT	NRMT
COMMON CARD	15.00	6.75
SEMISTARS	20.00	9.00

STATED ODDS 1:24

❑ AE Alex English	15.00	6.75
❑ BC Bob Cousy	25.00	11.00
❑ BL Bob Lanier	15.00	6.75
❑ BP Bob Pettit	20.00	9.00
❑ BR Bill Russell	400.00	180.00
❑ BS Bill Sharman	15.00	6.75
❑ BW Bill Walton	30.00	13.50
❑ CD Clyde Drexler	40.00	18.00
❑ DC Dave Cowens	15.00	6.75
❑ DD Dave DeBusschere	15.00	6.75
❑ DR Julius Erving	300.00	135.00
❑ DS Dolph Schayes	15.00	6.75
❑ DT David Thompson	15.00	6.75
❑ DW Dominique Wilkins	25.00	11.00
❑ EB Elgin Baylor	20.00	9.00
❑ EH Elvin Hayes	20.00	9.00
❑ EM Earl Monroe	25.00	11.00
❑ GA Gail Goodrich	15.00	6.75
❑ GG George Gervin	20.00	9.00
❑ HG Hal Greer	15.00	6.75
❑ IT Isiah Thomas	80.00	36.00
❑ JA Jamaal Wilkes	15.00	6.75
❑ JH John Havlicek	40.00	18.00
❑ JJ Jo Jo White	15.00	6.75
❑ JL Jerry Lucas	15.00	6.75
❑ JW Jerry West	40.00	18.00
❑ KA Kareem Abdul-Jabbar	100.00	45.00
❑ LB Larry Bird	700.00	325.00
❑ MG Magic Johnson	450.00	200.00
❑ MM Moses Malone	20.00	9.00
❑ NA Nate Archibald	15.00	6.75
❑ NT Nate Thurmond	15.00	6.75
❑ OR Oscar Robertson	40.00	18.00
❑ PA Paul Arizin	15.00	6.75
❑ PS Paul Silas	15.00	6.75
❑ RB Rick Barry	30.00	13.50
❑ SH Spencer Haywood	15.00	6.75
❑ WB Walt Bellamy	15.00	6.75
❑ WF Walt Frazier	20.00	9.00
❑ WR Willis Reed	15.00	6.75
❑ WU Wes Unseld	15.00	6.75

2000 Upper Deck Century Legends Legendary Signatures Gold

	MINT	NRMT
COMMON CARD	60.00	27.00

*GOLD: 1.5X TO 4X HI COLUMN
RANDOM INSERTS IN PACKS
STATED PRINT RUN 25 SERIAL #'d SETS

❑ BR Bill Russell	700.00	325.00
❑ DR Julius Erving	600.00	275.00
❑ KA Kareem Abdul-Jabbar	400.00	180.00
❑ LB Larry Bird	1000.00	450.00
❑ MG Magic Johnson	1000.00	450.00
❑ MJ Michael Jordan	5000.00	2200.00

2000 Upper Deck Century Legends MJ Final Floor Jumbos

	MINT	NRMT
COMPLETE SET (12)	500.00	220.00
COMMON CARD (FF1-FF12)	50.00	22.00

ONE PER BOX
COLOR PIECES CARRY PREMIUMS

	MINT	NRMT
❑ FF1 Michael Jordan	50.00	22.00
❑ FF2 Michael Jordan	50.00	22.00
❑ FF3 Michael Jordan	50.00	22.00
❑ FF4 Michael Jordan	50.00	22.00
❑ FF5 Michael Jordan	50.00	22.00
❑ FF6 Michael Jordan	50.00	22.00
❑ FF7 Michael Jordan	50.00	22.00
❑ FF8 Michael Jordan	50.00	22.00
❑ FF9 Michael Jordan	50.00	22.00
❑ FF10 Michael Jordan	50.00	22.00
❑ FF11 Michael Jordan	50.00	22.00
❑ FF12 Michael Jordan	50.00	22.00

2000 Upper Deck Century Legends NBA Originals

	MINT	NRMT
COMPLETE SET (6)	12.00	5.50
COMMON CARD (O1-O6)	.75	.35
UNLISTED STARS	1.00	.45
STATED ODDS 1:12		
❑ O1 Magic Johnson	5.00	2.20
❑ O2 Julius Erving	2.50	1.10
❑ O3 Michael Jordan	10.00	4.50
❑ O4 David Thompson	.75	.35
❑ O5 Kareem Abdul-Jabbar	2.50	1.10
❑ O6 Clyde Drexler	1.00	.45

2000 Upper Deck Century Legends Players of the Century

	MINT	NRMT
COMPLETE SET (20)	25.00	11.00
COMMON CARD (P1-P20)	.75	.35
UNLISTED STARS	1.00	.45
STATED ODDS 1:4		
❑ P1 Michael Jordan	10.00	4.50
❑ P2 Wilt Chamberlain	2.50	1.10
❑ P3 Magic Johnson	5.00	2.20
❑ P4 Larry Bird	6.00	2.70
❑ P5 Bill Russell	2.50	1.10
❑ P6 Jerry West	1.25	.55
❑ P7 Oscar Robertson	2.00	.90
❑ P8 John Havlicek	2.00	.90
❑ P9 Kareem Abdul-Jabbar	2.50	1.10
❑ P10 Pete Maravich	2.00	.90
❑ P11 Willis Reed	.75	.35
❑ P12 Bob Lanier	.75	.35
❑ P13 George Gervin	1.00	.45
❑ P14 Bill Walton	1.00	.45
❑ P15 Elvin Hayes	.75	.35
❑ P16 Julius Erving	2.50	1.10
❑ P17 Rick Barry	1.00	.45
❑ P18 Walt Frazier	1.00	.45
❑ P19 Nate Thurmond	.75	.35
❑ P20 Moses Malone	1.00	.45

2000 Upper Deck Century Legends Recollections

	MINT	NRMT
COMPLETE SET (7)	20.00	9.00
COMMON CARD (R1-R7)	1.50	.70
STATED ODDS 1:24		
❑ R1 Michael Jordan	15.00	6.75
❑ R2 Isiah Thomas	1.50	.70
❑ R3 Julius Erving	4.00	1.80
❑ R4 Wilt Chamberlain	4.00	1.80
❑ R5 Clyde Drexler	1.50	.70
❑ R6 Bill Walton	1.50	.70
❑ R7 Dominique Wilkins	1.50	.70

1998-99 Upper Deck Encore

	MINT	NRMT
COMPLETE SET (150)	200.00	90.00
COMMON CARD (1-90)	.15	.07
COMMON MJ (91-113)	3.00	1.35
COMMON RC (114-143)	1.00	.45
COMMON BONUS (144-150)	2.00	.90
SEMISTARS	.20	.09
SEMISTARS RC	1.25	.55
UNLISTED STARS	.40	.18
UNLISTED STARS RC	2.50	1.10
MJ SUBSET STATED ODDS 1:4		
ROOKIE SUBSET STATED ODDS 1:4		
BONUS SUBSET STATED ODDS 1:8		
MJ AU: 50 TOTAL AUTOGRAPHS		
❑ 1 Mookie Blaylock	.15	.07
❑ 2 Dikembe Mutombo	.20	.09
❑ 3 Steve Smith	.20	.09
❑ 4 Kenny Anderson	.20	.09
❑ 5 Antoine Walker	.60	.25
❑ 6 Ron Mercer	.60	.25
❑ 7 David Wesley	.15	.07
❑ 8 Elden Campbell	.15	.07
❑ 9 Eddie Jones	.75	.35
❑ 10 Ron Harper	.20	.09
❑ 11 Toni Kukoc	.50	.23
❑ 12 Brent Barry	.15	.07
❑ 13 Shawn Kemp	.60	.25
❑ 14 Brevin Knight	.15	.07
❑ 15 Derek Anderson	.50	.23
❑ 16 Shawn Bradley	.15	.07
❑ 17 Robert Pack	.15	.07
❑ 18 Michael Finley	.40	.18
❑ 19 Antonio McDyess	.40	.18
❑ 20 Nick Van Exel	.20	.09
❑ 21 Danny Fortson	.20	.09
❑ 22 Grant Hill	2.00	.90
❑ 23 Jerry Stackhouse	.20	.09
❑ 24 Bison Dele	.15	.07
❑ 25 Donyell Marshall	.15	.07
❑ 26 Tony Delk	.15	.07
❑ 27 Erick Dampier	.15	.07
❑ 28 John Starks	.15	.07
❑ 29 Charles Barkley	.60	.25
❑ 30 Hakeem Olajuwon	.60	.25
❑ 31 Othella Harrington	.15	.07
❑ 32 Scottie Pippen	1.25	.55
❑ 33 Rik Smits	.15	.07
❑ 34 Reggie Miller	.40	.18
❑ 35 Mark Jackson	.15	.07
❑ 36 Rodney Rogers	.15	.07
❑ 37 Lamond Murray	.15	.07
❑ 38 Maurice Taylor	.40	.18
❑ 39 Kobe Bryant	3.00	1.35
❑ 40 Shaquille O'Neal	2.00	.90
❑ 41 Derek Fisher	.20	.09
❑ 42 Glen Rice	.20	.09
❑ 43 Jamal Mashburn	.20	.09
❑ 44 Alonzo Mourning	.40	.18
❑ 45 Tim Hardaway	.40	.18
❑ 46 Ray Allen	.50	.23
❑ 47 Vinny Del Negro	.15	.07
❑ 48 Glenn Robinson	.20	.09
❑ 49 Joe Smith	.20	.09
❑ 50 Terrell Brandon	.20	.09
❑ 51 Kevin Garnett	2.50	1.10
❑ 52 Keith Van Horn	1.00	.45
❑ 53 Stephon Marbury	1.00	.45
❑ 54 Jayson Williams	.20	.09
❑ 55 Patrick Ewing	.40	.18
❑ 56 Allan Houston	.40	.18
❑ 57 Latrell Sprewell	.75	.35
❑ 58 Anfernee Hardaway	1.25	.55
❑ 59 Horace Grant	.20	.09
❑ 60 Nick Anderson	.15	.07
❑ 61 Allen Iverson	1.50	.70
❑ 62 Matt Geiger	.15	.07
❑ 63 Theo Ratliff	.15	.07
❑ 64 Jason Kidd	1.25	.55
❑ 65 Rex Chapman	.15	.07
❑ 66 Tom Gugliotta	.20	.09
❑ 67 Rasheed Wallace	.40	.18
❑ 68 Arvydas Sabonis	.20	.09
❑ 69 Damon Stoudamire	.40	.18
❑ 70 Vlade Divac	.15	.07
❑ 71 Corliss Williamson	.15	.07
❑ 72 Chris Webber	1.25	.55
❑ 73 Tim Duncan	2.00	.90
❑ 74 Sean Elliott	.15	.07
❑ 75 David Robinson	.60	.25
❑ 76 Vin Baker	.20	.09
❑ 77 Gary Payton	.60	.25
❑ 78 Detlef Schrempf	.20	.09
❑ 79 Tracy McGrady	1.50	.70
❑ 80 John Wallace	.15	.07
❑ 81 Doug Christie	.15	.07
❑ 82 Karl Malone	.60	.25
❑ 83 John Stockton	.40	.18
❑ 84 Jeff Hornacek	.20	.09
❑ 85 Bryant Reeves	.15	.07
❑ 86 Michael Smith	.15	.07
❑ 87 Shareef Abdur-Rahim	1.00	.45
❑ 88 Juwan Howard	.20	.09
❑ 89 Rod Strickland	.20	.09

❑ 90 Mitch Richmond .40 .18
❑ 91 Michael Jordan 3.00 1.35
❑ 92 Michael Jordan 3.00 1.35
❑ 93 Michael Jordan 3.00 1.35
❑ 94 Michael Jordan 3.00 1.35
❑ 95 Michael Jordan 3.00 1.35
❑ 96 Michael Jordan 3.00 1.35
❑ 97 Michael Jordan 3.00 1.35
❑ 98 Michael Jordan 3.00 1.35
❑ 99 Michael Jordan 3.00 1.35
❑ 100 Michael Jordan 3.00 1.35
❑ 101 Michael Jordan 3.00 1.35
❑ 102 Michael Jordan 3.00 1.35
❑ 103 Michael Jordan 3.00 1.35
❑ 104 Michael Jordan 3.00 1.35
❑ 105 Michael Jordan 3.00 1.35
❑ 106 Michael Jordan 3.00 1.35
❑ 107 Michael Jordan 3.00 1.35
❑ 108 Michael Jordan 3.00 1.35
❑ 109 Michael Jordan 3.00 1.35
❑ 110 Michael Jordan 3.00 1.35
❑ 111 Michael Jordan 3.00 1.35
❑ 112 Michael Jordan 3.00 1.35
❑ 113 Michael Jordan 3.00 1.35
❑ 114 Michael Olowokandi RC 4.00 1.80
❑ 115 Mike Bibby RC 8.00 3.60
❑ 116 Raef LaFrentz RC 5.00 2.20
❑ 117 Antawn Jamison RC 12.00 5.50
❑ 118 Vince Carter RC 60.00 27.00
❑ 119 Robert Traylor RC 2.50 1.10
❑ 120 Jason Williams RC 15.00 6.75
❑ 121 Larry Hughes RC 15.00 6.75
❑ 122 Dirk Nowitzki RC 10.00 4.50
❑ 123 Paul Pierce RC 12.00 5.50
❑ 124 Michael Doleac RC 2.50 1.10
❑ 125 Keon Clark RC 2.50 1.10
❑ 126 Michael Dickerson RC 5.00 2.20
❑ 127 Matt Harpring RC 2.50 1.10
❑ 128 Bryce Drew RC 2.50 1.10
❑ 129 Pat Garrity RC 1.25 .55
❑ 130 Roshown McLeod RC 1.25 .55
❑ 131 Ricky Davis RC 5.00 2.20
❑ 132 Predrag Stojakovic RC 4.00 1.80
❑ 133 Felipe Lopez RC 3.00 1.35
❑ 134 Al Harrington RC 8.00 3.60
❑ 135 Ruben Patterson RC 5.00 2.20
❑ 136 Cuttino Mobley RC 5.00 2.20
❑ 137 Tyronn Lue RC 1.25 .55
❑ 138 Brian Skinner RC 2.50 1.10
❑ 139 Nazr Mohammed RC 1.25 .55
❑ 140 Toby Bailey RC 1.00 .45
❑ 141 Casey Shaw RC 1.00 .45
❑ 142 Corey Benjamin RC 2.50 1.10
❑ 143 Rashard Lewis RC 10.00 4.50
❑ 144 Jason Williams BON 8.00 3.60
❑ 145 Paul Pierce BON 6.00 2.70
❑ 146 Vince Carter BON 30.00 13.50
❑ 147 Antawn Jamison BON 6.00 2.70
❑ 148 Raef LaFrentz BON 2.50 1.10
❑ 149 Mike Bibby BON 4.00 1.80
❑ 150 Michael Olowokandi BON 2.00 .90
❑ MJ Michael Jordan AU 2500.00 1100.00

1998-99 Upper Deck Encore F/X

	MINT	NRMT
COMMON CARD (1-90)	5.00	2.20
COMMON MJ (91-113)	50.00	22.00
COMMON RC (114-143)	4.00	1.80
COMMON BONUS (144-150)	25.00	11.00

*STARS: 12.5X TO 30X BASE CARD HI
*RCs: 1.5X TO 4X BASE HI
*BONUS: 3X TO 8X BASE HI
STATED PRINT RUN 125 SERIAL #'d SETS
RANDOM INSERTS IN PACKS

1998-99 Upper Deck Encore Driving Forces

	MINT	NRMT
COMPLETE SET (15)	60.00	27.00
COMMON CARD (F1-F15)	2.00	.90

STATED ODDS 1:23

COMP.FX SET (15)	200.00	90.00
COMMON FX (F1-F15)	6.00	2.70

*FX CARDS: 1.25X TO 3X HI COLUMN
FX: RANDOM INSERTS IN PACKS
FX: STATED PRINT RUN 500 SERIAL #'d SETS

❑ F1 Michael Jordan 25.00 11.00
❑ F2 Kobe Bryant 15.00 6.75
❑ F3 Keith Van Horn 5.00 2.20
❑ F4 Kevin Garnett 12.00 5.50
❑ F5 Tim Duncan 10.00 4.50
❑ F6 Gary Payton 3.00 1.35
❑ F7 Antoine Walker 3.00 1.35
❑ F8 Grant Hill 10.00 4.50
❑ F9 Scottie Pippen 6.00 2.70
❑ F10 Tim Hardaway 2.00 .90
❑ F11 Reggie Miller 2.00 .90
❑ F12 Shareef Abdur-Rahim 5.00 2.20
❑ F13 Anfernee Hardaway 6.00 2.70
❑ F14 Allen Iverson 8.00 3.60
❑ F15 Ray Allen 2.50 1.10

1998-99 Upper Deck Encore Intensity

	MINT	NRMT
COMPLETE SET (30)	40.00	18.00
COMMON CARD (I1-I30)	.40	.18
SEMISTARS	.60	.25
UNLISTED STARS	1.00	.45

STATED ODDS 1:11

❑ I1 Michael Jordan 12.00 5.50
❑ I2 Mitch Richmond 1.00 .45
❑ I3 Ron Mercer 1.50 .70
❑ I4 Terrell Brandon .60 .25
❑ I5 Brevin Knight .40 .18
❑ I6 Rasheed Wallace 1.00 .45
❑ I7 Keith Van Horn 2.50 1.10
❑ I8 Antawn Jamison 2.50 1.10
❑ I9 Antonio McDyess 1.00 .45
❑ I10 Allen Iverson 4.00 1.80
❑ I11 Anfernee Hardaway 3.00 1.35
❑ I12 Chris Webber 3.00 1.35
❑ I13 Lorenzen Wright .40 .18
❑ I14 Bryant Reeves .40 .18
❑ I15 Charles Barkley 1.50 .70
❑ I16 Tracy McGrady 4.00 1.80
❑ I17 Larry Johnson .60 .25
❑ I18 Jerry Stackhouse .60 .25
❑ I19 Derrick Coleman .60 .25
❑ I20 Detlef Schrempf .60 .25
❑ I21 John Stockton 1.00 .45
❑ I22 Kobe Bryant 8.00 3.60
❑ I23 Alonzo Mourning 1.00 .45
❑ I24 Dikembe Mutombo .60 .25
❑ I25 Jalen Rose 1.00 .45
❑ I26 Robert Pack .40 .18
❑ I27 Tom Gugliotta .60 .25
❑ I28 Shaquille O'Neal 5.00 2.20
❑ I29 Stephon Marbury 2.50 1.10
❑ I30 David Robinson 1.50 .70

1998-99 Upper Deck Encore MJ23

	MINT	NRMT
COMPLETE SET (20)	120.00	55.00
COMMON CARD (M1-M20)	8.00	3.60

STATED ODDS 1:23

COMMON FX (M1-M20)	400.00	180.00

FX: RANDOM INSERTS IN PACKS
FX: STATED PRINT RUN 23 SERIAL #'d SETS

❑ M1 Michael Jordan 8.00 3.60
❑ M2 Michael Jordan 8.00 3.60
❑ M3 Michael Jordan 8.00 3.60
❑ M4 Michael Jordan 8.00 3.60
❑ M5 Michael Jordan 8.00 3.60
❑ M6 Michael Jordan 8.00 3.60
❑ M7 Michael Jordan 8.00 3.60
❑ M8 Michael Jordan 8.00 3.60
❑ M9 Michael Jordan 8.00 3.60
❑ M10 Michael Jordan 8.00 3.60
❑ M11 Michael Jordan 8.00 3.60
❑ M12 Michael Jordan 8.00 3.60
❑ M13 Michael Jordan 8.00 3.60
❑ M14 Michael Jordan 8.00 3.60
❑ M15 Michael Jordan 8.00 3.60
❑ M16 Michael Jordan 8.00 3.60
❑ M17 Michael Jordan 8.00 3.60
❑ M18 Michael Jordan 8.00 3.60
❑ M19 Michael Jordan 8.00 3.60
❑ M20 Michael Jordan 8.00 3.60

1998-99 Upper Deck Encore PowerDeck

	MINT	NRMT
COMPLETE SET (9)	150.00	70.00
COMMON CARD (1-9)	10.00	4.50

STATED ODDS 1:47
NNO CARD LISTED BELOW ALPHABETICALLY

❑ 1 Charles Barkley	10.00	4.50
❑ 2 Kobe Bryant	25.00	11.00
❑ 3 Vince Carter	50.00	22.00
❑ 4 Julius Erving	10.00	4.50
❑ 5 Kevin Garnett	20.00	9.00
❑ 6 Michael Jordan	40.00	18.00
❑ 7 Shaquille O'Neal	15.00	6.75
❑ 8 Paul Pierce	10.00	4.50
❑ 9 Jason Williams	12.00	5.50

1998-99 Upper Deck Encore Rookie Encore

	MINT	NRMT
COMPLETE SET (10)	80.00	36.00
COMMON CARD (RE1-10)	2.00	.90
UNLISTED STARS	4.00	1.80
STATED ODDS 1:23		
COMP.FX SET (10)	150.00	70.00
COMMON FX (RE1-10)	4.00	1.80

*FX: .75X TO 2X HI COLUMN
FX: RANDOM INSERTS IN PACKS
FX: STATED PRINT RUN 1000 SERIAL #'d SETS

❑ RE1 Jason Williams	12.00	5.50
❑ RE2 Michael Olowokandi	4.00	1.80
❑ RE3 Paul Pierce	10.00	4.50
❑ RE4 Robert Traylor	2.00	.90
❑ RE5 Raef LaFrentz	4.00	1.80
❑ RE6 Mike Bibby	6.00	2.70
❑ RE7 Dirk Nowitzki	8.00	3.60
❑ RE8 Antawn Jamison	10.00	4.50
❑ RE9 Larry Hughes	12.00	5.50
❑ RE10 Vince Carter	50.00	22.00

1999-00 Upper Deck Encore

	MINT	NRMT
COMPLETE SET (120)	300.00	135.00
COMPLETE SET w/o RC (90)	25.00	11.00
COMMON CARD (1-90)	.15	.07
COMMON RC (91-120)	3.00	1.35
SEMISTARS	.20	.09
SEMISTARS RC	4.00	1.80

UNLISTED STARS	.40	.18
UNLISTED STARS RC	5.00	2.20

RCs: PRINT RUN 1999 SERIAL #'d SETS
RCs: RANDOM INSERTS IN PACKS
MJ FINAL FLOOR LISTED UNDER 99-00 UD

❑ 1 Dikembe Mutombo	.20	.09
❑ 2 Alan Henderson	.15	.07
❑ 3 Isaiah Rider	.20	.09
❑ 4 Kenny Anderson	.20	.09
❑ 5 Antoine Walker	.50	.23
❑ 6 Paul Pierce	.75	.35
❑ 7 Elden Campbell	.15	.07
❑ 8 Eddie Jones	.75	.35
❑ 9 David Wesley	.15	.07
❑ 10 Hersey Hawkins	.20	.09
❑ 11 Randy Brown	.15	.07
❑ 12 Toni Kukoc	.50	.23
❑ 13 Shawn Kemp	.60	.25
❑ 14 Bob Sura	.15	.07
❑ 15 Michael Finley	.40	.18
❑ 16 Dirk Nowitzki	.60	.25
❑ 17 Gary Trent	.15	.07
❑ 18 Antonio McDyess	.40	.18
❑ 19 Nick Van Exel	.20	.09
❑ 20 Raef LaFrentz	.40	.18
❑ 21 Christian Laettner	.20	.09
❑ 22 Grant Hill	2.00	.90
❑ 23 Lindsey Hunter	.15	.07
❑ 24 Jerry Stackhouse	.20	.09
❑ 25 John Starks	.15	.07
❑ 26 Antawn Jamison	.75	.35
❑ 27 Tony Farmer	.15	.07
❑ 28 Hakeem Olajuwon	.60	.25
❑ 29 Cuttino Mobley	.40	.18
❑ 30 Charles Barkley	.60	.25
❑ 31 Reggie Miller	.40	.18
❑ 32 Jalen Rose	.40	.18
❑ 33 Mark Jackson	.15	.07
❑ 34 Maurice Taylor	.40	.18
❑ 35 Derek Anderson	.40	.18
❑ 36 Michael Olowokandi	.20	.09
❑ 37 Kobe Bryant	3.00	1.35
❑ 38 Shaquille O'Neal	2.00	.90
❑ 39 Glen Rice	.20	.09
❑ 40 Tim Hardaway	.40	.18
❑ 41 Alonzo Mourning	.40	.18
❑ 42 Ray Allen	.40	.18
❑ 43 Glenn Robinson	.20	.09
❑ 44 Sam Cassell	.20	.09
❑ 45 Tim Thomas	.50	.23
❑ 46 Kevin Garnett	2.50	1.10
❑ 47 Terrell Brandon	.20	.09
❑ 48 Keith Van Horn	.75	.35
❑ 49 Stephon Marbury	.75	.35
❑ 50 Kendall Gill	.20	.09
❑ 51 Patrick Ewing	.40	.18
❑ 52 Allan Houston	.40	.18
❑ 53 Latrell Sprewell	.75	.35
❑ 54 Darrell Armstrong	.20	.09
❑ 55 John Amaechi RC	.50	.23
❑ 56 Michael Doleac	.15	.07
❑ 57 Allen Iverson	1.50	.70
❑ 58 Theo Ratliff	.15	.07
❑ 59 Larry Hughes	1.00	.45
❑ 60 Jason Kidd	1.25	.55
❑ 61 Tom Gugliotta	.20	.09
❑ 62 Anfernee Hardaway	1.25	.55
❑ 63 Rasheed Wallace	.40	.18
❑ 64 Steve Smith	.20	.09
❑ 65 Damon Stoudamire	.40	.18
❑ 66 Scottie Pippen	1.25	.55
❑ 67 Corliss Williamson	.15	.07
❑ 68 Jason Williams	1.00	.45
❑ 69 Vlade Divac	.15	.07
❑ 70 Chris Webber	1.25	.55
❑ 71 Tim Duncan	2.00	.90
❑ 72 David Robinson	.60	.25
❑ 73 Avery Johnson	.15	.07
❑ 74 Mario Elie	.15	.07
❑ 75 Gary Payton	.60	.25
❑ 76 Vin Baker	.20	.09
❑ 77 Ruben Patterson	.40	.18
❑ 78 Brent Barry	.15	.07
❑ 79 Vince Carter	4.00	1.80
❑ 80 Antonio Davis	.15	.07
❑ 81 Tracy McGrady	1.25	.55
❑ 82 Karl Malone	.60	.25
❑ 83 John Stockton	.40	.18
❑ 84 Bryon Russell	.15	.07
❑ 85 Shareef Abdur-Rahim	.75	.35
❑ 86 Mike Bibby	.50	.23
❑ 87 Othella Harrington	.15	.07
❑ 88 Juwan Howard	.20	.09
❑ 89 Rod Strickland	.20	.09
❑ 90 Mitch Richmond	.40	.18
❑ 91 Elton Brand RC	50.00	22.00
❑ 92 Steve Francis RC	80.00	36.00
❑ 93 Baron Davis RC	12.00	5.50
❑ 94 Lamar Odom RC	40.00	18.00
❑ 95 Jonathan Bender RC	25.00	11.00
❑ 96 Wally Szczerbiak RC	20.00	9.00
❑ 97 Richard Hamilton RC	12.00	5.50
❑ 98 Andre Miller RC	15.00	6.75
❑ 99 Shawn Marion RC	15.00	6.75
❑ 100 Jason Terry RC	8.00	3.60
❑ 101 Trajan Langdon RC	8.00	3.60
❑ 102 Kenny Thomas RC	8.00	3.60
❑ 103 Corey Maggette RC	20.00	9.00
❑ 104 William Avery RC	8.00	3.60
❑ 105 Ron Artest RC	12.00	5.50
❑ 106 Aleksandar Radojevic RC	3.00	1.35
❑ 107 James Posey RC	10.00	4.50
❑ 108 Quincy Lewis RC	5.00	2.20
❑ 109 Vonteego Cummings RC	8.00	3.60
❑ 110 Jeff Foster RC	5.00	2.20
❑ 111 Dion Glover RC	5.00	2.20
❑ 112 Devean George RC	10.00	4.50
❑ 113 Evan Eschmeyer RC	3.00	1.35
❑ 114 Tim James RC	6.00	2.70
❑ 115 Adrian Griffin RC	6.00	2.70
❑ 116 Anthony Carter RC	12.00	5.50
❑ 117 Obinna Ekezie RC	4.00	1.80
❑ 118 Todd MacCulloch RC	5.00	2.20
❑ 119 Chucky Atkins RC	6.00	2.70
❑ 120 Lazaro Borrell RC	3.00	1.35

1999-00 Upper Deck Encore Electric Currents

	MINT	NRMT
COMPLETE SET (20)	15.00	6.75
COMMON CARD (EC1-EC20)	.30	.14
UNLISTED STARS	.50	.23

STATED ODDS 1:3
COMMON F/X (EC1-EC20) 6.00 2.70
*F/X: 8X TO 20X HI COLUMN
F/X: PRINT RUN 150 SERIAL #'d SETS
F/X: RANDOM INSERTS IN PACKS

❑ EC1 Kevin Garnett	3.00	1.35
❑ EC2 Anfernee Hardaway	1.50	.70
❑ EC3 Shareef Abdur-Rahim	1.00	.45
❑ EC4 Allan Houston	.50	.23
❑ EC5 Michael Finley	.50	.23
❑ EC6 Tim Duncan	2.50	1.10
❑ EC7 Gary Payton	.75	.35
❑ EC8 Kobe Bryant	4.00	1.80
❑ EC9 Derek Anderson	.50	.23
❑ EC10 Reggie Miller	.50	.23
❑ EC11 Keith Van Horn	1.00	.45
❑ EC12 Jason Kidd	1.50	.70
❑ EC13 Ray Allen	.50	.23
❑ EC14 Tim Hardaway	.50	.23
❑ EC15 Darrell Armstrong	.30	.14
❑ EC16 Antonio McDyess	.50	.23
❑ EC17 Eddie Jones	1.00	.45
❑ EC18 Paul Pierce	1.00	.45
❑ EC19 Stephon Marbury	1.00	.45
❑ EC20 Chris Webber	1.50	.70

1999-00 Upper Deck Encore Future Charge

	MINT	NRMT
COMPLETE SET (15)	10.00	4.50
COMMON CARD (FC1-FC15)	.50	.23
UNLISTED STARS	.75	.35
STATED ODDS 1:6		
❑ FC1 Antawn Jamison	1.50	.70
❑ FC2 Mike Bibby	1.00	.45
❑ FC3 Antoine Walker	1.00	.45
❑ FC4 Baron Davis	1.00	.45
❑ FC5 Jason Terry	.75	.35
❑ FC6 Andre Miller	1.25	.55
❑ FC7 Ray Allen	.75	.35
❑ FC8 Wally Szczerbiak	1.50	.70
❑ FC9 Raef LaFrentz	.75	.35
❑ FC10 William Avery	.75	.35
❑ FC11 Jason Williams	2.00	.90
❑ FC12 Michael Olowokandi	.50	.23
❑ FC13 Stephon Marbury	1.50	.70
❑ FC14 Quincy Lewis	.50	.23
❑ FC15 Shawn Marion	1.25	.55

1999-00 Upper Deck Encore Game Jerseys

	MINT	NRMT
COMMON CARD	40.00	18.00
STATED ODDS 1:300		
AUTOS NOT INCLUDED IN SET PRICE		
KB-A UNPRICED DUE TO SCARCITY		
❑ MJ Michael Jordan Autographed to 23	11000.00	5000.00
❑ AI-J Allen Iverson	120.00	55.00
❑ AM-J Andre Miller	60.00	27.00
❑ BD-J Baron Davis	60.00	27.00
❑ GH-J Grant Hill	150.00	70.00
❑ JB-J Jonathan Bender	80.00	36.00
❑ JK-J Jason Kidd	150.00	70.00
❑ JT-J Jason Terry	40.00	18.00
❑ JW-J Jason Williams	120.00	55.00
❑ KB-A Kobe Bryant Autographed to 8		
❑ KB-J Kobe Bryant	300.00	135.00
❑ KG-A Kevin Garnett Autographed to 21	1200.00	550.00
❑ KG-J Kevin Garnett	150.00	70.00
❑ MC-J Antonio McDyess	40.00	18.00
❑ RH-J Richard Hamilton	80.00	36.00
❑ SF-J Steve Francis	300.00	135.00
❑ SM-J Shawn Marion	100.00	45.00
❑ SO-J Shaquille O'Neal	150.00	70.00
❑ TL-J Trajan Langdon	60.00	27.00
❑ WS-J Wally Szczerbiak	150.00	70.00

1999-00 Upper Deck Encore High Definition

	MINT	NRMT
COMPLETE SET (20)	50.00	22.00
COMMON CARD (HD1-HD20)	.75	.35
UNLISTED STARS	1.25	.55
STATED ODDS 1:15		
❑ HD1 Antonio McDyess	1.25	.55
❑ HD2 Kevin Garnett	8.00	3.60
❑ HD3 Vince Carter	12.00	5.50
❑ HD4 Shareef Abdur-Rahim	2.50	1.10
❑ HD5 Stephon Marbury	2.50	1.10
❑ HD6 Gary Payton	2.00	.90
❑ HD7 Glenn Robinson	.75	.35
❑ HD8 Kobe Bryant	10.00	4.50
❑ HD9 Antawn Jamison	2.50	1.10
❑ HD10 Chris Webber	4.00	1.80
❑ HD11 Corey Maggette	2.50	1.10
❑ HD12 Shawn Kemp	2.00	.90
❑ HD13 Derek Anderson	1.25	.55
❑ HD14 Michael Finley	1.25	.55
❑ HD15 Allan Houston	1.25	.55
❑ HD16 Anfernee Hardaway	4.00	1.80
❑ HD17 Grant Hill	6.00	2.70
❑ HD18 Shaquille O'Neal	6.00	2.70
❑ HD19 Paul Pierce	2.50	1.10
❑ HD20 Scottie Pippen	4.00	1.80

1999-00 Upper Deck Encore Jamboree

	MINT	NRMT
COMPLETE SET (15)	30.00	13.50
COMMON CARD (J1-J15)	.50	.23
UNLISTED STARS	.75	.35
STATED ODDS 1:6		
❑ J1 Michael Jordan	10.00	4.50
❑ J2 Karl Malone	1.25	.55
❑ J3 Kevin Garnett	5.00	2.20
❑ J4 Antonio McDyess	.75	.35
❑ J5 Shareef Abdur-Rahim	1.50	.70
❑ J6 David Robinson	1.25	.55
❑ J7 Marcus Camby	.75	.35
❑ J8 Kobe Bryant	6.00	2.70
❑ J9 Jason Kidd	2.50	1.10
❑ J10 Tim Duncan	4.00	1.80
❑ J11 Keith Van Horn	1.50	.70
❑ J12 Glenn Robinson	.50	.23
❑ J13 Grant Hill	4.00	1.80
❑ J14 Michael Finley	.75	.35
❑ J15 Vince Carter	8.00	3.60

1999-00 Upper Deck Encore MJ - A Higher Power

	MINT	NRMT
COMPLETE SET (10)	120.00	55.00
COMMON CARD (MJ1-MJ10)	15.00	6.75
STATED ODDS 1:90		
❑ MJ1 Michael Jordan	15.00	6.75
❑ MJ2 Michael Jordan	15.00	6.75
❑ MJ3 Michael Jordan	15.00	6.75
❑ MJ4 Michael Jordan	15.00	6.75
❑ MJ5 Michael Jordan	15.00	6.75
❑ MJ6 Michael Jordan	15.00	6.75
❑ MJ7 Michael Jordan	15.00	6.75
❑ MJ8 Michael Jordan	15.00	6.75
❑ MJ9 Michael Jordan	15.00	6.75
❑ MJ10 Michael Jordan	15.00	6.75

1999-00 Upper Deck Encore Upper Realm

	MINT	NRMT
COMPLETE SET (10)	15.00	6.75

COMMON CARD (UR1-UR10).... .75 .35
STATED ODDS 1:6
COMMON F/X (UR1-UR10).... 15.00 6.75
*F/X: 8X TO 20X HI COLUMN
F/X: PRINT RUN 150 SERIAL #'d SETS
F/X: RANDOM INSERTS IN PACKS

❑ UR1 Kevin Garnett 3.00 1.35
❑ UR2 Kobe Bryant 4.00 1.80
❑ UR3 Tim Duncan 2.50 1.10
❑ UR4 Vince Carter 5.00 2.20
❑ UR5 Gary Payton .... .75 .35
❑ UR6 Allen Iverson .... 2.00 .90
❑ UR7 Karl Malone .... .75 .35
❑ UR8 Jason Williams .... 1.25 .55
❑ UR9 Scottie Pippen .... 1.50 .70
❑ UR10 Shaquille O'Neal 2.50 1.10

1999-00 Upper Deck Gold Reserve

	MINT	NRMT
COMPLETE SET (270)	150.00	70.00
COMPLETE SET w/o RC (240)	40.00	18.00
COMMON CARD (1-240)	.15	.07
COMMON RC (241-270)	2.00	.90
SEMISTARS	.20	.09
SEMISTARS RC	2.50	1.10
UNLISTED STARS	.40	.18
UNLISTED STARS RC	3.00	1.35

RCs: PRINT RUN 3500 SERIAL #'d SETS
RCs: RANDOM INSERTS IN PACKS
MAXWELL CARD #294 SHOULD BE #204

❑ 1 Roshown McLeod .... .15 .07
❑ 2 Dikembe Mutombo .... .20 .09
❑ 3 Alan Henderson .... .15 .07
❑ 4 Chris Crawford .... .15 .07
❑ 5 Jim Jackson .... .15 .07
❑ 6 Isaiah Rider .... .20 .09
❑ 7 Lorenzen Wright .... .15 .07
❑ 8 Bimbo Coles .... .15 .07
❑ 9 Kenny Anderson .... .20 .09
❑ 10 Antoine Walker .... .50 .23
❑ 11 Paul Pierce .... .75 .35
❑ 12 Vitaly Potapenko .... .15 .07
❑ 13 Dana Barros .... .15 .07
❑ 14 Calbert Cheaney .... .15 .07
❑ 15 Pervis Ellison .... .15 .07
❑ 16 Eric Williams .... .15 .07
❑ 17 Tony Battie .... .15 .07
❑ 18 Elden Campbell .... .15 .07
❑ 19 Eddie Jones .... .75 .35
❑ 20 David Wesley .... .15 .07
❑ 21 Derrick Coleman .... .20 .09
❑ 22 Ricky Davis .... .40 .18
❑ 23 Anthony Mason .... .20 .09
❑ 24 Todd Fuller .... .15 .07
❑ 25 Brad Miller .... .15 .07
❑ 26 Corey Benjamin .... .15 .07
❑ 27 Randy Brown .... .15 .07
❑ 28 Dickey Simpkins .... .15 .07
❑ 29 Toni Kukoc .... .50 .23
❑ 30 Fred Hoiberg .... .15 .07
❑ 31 Hersey Hawkins .... .20 .09
❑ 32 Will Perdue .... .15 .07
❑ 33 Chris Anstey .... .15 .07
❑ 34 Shawn Kemp .... .60 .25
❑ 35 Wesley Person .... .15 .07
❑ 36 Brevin Knight .... .15 .07
❑ 37 Bob Sura .... .15 .07
❑ 38 Danny Ferry .... .15 .07
❑ 39 Lamond Murray .... .15 .07
❑ 40 Cedric Henderson .... .15 .07
❑ 41 Andrew DeClercq .... .15 .07
❑ 42 Michael Finley .... .40 .18
❑ 43 Shawn Bradley .... .15 .07
❑ 44 Dirk Nowitzki .... .60 .25
❑ 45 Erick Strickland .... .15 .07
❑ 46 Cedric Ceballos .... .15 .07
❑ 47 Hubert Davis .... .15 .07
❑ 48 Robert Pack .... .15 .07
❑ 49 Gary Trent .... .15 .07
❑ 50 Antonio McDyess .... .40 .18
❑ 51 Nick Van Exel .... .20 .09
❑ 52 Chauncey Billups .... .15 .07
❑ 53 Bryant Stith .... .15 .07
❑ 54 Raef LaFrentz .... .40 .18
❑ 55 Ron Mercer .... .50 .23
❑ 56 George McCloud .... .15 .07
❑ 57 Roy Rogers .... .15 .07
❑ 58 Keon Clark .... .15 .07
❑ 59 Grant Hill .... 2.00 .90
❑ 60 Lindsey Hunter .... .15 .07
❑ 61 Jerry Stackhouse .... .20 .09
❑ 62 Terry Mills .... .15 .07
❑ 63 Michael Curry .... .15 .07
❑ 64 Christian Laettner .... .20 .09
❑ 65 Jerome Williams .... .20 .09
❑ 66 Loy Vaught .... .15 .07
❑ 67 John Starks .... .15 .07
❑ 68 Antawn Jamison .... .75 .35
❑ 69 Erick Dampier .... .15 .07
❑ 70 Jason Caffey .... .15 .07
❑ 71 Terry Cummings .... .15 .07
❑ 72 Donyell Marshall .... .15 .07
❑ 73 Chris Mills .... .15 .07
❑ 74 Tony Farmer .... .15 .07
❑ 75 Adonal Foyle .... .15 .07
❑ 76 Hakeem Olajuwon .... .60 .25
❑ 77 Cuttino Mobley .... .40 .18
❑ 78 Charles Barkley .... .60 .25
❑ 79 Bryce Drew .... .15 .07
❑ 80 Shandon Anderson .... .15 .07
❑ 81 Kelvin Cato .... .15 .07
❑ 82 Walt Williams .... .15 .07
❑ 83 Carlos Rogers .... .15 .07
❑ 84 Reggie Miller .... .40 .18
❑ 85 Jalen Rose .... .40 .18
❑ 86 Mark Jackson .... .15 .07
❑ 87 Dale Davis .... .15 .07
❑ 88 Chris Mullin .... .40 .18
❑ 89 Al Harrington .... .50 .23
❑ 90 Rik Smits .... .15 .07
❑ 91 Sam Perkins .... .15 .07
❑ 92 Austin Croshere .... .40 .18
❑ 93 Maurice Taylor .... .40 .18
❑ 94 Tyrone Nesby RC .... .15 .07
❑ 95 Michael Olowokandi .... .20 .09
❑ 96 Eric Piatkowski .... .15 .07
❑ 97 Troy Hudson .... .15 .07
❑ 98 Derek Anderson .... .40 .18
❑ 99 Eric Murdock .... .15 .07
❑ 100 Brian Skinner .... .15 .07
❑ 101 Kobe Bryant 3.00 1.35
❑ 102 Shaquille O'Neal .... 2.00 .90
❑ 103 Glen Rice .... .20 .09
❑ 104 Robert Horry .... .15 .07
❑ 105 Ron Harper .... .20 .09
❑ 106 Derek Fisher .... .20 .09
❑ 107 Rick Fox .... .15 .07
❑ 108 A.C. Green .... .20 .09
❑ 109 Tim Hardaway .... .40 .18
❑ 110 Alonzo Mourning .... .40 .18
❑ 111 P.J. Brown .... .15 .07
❑ 112 Dan Majerle .... .20 .09
❑ 113 Jamal Mashburn .... .20 .09
❑ 114 Voshon Lenard .... .15 .07
❑ 115 Clarence Weatherspoon .15 .07
❑ 116 Rex Walters .... .15 .07
❑ 117 Ray Allen .... .40 .18
❑ 118 Glenn Robinson .... .20 .09
❑ 119 Sam Cassell .... .20 .09
❑ 120 Robert Traylor .... .15 .07
❑ 121 J.R. Reid .... .15 .07
❑ 122 Ervin Johnson .... .15 .07
❑ 123 Danny Manning .... .20 .09
❑ 124 Tim Thomas .... .50 .23
❑ 125 Kevin Garnett 2.50 1.10
❑ 126 Sam Mitchell .... .15 .07
❑ 127 Dean Garrett .... .15 .07
❑ 128 Bobby Jackson .... .15 .07
❑ 129 Radoslav Nesterovic .... .15 .07
❑ 130 Terrell Brandon .... .20 .09
❑ 131 Joe Smith .... .20 .09
❑ 132 Anthony Peeler .... .15 .07
❑ 133 Keith Van Horn .... .75 .35
❑ 134 Stephon Marbury .... .75 .35
❑ 135 Kendall Gill .... .20 .09
❑ 136 Scott Burrell .... .15 .07
❑ 137 Jayson Williams .... .20 .09
❑ 138 Jamie Feick RC .... .15 .07
❑ 139 Kerry Kittles .... .20 .09
❑ 140 Johnny Newman .... .15 .07
❑ 141 Patrick Ewing .... .40 .18
❑ 142 Allan Houston .... .40 .18
❑ 143 Latrell Sprewell .... .75 .35
❑ 144 Larry Johnson .... .20 .09
❑ 145 Marcus Camby .... .40 .18
❑ 146 Chris Childs .... .15 .07
❑ 147 Kurt Thomas .... .15 .07
❑ 148 Charlie Ward .... .15 .07
❑ 149 Darrell Armstrong .... .20 .09
❑ 150 Matt Harpring .... .15 .07
❑ 151 Michael Doleac .... .15 .07
❑ 152 Charles Outlaw .... .15 .07
❑ 153 Tariq Abdul-Wahad .... .15 .07
❑ 154 John Amaechi RC .... .50 .23
❑ 155 Ben Wallace .... .15 .07
❑ 156 Monty Williams .... .15 .07
❑ 157 Allen Iverson .... 1.50 .70
❑ 158 Theo Ratliff .... .15 .07
❑ 159 Larry Hughes .... 1.00 .45
❑ 160 Eric Snow .... .15 .07
❑ 161 George Lynch .... .15 .07
❑ 162 Tyrone Hill .... .15 .07
❑ 163 Billy Owens .... .15 .07
❑ 164 Aaron McKie .... .15 .07
❑ 165 Jason Kidd .... 1.25 .55
❑ 166 Clifford Robinson .... .15 .07
❑ 167 Tom Gugliotta .... .20 .09
❑ 168 Luc Longley .... .15 .07
❑ 169 Anfernee Hardaway .... 1.25 .55
❑ 170 Rex Chapman .... .15 .07
❑ 171 Oliver Miller .... .15 .07
❑ 172 Rodney Rogers .... .15 .07
❑ 173 Rasheed Wallace .... .40 .18
❑ 174 Arvydas Sabonis .... .20 .09
❑ 175 Damon Stoudamire .... .40 .18
❑ 176 Brian Grant .... .20 .09
❑ 177 Scottie Pippen .... 1.25 .55
❑ 178 Detlef Schrempf .... .20 .09
❑ 179 Steve Smith .... .20 .09
❑ 180 Jermaine O'Neal .... .20 .09
❑ 181 Bonzi Wells .... .60 .25
❑ 182 Jason Williams .... 1.00 .45
❑ 183 Vlade Divac .... .15 .07
❑ 184 Predrag Stojakovic .... .20 .09
❑ 185 Lawrence Funderburke .. .15 .07
❑ 186 Chris Webber .... 1.25 .55
❑ 187 Nick Anderson .... .15 .07
❑ 188 Darrick Martin .... .15 .07
❑ 189 Corliss Williamson .... .15 .07
❑ 190 Tim Duncan .... 2.00 .90
❑ 191 Sean Elliott .... .15 .07
❑ 192 David Robinson .... .60 .25
❑ 193 Mario Elie .... .15 .07
❑ 194 Avery Johnson .... .15 .07
❑ 195 Terry Porter .... .15 .07
❑ 196 Malik Rose .... .15 .07
❑ 197 Jaren Jackson .... .15 .07
❑ 198 Gary Payton .... .60 .25
❑ 199 Vin Baker .... .20 .09
❑ 200 Rashard Lewis .... .60 .25
❑ 201 Jelani McCoy .... .15 .07
❑ 202 Brent Barry .... .15 .07
❑ 203 Horace Grant .... .20 .09
❑ 204 Vernon Maxwell UER .... .15 .07
Listed as 294, should be 204
❑ 205 Ruben Patterson .... .40 .18

❑ 206	Vince Carter	4.00	1.80
❑ 207	Doug Christie	.15	.07
❑ 208	Kevin Willis	.15	.07
❑ 209	Dee Brown	.15	.07
❑ 210	Antonio Davis	.15	.07
❑ 211	Tracy McGrady	1.25	.55
❑ 212	Dell Curry	.15	.07
❑ 213	Charles Oakley	.15	.07
❑ 214	Karl Malone	.60	.25
❑ 215	John Stockton	.40	.18
❑ 216	Howard Eisley	.15	.07
❑ 217	Bryon Russell	.15	.07
❑ 218	Greg Ostertag	.15	.07
❑ 219	Jeff Hornacek	.20	.09
❑ 220	Olden Polynice	.15	.07
❑ 221	Adam Keefe	.15	.07
❑ 222	Shareef Abdur-Rahim	.75	.35
❑ 223	Mike Bibby	.50	.23
❑ 224	Felipe Lopez	.15	.07
❑ 225	Cherokee Parks	.15	.07
❑ 226	Michael Dickerson	.40	.18
❑ 227	Othella Harrington	.15	.07
❑ 228	Bryant Reeves	.15	.07
❑ 229	Brent Price	.15	.07
❑ 230	Michael Smith	.15	.07
❑ 231	Juwan Howard	.20	.09
❑ 232	Rod Strickland	.20	.09
❑ 233	Chris Whitney	.15	.07
❑ 234	Tracy Murray	.15	.07
❑ 235	Mitch Richmond	.40	.18
❑ 236	Aaron Williams	.15	.07
❑ 237	Isaac Austin	.15	.07
❑ 238	Kobe Bryant CL	.60	.25
❑ 239	Michael Jordan CL	1.00	.45
❑ 240	Kevin Garnett CL	.50	.23
❑ 241	Elton Brand RC	30.00	13.50
❑ 242	Steve Francis RC	40.00	18.00
❑ 243	Baron Davis RC	8.00	3.60
❑ 244	Lamar Odom RC	25.00	11.00
❑ 245	Jonathan Bender RC	15.00	6.75
❑ 246	Wally Szczerbiak RC	12.00	5.50
❑ 247	Richard Hamilton RC	8.00	3.60
❑ 248	Andre Miller RC	10.00	4.50
❑ 249	Shawn Marion RC	10.00	4.50
❑ 250	Jason Terry RC	5.00	2.20
❑ 251	Trajan Langdon RC	5.00	2.20
❑ 252	Aleksandar Radojevic RC	2.00	.90
❑ 253	Corey Maggette RC	12.00	5.50
❑ 254	William Avery RC	5.00	2.20
❑ 255	Ron Artest RC	8.00	3.60
❑ 256	Cal Bowdler RC	3.00	1.35
❑ 257	James Posey RC	6.00	2.70
❑ 258	Quincy Lewis RC	3.00	1.35
❑ 259	Dion Glover RC	3.00	1.35
❑ 260	Jeff Foster RC	3.00	1.35
❑ 261	Kenny Thomas RC	5.00	2.20
❑ 262	Devean George RC	6.00	2.70
❑ 263	Tim James RC	4.00	1.80
❑ 264	Vonteego Cummings RC	5.00	2.20
❑ 265	Jumaine Jones RC	2.50	1.10
❑ 266	Scott Padgett RC	3.00	1.35
❑ 267	Rodney Buford RC	2.00	.90
❑ 268	Adrian Griffin RC	4.00	1.80
❑ 269	Anthony Carter RC	8.00	3.60
❑ 270	Eddie Robinson RC	5.00	2.20

1999-00 Upper Deck Gold Reserve Gold Mine

	MINT	NRMT
COMPLETE SET (15)	30.00	13.50
COMMON CARD (R1-R15)	.75	.35
STATED ODDS 1:11		

❑ R1	Kobe Bryant	6.00	2.70
❑ R2	Vince Carter	8.00	3.60
❑ R3	Steve Francis	5.00	2.20
❑ R4	Kevin Garnett	5.00	2.20
❑ R5	Elton Brand	4.00	1.80
❑ R6	Gary Payton	1.25	.55
❑ R7	Lamar Odom	3.00	1.35
❑ R8	Grant Hill	4.00	1.80
❑ R9	Jason Williams	2.00	.90
❑ R10	Shareef Abdur-Rahim	1.50	.70
❑ R11	Tim Duncan	4.00	1.80
❑ R12	Keith Van Horn	1.50	.70
❑ R13	Tim Hardaway	.75	.35
❑ R14	Karl Malone	1.25	.55
❑ R15	Shaquille O'Neal	4.00	1.80

1999-00 Upper Deck Gold Reserve Gold Strike

	MINT	NRMT
COMPLETE SET (15)	20.00	9.00
COMMON CARD (GS1-GS15)	.50	.23
STATED ODDS 1:4		

❑ GS1	Kevin Garnett	3.00	1.35
❑ GS2	Kobe Bryant	4.00	1.80
❑ GS3	Tim Duncan	2.50	1.10
❑ GS4	Adrian Griffin	.50	.23
❑ GS5	Lamar Odom	3.00	1.35
❑ GS6	Jason Kidd	1.50	.70
❑ GS7	Wally Szczerbiak	1.50	.70
❑ GS8	Stephon Marbury	1.00	.45
❑ GS9	Shaquille O'Neal	2.50	1.10
❑ GS10	Elton Brand	4.00	1.80
❑ GS11	Allen Iverson	2.00	.90
❑ GS12	Shawn Marion	2.50	1.10
❑ GS13	Jason Williams	1.25	.55
❑ GS14	Antonio McDyess	.50	.23
❑ GS15	Vince Carter	5.00	2.20

1999-00 Upper Deck Gold Reserve UD Authentics

	MINT	NRMT
COMMON CARD	15.00	6.75
STATED ODDS 1:480		

❑ AH	Anfernee Hardaway	120.00	55.00
❑ AW	Antoine Walker	20.00	9.00
❑ BD	Baron Davis	20.00	9.00
❑ JB	Jonathan Bender	40.00	18.00
❑ JT	Jason Terry	20.00	9.00
❑ KB	Kobe Bryant	400.00	180.00
❑ KG	Kevin Garnett	250.00	110.00
❑ RH	Richard Hamilton	30.00	13.50
❑ SF	Steve Francis	120.00	55.00
❑ WS	Wally Szczerbiak	30.00	13.50

1998 Upper Deck Hardcourt

	MINT	NRMT
COMPLETE SET (90)	75.00	34.00
COMMON CARD (1-90)	.40	.18
SEMISTARS	.60	.25
UNLISTED STARS	1.00	.45

JORDAN SPEC. INSERTED EVERY TWO BOXES
JORDAN SPEC. NOT IN SET PRICE
ONE JORDAN JUMBO PER BOX

❑ 1	Kobe Bryant	8.00	3.60
❑ 2	Donyell Marshall	.40	.18
❑ 3	Bryant Reeves	.40	.18
❑ 4	Keith Van Horn	2.50	1.10
❑ 5	David Robinson	1.50	.70
❑ 6	Nick Anderson	.40	.18
❑ 7	Nick Van Exel	.60	.25
❑ 8	David Wesley	.40	.18
❑ 9	Alonzo Mourning	1.00	.45
❑ 10	Shawn Kemp	1.50	.70
❑ 11	Maurice Taylor	1.00	.45
❑ 12	Kenny Anderson	.60	.25
❑ 13	Jason Kidd	3.00	1.35
❑ 14	Marcus Camby	1.00	.45
❑ 15	Tim Hardaway	1.00	.45
❑ 16	Damon Stoudamire	1.00	.45
❑ 17	Detlef Schrempf	.60	.25
❑ 18	Dikembe Mutombo	.60	.25
❑ 19	Charles Barkley	1.50	.70
❑ 20	Ray Allen	1.25	.55
❑ 21	Ron Mercer	1.50	.70
❑ 22	Shawn Bradley	.40	.18
❑ 23	Michael Jordan	12.00	5.50
❑ 23A	Michael Jordan Spec.	20.00	9.00
❑ 24	Antonio McDyess	1.00	.45
❑ 25	Stephon Marbury	2.50	1.10
❑ 26	Rik Smits	.40	.18
❑ 27	Michael Stewart	.40	.18
❑ 28	Steve Smith	.60	.25
❑ 29	Glenn Robinson	.60	.25
❑ 30	Chris Webber	3.00	1.35
❑ 31	Antoine Walker	1.50	.70
❑ 32	Eddie Jones	2.00	.90
❑ 33	Mitch Richmond	1.00	.45
❑ 34	Kevin Garnett	6.00	2.70
❑ 35	Grant Hill	5.00	2.20

Card	MINT	NRMT
❑ 36 John Stockton	1.00	.45
❑ 37 Allan Houston	1.00	.45
❑ 38 Bobby Jackson	.40	.18
❑ 39 Sam Cassell	.60	.25
❑ 40 Allen Iverson	4.00	1.80
❑ 41 LaPhonso Ellis	.40	.18
❑ 42 Lorenzen Wright	.40	.18
❑ 43 Gary Payton	1.50	.70
❑ 44 Patrick Ewing	1.00	.45
❑ 45 Scottie Pippen	3.00	1.35
❑ 46 Hakeem Olajuwon	1.50	.70
❑ 47 Glen Rice	.60	.25
❑ 48 Antonio Daniels	.40	.18
❑ 49 Jayson Williams	.60	.25
❑ 50 Juwan Howard	.60	.25
❑ 51 Reggie Miller	1.00	.45
❑ 52 Joe Smith	.60	.25
❑ 53 Shaquille O'Neal	5.00	2.20
❑ 54 Dennis Rodman	2.00	.90
❑ 55 Vin Baker	.60	.25
❑ 56 Rod Strickland	.60	.25
❑ 57 Anfernee Hardaway	3.00	1.35
❑ 58 Zydrunas Ilgauskas	.40	.18
❑ 59 Chris Mullin	1.00	.45
❑ 60 Rasheed Wallace	1.00	.45
❑ 61 Shareef Abdur-Rahim	2.50	1.10
❑ 62 Tom Gugliotta	.60	.25
❑ 63 Tim Duncan	5.00	2.20
❑ 64 Michael Finley	1.00	.45
❑ 65 Jim Jackson	.40	.18
❑ 66 Chauncey Billups	.40	.18
❑ 67 Jerry Stackhouse	.60	.25
❑ 68 Jeff Hornacek	.60	.25
❑ 69 Clyde Drexler	1.00	.45
❑ 70 Karl Malone	1.50	.70
❑ 71 Tim Duncan RE	2.50	1.10
❑ 72 Keith Van Horn RE	1.25	.55
❑ 73 Chauncey Billups RE	.40	.18
❑ 74 Antonio Daniels RE	.40	.18
❑ 75 Tony Battie RE	.40	.18
❑ 76 Ron Mercer RE	1.00	.45
❑ 77 Tim Thomas RE	1.25	.55
❑ 78 Tracy McGrady RE	4.00	1.80
❑ 79 Danny Fortson RE	.40	.18
❑ 80 Derek Anderson RE	1.25	.55
❑ 81 Maurice Taylor RE	.60	.25
❑ 82 Kelvin Cato RE	.40	.18
❑ 83 Brevin Knight RE	.40	.18
❑ 84 Bobby Jackson RE	.40	.18
❑ 85 Rodrick Rhodes RE	.40	.18
❑ 86 Anthony Johnson RE	.40	.18
❑ 87 Cedric Henderson RE	.40	.18
❑ 88 Chris Anstey RE	.40	.18
❑ 89 Michael Stewart RE	.40	.18
❑ 90 Zydrunas Ilgauskas RE	.40	.18
❑ NNO Michael Jordan Jumbo	10.00	4.50

1998 Upper Deck Hardcourt Home Court Advantage

	MINT	NRMT
COMPLETE SET (90)	250.00	110.00
COMMON CARD (1-90)	1.00	.45

*STARS: 1X TO 2.5X BASE CARD HI
STATED ODDS 1:4

1998 Upper Deck Hardcourt Home Court Advantage Plus

	MINT	NRMT
COMMON CARD (1-90)	5.00	2.20

*STARS: 5X TO 12X BASE CARD HI
STATED PRINT RUN 500 SERIAL #'d SETS
RANDOM INSERTS IN PACKS

1998 Upper Deck Hardcourt High Court

	MINT	NRMT
COMPLETE SET (30)	300.00	135.00
COMMON CARD (H1-H30)	2.50	1.10
SEMISTARS	4.00	1.80
UNLISTED STARS	6.00	2.70

RANDOM INSERTS IN PACKS
STATED PRINT RUN 1300 SERIAL #'d SETS

Card	MINT	NRMT
❑ H1 Dikembe Mutombo	4.00	1.80
❑ H2 Ron Mercer	10.00	4.50
❑ H3 Glen Rice	4.00	1.80
❑ H4 Scottie Pippen	20.00	9.00
❑ H5 Shawn Kemp	10.00	4.50
❑ H6 Michael Finley	6.00	2.70
❑ H7 LaPhonso Ellis	2.50	1.10
❑ H8 Grant Hill	30.00	13.50
❑ H9 Erick Dampier	2.50	1.10
❑ H10 Hakeem Olajuwon	10.00	4.50
❑ H11 Chris Mullin	6.00	2.70
❑ H12 Lamond Murray	2.50	1.10
❑ H13 Kobe Bryant	50.00	22.00
❑ H14 Tim Hardaway	6.00	2.70
❑ H15 Ray Allen	8.00	3.60
❑ H16 Stephon Marbury	15.00	6.75
❑ H17 Keith Van Horn	15.00	6.75
❑ H18 Allan Houston	6.00	2.70
❑ H19 Anfernee Hardaway	20.00	9.00
❑ H20 Allen Iverson	25.00	11.00
❑ H21 Antonio McDyess	6.00	2.70
❑ H22 Rasheed Wallace	6.00	2.70
❑ H23 Mitch Richmond	6.00	2.70
❑ H24 Tim Duncan	30.00	13.50
❑ H25 Gary Payton	10.00	4.50
❑ H26 Chauncey Billups	2.50	1.10
❑ H27 John Stockton	6.00	2.70
❑ H28 Shareef Abdur-Rahim	15.00	6.75
❑ H29 Juwan Howard	4.00	1.80
❑ H30 Michael Jordan	80.00	36.00

1998 Upper Deck Hardcourt Jordan Holding Court Red

	MINT	NRMT
COMPLETE SET (30)	250.00	110.00
COMMON CARD (J1-J30)	2.00	.90
SEMISTARS	3.00	1.35
UNLISTED STARS	5.00	2.20

STATED ODDS 2300 SERIAL #'d SETS

	MINT	NRMT
COMMON BRONZE (J1-J30)	8.00	3.60

*BRONZE: 2X TO 4X HI COLUMN
BRONZE: RANDOM INSERTS IN PACKS
BRONZE: PRINT RUN 230 SERIAL #'d SETS
UNPRICED GOLD PARALLEL SERIAL #'d TO 1
GOLD: RANDOM INSERTS IN PACKS

Card	MINT	NRMT
❑ J1 Steve Smith Michael Jordan	3.00	1.35
❑ J2 Antoine Walker Michael Jordan	8.00	3.60
❑ J3 Glen Rice Michael Jordan	3.00	1.35
❑ J4 Scottie Pippen Michael Jordan	15.00	6.75
❑ J5 Shawn Kemp Michael Jordan	8.00	3.60
❑ J6 Michael Finley Michael Jordan	5.00	2.20
❑ J7 Bobby Jackson Michael Jordan	2.00	.90
❑ J8 Grant Hill Michael Jordan	25.00	11.00
❑ J9 Jim Jackson Michael Jordan	2.00	.90
❑ J10 Charles Barkley Michael Jordan	8.00	3.60
❑ J11 Reggie Miller Michael Jordan	5.00	2.20
❑ J12 Lorenzen Wright Michael Jordan	2.00	.90
❑ J13 Kobe Bryant Michael Jordan	40.00	18.00
❑ J14 Tim Hardaway Michael Jordan	5.00	2.20
❑ J15 Glenn Robinson Michael Jordan	3.00	1.35
❑ J16 Kevin Garnett Michael Jordan	30.00	13.50
❑ J17 Keith Van Horn Michael Jordan	12.00	5.50
❑ J18 Patrick Ewing Michael Jordan	5.00	2.20
❑ J19 Anfernee Hardaway Michael Jordan	15.00	6.75
❑ J20 Allen Iverson Michael Jordan	20.00	9.00
❑ J21 Jason Kidd Michael Jordan	15.00	6.75
❑ J22 Damon Stoudamire Michael Jordan	5.00	2.20
❑ J23 Mitch Richmond Michael Jordan	5.00	2.20
❑ J24 Tim Duncan Michael Jordan	25.00	11.00
❑ J25 Gary Payton Michael Jordan	8.00	3.60

		MINT	NRMT
❑ J26	Chauncey Billups / Michael Jordan	2.00	.90
❑ J27	Karl Malone / Michael Jordan	8.00	3.60
❑ J28	Shareef Abdur-Rahim / Michael Jordan	12.00	5.50
❑ J29	Chris Webber / Michael Jordan	15.00	6.75
❑ J30	Michael Jordan / Michael Jordan	60.00	27.00

1998 Upper Deck Hardcourt Jordan Holding Court Silver

	MINT	NRMT
COMMON CARD (J1-J30)	60.00	27.00
SEMISTARS	100.00	45.00
UNLISTED STARS	150.00	70.00

RANDOM INSERTS IN PACKS
STATED PRINT RUN 23 SERIAL #'d SETS

		MINT	NRMT
❑ J1	Steve Smith / Michael Jordan	100.00	45.00
❑ J2	Antoine Walker / Michael Jordan	250.00	110.00
❑ J3	Glen Rice / Michael Jordan	100.00	45.00
❑ J4	Scottie Pippen / Michael Jordan	500.00	220.00
❑ J5	Shawn Kemp / Michael Jordan	250.00	110.00
❑ J6	Michael Finley / Michael Jordan	150.00	70.00
❑ J7	Bobby Jackson / Michael Jordan	60.00	27.00
❑ J8	Grant Hill / Michael Jordan	800.00	350.00
❑ J9	Jim Jackson / Michael Jordan	60.00	27.00
❑ J10	Charles Barkley / Michael Jordan	250.00	110.00
❑ J11	Reggie Miller / Michael Jordan	150.00	70.00
❑ J12	Lorenzen Wright / Michael Jordan	60.00	27.00
❑ J13	Kobe Bryant / Michael Jordan	1200.00	550.00
❑ J14	Tim Hardaway / Michael Jordan	150.00	70.00
❑ J15	Glenn Robinson / Michael Jordan	100.00	45.00
❑ J16	Kevin Garnett / Michael Jordan	1000.00	450.00
❑ J17	Keith Van Horn / Michael Jordan	400.00	180.00
❑ J18	Patrick Ewing / Michael Jordan	150.00	70.00
❑ J19	Anfernee Hardaway / Michael Jordan	500.00	220.00
❑ J20	Allen Iverson / Michael Jordan	600.00	275.00
❑ J21	Jason Kidd / Michael Jordan	500.00	220.00
❑ J22	Damon Stoudamire / Michael Jordan	150.00	70.00
❑ J23	Mitch Richmond / Michael Jordan	150.00	70.00
❑ J24	Tim Duncan / Michael Jordan	800.00	350.00
❑ J25	Gary Payton / Michael Jordan	250.00	110.00
❑ J26	Chauncey Billups / Michael Jordan	60.00	27.00
❑ J27	Karl Malone / Michael Jordan	250.00	110.00
❑ J28	Shareef Abdur-Rahim / Michael Jordan	400.00	180.00
❑ J29	Chris Webber / Michael Jordan	500.00	220.00
❑ J30	Michael Jordan / Michael Jordan	2500.00	1100.00

1999-00 Upper Deck Hardcourt

	MINT	NRMT
COMPLETE SET (90)	100.00	45.00
COMPLETE SET w/o RC (60)	25.00	11.00
COMMON CARD (1-60)	.25	.11
COMMON RC (61-90)	1.00	.45
SEMISTARS	.30	.14
SEMISTARS RC	1.25	.55
UNLISTED STARS	.50	.23
UNLISTED STARS RC	1.50	.70

RC SUBSET: STATED ODDS 1:4
GF1: PRINT RUN 50 SERIAL #'d CARDS
GF1: RANDOM INSERTS IN PACKS
GF6: PRINT RUN 100 SERIAL #'d SETS
GF6: RANDOM INSERTS IN PACKS
MJ FINAL FLOOR LISTED UNDER 99-00 UD

		MINT	NRMT
❑ 1	Dikembe Mutombo	.30	.14
❑ 2	Alan Henderson	.25	.11
❑ 3	Antoine Walker	.60	.25
❑ 4	Paul Pierce	1.00	.45
❑ 5	Eddie Jones	1.00	.45
❑ 6	Elden Campbell	.25	.11
❑ 7	Toni Kukoc	.60	.25
❑ 8	Randy Brown	.25	.11
❑ 9	Shawn Kemp	.75	.35
❑ 10	Brevin Knight	.25	.11
❑ 11	Michael Finley	.50	.23
❑ 12	Dirk Nowitzki	.75	.35
❑ 13	Antonio McDyess	.50	.23
❑ 14	Nick Van Exel	.30	.14
❑ 15	Grant Hill	2.50	1.10
❑ 16	Jerry Stackhouse	.30	.14
❑ 17	Antawn Jamison	1.00	.45
❑ 18	John Starks	.25	.11
❑ 19	Hakeem Olajuwon	.75	.35
❑ 20	Scottie Pippen	1.50	.70
❑ 21	Reggie Miller	.50	.23
❑ 22	Jalen Rose	.50	.23
❑ 23	Maurice Taylor	.50	.23
❑ 24	Michael Olowokandi	.30	.14
❑ 25	Shaquille O'Neal	2.50	1.10
❑ 26	Kobe Bryant	4.00	1.80
❑ 27	Tim Hardaway	.50	.23
❑ 28	Alonzo Mourning	.50	.23
❑ 29	Glenn Robinson	.30	.14
❑ 30	Ray Allen	.50	.23
❑ 31	Kevin Garnett	3.00	1.35
❑ 32	Terrell Brandon	.30	.14
❑ 33	Stephon Marbury	1.00	.45
❑ 34	Keith Van Horn	1.00	.45
❑ 35	Latrell Sprewell	1.00	.45
❑ 36	Allan Houston	.50	.23
❑ 37	Patrick Ewing	.50	.23
❑ 38	Darrell Armstrong	.30	.14
❑ 39	Charles Outlaw	.25	.11
❑ 40	Allen Iverson	2.00	.90
❑ 41	Larry Hughes	1.25	.55
❑ 42	Jason Kidd	1.50	.70
❑ 43	Tom Gugliotta	.30	.14
❑ 44	Brian Grant	.30	.14
❑ 45	Damon Stoudamire	.50	.23
❑ 46	Jason Williams	1.25	.55
❑ 47	Vlade Divac	.25	.11
❑ 48	Tim Duncan	2.50	1.10
❑ 49	David Robinson	.75	.35
❑ 50	Avery Johnson	.25	.11
❑ 51	Gary Payton	.75	.35
❑ 52	Vin Baker	.30	.14
❑ 53	Vince Carter	5.00	2.20
❑ 54	Tracy McGrady	1.50	.70
❑ 55	Karl Malone	.75	.35
❑ 56	John Stockton	.50	.23
❑ 57	Shareef Abdur-Rahim	1.00	.45
❑ 58	Mike Bibby	.60	.25
❑ 59	Juwan Howard	.30	.14
❑ 60	Mitch Richmond	.50	.23
❑ 61	Elton Brand RC	15.00	6.75
❑ 62	Jason Terry RC	2.50	1.10
❑ 63	Kenny Thomas RC	2.50	1.10
❑ 64	Jonathan Bender RC	8.00	3.60
❑ 65	Aleksandar Radojevic RC	1.00	.45
❑ 66	Galen Young RC	1.00	.45
❑ 67	Baron Davis RC	4.00	1.80
❑ 68	Corey Maggette RC	6.00	2.70
❑ 69	Dion Glover RC	1.50	.70
❑ 70	Scott Padgett RC	1.50	.70
❑ 71	Steve Francis RC	20.00	9.00
❑ 72	Richard Hamilton RC	4.00	1.80
❑ 73	James Posey RC	3.00	1.35
❑ 74	Jumaine Jones RC	1.25	.55
❑ 75	Chris Herren RC	1.00	.45
❑ 76	Andre Miller RC	5.00	2.20
❑ 77	Lamar Odom RC	12.00	5.50
❑ 78	Wally Szczerbiak RC	6.00	2.70
❑ 79	William Avery RC	2.50	1.10
❑ 80	Devean George RC	3.00	1.35
❑ 81	Trajan Langdon RC	2.50	1.10
❑ 82	Cal Bowdler RC	1.50	.70
❑ 83	Kris Clack RC	1.00	.45
❑ 84	Tim James RC	2.00	.90
❑ 85	Shawn Marion RC	5.00	2.20
❑ 86	Ryan Robertson RC	1.25	.55
❑ 87	Quincy Lewis RC	1.50	.70
❑ 88	Vonteego Cummings RC	2.50	1.10
❑ 89	Obinna Ekezie RC	1.25	.55
❑ 90	Jeff Foster RC	1.50	.70
❑ GF1	Michael Jordan Floor	1200.00	550.00
❑ GF6	Wilt Chamberlain Floor	200.00	90.00

1999-00 Upper Deck Hardcourt Baseline Grooves Rainbow

	MINT	NRMT
COMMON CARD (1-90)	2.50	1.10

*STARS: 4X TO 10X BASE CARD HI

*RCs: .75X TO 2X BASE HI
STATED PRINT RUN 500 SERIAL #'d SETS
RANDOM INSERTS IN PACKS

1999-00 Upper Deck Hardcourt Baseline Grooves Silver

	MINT	NRMT
COMMON CARD (1-60)	25.00	11.00
COMMON CARD (61-90)	20.00	9.00

*STARS: 40X TO 100X BASE CARD HI
*RCs: 6X TO 15X BASE HI
STATED PRINT RUN 50 SERIAL #'d SETS
RANDOM INSERTS IN PACKS

1999-00 Upper Deck Hardcourt Court Authority

	MINT	NRMT
COMPLETE SET (10)	150.00	70.00
COMMON CARD (A1-A10)	5.00	2.20

STATED ODDS 1:99

	MINT	NRMT
❑ A1 Tim Duncan	20.00	9.00
❑ A2 Vince Carter	40.00	18.00
❑ A3 Allen Iverson	15.00	6.75
❑ A4 Jason Williams	10.00	4.50
❑ A5 Kevin Garnett	25.00	11.00
❑ A6 Keith Van Horn	8.00	3.60
❑ A7 Jason Kidd	12.00	5.50
❑ A8 Grant Hill	20.00	9.00
❑ A9 Antoine Walker	5.00	2.20
❑ A10 Michael Jordan	50.00	22.00

1999-00 Upper Deck Hardcourt Court Forces

	MINT	NRMT
COMPLETE SET (10)	6.00	2.70
COMMON CARD (CF1-CF10)	.50	.23
UNLISTED STARS	.60	.25

STATED ODDS 1:8

	MINT	NRMT
❑ CF1 Shareef Abdur-Rahim	1.25	.55
❑ CF2 Scottie Pippen	2.00	.90
❑ CF3 Latrell Sprewell	1.25	.55
❑ CF4 Tim Hardaway	.60	.25
❑ CF5 Shaquille O'Neal	3.00	1.35
❑ CF6 Mike Bibby	.75	.35
❑ CF7 Allen Iverson	2.50	1.10
❑ CF8 John Stockton	.60	.25
❑ CF9 Michael Finley	.50	.23
❑ CF10 Reggie Miller	.60	.25

1999-00 Upper Deck Hardcourt Legends of the Hardcourt

	MINT	NRMT
COMPLETE SET (10)	40.00	18.00
COMMON CARD (L1-L10)	1.25	.55
UNLISTED STARS	1.50	.70

STATED ODDS 1:19

	MINT	NRMT
❑ L1 Michael Jordan	20.00	9.00
❑ L2 Elgin Baylor	1.50	.70
❑ L3 Kevin McHale	1.50	.70
❑ L4 Julius Erving	5.00	2.20
❑ L5 Larry Bird	12.00	5.50
❑ L6 George Gervin	1.50	.70
❑ L7 Bob Cousy	2.00	.90
❑ L8 John Havlicek	4.00	1.80
❑ L9 Jerry West	2.50	1.10
❑ L10 Walt Frazier	1.25	.55

1999-00 Upper Deck Hardcourt MJ Records Almanac

	MINT	NRMT
COMPLETE SET (10)	50.00	22.00
COMMON CARD (J1-J10)	6.00	2.70

STATED ODDS 1:19

	MINT	NRMT
❑ J1 Michael Jordan	6.00	2.70
❑ J2 Michael Jordan	6.00	2.70
❑ J3 Michael Jordan	6.00	2.70
❑ J4 Michael Jordan	6.00	2.70
❑ J5 Michael Jordan	6.00	2.70
❑ J6 Michael Jordan	6.00	2.70
❑ J7 Michael Jordan	6.00	2.70
❑ J8 Michael Jordan	6.00	2.70
❑ J9 Michael Jordan	6.00	2.70
❑ J10 Michael Jordan	6.00	2.70

1999-00 Upper Deck Hardcourt New Court Order

	MINT	NRMT
COMPLETE SET (20)	15.00	6.75
COMMON CARD (NC1-NC20)	.30	.14
UNLISTED STARS	.50	.23

STATED ODDS 1:3

	MINT	NRMT
❑ NC1 Vince Carter	5.00	2.20
❑ NC2 Allan Houston	.50	.23
❑ NC3 Paul Pierce	1.00	.45
❑ NC4 Eddie Jones	1.00	.45
❑ NC5 Antawn Jamison	1.00	.45
❑ NC6 Mike Bibby	.60	.25
❑ NC7 Tim Duncan	2.50	1.10
❑ NC8 Kobe Bryant	4.00	1.80
❑ NC9 Maurice Taylor	.50	.23
❑ NC10 Darrell Armstrong	.30	.14
❑ NC11 Stephon Marbury	1.00	.45
❑ NC12 Gary Payton	.75	.35
❑ NC13 Brian Grant	.30	.14
❑ NC14 Jason Williams	1.25	.55
❑ NC15 Shareef Abdur-Rahim	1.00	.45
❑ NC16 Damon Stoudamire	.50	.23
❑ NC17 Keith Van Horn	1.00	.45
❑ NC18 Tom Gugliotta	.30	.14
❑ NC19 Antonio McDyess	.50	.23
❑ NC20 Ray Allen	.50	.23

1999-00 Upper Deck Hardcourt Power in the Paint

	MINT	NRMT
COMPLETE SET (12)	4.00	1.80
COMMON CARD (P1-P12)	.30	.14
UNLISTED STARS	.50	.23

STATED ODDS 1:6

	MINT	NRMT
❑ P1 Antoine Walker	.60	.25
❑ P2 Karl Malone	.75	.35
❑ P3 Hakeem Olajuwon	.75	.35
❑ P4 David Robinson	.75	.35
❑ P5 Antonio McDyess	.50	.23
❑ P6 Shawn Kemp	.75	.35
❑ P7 Glenn Robinson	.30	.14

❑ P8 Juwan Howard	.30	.14
❑ P9 Patrick Ewing	.50	.23
❑ P10 Alonzo Mourning	.50	.23
❑ P11 Antawn Jamison	1.00	.45
❑ P12 Dikembe Mutombo	.30	.14

1999-00 Upper Deck HoloGrFX

	MINT	NRMT
COMPLETE SET (90)	60.00	27.00
COMPLETE SET w/o RC (60)	20.00	9.00
COMMON CARD (1-60)	.15	.07
COMMON RC (61-90)	.60	.25
SEMISTARS	.20	.09
SEMISTARS RC	.75	.35
UNLISTED STARS	.40	.18
UNLISTED STARS RC	1.00	.45

RC SUBSET STATED ODDS 1:2
MJ FINAL FLOOR LISTED UNDER 99-00 UD

❑ 1 Dikembe Mutombo	.20	.09
❑ 2 Alan Henderson	.15	.07
❑ 3 Antoine Walker	.50	.23
❑ 4 Paul Pierce	.75	.35
❑ 5 Eddie Jones	.75	.35
❑ 6 David Wesley	.15	.07
❑ 7 Dickey Simpkins	.15	.07
❑ 8 Toni Kukoc	.50	.23
❑ 9 Shawn Kemp	.60	.25
❑ 10 Zydrunas Ilgauskas	.15	.07
❑ 11 Michael Finley	.40	.18
❑ 12 Cedric Ceballos	.15	.07
❑ 13 Antonio McDyess	.40	.18
❑ 14 Nick Van Exel	.20	.09
❑ 15 Grant Hill	2.00	.90
❑ 16 Bison Dele	.15	.07
❑ 17 Jerry Stackhouse	.20	.09
❑ 18 Antawn Jamison	.75	.35
❑ 19 John Starks	.15	.07
❑ 20 Scottie Pippen	1.25	.55
❑ 21 Charles Barkley	.60	.25
❑ 22 Hakeem Olajuwon	.60	.25
❑ 23 Reggie Miller	.40	.18
❑ 24 Rik Smits	.15	.07
❑ 25 Michael Olowokandi	.20	.09
❑ 26 Maurice Taylor	.40	.18
❑ 27 Shaquille O'Neal	2.00	.90
❑ 28 Kobe Bryant	3.00	1.35
❑ 29 Tim Hardaway	.40	.18
❑ 30 Alonzo Mourning	.40	.18
❑ 31 Ray Allen	.40	.18
❑ 32 Glenn Robinson	.20	.09
❑ 33 Kevin Garnett	2.50	1.10
❑ 34 Terrell Brandon	.20	.09
❑ 35 Stephon Marbury	.75	.35
❑ 36 Keith Van Horn	.75	.35
❑ 37 Allan Houston	.40	.18
❑ 38 Latrell Sprewell	.75	.35
❑ 39 Charles Outlaw	.15	.07
❑ 40 Darrell Armstrong	.20	.09
❑ 41 Allen Iverson	1.50	.70
❑ 42 Larry Hughes	1.00	.45
❑ 43 Jason Kidd	1.25	.55
❑ 44 Tom Gugliotta	.20	.09
❑ 45 Damon Stoudamire	.40	.18
❑ 46 Rasheed Wallace	.40	.18
❑ 47 Jason Williams	1.00	.45
❑ 48 Chris Webber	1.25	.55
❑ 49 Tim Duncan	2.00	.90
❑ 50 David Robinson	.60	.25
❑ 51 Gary Payton	.60	.25
❑ 52 Vin Baker	.20	.09
❑ 53 Vince Carter	4.00	1.80
❑ 54 Tracy McGrady	1.25	.55
❑ 55 John Stockton	.40	.18
❑ 56 Karl Malone	.60	.25
❑ 57 Mike Bibby	.50	.23
❑ 58 Shareef Abdur-Rahim	.75	.35
❑ 59 Juwan Howard	.20	.09
❑ 60 Mitch Richmond	.40	.18
❑ 61 Elton Brand RC	10.00	4.50
❑ 62 Lamar Odom RC	8.00	3.60
❑ 63 Kenny Thomas RC	1.50	.70
❑ 64 Scott Padgett RC	1.00	.45
❑ 65 Trajan Langdon RC	1.50	.70
❑ 66 James Posey RC	2.00	.90
❑ 67 Shawn Marion RC	3.00	1.35
❑ 68 Chris Herren RC	.60	.25
❑ 69 Tim James RC	1.25	.55
❑ 70 Evan Eschmeyer RC	.60	.25
❑ 71 Corey Maggette RC	4.00	1.80
❑ 72 Richard Hamilton RC	2.50	1.10
❑ 73 Baron Davis RC	2.50	1.10
❑ 74 Galen Young RC	.60	.25
❑ 75 Dion Glover RC	1.00	.45
❑ 76 Jumaine Jones RC	.75	.35
❑ 77 Wally Szczerbiak RC	4.00	1.80
❑ 78 Andre Miller RC	3.00	1.35
❑ 79 Devean George RC	2.00	.90
❑ 80 Obinna Ekezie RC	.75	.35
❑ 81 Steve Francis RC	12.00	5.50
❑ 82 Jason Terry RC	1.50	.70
❑ 83 Quincy Lewis RC	1.00	.45
❑ 84 Ryan Robertson RC	.75	.35
❑ 85 William Avery RC	1.50	.70
❑ 86 Aleksandar Radojevic RC	.60	.25
❑ 87 Jonathan Bender RC	5.00	2.20
❑ 88 Cal Bowdler RC	1.00	.45
❑ 89 Vonteego Cummings RC	1.50	.70
❑ 90 Jeff Foster RC	1.00	.45

1999-00 Upper Deck HoloGrFX AUSome

	MINT	NRMT
COMPLETE SET (90)	150.00	70.00
COMMON CARD (1-60)	.60	.25
COMMON CARD (61-90)	1.25	.55

*STARS: 1.5X TO 4X HI COLUMN
*RCs: .75X TO 2X HI
STATED ODDS 1:12

1999-00 Upper Deck HoloGrFX HoloFame

	MINT	NRMT
COMPLETE SET (9)	50.00	22.00
COMMON CARD (HF1-HF9)	1.25	.55

STATED ODDS 1:17

COMP.GOLD SET (9)	300.00	135.00
COMMON GOLD (HF1-HF9)	6.00	2.70

*GOLD: 2X TO 5X HI COLUMN
GOLD: STATED ODDS 1:210

❑ HF1 Michael Jordan	15.00	6.75
❑ HF2 Julius Erving	4.00	1.80
❑ HF3 Larry Bird	10.00	4.50
❑ HF4 George Gervin	1.25	.55
❑ HF5 Tim Duncan	6.00	2.70
❑ HF6 Kevin Garnett	8.00	3.60
❑ HF7 Kobe Bryant	10.00	4.50
❑ HF8 Jason Williams	3.00	1.35
❑ HF9 Vince Carter	12.00	5.50

1999-00 Upper Deck HoloGrFX Maximum Jordan

	MINT	NRMT
COMPLETE SET (6)	25.00	11.00
COMMON CARD (MJ1-MJ6)	6.00	2.70

STATED ODDS 1:34

COMP.GOLD SET (6)	200.00	90.00
COMMON GOLD (MJ1-MJ6)	40.00	18.00

GOLD: STATED ODDS 1:431

❑ MJ1 Michael Jordan	6.00	2.70
❑ MJ2 Michael Jordan	6.00	2.70
❑ MJ3 Michael Jordan	6.00	2.70
❑ MJ4 Michael Jordan	6.00	2.70
❑ MJ5 Michael Jordan	6.00	2.70
❑ MJ6 Michael Jordan	6.00	2.70

1999-00 Upper Deck HoloGrFX NBA 24-7

	MINT	NRMT
COMPLETE SET (15)	15.00	6.75

	MINT	NRMT
COMMON CARD (N1-N15)	.40	.18
STATED ODDS 1:3		
COMP.GOLD SET (15)	100.00	45.00
COMMON GOLD (N1-N15)	2.50	1.10
*GOLD: 2.5X TO 6X HI COLUMN		
GOLD: STATED ODDS 1:105		

	MINT	NRMT
❑ N1 Tim Duncan	2.00	.90
❑ N2 Allen Iverson	1.50	.70
❑ N3 Vince Carter	4.00	1.80
❑ N4 Kevin Garnett	2.50	1.10
❑ N5 Shaquille O'Neal	2.00	.90
❑ N6 Shareef Abdur-Rahim	.75	.35
❑ N7 Jason Williams	1.00	.45
❑ N8 Kobe Bryant	3.00	1.35
❑ N9 Grant Hill	2.00	.90
❑ N10 Antoine Walker	.50	.23
❑ N11 Stephon Marbury	.75	.35
❑ N12 Antonio McDyess	.40	.18
❑ N13 Jason Kidd	1.25	.55
❑ N14 Keith Van Horn	.75	.35
❑ N15 Karl Malone	.60	.25

1999-00 Upper Deck HoloGrFX NBA Shoetime

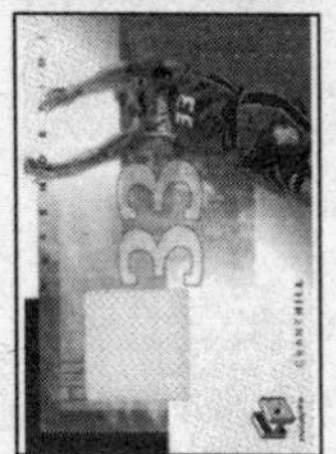

	MINT	NRMT
COMMON CARD	25.00	11.00
STATED ODDS 1:431		

	MINT	NRMT
❑ AI-S Allen Iverson	150.00	70.00
❑ BR-S Bryon Russell	25.00	11.00
❑ CB-S Charles Barkley	100.00	45.00
❑ CW-S Chris Webber	80.00	36.00
❑ DM-S Dikembe Mutombo	25.00	11.00
❑ DR-S David Robinson	80.00	36.00
❑ GH-S Grant Hill	100.00	45.00
❑ GP-S Gary Payton	100.00	45.00
❑ JK-S Jason Kidd	80.00	36.00
❑ JM-S Jamal Mashburn	25.00	11.00
❑ JS-S John Stockton	80.00	36.00
❑ KB-S Kobe Bryant	200.00	90.00
❑ KM-A Karl Malone Autographed to 32	600.00	275.00
❑ KM-S Karl Malone	50.00	22.00
❑ MJ-A Michael Jordan Autographed to 23	9000.00	4000.00
❑ MJ-S Michael Jordan	500.00	220.00
❑ PE-S Patrick Ewing	80.00	36.00
❑ SM-S Stephon Marbury	60.00	27.00
❑ SO-S Shaquille O'Neal	120.00	55.00
❑ SP-S Scottie Pippen	80.00	36.00
❑ TH-S Tim Hardaway	50.00	22.00

1999-00 Upper Deck HoloGrFX UD Authentics

	MINT	NRMT
COMMON CARD	8.00	3.60
SEMISTARS	12.00	5.50
STATED ODDS 1:431		

	MINT	NRMT
❑ AJ Antawn Jamison	30.00	13.50
❑ BD Baron Davis	20.00	9.00
❑ BG Brian Grant	15.00	6.75
❑ CM Corey Maggette	25.00	11.00
❑ DA Darrell Armstrong	12.00	5.50

	MINT	NRMT
❑ JO Michael Jordan	3500.00	1600.00
❑ JS Jerry Stackhouse	20.00	9.00
❑ JT Jason Terry	15.00	6.75
❑ LH Larry Hughes	40.00	18.00
❑ MB Mike Bibby	25.00	11.00
❑ MF Michael Finley	30.00	13.50
❑ MK Mark Jackson	12.00	5.50
❑ MT Maurice Taylor	12.00	5.50
❑ RD Richard Hamilton	20.00	9.00
❑ RH Wally Szczerbiak	50.00	22.00
❑ RL Raef LaFrentz	20.00	9.00
❑ RT Robert Traylor	8.00	3.60
❑ SF Steve Francis	100.00	45.00
❑ SM Sam Mack	8.00	3.60
❑ TG Tom Gugliotta	12.00	5.50
❑ SHM Shawn Marion	25.00	11.00

1999-00 Upper Deck MVP

	MINT	NRMT
COMPLETE SET (220)	40.00	18.00
COMMON CARD (1-178)	.10	.05
COMMON MJ (179-208)	1.50	.70
COMMON RC (209-218)	.60	.25
SEMISTARS	.15	.07
UNLISTED STARS	.25	.11

	MINT	NRMT
❑ 1 Dikembe Mutombo	.15	.07
❑ 2 Steve Smith	.15	.07
❑ 3 Mookie Blaylock	.10	.05
❑ 4 Alan Henderson	.10	.05
❑ 5 LaPhonso Ellis	.10	.05
❑ 6 Grant Long	.10	.05
❑ 7 Kenny Anderson	.15	.07
❑ 8 Antoine Walker	.30	.14
❑ 9 Ron Mercer	.30	.14
❑ 10 Paul Pierce	.50	.23
❑ 11 Vitaly Potapenko	.10	.05
❑ 12 Dana Barros	.10	.05
❑ 13 Elden Campbell	.10	.05
❑ 14 Eddie Jones	.50	.23
❑ 15 David Wesley	.10	.05
❑ 16 Bobby Phills	.10	.05
❑ 17 Derrick Coleman	.15	.07
❑ 18 Ricky Davis	.25	.11
❑ 19 Toni Kukoc	.30	.14
❑ 20 Brent Barry	.10	.05
❑ 21 Ron Harper	.15	.07
❑ 22 Kornel David RC	.10	.05
❑ 23 Mark Bryant	.10	.05
❑ 24 Dickey Simpkins	.10	.05
❑ 25 Shawn Kemp	.40	.18
❑ 26 Derek Anderson	.25	.11
❑ 27 Brevin Knight	.10	.05
❑ 28 Andrew DeClercq	.10	.05
❑ 29 Zydrunas Ilgauskas	.10	.05
❑ 30 Cedric Henderson	.10	.05
❑ 31 Shawn Bradley	.10	.05
❑ 32 A.C. Green	.15	.07
❑ 33 Gary Trent	.10	.05
❑ 34 Michael Finley	.25	.11
❑ 35 Dirk Nowitzki	.40	.18
❑ 36 Steve Nash	.10	.05
❑ 37 Antonio McDyess	.25	.11
❑ 38 Nick Van Exel	.15	.07
❑ 39 Chauncey Billups	.10	.05
❑ 40 Danny Fortson	.10	.05
❑ 41 Eric Washington	.10	.05
❑ 42 Raef LaFrentz	.25	.11
❑ 43 Grant Hill	1.25	.55
❑ 44 Bison Dele	.10	.05
❑ 45 Lindsey Hunter	.10	.05
❑ 46 Jerry Stackhouse	.15	.07
❑ 47 Don Reid	.10	.05
❑ 48 Christian Laettner	.15	.07
❑ 49 John Starks	.10	.05
❑ 50 Antawn Jamison	.50	.23
❑ 51 Erick Dampier	.10	.05
❑ 52 Donyell Marshall	.10	.05
❑ 53 Chris Mills	.10	.05
❑ 54 Bimbo Coles	.10	.05
❑ 55 Charles Barkley	.40	.18
❑ 56 Hakeem Olajuwon	.40	.18
❑ 57 Scottie Pippen	.75	.35
❑ 58 Othella Harrington	.10	.05
❑ 59 Bryce Drew	.10	.05
❑ 60 Michael Dickerson	.25	.11
❑ 61 Rik Smits	.10	.05
❑ 62 Reggie Miller	.25	.11
❑ 63 Mark Jackson	.10	.05
❑ 64 Antonio Davis	.10	.05
❑ 65 Jalen Rose	.25	.11
❑ 66 Dale Davis	.10	.05
❑ 67 Chris Mullin	.25	.11
❑ 68 Maurice Taylor	.25	.11
❑ 69 Lamond Murray	.10	.05
❑ 70 Rodney Rogers	.10	.05
❑ 71 Darrick Martin	.10	.05
❑ 72 Michael Olowokandi	.15	.07
❑ 73 Tyrone Nesby RC	.10	.05
❑ 74 Kobe Bryant	2.00	.90
❑ 75 Shaquille O'Neal	1.25	.55
❑ 76 Robert Horry	.10	.05
❑ 77 Glen Rice	.15	.07
❑ 78 J.R. Reid	.10	.05
❑ 79 Rick Fox	.10	.05
❑ 80 Derek Fisher	.15	.07
❑ 81 Tim Hardaway	.25	.11
❑ 82 Alonzo Mourning	.25	.11
❑ 83 Jamal Mashburn	.15	.07
❑ 84 P.J. Brown	.10	.05
❑ 85 Terry Porter	.10	.05
❑ 86 Dan Majerle	.15	.07
❑ 87 Ray Allen	.25	.11
❑ 88 Vinny Del Negro	.10	.05
❑ 89 Glenn Robinson	.15	.07
❑ 90 Dell Curry	.10	.05
❑ 91 Sam Cassell	.15	.07
❑ 92 Robert Traylor	.10	.05
❑ 93 Kevin Garnett	1.50	.70
❑ 94 Terrell Brandon	.15	.07
❑ 95 Joe Smith	.15	.07
❑ 96 Sam Mitchell	.10	.05
❑ 97 Anthony Peeler	.10	.05
❑ 98 Bobby Jackson	.10	.05
❑ 99 Keith Van Horn	.50	.23
❑ 100 Stephon Marbury	.50	.23
❑ 101 Jayson Williams	.15	.07
❑ 102 Kendall Gill	.15	.07
❑ 103 Kerry Kittles	.15	.07
❑ 104 Scott Burrell	.10	.05
❑ 105 Patrick Ewing	.25	.11
❑ 106 Allan Houston	.25	.11
❑ 107 Latrell Sprewell	.50	.23
❑ 108 Larry Johnson	.15	.07

☐ 109 Marcus Camby .25 .11
☐ 110 Charlie Ward .10 .05
☐ 111 Anfernee Hardaway .75 .35
☐ 112 Darrell Armstrong .15 .07
☐ 113 Nick Anderson .10 .05
☐ 114 Horace Grant .15 .07
☐ 115 Isaac Austin .10 .05
☐ 116 Matt Harpring .10 .05
☐ 117 Michael Doleac .10 .05
☐ 118 Allen Iverson 1.00 .45
☐ 119 Theo Ratliff .10 .05
☐ 120 Matt Geiger .10 .05
☐ 121 Larry Hughes .60 .25
☐ 122 Tyrone Hill .10 .05
☐ 123 George Lynch .10 .05
☐ 124 Jason Kidd .75 .35
☐ 125 Tom Gugliotta .15 .07
☐ 126 Rex Chapman .10 .05
☐ 127 Clifford Robinson .10 .05
☐ 128 Luc Longley .10 .05
☐ 129 Danny Manning .15 .07
☐ 130 Rasheed Wallace .25 .11
☐ 131 Arvydas Sabonis .15 .07
☐ 132 Damon Stoudamire .25 .11
☐ 133 Brian Grant .15 .07
☐ 134 Isaiah Rider .15 .07
☐ 135 Walt Williams .10 .05
☐ 136 Jim Jackson .10 .05
☐ 137 Jason Williams .60 .25
☐ 138 Vlade Divac .10 .05
☐ 139 Chris Webber .75 .35
☐ 140 Corliss Williamson .10 .05
☐ 141 Predrag Stojakovic .15 .07
☐ 142 Tariq Abdul-Wahad .10 .05
☐ 143 Tim Duncan 1.25 .55
☐ 144 Sean Elliott .10 .05
☐ 145 David Robinson .40 .18
☐ 146 Mario Elie .10 .05
☐ 147 Avery Johnson .10 .05
☐ 148 Steve Kerr .10 .05
☐ 149 Gary Payton .40 .18
☐ 150 Vin Baker .15 .07
☐ 151 Detlef Schrempf .15 .07
☐ 152 Hersey Hawkins .15 .07
☐ 153 Dale Ellis .10 .05
☐ 154 Olden Polynice .10 .05
☐ 155 Vince Carter 2.50 1.10
☐ 156 John Wallace .10 .05
☐ 157 Doug Christie .10 .05
☐ 158 Tracy McGrady .75 .35
☐ 159 Kevin Willis .10 .05
☐ 160 Charles Oakley .10 .05
☐ 161 Karl Malone .40 .18
☐ 162 John Stockton .25 .11
☐ 163 Jeff Hornacek .15 .07
☐ 164 Bryon Russell .10 .05
☐ 165 Howard Eisley .10 .05
☐ 166 Shandon Anderson .10 .05
☐ 167 Shareef Abdur-Rahim .50 .23
☐ 168 Mike Bibby .30 .14
☐ 169 Bryant Reeves .10 .05
☐ 170 Felipe Lopez .10 .05
☐ 171 Cherokee Parks .10 .05
☐ 172 Michael Smith .10 .05
☐ 173 Juwan Howard .15 .07
☐ 174 Rod Strickland .15 .07
☐ 175 Mitch Richmond .25 .11
☐ 176 Otis Thorpe .10 .05
☐ 177 Calbert Cheaney .10 .05
☐ 178 Tracy Murray .10 .05
☐ 179 Michael Jordan 1.50 .70
☐ 180 Michael Jordan 1.50 .70
☐ 181 Michael Jordan 1.50 .70
☐ 182 Michael Jordan 1.50 .70
☐ 183 Michael Jordan 1.50 .70
☐ 184 Michael Jordan 1.50 .70
☐ 185 Michael Jordan 1.50 .70
☐ 186 Michael Jordan 1.50 .70
☐ 187 Michael Jordan 1.50 .70
☐ 188 Michael Jordan 1.50 .70
☐ 189 Michael Jordan 1.50 .70
☐ 190 Michael Jordan 1.50 .70
☐ 191 Michael Jordan 1.50 .70
☐ 192 Michael Jordan 1.50 .70
☐ 193 Michael Jordan 1.50 .70
☐ 194 Michael Jordan 1.50 .70
☐ 195 Michael Jordan 1.50 .70
☐ 196 Michael Jordan 1.50 .70
☐ 197 Michael Jordan 1.50 .70
☐ 198 Michael Jordan 1.50 .70
☐ 199 Michael Jordan 1.50 .70
☐ 200 Michael Jordan 1.50 .70
☐ 201 Michael Jordan 1.50 .70
☐ 202 Michael Jordan 1.50 .70
☐ 203 Michael Jordan 1.50 .70
☐ 204 Michael Jordan 1.50 .70
☐ 205 Michael Jordan 1.50 .70
☐ 206 Michael Jordan 1.50 .70
☐ 207 Michael Jordan 1.50 .70
☐ 208 Michael Jordan 1.50 .70
☐ 209 Elton Brand RC 4.00 1.80
☐ 210 Steve Francis RC 5.00 2.20
☐ 211 Baron Davis RC 1.00 .45
☐ 212 Wally Szczerbiak RC 1.50 .70
☐ 213 Richard Hamilton RC 1.00 .45
☐ 214 Andre Miller RC 1.25 .55
☐ 215 Jason Terry RC .60 .25
☐ 216 Corey Maggette RC 1.50 .70
☐ 217 Shawn Marion RC 1.25 .55
☐ 218 Lamar Odom RC 3.00 1.35
☐ 219 Michael Jordan Checklist 1.00 .45
☐ 220 Michael Jordan Checklist 1.00 .45

1999-00 Upper Deck MVP Silver Script

	MINT	NRMT
COMPLETE SET (220)	200.00	90.00
COMMON CARD (1-220)	.40	.18
COMMON MJ (179-208)	5.00	2.20

*STARS: 1.5X TO 4X BASE CARD HI
*RCs: .75X TO 2X BASE HI
STATED ODDS 1:2 HOB/RET

1999-00 Upper Deck MVP Gold Script

	MINT	NRMT
COMMON CARD (1-220)	6.00	2.70
COMMON MJ (179-208)	50.00	22.00

*STARS: 25X TO 60X BASE CARD HI
*RCs: 12.5X TO 30X BASE HI
STATED PRINT RUN 100 SERIAL #'d SETS
RANDOM INSERTS IN HOBBY PACKS

1999-00 Upper Deck MVP Super Script

	MINT	NRMT
COMMON CARD (1-220)	20.00	9.00
COMMON MJ (179-208)	120.00	55.00
SEMISTARS	30.00	13.50
UNLISTED STARS	50.00	22.00

STATED PRINT RUN 25 SERIAL #'d SETS
RANDOM INSERTS IN HOBBY PACKS

☐ 1 Dikembe Mutombo 30.00 13.50
☐ 2 Steve Smith 30.00 13.50
☐ 3 Mookie Blaylock 20.00 9.00
☐ 4 Alan Henderson 20.00 9.00
☐ 5 LaPhonso Ellis 20.00 9.00
☐ 6 Grant Long 20.00 9.00
☐ 7 Kenny Anderson 30.00 13.50
☐ 8 Antoine Walker 60.00 27.00
☐ 9 Ron Mercer 60.00 27.00
☐ 10 Paul Pierce 100.00 45.00
☐ 11 Vitaly Potapenko 20.00 9.00
☐ 12 Dana Barros 20.00 9.00
☐ 13 Elden Campbell 20.00 9.00
☐ 14 Eddie Jones 100.00 45.00
☐ 15 David Wesley 20.00 9.00
☐ 16 Bobby Phills 20.00 9.00
☐ 17 Derrick Coleman 30.00 13.50
☐ 18 Ricky Davis 50.00 22.00
☐ 19 Toni Kukoc 80.00 36.00
☐ 20 Brent Barry 20.00 9.00
☐ 21 Ron Harper 30.00 13.50
☐ 22 Kornel David 20.00 9.00
☐ 23 Mark Bryant 20.00 9.00
☐ 24 Dickey Simpkins 20.00 9.00
☐ 25 Shawn Kemp 80.00 36.00
☐ 26 Derek Anderson 50.00 22.00
☐ 27 Brevin Knight 20.00 9.00
☐ 28 Andrew DeClercq 20.00 9.00
☐ 29 Zydrunas Ilgauskas 20.00 9.00
☐ 30 Cedric Henderson 20.00 9.00
☐ 31 Shawn Bradley 20.00 9.00
☐ 32 A.C. Green 30.00 13.50
☐ 33 Gary Trent 20.00 9.00
☐ 34 Michael Finley 50.00 22.00
☐ 35 Dirk Nowitzki 80.00 36.00
☐ 36 Steve Nash 20.00 9.00
☐ 37 Antonio McDyess 50.00 22.00
☐ 38 Nick Van Exel 30.00 13.50
☐ 39 Chauncey Billups 20.00 9.00
☐ 40 Danny Fortson 20.00 9.00
☐ 41 Eric Washington 20.00 9.00
☐ 42 Raef LaFrentz 50.00 22.00
☐ 43 Grant Hill 250.00 110.00
☐ 44 Bison Dele 20.00 9.00
☐ 45 Lindsey Hunter 20.00 9.00
☐ 46 Jerry Stackhouse 30.00 13.50
☐ 47 Don Reid 20.00 9.00
☐ 48 Christian Laettner 30.00 13.50
☐ 49 John Starks 20.00 9.00
☐ 50 Antawn Jamison 100.00 45.00
☐ 51 Erick Dampier 20.00 9.00
☐ 52 Donyell Marshall 20.00 9.00
☐ 53 Chris Mills 20.00 9.00
☐ 54 Bimbo Coles 20.00 9.00
☐ 55 Charles Barkley 80.00 36.00
☐ 56 Hakeem Olajuwon 80.00 36.00
☐ 57 Scottie Pippen 150.00 70.00

		MINT	NRMT
❑ 58	Othella Harrington	20.00	9.00
❑ 59	Bryce Drew	20.00	9.00
❑ 60	Michael Dickerson	50.00	22.00
❑ 61	Rik Smits	20.00	9.00
❑ 62	Reggie Miller	50.00	22.00
❑ 63	Mark Jackson	20.00	9.00
❑ 64	Antonio Davis	20.00	9.00
❑ 65	Jalen Rose	50.00	22.00
❑ 66	Dale Davis	20.00	9.00
❑ 67	Chris Mullin	50.00	22.00
❑ 68	Maurice Taylor	50.00	22.00
❑ 69	Lamond Murray	20.00	9.00
❑ 70	Rodney Rogers	20.00	9.00
❑ 71	Darrick Martin	20.00	9.00
❑ 72	Michael Olowokandi	30.00	13.50
❑ 73	Tyrone Nesby	20.00	9.00
❑ 74	Kobe Bryant	400.00	180.00
❑ 75	Shaquille O'Neal	250.00	110.00
❑ 76	Robert Horry	20.00	9.00
❑ 77	Glen Rice	30.00	13.50
❑ 78	J.R. Reid	20.00	9.00
❑ 79	Rick Fox	20.00	9.00
❑ 80	Derek Fisher	30.00	13.50
❑ 81	Tim Hardaway	50.00	22.00
❑ 82	Alonzo Mourning	50.00	22.00
❑ 83	Jamal Mashburn	30.00	13.50
❑ 84	P.J. Brown	20.00	9.00
❑ 85	Terry Porter	20.00	9.00
❑ 86	Dan Majerle	30.00	13.50
❑ 87	Ray Allen	50.00	22.00
❑ 88	Vinny Del Negro	20.00	9.00
❑ 89	Glenn Robinson	30.00	13.50
❑ 90	Dell Curry	20.00	9.00
❑ 91	Sam Cassell	30.00	13.50
❑ 92	Robert Traylor	20.00	9.00
❑ 93	Kevin Garnett	300.00	135.00
❑ 94	Terrell Brandon	30.00	13.50
❑ 95	Joe Smith	30.00	13.50
❑ 96	Sam Mitchell	20.00	9.00
❑ 97	Anthony Peeler	20.00	9.00
❑ 98	Bobby Jackson	20.00	9.00
❑ 99	Keith Van Horn	100.00	45.00
❑ 100	Stephon Marbury	100.00	45.00
❑ 101	Jayson Williams	30.00	13.50
❑ 102	Kendall Gill	30.00	13.50
❑ 103	Kerry Kittles	30.00	13.50
❑ 104	Scott Burrell	20.00	9.00
❑ 105	Patrick Ewing	50.00	22.00
❑ 106	Allan Houston	50.00	22.00
❑ 107	Latrell Sprewell	100.00	45.00
❑ 108	Larry Johnson	30.00	13.50
❑ 109	Marcus Camby	50.00	22.00
❑ 110	Charlie Ward	20.00	9.00
❑ 111	Anfernee Hardaway	150.00	70.00
❑ 112	Darrell Armstrong	30.00	13.50
❑ 113	Nick Anderson	20.00	9.00
❑ 114	Horace Grant	30.00	13.50
❑ 115	Isaac Austin	20.00	9.00
❑ 116	Matt Harpring	20.00	9.00
❑ 117	Michael Doleac	20.00	9.00
❑ 118	Allen Iverson	200.00	90.00
❑ 119	Theo Ratliff	20.00	9.00
❑ 120	Matt Geiger	20.00	9.00
❑ 121	Larry Hughes	120.00	55.00
❑ 122	Tyrone Hill	20.00	9.00
❑ 123	George Lynch	20.00	9.00
❑ 124	Jason Kidd	150.00	70.00
❑ 125	Tom Gugliotta	30.00	13.50
❑ 126	Rex Chapman	20.00	9.00
❑ 127	Clifford Robinson	20.00	9.00
❑ 128	Luc Longley	20.00	9.00
❑ 129	Danny Manning	30.00	13.50
❑ 130	Rasheed Wallace	50.00	22.00
❑ 131	Arvydas Sabonis	30.00	13.50
❑ 132	Damon Stoudamire	50.00	22.00
❑ 133	Brian Grant	30.00	13.50
❑ 134	Isaiah Rider	30.00	13.50
❑ 135	Walt Williams	20.00	9.00
❑ 136	Jim Jackson	20.00	9.00
❑ 137	Jason Williams	120.00	55.00
❑ 138	Vlade Divac	20.00	9.00
❑ 139	Chris Webber	150.00	70.00
❑ 140	Corliss Williamson	20.00	9.00
❑ 141	Predrag Stojakovic	30.00	13.50
❑ 142	Tariq Abdul-Wahad	20.00	9.00
❑ 143	Tim Duncan	250.00	110.00
❑ 144	Sean Elliott	20.00	9.00
❑ 145	David Robinson	80.00	36.00
❑ 146	Mario Elie	20.00	9.00
❑ 147	Avery Johnson	20.00	9.00
❑ 148	Steve Kerr	20.00	9.00
❑ 149	Gary Payton	80.00	36.00
❑ 150	Vin Baker	30.00	13.50
❑ 151	Detlef Schrempf	30.00	13.50
❑ 152	Hersey Hawkins	30.00	13.50
❑ 153	Dale Ellis	20.00	9.00
❑ 154	Olden Polynice	20.00	9.00
❑ 155	Vince Carter	500.00	220.00
❑ 156	John Wallace	20.00	9.00
❑ 157	Doug Christie	20.00	9.00
❑ 158	Tracy McGrady	150.00	70.00
❑ 159	Kevin Willis	20.00	9.00
❑ 160	Charles Oakley	20.00	9.00
❑ 161	Karl Malone	80.00	36.00
❑ 162	John Stockton	50.00	22.00
❑ 163	Jeff Hornacek	30.00	13.50
❑ 164	Bryon Russell	20.00	9.00
❑ 165	Howard Eisley	20.00	9.00
❑ 166	Shandon Anderson	20.00	9.00
❑ 167	Shareef Abdur-Rahim	100.00	45.00
❑ 168	Mike Bibby	60.00	27.00
❑ 169	Bryant Reeves	20.00	9.00
❑ 170	Felipe Lopez	20.00	9.00
❑ 171	Cherokee Parks	20.00	9.00
❑ 172	Michael Smith	20.00	9.00
❑ 173	Juwan Howard	30.00	13.50
❑ 174	Rod Strickland	30.00	13.50
❑ 175	Mitch Richmond	50.00	22.00
❑ 176	Otis Thorpe	20.00	9.00
❑ 177	Calbert Cheaney	20.00	9.00
❑ 178	Tracy Murray	20.00	9.00
❑ 179	Michael Jordan	120.00	55.00
❑ 180	Michael Jordan	120.00	55.00
❑ 181	Michael Jordan	120.00	55.00
❑ 182	Michael Jordan	120.00	55.00
❑ 183	Michael Jordan	120.00	55.00
❑ 184	Michael Jordan	120.00	55.00
❑ 185	Michael Jordan	120.00	55.00
❑ 186	Michael Jordan	120.00	55.00
❑ 187	Michael Jordan	120.00	55.00
❑ 188	Michael Jordan	120.00	55.00
❑ 189	Michael Jordan	120.00	55.00
❑ 190	Michael Jordan	120.00	55.00
❑ 191	Michael Jordan	120.00	55.00
❑ 192	Michael Jordan	120.00	55.00
❑ 193	Michael Jordan	120.00	55.00
❑ 194	Michael Jordan	120.00	55.00
❑ 195	Michael Jordan	120.00	55.00
❑ 196	Michael Jordan	120.00	55.00
❑ 197	Michael Jordan	120.00	55.00
❑ 198	Michael Jordan	120.00	55.00
❑ 199	Michael Jordan	120.00	55.00
❑ 200	Michael Jordan	120.00	55.00
❑ 201	Michael Jordan	120.00	55.00
❑ 202	Michael Jordan	120.00	55.00
❑ 203	Michael Jordan	120.00	55.00
❑ 204	Michael Jordan	120.00	55.00
❑ 205	Michael Jordan	120.00	55.00
❑ 206	Michael Jordan	120.00	55.00
❑ 207	Michael Jordan	120.00	55.00
❑ 208	Michael Jordan	120.00	55.00
❑ 209	Elton Brand	250.00	110.00
❑ 210	Steve Francis	300.00	135.00
❑ 211	Baron Davis	60.00	27.00
❑ 212	Wally Szczerbiak	100.00	45.00
❑ 213	Richard Hamilton	60.00	27.00
❑ 214	Andre Miller	80.00	36.00
❑ 215	Jason Terry	50.00	22.00
❑ 216	Corey Maggette	100.00	45.00
❑ 217	Shawn Marion	80.00	36.00
❑ 218	Lamar Odom	200.00	90.00
❑ 219	Michael Jordan CL	120.00	55.00
❑ 220	Michael Jordan CL	120.00	55.00

1999-00 Upper Deck MVP 21st Century NBA

	MINT	NRMT
COMPLETE SET (10)	12.00	5.50
COMMON CARD (N1-N10)	.75	.35
STATED ODDS 1:13 HOB/RET		

		MINT	NRMT
❑ N1	Jason Williams	1.50	.70
❑ N2	Paul Pierce	1.25	.55
❑ N3	Antoine Walker	.75	.35
❑ N4	Keith Van Horn	1.25	.55
❑ N5	Allen Iverson	2.50	1.10
❑ N6	Antawn Jamison	1.25	.55
❑ N7	Kobe Bryant	5.00	2.20
❑ N8	Shareef Abdur-Rahim	1.25	.55
❑ N9	Stephon Marbury	1.25	.55
❑ N10	Grant Hill	3.00	1.35

1999-00 Upper Deck MVP Dynamics

	MINT	NRMT
COMPLETE SET (6)	25.00	11.00
COMMON CARD (D1-D6)	2.00	.90
STATED ODDS 1:27 HOB/RET		

		MINT	NRMT
❑ D1	Michael Jordan	12.00	5.50
❑ D2	Kobe Bryant	8.00	3.60
❑ D3	Grant Hill	5.00	2.20
❑ D4	Shareef Abdur-Rahim	2.00	.90
❑ D5	Kevin Garnett	6.00	2.70
❑ D6	Vince Carter	10.00	4.50

1999-00 Upper Deck MVP Electrifying

	MINT	NRMT
COMPLETE SET (15)	10.00	4.50

COMMON CARD (E1-E15)	.40	.18
UNLISTED STARS	.60	.25
STATED ODDS 1:9 HOB/RET		

❑ E1 Shaquille O'Neal	3.00	1.35
❑ E2 Steve Smith	.40	.18
❑ E3 Toni Kukoc	.75	.35
❑ E4 Ron Mercer	.75	.35
❑ E5 Damon Stoudamire	.60	.25
❑ E6 Tim Hardaway	.60	.25
❑ E7 Paul Pierce	1.25	.55
❑ E8 Jason Kidd	2.00	.90
❑ E9 Stephon Marbury	1.25	.55
❑ E10 Terrell Brandon	.40	.18
❑ E11 Reggie Miller	.60	.25
❑ E12 Ray Allen	.60	.25
❑ E13 Maurice Taylor	.60	.25
❑ E14 Chris Webber	2.00	.90
❑ E15 Charles Barkley	1.00	.45

1999-00 Upper Deck MVP Game-Used Souvenirs

	MINT	NRMT
COMPLETE SET (15)	400.00	180.00
COMMON CARD	12.00	5.50
SEMISTARS	15.00	6.75
STATED ODDS 1:131 HOBBY		
AU CARDS NOT INCLUDED IN SET PRICE		
AH-A NOT PRICED DUE TO SCARCITY		

❑ AH-A Anfernee Hardaway AU/1		
❑ AH-S Anfernee Hardaway	40.00	18.00
❑ AJ-S Antawn Jamison	25.00	11.00
❑ AM-S Antonio McDyess	15.00	6.75
❑ GP-S Gary Payton	25.00	11.00
❑ JK-S Jason Kidd	40.00	18.00
❑ JW-S Jason Williams	40.00	18.00
❑ KB-S Kobe Bryant	80.00	36.00
❑ KG-S Kevin Garnett	50.00	22.00
❑ KM-A Karl Malone AU/32	600.00	275.00
❑ KM-S Karl Malone	30.00	13.50
❑ MB-S Mike Bibby	15.00	6.75
❑ MF-S Michael Finley	15.00	6.75
❑ MO-S Michael Olowokandi	12.00	5.50
❑ SO-S Shaquille O'Neal	60.00	27.00
❑ SP-S Scottie Pippen	40.00	18.00
❑ TD-S Tim Duncan	60.00	27.00

1999-00 Upper Deck MVP Jam Time

	MINT	NRMT
COMPLETE SET (14)	10.00	4.50
COMMON CARD (JT1-JT14)	.25	.11
UNLISTED STARS	.40	.18
STATED ODDS 1:6 HOB/RET		

❑ JT1 Michael Jordan	5.00	2.20
❑ JT2 Alonzo Mourning	.40	.18
❑ JT3 Shawn Kemp	.60	.25
❑ JT4 Juwan Howard	.25	.11
❑ JT5 Chris Webber	1.25	.55
❑ JT6 Tim Duncan	2.00	.90
❑ JT7 Keith Van Horn	.75	.35
❑ JT8 Eddie Jones	.75	.35
❑ JT9 Michael Finley	.40	.18
❑ JT10 Anfernee Hardaway	1.25	.55
❑ JT11 Antonio McDyess	.40	.18
❑ JT12 Charles Barkley	.60	.25
❑ JT13 Latrell Sprewell	.75	.35
❑ JT14 Hakeem Olajuwon	.60	.25

1999-00 Upper Deck MVP Jordan MVP Moments

	MINT	NRMT
COMPLETE SET (14)	100.00	45.00
COMMON CARD (MJ1-MJ14)	8.00	3.60
STATED ODDS 1:27 HOB/RET		

❑ MJ1 Michael Jordan	8.00	3.60
❑ MJ2 Michael Jordan	8.00	3.60
❑ MJ3 Michael Jordan	8.00	3.60
❑ MJ4 Michael Jordan	8.00	3.60
❑ MJ5 Michael Jordan	8.00	3.60
❑ MJ6 Michael Jordan	8.00	3.60
❑ MJ7 Michael Jordan	8.00	3.60
❑ MJ8 Michael Jordan	8.00	3.60
❑ MJ9 Michael Jordan	8.00	3.60
❑ MJ10 Michael Jordan	8.00	3.60
❑ MJ11 Michael Jordan	8.00	3.60
❑ MJ12 Michael Jordan	8.00	3.60
❑ MJ13 Michael Jordan	8.00	3.60
❑ MJ14 Michael Jordan	8.00	3.60

1999-00 Upper Deck MVP MVP Theatre

	MINT	NRMT
COMPLETE SET (15)	12.00	5.50
COMMON CARD (M1-M15)	.40	.18
UNLISTED STARS	.60	.25
STATED ODDS 1:9 HOB/RET		

❑ M1 Karl Malone	1.00	.45
❑ M2 Tom Gugliotta	.40	.18
❑ M3 Shaquille O'Neal	3.00	1.35
❑ M4 Mitch Richmond	.60	.25
❑ M5 David Robinson	1.00	.45
❑ M6 Gary Payton	1.00	.45
❑ M7 Allen Iverson	2.50	1.10
❑ M8 Glenn Robinson	.40	.18
❑ M9 Antoine Walker	.75	.35
❑ M10 Hakeem Olajuwon	1.00	.45
❑ M11 Patrick Ewing	.60	.25
❑ M12 Antonio McDyess	.60	.25
❑ M13 Tim Hardaway	.60	.25
❑ M14 Scottie Pippen	2.00	.90
❑ M15 Anfernee Hardaway	2.00	.90

1999-00 Upper Deck MVP ProSign

	MINT	NRMT
COMMON CARD	6.00	2.70
SEMISTARS	10.00	4.50
STATED ODDS 1:144 RETAIL		

❑ CH Charlie Ward	12.00	5.50
❑ CW Clarence Weatherspoon	6.00	2.70
❑ DA Darrell Armstrong	15.00	6.75
❑ DF Derek Fisher	15.00	6.75
❑ IA Isaac Austin	6.00	2.70
❑ JJ Jim Jackson	10.00	4.50
❑ JK Jaren Jackson	10.00	4.50
❑ JR Jalen Rose	25.00	11.00
❑ MD Michael Dickerson	15.00	6.75
❑ MJ Michael Jordan	6000.00	2700.00
❑ NV Nick Van Exel	15.00	6.75
❑ RT Robert Traylor	12.00	5.50
❑ SA Stacey Augmon	6.00	2.70
❑ TC Terry Cummings	6.00	2.70
❑ TR Theo Ratliff	6.00	2.70
❑ VC Vince Carter	300.00	135.00

1998-99 Upper Deck Ovation

	MINT	NRMT
COMPLETE SET (80)	125.00	55.00
COMPLETE SET w/o RC (70)	40.00	18.00
COMMON CARD (1-80)	.25	.11
COMMON RC	2.50	1.10
SEMISTARS	.40	.18
UNLISTED STARS	.60	.25
JORDAN BASKETBALL CARD NUMBERED TO 90		
RCs AVAILABLE VIA TRADE		

❑ 1 Steve Smith	.40	.18
❑ 2 Dikembe Mutombo	.40	.18
❑ 3 Antoine Walker	1.00	.45

Card	MINT	NRMT
❑ 4 Ron Mercer	1.00	.45
❑ 5 Glen Rice	.40	.18
❑ 6 Bobby Phills	.25	.11
❑ 7 Michael Jordan	8.00	3.60
❑ 8 Toni Kukoc	.75	.35
❑ 9 Dennis Rodman	1.25	.55
❑ 10 Scottie Pippen	2.00	.90
❑ 11 Shawn Kemp	1.00	.45
❑ 12 Derek Anderson	.75	.35
❑ 13 Brevin Knight	.25	.11
❑ 14 Michael Finley	.60	.25
❑ 15 Shawn Bradley	.25	.11
❑ 16 LaPhonso Ellis	.25	.11
❑ 17 Bobby Jackson	.25	.11
❑ 18 Grant Hill	3.00	1.35
❑ 19 Jerry Stackhouse	.40	.18
❑ 20 Donyell Marshall	.25	.11
❑ 21 Erick Dampier	.25	.11
❑ 22 Hakeem Olajuwon	1.00	.45
❑ 23 Charles Barkley	1.00	.45
❑ 24 Reggie Miller	.60	.25
❑ 25 Chris Mullin	.60	.25
❑ 26 Rik Smits	.25	.11
❑ 27 Maurice Taylor	.60	.25
❑ 28 Lorenzen Wright	.25	.11
❑ 29 Kobe Bryant	5.00	2.20
❑ 30 Eddie Jones	1.25	.55
❑ 31 Shaquille O'Neal	3.00	1.35
❑ 32 Alonzo Mourning	.60	.25
❑ 33 Tim Hardaway	.60	.25
❑ 34 Jamal Mashburn	.40	.18
❑ 35 Ray Allen	.75	.35
❑ 36 Terrell Brandon	.40	.18
❑ 37 Glenn Robinson	.40	.18
❑ 38 Kevin Garnett	4.00	1.80
❑ 39 Tom Gugliotta	.40	.18
❑ 40 Stephon Marbury	1.50	.70
❑ 41 Keith Van Horn	1.50	.70
❑ 42 Kerry Kittles	.40	.18
❑ 43 Jayson Williams	.40	.18
❑ 44 Patrick Ewing	.60	.25
❑ 45 Allan Houston	.60	.25
❑ 46 Larry Johnson	.40	.18
❑ 47 Anfernee Hardaway	2.00	.90
❑ 48 Nick Anderson	.25	.11
❑ 49 Allen Iverson	2.50	1.10
❑ 50 Joe Smith	.40	.18
❑ 51 Tim Thomas	1.00	.45
❑ 52 Jason Kidd	2.00	.90
❑ 53 Antonio McDyess	.60	.25
❑ 54 Damon Stoudamire	.60	.25
❑ 55 Isaiah Rider	.40	.18
❑ 56 Rasheed Wallace	.60	.25
❑ 57 Tariq Abdul-Wahad	.25	.11
❑ 58 Corliss Williamson	.25	.11
❑ 59 Tim Duncan	3.00	1.35
❑ 60 David Robinson	1.00	.45
❑ 61 Vin Baker	.40	.18
❑ 62 Gary Payton	1.00	.45
❑ 63 Chauncey Billups	.25	.11
❑ 64 Tracy McGrady	2.50	1.10
❑ 65 Karl Malone	1.00	.45
❑ 66 John Stockton	.60	.25
❑ 67 Shareef Abdur-Rahim	1.50	.70
❑ 68 Bryant Reeves	.25	.11
❑ 69 Juwan Howard	.40	.18
❑ 70 Rod Strickland	.40	.18
❑ 71 Michael Olowokandi RC	4.00	1.80
❑ 72 Mike Bibby RC	8.00	3.60
❑ 73 Raef LaFrentz RC	5.00	2.20
❑ 74 Antawn Jamison RC	12.00	5.50
❑ 75 Vince Carter RC	100.00	45.00
❑ 76 Robert Traylor RC	2.50	1.10
❑ 77 Jason Williams RC	15.00	6.75
❑ 78 Larry Hughes RC	15.00	6.75
❑ 79 Dirk Nowitzki RC	10.00	4.50
❑ 80 Paul Pierce RC	12.00	5.50
❑ BK1 Michael Jordan Game Used Basketball Card Serial #'d to 90	2000.00	900.00

1998-99 Upper Deck Ovation Gold

	MINT	NRMT
COMMON CARD (1-70)	2.00	.90
COMMON RC (71-80)	4.00	1.80

*STARS: 3X TO 8X BASE CARD HI
*RCs: 1.25X TO 3X BASE HI
STATED PRINT RUN 1000 SERIAL #'d SETS
RANDOM INSERTS IN PACKS

1998-99 Upper Deck Ovation Future Forces

	MINT	NRMT
COMPLETE SET (20)	100.00	45.00
COMMON CARD (F1-F20)	2.00	.90
UNLISTED STARS	3.00	1.35

STATED ODDS 1:29

Card	MINT	NRMT
❑ F1 Tim Duncan	15.00	6.75
❑ F2 Keith Van Horn	8.00	3.60
❑ F3 Kobe Bryant	25.00	11.00
❑ F4 Tracy McGrady	12.00	5.50
❑ F5 Maurice Taylor	3.00	1.35
❑ F6 Shareef Abdur-Rahim	8.00	3.60
❑ F7 Kevin Garnett	20.00	9.00
❑ F8 Brevin Knight	2.00	.90
❑ F9 Ron Mercer	5.00	2.20
❑ F10 Tim Thomas	5.00	2.20
❑ F11 Antoine Walker	5.00	2.20
❑ F12 Michael Finley	3.00	1.35
❑ F13 Grant Hill	15.00	6.75
❑ F14 Jerry Stackhouse	2.00	.90
❑ F15 Erick Dampier	2.00	.90
❑ F16 Lorenzen Wright	2.00	.90
❑ F17 Ray Allen	4.00	1.80
❑ F18 Stephon Marbury	8.00	3.60
❑ F19 Allen Iverson	12.00	5.50
❑ F20 Damon Stoudamire	3.00	1.35

1998-99 Upper Deck Ovation Jordan Rules

	MINT	NRMT
COMPLETE SET (15)	400.00	180.00
COMMON CARD (J1-J5)	15.00	6.75
COMMON CARD (J6-J10)	25.00	11.00
COMMON CARD (J11-J15)	50.00	22.00

J1-J5 STATED ODDS 1:23
J6-J10 STATED ODDS 1:45
J11-J15 STATED ODDS 1:99

Card	MINT	NRMT
❑ J1 Michael Jordan	15.00	6.75
❑ J2 Michael Jordan	15.00	6.75
❑ J3 Michael Jordan	15.00	6.75
❑ J4 Michael Jordan	15.00	6.75
❑ J5 Michael Jordan	15.00	6.75
❑ J6 Michael Jordan	25.00	11.00
❑ J7 Michael Jordan	25.00	11.00
❑ J8 Michael Jordan	25.00	11.00
❑ J9 Michael Jordan	25.00	11.00
❑ J10 Michael Jordan	25.00	11.00
❑ J11 Michael Jordan	50.00	22.00
❑ J12 Michael Jordan	50.00	22.00
❑ J13 Michael Jordan	50.00	22.00
❑ J14 Michael Jordan	50.00	22.00
❑ J15 Michael Jordan	50.00	22.00

1998-99 Upper Deck Ovation Superstars of the Court

	MINT	NRMT
COMPLETE SET (20)	40.00	18.00
COMMON CARD (S1-S20)	1.00	.45

STATED ODDS 1:2

Card	MINT	NRMT
❑ C1 Michael Jordan	12.00	5.50
❑ C2 Tim Duncan	5.00	2.20
❑ C3 Grant Hill	5.00	2.20
❑ C4 Karl Malone	1.50	.70
❑ C5 Dennis Rodman	2.00	.90
❑ C6 Hakeem Olajuwon	1.50	.70
❑ C7 Keith Van Horn	2.50	1.10
❑ C8 Kobe Bryant	8.00	3.60
❑ C9 Jason Kidd	3.00	1.35

Card	Player	MINT	NRMT
❏ C10	Stephon Marbury	2.50	1.10
❏ C11	Reggie Miller	1.00	.45
❏ C12	Damon Stoudamire	1.00	.45
❏ C13	Tracy McGrady	4.00	1.80
❏ C14	Scottie Pippen	3.00	1.35
❏ C15	Vin Baker	1.00	.45
❏ C16	Shaquille O'Neal	5.00	2.20
❏ C17	Anfernee Hardaway	3.00	1.35
❏ C18	Charles Barkley	1.50	.70
❏ C19	Kevin Garnett	6.00	2.70
❏ C20	Antoine Walker	1.50	.70

1999-00 Upper Deck Ovation

	MINT	NRMT
COMPLETE SET (90)	120.00	55.00
COMPLETE SET w/o RC (60)	25.00	11.00
COMMON CARD (1-60)	.25	.11
COMMON RC (61-90)	1.25	.55
SEMISTARS	.30	.14
SEMISTARS RC	1.50	.70
UNLISTED STARS	.50	.23
UNLISTED STARS RC	2.00	.90

RC SUBSET: STATED ODDS 1:4
MJ FINAL FLOOR LISTED UNDER 99-00 UD

Card	Player	MINT	NRMT
❏ 1	Dikembe Mutombo	.30	.14
❏ 2	Alan Henderson	.25	.11
❏ 3	Antoine Walker	.60	.25
❏ 4	Paul Pierce	1.00	.45
❏ 5	David Wesley	.25	.11
❏ 6	Eddie Jones	1.00	.45
❏ 7	Toni Kukoc	.60	.25
❏ 8	Randy Brown	.25	.11
❏ 9	Shawn Kemp	.75	.35
❏ 10	Zydrunas Ilgauskas	.25	.11
❏ 11	Michael Finley	.50	.23
❏ 12	Dirk Nowitzki	.75	.35
❏ 13	Nick Van Exel	.30	.14
❏ 14	Antonio McDyess	.50	.23
❏ 15	Grant Hill	2.50	1.10
❏ 16	Jerry Stackhouse	.30	.14
❏ 17	Antawn Jamison	1.00	.45
❏ 18	John Starks	.25	.11
❏ 19	Hakeem Olajuwon	.75	.35
❏ 20	Charles Barkley	.75	.35
❏ 21	Cuttino Mobley	.50	.23
❏ 22	Reggie Miller	.50	.23
❏ 23	Rik Smits	.25	.11
❏ 24	Maurice Taylor	.50	.23
❏ 25	Michael Olowokandi	.30	.14
❏ 26	Kobe Bryant	4.00	1.80
❏ 27	Shaquille O'Neal	2.50	1.10
❏ 28	Tim Hardaway	.50	.23
❏ 29	Alonzo Mourning	.50	.23
❏ 30	Glenn Robinson	.30	.14
❏ 31	Ray Allen	.50	.23
❏ 32	Kevin Garnett	3.00	1.35
❏ 33	Joe Smith	.30	.14
❏ 34	Stephon Marbury	1.00	.45
❏ 35	Keith Van Horn	1.00	.45
❏ 36	Patrick Ewing	.50	.23
❏ 37	Latrell Sprewell	1.00	.45
❏ 38	Darrell Armstrong	.30	.14
❏ 39	Charles Outlaw	.25	.11
❏ 40	Allen Iverson	2.00	.90
❏ 41	Larry Hughes	1.25	.55
❏ 42	Jason Kidd	1.50	.70
❏ 43	Anfernee Hardaway	1.50	.70
❏ 44	Brian Grant	.30	.14
❏ 45	Damon Stoudamire	.50	.23
❏ 46	Jason Williams	1.25	.55
❏ 47	Chris Webber	1.50	.70
❏ 48	Tim Duncan	2.50	1.10
❏ 49	David Robinson	.75	.35
❏ 50	Sean Elliott	.25	.11
❏ 51	Gary Payton	.75	.35
❏ 52	Vin Baker	.30	.14
❏ 53	Vince Carter	5.00	2.20
❏ 54	Tracy McGrady	1.50	.70
❏ 55	Karl Malone	.75	.35
❏ 56	John Stockton	.50	.23
❏ 57	Shareef Abdur-Rahim	1.00	.45
❏ 58	Mike Bibby	.60	.25
❏ 59	Juwan Howard	.30	.14
❏ 60	Mitch Richmond	.50	.23
❏ 61	Elton Brand RC	20.00	9.00
❏ 62	Steve Francis RC	25.00	11.00
❏ 63	Baron Davis RC	5.00	2.20
❏ 64	Lamar Odom RC	15.00	6.75
❏ 65	Jonathan Bender RC	10.00	4.50
❏ 66	Wally Szczerbiak RC	8.00	3.60
❏ 67	Richard Hamilton RC	5.00	2.20
❏ 68	Andre Miller RC	6.00	2.70
❏ 69	Shawn Marion RC	6.00	2.70
❏ 70	Jason Terry RC	3.00	1.35
❏ 71	Trajan Langdon RC	3.00	1.35
❏ 72	Aleksandar Radojevic RC	1.25	.55
❏ 73	Corey Maggette RC	8.00	3.60
❏ 74	William Avery RC	3.00	1.35
❏ 75	Galen Young RC	1.25	.55
❏ 76	Chris Herren RC	1.25	.55
❏ 77	Cal Bowdler RC	2.00	.90
❏ 78	James Posey RC	4.00	1.80
❏ 79	Quincy Lewis RC	2.00	.90
❏ 80	Dion Glover RC	2.00	.90
❏ 81	Jeff Foster RC	2.00	.90
❏ 82	Kenny Thomas RC	3.00	1.35
❏ 83	Devean George RC	4.00	1.80
❏ 84	Tim James RC	2.50	1.10
❏ 85	Vonteego Cummings RC	3.00	1.35
❏ 86	Jumaine Jones RC	1.50	.70
❏ 87	Scott Padgett RC	2.50	1.10
❏ 88	Obinna Ekezie RC	1.50	.70
❏ 89	Ryan Robertson RC	1.50	.70
❏ 90	Evan Eschmeyer RC	1.25	.55
❏ MJ-S	M.J Jordan AU/23	7000.00	3200.00

1999-00 Upper Deck Ovation Standing Ovation

	MINT	NRMT
COMMON CARD (1-60)	20.00	9.00
COMMON RC (61-90)	15.00	6.75

*STARS: 30X TO 80X BASE CARD HI
*RCs: 4X TO 10X BASE HI
STATED PRINT RUN 50 SERIAL #'d SETS
RANDOM INSERTS IN PACKS

1999-00 Upper Deck Ovation A Piece of History

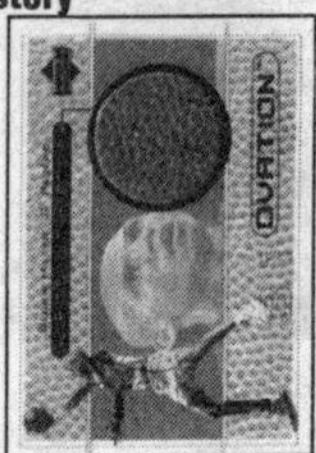

	MINT	NRMT
COMMON CARD	25.00	11.00

STATED ODDS 1:352
STATED PRINT RUN 4560 TOTAL CARDS

Card	Player	MINT	NRMT
❏ AM	Andre Miller	40.00	18.00
❏ BD	Baron Davis	30.00	13.50
❏ HO	Hakeem Olajuwon	50.00	22.00
❏ JB	Jonathan Bender	40.00	18.00
❏ JS	John Stockton	50.00	22.00
❏ JW	Jason Williams	40.00	18.00
❏ KB	Kobe Bryant	120.00	55.00
❏ KG	Kevin Garnett	60.00	27.00
❏ KM	Karl Malone	30.00	13.50
❏ RH	Richard Hamilton	25.00	11.00
❏ RM	Reggie Miller	50.00	22.00
❏ SF	Steve Francis	100.00	45.00
❏ SM	Shawn Marion	40.00	18.00
❏ WS	Wally Szczerbiak	50.00	22.00

1999-00 Upper Deck Ovation A Piece of History Autographs

	MINT	NRMT
COMMON CARD	250.00	110.00

PRINT RUN TO PLAYER'S JERSEY #
RANDOM INSERTS IN PACKS

Card	Player	MINT	NRMT
❏ KG-A	Kevin Garnett/21	1000.00	450.00
❏ KM-A	Karl Malone/32	600.00	275.00
❏ RH-A	Richard Hamilton/32	250.00	110.00
❏ SF-A	Steve Francis/3		
❏ SM-A	Shawn Marion/31	250.00	110.00
❏ WS-A	Wally Szczerbiak/10		

1999-00 Upper Deck Ovation Curtain Calls

	MINT	NRMT
COMPLETE SET (10)	8.00	3.60
COMMON CARD (CC1-CC10)	.60	.25

STATED ODDS 1:9

Card	Player	MINT	NRMT
❏ CC1	Hakeem Olajuwon	1.00	.45

	MINT	NRMT
❑ CC2 Karl Malone	1.00	.45
❑ CC3 Latrell Sprewell	1.25	.55
❑ CC4 Allen Iverson	2.50	1.10
❑ CC5 Tim Hardaway	.60	.25
❑ CC6 Shaquille O'Neal	3.00	1.35
❑ CC7 Jason Kidd	2.00	.90
❑ CC8 Charles Barkley	1.00	.45
❑ CC9 Antonio McDyess	.60	.25
❑ CC10 Gary Payton	1.00	.45

1999-00 Upper Deck Ovation Lead Performers

	MINT	NRMT
COMPLETE SET (10)	15.00	6.75
COMMON CARD (LP1-LP10)	.75	.35
STATED ODDS 1:9		

	MINT	NRMT
❑ LP1 Tim Duncan	3.00	1.35
❑ LP2 Kevin Garnett	4.00	1.80
❑ LP3 Keith Van Horn	1.25	.55
❑ LP4 Shareef Abdur-Rahim	1.25	.55
❑ LP5 Antoine Walker	.75	.35
❑ LP6 Shaquille O'Neal	3.00	1.35
❑ LP7 Grant Hill	3.00	1.35
❑ LP8 Kobe Bryant	5.00	2.20
❑ LP9 Allen Iverson	2.50	1.10
❑ LP10 Jason Williams	1.50	.70

1999-00 Upper Deck Ovation MJ Center Stage

	MINT	NRMT
COMPLETE SET (15)	150.00	70.00
COMMON CARD (CS1-CS5)	5.00	2.20
COMMON CARD (CS6-CS10)	10.00	4.50
COMMON CARD (CS11-CS15)	20.00	9.00
CS1-CS5: STATED ODDS 1:9		
CS6-CS10: STATED ODDS 1:39		
CS11-CS15: STATED ODDS 1:99		

	MINT	NRMT
❑ CS1 Michael Jordan	5.00	2.20
❑ CS2 Michael Jordan	5.00	2.20
❑ CS3 Michael Jordan	5.00	2.20
❑ CS4 Michael Jordan	5.00	2.20
❑ CS5 Michael Jordan	5.00	2.20
❑ CS6 Michael Jordan	10.00	4.50
❑ CS7 Michael Jordan	10.00	4.50
❑ CS8 Michael Jordan	10.00	4.50
❑ CS9 Michael Jordan	10.00	4.50
❑ CS10 Michael Jordan	10.00	4.50
❑ CS11 Michael Jordan	20.00	9.00
❑ CS12 Michael Jordan	20.00	9.00
❑ CS13 Michael Jordan	20.00	9.00
❑ CS14 Michael Jordan	20.00	9.00
❑ CS15 Michael Jordan	20.00	9.00

1999-00 Upper Deck Ovation Premiere Performers

	MINT	NRMT
COMPLETE SET (10)	25.00	11.00
COMMON CARD (PP1-PP10)	1.00	.45
STATED ODDS 1:19		

	MINT	NRMT
❑ PP1 Elton Brand	6.00	2.70
❑ PP2 Steve Francis	8.00	3.60
❑ PP3 Baron Davis	1.50	.70
❑ PP4 Lamar Odom	5.00	2.20
❑ PP5 Jonathan Bender	3.00	1.35
❑ PP6 Wally Szczerbiak	2.50	1.10
❑ PP7 Richard Hamilton	1.50	.70
❑ PP8 Andre Miller	2.00	.90
❑ PP9 Shawn Marion	2.00	.90
❑ PP10 Jason Terry	1.00	.45

1999-00 Upper Deck Ovation Spotlight

	MINT	NRMT
COMPLETE SET (10)	12.00	5.50
COMMON CARD (OS1-OS10)	.75	.35
STATED ODDS 1:3		

	MINT	NRMT
❑ OS1 Kevin Garnett	2.50	1.10
❑ OS2 Antawn Jamison	.75	.35
❑ OS3 Kobe Bryant	3.00	1.35
❑ OS4 Shareef Abdur-Rahim	.75	.35
❑ OS5 Keith Van Horn	.75	.35
❑ OS6 Vince Carter	4.00	1.80
❑ OS7 Stephon Marbury	.75	.35
❑ OS8 Paul Pierce	.75	.35
❑ OS9 Tim Duncan	2.00	.90
❑ OS10 Jason Williams	1.00	.45

1999-00 Upper Deck Ovation Superstar Theatre

	MINT	NRMT
COMPLETE SET (20)	80.00	36.00
COMMON CARD (ST1-ST20)	1.50	.70
STATED ODDS 1:19		

	MINT	NRMT
❑ ST1 Michael Jordan	20.00	9.00
❑ ST2 Vince Carter	15.00	6.75
❑ ST3 Kevin Garnett	10.00	4.50
❑ ST4 Paul Pierce	3.00	1.35
❑ ST5 Jason Williams	4.00	1.80
❑ ST6 Tim Duncan	8.00	3.60
❑ ST7 Allen Iverson	6.00	2.70
❑ ST8 Antawn Jamison	3.00	1.35
❑ ST9 Kobe Bryant	12.00	5.50
❑ ST10 Grant Hill	8.00	3.60
❑ ST11 Antoine Walker	2.00	.90
❑ ST12 Tracy McGrady	5.00	2.20
❑ ST13 Shareef Abdur-Rahim	3.00	1.35
❑ ST14 Stephon Marbury	3.00	1.35
❑ ST15 Jason Kidd	5.00	2.20
❑ ST16 Shaquille O'Neal	8.00	3.60
❑ ST17 Tim Hardaway	1.50	.70
❑ ST18 Keith Van Horn	3.00	1.35
❑ ST19 Gary Payton	2.50	1.10
❑ ST20 Karl Malone	2.50	1.10

1999-00 Upper Deck Retro

	MINT	NRMT
COMPLETE SET (110)	40.00	18.00
COMMON CARD (1-95)	.10	.05
COMMON RC (96-110)	.50	.23
SEMISTARS	.15	.07
UNLISTED STARS	.30	.14
UNPRICED PLATINUM SERIAL #'d TO 1		

	MINT	NRMT
❑ 1 Michael Jordan	4.00	1.80
❑ 2 John Havlicek	.75	.35
❑ 3 Antawn Jamison	.60	.25
❑ 4 Chris Webber	1.00	.45
❑ 5 Maurice Taylor	.30	.14
❑ 6 Kevin Garnett	2.00	.90
❑ 7 Walter Davis	.10	.05

❑ 8 Kobe Bryant 2.50 1.10
❑ 9 Tim Duncan 1.50 .70
❑ 10 Karl Malone .50 .23
❑ 11 Larry Bird 2.00 .90
❑ 12 Juwan Howard .15 .07
❑ 13 Bill Walton .30 .14
❑ 14 Bob Cousy .40 .18
❑ 15 Dave DeBusschere .10 .05
❑ 16 Toni Kukoc .40 .18
❑ 17 Allan Houston .30 .14
❑ 18 Grant Hill 1.50 .70
❑ 19 Rik Smits .10 .05
❑ 20 Glenn Robinson .15 .07
❑ 21 Dave Cowens .15 .07
❑ 22 Isaac Austin .10 .05
❑ 23 Derek Anderson .30 .14
❑ 24 Tracy McGrady 1.00 .45
❑ 25 Nate Thurmond .10 .05
❑ 26 Dikembe Mutombo .15 .07
❑ 27 Oscar Robertson .75 .35
❑ 28 Antonio McDyess .30 .14
❑ 29 Jamaal Wilkes .10 .05
❑ 30 Eddie Jones .60 .25
❑ 31 Nick Van Exel .15 .07
❑ 32 Reggie Miller .30 .14
❑ 33 David Thompson .10 .05
❑ 34 Ray Allen .30 .14
❑ 35 Anfernee Hardaway 1.00 .45
❑ 36 Brian Grant .15 .07
❑ 37 Allen Iverson 1.25 .55
❑ 38 Vince Carter 3.00 1.35
❑ 39 Mitch Richmond .30 .14
❑ 40 Kareem Abdul-Jabbar 1.00 .45
❑ 41 Alonzo Mourning .30 .14
❑ 42 Jonathan Bender RC 2.50 1.10
❑ 43 Scottie Pippen 1.00 .45
❑ 44 George Gervin .30 .14
❑ 45 Shawn Kemp .50 .23
❑ 46 Dave Bing .10 .05
❑ 47 John Starks .10 .05
❑ 48 Earl Monroe .30 .14
❑ 49 Stephon Marbury .60 .25
❑ 50 Cedric Maxwell .10 .05
❑ 51 Tom Gugliotta .15 .07
❑ 52 David Robinson .50 .23
❑ 53 Shareef Abdur-Rahim .60 .25
❑ 54 Elvin Hayes .15 .07
❑ 55 Wilt Chamberlain 1.00 .45
❑ 56 Willis Reed .15 .07
❑ 57 Kevin McHale .30 .14
❑ 58 Elden Campbell .10 .05
❑ 59 Steve Smith .15 .07
❑ 60 Brent Barry .10 .05
❑ 61 Jerry Stackhouse .15 .07
❑ 62 Otis Birdsong .10 .05
❑ 63 Michael Olowokandi .15 .07
❑ 64 Joe Smith .15 .07
❑ 65 Tim Thomas .40 .18
❑ 66 Rick Barry .15 .07
❑ 67 Jason Williams .75 .35
❑ 68 Julius Erving 1.00 .45
❑ 69 John Stockton .30 .14
❑ 70 Cal Bowdler RC .30 .14
❑ 71 Nate Archibald .30 .14
❑ 72 Elgin Baylor .40 .18
❑ 73 Ron Mercer .40 .18
❑ 74 Damon Stoudamire .30 .14
❑ 75 Jerry West .50 .23
❑ 76 Michael Finley .30 .14
❑ 77 Charles Barkley .50 .23
❑ 78 Shaquille O'Neal 1.50 .70
❑ 79 Paul Pierce .60 .25
❑ 80 Keith Van Horn .60 .25
❑ 81 Jason Kidd 1.00 .45
❑ 82 Gary Payton .50 .23
❑ 83 James Worthy .30 .14
❑ 84 Mike Bibby .40 .18
❑ 85 Bill Russell 1.00 .45
❑ 86 Wes Unseld .10 .05
❑ 87 Robert Parish .30 .14
❑ 88 Walt Frazier .30 .14
❑ 89 Antoine Walker .40 .18
❑ 90 Steve Nash .10 .05
❑ 91 Moses Malone .30 .14
❑ 92 Hakeem Olajuwon .50 .23
❑ 93 Tim Hardaway .30 .14
❑ 94 Patrick Ewing .30 .14
❑ 95 Vin Baker .15 .07
❑ 96 Trajan Langdon RC .75 .35
❑ 97 Ron Artest RC 1.25 .55
❑ 98 James Posey RC 1.00 .45
❑ 99 Shawn Marion RC 1.50 .70
❑ 100 Jumaine Jones RC .50 .23
❑ 101 William Avery RC .75 .35
❑ 102 Corey Maggette RC 2.00 .90
❑ 103 Andre Miller RC 1.50 .70
❑ 104 Jason Terry RC .75 .35
❑ 105 Wally Szczerbiak RC 2.00 .90
❑ 106 Richard Hamilton RC 1.25 .55
❑ 107 Elton Brand RC 5.00 2.20
❑ 108 Baron Davis RC 1.25 .55
❑ 109 Steve Francis RC 6.00 2.70
❑ 110 Lamar Odom RC 4.00 1.80

1999-00 Upper Deck Retro Gold

	MINT	NRMT
COMMON CARD (1-110)	2.00	.90

*STARS: 8X TO 20X BASE CARD HI
*RCs: 4X TO 10X BASE HI
STATED PRINT RUN 250 SERIAL #'d SETS
RANDOM INSERTS IN PACKS

1999-00 Upper Deck Retro Distant Replay

	MINT	NRMT
COMPLETE SET (10)	25.00	11.00
COMMON CARD (D1-D10)	1.00	.45

STATED ODDS 1:11

COMP.PARALLEL SET (10)	150.00	70.00
COMMON PARALLEL (D1-10)	6.00	2.70

*PARALLEL: 2.5X TO 6X HI COLUMN
PARALLEL: PRINT RUN 100 SERIAL #'d SETS
PARALLEL: RANDOM INSERTS IN PACKS

❑ D1 Michael Jordan 12.00 5.50
❑ D2 Kareem Abdul-Jabbar 3.00 1.35
❑ D3 Bill Russell 3.00 1.35
❑ D4 Julius Erving 3.00 1.35
❑ D5 George Gervin 1.00 .45
❑ D6 Moses Malone 1.00 .45
❑ D7 Larry Bird 12.00 5.50
❑ D8 Jerry West 1.50 .70
❑ D9 Oscar Robertson 2.50 1.10
❑ D10 Elgin Baylor 1.00 .45

1999-00 Upper Deck Retro Epic Jordan

	MINT	NRMT
COMPLETE SET (10)	60.00	27.00
COMMON CARD (J1-J10)	8.00	3.60

STATED ODDS 1:23

COMP.PARALLEL SET (10)	900.00	400.00
COMMON PARALLEL (J1-10)	100.00	45.00

PARALLEL: PRINT RUN 50 SERIAL #'d SETS
PARALLEL: RANDOM INSERTS IN PACKS

❑ J1 Michael Jordan 8.00 3.60
❑ J2 Michael Jordan 8.00 3.60
❑ J3 Michael Jordan 8.00 3.60
❑ J4 Michael Jordan 8.00 3.60
❑ J5 Michael Jordan 8.00 3.60
❑ J6 Michael Jordan 8.00 3.60
❑ J7 Michael Jordan 8.00 3.60
❑ J8 Michael Jordan 8.00 3.60
❑ J9 Michael Jordan 8.00 3.60
❑ J10 Michael Jordan 8.00 3.60

1999-00 Upper Deck Retro Fast Forward

	MINT	NRMT
COMPLETE SET (15)	50.00	22.00
COMMON CARD (F1-F15)	1.25	.55

STATED ODDS 1:23

❑ F1 Kevin Garnett	8.00	3.60
❑ F2 Kobe Bryant	10.00	4.50
❑ F3 Keith Van Horn	2.50	1.10
❑ F4 Allen Iverson	5.00	2.20
❑ F5 Vince Carter	12.00	5.50
❑ F6 Paul Pierce	2.50	1.10
❑ F7 Shareef Abdur-Rahim	2.50	1.10
❑ F8 Jason Williams	3.00	1.35
❑ F9 Tim Duncan	6.00	2.70
❑ F10 Shaquille O'Neal	6.00	2.70
❑ F11 Scottie Pippen	4.00	1.80
❑ F12 Anfernee Hardaway	4.00	1.80
❑ F13 Antawn Jamison	2.50	1.10
❑ F14 Antonio McDyess	1.25	.55
❑ F15 Stephon Marbury	2.50	1.10

1999-00 Upper Deck Retro Inkredible

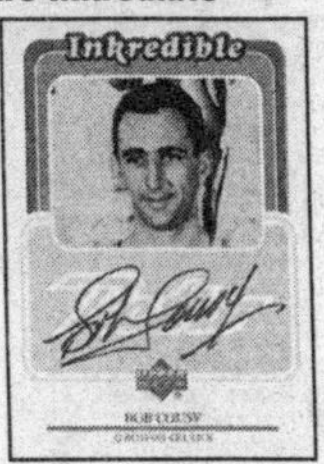

	MINT	NRMT
COMMON CARD	8.00	3.60
SEMISTARS	15.00	6.75

STATED ODDS 1:23

❑ AH Anfernee Hardaway	100.00	45.00
❑ AJ Antawn Jamison	30.00	13.50
❑ BC Bob Cousy	30.00	13.50
❑ BG Brian Grant	20.00	9.00
❑ BR Bill Russell	400.00	180.00
❑ CA Cory Alexander	8.00	3.60
❑ DA Darrell Armstrong	15.00	6.75
❑ EH Elvin Hayes	15.00	6.75
❑ ES Eric Snow	8.00	3.60
❑ GG George Gervin	15.00	6.75
❑ GR Glen Rice	30.00	13.50
❑ JH John Havlicek	25.00	11.00
❑ JR Jalen Rose	25.00	11.00
❑ JW Jerry West	30.00	13.50
❑ MB Mookie Blaylock	8.00	3.60
❑ MJ Mark Jackson	8.00	3.60
❑ MT Maurice Taylor	15.00	6.75
❑ NA Nate Archibald	15.00	6.75
❑ RL Raef LaFrentz	15.00	6.75
❑ RT Robert Traylor	8.00	3.60
❑ TK Toni Kukoc	25.00	11.00
❑ VC Vince Carter	200.00	90.00
❑ WC Wilt Chamberlain	400.00	180.00
❑ WF Walt Frazier	25.00	11.00

1999-00 Upper Deck Retro Inkredible Level 2

	MINT	NRMT
COMMON CARD	25.00	11.00

PRINT RUN TO PLAYER'S JERSEY #
LOWER PRINT RUNS UNPRICED
RANDOM INSERTS IN PACKS

❑ AH Anfernee Hardaway/1		
❑ AJ Antawn Jamison/7		
❑ BC Bob Cousy/14	120.00	55.00
❑ BG Brian Grant/44	60.00	27.00
❑ BR Bill Russell/6		
❑ CA Cory Alexander/7		
❑ DA Darrell Armstrong/10		
❑ EH Elvin Hayes/11		
❑ ES Eric Snow/20	60.00	27.00

❑ GG George Gervin/44	60.00	27.00
❑ GR Glen Rice/41	75.00	34.00
❑ JE Julius Erving/6		
❑ JH John Havlicek/17	100.00	45.00
❑ JR Jalen Rose/5		
❑ JW Jerry West/44	150.00	70.00
❑ MB Mookie Blaylock/10		
❑ MJ Mark Jackson/13	120.00	55.00
❑ MJ Michael Jordan/23	7000.00	3200.00
❑ MT Maurice Taylor/23	60.00	27.00
❑ NA Nate Archibald/7		
❑ RL Raef LaFrentz/45	60.00	27.00
❑ RT Robert Traylor/54	25.00	11.00
❑ TK Toni Kukoc/7		
❑ VC Vince Carter/15	1500.00	700.00
❑ WC Wilt Chamberlain/13	1500.00	700.00
❑ WF Walt Frazier/10		

1999-00 Upper Deck Retro Lunchboxes

	MINT	NRMT
COMPLETE SET (11)	150.00	70.00
COMMON BOX	8.00	3.60

NNO BOXES LISTED BELOW ALPHABETICALLY

❑ 1 Larry Bird	20.00	9.00
❑ 2 Julius Erving	8.00	3.60
❑ 3 Julius Erving Larry Bird	15.00	6.75
❑ 4 Michael Jordan #1	15.00	6.75
❑ 5 Michael Jordan #2	15.00	6.75
❑ 6 Michael Jordan #3	15.00	6.75
❑ 7 Michael Jordan Larry Bird	20.00	9.00
❑ 8 Michael Jordan Julius Erving	20.00	9.00
❑ 9 Michael Jordan #1 Michael Jordan #2	15.00	6.75
❑ 10 Michael Jordan #1 Michael Jordan #3	15.00	6.75
❑ 11 Michael Jordan #2 Michael Jordan #3	15.00	6.75

1999-00 Upper Deck Retro Old School/New School

	MINT	NRMT
COMPLETE SET (30)	40.00	18.00
COMMON CARD (S1-S30)	.30	.14
SEMISTARS	.40	.18
UNLISTED STARS	.50	.23

STATED ODDS 1:3

COMP.PARALLEL SET (30)	200.00	90.00
COMMON PARALLEL (S1-30)	1.50	.70

*PARALLEL: 2X TO 5X HI COLUMN
PARALLEL: PRINT RUN 500 SERIAL #'d SETS
PARALLEL: RANDOM INSERTS IN PACKS

❑ S1 Michael Jordan	6.00	2.70
❑ S2 Wilt Chamberlain	1.50	.70
❑ S3 Oscar Robertson	1.25	.55
❑ S4 Julius Erving	2.00	.90
❑ S5 George Gervin	.40	.18
❑ S6 John Havlicek	1.25	.55
❑ S7 Elgin Baylor	.60	.25
❑ S8 Earl Monroe	.30	.14
❑ S9 Jerry West	.75	.35
❑ S10 Larry Bird	5.00	2.20
❑ S11 Elvin Hayes	.30	.14
❑ S12 Moses Malone	.40	.18
❑ S13 Bill Walton	.40	.18
❑ S14 Kareem Abdul-Jabbar	1.50	.70
❑ S15 Bill Russell	1.50	.70
❑ S16 Kobe Bryant	4.00	1.80
❑ S17 Allen Iverson	2.00	.90
❑ S18 Stephon Marbury	1.00	.45
❑ S19 Shaquille O'Neal	2.50	1.10
❑ S20 Kevin Garnett	3.00	1.35
❑ S21 Keith Van Horn	1.00	.45
❑ S22 Jason Williams	1.25	.55
❑ S23 Paul Pierce	1.00	.45
❑ S24 Vince Carter	5.00	2.20
❑ S25 Tim Duncan	2.50	1.10
❑ S26 Antoine Walker	.60	.25
❑ S27 Shareef Abdur-Rahim	1.00	.45
❑ S28 Ray Allen	.50	.23
❑ S29 Anfernee Hardaway	1.50	.70
❑ S30 Grant Hill	2.50	1.10

1993-94 Upper Deck SE

	MINT	NRMT
COMPLETE SET (225)	15.00	6.75
COMMON CARD (1-225)	.05	.02
SEMISTARS	.15	.07
UNLISTED STARS	.30	.14

SUBSET CARDS HALF VALUE OF BASE CARDS
JK1/MJR1: STATED ODDS 1:72

❑ 1 Scottie Pippen	1.00	.45
❑ 2 Todd Day	.05	.02
❑ 3 Detlef Schrempf	.15	.07

❑ 4 Chris Webber RC	3.00	1.35
❑ 5 Michael Adams	.05	.02
❑ 6 Loy Vaught	.05	.02
❑ 7 Doug West	.05	.02
❑ 8 A.C. Green	.15	.07
❑ 9 Anthony Mason	.15	.07
❑ 10 Clyde Drexler	.30	.14
❑ 11 Popeye Jones RC	.05	.02
❑ 12 Vlade Divac	.15	.07
❑ 13 Armon Gilliam	.05	.02
❑ 14 Hersey Hawkins	.15	.07
❑ 15 Dennis Scott	.05	.02
❑ 16 Bimbo Coles	.05	.02
❑ 17 Blue Edwards	.05	.02
❑ 18 Negele Knight	.05	.02
❑ 19 Dale Davis	.05	.02
❑ 20 Isiah Thomas	.30	.14
❑ 21 Latrell Sprewell	.75	.35
❑ 22 Kenny Smith	.05	.02
❑ 23 Bryant Stith	.05	.02
❑ 24 Terry Porter	.05	.02
❑ 25 Spud Webb	.15	.07
❑ 26 John Battle	.05	.02
❑ 27 Jeff Malone	.05	.02
❑ 28 Olden Polynice	.05	.02
❑ 29 Kevin Willis	.05	.02
❑ 30 Robert Parish	.15	.07
❑ 31 Kevin Johnson	.15	.07
❑ 32 Shaquille O'Neal	1.50	.70
❑ 33 Willie Anderson	.05	.02
❑ 34 Micheal Williams	.05	.02
❑ 35 Steve Smith	.30	.14
❑ 36 Rik Smits	.15	.07
❑ 37 Pete Myers	.05	.02
❑ 38 Oliver Miller	.05	.02
❑ 39 Eddie Johnson	.05	.02
❑ 40 Calbert Cheaney RC	.15	.07
❑ 41 Vernon Maxwell	.05	.02
❑ 42 James Worthy	.30	.14
❑ 43 Dino Radja RC	.05	.02
❑ 44 Derrick Coleman	.15	.07
❑ 45 Reggie Williams	.05	.02
❑ 46 Dale Ellis	.05	.02
❑ 47 Clifford Robinson	.15	.07
❑ 48 Doug Christie	.05	.02
❑ 49 Ricky Pierce	.05	.02
❑ 50 Sean Elliott	.15	.07
❑ 51 Anfernee Hardaway RC	3.00	1.35
❑ 52 Dana Barros	.05	.02
❑ 53 Reggie Miller	.30	.14
❑ 54 Brian Williams	.05	.02
❑ 55 Otis Thorpe	.15	.07
❑ 56 Jerome Kersey	.05	.02
❑ 57 Larry Johnson	.30	.14
❑ 58 Rex Chapman	.05	.02
❑ 59 Kevin Edwards	.05	.02
❑ 60 Nate McMillan	.05	.02
❑ 61 Chris Mullin	.30	.14
❑ 62 Bill Cartwright	.05	.02
❑ 63 Dennis Rodman	.60	.25
❑ 64 Pooh Richardson	.05	.02
❑ 65 Tyrone Hill	.05	.02
❑ 66 Scott Brooks	.05	.02
❑ 67 Brad Daugherty	.05	.02
❑ 68 Joe Dumars	.30	.14
❑ 69 Vin Baker RC	.75	.35
❑ 70 Rod Strickland	.15	.07
❑ 71 Tom Chambers	.05	.02
❑ 72 Charles Oakley	.15	.07
❑ 73 Craig Ehlo	.05	.02
❑ 74 LaPhonso Ellis	.05	.02
❑ 75 Kevin Gamble	.05	.02
❑ 76 Shawn Bradley RC	.30	.14
❑ 77 Kendall Gill	.15	.07
❑ 78 Hakeem Olajuwon	.50	.23
❑ 79 Nick Anderson	.15	.07
❑ 80 Anthony Peeler	.05	.02
❑ 81 Wayman Tisdale	.05	.02
❑ 82 Danny Manning	.15	.07
❑ 83 John Starks	.15	.07
❑ 84 Jeff Hornacek	.15	.07
❑ 85 Victor Alexander	.05	.02
❑ 86 Mitch Richmond	.30	.14
❑ 87 Mookie Blaylock	.15	.07
❑ 88 Harvey Grant	.05	.02
❑ 89 Doug Smith	.05	.02
❑ 90 John Stockton	.30	.14
❑ 91 Charles Barkley	.50	.23
❑ 92 Gerald Wilkins	.05	.02
❑ 93 Mario Elie	.05	.02
❑ 94 Ken Norman	.05	.02
❑ 95 B.J. Armstrong	.05	.02
❑ 96 John Williams	.05	.02
❑ 97 Rony Seikaly	.05	.02
❑ 98 Sean Rooks	.05	.02
❑ 99 Shawn Kemp	.50	.23
❑ 100 Danny Ainge	.15	.07
❑ 101 Terry Mills	.05	.02
❑ 102 Doc Rivers	.15	.07
❑ 103 Chuck Person	.05	.02
❑ 104 Sam Cassell RC	.75	.35
❑ 105 Kevin Duckworth	.05	.02
❑ 106 Dan Majerle	.15	.07
❑ 107 Mark Jackson	.15	.07
❑ 108 Steve Kerr	.15	.07
❑ 109 Sam Perkins	.15	.07
❑ 110 Clarence Weatherspoon	.05	.02
❑ 111 Felton Spencer	.05	.02
❑ 112 Greg Anthony	.05	.02
❑ 113 Pete Chilcutt	.05	.02
❑ 114 Malik Sealy	.05	.02
❑ 115 Horace Grant	.15	.07
❑ 116 Chris Morris	.05	.02
❑ 117 Xavier McDaniel	.05	.02
❑ 118 Lionel Simmons	.05	.02
❑ 119 Dell Curry	.05	.02
❑ 120 Moses Malone	.30	.14
❑ 121 Lindsey Hunter RC	.30	.14
❑ 122 Buck Williams	.05	.02
❑ 123 Mahmoud Abdul-Rauf	.05	.02
❑ 124 Rumeal Robinson	.05	.02
❑ 125 Chris Mills RC	.30	.14
❑ 126 Scott Skiles	.05	.02
❑ 127 Derrick McKey	.05	.02
❑ 128 Avery Johnson	.05	.02
❑ 129 Harold Miner	.05	.02
❑ 130 Frank Brickowski	.05	.02
❑ 131 Gary Payton	.50	.23
❑ 132 Don MacLean	.05	.02
❑ 133 Thurl Bailey	.05	.02
❑ 134 Nick Van Exel RC	.75	.35
❑ 135 Matt Geiger	.05	.02
❑ 136 Stacey Augmon	.05	.02
❑ 137 Sedale Threatt	.05	.02
❑ 138 Patrick Ewing	.30	.14
❑ 139 Tyrone Corbin	.05	.02
❑ 140 Jim Jackson	.15	.07
❑ 141 Christian Laettner	.15	.07
❑ 142 Robert Horry	.15	.07
❑ 143 J.R. Reid	.05	.02
❑ 144 Eric Murdock	.05	.02
❑ 145 Alonzo Mourning	.50	.23
❑ 146 Sherman Douglas	.05	.02
❑ 147 Tom Gugliotta	.30	.14
❑ 148 Glen Rice	.15	.07
❑ 149 Mark Price	.05	.02
❑ 150 Dikembe Mutombo	.15	.07
❑ 151 Derek Harper	.15	.07
❑ 152 Karl Malone	.50	.23
❑ 153 Byron Scott	.15	.07
❑ 154 Reggie Jordan RC	.05	.02
❑ 155 Dominique Wilkins	.30	.14
❑ 156 Bobby Hurley RC	.15	.07
❑ 157 Ron Harper	.15	.07
❑ 158 Bryon Russell RC	.30	.14
❑ 159 Frank Johnson	.05	.02
❑ 160 Toni Kukoc RC	1.25	.55
❑ 161 Lloyd Daniels	.05	.02
❑ 162 Jeff Turner	.05	.02
❑ 163 Muggsy Bogues	.15	.07
❑ 164 Chris Gatling	.05	.02
❑ 165 Kenny Anderson	.15	.07
❑ 166 Elmore Spencer	.05	.02
❑ 167 Jamal Mashburn RC	.60	.25
❑ 168 Tim Perry	.05	.02
❑ 169 Antonio Davis RC	.15	.07
❑ 170 Isaiah Rider RC	.60	.25
❑ 171 Dee Brown	.05	.02
❑ 172 Walt Williams	.05	.02
❑ 173 Elden Campbell	.05	.02
❑ 174 Benoit Benjamin	.05	.02
❑ 175 Billy Owens	.05	.02
❑ 176 Andrew Lang	.05	.02
❑ 177 David Robinson	.50	.23
❑ 178 Checklist 1	.05	.02
❑ 179 Checklist 2	.05	.02
❑ 180 Checklist 3	.05	.02
❑ 181 Shawn Bradley AS	.15	.07
❑ 182 Calbert Cheaney AS	.05	.02
❑ 183 Toni Kukoc AS	.30	.14
❑ 184 Popeye Jones AS	.05	.02
❑ 185 Lindsey Hunter AS	.15	.07
❑ 186 Chris Webber AS	.75	.35
❑ 187 Bryon Russell AS	.15	.07
❑ 188 Anfernee Hardaway AS	1.50	.70
❑ 189 Nick Van Exel AS	.30	.14
❑ 190 P.J. Brown AS	.15	.07
❑ 191 Isaiah Rider AS	.30	.14
❑ 192 Chris Mills AS	.15	.07
❑ 193 Antonio Davis AS	.05	.02
❑ 194 Jamal Mashburn AS	.30	.14
❑ 195 Dino Radja AS	.05	.02
❑ 196 Sam Cassell AS	.30	.14
❑ 197 Isaiah Rider ASW	.30	.14
❑ 198 Mark Price ASW	.05	.02
❑ 199 Stacey Augmon TH	.05	.02
❑ 200 Celtics Team TH	.05	.02
❑ 201 Eddie Johnson TH	.05	.02
❑ 202 Scottie Pippen TH	.50	.23
❑ 203 Brad Daugherty TH	.05	.02
❑ 204 Jamal Mashburn TH	.30	.14
❑ 205 Dikembe Mutombo TH	.05	.02
(Oliver Miller on defense)		
❑ 206 Lindsey Hunter TH	.15	.07
❑ 207 Chris Webber TH	.50	.23
❑ 208 Rockets Team TH	.05	.02
❑ 209 Derrick McKey TH	.05	.02
❑ 210 Danny Manning TH	.05	.02
❑ 211 Doug Christie HDL	.05	.02
❑ 212 Glen Rice TH	.05	.02
❑ 213 Todd Day TH	.05	.02
Ken Norman TH		
Vin Baker TH		
Jon Barry TH		
❑ 214 Isaiah Rider TH	.30	.14
❑ 215 Kenny Anderson TH	.05	.02
❑ 216 Patrick Ewing TH	.15	.07
❑ 217 Anfernee Hardaway TH	1.00	.45
❑ 218 Moses Malone TH	.15	.07
❑ 219 Kevin Johnson TH	.05	.02
❑ 220 Clifford Robinson TH	.05	.02
❑ 221 Wayman Tisdale TH	.05	.02
❑ 222 David Robinson TH	.30	.14
❑ 223 Sonics Team TH	.05	.02
❑ 224 John Stockton TH	.15	.07
❑ 225 Don MacLean TH	.05	.02
❑ JK1 Johnny Kilroy	4.00	1.80
(Michael Jordan)		
❑ MJR1 Michael Jordan	8.00	3.60
Retirement Card		

1993-94 Upper Deck SE Electric Court

	MINT	NRMT
COMPLETE SET (225)	50.00	22.00
COMMON CARD (1-225)	.10	.05

*STARS: .75X TO 2X BASE CARD HI
*RCs: .6X TO 1.5X BASE HI
ONE PER PACK

1993-94 Upper Deck SE Electric Court Gold

	MINT	NRMT
COMPLETE SET (225)	400.00	180.00
COMMON GOLD (1-225)	1.25	.55

*STARS: 10X TO 20X BASE CARD HI
*RCs: 7.5X TO 15X BASE HI
STATED ODDS 1:36 HOB/RET

1993-94 Upper Deck SE Behind the Glass

	MINT	NRMT
COMPLETE SET (15)	40.00	18.00

*SINGLES: 2X TO 5X BASE CARD HI
STATED ODDS 1:30 RETAIL
ONE SET PER BHG TRADE CARD BY MAIL
BHG TRADE: STATED ODDS 1:360 HOBBY

❑ G1 Shawn Kemp	2.50	1.10
❑ G2 Patrick Ewing	1.50	.70
❑ G3 Dikembe Mutombo	.75	.35
❑ G4 Charles Barkley	2.50	1.10
❑ G5 Hakeem Olajuwon	2.50	1.10
❑ G6 Larry Johnson	1.50	.70
❑ G7 Chris Webber	10.00	4.50
❑ G8 John Starks	.75	.35
❑ G9 Kevin Willis	.25	.11
❑ G10 Scottie Pippen	5.00	2.20
❑ G11 Michael Jordan	20.00	9.00
❑ G12 Alonzo Mourning	2.50	1.10
❑ G13 Shaquille O'Neal	8.00	3.60
❑ G14 Shawn Bradley	1.50	.70
❑ G15 Ron Harper	.75	.35
❑ NNO Behind the Glass Trade Card	1.50	.70
❑ NNO Redeemed BHG Trade	.25	.11

1993-94 Upper Deck SE Die Cut All-Stars

	MINT	NRMT
COMPLETE SET (30)	400.00	180.00
COMP.EAST SET (15)	200.00	90.00
COMP.WEST SET (15)	200.00	90.00
COMMON EAST (E1-E15)	3.00	1.35
COMMON WEST (W1-W15)	3.00	1.35
SEMISTARS	6.00	2.70
UNLISTED STARS	10.00	4.50

STATED ODDS 1:30 HOBBY

❑ E1 Dominique Wilkins	10.00	4.50
❑ E2 Alonzo Mourning	15.00	6.75
❑ E3 B.J. Armstrong	3.00	1.35
❑ E4 Scottie Pippen	30.00	13.50
❑ E5 Mark Price	3.00	1.35
❑ E6 Isiah Thomas	10.00	4.50
❑ E7 Harold Miner	3.00	1.35
❑ E8 Vin Baker	20.00	9.00
❑ E9 Kenny Anderson	6.00	2.70
❑ E10 Derrick Coleman	6.00	2.70
❑ E11 Patrick Ewing	10.00	4.50
❑ E12 Anfernee Hardaway	60.00	27.00
❑ E13 Shaquille O'Neal	50.00	22.00
❑ E14 Shawn Bradley	10.00	4.50
❑ E15 Calbert Cheaney	6.00	2.70
❑ W1 Jim Jackson	6.00	2.70
❑ W2 Jamal Mashburn	15.00	6.75
❑ W3 Dikembe Mutombo	6.00	2.70
❑ W4 Latrell Sprewell	25.00	11.00
❑ W5 Chris Webber	60.00	27.00
❑ W6 Hakeem Olajuwon	15.00	6.75
❑ W7 Danny Manning	6.00	2.70
❑ W8 Nick Van Exel	20.00	9.00
❑ W9 Isaiah Rider	15.00	6.75
❑ W10 Charles Barkley	15.00	6.75
❑ W11 Clyde Drexler	10.00	4.50
❑ W12 Mitch Richmond	10.00	4.50
❑ W13 David Robinson	15.00	6.75
❑ W14 Shawn Kemp	15.00	6.75
❑ W15 Karl Malone	15.00	6.75

1993-94 Upper Deck SE USA Trade

	MINT	NRMT
COMPLETE SET (24)	40.00	18.00

*SINGLES: 2X TO 5X BASE CARD HI
ONE SET PER USA TRADE CARD BY MAIL
TRADE CARD: STATED ODDS 1:360 HOB/RET
USA PREFIX ON CARD NUMBER

❑ 1 Charles Barkley	2.50	1.10
❑ 2 Larry Bird	6.00	2.70
❑ 3 Clyde Drexler	1.50	.70
❑ 4 Patrick Ewing	1.50	.70
❑ 5 Michael Jordan	20.00	9.00
❑ 6 Christian Laettner	.75	.35
❑ 7 Karl Malone	2.50	1.10
❑ 8 Chris Mullin	1.50	.70
❑ 9 Scottie Pippen	5.00	2.20
❑ 10 David Robinson	2.50	1.10
❑ 11 John Stockton	1.50	.70
❑ 12 Dominique Wilkins	1.50	.70
❑ 13 Isiah Thomas	1.50	.70
❑ 14 Dan Majerle	.75	.35
❑ 15 Steve Smith	1.50	.70
❑ 16 Alonzo Mourning	2.50	1.10
❑ 17 Shawn Kemp	2.50	1.10
❑ 18 Larry Johnson	1.50	.70
❑ 19 Tim Hardaway	1.50	.70
❑ 20 Joe Dumars	1.50	.70
❑ 21 Mark Price	.25	.11
❑ 22 Derrick Coleman	.75	.35
❑ 23 Reggie Miller	1.50	.70
❑ 24 Shaquille O'Neal	8.00	3.60
❑ NNO Exp. USA Trade Card	1.00	.45
❑ NNO Red. USA Trade Card	.25	.11

1999-00 Upper Deck Ultimate Victory

	MINT	NRMT
COMPLETE SET (150)	150.00	70.00
COMPLETE SET w/o RC (120)	60.00	27.00
COMMON CARD (1-90)	.25	.11
COMMON MJ GH (91-120)	1.50	.70
COMMON RC (121-150)	1.50	.70
SEMISTARS	.30	.14
SEMISTARS RC	2.00	.90
UNLISTED STARS	.50	.23
UNLISTED STARS RC	2.50	1.10

MJ HITS SUBSET STATED ODDS 1:2
RC SUBSET STATED ODDS 1:4
UNPRICED PARALLEL SERIAL #'d TO 1
MJ FINAL FLOOR LISTED UNDER 99-00 UD

❑ 1 Dikembe Mutombo	.30	.14
❑ 2 Alan Henderson	.25	.11
❑ 3 LaPhonso Ellis	.25	.11
❑ 4 Kenny Anderson	.30	.14
❑ 5 Antoine Walker	.60	.25
❑ 6 Paul Pierce	1.00	.45
❑ 7 Elden Campbell	.25	.11
❑ 8 Eddie Jones	1.00	.45
❑ 9 David Wesley	.25	.11
❑ 10 Michael Jordan	5.00	2.20
❑ 11 Kornel David RC	.25	.11
❑ 12 Toni Kukoc	.60	.25
❑ 13 Shawn Kemp	.75	.35
❑ 14 Brevin Knight	.25	.11
❑ 15 Zydrunas Ilgauskas	.25	.11
❑ 16 Michael Finley	.50	.23
❑ 17 Shawn Bradley	.25	.11
❑ 18 Dirk Nowitzki	.75	.35
❑ 19 Antonio McDyess	.50	.23
❑ 20 Nick Van Exel	.30	.14
❑ 21 Ron Mercer	.60	.25
❑ 22 Grant Hill	2.50	1.10
❑ 23 Lindsey Hunter	.25	.11
❑ 24 Jerry Stackhouse	.30	.14
❑ 25 John Starks	.25	.11
❑ 26 Antawn Jamison	1.00	.45
❑ 27 Mookie Blaylock	.25	.11
❑ 28 Hakeem Olajuwon	.75	.35
❑ 29 Cuttino Mobley	.50	.23
❑ 30 Charles Barkley	.75	.35
❑ 31 Reggie Miller	.50	.23
❑ 32 Rik Smits	.25	.11

❑ 33 Jalen Rose	.50	.23
❑ 34 Maurice Taylor	.50	.23
❑ 35 Tyrone Nesby RC	.25	.11
❑ 36 Michael Olowokandi	.30	.14
❑ 37 Kobe Bryant	4.00	1.80
❑ 38 Shaquille O'Neal	2.50	1.10
❑ 39 Glen Rice	.30	.14
❑ 40 Robert Horry	.25	.11
❑ 41 Tim Hardaway	.50	.23
❑ 42 Alonzo Mourning	.50	.23
❑ 43 Jamal Mashburn	.30	.14
❑ 44 Ray Allen	.50	.23
❑ 45 Glenn Robinson	.30	.14
❑ 46 Robert Traylor	.25	.11
❑ 47 Kevin Garnett	3.00	1.35
❑ 48 Joe Smith	.30	.14
❑ 49 Bobby Jackson	.25	.11
❑ 50 Keith Van Horn	1.00	.45
❑ 51 Stephon Marbury	1.00	.45
❑ 52 Jayson Williams	.30	.14
❑ 53 Patrick Ewing	.50	.23
❑ 54 Allan Houston	.50	.23
❑ 55 Latrell Sprewell	1.00	.45
❑ 56 Marcus Camby	.50	.23
❑ 57 Darrell Armstrong	.30	.14
❑ 58 Matt Harpring	.25	.11
❑ 59 Charles Outlaw	.25	.11
❑ 60 Allen Iverson	2.00	.90
❑ 61 Theo Ratliff	.25	.11
❑ 62 Larry Hughes	1.25	.55
❑ 63 Jason Kidd	1.50	.70
❑ 64 Tom Gugliotta	.30	.14
❑ 65 Anfernee Hardaway	1.50	.70
❑ 66 Scottie Pippen	1.50	.70
❑ 67 Damon Stoudamire	.50	.23
❑ 68 Brian Grant	.30	.14
❑ 69 Jason Williams	1.25	.55
❑ 70 Vlade Divac	.25	.11
❑ 71 Chris Webber	1.50	.70
❑ 72 Tim Duncan	2.50	1.10
❑ 73 Sean Elliott	.25	.11
❑ 74 David Robinson	.75	.35
❑ 75 Avery Johnson	.25	.11
❑ 76 Gary Payton	.75	.35
❑ 77 Vin Baker	.30	.14
❑ 78 Brent Barry	.25	.11
❑ 79 Vince Carter	5.00	2.20
❑ 80 Doug Christie	.25	.11
❑ 81 Tracy McGrady	1.50	.70
❑ 82 Karl Malone	.75	.35
❑ 83 John Stockton	.50	.23
❑ 84 Bryon Russell	.25	.11
❑ 85 Shareef Abdur-Rahim	1.00	.45
❑ 86 Mike Bibby	.60	.25
❑ 87 Felipe Lopez	.25	.11
❑ 88 Juwan Howard	.30	.14
❑ 89 Rod Strickland	.30	.14
❑ 90 Mitch Richmond	.50	.23
❑ 91 Michael Jordan GH	1.50	.70
❑ 92 Michael Jordan GH	1.50	.70
❑ 93 Michael Jordan GH	1.50	.70
❑ 94 Michael Jordan GH	1.50	.70
❑ 95 Michael Jordan GH	1.50	.70
❑ 96 Michael Jordan GH	1.50	.70
❑ 97 Michael Jordan GH	1.50	.70
❑ 98 Michael Jordan GH	1.50	.70
❑ 99 Michael Jordan GH	1.50	.70
❑ 100 Michael Jordan GH	1.50	.70
❑ 101 Michael Jordan GH	1.50	.70
❑ 102 Michael Jordan GH	1.50	.70
❑ 103 Michael Jordan GH	1.50	.70
❑ 104 Michael Jordan GH	1.50	.70
❑ 105 Michael Jordan GH	1.50	.70
❑ 106 Michael Jordan GH	1.50	.70
❑ 107 Michael Jordan GH	1.50	.70
❑ 108 Michael Jordan GH	1.50	.70
❑ 109 Michael Jordan GH	1.50	.70
❑ 110 Michael Jordan GH	1.50	.70
❑ 111 Michael Jordan GH	1.50	.70
❑ 112 Michael Jordan GH	1.50	.70
❑ 113 Michael Jordan GH	1.50	.70
❑ 114 Michael Jordan GH	1.50	.70
❑ 115 Michael Jordan GH	1.50	.70
❑ 116 Michael Jordan GH	1.50	.70
❑ 117 Michael Jordan GH	1.50	.70
❑ 118 Michael Jordan GH	1.50	.70
❑ 119 Michael Jordan GH	1.50	.70
❑ 120 Michael Jordan GH	1.50	.70
❑ 121 Elton Brand RC	25.00	11.00
❑ 122 Steve Francis RC	30.00	13.50
❑ 123 Baron Davis RC	6.00	2.70
❑ 124 Lamar Odom RC	20.00	9.00
❑ 125 Jonathan Bender RC	12.00	5.50
❑ 126 Wally Szczerbiak RC	10.00	4.50
❑ 127 Richard Hamilton RC	6.00	2.70
❑ 128 Andre Miller RC	8.00	3.60
❑ 129 Shawn Marion RC	8.00	3.60
❑ 130 Jason Terry RC	4.00	1.80
❑ 131 Trajan Langdon RC	4.00	1.80
❑ 132 Aleksandar Radojevic RC	1.50	.70
❑ 133 Corey Maggette RC	10.00	4.50
❑ 134 William Avery RC	4.00	1.80
❑ 135 Ron Artest RC	6.00	2.70
❑ 136 Cal Bowdler RC	2.50	1.10
❑ 137 James Posey RC	5.00	2.20
❑ 138 Quincy Lewis RC	2.50	1.10
❑ 139 Dion Glover RC	2.50	1.10
❑ 140 Jeff Foster RC	2.50	1.10
❑ 141 Kenny Thomas RC	4.00	1.80
❑ 142 Devean George RC	5.00	2.20
❑ 143 Tim James RC	3.00	1.35
❑ 144 Vonteego Cummings RC	4.00	1.80
❑ 145 Jumaine Jones RC	2.00	.90
❑ 146 Scott Padgett RC	2.50	1.10
❑ 147 John Celestand RC	2.50	1.10
❑ 148 Adrian Griffin RC	3.00	1.35
❑ 149 Chris Herren RC	1.50	.70
❑ 150 Anthony Carter RC	6.00	2.70

1999-00 Upper Deck Ultimate Victory Victory Collection

	MINT	NRMT
COMPLETE SET (150)	400.00	180.00
COMMON CARD (1-90)	.75	.35
COMMON MJ GH (91-120)	5.00	2.20
COMMON RC (121-150)	2.50	1.10

*STARS: 1.25X TO 3X BASE CARD HI
*RCs: .6X TO 1.5X BASE HI
STARS: STATED ODDS 1:12
RCs: STATED ODDS 1:24

1999-00 Upper Deck Ultimate Victory Ultimate Collection

	MINT	NRMT
COMMON CARD (1-90)	8.00	3.60
COMMON MJ GH (91-120)	50.00	22.00
COMMON RC (121-150)	8.00	3.60

*STARS: 12.5X TO 30X BASE CARD HI
*RCs: 2X TO 5X BASE HI
RANDOM INSERTS IN PACKS
STATED PRINT RUN 100 SERIAL #'d SETS

1999-00 Upper Deck Ultimate Victory Court Impact

	MINT	NRMT
COMPLETE SET (10)	50.00	22.00
COMMON CARD (C1-C10)	2.00	.90

STATED ODDS 1:24

Card		
❑ C1 Michael Jordan	15.00	6.75
❑ C2 Vince Carter	12.00	5.50
❑ C3 Kobe Bryant	10.00	4.50
❑ C4 Kevin Garnett	8.00	3.60
❑ C5 Tim Duncan	6.00	2.70
❑ C6 Jason Williams	3.00	1.35
❑ C7 Grant Hill	6.00	2.70
❑ C8 Keith Van Horn	2.50	1.10
❑ C9 Allen Iverson	5.00	2.20
❑ C10 Karl Malone	2.00	.90

1999-00 Upper Deck Ultimate Victory Dr. J Glory Days

	MINT	NRMT
COMPLETE SET (8)	30.00	13.50
COMMON CARD (DR1-DR8)	5.00	2.20

STATED ODDS 1:24

Card		
❑ DR1 Julius Erving	5.00	2.20
❑ DR2 Julius Erving	5.00	2.20

❑ DR3 Julius Erving	5.00	2.20
❑ DR4 Julius Erving	5.00	2.20
❑ DR5 Julius Erving	5.00	2.20
❑ DR6 Julius Erving	5.00	2.20
❑ DR7 Julius Erving	5.00	2.20
❑ DR8 Julius Erving	5.00	2.20

1999-00 Upper Deck Ultimate Victory Got Skills?

	MINT	NRMT
COMPLETE SET (8)	12.00	5.50
COMMON CARD (GS1-GS8)	1.00	.45
STATED ODDS 1:24		
❑ GS1 Kevin Garnett	6.00	2.70
❑ GS2 Tim Hardaway	1.00	.45
❑ GS3 Mike Bibby	1.25	.55
❑ GS4 Stephon Marbury	2.00	.90
❑ GS5 Reggie Miller	1.00	.45
❑ GS6 Jason Williams	2.50	1.10
❑ GS7 Antoine Walker	1.25	.55
❑ GS8 Jason Kidd	3.00	1.35

1999-00 Upper Deck Ultimate Victory MJ's World Famous

	MINT	NRMT
COMPLETE SET (12)	60.00	27.00
COMMON CARD (MJ1-MJ12)	6.00	2.70
STATED ODDS 1:24		
❑ MJ1 Michael Jordan	6.00	2.70
❑ MJ2 Michael Jordan	6.00	2.70
❑ MJ3 Michael Jordan	6.00	2.70
❑ MJ4 Michael Jordan	6.00	2.70
❑ MJ5 Michael Jordan	6.00	2.70
❑ MJ6 Michael Jordan	6.00	2.70
❑ MJ7 Michael Jordan	6.00	2.70
❑ MJ8 Michael Jordan	6.00	2.70
❑ MJ9 Michael Jordan	6.00	2.70
❑ MJ10 Michael Jordan	6.00	2.70
❑ MJ11 Michael Jordan	6.00	2.70
❑ MJ12 Michael Jordan	6.00	2.70

1999-00 Upper Deck Ultimate Victory Scorin' Legion

	MINT	NRMT
COMPLETE SET (10)	15.00	6.75
COMMON CARD (SL1-SL10)	.75	.35
STATED ODDS 1:12		
❑ SL1 Tim Duncan	4.00	1.80
❑ SL2 Karl Malone	1.25	.55
❑ SL3 Stephon Marbury	1.50	.70
❑ SL4 Shaquille O'Neal	4.00	1.80
❑ SL5 Antonio McDyess	.75	.35
❑ SL6 Gary Payton	1.25	.55
❑ SL7 Allen Iverson	3.00	1.35
❑ SL8 Keith Van Horn	1.50	.70
❑ SL9 Shareef Abdur-Rahim	1.50	.70
❑ SL10 Grant Hill	4.00	1.80

1999-00 Upper Deck Ultimate Victory Surface to Air

	MINT	NRMT
COMPLETE SET (12)	12.00	5.50
COMMON CARD (SA1-SA12)	.50	.23
UNLISTED STARS	.60	.25
STATED ODDS 1:6		
❑ SA1 Vince Carter	6.00	2.70
❑ SA2 Antawn Jamison	1.25	.55
❑ SA3 Eddie Jones	1.25	.55
❑ SA4 Anfernee Hardaway	2.00	.90
❑ SA5 Latrell Sprewell	1.25	.55
❑ SA6 Antonio McDyess	.60	.25
❑ SA7 Michael Finley	.50	.23
❑ SA8 Kobe Bryant	5.00	2.20
❑ SA9 Chris Webber	2.00	.90
❑ SA10 Shawn Kemp	1.00	.45
❑ SA11 Ray Allen	.60	.25
❑ SA12 Shaquille O'Neal	3.00	1.35

1999-00 Upper Deck Ultimate Victory Ultimate Fabrics

	MINT	NRMT
COMMON CARD (UF1-UF3)	150.00	70.00
RANDOM INSERTS IN PACKS		
CARD UF1A NOT PRICED DUE TO SCARCITY		
❑ UF1 Julius Erving/300	150.00	70.00
❑ UF1A Julius Erving AU/6		
❑ UF2 Wilt Chamberlain/100	500.00	220.00
❑ UF3 J.Erving/K.Bryant/25	1000.00	450.00

1999-00 Upper Deck Victory

	MINT	NRMT
COMPLETE SET (440)	60.00	27.00
COMMON CARD (1-380)	.05	.02
COMMON MJ HITS (381-430)	1.00	.45
COMMON RC (431-440)	.75	.35
SEMISTARS	.10	.05
UNLISTED STARS	.20	.09
SUBSET CARDS HALF VALUE OF BASE CARDS		
❑ 1 Dikembe Mutombo CL	.05	.02
❑ 2 Steve Smith	.10	.05
❑ 3 Dikembe Mutombo	.10	.05
❑ 4 Ed Gray	.05	.02
❑ 5 Alan Henderson	.05	.02
❑ 6 LaPhonso Ellis	.05	.02
❑ 7 Roshown McLeod	.05	.02
❑ 8 Bimbo Coles	.05	.02
❑ 9 Chris Crawford	.05	.02
❑ 10 Anthony Johnson	.05	.02
❑ 11 Antoine Walker CL	.20	.09
❑ 12 Kenny Anderson	.10	.05
❑ 13 Antoine Walker	.25	.11
❑ 14 Greg Minor	.05	.02
❑ 15 Tony Battie	.05	.02
❑ 16 Ron Mercer	.25	.11
❑ 17 Paul Pierce	.40	.18
❑ 18 Vitaly Potapenko	.05	.02
❑ 19 Dana Barros	.05	.02
❑ 20 Walter McCarty	.05	.02
❑ 21 Elden Campbell CL	.05	.02
❑ 22 Elden Campbell	.05	.02

❑ 23 Eddie Jones .40 .18
❑ 24 David Wesley .05 .02
❑ 25 Bobby Phills .05 .02
❑ 26 Derrick Coleman .10 .05
❑ 27 Anthony Mason .10 .05
❑ 28 Brad Miller .05 .02
❑ 29 Eldridge Recasner .05 .02
❑ 30 Ricky Davis .20 .09
❑ 31 Toni Kukoc CL .20 .09
❑ 32 Michael Jordan 2.50 1.10
❑ 33 Brent Barry .05 .02
❑ 34 Randy Brown .05 .02
❑ 35 Keith Booth .05 .02
❑ 36 Kornel David RC .05 .02
❑ 37 Mark Bryant .05 .02
❑ 38 Toni Kukoc .25 .11
❑ 39 Rusty LaRue .05 .02
❑ 40 Brevin Knight CL .05 .02
❑ 41 Shawn Kemp .30 .14
❑ 42 Wesley Person .05 .02
❑ 43 Johnny Newman .05 .02
❑ 44 Derek Anderson .20 .09
❑ 45 Brevin Knight .05 .02
❑ 46 Bob Sura .05 .02
❑ 47 Andrew DeClercq .05 .02
❑ 48 Zydrunas Ilgauskas .05 .02
❑ 49 Danny Ferry .05 .02
❑ 50 Steve Nash CL .05 .02
❑ 51 Michael Finley .20 .09
❑ 52 Robert Pack .05 .02
❑ 53 Shawn Bradley .05 .02
❑ 54 John Williams .05 .02
❑ 55 Hubert Davis .05 .02
❑ 56 Dirk Nowitzki .30 .14
❑ 57 Steve Nash .05 .02
❑ 58 Chris Anstey .05 .02
❑ 59 Erick Strickland .05 .02
❑ 60 Nick Van Exel CL .05 .02
❑ 61 Antonio McDyess .20 .09
❑ 62 Nick Van Exel .10 .05
❑ 63 Bryant Stith .05 .02
❑ 64 Chauncey Billups .05 .02
❑ 65 Danny Fortson .05 .02
❑ 66 Eric Williams .05 .02
❑ 67 Eric Washington .05 .02
❑ 68 Raef LaFrentz .20 .09
❑ 69 Johnny Taylor .05 .02
❑ 70 Jerry Stackhouse CL .05 .02
❑ 71 Grant Hill 1.00 .45
❑ 72 Lindsey Hunter .05 .02
❑ 73 Bison Dele .05 .02
❑ 74 Loy Vaught .05 .02
❑ 75 Jerome Williams .10 .05
❑ 76 Jerry Stackhouse .10 .05
❑ 77 Christian Laettner .10 .05
❑ 78 Jud Buechler .05 .02
❑ 79 Don Reid .05 .02
❑ 80 Antawn Jamison CL .20 .09
❑ 81 John Starks .05 .02
❑ 82 Antawn Jamison .40 .18
❑ 83 Adonal Foyle .05 .02
❑ 84 Jason Caffey .05 .02
❑ 85 Donyell Marshall .05 .02
❑ 86 Chris Mills .05 .02
❑ 87 Tony Delk .05 .02
❑ 88 Mookie Blaylock .05 .02
❑ 89 Charles Barkley CL .20 .09
❑ 90 Hakeem Olajuwon .30 .14
❑ 91 Scottie Pippen .60 .25
❑ 92 Charles Barkley .30 .14
❑ 93 Bryce Drew .05 .02
❑ 94 Cuttino Mobley .20 .09
❑ 95 Othella Harrington .05 .02
❑ 96 Matt Maloney .05 .02
❑ 97 Michael Dickerson .20 .09
❑ 98 Matt Bullard .05 .02
❑ 99 Jalen Rose CL .10 .05
❑ 100 Reggie Miller .20 .09
❑ 101 Rik Smits .05 .02
❑ 102 Jalen Rose .20 .09
❑ 103 Antonio Davis .05 .02
❑ 104 Mark Jackson .05 .02
❑ 105 Sam Perkins .05 .02
❑ 106 Travis Best .05 .02
❑ 107 Dale Davis .05 .02
❑ 108 Chris Mullin .20 .09
❑ 109 Michael Olowokandi CL .05 .02
❑ 110 Maurice Taylor .20 .09
❑ 111 Tyrone Nesby RC .05 .02
❑ 112 Lamond Murray .05 .02
❑ 113 Darrick Martin .05 .02
❑ 114 Michael Olowokandi .10 .05
❑ 115 Rodney Rogers .05 .02
❑ 116 Eric Piatkowski .05 .02
❑ 117 Lorenzen Wright .05 .02
❑ 118 Brian Skinner .05 .02
❑ 119 Kobe Bryant CL .75 .35
❑ 120 Kobe Bryant 1.50 .70
❑ 121 Shaquille O'Neal 1.00 .45
❑ 122 Derek Fisher .10 .05
❑ 123 Tyronn Lue .05 .02
❑ 124 Travis Knight .05 .02
❑ 125 Glen Rice .10 .05
❑ 126 Derek Harper .10 .05
❑ 127 Robert Horry .05 .02
❑ 128 Rick Fox .05 .02
❑ 129 Tim Hardaway CL .10 .05
❑ 130 Tim Hardaway .20 .09
❑ 131 Alonzo Mourning .20 .09
❑ 132 Keith Askins .05 .02
❑ 133 Jamal Mashburn .10 .05
❑ 134 P.J. Brown .05 .02
❑ 135 Clarence Weatherspoon .05 .02
❑ 136 Terry Porter .05 .02
❑ 137 Dan Majerle .10 .05
❑ 138 Voshon Lenard .05 .02
❑ 139 Ray Allen CL .10 .05
❑ 140 Ray Allen .20 .09
❑ 141 Vinny Del Negro .05 .02
❑ 142 Glenn Robinson .10 .05
❑ 143 Dell Curry .05 .02
❑ 144 Sam Cassell .10 .05
❑ 145 Haywoode Workman .05 .02
❑ 146 Armon Gilliam .05 .02
❑ 147 Robert Traylor .05 .02
❑ 148 Chris Gatling .05 .02
❑ 149 Kevin Garnett CL .60 .25
❑ 150 Kevin Garnett 1.25 .55
❑ 151 Malik Sealy .05 .02
❑ 152 Radoslav Nesterovic .05 .02
❑ 153 Joe Smith .10 .05
❑ 154 Sam Mitchell .05 .02
❑ 155 Dean Garrett .05 .02
❑ 156 Anthony Peeler .05 .02
❑ 157 Tom Hammonds .05 .02
❑ 158 Bobby Jackson .05 .02
❑ 159 Jayson Williams CL .05 .02
❑ 160 Keith Van Horn .40 .18
❑ 161 Stephon Marbury .40 .18
❑ 162 Jayson Williams .10 .05
❑ 163 Kendall Gill .10 .05
❑ 164 Kerry Kittles .10 .05
❑ 165 Jamie Feick RC .05 .02
❑ 166 Scott Burrell .05 .02
❑ 167 Lucious Harris .05 .02
❑ 168 Marcus Camby CL .10 .05
❑ 169 Patrick Ewing .20 .09
❑ 170 Allan Houston .20 .09
❑ 171 Latrell Sprewell .40 .18
❑ 172 Kurt Thomas .05 .02
❑ 173 Larry Johnson .10 .05
❑ 174 Chris Childs .05 .02
❑ 175 Marcus Camby .20 .09
❑ 176 Charlie Ward .05 .02
❑ 177 Chris Dudley .05 .02
❑ 178 Bo Outlaw CL .05 .02
❑ 179 Anfernee Hardaway .60 .25
❑ 180 Darrell Armstrong .10 .05
❑ 181 Nick Anderson .05 .02
❑ 182 Horace Grant .10 .05
❑ 183 Isaac Austin .05 .02
❑ 184 Matt Harpring .05 .02
❑ 185 Michael Doleac .05 .02
❑ 186 Bo Outlaw .05 .02
❑ 187 Allen Iverson CL .40 .18
❑ 188 Allen Iverson .75 .35
❑ 189 Theo Ratliff .05 .02
❑ 190 Matt Geiger .05 .02
❑ 191 Larry Hughes .50 .23
❑ 192 Tyrone Hill .05 .02
❑ 193 George Lynch .05 .02
❑ 194 Eric Snow .05 .02
❑ 195 Aaron McKie .05 .02
❑ 196 Harvey Grant .05 .02
❑ 197 Jason Kidd CL .25 .11
❑ 198 Jason Kidd .60 .25
❑ 199 Tom Gugliotta .10 .05
❑ 200 Rex Chapman .05 .02
❑ 201 Clifford Robinson .05 .02
❑ 202 Luc Longley .05 .02
❑ 203 Danny Manning .10 .05
❑ 204 Pat Garrity .05 .02
❑ 205 George McCloud .05 .02
❑ 206 Toby Bailey .05 .02
❑ 207 Brian Grant CL .05 .02
❑ 208 Rasheed Wallace .20 .09
❑ 209 Arvydas Sabonis .10 .05
❑ 210 Damon Stoudamire .20 .09
❑ 211 Brian Grant .10 .05
❑ 212 Isaiah Rider .10 .05
❑ 213 Walt Williams .05 .02
❑ 214 Jim Jackson .05 .02
❑ 215 Greg Anthony .05 .02
❑ 216 Stacey Augmon .05 .02
❑ 217 Vlade Divac CL .05 .02
❑ 218 Jason Williams .50 .23
❑ 219 Vlade Divac .05 .02
❑ 220 Chris Webber .60 .25
❑ 221 Nick Anderson .05 .02
❑ 222 Predrag Stojakovic .10 .05
❑ 223 Tariq Abdul-Wahad .05 .02
❑ 224 Vernon Maxwell .05 .02
❑ 225 Lawrence Funderburke .05 .02
❑ 226 Jon Barry .05 .02
❑ 227 David Robinson CL .20 .09
❑ 228 Tim Duncan 1.00 .45
❑ 229 Sean Elliott .05 .02
❑ 230 David Robinson .30 .14
❑ 231 Mario Elie .05 .02
❑ 232 Avery Johnson .05 .02
❑ 233 Steve Kerr .05 .02
❑ 234 Malik Rose .05 .02
❑ 235 Jaren Jackson .05 .02
❑ 236 Vin Baker CL .05 .02
❑ 237 Gary Payton .30 .14
❑ 238 Vin Baker .10 .05
❑ 239 Detlef Schrempf .10 .05
❑ 240 Hersey Hawkins .10 .05
❑ 241 Dale Ellis .05 .02
❑ 242 Rashard Lewis .30 .14
❑ 243 Billy Owens .05 .02
❑ 244 Aaron Williams .05 .02
❑ 245 Vince Carter CL .60 .25
❑ 246 Vince Carter 2.00 .90
❑ 247 John Wallace .05 .02
❑ 248 Doug Christie .05 .02
❑ 249 Tracy McGrady .60 .25
❑ 250 Kevin Willis .05 .02
❑ 251 Michael Stewart .05 .02
❑ 252 Dee Brown .05 .02
❑ 253 John Thomas .05 .02
❑ 254 Alvin Williams .05 .02
❑ 255 Karl Malone CL .20 .09
❑ 256 Karl Malone .30 .14
❑ 257 John Stockton .20 .09
❑ 258 Jacque Vaughn .05 .02
❑ 259 Bryon Russell .05 .02
❑ 260 Howard Eisley .05 .02
❑ 261 Greg Ostertag .05 .02
❑ 262 Adam Keefe .05 .02
❑ 263 Todd Fuller .05 .02
❑ 264 Mike Bibby CL .20 .09
❑ 265 Shareef Abdur-Rahim .40 .18
❑ 266 Mike Bibby .25 .11
❑ 267 Bryant Reeves .05 .02
❑ 268 Felipe Lopez .05 .02
❑ 269 Cherokee Parks .05 .02
❑ 270 Michael Smith .05 .02
❑ 271 Tony Massenburg .05 .02
❑ 272 Rodrick Rhodes .05 .02
❑ 273 Juwan Howard CL .05 .02
❑ 274 Juwan Howard .10 .05
❑ 275 Rod Strickland .10 .05
❑ 276 Mitch Richmond .20 .09
❑ 277 Otis Thorpe .05 .02
❑ 278 Calbert Cheaney .05 .02
❑ 279 Tracy Murray .05 .02
❑ 280 Ben Wallace .05 .02

❑ 281 Terry Davis .05 .02
❑ 282 Michael Jordan RF 1.25 .55
❑ 283 Reggie Miller RF .10 .05
❑ 284 Dikembe Mutombo RF .05 .02
❑ 285 Patrick Ewing RF .10 .05
❑ 286 Allan Houston RF .10 .05
❑ 287 Danny Manning RF .05 .02
❑ 288 Jalen Rose RF .10 .05
❑ 289 Rasheed Wallace RF .10 .05
❑ 290 Jerry Stackhouse RF .05 .02
❑ 291 Damon Stoudamire RF .10 .05
❑ 292 Kenny Anderson RF .05 .02
❑ 293 Shawn Kemp RF .20 .09
❑ 294 Vlade Divac RF .05 .02
❑ 295 Larry Johnson RF .05 .02
❑ 296 Jamal Mashburn RF .05 .02
❑ 297 Ron Harper RF .05 .02
❑ 298 Steve Smith RF .05 .02
❑ 299 Kendall Gill RF .05 .02
❑ 300 Chris Mullin RF .10 .05
❑ 301 Robert Horry RF .05 .02
❑ 302 Dikembe Mutombo DD .05 .02
❑ 303 Ron Mercer DD .10 .05
❑ 304 Eddie Jones DD .20 .09
❑ 305 Toni Kukoc DD .20 .09
❑ 306 Derek Anderson DD .10 .05
❑ 307 Shawn Bradley DD .05 .02
❑ 308 Danny Fortson DD .05 .02
❑ 309 Bison Dele DD .05 .02
❑ 310 Antawn Jamison DD .20 .09
❑ 311 Scottie Pippen DD .30 .14
❑ 312 Reggie Miller DD .10 .05
❑ 313 Maurice Taylor DD .10 .05
❑ 314 Glen Rice DD .05 .02
❑ 315 Alonzo Mourning DD .10 .05
❑ 316 Glenn Robinson DD .05 .02
❑ 317 Anthony Peeler DD .05 .02
❑ 318 Kerry Kittles DD .05 .02
❑ 319 Latrell Sprewell DD .20 .09
❑ 320 Darrell Armstrong DD .05 .02
❑ 321 Larry Hughes DD .10 .05
❑ 322 Tom Gugliotta DD .05 .02
❑ 323 Brian Grant DD .05 .02
❑ 324 Chris Webber DD .25 .11
❑ 325 David Robinson DD .20 .09
❑ 326 Vin Baker DD .05 .02
❑ 327 Vince Carter DD .60 .25
❑ 328 Bryon Russell DD .05 .02
❑ 329 Felipe Lopez DD .05 .02
❑ 330 Juwan Howard DD .05 .02
❑ 331 Michael Jordan DD 1.25 .55
❑ 332 Jason Kidd CC .25 .11
❑ 333 Rod Strickland CC .05 .02
❑ 334 Stephon Marbury CC .20 .09
❑ 335 Gary Payton CC .20 .09
❑ 336 Mark Jackson CC .05 .02
❑ 337 John Stockton CC .10 .05
❑ 338 Brevin Knight CC .05 .02
❑ 339 Bobby Jackson CC .05 .02
❑ 340 Nick Van Exel CC .05 .02
❑ 341 Tim Hardaway CC .10 .05
❑ 342 Darrell Armstrong CC .05 .02
❑ 343 Avery Johnson CC .05 .02
❑ 344 Mike Bibby CC .20 .09
❑ 345 Damon Stoudamire CC .10 .05
❑ 346 Jason Williams CC .40 .18
❑ 347 Allen Iverson PC .40 .18
❑ 348 Kobe Bryant PC .75 .35
❑ 349 Karl Malone PC .20 .09
❑ 350 Keith Van Horn PC .20 .09
❑ 351 Kevin Garnett PC .60 .25
❑ 352 Antoine Walker PC .20 .09
❑ 353 Tim Duncan PC .60 .25
❑ 354 Scottie Pippen PC .30 .14
❑ 355 Paul Pierce PC .20 .09
❑ 356 Michael Finley PC .10 .05
❑ 357 Shaquille O'Neal PC .40 .18
❑ 358 Grant Hill PC .60 .25
❑ 359 Jason Williams PC .40 .18
❑ 360 Antonio McDyess PC .10 .05
❑ 361 Shareef Abdur-Rahim PC .20 .09
❑ 362 Allen Iverson SC .40 .18
❑ 363 Shaquille O'Neal SC .40 .18
❑ 364 Karl Malone SC .20 .09
❑ 365 Shareef Abdur-Rahim SC .20 .09
❑ 366 Keith Van Horn SC .20 .09
❑ 367 Tim Duncan SC .60 .25
❑ 368 Gary Payton SC .20 .09
❑ 369 Stephon Marbury SC .20 .09
❑ 370 Antonio McDyess SC .10 .05
❑ 371 Grant Hill SC .60 .25
❑ 372 Kevin Garnett SC .60 .25
❑ 373 Shawn Kemp SC .20 .09
❑ 374 Kobe Bryant SC .75 .35
❑ 375 Michael Finley SC .10 .05
❑ 376 Vince Carter SC .60 .25
❑ 377 Checklist .05 .02
❑ 378 Checklist .05 .02
❑ 379 Checklist .05 .02
❑ 380 Checklist .05 .02
❑ 381 Michael Jordan GH 1.00 .45
❑ 382 Michael Jordan GH 1.00 .45
❑ 383 Michael Jordan GH 1.00 .45
❑ 384 Michael Jordan GH 1.00 .45
❑ 385 Michael Jordan GH 1.00 .45
❑ 386 Michael Jordan GH 1.00 .45
❑ 387 Michael Jordan GH 1.00 .45
❑ 388 Michael Jordan GH 1.00 .45
❑ 389 Michael Jordan GH 1.00 .45
❑ 390 Michael Jordan GH 1.00 .45
❑ 391 Michael Jordan GH 1.00 .45
❑ 392 Michael Jordan GH 1.00 .45
❑ 393 Michael Jordan GH 1.00 .45
❑ 394 Michael Jordan GH 1.00 .45
❑ 395 Michael Jordan GH 1.00 .45
❑ 396 Michael Jordan GH 1.00 .45
❑ 397 Michael Jordan GH 1.00 .45
❑ 398 Michael Jordan GH 1.00 .45
❑ 399 Michael Jordan GH 1.00 .45
❑ 400 Michael Jordan GH 1.00 .45
❑ 401 Michael Jordan GH 1.00 .45
❑ 402 Michael Jordan GH 1.00 .45
❑ 403 Michael Jordan GH 1.00 .45
❑ 404 Michael Jordan GH 1.00 .45
❑ 405 Michael Jordan GH 1.00 .45
❑ 406 Michael Jordan GH 1.00 .45
❑ 407 Michael Jordan GH 1.00 .45
❑ 408 Michael Jordan GH 1.00 .45
❑ 409 Michael Jordan GH 1.00 .45
❑ 410 Michael Jordan GH 1.00 .45
❑ 411 Michael Jordan GH 1.00 .45
❑ 412 Michael Jordan GH 1.00 .45
❑ 413 Michael Jordan GH 1.00 .45
❑ 414 Michael Jordan GH 1.00 .45
❑ 415 Michael Jordan GH 1.00 .45
❑ 416 Michael Jordan GH 1.00 .45
❑ 417 Michael Jordan GH 1.00 .45
❑ 418 Michael Jordan GH 1.00 .45
❑ 419 Michael Jordan GH 1.00 .45
❑ 420 Michael Jordan GH 1.00 .45
❑ 421 Michael Jordan GH 1.00 .45
❑ 422 Michael Jordan GH 1.00 .45
❑ 423 Michael Jordan GH 1.00 .45
❑ 424 Michael Jordan GH 1.00 .45
❑ 425 Michael Jordan GH 1.00 .45
❑ 426 Michael Jordan GH 1.00 .45
❑ 427 Michael Jordan GH 1.00 .45
❑ 428 Michael Jordan GH 1.00 .45
❑ 429 Michael Jordan GH 1.00 .45
❑ 430 Michael Jordan GH 1.00 .45
❑ 431 Elton Brand RC 5.00 2.20
❑ 432 Steve Francis RC 6.00 2.70
❑ 433 Baron Davis RC 1.25 .55
❑ 434 Lamar Odom RC 4.00 1.80
❑ 435 Wally Szczerbiak RC 2.00 .90
❑ 436 Richard Hamilton RC 1.25 .55
❑ 437 Andre Miller RC 1.50 .70
❑ 438 Shawn Marion RC 1.50 .70
❑ 439 Jason Terry RC .75 .35
❑ 440 Corey Maggette RC 2.00 .90

1996-97 Z-Force

	MINT	NRMT
COMPLETE SET (200)	40.00	18.00
COMPLETE SERIES 1 (100)	20.00	9.00
COMPLETE SERIES 2 (100)	20.00	9.00
COMMON CARD (1-200)	.10	.05
SEMISTARS	.15	.07
UNLISTED STARS	.30	.14

SUBSET CARDS HALF VALUE OF BASE CARDS

HILL Z: SER.2 STATED ODDS 1:900 HOB/RET

❑ 1 Mookie Blaylock .10 .05
❑ 2 Alan Henderson .10 .05
❑ 3 Christian Laettner .15 .07
❑ 4 Steve Smith .15 .07
❑ 5 Rick Fox .10 .05
❑ 6 Dino Radja .10 .05
❑ 7 Eric Williams .10 .05
❑ 8 Muggsy Bogues .10 .05
❑ 9 Larry Johnson .15 .07
❑ 10 Glen Rice .15 .07
❑ 11 Michael Jordan 4.00 1.80
❑ 12 Toni Kukoc .40 .18
❑ 13 Scottie Pippen 1.00 .45
❑ 14 Dennis Rodman .60 .25
❑ 15 Terrell Brandon .15 .07
❑ 16 Bobby Phills .10 .05
❑ 17 Bob Sura .10 .05
❑ 18 Jim Jackson .10 .05
❑ 19 Jason Kidd 1.00 .45
❑ 20 Jamal Mashburn .15 .07
❑ 21 George McCloud .10 .05
❑ 22 Mahmoud Abdul-Rauf .10 .05
❑ 23 Antonio McDyess .50 .23
❑ 24 Dikembe Mutombo .15 .07
❑ 25 Joe Dumars .30 .14
❑ 26 Grant Hill 1.50 .70
❑ 27 Allan Houston .30 .14
❑ 28 Otis Thorpe .10 .05
❑ 29 Chris Mullin .30 .14
❑ 30 Joe Smith .30 .14
❑ 31 Latrell Sprewell .60 .25
❑ 32 Sam Cassell .15 .07
❑ 33 Clyde Drexler .30 .14
❑ 34 Robert Horry .10 .05
❑ 35 Hakeem Olajuwon .50 .23
❑ 36 Travis Best .10 .05
❑ 37 Dale Davis .10 .05
❑ 38 Reggie Miller .30 .14
❑ 39 Rik Smits .10 .05
❑ 40 Brent Barry .10 .05
❑ 41 Loy Vaught .10 .05
❑ 42 Brian Williams .10 .05
❑ 43 Cedric Ceballos .10 .05
❑ 44 Eddie Jones .60 .25
❑ 45 Nick Van Exel .15 .07
❑ 46 Tim Hardaway .30 .14
❑ 47 Alonzo Mourning .30 .14
❑ 48 Kurt Thomas .10 .05
❑ 49 Walt Williams .10 .05
❑ 50 Vin Baker .15 .07
❑ 51 Glenn Robinson .30 .14
❑ 52 Kevin Garnett 2.00 .90
❑ 53 Tom Gugliotta .15 .07
❑ 54 Isaiah Rider .15 .07
❑ 55 Shawn Bradley .10 .05
❑ 56 Chris Childs .10 .05
❑ 57 Jayson Williams .15 .07
❑ 58 Patrick Ewing .30 .14
❑ 59 Anthony Mason .15 .07
❑ 60 Charles Oakley .10 .05
❑ 61 Nick Anderson .10 .05
❑ 62 Horace Grant .15 .07
❑ 63 Anfernee Hardaway 1.00 .45
❑ 64 Shaquille O'Neal 1.50 .70
❑ 65 Dennis Scott .10 .05
❑ 66 Jerry Stackhouse .30 .14

❑ 67 Clarence Weatherspoon .. .10 .05
❑ 68 Charles Barkley .... .50 .23
❑ 69 Michael Finley .... .40 .18
❑ 70 Kevin Johnson................. .15 .07
❑ 71 Clifford Robinson............. .10 .05
❑ 72 Arvydas Sabonis .... .15 .07
❑ 73 Rod Strickland................. .15 .07
❑ 74 Tyus Edney .... .10 .05
❑ 75 Brian Grant .... .30 .14
❑ 76 Billy Owens .... .10 .05
❑ 77 Mitch Richmond .... .30 .14
❑ 78 Vinny Del Negro .... .10 .05
❑ 79 Sean Elliott .... .10 .05
❑ 80 Avery Johnson .... .10 .05
❑ 81 David Robinson............... .50 .23
❑ 82 Hersey Hawkins .... .15 .07
❑ 83 Shawn Kemp................... .50 .23
❑ 84 Gary Payton .... .50 .23
❑ 85 Detlef Schrempf .... .15 .07
❑ 86 Doug Christie .... .10 .05
❑ 87 Damon Stoudamire .... .50 .23
❑ 88 Sharone Wright .... .10 .05
❑ 89 Jeff Hornacek .... .15 .07
❑ 90 Karl Malone .... .50 .23
❑ 91 John Stockton .... .30 .14
❑ 92 Greg Anthony .... .10 .05
❑ 93 Bryant Reeves.................. .10 .05
❑ 94 Byron Scott .... .10 .05
❑ 95 Juwan Howard .... .15 .07
❑ 96 Gheorghe Muresan .... .10 .05
❑ 97 Rasheed Wallace .... .40 .18
❑ 98 Chris Webber .... 1.00 .45
❑ 99 Checklist .... .10 .05
❑ 100 Checklist .... .10 .05
❑ 101 Dikembe Mutombo .... .15 .07
❑ 102 Dee Brown .... .10 .05
❑ 103 Dell Curry .... .10 .05
❑ 104 Vlade Divac.................... .10 .05
❑ 105 Anthony Mason .... .15 .07
❑ 106 Robert Parish .... .15 .07
❑ 107 Oliver Miller .... .10 .05
❑ 108 Eric Montross .... .10 .05
❑ 109 Ervin Johnson .... .10 .05
❑ 110 Stacey Augmon............. .10 .05
❑ 111 Charles Barkley............. .50 .23
❑ 112 Jalen Rose .... .30 .14
❑ 113 Rodney Rogers .... .10 .05
❑ 114 Shaquille O'Neal .... 1.50 .70
❑ 115 Dan Majerle................... .15 .07
❑ 116 Kendall Gill .... .15 .07
❑ 117 Khalid Reeves .... .10 .05
❑ 118 Allan Houston .... .30 .14
❑ 119 Larry Johnson .... .15 .07
❑ 120 John Starks .... .10 .05
❑ 121 Rony Seikaly .... .10 .05
❑ 122 Gerald Wilkins............... .10 .05
❑ 123 Michael Cage .... .10 .05
❑ 124 Derrick Coleman .... .15 .07
❑ 125 Sam Cassell .... .15 .07
❑ 126 Danny Manning.............. .15 .07
❑ 127 Robert Horry .... .10 .05
❑ 128 Kenny Anderson .... .15 .07
❑ 129 Isaiah Rider................... .15 .07
❑ 130 Rasheed Wallace .... .40 .18
❑ 131 Mahmoud Abdul-Rauf ..... .10 .05
❑ 132 Vernon Maxwell.............. .10 .05
❑ 133 Dominique Wilkins.......... .30 .14
❑ 134 Hubert Davis .... .10 .05
❑ 135 Popeye Jones .... .10 .05
❑ 136 Anthony Peeler .... .10 .05
❑ 137 Tracy Murray .... .10 .05
❑ 138 Rod Strickland............... .15 .07
❑ 139 Shareef Abdur-Rahim RC 2.00 .90
❑ 140 Ray Allen RC.............. 1.25 .55
❑ 141 Shandon Anderson RC .. .40 .18
❑ 142 Kobe Bryant RC 10.00 4.50
❑ 143 Marcus Camby RC ...... 1.00 .45
❑ 144 Erick Dampier RC .... .15 .07
❑ 145 Emanual Davis RC .... .10 .05
❑ 146 Tony Delk RC .... .15 .07
❑ 147 Todd Fuller RC .... .10 .05
❑ 148 Darvin Ham RC.............. .10 .05
❑ 149 Othella Harrington RC..... .30 .14
❑ 150 Shane Heal RC .... .10 .05
❑ 151 Allen Iverson RC 3.00 1.35
❑ 152 Dontae' Jones RC.......... .10 .05
❑ 153 Kerry Kittles RC............. .60 .25
❑ 154 Priest Lauderdale RC .... .10 .05
❑ 155 Matt Maloney RC .... .15 .07
❑ 156 Stephon Marbury RC .. 2.00 .90
❑ 157 Walter McCarty RC .... .10 .05
❑ 158 Steve Nash RC .... .15 .07
❑ 159 Jermaine O'Neal RC ...... .60 .25
❑ 160 Ray Owes RC .... .10 .05
❑ 161 Vitaly Potapenko RC...... .10 .05
❑ 162 Roy Rogers RC.............. .10 .05
❑ 163 Antoine Walker RC ...... 1.25 .55
❑ 164 Samaki Walker RC .... .10 .05
❑ 165 Ben Wallace RC .... .10 .05
❑ 166 John Wallace RC .... .30 .14
❑ 167 Jerome Williams RC ...... .50 .23
❑ 168 Lorenzen Wright RC ...... .15 .07
❑ 169 Vin Baker ZUP .... .10 .05
❑ 170 Charles Barkley ZUP...... .30 .14
❑ 171 Patrick Ewing ZUP .... .15 .07
❑ 172 Michael Finley ZUP .... .30 .14
❑ 173 Kevin Garnett ZUP ...... 1.00 .45
❑ 174 Anfernee Hardaway ZUP .60 .25
❑ 175 Grant Hill ZUP .... 1.00 .45
❑ 176 Juwan Howard ZUP ...... .10 .05
❑ 177 Jim Jackson ZUP .... .10 .05
❑ 178 Eddie Jones ZUP .... .30 .14
❑ 179 Michael Jordan ZUP .... 2.00 .90
❑ 180 Shawn Kemp ZUP.......... .30 .14
❑ 181 Jason Kidd ZUP .... .30 .14
❑ 182 Karl Malone ZUP............ .30 .14
❑ 183 Antonio McDyess ZUP .. .30 .14
❑ 184 Reggie Miller ZUP.......... .15 .07
❑ 185 Alonzo Mourning ZUP.... .15 .07
❑ 186 Hakeem Olajuwon ZUP.. .30 .14
❑ 187 Shaquille O'Neal ZUP .... .60 .25
❑ 188 Gary Payton ZUP .... .30 .14
❑ 189 Mitch Richmond ZUP .... .15 .07
❑ 190 Clifford Robinson ZUP .. .10 .05
❑ 191 David Robinson ZUP...... .30 .14
❑ 192 Glenn Robinson ZUP .... .15 .07
❑ 193 Dennis Rodman ZUP .... .30 .14
❑ 194 Joe Smith ZUP .... .15 .07
❑ 195 Jerry Stackhouse ZUP .. .15 .07
❑ 196 John Stockton ZUP .... .15 .07
❑ 197 Damon Stoudamire ZUP .30 .14
❑ 198 Chris Webber ZUP .... .40 .18
❑ 199 Checklist (101-157)........ .10 .05
❑ 200 Checklist (158-200/ins.) .10 .05
❑ NNO Grant Hill 5.00 2.20
Jerry Stackhouse Promo
❑ NNO Grant Hill Promo 5.00 2.20
❑ NNO Grant Hill Total Z 25.00 11.00

1996-97 Z-Force Z-Cling

	MINT	NRMT
COMPLETE SET (100)	50.00	22.00
COMMON CARD (1-100)...........	.20	.09
SEMISTARS...........................	.40	.18
UNLISTED STARS...................	1.00	.45

*Z-CLING: 1.25X TO 2.5X BASIC
ONE IN EVERY SER.1 PACK
TWO PER SPECIAL SER.1 RETAIL PACK
NUMBER 94 NEVER ISSUED

❑ 64 Shaquille O'Neal 6.00 2.70
Lakers uniform
❑ R1 Ray Allen 4.00 1.80
❑ R2 Stephon Marbury 6.00 2.70
❑ R3 Shareef Abdur-Rahim.... 6.00 2.70

1996-97 Z-Force Big Men on the Court

	MINT	NRMT
COMPLETE SET (10)	400.00	180.00
COMMON CARD (1-10).........	12.00	5.50

SER.2 STATED ODDS 1:240 HOBBY/RETAIL

COMP.BMOC Z-P.SET (10)..	800.00	350.00
COMMON BMOC Z-P.(1-10) ..	25.00	11.00

*BMOC Z-PEAT STARS: 1.25X TO 2X
BMOC Z-P: SER.2 STATED ODDS 1:1,120 H/R

❑ 1 Charles Barkley............. 20.00 9.00
❑ 2 Anfernee Hardaway 40.00 18.00
❑ 3 Grant Hill 60.00 27.00
❑ 4 Michael Jordan 150.00 70.00
❑ 5 Shawn Kemp.................. 20.00 9.00
❑ 6 Alonzo Mourning............ 12.00 5.50
❑ 7 Hakeem Olajuwon.......... 20.00 9.00
❑ 8 Shaquille O'Neal 60.00 27.00
❑ 9 Scottie Pippen 40.00 18.00
❑ 10 David Robinson............ 20.00 9.00

1996-97 Z-Force Little Big Men

	MINT	NRMT
COMPLETE SET (10)	40.00	18.00
COMMON CARD (1-10)............	2.00	.90
SEMISTARS............................	2.50	1.10
UNLISTED STARS....................	4.00	1.80

SER.2 STATED ODDS 1:36 RETAIL

❑ 1 Kenny Anderson 2.50 1.10
❑ 2 Mookie Blaylock .... 2.00 .90
❑ 3 Muggsy Bogues .... 2.00 .90
❑ 4 Terrell Brandon 2.50 1.10
❑ 5 Allen Iverson 20.00 9.00
❑ 6 Avery Johnson .... 2.00 .90
❑ 7 Kevin Johnson................ 2.50 1.10
❑ 8 Stephon Marbury........... 12.00 5.50
❑ 9 Gary Payton 6.00 2.70
❑ 10 Nick Van Exel 2.50 1.10

1996-97 Z-Force Slam Cam

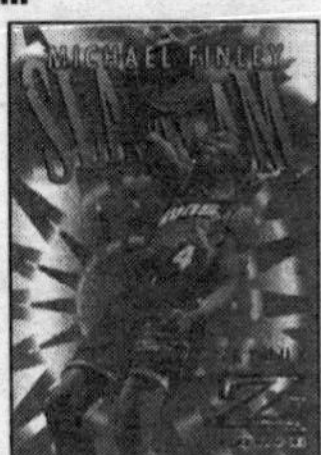

	MINT	NRMT
COMPLETE SET (9)	350.00	160.00
COMMON CARD (SC1-SC9)	12.00	5.50

SER.1 STATED ODDS 1:240 HOBBY/RETAIL

	MINT	NRMT
❑ SC1 Clyde Drexler	12.00	5.50
❑ SC2 Michael Finley	15.00	6.75
❑ SC3 Anfernee Hardaway	40.00	18.00
❑ SC4 Grant Hill	60.00	27.00
❑ SC5 Michael Jordan	150.00	70.00
❑ SC6 Shawn Kemp	20.00	9.00
❑ SC7 Karl Malone	20.00	9.00
❑ SC8 Antonio McDyess	20.00	9.00
❑ SC9 Shaquille O'Neal	60.00	27.00

1996-97 Z-Force Swat Team

	MINT	NRMT
COMPLETE SET (9)	80.00	36.00
COMMON CARD (ST1-ST9)	3.00	1.35
SEMISTARS	6.00	2.70

SER.1 STATED ODDS 1:72 HOBBY

	MINT	NRMT
❑ ST1 Patrick Ewing	6.00	2.70
❑ ST2 Kevin Garnett	40.00	18.00
❑ ST3 Alonzo Mourning	6.00	2.70
❑ ST4 Dikembe Mutombo	3.00	1.35
❑ ST5 Hakeem Olajuwon	10.00	4.50
❑ ST6 Shaquille O'Neal	30.00	13.50
❑ ST7 David Robinson	10.00	4.50
❑ ST8 Dennis Rodman	12.00	5.50
❑ ST9 Joe Smith	6.00	2.70

1996-97 Z-Force Vortex

	MINT	NRMT
COMPLETE SET (15)	100.00	45.00
COMMON CARD (V1-V15)	2.00	.90
SEMISTARS	2.50	1.10
UNLISTED STARS	4.00	1.80

SER.1 STATED ODDS 1:36 RETAIL

	MINT	NRMT
❑ V1 Charles Barkley	6.00	2.70
❑ V2 Anfernee Hardaway	12.00	5.50
❑ V3 Grant Hill	20.00	9.00
❑ V4 Juwan Howard	2.50	1.10
❑ V5 Michael Jordan	50.00	22.00
❑ V6 Jason Kidd	12.00	5.50
❑ V7 Reggie Miller	4.00	1.80
❑ V8 Gary Payton	6.00	2.70
❑ V9 Scottie Pippen	12.00	5.50
❑ V10 Mitch Richmond	4.00	1.80
❑ V11 Glenn Robinson	4.00	1.80
❑ V12 Arvydas Sabonis	2.00	.90
❑ V13 Jerry Stackhouse	4.00	1.80
❑ V14 John Stockton	4.00	1.80
❑ V15 Damon Stoudamire	6.00	2.70

1996-97 Z-Force Zebut

	MINT	NRMT
COMPLETE SET (20)	100.00	45.00
COMMON CARD (1-20)	1.25	.55
SEMISTARS	2.50	1.10
UNLISTED STARS	4.00	1.80

SER.2 STATED ODDS 1:24 HOBBY

COMP.ZEBUT Z-P.SET (20)	400.00	180.00
COMMON ZEBUT Z-P. (1-20)	5.00	2.20

*ZEBUT Z-PEAT RC's: 2X TO 4X
ZEBUT Z-P: SER.2 STATED ODDS 1:240 HOB

	MINT	NRMT
❑ 1 Shareef Abdur-Rahim	12.00	5.50
❑ 2 Ray Allen	8.00	3.60
❑ 3 Kobe Bryant	40.00	18.00
❑ 4 Marcus Camby	6.00	2.70
❑ 5 Erick Dampier	1.25	.55
❑ 6 Todd Fuller	1.25	.55
❑ 7 Othella Harrington	2.50	1.10
❑ 8 Allen Iverson	20.00	9.00
❑ 9 Kerry Kittles	4.00	1.80
❑ 10 Priest Lauderdale	1.25	.55
❑ 11 Stephon Marbury	12.00	5.50
❑ 12 Steve Nash	1.25	.55
❑ 13 Jermaine O'Neal	4.00	1.80
❑ 14 Ray Owes	1.25	.55
❑ 15 Vitaly Potapenko	1.25	.55
❑ 16 Roy Rogers	1.25	.55
❑ 17 Antoine Walker	8.00	3.60
❑ 18 Samaki Walker	1.25	.55
❑ 19 John Wallace	2.50	1.10
❑ 20 Lorenzen Wright	1.25	.55

1996-97 Z-Force Zensations

	MINT	NRMT
COMPLETE SET (20)	25.00	11.00

COMMON CARD (1-20)	.60	.25
SEMISTARS	.75	.35
UNLISTED STARS	1.25	.55

SER.2 STATED ODDS 1:6 HOBBY/RETAIL

❑ 1 Shareef Abdur-Rahim	5.00	2.20
❑ 2 Ray Allen	3.00	1.35
❑ 3 Nick Anderson	.60	.25
❑ 4 Vin Baker	.75	.35
❑ 5 Mookie Blaylock	.60	.25
❑ 6 Calbert Cheaney	.60	.25
❑ 7 Kevin Garnett	8.00	3.60
❑ 8 Horace Grant	.75	.35
❑ 9 Tim Hardaway	1.25	.55
❑ 10 Allen Iverson	8.00	3.60
❑ 11 Avery Johnson	.60	.25
❑ 12 Kevin Johnson	.75	.35
❑ 13 Danny Manning	.75	.35
❑ 14 Stephon Marbury	5.00	2.20
❑ 15 Jamal Mashburn	.75	.35
❑ 16 Glen Rice	.75	.35
❑ 17 Isaiah Rider	.75	.35
❑ 18 Latrell Sprewell	2.50	1.10
❑ 19 Rod Strickland	.75	.35
❑ 20 Nick Van Exel	.75	.35

1997-98 Z-Force

	MINT	NRMT
COMPLETE SET (210)	25.00	11.00
COMPLETE SERIES 1 (110)	10.00	4.50
COMPLETE SERIES 2 (100)	15.00	6.75
COMMON CARD (1-210)	.10	.05
SEMISTARS	.15	.07
UNLISTED STARS	.25	.11

SUBSET CARDS HALF VALUE OF BASE CARDS
CARD NUMBER 143 DOES NOT EXIST
BAKER AND MCGRADY BOTH #'d 172

	MINT	NRMT
❑ 1 Anfernee Hardaway	.75	.35
❑ 2 Mitch Richmond	.25	.11
❑ 3 Stephon Marbury	.75	.35
❑ 4 Charles Barkley	.40	.18
❑ 5 Juwan Howard	.15	.07
❑ 6 Avery Johnson	.10	.05
❑ 7 Rex Chapman	.10	.05
❑ 8 Antoine Walker	.50	.23
❑ 9 Nick Van Exel	.15	.07
❑ 10 Tim Hardaway	.25	.11
❑ 11 Clarence Weatherspoon	.10	.05

❑ 12 John Stockton .25 .11
❑ 13 Glenn Robinson .15 .07
❑ 14 Anthony Mason .15 .07
❑ 15 Latrell Sprewell .50 .23
❑ 16 Kendall Gill .15 .07
❑ 17 Terry Mills .10 .05
❑ 18 Mookie Blaylock .10 .05
❑ 19 Michael Finley .25 .11
❑ 20 Gary Payton .40 .18
❑ 21 Kevin Garnett 1.50 .70
❑ 22 Clyde Drexler .25 .11
❑ 23 Michael Jordan 3.00 1.35
❑ 24 Antonio McDyess .30 .14
❑ 25 Nick Anderson .10 .05
❑ 26 Patrick Ewing .25 .11
❑ 27 Anthony Peeler .10 .05
❑ 28 Doug Christie .10 .05
❑ 29 Bobby Phills .10 .05
❑ 30 Kerry Kittles .25 .11
❑ 31 Reggie Miller .25 .11
❑ 32 Karl Malone .40 .18
❑ 33 Grant Hill 1.25 .55
❑ 34 Shaquille O'Neal 1.25 .55
❑ 35 Loy Vaught .10 .05
❑ 36 Kenny Anderson .15 .07
❑ 37 Wesley Person .10 .05
❑ 38 Jamal Mashburn .15 .07
❑ 39 Christian Laettner .15 .07
❑ 40 Shawn Kemp .40 .18
❑ 41 Glen Rice .15 .07
❑ 42 Vin Baker .15 .07
❑ 43 Popeye Jones .10 .05
❑ 44 Derrick Coleman .15 .07
❑ 45 Rik Smits .10 .05
❑ 46 Dale Ellis .10 .05
❑ 47 Rod Strickland .15 .07
❑ 48 Mark Price .10 .05
❑ 49 Toni Kukoc .30 .14
❑ 50 David Robinson .40 .18
❑ 51 John Wallace .10 .05
❑ 52 Samaki Walker .10 .05
❑ 53 Shareef Abdur-Rahim .75 .35
❑ 54 Rodney Rogers .10 .05
❑ 55 Dikembe Mutombo .15 .07
❑ 56 Rony Seikaly .10 .05
❑ 57 Matt Maloney .10 .05
❑ 58 Chris Webber .75 .35
❑ 59 Robert Horry .10 .05
❑ 60 Rasheed Wallace .25 .11
❑ 61 Jeff Hornacek .15 .07
❑ 62 Walt Williams .10 .05
❑ 63 Detlef Schrempf .15 .07
❑ 64 Dan Majerle .15 .07
❑ 65 Dell Curry .10 .05
❑ 66 Scottie Pippen .75 .35
❑ 67 Greg Anthony .10 .05
❑ 68 Mahmoud Abdul-Rauf .10 .05
❑ 69 Cedric Ceballos .10 .05
❑ 70 Terrell Brandon .15 .07
❑ 71 Arvydas Sabonis .15 .07
❑ 72 Malik Sealy .10 .05
❑ 73 Dean Garrett .10 .05
❑ 74 Joe Dumars .25 .11
❑ 75 Joe Smith .15 .07
❑ 76 Shawn Bradley .10 .05
❑ 77 Gheorghe Muresan .10 .05
❑ 78 Dale Davis .10 .05
❑ 79 Bryant Stith .10 .05
❑ 80 Lorenzen Wright .10 .05
❑ 81 Chris Childs .10 .05
❑ 82 Bryon Russell .10 .05
❑ 83 Steve Smith .15 .07
❑ 84 Jerry Stackhouse .15 .07
❑ 85 Hersey Hawkins .15 .07
❑ 86 Ray Allen .40 .18
❑ 87 Dominique Wilkins .25 .11
❑ 88 Kobe Bryant 2.00 .90
❑ 89 Tom Gugliotta .15 .07
❑ 90 Dennis Scott .10 .05
❑ 91 Dennis Rodman .50 .23
❑ 92 Bryant Reeves .10 .05
❑ 93 Vlade Divac .10 .05
❑ 94 Jason Kidd .75 .35
❑ 95 Mario Elie .10 .05
❑ 96 Lindsey Hunter .10 .05
❑ 97 Olden Polynice .10 .05
❑ 98 Allan Houston .25 .11
❑ 99 Alonzo Mourning .25 .11
❑ 100 Allen Iverson 1.25 .55
❑ 101 LaPhonso Ellis .10 .05
❑ 102 Bob Sura .10 .05
❑ 103 Chris Mullin .25 .11
❑ 104 Sam Cassell .15 .07
❑ 105 Eric Williams .10 .05
❑ 106 Antonio Davis .10 .05
❑ 107 Marcus Camby .30 .14
❑ 108 Isaiah Rider .15 .07
❑ 109 Checklist .10 .05
(Atlanta Hawks-Phoenix Suns)
❑ 110 Checklist .10 .05
(Portland-inserts)
❑ 111 Tim Duncan RC 3.00 1.35
❑ 112 Joe Smith .15 .07
❑ 113 Shawn Kemp .40 .18
❑ 114 Terry Mills .10 .05
❑ 115 Jacque Vaughn RC .15 .07
❑ 116 Ron Mercer RC .75 .35
❑ 117 Brian Williams .10 .05
❑ 118 Rik Smits .10 .05
❑ 119 Eric Williams .10 .05
❑ 120 Tim Thomas RC .75 .35
❑ 121 Damon Stoudamire .30 .14
❑ 122 God Shammgod RC .10 .05
❑ 123 Tyrone Hill .10 .05
❑ 124 Elden Campbell .10 .05
❑ 125 Keith Van Horn RC 1.25 .55
❑ 126 Brian Grant .15 .07
❑ 127 Antonio McDyess .30 .14
❑ 128 Darrell Armstrong .15 .07
❑ 129 Sam Perkins .15 .07
❑ 130 Chris Mills .10 .05
❑ 131 Reggie Miller .25 .11
❑ 132 Chris Gatling .10 .05
❑ 133 Ed Gray RC .10 .05
❑ 134 Hakeem Olajuwon .40 .18
❑ 135 Chris Webber .75 .35
❑ 136 Kendall Gill .15 .07
❑ 137 Wesley Person .10 .05
❑ 138 Derrick Coleman .15 .07
❑ 139 Dana Barros .10 .05
❑ 140 Dennis Scott .10 .05
❑ 141 Paul Grant RC .10 .05
❑ 142 Scott Burrell .10 .05
❑ 143 Does not Exist
❑ 144 Austin Croshere RC .60 .25
❑ 145 Maurice Taylor RC .50 .23
❑ 146 Kevin Johnson .15 .07
❑ 147 Tony Battie RC .25 .11
❑ 148 Tariq Abdul-Wahad RC .15 .07
❑ 149 Johnny Taylor RC .10 .05
❑ 150 Allen Iverson 1.25 .55
❑ 151 Terrell Brandon .15 .07
❑ 152 Derek Anderson RC .60 .25
❑ 153 Calbert Cheaney .10 .05
❑ 154 Jayson Williams .15 .07
❑ 155 Rick Fox .10 .05
❑ 156 John Thomas RC .10 .05
❑ 157 David Wesley .10 .05
❑ 158 Bobby Jackson RC .15 .07
❑ 159 Kelvin Cato RC .25 .11
❑ 160 Vinny Del Negro .10 .05
❑ 161 Adonal Foyle RC .15 .07
❑ 162 Larry Johnson .15 .07
❑ 163 Brevin Knight RC .40 .18
❑ 164 Rod Strickland .15 .07
❑ 165 Rodrick Rhodes RC .10 .05
❑ 166 Scot Pollard RC .15 .07
❑ 167 Sam Cassell .15 .07
❑ 168 Jerry Stackhouse .15 .07
❑ 169 Mark Jackson .10 .05
❑ 170 John Wallace .10 .05
❑ 171 Horace Grant .15 .07
❑ 172A Vin Baker .15 .07
❑ 172B T. McGrady RC ERR 2.50 1.10
❑ 173 Eddie Jones .50 .23
❑ 174 Kerry Kittles .25 .11
❑ 175 Antonio Daniels RC .25 .11
❑ 176 Alan Henderson .10 .05
❑ 177 Sean Elliott .10 .05
❑ 178 John Starks .10 .05
❑ 179 Chauncey Billups RC .30 .14
❑ 180 Juwan Howard .15 .07
❑ 181 Bobby Phills .10 .05
❑ 182 Latrell Sprewell .50 .23
❑ 183 Jim Jackson .10 .05
❑ 184 Danny Fortson RC .25 .11
❑ 185 Zydrunas Ilgauskas .10 .05
❑ 186 Clifford Robinson .10 .05
❑ 187 Chris Mullin .25 .11
❑ 188 Greg Ostertag .10 .05
❑ 189 Antoine Walker ZUP .25 .11
❑ 190 Michael Jordan ZUP 1.50 .70
❑ 191 Scottie Pippen ZUP .40 .18
❑ 192 Dennis Rodman ZUP .25 .11
❑ 193 Grant Hill ZUP .75 .35
❑ 194 Clyde Drexler ZUP .15 .07
❑ 195 Kobe Bryant ZUP 1.00 .45
❑ 196 Shaquille O'Neal ZUP .50 .23
❑ 197 Alonzo Mourning ZUP .15 .07
❑ 198 Ray Allen ZUP .25 .11
❑ 199 Kevin Garnett ZUP .75 .35
❑ 200 Stephon Marbury ZUP .60 .25
❑ 201 Anfernee Hardaway ZUP .50 .23
❑ 202 Jason Kidd ZUP .25 .11
❑ 203 David Robinson ZUP .25 .11
❑ 204 Gary Payton ZUP .25 .11
❑ 205 Marcus Camby ZUP .15 .07
❑ 206 Karl Malone ZUP .25 .11
❑ 207 John Stockton ZUP .15 .07
❑ 208 S. Abdur-Rahim ZUP .40 .18
❑ 209 Charles Barkley CL .25 .11
❑ 210 Gary Payton CL .25 .11

1997-98 Z-Force Rave

	MINT	NRMT
COMPLETE SET (208)	2500.00	1100.00
COMPLETE SERIES 1 (108)	1500.00	700.00
COMPLETE SERIES 2 (100)	1000.00	450.00
COMMON CARD	5.00	2.20

*STARS: 20X TO 50X BASE CARD HI
*RCs: 10X TO 25X BASE HI
STATED PRINT RUN 399 SERIAL #'d SETS
RANDOM INSERTS IN SER.1/2 HOBBY PACKS
CARD NUMBER 143 DOES NOT EXIST
BAKER AND MCGRADY BOTH #'d 172

1997-98 Z-Force Super Rave

	MINT	NRMT
COMMON CARD (111-210)	30.00	13.50

*STARS: 100X TO 250X BASE CARD HI

*RCs: 50X TO 125X BASE HI
RANDOM INSERTS IN SER.2 HOBBY PACKS
STATED PRINT RUN 50 SERIAL #'d SETS
CARD NUMBER 143 DOES NOT EXIST
BAKER AND MCGRADY BOTH #'d 172

- ❑ 111 Tim Duncan 300.00 135.00
- ❑ 190 Michael Jordan ZUP 1500.00 700.00
- ❑ 195 Kobe Bryant ZUP 600.00 275.00
- ❑ 209 Charles Barkley CL 70.00 32.00
- ❑ 210 Gary Payton CL.......... 70.00 32.00

1997-98 Z-Force Big Men on Court

	MINT	NRMT
COMPLETE SET (15)	550.00	250.00
COMMON CARD (1-15)..........	12.00	5.50

SER.2 STATED ODDS 1:288 HOB/RET

- ❑ 1 Shareef Abdur-Rahim 30.00 13.50
- ❑ 2 Kobe Bryant 80.00 36.00
- ❑ 3 Marcus Camby 12.00 5.50
- ❑ 4 Tim Duncan..................... 50.00 22.00
- ❑ 5 Kevin Garnett 60.00 27.00
- ❑ 6 Anfernee Hardaway 30.00 13.50
- ❑ 7 Grant Hill 50.00 22.00
- ❑ 8 Allen Iverson 50.00 22.00
- ❑ 9 Michael Jordan 125.00 55.00
- ❑ 10 Shawn Kemp................ 15.00 6.75
- ❑ 11 Stephon Marbury.......... 30.00 13.50
- ❑ 12 Shaquille O'Neal 50.00 22.00
- ❑ 13 Scottie Pippen.............. 30.00 13.50
- ❑ 14 Dennis Rodman 20.00 9.00
- ❑ 15 Antoine Walker 20.00 9.00

1997-98 Z-Force Boss

	MINT	NRMT
COMPLETE SET (20)	30.00	13.50
COMMON CARD (1-20)..........	.60	.25

SER.1 STATED ODDS 1:6 HOBBY/RETAIL

COMP.SUP.BOSS SET (20)	100.00	45.00
COMMON SUP.BOSS (1-20)....	2.00	.90

*SUP.BOSS: 1.25X TO 3X HI COLUMN
SUP.BOSS: SER.1 STATED ODDS 1:36 H/R

- ❑ 1 Shareef Abdur-Rahim ...... 2.00 .90
- ❑ 2 Ray Allen........................ 1.00 .45
- ❑ 3 Kobe Bryant 5.00 2.20
- ❑ 4 Marcus Camby .... .75 .35
- ❑ 5 Kevin Garnett 4.00 1.80
- ❑ 6 Anfernee Hardaway .... 2.00 .90
- ❑ 7 Grant Hill 3.00 1.35
- ❑ 8 Allen Iverson 3.00 1.35
- ❑ 9 Eddie Jones .... 1.25 .55
- ❑ 10 Michael Jordan 8.00 3.60
- ❑ 11 Shawn Kemp.................. 1.00 .45
- ❑ 12 Kerry Kittles..................... .60 .25
- ❑ 13 Stephon Marbury........... 2.00 .90
- ❑ 14 Shaquille O'Neal 3.00 1.35
- ❑ 15 Hakeem Olajuwon.......... 1.00 .45
- ❑ 16 Scottie Pippen................ 2.00 .90
- ❑ 17 Dennis Rodman .... 1.25 .55
- ❑ 18 Joe Smith .... .60 .25
- ❑ 19 Damon Stoudamire.......... .75 .35
- ❑ 20 Antoine Walker .... 1.25 .55

1997-98 Z-Force Fast Track

	MINT	NRMT
COMPLETE SET (12)	30.00	13.50
COMMON CARD (1-12)...........	2.00	.90

SER.1 STATED ODDS 1:24 HOBBY/RETAIL

- ❑ 1 Ray Allen.......................... 3.00 1.35
- ❑ 2 Kobe Bryant 15.00 6.75
- ❑ 3 Marcus Camby 2.50 1.10
- ❑ 4 Juwan Howard .... 2.00 .90
- ❑ 5 Eddie Jones 4.00 1.80
- ❑ 6 Kerry Kittles..................... 2.00 .90
- ❑ 7 Antonio McDyess 2.50 1.10
- ❑ 8 Joe Smith .... 2.00 .90
- ❑ 9 Jerry Stackhouse .... 2.00 .90
- ❑ 10 Damon Stoudamire........ 2.50 1.10
- ❑ 11 Antoine Walker 4.00 1.80
- ❑ 12 Chris Webber 6.00 2.70

1997-98 Z-Force Limited Access

	MINT	NRMT
COMPLETE SET (10)	50.00	22.00
COMMON CARD (1-10)...........	1.50	.70

SER.1 STATED ODDS 1:18 RETAIL

- ❑ 1 Shareef Abdur-Rahim 6.00 2.70
- ❑ 2 Ray Allen.......................... 3.00 1.35
- ❑ 3 Charles Barkley................ 3.00 1.35
- ❑ 4 Anfernee Hardaway 6.00 2.70
- ❑ 5 Juwan Howard .... 1.50 .70
- ❑ 6 Michael Jordan 25.00 11.00
- ❑ 7 Stephon Marbury............ 6.00 2.70
- ❑ 8 Shaquille O'Neal 10.00 4.50
- ❑ 9 Dennis Rodman 4.00 1.80
- ❑ 10 Antoine Walker 4.00 1.80

1997-98 Z-Force Quick Strike

	MINT	NRMT
COMPLETE SET (12)	120.00	55.00
COMMON CARD (1-12)..........	5.00	2.20

SER.2 STATED ODDS 1:96 HOB/RET

- ❑ 1 Shareef Abdur-Rahim 12.00 5.50
- ❑ 2 Anfernee Hardaway 12.00 5.50
- ❑ 3 Grant Hill 20.00 9.00
- ❑ 4 Allen Iverson 20.00 9.00
- ❑ 5 Michael Jordan 50.00 22.00
- ❑ 6 Stephon Marbury........... 12.00 5.50
- ❑ 7 Hakeem Olajuwon........... 6.00 2.70
- ❑ 8 Scottie Pippen............... 12.00 5.50
- ❑ 9 Damon Stoudamire 5.00 2.20
- ❑ 10 Keith Van Horn 10.00 4.50
- ❑ 11 Antoine Walker 8.00 3.60
- ❑ 12 Chris Webber 12.00 5.50

1997-98 Z-Force Rave Reviews

	MINT	NRMT
COMPLETE SET (12)	350.00	160.00
COMMON CARD (1-12)..........	12.00	5.50

SER.1 STATED ODDS 1:288 HOBBY/RETAIL

- ❑ 1 Shareef Abdur-Rahim 25.00 11.00
- ❑ 2 Kevin Garnett 50.00 22.00
- ❑ 3 Anfernee Hardaway 25.00 11.00
- ❑ 4 Grant Hill 40.00 18.00
- ❑ 5 Allen Iverson 40.00 18.00
- ❑ 6 Michael Jordan 100.00 45.00
- ❑ 7 Shawn Kemp................. 12.00 5.50
- ❑ 8 Stephon Marbury........... 25.00 11.00
- ❑ 9 Shaquille O'Neal 40.00 18.00
- ❑ 10 Hakeem Olajuwon........ 12.00 5.50
- ❑ 11 Scottie Pippen.............. 25.00 11.00
- ❑ 12 Dennis Rodman 15.00 6.75

1997-98 Z-Force Slam Cam

	MINT	NRMT
COMPLETE SET (12)	80.00	36.00
COMMON CARD (1-12)	2.50	1.10
SER.2 STATED ODDS 1:36 HOB/RET		

	MINT	NRMT
❑ 1 Kobe Bryant	20.00	9.00
❑ 2 Marcus Camby	3.00	1.35
❑ 3 Tim Duncan	12.00	5.50
❑ 4 Kevin Garnett	15.00	6.75
❑ 5 Michael Jordan	30.00	13.50
❑ 6 Shawn Kemp	4.00	1.80
❑ 7 Karl Malone	4.00	1.80
❑ 8 Antonio McDyess	3.00	1.35
❑ 9 Shaquille O'Neal	12.00	5.50
❑ 10 Joe Smith	2.50	1.10
❑ 11 Jerry Stackhouse	2.50	1.10
❑ 12 Chris Webber	8.00	3.60

1997-98 Z-Force Star Gazing

	MINT	NRMT
COMPLETE SET (15)	80.00	36.00
COMMON CARD (1-15)	2.50	1.10
SER.2 STATED ODDS 1:18 RETAIL		

	MINT	NRMT
❑ 1 Shareef Abdur-Rahim	6.00	2.70
❑ 2 Kobe Bryant	15.00	6.75
❑ 3 Marcus Camby	2.50	1.10
❑ 4 Kevin Garnett	12.00	5.50
❑ 5 Anfernee Hardaway	6.00	2.70
❑ 6 Grant Hill	10.00	4.50
❑ 7 Allen Iverson	10.00	4.50
❑ 8 Stephon Marbury	6.00	2.70
❑ 9 Hakeem Olajuwon	3.00	1.35
❑ 10 Shaquille O'Neal	10.00	4.50
❑ 11 Scottie Pippen	6.00	2.70
❑ 12 Dennis Rodman	4.00	1.80
❑ 13 Damon Stoudamire	2.50	1.10
❑ 14 Keith Van Horn	5.00	2.20
❑ 15 Antoine Walker	4.00	1.80

1997-98 Z-Force Total Impact

	MINT	NRMT
COMPLETE SET (12)	60.00	27.00
COMMON CARD (1-12)	2.50	1.10
SER.1 STATED ODDS 1:48 HOBBY/RETAIL		

	MINT	NRMT
❑ 1 Kobe Bryant	20.00	9.00
❑ 2 Marcus Camby	3.00	1.35
❑ 3 Kevin Garnett	15.00	6.75
❑ 4 Grant Hill	12.00	5.50
❑ 5 Allen Iverson	12.00	5.50
❑ 6 Eddie Jones	5.00	2.20
❑ 7 Shawn Kemp	4.00	1.80
❑ 8 Kerry Kittles	2.50	1.10
❑ 9 Hakeem Olajuwon	4.00	1.80
❑ 10 Scottie Pippen	8.00	3.60
❑ 11 Joe Smith	2.50	1.10
❑ 12 Chris Webber	8.00	3.60

1997-98 Z-Force Zebut

	MINT	NRMT
COMPLETE SET (12)	25.00	11.00
COMMON CARD (1-12)	1.00	.45
SEMISTARS	1.25	.55
UNLISTED STARS	2.00	.90
SER.2 STATED ODDS 1:24 HOB/RET		

	MINT	NRMT
❑ 1 Derek Anderson	2.50	1.10
❑ 2 Tony Battie	1.00	.45
❑ 3 Chauncey Billups	1.25	.55
❑ 4 Austin Croshere	2.50	1.10
❑ 5 Antonio Daniels	1.25	.55
❑ 6 Tim Duncan	10.00	4.50
❑ 7 Danny Fortson	1.00	.45
❑ 8 Tracy McGrady	10.00	4.50
❑ 9 Ron Mercer	3.00	1.35
❑ 10 Tariq Abdul-Wahad	1.00	.45
❑ 11 Tim Thomas	3.00	1.35
❑ 12 Keith Van Horn	5.00	2.20

1997-98 Z-Force Zensations

	MINT	NRMT
COMPLETE SET (25)	12.00	5.50
COMMON CARD (1-25)	.40	.18
SEMISTARS	.50	.23

	MINT	NRMT
UNLISTED STARS	.75	.35
SER.2 STATED ODDS 1:6 HOB/RET		

	MINT	NRMT
❑ 1 Ray Allen	1.25	.55
❑ 2 Vin Baker	.50	.23
❑ 3 Charles Barkley	1.25	.55
❑ 4 Clyde Drexler	.75	.35
❑ 5 Patrick Ewing	.75	.35
❑ 6 Juwan Howard	.50	.23
❑ 7 Eddie Jones	1.50	.70
❑ 8 Shawn Kemp	1.25	.55
❑ 9 Jason Kidd	2.50	1.10
❑ 10 Kerry Kittles	.75	.35
❑ 11 Karl Malone	1.25	.55
❑ 12 Antonio McDyess	1.00	.45
❑ 13 Hakeem Olajuwon	1.25	.55
❑ 14 Gary Payton	1.25	.55
❑ 15 Glen Rice	.50	.23
❑ 16 Mitch Richmond	.75	.35
❑ 17 David Robinson	1.25	.55
❑ 18 Dennis Rodman	1.50	.70
❑ 19 Joe Smith	.50	.23
❑ 20 Latrell Sprewell	1.50	.70
❑ 21 Jerry Stackhouse	.50	.23
❑ 22 John Stockton	.75	.35
❑ 23 Damon Stoudamire	1.00	.45
❑ 24 Rasheed Wallace	.75	.35
❑ 25 Chris Webber	2.50	1.10

Acknowledgments

Each year we refine the process of developing the most accurate and up-to-date information for this book. We believe this year's Price Guide is our best yet. Thanks again to all the contributors nationwide (listed below) as well as our staff here in Dallas.

Those who have worked closely with us on this and many other books, have again proven themselves invaluable in every aspect of producing this book: Rich Altman, Randy Archer, Mike Aronstein, Jerry Bell, Chris Benjamin, Mike Blaisdell, Bill Bossert (Mid-Atlantic Coin Exchange), Todd Crosner (California Sportscard Exchange), Bud Darland, Bill and Diane Dodge, Rick Donohoo, Willie Erving, Fleer (Josh Perlman), Gervise Ford, Steve Freedman, Larry and Jeff Fritsch, Jim Galusha, Dick Gariepy, Dick Gilkeson, Mike and Howard Gordon, Sally Grace, Oscar Garcia, George Grauer, John Greenwald, Jess Guffey, Bill Haber, George Henn, Mike Hersh, John Inouye, Steven Judd, Edward J. Kabala, Judy and Norman Kay, Lon Levitan, Lew Lipset, Dave Lucey, Paul Marchant, Brian Marcy (Scottsdale Baseball Cards), Dr. John McCue, Mike Mosier (Columbia City Collectibles Co.), Clark Muldavin, B.A. Murry, Pacific Trading Cards (Mike Cramer and Mike Monson), Steven Panet, Earl N. Petersen (U.S.A. Coins), J.C (Boo) Phillips, Jack Pollard, Racing Champions (Bill Surdock), Pat Quinn, Tom Reid, Henry M. Reizes, Gavin Riley, Rotman Productions, John Rumierz, Kevin Savage and Pat Blandford (Sports Gallery), Mike Schechter (MSA), Dan Sherlock, Bill Shonscheck, Glen J. Sidler, John Spalding, Spanky's, Nigel Spill (Oldies and Goodies), Murvin Sterling, Dan Stickney, Steve Taft, Ed Taylor, Lee Temanson, Topps (Marty Appel), Upper Deck (Justin Kanoya), Bill Vizas, Bill Wesslund (Portland Sports Card Co.), Jim Woods, Kit Young, Robert Zanze, Bill Zimpleman and Dean Zindler.

Many other individuals have provided price input, illustrative material, checklist verifications, errata, and/or background information. At the risk of inadvertently overlooking or omitting these many contributors, we should like to personally thank Joseph Abram, Darren Adams, Brett Allen, Alan Applegate, Randy Archer, Jeremy Bachman, Fran Bailey, Dean Bedell, Bubba Bennett, Eric Berger, Stanley Bernstein, Mike Blair, Andrew Bosarge, Naed Bou, David Bowlby, Gary Boyd, Terry Boyd, Nelson Brewart, Ray Bright, Britt Britton, Jacey Buel, Terry Bunt, David Cadelina, Danny Cariseo, Sally Carves, Tom Cavalierre, Garrett Chan, Lance Churchill, Craig Coddling, H. William Cook, Dave Cooper, Ron Cornell, Paul Czuchna, Jeff Daniels, Robert DeSalvatore, Robert Dichiara, Pat Dorsey, Joe Drelich, Brad Drummond, Charles Easterday Jr., Al Eng, Brad Engelhardt, Darrell Ereth, F&F Fast Break Cards, Gary Farbstein, Anthony Fernando, Joe Filas, Tom Freeman, Bob Frye, Chris Gala, Greg George, Pete George, Arthur Goyette, Dina Gray, Bob Grissett, Jess Guffey, Simon Gutis, Steve Hart, John Haupt, Sol Hauptman, Brian Headrick, Steven Hecht, Rod Heffem, Kevin Heffner, Stpehen Hils, Neil Hoppenworth, Bill Huggins, Wendell Hunter, Frank Hurtado, Brett Hyle, John Inouye, Brian Jaccoma, Mike Jardina, David Johnson, Craig Jones, Carmen Jordan, Loyd Jungling, Nick Kardoulias, Scott Kashner, Glenn Kasnuba, Jan Kemplin, Kal Kenfield, John Kilian, Tim Kirk, John Klassnik, Steve (DJ) Kluback, Mike Knoll, Don Knutsen, Mike Kohlhas, Bob and Bryan Kornfeld, George Kruk, Tom Kummer, Tim Landis, Jeff La Scala, Howard Lau, John Law, Ed Lim, Neil Lopez, Kendall Loyd, Fernando Mercado, Bruce Margulies, Scott Martinez, Bill McAvoy, Steve McHenry, Chris Merrill, Robert Merrill, Blake Meyer, Chad Meyer, Mark Meyer, Midwest Sports Cards, Jeff Mimick, Jeff Monaco, Jeff Morris, Don Olson Jr., Michael Olsen, Glenn Olson, Michael Parker, Jeff Patton, Jeff Prillaman, Paul Purves, Don Ras, Ron Resling, Carson Ritchey, Brent Ruland, Erik Runge, Mark Samarin, Bob Santos, Eric Shilito, Masa Shinohara, Bob Shurtleff, Sam Sliheet, Doug Smith, Don Spagnolo, Doug Spooner, Dan Statman, Geoff Stevers, Brad Stiles, Andy Stoltz, Nick Teresi, Jim Tripodi, Rob Veres, Bill Vizas, Kevin Vo, Mark Watson, Brian Wentz, Brian White, Doc White, Jeff Wiedenfeld, Mike Wiggins, Douglas Wilding, Steve Yeh, Diamond Zaferis, Zario Zigler, and Mark Zubrensky.

Every year we make active solicitations for expert input. We are particularly appreciative of help (however extensive or cursory) provided for this volume. We receive many inquiries, comments and questions regarding material within this book. In fact, each and every one is read and digested. Time constraints, however, prevent us from personally replying. But keep sharing your knowledge. Your letters and input are part of the "big picture" of hobby information we can pass along to readers in our books and magazines. Even though we cannot respond to each letter, you are making significant contributions to the hobby through your interest and comments.

The effort to continually refine and improve this book also involves a growing number of people and types of expertise on our home team. Our company boasts a substantial Collectibles Data Publishing team, which strengthens our ability to provide comprehensive analysis of the marketplace. Collectibles Data Publishing capably handled numerous technical details and provided able assistance and leadership in the preparation of this edition.

Our basketball analysts played a major part in compiling this year's book, traveling thousands of miles during the past year to attend sports card shows and visit card shops around the United States and Canada. The Beckett basketball specialists are Clint Hall, Scott Prusha, Joe White and Rob Springs (Price Guide Editor.) Their gathering information, entering sets, pricing analysis and careful proofreading were key contributors to the accuracy of this annual.

Rob Springs' coordination of input as the Beckett Basketball Monthly Price Guide Editor helped immeasurably. He would like to thank his wife, Amy, for her patience and understanding during the whole process. He was the key person in the organization of both technological and people resources for the book. He set up initial schedules and ensured that all deadlines were met. Also key contributors to endless hours of information gathering, pricing and analysis were Wayne Grove and Rich Klein.

They were ably assisted by Brad Grmela, who helped enter new sets and pricing information.